Chambers
Thesaurus

Chambers
Thesaurus

A comprehensive
word-finding dictionary

Edited by
Anne Seaton, George Davidson,
Catherine Schwarz, John Simpson

CAMBRIDGE   EDINBURGH

NEW YORK   PORT CHESTER   MELBOURNE   SYDNEY

Published jointly by W & R Chambers Limited
43-45 Annandale Street, Edinburgh EH7 4AZ, and
The Press Syndicate of the University of Cambridge,
The Pitt Building, Trumpington Street, Cambridge CB2 1RP
40 West 20th Street, New York, N.Y. 10011, USA
10 Stamford Road, Oakleigh, Melbourne 3166, Australia

© W & R Chambers Ltd and Cambridge University Press 1988

First published as *Chambers 20th Century Thesaurus* 1986
Published as *Chambers Thesaurus* 1988
First paperback edition 1989

British Library Cataloguing in Publication Data

[Chambers 20th century thesaurus]. Chambers
  thesaurus : a comprehensive word-finding
  dictionary.
  1. English language – Thesauri
  I. Seaton, M.A.
  423'.1

ISBN 1-85296-017-5

Typeset by Hewer Text Composition Services, Edinburgh.
Printed and bound in Great Britain by
William Clowes Limited, Beccles and London.

Contents

air and space vehicles; alphabets and writing
systems; anatomical; architecture and building; art;
canonical hours; cattle breeds; cheeses; chemical
elements; cloths, fabrics; coins, currencies; collective
nouns; collectors, enthusiasts; colours; confections,
dishes, foods; dances; dog breeds; drinks, alcoholic;
French Revolutionary calendar; furniture,
furnishings; garments, vestments; heraldry; herbs,
spices; jewels, gems; Jewish calendar; languages;
legal; minerals; musical instruments; parliaments;
prosody; ranks in armed forces; rhetoric; titles of
rulers; tools; units of measurement; vehicles; vessels,
ships; weapons, armour; wine-bottle sizes; zodiac
signs.

Preface

What is a thesaurus?

Clearly it is a kind of dictionary; but whereas an ordinary dictionary gives the meanings of a word, a thesaurus supplies alternatives for it. It is the essential companion for anyone who wants to create something satisfying out of words – a quick, convenient source of synonymous and related terms that will help the user to express himself in as precise, succinct, and yet varied a manner as possible.

It is 130 years since Peter Mark Roget published his *Thesaurus*. His purpose was to provide the reader not only with synonyms for a word, but, more generally, with a wide choice of expressions relevant to a particular concept. His method was to classify these within a framework of ideas on seventeenth-century philosophical and scientific principles. This meant that a very full alphabetical index was needed to open up the classified lists to the user. It was probably the complications of this system that ensured the continued popularity of the more 'user-friendly' type of word-finding book already in production in Roget's time – the simple alphabetical list of words, each followed by its own group of synonyms. More recently there has emerged the type of thesaurus that, while preserving the alphabetical arrangements, acknowledges the value of Roget's approach by supplying with each entry related vocabulary on a rather broader, more comprehensive basis than that of mere synonymity.

Chambers Thesaurus belongs to this last type – it contains 18 000 of the commonest, most synonym-rich words in the language, alphabetically listed, each with a plentiful supply of alternative and connected expressions; selected antonyms have also been added wherever appropriate. It has all the recognised usefulness of any thesaurus – but its special advantage is that it draws on the resources of *Chambers English Dictionary*, known to dictionary connoisseurs and word-game enthusiasts alike as a mine of useful, interesting and diverting items of vocabulary.

What are the advantages of a thesaurus?

To a regular thesaurus-user they become ever more apparent. A thesaurus jogs the memory – it offers help to the person struggling to encapsulate his meaning in a forgotten *mot juste* that might remain tantalisingly on the tip of his tongue. It is indispensable to the journalist, writer and reporter. A thesaurus is fun to use, and with the fun comes the opportunity to enhance one's personal command of words and increase one's general knowledge; words that may not be well known to the reader will trigger off investigations of his dictionary and lead him to explore the remoter corners of the language. Finally, a thesaurus is a tool that the word-gamester – compiler, player or solver – cannot do without.

The thing one notices about a thesaurus is that it rarely yields completely interchangeable alternatives for a word – but this is one of its beauties. What it gives is a list of possibilities that have more or less of a particular ingredient, are more or less formal, are more or less euphonious, that, in short, have more or less of the precise flavour sought by the user. English has its international origins largely to thank for its richness and subtle variety, and a thesaurus of English words, with their diversity of shape, size, sound and association, will surely yield that ideal unmistakably usable expression to fit a particular context.

The bias towards abstract terms in the main text has been balanced by the addition of a section that is a newcomer to this type of thesaurus: an appendix of concrete and technical terms drawn from the *Chambers English Dictionary* and collected alphabetically into categories such as architecture, furniture, vehicles, garments, rhetorical terms, legal terms, anatomical terms. There are also lists of collective nouns, names for collectors and enthusiasts, ranks in the armed forces, and wine-bottle sizes. Such words do not fit readily into synonym lists but may be no less sought-after for that. A list of the categories included appears on the Contents page.

A second appendix contains words listed by suffix. The *Chambers English Dictionary* has been combed to produce exhaustive lists of -ologies, -ocracies, -ographies, -philias, -phobias, -manias, -therapies, -hoods, -doms and some seventy other such groups. This is another innovative and intriguing addition to the standard thesaurus. These two appendices will be invaluable extras not only for the crossword-solver, but for all types of thesaurus-user.

How to use this thesaurus

Little explanation is needed, as the arrangement is deliberately simple. To take the word **ailment** as an example: the part of speech, *n*, is given, and then a list of related and synonymous words in straightforward alphabetical order – affliction, complaint, disability, disease, disorder, illness, indisposition, infection, infirmity, malady, sickness, weakness. If none of the synonyms will do, many (in this case all) have entries of their own, providing further alternatives. It is the same with the antonyms: at **abiding** the word 'transient' is supplied as an antonym; the entry **transient** will give further opposites to 'abiding'.

Separate parts of speech have separate lists of synonyms: thus at **act**, two distinct lists are provided for the word as noun and as verb; the list for each new part of speech begins on a new line.

There is coverage of phrases too: again at **act**, there are the sub-entries **act up** and **act upon**, each with its lists of synonymous expressions. Some phrases occur as independent entries rather than as sub-entries, and are ordered according to their first word. This means that all the phrases beginning with the word **in**, for example, will be found in an alphabetically arranged group *before* the word **inability**, and the phrase **de trop** must be looked for *before* the word **dead**.

Among the listed synonyms the user will find the occasional abstruse or colourfully unusual word, reflecting the broad coverage of *Chambers English Dictionary*. At **aftermath**, for instance, the words 'lattermath' and 'rowen', which correspond to the original meaning of aftermath (a second crop of grass), are included in the synonym list. As a general policy, however, the editors have excluded dialect and obsolete terms, unless such terms make an appearance in, say, a well-known song, poem or play.

The simple alphabetical arrangement of synonyms means that there is no classification of meanings within an entry, but many words that have strongly distinct senses are given two or more entries. For example, **bear** (carry . . . transport . . . sustain . . . endure . . . weather, etc) and **bear** (breed . . . engender . . . give birth to . . . produce . . . propagate, etc) have been entered as **bear**[1] and **bear**[2].

It is recommended that the thesaurus should be used in conjunction with a dictionary. *Chambers Concise Dictionary* will be a useful standard companion; the obscurer terms will be found in the fuller *Chambers English Dictionary*.

The editors hope that the reader will get as much enjoyment out of using this thesaurus as they have had in compiling it, and that it will be found to live up to the definition of **thesaurus** in the *Chambers English Dictionary* – 'a treasury, a storehouse of knowledge'.

Acknowledgement
W & R Chambers would like to thank Peter Schwarz for the invaluable contribution in time and technical expertise that he has made to this project.

A

abandon v. abdicate, back-pedal, cede, chuck, desert, desist, discontinue, ditch, drop, evacuate, forgo, forsake, give up, jilt, leave, leave behind, leave in the lurch, quit, relinquish, renounce, repudiate, resign, scrap, sink, surrender, vacate, waive, withdraw from, yield.
antonyms continue, persist, support.
n. dash, recklessness, unrestraint, wantonness, wildness.
antonym restraint.

abandoned adj. cast aside, cast away, cast out, corrupt, debauched, depraved, derelict, deserted, desolate, discarded, dissipated, dissolute, dropped, forlorn, forsaken, jilted, left, neglected, outcast, profligate, rejected, relinquished, reprobate, scorned, sinful, unoccupied, vacant, wanton, wicked.
antonyms cherished, restrained.

abandonment n. apostasy, cession, decampment, dereliction, desertion, desistance, discontinuance, discontinuation, dropping, evacuation, forsaking, giving up, jilting, leaving, neglect, relinquishment, renegation, renunciation, resignation, sacrifice, scrapping, surrender, waiver.

abase v. belittle, cast down, debase, degrade, demean, discredit, disgrace, dishonour, downgrade, humble, humiliate, lower, malign, mortify, reduce, vitiate.
antonyms elevate, honour.

abasement n. belittlement, debasement, degradation, demotion, depravation, deterioration, disgrace, dishonour, downgrading, humbling, humiliation, lowering, mortification, reduction, shame, vitiation.
antonyms elevation, promotion.

abashed adj. affronted, ashamed, astounded, bewildered, chagrined, confounded, confused, cowed, discomfited, discomposed, disconcerted, discountenanced, discouraged, dismayed, dum(b)founded, embarrassed, floored, humbled, humiliated, mortified, nonplussed, perturbed, shamefaced, taken aback.
antonyms at ease, audacious, composed.

abate v. alleviate, appease, attenuate, bate, decline, decrease, deduct, diminish, discount, dull, dwindle, ease, ebb, fade, faik, fall off, lessen, let up, mitigate, moderate, mollify, pacify, quell, rebate, reduce, relieve, remit, sink, slacken, slake, slow, subside, subtract, taper off, wane, weaken.
antonyms increase, strengthen.

abatement n. alleviation, allowance, assuagement, attenuation, cessation, decline, decrease, deduction, diminution, discount, dulling, dwindling, easing, ebb, extenuation, fading, fall-off, lessening, let-up, mitigation, moderation, mollification, palliation, quelling, rebatement, reduction, relief, remission, slackening, slowing, softening, subsidence, subtraction, tapering off, tempering, waning, weakening.
antonyms crescendo, increase.

abbey n. abbacy, cloister, convent, friary, monastery, nunnery, priory, seminary.

abbot n. abbé, archimandrite, general, head, prior, superior.

abbreviate v. abridge, abstract, clip, compress, condense, contract, curtail, cut, digest, epitomise, lessen, précis, reduce, shorten, shrink, summarise, trim, truncate.
antonyms amplify, extend.

abbreviation n. abridgement, abstract, abstraction, clipping, compendium, compression, condensation, conspectus, contraction, curtailment, digest, epitome, précis, reduction, résumé, shortening, summarisation, summary, summation, synopsis, trimming, truncation.
antonyms expansion, extension.

abdicate v. abandon, abjure, abnegate, cede, demit, forgo, give up, quit, relinquish, renounce, repudiate, resign, retire, surrender, vacate, yield.

abdication n. abandonment, abjuration, abnegation, cession, giving up, quitting, relinquishment, renunciation, resignation, retiral, retirement, surrender.

abdomen n. belly, bread-basket, corporation, guts, hind-body, midriff, paunch, pot, stomach, tum, tummy, venter.

abdominal adj. coeliac, gastric, intestinal, stomachic(al), ventral, ventricular, visceral.

abduct v. abduce, appropriate, carry off, kidnap, lay hold of, make off with, rape, run away with, run off with, seduce, seize, snatch, spirit away.

abducted adj. appropriated, enlevé, kidnapped, seduced, seized, snatched, stolen.

abduction n. appropriation, enlevement, kidnap, rape, seduction, seizure, theft.

aberrant adj. abnormal, anomalous, atypical, corrupt, corrupted, defective, degenerate, depraved, deviant, different, divergent, eccentric, egregious, erroneous, incongruous, irregular, odd, peculiar, perverse, perverted, queer, quirky, rambling, roving, straying, untypical, wandering, wrong.
antonyms normal, straight.

aberration n. aberrancy, abnormality, anomaly, defect, delusion, deviation, divergence,

eccentricity, freak, hallucination, illusion, irregularity, lapse, nonconformity, oddity, peculiarity, quirk, rambling, rogue, straying, vagary, wandering.
antonym conformity.

abet *v.* aid, assist, back, condone, connive, egg on, encourage, goad, help, incite, promote, prompt, sanction, second, spur, succour, support, sustain, uphold, urge.
antonym discourage.

abettor *n.* accessory, accomplice, assistant, associate, backer, confederate, conniver, co-operator, encourager, fautor, fomenter, goad, helper, henchman, inciter, instigator, particeps criminis, prompter, second, supporter.

abeyance *n.* adjournment, deferral, discontinuation, inactivity, intermission, lull, postponement, recess, remission, reservation, suspension, waiting.
antonyms activity, continuation.

abhor *v.* abominate, despise, detest, execrate, hate, loathe, recoil from, shrink from, shudder at, spurn.
antonyms adore, love.

abhorrence *n.* abomination, animosity, aversion, despite, detestation, disgust, distaste, enmity, execration, hate, hatred, horror, loathing, malice, odium, repugnance, revulsion.
antonyms adoration, love.

abhorrent *adj.* abominable, absonant, despiteful, detestable, disgusting, distasteful, execrable, hated, hateful, heinous, horrible, horrid, loathsome, nauseating, obnoxious, odious, offensive, repellent, repugnant, repulsive, revolting.
antonym attractive.

abide *v.* accept, bear, brook, continue, endure, last, outlive, persist, put up with, remain, stand, stay, stomach, submit to, suffer, survive, tarry, tolerate.
antonyms dispute, quit.

abide by acknowledge, acquiesce in, adhere to, agree to, carry out, comply with, conform to, discharge, follow, fulfil, go along with, hold to, keep to, obey, observe, stand by, submit to.

abiding *adj.* constant, continual, continuing, continuous, durable, enduring, eternal, everlasting, fast, firm, immortal, immutable, indissoluble, lasting, permanent, persistent, persisting, stable, steadfast, surviving, tenacious, unchangeable, unchanging, unending.
antonyms ephemeral, transient.

ability *n.* adeptness, adroitness, aptitude, capability, capacity, competence, competency, deftness, dexterity, endowment, energy, expertise, expertness, facility, faculty, flair, forte, genius, gift, knack, know-how, long suit, nous, potentiality, power, proficiency, qualification, savoir-faire, savvy, skill, strength, talent, touch.
antonyms inability, incompetence.

abject *adj.* base, contemptible, cringing, debased, degenerate, degraded, deplorable, despicable, dishonourable, execrable, fawning, forlorn, grovelling, hopeless, humiliating, ignoble, ignominious, low, mean, miserable, outcast, pathetic, pitiable, servile, slavish, sordid, submissive, vile, worthless, wretched.
antonym exalted.

abjuration *n.* abnegation, abstention, denial, disavowal, disclaiming, disclamation, eschewal, forswearing, recantation, refusal, rejection, relinquishment, renunciation, retraction, self-denial.
antonyms agreement, assent, support.

abjure *v.* abandon, abnegate, abstain from, deny, disavow, discard, disclaim, disown, eschew, forsake, forswear, give up, recant, refrain from, reject, relinquish, renegue on, renounce, retract.
antonyms agree, assent, support.

ablaze *adj.* afire, aflame, aglow, alight, angry, aroused, blazing, brilliant, burning, enthusiastic, excited, exhilarated, fervent, fiery, flaming, flashing, frenzied, fuming, furious, glaring, gleaming, glowing, ignited, illuminated, impassioned, incandescent, incensed, lighted, luminous, on fire, passionate, radiant, raging, sparkling, stimulated.

able *adj.* accomplished, adept, adequate, adroit, capable, clever, competent, deft, dexterous, effective, efficient, experienced, expert, fere, fit, fitted, gifted, ingenious, masterful, masterly, powerful, practised, proficient, qualified, skilful, skilled, strong, talented.
antonyms incapable, incompetent.

able-bodied *adj.* firm, fit, hale, hardy, healthy, hearty, lusty, powerful, robust, sound, stalwart, staunch, stout, strapping, strong, sturdy, tough, vigorous.
antonyms delicate, infirm.

ablution *n.* bath, bathing, cleansing, lavation, purgation, purging, purification, shower, wash, washing.

abnegate *v.* abandon, abdicate, abjure, abstain from, acquiesce, concede, decline, deny, disallow, eschew, forbear, forgo, forsake, give up, refrain from, reject, relinquish, renounce, sacrifice, submit, surrender, yield.

abnegation *n.* abandonment, abjuration, abstinence, acquiescence, continence, disallowance, eschewal, forbearance, giving up, refusal, rejection, relinquishment, renunciation, sacrifice, self-denial, submission, surrender, temperance.
antonyms acceptance, support.

abnormal *adj.* aberrant, anomalous, atypical, curious, deviant, different, divergent, eccentric, erratic, exceptional, extraordinary, irregular, monstrous, odd, paranormal, peculiar, queer, singular, strange, uncanny, uncommon, unexpected, unnatural, untypical, unusual, wayward, weird.
antonyms normal, straight.

abnormality *n.* aberration, anomaly, atypicalness, bizarreness, deformity, deviation, difference, divergence, dysfunction, eccentricity, exception, flaw, irregularity,

monstrosity, oddity, peculiarity, queerness, singularity, strangeness, uncommonness, unexpectedness, unnaturalness, untypicalness, unusualness, weirdness.
antonym normality.

abode *n.* domicile, dwelling, dwelling-place, habitat, habitation, home, house, lodging, pad, place, quarters, residence.

abolish *v.* abrogate, annihilate, annul, blot out, cancel, destroy, do away with, eliminate, end, eradicate, expunge, exterminate, extinguish, extirpate, get rid of, invalidate, kibosh, nullify, obliterate, overthrow, overturn, put an end to, put the kibosh on, quash, repeal, repudiate, rescind, revoke, sink, stamp out, subvert, suppress, terminate, vitiate, void, wipe out.
antonyms continue, retain.

abolition *n.* abolishment, abrogation, annihilation, annulment, cancellation, destruction, dissolution, elimination, end, ending, eradication, expunction, extermination, extinction, extirpation, invalidation, nullification, obliteration, overthrow, overturning, quashing, repeal, repudiation, rescission, revocation, subversion, suppression, termination, vitiation, voiding, withdrawal.
antonyms continuance, retention.

abominable *adj.* abhorrent, accursed, appalling, atrocious, base, beastly, contemptible, despicable, detestable, disgusting, execrable, foul, hateful, heinous, hellish, horrible, horrid, loathsome, nauseating, nauseous, nefandous, nefast, obnoxious, odious, repellent, reprehensible, repugnant, repulsive, revolting, terrible, vile, villainous, wretched.
antonyms delightful, desirable.

abominate *v.* abhor, condemn, despise, detest, execrate, hate, loathe.
antonyms adore, esteem, love.

abomination *n.* abhorrence, anathema, animosity, animus, antipathy, aversion, bête noire, bugbear, curse, detestation, disgrace, disgust, distaste, evil, execration, hate, hatred, horror, hostility, loathing, odium, offence, plague, repugnance, revulsion, torment.
antonyms adoration, delight.

aboriginal *adj.* ancient, autochthonic, autochthonous, domestic, earliest, enchorial, endemic, first, indigenous, native, original, primal, primary, primeval, primitive, primordial, pristine.

aborigine *n.* aboriginal, autochthon, indigene, native, warragal.
antonyms immigrant, incomer.

abort *v.* arrest, call off, check, end, fail, frustrate, halt, miscarry, nullify, stop, terminate, thwart.
antonym continue.

abortion *n.* aborticide, disappointment, failure, fiasco, foeticide, freak, frustration, misadventure, misbirth, miscarriage, monster, monstrosity, termination, thwarting.
antonyms continuation, success.

abortive *adj.* barren, bootless, failed, failing, fruitless, futile, idle, ineffective, ineffectual,

misborn, miscarried, sterile, unavailing, unproductive, unsuccessful, useless, vain.
antonym successful.

abound *v.* be plentiful, brim over, crowd, exuberate, flourish, increase, infest, luxuriate, overflow, proliferate, run riot, superabound, swarm, swell, teem, thrive.
antonym be in short supply.

abounding *adj.* abundant, bountiful, copious, filled, flourishing, flowing, flush, full, lavish, luxuriant, overflowing, plenteous, plentiful, prodigal, profuse, prolific, rank, replete, rich, superabundant, teeming, unstinting.
antonym lacking.

about *prep.* adjacent to, all over, anent, around, as regards, beside, busy with, circa, close to, concerned with, connected with, encircling, encompassing, engaged on, in respect to, in the matter of, near, nearby, on, over, re, referring to, regarding, relating to, relative to, respecting, round, surrounding, through, throughout, touching, with reference to, with regard to, with respect to.
adv. active, almost, approaching, approximately, around, astir, close to, from place to place, here and there, hither and thither, in motion, in the region of, more or less, nearing, nearly, present, roughly, stirring, to and fro.

about to all but, intending to, on the point of, on the verge of, preparing to, ready to.

about-turn *n.* about-face, apostasy, backtrack, enantiodromia, reversal, right-about (face), turnabout, turn(a)round, uey, U-turn, volteface.

above *prep.* atop, before, beyond, exceeding, higher than, in excess of, on top of, over, prior to, superior to, surpassing, upon.
antonyms below, under.
adv. aloft, atop, earlier, heavenwards, in heaven, on high, overhead, supra.
antonym below.
adj. above-mentioned, above-stated, aforementioned, aforesaid, earlier, foregoing, preceding, previous, prior.

above suspicion above reproach, blameless, guiltless, honourable, innocent, irreproachable, pure, sinless, unimpeachable, virtuous.

above-board *adj.* candid, fair, fair and square, forthright, frank, guileless, honest, honourable, legitimate, on the level, open, overt, reputable, square, straight, straightforward, true, trustworthy, truthful, upright, veracious.
antonyms shady, underhand.

abrade *v.* chafe, erase, erode, file, grind, levigate, rub off, scour, scrape, triturate, wear away, wear down, wear off.

abrasion *n.* abrading, chafe, chafing, erosion, friction, grating, graze, grinding, levigation, rubbing, scouring, scrape, scraping, scratch, scratching, scuff, scuffing, trituration, wearing away, wearing down.

abrasive *adj.* abradant, annoying, attritional, biting, caustic, chafing, erodent, erosive, frictional, galling, grating, hurtful, irritating,

nasty, rough, scraping, scratching, scratchy, scuffing, sharp, unpleasant.
antonyms pleasant, smooth.

abreast *adj.* acquainted, au courant, au fait, conversant, familiar, in the picture, in touch, informed, knowledgeable, on the ball, up to date.
antonyms out of touch, unaware.

abridge *v.* abbreviate, abstract, circumscribe, clip, compress, concentrate, condense, contract, curtail, cut, cut down, decrease, digest, diminish, dock, epitomise, lessen, lop, précis, prune, reduce, shorten, summarise, synopsise, trim, truncate.
antonyms amplify, pad.

abridgement *n.* abbreviation, abrégé, abstract, compendium, compression, concentration, condensation, conspectus, contraction, curtailment, cutting, decrease, digest, diminishing, diminution, epitome, lessening, limitation, outline, précis, pruning, reduction, restriction, résumé, shortening, summary, synopsis, truncation.
antonyms expansion, padding.

abroad *adv.* about, at large, away, circulating, current, elsewhere, extensively, far, far and wide, forth, in circulation, in foreign parts, out, out of the country, out-of-doors, outside, overseas, publicly, widely.

abrogate *v.* abolish, annul, cancel, countermand, disannul, discontinue, disenact, dissolve, end, invalidate, nullify, override, overrule, quash, recall, repeal, repudiate, rescind, retract, reverse, revoke, scrap, set aside, terminate, void, withdraw.
antonyms establish, institute.

abrogation *n.* abolition, annulling, annulment, cancellation, countermanding, defeasance, disannulment, discontinuation, ending, invalidation, nullification, overriding, overruling, quashing, repeal, repudiation, rescission, retraction, reversal, revocation, scrapping, setting aside, termination, voiding, withdrawal.
antonyms continuation, retention.

abrupt *adj.* blunt, brief, brisk, broken, brusque, curt, direct, disconnected, discontinuous, discourteous, gruff, hasty, headlong, hurried, impolite, irregular, jerky, precipitate, precipitous, prerupt, quick, rapid, rough, rude, sharp, sheer, short, snappy, steep, sudden, surprising, swift, terse, unannounced, unceremonious, uncivil, uneven, unexpected, unforeseen, ungracious.
antonyms ceremonious, expansive, leisurely.

abscond *v.* absquatulate, beat it, bolt, clear out, decamp, disappear, do a bunk, escape, flee, flit, fly, hightail it, levant, make off, quit, run off, scram, skedaddle, skive, take French leave, vamoose.

absconder *n.* absentee, bolter, escapee, levanter, quitter, truant.

absence *n.* absenteeism, absent-mindedness, abstraction, dearth, default, defect, deficiency, distraction, inattention, lack, need, non-appearance, non-attendance, non-existence, omission, paucity, preoccupation, privation, reverie, scarcity, truancy, unavailability, vacancy, vacuity, want.
antonyms existence, presence.

absent *adj.* absent-minded, absorbed, abstracted, away, bemused, blank, daydreaming, distracted, distrait(e), dreamy, elsewhere, empty, faraway, gone, heedless, inattentive, lacking, missing, musing, non-existent, not present, oblivious, out, preoccupied, truant, unavailable, unaware, unconscious, unheeding, unthinking, vacant, vague, wanting, withdrawn, wool-gathering.
antonyms aware, present.

absent-minded *adj.* absent, absorbed, abstracted, bemused, distracted, distrait(e), dreaming, dreamy, engrossed, faraway, forgetful, heedless, impractical, inattentive, musing, oblivious, otherwordly, pensive, preoccupied, scatterbrained, unaware, unconscious, unheeding, unthinking, withdrawn, wool-gathering.
antonyms matter-of-fact, attentive, practical.

absent-mindedness *n.* absence, absorption, abstraction, distraction, dreaminess, forgetfulness, heedlessness, inattention, muse, preoccupation, unawareness, vacancy, vagueness.
antonym alertness.

absolute *adj.* absolutist, actual, almighty, arbitrary, autarchical, autocratic, autonomous, categorical, certain, complete, conclusive, consummate, decided, decisive, definite, definitive, despotic, dictatorial, downright, entire, exact, exhaustive, final, flawless, free, full, genuine, independent, indubitable, infallible, omnipotent, out-and-out, outright, peremptory, perfect, positive, precise, pure, sheer, sovereign, supreme, sure, terminative, thorough, total, totalitarian, tyrannical, unadulterated, unalloyed, unambiguous, unbounded, unconditional, uncontrolled, undivided, unequivocal, unlimited, unmitigated, unmixed, unqualified, unquestionable, unrestrained, unrestricted, utter.
antonyms conditional, partial.

absolutely *adv.* actually, arbitrarily, autocratically, autonomously, bang, categorically, certainly, completely, conclusively, consummately, dead, decidedly, decisively, definitely, despotically, diametrically, dictatorially, entirely, exactly, exhaustively, finally, fully, genuinely, indubitably, infallibly, peremptorily, perfectly, positively, precisely, purely, sovereignly, supremely, surely, thoroughly, totally, truly, tyrannically, unambiguously, unconditionally, unequivocally, unmitigatedly, unquestionably, unrestrainedly, utterly, wholly.

absolution *n.* acquittal, acquittance, amnesty, compurgation, deliverance, discharge, dispensation, emancipation, exculpation, exemption, exoneration, forgiveness, forgiving, freeing, indulgence, liberation, mercy, pardon, purgation, redemption, release, remission, shriving, vindication.

antonym condemnation.

absolve *v.* acquit, clear, deliver, discharge, emancipate, exculpate, excuse, exempt, exonerate, forgive, free, justify, let off, liberate, loose, pardon, ransom, redeem, release, remit, set free, shrive, vindicate.

antonym charge.

absorb *v.* adsorb, apprehend, assimilate, captivate, consume, co-opt, devour, digest, drink in, engage, engross, engulf, enthrall, enwrap, exhaust, fascinate, fill (up), fix, grip, hold, imbibe, immerse, incorporate, ingest, involve, monopolise, occupy, osmose, pre-occupy, receive, retain, rivet, soak up, sorb, submerge, suck up, take in, understand, utilise.

antonyms dissipate, exude.

absorbed *adj.* captivated, concentrating, engaged, engrossed, enthralled, fascinated, fixed, gripped, held, immersed, intent, involved, lost, obsessed, occupied, pre-occupied, rapt, riveted, wrapped up.

antonyms bored, distracted.

absorbent *adj.* absorptive, assimilative, blotting, penetrable, permeable, pervious, porous, receptive, resorbent, retentive, sorbefacient, sorbent, spongy.

antonym impermeable.

absorbing *adj.* amusing, arresting, captivating, compulsive, diverting, engrossing, entertaining, enthralling, fascinating, gripping, interesting, intriguing, preoccupying, riveting, spellbinding, unputdownable.

antonyms boring, off-putting.

absorption *n.* adsorption, assimilation, attentiveness, captivation, concentration, consumption, digestion, engagement, exhaustion, fascination, holding, imbibition, immersion, incorporation, ingestion, intentness, involvement, occupation, osmosis, preoccupation, raptness, soaking up, sucking up.

abstain *v.* avoid, cease, decline, deny, desist, eschew, forbear, forgo, give up, keep from, refrain, refuse, reject, renounce, resist, shun, stop, swear off, withhold.

antonym indulge.

abstemious *adj.* abstinent, ascetic, austere, continent, disciplined, frugal, moderate, restrained, self-denying, self-disciplined, sober, sparing, temperate.

antonyms gluttonous, intemperate, luxurious.

abstention *n.* abstaining, abstinence, avoidance, continence, desistance, eschewal, forbearance, frugality, nephalism, non-indulgence, refraining, refusal, restraint, self-control, self-denial, self-discipline, self-restraint, sobriety.

abstinence *n.* abstemiousness, abstinency, asceticism, avoidance, continence, forbearance, frugality, moderation, nephalism, non-indulgence, refraining, self-denial, self-discipline, self-restraint, soberness, sobriety, teetotalism, temperance.

antonym self-indulgence.

abstinent *adj.* abstaining, abstemious, continent, disciplined, forbearing, frugal, moderate, self-controlled, self-denying, self-disciplined, self-restrained, sober, temperate.

antonyms self-indulgent, voluptuous, wanton.

abstract *adj.* abstruse, academic, arcane, complex, conceptual, deep, discrete, general, generalised, hypothetical, indefinite, intellectual, metaphysical, non-concrete, occult, philosophical, profound, recondite, separate, subtle, theoretic, theoretical, unpractical, unrealistic.

antonym concrete.

n. abbreviation, abridgement, abstractive, compendium, compression, condensation, conspectus, digest, epitome, essence, outline, précis, recapitulation, résumé, summary, synopsis.

v. abbreviate, abridge, compress, condense, detach, digest, dissociate, epitomise, extract, isolate, outline, précis, purloin, remove, separate, shorten, steal, summarise, withdraw.

antonyms expand, insert.

abstracted *adj.* absent, absent-minded, bemused, distrait(e), dreamy, faraway, inattentive, pensive, preoccupied, remote, withdrawn, wool-gathering.

antonyms alert, on the ball.

abstraction *n.* absence, absent-mindedness, absorption, bemusedness, concept, conception, dissociation, distraction, dream, dreaminess, formula, generalisation, generality, hypothesis, idea, inattention, notion, pensiveness, preoccupation, remoteness, separation, theorem, theory, thought, withdrawal, wool-gathering.

abstruse *adj.* abstract, arcane, complex, cryptic, dark, deep, devious, difficult, enigmatic, esoteric, hermetic, hidden, incomprehensible, mysterious, mystical, obscure, occult, perplexing, profound, puzzling, recondite, subtle, tortuous, unfathomable, unobvious, vague.

antonyms concrete, obvious.

absurd *adj.* anomalous, comical, crazy, daft, derisory, fantastic, farcical, foolish, funny, humorous, idiotic, illogical, implausible, incongruous, irrational, laughable, ludicrous, meaningless, nonsensical, paradoxical, preposterous, ridiculous, risible, senseless, silly, stupid, unreasonable, untenable.

antonyms logical, rational, sensible.

absurdity *n.* comicality, craziness, daftness, farce, farcicality, farcicalness, fatuity, fatuousness, folly, foolery, foolishness, idiocy, illogicality, illogicalness, incongruity, irrationality, joke, ludicrousness, meaninglessness, nonsense, nonsensicality, preposterousness, ridiculousness, senselessness, silliness, stupidity, unreasonableness.

abundance *n.* affluence, ampleness, amplitude, bonanza, bounty, copiousness, exuberance, fortune, fullness, glut, heap, lavishness,

luxuriance, luxuriancy, milk and honey, munificence, oodles, opulence, plenitude, plenteousness, plenty, pleroma, plethora, prodigality, profusion, riches, richness, routh, uberty, wealth.
antonyms dearth, scarcity.

abundant *adj.* ample, bounteous, bountiful, copious, exuberant, filled, full, generous, in plenty, lavish, luxuriant, overflowing, plenteous, plentiful, prodigal, profuse, rank, rich, superabundant, teeming, uberous, unstinted, well-provided, well-supplied.
antonyms scarce, sparse.

abuse *v.* batter, calumniate, castigate, curse, damage, deceive, defame, denigrate, disparage, exploit, harm, hurt, ill-treat, impose on, injure, insult, inveigh against, libel, malign, maltreat, manhandle, mar, misapply, miscall, misemploy, misuse, molest, objurgate, oppress, oppugn, revile, scold, slander, slate, smear, spoil, swear at, take advantage of, traduce, upbraid, vilify, violate, vituperate, wrong.
antonyms cherish, compliment, praise.
n. affront, blame, calumniation, calumny, castigation, censure, contumely, curses, cursing, damage, defamation, denigration, derision, diatribe, disparagement, execration, exploitation, flyting, harm, hurt, ill-treatment, imposition, injury, insults, invective, libel, malediction, maltreatment, manhandling, misapplication, misconduct, misdeed, misuse, obloquy, offence, oppression, opprobrium, reproach, revilement, scolding, sin, slander, spoiling, swearing, tirade, traducement, upbraiding, vilification, violation, vitriol, vituperation, wrong, wrong-doing.
antonyms attention, care.

abusive *adj.* brutal, calumniating, calumnious, castigating, censorious, contumelious, cruel, defamatory, denigrating, derisive, derogatory, destructive, disparaging, harmful, hurtful, injurious, insulting, invective, libellous, maligning, objurgatory, offensive, opprobrious, pejorative, reproachful, reviling, rough, rude, scathing, scolding, slanderous, traducing, upbraiding, vilifying, vituperative.
antonym complimentary.

abut *v.* adjoin, border, conjoin, connect, impinge, join, meet, touch, verge.

abysmal *adj.* abyssal, bottomless, boundless, complete, deep, endless, extreme, immeasurable, incalculable, infinite, profound, thorough, unending, unfathomable, vast, yawning.

abyss *n.* abysm, Avernus, barathrum, canyon, chasm, crater, crevasse, depth, fissure, gorge, gulf, pit, profound, swallow, void.

academic *adj.* abstract, bookish, collegiate, conjectural, donnish, educational, erudite, highbrow, hypothetical, impractical, instructional, learned, lettered, literary, notional, pedagogical, scholarly, scholastic, speculative, studious, theoretical, well-read.
n. academe, academician, don, fellow, lecturer, man of letters, master, pedant, professor, pundit, savant, scholar, scholastic, schoolman, student, tutor.

accede *v.* accept, acquiesce, admit, agree, assent, assume, attain, capitulate, comply, concede, concur, consent, defer, endorse, grant, inherit, submit, succeed (to), yield.
antonyms demur, object.

accelerate *v.* advance, antedate, dispatch, expedite, facilitate, festinate, forward, further, hasten, hurry, pick up speed, precipitate, promote, quicken, speed, speed up, spur, step on the gas, step on the juice, step up, stimulate.
antonyms delay, slow down.

accent *n.* accentuation, arsis, articulation, beat, cadence, emphasis, enunciation, force, ictus, inflection, intensity, intonation, modulation, pitch, pronunciation, pulsation, pulse, rhythm, stress, thesis, timbre, tonality, tone.
v. accentuate, emphasise, stress, underline, underscore.

accentuate *v.* accent, deepen, emphasise, highlight, intensify, italicise, spotlight, strengthen, stress, underline, underscore.
antonyms play down, weaken.

accept *v.* abide by, accede, acknowledge, acquiesce, acquire, admit, adopt, affirm, agree to, approve, assume, avow, bear, believe, bow to, brook, concur with, consent to, co-operate with, defer to, gain, get, have, jump at, obtain, put up with, receive, recognise, secure, stand, stomach, submit to, suffer, swallow, take, take on, tolerate, undertake, wear, yield to.
antonyms demur, reject.

acceptable *adj.* adequate, admissible, agreeable, all right, conventional, correct, delightful, desirable, done, grateful, gratifying, moderate, passable, pleasant, pleasing, satisfactory, standard, suitable, tolerable, U, unexceptionable, unobjectionable, welcome.
antonyms unsatisfactory, unwelcome.

acceptance *n.* accedence, accepting, accession, acknowledgement, acquiescence, acquiring, admission, adoption, affirmation, agreement, approbation, approval, assent, belief, compliance, concession, concurrence, consent, credence, gaining, getting, having, obtaining, OK, permission, ratification, receipt, recognition, seal of approval, securing, stamp of approval, taking, tolerance, toleration, undertaking.
antonyms dissent, refusal.

accepted *adj.* acceptable, acknowledged, admitted, agreed, agreed upon, approved, authorised, common, confirmed, consuetudinary, conventional, correct, customary, established, normal, ratified, received, recognised, regular, sanctioned, standard, time-honoured, traditional, universal, unwritten, usual.
antonym unorthodox.

access *n.* adit, admission, admittance, approach, avenue, course, door, entering, entrance,

entrée, entry, gateway, increase, ingress, key, onset, passage, passageway, path, road, upsurge, upsurgence.
antonyms egress, outlet.

accessible *adj.* achievable, affable, approachable, at hand, attainable, available, come-at-able, conversable, cordial, exposed, friendly, get-at-able, handy, informal, liable, near, nearby, obtainable, on hand, open, possible, procurable, reachable, ready, sociable, subject, susceptible, vulnerable, wide-open.
antonym inaccessible.

accession *n.* accedence, acceptance, acquiescence, acquisition, addition, agreement, assumption, attaining, attainment, augmentation, concurrence, consent, enlargement, entering upon, extension, increase, installation, purchase, submission, succession, taking over, yielding.

accessory *n.* abettor, accompaniment, accomplice, addition, adjunct, adjuvant, adornment, aid, appendage, assistant, associate, attachment, colleague, component, confederate, conniver, convenience, decoration, embellishment, extension, extra, frill, help, helper, particeps criminis, partner, supplement, trim, trimming.
adj. abetting, additional, adjuvant, adventitious, aiding, ancillary, assisting, auxiliary, contributory, extra, incidental, secondary, subordinate, subsidiary, supplemental, supplementary.

accident *n.* blow, calamity, casualty, chance, collision, contingency, contretemps, crash, disaster, fate, fluke, fortuity, fortune, happenstance, hazard, luck, misadventure, miscarriage, mischance, misfortune, mishap, pile-up, prang, serendipity, shunt.

accidental *adj.* adventitious, adventive, casual, chance, contingent, fluky, fortuitous, haphazard, inadvertent, incidental, random, serendipitous, unanticipated, uncalculated, uncertain, unexpected, unforeseen, unintended, unintentional, unlooked-for, unplanned, unpremeditated, unwitting.
antonyms intentional, premeditated.

accidentally *adv.* adventitiously, bechance, by accident, by chance, by mistake, casually, fortuitously, haphazardly, inadvertently, incidentally, involuntarily, randomly, serendipitously, unconsciously, undesignedly, unexpectedly, unintentionally, unwittingly.
antonym intentionally.

acclaim *v.* announce, applaud, approve, celebrate, cheer, clap, commend, crown, declare, eulogise, exalt, extol, hail, honour, laud, praise, salute, welcome.
antonym demean.
n. acclamation, applause, approbation, approval, celebration, cheering, clapping, commendation, eulogising, eulogy, exaltation, honour, laudation, ovation, plaudits, praise, welcome.
antonyms brickbats, criticism, vituperation.

acclamation *n.* acclaim, adulation, applause,

approbation, bravos, cheer, cheering, cheers, commendation, declaration, éclat, endorsement, enthusiasm, extolment, homage, laudation, ovation, paean, panegyric, plaudit, praise, salutation, shouting, tribute.
antonym disapproval.

acclimatise *v.* accommodate, acculturate, accustom, adapt, adjust, attune, conform, familiarise, find one's legs, get used to, habituate, inure, naturalise.

acclivity *n.* ascent, gradient, hill, rise, rising ground, slope.

accolade *n.* award, honour, kudos, laurels, praise.

accommodate *v.* acclimatise, accustom, adapt, adjust, afford, aid, assist, attune, billet, board, cater for, comply, compose, conform, domicile, entertain, fit, furnish, harbour, harmonise, help, house, lodge, modify, oblige, provide, put up, quarter, reconcile, serve, settle, shelter, supply.

accommodating *adj.* complaisant, considerate, co-operative, friendly, helpful, hospitable, indulgent, kind, obliging, polite, sympathetic, unselfish, willing.
antonym disobliging.

accommodation[1] *n.* adaptation, adjustment, assistance, compliance, composition, compromise, conformity, fitting, harmonisation, harmony, help, modification, reconciliation, settlement.

accommodation[2] *n.* bed and breakfast, billet, board, digs, domicile, dwelling, harbouring, house, housing, lodgings, quartering, quarters, residence, shelter, sheltering.

accompaniment *n.* accessory, attendance, background, back-up, complement, concomitant, obligato, support, vamp.

accompany *v.* attend, belong to, chaperon, co-exist, coincide, complement, conduct, consort, convoy, escort, follow, go with, occur with, squire, supplement, usher.

accompanying *adj.* accessory, added, additional, appended, associate, associated, attached, attendant, background, complementary, concomitant, concurrent, connected, fellow, joint, related, subsidiary, supplemental, supplementary.

accomplice *n.* abettor, accessory, ally, assistant, associate, coadjutor, collaborator, colleague, confederate, conspirator, helper, helpmate, henchman, mate, particeps criminis, participator, partner, practisant.

accomplish *v.* achieve, attain, bring about, bring off, carry out, compass, complete, conclude, consummate, discharge, do, effect, effectuate, engineer, execute, finish, fulfil, manage, obtain, perform, produce, realise.

accomplished *adj.* adept, adroit, consummate, cultivated, expert, facile, gifted, masterly, polished, practised, professional, proficient, skilful, skilled, talented.
antonym inexpert.

accomplishment *n.* ability, achievement, act, aptitude, art, attainment, capability, carrying out, completion, conclusion, consummation, coup, deed, discharge, doing, effecting, execution, exploit, faculty, feat, finishing, forte, fruition, fulfilment, futurition, gift, management, perfection, performance, production, proficiency, realisation, skill, stroke, talent, triumph.

accord *v.* agree, allow, assent, bestow, concede, concur, confer, conform, correspond, endow, fit, give, grant, harmonise, jibe, match, present, render, suit, tally, tender, vouchsafe. *antonym* disagree.

n. accordance, agreement, assent, concert, concurrence, conformity, congruence, congruity, consort, correspondence, harmony, rapport, symmetry, sympathy, unanimity, unity. *antonym* discord.

accordance *n.* accord, agreement, assent, concert, concurrence, conformity, congruence, consistency, consonance, correspondence, harmony, rapport, sympathy, unanimity.

accordingly *adv.* appropriately, as a result, as requested, consequently, correspondingly, ergo, fitly, hence, in accord with, in accordance, in consequence, properly, so, suitably, therefore, thus.

according to after, after the manner of, agreeably to, commensurate with, consistent with, in accordance with, in compliance with, in conformity with, in keeping with, in line with, in obedience to, in proportion, in relation, in the light of, in the manner of, obedient to.

accost *v.* address, approach, button-hole, confront, detain, greet, hail, halt, importune, salute, solicit, stop, waylay.

account[1] *n.* advantage, basis, battels, benefit, cause, chronicle, communiqué, concern, consequence, consideration, description, detail, distinction, esteem, estimation, explanation, ground, grounds, history, honour, import, importance, interest, memoir, merit, motive, narration, narrative, note, performance, portrayal, presentation, profit, rank, reason, recital, record, regard, relation, report, reputation, repute, sake, score, significance, sketch, standing, statement, story, tale, use, value, version, worth, write-up.

v. adjudge, appraise, assess, believe, consider, count, deem, esteem, estimate, explain, gauge, hold, judge, rate, reckon, regard, think, value, weigh.

account for answer for, clarify, clear up, destroy, elucidate, explain, illuminate, incapacitate, justify, kill, put paid to, rationalise, vindicate.

account[2] *n.* balance, battels, bill, book, books, charge, check, computation, inventory, invoice, ledger, reckoning, register, score, statement, tab, tally, tick.

accountability *n.* amenability, answerability, blamableness, blameworthiness, chargeability, liability, responsibility.

accountable *adj.* amenable, answerable, blamable, bound, charged with, liable, obligated, obliged, responsible.

accoutrements *n.* adornments, apparel, appurtenances, array, attire, caparison, clothes, clothing, decorations, dress, equipage, equipment, fittings, fixtures, furnishings, garb, gear, habiliments, kit, ornamentation, outfit, paraphernalia, tackle, trappings, traps, trimmings.

accredit *v.* appoint, approve, ascribe, assign, attribute, authorise, certificate, certify, commission, credit, depute, empower, enable, endorse, entrust, guarantee, license, okay, qualify, recognise, sanction, vouch for.

accredited *adj.* appointed, approved, attested, authorised, certificated, certified, commissioned, deputed, deputised, empowered, endorsed, guaranteed, licensed, official, qualified, recognised, sanctioned, vouched for. *antonym* unauthorised.

accretion *n.* accession, accrual, accumulation, addition, amplification, augmentation, coherence, cohesion, enlargement, fusion, growth, increase, increment, supplement. *antonyms* decrease, deduction.

accrue *v.* accumulate, amass, arise, be added, build up, collect, emanate, enlarge, ensue, fall due, flow, follow, gather, grow, increase, issue, proceed, redound, result, spring up.

accumulate *v.* accrue, agglomerate, aggregate, amass, assemble, build up, collect, cumulate, gather, grow, hoard, increase, multiply, pile up, stash, stockpile, store. *antonyms* diffuse, disseminate.

accumulation *n.* accretion, aggregation, assemblage, augmentation, backlog, build-up, collection, conglomeration, gathering, growth, heap, hoard, increase, mass, pile, reserve, stack, stock, stockpile, store.

accuracy *n.* accurateness, actuality, authenticity, carefulness, closeness, correctness, exactitude, exactness, faithfulness, faultlessness, fidelity, meticulousness, minuteness, niceness, nicety, precision, rigorousness, scrupulosity, scrupulousness, strictness, truth, truthfulness, veracity, veridicality, verity. *antonym* inaccuracy.

accurate *adj.* authentic, careful, close, correct, exact, factual, faithful, faultless, just, letter-perfect, mathematical, meticulous, minute, nice, perfect, precise, proper, regular, right, rigorous, scrupulous, sound, spot-on, strict, true, truthful, unerring, veracious, veridical, well-aimed, well-directed, well-judged, word-perfect. *antonyms* inaccurate, wrong.

accursed *adj.* abominable, anathematised, bedevilled, bewitched, blighted, condemned, cursed, damned, despicable, detestable, doomed, execrable, foredoomed, hateful, hellish, hopeless, horrible, ill-fated, ill-omened, jinxed, luckless, maledict, ruined, star-crossed, undone, unfortunate, unholy, unlucky, wretched. *antonym* blessed.

accusation *n.* accusal, allegation, arraignment, attribution, charge, citation, complaint, crimination, delation, denunciation, gravamen, impeachment, imputation, incrimination, indictment, plaint, recrimination, threap.

accuse *v.* allege, arraign, attaint, attribute, blame, censure, charge, cite, criminate, delate, denounce, impeach, impugn, impute, incriminate, indict, inform against, recriminate, tax.

accustom *v.* acclimatise, acculturate, acquaint, adapt, adjust, discipline, exercise, familiarise, habituate, harden, inure, season, train.

accustomed *adj.* acclimatised, acquainted, adapted, common, confirmed, consuetudinary, conventional, customary, disciplined, established, everyday, exercised, expected, familiar, familiarised, fixed, general, given to, habitual, habituated, in the habit of, inured, normal, ordinary, prevailing, regular, routine, seasoned, set, traditional, trained, used, usual, wonted.
antonym unaccustomed.

ace *n.* adept, champion, dab hand, dabster, expert, genius, maestro, master, nonpareil, star, talent, virtuoso, winner, wizard.
antonyms colt, novice.
adj. brilliant, champion, excellent, expert, fine, first-class, great, masterly, matchless, nonpareil, outstanding, superb, superlative, tiptop, virtuoso.

acerbic *adj.* abrasive, acid, acidulous, acrid, acrimonious, astringent, bitter, brusque, caustic, churlish, corrosive, harsh, incisive, mordant, nasty, rancorous, rude, severe, sharp, sour, stern, tart, trenchant, unfriendly, unkind.
antonym mild.

acerbity *n.* acidity, acidulousness, acridity, acridness, acrimoniousness, acrimony, asperity, astringency, bitterness, brusqueness, causticity, churlishness, harshness, mordacity, mordancy, nastiness, rancour, rudeness, severity, sharpness, sourness, sternness, tartness, trenchancy, unfriendliness, unkindness.
antonym mildness.

ache *v.* agonise, covet, crave, desire, grieve, hanker, hunger, hurt, itch, long, mourn, need, pain, pine, pound, rack, smart, sorrow, suffer, throb, twinge, yearn.
n. anguish, craving, desire, grief, hankering, hunger, hurt, itch, longing, misery, mourning, need, pain, pang, pining, pounding, smart, smarting, soreness, sorrow, suffering, throb, throbbing, yearning.

achieve *v.* accomplish, acquire, attain, bring about, carry out, compass, complete, consummate, do, earn, effect, effectuate, execute, finish, fulfil, gain, get, manage, obtain, perform, procure, produce, reach, realise, score, strike, succeed, win.
antonyms fail, miss.

achievement *n.* accomplishment, acquirement, act, attainment, completion, deed, effort, execution, exploit, feat, fruition, fulfilment,

magnum opus, performance, production, qualification, realisation, stroke, success.

achiever *n.* doer, goer, go-getter, performer, succeeder.

acid *adj.* acerbic, acidulous, acrid, astringent, biting, bitter, caustic, corrosive, cutting, harsh, hurtful, ill-natured, incisive, mordant, morose, pungent, sharp, sour, stinging, tart, trenchant, vinegarish, vinegary, vitriolic.

acid test experimentum crucis, proof of the pudding.

acidity *n.* acerbity, acidulousness, acridity, acridness, asperity, astringency, bitterness, causticity, causticness, corrosiveness, harshness, hurtfulness, incisiveness, mordancy, pungency, sharpness, sourness, tartness, trenchancy, vinegariness, vinegarishness.

acidulous *adj.* acerbic, acid, astringent, biting, bitter, caustic, cutting, harsh, incisive, pungent, sharp, sour, tart, vinegarish, vinegary.
antonyms saccharine, sugary, sweet.

acknowledge *v.* accede, accept, acquiesce, address, admit, affirm, agnise, allow, answer, attest, avouch, concede, confess, confirm, declare, endorse, grant, greet, hail, notice, own, profess, react to, recognise, reply to, respond to, return, salute, vouch for, witness, yield.

acknowledged *adj.* accepted, accredited, admitted, affirmed, answered, approved, attested, avowed, conceded, confessed, declared, endorsed, professed, recognised, returned.

acknowledgement *n.* acceptance, accession, acquiescence, addressing, admission, affirmation, allowing, answer, appreciation, confession, credit, declaration, endorsement, gratitude, greeting, hail, hailing, honour, notice, profession, reaction, realisation, recognition, recompense, reply, response, return, salutation, salute, thanks, tribute, yielding.

acme *n.* apex, apogee, climax, crest, crown, culmination, height, high point, maximum, optimum, peak, pinnacle, sublimation, sublimity, summit, top, vertex, zenith.
antonym nadir.

acolyte *n.* acolyth, adherent, admirer, altar boy, assistant, attendant, follower, helper, lackey, slave.

acoustic *adj.* audile, auditory, aural.

acquaint *v.* accustom, advise, announce, apprise, brief, disclose, divulge, enlighten, familiarise, inform, notify, reveal, tell.

acquaintance *n.* associate, association, awareness, chum, cognisance, colleague, companionship, confrère, consociate, contact, conversance, conversancy, experience, familiarity, fellowship, intimacy, knowledge, relationship, understanding.

acquainted *adj.* abreast, conversant, familiar, in the know, informed.

acquiesce *v.* accede, accept, agree, allow, approve, assent, comply, concur, conform, consent, defer, give in, submit, yield.
antonyms disagree, object.

acquiescence *n.* acceptance, accession, agreement, approval, assent, compliance, concurrence, conformity, consent, deference, giving in, obedience, sanction, submission, yielding.
antonyms disagreement, rebelliousness.

acquiescent *adj.* acceding, accepting, agreeable, amenable, approving, assenting, biddable, complaisant, compliant, concurrent, conforming, consenting, obedient, submissive, yielding.

acquire *v.* achieve, amass, appropriate, attain, buy, collect, cop, earn, gain, gather, get, net, obtain, pick up, procure, realise, receive, secure, win.
antonyms forfeit, forgo, relinquish.

acquirements *n.* accomplishments, achievements, acquisitions, attainments, attributes, culture, erudition, knowledge, learning, mastery, qualifications, skills.

acquisition *n.* accession, achievement, acquest, acquirement, appropriation, attainment, buy, gain, gaining, learning, obtainment, possession, prize, procurement, property, purchase, pursuit, securing, take-over.

acquisitive *adj.* avaricious, avid, covetous, grabbing, grasping, greedy, insatiable, mercenary, possessive, predatory, rapacious, voracious.
antonym generous.

acquisitiveness *n.* avarice, avidity, avidness, covetousness, graspingness, greed, predatoriness, rapaciousness, rapacity, voracity.

acquit *v.* absolve, bear, behave, clear, comport, conduct, deliver, discharge, dismiss, exculpate, excuse, exonerate, free, fulfil, liberate, pay, pay off, perform, release, relieve, repay, reprieve, satisfy, settle, vindicate.
antonym convict.

acquittal *n.* absolution, clearance, compurgation, deliverance, discharge, dismissal, dispensation, exculpation, excusing, exoneration, freeing, liberation, release, relief, reprieve, vindication.
antonym conviction.

acquittance *n.* discharge, dispensation, payment, quittance, release, satisfaction, settlement.

acrid *adj.* acerbic, acid, acrimonious, astringent, biting, bitter, burning, caustic, cutting, empyreumatic, harsh, incisive, irritating, malicious, mordant, nasty, pungent, sarcastic, sardonic, sharp, stinging, trenchant, venomous, virulent, vitriolic.

acridity *n.* acidity, acrimoniousness, acrimony, astringency, bitterness, causticity, empyreuma, harshness, mordancy, sharpness, trenchancy.

acrimonious *adj.* abusive, acerbic, astringent, atrabilious, biting, bitter, caustic, censorious, churlish, crabbed, cutting, ill-tempered, irascible, mordant, peevish, petulant, pungent, rancorous, sarcastic, severe, sharp, spiteful, splenetic, tart, testy, trenchant, virulent, waspish.

antonyms irenic, kindly, peaceable.

acrimony *n.* acerbity, asperity, astringency, bitterness, churlishness, gall, harshness, ill-temper, ill-will, irascibility, mordancy, peevishness, petulance, rancour, resentment, sarcasm, spleen, tartness, trenchancy, virulence, waspishness.

acrobat *n.* aerialist, balancer, contortionist, equilibrist, funambulist, gymnast, somersaulter, stunt-girl, stuntman, tumbler, voltigeur.

act *n.* accomplishment, achievement, action, affectation, attitude, bill, blow, counterfeit, decree, deed, dissimulation, doing, edict, enactment, enterprise, execution, exertion, exploit, fake, feat, feigning, front, gest, gig, law, make-believe, manoeuvre, measure, move, operation, ordinance, performance, pose, posture, pretence, proceeding, resolution, routine, sham, show, sketch, spiel, stance, statute, step, stroke, transaction, turn, undertaking.
v. acquit, act out, affect, assume, bear, behave, carry, carry out, characterise, comport, conduct, counterfeit, dissimulate, do, enact, execute, exert, feign, function, go about, imitate, impersonate, make, mime, mimic, move, operate, perform, personate, personify, play, portray, pose, posture, pretend, put on, react, represent, seem, serve, sham, simulate, strike, take effect, undertake, work.

act up carry on, cause trouble, give bother, give trouble, horse around, make waves, malfunction, mess about, misbehave, muck about, play up, rock the boat.

act (up)on affect, alter, carry out, change, comply with, conform to, execute, follow, fulfil, heed, influence, modify, obey, sway, transform, yield to.

acting *adj.* interim, pro tem, provisional, reserve, stand-by, stop-gap, substitute, supply, surrogate, temporary.
n. affectation, assuming, bluff, characterisation, counterfeiting, dissimulation, dramatics, enacting, feigning, histrionicism, histrionics, histrionism, imitating, imitation, impersonation, imposture, melodrama, performance, performing, play-acting, playing, portrayal, portraying, posing, posturing, pretence, pretending, putting on, seeming, shamming, stagecraft, theatre, theatricals.

action *n.* accomplishment, achievement, act, activity, affray, agency, battle, case, cause, clash, combat, conflict, contest, deed, effect, effort, encounter, endeavour, energy, engagement, enterprise, exercise, exertion, exploit, feat, fight, fighting, force, fray, functioning, influence, lawsuit, litigation, liveliness, mechanism, motion, move, movement, operation, performance, power, proceeding, process, prosecution, skirmish, sortie, spirit, stop, stroke, suit, undertaking, vigour, vim, vitality, warfare, work, working, works.

actions *n.* address, air, bearing, behaviour, comportment, conduct, demeanour, deportment, manners, mein, port, ways.

activate *v.* actuate, animate, arouse, bestir, energise, excite, fire, galvanise, impel, initiate, mobilise, motivate, move, prompt, propel, rouse, set in motion, set off, start, stimulate, stir, switch on, trigger. *antonyms* arrest, deactivate, stop.

active *adj.* acting, activist, aggressive, agile, alert, ambitious, animated, assertive, assiduous, astir, bustling, busy, committed, deedy, devoted, diligent, doing, effectual, energetic, engaged, enterprising, enthusiastic, forceful, forward, full, functioning, hardworking, in force, in operation, industrious, involved, light-footed, live, lively, militant, moving, nimble, occupied, on the go, on the move, operate, quick, running, sedulous, spirited, sprightly, spry, stirabout, stirring, strenuous, through-going, vibrant, vigorous, vital, vivacious, working, zealous. *antonyms* dormant, inactive, inert, passive.

activity *n.* act, action, activeness, animation, avocation, bustle, commotion, deed, endeavour, enterprise, exercise, exertion, hobby, hurly-burly, hustle, industry, interest, job, kerfuffle, labour, life, liveliness, motion, movement, occupation, pastime, project, pursuit, scheme, stir, task, undertaking, venture, work.

actor *n.* actress, agent, artist, comedian, doer, executor, factor, functionary, guiser, ham, hamfatter, histrio, histrion, impersonator, masquerader, mime, mummer, operative, operator, participant, participator, performer, perpetrator, personator, play-actor, player, practitioner, Roscius, Thespian, tragedian, trouper, worker.

actual *adj.* absolute, authentic, bona fide, categorical, certain, concrete, confirmed, corporeal, current, de facto, definite, existent, extant, factual, genuine, indisputable, indubitable, legitimate, live, living, material, physical, positive, present, present-day, prevailing, real, realistic, substantial, tangible, thingy, true, truthful, unquestionable, verified, veritable. *antonyms* apparent, imaginary, theoretical.

actuality *n.* corporeality, fact, factuality, historicity, materiality, reality, realness, substance, substantiality, truth, verity.

actually *adv.* absolutely, as a matter of fact, de facto, essentially, in fact, in reality, in truth, indeed, literally, really, truly, verily, veritably.

actuate *v.* activate, animate, arouse, cause, circulate, dispose, drive, excite, impel, incite, induce, influence, inspire, instigate, lead, mobilise, motivate, move, prod, prompt, propel, quicken, rouse, spur, stimulate, stir, urge.

acumen *n.* acuteness, astuteness, cleverness, discernment, discrimination, gumption, ingenuity, insight, intelligence, intuition,

judgement, judiciousness, keenness, penetration, perception, perceptiveness, percipience, perspicacity, perspicuity, quickness, sagacity, sapience, sharpness, shrewdness, smartness, wisdom, wit. *antonym* obtuseness.

acute[1] *adj.* astute, canny, clever, critical, crucial, cutting, dangerous, decisive, discerning, discriminating, distressing, essential, excruciating, exquisite, extreme, fierce, grave, important, incisive, ingenious, insightful, intense, intuitive, judicious, keen, lancinating, observant, overpowering, overwhelming, penetrating, perceptive, percipient, perspicacious, piercing, poignant, pointed, powerful, racking, sagacious, sapient, sensitive, serious, severe, sharp, shooting, shrewd, shrill, smart, stabbing, subtle, sudden, urgent, violent, vital. *antonyms* chronic, mild, obtuse.

acute[2] *adj.* acicular, apiculate, cuspate, cuspidate, needle-shaped, peaked, pointed, sharp, sharpened. *antonym* obtuse.

acuteness *n.* acuity, astuteness, canniness, cleverness, criticality, danger, dangerousness, discernment, discrimination, fierceness, gravity, importance, ingenuity, insight, intensity, intuition, intuitiveness, keenness, perception, perceptiveness, percipience, perspicacity, poignancy, powerfulness, sagacity, sapience, sensitivity, seriousness, severity, sharpness, shrewdness, shrillness, smartness, subtlety, suddenness, urgency, violence, wit.

adage *n.* aphorism, apophthegm, axiom, byword, dictum, gnome, maxim, motto, paroemia, precept, proverb, saw, saying, sentence.

adamant *adj.* adamantine, determined, firm, fixed, flinty, hard, immovable, impenetrable, indestructible, inexorable, inflexible, infrangible, insistent, intransigent, obdurate, resolute, rigid, rock-like, rocky, set, steely, stiff, stony, stubborn, tough, unbending, unbreakable, uncompromising, unrelenting, unshakable, unyielding. *antonyms* flexible, pliant, yielding.

adapt *v.* acclimatise, accommodate, adjust, alter, apply, attemper, change, comply, conform, contemper, convert, customise, familiarise, fashion, fit, habituate, harmonise, match, metamorphose, modify, prepare, proportion, qualify, refashion, remodel, shape, suit, tailor.

adaptable *adj.* adjustable, alterable, amenable, changeable, compliant, conformable, convertible, easy-going, flexible, malleable, modifiable, plastic, pliant, resilient, tractable, variable, versatile. *antonyms* inflexible, refractory.

adaptation *n.* acclimatisation, accommodation, accustomedness, adaption, adjustment, alteration, change, conversion, familiarisation, habituation, modification, naturalisation, refashioning, refitting, remodelling, reshaping, reworking, shift, transformation, variation, version.

add *v.* adjoin, affix, amplify, annex, append, attach, augment, combine, compute, count, include, join, reckon, subjoin, sum up, superimpose, supplement, tack on, tot up, total.
antonym subtract.

add up add, amount, be consistent, be plausible, be reasonable, come to, compute, count, count up, hang together, hold water, imply, indicate, make sense, mean, reckon, reveal, ring true, signify, stand to reason, sum up, tally, tot up, total.

added *adj.* additional, adjective, adjunct, extra, fresh, further, increased, new, supplementary.

addendum *n.* addition, adjunct, affix, allonge, appendage, appendix, attachment, augmentation, codicil, endorsement, epilogue, extension, extra, postscript, supplement.

addict *n.* acid-head, adherent, buff, devotee, dope-fiend, enthusiast, fan, fiend, follower, freak, head, hop-head, junkie, mainliner, nut, pot-head, tripper, user.

addicted *adj.* absorbed, accustomed, dedicated, dependent, devoted, disposed, enslaved, fond, habituated, hooked, inclined, obsessed, prone, spaced out.

addiction *n.* a monkey on one's back, craving, dependence, enslavement, habit, monkey, obsession.

addition *n.* accession, accessory, accretion, addend, addendum, adding, additament, additive, adjoining, adjunct, adjunction, affix, affixing, amplification, annexation, annexure, appendage, appendix, appurtenance, attachment, augmentation, computation, counting, enlargement, extension, extra, gain, inclusion, increase, increasing, increment, inpouring, reckoning, summation, summing-up, supplement, totalling, totting-up.

additional *adj.* added, additive, adscititious, adventitious, adventive, affixed, appended, excrescent, extra, fresh, further, increased, more, new, other, spare, supplementary.

addled *adj.* bad, bamboozled, befuddled, bewildered, confused, flustered, foolish, gone bad, mixed-up, muddled, off, perplexed, putrid, rancid, rotten, silly, turned, unbalanced.
antonyms clear, fresh.

address[1] *n.* abode, department, direction, domicile, dwelling, home, house, inscription, location, lodging, place, residence, situation, superscription, whereabouts.

address[2] *n.* adroitness, air, allocution, application, art, bearing, declamation, deftness, dexterity, discourse, discretion, dispatch, disquisition, dissertation, expedition, expertise, expertness, facility, harangue, ingenuity, lecture, manner, oration, sermon, skilfulness, skill, speech, tact, talk.
v. accost, address (oneself) to, apostrophise, apply (oneself) to, approach, attend to,

bespeak, button-hole, concentrate on, devote (oneself) to, discourse, engage in, focus on, greet, hail, harangue, invoke, lecture, orate, salute, sermonise, speak, speak to, take care of, talk, talk to, turn to, undertake.

addresses *n.* advances, approaches, attentions, courting, courtship, lovemaking, proposals, wooing.

adept *adj.* able, accomplished, ace, adroit, deft, dexterous, experienced, expert, masterful, masterly, nimble, polished, practised, proficient, skilful, skilled, versed.
antonyms bungling, incompetent, inept.
n. ace, dab hand, dabster, deacon, don, expert, genius, maestro, mahatma, master, old hand, pastmaster, wizard.
antonyms bungler, incompetent.

adequacy *n.* adequateness, capability, commensurateness, competence, competency, efficacy, fairness, fitness, passability, requisiteness, satisfactoriness, serviceability, sufficiency, suitability, tolerability.
antonyms inadequacy, insufficiency.

adequate *adj.* able, acceptable, capable, commensurate, competent, condign, efficacious, enough, fair, fit, passable, presentable, requisite, respectable, satisfactory, serviceable, sufficient, suitable, tolerable.
antonyms inadequate, insufficient.

adhere *v.* abide by, accrete, agree, attach, cement, cleave, cleave to, cling, coalesce, cohere, combine, comply with, fasten, fix, follow, fulfil, glue, heed, hold, hold fast, join, keep, link, maintain, mind, obey, observe, paste, respect, stand by, stick, stick fast, support, unite.

adherent *n.* admirer, advocate, aficionado, devotee, disciple, enthusiast, fan, follower, freak, hanger-on, henchman, nut, partisan, satellite, sectary, supporter, upholder, votary.

adhering *adj.* adherent, clinging, coalescent, cohering, cohesive, holding, osculant, tenacious.

adhesion *n.* adherence, adhesiveness, allegiance, attachment, bond, coherence, cohesion, constancy, devotion, faithfulness, fidelity, fulfilment, grip, heed, holding fast, loyalty, obedience, observation, respect, sticking, support, union.

adhesive *adj.* adherent, adhering, attaching, clinging, cohesive, emplastic, gluey, glutinous, gummy, holding, mucilaginous, sticking, sticky, tacky, tenacious.
n. cement, glue, gum, mountant, mucilage, paste, tape.

adieu *n.* bon voyage, cheerio, congé, departure, farewell, goodbye, leave-taking, parting, valediction, valedictory.

adjacent *adj.* abutting, adjoining, alongside, beside, bordering, close, conterminant, conterminate, conterminous, contiguous, juxtaposed, near, neighbouring, next, proximate, touching, vicinal.

adjoin *v.* abut, add, affix, annex, append, approximate, attach, border, combine, communicate with, connect, couple, impinge, interconnect, join, juxtapose, link, meet, neighbour, touch, unite, verge.

adjoining *adj.* abutting, adjacent, bordering, connecting, contiguous, impinging, interconnecting, joined, juxtaposed, near, neighbouring, next, next door, proximate, touching, verging, vicinal.

adjourn *v.* continue, defer, delay, discontinue, interrupt, postpone, prorogue, put off, recess, stay, suspend.
antonym convene.

adjournment *n.* break, deferment, deferral, delay, discontinuation, dissolution, interruption, pause, postponement, prorogation, putting off, recess, stay, suspension.

adjudicate *v.* adjudge, arbitrate, decide, determine, judge, pronounce, ref, referee, settle, umpire.

adjudication *n.* adjudgement, arbitration, conclusion, decision, determination, finding, judgement, pronouncement, reffing, ruling, settlement, verdict.

adjunct *n.* accessory, addendum, addition, appanage, appendage, appendix, appurtenance, auxiliary, complement, extension, supplement.

adjure *v.* appeal to, beg, beseech, charge, command, conjure, direct, enjoin, entreat, implore, importune, invoke, order, plead with, pray, request, supplicate.

adjust *v.* acclimatise, accommodate, accustom, adapt, alter, arrange, balance, change, coapt, compose, concert, conform, convert, dispose, fine-tune, fit, fix, harmonise, jiggle, measure, modify, order, proportion, reconcile, rectify, redress, refashion, regulate, remodel, reshape, set, settle, shape, square, suit, temper, tune.
antonyms derange, disarrange, upset.

adjustable *adj.* adaptable, alterable, flexible, malleable, modifiable, mouldable, movable, tractable.
antonyms fixed, inflexible.

adjustment *n.* acclimatisation, accommodation, adaptation, alteration, arrangement, arranging, conforming, conversion, fitting, fixing, harmonisation, modification, naturalisation, ordering, orientation, reconciliation, rectification, redress, refashioning, regulation, remodelling, setting, settlement, settling in, shaping, tuning.

ad-lib *v.* extemporise, improvise, invent, make up.
adj. extemporaneous, extempore, extemporised, impromptu, improvised, made up, off-the-cuff, spontaneous, unpremeditated, unprepared, unrehearsed.
antonym prepared.
adv. extemporaneously, extempore, impromptu, impulsively, off the cuff, off the top of one's head, spontaneously.

administer *v.* adhibit, apply, assign, conduct, contribute, control, direct, disburse, dispense, dispose, distribute, dole out, execute, give, govern, head, impose, lead, manage, measure out, mete out, officiate, organise, oversee, perform, preside over, provide, regulate, rule, run, superintend, supervise, supply.

administration *n.* adhibition, administering, application, conduct, control, direction, directorship, disbursement, dispensation, disposal, distribution, execution, executive, governing, governing body, government, leadership, management, ministry, organisation, overseeing, performance, provision, regime, regulation, rule, ruling, running, settlement, superintendence, supervision, supply, term of office.

administrative *adj.* authoritative, directorial, executive, governmental, gubernatorial, legislative, management, managerial, organisational, regulatory, supervisory.

administrator *n.* boss, controller, curator, custodian, director, factor, governor, guardian, leader, manager, organiser, overseer, ruler, superintendent, supervisor, trustee.

admirable *adj.* choice, commendable, creditable, deserving, estimable, excellent, exquisite, fine, laudable, meritorious, praiseworthy, rare, respected, superior, valuable, wonderful, worthy.
antonym despicable.

admiration *n.* adoration, affection, amazement, appreciation, approbation, approval, astonishment, awe, delight, esteem, fureur, idolism, pleasure, praise, regard, respect, reverence, surprise, veneration, wonder, wonderment, worship.
antonym contempt.

admire *v.* adore, applaud, appreciate, approve, esteem, iconise, idolise, laud, praise, prize, respect, revere, value, venerate, worship.
antonym despise.

admirer *n.* adherent, aficionado, beau, boyfriend, devotee, disciple, enthusiast, fan, follower, gallant, idolator, idoliser, lover, partisan, suitor, supporter, sweetheart, votary, wooer, worshipper.
antonyms critic, opponent.

admissible *adj.* acceptable, allowable, allowed, equitable, justifiable, lawful, legitimate, licit, passable, permissible, permitted, tolerable, tolerated.
antonyms illegitimate, inadmissible.

admission *n.* acceptance, access, acknowledgement, adhibition, admittance, admitting, affirmation, allowance, avowal, concession, confession, declaration, disclosure, divulgence, entrance, entrée, entry, exposé, granting, inclusion, ingress, initiation, introduction, owning, profession, revelation.
antonyms denial, exclusion.

admit *v.* accept, acknowledge, adhibit, affirm, agree, allow, allow to enter, avow, concede, confess, declare, disclose, divulge, give access, grant, initiate, introduce, intromit, let, let in, permit, profess, receive, recognise, reveal, take in.

antonyms exclude, gainsay.

admittance *n.* acceptance, access, admitting, allowing, entrance, entrée, entry, ingress, letting in, passage, reception.

admixture *n.* addition, amalgamation, blend, combination, commixture, fusion, intermixture, mingling, tincture, trace.

admonish *v.* advise, berate, caution, censure, check, chide, counsel, enjoin, exhort, forewarn, rebuke, reprehend, reprimand, reproach, reprove, scold, upbraid, warn.

admonition *n.* advice, berating, caution, censure, counsel, pi-jaw, rebuke, reprehension, reprimand, reproach, reproof, scolding, warning.

admonitory *adj.* admonishing, advisory, cautionary, censorious, rebuking, reprimanding, reproachful, reproving, scolding, warning.

ado *n.* agitation, bother, business, bustle, ceremony, commotion, confusion, delay, disturbance, excitement, ferment, flurry, fuss, hassle, hurly-burly, kerfuffle, labour, pother, romage, stir, to-do, trouble, tumult, turmoil. *antonyms* calm, tranquillity.

adolescence *n.* boyhood, boyishness, childishness, development, girlhood, girlishness, immaturity, juvenescence, juvenility, minority, puberty, puerility, teens, transition, youth, youthfulness. *antonym* senescence.

adolescent *adj.* boyish, girlish, growing, immature, juvenescent, juvenile, maturing, puerile, teenage, young, youthful.
n. bobbysoxer, Halbstarker, halfling, juvenile, minor, teenager, youngster, youth.

Adonis *n.* charmer, dish, Ganymede, god, golden boy, good-looker, he-man, idol, knockout, matinee idol.

adopt *v.* accept, affect, appropriate, approve, assume, back, choose, embrace, endorse, espouse, follow, foster, maintain, ratify, sanction, select, support, take in, take on, take up. *antonyms* disown, repudiate.

adoption *n.* acceptance, affectation, approbation, appropriation, approval, assumption, cherishment, choice, embracement, embracing, endorsement, espousal, following, fosterage, fostering, maintenance, ratification, sanction, select, selection, support.

adorable *adj.* appealing, attractive, bewitching, captivating, charming, darling, dear, delightful, enchanting, fetching, lovable, pleasing, precious, winning, winsome. *antonym* hateful.

adoration *n.* admiration, esteem, estimation, exaltation, glorification, honour, idolatry, idolisation, love, magnification, reverence, veneration, worship. *antonyms* abhorrence, detestation.

adore *v.* admire, cherish, dote on, esteem, exalt, glorify, honour, idolatrise, idolise, love, magnify, revere, reverence, venerate, worship. *antonyms* abhor, hate.

adorn *v.* adonise, apparel, array, beautify, bedeck, bedight, bedizen, begem, bejewel, bestick, crown, deck, decorate, dight, doll up, embellish, emblazon, enhance, enrich, furbish, garnish, gild, grace, impearl, miniate, ornament, tart up, trick out, trim.

adornment *n.* accessory, beautification, bedizenment, decorating, decoration, embellishment, falbala, fallal, fallalery, fandangle, figgery, flounce, frill, frippery, furbelow, garnish, garnishry, garniture, gilding, ornament, ornamentation, ornateness, trappings, trimming.

adrift *adj.* aimless, amiss, anchorless, astray, at sea, directionless, goalless, insecure, off course, purposeless, rootless, rudderless, unsettled, wrong. *antonyms* anchored, stable.

adroit *adj.* able, adept, apt, artful, clever, cunning, deft, dexterous, expert, habile, ingenious, masterful, neat, nimble, proficient, quick, resourceful, skilful, skilled, slick. *antonyms* clumsy, inept, maladroit.

adroitness *n.* ability, ableness, address, adeptness, aptness, artfulness, cleverness, cunning, deftness, dexterity, expertise, facility, finesse, ingeniousness, ingenuity, legerdemain, masterfulness, mastery, neatness, nimbleness, proficiency, quickness, resourcefulness, skilfulness, skill. *antonyms* clumsiness, ineptitude.

adulation *n.* blandishment, bootlicking, fawning, flattery, idolatory, idolisation, personality cult, sycophancy, worship. *antonym* abuse.

adulatory *adj.* blandishing, bootlicking, fawning, flattering, fulsome, grovelling, idolatrous, obsequious, praising, servile, slavish, sycophantic, unctuous, worshipping. *antonym* unflattering.

adult *adj.* developed, full-grown, fully grown, grown-up, mature, of age, ripe, ripened. *antonym* immature.

adulterate *v.* attenuate, bastardise, contaminate, corrupt, dash, debase, defile, depreciate, deteriorate, devalue, dilute, doctor, infect, load, pollute, taint, thin, vitiate, water down, weaken. *antonym* refine.

adumbrate *v.* augur, bedim, chart, conceal, darken, delineate, draft, eclipse, forecast, foreshadow, foretell, hint at, indicate, obfuscate, obscure, outline, overshadow, portend, predict, prefigure, presage, prognosticate, prophesy, silhouette, sketch, suggest, trace, veil.

advance *v.* accelerate, adduce, allege, ameliorate, assist, benefit, bring forward, cite, elevate, expedite, facilitate, foster, furnish, further, go ahead, go forward, grow, hasten, improve, increase, lend, move on, multiply, offer, pay beforehand, present, press on, proceed, proffer, profit, progress, promote, prosper, provide, raise, send forward, speed, submit, suggest, supply, thrive, upgrade.

antonyms impede, retard, retreat.

n. advancement, amelioration, betterment, breakthrough, credit, deposit, development, down payment, furtherance, gain, growth, headway, improvement, increase, loan, preferment, prepayment, profit, progress, promotion, retainer, rise, step.
antonym recession.

adj. beforehand, early, foremost, forward, in front, leading, preliminary, prior.

advanced *adj.* ahead, avant-garde, extreme, foremost, forward, forward-looking, higher, imaginative, late, leading, original, precocious, progressive.
antonyms backward, retarded.

advancement *n.* advance, amelioration, betterment, development, forward movement, gain, growth, headway, improvement, maturation, onward movement, preferment, progress, promotion, rise.
antonyms demotion, retardation.

advances *n.* addresses, approach, approaches, attentions, moves, overtures, proposals, proposition.

advantage *n.* account, aid, ascendancy, asset, assistances, avail, benefit, blessing, boon, boot, convenience, dominance, edge, expediency, fruit, gain, good, help, hold, interest, lead, leverage, precedence, preeminence, profit, purchase, service, start, superiority, sway, upper hand, use, usefulness, utility, welfare.
antonyms disadvantage, hindrance.

advantageous *adj.* beneficial, convenient, favourable, furthersome, gainful, helpful, opportune, profitable, propitious, remunerative, rewarding, superior, useful, valuable, worthwhile.
antonym disadvantageous.

advent *n.* accession, appearance, approach, arrival, coming, dawn, entrance, inception, introduction, occurrence, onset, visitation.

adventitious *adj.* accidental, casual, chance, contingent, extraneous, extrinsic, foreign, fortuitous, incidental, non-essential, serendipitous, supervenient, unexpected.
antonyms inherent, intrinsic.

adventure *n.* chance, contingency, enterprise, experience, exploit, gest, hazard, incident, occurrence, risk, speculation, undertaking, venture.

adventurer *n.* cowboy, daredevil, derring-doer, filibuster, fortune-hunter, freebooter, freelancer, gambler, hero, heroine, knight-errant, madcap, mercenary, opportunist, rogue, soldier of fortune, speculator, swashbuckler, traveller, venturer, voyager, wanderer.

adventuress *n.* bloodsucker, gold-digger, harpy, man-eater, seductress, siren, temptress, vamp.

adventurous *adj.* adventuresome, audacious, bold, dangerous, daredevil, daring, dauntless, doughty, enterprising, foolhardy, game, hazardous, headstrong, impetuous, intrepid,

perilous, plucky, rash, reckless, risky, spunky, swashbuckling, temerarious, venturesome.
antonyms cautious, chary, prudent.

adversary *n.* antagonist, assailant, attacker, competitor, contestant, enemy, foe, foeman, opponent, opposer, rival.
antonyms ally, supporter.

adverse *adj.* antagonistic, conflicting, contrary, counter, counter-productive, detrimental, disadvantageous, hostile, hurtful, inauspicious, inexpedient, inimical, injurious, inopportune, negative, noxious, opposing, opposite, reluctant, repugnant, uncongenial, unfavourable, unfortunate, unfriendly, unlucky, unpropitious, untoward, unwilling.
antonyms advantageous, propitious.

adversity *n.* affliction, ambs-ace, bad luck, calamity, catastrophe, contretemps, disaster, distress, hard times, hardship, ill-fortune, ill-luck, mischance, misery, misfortune, mishap, reverse, sorrow, suffering, trial, tribulation, trouble, woe, wretchedness.
antonym prosperity.

advertise *v.* advise, announce, apprise, blazon, broadcast, bruit, declare, display, flaunt, herald, inform, make known, notify, plug, praise, proclaim, promote, promulgate, publicise, publish, puff, push, tout, trumpet.

advertisement *n.* ad, advert, announcement, bill, blurb, circular, commercial, display, handbill, handout, hype, leaflet, notice, placard, plug, poster, promotion, propaganda, propagation, publicity, puff, puffery.

advice *n.* admonition, caution, communication, conseil, counsel, direction, do's and don'ts, guidance, help, information, injunction, instruction, intelligence, memorandum, notice, notification, opinion, recommendation, rede, suggestion, view, warning, wisdom, word.

advisable *adj.* advantageous, appropriate, apt, beneficial, correct, desirable, expedient, fit, fitting, judicious, meet, politic, profitable, proper, prudent, recommended, seemly, sensible, sound, suggested, suitable, wise.
antonyms inadvisable, injudicious.

advise *v.* acquaint, apprise, bethink, caution, commend, counsel, enjoin, forewarn, guide, inform, instruct, make known, notify, recommend, report, suggest, teach, tell, tutor, urge, warn.

adviser *n.* admonitor, aide, authority, coach, confidant, consultant, counsel, counsellor, éminence grise, guide, helper, instructor, lawyer, mentor, monitor, preceptor, right-hand man, solicitor, teacher, therapist, tutor.

advisory *adj.* advising, consultative, consultatory, consulting, counselling, helping, hortatory, recommending.

advocacy *n.* adoption, advancement, backing, campaigning, championing, championship, defence, encouragement, espousal, justification, patronage, pleading, promotion, promulgation, propagation, proposal, recommendation, spokesmanship, support, upholding, urging.

advocate v. adopt, advise, argue for, campaign for, champion, countenance, defend, encourage, endorse, espouse, favour, justify, patronise, plead for, press for, promote, propose, recommend, subscribe to, support, uphold, urge.
antonyms deprecate, disparage, impugn.
n. apologist, apostle, attorney, backer, barrister, campaigner, champion, counsel, counsellor, defender, interceder, intercessor, lawyer, mediator, paraclete, patron, pleader, promoter, proponent, proposer, solicitor, speaker, spokesman, supporter, upholder, vindicator.
antonyms critic, opponent.

aegis n. advocacy, auspices, backing, championship, favour, guardianship, patronage, protection, shelter, sponsorship, support, wing.

aerial adj. aeolian, aery, atmospheric, elevated, ethereal, incorporeal, insubstantial, lofty, unreal.

affability n. accessibility, amiability, amicability, approachability, benevolence, benignity, civility, congeniality, conversableness, cordiality, courtesy, easiness, friendliness, geniality, good humour, good nature, graciousness, kindliness, mildness, obligingness, openness, pleasantness, sociability, suavity, urbanity, warmth.
antonyms coolness, reserve, reticence.

affable adj. agreeable, amiable, amicable, approachable, benevolent, benign, civil, congenial, cordial, courteous, expansive, free, friendly, genial, good-humoured, good-natured, gracious, kindly, mild, obliging, open, pleasant, sociable, suave, urbane, warm.
antonyms cool, reserved, reticent, unfriendly.

affair n. activity, adventure, amour, amourette, business, circumstance, concern, connection, episode, event, happening, incident, interest, intrigue, liaison, matter, occurrence, operation, organisation, party, proceeding, project, question, reception, relationship, responsibility, romance, subject, topic, transaction, undertaking.

affect[1] v. act on, agitate, alter, apply to, attack, bear upon, change, concern, disturb, grieve, grip, impinge upon, impress, influence, interest, involve, melt, modify, move, overcome, penetrate, pertain to, perturb, prevail over, regard, relate to, seize, soften, stir, strike, sway, touch, transform, trouble, upset.

affect[2] v. adopt, aspire to, assume, contrive, counterfeit, fake, feign, imitate, pretend, profess, put on, sham, simulate.

affectation n. act, affectedness, appearance, artificiality, euphuism, façade, fakery, false display, imitation, insincerity, ladyism, mannerism, minanderie, pose, pretence, pretension, pretentiousness, sham, show, simulation, staginess, theatricality, theatricism, unnaturalness.
antonyms artlessness, ingenuousness.

affected[1] adj. afflicted, agitated, altered, changed, concerned, damaged, distressed, gripped, hurt, impaired, impressed, influenced, injured, melted, moved, perturbed, smitten, stimulated, stirred, swayed, touched, troubled, upset.

affected[2] adj. alembicated, artificial, assumed, bogus, chichi, conceited, contrived, counterfeit, debby, euphuistic, fake, feigned, fussy, greenery-yallery, hyperaesthesic, hyperaesthetic, insincere, lah-di-dah, literose, mannered, mincing, minikin, namby-pamby, niminy-piminy, phoney, pompous, precious, pretended, pretentious, put-on, sham, simulated, spurious, stiff, studied, unnatural.
antonyms genuine, natural.

affecting adj. impressive, moving, pathetic, piteous, pitiable, pitiful, poignant, sad, saddening, stirring, touching, troubling.

affection n. amity, attachment, care, desire, devotion, favour, feeling, fondness, friendliness, good will, inclination, kindness, liking, love, partiality, passion, penchant, predilection, predisposition, proclivity, propensity, regard, tenderness, warmth.
antonyms antipathy, dislike.

affectionate adj. amiable, amorous, attached, caring, cordial, devoted, doting, fond, friendly, kind, loving, passionate, responsive, solicitous, tender, warm, warm-hearted.
antonyms cold, undemonstrative.

affiliate v. ally, amalgamate, annex, associate, band together, combine, confederate, conjoin, connect, federate, incorporate, join, merge, syndicate, unite.

affiliation n. alliance, amalgamation, association, coalition, combination, confederation, connection, federation, incorporation, joining, league, merger, merging, relationship, syndication, union.

affinity n. alliance, analogy, attraction, closeness, compatibility, connection, correspondence, fondness, homogeneity, inclination, kinship, leaning, likeness, liking, partiality, predisposition, proclivity, propensity, rapport, relation, relationship, resemblance, similarity, similitude, sympathy.
antonym dissimilarity.

affirm v. assert, asseverate, attest, aver, avouch, avow, certify, confirm, corroborate, declare, depose, endorse, maintain, pronounce, ratify, state, swear, testify, witness.

affirmation n. affirmance, assertion, asseveration, attestation, averment, avouchment, avowal, certification, confirmation, corroboration, declaration, deposition, endorsement, oath, pronouncement, ratification, statement, testimony, witness.

affirmative adj. affirmatory, agreeing, approving, assenting, assertory, asseverative, concurring, confirming, consenting, corroborative, emphatic, positive.
antonyms dissenting, negative.

affix v. add, adjoin, annex, append, assign, attach, attribute, bind, connect, fasten, glue, join, paste, pin on, stick, subjoin, tack, tag.
antonym detach.

afflict *v.* beset, burden, distress, grieve, harass, harm, harrow, hurt, oppress, pain, plague, rack, smite, strike, torment, torture, trouble, try, visit, wound, wring.
antonyms comfort, solace.

affliction *n.* adversity, calamity, cross, curse, depression, disaster, disease, distress, grief, hardship, illness, misery, misfortune, ordeal, pain, plague, scourge, sickness, sorrow, suffering, torment, trial, tribulation, trouble, visitation, woe, wretchedness.
antonyms comfort, consolation, solace.

affluence *n.* abundance, exuberance, fortune, opulence, plenty, profusion, property, prosperity, riches, substance, wealth, wealthiness.
antonym poverty.

affluent *adj.* comfortable, flourishing, flush, loaded, moneyed, opulent, pecunious, prosperous, rich, wealthy, well-heeled, well-off, well-to-do.
antonyms impecunious, impoverished, poor.

afford *v.* bear, bestow, cope with, engender, furnish, generate, give, grant, impart, manage, offer, produce, provide, render, spare, stand, supply, sustain, yield.

affray *n.* brawl, brush, contest, disturbance, dogfight, Donnybrook, encounter, feud, fight, fisticuffs, fracas, fray, free-for-all, mêlée, quarrel, riot, row, scrap, scrimmage, scuffle, set-to, skirmish, squabble, tussle, wrangle.

affront *v.* abuse, anger, annoy, displease, gall, incense, insult, irritate, nettle, offend, outrage, pique, provoke, slight, snub, vex.
antonyms appease, compliment.
n. abuse, discourtesy, disrespect, facer, indignity, injury, insult, offence, outrage, provocation, rudeness, slap in the face, slight, slur, snub, vexation, wrong.
antonym compliment.

afoot *adv.* about, abroad, afloat, agate, astir, brewing, circulating, current, going about, in preparation, in progress, in the air, in the wind, up.

afraid *adj.* aghast, alarmed, anxious, apprehensive, cowardly, diffident, distrustful, faint-hearted, fearful, frightened, intimidated, nervous, regretful, reluctant, scared, sorry, suspicious, timid, timorous, tremulous, unhappy.
antonyms confident, unafraid.

afresh *adv.* again, anew, da capo, de integro, de novo, newly, once again, once more, over again.

after *adv.* afterwards, as a result of, behind, below, following, in consequence of, later, post, subsequent to, subsequently, succeeding, thereafter.
antonym before.

aftermath *n.* afterclap, after-effects, backwash, consequences, effects, end, fall-out, lattermath, outcome, repercussion, results, rowen, upshot, wake.

afternoon *n.* mid-life, pip-emma, pm, post meridiem, siesta.

again *adv.* afresh, also, anew, another time, au contraire, besides, bis, conversely, da capo, de integro, de novo, ditto, encore, furthermore, in addition, moreover, on the contrary, on the other hand, once more.

against *prep.* abutting, across, adjacent to, athwart, close up to, confronting, contra, counter to, facing, fronting, hostile to, in contact with, in contrast to, in defiance of, in exchange for, in opposition to, in the face of, on, opposed to, opposing, opposite to, resisting, touching, versus.
antonyms for, pro.

age *n.* (a)eon, agedness, anility, caducity, date, day, days, decline, decrepitude, dotage, duration, eld, elderliness, epoch, era, generation, lifetime, majority, maturity, old age, period, senescence, senility, seniority, span, the sere and yellow, time, years.
antonyms salad days, youth.
v. decline, degenerate, deteriorate, grow old, mature, mellow, obsolesce, ripen, season.

aged *adj.* advanced, age-old, ancient, antiquated, antique, decrepit, elderly, geriatric, grey, hoary, old, patriarchal, senescent, sere, superannuated, time-worn, venerable, worn-out.
antonyms young, youthful.

agency *n.* action, activity, bureau, business, department, effect, effectuation, efficiency, finger, force, handling, influence, instrumentality, intercession, intervention, means, mechanism, mediation, medium, office, offices, operation, organisation, power, work, workings.

agenda *n.* calendar, diary, list, menu, plan, programme, schedule, timetable.

agent *n.* actor, agency, author, cause, channel, delegate, deputy, doer, emissary, envoy, executor, factor, force, functionary, go-between, instrument, intermediary, legate, means, middleman, mover, negotiator, operative, operator, organ, performer, power, practisant, rep, representative, substitute, surrogate, vehicle, vicar, worker.

ages *n.* (a)eons, centuries, decades, donkey's years, years, yonks.

aggrandise *v.* advance, amplify, augment, dignify, elevate, enhance, enlarge, ennoble, enrich, exaggerate, exalt, glamorise, glorify, increase, inflate, magnify, promote, upgrade, widen.
antonyms belittle, debase.

aggravate *v.* annoy, exacerbate, exaggerate, exasperate, harass, hassle, heighten, incense, increase, inflame, intensify, irk, irritate, magnify, needle, nettle, peeve, pester, provoke, tease, vex, worsen.
antonyms alleviate, appease, mollify.

aggravation *n.* annoyance, bore, drag, exacerbation, exacerbescence, exaggeration, exasperation, hassle, heightening, increase, inflammation, intensification, irksomeness, irritant, irritation, magnification,

18

provocation, teasing, thorn in the flesh, vexation, worsening.

aggregate *n.* accumulation, agglomeration, aggregation, amount, assemblage, body, bulk, collection, combination, entirety, generality, heap, herd, lump, mass, mixture, pile, sum, throng, total, totality, whole.
adj. accumulated, added, assembled, collected, collective, combined, complete, composite, corporate, cumulative, mixed, total, united.
antonyms individual, particular.
v. accumulate, add up, agglomerate, amass, amount to, assemble, cluster, collect, combine, conglomerate, heap, mix, pile, total.

aggregation *n.* accumulation, agglomeration, amassment, asemblage, cluster, collection, combination, congeries, conglomeration, heap, mass, pile, stack.

aggression *n.* aggressiveness, antagonism, assault, attack, bellicosity, belligerence, combativeness, destructiveness, encroachment, hostility, impingement, incursion, injury, intrusion, invasion, jingoism, militancy, offence, offensive, onslaught, provocation, pugnacity, raid.

aggressive *adj.* argumentative, assertive, bellicose, belligerent, bold, butch, combative, contentious, destructive, disputatious, dynamic, energetic, enterprising, forceful, go-ahead, hostile, intrusive, invasive, jingoistic, militant, offensive, provocative, pugnacious, pushful, pushing, pushy, quarrelsome, scrappy, vigorous, zealous.
antonyms peaceable, submissive.

aggressor *n.* assailant, assaulter, attacker, intruder, invader, offender, provoker.
antonym victim.

aggrieved *adj.* afflicted, affronted, distressed, disturbed, harmed, hurt, ill-used, injured, insulted, maltreated, offended, pained, peeved, saddened, unhappy, woeful, wronged.
antonym pleased.

aghast *adj.* afraid, amazed, appalled, astonished, astounded, awestruck, confounded, dismayed, frightened, horrified, horror-struck, shocked, startled, stunned, stupefied, terrified, thunder-struck.

agile *adj.* active, acute, adroit, alert, brisk, clever, fleet, flexible, limber, lissome, lithe, lively, mobile, nimble, prompt, quick, quick-witted, sharp, sprightly, spry, supple, swift, withy.
antonyms clumsy, stiff, torpid.

agility *n.* activity, acuteness, adroitness, alertness, briskness, cleverness, flexibility, lissomeness, litheness, liveliness, mobility, nimbleness, promptitude, promptness, quickness, quick-wittedness, sharpness, sprightliness, spryness, suppleness, swiftness.
antonyms sluggishness, stiffness, torpidity.

aging *adj.* elderly, gerontic, obsolescent, senescent.

agitate *v.* alarm, arouse, beat, churn, confuse, convulse, discompose, disconcert, disquiet, distract, disturb, excite, ferment, flurry, fluster, incite, inflame, perturb, rattle, rock, rouse, ruffle, shake, stimulate, stir, toss, trouble, unnerve, unsettle, upset, work up, worry.
antonyms calm, tranquillise.

agitated *adj.* anxious, discomposed, distracted, feverish, flurried, flustered, in a lather, insecure, jumpy, nervous, perturbed, restive, restless, ruffled, tumultuous, twitchy, uneasy, unnerved, unsettled, upset, wrought-up.
antonyms calm, composed.

agitation *n.* agitprop, alarm, anxiety, arousal, churning, clamour, commotion, confusion, controversy, convulsion, discomposure, disquiet, distraction, disturbance, doodah, ebullition, excitement, ferment, flurry, fluster, fomentation, hassle, incitement, inflammation, outcry, rocking, shake, shaking, solicitude, stimulation, stir, stirring, tail-spin, taking, tizz(y), tossing, trepidation, trouble, tumult, turbulence, turmoil, uneasiness, unrest, upset, welter, worry.
antonyms calm, tranquillity.

agitator *n.* agent provocateur, bell-wether, demagogue, firebrand, fomenter, inciter, instigator, mob orator, rabble-rouser, revolutionary, soap-box orator, stirrer, troublemaker, tub-thumper.

agog *adj.* avid, breathless, curious, desirous, eager, enthralled, enthusiastic, excited, expectant, impatient, in suspense, keen, on tenterhooks.
antonyms incurious, laid-back.

agonise *v.* afflict, anguish, bleed, distress, excruciate, harrow, labour, pain, rack, strain, strive, struggle, suffer, toil, torment, torture, trouble, worry, wrestle, writhe.

agony *n.* affliction, anguish, distress, misery, pain, pangs, paroxysm, spasm, suffering, throes, torment, torture, tribulation, woe, wretchedness.

agrarian *adj.* agricultural, agronomic, farming, geoponic, georgic, praedial.

agree *v.* accede, accord, acquiesce, admit, allow, answer, assent, chime, coincide, comply, concede, concord, concur, conform, consent, consort, contract, correspond, cotton, covenant, engage, fadge, fit, fix, get on, grant, harmonise, homologate, jibe, match, permit, promise, see eye to eye, settle, side with, square, suit, tally, yield.
antonyms conflict, disagree.

agreeable *adj.* acceptable, acquiescent, amenable, amicable, appropriate, approving, attractive, befitting, compatible, complying, concurring, conformable, congenial, consenting, consistent, d'accord, delectable, delightful, enjoyable, fitting, gemütlich, gratifying, in accord, likeable, palatable, pleasant, pleasing, pleasurable, proper, responsive, satisfying, suitable, sympathetic, well-disposed, willing.

antonyms disagreeable, distasteful, incompatible, nasty.

agreement[1] *n.* acceptance, accord, accordance, adherence, affinity, analogy, closing, compact, compatibility, complaisance, compliance, concert, concord, concordat, concurrence, conformity, congruence, congruity, consentience, consistency, consonance, consort, convention, correspondence, harmony, modus vivendi, preconcert, resemblance, respondence, similarity, suitableness, sympathy, unanimity, union, unison.
antonym disagreement.

agreement[2] *n.* arrangement, bargain, compact, concordat, contract, covenant, deal, pact, settlement, treaty, understanding.

agricultural *adj.* agrarian, agronomic, farming, geoponic, georgic, praedial.

agriculture *n.* agribusiness, agronomics, agronomy, cultivation, culture, farming, geoponics, husbandry, tillage.

aground *adj., adv.* ashore, beached, foundered, grounded, high and dry, marooned, on the rocks, stranded, stuck, wrecked.
antonym afloat.

ague *n.* fever, fit, malaria, quaking, shivering, trembling, tremor.

ahead *adj., adv.* advanced, along, at an advantage, at the head, before, earlier on, forwards, in advance, in front, in the forefront, in the lead, in the vanguard, leading, onwards, superior, to the fore, winning.

aid *v.* abet, accommodate, adminiculate, assist, befriend, boost, ease, encourage, expedite, facilitate, favour, help, oblige, promote, prop, rally round, relieve, second, serve, subsidise, succour, support, sustain.
antonyms impede, obstruct.
n. a leg up, adminicle, aidance, assistance, assistant, benefit, contribution, donation, encouragement, favour, help, helper, patronage, prop, relief, service, sponsorship, subsidy, subvention, succour, support, supporter.
antonyms impediment, obstruction.

aide *n.* adjutant, adviser, advocate, aide de camp, assistant, attaché, confidant, disciple, follower, galloper, henchman, right-hand man, supporter.

ail *v.* afflict, annoy, be indisposed, bother, decline, distress, droop, fail, irritate, languish, pain, pine, sicken, trouble, upset, weaken, worry.
antonyms comfort, flourish.

ailing *adj.* debilitated, diseased, feeble, frail, ill, indisposed, infirm, invalid, languishing, off-colour, out of sorts, peaky, poorly, sick, sickly, suffering, under the weather, unsound, unwell, weak, weakly.
antonyms flourishing, healthy.

ailment *n.* affliction, complaint, disability, disease, disorder, illness, indisposition, infection, infirmity, malady, sickness, weakness.

aim *v.* address, aspire, attempt, beam, design, direct, draw a bead, endeavour, essay, ettle, intend, level, mean, plan, point, propose, purpose, resolve, seek, set one's sights on, sight, strive, take aim, target, train, try, want, wish, zero in on.
n. ambition, aspiration, course, desideratum, design, desire, direction, dream, end, goal, hope, intent, intention, mark, motive, object, objective, plan, purpose, scheme, target, telos, wish.

aimless *adj.* chance, desultory, directionless, erratic, feckless, frivolous, goalless, haphazard, irresolute, pointless, purposeless, rambling, random, stray, undirected, unguided, unmotivated, unpredictable, vagrant, wayward.
antonyms determined, positive, purposeful.

air *n.* ambience, ambient, appearance, aria, atmosphere, aura, bearing, blast, breath, breeze, character, demeanour, draught, effect, ether, feeling, flavour, heavens, impression, lay, look, manner, melody, mood, motif, oxygen, puff, quality, sky, song, strain, style, theme, tone, tune, waft, welkin, whiff, wind, zephyr.
v. aerate, broadcast, circulate, communicate, declare, disclose, display, disseminate, divulge, exhibit, expose, express, freshen, give vent to, make known, make public, parade, proclaim, publicise, publish, reveal, tell, utter, vaunt, ventilate, voice.

airily *adv.* animatedly, blithely, breezily, brightly, buoyantly, cheerfully, daintily, delicately, ethereally, flippantly, gaily, gracefully, happily, high-spiritedly, insouciantly, jauntily, light-heartedly, lightly, nonchalantly, unconcernedly.
antonyms concernedly, thoughtfully.

airless *adj.* breathless, close, frowsty, frowsy, fusty, heavy, muggy, musty, oppressive, stale, stifling, stuffy, suffocating, sultry, unventilated.
antonyms airy, fresh.

airman *n.* ace, aviator, erk, flyer, pilot.

airs *n.* affectation, affectedness, arrogance, artificiality, haughtiness, hauteur, pomposity, posing, pretensions, pretentiousness, staginess, superciliousness, swank.

air-tight *adj.* closed, impenetrable, impermeable, sealed, tight-fitting, wind-tight.

airy *adj.* aerial, blithe, blowy, bodiless, breezy, buoyant, cheerful, cheery, debonair, delicate, disembodied, draughty, ethereal, fanciful, flimsy, fresh, frolicsome, gay, graceful, gusty, happy, high-spirited, illusory, imaginary, immaterial, incorporeal, insouciant, insubstantial, jaunty, light, light-hearted, lively, lofty, merry, nimble, nonchalant, offhand, open, roomy, spacious, spectral, sportive, sprightly, trifling, uncluttered, unreal, unsubstantial, vaporous, visionary, weightless, well-ventilated, windy.
antonyms close, heavy, oppressive, stuffy.

aisle *n.* alleyway, ambulatory, corridor, de-ambulatory, division, gangway, lane, passage, passageway, path, walkway.

akin *adj.* affiliated, agnate, alike, allied, analogous, cognate, comparable, congenial, connected, consanguineous, consonant, corresponding, kin, kindred, like, parallel, related, similar.
antonym alien.

alacrity *n.* alertness, avidity, briskness, celerity, cheerfulness, dispatch, eagerness, enthusiasm, gaiety, liveliness, promptitude, promptness, quickness, readiness, speed, sprightliness, swiftness, willingness, zeal.
antonyms dilatoriness, slowness.

alarm *v.* affright, agitate, daunt, dismay, distress, frighten, give (someone) a turn, panic, put the wind up (someone), scare, startle, terrify, terrorise, unnerve.
antonyms calm, reassure, soothe.
n. alarm-bell, alert, anxiety, apprehension, bell, consternation, danger signal, dismay, distress, distress signal, fear, fright, horror, larum, larum-bell, nervousness, panic, scare, siren, terror, tocsin, trepidation, unease, uneasiness, warning.
antonym composure.

alarming *adj.* daunting, direful, dismaying, distressing, disturbing, dreadful, frightening, ominous, scaring, shocking, startling, terrifying, threatening, unnerving.
antonym reassuring.

alarmist *n.* doomsman, doomwatcher, jitterbug, pessimist, scaremonger.
antonym optimist.

alas *interj.* alack, alack-a-day, ewhow, good lack, waesucks, welladay, wel(l)away, woe.

albeit *conj.* although, even if, even though, howbeit, notwithstanding that, though.

albumen *n.* glair.

alchemy *n.* hermetics, magic, sorcery, thaumaturgy, witchcraft, wizardry.

alcohol *n.* bev(v)y, booze, firewater, hard stuff, hooch, John Barleycorn, (jungle) juice, liquor, medicine, moonshine, mountain dew, rotgut, spirits.

alcoholic *adj.* ardent, brewed, distilled, fermented, hard, inebriant, inebriating, intoxicating, spirituous, strong, vinous.
n. bibber, boozer, dipso, dipsomaniac, drunk, drunkard, hard drinker, inebriate, lush, piss artist, soak, sot, sponge, tippler, toper, tosspot, wino.

alcoholism *n.* alcohol-addiction, crapulence, dipsomania, drunkenness, methomania, vinosity.

alcove *n.* bay, booth, bower, carrel, compartment, corner, cubby-hole, cubicle, niche, nook, recess.

ale *n.* beer, bitter, mild, morocco, nappy, swipes, wallop.

alert *adj.* active, agile, attentive, brisk, careful, circumspect, gleg, heedful, lively, nimble, observant, on the ball, on the lookout, on the qui vive, perceptive, prepared, quick, ready, sharp-eyed, sharp-witted, spirited, sprightly, vigilant, wary, watchful, wide-awake.
antonyms listless, slow.
n. alarm, signal, siren, tocsin, warning.
v. alarm, forewarn, inform, notify, signal, tip off, warn.

alertness *n.* activeness, agility, attention, attentiveness, briskness, carefulness, circumspection, heedfulness, liveliness, nimbleness, perceptiveness, preparedness, promptitude, quickness, readiness, spiritedness, sprightliness, vigilance, wakefulness, wariness, watchfulness.
antonyms listlessness, slowness.

alias *n.* allonym, anonym, assumed name, false name, nickname, nom de guerre, nom de plume, pen name, pseudonym, soubriquet, stage name.
adv. alias dictus, also, also called, also known as, formerly, otherwise, otherwise called.

alibi *n.* cover-up, defence, excuse, explanation, justification, plea, pretext, reason, story.

alien *adj.* adverse, antagonistic, conflicting, contrary, estranged, exotic, extraneous, foreign, inappropriate, incompatible, incongruous, inimical, opposed, outlandish, remote, repugnant, separated, strange, unfamiliar.
antonym akin.
n. emigrant, foreigner, immigrant, metic, newcomer, outlander, outsider, stranger.
antonym native.

alienate *v.* antagonise, disaffect, divert, divorce, estrange, separate, set against, turn away, turn off, withdraw.
antonyms disarm, unite.

alienation *n.* antagonisation, disaffection, disjunction, disunion, diversion, divorce, estrangement, indifference, remoteness, rupture, separation, severance, turning away, withdrawal.
antonym endearment.

alight[1] *v.* come down, come to rest, debark, descend, detrain, disembark, disentrain, dismount, get down, get off, land, light, perch, settle, touch down.
antonyms ascend, board, rise.

alight[2] *adj.* ablaze, afire, aflame, blazing, bright, brilliant, burning, fiery, flaming, flaring, ignited, illuminated, illumined, lighted, lit, lit up, on fire, radiant, shining.
antonym dark.

align *v.* affiliate, agree, ally, arrange in line, associate, co-operate, co-ordinate, even, even up, join, line up, make parallel, order, range, regularise, regulate, side, straighten, sympathise.

alignment *n.* adjustment, affiliation, agreement, alliance, arrangement, association, conformity, co-operation, co-ordination, evening, evening up, line, lining up, order, ranging, regularisation, regulating, regulation, sequence, straightening, sympathy, union.

alike *adj.* akin, analogous, cognate, comparable, corresponding, duplicate, equal, equivalent,

even, homologous, identical, parallel, resembling, similar, the same, uniform.
antonyms different, unlike.
adv. analogously, correspondingly, equally, evenly, identically, in common, similarly, uniformly.

alive *adj.* active, alert, animate, animated, awake, breathing, brisk, cheerful, eager, energetic, existent, existing, extant, functioning, having life, in existence, in force, life-like, live, lively, living, operative, quick, real, spirited, sprightly, spry, subsisting, vibrant, vigorous, vital, vivacious, zestful.
antonyms dead, lifeless.
alive with abounding in, bristling with, bustling with, buzzing with, crawling with, crowded with, infested with, lousy with, overflowing with, overrun by, stiff with, swarming with, teeming with, thronged with.

all *adj.* complete, each, each and every, entire, every, every bit of, every one of, every single, full, greatest, gross, outright, perfect, the complete, the entire, the sum of, the total of, the totality of, the whole of, total, utter.
antonym none.
n. aggregate, comprehensiveness, entirety, everything, sum, sum total, total, total amount, totality, universality, utmost, whole, whole amount.
adv. altogether, completely, entirely, fully, holus-bolus, totally, utterly, wholesale, wholly.
all being well Deo volente, DV, God willing, if I'm spared, volente Deo.
all right *adj.* acceptable, adequate, allowable, average, fair, hale, healthy, OK, passable, permissible, right as rain, safe, satisfactory, secure, sound, standard, unharmed, unhurt, unimpaired, uninjured, unobjectionable, well, whole.
antonyms unacceptable, uninjured.
adv. acceptably, adequately, appropriately, OK, passably, reasonably, satisfactorily, suitably, unobjectionably, well enough.
antonyms unacceptably, unsatisfactorily.
all the time always, constantly, continually, continuously, ever, everlastingly, perpetually, unceasingly.
all thumbs butter-fingered, cack-handed, clumsy, ham-fisted, ham-handed, inept, maladroit, unhandy.

allay *v.* allege, alleviate, appease, assuage, blunt, calm, check, compose, diminish, dull, ease, lessen, lull, mitigate, moderate, mollify, pacify, quell, quiet, reduce, relieve, slake, smooth, soften, soothe, subdue, tranquillise.
antonyms exacerbate, intensify.

allegation *n.* accusation, affirmation, assertion, asseveration, attestation, averment, avowal, charge, claim, declaration, deposition, plea, profession, statement, testimony.

allege *v.* adduce, advance, affirm, assert, asseverate, attest, aver, avow, charge, claim, contend, declare, depose, hold, insist, maintain, plead, profess, put forward, state.

alleged *adj.* affirmed, asserted, averred, claimed, declared, described, designated, doubtful, dubious, inferred, ostensible, professed, purported, reputed, so-called, stated, supposed, suspect, suspicious.

allegiance *n.* adherence, constancy, devotion, duty, faithfulness, fealty, fidelity, friendship, homage, loyalty, obedience, obligation, support.
antonyms disloyalty, enmity.

allegorical *adj.* emblematic, figurative, parabolic, representative, significative, symbolic, symbolising, typical.

allegory *n.* analogy, apologue, comparison, emblem, fable, metaphor, myth, parable, story, symbol, symbolism, tale.

allergic *adj.* affected, antipathetic, averse, disinclined, dyspathetic, hostile, hypersensitive, loath, opposed, sensitised, sensitive, susceptible.
antonym tolerant.

allergy *n.* antipathy, aversion, disinclination, dislike, dyspathy, hostility, hypersensitivity, loathing, opposition, sensitivity, susceptibility, vulnerability, weakness.
antonyms affinity, tolerance.

alleviate *v.* abate, allay, assuage, blunt, check, cushion, deaden, diminish, dull, ease, lessen, lighten, mitigate, moderate, modify, mollify, palliate, quell, quench, quiet, reduce, relieve, slacken, slake, smooth, soften, soothe, subdue, temper.
antonym aggravate.

alleviation *n.* abatement, allegeance, assuagement, diminution, dulling, easing, lessening, lightening, mitigation, moderation, mollification, palliation, quelling, quenching, reduction, relief, slackening, slaking.
antonym aggravation.

alley *n.* alleyway, back street, close, entry, gate, ginnel, lane, mall, passage, passageway, pathway, walk.

alliance *n.* affiliation, affinity, agreement, association, bloc, bond, cartel, coalition, combination, compact, concordat, confederacy, confederation, conglomerate, connection, consociation, consortium, faction, federation, guild, league, marriage, pact, partnership, syndicate, treaty, union.
antonyms divorce, enmity, estrangement, hostility.

allied *adj.* affiliated, agnate, amalgamated, associate, associated, bound, combined, confederate, congeric, connected, correlate(d), hand in glove, in cahoots, in league, joined, joint, kindred, leagued, linked, married, related, unified, united, wed.
antonym estranged.

allocate *v.* allot, apportion, appropriate, assign, budget, designate, disperse, distribute, earmark, mete, ration, set aside, share out.

allocation *n.* allotment, allowance, apportionment, appropriation, budget, grant, lot, measure, portion, quota, ration, share, stint.

allot v. allocate, apportion, appropriate, assign, budget, designate, dispense, distribute, earmark, grant, mete, render, set aside, share out.

allotment n. allocation, allowance, apportionment, appropriation, division, grant, lot, measure, partition, percentage, portion, quota, ration, share, stint.

all-out adj. complete, determined, energetic, exhaustive, full, full-scale, intensive, maximum, no-holds-barred, optimum, powerful, resolute, supreme, thorough, thoroughgoing, total, undivided, unlimited, unremitting, unrestrained, unstinted, utmost, vigorous, wholesale.
antonyms half-hearted, perfunctory.

allow v. accord, acknowledge, acquiesce, admeasure, admit, allocate, allot, apportion, approve, assign, authorise, bear, brook, concede, confess, deduct, endure, give, give leave, grant, let, own, permit, provide, put up with, remit, sanction, spare, stand, suffer, tolerate.
antonyms deny, forbid.

allow for arrange for, bear in mind, consider, foresee, include, keep in mind, keep in view, make allowances for, make concessions for, make provision for, plan for, provide for, take into account.
antonym discount.

allowable adj. acceptable, admissible, all right, appropriate, approved, apt, legal(ised), legitimate, licit, permissible, sanctionable, sufferable, suitable, supportable, tolerable.
antonym unacceptable.

allowance n. admission, allocation, allotment, amount, annuity, apportionment, batta, concession, deduction, discount, grant, lot, measure, pension, portion, quota, ration, rebate, reduction, remittance, sanction, share, stint, stipend, subsidy, sufferance, tolerance, weighting, X-factor.

alloy n. admixture, amalgam, blend, coalescence, combination, composite, compound, fusion, hybrid, mix, mixture.
v. admix, amalgamate, blend, combine, compound, debase, fuse, impair, mix, qualify, temper.

all-rounder n. generalist, pancratist, Renaissance man.
antonym specialist.

allude v. adumbrate, advert, cite, glance, hint, imply, infer, insinuate, intimate, mention, refer, remark, speak of, suggest, touch upon.

allure v. attract, beguile, cajole, captivate, charm, coax, decoy, disarm, enchant, enrapture, entice, entrance, fascinate, interest, inveigle, lead on, lure, persuade, seduce, tempt, win over.
antonym repel.
n. appeal, attraction, captivation, charm, enchantment, enticement, fascination, glamour, lure, magnetism, persuasion, seductiveness, temptation.

alluring adj. agaçant(e), arousing, attractive, beguiling, bewitching, captivating, come-hither, enchanting, engaging, enticing, fascinating, fetching, intriguing, seductive, sensuous, sexy, tempting, voluptuous, winning.
antonyms repellant, unattractive.

allusion n. citation, glance, hint, implication, innuendo, insinuation, intimation, mention, observation, quotation, reference, remark, suggestion.

ally n. abettor, accessory, accomplice, associate, coadjutor, collaborator, colleague, confederate, confrere, consort, co-worker, friend, helper, helpmate, leaguer, partner, side-kick.
antonyms antagonist, enemy.
v. affiliate, amalgamate, associate, band together, collaborate, combine, confederate, conjoin, connect, fraternise, join, join forces, league, marry, team up, unify, unite.
antonym estrange.

almanac n. annual, calendar, ephemeris, register, yearbook.

almighty adj. absolute, all-powerful, awful, desperate, enormous, excessive, great, intense, invincible, loud, omnipotent, overpowering, overwhelming, plenipotent, severe, supreme, terrible, unlimited.
antonyms impotent, insignificant, weak.

almost adv. about, all but, approaching, approximately, as good as, close to, just about, nearing, nearly, not far from, not quite, practically, towards, virtually, well-nigh.

alms n. benefaction, beneficence, bounty, charity, donation, gift, largess(e), offerings, relief.

alone adj., adv. abandoned, apart, by itself, by oneself, deserted, desolate, detached, discrete, forlorn, forsaken, incomparable, isolated, just, lonely, lonesome, matchless, mere, nonpareil, on one's own, on one's tod, only, peerless, separate, simply, single, single-handed, singular, sole, solitary, unaccompanied, unaided, unassisted, unattended, uncombined, unconnected, unequalled, unescorted, unique, unparalleled, unsurpassed.

aloof adj. chilly, cold, cool, detached, distant, forbidding, formal, haughty, inaccessible, indifferent, offish, remote, reserved, reticent, stand-offish, supercilious, unapproachable, uncompanionable, unforthcoming, unfriendly, uninterested, unresponsive, unsociable, unsympathetic.
antonyms concerned, sociable.

aloofness n. coolness, distance, indifference, offishness, remoteness, reservation, reserve, uncompanionability.
antonyms concern, sociability.

aloud adj. audibly, clamorously, clangorously, clearly, distinctly, intelligibly, loudly, noisily, out loud, plainly, resoundingly, sonorously, vociferously.
antonym silently.

already adv. at present, before now, beforehand, by now, by that time, by then, by this time, even now, heretofore, hitherto, just now, previously.

also *adv.* additionally, along with, and, as well, as well as, besides, ditto, eke, further, furthermore, in addition, including, moreover, plus, therewithal, to boot, too.

alter *v.* adapt, adjust, amend, bushel, castrate, change, convert, diversify, emend, metamorphose, modify, qualify, recast, reform, remodel, reshape, revise, shift, take liberties with, transform, transmute, transpose, turn, vary.
antonym fix.

alteration *n.* adaptation, adjustment, amendment, castration, change, conversion, difference, diversification, emendation, interchanging, metamorphosis, modification, reciprocation, reformation, remodelling, reshaping, revision, rotation, shift, transfiguration, transformation, transmutation, transposition, variance, variation, vicissitude.
antonym fixity.

altercation *n.* argument, bickering, clash, contention, controversy, debate, disagreement, discord, dispute, dissension, fracas, logomachy, quarrel, row, sparring, squabble, wrangle.

alternate *v.* alter, change, fluctuate, follow one another, interchange, intersperse, oscillate, reciprocate, rotate, substitute, take turns, transpose, vary.
adj. alternating, alternative, another, different, every other, every second, interchanging, reciprocal, reciprocating, reciprocative, rotating, second, substitute.

alternative *n.* back-up, choice, option, other, preference, recourse, selection, substitute.
adj. alternate, another, different, fall-back, fringe, other, second, substitute, unconventional, unorthodox.

although *conj.* admitting that, albeit, conceding that, even if, even supposing, even though, granted that, howbeit, notwithstanding, though, while.

altitude *n.* elevation, height, loftiness, stature, tallness.
antonym depth.

altogether *adv.* absolutely, all in all, all told, as a whole, collectively, completely, entirely, fully, generally, holus-bolus, in all, in general, in sum, in toto, on the whole, perfectly, quite, thoroughly, totally, utterly, wholesale, wholly.

altruistic *adj.* benevolent, charitable, considerate, disinterested, generous, humane, humanitarian, philanthropic, public-spirited, self-abnegating, self-sacrificing, unselfish.

altruism *n.* considerateness, disinterestedness, generosity, humanity, philanthropy, public spirit, self-abnegation, self-sacrifice, social conscience, unself, unselfishness.
antonym selfishness.

always *adv.* aye, consistently, constantly, continually, endlessly, eternally, ever, everlastingly, evermore, every time, forever, in perpetuum, invariably, perpetually, regularly, repeatedly, sempiternally, unceasingly, unfailingly, without exception.
antonym never.

amalgam *n.* admixture, aggregate, alloy, amalgamation, blend, coalescence, combination, commixture, composite, compound, fusion, mixture, union.

amalgamate *v.* alloy, ally, blend, coalesce, coalise, combine, commingle, compound, fuse, homogenise, incorporate, integrate, intermix, merge, mingle, synthesise, unify, unite.
antonym separate.

amalgamation *n.* admixture, alliance, alloy, amalgam, amalgamating, blend, coalescence, coalition, combination, commingling, composite, compound, fusion, homogenisation, incorporation, integration, joining, merger, mingling, mixing, mixture, synthesis, unification, union.

amass *v.* accumulate, agglomerate, agglutinate, aggregate, assemble, collect, compile, foregather, garner, gather, heap up, hoard, pile up, rake up, scrape together.

amateur *n.* buff, dabbler, dilettante, do-it-yourselfer, fancier, ham, layman, nonprofessional.
antonym professional.

amateurish *adj.* amateur, clumsy, crude, dilettantism, incompetent, inept, inexpert, unaccomplished, unprofessional, unskilful, untrained.
antonyms professional, skilled.

amatory *adj.* amatorial, amatorious, amorous, aphrodisiac, erogenous, erotic, erotogenous, lascivious, libidinous, love, passionate, romantic, sensual, sexual, sexy.

amaze *v.* alarm, astonish, astound, bewilder, confound, daze, disconcert, dismay, dumbfound, electrify, flabbergast, floor, shock, stagger, startle, stun, stupefy, surprise, wow.

amazement *n.* admiration, astonishment, bewilderment, confusion, dismay, incomprehension, marvel, perplexity, shock, stupefaction, surprise, wonder, wonderment.

ambassador *n.* agent, apostle, consul, deputy, diplomat, elchi, embassador, emissary, envoy, legate, minister, nuncio, plenipotentiary, representative.

ambassadorial *adj.* diplomatic, fetial, legatine, plenipotentiary, representative.

ambience *n.* air, atmosphere, aura, character, climate, environment, feel, feeling, flavour, impression, milieu, mood, quality, setting, spirit, surroundings, tenor, tone, vibes, vibrations.

ambiguity *n.* ambivalence, confusion, doubt, doubtfulness, dubiety, dubiousness, enigma, equivocacy, equivocality, equivocation, inconclusiveness, indefiniteness, indeterminateness, obscurity, puzzle, tergiversation, uncertainty, unclearness, vagueness, weasel word(s), woolliness.
antonym clarity.

ambiguous *adj.* ambivalent, amphibolic, amphibological, amphibolous, confused, confusing, cryptic, Delphic, double-barrelled, double-meaning, doubtful, dubious, enigmatic, enigmatical, equivocal, inconclusive, indefinite, indeterminate, louche, multivocal, obscure, oracular, puzzling, uncertain, unclear, vague, woolly.
antonym clear.

ambit *n.* circuit, compass, confines, environs, precints, scope.

ambition *n.* aim, aspiration, avidity, craving, design, desire, dream, drive, eagerness, end, enterprise, goal, hankering, hope, hunger, ideal, intent, longing, object, objective, purpose, push, striving, target, wish, yearning, zeal.
antonyms apathy, diffidence.

ambitious *adj.* arduous, aspiring, assertive, avid, bold, challenging, demanding, desirous, difficult, driving, eager, elaborate, energetic, enterprising, enthusiastic, exacting, fervid, formidable, go-ahead, grandiose, hard, hopeful, impressive, industrious, intent, keen, pretentious, purposeful, pushy, severe, strenuous, striving, zealous.
antonym unassuming.

ambivalence *n.* ambiguity, clash, conflict, confusion, contradiction, doubt, equivocation, fluctuation, hesitancy, inconsistency, indecision, instability, irresolution, opposition, uncertainty, vacillation, wavering.
antonym certainty.

ambivalent *adj.* ambiguous, clashing, conflicting, confused, contradictory, debatable, doubtful, equivocal, fluctuating, hesitant, inconclusive, inconsistent, irresolute, mixed, opposed, uncertain, undecided, unresolved, unsettled, unsure, vacillating, warring, wavering.
antonym unequivocal.

amble *v.* dawdle, drift, meander, mosey, perambulate, promenade, ramble, saunter, stroll, toddle, walk, wander.
antonyms march, stride.

ambush *n.* ambuscade, concealment, cover, emboscata, hiding, hiding-place, retreat, shelter, snare, trap, waylaying.
v. ambuscade, bushwhack, ensnare, entrap, surprise, trap, waylay.

ameliorate *v.* advance, alleviate, amend, assuage, benefit, better, ease, elevate, emend, enhance, improve, meliorate, mend, mitigate, promote, raise, redress, reform, relieve, revise.
antonyms exacerbate, worsen.

amenable *adj.* accountable, acquiescent, agreeable, answerable, biddable, chargeable, complaisant, conformable, docile, flexible, liable, open, persuadable, responsible, responsive, submissive, susceptible, tractable.
antonym intractable.

amend *v.* adjust, alter, ameliorate, better, change, correct, emend, emendate, enhance, fix, improve, mend, modify, qualify, rectify,

redress, reform, remedy, repair, revise.
antonyms impair, worsen.

amendment *n.* addendum, addition, adjunct, adjustment, alteration, amelioration, betterment, change, clarification, correction, corrigendum, emendation, enhancement, improvement, mending, modification, qualification, rectification, redress, reform, remedy, repair, revision.
antonyms deterioration, impairment.

amends *n.* atonement, compensation, expiation, indemnification, indemnity, mitigation, quittance, recompense, redress, reparation, requital, restitution, restoration, satisfaction.

amenity *n.* advantage, attraction, beauty, charm, comfort, convenience, facility, pleasantness, refinement, service.
antonyms eyesore, inconvenience.

amiable *adj.* accessible, affable, agreeable, approachable, attractive, benign, biddable, charming, cheerful, companionable, complaisant, congenial, conversable, couthie, delightful, engaging, friendly, gemütlich, genial, good-humoured, good-natured, good-tempered, kind, kindly, likable, lovable, obliging, pleasant, pleasing, sociable, sweet, winning, winsome.
antonyms hostile, unfriendly.

amicable *adj.* amiable, brotherly, civil, civilised, cordial, courteous, easy, frank, fraternal, friendly, good-natured, harmonious, kind, kindly, neighbourly, open, peaceable, peaceful, polite, sociable, unreserved.
antonym hostile.

amid *conj.* amidst, among, amongst, in the middle of, in the midst of, in the thick of, surrounded by.

amiss *adj.* awry, defective, erroneous, fallacious, false, faulty, improper, inaccurate, inappropriate, incorrect, out of order, unsuitable, untoward, wonky, wrong.
adv. ill, imperfect, imprecise, out of kilter.
antonyms right, well.

amity *n.* accord, amicability, brotherhood, brotherliness, comity, comradeship, concord, cordiality, fellowship, fraternity, friendliness, friendship, goodwill, harmony, kindliness, kindness, peace, peacefulness, sympathy, tranquillity, understanding.
antonyms discord, hostility.

amnesty *n.* absolution, condonation, dispensation, forgiveness, immunity, indulgence, lenience, mercy, oblivion, pardon, remission, reprieve.

amok *adv.* amuck, berserk, crazy, in a frenzy, in a fury, insane, like a madman, mad, wild.

among *prep.* amid, amidst, amongst, between, in the middle of, in the midst of, in the thick of, midst, mongst, surrounded by, together with, with.

amoral *adj.* abandoned, free-living, intemperate, lax, loose, non-moral, uninhibited, unmoral, unrestrained.
antonym moral.

amorous *adj.* affectionate, amatory, ardent,

attached, doting, enamoured, erotic, fond, impassioned, in love, lovesick, loving, lustful, passionate, randy, tender, uxorious.
antonyms cold, indifferent.

amorphous *adj.* chaotic, characterless, featureless, formless, inchoate, indeterminate, indistinct, irregular, nebulous, nondescript, shapeless, undefined, unformed, unshaped, unshapen, unstructured, vague.
antonyms definite, distinctive, shapely.

amount *n.* addition, aggregate, bulk, entirety, expanse, extent, lot, magnitude, mass, measure, number, quantity, quantum, quota, sum, sum total, supply, total, volume, whole.
amount to add up to, aggregate, approximate to, be equivalent to, be tantamount to, become, come to, equal, grow, mean, purport, run to, total.

amour *n.* affair, affaire de coeur, entanglement, intimacy, intrigue, liaison, love affair, relationship, romance.

ample *adj.* abundant, big, bountiful, broad, capacious, commodious, considerable, copious, expansive, extensive, full, generous, goodly, great, handsome, large, lavish, liberal, munificent, plenteous, plentiful, plenty, profuse, rich, roomy, spacious, substantial, sufficient, unrestricted, voluminous, wide.
antonyms insufficient, meagre.

amplify *v.* add to, augment, boost, broaden, bulk out, deepen, develop, dilate, elaborate, enhance, enlarge, expand, expatiate, extend, fill out, heighten, increase, intensify, lengthen, magnify, raise, strengthen, supplement, widen.
antonym reduce.

amplitude *n.* abundance, ampleness, bigness, breadth, bulk, capaciousness, capacity, compass, completeness, copiousness, dimension, expanse, extent, fullness, greatness, hugeness, largeness, magnitude, mass, plenitude, plentifulness, plethora, profusion, range, reach, richness, scope, size, spaciousness, sweep, vastness, volume, width.

amply *adv.* abundantly, bountifully, completely, copiously, extensively, fully, generously, greatly, handsomely, lavishly, liberally, munificently, plenteously, plentifully, profusely, richly, substantially, sufficiently, thoroughly, unstintingly, well.
antonym inadequately.

amputate *v.* curtail, cut off, dissever, dock, excise, lop, remove, separate, sever, truncate.

amulet *n.* abraxas, charm, fetish, juju, lucky charm, pentacle, periapt, phylactery, talisman, telesm.

amuse *v.* absorb, beguile, charm, cheer, cheer up, delight, disport, divert, engross, enliven, entertain, enthral, gladden, interest, occupy, please, popjoy, recreate, regale, relax, slay, tickle.
antonym bore.

amusement *n.* beguilement, delight, disportment, distraction, diversion, enjoyment, entertainment, fun, game, gladdening, hilarity, hobby, interest, joke, lark, laughter, merriment, mirth, pastime, pleasure, prank, recreation, regalement, sport.
antonyms bore, boredom.

amusing *adj.* amusive, charming, cheerful, cheering, comical, delightful, diverting, droll, enjoyable, entertaining, facetious, funny, gladdening, hilarious, humorous, interesting, jocular, jolly, killing, laughable, lively, ludicrous, merry, pleasant, pleasing, risible, sportive, witty.
antonym boring.

an eye for an eye justice, reciprocation, repayment, reprisal, requital, retaliation, retribution, revenge, tit for tat, vengeance.

anachronism *n.* antique, archaism, back number, dinosaur, fogey, fossil, metachronism, parachronism, prochronism.

anaemic *adj.* ashen, bloodless, chalky, characterless, colourless, dull, enervated, exsanguine, exsanguine(e)ous, feeble, frail, ineffectual, infirm, insipid, pale, pallid, pasty, peelie-wally, sallow, sickly, spiritless, wan, weak, whey-faced.
antonyms full-blooded, ruddy, sanguine.

anaesthetic *n.* analgesic, anodyne, narcotic, opiate, pain-killer, palliative, sedative, soporific, stupefacient, stupefactive.

anaesthetise *v.* benumb, deaden, desensitise, dope, dull, etherise, lull, mull, numb, stupefy.

analogous *adj.* agreeing, akin, alike, comparable, correlative, corresponding, equivalent, homologous, like, matching, parallel, reciprocal, related, resembling, similar.
antonym disparate.

analogy *n.* agreement, comparison, correlation, correspondence, equivalence, homologue, homology, likeness, parallel, parallelism, relation, resemblance, semblance, similarity, similitude.

analyse *v.* anatomise, assay, break down, consider, dissect, dissolve, divide, estimate, evaluate, examine, interpret, investigate, judge, reduce, resolve, review, scrutinise, separate, sift, study, test.

analysis *n.* anatomisation, anatomy, assay, breakdown, dissection, dissolution, division, enquiry, estimation, evaluation, examination, exegesis, explanation, explication, exposition, interpretation, investigation, judgement, opinion, reasoning, reduction, resolution, review, scrutiny, separation, sifting, study, test.

analytic *adj.* analytical, anatomical, critical, detailed, diagnostic, discrete, dissecting, explanatory, expository, inquiring, inquisitive, interpretative, interpretive, investigative, investigatory, logical, methodical, questioning, rational, searching, studious, systematic.

anarchic *adj.* anarchical, anarchistic, chaotic, confused, disordered, disorganised, iconoclastic, lawless, libertarian, nihilist, rebellious, revolutionary, riotous, ungoverned.
antonyms orderly, submissive.

anarchist *n.* anarch, apostate, iconoclast, insurgent, libertarian, nihilist, rebel, revolutionary, terrorist.

anarchy *n.* anarchism, apostasy, bedlam, chaos, confusion, disorder, disorganisation, iconoclasm, insurrection, lawlessness, libertarianism, misgovernment, misrule, mutiny, nihilism, pandemonium, rebellion, revolution, riot, unrule.
antonyms control, order, rule.

anathema *n.* abhorrence, abomination, aversion, ban, bane, bête noire, bugbear, condemnation, curse, damnation, denunciation, excommunication, execration, imprecation, malediction, object of loathing, pariah, proscription, taboo.

anatomise *v.* analyse, break down, dissect, dissolve, divide, examine, pull apart, resolve, scrutinise, separate, study, vivisect.

anatomy *n.* analysis, build, composition, constitution, construction, dissection, frame, framework, make-up, structure, vivisection, zootomy.

ancestor *n.* antecedent, antecessor, forebear, forefather, forerunner, precursor, predecessor, primogenitor, progenitor, progenitress, progenitrix.
antonym descendant.

ancestral *adj.* atavistic, avital, familial, genealogical, genetic, hereditary, lineal, parental.

ancestry *n.* ancestors, antecedents, antecessors, blood, derivation, descent, extraction, family, forebears, forefathers, genealogy, heredity, heritage, house, line, lineage, origin, parentage, pedigree, progenitors, race, roots, stirps, stock.

anchor *n.* grapnel, kedge, killick, mainstay, mud-hook, pillar of strength, prop, security, staff, support.
v. affix, attach, fasten, fix, make fast, moor.

anchorage *n.* bield, harbour, harbourage, haven, mooring, port, protection, refuge, sanctuary, shelter.

anchorite *n.* anchoress, anchoret, ancress, ascetic, eremite, hermit, holy man, marabout, recluse, solitaire, solitarian, solitary, stylite.

ancient *adj.* aged, age-old, antediluvian, antiquated, antique, archaic, bygone, démodé, early, fossilised, hoary, immemorial, obsolete, old, olden, old-fashioned, original, outmoded, out-of-date, preadamic, prehistoric, primeval, primordial, pristine, superannuated, time-worn, venerable, world-old.
antonym modern.

ancillary *adj.* accessory, additional, adjuvant, adminicular, auxiliary, contributory, extra, secondary, subordinate, subsidiary, supplementary.

androgynous *adj.* bisexual, epicene, gynandrous, hermaphrodite, hermaphroditic.

anecdote *n.* exemplum, fable, reminiscence, sketch, story, tale, yarn.

angel *n.* archangel, backer, benefactor, cherub, darling, divine messenger, fairy godmother, guardian spirit, ideal, paragon, principality, saint, seraph, supporter, treasure.
antonyms devil, fiend.

angelic *adj.* adorable, beatific, beautiful, celestial, cherubic, divine, entrancing, ethereal, exemplary, heavenly, holy, innocent, lovely, pious, pure, saintly, seraphic, unworldly, virtuous.
antonyms devilish, fiendish.

anger *n.* annoyance, antagonism, bad blood, bile, bitterness, choler, dander, displeasure, dudgeon, exasperation, fury, gall, indignation, ire, irritability, irritation, monkey, outrage, passion, pique, rage, rancour, resentment, spleen, temper, vexation, wrath.
antonym forbearance.
v. affront, aggravate, annoy, antagonise, bother, bug, displease, enrage, exasperate, fret, frustrate, gall, incense, infuriate, irk, irritate, madden, miff, needle, nettle, offend, outrage, pique, provoke, rile, ruffle, vex.
antonyms appease, calm, please.

angle *n.* approach, aspect, bend, corner, crook, crotch, cusp, direction, edge, elbow, facet, flexure, hook, nook, outlook, perspective, point, point of view, position, side, slant, standpoint, turn, viewpoint.
angle for aim for, be after, be out for, contrive, fish for, have one's beady eye on, hunt, invite, scheme, seek, solicit.

angler *n.* fisherman, piscator, piscatrix, rodman, rodsman, rodster.

angling *n.* ars piscatoria, fishing, gentle craft.

angry *adj.* aggravated, annoyed, antagonised, bitter, burned up, choked, choleric, chuffed, disgruntled, displeased, enraged, exasperated, furious, heated, hot, incensed, indignant, infuriated, irascible, irate, ireful, irked, irritable, irritated, mad, miffed, needled, nettled, outraged, passionate, piqued, provoked, raging, rancorous, ratty, red-headed, resentful, riled, shirty, splenetic, stomachful, tumultuous, uptight, waxy, wrathful, wroth.
antonyms calm, content.

angst *n.* agony, angoisse, anguish, anxiety, apprehension, depression, dread, foreboding, future shock, mal du siècle, malaise, mid-life crisis, Weltschmerz, worry.

anguish *n.* agony, angst, anxiety, desolation, distress, dole, dolour, grief, heartache, heartbreak, misery, pain, pang, rack, sorrow, suffering, torment, torture, tribulation, woe, wretchedness.
antonyms happiness, solace.

anguished *adj.* afflicted, agonised, angst-ridden, distressed, dolorous, harrowed, miserable, racked, stricken, suffering, tormented, tortured, wretched.

angular *adj.* bony, gauche, gaunt, gawky, lank, lanky, lean, rangy, rawboned, scrawny, skinny, spare, ungainly.

animal *n.* barbarian, beast, brute, creature, critter, cur, hound, mammal, monster, pig, savage, swine.
adj. bestial, bodily, brutish, carnal, faunal, feral, ferine, fleshly, gross, inhuman, instinctive, physical, piggish, savage, sensual, wild, zoic.

animate v. activate, arouse, embolden, encourage, energise, enliven, excite, fire, galvanise, goad, impel, incite, inspire, inspirit, instigate, invest, invigorate, irradiate, kindle, move, quicken, reactivate, revive, revivify, rouse, spark, spur, stimulate, stir, suffuse, urge, vitalise, vivify.
antonyms dull, inhibit.
adj. alive, breathing, conscious, live, living, sentient.
antonyms dull, spiritless.

animated *adj.* active, airy, alive, ardent, brisk, buoyant, eager, ebullient, energetic, enthusiastic, excited, fervent, gay, glowing, impassioned, lively, passionate, quick, radiant, spirited, sprightly, vehement, vibrant, vigorous, vital, vivacious, vivid, zestful.
antonyms inert, sluggish.

animation *n.* action, activity, ardour, briskness, buoyancy, ebullience, elation, energy, enthusiasm, excitement, exhilaration, fervour, gaiety, high spirits, life, liveliness, passion, pep, radiance, sparkle, spirit, sprightliness, verve, vibrancy, vigour, vitality, vivacity, zeal, zest, zing.
antonyms dullness, inertia.

animosity *n.* acrimony, animus, antagonism, antipathy, bad blood, bitterness, enmity, feud, feuding, hate, hatred, hostility, ill-will, loathing, malevolence, malice, malignity, odium, rancour, resentment, spite.
antonym goodwill.

animus *n.* acrimony, animosity, antagonism, antipathy, bad blood, bitterness, enmity, hate, hatred, hostility, ill-feeling, ill-will, impetus, intention, loathing, malevolence, malice, malignance, malignity, motive, odium, purpose, rancour, resentment, will.
antonym sympathy.

annals *n.* accounts, archives, chronicles, history, journals, memoirs, memorials, records, registers, reports.

annex v. acquire, add, adjoin, affix, append, appropriate, arrogate, attach, connect, conquer, expropriate, fasten, incorporate, join, occupy, purloin, seize, subjoin, tack, take over, unite, usurp.
n. addendum, additament, addition, adjunct, appendix, attachment, supplement.

annexation *n.* amalgamation, annexing, appropriation, arrogation, augmentation, combination, conquest, expropriation, occupation, seizure, takeover, usurpation.

annexe *n.* addition, ell, expansion, extension, wing.

annihilate v. abolish, assassinate, destroy, eliminate, eradicate, erase, exterminate, extinguish, extirpate, liquidate, murder, nullify, obliterate, raze, rub out, thrash, trounce, wipe out.

annihilation *n.* abolition, assassination, defeat, destruction, elimination, eradication, erasure, extermination, extinction, extirpation, liquidation, nullification, obliteration.

annotate v. comment, commentate, elucidate, explain, gloss, gloze, interpret, marginalise, note.

annotation *n.* apparatus criticus, comment, commentary, elucidation, exegesis, explanation, explication, footnote, gloss, interpretation, marginalia, note, scholia, scholion, scholium.

announce v. advertise, blazon, broadcast, declare, disclose, divulge, intimate, leak, make known, notify, preconise, proclaim, promulgate, propound, publicise, publish, report, reveal, state.
antonym suppress.

announcement *n.* advertisement, broadcast, bulletin, communiqué, declaration, despatch, disclosure, divulgation, divulgence, intimation, notification, proclamation, promulgation, publication, report, revelation, statement.

announcer *n.* anchor man, broadcaster, commentator, commère, compère, crier, harbinger, herald, messenger, newscaster, news-reader, reporter.

annoy v. aggravate, anger, badger, bore, bother, bug, chagrin, contrary, displease, disturb, exasperate, fash, gall, get, give the pigs, harass, harm, harry, hip, hump, incommode, irk, irritate, madden, molest, needle, nettle, peeve, pester, pique, plague, provoke, rile, ruffle, tease, trouble, vex.
antonyms gratify, please.

annoyance *n.* aggravation, anger, bind, bore, bother, désagrément, displeasure, disturbance, exasperation, fash, gêne, harassment, headache, irritant, irritation, nuisance, pain, pest, pique, plague, provocation, tease, trouble, vexation.
antonym pleasure.

annoyed *adj.* bored, bugged, chagrined, displeased, exasperated, galled, harassed, hipped, irked, irritated, narked, peeved, piqued, provoked, shirty, vexed.
antonym pleased.

annoying *adj.* aggravating, boring, bothersome, displeasing, disturbing, exasperating, fashious, galling, harassing, irksome, irritating, maddening, offensive, peeving, pesky, pesterous, pestful, pestiferous, pestilent, pestilential, plaguesome, plaguey, provoking, teasing, troublesome, vexatious.
antonyms pleasing, welcome.

annual *n.* almanac, annal, ephemeris, yearbook.

annul v. abolish, abrogate, cancel, cashier, countermand, disannul, invalidate, negate, nullify, quash, recall, repeal, rescind, retract, reverse, revoke, suspend, void.
antonyms enact, restore.

annulment *n.* abolition, abrogation, cancellation, cassation, countermanding, disannulment, invalidation, negation, nullification, quashing, recall, repeal, rescindment, rescission, retraction, reversal, revocation, suspension, voiding.
antonyms enactment, restoration.

anodyne *adj.* analgesic, bland, blunting, calmative, deadening, desensitising, dulling, febrifugal, inoffensive, narcotic, numbing, pain-killing, pain-relieving, palliative, sedative.
antonym irritant.
n. alleviative, analgesic, febrifuge, narcotic, pain-killer, pain-reliever, palliative, sedative.
antonym irritant.

anoint *v.* anele, bless, consecrate, daub, dedicate, embrocate, grease, hallow, lard, lubricate, oil, rub, sanctify, smear.

anointing *n.* aneling, blessing, consecration, dedication, embrocation, hallowing, sanctification, unction.

anomalous *adj.* aberrant, abnormal, atypical, bizarre, deviant, eccentric, exceptional, freakish, incongruous, inconsistent, irregular, odd, peculiar, quirky, rare, singular, untypical, unusual.
antonyms normal, regular.

anomaly *n.* aberration, abnormality, departure, deviant, deviation, divergence, eccentricity, exception, freak, incongruity, inconsistency, irregularity, misfit, oddity, peculiarity, rarity.

anonymous *adj.* characterless, faceless, impersonal, incognito, innominate, nameless, nondescript, unacknowledged, unattested, unauthenticated, uncredited, unexceptional, unidentified, unknown, unnamed, unsigned, unspecified.
antonyms distinctive, identifiable, named.

anorak *n.* blouson, golf-jacket, jerkin, lumber-jacket, parka, waterproof, windcheater, windjammer.

answer *n.* acknowledgement, apology, comeback, counterbuff, countercharge, defence, explanation, outcome, plea, reaction, rebuttal, reciprocation, refutation, rejoinder, reply, report, resolution, response, retaliation, retort, return, riposte, solution, vindication.
v. acknowledge, agree, balance, conform, correlate, correspond, do, echo, explain, fill, fit, fulfil, match up to, meet, pass, qualify, react, reciprocate, refute, rejoin, reply, resolve, respond, retaliate, retort, return, satisfy, serve, solve, succeed, suffice, suit, work.
answer back argue, cheek, contradict, disagree, dispute, rebut, retaliate, retort, riposte, talk back.
antonym acquiesce.

answerable[1] *adj.* accountable, amenable, blameable, blameworthy, chargeable, liable, responsible, to blame.

answerable[2] *adj.* defensible, deniable, disprovable, explicable, rebuttable, refutable, repudiable.

answering *adj.* respondent, responsory.

ant *n.* emmet, hymenopteran, pismire, termite.

antagonise *v.* alienate, anger, annoy, disaffect, embitter, estrange, incense, insult, irritate, offend, provoke, repel.
antonym disarm.

antagonism *n.* animosity, animus, antipathy, competition, conflict, contention, discord, dissension, friction, hostility, ill-feeling, ill-will, opposition, rivalry.
antonyms rapport, sympathy.

antagonist *n.* adversary, competitor, contender, contestant, disputant, enemy, foe, opponent, opposer, rival.
antonyms ally, supporter.

antagonistic *adj.* adverse, antipathetic, at variance, averse, bellicose, belligerent, conflicting, contentious, hostile, ill-disposed, incompatible, inimical, opposed, pugnacious, unfriendly.
antonyms friendly, sympathetic.

antecedents *n.* ancestors, ancestry, antecessors, background, blood, descent, dossier, extraction, family, forebears, forefathers, genealogy, history, line, lineage, past, pedigree, prodromi, progenitors, record, stock.

antedate *v.* antecede, anticipate, forego, forerun, go before, precede, predate.
antonym follow.

antediluvian *adj.* anachronistic, ancient, antiquated, antique, archaic, bygone, démodé, fossilised, obsolete, old-fashioned, out of the ark, out-of-date, passé, prehistoric, primal, primeval, primitive, primordial, superannuated.
antonyms up-to-date, with it.

anterior *adj.* antecedent, earlier, foregoing, former, introductory, preceding, previous, prior, prodromal, prodromic.
antonym subsequent.

anthem *n.* canticle, chant, chorale, hymn, introit, paean, psalm, song.

anthology *n.* analects, choice, collection, compendium, compilation, digest, divan, florilegium, garland, miscellany, selection, spicilegium, treasury.

anticipate *v.* antedate, apprehend, await, bank on, beat to it, count upon, earlierise, expect, forecast, foredate, foresee, forestall, foretaste, foretell, forethink, hope for, intercept, look for, look forward to, predict, pre-empt, prevent.

anticipation *n.* apprehension, awaiting, expectancy, expectation, foresight, foretaste, forethought, forewarning, hope, preconception, premonition, prescience, presentiment, prodrome, prolepsis.

anticipatory *adj.* anticipative, expectant, hopeful, intuitive, preparatory, proleptic, proleptical.

anticlimax *n.* bathos, comedown, damp squib, disappointment, disenchantment, fiasco, letdown.

anticlockwise *adj.* dextrorse, l(a)evorotatory.

antics *n.* buffoonery, capers, clownery, clowning, didoes, doings, escapades, foolery, foolishness, frolics, larks, mischief, monkey tricks, playfulness, pranks, silliness, skylarking, stunts, tomfoolery, tricks, zanyism.

antidote *n.* antitoxin, antivenin, corrective, counter-agent, countermeasure, cure, detoxicant, mithridate, neutraliser, preventive, remedy, specific, theriac, treacle.

antipathetic *adj.* abhorrent, allergic, anathematical, antagonistic, antipathetical, averse, disgusting, distasteful, hateful, horrible, hostile, incompatible, inimical, invidious, loathsome, obnoxious, odious, offensive, repellent, repugnant, repulsive, revolting. *antonyms* agreeable, harmonious, sympathetic.

antipathy *n.* abhorrence, allergy, animosity, animus, antagonism, aversion, bad blood, contrariety, disgust, dislike, distaste, enmity, hate, hatred, hostility, ill-will, incompatibility, loathing, odium, opposition, rancour, repugnance, repulsion, resentment. *antonyms* rapport, sympathy.

antipodes *n.* underworld.

antiquary *n.* antiquarian, archaeologist, archaist, bibliophile, collector, Dryasdust, palaeologist, virtuoso.

antiquated *adj.* anachronistic, ancient, antediluvian, antique, archaic, dated, démodé, elderly, fogeyish, fogram, fossilised, obsolete, old, old hat, old-fashioned, old-fogeyish, outdated, outmoded, out-of-date, outworn, passé, quaint, superannuated, unfashionable. *antonyms* forward-looking, modern.

antique *adj.* aged, ancient, antiquarian, archaic, elderly, obsolete, old, old-fashioned, outdated, quaint, superannuated, vintage.
n. antiquity, bibelot, bygone, curio, curiosity, heirloom, knick-knack, museum-piece, object of virtu, period piece, rarity, relic.

antiquity *n.* age, agedness, ancient times, ancientness, antique, distant past, e(i)ld, elderliness, fogramity, hoariness, old age, olden days, oldness, time immemorial, venerableness. *antonyms* modernity, novelty.

antiseptic *adj.* aseptic, bactericidal, clean, disinfectant, germ-free, germicidal, hygienic, medicated, pure, sanitary, sanitised, sterile, uncontaminated, unpolluted.
n. bactericide, cleanser, decontaminant, disinfectant, germicide, purifier.

antisocial *adj.* alienated, anarchic, antagonistic, asocial, belligerent, disorderly, disruptive, hostile, menacing, misanthropic, rebellious, reserved, retiring, unacceptable, unapproachable, uncommunicative, unfriendly, unsociable, withdrawn. *antonyms* acceptable, sociable.

antithesis *n.* antipode, contradiction, contradistinction, contraposition, contrariety, contrary, contrast, converse, inverse, inversion, opposite, opposite extreme, opposition, polarity, reversal, reverse.

antithetical *adj.* antipodal, antipodean, antithetic, contradictory, contrary, contrasted, contrasting, converse, counter, inverse, opposed, opposite, polarised, poles apart, reverse.

anxiety *n.* angst, anxiousness, apprehension, care, concern, craving, desire, disquiet, disquietude, distress, dread, dysthymia, eagerness, foreboding, fretfulness, impatience, keenness, misgiving, nervousness, presentiment, restlessness, solicitude, suspense, tension, torment, torture, unease, uneasiness, watchfulness, willingness, worriment, worry. *antonym* composure.

anxious *adj.* afraid, angst-ridden, apprehensive, avid, careful, concerned, desirous, disquieted, distressed, disturbed, eager, expectant, fearful, fretful, impatient, in suspense, intent, itching, keen, nervous, on tenterhooks, overwrought, restless, solicitous, taut, tense, tormented, tortured, troubled, uneasy, unquiet, watchful, worried, yearning. *antonym* composed.

apace *adv.* at full speed, at top speed, doublequick, expeditiously, fast, hastily, posthaste, quickly, rapidly, speedily, swiftly, without delay.

apart *adv.* afar, alone, aloof, aside, asunder, away, by oneself, cut off, distant, distinct, divorced, excluded, in bits, in pieces, independent, independently, individually, into parts, isolated, on one's own, piecemeal, privately, separate, separated, separately, singly, to bits, to one side, to pieces.

apartment *n.* accommodation, chambers, compartment, condominium, flat, living quarters, lodgings, maisonette, pad, penthouse, quarters, room, rooms, suite, tenement.

apathetic *adj.* cold, cool, dispassionate, emotionless, impassive, indifferent, insensible, insentient, listless, numb, passive, phlegmatic, sluggish, stoic, torpid, unambitious, unconcerned, unemotional, unfeeling, uninterested, uninvolved, unmotivated, unmoved, unresponsive. *antonyms* concerned, responsive.

apathy *n.* accidie, acedia, coldness, coolness, emotionlessness, impassibility, impassivity, incuriousness, indifference, inertia, insensibility, lethargy, listlessness, passiveness, passivity, phlegm, sluggishness, torpor, unconcern, unfeelingness, uninterestedness, unresponsiveness. *antonyms* concern, warmth.

ape *v.* affect, caricature, copy, counterfeit, echo, imitate, mimic, mirror, mock, parody, parrot, take off.
n. baboon, boor, brute, chimpanzee, gibbon, gorilla, jocko, monkey, oaf, orang-utan, pongid, pongo, savage.

aperture *n.* breach, chink, cleft, crack, eye, eyelet, fissure, foramen, gap, hole, interstice, opening, orifice, passage, perforation, rent, rift, slit, slot, space, vent.

apex *n.* acme, apogee, climax, consummation, crest, crown, crowning point, culmination, fastigium, height, high point, peak, pinnacle, point, summit, tip, top, vertex, zenith. *antonym* nadir.

aphorism *n.* adage, apothegm, axiom, dictum, epigram, gnome, maxim, mot, precept, proverb, saw, saying, sentence.

aphrodisiac *adj.* amative, amatory, erogenous, erotic, erotogenous, venerous.

aplomb *n.* assurance, audacity, balance, calmness, composure, confidence, coolness, equanimity, poise, sang-froid, savoir faire, self-assurance, self-confidence, self-possession.
antonym discomposure.

apocalyptic *adj.* fatidic, ominous, oracular, portentous, prophetic, revelational, revelatory, signal, threatening, vatic.

apocryphal *adj.* concocted, doubtful, dubious, equivocal, fabricated, fictitious, imaginary, legendary, mythical, phony, questionable, spurious, unauthenticated, uncanonical, unsubstantiated, unsupported, unverified.
antonym true.

apogee *n.* acme, apex, climax, consummation, crest, crown, culmination, height, high point, meridian, peak, pinnacle, summit, tip, top, vertex, zenith.
antonyms nadir, perigee.

apologetic *adj.* compunctious, conscience-stricken, contrite, excusatory, penitent, regretful, remorseful, repentant, rueful, sorry.
antonym defiant.

apologist *n.* advocate, champion, defender, endorser, justifier, pleader, seconder, spokesman, supporter, upholder, vindicator.
antonym critic.

apology *n.* acknowledgement, apologia, confession, defence, excuse, explanation, extenuation, justification, palliation, plea, semblance, substitute, travesty, vindication.
antonym defiance.

apophthegm *n.* adage, aphorism, axiom, dictum, epigram, gnome, maxim, precept, proverb, saw, saying, sentence.

apostasy *n.* defection, desertion, disloyalty, faithlessness, falseness, heresy, perfidy, rattery, ratting, recidivism, recreance, recreancy, renegation, renunciation, treachery, unfaithfulness.
antonyms loyalty, orthodoxy.

apostate *n.* defector, deserter, heretic, recidivist, recreant, renegade, renegado, runagate, tergiversator, traitor, turncoat.
antonyms adherent, convert, loyalist.
adj. disloyal, faithless, false, heretical, perfidious, recreant, renegate, traitorous, treacherous, unfaithful, unorthodox, untrue.
antonym faithful.

apostatise *v.* backslide, defect, lapse, recant, renegue, renig, tergiversate, withdraw.

apostle *n.* advocate, champion, crusader, evangelist, exponent, herald, messenger, missionary, pioneer, preacher, promoter, propagandist, propagator, proponent, proselytiser.

apotheosis *n.* deification, elevation, exaltation, glorification, godding, idealisation, idolisation, immortalisation.

apotheosise *v.* deify, elevate, exalt, glorify, god, idealise, idolise, immortalise.

appal *v.* alarm, astound, daunt, disconcert, disgust, dishearten, dismay, frighten, harrow, horrify, intimidate, outrage, petrify, scare, shock, terrify, unnerve.
antonyms encourage, reassure.

appalling *adj.* alarming, astounding, awful, daunting, dire, disheartening, dismaying, dreadful, fearful, frightening, frightful, ghastly, grim, harrowing, hideous, horrible, horrid, horrific, horrifying, intimidating, loathsome, petrifying, scaring, shocking, startling, terrible, terrifying, unnerving, wretched.
antonym reassuring.

apparatus *n.* appliance, bureaucracy, contraption, device, equipment, framework, gadget, gear, gismo, hierarchy, implements, machine, machinery, materials, means, mechanism, network, organisation, outfit, set-up, structure, system, tackle, tools, utensils.

apparel *n.* accoutrements, array, attire, clothes, clothing, costume, dress, equipment, garb, garments, garniture, gear, guise, habiliments, habit, outfit, raiment, rig-out, robes, suit, trappings, vesture, vestments, wardrobe, weeds.

apparent *adj.* clear, conspicuous, declared, discernible, distinct, evident, indubitable, manifest, marked, noticeable, obvious, on paper, open, ostensible, outward, overt, patent, perceptible, plain, seeming, specious, superficial, unmistakable, visible.
antonyms obscure, real.

apparently *adv.* clearly, manifestly, obviously, ostensibly, outwardly, patently, plainly, seemingly, speciously, superficially.

apparition *n.* chimera, eidolon, ghost, manifestation, materialisation, phantasm, phantom, presence, revenant, shade, spectre, spirit, spook, umbra, vision, visitant, visitation, wraith.

appeal[1] *n.* adjuration, application, entreaty, imploration, invocation, orison, petition, plea, prayer, request, solicitation, suit, supplication.
v. address, adjure, apply, ask, beg, beseech, call, call upon, entreat, implore, invoke, petition, plead, pray, refer, request, resort to, solicit, sue, supplicate.

appeal[2] *n.* allure, attraction, attractiveness, beauty, charisma, charm, enchantment, fascination, interest, magnetism, winsomeness.
v. allure, attract, charm, draw, engage, entice, fascinate, interest, invite, lure, please, tempt.

appear *v.* act, arise, arrive, attend, be published, bob up, come into sight, come into view, come out, come to light, crop up, develop, emerge, enter, issue, leak out, look, loom, materialise, occur, perform, play, rise, seem, show, show up, surface, take part, transpire, turn out, turn up.
antonym disappear.

appearance *n.* advent, air, appearing, arrival, aspect, bearing, brow, cast, character, coming, début, demeanour, emergence, expression, face, facies, favour, figure, form, front,

guise, illusion, image, impression, introduction, look, looks, manner, mien, physiognomy, presence, pretence, seeming, semblance, show, the cut of one's jib.
antonyms disappearance, reality.

appease *v.* allay, assuage, blunt, calm, compose, conciliate, diminish, ease, give a sop to, humour, lessen, lull, mitigate, mollify, pacify, placate, propitiate, quell, quench, quiet, reconcile, satisfy, soften, soothe, subdue, tranquillise.
antonym aggravate.

appeasement *n.* acceding, accommodation, assuagement, compromise, concession, conciliation, humouring, lessening, mitigation, mollification, Munich, Munichism, pacification, placation, propitiation, quelling, quieting, satisfaction, softening, sop.
antonyms aggravation, resistance.

appellation *n.* address, denomination, description, designation, epithet, label, monicker, name, nickname, sobriquet, style, term, title.

append *v.* add, adjoin, affix, annex, attach, conjoin, fasten, join, subjoin, tack on.

appendage *n.* accessory, addendum, addition, adjunct, affix, ancillary, annexe, appendix, appurtenance, attachment, auxiliary, excrescence, extremity, limb, member, projection, prosthesis, protuberance, supplement, tab, tag.

appendix *n.* addendum, additament, addition, adjunct, appendage, codicil, epilogue, excursus, postscript, rider, supplement.

appertaining *adj.* applicable, applying, belonging, characteristic, connected, germane, pertinent, related, relevant.

appetiser *n.* antipasto, apéritif, bonne bouche, canapé, cocktail, foretaste, hors d'oeuvre, preview, sample, taste, taster, titbit, whet.

appetising *adj.* appealing, delicious, inviting, moreish, mouthwatering, palatable, piquant, savoury, scrumptious, succulent, tasty, tempting, toothsome, yummy.
antonym disgusting.

appetite *n.* appetence, appetency, craving, demand, desire, eagerness, hankering, hunger, inclination, keenness, liking, limosis, longing, orexis, passion, predilection, proclivity, propensity, relish, stomach, taste, willingness, yearning, zeal, zest.
antonym distaste.

applaud *v.* acclaim, approve, cheer, clap, commend, compliment, congratulate, encourage, eulogise, extol, laud, ovate, praise.
antonyms censure, disparage.

applauding *adj.* acclamatory, adulatory, approving, commendatory, complimentary, congratulatory, laudatory, plauditory, plausive.
antonym abusive.

applause *n.* acclaim, acclamation, accolade, approbation, approval, cheering, cheers, commendation, congratulation, encomium, eulogies, eulogising, hand, laudation, ovation, plaudits, praise.
antonyms censure, disparagement.

appliance *n.* apparatus, contraption, contrivance, device, gadget, gismo, implement, instrument, machine, mechanism, tool.

applicable *adj.* apposite, appropriate, apropos, apt, befitting, fit, fitting, germane, legitimate, pertinent, proper, related, relevant, suitable, suited, useful, valid.
antonym inapplicable.

applicant *n.* aspirant, candidate, claimant, competitor, contestant, inquirer, interviewee, petitioner, postulant, suitor.

application[1] *n.* adhibition, appeal, appositeness, apposition, assiduity, attention, attentiveness, claim, commitment, dedication, diligence, effort, exercise, extension, function, germaneness, industry, inquiry, keenness, lesson, moral, perseverance, pertinence, petition, practice, purpose, reference, relevance, request, requisition, sedulity, sedulousness, solicitation, suit, use, value.

application[2] *n.* balm, cream, dressing, emollient, lotion, medication, ointment, poultice, preparation, salve, unguent.

apply[1] *v.* adhibit, administer, appose, assign, bring into play, bring to bear, direct, employ, engage, execute, exercise, implement, ply, practise, resort to, set, use, utilise, wield.

apply[2] *v.* appertain, be relevant, fit, have force, pertain, refer, relate, suit.

apply[3] *v.* anoint, cover with, lay on, paint, place, put on, rub, smear, spread on, use.

apply[4] *v.* appeal, ask for, claim, indent for, inquire, petition, put in, request, requisition, solicit, sue.

apply[5] *v.* address, bend, buckle down, commit, concentrate, dedicate, devote, direct, give, persevere, settle down, study, throw.

appoint *v.* allot, arrange, assign, charge, choose, command, commission, constitute, co-opt, decide, decree, delegate, designate, destine, detail, determine, devote, direct, elect, engage, enjoin, equip, establish, fit out, fix, furnish, install, name, nominate, ordain, outfit, plenish, provide, select, set, settle, supply.
antonyms dismiss, reject.

appointed *adj.* allotted, arranged, assigned, chosen, commanded, commissioned, coopted, dative, decided, decreed, delegated, designated, determined, directed, elected, enjoined, equipped, established, fitted out, fixed, furnished, installed, invested, named, nominated, ordained, plenished, preordained, provided, selected, set, settled, supplied.

appointment *n.* allotment, arrangement, assignation, assignment, choice, choosing, commissioning, consultation, date, delegation, election, engagement, installation, interview, job, meeting, naming, nomination, office, place, position, post, rendezvous, selection, session, situation, station, tryst.

appointments *n.* accoutrements, appurtenances, equipage, fittings, fixtures, furnishings, furniture, gear, outfit, paraphernalia, plenishings, trappings.

apportion v. accord, admeasure, allocate, allot, assign, award, deal, dispense, distribute, divide, dole out, grant, measure out, mete, morsel, portion out, ration, share.

apportionment n. allocation, allotment, assignment, dealing, dispensation, dispensing, distribution, division, divvying up, doling, measuring, meting, partitioning, sharing.

apposite adj. applicable, appropriate, apropos, apt, befitting, condign, felicitous, germane, in point, pertinent, proper, relevant, suitable, suited, to the point, to the purpose.
antonym inapposite.

appraisal n. appreciation, assay, assaying, assessment, estimate, estimation, evaluation, examination, inspection, judgement, once-over, opinion, pricing, rating, reckoning, review, sizing-up, survey, valuation.

appraise v. assay, assess, estimate, evaluate, examine, gauge, inspect, judge, price, rate, review, size up, survey, valuate, value.

appreciable adj. apparent, ascertainable, clear-cut, considerable, definite, detectable, discernible, distinguishable, evident, marked, material, measurable, noticeable, obvious, perceivable, perceptible, pronounced, recognisable, significant, substantial, undeniable, visible.
antonyms imperceptible, negligible.

appreciate[1] v. acknowledge, admire, be sensible of, be sensitive to, cherish, comprehend, dig, do justice to, enjoy, esteem, estimate, know, like, perceive, prize, realise, recognise, regard, relish, respect, savour, sympathise with, take kindly to, treasure, understand, value.
antonyms despise, overlook.

appreciate[2] v. enhance, gain, grow, improve, increase, inflate, mount, rise, strengthen.
antonym depreciate.

appreciation[1] n. acclamation, acknowledgement, admiration, appraisal, assessment, awareness, cognisance, comprehension, criticism, critique, enjoyment, esteem, estimation, gratefulness, gratitude, indebtedness, judgement, knowledge, liking, notice, obligation, perception, praise, realisation, recognition, regard, relish, respect, responsiveness, review, sensitivity, sympathy, thankfulness, thanks, tribute, understanding, valuation.
antonyms ingratitude, neglect.

appreciation[2] n. climb, enhancement, gain, growth, improvement, increase, inflation, rise, the up-and-up.
antonym depreciation.

appreciative adj. admiring, aware, beholden, cognisant, conscious, encouraging, enthusiastic, grateful, indebted, knowledgeable, mindful, obliged, perceptive, pleased, regardful, respectful, responsive, sensible, sensitive, supportive, sympathetic, thankful, understanding.
antonym ungrateful.

apprehend[1] v. arrest, bust, capture, catch, collar, detain, get, grab, nab, nick, pinch, run in, seize, take.

apprehend[2] v. appreciate, believe, comprehend, conceive, consider, discern, grasp, imagine, know, perceive, realise, recognise, see, twig, understand.

apprehension[1] n. arrest, capture, catching, seizure, taking.

apprehension[2] n. alarm, anxiety, apprehensiveness, awareness, belief, comprehension, concept, conception, concern, conjecture, discernment, disquiet, doubt, dread, fear, foreboding, grasp, idea, impression, intellect, intellection, intelligence, ken, knowledge, misgiving, mistrust, nervousness, notion, opinion, perception, premonition, presentiment, qualm, sentiment, suspicion, thought, understanding, unease, uneasiness, uptake, view, worry.

apprehensive adj. afraid, alarmed, anxious, concerned, disquieted, distrustful, disturbed, doubtful, fearful, mistrustful, nervous, solicitous, suspicious, uneasy, worried.
antonym confident.

apprentice n. beginner, cub, learner, neophyte, newcomer, novice, probationer, pupil, recruit, starter, student, trainee, tyro.
antonym expert.

apprise v. acquaint, advise, brief, communicate, enlighten, inform, intimate, notify, tell, tip off, warn.

approach v. advance, anear, appeal to, apply to, approximate, be like, begin, broach, catch up, come close, come near to, commence, compare with, draw near, embark on, gain on, introduce, make advances, make overtures, meet, mention, near, reach, resemble, set about, sound out, undertake.
n. access, advance, advent, appeal, application, approximation, arrival, attitude, avenue, course, doorway, entrance, gesture, invitation, landfall, likeness, manner, means, method, mode, modus operandi, motion, nearing, offer, overture, passage, procedure, proposal, proposition, resemblance, road, semblance, style, system, technique, threshold, way.

approachable adj. accessible, affable, agreeable, attainable, congenial, conversable, cordial, easy, friendly, informal, open, reachable, sociable.
antonym unapproachable.

approbation n. acceptance, acclaim, acclamation, applause, approval, assent, commendation, congratulation, encouragement, endorsement, esteem, favour, kudos, laudation, praise, ratification, recognition, regard, sanction, support.
antonym disapprobation.

appropriate adj. applicable, apposite, appurtenant, apropos, apt, becoming, befitting, belonging, condign, congruous, correct, felicitous, fit, fitting, germane, meet, merited, opportune, pertinent, proper, relevant, right, seasonable, seemly, spot-on, suitable, timely, to the point, well-chosen, well-suited, well-timed.
antonym inappropriate.

v. allocate, allot, annex, apportion, arrogate, assign, assume, commandeer, confiscate, devote, earmark, embezzle, expropriate, filch, impound, impropriate, misappropriate, pilfer, pocket, possess oneself of, pre-empt, purloin, seize, set apart, steal, take, usurp.

appropriateness *n.* applicability, appositeness, aptness, becomingness, condignness, congruousness, correctness, felicitousness, felicity, fitness, germaneness, justness, opportuneness, pertinence, properness, propriety, relevance, rightness, seemliness, suitability, timeliness.

appropriation *n.* allocation, allotment, annexation, apportionment, arrogation, assignment, assumption, commandeering, confiscation, dispensation, earmarking, expropriation, impoundment, misappropriation, pre-emption, seizure, setting apart, usurpation.

approval *n.* acclaim, acclamation, acquiescence, admiration, adoption, agreement, applause, appreciation, approbation, approof, assent, authorisation, blessing, certification, commendation, compliance, concurrence, confirmation, consent, countenance, endorsement, esteem, favour, go-ahead, good opinion, green light, honour, imprimatur, leave, licence, liking, mandate, OK, permission, plaudits, praise, ratification, recommendation, regard, respect, sanction, support, validation.
antonym disapproval.

approve *v.* accede to, accept, acclaim, admire, adopt, advocate, agree to, allow, applaud, appreciate, assent to, authorise, back, bless, commend, comply with, concur in, confirm, consent to, countenance, dig, endorse, esteem, favour, homologate, like, mandate, OK, pass, permit, praise, ratify, recommend, regard, respect, rubber-stamp, sanction, second, support, take kindly to, uphold, validate.
antonym disapprove.

approved *adj.* acceptable, accepted, authorised, comme il faut, correct, favoured, official, permissible, permitted, preferred, proper, recognised, recommended, sanctioned.
antonym unorthodox.

approximate *adj.* close, comparable, conjectural, estimated, extrapolated, guessed, inexact, like, loose, near, relative, rough, similar, verging on.
antonym exact.
v. approach, be tantamount to, border on, resemble, verge on.

approximately *adv.* about, almost, around, circa, close to, coming up to, in round numbers, in the region of, in the vicinity of, just about, loosely, more or less, nearly, not far off, pushing, relatively, roughly, round about, well-nigh.
antonym exactly.

approximation *n.* approach, conjecture, correspondence, estimate, estimation, extrapolation, guess, guesstimate, guesswork, likeness, proximity, resemblance, rough calculation, rough idea, semblance.
antonyms exactitude, precision.

appurtenance *n.* accessory, accompaniment, addition, adjunct, annexe, appanage, appendage, appurtenant, attachment, auxiliary, concomitant, incidental, subordinate, subsidiary, supplement.

appurtenances *n.* accessories, accompaniments, accoutrements, appendages, equipment, gear, impedimenta, kit, paraphernalia, trappings, traps.

apropos *adj.* applicable, apposite, appropriate, apt, befitting, belonging, condign, correct, fit, fitting, germane, meet, opportune, pertinent, proper, related, relevant, right, seemly, suitable, timely, to the point.
antonym inappropriate.
adv. appositely, appropriately, aptly, by the bye, by the way, en passant, in passing, incidentally, opportunely, pat, pertinently, properly, relevantly, suitably, to the point.
antonym inappropriately.

apropos of in connection with, in relation to, in respect of, on the subject of, re, regarding, respecting, with reference to, with regard to, with respect to.

apt *adj.* accurate, adept, applicable, apposite, appropriate, apropos, astute, befitting, bright, clever, condign, correct, disposed, expert, fair, fit, fitting, germane, gifted, given, gleg, inclined, ingenious, intelligent, liable, likely, meet, pertinent, prompt, prone, proper, quick, ready, relevant, seasonable, seemly, sharp, skilful, smart, spot-on, suitable, talented, teachable, tending, timely.
antonym inapt.

aptitude *n.* ability, aptness, bent, capability, capacity, cleverness, disposition, facility, faculty, flair, gift, inclination, intelligence, knack, leaning, penchant, predilection, proclivity, proficiency, proneness, propensity, quickness, talent, tendency.
antonym inaptitude.

aptness *n.* ability, accuracy, applicability, appositeness, appropriateness, aptitude, becomingness, bent, capability, capacity, cleverness, condignness, congruousness, correctness, disposition, facility, faculty, felicitousness, felicity, fitness, fittingness, flair, germaneness, gift, inclination, intelligence, knack, leaning, liability, likelihood, likeliness, opportuneness, pertinence, predilection, proclivity, proficiency, proneness, propensity, properness, quickness, readiness, relevance, rightness, seemliness, suitability, talent, tendency, timeliness.

arbiter *n.* adjudicator, arbiter elegantiarum, arbitrator, authority, controller, dictator, expert, intermediary, judge, master, mediator, negotiator, pundit, referee, ruler, umpire.

arbitrariness *n.* absoluteness, capriciousness, despotism, dogmatism, fancifulness, highhandedness, imperiousness, inconsistency, irrationality, irresponsibility, peremptoriness, randomness, subjectivity, summariness, tyranny, unreasonableness, waywardness, whimsicality, wilfulness.

arbitrary *adj.* absolute, autocratic, capricious, chance, despotic, dictatorial, discretionary, dogmatic, domineering, erratic, fanciful, high-handed, imperious, inconsistent, instinctive, magisterial, optional, overbearing, peremptory, personal, random, subjective, summary, tyrannical, tyrannous, unreasonable, unreasoned, unsupported, whimsical, wilful.

antonyms circumspect, rational, reasoned.

arbitrate *v.* adjudge, adjudicate, decide, determine, judge, pass judgement, referee, settle, umpire.

arbitration *n.* adjudication, arbitrament, decision, determination, intervention, judgement, mediation, negotiation, settlement.

arbitrator *n.* adjudicator, arbiter, intermediary, judge, mediator, moderator, negotiator, referee, umpire.

arcade *n.* cloister, colonnade, covered way, gallery, loggia, mall, peristyle, portico, precinct, stoa.

arcane *adj.* abstruse, cabbalistic, cryptic, enigmatic, esoteric, hidden, mysterious, mystical, obscure, occult, profound, recondite, secret.

antonym commonplace.

arch[1] *n.* arc, archway, bend, bow, concave, cupola, curvature, curve, dome, flexure, semicircle, span, vault.

v. arc, bend, bow, camber, curve, embow, extend, vault.

arch[2] *adj.* accomplished, chief, consummate, coy, egregious, espiègle, expert, finished, first, first-class, foremost, frolicsome, greatest, highest, knowing, leading, main, major, master, mischievous, pert, playful, pre-eminent, primary, principal, provocative, roguish, saucy, sly, top, waggish, wily.

archaic *adj.* ancient, antediluvian, antiquated, antique, bygone, démodé, fogram, obsolete, old, old hat, old-fashioned, outdated, outmoded, out-of-date, passé, primitive, quaint, superannuated, Wardour Street.

antonym modern.

archetype *n.* classic, conception, exemplar, form, idea, ideal, model, original, paradigm, pattern, precursor, prototype, standard, type.

architect *n.* artist, author, constructor, contriver, creator, designer, deviser, engineer, fabricator, fashioner, founder, instigator, inventor, maker, master builder, originator, planner, prime mover, shaper.

architecture *n.* architectonics, arrangement, building, composition, construction, design, framework, make-up, planning, structure, style.

archive *n.* library, muniment room, museum, record office, registry, repository.

archives *n.* annals, chronicles, deeds, documents, ledgers, memorabilia, memorials, muniments, papers, records, registers, roll.

ardent *adj.* amorous, avid, devoted, eager, enthusiastic, fervent, fervid, fierce, fiery, hot, hot-blooded, impassioned, intense, keen, lusty, passionate, perfervid, spirited, vehement, warm, zealous.

antonym dispassionate.

ardour *n.* animation, avidity, devotion, eagerness, earnestness, empressement, enthusiasm, feeling, fervour, fire, heat, intensity, keenness, lust, passion, spirit, vehemence, warmth, zeal, zest.

antonyms coolness, indifference.

arduous *adj.* backbreaking, burdensome, daunting, difficult, exhausting, fatiguing, formidable, gruelling, hard, harsh, herculean, laborious, onerous, punishing, rigorous, severe, strenuous, taxing, tiring, toilsome, tough, troublesome, trying, uphill, wearisome.

antonym easy.

area *n.* arena, bailiwick, ball-park, breadth, canvas, compass, department, district, domain, environs, expanse, extent, field, locality, neighbourhood, part, patch, pidgin, portion, province, range, realm, region, scope, section, sector, size, sphere, stretch, terrain, territory, tract, width, zone.

arena *n.* amphitheatre, area, battlefield, battleground, bowl, coliseum, field, ground, lists, park, ring, scene, stadium, stage.

argot *n.* cant, dialect, idiom, jargon, lingo, parlance, patois, slang, terminology, usage, vernacular, vocabulary.

argue *v.* altercate, argufy, assert, bicker, chop logic, claim, contend, convince, debate, demonstrate, denote, disagree, discuss, display, dispute, evidence, evince, exhibit, expostulate, fall out, fence, feud, fight, haggle, hold, imply, indicate, join issue, logicise, maintain, manifest, moot, persuade, plead, prevail upon, prove, quarrel, question, reason, remonstrate, show, squabble, suggest, talk into, wrangle.

argument *n.* abstract, altercation, argumentation, assertion, barney, beef, bickering, case, claim, clash, contention, controversy, debate, defence, demonstration, dialectic, difference, disagreement, discussion, dispute, exposition, expostulation, feud, fight, gist, ground, lemma, logic, logomachy, outline, plea, pleading, plot, polemic, quarrel, questioning, quodlibet, reason, reasoning, remonstrance, remonstration, row, set-to, shouting-match, squabble, story, story line, subject, summary, synopsis, theme, thesis, wrangle.

argumentative *adj.* belligerent, captious, combative, contentious, contrary, disputatious, disputative, dissentious, litigious, opinionated, perverse, polemical, quarrelsome, wranglesome.

antonym complaisant.

arid *adj.* baked, barren, boring, colourless, desert, desiccated, dreary, droughty, dry, dull, empty, flat, infertile, jejune, lifeless, moistureless, monotonous, parched, spiritless, sterile, tedious, torrid, torrefied,

uninspired, uninteresting, unproductive, vapid, waste, waterless.
antonyms fertile, lively.

aridity *n.* aridness, barrenness, boredom, colourlessness, dreariness, dryness, dullness, emptiness, flatness, infertility, jejuneness, jejunity, lifelessness, monotony, sterility, tedium, vapidity, vapidness.
antonyms fertility, liveliness, productivity, variety.

aright *adv.* accurately, aptly, correctly, de règle, deasil, duly, en règle, exactly, fitly, justly, properly, rightly, suitably, truly.

arise *v.* appear, ascend, begin, climb, come to light, commence, crop up, derive, emanate, emerge, ensue, flow, follow, get up, go up, grow, happen, issue, lift, mount, occur, originate, proceed, result, rise, set in, soar, spring, stand up, start, stem, tower, wake up.

aristocracy *n.* élite, gentility, gentry, haut monde, nobility, noblemen, noblesse, optimates, patricians, patriciate, peerage, quality, ruling class, top drawer, upper class, upper crust.
antonyms canaille, the plebs.

aristocrat *n.* eupatrid, grand seigneur, grande dame, grandee, lady, lord, lordling, nob, noble, nobleman, noblewoman, optimate, patrician, peer, peeress, swell, toff.
antonym commoner.

aristocratic *adj.* blue-blooded, courtly, dignified, elegant, élite, fine, gentle, gentlemanly, haughty, highborn, lordly, noble, patricianly, polished, refined, supercilious, thoroughbred, titled, upper-class, uppercrust, well-born, well-bred.
antonyms plebeian, vulgar.

arithmetic *n.* algorism, algorithm, calculation, ciphering, computation, count, counting, mathematics, numeration, reckoning.

arm[1] *n.* appendage, authority, bough, brachium, branch, channel, department, detachment, division, estuary, extension, firth, inlet, limb, offshoot, projection, section, sector, sound, strait, sway, tributary, upper limb.

arm[2] *v.* accoutre, ammunition, array, brace, empanoply, equip, forearm, fortify, furnish, gird, issue with, munition, outfit, prepare, prime, protect, provide, reinforce, rig, steel, strengthen, supply.

armaments *n.* ammunition, arms, artillery, cannon, guns, matériel, munitions, ordnance, weaponry, weapons.

armed *adj.* accoutred, armoured, arrayed, braced, briefed, equipped, fitted out, forearmed, fortified, furnished, girded, guarded, prepared, primed, protected, provided, steeled, strengthened, thorny.
antonyms unarmed, unprepared.

armour *n.* armature, carapace, chain-mail, garniture, iron-cladding, mail, shell, steel-plating.

armoured *adj.* armour-plated, bomb-proof, bullet-proof, iron-clad, mail-clad, mailed, protected, steel-plated.

armoury *n.* ammunition dump, arsenal, depot, garderobe, magazine, ordnance depot, repertoire, repository, stock, stock-in-trade, stockpile.

arms[1] *n.* armaments, firearms, guns, instruments of war, ordnance, weaponry, weapons.

arms[2] *n.* armorial bearings, blazonry, crest, escutcheon, hatchment, heraldry, insignia, scutcheon, shield.

army *n.* armed force, array, arrière-ban, cohorts, fyrd, gang, horde, host, land forces, legions, military, militia, mob, multitude, pack, soldiers, soldiery, swarm, the junior service, throng, troops.

aroma *n.* bouquet, fragrance, fumet(te), odour, perfume, redolence, savour, scent, smell.

aromatic *adj.* balmy, fragrant, odoriferous, perfumed, pungent, redolent, savoury, spicy, sweet-smelling.
antonym acrid.

around *prep.* about, approximately, circa, circling, circumambient, circumjacent, encircling, enclosing, encompassing, environing, more or less, on all sides of, on every side of, roughly, surrounding.
adv. about, abroad, all over, at hand, close, close by, everywhere, here and there, in all directions, in the air, near, nearby, nigh, on all sides, to and fro.

arouse *v.* agitate, animate, awaken, bestir, call forth, disentrance, enliven, evoke, excite, foment, foster, galvanise, goad, incite, inflame, instigate, kindle, move, prompt, provoke, quicken, rouse, sharpen, spark, spur, startle, stimulate, stir up, summon up, wake up, waken, warm, whet, whip up.
antonyms calm, lull, quieten.

arraign *v.* accuse, attack, call to account, charge, denounce, impeach, impugn, incriminate, indict, prosecute.

arrange[1] *v.* adjust, align, array, categorise, class, classify, collocate, concert, construct, contrive, co-ordinate, design, determine, devise, dispose, distribute, fettle, file, fix, form, group, lay out, marshal, methodise, order, organise, plan, position, prepare, project, range, rank, regulate, schedule, set out, settle, sift, sort, sort out, stage-manage, style, swing, systematise, tidy, trim.

arrange[2] *v.* adapt, harmonise, instrument, orchestrate, score, set.

arrangement[1] *n.* adjustment, agreement, alignment, array, Ausgleich, battery, classification, compact, compromise, construction, deal, design, display, disposition, form, grouping, layout, line-up, marshalling, method, modus vivendi, order, ordering, organisation, plan, planning, preconcert, preparation, provision, ranging, rank, schedule, scheme, settlement, set-up, spacing, structure, system, tabulation, taxis, terms.

arrangement[2] *n.* adaptation, harmonisation, instrumentation, interpretation, orchestration, score, setting, version.

arrant *adj.* absolute, atrocious, barefaced, blatant, brazen, complete, downright, egregious, extreme, flagrant, gross, incorrigible, infamous, monstrous, notorious, out-and-out, outright, rank, thorough, thoroughgoing, undisguised, unmitigated, unregenerate, utter, vile.

array *n.* apparel, arrangement, assemblage, attire, battery, clothes, collection, display, disposition, dress, equipage, exhibition, exposition, finery, formation, garb, garments, line-up, marshalling, muster, order, parade, raiment, regalia, robes, show, supply.
v. accoutre, adorn, align, apparel, arrange, assemble, attire, bedeck, bedizen, caparison, clothe, deck, decorate, display, dispose, draw up, dress, equip, exhibit, form up, garb, group, habilitate, line up, marshal, muster, order, outfit, parade, range, rig out, robe, show, supply, trick out, wrap.

arrest *v.* absorb, apprehend, block, bust, capture, catch, check, collar, delay, detain, divert, end, engage, engross, fascinate, grip, halt, hinder, hold, impede, inhibit, interrupt, intrigue, lay, nab, nick, nip, obstruct, occupy, pinch, prevent, restrain, retard, run in, seize, slow, stall, stanch, stay, stem, stop, suppress.
n. apprehension, blockage, bust, caption, capture, cessation, check, cop, delay, detention, end, halt, hindrance, inhibition, interruption, obstruction, prevention, restraint, seizure, stalling, stay, stoppage, suppression, suspension.

arresting *adj.* amazing, conspicuous, engaging, extraordinary, impressive, notable, noteworthy, noticeable, outstanding, remarkable, striking, stunning, surprising.
antonyms inconspicuous, unremarkable.

arrival *n.* accession, advent, appearance, approach, caller, comer, coming, débutant(e), entrance, entrant, happening, incomer, landfall, newcomer, occurrence, visitant, visitor.
antonym departure.

arrive *v.* alight, appear, attain, befall, come, enter, fetch, get to the top, happen, land, make it, materialise, occur, reach, show, show up, succeed, turn up.
antonym depart.

arrogance *n.* airs, conceit, conceitedness, condescension, contempt, contemptuousness, contumely, disdain, disdainfulness, haughtiness, hauteur, high-handedness, hubris, imperiousness, insolence, loftiness, lordliness, morgue, presumption, presumptuousness, pretension, pretentiousness, pride, scorn, scornfulness, superciliousness, superiority, uppishness.
antonym humility.

arrogant *adj.* assuming, conceited, condescending, contemptuous, contumelious, disdainful, fastuous, haughty, high and mighty, high-handed, hubristic, imperious, insolent, lordly, on the high ropes, overbearing, overweening, presumptuous, proud, scornful, supercilious, superior, uppish.

antonym humble.

arrogate *v.* appropriate, assume, commandeer, confiscate, demand, expropriate, misappropriate, possess oneself of, presume, seize, usurp.

arrow *n.* bolt, dart, flight, indicator, pointer, shaft.

arsenal *n.* ammunition dump, armoury, depot, magazine, ordnance depot, repository, stock, stockpile, store, storehouse, supply, warehouse.

arson *n.* fire-raising, incendiarism, pyromania.

arsonist *n.* fire-bug, fire-raiser, incendiary, pyromaniac.

art *n.* address, adroitness, aptitude, artfulness, artifice, artistry, artwork, astuteness, contrivance, craft, craftiness, craftsmanship, cunning, deceit, dexterity, draughtsmanship, drawing, expertise, facility, finesse, guile, ingenuity, knack, knowledge, mastery, method, métier, painting, profession, sculpture, skill, slyness, subtlety, trade, trick, trickery, virtu, virtuosity, visuals, wiliness.

artful *adj.* adept, adroit, canny, clever, crafty, cunning, deceitful, designing, devious, dexterous, fly, foxy, ingenious, masterly, politic, resourceful, rusé, scheming, sharp, shrewd, skilful, sly, smart, subtle, tricksy, tricky, vulpine, wily.
antonyms artless, ingenuous, naïve.

article *n.* account, bit, clause, commodity, composition, constituent, count, detail, discourse, division, element, essay, feature, head, heading, item, matter, object, paper, paragraph, part, particular, piece, point, portion, report, review, section, story, thing, unit.

articulate[1] *adj.* clear, coherent, comprehensible, distinct, eloquent, expressive, facile, fluent, intelligible, lucid, meaningful, understandable, vocal, well-spoken.
v. breathe, elocute, enounce, enunciate, express, pronounce, say, speak, state, talk, utter, verbalise, vocalise, voice.

articulate[2] *v.* attach, connect, couple, fasten, fit together, hinge, interlock, join, joint, link.

articulation[1] *n.* delivery, diction, enunciation, expression, pronunciation, saying, speaking, talking, utterance, verbalisation, vocalisation, voicing.

articulation[2] *n.* arthrosis, conjunction, connection, coupling, hinge, interlinking, interlock, joint, jointing, juncture, link.

artifice *n.* adroitness, artfulness, chicanery, cleverness, contrivance, cozenage, craft, craftiness, cunning, deception, deftness, device, dodge, duplicity, expedient, facility, finesse, fraud, guile, hoax, invention, machination, manipulation, manoeuvre, ruse, scheme, shift, skill, slyness, stratagem, strategy, subterfuge, subtlety, tactic, trick, trickery, wile.

artificer *n.* architect, artisan, builder, constructer, contriver, craftsman, creator, designer, deviser, fabricator, fashioner, framer, inventor, maker, mechanic, opificer, originator.

artificial *adj.* affected, assumed, bogus, contrived, counterfeit, ersatz, factitious, fake, false, feigned, forced, hyped up, imitation, insincere, made-up, man-made, mannered, manufactured, meretricious, mock, nonnatural, phoney, plastic, pretended, pseudo, sham, simulated, specious, spurious, stagey, synthetic, unnatural.
antonyms genuine, natural.

artillery *n.* battery, cannon, cannonry, enginery, field-guns, field-pieces, gunnage, gunnery, guns, heavy metal, ordnance.

artisan *n.* artificer, craftsman, expert, handicraftsman, journeyman, mechanic, operative, technician, workman.

artist *n.* colourist, craftsman, draughtsman, expert, maestro, master, painter, portraitist, portrait-painter, sculptor, water-colourist.

artiste *n.* actor, comedian, comedienne, comic, entertainer, moke, performer, player, trouper, variety artist, vaudevillian.

artistic *adj.* aesthetic, beautiful, bohemian, creative, cultivated, cultured, decorative, elegant, exquisite, graceful, harmonious, imaginative, ornamental, refined, sensitive, skilled, stylish, talented, tasteful.
antonym inelegant.

artistry *n.* accomplishment, art, brilliance, craft, craftsmanship, creativity, deftness, expertise, finesse, flair, genius, mastery, proficiency, sensibility, sensitivity, skill, style, talent, taste, touch, virtuosity, workmanship.
antonym ineptitude.

artless *adj.* candid, childlike, direct, frank, genuine, guileless, honest, humble, ingenuous, innocent, naïf, naïve, naked, natural, open, plain, primitive, pure, simple, sincere, straightforward, true, trustful, trusting, unadorned, unaffected, uncontrived, undesigning, unpretentious, unsophisticated, unwary, unworldly.
antonym artful.

artlessness *n.* candour, directness, frankness, genuineness, honesty, humbleness, humility, ingenuousness, innocence, naïveté, naïvety, naturalness, openness, purity, simplicity, sincerity, straightforwardness, trustfulness, unpretentiousness, unwariness, unworldliness.
antonym cunning.

as *conj,prep.* because, being, considering that, for example, for instance, in that, in the character of, in the manner of, in the part of, in the role of, inasmuch as, like, seeing that, since, such as, that, to wit, what, when, which, while.

as a rule characteristically, customarily, generally, habitually, mainly, normally, ordinarily, regularly, typically, usually.

as for as regards, in connection with, in reference to, on the subject of, with reference to, with regard to, with relation to, with respect to.

as it were as it might be, in a manner of speaking, in a way, in some way, so to say, so to speak.

as long as assuming, on condition that, provided, supposing, with the provision that.

ascend *v.* climb, float up, fly up, go up, lift off, mount, move up, rise, scale, slope upwards, soar, take off, tower.
antonym descend.

ascendancy *n.* authority, command, control, dominance, domination, dominion, edge, hegemony, influence, leadership, lordship, mastery, power, predominance, preeminence, prestige, prevalence, reign, rule, sovereignty, superiority, supremacy, sway, upper hand.
antonyms decline, subordination.

ascendant *adj.* ascending, authoritative, climbing, commanding, controlling, dominant, influential, levitating, lifting, mounting, powerful, predominant, pre-eminent, prevailing, rising, ruling, superior, supreme, upgoing, uphill, uppermost.
antonyms descending, subordinate.

ascension *n.* arising, ascent, climb, levitation, lifting, mounting, raising, rise, rising.
antonym descent.

ascent *n.* acclivity, advancement, anabasis, ascending, ascension, brae, clamber, clambering, climb, climbing, elevation, escalation, gradient, hill, incline, mounting, ramp, rise, rising, scaling, slope.
antonym descent.

ascertain *v.* confirm, detect, determine, discover, establish, find out, fix, identify, learn, locate, make certain, settle, verify.

ascetic *n.* abstainer, anchorite, celibate, flagellant, hermit, monk, nun, puritan, recluse, solitary, Spartan, stylite.
antonym voluptuary.
adj. abstemious, abstinent, austere, celibate, continent, frugal, harsh, plain, puritanical, rigorous, self-controlled, self-denying, self-disciplined, severe, Spartan, stern, strict, temperate.
antonym voluptuous.

asceticism *n.* abstemiousness, abstinence, ascesis, austerity, celibacy, continence, frugality, harshness, moderation, monasticism, plainness, puritanism, rigorousness, rigour, self-abnegation, self-control, self-denial, self-discipline, temperance.
antonym voluptuousness.

ascribe *v.* accredit, arrogate, assign, attribute, chalk up to, charge, credit, impute, put down.

ashamed *adj.* abashed, apologetic, bashful, blushing, chagrined, confused, conscience-stricken, crestfallen, discomfited, discomposed, distressed, embarrassed, guilty, hesitant, humbled, humiliated, modest, mortified, prudish, red in the face, redfaced, reluctant, remorseful, self-conscious, shamefaced, sheepish, shy, sorry, unwilling, verecund.
antonyms defiant, shameless.

ashen *adj.* anaemic, ashy, blanched, bleached, colourless, ghastly, grey, leaden, livid, pale, pallid, pasty, wan, white.
antonym ruddy.

aside *adv.* alone, apart, away, in isolation, in reserve, on one side, out of the way, privately, secretly, separately.
n. departure, digression, excursion, excursus, interpolation, interposition, parenthesis, soliloquy, whisper.

asinine *adj.* absurd, brainless, cretinous, daft, doltish, dunderheaded, fatuous, foolish, goofy, gormless, half-witted, idiotic, imbecile, imbecilic, inane, moronic, obstinate, potty, senseless, silly, stupid, witless.
antonyms intelligent, sensible.

ask *v.* appeal, apply, beg, beseech, bid, catechise, claim, clamour, crave, demand, entreat, implore, importune, indent, inquire, interrogate, invite, order, petition, plead, pray, press, query, question, quiz, request, require, seek, solicit, sue, summon, supplicate.

askance *adv.* contemptuously, disapprovingly, disdainfully, distrustfully, doubtfully, dubiously, indirectly, mistrustfully, obliquely, sceptically, scornfully, sideways, suspiciously.

askew *adv, adj.* aglee, agley, aslant, asymmetric, awry, cock-eyed, crooked, crookedly, lopsided, oblique, off-centre, out of line, skew, skew-whiff, squint.

asleep *adj.* benumbed, comatose, dead to the world, dormant, dormient, dozing, fast asleep, inactive, inert, napping, numb, reposing, sleeping, slumbering, snoozing, sound asleep, unconscious.

aspect *n.* air, angle, appearance, attitude, bearing, condition, countenance, demeanour, direction, elevation, exposure, expression, face, facet, feature, look, manner, mien, outlook, physiognomy, point of view, position, prospect, scene, side, situation, standpoint, view, visage.

asperity *n.* acerbity, acidity, acrimony, astringency, bitterness, causticity, churlishness, crabbedness, crossness, harshness, irascibility, irritability, peevishness, roughness, severity, sharpness, sourness.
antonym mildness.

aspersion *n.* abuse, animadversion, calumny, censure, criticism, defamation, denigration, derogation, detraction, disparagement, mudslinging, obloquy, reproach, slander, slur, smear, traducement, vilification, vituperation.
antonyms commendation, compliment.

asphyxiate *v.* burke, choke, garrotte, smother, stifle, strangle, strangulate, suffocate, throttle.

aspirant *n.* applicant, aspirer, candidate, competitor, contestant, hopeful, postulant, seeker, striver, suitor.

aspiration *n.* aim, ambition, craving, desire, dream, eagerness, endeavour, goal, hankering, hope, ideal, intent, longing, object, objective, purpose, wish, yearning.

aspire *v.* aim, crave, desire, dream, ettle, hanker, hope, intend, long, purpose, pursue, seek, wish, yearn.

aspiring *adj.* ambitious, aspirant, eager, endeavouring, enterprising, hopeful, keen, longing, optimistic, striving, wishful, would-be.

ass[1] *n.* blockhead, bonehead, cretin, dolt, dope, dunce, fool, half-wit, idiot, moron, nincompoop, ninny, nitwit, numskull, schmuck, simpleton, twerp, twit.

ass[2] *n.* burro, cardophagus, cuddy, donkey, hinny, jackass, jenny, Jerusalem pony, moke, mule.

assail *v.* abuse, assault, attack, belabour, berate, beset, bombard, charge, criticise, encounter, fall upon, impugn, invade, lay into, malign, maltreat, pelt, revile, set about, set upon, strike, vilify.

assailant *n.* abuser, adversary, aggressor, assailer, assaulter, attacker, invader, opponent, reviler.

assassin *n.* bravo, cut-throat, eliminator, executioner, hatchet man, hit-man, homicide, killer, liquidator, murderer, slayer, thug.

assassinate *v.* dispatch, eliminate, hit, kill, liquidate, murder, rub out, slay.

assault *n.* aggression, attack, blitz, charge, incursion, invasion, offensive, onset, onslaught, raid, storm, storming, strike.
v. assail, attack, beset, charge, fall on, hit, invade, lay violent hands on, set upon, storm, strike.

assay *v.* analyse, appraise, assess, estimate, evaluate, examine, inspect, investigate, prove, test, try, weigh.
n. analysis, assaying, attempt, docimasy, endeavour, essay, examination, inspection, investigation, test, trial, try, valuation, venture.

assemblage *n.* accumulation, aggregation, array, assembly, body, collection, company, congeries, conglomeration, crowd, flock, galaxy, gathering, group, mass, multitude, rally, throng.

assemble *v.* accumulate, amass, build, collect, compose, congregate, construct, convene, convocate, convoke, erect, fabricate, flock, forgather, gather, group, join up, levy, make, manufacture, marshal, meet, mobilise, muster, muster (up), piece, rally, round up, set up, summon, together.
antonym disperse.

assembly *n.* agora, assemblage, ball, body, building, collection, company, conclave, conference, congregation, congress, consistory, construction, convocation, council, crowd, diet, divan, ecclesia, erection, fabrication, fitting, flock, folkmoot, gathering, gemot, gorsedd, group, indaba, joining, kgotla, levy, manufacture, mass, meeting, moot, multitude, panegyry, rally, reception, setting up, soirée, synod, throng.

assent *v.* accede, accept, acquiesce, agree, allow, approve, comply, concede, concur, consent, grant, permit, sanction, submit, subscribe, yield.
antonym disagree.

n. acceptance, accession, accord, acquiescence, agreement, approval, capitulation, compliance, concession, concurrence, consent, permission, sanction, submission.

assert *v.* advance, affirm, allege, asseverate, attest, aver, avouch, avow, claim, constate, contend, declare, defend, dogmatise, insist, lay down, maintain, predicate, press, profess, promote, pronounce, protest, state, stress, swear, testify to, thrust forward, uphold, vindicate.
antonym deny.

assertion *n.* affirmance, affirmation, allegation, asseveration, attestation, averment, avowal, claim, constatation, contention, declaration, dictum, gratis dictum, ipse dixit, predication, profession, pronouncement, statement, vindication, vouch, word.
antonym denial.

assertive *adj.* aggressive, assuming, bold, bumptious, confident, decided, dogmatic, domineering, emphatic, firm, forceful, forward, insistent, opinionated, overbearing, presumptuous, pushy, self-assured, strongwilled.
antonym diffident.

assertiveness *n.* aggressiveness, boldness, bumptiousness, decisiveness, dogmatism, forcefulness, forwardness, insistence, overbearingness, positiveness, presumption, presumptuousness, pushiness, self-assurance, selfconfidence.

assess *v.* affeer, appraise, compute, consider, demand, determine, estimate, evaluate, fix, gauge, impose, investigate, judge, levy, rate, review, size up, tax, value, weigh.

assessment *n.* affeerment, appraisal, calculation, consideration, determination, estimate, estimation, evaluation, gauging, judgement, opinion, rating, review, taxation, valuation.

asset *n.* advantage, aid, benefit, blessing, help, plus, resource, service, strength, virtue.
antonym liability.

assets *n.* capital, estate, funds, goods, holdings, means, money, possessions, property, reserves, resources, securities, wealth, wherewithal.

asseverate *v.* affirm, assert, attest, aver, avouch, avow, certify, declare, maintain, profess, pronounce, protest, state, swear, testify.

asseveration *n.* affirmation, assertion, assurance, attestation, averment, avowal, declaration, deposition, predication, profession, pronouncement, protestation, statement, vow.

assiduity *n.* application, assiduousness, attentiveness, conscientiousness, constancy, dedication, devotion, diligence, indefatigability, industriousness, industry, labour, perseverance, persistence, sedulity, sedulousness, steadiness, tirelessness.
antonym negligence.

assiduous *adj.* attentive, conscientious, constant, dedicated, devoted, diligent, hard-working, indefatigable, industrious, persevering,

persistent, sedulous, steady, studious, unflagging, untiring.
antonym negligent.

assign *v.* accredit, adjudge, allocate, allot, apart, appoint, apportion, arrogate, ascribe, attribute, choose, consign, delegate, designate, determine, dispense, distribute, fix, give, grant, name, nominate, put down, select, set, specify, stipulate.

assignation *n.* allocation, allotment, appointment, arrangement, date, engagement, meeting, rendezvous, tryst.

assignment *n.* allocation, allotment, appointment, apportionment, ascription, attribution, charge, commission, consignment, delegation, designation, determination, dispensation, distribution, duty, errand, giving, grant, imposition, job, mission, nomination, position, post, responsibility, selection, specification, task.

assimilate *v.* absorb, accept, acclimatise, accommodate, acculturate, accustom, adapt, adjust, blend, conform, digest, fit, homogenise, imbibe, incorporate, ingest, intermix, learn, merge, mingle, take in, tolerate.
antonym reject.

assimilation *n.* absorption, acceptance, acclimatisation, accommodation, acculturation, adaptation, adjustment, conformity, homogenisation, incorporation, ingestion, learning, toleration.
antonym rejection.

assist *v.* abet, accommodate, aid, back, benefit, bestead, boost, collaborate, co-operate, enable, expedite, facilitate, further, help, rally round, reinforce, relieve, second, serve, succour, support, sustain.
antonym thwart.

assistance *n.* a leg up, abetment, accommodation, adjutancy, aid, backing, benefit, boost, collaboration, comfort, co-operation, furtherance, help, reinforcement, relief, succour, support, sustainment.
antonym hindrance.

assistant *n.* abettor, accessory, accomplice, adjutant, aide, ally, ancillary, associate, auxiliary, backer, coadjutor, collaborator, colleague, confederate, co-operator, Girl Friday, helper, helpmate, henchman, Man Friday, partner, Person Friday, right-hand man, second, subordinate, subsidiary, supporter.

associate *v.* accompany, affiliate, ally, amalgamate, combine, company, confederate, conjoin, connect, consort, correlate, couple, fraternise, hang around, hobnob, identify, join, league, link, mingle, mix, pair, relate, socialise, unite, yoke.
n. affiliate, ally, assistant, bedfellow, co-adjutor, collaborator, colleague, companion, compeer, comrade, confederate, confrère, co-worker, fellow, follower, friend, leaguer, mate, partner, peer, side-kick.

association *n.* affiliation, alliance, analogy, band, blend, bloc, bond, cartel, clique, club, coalition, combination, combine, companionship, company, compound, comradeship, concomitance, confederacy, confederation, connection, consociation, consortium, conspiracy, co-operative, corporation, correlation, familiarity, federation, fellowship, fraternisation, fraternity, friendship, Gesellschaft, group, intimacy, joining, juxtaposition, league, linkage, mixture, organisation, pairing, partnership, relation, relations, relationship, resemblance, society, syndicate, syndication, tie, trust, union, Verein.

assorted *adj.* different, differing, divergent, divers, diverse, diversified, heterogeneous, manifold, miscellaneous, mixed, motley, multifarious, multiform, several, sundry, varied, variegated, various.

assortment *n.* arrangement, array, assemblage, categorisation, choice, classification, collection, disposition, distribution, diversity, farrago, grading, grouping, hotchpotch, jumble, medley, mélange, miscellany, mishmash, mixture, olio, olla-podrida, pot-pourri, ranging, salad, salmagundi, selection, sift, sifting, sorting, variety.

assuage *v.* allay, alleviate, appease, calm, dull, ease, lessen, lighten, lower, lull, mitigate, moderate, mollify, pacify, palliate, quench, quieten, reduce, relieve, satisfy, slake, soften, soothe, still, temper, tranquillise.
antonym exacerbate.

assume *v.* accept, acquire, adopt, affect, appropriate, arrogate, believe, commandeer, counterfeit, deduce, don, embrace, expect, expropriate, fancy, feign, guess, imagine, infer, opine, postulate, pre-empt, premise, presume, presuppose, pretend to, put on, seize, sham, shoulder, simulate, strike, suppose, surmise, suspect, take, take for granted, take on, take over, take up, think, understand, undertake, usurp.

assumed *adj.* accepted, adopted, affected, bogus, conjectural, counterfeit, expected, fake, false, feigned, fictitious, fiducial, hyphothetical, made-up, phoney, presumed, presupposed, pretended, pseudonymous, seized, sham, simulated, specious, spurious, supposed, suppositional, surmised, usurped.

assuming *adj.* arrogant, assertive, audacious, bold, brazen, bumptious, conceited, forward, impertinent, impudent, overconfident, presumptuous, pretentious, pushy, self-assertive, self-important, uppish.
antonym unassuming.

assumption *n.* acceptance, acquisition, adoption, appropriation, arrogance, arrogation, audacity, belief, bumptiousness, conceit, conjecture, expectation, expropriation, fancy, guess, guesswork, hypothesis, impudence, inference, postulate, postulation, pre-emption, premise, premiss, presumption, presumptuousness, presupposition, pride, seizure, self-importance, supposition, surmise, suspicion, theory, understanding, undertaking, usurpation.

assurance *n.* affirmation, aplomb, assertion, asseveration, assuredness, audacity, boldness, certainty, certitude, chutzpah, confidence, conviction, coolness, courage, declaration, firmness, gall, guarantee, nerve, oath, pledge, plerophory, poise, positiveness, profession, promise, protestation, security, self-confidence, self-reliance, sureness, vow, word.
antonym uncertainty.

assure *v.* affirm, attest, boost, certify, clinch, comfort, confirm, convince, embolden, encourage, ensure, guarantee, hearten, persuade, pledge, promise, reassure, seal, secure, soothe, strengthen, swear, tell, vow, warrant.

assured *adj.* assertive, audacious, bold, certain, clinched, cocksure, confident, confirmed, definite, ensured, fixed, guaranteed, indisputable, indubitable, irrefutable, overconfident, pert, poised, positive, secure, self-assured, self-confident, self-possessed, settled, sure, unquestionable.
antonym uncertain.

assuredly *adv.* certainly, definitely, indisputably, indubitably, surely, truly, unquestionably.

astir *adj., adv.* about, active, afoot, awake, circulating, in motion, in the air, roused, up.

astonish *v.* amaze, astound, baffle, bewilder, confound, daze, dumbfound, electrify, flabbergast, floor, nonplus, shock, stagger, startle, stun, stupefy, surprise, wow.

astonished *adj.* amazed, astounded, baffled, bewildered, bug-eyed, confounded, dazed, dumbfounded, electrified, flabbergasted, incredulous, staggered, startled, stunned, surprised, thunder-struck.

astonishing *adj.* amazing, astounding, baffling, bewildering, breathtaking, dazzling, impressive, incredible, prodigious, staggering, startling, striking, stunning, stupefying, surprising.

astonishment *n.* amazement, awe, bafflement, bewilderment, confusion, consternation, dismay, shock, stupefaction, surprise, wonder, wonderment.

astound *v.* abash, amaze, astonish, baffle, bewilder, confound, daze, dumbfound, electrify, flabbergast, overwhelm, shake, shock, stagger, stun, stupefy, surprise, wow.

astounded *adj.* abashed, amazed, baffled, bewildered, confounded, dazed, dumbfounded, electrified, flabbergasted, incredulous, overwhelmed, shaken, shocked, staggered, stunned, stupefied, wowed.

astounding *adj.* amazing, astonishing, baffling, bewildering, breathtaking, electrifying, impressive, incredible, overwhelming, shocking, staggering, striking, stunning, stupefying, surprising.

astray *adv.* adrift, amiss, awry, lost, off course, off the mark, off the rails, to the bad, wrong.

astringent *adj.* acerb, acerbic, acid, astrictive, austere, biting, caustic, contractile, contractive, exacting, grim, hard, harsh, puckery,

restringent, rigorous, scathing, severe, stern, strict, stringent, styptic, trenchant.
antonym bland.

astrology *n.* astromancy, horoscopy, star-gazing.

astronomical *adj.* astrophysical, celestial, cosmological, enormous, high, huge, Uranian.

astronomy *n.* astrodynamics, astrography, astrophysics, cosmography, cosmology, star-gazing, uranography, uranology.

astute *adj.* acute, adroit, artful, astucious, calculating, canny, clever, crafty, cunning, discerning, fly, foxy, intelligent, keen, knowing, penetrating, perceptive, percipient, perspicacious, politic, prudent, sagacious, sharp, shrewd, sly, subtle, wily, wise.
antonym stupid.

astuteness *n.* acumen, acuteness, adroitness, artfulness, astucity, canniness, cleverness, craftiness, cunning, discernment, insight, intelligence, penetration, perceptiveness, percipience, perspicacity, sagacity, sharpness, shrewdness, slyness, subtlety, wiliness.
antonym stupidity.

asunder *adv.* apart, in half, in pieces, in twain, in two, into pieces, to bits, to pieces.

asylum *n.* bedlam, bughouse, cover, funny farm, harbour, haven, hospital, institution, loony-bin, madhouse, mental hospital, nuthouse, preserve, refuge, reserve, retreat, safety, sanctuary, shelter.

asymmetrical *adj.* asymmetric, awry, crooked, disproportionate, disymmetric, gibbous, irregular, unbalanced, unequal, uneven, unsymmetrical.
antonym symmetrical.

asymmetry *n.* disproportion, disymmetry, imbalance, inequality, irregularity, misproportion, unevenness, unsymmetry.
antonym symmetry.

at a loss baffled, bewildered, confounded, confused, helpless, nonplussed, perplexed, puzzled, resourceless, stuck, stumped.

at bay caught, cornered, trapped, up against it, with one's back to the wall.

at fault accountable, answerable, blamable, blameworthy, culpable, guilty, responsible.

at first sight on first acquaintance, on the surface, prima facie, superficially, to the outsider.

at hand approaching, at one's elbow, available, close, handy, immediate, imminent, impending, near, nearby, on tap, ready.

at home at ease, comfortable, contented, conversant, experienced, familiar, knowledgeable, proficient, relaxed, skilled, well-versed.

at large at liberty, footloose, free, independent, liberated, on the loose, on the run, roaming, unconfined, unconstrained.

at last at length, at long last, eventually, finally, in conclusion, in due course, in the end, in time, ultimately.

at leisure at ease, at liberty, disengaged, free, idle, off the hook, unbusy, unengaged.

at length at last, at long last, completely, eventually, exhaustively, finally, for ages, for hours, fully, in depth, in detail, in the end, in time, interminably, thoroughly, to the full, ultimately.

at liberty at large, at leisure, disengaged, footloose, free, idle, not confined, on the loose, unconstrained, unrestricted.

at odds at daggers drawn, at enmity, at loggerheads, at one another's throats, at outs, at variance, feuding, in conflict, in dispute, opposed, quarrelling.

at once at one go, at the same time, directly, ek dum, forthwith, immediately, in concert, in unison, incontinent, instantly, now, promptly, right away, simultaneously, straight away, straightway, this minute, together, unhesitatingly, without delay.

at one's wits' end at a loss, at the end of one's tether, baffled, bewildered, desperate, in despair, in dire straits, lost, resourceless, stuck, stumped.

at random accidentally, adventitiously, aimlessly, arbitrarily, casually, desultorily, fortuitously, haphazardly, indiscriminately, irregularly, purposelessly, randomly, unsystematically.

at rest asleep, at a standstill, calm, dead, idle, inactive, motionless, peaceful, resting, sleeping, still, stopped, tranquil, unmoving.

at sea adrift, astray, baffled, bewildered, confused, disoriented, insecure, lost, mystified, perplexed, puzzled, upset.

at the double at full speed, at once, briskly, immediately, in double-quick time, lickety-split, like lightning, posthaste, quickly, quick-sticks, without delay.

at work on the job.

atheism *n.* disbelief, free-thinking, godlessness, heathenism, impiety, infidelity, irreligion, non-belief, paganism, rationalism, scepticism, unbelief, ungodliness.

atheist *n.* disbeliever, free-thinker, heathen, infidel, irreligionist, non-believer, nullifidian, pagan, sceptic, unbeliever.

atheistic *adj.* atheistical, disbelieving, free-thinking, heathen, impious, irreligious, irreverent, rationalistic, sceptical, unbelieving, ungodly, unreligious.
antonym religious.

athlete *n.* agonist, competitor, contender, contestant, gymnast, jock, runner, sportsman, sportswoman.

athletic *adj.* active, brawny, energetic, fit, husky, muscular, powerful, robust, sinewy, strapping, strong, sturdy, thewy, vigorous, well-knit, well-proportioned, wiry.
antonym puny.

athletics *n.* agonistics, callisthenics, contests, events, exercises, games, gymnastics, races, sports, track events.

atmosphere *n.* aerospace, aerosphere, air, ambience, aura, character, climate, environment, feel, feeling, flavour, heavens, milieu, mood, quality, sky, spirit, surroundings, tenor, tone, vibrations.

atmospheric *adj.* aerial, climatic, epedaphic, meteorological.

atom *n.* atomy, bit, crumb, grain, hint, iota, jot, mite, molecule, morsel, particle, scintilla, scrap, shred, smidgen, speck, spot, tittle, trace, whit.

atone *v.* aby(e), compensate, expiate, make amends, make up for, offset, pay for, propitiate, recompense, reconcile, redeem, redress, remedy.

atonement *n.* amends, compensation, expiation, indemnity, payment, penance, propitiation, recompense, redress, reparation, repayment, restitution, restoration, satisfaction.

atrocious *adj.* abominable, barbaric, brutal, cruel, diabolical, execrable, fell, fiendish, flagitious, ghastly, grievous, heinous, hideous, horrible, horrifying, infamous, infernal, inhuman, monstrous, piacular, ruthless, savage, shocking, terrible, vicious, vile, villainous, wicked.

atrocity *n.* abomination, atrociousness, barbarity, barbarousness, brutality, crime, cruelty, enormity, evil, flagitiousness, ghastliness, heinousness, hideousness, horror, infamy, inhumanity, monstrousness, outrage, ruthlessness, savagery, viciousness, vileness, villainy, wickedness.

atrophy *n.* decay, decline, degeneration, deterioration, diminution, emaciation, marasmus, shrivelling, tabefaction, tabes, wasting, withering.

v. decay, decline, degenerate, deteriorate, diminish, dwindle, emaciate, fade, shrink, shrivel, tabefy, waste, wither.

attach *v.* add, adhere, adhibit, affix, annex, append, articulate, ascribe, assign, associate, attract, attribute, belong, bind, captivate, combine, connect, couple, fasten, fix, impute, join, link, place, put, relate to, secure, stick, tie, unite, weld.

antonyms detach, unfasten.

attached *adj.* affectionate, affiliated, associated, connected, fond, loving.

attachment *n.* accessory, accoutrement, adapter, addition, adhesion, adhibition, adjunct, affection, affinity, appendage, appurtenance, attraction, bond, codicil, cohesion, confiscation, connection, connector, coupling, devotion, esteem, extension, extra, fastener, fastening, fidelity, fitting, fixture, fondness, friendship, joint, junction, liking, link, love, loyalty, partiality, predilection, regard, seizure, supplement, tenderness, tie.

attack *n.* abuse, access, aggression, assailment, assault, battery, blitz, bombardment, bout, broadside, censure, charge, convulsion, criticism, fit, foray, impugnment, incursion, inroad, invasion, invective, kamikaze, offensive, onset, onslaught, paroxysm, raid, rush, seizure, spasm, spell, stroke, stroke.

v. abuse, assail, assault, belabour, berate, blame, censure, charge, chastise, criticise, denounce, do over, fake, fall on, flay, have one's knife in, impugn, invade, inveigh

against, lash, lay into, light into, make at, malign, mob, put the boot in, raid, rate, revile, rush, set about, set on, snipe, storm, strafe, strike, vilify, visit, wade into.

attacker *n.* abuser, aggressor, assailant, assaulter, critic, invader, mugger, persecutor, raider, reviler, traducer.

antonyms defender, supporter.

attain *v.* accomplish, achieve, acquire, arrive at, bag, compass, complete, earn, effect, fulfil, gain, get, grasp, net, obtain, procure, reach, realise, reap, secure, touch, win.

attainability *n.* accessibility, availability, feasibility, obtainability, practicalness, procurability, realisability.

attainable *adj.* accessible, achievable, available, feasible, manageable, obtainable, possible, potential, practicable, probable, procurable, reachable, realistic, within reach.

antonym unattainable.

attainment *n.* ability, accomplishment, achievement, acquirement, acquisition, aptitude, art, capability, competence, completion, consummation, facility, feat, fulfilment, gift, mastery, procurement, proficiency, reaching, realisation, skill, success, talent.

attempt *n.* assault, assay, attack, bash, bid, coup d'essai, crack, effort, endeavour, essay, experiment, go, move, push, shot, shy, stab, struggle, trial, try, undertaking, venture.

v. aspire, endeavour, essay, experiment, have a bash, have a crack, have a go, have a shot, seek, strive, tackle, try, try one's hand at, try one's luck at, undertake, venture.

attend *v.* accompany, appear, arise from, assist, be all ears, be present, care for, chaperon, companion, convoy, escort, follow, frequent, give ear, guard, hear, hearken, heed, help, lend an ear, listen, look after, mark, mind, minister to, note, notice, nurse, observe, pay attention, pay heed, pin back one's ears, regard, result from, serve, squire, succour, take care of, tend, usher, visit, wait upon, watch.

attend to concentrate on, control, cope with, deal with, direct, look after, manage, oversee, see to, supervise, take care of.

attendance *n.* appearance, assistance, attending, audience, crowd, escortage, gate, house, ministration, presence, turn-out.

attendant *n.* acolyte, aide, assistant, auxiliary, batman, bed captain, chaperon, companion, custodian, equerry, escort, famulus, flunkey, follower, ghillie, guard, guide, helper, jäger, Jeames, kavass, lackey, lady-help, lady-in-waiting, lady's-maid, livery-servant, marshal, menial, page, poursuivant, retainer, servant, steward, underling, usher, waiter.

adj. accessory, accompanying, associated, attached, concomitant, consequent, incidental, related, resultant, subsequent.

attention *n.* advertence, advertency, alertness, attentiveness, awareness, care, civility, concentration, concern, consciousness, consideration, contemplation, courtesy, deference, ear, gallantry, heed, heedfulness, intentness, mindfulness, ministration, notice, observation, politeness, recognition, regard, respect, service, thought, thoughtfulness, treatment, vigilance.

antonyms disregard, inattention.

attentive *adj.* accommodating, advertent, alert, awake, careful, civil, concentrating, conscientious, considerate, courteous, deferential, devoted, gallant, gracious, heedful, intent, kind, mindful, obliging, observant, polite, regardant, studious, thoughtful, vigilant, watchful.

antonyms heedless, inattentive, inconsiderate.

attenuate *v.* adulterate, debase, decrease, devaluate, dilute, diminish, draw out, elongate, enervate, enfeeble, extend, lengthen, rarefy, reduce, refine, sap, stretch out, taper, thin, thin out, water down, weaken.

antonyms expand, intensify, thicken.

attenuated *adj.* adulterated, attenuate, debased, decreased, devalued, dilute, diluted, diminished, drawn out, elongated, enervated, enfeebled, extended, lengthened, rarefied, reduced, refined, sapped, slender, spun out, stretched out, tapering, thinned, watered down, weakened.

attest *v.* adjure, affirm, assert, authenticate, aver, certify, confirm, corroborate, declare, demonstrate, depose, display, endorse, evidence, evince, exhibit, manifest, prove, ratify, seal, show, substantiate, swear, testify, verify, vouch, warrant, witness.

attestation *n.* affirmation, asseveration, assurance, averment, avowal, certification, confirmation, corroboration, declaration, deposition, endorsement, evidence, evincement, testification, testimony, vouch, witness.

attire *n.* accoutrements, apparel, array, clothes, clothing, costume, dress, finery, garb, garments, gear, get-up, habiliments, habit, outfit, raiment, rig-out, robes, togs, uniform, vestment, wear, weeds.

v. accoutre, adorn, apparel, array, caparison, clothe, costume, deck out, dress, equip, garb, habilitate, outfit, prepare, rig out, robe, turn out.

attitude *n.* affectation, air, Anschauung, approach, aspect, bearing, carriage, condition, demeanour, disposition, feeling, manner, mien, mood, opinion, outlook, perspective, point of view, pose, position, posture, stance, view, Weltanschauung.

attract *v.* allure, appeal to, bewitch, captivate, charm, decoy, draw, enchant, engage, entice, fascinate, incline, induce, interest, inveigle, invite, lure, pull, seduce, tempt.

antonym repel.

attraction *n.* allure, amenity, appeal, attractiveness, bait, captivation, charm, draw, enchantment, entertainment, enticement, event, fascination, inducement, interest, invitation, lure, magnetism, pull, seduction, show, temptation.

antonym repulsion.

attractive *adj.* agreeable, alluring, appealing, appetible, beautiful, beddable, captivating, catching, catchy, charming, comely, enchanting, engaging, enticing, epigamous, fair, fascinating, fetching, glamorous, good-looking, gorgeous, handsome, interesting, inviting, jolie laide, lovely, magnetic, nubile, personable, pleasant, pleasing, prepossessing, pretty, seductive, snazzy, stunning, taky, tempting, toothsome, voluptuous, winning, winsome.

antonyms repellent, unattractive.

attribute *v.* accredit, apply, arrogate, ascribe, assign, blame, charge, credit, impute, put down, refer.

n. affection, aspect, character, characteristic, facet, feature, idiosyncrasy, mark, note, peculiarity, point, property, quality, quirk, sign, symbol, trait, virtue.

attribution *n.* accreditation, application, ascription, assignment, charge, crediting, imputation.

attrition *n.* abrasion, attenuation, chafing, debilitation, detrition, erosion, fretting, friction, grinding, harassment, harrying, rubbing, scraping, weakening, wear, wearing away, wearing down.

attune *v.* acclimatise, accustom, adapt, adjust, assimilate, co-ordinate, familiarise, harmonise, homologise, modulate, reconcile, regulate, set, tune.

atypical *adj.* aberrant, abnormal, anomalous, deviant, divergent, eccentric, exceptional, extraordinary, freakish, untypical, unusual.

antonym typical.

au fait abreast of, acquainted, au courant, clued-up, conversant, hep, in the know, in the stream, in the swim, in touch, knowledgeable, on the ball, posted, up-to-date, well up, well-informed.

auburn *adj.* chestnut, copper, henna, nutbrown, red, russet, rust, tawny, titian.

auction *n.* cant, roup, sale, vendue.

audacious *adj.* adventurous, assuming, assured, bold, brave, brazen, cheeky, courageous, dare-devil, daring, dauntless, death-defying, der-doing, disrespectful, enterprising, fearless, forward, impertinent, impudent, insolent, intrepid, pert, plucky, presumptuous, rash, reckless, risky, rude, shameless, unabashed, valiant, venturesome.

antonyms cautious, reserved, timid.

audacity *n.* adventurousness, assurance, audaciousness, boldness, brass neck, bravery, brazenness, cheek, chutzpah, courage, daring, dauntlessness, defiance, derring-do, disrespectfulness, effrontery, enterprise, fearlessness, foolhardiness, forwardness, gall, guts, impertinence, impudence, insolence, intrepidity, nerve, pertness, presumption, rashness, recklessness, rudeness, shamelessness, valour, venturesomeness.

antonyms caution, reserve, timidity.

audible *adj.* appreciable, clear, detectable, discernible, distinct, hearable, perceptible, recognisable.
antonym inaudible.

audience *n.* assemblage, assembly, auditorium, congregation, crowd, devotees, fans, following, gallery, gathering, hearing, house, interview, listeners, market, meeting, onlookers, public, ratings, reception, regulars, spectators, turn-out, viewers.

audit *n.* analysis, balancing, check, checking, examination, inspection, investigation, review, scrutiny, statement, verification.
v. analyse, balance, check, examine, inspect, investigate, review, scrutinise, verify.

auditor *n.* accountant, actuary, analyst, examiner, inspector, scrutator, scrutiniser.

augment *v.* add to, amplify, boost, dilate, eke out, enhance, enlarge, expand, extend, grow, heighten, increase, inflate, intensify, magnify, multiply, raise, reinforce, strengthen, supplement, swell.
antonym decrease.

augur *n.* auspex, divinator, diviner, haruspex, oracle, prognosticator, prophet, seer, soothsayer.
v. auspicate, bespeak, betoken, bode, forebode, foreshadow, foretoken, harbinger, haruspicate, herald, import, portend, predict, prefigure, presage, promise, prophesy, signify.

augury *n.* auspice, divination, foreboding, forerunner, forewarning, harbinger, haruspication, herald, omen, portent, precursor, prediction, presage, prodrome, prognostication, promise, prophecy, sign, soothsaying, token, warning.

august *adj.* awful, dignified, exalted, glorious, grand, imposing, impressive, lofty, magnificent, majestic, monumental, noble, portentous, regal, revered, solemn, splendid, stately, venerable.

aura *n.* air, ambience, aroma, atmosphere, effluvium, emanation, feel, feeling, hint, mood, nimbus, odour, quality, scent, suggestion, vibes, vibrations.

auspices *n.* aegis, authority, backing, care, championship, charge, control, guidance, influence, patronage, protection, responsibility, sponsorship, superintendence, supervision, support, tutelage.

auspicious *adj.* bright, cheerful, encouraging, favourable, felicitous, fortunate, happy, hopeful, lucky, opportune, optimistic, promising, propitious, prosperous, rosy, white.
antonyms inauspicious, ominous.

austere *adj.* abstemious, abstinent, ascetic, astringent, bitter, bleak, chaste, cold, conservative, continent, Dantean, Dantesque, economical, exacting, forbidding, formal, grave, grim, hard, harsh, plain, puritanical, restrained, rigid, rigorous, self-denying, self-disciplined, serious, severe, simple, sober, solemn, sour, spare, Spartan, stark, stern,

strict, stringent, unadorned, unembellished, unornamented, unrelenting.
antonyms elaborate, extravagant, genial.

austerity *n.* abstemiousness, abstinence, asceticism, chasteness, chastity, coldness, continence, economy, formality, gravity, grimness, hardness, harshness, inflexibility, plainness, puritanism, reserve, restraint, rigidity, rigour, self-control, self-denial, self-discipline, seriousness, severity, simplicity, sobriety, solemnity, spareness, Spartanism, starkness, sternness, strictness.
antonyms elaborateness, extravagant, geniality.

authentic *adj.* accurate, actual, authoritative, bona fide, certain, dependable, dinkum, factual, faithful, genuine, honest, kosher, legitimate, original, pure, real, reliable, simon-pure, true, true-to-life, trustworthy, valid, veracious, veritable.
antonyms counterfeit, inauthentic, spurious.

authenticate *v.* accredit, attest, authorise, avouch, certify, confirm, corroborate, endorse, guarantee, validate, verify, vouch for, warrant.

authentication *n.* accreditation, attestation, authorisation, certification, confirmation, corroboration, endorsement, guarantee, validation, verification, voucher, warrant.

authenticity *n.* accuracy, actuality, authoritativeness, certainty, correctness, dependability, factualness, faithfulness, fidelity, genuineness, honesty, legitimacy, purity, reality, realness, reliability, trustworthiness, truth, truthfulness, validity, veracity, veritableness, verity.
antonyms invalidity, spuriousness.

author *n.* architect, begetter, composer, creator, designer, fabricator, fashioner, father, forger, founder, framer, initiator, inventor, maker, mover, originator, paper-stainer, parent, pen, penman, penwoman, planner, prime mover, producer, volumist, writer.

authorisation *n.* accreditation, approval, certification, credentials, go-ahead, green light, leave, licence, permission, permit, sanction, warrant.

authorise *v.* accredit, allow, approve, commission, confirm, consent to, countenance, empower, enable, entitle, legalise, license, permit, ratify, sanction, validate, warrant.

authoritarian *adj.* absolute, autocratic, despotic, dictatorial, disciplinarian, doctrinaire, dogmatic, domineering, harsh, heavy, imperious, inflexible, oppressive, repressive, rigid, severe, strict, tyrannical, unyielding.
antonym liberal.
n. absolutist, autocrat, despot, dictator, disciplinarian, fascist, Hitler, tyrant.

authoritarianism *n.* absolutism, autocracy, despotism, dictatorship, fascism, fascismo, Hildebrandism, Hitlerism, totalitarianism, tyranny.
antonyms laissez faire, liberalism.

authoritative *adj.* accepted, accurate, approved,

assured, authentic, authorised, cathedratic, commanding, confident, convincing, decisive, definitive, dependable, factual, faithful, learned, legitimate, magisterial, magistral, masterly, official, reliable, sanctioned, scholarly, sound, sovereign, true, trustworthy, truthful, valid, veritable.
antonym unreliable.

authoritatively *adv.* confidently, decisively, ex cathedra, legitimately, reliably, soundly.

authority[1] *n.* administration, ascendancy, attestation, authorisation, avowal, charge, command, control, declaration, domination, dominion, evidence, force, government, imperium, influence, jurisdiction, justification, licence, management, might, officialdom, permission, permit, power, prerogative, profession, right, rule, sanction, sovereignty, statement, strength, supremacy, sway, testimony, textbook, warrant, weight, word.

authority[2] *n.* arbiter, bible, connoisseur, expert, judge, master, professional, pundit, sage, scholar, specialist.

autocracy *n.* absolutism, authoritarianism, despotism, dictatorship, fascism, Hitlerism, totalitarianism, tyranny.
antonym democracy.

autocrat *n.* absolutist, authoritarian, Caesar, cham, despot, dictator, fascist, Hitler, panjandrum, totalitarian, tyrant.

autocratic *adj.* absolute, all-powerful, authoritarian, despotic, dictatorial, dictatory, domineering, imperious, overbearing, totalitarian, tyrannical, tyrannous.
antonyms democratic, liberal.

automatic *adj.* automated, certain, habitual, inescapable, inevitable, instinctive, involuntary, mechanical, mechanised, natural, necessary, perfunctory, push-button, reflex, robot, robot-like, routine, self-acting, self-activating, self-moving, self-propelling, self-regulating, spontaneous, unavoidable, unbidden, unconscious, unthinking, unwilled, vegetative.

automaton *n.* Dalek, machine, mechanical man, robot.

autonomous *adj.* autarkic, free, independent, self-determining, self-governing, sovereign, voluntary.
antonym subject.

autonomy *n.* autarky, free will, freedom, home rule, independence, self-determination, self-government, self-rule, sovereignty.
antonyms compulsion, subjection.

auxiliary *adj.* accessory, adjuvant, adminicular, aiding, ancillary, assistant, assisting, back-up, emergency, helping, reserve, secondary, subsidiary, substitute, supplementary, supporting, supportive.
n. accessory, accomplice, adminicle, ally, ancillary, assistant, associate, companion, confederate, foederatus, helper, partner, reserve, subordinate, supporter.

avail *v.* advance, advantage, aid, assist, benefit, boot, dow, exploit, help, make the most of, profit, serve, work.
n. advantage, aid, assistance, benefit, boot, good, help, profit, purpose, service, use, value.

avail oneself of capitalise on, make use of, profit by, profit from, take advantage of, turn to account, use, utilise.

available *adj.* accessible, at hand, attainable, convenient, disengaged, free, handy, obtainable, on hand, on tap, procurable, ready, to hand, vacant, within reach.
antonym unavailable.

avalanche *n.* barrage, cascade, cataclysm, deluge, flood, inundation, landslide, landslip, laurine, torrent.

avant-garde *adj.* advanced, enterprising, experimental, far-out, forward-looking, goey, innovative, innovatory, inventive, pioneering, progressive, unconventional, way-out.
antonyms conservative, dyed-in-the-wool.

avarice *n.* acquisitiveness, cheese-paring, covetousness, cupidity, greed, greediness, meanness, miserliness, niggardliness, parsimoniousness, parsimony, penny-pinching, penuriousness, predatoriness, rapacity, stinginess, tight-fistedness.
antonym generosity.

avaricious *adj.* acquisitive, cheese-paring, covetous, gare, grasping, greedy, gripple, mean, miserable, miserly, niggardly, parsimonious, penny-pinching, penurious, predatory, rapacious, stingy, tight-fisted.
antonym generous.

avenge *v.* punish, repay, requite, take revenge for, take vengeance for, vindicate.

avengement *n.* punishment, repayment, reprisal, requital, retaliation, retribution, revenge, ultion, vengeance.

avenger *n.* retributor, vindicator.

avenging *adj.* retaliatory, retributive, vengeful, vindictive, wreakful.

avenue *n.* access, alley, approach, boulevard, channel, course, drive, driveway, entrance, entrée, entry, means, pass, passage, path, pathway, road, route, street, thoroughfare, vista, walk, way.

aver *v.* affirm, allege, assert, asseverate, attest, avouch, avow, declare, insist, maintain, proclaim, profess, pronounce, protest, say, state, swear, testify, witness.

average *n.* mean, mediocrity, medium, midpoint, norm, par, rule, run, standard.
antonyms exception, extreme.
adj. common, commonplace, everyday, fair, general, indifferent, intermediate, mean, medial, median, mediocre, medium, middle, middling, moderate, normal, ordinary, passable, regular, run-of-the-mill, satisfactory, so-so, standard, tolerable, typical, undistinguished, unexceptional, unremarkable, usual.
antonyms exceptional, extreme.

averse *adj.* antagonistic, antipathetic, disapproving, disinclined, hostile, ill-disposed, inimical,

loath, opposed, reluctant, unfavourable, unwilling.
antonyms sympathetic, willing.

aversion *n.* abhorrence, abomination, anathema, animosity, antagonism, antipathy, detestation, disapproval, disgust, disinclination, dislike, distaste, hate, hatred, horror, hostility, loathing, odium, opposition, phobia, phobism, reluctance, repugnance, repulsion, revulsion, unwillingness.
antonyms liking, sympathy.

avert *v.* avoid, deflect, evade, fend off, forestall, frustrate, obviate, parry, preclude, prevent, stave off, turn, turn aside, turn away, ward off.

aviary *n.* birdcage, birdhouse, volary.

aviation *n.* aeronautics, flight, flying.

aviator *n.* ace, aeronaut, airman, erk, flier, pilot.

avid *adj.* acquisitive, ardent, avaricious, covetous, dedicated, devoted, eager, earnest, enthusiastic, fanatical, fervent, grasping, greedy, hungry, insatiable, intense, keen, passionate, rapacious, ravenous, thirsty, voracious, zealous.
antonym indifferent.

avidity *n.* acquisitiveness, ardour, avarice, covetousness, craving, cupidity, desire, devotion, eagerness, enthusiasm, fervour, greed, greediness, hankering, hunger, insatiability, keenness, longing, rapacity, ravenousness, thirst, voracity, zeal.
antonym indifference.

avocation *n.* business, calling, distraction, diversion, employment, hobby, interest, job, occupation, pastime, profession, pursuit, recreation, relaxation, sideline, trade, vocation, work.

avoid *v.* abstain from, avert, balk, bypass, circumvent, dodge, duck, elude, escape, eschew, evade, evite, funk, get out of, obviate, prevent, refrain from, shirk, shun, side-step, steer clear of.

avoidable *adj.* avertible, eludible, escapable, evadable, evitable, preventable, voidable.
antonym inevitable.

avoidance *n.* abstention, abstinence, circumvention, dodge, dodging, eluding, elusion, escape, eschewal, evasion, evitation, prevention, refraining, shirking, shunning.

avow *v.* acknowledge, admit, affirm, allege, assert, asseverate, attest, aver, confess, declare, maintain, own, proclaim, profess, recognise, state, swear, testify.

avowal *n.* acknowledgment, admission, affirmation, allegation, assertion, asseveration, attestation, averment, confession, declaration, oath, owning, proclamation, profession, recognition, statement, swearing, testimony.

avowed *adj.* acknowledged, admitted, confessed, declared, open, overt, professed, self-confessed, self-proclaimed, sworn.

avowedly *adv.* admittedly, candidly, confessedly, ex professo, frankly, openly, overtly, professedly.
antonym secretly.

await *v.* anticipate, attend, be in store for, expect, hope for, lie in wait, look for, look forward to, wait for.

awake *v.* arouse, awaken, rouse, wake, wake up.
adj. alert, alive, aroused, astir, attentive, awakened, aware, conscious, heedful, observant, sensitive, vigilant, wakeful, waking, watchful, wide-awake.

awaken *v.* activate, alert, animate, arouse, awake, call forth, enliven, evoke, excite, fan, kindle, prompt, provoke, revive, rouse, stimulate, stir up, vivify, wake, waken.
antonyms lull, quell, quench.

awakening *n.* activation, animating, arousal, awaking, birth, enlivening, evocation, kindling, prompting, provocation, revival, rousing, stimulation, vivification, wakening, waking.

award *v.* accord, adjudge, allot, allow, apportion, assign, bestow, confer, determine, dispense, distribute, endow, gift, give, grant, present.
n. adjudication, allotment, allowance, bestowal, conferment, conferral, decision, decoration, dispensation, endowment, gift, grant, judgement, order, presentation, prize, trophy.

aware *adj.* acquainted, alive to, appreciative, apprised, attentive, au courant, cognisant, conscient, conscious, conversant, enlightened, familiar, heedful, hep, hip, informed, knowing, knowledgeable, mindful, observant, on the ball, on the qui vive, sensible, sensitive, sentient, sharp, shrewd.
antonyms insensitive, unaware.

awareness *n.* acquaintance, appreciation, attention, cognisance, consciousness, enlightenment, familiarity, knowledge, observation, perception, realisation, recognition, sensibility, sensitivity, sentience, understanding.
antonyms insensitivity, unawareness.

awe *n.* admiration, amazement, apprehension, astonishment, dread, fear, respect, reverence, terror, veneration, wonder, wonderment.
antonym contempt.
v. amaze, astonish, cow, daunt, frighten, horrify, impress, intimidate, overwhelm, stun, terrify.

awe-inspiring *adj.* amazing, astonishing, awesome, awful, breathtaking, daunting, fearsome, formidable, impressive, intimidating, magnificent, overwhelming, wonderful, wondrous.
antonyms contemptible, tame.

awesome *adj.* alarming, amazing, astonishing, august, awe-inspiring, awful, breathtaking, daunting, dread, dreadful, fearful, fearsome, formidable, frightening, imposing, impressive, intimidating, magnificent, majestic, moving, overwhelming, redoubtable, solemn, stunning, stupefying, stupendous, terrible, terrifying, wonderful, wondrous.

awe-struck *adj.* afraid, amazed, astonished, awed, awe-inspired, awe-stricken, cowed, daunted, dumbfounded, fearful, frightened, impressed, intimidated, speechless, struck dumb, stunned, terrified, wonder-struck.

awful *adj.* abysmal, alarming, amazing, atrocious, august, awe-inspiring, awesome, blood-curdling, dire, dread, dreadful, eldritch, fearful, fearsome, frightful, ghastly, gruesome, harrowing, hideous, horrendous, horrible, horrific, horrifying, majestic, nasty, portentous, shocking, solemn, spine-chilling, terrible, tremendous, ugly, unpleasant.

awfully *adv.* abysmally, badly, disgracefully, disputably, dreadfully, exceedingly, exceptionally, excessively, extremely, greatly, immensely, inadequately, quite, reprehensibly, shockingly, shoddily, terribly, unforgivably, unpleasantly, very, wickedly, woefully, wretchedly.

awkward *adj.* annoying, bloody-minded, blundering, bungling, chancy, clownish, clumsy, coarse, compromising, cubbish, cumbersome, delicate, difficult, disobliging, embarrassed, embarrassing, exasperating, farouche, fiddly, gauche, gawky, graceless, ham-fisted, ham-handed, hazardous, ill at ease, inconvenient, inelegant, inept, inexpedient, inexpert, inopportune, intractable, intransigent, irritable, left-handed, maladroit, obstinate, painful, perplexing, perverse, prickly, risky, rude, spastic, sticky, stubborn, thorny, ticklish, touchy, troublesome, trying, uncomfortable, unco-operative, unco-ordinated, uncouth, ungainly, ungraceful, unhandy, unhelpful, unmanageable, unpleasant, unrefined, unskilful, untimely, untoward, unwieldy, vexatious, vexing.
antonyms amenable, convenient, elegant, graceful, straightforward.

awkwardness *n.* bloody-mindedness, clumsiness, coarseness, cumbersomeness, delicacy, difficulty, discomfort, embarrassment, gaucheness, gaucherie, gawkihood, gracelessness, inconvenience, inelegance, ineptness, inexperience, intractability, intransigence, irritability, left-handedness, left-handiness, maladresse, maladroitness, obstinacy, painfulness, perilousness, perversity, prickliness, risk, riskiness, rudeness, stiffness, stubbornness, touchiness, troublesomeness, uncooperativeness, ungainliness, unhandiness, unhelpfulness, unmanageability, unpleasantness, untimeliness, unwieldiness.
antonyms amenability, convenience, elegance, grace, straightforwardness.

awning *n.* baldachin, canopy, covering, sunshade, tarpaulin, velarium, wind-break.

awry *adv. adj.* aglee, amiss, askew, asymmetrical, cock-eyed, crooked, misaligned, oblique, off-centre, out of kilter, skew-whiff, twisted, uneven, unevenly, wonky, wrong.
antonyms straight, symmetrical.

axe *v.* cancel, chop, cleave, cut, cut down, discharge, discontinue, dismiss, eliminate, fell, fire, get rid of, hew, remove, sack, split, terminate, throw out, withdraw.

axiom *n.* adage, aphorism, apophthegm, byword, dictum, fundamental, gnome, maxim, postulate, precept, principle, truism, truth.

axiomatic *adj.* absolute, accepted, aphoristic, apodictic, apophthegmatic, assumed, certain, fundamental, given, gnomic, granted, indubitable, manifest, presupposed, proverbial, self-evident, understood, unquestioned.

axis *n.* alliance, arbor, axle, bloc, centre-line, coalition, compact, entente, league, longitude, pact, pivot, plumb-line, shaft, spindle, vertical.

axle *n.* arbor, axis, hinge, mandrel, pin, pivot, shaft, spindle.

B

babble v. blab, burble, cackle, chatter, gabble, gibber, gurgle, jabber, mumble, murmur, mutter, prate, prattle, purl, twattle.
n. burble, clamour, drivel, gabble, gibberish, lallation, lalling, murmur, purl, purling, twattle.

babbling adj. burbling, cackling, chattering, drivelling, drooling, gabbling, gibbering, gurgling, incoherent, jabbering, long-tongued, murmuring, prattling, rambling, unco-ordinated, unintelligible.

babe n. bab, baby, bairn, child, infant, nursling, papoose, suckling, wean, weanling, youngling.

babel n. bedlam, chaos, clamour, commotion, confusion, din, disorder, hubbub, hullabaloo, pandemonium, tumult, turmoil, uproar.
antonyms calm, order.

baby n. babe, bairn, child, infant, nursling, papoose, suckling, tiny, toddler, wean, weanling, youngling.
adj. diminutive, dwarf, Lilliputian, little, midget, mini, miniature, minute, pygmy, small, small-scale, tiny, toy, wee.
v. cocker, coddle, cosset, humour, indulge, mollycoddle, overindulge, pamper, pander to, pet, spoil, spoon-feed.

babyish adj. baby, childish, foolish, immature, infantile, jejune, juvenile, naïve, namby-pamby, puerile, silly, sissy, soft, spoilt.
antonyms mature, precocious.

bacchanalian adj. bacchaic, debauched, Dionysian, dissolute, drunken, frenzied, intemperate, licentious, maenadic, orgiastic, riotous, saturnalian, wanton.

back¹ v. advocate, assist, boost, buttress, champion, countenance, countersign, encourage, endorse, favour, finance, sanction, second, side with, sponsor, subsidise, support, sustain, underwrite.
antonym discourage.
back up aid, assist, bolster, champion, confirm, corroborate, endorse, reinforce, second, substantiate, support.
antonym let down.

back² n. backside, end, hind part, hindquarters, posterior, rear, reverse, stern, tail, tail end, tergum, verso.
adj. end, hind, hindmost, posterior, rear, reverse, tail.

back³ v. backtrack, recede, recoil, regress, retire, retreat, reverse, withdraw.
back down accede, back-pedal, concede, give in, retreat, submit, surrender, withdraw, yield.
back out abandon, apostatise, bunk off, cancel, chicken out, give up, go back on, recant, renegue, resign, withdraw.

back⁴ adj. delayed, earlier, elapsed, former, outdated, overdue, past, previous, prior, superseded.

backbite v. abuse, attack, calumniate, criticise, defame, denigrate, disparage, libel, malign, revile, slag, slander, traduce, vilify, vituperate.
antonym praise.

backbiting n. abuse, aspersion, bitchiness, calumniation, calumny, cattiness, criticism, defamation, denigration, detraction, disparagement, gossip, malice, revilement, scandalmongering, slagging, slander, spite, spitefulness, vilification, vituperation.
antonym praise.

backbone n. basis, bottle, character, core, courage, determination, firmness, foundation, grit, hardihood, mainstay, mettle, nerve, pluck, power, resolution, resolve, spine, stamina, staunchness, steadfastness, strength, support, tenacity, toughness, vertebral column, will.
antonyms spinelessness, weakness.

backbreaking adj. arduous, crushing, exhausting, gruelling, hard, heavy, killing, laborious, punishing, strenuous, tiring, toilsome, wearing, wearisome.
antonym easy.

backer n. advocate, benefactor, bottle-holder, champion, patron, promoter, second, seconder, sponsor, subscriber, supporter, underwriter, well-wisher.

backfire v. boomerang, come home to roost, fail, flop, miscarry, rebound, recoil, ricochet.

background n. breeding, circumstances, credentials, culture, dossier, education, environment, experience, fond, grounding, history, milieu, preparation, record, surroundings, tradition, upbringing.

back-handed adj. ambiguous, double-edged, doubtful, dubious, equivocal, ironic, oblique, sarcastic, sardonic, two-edged.
antonyms sincere, wholehearted.

backing n. accompaniment, advocacy, aid, assistance, championing, championship, encouragement, endorsement, favour, funds, grant, helpers, moral support, patronage, sanction, seconding, sponsorship, subsidy, support.

backlash n. backfire, boomerang, counterblast, kickback, reaction, recoil, repercussion, reprisal, resentment, response, retaliation.

backlog n. accumulation, excess, hoard, leeway, mountain, reserve, reserves, resources, stock, supply.

backslide v. apostatise, default, defect, fall from grace, lapse, regress, relapse, renegue, retrogress, revert, sin, slip, stray, weaken.
antonym persevere.

backslider n. apostate, defaulter, defector, deserter, recidivist, recreant, renegade, reneguer, turncoat.

backsliding n. apostasy, defaulting, defection, desertion, lapse, recidivism, recreancy, relapse, renegation.

backward adj. bashful, behind, behindhand, diffident, dull, hesitant, hesitating, immature, late, reluctant, retarded, shy, slow, sluggish, stupid, subnormal, tardy, underdeveloped, unwilling, wavering.
antonyms forward, precocious.

backwoods n. back of beyond, boondocks, bush, outback, sticks.

bacteria n. bacilli, bugs, germs, microbes, microorganisms, pathogens, schizomycetes, viruses.

bad adj. adverse, ailing, base, blameworthy, conscience-stricken, contrite, corrupt, criminal, damaging, dangerous, decayed, defective, deficient, deleterious, delinquent, despondent, detrimental, disastrous, discouraged, discouraging, diseased, disobedient, distressed, distressing, evil, fallacious, faulty, gloomy, grave, grim, grotty, guilty, harmful, harsh, ill, illaudable, immoral, imperfect, inadequate, incorrect, inferior, injurious, mean, melancholy, mischievous, mouldy, naughty, noxious, off, offensive, onkus, painful, piacular, poor, putrid, rancid, regretful, remorseful, ropy, rotten, rueful, ruinous, sad, serious, severe, shoddy, sick, sinful, sombre, sorry, sour, spoilt, stormy, substandard, terrible, troubled, unfortunate, unhealthy, unpleasant, unruly, unsatisfactory, unwell, upset, vile, wicked, wrong.

bad blood acrimony, anger, animosity, antagonism, bad feeling, dislike, distrust, enmity, feud, hatred, hostility, malevolence, malice, nastiness, odium, rancour, resentment, upset, vendetta.

bad form bad style, barbarism, gaucherie, impropriety, indecorum, inelegance, infelicity, mauvais ton, solecism.

bad luck adversity, blow, deuce-ace, hard cheese, hard lines, hard luck, hoodoo, ill luck, mischance, misfortune, misluck, reverse, setback.
antonym luck.

bad manners boorishness, coarseness, discourtesy, disrespect, gaucherie, impoliteness, incivility, inconsideration, indelicacy, mismanners, unmannerliness.
antonym politeness.

bad taste coarseness, crudeness, grossness, indecency, indelicacy, mauvais goût, obscenity, offensiveness, poor taste, smuttiness, tactlessness, tastelessness, vulgarity.
antonyms delicacy, tastefulness.

bad time agony, going-over, grilling, mauvais moment, mauvais quart d'heure, nasty moment, suspense, third degree, torture.

badge n. brand, cognisance, device, emblem, episemon, identification, insignia, logo, mark, sign, stamp, token, trademark.

badger v. bait, bully, bullyrag, chivvy, goad, harass, harry, hassle, hound, importune, nag, pester, plague, torment.

badinage n. banter, chaff, dicacity, drollery, give and take, humour, jocularity, mockery, persiflage, raillery, repartee, ribbing, teasing, waggery, word-play.

badly[1] adv. carelessly, criminally, defectively, faultily, immorally, imperfectly, improperly, inadequately, incompetently, incorrectly, ineptly, negligently, poorly, shamefully, shoddily, unethically, unfairly, unfavourably, unfortunately, unsatisfactorily, unsuccessfully, wickedly, wrong, wrongly.
antonym mildly.

badly[2] adv. acutely, bitterly, critically, crucially, deeply, desperately, exceedingly, extremely, gravely, greatly, intensely, painfully, seriously, severely.
antonym mildly.

bad-tempered adj. cantankerous, captious, choleric, crabbed, cross, crotchety, dyspeptic, fractious, franzy, girnie, impatient, irascible, irritable, peevish, petulant, querulous, snappy, splenetic, stroppy, testy, vixenish, vixenly.
antonyms equable, genial.

baffle v. amaze, astound, balk, bamboozle, bemuse, bewilder, check, confound, confuse, daze, defeat, disconcert, dumbfound, flabbergast, floor, flummox, foil, frustrate, hinder, mystify, nonplus, perplex, puzzle, stump, stun, stymie, thwart, upset.
antonyms enlighten, help.

baffling adj. amazing, astounding, bemusing, confusing, extraordinary, frustrating, mysterious, perplexing, stupefying, surprising, thwarting, unfathomable.
antonyms enlightening, explanatory.

bag v. acquire, appropriate, capture, catch, commandeer, corner, gain, get, grab, kill, land, obtain, reserve, shoot, take, trap.
n. carrier, container, dorlach, Dorothy bag, dressing-case, Gladstone bag, grab-bag, grip, gripsack, handbag, haversack, hold-all, holder, pack, poke, reticule, rucksack, sack, satchel, satchet, scrip, shoulder-bag, tote-bag, valise.

baggage n. accoutrements, bags, belongings, equipment, gear, impedimenta, luggage, paraphernalia, suit-cases, things, traps, viaticals.

baggy adj. billowing, bulging, droopy, flaccid, floppy, ill-fitting, loose, oversize, pouchy, roomy, sagging, slack.
antonyms firm, tight.

bail n. bond, guarantee, guaranty, pledge, security, surety, warranty.

bail out[1] aid, assist, finance, help, relieve, rescue.

bail out[2], **bale out** back out, cop out, escape, quit, retreat, withdraw.

bailiff n. agent, beagle, constable, deputy, factor, huissier, magistrate, office, Philistine, sheriff.

bait *n.* allurement, attraction, bribe, carrot, decoy, enticement, inducement, lure, temptation.
antonym disincentive.
v. annoy, gall, goad, harass, hound, irk, irritate, needle, persecute, provoke, tease, torment.

balance *v.* adjust, assess, calculate, compare, compute, consider, counteract, counterbalance, counterpoise, deliberate, equalise, equate, equilibrate, equipoise, equiponderate, estimate, evaluate, level, librate, match, neutralise, offset, parallel, poise, settle, square, stabilise, steady, tally, total, weigh.
antonyms overbalance, unbalance.
n. composure, correspondence, difference, equality, equanimity, equilibrium, equipoise, equity, equivalence, evenness, parity, poise, remainder, residue, rest, self-possession, stability, stasis, steadiness, surplus, symmetry.
antonyms imbalance, instability.

balanced *adj.* calm, equitable, even-handed, fair, impartial, just, self-possessed, sensible, unbiased, unprejudiced, well-rounded.
antonyms prejudiced, unbalanced.

balcony *n.* gallery, gods, moucharaby, terrace, upper circle, veranda.

bald *adj.* bald-headed, baldpated, bare, barren, bleak, depilated, direct, downright, exposed, forthright, glabrate, glabrous, hairless, naked, outright, peeled, plain, severe, simple, stark, straight, straightforward, treeless, unadorned, uncompromising, uncovered, undisguised, unvarnished.
antonyms adorned, hirsute.

balderdash *n.* balls, bollocks, bullshit, bunk, bunkum, claptrap, drivel, gibberish, nonsense, poppycock, rot, rubbish, tommyrot, trash, tripe, twaddle.

baldness *n.* alopecia, bald-headedness, bareness, calvities, calvousness, directness, glabrousness, hairlessness, psilosis, starkness.
antonym hirsuteness.

bale *n.* bundle, fardel, pack, package, parcel, truss.

bale out *see* **bail out** .

baleful *adj.* deadly, destructive, evil, fell, harmful, hurtful, injurious, malevolent, malignant, menacing, mournful, noxious, ominous, pernicious, ruinous, sad, sinister, venomous, woeful.
antonyms auspicious, favourable.

balk, baulk *v.* baffle, bar, boggle, check, counteract, defeat, demur, disconcert, dodge, evade, flinch, foil, forestall, frustrate, hesitate, hinder, jib, make difficulties, obstruct, prevent, recoil, refuse, resist, shirk, shrink, stall, thwart.

ball¹ *n.* bauble, bobble, bullet, clew, conglomeration, drop, globe, globule, orb, pellet, pill, shot, slug, sphere, spheroid.

ball² *n.* assembly, carnival, dance, dinnerdance, fandango, hop, masquerade, party, ridotto, rout, soirée.

ballad *n.* carol, composition, ditty, folk-song, forebitter, lay, poem, shanty, song.

ballet *n.* ballet-dancing, dancing, leg-business.

balloon *v.* bag, belly, billow, blow up, bulge, dilate, distend, enlarge, expand, inflate, puff out, swell.

ballot *n.* election, plebiscite, poll, polling, referendum, vote, voting.

ballyhoo *n.* advertising, agitation, build-up, clamour, commotion, disturbance, excitement, fuss, hubbub, hue and cry, hullabaloo, hype, noise, promotion, propaganda, publicity, racket, tumult.

balm *n.* anodyne, balsam, bromide, calmative, comfort, consolation, cream, curative, embrocation, emollient, lenitive, lotion, ointment, palliative, restorative, salve, sedative, solace, unguent.
antonyms irritant, vexation.

balmy¹ *adj.* clement, gentle, mild, pleasant, soft, summery, temperate.
antonym inclement.

balmy² *adj.* barmy, crazy, daft, dippy, dotty, foolish, idiotic, insane, loony, mad, nuts, nutty, odd, round the bend, silly, stupid.
antonyms rational, sane, sensible.

bamboozle *v.* baffle, befool, befuddle, bemuse, cheat, con, confound, confuse, cozen, deceive, defraud, delude, dupe, fool, hoax, hoodwink, mystify, perplex, puzzle, stump, swindle, trick.

ban *v.* anathematise, banish, bar, debar, disallow, exclude, forbid, interdict, ostracise, outlaw, prohibit, proscribe, restrict, suppress.
antonym permit.
n. anathematisation, boycott, censorship, condemnation, curse, denunciation, embargo, interdiction, outlawry, prohibition, proscription, restriction, stoppage, suppression, taboo.
antonyms dispensation, permission.

banal *adj.* boring, clichéd, cliché-ridden, commonplace, corny, empty, everyday, hackneyed, humdrum, jejune, old hat, ordinary, pedestrian, platitudinous, stale, stereotyped, stock, threadbare, tired, trite, unimaginative, unoriginal, vapid.
antonym original.

banality *n.* bromide, cliché, commonplace, dullness, platitude, prosaicism, triteness, triviality, truism, vapidity.
antonym originality.

band¹ *n.* bandage, bandeau, belt, binding, bond, chain, cord, fascia, fasciole, fetter, fillet, ligature, manacle, ribbon, shackle, strap, strip, swath, tape, tie, vitta.

band² *n.* association, body, clique, club, combo, company, coterie, crew, ensemble, flock, gang, group, herd, horde, orchestra, party, range, society, troop, waits.
v. affiliate, ally, amalgamate, collaborate, consolidate, federate, gather, group, join, merge, unite.
antonyms disband, disperse.

bandage *n.* compress, dressing, gauze, ligature, plaster, swaddle, swathe, tourniquet.
v. bind, cover, dress, swaddle, swathe.

bandit *n.* brigand, buccaneer, cowboy, dacoit, desperado, footpad, freebooter, gangster, gunman, highwayman, hijacker, marauder, outlaw, pirate, racketeer, robber, ruffian, thief.

banditry *n.* brigandage, dacoitage, dacoity, freebooting, heist, hijacking, hold-up, latrociny, robbery, stickup, theft.

bandy[1] *v.* barter, exchange, interchange, pass, reciprocate, swap, throw, toss, trade.

bandy[2] *adj.* bandy-legged, bent, bowed, bowlegged, crooked, curved, valgous.

bane *n.* adversity, affliction, annoyance, bête noire, blight, burden, calamity, curse, despair, destruction, disaster, distress, downfall, evil, irritation, misery, misfortune, nuisance, ordeal, pest, pestilence, plague, ruin, scourge, sorrow, torment, trial, trouble, vexation, woe.
antonym blessing.

baneful *adj.* deadly, deleterious, destructive, disastrous, fell, harmful, hurtful, injurious, malevolent, noxious, pernicious, pestilential, ruinous, sinister, venomous.
antonym beneficent.

bang *n.* blow, boom, box, bump, clang, clap, clash, collision, crash, cuff, detonation, explosion, hit, knock, noise, peal, pop, punch, report, shot, slam, smack, stroke, thud, thump, wallop, whack.
v. bash, boom, bump, burst, clang, clatter, crash, detonate, drum, echo, explode, hammer, knock, peal, pound, pummel, rap, resound, slam, stamp, strike, thump, thunder.
adv. directly, hard, headlong, noisily, plumb, precisely, right, slap, smack, straight, suddenly.

banish *v.* ban, bar, blacklist, debar, deport, discard, dislodge, dismiss, dispel, eject, eliminate, eradicate, evict, exclude, excommunicate, exile, expatriate, expel, get rid of, ostracise, oust, outlaw, remove, shut out, transport.
antonyms recall, welcome.

banishment *n.* deportation, eviction, exile, exilement, expatriation, expulsion, ostracisation, outlawry, proscription, transportation.
antonyms recall, return, welcome.

bank[1] *n.* accumulation, cache, depository, fund, hoard, pool, repository, reserve, reservoir, savings, stock, stockpile, store, storehouse, treasury.
v. accumulate, deposit, keep, save, stockpile, store.
antonym spend.

bank[2] *n.* acclivity, banking, brink, bund, earthwork, edge, embankment, fail-dike, heap, margin, mass, mound, pile, rampart, ridge, rivage, shallow, shoal, shore, side, slope, tilt.
v. accumulate, aggrade, amass, camber, cant, drift, heap, incline, mass, mound, pile, pitch, slant, slope, stack, tilt, tip.

bank[3] *n.* array, bench, echelon, file, group, line, rank, row, sequence, series, succession, tier, train.

bank-note *n.* bill, flimsy, greenback, note, paper money, treasury note.

bankrupt *adj.* beggared, broke, depleted, destitute, exhausted, failed, impecunious, impoverished, insolvent, lacking, penurious, ruined, spent.
antonyms solvent, wealthy.
n. debtor, duck, dyvour, insolvent, pauper.

bankruptcy *n.* beggary, disaster, dyvoury, exhaustion, failure, indebtedness, insolvency, lack, liquidation, penury, ruin, ruination.
antonyms solvency, wealth.

banner *n.* banderol(e), bannerol, burgee, colours, ensign, fanion, flag, gonfalon, labarum, oriflamme, pennant, pennon, standard, streamer, vexillum.

banquet *n.* binge, dinner, feast, meal, repast, revel, treat, wayzgoose.

banter *n.* badinage, chaff, chaffing, cross-talk, derision, dicacity, jesting, joking, kidding, mockery, persiflage, pleasantry, quiz, raillery, repartee, ribbing, ridicule, word play.

baptise *v.* admit, call, christen, cleanse, dub, enrol, immerse, initiate, introduce, name, purify, recruit, sprinkle, style, term, title.

baptism *n.* beginning, chrism, christening, début, dedication, immersion, initiation, introduction, launch, launching, purification, sprinkling.

bar[1] *n.* barricade, barrier, batten, check, crosspiece, deterrent, deterrment, hindrance, impediment, obstacle, obstruction, overslaugh, paling, pole, preventive, rail, railing, rod, shaft, stake, stanchion, stick, stop.
v. ban, barricade, blackball, bolt, debar, exclude, fasten, forbid, hinder, latch, lock, obstruct, preclude, prevent, prohibit, restrain, secure.

bar[2] *n.* bierkeller, boozer, canteen, counter, dive, doggery, dram-shop, estaminet, exchange, gin-palace, ginshop, groggery, grogshop, honky-tonk, howff, inn, joint, lounge, nineteenth hole, pub, public house, saloon, tavern, vaults, watering-hole.

bar[3] *n.* advocates, attorneys, barristers, bench, counsel, court, courtroom, dock, law court, tribunal.

bar[4] *n.* block, chunk, ingot, lump, nugget, slab, wedge.

barb *n.* affront, arrow, barbule, bristle, cut, dig, fluke, gibe, home-thrust, home-truth, insult, point, prickle, prong, quill, rebuff, sarcasm, sneer, spicule, spike, spur, stab, thorn, thrust.

barbarian *n.* ape, boor, brute, clod, hooligan, hottentot, hun, ignoramus, illiterate, lout, lowbrow, oaf, philistine, ruffian, savage, tramontane, vandal, vulgarian, yahoo.
adj. boorish, brutish, coarse, crude, lowbrow, philistine, rough, tramontane, uncivilised, uncouth, uncultivated, uncultured, unsophisticated, vulgar.

barbaric *adj.* barbarous, boorish, brutal, brutish, coarse, crude, cruel, ferocious, fierce, inhuman, primitive, rude, savage, uncivilised, uncouth, vulgar, wild.

antonyms civilised, humane.

barbarism *n.* abuse, atrocity, barbarity, brutishness, coarseness, corruption, crudity, cruelty, enormity, misuse, outrage, savagery, solecism, vulgarism.

barbarity *n.* barbarousness, boorishness, brutality, brutishness, cruelty, ferocity, inhumanity, rudeness, ruthlessness, savagery, viciousness, wildness.

antonyms civilisation, civility, humanity.

barbarous *adj.* barbarian, barbaric, brutal, brutish, coarse, crude, cruel, ferocious, heartless, heathenish, ignorant, inhuman, monstrous, philistine, primitive, rough, rude, ruthless, savage, uncivilised, uncouth, uncultured, unlettered, unrefined, vicious, vulgar, wild.

antonyms civilised, cultured, educated.

barbed *adj.* acerbic, acid, catty, caustic, critical, cutting, hooked, hostile, hurtful, jagged, nasty, pointed, prickly, pronged, snide, spiked, spiny, thorny, toothed, unkind.

bare *adj.* austere, bald, barren, basic, blank, defoliate, defoliated, denudated, denuded, disfurnished, empty, essential, explicit, exposed, hard, lacking, literal, mean, naked, napless, nude, open, peeled, plain, poor, scanty, scarce, severe, sheer, shorn, simple, spare, stark, stripped, unadorned, unarmed, unclad, unclothed, uncovered, undisguised, undressed, unembellished, unforested, unfurnished, unprovided, unsheathed, untimbered, unvarnished, unwooded, vacant, void, wanting, woodless.

barefaced *adj.* arrant, audacious, bald, blatant, bold, brash, brazen, flagrant, glaring, impudent, insolent, manifest, naked, obvious, open, palpable, patent, shameless, transparent, unabashed, unconcealed.

barefooted *adj.* barefoot, discalced, shoeless, unshod.

antonym shod.

barely¹ *adv.* almost, hardly, just, scarcely, sparingly, sparsely.

barely² *adv.* explicitly, nakedly, openly, plainly.

bargain *n.* agreement, arrangement, compact, contract, discount, giveaway, negotiation, pact, pledge, promise, reduction, snip, steal, stipulation, transaction, treaty, understanding.

v. agree, barter, broke, buy, chaffer, contract, covenant, deal, dicker, haggle, higgle, negotiate, promise, sell, stipulate, trade, traffic, transact.

bargain for anticipate, consider, contemplate, expect, foresee, imagine, include, look for, plan for, reckon on.

bargaining *n.* barter, bartering, dealing, dicker, haggling, higgling, negotiation, trading, trafficking, wheeler-dealing.

barge¹ *v.* bump, butt in, cannon, collide, elbow, encroach, gatecrash, hit, impinge, interfere, interrupt, intrude, muscle in, push, push in, shove.

barge² *n.* birlinn, Bucentaur, canal boat, flatboat, house-boat, lighter, narrow-boat, transport.

bark *n.* bawl, bay, growl, shout, snap, snarl, woof, yap, yell, yelp.

v. advertise, bawl, bay, bluster, cough, growl, shout, snap, snarl, yap, yell, yelp.

barking *n.* latration.

adj. latrant.

barmy *adj.* balmy, crazy, daft, dippy, dotty, foolish, idiotic, insane, loony, mad, nuts, nutty, odd, silly, stupid.

antonyms rational, sane, sensible.

baroque *adj.* bizarre, bold, convoluted, elaborate, extravagant, exuberant, fanciful, fantastic, flamboyant, florid, grotesque, ornate, overdecorated, overwrought, rococo, vigorous, whimsical.

antonym plain.

barracks *n.* accommodation, billet, camp, cantonment, caserne, encampment, garrison, guard-house, lodging, quarters.

barrage *n.* assault, attack, battery, bombardment, broadside, burst, cannonade, deluge, fusillade, gunfire, hail, mass, onset, onslaught, plethora, profusion, rain, salvo, shelling, shower, storm, stream, torrent, volley.

barred *adj.* banned, blackballed, disallowed, excluded, forbidden, outlawed, prohibited, proscribed, taboo.

antonym permissible.

barrel *n.* butt, cade, cask, hogshead, keg, kilderkin, puncheon, rundlet, tierce, tun, water-butt, wood.

barren *adj.* arid, boring, childless, desert, desolate, dry, dull, empty, flat, fruitless, infecund, infertile, jejune, lacklustre, pointless, profitless, stale, sterile, unbearing, unfruitful, uninformative, uninspiring, uninstructive, uninteresting, unproductive, unprolific, unrewarding, useless, vapid, waste.

antonyms fertile, productive, useful.

barricade *n.* barrier, blockade, bulwark, fence, obstruction, palisade, protection, rampart, screen, stockade.

v. bar, block, blockade, defend, fortify, obstruct, palisade, protect, screen.

barrier *n.* bail, bar, barricade, blockade, boom, boundary, bulkhead, check, difficulty, ditch, drawback, fence, fortification, handicap, hindrance, hurdle, impediment, limitation, obstacle, obstruction, railing, rampart, restriction, stop, stumbling-block, transverse, wall.

barrow *n.* hand-barrow, handcart, hurly, push-cart, wheelbarrow.

bartender *n.* bar-keeper, barmaid, barman, publican, tapster.

barter *v.* bargain, chaffer, deal, dicker, exchange, haggle, higgle, negotiate, niffer, sell, swap, trade, traffic, truck.

base¹ *n.* basis, bed, bottom, camp, centre, core, essence, essential, foot, foundation, fundamental, groundwork, headquarters, heart, home, key, origin, pedestal, plinth, post, principal, rest, root, settlement, socle, source, stand, standard, starting-point, station, substrate, substructure, support, underpinning, understructure.

v. build, construct, depend, derive, establish, found, ground, hinge, locate, station.

base² *adj.* abject, contemptible, corrupt, counterfeit, depraved, disgraceful, disreputable, dog, evil, grovelling, humble, ignoble, ignominious, immoral, infamous, low, lowly, low-minded, low-thoughted, mean, menial, miserable, paltry, pitiful, poor, scandalous, servile, shameful, slavish, sordid, sorry, valueless, vile, villainous, vulgar, wicked, worthless, wretched.

base³ *adj.* adulterated, alloyed, artificial, bastard, counterfeit, debased, fake, forged, fraudulent, impure, inferior, pinchbeck, spurious.

base-born *adj.* bastard, common, humble, illegitimate, low-born, low-bred, lowly, misborn, plebeian, proletarian, vulgar.
antonym highborn.

baseless *adj.* gratuitous, groundless, unattested, unauthenticated, uncalled-for, unconfirmed, uncorroborated, unfounded, ungrounded, unjustifiable, unjustified, unsubstantiated, unsupported.
antonym justifiable.

baseness *n.* contemptibility, degradation, depravation, depravity, despicability, ignominy, infamy, knavery, lowliness, meanness, misery, poverty, servility, slavishness, sordidness, sorriness, subservience, turpitude, vileness, villainy, worthlessness, wretchedness.

bash *v.* belt, biff, break, crash, crush, ding, dunt, hit, punch, slosh, slug, smack, smash, sock, strike, swipe, wallop.
n. attempt, crack, go, shot, stab, try, turn, whirl.

bashful *adj.* abashed, backward, blushing, confused, coy, diffident, embarrassed, hesitant, inhibited, modest, nervous, reserved, reticent, retiring, self-conscious, self-effacing, shamefaced, sheepish, shrinking, shy, timid, timorous, unforthcoming, verecund.
antonym confident.

bashfulness *n.* coyness, diffidence, embarrassment, hesitancy, inhibition, mauvaise honte, modesty, reserve, self-consciousness, shamefacedness, sheepishness, shyness, timidity, timorousness.
antonym confidence.

basic *adj.* central, elementary, essential, fundamental, important, indispensable, inherent, intrinsic, key, necessary, primary, radical, root, underlying, vital.
antonyms inessential, peripheral.

basically *adv.* à fond, at bottom, at heart, au fond, essentially, fundamentally, inherently, intrinsically, primarily, principally, radically.

basics *n.* bedrock, brass tacks, core, essentials, facts, fundamentals, grass roots, necessaries, nitty-gritty, nuts and bolts, practicalities, principles, rock bottom, rudiments.

basin *n.* aquamanile, bowl, cavity, crater, depression, dip, dish, hollow, porringer, sink.

basis *n.* approach, base, bottom, core, essential, fond, footing, foundation, fundamental, ground, groundwork, heart, keynote, pedestal, premise, principle, support, thrust.

bask *v.* apricate, delight in, enjoy, laze, lie, lounge, luxuriate, relax, relish, revel, savour, sunbathe, wallow.

basket *n.* bassinet, creel, dosser, frail, hamper, junket, pannier, pottle, punnet, skep.

bass *adj.* deep, deep-toned, grave, low, low-pitched, low-toned, resonant, sepulchral, sonorous.

bastard *n.* by-blow, filius nullius, git, illegitimate, love child, love-child, lucky-piece, misfortune, mother-fucker, natural child, whoreson.
adj. abnormal, adulterated, anomalous, artificial, base, baseborn, counterfeit, false, illegitimate, imperfect, impure, inferior, irregular, misbegotten, sham, spurious, synthetic.
antonyms genuine, legitimate.

bastardise *v.* adulterate, cheapen, corrupt, debase, defile, degrade, demean, depreciate, devalue, distort, pervert, vitiate.

bastion *n.* bulwark, citadel, defence, fastness, fortress, mainstay, pillar, prop, redoubt, rock, stronghold, support, tower of strength.

batch *n.* amount, assemblage, assortment, bunch, collection, consignment, contingent, group, lot, pack, parcel, quantity, set.

bath *n.* ablution, balneary, cleansing, douche, douse, hamman, Jacuzzi®, scrubbing, shower, soak, tub, wash.
v. bathe, clean, douse, lave, shower, soak, tub, wash.

bathe *v.* cleanse, cover, dook, dunk, encompass, flood, immerse, moisten, rinse, soak, steep, stew, suffuse, swim, wash, wet.
n. dip, dook, rinse, soak, swim, wash.

bathetic *adj.* anticlimactic, sublime to ridiculous.

bathos *n.* anticlimax, comedown, let-down.

battalion *n.* army, brigade, company, contingent, division, force, herd, horde, host, legion, mass, multitude, phalanx, platoon, regiment, squadron, throng.

batten *v.* barricade, board up, clamp down, fasten, fix, nail down, secure, tighten.

batter *v.* abuse, assault, bash, beat, belabour, bruise, buffet, crush, dash, deface, demolish, destroy, disfigure, distress, hurt, injure, lash, maltreat, mangle, manhandle, mar, maul, pelt, pound, pummel, ruin, shatter, smash, thrash, wallop.

battered *adj.* abused, beaten, bruised, crumbling, crushed, damaged, delapidated, ill-treated, injured, ramshackle, tumbledown, weather-beaten.

battery *n.* artillery, assault, attack, barrage, beating, cannon, cannonry, emplacements, guns, mayhem, onslaught, progression, sequence, series, set, thrashing, violence.

battle *n.* action, attack, campaign, clash, combat, conflict, contest, controversy, crusade, debate, disagreement, dispute, encounter,

engagement, fight, fray, hostilities, row, skirmish, stour, strife, struggle, war, warfare.
v. agitate, argue, campaign, clamour, combat, contend, contest, crusade, dispute, feud, fight, strive, struggle, war.

battle-axe *n.* disciplinarian, harridan, martinet, Tartar, termagant, virago.

battle-cry *n.* catchword, motto, slogan, war cry, war whoop, warsong, watchword.

batty *adj.* barmy, bats, bonkers, cracked, crackers, crazy, daffy, daft, demented, dippy, dotty, eccentric, idiotic, insane, loony, lunatic, mad, nuts, nutty, odd, off one's rocker, peculiar, potty, queer, screwy, touched. *antonym* sane.

bauble *n.* bagatelle, flamfew, gewgaw, gimcrack, kickshaw, knick-knack, plaything, tinsel, toy, trifle, trinket.

baulk, balk *v.* baffle, bar, boggle, check, counteract, defeat, demur, disconcert, dodge, evade, flinch, foil, forestall, frustrate, hesitate, hinder, jib, make difficulties, obstruct, prevent, recoil, refuse, resist, shirk, shrink, stall, thwart.

bawd *n.* brothel-keeper, madam, panderess, pimp, procuress.

bawdy *adj.* blue, coarse, dirty, erotic, gross, improper, indecent, indecorous, indelicate, lascivious, lecherous, lewd, libidinous, licentious, lustful, obscene, pornographic, prurient, ribald, risqué, rude, salacious, smutty, suggestive, vulgar. *antonyms* chaste, clean.

bawl *v.* bellow, blubber, call, caterwaul, clamour, cry, halloo, howl, roar, shout, sob, squall, vociferate, wail, waul, weep, yell.

bay[1] *n.* arm, bight, cove, embayment, gulf, inlet, voe.

bay[2] *n.* alcove, booth, carrel, compartment, cubicle, embrasure, niche, nook, opening, recess, stall.

bay[3] *v.* bark, bawl, bell, bellow, cry, holler, howl, roar.

bayonet *v.* impale, knife, pierce, spear, stab, stick.

bazaar *n.* agora, alcaicería, alcázar, bring-and-buy, exchange, fair, fête, market, market-place, mart, sale.

be *v.* abide, arise, befall, breathe, come about, come to pass, continue, develop, dwell, endure, exist, happen, inhabit, inhere, last, live, obtain, occur, persist, prevail, remain, reside, stand, stay, survive, take place.

beach *n.* coast, foreshore, lido, littoral, machair, margin, plage, sand, sands, seaboard, seashore, seaside, shingle, shore, strand, water's edge.

beachcomber *n.* Autolycus, forager, loafer, loiterer, scavenger, scrounger, wayfarer.

beacon *n.* beam, bonfire, fanal, flare, lighthouse, pharos, rocket, sign, signal, watch-fire.

bead *n.* blob, bubble, dot, drop, droplet, glob, globule, pearl, pellet, pill, spherule.

beak *n.* bill, bow, mandibles, neb, nib, nose,

nozzle, proboscis, projection, prow, ram, rostrum, snout, stem.

beaked *adj.* curved, hooked, pointed, rostrate, rostrated, sharp.

beam *n.* arbor, bar, boom, girder, gleam, glimmer, glint, glow, joist, plank, radiation, rafter, ray, shaft, spar, stanchion, stream, support, timber.
v. broadcast, effulge, emit, fulgurate, glare, glimmer, glitter, glow, grin, laugh, radiate, shine, smile, transmit.

beaming *adj.* beautiful, bright, brilliant, cheerful, effulgent, flashing, gleaming, glistening, glittering, glowing, grinning, happy, joyful, lambent, radiant, refulgent, scintillating, shining, smiling, sparkling, sunny. *antonyms* lowering, sullen.

bear[1] *v.* abide, admit, allow, beget, bring, brook, carry, cherish, convey, endure, entertain, exhibit, hack, harbour, have, hold, maintain, move, permit, possess, put up with, shoulder, stomach, suffer, support, sustain, take, tolerate, tote, transport, undergo, uphold, weather, weigh upon.

bear down advance on, approach, attack, burden, close in, compress, converge on, encumber, near, oppress, press down, push, strain, weigh down.

bear in mind be cognisant of, be mindful of, beware, consider, heed, include, mind out for, note, remember.

bear on affect, appertain to, concern, connect with, involve, pertain to, refer to, relate to, touch on.

bear oneself acquit oneself, act, behave, comport oneself, demean oneself, deport oneself, perform.

bear out confirm, corroborate, demonstrate, endorse, justify, prove, substantiate, support, testify, uphold, vindicate.

bear up carry on, endure, keep one's pecker up, persevere, soldier on, suffer, withstand.

bear with be patient with, endure, forbear, make allowances for, put up with, suffer, tolerate.

bear witness attest, confirm, corroborate, demonstrate, depone, depose, evidence, evince, prove, show, testify, testify to, vouch for.

bear[2] *v.* breed, bring forth, develop, drop, engender, generate, give birth to, give up, produce, propagate, yield.

bearable *adj.* acceptable, endurable, livable(-with), manageable, sufferable, supportable, sustainable, tolerable.

beard *v.* brave, challenge, confront, dare, defy, face, oppose.
n. beaver, excrement, goatee, imperial, moustache, mutton chops, sideburns, tuft, vandyke, whiskers.

bearded *adj.* awned, bewhiskered, bristly, bushy, hairy, hirsute, shaggy, tufted, unshaven, whiskered. *antonyms* beardless, cleanshaven, smooth.

bearer *n.* beneficiary, carrier, consignee,

conveyor, courier, holder, messenger, payee, porter, possessor, post, runner, servant.

bearing *n.* air, application, aspect, attitude, behaviour, carriage, comportment, connection, course, demeanour, deportment, direction, import, manner, mien, pertinence, poise, posture, presence, reference, relation, relevance, significance.

bearings *n.* aim, course, direction, inclination, location, orientation, position, situation, tack, track, way, whereabouts.

beast *n.* animal, ape, barbarian, brute, creature, devil, fiend, monster, pig, sadist, savage, swine.

beastly *adj.* barbarous, bestial, brutal, brutish, coarse, cruel, depraved, disagreeable, foul, inhuman, mean, monstrous, nasty, repulsive, rotten, sadistic, savage, sensual, swinish, terrible, unpleasant, vile.

beat[1] *v.* bang, bash, baste, bastinade, bastinado, batter, belabour, bethump, bethwack, bless, bludgeon, bruise, buffet, cane, contuse, cudgel, curry, ding, drub, dunt, fashion, flog, forge, form, fustigate, hammer, hit, impinge, knobble, knock, knout, knubble, lam, lash, lay into, malleate, maul, mill, model, nubble, pelt, pound, punch, shape, slat, strap, strike, swipe, tan, thrash, thwack, trounce, vapulate, verberate, warm, welt, whale, wham, whip, work.

n. blow, hit, lash, punch, shake, slap, strike, swing, thump.

adj. exhausted, fatigued, jiggered, tired, wearied, worn out, zonked.

beat it go away, hop it, leave, scarper, scram, shoo, skedaddle, vamoose.

beat up assault, attack, batter, do over, duff over, duff up, fill in, hammer, knock about, knock around, thrash.

beat[2] *v.* best, conquer, defeat, excel, hammer, outdo, outrun, outstrip, overcome, overwhelm, slaughter, subdue, surpass, trounce, vanquish.

beat[3] *v.* flutter, palpitate, patter, pound, pulsate, pulse, quake, quiver, race, shake, throb, thump, tremble, vibrate.

n. accent, cadence, flutter, measure, metre, palpitation, pulsation, pulse, rhyme, rhythm, stress, throb, time.

beat[4] *n.* circuit, course, journey, path, round, rounds, route, territory, way.

beaten[1] *adj.* baffled, cowed, defeated, disappointed, disheartened, frustrated, overcome, ruined, surpassed, thwarted, vanquished, worsted.

beaten[2] *adj.* fashioned, forged, formed, hammered, malleated, shaped, stamped, worked.

beaten[3] *adj.* blended, foamy, frothy, mixed, pounded, stirred, tenderised, whipped, whisked.

beatific *adj.* angelic, blessed, blissful, divine, ecstatic, exalted, glorious, heavenly, joyful, rapturous, seraphic, serene, sublime.

beatify *v.* bless, exalt, glorify, macarise, sanctify.

beating *n.* belting, caning, chastisement,

conquest, corporal punishment, defeat, downfall, dressing, drubbing, flogging, laldie, lamming, overthrow, rout, ruin, slapping, smacking, thrashing, vapulation, verberation, warming, whaling, whipping.

adj. pounding, pulsatile, pulsating, pulsative, pulsatory, pulsing, racing, throbbing, thumping.

beatitude *n.* beatification, blessedness, bliss, ecstasy, exaltation, felicity, happiness, holiness, joy, macarism, saintliness, sanctity.

beau *n.* admirer, Adonis, boyfriend, cavalier, coxcomb, dandy, escort, fancy man, fiancé, fop, gallant, Jack-a-dandy, ladies' man, lover, popinjay, suitor, swain, sweetheart, swell.

beautician *n.* beauty specialist, cosmetician, friseur, hairdresser, visagiste.

beautiful *adj.* alluring, appealing, attractive, beau, beauteous, belle, charming, comely, delightful, exquisite, fair, fine, good-looking, gorgeous, graceful, handsome, lovely, pleasing, pulchritudinous, radiant, ravishing, stunning.

antonyms plain, ugly.

beautify *v.* adorn, array, bedeck, bedizen, deck, decorate, embellish, enhance, garnish, gild, glamorise, grace, improve, ornament, tart up, titivate.

antonyms disfigure, spoil.

beauty[1] *n.* allure, attractiveness, bloom, charm, comeliness, elegance, excellence, exquisiteness, fairness, glamour, grace, handsomeness, loveliness, pleasure, pulchritude, seemliness, symmetry.

antonym ugliness.

beauty[2] *n.* belle, charmer, corker, cracker, femme fatale, goddess, good-looker, knockout, lovely, siren, stunner, Venus.

antonym frump.

becalmed *adj.* at a standstill, idle, motionless, still, stranded, stuck.

because *conj.* as, by reason of, for, forasmuch, forwhy, in that, inasmuch as, on account of, owing to, since, thanks to.

beckon *v.* allure, attract, bid, call, coax, decoy, draw, entice, gesticulate, gesture, invite, lure, motion, nod, pull, signal, summon, tempt, waft.

become *v.* befit, behove, embellish, enhance, fit, flatter, grace, harmonise, ornament, set off, suit.

becoming *adj.* appropriate, attractive, befitting, charming, comely, comme il faut, compatible, congruous, decent, decorous, enhancing, fit, fitting, flattering, graceful, maidenly, meet, neat, pretty, proper, seemly, suitable, tasteful, worthy.

antonym unbecoming.

bed[1] *n.* bedstead, berth, bunk, cot, cote, couch, divan, kip, mattress, pallet, palliasse, sack, the downy.

bed[2] *n.* base, border, bottom, channel, foundation, garden, groundwork, layer, matrix, patch, plot, row, stratus, strip, substratum, wadi, watercourse.

v. base, embed, establish, fix, found, ground, implant, insert, plant, settle.

bedaub *v.* begrime, besmear, blotch, daub, smear, smirch, soil, spatter, splash, stain.

bedclothes *n.* bedding, bed-linen, blankets, counterpanes, coverlets, covers, downies, eiderdowns, pillows, quilts, sheets.

bedeck *v.* adorn, array, beautify, bedight, bedizen, decorate, embellish, festoon, garnish, ornament, trick out, trim.
antonym strip.

bedevil *v.* afflict, annoy, besiege, confound, distress, fret, frustrate, harass, irk, irritate, pester, plague, tease, torment, torture, trouble, vex, worry.

bedew *v.* dampen, drench, imbue, moisten, shower, soak, spray, sprinkle, water, wet.

bedim *v.* becloud, bedarken, befog, cloak, cloud, darken, dim, fog, obscure, overcast, shade, shadow, veil.

bedlam *n.* anarchy, babel, chaos, clamour, commotion, confusion, furore, hubbub, hullabaloo, madhouse, noise, pandemonium, tumult, turmoil, uproar.
antonym calm.

bedraggled *adj.* dirty, dishevelled, disordered, messy, muddied, muddy, scruffy, slovenly, sodden, soiled, stained, sullied, unkempt, untidy.
antonym tidy.

beef[1] *n.* beefiness, brawn, bulk, flesh, fleshiness, heftiness, muscle, robustness, sinew, strength.

beef[2] *n.* complaint, criticism, dispute, dissatisfaction, grievance, gripe, grouse, grumble, objection, protest.
v. complain, criticise, gripe, grumble, moan, object.
antonym approve.

beefy *adj.* brawny, bulky, burly, corpulent, fat, fleshy, heavy, hefty, hulking, muscular, plump, podgy, pudgy, rotund, stalwart, stocky, strapping, sturdy.
antonym slight.

beetle *v.* dash, hurry, nip, run, rush, scamper, scoot, scurry, tear, zip.

beetling *adj.* beetle, jutting, overhanging, pendent, poking, projecting, prominent, protruding.

befall *v.* arrive, betide, chance, ensue, fall, follow, happen, materialise, occur, supervene, take place.

befitting *adj.* appropriate, becoming, correct, decent, fit, fitting, meet, proper, right, seemly, suitable.
antonym unbecoming.

befoul *v.* bedung, begrime, besmirch, bespatter, defile, dirty, foul, muddy, pollute, soil, stain, sully, tarnish.

before *adv.* ahead, earlier, formerly, in advance, in front, previously, sooner.
antonyms after, later.
prep. ahead of, earlier than, in advance of, in anticipation of, in front of, in preparation for, previous to, prior to, sooner than.

conj. in case, rather than.

beforehand *adv.* already, before, earlier, in advance, preliminarily, previously, sooner.

befriend *v.* aid, assist, back, benefit, comfort, encourage, favour, help, patronise, stand by, succour, support, sustain, take a liking to, take under one's wing, uphold, welcome.
antonym neglect.

befuddle *v.* baffle, bamboozle, befog, bewilder, confuse, daze, disorient, hocus, muddle, puzzle, stupefy.

befuddled *adj.* baffled, bewildered, confused, dazed, fuddled, groggy, hazy, inebriated, intoxicated, muddled, woozy.
antonym lucid.

beg *v.* beseech, cadge, crave, desire, entreat, fleech, implore, importune, petition, plead, pray, prog, request, require, schnorr, scrounge, shool, skelder, solicit, sponge on, supplicate, touch.

beg the question avoid, dodge, duck, equivocate, evade, hedge, shirk, shun, side-step, take for granted.

beget *v.* breed, bring, cause, create, effect, engender, father, gender, generate, get, give rise to, occasion, procreate, produce, propagate, result in, sire, spawn.

beggar *n.* Abraham-man, bankrupt, beadsman, besognio, bluegown, cadger, canter, craver, down-and-out, gaberlunzie, lazzarone, mendicant, pauper, schnorrer, scrounger, sponger, starveling, supplicant, toe-rag, toe-ragger, tramp, vagrant.

beggar[2] *v.* baffle, challenge, defy, exceed, surpass, transcend.

beggarly *adj.* abject, contemptible, despicable, destitute, impoverished, inadequate, indigent, low, meagre, mean, miserly, needy, niggardly, paltry, pathetic, penurious, pitiful, poor, poverty-stricken, stingy, vile, wretched.
antonyms affluent, generous.

beggary *n.* bankruptcy, destitution, indigence, mendicancy, need, neediness, pauperism, penury, poverty, vagrancy, want, wretchedness.
antonyms affluence, plenty.

begging *adj.* beseeching, entreating, imploratory, imploring, longing, pleading, precative, precatory, wistful.
n. cadging, entreaty, mendicancy, mendicity, petitioning, prayers, scrounging, soliciting, sponging, supplication.

begin *v.* activate, actuate, appear, arise, commence, crop up, dawn, emerge, happen, inaugurate, initiate, instigate, institute, introduce, originate, prepare, set about, set in, spring, start.
antonyms end, finish.

beginner *n.* abecedarian, alphabetarian, amateur, apprentice, cheechako, cub, fledgling, freshman, greenhorn, initiate, Johnny-raw, learner, neophyte, novice, recruit, rookie, rooky, starter, student, tenderfoot, tiro, trainee.
antonyms expert, old hand, veteran.

beginning n. birth, commencement, embryo, establishment, fons et origo, fountainhead, germ, inauguration, inception, inchoation, initiation, introduction, onset, opening, origin, outset, preface, prelude, prime, rise, root, rudiments, seed, source, start, starting point.
antonyms end, finish.
adj. early, elementary, inaugural, inauguratory, inceptive, inchoative, incipient, initial, introductory, nascent, primal, primary, primeval.

begrudge v. covet, envy, grudge, mind, resent, stint.
antonym allow.

beguile v. amuse, charm, cheat, cheer, cozen, deceive, delight, delude, distract, divert, dupe, engross, entertain, fool, hoodwink, mislead, occupy, pass, solace, trick, wile.

beguiling adj. alluring, appealing, attractive, bewitching, captivating, charming, diverting, enchanting, entertaining, enticing, interesting, intriguing.
antonyms offensive, repulsive.

behalf n. account, advantage, authority, benefit, defence, good, interest, name, part, profit, sake, side, support.

behave v. acquit, act, bear, comport, conduct, demean, deport, function, operate, perform, react, respond, run, work.

behaviour n. action, actions, bearing, carriage, comportment, conduct, dealings, demeanour, deportment, doings, functioning, habits, manner, manners, operation, performance, reaction, response, ways.

behead v. decapitate, decollate, execute, guillotine, unhead.

behest n. authority, bidding, charge, command, commandment, decree, dictate, direction, fiat, injunction, instruction, mandate, order, ordinance, precept, wish.

behind prep. after, backing, causing, following, for, initiating, instigating, later than, responsible for, supporting.
adv. after, afterwards, behindhand, en arrière, following, in arrears, in debt, in the wake of, next, overdue, subsequently.
n. backside, bottom, butt, buttocks, derrière, posterior, prat, rear, rump, seat, sit-upon, tail.

behind one's back covertly, deceitfully, secretly, sneakily, sub rosa, surreptitiously, treacherously.

behind the times antiquated, dated, démodé, fogram, obsolete, old hat, old-fashioned, out of date, outdated, outmoded, passé, square.

behind-hand adj. backward, dilatory, ill-provided, lag, late, remiss, slow, tardy.
antonym provident.

behold v. consider, contemplate, descry, discern, espy, eye, look at, note, observe, perceive, regard, scan, survey, view, watch, witness.
interj. ecce, lo, look, mark, observe, see, voici, voilà, watch.

beholden adj. bound, grateful, indebted, obligated, obliged, owing, thankful.

behove v. advance, be to one's advantage, befit, benefit, beseem, profit.

beige adj. biscuit, buff, café au lait, camel, cinnamon, coffee, cream, ecru, fawn, greige, khaki, mushroom, neutral, oatmeal, sand, tan.

being[1] n. actuality, animation, entity, essence, existence, haecceity, life, living, nature, quiddity, reality, soul, spirit, substance.

being[2] n. animal, beast, body, creature, human being, individual, mortal, sentient, thing.

belabour v. attack, bash, batter, beat, belt, berate, castigate, censure, chastise, criticise, flay, flog, lambast, lay into, thrash, whip.

belated adj. behind-hand, delayed, late, overdue, retarded, tardy, unpunctual.
antonyms punctual, timely.

belch v. burp, discharge, disgorge, emit, eruct, eructate, erupt, gush, hiccup, spew, vent.
n. burp, eructation, eruption, hiccup.

beleaguered adj. badgered, beset, besieged, bothered, harassed, hedged about, hedged in, persecuted, plagued, surrounded, vexed, worried.

belie v. conceal, confute, contradict, deceive, deny, disguise, disprove, falsify, gainsay, mislead, misrepresent, negate, refute, repudiate, run counter to, understate.
antonym attest.

belief n. assurance, confidence, conviction, credence, credit, credo, creed, doctrine, dogma, expectation, faith, feeling, ideology, impression, intuition, ism, judgement, notion, opinion, persuasion, presumption, principle, principles, reliance, sureness, surety, tenet, theory, trust, view.
antonym disbelief.

believable adj. acceptable, authentic, authoritative, conceivable, credible, creditable, imaginable, likely, plausible, possible, probable, reliable, thinkable, trustworthy.
antonym unconvincing.

believe v. accept, assume, be under the impression, conjecture, consider, count on, credit, deem, depend on, gather, guess, hold, imagine, judge, maintain, postulate, presume, reckon, rely on, speculate, suppose, swallow, swear by, think, trust, wear.
antonym disbelieve.

believer n. adherent, catechumen, convert, devotee, disciple, follower, proselyte, supporter, upholder, votary, zealot.
antonyms apostate, sceptic, unbeliever.

belittle v. decry, deprecate, depreciate, deride, derogate, detract, diminish, dismiss, disparage, downgrade, lessen, minimise, ridicule, run down, scorn, underestimate, underrate, undervalue, vilipend.
antonym exaggerate.

bellicose adj. aggressive, antagonistic, argumentative, belligerent, combative, contentious, defiant, hawkish, hostile, jingoistic, militant, militaristic, provocative, pugnacious,

quarrelsome, sabre-rattling, warlike, war-loving, warmongering.
antonym peaceable.

belligerence *n.* aggression, aggressiveness, animosity, antagonism, bellicosity, combativeness, contentiousness, pugnacity, quarrelsomeness, unfriendliness, violence.
antonym complaisance.

belligerent *adj.* aggressive, antagonistic, argumentative, bellicose, bullying, combative, contentious, forceful, militant, pugnacious, quarrelsome, violent, warlike, warring.
antonym peaceable.

bellow *v.* bell, call, clamour, cry, howl, roar, scream, shout, shriek, troat, yell.

belly *n.* abdomen, bowels, bread-basket, corporation, gut, guts, insides, paunch, pot, soundboard, stomach, tummy, uterus, venter, vitals, womb.
v. bag, balloon, billow, blow up, bulge, dilate, distend, expand, fill out, inflate, swell.
antonyms deflate, shrink.

belong *v.* attach to, be connected with, be part of, be relevant to, be tied to, fit, go with, inhere, link up with, pertain to, relate to, tie up with.

belonging *n.* acceptance, affinity, association, attachment, closeness, compatibility, fellow-feeling, fellowship, inclusion, kinship, link, linkage, loyalty, rapport, relationship.
antonym antipathy.
belonging to affiliated to, associated with, essential to, held by, included in, inherent in, intrinsic in, native to, owned by.
antonym alien to.

belongings *n.* accoutrements, chattels, effects, gear, goods, impedimenta, paraphernalia, possessions, stuff, things, traps.

beloved *adj.* admired, adored, cherished, darling, dear, dearest, favourite, loved, pet, precious, prized, revered, sweet, treasured.
n. adored, darling, dear, dearest, favourite, inamorata, inamorato, lover, pet, precious, sweet, sweetheart.

below *adv.* beneath, down, infra, lower, lower down, under, underneath.
prep. inferior to, lesser than, 'neath, subject to, subordinate to, under, underneath, unworthy of.
below par below average, imperfect, inferior, lacking, not oneself, off, off-colour, off-form, poor, poorly, second-rate, substandard, under the weather, unfit, unhealthy, wanting.
below the belt cowardly, dirty, dishonest, foul, unfair, unjust, unscrupulous, unsporting, unsportsmanlike.

belt[1] *n.* area, band, ceinture, cincture, cingulum, cummerbund, district, girdle, girth, layer, region, sash, strait, stretch, strip, swathe, tract, waistband, zone, zonule, zonulet.
v. circle, encircle, girdle, ring, surround.
belt up be quiet, cut it out, leave it out, put a sock in, shut one's mouth, shut up, stow it.

belt[2] *v.* bolt, career, charge, dash, hurry, race, rush, speed.

bemoan *v.* bewail, deplore, grieve for, lament, mourn, regret, rue, sigh for, sorrow over, weep for.
antonym gloat.

bemuse *v.* amaze, bewilder, confuse, daze, distract, muddle, overwhelm, perplex, pixillate, puzzle, stun.
antonyms enlighten, illuminate.

bemused *adj.* absent-minded, befuddled, bewildered, confused, dazed, distracted, engrossed, fuddled, half-drunk, muddled, mused, perplexed, pixillated, stunned, stupefied, tipsy.
antonyms clear, clear-headed, lucid.

bench[1] *n.* bleachers, board, counter, form, ledge, pew, seat, settle, stall, table, terrace, tier, work-bench, work-table.

bench[2] *n.* court, courtroom, judge, judges, judicature, judiciary, magistrate, magistrates, tribunal.

benchmark *n.* criterion, example, level, model, norm, reference, reference-point, standard, touchstone, yardstick.

bend *v.* aim, bow, brace, buckle, compel, constrain, contort, couch, crankle, crimp, crouch, curve, deflect, direct, dispose, diverge, embow, fasten, flex, incline, incurvate, incurve, influence, lean, mould, nerve, persuade, shape, stoop, string, subdue, submit, sway, swerve, turn, twist, veer, warp, yield.
n. angle, arc, bight, bought, bow, corner, crank, crook, curvature, curve, elbow, flexure, genu, hook, incurvation, incurvature, incurve, inflexure, loop, turn, twist, zigzag.

beneath *adv.* below, lower, lower down, under, underneath.
prep. below, inferior to, infra dig(nitatem), lower than, 'neath, subject to, subordinate to, unbefitting, under, underneath, unworthy of.

benediction *n.* beatitude, Benedictus, benison, blessing, consecration, favour, grace, invocation, orison, prayer, thanksgiving.
antonyms anathema, curse, execration.

benefaction *n.* aid, alms-giving, backing, beneficence, benevolence, bequest, boon, bounty, charity, contribution, donation, endowment, generosity, gift, grant, gratuity, help, legacy, liberality, munificence, offering, philanthropy, present, sponsorship, subsidy.

benefactor *n.* angel, backer, contributor, donor, endower, friend, helper, patron, philanthropist, promoter, provider, sponsor, subscriber, subsidiser, supporter, well-wisher.
antonyms opponent, persecutor.

beneficence *n.* aid, altruism, benefaction, benevolence, bestowal, bounty, charity, compassion, donation, generosity, gift, goodness, helpfulness, kindness, largess, largition, liberality, love, munificence, present, relief, succour, unselfishness, virtue.
antonym meanness.

beneficent *adj.* altruistic, benevolent, benign, bounteous, bountiful, charitable, compassionate, generous, helpful, kind, liberal, munificent, unselfish.
antonym mean.

beneficial *adj.* advantageous, benign, benignant, edifying, favourable, gainful, healthful, helpful, improving, nourishing, nutritious, profitable, restorative, rewarding, salubrious, salutary, serviceable, useful, valuable, wholesome. *antonym* harmful.

beneficiary *n.* assignee, devisee, donee, fructuary, heir, heiress, heritor, inheritor, legatee, payee, receiver, recipient, successor.

benefit *n.* advantage, aid, asset, assistance, avail, betterment, blessing, boon, favour, gain, good, help, interest, profit, service, use, weal, welfare.
antonym harm.
v. advance, advantage, aid, ameliorate, amend, assist, avail, better, enhance, further, improve, profit, promote, serve.
antonyms harm, hinder, undermine.

benefits *n.* advantages, bonuses, extras, freebies, loaves and fishes, perks, perquisites, pluses. *antonym* disadvantages.

benevolence *n.* altruism, benignity, bounty, charity, compassion, fellow-feeling, generosity, goodness, goodwill, humanity, kindheartedness, kindliness, kindness, munificence, sympathy.
antonym meanness.

benevolent *adj.* altruistic, beneficent, benign, bounteous, bountiful, caring, charitable, compassionate, considerate, generous, good-will, Grandisonian, humane, humanitarian, kind, kind-hearted, kindly, liberal, loving, philanthropic, solicitous, well-disposed.
antonym mean.

benign *adj.* advantageous, amiable, auspicious, balmy, benefic, beneficent, beneficial, benevolent, complaisant, curable, curative, encouraging, favourable, friendly, generous, genial, gentle, good, gracious, harmless, healthful, kind, kindly, liberal, lucky, mild, obliging, propitious, refreshing, restorative, salubrious, salutary, sympathetic, temperate, warm, wholesome.
antonyms harmful, hostile, malign, malignant.

bent *adj.* angled, arched, bowed, coudé, criminal, crooked, curved, dishonest, doubled, falcate, folded, homosexual, hunched, inbent, inflexed, retorted, retroverted, stolen, stooped, twisted, untrustworthy.
antonym straight.
n. ability, aptitude, capacity, facility, faculty, flair, forte, gift, inclination, knack, leaning, penchant, preference, proclivity, propensity, talent, tendency.

bent on determined, disposed, fixed, heading for, inclined, insistent, resolved, set on.

benumbed *adj.* anaesthetised, dazed, deadened, desensitised, dull, frozen, immobilised, insensible, insensitive, numb, numbed, paralysed, stunned, stupefied, unfeeling, unresponsive.

bequeath *v.* assign, bestow, commit, demise, devise, endow, entrust, gift, give, grant, hand down, impart, pass on, settle, transmit, will.

bequest *n.* bequeathal, bequeathment, bestowal, devisal, devise, donation, dower, endowment, estate, gift, heritage, inheritance, legacy, patrimony, settlement, trust.

berate *v.* castigate, censure, chastise, chide, criticise, flyte, jump down the throat of, rail at, rate, rebuke, reprimand, reproach, reprove, revile, scold, tell off, upbraid, vituperate.
antonym praise.

bereave *v.* afflict, deprive, despoil, dispossess, divest, orphan, rob, strip, widow.

bereavement *n.* death, defiliation, deprivation, despoliation, dispossession, loss.
antonyms addition, increase.

bereft *adj.* denuded, deprived, despoiled, destitute, devoid, lacking, minus, robbed, shorn, stripped, wanting.

berserk *adj.* amok, crazy, demented, deranged, enraged, frantic, frenetic, frenzied, furious, insane, mad, maniacal, manic, rabid, raging, raving, uncontrollable, violent, wild.
antonyms calm, sane.

berth *n.* anchorage, bed, billet, bunk, cot, dock, employment, hammock, harbour, harbourage, haven, job, landfall, pier, port, position, post, quay, shelter, sinecure, situation, slip, wharf.
v. anchor, dock, drop anchor, land, moor, tie up.
antonym weigh anchor.

beseech *v.* adjure, ask, beg, call on, conjure, crave, desire, entreat, implore, importune, obsecrate, petition, plead, pray, solicit, sue, supplicate.

beset *v.* assail, attack, badger, bamboozle, bedevil, besiege, embarrass, encircle, enclose, encompass, entangle, environ, faze, harass, hassle, hem in, perplex, pester, plague, surround.

besetting *adj.* compulsive, constant, dominant, habitual, harassing, inveterate, irresistible, obsessive, persistent, prevalent, recurring, troublesome, uncontrollable.

beside *prep.* abreast of, abutting on, adjacent, bordering on, close to, near, neighbouring, next door to, next to, overlooking, upsides with.
beside oneself berserk, crazed, delirious, demented, deranged, distracted, distraught, frantic, frenetic, frenzied, furious, insane, mad, unbalanced, unhinged.
beside the point extraneous, immaterial, inapplicable, incidental, inconsequential, irrelevant, pointless, unimportant, unrelated.
antonym relevant.

besides *adv.* additionally, also, as well, extra, further, furthermore, in addition, into the bargain, moreover, otherwise, to boot, too, withal.
prep. apart from, in addition to, other than, over and above.

besiege *v.* assail, badger, belay, beleaguer, beset, blockade, bother, confine, dun, encircle, encompass, environ, harass, harry, hound, importune, nag, pester, plague, surround, trouble.

besmirch v. begrime, bespatter, daub, defame, defile, dirty, dishonour, muddy, slander, smear, soil, spatter, stain, sully, tarnish. *antonym* enhance.

besotted *adj.* befuddled, bewitched, confused, doting, drunk, foolish, hypnotised, inebriated, infatuated, intoxicated, muddled, obsessed, smitten, stupefied, witless. *antonyms* disenchanted, indifferent, sober.

bespeak v. attest, betoken, demonstrate, denote, display, evidence, evince, exhibit, forebode, foretell, imply, indicate, predict, proclaim, reveal, show, signify, suggest, testify to.

best *adj.* advantageous, apt, correct, excellent, finest, first, first-class, first-rate, foremost, greatest, highest, incomparable, largest, leading, makeless, matchless, nonpareil, optimal, optimum, outstanding, perfect, pre-eminent, preferable, principal, right, superlative, supreme, transcendent, unequalled, unsurpassed. *antonym* worst.

adv. excellently, exceptionally, extremely, greatly, superlatively, surpassingly. *antonym* worst.

n. choice, cream, crème de la crème, élite, favourite, finest, first, flower, hardest, nonpareil, pick, prime, the tops, top, utmost. *antonym* worst.

v. beat, conquer, defeat, get the better of, have the laugh of, lick, outclass, outdo, outwit, surpass, thrash, trounce, vanquish, worst.

bestial *adj.* animal, barbaric, barbarous, beastly, brutal, brutish, carnal, degraded, depraved, feral, gross, inhuman, savage, sensual, sordid, subhuman, swinish, vile. *antonyms* civilised, humane.

bestir v. activate, actuate, animate, arouse, awaken, energise, exert, galvanise, incite, motivate, rouse, stimulate. *antonyms* calm, lull, quell.

bestow v. accord, allot, apportion, award, bequeath, commit, confer, donate, dower, endow, entrust, give, grant, impart, lavish, lend, present, transmit, wreak. *antonym* deprive.

bestowal *n.* benefaction, bequeathal, bequeathment, conferring, distribution, donation, gift, giving, imparting, largition, presentation, transmission.

bestride v. bestraddle, command, dominate, horse, overshadow, sit astride, stand astride, straddle.

bet *n.* accumulator, ante, bid, flutter, gamble, hazard, pledge, risk, speculation, stake, venture, wager.

v. ante, bid, chance, gamble, hazard, lay, pledge, punt, risk, speculate, stake, venture, wager.

bête noire abomination, anathema, aversion, bane, bogey, bugbear, curse, pet hate.

antonym favourite.

betide v. bechance, befall, chance, develop, ensue, hap, happen, occur, overtake, supervene.

betimes *adv.* early, expeditiously, punctually, seasonably, soon, speedily, timeously. *antonym* late.

betoken v. augur, bespeak, bode, declare, denote, evidence, forebode, foreshow, import, indicate, manifest, mark, portend, presage, prognosticate, promise, represent, signify, suggest.

betray v. abandon, beguile, corrupt, deceive, delude, desert, disclose, discover, divulge, dob in, double-cross, dupe, ensnare, entrap, evince, expose, forsake, give away, grass, inform on, jilt, manifest, mislead, reveal, seduce, sell, sell down the river, sell out, shop, show, tell, turn Queen's (King's) evidence, undo. *antonyms* defend, fulfil, protect.

betrayal *n.* deception, disclosure, discovery, disloyalty, divulgence, double-dealing, duplicity, exposure, falseness, Judas-kiss, perfidy, rattery, ratting, revelation, sell-out, treachery, treason, trickery, unfaithfulness. *antonyms* loyalty, protection.

betrayer *n.* apostate, conspirator, deceiver, double-crosser, grass, informer, renegade, supergrass, traitor. *antonyms* protector, supporter.

betroth v. affiance, contract, espouse, plight, plight one's troth, promise.

betrothal *n.* engagement, espousal, fiançailles, handfast, plight, promise, troth, vow.

better *adj.* bigger, cured, finer, fitter, greater, healthier, improving, larger, longer, on the mend, preferable, progressing, recovered, recovering, restored, stronger, superior, surpassing, worthier. *antonym* worse.

v. advance, ameliorate, amend, beat, cap, correct, enhance, exceed, excel, forward, further, go one further than, improve, improve on, increase, meliorate, mend, outdo, outstrip, overtake, overtop, promote, raise, rectify, redress, reform, strengthen, surpass, top, transcend. *antonyms* deteriorate, worsen.

betterment *n.* advancement, amelioration, edification, enhancement, furtherance, improvement, melioration. *antonyms* deterioration, impairment.

betterness *n.* advantage, ascendancy, meliority, preferability, superiority, transcendancy.

between *prep.* amidst, among, amongst, betwixt, inter-, mid.

between ourselves entre nous, in confidence, in secret, privately, within these four walls.

bevel *n.* angle, basil, bezel, bias, cant, chamfer, diagonal, mitre, oblique, slant, slope.

v. bias, cant, chamfer, mitre, slant.

beverage *n.* bevvy, draught, drink, libation, liquid, liquor, poison, potable, potation.

bevy *n.* band, bunch, collection, company,

crowd, flock, gaggle, gathering, group, pack, phalanx, throng, troupe.

bewail v. bemoan, cry over, deplore, greet, grieve for, keen, lament, moan, mourn, regret, repent, rue, sigh over, sorrow over. *antonyms* gloat, glory, vaunt.

beware v. avoid, give a wide berth to, guard against, heed, look out, mind, shun, steer clear of, take heed, watch out. *antonym* court. *interj.* fore, nix.

bewilder v. baffle, bamboozle, befuddle, bemuse, buffalo, confound, confuse, daze, disconcert, disorient, fuddle, maze, muddle, mystify, perplex, puzzle, stupefy, tie in knots.

bewildered adj. awed, baffled, bamboozled, bemused, confused, désorienté, disconcerted, disoriented, dizzy, giddy, muddled, mystified, nonplussed, perplexed, pixillated, pixy-led, puzzled, stunned, surprised, uncertain. *antonyms* collected, unperturbed.

bewilderment n. awe, confusion, daze, disconcertion, disorientation, mizmaze, mystification, perplexity, puzzledom, puzzlement, stupefaction, surprise, uncertainty. *antonyms* composure, confidence.

bewitch v. allure, attract, beguile, captivate, charm, elf-shoot, enchant, enrapture, ensorcell, entrance, fascinate, forspeak, hex, hoodoo, hypnotise, jinx, obsess, possess, spellbind, voodoo, witch.

bewitched adj. charmed, elf-shot, enchanted, enthralled, entranced, fascinated, hexed, jinxed, mesmerised, obsessed, possessed, spellbound, transfixed, transformed. *antonym* disenchanted.

bewitching adj. beguiling, charming, enchanting, entrancing, fascinating, glamorous, hypnotic, intriguing, seductive, tantalising, witching. *antonym* repellent.

beyond prep. above, across, apart from, away from, before, further than, out of range, out of reach of, over, past, remote from, superior to, yonder.

beyond price inestimable, invaluable, irreplaceable, precious, priceless.

bias n. angle, bent, bigotry, distortion, editorialisation, favouritism, inclination, intolerance, leaning, one-sidedness, parti pris, partiality, penchant, predilection, predisposition, prejudice, proclivity, proneness, propensity, slant, tendency, tendentiousness, turn, unfairness, viewiness. *antonyms* fairness, impartiality.

v. angle, distort, earwig, editorialise, influence, jaundice, load, load the dice, predispose, prejudice, slant, sway, twist, warp, weight.

biased adj. angled, bigoted, blinkered, distorted, embittered, jaundiced, loaded, one-sided, partial, predisposed, prejudiced, slanted, swayed, tendentious, twisted, unfair, verkrampte, viewy, warped, weighted. *antonyms* fair, impartial.

bibulous adj. alcoholic, crapulous, dipsomaniac, drunken, inebriate, intemperate, sottish, thirsty, tipsy. *antonyms* sober, temperate.

bicker v. altercate, argue, clash, disagree, dispute, feud, fight, quarrel, row, scrap, spar, squabble, wrangle. *antonym* agree.

bicycle n. bike, boneshaker, cycle, ordinary, penny-farthing, push-bike, racer, safety bicycle, tandem, two-wheeler, velocipede.

bid v. ask, call, charge, command, desire, direct, enjoin, greet, instruct, invite, offer, proclaim, propose, request, require, say, solicit, summon, tell, wish.

n. advance, amount, ante, attempt, crack, effort, endeavour, go, offer, price, proposal, proposition, submission, sum, tender, try, venture.

biddable adj. acquiescent, agreeable, amenable, complaisant, co-operative, docile, obedient, responsive, teachable, tractable. *antonym* recalcitrant.

bidding n. behest, call, charge, command, demand, dictate, direction, injunction, instruction, invitation, order, request, requirement, summons.

big adj. adult, altruistic, beefy, benevolent, boastful, bombastic, bulky, burly, buxom, colossal, considerable, corpulent, elder, elephantine, eminent, enormous, extensive, gargantuan, generous, gigantic, gracious, great, grown, grown-up, heroic, huge, hulking, immense, important, influential, large, mammoth, man-sized, massive, mature, momentous, noble, paramount, plonking, ponderous, powerful, prime, principal, prodigious, prominent, serious, significant, sizable, skelping, spacious, stout, substantial, titanic, tolerant, unselfish, valuable, vast, voluminous, weighty. *antonyms* little, small.

big shot big noise, bigwig, celebrity, dignitary, heavyweight, mogul, mugwump, nob, notability, notable, panjandrum, personage, somebody, VIP. *antonym* nonentity.

bigamy n. diandry.

bigot n. chauvinist, dogmatist, fanatic, racist, religionist, sectarian, sexist, verkrampte, zealot. *antonyms* humanitarian, liberal.

bigoted adj. biased, blinkered, chauvinist, closed, dogmatic, illiberal, intolerant, narrow, narrow-minded, obstinate, opinionated, prejudiced, sectarian, twisted, verkrampte, warped. *antonyms* broad-minded, enlightened, liberal.

bigotry n. bias, chauvinism, discrimination, dogmatism, fanaticism, ignorance, illiberality, injustice, intolerance, jingoism, mindlessness, narrow-mindedness, prejudice, racialism, racism, religionism, sectarianism, sexism, unfairness.

bigwig *n.* big gun, big noise, big shot, celebrity, dignitary, heavyweight, huzoor, mogul, mugwump, nabob, nob, notability, notable, panjandrum, personage, somebody, VIP.
antonym nobody.

bile *n.* anger, bitterness, choler, gall, ill-humour, irascibility, irritability, peevishness, rancour, spleen, testiness.

bilingual *adj.* diglot.

bilious *adj.* choleric, crabby, cross, crotchety, grouchy, grumpy, irritable, liverish, nauseated, out of sorts, peevish, queasy, sick, sickly, testy.

bilk *v.* balk, bamboozle, cheat, con, cozen, deceive, defraud, do, do out of, fleece, foil, rook, sting, swindle, thwart, trick.

bill[1] *n.* account, advertisement, battels, broadsheet, broadside, bulletin, card, catalogue, charges, chit, circular, greenback, handbill, hand-out, inventory, invoice, leaflet, legislation, list, listing, measure, note, notice, placard, playbill, poster, programme, proposal, reckoning, roster, schedule, score, sheet, statement, syllabus, tab, tally.
v. advertise, announce, charge, debit, invoice, list, post, reckon, record.

bill[2] *n.* beak, mandible, neb, nib, rostrum.

billet *n.* accommodation, barracks, berth, employment, housing, lodgement, lodging, occupation, post, quarterage, quarters.
v. accommodate, berth, lodge, quarter, station.

billow *v.* balloon, belly, expand, fill out, heave, puff out, roll, seethe, spread, surge, swell, undulate.

billowy *adj.* billowing, heaving, rippling, rolling, surging, swelling, swirling, tossing, undulating, waving.

bind *v.* astrict, astringe, attach, bandage, border, cinch, clamp, colligate, compel, complain, confine, constipate, constrain, cover, detain, dress, edge, encase, engage, fasten, finish, force, glue, hamper, harden, hinder, hitch, indenture, lash, necessitate, obligate, oblige, prescribe, require, restrain, restrict, rope, seal, secure, stick, strap, swathe, thirl, tie, trim, truss, wrap.
n. bore, difficulty, dilemma, embarrassment, hole, impasse, nuisance, predicament, quandary.

binding *adj.* compulsory, conclusive, imperative, indissoluble, irrevocable, mandatory, necessary, obligatory, permanent, requisite, strict, unalterable, unbreakable.
n. bandage, border, covering, deligation, edging, stricture, syndesis, tape, trimming, wrapping.

binge *n.* banquet, beano, bender, blind, bout, do, feast, fling, guzzle, jag, orgy, spree.
antonym fast.

biographical *adj.* prosopographical.

biography *n.* account, adventures, autobiography, biopic, curriculum vitae, exposé, fortunes, history, life, life story, memoir, memoirs, prosopography, recollections, record.

bird-like *adj.* aquiline, avian, aviform, avine, hawk-like, ornithoid, volucrine.

birth *n.* ancestry, background, beginning, birthright, blood, breeding, childbirth, delivery, derivation, descent, emergence, extraction, family, fell, genealogy, genesis, geniture, line, lineage, nativity, nobility, origin, parentage, parturition, pedigree, race, rise, source, stirps, stock, strain.

birthday *n.* anniversary, day of birth, (dies) natalis, natalitium.
adj. anniversary, genethliac, genethliacal, natal, natalitial.

birthmark *n.* angioma, mole, mother's mark, motherspot, naevus, port wine stain.

birthplace *n.* fount, incunabula, native country, native town, place of origin, provenance, roots, source.

biscuit *n.* cake, cookie, cracker, hardtack, rusk, wafer.

bisect *v.* bifurcate, cross, divide, fork, furcate, halve, intersect, separate, split.

bisexual *adj.* androgynous, epicene, gynandromorphic, gynandromorphous, gynandrous, hermaphrodite, hermaphroditic, monoclinous.
antonyms heterosexual, homosexual.

bishop *n.* abba, archbishop, diocesan, exarch, metropolitan, patriarch, prelate, primate, suffragan.

bit *n.* atom, chip, crumb, fragment, grain, instant, iota, jiffy, jot, mammock, minute, mite, moment, morsel, part, period, piece, scrap, second, segment, sippet, slice, snippet, speck, spell, tick, time, tittle, while, whit.
bit by bit gradatim, gradually, insidiously, little by little, piecemeal, seriatim, step by step.
antonym wholesale.

bitch *n.* back-biter, cat, doggess, fury, harridan, shrew, termagant, virago, vixen.

bitchy *adj.* back-biting, catty, cruel, malicious, mean, nasty, poisonous, snide, spiteful, venomous, vicious, vindictive, vixenish, vixenly, waspish.
antonym kind.

bite *v.* burn, champ, chew, clamp, corrode, crunch, crush, cut, gnaw, knap, masticate, nibble, nip, pierce, pinch, rend, seize, smart, snap, sting, tear, tingle, wound.
n. edge, food, grip, kick, morsel, morsure, mouthful, nip, piece, pinch, piquancy, prick, punch, pungency, refreshment, smarting, snack, spice, sting, taste, wound.
bite the dust crumple, die, drop, drop dead, expire, fall, perish.

biting *adj.* astringent, bitter, blighting, caustic, cold, cutting, cynical, freezing, harsh, hurtful, incisive, mordant, nipping, penetrating, piercing, raw, sarcastic, scathing, severe, sharp, stinging, tart, trenchant, withering.
antonyms bland, mild.

bitter *adj.* acerb, acerbic, acid, acrid, acrimonious, astringent, begrudging, biting, calamitous, crabbed, cruel, cynical, dire, distressing, embittered, fierce, freezing, galling, grievous, harsh, hateful, heartbreaking, hostile, intense, ironic, jaundiced, merciless, morose, odious, painful, poignant, rancorous, raw, resentful, ruthless, sarcastic, savage, severe, sharp, sore, sour, stinging, sullen, tart, unsweetened, vexatious, vinegary, waspish. *antonyms* contented, genial, sweet.

bitterness *n*. acerbity, acidity, acrimoniousness, animosity, asperity, astringency, causticity, grudge, hostility, irony, mordancy, pique, rancour, resentment, sarcasm, sharpness, sourness, tartness, venom, virulence, wormwood. *antonyms* contentment, geniality, sweetness.

bizarre *adj*. abnormal, comical, curious, deviant, eccentric, extraordinary, extravagant, fantastic, freakish, grotesque, ludicrous, odd, off-beat, outlandish, outré, peculiar, quaint, queer, ridiculous, strange, unusual, way-out, weird. *antonym* normal.

bizarreness *n*. bizarrerie, curiousness, eccentricity, freakishness, grotesqueness, grotesquerie, oddity, oddness, outlandishness, queerness, singularity, strangeness, weirdness. *antonym* normality.

blab *v*. blurt, disclose, divulge, gossip, leak, reveal, squeal, tattle, tell. *antonyms* hide, hush up.

blabber *v*. blather, blether, chatter, chinwag, earbash, gab, gabble, jabber, natter, prattle, whitter.

black *adj*. angry, atrocious, bad, begrimed, coal-black, collied, dark, darksome, depressing, dingy, dirty, dismal, doleful, dusky, ebony, evil, filthy, funereal, furious, gloomy, grim, grimy, grubby, hopeless, horrible, hostile, inky, jet, jet-black, jetty, lugubrious, menacing, moonless, morel, mournful, murky, nefarious, ominous, overcast, pitchy, raven, resentful, sable, sad, sloe, soiled, sombre, sooty, stained, starless, Stygian, sullen, swarthy, threatening, thunderous, villainous, wicked.

v. ban, bar, blacklist, boycott, taboo.

black eye keeker, mouse, shiner.

black magic black art, demonolatry, devil-worship, diabolism, hoodoo, necromancy, sorcery, voodoo, witchcraft, wizardry.

black out censor, collapse, conceal, cover up, darken, eclipse, extinguish, faint, flake out, gag, keel over, obfuscate, obliterate, pass out, shade, suppress, swoon, withhold.

black sheep disgrace, drop-out, ne'er-do-well, outcast, pariah, prodigal, reject, renegade, reprobate, wastrel. *antonym* pride.

blackball *v*. ban, bar, blacklist, debar, exclude, expel, ostracise, oust, pip, reject, repudiate, snub, veto.

blacken *v*. befoul, begrime, besmirch, calumniate, cloud, colly, darken, decry, defame, defile, denigrate, detract, dishonour, malign,

nigrify, revile, slander, smear, smirch, smudge, soil, stain, sully, taint, tarnish, traduce, vilify. *antonyms* enhance, praise.

blackguard *n*. bleeder, blighter, bounder, cur, devil, knave, miscreant, rascal, reprobate, rogue, rotter, scoundrel, stinker, swine, villain, wretch.

blackhead *n*. comedo.

blackleg *n*. fink, strike-breaker.

blacklist *v*. ban, bar, blackball, boycott, debar, disallow, exclude, expel, ostracise, preclude, proscribe, reject, repudiate, snub, taboo, veto. *antonyms* accept, allow.

blackmail *n*. blood-sucking, chantage, exaction, extortion, hush money, intimidation, milking, pay-off, protection, ransom.
v. bleed, bribe, coerce, compel, demand, force, hold to ransom, lean on, milk, put the black on, squeeze, threaten.

blackmailer *n*. bloodsucker, extortioner, extortionist, highbinder, vampire.

blackness *n*. darkness, duskiness, filthiness, gloom, griminess, inkiness, melanism, murkiness, nigrescence, nigritude, swarthiness, wickedness.

blackout *n*. censorship, coma, concealment, cover-up, faint, oblivion, power cut, secrecy, suppression, swoon, syncope, unconsciousness.

bladder *n*. aveole, bag, bursa, caecum, capsule, cell, cyst, pocket, pouch, receptacle, sac, saccule, theca, utricle, vesica, vesicle, vesicula.

blade *n*. dagger, edge, knife, rapier, scalpel, sword, vane.

blamable *adj*. accountable, answerable, at fault, blameworthy, culpable, guilty, liable, reprehensible, reproachable, reprovable, responsible, wrong.

blame *n*. accountability, accusation, animadversion, castigation, censure, charge, complaint, condemnation, criticism, culpability, discommendation, fault, guilt, incrimination, liability, obloquy, onus, rap, recrimination, reprimand, reproach, reproof, responsibility, stick, stricture.
v. accuse, admonish, censure, charge, chide, condemn, criticise, disapprove, discommend, dispraise, find fault with, rebuke, reprehend, reprimand, reproach, reprove, tax, upbraid. *antonym* exonerate.

blameless *adj*. above reproach, clean, clear, faultless, guiltless, immaculate, impeccable, inculpable, innocent, irreprehensible, irreproachable, irreprovable, perfect, sinless, stainless, unblamable, unblemished, unimpeachable, unspotted, unsullied, untarnished, upright, virtuous. *antonym* guilty.

blameworthy *adj*. censurable, culpable, discreditable, disreputable, flagitious, guilty, indefensible, inexcusable, reprehensible, reproachable, shameful, unworthy. *antonym* blameless.

blanch v. bleach, blench, drain, etiolate, fade, pale, wan, whiten.
antonyms blush, colour, redden.

bland *adv.* affable, amiable, balmy, boring, calm, characterless, congenial, courteous, demulcent, dull, fair-spoken, flat, friendly, gentle, gracious, humdrum, hypo-allergenic, impassive, inscrutable, insipid, mild, mollifying, monotonous, nondescript, non-irritant, smooth, soft, soothing, suave, tasteless, tedious, temperate, unexciting, uninspiring, uninteresting, urbane, vapid, weak.
antonyms piquant, sharp.

blandishments *n.* blarney, cajolery, coaxing, compliments, enticements, fawning, flattery, inducements, ingratiation, inveiglement, lip-salve, persuasiveness, soft soap, sweet talk, sycophancy, wheedling.

blank *adj.* apathetic, bare, bewildered, clean, clear, confounded, confused, deadpan, disconcerted, dull, dumbfounded, empty, expressionless, featureless, glazed, hollow, immobile, impassive, inane, inscrutable, lifeless, muddled, nonplussed, plain, poker-faced, sheer, spotless, staring, uncomprehending, unfilled, unmarked, unrhymed, vacant, vacuous, vague, void, white.
n. break, emptiness, gap, nothingness, space, tabula rasa, vacancy, vacuity, vacuum, void.

blanket *n.* carpet, cloak, coat, coating, cover, covering, coverlet, envelope, film, housing, layer, mackinaw, manta, mantle, rug, sheet, wrapper, wrapping.
adj. across-the-board, all-embracing, all-inclusive, comprehensive, inclusive, overall, sweeping, wide-ranging.
v. cloak, cloud, coat, conceal, cover, deaden, eclipse, hide, mask, muffle, obscure, surround.

blankness *n.* abstraction, bareness, emptiness, immobility, impassivity, inanity, incomprehension, indifference, inscrutability, obliviousness, vacancy, vacuity, void.

blare *v.* blast, boom, clamour, clang, honk, hoot, peal, resound, ring, roar, scream, shriek, toot, trumpet.

blarney *n.* blandishment, cajolery, coaxing, eloquence, flattery, persuasiveness, plausibility, soft soap, spiel, sweet talk, wheedling.

blasé *adj.* apathetic, bored, dulled, glutted, indifferent, jaded, nonchalant, offhand, sated, satiated, surfeited, unconcerned, unexcited, unimpressed, unimpressible, uninspired, uninterested, unmoved, weary, world-weary.
antonyms enthusiastic, excited.

blaspheme *v.* abuse, curse, damn, defile, desecrate, execrate, imprecate, profane, revile, swear.

blasphemous *adj.* execrative, godless, hubristic, impious, imprecatory, irreligious, irreverent, profane, sacrilegious, ungodly.

blasphemy *n.* curse, cursing, defilement, desecration, execration, expletive, hubris, impiety, impiousness, imprecation, irreverence, outrage, profanation, profaneness, profanity, sacrilege, swearing, violation.

blast[1] *n., v.* blare, blow, boom, honk, hoot, peal, roar, scream, shriek, sound, wail.

blast[2] *n.* bang, bluster, burst, clap, crack, crash, detonation, discharge, draught, eruption, explosion, flatus, gale, gust, hail, outburst, salvo, squall, storm, tempest, volley.
v. assail, attack, blight, blow up, burst, castigate, demolish, destroy, explode, flay, kill, lash, ruin, shatter, shrivel, storm at, wither.

blasted *adj.* blighted, desolated, destroyed, devastated, ravaged, ruined, scorched, shattered, wasted, withered.

blatant *adj.* arrant, bald, barefaced, brazen, clamorous, conspicuous, egregious, flagrant, flaunting, glaring, harsh, loud, naked, noisy, obtrusive, obvious, ostentatious, outright, overt, prominent, pronounced, sheer, unmitigated.

blaze *n.* blast, bonfire, brilliance, burst, conflagration, eruption, explosion, fire, flame, flames, flare, flare-up, flash, fury, glare, gleam, glitter, glow, light, outbreak, outburst, radiance, rush, storm.
v. beam, burn, burst, erupt, explode, fire, flame, flare, flare up, flash, fume, glare, gleam, glow, seethe, shine.

blazon *v.* announce, broadcast, bruit, celebrate, flaunt, flourish, proclaim, publicise, trumpet, vaunt.
antonyms deprecate, hush up.

bleach *v.* blanch, decolorise, etiolate, fade, lighten, pale, peroxide, whiten.

bleak *adj.* bare, barren, blae, blasted, cheerless, chilly, cold, colourless, comfortless, delightless, depressing, desolate, discouraging, disheartening, dismal, dreary, empty, exposed, gaunt, gloomy, grim, hopeless, joyless, leaden, loveless, open, raw, sombre, unsheltered, weather-beaten, windswept, windy.
antonyms cheerful, congenial.

bleary *adj.* blurred, blurry, cloudy, dim, fogged, foggy, fuzzy, hazy, indistinct, misty, muddy, murky, obscured, rheumy, watery.

bleat *v.* baa, bitch, blat, complain, growl, grumble, moan, whine, whinge.

bleed *v.* blackmail, deplete, drain, exhaust, exploit, extort, extract, extravasate, exude, fleece, flow, gush, haemorrhage, leech, milk, ooze, reduce, run, sap, seep, spurt, squeeze, suck dry, trickle, weep.

blemish *n.* birthmark, blot, blotch, blur, botch, defect, deformity, disfigurement, disgrace, dishonour, fault, flaw, imperfection, mackle, macula, maculation, mark, naevus, smudge, speck, spot, stain, taint.
v. besmirch, blot, blotch, blur, damage, deface, disfigure, flaw, impair, injure, maculate, mar, mark, smirch, smudge, spoil, spot, stain, sully, taint, tarnish.

blench *v.* balk, boggle, cower, falter, flinch, hesitate, jib, quail, quake, quiver, recoil, shrink, shudder, shy, start, wince.

blend v. amalgamate, coalesce, combine, complement, compound, contemper, fit, fuse, harmonise, intermix, meld, merge, mingle, mix, synthesise, unite.
antonym separate.
n. alloy, amalgam, amalgamation, combination, composite, compound, concoction, fusion, interunion, meld, mix, mixture, synthesis, union.

bless v. anoint, approve, bestow, consecrate, countenance, dedicate, endow, exalt, extol, favour, glorify, grace, hallow, magnify, ordain, praise, provide, sanctify, thank.
antonyms condemn, curse.

blessed adj. adored, beatified, blissful, contented, divine, endowed, favoured, fortunate, glad, hallowed, happy, holy, joyful, joyous, lucky, prosperous, revered, sacred, sanctified, seely.
antonym cursed.

blessedness n. beatitude, bliss, blissfulness, content, felicity, happiness, joy, sanctity, seel.

blessing n. advantage, approbation, approval, authority, backing, benedicite, benediction, benefit, benison, boon, bounty, commendation, concurrence, consecration, consent, countenance, darshan, dedication, favour, gain, gift, godsend, grace, help, invocation, kindness, leave, permission, profit, sanction, service, support, thanksgiving, windfall.
antonyms blight, condemnation, curse.

blether n. blather, chatter, chatterbox, chatterer, chit-chat, claptrap, drivel, gibberish, gibble-gabble, gobbledegook, haverel, jabbering, loquacity, moonshine, nonsense, prattle, prattler, twaddle.
v. blabber, chatter, gab, gabble, haver, jabber, prattle.

blight n. affliction, bane, cancer, canker, check, contamination, corruption, curse, decay, depression, disease, evil, fungus, infestation, mildew, pest, pestilence, plague, pollution, rot, scourge, set-back, woe.
antonyms blessing, boon.
v. annihilate, blast, crush, dash, destroy, disappoint, frustrate, injure, mar, ruin, shatter, shrivel, spoil, undermine, wither, wreck.
antonym bless.

blind adj. amaurotic, beetle-eyed, blinkered, careless, closed, concealed, dark, dim, eyeless, hasty, heedless, hidden, ignorant, impetuous, inattentive, inconsiderate, indifferent, indiscriminate, injudicious, insensate, insensitive, irrational, mindless, neglectful, oblivious, obscured, obstructed, prejudiced, purblind, rash, reckless, sand-blind, senseless, sightless, stone-blind, thoughtless, unaware, uncontrollable, uncritical, undiscerning, unobservant, unobserving, unreasoning, unseeing, unsighted, unthinking, violent, visionless, wild.
antonyms aware, clear, sighted.
n. camouflage, cloak, cover, cover-up, distraction, façade, feint, front, mask, masquerade, screen, smoke-screen.

blindfold v. bamboozle, beguile, blind, deceive, delude, fool, hoodwink, mislead.
antonym enlighten.

blindly adv. aimlessly, carelessly, confusedly, frantically, headlong, heedlessly, impetuously, impulsively, incautiously, inconsiderately, indiscriminately, madly, passionately, precipitately, purposelessly, recklessly, regardlessly, senselessly, thoughtlessly, wildly, wilfully.
antonym cautiously.

blindness n. cecity, ignorance, indifference, insensitivity, narrow-mindedness, neglect, prejudice, prestriction, sightlessness, unawareness.
antonyms awareness, sight, sightedness.

blink v. bat, condone, connive at, disregard, flash, flicker, flutter, gleam, glimmer, glimpse, ignore, nictate, nictitate, overlook, peer, pink, scintillate, shine, sparkle, squint, twinkle, wink.

bliss n. beatitude, blessedness, blissfulness, ecstasy, euphoria, felicity, gladness, happiness, heaven, joy, nirvana, paradise, rapture, seel.
antonyms damnation, misery.

blissful adj. beatific, delighted, ecstatic, elated, enchanted, enraptured, euphoric, happy, heavenly, joyful, joyous, rapturous.
antonym wretched.

blister n. abscess, blain, bleb, boil, bubble, bulla, canker, carbuncle, cyst, furuncle, papilla, papula, papule, pimple, pompholyx, pustule, sore, swelling, ulcer, vesicle, vesicula, welt, wen.

blistering adj. cruel, excoriating, hot, intense, sarcastic, savage, scathing, scorching, strenuous, vesicant, vesicatory, vicious, virulent, withering.
antonym mild.

blithe adj. animated, buoyant, carefree, careless, casual, cheerful, cheery, debonair, gay, gladsome, happy, heedless, jaunty, lighthearted, lightsome, lively, merry, mirthful, nonchalant, sprightly, sunny, thoughtless, unconcerned, untroubled, vivacious.
antonym morose.

blizzard n. snow-squall, snowstorm, squall, storm, tempest.

bloated adj. blown up, bombastic, dilated, distended, dropsical, enlarged, expanded, inflated, oedematous, sated, swollen, tumescent, tumid, turgid.
antonyms shrivelled, shrunken, thin.

blob n. ball, bead, bobble, bubble, dab, dew-drop, drop, droplet, glob, globule, gob, lump, mass, pearl, pellet, pill, spot.

bloc n. alliance, axis, cabal, cartel, clique, coalition, combine, entente, faction, group, league, ring.

block n. bar, barrier, blockage, brick, cake, chunk, cube, delay, hang-up, hindrance, hunk, impediment, ingot, jam, let, lump, mass, obstacle, obstruction, piece, resistance, square, stoppage, tranche.

v. arrest, bar, check, choke, clog, close, dam up, deter, halt, hinder, impede, obstruct, obturate, oppilate, plug, scotch, stonewall, stop, stop up, thwart, trig.

blockade *n.* barricade, barrier, beleaguerment, closure, encirclement, obstruction, restriction, siege, stoppage.

blockage *n.* block, blocking, clot, embolism, hindrance, impediment, jam, log-jam, obstruction, occlusion, stoppage.

blockhead *n.* bonehead, boodle, chump, dolt, dullard, dunce, fool, idiot, ignoramus, jobernowl, leather-head, loggerhead, log-head, noodle, numskull, pigsconce, pinhead, pot-head, thickhead, thickskin, thick-skull.
antonyms brain, genius.

bloke *n.* bastard, bod, body, bugger, chap, character, cove, customer, fellow, individual, Johnny, oik, personage, punter.

blond, blonde *adj.* bleached, fair, fair-haired, fair-skinned, flaxen, golden-haired, light-coloured, tow-headed.

blood *n.* ancestry, anger, birth, bloodshed, consanguinity, descendants, descent, extraction, family, kindred, kinship, lineage, murder, relations, relationship, temper, temperament.

bloodcurdling *adj.* appalling, chilling, dreadful, eldritch, fearful, frightening, hair-raising, horrendous, horrible, horrid, horrifying, scaring, spine-chilling, terrifying, weird.

bloodless *adj.* anaemic, ashen, chalky, cold, colourless, drained, feeble, insipid, languid, lifeless, listless, pale, pallid, passionless, pasty, sallow, sickly, spiritless, torpid, unemotional, unfeeling, wan.
antonyms bloody, ruddy, vigorous.

bloodshed *n.* bloodletting, butchery, carnage, gore, killing, massacre, murder, slaughter, slaying.

blood-sucker *n.* blackmailer, extortioner, extortionist, leech, parasite, sponger.

bloodthirsty *adj.* barbaric, barbarous, brutal, cruel, ferocious, inhuman, murderous, ruthless, sanguinary, savage, slaughterous, vicious, warlike.

bloody *adj.* bleeding, bloodstained, blooming, brutal, cruel, ferocious, fierce, gaping, murderous, raw, sanguinary, sanguine, sanguineous, sanguinolent, savage.

bloom *n.* beauty, blossom, blossoming, blow, blush, bud, efflorescence, florescence, flourishing, flower, flush, freshness, glaucescence, glow, health, heyday, lustre, perfection, prime, radiance, rosiness, vigour.
v. blossom, blow, bud, burgeon, develop, flourish, grow, open, prosper, sprout, succeed, thrive, wax.
antonym wither.

blooming *adj.* blossoming, bonny, florescent, flowering, healthful, healthy, rosy, ruddy.
antonym ailing.

blossom *n.* bloom, bud, floret, flower, flowers.
v. bloom, blow, burgeon, develop, effloresce,

flourish, flower, grow, mature, progress, prosper, thrive.
antonym wither.

blot *n.* blemish, blotch, defect, disgrace, fault, flaw, mackle, macula, mark, patch, smear, smudge, speck, splodge, spot, stain, taint.
v. bespatter, blur, disfigure, disgrace, maculate, mar, mark, smudge, spoil, spot, stain, sully, taint, tarnish.

blot out cancel, darken, delete, destroy, eclipse, efface, erase, expunge, obliterate, obscure, shadow.

blotch *n.* blemish, blot, mark, patch, pustule, smudge, splash, splodge, spot, stain.

blotchy *adj.* blemished, macular, maculose, patchy, reddened, smeary, spotted, spotty, uneven.

blow[1] *v.* bear, blare, blast, breathe, buffet, drive, exhale, fan, fling, flow, flutter, mouth, pant, pipe, play, puff, rush, sound, stream, sweep, toot, trumpet, vibrate, waft, whirl, whisk, wind.
n. blast, draught, flurry, gale, gust, puff, squall, tempest, wind.

blow in(to) insufflate.

blow over cease, die down, disappear, dissipate, end, finish, fizzle out, pass, peter out, subside, vanish.

blow up balloon, belly out, bloat, dilate, distend, enlarge, exaggerate, expand, fill, fill out, heighten, inflate, magnify, overstate, puff up, pump up, swell.

blow[2] *n.* affliction, bang, bash, bat, belt, biff, bombshell, bop, box, buff, buffet, calamity, catastrophe, clap, clip, clout, clump, comedown, concussion, counterbluff, devvel, disappointment, disaster, douse, fourpenny one, haymaker, jolt, knock, knuckle sandwich, misfortune, oner, paik, punch, rap, reverse, setback, shock, siserary, slap, slat, slosh, smack, sock, sockdologer, souse, stroke, swash, swat, swipe, thump, upset, wallop, wap, welt, whack, whang, winder.

blow up blast, blow one's top, bomb, burst, castigate, detonate, dynamite, erupt, explode, go off, go off the deep end, hit the roof, lose one's cool, lose one's rag, lose one's temper, rage, reprimand, rupture, scold, shatter.

blown *adj.* breathless, effete, jaded, stale, tired, worthless.

blow-out *n.* beanfeast, binge, blast, burst, carousal, detonation, eruption, escape, explosion, feast, fuse, leak, party, puncture, rupture, spree, tear.

blowy *adj.* blustery, breezy, draughty, fresh, gusty, squally, stormy, windy.

blowzy *adj.* bedraggled, dishevelled, draggletailed, flushed, frowzy, messy, ruddy, slatternly, slipshod, sloppy, slovenly, sluttish, tousled, ungroomed, unkempt, untidy.
antonyms neat, smart.

bludgeon *n.* baton, club, cosh, cudgel, knobkerrie, life-preserver, night-stick, sap, shillelagh, truncheon.

v. badger, batter, beat, browbeat, bulldoze, bully, club, coerce, cosh, cudgel, force, harass, hector, intimidate, sap, steam-roller, strike, terrorise, torment.

blue[1] *adj.* aquamarine, azure, cerulean, cobalt, cyan, indigo, navy, sapphire, turquoise, ultramarine, watchet.

blue[2] *adj.* black, bleak, dejected, depressed, despondent, dismal, dispirited, doleful, down in the dumps, downcast, down-hearted, fed up, gloomy, glum, low, melancholy, miserable, morose, sad, unhappy.
antonym cheerful.

blue[3] *adv.* bawdy, coarse, dirty, improper, indecent, lewd, naughty, near the bone, near the knuckle, obscene, offensive, pornographic, risqué, smutty, vulgar.
antonym decent.

blue-pencil *v.* bowdlerise, censor, clean up, correct, edit, expurgate, purge.

blueprint *n.* archetype, design, draft, guide, model, outline, pattern, pilot, plan, project, prototype, sketch.

blues *n.* blue devils, dejection, depression, despondency, doldrums, dumps, gloom, gloominess, glumness, melancholy, miseries, moodiness.
antonym euphoria.

blue-stocking *n.* bas-bleu, femme savante, learned lady.

bluff[1] *n.* bank, brow, cliff, crag, escarp, escarpment, foreland, headland, height, knoll, peak, precipice, promontory, ridge, scarp, slope.
adj. affable, blunt, candid, direct, downright, frank, genial, good-natured, hearty, open, outspoken, plain-spoken, straightforward.
antonyms diplomatic, refined.

bluff[2] *v.* bamboozle, blind, deceive, defraud, delude, fake, feign, grift, hoodwink, humbug, lie, mislead, pretend, sham.
n. bluster, boast, braggadocio, bravado, deceit, deception, fake, fanfaronade, feint, fraud, grift, humbug, idle boast, lie, pretence, sham, show, subterfuge, trick.

blunder *n.* bêtise, bevue, bish, bloomer, boner, boob, boo-boo, clanger, clinker, error, fault, faux pas, floater, fluff, gaffe, gaucherie, goof, howler, impropriety, inaccuracy, indiscretion, mistake, oversight, pratfall, slip, slip-up, solecism.
v. blow it, botch, bumble, bungle, err, flounder, flub, fluff, fumble, goof, miscalculate, misjudge, mismanage, muff it, slip up, stumble.

blunderer *n.* botcher, bungler, duffer, fool, goof, incompetent, josser.

blunt *adj.* abrupt, bluff, brusque, candid, curt, direct, discourteous, downright, dull, dulled, edgeless, explicit, forthright, frank, honest, impolite, insensitive, obtuse, outspoken, plain-spoken, pointless, retuse, rounded, rude, straightforward, stubbed, stumpy, tactless, thick, trenchant, unceremonious, uncivil, unpolished, unsharpened.
antonyms sharp, tactful.

v. abate, allay, alleviate, anaesthetise, bate, dampen, deaden, disedge, dull, hebetate, numb, obtund, palliate, rebate, retund, soften, stupefy, unedge, weaken.
antonyms intensify, sharpen.

bluntness *n.* abruptness, brusqueness, candidness, dullness, forthrightness, frankness, hebetude, hebetudinarity, insensitivity, lack of ceremony, obtuseness, obtusity, tactlessness.
antonyms sharpness, tact.

blur *v.* becloud, befog, blear, blemish, blot, blotch, cloud, darken, dim, fog, mask, obfuscate, obscure, scumble, smear, smutch, soften, spot, stain.
n. blear, blot, blotch, cloudiness, confusion, dimness, fog, fuzziness, haze, indistinctness, muddle, obscurity, smear, smudge, spot, stain.

blurb *n.* advertisement, commendation, copy, hype, puff, spiel.

blurred *adj.* beclouded, bleary, blurry, clouded, confused, dim, faint, foggy, fuzzy, hazy, ill-defined, indistinct, misty, nebulous, unclear, vague.
antonym distinct.

blurt *v.* babble, blab, cry, disclose, divulge, ejaculate, exclaim, gush, leak, let slip, let the cat out of the bag, reveal, spill, spill the beans, spout, utter.
antonym hush up.

blush *v.* colour, crimson, flush, glow, mantle, redden.
antonym blanch.
n. colour, erubescence, flush, glow, reddening, rosiness, ruddiness, suffusion.

blushing *adj.* confused, discomfited, embarrassed, erubescent, flushed, glowing, red, rosy, rubescent, suffused.
antonyms composed, pale.

bluster *v.* boast, brag, bully, domineer, fanfaronade, hector, rant, roar, rodomontade, roist, roister, storm, strut, swagger, swell, talk big, vapour, vaunt.
n. bluff, boasting, bombast, braggadocio, bragging, bravado, crowing, fanfaronade, parade, racket, rodomontade, swagger, swaggering, vapour, vauntery.

blusterer *n.* big mouth, big talker, boaster, braggart, fanfaron, rodomontader, roister, roisterer, show-off, swaggerer, swank, swashbuckler, swasher, vapourer, windbag.

blustery *adj.* boisterous, gusty, noisy, squally, stormy, tempestuous, tumultuous, violent, wild, windy.
antonym calm.

board[1] *n.* beam, clapboard, deal, lath, panel, plank, sheet, slab, slat, timber, two-by-four.

board[2] *n.* commons, food, grub, meals, provisions, rations, repasts, table, victuals.
v. accommodate, bed, billet, feed, house, lodge, put up, quarter, room, table.

board[3] *n.* advisers, chamber, commission, committee, conclave, council, directorate, directors, jury, panel, trustees.

board[4] *v.* catch, embark, embus, emplane, enter, entrain, mount.

boarding-house *n.* pension.

boast *v.* be all mouth, blazon, blow, bluster, bounce, brag, claim, crow, exaggerate, exhibit, gasconade, possess, puff, rodomontade, show off, strut, swagger, talk big, trumpet, vaunt.

antonym deprecate.

n. avowal, brag, claim, fanfaronade, gasconade, gem, joy, pride, rodomontade, swank, treasure, vaunt.

boaster *n.* bangster, big mouth, big talker, Bobadil, braggart, fanfaron, galah, gascon, gasconader, rodomontader, show-off, swaggerer, swank, vapourer, vaunter.

boastful *adj.* braggart, bragging, cocky, conceited, crowing, egotistical, proud, puffed-up, self-glorious, swaggering, swanky, swollenheaded, thrasonic, thrasonical, vain, vainglorious, vaunting, windy.

antonym modest.

boasting *n.* bluster, bragging, conceit, fanfaronade, gasconade, gasconism, jactation, jactitation, ostentation, rodomontade, swagger, swank, vaingloriousness, vainglory, vauntery, vaunting, windiness.

antonym modesty.

boat *n.* bateau, canoe, dahabiyah, dinghy, funny, gondola, ketch, punt, rowing-boat, speed-boat, water-craft.

boatman *n.* ferryman, gondolier, oarsman, rower, sailor, voyageur, waterman, water-rat, wet bob, yachtsman.

bob *v.* bounce, duck, hop, jerk, jolt, jounce, jump, leap, nod, oscillate, popple, quiver, shake, skip, spring, twitch, waggle, weave, wobble.

bob up appear, arise, arrive, crop up, emerge, materialise, pop up, rise, show up, spring up, surface.

bode *v.* adumbrate, augur, betoken, forebode, foreshadow, foreshow, foretell, forewarn, import, indicate, intimate, omen, portend, predict, presage, prophesy, signify, threaten, warn.

bodily *adj.* actual, carnal, concrete, corporal, corporeal, earthly, fleshly, incarnate, material, physical, real, somatic, substantial, tangible.

antonym spiritual.

adv. altogether, as a whole, bag and baggage, collectively, completely, en masse, entirely, fully, in toto, totally, wholly.

antonym piecemeal.

body[1] *n.* being, bod, build, bulk, cadaver, carcass, consistency, corpse, corpus, creature, density, essence, figure, firmness, form, frame, human, individual, mass, material, matter, mortal, opacity, person, physique, relics, remains, richness, shape, solidity, stiff, substance, substantiality, tabernacle, torso, trunk.

body[2] *n.* association, band, bevy, bloc, cartel, collection, company, confederation, congress, corporation, crowd, group, horde, majority, mass, mob, multitude, society, syndicate, throng.

bodyguard *n.* minder, praetorian, protector.

body-snatcher *n.* desecrator, resurrectionist, resurrection-man.

boffin *n.* backroom-boy, brain, designer, egghead, engineer, genius, headpiece, intellect, intellectual, inventor, mastermind, planner, scientist, thinker, wizard.

bog *n.* fen, marsh, marshland, mire, morass, moss, muskeg, quag, quagmire, quicksands, slough, swamp, swampland, wetlands.

bog down delay, deluge, halt, hinder, impede, overwhelm, retard, sink, slow down, slow up, stall, stick.

boggle *v.* blench, demur, dither, doubt, equivocate, falter, fight shy, flinch, funk, hang back, hesitate, hover, jib, jump, pause, recoil, shillyshally, shrink, shy, stagger, start, startle, vacillate, waver.

boggy *adj.* fennish, fenny, marshy, miry, morassy, muddy, oozy, paludal, quaggy, soft, spongy, swampy, waterlogged.

antonym arid.

bogus *adj.* artificial, counterfeit, dummy, ersatz, fake, false, forged, fraudulent, imitation, phoney, pinchbeck, pseudo, sham, spoof, spurious, unauthentic.

antonym genuine.

bogy, bogey *n.* bête noire, bogeyman, boggart, bogle, bugaboo, bugbear, goblin, hobgoblin, imp, incubus, nightmare, spectre, spook.

bohemian *adj.* alternative, artistic, arty, bizarre, eccentric, exotic, irregular, left-bank, nonconformist, offbeat, outré, unconventional, unorthodox, way-out.

antonyms bourgeois, conventional.

n. beatnik, drop-out, hippie, iconoclast, nonconformist.

antonyms bourgeois, conformist.

boil[1] *v.* agitate, brew, bubble, churn, decoct, effervesce, erupt, explode, fizz, foam, froth, fulminate, fume, gurgle, mantle, parboil, rage, rave, seethe, simmer, sizzle, spume, steam, stew, storm, wallop.

boil down abridge, abstract, concentrate, condense, decrease, digest, distil, epitomise, reduce, summarise, synopsise.

boil[2] *n.* abscess, anthrax, blain, bleb, blister, carbuncle, furuncle, gathering, gumboil, inflammation, papule, parulis, pimple, pock, pustule, tumour, ulcer, whelk.

boiling *adj.* angry, baking, blistering, bubbling, enraged, flaming, fuming, furious, gurgling, hot, incensed, indignant, infuriated, roasting, scorching, seething, torrid, turbulent.

boisterous *adj.* blusterous, blustery, bouncy, clamorous, disorderly, exuberant, gusty, impetuous, loud, noisy, obstreperous, rackety, raging, rambunctious, riotous, roisting, rollicking, rough, rowdy, rumbustious, squally, tempestuous, termagant, tumultous, turbulent, unrestrained, unruly, uproarious, vociferous, wild.

antonyms calm, quiet, restrained.

bold *adj.* adventurous, audacious, brash, brave, brazen, bright, cheeky, colourful, confident, conspicuous, courageous, daring, dauntless, enterprising, extravert, eye-catching, fearless, flamboyant, flashy, forceful, forward, fresh, gallant, heroic, impudent, insolent, intrepid, jazzy, lively, loud, malapert, outgoing, pert, plucky, prominent, pronounced, saucy, shameless, showy, spirited, striking, strong, unabashed, unashamed, unbashful, valiant, valorous, venturesome, vivid.
antonyms diffident, restrained.

bolster *v.* aid, assist, augment, boost, brace, buoy up, buttress, firm up, help, maintain, prop, reinforce, shore up, stay, stiffen, strengthen, supplement, support.
antonym undermine.

bolt *n.* arrow, bar, bound, catch, dart, dash, elopement, escape, fastener, flight, flit, latch, lock, missile, peg, pin, projectile, rivet, rod, rush, shaft, sneck, sprint, thunderbolt.
v. abscond, bar, bound, cram, dart, dash, devour, discharge, elope, escape, expel, fasten, fetter, flee, fly, gobble, gorge, gulp, guzzle, hurtle, jump, latch, leap, lock, run, rush, secure, spring, sprint, stuff, wolf.

bomb *n.* A-bomb, bombshell, charge, egg, explosive, grenade, mine, missile, mortar-bomb, petrol bomb, projectile, rocket, shell, torpedo.
v. attack, blow up, bombard, collapse, come a cropper, come to grief, destroy, fail, flop, misfire, shell, strafe, torpedo.

bombard *v.* assail, assault, attack, barrage, batter, beset, besiege, blast, blitz, bomb, cannonade, dun, harass, hound, importune, pelt, pester, pound, shell, strafe.

bombardment *n.* air-raid, assault, attack, barrage, blitz, bombing, cannonade, fire, flak, fusillade, salvo, shelling, strafe.

bombast *n.* ampollosity, bluster, brag, braggadocio, euphuism, fustian, gasconade, Gongorism, grandiloquence, grandiosity, heroics, magniloquence, pomposity, portentousness, pretentiousness, rant, rodomontade, verbosity, wordiness.
antonyms reserve, restraint.

bombastic *adj.* bloated, declamatory, euphuistic, fustian, Gongoristic, grandiloquent, grandiose, high-flown, histrionic, inflated, magniloquent, pompous, turgid, verbose, windy, wordy.

bon viveur bon vivant, epicure, epicurean, gastronome, gourmet, hedonist, luxurist, pleasure-seeker, voluptuary.
antonym ascetic.

bona fide actual, authentic, genuine, honest, kosher, lawful, legal, legitimate, real, true, valid.
antonym bogus.

bond *n.* affiliation, affinity, agreement, attachment, band, binding, chain, compact, connection, contract, copula, cord, covenant, fastening, fetter, ligament, ligature, link, manacle, obligation, pledge, promise, relation, shackle, tie, union, vinculum, word.
v. bind, connect, fasten, fuse, glue, gum, paste, seal, unite.

bondage *n.* captivity, confinement, durance, duress, enslavement, enthralment, imprisonment, incarceration, restraint, serfdom, servitude, slavery, subjection, subjugation, subservience, thraldom, vassalage, yoke.
antonyms freedom, independence.

bonfire *n.* beacon, conflagration, feu de joie, pyre.

bonny *adj.* attractive, beautiful, blithe, blooming, bouncing, buxom, cheerful, cheery, chubby, comely, fair, fine, gay, goodly, handsome, joyful, lovely, merry, pretty, shapely, sunny, sweet, wholesome, winsome.
antonym ill-favoured.

bonus *n.* advantage, benefit, bounty, bribe, commission, dividend, douceur, extra, freebie, gift, gratuity, hand-out, honorarium, lagniappe, perk, perquisite, plus, premium, prize, profit, reward, tip.
antonyms disadvantage, disincentive, liability.

bony *adj.* angular, drawn, emaciated, gangling, gaunt, gawky, knobbly, lanky, lean, osseous, rawboned, sclerous, scrawny, skinny, thin.
antonym plump.

boob *n.* balls-up, bêtise, blunder, botch, clanger, error, fault, faux pas, gaffe, gaucherie, howler, inaccuracy, indiscretion, mistake, oversight, pratfall, slip, slip-up, solecism.

booby *n.* blockhead, clod, clodpate, clodpoll, clot, dimwit, duffer, dunce, dunderhead, fool, goof, halfwit, idiot, muggins, nickumpoop, ni(n)compoop, ninny, palooka, prat, schmuck, simpleton.
antonym genius.

booby prize consolation prize, wooden spoon.

book *n.* album, booklet, codex, companion, diary, hornbook, incunable, incunabulum, jotter, lectionary, manual, manuscript, notebook, pad, paperback, publication, roll, scroll, textbook, tome, tract, volume, work.
v. arrange, arrest, bag, charter, engage, enter, insert, list, log, note, organise, post, procure, programme, record, register, reserve, schedule.
antonym cancel.

bookish *adj.* academic, cultured, donnish, erudite, highbrow, intellectual, learned, lettered, literary, pedantic, scholarly, scholastic, studious, well-read.
antonyms lowbrow, unlettered.

boom[1] *v.* bang, blare, blast, crash, explode, resound, reverberate, roar, roll, rumble, sound, thunder.
n. bang, blast, burst, clang, clap, crash, explosion, reverberation, roar, rumble, thunder.

boom[2] *v.* develop, escalate, expand, explode, flourish, gain, go from strength to strength, grow, increase, intensify, prosper, spurt, strengthen, succeed, swell, thrive.

antonyms collapse, fail.

n. advance, boost, development, escalation, expansion, explosion, gain, growth, improvement, increase, jump, spurt, upsurge, upturn. *antonyms* collapse, failure.

boon *n.* advantage, benefaction, benefit, blessing, donation, favour, gift, godsend, grant, gratification, gratuity, kindness, petition, present, windfall.
antonyms blight, disadvantage.

boor *n.* barbarian, brute, bumpkin, chuff, churl, clodhopper, goop, Goth, Grobian, hedgehog, hog, keelie, kerne, lout, oaf, peasant, philistine, rustic, vulgarian.
antonyms aesthete, charmer.

boorish *adj.* awkward, barbaric, bearish, churlish, clodhopping, clownish, coarse, crude, goustrous, gross, gruff, ill-bred, jungli, kernish, loutish, lubberly, lumpen, oafish, rude, rustic, swailish, uncivilised, uncouth, uneducated, unrefined, vulgar.
antonyms cultured, polite, refined.

boorishness *n.* awkwardness, barbarity, bluntness, coarseness, crudeness, gaucherie, Gothicism, grossièreté, grossness, hoggery, ignorance, impoliteness, loutishness, lubberliness, philistinism, roughness, rudeness, rudery, rusticity, uncouthness, vulgarity.
antonyms politeness, refinement.

boost *n.* addition, advancement, ego-trip, encouragement, enhancement, expansion, fillip, heave, help, hoist, hype, improvement, increase, increment, jump, lift, praise, promotion, push, rise, supplement, thrust.
antonyms blow, setback.

v. advance, advertise, aid, amplify, assist, augment, bolster, develop, elevate, encourage, enhance, enlarge, expand, foster, further, heave, heighten, hoist, improve, increase, inspire, jack up, lift, plug, praise, promote, push, raise, supplement, support, sustain, thrust.
antonyms hinder, undermine.

boot[1] *n.* bootee, galosh, gumboot, jemima, Kletterschuh, larrigan, moon-boot, muckluck, overshoe, riding-boot, rubber, top-boot, wader, wellie, wellington.

v. bounce, dismiss, eject, expel, fire, give the bum's rush, give the heave, kick, kick out, knock, oust, punt, sack, shove.

boot[2] *v.* advantage, aid, avail, benefit, help, profit, serve.

booth *n.* bay, carrel, cart, compartment, guichet, hut, kiosk, stall, stand, ticket-office.

bootless *adj.* barren, fruitless, futile, ineffective, on a hiding to nothing, pointless, profitless, sterile, unavailing, unproductive, unsuccessful, useless, vain, worthless.
antonyms profitable, useful.

bootlicking *n.* arse-licking, back-scratching, crawling, cringing, deference, faggery, fagging, fawning, flattery, grovelling, heepishness, ingratiation, lackeying, obsequiousness, servility, sycophancy, toadying.

booty *n.* boodle, bunce, gains, haul, loot, pickings, pillage, plunder, spoil, spoils, swag, takings, winnings.

border *n.* borderline, bound, boundary, bounds, brim, brink, circumference, confine, confines, demarcation, edge, fringe, frontier, hem, limit, limits, lip, list, march, margin, perimeter, periphery, rand, rim, screed, selvage, skirt, surround, trimming, valance, verge.
adj. boundary, circumscriptive, dividing, frontier, limitary, limitrophe, marginal, perimeter, separating, side.

border on abut, adjoin, appear like, approach, approximate, communicate with, connect, contact, impinge, join, march, neighbour, resemble, touch, verge on.

bordered *adj.* bounded, circumscribed, edged, fringed, hemmed, limbate, marginate, margined, rimmed, skirted, surrounded, trimmed.

borderline *adj.* ambivalent, doubtful, iffy, indecisive, indefinite, indeterminate, marginal, problematic, uncertain.
antonyms certain, definite.

bore[1] *v.* burrow, countermine, drill, gouge, mine, penetrate, perforate, pierce, sap, sink, thirl, thrill, tunnel, undermine.

bore[2] *v.* annoy, bother, bug, fatigue, irk, irritate, jade, pester, tire, trouble, vex, weary, worry.
antonyms charm, interest.

n. annoyance, bind, bother, drag, dullard, headache, nuisance, pain, pain in the neck, pest, schmo, terebrant, trial, vexation, vieux jeu, yawn.
antonym pleasure.

bored *adj.* brassed off, browned off, ennuied, ennuyé.
antonym interested.

boredom *n.* acedia, apathy, doldrums, dullness, ennui, flatness, irksomeness, listlessness, monotony, sameness, tediousness, tedium, vapours, weariness, wearisomeness, world-weariness.
antonym interest.

boring *adj.* commonplace, dead, dreary, dry, dull, ennuying, flat, ho-hum, humdrum, insipid, irksome, monotonous, repetitious, routine, stale, stupid, tedious, tiresome, tiring, trite, unamusing, undiverting, unedifying, uneventful, unexciting, unfunny, unimaginative, uninspired, uninteresting, unvaried, unwitty, vapid, wearisome.
antonyms interesting, original.

borrow *v.* adopt, ape, appropriate, cadge, copy, crib, derive, draw, echo, filch, imitate, list, mimic, obtain, pilfer, pirate, plagiarise, scrounge, sponge, steal, take, use, usurp.

borrowing *n.* adoption, appropriation, cadging, calque, copy, copying, crib, imitation, loan, loan-translation, loan-word, plagiarisation, scrounging, sponging.

bosom *n.* breast, bust, centre, chest, circle, core, heart, midst, protection, sanctuary, shelter.
adj. boon, cherished, close, confidential, dear, favourite, inseparable, intimate.

boss[1] *n.* administrator, baron, captain, chief, director, employer, executive, foreman, gaffer, governor, head, leader, manager, master, overseer, owner, superintendent, supervisor, supremo.
v. administrate, command, control, direct, employ, manage, oversee, run, superintend, supervise.
boss around browbeat, bulldoze, bully, dominate, domineer, dragoon, hector, oppress, order about, overbear, push around, tyrannise.

boss[2] *n.* knob, knub, knubble, nub, nubble, omphalos, point, protuberance, stud, tip, umbo.

bossy *adj.* arrogant, authoritarian, autocratic, demanding, despotic, dictatorial, domineering, exacting, hectoring, high-handed, imperious, insistent, lordly, oppressive, overbearing, tyrannical.
antonym unassertive.

botch *v.* balls up, blunder, bungle, butcher, cobble, cock up, corpse, flub, fuck up, fudge, fumble, goof, louse up, mar, mend, mess, mismanage, muff, patch, ruin, screw up, spoil.
antonyms accomplish, succeed.
n. balls-up, blunder, bungle, cock-up, failure, farce, hash, mess, miscarriage, muddle, shambles.
antonym success.

bother *v.* alarm, annoy, bore, chivvy, concern, dismay, distress, disturb, dog, harass, harry, hassle, inconvenience, irk, irritate, molest, nag, pester, plague, pother, pudder, trouble, upset, vex, worry.
n. aggravation, annoyance, bustle, consternation, difficulty, flurry, fuss, hassle, inconvenience, irritation, kerfuffle, molestation, nuisance, palaver, perplexity, pest, pother, problem, pudder, strain, trouble, vexation, worry.

bothersome *adj.* aggravating, annoying, boring, distressing, exasperating, inconvenient, infuriating, irksome, irritating, laborious, tedious, tiresome, troublesome, vexatious, vexing, wearisome.

bottle *n.* carafe, carboy, dead-man, decanter, demijohn, flacket, flacon, flagon, flask, jack, jar, phial, vial.
bottle up check, conceal, contain, curb, enclose, hide, hold in, inhibit, quell, restrain, restrict, suppress.
antonyms unbosom, unburden.

bottleneck *n.* block, blockage, clogging, congestion, hindrance, hold-up, jam, obstacle, obstruction, snarl-up, traffic-jam.

bottom *n.* backside, base, basis, bed, behind, bum, butt, buttocks, core, depths, derrière, essence, floor, foot, foundation, fundament, fundus, ground, groundwork, heart, nadir, origin, pedestal, plinth, posterior, principle, rear, rear end, root, rump, seat, sit-upon, socle, sole, source, substance, substratum, substructure, support, tail, underneath, underside, understratum.

bottom drawer hope chest.

bottomless *adj.* abysmal, abyssal, boundless, deep, fathomless, immeasurable, inexhaustible, infinite, limitless, measureless, profound, unfathomable, unfathomed, unlimited, unplumbed.
antonym shallow.

bottomless pit Abaddon, abode of the damned, abysm, abyss, chasm, crevasse, fire and brimstone, Gehenna, gulf, Hades, Hell, hellfire, infernal regions, inferno, maw.

boulevard *n.* avenue, mall, parade, promenade, prospect, row, street, terrace, thoroughfare.

bounce *v.* bob, bound, bump, dap, dismiss, eject, jounce, jump, kick out, leap, oust, rebound, recoil, resile, ricochet, spring, stot, throw out.
n. animation, bound, dap, dynamism, ebullience, elasticity, energy, exuberance, give, go, life, liveliness, pep, rebound, recoil, resilience, spring, springiness, vigour, vitality, vivacity, zip.

bouncing *adj.* blooming, bonny, healthy, lively, robust, strong, thriving, vigorous.

bound[1] *adj.* bandaged, beholden, cased, certain, chained, committed, compelled, constrained, destined, doomed, duty-bound, fastened, fated, fixed, forced, held, liable, manacled, obligated, obliged, pinioned, pledged, required, restricted, secured, sure, tied, tied up.

bound[2] *v.* bob, bounce, caper, frisk, gallumph, gambol, hurdle, jump, leap, lope, loup, lunge, pounce, prance, skip, spring, vault.
n. bob, bounce, caper, dance, frisk, gambado, gambol, jump, leap, lope, loup, lunge, pounce, prance, scamper, skip, spring, vault.

boundary *n.* abuttal, barrier, border, borderline, bounds, bourne, brink, confines, demarcation, edge, extremity, fringe, frontier, junction, limes, limits, line, march, margin, mete, perimeter, termination, verge.
adj. border, demarcation, frontier, limitary, limitrophe, perimeter.

bounded *adj.* bordered, circumscribed, confined, controlled, defined, delimited, demarcated, edged, encircled, enclosed, encompassed, hemmed in, limit ed, restrained, restricted, surrounded, terminated.

bounder *n.* blackguard, blighter, cad, cheat, cur, dastard, dirty dog, heel, knave, miscreant, oik, pig, rat, rip, rogue, rotter, swine.

boundless *adj.* countless, endless, illimitable, immeasurable, immense, incalculable, indefatigable, inexhaustible, infinite, interminable, interminate, limitless, measureless, prodigious, unbounded, unconfined, unending, unflagging, unlimited, untold, vast.
antonym limited.

bounds *n.* borders, boundaries, circumference, confines, edges, extremities, fringes, frontiers, limits, marches, margins, periphery, rim, verges.

bountiful *adj.* abundant, ample, boundless, bounteous, copious, exuberant, generous, lavish, liberal, luxuriant, magnanimous,

munificent, open-handed, overflowing, plenteous, plentiful, princely, profuse, prolific, ungrudging, unstinting.
antonyms meagre, mean, sparse.

bounty *n.* allowance, almsgiving, annuity, assistance, beneficence, benevolence, bonus, charity, donation, generosity, gift, grace, grant, gratuity, kindness, largesse, liberality, philanthropy, premium, present, recompense, reward.

bouquet *n.* anthology, aroma, boutonnière, bunch, buttonhole, corsage, florilegium, fragrance, garland, nosegay, odour, perfume, posy, redolence, savour, scent, smell, spray, wreath.

bourgeois *adj.* Biedermeier, circumscribed, commonplace, conformist, conservative, conventional, dull, hide-bound, humdrum, kitsch, materialistic, middle-class, pedestrian, tawdry, traditional, trite, trivial, unadventurous, unimaginative, uninspired, unoriginal, vulgar.
antonyms bohemian, original, unconventional.
n. conformist, petit bourgeois, philistine, plebeian, Pooter, stick-in-the-mud.
antonyms bohemian, nonconformist.

bout *n.* battle, competition, contest, course, encounter, engagement, fight, fit, go, heat, match, period, round, run, session, set-to, spell, spree, stint, stretch, struggle, term, time, turn, venue.

bovine *adj.* beefy, dense, dull, dumb, heavy, hulking, obtuse, slow, slow-witted, sluggish, stolid, stupid, thick.
antonym quick.

bow[1] *v.* accept, acquiesce, bend, bob, capitulate, comply, concede, conquer, consent, crush, curtsey, defer, depress, droop, genuflect, give in, incline, kowtow, nod, overpower, stoop, subdue, subjugate, submit, surrender, vanquish, yield.
n. acknowledgement, bending, bob, curtsey, genuflexion, inclination, kowtow, nod, obeisance, salaam, salutation.
bow out abandon, back out, bunk off, chicken out, defect, desert, give up, opt out, pull out, quit, resign, retire, stand down, step down, withdraw.

bow[2] *n.* beak, head, prow, rostrum, stem.

bowdlerise *v.* blue-pencil, censor, clean up, cut, edit, excise, expunge, expurgate, launder, modify, mutilate, purge, purify.

bowels *n.* belly, centre, core, depths, entrails, guts, heart, hold, innards, inside, insides, interior, intestines, middle, viscera, vitals.

bower *n.* alcove, arbour, bay, belvedere, boudoir, dwelling, gazebo, grot, grotto, hideaway, pleasance, recess, retreat, sanctuary, shelter, summer-house.

bowl[1] *n.* basin, bicker, cruse, dish, pan, piggin, porringer, quaich, receptacle, sink, tureen, vessel.

bowl[2] *n.* jack, wood.
v. fling, hurl, pitch, revolve, roll, rotate, spin, throw, trundle, whirl.

bowl over amaze, astonish, astound, dumbfound, fell, flabbergast, floor, stagger, startle, stun, surprise, topple, unbalance.

bow-legs *n.* bandiness, bandy legs, valgus.

bowler *n.* billycock, bowler hat, hard hat, pot-hat.

box[1] *n.* bijou, carton, case, casket, chest, coffer, coffin, coffret, consignment, container, coop, fund, pack, package, portmanteau, present, pyx, pyxis, receptacle, trunk.
v. case, embox, encase, pack, package, wrap.
box in cage, circumscribe, confine, contain, coop up, cordon off, corner, enclose, hem in, imprison, restrict, surround, trap.

box[2] *v.* buffet, butt, clout, cuff, fight, hit, punch, slap, sock, spar, strike, thwack, wallop, whack, wham, whang.
n. blow, buffet, clout, cuff, punch, slap, stroke, thump, wallop, wham, whang.

boxing *n.* fisticuffs, prize-fighting, pugilism, sparring, the noble art.
adj. fistic, fistical, pugilistic.

boxing-match *n.* bout, mill.

boy *n.* callant, cub, dandiprat, fellow, gamin, gossoon, halfling, imp, junior, kid, lad, loon, loonie, man-child, nipper, puppy, schoolboy, spalpeen, stripling, urchin, whippersnapper, youngster, youth.

boycott *v.* ban, bar, black, blackball, blacklist, cold-shoulder, disallow, embargo, exclude, ignore, ostracise, outlaw, prohibit, proscribe, refuse, reject, spurn.
antonyms encourage, support.

boyfriend *n.* admirer, beau, date, fancy man, follower, lover, man, steady, suitor, swain, sweetheart, young man.

boyish *adj.* adolescent, childish, gamine, immature, innocent, juvenile, puerile, tomboy, unfeminine, unmaidenly, young, youthful.

brace[1] *n.* binder, bracer, bracket, buttress, cleat, corset, nogging, prop, reinforcement, shoring, stanchion, stay, strap, strut, support, truss.
v. bandage, bind, bolster, buttress, fasten, fortify, prop, reinforce, shore (up), steady, strap, strengthen, support, tie, tighten.

brace[2] *n.* couple, doubleton, duo, pair, twosome.

braces *n.* gallowses, galluses, suspenders.

bracing *adj.* brisk, crisp, energetic, energising, enlivening, exhilarating, fortifying, fresh, invigorating, refreshing, restorative, reviving, rousing, stimulating, strengthening, tonic, vigorous.
antonym debilitating.

brackish *adj.* bitter, briny, saline, salt, saltish, salty.
antonym fresh.

brag *v.* bluster, boast, crow, fanfaronade, rodomontade, swagger, talk big, trumpet, vapour, vaunt.
antonym deprecate.

braggart *n.* bangster, big mouth, bluffer, blusterer, boaster, braggadocio, Brobadil, fanfaron, gascon, gasconader, rodomontader, show-off, swaggerer, swashbuckler, vapourer, whiffler.

bragging *n.* bluster, boastfulness, boasting, bravado, exaggeration, fanfaronade, gasconade, jactation, jactitation, rodomontade, showing off, strutting, swagger, swank, talk, vauntery.

antonyms modesty, unobtrusiveness.

braid *v.* entwine, interlace, intertwine, interweave, lace, plait, ravel, twine, twist, weave, wind.

antonyms undo, untwist.

brain[1] *n.* boffin, egghead, expert, genius, highbrow, intellect, intellectual, mastermind, prodigy, pundit, sage, savant, scholar, wizard.

antonym simpleton.

brain[2] *n.* cerebrum, grey matter, intellect, mind, sensorium, sensory.

brainless *adj.* crazy, daft, foolish, half-witted, hen-witted, idiotic, incompetent, inept, mindless, senseless, stupid, thoughtless, unintelligent, witless.

antonyms sensible, shrewd, wise.

brains *n.* capacity, common sense, grey matter, head, intellect, intelligence, mind, nous, reason, sagacity, savvy, sense, shrewdness, understanding, wit.

brain-teaser *n.* conundrum, mind-bender, poser, problem, puzzle, riddle.

brainwash *v.* alter, bludgeon, condition, grill, indoctrinate, persuade, pressure, pressurise, re-educate, verbal.

brainwashing *n.* conditioning, double-think, grilling, indoctrination, menticide, mind-bending, persuasion, pressure, pressurisation, re-education, unlearning, verballing.

brainy *adj.* bright, brilliant, clever, intellectual, intelligent, sapient, smart.

antonym dull.

brake *n.* check, constraint, control, curb, drag, rein, restraint, restriction, retardment.

v. check, decelerate, drag, halt, moderate, pull up, retard, slacken, slow, stop.

antonym accelerate.

branch *n.* arm, bough, chapter, department, division, grain, limb, lodge, office, offshoot, part, prong, ramification, ramus, section, shoot, sprig, subdivision, subsection, whip, wing, witty.

branch out bifurcate, broaden out, develop, divaricate, diversify, enlarge, expand, extend, increase, move on, multiply, proliferate, ramify, vary.

brand *n.* brand-name, class, emblem, grade, hallmark, kind, label, line, logo, make, mark, marker, marque, quality, sign, sort, species, stamp, symbol, trademark, type, variety.

v. burn, censure, denounce, discredit, disgrace, label, mark, scar, stain, stamp, stigmatise, taint, type.

brandish *v.* display, exhibit, flash, flaunt, flourish, parade, raise, shake, swing, wave, wield.

brand-new *adj.* fire-new, fresh.

brash *adj.* assuming, assured, audacious, bold, brazen, bumptious, cocky, foolhardy, forward, hasty, heedless, impertinent, impetuous, impudent, impulsive, incautious, indiscreet, insolent, precipitate, rash, reckless, rude, temerarious.

antonyms cautious, reserved, unobtrusive.

brass *n.* assurance, audacity, brass neck, brazenness, cheek, effrontery, gall, impertinence, impudence, insolence, nerve, presumption, rudeness, self-assurance, temerity.

antonyms circumspection, timidity.

brassy *adj.* blaring, blatant, bold, brash, brazen, cheap, dissonant, flamboyant, flashy, forward, garish, gaudy, grating, hard, harsh, jangling, jarring, jazzy, loud, loud-mouthed, meretricious, noisy, obtrusive, pert, piercing, raucous, saucy, showy, shrill, strident, tawdry, vulgar.

brat *n.* cub, gamin, get, guttersnipe, jackanapes, kid, nipper, puppy, rascal, ruffian, toe-rag, urchin, varmint, whippersnapper, youngster.

bravado *n.* bluster, boast, boastfulness, boasting, bombast, brag, braggadocio, bragging, fanfaronade, parade, pretence, rodomontade, show, showing off, swagger, swaggering, swank, swashbuckling, talk, vauntery, vaunting.

antonyms modesty, restraint.

brave *adj.* audacious, bold, courageous, daring, dauntless, doughty, fearless, fine, gallant, game, glorious, hardy, heroic, indomitable, intrepid, plucky, resolute, resplendent, splendid, stalwart, stoic, stoical, stout-hearted, unafraid, undaunted, unflinching, valiant, valorous.

antonyms cowardly, timid.

v. accost, bear, beard, challenge, confront, dare, defy, encounter, endure, face, face up to, stand up to, suffer, withstand.

antonyms capitulate, crumple.

bravely *adv.* courageously, dauntlessly, fearlessly, gallantly, gamely, heroically, intrepidly, manfully, pluckily, resolutely, splendidly, stoically, unflinchingly, valiantly, womanfully.

antonym cravenly.

bravery *n.* audacity, boldness, courage, daring, dauntlessness, doughtiness, fearlessness, fortitude, gallantry, grit, guts, hardihood, hardiness, heroism, indomitability, intrepidity, mettle, pluck, pluckiness, resoluteness, resolution, spirit, spunk, stalwartness, stoicism, stout-heartedness, valiance, valour.

antonyms cowardice, timidity.

bravura *n.* animation, audacity, boldness, brilliance, brio, daring, dash, display, élan, energy, exhibitionism, extravagance, flamboyance, liveliness, ostentation, panache, pizzazz, punch, spirit, verve, vigour, virtuosity.

antonym restraint.

brawl *n.* affray, altercation, argument, bagarre, battle, broil, bust-up, clash, disorder, dispute, dog-fight, Donnybrook, dust-up, fight, fracas, fray, free-for-all, mêlée, punch-up, quarrel, row, ruckus, rumpus, scrap, scuffle, squabble, tumult, uproar, wrangle.

v. altercate, argue, argy-bargy, battle, dispute, fight, flyte, quarrel, row, scrap, scuffle, squabble, tussle, wrangle, wrestle.

brawn *n.* beef, beefiness, brawniness, bulk, bulkiness, flesh, meat, might, muscle, muscles, muscularity, power, robustness, sinews, strength, thews.

brawny *adj.* athletic, beefy, bovine, bulky, burly, fleshy, hardy, hefty, herculean, hulking, husky, lusty, massive, muscular, powerful, robust, sinewy, solid, stalwart, strapping, strong, sturdy, thewy, vigorous, well-built, well-knit.

antonyms frail, slight.

bray *v.* blare, hoot, roar, screech, trumpet.
n. bawl, bellow, blare, blast, cry, hoot, roar, screech, shout, shriek.

brazen *adj.* assured, audacious, barefaced, blatant, bold, brash, brassy, defiant, flagrant, forward, immodest, impudent, insolent, malapert, pert, saucy, shameless, unabashed, unashamed.

antonym shamefaced.

breach *n.* alienation, aperture, break, break-up, chasm, cleft, contravention, crack, crevice, difference, disaffection, disagreement, discontinuity, disobedience, disruption, dissension, dissociation, division, estrangement, fissure, gap, hole, infraction, infringement, lapse, offence, opening, parting, quarrel, rent, rift, rupture, schism, scission, scissure, secession, separation, severance, split, transgression, trespass, variance, violation.

bread *n.* aliment, cash, diet, dough, fare, finance, food, funds, money, moolah, necessities, nourishment, nutriment, provisions, rooty, spondulicks, subsistence, sustenance, viands, victuals, wherewithal.

breadth *n.* amplitude, area, beam, broadness, bulk, compass, comprehensiveness, dimension, expanse, extensiveness, extent, latitude, magnitude, measure, range, reach, scale, scope, size, space, span, spread, sweep, thickness, vastness, volume, wideness, width.

break *v.* abandon, absorb, announce, appear, bankrupt, batter, beat, better, breach, burst, bust, contravene, cow, crack, crash, cripple, cushion, cut, dash, defeat, degrade, demolish, demoralise, destroy, diminish, discharge, disclose, discontinue, disintegrate, disobey, dispirit, disregard, divide, divulge, emerge, enervate, enfeeble, erupt, escape, exceed, excel, explode, flee, flout, fly, fract, fracture, fragment, go phut, happen, humiliate, impair, impart, incapacitate, inform, infract, infringe, interrupt, jigger, knacker, knap, lessen, moderate, modify, occur, outdo, outstrip, part, pause, proclaim, reduce, rend, rest, retard, reveal, ruin, separate, sever, shatter, shiver, smash, snap, soften, splinter, split, stave, stop, subdue, surpass, suspend, tame, tear, tell, transgress, undermine, undo, violate, weaken, worst.

n. abruption, advantage, alienation, breach, breather, chance, cleft, crack, crevice, disaffection, discontinuity, dispute, disruption, divergence, division, estrangement, fissure, fortune, fracture, gap, gash, halt, hiatus, hole, interlude, intermission, interruption, interval, lapse, let-up, lull, opening, opportunity, pause, quarrel, recess, rent, respite, rest, rift, rupture, schism, separation, split, suspension, tear, time-out.

break away apostasise, depart, detach, escape, flee, fly, leave, part company, quit, renegue, revolt, run away, secede, separate, split.

break down analyse, anatomise, collapse, conk out, crack up, crush, demolish, dissect, fail, give way, go phut, seize up, stop.

break in burgle, encroach, impinge, interfere, interject, interpose, interrupt, intervene, intrude, invade, irrupt.

break off cease, desist, detach, disconnect, discontinue, dissever, divide, end, finish, halt, interrupt, part, pause, separate, sever, snap off, splinter, stop, suspend, terminate.

break out abscond, arise, begin, bolt, burst, commence, emerge, erupt, escape, flare up, flee, happen, occur, start.

break the ice begin, lead the way, oil the works, relax, set at ease, start the ball rolling, unbend.

break through achieve, emerge, gain ground, leap forward, make headway, pass, penetrate, progress, succeed.

break up adjourn, analyse, anatomise, demolish, destroy, disband, dismantle, disperse, disrupt, dissolve, divide, divorce, part, scatter, separate, sever, split, stop, suspend, terminate.

break with ditch, drop, finish with, jilt, part with, reject, renounce, repudiate, separate.

breakable *adj.* brittle, crumbly, delicate, flimsy, fragile, frail, frangible, friable, insubstantial, murly.

antonyms durable, sturdy.

breakaway *adj.* apostate, dissenting, heretical, rebel, renegade, schismatic, seceding, secessionist.

breakdown *n.* analysis, cataclasm, categorisation, classification, collapse, disintegration, disruption, dissection, failure, interruption, itemisation, mishap, stoppage.

breakfast *n.* dejeune, déjeuner, disjune, petit déjeuner.

break-in *n.* burglary, housebreaking, intrusion, larceny, robbery, theft.

breakthrough *n.* advance, development, discovery, find, finding, gain, headway, improvement, invention, leap, progress, step.

break-up *n.* breakdown, crack-up, crumbling, disintegration, dispersal, dissolution, divorce, finish, parting, rift, separation, split, splitting, termination.

breakwater *n.* dock, groyne, jetty, mole, pier, quay, wharf.

breast *n.* bosom, bust, chest, front, heart, thorax.

breasts *n.* boobs, bristols, bust, cans, dugs, knockers, paps, teats, tits.

breath *n.* air, animation, aroma, breathing, breeze, energy, exhalation, existence, flatus, flutter, gasp, gulp, gust, hint, inhalation, life, murmur, odour, pant, pneuma, puff, respiration, sigh, smell, spirit, suggestion, suspicion, undertone, vapour, vitality, waft, wheeze, whiff, whisper.

breathe *v.* articulate, exercise, exhale, expire, express, imbue, impart, infuse, inhale, inject, inspire, instil, live, murmur, pant, puff, respire, say, sigh, suspire, tire, transfuse, utter, voice, whisper.

breather *n.* break, breathing-space, constitutional, halt, pause, recess, relaxation, respite, rest, walk.

breathless *adj.* agog, anxious, avid, choking, eager, excited, exhausted, expectant, gasping, gulping, hushed, impatient, panting, peching, puffing, short-winded, spent, wheezing, wheezy, winded.

breathlessness *n.* air-hunger, dyspnoea, gasping, panting, short-windedness, wheeziness.

breathtaking *adj.* affecting, amazing, astonishing, awe-inspiring, awesome, exciting, impressive, magnificent, moving, overwhelming, stirring, stunning, thrilling.

breeches *n.* galligaskins, knee-breeches, knee-cords, knickerbockers, knickers, moleskins, pantaloons, pants, plus-fours, trews, trousers.

breed *v.* arouse, bear, beget, bring forth, bring up, cause, create, cultivate, develop, discipline, educate, engender, foster, generate, hatch, induce, instruct, make, multiply, nourish, nurture, occasion, originate, procreate, produce, propagate, raise, rear, reproduce, train.
n. family, ilk, kind, line, lineage, pedigree, progeny, race, sort, species, stamp, stock, strain, type, variety.

breeding *n.* ancestry, background, civility, courtesy, cultivation, culture, development, education, gentility, lineage, manners, nurture, polish, politeness, raising, rearing, refinement, reproduction, stock, strain, training, upbringing, urbanity.
antonym vulgarity.

breeding-ground *n.* hotbed, nest, nursery, school, training ground.

breeze *n.* air, breath, cat's-paw, draught, flurry, gale, gust, waft, whiff, wind, zephyr.
v. flit, glide, hurry, sail, sally, sweep, trip, wander.

breezy *adj.* airy, animated, blithe, blowing, blowy, blustery, bright, buoyant, carefree, careless, casual, cheerful, debonair, easygoing, exhilarating, fresh, gusty, informal, insouciant, jaunty, light, light-hearted, lively, nonchalant, sprightly, squally, sunny, untroubled, vivacious, windy.
antonyms calm, staid.

brevity *n.* abruptness, briefness, brusqueness, conciseness, concision, crispness, curtness, economy, ephemerality, evanescence, fugacity, impermanence, incisiveness, laconicism, laconism, pithiness, shortness, succinctness, summariness, terseness, transience, transitoriness.
antonyms longevity, permanence, verbosity.

brew *v.* boil, build up, concoct, contrive, cook, decoct, develop, devise, excite, ferment, foment, gather, hatch, infuse, mix, plan, plot, prepare, project, scheme, seethe, soak, steep, stew.
n. beverage, blend, bouillon, brewage, broth, concoction, distillation, drink, fermentation, gruel, infusion, liquor, mixture, potion, preparation, stew.

bribable *adj.* bent, buyable, corrupt, corruptible, purchasable, venal.
antonym incorruptible.

bribe *n.* allurement, back-hander, baksheesh, boodle, dash, enticement, graft, grease, hush money, incentive, inducement, kickback, pay-off, payola, protection money, refresher, slush fund, sweetener.
v. buy off, buy over, corrupt, reward, square, suborn.

bribery *n.* corruption, graft, greasing, inducement, lubrication, palm-greasing, payola, protection, subornation.

bric-à-brac *n.* antiques, baubles, bibelots, curios, curiosities, gewgaws, kickshaws, knick-knacks, ornaments, rattle-trap, trinkets, virtu.

brick *n.* adobe, block, breeze block, brickbat, clanger, closer, faux pas, firebrick, fletton, gaffe, gaucherie, header, klinker, nogging, quoin, stretcher.

bridal *adj.* conjugal, connubial, hymeneal, hymenean, marital, marriage, matrimonial, nuptial, sponsal, spousal, wedding.

bridge *n.* arch, band, bond, causeway, connection, flyover, link, overpass, pontoon bridge, span, tie, viaduct, yoke.
v. attach, bind, connect, couple, cross, fill, join, link, span, traverse, unite, yoke.

bridle *v.* check, contain, control, curb, govern, master, moderate, rein in, repress, restrain, subdue.

brief *adj.* abrupt, aphoristic, blunt, brusque, capsular, compendious, compressed, concise, crisp, cursory, curt, ephemeral, fast, fleeting, fugacious, fugitive, hasty, laconic, limited, momentary, passing, pithy, quick, sharp, short, short-lived, succinct, surly, swift, temporary, terse, thumbnail, transient, transitory.
antonyms long, long-lived, verbose.
n. advice, argument, briefing, case, contention, data, defence, demonstration, directions, directive, dossier, instructions, mandate, orders, outline, précis, remit, summary.
v. advise, direct, explain, fill in, gen up, guide, inform, instruct, prepare, prime.

briefing *n.* advice, conference, directions, filling-in, gen, guidance, information, instruction, instructions, intimation, low-down, meeting, notification, orders, preamble, preparation, priming.

briefly *adv.* abruptly, brusquely, concisely, cursorily, curtly, fleetingly, hastily, hurriedly, laconically, momentarily, precisely, quickly, shortly, summarily, temporarily, tersely.
antonyms fully, permanently.

brigade *n.* band, body, company, contingent, corps, crew, force, group, guard, outfit, party, squad, team, troop, unit.

brigand *n.* bandit, cateran, dacoit, desperado, footpad, freebooter, gangster, haiduk, heister, highwayman, klepht, marauder, outlaw, plunderer, robber, ruffian.

brigandage *n.* banditry, brigandry, dacoitage, dacoity, freebootery, freebooting, gangsterism, heist, hold-up, robbery.

bright *adj.* ablaze, acute, astute, auspicious, beaming, blazing, brainy, breezy, brilliant, burnished, cheerful, clear, clear-headed, clever, cloudless, dazzling, effulgent, encouraging, excellent, favourable, flashing, fulgent, gay, genial, glad, glaring, gleaming, glistening, glittering, glorious, glowing, golden, happy, hopeful, illuminated, illustrious, ingenious, intelligent, intense, inventive, jolly, joyful, joyous, keen, lambent, lamping, light-hearted, limpid, lively, lucent, lucid, luculent, luminous, lustrous, magnificent, merry, observant, optimistic, pellucid, perceptive, percipient, perspicacious, polished, prefulgent, promising, propitious, prosperous, quick, quick-witted, radiant, resplendent, rosy, scintillating, sharp, sheeny, shimmering, shining, smart, sparkling, splendid, sunny, translucent, transparent, twinkling, unclouded, undulled, untarnished, vivacious, vivid, wide-awake.
antonyms depressing, dull, stupid.

brighten *v.* burnish, cheer up, clear up, encourage, enliven, flash, gladden, gleam, glow, hearten, illuminate, light up, lighten, perk up, polish, rub up, shine.
antonyms darken, dull, tarnish.

brightness *n.* blaze, braininess, brains, breeziness, brilliance, brilliancy, cheer, cheerfulness, cleverness, effulgence, fulgency, fulgor, gladness, glare, glitter, glory, hopefulness, illumination, joy, liveliness, lucency, luminance, luminosity, lustre, magnificence, optimism, promise, propitiousness, radiance, refulgence, resplendence, sheen, sparkle, splendour, vivacity, vividness.
antonyms cheerlessness, darkness, dullness.

brilliance *n.* animation, aptitude, blaze, braininess, bravura, brightness, brilliancy, cleverness, coruscation, dazzle, distinction, éclat, effulgence, excellence, fulgency, gaiety, genius, giftedness, glamour, glare, gleam, glitter, glory, gloss, gorgeousness, grandeur, greatness, illustriousness, intensity, inventiveness, lambency, lucency, luminosity, lustre, magnificence, pizzazz, radiance, refulgence, resplendence, scintillation, sheen, sparkle, splendour, talent, vivacity, vividness, wit.

brilliant *adj.* ablaze, accomplished, adroit, animated, astute, blazing, brainy, bright, celebrated, clever, coruscating, dazzling, effulgent, eminent, exceptional, expert, famous, gemmy, gifted, glaring, glittering, glorious, glossy, illustrious, ingenious, intellectual, intelligent, intense, inventive, lambent, luminous, magnificent, masterly, outstanding, quick, refulgent, scintillating, shining, showy, skilful, sparkling, splendid, star, star-like, superb, talented, vivacious, vivid, witty.
antonyms dull, restrained, stupid, undistinguished.

brim *n.* border, brink, circumference, edge, lip, marge, margin, perimeter, periphery, rim, skirt, verge.

bring *v.* accompany, accustom, add, attract, bear, carry, cause, command, conduct, convey, convince, create, deliver, dispose, draw, earn, effect, engender, escort, fetch, force, gather, generate, get beget, gross, guide, induce, inflict, influence, introduce, lead, make, move, net, occasion, persuade, produce, prompt, return, sway, take, transfer, transport, usher, wreak, yield.

bring about accomplish, achieve, cause, compass, create, effect, effectuate, engender, engineer, fulfil, generate, manage, manipulate, manoeuvre, occasion, produce, realise.

bring down abase, break, debase, degrade, fell, floor, humble, lay low, level, lower, overthrow, overturn, reduce, ruin, shoot, topple, undermine.

bring forth afford, bear, beget, engender, furnish, generate, produce, provide, supply, yield.

bring home to convince, drive home, emphasise, impress upon, persuade, prove.

bring in accrue, earn, fetch, gross, introduce, net, produce, profit, realise, return, yield.

bring off accomplish, achieve, bring about, compass, discharge, execute, fulfil, perform, rescue.

bring on accelerate, advance, cause, expedite, generate, give rise to, induce, inspire, lead to, occasion, precipitate, prompt, provoke.
antonym inhibit.

bring out draw out, emphasise, enhance, highlight, introduce, issue, print, publish, utter.

bring to light dig up, disclose, discover, disinter, exhume, expose, reveal, show, uncover, unearth, unveil.

bring to nothing destroy, knock the bottom out of, mar, nullify, ruin, scupper, spoil, undermine, vitiate.

bring up advance, broach, disgorge, educate, form, foster, introduce, mention, nurture, propose, puke, raise, rear, regurgitate, submit, succeed, succour, support, teach, throw up, train, vomit.

brink *n.* bank, border, boundary, brim, edge, extremity, fringe, limit, lip, marge, margin, point, rim, skirt, threshold, verge, waterside.

briny *adj.* muriatic, salty.

brisk *adj.* active, agile, alert, allegro, bracing, bright, brushy, bustling, busy, crank, crisp, effervescing, energetic, exhilarating, expeditious, fresh, galliard, invigorating, keen, lively, nimble, nippy, no-nonsense, prompt, quick, refreshing, sharp, snappy, speedy, spirited, sprightly, spry, stimulating, vigorous.
antonym sluggish.

briskly *adv.* abruptly, actively, allegro, brightly, decisively, efficiently, energetically, expeditiously, incisively, nimbly, promptly, quickly, rapidly, readily, smartly, vigorously.
antonym sluggishly.

bristle *n.* barb, hair, prickle, spine, stubble, thorn, vibrissa, whisker.
v. bridle, draw oneself up, horripilate, prickle, react, rise, seethe, spit.

bristling *adj.* abounding, crawling, horrent, horrid, horripilant, humming, incensed, indignant, seething, spitting, swarming, teeming.

bristly *adj.* bearded, bewhiskered, bristling, hairy, hirsute, hispid, horrent, horripilant, prickly, rough, stubbly, thorny, unshaven, whiskered.
antonyms clean-shaven, smooth.

brittle *adj.* anxious, breakable, crackly, crisp, crumbling, crumbly, curt, delicate, edgy, fragile, frail, frangible, friable, frush, irritable, nervous, nervy, shattery, shivery, short, tense.
antonyms durable, resilient, sturdy.

broach *v.* crack open, introduce, launch into, mention, pierce, propose, puncture, raise, start, suggest, tap, uncork, utter.

broad *adj.* all-embracing, ample, beamy, blue, capacious, catholic, coarse, comprehensive, eclectic, encyclopaedic, enlightened, expansive, extensive, far-reaching, general, generous, gross, improper, inclusive, indecent, indelicate, large, latitudinous, roomy, spacious, square, sweeping, tolerant, universal, unlimited, unrefined, vast, voluminous, vulgar, wide, wide-ranging, widespread.
antonym narrow.

broadcast *v.* advertise, air, announce, beam, cable, circulate, disseminate, proclaim, promulgate, publicise, publish, radio, relay, report, show, spread, televise, transmit.
n. programme, relay, show, telecast, transmission.

broaden *v.* augment, branch out, develop, diversify, enlarge, enlighten, expand, extend, increase, open up, spread, stretch, supplement, swell, thicken, widen.

broad-minded *adj.* catholic, cosmopolitan, dispassionate, enlightened, flexible, free-thinking, indulgent, liberal, open-minded, permissive, receptive, tolerant, unbiased, unprejudiced, verligte.

broadside *n.* assault, attack, battering, blast, bombardment, brickbat, broadsheet, cannonade, counterblast, denunciation, diatribe,

fulmination, harangue, invective, pamphlet, philippic.

brochure *n.* advertisement, booklet, broadsheet, broadside, circular, folder, handbill, hand-out, leaflet, pamphlet.

broil *n.* affray, altercation, argument, brawl, brouhaha, dispute, disturbance, fracas, fray, imbraglio, quarrel, scrimmage, scrum, stramash, strife, tumult, wrangle.

broke *adj.* bankrupt, bust, destitute, impecunious, impoverished, insolvent, penniless, penurious, ruined, skint, stony-broke, strapped.
antonyms affluent, solvent.

broken *adj.* bankrupt, beaten, betrayed, browbeaten, burst, crippled, crushed, defeated, defective, demolished, demoralised, destroyed, disconnected, discontinuous, dishonoured, disjointed, dismantled, dispersed, disregarded, disturbed, down, dud, duff, erratic, exhausted, faulty, feeble, forgotten, fracted, fractured, fragmentary, fragmented, halting, hesitating, humbled, ignored, imperfect, incoherent, incomplete, infirm, infringed, intermittent, interrupted, isolated, jiggered, kaput, knackered, oppressed, out of order, overpowered, prerupt, rent, retracted, routed, ruined, run-down, ruptured, separated, severed, shattered, shivered, spasmodic, spent, stammering, subdued, tamed, traduced, transgressed, uncertain, vanquished, variegated, weak.

broken-down *adj.* collapsed, decayed, dilapidated, disintegrated, inoperative, kaput, out of order, ruined.

broken-hearted *adj.* crestfallen, dejected, desolate, despairing, despondent, devastated, disappointed, disconsolate, grief-stricken, hard-hit, heartbroken, heart-sick, heartsore, inconsolable, miserable, mournful, prostrated, sorrowful, unhappy, wretched.

broker *n.* agent, dealer, factor, handler, intermediary, middleman, negotiator, stockbroker.

bromide *n.* anodyne, banality, cliché, commonplace, platitude, stereotype, truism.

bronze *adj.* auburn, brazen, chestnut, copper, copper-coloured, reddish-brown, rust, tan, titian.

brooch *n.* badge, breastpin, clasp, clip, pin, prop.

brood *v.* agonise, cover, dwell on, fret, go over, hatch, incubate, meditate, mope, mull over, muse, ponder, rehearse, repine, ruminate.
n. birth, chicks, children, clutch, family, get, hatch, issue, litter, nide, offspring, progeny, young.

brook[1] *n.* beck, burn, channel, freshet, gill, inlet, mill, rill, rivulet, runnel, stream, streamlet, watercourse.

brook[2] *v.* abide, accept, allow, bear, countenance, endure, permit, stand, stomach, submit to, suffer, support, swallow, thole, tolerate, withstand.

broom *n.* besom, brush, sweeper, wisp.

brothel *n.* bagnio, bawdy-house, bordello, cathouse, flash-house, house of ill fame, house of ill repute, kip, kip-shop, knocking-shop, red light, stews, vaulting-house, whorehouse.

brother *n.* associate, blood-brother, brer, chum, colleague, companion, compeer, comrade, confrère, cousin, fellow, fellow-creature, friar, friend, kin, kinsman, mate, monk, pal, partner, relation, relative, religieux, religious, sibling.

brotherhood *n.* affiliation, alliance, association, clan, clique, community, confederacy, confederation, confraternity, confrèrie, coterie, fraternity, guild, league, society, union.

brotherly *adj.* affectionate, amicable, benevolent, caring, concerned, cordial, fraternal, friendly, kind, loving, neighbourly, philanthropic, supervisory, sympathetic.
antonyms callous, unbrotherly.

brow *n.* appearance, aspect, bearing, brink, cliff, countenance, crown, edge, eyebrow, face, forehead, front, mien, peak, ridge, rim, summit, temples, tip, top, verge, visage.

browbeat *v.* awe, batter, bludgeon, bulldoze, bully, coerce, cow, domineer, dragoon, hector, hound, intimidate, oppress, overbear, threaten, tyrannise.
antonym coax.

brown *adj.* auburn, bay, brick, bronze, bronzed, browned, brunette, chestnut, chocolate, coffee, dark, donkey, dun, dusky, fuscous, ginger, hazel, mahogany, russet, rust, rusty, sunburnt, tan, tanned, tawny, titian, toasted, umber, vandyke brown.

brown study absence, absent-mindedness, absorption, abstraction, contemplation, meditation, musing, pensiveness, preoccupation, reflection, reverie, rumination.

browned off bored, bored stiff, brassed off, cheesed off, discontented, discouraged, disgruntled, disheartened, fed up, pissed off, weary.
antonyms fascinated, interested.

brownie *n.* elf, fairy, goblin, hob, kobold, leprechaun, lob-lie-by-the-fire, lubber fiend, nix, nixie, pixie, Puck, Robin Goodfellow, sprite.

browse *v.* crop, dip into, eat, feed, flick through, graze, leaf through, nibble, pasture, peruse, scan, skim, survey.

bruise *v.* blacken, blemish, contund, contuse, crush, discolour, grieve, hurt, injure, insult, mar, mark, offend, pound, pulverise, stain, wound.
n. blemish, contusion, discoloration, injury, mark, rainbow, shiner, swelling.

brunt *n.* burden, force, impact, impetus, pressure, shock, strain, stress, thrust, violence, weight.

brush¹ *n.* besom, broom, sweeper.
v. buff, burnish, caress, clean, contact, flick, glance, graze, kiss, paint, polish, rub, scrape, shine, stroke, sweep, touch, wash.
brush aside belittle, dismiss, disregard, flout, ignore, override, pooh-pooh.

brush off cold-shoulder, discourage, disdain, dismiss, disown, disregard, ignore, rebuff, refuse, reject, repudiate, repulse, scorn, slight, snub, spurn.
antonyms cultivate, encourage.

brush up cram, freshen up, improve, read up, refresh, relearn, revise, study, swot.

brush² *n.* brushwood, bushes, frith, ground cover, scrub, shrubs, thicket, undergrowth, underwood.

brush³ *n.* clash, conflict, confrontation, dust-up, encounter, fight, fracas, incident, run-in, scrap, set-to, skirmish, tussle.

brush-off *n.* cold shoulder, discouragement, dismissal, go-by, rebuff, refusal, rejection, repudiation, repulse, slight, snub.
antonym encouragement.

brusque *adj.* abrupt, blunt, curt, discourteous, gruff, hasty, impolite, sharp, short, surly, tactless, tart, terse, uncivil, undiplomatic.
antonyms courteous, tactful.

brutal *adj.* animal, barbarous, bearish, beastly, bestial, bloodthirsty, boarish, brute, brutish, callous, carnal, coarse, crude, cruel, doggish, ferocious, gruff, harsh, heartless, impolite, inhuman, inhumane, insensitive, merciless, pitiless, remorseless, rough, rude, ruthless, savage, sensual, severe, uncivil, uncivilised, unfeeling, unmannerly, unsympathetic, vicious.
antonyms humane, kindly.

brutalise *v.* decivilise, dehumanise, desensitise, harden, inure.
antonym civilise.

brutality *n.* atrocity, barbarism, barbarity, bloodthirstiness, brutishness, callosity, callousness, coarseness, cruelty, ferocity, inhumanity, roughness, ruthlessness, savageness, savagery, viciousness.
antonyms gentleness, kindness.

brutally *adv.* barbarically, barbarously, brutishly, callously, coarsely, cruelly, ferociously, fiercely, hard-heartedly, harshly, heartlessly, inhumanly, meanly, mercilessly, murderously, pitilessly, remorselessly, roughly, ruthlessly, savagely, unkindly, viciously.
antonyms gently, kindly.

brute *n.* animal, barbarian, beast, bête, boor, creature, devil, fiend, lout, monster, ogre, sadist, savage, swine.
antonym gentleman.
adj. bestial, bodily, carnal, coarse, depraved, fleshly, gross, instinctive, mindless, physical, senseless, sensual, unthinking.
antonym refined.

brutish *adj.* barbarian, barbaric, barbarous, boorish, coarse, crass, crude, cruel, feral, ferine, gross, loutish, savage, stupid, subhuman, swinish, uncouth, vulgar.
antonym refined.

bubble¹ *n.* ball, bead, bladder, blister, blob, drop, droplet, globule, vesicle.
v. babble, boil, burble, effervesce, fizz, foam, froth, gurgle, murmur, percolate, purl, ripple, seethe, sparkle, trickle, trill, wallop.

bubble[2] *n.* bagatelle, delusion, fantasy, fraud, illusion, sting, toy, trifle, vanity.

bubbles *n.* effervescence, fizz, foam, froth, head, lather, spume, suds.

bubbly *adj.* animated, bouncy, carbonated, curly, effervescent, elated, excited, fizzy, happy, lively, merry, sudsy.
antonym flat.

buccaneer *n.* corsair, filibuster, freebooter, pirate, privateer, sea-robber, sea-rover, sea-wolf.

buck[1] *n.* beau, blade, blood, coxcomb, dandy, fop, gallant, playboy, popinjay, spark, swell.

buck[2] *v.* bound, cheer, dislodge, encourage, gladden, gratify, hearten, inspirit, jerk, jump, leap, please, prance, spring, start, throw, unseat, vault.
buck up brighten, cheer, cheer up, encourage, hearten, improve, inspirit, perk up, rally, stimulate, take heart.
antonym dishearten.

bucket *n.* bail, barrel, basin, can, cask, kibble, pail, pan, pitcher, vessel.

buckle *n.* bend, bulge, catch, clasp, clip, contortion, distortion, fastener, hasp, kink, twist, warp.
v. bend, bulge, catch, cave in, clasp, close, collapse, connect, contort, crumple, distort, fasten, fold, hitch, hook, secure, twist, warp, wrinkle.

bucolic *adj.* agrarian, agricultural, countrified, country, pastoral, rural, rustic.
antonyms industrial, urban.

bud *n.* embryo, germ, knosp, shoot, sprig, sprout.
v. burgeon, develop, grow, pullulate, shoot, sprout.
antonyms waste away, wither.

budding *adj.* burgeoning, developing, embryonic, fledgling, flowering, germinal, growing, hopeful, incipient, intending, nascent, potential, promising.
antonym experienced.

budge *v.* bend, change, convince, dislodge, give (way), inch, influence, move, persuade, propel, push, remove, roll, shift, slide, stir, sway, yield.

budget *n.* allocation, allotment, allowance, cost, estimate, finances, fonds, funds, means, resources.
v. allocate, apportion, cost, estimate, plan, ration.

buff[1] *adj.* fawn, fulvid, fulvous, khaki, sandy, straw, tan, yellowish, yellowish-brown.
v. brush, burnish, polish, polish up, rub, shine, smooth.

buff[2] *n.* addict, admirer, aficionado, bug, cognoscente, connoisseur, devotee, enthusiast, expert, fan, fiend, freak.

buffer *n.* bulwark, bumper, cushion, fender, intermediary, pad, pillow, safeguard, screen, shield, shock-absorber.

buffet[1] *n.* café, cafeteria, counter, snack-bar, snack-counter.

buffet[2] *v.* bang, batter, beat, box, bump, clobber, clout, cuff, flail, hit, jar, knock, pound, pummel, push, rap, shove, slap, strike, thump, wallop.
n. bang, blow, box, bump, clout, cuff, jar, jolt, knock, push, rap, shove, slap, smack, thump, wallop.

buffoon *n.* clown, comedian, comic, droll, fool, goliard, harlequin, jester, joker, merry-andrew, mountebank, scaramouch, Scoggin, tomfool, vice, wag, zany.

buffoonery *n.* clowning, drollery, harlequinade, jesting, nonsense, pantomime, silliness, tomfoolery, waggishness, zanyism.

bug *n.* addict, admirer, bacterium, blemish, buff, catch, craze, defect, disease, enthusiast, error, fad, failing, fan, fault, fiend, flaw, freak, germ, gremlin, imperfection, infection, mania, micro-organism, obsession, rage, snarl-up, virus.
v. annoy, badger, bother, disturb, get, harass, irk, irritate, needle, nettle, pester, plague, vex.

bugbear *n.* anathema, bane, bête noire, bloody-bones, bogey, bugaboo, devil, dread, fiend, horror, Mumbo-jumbo, nightmare, pet hate, poker, rawhead.

build *v.* assemble, augment, base, begin, big, constitute, construct, develop, edify, enlarge, erect, escalate, establish, extend, fabricate, form, formulate, found, improve, inaugurate, increase, initiate, institute, intensify, knock together, make, originate, raise, strengthen.
antonyms destroy, knock down, lessen, weaken.
n. body, figure, form, frame, physique, shape, size, structure.
build up advertise, amplify, assemble, boost, develop, enhance, expand, extend, fortify, heighten, hype, improve, increase, intensify, plug, promote, publicise, reinforce, strengthen.
antonyms lessen, weaken.

building *n.* architecture, construction, domicile, dwelling, edifice, erection, fabric, fabrication, house, pile, structure.
antonym destruction.

build-up *n.* accretion, accumulation, ballyhoo, development, enlargement, escalation, expansion, gain, growth, heap, hype, increase, load, mass, plug, promotion, publicity, puff, stack, stockpile, store.
antonyms decrease, reduction.

built-in *adj.* essential, fundamental, implicit, in-built, included, incorporated, inherent, inseparable, integral, intrinsic, necessary.

bulbous *adj.* bellied, bellying, bloated, bulging, convex, distended, pulvinate(d), rounded, swelling, swollen.

bulge *n.* belly, boost, bump, distension, hump, increase, intensification, lump, projection, protrusion, protuberance, rise, surge, swelling, upsurge.
v. bag, belly, bulb, dilate, distend, enlarge, expand, hump, project, protrude, sag, strout, swell.

bulging *adj.* bellied, bulbous, bunchy, convex, pulvinate, pulvinated, rounded, swelling, swollen.

bulk *n.* amplitude, bigness, body, dimensions, extensity, extent, generality, immensity, largeness, magnitude, majority, mass, most, plurality, preponderance, size, substance, volume, weight.

bulky *adj.* big, colossal, cumbersome, enormous, heavy, hefty, huge, hulking, immense, large, lumping, mammoth, massive, massy, ponderous, substantial, unmanageable, unwieldy, volumed, voluminous, weighty.
antonyms handy, insubstantial, small.

bulldoze *v.* browbeat, buffalo, bully, clear, coerce, cow, demolish, drive, flatten, force, hector, intimidate, knock down, level, propel, push, push through, raze, shove, thrust.

bullet *n.* ball, missile, pellet, plumb, projectile, shot, sinker, slug, weight.

bulletin *n.* announcement, communication, communiqué, dispatch, dope, message, newsflash, notification, report, sitrep, statement.

bull's-eye *n.* bull, centre, gold.
antonym miss.

bully *n.* bouncer, browbeater, bucko, bully-boy, bully-rook, coercionist, Drawcansir, intimidator, killcrow, oppressor, persecutor, ruffian, termagant, tormentor, tough, tyrant.
v. bluster, browbeat, bulldoze, bullyrag, coerce, cow, domineer, haze, hector, intimidate, oppress, overbear, persecute, push around, swagger, terrorise, tyrannise.
antonyms coax, persuade.

bulwark *n.* bastion, buffer, buttress, defence, embankment, fortification, guard, mainstay, outwork, partition, rampart, redoubt, safeguard, security, support.

bumbling *adj.* awkward, blundering, botching, bungling, clumsy, footling, foozling, incompetent, inefficient, inept, lumbering, maladroit, muddled, stumbling.
antonyms competent, efficient.

bump *v.* bang, bounce, budge, collide (with), crash, dislodge, displace, hit, jar, jerk, jolt, jostle, jounce, knock, move, rattle, remove, shake, shift, slam, strike.
n. bang, blow, bulge, collision, contusion, crash, hit, hump, impact, jar, jolt, knob, knock, knot, lump, node, nodule, protuberance, rap, shock, smash, swelling, thud, thump.

bump off assassinate, dispatch, do in, eliminate, kill, liquidate, murder, remove, rub out, top.

bumper *adj.* abundant, bountiful, enormous, excellent, exceptional, great, huge, jumbo, large, massive, prodigal, spanking, teeming, unusual, whacking, whopping.
antonyms miserly, small.

bumpkin *n.* boor, chaw-bacon, clodhopper, clown, corn-ball, hick, hillbilly, jake, looby, lout, lubbard, lubber, lummox, oaf, peasant, provincial, rustic, yokel.
antonym man of the world.

bumptious *adj.* arrogant, boastful, brash, cocky, conceited, egotistic, forward, full of oneself, impudent, overbearing, over-confident, pompous, presumptuous, pushy, self-assertive, self-important, showy, swaggering, vainglorious, vaunting.
antonyms humble, modest.

bumpy *adj.* bouncy, choppy, irregular, jarring, jerky, jolting, jolty, knobbly, knobby, lumpy, rough, rutted, uneven.
antonym smooth.

bunch *n.* assortment, band, batch, bouquet, bundle, clump, cluster, collection, crew, crowd, fascicle, fascicule, flock, gang, gathering, group-knot, heap, lot, mass, mob, multitude, number, parcel, party, pile, quantity, sheaf, spray, stack, swarm, team, troop, tuft.
v. assemble, bundle, cluster, collect, congregate, crowd, flock, group, herd, huddle, mass, pack.
antonyms scatter, spread out.

bunched *adj.* clustered, concentrated, fascicled, fascicular, fascicule(d), gathered, grouped.
antonyms scattered, spread out.

bundle *n.* accumulation, assortment, bag, bale, batch, box, bunch, carton, collection, consignment, crate, dorlach, drum, fascicle, fascicule, group, heap, mass, Matilda, pack, package, packet, pallet, parcel, pile, quantity, roll, shock, shook, stack, stook, swag.
v. bale, bind, fasten, pack, palletise, tie, truss, wrap.

bundled *adj.* clustered, fascicled, fascicular, fasciculate(d), gathered, grouped, parcelled, tied.
antonyms loose, scattered.

bung *n.* cork, dook, stopper.

bungle *v.* blunder, bodge, boob, botch, bumble, cock up, duff, flub, footle, foozle, foul up, fuck up, fudge, goof, louse up, mar, mess up, miscalculate, mismanage, muff, mull, ruin, screw up, spoil.
n. blunder, boob, boo-boo, botch-up, cock-up, foul-up, mull.

bungler *n.* blunderer, botcher, butterfingers, duffer, footler, foozler, fumbler, incompetent, lubber, muddler, muff.

bungling *adj.* awkward, blundering, botching, cack-handed, clumsy, footling, foozling, hamfisted, ham-handed, incompetent, inept, maladroit, unskilful.

bunkum *n.* balderdash, baloney, bilge, bosh, bunk, garbage, havers, hooey, horsefeathers, nonsense, piffle, poppycock, rot, rubbish, stuff and nonsense, tar(r)adiddle, tomfoolery, tommyrot, tosh, trash, tripe, twaddle.
antonym sense.

buoy *n.* beacon, dolphin, float, marker, signal.
buoy up boost, cheer, encourage, hearten, lift, raise, support, sustain.
antonym depress.

buoyant *adj.* afloat, animated, blithe, bouncy, breezy, bright, bullish, carefree, cheerful, debonair, floatable, floating, happy, jaunty,

joyful, light, light-hearted, lively, peppy, rising, sprightly, sunny, weightless.
antonym depressed.

burble *n.* babble, gurgle, lapping, murmur, purl, purling.

v. babble, gurgle, lap, murmur, purl.

burden *n.* affliction, anxiety, bear, care, cargo, clog, dead weight, encumbrance, grievance, load, millstone, obligation, obstruction, onus, responsibility, sorrow, strain, stress, trial, trouble, weight, worry.

v. bother, encumber, handicap, lade, lie hard on, lie heavy on, load, oppress, overload, overwhelm, strain, tax, worry.

antonyms disburden, lighten, relieve.

burdensome *adj.* crushing, difficult, distressing, exacting, heavy, irksome, onerous, oppressive, taxing, troublesome, trying, wearisome, weighty.

antonyms easy, light.

bureau *n.* agency, branch, counter, department, desk, division, office, service.

bureaucracy *n.* administration, city hall, civil service, directorate, government, ministry, officialdom, officialese, officials, red tape, regulations, the authorities, the system.

bureaucrat *n.* administrator, apparatchik, bureaucratist, chinovnik, civil servant, functionary, mandarin, minister, office-holder, officer, official.

burglar *n.* cat-burglar, cracksman, housebreaker, picklock, pilferer, robber, thief, yegg.

burglary *n.* break-in, cat-burglary, housebreaking, larceny, pilferage, robbery, stealing, theft, thieving.

burial *n.* burying, entombment, exequies, funeral, inhumation, interment, obsequies, sepulchre, sepulture.

burlesque *n.* caricature, mickey-taking, mock, mockery, parody, ridicule, satire, send-up, spoof, take-off, travesty.

adj. caricatural, comic, derisive, droll, farcical, hudibrastic, mocking, parodying, satirical.

antonym serious.

v. ape, caricature, exaggerate, imitate, lampoon, mock, parody, ridicule, satirise, send up, spoof, take off, travesty.

burly *adj.* athletic, beefy, big, brawny, bulky, heavy, hefty, hulking, husky, muscular, powerful, stocky, stout, strapping, strong, sturdy, thickset, well-built.

antonyms puny, slim, small, thin.

burn *v.* bite, blaze, brand, calcine, cauterise, char, combust, conflagrate, consume, corrode, deflagrate, desire, expend, flame, flare, flash, flicker, fume, glow, hurt, ignite, incinerate, kindle, light, oxidise, pain, parch, scorch, seethe, shrivel, simmer, singe, smart, smoke, smoulder, sting, tingle, toast, use, wither, yearn.

burning *adj.* acrid, acute, ardent, biting, blazing, caustic, compelling, consuming, corrosive, critical, crucial, eager, earnest, essential, excessive, fervent, fiery, flaming, flashing, frantic, frenzied, gleaming, glowing, hot, illuminated, impassioned, important, intense, irritating, painful, passionate, piercing, pressing, prickling, pungent, reeking, scorching, significant, smarting, smouldering, stinging, tingling, urent, urgent, vehement, vital, zealous.

antonyms apathetic, cold, mild, unimportant.

burnish *v.* brighten, buff, furbish, glaze, polish, polish up, rub, shine.

antonym tarnish.

n. gloss, lustre, patina, polish, sheen, shine.

burrow *n.* den, earth, hole, lair, retreat, set(t), shelter, tunnel, warren.

v. delve, dig, earth, excavate, mine, tunnel, undermine.

burst *v.* barge, blow up, break, crack, dehisce, disintegrate, erupt, explode, fragment, gush, puncture, run, rupture, rush, shatter, shiver, split, spout, tear.

n. bang, blast, blasting, blow-out, blow-up, breach, break, crack, discharge, eruption, explosion, fit, gallop, gush, gust, outbreak, outburst, outpouring, rupture, rush, spate, split, spurt, surge, torrent.

adj. broken, burst, flat, kaput, punctured, rent, ruptured, split, torn.

burst-up *n.* break, collapse, commotion, disruption, failure, separation.

bury *v.* absorb, conceal, cover, embed, enclose, engage, engross, engulf, enshroud, entomb, hide, immerse, implant, inearth, inhume, inter, interest, lay to rest, occupy, secrete, sepulchre, shroud, sink, submerge.

antonyms disinter, uncover.

bus *n.* charabanc, coach, jitney, mammy-wagon, omnibus.

bush *n.* backwoods, brush, hedge, plant, scrub, scrubland, shrub, shrubbery, thicket, wilds, woodland.

bushy *adj.* bosky, bristling, bristly, dasyphyllous, dumose, dumous, fluffy, fuzzy, luxuriant, rough, shaggy, spreading, stiff, thick, unruly, wiry.

antonyms neat, tidy, trim, well-kept.

busily *adv.* actively, assiduously, briskly, diligently, earnestly, energetically, hard, industriously, intently, purposefully, speedily, strenuously.

business *n.* affair, assignment, bargaining, calling, career, commerce, company, concern, corporation, craft, dealings, duty, employment, enterprise, establishment, firm, function, industry, issue, job, line, line of country, manufacturing, matter, merchandising, métier, occupation, organisation, palaver, point, problem, profession, pursuit, question, responsibility, selling, subject, task, topic, trade, trading, transaction(s), venture, vocation, work.

business-like *adj.* correct, efficient, formal, impersonal, matter-of-fact, methodical, orderly, organised, practical, precise, professional, regular, routine, systematic, thorough, well-ordered.

antonyms disorganised, inefficient.

businessman *n.* capitalist, employer, entrepreneur, executive, financier, homme d'affaires, industrialist, merchant, trader, tradesman, tycoon.

buskers *n.* German-band, mariachi, street-entertainers, street-musicians.

bust *n.* bosom, breast, carving, chest, head, statue, statuette, torso.

bustle *v.* dash, flutter, fuss, hasten, hurry, rush, scamper, scramble, scurry, scuttle, stir, tear.
n. activity, ado, agitation, commotion, excitement, flurry, fuss, haste, hurly-burly, hurry, palaver, pother, stir, to-do, toing and froing, tumult.

bustling *adj.* active, astir, busy, buzzing, crowded, energetic, eventful, full, humming, lively, restless, rushing, stirring, swarming, teeming, thronged.
antonym quiet.

bust-up *n.* brawl, disruption, disturbance, quarrel, separation.

busy *adj.* active, assiduous, brisk, diligent, eident, employed, energetic, engaged, engrossed, exacting, full, fussy, hectic, industrious, inquisitive, interfering, lively, meddlesome, meddling, nosy, occupied, officious, persevering, prying, restless, slaving, stirabout, stirring, strenuous, tireless, tiring, troublesome, unleisured, versant, working.
antonyms idle, quiet.
v. absorb, bother, concern, employ, engage, engross, immerse, interest, occupy.

busybody *n.* eavesdropper, gossip, intriguer, intruder, meddler, nosey parker, pantopragmatic, pry, scandalmonger, snoop, snooper, troublemaker.

butcher *n.* destroyer, killcow, killer, murderer, slaughterer, slayer.
v. assassinate, botch, carve, clean, cut, destroy, dress, exterminate, joint, kill, liquidate, massacre, mutilate, prepare, ruin, slaughter, slay, spoil, wreck.

butchery *n.* blood-letting, bloodshed, carnage, killing, mass destruction, massacre, murder, slaughter.

butler *n.* sommelier, wine-waiter.

butt[1] *n.* base, end, foot, haft, handle, hilt, shaft, shank, stock, stub, tail, tip.

butt[2] *n.* dupe, laughing-stock, mark, object, point, subject, target, victim.

butt[3] *v., n.* buck, buffet, bump, bunt, hit, jab, knock, poke, prod, punch, push, ram, shove, thrust.

butt in cut in, interfere, interpose, interrupt, intrude, meddle.

butter up blarney, cajole, coax, flatter, softsoap, wheedle.

buttocks *n.* arse, backside, beam end, behind, bottom, breach, bum, derrière, doup, fanny, fud, haunches, hinder-end, hinderlin(g)s, hindquarters, hurdies, natch, nates, posterior, prat, rear, rump, seat.

button *n.* bud, catch, clasp, fastening, frog, knob, pimple.

buttonhole *v.* accost, bore, catch, detain, grab, importune, nab, pin, waylay.

buttress *n.* abutment, brace, mainstay, pier, prop, reinforcement, shore, stanchion, stay, strut, support.
v. bolster up, brace, hold up, prop up, reinforce, shore up, strengthen, support, sustain, uphold.
antonym weaken.

buxom *adj.* ample, bosomy, busty, chesty, comely, debonair, hearty, jocund, jolly, lively, lusty, merry, plump, robust, voluptuous, well-rounded, winsome.
antonyms petite, slim, small.

buy *v.* acquire, bribe, corrupt, fix, get, obtain, procure, purchase, square, suborn.
antonym sell.
n. acquisition, bargain, deal, purchase.

buyer *n.* emptor, purchaser, vendee.
antonyms seller, vendor.

buying *n.* acquisition, emption, purchase.

buzz *n.* bombilation, bombination, buzzing, drone, gossip, hearsay, hiss, hum, murmur, news, purr, report, ring, ringing, rumour, scandal, susurration, susurrus, whir(r), whisper, whizz.
v. bombilate, bombinate, drone, hum, murmur, reverberate, ring, susurrate, whir(r), whisper, whizz.

by *prep.* along, beside, near, next to, over, past, through, via.
adv. aside, at hand, away, beyond, close, handy, near, past.

by all means absolutely, certainly, doubtlessly, of course, positively, surely.

by any means anyhow.

by chance perchance.

by degrees bit by bit, gently, gradually, imperceptibly, inch by inch, little by little, slowly, step by step.
antonyms all at one go, quickly, suddenly.

by far by a long chalk, by a long shot, easily, far and away, immeasurably, incomparably, much.

by fits and starts erratically, fitfully, intermittently, irregularly, now and again, on and off, spasmodically, sporadically, unsystematically.
antonyms constantly, continuously.

by force vi et armis.

by halves imperfectly, incompletely, scrappily, skimpily.
antonyms completely, totally.

by heart by rote, memoriter, off pat, parrot-fashion, pat, word for word.

by mistake in error, misapprehensively, mistakenly.

by no means in no way, not at all, not in the least, not the least bit, on no account.

by repute reputatively, reputedly, supposedly.

by the way en passant, in passing.

bygone *adj.* ancient, antiquated, departed, erstwhile, forepast, forgotten, former, lost, olden, past, previous.
antonyms modern, recent.
n. antique, grievance, oldie.

bypass *v.* avoid, circumvent, ignore, neglect, outflank.
n. detour, ring road.

by-product *n.* after-effect, consequence, epiphenomenon, fall-out, repercussion, result, side-effect.

bystander *n.* eye-witness, looker-on, observer, onlooker, passer-by, spectator, watcher, witness.

byword *n.* adage, aphorism, apophthegm, catch-word, dictum, epithet, gnome, maxim, motto, precept, proverb, saw, saying, slogan.

C

cab *n*. hackney carriage, minicab, taxi, taxicab, vettura.

cabal *n*. caucus, clique, coalition, conclave, confederacy, conspiracy, coterie, faction, intrigue, junta, junto, league, machination, party, plot, plotters, scheme, set.

cabin *n*. berth, bothy, chalet, compartment, cot, cot-house, cottage, crib, deck-house, hovel, hut, lodge, quarters, room, shack, shanty, shed.

cabin boy grummet.

cabinet *n*. almirah, case, chiffonier, closet, commode, cupboard, dresser, escritoire, locker.

cabinetmaker *n*. ébéniste.

cable *n*. chain, cord, hawser, line, mooring, rope.

cabman *n*. cabby, taxi-driver, vetturino.

cache *n*. accumulation, fund, garner, hoard, repository, reserve, stockpile, store, storehouse, supply, treasure-store.
v. bury, conceal, hide, secrete, stash, store, stow.

cackle *v.,n*. babble, chatter, chuckle, crow, gabble, gibber, giggle, jabber, laugh, prattle, snicker, snigger, titter.

cacophonous *adj*. discordant, dissonant, grating, harsh, horrisonant, inharmonious, jarring, raucous, strident.
antonyms harmonious, pleasant.

cacophony *n*. caterwauling, discord, disharmony, dissonance, horrisonance, stridency.
antonym harmony.

cad *n*. blackguard, bounder, caitiff, churl, cur, dastard, heel, knave, oik, poltroon, rat, rotter, skunk, swine, worm.
antonym gentleman.

cadence *n*. accent, beat, inflection, intonation, lilt, measure, metre, modulation, pattern, pulse, rate, rhythm, stress, swing, tempo, throb.

cadge *v*. beg, bum, freeload, hitch, scrounge, sponge.

cadre *n*. basis, core, framework, hierarchy, infrastructure, nucleus, official.

café *n*. cafeteria, coffee bar, coffee shop, estaminet, greasy spoon, restaurant, snack bar, tea-room.

cage *v*. confine, coop up, encage, fence in, immure, impound, imprison, incarcerate, lock up, mew, restrain, shut up.
antonyms free, let out.
n. aviary, coop, corral, enclosure, pen, pound.

cag(e)y *adj*. careful, chary, circumspect, discreet, guarded, non-committal, secretive, shrewd, wary, wily.
antonyms frank, indiscreet, open.

cajole *v*. beguile, blandish, blarney, coax, decoy, dupe, entice, entrap, flatter, fleech, inveigle, lure, manoeuvre, mislead, seduce, soothe, sweet-talk, tempt, wheedle, whillywha(w), wile.
antonyms bully, force.

cajolery *n*. beguilement, blandishments, blarney, coaxing, enticement, flattery, inducement(s), inveigling, persuasion, soft soap, sweet talk, wheedling.
antonyms bullying, force.

cake *v*. bake, cement, coagulate, coat, condense, congeal, consolidate, cover, dry, encrust, harden, inspissate, ossify, solidify, thicken.
n. block, jumbal, loaf, lump, madeleine, mass, slab.

calamitous *adj*. cataclysmic, catastrophic, deadly, devastating, dire, disastrous, dreadful, fatal, ghastly, grievous, pernicious, ruinous, tragic, woeful.
antonyms fortunate, happy.

calamity *n*. adversity, affliction, cataclysm, catastrophe, desolation, disaster, distress, downfall, misadventure, mischance, misfortune, mishap, reverse, ruin, scourge, tragedy, trial, tribulation, woe, wretchedness.
antonyms blessing, godsend.

calculate *v*. aim, cipher, compute, consider, count, determine, enumerate, estimate, figure, gauge, intend, judge, plan, rate, reckon, value, weigh, work out.

calculated *adj*. considered, deliberate, intended, intentional, planned, premeditated, purposed, purposeful, purposive, wilful.
antonyms unintended, unplanned.

calculating *adj*. canny, cautious, contriving, crafty, cunning, designing, devious, Machiavellian, manipulative, politic, scheming, sharp, shrewd, sly.
antonyms artless, naïve, open.

calculation *n*. answer, caution, ciphering, circumspection, computation, deliberation, estimate, estimation, figuring, forecast, foresight, forethought, judgement, planning, precaution, reckoning, result.

calibre *n*. ability, bore, capacity, character, diameter, distinction, endowment, faculty, force, gauge, gifts, league, measure, merit, parts, quality, scope, size, stature, strength, talent, worth.

call *v*. announce, appoint, arouse, assemble, awaken, bid, christen, collect, consider, contact, convene, convoke, cry, declare, decree, denominate, designate, dub, elect, entitle, estimate, gather, hail, halloo, invite, judge, label, muster, name, ordain, order, phone, proclaim, rally, regard, rouse, shout, style, summon, telephone, term, think, waken, yell.

n. announcement, appeal, cause, claim, command, cry, demand, excuse, grounds, hail, invitation, justification, need, notice, occasion, order, plea, reason, request, right, ring, scream, shout, signal, summons, supplication, urge, visit, whoop, yell.

call for[1] demand, entail, involve, necessitate, need, occasion, require, suggest.

call for[2] collect, fetch, pick up, uplift.

call it a day finish, knock off, leave off, pack it in, pack up, shut up shop, stop, throw in the towel.

call off abandon, break off, cancel, desist, discontinue, drop, withdraw.

call on appeal, appeal to, ask, bid, call round, entreat, gam, go and see, invite, invoke, request, summon, supplicate, visit.

call the tune call the shots, command, dictate, give the orders, govern, lead, rule, rule the roost.

calling *n.* business, career, employment, field, job, line, line of country, métier, mission, occupation, profession, province, pursuit, trade, vocation, work.

callous *adj.* case-hardened, cold, hard-bitten, hard-boiled, hardened, hard-hearted, heartless, indifferent, indurated, insensate, insensible, insensitive, inured, obdurate, soulless, thick-skinned, uncaring, unfeeling, unresponsive, unsouled, unsusceptible, unsympathetic.
antonyms kind, sensitive, sympathetic.

callow *adj.* fledgling, green, guileless, immature, inexperienced, jejune, juvenile, naïve, puerile, raw, unfledged, uninitiated, unsophisticated, untried.
antonym experienced.

calm *adj.* balmy, collected, composed, cool, dispassionate, equable, halcyon, impassive, imperturbable, laid back, mild, pacific, passionless, peaceful, placid, quiet, relaxed, restful, sedate, self-collected, self-possessed, serene, smooth, still, stilly, tranquil, unapprehensive, unclouded, undisturbed, unemotional, uneventful, unexcitable, unexcited, unflappable, unflustered, unmoved, unperturbed, unruffled, untroubled, windless.
antonyms excitable, rough, stormy, wild, worried.

v. compose, hush, mollify, pacify, placate, quieten, relax, soothe.
antonyms excite, irritate, worry.

n. calmness, dispassion, hush, peace, peacefulness, quiet, repose, serenity, stillness.
antonyms restlessness, storminess.

calmness *n.* ataraxia, ataraxy, calm, composure, cool, coolness, dispassion, equability, equanimity, hush, impassiveness, impassivity, imperturbability, motionless, peace, peacefulness, placidity, poise, quiet, repose, restfulness, sang-froid, self-possession, serenity, smoothness, stillness, tranquillity, unexcitableness, unflappableness.
antonyms excitability, restlessness, storminess.

calumniate *v.* asperse, backbite, blacken, defame, denigrate, detract, disparage, lampoon, libel, malign, misrepresent, revile, slag, slander, stigmatise, traduce, vilify, vilipend.

calumny *n.* abuse, aspersion, backbiting, calumniation, defamation, denigration, derogation, detraction, disparagement, insult, libel, lying, misrepresentation, obloquy, revilement, slagging, slander, smear, stigma, vilification, vituperation.

camaraderie *n.* brotherhood, brotherliness, companionship, comradeship, esprit de corps, fellowship, fraternisation, good-fellowship, intimacy, togetherness.

camouflage *n.* blind, cloak, concealment, cover, covering, deception, disguise, front, guise, mask, masquerade, screen, subterfuge.
v. cloak, conceal, cover, disguise, hide, mask, obfuscate, obscure, screen, veil.
antonyms reveal, uncover.

camp[1] *adj.* affected, artificial, campy, effeminate, exaggerated, homosexual, mannered, ostentatious, over the top, poncy, posturing, theatrical.

camp[2] *n.* caucus, clique, crowd, faction, group, party, section, set, side.

campaign *n.* attack, crusade, drive, excursion, expedition, jihad, movement, offensive, operation, promotion, push.
v. advocate, attack, crusade, fight, promote, push.

camp-follower *n.* hanger-on, henchman, lackey, lascar, leaguer-lady, leaguer-lass, toady.

can *n.* canister, cannikin, container, jar, jerrycan, pail, receptacle, tin.

canal *n.* waterway, zanja.

cancel *v.* abolish, abort, abrogate, adeem, annul, compensate, counterbalance, countermand, delete, efface, eliminate, erase, expunge, neutralise, nullify, obliterate, offset, quash, redeem, repeal, repudiate, rescind, revoke, scrub, strike.

cancellation *n.* abandoning, abandonment, abolition, ademption, annulment, deletion, elimination, neutralisation, nullifying, quashing, repeal, revocation.

cancer *n.* blight, canker, carcinoma, corruption, evil, growth, malignancy, melanoma, pestilence, rot, sickness, tumour.

candelabrum *n.* candlestick, menorah.

candid *adj.* blunt, clear, fair, forthright, frank, free, guileless, ingenuous, just, open, outspoken, plain, shining, sincere, straightforward, truthful, unbiased, uncontrived, unequivocal, unposed, unprejudiced.
antonyms cagey, devious, evasive.

candidate *n.* applicant, aspirant, claimant, competitor, contender, contestant, doctorand, entrant, nominee, possibility, pretendant, pretender, runner, solicitant, suitor.

candle *n.* cerge, taper, wax-light.
candour *n.* artlessness, directness, fairness, forthrightness, franchise, frankness, guilelessness, honesty, ingenuousness, naïvety, openness, outspokenness, plain-dealing, simplicity, sincerity, straightforwardness, truthfulness, unequivocalness.
antonyms cageyness, deviousness, evasiveness.
cane *n.* ferula, ferule, Malacca-cane, Penang-lawyer, stick, walking-stick.
canker *n.* bane, blight, boil, cancer, corrosion, corruption, infection, lesion, rot, scourge, sore, ulcer.
cannabis *n.* benj, bhang, grass, hash, hashish, marijuana, pot.
cannibal *n.* anthropophagite, man-eater.
cannibalism *n.* anthropophagy, endophagy, exophagy.
canny *adj.* acute, artful, astute, careful, cautious, circumspect, clever, comfortable, gentle, harmless, innocent, judicious, knowing, lucky, perspicacious, prudent, sagacious, sharp, shrewd, skilful, sly, subtle, wise, worldly-wise.
antonyms foolish, imprudent.
canon *n.* catalogue, criterion, dictate, formula, list, precept, principle, regulation, roll, rule, standard, statute, yardstick.
canonical *adj.* accepted, approved, authorised, authoritative, orthodox, recognised, regular, sanctioned.
antonym uncanonical.
canopy *n.* awning, baldachin, covering, dais, shade, sunshade, tabernacle, tester, umbrella.
cant[1] *n.* argot, humbug, hypocrisy, insincerity, jargon, lingo, pretentiousness, sanctimoniousness, slang, thieves' Latin, vernacular.
cant[2] *n.* angle, bevel, incline, jerk, rise, slant, slope, tilt, toss.
cantankerous *adj.* bad-tempered, captious, carnaptious, choleric, contrary, crabbed, crabby, cranky, crotchety, crusty, difficult, disagreeable, feisty, grouchy, grumpy, ill-humoured, ill-natured, irascible, irritable, peevish, perverse, piggish, quarrelsome, testy.
antonyms good-natured, pleasant.
canter *n.* amble, dogtrot, jog, jog-trot, lope.
v. amble, jog, lollop, lope, run.
canvass *v.* agitate, analyse, ask for, campaign, debate, discuss, dispute, electioneer, examine, inspect, investigate, poll, scan, scrutinise, seek, sift, solicit, study.
n. examination, investigation, poll, scrutiny, survey, tally.
canyon *n.* box-canyon, cañon, coulée, gorge, gulch, gully, ravine.
cap *v.* beat, better, complete, cover, crown, eclipse, exceed, excel, finish, outdo, outstrip, surpass, top, transcend.
n. beret, biretta, bonnet, chapka, cowl, fez, hat, shako, skullcap, yarmulka.
capability *n.* ability, capacity, competence, facility, faculty, means, potential, potential-ity, power, proficiency, qualification, skill, talent.
capable *adj.* able, accomplished, adept, adequate, apt, clever, competent, disposed, efficient, experienced, fitted, gifted, intelligent, liable, masterly, predisposed, proficient, qualified, skilful, suited, susceptible, talented.
antonyms incapable, incompetent, useless.
capacious *adj.* ample, big, broad, comfortable, commodious, comprehensive, expansive, extensive, generous, huge, large, liberal, roomy, sizable, spacious, substantial, vast, voluminous, wide.
antonyms cramped, small.
capacity *n.* ability, amplitude, appointment, aptitude, aptness, brains, calibre, capability, cleverness, compass, competence, competency, dimensions, efficiency, extent, facility, faculty, forte, function, genius, gift, intelligence, magnitude, office, position, post, power, province, range, readiness, role, room, scope, service, size, space, sphere, strength, volume.
cape[1] *n.* chersonese, head, headland, ness, peninsula, point, promontory, tongue.
cape[2] *n.* cloak, coat, cope, mantle, pelerine, pelisse, poncho, robe, shawl, wrap.
caper *v.* bounce, bound, capriole, cavort, dance, frisk, frolic, gambol, hop, jump, leap, romp, skip, spring.
n. affair, antic, business, capriole, dido, escapade, gambado, gambol, high jinks, hop, jape, jest, jump, lark, leap, mischief, prank, revel, sport, stunt.
capital[1] *adj.* cardinal, central, chief, controlling, essential, excellent, fine, first, first-rate, foremost, great, important, leading, main, major, overruling, paramount, pre-eminent, primary, prime, principal, splendid, superb, upper-case.
antonyms minor, sad, unfortunate.
capital[2] *n.* assets, cash, finance, finances, financing, fonds, funds, investment(s), means, money, principal, property, resources, stock, wealth, wherewithal.
capitulate *v.* give in, relent, submit, succumb, surrender, throw in the towel/sponge, yield.
antonym fight on.
capitulation *n.* accedence, relentment, submission, surrender, yielding.
caprice *n.* boutade, changeableness, concetto, fad, fancy, fantasia, fantasy, fickleness, fitfulness, freak, humoresque, humour, impulse, inconstancy, notion, quirk, vagary, vapour, whim, whimsy.
capricious *adj.* changeable, crotchety, erratic, fanciful, fickle, fitful, freakish, humorous, impulsive, inconstant, mercurial, odd, queer, quirky, uncertain, unpredictable, variable, wayward, whimsical.
antonyms sensible, steady.
capsize *v.* invert, keel over, overturn, turn over, turn turtle, upset.
capsule *n.* bolus, case, lozenge, module, pericarp, pill, pod, receptacle, sheath, shell,

space-ship, tablet, troche, vessel.
captain *n.* boss, chief, chieftain, commander, head, leader, master, officer, patron, pilot, skip, skipper.
captious *adj.* acrimonious, cantankerous, carping, cavilling, censorious, crabbed, critical, cross, disparaging, exceptious, fault-finding, hypercritical, irritable, nagging, narky, nit-picking, peevish, testy, touchy.
antonyms amiable, good-natured, pleasant.
captivate *v.* allure, attract, beguile, besot, bewitch, charm, dazzle, enamour, enchain, enchant, enrapture, enslave, ensnare, enthrall, entrance, fascinate, hypnotise, infatuate, lure, mesmerise, seduce, win.
antonyms appal, repel.
captivated *adj.* beguiled, besotted, bewitched, crazy, enchanted, épris, infatuated.
captivating *adj.* attractive, beautiful, beguiling, bewitching, catching, dazzling, enchanting.
antonyms ugly, unattractive.
captive *n.* convict, detainee, hostage, internee, prisoner, slave.
adj. caged, confined, enchained, enslaved, ensnared, imprisoned, incarcerated, restricted, secure, subjugated.
antonym free.
captivity *n.* bondage, confinement, custody, detention, durance, duress, enchainment, enthralment, imprisonment, incarceration, internment, restraint, servitude, slavery, thraldom, vassalage.
antonym freedom.
capture *v.* apprehend, arrest, bag, catch, collar, cop, feel someone's collar, lift, nab, secure, seize, snaffle, take.
n. apprehension, arrest, catch, imprisonment, seizure, taking, trapping.
car *n.* auto, autocar, automobile, banger, buggy, crate, drag, dragster, flivver, horseless carriage, hot rod, jalop(p)y, jalopy, machine, motor, motor-car, vehicle, vettura.
carafe *n.* bottle, decanter, flagon, flask, jug, pitcher.
caravan *n.* camel train, kafila.
carbuncle *n.* anthrax, boil, inflammation, pimple, sore.
carcass *n.* body, cadaver, corpse, framework, hulk, relics, remains, shell, skeleton, stiff.
card[1] *n.* dial, domino, map, playing-card, programme.
card[2] *n.* eccentric, person, wag.
cardinal *adj.* capital, central, chief, essential, first, foremost, fundamental, greatest, highest, important, key, leading, main, paramount, pre-eminent, primary, prime, principal.
cardinal *n.* red-hat.
cards *n.* devil's (picture-)books.
care *n.* affliction, anxiety, attention, burden, carefulness, caution, charge, circumspection, concern, consideration, control, custody, direction, disquiet, forethought, guardianship, hardship, heed, interest, keeping, leading-strings, management, meticulous-

ness, ministration, pains, perplexity, pressure, protection, prudence, regard, responsibility, solicitude, stress, supervision, tribulation, trouble, vexation, vigilance, ward, watchfulness, woe, worry.
antonyms carelessness, inattention, thoughtlessness.
care for attend, delight in, desire, enjoy, foster, like, love, mind, nurse, prize, protect, take pleasure in, tend, want, watch over.
career *n.* calling, course, employment, job, life-work, livelihood, occupation, passage, path, procedure, progress, pursuit, race, vocation, walk.
v. bolt, dash, gallop, hurtle, race, run, rush, shoot, speed, tear.
carefree *adj.* airy, blithe, breezy, buoyant, careless, cheerful, cheery, easy-going, happy, happy-go-lucky, insouciant, jaunty, laid-back, light-hearted, lightsome, radiant, sunny, untroubled, unworried.
antonyms anxious, worried.
careful *adj.* accurate, alert, attentive, cautious, chary, circumspect, concerned, conscientious, discreet, fastidious, heedful, judicious, meticulous, mindful, painstaking, particular, precise, protective, prudent, punctilious, scrupulous, softly-softly, solicitous, thoughtful, thrifty, vigilant, wary, watchful.
antonyms careless, inattentive, thoughtless.
carefully *adv.* cautiously, painstakingly, point-device, punctiliously, warily.
antonym carelessly.
careless *adj.* absent-minded, casual, cursory, derelict, forgetful, heedless, hit-or-miss, inaccurate, incautious, inconsiderate, indiscreet, irresponsible, lackadaisical, messy, neglectful, negligent, nonchalant, offhand, perfunctory, regardless, remiss, slap-dash, slipshod, sloppy, thoughtless, uncaring, unconcerned, unguarded, unmindful, unstudied, untenty, unthinking.
antonyms accurate, careful, meticulous, thoughtful.
carelessness *n.* absent-mindedness, heedlessness, inaccuracy, inattention, inconsiderateness, indiscretion, irresponsibility, messiness, neglect, negligence, omission, remissness, slackness, slipshodness, sloppiness, thoughtlessness.
antonyms accuracy, care, thoughtfulness.
caress *v.* canoodle, cuddle, embrace, fondle, hug, kiss, lallygag (lollygag), nuzzle, paw, pet, rub, stroke, touch.
n. cuddle, embrace, fondle, hug, kiss, pat, stroke.
caretaker *n.* concierge, curator, custodian, dvornik, janitor, keeper, porter, superintendent, warden, watchman.
careworn *adj.* exhausted, fatigued, gaunt, haggard, tired, weary, worn, worn-out.
antonyms lively, sprightly.
cargo *n.* baggage, consignment, contents, freight, goods, haul, lading, load, merchandise, pay-load, shipment, tonnage, ware.

caricature *n.* burlesque, cartoon, distortion, farce, lampoon, mimicry, parody, Pasquil, Pasquin, pasquinade, representation, satire, send-up, take-off, travesty.

v. burlesque, distort, lampoon, mimic, mock, parody, pasquinade, ridicule, satirise, send up, take off.

carnage *n.* blood-bath, bloodshed, butchery, havoc, holocaust, massacre, murder, shambles, slaughter.

carnal *adj.* animal, bodily, corporeal, earthly, erotic, fleshly, human, impure, lascivious, lecherous, lewd, libidinous, licentious, lustful, mundane, natural, physical, profane, prurient, salacious, secular, sensual, sensuous, sexual, sublunary, temporal, unchaste, unregenerate, unspiritual, voluptuous, wanton, worldly.

antonyms chaste, pure, spiritual.

carnality *n.* bestiality, brutishness, corporeality, fleshliness, lasciviousness, lechery, lust, lustfulness, prurience, salaciousness, sensuality, voluptuousness, worldliness.

antonyms chastity, purity, spirituality.

carnival *n.* celebration, fair, Fasching, festival, fête, fiesta, gala, holiday, jamboree, jubilee, Mardi Gras, merrymaking, revelry, wassail, wassail-bout, wassailry.

carnivorous *adj.* creophagous, meat-eating, zoophagous.

carol *n.* canticle, canzonet, chorus, ditty, hymn, lay, noel, song, strain, wassail.

carouse *v.* booze, drink, imbibe, quaff, revel, roister, wassail.

n. drinking-bout, party, wassail.

carousing *n.* celebrating, drinking, mallemaroking, party, partying.

carp *v.* cavil, censure, complain, criticise, hypercriticise, knock, nag, quibble, reproach, ultracrepidate.

antonym praise.

carpet *n.* Axminster, kali, mat, rug, Wilton.

carping *adj.* biting, bitter, captious, cavilling, critical, fault-finding, grouchy, hypercritical, nagging, nit-picking, picky, reproachful, Zoilean.

n. censure, complaints, criticism, disparagement, knocking, reproofs, Zoilism.

antonyms compliments, praise.

carriage *n.* air, bearing, behaviour, cab, carrying, coach, comportment, conduct, conveyance, conveying, delivery, demeanour, deportment, freight, gait, manner, mien, posture, presence, transport, transportation, vehicle, vettura, voiture, wagon, wagonette.

carrier *n.* bearer, conveyor, delivery-man, messenger, porter, runner, transmitter, transporter, vector.

carry *v.* accomplish, bear, bring, broadcast, capture, chair, communicate, conduct, convey, display, disseminate, drive, effect, fetch, gain, give, haul, hip, impel, influence, lift, lug, maintain, motivate, move, offer, publish, relay, release, secure, shoulder, spur, stand, stock, suffer, support, sustain, take, tote,

transfer, transmit, transport, underpin, uphold, urge, win.

carry on administer, continue, endure, flirt, last, maintain, manage, misbehave, operate, perpetuate, persevere, persist, proceed, run.

carry out accomplish, achieve, bring off, discharge, do, effect, execute, fulfil, implement, perform, realise.

cart *n.* barrow, buggy, chaise, curricle, float, gig, shay, trap, tray, truck, tumbrel, wagon, wain, wheel-barrow.

v. bear, carry, convey, haul, hump, humph, jag, lug, move, tote, transport.

carton *n.* box, case, container, pack, package, packet, parcel.

cartoon *n.* animation, caricature, comic strip, drawing, lampoon, parody, representation, sketch, take-off.

cartridge *n.* canister, capsule, case, cassette, charge, container, cylinder, magazine, round, shell.

carve *v.* chip, chisel, cut, divide, engrave, etch, fashion, form, grave, hack, hew, incise, indent, make, mould, sculp(t), sculpture, slash, slice, tool, whittle.

carving *n.* bust, dendroglyph, incision, lithoglyph, petroglyph, sculpture, statue, statuette.

cascade *n.* avalanche, cataract, deluge, falls, flood, force, fountain, outpouring, rush, shower, torrent, waterfall, water-works.

antonym trickle.

v. descend, flood, gush, overflow, pitch, plunge, pour, rush, shower, spill, surge, tumble.

case[1] *n.* box, cabinet, canister, capsule, carton, cartridge, casing, casket, chest, compact, container, cover, covering, crate, envelope, étui, folder, holder, integument, jacket, receptacle, sheath, shell, showcase, suit-case, tray, trunk, wrapper, wrapping.

v. encase, enclose, skin.

case[2] *n.* argument, circumstances, condition, context, contingency, dilemma, event, example, illustration, instance, occasion, occurrence, plight, point, position, predicament, situation, specimen, state, thesis.

v. investigate, reconnoitre.

case[3] *n.* action, argument, cause, dispute, lawsuit, proceedings, process, suit, trial.

cash *n.* bank-notes, bread, bullion, change, coin, coinage, currency, dough, funds, hard currency, hard money, money, notes, payment, readies, ready, ready money, resources, specie, wherewithal.

v. encash, liquidate, realise.

cashier[1] *n.* accountant, assistant, banker, bursar, check-out girl, clerk, purser, teller, treasurer.

cashier[2] *v.* break, discard, discharge, dismiss, drum out, expel, sack, unfrock.

cask *n.* barrel, barrico, butt, cade, firkin, hogshead, puncheon, tub, tun, vat, wood.

casket *n.* box, case, chest, coffer, jewel-box, kist, pyxis.

casserole *n.* pot-au-feu, stew-pan.

cast¹ *v.* abandon, add, allot, appoint, assign, bestow, calculate, categorise, choose, chuck, compute, deposit, diffuse, distribute, drive, drop, emit, figure, fling, forecast, form, found, give, hurl, impel, launch, lob, model, mould, name, pick, pitch, project, radiate, reckon, reject, scatter, select, set, shape, shed, shy, sling, spread, throw, thrust, toss, total.

n. air, appearance, complexion, demeanour, fling, form, lob, look, manner, mien, quality, semblance, shade, stamp, style, throw, thrust, tinge, tone, toss, turn.

cast down crush, deject, depress, desolate, discourage, dishearten, dispirit, sadden.

antonyms encourage, lift up.

cast² *n.* actors, artistes, characters, company, dramatis personae, entertainers, performers, players, troupe.

caste *n.* class, degree, estate, grade, lineage, order, position, race, rank, species, station, status, stratum.

castigate *v.* beat, berate, cane, censure, chasten, chastise, chide, correct, discipline, flail, flay, flog, flyte, lash, rebuke, reprimand, scold, scourge, whip.

castle *n.* casbah (kasba, kasbah), château, citadel, donjon, fastness, fortress, keep, mansion, motte and bailey, palace, peel, schloss, stronghold, tower.

castrate *v.* emasculate, evirate, geld, neuter, unman, unsex.

casual *adj.* accidental, apathetic, blasé, chance, contingent, cursory, fortuitous, incidental, indifferent, informal, insouciant, irregular, lackadaisical, negligent, nonchalant, occasional, offhand, perfunctory, random, relaxed, serendipitous, stray, unceremonious, uncertain, unconcerned, unexpected, unforeseen, unintentional, unpremeditated.

antonyms deliberate, painstaking, planned.

casualty *n.* death, injured, injury, loss, sufferer, victim, wounded.

casuistry *n.* chicanery, equivocation, Jesuitism, Jesuitry, sophism, sophistry, speciousness.

cat *n.* feline, gib, grimalkin, malkin, mawkin, mog, moggy, mouser, puss, pussy, tabby.

cataclysm *n.* blow, calamity, catastrophe, collapse, convulsion, debacle (débâcle), devastation, disaster, upheaval.

catacomb *n.* burial-vault, crypt, ossuary, tomb, vault.

catalogue *n.* directory, gazetteer, index, inventory, list, litany, record, register, roll, roster, schedule, table.

v. accession, alphabetise, classify, codify, file, index, inventory, list, record, register.

catapult *v.* heave, hurl, hurtle, launch, pitch, plunge, propel, shoot, throw, toss.

cataract *n.* cascade, deluge, downpour, falls, force, rapids, torrent, waterfall.

catastrophe *n.* adversity, affliction, blow, calamity, cataclysm, conclusion, culmination, curtain, debacle (débâcle), dénouement, devastation, disaster, end, failure, fiasco, finale, ill,

mischance, misfortune, mishap, reverse, ruin, termination, tragedy, trial, trouble, upheaval, upshot, winding-up.

catcall *n.* barracking, boo, gibe, hiss, jeer, raspberry, whistle.

v. barrack, boo, deride, gibe, give (someone) the bird, hiss, jeer, whistle.

catch *v.* apprehend, arrest, benet, bewitch, captivate, capture, charm, clutch, contract, cop, delight, detect, develop, discern, discover, enchant, enrapture, ensnare, entangle, entrap, expose, fascinate, feel, follow, grab, grasp, grip, hear, incur, nab, nail, perceive, recognise, seize, sense, snare, snatch, surprise, take, twig, unmask.

antonyms drop, free, miss.

n. bolt, clasp, clip, detent, disadvantage, drawback, fastener, hasp, hitch, hook, latch, obstacle, parti, snag, sneck, snib, trap, trick.

catch sight of espy, glimpse, notice, recognise, spot, view.

catch up draw level with, gain on, make up leeway, overtake.

catching *adj.* attractive, captivating, charming, communicable, contagious, enchanting, fascinating, fetching, infectious, infective, taking, transferable, transmissible, transmittable, winning, winsome.

antonyms boring, ugly, unattractive.

catchword *n.* byword, catch-phrase, motto, parrot-cry, password, refrain, slogan, watchword.

catchy *adj.* attractive, captivating, confusing, deceptive, haunting, memorable, popular.

antonyms boring, dull.

catechise *v.* cross-examine, drill, examine, grill, instruct, interrogate, question, test.

catechumen *v.* convert, disciple, initiate, learner, neophyte, novice, probationer, proselyte, pupil, tyro.

categorical *adj.* absolute, clear, direct, downright, emphatic, explicit, express, positive, total, unambiguous, unconditional, unequivocal, unqualified, unquestionable, unreserved.

antonyms qualified, tentative, vague.

categorise *v.* class, classify, grade, group, list, order, pigeonhole, rank, sort.

category *n.* chapter, class, classification, department, division, grade, grouping, head, heading, list, order, rank, section, sort, type.

cater *v.* furnish, humour, indulge, outfit, pander, provide, provision, purvey, supply, victual.

caterwaul *v.* bawl, cry, howl, miaow, miaul, scream, screech, shriek, squall, wail, yowl.

catharsis *n.* abreaction, abstersion, cleansing, epuration, lustration, purgation, purging, purification, purifying, release.

cathedral *n.* dome, duomo, minster.

catholic *adj.* all-embracing, all-inclusive, broad, broad-minded, charitable, comprehensive, eclectic, ecumenical, general, global, inclusive, liberal, tolerant, universal, whole, wide, wide-ranging, world-wide.

antonyms narrow, narrow-minded.

cattle *n.* beasts, cows, kine, livestock, neat, nowt, stock.

catty *adj.* back-biting, bitchy, ill-natured, malevolent, malicious, mean, rancorous, spiteful, venomous, vicious.
antonyms kind, pleasant.

caucus *n.* assembly, clique, conclave, convention, gathering, get-together, meeting, parley, session, set.

causative *adj.* factitive, factive, root.

cause *n.* account, agency, agent, aim, attempt, basis, beginning, belief, causation, consideration, conviction, creator, end, enterprise, genesis, grounds, ideal, impulse, incentive, inducement, mainspring, maker, motivation, motive, movement, object, origin, originator, producer, purpose, reason, root, source, spring, stimulus, undertaking.
antonyms effect, result.
v. begin, compel, create, effect, engender, gar, generate, give rise to, incite, induce, motivate, occasion, precipitate, produce, provoke, result in.

caustic *adj.* acidulous, acrid, acrimonious, astringent, biting, bitter, burning, corroding, corrosive, cutting, escharotic, keen, mordant, pungent, sarcastic, scathing, severe, stinging, trenchant, virulent, waspish.
antonyms mild, soothing.

caution *n.* admonition, advice, alertness, care, carefulness, circumspection, counsel, deliberation, discretion, forethought, heed, heedfulness, injunction, prudence, via trita, via tuta, vigilance, wariness, warning, watchfulness.
v. admonish, advise, urge, warn.

cautious *adj.* alert, cagey, careful, chary, circumspect, discreet, Fabian, guarded, heedful, judicious, prudent, scrupulous, softly-softly, tentative, unadventurous, vigilant, wary, watchful.
antonyms heedless, imprudent, incautious.

cautiousness *n.* caginess, care, carefulness, caution, chariness, via trita, via tuta, wariness.
antonym heedlessness.

cavalcade *n.* array, march-past, parade, procession, retinue, spectacle, train, troop.

cavalier *n.* attendant, beau, blade, chevalier, equestrian, escort, gallant, gentleman, horseman, knight, partner, royalist.
adj. arrogant, cavalierish, condescending, curt, disdainful, free-and-easy, gay, haughty, insolent, lofty, lordly, misproud, off-hand, scornful, supercilious, swaggering.

cave *n.* antre, cavern, cavity, den, grotto, hollow, mattamore, pothole.
cave in collapse, fall, give way, slip, subside, yield.

caveat *n.* admonition, alarm, caution, warning.

cavern *n.* cave, cavity, den, grotto, hollow, pothole, vault.

cavernous *adj.* concave, deep, deep-set, echoing, gaping, hollow, resonant, reverberant, sepulchral, sunken, yawning.

cavil *v.* carp, censure, complain, hypercriticise, nit-pick, object, quibble.

n. complaint, criticism, objection, quibble, quiddit, quiddity.

cavilling *adj.* captious, carping, censorious, critical, fault-finding, hypercritical, nit-picking, quibbling, quidditative.

cavity *n.* antrum, belly, caries, crater, dent, gap, hole, hollow, pit, pot-hole, sinus, vacuole, ventricle, well, womb.

cavort *v.* caper, caracole, dance, frisk, frolic, gambol, hop, prance, romp, skip, sport.

cease *v.* call a halt, call it a day, conclude, culminate, desist, die, discontinue, end, fail, finish, halt, pack in, poop out, refrain, stay, stop, terminate.
antonyms begin, start.

ceaseless *adj.* constant, continual, continuous, endless, eternal, everlasting, incessant, indefatigable, interminable, never-ending, nonstop, perennial, perpetual, persistent, unending, unremitting, untiring.
antonyms irregular, occasional.

cede *v.* abandon, abdicate, allow, concede, convey, give up, grant, relinquish, renounce, resign, surrender, transfer, yield.

celebrate *v.* bless, commemorate, commend, emblazon, eulogise, exalt, extol, glorify, honour, keep, laud, live it up, observe, perform, praise, proclaim, publicise, rejoice, reverance, solemnise, toast, wassail, whoop it up.

celebrated *adj.* acclaimed, big, distingué, distinguished, eminent, exalted, famed, famous, glorious, illustrious, lionised, notable, outstanding, popular, pre-eminent, prominent, renowned, revered, well-known.
antonyms obscure, unknown.

celebration *n.* anniversary, carousal, commemoration, festival, festivity, gala, honouring, jollification, jubilee, junketing, merrymake, merrymaking, observance, orgy, party, performance, rave-up, rejoicings, remembrance, revelry, shindig, solemnisation.

celebrity *n.* big name, big shot, bigwig, dignitary, distinction, éclat, eminence, fame, glory, honour, lion, luminary, name, notability, personage, personality, popularity, preeminence, prestige, prominence, renown, reputation, repute, star, stardom, superstar, VIP.
antonyms nobody, obscurity.

celerity *n.* dispatch, expedition, fastness, fleetness, haste, promptness, quickness, rapidity, speed, swiftness, velocity.
antonyms sloth, slowness.

celestial *adj.* angelic, astral, divine, elysian, empyrean, eternal, ethereal, godlike, heavenly, immortal, paradisaic(al), seraphic, spiritual, starry, sublime, supernatural, transcendental.
antonyms earthly, mundane.

celibacy *n.* bachelorhood, chastity, continence, singleness, spinsterhood, virginity.

cell *n.* caucus, cavity, chamber, compartment, coterie, cubicle, dungeon, group, little-ease, nucleus, peter, stall, unit.

cellar *n.* basement, crypt, store-room, vault, wine-store.

cement *v.* attach, bind, bond, cohere, combine, fix together, glue, gum, join, plaster, seal, solder, stick, unite, weld.
n. adhesive, concrete, glue, gum, mortar, paste, plaster, sealant.

cemetery *n.* boneyard, burial-ground, church-yard, God's acre, graveyard, necropolis.

censor *v.* amend, blue-pencil, bowdlerise, cut, edit, expurgate.

censorious *adj.* captious, carping, cavilling, condemnatory, critical, disapproving, disparaging, fault-finding, hypercritical, severe.
antonyms approving, complimentary, laudatory.

censure *n.* admonishment, admonition, blame, castigation, condemnation, criticism, disapproval, obloquy, rebuke, remonstrance, reprehension, reprimand, reproach, reprobation, reproof, stricture, telling-off, vituperation.
antonyms approval, compliments, praise.
v. abuse, admonish, animadvert, berate, blame, castigate, chide, condemn, criticise, decry, denounce, jump on, rebuke, reprehend, reprimand, reproach, reprobate, reprove, scold, slam, tell off, upbraid.
antonyms approve, compliment, praise.

central *adj.* chief, essential, focal, fundamental, important, inner, interior, key, main, mean, median, mid, middle, pivotal, primary, principal, vital.
antonyms minor, peripheral.

centralise *v.* amalgamate, compact, concentrate, condense, converge, gather together, incorporate, rationalise, streamline, unify.
antonym decentralise.

centre *n.* bull's-eye, core, crux, focus, heart, hub, Mecca, mid, middle, mid-point, nave, nucleus, omphalos, pivot.
antonyms edge, outskirts, periphery.
v. cluster, concentrate, converge, focus, gravitate, hinge, pivot, revolve.

centre-piece *n.* cynosure, epergne, focus, highlight, ornament.

centrifugal *adj.* diffusive, divergent, diverging, efferent, radial, radiating, scattering, spreading.
antonym centripetal.

centripetal *adj.* afferent, clustering, concentrating, convergent, converging.
antonym centrifugal.

ceremonial *adj.* dress, formal, liturgical, ritual, ritualistic, solemn, stately.
antonym informal.
n. ceremony, formality, protocol, rite, ritual, solemnity.

ceremonious *adj.* civil, courteous, courtly, deferential, dignified, exact, formal, grand, polite, pompous, precise, punctilious, ritual, solemn, starchy, stately, stiff.
antonyms informal, relaxed, unceremonious.

ceremony *n.* celebration, ceremonial, commemoration, decorum, etiquette, event, form, formality, function, niceties, observance, parade, pomp, propriety, protocol, rite, ritual, service, show, solemnities.

certain *adj.* ascertained, assured, bound, conclusive, confident, constant, convinced, convincing, decided, definite, dependable, destined, determinate, established, express, fated, fixed, incontrovertible, individual, indubitable, ineluctable, inescapable, inevitable, inexorable, irrefutable, known, one, particular, plain, positive, precise, regular, reliable, resolved, satisfied, settled, some, special, specific, stable, steady, sure, true, trustworthy, undeniable, undoubted, unequivocal, unfailing, unmistakable, unquestionable, valid.
antonyms doubtful, hesitant, uncertain, unsure.

certainly *adj.* doubtlessly, naturally, of course, questionless.

certainty *n.* assurance, authoritativeness, certitude, confidence, conviction, fact, faith, indubitableness, inevitability, nap, plerophoria, plerophory, positiveness, reality, sure thing, sureness, surety, trust, truth, validity.
antonyms doubt, hesitation, uncertainty.

certificate *n.* attestation, authorisation, award, credentials, diploma, document, endorsement, guarantee, licence, pass, qualification, testimonial, validation, voucher, warrant.

certify *v.* ascertain, assure, attest, authenticate, authorise, aver, avow, confirm, corroborate, declare, endorse, evidence, guarantee, notify, show, testify, validate, verify, vouch, witness.

certitude *n.* assurance, certainty, confidence, conviction, plerophoria, plerophory.
antonym doubt.

cessation *n.* abeyance, arrest, arresting, break, ceasing, desistance, discontinuance, discontinuation, discontinuing, end, ending, halt, halting, hiatus, intermission, interruption, interval, let-up, pause, recess, remission, respite, rest, standstill, stay, stoppage, stopping, suspension, termination.
antonym commencement.

cession *n.* abandoning, abandonment, abnegation, capitulation, ceding, conceding, concession, conveyance, grant, relinquishing, relinquishment, renouncing, renunciation, surrender, yielding.

chafe *v.* abrade, anger, annoy, enrage, exasperate, fret, fume, gall, get, grate, heat, incense, inflame, irritate, offend, provoke, rage, rasp, rub, scrape, scratch, vex, wear, worry.

chaff *n.* badinage, banter, jesting, jokes, joking, persiflage, raillery, teasing.
v. banter, chip, deride, jeer, laugh at, mock, pull (someone's) leg, rib, ridicule, scoff, taunt, tease.

chagrin *n.* annoyance, discomfiture, discomposure, displeasure, disquiet, dissatisfaction, embarrassment, exasperation, fretfulness, humiliation, indignation, irritation, mortification, peevishness, spleen, vexation.
antonyms delight, pleasure.

v. annoy, displease, disquiet, dissatisfy, embarrass, exasperate, humiliate, irk, irritate, mortify, peeve, vex.

chain *n.* bond, catena, concatenation, coupling, fetter, fob, link, manacle, progression, restraint, sequence, series, set, shackle, string, succession, train, union, vinculum.
v. bind, confine, enslave, fasten, fetter, gyve, handcuff, manacle, restrain, secure, shackle, tether, trammel.
antonyms free, release.

chairman *n.* chair, chairperson, chairwoman, convenor, director, master of ceremonies, MC, president, presider, speaker, spokesman, toastmaster.

chalk up accumulate, achieve, ascribe, attain, attribute, charge, credit, enter, gain, log, mark, record, register, score, tally, win.

chalky *adj.* ashen, calcareous, cretaceous, pale, pallid, powdery, wan, white.

challenge *v.* accost, beard, brave, confront, dare, defy, demand, dispute, impugn, provoke, query, question, stimulate, summon, tax, test, throw down the gauntlet, try.
n. confrontation, dare, defiance, gauntlet, hurdle, interrogation, obstacle, poser, provocation, question, test, trial, ultimatum.

chamber *n.* apartment, assembly, bed-chamber, bedroom, boudoir, camera, cavity, closet, compartment, council, cubicle, enclosure, hall, legislature, parliament, room, vault.

chamberpot *n.* jerry, po, pot, potty.

champion *n.* backer, challenger, conqueror, defender, guardian, hero, kemper, kemperyman, nonpareil, paladin, Palmerin, patron, peer, promachos, protector, Roland, upholder, victor, vindicator, warrior, winner.
v. advocate, back, defend, espouse, maintain, promote, stand up for, support, uphold.

chance *n.* accident, act of God, coincidence, contingency, destiny, fate, fortuity, fortune, gamble, happenstance, hazard, jeopardy, liability, likelihood, luck, misfortune, occasion, odds, opening, opportunity, peril, possibility, probability, prospect, providence, risk, scope, speculation, time, uncertainty.
antonyms certainty, law, necessity.
v. befall, gamble, happen, hazard, occur, risk, stake, transpire, try, venture, wager.
adj. accidental, casual, contingent, fortuitous, inadvertent, incidental, random, serendipitous, unforeseeable, unforeseen, unintended, unintentional, unlooked-for.
antonyms certain, deliberate, intentional.

chancy *adj.* dangerous, dicey, dodgy, fraught, hazardous, problematical, risky, speculative, tricky, uncertain.
antonyms safe, secure.

chandelier *n.* corona, girandole, lustre.

change *v.* alter, alternate, barter, convert, denature, displace, diversify, exchange, fluctuate, interchange, metamorphose, moderate, modify, mutate, reform, remodel, remove, reorganise, replace, restyle, shift, substitute, swap, take liberties with, trade,

transfigure, transform, transmit, transmute, transpose, vacillate, vary, veer.
n. alteration, break, chop, conversion, difference, diversion, exchange, innovation, interchange, metamorphosis, metanoia, modification, mutation, novelty, permutation, revolution, satisfaction, sea-change, shift, substitution, trade, transformation, transition, transmutation, transposition, upheaval, variation, variety, vicissitude.

change of heart metanoia.

changeable *adj.* capricious, chameleonic, changeful, erratic, fickle, fitful, fluid, inconstant, irregular, kaleidoscopic, labile, mercurial, mobile, mutable, protean, shifting, uncertain, unpredictable, unreliable, unsettled, unstable, unsteady, vacillating, variable, vicissitudinous, volatile, wavering, windy.
antonyms constant, reliable, unchangeable.

changeling *n.* elf-child, killcrop.

changing *adj.* different, diverse, fluctuating, fluid, inconstant, kaleidoscopic, mobile, unstable, various, varying.

channel *n.* approach, artery, avenue, canal, chamber, chamfer, communication, conduit, course, duct, euripus, fairway, fleet, flume, fluting, furrow, gat, groove, gullet, gut, gutter, level, main, means, medium, overflow, passage, path, route, sound, start, strait, trough, watercourse, waterway, way.
v. conduct, convey, direct, force, furrow, guide, send, transmit.

chant *n.* carol, chorus, mantra(m), melody, psalm, slogan, song, war-cry.
v. cantillate, carol, chorus, croon, decantate, descant, intone, recite, sing.

chaos *n.* anarchy, bedlam, confusion, disorder, disorganisation, entropy, lawlessness, pandemonium, snafu, tohu bohu, tumult, unreason.
antonym order.

chaotic *adj.* anarchic, confused, deranged, disordered, disorganised, lawless, purposeless, rampageous, riotous, shambolic, snafu, topsy-turvy, tumultous, tumultuary, uncontrolled.
antonyms organised, purposive.

chap *n.* bloke, buffer, character, codger, cove, customer, fellow, guy, individual, Johnny, josser, oik, person, punter, shaver, sort, type.

chapel *n.* bethel, Bethesda, Beulah, church, ebenezer, meeting-house, sacellum.

chaperon *n.* companion, duenna, escort, gooseberry, gouvernante, governess.
v. accompany, attend, escort, guard, matronise, protect, safeguard, shepherd, watch over.

chapter *n.* assembly, branch, chapel, clause, division, episode, part, period, phase, section, stage, topic.

char *v.* brown, burn, carbonise, cauterise, scorch, sear, singe.

character[1] *n.* attributes, bent, calibre, cast, complexion, constitution, disposition, feature, honour, individuality, integrity, kidney, make-up, nature, peculiarity, personality, physiognomy, position, quality, rank, rectitude, reputation, stamp, status, strength, temper, temperament, type, uprightness.

character[2] *n.* card, cove, customer, eccentric, fellow, guy, individual, oddball, oddity, original, part, person, persona, portrayal, role, sort, type.

character[3] *n.* cipher, device, emblem, figure, hieroglyph, ideogram, ideograph, letter, logo, mark, rune, sign, symbol, type.

characterise *v.* brand, distinguish, identify, indicate, inform, mark, represent, stamp, symptomise, typify.

characteristic *adj.* discriminative, distinctive, distinguishing, idiosyncratic, individual, peculiar, representative, singular, special, specific, symbolic, symptomatic, typical, vintage. *antonyms* uncharacteristic, untypical.

n. attribute, faculty, feature, hallmark, idiosyncrasy, lineament, mannerism, mark, peculiarity, property, quality, symptom, thing, trait.

charade *n.* fake, farce, mockery, pantomime, parody, pasquinade, pretence, travesty.

charge *v.* accuse, adjuration, afflict, arraign, ask, assail, assault, attack, behest, bid, blame, burden, command, commit, count, demand, enjoin, entrust, exact, exhort, fill, impeach, incriminate, inculpate, indict, instil, instruct, involve, lade, load, onset, order, require, rush, storm, suffuse, tax, terms.

n. accusation, allegation, amount, assault, attack, burden, care, command, concern, cost, custody, damage, demand, dictate, direction, duty, exhortation, expenditure, expense, imputation, indictment, injunction, instruction, mandate, office, onset, onslaught, order, outlay, payment, precept, price, rate, responsibility, rush, safekeeping, sortie, trust, ward.

charitable *adj.* accommodating, beneficent, benevolent, benign, benignant, bountiful, broad-minded, clement, compassionate, considerate, eleemosynary, favourable, forgiving, generous, gracious, humane, indulgent, kind, kindly, lavish, lenient, liberal, magnanimous, mild, philanthropic, sympathetic, tolerant, understanding. *antonyms* uncharitable, unforgiving.

charity *n.* affection, agape, alms-giving, altruism, assistance, benefaction, beneficence, benevolence, benignity, benignness, bountifulness, bounty, clemency, compassion, endowment, fund, generosity, gift, goodness, hand-out, humanity, indulgence, love, philanthropy, relief, tender-heartedness.

charlatan *n.* cheat, con man, fake, fraud, impostor, mountebank, phoney, pretender, quack, quacksalver, sham, swindler, trickster.

charm *v.* allure, attract, becharm, beguile, bewitch, cajole, captivate, delight, enamour, enchant, enrapture, entrance, fascinate, mesmerise, please, win.

n. abraxas, allure, allurement, amulet, appeal, attraction, attractiveness, desirability, enchantment, fascination, fetish, grisgris, idol, ju-ju, magic, magnetism, medicine, obeah, obi, phylactery, porte-bonheur, sorcery, spell, talisman, trinket, weird.

charming *adj.* appealing, attractive, bewitching, captivating, delectable, delightful, engaging, eye-catching, fetching, honeyed, irresistible, lovely, pleasant, pleasing, seductive, sweet, winning, winsome. *antonyms* ugly, unattractive.

chart *n.* abac, alignment chart, blueprint, diagram, graph, map, nomograph, plan, table, tabulation.

v. delineate, draft, draw, graph, map out, mark, outline, place, plot, shape, sketch.

charter *n.* accreditation, authorisation, bond, concession, contract, deed, document, franchise, indenture, licence, permit, prerogative, privilege, right.

v. authorise, commission, employ, engage, hire, lease, rent, sanction.

chary *adj.* careful, cautious, circumspect, guarded, heedful, leery, prudent, reluctant, slow, suspicious, uneasy, unwilling, wary. *antonyms* heedless, unwary.

chase *v.* course, drive, expel, follow, hunt, hurry, pursue, rush, track.

n. coursing, hunt, hunting, pursuit, race, run, rush, venery.

chasm *n.* abysm, abyss, breach, canyon, cavity, cleft, crater, crevasse, fissure, gap, gorge, gulf, hiatus, hollow, opening, ravine, rent, rift, split, void.

chassis *n.* anatomy, bodywork, bones, frame, framework, fuselage, skeleton, structure, substructure, undercarriage.

chaste *adj.* austere, decent, decorous, elegant, immaculate, incorrupt, innocent, maidenly, modest, moral, neat, pure, refined, restrained, simple, unaffected, undefiled, unsullied, unvulgar, vestal, virginal, virginly, virtuous, wholesome. *antonyms* indecorous, lewd.

chasten *v.* admonish, afflict, castigate, chastise, correct, cow, curb, discipline, humble, humiliate, repress, reprove, soften, subdue, tame.

chastise *v.* beat, berate, castigate, censure, correct, discipline, flog, flyte, lash, punish, reprove, scold, scourge, smack, spank, upbraid, whip.

chastity *n.* abstinence, celibacy, continence, innocence, maidenhood, modesty, purity, restraint, self-restraint, temperateness, virginity, virtue. *antonym* lechery.

chat *n.* chatter, chinwag, confab, coze, crack, gossip, heart-to-heart, natter, rap, talk, tête-à-tête, visit.

v. chatter, chew the fat, crack, gossip, jaw, natter, rabbit (on), talk, visit, yackety-yak.

chatter *n.* babble, blather, blether, chat, gab, gabnash, gossip, jabber, nashgab, natter, prate, prattle, prattlement, tattle, tongue-work, twaddle.

v. babble, blather, blether, chat, clack,

clatter, gab, gossip, jabber, natter, prate, prattle, prittle-prattle, talk like a pen-gun, tattle, twaddle, yackety-yak.

chatterer *n.* big mouth, blabber, blatherskite, bletherskate, chatterbox, gabber, gabnash, gossip, loudmouth, nashgab, pie, prattlebox, windbag.

chattering *adj.* blathering, blethering, clacking, long-tongued, prattling, tattling.

chatty *adj.* colloquial, familiar, friendly, gossipy, informal, long-tongued, newsy, prattling, talkative.

antonym quiet.

chauvinist *adj.* flag-flapping, jingoish, jingoistic, nationalistic, parochial.

cheap *adj.* à bon marché, bargain, base, budget, common, contemptible, cut-price, despicable, dirt-cheap, dog-cheap, economical, economy, inexpensive, inferior, jitney, keen, knock-down, low, low-cost, low-priced, mean, paltry, poor, reasonable, reduced, sale, scurvy, second-rate, shoddy, sordid, tatty, tawdry, uncostly, vulgar, worthless.

antonyms costly, excellent, noble, superior.

cheapen *v.* belittle, debase, degrade, demean, denigrate, depreciate, derogate, devalue, discredit, disparage, downgrade, lower, prostitute.

antonym enhance.

cheat *v.* baffle, bam, bamboozle, beguile, bilk, check, chisel, chouse, cog, con, cozen, deceive, defeat, defraud, deprive, diddle, do, double-cross, dupe, finagle, fleece, fob, foil, fool, frustrate, fudge, grift, gudgeon, gull, gyp, hand (someone) a lemon, hoax, hocus, hoodwink, mislead, prevent, queer, rip off, screw, short-change, skin, smouch, swindle, thwart, touch, trick, trim, victimise.

n. artifice, bilker, charlatan, cheater, chouse, cogger, con man, cozener, deceit, deceiver, deception, dodger, double-crosser, extortioner, fraud, grifter, impostor, imposture, knave, picaroon, rip-off, rogue, shark, sharp, sharper, short-changer, snap, swindle, swindler, trickery, trickster, welsher.

check[1] *v.* compare, confirm, examine, give the once-over, inspect, investigate, monitor, note, probe, research, scrutinise, study, test, verify.

n. audit, examination, inspection, investigation, research, scrutiny, tab, test.

check out examine, investigate, test.

check[2] *v.* arrest, bar, blame, bridle, chide, control, curb, damp, delay, halt, hinder, impede, inhibit, limit, obstruct, pause, rebuke, repress, reprimand, reprove, restrain, retard, scold, stop, thwart.

n. blow, constraint, control, curb, damp, damper, disappointment, frustration, hindrance, impediment, inhibition, limitation, obstruction, rejection, restraint, reverse, setback, stoppage.

check[3] *n.* bill, counterfoil, token.

cheek[1] *n.* audacity, brass, brass neck, brazenness, brazenry, disrespect, effrontery, gall,

impertinence, impudence, insolence, lip, nerve, sauce, temerity.

cheek[2] *n.* chap, face, gena, jowl.

cheeky *adj.* audacious, disrespectful, forward, impertinent, impudent, insolent, insulting, lippy, malapert, pert, saucy.

antonyms polite, respectful.

cheer *v.* acclaim, animate, applaud, brighten, clap, comfort, console, elate, elevate, encheer, encourage, enhearten, enliven, exhilarate, gladden, hail, hearten, hurrah, incite, inspirit, solace, uplift, warm.

antonyms boo, dishearten, jeer.

n. acclamation, animation, applause, bravo, buoyancy, cheerfulness, comfort, gaiety, gladness, glee, hoorah, hopefulness, hurrah, joy, liveliness, merriment, merry-making, mirth, optimism, ovation, plaudits, solace.

cheerful *adj.* animated, blithe, bobbish, bright, bucked, buoyant, canty, cheery, chipper, chirpy, chirrupy, contented, enlivening, enthusiastic, eupeptic, gay, gaysome, genial, glad, gladsome, happy, hearty, jaunty, jolly, jovial, joyful, joyous, light-hearted, lightsome, light-spirited, merry, optimistic, perky, pleasant, sparkling, sprightly, sunny, upbeat, winsome.

antonym sad.

cheerfulness *n.* blitheness, buoyancy, cheeriness, exuberance, gaiety, geniality, gladness, happiness, jauntiness, joyfulness, joyousness, light-heartedness, sprightliness.

antonym sadness.

cheering *adj.* auspicious, bright, comforting, encouraging, heartening, inspiring, promising, propitious, reassuring, stirring.

antonyms depressing, disheartening.

cheerless *adj.* austere, barren, bleak, cold, comfortless, dank, dark, dejected, depressed, desolate, despondent, dingy, disconsolate, dismal, dolorous, drab, dreary, dull, forlorn, gloomy, grim, joyless, lonely, melancholy, miserable, mournful, sad, sombre, sorrowful, sullen, sunless, unhappy, uninviting, winterly, woebegone, woeful.

antonyms bright, cheerful.

cheers *interj.* bottoms up, drink-hail, prosit, skoal, skol, slàinte.

cheery *adj.* blithe, breezy, bright, carefree, cheerful, chipper, gay, good-humoured, happy, jovial, lightsome, light-spirited, lively, merry, pleasant, sparkling, sunny.

antonyms downcast, sad.

chemical *n.* compound, element, substance, synthetic.

cherish *v.* comfort, cosset, encourage, entertain, foster, harbour, make much of, nourish, nurse, nurture, prize, shelter, support, sustain, tender, treasure, value.

cherubic *adj.* adorable, angelic, appealing, cute, heavenly, innocent, lovable, lovely, seraphic, sweet.

chest *n.* ark, box, case, casket, coffer, crate, kist, strongbox, trunk.

chestnut *n.* cliché, vieux jeu, war-horse.

chew *v.* champ, crunch, gnaw, grind, manducate, masticate, munch.

chic *adj.* à la mode, chichi, elegant, fashionable, modish, smart, stylish, trendy.
antonyms out-moded, unfashionable.

chicanery *n.* artifice, cheating, chicane, deception, deviousness, dodge, double-dealing, duplicity, intrigue, jiggery-pokery, sharp practice, skulduggery, sophistry, stratagems, subterfuge, trickery, underhandedness, wiles, wire-pulling.

chick *n.* baby, broad, chicken, girl, girlfriend, peeper.

chicken *n.* chick, chook(ie), chuck(ie), fowl, hen, pullet.

chicken-feed *n.* coppers, peanuts, pennies, pin money, pittance.

chide *v.* admonish, berate, blame, censure, check, criticise, lecture, objurgate, rate, rebuke, reprehend, reprimand, reproach, reprove, scold, tell off, upbraid.
antonym praise.

chief *adj.* capital, cardinal, central, especial, essential, foremost, grand, highest, key, leading, main, outstanding, paramount, predominant, pre-eminent, premier, prevailing, primal, primary, prime, principal, superior, supreme, uppermost, vital.
antonyms junior, minor, unimportant.
n. boss, captain, chieftain, cock of the loft, commander, coryphaeus, director, duke, gaffer, governor, head, kaid, leader, lord, manager, master, paramount, paramount chief, principal, ringleader, ruler, superintendent, superior, supremo, suzerain.

chiefly *adv.* especially, essentially, for the most part, generally, mainly, mostly, predominantly, primarily, principally, usually.

child *n.* babe, baby, bairn, bambino, bantling, brat, chit, dandiprat, descendant, elf, get, git, gyte, infant, issue, juvenile, kid, kiddiewinkie, kiddywink, kinchin, littling, minor, nipper, nursling, offspring, papoose, pickaninny, progeny, shaver, sprog, suckling, toddler, tot, wean, youngling, youngster.

child prodigy wunderkind.

childbirth *n.* accouchement, child-bearing, childbed, confinement, delivery, labour, lying-in, parturition, travail.

childhood *n.* adolescence, babyhood, boyhood, girlhood, immaturity, infancy, minority, schooldays, youth.

childish *adj.* boyish, foolish, frivolous, girlish, hypocoristic, hypocoristical, immature, infantile, juvenile, puerile, silly, simple, trifling, weak, young.
antonyms adult, sensible.

childlike *adj.* artless, credulous, guileless, ingenuous, innocent, naive, natural, simple, trustful, trusting.

children *n.* line, offspring, progeny.

chill *adj.* aloof, biting, bleak, chilly, cold, cool, depressing, distant, freezing, frigid, hostile, parky, raw, sharp, stony, unfriendly, unresponsive, unwelcoming, wintry.

antonyms friendly, warm.
v. congeal, cool, dampen, depress, discourage, dishearten, dismay, freeze, frighten, refrigerate, terrify.
n. bite, cold, coldness, coolness, coolth, crispness, frigidity, nip, rawness, sharpness.

chilly *adj.* aloof, blowy, breezy, brisk, cold, cool, crisp, draughty, fresh, frigid, hostile, nippy, parky, penetrating, sharp, stony, unfriendly, unresponsive, unsympathetic, unwelcoming.
antonyms friendly, warm.

chime *v.* clang, dong, jingle, mark, peal, ping, ring, sound, strike, tell, ting, tinkle, tintinnabulate, toll.

chimera *n.* bogy, delusion, dream, fancy, fantasy, figment, hallucination, idle fancy, ignis fatuus, illusion, monster, monstrosity, snare, spectre, will-o'-the-wisp.

chimeric *adj.* chimerical, delusive, fabulous, fanciful, fantastic, hallucinatory, illusive, illusory, imaginary, quixotic, unfounded, unreal, vain, visionary, whimsical, wild.
antonym real.

chimney *n.* cleft, crevice, femerall, funnel, lum, shaft, vent.

chimpanzee *n.* ape, jocko, pongo.

china *adj.* ceramic, earthenware, porcelain, pottery, terracotta, wally.

chink[1] *n.* aperture, cleft, crack, crevice, cut, fissure, flaw, gap, opening, rift, slot, space.

chink[2] *n.* clink, ding, jangle, jingle, ping, ring, ting, tinkle.

chip *n.* dent, flake, flaw, fragment, nick, notch, paring, scrap, scratch, shard, shaving, sliver, spall, wafer.
v. chisel, damage, gash, nick, notch, spall, whittle.

chip in contribute, donate, interpose, interrupt, participate, pay, subscribe.

chiropodist *n.* pedicurist.

chiropody *n.* pedicure.

chirp *v., n.* cheep, chirrup, peep, pipe, tweet, twitter, warble, whistle.

chirpy *adj.* blithe, bright, cheerful, cheery, chipper, gay, happy, jaunty, merry, perky, sunny.
antonyms downcast, sad.

chivalrous *adj.* bold, brave, chivalric, courageous, courteous, courtly, gallant, gentlemanly, Grandisonian, heroic, honourable, knightly, polite, true, valiant.
antonyms cowardly, ungallant.

chivalry *n.* boldness, bravery, courage, courtesy, courtliness, gallantry, gentlemanliness, knight-errantry, knighthood, politeness.

chivvy *v.* badger, harass, hassle, hound, importune, nag, pester, plague, pressure, prod, torment.

choice *n.* alternative, choosing, decision, dilemma, discrimination, election, espousal, opting, option, pick, preference, say, selection, variety.
adj. best, dainty, elect, élite, excellent, exclusive, exquisite, hand-picked, nice, plum, precious, prime, prize, rare, select, special,

superior, uncommon, unusual, valuable.
antonym inferior.

choke *v.* asphyxiate, bar, block, clog, close, congest, constrict, dam, gag, obstruct, occlude, overpower, reach, retch, smother, stifle, stop, strangle, suffocate, suppress, throttle.

choleric *adj.* angry, bad-tempered, crabbed, crabby, crotchety, fiery, hasty, hot, hot-tempered, ill-tempered, irascible, irritable, petulant, quick-tempered, testy, touchy.
antonyms calm, placid.

choose *v.* adopt, cull, designate, desire, elect, espouse, fix on, opt for, pick, plump for, predestine, prefer, see fit, select, settle on, single out, take, vote for, wish.

choosing *n.* proairesis.

choosy *adj.* discriminating, exacting, faddy, fastidious, fikish, fiky, finicky, fussy, particular, picky, selective.
antonym undemanding.

chop *v.* cleave, cut, divide, fell, hack, hew, lop, sever, shear, slash, slice, truncate.
chop up cube, cut up, dice, divide, fragment, mince, slice (up).

choppy *adj.* blustery, broken, rough, ruffled, squally, stormy, tempestuous, wavy, white.
antonym calm.

chore *n.* burden, duty, errand, fag, job, stint, task, trouble.

chortle *v.* cackle, chuckle, crow, guffaw, laugh, snigger.

chorus *n.* burden, call, choir, choristers, ensemble, refrain, response, shout, singers, strain, vocalists.

chosen *adj.* elect, élite, peculiar, predilect, predilected, selected.

christen *v.* baptise, besprinkle, call, designate, dub, inaugurate, name, sprinkle, style, term, title, use.

Christmas *n.* Noel (Nowell), Xmas, Yule, Yuletide.

chronic *adj.* appalling, atrocious, awful, confirmed, deep-rooted, deep-seated, dreadful, habitual, incessant, incurable, ineradicable, ingrained, inveterate, persistent, terrible.
antonym temporary.

chronicle *n.* account, annals, chanson de geste, diary, epic, gest(e), history, journal, narrative, record, register, saga, story.
v. enter, list, narrate, record, recount, register, relate, report, tell, write down.

chronicler *n.* annalist, chronographer, chronologer, diarist, historian, historiographer, narrator, recorder, reporter, scribe.

chronological *adj.* consecutive, historical, ordered, progressive, sequential.

chubby *adj.* buxom, flabby, fleshy, paunchy, plump, podgy, portly, rotund, round, stout, tubby.
antonyms skinny, slim.

chuck *v.* cast, discard, fling, heave, hurl, jettison, pitch, reject, shy, sling, throw, toss.

chuckle *v.* chortle, crow, exult, giggle, laugh, snigger, snort, titter.

chum *n.* china, cobber, companion, comrade, crony, friend, mate, pal.
antonym enemy.

chummy *adj.* affectionate, close, friendly, intimate, matey, pally, sociable, thick.

chunk *n.* block, chuck, dod, dollop, hunk, lump, mass, piece, portion, slab, wad, wodge.

chunky *adj.* beefy, brawny, dumpy, fat, square, stocky, stubby, thick, thickset.
antonym slim.

church *n.* basilica, bethel, Bethesda, Beulah, cathedral, house of God, house of prayer, kirk, minster, preaching-house, steeple-house.
adj. ecclesiastic, ecclesiastical, ecclesiological.

churl *n.* boor, bumpkin, clodhopper, clown, curmudgeon, hill-billy, labourer, lout, oaf, peasant, rustic, yokel.

churlish *adj.* boorish, brusque, crabbed, doggish, harsh, ill-tempered, impolite, loutish, morose, oafish, rude, sullen, surly, uncivil, unmannerly, unneighbourly, unsociable, vulgar.
antonyms polite, urbane.

churn *v.* agitate, beat, boil, convulse, foam, froth, knot, seethe, swirl, toss, writhe.

chute *n.* channel, funnel, gutter, incline, ramp, runway, shaft, slide, slope, trough.

cigarette *n.* cancer-stick, cig, ciggy, coffin-nail, fag, gasper, joint, smoke, snout, whiff.

cinch *n.* doddle, piece of cake, snip, stroll, walk-over.

cinema *n.* big screen, filmhouse, flicks, movies, picture-house, picture-palace.

cipher *n.* character, code, cryptograph, device, digit, figure, logo, mark, monogram, nil, nobody, nonentity, nothing, nought, number, numeral, symbol, yes-man, zero.

circle *n.* area, assembly, band, bounds, circuit, circumference, class, clique, club, coil, company, compass, cordon, coterie, crowd, cycle, disc, domain, enclosure, fellowship, field, fraternity, globe, group, gyre, lap, loop, orb, orbit, perimeter, periphery, province, range, realm, region, revolution, ring, round, roundance, roundel, roundlet, rundle, scene, school, set, society, sphere, turn.
v. belt, circumambulate, circumnavigate, circumscribe, coil, compass, curl, curve, encircle, enclose, encompass, envelop, gird, girdle, hem in, loop, pivot, revolve, ring, rotate, surround, tour, whirl.

circling *adj.* eddying, vortical, wheeling, whirling.

circuit *n.* ambit, area, boundary, bounds, circumference, compass, course, district, eyre, journey, limit, orbit, perambulation, range, region, revolution, round, route, tour, track, tract.

circuitous *adj.* ambagious, anfractuous, cagey, devious, indirect, labyrinthine, meandering, oblique, periphrastic, rambling, roundabout, tortuous, winding.
antonyms direct, straight.

circular *adj.* annular, discoid(al), disc-shaped,

hoop-shaped, ring-shaped, round.

n. advert, announcement, handbill, leaflet, letter, notice, pamphlet.

circulate *v.* broadcast, diffuse, disseminate, distribute, flow, go around, go the rounds, gyrate, issue, promulgate, propagate, publicise, publish, radiate, revolve, rotate, spread, spread abroad, swirl, whirl.

circulation *n.* blood-flow, circling, currency, dissemination, distribution, flow, motion, rotation, spread, spreading, transmission.

circumference *n.* border, boundary, bounds, circuit, edge, extremity, fringe, limits, margin, outline, perimeter, periphery, rim, verge.

circumlocution *n.* diffuseness, discursiveness, euphemism, indirectness, periphrasis, prolixity, redundancy, roundaboutness, wordiness.

circumscribe *v.* bound, confine, curtail, define, delimit, delineate, demarcate, encircle, enclose, encompass, environ, hem in, limit, pen in, restrain, restrict, surround, trim.

circumspect *adj.* attentive, canny, careful, cautious, chary, deliberate, discreet, discriminating, guarded, heedful, judicious, leery, observant, politic, sagacious, sage, vigilant, wary, watchful.

antonyms unguarded, unwary.

circumspection *n.* canniness, care, caution, chariness, deliberation, discretion, guardedness, prudence, wariness.

circumstance *n.* accident, condition, contingency, detail, element, event, fact, factor, happening, happenstance, incident, item, occurrence, particular, position, respect, situation.

circumstances *n.* conditions, galère, lifestyle, means, position, resources, situation, state, state of affairs, station, status, times.

circumstantial *adj.* conjectural, contingent, detailed, evidential, exact, hearsay, incidental, indirect, inferential, minute, particular, presumptive, provisional, specific.

antonyms hard, inexact, vague.

circumvent *v.* beguile, bypass, deceive, dupe, elude, ensnare, entrap, evade, get out of, get past, hoodwink, mislead, outflank, outgeneral, outwit, overreach, sidestep, steer clear of, thwart, trick.

circumvention *n.* bypassing, chicanery, deceit, deception, dodge, duplicity, evasion, fraud, guile, imposition, imposture, thwarting, trickery, wiles.

cistern *n.* basin, pool, reservoir, sink, tank, vat.

citadel *n.* acropolis, bastion, castle, fortification, fortress, keep, stronghold, tower.

citation *n.* award, commendation, cutting, excerpt, illustration, mention, passage, quotation, quote, reference, source.

cite *v.* accite, adduce, advance, call, enumerate, evidence, extract, mention, name, quote, specify, subpoena, summon.

citizen *n.* burgess, burgher, city-dweller, denizen, dweller, freeman, inhabitant, oppidan, ratepayer, resident, subject, townsman, urbanite.

city *n.* conurbation, megalopolis, metropolis, municipality, town.

civic *adj.* borough, city, communal, community, local, municipal, oppidan, public, urban.

civil *adj.* accommodating, affable, civic, civilised, complaisant, courteous, courtly, domestic, home, interior, internal, internecine, lay, municipal, obliging, polished, polite, political, refined, secular, temporal, urbane, well-bred, well-mannered.

antonym uncivil.

civil servant bureaucrat, fonctionnaire.

civilisation *n.* advancement, cultivation, culture, development, education, enlightenment, kultur, progress, refinement, sophistication, urbanity.

antonyms barbarity, primitiveness.

civilise *v.* ameliorate, cultivate, educate, enlighten, humanise, improve, meliorate, perfect, polish, refine, sophisticate, tame.

civilised *adj.* advanced, cultured, educated, enlightened, humane, polite, refined, sophisticated, tolerant, urbane.

antonyms barbarous, primitive.

civility *n.* affability, amenity, amiability, attention, breeding, comity, complaisance, cordiality, courteousness, courtesy, graciousness, politeness, politesse, tact, urbanity.

antonyms rudeness, uncouthness.

claim *v.* affirm, allege, arrogate, ask, assert, challenge, collect, demand, exact, hold, insist, maintain, need, profess, request, require, state, take, uphold.

n. affirmation, allegation, application, assertion, call, demand, insistence, petition, pretension, privilege, protestation, request, requirement, right, title.

claimant *n.* applicant, petitioner, pretendant, pretender, suppliant, supplicant.

clairvoyant *adj.* extra-sensory, fey, oracular, prescient, prophetic, psychic, second-sighted, sibylline, telepathic, vatic, visionary.

n. augur, diviner, fortune-teller, haruspex, oracle, prophet, prophetess, seer, sibyl, soothsayer, spaeman, spaer, spaewife, telepath, telepathist, visionary.

clamber *v.* ascend, claw, climb, crawl, descend, scale, scrabble, scramble, shin.

clammy *adj.* close, damp, dank, heavy, moist, muggy, pasty, slimy, sticky, sweating, sweaty, viscid.

clamorous *adj.* blaring, deafening, insistent, lusty, noisy, riotous, tumultuous, uproarious, vehement, vociferant, vociferous.

antonym silent.

clamour *n.* agitation, babel, blare, brouhaha, commotion, complaint, din, exclamation, hubbub, hue, hullabaloo, katzenjammer, noise, outcry, racket, shout, shouting, uproar, vociferation.

antonym silence.

clamp *n.* brace, bracket, fastener, grip, press, vice.

v. brace, clinch, fasten, fix, impose, secure.

clan *n.* band, brotherhood, clique, confraternity,

coterie, faction, family, fraternity, gens, group, house, phratry, race, sect, sept, set, society, sodality, tribe.

clandestine *adj.* backroom, behind-door, cloak-and-dagger, closet, concealed, covert, fraudulent, furtive, hidden, private, secret, sly, sneaky, stealthy, subreptitious, surreptitious, underground, underhand, under-the-counter.
antonym open.

clandestinely *adv.* covertly, furtively, on the q.t., on the quiet, quietly, secretly, surreptitiously.

clang *v.* bong, chime, clank, clash, jangle, peal, resound, reverberate, ring, toll.
n. bong, clank, clash, clatter, jangle, peal.

clannish *adj.* cliqu(e)y, cliquish, close, exclusive, insular, narrow, parochial, sectarian, select, unfriendly.
antonyms friendly, open.

clap *v.* acclaim, applaud, bang, cheer, pat, slap, smack, thrust, thwack, wallop, whack.

claptrap *n.* affectation, balderdash, blarney, bombast, bunk, bunkum, codswallop, drivel, flannel, guff, hokum, hot air, humbug, nonsense, rodomontade, rubbish, tripe.

clarification *n.* definition, elucidation, explanation, exposition, gloss, illumination, interpretation, simplification.
antonym obfuscation.

clarify *v.* cleanse, define, elucidate, explain, gloss, illuminate, purify, refine, resolve, shed/throw light on, simplify.
antonym obscure.

clarity *n.* clearness, comprehensibility, definition, explicitness, intelligibility, limpidity, lucidity, lucidness, obviousness, precision, simplicity, transparency, unambiguousness.
antonyms obscurity, vagueness.

clash *v.* bang, clang, clank, clatter, conflict, crash, disagree, feud, fight, grapple, jangle, jar, quarrel, rattle, war, wrangle.
n. brush, clank, clatter, collision, conflict, confrontation, disagreement, fight, jangle, jar, noise, show-down.

clasp *n.* agraffe, brooch, buckle, catch, clip, embrace, fastener, fastening, grasp, grip, hasp, hold, hook, hug, pin, snap, tach(e).
v. attach, clutch, concatenate, connect, embrace, enclasp, enfold, fasten, grapple, grasp, grip, hold, hug, press, seize, squeeze.

class[1] *n.* calibre, caste, category, classification, collection, denomination, department, description, division, genre, genus, grade, group, grouping, ilk, kidney, kind, kingdom, league, order, phylum, quality, rank, section, set, sort, species, sphere, status, style, taxon, type, value.
v. assort, brand, categorise, classify, codify, designate, grade, group, rank, rate.

class[2] *n.* course, lecture, seminar, teach-in, tutorial.

classic *adj.* abiding, ageless, archetypal, Augustan, best, characteristic, chaste, consummate, deathless, definitive, enduring, established, excellent, exemplary, finest, first-rate, ideal, immortal, lasting, master, masterly, model,

paradigmatic, quintessential, refined, regular, restrained, standard, time-honoured, traditional, typical, undying, usual.
antonym second-rate.
n. chef d'oeuvre, exemplar, masterpiece, masterwork, model, paradigm, pièce de résistance, prototype, standard.

classical *adj.* attic, Attic, Augustan, chaste, elegant, established, excellent, grecian, Greek, harmonious, Hellenic, Latin, pure, refined, restrained, Roman, standard, symmetrical, traditional, well-proportioned.

classification *n.* analysis, arrangement, cataloguing, categorisation, codification, digestion, grading, pigeon-holing, sorting, taxis, taxonomy.

classify *v.* arrange, assort, catalogue, categorise, codify, digest, dispose, distribute, file, grade, pigeon-hole, rank, sort, systematise, tabulate.

classy *adj.* elegant, exclusive, exquisite, fine, gorgeous, grand, high-class, posh, select, stylish, superior, swanky, up-market.
antonyms dowdy, plain, unstylish.

clause *n.* article, chapter, condition, demand, heading, item, paragraph, part, passage, point, provision, proviso, section, specification, stipulation, subsection.

claw *n.* griff(e), gripper, nail, nipper, pincer, pounce, talon, tentacle, unguis.
v. dig, graze, lacerate, mangle, maul, rip, scrabble, scrape, scratch, tear.

clean *adj.* antiseptic, chaste, clarified, complete, conclusive, decent, decisive, decontaminated, delicate, elegant, entire, exemplary, faultless, final, flawless, fresh, good, graceful, guiltless, honest, honourable, hygienic, immaculate, innocent, laundered, moral, natural, neat, perfect, pure, purified, respectable, sanitary, simple, spotless, sterile, sterilised, thorough, tidy, total, trim, umblemished, unadulterated, uncluttered, uncontaminated, undefiled, unimpaired, unpolluted, unsoiled, unspotted, unstained, unsullied, upright, virtuous, washed, whole.
antonyms dirty, indecent, polluted, unsterile.
v. bath, cleanse, deodorise, deterge, disinfect, dust, launder, lave, mop, purge, purify, rinse, sanitise, scour, scrub, sponge, swab, sweep, vacuum, wash, wipe.
antonyms defile, dirty.

clean up sanitise, tidy, wash.

cleaner *n.* char, charlady, charwoman, daily.

cleanse *v.* absolve, absterge, catharise, clean, clear, deterge, detoxicate, detoxify, lustrate, purge, purify, rinse, scavenge, scour, scrub, wash.
antonyms defile, dirty.

cleanser *n.* abstergent, detergent, detersive, disinfectant, purifier, scourer, scouring-powder, soap, solvent.

cleansing *n.* abstersion, detergence, detergency, detersion.
adj. abstergent, abstersive, cathartic(al), detergent, detersive, purgative, purgatory.

clear *adj.* apparent, audible, bright, certain,

clean, cloudless, coherent, comprehensible, conspicuous, convinced, crystalline, decided, definite, diaphanous, disengaged, distinct, eidetic, empty, evident, explicit, express, fair, fine, free, glassy, guiltless, halcyon, hyaline, immaculate, incontrovertible, innocent, intelligible, light, limpid, lucid, luculent, luminous, manifest, obvious, open, palpable, patent, pellucid, perceptible, perspicuous, plain, positive, pronounced, pure, recognisable, resolved, satisfied, see-through, serene, sharp, shining, smooth, stainless, sunny, sure, translucent, transparent, unambiguous, unblemished, unclouded, undefiled, undimmed, undulled, unequivocal, unhampered, unhindered, unimpeded, unlimited, unmistakable, unobstructed, unquestionable, untarnished, untroubled, well-defined.
antonyms cloudy, fuzzy, guilty, vague.

v. absolve, acquire, acquit, brighten, clarify, clean, cleanse, decode, decongest, deoppilate, disengage, disentangle, earn, emancipate, erase, excuse, exonerate, extricate, fix, free, gain, jump, justify, leap, liberate, lighten, loosen, make, miss, open, pass over, purify, reap, refine, rid, secure, strip, tidy, unblock, unclog, uncloud, unload, unpack, unscramble, vault, vindicate, wipe.
antonyms block, condemn, defile, dirty.

clear out beat it, clear off, decamp, depart, empty, exhaust, leave, retire, sort, throw out, withdraw.

clear up answer, clarify, elucidate, explain, fix, order, rearrange, remove, resolve, solve, sort, tidy, unravel.

clearance *n.* allowance, authorisation, consent, endorsement, gap, go-ahead, headroom, leave, margin, OK, permission, riddance, sanction, space, the green light.

clear-cut *adj.* clear, definite, distinct, explicit, plain, precise, specific, straightforward, unambiguous, unequivocal, well-defined.
antonyms ambiguous, vague.

clearing *n.* dell, glade, hollow, opening, space.
adj. deobstruent.

clearly *adv.* distinctly, evidently, incontestably, incontrovertibly, manifestly, markedly, obviously, openly, plainly, undeniably, undoubtedly.
antonyms indistinctly, vaguely.

clearness *n.* audibility, brightness, clarity, coherence, distinctness, explicitness, glassiness, intelligibility, limpidity, lucidity, lucidness, luminosity, transparency, transparentness, unambiguousness.

cleave[1] *v.* adhere, attach, cling, cohere, hold, remain, stick, unite.

cleave[2] *v.* chop, crack, dissever, disunite, divide, halve, hew, open, part, pierce, rend, rive, separate, sever, slice, split, sunder.
antonyms join, unite.

cleft *n.* breach, break, chasm, chink, crack, cranny, crevice, fissure, fracture, gap, opening, rent, split.
adj. cloven, divided, parted, rent, riven,

ruptured, separated, split, sundered, torn.
antonym solid.

clemency *n.* compassion, forebearance, forgiveness, generosity, humanity, indulgence, kindness, lenience, leniency, lenity, magnanimity, mercifulness, mercy, mildness, moderation, soft-heartedness, tenderness.
antonyms harshness, ruthlessness.

clement *adj.* balmy, calm, compassionate, fair, fine, forbearing, forgiving, generous, gentle, humane, indulgent, kind, kind-hearted, lenient, magnanimous, merciful, mild, soft-hearted, temperate, tender.
antonyms harsh, ruthless.

clench *v.* clasp, close, clutch, double, grasp, grip, grit, hold.

clergy *n.* churchmen, clergymen, clerics, ecclesiastics, ministry, presbyterate, priesthood, the church, the cloth.

clergyman *n.* chaplain, churchman, cleric, curate, deacon, dean, divine, father, levite, man of God, minister, padre, parson, pastor, presbyter, priest, rabbi, rector, reverend, sky-pilot, vicar.

clerical *adj.* ecclesiastical, pastoral, priestly, sacerdotal.

clerk *n.* account-keeper, assistant, copyist, official, pen-driver, pen-pusher, protocolist, quill-driver, quillman, receptionist, shop-assistant, writer.

clever *adj.* able, adroit, apt, astute, brainy, bright, canny, capable, cunning, deep, dexterous, discerning, elegant, expert, gifted, gleg, good-natured, habile, ingenious, intelligent, inventive, keen, knowing, knowledgeable, quick, quick-witted, rational, resourceful, sagacious, sensible, shrewd, skilful, smart, talented, witty.
antonyms foolish, naïve, senseless.

clever dick smart Alec, smart-ass, smarty-pants, wiseling, witling, wit-monger.

cleverness *n.* ability, adroitness, astuteness, brains, brightness, canniness, cunning, dexterity, flair, gift, gumption, ingenuity, intelligence, nous, quickness, resourcefulness, sagacity, sense, sharpness, shrewdness, smartness, smeddum, talent, wit.
antonyms foolishness, naïvety, senselessness.

cliché *n.* banality, bromide, chestnut, penny-a-lineism, platitude, stereotype, tag, truism.

click *n., v.* beat, clack, snap, snick, snip, tick.

client *n.* applicant, buyer, consumer, customer, dependant, habitué, patient, patron, protégé, shopper.

clientèle *n.* business, clients, customers, following, market, patronage, patrons, regulars, trade.

cliff *n.* bluff, crag, escarpment, face, overhang, precipice, rock-face, scar, scarp.

climactic *adj.* climactical, critical, crucial, decisive, exciting, orgasmic, orgastic, paramount.
antonyms bathetic, trivial.

climate *n.* ambience, atmosphere, clime, country, disposition, feeling, milieu, mood, region, setting, temper, temperature, tendency, trend, weather.

climax *n.* acme, apogee, culmination, head, height, high point, highlight, orgasm, peak, summit, top, zenith.

antonyms bathos, low point, nadir.

climb *v.* ascend, clamber, mount, rise, scale, shin up, soar, swarm (up), top.

climb down back down, clamber down, descend, dismount, eat crow, eat one's words, retract, retreat.

clinch *v.* assure, bolt, cap, clamp, conclude, confirm, cuddle, decide, determine, embrace, fasten, fix, grasp, hug, nail, neck, rivet, seal, secure, settle, squeeze, verify.

cling *v.* adhere, clasp, cleave, clutch, embrace, fasten, grasp, grip, hug, stick.

clinical *adj.* analytic, business-like, cold, detached, disinterested, dispassionate, emotionless, impersonal, objective, scientific, unemotional.

antonyms biased, subjective.

clip[1] *v.* crop, curtail, cut, dock, pare, poll, pollard, prune, shear, shorten, snip, trim.

clip[2] *v.* box, clobber, clout, cuff, hit, knock, punch, skelp, slap, smack, sock, thump, wallop, whack.

n. blow, box, clout, cuff, hit, knock, punch, skelp, slap, smack, sock, thump, wallop, whack.

clip[3] gallop, lick, rate, speed.

clip[4] *v.* attach, fasten, fix, hold, pin, staple.

clipping *adj.* citation, cutting, excerpt, extract, piece.

clique *n.* bunch, circle, clan, coterie, crew, crowd, faction, gang, group, mates, mob, pack, set.

cloak *n.* blind, cape, coat, cover, front, mantle, mask, pretext, shield, wrap.

v. camouflage, conceal, cover, disguise, hide, mask, obscure, screen, veil.

clodhopper *n.* booby, boor, bumpkin, galoot, lout, lummox, lumpkin, oaf, ox, yokel.

clog *v.* ball, block, burden, congest, dam up, gaum, hamper, hinder, impede, jam, obstruct, occlude, shackle, stop up, stuff.

antonym unblock.

n. burden, dead-weight, drag, encumbrance, hindrance, impediment, obstruction.

cloistered *adj.* cloistral, confined, enclosed, hermitic, insulated, protected, reclusive, restricted, secluded, sequestered, sheltered, shielded, withdrawn.

antonyms open, urbane.

close[1] *v.* bar, block, cease, choke, clog, cloture, complete, conclude, confine, connect, cork, couple, culminate, discontinue, end, fill, finish, fuse, grapple, join, lock, mothball, obstruct, plug, seal, secure, shut, stop, terminate, unite, wind up.

n. cadence, cessation, completion, conclusion, culmination, denouement, end, ending, finale, finish, junction, pause, stop, termination, wind-up.

close[2] *adj.* accurate, adjacent, adjoining, airless, alert, approaching, approximative, assiduous, at hand, attached, attentive, careful, compact, concentrated, confidential, confined, congested, conscientious, cramped, cropped, crowded, dear, dense, detailed, devoted, dogged, earnest, exact, faithful, familiar, fixed, frowsty, fuggy, handy, hard by, heavy, hidden, humid, illiberal, imminent, impending, impenetrable, inseparable, intense, intent, intimate, jam-packed, keen, literal, loving, mean, mingy, minute, miserly, muggy, narrow, near, near-by, neighbouring, niggardly, nigh, oppressive, packed, painstaking, parsimonious, penurious, precise, private, reserved, reticent, retired, rigorous, searching, secluded, secret, secretive, short, solid, stale, stifling, stingy, strict, stuffy, suffocating, sweltering, taciturn, thick, thorough, tight, tight-fisted, uncommunicative, unforthcoming, ungenerous, unventilated.

antonyms careless, cool, far, unfriendly.

closed *adj.* concluded, decided, ended, exclusive, fastened, finished, locked, over, resolved, restricted, sealed, settled, shut, terminated, wound-up.

antonyms open, unfastened, unsettled.

closure *n.* cap, cessation, closing, cloture, conclusion, end, finish, guillotine, lid, plug, seal, stoppage, stopper, stricture, winding-up.

antonym opening.

clot[1] *n.* clotting, coagulation, curdling, embolism, embolus, gob, grume, lump, mass, occlusion, thrombus.

v. coagulate, coalesce, congeal, curdle, jell, thicken.

clot[2] *n.* ass, buffoon, dolt, dope, dunderhead, fathead, fool, idiot, nincompoop, nit, nitwit, numbskull, twerp.

cloth *n.* dish-cloth, duster, fabric, face-cloth, material, rag, stuff, textiles, tissue, towel.

clothe *v.* accoutre, apparel, array, attire, bedizen, caparison, cover, deck, drape, dress, enclothe, endow, enwarp, equip, garb, habilitate, habit, invest, outfit, rig, robe, swathe, vest.

antonyms unclothe, undress.

clothes *n.* apparel, attire, clobber, clothing, costume, dress, duds, ensemble, garb, garments, garmenture, gear, get-up, habiliments, habit(s), outfit, raiment, rig-out, threads, toggery, togs, vestiture, vestments, vesture, wardrobe, wear, weeds.

cloud *n.* billow, crowd, darkness, flock, fog, gloom, haze, horde, host, mist, multitude, murk, nebula, nebulosity, obscurity, shower, swarm, throng, vapour, water-dog, weft, woolpack.

v. becloud, confuse, darken, defame, dim, disorient, distort, dull, eclipse, impair, muddle, obfuscate, obscure, overcast, overshadow, shade, shadow, stain, veil.

antonym clear.

cloudiness *n.* blurredness, dimness, haziness, murkiness, nebula, opacity.

antonym clearness.

cloudy *adj.* blurred, blurry, confused, dark, dim, dismal, dull, emulsified, hazy, indistinct, leaden, lightless, lowering, muddy, murky, nebulous, nubilous, obscure, opaque, overcast, sombre, sullen, sunless.
antonyms clear, sunny.

clout *v.* box, clobber, cuff, hit, skelp, slap, smack, sock, strike, thump, wallop, whack, wham.
n. authority, cuff, influence, power, prestige, pull, skelp, slap, smack, sock, standing, thump, wallop, weight, whack.

cloven *adj.* bisected, cleft, divided, split.
antonym solid.

clown *n.* august(e), boor, buffoon, chuff, clodhopper, clout-shoe, comedian, dolt, fool, gracioso, harlequin, hob, jester, Joey, joker, joskin, merry-andrew, mountebank, peasant, pierrot, Pierrot, prankster, punchinello, swain, yahoo, yokel, zany.

clowning *n.* buffoonery, jesting, joking, messing about, pantaloonery, pranks, skylarking.

clownish *adj.* awkward, clumsy, comic, foolish, galumphing, hobbish, ill-bred, rough, rude, rustic, slapstick, uncivil, ungainly, vulgar, zany.
antonyms graceful, sophisticated.

cloy *v.* choke, disgust, glut, gorge, nauseate, sate, satiate, sicken, surfeit, tire, weary.
antonyms please, whet.

cloying *adj.* excessive, nauseating, oversweet, sickening, sickly.

club¹ *n.* bat, bludgeon, cosh, cudgel, mace, mere, stick, truncheon, waddy.
v. bash, baste, batter, beat, bludgeon, clobber, clout, cosh, hammer, hit, pummel, strike.

club² *n.* association, bunch, circle, clique, combination, company, fraternity, group, guild, lodge, order, set, society, sodality, union.

clue *n.* clavis, evidence, hint, idea, indication, inkling, intimation, lead, notion, pointer, sign, suggestion, suspicion, tip, tip-off, trace.

clump *n.* bunch, bundle, cluster, mass, shock, thicket, tuffet, tuft.
v. clomp, lumber, plod, stamp, stomp, stump, thud, thump, tramp, tread.

clumsiness *n.* awkwardness, bungling, gaucheness, indexterity, maladdress, maladroitness, unhandiness.

clumsy *adj.* awkward, blundering, bumbling, bungling, cack-handed, chuckle, clumping, crude, gauche, gawky, ham-fisted, ham-handed, heavy, hulking, ill-made, inept, inexpert, lubber, lubberly, lumbering, maladroit, ponderous, rough, shapeless, spastic, squab, unco-ordinated, uncouth, ungainly, ungraceful, unhandy, unskilful, unwieldy.
antonym graceful.

cluster *n.* assemblage, batch, bunch, clump, collection, gathering, glomeration, group, knot, mass.
v. assemble, bunch, collect, flock, gather, group.

clustered *adj.* assembled, bunched, gathered, glomerate, grouped, massed.

clutch *v.* catch, clasp, embrace, fasten, grab, grapple, grasp, grip, hang on to, seize, snatch.

clutches *n.* claws, control, custody, dominion, embrace, grasp, grip, hands, keeping, mercy, possession, power, sway.

clutter *n.* confusion, disarray, disorder, hotchpotch, jumble, litter, mess, muddle, untidiness.
v. cover, encumber, fill, litter, scatter, strew.

coach¹ *n.* grinder, instructor, répétiteur, teacher, trainer, tutor.
v. cram, drill, instruct, prepare, teach, train, tutor.

coach² *n.* bus, carriage, charabanc, landau, motor-bus, motor-coach, omnibus.

coagulate *v.* clot, congeal, curdle, jell, solidify, thicken.
antonym melt.

coal *n.* black diamonds.

coalesce *v.* amalgamate, blend, cohere, combine, commingle, commix, consolidate, fuse, incorporate, integrate, merge, mix, unite.

coalition *n.* affiliation, alliance, amalgam, amalgamation, association, bloc, coadunation, combination, compact, confederacy, confederation, conjunction, federation, fusion, integration, league, merger, union.

coal-scuttle *n.* purdonium.

coarse *adj.* bawdy, blowzy, boorish, brutish, coarse-grained, crude, earthly, foul-mouthed, homespun, immodest, impolite, improper, impure, indelicate, inelegant, loutish, mean, offensive, porterly, Rabelaisian, ribald, rough, rude, smutty, Sotadic, uncivil, unfinished, unpolished, unprocessed, unpurified, unrefined, vulgar.
antonyms fine, polite, refined, sophisticated.

coarsen *v.* anaesthetise, blunt, deaden, desensitise, dull, harden, indurate, roughen.
antonyms civilise, sensitise.

coarseness *n.* bawdiness, boorishness, crassitude, crudity, earthiness, grossièreté, indelicacy, offensiveness, ribaldry, roughness, smut, smuttiness, uncouthness, unevenness.
antonyms delicacy, politeness, sophistication.

coast *n.* coastline, littoral, seaboard, seaside, shore.
v. cruise, drift, free-wheel, glide, sail.

coat *n.* Burberry, cloak, coating, covering, fleece, fur, hair, hide, layer, mac, mackinaw, mackintosh, mantle, overlay, pelt, raincoat, skin, wash, wool.
v. apply, cover, plaster, smear, spread.

coated *adj.* covered, furred, painted, proofed.

coating *n.* blanket, coat, covering, dusting, film, finish, fur, glaze, lamination, layer, membrane, patina, pellicle, sheet, skin, varnish, veneer, wash.

coax *v.* allure, beguile, cajole, decoy, entice, flatter, inveigle, persuade, soft-soap, sweet-talk, wheedle, whilly, whillywha(w), wile.
antonym force.

cobble *v.* botch, bungle, knock up, mend, patch,

put together, tinker.

cock *n.* capon, chanticleer, rooster.

cock-eyed *adj.* absurd, askew, asymmetrical, awry, crazy, crooked, daft, lop-sided, ludicrous, nonsensical, preposterous, skew-whiff, squint, tiddly, tipsy.
antonyms sensible, sober.

cocksure *adj.* arrogant, brash, bumptious, cocky, hubristic, overconfident, presumptuous, self-confident.
antonym modest.

cocky *adj.* arrogant, bouncy, brash, cocksure, conceited, egotistical, fresh, pert, swaggering, swollen-headed, vain.

cocoon *v.* cover, cushion, envelop, insulate, pad, preserve, protect, sheathe, swaddle, swathe, wrap.

coddle *v.* baby, cocker, cosset, humour, indulge, mollycoddle, nurse, pamper, pet, spoil.

code *n.* canon, cipher, convention, cryptograph, custom, ethics, etiquette, manners, maxim, regulations, rules, system.
v. encipher, encode.

coded *adj.* cryptic, encrypted, hidden, secret.

codify *v.* catalogue, classify, code, digest, organise, summarise, systematise, tabulate, write down.

coding *n.* encryption.

coerce *v.* bludgeon, browbeat, bulldoze, bully, compel, constrain, dragoon, drive, drum, force, intimidate, press-gang, pressurise.
antonyms coax, persuade.

coercion *n.* browbeating, bullying, compulsion, constraint, direct action, duress, force, intimidation, pressure, threats.
antonym persuasion.

co-existent *adj.* coetaneous, coeval, co-existing, concomitant, contemporaneous, contemporary, synchronous.

coffer *n.* ark, case, casket, chest, kist, repository, strongbox, treasure, treasury.

cogency *n.* conviction, force, persuasion, potency, power, strength.
antonym weakness.

cogent *adj.* compelling, conclusive, convincing, effective, forceful, forcible, influential, irresistible, persuasive, potent, powerful, strong, unanswerable, urgent, weighty.
antonyms ineffective, unsound.

cogitate *v.* cerebrate, consider, contemplate, deliberate, meditate, muse, ponder, reflect, ruminate, think.

cogitation *n.* cerebration, consideration, contemplation, deliberation, meditation, reflection, rumination, thought.

cognate *adj.* affiliated, agnate, akin, alike, allied, analogous, associated, connected, kindred, related, similar.
antonym unconnected.

cognisance *n.* acknowledgement, apprehension, cognition, knowledge, notice, perception, percipience, recognition, regard.
antonym unawareness.

cognisant *adj.* acquainted, aware, conscious, conversant, familiar, informed, knowledgeable, versed, witting.
antonym unaware.

cognition *n.* apprehension, awareness, comprehension, discernment, insight, intelligence, perception, reasoning, understanding.

cohere *v.* adhere, agree, bind, cling, coalesce, combine, consolidate, correspond, fuse, glue, hang together, harmonise, hold, square, stick, unite.
antonym separate.

coherence *n.* agreement, comprehensibility, concordance, congruity, connection, consistency, consonance, correspondence, intelligibility, rationality, sense, union, unity.
antonym incoherence.

coherent *adj.* articulate, comprehensible, consistent, intelligible, logical, lucid, meaningful, orderly, organised, rational, reasoned, sensible, systematic.

cohort *n.* accomplice, assistant, associate, band, companion, company, comrade, contingent, crony, division, follower, henchman, legion, mate, myrmidon, partner, regiment, sidekick, squadron, supporter, toady, troop.

coil *v.* convolute, curl, entwine, loop, snake, spiral, twine, twist, wind, wreathe, writhe.
n. bight, convolution, curl, fank, loop, spiral, twist.

coin *v.* conceive, create, devise, fabricate, forge, form, formulate, frame, introduce, invent, make up, mint, mould, originate, produce, think up.
n. bit, cash, change, copper, jitney, loose change, lucky-piece, money, piece, silver, small change, specie.

coincide *v.* accord, agree, co-exist, concur, correspond, harmonise, match, square, tally.

coincidence *n.* accident, chance, concomitance, concurrence, conjunction, correlation, correspondence, eventuality, fluke, fortuity, luck, synchronism.

coincidental *adj.* accident, casual, chance, coincident, concomitant, concurrent, fluky, fortuitous, lucky, simultaneous, synchronous, unintentional, unplanned.
antonyms deliberate, planned.

coitus *n.* coition, congress, copulation, coupling, love-making, marriage-bed, mating, sexual intercourse, union.

cold *adj.* agued, algid, aloof, apathetic, arctic, benumbed, biting, bitter, bleak, brumal, chill, chilled, chilly, cold-blooded, cool, dead, distant, freezing, frigid, frosty, frozen, gelid, glacial, icy, inclement, indifferent, inhospitable, lukewarm, numbed, parky, passionless, phlegmatic, raw, reserved, shivery, spiritless, stand-offish, stony, undemonstrative, unfeeling, unfriendly, unheated, unmoved, unresponsive, unsympathetic, wintry.
antonyms friendly, warm.
n. catarrh, chill, chilliness, coldness, frigidity, frostiness, hypothermia, iciness, inclemency.
antonyms friendliness, warmth.

cold fish iceberg.

cold-blooded *adj.* barbaric, barbarous, brutal,

callous, cruel, dispassionate, fell, flinty, heartless, inhuman, merciless, obdurate, pitiless, ruthless, savage, steely, stony-hearted, uncompassionate, unemotional, unfeeling, unmoved.

antonyms compassionate, merciful.

cold-hearted *adj.* callous, cold, detached, flinty, frigid, frozen, heartless, indifferent, inhuman, insensitive, stony-hearted, uncaring, uncompassionate, unfeeling, unkind, unsympathetic.

antonym warm-hearted.

collaborate *v.* coact, collude, conspire, co-operate, co-produce, fraternise, participate, team up.

collaboration *n.* alliance, association, coactivity, concert, co-operation, partnership, teamwork.

collaborator *n.* assistant, associate, caballer, collaborationist, colleague, confederate, co-worker, fellow-traveller, partner, quisling, team-mate, traitor, turncoat.

collapse *v.* crumple, fail, faint, fall, fold, founder, peg out, sink, subside.

n. breakdown, cave-in, debacle (débâcle), detumescence, disintegration, downfall, éfoulement, exhaustion, failure, faint, flop, subsidence.

collar *v.* apprehend, appropriate, arrest, capture, catch, grab, nab, nick, seize.

n. dog-collar, gorget, neckband, ring, ruff.

collate *v.* adduce, analogise, arrange, collect, compare, compose, gather, sort.

collateral *n.* assurance, deposit, funds, guarantee, pledge, security, surety.

adj. concurrent, confirmatory, corroborative, indirect, parallel, related, supporting.

colleague *n.* aide, aider, ally, assistant, associate, auxiliary, bedfellow, coadjutor, collaborator, companion, comrade, confederate, confrère, helper, partner, team-mate, workmate.

collect *v.* accumulate, acquire, aggregate, amass, assemble, cluster, congregate, convene, converge, forgather, gather, gather together, heap, hoard, muster, obtain, raise, rally, save, secure, stockpile, uplift.

collected *adj.* assembled, calm, composed, confident, cool, efficient, gathered, placid, poised, self-possessed, serene, together, unperturbable, unperturbed, unruffled.

antonyms disorganised, dithery, worried.

collection *n.* accumulation, anthology, assemblage, assembly, assortment, caboodle, cluster, company, compilation, congeries, conglomerate, conglomeration, congregation, convocation, crowd, festschrift, gathering, group, harvesting, heap, hoard, ingathering, inning, jingbang, job-lot, mass, pile, set, spicilege, stockpile, store, whip-round.

collective *adj.* aggregate, combined, common, composite, concerted, congregated, co-operative, corporate, cumulative, joint, shared, unified, united.

n. aggregate, assemblage, corporation, gathering, group.

collision *n.* accident, bump, clash, clashing, conflict, confrontation, crash, encounter, impact, opposition, pile-up, prang, rencontre, rencounter, skirmish, smash.

colloquial *adj.* conversational, demotic, everyday, familiar, idiomatic, informal, non-technical, vernacular.

antonym formal.

collude *v.* abet, cabal, coact, colloborate, complot, connive, conspire, contrive, intrigue, machinate, plot, scheme.

collusion *n.* artifice, cahoots, coactivity, complicity, connivance, conspiracy, craft, deceit, fraudulent, intrigue.

colonise *v.* people, pioneer, populate, settle.

colonist *n.* colonial, coloniser, emigrant, frontiersman, homesteader, immigrant, oecist, oikist, pioneer, planter, settler.

colonnade *n.* arcade, cloisters, columniation, peristyle, portico.

colony *n.* dependency, dominion, outpost, possession, province, settlement, territory.

colossal *adj.* Brobdingnagian, elephantine, enormous, gargantuan, gigantic, herculean, heroic, huge, immense, leviathan, mammoth, massive, monstrous, monumental, mountainous, prodigious, titanic, vast.

antonym tiny.

colour[1] *n.* animation, appearance, bloom, blush, brilliance, chroma, colorant, coloration, complexion, disguise, dye, façade, flush, glow, guise, hue, liveliness, paint, pigment, pigmentation, plausibility, pretence, pretext, race, reason, rosiness, ruddiness, semblance, shade, timbre, tincture, tinge, tint, variety, vividness, wash, water-colour.

v. blush, burn, colourwash, disguise, distort, dye, embroider, encolour, exaggerate, falsify, flush, misrepresent, paint, pervert, prejudice, redden, slant, stain, strain, taint, tinge, tint.

colour[2] *n.* colours, ensign, flag, standard.

colour-blind *adj.* dichromatic.

coloured *n.* Asian, black, Hottentot, Negro.

adj. Asian, black, brown-skinned, dark-skinned, Negro.

colourful *adj.* bright, brilliant, distinctive, graphic, intense, interesting, jazzy, kaleidoscopic, lively, motley, multicoloured, parti-coloured, picturesque, psychedelic, rich, stimulating, unusual, variegated, vibrant, vivid.

antonyms colourless, drab, plain.

colourless *adj.* achromatic, achromic, anaemic, ashen, bleached, characterless, drab, dreary, fade, faded, insipid, lacklustre, livid, neutral, pale, sickly, tame, transparent, uninteresting, unmemorable, vacuous, vapid, wan, washed out.

antonym colourful.

colours *n.* banner, colour, emblem, ensign, flag, standard.

column *n.* anta, cavalcade, file, line, list, obelisk, pilaster, pillar, post, procession, queue, rank, row, shaft, string, support, train, upright.

columnist *n.* correspondent, critic, editor, journalist, reporter, reviewer, writer.

coma *n.* catalepsy, drowsiness, hypnosis, insensibility, lethargy, oblivion, somnolence, sopor, stupor, torpor, trance, unconsciousness.

comatose *adj.* cataleptic, drowsy, insensible, lethargic, sleepy, sluggish, somnolent, soporose, stupefied, torpid, unconscious.
antonym conscious.

comb *v.* hackle, hunt, rake, ransack, rummage, scour, screen, search, sift, sweep.
n. crest, hackle.

combat *n.* action, battle, bout, clash, conflict, contest, duel, encounter, engagement, fight, hostilities, j(i)u-jitsu, judo, karate, kendo, kung fu, skirmish, struggle, war, warfare.
v. battle, contend, contest, defy, engage, fight, oppose, resist, strive, struggle, withstand.

combatant *n.* adversary, antagonist, belligerent, contender, enemy, fighter, opponent, serviceman, soldier, warrior.
adj. active, battling, belligerent, combating, contending, fighting, opposing, warring.

combative *adj.* aggressive, antagonistic, argumentative, bellicose, belligerent, contentious, militant, pugnacious, quarrelsome, truculent, warlike.
antonym pacific, peaceful.

combination *n.* alliance, amalgam, amalgamation, association, blend, cabal, cartel, coalescence, coalition, combine, composite, composition, compound, confederacy, confederation, conjunction, connection, consortium, conspiracy, federation, meld, merger, mix, mixture, syndicate, unification, union.

combine *v.* amalgamate, associate, bind, blend, bond, coadunate, compound, conjoin, connect, cooperate, fuse, incorporate, integrate, join, link, marry, meld, merge, mix, peace, pool, sythesise, unify, unite.
antonym separate.

combustible *adj.* excitable, explosive, flammable, incendiary, inflammable.
antonyms incombustible, non-inflammable.

come *v.* advance, appear, approach, arrive, attain, become, draw near, ejaculate, enter, happen, materialise, move, near, occur, originate, reach.
antonyms depart, go, leave.

come about arise, befall, come to pass, happen, occur, result, transpire.

come across bump into, chance upon, discover, encounter, find, happen on, meet, notice, unearth.

come along arise, arrive, develop, happen, improve, mend, progress, rally, recover, recuperate.

come apart break, crumble, disintegrate, fall to bits, separate, split, tear.

come between alienate, disunite, divide, estrange, interfere, meddle, part, separate, split up.

come by acquire, get, obtain, procure, secure.
antonyms give, lose.

come clean acknowledge, admit, confess, own, own up, reveal, spill the beans.

come down decline, degenerate, descend, deteriorate, fall, reduce, worsen.

come in appear, arrive, enter, finish, show up.

come on advance, appear, begin, develop, improve, proceed, progress, take place, thrive.

come out conclude, end, result, terminate.

come out with affirm, declare, disclose, divulge, own, say, state.

come round accede, acquiesce, allow, awake, awaken, concede, grant, mellow, recover, relent, revive, wake, waken, yield.

come through accomplish, achieve, endure, prevail, succeed, survive, triumph, withstand.

come to grief bomb, come unstuck, fail, miscarry.
antonyms succeed, triumph.

come to life revive, rouse.
antonym collapse.

come to light appear, come out, transpire, turn up.

come up with advance, create, discover, find, furnish, offer, present, produce, propose, provide, submit, suggest, think of, think out.

come-back *n.* quip, rally, rebound, recovery, rejoinder, repartee, reply, response, resurgence, retaliation, retort, return, revival, riposte, triumph.

comedian *n.* card, clown, comic, droll, funny man, gagster, humorist, jester, joker, jokesmith, laugh, wag, wit.

come-down *n.* anticlimax, blow, decline, deflation, degradation, demotion, descent, disappointment, humiliation, let-down, reverse.

comedy *n.* chaffing, clowning, drollery, facetiousness, farce, fun, hilarity, humour, jesting, joking, sitcom, slapstick, wisecracking, witticisms.

comely *adj.* attractive, beautiful, becoming, blooming, bonny, buxom, callipygian, callipygous, decent, decorous, fair, fit, fitting, gainly, good-looking, graceful, handsome, lovely, pleasing, pretty, proper, pulchritudinous, seemly, suitable, wholesome, winsome.

come-uppance *n.* chastening, deserts, dues, merit, punishment, rebuke, recompense, requital, retribution.

comfort *v.* alleviate, assuage, cheer, console, ease, encheer, encourage, enliven, gladden, hearten, inspirit, invigorate, reassure, refresh, relieve, solace, soothe, strengthen.
n. aid, alleviation, cheer, compensation, consolation, cosiness, ease, easy street, encouragement, enjoyment, help, luxury, opulence, relief, satisfaction, snugness, succour, support, well-being.
antonyms distress, torment.

comfortable *adj.* adequate, affluent, agreeable, ample, canny, commodious, contented, convenient, cosy, delightful, easy, enjoyable, gemütlich, gratified, happy, homely, loose, loose-fitting, pleasant, prosperous, relaxed, relaxing, restful, roomy, serene, snug, well-

off, well-to-do.
antonyms poor, uncomfortable.

comforting *adj.* analeptic, cheering, consolatory, consoling, encouraging, heart-warming, inspiriting, reassuring, soothing.
antonym worrying.

comic *adj.* amusing, comical, droll, facetious, farcical, funny, humorous, jocular, joking, light, rich, waggish, witty.
antonyms serious, tragic, unfunny.
n. buffoon, clown, comedian, droll, funny, gagster, humorist, jester, joker, jokesmith, man, wag, wit.

comical *adj.* absurd, amusing, comic, diverting, droll, entertaining, farcical, funny, hilarious, humorous, laughable, ludicrous, priceless, ridiculous, risible, side-splitting, silly, whimsical.
antonyms sad, unamusing.

coming *adj.* approaching, aspiring, due, forthcoming, future, imminent, impending, near, next, nigh, promising, rising, up-and-coming.
n. accession, advent, approach, arrival.

command *v.* bid, charge, compel, control, demand, direct, dominate, enjoin, govern, head, lead, manage, order, reign over, require, rule, supervise, sway.
n. authority, behest, bidding, charge, commandment, control, decree, dictation, diktat, direction, directive, domination, dominion, edict, fiat, government, grasp, injunction, instruction, management, mandate, mastery, order, power, precept, requirement, rule, supervision, sway, ukase, ultimatum.

commandeer *v.* appropriate, confiscate, expropriate, hijack, requisition, seize, sequester, sequestrate, usurp.

commander *n.* admiral, boss, captain, chief, commander-in-chief, commanding officer, director, general, head, imperator, leader, marshal, officer, ruler.

commanding *adj.* advantageous, assertive, authoritative, autocratic, compelling, controlling, decisive, dominant, dominating, forceful, imposing, impressive, peremptory, superior.

commando *n.* fedayee, Green Beret, soldier.

commemorate *v.* celebrate, honour, immortalise, keep, memorialise, observe, remember, salute, solemnise.

commemoration *n.* ceremony, honouring, observance, recordation, remembrance, tribute.

commemorative *adj.* celebratory, dedicatory, in memoriam, memorial.

commence *v.* begin, embark on, inaugurate, initiate, open, originate, start.
antonyms cease, finish.

commend *v.* acclaim, applaud, approve, commit, compliment, confide, consign, deliver, entrust, eulogise, extol, praise, recommend, yield.
antonym criticise.

commendable *adj.* admirable, creditable, deserving, estimable, excellent, exemplary, laudable, meritorious, noble, praiseworthy,

worthy.
antonyms blameworthy, poor.

commendation *n.* acclaim, acclamation, accolade, applause, approbation, approval, credit, encomium, encouragement, panegyric, praise, recommendation.
antonyms blame, criticism.

commensurate *adj.* acceptable, adequate, appropriate, co-extensive, comparable, compatible, consistent, corresponding, due, equivalent, fitting, just, meet, proportionate, sufficient.
antonym inappropriate.

comment *v.* animadvert, annotate, criticise, descant, elucidate, explain, gloss, interpose, interpret, mention, note, observe, opine, remark, say.
n. animadversion, annotation, commentary, criticism, elucidation, explanation, exposition, footnote, illustration, marginal note, marginalia, note, observation, remark, statement.

commentary *n.* analysis, critique, description, elucidation, exegesis, explanation, narration, notes, postil, review, treatise, voice-over.

commentator *n.* annotator, commenter, critic, expositor, glossator, glosser, glossographer, interpreter, reporter, scholiast.

commerce *n.* business, communication, dealing(s), exchange, intercourse, merchandising, relations, trade, traffic.

commercial *adj.* business, exploited, marketable, materialistic, mercantile, mercenary, monetary, pecuniary, popular, profitable, profit-making, saleable, sales, sellable, trade, trading, venal.

commiseration *n.* compassion, condolence, consolation, pity, sympathy.

commission *n.* allowance, appointment, authority, board, brokerage, brok(er)age, charge, committee, compensation, cut, delegation, deputation, duty, employment, errand, fee, function, mandate, mission, percentage, rake-off, representative, task, trust, warrant.
v. appoint, ask for, authorise, contract, delegate, depute, empower, engage, nominate, order, request, select, send.

commit *v.* align, bind, commend, compromise, confide, confine, consign, deliver, deposit, do, enact, endanger, engage, entrust, execute, give, imprison, involve, obligate, perform, perpetrate, pledge.
commit oneself bind oneself, decide, promise, take the plunge, undertake.

commitment *n.* adherence, assurance, dedication, devotion, duty, engagement, guarantee, involvement, liability, loyalty, obligation, pledge, promise, responsibility, tie, undertaking, vow, word.

committed *adj.* active, card-carrying, engagé, fervent, red-hot.
antonyms apathetic, uncommitted.

committee *n.* advisory group, board, cabinet, commission, council, jury, panel, table, task force, think-tank, working party.

commodious *adj.* ample, capacious, comfortable, expansive, extensive, large, loose, roomy, spacious.
antonym cramped.

commodities *n.* goods, merchandise, output, produce, products, stock, things, wares.

common *adj.* accepted, average, coarse, collective, commonplace, communal, conventional, customary, daily, everyday, familiar, flat, frequent, general, habitual, hackneyed, humdrum, inferior, low, mutual, obscure, ordinary, pedestrian, plain, plebby, plebeian, popular, prevailing, prevalent, public, regular, routine, run-of-the-mill, simple, social, stale, standard, stock, trite, tritical, undistinguished, unexceptional, universal, usual, vulgar, widespread, workaday.
antonyms noteworthy, uncommon.

common sense gumption, judgement, levelheadedness, mother-wit, nous, practicality, prudence, soundness, wit.

commonly *adv.* for the most part, generally, normally, usually, vulgo.
antonym rarely.

commonplace *adj.* common, customary, everyday, humdrum, obvious, ordinary, pedestrian, quotidian, stale, threadbare, trite, uninteresting, widespread, worn out.
antonyms exceptional, rare.
n. banality, cliché, platitude, truism.

common-sense *adj.* astute, common-sensical, down-to-earth, hard-headed, judicious, levelheaded, matter-of-fact, practical, pragmatical, realistic, reasonable, sane, sensible, shrewd, sound.
antonym foolish.

commotion *n.* ado, agitation, ballyhoo, bobbery, brouhaha, burst-up, bustle, bust-up, carfuffle, disorder, disturbance, excitement, ferment, fracas, fraise, furore, fuss, hubbub, hullaballoo, hurly-burly, perturbation, pother, pudder, racket, riot, rumpus, to-do, toss, tumult, turmoil, uproar.

communal *adj.* collective, common, communistic, community, general, joint, public, shared.
antonyms personal, private.

commune *n.* collective, colony, community, co-operative, encampment, fellowship, kibbutz, settlement.
v. communicate, confer, converse, discourse, hold converse with, make contact with.

communicable *adj.* catching, contagious, conveyable, impartible, infectious, infective, spreadable, transferable, transmittable.

communicate *v.* acquaint, announce, bestow, connect, contact, convey, correspond, declare, diffuse, disclose, disseminate, divulge, impart, inform, intimate, notify, proclaim, promulgate, publish, report, reveal, signify, spread, transmit, unfold.

communication *n.* announcement, bulletin, communiqué, connection, contact, conversation, converse, correspondence, disclosure, dispatch, dissemination, information, intelligence, intercourse, intimation, message, news, promulgation, report, statement, transmission, word.

communicative *adj.* candid, chatty, conversable, conversational, expansive, extravert, forthcoming, frank, free, friendly, informative, loquacious, open, outgoing, sociable, talkative, unreserved, voluble.
antonym reticent.

communion *n.* accord, affinity, agreement, closeness, communing, concord, converse, empathy, Eucharist, fellow-feeling, fellowship, harmony, Holy Communion, housel, intercourse, Lord's Supper, Mass, participation, rapport, Sacrament, sympathy, togetherness, unity.

communiqué *n.* announcement, bulletin, communication, dispatch, message, report, statement.

communism *n.* Bolshevism, collectivism, Leninism, Marxism, socialism, sovietism, Stalinism, totalitarianism, Trotskyism.

communist *n.* Bolshevik, collectivist, Leninist, Marxist, Red, socialist, soviet, Stalinist, totalitarian, Trot, Trotskyist, Trotskyite.

community *n.* affinity, agreement, association, body politic, brotherhood, coincidence, colony, commonness, commonwealth, company, concurrence, confraternity, confrérie, correspondence, district, fellowship, fraternity, identity, kibbutz, kindredness, likeness, locality, nest, people, populace, population, public, residents, sameness, similarity, society, state.

commute[1] *v.* adjust, alter, curtail, decrease, lighten, mitigate, modify, reduce, remit, shorten, soften.

commute[2] *v.* alternate, journey, strap-hang, travel.

commuter *n.* exurbanite, strap-hanger, suburbanite, traveller.
antonym urbanite.

compact[1] *adj.* brief, close, compendious, compressed, concise, condensed, dense, firm, impenetrable, solid, stocky, succinct, thick, well-knit.
antonyms diffuse, rambling, rangy.
v. compress, condense, consolidate, cram, flatten, ram, squeeze, tamp.

compact[2] *n.* agreement, alliance, arrangement, bargain, bond, concordat, contract, covenant, deal, entente, pact, settlement, treaty, understanding.

companion *n.* accomplice, aide, ally, assistant, associate, attendant, attender, buddy, chaperon, cohort, colleague, compeer, complement, comrade, confederate, confidant, confidante, consort, counterpart, crony, duenna, escort, fellow, fere, follower, friend, intimate, mate, partner, satellite, shadow, squire, twin.

companionable *adj.* affable, amiable, approachable, congenial, conversable, convivial, extravert, familiar, friendly, genial, gregarious, informal, neighbourly, outgoing, sociable, sympathetic.
antonym unfriendly.

companionship *n.* camaraderie, companionhood, company, comradeship, confraternity, consociation, conviviality, esprit de corps, fellowship, fraternity, friendship, rapport, support, sympathy, togetherness.

company[1] *n.* assemblage, assembly, association, band, body, business, cartel, circle, collection, community, concern, concourse, consociation, consortium, convention, corporation, coterie, crew, crowd, ensemble, establishment, firm, fraternity, gathering, group, house, league, line, partnership, party, set, set-out, syndicate, throng, troop, troupe.

company[2] *n.* attendance, callers, companionhood, companionship, fellowship, guests, party, presence, society, support, visitors.

comparable *adj.* akin, alike, analogous, cognate, commensurate, correspondent, corresponding, equal, equivalent, kindred, parallel, proportionate, related, similar, tantamount.
antonym unlike.

compare *v.* balance, collate, confront, contrast, correlate, emulate, equal, equate, juxtapose, liken, match, parallel, resemble, similise, vie, weigh.

comparison *n.* analogy, collation, comparability, contrast, correlation, distinction, juxtaposition, likeness, parallel, parallelism, resemblance, similarity, similitude.

compartment *n.* alcove, area, bay, berth, booth, box, carrel, carriage, category, cell, chamber, cubby-hole, cubicle, department, division, locker, niche, pigeon-hole, section, stall, subdivision.

compass *n.* area, boundary, bounds, circle, circuit, circumference, diapason, enclosure, extent, field, gamut, girth, limit, range, reach, realm, round, scale, scope, space, sphere, stretch, zone.
v. accomplish, achieve, beset, besiege, blockade, circumscribe, contrive, devise, effect, encircle, enclose, encompass, environ, manage, realise, surround.

compassion *n.* charity, clemency, commiseration, concern, condolence, fellow-feeling, heart, humanity, kindness, loving-kindness, mercy, pity, ruth, sorrow, sympathy, tenderness, understanding, weltschmerz, yearning.
antonym indifference.

compassionate *adj.* benevolent, caring, charitable, clement, humane, humanitarian, indulgent, kind-hearted, kindly, lenient, merciful, piteous, pitying, supportive, sympathetic, tender, tender-hearted, understanding, warm-hearted.
antonym indifferent.

compatibility *n.* accord, affinity, agreement, amity, concord, congeniality, consistency, consonance, correspondence, empathy, fellowship, harmony, like-mindedness, rapport, reconcilability, sympathy, understanding, unity.
antonyms antagonism, antipathy, incompatibility.

compatible *adj.* accordant, adaptable, agree-able, conformable, congenial, congruent, congruous, consistent, consonant, harmonious, kindred, like-minded, reconcilable, suitable, sympathetic.
antonyms antagonistic, antipathetic, incompatible.

compel *v.* browbeat, bulldoze, bully, coact, coerce, constrain, dragoon, drive, enforce, exact, force, gar, hustle, impel, make, necessitate, obligate, oblige, press-gang, pressurise, strongarm, urge.

compelling *adj.* binding, coercive, cogent, compulsive, conclusive, convincing, enchanting, enthralling, forceful, gripping, hypnotic, imperative, incontrovertible, irrefragable, irrefutable, irresistible, mesmeric, overriding, peremptory, persuasive, powerful, pressing, spellbinding, telling, unanswerable, unavoidable, unputdownable, urgent, weighty.

compendious *adj.* abbreviated, abridged, brief, compact, comprehensive, concise, condensed, contracted, epitomised, short, shortened, succinct, summarised, summary, synoptic.
antonym enlarged.

compendium *n.* abbreviation, abridgement, abstract, brief, companion, condensation, conspectus, digest, encapsulation, epitome, handbook, manual, précis, recapitulation, summary, synopsis, vade-mecum.

compensate *v.* atone, balance, cancel, counteract, counterbalance, countervail, expiate, guerdon, indemnify, offset, recompense, recover, recuperate, redeem, redress, refund, reimburse, remunerate, repay, requite, restore, reward, satisfy.

compensation *n.* amends, atonement, comfort, consolation, damages, guerdon, indemnification, indemnity, payment, quittance, recompense, redress, refund, reimbursement, remuneration, reparation, repayment, requital, restitution, restoration, return, reward, satisfaction, solatium.

compère *n.* anchor-man, announcer, commère, emcee, host, link man, master of ceremonies, MC, presenter, ringmaster.

compete *v.* battle, challenge, contend, contest, duel, emulate, fight, oppose, rival, strive, struggle, tussle, vie.

competence *n.* ability, adequacy, appropriateness, aptitude, capability, capacity, competency, experience, expertise, facility, fitness, proficiency, skill, suitability, technique.
antonym incompetence.

competent *adj.* able, adapted, adequate, appropriate, belonging, capable, clever, efficient, endowed, equal, fit, legitimate, masterly, pertinent, proficient, qualified, satisfactory, strong, sufficient, suitable, trained, well-qualified.
antonym incompetent.

competition *n.* challenge, challengers, championship, combativeness, competitiveness, competitors, contention, contest, corrivalry,

cup, emulation, event, field, match, opposition, quiz, race, rivalry, rivals, series, strife, struggle, tournament, tourney, trial.
competitive *adj.* aggressive, ambitious, antagonistic, combative, contentious, cut-throat, emulative, emulous, keen, pushy, vying.
antonyms sluggish, unambitious.
competitiveness *n.* aggression, aggressiveness, ambition, ambitiousness, antagonism, assertiveness, challenge, combativeness, contention, contentiousness, emulation, keenness, pugnacity, pushiness, rivalry, self-assertion.
antonyms backwardness, sluggishness.
competitor *n.* adversary, agonist, antagonist, challenger, competition, contender, contestant, corrival, emulator, entrant, opponent, opposition, rival.
compilation *n.* accumulation, amassment, anthology, arrangement, assemblage, assortment, collection, composition, florilegium, opus, selection, thesaurus, treasury, work.
compile *v.* accumulate, amass, anthologise, arrange, assemble, collect, compose, cull, garner, gather, marshal, organise.
complacency *n.* content, contentment, gloating, gratification, pleasure, pride, satisfaction, self-content, self-satisfaction, serenity, smugness, triumph.
antonyms diffidence, discontent.
complacent *adj.* contented, gloating, gratified, pleased, proud, satisfied, self-assured, self-congratulatory, self-contented, self-righteous, self-satisfied, serene, smug, triumphant, unconcerned.
antonyms diffident, discontented.
complain *v.* beef, belly-ache, bemoan, bewail, bind, bitch, bleat, carp, deplore, fuss, girn, grieve, gripe, groan, grouse, growl, grumble, kvetch, lament, moan, squeal, whine, whinge.
complainer *n.* belly-acher, fuss-pot, girner, grouser, grumbler, kvetch(er), moaner, nitpicker, whiner, whinger, winger.
complaining *adj.* bleating, cantankerous, captious, critical, fault-finding, fussy, hypercritical, moaning, nagging, nit-picking, peevish, querimonious, querulous, whingeing.
antonym contented.
complaint[1] *n.* accusation, annoyance, beef, belly-ache, bitch, bleat, censure, charge, criticism, dissatisfaction, fault-finding, girn, gravamen, grievance, gripe, grouse, grumble, lament, moan, nit-picking, plaint, querimony, remonstrance, squawk, stricture, wail, whinge, winge.
complaint[2] *n.* affliction, ailment, disease, disorder, illness, indisposition, malady, malaise, sickness, trouble, upset.
complaisance *n.* acquiescence, agreeableness, amenability, biddableness, compliance, conformability, deference, docility, obligingness.
antonyms obstinacy, perversity.
complaisant *adj.* accommodating, agreeable, amenable, amiable, biddable, compliant, conciliatory, conformable, deferential, docile, douce, obedient, obliging, solicitous,

tractable.
antonyms obstinate, perverse.
complement *n.* aggregate, capacity, companion, completion, consummation, counterpart, entirety, fellow, quota, sum, supplement, total, totality, wholeness.
complementary *adj.* companion, correlative, corresponding, dove-tailed, fellow, interdependent, interrelated, interrelating, interwoven, matched, reciprocal, reciprocative, reciprocatory.
complete *adj.* absolute, accomplished, achieved, all, concluded, consummate, ended, entire, equipped, faultless, finished, full, intact, integral, integrate, out-and-out, perfect, plenary, root-and-branch, self-contained, thorough, thoroughgoing, thorough-paced, total, unabbreviated, unabridged, unbroken, uncut, undivided, unedited, unexpurgated, unimpaired, utter, whole, whole-hog.
antonyms imperfect, incomplete.
v. accomplish, achieve, cap, clinch, close, conclude, consummate, crown, discharge, do, effect, end, execute, finalise, finish, fulfil, perfect, perform, realise, settle, terminate, wind up.
completely *adv.* absolutely, altogether, diametrically, en bloc, en masse, entirely, every inch, from first to last, fully, heart and soul, in full, in toto, lock stock and barrel, perfectly, quite, root and branch, solidly, thoroughly, totally, utterly, wholly.
completion *n.* accomplishment, achievement, attainment, close, conclusion, consummation, crowning, culmination, discharge, end, expiration, finalisation, finish, fruition, fulfilment, perfection, plenitude, realisation, settlement, telos, termination.
complex *adj.* ambagious, Byzantine, circuitous, complicated, composite, compound, compounded, convoluted, Daedalian, devious, diverse, elaborate, heterogeneous, intricate, involved, knotty, labyrinthine, manifold, mingled, mixed, multifarious, multipartite, multiple, plexiform, polymerous, ramified, tangled, tortuous.
antonym simple.
n. aggregate, composite, establishment, fixation, hang-up, idée fixe, institute, network, obsession, organisation, phobia, preoccupation, scheme, structure, syndrome, synthesis, system.
complexion *n.* appearance, aspect, cast, character, colour, colouring, composition, countenance, disposition, guise, hue, kind, light, look, make-up, nature, pigmentation, rud, skin, stamp, temperament, type.
complexity *n.* complication, convolution, deviousness, diversity, elaboration, entanglement, intricacy, involution, involvement, multifariousness, multiplicity, ramification, repercussion, tortuousness, variation, variety.
antonym simplicity.
compliance *n.* acquiescence, agreement, assent, complaisance, concession, concurrence,

conformability, conformity, consent, co-operation, deference, obedience, observance, passivity, submission, submissiveness, yielding.
antonyms defiance, disobedience.
compliant *adj.* accommodating, acquiescent, agreeable, amenable, biddable, complaisant, conformable, deferential, docile, obedient, obliging, passive, submissive, tractable, yielding.
antonyms disobedient, intractable.
complicate *v.* compound, confuse, elaborate, embroil, entangle, foul up, involve, mix up, muddle, tangle.
antonym simplify.
complicated *adj.* ambivalent, baroque, Byzantine, complex, convoluted, devious, difficult, elaborate, entangled, Heath-Robinson, intricate, involved, labyrinthine, perplexing, problematic, puzzling, rigmarole, tangled, tortuous, troublesome.
antonyms easy, simple.
complication *n.* aggravation, ambage, complexity, complicatedness, confusion, difficulty, drawback, elaboration, embarrassment, entanglement, factor, intricacy, mixture, obstacle, problem, ramification, repercussion, snag, web.
complicity *n.* abetment, agreement, approval, collaboration, collusion, concurrence, connivance, involvement, knowledge.
antonyms ignorance, innocence.
compliment *n.* accolade, admiration, bouquet, commendation, congratulations, courtesy, douceur, encomium, eulogy, favour, felicitation, flattery, honour, plaudit, praise, tribute.
antonyms criticism, insult.
v. admire, applaud, commend, congratulate, eulogise, extol, felicitate, flatter, laud, praise, salute.
antonyms condemn, insult.
complimentary *adj.* admiring, appreciative, approving, commendatory, congratulatory, courtesy, encomiastic, eulogistic, favourable, flattering, free, gratis, honorary, laudatory, panegyrical.
antonyms critical, insulting, unflattering.
compliments *n.* best wishes, congratulations, devoirs, greetings, regards, remembrances, respects, salutation.
comply *v.* accede, accommodate, accord, acquiesce, agree, assent, conform, consent, defer, discharge, fall in, follow, fulfil, obey, oblige, observe, perform, respect, satisfy, submit, yield.
antonyms disobey, resist.
component *n.* bit, constituent, element, factor, ingredient, item, part, piece, spare part, unit.
comport *v.* acquit, act, bear, behave, carry, conduct, demean, deport, perform.
compose *v.* adjust, arrange, build, calm, collect, compound, comprise, constitute, construct, contrive, control, create, devise, fashion, form, frame, govern, imagine, indite, invent, make, meditate the muse, pacify, produce,

quell, quiet, recollect, reconcile, regulate, resolve, settle, soothe, still, structure, tranquillise, write.
composed *adj.* calm, collected, complacent, confident, cool, imperturbable, level-headed, placid, poised, relaxed, self-possessed, serene, together, tranquil, unflappable, unruffled, unworried.
antonym agitated.
composer *n.* arranger, author, bard, creator, makar, maker, originator, poet, songsmith, songwriter, tunesmith, writer.
composite *adj.* agglutinate, blended, combined, complex, compound, conglomerate, fused, mixed, patchwork, synthesised.
antonyms homogeneous, uniform.
n. agglutination, alloy, amalgam, blend, combination, compound, conglomerate, fusion, mixture, pastiche, patchwork, synthesis.
composition *n.* arrangement, balance, combination, compilation, compromise, concord, confection, configuration, congruity, consonance, constitution, creation, design, essay, exaration, exercise, form, formation, formulation, harmony, invention, lay-out, lucubration, make-up, making, mixture, opus, organisation, piece, placing, production, proportion, structure, study, symmetry, work, writing.
composure *n.* aplomb, assurance, calm, calmness, confidence, cool, coolness, dignity, dispassion, ease, equanimity, impassivity, imperturbability, placidity, poise, sang-froid, savoir-faire, sedateness, self-assurance, self-possession, serenity, tranquillity.
antonym discomposure.
compound *v.* aggravate, alloy, amalgamate, augment, blend, coalesce, combine, complicate, compose, concoct, exacerbate, fuse, heighten, increase, intensify, intermingle, magnify, mingle, mix, synthesise, unite, worsen.
n. alloy, amalgam, amalgamation, blend, combination, composite, composition, confection, conglomerate, conglomeration, fusion, medley, mixture, synthesis.
adj. complex, complicated, composite, conglomerate, intricate, mixed, multiple.
comprehend *v.* appreciate, apprehend, assimilate, compass, comprise, conceive, cover, discern, embrace, encompass, fathom, grasp, include, know, penetrate, perceive, see, see daylight, tumble to, twig, understand.
antonym misunderstand.
comprehensible *adj.* clear, coherent, conceivable, explicit, graspable, intelligible, knowable, lucid, plain, rational, simple, straightforward, understandable.
antonym incomprehensible.
comprehension *n.* appreciation, apprehension, capacity, conception, discernment, grasp, intellection, intelligence, intension, judgement, knowledge, perception, realisation, sense, understanding.
antonym incomprehension.

comprehensive *adj.* across-the-board, all-embracing, all-inclusive, blanket, broad, catholic, compendious, complete, encyclopedic, exhaustive, extensive, full, general, inclusive, omnibus, sweeping, thorough, wide.
antonyms incomplete, selective.

compress *v.* abbreviate, astrict, astringe, compact, concentrate, condense, constrict, contract, cram, crowd, crush, flatten, impact, jam, précis, press, shorten, squash, squeeze, stuff, summarise, synopsise, telescope, wedge.
antonyms diffuse, expand, separate.

compressed *adj.* abridged, coarctate, compact, compacted, compendious, concentrated, concise, condensed, consolidated, constricted, flattened, impacted, pressed, reduced, shortened, squashed, squeezed, synopsised.

compression *n.* abbreviation, abridgement, astriction, concentration, condensation, consolidation, constriction, crushing, digest, impaction, pressure, reduction, squeezing, thlipsis.
antonyms enlargement, expansion.

comprise *v.* comprehend, consist of, contain, cover, embody, embrace, encompass, include, incorporate, involve, subsume.

compromise[1] *v.* adapt, adjust, agree, arbitrate, bargain, concede, make concessions, negotiate, retire, retreat, settle.
antonyms differ, quarrel.
n. accommodation, accord, adjustment, agreement, bargain, concession, co-operation, settlement, trade-off, via media.
antonyms disagreement, intransigence.

compromise[2] *v.* discredit, dishonour, embarrass, embroil, expose, hazard, imperil, implicate, involve, jeopardise, prejudice, undermine, weaken.

compulsion *n.* coercion, constraint, demand, distress, drive, duress, exigency, force, impulse, necessity, need, obligation, obsession, preoccupation, pressure, urge, urgency.
antonyms freedom, liberty.

compulsive *adj.* besetting, compelling, driving, hardened, hopeless, incorrigible, incurable, irredeemable, irresistible, obsessive, over-mastering, overpowering, overwhelming, uncontrollable, unputdownable, urgent.

compulsory *adj.* binding, de rigueur, forced, imperative, mandatory, obligatory, required, requisite, stipulated, stipulatory.
antonyms optional, voluntary.

compunction *n.* contrition, hesitance, hesitation, misgiving, penitence, qualm, regret, reluctance, remorse, repentance, sorrow, unease, uneasiness.
antonyms callousness, defiance.

compute *v.* assess, calculate, count, enumerate, estimate, evaluate, figure, measure, rate, reckon, sum, tally, total.

computer *n.* adding machine, analogue computer, calculator, data processor, digital computer, mainframe, processor, word processor.

comrade *n.* Achates, ally, associate, brother, buddy, bully-rook, butty, china, cobber, colleague, companion, compatriot, compeer, confederate, co-worker, crony, fellow, frater, friend, mate, pal, partner, sidekick.

con *v.* bamboozle, beguile, bilk, bluff, bunko, cheat, cozen, deceive, defraud, double-cross, dupe, fiddle, grift, gull, hoax, hoodwink, humbug, inveigle, mislead, racket, rip off, rook, swindle, trick.
n. bluff, deception, fraud, grift, kidology, scam, swindle, trick.

concatenation *n.* chain, connection, course, interlinking, interlocking, linking, nexus, procession, progress, progression, sequence, series, string, succession, thread, trail, train.

concave *adj.* cupped, depressed, emaciated, excavated, hollow, hollowed, incurved, indented, scooped, sunken.
antonym convex.

concavity *n.* basin, bowl, cavity, depression, dimple, dint, dip, dish, fossa, fossula, fovea, foveola, foveole, hole, hollow, hollowness, indentation, invagination, pit, recess, sag, sink, umbilicus, vacuity.
antonyms convexity, mound, protuberance.

conceal *v.* bury, camouflage, cloak, cover, disguise, dissemble, hide, keep dark, mask, obscure, screen, secrete, shelter, sink, smother, submerge, suppress, veil.
antonym reveal.

concealed *adj.* clandestine, covered, covert, disguised, hidden, inconspicuous, masked, perdu(e), screened, secret, secreted, ulterior, unseen, veiled.
antonyms clear, plain.

concealment *n.* ambush, camouflage, cloak, cover, disguise, hide-away, hideout, hiding, protection, screen, secrecy, shelter.
antonyms openness, revelation.

concede *v.* accept, acknowledge, admit, allow, cede, confess, forfeit, grant, own, recognise, relinquish, sacrifice, surrender, yield.
antonyms deny, dispute.

conceit[1] *n.* arrogance, assumption, cockiness, complacency, conceitedness, egotism, narcissism, pride, self-assumption, self-conceit, self-importance, self-love, self-pride, self-satisfaction, swagger, vainglory, vainness, vanity.
antonyms diffidence, modesty.

conceit[2] *n.* belief, caprice, concetto, fancy, fantasy, freak, humour, idea, image, imagination, impulse, jeu d'esprit, judgement, notion, opinion, quip, quirk, thought, vagary, whim, whimsy, wit.

conceited *adj.* arrogant, assuming, bigheaded, cocky, complacent, egotistical, highty-tighty, hoity-toity, immodest, narcissistic, overweening, self-important, self-satisfied, stuck-up, swell-headed, swollen-headed, toffee-nose(d), uppist, uppity, vain, vainglorious, windy.
antonyms diffident, modest.

conceivable *adj.* believable, credible, imagin-

able, likely, possible, probable, supposable, tenable, thinkable.
antonym inconceivable.

conceive *v.* appreciate, apprehend, believe, comprehend, contrive, create, design, develop, devise, envisage, fancy, form, formulate, germinate, grasp, ideate, imagine, invent, originate, produce, project, purpose, realise, suppose, think, understand, visualise.

concentrate *v.* absorb, accumulate, attend, attract, centre, cluster, collect, condense, congregate, converge, crowd, draw, engross, focus, foregather, gather, huddle, intensify.
antonyms disperse, distract, separate.
n. apozem, decoction, decocture, distillate, distillation, elixir, essence, extract, juice, quintessence.

concentrated *adj.* all-out, compact, condensed, deep, dense, evaporated, hard, intense, intensive, reduced, rich, thickened, undiluted.
antonyms desultory, diffuse, diluted.

concentration *n.* absorption, accumulation, agglomeration, aggregation, application, centralisation, centring, cluster, collection, combination, compression, conglomeration, consolidation, convergence, crowd, denseness, focusing, grouping, heed, horde, intensification, intensity, mass, single-mindedness.
antonyms dilution, dispersal, distraction.

concept *n.* abstraction, conception, conceptualisation, construct, hyphothesis, idea, image, impression, invention, notion, pattern, picture, plan, theory, type, view, visualisation.

conception *n.* appreciation, apprehension, beginning, birth, clue, comprehension, concept, design, envisagement, fertilisation, formation, germination, idea, image, impregnation, impression, inauguration, inception, initiation, inkling, insemination, invention, knowledge, launching, notion, origin, outset, perception, picture, plan, understanding, visualisation.

concern *v.* affect, bother, disquiet, distress, disturb, interest, involve, pertain to, perturb, refer to, regard, relate to, touch, trouble, upset, worry.
n. affair, anxiety, apprehension, attention, bearing, burden, business, care, charge, company, consideration, corporation, disquiet, disquietude, distress, enterprise, establishment, field, firm, heed, house, importance, interest, involvement, job, matter, mission, occupation, organisation, perturbation, reference, relation, relevance, responsibility, solicitude, stake, task, transaction, unease, uneasiness, worry.
antonym unconcern.

concerned *adj.* active, anxious, apprehensive, attentive, bothered, caring, connected, disquieted, distressed, disturbed, exercised, implicated, interested, involved, perturbed, solicitous, troubled, uneasy, unhappy, upset, worried.
antonym unconcerned.

concerning *prep.* about, anent, apropos of, as regards, germane to, in regard to, in the matter of, re, regarding, relating to, relevant to, respecting, touching, with reference to, with regard to.

concert[1] *n.* accord, agreement, concord, concordance, consonance, diapason, harmony, unanimity, union, unison.
antonym disunity.

concert[2] *n.* appearance, engagement, gig, performance, presentation, production, recital, rendering, rendition, show.

concerted *adj.* collaborative, collective, combined, co-ordinated, joint, organised, planned, prearranged, shared, united.
antonyms disorganised, separate, uncoordinated.

concert-hall *n.* assembly room, auditorium, chamber, music hall, odeon, town hall.

concession *n.* acknowledgement, adjustment, admission, allowance, assent, boon, compromise, exception, favour, grant, indulgence, permit, privilege, relaxation, sacrifice, surrender, yielding.

conciliate *v.* appease, disarm, disembitter, mollify, pacify, placate, propitiate, satisfy, soften, soothe.
antonym antagonise.

conciliation *n.* appeasement, indulgence, mollification, pacification, peace-making, placation, propitiation, reconciliation, satisfaction.
antonyms alienation, antagonisation.

conciliator *n.* dove, intercessor, intermediary, mediator, negotiator, peace-maker, reconciler.
antonym trouble-maker.

conciliatory *adj.* disarming, irenic, mollifying, pacific, pacificatory, peaceable, placatory, propitiative, propitiatory, reconciliatory.
antonym antagonistic.

concise *adj.* abbreviated, abridged, aphoristic, brief, compact, compendious, compressed, condensed, epigrammatic, gnomic, laconic, pithy, short, succinct, summary, synoptic, terse, thumbnail.
antonyms diffuse, expansive.

conclave *n.* assembly, cabal, cabinet, confabulation, conference, conspiracy, conventicle, council, meeting, parley, powwow, session.

conclude *v.* accomplish, assume, cease, clinch, close, complete, consummate, culminate, decide, deduce, determine, effect, end, establish, finish, fix, gather, infer, judge, opine, reckon, resolve, settle, suppose, surmise, terminate.

concluding *adj.* closing, epilogic, epilogistic, final, last, perorating, terminal, ultimate.
antonym introductory.

conclusion *n.* answer, assumption, clincher, close, come-off, completion, consequence, consummation, conviction, culmination, decision, deduction, end, explicit, finale, fine, finis, finish, illation, inference, issue, judgement, opinion, outcome, resolution, result, settlement, solution, termination, upshot, verdict.

conclusive *adj.* clear, clinching, convincing, decisive, definite, definitive, final, incontrovertible, irrefragable, irrefutable, manifest, ultimate, unanswerable, unappealable, unarguable, undeniable.
antonym inconclusive.

concoct *v.* brew, contrive, decoct, design, develop, devise, digest, fabricate, form, formulate, hatch, invent, mature, plan, plot, prepare, project, refine.

concoction *n.* blend, brew, combination, compound, contrivance, creation, decoction, fable, mixture, myth, potion, preparation, story.

concomitant *adj.* accompanying, associative, attendant, co-existent, coincidental, collateral, complementary, concurrent, contemporaneous, conterminous, contributing, incidental, simultaneous, synchronous, syndromic.
antonyms accidental, unrelated.
n. accompaniment, by-product, epiphenomenon, incidental, secondary, symptom.

concord *n.* accord, agreement, amicability, amity, brotherliness, compact, concert, concordat, consensus, consonance, convention, diapason, entente, friendship, harmony, peace, protocol, rapport, treaty, unanimity, unison.
antonym discord.

concourse *n.* assemblage, assembly, collection, confluence, convergence, crowd, crush, entrance, foyer, frequence, gathering, hall, lobby, lounge, meeting, multitude, piazza, plaza, press, swarm, throng.

concrete *adj.* actual, calcified, compact, compressed, conglomerated, consolidated, definite, explicit, factual, firm, material, perceptible, petrified, physical, real, seeable, sensible, solid, solidified, specific, substantial, tactile, tangible, touchable, visible.
antonym abstract.

concubine *n.* apple-squire, courtesan, hetaira, leman, lorette, lover, mistress, odalisque, paramour.

concupiscence *n.* appetite, desire, horniness, lasciviousness, lechery, lewdness, libidinousness, libido, lickerishness, lubricity, lust, lustfulness, randiness, ruttishness.

concupiscent *adj.* horny, lascivious, lecherous, lewd, libidinous, lickerish, lubricious, lustful, randy, ruttish.

concur *v.* accede, accord, acquiesce, agree, approve, assent, coincide, combine, comply, consent, co-operate, harmonise, join, meet, unite.
antonym disagree.

concurrence *n.* acquiescence, agreement, assent, association, co-existence, coincidence, common ground, community, concomitance, conjunction, consilience, contemporaneity, convergence, juxtaposition, simultaneity, synchrony, syndrome.
antonyms difference, disagreement.

concurrent *adj.* co-existing, coincident, coincid-ing, concerted, concomitant, confluent, consilient, contemporaneous, convergent, converging, simultaneous, synchronous, syndromic, uniting.

condemn *v.* ban, blame, castigate, censure, convict, damn, decry, denounce, disapprove, disparage, doom, pan, proscribe, reprehend, reproach, reprobate, reprove, revile, sentence, slam, slate, upbraid.
antonyms approve, praise.

condemnation *n.* ban, blame, castigation, censure, conviction, damnation, denouncement, denunciation, disapproval, disparagement, judgement, proscription, reproach, reprobation, reproof, sentence, slating, stricture, thumbs-down.
antonyms approval, praise.

condemnatory *adj.* accusatory, accusing, censorious, critical, damnatory, denunciatory, deprecatory, disapproving, discouraging, incriminating, proscriptive, reprobative, reprobatory, unfavourable.
antonyms approving, complimentary, indulgent, laudatory.

condensation *n.* abridgement, compression, concentrate, concentration, condensate, consolidation, contraction, crystallisation, curtailment, decoction, deliquescence, digest, distillate, distillation, encapsulation, liquefaction, precipitate, precipitation, précis, reduction, synopsis.

condense *v.* abbreviate, abridge, capsulise, coagulate, compact, compress, concentrate, contract, crystallise, curtail, decoct, distil, encapsulate, epitomise, evaporate, inspissate, precipitate, précis, reduce, shorten, solidify, summarise, synopsise, thicken.
antonyms dilute, expand.

condensed *adj.* abbreviated, abridged, abstracted, capsular, clotted, coagulated, compact, compressed, concentrated, concise, contracted, crystallised, curtailed, distilled, epitomised, evaporated, precipitated, reduced, shortened, shrunken, summarised, thickened.
antonyms diluted, expanded.

condescend *v.* bend, deign, patronise, see fit, stoop, submit, unbend, vouchsafe.

condescending *adj.* de haut en bas, disdainful, gracious, haughty, imperious, lofty, lordly, patronising, snooty, stooping, supercilious, superior, unbending.
antonyms approachable, humble.

condescension *n.* affability, airs, civility, courtesy, deference, disdain, favour, generosity, graciousness, haughtiness, loftiness, lordliness, superciliousness, superiority.
antonym humility.

condign *adj.* adequate, apposite, appropriate, deserved, earned, fitting, just, meet, merited, suitable, well-earned, well-merited.
antonym unjust.

condition *n.* ailment, arrangement, article, case, caste, circumstances, class, complaint, defect, demand, diathesis, disease, disorder, estate, fettle, fitness, grade, health, infirmity, kilter, level, liability, limitation, malady, modification, nick, obligation, order, plight, position, predicament, prerequisite, problem, provision, proviso, qualification, rank, requirement, requisite, restriction, rule, shape, situation, state, status, stipulation, stratum, terms, trim, understanding, weakness.

v. accustom, adapt, adjust, attune, determine, educate, equip, groom, habituate, hone, indoctrinate, inure, limit, prepare, prime, ready, restrict, season, temper, train, tune.

conditional *adj.* contingent, dependent, limited, provisional, qualified, relative, restricted, tied.

antonym unconditional.

conditioned *adj.* acclimatised, accustomed, adapted, adjusted, attuned, familiarised, groomed, habituated, honed, indoctrinated, inured, prepared, primed, seasoned, tempered, trained, tuned, used.

conditioning *n.* acculturation, adjustment, education, familiarisation, grooming, hardening, honing, indoctrination, inurement, preparation, priming, reorientation, seasoning, tempering, training, tuning.

conditions *n.* atmosphere, background, circumstances, context, environment, habitat, medium, milieu, setting, situation, state, surroundings.

condolence *n.* commiseration, compassion, condolences, consolation, pity, support, sympathy.

antonym congratulation.

condom *n.* French letter, johnnie, johnny, protective, rubber, safe, sheath.

condone *v.* allow, brook, disregard, excuse, forgive, ignore, indulge, overlook, pardon, tolerate.

antonyms censure, disallow.

conducive *adj.* advantageous, beneficial, contributive, contributory, encouraging, favourable, helpful, leading, productive, promotive, stimulative, tending.

antonyms adverse, unfavourable.

conduct *n.* actions, administration, attitude, bearing, behaviour, carriage, comportment, control, co-ordination, demeanour, deportment, direction, discharge, escort, guidance, guide, leadership, management, manners, mien, orchestration, organisation, running, supervision, ways.

v. accompany, acquit, act, administer, attend, bear, behave, carry, chair, comport, control, convey, demean, deport, direct, escort, govern, guide, handle, lead, manage, orchestrate, organise, pilot, regulate, run, solicit, steer, supervise, transact, usher.

conduit *n.* canal, channel, chute, culvert, ditch, drain, duct, flume, gutter, lade, main, passage, pipe, rhine, tube, water-course, waterway.

confab *n.* blether, chat, chinwag, conclave, confabulation, conference, conversation, discussion, gossip, jaw, natter, powwow, session, talk.

confabulate *v.* blether, chat, clash, claver, confer, converse, discuss, gossip, natter, talk.

confederacy *n.* alliance, Bund, cabal, coalition, compact, confederation, conspiracy, covenant, federation, junta, league, partnership, union.

confederate *adj.* allied, associated, combined, federal, federated.

n. abettor, accessory, accomplice, ally, assistant, associate, collaborator, colleague, conspirator, friend, leaguer, partner, practisant, supporter.

v. ally, amalgamate, associate, bind, combine, federate, join, merge, unite, weld.

confer *v.* accord, award, bestow, consult, converse, deliberate, discourse, discuss, give, grant, impart, lay heads together, lend, parley, powwow, present, talk, vouchsafe.

conference *n.* colloquium, confab, confabulation, congress, consultation, convention, convocation, debate, diet, discussion, forum, indaba, meeting, moot, powwow, seminar, symposium, synod, teach-in.

confess *v.* acknowledge, admit, affirm, agnise, allow, assert, attest, aver, betray, concede, confide, confirm, declare, disclose, divulge, evince, expose, grant, manifest, own, own up, profess, prove, recognise, reveal, show.

antonyms conceal, deny.

confession *n.* acknowledgement, admission, affirmation, assertion, attestation, averment, avowal, confidences, confiteor, declaration, disclosure, divulgence, exposé, exposure, profession, revelation, unbosoming, unburdening, verbal.

antonyms concealment, denial.

confidant *n.* companion, confidante, crony, duenna, familiar, friend, inseparable, intimate, repository.

confide *v.* admit, breathe, confess, disclose, divulge, impart, reveal, unburden, whisper.

antonyms hide, suppress.

confidence *n.* aplomb, assurance, belief, boldness, calmness, communication, composure, confession, coolness, courage, credence, dependence, disclosure, divulgence, faith, firmness, nerve, reliance, savoir-faire, secret, self-assurance, self-confidence, self-possession, self-reliance, trust.

antonyms diffidence, distrust.

confident *adj.* assured, bold, certain, composed, convinced, cool, dauntless, fearless, persuaded, positive, sanguine, satisfied, secure, self-assured, self-confident, self-possessed, self-reliant, sure, unabashed, unbashful, unselfconscious.

antonyms diffident, sceptical.

confidential *adj.* classified, close, closed, faithful, familiar, hush-hush, in camera, intimate, private, privy, secret, tête-à-tête, trusted, trustworthy, trusty.

antonyms common, public.

confidentially *adv.* behind closed doors, between you me and the bed-post (lamp-post,

gate-post), in camera, in confidence, in privacy, in private, in secret, on the quiet, personally, privately, under the rose, within these four walls.
antonym openly.

configuration *n.* arrangement, cast, composition, conformation, contour, deployment, disposition, figure, form, Gestalt, outline, shape.

confine *v.* bind, bound, cage, chamber, circumscribe, constrain, cramp, crib, emmew, enclose, immew, immure, imprison, incarcerate, inhibit, intern, keep, keep prisoner, limit, mew, repress, restrain, restrict, shackle, shut up, thirl, trammel.
antonym free.

confined *adj.* circumscribed, enclosed, housebound, limited, pokey, poking, restricted.
antonyms free, unrestricted.

confinement *n.* accouchement, birth, childbed, childbirth, constraint, custody, delivery, detention, down-lying, gander-month, gander-moon, house-arrest, imprisonment, incarceration, internment, labour, lying-in, parturition, time, travail.
antonym freedom.

confines *n.* border, boundaries, bounds, circumference, edge, frontier, limits, perimeter, periphery, precincts.

confirm *v.* approve, assure, attest, authenticate, back, buttress, clinch, corroborate, endorse, establish, evidence, fix, fortify, homologate, prove, ratify, reinforce, sanction, settle, strengthen, substantiate, support, validate, verify, witness to.
antonym deny.

confirmation *n.* acceptance, agreement, approval, assent, attestation, authentication, backing, clincher, corroboration, endorsement, evidence, proof, ratification, sanction, substantiation, support, testimony, validation, verification, witness.
antonym denial.

confirmed *adj.* authenticated, chronic, committed, corroborated, deep-dyed, dyed-in-the-wool, entrenched, established, habitual, hardened, incorrigible, incurable, ingrained, inured, inveterate, irredeemable, long-established, long-standing, proved, proven, rooted, seasoned, substantiated, unredeemed.
antonyms uncommitted, unconfirmed.

confiscate *v.* appropriate, commandeer, distrain, escheat, expropriate, impound, remove, seize, sequester, sequestrate.
antonym restore.

confiscation *n.* appropriation, distrainment, distraint, escheat, expropriation, forfeiture, impounding, seizure, sequestration, takeover.
antonym restoration.

conflagration *n.* blaze, deflagration, fire, hellfire, holocaust, inferno, wildfire.

conflict *n.* agony, ambivalence, antagonism, antipathy, Armageddon, battle, brawl, clash, collision, combat, confrontation, contention, contest, difference, disagreement, discord, dissension, encounter, engagement, feud, fight, fracas, friction, hostility, interference, opposition, quarrel, set-to, skirmish, strife, turmoil, unrest, variance, war, warfare.
antonyms agreement, concord.
v. battle, clash, collide, combat, contend, contest, contradict, differ, disagree, fight, interfere, oppose, strive, struggle, war, wrangle.
antonym agree.

conflicting *adj.* ambivalent, antagonistic, clashing, contradictory, contrary, discordant, inconsistent, opposed, opposing, opposite, paradoxical, turbulent, warring.
antonym compatible.

confluence *n.* assemblage, assembly, concourse, concurrence, conflux, conjunction, convergence, crowd, disemboguement, host, junction, meeting, multitude, union, watersmeet.

conform *v.* accommodate, accord, adapt, adjust, agree, assimilate, comply, correspond, follow, harmonise, match, obey, quadrate, square, suit, tally, yield.
antonym differ.

conformation *n.* anatomy, arrangement, build, composition, configuration, form, framework, Gestalt, outline, shape, structure.

conformist *n.* Babbit, bourgeois, conventionalist, rubber-stamp, stick-in-the-mud, traditionalist, yes-man.
antonyms bohemian, nonconformist.

conformity *n.* affinity, agreement, allegiance, Babbitry, compliance, congruity, consonance, conventionalism, conventionality, correspondence, Gleichschaltung, harmony, likeness, observance, orthodoxy, resemblance, similarity, traditionalism.
antonyms difference, nonconformity.

confound *v.* abash, amaze, astonish, astound, baffle, bamboozle, bewilder, confuse, contradict, demolish, destroy, discombobulate, dismay, dumbfound, flabbergast, mystify, nonplus, overthrow, overwhelm, perplex, ruin, spif(f)licate, startle, stupefy, surprise, thwart, unshape, upset.

confounded *adj.* arrant, astounded, baffled, bewildered, confused, consummate, cursed, discomfited, dismayed, dumbfounded, egregious, embarrassed, flabbergasted, frustrated, insufferable, mystified, nonplussed, notorious, outrageous, perplexed, rank, thwarted.

confront *v.* accost, address, appose, beard, brave, challenge, defy, encounter, face, front, oppose.
antonym evade.

confrontation *n.* battle, collision, conflict, contest, crisis, disagreement, encounter, engagement, face-off, fight, quarrel, set-to, showdown.

confuse *v.* abash, addle, baffle, befuddle, bemuse, bewilder, buffalo, burble, confound, darken, demoralise, disarrange, discomfit, discompose, disconcert, discountenance, disorder, disorient, disorientate, embarrass, embrangle, flummox, fluster, intermingle, involve, jumble, maze, mingle, mistake, mix up, mortify, muddle, mystify, nonplus, obscure, perplex, puzzle, rattle, shame, tangle, tie in knots, upset.

antonyms clarify, enlighten, reassure.

confused *adj.* addle-brained, addle(d), addle-headed, addle-pated, baffled, bewildered, bushed, chaotic, dazed, désorienté, disarranged, discombobulated, disordered, disorderly, disorganised, disorientated, distracted, embarrassed, flummoxed, fuddled, higgledy-piggledy, jumbled, maffled, mistaken, misunderstood, muddled, muddle-headed, muzzy, nonplussed, perplexed, puzzled, puzzle-headed, streaked, topsy-turvy, tosticated, untidy, upset.

antonym clear.

confusing *adj.* ambiguous, baffling, bewildering, complicated, contradictory, cryptic, difficult, inconclusive, inconsistent, involved, misleading, muddling, perplexing, puzzling, tortuous, unclear.

antonyms clear, definite.

confusion *n.* abashment, Babel, balls-up, befuddlement, bemusement, bewilderment, bustle, chagrin, chaos, clutter, cock-up, combustion, commotion, demoralisation, disarrangement, discomfiture, disorder, disorganisation, disorientation, distraction, dudder, égarement, embarrassment, embroglio, embroilment, fluster, hotchpotch, hubble-bubble, huggermugger, imbroglio, jumble, mess, mix-up, muddle, mystification, overthrow, palaver, perdition, perplexity, perturbation, pie, puzzlement, shambles, shame, tangle, tizz(y), topsyturviness, topsyturvy, topsyturvydom, toss, turmoil, untidiness, upheaval, welter.

antonyms clarity, composure, order.

confute *v.* annihilate, confound, controvert, disprove, give the lie to, impune, invalidate, nullify, oppugn, overthrow, overturn, rebut, refute, vitiate.

antonyms confirm, prove.

congeal *v.* clot, coagulate, coalesce, concrete, condense, curdle, freeze, fuse, geal, gelatinate, gelatinise, harden, jell, jelly, pectise, set, solidify, stiffen, thicken.

antonyms dissolve, melt, separate.

congealment *n.* clotting, coalescence, concretion, condensing, congelation, curdling, freezing, fusion, gelatination, gelatinisation, hardening, jelling, setting, solidification, stiffening, thickening.

antonyms liquefaction, melting, separation.

congenial *adj.* agreeable, companionable, compatible, complaisant, cosy, delightful, favourable, friendly, gemütlich, genial, homely, kindly, kindred, like-minded, pleasant, pleasing, relaxing, suitable, sympathetic, well-suited.

antonym disagreeable.

congenital *adj.* complete, connate, constitutional, hereditary, inborn, inbred, ingenerate,

inherent, inherited, innate, inveterate, natural, thorough, utter.

congested *adj.* blocked, clogged, crammed, engorged, full, jammed, overcharged, overcrowded, overfilled, overflowing, overfull, packed, saturated, stuffed, swollen, teeming.

antonym clear.

congestion *n.* bottle-neck, clogging, engorgement, fullness, gridlock, jam, log-jam, mass, overcrowding, overfullness, snarl-up, surfeit, traffic-jam.

conglomerate *adj.* agglutinated, amassed, clustered, coherent, composite, conglutinated, heterogeneous, massed.

v. accumulate, agglomerate, agglutinate, aggregate, amass, assemble, clump, cohere, collect, congregate, foregather, gather, mass.

antonym separate.

n. agglomerate, aggregate, composite, congeries, mass, multinational.

conglomeration *n.* accumulation, agglomeration, agglutination, aggregation, assemblage, combination, composite, congeries, hotchpotch, mass, medley.

congratulate *v.* compliment, felicitate, gratulate.

antonym commiserate.

congratulations *n.* compliments, felicitations, good wishes, greetings.

antonyms commiserations, condolences.

congregate *v.* accumulate, assemble, bunch, clump, cluster, collect, concentrate, conglomerate, convene, converge, convoke, crowd, flock, foregather, gather, mass, meet, muster, rally, rendezvous, throng.

antonyms dismiss, disperse.

congregation *n.* assemblage, assembly, brethren, concourse, crowd, fellowship, flock, host, laity, multitude, parish, parishioners, throng.

congress *n.* assembly, conclave, conference, convention, convocation, council, diet, forum, legislature, meeting, parliament, synod.

congruity *n.* agreement, coincidence, compatibility, concinnity, concurrence, conformity, congruence, congruousness, consistency, correspondence, harmony, identity, match, parallelism.

antonym incongruity.

conical *adj.* cone-shaped, conic, conoid, fastigiate(d), funnel-shaped, infundibular, infundibulate, infundibuliform, pointed, pyramidal, tapered, tapering.

conjectural *adj.* academic, assumed, hypothetical, posited, postulated, speculative, supposed, suppositional, surmised, tentative, theoretical.

antonyms factual, real.

conjecture *v.* assume, estimate, extrapolate, fancy, guess, hypothesise, imagine, infer, opine, reckon, speculate, suppose, surmise, suspect, theorise.

n. assumption, conclusion, estimate, extrapolation, fancy, guess, guesstimate, guesswork, hypothesis, inference, notion, opinion, presumption, projection, speculation, supposition, surmise, theorising, theory.

conjugal *adv.* bridal, connubial, epithalamic, hymeneal, marital, married, matrimonial, nuptial, spousal, wedded.

conjunction *n.* amalgamation, association, coincidence, combination, concurrence, juxtaposition, syzygy, unification, union, unition.

conjuncture *n.* combination, concomitance, concurrence, connection, crisis, crossroads, emergency, exigency, juncture, pass, predicament, simultaneity, stage.

conjure *v.* adjure, beseech, bewitch, charm, compel, crave, enchant, entreat, fascinate, implore, importune, invoke, juggle, pray, raise, rouse, summon, supplicate.
   conjure up awaken, contrive, create, evoke, excite, produce, recall, recollect.

conjuror, conjurer *n.* illusionist, magician, miracle-worker, prestidigitator, prestigiator, sorcerer, thaumaturge, wizard.

conk out break down, collapse, fail, fall asleep.

connect *v.* affix, ally, associate, cohere, combine, compaginate, concatenate, couple, enlink, fasten, join, link, relate, unite.
   antonym disconnect.

connected *adj.* affiliated, akin, allied, associate, associated, bracketed, combined, confederate, coupled, joined, linked, related, united.
   antonyms disconnected, unconnected.

connection *n.* acquaintance, affinity, alliance, ally, arthrosis, associate, association, attachment, bond, catenation, coherence, commerce, communication, compagination, conjunction, contact, context, correlation, correspondence, coupling, fastening, friend, hook-up, intercourse, interrelation, intimacy, junction, kin, kindred, kinsman, kith, link, marriage, reference, relation, relationship, relative, relevance, sponsor, tie, tie-in, union.
   antonym disconnection.

connivance *n.* abetment, abetting, collusion, complicity, condoning, consent, jobbery.

connive *v.* cabal, coact, collude, complot, conspire, intrigue, plot, scheme.
   connive at abet, aid, blink at, condone, disregard, let go, overlook, turn a blind eye to, wink at.

connoisseur *n.* aficionado, appreciator, arbiter, authority, buff, cognoscente, devotee, expert, iconophilist, judge, savant, specialist, virtuoso.

connoisseurship *n.* virtuosity.

connotation *n.* association, colouring, hint, implication, nuance, overtone, significance, suggestion, undertone.

connote *v.* betoken, hint at, imply, import, indicate, intimate, involve, purport, signify, suggest.

connubial *adj.* conjugal, epithalamic, hymeneal, marital, married, matrimonial, nuptial, wedded.

conquer *v.* acquire, annex, beat, best, checkmate, crush, defeat, discomfit, get the better of, humble, master, obtain, occupy, overcome, overpower, overrun, overthrow, prevail, quell, rout, seize, subdue, subjugate, succeed, surmount, triumph, vanquish, win, worst.
   antonyms surrender, yield.

conqueror *n.* champ, champion, conquistador, defeater, hero, lord, master, number one, subjugator, vanquisher, victor, winner.

conquest *n.* acquisition, annexation, appropriation, captivation, coup, defeat, discomfiture, enchantment, enthralment, enticement, invasion, inveiglement, mastery, occupation, overthrow, rout, seduction, subjection, subjugation, takeover, triumph, vanquishment, victory.

conscience *n.* ethics, morals, principles, scruples, standards.

conscience-stricken *adj.* ashamed, compunctious, contrite, disturbed, guilt-ridden, guilty, penitent, regretful, remorseful, repentant, sorry, troubled.
   antonyms unashamed, unrepentant.

conscientious *adj.* careful, diligent, exact, faithful, hard-working, high-minded, high-principled, honest, honourable, incorruptible, just, meticulous, moral, painstaking, particular, punctilious, responsible, scrupulous, solicitous, straightforward, strict, thorough, upright.
   antonyms careless, irresponsible.

conscious *adj.* alert, alive, awake, aware, calculated, cognisant, deliberate, heedful, intentional, knowing, mindful, percipient, premeditated, rational, reasoning, reflective, regardful, responsible, responsive, self-conscious, sensible, sentient, studied, wilful, witting.
   antonym unconscious.

consciousness *n.* apprehension, awareness, intuition, knowledge, realisation, recognition, sensibility, sentience.
   antonym unconciousness.

consecrate *v.* beatify, dedicate, devote, exalt, hallow, ordain, revere, sanctify, venerate.

consecutive *adj.* chronological, continuous, following, running, sequential, seriatim, succeeding, successive, unbroken, uninterrupted.
   antonym discontinuous.

consensus *n.* agreement, concord, concurrence, consent, consentience, harmony, unanimity, unity.
   antonym disagreement.

consent *v.* accede, acquiesce, admit, agree, allow, approve, assent, comply, concede, concur, grant, homologate, permit, yield.
   antonyms oppose, refuse.
   n. accordance, acquiescence, agreement, approval, assent, compliance, concession, concurrence, consentience, go-ahead, green light, permission, sanction.
   antonyms opposition, refusal.

consequence *n.* account, concern, distinction, effect, eminence, end, event, fall-out, import, importance, interest, issue, moment, notability, note, outcome, portent, rank, repercussion,

repute, result, side effect, significance, standing, status, upshot, value, weight.
antonym cause.

consequent *adj.* ensuing, following, resultant, resulting, sequent, sequential, subsequent, successive.

consequential *adj.* arrogant, bumptious, conceited, consequent, eventful, far-reaching, grave, important, impressive, indirect, inflated, momentous, noteworthy, pompous, pretentious, resultant, self-important, serious, significant, supercilious, vainglorious, weighty.
antonyms inconsequential, unimportant.

consequently *adv.* accordingly, consequentially, ergo, hence, inferentially, necessarily, subsequently, therefore, thus.

conservation *n.* custody, ecology, economy, guardianship, husbandry, keeping, maintenance, preservation, protection, safeguarding, safe-keeping, saving, upkeep.
antonyms destruction, neglect, waste.

conservatism *n.* conservativeness, conventionalism, orthodoxy, traditionalism, via trita, via truta.
antonym radicalism.

conservative *adj.* cautious, conventional, diehard, establishmentarian, guarded, hidebound, middle-of-the-road, moderate, quiet, reactionary, right-wing, sober, Tory, traditional, unexaggerated, unprogressive, verkrampte.
antonyms left-wing, radical.
n. diehard, moderate, moss-back, reactionary, right-winger, stick-in-the-mud, Tory, traditionalist.
antonyms left-winger, radical.

conservatory *n.* academy, conservatoire, glasshouse, greenhouse, hothouse, institute.

conserve *v.* guard, hoard, husband, keep, maintain, nurse, preserve, protect, save.
antonyms squander, use, waste.

consider *v.* believe, bethink, cogitate, consult, contemplate, count, deem, deliberate, discuss, examine, judge, meditate, mull over, muse, perpend, ponder, rate, reflect, regard, remember, respect, revolve, ruminate, study, think, weigh.
antonym ignore.

considerable *adj.* abundant, ample, appreciable, big, comfortable, distinguished, goodly, great, important, influential, large, lavish, marked, much, noteworthy, noticeable, plentiful, reasonable, renowned, significant, siz(e)able, substantial, tidy, tolerable, venerable.
antonyms insignificant, slight.

considerably *adv.* abundantly, appreciably, greatly, markedly, much, noticeably, remarkably, significantly, substantially.
antonym slightly.

considerate *adj.* attentive, charitable, circumspect, concerned, discreet, forbearing, gracious, kind, kindly, mindful, obliging, patient, solicitous, tactful, thoughtful, unselfish.
antonyms selfish, thoughtless.

consideration *n.* analysis, attention, cogitation, concern, considerateness, contemplation, deliberation, discussion, examination, factor, fee, friendliness, issue, kindliness, kindness, meditation, payment, perquisite, point, recompense, reflection, regard, remuneration, respect, review, reward, rumination, scrutiny, solicitude, study, tact, thought, thoughtfulness, tip.
antonyms disdain, disregard.

consign *v.* commit, convey, deliver, devote, entrust, hand over, relegate, seal, ship, sign, transfer, transmit.

consignment *n.* assignment, batch, cargo, committal, delivery, dispatch, distribution, goods, load, relegation, sending, shipment, transmittal.

consist of amount to, comprise, contain, embody, embrace, include, incorporate, involve.

consist in inhere, lie, reside.

consistency *n.* accordance, agreement, coherence, compactness, compatibility, concordance, congruity, constancy, correspondence, density, evenness, firmness, harmony, identity, regularity, sameness, steadfastness, steadiness, thickness, uniformity, viscosity.
antonym inconsistency.

consistent *adj.* accordant, agreeing, coherent, compatible, congruous, consonant, constant, dependable, harmonious, logical, of a piece, persistent, regular, steady, unchanging, undeviating, unfailing, uniform.
antonyms erratic, inconsistent.

consolation *n.* aid, alleviation, assuagement, cheer, comfort, ease, easement, encouragement, help, relief, solace, succour, support.
antonym discouragement.

console *v.* assuage, calm, cheer, comfort, encourage, hearten, solace, soothe.
antonyms agitate, upset.

consolidate *v.* affiliate, amalgamate, cement, combine, compact, condense, confederate, conjoin, federate, fortify, fuse, harden, join, reinforce, secure, solidify, stabilise, strengthen, thicken, unify, unite.

consolidation *n.* affiliation, alliance, amalgamation, association, compression, condensation, confederation, federation, fortification, fusion, reinforcement, strengthening.

consonance *n.* accord, agreement, compatibility, concord, conformity, congruence, congruity, consistency, correspondence, harmony, suitableness.
antonym dissonance.

consonant *adj.* accordant, according, compatible, concordant, congruous, consistent, correspondent, harmonious, suitable.
antonym dissonant.

consort *n.* associate, companion, fellow, helpmate, helpmeet, husband, partner, spouse, wife.
v. accord, agree, associate, correspond, fraternise, harmonise, jibe, mingle, mix, square, tally.

conspectus n. abstract, compendium, digest, epitome, outline, précis, report, résumé, review, statement, summary, survey, syllabus, synopsis.

conspicuous adj. apparent, blatant, clear, discernible, evident, flagrant, flashy, garish, glaring, kenspeck(le), manifest, noticeable, obvious, patent, perceptible, remarked, showy, visible.
antonym inconspicuous.

conspiracy n. cabal, collusion, complot, confederacy, fix, frame-up, intrigue, league, machination, plot, scheme, treason.

conspirator n. caballer, conspirer, highbinder, intriguer, plotter, practisant, schemer, traitor.

conspire v. cabal, collude, combine, complot, concur, conduce, confederate, contribute, contrive, co-operate, devise, hatch, intrigue, machinate, manoeuvre, plot, scheme, tend, treason.

constancy n. determination, devotion, faithfulness, fidelity, firmness, fixedness, loyalty, permanence, perseverance, regularity, resolution, stability, steadfastness, steadiness, tenacity, uniformity.
antonyms inconstancy, irregularity.

constant adj. attached, ceaseless, changeless, continual, continuous, dependable, determined, devoted, dogged, endless, eternal, even, everlasting, faithful, firm, fixed, habitual, immutable, incessant, interminable, invariable, loyal, never-ending, non-stop, permanent, perpetual, persevering, persistent, regular, relentless, resolute, stable, staunch, steadfast, steady, sustained, tried-and-true, true, trustworthy, trusty, unalterable, unbroken, unchangeable, unfailing, unflagging, uniform, uninterrupted, unrelenting, unremitting, unshaken, unvarying, unwavering.
antonyms fickle, fitful, irregular, occasional, variable.

constantly adv. always, continually, continuously, endlessly, everlastingly, incessantly, interminably, invariably, non-stop, perpetually, relentlessly, steadfastly, uniformly.
antonym occasionally.

consternation n. alarm, amazement, anxiety, awe, bewilderment, confusion, dismay, disquietude, distress, dread, fear, fright, horror, panic, perturbation, shock, terror, trepidation.
antonym composure.

constituent adj. basic, component, elemental, essential, inherent, integral, intrinsic.
n. bit, component, element, essential, factor, ingredient, part, portion, principle, section, unit.
antonym whole.

constitute v. appoint, authorise, commission, compose, comprise, create, delegate, depute, empower, enact, establish, fix, form, found, inaugurate, make, name, nominate, ordain.

constitution n. build, character, composition, configuration, construction, disposition, establishment, form, formation, habit, health, make-up, nature, organisation, physique, structure, temper, temperament.

constitutional adj. chartered, congenital, immanent, inborn, inherent, innate, intrinsic, organic, statutory, vested.
n. airing, promenade, stroll, turn, walk.

constrain v. bind, bulldoze, chain, check, coerce, compel, confine, constrict, curb, drive, force, impel, necessitate, oblige, pressure, pressurise, railroad, restrain, urge.

constrained adj. embarrassed, forced, guarded, inhibited, reserved, reticent, stiff, subdued, uneasy, unnatural.
antonyms free, relaxed.

constraint n. check, coaction, coercion, compulsion, curb, damper, deterrent, duress, force, hindrance, limitation, necessity, pressure, restraint, restriction.

constrict v. choke, compact, compress, constringe, contract, cramp, inhibit, limit, narrow, pinch, restrict, shrink, squeeze, strangle, strangulate, tighten.
antonym expand.

constriction n. blockage, compression, constraint, constringency, cramp, impediment, limitation, narrowing, pressure, reduction, restriction, squeezing, stenosis, stricture, tightening, tightness.
antonym expansion.

construct v. assemble, build, compose, create, design, elevate, engineer, erect, establish, fabricate, fashion, form, formulate, found, frame, knock together, make, manufacture, model, organise, raise, shape.
antonyms demolish, destroy.

construction n. assembly, building, composition, constitution, creation, edifice, erection, fabric, fabrication, figure, form, formation, model, organisation, shape, structure.
antonym destruction.

constructive adj. advantageous, beneficial, helpful, positive, practical, productive, useful, valuable.
antonyms destructive, negative, unhelpful.

construe v. analyse, decipher, deduce, explain, expound, infer, interpret, parse, read, render, take, translate.

consult v. ask, commune, confer, consider, debate, deliberate, interrogate, parley, pow-wow, question, regard, respect.

consultant n. adviser, authority, expert, specialist.

consultation n. appointment, colloquy, conference, council, deliberation, dialogue, discussion, examination, hearing, interview, meeting, parley, session.

consumables n. comestibles, eatables, fungibles.

consume v. absorb, annihilate, decay, demolish, deplete, destroy, devastate, devour, discuss, dissipate, drain, eat, employ, engulf, envelop, exhaust, expend, gobble, guzzle, lessen, ravage, spend, squander, swallow, use (up), utilise, vanish, waste, wear out.

consumed adj. absorbed, devoured, dominated,

engrossed, monopolised, obsessed, preoccupied.

consumer *n.* buyer, customer, end-user, purchaser, shopper, user.

consuming *adj.* absorbing, compelling, devouring, dominating, engrossing, excruciating, gripping, immoderate, monopolising, overwhelming, tormenting.

consummate *v.* accomplish, achieve, cap, compass, complete, conclude, crown, effectuate, end, finish, fulfil, perfect, perform, terminate.
adj. absolute, accomplished, complete, conspicuous, distinguished, finished, matchless, perfect, polished, practised, skilled, superb, superior, supreme, total, transcendent, ultimate, unqualified, utter.
antonym imperfect.

consummation *n.* achievement, actualisation, completion, culmination, end, fulfilment, perfection, realisation, termination.

consumption *n.* consuming, decay, decline, decrease, depletion, destruction, diminution, dissipation, emaciation, exhaustion, expenditure, loss, phthisis, tabefaction, tabes, TB, tuberculosis, use, utilisation, waste.

contact *n.* acquaintance, approximation, association, communication, connection, contiguity, contingence, impact, junction, juxtaposition, meeting, tangency, touch, union.
v. approach, call, get hold of, notify, phone, reach, ring.

contagious *adj.* catching, communicable, epidemic, epizootic, infectious, pestiferous, pestilential, spreading, transmissible, zymotic.

contain *v.* accommodate, check, comprehend, comprise, control, curb, embody, embrace, enclose, entomb, hold, include, incorporate, involve, limit, repress, restrain, seat, stifle.
antonym exclude.

container *n.* holder, hopper, receptacle, repository, vessel.

contaminate *v.* adulterate, befoul, besmirch, corrupt, debase, defile, deprave, infect, pollute, soil, stain, sully, taint, tarnish, vitiate.
antonym purify.

contamination *n.* adulteration, contagion, corruption, decay, defilement, desecration, filth, foulness, impurity, infection, poisoning, pollution, rottenness, taint, vitiation.
antonym purification.

contemplate *v.* behold, cerebrate, consider, deliberate, design, envisage, examine, expect, eye, foresee, inspect, intend, mean, meditate, mull over, observe, plan, ponder, propose, reflect on, regard, ruminate, scrutinise, study, survey, view.

contemplation *n.* cerebration, cogitation, consideration, deliberation, examination, inspection, meditation, musing, observation, pondering, reflection, reverie, rumination, scrutiny, survey, thought, viewing.

contemplative *adj.* cerebral, intent, introspective, meditative, musing, pensive, rapt, reflective, ruminative, thoughtful.

antonyms impulsive, thoughtless.

contemporary *adj.* à la mode, coetaneous, coeval, co-existent, co-existing, concurrent, contemporaneous, conterminous, coterminous, current, latest, modern, newfangled, present, present-day, recent, synchronous, ultra-modern, up-to-date, up-to-the-minute, with it.
antonyms preceding, succeeding.

contempt *n.* condescension, contumely, derision, despite, detestation, disdain, disgrace, dishonour, disregard, disrespect, floccinaucinihilipilification, humiliation, loathing, mockery, neglect, scorn, shame, slight.
antonyms admiration, regard.

contemptible *adj.* abject, base, cheap, degenerate, despicable, detestable, ignominious, loathsome, low, low-down, mean, paltry, pitiful, scurvy, shabby, shameful, vile, worthless, wretched.
antonyms admirable, honourable.

contemptuous *adj.* arrogant, cavalier, condescending, contumacious, contumelious, cynical, derisive, disdainful, haughty, high and mighty, insolent, insulting, scornful, sneering, supercilious, tossy, withering.
antonyms humble, polite, respectful.

contemptuously *adv.* arrogantly, de haut en bas, derisively, disdainfully, haughtily, insolently, pompously, scornfully, superciliously.
antonyms humbly, politely, respectfully.

contend *v.* affirm, allege, argue, assert, aver, avow, clash, compete, contest, cope, debate, declare, dispute, emulate, grapple, hold, jostle, litigate, maintain, skirmish, strive, struggle, vie, wrestle.

content[1] *v.* appease, delight, gladden, gratify, humour, indulge, mollify, pacify, placate, please, reconcile, satisfy, suffice.
antonym displease.
n. comfort, contentment, delight, ease, gratification, happiness, peace, pleasure, satisfaction.
antonym discontent.
adj. agreeable, comfortable, contented, fulfilled, pleased, satisfied, untroubled.
antonym dissatisfied.

content[2] *n.* burden, capacity, essence, gist, ideas, load, matter, meaning, measure, significance, size, subject matter, substance, text, thoughts, volume.

contented *adj.* cheerful, comfortable, complacent, content, glad, gratified, happy, placid, pleased, relaxed, satisfied, serene, thankful.
antonym discontented.

contention *n.* affirmation, allegation, argument, assertion, asseveration, belief, claim, competition, contest, controversy, debate, declaration, discord, dispute, dissension, enmity, feuding, ground, hostility, idea, opinion, position, profession, rivalry, stand, strife, struggle, thesis, view, wrangling.

contentious *adj.* antagonistic, argumentative, bickering, captious, cavilling, combative, controversial, cross, debat(e)able, disputatious, factious, hostile, litigious, peevish, perverse, pugnacious, quarrelsome, querulous, wrangling.

antonyms co-operative, peaceable, uncontroversial.

contentment *n.* comfort, complacency, content, contentedness, ease, equanimity, fulfilment, gladness, gratification, happiness, peace, peacefulness, placidity, pleasure, repletion, satisfaction, serenity.

antonym dissatisfaction.

contents *n.* chapters, constituents, divisions, elements, ingredients, items, load, parts, subjects, themes, topics.

contest *n.* affray, altercation, battle, combat, competition, concours, conflict, controversy, debate, discord, dispute, encounter, fight, game, match, olympiad, set-to, shock, struggle, tournament, trial.

v. argue against, challenge, compete, contend, debate, deny, dispute, doubt, fight, litigate, oppose, question, refute, strive, vie.

contestant *n.* agonist, aspirant, candidate, competitor, contender, entrant, participant, player.

context *n.* ambience, associations, background, circumstances, conditions, connection, frame of reference, framework, relation, situation.

contiguous *adj.* abutting, adjacent, adjoining, beside, bordering, conjoining, conterminous, juxtaposed, juxtapositional, near, neighbouring, next, tangential, touching.

antonyms distort, separate.

continence *n.* abstemiousness, abstinence, asceticism, celibacy, chastity, moderation, self-control, self-restraint, sobriety, temperance.

antonym incontinence.

continent *adj.* abstemious, abstinent, ascetic, austere, celibate, chaste, pure, restrained, self-restrained, sober, virginal.

antonym incontinent.

contingency *n.* accident, arbitrariness, chance, emergency, event, eventuality, fortuity, happening, incident, juncture, possibility, randomness, uncertainty.

contingent *n.* batch, body, bunch, company, complement, deputation, detachment, group, mission, quota, section, set.

continual *adj.* ceaseless, constant, continuous, endless, eternal, everlasting, frequent, incessant, interminable, oft-repeated, perpetual, recurrent, regular, repeated, repetitive, unbroken, unceasing, uninterrupted, unremitting.

antonyms intermittent, occasional, temporary.

continually *adv.* always, ceaselessly, constantly, endlessly, eternally, everlastingly, forever, incessantly, interminably, non-stop, perpetually, persistently, repeatedly.

antonym occasionally.

continuance *n.* continuation, duration, endurance, period, permanence, protraction, term.

continuation *n.* addition, appendix, epilogue, extension, furtherance, maintenance, perpetuation, postscript, prolongation, resumption, sequel, supplement.

antonyms cessation, termination.

continue *v.* abide, aby(e), adjourn, carry on, endure, extend, go on, last, lengthen, maintain, persevere, persist, proceed, project, prolong, pursue, reach, recommence, remain, rest, resume, stay, stick at, survive, sustain.

antonyms discontinue, stop.

continuing *adj.* abiding, enduring, lasting, on-going, progressing, sustained.

continuity *n.* cohesion, connection, extension, flow, interrelationship, linkage, progression, sequence, succession.

antonym discontinuity.

continuous *adj.* connected, consecutive, constant, continued, extended, non-stop, prolonged, unbroken, unceasing, undivided, uninterrupted.

antonyms discontinuous, intermittent, sporadic.

contort *v.* convolute, deform, disfigure, distort, gnarl, knot, misshape, squirm, twist, warp, wrench, wriggle, writhe.

contortionist *n.* acrobat, gymnast, posture-maker, posture-master, tumbler.

contour *n.* aspect, character, contorno, curve, figure, form, lines, outline, profile, relief, shape, silhouette.

contraband *adj.* banned, black-market, bootleg, forbidden, hot, illegal, illicit, interdicted, prohibited, proscribed, smuggled, unlawful, verboten.

contract *v.* abbreviate, abridge, acquire, agree, arrange, bargain, catch, clinch, close, compress, condense, confine, constrict, constringe, covenant, curtail, develop, dwindle, engage, epitomise, incur, lessen, narrow, negotiate, pledge, purse, reduce, shrink, shrivel, stipulate, tighten, wither, wrinkle.

antonyms enlarge, expand, lengthen.

n. agreement, arrangement, bargain, bond, commission, commitment, compact, concordat, convention, covenant, deal, engagement, handfast, instrument, pact, settlement, stipulation, transaction, treaty, understanding.

contraction *n.* abbreviation, astringency, compression, constriction, diminution, elision, narrowing, reduction, retrenchment, shortening, shrinkage, shrivelling, tensing, tightening.

antonyms expansion, growth.

contradict *v.* belie, challenge, contravene, controvert, counter, counteract, deny, disaffirm, dispute, gainsay, impugn, negate, oppose.

antonyms agree, confirm, corroborate.

contradiction *n.* conflict, confutation, contravention, denial, disaffirmance, disaffirmation, gainsay, Hibernicism, incongruity, inconsistency, negation, opposite.

antonyms agreement, confirmation, corroboration.

contradictory *adj.* antagonistic, antithetical, conflicting, contrary, discrepant, dissident, double-mouthed, incompatible, inconsistent, irreconcilable, opposed, opposite, paradoxical, repugnant, unreconciled.
antonym consistent.

contraption *n.* apparatus, contrivance, device, gadget, gizmo, mechanism, rig, thingumajig, widget.

contrary *adj.* adverse, antagonistic, arsy-versy, awkward, balky, cantankerous, clashing, contradictory, counter, cross-grained, cussed, difficult, discordant, disobliging, froward, hostile, inconsistent, inimical, intractable, intractible, obstinate, opposed, opposite, paradoxical, perverse, stroppy, thrawn, unaccommodating, wayward, wilful.
antonyms like, obliging, similar.
n. antithesis, converse, opposite, reverse.

contrast *n.* comparison, contraposition, contrariety, counter-view, difference, differentiation, disparity, dissimilarity, distinction, divergence, foil, opposition, set-off.
antonym similarity.
v. compare, differ, differentiate, discriminate, distinguish, oppose, set off.

contravene *v.* break, contradict, counteract, cross, disobey, hinder, infract, infringe, interfere, oppose, refute, thwart, transgress, trespass, violate.
antonym uphold.

contretemps *n.* accident, calamity, difficulty, hitch, misadventure, misfortune, mishap, mistake, predicament.

contribute *v.* add, afford, bestow, conduce, dob in, donate, furnish, give, help, kick in, lead, provide, subscribe, supply, tend.
antonyms subtract, withhold.

contribution *n.* addition, bestowal, donation, gift, grant, gratuity, handout, input, offering, subscription.

contributor *n.* backer, benefactor, bestower, conferrer, correspondent, donor, freelance, freelancer, giver, journalist, patron, reporter, subscriber, supporter.

contrite *adj.* chastened, conscience-stricken, guilt-ridden, humble, penitent, penitential, penitentiary, regretful, remorseful, repentant, sorrowful, sorry.

contrition *n.* compunction, humiliation, penitence, remorse, repentance, sackcloth and ashes, self-reproach, sorrow.

contrivance *n.* apparatus, appliance, artifice, contraption, design, device, dodge, equipment, excogitation, expedient, fabrication, formation, gadget, gear, implement, intrigue, invention, inventiveness, knack, machination, machine, measure, mechanism, plan, plot, project, ruse, scheme, stratagem, trick.

contrive *v.* arrange, compass, concoct, construct, create, design, devise, effect, engineer, excogitate, fabricate, frame, improvise, invent, manage, manoeuvre, plan, plot, scheme, wangle.

contrived *adj.* artificial, elaborate, false, forced, laboured, mannered, overdone, planned, recherché, strained, unnatural.
antonym natural.

control *v.* boss, bridle, check, command, conduct, confine, constrain, contain, curb, determine, direct, dominate, govern, lead, limit, manage, manipulate, master, monitor, oversee, pilot, regiment, regulate, repress, restrain, rule, run, stage-manage, steer, subdue, superintend, supervise, suppress, verify.
n. authority, brake, charge, check, clutches, command, curb, direction, dirigism(e), discipline, governance, government, guidance, jurisdiction, leading-strings, leash, limitation, management, mastery, oversight, regulation, rule, superintendence, supervision, supremacy.

controller *n.* administrator, captain, compère, director, executive, executor, gerent, governor, gubernator, manager, marshal, navigator, pilot, ringmaster, ruler, steward.

controversial *adj.* attacking, contentious, controvertible, debatable, disputable, disputed, doubtful, polemic, polemical, questionable.

controversy *n.* altercation, argument, contention, debate, disagreement, discussion, dispute, dissension, polemic, quarrel, squabble, strife, war of words, wrangle, wrangling.
antonyms accord, agreement.

controvert *v.* argue, challenge, contest, contradict, counter, debate, deny, disaffirm, discuss, dispute, gainsay, oppose, refute, wrangle.

contumacious *adj.* haughty, headstrong, insubordinate, intractable, intransigent, mulish, obdurate, obstinate, perverse, pig-headed, rebellious, recalcitrant, refractory, stiff-necked, stubborn, wilful.
antonym obedient.

contumely *n.* abuse, affront, arrogance, contempt, derision, disdain, humiliation, incivility, indignity, insolence, insult, invective, obloquy, opprobrium, rudeness, scorn, superciliousness.

contusion *n.* bruise, bump, discolouration, injury, knock, lump, swelling.

conundrum *n.* anagram, brain-teaser, enigma, poser, problem, puzzle, riddle.

convalescence *n.* improvement, recovery, recuperation, rehabilitation, restoration.

convene *v.* assemble, call, collect, congregate, convoke, gather, meet, muster, rally, summon.

convenience *n.* accessibility, accommodation, advantage, amenity, appliance, appropriateness, availability, benefit, chance, comfort, ease, enjoyment, facility, fitness, handiness, help, leisure, opportuneness, opportunity, satisfaction, service, serviceability, suitability, timeliness, use, usefulness, utility.

convenient *adj.* accessible, adapted, advantageable, appropriate, at hand, available, beneficial, commodious, fit, fitted, handy, helpful, labour-saving, nearby, opportune, seasonable, serviceable, suitable, suited, timely, useful, utile, well-timed.

antonyms awkward, inconvenient.

convention *n.* agreement, assembly, bargain, code, compact, conclave, concordat, conference, congress, contract, convocation, council, custom, delegates, etiquette, formality, matter of form, meeting, pact, practice, propriety, protocol, representatives, stipulation, synod, tradition, treaty, understanding, usage.

conventional *adj.* accepted, arbitrary, bourgeois, common, commonplace, copybook, correct, customary, decorous, expected, formal, habitual, hackneyed, hidebound, iconic, nomic, normal, ordinary, orthodox, pedestrian, prevailing, prevalent, proper, prosaic, regular, ritual, routine, run-of-the-mill, standard, stereotyped, straight, stylised, traditional, unoriginal, uptight, usual, wonted.

antonyms exotic, unconventional, unusual.

converge *v.* approach, coincide, combine, concentrate, concur, focus, gather, join, meet, merge, mingle.

antonyms disperse, diverge.

convergence *n.* approach, blending, coincidence, concentration, concurrence, confluence, conflux, conjunction, intersection, junction, meeting, merging, mingling, union.

antonym divergence.

conversant with acquainted with, apprised of, au fait with, experienced in, familiar with, informed about, knowledgeable about, practised in, proficient in, skilled in, versant with, versed in.

antonym ignorant of.

conversation *n.* chat, chinwag, chitchat, colloquy, communication, communion, confab, confabulation, conference, converse, dialogue, discourse, discussion, exchange, gossip, intercourse, interlocution, powwow, talk, tête-à-tête.

conversational *adj.* chatty, colloquial, communicative, confabulatory, informal, relaxed.

conversationalist *n.* deipnosophist, table-philosopher.

converse[1] *v.* chat, colloquise, commune, confabulate, confer, discourse, talk.

converse[2] *n.* antithesis, contrary, counterpart, obverse, opposite, reverse.

adj. antipodal, antipodean, contrary, counter, opposite, reverse, reversed, transposed.

conversion *n.* adaptation, alteration, change, metamorphosis, metanoia, modification, permutation, proselytisation, rebirth, reconstruction, reformation, regeneration, remodelling, reorganisation, transfiguration, transformation, transmogrification, transmutation.

convert *v.* adapt, alter, apply, appropriate, baptise, change, convince, interchange, metamorphose, modify, permute, proselytise, reform, regenerate, remodel, reorganise, restyle, revise, save, transform, transmogrify, transmute, transpose, turn.

n. catechumen, disciple, neophyte, proselyte, vert.

convertible *adj.* adaptable, adjustable, exchangeable, interchangeable, permutable.

convex *adj.* bulging, gibbous, protuberant, rounded, tumid.

antonym concave.

convey *v.* bear, bequeath, bring, carry, cede, communicate, conduct, deliver, demise, devolve, disclose, fetch, forward, grant, guide, impart, lease, move, relate, reveal, send, steal, support, tell, transfer, transmit, transport, waft, will.

conveyance *n.* carriage, movement, shipment, transfer, transference, transmission, transport, transportation, tran(s)shipment, vehicle, wagonage.

convict *v.* attaint, condemn, imprison, sentence. *n.* con, criminal, culprit, felon, forçat, jail-bird, lag, malefactor, prisoner.

conviction *n.* assurance, belief, certainty, certitude, confidence, convincement, creed, earnestness, faith, fervour, firmness, opinion, persuasion, plerophory, principle, reliance, tenet, view.

convince *v.* assure, confirm, persuade, reassure, satisfy, sway, win over.

convincing *adj.* cogent, conclusive, credible, impressive, incontrovertible, likely, luculent, persuasive, plausible, powerful, probable, telling, verisimiliar.

antonyms dubious, improbable.

convivial *adj.* back-slapping, cheerful, festive, friendly, fun-loving, gay, genial, hearty, hilarious, jolly, jovial, lively, merry, mirthful, sociable.

antonym taciturn.

conviviality *n.* bonhomie, cheer, cordiality, festivity, gaiety, geniality, jollification, jollity, joviality, liveliness, merrymaking, mirth, sociability.

convocation *n.* assemblage, assembly, conclave, concourse, congregation, congress, convention, council, diet, for(e)gathering, meeting, muster, synod.

convoke *v.* assemble, collect, convene, gather, muster, rally, round up, summon.

convoluted *adj.* complex, complicated, gyrose, involved, meandering, tangled, twisting, winding.

antonym straightforward.

convolution *n.* coil, coiling, complexity, contortion, curlicue, gyrus, helix, intricacy, involution, loop, sinuousness, sinuosity, spiral, tortuousness, twist, undulation, volution, whorl, winding.

convoy *n.* attendance, attendant, escort, fleet, guard, protection, train.

convulsion *n.* agitation, commotion, contortion, contraction, cramp, disturbance, eruption, fit, furore, outburst, paroxysm, seizure, shaking, spasm, throe, tremor, tumult, turbulence, upheaval.

convulsive *adj.* churning, fitful, jerky, paroxysmal, spasmodic, spastic, sporadic, twitchy, violent.

cook *n.* chef, chef de cuisine, confectioner,

cuisinier, pastrycook.

v. bake, boil, braise, broil, fry, grill, heat, prepare, roast, sauté, simmer, steam, stew, toast.

cook up brew, concoct, contrive, devise, fabricate, improvise, invent, plan, plot, prepare, scheme.

cool *adj.* aloof, apathetic, audacious, bold, brazen, calm, cheeky, chilled, chilling, chilly, coldish, collected, composed, cosmopolitan, dégagé, deliberate, dispassionate, distant, down-beat, elegant, frigid, impertinent, imperturbable, impudent, incurious, indifferent, laid-back, level-headed, lukewarm, nippy, offhand, placid, pleasant, presumptuous, quiet, refreshing, relaxed, reserved, satisfying, self-controlled, self-possessed, serene, shameless, sophisticated, stand-offish, together, uncommunicative, unconcerned, unemotional, unenthusiastic, unexcited, unfriendly, unheated, uninterested, unresponsive, unruffled, unwelcoming, urbane.

antonyms excited, friendly, hot, warm.

v. abate, allay, assuage, calm, chill, dampen, defuse, fan, freeze, lessen, moderate, quiet, refrigerate, temper.

antonyms excite, heat, warm.

n. calmness, collectedness, composure, control, poise, sangfroid, self-control, self-discipline, self-possession, temper.

cooling *n.* air-conditioning, chilling, defervescence, defervescency, refrigeration, ventilation.

antonyms heating, warming.

adj. freezing, refrigerant, refrigerative, refrigeratory.

antonym warming.

coop *n.* box, cage, enclosure, hutch, mew, pen, pound.

v. cage, confine, immure, impound, imprison, intern, pen.

co-operate *v.* abet, aid, assist, collaborate, combine, concur, conduce, conspire, contribute, co-ordinate, help, play along, play ball.

co-operation *n.* assistance, coaction, collaboration, concert, concurrence, give-and-take, helpfulness, participation, responsiveness, synergy, teamwork, unity.

co-operative *adj.* accommodating, coactive, collective, combined, concerted, coordinated, helpful, joint, obliging, responsive, shared, supportive, synergetic, synergic, unified, united.

antonym unco-operative.

co-ordinate *v.* codify, correlate, grade, graduate, harmonise, integrate, match, mesh, organise, relate, synchronise, systematise, tabulate.

adj. coequal, correlative, correspondent, equal, equipotent, equivalent, parallel, reciprocal.

cop out abandon, desert, dodge, evade, quit, renege, renounce, revoke, shirk, skip, skive, withdraw.

cope *v.* carry on, get by, make (a) shift, make do, manage, survive.

cope with contend with, deal with, dispatch, encounter, grapple with, handle, manage, struggle with, tangle with, tussle with, weather, wrestle with.

copious *adj.* abundant, ample, bounteous, bountiful, extensive, exuberant, full, generous, great, huge, inexhaustible, lavish, liberal, luxuriant, overflowing, plenteous, plentiful, profuse, rich, superabundant.

antonyms meagre, scarce.

copiousness *n.* abundance, amplitude, bountifulness, bounty, cornucopia, exuberance, fullness, lavishness, luxuriance, plenitude, plentifulness, plenty, prodigality, profusion, richness, superabundance.

antonym scarcity.

cop-out *n.* alibi, dodge, evasion, fraud, pretence, pretext.

copulate *v.* cover, enjoy, fuck, gender, horse, line, make love, mate, serve, tread.

copulation *n.* carnal knowledge, coition, coitus, congress, coupling, covering, joining, love, lovemaking, mating, serving, sex, sexual intercourse, treading.

copy *n.* apograph, archetype, autotype, borrowing, calque, carbon copy, counterfeit, crib, duplicate, ectype, engrossment, exemplar, facsimile, flimsy, forgery, image, imitation, likeness, loan translation, loan-word, model, Ozalid®, pattern, photocopy, Photostat®, plagiarisation, print, replica, replication, representation, reproduction, tracing, transcript, transcription, Xerox®.

antonym original.

v. ape, borrow, counterfeit, crib, duplicate, echo, emulate, engross, exemplify, extract, facsimile, follow, imitate, mimic, mirror, parrot, personate, photocopy, Photostat®, plagiarise, repeat, replicate, reproduce, simulate, transcribe, Xerox®.

coquettish *adj.* amorous, arch, come-hither, coy, dallying, flighty, flirtatious, flirty, inviting, teasing, vampish.

cord *n.* bond, connection, funicle, gimp, line, link, rope, strand, string, tie, twine.

cordial *adj.* affable, affectionate, agreeable, cheerful, earnest, friendly, genial, heartfelt, hearty, invigorating, pleasant, restorative, sociable, stimulating, warm, warm-hearted, welcoming, whole-hearted.

antonyms aloof, cool, hostile.

cordiality *n.* affability, affection, amiability, friendliness, geniality, goodwill, heartiness, sincerity, warmth, whole-heartedness.

antonyms coolness, hostility.

cordon *n.* barrier, chain, fence, line, ring.

cordon off encircle, enclose, fence off, isolate, separate, surround.

core *n.* centre, crux, essence, germ, gist, heart, kernel, nitty-gritty, nub, nucleus, pith.

antonyms exterior, perimeter, surface.

corner *n.* angle, bend, cantle, cavity, cranny, crook, hide-away, hideout, hidey-hole, hole, joint, neuk, niche, nook, pickle, predicament, recess, retreat, spot.

corny *adj.* banal, clichéd, commonplace, dull, feeble, hackneyed, maudlin, mawkish, old-fashioned, platitudinous, sentimental, stale, stereotyped, trite.
antonyms new, original.

corollary *n.* conclusion, consequence, deduction, fall-out, illation, induction, inference, result, upshot.

corporal *adj.* anatomical, bodily, carnal, concrete, corporeal, fleshly, material, physical, somatic, tangible.
antonym spiritual.

corporate *adj.* allied, amalgamated, collaborative, collective, combined, communal, concerted, joint, merged, pooled, shared, united.

corporation[1] *n.* association, authorities, body, combine, conglomerate, council, society.

corporation[2] *n.* beer belly, paunch, pod, pot, pot-belly, spare tyre.

corporeal *adj.* actual, bodily, fleshly, human, hylic, material, mortal, physical, substantial, tangible.
antonym spiritual.

corps *n.* band, body, brigade, company, contingent, crew, detachment, division, phalanx, regiment, squad, squadron, team, troop, unit.

corpse *n.* body, cadaver, carcass, deader, remains, skeleton, stiff.

corpulence *n.* adiposity, blubber, burliness, embonpoint, fatness, fleshiness, obesity, plumpness, portliness, rotundity, stoutness, tubbiness.
antonym thinness.

corpulent *adj.* adipose, beefy, bulky, burly, fat, fattish, fleshy, large, lusty, obese, overweight, plump, poddy, podgy, portly, pot-bellied, pudgy, roly-poly, rotund, stout, tubby, well-padded.
antonym thin.

corpus *n.* aggregation, body, collection, compilation, entirety, oeuvre, whole.

corral *n.* coop, enclosure, fold, kraal, pound, stall, sty.

correct *v.* adjust, admonish, amend, blue-pencil, chasten, chastise, chide, counterbalance, cure, debug, discipline, emend, emendate, improve, punish, rectify, redress, reform, regulate, remedy, reprimand, reprove, right.
adj. acceptable, accurate, appropriate, comme il faut, diplomatic, equitable, exact, faultless, fitting, flawless, jake, just, OK, precise, proper, regular, right, seemly, standard, strict, true, well-formed, word-perfect.
antonyms inaccurate, incorrect, wrong.

correction *n.* adjustment, admonition, alteration, amendment, castigation, chastisement, discipline, emendation, improvement, modification, punishment, rectification, reformation, reproof, righting.

corrective *adj.* curative, disciplinary, emendatory, medicinal, palliative, penal, punitive, reformatory, rehabilitative, remedial, restorative, therapeutic.

correctly *adv.* accurately, aright, faithfully, faultlessly, perfectly, precisely, properly, right, rightly.
antonyms incorrectly, wrongly.

correctness *n.* accuracy, breeding, civility, decorum, exactitude, exactness, faithfulness, faultlessness, fidelity, perfection, preciseness, precision, propriety, regularity, seemliness, truth.

correlate *v.* associate, compare, connect, co-ordinate, correspond, equate, interact, link, parallel, relate, tie in.

correlation *n.* alternation, correspondence, equivalence, interaction, interchange, interdependence, interrelationship, link, reciprocity, relationship.

correspond *v.* accord, agree, answer, coincide, communicate, complement, concur, conform, correlate, dovetail, fit, harmonise, match, square, tally, write.

correspondence *n.* agreement, analogy, assonance, coincidence, communication, comparability, comparison, concurrence, conformity, congruity, correlation, equivalence, fitness, harmony, homology, homotypy, letters, mail, match, post, relation, resemblance, respondence, responding, similarity, writing.
antonyms divergence, incongruity.

correspondent *n.* contributor, journalist, penpal, reporter, writer.
adj. analogous, comparable, equivalent, like, matching, parallel, reciprocal, similar.

corresponding *adj.* accordant, analogous, answering, collateral, complementary, correlative, correspondent, equivalent, homologous, homotypal, homotypic, identical, interrelated, matching, reciprocal, similar, synonymous.

corridor *n.* aisle, ambulatory, foyer, hallway, lobby, passage, passageway, vestibule.

corroborate *v.* authenticate, bear out, confirm, document, endorse, establish, prove, ratify, substantiate, support, sustain, underpin, validate.
antonym contradict.

corroborative *adj.* confirmative, confirmatory, evidential, evidentiary, supportive, verificatory.

corrode *v.* canker, consume, corrupt, crumble, deteriorate, disintegrate, eat away, erode, fret, impair, oxidise, rust, waste, wear away.

corrosive *adj.* abrasive, acid, acrid, biting, caustic, consuming, corroding, cutting, incisive, mordant, sarcastic, trenchant, venomous, virulent, wasting, wearing.

corrugated *adj.* channelled, creased, crinkled, fluted, furrowed, grooved, puckered, ribbed, ridged, rumpled, striate(d), wrinkled.

corrupt *adj.* abandoned, adulterate(d), altered, bent, bribed, contaminated, crooked, debased, decayed, defiled, degenerate, demoralised, depraved, dishonest, dishonoured, dissolute, distorted, doctored, falsified, fraudulent, honest, infected, polluted, profligate, putrescent, putrid, rotten, shady, tainted, trustworthy, unethical, unprincipled, unscrupulous, upright, venal, vicious.

v. adulterate, barbarise, bribe, canker, contaminate, debase, debauch, defile, demoralise, deprave, doctor, empoison, entice, fix, infect, lure, pervert, putrefy, seduce, spoil, square, suborn, subvert, taint, vitiate.
antonym purify.

corruption *n.* adulteration, baseness, bribery, bribing, crookedness, debasement, decadence, decay, defilement, degeneration, degradation, demoralisation, depravity, dishonesty, distortion, doctoring, evil, extortion, falsification, fiddling, foulness, fraud, fraudulence, fraudulency, graft, immorality, impurity, infection, iniquity, jobbery, leprosy, malversation, perversion, pollution, profiteering, profligacy, putrefaction, putrescence, rot, rottenness, shadiness, sinfulness, turpitude, ulcer, unscrupulousness, venality, vice, viciousness, virus, wickedness.
antonyms honesty, purification.

corset *n.* belt, bodice, check, corselet, curb, curtailment, foundation garment, girdle, limit, limitation, panty girdle, restriction, stays.

cortège *n.* cavalcade, column, entourage, parade, procession, retinue, suite, train.

cosmetic *adj.* non-essential, superficial, surface.
antonym essential.

cosmetics *n.* grease paint, make-up, maquillage, pancake.

cosmic *adj.* boundless, grandiose, huge, illimitable, immense, infinite, limitless, measureless, universal, vast.

cosmopolitan *adj.* catholic, international, sophisticated, universal, unprejudiced, urbane, well-travelled, worldly, worldy-wise.
antonyms insular, parochial, rustic.

cosmos *n.* creation, galaxy, system, universe, world.

cosset *v.* baby, cherish, coddle, cuddle, mollycoddle, pamper, pet.

cost *n.* amount, charge, damage, deprivation, detriment, disbursement, expenditure, expense, figure, harm, hurt, injury, loss, outlay, payment, penalty, price, rate, sacrifice, worth.

costly *adj.* catastrophic, damaging, dear, deleterious, disastrous, excessive, exorbitant, expensive, extortionate, gorgeous, harmful, highly-priced, lavish, loss-making, luxurious, opulent, precious, priceless, pricy, rich, ruinous, sacrificial, splendid, steep, sumptuous, valuable.
antonyms cheap, inexpensive.

costs *n.* budget, expenses, oncosts, outgoings, overheads.

costume *n.* apparel, attire, clothing, dress, ensemble, garb, get-up, livery, outfit, raiment, robes, uniform, vestment.

cosy *adj.* comfortable, comfy, homelike, homely, intimate, secure, sheltered, snug, warm.
antonyms cold, uncomfortable.

coterie *n.* camp, caucus, cenacle, circle, clique,

galère, gang, group, outfit, set.

cottage *n.* bothy, bungalow, but-and-ben, cabin, chalet, cot, hut, lodge, shack.

couch *v.* bear, cradle, express, frame, phrase, support, utter, word.
n. bed, chaise-longue, chesterfield, day-bed, divan, lounge, ottoman, settee, sofa.

cough *n.* bark, hack, tussis.
v. bark, hack, harrumph, hawk, hem, hoast.

cough up deliver, fork out, give, hand over, pay, pay out, shell out, surrender.

council *n.* assembly, board, cabinet, chamber, committee, conclave, conference, congress, consistory, consult, convention, convocation, diet, divan, ministry, panchayat, panel, parliament, soviet, syndicate, synod, volost.

counsel *n.* admonition, advice, advocate, attorney, barrister, caution, consideration, consultation, deliberation, direction, forethought, guidance, information, lawyer, plan, purpose, recommendation, solicitor, suggestion, warning.
v. admonish, advise, advocate, caution, direct, exhort, guide, instruct, recommend, suggest, urge, warn.

counsellor *n.* adviser, attorney, councillor, lawyer, representative, vizier, wazir.

count *v.* add, ascribe, calculate, check, compute, consider, deem, enumerate, esteem, estimate, hold, impute, include, judge, list, matter, number, rate, reckon, regard, score, signify, tally, tell, think, tot up, total, weigh.
n. addition, calculation, computation, enumeration, numbering, poll, reckoning, sum, tally, total.

count for nothing cut no ice, make no difference.

count on bank on, believe, depend on, expect, reckon on, rely on, trust.

count out exclude, include out.
antonym include.

countenance *n.* acquiescence, aid, air, appearance, approval, aspect, assistance, backing, demeanour, endorsement, expression, face, favour, features, help, look, mien, physiognomy, sanction, support, visage.
v. abet, acquiesce, agree to, aid, approve, back, brook, champion, condone, encourage, endorse, endure, help, sanction, support, tolerate.

counter[1] *adv.* against, contrarily, contrariwise, conversely, in opposition.
adj. adverse, against, antithetical, conflicting, contradictory, contrary, contrasting, obverse, opposed, opposing, opposite.
antonyms concurring, corroborating.
v. answer, meet, offset, parry, resist, respond, retaliate, retort, return.

counter[2] *n.* coin, disc, jet(t)on, marker, tiddlywink, token.

counteract *v.* act against, annul, check, contravene, counterbalance, countervail, cross, defeat, foil, frustrate, hinder, invalidate, negate, neutralise, offset, oppose, resist, thwart, undo.

antonyms assist, support.

counterbalance *v.* balance, compensate for, counterpoise, countervail, equalise, neutralise, offset.

counterfeit *v.* copy, fabricate, fake, feign, forge, imitate, impersonate, phoney, pretend, sham, simulate.
adj. bogus, Brummagem, copied, ersatz, faked, false, feigned, forged, fraudulent, imitation, phoney, postiche, pretend(ed), pseud, pseudo, sham, simular, simulated, simulate(d), spurious, supposititious.
antonym genuine.
n. copy, fake, forgery, fraud, imitant, imitation, phantasm(a), phoney, reproduction, sham.

countermand *v.* abrogate, annul, cancel, override, repeal, rescind, reverse, revoke.

counterpart *n.* complement, copy, correlative, duplicate, equal, fellow, homologue, homotype, match, mate, opposite number, supplement, tally, twin, vis-à-vis.

countless *adj.* endless, immeasurable, incalculable, infinite, innumerable, legion, limitless, measureless, multitudinous, myriad, numberless, uncounted, unnumbered, unsummed, untold.
antonym limited.

countrified *adj.* agrestic, arcadian, bucolic, hick, homespun, idyllic, pastoral, provincial, rural, rustic.
antonyms oppidan, urban.

country *n.* backwoods, boondocks, citizenry, citizens, clime, commonwealth, community, countryside, electors, farmland, fatherland, green belt, homeland, inhabitants, kingdom, land, motherland, nation, nationality, outback, outdoors, part, people, populace, provinces, public, realm, region, society, sovereign state, state, sticks, terrain, territory, voters.
adj. agrarian, agrestic, arcadian, bucolic, georgic, landed, pastoral, provincial, rude, rural, rustic.
antonyms oppidan, urban.

countryman *n.* bumpkin, compatriot, farmer, fellow countryman, hayseed, hind, husbandman, peasant, provincial, rustic, swain, yokel.

countryside *n.* country, farmland, green belt, landscape, outback, outdoors, panorama, sticks.

county *n.* airt, comitatus, district, province, region, shire.

coup *n.* accomplishment, action, blow, coup d'état, deed, exploit, feat, manoeuvre, masterstroke, putsch, revolution, stratagem, stroke, stunt, tour de force.
coup de grâce clincher, come-uppance, death-blow, kibosh, kill, quietus.
coup d'état coup, overthrow, palace revolution, putsch, rebellion, revolt, revolution, takeover, uprising.

couple *n.* brace, Darby and Joan, duo, dyad, pair, span, team, twain, twosome, yoke.
v. accompany, buckle, clasp, conjoin, connect, copulate, fornicate, hitch, join, link, marry, pair, unite, wed, yoke.

coupon *n.* billet, card, certificate, check, slip, ticket, token, voucher.

courage *n.* boldness, bottle, bravery, daring, dauntlessness, fearlessness, firmness, fortitude, gallantry, grit, guts, hardihood, heroism, mettle, nerve, pluck, resolution, spirit, spunk, stomach, valour.
antonym cowardice.

courageous *adj.* audacious, bold, brave, daring, dauntless, dreadless, fearless, gallant, gutsy, hardy, heroic, high-hearted, indomitable, intrepid, lion-hearted, plucky, resolute, stouthearted, valiant, valorous.
antonym cowardly.

courier *n.* bearer, carrier, emissary, envoy, estafette, guide, herald, legate, messenger, nuncio, pursuivant, representative, runner.

course *n.* advance, advancement, channel, circuit, circus, classes, continuity, current, curriculum, development, diadrom, direction, duration, flight-path, flow, furtherance, hippodrome, lap, lapse, lectures, line, march, method, mode, movement, orbit, order, passage, passing, path, piste, plan, policy, procedure, programme, progress, progression, race, race-course, race-track, raik, regimen, road, round, route, schedule, sequence, series, studies, succession, sweep, syllabus, tack, term, time, track, trail, trajectory, unfolding, vector, voyage, way, wheel.
v. chase, dash, flow, follow, gush, hunt, move, pour, pursue, race, run, scud, scurry, speed, stream, surge, tumble.

court *n.* attendants, bailey, bar, bench, cloister, cortège, courtyard, durbar, entourage, hall, Hof, law-court, manor, palace, piazza, plaza, quad, quadrangle, retinue, square, suite, train, tribunal, yard.
v. attract, chase, cultivate, date, flatter, incite, invite, lionise, pander to, prompt, provoke, pursue, seek, serenade, solicit, woo.

courteous *adj.* affable, attentive, ceremonious, civil, considerate, courtly, debonair, elegant, gallant, gracious, mannerly, obliging, polished, polite, refined, respectful, urbane, well-bred, well-mannered.
antonyms discourteous, rude.

courtesan *n.* call girl, Delilah, demi-mondaine, fille de joie, harlot, hetaira, kept woman, lorette, mistress, paramour, prostitute, scarlet woman, whore, woman of easy virtue, woman of the night, woman of the town.

courtesy *n.* affability, attention, benevolence, breeding, civility, comity, consent, consideration, courteousness, courtliness, elegance, favour, gallantness, gallantry, generosity, gentilesse, graciousness, indulgence, kindness, manners, polish, politeness, urbanity.
antonyms discourtesy, rudeness.

courtier *n.* attendant, chamberlain, follower, henchman, lady, lord, major-domo, noble, nobleman, page, pursuivant, squire, steward, sycophant, toady, train-bearer.

courtly *adj.* affable, aristocratic, aulic, ceremonious, chivalric, chivalrous, civil, decorous, dignified, elegant, flattering, formal, gallant, high-bred, lordly, obliging, polished, polite, refined, stately.
antonyms inelegant, provincial, rough.

courtyard *n.* area, cortile, enclosure, patio, peristyle, playground, quad, quadrangle, yard.

cove *n.* anchorage, bay, bight, creek, estuary, fiord, firth, frith, harbour, inlet, sound.

covenant *n.* arrangement, bargain, bond, commitment, compact, concordat, contract, convention, deed, engagement, pact, pledge, promise, stipulation, treaty, trust, undertaking.
v. agree, bargain, contract, engage, pledge, promise, stipulate, undertake.

cover *v.* balance, camouflage, canopy, clad, cloak, clothe, coat, compensate, comprehend, comprise, conceal, consider, contain, counterbalance, curtain, daub, defend, describe, detail, disguise, dress, eclipse, embody, embrace, encase, encompass, enshroud, envelop, examine, guard, hide, hood, house, include, incorporate, insure, invest, investigate, involve, layer, mantle, mask, narrate, obscure, offset, overlay, overspread, protect, recount, reinforce, relate, report, screen, secrete, shade, sheathe, shelter, shield, shroud, suffuse, survey, veil.
n. bedspread, binding, camouflage, canopy, cap, case, cloak, clothing, coating, compensation, concealment, confederate, covering, cover-up, defence, disguise, dress, envelope, façade, front, guard, indemnity, insurance, jacket, lid, mask, payment, pretence, pretext, protection, refuge, reimbursement, sanctuary, screen, sheath, shelter, shield, smoke, spread, top, undergrowth, veil, woods, wrapper.

cover up coat, conceal, cover, dissemble, dissimulate, encrust, envelop, hide, hush up, plaster, repress, stonewall, suppress, swathe, whitewash.
antonym uncover.

coverage *n.* analysis, assurance, description, insurance, protection, reportage, reporting, treatment.

covering *n.* blanket, capping, casing, cloak, clothing, coating, cocoon, cope, cover, exoskeleton, housing, integument, layer, mask, masking, overlay, protection, sheath, shelter, tegmen, tegument, top, umbrella, wash, wrap, wrappage, wrapper, wrapping.
adj. accompanying, descriptive, explanatory, introductory, masking, obscuring, protective.

covert *adj.* clandestine, concealed, disguised, dissembled, hidden, private, secret, sneaky, stealthy, subreptitious, surreptitious, ulterior, under the table, underhand, unsuspected, veiled.
antonym open.

cover-up *n.* complicity, concealment, conspiracy,

dissemblance, dissimulation, front, pretence, smoke-screen, whitewash.

covet *v.* after, begrudge, crave, desire, envy, fancy, hanker, long for, lust after, thirst for, want, yearn for, yen for.
antonym abjure.

covetous *adj.* acquisitive, avaricious, close-fisted, envious, grasping, greedy, insatiable, jealous, mercenary, rapacious, thirsting, yearning.
antonyms generous, temperate.

covey *n.* bevy, cluster, flight, flock, group, nide, nye, skein.

cow *v.* awe, break, browbeat, bulldoze, bully, daunt, dishearten, dismay, domineer, frighten, intimidate, overawe, scare, subdue, terrorise, unnerve.
antonym encourage.

coward *n.* caitiff, chicken, craven, dastard, faint-heart, funk, hilding, nithing, poltroon, recreant, renegade, scaredy-cat, skulker, sneak, viliaco, viliago, yellow-belly, yellow-dog.
antonym hero.

cowardice *n.* faint-heartedness, fear, funk, gutlessness, pusillanimity, spinelessness.
antonyms courage, valour.

cowardly *adj.* base, caitiff, chicken, chicken-hearted, chicken-livered, craven, dastard(ly), faint-hearted, fearful, gutless, hilding, lily-livered, nesh, nithing, pusillanimous, recreant, scared, shrinking, soft, spineless, timorous, unheroic, weak, weak-kneed, white-livered, yellow, yellow-bellied.
antonym courageous.

cowboy *n.* bronco-buster, buckaroo, cattleman, cowhand, cowpoke, cowpuncher, drover, gaucho, herder, herdsman, rancher, ranchero, stockman, vaquero, waddy, wrangler.

cower *v.* cringe, crouch, flinch, grovel, quail, ruck, shake, shiver, shrink, skulk, tremble.

coxcomb *n.* beau, Beau Brummell, dandy, dude, exquisite, fop, Jack-a-dandy, jackanapes, macaroni, peacock, popinjay, princox, swell.

coy *adj.* arch, backward, bashful, coquettish, demure, diffident, evasive, flirtatious, kittenish, maidenly, modest, prudish, reserved, retiring, self-effacing, shrinking, shy, skittish, timid, virginal.
antonyms forward, impudent, sober.

coyness *n.* affectation, archness, bashfulness, coquettishness, demureness, diffidence, evasiveness, modesty, primness, prudery, prudishness, reserve, shyness, skittishness, timidity.
antonyms forwardness, impudence.

cozen *v.* bamboozle, bilk, cheat, circumvent, con, deceive, diddle, double-cross, dupe, finagle, gull, hoodwink, inveigle, swindle, trick.

crabbed *adj.* acid, acrid, acrimonious, awkward, bad-tempered, captious, churlish, crabby, cross, cross-grained, crotchety, cynical, difficult, fretful, grouchy, harsh, ill-humoured, ill-tempered, iracund, iracundulous, irascible, irritable, misanthropic, morose, perverse, petulant, prickly, snappish, snappy, sour, splenetic, surly, tart, testy, tough, trying. *antonyms* calm, placid.

crack *v.* break, buffet, burst, chap, chip, chop, cleave, clip, clout, collapse, crackle, crash, craze, cuff, decipher, detonate, explode, fathom, fracture, pop, ring, rive, slap, snap, solve, splinter, split, succumb, thump, wallop, whack, yield.

n. attempt, blow, breach, break, buffet, burst, chap, chink, chip, clap, cleft, clip, clout, cranny, crash, craze, crevasse, crevice, cuff, dig, expert, explosion, fent, fissure, flaw, fracture, gag, gap, go, insult, interstice, jibe, joke, moment, opportunity, pop, quip, report, rift, slap, smack, snap, stab, thump, try, wallop, whack, wisecrack, witticism.

adj. ace, choice, élite, excellent, first-class, first-rate, hand-picked, superior, top-notch.

crack down on act against, check, clamp down on, end, put a stop to, stop.

crack up break down, collapse, go crackers, go crazy, go to pieces.

crackdown *n.* clampdown, crushing, end, repression, stop, suppression.

cracked *adj.* bats, batty, broken, chipped, crackbrained, crackpot, crazed, crazy, daft, damaged, defective, deranged, eccentric, faulty, fissured, flawed, imperfect, insane, loony, nuts, nutty, rent, split, torn. *antonyms* flawless, perfect, sane.

crackers *adj.* cracked, crazy, daft, foolish, idiotic, loony, mad, nuts. *antonym* sane.

crackle *v.* crepitate, decrepitate, rustle. *n.* crepitation, crepitus, decrepitation, rustle.

crackpot *n.* crackbrain, idiot, loony, nut, nutter.

cradle *n.* bassinet, bed, beginning, berceau, birthplace, cot, crib, fount, fountain-head, holder, incunabula, origin, rest, source, spring, stand, well-spring.

v. bear, couch, hold, lull, nestle, nurse, rock, support, tend.

craft *n.* ability, aircraft, aptitude, art, artfulness, artifice, artistry, barque, boat, business, calling, cleverness, contrivance, craftiness, cunning, deceit, dexterity, duplicity, employment, expertise, expertness, guile, handicraft, handiwork, ingenuity, knack, know-how, line, occupation, plane, pursuit, ruse, scheme, ship, shrewdness, skill, spacecraft, spaceship, stratagem, subterfuge, subtlety, technique, trade, trickery, vessel, vocation, wiles, work, workmanship.

antonyms naïvety, openness.

craftiness *n.* artfulness, astuteness, canniness, cunning, deceit, deviousness, double-dealing, duplicity, foxiness, guile, shrewdness, slyness, subtlety, trickiness, underhandedness, vulpinism, wiliness.

antonyms naïvety, openness.

craftsman *n.* artificer, artisan, maker, master, opificer, smith, technician, wright.

craftsmanship *n.* artistry, expertise, facture, mastery, technique, workmanship.

crafty *adj.* artful, astute, calculating, canny, cunning, deceitful, designing, devious, duplicitous, foxy, fraudulent, guileful, insidious, knowing, machiavellian, scheming, sharp, shrewd, sly, subtle, tricksy, tricky, versute, vulpine, wily.

antonyms naïve, open.

crag *n.* aiguille, bluff, cliff, peak, pinnacle, rock, tor(r).

craggy *adj.* broken, brusque, cragged, jagged, jaggy, precipitous, rocky, rough, rugged, stony, surly, uneven.

antonyms pleasant, smooth.

cram *v.* bag, compact, compress, con, crowd, crush, force, glut, gorge, gormandise, grind, guzzle, jam, mug up, overcrowd, overeat, overfeed, overfill, pack, press, ram, satiate, shove, squeeze, stodge, study, stuff, swot.

cramming *n.* gavage, gluttony, gormandise, gourmandise, greed, packing, pressing, stuffing.

cramp[1] *v.* check, circumscribe, clog, confine, constrain, encumber, frustrate, hamper, hamstring, handicap, hinder, impede, inhibit, obstruct, restrict, shackle, stymie, thwart, tie.

cramp[2] *n.* ache, contraction, convulsion, crick, pain, pang, pins and needles, spasm, stiffness, stitch, twinge.

cramped *adj.* awkward, circumscribed, confined, congested, crowded, incapacious, jampacked, narrow, overcrowded, packed, restricted, riggling, squashed, squeezed, squeezy, tight, uncomfortable.

antonym spacious.

crane *n.* block and tackle, davit, derrick, hoist, tackle, winch.

crank *n.* eccentric, loony, madman, nutter.

cranky *adj.* bizarre, capricious, crabbed, cross, crotchety, dotty, eccentric, erratic, Fifish, freakish, freaky, funny, idiosyncratic, irritable, odd, peculiar, prickly, queer, quirky, strange, surly, viewy, wacky.

antonyms normal, placid, sensible.

cranny *n.* chink, cleavage, cleft, crack, crevice, fissure, gap, hole, interstice, nook, opening.

crash *n.* accident, bang, bankruptcy, boom, bump, clang, clash, clatter, clattering, collapse, collision, debacle (débâcle), depression, din, downfall, failure, fragor, jar, jolt, pile-up, prang, racket, ruin, smash, smashing, smash-up, thud, thump, thunder, wreck.

v. bang, break, bump, collapse, collide, dash, disintegrate, fail, fall, fold (up), fracture, fragment, go bust, go under, hurtle, lurch, overbalance, pitch, plunge, prang, shatter, shiver, smash, splinter, sprawl, topple.

adj. concentrated, emergency, immediate, intensive, round-the-clock, telescoped, urgent.

crass *adj.* asinine, blundering, boorish, bovine, coarse, dense, doltish, gross, indelicate, insensitive, lumpish, oafish, obtuse, stupid, tactless, unrefined, unsubtle, witless.

antonyms refined, sensitive.

crate *n.* box, case, container, packing case, packing-box, tea-chest.

crave *v.* ask, beg, beseech, desire, entreat, fancy, hanker after, hunger after, implore, long for, need, petition, pine for, require, seek, solicit, supplicate, thirst for, want, yearn for, yen for.
antonyms dislike, spurn.

craven *adj.* caitiff, chicken-hearted, cowardly, dastardly, fearful, lily-livered, mean-spirited, nithing, pusillanimous, scared, spiritless, timorous, unheroic, weak, whey-faced, yellow.
antonym courageous.
n. caitiff, coward, dastard, nithing, poltroon, recreant.
antonyms hero, renegade, yellow-belly.

craving *n.* appetence, appetency, appetite, cacoethes, desire, hankering, hunger, longing, lust, thirst, urge, yearning, yen.
antonyms dislike, distaste.

craw *n.* crop, gizzard, gullet, maw, oesophagous, throat.

crawl *v.* creep, cringe, drag, eat crow, eat dirt, eat humble pie, fawn, grovel, inch, slither, swarm, teem, toady, truckle, wriggle, writhe.

craze *n.* dernier cri, enthusiasm, fad, fashion, frenzy, infatuation, mania, mode, novelty, obsession, passion, preoccupation, rage, thing, trend, vogue.
v. bewilder, confuse, dement, derange, distemper, distract, enrage, infatuate, inflame, madden, unbalance, unhinge.

crazed *adj.* demented, maddened, maenadic, possessed.
antonym sane.

crazy *adj.* absurd, ardent, bananas, barmy, bats, batty, berserk, bird-brained, bizarre, bonkers, cockeyed, cracked, crazed, cuckoo, daffy, daft, delirious, demented, deranged, derisory, devoted, dippy, eager, eccentric, enamoured, enthusiastic, fanatical, fantastic, fatuous, foolhardy, foolish, fruity, half-baked, hysterical, idiotic, ill-conceived, impracticable, imprudent, inane, inappropriate, infatuated, insane, irresponsible, ludicrous, lunatic, mad, maniacal, mental, nonsensical, nuts, nutty, odd, off one's rocker, outrageous, passionate, peculiar, pixil(l)ated, potty, preposterous, puerile, quixotic, ridiculous, scatty, senseless, short-sighted, silly, smitten, strange, touched, unbalanced, unhinged, unrealistic, unwise, unworkable, up the pole, wacky, weird, wild, zany, zealous.
antonyms sane, sensible.

creak *v.* grate, grind, groan, rasp, scrape, scratch, screak, screech, squeak, squeal.

creaky *adj.* creaking, grating, rasping, rusty, screaky, squeaking, squeaky, unoiled.

cream *n.* best, cosmetic, crème de la crème, élite, emulsion, essence, flower, liniment, lotion, oil, ointment, paste, pick, prime, salve, the four hundred, unguent.

creamy *adj.* buttery, cream-coloured, creamed, lush, milky, off-white, oily, rich, smooth, soft, velvety.

crease *v.* corrugate, crimp, crinkle, crumple, fold, pucker, ridge, ruckle, rumple, wrinkle.
n. bulge, corrugation, crumple, fold, groove, line, overlap, pucker, ridge, ruck, ruckle, rumple, tuck, wrinkle.

create *v.* appoint, beget, cause, coin, compose, concoct, constitute, design, develop, devise, engender, establish, form, formulate, found, generate, hatch, initiate, install, institute, invent, invest, make, occasion, originate, produce, set up, sire, spawn.
antonym destroy.

creation *n.* achievement, brainchild, chef d'oeuvre, concept, conception, concoction, constitution, cosmos, development, establishment, fathering, formation, foundation, generation, genesis, handiwork, inception, institution, invention, life, magnum opus, making, nature, origination, pièce de résistance, procreation, production, siring, universe, world.
antonym destruction.

creative *adj.* adept, artistic, clever, fertile, gifted, imaginative, ingenious, inspired, inventive, original, productive, resourceful, stimulating, talented, visionary.
antonym unimaginative.

creativity *n.* artistry, cleverness, fecundity, fertility, imagination, imaginativeness, ingenuity, inspiration, inventiveness, originality, resourcefulness, talent, vision.
antonym unimaginativeness.

creator *n.* architect, auteur, author, begetter, demiurge, demiurgus, designer, father, framer, God, initiator, inventor, maker, originator.

creature *n.* animal, beast, being, body, brute, character, critter, dependant, fellow, hanger-on, henchman, hireling, individual, instrument, lackey, man, minion, mortal, person, puppet, retainer, soul, toady, tool, wight, woman, wretch.

credence *n.* belief, confidence, credit, dependence, faith, reliance, support, trust.
antonym distrust.

credentials *n.* accreditation, attestation, authorisation, card, certificate, deed, diploma, docket, endorsement, letters of credence, licence, missive, passport, permit, recommendation, reference, testament, testimonial, title, voucher, warrant.

credibility *n.* believableness, integrity, likeliness, plausibility, probability, reliability, tenability, trustworthiness.
antonym implausibility.

credible *adj.* believable, conceivable, convincing, dependable, honest, imaginable, likely, persuasive, plausible, possible, probable, reasonable, reliable, sincere, supposable, tenable, thinkable, trustworthy, trusty.
antonyms implausible, unreliable.

credit *n.* acclaim, acknowledgement, approval, belief, character, clout, commendation, confidence, credence, distinction, esteem, estimation, faith, fame, glory, honour, influence, kudos, merit, position, praise, prestige, recognition, regard, reliance, reputation, repute, standing, status, thanks, tribute, trust. *antonym* discredit.

v. accept, believe, buy, subscribe to, swallow, trust. *antonym* disbelieve.

creditable *adj.* admirable, commendable, deserving, estimable, excellent, exemplary, good, honourable, laudable, meritorious, praiseworthy, reputable, respectable, sterling, worthy. *antonyms* blameworthy, shameful.

creditor *n.* debtee, dun, lender.

credulity *n.* credulousness, dupability, gullibility, naïvety, silliness, simplicity, stupidity. *antonym* scepticism.

credulous *adj.* dupable, green, gullible, naïve, trusting, uncritical, unsuspecting, unsuspicious, wide-eyed. *antonym* sceptical.

creed *n.* articles, belief, canon, catechism, confession, credo, doctrine, dogma, faith, persuasion, principles, tenets.

creek *n.* bay, bight, brook, cove, fiord, firth, frith, inlet, rivulet, stream, streamlet, tributary, voe, watercourse.

creep *v.* bootlick, cower, crawl, cringe, dawdle, drag, edge, fawn, grovel, inch, insinuate, kowtow, scrape, skulk, slink, slither, snail, sneak, squirm, steal, tiptoe, toady, truckle, worm, wriggle, writhe. *n.* bootlicker, Jack Nasty, jerk, sneak, sycophant, toady.

creeper *n.* climber, liana, plant, rambler, runner, trailing, vine.

creepy *adj.* awful, direful, disturbing, eerie, frightening, ghoulish, gruesome, hair-raising, horrible, macabre, menacing, nightmarish, ominous, scary, sinister, spookish, spooky, terrifying, threatening, unearthly, unpleasant, weird. *antonyms* normal, pleasant.

crescent-shaped *adj.* bow-shaped, falcate(d), falciform, lunate(d), lunular, sickle-shaped.

crest *n.* aigrette, apex, badge, caruncle, cockscomb, coma, comb, crown, device, emblem, head, height, insignia, mane, panache, peak, pinnacle, plume, ridge, summit, symbol, tassel, top, topknot, tuft.

crestfallen *adj.* chopfallen, dejected, depressed, despondent, disappointed, disconsolate, discouraged, disheartened, dispirited, downcast, downhearted, woebegone. *antonym* elated.

crevasse *n.* abyss, bergschrund, chasm, cleavage, cleft, crack, fissure, gap.

crevice *n.* chink, cleavage, cleft, crack, cranny, fissure, fracture, gap, hole, interstice, opening, rent, rift, slit, split.

crew *n.* assemblage, band, bunch, company, complement, corps, crowd, galère, gang, hands, henchmen, herd, horde, lot, lower

deck, mob, pack, party, posse, set, squad, swarm, team, troop.

crib *n.* bassinet, bed, bin, borrowing, box, bunker, cot, cradle, key, manger, plagiarism, rack, stall, translation. *v.* borrow, cheat, copy, pinch, pirate, plagiarise, purloin, steal.

crick *n.* convulsion, cramp, pain, spasm, stiffness, twinge. *v.* jar, rax, rick, sprain, twist, wrench.

crime *n.* atrocity, corruption, delinquency, fault, felony, flagitiousness, guilt, illegality, iniquity, law-breaking, malefaction, malfeasance, misconduct, misdeed, misdemeanour, offence, outrage, sin, transgression, trespass, unrighteousness, vice, villainy, violation, wickedness, wrong, wrong-doing.

criminal *n.* con, convict, crook, culprit, delinquent, evil-doer, felon, infractor, jailbird, law-breaker, malefactor, offender, sinner, transgressor. *adj.* bent, corrupt, crooked, culpable, deplorable, felonious, flagitious, foolish, illegal, immoral, indictable, iniquitous, lawless, malfeasant, nefarious, peccant, preposterous, ridiculous, scandalous, senseless, unlawful, unrighteous, vicious, villainous, wicked, wrong. *antonyms* honest, upright.

cringe *v.* bend, blench, bootlick, bow, cower, crawl, creep, crouch, dodge, duck, fawn, flinch, grovel, kneel, kowtow, quail, quiver, recoil, shrink, shy, sneak, start, stoop, submit, toady, tremble, truckle, wince.

crinkle *n.* curl, fold, pucker, ruffle, rumple, rustle, scallop, twist, wave, wrinkle. *v.* crimp, crimple, crumple, curl, fold, pucker, ruffle, rumple, rustle, scallop, twist, wrinkle.

crinkly *adj.* curly, fluted, frizzy, furrowed, gathered, kinky, puckered, ruffled, scalloped, wrinkled, wrinkly. *antonyms* smooth, straight.

cripple *v.* cramp, damage, debilitate, destroy, disable, enfeeble, halt, hamstring, impair, incapacitate, lame, maim, mutilate, paralyse, ruin, sabotage, spoil, vitiate, weaken.

crippled *adj.* deformed, disabled, enfeebled, handicapped, incapacitated, invalid, lame, paralysed.

crisis *n.* calamity, catastrophe, climacteric, climax, confrontation, conjuncture, crunch, crux, culmination, difficulty, dilemma, disaster, emergency, exigency, extremity, height, impasse, mess, pinch, plight, predicament, quandary, strait, trouble.

crisp *adj.* bracing, brief, brisk, brittle, brusque, clear, crispy, crumbly, crunchy, decisive, firm, forthright, fresh, incisive, invigorating, neat, orderly, pithy, refreshing, short, smart, snappy, spruce, succinct, tart, terse, tidy, vigorous. *antonyms* flabby, limp, vague.

criterion *n.* bench-mark, canon, gauge, measure, norm, precedent, principle, proof, rule, shibboleth, standard, test, touchstone, yardstick.

critic *n.* analyst, animadverter, arbiter, Aristarch, attacker, authority, carper, caviller, censor, censurer, commentator, connoisseur, detractor, expert, expositor, fault-finder, feuilletonist, judge, knocker, Momus, pundit, reviewer, reviler, vilifier, Zoilist.

critical *adj.* accurate, all-important, analytical, captious, carping, cavilling, censorious, climacteric, crucial, dangerous, deciding, decisive, derogatory, diagnostic, disapproving, discerning, discriminating, disparaging, fastidious, fault-finding, grave, hairy, high-priority, judicious, momentous, nagging, niggling, nit-picking, penetrating, perceptive, perilous, pivotal, precarious, precise, pressing, psychological, risky, serious, sharp-tongued, uncomplimentary, urgent, vital, Zoilean.

antonyms uncritical, unimportant.

criticise *v.* analyse, animadvert, appraise, assess, badmouth, blame, carp, censure, condemn, crab, decry, disparage, evaluate, excoriate, judge, knock, pan, review, roast, scarify, slag, slam, slash, slate, snipe.

antonym praise.

criticism *n.* analysis, animadversion, appraisal, appreciation, assessment, blame, brickbat, censure, comment, commentary, critique, disapproval, disparagement, elucidation, evaluation, fault-finding, flak, judgement, knocking, knocking-copy, notice, panning, review, slating, stick, stricture, vivisection, Zoilism.

antonym praise.

critique *n.* analysis, appraisal, assessment, commentary, essay, evaluation, examination, review.

croak *v.* caw, die, expire, gasp, grunt, kick the bucket, pass away, perish, snuff it, squawk, wheeze.

crockery *n.* ceramics, china, dishes, earthenware, holloware, pottery, stoneware, whiteware.

croft *n.* farm, pightle, plot, smallholding.

crone *n.* bag, bat, beldam, gammer, grandam, grannam, hag, witch.

crony *n.* accomplice, ally, associate, buddy, china, chum, colleague, companion, comrade, follower, friend, henchman, mate, pal, sidekick.

crook *n.* cheat, criminal, knave, racketeer, robber, rogue, shark, shyster, swindler, thief, villain.

crooked[1] *adj.* bent, corrupt, crafty, criminal, deceitful, discreditable, dishonest, dishonourable, dubious, fraudulent, illegal, knavish, nefarious, questionable, shady, shifty, treacherous, underhand, unethical, unlawful, unprincipled, unscrupulous.

antonym honest.

crooked[2] *adj.* anfractuous, angled, askew, asymmetric, awry, bent, bowed, crank, cranky, crippled, crump, curved, deformed, deviating, disfigured, distorted, hooked, irregular, lopsided, meandering, misshapen,

off-centre, skew-whiff, slanted, slanting, squint, tilted, tortuous, twisted, twisting, uneven, warped, winding, zigzag.

antonym straight.

crookedness *n.* distortion, squintness, twistedness, warp.

antonym straightness.

crop[1] *n.* fruits, gathering, growth, harvest, ingathering, produce, vintage, yield.

v. browse, clip, collect, curtail, cut, garner, gather, graze, harvest, lop, mow, nibble, pare, pick, prune, reap, reduce, shear, shingle, shorten, snip, top, trim, yield.

crop up appear, arise, arrive, emerge, happen, occur.

crop[2] *n.* craw, gizzard, gullet, maw, oesophagus, throat.

cross *adj.* adverse, angry, annoyed, cantankerous, captious, churlish, contrary, cranky, crosswise, crotchety, crusty, disagreeable, displeased, fractious, fretful, grouchy, grumpy, hybrid, ill-humoured, ill-tempered, impatient, interchanged, intersecting, irascible, irritable, oblique, opposed, opposing, opposite, peeved, peevish, pettish, petulant, querulous, reciprocal, shirty, short, snappish, snappy, splenetic, sullen, surly, testy, transverse, unfavourable, vexed, waspish.

antonyms calm, placid, pleasant.

v. annoy, bestride, blend, block, bridge, cancel, criss-cross, crossbreed, cross-fertilise, cross-pollinate, decussate, deny, foil, ford, frustrate, hinder, hybridise, impede, interbreed, intercross, interfere, intersect, intertwine, lace, meet, mix, mongrelise, obstruct, oppose, resist, span, thwart, traverse, zigzag.

n. affliction, amalgam, blend, burden, combination, crossbreed, crossing, crossroads, crucifix, cur, grief, holy-rood, hybrid, hybridisation, intersection, load, misery, misfortune, mixture, mongrel, rood, trial, tribulation, trouble, woe, worry.

cross swords argue, dispute, fight, spar, take issue, wrangle.

cross-examine *v.* catechise, give (someone) the third degree, grill, interrogate, pump, question, quiz.

crosspatch *n.* bear, crank, crotcheteer, curmudgeon, grump, kill-joy, scold, shrew, sorehead, sourpuss.

cross-question *v.* cross-examine, debrief, examine, grill.

crosswise *adv.* across, aslant, athwart, awry, crisscross, crossways, diagonally, over, sideways, transversely.

crotchety *adj.* awkward, bad-tempered, cantankerous, contrary, crabbed, crabby, cross, crusty, curmudgeonly, difficult, disagreeable, fractious, grumpy, iracund, iracundulous, irascible, irritable, obstreperous, peevish, prickly, surly, testy.

antonyms clam, placid, pleasant.

crouch *v.* bend, bow, cower, cringe, duck, hunch, kneel, ruck, squat, stoop.

crow *v.* bluster, boast, brag, exult, flourish,

gloat, prate, rejoice, triumph, vaunt.

crowbar *n.* gavelock, jemmy, jimmy.

crowd *n.* army, assembly, attendance, audience, boodle, bunch, caboodle, circle, clique, company, concourse, flock, gate, group, herd, hoi polloi, horde, host, house, lot, many-headed beast/monster, mass, masses, mob, multitude, pack, people, populace, press, proletariat, public, rabble, riff-raff, set, spectators, squash, swarm, the many, throng, troupe.

v. bundle, cluster, compress, congest, congregate, cram, elbow, flock, for(e)gather, gather, huddle, jostle, mass, muster, pack, pile, press, push, shove, squeeze, stream, surge, swarm, throng.

crowded *adj.* busy, congested, cramped, crushed, filled, full, huddled, jammed, jam-packed, mobbed, overflowing, packed, populous, swarming, teeming, thronged. *antonym* empty.

crown *n.* acme, apex, bays, chaplet, circlet, coronal, coronet, crest, diadem, distinction, forehead, garland, head, honour, kudos, laurel wreath, laurels, monarch, monarchy, pate, perfection, pinnacle, prize, royalty, ruler, skull, sovereign, sovereignty, summit, tiara, tip, top, trophy, ultimate, zenith.

v. adorn, biff, box, cap, clout, complete, consummate, cuff, dignify, festoon, finish, fulfil, honour, instal, perfect, punch, reward, surmount, terminate, top.

crowned *adj.* capped, incoronate(d), royal, ruling, sovereign, surmounted, topped, wreathed.

crowning *adj.* climactic, consummate, culminating, final, paramount, perfect, sovereign, supreme, top, ultimate, unmatched, unsurpassed.

n. coronation, incoronation, installation.

crucial *adj.* central, critical, decisive, essential, important, key, momentous, pivotal, pressing, psychological, searching, testing, trying, urgent, vital. *antonym* unimportant.

crucifix *n.* cross, holy-rood, rood.

crucify *v.* criticise, execute, harrow, lampoon, mock, pan, persecute, rack, ridicule, slam, torment, torture.

crude *adj.* amateurish, blue, boorish, clumsy, coarse, crass, dirty, earthy, gross, half-baked, immature, inartistic, indecent, lewd, makeshift, natural, obscene, outline, primitive, raw, rough, rough-hewn, rude, rudimentary, sketchy, smutty, tactless, tasteless, uncouth, undeveloped, undigested, unfinished, unformed, unpolished, unprepared, unprocessed, unrefined, unsubtle, vulgar. *antonyms* finished, polite, refined, tasteful.

crudity *n.* bawdiness, clumsiness, coarseness, crudeness, impropriety, indecency, indelicacy, lewdness, loudness, obscenity, offensiveness, primitiveness, roughness, rudeness, smuttiness, vulgarity. *antonyms* polish, politeness, tastefulness.

cruel *adj.* atrocious, barbarous, bitter, bloodthirsty, brutal, brutish, butcherly, callous, cold-blooded, cutting, depraved, excruciating, fell, ferocious, fierce, flinty, grim, hard, hard-hearted, harsh, heartless, heathenish, hellish, immane, implacable, inclement, inexorable, inhuman, inhumane, malevolent, marble-breasted, merciless, murderous, painful, pitiless, poignant, ravening, raw, relentless, remorseless, ruthless, sadistic, sanguinary, savage, severe, spiteful, stony-hearted, unfeeling, ungentle, unkind, unmerciful, unnatural, unrelenting, vengeful, vicious. *antonyms* compassionate, kind, merciful.

cruelty *n.* barbarity, bestiality, bloodthirstiness, brutality, brutishness, callousness, depravity, ferocity, fiendishness, hard-heartedness, harshness, heartlessness, immanity, inhumanity, mercilessness, murderousness, ruthlessness, sadism, savagery, severity, spite, spitefulness, tyranny, ungentleness, venom, viciousness. *antonyms* compassion, kindness, mercy.

crumb *n.* atom, bit, grain, iota, jot, mite, morsel, nirl, particle, scrap, shred, sliver, snippet, soupçon, speck.

crumble *v.* break up, collapse, comminute, crumb, crush, decay, decompose, degenerate, deteriorate, disintegrate, fragment, granulate, grind, levigate, moulder, murl, perish, pound, powder, pulverise, triturate.

crumbly *adj.* brittle, friable, murly, powdery, pulverulent, short.

crummy *adj.* cheap, contemptible, grotty, half-baked, inferior, miserable, pathetic, poor, rotten, rubbishy, second-rate, shoddy, third-rate, trashy, useless, weak, worthless. *antonym* excellent.

crumple *v.* collapse, crease, crunkle, crush, fall, pucker, raffle, rumple, wrinkle.

crunch *v.* champ, chomp, grind, masticate, munch, scranch.

n. crisis, crux, emergency, pinch, test.

crusade *n.* campaign, cause, drive, expedition, holy war, jihad, movement, push, undertaking.

crusader *n.* advocate, campaigner, champion, enthusiast, fighter, missionary, reformer, zealot.

crush *v.* abash, break, browbeat, bruise, chagrin, champ, comminute, compress, conquer, contuse, crease, crumble, crumple, crunch, embrace, enfold, extinguish, hug, humiliate, mash, mortify, overcome, overpower, overwhelm, pound, press, pulverise, quash, quell, rumple, shame, smash, squabash, squeeze, squelch, steam-roller, subdue, vanquish, wrinkle.

n. check, crowd, huddle, jam.

crust *n.* caking, coat, coating, concretion, covering, exterior, film, heel, impertinence, incrustation, layer, outside, rind, scab, shell, skin, surface.

crusty *adj.* brittle, brusque, cantankerous, captious, choleric, crabbed, crabby, crisp, crispy, cross, curt, friable, grouchy, gruff,

hard, ill-humoured, irritable, peevish, prickly, short, short-tempered, snappish, snappy, snarling, splenetic, surly, testy, touchy.
antonyms calm, pleasant, soft, soggy.

crux *n.* core, essence, heart, nub, vexata quaestio, vexed question.

cry *v.* advertise, announce, bark, bawl, beg, bellow, beseech, bewail, blubber, boo-hoo, broadcast, bruit, call, caterwaul, clamour, ejaculate, entreat, exclaim, greet, hail, halloo, hawk, holler, howl, implore, keen, lament, mewl, miaow, miaul, noise, plead, pray, proclaim, promulgate, pule, roar, scream, screech, shout, shriek, snivel, sob, squall, squeal, trumpet, vociferate, wail, weep, whimper, whine, whinge, whoop, yell, yowl.
n. announcement, appeal, battle-cry, bawl-(ing), bellow, blubber(ing), call, caterwaul, caterwaul(ing), ejaculation, entreaty, exclamation, greet, holler, hoot, howl, keening, lament, lamentation, miaow, miaul, outcry, petition, plaint, plea, prayer, proclamation, report, roar, rumour, scream, screech, shriek, slogan, snivel(ling), sob(bing), sorrowing, squall, squawk, squeal, supplication, utterance, wail(ing), watch-word, weep(ing), whoop, yell, yelp, yoo-hoo.

cry-baby *n.* cissy, mardy, softy.

crypt *n.* catacomb, mausoleum, tomb, undercroft, vault.

cryptic *adj.* abstruse, ambiguous, aprocryphal, arcane, bizarre, cabbalistic, dark, Delphic, enigmatic, equivocal, esoteric, hidden, mysterious, obscure, occult, oracular, perplexing, puzzling, recondite, secret, strange, vague, veiled.
antonyms clear, obvious, straightforward.

crystallise *v.* appear, coalesce, emerge, form, harden, materialise, solidify.

cub *n.* babe, beginner, fledgling, greenhorn, lad, learner, offspring, pup, puppy, recruit, tenderfoot, trainee, whelp, whippersnapper, young, youngster, youth.
antonym adult.

cubby-hole *n.* compartment, den, hide-away, hole, niche, pigeonhole, priest hole, recess, slot, snug.

cube *n.* cuboid, dice, die, hexahedron, solid.

cuddle *v.* canoodle, clasp, cosset, dandle, doodle, embrace, fondle, hug, nestle, pet, smuggle, snuggle.

cuddly *adj.* buxom, cosy, cuddlesome, curvaceous, huggable, lovable, plump, soft, warm.

cudgel *n.* alpeen, bastinado, baton, bludgeon, club, cosh, plant, shillelagh, stick, truncheon.
v. bang, baste, bastinado, batter, beat, bludgeon, cane, clobber, cosh, drub, maul, pound, pummel, thrash, thump, thwack.

cue *n.* catchword, hint, incentive, key, nod, prompt(ing), reminder, sign, signal, stimulus, suggestion.

cuff *v.* bat, beat, belt, biff, box, buffet, clap, clobber, clout, knock, pummel, punch, slap, smack, smite, strike, thump, whack.
n. belt, biff, blow, box, buffet, clout, knock, punch, rap, slap, smack, swat, thump, whack.

cull *v.* amass, choose, collect, decimate, destroy, gather, glean, kill, pick, pick out, pluck, select, sift, thin, winnow.

culminate *v.* climax, close, conclude, consummate, end (up), finish, peak, terminate.
antonyms begin, start.

culmination *n.* acme, apex, apogee, climax, completion, conclusion, consummation, crown, finale, height, meridian, ne plus ultra, peak, perfection, pinnacle, summit, top, zenith.
antonyms beginning, start.

culpable *adj.* answerable, blam(e)able, blameworthy, censurable, guilty, liable, offending, peccant, reprehensible, sinful, to blame, wrong.
antonyms blameless, innocent.

culprit *n.* criminal, delinquent, evil-doer, felon, guilty party, law-breaker, malefactor, miscreant, offender, rascal, sinner, transgressor, wrong-doer.

cult *n.* admiration, believers, body, clique, craze, denomination, devotion, faith, following, idolisation, party, religion, reverence, school, sect, veneration, worship.

cultivate *v.* aid, ameliorate, better, cherish, civilise, court, develop, discipline, elevate, encourage, enrich, farm, fertilise, forward, foster, further, harvest, help, improve, patronise, plant, plough, polish, prepare, promote, pursue, refine, school, support, tend, till, train, work.
antonym neglect.

cultivation *n.* advancement, advocacy, agronomy, breeding, civilisation, civility, culture, development, discernment, discrimination, education, encouragement, enhancement, enlightenment, farming, fostering, furtherance, gardening, gentility, help, husbandry, learning, letters, manners, nurture, patronage, planting, ploughing, polish, promotion, pursuit, refinement, schooling, study, support, taste, tillage, tilling, tilth, working.

cultural *adj.* aesthetic, artistic, arty, broadening, civilising, developmental, edifying, educational, educative, elevating, enlightening, enriching, humane, humanising, liberal.

culture *n.* accomplishment, aestheticism, agriculture, agronomy, art, breeding, civilisation, cultivation, customs, education, elevation, enlightenment, erudition, farming, gentility, husbandry, improvement, Kultur, lifestyle, mores, polish, politeness, refinement, society, taste, the arts, urbanity.

cultured *adj.* accomplished, advanced, aesthetic, arty, civilised, educated, enlightened, erudite, genteel, highbrow, knowledgeable, polished, refined, scholarly, urbane, versed, well-bred, well-informed, well-read.
antonyms ignorant, uncultured.

culvert *n.* channel, conduit, drain, duct, gutter, sewer, watercourse.

cumbersome *adj.* awkward, bulky, burdensome, clumsy, cumbrous, embarrassing, heavy, hefty, incommodious, inconvenient, onerous, oppressive, ponderous, unmanageable, unwieldy, weighty.
antonyms convenient, manageable.

cumulative *adj.* accumulative, additive, aggregate, collective, increasing.

cunning *adj.* adroit, arch, artful, astute, canny, crafty, deep, deft, devious, dexterous, foxy, guileful, imaginative, ingenious, knowing, leery, Machiavellian, rusé, sharp, shifty, shrewd, skilful, sneaky, subtle, tricky, vulpine, wily.
antonyms gullible, naïve.
n. ability, adroitness, art, artfulness, artifice, astuteness, cleverness, craftiness, deceitfulness, deftness, deviousness, dexterity, finesse, foxiness, guile, ingenuity, policy, shrewdness, skill, slyness, subtlety, trickery, vulpinism, wiliness.
antonyms openness, simplicity.

cup *n.* beaker, cannikin, cantharus, chalice, cupful, cylix, demitasse, dish, draught, drink, fingan, goblet, mazer, pokal, potion, tankard, tass, tazza, teacup, tig, trophy.

cupboard *n.* almirah, ambry, armoire, cabinet, closet, locker, press.

cupidity *n.* acquisitiveness, avarice, avidity, covetousness, eagerness, graspingness, greed, greediness, hankering, hunger, itching, longing, rapaciousness, rapacity, voracity, yearning.

cur *n.* blackguard, canine, coward, dastard, good-for-nothing, heel, hound, mongrel, mutt, rat, rotter, scoundrel, stray, swine, villain, wretch.

curative *adj.* alleviative, corrective, febrifugal, healing, healthful, health-giving, medicinal, remedial, restorative, salutary, therapeutic, tonic, vulnerary.

curb *v.* bit, bridle, check, constrain, contain, control, hamper, hinder, hobble, impede, inhibit, moderate, muzzle, repress, restrain, restrict, retard, subdue, suppress.
antonyms encourage, foster, goad.
n. brake, bridle, check, control, deterrent, hamper, hobble, limitation, rein, restraint.

curdle *v.* clot, coagulate, condense, congeal, earn, ferment, sour, thicken, turn.

cure[1] *v.* alleviate, correct, ease, heal, help, mend, rehabilitate, relieve, remedy, restore.
n. alleviation, antidote, corrective, detoxicant, febrifuge, healing, medicine, panacea, panpharmacon, recovery, remedy, restorative, specific, treatment, vulnerary.

cure[2] *v.* brine, dry, kipper, pickle, preserve, salt, smoke.

curio *n.* antique, bibelot, bygone, curiosity, knick-knack, object of virtu, objet de vertu, trinket.

curiosity *n.* bibelot, bygone, celebrity, curio, freak, inquisitiveness, interest, knick-knack, marvel, nosiness, novelty, object of virtu, objet d'art, objet de vertu, oddity, phenome-

non, prying, rarity, sight, snooping, spectacle, trinket, wonder.

curiosities *n.* exotica, novelties, virtu.

curious *adj.* bizarre, exotic, extraordinary, ferly, funny, inquiring, inquisitive, interested, marvellous, meddling, mysterious, nosy, novel, odd, peculiar, peeping, peering, prying, puzzled, puzzling, quaint, queer, questioning, rare, searching, singular, snoopy, strange, unconventional, unexpected, unique, unorthodox, unusual, wonderful.
antonyms incurious, indifferent, normal, ordinary, uninterested.

curl *v.* bend, coil, convolute, corkscrew, crimp, crimple, crinkle, crisp, curve, entwine, frizz, loop, meander, ripple, scroll, spiral, turn, twine, twirl, wind, wreathe, writhe.
antonym uncurl.
n. coil, curlicue, kink, ringlet, spiral, swirl, tress, twist, whorl.

curly *adj.* corkscrew, crimped, crimpy, crinkly, curled, curling, frizzy, fuzzy, kinky, spiralled, waved, wavy, whorled, winding.
antonym straight.

currency *n.* acceptance, bills, circulation, coinage, coins, exposure, legal tender, money, notes, popularity, prevalence, publicity, reign, transmission, vogue.

current *adj.* accepted, circulating, common, contemporary, customary, extant, fashionable, general, on-going, popular, present, present-day, prevailing, prevalent, reigning, rife, trendy, up-to-date, up-to-the-minute, widespread.
antonyms antiquated, old-fashioned.
n. atmosphere, course, draught, drift, feeling, flow, inclination, jet, juice, mood, progression, river, stream, tendency, thermal, tide, trend, undercurrent.

curse *n.* affliction, anathema, ban, bane, blasphemy, burden, calamity, cross, damn, denunciation, disaster, evil, excommunication, execration, expletive, imprecation, jinx, malediction, malison, misfortune, oath, obscenity, ordeal, plague, scourge, swearing, swear-word, torment, tribulation, trouble, vexation, woe.
antonyms advantage, blessing.
v. accurse, afflict, anathematise, blaspheme, blight, blind, blow, burden, cuss, damn, destroy, doom, excommunicate, execrate, fulminate, imprecate, plague, scourge, swear, torment, trouble, vex.
antonym bless.

cursed *adj.* abominable, accursed, bedevilled, bewitched, blessed, blighted, confounded, damnable, damned, destestable, devilish, doomed, excommunicate, execrable, fell, fey, fiendish, foredoomed, hateful, hexed, ill-fated, infamous, infernal, loathsome, odious, pernicious, pestilential, star-crossed, unholy, unsanctified, vile, villainous.

cursory *adj.* brief, careless, casual, desultory, fleeting, hasty, hurried, offhand, passing, perfunctory, quick, rapid, slap-dash, slight, summary, superficial.

antonyms painstaking, thorough.

curt *adj.* abrupt, blunt, brief, brusque, concise, gruff, laconic, offhand, pithy, rude, sharp, short, short-spoken, snappish, succinct, summary, tart, terse, unceremonious, uncivil, ungracious.

antonym voluble.

curtail *v.* abbreviate, abridge, circumscribe, contract, cut, decrease, dock, lessen, lop, pare, prune, reduce, restrict, retrench, shorten, trim, truncate.

antonyms extend, lengthen, prolong.

curtailment *n.* abbreviation, abridgement, contraction, cutback, cutting, docking, guillotine, pruning, restriction, retrenchment, truncation.

antonyms extension, lengthening, prolongation.

curtain *v.* conceal, drape, hide, screen, shield, shroud, shutter, veil.

n. arras, backdrop, drapery, hanging, portière, tab, tapestry, vitrage.

curtsy *n.* bob, bow, genuflection, kowtow, salaam.

curvaceous *adj.* bosomy, buxom, comely, curvy, Junoesque, shapely, voluptuous, well-proportioned, well-rounded, well-stacked.

curve *v.* arc, arch, bend, bow, coil, hook, incurvate, incurve, inflect, spiral, swerve, turn, twist, wind.

n. arc, bend, camber, curvature, half-moon, incurvation, incurvature, inflexure, loop, trajectory, turn.

curved *adj.* arched, arc(k)ed, arcuate, bent, bowed, crooked, falcate, humped, inbent, incurvate, incurved, inflexed, rounded, serpentine, sinuous, sweeping, turned, twisted.

antonym straight.

cushion *n.* bean-bag, bolster, buffer, hassock, headrest, pad, pillion, pillow, shock absorber, squab.

v. allay, bolster, buttress, cradle, dampen, deaden, lessen, mitigate, muffle, pillow, protect, soften, stifle, support, suppress.

cushy *adj.* comfortable, easy, jammy, plum, soft, undemanding.

antonyms demanding, tough.

custodian *n.* caretaker, castellan, chatelaine, claviger, conservator, curator, guardian, keeper, overseer, protector, superintendent, warden, warder, watch-dog, watchman.

custody *n.* aegis, arrest, auspices, care, charge, confinement, custodianship, detention, durance, duress, guardianship, holding, imprisonment, incarceration, keeping, observation, possession, preservation, protection, retention, safe-keeping, supervision, trusteeship, tutelage, ward, wardship, watch.

custom *n.* consuetude, convention, customers, etiquette, fashion, form, formality, habit, habitude, manner, mode, observance, observation, patronage, policy, practice, praxis, procedure, ritual, routine, rule, style, thew, trade, tradition, usage, use, way, wont.

customarily *adv.* commonly, generally, habitually, normally, ordinarily, popularly, regularly, routinely, traditionally, usually.

antonyms occasionally, rarely.

customary *adj.* accepted, accustomed, acknowledged, common, confirmed, conventional, established, everyday, familiar, fashionable, favourite, general, habitual, nomic, normal, ordinary, popular, prevailing, regular, routine, traditional, usual, wonted.

antonyms occasional, rare, unusual.

customer *n.* buyer, client, consumer, habitué, patron, prospect, punter, purchaser, regular, shopper, vendee.

cut *v.* abbreviate, abridge, avoid, bisect, carve, castrate, chip, chisel, chop, cleave, clip, cold-shoulder, condense, contract, cross, curtail, decrease, delete, dissect, divide, dock, dod, edit, engrave, excise, fashion, fell, form, gash, gather, gride, grieve, hack, harvest, hew, hurt, ignore, incise, insult, interrupt, intersect, lacerate, lop, lower, mow, nick, notch, pain, pare, part, penetrate, pierce, précis, prune, rationalise, reap, reduce, saw, scissor, score, sculpt, sculpture, segment, sever, shape, share, shave, shorten, slash, slice, slight, slim, slit, sned, snub, split, spurn, sting, sunder, trim, truncate, whittle, wound.

n. abscission, blow, chop, configuration, cutback, decrease, decrement, diminution, division, economy, fall, fashion, form, gash, graze, groove, incision, incisure, insection, kerf, kickback, laceration, look, lowering, mode, nick, percentage, piece, portion, race, rake-off, reduction, rent, rip, saving, section, shape, share, slash, slice, slit, snick, stroke, style, wound.

cut and dried automatic, fixed, organised, prearranged, predetermined, settled, sewn up.

cut back check, crop, curb, decrease, economise, lessen, lop, lower, prune, reduce, retrench, slash, trim.

cut down decrease, diminish, dispatch, fell, hew, kill, lessen, level, lop, lower, massacre, raze, reduce, slaughter, slay.

cut in interjaculate, interject, interpose, interrupt, intervene, intrude.

cut off abscind, block, disconnect, discontinue, disinherit, disown, end, excide, excise, exscind, halt, intercept, interclude, interrupt, intersect, isolate, obstruct, prescind, renounce, separate, sever, stop, suspend.

cut out cease, contrive, debar, delete, displace, eliminate, excise, exclude, exsect, extract, oust, remove, sever, shape, stop, supersede, supplant.

cut out for adapted, adequate, competent, designed, equipped, fitted, made, qualified, right, suitable, suited.

cut short abbreviate, abort, arrest, check, crop, curtail, dock, halt, interrupt, postpone, prune, reduce, stop, terminate.

antonym prolong.

cut up carve, chop, criticise, crucify, dice, divide, injure, knife, lacerate, mince, pan, ridicule, slash, slate, slice, vilify, wound.

cutback *n.* cut, decrease, decrement, economy, lessening, reduction, retrenchment.

cut-price *adj.* bargain, cheap, cut-rate, low-priced, reduced, sale.

cut-throat *n.* assassin, bravo, butcher, executioner, hatchet man, hit-man, homicide, killer, liquidator, murderer, slayer, thug.
adj. barbarous, bloodthirsty, bloody, brutal, competitive, cruel, dog-eat-dog, ferine, ferocious, fierce, homicidal, murderous, relentless, ruthless, savage, thuggish, unprincipled, vicious, violent.

cutting *adj.* acid, acrimonious, barbed, biting, bitter, caustic, chill, hurtful, incisive, keen, malicious, mordant, numbing, penetrating, piercing, pointed, raw, sarcastic, sardonic, scathing, severe, sharp, stinging, trenchant, wounding.
n. bit, cleavage, clipping, piece, scion, scission, slice.

cycle *n.* aeon, age, circle, epoch, era, period, phase, revolution, rotation, round, sequence.

cyclist *n.* velocipedean, velocipeder, velocipedestrian, velocipedian, velocipedist, wheeler.

cyclone *n.* hurricane, monsoon, tempest, tornado, twister, typhoon, whirlwind.

cylinder *n.* barrel, bobbin, column, drum, reel, spindle, spool, trunk.

cynic *n.* doubter, killjoy, knocker, misanthrope, misanthropist, pessimist, sceptic, scoffer, spoilsport.

cynical *adj.* contemptuous, derisive, distrustful, ironic, mephistophelian, mephistophilic, misanthropic(al), mocking, mordant, pessimistic, sarcastic, sardonic, sceptical, scoffing, scornful, sharp-tongued, sneering.

cynicism *n.* disbelief, distrust, doubt, misanthropy, pessimism, sarcasm, scepticism.

cyst *n.* atheroma, bladder, bleb, blister, growth, sac, vesicle, wen.

D

dab[1] *v.* blot, daub, pat, stipple, swab, tap, touch, wipe.
n. bit, dollop, drop, fingerprint, fleck, flick, pat, peck, smear, smidgen, smudge, speck, spot, stroke, tap, touch, trace.

dab[2] ace, adept, dab hand, dabster, expert, pastmaster, wizard.

dabble *v.* dally, dip, fiddle, guddle, moisten, paddle, potter, spatter, splash, sprinkle, tinker, toy, trifle, wet.

dabbler *n.* amateur, dilettante, potterer, sciolist, tinkerer, trifler.
antonyms connoisseur, expert, professional.

daft *adj.* absurd, asinine, berserk, besotted, crackers, crazy, daffy, delirious, demented, deranged, dop(e)y, doting, dotty, foolish, giddy, hysterical, idiotic, inane, infatuated, insane, lunatic, mad, mental, nuts, nutty, potty, scatty, screwy, silly, simple, stupid, touched, unhinged, witless.
antonyms bright, sane.

dagger *n.* bayonet, dah, dirk, jambiya(h), kris, kukri, misericord(e), poniard, skean, skeandhu, stiletto, whinger, whiniard, yatag(h)an.

daily *adj.* circadian, common, commonplace, customary, day-to-day, diurnal, everyday, normal, ordinary, quotidian, regular, routine.

dainty *adj.* charming, choice, choos(e)y, delectable, delicate, delicious, dinky, elegant, exquisite, fastidious, fine, finical, finicking, finicky, friand(e), fussy, genty, graceful, lickerish, liquorish, meticulous, mignon(ne), mincing, minikin, neat, nice, palatable, particular, petite, pretty, refined, savoury, scrupulous, tasty, tender, toothsome.
antonyms clumsy, gross.
n. bonbon, bonne-bouche, delicacy, fancy, sweetmeat, titbit.

dale *n.* bottom, clough, coomb, dell, dingle, ghyll, gill, glen, strath, vale, valley.

dally *v.* canoodle, dawdle, delay, dilly-dally, fiddle-faddle, flirt, frivol, linger, loiter, play, procrastinate, sport, tamper, tarry, toy, trifle.
antonyms hasten, hurry.

dam *n.* an(n)icut, barrage, barrier, blockage, embankment, hindrance, obstruction, wall.
v. barricade, block, check, choke, confine, obstruct, restrict, stanch, staunch, stem.

damage *n.* destruction, detriment, devastation, disprofit, harm, hurt, impairment, injury, loss, mischief, mutilation, scathe, suffering.
antonym repair.
v. deface, harm, hurt, impair, incapacitate, injure, mar, mutilate, play havoc with, play hell with, ruin, spoil, tamper with, weaken, wreck.

antonyms fix, repair.

damages *n.* amercement, compensation, fine, indemnity, reimbursement, reparation, satisfaction.

damaging *adj.* deleterious, detrimental, disadvantageous, harmful, hurtful, injurious, pernicious, prejudicial, ruinous, unfavourable.
antonyms favourable, helpful.

dame *n.* baroness, broad, dowager, female, lady, matron, noblewoman, peeress, woman.

damn *v.* abuse, anathematise, blaspheme, blast, castigate, censure, condemn, criticise, curse, dang, darn, dash, denounce, denunciate, doom, excoriate, execrate, imprecate, pan, revile, sentence, slam, slate, swear.
antonym bless.
n. brass farthing, darn, dash, hoot, iota, jot, monkey's, tinker's cuss, two hoots, whit.

damnable *adj.* abominable, accursed, atrocious, culpable, cursed, despicable, detestable, execrable, hateful, horrible, iniquitous, offensive, sinful, wicked.
antonyms admirable, praiseworthy.

damnation *n.* anathema, ban, condemnation, denunciation, doom, excommunication, malison, objurgation, perdition, proscription.

damned *adj.* accursed, anathematised, condemned, confounded, danged, darned, dashed, despicable, detestable, deuced, doggone(d), doomed, dratted, effing, flipping, fucking, goddam(n), goddamned, hateful, infamous, infernal, loathsome, lost, reprobate, revolting, unhappy.
antonym blessed.

damning *adj.* accusatorial, condemnatory, damnatory, dooming, implicative, incriminating, inculpatory.

damp *n.* clamminess, dampness, dankness, dew, drizzle, fog, humidity, mist, moisture, muzziness, vapour, wet.
antonym dryness.
adj. clammy, dank, dewy, dripping, drizzly, humid, misty, moist, muggish, muggy, sodden, soggy, sopping, vaporous, vapourish, vapoury, wet.
antonyms arid, dry.
v. allay, bedew, check, chill, cool, curb, dampen, dash, deaden, deject, depress, diminish, discourage, dispirit, dull, inhibit, moderate, moisten, restrain, stifle, wet.
antonym dry.

dampen *v.* bedew, besprinkle, check, dash, deaden, decrease, depress, deter, diminish, dishearten, dismay, dull, lessen, moderate, moisten, muffle, reduce, restrain, smother,

spray, stifle, wet.
antonyms dry, encourage.
dance *v.* caper, frolic, gambol, hoof it, hop, jig, juke, kantikoy, prance, rock, skip, spin, stomp, sway, swing, tread a measure, whirl.
n. bal masqué, bal paré, ball, hop, kantikoy, kick-up, knees-up, prom, shindig, social.
dancer *n.* ballerina, ballet dancer, belly-dancer, coryphée, danseur, danseuse, hoofer, prima ballerina, tap-dancer.
dandy *n.* Adonis, beau, blade, blood, buck, Corinthian, coxcomb, dapperling, dude, exquisite, fop, Jack-a-dandy, jay, macaroni, man-about-town, masher, muscadin, musk-cat, peacock, popinjay, swell, toff.
adj. capital, dinky, excellent, fine, first-rate, great, splendid.
danger *n.* endangerment, hazard, insecurity, jeopardy, liability, menace, peril, precariousness, risk, threat, trouble, venture, vulnerability.
antonyms safety, security.
dangerous *adj.* alarming, breakneck, chancy, critical, daring, exposed, grave, hairy, harmful, hazardous, insecure, menacing, nasty, parlous, perilous, precarious, reckless, risky, serious, severe, threatening, tickly, treacherous, ugly, unsafe, vulnerable.
antonyms harmless, safe, secure.
dangle *v.* droop, flap, flaunt, flourish, hang, lure, sway, swing, tantalise, tempt, trail, wave.
dangling *adj.* disconnected, drooping, hanging, loose, pendulous, swaying, swinging, trailing.
dank *adj.* chilly, clammy, damp, dewy, dripping, moist, rheumy, slimy, soggy.
antonym dry.
dapper *adj.* active, brisk, chic, dainty, natty, neat, nimble, smart, spiffy, spruce, spry, stylish, trig, trim, well-dressed, well-groomed.
antonyms dishevelled, dowdy, scruffy, shabby, sloppy.
dappled *adj.* bespeckled, brindled, checkered, dotted, flecked, freckled, mottled, piebald, pied, speckled, spotted, stippled, variegated.
dare *v.* adventure, brave, challenge, defy, endanger, gamble, goad, have the gall, hazard, presume, provoke, risk, stake, taunt, venture.
n. challenge, gauntlet, provocation, taunt.
daredevil *n.* adventurer, desperado, exhibitionist, Hotspur, madcap, stuntman.
antonym coward.
adj. adventurous, audacious, bold, daring, death-defying, fearless, madcap, rash, reckless.
antonyms cautious, prudent, timid.
daring *adj.* adventurous, audacious, bold, brave, brazen, dauntless, fearless, game, impulsive, intrepid, plucky, rash, reckless, valiant, venturesome.
antonyms afraid, timid.
n. audacity, boldness, bottle, bravery, bravura, courage, defiance, derring-do, fearlessness, gall, grit, guts, intrepidity, nerve, pluck,

prowess, rashness, spirit, spunk, temerity.
antonyms cowardice, timidity.
dark *adj.* abstruse, angry, aphotic, arcane, atrocious, benighted, black, bleak, brunette, caliginous, cheerless, cloudy, concealed, cryptic, damnable, darkling, dark-skinned, darksome, deep, dim, dingy, dismal, doleful, dour, drab, dusky, ebony, enigmatic, evil, forbidding, foul, frowning, gloomy, glowering, glum, grim, hellish, hidden, horrible, ignorant, indistinct, infamous, infernal, joyless, lightless, melanic, melanous, midnight, mirk, mirky, morbid, morose, mournful, murk, murky, mysterious, mystic, nefarious, obscure, occult, ominous, overcast, pitch-black, pitchy, puzzling, recondite, sable, satanic, scowling, secret, shadowy, shady, sinful, sinister, sombre, sulky, sullen, sunless, swarthy, tenebr(i)ous, threatening, uncultivated, unenlightened, unillumed, unilluminated, unlettered, unlit, vile, wicked.
antonyms bright, happy, light, lucid.
n. concealment, darkness, dimness, dusk, evening, gloom, ignorance, mirk, mirkiness, murk, murkiness, night, nightfall, night-time, obscurity, secrecy, twilight, yin.
antonyms brightness, light.
darken *v.* becloud, blacken, cloud, cloud over, darkle, deepen, deject, depress, dim, disilluminate, dispirit, dusken, eclipse, embrown, obscure, overshade, overshadow, sadden, shade, shadow.
antonyms brighten, lighten.
darkness *n.* blackness, blindness, concealment, dark, dimness, dusk, duskiness, gloom, ignorance, mirk, mirkiness, murk, murkiness, mystery, nightfall, obscurity, privacy, secrecy, shade, shadiness, shadows, tenebr(os)ity.
antonyms brightness, daylight, lightness.
darling *n.* acushla, apple of one's eye, asthore, beloved, blue-eyed boy, dear, dearest, fair-haired boy, favourite, jo(e), lady-love, love, lovey, machree, mavourneen, minikin, pet, poppet, sweetheart, true-love.
adj. adored, beloved, cherished, dear, precious, treasured, white-headed.
dart *v.* bound, cast, dartle, dash, flash, fling, flit, fly, hurl, launch, propel, race, run, rush, scoot, send, shoot, sling, spring, sprint, start, tear, throw, whistle, whiz.
n. arrow, barb, bolt, flight, shaft.
dash[1] *v.* abash, blight, break, cast, chagrin, confound, crash, dampen, destroy, ding, disappoint, discomfort, discourage, fling, foil, frustrate, hurl, ruin, shatter, shiver, slam, sling, smash, splinter, spoil, throw, thwart.
n. bit, bravura, brio, da(u)d, drop, élan, flair, flavour, flourish, hint, little, panache, pinch, smack, soupçon, spirit, sprinkling, style, suggestion, tinge, touch, verve, vigour, vivacity.
dash[2] *v.* be off like a shot, bolt, bound, dart, dartle, fly, haste(n), hurry, race, run, rush, speed, spring, sprint, tear.
n. bolt, dart, race, run, rush, sprint, spurt.

dashing *adj.* bold, dapper, daring, dazzling, debonair, doggy, elegant, exuberant, flamboyant, gallant, impressive, jaunty, lively, plucky, showy, smart, spirited, sporty, stylish, swashbuckling, swish.
antonym drab.

dastard *n.* caitiff, coward, craven, cur, milksop, poltroon, worm.

dastardly *adj.* base, caitiff, contemptible, cowardly, craven, despicable, faint-hearted, lily-livered, low, mean, niddering, pusillanimous, recreant, sneaking, sneaky, spiritless, timorous, underhand, vile.
antonyms heroic, noble.

data *n.* details, documents, dope, facts, figures, info, information, input, materials, statistics.

date[1] *n.* age, epoch, era, period, point, point in time, stage, time.

date[2] *n.* appointment, assignation, engagement, escort, friend, meeting, partner, rendezvous, steady, tryst.

dated *adj.* antiquated, archaic, démodé, obsolescent, obsolete, old hat, old-fashioned, out, outdated, outmoded, out-of-date, passé, superseded, unfashionable.
antonyms fashionable, up-to-the-minute.

daub *v.* begrime, besmear, blur, coat, cover, dedaub, deface, dirty, gaum, grime, paint, plaster, smear, smirch, smudge, spatter, splatter, stain, sully.
n. blot, blotch, smear, splash, splodge, splotch, spot, stain.

daunt *v.* alarm, appal, cow, deter, discourage, dishearten, dismay, dispirit, frighten, intimidate, overawe, put off, scare, shake, subdue, terrify, unnerve.
antonyms encourage, hearten.

daunted *adj.* alarmed, cowed, demoralised, deterred, discouraged, disheartened, disillusioned, dismayed, dismayful, dispirited, downcast, frightened, hesitant, intimidated, overcome, put off, unnerved.
antonyms encouraged, heartened.

dauntless *adj.* bold, brave, courageous, daring, doughty, fearless, gallant, game, heroic, indomitable, intrepid, lion-hearted, plucky, resolute, stout-hearted, undaunted, unflinching, valiant, valorous.
antonyms discouraged, disheartened.

dawdle *v.* daidle, dally, delay, dilly-dally, fiddle, fritter, hang about, idle, lag, loaf, loiter, potter, shilly-shally, trail.
antonym hurry.

dawdler *n.* laggard, lingerer, loafer, loiterer, shilly-shallier, slowcoach, snail, tortoise.

dawn *n.* advent, aurora, beginning, birth, cock-crow(ing), dawning, daybreak, daylight, day-peep, dayspring, emergence, genesis, inception, morning, onset, origin, outset, peep of day, rise, start, sunrise, sun-up.
antonyms dusk, sundown, sunset.
v. appear, begin, break, brighten, develop, emerge, gleam, glimmer, hit, initiate, lighten, occur, open, originate, register, rise, strike, unfold.

day *n.* age, ascendancy, childhood, cycle, date, daylight, daytime, epoch, era, generation, height, heyday, period, prime, time, young days, youth, zenith.
antonym night.

day after day continually, endlessly, forever, monotonously, perpetually, persistently, regularly, relentlessly.

day by day daily, gradually, progressively, slowly but surely, steadily.

daybreak *n.* break of day, cock-crow(ing), crack of dawn, dawn, day-peep, dayspring, first light, morning, peep of day, sunrise, sun-up.
antonyms sundown, sunset.

daydream *n.* castles in Spain, castles in the air, dream, dwa(l)m, fantasy, figment, fond hope, imagining, musing, phantasm, pipe dream, reverie, star-gazing, vision, wish, woolgathering.
v. dream, fancy, fantasise, hallucinate, imagine, muse, stargaze.

daydreamer *n.* fantasiser, rêveur, rêveuse, stargazer.

daze *v.* amaze, astonish, astound, befog, benumb, bewilder, blind, confuse, dazzle, dumbfound, flabbergast, numb, paralyse, perplex, shock, stagger, startle, stun, stupefy, surprise.
n. bewilderment, confusion, distraction, dwa(l)m, shock, stupor, trance.

dazed *adj.* baffled, bemused, bewildered, confused, disorien(ta)ted, dizzy, dop(e)y, dumbstruck, flabbergasted, fuddled, groggy, light-headed, muddled, nonplussed, numbed, perplexed, punch-drunk, shocked, staggered, stunned, stupefied, totty, woozy.

dazzle *v.* amaze, astonish, awe, bedazzle, blind, blur, confuse, daze, fascinate, hypnotise, impress, overawe, overpower, overwhelm, scintillate, sparkle, stupefy.
n. brilliance, glitter, magnificence, razzle-dazzle, razzmatazz, scintillation, sparkle, splendour.

dazzling *adj.* brilliant, foudroyant, glaring, glary, glittering, glorious, radiant, ravishing, scintillating, sensational, shining, sparkling, splendid, stunning, sublime, superb, virtuoso.

de facto *adv.* actually, in effect, really.
adj. actual, existing, real.

de jure legally, rightfully.

de luxe choice, costly, elegant, exclusive, expensive, grand, luxurious, opulent, palatial, plush, rich, select, special, splendid, sumptuous, superior.

de rigueur comme il faut, conventional, correct, decent, decorous, done, fitting, necessary, proper, required, right, the done thing.

de trop needless, redundant, supererogatory, superfluous, supernumerary, surplus, unnecessary, unneeded, unwanted, unwelcome.

dead[1] *adj.* ad patres, apathetic, barren, boring, breathless, callous, cold, dead-and-alive, dead-beat, deceased, defunct, departed, dull, exhausted, extinct, flat, frigid, glassy, glazed, gone, inactive, inanimate, indifferent, inert,

inoperative, insipid, late, lifeless, lukewarm, napoo, numb, obsolete, paralysed, perished, spent, spiritless, stagnant, stale, sterile, stiff, still, tasteless, tired, torpid, unemployed, uninteresting, unprofitable, unresponsive, useless, vapid, wooden, worn out.
antonyms active, alive, animated.

dead[2] *adj.* absolute, complete, downright, entire, outright, perfect, thorough, total, unqualified, utter.
adv. absolutely, completely, entirely, exactly, perfectly, quite, totally.

deaden *v.* abate, allay, alleviate, anaesthetise, benumb, blunt, check, cushion, damp, dampen, desensitise, diminish, dull, hush, impair, lessen, muffle, mute, numb, obtund, paralyse, quieten, reduce, smother, stifle, suppress, weaken.
antonym enliven.

deadlock *n.* halt, impasse, stalemate, standstill.

deadly *adj.* accurate, ashen, baleful, baneful, boring, cruel, dangerous, death-dealing, deathful, deathlike, deathly, destructive, devastating, dull, effective, exact, fatal, feral, funest, ghastly, ghostly, grim, implacable, lethal, malignant, monotonous, mortal, noxious, pallid, pernicious, pestilent, poisonous, precise, ruthless, savage, sure, tedious, thanatoid, true, unerring, unfailing, uninteresting, unrelenting, venomous, wearisome, white.
antonyms harmless, healthy.

deadpan *adj.* blank, dispassionate, empty, expressionless, impassive, inexpressive, inscrutable, poker-faced, straight-faced, unexpressive.

deaf *adj.* hard of hearing, heedless, indifferent, oblivious, stone-deaf, unconcerned, unmindful, unmoved.
antonyms aware, conscious.

deafening *adj.* booming, dinning, ear-piercing, ear-splitting, fortissimo, piercing, resounding, ringing, roaring, thunderous.
antonyms pianissimo, quiet.

deal *v.* allot, apportion, assign, bargain, bestow, dispense, distribute, divide, dole out, give, mete out, negotiate, reward, sell, share, stock, trade, traffic, treat.
n. agreement, amount, arrangement, bargain, buy, contract, degree, distribution, extent, hand, pact, portion, quantity, round, share, transaction, understanding.
deal with attend to, concern, consider, cope with, handle, manage, oversee, see to, treat.

dealer *n.* chandler, chapman, marketer, merchandiser, merchant, monger, trader, tradesman, wholesaler.

dealings *n.* business, commerce, intercourse, intertraffic, trade, traffic, transactions, truck.

dear *adj.* beloved, cherished, close, costly, darling, esteemed, expensive, familiar, favourite, high-priced, intimate, loved, overpriced, precious, pric(e)y, prized, respected, treasured, valued.
antonyms cheap, hateful.

n. angel, beloved, darling, dearie, deary, loved one, precious, treasure.

dearly *adv.* affectionately, devotedly, extremely, fondly, greatly, lovingly, profoundly, tenderly.

dearth *n.* absence, barrenness, deficiency, exiguousness, famine, inadequacy, insufficiency, lack, need, paucity, poverty, scantiness, scarcity, shortage, sparseness, sparsity, want.
antonyms abundance, excess.

death *n.* annihilation, bane, bereavement, cessation, curtains, decease, demise, departure, destruction, dissolution, dormition, downfall, dying, end, eradication, exit, expiration, extermination, extinction, fatality, finish, grave, loss, obliteration, passing, quietus, release, ruin, ruination, undoing.
antonyms birth, life.

deathless *adj.* eternal, everlasting, immortal, imperishable, incorruptible, never-ending, timeless, undying, unforgettable.

deathly *adj.* ashen, cadaverous, deadly, deathlike, fatal, gaunt, ghastly, grim, haggard, intense, mortal, pale, pallid, terrible, wan.

debacle *n.* cataclysm, catastrophe, collapse, defeat, devastation, disaster, downfall, farce, fiasco, havoc, overthrow, reversal, rout, ruin, ruination, stampede.

debar *v.* bar, blackball, deny, eject, exclude, expel, hamper, hinder, obstruct, preclude, prevent, prohibit, restrain, segregate, shut out, stop.
antonym admit.

debase *v.* abase, adulterate, allay, bastardise, cheapen, contaminate, corrupt, defile, degrade, demean, depreciate, devalue, diminish, disgrace, dishonour, embase, humble, humiliate, impair, lower, pollute, reduce, shame, taint, vitiate.
antonyms elevate, upgrade.

debased *adj.* abandoned, adulterated, base, corrupt, debauched, degenerate, degraded, depraved, depreciated, devalued, diminished, fallen, impure, low, lowered, mixed, perverted, polluted, reduced, sordid, vile.
antonyms elevated, pure.

debasement *n.* abasement, adulteration, baseness, contamination, corruption, degeneration, degradation, depravation, depreciation, devaluation, dishonour, perversion, pollution, reduction.
antonyms elevation, purification.

debatable *adj.* arguable, borderline, contentious, contestable, controversial, controvertible, disputable, doubtful, dubious, moot, open to question, problematical, questionable, uncertain, undecided, unsettled.
antonyms certain, questionable.

debate *v.* argue, cogitate, consider, contend, contest, controvert, deliberate, discuss, dispute, logicise, meditate on, mull over, ponder, question, reflect, revolve, ruminate, weigh, wrangle.
antonym agree.

n. altercation, argument, cogitation, consideration, contention, controversy, deliberation, discussion, disputation, dispute, meditation, polemic, quodlibet, reflection.
antonym agreement.

debauch *v.* corrupt, deflower, demoralise, deprave, over-indulge, pervert, pollute, ravish, ruin, seduce, subvert, violate, vitiate.
antonyms cleanse, purge, purify.
n. bacchanalia, bender, bevvy, binge, booze-up, bout, fling, orgy, pub-crawl, saturnalia, spree, wet.

debauched *adj.* abandoned, corrupt, corrupted, debased, degenerate, degraded, depraved, dissipated, dissolute, immoral, intemperate, lewd, licentious, perverted, profligate, raddled, rakehell, rakehelly, wanton.
antonyms decent, pure, virtuous.

debauchee *n.* hell-bender, libertine, Lothario, playboy, profligate, rake, rake-hell, roué, sensualist, wanton.

debauchery *n.* carousal, debauchedness, debauchment, depravity, dissipation, dissoluteness, excess, gluttony, immorality, incontinence, indulgence, intemperance, lewdness, licentiousness, lust, orgy, overindulgence, rakery, revel, riot, wantonness.

debilitate *v.* devitalise, enervate, enfeeble, exhaust, impair, incapacitate, prostrate, relax, sap, undermine, unman, weaken, wear out.
antonyms energise, invigorate, strengthen.

debilitating *adj.* enervating, enervative, enfeebling, exhausting, fatiguing, tiring, weakening.
antonyms invigorating, strengthening.

debility *n.* asthenia, atonicity, atony, decrepitude, enervation, enfeeblement, exhaustion, faintness, feebleness, frailty, incapacity, infirmity, languor, malaise, sickliness, weakness.
antonyms strength, vigour.

debonair *adj.* affable, breezy, buoyant, charming, cheerful, courteous, dashing, elegant, gay, jaunty, light-hearted, refined, smooth, sprightly, suave, urbane, well-bred.

debris *n.* bits, brash, detritus, drift, dross, duff, eluvium, exuviae, fragments, litter, moraine, pieces, remains, rubbish, rubble, ruins, sweepings, trash, waste, wreck, wreckage.

debt *n.* arrears, bill, claim, commitment, debit, due, duty, indebtedness, liability, obligation, score, sin.
antonyms asset, credit.

debtor *n.* bankrupt, borrower, defaulter, insolvent, mortgagee, mortgagor.
antonym creditor.

debunk *v.* deflate, disparage, explode, expose, lampoon, mock, puncture, ridicule, show up.

debut *n.* appearance, beginning, bow, entrance, inauguration, initiation, introduction, launching, première, presentation.

decadence *n.* corruption, debasement, decadency, decay, decline, degenerateness, degeneration, deterioration, dissipation, dissolution, fall, perversion, retrogression, symbolism.

antonyms flourishing, rise.

decadent *adj.* corrupt, debased, debauched, decaying, declining, degenerate, degraded, depraved, dissolute, effete, fin-de-siècle, immoral, self-indulgent, symbolist.
antonym moral.

decamp *v.* abscond, absquatulate, bolt, desert, do a bunk, escape, flee, flit, fly, guy, hightail it, levant, make off, mizzle, run away, scarper, skedaddle.

decapitate *v.* behead, execute, guillotine, unhead.

decay *v.* atrophy, canker, corrode, crumble, decline, decompose, decompound, degenerate, deteriorate, disintegrate, dissolve, dote, dwindle, mortify, moulder, perish, putrefy, rot, shrivel, sink, spoil, wane, waste away, wear away, wither.
antonyms flourish, grow, ripen.
n. atrophy, caries, collapse, consenescence, decadence, decline, decomposition, decrepitness, decrepitude, degeneracy, degeneration, deterioration, disintegration, dying, fading, failing, gangrene, labefactation, labefaction, mortification, perishing, putrefaction, putrescence, putridity, putridness, rot, rotting, wasting, withering.

decayed *adj.* addled, bad, carious, carrion, corroded, decomposed, off, perished, putrefied, putrid, rank, rotten, spoiled, wasted, withered.

decaying *adj.* crumbling, decrepit, deteriorating, disintegrating, doty, dricksie, druxy, gangrenous, perishing, putrescent, rotting.

decease *n.* death, demise, departure, dissolution, dying, passing, release.
v. cease, croak, die, expire, give up the ghost, kick the bucket, pass away, pass on, pass over, perish.

deceased *adj.* dead, defunct, departed, expired, extinct, finished, former, gone, late, lifeless, lost.
n. dead, decedent, departed.

deceit *n.* abuse, artifice, blind, cheat, cheating, chicanery, con, cozenage, craftiness, cunning, deceitfulness, deception, dissimulation, double-dealing, duplicity, fake, feint, fraud, fraudulence, guile, hypocrisy, imposition, imposture, misrepresentation, phenakism, pretence, ruse, sham, shift, slyness, stratagem, subterfuge, swindle, treachery, trick, trickery, underhandedness, wile.
antonyms honesty, openness.

deceitful *adj.* collusive, counterfeit, crafty, deceiving, deceptive, designing, dishonest, disingenuous, double-dealing, duplicitous, elusory, fallacious, false, fraudulent, guileful, hypocritical, illusory, insincere, knavish, prestigious, Punic, rusé, sneaky, treacherous, tricky, two-faced, underhand, untrustworthy.
antonyms honest, open, trustworthy.

deceive *v.* abuse, bamboozle, befool, beguile, betray, camouflage, cheat, cog, con, cozen, delude, diddle, disappoint, dissemble, dissimulate, double-cross, dupe, ensnare,

entrap, flam, fool, gag, gammon, gloze, gull, have on, hoax, hoodwink, impose upon, lead on, mislead, outwit, seel, swindle, take for a ride, take in, trick, two-time.
antonym enlighten.

deceiver *n.* abuser, betrayer, charlatan, cheat, con man, cozener, crook, deluder, diddler, dissembler, dissimulator, double-dealer, fake, fraud, hypocrite, impostor, inveigler, mountebank, pretender, sharper, swindler, trickster.

decency *n.* appropriateness, civility, correctness, courtesy, decorum, etiquette, fitness, good form, good manners, helpfulness, modesty, propriety, respectability, seemliness, thoughtfulness.
antonyms discourtesy, indecency.

decent *adj.* acceptable, accommodating, adequate, ample, appropriate, average, becoming, befitting, chaste, comely, comme il faut, competent, courteous, decorous, delicate, fair, fit, fitting, friendly, generous, gracious, gradely, helpful, kind, modest, nice, obliging, passable, polite, presentable, proper, pure, reasonable, respectable, satisfactory, seemly, sufficient, suitable, thoughtful, tolerable.
antonyms disobliging, indecent, poor.

decentralisation *n.* delegation, development, devolution.
antonym centralisation.

deception *n.* artifice, bluff, cheat, conning, craftiness, cunning, deceifulness, deceit, deceptiveness, decoy, defraudation, defraudment, dissembling, dissimulation, duplicity, false-pretences, feint, flim-flam, fraud, fraudulence, guile, gullery, hoax, hype, hypocrisy, illusion, imposition, imposture, insincerity, legerdemain, leg-pull, lie, ruse, sell, sham, snare, stratagem, subterfuge, take-in, treachery, trick, trickery, wile.
antonyms artlessness, openness.

deceptive *adj.* ambiguous, catchy, delusive, delusory, dishonest, elusory, fake, fallacious, false, fraudulent, illusive, illusory, misleading, mock, specious, spurious, unreliable.
antonyms artless, genuine, open.

decide *v.* adjudge, adjudicate, choose, conclude, decree, determine, dijudicate, elect, end, fix, judge, opt, purpose, reach a decision, resolve, settle.

decided *adj.* absolute, assertive, categorical, certain, clear-cut, decisive, definite, deliberate, determined, distinct, emphatic, express, firm, forthright, indisputable, marked, noticeable, positive, pronounced, resolute, strongwilled, unambiguous, undeniable, undisputed, unequivocal, unfaltering, unhesitating, unmistakable, unquestionable.
antonyms indecisive, undecided.

decidedly *adv.* absolutely, certainly, clearly, decisively, definitely, distinctly, downright, positively, quite, unequivocally, unmistakably, very.

decider *n.* clincher, coup de grâce, determiner, floorer.

deciding *adj.* chief, conclusive, critical, crucial, crunch, decisive, determining, final, influential, prime, principal, significant, supreme.
antonym insignificant.

decipher *v.* construe, crack, decode, decrypt, deduce, explain, figure out, interpret, make out, read, solve, transliterate, uncipher, understand, unfold, unravel, unscramble.
antonym encode.

decipherment *n.* decryption, interpretation, translation, transliteration, unscrambling.
antonym encoding.

decision *n.* arbitrament, arbitration, arrêt, conclusion, decisiveness, determination, fetwa, finding, firmness, judgement, outcome, parti, purpose, purposefulness, resoluteness, resolution, resolve, result, ruling, settlement, verdict.

decisive *adj.* absolute, conclusive, critical, crucial, crunch, decided, definite, definitive, determinate, determined, fateful, final, firm, forceful, forthright, incisive, influential, momentous, positive, resolute, significant, strong-minded, supreme, trenchant.
antonyms indecisive, insignificant.

deck *v.* adorn, apparel, array, attire, beautify, bedeck, bedight, bedizen, betrim, clothe, decorate, doll up, dress, embellish, festoon, garland, grace, ornament, prettify, pretty up, primp, prink, rig out, smarten, titivate, tog out, tog up, trick out, trim.

declaim *v.* bespout, harangue, hold forth, lecture, mouth, orate, perorate, preach, proclaim, rant, recite, rhetorise, speak, speechify, spiel, spout.

declamation *n.* address, harangue, lecture, oration, rant, recitation, rhetoric, speech, speechifying, tirade.

declamatory *adj.* bombastic, discursive, fustian, grandiloquent, grandiose, high-flown, inflated, magniloquent, oratorical, oro(ro)tund, overblown, pompous, rhetorical, stagy, stilted, theatrical, turgid.

declaration *n.* acknowledgement, affirmation, announcement, assertion, asseveration, attestation, averment, avouchment, avowal, deposition, disclosure, edict, manifesto, notification, proclamation, profession, promulgation, pronouncement, pronunciamento, protestation, revelation, statement, testimony.

declare *v.* affirm, announce, assert, attest, aver, avouch, avow, certify, claim, confess, confirm, convey, disclose, maintain, manifest, nuncupate, proclaim, profess, pronounce, reveal, show, state, swear, testify, validate, witness.

decline[1] *v.* avoid, balk, decay, decrease, degenerate, deny, deteriorate, deviate, diminish, droop, dwindle, ebb, fade, fail, fall, fall off, flag, forgo, languish, lessen, pine, refuse, reject, shrink, sink, turn down, wane, weaken, worsen.
n. abatement, consumption, decay, declension, decrepitude, degeneration, deterioration, deviation, diminution, downturn,

dwindling, enfeeblement, failing, falling off, falling-off, lessening, paracme, phthisis, recession, senility, slump, tuberculosis, weakening, worsening.

decline[2] *v.* descend, dip, sink, slant, slope.
n. brae, declination, declivity, descent, deviation, dip, divergence, hill, incline, obliqueness, obliquity, slope.

declivity *n.* brae, declination, decline, descent, incline, slant, slope.
antonym acclivity.

decode *v.* decipher, decrypt, interpret, translate, transliterate, uncipher, unscramble.
antonym encode.

decomposable *adj.* biodegradable, decompoundable, degradable, destructible.

decompose *v.* analyse, atomise, break down, break up, crumble, decay, decompound, degrade, disintegrate, dissolve, distil, fall apart, fester, fractionate, putrefy, rot, separate, spoil.
antonyms combine, unite.

decomposition *n.* atomisation, breakdown, corruption, decay, degradation, disintegration, dissolution, distillation, division, electrolysis, fractionation, hydrolysis, putrefaction, putrescence, putridity, rot.
antonyms combination, unification.

décor *n.* colour-scheme, decoration, embellishments, furnishings, ornamentation, scenery.

decorate[1] *v.* adorn, beautify, bedeck, colour, daiker, deck, do up, embellish, enrich, furbish, grace, impearl, miniate, ornament, paint, paper, prettify, renovate, tart up, trick out, trim, wallpaper.

decorate[2] *v.* bemedal, cite, crown, garland, honour.

decorated *adj.* baroque, elaborate, embellished, figured, garnished, ornate, rococo.
antonym plain.

decoration[1] *n.* adornment, arabesque, bauble, beautification, curlicue, elaboration, embellishment, enrichment, falderal, flounce, flourish, frill, frou-frou, furbelow, garnish, ornament, ornamentation, pass(e)ment, passementerie, scroll, spangle, trimming, trinket.

decoration[2] *n.* award, badge, colours, crown, emblem, garland, garter, laurel, laurel-wreath, medal, order, ribbon, star.

decorative *adj.* adorning, arty-crafty, baroque, beautifying, embellishing, enhancing, fancy, non-functional, ornamental, ornate, pretty, rococo, superfluous.
antonyms plain, ugly.

decorous *adj.* appropriate, becoming, befitting, comely, comme il faut, correct, courtly, decent, dignified, fit, maidenly, mannerly, modest, polite, proper, refined, sedate, seemly, staid, suitable, well-behaved.
antonym indecorous.

decorum *n.* behaviour, breeding, courtliness, decency, deportment, dignity, etiquette, gentility, good manners, grace, gravity, modesty, politeness, politesse, propriety, protocol, punctilio, respectability, restraint,

seemliness.
antonyms bad manners, indecorum.

decoy *n.* attraction, bait, ensnarement, enticement, inducement, lure, pretence, roper(-in), trap.
v. allure, attract, bait, beguile, deceive, draw, ensnare, entice, entrap, inveigle, lead, lure, seduce, tempt.

decrease *v.* abate, ablate, contract, curtail, cut down, decline, diminish, drop, dwindle, ease, fall off, lessen, lower, peter out, reduce, shrink, slacken, slim, subside, taper, wane.
antonym increase.
n. abatement, ablation, contraction, cutback, decline, decrement, degression, diminution, downturn, dwindling, ebb, falling off, lessening, loss, reduction, shrinkage, step down, subsidence.
antonym increase.

decree *n.* act, command, decretal, dictum, edict, enactment, firman, hatti-sherif, indiction, interlocution, interlocutor, law, mandate, order, ordinance, precept, proclamation, regulation, ruling, statute, ukase.
v. command, decide, determine, dictate, enact, lay down, ordain, order, prescribe, proclaim, pronounce, rescript, rule.

decreed *adj.* enacted, ordained, proclaimed, stated, writ, written.

decrepit *adj.* aged, antiquated, battered, broken-backed, broken-down, crippled, debilitated, deteriorated, dilapidated, doddering, doddery, feeble, frail, incapacitated, infirm, ramshackle, rickety, run-down, superannuated, tumble-down, warby, wasted, weak, worn-out.
antonyms fit, well-cared-for, youthful.

decrepitude *n.* debility, decay, degeneration, deterioration, dilapidation, disability, dotage, feebleness, incapacity, infirmity, invalidity, old age, senescence, senility, wasting, weakness.
antonyms good repair, youth.

decry *v.* abuse, belittle, blame, censure, condemn, criticise, cry down, declaim against, denounce, depreciate, derogate, detract, devalue, discredit, disparage, inveigh against, rail against, run down, traduce, underestimate, underrate, undervalue.
antonyms praise, value.

dedicate *v.* address, assign, bless, commit, consecrate, devote, give over to, hallow, inscribe, offer, pledge, present, sacrifice, sanctify, set apart, surrender.

dedicated *adj.* committed, devoted, enthusiastic, given over to, purposeful, single-hearted, single-minded, sworn, whole-hearted, zealous.
antonyms apathetic, uncommitted.

dedication[1] *n.* adherence, allegiance, attachment, commitment, devotedness, devotion, faithfulness, loyalty, self-sacrifice, single-mindedness, whole-heartedness.
antonym apathy.

dedication[2] *n.* address, consecration, donation,

hallowing, inscription, presentation, sanctification.
antonym praise.

deduce *v.* conclude, derive, draw, gather, glean, infer, reason, surmise, understand.

deducible *adj.* a fortiori, a posteriori, derivable, inferable, traceable.

deduct *v.* decrease by, knock off, reduce by, remove, subduct, subtract, take away, withdraw.
antonym add.

deduction [1] *n.* assumption, conclusion, consectary, corollary, finding, inference, reasoning, result.

deduction [2] *n.* abatement, allowance, decrease, diminution, discount, reduction, subduction, subtraction, withdrawal.
antonyms addition, increase.

deed [1] *n.* achievement, act, action, exploit, fact, factum, feat, gest(e), performance, reality, truth.

deed [2] *n.* contract, document, indenture, instrument, record, title, transaction.

deem *v.* account, adjudge, believe, conceive, consider, esteem, estimate, hold, imagine, judge, reckon, regard, suppose, think.

deep *adj.* absorbed, abstract, abstruse, abyssal, acute, arcane, artful, astute, bass, booming, bottomless, broad, canny, cryptic, cunning, dark, designing, devious, discerning, engrossed, esoteric, extreme, far, fathomless, full-toned, grave, great, hidden, immersed, insidious, intense, knowing, learned, lost, low, low-pitched, mysterious, obscure, penetrating, preoccupied, profound, rapt, recondite, resonant, rich, sagacious, scheming, secret, shrewd, sonorous, strong, unfathomable, unfathomed, unplumbed, unsoundable, unsounded, vivid, wide, wise, yawning.
antonyms open, shallow.
n. briny, drink, high seas, main, ocean, sea.

deepen *v.* dredge, excavate, grow, hollow, increase, intensify, magnify, reinforce, scoop out, strengthen.
antonym fill in.

deeply *adv.* acutely, affectingly, completely, distressingly, feelingly, gravely, intensely, mournfully, movingly, passionately, profoundly, sadly, seriously, severely, thoroughly, to the quick, very much.
antonym slightly.

deep-seated *adj.* confirmed, deep, deep-rooted, entrenched, fixed, ineradicable, ingrained, inveterate, rooted, settled, subconscious, unconscious.
antonyms eradicable, temporary.

deer *n.* buck, doe, hart, reindeer, roe, stag.

deface *v.* blemish, damage, deform, destroy, disfeature, disfigure, impair, injure, mar, mutilate, obliterate, spoil, sully, tarnish, vandalise.
antonym repair.

defamation *n.* aspersion, calumny, denigration, derogation, disparagement, innuendo, libel, mud-slinging, obloquy, opprobrium, scandal, slander, slur, smear, traducement, vilification.
antonym praise.

defamatory *adj.* abusive, calumnious, contumelious, denigrating, derogatory, disparaging, injurious, insulting, libellous, pejorative, slanderous, vilifying, vituperative.
antonym complimentary.

defame *v.* asperse, belie, besmirch, blacken, calumniate, cast aspersions on, cloud, denigrate, detract, discredit, disgrace, dishonour, disparage, infame, libel, malign, slander, smear, speak evil of, stigmatise, traduce, vilify, vituperate.
antonyms compliment, praise.

default *n.* absence, defalcation, defect, deficiency, dereliction, failure, fault, lack, lapse, neglect, non-payment, omission, want.
v. backslide, bilk, defraud, dodge, evade, fail, levant, neglect, rat, swindle, waddle, welsh.

defaulter *n.* defalcator, defector, delinquent, duck, embezzler, levanter, non-payer, offender, peculator, welsher.

defeat *v.* baffle, balk, beat, best, checkmate, clobber, confound, conquer, counteract, crush, disappoint, discomfit, down, foil, frustrate, get the better of, outbargain, overpower, overthrow, overwhelm, psych out, quell, repulse, rout, ruin, stump, subdue, subjugate, tank, thump, thwart, trounce, vanquish, vote down, whop.
n. beating, conquest, débâcle, disappointment, discomfiture, failure, frustration, overthrow, rebuff, repulse, reverse, rout, setback, thwarting, trouncing, vanquishment, Waterloo.

defeated *adj.* balked, beaten, bested, checkmated, confounded, conquered, crushed, licked, nonplussed, overcome, overpowered, overwhelmed, routed, thrashed, thwarted, trounced, vanquished, worsted.
antonyms conquering, triumphant.

defeatist *n.* futilitarian, pessimist, prophet of doom, quitter.
antonym optimist.
adj. cynical, despairing, despondent, fatalistic, gloomy, helpless, hopeless, pessimistic, resigned, resourceless.
antonym optimistic.

defecate *v.* ease oneself, egest, empty, evacuate, excrete, pass a motion, relieve oneself, void (excrement).

defecation *n.* dejection, egestion, elimination, evacuation, excrement, excretion, motion, movement, voiding.

defect *n.* absence, blemish, bug, default, deficiency, error, failing, fault, flaw, frailty, hamartia, imperfection, inadequacy, lack, mistake, shortcoming, spot, taint, want, weakness.
v. apostatise, break faith, desert, rebel, renegue, revolt, tergiversate.

defection *n.* abandonment, apostasy, backsliding, defalcation, dereliction, desertion, rebellion, renegation, revolt.

defective *adj.* abnormal, broken, deficient,

faulty, flawed, imperfect, inadequate, incomplete, insufficient, kaput, out of order, retarded, scant, short, subnormal.
antonyms normal, operative.

defector *n.* apostate, deserter, Grenzgänger, Judas, quisling, rat, recreant, renegade, runagate, tergiversator, turncoat.

defence[1] *n.* aegis, armament, barricade, bastion, buckler, bulwark, buttress, cover, deterrence, fastness, fortification, guard, immunity, muniment, munition, protection, rampart, resistance, safeguard, security, shelter, shield.
antonym attack.

defence[2] *n.* alibi, apologia, apology, argument, case, declaration, denial, excuse, exoneration, explanation, extenuation, justification, palliation, plea, pleading, rebuttal, testimony, vindication.

defenceless *adj.* endangered, exposed, helpless, imperilled, naked, powerless, unarmed, undefended, unguarded, unprotected, unshielded, vulnerable, wide open.
antonym protected.

defend *v.* assert, bulwark, champion, contest, cover, endorse, espouse, fortify, guard, justify, maintain, plead, preserve, protect, safeguard, screen, secure, shelter, shield, speak up for, stand by, stand up for, support, sustain, uphold, vindicate, watch over.
antonym attack.

defendant *n.* accused, appellant, defender, litigant, offender, prisoner, respondent.

defender *n.* advocate, bodyguard, champion, counsel, escort, guard, patron, promachos, protector, sponsor, supporter, vindicator.
antonym attacker.

defensible *adj.* arguable, holdable, impregnable, justifiable, pardonable, permissible, plausible, safe, secure, tenable, unassailable, valid, vindicable.
antonyms indefensible, insecure.

defensive *adj.* apologetic, aposematic, averting, cautious, defending, opposing, protective, safeguarding, self-justifying, wary, watchful, withstanding.
antonym bold.

defer[1] *v.* adjourn, delay, hold over, postpone, procrastinate, prorogue, protract, put off, put on ice, shelve, suspend, waive.

defer[2] *v.* accede, bow, capitulate, comply, give way, kowtow, respect, submit, yield.

deference *n.* acquiescence, attention, capitulation, civility, complaisance, compliance, consideration, courtesy, esteem, homage, honour, morigeration, obedience, obeisance, obsequiousness, politeness, regard, respect, reverence, submission, submissiveness, thoughtfulness, veneration, yielding.

deferential *adj.* civil, complaisant, considerate, courteous, dutiful, ingratiating, morigerous, obedient, obeisant, obsequious, polite, regardful, respectful, reverential, submissive.
antonyms arrogant, immodest.

deferment *n.* adjournment, deferral, delay, moratorium, postponement, procrastination,

putting off, stay, suspension.

defiance *n.* challenge, confrontation, contempt, contumacy, disobedience, disregard, insolence, insubordination, obstinacy, opposition, provocation, rebelliousness, recalcitrance, spite.
antonyms acquiescence, submissiveness.

defiant *adj.* aggressive, audacious, bold, challenging, contumacious, daring, disobedient, insolent, insubordinate, intransigent, mutinous, obstinate, provocative, rebellious, recalcitrant, refractory, truculent, uncooperative.
antonyms acquiescent, submissive.

deficiency *n.* absence, dearth, defalcation, defect, deficit, demerit, failing, fault, flaw, frailty, imperfection, inadequacy, insufficiency, lack, paucity, scantiness, scarcity, shortage, shortcoming, want, wantage, weakness.
antonym superfluity.

deficient *adj.* defectible, defective, exiguous, faulty, flawed, impaired, imperfect, inadequate, incomplete, inferior, insufficient, lacking, meagre, scanty, scarce, short, skimpy, unsatisfactory, wanting, weak.
antonyms excessive, superfluous.

deficit *n.* arrears, defalcation, default, deficiency, lack, loss, shortage, shortfall.
antonym excess.

defile[1] *v.* abuse, befoul, besmirch, contaminate, corrupt, debase, deflower, defoul, degrade, desecrate, dirty, disgrace, dishonour, inquinate, make foul, molest, pollute, profane, rape, ravish, seduce, smear, soil, stain, sully, taint, tarnish, violate, vitiate.
antonym cleanse.

defile[2] *n.* gorge, gulch, gully, pass, passage, ravine.

defiled *adj.* besmirched, desecrated, dishonoured, impure, maculate, polluted, profaned, ravished, spoilt, sullied, tainted, unclean.
antonyms clean, cleansed, pure.

definable *adj.* ascertainable, definite, describable, determinable, explicable, perceptible, specific.
antonym indefinable.

define *v.* bound, characterise, circumscribe, delimit, delimitate, delineate, demarcate, describe, designate, detail, determine, explain, expound, interpret, limit, mark out, outline, specify, spell out.

definite *adj.* assured, certain, clear, clear-cut, decided, determined, exact, explicit, express, fixed, guaranteed, marked, obvious, particular, positive, precise, settled, specific, substantive, sure.
antonyms indefinite, vague.

definitely *adv.* absolutely, beyond doubt, categorically, certainly, clearly, decidedly, doubtless, doubtlessly, easily, finally, indeed, indubitably, obviously, plainly, positively, surely, undeniably, unequivocally, unmistakably, unquestionably, without doubt, without fail.

definition[1] *n.* clarification, delimitation, delineation, demarcation, description, determination, elucidation, explanation, exposition, interpretation, outlining, settling.

definition[2] *n.* clarity, clearness, contrast, distinctness, focus, precision, sharpness.

definitive *adj.* absolute, authoritative, complete, conclusive, correct, decisive, exact, exhaustive, final, perfect, reliable, standard, ultimate.
antonym interim.

deflate[1] *v.* chasten, collapse, contract, dash, debunk, disconcert, dispirit, empty, exhaust, flatten, humble, humiliate, mortify, press, puncture, put down, shrink, squash, squeeze, void.
antonym inflate.

deflate[2] *v.* decrease, depreciate, depress, devalue, diminish, lessen, lower, reduce.
antonym increase.

deflect *v.* avert, bend, deviate, diverge, glance off, ricochet, shy, sidetrack, slew, swerve, turn, turn aside, twist, veer, wind.

deflection *n.* aberration, bend, bending, declination, deviation, divergence, drift, refraction, swerve, turning, veer.

deflower *v.* assault, defile, deflorate, desecrate, despoil, force, harm, mar, molest, rape, ravish, ruin, seduce, spoil, violate.

deflowering *n.* defloration, green gown, rape, ravishment, violation.

deform *v.* corrupt, disfigure, distort, mangle, mar, pervert, ruin, spoil, twist, warp.

deformation *n.* bend, curve, diastrophism, distortion, malformation, twist, warp.

deformed *adj.* bent, blemished, buckled, contorted, corrupted, crippled, crooked, defaced, depraved, disfigured, distorted, gnarled, maimed, malformed, mangled, marred, misbegotten, misborn, miscreate(d), misshapen, mutilated, perverted, ruined, spoilt, twisted, warped.

deformity *n.* abnormality, corruption, defect, depravity, disfigurement, distortion, dysmelia, irregularity, malformation, misfeature, misproportion, misshape, misshapenness, ugliness.

defraud *v.* beguile, bilk, cheat, con, cozen, deceive, delude, diddle, do, dupe, embezzle, fleece, gull, gyp, outwit, rip off, rob, rock, sting, swindle, trick.

defray *v.* clear, cover, discharge, foot, meet, pay, refund, repay, settle.
antonym incur.

defrayal *n.* clearance, defrayment, discharge, payment, refund, settlement.
antonym incurrence.

deft *adj.* able, adept, adroit, agile, clever, dexterous, expert, feat, habile, handy, neat, nifty, nimble, proficient, skilful.
antonym clumsy.

defunct *adj.* dead, deceased, departed, expired, extinct, gone, inoperative, invalid, kaput, non-existent, obsolete, passé.
antonyms alive, live, operative.

defy *v.* baffle, beard, beat, brave, challenge,

confront, contemn, dare, defeat, despise, disregard, elude, face, flout, foil, frustrate, outdare, provoke, repel, repulse, resist, scorn, slight, spurn, thwart, withstand.
antonyms flinch, quail, yield.

degeneracy *n.* corruption, debasement, decadence, decay, decline, decrease, degradation, depravation, depravity, deterioration, dissoluteness, effeteness, falling-off, immorality, inferiority, lapsing, meanness, poorness, turpitude.
antonyms morality, uprightness.

degenerate *adj.* base, corrupt, debased, debauched, decadent, degenerated, degraded, depraved, deteriorated, dissolute, effete, fallen, immoral, low, mean, perverted.
antonyms upright, virtuous.
v. age, decay, decline, decrease, deteriorate, fall off, lapse, regress, retrogress, rot, sink, slip, worsen.
antonym improve.

degeneration *n.* debasement, decline, degeneracy, descent, deterioration, dissipation, dissolution, falling-off, lapse, lapsing, regression, retrogress, retrogression.
antonyms improvement, uprightness, virtue.

degradation *n.* abasement, debasedness, debasement, decadence, decline, degeneracy, degeneration, demission, demotion, derogation, destitution, deterioration, discredit, disgrace, dishonour, downgrading, humiliation, ignominy, mortification, perversion, shame.
antonyms enhancement, virtue.

degrade *v.* abase, adulterate, break, brutalise, cashier, cheapen, corrupt, debase, declass, demean, demote, depose, deprive, deteriorate, discredit, disennoble, disgrace, disgrade, dishonour, disrank, disrate, downgrade, embase, humble, humiliate, impair, injure, lower, pervert, shame, unfrock, ungown, vitiate, weaken.
antonyms enhance, improve.

degraded *adj.* abandoned, abased, base, corrupt, debased, debauched, decadent, déclassé, depraved, despicable, disgraced, disreputable, dissolute, low, mean, profligate, sordid, vicious, vile.
antonyms moral, upright.

degrading *adj.* base, cheapening, contemptible, debasing, demeaning, disgraceful, dishonourable, humiliating, ignoble, infra dig, lowering, shameful, undignified, unworthy.
antonym enhancing.

degree *n.* calibre, class, division, doctorate, extent, gradation, grade, intensity, interval, level, limit, mark, masterate, measure, notch, order, point, position, proportion, quality, quantity, range, rank, rate, ratio, run, scale, scope, severity, stage, standard, standing, station, status, step, unit.

dehydrate *v.* desiccate, drain, dry out, dry up, effloresce, evaporate, exsiccate, parch.

deification *n.* apotheosis, divinification, divinisation, elevation, ennoblement, exaltation, glorification, idolisation,

deify v. apotheosise, divinify, divinise, elevate, ennoble, enthrone, exalt, extol, glorify, idealise, idolise, immortalise, venerate, worship.

deign v. condescend, consent, demean oneself, lower oneself, stoop, vouchsafe.

deity n. Allah, demigod, demigoddess, deva, divinity, god, goddess, godhead, godhood, idol, immortal, Jehovah, kami, power.

deject v. cast down, crush, dampen, daunt, demoralise, depress, discourage, dishearten, dismay, dispirit, sadden.

dejected adj. abattu, alamort, blue, cast down, crestfallen, depressed, despondent, disconsolate, disheartened, dismal, doleful, down, downcast, downhearted, gloomy, glum, jaw-fallen, low, low-spirited, melancholy, miserable, morose, sad, spiritless, woebegone, wretched.
antonyms bright, happy, high-spirited.

dejection n. blues, depression, despair, despondency, disconsolateness, disconsolation, doldrums, downheartedness, dumps, gloom, gloominess, low spirits, melancholy, sadness, sorrow, unhappiness.
antonyms happiness, high spirits.

delay v. arrest, bog down, check, dawdle, defer, detain, dilly-dally, drag, halt, hinder, hold back, hold over, hold up, impede, lag, linger, loiter, obstruct, play for time, postpone, procrastinate, prolong, protract, put off, retard, set back, shelve, stall, stave off, stop, suspend, table, tarry, temporise.
antonyms accelerate, expedite, hurry.
n. ambage, check, cunctation, dawdling, deferment, detention, dilly-dallying, hindrance, hold-up, impediment, interruption, interval, lingering, loitering, obstruction, postponement, procrastination, setback, stay, stoppage, suspension, tarrying, wait.
antonyms hastening, hurry.

delaying adj. cunctatious, cunctative, cunctatory, filibusterous, retardative, retardatory.
antonyms advancing, expediting.

delectable adj. adorable, agreeable, ambrosial, ambrosian, appetising, charming, dainty, delicious, delightful, enjoyable, enticing, flavoursome, gratifying, inviting, luscious, lush, palatable, pleasant, pleasurable, satisfying, scrumptious, tasty, toothsome, yummy.
antonyms horrid, unpleasant.

delectation n. amusement, comfort, contentment, delight, diversion, enjoyment, entertainment, gratification, happiness, pleasure, refreshment, relish, satisfaction.
antonym distaste.

delegate n. agent, ambassador, commissioner, deputy, envoy, legate, messenger, nuncio, representative.
v. accredit, appoint, assign, authorise, charge, commission, consign, depute, designate, devolve, empower, entrust, give, hand over, mandate, name, nominate, pass on, relegate, transfer.

delegated adj. assigned, devolved, relegated, vicarate, vicarial, vicariate.

delegation n. commission, contingent, deputation, embassy, legation, mission.

delete v. blot out, blue-pencil, cancel, cross out, dele, edit, edit out, efface, erase, expunge, obliterate, remove, rub out, strike, strike out.
antonym add in.

deleterious adj. bad, damaging, destructive, detrimental, harmful, hurtful, injurious, noxious, pernicious, prejudicial, ruinous.
antonyms enhancing, helpful.

deliberate v. cogitate, consider, consult, debate, discuss, meditate, mull over, ponder, reflect, ruminate, think, weigh.
adj. advised, calculated, careful, cautious, circumspect, conscious, considered, designed, heedful, intentional, measured, methodical, planned, ponderous, prearranged, premeditated, prudent, purposeful, slow, studied, thoughtful, unhurried, volitive, voulu, wary, wilful, willed, witting.
antonyms chance, unintentional.

deliberately adv. by design, calculatingly, consciously, determinedly, emphatically, in cold blood, intentionally, knowingly, on purpose, pointedly, resolutely, wilfully, with malice aforethought, wittingly.
antonym unintentionally.

deliberation n. calculation, canniness, care, carefulness, caution, circumspection, cogitation, conference, consideration, consultation, coolness, debate, discussion, forethought, meditation, prudence, purpose, reflection, rumination, speculation, study, thought, wariness.

delicacy n. accuracy, bonne bouche, daintiness, dainty, discrimination, elegance, exquisiteness, fastidiousness, fineness, finesse, lightness, luxury, niceness, nicety, precision, purity, refinement, relish, savoury, sensibility, sensitiveness, sensitivity, subtlety, sweetmeat, tact, taste, titbit, treat.
antonyms indelicacy, tactlessness.

delicate adj. accurate, ailing, careful, choice, considerate, critical, dainty, debilitated, deft, delicious, detailed, diaphanous, difficult, diplomatic, discreet, discriminating, eggshell, elegant, elfin, exquisite, faint, fastidious, fine, flimsy, fragile, frail, friand(e), gauzy, graceful, hazardous, kid-glove, minikin, minute, muted, nesh, pastel, precarious, precise, prudish, pure, refined, risky, savoury, scrupulous, sensible, sensitive, sickly, skilled, slender, slight, soft, softly-softly, squeamish, sticky, subdued, subtle, tactful, tender, ticklish, touchy, weak.
antonyms harsh, imprecise, strong.

delicious adj. agreeable, ambrosial, ambrosian, appetising, charming, choice, dainty, delectable, delightful, enjoyable, entertaining, exquisite, flavoursome, goluptious, luscious, mouthwatering, nectareous, palatable, pleasant, pleasing, savoury, scrummy, scrumptious, tasty, toothsome, yummy.
antonym unpleasant.

delight *n*. bliss, ecstasy, enjoyment, felicity, gladness, gratification, happiness, heaven, joy, jubilation, pleasure, rapture, transport.
antonyms dismay, displeasure.
v. amuse, charm, cheer, divert, enchant, gladden, gratify, please, ravish, rejoice, satisfy, thrill, tickle.
antonyms dismay, displease.
delight in appreciate, enjoy, gloat over, glory in, indulge in, like, love, relish, revel in, savour, take pride in.
delighted *adj*. captivated, charmed, cock-a-hoop, ecstatic, elated, enchanted, gladdened, happy, joyous, jubilant, overjoyed, pleased, pleased as Punch, thrilled.
antonyms dismayed, displeased.
delightful *adj*. agreeable, amusing, captivating, charming, congenial, delectable, delightsome, enchanting, engaging, enjoyable, entertaining, fascinating, fetching, gratifying, heavenly, pleasant, pleasing, pleasurable, rapturous, ravishing, scrummy, scrumptious, sweet, thrilling, wizard.
antonym horrible.
delimit *v*. bound, define, demarcate, determine, establish, fix, mark.
delineate *v*. characterise, chart, depict, describe, design, draw, figure, limn, outline, paint, picture, portray, render, represent, sketch, trace.
delineation *n*. account, characterisation, chart, depiction, description, design, diagram, drawing, outline, picture, portrait, portrayal, representation, sketch, tracing.
delinquency *n*. crime, criminality, fault, law-breaking, misbehaviour, misconduct, misdeed, misdemeanour, offence, wrong-doing.
delinquent *n*. criminal, culprit, defaulter, hooligan, law-breaker, malefactor, miscreant, offender, rough, tough, wrong-doer, young offender.
adj. careless, culpable, guilty, neglectful, negligent, remiss.
antonyms blameless, careful.
delirious *adj*. bacchic, beside oneself, corybantic, crazy, demented, deranged, ecstatic, excited, frantic, frenzied, hysterical, incoherent, insane, light-headed, mad, maenadic, raving, unhinged, wild.
antonym sane.
delirium *n*. derangement, ecstasy, fever, frenzy, fury, hallucination, hysteria, insanity, jim-jams, lunacy, madness, passion, rage, raving.
deliver *v*. acquit, administer, aim, announce, bear, bring, carry, cart, cede, commit, convey, deal, declare, direct, discharge, dispense, distribute, emancipate, feed, free, give, give forth, give up, grant, hand over, inflict, launch, liberate, loose, make over, pass, present, proclaim, pronounce, publish, ransom, read, redeem, release, relinquish, rescue, resign, save, strike, supply, surrender, throw, transfer, transport, turn over, utter, yield.
deliverance *n*. emancipation, escape, extrica-

tion, liberation, ransom, redemption, release, rescue, salvation.
delivery[1] *n*. consignment, conveyance, dispatch, distribution, shipment, surrender, transfer, transmission, transmittal, transport.
delivery[2] *n*. articulation, elocution, enunciation, intonation, presentation, speech, utterance.
delivery[3] *n*. accouchement, childbirth, confinement, labour, parturition, travail.
dell *n*. dargle, dean, dimble, dingle, hollow, vale, valley.
delude *v*. bamboozle, beguile, cheat, con, cozen, deceive, dupe, fool, gull, hoax, hoodwink, impose on, misguide, misinform, mislead, snow, take in, trick.
deluge *n*. avalanche, barrage, cataclysm, downpour, flood, hail, inundation, rush, spate, torrent.
v. bury, douse, drench, drown, engulf, flood, inundate, overload, overrun, overwhelm, soak, submerge, swamp.
delusion *n*. deception, error, fallacy, fancy, fata Morgana, hallucination, illusion, mirage, misapprehension, misbelief, misconception, mistake, phantasm.
delve *v*. burrow, dig into, examine, explore, investigate, poke, probe, ransack, research, root, rummage, search.
demagogue *n*. agitator, Boanerges, firebrand, haranguer, mob-orator, orator, rabble-rouser, tub-thumper.
demand *v*. ask, call for, challenge, claim, exact, expect, inquire, insist on, interrogate, involve, necessitate, need, order, question, request, require, take, want.
antonyms cede, supply.
n. bidding, call, charge, claim, desire, inquiry, interrogation, necessity, need, order, question, request, requirement, requisition, want.
antonym supply.
demanding *adj*. back-breaking, challenging, clamorous, difficult, exacting, exhausting, exigent, fatiguing, hard, imperious, importunate, insistent, nagging, pressing, taxing, tough, trying, urgent, wearing.
antonyms easy, easy-going, undemanding.
demarcate *v*. define, delimit, determine, differentiate, distinguish, establish, fix, mark, mark out, separate.
demarcation *n*. bound, boundary, bourn, confine, delimitation, differentiation, distinction, division, enclosure, limit, line, margin, pale, separation.
demean *v*. abase, condescend, debase, degrade, deign, descend, humble, lower, stoop.
antonym enhance.
demeanour *n*. air, bearing, behaviour, carriage, comportment, conduct, deportment, manner, mien, port.
demented *adj*. crazed, crazy, deranged, distracted, distraught, dotty, foolish, frenzied, idiotic, insane, lunatic, mad, maenadic, maniacal, manic, non compos mentis, nutty, unbalanced, unhinged.
antonym sane.

demigod *n.* demigoddess, kami, power, spirit.

demise[1] *n.* collapse, death, decease, departure, dissolution, downfall, end, expiration, failure, fall, passing, ruin, termination.

demise[2] *n.* alienation, conveyance, inheritance, transfer, transmission.

v. bequeath, convey, grant, leave, transfer, will.

democracy *n.* autonomy, commonwealth, populism, republic, self-government.

democratic *adj.* autonomous, egalitarian, popular, populist, representative, republican, self-governing.

demolish *v.* annihilate, bulldoze, consume, defeat, delapidate, destroy, devour, dismantle, down, eat, flatten, gobble, gulp, guzzle, knock down, level, overthrow, overturn, pull down, pulverize, raze, ruin, tear down, unbuild, undo, wreck.
antonym build up.

demolition *n.* bulldozing, destruction, dismantling, levelling, razing, wrecking.

demon[1] *n.* afrit, daemon, daimon, devil, evil spirit, fallen angel, fiend, genius, goblin, guardian spirit, incubus, monster, numen, rakshas, rakshasa, succubus, villain, warlock.

demon[2] *n.* ace, addict, dab hand, fanatic, fiend, master, pastmaster, wizard.

demoniac *adj.* crazed, d(a)emonic, demoniacal, devilish, diabolic, diabolical, fiendish, frantic, frenetic, frenzied, furious, hectic, hellish, infernal, mad, maniacal, manic, possessed, satanic.

demonstrable *adj.* arguable, attestable, axiomatic, certain, clear, evident, evincible, incontrovertible, indubitable, irrefutable, obvious, palpable, positive, provable, self-evident, substantiable, undeniable, unmistakable, verifiable.
antonyms untestable, unverifiable.

demonstrate[1] *v.* describe, display, establish, evidence, evince, exhibit, explain, expound, illustrate, indicate, manifest, prove, show, substantiate, teach, testify to.

demonstrate[2] *v.* march, parade, picket, protest, rally, sit in.

demonstration[1] *n.* affirmation, confirmation, deixis, description, display, evidence, exhibition, explanation, exposition, expression, illustration, manifestation, presentation, proof, substantiation, test, testimony, trial, validation.

demonstration[2] *v.* demo, march, parade, picket, protest, rally, sit-in, work-in.

demonstrative *adj.* affectionate, deictic, effusive, emotional, endeictic, evincive, expansive, explanatory, expository, expressive, illustrative, indicative, loving, open, symptomatic, unreserved, unrestrained.
antonyms cold, undemonstrative.

demoralisation *n.* agitation, corruption, crushing, debasement, dejection, depravation, depression, despondency, devitalisation, discomfiture, enervation, lowering, panic, perturbation, perversion, trepidation, unmanning, vitiation, weakening.
antonym encouragement.

demoralise *v.* corrupt, cripple, crush, daunt, debase, debauch, deject, deprave, depress, disconcert, discourage, dishearten, dispirit, enfeeble, lower, panic, pervert, rattle, sap, shake, undermine, unnerve, vitiate, weaken.
antonym encourage.

demoralised *adj.* bad, base, broken, corrupt, crushed, degenerate, dejected, depraved, depressed, despondent, discouraged, disheartened, dispirited, dissolute, downcast, immoral, low, reprobate, sinful, subdued, unmanned, unnerved, weakened, wicked.
antonyms encouraged, heartened.

demote *v.* declass, degrade, disrate, downgrade, reduce, relegate.
antonyms promote, upgrade.

demotic *adj.* enchorial, enchoric, popular, vernacular, vulgar.

demur *v.* balk, cavil, disagree, dispute, dissent, doubt, hesitate, object, pause, protest, refuse, take exception, waver.
n. arrière pensée, compunction, demurral, demurrer, dissent, hesitation, misgiving, objection, protest, qualm, reservation, scruple.

demure *adj.* coy, decorous, diffident, grave, maidenly, modest, priggish, prim, prissy, prudish, reserved, reticent, retiring, sedate, shy, sober, staid, strait-laced.
antonym forward.

den *n.* cave, cavern, cloister, cubby-hole, earth, haunt, hide-away, hide-out, hole, lair, retreat, sanctuary, sanctum, set(t), shelter, study.

denial *n.* abjuration, abnegation, contradiction, denegation, disaffirmance, disaffirmation, disavowal, disclaimer, dismissal, dissent, gainsay, negation, prohibition, rebuff, refusal, rejection, renunciation, repudiation, repulse, retraction, veto.

denigrate *v.* abuse, assail, belittle, besmirch, blacken, calumniate, criticise, decry, defame, disparage, impugn, malign, revile, run down, slander, vilify, vilipend.
antonym praise.

denigration *n.* aspersion, backbiting, decrial, defamation, derogation, detraction, disparagement, mud-slinging, obloquy, scandal, scurrility, slander, vilification.
antonym praise.

denizen *n.* citizen, dweller, habitant, habitué, inhabitant, occupant, resident.

denominate *v.* baptise, call, christen, designate, dub, entitle, name, phrase, style, term, title.

denomination *n.* appellation, belief, body, category, class, classification, communion, creed, designation, grade, group, label, name, persuasion, religious, school, sect, size, style, taxon, term, title, unit, value.

denote *v.* betoken, designate, express, imply, import, indicate, mark, mean, show, signify, stand for, symbolise, typify.

dénouement *n.* climax, close, conclusion, culmination, finale, finish, outcome, pay-off, resolution, solution, termination, upshot.

denounce v. accuse, anathematise, arraign, assail, attack, brand, castigate, censure, condemn, declaim against, decry, denunciate, fulminate, hereticate, impugn, inveigh against, proscribe, revile, stigmatise, vilify, vilipend.
antonym praise.

dense adj. blockish, close, close-knit, compact, compressed, condensed, crass, crowded, dull, heavy, impenetrable, jam-packed, obtuse, opaque, packed, slow, slow-witted, solid, stolid, stupid, substantial, thick, thickset, thick-witted.
antonyms clever, sparse.

denseness n. crassness, density, dullness, obtuseness, slowness, stolidity, stupidity, thickness.
antonym acuteness.

density n. body, bulk, closeness, compactness, consistency, crassitude, denseness, impenetrability, mass, solidity, solidness, spissitude, thickness, tightness.
antonym sparseness.

dent n. bang, chip, concavity, crater, depression, dimple, dint, dip, dunt, hollow, impression, indentation, pit.
v. depress, dint, gouge, indent, push in.

dentures n. false teeth, wallies.

denude v. bare, defoliate, deforest, divest, expose, strip, uncover.
antonym cover.

denunciation n. accusation, assailment, castigation, censure, condemnation, criticism, decrial, decrying, denouncement, fulmination, incrimination, invective, obloquy, stigmatisation.
antonyms compliment, praise.

denunciatory adj. accusatory, censorious, comminatory, condemnatory, decrying, execrative, fulminatory, incriminatory, recriminatory, reproachful.
antonym complimentary.

deny v. abjure, begrudge, contradict, decline, disaffirm, disagree with, disallow, disavow, discard, disclaim, disown, disprove, forbid, gainsay, negative, oppose, rebuff, recant, refuse, refute, reject, renounce, repudiate, revoke, traverse, turn down, veto, withhold.
antonyms admit, allow.

deodorant n. air-freshener, antiperspirant, deodoriser, disinfectant, fumigant, fumigator.

deodorise v. aerate, disinfect, freshen, fumigate, purify, refresh, sweeten, ventilate.

depart v. absent oneself, decamp, deviate, differ, digress, disappear, diverge, escape, exit, go, leave, levant, make off, migrate, mizzle, quit, remove, retire, retreat, set forth, stray, swerve, take one's leave, toddle, vanish, vary, veer, withdraw.
antonyms arrive, keep to.

departed adj. dead, deceased, defunct, expired, late.

department n. area, branch, bureau, district, division, domain, field, function, line, line of country, office, province, realm, region, responsibility, section, sector, speciality, sphere, station, subdivision, unit.

departure n. abandonment, branching, branching out, change, decession, departure, deviation, difference, digression, divergence, exit, exodus, going, innovation, leave-taking, leaving, lucky, novelty, removal, retirement, shift, variation, veering, withdrawal.
antonym arrival.

depend on anticipate, bank on, build upon, calculate on, count on, expect, hang on, hinge on, lean on, reckon on, rely upon, rest on, revolve around, trust in, turn to.

dependable adj. certain, conscientious, faithful, gilt-edged, honest, reliable, responsible, steady, sure, trustworthy, trusty, unfailing.
antonyms undependable, unreliable.

dependant n. child, client, galloglass, hanger-on, henchman, minion, minor, protégé, relative, retainer, subordinate, vassal.

dependence n. addiction, assurance, attachment, belief, confidence, craving, dependency, expectation, faith, helplessness, hope, need, reliance, subordination, subservience, trust, vassalage, vulnerability, weakness.
antonym independence.

dependent adj. adjective, conditional, contingent, defenceless, depending, determined by, feudal, helpless, immature, liable to, relative, reliant, relying on, subject, subject to, subordinate, tributary, vulnerable, weak.
antonym independent.

depict v. caricature, characterise, delineate, describe, detail, draw, illustrate, limn, narrate, outline, paint, picture, portray, render, reproduce, sculpt, sketch, trace.

depiction n. caricature, delineation, description, drawing, illustration, image, likeness, outline, picture, portrayal, representation, sketch.

depilation n. electrolysis, epilation, hair-removing.

deplete v. attenuate, bankrupt, consume, decrease, drain, empty, evacuate, exhaust, expend, impoverish, lessen, reduce, use up.

depleted adj. attenuated, consumed, decreased, depreciated, drained, emptied, exhausted, lessened, reduced, spent, wasted, weakened, worn out.
antonyms augmented, increased.

depletion n. attenuation, consumption, decimation, decrease, deficiency, diminution, dwindling, exhaustion, expenditure, lessening, lowering, reduction, shrinkage.
antonyms increase, supply.

deplorable adj. blameworthy, calamitous, dire, disastrous, disgraceful, dishonourable, disreputable, distressing, execrable, grievous, heartbreaking, lamentable, melancholy, miserable, opprobrious, pitiable, regrettable, reprehensible, sad, scandalous, shameful, unfortunate, wretched.
antonyms excellent, praiseworthy.

deplore v. abhor, bemoan, bewail, censure, condemn, denounce, deprecate, grieve for, lament, mourn, regret, repent of, rue.

antonym praise.

deploy *v.* arrange, darraign, dispose, distribute, embattle, extend, position, station, use, utilise.

depopulate *v.* dispeople, empty, unpeople.

deport[1] *v.* banish, exile, expatriate, expel, extradite, ostracise, oust.

deport[2] *v.* acquit, act, bear, behave, carry, comport, conduct, hold, manage.

deportation *n.* banishment, eviction, exile, expatriation, expulsion, extradition, ostracism, transportation.

deportment *n.* air, appearance, aspect, bearing, behaviour, carriage, cast, comportment, conduct, demeanour, etiquette, manner, mien, pose, posture, stance.

depose *v.* break, cashier, decrown, degrade, demote, dethrone, discrown, disestablish, dismiss, displace, downgrade, oust, topple, unking.

deposit[1] *v.* drop, dump, lay, locate, park, place, precipitate, put, settle, sit.
n. accumulation, alluvium, deposition, dregs, hypostasis, lees, precipitate, sediment, silt.

deposit[2] *v.* amass, bank, consign, depone, entrust, file, hoard, lodge, reposit, save, store.
n. bailment, down payment, instalment, money, part payment, pledge, retainer, security, stake, warranty.

deposition[1] *n.* dethronement, dismissal, displacement, ousting, removal, toppling.

deposition[2] *n.* affidavit, declaration, denunciation, evidence, information, statement, testimony.

depository *n.* bond, depot, dump, godown, repository, store, storehouse, warehouse.

depot *n.* arsenal, bond, depository, dump, garage, receiving-house, repository, station, storehouse, terminus, warehouse.

deprave *v.* brutalise, contaminate, corrupt, debase, debauch, degrade, demoralise, infect, pervert, seduce, subvert, vitiate.
antonym improve.

depraved *adj.* abandoned, base, corrupt, debased, debauched, degenerate, degraded, dissolute, evil, immoral, lewd, libertine, licentious, perverted, profligate, reprobate, shameless, sinful, vicious, vile, wicked.
antonym upright.

depravity *n.* baseness, contamination, corruption, criminality, debasement, debauchery, degeneracy, degradation, depravation, depravedness, depravement, dissoluteness, evil, immorality, iniquity, lewdness, libertinage, licence, perversion, profligacy, reprobacy, sinfulness, turpitude, vice, viciousness, vileness, wickedness.
antonym uprightness.

deprecate *v.* condemn, deplore, disapprove of, disparage, object to, protest at, reject.
antonyms approve, commend.

deprecation *n.* condemnation, deploration, disapproval, dismissal, disparagement, protestation, rejection.
antonyms commendation, encouragement.

deprecatory *adj.* apologetic, censorious, condemnatory, disapproving, dismissive, protesting, regretful, reproachful.
antonyms commendatory, encouraging.

depreciate *v.* belittle, decrease, decry, deflate, denigrate, deride, derogate, detract, devaluate, devalue, disparage, downgrade, drop, fall, lessen, lower, minimise, misprise, reduce, ridicule, scorn, slump, traduce, underestimate, underrate, undervalue.
antonyms appreciate, overrate, praise.

depreciation *n.* belittlement, deflation, depression, derogation, detraction, devaluation, disparagement, downgrading, drop, fall, misprising, misprision, pejoration, slump.
antonyms appreciation, exaggeration, praise.

depredation *n.* denudation, desolation, despoiling, despoliation, destruction, devastation, harrying, laying waste, looting, marauding, pillage, plunder, raiding, ransacking, rapine, ravaging, ravin, robbery, spoliation, stripping, theft.

depress *v.* burden, cheapen, chill, damp, daunt, debilitate, deject, depreciate, devaluate, devalue, devitalise, diminish, discourage, dishearten, dispirit, downgrade, drain, enervate, engloom, exhaust, flatten, hip, impair, lessen, level, lower, oppress, overburden, press, reduce, sadden, sap, squash, tire, undermine, upset, weaken, weary.
antonym cheer.

depressant *n.* calmant, calmative, downer, relaxant, sedative, tranquilliser.
antonym stimulant.

depressed[1] *adj.* a peg too low, accablé, blue, cast down, crestfallen, debilitated, dejected, deprived, despondent, desponding, destitute, disadvantaged, discouraged, disheartened, dispirited, distressed, down, down-beat, downcast, downhearted, exanimate, fed up, glum, jaw-fallen, low, low-spirited, melancholy, miserable, Mondayish, moody, morose, needy, pessimistic, poor, sad, unhappy.
antonym cheerful.

depressed[2] *adj.* concave, dented, dinted, dished, hollow, indented, invaginated, recessed, sunken.
antonyms convex, prominent, protuberant.

depressing *adj.* black, bleak, cheerless, daunting, dejecting, discouraging, disheartening, dismal, dispiriting, distressing, dreary, gloomy, grey, heartbreaking, hopeless, lugubrious, melancholy, Mondayish, sad, saddening, sombre.
antonym encouraging.

depression[1] *n.* blues, cafard, decline, dejection, demission, despair, despondency, doldrums, dolefulness, downheartedness, dullness, dumps, exanimation, gloominess, glumness, hard times, heart-heaviness, hopelessness, inactivity, low spirits, lowness, mal du siècle, megrims, melancholia, melancholy, panophobia, recession, sadness, slump, stagnation, vapours.

antonyms cheerfulness, prosperity.

depression² *n.* basin, bowl, cavity, concavity, dent, dimple, dint, dip, dish, excavation, fossa, fossula, fovea, foveola, hollow, hollowness, impression, indentation, pit, sag, sink, umbilicus, valley.
antonyms convexity, prominence, protuberance.

deprivation *n.* degradation, denial, denudation, deprival, despoliation, destitution, disadvantage, dispossession, distress, divestment, expropriation, hardship, need, privation, removal, want, withdrawal, withholding.
antonym bestowal.

deprive *v.* amerce, bereave, denude, deny, despoil, dispossess, divest, expropriate, mulct, rob, starve, strip.
antonym bestow.

deprived *adj.* benighted, bereft, denuded, depressed, destitute, disadvantaged, forlorn, impoverished, lacking, necessitous, needy, poor.
antonyms fortunate, prosperous.

depth *n.* abstruseness, abysm, abyss, complexity, deepness, discernment, drop, exhaustiveness, extent, gulf, insight, intensity, measure, obscurity, penetration, pit, profoundness, profundity, reconditeness, richness, sagacity, shrewdness, strength, thoroughness, wisdom.

deputation *n.* appointment, assignment, commission, delegates, delegation, deputies, deputing, designation, embassy, legation, mission, nomination, representatives.

depute *v.* accredit, appoint, authorise, charge, commission, delegate, empower, entrust, mandate, nominate.

deputise *n.* commission, delegate, depute, double, replace, represent, stand in for, substitute, understudy.

deputy *n.* agent, alternate, ambassador, commis, commissary, commissioner, delegate, henchman, legate, lieutenant, nuncio, proxy, representative, second-in-command, substitute, suffragan, surrogate, vicar, vicegerent.
adj. assistant, coadjutor, depute, subordinate, suffragan.

derange *v.* confound, confuse, craze, dement, disarrange, disarray, discompose, disconcert, disorder, displace, disturb, drive crazy, madden, ruffle, unbalance, unhinge, unsettle, upset.

deranged *adj.* aberrant, batty, berserk, brainsick, confused, crazed, crazy, delirious, demented, disarranged, disordered, distracted, distraught, disturbed, frantic, frenzied, insane, irrational, loony, lunatic, mad, maddened, nutty, unbalanced, unhinged.
antonyms calm, sane.

derangement *n.* aberration, agitation, alienation, confusion, delirium, dementia, disarrangement, disarray, disorder, distraction, disturbance, frenzy, hallucination, insanity, irregularity, jumble, lunacy, madness, mania, muddle.
antonyms order, sanity.

derelict *adj.* abandoned, deserted, desolate, dilapidated, discarded, forlorn, forsaken, neglected, ruined.
n. dosser, down-and-out, drifter, hobo, outcast, toe-rag, tramp, vagrant, wastrel.

dereliction *n.* abandonment, abdication, apostasy, betrayal, delinquency, desertion, evasion, failure, faithlessness, fault, forsaking, neglect, negligence, relinquishment, remissness, renegation, renunciation.
antonyms devotion, faithfulness, fulfilment.

deride *v.* belittle, condemn, detract, disdain, disparage, flout, gibe, insult, jeer, knock, mock, pillory, pooh-pooh, rail at, ridicule, satirise, scoff, scorn, sneer, taunt, vilipend.
antonym praise.

derision *n.* contempt, contumely, dicacity, disdain, disparagement, disrespect, insult, irrision, laughter, mockery, raillery, ridicule, satire, scoffing, scorn, sneering.
antonym praise.

derisive *adj.* contemptuous, disdainful, disrespectful, irreverent, irrisory, jeering, mocking, scornful, taunting.
antonyms appreciative, flattering.

derisory *adj.* absurd, contemptible, insulting, laughable, ludicrous, mockable, outrageous, paltry, preposterous, ridiculous, risible.

derivation *n.* acquisition, ancestry, basis, beginning, deduction, descent, etymology, extraction, foundation, genealogy, inference, origin, root, source.

derivative *adj.* acquired, borrowed, copied, cribbed, daughter, derived, hackneyed, imitative, inferred, obtained, plagiarised, plagiaristic, procured, regurgitated, rehashed, secondary, second-hand, transmitted, trite, unadventurous, uninventive, unoriginal.
n. branch, by-product, derivation, descendant, development, formative, offshoot, outgrowth, product, refinement, spin-off.

derive *v.* acquire, arise, borrow, collect, crib, deduce, descend, develop, draw, elicit, emanate, extract, flow, follow, gain, gather, get, glean, grow, infer, issue, lift, obtain, originate, proceed, procure, receive, spring, stem, trace.

derogate *v.* belittle, decry, defame, denigrate, depreciate, detract, devalue, diminish, disparage, insult, lessen, misprise, slight, take away from.
antonyms add to, appreciate, praise.

derogatory *adj.* aspersory, belittling, critical, damaging, defamatory, depreciative, destructive, detractive, detractory, disparaging, injurious, insulting, offensive, pejorative, slighting, snide, uncomplimentary, unfavourable, unflattering.
antonyms appreciative, favourable, flattering.

descend *v.* alight, arrive, assail, assault, attack, condescend, degenerate, dégringoler, deign, derive, deteriorate, develop, dip, dismount, drop, fall, gravitate, incline, invade, issue, leap, originate, plummet, plunge, pounce, proceed, raid, sink, slant, slope, spring, stem, stoop, subside, swoop, tumble.

descendants *n.* children, epigones, epigoni, epigons, family, issue, line, lineage, offspring, posterity, progeny, race, scions, seed, sons and daughters, successors.

descent *n.* ancestry, assault, attack, comedown, debasement, decadence, declination, decline, declivity, degradation, dégringolade, deterioration, dip, drop, extraction, fall, family tree, foray, genealogy, heredity, incline, incursion, invasion, lineage, origin, parentage, plunge, pounce, raid, slant, slope, stoop, swoop.
antonyms ascent, improvement.

describe *v.* characterise, define, delineate, depict, detail, draw, enlarge on, explain, express, illustrate, mark out, narrate, outline, portray, present, recount, relate, report, sketch, specify, tell, trace.

description *n.* account, brand, breed, category, characterisation, class, delineation, depiction, detail, explanation, exposition, genre, genus, hypotyposis, ilk, kidney, kind, narration, narrative, order, outline, portrayal, presentation, report, representation, sketch, sort, species, specification, type, variety, word-painting, word-picture.

descriptive *adj.* blow-by-blow, circumstantial, colourful, depictive, detailed, explanatory, expressive, graphic, illustrative, immediate, pictorial, picturesque, specific, vivid.
antonyms cursory, laconic.

descry *v.* detect, discern, discover, distinguish, espy, glimpse, mark, notice, observe, perceive, recognise, see, sight, spot, spy.

desecrate *v.* abuse, blaspheme, contaminate, debase, defile, despoil, dishallow, dishonour, insult, invade, pervert, pollute, profane, vandalise, violate.

desecration *n.* blasphemy, debasement, defilement, dishonouring, impiety, insult, invasion, pollution, profanation, sacrilege, violation.

desert[1] *n.* solitude, vacuum, vast, void, waste, wasteland, wilderness, wilds.
adj. arid, bare, barren, desolate, droughty, dry, eremic, infertile, lonely, solitary, sterile, uncultivated, uninhabited, unproductive, untilled, waste, waterless, wild.

desert[2] *v.* abandon, abscond, apostatise, backslide, betray, decamp, deceive, defect, forsake, give up, jilt, leave, leave in the lurch, maroon, quit, rat on, relinquish, renegue, renounce, resign, strand, tergiversate, vacate.

desert[3] *n.* come-uppance, demerit, deserts, due, guerdon, meed, merit, payment, recompense, remuneration, requital, retribution, return, reward, right, virtue, worth.

deserted *adj.* abandoned, benighted, bereft, betrayed, derelict, desolate, empty, forlorn, forsaken, friendless, godforsaken, isolated, left in the lurch, lonely, neglected, solitary, stranded, underpopulated, unfriended, unoccupied, unpopulous, vacant, vacated.
antonym populous.

deserter *n.* absconder, apostate, backslider,

betrayer, defector, delinquent, escapee, fugitive, rat, renegade, runaway, traitor, truant.

desertion *n.* abandonment, absconding, apostasy, betrayal, defection, delinquency, departure, dereliction, escape, evasion, flight, forsaking, relinquishment, renegation, tergiversation, truancy.

deserve *v.* ask for, earn, gain, incur, justify, merit, procure, rate, warrant, win.

deserved *adj.* apposite, appropriate, apt, condign, due, earned, fair, fitting, just, justifiable, justified, legitimate, meet, merited, proper, right, rightful, suitable, warranted, well-earned.
antonyms gratuitous, undeserved.

deserving *adj.* admirable, commendable, creditable, estimable, exemplary, laudable, meritorious, praiseworthy, righteous, worthy.
antonyms undeserving, unworthy.

desiccated *adj.* arid, dead, dehydrated, drained, dried, dry, dry-as-dust, exsiccated, lifeless, parched, passionless, powdered, spiritless, sterile.

desiccation *n.* aridity, dehydration, dryness, exsiccation, parching, sterility, xeransis.

desideratum *n.* aim, aspiration, besoin, dream, essential, gap, goal, heart's desire, hope, ideal, lack, lacuna, need, object, objective, sine qua non, want, wish.

design *n.* aim, arrangement, blueprint, composition, configuration, conformation, conspiracy, construction, contrivance, delineation, draft, drawing, end, enterprise, exemplar, figure, form, goal, guide, intent, intention, intrigue, machination, manoeuvre, meaning, model, motif, object, objective, organisation, outline, pattern, plan, plot, project, prototype, purpose, schema, scheme, shape, sketch, structure, style, target, undertaking.
v. aim, conceive, construct, contrive, create, delineate, describe, destine, develop, devise, draft, draw, draw up, fabricate, fashion, form, intend, invent, make, mean, model, originate, outline, plan, project, propose, purpose, scheme, shape, sketch, structure, tailor, trace.

designate *v.* allot, appoint, assign, bill, call, characterise, choose, christen, code-name, deem, define, delegate, denominate, denote, depute, describe, docket, dub, earmark, entitle, indicate, label, name, nickname, nominate, select, show, specify, stipulate, style, term, ticket, title.

designation *n.* appointment, category, characterisation, classification, code-name, definition, delegation, denomination, description, docket, epithet, indication, label, mark, name, nickname, nomination, selection, specification, title.

designedly *adv.* calculatedly, consciously, deliberately, intentionally, knowingly, on purpose, premeditatedly, purposely, studiously, wilfully, willingly, with malice aforethought, wittingly.
antonyms innocently, unwittingly.

designer *n.* architect, artificer, author, contriver,

couturier, creator, deviser, fashioner, framer, inventor, maker, originator, stylist.

designing *adj.* artful, conniving, conspiring, contriving, crafty, cunning, deceitful, devious, disingenuous, guileful, insidious, intriguing, Machiavellian, plotting, scheming, sharp, shrewd, sly, treacherous, tricky, underhand, unscrupulous, wily.
antonym artless.

desirability *n.* advantage, advisability, attraction, attractiveness, beauty, benefit, merit, profit, seductiveness, usefulness, value, worth.
antonyms disadvantage, inadvisability, undesirability.

desirable *adj.* adorable, advantageous, advisable, agreeable, alluring, appetible, appropriate, attractive, beneficial, captivating, covetable, eligible, enviable, expedient, fascinating, fetching, good, nubile, pleasing, plummy, preferable, profitable, seductive, sensible, sexy, tempting, worthwhile.
antonym undesirable.

desire *v.* ask, aspire to, beg, covet, crave, desiderate, entreat, fancy, hanker after, hunger for, importune, lack, long for, need, petition, request, solicit, want, wish for, yearn for.
n. appeal, appetence, appetency, appetite, ardour, aspiration, besoin, concupiscence, covetousness, craving, cupidity, desideration, entreaty, greed, hankering, hot pants, importunity, kama, kamadeva, lasciviousness, lechery, libido, longing, lust, lustfulness, month's mind, need, passion, petition, request, solicitation, supplication, velleity, want, wish, yearning, yen.

desired *adj.* accurate, appropriate, correct, exact, expected, express, fitting, longed-for, looked-for, necessary, particular, proper, required, right, sought-after, wanted, wished-for.
antonyms undesired, unintentional.

desirous *adj.* ambitious, anxious, appetent, aspiring, avid, burning, craving, cupidinous, eager, enthusiastic, hopeful, hoping, itching, keen, longing, ready, willing, wishing, yearning.
antonyms reluctant, unenthusiastic.

desist *v.* abstain, break off, cease, come to a halt, discontinue, end, forbear, give over, give up, halt, leave off, pause, peter out, refrain, remit, stop, suspend.
antonyms continue, resume.

desk *n.* bureau, davenport, écritoire, lectern, prie-dieu, secretaire, writing-table.

desolate *adj.* abandoned, arid, bare, barren, benighted, bereft, bleak, cheerless, comfortless, companionless, dejected, depopulated, depressed, depressing, desert, desolated, despondent, disconsolate, disheartened, dismal, dismayed, distressed, downcast, dreary, forlorn, forsaken, gloomy, god-forsaken, grieved, inconsolable, lonely, melancholy, miserable, ravaged, ruined, solitary, unfrequented, uninhabited, unpopulous, unsolaced, waste, wild, wretched.
antonym cheerful.
v. denude, depopulate, despoil, destroy, devastate, lay waste, pillage, plunder, ravage, ruin, spoil, waste, wreck.

desolation *n.* anguish, barrenness, bleakness, dejection, depopulation, desolateness, despair, desperation, despondency, destruction, devastation, disconsolateness, distress, emptiness, forlornness, gloom, gloominess, grief, havoc, isolation, loneliness, melancholy, misery, ravages, ruin, ruination, sadness, solitariness, solitude, sorrow, unhappiness, wildness, woe, wretchedness.

despair *v.* capitulate, collapse, crumple, despond, give in, give up, lose heart, lose hope, quit, surrender.
antonym hope.
n. anguish, dejection, depression, desperation, despond, despondency, emptiness, gloom, hopelessness, inconsolableness, melancholy, misery, ordeal, pain, resourcelessness, sorrow, trial, tribulation, wretchedness.
antonyms cheerfulness, resilience.

despairing *adj.* anxious, broken-hearted, dejected, depressed, desolate, desperate, despondent, disconsolate, disheartened, distracted, distraught, downcast, frantic, grief-stricken, hopeless, inconsolable, melancholy, miserable, sorrowful, suicidal, wretched.
antonyms cheerful, resilient.

despatch *see* **dispatch** .

desperado *n.* bandit, brigand, cateran, criminal, cut-throat, dacoit, gangster, gunman, heavy, hood, hoodlum, law-breaker, mugger, outlaw, ruffian, thug.

desperate *adj.* grave, abandoned, acute, audacious, critical, dangerous, daring, despairing, despondent, determined, dire, do-or-die, drastic, extreme, foolhardy, forlorn, frantic, frenzied, furious, great, hasty, hazardous, headlong, headstrong, hopeless, impetuous, inconsolable, irremediable, irretrievable, madcap, precipitate, rash, reckless, risky, serious, severe, temerarious, urgent, violent, wild, wretched.

desperately *adv.* appallingly, badly, critically, dangerously, distractedly, fearfully, frantically, frenziedly, frightfully, gravely, hopelessly, perilously, seriously, severely, shockingly.

desperation *n.* agony, anguish, anxiety, defiance, despair, despondency, disconsolateness, distraction, distress, foolhardiness, franticness, frenzy, hastiness, heedlessness, hoplessness, madness, misery, pain, rashness, recklessness, sorrow, trouble, unhappiness, worry.

despicable *adj.* abhorrent, abject, base, cheap, contemptible, degrading, detestable, disgraceful, disgusting, disreputable, hateful, ignoble, ignominious, infamous, low, mean, reprehensible, reprobate, scurvy, shameful, sordid, unprincipled, vile, worthless, wretched.

antonyms laudable, noble.

despise *v.* abhor, condemn, deplore, deride, detest, disdain, dislike, disregard, ignore, loathe, misprise, revile, scorn, slight, spurn, undervalue, vilipend.
antonyms appreciate, prize.

despite *prep.* against, defying, heedless of, in spite of, in the face of, in the teeth of, notwithstanding, regardless of, undeterred by.

despoil *v.* bereave, denude, depredate, deprive, destroy, devastate, disgarnish, dispossess, divest, loot, maraud, pillage, plunder, ransack, ravage, rifle, rob, spoliate, strip, vandalise, wreck.
antonyms adorn, enrich.

despoliation *n.* depredation, despoilment, destruction, devastation, havoc, looting, marauding, pillage, plunder, rapine, ravaging, ravin, ruin, spoliation, vandalism, wreckage.
antonyms adornment, enrichment.

despond *v.* capitulate, despair, lose courage, lose heart, lose hope, mourn, quit, sorrow, surrender.
antonym hope.

despondency *n.* broken-heartedness, dejection, depression, despair, desperation, disconsolateness, discouragement, dispiritedness, downheartedness, gloom, glumness, hopelessness, inconsolability, melancholia, melancholy, misery, sadness, sorrow, wretchedness.
antonyms cheerfulness, hopefulness.

despondent *adj.* blue, broken-hearted, dejected, depressed, despairing, disconsolate, discouraged, disheartened, dispirited, doleful, down, downcast, downhearted, gloomy, glum, hopeless, inconsolable, low, low-spirited, melancholy, miserable, morose, mournful, overwhelmed, sad, sorrowful, woebegone, wretched.
antonyms cheerful, hopeful.

despot *n.* absolutist, autocrat, boss, dictator, monocrat, oppressor, tyrant.
antonyms democrat, egalitarian, liberal.

despotic *adj.* absolute, absolutist, arbitrary, arrogant, authoritarian, autocratic, bossy, dictatorial, domineering, imperious, monocratic, oppressive, overbearing, peremptory, tyrannical.
antonyms democratic, egalitarian, liberal, tolerant.

despotism *n.* absolutism, autarchy, autocracy, dictatorship, monarchism, monocracy, oppression, repression, totalitarianism, tyranny.
antonyms democracy, egalitarianism, liberalism, tolerance.

dessert *n.* afters, doucet, pudding, sweet, sweet course.

destination *n.* aim, ambition, aspiration, design, end, end in view, goal, harbour, haven, intention, journey's end, object, objective, port of call, purpose, station, stop, target, terminus.

destine *v.* allot, appoint, assign, consecrate, decree, design, designate, devote, doom, earmark, fate, foredoom, head, intend, mark out, mean, ordain, predetermine, preordain, purpose, reserve.

destined *adj.* assigned, booked, bound, certain, designed, directed, doomed, en route, fated, foreordained, headed, heading, ineluctable, inescapable, inevitable, intended, meant, ordained, predestined, predetermined, preordained, routed, scheduled, unavoidable.

destiny *n.* cup, doom, fate, fortune, joss, karma, kismet, lot, Moira, portion, predestiny, weird.

destitute *adj.* bankrupt, beggared, bereft, deficient, depleted, deprived, devoid of, distressed, down and out, impecunious, impoverished, indigent, innocent of, insolvent, lacking, necessitous, needy, penniless, penurious, poor, poverty-stricken, skint, strapped, wanting.
antonyms prosperous, wealthy.

destitution *n.* bankruptcy, beggary, distress, impecuniousness, indigence, neediness, pauperdom, pauperism, pennilessness, penury, poverty, privation, starvation, straits, want.
antonyms prosperity, wealth.

destroy *v.* annihilate, banjax, break, canker, crush, demolish, destruct, devastate, dismantle, dispatch, eliminate, eradicate, extinguish, extirpate, gut, kill, level, nullify, overthrow, ravage, raze, ruin, sabotage, scuttle, shatter, slay, slight, smash, stonker, thwart, torpedo, undermine, undo, unshape, vaporise, waste, wreck, zap.
antonym create.

destroyer *n.* annihilator, demolisher, desolater, despoiler, iconoclast, Juggernaut, kiss of death, locust, Luddite, maelstrom, ransacker, ravager, vandal, wrecker.
antonym creator.

destruction *n.* annihilation, bane, confutation, crushing, defeat, demolition, depopulation, desolation, devastation, downfall, elimination, end, eradication, estrepement, extermination, extinction, extirpation, havoc, liquidation, massacre, nullification, overthrow, ravagement, ruin, ruination, shattering, slaughter, undoing, wastage, wrack, wreckage.
antonym creation.

destructive *adj.* adverse, antagonistic, baleful, baneful, calamitous, cataclysmic, catastrophic, contrary, damaging, deadly, deathful, deleterious, derogatory, detrimental, devastating, disastrous, discouraging, disparaging, disruptive, fatal, harmful, hostile, hurtful, injurious, invalidating, lethal, malignant, mischievous, negative, noxious, nullifying, pernicious, pestful, pestiferous, pestilent, pestilential, ruinous, slaughterous, subversive, undermining, vexatious, vicious.
antonyms creative, positive, productive.

desultory *adj.* aimless, capricious, cursory, disconnected, discursive, disorderly, disorganised, erratic, fitful, haphazard, inconsistent, inconstant, inexact, irregular, loose, maundering, random, spasmodic, unco-ordinated, undirected, unmethodical, unsystematic.

antonyms concerted, methodical, systematic.

detach *v.* abstract, alienate, cut off, deglutinate, disconnect, disengage, disentangle, disjoin, dissociate, disunite, divide, estrange, free, isolate, loosen, remove, segregate, separate, sever, uncouple, undo, unfasten, unfix, unhitch.

antonym attach.

detached *adj.* aloof, disconnected, discrete, disinterested, disjoined, dispassionate, dissociated, divided, free, free-standing, impartial, impassive, impersonal, independent, loosened, neutral, objective, reserved, separate, severed, unattached, unbiased, uncommitted, unconcerned, unconnected, unimpassioned, uninvolved, unprejudiced.

antonyms concerned, connected, involved.

detachment[1] *n.* aloofness, coolness, disconnection, disengagement, disinterestedness, disjoining, fairness, impartiality, impassivity, indifference, laissez-faire, neutrality, nonpartisanship, objectivity, remoteness, separation, severance, severing, unconcern.

antonym concern.

detachment[2] *n.* body, brigade, corps, detail, force, party, patrol, squad, task force, unit.

detail *n.* aspect, attribute, complexity, complication, component, count, elaborateness, elaboration, element, fact, factor, feature, ingredient, intricacy, item, meticulousness, nicety, particular, particularity, point, refinement, respect, specific, specificity, technicality, thoroughness, triviality.

v. allocate, appoint, assign, catalogue, charge, commission, delegate, delineate, depict, depute, describe, detach, enarrate, enumerate, individualise, itemise, list, narrate, overname, particularise, portray, recount, rehearse, relate, send, specify.

detailed *adj.* blow-by-blow, circumstantial, complex, complicated, comprehensive, descriptive, elaborate, exact, exhaustive, fine, full, intricate, itemised, meticulous, minute, particular, particularised, refined, specific, thorough, unsparing.

antonyms brief, cursory, summary.

details *n.* complexities, complications, ins and outs, intricacies, minutiae, niceties, particularities, particulars, specifics, trivia, trivialities.

detain *v.* arrest, buttonhole, check, confine, delay, hinder, hold, hold up, impede, intern, keep, prevent, restrain, retard, slow, stay, stop.

antonym release.

detect *v.* ascertain, catch, descry, discern, disclose, discover, distinguish, espy, expose, find, identify, note, notice, observe, perceive, recognise, reveal, scent, sight, spot, spy, track down, uncover, unmask.

detection *n.* discernment, discovery, exposé, exposure, identification, revelation, smelling out, sniffing out, tracking down, uncovering, unearthing, unmasking.

detective *n.* busy, constable, cop, copper, dick, gumshoe, investigator, jack, private dick, private eye, private investigator, shamus, sleuth, sleuth-hound, tec, thief-catcher, thief-taker.

detention *n.* confinement, constraint, custody, delay, detainment, duress, hindrance, holding back, imprisonment, incarceration, quarantine, restraint, withholding.

antonym release.

deter *v.* caution, check, damp, daunt, debar, discourage, disincline, dissuade, frighten, hinder, inhibit, intimidate, prevent, prohibit, put off, repel, restrain, stop, turn off, warn.

antonym encourage.

detergent *n.* abstergent, cleaner, cleanser, soap.

adj. abstergent, abstersive, cleaning, cleansing, detersive.

deteriorate *v.* backslide, crumble, decay, decline, decompose, degenerate, depreciate, disintegrate, ebb, fade, fail, fall off, go downhill, lapse, relapse, slide, slip, weaken, worsen.

antonym improve.

deterioration *n.* atrophy, corrosion, debasement, decline, degeneration, degradation, dégringolade, depreciation, descent, dilapidation, disintegration, downturn, drop, failing, fall, falling-off, lapse, pejoration, retrogression, slump, tabes, tabescence, vitiation, wastage, worsening.

antonym improvement.

determinate *adj.* absolute, certain, clear-cut, conclusive, decided, decisive, defined, definite, definitive, delimited, determined, distinct, established, explicit, express, fixed, limited, positive, precise, quantified, settled, specific, specified.

antonym indeterminate.

determination *n.* backbone, conclusion, constancy, conviction, decision, dedication, doggedness, drive, firmness, fortitude, indomitability, insistence, intention, judgement, obstinacy, perseverance, persistence, pertinacity, purpose, resoluteness, resolution, resolve, result, settlement, single-mindedness, solution, steadfastness, stubbornness, tenacity, verdict, will, will-power.

antonym irresolution.

determine *v.* affect, arbitrate, ascertain, certify, check, choose, conclude, control, decide, detect, dictate, direct, discover, elect, end, establish, finish, fix, govern, guide, identify, impel, impose, incline, induce, influence, intend, lead, learn, modify, ordain, point, purpose, regulate, resolve, rule, settle, shape, terminate, undertake, verify.

determined *adj.* bent, constant, convinced, decided, dogged, firm, fixed, indivertible, insistent, intent, obstinate, persevering, persistent, pertinacious, purposeful, resolute, set, single-minded, steadfast, strong-minded,

strong-willed, stubborn, tenacious, tough-minded, undissuadable, unflinching, unhesitating, unwavering.
antonym irresolute.

deterrent *n.* bar, barrier, check, curb, determent, difficulty, discouragement, disincentive, hindrance, impediment, obstacle, obstruction, repellent, restraint, turn-off.
antonym incentive.

detest *v.* abhor, abominate, deplore, despise, dislike, execrate, hate, loathe, recoil from.
antonym adore.

detestable *adj.* abhorred, abhorrent, abominable, accursed, despicable, disgusting, execrable, foul, hated, hateful, heinous, loathsome, nauseating, noisome, obnoxious, odious, offensive, pestiferous, pestilent, pestilential, repellent, repugnant, repulsive, revolting, rotten, shocking, sordid, swinish, vile, villainous.
antonyms admirable, adorable, pleasant.

detestation *n.* abhorrence, abomination, anathema, animosity, animus, antipathy, aversion, despite, disgust, dislike, enmity, execration, hate, hatred, hostility, loathing, odium, repugnance, revulsion.
antonyms adoration, approval, love.

dethrone *v.* depose, oust, topple, uncrown, unking, unseat, unthrone.
antonyms crown, enthrone.

detonate *v.* blast, blow up, discharge, displode, explode, fulminate, ignite, kindle, set off, spark off.

detonation *n.* bang, blast, blow-up, boom, burst, discharge, displosion, explosion, fulmination, igniting, ignition, report.

detour *n.* bypass, bypath, byroad, byway, circumbendibus, deviation, digression, diversion, excursus.

detract *v.* belittle, depreciate, derogate, devaluate, diminish, lessen, lower, negate, nullify, reduce, vilipend, vitiate.
antonyms add to, praise.

detraction *n.* abuse, aspersion, belittlement, calumniation, calumny, defamation, denigration, depreciation, derogation, disparagement, innuendo, insinuation, misprision, misrepresentation, muck-raking, revilement, scandalmongering, scurrility, slander, traducement, vituperation.
antonyms appreciation, praise.

detractor *n.* backbiter, belittler, defamer, denigrator, disparager, enemy, muck-raker, reviler, scandalmonger, slanderer, traducer, vilifier.
antonyms flatterer, supporter.

detriment *n.* damage, disadvantage, disservice, evil, harm, hurt, ill, impairment, injury, loss, mischief, prejudice.
antonym advantage.

detrimental *adj.* adverse, baleful, damaging, deleterious, destructive, disadvantageous, harmful, hurtful, inimical, injurious, mischievous, noxious, pernicious, prejudicial, unfavourable, untoward.

antonym advantageous.

detritus *n.* debris, fragments, garbage, junk, litter, remains, rubbish, scum, waste, wreckage.

devaluation *n.* decrease, deflation, devalorisation, lowering, reduction.

devalue *v.* decrease, deflate, devalorise, devaluate, lower, reduce.

devastate *v.* confound, demolish, depredate, desolate, despoil, destroy, discomfit, discompose, disconcert, floor, lay waste, level, maraud, nonplus, overwhelm, pillage, plunder, ransack, ravage, raze, ruin, sack, spoil, spoliate, waste, wreck.

devastation *n.* annihilation, demolition, denudation, depredation, desolation, despoliation, destruction, havoc, pillage, plunder, ravages, ruin, ruination, spoliation, wrack, wreckage.

devastator *n.* demolisher, desolater, despoiler, destroyer, devourer, locust, plunderer, ravager, spoliator, vandal, wrecker.

develop *v.* acquire, advance, amplify, augment, begin, bloom, blossom, branch out, breed, broaden, commence, contract, cultivate, dilate, diversify, elaborate, engender, enlarge, ensue, establish, evolve, expand, flourish, follow, form, foster, generate, grow, happen, invent, make headway, mature, move on, originate, pick up, progress, promote, prosper, result, ripen, sprout, start, unfold.

development *n.* advance, advancement, blooming, blossoming, change, circumstance, detail, elaboration, event, evolution, expansion, extension, furtherance, growth, happening, improvement, incident, increase, issue, maturation, maturity, occurrence, outcome, phenomenon, phylogenesis, phylogeny, progress, progression, promotion, refinement, result, ripening, situation, spread, unfolding, unravelling, upbuilding, upshot.

deviant *adj.* aberrant, abnormal, anomalous, bent, bizarre, deviate, devious, divergent, freakish, freaky, heretical, heteromorphic, heteromorphous, heterotypic, irregular, kinky, perverse, perverted, queer, twisted, wayward.
antonym normal.
n. deviate, freak, kook, misfit, oddball, pervert, queer, vert.
antonym straight.

deviate *v.* aberrate, depart, differ, digress, divagate, diverge, drift, err, go astray, go off the rails, part, stray, swerve, turn, turn aside, vary, veer, wander, yaw.

deviation *n.* aberrance, aberrancy, aberration, abnormality, alteration, ambage, anomaly, change, deflection, departure, detour, digression, discrepancy, disparity, divagation, divergence, driftage, eccentricity, fluctuation, freak, heteromorphism, heteromorphy, inconsistency, irregularity, kinkiness, quirk, shift, variance, variation, wandering.
antonym conformity.

device *n.* apparatus, appliance, artifice, badge,

blazon, colophon, contraption, contrivance, crest, design, dodge, emblem, episemon, expedient, figure, gadget, gambit, gimmick, gismo, implement, improvisation, insignia, instrument, invention, logo, machination, manoeuvre, motif, motto, plan, plot, ploy, project, ruse, scheme, shield, shift, stratagem, strategy, stunt, symbol, tactic, token, tool, trick, utensil, wile.

devil *n.* Abaddon, Adversary, Apollyon, archfiend, bastard, beast, Beelzebub, Belial, bog(e)y-man, brute, bugger, cad, Clootie, creature, deil, demon, enthusiast, Evil One, fiend, goodman, Hornie, imp, incubus, jumpy, Lucifer, Mahoun(d), man of sin, Mephisto, Mephistopheles, monkey, monster, ogre, Old Harry, Old Nick, Old Scratch, Prince of Darkness, ragman, rascal, rogue, rotter, Satan, savage, scamp, scoundrel, shaitan, Slanderer, succubus, swine, terror, unfortunate, villain, wirricow, worricow, wretch.

devilish *adj.* accursed, black-hearted, damnable, demoniac, demoniacal, diabolic, diabolical, execrable, fiendish, hellish, impious, infernal, iniquitous, mischievous, monstrous, nefarious, satanic, wicked.

devil-may-care *adj.* careless, casual, cavalier, easy-going, flippant, frivolous, happy-go-lucky, heedless, insouciant, jaunty, lackadaisical, nonchalant, pococurante, reckless, swaggering, swashbuckling, unconcerned, unworried.

devilment *n.* devilry, knavery, mischief, mischievousness, naughtiness, rascality, roguery, roguishness, sport, teasing.

devilry *n.* black magic, chicanery, cruelty, devilment, deviltry, diablerie, diabolism, evil, jiggery-pokery, knavery, malevolence, malice, mischief, mischievousness, monkey-business, rascality, roguery, sorcery, trickiness, vice, viciousness, villainy, wickedness.

devious *adj.* calculating, circuitous, confusing, crooked, cunning, deceitful, deviating, dishonest, disingenuous, double-dealing, erratic, evasive, excursive, indirect, insidious, insincere, misleading, rambling, roundabout, scheming, slippery, sly, subtle, surreptitious, tortuous, treacherous, tricky, underhand, wandering, wily, winding.
antonyms artless, candid, straightforward.

deviousness *n.* cunning, deceit, dishonesty, disingenuity, evasion, evasiveness, indirectness, insincerity, slipperiness, slyness, subtlety, trickiness.
antonyms artlessness, openness.

devise *v.* arrange, compass, compose, conceive, concoct, construct, contrive, design, excogitate, forge, form, formulate, frame, imagine, invent, plan, plot, prepare, project, scheme, shape.

devoid *adj.* barren, bereft, deficient, denuded, destitute, empty, free, innocent, lacking, sans, vacant, void, wanting, without.
antonyms blessed, endowed.

devolution *n.* decentralisation, delegation, dispersal, distribution, transference.
antonym centralisation.

devolve *v.* alienate, be handed down, commission, consign, convey, delegate, deliver, depute, entrust, fall to, hand down, rest with, transfer.

devote *v.* allocate, allot, apply, appropriate, assign, commit, consecrate, dedicate, enshrine, give, oneself, pledge, reserve, sacrifice, set apart, set aside, surrender.

devoted *adj.* ardent, attentive, caring, committed, concerned, constant, dedicated, devout, faithful, fond, loving, loyal, staunch, steadfast, tireless, true, unremitting, unswerving.
antonyms inconstant, indifferent, negligent.

devotee *n.* addict, adherent, admirer, aficionado, buff, devil, disciple, enthusiast, fan, fanatic, fiend, follower, hound, merchant, supporter, votary, voteen, zealot.
antonyms adversary, sceptic.

devotion *n.* adherence, adoration, affection, allegiance, ardour, assiduity, attachment, commitment, consecration, constancy, dedication, devoutness, earnestness, faith, faithfulness, fervour, fidelity, fondness, godliness, holiness, indefatigability, love, loyalty, partiality, passion, piety, prayer, regard, religiousness, reverence, sanctity, sedulousness, spirituality, steadfastness, support, worship, zeal.
antonyms inconstancy, negligence.

devotional *adj.* devout, dutiful, holy, pietistic, pious, religious, reverential, sacred, solemn, spiritual.

devour *v.* absorb, annihilate, bolt, consume, cram, destroy, dispatch, down, eat, engulf, feast on, feast one's eyes on, gluttonise, gobble, gorge, gormandise, gulp, guzzle, polish off, ravage, ravin, relish, revel in, spend, stuff, swallow, waste, wolf.

devourer *n.* consumer, glutton, gobbler, gormandiser, gourmand, guzzler, locust, waster.

devout *adj.* ardent, constant, deep, devoted, earnest, faithful, fervent, genuine, godly, heartfelt, holy, intense, orthodox, passionate, pious, prayerful, profound, pure, religious, reverent, saintly, serious, sincere, staunch, steadfast, unswerving, whole-hearted, zealous.
antonyms insincere, uncommitted.

devoutly *adv.* deeply, faithfully, fervently, profoundly, sincerely, staunchly, steadfastly, whole-heartedly.

dewy *adj.* blooming, innocent, roral, roric, rorid, roscid, starry-eyed, youthful.

dexterity *n.* ability, address, adroitness, agility, aptitude, art, artistry, cleverness, cunning, deftness, effortlessness, expertise, expertness, facility, finesse, handiness, ingenuity, knack, legerdemain, mastery, neatness, nimbleness, proficiency, readiness, skilfulness, skill, smoothness, tact, touch.
antonyms clumsiness, ineptitude.

dexterous *adj.* able, active, acute, adept, adroit,

agile, apt, clever, cunning, deft, expert, facile, feat, habile, handy, ingenious, light-handed, masterly, neat, neat-handed, nifty, nimble, nimble-fingered, nippy, proficient, prompt, quick, skilful.
antonyms clumsy, inept.

diabolical *adj.* damnable, devilish, diabolic, difficult, disastrous, dreadful, excruciating, fiendish, hellish, infernal, knavish, nasty, outrageous, shocking, tricky, unpleasant, vile, villainous, wicked.

diadem *n.* circlet, coronet, crown, mitre, round, tiara.

diagnose *v.* analyse, determine, distinguish, explain, identify, interpret, investigate, isolate, pinpoint, pronounce, recognise.

diagnosis *n.* analysis, answer, conclusion, examination, explanation, identification, interpretation, investigation, isolation, opinion, pronouncement, scrutiny, verdict.

diagnostic *adj.* analytical, demonstrative, distinctive, distinguishing, idiosyncratic, indicative, interpretative, interpretive, particular, peculiar, recognisable, symptomatic.

diagonal *adj.* angled, cater-cornered, cornerways, crooked, cross, crossways, crosswise, oblique, slanting, slantwise, sloping.

diagonally *adv.* aslant, at an angle, cornerwise, crosswise, obliquely, on the bias, on the cross, on the slant, slantwise.

diagram *n.* abac, chart, drawing, figure, graph, illustration, lay-out, nomogram, outline, picture, plan, representation, schema, sketch, table.

diagrammatic *adj.* diagrammatical, graphic, illustrative, representational, schematic, tabular.
antonyms imaginative, impressionistic.

dialect *n.* accent, diction, Doric, idiom, jargon, language, lingo, localism, patois, pronunciation, provincialism, regionalism, speech, tongue, vernacular.

dialectic *adj.* analytic, argumentative, deductive, dialectical, disceptatorial, inductive, logical, logistic, polemical, ratiocinative, ratiocinatory, rational, rationalistic.
n. analysis, argumentation, casuistry, contention, debate, deduction, dialectics, disceptation, discussion, disputation, induction, logic, polemics, ratiocination, rationale, reasoning, sophistry.

dialogue *n.* causerie, colloquy, communication, confabulation, conference, conversation, converse, debate, discourse, discussion, duologue, exchange, interchange, interlocution, lines, script, stichomythia, table talk, talk.

diametric *adj.* antipodal, antithetical, contrary, contrasting, counter, diametral, diametrical, opposed, opposite.

diaphanous *adj.* cobwebby, delicate, filmy, fine, gauzy, gossamer, gossamery, light, pellucid, see-through, sheer, thin, translucent, transparent, veily.
antonyms heavy, opaque, thick.

diarrhoea *n.* dysentery, gippy tummy, holiday tummy, looseness, Montezuma's revenge, Spanish tummy, the runs, the trots.
antonym constipation.

diary *n.* appointment book, chronicle, commonplace book, day-book, diurnal, engagement book, journal, journal intime, logbook, year-book.

diatribe *n.* abuse, attack, castigation, criticism, denunciation, flyting, harangue, insult, invective, onslaught, philippic, reviling, stricture, tirade, upbraiding, vituperation.
antonyms bouquet, encomium, praise.

dice *n.* astragals, bones, cubes, devil's bones, die, hazard.

dicey *adj.* chancy, dangerous, difficult, dubious, hairy, iffy, problematic, risky, ticklish, tricky.
antonyms certain, easy.

dicky *adj.* ailing, frail, infirm, queer, shaky, unreliable, unsound, unsteady, weak.
antonyms healthy, robust.

dictate *v.* announce, command, decree, direct, enjoin, impose, instruct, ordain, order, prescribe, pronounce, rule, say, speak, transmit, utter.
n. behest, bidding, code, command, decree, dictation, dictum, direction, edict, fiat, injunction, law, mandate, order, ordinance, precept, principle, requirement, rule, ruling, statute, ultimatum, word.

dictator *n.* autarch, autocrat, Big Brother, boss, despot, supremo, tyrant.

dictatorial *adj.* absolute, almighty, arbitrary, autarchic, authoritarian, autocratic, bossy, despotic, dogmatic, domineering, imperious, magisterial, oppressive, overbearing, peremptory, repressive, totalitarian, tyrannical.
antonyms democratic, egalitarian, liberal, tolerant.

dictatorship *n.* absolute rule, absolutism, autarchy, authoritarianism, autocracy, despotism, dictature, fascism, Hitlerism, totalitarianism, tyranny.
antonyms democracy, egalitarianism.

diction *n.* articulation, delivery, elocution, enunciation, expression, fluency, idiom, inflection, intonation, language, phraseology, phrasing, pronunciation, speech, style, terminology, usage, vocabulary, wording.

dictionary *n.* concordance, encyclopaedia, glossary, idioticon, lexicon, onomasticon, thesaurus, vocabulary, wordbook.

dictum *n.* adage, axiom, command, decree, dictate, edict, fiat, gnome, maxim, order, precept, pronouncement, proverb, ruling, saw, saying, utterance.

didactic *adj.* didascalic, educational, educative, homiletic, instructive, moral, moralising, pedagogic, pedantic, preceptive, prescriptive.

die *v.* breathe one's last, croak, decay, decease, decline, depart, desire, disappear, dwindle, ebb, end, expire, fade, finish, fizzle out, gangrene, go over to the majority, go to one's (long) account, hunger, kick in, kick it, kick the bucket, languish, lapse, long for, pass,

pass away, pass over, peg out, perish, peter out, pine for, pop off, run down, sink, slip the cable, snuff it, starve, stop, subside, succumb, suffer, vanish, wane, wilt, wither, yearn.

die-hard *n.* blimp, Colonel Blimp, fanatic, fogey, hardliner, intransigent, reactionary, rightist, stick-in-the-mud, ultra-conservative, zealot.

adj. blimpish, confirmed, dyed-in-the-wool, entrenched, hardcore, hardline, immovable, incorrigible, incurable, inflexible, intransigent, irreconcilable, obstinate, reactionary, rigid, stubborn, ultra-conservative, uncompromising, unyielding.

antonyms enlightened, flexible, progressive.

diet¹ *n.* abstinence, aliment, board, comestibles, commons, dietary, edibles, fare, fast, food, foodstuffs, nourishment, nutriment, nutrition, provisions, rations, regime, regimen, subsistence, sustenance, viands, victuals.

v. abstain, bant, fast, lose weight, reduce, slim, weight-watch.

diet² *n.* assembly, chamber, congress, convention, convocation, council, divan, legislature, meeting, parliament, session, sitting, synod.

differ *v.* argue, be at odds with, clash, conflict, contend, contradict, contrast, debate, demur, depart from, deviate, disagree, dispute, dissent, diverge, fall out, oppose, part company with, quarrel, take issue, vary.

antonyms agree, conform.

difference *n.* alteration, argument, balance, change, clash, conflict, contention, contrariety, contrast, contretemps, controversy, debate, deviation, differentia, differentiation, difformity, disagreement, discordance, discrepancy, discreteness, disparateness, disparity, dispute, dissimilarity, distinction, distinctness, divergence, diversity, exception, idiosyncrasy, jizz, particularity, peculiarity, quarrel, remainder, rest, set-to, singularity, strife, tiff, unlikeness, variation, variety, wrangle.

antonyms agreement, conformity, uniformity.

different *adj.* altered, anomalous, assorted, at odds, at variance, atypical, bizarre, changed, clashing, contrasting, deviating, discrepant, discrete, disparate, dissimilar, distinct, distinctive, divergent, divers, diverse, eccentric, extraordinary, inconsistent, individual, manifold, many, miscellaneous, multifarious, numerous, opposed, original, other, peculiar, rare, separate, several, singular, special, strange, sundry, unalike, uncommon, unconventional, unique, unlike, unusual, varied, various.

antonyms conventional, normal, same, similar, uniform.

differentiate *v.* adapt, alter, change, contrast, convert, demarcate, discern, discriminate, distinguish, individualise, mark off, modify, particularise, separate, tell apart, transform.

antonyms assimilate, associate, confuse, link.

differentiation *n.* contrast, demarcation, differentia, discrimination, distinction,

distinguishing, individualisation, jizz, modification, particularisation, separation.

antonyms assimilation, association, confusion, connection.

difficult *adj.* abstract, abstruse, arduous, Augean, baffling, burdensome, captious, complex, complicated, dark, delicate, demanding, difficile, disruptive, enigmatical, fastidious, formidable, fractious, fussy, Gordian, grim, hard, herculean, iffy, intractable, intricate, involved, knotty, laborious, obscure, obstinate, obstreperous, onerous, painful, perplexing, perverse, problematic, problematical, recalcitrant, refractory, rigid, steep, sticky, stiff, straitened, strenuous, stubborn, thorny, ticklish, tiresome, toilsome, tough, troublesome, trying, unamenable, unco-operative, unmanageable, uphill, wearisome.

antonyms easy, straightforward.

difficulty *n.* a bad patch, arduousness, awkwardness, block, complication, dilemma, distress, embarrassment, fix, hang-up, hardship, hiccup, hindrance, hole, hurdle, impediment, jam, laboriousness, labour, mess, nineholes, objection, obstacle, opposition, pain, painfulness, perplexity, pickle, pinch, pitfall, plight, predicament, problem, protest, quandary, scruple, spot, strain, strait, straits, strenuousness, stumbling-block, trial, tribulation, trouble, vexata quaestio, vexed question.

antonyms advantage, ease.

diffidence *n.* abashment, backwardness, bashfulness, constraint, doubt, fear, hesitancy, hesitation, humility, inhibition, insecurity, meekness, modesty, reluctance, reserve, self-consciousness, self-distrust, self-doubt, self-effacement, shamefacedness, shamefast, sheepishness, shyness, tentativeness, timidity, timidness, timorousness, unassertiveness.

antonym confidence.

diffident *adj.* abashed, backward, bashful, constrained, distrustful, doubtful, hesitant, inhibited, insecure, meek, modest, reluctant, reserved, self-conscious, self-effacing, shamefaced, shamefast, sheepish, shrinking, shy, suspicious, tentative, timid, timorous, unadventurous, unassertive, unassuming, unobtrusive, unsure, withdrawn.

antonym confident.

diffuse *adj.* ambagious, circuitous, circumlocutory, copious, diffused, digressive, disconnected, discursive, dispersed, long-winded, loose, maundering, meandering, prolix, rambling, scattered, unconcentrated, uncoordinated, vague, verbose, waffling, wordy.

antonyms concentrated, succinct.

v. circulate, dispense, disperse, disseminate, dissipate, distribute, propagate, scatter, spread, winnow.

antonyms concentrate, suppress.

dig¹ *v.* burrow, delve, drive, excavate, go into, gouge, graft, grub, hoe, howk, investigate, jab, mine, penetrate, pierce, poke, probe, prod, punch, quarry, research, scoop, search, spit, thrust, till, tunnel.

n. aspersion, barb, crack, cut, gibe, insinuation, insult, jab, jeer, poke, prod, punch, quip, sneer, taunt, thrust, wisecrack.
antonym compliment.

dig up *v.* discover, disinter, dredge, exhumate, exhume, expose, extricate, find, retrieve, track down, uncover, unearth.
antonyms bury, obscure.

dig² *v.* adore, appreciate, be into, enjoy, fancy, follow, get a kick out of, get off on, go a bundle on, go for, go overboard about, groove, have the hots for, like, love, understand, warm to.
antonym hate.

digest *v.* abridge, absorb, arrange, assimilate, classify, codify, compress, condense, consider, contemplate, dispose, dissolve, grasp, incorporate, ingest, macerate, master, meditate, methodise, ponder, process, reduce, shorten, stomach, study, summarise, systematise, tabulate, take in, understand.
n. abbreviation, abridgement, abstract, compendium, compression, condensation, epitome, précis, reduction, résumé, summary, synopsis.

digestion *n.* absorption, assimilation, dyspepsia, eupepsia, ingestion, transformation.

dignified *adj.* august, decorous, distinguished, exalted, formal, grave, honourable, imposing, impressive, lofty, lordly, majestic, noble, oro(ro)tund, reserved, solemn, stately, upright.
antonym undignified.

dignify *v.* adorn, advance, aggrandise, apotheosise, distinguish, elevate, ennoble, exalt, glorify, honour, promote, raise.
antonyms degrade, demean.

dignitary *n.* bigwig, dignity, high-up, notability, notable, personage, pillar of society, VIP, worthy.

dignity *n.* amour-propre, courtliness, decorum, elevation, eminence, excellence, glory, grandeur, gravitas, gravity, greatness, hauteur, honour, importance, loftiness, majesty, nobility, nobleness, pride, propriety, rank, respectability, self-esteem, self-importance, self-possession, self-regard, self-respect, solemnity, standing, stateliness, station, status.

digress *v.* depart, deviate, divagate, diverge, drift, excurse, expatiate, go off at a tangent, ramble, stray, wander.

digression *n.* apostrophe, aside, departure, detour, deviation, divagation, divergence, diversion, evagation, excursion, footnote, obiter dictum, parenthesis, straying, vagary, wandering.

dilapidated *adj.* battered, broken-down, crumbling, decayed, decaying, decrepit, mouldering, neglected, ramshackle, rickety, ruined, ruinous, run-down, shabby, shaky, tumbledown, uncared-for, worn-out.

dilapidation *n.* collapse, decay, demolition, destruction, deterioration, disintegration, disrepair, dissolution, downfall, ruin, ruination, waste.

dilate *v.* amplify, broaden, descant, detail, develop, distend, dwell on, elaborate, enlarge, expand, expatiate, expound, extend, increase, puff out, spin out, stretch, swell, widen.
antonyms abbreviate, constrict, curtail.

dilated *adj.* bloated, distended, enlarged, expanded, extended, inflated, outspread, swollen, tumescent, varicose.
antonyms contracted, shortened.

dilation *n.* broadening, dilatation, distension, enlargement, expansion, extension, increase, spread, swelling, widening.
antonyms constriction, contraction.

dilatory *adj.* backward, behind-hand, dallying, delaying, indolent, lackadaisical, laggard, lingering, loitering, procrastinating, slack, slothful, slow, sluggish, tardy, tarrying.
antonym diligent.

dilemma *n.* bind, corner, difficulty, embarrassment, fix, jam, mess, perplexity, pickle, pinch, plight, predicament, problem, puzzle, quandary, spot, strait.

dilettante *n.* aesthete, amateur, dabbler, sciolist, trifler.

diligence *n.* activity, application, assiduity, assiduousness, attention, attentiveness, care, constancy, earnestness, heedfulness, industry, intentness, laboriousness, perseverance, pertinacity, sedulousness.
antonym laziness.

diligent *adj.* active, assiduous, attentive, busy, careful, conscientious, constant, dogged, earnest, hard-working, indefatigable, industrious, laborious, painstaking, persevering, persistent, pertinacious, sedulous, studious, tireless.
antonyms dilatory, lazy.

dilly-dally *v.* dally, dawdle, delay, dither, falter, hesitate, hover, linger, loiter, potter, procrastinate, shilly-shally, swither, tarry, trifle, vacillate, waver.

dilute *v.* adulterate, allay, attenuate, cut, dash, decrease, diffuse, diminish, lessen, mitigate, reduce, temper, thin (out), water down, weaken.
antonym concentrate.
adj. adulterated, attenuate(d), cut, diluted, thin, watered (down), waterish, weak.
antonym concentrated.

dim *adj.* bleary, blurred, caliginous, cloudy, confused, dark, darkish, dense, depressing, dingy, discouraging, dull, dumb, dusky, faint, feeble, foggy, fuzzy, gloomy, grey, hazy, ill-defined, imperfect, indistinct, intangible, lack-lustre, misty, muted, obscure, obscured, obtuse, opaque, overcast, pale, remote, shadowy, slow, sombre, stupid, sullied, tarnished, tenebrious, thick, unclear, unfavourable, unilluminated, unpromising, vague, weak.
antonyms bright, distinct.
v. becloud, bedim, blear, blur, cloud, darken, dull, fade, lower, obscure, tarnish.

antonyms brighten, illuminate.

dimension(s) *n.* amplitude, bulk, capacity, extent, greatness, importance, largeness, magnitude, measure, range, scale, scope, size.

diminish *v.* abate, bate, belittle, cheapen, contract, curtail, cut, deactivate, decline, decrease, demean, depreciate, devalue, dwindle, ebb, fade, lessen, lower, minify, peter out, recede, reduce, retrench, shrink, shrivel, sink, slacken, subside, taper off, wane, weaken.
antonyms enhance, enlarge, increase.

diminishing *adj.* abating, contracting, declining, decreasing, decrescent, dwindling, ebbing, fading, lessening, lowering, receding, reducing, shrinking, shrivelling, subsiding, waning.
antonyms growing, increasing.

diminution *n.* abatement, contraction, curtailment, cut, cutback, deactivation, decay, decline, decrease, deduction, ebb, lessening, reduction, retrenchment, shortening, shrinkage, subsidence, weakening.
antonyms enlargement, increase.

diminutive *adj.* bantam, dinky, Lilliputian, little, midget, mini, miniature, minute, petite, pint-size(d), pocket(-sized), pygmy, small, tiny, undersized, wee.
antonyms big, great, huge, large.
n. hypocorisma, pet-name.

dimple *n.* concavity, depression, dint, fovea, hollow, umbilicus.

dimwit *n.* blockhead, bonehead, booby, dullard, dunce, dunderhead, ignoramus, nitwit, numskull, thick, thick-skull, twit.

din *n.* babble, chirm, clamour, clangour, clash, clatter, commotion, crash, hubbub, hullabaloo, noise, outcry, pandemonium, racket, randan, row, shout, uproar.
antonyms calm, quiet.

dine *v.* banquet, break bread, eat, feast, feed, lunch, sup.

dine on banquet, consume, dine off, eat, feast, feed, regale oneself.

dingy *adj.* bedimmed, colourless, dark, dim, dirty, discoloured, drab, dreary, dull, dusky, faded, fuscous, gloomy, grimy, murky, obscure, run-down, seedy, shabby, soiled, sombre, tacky, worn.
antonyms bright, clean.

dining-room *n.* dinette, frater, mess, refectory, triclinium.

dinky *adj.* dainty, fine, mini, miniature, natty, neat, petite, small, trig, trim.

dinner *n.* banquet, beanfeast, blow-out, collation, feast, meal, refection, repast, spread, supper, tea.

dint *n.* blow, concavity, dent, depression, hollow, impression, indentation, stroke.

dip *v.* bathe, decline, descend, disappear, dook, dop, douse, droop, drop, duck, dunk, fade, fall, immerse, ladle, lower, plunge, rinse, sag, scoop, set, sink, slope, slump, souse, spoon, subside, tilt.
n. basin, bathe, concavity, concoction, decline, depression, dilution, dive, dook,

douche, drenching, ducking, fall, hole, hollow, immersion, incline, infusion, lowering, mixture, plunge, preparation, sag, slip, slope, slump, soaking, solution, suspension, swim.

dip into browse, dabble, peruse, sample, skim, try.

diplomacy *n.* artfulness, craft, delicacy, discretion, finesse, manoeuvring, savoir-faire, skill, statecraft, statesmanship, subtlety, tact, tactfulness.

diplomat *n.* conciliator, go-between, mediator, moderator, negotiator, peacemaker, politician, tactician.

diplomatic *adj.* discreet, judicious, polite, politic, prudent, sagacious, sensitive, subtle, tactful.
antonyms rude, tactless, thoughtless.

dire *adj.* alarming, appalling, awful, calamitous, cataclysmic, catastrophic, critical, crucial, cruel, crying, desperate, disastrous, dismal, distressing, drastic, dreadful, exigent, extreme, fearful, gloomy, grave, grim, horrible, horrid, ominous, portentous, pressing, ruinous, terrible, urgent, woeful.

direct[1] *v.* address, administer, advise, aim, bid, case, charge, command, conduct, control, dictate, direct, dispose, enjoin, fix, focus, govern, guide, handle, indicate, instruct, intend, label, lead, level, mail, manage, mastermind, mean, order, oversee, point, regulate, route, rule, run, send, show, stage-manage, superintend, superscribe, supervise, train, turn.

direct[2] *adj.* absolute, blunt, candid, categorical, downright, explicit, express, face-to-face, first-hand, frank, head-on, honest, immediate, man-to-man, matter-of-fact, non-stop, open, outright, outspoken, personal, plain, plain-spoken, point-blank, shortest, sincere, straight, straightforward, through, unambiguous, unbroken, undeviating, unequivocal, uninterrupted.
antonyms crooked, devious, indirect.

direction *n.* address, administration, aim, approach, bearing, bent, bias, charge, command, control, course, current, drift, end, government, guidance, label, leadership, line, management, mark, order, orientation, oversight, path, proclivity, purpose, road, route, superintendence, superscription, supervision, tack, tendency, tenor, track, trend, way.

directions *n.* briefing, guidance, guidelines, indication, instructions, orders, plan, recipe, recommendations, regulations.

directive *n.* charge, command, decree, dictate, diktat, edict, fiat, imperative, injunction, instruction, mandate, notice, order, ordinance, regulation, ruling.

directly *adv.* bluntly, candidly, dead, due, exactly, face-to-face, forthwith, frankly, honestly, immediately, instantaneously, instantly, openly, personally, plainly, point-blank, precisely, presently, promptly, pronto, quickly, right away, soon, speedily, straight,

straightaway, straightforwardly, truthfully, unequivocally, unerringly, unswervingly.
antonym indirectly.

directness *n.* bluffness, bluntness, candour, forthrightness, frankness, honesty, outspoken-ness, plain-speaking, sincerity, straightforwardness.

director *n.* administrator, auteur, boss, chairman, chief, conductor, controller, corrector, executive, governor, head, leader, manager, monitor, organiser, principal, producer, supervisor.

dirge *n.* coronach, dead-march, dirge, elegy, lament, monody, requiem, threnody.

dirt *n.* clay, crud, dust, earth, excrement, filth, grime, impurity, indecency, loam, mire, muck, mud, obscenity, ordure, pornography, slime, smudge, smut, smutch, soil, sordor, stain, tarnish, vomit, yuck.
antonyms cleanliness, cleanness.

dirty *adj.* angry, base, beggarly, begrimed, bitter, blue, clouded, contemptible, corrupt, cowardly, crooked, cruddy, dark, despicable, dishonest, dull, filthy, foul, fraudulent, grimy, grubby, ignominious, illegal, indecent, low, low-down, maculate, manky, mean, messy, miry, mucky, muddy, nasty, obscene, off-colour, piggish, polluted, pornographic, risqué, salacious, scruffy, scurvy, shabby, sluttish, smutty, soiled, sordid, squalid, sullied, treacherous, unclean, unfair, unscrupulous, unsporting, unsterile, unswept, vile, vulgar, yucky.
antonyms clean, spotless.
v. bedaub, begrime, besmear, besmirch, besmut, bespatter, blacken, defile, foul, mess up, muddy, pollute, smear, smirch, smudge, soil, soss, spoil, stain, sully.
antonyms clean, cleanse.

disability *n.* affliction, ailment, complaint, crippledom, defect, disablement, disorder, disqualification, handicap, impairment, impotency, inability, incapacitation, incapacity, incompetency, infirmity, malady, unfitness, weakness.

disable *v.* cripple, damage, debilitate, disenable, disqualify, enfeeble, hamstring, handicap, immobilise, impair, incapacitate, invalidate, lame, paralyse, prostrate, unfit, unman, weaken.

disabled *adj.* bedridden, crippled, handicapped, hors de combat, immobilised, incapacitated, infirm, lame, maimed, mangled, mutilated, paralysed, weak, weakened, wrecked.
antonyms able, able-bodied.

disadvantage *n.* burden, damage, debit, detriment, disservice, drawback, flaw, fly in the ointment, handicap, hardship, harm, hindrance, hurt, impediment, inconvenience, injury, liability, loss, minus, nuisance, prejudice, privation, snag, trouble, unfavourableness, weakness.
antonyms advantage, benefit.
v. hamper, handicap, hinder, inconvenience, wrong-foot.

antonyms aid, help.

disadvantaged *adj.* deprived, handicapped, hindered, impeded, impoverished, struggling, underprivileged.
antonym privileged.

disadvantageous *adj.* adverse, burdensome, damaging, deleterious, detrimental, harmful, hurtful, ill-timed, inauspicious, inconvenient, inexpedient, injurious, inopportune, prejudicial, unfavourable.
antonym advantageous.

disaffected *adj.* alienated, antagonistic, antipathetic(al), discontented, disgruntled, disloyal, dissatisfied, estranged, hostile, mutinous, rebellious, seditious.
antonym contented.

disaffection *n.* alienation, animosity, antagonism, antipathy, aversion, breach, coolness, disagreement, discontentment, discord, disharmony, dislike, disloyalty, dissatisfaction, estrangement, hostility, ill-will, repugnance, resentment, unfriendliness.
antonym contentment.

disagree *v.* altercate, argue, bicker, bother, clash, conflict, contend, contest, contradict, counter, depart, deviate, differ, discomfort, dissent, distress, diverge, fall out, hurt, nauseate, object, oppose, quarrel, run counter to, sicken, spat, squabble, take issue with, tiff, trouble, upset, vary, wrangle.
antonym agree.

disagreeable *adj.* bad-tempered, brusque, churlish, contrary, cross, difficult, disgusting, dislik(e)able, disobliging, displeasing, distasteful, ill-natured, irritable, nasty, objectionable, obnoxious, offensive, peevish, repellent, repugnant, repulsive, rude, surly, unamiable, unappetising, unfriendly, ungracious, uninviting, unpalatable, unpleasant, unsavoury.
antonyms agreeable, friendly, pleasant.

disagreement *n.* altercation, argument, clash, conflict, debate, difference, discord, discrepancy, disparity, dispute, dissent, dissimilarity, dissimilitude, divergence, diversity, division, falling-out, incompatibility, incongruity, misunderstanding, quarrel, squabble, strife, tiff, unlikeness, variance, wrangle.
antonym agreement.

disallow *v.* abjure, ban, cancel, chalk off, debar, disaffirm, disavow, disclaim, dismiss, disown, embargo, forbid, prohibit, proscribe, rebuff, refuse, reject, repudiate, veto.
antonyms allow, permit.

disallowed *adj.* debarred, excepted, excluded, forbidden, impermissible, interdicted, prohibited, proscribed, rejected.
antonyms allowed, permissible.

disappear *v.* cease, dematerialise, depart, dissolve, ebb, end, escape, evanesce, evaporate, expire, fade, flee, fly, go, pass, perish, recede, retire, scarper, vamoose, vanish, wane, withdraw.
antonym appear.

disappearance *n.* dematerialisation, departure,

desertion, disappearing, dispersal, dispersion, dissipation, eclipse, evanescence, evaporation, fading, flight, going, loss, melting, passing, vanishing.
antonym appearance.

disappoint *v.* baffle, balk, chagrin, dash, deceive, defeat, delude, disconcert, disenchant, disgruntle, dishearten, disillusion, dismay, dissatisfy, fail, foil, frustrate, hamper, hinder, let down, miff, sadden, thwart, vex.
antonyms delight, please, satisfy.

disappointed *adj.* balked, depressed, despondent, discontented, discouraged, disenchanted, disgruntled, disillusioned, dissatisfied, distressed, down-hearted, foiled, frustrated, let down, miffed, saddened, thwarted, upset.
antonyms delighted, pleased, satisfied.

disappointing *adj.* anti-climactic, depressing, disagreeable, disconcerting, discouraging, inadequate, inferior, insufficient, pathetic, sad, sorry, unhappy, unsatisfactory, unworthy.
antonyms encouraging, pleasant, satisfactory.

disappointment[1] *n.* bafflement, chagrin, discontent, discouragement, disenchantment, disillusionment, displeasure, dissatisfaction, distress, failure, frustration, mortification, regret.
antonyms delight, pleasure, satisfaction.

disappointment[2] *n.* blow, calamity, comedown, disaster, drop, failure, fiasco, frost, lemon, let-down, misfortune, setback, swiz, swizzle.
antonyms boost, success.

disapprobation *n.* blame, censure, condemnation, denunciation, disapproval, disfavour, dislike, displeasure, dissatisfaction, objection, reproach, reproof.
antonyms approbation, approval.

disapproval *n.* censure, condemnation, criticism, denunciation, deprecation, disapprobation, disfavour, dislike, disparagement, displeasure, dissatisfaction, objection, reproach.
antonyms approbation, approval.

disapprove of blame, censure, condemn, denounce, deplore, deprecate, disallow, discountenance, dislike, disparage, object to, reject, spurn, take exception to.
antonym approve of.

disapproving *adj.* censorious,[1] condemnatory, critical, deprecatory, disapprobative, disapprobatory, disparaging, improbative, improbatory, reproachful.

disarm[1] *v.* deactivate, demilitarise, demobilise, disable, disband, unarm, unweapon.
antonym arm.

disarm[2] appease, conciliate, modify, persuade, win over.

disarming *adj.* charming, conciliatory, irresistible, likeable, mollifying, persuasive, winning.

disarrange *v.* confuse, derange, disarray, discompose, dislocate, disorder, disorganise, disrank, disturb, jumble, muss(e), shuffle, unsettle, untidy.
antonym arrange.

disarray *n.* chaos, clutter, confusion, discompo-

sure, disharmony, dishevelment, dislocation, dismay, disorder, disorderliness, disorganisation, displacement, disunity, guddle, indiscipline, jumble, mess, muddle, shambles, tangle, unruliness, untidiness, upset.
antonyms array, order.

disaster *n.* accident, act of God, blow, calamity, cataclysm, catastrophe, curtains, debacle, misadventure, mischance, misfortune, mishap, reverse, ruin, ruination, stroke, tragedy, trouble.
antonyms success, triumph.

disastrous *adj.* adverse, calamitous, cataclysmal, cataclysmic, catastrophic, destructive, detrimental, devastating, dire, dreadful, fatal, grievous, hapless, harmful, ill-fated, ill-starred, miserable, ruinous, terrible, tragic, unfortunate, unlucky.
antonyms successful, triumphant.

disband *v.* break up, demobilise, dismiss, disperse, dissolve, part company, retire, scatter, separate.
antonyms assemble, band, combine.

disbelief *n.* distrust, doubt, dubiety, incredulity, mistrust, rejection, scepticism, suspicion, unbelief.
antonym belief.

disbelieve *v.* discount, discredit, miscredit, mistrust, reject, repudiate, suspect, unbelieve.
antonyms believe, trust.

disbeliever *n.* agnostic, atheist, doubter, doubting Thomas, nullifidian, questioner, sceptic, scoffer, unbeliever.
antonym believer.

disbursement *n.* disbursal, disposal, expenditure, outlay, payment, spending.

disc *n.* circle, disk, diskette, face, plate, record, ring, roundel, roundlet, rundle.

discard *v.* abandon, cashier, cast aside, dispense with, dispose of, ditch, drop, dump, jettison, leave off, reject, relinquish, remove, repudiate, scrap, shed.
antonyms adopt, embrace, espouse.

discern *v.* ascertain, behold, descry, detect, determine, differentiate, discover, discriminate, distinguish, espy, judge, make out, notice, observe, perceive, recognise, see, wot.

discernible *adj.* apparent, appreciable, clear, detectable, discoverable, distinct, distinguishable, manifest, noticeable, observable, obvious, patent, perceptible, plain, recognisable, sensible, visible.
antonym invisible.

discerning *adj.* acute, astute, clear-sighted, critical, discriminating, eagle-eyed, eagle-sighted, ingenious, intelligent, judicious, knowing, penetrating, perceptive, percipient, perspicacious, piercing, sagacious, sensitive, sharp, shrewd, subtle, wise.
antonym obtuse.

discernment *n.* acumen, acuteness, ascertainment, astuteness, awareness, clear-sightedness, cleverness, discrimination, ingenuity, insight, intelligence, judgement, keenness, penetration, perception, perceptiveness, percipience, perspicacity, sagacity, sharpness, understanding, wisdom.

discharge *v.* absolve, accomplish, acquit, carry out, cashier, clear, detonate, disburden, discard, disembogue, dismiss, dispense, drum out, effectuate, egest, eject, emit, empty, excrete, execute, exonerate, expel, explode, exude, fire, free, fulfil, give off, gush, honour, leak, let off, liberate, meet, offload, ooze, oust, pardon, pay, perform, release, relieve, remove, sack, satisfy, set off, settle, shoot, unburden, unload, vent, void, volley.
antonyms employ, engage, hire.
n. accomplishment, achievement, acquittal, acquittance, blast, burst, clearance, congé, defluxion, demobilisation, detonation, disburdening, discharging, dismissal, effluent, ejecta, ejectamenta, ejection, emission, emptying, excretion, execution, exoneration, explosion, firing, flight, flow, flux, fluxion, fulfilment, fusillade, gleet, glit, liberation, mittimus, observance, ooze, pardon, payment, performance, pus, quietus, quittance, release, remittance, report, salvo, satisfaction, secretion, seepage, settlement, shot, suppuration, the boot, the sack, unburdening, unloading, vent, voidance, voiding, volley, whiff.

disciple *n.* acolyte, adherent, apostle, believer, catechumen, chela, convert, devotee, follower, learner, partisan, proselyte, pupil, student, supporter, votary.

disciplinarian *n.* authoritarian, autocrat, despot, martinet, stickler, taskmaster, tyrant.

discipline *n.* castigation, chastisement, conduct, control, correction, course, curriculum, drill, exercise, martinetism, method, orderliness, practice, punishment, regimen, regulation, restraint, self-control, speciality, strictness, subject, training.
antonyms carelessness, negligence.
v. break in, castigate, chasten, chastise, check, control, correct, drill, educate, exercise, form, govern, habituate, instruct, inure, penalise, prepare, punish, regulate, reprimand, reprove, restrain, toughen, train.

disclaim *v.* abandon, abjure, abnegate, decline, deny, disacknowledge, disaffirm, disallow, disavow, disown, forswear, reject, renounce, repudiate.
antonyms accept, acknowledge, claim.

disclaimer *n.* abjuration, abnegation, contradiction, denial, disavowal, disownment, rejection, renunciation, repudiation, retraction.

disclose *v.* broadcast, communicate, confess, discover, divulge, exhibit, expose, impart, lay, lay bare, leak, let slip, propale, publish, relate, reveal, show, tell, unbare, unbosom, unburden, uncover, unfold, unveil, utter.
antonyms conceal, hide.

disclosure *n.* acknowledgement, admission, announcement, Apocalypse, broadcast, confession, declaration, discovery, divulgence, exposé, exposure, leak, publication, revela-

tion, uncovering.

discoloration *n.* blemish, blot, blotch, dyschroa, ecchymosis, mark, patch, splotch, spot, stain.

discolour *v.* disfigure, fade, mar, mark, rust, soil, stain, streak, tarnish, tinge, weather.

discomfit *v.* abash, baffle, balk, beat, checkmate, confound, confuse, defeat, demoralise, discompose, disconcert, embarrass, faze, flurry, fluster, foil, frustrate, humble, humiliate, outwit, overcome, perplex, perturb, rattle, ruffle, thwart, trump, unsettle, vanquish, worry, worst.

discomfiture *n.* abashment, beating, chagrin, confusion, defeat, demoralisation, disappointment, discomposure, embarrassment, failure, frustration, humiliation, overthrow, repulse, rout, ruin, shame, undoing, unease, vanquishment.

discomfort *n.* ache, annoyance, disquiet, distress, hardship, hurt, inquietude, irritant, irritation, malaise, trouble, uneasiness, unpleasantness, unpleasantry, vexation.
antonyms comfort, ease.

discompose *v.* agitate, annoy, bewilder, confuse, discomfit, disconcert, dishevel, displease, disturb, embarrass, faze, flurry, fluster, fret, irritate, perturb, rattle, ruffle, rumple, tousle, unsettle, upset, vex, worry.
antonym compose.

discomposure *n.* agitation, anxiety, confusion, discomfiture, dislocation, disorder, disquiet, disquietude, distraction, disturbance, embarrassment, fluster, inquietude, malaise, nervousness, perturbation, uneasiness.
antonym composure.

disconcert *v.* abash, agitate, baffle, balk, bewilder, confuse, discombobulate, discomfit, discompose, disturb, flurry, fluster, frustrate, hinder, nonplus, perplex, perturb, put someone's nose out of joint, rattle, ruffle, thwart, trouble, unbalance, undo, unsettle, upset, worry.

disconcerted *adj.* annoyed, bewildered, confused, discombobulated, discomfited, distracted, disturbed, embarrassed, fazed, flurried, flustered, mixed-up, nonplussed, perturbed, rattled, ruffled, taken aback, thrown, troubled, unsettled, upset.

disconcerting *adj.* alarming, awkward, baffling, bewildering, bothersome, confusing, discombobulating, dismaying, distracting, disturbing, embarrassing, off-putting, perplexing, upsetting.

disconnect *v.* cut off, detach, disengage, divide, part, separate, sever, uncouple, ungear, unhitch, unhook, unlink, unplug, unyoke.
antonyms attach, connect, engage.

disconnected *adj.* confused, disjointed, free, garbled, illogical, incoherent, irrational, jumbled, loose, rambling, unco-ordinated, unintelligible, wandering.
antonyms attached, coherent, connected.

disconsolate *adj.* crushed, dejected, desolate, despairing, dispirited, forlorn, gloomy, grief-stricken, heartbroken, heavy-hearted,

hopeless, inconsolable, melancholy, miserable, sad, unhappy, unsolaced, woeful, wretched.
antonyms cheerful, cheery.

discontent *n.* discontentment, displeasure, disquiet, dissatisfaction, envy, fretfulness, impatience, regret, restlessness, uneasiness, unhappiness, unrest, vexation.
antonym content.

discontented *adj.* brassed off, browned off, cheesed off, complaining, disaffected, disgruntled, displeased, dissatisfied, exasperated, fed up, fretful, impatient, miserable, scunnered, unhappy, vexed.
antonyms contented, happy, satisfied.

discontinue *v.* abandon, break off, cancel, cease, drop, end, finish, halt, interrupt, pause, quit, stop, suspend, terminate.
antonym continue.

discontinuity *n.* breach, disconnectedness, disconnection, disjointedness, disruption, disunion, incoherence, interruption, rupture.
antonym continuity.

discontinuous *adj.* broken, disconnected, fitful, intermittent, interrupted, irregular, periodic, punctuated, spasmodic.
antonym continuous.

discord *n.* cacophony, clashing, conflict, contention, difference, din, disagreement, discordance, disharmony, dispute, dissension, dissonance, disunity, division, friction, harshness, incompatibility, jangle, jarring, opposition, racket, rupture, split, strife, tumult, variance, wrangling.
antonyms agreement, concord, harmony.

discordant *adj.* absonant, at odds, cacophonous, clashing, conflicting, contradictory, contrary, different, disagreeing, disharmonic, disharmonious, dissonant, grating, harsh, incompatible, incongruous, inconsistent, inharmonious, jangling, jarring, opposite, shrill, strident, unmelodious, untuneful.
antonyms concordant, harmonious.

discount[1] *v.* disbelieve, disregard, gloss over, ignore, overlook.

discount[2] *n.* abatement, allowance, concession, cut, deduction, mark-down, rebate, rebatement, reduction.

discountenance *v.* abash, chagrin, confuse, discompose, disconcert, discourage, embarrass, humble, humiliate, shame.
antonyms countenance, support.

discourage *v.* abash, awe, check, chill, cow, curb, damp, dampen, dash, daunt, deject, demoralise, deprecate, depress, deter, discountenance, disfavour, dishearten, dismay, dispirit, dissuade, frighten, hinder, inhibit, intimidate, overawe, prevent, put off, restrain, scare, unman, unnerve.
antonyms encourage, favour, hearten, inspire.

discouraged *adj.* chopfallen, crestfallen, dashed, daunted, depressed, deterred, disheartened, dismayed, dispirited, downcast, glum, pessimistic.
antonyms encouraged, heartened.

discouragement *n.* constraint, curb, damp, damper, dejection, depression, despair, despondency, deterrent, disappointment, discomfiture, disincentive, dismay, dismayedness, downheartedness, hindrance, hopelessness, impediment, obstacle, opposition, pessimism, rebuff, restraint, setback.
antonym encouragement, incentive.

discouraging *adj.* dampening, daunting, dehortatory, depressing, disappointing, disheartening, dispiriting, dissuasive, dissuasory, inauspicious, off-putting, unfavourable, unpropitious.
antonyms encouraging, heartening.

discourse *n.* address, chat, communication, conversation, converse, descant, dialogue, discussion, disquisition, dissertation, essay, exercitation, homily, lecture, oration, sermon, speech, talk, treatise.
v. confer, converse, debate, declaim, descant, dialogise, discuss, dissent, dissertate, expatiate, jaw, lecture, lucubrate, talk.

discourteous *adj.* abrupt, bad-mannered, boorish, brusque, curt, disrespectful, ill-bred, ill-mannered, impolite, insolent, offhand, rude, slighting, unceremonious, uncivil, uncourteous, ungracious, unmannerly.
antonyms courteous, polite, respectful.

discourtesy *n.* affront, bad manners, disrespectfulness, ill-breeding, impertinence, impoliteness, incivility, indecorousness, indecorum, insolence, insult, rebuff, rudeness, slight, snub, ungraciousness, unmannerliness.
antonyms courtesy, politeness.

discover *v.* ascertain, conceive, contrive, descry, design, detect, determine, devise, dig up, discern, disclose, espy, find, invent, learn, light on, locate, notice, originate, perceive, pioneer, realise, recognise, reveal, see, spot, suss out, uncover, unearth.
antonyms conceal, hide.

discoverer *n.* author, explorer, finder, founder, initiator, inventor, originator, pioneer.

discovery *n.* ascertainment, breakthrough, coup, detection, disclosure, espial, eureka, exploration, find, finding, innovation, introduction, invention, locating, location, origination, revelation, uncovering.
antonym concealment.

discredit *v.* blame, censure, challenge, defame, degrade, deny, disbelieve, discount, disgrace, dishonour, disparage, dispute, distrust, doubt, explode, mistrust, question, reproach, slander, slur, smear, vilify.
antonyms believe, credit.
n. aspersion, blame, censure, disgrace, dishonour, disrepute, distrust, doubt, ignominy, ill-repute, imputation, mistrust, odium, opprobrium, question, reproach, scandal, scepticism, shame, slur, smear, stigma, suspicion.
antonym credit.

discreditable *adj.* blameworthy, degrading, disgraceful, dishonourable, humiliating, ignoble, ignominious, improper, infamous,

reprehensible, scandalous, shameful, unbecoming, unprincipled, unworthy.
antonyms creditable, worthy.
discredited *adj.* debunked, discarded, disgraced, dishonoured, exploded, exposed, outworn, refuted, rejected.
discreet *adj.* careful, cautious, circumspect, considerate, delicate, diplomatic, discerning, guarded, judicious, politic, prudent, reserved, sagacious, sensible, softly-softly, tactful, wary.
antonyms careless, indiscreet, tactless.
discrepancy *n.* conflict, contrariety, difference, disagreement, discordance, disparity, dissimilarity, dissonance, divergence, imparity, incongruity, inconsistency, inequality, variance, variation.
discrete *adj.* detached, disconnected, discontinuous, disjoined, disjunct, distinct, individual, separate, unattached.
discretion *n.* acumen, care, carefulness, caution, choice, circumspection, consideration, diplomacy, discernment, disposition, heedfulness, inclination, judgement, judiciousness, liking, maturity, mind, option, pleasure, predilection, preference, prudence, responsibility, sagacity, tact, volition, wariness, will, wisdom, wish.
antonym indiscretion.
discriminate[1] *v.* assess, differentiate, discern, distinguish, evaluate, make a distinction, segregate, separate, sift, tell apart.
antonyms confound, confuse.
discriminate[2] **(against)** *v.* be biased, be prejudiced, disfavour, victimise.
discriminating *adj.* acute, astute, critical, cultivated, discerning, discriminant, fastidious, nasute, particular, perceptive, selective, sensitive, tasteful.
discrimination[1] *n.* bias, bigotry, favouritism, inequity, intolerance, Jim Crow, prejudice, unfairness.
discrimination[2] *n.* acumen, acuteness, discernment, insight, judgement, keenness, penetration, perception, percipience, refinement, sagacity, subtlety, taste.
discriminatory[1] *adj.* biased, discriminative, favouring, inequitable, loaded, one-sided, partial, partisan, preferential, prejudiced, prejudicial, unfair, unjust, weighted.
antonyms fair, impartial, unbiased.
discriminatory[2] *adj.* analytical, astute, differentiating, discerning, discriminating, perceptive, percipient, perspicacious.
discursive *adj.* circuitous, desultory, diffuse, digressive, discursory, erratic, long-winded, loose, meandering, prolix, rambling, wideranging.
antonyms brief, short.
discuss *v.* argue, confer, consider, consult, converse, debate, deliberate, examine, lay heads together, rap.
discussion *n.* analysis, argument, colloquium, colloquy, confabulation, conference, consideration, consultation, conversation,

debate, deliberation, dialogue, discourse, examination, exchange, gabfest, moot, quodlibet, rap, review, scrutiny, seminar, symposium, talkfest.
disdain *v.* belittle, contemn, deride, despise, disavow, disregard, misprise, pooh-pooh, rebuff, reject, scorn, slight, sneer at, spurn, undervalue.
antonyms admire, respect.
n. arrogance, contempt, contumely, deprecation, derision, dislike, haughtiness, hauteur, imperiousness, indifference, scorn, sneering, snobbishness, superciliousness.
antonyms admiration, respect.
disdainful *adj.* aloof, arrogant, contemptuous, derisive, haughty, hoity-toity, imperious, insolent, proud, scornful, sneering, supercilious, superior, uppish.
antonyms admiring, respectful.
disease *n.* affection, affliction, ailment, blight, cancer, canker, complaint, condition, contagion, contamination, disorder, distemper, epidemic, epizootic, idiopathy, ill-health, illness, indisposition, infection, infirmity, malady, malaise, murrain, pest, plague, sickness, upset.
antonym health.
diseased *adj.* ailing, contaminated, distemperate, infected, poisoned, rotten, sick, sickly, tainted, unhealthy, unsound, unwell, unwholesome.
antonym healthy.
disembark *v.* alight, arrive, debark, detrain, disbark, land.
antonym embark.
disembodied *adj.* bodiless, disbodied, discorporate, disfleshed, ghostly, immaterial, incorporeal, intangible, phantom, spectral, spiritual, unbodied.
disembowel *v.* disbowel, draw, embowel, eviscerate, exenterate, gralloch, gut, paunch.
disenchanted *adj.* blasé, cynical, disappointed, disillusioned, fed up, indifferent, jaundiced, scunnered, soured, undeceived.
disenchantment *n.* cynicism, disappointment, disillusion, disillusionment, revulsion, scunner.
disengage *v.* detach, disconnect, disentangle, disentwine, disinvolve, disjoin, disunite, divide, ease, extricate, free, liberate, loosen, release, separate, undo, unloose, untie, untwine, withdraw.
antonyms attach, connect, engage.
disengaged *adj.* disentangled, free(d), heart-free, heart-whole, inactive, liberated, loose, released, separate(d), unattached, unconnected, unhitched, unoccupied.
antonyms connected, joined, united.
disentangle *v.* clarify, debarrass, detach, disconnect, disembarrass, disengage, disentwine, disinvolve, extricate, free, loose, ravel out, resolve, separate, sever, simplify, unfold, unravel, unsnarl, untangle, untwine, untwist.
antonym entangle.
disfavour *n.* disapprobation, disapproval,

discredit, disesteem, disgrace, disgust, dislike, displeasure, unpopularity.
antonym favour.

disfigure *v.* blemish, damage, deface, deform, disfeature, distort, injure, maim, mar, mutilate, scar, spoil, uglify.
antonym adorn.

disfigured *adj.* damaged, defaced, deformed, flawed, ruined, scarred, spoilt, ugly.
antonym adorned.

disfigurement *n.* blemish, defacement, defect, deformity, disgrace, distortion, impairment, injury, mutilation, scar, spot, stain, uglification.
antonym adornment.

disgorge *v.* belch, discharge, effuse, eject, empty, expel, regorge, regurgitate, relinquish, renounce, spew, spout, surrender, throw up, vomit.

disgrace *n.* aspersion, attaint, baseness, blemish, blot, contempt, defamation, degradation, discredit, disesteem, disfavour, dishonour, disrepute, dog-house, ignominy, infamy, obloquy, odium, opprobium, reproach, scandal, shame, slur, stain, stigma.
antonyms esteem, honour, respect.
v. abase, attaint, defame, degrade, discredit, disfavour, dishonour, disparage, humiliate, reproach, scandalise, shame, slur, stain, stigmatise, sully, taint.
antonyms honour, respect.

disgraced *adj.* branded, degraded, discredited, dishonoured, humiliated, in the doghouse, stigmatised.
antonyms honoured, respected.

disgraceful *adj.* appalling, blameworthy, contemptible, degrading, detestable, discreditable, dishonourable, disreputable, dreadful, ignominious, infamous, low, mean, opprobrious, scandalous, shameful, shocking, unworthy.
antonyms honourable, respectable.

disgruntled *adj.* annoyed, brassed off, browned off, cheesed off, discontented, displeased, dissatisfied, grumpy, irritated, malcontent, peeved, peevish, petulant, put out, scunnered, sulky, sullen, testy, vexed.
antonyms pleased, satisfied.

disguise *v.* camouflage, cloak, conceal, cover, deceive, dissemble, dissimulate, dress up, explain away, fake, falsify, fudge, hide, mask, misrepresent, screen, secrete, shroud, veil.
antonyms expose, reveal, uncover.
n. camouflage, cloak, concealment, costume, cover, coverture, deception, dissimulation, façade, front, get-up, mask, masquerade, pretence, screen, semblance, travesty, trickery, veil, veneer, visor.

disguised *adj.* camouflaged, cloaked, covert, fake, false, feigned, incognito, made up, masked, undercover, unrecognisable, visored.

disgust *v.* displease, nauseate, offend, outrage, put off, repel, revolt, scandalise, scunner, sicken.

antonyms delight, gratify, tempt.
n. abhorrence, abomination, antipathy, aversion, detestation, dislike, disrelish, distaste, hatefulness, hatred, loathing, nausea, odium, repugnance, repulsion, revulsion.
antonyms admiration, liking.

disgusted *adj.* appalled, nauseated, offended, outraged, repelled, repulsed, scandalised, scunnered, sick (and tired), sickened.
antonyms attracted, delighted.

disgusting *adj.* abominable, detestable, distasteful, foul, gross, hateful, loathsome, nasty, nauseating, nauseous, objectionable, obnoxious, obscene, odious, offensive, repellent, repugnant, revolting, shameless, sickening, sick-making, stinking, ugsome, unappetising, vile, vulgar.
antonyms attractive, delightful, pleasant.

dish[1] *n.* bowl, fare, food, plate, platter, porringer, ramekin, recipe, salver, trencher.
dish out allocate, distribute, dole out, give out, hand out, hand round, inflict, mete out.
dish up dispense, ladle, prepare, present, produce, scoop, serve, spoon.
dish[2] *v.* finish, ruin, spoil, torpedo, wreck.

disharmony *n.* clash, conflict, disaccord, discord, discordance, dissonance, friction, incompatibility.
antonym harmony.

dishearten *v.* cast down, crush, damp, dampen, dash, daunt, deject, depress, deter, discourage, dismay, dispirit, frighten, weary.
antonyms encourage, hearten.

disheartened *adj.* crestfallen, crushed, daunted, dejected, depressed, disappointed, discouraged, dismayed, dispirited, downcast, downhearted, frightened, weary.
antonyms encouraged, heartened.

dishevelled *adj.* bedraggled, blowsy, disarranged, disordered, frowsy, messy, mussy, ruffled, rumpled, slovenly, tousled, uncombed, unkempt, untidy.
antonyms neat, spruce, tidy.

dishonest *adj.* bent, cheating, corrupt, crafty, crooked, deceitful, deceiving, deceptive, designing, disreputable, double-dealing, false, fraudulent, guileful, immoral, knavish, lying, mendacious, perfidious, shady, snide, swindling, treacherous, unethical, unfair, unprincipled, unscrupulous, untrustworthy, untruthful, wrongful.
antonyms fair, honest, scrupulous, trustworthy.

dishonesty *n.* cheating, chicanery, corruption, craft, criminality, crookedness, deceit, duplicity, falsehood, falsity, fraud, fraudulence, graft, immorality, improbity, insincerity, mendacity, perfidy, stealing, treachery, trickery, unscrupulousness, wiliness.
antonyms honesty, truthfulness.

dishonour *v.* abase, blacken, corrupt, debase, debauch, defame, defile, deflower, degrade, demean, discredit, disgrace, disparage, pollute, rape, ravish, seduce, shame, sully.
antonym honour.

n. abasement, abuse, affront, aspersion, degradation, discourtesy, discredit, disfavour, disgrace, disrepute, ignominy, imputation, indignity, infamy, insult, obloquy, odium, offence, opprobrium, outrage, reproach, scandal, shame, slight, slur.
antonym honour.

dishonourable *adj.* base, blackguardly, contemptible, corrupt, despicable, discreditable, disgraceful, disreputable, ignoble, ignominous, infamous, scandalous, shameful, shameless, treacherous, unethical, unprincipled, unscrupulous, untrustworthy, unworthy.
antonym honourable.

disillusioned *adj.* disabused, disappointed, disenchanted, enlightened, indifferent, undeceived, unenthusiastic.

disincentive *n.* barrier, constraint, damper, determent, deterrent, discouragement, dissuasion, hindrance, impediment, obstacle, repellent, restriction, turn-off.
antonyms encouragement, incentive.

disinclination *n.* alienation, antipathy, averseness, aversion, demur, dislike, loathness, objection, opposition, reluctance, repugnance, resistance, unwillingness.
antonym inclination.

disinclined *adj.* antipathetic, averse, hesitant, indisposed, loath, opposed, reluctant, resistant, undisposed, unenthusiastic, unwilling.
antonyms inclined, willing.

disinfect *v.* clean, cleanse, decontaminate, deodorise, depurate, fumigate, purge, purify, sanitise, sterilise.
antonyms contaminate, infect.

disinfectant *n.* antiseptic, decontaminative, depurant, germicide, sanitiser, steriliser.

disinfection *n.* cleansing, decontamination, depuration, fumigation, purification, sanitisation, sterilisation.

disingenuous *adj.* artful, cunning, deceitful, designing, devious, dishonest, duplicitous, guileful, insidious, insincere, shifty, two-faced, uncandid, wily.
antonyms artless, frank, ingenuous, naive.

disintegrate *v.* break up, crumble, decompose, disunite, fall apart, moulder, rot, separate, shatter, splinter.
antonyms combine, merge, unite.

disinterest *n.* candidness, detachment, disinterestedness, dispassionateness, equitableness, equity, fairness, impartiality, justice, neutrality, unbiasedness.
antonym interest.

disinterested *adj.* candid, detached, dispassionate, equitable, even-handed, impartial, impersonal, neutral, open-minded, unbiased, uninvolved, unprejudiced, unselfish.
antonyms biased, concerned, interested, prejudiced.

disjoin *v.* detach, disannex, disconnect, disengage, dismember, dissociate, disunite, divide, divorce, isolate, partition, segregate, separate, sever, split, uncouple.
antonyms connect, join.

disjoint *v.* anatomise, disarrange, disarticulate, discompose, dislocate, dismember, disorder, displace, dissect, unjoint.

disjointed *adj.* aimless, broken, confused, dearticulated, disarticulated, disconnected, dislocated, disordered, displaced, disunited, divided, fitful, incoherent, loose, rambling, separated, spasmodic, split, unconnected, unjointed.
antonym coherent.

dislike *n.* animosity, animus, antagonism, antipathy, aversion, detestation, disapprobation, disapproval, disgust, disinclination, displeasure, disrelish, distaste, dyspathy, enmity, hatred, hostility, loathing, repugnance.
antonyms attachment, liking, predilection.
v. abhor, abominate, despise, detest, disapprove, disfavour, disrelish, hate, keck, loathe, scorn, shun.
antonyms favour, like, prefer.

dislocate *v.* derange, disarray, disarticulate, disconnect, disengage, disjoint, disorder, displace, disrupt, disturb, disunite, luxate, misplace, shift, unhinge.

dislocation *n.* derangement, disarray, disarticulation, disconnection, disengagement, disorder, disorganisation, disruption, disturbance, luxation, misarrangement, misarray, misplacement, unhingement, unhinging.
antonym order.

dislodge *v.* displace, disturb, eject, extricate, move, oust, remove, shift, uproot.

disloyal *adj.* apostate, disaffected, faithless, false, perfidious, seditious, subversive, traitorous, treacherous, treasonable, two-faced, unfaithful, unleal, unpatriotic, untrustworthy, unwifely.
antonym loyal.

disloyalty *n.* apostasy, betrayal, double-dealing, falseness, falsity, inconstancy, infidelity, lese-majesty, perfidiousness, perfidy, sedition, treachery, treason, unfaithfulness.
antonym loyalty.

dismal *adj.* black, bleak, burdan, cheerless, dark, depressing, despondent, discouraging, doleful, dolorous, dowie, dreary, dreich, forlorn, funereal, ghostful, gloomy, gruesome, hopeless, incompetent, inept, lac(h)rymose, lonesome, long-faced, long-visaged, lowering, low-spirited, lugubrious, melancholy, poor, sad, sepulchral, sombre, sorrowful, stupid, thick, useless.
antonyms bright, cheerful.

dismantle *v.* demolish, demount, disassemble, dismount, raze, strike, strip, unrig.
antonym assemble.

dismay *v.* affright, alarm, appal, consternate, daunt, depress, disappoint, disconcert, discourage, dishearten, disillusion, dispirit, distress, frighten, horrify, paralyse, put off, scare, terrify, unnerve, unsettle.
antonym encourage.
n. agitation, alarm, anxiety, apprehension, consternation, disappointment, distress,

dread, fear, fright, funk, horror, panic, terror, trepidation, upset.
antonyms boldness, encouragement.

dismember *v.* amputate, anatomise, disject, disjoint, dislimb, dislocate, dissect, divellicate, divide, mutilate, piecemeal, rend, sever.
antonyms assemble, join.

dismemberment *n.* amputation, anatomisation, disjection, dislocation, dissection, division, mutilation.
antonyms assembly, joining, unifying.

dismiss *v.* axe, banish, bounce, bowler-hat, cashier, chassé, chuck, disband, discharge, discount, dispel, disperse, disregard, dissolve, drop, fire, free, give (someone) the push, lay off, let go, oust, pooh-pooh, reject, release, relegate, remove, repudiate, sack, send packing, set aside, shelve, spurn.
antonyms accept, appoint.

dismissal *n.* adjournment, cards, congé, dear John letter, discharge, dismission, end, expulsion, marching orders, mittimus, notice, release, removal, the boot, the bum's rush, the elbow, the mitten, the push, the sack, walking-orders, walking-papers, walking-ticket.
antonym appointment.

dismissive *adj.* contemptuous, disdainful, dismissory, off-hand, scornful, sneering.
antonyms concerned, interested.

dismount *v.* alight, descend, get down, light, unmount.
antonym mount.

disobedience *n.* contrariness, contumacity, contumacy, indiscipline, infraction, insubordination, mutiny, non-observance, recalcitrance, revolt, unruliness, waywardness.
antonym obedience.

disobedient *adj.* contrary, contumacious, defiant, disorderly, froward, insubordinate, intractable, mischievous, naughty, obstreperous, refractory, unruly, wayward, wilful.
antonym obedient.

f19**disobey** *v.* contravene, defy, disregard, flout, ignore, infringe, overstep, rebel, resist, transgress, violate.
antonym obey.

disoblige *v.* deny, disserve, refuse.
antonym oblige.

disobliging *adj.* awkward, bloody-minded, cussed, disagreeable, discourteous, inaccommodating, rude, unaccommodating, uncivil, unco-operative, unhelpful.
antonym obliging.

disorder *n.* affliction, ailment, brawl, chaos, clamour, clutter, commotion, complaint, confusion, derangement, disarray, disease, disorderliness, disorganisation, disturbance, fight, fracas, hubbub, hullabaloo, illness, indisposition, irregularity, jumble, malady, mess, misarrangement, misarray, misorder, misrule, muddle, muss(e), mussiness, quarrel, riot, rumpus, shambles, sickness, tumult, untidiness, uproar.
antonym order.

v. clutter, confound, confuse, derange, disarrange, discompose, disorganise, disrank, disturb, jumble, mess up, misorder, mix up, muddle, scatter, unsettle, upset.
antonyms arrange, organise.

disordered *adj.* confused, deranged, disarranged, dislocated, disorganised, displaced, higgledy-piggledy, indigest, jumbled, misplaced, muddle, mussy, onkus, out of kilter, turbid, untidy.
antonyms ordered, tidy.

disorderly *adj.* chaotic, confused, disordinate, disorganised, disruptive, higgledy-piggledy, indiscriminate, irregular, jumbled, lawless, messy, obstreperous, rebellious, refractory, riotous, rowdy, shambolic, stormy, tumultuous, turbulent, undisciplined, ungovernable, unlawful, unmanageable, unruly, unsystematic, untidy.
antonyms tidy, well-behaved.

disorganisation *n.* chaos, confusion, derangement, disarray, disjointedness, dislocation, disorder, disruption, incoherence, unconnectedness.
antonyms order, tidiness.

disorganise *v.* break up, confuse, derange, destroy, disarrange, discompose, disorder, disrank, disrupt, disturb, jumble, muddle, play havoc with, play hell with, unsettle, upset.
antonym organise.

disorganised *adj.* chaotic, confused, disordered, haphazard, jumbled, muddled, shambolic, shuffled, topsy-turvy, unmethodical, unorganised, unregulated, unsifted, unsorted, unstructured, unsystematic, unsystematised.
antonyms organised, tidy.

disorientate *v.* confuse, dislocate, disorient, faze, feeze, mislead, muddle, perplex, puzzle, upset.

disorientated *adj.* adrift, astray, at sea, bewildered, confused, disoriented, lost, mixed up, muddled, perplexed, puzzled, unbalanced, unsettled, upset.

disown *v.* abandon, abnegate, cast off, deny, disacknowledge, disallow, disavow, disclaim, reject, renounce, repudiate, unget.
antonym accept.

disparage *v.* belittle, criticise, decry, defame, degrade, denigrate, deprecate, depreciate, deride, derogate, detract from, discredit, disdain, dishonour, dismiss, disvalue, malign, minimise, ridicule, run down, scorn, slander, traduce, underestimate, underrate, undervalue, vilify, vilipend.
antonym praise.

disparagement *n.* aspersion, belittlement, condemnation, contempt, contumely, criticism, debasement, decrial, decrying, degradation, denunciation, deprecation, depreciation, derision, derogation, detraction, discredit, disdain, ridicule, scorn, slander, underestimation, vilification.
antonym praise.

disparate *adj.* contrary, contrasting, different,

discordant, discrepant, dissimilar, distinct, diverse, unequal, unlike.
antonyms equal, similar.

disparity *n.* contrast, difference, discrepancy, disproportion, dissimilarity, dissimilitude, distinction, gap, imbalance, imparity, incongruity, inequality, unevenness, unlikeness.
antonyms equality, similarity.

dispassionate *adj.* calm, candid, collected, composed, cool, detached, disinterested, fair, impartial, impersonal, imperturbable, indifferent, moderate, neutral, objective, quiet, serene, sober, temperate, unbiased, unemotional, unexcitable, unexcited, uninvolved, unmoved, unprejudiced, unruffled.
antonyms biased, emotional.

dispatch[1], **despatch** *v.* accelerate, conclude, discharge, dismiss, dispose of, expedite, finish, hasten, hurry, perform, quicken, settle.
antonym impede.
n. alacrity, celerity, dépêche, expedition, haste, precipitateness, promptitude, promptness, quickness, rapidity, speed, swiftness.
antonym slowness.

dispatch[2], **despatch** *v.* consign, express, forward, remit, send, transmit.
n. account, bulletin, communication, communiqué, document, instruction, item, letter, message, missive, news, piece, report, story.

dispatch[3], **despatch** *v.* assassinate, bump off, execute, kill, murder, rub out, slaughter, slay, waste.

dispel *v.* allay, banish, discuss, dismiss, disperse, dissipate, drive off, eliminate, expel, melt away, resolve, rout, scatter.
antonym give rise to.

dispensable *adj.* disposable, expendable, inessential, needless, non-essential, replaceable, superfluous, unnecessary, useless.
antonym indispensable.

dispensation *n.* administration, allotment, appointment, apportionment, award, bestowal, conferment, consignment, derogation, direction, disbursement, distribution, dole, economy, endowment, exception, exemption, immunity, indulgence, licence, management, part, permission, plan, portion, privilege, quota, regulation, relaxation, relief, remission, reprieve, scheme, share, stewardship, supplying, system.

dispensatory *adj.* derogative, disobligatory, dispensative.

dispense *v.* administer, allocate, allot, apply, apportion, assign, deal out, direct, disburse, discharge, distribute, dole out, enforce, except, excuse, execute, exempt, exonerate, implement, let off, measure, mete out, mix, operate, prepare, release, relieve, reprieve, share, supply, undertake.

dispense with abolish, cancel, dispose of, disregard, forgo, ignore, omit, pass over, relinquish, waive.
antonyms accept, use.

disperse *v.* broadcast, circulate, diffuse, disappear, disband, dismiss, dispel, disseminate,

dissipate, dissolve, distribute, drive off, evanesce, melt away, rout, scatter, separate, spread, strew, vanish.
antonym gather.

dispersion *n.* broadcast, circulation, diaspora, diffusion, discussion, dispersal, dissemination, dissipation, distribution, galut(h), scattering, spread.

dispirit *v.* damp, dampen, dash, deject, depress, deter, discourage, dishearten, put a damper on, sadden.
antonym encourage.

dispirited *adj.* brassed off, browned off, cast down, crestfallen, dejected, depressed, despondent, discouraged, disheartened, down, downcast, fed up, gloomy, glum, low, morose, sad.
antonym encouraged.

displace *v.* cashier, crowd out, depose, derange, disarrange, discard, discharge, dislocate, dislodge, dismiss, dispossess, disturb, eject, evict, fire, luxate, misplace, move, oust, remove, replace, sack, shift, succeed, supersede, supplant, transpose, unsettle.

displaced *adj.* disarranged, ectopic, misplaced.

displacement *n.* disarrangement, disturbance, ectopia, ectopy, heterotaxis, heterotopia, misplacement.
antonym order.

display *v.* betray, blazon, boast, demonstrate, disclose, evidence, evince, exhibit, expand, expose, extend, flash, flaunt, flourish, manifest, model, parade, present, reveal, show, show off, showcase, splash, sport, unfold, unfurl, unveil, vaunt, wear.
antonym hide.
n. array, demonstration, étalage, exhibition, exposition, exposure, flourish, manifestation, ostentation, pageant, parade, pomp, presentation, revelation, show, spectacle, splurge.

displease *v.* aggravate, anger, annoy, disgust, dissatisfy, exasperate, gall, get, incense, infuriate, irk, irritate, nettle, offend, peeve, pique, provoke, put out, rile, upset, vex.
antonyms calm, please.

displeased *n.* aggravated, angry, annoyed, chuffed, exasperated, furious, irritated, peeved, piqued, put out, upset.
antonym pleased.

displeasure *n.* anger, annoyance, disapprobation, disapproval, discontent, disfavour, disgruntlement, dudgeon, huff, indignation, irritation, offence, pique, resentment, vexation, wrath.
antonyms gratification, pleasure.

disport *v.* amuse, beguile, bound, caper, cavort, cheer, delight, divert, entertain, frisk, frolic, gambol, play, revel, romp, sport.

disposal *n.* arrangement, array, assignment, authority, bequest, bestowal, clearance, conduct, consignment, control, conveyance, determination, direction, discarding, discretion, dispensation, disposition, distribution, dumping, ejection, gift, government, jettisoning, management, ordering, position, regula-

tion, relinquishment, removal, responsibility, riddance, scrapping, settlement, transfer.
antonym provision.

dispose *v.* actuate, adapt, adjust, align, arrange, array, bias, condition, determine, dispone, distribute, fix, group, incline, induce, influence, lay, lead, marshal, motivate, move, order, place, position, predispose, prompt, put, range, rank, regulate, set, settle, situate, stand, tempt.

dispose of bestow, deal with, decide, destroy, determine, discard, dump, end, get rid of, give, jettison, kibosh, make over, put the kibosh on, scrap, sell, settle, transfer, unload.
antonym provide.

disposed *adj.* apt, given, inclined, liable, likely, minded, moved, predisposed, prone, ready, subject, willing.
antonym disinclined.

disposition *n.* adjustment, arrangement, bent, bias, character, classification, constitution, control, direction, disposal, distribution, grain, grouping, habit, inclination, kidney, leaning, make-up, management, nature, ordering, organisation, placement, predisposition, proclivity, proneness, propensity, readiness, regulation, spirit, temper, temperament, tendency, velleity.

dispossess *v.* deprive, dislodge, disseise, divest, eject, evict, expel, oust, rob, strip, unhouse.
antonyms give, provide.

dispossession *n.* dethronement, dethroning, disseisin, ejection, ejectment, eviction, expulsion, ousting.
antonym possession.

disproportion *n.* asymmetry, discrepancy, disparity, imbalance, imparity, inadequacy, inequality, insufficiency, lopsidedness, unevenness.
antonyms balance, equality.

disproportionate *adj.* excessive, inappropriate, incommensurate, inordinate, unbalanced, unequal, uneven, unreasonable.
antonyms appropriate, balanced.

disprove *v.* answer, confute, contradict, controvert, discredit, explode, expose, invalidate, negate, rebut, refute.
antonym prove.

disputable *adj.* arguable, controversial, debatable, doubtful, dubious, litigious, moot, questionable, uncertain.
antonym indisputable.

disputation *n.* argumentation, controversy, debate, dispute, dissension, polemics, quodlibet.

disputatious *adj.* argumentative, cantankerous, captious, cavilling, contentious, litigious, polemical, pugnacious, quarrelsome, wranglesome.

dispute *v.* altercate, argue, brawl, challenge, clash, contend, contest, contradict, controvert, debate, deny, discuss, doubt, gainsay, impugn, litigate, moot, oppugn, quarrel, question, spar, squabble, traverse, wrangle.
antonym agree.

n. altercation, argument, brawl, conflict, contention, controversy, debate, disagreement, discord, discussion, dissension, disturbance, feud, friction, quarrel, spar, squabble, strife, wrangle.
antonym agreement.

disputer *n.* adversary, antagonist, arguer, contender, contestant, debater, discursist, discutant, opponent.

disqualified *adj.* debarred, eliminated, ineligible.
antonyms accepted, eligible, qualified.

disqualify *v.* debar, disable, disauthorise, disentitle, dishabilitate, disprivilege, incapacitate, invalidate, preclude, prohibit, rule out, unfit.
antonyms accept, allow.

disquiet *n.* alarm, angst, anxiety, concern, disquietude, distress, disturbance, fear, foreboding, fretfulness, nervousness, restlessness, trouble, uneasiness, unrest, worry.
antonym calmness.

v. agitate, annoy, bother, concern, discompose, distress, disturb, fret, harass, hassle, incommode, perturb, pester, plague, shake, trouble, unsettle, upset, vex, worry.
antonym calm.

disquieting *adj.* annoying, bothersome, disconcerting, disquietful, disquietive, distressing, disturbing, irritating, perturbing, troubling, unnerving, unsettling, upsetting, vexing, worrying.
antonym calming.

disquisition *n.* descant, discourse, dissertation, essay, exposition, monograph, paper, sermon, thesis, treatise.

disregard *v.* brush aside, cold-shoulder, contemn, despise, discount, disdain, disobey, disparage, ignore, laugh off, make light of, neglect, overlook, pass over, pooh-pooh, slight, snub, turn a blind eye to.
antonyms note, pay attention to.

n. brush-off, contempt, disdain, disesteem, disrespect, heedlessness, ignoring, inattention, indifference, neglect, negligence, oversight, slight.
antonym attention.

disrepair *n.* collapse, decay, deterioration, dilapidation, ruin, ruination, shabbiness, unrepair.
antonyms good repair, restoration.

disreputable *adj.* base, contemptible, derogatory, discreditable, disgraceful, dishonourable, disorderly, disrespectable, ignominious, infamous, louche, low, mean, notorious, opprobrious, scandalous, seedy, shady, shameful, shocking, unprincipled.
antonyms decent, honourable.

disrepute *n.* discredit, disesteem, disfavour, disgrace, dishonour, disreputation, ignominy, infamy, obloquy, shame.
antonyms esteem, honour.

disrespect *n.* cheek, contempt, discourtesy, dishonour, disregard, impertinence, impoliteness, impudence, incivility, insolence, irrever-

ence, misesteem, rudeness, unmannerliness.
antonym respect.

disrespectful *adj.* bad-tempered, cheeky, contemptuous, discourteous, impertinent, impolite, impudent, insolent, insulting, irreverent, rude, uncivil, unmannerly.
antonym respectful.

disrobe *v.* bare, denude, disapparel, divest, remove, shed, strip, take off, unclothe, uncover, undress.
antonyms cover, dress.

disrupt *v.* agitate, break into, break up, confuse, derange, dislocate, disorder, disorganise, disturb, interrupt, intrude, obstruct, spoil, unsettle, upset.

disruption *n.* burst-up, bust-up, cataclasm, confusion, disarray, disorder, disorderliness, dissembly, dissolution, disturbance, interference, interruption, stoppage, upheaval.

disruptive *adj.* boisterous, disorderly, distracting, disturbing, obstreperous, troublesome, turbulent, undisciplined, unruly, unsettling, upsetting.
antonym well-behaved.

dissatisfaction *n.* annoyance, chagrin, disappointment, discomfort, discontent, dislike, dismay, displeasure, distress, exasperation, frustration, irritation, non-fulfilment, regret, resentment, unfulfilment, unhappiness.
antonyms fulfilment, satisfaction.

dissatisfied *adj.* chuffed, disappointed, discontented, disgruntled, displeased, fed up, frustrated, unfulfilled, unhappy, unsatisfied.
antonyms fulfilled, satisfied.

dissatisfy *v.* annoy, disappoint, discontent, disgruntle, displease, exasperate, frustrate, irritate, put out, vex.

dissect *v.* analyse, anatomise, break down, dismember, examine, explore, inspect, investigate, pore over, scrutinise, study.

dissection *n.* analysis, anatomisation, anatomy, autopsy, breakdown, dismemberment, examination, inspection, investigation, necropsy, scrutiny, study.

dissemble *v.* affect, camouflage, cloak, conceal, counterfeit, cover up, disguise, dissimulate, fake, falsify, feign, hide, mask, play possum, pretend, sham, simulate.
antonym admit.

dissembler *n.* charlatan, con man, deceiver, dissimulator, fake, feigner, fraud, humbug, hypocrite, impostor, pretender, trickster, whited sepulchre.

disseminate *v.* broadcast, circulate, diffuse, disperse, dissipate, distribute, evangelise, proclaim, promulgate, propagate, publicise, publish, scatter, sow, spread.

dissemination *n.* broadcasting, circulation, diffusion, dispersion, distribution, evangelisation, evangelism, promulgation, propagation, publication, publishing, spread.

dissension *n.* conflict, contention, difference, disagreement, discord, discordance, dispeace, dispute, dissent, friction, quarrel, strife, variance.

antonyms agreement, peace.

dissent *v.* decline, differ, disagree, disconsent, object, protest, quibble, refuse.
antonyms agree, consent.
n. difference, disagreement, discord, dissension, dissidence, nonconformity, objection, opposition, quibble, refusal, resistance.
antonym agreement.

dissenter *n.* disputant, dissident, nonconformist, objector, protestant, protestor, recusant, schismatic, sectary.

dissentient *adj.* conflicting, differing, disagreeing, dissenting, dissident, opposing, protesting, recusant.
antonym arguing.

dissertation *n.* critique, discourse, disquisition, essay, exposition, monograph, paper, prolegomena, propaedeutic, thesis, treatise.

disservice *n.* bad turn, disfavour, harm, injury, injustice, unkindness, wrong.
antonym favour.

dissever *v.* cleave, disunite, divorce, part, rend, rift, rive, separate, sever, split, sunder.

dissidence *n.* disagreement, discordance, dispute, dissent, feud, recusancy, rupture, schism, variance.
antonyms agreement, peace.

dissident *adj.* differing, disagreeing, discordant, dissentient, dissenting, heterodox, nonconformist, recusant, schismatic.
antonyms acquiescent, agreeing.
n. agitator, dissenter, protestor, rebel, recusant, refus(e)nik, schismatic.
antonym assenter.

dissimilar *adj.* different, disparate, divergent, diverse, heterogeneous, incompatible, mismatched, unlike, unrelated, various.
antonyms compatible, similar.

dissimilarity *n.* difference, discrepancy, disparity, dissimilitude, distinction, divergence, diversity, heterogeneity, incomparability, incompatibility, unlikeness, unrelatedness.
antonyms compatibility, similarity.

dissimulate *v.* camouflage, cloak, conceal, disguise, dissemble, fake, feign, hide, mask, pretend.

dissimulation *n.* act, affectation, concealment, deceit, deception, dissembling, double-dealing, duplicity, feigning, hypocrisy, play-acting, pretence, sham, wile.
antonym openness.

dissipate *v.* burn up, consume, deplete, disappear, dispel, disperse, dissolve, evaporate, expend, fritter away, lavish, rig, scatter, spend, squander, vanish, wanton, waste.
antonym accumulate.

dissipated *adj.* abandoned, consumed, debauched, destroyed, dissolute, exhausted, intemperate, profligate, rakehell, rakehelly, rakish, scattered, squandered, wasted.
antonyms conserved, virtuous.

dissipation *n.* abandonment, debauchery, disappearance, disintegration, dispersion, dissemination, dissoluteness, dissolution, excess, extravagance, intemperance, prodigality,

profligacy, rakery, rakishness, scattering, squandering, vanishing, wantonness, waste.
antonyms conservation, virtue.

dissociate *v.* break off, detach, disband, disconnect, disrupt, distance, divorce, isolate, leave, quit, segregate, separate.
antonyms attach, share.

dissociation *n.* break, detachment, disconnection, disengagement, dissevering, distancing, disunion, division, divorce, isolation, segregation, separation, severance, severing, split.
antonyms association, union.

dissolute *adj.* abandoned, corrupt, debauched, degenerate, depraved, dissipated, immoral, lax, lewd, libertine, licentious, loose, profligate, rakehell, rakehelly, rakish, unrestrained, vicious, wanton, wide, wild.
antonym virtuous.

dissoluteness *n.* abandon, corruption, debauchery, degeneracy, depravity, dissipation, immorality, lewdness, licence, licentiousness, profligacy, rakery, vice, wantonness.
antonym virtue.

dissolution *n.* adjournment, break-up, conclusion, death, decay, decomposition, demise, destruction, disappearance, disbandment, discontinuation, disintegration, dismissal, dispersal, disruption, dissembly, division, divorce, end, ending, evaporation, extinction, finish, liquefaction, melting, overthrow, parting, resolution, ruin, separation, solution, suspension, termination.
antonym unification.

dissolve *v.* break up, crumble, decompose, deliquesce, destroy, diffuse, disappear, discontinue, disintegrate, dismiss, disorganise, disperse, dissipate, disunite, divorce, dwindle, end, evanesce, evaporate, fade, flux, fuse, liquefy, loose, melt, overthrow, perish, ruin, separate, sever, soften, suspend, terminate, thaw, vanish, wind up.

dissonance *n.* cacophony, difference, disagreement, discord, discordance, discrepancy, disharmony, disparity, dissension, harshness, incongruity, inconsistency, jangle, jarring, variance.
antonym harmony.

dissonant *adj.* anomalous, cacophonous, different, differing, disagreeing, discordant, discrepant, disharmonious, dissentient, grating, harsh, incompatible, incongruous, inconsistent, inharmonious, irreconcilable, irregular, jangling, jarring, raucous, strident, tuneless, unmelodious.
antonyms compatible, harmonious.

dissuade *v.* dehort, deter, discourage, disincline, divert, expostulate, put off, remonstrate, warn.
antonym persuade.

dissuasion *n.* caution, dehortation, determent, deterrence, deterring, discouragement, expostulation, remonstrance, remonstration, setback.
antonym persuasion.

distance *n.* absence, aloofness, coldness, coolness, extent, farness, frigidity, gap, interval, isolation, lapse, length, range, reach, remoteness, remove, reserve, restraint, separation, space, span, stand-offishness, stiffness, stretch, width.

distant *adj.* abroad, afar, aloof, apart, ceremonious, cold, cool, disparate, dispersed, distinct, faint, far, faraway, far-flung, far-off, formal, haughty, indirect, indistinct, isolated, obscure, outlying, out-of-the-way, remote, removed, reserved, restrained, reticent, scattered, separate, slight, stand-offish, stiff, unapproachable, uncertain, unfriendly, withdrawn.
antonyms close, friendly.

distaste *n.* abhorrence, antipathy, aversion, detestation, discontent, discontentment, disfavour, disgust, disinclination, dislike, displeasure, disrelish, dissatisfaction, horror, loathing, repugnance, revulsion.
antonym inclination.

distasteful *adj.* abhorrent, aversive, disagreeable, displeasing, dissatisfying, loathsome, nasty, nauseous, objectionable, obnoxious, offensive, repugnant, repulsive, undesirable, uninviting, unpalatable, unpleasant, unsavoury.
antonym pleasing.

distend *v.* balloon, bloat, bulge, dilate, enlarge, expand, fill out, increase, inflate, intumesce, puff, stretch, swell, widen.
antonym deflate.

distended *adj.* astrut, bloated, dilated, emphysematous, enlarged, expanded, inflated, puffed-out, puffy, stretched, swollen, tumescent, varicose.
antonym deflated.

distension *n.* dilatation, dilation, emphysema, enlargement, expansion, extension, inflation, intumescence, spread, swelling, tumescence.

distil *v.* condense, drip, evaporate, extract, flow, purify, rectify, refine, sublimate, trickle, vaporise.

distinct *adj.* apparent, clear, clear-cut, decided, definite, detached, different, discrete, dissimilar, evident, individual, lucid, manifest, marked, noticeable, obvious, palpable, patent, plain, recognisable, separate, several, sharp, unambiguous, unconnected, unmistakable, well-defined.
antonyms fuzzy, hazy, indistinct.

distinction[1] *n.* characteristic, contradistinction, contrast, difference, differential, differentiation, diorism, discernment, discrimination, dissimilarity, distinctiveness, division, feature, individuality, mark, nuance, particularity, peculiarity, penetration, perception, quality, separation.

distinction[2] *n.* account, celebrity, consequence, credit, eminence, excellence, fame, glory, greatness, honour, importance, merit, name, note, prestige, prominence, quality, rank, renown, reputation, repute, significance, superiority, worth.
antonym insignificance.

distinctive 175 **distrust**

distinctive *adj.* characteristic, different, discriminative, discriminatory, distinguishing, extraordinary, idiosyncratic, individual, inimitable, original, peculiar, singular, special, typical, uncommon, unique.
antonym common.
distinctness *n.* clarity, clearness, difference, discreteness, disparateness, dissimilarity, dissociation, distinctiveness, individuality, lucidity, obviousness, plainness, sharpness, vividness.
antonyms fuzziness, haziness, indistinctness.
distinguish *v.* ascertain, categorise, celebrate, characterise, classify, decide, determine, differentiate, dignify, discern, discriminate, honour, immortalise, individualise, judge, know, make out, mark, perceive, pick out, recognise, see, separate, signalise, tell, tell apart.
distinguishable *adj.* appreciable, clear, conspicuous, discernible, evident, manifest, noticeable, observable, obvious, perceptible, plain, recognisable.
antonym indistinguishable.
distinguished *adj.* acclaimed, celebrated, conspicuous, distingué, eminent, eximious, extraordinary, famed, famous, illustrious, marked, nameworthy, notable, noted, outstanding, renowned, signal, striking, well-known.
antonyms insignificant, ordinary.
distinguishing *adj.* characteristic, different, differentiating, discriminative, discriminatory, distinctive, individual, individualistic, marked, peculiar, typical, unique.
distort *v.* bend, bias, buckle, colour, contort, deform, disfigure, falsify, garble, miscolour, misrepresent, misshape, pervert, skew, slant, torture, twist, warp, wrench, wrest, wring.
distorted *adj.* awry, biased, deformed, false, misshapen, skew, skewed, twisted, warped, wry.
antonym straight.
distortion *n.* bend, bias, buckle, colouring, contortion, crookedness, deformity, falsification, malformation, misrepresentation, obliquity, perversion, skew, slant, twist, warp.
distract *v.* agitate, amuse, beguile, bewilder, confound, confuse, derange, discompose, disconcert, disturb, divert, engross, entertain, faze, feeze, harass, madden, occupy, perplex, puzzle, sidetrack, torment, trouble.
distracted *adj.* agitated, bemused, bewildered, confounded, confused, crazy, deranged, distraught, éperdu(e), flustered, frantic, frenzied, grief-stricken, harassed, hassled, insane, mad, maddened, overwrought, perplexed, puzzled, raving, troubled, wild, worked up, wrought up.
antonyms calm, untroubled.
distracting *adj.* annoying, bewildering, confusing, disconcerting, disturbing, irritating, offputting, perturbing.
distraction *n.* aberration, abstraction, agitation, alienation, amusement, beguilement, bewilderment, commotion, confusion, delirium,

derangement, desperation, discord, disorder, disturbance, diversion, divertissement, entertainment, frenzy, hallucination, harassment, incoherence, insanity, interference, interruption, mania, pastime, recreation.
distraught *adj.* agitated, anxious, beside oneself, crazed, crazy, distracted, distressed, frantic, hysterical, mad, overwrought, raving, wild, worked up, wrought up.
antonyms calm, untroubled.
distress *n.* adversity, affliction, agony, anguish, anxiety, calamity, depravation, desolation, destitution, difficulties, discomfort, grief, hardship, heartache, indigence, katzenjammer, misery, misfortune, need, pain, pauperism, poverty, privation, sadness, sorrow, strait(s), suffering, torment, torture, trial, trouble, woe, worry, wretchedness.
antonyms comfort, ease, security.
v. afflict, agonise, bother, constrain, cut up, disturb, grieve, harass, harrow, pain, perplex, sadden, straiten, torment, trouble, upset, worry, wound.
antonyms assist, comfort.
distressed *adj.* afflicted, agitated, anxious, cut up, destitute, distracted, distraught, indigent, needy, poor, poverty-stricken, saddened, straitened, tormented, troubled, upset, worried, wretched.
antonyms calm, untroubled.
distressing *adj.* affecting, afflicting, afflictive, disquieting, distressful, disturbing, grievous, heart-breaking, hurtful, lamentable, nerveracking, painful, perturbing, sad, trying, unnerving, upsetting, worrying.
antonyms assuaging, pleasant.
distribute *v.* administer, allocate, allot, apportion, arrange, assign, assort, bestow, carve up, categorise, circulate, class, classify, convey, deal, deliver, diffuse, dish out, dispense, disperse, dispose, disseminate, divide, dole, file, give, group, hand out, mete, scatter, share, spread, strew.
antonyms collect, gather in.
distribution *n.* allocation, allotment, apportionment, arrangement, assortment, bestowal, bestowing, circulation, classification, dealing, delivery, diffusion, dispensation, dispersal, dispersion, disposition, dissemination, division, dole, handling, largition, location, mailing, marketing, partition, placement, propagation, scattering, sharing, spreading, trading, transport, transportation.
antonyms collection, gathering.
district *n.* area, canton, cantred, cantret, community, gau, hundred, locale, locality, neighbourhood, parish, precinct, quarter, region, sector, vicinity, ward.
distrust *v.* disbelieve, discredit, doubt, misbelieve, miscredit, misdeem, mistrust, question, suspect.
antonym trust.
n. disbelief, doubt, misfaith, misgiving, mistrust, qualm, question, scepticism, suspicion, untrust, wariness.

antonym trust.

distrustful *adj.* chary, cynical, disbelieving, distrusting, doubtful, doubting, dubious, mistrustful, sceptical, suspicious, uneasy, untrustful, untrusting, wary.
antonyms trustful, unsuspecting.

disturb *v.* affray, agitate, alarm, annoy, bother, concuss, confound, confuse, derange, disarrange, discompose, disorder, disorganise, disrupt, distract, distress, excite, fluster, harass, interrupt, muddle, perturb, pester, rouse, ruffle, shake, startle, trouble, unsettle, upset, worry.
antonyms calm, quiet, reassure.

disturbance *n.* agitation, annoyance, bother, brawl, breeze, broil, burst-up, bust-up, commotion, confusion, derangement, disorder, distraction, fracas, fray, hindrance, hubbub, interruption, intrusion, katzenjammer, kick-up, misarrangement, molestation, muss(e), perturbation, riot, ruckus, ruction, shake-up, stour, stramash, tumult, turmoil, unrest, upheaval, uproar, upset, upturn.
antonyms peace, quiet.

disturbed *adj.* agitated, anxious, apprehensive, bothered, concerned, confused, discomposed, disordered, disquieted, flustered, maladjusted, neurotic, troubled, unbalanced, uneasy, unrestful, upset, worried.
antonyms calm, sane.

disturbing *adj.* agitating, alarming, disconcerting, discouraging, dismaying, disquieting, distressful, distressing, disturbant, disturbative, frightening, perturbing, startling, threatening, troubling, unsettling, upsetting, worrying.
antonym reassuring.

disunion *n.* alienation, breach, detachment, disagreement, disconcert, disconnection, discord, disjunction, dissension, dissevering, dissidence, division, estrangement, feud, partition, rift, rupture, schism, separation, severance, split.
antonym unification.

disunite *v.* alienate, detach, disband, disconnect, disengage, disjoin, disrupt, divide, estrange, part, segregate, separate, sever, split, sunder.
antonym unify.

disunity *n.* alienation, breach, conflict, disagreement, discord, discordance, dissension, dissent, estrangement, rupture, schism, split, strife, variance.
antonym unity.

disuse *n.* abandonment, decay, desuetude, discontinuance, disusage, idleness, neglect.
antonym use.

ditch *n.* channel, drain, dyke, furrow, gully, ha-ha, level, moat, rhine, stank, trench, watercourse.
v. abandon, discard, dispose of, drop, dump, jettison, scrap.

dither *v.* faff about, falter, footer, haver, hesitate, oscillate, shilly-shally, swither, teeter, vacillate, waver.
antonym decide.

n. bother, flap, fluster, flutter, indecision, panic, pother, stew, tizzy, twitter.
antonym decision.

diuretic *adj.* emictory.

divan *n.* chaise-longue, couch, lounger, ottoman, settee, sofa.

dive[1] *v.* descend, dip, drop, duck, fall, jump, leap, nose-dive, pitch, plummet, plunge, rush, sound, submerge, swoop.
n. dash, header, jump, leap, lunge, nose-dive, plunge, rush, spring, swoop.

dive[2] *n.* den, honky-tonk, joint, lush-house.

diverge *v.* bifurcate, branch, conflict, depart, deviate, differ, digress, disagree, dissent, divaricate, divide, fork, part, radiate, separate, split, spread, stray, vary, wander.
antonyms agree, come together, join.

divergence *n.* branching-out, deflection, departure, deviation, difference, digression, disparity, divagation, parting, radiating, ramification, separation, variation.
antonym convergence.

divergent *adj.* conflicting, deviating, different, differing, disagreeing, dissimilar, diverging, diverse, forking, parting, radial, radiating, separate, spreading, variant, varying.
antonym convergent.

divers *adj.* different, manifold, many, miscellaneous, multifarious, numerous, several, some, sundry, varied, various.

diverse *adj.* assorted, different, differing, discrete, disparate, dissimilar, distinct, divergent, diversified, heterogeneous, manifold, many, miscellaneous, multifarious, multiform, numerous, separate, several, some, sundry, unlike, varied, various, varying.
antonym identical.

diversify *v.* alter, assort, branch out, change, expand, mix, spread out, variegate, vary.

diversion *n.* alteration, amusement, beguilement, change, deflection, delight, departure, detour, deviation, digression, disportment, distraction, divertissement, enjoyment, entertainment, game, gratification, pastime, play, pleasure, recreation, relaxation, sport, variation.

diversionary *adj.* distracting, divertive.

diversity *n.* assortment, difference, dissimilarity, distinctiveness, divergence, diverseness, diversification, heterogeneity, medley, multifariousness, multiplicity, range, unlikeness, variance, variegation, variety.
antonyms sameness, similarity.

divert *v.* amuse, avert, beguile, deflect, delight, detract, distract, entertain, gratify, hive off, recreate, redirect, regale, side-track, switch, tickle.
antonyms direct, irritate.

diverting *adj.* amusing, beguiling, enjoyable, entertaining, fun, funny, humorous, pleasant, witty.
antonym irritating.

divest *v.* denude, deprive, despoil, disinvest, dispossess, disrobe, disseise, doff, remove, strip, unclothe, undress.

antonym clothe.

divide *v.* alienate, allocate, allot, apportion, arrange, bisect, break up, categorise, classify, cleave, cut, deal out, detach, disconnect, dispense, distribute, disunite, divvy, estrange, grade, group, part, partition, portion, segment, segregate, separate, sever, share, shear, sort, split, subdivide, sunder.
antonyms collect, gather, join.

divide out allocate, allot, apportion, dole out, measure out, morsel, parcel out, share, share out.

dividend *n.* bonus, cut, divvy, extra, gain, gratuity, interest, lagniappe, plus, portion, share, surplus, whack.

divination *n.* augury, clairvoyance, divining, dukkeripen, foretelling, fortune-telling, hariolation, -mancy, prediction, presage, prognostication, prophecy, second sight, soothsaying, taghairm.

divine *adj.* angelic, beatific, beautiful, blissful, celestial, consecrated, exalted, excellent, glorious, godlike, heavenly, holy, marvellous, mystical, perfect, rapturous, religious, sacred, sanctified, spiritual, splendid, superhuman, superlative, supernatural, supreme, transcendent, transcendental, transmundane, wonderful.
n. churchman, clergyman, cleric, ecclesiastic, minister, parson, pastor, prelate, priest, reverend.
v. apprehend, conjecture, deduce, foretell, guess, hariolate, haruspicate, infer, intuit, perceive, prognosticate, suppose, surmise, suspect, understand.

diviner *n.* astrologer, augur, divinator, dowser, haruspex, oracle, prophet, seer, sibyl, soothsayer, water-finder.

divinity *n.* daemon, deity, deva, genius, god, goddess, godhead, godhood, godliness, godship, holiness, kami, sanctity, spirit.

divisible *adj.* dividable, dividual, fractional, partible, separable, splittable.

division *n.* allotment, apportionment, bisection, border, boundary, branch, breach, category, class, compartment, cutting, demarcation, department, detaching, dichotomy, disagreement, discord, distribution, disunion, divide, divider, dividing, estrangement, feud, group, head, part, partition, portion, rupture, schism, scission, section, sector, segment, separation, sept, sharing, side, split, splitting, stream, variance, wapentake, ward, watershed, wing.
antonyms agreement, multiplication, unification.

divisive *adj.* alienating, discordant, disruptive, inharmonious.
antonyms harmonious, unifying.

divorce *n.* annulment, breach, break, break-up, decree nisi, diffarreation, dissolution, disunion, rupture, separation, severance, split-up.
v. annul, cancel, disconnect, dissever, dissociate, dissolve, disunite, divide, part, separate, sever, split up, sunder.

antonyms marry, unify.

divulge *v.* betray, broadcast, communicate, confess, declare, disclose, evulgate, exhibit, expose, impart, leak, let slip, proclaim, promulgate, publish, reveal, spill, tell, uncover.

divvy *n.* bit, cut, dividend, lagniappe, percentage, portion, quota, share, whack.
v. apportion, cut, distribute, divide, parcel out, share, share out, split.

dizzy *adj.* befuddled, bemused, bewildered, capricious, confused, dazed, dazzled, faint, fickle, flighty, foolish, frivolous, giddy, light-headed, lofty, muddled, reeling, scatter-brained, shaky, staggering, steep, swimming, vertiginous, wobbly, woozy.

do *v.* accomplish, achieve, act, adapt, answer, arrange, behave, carry out, cause, cheat, complete, con, conclude, cover, cozen, create, deceive, decipher, decode, defraud, discharge, dupe, effect, end, execute, explore, fare, fix, fleece, give, hoax, implement, make, manage, organise, pass muster, perform, prepare, present, proceed, produce, put on, render, resolve, satisfy, serve, solve, suffice, suit, swindle, tour, transact, translate, transpose, travel, trick, undertake, visit, work, work out.
n. affair, event, function, gathering, occasion, party.

do away with abolish, bump off, destroy, discard, discontinue, do in, eliminate, exterminate, get rid of, kill, liquidate, murder, remove, slay.

do for defeat, destroy, finish (off), kill, ruin, shatter, slay.

do in butcher, dispatch, eliminate, execute, exhaust, fag, fatigue, kill, knacker, liquidate, murder, rub out, shatter, slaughter, slay, tire, waste, wear out, weary.

do out of balk, bilk, cheat, con, deprive, diddle, fleece, rook, swindle, trick.

do's and don'ts code, customs, etiquette, instructions, niceties, p's and q's, punctilios, regulations, rules, standards.

do without abstain from, dispense with, forgo, give up, relinquish, waive.

docile *adj.* amenable, biddable, complaisant, compliant, ductile, manageable, obedient, obliging, pliable, pliant, submissive, teachable, tractable, unmurmuring, unprotesting, unquestioning.
antonyms truculent, unco-operative.

docility *n.* amenability, biddableness, complaisance, compliance, ductility, manageability, meekness, obedience, pliability, pliancy, submissiveness, tractability.
antonyms truculence, unco-operativeness.

dock[1] *n.* boat-yard, harbour, marina, pier, quay, waterfront, wharf.
v. anchor, berth, drop anchor, join up, land, link up, moor, put in, rendezvous, tie up, unite.

dock[2] *v.* clip, crop, curtail, cut, decaudate, decrease, deduct, diminish, lessen, reduce, shorten, subtract, truncate, withhold.

docket *n*. bill, certificate, chit, chitty, counterfoil, label, receipt, tab, tag, tally, ticket.
v. catalogue, file, index, label, mark, register, tab, tag, ticket.

doctor *n*. clinician, doctoress, doctress, general practitioner, GP, hakim, internist, leech, medic, medical officer, medical practitioner, medicaster, medico, physician, pill(s).
v. adulterate, alter, botch, change, cobble, cook, cut, dilute, disguise, falsify, fix, fudge, hocus, load, medicate, mend, misrepresent, patch, pervert, repair, spike, tamper with, treat.

doctrinaire *adj*. biased, doctrinarian, dogmatic, fanatical, hypothetical, ideological, impractical, inflexible, insistent, opinionated, pedantic, rigid, speculative, theoretical, unrealistic.
antonym flexible.

doctrine *n*. belief, canon, concept, conviction, creed, dogma, ism, opinion, precept, principle, teaching, tenet.

document *n*. certificate, chirograph, deed, form, instrument, paper, parchment, record, report.
v. authenticate, back, certify, cite, corroborate, detail, enumerate, instance, list, particularise, prove, substantiate, support, validate, verify.

documentary *n*. faction, feature, programme.

doddery *adj*. aged, decrepit, doddering, doited, faltering, feeble, infirm, rambling, senile, shaky, shambling, tottery, trembly, unsteady, weak.
antonyms hale, youthful.

dodge *v*. avoid, dart, deceive, duck, elude, equivocate, evade, fend off, fudge, hedge, parry, shift, shirk, shuffle, side-step, skive, swerve, swing the lead, trick.
n. chicane, contrivance, device, feint, machination, manoeuvre, ploy, ruse, scheme, stratagem, subterfuge, trick, wheeze, wile.

dodger *n*. evader, lead-swinger, shirker, skiver, slacker, slyboots, trickster.

dodgy *adj*. chancy, dangerous, delicate, dicey, dicky, difficult, problematical, risky, ticklish, tricky, uncertain, unreliable, unsafe.
antonyms easy, safe.

doer *n*. accomplisher, achiever, activist, bustler, dynamo, executer, go-getter, live wire, organiser, power-house, wheeler-dealer.

doff *v*. discard, lift, raise, remove, shed, take off, throw off, tip, touch, undress.
antonym don.

dog *n*. beast, bitch, blackguard, bowwow, canid, canine, cur, heel, hound, knave, mongrel, moppet, mutt, pooch, pup, puppy, scoundrel, tyke, villain, yapper, yapster.
v. harry, haunt, hound, plague, pursue, shadow, tail, track, trail, trouble, worry.

dogged *adj*. determined, firm, indefatigable, indomitable, obstinate, persevering, persistent, pertinacious, relentless, resolute, single-minded, staunch, steadfast, steady, stubborn, tenacious, unflagging, unshakable,

unyielding.
antonym irresolute.

doggedness *n*. determination, endurance, indomitablity, obstinacy, perseverance, persistence, pertinacity, relentlessness, resolution, single-mindedness, steadfastness, steadiness, stubbornness, tenaciousness, tenacity.

dogma *n*. article, article of faith, belief, conviction, credendum, credo, creed, doctrine, opinion, precept, principle, teaching, tenet.

dogmatic *adj*. affirmative, arbitrary, assertive, authoritative, canonical, categorical, dictatorial, didactic, doctrinaire, doctrinal, downright, emphatic, ex cathedra, high-dried, imperious, magisterial, obdurate, opinionated, oracular, overbearing, peremptory, pontific(al), positive.

dogmatism *n*. arbitrariness, assertiveness, bigotry, dictatorialness, imperiousness, opinionatedness, peremptoriness, positiveness, presumption.

dogsbody *n*. doormat, drudge, factotum, galleyslave, lackey, maid-of-all-work, man-of-all-work, menial, skivvy, slave.

doings *n*. actions, activities, acts, adventures, affairs, concerns, dealings, deeds, events, exploits, goings-on, handiwork, happenings, proceedings, transactions.

doldrums *n*. accidie, acedia, apathy, blues, boredom, depression, dullness, dumps, ennui, gloom, inertia, lassitude, listlessness, low-spiritedness, malaise, stagnation, tedium, torpor.

dole *n*. allocation, allotment, allowance, alms, apportionment, benefit, dispensation, dispersal, distribution, division, donation, gift, grant, gratuity, issuance, modicum, parcel, pittance, portion, quota, share.

dole out administer, allocate, allot, apportion, assign, deal, dispense, distribute, divide, give, hand out, issue, mete, ration, share.

doleful *adj*. blue, cheerless, depressing, dismal, distressing, dolorous, dreary, forlorn, funereal, gloomy, lugubrious, melancholy, mournful, painful, pathetic, pitiful, rueful, sad, sombre, sorrowful, woebegone, woeful, wretched.
antonym cheerful.

doll *n*. dolly, figurine, kewpie doll, marionette, moppet, plaything, puppet, toy.

doll up deck out, dress up, preen, primp, prink, tart up, titivate, trick out.

dollar *n*. buck, greenback, smacker, wheel.

dollop *n*. ball, blob, bunch, clump, glob, gob, gobbet, lump.

dolorous *adj*. anguished, distressing, doleful, grievous, harrowing, heart-rending, lugubrious, melancholy, miserable, mournful, painful, rueful, sad, sombre, sorrowful, woebegone, woeful, wretched.
antonym happy.

dolour *n*. anguish, distress, grief, heartache, heartbreak, lamentation, misery, mourning, ruth, sadness, sorrow, suffering.

antonym beatitude.

dolt *n.* ass, beetlebrain, beetlehead, besom-head, blockhead, bonehead, booby, boodle, bufflehead, bull-calf, calf, chump, clod, clodhopper, clodpate, clodpoll, clot, clunk, dimwit, dope, dullard, dunce, fool, galoot, half-wit, idiot, ignoramus, leather-head, log-gerhead, log-head, lurdan(e), lurden, mutt, mutton-head, nitwit, nutcase, palooka, sheep's-head, simpleton, turnip.

doltish *adj.* boneheaded, brainless, clottish, daffy, dense, dimwitted, dopey, dumb, foolish, half-witted, idiotic, mindless, obtuse, silly, stupid, thick.

antonyms brainy, clever.

domain *n.* area, authority, bailiwick, business, concern, demesne, department, discipline, dominion, empire, estate, field, jurisdiction, kingdom, lands, orbit, pidgin, policies, power, province, realm, region, scope, speciality, sphere, sway, territory.

domestic *adj.* autochthonic, domal, domesti-cated, domiciliary, family, home, home-bred, home-loving, homely, house, household, house-trained, housewifely, indigenous, in-ternal, native, pet, private, stay-at-home, tame, trained.

n. au pair, char, charwoman, daily, daily help, help, maid, scullery maid, servant, slavey, woman.

domesticate *v.* acclimatise, accustom, break, domesticise, familiarise, habituate, house-train, naturalise, tame, train.

domesticated *adj.* broken (in), domestic, home-loving, homely, house-proud, housewifely, naturalised, tame, tamed.

antonyms feral, wild.

domesticity *n.* domestic science, domestication, familism, home economics, homecraft, home-making, housecraft, housekeeping, house-wifery, housewifeship.

domicile *n.* abode, dwelling, habitation, home, house, lodging(s), mansion, quarters, resi-dence, residency, settlement.

dominance *n.* ascendancy, authority, command, control, domination, government, hegemony, leadership, mastery, paramountcy, power, rule, supremacy, sway.

dominant *adj.* ascendant, assertive, authorita-tive, besetting, chief, commanding, controll-ing, governing, influential, leading, main, outstanding, paramount, predominant, pre-eminent, presiding, prevailing, prevalent, primary, prime, principal, prominent, ruling, superior, supreme.

antonym subordinate.

dominate *v.* bestride, control, direct, domineer, dwarf, eclipse, govern, have the whip hand, keep under one's thumb, lead, master, monopolise, outshine, overbear, overgang, overlook, overrule, overshadow, predomin-ate, prevail, rule, tyrannise.

domination *n.* ascendancy, authority, command, control, despotism, dictatorship, hegemony, influence, leadership, mastery, oppression,

power, repression, rule, subjection, subordi-nation, superiority, suppression, supremacy, sway, tyranny.

domineer *v.* bluster, boss, browbeat, bully, command, hector, intimidate, lord it over, menace, overbear, ride roughshod, rule, swagger, threaten, tyrannise.

domineering *adj.* arrogant, authoritarian, auto-cratic, bossy, coercive, despotic, dictatorial, harsh, high-handed, imperious, iron-handed, magisterial, masterful, oppressive, overbear-ing, severe, tyrannical.

antonyms meek, obsequious, servile.

dominion *n.* ascendancy, authority, colony, command, control, country, domain, domina-tion, empire, government, hegemony, juris-diction, kingdom, lordship, mastery, power, province, realm, region, rule, sovereignty, supremacy, sway, territory.

don *v.* affect, assume, clothe oneself in, dress in, get into, put on.

antonym doff.

Don Juan *n.* amoretto, amoroso, amourette, Casanova, gigolo, ladies' man, lady-killer, lover, muff, philander(er), romeo.

donate *v.* bequeath, bestow, chip in, confer, contribute, cough up, fork out, gift, give, impart, present, proffer, subscribe.

donation *n.* alms, benefaction, boon, confer-ment, contribution, gift, grant, gratuity, largess(e), offering, present, presentation, subscription.

done *adj.* acceptable, accomplished, advised, agreed, completed, concluded, consum-mated, conventional, cooked, cooked to a turn, de rigueur, depleted, drained, ended, executed, exhausted, fatigued, finished, OK, over, perfected, proper, ready, realised, settled, spent, terminated, through, U, used up.

done for beaten, broken, dashed, defeated, destroyed, doomed, finished, foiled, for the high jump, lost, ruined, undone, vanquished, wrecked.

done in all in, bushed, dead, dead beat, dog-tired, exhausted, fagged, jiggered, knackered, pooped, worn to a frazzle, zonked.

donkey *n.* ass, burro, cardophagus, cuddy, hinny, jackass, jennet, jenny, moke, mule.

donnish *adj.* academic, bookish, erudite, forma-listic, learned, pedagogic, pedantic, precise, scholarly, scholastic.

donor *n.* benefactor, contributor, donator, fairy godmother, giver, granter, philanthropist, provider.

antonym beneficiary.

doom *n.* Armageddon, catastrophe, condemna-tion, death, death-knell, decision, decree, destiny, destruction, Doomsday, downfall, fate, fortune, judgement, Judgement Day, karma, kismet, lot, portion, ruin, sentence, the Last Judgement, the last trump, verdict.

v. condemn, consign, damn, decree, destine, foredoom, foreordain, judge, predestine, preordain, sentence, threaten.

doomed adj. accursed, bedevilled, bewitched, condemned, cursed, fated, fey, hopeless, ill-fated, ill-omened, ill-starred, luckless, star-crossed.

door n. doorstead, doorway, egress, entrance, entry, exit, ingress, opening, portal, vomitorium, vomitory.

doorkeeper n. commissionaire, gate-keeper, huissier, janitor, jobsworth, ostiary, porter.

dope[1] n. details, drugs, facts, gen, hallucinogen, info, information, low-down, narcotic, news, opiate, tip.
v. anaesthetise, doctor, drug, inject, load, medicate, narcotise, sedate, stupefy.

dope[2] n. blockhead, bonehead, clot, dimwit, dolt, dullard, dunce, fool, half-wit, idiot, simpleton.

dop(e)y adj. dazed, dense, doltish, dozy, drowsy, drugged, dumb, foolish, groggy, hazy, idiotic, muzzy, senseless, silly, simple, slow, stupefied, stupid, thick, woozy.
antonyms alert, bright.

dormant adj. asleep, comatose, fallow, hibernating, inactive, inert, inoperative, latent, latescent, quiescent, sleeping, sluggish, slumbering, suspended, torpid, undeveloped, unrealised.
antonym active.

dose n. dosage, draught, drench, hit, measure, portion, potion, prescription, quantity, shot, slug.
v. administer, dispense, drench, medicate, treat.

dot n. atom, circle, dab, decimal point, dit, fleck, full stop, iota, jot, mark, mite, mote, pin-point, point, speck, spot.
v. bespeckle, dab, dabble, fleck, punctuate, spot, sprinkle, stipple, stud.

dotage n. anility, decrepitude, feebleness, imbecility, old age, second childhood, senility, weakness.
antonym youth.

dote on admire, adore, idolise, indulge, pamper, prize, spoil, treasure.

doting adj. adoring, devoted, fond, foolish, indulgent, lovesick, soft.

dotty adj. batty, crazy, eccentric, feeble-minded, loopy, peculiar, potty, touched, weird.
antonym sensible.

double adj. bifarious, bifold, binate, coupled, diploid, doubled, dual, duple, duplex, duplicate, paired, twice, twin, twofold.
v. duplicate, enlarge, fold, geminate, grow, increase, magnify, multiply, repeat.
n. clone, copy, counterpart, dead ringer, dead spit, Doppelgänger, duplicate, fellow, image, impersonator, lookalike, mate, replica, ringer, spitting image, twin.
double back backtrack, circle, dodge, evade, loop, retrace one's steps, return, reverse.
double entendre ambiguity, double meaning, innuendo, play on words, pun, suggestiveness, word-play.

double-cross v. betray, cheat, con, cozen,

defraud, hoodwink, mislead, swindle, trick, two-time.

double-dealer n. betrayer, cheat, con man, cozener, deceiver, dissembler, double-crosser, fraud, hypocrite, Machiavellian, rogue, swindler, traitor, two-timer.

double-dealing n. bad faith, betrayal, cheating, deceit, deception, dishonesty, duplicity, foul play, hypocrisy, Machiavellianism, mendacity, perfidy, treachery, trickery, two-timing.
adj. cheating, crooked, deceitful, dishonest, duplicitous, fraudulent, hypocritical, lying, Machiavellian, perfidious, scheming, shifty, sneaky, swindling, treacherous, tricky, two-faced, two-timing, underhanded, unscrupulous, untrustworthy, wily.

doubly adv. again, bis, twice, twofold.

doubt v. be dubious, be uncertain, demur, discredit, distrust, dubitate, fear, fluctuate, hesitate, misgive, mistrust, query, question, scruple, suspect, vacillate, waver.
antonyms believe, trust.
n. ambiguity, apprehension, arrière pensée, confusion, difficulty, dilemma, disquiet, distrust, dubiety, fear, hesitancy, hesitation, incredulity, indecision, irresolution, misgiving, mistrust, perplexity, problem, qualm, quandary, reservation, scepticism, suspense, suspicion, uncertainty, vacillation.
antonyms belief, certainty, confidence, trust.

doubter n. agnostic, cynic, disbeliever, doubting Thomas, questioner, questionist, sceptic, scoffer, unbeliever.
antonym believer.

doubtful adj. ambiguous, debatable, disreputable, distrustful, dubious, dubitable, equivocal, hazardous, hesitant, hesitating, inconclusive, indefinite, indeterminate, irresolute, litigious, obscure, perplexed, precarious, problematic, problematical, questionable, sceptical, shady, suspect, suspicious, tentative, uncertain, unclear, unconfirmed, unconvinced, undecided, unresolved, unsettled, unsure, vacillating, vague, wavering.
antonyms certain, definite.

doubtless adv. apparently, assuredly, certainly, clearly, indisputably, most likely, of course, ostensibly, out of question, precisely, presumably, probably, questionless, seemingly, supposedly, surely, truly, undoubtedly, unquestionably, without doubt.

doughty adj. able, bold, brave, courageous, daring, dauntless, fearless, gallant, game, hardy, heroic, intrepid, redoubtable, resolute, stout-hearted, strong, valiant, valorous.
antonyms cowardly, weak.

dour adj. austere, dismal, dreary, forbidding, gloomy, grim, hard, humourless, inflexible, morose, obstinate, rigid, rigorous, severe, sour, Spartan, strict, sullen, uncompromising, unfriendly, unyielding.
antonyms bright, cheery, easy-going.

douse, dowse v. blow out, dip, drench, duck, dunk, extinguish, immerge, immerse, plunge, put out, saturate, smother, snuff, soak, souse, steep, submerge.

dovetail v. accord, agree, coincide, conform, correspond, fit, harmonise, interlock, join, link, match, mortise, splice, tailor, tally, tenon, unite.

dowdy adj. dingy, drab, frowzy, frumpish, frumpy, ill-dressed, old-fashioned, scrubby, shabby, slovenly, tacky, tatty, unfashionable, unmodish, unsmart.

antonyms dressy, smart, spruce.

down[1] n. bloom, floccus, floss, flue, fluff, fuzz, nap, pile, shag, thistledown, wool.

down[2] v. drink, fell, floor, gulp, knock back, swallow, throw, topple, toss off.

down and out derelict, destitute, impoverished, on one's uppers, penniless, ruined.

down at heel dowdy, impoverished, out at elbows, run-down, seedy, shabby, slipshod, slovenly, slummy, worn.

down in the mouth blue, chopfallen, crestfallen, dejected, depressed, disheartened, dispirited, down, down in the dumps, downcast, in low spirits, in the doldrums, melancholy, sad, unhappy.

down the drain lost, out of the window, ruined, up the spout, wasted.

down with away with, exterminate, get rid of.

down-and-out n. beggar, bum, derelict, dosser, loser, outcast, pauper, tramp, vagabond, vagrant.

downcast adj. cheerless, chopfallen, crestfallen, daunted, dejected, depressed, despondent, disappointed, disconsolate, discouraged, disheartened, dismayed, dispirited, down, miserable, sad, unhappy.

antonyms cheerful, elated, happy.

downfall n. breakdown, cloudburst, collapse, comedown, come-uppance, debacle, deluge, descent, destruction, disgrace, downpour, failure, fall, humiliation, overthrow, rainstorm, ruin, undoing, Waterloo.

downgrade v. belittle, decry, degrade, demote, denigrate, detract from, disparage, humble, lower, reduce in rank, run down.

antonyms improve, upgrade.

downhearted adj. blue, chopfallen, crestfallen, dejected, depressed, despondent, discouraged, disheartened, dismayed, dispirited, downcast, gloomy, glum, jaw-fallen, low-spirited, sad, sorrowful, unhappy.

antonyms cheerful, enthusiastic, happy.

downpour n. cloudburst, deluge, downcome, flood, inundation, rainstorm, torrent, waterspout.

downright adj. absolute, blatant, blunt, candid, categorical, clear, complete, explicit, forthright, frank, honest, open, out-and-out, outright, outspoken, plain, positive, simple, sincere, straightforward, thoroughgoing, total, undisguised, unequivocal, unqualified, utter, wholesale.

down-to-earth adj. commonsense, commonsensical, hard-headed, matter-of-fact, mundane, no-nonsense, plain-spoken, practical, realistic, sane, sensible, unsentimental.

antonyms fantastic, impractical.

down-trodden adj. abused, afflicted, distressed, exploited, helpless, oppressed, subjugated, subservient, trampled on, trampled underfoot, tyrannised, victimised.

downward adj. declining, descending, downhill, sliding, slippery, slipping.

antonym upward.

downy adj. eriophorous, feathery, fleecy, floccose, fluffy, lanuginose, lanuginous, nappy, plumate, plumulate, silky, soft, velvety, woolly.

dowry n. dot, dower, endowment, faculty, gift, inheritance, legacy, portion, provision, share, talent, wedding-dower.

dowse see **douse**.

doze v. catnap, dove, dover, drop off, drowse, kip, nap, nod, nod off, sleep, slumber, snooze, zizz.

n. catnap, dogsleep, forty winks, kip, nap, shut-eye, siesta, snooze, zizz.

drab adj. cheerless, colourless, dingy, dismal, dreary, dull, dun-coloured, flat, gloomy, grey, lack-lustre, mous(e)y, shabby, sombre, uninspired, vapid.

antonym bright.

draft[1] v. compose, delineate, design, draw, draw up, formulate, outline, plan, sketch.

n. abstract, delineation, ébauche, outline, plan, protocol, rough, sketch, version.

draft[2] n. bill, cheque, order, postal order.

drag v. crawl, creep, dawdle, draggle, draw, hale, harl, haul, inch, lag, linger, loiter, lug, pull, schlep, shamble, shuffle, straggle, sweep, tow, trail, tug, yank.

n. annoyance, bore, bother, brake, drogue, nuisance, pain, pest, pill.

drag on, drag out draw out, extend, hang on, lengthen, persist, prolong, protract, spin out.

drag one's feet delay, obstruct, procrastinate, stall.

dragoon v. browbeat, bully, coact, coerce, compel, constrain, drive, force, impel, intimidate, strong-arm.

drain v. bleed, consume, deplete, discharge, dissipate, down, draw off, drink up, dry, effuse, empty, emulge, evacuate, exhaust, exude, finish, flow out, lade, leak, milk, ooze, quaff, remove, sap, seep, strain, swallow, tap, tax, trickle, use up, weary, withdraw.

antonym fill.

n. channel, conduit, culvert, depletion, ditch, drag, duct, exhaustion, expenditure, grip, outlet, pipe, reduction, sap, sewer, sink, sough, stank, strain, trench, watercourse, withdrawal.

drainage n. bilge, leaching, seepage, sewage, sewerage, waste.

dram n. caulker, drop, glass, measure, nobbler, shot, slug, snifter, snort, tot.

drama n. acting, crisis, dramatics, dramatisation, dramaturgy, excitement, histrionics, kabuki, kathakali, melodrama, play, scene, show, spectacle, stage-craft, theatre, theatricals, Thespian art, turmoil.

dramatic *adj.* affecting, breathtaking, climactic, dramaturgic, dramaturgical, effective, electrifying, emotional, exciting, expressive, graphic, impressive, meaningful, melodramatic, moving, powerful, sensational, startling, striking, sudden, suspenseful, tense, theatrical, Thespian, thrilling, vivid.
antonyms normal, ordinary.

dramatise *v.* act, exaggerate, overdo, overstate, play-act, put on, stage.

dramatist *n.* comedian, dramaturge, dramaturgist, playwright, play-writer, screen-writer, scriptwriter, tragedian.

drape *v.* adorn, array, cloak, cover, dangle, droop, drop, enrap, fold, hang, suspend, swathe, vest, wrap.

drapery *n.* arras, backdrop, blind(s), covering(s), curtain(s), hanging(s), portière, tapestry, valance.

drastic *adj.* desperate, dire, draconian, extreme, far-reaching, forceful, harsh, heroic, radical, severe, strong.
antonym mild.

draught *n.* cup, current, dose, dragging, drawing, drench, drink, flow, haulage, influx, movement, portion, potation, puff, pulling, quantity, traction.

draw[1] *v.* allure, attenuate, attract, borrow, breathe in, bring forth, choose, deduce, delineate, depict, derive, design, drag, drain, elicit, elongate, engage, entice, entrain, evoke, extend, extort, extract, get, haul, induce, infer, influence, inhale, inspire, invite, lengthen, make, map out, mark out, outline, paint, pencil, persuade, pick, portray, puff, pull, respire, select, sketch, stretch, suck, take, tow, trace, tug, unsheathe.
antonyms propel, push.
n. appeal, attraction, bait, enticement, interest, lure, pull.

draw back recoil, resile, retract, retreat, shrink, start back, withdraw.

draw lots choose, decide, draw straws, pick, select, spin a coin, toss up.

draw on employ, exploit, extract, make use of, quarry, rely on, take from, use.

draw out drag out, elongate, extend, lengthen, prolong, prolongate, protract, spin out, stretch, string out.
antonym curtail.

draw the line lay down the law, object, put one's foot down, restrict, say no, set a limit.

draw up compose, draft, embattle, formulate, frame, halt, prepare, pull up, run in, stop, stop short, write out.

draw[2] *v.* be equal, be even, be neck and neck, dead-heat, tie.
n. dead-heat, deadlock, impasse, stalemate, tie.

drawback *n.* block, defect, deficiency, désagrément, detriment, difficulty, disability, disadvantage, fault, flaw, fly in the ointment, handicap, hindrance, hitch, impediment, imperfection, nuisance, obstacle, pull-back,

snag, stumbling, trouble.
antonym advantage.

drawing *n.* cartoon, delineation, depiction, graphic, illustration, outline, picture, portrait, portrayal, representation, sketch, study.

drawl *v.* dra(u)nt, drone, haw-haw, protract, twang.

drawn *adj.* fatigued, fraught, haggard, harassed, harrowed, hassled, pinched, sapped, strained, stressed, taut, tense, tired, worn.

dread *v.* cringe at, fear, flinch, quail, shrink from, shudder, shy, tremble.
n. alarm, apprehension, aversion, awe, dismay, disquiet, fear, fright, funk, heebie-jeebies, horror, misgiving, terror, trepidation, worry.
antonyms confidence, security.
adj. alarming, awe-inspiring, awful, dire, dreaded, dreadful, frightening, frightful, ghastly, grisly, gruesome, horrible, terrible, terrifying.

dreadful *adj.* alarming, appalling, awful, dire, distressing, fearful, formidable, frightful, ghastly, grievous, grisly, gruesome, harrowing, hideous, horrendous, horrible, monstrous, shocking, terrible, tragic, tremendous.
antonym comforting.

dream *n.* ambition, aspiration, beauty, castle in Spain, castle in the air, daydream, delight, delusion, design, desire, fantasy, goal, hallucination, hope, illusion, imagination, joy, marvel, notion, phantasm, pipe-dream, pleasure, reverie, speculation, trance, treasure, vagary, vision, wish.
v. conjure, daydream, envisage, fancy, fantasise, hallucinate, imagine, muse, stargaze, think, visualise.

dream up conceive, concoct, contrive, cook up, create, devise, hatch, imagine, invent, spin, think up.

dreamer *n.* daydreamer, Don Quixote, fantasiser, fantasist, fantast, idealist, John o'dreams, Johnny-head-in-the-air, romancer, stargazer, theoriser, utopian, visionary, Walter Mitty, wool-gatherer.
antonyms pragmatist, realist.

dreaminess *n.* absent-mindedness, abstraction, dimness, dwam, ethereality, fancifulness, insubstantiality, kef, preoccupation, vagueness, whimsicality.

dreamlike *adj.* chimerical, hallucinatory, illusory, insubstantial, phantasmagoric, phantasmagorical, phantom, surreal, trance-like, unreal, unsubstantial, visionary.

dreamy *adj.* absent, abstracted, chimerical, daydreaming, dreamlike, fanciful, fantastic, faraway, gentle, imaginary, impractical, intangible, lulling, misty, musing, pensive, phantasmagoric, phantasmagorical, phantasmal, preoccupied, quixotic, romantic, shadowy, speculative, unreal, vague, visionary.
antonyms down-to-earth, realistic.

dreary *adj.* bleak, boring, cheerless, colourless, comfortless, commonplace, depressing, dismal, doleful, downcast, drab, drear, dreich,

dull, forlorn, gloomy, glum, gousty, humdrum, joyless, lifeless, lonely, lonesome, melancholy, monotonous, mournful, routine, sad, solitary, sombre, sorrowful, tedious, trite, uneventful, uninteresting, wearisome, wretched.
antonyms bright, interesting.
dredge *v.* dig up, discover, drag up, draw up, expose, fish up, raise, rake up, scoop up, uncover, unearth.
dregs *n.* canaille, deposit, draff, dross, excrement, faeces, fag-end, fecula, grounds, lags, lees, left-overs, mother, outcasts, rabble, residue, residuum, riff-raff, scourings, scum, sediment, tailings, trash, waste.
drench *v.* douse, drouk, drown, duck, flood, imbrue, imbue, immerse, inundate, saturate, soak, souse, steep, wet.
dress *n.* apparel, attire, caparison, clothes, clothing, costume, ensemble, frock, garb, garment, garments, gear, get-up, gown, guise, habiliments, habit, outfit, raiment, rig-out, robe, suit, togs, vestment.
v. accoutre, adjust, adorn, align, apparel, arrange, array, attire, bandage, bedeck, bedizen, betrim, bind up, boun, busk, caparison, change, clothe, deck, decorate, dispose, don, drape, embellish, fit, furbish, garb, garnish, groom, habilitate, habit, ornament, plaster, prepare, put on, rig, robe, set, straighten, tend, treat, trim.
antonyms disrobe, strip, undress.
dress down berate, carpet, castigate, chide, flyte, haul over the coals, rebuke, reprimand, reprove, scold, tear off a strip, tell off, upbraid.
dress up adorn, beautify, dandify, deck, disguise, doll up, embellish, fig out, gild, improve, play-act, tart up, titivate, trick out.
dressing *n.* bandage, compress, emplastron, emplastrum, ligature, pad, plaster, pledget, poultice, spica, tourniquet.
dressing-gown *n.* housecoat, negligee, peignoir.
dressmaker *n.* couturier, midinette, modiste, seamstress, sewing woman, tailor, tailoress.
dressy *adj.* classy, elaborate, elegant, formal, natty, ornate, ritzy, smart, stylish, swanky, swish.
antonyms dowdy, scruffy.
dribble *v.* drip, drivel, drool, drop, leak, ooze, run, saliva, seep, slaver, slobber, sprinkle, trickle.
n. drip, droplet, gobbet, leak, seepage, sprinkling, trickle.
dried *adj.* arid, dehydrated, desiccated, drained, exsiccated, mummified, parched, shrivelled, wilted, withered, wizened.
drift *v.* accumulate, amass, coast, drive, float, freewheel, gather, meander, pile up, stray, waft, wander.
n. accumulation, aim, bank, course, current, design, direction, dune, flow, gist, heap, implication, import, impulse, intention, mass, meaning, mound, movement, object, pile,

purport, ridge, rush, scope, significance, sweep, tendency, tenor, thrust, trend.
drifter *n.* beachcomber, hobo, intinerant, rolling stone, rover, swagman, tramp, vagabond, vagrant, wanderer.
drill[1] *v.* coach, discipline, exercise, instruct, practise, rehearse, teach, train, tutor.
n. coaching, discipline, exercise, instruction, practice, preparation, repetition, training, tuition.
drill[2] *v.* bore, penetrate, perforate, pierce, puncture, transpierce.
n. awl, bit, borer, gimlet.
drink *v.* absorb, bib, booze, carouse, down, drain, dram, gulp, guzzle, hit the bottle, imbibe, indulge, knock back, liquefy, liquor up, partake of, quaff, revel, sip, suck, sup, swallow, swig, swill, tank up, tipple, tope, toss off, wassail, water.
n. alcohol, ambrosia, beverage, bev(v)y, booze, deoch-an-doris, dose, dram, draught, glass, gulp, hooch, liquid, liquor, noggin, plonk, potion, refreshment, sensation, sip, slug, snifter, snort, spirits, stiffener, suck, swallow, swig, swizzle, taste, the bottle, tickler, tiff, tipple, toss, tot.
drink in absorb, assimilate, attend to, be absorbed by, ingest, soak up.
drink to pledge (the health of), salute, toast.
drinker *n.* alcoholic, bibber, boozer, carouser, dipso, dipsomaniac, drunk, drunkard, guzzler, inebriate, lush, soak, sot, souse, sponge, tippler, toper, wino.
antonyms abstainer, teetotaller.
drip *v.* dribble, drizzle, drop, exude, filter, plop, splash, sprinkle, trickle, weep.
n. dribble, dripping, drop, leak, milk-sop, ninny, softy, stillicide, trickle, weakling, weed, wet.
drive *v.* actuate, bear, coerce, compel, constrain, dash, dig, direct, force, goad, guide, hammer, handle, harass, herd, hurl, impel, manage, motivate, motor, oblige, operate, overburden, overwork, plunge, press, prod, propel, push, ram, ride, rush, send, sink, spur, stab, steer, task, tax, thrust, travel, urge.
n. action, advance, ambition, appeal, campaign, crusade, determination, effort, energy, enterprise, excursion, get-up-and-go, hurl, initiative, jaunt, journey, motivation, outing, pressure, push, ride, run, spin, surge, trip, turn, vigour, vim, zip.
drive at aim, allude to, get at, imply, indicate, insinuate, intend, intimate, mean, refer to, signify, suggest.
drive up the wall annoy, dement, derange, drive round the bend, exasperate, infuriate, irritate, madden.
drivel *n.* blathering, bunkum, eyewash, fosh, gibberish, gobbledegook, guff, gush, jive, mumbo-jumbo, nonsense, slush, stultiloquy, twaddle, waffle.
driver *n.* cabbie, cabman, charioteer, chauffeur, coachman, Jehu, motorist, trucker, vetturino, voiturier, wag(g)oner.

driving *adj.* compelling, dynamic, energetic, forceful, forthright, galvanic, heavy, sweeping, vigorous, violent.

drizzle *n.* drow, mizzle, Scotch mist, serein.
v. dribble, mizzle, rain, shower, spit, spot, spray, sprinkle.

droll *adj.* amusing, clownish, comic, comical, diverting, eccentric, entertaining, farcical, funny, humorous, jocular, laughable, ludicrous, pawky, quaint, ridiculous, risible, waggish, whimsical, witty.

drollery *n.* absurdity, archness, banter, buffoonery, comicality, farce, fun, humour, jocularity, pleasantry, waggery, waggishness, whimsicality, wit.

drone *v.* bombilate, bombinate, buzz, chant, drawl, hum, intone, purr, thrum, vibrate, whirr.
n. buzz, chant, hum, murmuring, purr, thrum, vibration, whirr, whirring.

drool *v.* dote, dribble, drivel, enthuse, fondle, gloat, gush, rave, salivate, slaver, slobber, water at the mouth.

droop *v.* bend, dangle, decline, despond, diminish, drop, fade, faint, fall down, falter, flag, hang (down) sag, languish, lose heart, sink, slouch, slump, stoop, wilt, wither.
antonyms rise, straighten.

drooping *adj.* blue, dejected, disheartened, dispirited, doleful, downcast, droopy, flabby, flaccid, floppy, languid, languorous, lassitudinous, limp, pendulous, sagging, stooped, wilting.
antonyms stiff, straight.

drop *n.* abyss, bead, bubble, chasm, cut, dab, dash, decline, declivity, decrease, descent, deterioration, downturn, drib, driblet, drip, droplet, fall, falling-off, glob, globule, globulet, goutte, gutta, lowering, mouthful, nip, pearl, pinch, plunge, precipice, reduction, shot, sip, slope, slump, spot, taste, tear, tot, trace, trickle.
v. abandon, cease, chuck, decline, depress, descend, desert, diminish, discontinue, disown, dive, dribble, drip, droop, fall, forsake, give up, jilt, kick, leave, lower, plummet, plunge, quit, reject, relinquish, remit, renounce, repudiate, sink, stop, terminate, throw over, trickle, tumble.
antonyms mount, rise.

drop off catnap, decline, decrease, deliver, depreciate, diminish, doze, drowse, dwindle, fall off, have forty winks, leave, lessen, nod, nod off, set down, slacken, snooze.
antonym increase.

drop out abandon, back out, cry off, forsake, leave, quit, renegue, stop, withdraw.

drop-out *n.* Bohemian, deviant, dissenter, dissentient, hippie, loner, malcontent, nonconformist, rebel, renegade.

droppings *n.* dung, egesta, excrement, excreta, faeces, fumet, guano, manure, ordure, spraint, stools.

dross *n.* crust, debris, dregs, impurity, lees, recrement, refuse, remains, rubbish, scoria, scum, trash, waste.

drought *n.* aridity, dearth, deficiency, dehydration, desiccation, drouth, dryness, insufficiency, lack, need, parchedness, scarcity, shortage, want.

drove *n.* collection, company, crowd, drift, flock, gathering, herd, horde, mob, multitude, press, swarm, throng.

drown *v.* deaden, deluge, drench, engulf, extinguish, flood, go under, immerse, inundate, muffle, obliterate, overcome, overpower, overwhelm, silence, sink, stifle, submerge, swallow up, swamp, wipe out.

drowsiness *n.* dopeyness, doziness, grogginess, lethargy, narcosis, oscitancy, sleepiness, sluggishness, somnolence, torpor.

drowsy *adj.* comatose, dazed, dopey, dozy, dreamy, drugged, heavy, lethargic, lulling, nodding, restful, sleepy, somniculous, somnolent, soothing, soporific, tired, torpid.
antonyms alert, awake.

drubbing *n.* beating, clobbering, defeat, flogging, hammering, licking, pounding, pummelling, thrashing, trouncing, walloping, whipping, whitewash.

drudge *n.* afterguard, devil, dogsbody, factotum, galley-slave, hack, jackal, lackey, maid-of-all-work, man-of-all-work, menial, scullion, servant, skivvy, slave, toiler, worker.
v. beaver, droil, grind, labour, moil, plod, plug away, slave, toil, work.
antonyms idle, laze.

drudgery *n.* chore, collar-work, donkey-work, drudgism, fag, faggery, grind, hack-work, labor improbus, labour, skivvying, slavery, slog, sweat, sweated labour, toil.

drug *n.* depressant, dope, kef, medicament, medication, medicine, Mickey, Mickey Finn, narcotic, opiate, physic, poison, potion, remedy, stimulant.
v. anaesthetise, deaden, dope, dose, drench, knock out, load, medicate, numb, poison, stupefy, treat.

drug-addict *n.* acid head, dope-fiend, head, hop-head, hype, junkie, tripper.

drugged *adj.* comatose, doped, dopey, high, looped, spaced out, stoned, stupefied, tripping, turned on, zonked.

drum *v.* beat, pulsate, rap, reverberate, tap, tattoo, throb, thrum.

drum into din into, drive home, hammer, harp on, instil, reiterate.

drum up attract, canvass, collect, gather, obtain, petition, round up, solicit.

drunk *adj.* a peg too low, a sheet (three sheets) in the wind, bevvied, blind, blotto, bonkers, bottled, canned, cockeyed, corked, corny, drunken, fou, fuddled, half-seas-over, in liquor, inebriate, inebriated, intoxicated, legless, liquored, lit up, loaded, lushy, maggoty, maudlin, merry, moony, moppy, mops and brooms, mortal, muddled, nappy, obfuscated, paralytic, pickled, pie-eyed, pissed, pixil(l)ated, plastered, shickered, sloshed, soaked, sottish, soused, sow-drunk,

sozzled, stewed, stoned, stotious, tanked up, temulent, tiddly, tight, tipsy, up the pole, well-oiled, wet.
antonym sober.

n. boozer, drunkard, inebriate, lush, soak, sot, toper, wino.

drunkard *n.* alcoholic, bacchant, carouser, dipsomaniac, drinker, drunk, lush, soak, sot, souse, sponge, tippler, toper, tosspot, wino.

drunken *adj.* bacchanalian, bacchic, bibulous, boozing, boozy, crapulent, crapulous, debauched, Dionysiac, dissipated, drunk, inebriate, intoxicated, orgiastic, riotous, saturnalian, sodden, sottish, spongy, tippling, toping, under the influence.
antonym sober.

drunkenness *n.* alcoholism, bibulousness, dipsomania, inebriety, insobriety, intemperance, intoxication, ivresse, methysis, sottishness, tipsiness.
antonym sobriety.

dry *adj.* arid, barren, boring, cutting, cynical, deadpan, dehydrated, desiccated, dreary, dried up, droll, droughty, drouthy, dull, juiceless, keen, low-key, moistureless, monotonous, parched, pawky, plain, sapless, sarcastic, sec, secco, sharp, sly, tedious, thirsty, tiresome, torrid, uninteresting, waterless, withered, xeric.
antonyms interesting, sweet, wet.

v. dehumidify, dehydrate, desiccate, drain, exsiccate, harden, mummify, parch, sear, shrivel, welt, wilt, wither, wizen.
antonyms soak, wet.

drying *n.* dehumidification, dehydration, desiccation, exsiccation.

dryness *n.* aridity, aridness, cynicality, dehydration, drought, drouth, pawkiness, sarcasm, thirst, thirstiness, xerosis.
antonym wetness.

dual *adj.* binary, combined, coupled, double, duplex, duplicate, geminate, matched, paired, twin, twofold.

dub *v.* bestow, call, christen, confer, denominate, designate, entitle, knight, label, name, nickname, style, tag, term.

dubiety *n.* doubt, doubtfulness, dubiosity, dubiousness, incertitude, indecision, misgiving, mistrust, qualm, scepticism, suspicion, uncertainty.
antonym certainty.

dubious *adj.* ambiguous, debatable, doubtful, equivocal, fishy, hesitant, iffy, indefinite, indeterminate, obscure, problematical, questionable, sceptical, shady, speculative, suspect, suspicious, uncertain, unclear, unconvinced, undecided, undependable, unreliable, unsettled, unsure, untrustworthy, wavering.
antonyms certain, reliable, trustworthy.

duck[1] *v.* avoid, bend, bob, bow, crouch, dodge, drop, escape, evade, lower, shirk, shun, sidestep, squat, stoop.

duck[2] *v.* dip, dive, dook, douse, dunk, immerse, plunge, souse, submerge, wet.

duct *n.* blood, canal, channel, conduit, fistula, funnel, passage, pipe, tube, vas, vessel.

ductile *adj.* amenable, biddable, complaint, docile, extensible, flexible, malleable, manageable, manipul(at)able, plastic, pliable, pliant, tractable, yielding.
antonyms intractable, refractory.

dud *n.* bum steer, failure, flop, lemon, stumer, wash-out.

adj. broken, bust, duff, failed, inoperative, kaput, nugatory, valueless, worthless.

due *adj.* adequate, ample, appropriate, becoming, bounden, deserved, enough, expected, fit, fitting, in arrears, just, justified, mature, merited, obligatory, outstanding, owed, owing, payable, plenty of, proper, requisite, returnable, right, rightful, scheduled, sufficient, suitable, unpaid, well-earned.

n. birthright, come-uppance, deserts, merits, prerogative, privilege, right(s).

adv. dead, direct, directly, exactly, precisely, straight.

duel *n.* affair of honour, clash, competition, contest, duello, encounter, engagement, fight, monomachia, monomachy, rivalry, single combat, struggle.
v. battle, clash, compete, contend, contest, fight, rival, struggle, vie.

dues *n.* charge(s), contribution, fee, levy, subscription.

duffer *n.* blunderer, bonehead, booby, bungler, clod, clot, dolt, galoot, lubber, lummox, muff, oaf.

dull *adj.* apathetic, blank, blockish, blunt, blunted, Boeotian, boring, bovine, callous, cloudy, commonplace, corny, dead, dead-and-alive, dense, depressed, dim, dimwitted, dismal, doltish, dowie, drab, dreary, dry, dulled, edgeless, empty, faded, featureless, feeble, flat, gloomy, heavy, humdrum, inactive, indifferent, indistinct, insensible, insensitive, insipid, lack-lustre, leaden, lifeless, listless, monotonous, mopish, muffled, mumpish, murky, muted, opaque, overcast, passionless, pedestrian, plain, prosaic, run-of-the-mill, slack, sleepy, slow, sluggish, sombre, stodgy, stolid, stultifying, stupid, subdued, subfusc, sullen, sunless, tame, tedious, thick, tiresome, toneless, torpid, turbid, uneventful, unexciting, unfunny, ungifted, unidea'd, unimaginative, unintelligent, uninteresting, unlively, unresponsive, unsharpened, unsunny, unsympathetic, untalented, vacuous, vapid.
antonyms alert, bright, clear, exciting, sharp.

v. allay, alleviate, assuage, blunt, cloud, dampen, darken, deject, depress, dim, discourage, disedge, dishearten, dispirit, fade, hebetate, lessen, mitigate, moderate, muffle, obscure, obtund, opiate, palliate, paralyse, rebate, relieve, sadden, soften, stain, stupefy, subdue, sully, tarnish.
antonyms brighten, sharpen, stimulate.

dullard *n.* blockhead, bonehead, chump, clod, clot, dimwit, dolt, dope, dummy, dunce,

dunderhead, flat tyre, idiot, ignoramus, imbecile, moron, nitwit, noodle, numskull, oaf, simpleton, vegetable.
antonym brain.

dullness *n.* dreariness, dryness, emptiness, fadeur, flatness, hebetude, hebetudinosity, monotony, plainness, slowness, sluggishness, stolidity, stupidity, tedium, torpor, vacuity, vapidity.
antonyms brightness, clarity, excitement, interest, sharpness.

duly *adv.* accordingly, appropriately, befittingly, condignly, correctly, decorously, deservedly, fitly, fittingly, properly, punctually, rightfully, suitably, sure enough.

dumb *adj.* aphonic, aphonous, dense, dimwitted, dull, foolish, inarticulate, mum, mute, silent, soundless, speechless, stupid, thick, tongue-tied, unintelligent, voiceless, wordless.
antonym intelligent.

dum(b)founded *adj.* amazed, astonished, astounded, bewildered, bowled over, breathless, confounded, confused, dumb, flabbergasted, floored, knocked sideways, nonplussed, overcome, overwhelmed, paralysed, speechless, staggered, startled, stunned, taken aback, thrown, thunderstruck.

dummy *n.* blockhead, copy, counterfeit, dimwit, dolt, dullard, dunce, duplicate, figure, fool, form, imitation, lay-figure, manikin, mannequin, model, numskull, pacifier, sham, simpleton, substitute, teat.
adj. artificial, bogus, dry, fake, false, imitation, mock, phoney, practice, sham, simulated, trial.

dump *v.* deposit, discharge, dispose of, ditch, drop, empty out, get rid of, jettison, let fall, offload, park, scrap, throw away, throw down, tip, unload.
n. coup, hole, hovel, joint, junk-yard, landhill, mess, midden, pigsty, rubbish-heap, rubbish-tip, shack, shanty, slum, tip.

dumpy *adj.* chubby, chunky, fatling, homely, plump, podgy, pudgy, roly-poly, short, squab, squat, stout, stubby, tubby.
antonyms rangy, tall.

dun *v.* beset, harass, harry, importune, pester, plague, press, urge.

dunce *n.* ass, blockhead, bonehead, dimwit, dolt, donkey, duffer, dullard, dunderhead, goose, half-wit, ignoramus, loggerhead, loghead, loon, moron, nincompoop, numskull, simpleton.
antonyms brain, intellectual.

dung *n.* excrement, faeces, fumet, guano, manure, ordure, spraint.

dungeon *n.* cage, cell, donjon, lock-up, oubliette, pit, prison, vault.

dunghill *n.* midden, middenstead, mixen, muck-heap, muck-midden.

dupe *n.* cat's-paw, fall guy, flat, geck, gull, instrument, mug, pawn, pigeon, puppet, push-over, sap, simpleton, sitter, soft mark, stooge, sucker, tool, victim.

v. bamboozle, beguile, cheat, con, cozen, deceive, defraud, delude, gammon, grift, gudgeon, gull, hoax, hoodwink, humbug, outwit, overreach, pigeon, rip off, swindle, trick.

duplicate *adj.* corresponding, geminate, identical, matched, matching, twin, twofold.
n. carbon copy, copy, facsimile, match, photocopy, Photostat®, replica, reproduction, Xerox®.
v. clone, copy, ditto, double, echo, geminate, photocopy, Photostat®, repeat, replicate, reproduce, Xerox®.

duplication *n.* clone, cloning, copy(ing), dittography, gemination, photocopy(ing), repetition, replication, reproduction.

duplicity *n.* artifice, chicanery, deceit, deception, dishonesty, dissimulation, double-dealing, falsehood, fraud, guile, hypocrisy, mendacity, perfidy, treachery.

durability *n.* constancy, durableness, endurance, imperishability, lastingness, longevity, permanence, persistence, stability, strength.
antonyms fragility, impermanence, weakness.

durable *adj.* abiding, constant, dependable, enduring, fast, firm, fixed, hard-wearing, lasting, long-lasting, perdurable, permanent, persistent, reliable, resistant, sound, stable, strong, sturdy, substantial, tough, unfading.
antonyms fragile, impermanent, perishable, weak.

duration *n.* continuance, continuation, extent, fullness, length, period, perpetuation, prolongation, span, spell, stretch, term-time.
antonym shortening.

duress *n.* bullying, captivity, coaction, coercion, compulsion, confinement, constraint, force, hardship, imprisonment, incarceration, pressure, restraint, threat.

dusk *n.* crepuscle, crepuscule, dark, darkness, evening, eventide, gloaming, gloom, murk, nightfall, obscurity, shade, shadowiness, sundown, sunset, twilight.
antonyms brightness, dawn.

duskiness *n.* caliginosity, darkness, fuliginosity, murkiness, swarthiness.
antonyms brightness, lightness, whiteness.

dusky *adj.* caliginous, cloudy, crepuscular, dark, dark-hued, darkish, dim, fuliginous, gloomy, murky, obscure, overcast, sable, shadowy, shady, sooty, subfusc, swarthy, tenebr(i)ous, twilight, twilit, umbrose, veiled.
antonyms bright, light, white.

dust *n.* coom, dirt, earth, grime, grit, ground, particles, powder, soil.
v. burnish, clean, cover, dredge, polish, powder, scatter, sift, spray, spread, sprinkle, wipe.

dustman *n.* garbo, garbologist.

dust-storm *n.* dust-devil, sand-storm.

dust-up *n.* argument, argy-bargy, brawl, brush, commotion, conflict, disagreement, disturbance, encounter, fight, fracas, punch-up, quarrel, scrap, scuffle, set-to, shindig, skirmish, tussle.

dusty *adj.* chalky, crumbly, dirty, filthy, friable, granular, grubby, powdery, pulverous, sandy, sooty, unswept.
antonyms clean, hard, polished, solid.
dutiful *adj.* acquiescent, complaisant, compliant, conscientious, deferential, devoted, docile, duteous, filial, obedient, punctilious, regardful, respectful, reverential, submissive.
duty *n.* allegiance, assignment, business, calling, charge, chore, customs, debt, deference, devoir, due, engagement, excise, function, impost, job, levy, loyalty, mission, obedience, obligation, office, onus, province, respect, responsibility, reverence, role, service, tariff, task, tax, toll, work.
dwarf *n.* droich, durgan, elf, gnome, goblin, homuncle, homuncule, homunculus, hop-o'-my-thumb, Lilliputian, man(n)ikin, midget, pygmy, Tom Thumb.
adj. baby, bonsai, diminutive, dwarfed, dwarfish, Lilliputian, mini, miniature, petite, pint-size(d), pocket, small, tiny, undersized.
antonym large.
v. check, dim, diminish, dominate, lower, minimise, overshadow, retard, stunt.
dwarfish *adj.* diminutive, durgy, pocket, pygmean, pygmy, small, stunted, undersized.
antonym large.
dwell *v.* abide, bide, hang out, inhabit, live, lodge, people, populate, quarter, remain, reside, rest, settle, sojourn, stay, stop, tenant.
dwell on elaborate, emphasise, expatiate, harp on, harp on about, linger over, mull over.
antonym pass over.
dweller *n.* denizen, inhabitant, occupant, occupier, resident.
dwelling *n.* abode, domicile, dwelling-house, establishment, habitation, home, house, lodge, lodging, quarters, residence, tent, tepee, woning.
dwindle *v.* abate, contract, decay, decline, decrease, die, die out, diminish, disappear, ebb, fade, fall, lessen, peter out, pine, shrink, shrivel, sink, subside, tail off, taper off, vanish, wane, waste away, weaken, wither.
antonym increase.
dye *n.* colorant, colour, colouring, grain, pigment, stain, tinge, tint.
v. colour, grain, imbue, pigment, stain, tincture, tinge, tint.
dyed-in-the-wool *adj.* card-carrying, complete, confirmed, deep-rooted, die-hard, entrenched, established, fixed, hard-core, hardened, inflexible, inveterate, long-standing, settled, unchangeable, uncompromising, unshakable.
antonym superficial.
dying *adj.* at death's door, declining, disappearing, ebbing, expiring, fading, failing, final, going, in articulo mortis, in extremis, moribund, mortal, not long for this world, obsolescent, passing, perishing, sinking, vanishing.
antonyms coming, reviving.
dynamic *adj.* active, driving, electric, energetic, forceful, go-ahead, go-getting, high-powered, lively, powerful, self-starting, spirited, vigorous, vital, zippy.
antonyms apathetic, inactive, slow.
dynamism *n.* drive, energy, enterprise, forcefulness, get-up-and-go, go, initiative, liveliness, pep, pizzazz, push, vigour, vim, zap, zip.
antonyms apathy, inactivity, slowness.
dynasty *n.* ascendancy, authority, dominion, empire, government, house, regime, rule, sovereignty, succession, sway.
dyspeptic *adj.* bad-tempered, crabbed, crabby, crotchety, gloomy, grouchy, indigested, peevish, short-tempered, snappish, testy, touchy.

E

each *adv.* apiece, individually, per capita, per head, per person, respectively, separately, singly.

eager *adj.* agog, anxious, ardent, athirst, avid, desirous, earnest, empressé, enthusiastic, fervent, fervid, fervorous, freck, greedy, gung-ho, hot, hungry, impatient, intent, keen, longing, perfervid, raring, unshrinking, vehement, yearning, zealous.
antonyms apathetic, unenthusiastic.

eagerly *adv.* ardently, avidly, earnestly, enthusiastically, fain, fervently, greedily, intently, keenly, zealously.
antonyms apathetically, listlessly.

eagerness *n.* ardour, avidity, earnestness, enthusiasm, fainness, fervency, fervidity, fervour, greediness, heartiness, hunger, impatience, impetuosity, intentness, keenness, longing, thirst, vehemence, yearning, zeal.
antonyms apathy, disinterest.

ear *n.* ability, appreciation, attention, consideration, discrimination, hearing, heed, notice, perception, regard, sensitivity, skill, taste.

early *adj.* advanced, forward, matutinal, matutine, prehistoric, premature, primeval, primitive, primordial, undeveloped, untimely, young.
adv. ahead of time, beforehand, betimes, in advance, in good time, prematurely, too soon.
antonym late.

earmark *v.* allocate, designate, keep back, label, put aside, reserve, set aside, tag.

earn *v.* acquire, attain, bring in, collect, deserve, draw, gain, get, gross, make, merit, net, obtain, procure, rate, realise, reap, receive, warrant, win.
antonyms lose, spend.

earnest *adj.* ardent, close, constant, determined, devoted, eager, enthusiastic, fervent, fervid, firm, fixed, grave, heartfelt, impassioned, intent, keen, passionate, purposeful, resolute, resolved, serious, sincere, solemn, stable, staid, steady, thoughtful, urgent, vehement, warm, zealous.
antonyms apathetic, flippant, unenthusiastic.
n. assurance, deposit, determination, down payment, guarantee, pledge, promise, resolution, security, seriousness, sincerity, token, truth.

earnestly *adv.* eagerly, ex animo, fervently, firmly, intently, keenly, resolutely, seriously, sincerely, warmly, zealously.
antonyms flippantly, listlessly.

earnestness *n.* ardour, determination, devotion, eagerness, enthusiasm, fervency, fervour, gravity, intentness, keenness, passion, purposefulness, resolution, seriousness, sincerity, urgency, vehemence, warmth, zeal.
antonyms apathy, flippancy.

earnings *n.* emoluments, gain, income, pay, proceeds, profits, receipts, remuneration, return, revenue, reward, salary, stipend, takings, wages.
antonyms expenses, outgoings.

earring *n.* earbob, ear-drop.

earth[1] *n.* geosphere, globe, middle-earth, middle-world, Midgard, orb, planet, sphere, world.

earth[2] *n.* clay, clod, dirt, ground, humus, land, loam, mould, sod, soil, topsoil.

earthenware *n.* ceramics, crockery, crocks, pots, pottery.
adj. ceramic, clay, fictile, figuline, terra-cotta, wally.

earthly *adj.* base, carnal, conceivable, earthern, feasible, fleshly, gross, human, imaginable, likely, low, material, materialistic, mortal, mundane, physical, possible, practical, profane, secular, sensual, slight, slightest, sordid, sublunar, sublunary, tellurian, telluric, temporal, terrene, terrestrial, vile, worldly.
antonyms heavenly, spiritual.

earthquake *n.* earth-tremor, quake, seism, shake, upheaval.

earthy *adj.* bawdy, blue, coarse, crude, down-to-earth, homely, indecorous, lusty, natural, raunchy, ribald, robust, rough, simple, uninhibited, unrefined, unsophisticated, vulgar.
antonyms cultured, refined.

ease *n.* affluence, aplomb, calmness, comfort, composure, content, contentment, deftness, dexterity, easiness, effortlessness, enjoyment, facileness, facility, flexibility, freedom, happiness, informality, insouciance, leisure, liberty, naturalness, nonchalance, peace, peace of mind, poise, quiet, quietude, readiness, relaxation, repose, rest, restfulness, serenity, simplicity, solace, tranquillity, unaffectedness, unconstraint, unreservedness.
antonyms difficulty, discomfort.
v. abate, aid, allay, alleviate, appease, assist, assuage, calm, comfort, disburden, edge, expedite, facilitate, forward, further, guide, inch, lessen, lighten, manoeuvre, mitigate, moderate, mollify, pacify, palliate, quiet, relax, relent, relieve, simplify, slacken, slide, slip, smooth, solace, soothe, speed up, squeeze, steer, still, tranquillise.
antonyms hinder, retard, torment.

ease off abate, decrease, die away, die down, moderate, relent, slacken, subside, wane.

antonym increase.

easily[1] *adv.* comfortably, effortlessly, facilely, readily, simply, smoothly, standing on one's head, with one arm tied behind one's back. *antonym* laboriously.

easily[2] *adv.* absolutely, by far, certainly, clearly, definitely, doubtlessly, far and away, indisputably, indubitably, plainly, probably, simply, surely, undeniably, undoubtedly, unequivocally, unquestionably, well.

easy *adj.* a doddle, a piece of cake, a pushover, accommodating, affable, amenable, biddable, calm, carefree, casual, child's play, clear, comfortable, compliant, contented, cushy, docile, easeful, easy-going, effortless, facile, flexible, friendly, gentle, graceful, gracious, gullible, idiot-proof, indulgent, informal, leisurely, lenient, liberal, light, manageable, mild, moderate, natural, no bother, open, painless, peaceful, permissive, pleasant, pliant, quiet, relaxed, satisfied, serene, simple, smooth, soft, straightforward, submissive, suggestible, susceptible, temperate, tolerant, tractable, tranquil, trusting, unaffected, unburdensome, unceremonious, uncomplicated, unconstrained, undemanding, undisturbed, unexacting, unforced, unhurried, unlaboured, unoppressive, unpretentious, untroubled, unworried, well-to-do, yielding. *antonyms* demanding, difficult, fast, impossible, intolerant.

easy-going *adj.* amenable, calm, carefree, casual, complacent, easy, easy-osy, even-tempered, flexible, happy-go-lucky, indulgent, insouciant, laid-back, lenient, liberal, mild, moderate, nonchalant, permissive, placid, relaxed, serene, tolerant, unconcerned, uncritical, undemanding, unhurried, unworried. *antonyms* fussy, intolerant.

eat *v.* banquet, break bread, chew, chop, consume, corrode, crumble, decay, devour, dine, dissolve, erode, feed, grub, ingest, knock back, manducate, munch, pig, rot, scoff, swallow, wear away.

eat one's words abjure, recant, rescind, retract, take back, unsay.

eatable *adj.* comestible, digestible, edible, esculent, good, harmless, palatable, wholesome. *antonym* unpalatable.

eatables *n.* comestibles, food, grub, nosh, scoff.

eavesdrop *v.* bug, earwig, listen in, monitor, overhear, snoop, spy, tap.

eavesdropper *n.* listener, monitor, snoop, snooper, spy.

ebb *v.* abate, decay, decline, decrease, degenerate, deteriorate, diminish, drop, dwindle, fade away, fall away, fall back, flag, flow back, go out, lessen, peter out, recede, reflow, retire, retreat, retrocede, shrink, sink, slacken, subside, wane, weaken, withdraw. *antonyms* increase, rise.

n. decay, decline, decrease, degeneration, deterioration, diminution, drop, dwindling, ebb tide, flagging, lessening, low tide, low water, reflow, refluence, reflux, regression, retreat, retrocession, shrinkage, sinking, slackening, subsidence, wane, waning, weakening, withdrawal. *antonyms* flow, increase, rising.

ebony *adj.* black, dark, jet, jet-black, jetty, sable, sooty.

ebullience *n.* boiling, breeziness, brightness, bubbling, buoyancy, chirpiness, ebullition, effervescence, effusiveness, elation, enthusiasm, excitement, exhilaration, exuberance, ferment, fermentation, foaming, frothing, high spirits, seething, vivacity, zest. *antonyms* apathy, dullness, lifelessness.

ebullient *adj.* boiling, breezy, bright, bubbling, buoyant, chirpy, effervescent, effusive, elated, enthusiastic, excited, exhilarated, exuberant, foaming, frothing, frothy, gushing, irrepressible, seething, vivacious, zestful. *antonyms* apathetic, dull, lifeless.

eccentric *adj.* aberrant, abnormal, anomalous, bizarre, capricious, dotty, erratic, fey, freakish, fruity, idiosyncratic, irregular, nuts, nutty, odd, offbeat, outlandish, peculiar, queer, quirky, screwball, screwy, singular, spac(e)y, strange, uncommon, unconventional, way-out, weird, whimsical. *antonyms* normal, sane.

n. case, character, crank, freak, fruit-cake, nonconformist, nut, nutter, oddball, oddity, queer fish, screwball, weirdie, weirdo.

eccentricity *n.* aberration, abnormality, anomaly, bizarreness, bizarrerie, caprice, capriciousness, foible, freakishness, idiosyncrasy, irregularity, nonconformity, oddity, outlandishness, peculiarity, queerness, quirk, singularity, strangeness, unconventionality, waywardness, weirdness, whimsicality. *antonyms* normalcy, normality, ordinariness.

ecclesiastic *n.* abbé, churchman, clergyman, cleric, divine, man of the cloth, minister, parson, priest.

ecclesiastic(al) *adj.* church, churchly, churchy, clerical, divine, holy, pastoral, priestly, religious, spiritual, templar.

echelon *n.* degree, grade, level, place, position, rank, status, step, tier.

echo *v.* ape, copy, echoise, imitate, mimic, mirror, parallel, parrot, recall, reflect, reiterate, repeat, reproduce, resemble, resound, reverberate, ring, second.

n. allusion, answer, copy, evocation, hint, image, imitation, intimation, memory, mirror image, parallel, reflection, reiteration, reminder, repetition, reproduction, reverberation, suggestion, sympathy, trace.

echoic *adj.* imitative, onomatopoeic, onomatopoetic.

éclat *n.* acclaim, acclamation, applause, approval, brilliance, celebrity, display, distinction, effect, fame, glory, lustre, ostentation, plaudits, pomp, renown, show, showmanship, splendour, success.

antonyms disapproval, dullness.

eclectic *adj.* all-embracing, broad, catholic, comprehensive, dilettantish, diverse, diversified, general, heterogeneous, liberal, many-sided, multifarious, selective, varied, wide-ranging.

antonyms narrow, one-sided.

eclipse *v.* blot out, cloud, darken, dim, dwarf, exceed, excel, extinguish, obscure, outdo, outshine, overshadow, shroud, surpass, transcend, veil.

n. darkening, decline, deliquium, diminution, dimming, extinction, failure, fall, loss, obscuration, occultation, overshadowing, shading.

economic *adj.* budgetary, business, cheap, commercial, cost-effective, economical, economy-size, fair, financial, fiscal, industrial, inexpensive, low, low-priced, mercantile, modest, monetary, money-making, pecuniary, productive, profitable, profit-making, reasonable, remunerative, solvent, trade, viable.

antonyms expensive, uneconomic.

economical *adj.* careful, cheap, cost-effective, economic, economising, efficient, fair, frugal, inexpensive, labour-saving, low, low-priced, modest, prudent, reasonable, saving, scrimping, sparing, thrifty, time-saving.

antonyms expensive, uneconomical.

economics *n.* plutology, plutonomy, political economy.

economise *v.* cut back, cut corners, husband, retrench, save, scrimp, tighten one's belt.

antonym squander.

economy *n.* frugality, frugalness, husbandry, parsimony, providence, prudence, restraint, retrenchment, saving, scrimping, sparingness, thrift, thriftiness.

antonym improvidence.

ecstasy *n.* bliss, delight, ecstasis, elation, enthusiasm, euphoria, exaltation, fervour, frenzy, joy, rapture, ravishment, rhapsody, seventh heaven, sublimation, trance, transport.

antonym torment.

ecstatic *adj.* blissful, delirious, elated, enraptured, enthusiastic, entranced, euphoric, exultant, fervent, frenzied, joyful, joyous, on cloud nine, over the moon, overjoyed, rapturous, rhapsodic, transported.

antonym downcast.

eddy *n.* counter-current, counterflow, pirl, purl, swirl, vortex, well, whirlpool.

v. swirl, whirl.

edge *n.* acuteness, advantage, animation, arris, ascendancy, bezel, bite, border, bound, boundary, brim, brink, cantle, contour, dominance, effectiveness, force, fringe, incisiveness, interest, keenness, lead, limit, line, lip, margin, outline, perimeter, periphery, point, pungency, rim, sharpness, side, sting, superiority, threshold, upper hand, urgency, verge, zest.

v. bind, border, creep, drib, ease, fringe,

gravitate, hem, hone, inch, rim, shape, sharpen, sidle, steal, strop, trim, verge, whet, work, worm.

edgy *adj.* anxious, ill at ease, irascible, irritable, keyed-up, nervous, on edge, prickly, restive, tense, testy, touchy.

antonym calm.

edible *adj.* comestible, digestible, eatable, esculent, good, harmless, palatable, safe, wholesome.

antonym inedible.

edict *n.* act, command, decree, dictate, dictum, enactment, fiat, injunction, law, mandate, manifesto, order, ordinance, proclamation, pronouncement, pronunciamento, regulation, rescript, ruling, statute, ukase.

edification *n.* enlightenment, guidance, improvement, instruction, upbuilding.

edifice *n.* building, construction, erection, structure.

edify *v.* educate, elevate, enlighten, guide, improve, inform, instruct, nurture, school, teach, train, tutor.

edit *v.* adapt, annotate, assemble, blue-pencil, bowdlerise, censor, check, compose, condense, correct, emend, polish, rearrange, redact, reorder, rephrase, revise, rewrite, select.

edition *n.* copy, exemplar, impression, issue, number, printing, programme, version, volume.

educable *adj.* instructible, teachable, trainable.

antonym ineducable.

educate *v.* catechise, civilise, coach, cultivate, develop, discipline, drill, edify, exercise, improve, indoctrinate, inform, instruct, learn, mature, rear, school, teach, train, tutor.

educated *adj.* civilised, coached, cultivated, cultured, enlightened, experienced, informed, instructed, knowledgeable, learned, lettered, literary, nurtured, polished, refined, schooled, sophisticated, taught, trained, tutored, well-bred.

antonyms uncultured, uneducated.

education *n.* breeding, civilisation, coaching, cultivation, culture, development, discipline, drilling, edification, enlightenment, erudition, guidance, improvement, indoctrination, instruction, knowledge, nurture, scholarship, schooling, teaching, training, tuition, tutelage, tutoring.

educational *adj.* cultural, didactic, edifying, educative, enlightening, improving, informative, instructive, scholastic.

antonym uninformative.

educative *adj.* catechetic, catechismal, catechistic(al), didactic, edifying, educational, enlightening, improving, informative, instructive.

antonym uninformative.

educator *n.* coach, dominie, edifier, educationalist, educationist, instructor, lecturer, pedagogue, schoolmaster, schoolmistress, schoolteacher, teacher, trainer, tutor.

eerie *adj.* awesome, chilling, creepy, eldritch,

fearful, frightening, ghastly, ghostly, mysterious, scary, spectral, spine-chilling, spooky, strange, uncanny, unearthly, unnatural, weird.
antonyms natural, ordinary.
efface *v.* annihilate, blank out, blot out, blue-pencil, cancel, cross out, delete, destroy, dim, eliminate, eradicate, erase, excise, expunge, extirpate, humble, lower, obliterate, raze, remove, rub out, wipe out, withdraw.
effect *n.* action, aftermath, clout, conclusion, consequence, drift, éclat, effectiveness, efficacy, efficiency, enforcement, essence, event, execution, fact, force, fruit, impact, implementation, import, impression, influence, issue, meaning, operation, outcome, power, purport, purpose, reality, result, sense, significance, strength, tenor, upshot, use, validity, vigour, weight, work.
v. accomplish, achieve, actuate, cause, complete, consummate, create, effectuate, execute, fulfil, initiate, make, perform, produce, wreak.
effective *adj.* able, active, adequate, capable, cogent, compelling, competent, convincing, current, effectual, efficacious, efficient, emphatic, energetic, forceful, forcible, implemental, impressive, moving, operative, perficient, persuasive, potent, powerful, productive, real, serviceable, striking, telling, useful.
antonyms ineffective, useless.
effectiveness *n.* ability, capability, clout, cogency, effect, efficacy, efficiency, force, influence, potency, power, strength, success, use, validity, vigour, weight.
antonyms ineffectiveness, uselessness.
effects *n.* belongings, chattels, gear, goods, movables, paraphernalia, possessions, property, things, trappings, traps.
effectual *adj.* authoritative, binding, capable, effective, efficacious, efficient, forcible, influential, lawful, legal, licit, operative, perficient, potent, powerful, productive, serviceable, sound, successful, telling, useful, valid.
antonyms ineffective, useless.
effeminate *adj.* delicate, epicene, feminine, pansy, poofy, sissy, soft, tender, unmanly, weak, womanish, womanlike, womanly.
antonym manly.
effervesce *v.* boil, bubble, ferment, fizz, foam, froth, sparkle.
effervescence *n.* animation, bubbles, bubbling, buoyancy, ebullience, ebulliency, enthusiasm, excitedness, excitement, exhilaration, exuberance, ferment, fermentation, fizz, foam, foaming, froth, frothing, gaiety, high spirits, liveliness, sparkle, vim, vitality, vivacity, zing, zip.
effervescent *adj.* animated, bubbling, bubbly, buoyant, carbonated, ebullient, enthusiastic, excited, exhilarated, exuberant, fermenting, fizzing, fizzy, foaming, frothing, frothy, gay, irrepressible, lively, merry, sparkling, vital,

vivacious, zingy.
antonyms apathetic, dull, flat.
effete *adj.* barren, corrupt, debased, debilitated, decadent, decayed, decrepit, degenerate, dissipated, drained, enervated, enfeebled, exhausted, feeble, fruitless, incapable, ineffectual, infecund, infertile, overrefined, played out, spent, spoiled, sterile, tired out, unfruitful, unproductive, unprolific, used up, wasted, weak, worn out.
antonym vigorous.
efficacious *adj.* active, adequate, capable, competent, effective, effectual, efficient, energetic, operative, potent, powerful, productive, serviceable, strong, successful, sufficient, useful.
antonyms ineffective, useless.
efficacy *n.* ability, capability, competence, effect, effectiveness, efficaciousness, efficiency, energy, force, influence, potency, power, strength, success, use, virtue.
antonyms ineffectiveness, uselessness.
efficiency *n.* ability, adeptness, capability, competence, competency, economy, effectiveness, efficacy, mastery, power, productivity, proficiency, readiness, skilfulness, skill.
antonym inefficiency.
efficient *adj.* able, adept, businesslike, capable, competent, economic, effective, effectual, powerful, productive, proficient, ready, skilful, streamlined, well-conducted, well-ordered, well-organised, well-regulated, workmanlike.
antonym inefficient.
effigy *n.* carving, dummy, figure, guy, icon, idol, image, likeness, mumbo-jumbo, picture, portrait, representation, statue.
effluent *n.* discharge, effluence, effluvium, efflux, emanation, emission, exhalation, outflow, pollutant, pollution, sewage, waste.
effort *n.* accomplishment, achievement, application, attempt, conatus, creation, deed, endeavour, energy, essay, exertion, feat, force, go, job, labour, molimen, nisus, pains, power, product, production, shot, stab, strain, stress, stretch, striving, struggle, toil, travail, trouble, try, work.
effortless *adj.* easy, facile, painless, simple, smooth, uncomplicated, undemanding, unlaboured.
antonym difficult.
effrontery *n.* arrogance, assurance, audacity, boldness, brashness, brass (neck), brazenness, cheek, cheekiness, disrespect, face, front, gall, impertinence, impudence, incivility, insolence, neck, nerve, presumption, rudeness, shamelessness, temerity.
effusion *n.* address, discharge, effluence, efflux, emission, gush, outflow, outpouring, shedding, speech, stream, talk, utterance, voidance, word salad, writing.
effusive *adj.* demonstrative, ebullient, enthusiastic, expansive, extravagant, exuberant, fulsome, gushing, gushy, lavish, overflowing, profuse, talkative, unreserved, unrestrained,

voluble, wordy.

antonyms quiet, restrained.

egg on coax, encourage, exhort, goad, incite, prick, prod, prompt, push, spur, stimulate, urge, wheedle.

antonym discourage.

egghead *n.* brain, Einstein, genius, headpiece, intellect, intellectual, scholar.

egoism *n.* amour-propre, egocentricity, egomania, egotism, narcissism, self-absorption, self-centredness, self-importance, self-interest, selfishness, self-love, self-regard, self-seeking.

antonym altruism.

egoist *n.* egomaniac, egotist, narcissist, self-seeker.

egoistic *adj.* egocentric, egoistical, egomaniacal, egotistic, egotistical, narcissistic, self-absorbed, self-centred, self-important, self-involved, self-pleasing, self-seeking.

antonym altruistic.

egotism *n.* bigheadedness, conceitedness, egocentricity, egoism, egomania, narcissism, self-admiration, self-centredness, self-conceit, self-esteem, self-importance, self-love, self-praise, self-pride, superiority, vainglory, vanity.

antonym humility.

egotist *n.* bighead, boaster, braggadocio, braggart, egoist, egomaniac, swaggerer.

egotistic *adj.* bigheaded, boasting, bragging, conceited, egocentric, egoistic, egoistical, egomaniacal, egotistical, narcissistic, opinionated, self-centred, self-important, superior, swollen-headed, vain, vainglorious.

antonym humble.

egregious *adj.* arrant, flagrant, frabjous, glaring, grievous, gross, heinous, infamous, insufferable, intolerable, monstrous, notorious, outrageous, rank, scandalous, shocking.

antonym slight.

egress *n.* emergence, escape, exit, exodus, issue, outlet, vent.

ejaculate[1] *v.* discharge, eject, emit, spurt.

ejaculate[2] *v.* blurt, call, cry, exclaim, scream, shout, utter, yell.

ejaculation[1] *n.* discharge, ejection, emission, spurt.

ejaculation[2] *n.* call, cry, exclamation, scream, shout, utterance, yell.

eject *v.* banish, belch, boot out, bounce, deport, discharge, disgorge, dislodge, dismiss, dispossess, drive out, emit, evacuate, evict, exile, expel, fire, kick out, oust, remove, sack, spew, spout, throw out, turn out, unhouse, vomit.

ejection *n.* banishment, defenestration, deportation, discharge, disgorgement, dislodgement, dismissal, dispossession, evacuation, eviction, exile, expulsion, firing, ouster, ousting, removal, sacking, spouting, the boot, the sack.

eke out add to, economise on, husband, increase, make (something) stretch, stretch, supplement.

elaborate *adj.* careful, complex, complicated,

daedal(ic), decorated, dedal(ian), detailed, exact, extravagant, fancy, fussy, Heath-Robinson, intricate, involved, laboured, minute, ornamental, ornate, ostentatious, painstaking, perfected, precise, showy, skilful, studied, thorough.

antonyms plain, simple.

v. amplify, complicate, decorate, detail, develop, devise, embellish, enhance, enlarge, expand, expatiate, explain, flesh out, garnish, improve, ornament, polish, refine.

antonyms précis, simplify.

élan *n.* animation, brio, dash, esprit, flair, flourish, impetuosity, liveliness, oomph, panache, pizzazz, spirit, style, verve, vigour, vivacity, zest.

antonyms apathy, lifelessness.

elapse *v.* go by, lapse, pass, slip away.

elastic *adj.* accommodating, adaptable, adjustable, bouncy, buoyant, complaisant, compliant, distensible, ductile, flexible, irrepressible, plastic, pliable, pliant, resilient, rubbery, springy, stretchable, stretchy, supple, tolerant, variable, yielding.

antonym rigid.

elasticity *n.* adaptability, adjustability, bounce, buoyancy, complaisance, compliance, compliancy, compliantness, ductileness, ductility, flexibility, give, irrepressibility, plasticity, pliability, pliancy, resilience, rubberiness, springiness, stretch, stretchiness, suppleness, tolerance, variability.

antonym rigidity.

elated *adj.* animated, blissful, cheered, delighted, ecstatic, euphoric, excited, exhilarated, exultant, gleeful, joyful, joyous, jubilant, on the high ropes, over the moon, overjoyed, pleased, proud, roused.

antonym downcast.

elation *n.* bliss, delight, ecstasy, euphoria, exaltation, exhilaration, exultation, glee, high spirits, joy, joyfulness, joyousness, jubilation, rapture, transports of delight.

antonym depression.

elbow *v.* bulldoze, bump, crowd, hustle, jostle, knock, nudge, plough, push, shoulder, shove.

elbow-room *n.* freedom, latitude, Lebensraum, leeway, play, room, scope, space.

elder *adj.* aîné(e), ancient, eigne, first-born, older, senior.

antonym younger.

n. deacon, presbyter, senior.

elderly *adj.* aged, aging, badgerly, hoary, old, senile.

antonyms young, youthful.

eldest *adj.* first, first-begotten, first-born, oldest.

antonym youngest.

elect *v.* adopt, appoint, choose, designate, determine, opt for, pick, prefer, select, vote. *adj.* choice, chosen, designate, designated, elite, hand-picked, picked, preferred, presumptive, prospective, select, selected, to be.

election *n.* appointment, ballot-box, choice, choosing, decision, determination, judgement, preference, selection, vote, voting.

elector *n.* constituent, selector, voter.

electric *adj.* charged, dynamic, electrifying, exciting, rousing, stimulating, stirring, tense, thrilling.
antonyms tedious, unexciting.

electrify *v.* amaze, animate, astonish, astound, excite, fire, galvanise, invigorate, jolt, rouse, shock, stagger, startle, stimulate, stir, stun, thrill.
antonym bore.

elegance *n.* beauty, chic, concinnity, courtliness, dignity, discernment, distinction, exquisiteness, gentility, grace, gracefulness, grandeur, luxury, polish, politeness, propriety, refinement, style, sumptuousness, taste.
antonym inelegance.

elegant *adj.* à la mode, appropriate, apt, artistic, beautiful, chic, choice, clever, comely, concinnous, courtly, cultivated, debonair, delicate, effective, exquisite, fashionable, fine, genteel, graceful, handsome, ingenious, luxurious, modish, neat, nice, polished, refined, simple, smooth, stylish, sumptuous, tasteful.
antonym inelegant.

elegiac *adj.* doleful, funereal, keening, lamenting, melancholy, mournful, nostalgic, plaintive, sad, threnetic, threnetical, threnodial, threnodic, valedictory.
antonym happy.

elegy *n.* coronach, dirge, keen, lament, plaint, requiem, threnode, threnody.

element *n.* basis, component, constituent, domain, environment, factor, feature, field, fragment, habitat, hint, ingredient, medium, member, milieu, part, piece, section, sphere, subdivision, trace, unit.

elementary *adj.* basic, clear, easy, elemental, facile, fundamental, initial, introductory, original, plain, primary, principial, rudimentary, simple, straightforward, uncomplicated.
antonyms advanced, complex.

elements *n.* basics, essentials, foundations, fundamentals, introduction, principia, principles, rudiments, weather.

elevate *v.* advance, aggrandise, animate, augment, boost, brighten, buoy up, cheer, elate, exalt, excite, exhilarate, hearten, heighten, hoist, increase, intensify, lift, magnify, prefer, promote, raise, rouse, sublimate, swell, upgrade, uplift, upraise.
antonyms lessen, lower.

elevated *adj.* animated, cheerful, cheery, dignified, elated, exalted, excited, exhilarated, grand, high, high-flown, high-minded, inflated, lofty, noble, overjoyed, raised, sublime, tipsy.
antonyms base, informal, lowly.

elevation *n.* acclivity, advancement, aggrandisement, altitude, eminence, exaltation, exaltedness, grandeur, height, hill, hillock, loftiness, mountain, nobility, nobleness, preferment, promotion, rise, sublimation, sublimity, upgrading, uplift.
antonyms baseness, informality.

elfin *adj.* arch, charming, delicate, elfish, elflike, elvish, frolicsome, impish, mischievous, petite, playful, puckish, small, sprightly.

elicit *v.* cause, derive, draw out, educe, evoke, evolve, exact, extort, extract, fish, mole out, obtain, wrest, wring.

eligible *adj.* acceptable, appropriate, available, desirable, fit, proper, qualified, suitable, suited, worthy.
antonym ineligible.

eliminate *v.* annihilate, bump off, cut out, delete, dispense with, dispose of, disregard, do away with, drop, eject, eradicate, exclude, expel, expunge, exterminate, extinguish, get rid of, ignore, kill, knock out, liquidate, murder, omit, reject, remove, rub out, slay, stamp out, take out, terminate, waste.
antonym accept.

elite *n.* aristocracy, best, cream, crème de la crème, elect, establishment, flower, gentry, high society, meritocracy, nobility, pick.
adj. aristocratic, best, choice, crack, exclusive, first-class, noble, pick, selected, top, top-class, upper-class.
antonyms ordinary, run-of-the-mill.

elixir *n.* concentrate, cure-all, daffy, essence, extract, mixture, nostrum, panacea, pith, potion, principle, quintessence, remedy, solution, syrup, tincture, treacle.

elliptical[1] *adj.* egg-shaped, oval, oviform, ovoid(al).

elliptical[2] *adj.* abstruse, ambiguous, concentrated, concise, condensed, cryptic, incomprehensible, laconic, obscure, recondite, terse, unfathomable.
antonym clear.

elocution *n.* articulation, declamation, delivery, diction, enunciation, oratory, pronunciation, rhetoric, speech, speechmaking, utterance.

elongated *adj.* extended, lengthened, long, prolonged, protracted, stretched.

elope *v.* abscond, bolt, decamp, disappear, do a bunk, escape, leave, run away, run off, slip away, steal away.

eloquence *n.* dick, expression, expressiveness, facundity, fluency, forcefulness, oratory, persuasiveness, rhetoric.
antonym inarticulateness.

eloquent *adj.* articulate, Demosthenic, expressive, fluent, forceful, graceful, honeyed, meaningful, moving, persuasive, plausible, pregnant, revealing, silver-tongued, stirring, suggestive, telling, vivid, vocal, voluble, well-expressed.
antonyms inarticulate, tongue-tied.

elucidate *v.* annotate, clarify, explain, explicate, expound, gloss, illuminate, illustrate, interpret, spell out, unfold.
antonyms confuse, obscure.

elucidation *n.* annotation, clarification, comment, commentary, explanation, explication, exposition, foot-note, gloss, illumination, illustration, interpretation, marginalia.

elude *v.* avoid, baffle, beat, circumvent, confound, dodge, duck, escape, evade, flee, foil, frustrate, outrun, puzzle, shirk, shun, stump, thwart.

elusive *adj.* ambiguous, baffling, deceitful, deceptive, elusory, equivocal, evasive, fallacious, fleeting, fraudulent, fugitive, illusory, indefinable, intangible, misleading, puzzling, shifty, slippery, subtle, transient, transitory, tricky, unanalysable.

emaciated *adj.* atrophied, attenuate, attenuated, cadaverous, gaunt, haggard, lank, lean, meagre, pinched, scrawny, skeletal, tabefied, tabescent, thin, wasted.
antonyms plump, well-fed.

emaciation *n.* atrophy, attenuation, gauntness, haggardness, leanness, meagreness, scrawniness, tabefaction, tabes, tabescence, thinness.
antonym plumpness.

emanate *v.* arise, come, derive, discharge, emerge, emit, exhale, flow, give off, give out, issue, originate, proceed, radiate, send out, spring, stem.

emanation *n.* arising, derivation, discharge, ectoplasm, effluence, effluent, effluvium, efflux, effluxion, effusion, emergence, emission, exhalation, exoplasm, flow, generation, mephitis, origination, proceeding, procession, radiation.

emancipate *v.* deliver, discharge, disencumber, disenthral, enfranchise, free, liberate, manumit, release, set free, unbind, unchain, unfetter, unshackle.
antonym enslave.

emancipation *n.* deliverance, discharge, enfranchisement, freedom, liberation, liberty, manumission, release, unbinding, unchaining.
antonym enslavement.

emasculate *v.* castrate, cripple, debilitate, enervate, geld, impoverish, neuter, soften, spay, weaken.
antonyms boost, vitalise.

embalm *v.* cherish, consecrate, conserve, enshrine, immortalise, mummify, preserve, store, treasure.

embankment *n.* bund, causeway, causey, defences, earthwork, levee, rampart.

embargo *n.* ban, bar, barrier, blockage, check, hindrance, impediment, interdict, interdiction, prohibition, proscription, restraint, restriction, seizure, stoppage.
v. ban, bar, block, check, embar, impede, interdict, prohibit, proscribe, restrict, seize, stop.
antonym allow.

embark *v.* board ship, emplane, entrain, take ship.
antonym disembark.
embark on begin, broach, commence, engage, enter, initiate, launch, start, undertake.
antonym finish.

embarkation *n.* boarding, entrainment.
antonym disembarkation.

embarrass *v.* abash, chagrin, confuse, discomfit, discomfort, discompose, disconcert, discountenance, distress, fluster, mortify, shame, show up.

embarrassed *adj.* abashed, constrained, discomfited, disconcerted, mortified, shamed, shown up, uncomfortable.
antonym unembarrassed.

embarrassing *adj.* awkward, compromising, discomfiting, discomfortable, disconcerting, distressing, humiliating, mortifying, sensitive, shameful, shaming, touchy, tricky, uncomfortable.

embarrassment *n.* awkwardness, bashfulness, bind, chagrin, confusion, constraint, difficulty, discomfiture, discomfort, discomposure, distress, excess, gêne, humiliation, mess, mortification, overabundance, pickle, predicament, scrape, self-consciousness, shame, superabundance, superfluity, surfeit, surplus.

embassy *n.* consulate, delegation, deputation, embassade, embassage, legation, mission.

embed *v.* fix, imbed, implant, insert, plant, root, set, sink.

embellish *v.* adorn, beautify, bedeck, deck, decorate, dress up, elaborate, embroider, enhance, enrich, exaggerate, festoon, garnish, gild, grace, ornament, trim, varnish.
antonyms denude, simplify.

embellishment *n.* adornment, decoration, elaboration, embroidery, enhancement, enrichment, exaggeration, fioritura, garnish, gilding, melisma, ornament, ornamentation, trimming, vignette.

embers *n.* ashes, cinders.

embezzle *v.* abstract, appropriate, defalcate, filch, misapply, misappropriate, misuse, peculate, pilfer, pinch, purloin, steal, sting.

embezzlement *n.* abstraction, appropriation, defalcation, filching, fraud, larceny, misapplication, misappropriation, misuse, peculation, pilferage, pilfering, purloining, stealing, sting, theft, thieving.

embezzler *n.* cheat, defalcator, fraud, peculator, thief.

embitter *v.* acerbate, aggravate, alienate, anger, disaffect, disillusion, empoison, envenom, exacerbate, exasperate, poison, sour, worsen.
antonym pacify.

embittered *adj.* bitter, disaffected, disillusioned, empoisoned, sour, soured.
antonym pacified.

emblazon *v.* adorn, blazon, colour, decorate, depict, embellish, extol, glorify, illuminate, laud, ornament, paint, praise, proclaim, publicise, publish, trumpet.

emblem *n.* badge, crest, device, figure, ichthys, image, insignia, mark, representation, sigil, sign, symbol, token, type.

emblematic *adj.* emblematical, figurative, representative, representing, symbolic, symbolical.

embodiment *n.* codification, collection, combination, comprehension, concentration, consolidation, example, exemplar, exemplification, expression, incarnation, inclusion, incorporation, integration, manifestation, organisation, personification, realisation, reification, representation, symbol, systematisation, type.

embody v. codify, collect, combine, comprehend, comprise, concentrate, concretise, consolidate, contain, encarnalise, exemplify, express, incarnate, include, incorporate, integrate, manifest, organise, personify, realise, reify, represent, stand for, symbolise, systematise, typify.

embolden v. animate, cheer, encourage, enhearten, fire, hearten, inflame, inspire, inspirit, invigorate, nerve, reassure, rouse, stimulate, stir, strengthen, vitalise.
antonym dishearten.

embrace v. accept, canoodle, clasp, complect, comprehend, comprise, contain, cover, cuddle, dally, embody, embosom, encircle, enclose, encompass, enfold, enlace, espouse, grab, grasp, halse, hold, hug, inarm, include, incorporate, involve, neck, receive, seize, snog, squeeze, subsume, take up, welcome.
n. accolade, clasp, clinch, cuddle, hug, squeeze.

embrocation n. cream, epithem, lotion, ointment, salve.

embroglio *see* **imbroglio** .

embroidery n. fancywork, needle-point, needlework, sewing, tapestry, tatting.

embroil v. confound, confuse, distract, disturb, encumber, enmesh, ensnare, entangle, implicate, incriminate, involve, mire, mix up, muddle, perplex, trouble.

embryo n. beginning, embryon, germ, nucleus, root, rudiment.

embryonic adj. beginning, early, germinal, immature, inchoate, incipient, primary, rudimentary, seminal, underdeveloped.
antonyms advanced, developed.

emend v. alter, amend, correct, edit, improve, rectify, redact, revise, rewrite.

emendation n. alteration, amendment, correction, corrigendum, editing, improvement, rectification, redaction, revision.

emerge v. appear, arise, crop up, debouch, develop, eclose, emanate, issue, materialise, proceed, rise, surface, transpire, turn up.
antonyms disappear, fade.

emergence n. advent, apparition, appearance, arrival, coming, dawn, development, disclosure, eclosion, emanation, emersion, issue, materialisation, rise.
antonyms decline, disappearance.

emergency n. crisis, crunch, danger, difficulty, exigency, extremity, necessity, pass, pinch, plight, predicament, quandary, scrape, strait.
adj. alternative, back-up, extra, fall-back, reserve, spare, substitute.

emergent adj. budding, coming, developing, emerging, independent, rising.
antonyms declining, disappearing.

emetic adj. emetical, vomitive, vomitory.
n. vomit, vomitary, vomitive.

emigration n. departure, exodus, journey, migration, removal.

eminence n. celebrity, dignity, distinction, elevation, esteem, fame, greatness, height, hill, hillock, illustriousness, importance, knob, knoll, notability, note, peak, preeminence, prestige, prominence, rank, renown, reputation, repute, ridge, rise, summit, superiority.

eminent adj. august, celebrated, conspicuous, distinguished, elevated, esteemed, exalted, famous, grand, great, high, high-ranking, illustrious, important, notable, noted, noteworthy, outstanding, paramount, preeminent, prestigious, prominent, renowned, reputable, respected, revered, signal, superior, well-known.
antonyms unimportant, unknown.

eminently adv. conspicuously, exceedingly, exceptionally, extremely, greatly, highly, notably, outstandingly, par excellence, prominently, remarkably, signally, strikingly, surpassingly.

emissary n. agent, ambassador, courier, delegate, deputy, envoy, herald, legate, messenger, nuncio, plenipotentiary, representative, scout, spy.

emission n. diffusion, discharge, ejaculation, ejection, emanation, exhalation, exudation, issuance, issue, mephitis, radiation, release, shedding, transmission, utterance, vent, venting.

emit v. diffuse, discharge, eject, emanate, exhale, exude, give off, give out, issue, radiate, shed, vent.
antonym absorb.

emollient adj. assuaging, assuasive, balsamic, demulcent, lenitive, mitigative, mollifying, softening, soothing.
n. balm, cream, lenitive, liniment, lotion, moisturiser, oil, ointment, poultice, salve, unguent.

emolument n. allowance, benefit, compensation, earnings, fee, gain, hire, honorarium, pay, payment, profits, recompense, remuneration, return, reward, salary, stipend, wages.

emotion n. affect, agitation, ardour, excitement, feeling, fervour, passion, perturbation, reaction, sensation, sentiment, vehemence, warmth.

emotional adj. affecting, ardent, demonstrative, emotive, enthusiastic, excitable, exciting, feeling, fervent, fervid, fiery, heart-warming, heated, hot-blooded, impassioned, moved, moving, overcharged, passionate, pathetic, poignant, responsive, roused, sensitive, sentimental, stirred, stirring, susceptible, tearjerking, temperamental, tempestuous, tender, thrilling, touching, volcanic, warm, zealous.
antonyms calm, cold, detached, emotionless, unemotional.

emotionless adj. blank, cold, cold-blooded, cool, detached, distant, frigid, glacial, impassive, imperturbable, indifferent, phlegmatic, remote, toneless, undemonstrative, unemotional, unfeeling.
antonym emotional.

emotive adj. affecting, ardent, controversial,

delicate, emotional, enthusiastic, exciting, fervent, fervid, fiery, heart-warming, heated, impassioned, inflammatory, moving, passionate, pathetic, poignant, roused, sensitive, sentimental, stirred, stirring, tear-jerking, thrilling, touching, touchy, zealous.

emperor n. imperator, kaiser, mikado, ruler, shogun, sovereign, tsar.

emphasis n. accent, accentuation, attention, force, import, importance, impressiveness, insistence, intensity, mark, moment, positiveness, power, pre-eminence, priority, prominence, significance, strength, stress, underscoring, urgency, weight.

emphasise v. accent, accentuate, dwell on, feature, highlight, insist on, intensify, play up, point up, press home, punctuate, spotlight, strengthen, stress, underline, underscore, weight.
antonyms depreciate, play down, understate.

emphatic adj. absolute, categorical, certain, decided, definite, direct, distinct, earnest, energetic, forceful, forcible, graphic, important, impressive, insistent, marked, momentous, positive, powerful, pronounced, punctuated, resounding, significant, striking, strong, telling, trenchant, unequivocal, unmistakable, vigorous, vivid.
antonyms quiet, understated, unemphatic.

empire n. authority, bailiwick, command, commonwealth, control, domain, dominion, government, imperium, jurisdiction, kingdom, power, realm, rule, sovereignty, supremacy, sway, territory.

empirical adj. empiric, experiential, experimental, observed, practical, pragmatic.
antonyms conjectural, speculative, theoretical.

employ v. apply, apprentice, bring to bear, commission, engage, enlist, exercise, exert, fill, hire, indent(ure), occupy, ply, retain, spend, take on, take up, use, utilise.
n. employment, hire, pay, service.

employed adj. active, busy, earning, engaged, hired, occupied, working.
antonym unemployed.

employee n. hand, job-holder, member of staff, staffer, wage-earner, worker, workman.

employer n. boss, business, company, establishment, firm, gaffer, organisation, outfit, owner, padrone, patron, proprietor, taskmaster, workmaster, workmistress.

employment n. application, avocation, business, calling, craft, employ, engagement, enlistment, errand, exercise, exercitation, exertion, hire, job, line, métier, occupation, profession, pursuit, service, trade, use, utilisation, vocation, work.
antonym unemployment.

emporium n. bazaar, establishment, market, mart, shop, store.

empower v. accredit, allow, authorise, commission, delegate, enable, enfranchise, entitle, license, permit, qualify, sanction, warrant.

emptiness n. absentness, aimlessness, banality,

bareness, barrenness, blankness, cheapness, desertedness, desire, desolation, destitution, expressionlessness, frivolity, futility, hollowness, hunger, idleness, inanity, ineffectiveness, insincerity, insubstantiality, meaninglessness, purposelessness, ravening, senselessness, silliness, triviality, trivialness, unreality, unsatisfactoriness, vacancy, vacantness, vacuity, vacuousness, vacuum, vainness, valuelessness, vanity, void, waste, worthlessness.
antonym fullness.

empty adj. absent, aimless, banal, bare, blank, bootless, cheap, clear, deserted, desolate, destitute, expressionless, famished, frivolous, fruitless, futile, hollow, hungry, idle, inane, ineffective, insincere, insubstantial, meaningless, purposeless, ravenous, senseless, silly, starving, superficial, trivial, unfed, unfilled, unfrequented, unfurnished, uninhabited, unintelligent, unoccupied, unreal, unsatisfactory, unsubstantial, untenanted, vacant, vacuous, vain, valueless, viduous, void, waste, worthless.
antonyms filled, full, replete.
v. clear, consume, deplete, discharge, drain, dump, evacuate, exhaust, gut, lade, pour out, unburden, unload, vacate, void.
antonym fill.

empty-headed adj. batty, brainless, dizzy, dotty, flighty, frivolous, giddy, hare-brained, inane, scatter-brained, scatty, silly, skittish, vacuous.

emulate v. challenge, compete with, contend with, copy, echo, follow, imitate, match, mimic, rival, vie with.

emulation n. challenge, competition, contention, contest, copying, echoing, envy, following, imitation, jealousy, matching, mimicry, rivalry, strife.

en masse all at once, all together, as a group, as a whole, as one, en bloc, ensemble, in a body, together, wholesale.

enable v. accredit, allow, authorise, capacitate, commission, empower, endue, equip, facilitate, fit, license, permit, prepare, qualify, sanction, warrant.
antonyms inhibit, prevent.

enact v. act (out), authorise, command, decree, depict, establish, impersonate, legislate, ordain, order, pass, perform, personate, play, portray, proclaim, ratify, represent, sanction.
antonym repeal.

enactment n. acting, authorisation, command, commandment, decree, depiction, dictate, edict, impersonation, law, legislation, order, ordinance, performance, personation, playacting, playing, portrayal, proclamation, ratification, regulation, representation, statute.
antonym repeal.

enamoured adj. besotted, bewitched, captivated, charmed, enchanted, enraptured, entranced, fascinated, fond, infatuated, smitten, taken.

encampment n. base, bivouac, camp, camping-ground, campsite, cantonment, duar, hutment, quarters, tents.

encapsulate v. abridge, capture, compress, condense, digest, epitomise, exemplify, incapsulate, précis, represent, sum up, summarise, typify.

enchant v. becharm, beguile, bewitch, captivate, charm, delight, enamour, enrapture, enravish, ensorcell, enthral, fascinate, hypnotise, mesmerise, spellbind.
antonyms bore, disenchant.

enchanter n. conjurer, magician, magus, mesmerist, necromancer, reim-kennar, sorcerer, spellbinder, warlock, witch, wizard.

enchanting adj. alluring, appealing, attractive, bewitching, captivating, charming, delightful, endearing, entrancing, fascinating, lovely, mesmerising, pleasant, ravishing, winsome, wonderful.
antonyms boring, repellent.

enchantment n. allure, allurement, beguilement, bliss, charm, conjuration, delight, fascination, glamour, gramary(e), hypnotism, incantation, magic, mesmerism, necromancy, rapture, ravishment, sorcery, spell, transport, witchcraft, wizardry.
antonym disenchantment.

enchantress n. charmer, Circe, conjurer, femme fatale, lamia, magician, necromancer, reim-kennar, seductress, siren, sorceress, spellbinder, vamp, witch.

encircle v. begird, circle, circumscribe, compass, enclose, encompass, enfold, engird, engirdle, enlace, enring, envelop, environ, enwreathe, gird, girdle, hem in, ring, surround.

enclose v. bound, circumscribe, compass, comprehend, confine, contain, cover, embale, embosom, embrace, encase, encircle, encompass, enlock, environ, fence, hedge, hem in, hold, inclose, include, incorporate, insert, pen, shut in, wall in, wrap.

enclosed adj. bound, caged, cocooned, confined, contained, corralled, encased, encircled, encompassed, ensheathed, immured, imprisoned, included, sacculated, surrounded.
antonyms open, unenclosed.

enclosure n. arena, bawn, boma, cloister, compound, corral, court, encasement, enceinte, fold, haining, hope, kraal, paddock, pen, pightle, pinfold, pound, ring, sept, seraglio, stockade, sty.

encompass v. admit, begird, bring about, cause, circle, circumscribe, comprehend, comprise, contain, contrive, cover, devise, effect, embody, embrace, encircle, enclose, envelop, environ, girdle, hem in, hold, include, incorporate, involve, manage, ring, subsume, surround.

encounter v. chance upon, clash with, combat, come upon, confront, contend, cross swords with, engage, experience, face, fight, grapple with, happen on, meet, rencontre, rencounter, run across, run into, strive, struggle.
n. action, battle, brush, clash, collision, combat, conflict, confrontation, contest,

dispute, engagement, fight, meeting, rencontre, rencounter, run-in, set-to, skirmish.

encourage v. abet, advance, advocate, aid, animate, boost, buoy up, cheer, comfort, console, egg on, embolden, embrave, favour, forward, foster, further, hearten, help, incite, inspire, inspirit, promote, rally, reassure, rouse, second, spirit, spur, stimulate, strengthen, succour, support, urge.
antonyms depress, discourage, dissuade.

encouragement n. advocacy, aid, boost, cheer, come-on, consolation, favour, help, hortation, incentive, incitement, inspiration, promotion, reassurance, stimulation, stimulus, succour, support, urging.
antonyms disapproval, discouragement.

encouraging adj. auspicious, bright, cheerful, cheering, cohortative, comforting, heartening, hopeful, hortatory, incentive, proceleusmatic, promising, protreptic, reassuring, rosy, satisfactory, stimulating, uplifting.
antonym discouraging.

encroach v. appropriate, arrogate, impinge, infringe, intrude, invade, make inroads, muscle in, obtrude, overstep, trench, trespass, usurp.

encroachment n. appropriation, arrogation, impingement, incursion, infringement, inroad, intrusion, invasion, obtrusion, trespass, usurpation, violation.

encumber v. burden, clog, cramp, cumber, embarrass, hamper, handicap, hinder, impede, incommode, inconvenience, lumber, obstruct, oppress, overload, retard, saddle, slow down, trammel, weigh down.

encumbrance n. burden, clog, cumbrance, difficulty, drag, embarrassment, handicap, hindrance, impediment, inconvenience, liability, load, lumber, millstone, obstacle, obstruction, onus.
antonym aid.

encyclopaedic adj. all-embracing, all-encompassing, all-inclusive, broad, compendious, complete, comprehensive, exhaustive, thorough, universal, vast, wide-ranging.
antonyms incomplete, narrow.

end n. aim, annihilation, aspiration, attainment, bit, bound, boundary, butt, cessation, close, closure, completion, conclusion, consequence, consummation, culmination, curtain, death, demise, dénouement, design, destruction, dissolution, doom, downfall, drift, edge, ending, expiration, expiry, extent, extermination, extinction, extreme, extremity, finale, fine, finis, finish, fragment, goal, intent, intention, issue, left-over, limit, object, objective, outcome, part, pay-off, piece, point, portion, purpose, reason, remainder, remnant, resolution, responsibility, result, ruin, ruination, scrap, share, side, stop, stub, telos, termination, terminus, tip, upshot, wind-up.
antonyms beginning, opening, start.
v. abate, abolish, annihilate, cease, close, complete, conclude, culminate, destroy,

dissolve, expire, exterminate, extinguish, fetch up, finish, resolve, ruin, sopite, stop, terminate, wind up.
antonyms begin, start.

endanger *v.* compromise, expose, hazard, imperil, jeopardise, risk, threaten.
antonyms protect, shelter, shield.

endearing *adj.* adorable, attractive, captivating, charming, delightful, enchanting, engaging, lovable, sweet, winning, winsome.

endearment *n.* affection, attachment, diminutive, fondness, hypocorisma, love, pet-name, sweet nothing.

endeavour *n.* aim, attempt, conatus, crack, effort, enterprise, essay, go, nisus, shot, stab, trial, try, undertaking, venture.
v. aim, aspire, attempt, essay, labour, strive, struggle, take pains, try, undertake, venture.

ending *n.* catastrophe, cessation, climax, close, completion, conclusion, consummation, culmination, dénouement, desinence, end, epilogue, finale, finish, resolution, termination, wind-up.
antonyms beginning, start.

endless *adj.* boundless, ceaseless, constant, continual, continuous, eternal, everlasting, immortal, incessant, infinite, interminable, interminate, limitless, measureless, monotonous, overlong, perpetual, Sisyphean, termless, unbounded, unbroken, undivided, undying, unending, uninterrupted, unlimited, whole.

endorse *v.* adopt, advocate, affirm, approve, authorise, back, champion, confirm, countenance, countersign, favour, indorse, ratify, recommend, sanction, sign, subscribe to, superscribe, support, sustain, undersign, vouch for, warrant.
antonyms denounce, disapprove.

endorsement *n.* advocacy, affirmation, approbation, approval, authorisation, backing, championship, commendation, comment, confirmation, corroboration, countersignature, favour, fiat, indorsement, OK, qualification, ratification, recommendation, sanction, seal of approval, signature, superscription, support, testimonial, warrant.
antonyms denouncement, disapproval.

endow *v.* award, bequeath, bestow, confer, donate, dower, endue, enrich, favour, finance, fund, furnish, give, grant, invest, leave, make over, present, provide, settle on, supply, will.
antonym divest.

endowment *n.* ability, aptitude, attribute, award, benefaction, bequest, bestowal, boon, capability, capacity, donation, dotation, dowry, faculty, flair, fund, genius, gift, grant, income, largesse, legacy, power, presentation, property, provision, qualification, quality, revenue, talent.

endurable *adj.* bearable, sufferable, supportable, sustainable, tolerable.
antonyms intolerable, unbearable.

endurance *n.* bearing, continuation, continuity,

durability, fortitude, immutability, lastingness, longevity, patience, permanence, perseverance, persistence, pertinacity, resignation, resolution, stability, stamina, staying power, strength, submission, sufferance, sustainment, sustenance, tenacity, toleration.

endure *v.* abear, abide, aby(e), allow, bear, brave, brook, continue, cope with, countenance, digest, dree, experience, go through, hold, last, live, perdure, permit, persist, prevail, put up with, remain, stand, stay, stick, stomach, submit to, suffer, support, survive, sustain, swallow, thole, tolerate, undergo, weather, withstand.
antonyms cease, end.

enduring *adj.* abiding, continuing, durable, eternal, firm, immortal, imperishable, lasting, living, long(a)evous, long-lasting, perennial, permanent, persistent, persisting, prevailing, remaining, steadfast, steady, surviving, unfaltering, unwavering.
antonyms changeable, fleeting.

enemy *n.* adversary, antagonist, competitor, foe, foeman, opponent, opposer, Philistine, rival, the opposition.
antonyms ally, friend.

energetic *adj.* active, animated, brisk, dynamic, forceful, forcible, high-powered, indefatigable, lively, pithy, potent, powerful, spirited, strenuous, strong, throughgoing, tireless, vigorous, zippy.
antonyms idle, inactive, lazy, sluggish.

energise *v.* activate, animate, electrify, enliven, galvanise, inspirit, invigorate, liven, motivate, pep up, quicken, stimulate, vitalise, vivify.
antonym daunt.

energy *n.* activity, animation, ardour, brio, drive, efficiency, élan, exertion, fire, force, forcefulness, get-up-and-go, intensity, inworking, jism, juice, life, liveliness, pluck, power, spirit, stamina, steam, strength, strenuousness, verve, vigour, vim, vitality, vivacity, vroom, zeal, zest, zip.
antonyms inertia, lethargy, weakness.

enervate *v.* debilitate, deplete, devitalise, enfeeble, exhaust, fatigue, incapacitate, paralyse, prostrate, sap, tire, unman, unnerve, weaken, wear out.
antonyms activate, energise.

enervated *adj.* debilitated, depleted, devitalised, done in, effete, enervate, enfeebled, exhausted, fatigued, feeble, incapacitated, limp, paralysed, prostrate, prostrated, run-down, sapped, spent, tired, undermined, unmanned, unnerved, washed out, weak, weakened, worn out.
antonyms active, energetic.

enervation *n.* debilitation, debility, depletion, effeteness, enfeeblement, exhaustedness, exhaustion, fatigue, feebleness, impotence, incapacity, infirmity, lassitude, paralysis, powerlessness, prostration, tiredness, unmanning, weakening, weakness.

enfeeble *v.* debilitate, deplete, devitalise, dimin-

ish, enervate, exhaust, fatigue, geld, reduce, sap, undermine, unhinge, unnerve, weaken, wear out.
antonym strengthen.

enfold *v.* clasp, embrace, encircle, enclose, encompass, envelop, enwrap, fold, hold, hug, shroud, swathe, wimple, wrap (up).

enforce *v.* administer, apply, carry out, coact, coerce, compel, constrain, discharge, exact, execute, implement, impose, insist on, oblige, prosecute, reinforce, require, urge.

enforced *adj.* binding, compelled, compulsory, constrained, dictated, imposed, involuntary, necessary, ordained, prescribed, required, unavoidable.

enforcement *n.* administration, application, coaction, coercion, compulsion, constraint, execution, implementation, imposition, insistence, obligation, pressure, prosecution, requirement.

enfranchise *v.* affranchise, emancipate, free, liberate, manumit, release.
antonym disenfranchise.

enfranchisement *n.* affranchisement, emancipation, freedom, freeing, liberating, liberation, manumission, release, suffrage.
antonym disenfranchisement.

engage *v.* absorb, activate, affiance, agree, allure, apply, appoint, arrest, assail, attach, attack, attract, bespeak, betroth, bind, book, busy, captivate, catch, charm, charter, combat, commission, commit, contract, covenant, draw, embark, employ, enamour, enchant, encounter, energise, engross, enlist, enrol, enter, fascinate, fit, fix, gain, grip, guarantee, hire, interact, interconnect, interlock, involve, join, lease, meet, mesh, obligate, oblige, occupy, operate, partake, participate, pledge, practise, prearrange, preoccupy, promise, rent, reserve, retain, secure, take on, tie up, undertake, vouch, vow, win.
antonyms discharge, disengage, dismiss.

engaged *adj.* absorbed, affianced, betrothed, busy, committed, employed, engrossed, immersed, involved, occupied, pledged, preoccupied, promised, spoken for, tied up, unavailable.

engagement *n.* action, affiance, appointment, arrangement, assurance, battle, bethrothal, bond, combat, commission, commitment, compact, conflict, confrontation, contest, contract, date, employment, encounter, fight, gig, job, meeting, oath, obligation, pact, pledge, post, promise, situation, stint, subarr(h)ation, troth, undertaking, vow, word, work.
antonym disengagement.

engaging *adj.* agreeable, appealing, attractive, beguiling, captivating, charming, enchanting, fascinating, fetching, lik(e)able, lovable, pleasant, pleasing, prepossessing, winning, winsome.
antonyms boring, loathsome.

engender *v.* beget, breed, bring about, cause, create, encourage, excite, father, foment,

generate, give rise to, hatch, incite, induce, instigate, lead to, make, nurture, occasion, precipitate, procreate, produce, propagate, provoke, sire, spawn.

engine *n.* agency, agent, apparatus, appliance, contraption, contrivance, device, dynamo, implement, instrument, machine, means, mechanism, motor, tool, turbine, weapon.

engineer *n.* architect, contriver, designer, deviser, driver, inventor, operator, originator, planner.
v. cause, concoct, contrive, control, create, devise, effect, encompass, finagle, machinate, manage, manipulate, manoeuvre, mastermind, originate, plan, plot, scheme, wangle.

engrave *v.* blaze, carve, chase, chisel, cut, embed, enchase, etch, fix, grave, impress, imprint, infix, ingrain, inscribe, lodge, mark, print.

engraved *adj.* carved, chased, chiselled, cut, enchased, etched, graven, imprinted, incised, intagliated, marked, printed.

engraving *n.* blaze, block, carving, chasing, chiselling, cutting, dendroglyph, dry-point, enchasing, etching, impression, inscribing, inscription, lithoglyph, mark, plate, print, woodcut.

engross *v.* absorb, arrest, corner, engage, engulf, fixate, hold, immerse, involve, monopolise, occupy, preoccupy, rivet.

engrossed *adj.* absorbed, captivated, caught up, enthralled, fascinated, fixated, gripped, immersed, intent, intrigued, lost, preoccupied, rapt, riveted, taken.
antonyms bored, disinterested.

engrossing *adj.* absorbing, captivating, compelling, enthralling, fascinating, gripping, interesting, intriguing, riveting, suspenseful, taking, unputdownable.
antonym boring.

engulf *v.* absorb, bury, consume, deluge, drown, encompass, engross, envelop, flood, immerse, ingulf, inundate, overrun, overwhelm, plunge, submerge, swallow up, swamp.

enhance *v.* amplify, augment, boost, complement, elevate, embellish, escalate, exalt, heighten, improve, increase, intensify, lift, magnify, raise, reinforce, strengthen, swell.
antonyms decrease, minimise.

enigma *n.* brain-teaser, conundrum, mystery, poser, problem, puzzle, riddle.

enigmatic *adj.* ambiguous, cryptic, Delphic, doubtful, enigmatical, equivocal, impenetrable, incomprehensible, indecipherable, inexplicable, inscrutable, mysterious, obscure, perplexing, puzzling, recondite, riddling, strange, uncertain, unfathomable, unintelligible.
antonyms simple, straightforward.

enjoin *v.* advise, ban, bar, bid, call upon, charge, command, comply, counsel, demand, direct, disallow, forbid, instruct, interdict, obey, order, preclude, prescribe, prohibit, proscribe, require, restrain, urge, warn.

enjoy *v.* appreciate, delight in, dig, experience,

have, like, make a meal of, own, possess, rejoice in, relish, revel in, savour, take pleasure in, use.

antonyms abhor, detest.

enjoy oneself have a ball, have a good time, have fun, make merry, party.

enjoyable *adj.* agreeable, amusing, delectable, delicious, delightful, entertaining, fun, good, gratifying, pleasant, pleasing, pleasurable, satisfying.

antonyms disagreeable, unpleasant.

enjoyment *n.* advantage, amusement, benefit, comfort, delectation, delight, diversion, ease, entertainment, exercise, fun, gaiety, gladness, gratification, gusto, happiness, indulgence, jollity, joy, ownership, pleasure, possession, recreation, relish, satisfaction, use, zest.

antonyms displeasure, dissatisfaction.

enlarge *v.* add to, amplify, augment, blow up, broaden, descant, develop, diffuse, dilate, distend, elaborate, elongate, expand, expatiate, extend, greaten, grow, heighten, increase, inflate, intumesce, jumboise, lengthen, magnify, multiply, stretch, swell, wax, widen.

antonyms decrease, diminish, shrink.

enlargement *n.* ampliation, amplification, aneurysm, augmentation, blow-up, dilation, distension, emphysema, expansion, extension, growth, increase, increment, intumescence, magnification, oedema, protuberation, supplementation, swelling.

antonyms contraction, decrease.

enlighten *v.* advise, apprise, civilise, counsel, edify, educate, illuminate, indoctrinate, inform, instruct, teach, undeceive.

antonyms confuse, puzzle.

enlightened *adj.* aware, broad-minded, civilised, conversant, cultivated, educated, informed, knowledgeable, liberal, literate, open-minded, reasonable, refined, sophisticated, verligte, wise.

antonyms confused, ignorant.

enlightenment *n.* awareness, broad-mindedness, civilisation, comprehension, cultivation, edification, education, erudition, information, insight, instruction, knowledge, learning, literacy, open-mindedness, refinement, sapience, sophistication, teaching, understanding, wisdom.

antonyms confusion, ignorance.

enlist *v.* conscript, employ, engage, enrol, enter, gather, join (up), muster, obtain, procure, recruit, register, secure, sign up, volunteer.

enliven *v.* animate, brighten, buoy up, cheer (up), excite, exhilarate, fire, gladden, hearten, inspire, inspirit, invigorate, kindle, liven (up), pep up, perk up, quicken, rouse, spark, stimulate, vitalise, vivify, wake up.

antonym subdue.

enmity *n.* acrimony, animosity, animus, antagonism, antipathy, aversion, bad blood, bitterness, feud, hate, hatred, hostility, ill-will, invidiousness, malevolence, malice, malignity, rancour, spite, venom.

antonyms amity, friendship.

ennoble *v.* aggrandise, dignify, elevate, enhance, exalt, gentle, glorify, honour, magnify, nobilitate, raise.

ennoblement *n.* aggrandisement, dignification, elevation, exaltation, glorification, lionisation, magnification, nobilitation.

ennui *n.* accidie, acedia, boredom, dissatisfaction, lassitude, listlessness, tedium, the doldrums.

enormity *n.* abomination, atrociousness, atrocity, crime, depravity, disgrace, evil, evilness, flagitiousness, heinousness, horror, iniquity, monstrosity, monstrousness, nefariousness, outrage, outrageousness, turpitude, viciousness, vileness, villainy, wickedness.

antonyms triviality, unimportance.

enormous *adj.* abominable, astronomic(al), atrocious, Brobdingnagian, colossal, cyclopean, depraved, disgraceful, evil, excessive, gargantuan, gigantic, gross, heinous, herculean, huge, hulking, immense, jumbo, leviathan, mammoth, massive, monstrous, mountainous, nefarious, odious, outrageous, prodigious, titanic, tremendous, vast, vasty, vicious, vile, villainous, wicked.

antonyms small, tiny.

enough *adj.* abundant, adequate, ample, enow, plenty, sufficient.

n. abundance, adequacy, plenitude, plenty, repletion, sufficiency.

adv. abundantly, adequately, amply, aplenty, enow, fairly, moderately, passably, reasonably, satisfactorily, sufficiently, tolerably.

enquire, inquire *v.* ask, examine, explore, inspect, investigate, probe, query, question, quiz, scrutinise, search, speir.

enquiry, inquiry *n.* examination, exploration, inquest, inspection, investigation, probe, query, quest, question, research, scrutiny, search, study, survey.

enrage *v.* acerbate, aggravate, anger, exasperate, incense, incite, inflame, infuriate, irritate, madden, make someone's hackles rise, provoke.

antonyms calm, placate, soothe.

enraged *adj.* aggravated, angered, angry, exasperated, fizzing, fuming, furious, incensed, inflamed, infuriated, irate, irritated, livid, mad, raging, storming, wild.

antonym calm.

enrapture *v.* beguile, bewitch, captivate, charm, delight, enchant, enravish, enthrall, entrance, fascinate, ravish, spellbind, thrill, transport.

enrich *v.* adorn, aggrandise, ameliorate, augment, cultivate, decorate, develop, embellish, endow, enhance, fortify, grace, improve, ornament, prosper, refine, supplement.

antonym impoverish.

enrol *v.* accept, admit, chronicle, empanel, engage, enlist, enregister, inscribe, join up, list, matriculate, note, record, recruit, register, sign on, sign up, take on.

antonyms leave, reject.

enrolment *n.* acceptance, admission, empanelment, engagement, enlistment, matriculation, recruitment, register, registration.

ensconce v. entrench, establish, install, locate, lodge, nestle, place, protect, put, screen, settle, shelter, shield.

ensemble n. aggregate, assemblage, band, case, chorus, collection, company, corps de ballet, costume, entirety, get-up, group, outfit, rig-out, set, suit, sum, total, totality, troupe, whole.

enshrine v. apotheosise, cherish, consecrate, dedicate, embalm, exalt, hallow, idolise, preserve, revere, sanctify, treasure.

enshroud v. cloak, cloud, conceal, cover, enclose, enfold, envelop, enwrap, enwreathe, hide, obscure, pall, shroud, veil, wrap.

ensign n. badge, banner, colours, flag, gonfalon, jack, oriflamme, pennant, pennon, standard, streamer.

enslave v. bind, conquer, dominate, enchain, enthrall, overcome, subject, subjugate, yoke.
antonyms emancipate, free.

enslavement n. bondage, captivity, dulosis, duress, enthralment, oppression, repression, serfdom, servitude, slavery, subjection, subjugation, thraldom, vassalage.
antonym emancipation.

ensnare v. catch, embroil, enmesh, entangle, entrap, gin, illaqueate, net, snare, snarl, trap, trepan.

ensue v. arise, attend, befall, derive, eventuate, flow, follow, happen, issue, proceed, result, stem, succeed, supervene, turn out, turn up.
antonym precede.

ensure v. certify, clinch, confirm, effect, guarantee, guard, insure, protect, safeguard, secure, warrant.

entail v. cause, demand, encompass, give rise to, impose, involve, lead to, necessitate, occasion, predetermine, require, result in.

entangle v. ball, bewilder, catch, complicate, compromise, confuse, embroil, enlace, enmesh, ensnare, entoil, entrap, foul, implicate, involve, jumble, knot, mat, mix up, muddle, perplex, puzzle, ravel, snag, snare, snarl, tangle, trammel, trap, twist.
antonym disentangle.

entanglement n. complication, confusion, difficulty, embarrassment, ensnarement, entoilment, entrapment, imbroglio, involvement, jumble, knot, liaison, mesh, mess, mix-up, muddle, predicament, snare, snarl-up, tangle, tie, toils, trap.
antonym disentanglement.

entente n. agreement, arrangement, compact, deal, entente cordiale, friendship, pact, treaty, understanding.

enter v. arrive, begin, board, commence, embark upon, enlist, enrol, inscribe, insert, introduce, join, list, log, note, offer, participate, participate in, penetrate, pierce, present, proffer, record, register, set about, set down, sign up, start, submit, take down, take up, tender.
antonyms delete, issue, leave.

enterprise n. activity, adventure, adventurousness, alertness, audacity, boldness, business, company, concern, daring, dash, drive, eagerness, effort, emprise, endeavour, energy, enthusiasm, essay, establishment, firm, get-up-and-go, gumption, imagination, initiative, operation, plan, programme, project, push, readiness, resource, resourcefulness, spirit, undertaking, venture, vigour, zeal.
antonyms apathy, inertia.

enterprising adj. active, adventurous, alert, ambitious, aspiring, audacious, bold, daring, dashing, eager, energetic, enthusiastic, go-ahead, imaginative, intrepid, keen, pushful, ready, resourceful, self-reliant, spirited, stirring, up-and-coming, venturesome, vigorous, zealous.
antonyms lethargic, unadventurous.

entertain v. accommodate, accourt, amuse, charm, cheer, cherish, conceive, consider, contemplate, countenance, delight, divert, fête, foster, harbour, hold, imagine, lodge, maintain, occupy, please, ponder, put up, recreate, regale, support, treat.
antonyms bore, reject.

entertainer n. artiste, diseur, diseuse, performer, troubadour, trouper.

entertaining adj. amusing, charming, cheering, delightful, diverting, droll, fun, funny, humorous, interesting, pleasant, pleasing, pleasurable, recreative, witty.
antonym boring.

entertainment n. amusement, cheer, distraction, diversion, enjoyment, extravaganza, fun, pastime, play, pleasure, recreation, satisfaction, show, spectacle, sport, table, treat.

enthrall v. beguile, captivate, charm, enchant, enrapture, enravish, entrance, fascinate, grip, hypnotise, intrigue, mesmerise, rivet, spellbind, thrill.
antonyms bore, weary.

enthralling adj. beguiling, captivating, charming, compelling, compulsive, enchanting, entrancing, fascinating, gripping, hypnotising, intriguing, mesmeric, mesmerising, riveting, spellbinding, thrilling.
antonym boring.

enthuse v. absorb, drool, ecstasise, effervesce, emote, excite, gush, impassion, inflame, involve, possess, wax lyrical.

enthusiasm n. ardour, avidity, craze, devotion, eagerness, earnestness, empressement, entraînement, estro, excitement, fad, fervour, frenzy, hobby, hobby-horse, interest, keenness, mania, oomph, passion, rage, relish, spirit, vehemence, warmth, zeal, zest.
antonym apathy.

enthusiast n. admirer, aficionado, buff, bug, devotee, eager beaver, fan, fanatic, fiend, follower, freak, lover, supporter, wholehogger, zealot.
antonym detractor.

enthusiastic adj. ardent, avid, devoted, eager, earnest, ebullient, empressé, excited, exuberant, fervent, fervid, forceful, gung-ho, hearty,

keen, keen as mustard, lively, passionate, spirited, unstinting, vehement, vigorous, warm, whole-hearted, zealous.
antonyms apathetic, reluctant, unenthusiastic.

entice *v.* allure, attract, beguile, blandish, cajole, coax, decoy, draw, induce, inveigle, lead on, lure, persuade, prevail on, seduce, sweet-talk, tempt, wheedle.

enticement *n.* allurement, attraction, bait, beguilement, blandishments, cajolery, coaxing, come-on, decoy, inducement, inveiglement, lure, persuasion, seduction, sweet-talk, temptation.

entire *adj.* absolute, all-in, complete, continuous, full, intact, integrated, outright, perfect, sound, thorough, total, unabridged, unbroken, uncut, undamaged, undiminished, undivided, unified, unmarked, unmarred, unmitigated, unreserved, unrestricted, whole.
antonyms impaired, incomplete, partial.

entirely *adv.* absolutely, altogether, completely, every inch, exclusively, fully, hook line and sinker, in toto, lock stock and barrel, only, perfectly, solely, thoroughly, totally, unreservedly, utterly, wholly, without exception, without reservation.
antonym partially.

entirety *n.* absoluteness, aggregate, completeness, fullness, sum, total, totality, unity, universality, whole, wholeness.
antonyms element, incompleteness, part.

entitle *v.* accredit, allow, authorise, call, christen, denominate, designate, dub, empower, enable, enfranchise, label, license, name, permit, style, term, title, warrant.

entity *n.* being, body, creature, essence, existence, haecceity, individual, individuum, object, organism, presence, quantity, quiddity, quintessence, substance, thing.

entombment *n.* burial, inhumation, interment, inurnment, sepulture.

entourage *n.* associates, attendants, claque, companions, company, cortège, coterie, court, escort, followers, following, retainers, retinue, staff, suite, train.

entrails *n.* bowels, entera, gralloch, guts, harigal(d)s, ha(r)slet, innards, insides, intestines, offal, umbles, viscera.

entrance¹ *n.* access, admission, admittance, appearance, arrival, atrium, avenue, beginning, commencement, debut, door, doorway, entrée, entry, gate, ingress, initiation, inlet, introduction, opening, outset, passage, portal, start.
antonyms departure, exit.

entrance² *v.* bewitch, captivate, charm, delight, enchant, enrapture, enravish, enthrall, fascinate, gladden, hypnotise, magnetise, mesmerise, ravish, spellbind, transport.
antonyms bore, repel.

entrant *n.* beginner, candidate, competitor, contender, contestant, convert, entry, initiate, neophyte, newcomer, novice, participant, player, probationer, tyro.

entrap *v.* allure, beguile, capture, catch, decoy, embroil, enmesh, ensnare, entangle, entice, gin, implicate, inveigle, involve, lure, net, seduce, snare, trap, trepan, trick.

entreat *v.* appeal to, ask, beg, beseech, conjure, crave, enjoin, exhort, flagitate, implore, importune, invoke, petition, plead with, pray, request, sue, supplicate.

entreaty *n.* appeal, entreatment, exhortation, importunity, invocation, petition, plea, prayer, request, solicitation, suing, suit, supplication.

entrench *v.* anchor, dig in, embed, encroach, ensconce, establish, fix, fortify, impinge, infix, infringe, ingrain, install, interlope, intrench, intrude, lodge, plant, root, seat, set, settle, trespass.
antonym dislodge.

entrenched *adj.* deep-rooted, deep-seated, firm, fixed, implanted, inbred, indelible, ineradicable, ingrained, rooted, set, unshakable, well-established.

entrepreneur *n.* businessman, businesswoman, contractor, financier, impresario, industrialist, magnate, tycoon, undertaker.

entrust *v.* assign, authorise, charge, commend, commit, confide, consign, delegate, deliver, depute, invest, trust, turn over.

entry¹ *n.* access, admission, admittance, appearance, avenue, door, doorway, entering, entrance, entrée, gate, ingress, initiation, inlet, introduction, opening, passage, passageway, portal, threshold.
antonym exit.

entry² *n.* account, attempt, bulletin, candidate, competitor, contestant, effort, entrant, item, jotting, listing, memo, memorandum, minute, note, participant, player, record, registration, statement, submission.

entwine *v.* braid, embrace, encircle, enlace, entwist, interlace, interlink, intertwine, interweave, intwine, knit, plait, splice, surround, thatch, twine, twist, weave, wind.
antonym unravel.

enumerate *v.* calculate, cite, count, detail, itemise, list, mention, name, number, quote, recapitulate, recite, reckon, recount, rehearse, relate, specify, spell out, tell.

enunciate *v.* articulate, broadcast, declare, enounce, proclaim, promulgate, pronounce, propound, publish, say, sound, speak, state, utter, vocalise, voice.

envelop *v.* blanket, cloak, conceal, cover, embrace, encase, encircle, enclose, encompass, enfold, engulf, enshroud, enwrap, enwreathe, hide, obscure, sheathe, shroud, surround, swaddle, swathe, veil, wrap.

envelope *n.* case, casing, coating, cover, covering, integument, jacket, sheath, shell, skin, theca, wrapper, wrapping.

enviable *adj.* advantageous, blessed, covetable, desirable, excellent, favoured, fine, fortunate, good, lucky, privileged.
antonym unenviable.

envious *adj.* begrudging, covetous, dissatisfied,

green, green with envy, green-eyed, grudging, jaundiced, jealous, malcontent, malicious, resentful, spiteful.

environment *n.* ambience, atmosphere, background, conditions, context, domain, element, entourage, habitat, locale, medium, milieu, scene, setting, situation, surroundings, territory.

environmentalist *n.* conservationist, doomwatcher, ecofreak, econut, green.

environs *n.* circumjacencies, district, locality, neighbourhood, outskirts, precincts, purlieus, suburbs, surround(ing)s, vicinage, vicinity.

envisage *v.* anticipate, conceive of, conceptualise, contemplate, envision, fancy, foresee, ideate, image, imagine, picture, preconceive, predict, see, visualise.

envoy *n.* agent, ambassador, courier, delegate, deputy, diplomat, elchi, emissary, intermediary, legate, messenger, minister, nuncio, plenipotentiary, representative.

envy *n.* covetousness, cupidity, dissatisfaction, enviousness, grudge, hatred, ill-will, jealousy, malice, malignity, resentfulness, resentment, spite.
v. begrudge, covet, crave, grudge, resent.

enwrap *v.* encase, enclose, enfold, enshroud, envelop, enwind, enwreathe, parcel, sheathe, sheet, shroud, swaddle, swathe, wimple, wind.

ephemeral *adj.* brief, evanescent, fleeting, flitting, fugacious, fugitive, fungous, impermanent, momentary, passing, short, short-lived, temporary, transient, transitory.
antonyms enduring, lasting, perpetual.

epic *adj.* colossal, elevated, exalted, grand, grandiloquent, great, heroic, Homeric, huge, imposing, impressive, lofty, majestic, sublime, vast.
antonym ordinary.

epicure *n.* arbiter elegantiae, bon vivant, bon viveur, connoisseur, epicurean, gastronome, glutton, gourmand, gourmet, hedonist, sensualist, sybarite, voluptuary.

epicurean *adj.* gluttonous, gourmandising, hedonistic, libertine, luscious, lush, luxurious, self-indulgent, sensual, sybaritic, unrestrained, voluptuous.
n. bon vivant, bon viveur, epicure, gastronome, gourmet, hedonist, sensualist, voluptuary.

epidemic *adj.* epizootic, general, pandemic, prevailing, prevalent, rampant, rife, sweeping, wide-ranging, widespread.
n. growth, outbreak, pandemic, plague, rash, spread, upsurge, wave.

epigram *n.* aphorism, apophthegm, bon mot, gnome, quip, witticism.

epigrammatic *adj.* aphoristic, apophthegmatic, concise, gnomic, laconic, piquant, pithy, pointed, pungent, sharp, short, succinct, terse, witty.

epilogue *n.* afterword, coda, conclusion, exode, postscript.
antonyms foreword, preface, prologue.

episode *n.* adventure, affaire, business, chapter, circumstance, event, experience, happening, incident, instalment, matter, occasion, occurrence, part, passage, scene, section.

episodic *adj.* anecdotal, digressive, disconnected, disjointed, episod(i)al, intermittent, irregular, occasional, picaresque, spasmodic, sporadic.

epistle *n.* communication, encyclical, letter, line, message, missive, note.

epithet *n.* appellation, denomination, description, designation, epitheton, name, nickname, so(u)briquet, tag, title.

epitome *n.* abbreviation, abridgement, abstract, archetype, compendium, compression, condensation, conspectus, contraction, digest, embodiment, essence, exemplar, personification, préis, quintessence, reduction, representation, résumé, summary, syllabus, synopsis, type.

epitomise *v.* abbreviate, abridge, abstract, compress, condense, contract, curtail, cut, embody, encapsulate, exemplify, illustrate, incarnate, personify, précis, reduce, represent, shorten, summarise, symbolise, typify.
antonyms elaborate, expand.

epoch *n.* age, date, epocha, era, period, time.

equable *adj.* agreeable, calm, composed, consistent, constant, easy-going, even, even-tempered, imperturbable, level-headed, phlegmatic, placid, regular, serene, smooth, stable, steady, temperate, tranquil, unchanging, unexcitable, unflappable, uniform, unruffled, unvarying, unworrying.
antonyms excitable, variable.

equal *adj.* able, adequate, alike, balanced, capable, commensurate, competent, corresponding, egalitarian, equable, equivalent, even, even-handed, evenly-balanced, evenly-matched, evenly-proportioned, fair, fifty-fifty, fit, identical, impartial, just, level-pegging, like, matched, proportionate, ready, regular, sufficient, suitable, symmetrical, tantamount, the same, unbiased, uniform, unvarying, up to.
antonyms different, inequitable, unequal.
n. brother, coequal, compeer, counterpart, equivalent, fellow, match, mate, parallel, peer, rival, twin.
v. balance, commeasure, correspond to, equalise, equate, even, level, match, parallel, rival, square with, tally with.

equalise *v.* balance, compensate, draw level, equal, equate, even up, level, match, regularise, smooth, square, standardise.

equality *n.* balance, coequality, correspondence, egalitarianism, equitability, equivalence, evenness, fairness, identity, likeness, par, parity, proportion, sameness, similarity, uniformity.
antonym inequality.

equanimity *n.* aplomb, calm, calmness, composure, coolness, equability, equableness, imperturbability, level-headedness, peace, phlegm, placidity, poise, presence of mind,

sang-froid, self-possession, serenity, steadiness, tranquillity.
antonyms alarm, anxiety, discomposure.

equate *v.* agree, balance, compare, correspond to, correspond with, equalise, juxtapose, liken, match, offset, pair, parallel, square, tally.

equation *n.* agreement, balancing, bracketing, comparison, correspondence, equalisation, equality, equating, equivalence, juxtaposition, likeness, match, pairing, parallel.

equestrian *n.* cavalier, horseman, knight, postilion, rider.

equilibrium *n.* balance, calm, calmness, collectedness, composure, cool, coolness, counterpoise, equanimity, equipoise, equiponderance, evenness, poise, rest, self-possession, serenity, stability, steadiness, symmetry.
antonym imbalance.

equip *v.* accoutre, arm, array, attire, bedight, deck out, dight, dress, endow, fit out, fit up, furnish, habilitate, kit out, outfit, prepare, provide, rig, stock, supply.

equipage *n.* accoutrements, apparatus, baggage, carriage, coach, equipment, gear, impedimenta, material, munitions, outfit, retinue, stores, suite, train, traps, turn-out.

equipment *n.* accessories, accoutrements, apparatus, appurtenances, baggage, equipage, furnishings, furniture, gear, graith, impedimenta, implements, material, matériel, muniments, outfit, paraphernalia, rig-out, stuff, supplies, tackle, things, tools, traps.

equipoise *n.* balance, ballast, counterbalance, counterpoise, counter-weight, equibalance, equilibrium, equiponderance, evenness, offset, poise, stability, steadiness, symmetry.
antonym imbalance.

equitable *adj.* disinterested, dispassionate, due, ethical, even-handed, fair, fair-and-square, honest, impartial, just, legitimate, objective, proper, proportionate, reasonable, right, rightful, square, unbiased, unprejudiced.
antonyms inequitable, unfair.

equitably *adv.* disinterestedly, dispassionately, even-handedly, ex aequo, fairly, fairly and squarely, honestly, impartially, justly, objectively, properly, reasonably, rightly.
antonym inequitably.

equity *n.* disinterestedness, equality, equitableness, even-handedness, fair play, fair-mindedness, fairness, honesty, impartiality, integrity, justice, justness, objectivity, reasonableness, rectitude, righteousness, uprightness.
antonym inequity.

equivalence *n.* agreement, alikeness, conformity, correspondence, equality, evenness, homology, identity, interchangeability, interchangeableness, likeness, match, parallel, parity, sameness, similarity, substitutability, synonymy.
antonyms dissimilarity, inequality, unlikeness.

equivalent *adj.* alike, commensurate, comparable, convertible, correlative, correspondent, corresponding, equal, equipollent, equipotent, even, homologous, homotypal, homotypic, interchangeable, same, similar, substitutable, synonymous, tantamount, twin.
antonyms dissimilar, unlike.
n. correlative, correspondent, counterpart, equal, homologue, homotype, match, opposite number, parallel, peer, twin.

equivocal *adj.* ambiguous, ambivalent, casuistical, confusing, Delphic, doubtful, dubious, evasive, indefinite, indeterminate, misleading, oblique, obscure, oracular, questionable, suspicious, uncertain, vague.
antonyms clear, unequivocal.

equivocate *v.* dodge, evade, fence, fudge, hedge, mislead, palter, parry, prevaricate, pussyfoot, quibble, shift, shuffle, sidestep, tergiversate, weasel.

equivocation *n.* ambiguity, casuistry, confusion, double talk, doubtfulness, equivocacy, equivocality, equivocalness, equivoke, evasion, hedging, prevarication, quibbling, shifting, shuffling, sophistry, tergiversation, waffle, weasel-words.
antonym directness.

era *n.* aeon, age, century, cycle, date, day, days, epoch, generation, period, stage, time.

eradicable *adj.* destroyable, destructible, effaceable, eliminable, erasable, exterminable, extinguishable, extirpable, removable, washable.
antonyms ineradicable, permanent.

eradicate *v.* abolish, annihilate, deracinate, destroy, efface, eliminate, erase, expunge, exterminate, extinguish, extirpate, get rid of, obliterate, rase, remove, root out, stamp out, suppress, unroot, uproot, weed out.

eradication *n.* abolition, annihilation, deracination, destruction, effacement, elimination, erasure, expunction, extermination, extinction, extirpation, obliteration, removal, riddance, suppression.

erasable *adj.* effaceable, eradicable, removable, washable.
antonyms ineradicable, permanent.

erase *v.* blot out, cancel, cleanse, delete, efface, eliminate, eradicate, expunge, get rid of, obliterate, remove, rub out.

erasure *n.* cancellation, cleansing, deletion, effacement, elimination, eradication, erasement, expunction, obliteration, rasure, razure, removal.

erect *adj.* elevated, engorged, firm, hard, perpendicular, pricked, raised, rigid, standing, stiff, straight, taut, tense, tumescent, upright, upstanding, vertical.
antonyms limp, relaxed.
v. assemble, build, constitute, construct, create, elevate, establish, fabricate, form, found, initiate, institute, lift, mount, organise, pitch, put up, raise, rear, set up.

erection *n.* assembly, building, construction, creation, edifice, elevation, establishment, fabrication, manufacture, pile, raising, rigidity, stiffness, structure, tumescence.

ergo *adv.* accordingly, consequently, for this reason, hence, in consequence, so, then, therefore, this being the case, thus.

erode *v.* abrade, consume, corrade, corrode, denude, destroy, deteriorate, disintegrate, eat away, grind down, spoil, wear away, wear down.

eroded *adj.* abraded, attrite, corraded, denuded, destroyed, disintegrated, eaten away, fragmented, ground down, undermined, worn away.

erosion *n.* abrasion, attrition, consumption, corrasion, corrosion, denudation, destruction, deterioration, diminishment, disintegration, fragmentation, undermining.

erosive *adj.* caustic, corrosive, denuding, destructive, disruptive, erodent, gnawing, nibbling, undermining.

erotic *adj.* amatorial, amatorious, amatory, amorous, aphrodisiac, carnal, concupiscent, erogenic, erogenous, erotogenic, erotogenous, libidinous, lustful, rousing, seductive, sensual, sexy, stimulating, suggestive, titillating, venereal, voluptuous.

err *v.* blunder, deviate, fail, go astray, lapse, misapprehend, misbehave, miscalculate, misjudge, mistake, misunderstand, offend, sin, slip up, stray, stumble, transgress, trespass, trip up, wander.

errand *n.* assignment, charge, commission, duty, job, message, mission, task.

errant *adj.* aberrant, deviant, erring, itinerant, journeying, loose, nomadic, offending, peccant, peripatetic, rambling, roaming, roving, sinful, sinning, stray, straying, vagrant, wandering, wayward, wrong.

erratic *adj.* aberrant, abnormal, capricious, changeable, desultory, directionless, eccentric, fitful, fluctuating, inconsistent, inconstant, irregular, meandering, planetary, shifting, unpredictable, unreliable, unstable, variable, wandering, wayward.
antonyms consistent, reliable, stable, straight.

erring *adj.* aberrant, backsliding, delinquent, disobedient, errant, faithless, guilty, peccant, sinful, sinning, straying, wandering, wayward.

erroneous *adj.* amiss, fallacious, false, faulty, flawed, illogical, inaccurate, incorrect, inexact, invalid, mistaken, specious, spurious, unfounded, unsound, untrue, wrong.
antonym correct.

error *n.* barbarism, bêtise, bish, bloomer, blunder, boner, boob, corrigendum, delinquency, delusion, deviation, erratum, fallacy, fault, faux pas, flaw, gaucherie, howler, ignorance, ignoratio elenchi, illusion, inaccuracy, inexactitude, lapse, lapsus calami, lapsus linguae, lapsus memoriae, literal, malapropism, misapprehension, miscalculation, misconception, miscopy, miscorrection, misdeed, misprint, mistake, misunderstanding, mumpsimus, offence, omission, oversight, overslip, sin, slip, slip-up, solecism, transgression,

trespass, wrong, wrongdoing.

erstwhile *adj.* bygone, ex, former, late, old, once, one-time, past, previous, quondam, sometime, umwhile, whilom.

erudite *adj.* academic, cultivated, cultured, educated, highbrow, knowledgeable, learned, lettered, literate, profound, recondite, scholarly, scholastic, well-educated, well-read, wise.
antonym unlettered.

erudition *n.* culture, data, education, facts, knowledge, knowledgeableness, learnedness, learning, letters, lore, profoundness, profundity, reconditeness, scholarliness, scholarship, wisdom.

erupt *v.* belch, break, break out, burst, discharge, eruct, eructate, explode, flare, gush, rift, spew, spout, vent, vomit.

eruption *n.* discharge, ejection, emphysis, empyesis, eructation, explosion, imflammation, outbreak, outburst, rash, sally, venting.

escalate *v.* accelerate, amplify, ascend, climb, enlarge, expand, extend, grow, heighten, increase, intensify, magnify, mount, raise, rise, spiral, step up.
antonym diminish.

escalator *n.* elevator, lift, moving staircase.

escapable *adj.* avertible, avoidable, eludible, evadable, evitable.
antonym inevitable.

escapade *n.* adventure, antic, caper, doing, escapado, exploit, fling, fredaine, gest, lark, prank, romp, scrape, spree, stunt, trick.

escape *v.* abscond, avoid, baffle, bolt, break free, break loose, break off, break out, circumvent, decamp, discharge, do a bunk, dodge, drain, duck, elude, emanate, evade, flee, flit, flow, fly, foil, get away, gush, issue, leak, ooze, pass, pour forth, scape, scarper, seep, shake off, shun, skedaddle, skip, slip, slip away, spurt, take it on the run, take to one's heels, trickle, vamoose.
n. abscondence, avoidance, bolt, break, break-out, circumvention, decampment, discharge, distraction, diversion, drain, effluence, effluent, efflux, effluxion, elusion, emanation, emission, escapism, evasion, flight, flit, getaway, gush, jail-break, leak, leakage, meuse, out, outflow, outlet, outpour, pastime, recreation, relaxation, relief, safety-valve, seepage, spurt, vent.
  escape route bolthole, egress, escape road, exit, loophole, meuse, out, outlet, secret passage, slip road, vent.

escapee *n.* absconder, defector, deserter, fugitive, jail-breaker.

escapist *n.* daydreamer, dreamer, fantasiser, non-realist, ostrich, Walter Mitty, wishful thinker.
antonym realist.

eschew *v.* abandon, abjure, abstain from, avoid, disdain, forgo, forswear, give up, keep clear of, refrain from, renounce, repudiate, shun, spurn, swear off.
antonym embrace.

escort *n.* aide, attendant, beau, bodyguard, chaperon, cicisbeo, companion, company, convoy, cortège, entourage, gigolo, guard, guardian, guide, partner, pilot, procession, protection, protector, retinue, safeguard, squire, suite, train.

v. accompany, chaperon, chum, company, conduct, convoy, guard, guide, lead, partner, protect, shepherd, squire, usher.

esoteric *adj.* abstruse, acroamatic, acroamatical, arcane, cabbalistic, confidential, cryptic, hermetic, hidden, inner, inscrutable, inside, mysterious, mystic, mystical, obscure, occult, private, recondite, secret.

antonyms familiar, popular.

especial *adj.* chief, conspicuous, distinguished, eminent, exceptional, exclusive, express, extraordinary, individual, marked, notable, noteworthy, outstanding, particular, peculiar, personal, pre-eminent, principal, private, proper, remarkable, signal, singular, special, specific, striking, uncommon, unique, unusual.

especially *adv.* chiefly, conspicuously, eminently, exceedingly, exceptionally, exclusively, expressly, extraordinarily, mainly, markedly, notably, noticeably, outstandingly, particularly, passing, peculiarly, pre-eminently, principally, remarkably, signally, singularly, specially, specifically, strikingly, supremely, uncommonly, uniquely, unusually, very.

espionage *n.* counter-intelligence, infiltration, intelligence, investigation, probing, reconnaissance, spying, surveillance, undercover operations.

espousal *n.* adoption, advocacy, affiance, alliance, backing, betrothal, betrothing, bridal, championing, championship, defence, embracing, engagement, espousing, maintenance, marriage, matrimony, nuptials, plighting, spousal, support, wedding.

espouse *v.* adopt, advocate, affiance, back, befriend, betroth, champion, choose, defend, embrace, maintain, marry, opt for, patronise, support, take to wife, take up, wed.

espy *v.* behold, descry, detect, discern, discover, distinguish, glimpse, make out, notice, observe, perceive, see, sight, spot, spy.

essay[1] *n.* article, assignment, commentary, composition, critique, discourse, disquisition, dissertation, essayette, leader, paper, piece, review, thesis, tract, treatise.

essay[2] *n.* attempt, bash, bid, crack, effort, endeavour, exertion, experiment, go, shot, stab, struggle, test, trial, try, undertaking, venture, whack, whirl.

v. attempt, endeavour, go for, have a bash, have a crack, have a go, have a stab, strain, strive, struggle, tackle, take on, test, try, undertake.

essence *n.* alma, attar, attributes, being, centre, character, characteristics, concentrate, core, crux, decoction, decocture, distillate, elixir, ens, entity, esse, extract, fragrance, haecceity, heart, hypostasis, inscape, kernel, life, lifeblood, marrow, meaning, nature, perfume, pith, principle, properties, qualities, quality, quiddit, quiddity, quintessence, scent, significance, soul, spirit, spirits, substance, tincture, virtuality, whatness.

essential[1] *adj.* absolute, basic, cardinal, characteristic, complete, constituent, constitutional, constitutive, crucial, definitive, elemental, elementary, formal, fundamental, ideal, important, indispensable, inherent, innate, intrinsic, key, main, necessary, needed, perfect, principal, quintessential, required, requisite, typical, vital.

antonym inessential.

n. basic, fundamental, must, necessary, necessity, prerequisite, principle, qualification, quality, requirement, requisite, rudiment, sine qua non.

antonym inessential.

essential[2] *adj.* concentrated, decocted, distilled, ethereal, extracted, pure, purified, rectified, refined, volatile.

establish *v.* affirm, attest to, authenticate, authorise, base, certify, confirm, constitute, corroborate, create, decree, demonstrate, enact, ensconce, entrench, fix, form, found, ground, implant, inaugurate, install, institute, introduce, invent, lodge, ordain, organise, plant, prove, radicate, ratify, root, sanction, seat, secure, set up, settle, show, start, station, substantiate, validate, verify.

established *adj.* accepted, attested, confirmed, conventional, ensconced, entrenched, experienced, fixed, proved, proven, radicate, radicated, respected, routed, secure, settled, stated, steadfast, traditional.

antonyms impermanent, unreliable.

establishment *n.* abode, building, business, company, concern, construction, corporation, creation, domicile, dwelling, edifice, enactment, enterprise, erection, factory, firm, formation, foundation, founding, hacienda, home, house, household, implantation, inauguration, inception, installation, institute, institution, introduction, invention, office, ordination, organisation, outfit, plant, quarters, radication, residence, ruling class, set-up, structure, system, the powers that be, the system.

estate *n.* area, assets, barony, belongings, caste, class, condition, demesne, domain, effects, estancia, fortune, goods, grade, hacienda, holdings, lands, latifundium, lot, manor, order, period, place, position, possessions, property, quality, ranch, rank, situation, standing, state, station, status, wealth.

esteem *v.* account, adjudge, admire, believe, calculate, cherish, consider, count, deem, estimate, hold, honour, include, judge, like, love, prize, rate, reckon, regard, regard highly, respect, revere, reverence, think, treasure, value, venerate, view.

n. account, admiration, consideration, count, credit, estimation, good opinion, honour, judgement, love, reckoning, regard, respect, reverence, veneration.

esteemed *adj.* admirable, admired, distinguished, excellent, highly-regarded, honourable, honoured, prized, reputable, respectable, respected, revered, treasured, valued, venerated, well-respected, well-thought-of, worthy.

estimable *adj.* admirable, commendable, considerable, distinguished, egregious, esteemed, excellent, good, honourable, laudable, meritorious, notable, noteworthy, praiseworthy, reputable, respectable, respected, valuable, valued, worthy.
antonyms despicable, insignificant.

estimate *v.* appraise, approximate, assess, believe, calculate, compute, conjecture, consider, count, evaluate, gauge, guess, judge, number, opine, rank, rate, reckon, surmise, think, value.
n. appraisal, appraisement, approximation, assessment, belief, computation, conceit, conception, conjecture, estimation, evaluation, guess, guesstimate, judgement, opinion, reckoning, surmise, valuation.

estimation *n.* account, admiration, appraisal, appreciation, assessment, belief, calculation, computation, conception, consideration, credit, esteem, estimate, evaluation, good opinion, honour, judgement, opinion, rating, reckoning, regard, respect, reverence, veneration, view.

estrange *v.* alienate, antagonise, disaffect, disunite, divide, drive a wedge between, drive apart, part, put a barrier between, separate, set at variance, sever, sunder, withdraw, withhold.
antonyms ally, attract, bind, unite.

estrangement *n.* alienation, antagonisation, antipathy, breach, break-up, disaffection, dissociation, disunity, division, hostility, parting, separation, severance, split, sunderance, sundering, unfriendliness, withdrawal, withholding.

estuary *n.* arm, creek, firth, fjord, inlet, mouth, sea-loch, wash, wick.

et cetera and so forth, and so on, and the like, and the rest, &c, et ainsi de suite, et al, et alia, et alii, et hoc genus omne, et sequentia, et sic de ceteris, et sic de similibus, etc, kai ta leipomena, kai ta loipa, ktl, und so weiter, usw.

etch *v.* bite, burn, carve, corrode, cut, dig, engrave, furrow, grave, groove, hatch, impress, imprint, incise, ingrain, inscribe, stamp.

etching *n.* carving, cut, engraving, impression, imprint, print, sketch.

eternal *adj.* abiding, aeonian, ceaseless, changeless, constant, deathless, durable, endless, enduring, eterne, everlasting, eviternal, illimitable, immortal, immutable, imperishable, incessant, indestructible, infinite, interminable, lasting, limitless, never-ending, perennial, permanent, perpetual, sempiternal, timeless, unbegotten, unceasing, unchanging, undying, unending, unextinguishable, unremitting.
antonyms changeable, ephemeral, temporary.

eternally *adv.* ceaselessly, constantly, endlessly, everlastingly, immutably, incessantly, indestructibly, interminably, lastingly, neverendingly, perennially, permanently, perpetually, unendingly.
antonyms briefly, temporarily.

eternity *n.* aeon, afterlife, age, ages, changelessness, endlessness, everlasting, everlastingness, eviternity, Ewigkeit, heaven, hereafter, illimitability, immortality, immutability, imperishability, incorruptibility, incorruption, infinitude, infinity, next world, paradise, perpetuity, sempiternity, timelessness, world to come.

ethereal *adj.* aerial, airy, celestial, dainty, delicate, diaphanous, elemental, empyreal, empyrean, essential, etheric, etherical, exquisite, fairy, fine, gossamer, heavenly, impalpable, insubstantial, intangible, light, rarefied, rectified, refined, spiritual, subtle, tenuous, unearthly, unworldly.
antonyms earthly, solid.

ethical *adj.* commendable, conscientious, correct, decent, fair, fitting, good, honest, honourable, just, meet, moral, noble, principled, proper, right, righteous, seemly, upright, virtuous.
antonym unethical.

ethics *n.* code, conscience, deontics, deontology, equity, mind philosophy, moral ethology, moral philosophy, moral values, morality, principles, probity, propriety, rule, rules, seemliness, standards.

ethnic *adj.* aboriginal, ancestral, autochthonous, cultural, folk, gentilic, historic, indigenous, national, native, racial, traditional, traditive, tribal.

ethos *n.* attitude, beliefs, character, code, disposition, ethic, geist, manners, moeurs, morality, principles, rationale, spirit, standards, tenor.

etiquette *n.* ceremony, civility, code, convention, conventionalities, correctness, courtesy, customs, decency, decorum, formalities, manners, politeness, politesse, propriety, protocol, rules, seemliness, usage, use.

etymology *n.* derivation, descent, lexicology, linguistics, origin, pedigree, philology, semantics, source, word history, word-lore.

eulogise *v.* acclaim, adulate, applaud, approve, belaud, celebrate, commend, compliment, congratulate, cry up, exalt, extol, flatter, glorify, honour, laud, magnify, panegyrise, praise.
antonym condemn.

eulogistic *adj.* adulatory, approbatory, commendatory, complimentary, encomiastic, epaenetic, favourable, flattering, laudatory, panegyrical.
antonym unfavourable.

eulogy *n.* acclaim, acclamation, accolade, applause, commendation, compliment,

encomium, exaltation, glorification, laud, laudation, laudatory, paean, panegyric, plaudit, praise, tribute.
antonym condemnation.

euphemism *n.* evasion, fig-leaf, genteelism, hypocorism, hypocorisma, polite term, politeness, substitution, understatement.

euphonious *adj.* canorous, clear, consonant, dulcet, dulcifluous, dulciloquent, euphonic, harmonious, honeyed, mellifluent, mellifluous, mellow, melodic, melodious, musical, silvery, soft, sugared, sweet, sweet-sounding, sweet-toned, symphonious, tunable, tuneful.
antonym cacophonous.

euphony *n.* consonance, dulciloquy, euphoniousness, harmoniousness, harmony, mellifluousness, mellowness, melodiousness, melody, music, musicality, tunefulness.
antonym cacophony.

euphoria *n.* bliss, buoyancy, cheerfulness, cloud nine, ecstasy, elation, enthusiasm, euphory, exaltation, exhilaration, exultation, glee, high, high spirits, intoxication, joy, joyousness, jubilation, rapture, transport.
antonym depression.

euphoric *adj.* blissful, buoyant, cheerful, ecstatic, elated, enraptured, enthusiastic, exhilarated, exultant, exulted, gleeful, happy, high, intoxicated, joyful, joyous, jubilant, rapturous.
antonym depressed.

euthanasia *n.* euthanasy, mercy killing, quietus.

evacuate[1] *v.* abandon, clear, clear out, decamp, depart, desert, forsake, leave, quit, relinquish, remove, retire from, vacate, withdraw.

evacuate[2] *v.* defecate, discharge, eject, eliminate, empty, excrete, expel, purge, void.

evacuation[1] *n.* abandonment, clearance, departure, desertion, exodus, quitting, relinquishment, removal, retiral, retreat, vacation, withdrawal.

evacuation[2] *n.* defecation, discharge, ejection, elimination, emptying, excretion, expulsion, purgation, purging, urination, voidance.

evade *v.* avert, avoid, balk, blink, chicken out of, circumvent, cop out, decline, dodge, duck, elude, equivocate, escape, fence, fend off, fudge, hedge, parry, prevaricate, quibble, scrimshank, shirk, shun, sidestep, skive, steer clear of, temporise.
antonym face.

evaluate *v.* appraise, assay, assess, calculate, compute, estimate, gauge, judge, rank, rate, reckon, size up, value, weigh.

evaluation *n.* appraisal, assessment, calculation, computation, estimate, estimation, judgement, opinion, rating, reckoning, valuation.

evanescence *n.* brevity, briefness, ephemerality, ephemeralness, fleetingness, fugaciousness, fugacity, fugitiveness, impermanence, inconstancy, instability, momentariness, temporariness, transience, transitoriness.
antonym permanence.

evanescent *adj.* brief, changing, disappearing,

ephemeral, fading, fleeting, fugacious, fugitive, impermanent, insubstantial, momentary, passing, perishable, short-lived, temporary, transient, transitory, unstable, vanishing.
antonym permanent.

evangelical *adj.* campaigning, crusading, evangelistic, missionary, propagandising, propagandist, proselytising, zealous.

evangelise *v.* baptise, campaign, convert, crusade, gospelise, missionarise, missionise, preach, propagandise, proselytise.

evaporate *v.* condense, dehydrate, dematerialise, desiccate, disappear, dispel, disperse, dissipate, dissolve, distil, dry, evanesce, exhale, fade, melt (away), vanish, vaporise, vapour.

evaporation *n.* condensation, dehydration, dematerialisation, desiccation, disappearance, dispelling, dispersal, dissipation, dissolution, distillation, drying, evanescence, fading, melting, vanishing, vaporisation, watersmoke.

evasion *n.* artifice, avoidance, casuistry, circumvention, cop-out, cunning, dodge, elusion, equivocation, escape, euphemism, evasiveness, excuse, fudging, obfuscation, obliqueness, pretext, prevarication, put-off, ruse, shift, shirking, shuffling, sophism, sophistry, subterfuge, trickery, weasel-words.
antonyms directness, frankness.

evasive *adj.* ambiguous, cag(e)y, casuistic, casuistical, cunning, deceitful, deceptive, devious, disingenuous, dissembling, elusive, elusory, equivocating, indirect, misleading, oblique, prevaricating, secretive, shifty, shuffling, slippery, sophistical, tricky, unforthcoming, vacillating.
antonyms direct, frank.

eve *n.* brink, edge, evening, moment, point, threshold, verge, vigil.

even *adj.* abreast, alongside, balanced, calm, coequal, commensurate, comparable, complanate, composed, constant, cool, disinterested, dispassionate, drawn, equable, equal, equalised, equanimous, equitable, even-tempered, fair, fair and square, fifty-fifty, flat, fluent, flush, horizontal, identical, impartial, impassive, imperturbable, just, level, level-pegging, like, matching, metrical, monotonous, neck and neck, on a par, parallel, peaceful, placid, plane, plumb, proportionate, quits, regular, rhythmical, serene, side by side, similar, smooth, square, stable, steady, straight, symmetrical, tied, tranquil, true, unbiased, unbroken, undisturbed, unexcitable, unexcited, uniform, uninterrupted, unprejudiced, unruffled, unvarying, unwavering, well-balanced.
antonyms unequal, uneven.
adv. all the more, also, although, as well, at all, directly, exactly, hardly, including, just, much, scarcely, so much as, still, yet.
v. align, balance, equal, equalise, flatten, flush, level, match, regularise, regulate, smooth, square, stabilise, steady, straighten.

even so all the same, despite that, however, however that may be, in spite of that, natheless, nevertheless, nonetheless, notwithstanding that, still, yet.

even-handed *adj.* balanced, disinterested, dispassionate, equitable, fair, fair and square, impartial, just, neutral, non-discriminatory, reasonable, square, unbiased, unprejudiced, without fear or favour.
antonym inequitable.

evening *n.* crepuscule, dusk, eve, even, eventide, forenight, gloaming, Hesper, Hesperus, nightfall, sundown, sunset, twilight, vesper.
adj. crepuscular, twilight, vesperal, vespertinal, vespertine.

evenness *n.* alikeness, balance, calmness, commensurateness, comparability, composure, constancy, coolness, equability, equableness, equality, equanimity, flatness, fluency, identicalness, impassivity, imperturbability, levelness, monotony, peacableness, placidity, proportion, regularity, rhythmicality, serenity, similarity, smoothness, stability, steadiness, straightness, symmetry, tranquillity, trueness, uniformity.
antonyms inequality, unevenness.

event *n.* adventure, affair, bout, business, case, circumstance, competition, conclusion, consequence, contest, effect, end, engagement, episode, eventuality, experience, fact, game, happening, incident, issue, match, matter, milestone, occasion, occurrence, outcome, possibility, result, termination, tournament, upshot.

even-tempered *adj.* calm, composed, cool, cool-headed, equable, equanimous, impassive, imperturbable, level-headed, peaceable, peaceful, placid, serene, stable, steady, tranquil, unexcitable, unfussed, unruffled.
antonym excitable.

eventful *adj.* active, busy, consequential, critical, crucial, decisive, epochal, exciting, fateful, full, historic, important, interesting, lively, memorable, momentous, notable, noteworthy, portentous, remarkable, significant, unforgettable.
antonyms dull, ordinary, uneventful.

eventual *adj.* concluding, consequent, ensuing, final, future, impending, last, later, overall, planned, projected, prospective, resulting, subsequent, ultimate.

eventuality *n.* case, chance, circumstance, contingency, crisis, emergency, event, happening, happenstance, likelihood, mishap, outcome, possibility, probability.

eventually *adv.* after all, at last, at length, finally, in one's own good time, sooner or later, subsequently, ultimately.

ever *adv.* always, at all, at all times, at any time, ceaselessly, constantly, continually, endlessly, eternally, everlastingly, evermore, for ever, in any case, in any circumstances, incessantly, on any account, perpetually, unceasingly, unendingly.

everlasting *adj.* abiding, boring, ceaseless, changeless, constant, continual, continuous, deathless, durable, endless, enduring, eternal, immarcescible, immortal, imperishable, incessant, indestructible, infinite, interminable, lasting, monotonous, never-ending, perdurable, permanent, perpetual, relentless, tedious, timeless, unceasing, unchanging, undying, unfading, uninterrupted, unremitting.
antonyms temporary, transient.

evermore *adv.* always, eternally, ever, ever after, for aye, for ever, for ever and a day, for ever and ever, henceforth, hereafter, in perpetuum, in saecula saeculorum, till doomsday, to the end of time, unceasingly.

evert *v.* evaginate, turn inside out, turn out.

everted *adj.* evaginated, extrorse, turned inside out.

everybody *n.* all and sundry, each one, everyone, one and all, the whole world, tout le monde.

everyday *adj.* accustomed, banal, boring, circadian, common, common-or-garden, commonplace, conventional, customary, daily, diurnal, dull, familiar, frequent, habitual, informal, monotonous, mundane, normal, ordinary, plain, prosaic, quotidian, regular, routine, run-of-the-mill, simple, stock, unexceptional, unimaginative, usual, wonted, workaday.
antonyms exceptional, special.

everyone *n.* all and sundry, each one, every man-jack, every mother's son, everybody, one and all, the whole jingbang, the whole world, tout le monde.

everything *n.* all, lock stock and barrel, the aggregate, the entirety, the lot, the sum, the total, the whole caboodle, the whole lot, the whole shoot, the whole shooting-match.

everywhere *adv.* all along the line, all around, all over, far and near, far and wide, high and low, left right and centre, omnipresent, passim, ubique, ubiquitous.

evict *v.* boot out, cast out, chuck out, defenestrate, dislodge, dispossess, disseise, eject, expel, expropriate, give the bum's rush, kick out, oust, put out, remove, show the door, turf out.

eviction *n.* clearance, defenestration, dislodgement, dispossession, disseisin, ejection, expropriation, expulsion, ouster, removal, the bum's rush.

evidence *n.* affirmation, attestation, betrayal, confirmation, corroboration, data, declaration, demonstration, deposition, documentation, grounds, hint, indication, manifestation, mark, pledge, proof, sign, substantiation, suggestion, testimony, token, voucher, witness.
v. affirm, attest, betray, confirm, demonstrate, denote, display, establish, evince, exhibit, indicate, manifest, prove, reveal, show, signify, testify to, witness.

evident *adj.* apparent, clear, clear-cut, confessed, conspicuous, detectable, discernible, distinct, incontestable, incontrovertible,

indisputable, manifest, noticeable, obvious, ostensible, palpable, patent, perceptible, plain, tangible, undeniable, unmistakable, visible.
antonym uncertain.

evidently *adv.* apparently, clearly, distinctly, doubtless, doubtlessly, incontestably, incontrovertibly, indisputably, indubitably, irrefragably, manifestly, obviously, ostensibly, outwardly, patently, plainly, seemingly, undoubtedly, unmistakably, unquestionably.

evil *adj.* adverse, bad, baleful, baneful, base, blackguardly, black-hearted, calamitous, catastrophic, corrupt, cruel, deadly, deleterious, depraved, destructive, detrimental, devilish, dire, disastrous, facinorous, flagitious, foul, ghastly, grim, harmful, heinous, hurtful, immoral, inauspicious, inimical, iniquitous, injurious, knavish, malefactory, malefic, maleficent, malevolent, malicious, malignant, mephitic, mischievous, miscreant, nefarious, nefast, nocuous, noisome, noxious, offensive, painful, perfidious, pernicious, pestiferous, pestilential, poisonous, putrid, reprobate, ruinous, sinful, sorrowful, ugly, unfortunate, unlucky, unpleasant, unspeakable, vicious, vile, villainous, wicked, woeful, wrong.
n. adversity, affliction, amiss, badness, bane, baseness, blow, calamity, catastrophe, corruption, curse, demonry, depravity, disaster, distress, facinorousness, flagitiousness, foulness, harm, heinousness, hurt, hydra, ill, immorality, impiety, improbity, iniquity, injury, knavery, maleficence, malignity, mischief, misery, misfortune, pain, perfidy, ruin, sin, sinfulness, sorrow, suffering, turpitude, ulcer, vice, viciousness, villainy, wickedness, woe, wrong, wrong-doing.
evil eye blight, cantrip, charm, curse, hoodoo, jettatura, jinx, malocchio, spell, voodoo.
evil spirit bogey, bogle, cacodaemon, demon, devil, fiend, ghost, goblin, gremlin, hobgoblin, imp, incubus, jumby, kelpie, kobold, nicker, nightmare, nix, nixie, succubus, troll.

evil-doer *n.* blackguard, caitiff, criminal, delinquent, knave, malefactor, malfeasant, miscreant, offender, reprobate, rogue, scamp, scapegrace, scoundrel, sinner, villain, wrongdoer.

evince *v.* attest, bespeak, betoken, betray, confess, declare, demonstrate, display, establish, evidence, exhibit, express, indicate, manifest, reveal, show, signify.
antonyms conceal, suppress.

eviscerate *v.* disembowel, draw, exenterate, gralloch, gut.

evisceration *n.* disembowelment, drawing, exenteration, gralloching, gutting.

evocation *n.* activation, actuation, arousal, echo, eduction, elicitation, excitation, kindling, recall, stimulation, stirring, suggestion, summoning-up.

evoke *v.* activate, actuate, arouse, awaken, call, call forth, call up, conjure up, educe, elicit,

excite, induce, invoke, produce, provoke, raise, recall, rekindle, stimulate, stir, summon, summon up.
antonyms quell, suppress.

evolution *n.* convolution, Darwinism, derivation, descent, development, evolvement, expansion, growth, gyration, increase, maturation, progress, progression, ripening, unfolding, unrolling.

evolve *v.* derive, descend, develop, disclose, elaborate, emerge, enlarge, expand, grow, increase, mature, progress, result, unravel.

exacerbate *v.* aggravate, deepen, embitter, enrage, envenom, exaggerate, exasperate, excite, heighten, increase, inflame, infuriate, intensify, irritate, provoke, sharpen, vex, worsen.
antonym soothe.

exact *adj.* accurate, blow-by-blow, careful, close, correct, definite, detailed, explicit, express, factual, faithful, faultless, finical, finicky, flawless, identical, letter-perfect, literal, methodical, meticulous, nice, orderly, painstaking, particular, perfectionist, perjink, precise, punctilious, right, rigorous, scrupulous, severe, specific, square, strict, true, unambiguous, unequivocal, unerring, veracious, very, word-perfect.
antonym inexact.
v. bleed, claim, command, compel, demand, extort, extract, force, impose, insist on, milk, require, requisition, squeeze, wrest, wring.

exactable *adj.* demandable, exigible, imposable, requirable.

exacting *adj.* arduous, demanding, difficult, exig(e)ant, exigent, hard, harsh, imperious, laborious, oppressive, painstaking, rigid, rigorous, severe, stern, strict, stringent, taxing, toilsome, tough, trying, tyrannical, unsparing, uphill.
antonyms easy, tolerant.

exaction *n.* blackmail, bleeding, compulsion, contribution, demand, extortion, imposition, milking, rapacity, requirement, requisition, tribute.

exactitude *n.* accuracy, authenticity, care, carefulness, clarity, conscientiousness, correctness, detail, exactness, faithfulness, faultlessness, fidelity, meticulousness, nicety, orderliness, painstakingness, perfectionism, preciseness, precision, promptitude, promptness, punctilio, punctuality, regularity, rigorousness, rigour, scrupulosity, scrupulousness, strictness, thoroughness, truth, veracity.
antonyms carelessness, inaccuracy.

exactly *adv.* absolutely, accurately, bang, carefully, correctly, dead, definitely, explicitly, expressly, faithfully, faultlessly, just, literally, literatim, methodically, particularly, plumb, precisely, punctiliously, quite, rigorously, scrupulously, severely, specifically, strictly, to the letter, truly, truthfully, unambiguously, unequivocally, unerringly, veraciously, verbatim.
interj. absolutely, agreed, certainly, indeed,

just so, of course, precisely, quite, right, true.

exactness *n.* accuracy, authenticity, carefulness, correctness, detail, exactitude, faithfulness, faultlessness, fidelity, meticulousness, nicety, orderliness, painstakingness, perfectionism, preciseness, precision, promptitude, punctilio, regularity, rigorousness, rigour, scrupulousness, strictness, truth, veracity, verity.
antonyms carelessness, inaccuracy.

exaggerate *v.* amplify, bounce, caricature, distend, embellish, embroider, emphasise, enlarge, exalt, hyperbolise, inflate, magnify, overdo, overdraw, overemphasise, overestimate, oversell, overstate, pile it on.
antonyms belittle, understate.

exaggerated *adj.* amplified, bloated, bombastic, burlesqued, caricatured, embellished, euphuistic, exalted, excessive, extravagant, hyperbolic, hyperbolical, inflated, overblown, overcharged, overdone, overestimated, overstated, pretentious, tall, turgid.
antonym understated.

exaggeration *n.* amplification, burlesque, caricature, embellishment, emphasis, enlargement, exaltation, excess, extravagance, hyperbole, inflation, magnification, overemphasis, overestimation, overstatement, parody, pretension, pretentiousness, stretcher.
antonyms meiosis, understatement.

exalt *v.* acclaim, advance, aggrandise, animate, apotheosise, applaud, arouse, bless, crown, deify, delight, dignify, elate, electrify, elevate, enliven, ennoble, enthrone, excite, exhilarate, extol, fire, glorify, heighten, honour, idolise, inspire, inspirit, laud, magnify, praise, promote, raise, revere, reverence, stimulate, sublimise, thrill, upgrade, uplift, venerate, worship.
antonym debase.

exaltation *n.* acclaim, acclamation, adoration, adulation, advancement, aggrandisement, animation, apotheosis, applause, blessing, bliss, canonisation, deification, delight, dignification, dignity, ecstasy, elation, elevation, eminence, ennoblement, enthusiasm, excitement, exhilaration, extolment, exultation, glorification, glory, grandeur, homage, honour, idealisation, idolisation, inspiration, joy, joyfulness, joyousness, jubilation, laudation, lionisation, loftiness, magnification, panegyric, plaudits, praise, prestige, promotion, rapture, reverence, rise, stimulation, transport, tribute, upgrading, uplift, veneration, worship.
antonym debasement.

exalted *adj.* animated, august, blissful, dignified, ecstatic, elate, elated, elevated, eminent, enhanced, enlivened, enthusiastic, exaggerated, excessive, excited, exhilarated, exultant, glorified, glorious, grand, happy, high, high-minded, high-ranking, honoured, ideal, idealised, in high spirits, in seventh heaven, inflated, inspired, inspirited, intellectual, joyful, joyous, jubilant, lofty, lordly, noble, overblown, prestigious, pretentious, princely,

rapturous, stately, stimulated, sublime, superior, transcendent, transported, uplifted, uplifting.
antonym debased.

examination *n.* analysis, appraisal, assay, audit, catechism, check, check-up, critique, cross-examination, cross-questioning, docimasy, exam, exploration, inquiry, inquisition, inspection, interrogation, investigation, observation, once-over, perusal, probe, questioning, quiz, research, review, scan, scrutinisation, scrutiny, search, sift, study, survey, test, trial, visitation, viva.

examine *v.* analyse, appraise, assay, audit, case, catechise, check (out), consider, cross-examine, cross-question, explore, grill, inquire, inspect, interrogate, investigate, jerque, peruse, ponder, pore over, probe, question, quiz, review, scan, scrutinise, sift, study, survey, sus out, test, vet, visit, weigh.

examinee *n.* applicant, candidate, competitor, contestant, entrant, examinant, examinate, interviewee.

examiner *n.* adjudicator, analyst, arbiter, assayer, assessor, auditor, censor, critic, examinant, examinator, inspector, interlocutor, interviewer, judge, marker, questioner, reader, reviewer, scrutator, scrutineer, scrutiniser, tester.

example *n.* admonition, archetype, case, case in point, caution, citation, ensample, exemplar, exemplification, exemplum, ideal, illustration, instance, lesson, mirror, model, occurrence, paradigm, paragon, parallel, pattern, praxis, precedent, prototype, sample, specimen, standard, type, warning.

exasperate *v.* aggravate, anger, annoy, bug, enrage, exacerbate, excite, exulcerate, gall, get, get in someone's hair, get on someone's nerves, get on someone's wick, get to, goad, incense, inflame, infuriate, irk, irritate, madden, needle, nettle, peeve, pique, plague, provoke, rankle, rile, rouse, vex.
antonyms calm, soothe.

exasperated *adj.* aggravated, angered, angry, annoyed, at the end of one's tether, bored, bugged, fed up, galled, goaded, incensed, indignant, infuriated, irked, irritated, maddened, needled, nettled, peeved, piqued, provoked, riled, vexed.

exasperating *adj.* aggravating, annoying, boring, bothersome, disagreeable, galling, infuriating, irksome, irritating, maddening, pernicious, pesky, pestiferous, pestilential, provoking, troublesome, vexatious, vexing.

exasperation *n.* aggravation, anger, annoyance, arousal, discontent, disgust, displeasure, dissatisfaction, enragement, exacerbation, exulceration, fury, gall, indignation, inflammation, ire, irritation, passion, pique, provocation, rage, resentment, vexation, wrath.
antonym calmness.

excavate *v.* burrow, cut, delve, dig, dig out, dig up, disinter, drive, exhume, gouge, hollow, mine, quarry, sap, scoop, stope, trench, tunnel, uncover, undermine, unearth.

excavation *n.* burrow, cavity, cut, cutting, delf, dig, diggings, ditch, dugout, hole, hollow, mine, pit, quarry, sap, sapping, shaft, souterrain, stope, trench, trough, undermining.

exceed *v.* beat, better, cap, contravene, eclipse, excel, outdistance, outdo, outreach, outrival, outrun, outshine, outstrip, overdo, overstep, overtake, pass, surmount, surpass, take liberties with, top, transcend, transgress.

exceeding *adj.* amazing, astonishing, enormous, exceptional, excessive, extraordinary, great, huge, outstanding, pre-eminent, superior, superlative, surpassing, transcendent, unequalled, unprecedented, unusual, vast.

exceedingly *adv.* amazingly, astonishingly, enormously, especially, exceeding, exceptionally, excessively, extraordinarily, extremely, greatly, highly, hugely, inordinately, passing, superlatively, surpassingly, unprecedentedly, unusually, vastly, very.

excel *v.* beat, better, cap, eclipse, exceed, outclass, outdo, outperform, outrank, outrival, outshine, outstrip, overshadow, pass, predominate, shine, stand out, surmount, surpass, top, transcend, trump.

excellence *n.* distinction, eminence, fineness, goodness, greatness, merit, perfection, pre-eminence, purity, quality, superiority, supremacy, transcendence, virtue, water, worth. *antonym* inferiority.

excellent *adj.* A1, admirable, beaut, bonzer, boshta, bosker, boss, brave, bully, capital, champion, choice, commendable, copacetic, corking, crack, cracking, distinguished, estimable, exemplary, eximious, exquisite, fine, first-class, first-rate, good, great, hot stuff, laudable, meritorious, nonpareil, notable, noted, noteworthy, outstanding, peerless, prime, remarkable, ripping, select, splendid, sterling, stunning, superb, supereminent, superior, superlative, surpassing, tipping, tiptop, top-flight, top-notch, topping, unequalled, unexceptionable, up to dick, wayout, wonderful, worthy. *antonym* inferior.

except *prep.* apart from, bar, barring, besides, but, except for, excepting, excluding, exclusive of, leaving out, less, minus, not counting, omitting, other than, save, saving. *v.* ban, bar, debar, disallow, eliminate, exclude, leave out, omit, pass over, reject, rule out.

exception *n.* abnormality, anomaly, curiosity, debarment, departure, deviation, disallowment, eccentricity, excepting, exclusion, exemption, freak, inconsistency, irregularity, oddity, omission, peculiarity, prodigy, quirk, rarity, rejection, special case.

exceptional *adj.* aberrant, abnormal, anomalous, atypical, curious, deviant, eccentric, excellent, extraordinary, freakish, inconsistent, irregular, marvellous, notable, noteworthy,

odd, outstanding, peculiar, phenomenal, prodigious, quirky, rare, remarkable, singular, special, strange, superior, superlative, uncommon, unconventional, unequalled, unexpected, unusual. *antonyms* mediocre, unexceptional.

exceptionally *adv.* amazingly, especially, excellently, extraordinarily, marvellously, notably, outstandingly, peculiarly, phenomenally, prodigiously, remarkably, singularly, specially, splendidly, superlatively, uncommonly, unusually, wonderfully.

excerpt *n.* citation, extract, fragment, gobbet, part, passage, pericope, portion, quotation, quote, scrap, section, selection. *v.* borrow, cite, crib, cull, extract, lift, mine, quarry, quote, select.

excess *n.* debauchery, diarrhoea, dissipation, dissoluteness, excesses, exorbitance, extravagance, glut, gluttony, immoderateness, immoderation, intemperance, left-over, libertinism, licentiousness, nimiety, overabundance, overdose, overflow, overflush, overindulgence, overkill, overload, plethora, prodigality, remainder, superabundance, superfluity, surfeit, surplus, unrestraint. *antonym* dearth. *adj.* additional, extra, left-over, redundant, remaining, residual, spare, superfluous, supernumerary, surplus.

excessive *adj.* disproportionate, exaggerated, exorbitant, extravagant, extreme, fanatical, immoderate, inordinate, intemperate, needless, nimious, overdone, overmuch, prodigal, profligate, steep, stiff, supererogatory, superfluous, unasked-for, uncalled-for, unconscionable, undue, unnecessary, unneeded, unreasonable. *antonym* insufficient.

excessively *adv.* disproportionately, exaggeratedly, exorbitantly, extravagantly, extremely, fanatically, immoderately, inordinately, intemperately, needlessly, overly, overmuch, prodigally, superfluously, unconscionably, unduly, unnecessarily, unreasonably. *antonym* insufficiently.

exchange *v.* bandy, bargain, barter, change, commute, convert, interchange, reciprocate, replace, substitute, swap, switch, toss about, trade, truck. *n.* bargain, barter, bourse, brush, chat, commerce, conversation, converse, conversion, dealing, interchange, intercourse, market, quid pro quo, reciprocity, replacement, substitution, swap, switch, tit for tat, trade, traffic, truck.

excise[1] *n.* customs, duty, impost, levy, surcharge, tariff, tax, toll, VAT.

excise[2] *v.* bowdlerise, cut, cut out, delete, destroy, eradicate, erase, expunge, expurgate, exterminate, extirpate, extract, remove, rescind.

excision *n.* bowdlerisation, deletion, destruction, eradication, expunction, expurgation, extermination, extirpation, removal.

excitable *adj.* edgy, emotional, explosive, feisty, fiery, hasty, highly-strung, high-strung, hot-headed, hot-tempered, inflammable, irascible, mercurial, nervous, nervy, passionate, quick-tempered, restive, restless, sensitive, susceptible, temperamental, unstable, violent, volatile.
antonyms calm, impassive.

excite *v.* activate, actuate, aerate, affect, agitate, animate, arouse, awaken, discompose, disturb, elate, electrify, elicit, engender, evoke, fire, foment, galvanise, generate, ignite, impress, incite, induce, inflame, initiate, inspire, instigate, kindle, motivate, move, provoke, quicken, rouse, stimulate, stir up, suscitate, sway, thrill, titillate, touch, turn on, upset, waken, warm, whet.
antonyms bore, quell.

excited *adj.* aflame, agitated, animated, aroused, awakened, breathless, corybantic, discomposed, disturbed, eager, elated, enthused, enthusiastic, feverish, flurried, flustered, fluttered, frantic, frenzied, high, impassioned, moved, nervous, overwrought, restive, restless, roused, ruffled, stimulated, stirred, thrilled, titillated, upset, wild, worked up, wrought-up.
antonyms apathetic, bored.

excitement *n.* action, activity, ado, adventure, agitation, animation, brouhaha, clamour, commotion, deliriousness, delirium, discomposure, eagerness, elation, enthusiasm, excitation, ferment, fever, flurry, furore, fuss, heat, hubbub, hue and cry, hurly-burly, kerfuffle, kicks, passion, perturbation, restlessness, stimulation, stimulus, tew, thrill, titillation, tumult, unrest, urge.
antonyms apathy, calm.

exciting *adj.* cliff-hanging, electrifying, encouraging, enthralling, exhilarating, impressive, inspiring, intoxicating, moving, nail-biting, promising, provocative, rousing, sensational, stimulating, stirring, striking, suspenseful, swashbuckling, thrilling, titillating.
antonyms boring, unexciting.

exclaim *v.* blurt, call, cry, declare, ejaculate, interject, proclaim, shout, utter, vociferate.

exclamation *n.* call, cry, ecphonesis, ejaculation, expletive, interjection, outcry, shout, utterance, vociferation.

exclamatory *adj.* dramatic, ejaculatory, exclamative, interjaculatory, interjectional, interjectionary, interjectural, melodramatic, sensationalist.

exclude *v.* anathematise, ban, bar, blackball, blacklist, bounce, boycott, debar, disallow, eject, eliminate, embargo, evict, except, excommunicate, expel, forbid, ignore, include out, interclude, interdict, keep out, leave out, omit, ostracise, oust, preclude, prohibit, proscribe, refuse, reject, remove, repudiate, rule out, shut out, veto.
antonyms admit, allow, include.

exclusion *n.* ban, bar, boycott, debarment,

disfellowship, ejection, elimination, embargo, eviction, exception, expulsion, forbiddal, forbiddance, interdict, non-admission, omission, ostracisation, preclusion, prohibition, proscription, refusal, rejection, removal, repudiation, veto.
antonyms admittance, allowance, inclusion.

exclusive *adj.* absolute, arrogant, chic, choice, clannish, classy, cliquey, cliquish, closed, complete, confined, discriminative, elegant, entire, esoteric, exclusory, fashionable, full, limited, luxurious, monopolistic, narrow, only, peculiar, posh, private, restricted, restrictive, select, selective, selfish, single, snobbish, sole, total, undivided, unique, unshared, whole.

exclusive of barring, debarring, except, except for, excepting, excluding, omitting, ruling out.
antonym inclusive of.

excommunicate *v.* anathematise, ban, banish, bar, blacklist, debar, denounce, disfellowship, eject, exclude, execrate, expel, outlaw, proscribe, remove, repudiate, unchurch.

excrescence *n.* appendage, bump, excrement, growth, intumescence, knob, lump, misgrowth, outgrowth, process, projection, prominence, protrusion, protuberance, swelling, tumour, wart.

excrete *v.* crap, defecate, discharge, egest, eject, eliminate, evacuate, expel, exude, secrete, shit, urinate, void.

excretion *n.* crap, defecation, discharge, droppings, dung, eccrisis, egesta, ejection, elimination, evacuation, excrement, excreta, expulsion, exudation, ordure, perspiration, rejectamenta, shit(e), skat, stool, sudation, urination, voidance.

excretory *adj.* defecatory, egestive, emunctory, excremental, excrementitial, excrementitious, exudative, faecal, perspiratory, sudatory, urinary, urinative.

excruciating *adj.* acute, agonising, atrocious, bitter, burning, exquisite, extreme, harrowing, insufferable, intense, intolerable, painful, piercing, racking, savage, searing, severe, sharp, tormenting, torturing, torturous, unbearable, unendurable.

exculpate *v.* absolve, acquit, clear, deliver, discharge, disculpate, excuse, exonerate, forgive, free, justify, let off, pardon, release, vindicate.
antonyms blame, condemn.

exculpation *n.* absolution, acquittal, clearance, discharge, excuse, exoneration, expurgation, freedom, justification, pardon, release, vindication.
antonym condemnation.

excursion *n.* airing, breather, day trip, detour, deviation, digression, divagation, ecbole, episode, excursus, expedition, jaunt, journey, outing, ramble, ride, sashay, tour, trip, walk, wandering, wayzgoose.

excusable *adj.* allowable, defensible, explainable, explicable, forgivable, ignorable, justifiable, minor, pardonable, permissible, slight, understandable, venial, vindicable, warrantable.

antonym blameworthy.

excuse *v.* absolve, acquit, apologise for, condone, defend, discharge, exculpate, exempt, exonerate, explain, extenuate, forgive, free, ignore, indulge, justify, let off, liberate, mitigate, overlook, palliate, pardon, release, relieve, sanction, spare, tolerate, vindicate, warrant, wink at.

n. alibi, apology, cop-out, defence, disguise, evasion, exculpation, exoneration, expedient, explanation, extenuation, grounds, justification, makeshift, mitigation, mockery, palliation, parody, plea, pretence, pretext, put-off, reason, semblance, shift, substitute, subterfuge, travesty, vindication.

ex-directory *adj.* unlisted.

execrable *adj.* abhorrent, abominable, accursed, appalling, atrocious, damnable, deplorable, despicable, detestable, disgusting, foul, hateful, heinous, horrible, loathsome, nauseous, obnoxious, odious, offensive, repulsive, revolting, shocking, sickening, vile.

antonyms admirable, esteemable.

execrate *v.* abhor, abominate, anathematise, blast, condemn, curse, damn, denounce, denunciate, deplore, despise, detest, excoriate, fulminate, hate, imprecate, inveigh against, loathe, revile, vilify.

antonyms commend, praise.

execration *n.* abhorrence, abomination, anathema, condemnation, contempt, curse, damnation, detestation, excoriation, fulmination, hate, hatred, imprecation, invective, loathing, malediction, odium, revilement, vilification, vituperation.

antonyms commendation, praise.

execute¹ *v.* behead, burn, crucify, decapitate, decollate, electrocute, guillotine, hang, kill, liquidate, put to death, shoot.

execute² *v.* accomplish, achieve, administer, complete, consummate, deliver, discharge, dispatch, do, effect, effectuate, enact, enforce, expedite, finish, fulfil, implement, perform, prosecute, realise, render, seal, serve, sign, validate.

execution¹ *n.* auto-da-fé, beheading, burning, capital punishment, crucifixion, death, death penalty, decapitation, decollation, electrocution, firing squad, fusillation, guillotining, hanging, killing, shooting.

execution² *n.* accomplishment, achievement, administration, completion, consummation, delivery, discharge, dispatch, effect, effectuation, enactment, enforcement, exercitation, implementation, manner, mode, operation, performance, prosecution, realisation, rendering, rendition, style, technique, warrant, writ.

executioner *n.* assassin, exterminator, hangman, headsman, hit man, killer, liquidator, murderer, slayer.

executive *n.* administration, administrator, controller, director, directorate, directors, government, hierarchy, leadership, management, manager, official, organiser.

adj. administrative, controlling, decision-making, directing, directorial, governing, gubernatorial, guiding, leading, managerial, organisational, organising, regulating, supervisory.

exemplar *n.* archetype, copy, criterion, embodiment, epitome, example, exemplification, ideal, illustration, instance, model, paradigm, paragon, pattern, prototype, specimen, standard, type, yardstick.

exemplary *adj.* admirable, admonitory, cautionary, commendable, correct, estimable, excellent, faultless, flawless, good, honourable, ideal, laudable, meritorious, model, monitory, perfect, praiseworthy, punctilious, sterling, unerring, unexceptionable, warning, worthy.

antonyms imperfect, unworthy.

exemplify *v.* demonstrate, depict, display, embody, ensample, epitomise, evidence, example, exhibit, illustrate, instance, manifest, represent, show, typify.

exempt *v.* absolve, discharge, dismiss, except, excuse, exonerate, free, let off, liberate, make an exception of, release, relieve, spare.

adj. absolved, clear, discharged, excepted, excluded, excused, favoured, free, immune, liberated, released, spared.

antonym liable.

exemption *n.* absolution, discharge, dispensation, exception, exclusion, exoneration, freedom, immunity, indulgence, overslaugh, privilege, release.

antonym liability.

exercise *v.* afflict, agitate, annoy, apply, burden, discharge, discipline, distress, disturb, drill, employ, enjoy, exert, habituate, inure, occupy, operate, pain, perturb, practise, preoccupy, train, trouble, try, upset, use, utilise, vex, wield, work out, worry.

n. accomplishment, action, activity, aerobics, application, assignment, daily dozen, discharge, discipline, drill, drilling, effort, employment, enjoyment, exercitation, exertion, fulfilment, implementation, krieg(s)spiel, labour, lesson, operation, physical jerks, practice, problem, schooling, schoolwork, task, toil, training, use, utilisation, war-game, work, work-out.

exert *v.* apply, bring to bear, employ, exercise, expend, use, utilise, wield.

exert oneself apply oneself, concentrate, endeavour, labour, strain, strive, struggle, sweat, take pains, toil, work.

exertion *n.* action, application, assiduity, attempt, diligence, effort, employment, endeavour, exercise, industry, labour, operation, pains, perseverance, sedulousness, strain, stretch, struggle, toil, travail, trial, use, utilisation, work.

antonyms idleness, rest.

exhalation *n.* air, aura, breath, discharge,

ectoplasm, effluvium, efflux, emanation, emission, evaporation, exhaust, expiration, flow, fog, fume, fumes, mist, respiration, smoke, steam, vapour, vapours.
antonym inhalation.

exhale *v.* breathe (out), discharge, eject, emanate, emit, evaporate, expel, expire, give off, issue, respire, steam.
antonym inhale.

exhaust *v.* bankrupt, beggar, bugger, consume, cripple, debilitate, deplete, disable, dissipate, drain, dry, empty, enervate, enfeeble, expend, fatigue, finish, impoverish, overtax, overtire, overwork, prostrate, run through, sap, spend, squander, strain, tax, tire (out), use up, void, waste, weaken, wear out, weary.
antonym refresh.
n. discharge, eduction, effluvium, emanation, emission, exhalation, fumes.

exhausted *adj.* all in, bare, beat, buggered, burned out, clapped-out, consumed, crippled, dead, dead tired, dead-beat, debilitated, depleted, disabled, dissipated, dog-tired, done, done in, drained, dry, effete, empty, enervated, enfeebled, expended, fatigued, finished, fogged out, forjeskit, forswunk, gone, jaded, jiggered, knackered, out for the count, outspent, pooped, prostrated, sapped, spent, squandered, tired out, used up, void, washed-out, washed-up, wasted, weak, whacked, worn out, zonked.
antonyms conserved, fresh, vigorous.

exhausting *adj.* arduous, backbreaking, crippling, debilitating, difficult, draining, enervating, fatiguing, formidable, gruelling, hard, knackering, laborious, punishing, sapping, severe, strenuous, taxing, testing, tiring, vigorous.
antonym refreshing.

exhaustion *n.* consumption, debilitation, depletion, effeteness, emptying, enervation, fatigue, feebleness, inanition, jet-lag, lassitude, prostration, tiredness, weariness.
antonym freshness.

exhaustive *adj.* all-embracing, all-inclusive, all-out, complete, comprehensive, definitive, detailed, encyclopaedic, expansive, extensive, far-reaching, full, full-scale, in-depth, intensive, sweeping, thorough, thoroughgoing, total.
antonym incomplete.

exhibit *v.* air, demonstrate, disclose, display, evidence, evince, expose, express, flaunt, indicate, manifest, offer, parade, present, reveal, show, showcase, sport.
antonym hide.
n. display, exhibition, illustration, model, show.

exhibition *n.* airing, array, demonstration, display, exhibit, expo, exposition, fair, manifestation, panopticon, performance, presentation, representation, show, showcase, showing, spectacle.

exhibitionist *n.* extrovert, flasher, pervert, self-advertiser, show-off.

exhilarate *v.* animate, cheer, delight, elate, energise, enhearten, enliven, exalt, excite, gladden, hearten, inspirit, invigorate, lift, stimulate, thrill, vitalise.
antonyms bore, discourage.

exhilarating *adj.* breathtaking, cheering, enlivening, euphoriant, exalting, exciting, exhilarant, exhilarative, exhilaratory, gladdening, heartsome, invigorating, mind-blowing, stimulating, thrilling, vitalising.
antonyms boring, discouraging.

exhilaration *n.* animation, ardour, cheerfulness, dash, delight, élan, elation, exaltation, excitement, gaiety, gladness, glee, gleefulness, gusto, high spirits, hilarity, joy, joyfulness, liveliness, mirth, sprightliness, vivacity, zeal.
antonyms boredom, discouragement.

exhort *v.* admonish, advise, beseech, bid, call upon, caution, counsel, encourage, enjoin, entreat, goad, implore, incite, inflame, inspire, instigate, persuade, press, spur, urge, warn.

exhortation *n.* admonition, advice, allocution, beseeching, bidding, caution, counsel, encouragement, enjoinder, entreaty, goading, incitement, lecture, paraenesis, persuasion, protreptic, sermon, urging, warning.

exhortative *adj.* begging, beseeching, imploring, paraenetic(al), persuasive, protreptic, protreptical.

exhume *v.* dig up, disentomb, disinhume, disinter, excavate, unbury, unearth.
antonym bury.

exigency *n.* acuteness, bind, constraint, crisis, criticalness, crunch, demand, difficulty, distress, emergency, exigence, extremity, fix, hardship, imperativeness, jam, juncture, necessity, need, needfulness, pass, pickle, pinch, plight, predicament, pressure, quandary, requirement, scrape, stew, strait, stress, urgency.

exigent *adj.* acute, arduous, constraining, critical, crucial, demanding, difficult, exacting, exhausting, hard, harsh, imperative, importunate, insistent, necessary, needful, pressing, rigorous, severe, stiff, strict, stringent, taxing, tough, urgent.
antonym mild.

exile *n.* banishment, deportation, deportee, émigré, exilement, expatriate, expatriation, expulsion, galut(h), ostracism, outcast, proscription, refugee, separation.
v. banish, deport, drive out, expatriate, expel, ostracise, oust, proscribe.

exist *v.* abide, be, be available, be extant, breathe, continue, endure, happen, have one's being, last, live, obtain, occur, prevail, remain, stand, subsist, survive.

existence *n.* actuality, animation, being, breath, continuance, continuation, creation, creature, duration, endurance, entity, esse, haecceity, inbeing, life, reality, subsistence, survival, the world, thing.
antonym non-existence.

existent *adj.* abiding, actual, around, current, enduring, existing, extant, living, obtaining, present, prevailing, real, remaining, standing, surviving.
antonym non-existent.

exit *n.* adieu, aperture, congé, departure, door, doorway, egress, evacuation, exodus, farewell, gate, going, leave-taking, outlet, retirement, retreat, vent, way out, withdrawal.
antonym entrance.
v. arrive, depart, enter, issue, leave, retire, retreat, take one's leave, withdraw.

exodus *n.* departure, evacuation, exit, flight, hegira, leaving, long march, migration, retirement, retreat, withdrawal.

exonerate *v.* absolve, acquit, clear, discharge, disculpate, dismiss, except, exculpate, excuse, exempt, free, justify, let off, liberate, pardon, release, relieve, vindicate.
antonym incriminate.

exoneration *n.* absolution, acquittal, amnesty, deliverance, discharge, dismissal, exception, exculpation, exemption, freeing, immunity, indemnity, justification, liberation, pardon, release, relief, vindication.
antonym incrimination.

exorbitance *n.* excess, excessiveness, extravagance, immoderateness, immoderation, inordinateness, monstrousness, nimiety, preposterousness, unreasonableness.
antonyms fairness, reasonableness.

exorbitant *adj.* enormous, excessive, extortionate, extravagant, extreme, immoderate, inordinate, monstrous, outrageous, preposterous, unconscionable, undue, unreasonable, unwarranted.
antonyms fair, reasonable.

exorcise *v.* adjure, cast out, drive out, expel, exsufflate, purify.

exorcism *n.* adjuration, deliverance, expulsion, exsufflation, purification.

exotic *adj.* alien, bizarre, colourful, curious, different, external, extraneous, extraordinary, extrinsic, fascinating, foreign, foreign-looking, glamorous, imported, introduced, mysterious, naturalised, outlandish, outré, peculiar, recherché, strange, striking, unfamiliar, unusual.
antonym ordinary.

expand *v.* amplify, augment, bloat, blow up, branch out, broaden, develop, diffuse, dilate, dispread, distend, diversify, elaborate, embellish, enlarge, expatiate, expound, extend, fatten, fill out, flesh out, grow, heighten, increase, inflate, lengthen, magnify, multiply, open, outspread, prolong, protract, snowball, spread, stretch, swell, thicken, unfold, unfurl, unravel, unroll, wax, widen.
antonyms contract, précis.

expanded *adj.* bloated, blown out, blown up, dilated, distended, enlarged, increased, inflated, puffed out, swollen.

expanse *n.* area, breadth, extent, field, plain, range, space, stretch, sweep, tract, vast, vastness.

expansible *adj.* distensible, distensile, expansile, inflatable.

expansion *n.* amplification, augmentation, development, diffusion, dilatation, dilation, distension, diversification, enlargement, expanse, extension, growth, increase, inflation, magnification, multiplication, spread, swelling, unfolding, unfurling.
antonym contraction.

expansive *adj.* affable, all-embracing, broad, communicative, comprehensive, dilating, distending, easy, effusive, elastic, expanding, expatiative, expatiatory, extendable, extensive, far-reaching, free, friendly, garrulous, genial, inclusive, loquacious, open, outgoing, sociable, stretching, stretchy, swelling, talkative, thorough, unreserved, voluminous, warm, wide, wide-ranging, widespread.
antonyms cold, reserved.

expatiate *v.* amplify, descant, develop, dilate, dwell on, elaborate, embellish, enlarge, expound.

expatriate *n.* displaced person, emigrant, émigré, exile, ex-pat, refugee.
v. banish, deport, exile, expel, ostracise, oust, proscribe.
adj. banished, emigrant, émigré, exiled.

expect *v.* anticipate, assume, await, bank on, bargain for, believe, calculate, conjecture, contemplate, count on, demand, envisage, forecast, foresee, hope for, imagine, insist on, look for, look forward to, predict, presume, project, reckon, rely on, require, suppose, surmise, think, trust, want, wish.

expectancy *n.* anticipation, assumption, belief, conjecture, curiosity, eagerness, expectation, hope, likelihood, outlook, prediction, presumption, probability, prospect, supposition, surmise, suspense, waiting.

expectant *adj.* agog, anticipating, anxious, apprehensive, awaiting, curious, eager, enceinte, expecting, gravid, hopeful, in suspense, pregnant, ready, watchful.

expectantly *adv.* eagerly, expectingly, hopefully, in anticipation, optimistically.

expectation *n.* anticipation, apprehension, assumption, assurance, belief, calculation, chance, confidence, conjecture, demand, eagerness, expectancy, fear, forecast, hope, insistence, likelihood, optimism, outlook, possibility, prediction, presumption, probability, projection, promise, prospect, reliance, requirement, supposition, surmise, suspense, trust, want, wish.

expected *adj.* anticipated, awaited, en l'aire, hoped-for, longed-for, predicted, promised.
antonym unexpected.

expecting *adj.* enceinte, expectant, gravid, in the club, in the family way, pregnant, with child.

expedience *n.* advantage, advantageousness, advisability, appropriateness, aptness, benefit, convenience, desirability, effectiveness, expediency, fitness, gainfulness, helpfulness, judiciousness, meetness, practicality, pragmatism, profitability, profitableness, properness, propriety, prudence, suitability, usefulness, utilitarianism, utility.

expedient adj. advantageous, advisable, appropriate, beneficial, convenient, desirable, effective, fit, helpful, judicious, meet, opportune, politic, practical, pragmatic, profitable, proper, prudent, serviceable, suitable, useful, utilitarian, worthwhile.
antonym inexpedient.
n. contrivance, device, dodge, makeshift, manoeuvre, means, measure, method, resort, resource, ruse, scheme, shift, stop-gap, stratagem, substitute.

expedite v. accelerate, advance, aid, assist, dispatch, facilitate, forward, further, hasten, hurry, precipitate, press, promote, quicken, rush, speed.
antonym delay.

expedition[1] n. company, crusade, enterprise, excursion, exploration, explorers, hike, journey, mission, pilgrimage, quest, raid, ramble, safari, sail, team, tour, travellers, trek, trip, undertaking, voyage, voyagers.

expedition[2] n. alacrity, briskness, celerity, dispatch, expeditiousness, haste, hurry, immediacy, promptness, quickness, rapidity, readiness, speed, swiftness.
antonym delay.

expeditious adj. active, alert, brisk, diligent, efficient, fast, hasty, immediate, instant, meteoric, prompt, quick, rapid, ready, speedy, swift.
antonym slow.

expel v. ban, banish, bar, belch, blackball, cast out, disbar, discharge, dislodge, dismiss, drive out, drum out, egest, eject, evict, exclude, exile, expatriate, hoof out, oust, proscribe, remove, send packing, spew, throw out, turf out.
antonym admit.

expend v. consume, disburse, dissipate, employ, exhaust, fork out, pay, shell out, spend, use, use up.
antonym save.

expendable adj. dispensable, disposable, inessential, non-essential, replaceable, unimportant, unnecessary.
antonyms indispensable, necessary.

expenditure n. application, charge, consumption, cost, disbursement, expense, outgo, outgoings, outlay, output, payment, spending.
antonyms profit, savings.

expense n. charge, consumption, cost, damage, disbursement, expenditure, loss, outlay, output, payment, sacrifice, spending, toll, use.

expenses n. costs, incidentals, outgoings, outlay, overheads.

expensive adj. costly, dear, excessive, exorbitant, extortionate, extravagant, high-priced, inordinate, lavish, overpriced, rich, steep, stiff.
antonyms cheap, inexpensive.

experience n. adventure, affair, assay, contact,

doing, encounter, episode, event, evidence, exposure, familiarity, happening, incident, involvement, know-how, knowledge, observation, occurrence, ordeal, participation, practice, proof, taste, test, training, trial, understanding.
antonym inexperience.
v. apprehend, behold, empathise, encounter, endure, face, feel, have, know, meet, observe, perceive, sample, sense, suffer, sustain, taste, try, undergo.

experienced adj. accomplished, adept, capable, competent, expert, familiar, knowing, knowledgeable, master, mature, practised, professional, qualified, schooled, seasoned, skilful, sophisticated, tested, trained, travailed, travelled, tried, veteran, well-versed, wise, worldly, worldly-wise.
antonym inexperienced.

experiment n. assay, attempt, ballon d'essai, examination, experimentation, heurism, investigation, procedure, proof, research, test, trial, trial and error, trial run, venture.
v. assay, examine, investigate, research, sample, test, try, verify.

experimental adj. empiric(al), exploratory, heuristic, peirastic, pilot, preliminary, probationary, provisional, speculative, tentative, test, trial, trial-and-error.

expert n. ace, adept, authority, boffin, connoisseur, dab hand, dabster, deacon, dean, maestro, master, pastmaster, pro, professional, specialist, virtuoso, wizard.
adj. able, adept, adroit, apt, clever, crack, deft, dexterous, experienced, facile, handy, knowledgeable, master, masterly, practised, professional, proficient, qualified, skilful, skilled, trained, virtuoso.
antonym novice.

expertise n. ableness, adroitness, aptness, cleverness, command, deftness, dexterity, expertness, facility, judgement, knack, know-how, knowledge, masterliness, mastery, proficiency, skilfulness, skill, virtuosity.
antonym inexpertness.

expertness n. ableness, adroitness, aptness, command, deftness, dexterity, expertise, facility, finesse, judgement, know-how, knowledge, masterliness, mastery, proficiency, savoir-faire, skilfulness, skill.
antonym inexpertness.

expiation n. amends, atonement, penance, ransom, redemption, redress, shrift.

expiatory adj. atoning, piacular, purgative, purgatory, redemptive.

expire v. cease, close, conclude, decease, depart, die, discontinue, emit, end, exhale, finish, lapse, perish, run out, stop, terminate.
antonyms begin, continue.

expiry n. cease, cessation, close, conclusion, death, decease, demise, departure, end, expiration, finis, finish, termination.
antonyms beginning, continuation.

explain v. account for, clarify, clear up, construe, decipher, decode, define, demonstrate,

describe, disclose, elucidate, enucleate, excuse, explicate, expound, gloss, gloze, illustrate, interpret, justify, resolve, simplify, solve, spell out, teach, translate, unfold, unravel, untangle.
antonyms obfuscate, obscure.

explanation *n.* account, answer, cause, clarification, definition, demonstration, description, éclaircissement, elucidation, enucleation, excuse, exegesis, explication, exposition, gloss, illustration, interpretation, justification, legend, meaning, mitigation, motive, reason, resolution, sense, significance, solution, vindication, voice-over.

explanatory *adj.* demonstrative, descriptive, elucidative, elucidatory, exegetic, exegetical, explicative, expositive, expository, illuminative, illustrational, illustrative, illustratory, interpretive, justifying.

explicable *adj.* accountable, definable, determinable, explainable, exponible, intelligible, interpretable, justifiable, resolvable, solvable, understandable.

explicate *v.* clarify, construct, develop, devise, elucidate, evolve, explain, expound, formulate, interpret, set forth, unfold, unravel, untangle, work out.
antonyms confuse, obscure.

explicit *adj.* absolute, accurate, categorical, certain, clear, declared, definite, detailed, direct, distinct, exact, express, frank, open, outspoken, patent, plain, positive, precise, specific, stated, straightforward, unambiguous, unequivocal, unqualified, unreserved.
antonyms inexplicit, vague.

explode *v.* belie, blow up, burst, debunk, detonate, discharge, discredit, disprove, erupt, give the lie to, go off, invalidate, rebut, refute, repudiate, set off, shatter, shiver.
antonym prove.

exploit *n.* accomplishment, achievement, adventure, attainment, deed, feat, gest(e), stunt.
v. abuse, bleed, capitalise on, cash in on, fleece, impose on, make capital out of, manipulate, milk, misuse, profit by, rip off, skin, soak, take advantage of, turn to account, use, utilise.

exploitation *n.* abuse, imposition, manipulation, misuse, rip-off, sexploitation.

exploration *n.* analysis, examination, expedition, inquiry, inquisition, inspection, investigation, probe, reconnaissance, research, safari, scrutiny, search, study, survey, tour, travel, trip, voyage.

exploratory *adj.* analytic(al), experimental, fact-finding, investigative, pilot, probing, searching, tentative, trial, wildcat.

explore *v.* analyse, case, examine, inspect, investigate, probe, prospect, reconnoitre, research, scout, scrutinise, search, survey, tour, travel, traverse.

explosion *n.* bang, blast, burst, clap, crack, debunking, detonation, discharge, discrediting, eruption, fit, outbreak, outburst, paroxysm, refutation, report.

explosive *adj.* charged, dangerous, fiery, hazardous, overwrought, perilous, stormy, tense, touchy, ugly, unstable, vehement, violent, volatile, volcanic.
antonym calm.
n. cordite, dynamite, gelignite, gun-powder, jelly, lyddite, melinite, nitroglycerine, TNT.

exponent *n.* advocate, backer, champion, commentator, defender, demonstrator, elucidator, example, executant, exegetist, exemplar, expositor, expounder, illustration, illustrator, indication, interpreter, model, performer, player, presenter, promoter, propagandist, proponent, representative, sample, specimen, spokesman, spokeswoman, supporter, type, upholder.

expose *v.* air, betray, bring to light, denounce, detect, disclose, display, divulge, endanger, exhibit, hazard, imperil, jeopardise, manifest, present, reveal, risk, show, uncover, unearth, unmask, unveil, wash one's dirty linen in public.
antonym cover.

expose to acquaint with, bring into contact with, familiarise with, introduce to, lay open to, subject to.
antonym protect.

exposé *n.* account, article, disclosure, divulgence, expose, exposure, revelation, uncovering.

exposed *adj.* bare, exhibited, laid bare, liable, on display, on show, on view, open, prey to, revealed, shown, susceptible, unconcealed, uncovered, unprotected, unsheltered, unveiled, vulnerable.
antonyms covered, sheltered.

exposition *n.* account, commentary, critique, demonstration, description, discourse, display, elucidation, exegesis, exhibition, explanation, explication, expo, fair, illustration, interpretation, monograph, paper, presentation, show, study, thesis.

expository *adj.* declaratory, descriptive, elucidative, exegetic, explanatory, explicative, explicatory, hermeneutic, illustrative, interpretative, interpretive.

expostulate *v.* argue, dissuade, plead, protest, reason, remonstrate.

exposure *n.* acquaintance, airing, aspect, betrayal, cold, contact, conversance, conversancy, danger, denunciation, detection, disclosure, discovery, display, divulgence, divulging, exhibition, experience, exposé, familiarity, frontage, hazard, introduction, jeopardy, knowledge, lack of shelter, location, manifestation, outlook, position, presentation, publicity, revelation, risk, setting, showing, uncovering, unmasking, unveiling, view, vulnerability.

expound *v.* describe, elucidate, explain, explicate, illustrate, interpet, preach, sermonise, set forth, spell out, unfold.

express *v.* articulate, assert, asseverate, bespeak, communicate, conceive, convey, couch, declare, denote, depict, designate, disclose, divulge, embody, enunciate, evince, exhibit, extract, force out, formulate, formulise, indicate, intimate, manifest, phrase, pronounce, put, put across, represent, reveal, say, show, signify, speak, stand for, state, symbolise, tell, testify, utter, verbalise, voice, word.

adj. accurate, categorical, certain, clear, clear-cut, definite, direct, distinct, especial, exact, explicit, fast, high-speed, manifest, non-stop, outright, particular, plain, pointed, precise, quick, rapid, singular, special, speedy, stated, swift, unambiguous, unqualified.

antonym vague.

expression *n.* air, announcement, appearance, aspect, assertion, asseveration, communication, countenance, declaration, delivery, demonstration, diction, embodiment, emphasis, enunciation, execution, exhibition, face, idiom, indication, intonation, language, locution, look, manifestation, mention, mien, phrase, phraseology, phrasing, pronouncement, reflex, remark, representation, set phrase, show, sign, speaking, speech, statement, style, symbol, term, token, turn of phrase, utterance, verbalisation, verbalism, voicing, word, wording.

expressionless *adj.* blank, dead-pan, dull, empty, glassy, impassive, inscrutable, poker-faced, straight-faced, vacuous, wooden.

antonym expressive.

expressive *adj.* allusive, demonstrative, eloquent, emphatic, energetic, forcible, indicative, informative, lively, meaningful, mobile, moving, poignant, pointed, pregnant, representative, revealing, significant, striking, strong, suggestive, sympathetic, telling, thoughtful, vivid.

antonyms expressionless, poker-faced.

expressly *adv.* absolutely, categorically, clearly, decidedly, definitely, distinctly, especially, exactly, explicitly, intentionally, manifestly, on purpose, outright, particularly, plainly, pointedly, positively, precisely, purposely, specially, specifically, unambiguously, unequivocally.

expropriate *v.* annex, appropriate, arrogate, assume, commandeer, confiscate, dispossess, disseise, impound, requisition, seize, sequester, take, unhouse.

expulsion *n.* banishment, debarment, disbarment, discharge, dislodgement, dislodging, dismissal, ejection, ejectment, eviction, exclusion, exile, expatriation, extrusion, proscription, removal.

expunge *v.* abolish, annihilate, annul, blot out, cancel, delete, destroy, efface, eradicate, erase, exterminate, extinguish, extirpate, obliterate, raze, remove, uncreate, unmake, wipe out.

expurgate *v.* blue-pencil, bowdlerise, censor, clean up, cut, emend, purge, purify, sanitise.

exquisite *adj.* acute, admirable, alembicated, appreciative, attractive, beautiful, charming,

choice, comely, consummate, cultivated, dainty, delicate, delicious, discerning, discriminating, elegant, excellent, excruciating, fastidious, fine, flawless, impeccable, incomparable, intense, keen, lovely, matchless, meticulous, outstanding, peerless, perfect, piercing, pleasing, poignant, polished, precious, rare, refined, select, selective, sensitive, sharp, splendid, striking, superb, superlative, too-too.

antonyms flawed, imperfect, poor, ugly.

extant *adj.* alive, existent, existing, in existence, living, remaining, subsistent, subsisting, surviving.

antonyms dead, extinct, non-existent.

extemporary *adj.* ad-lib, expedient, extemporaneous, extempore, free, impromptu, improvisatory, improvised, jazz, made-up, makeshift, offhand, off-the-cuff, on-the-spot, spontaneous, temporary, unplanned, unpremeditated, unprepared, unrehearsed.

antonym planned.

extemporise *v.* ad-lib, autoschediaze, improvise, make up, play by ear.

extend *v.* advance, amplify, attain, augment, bestow, broaden, confer, continue, develop, dilate, drag out, draw out, elongate, enhance, enlarge, expand, give, grant, hold out, impart, increase, last, lengthen, offer, present, proffer, prolong, protract, pull out, reach, spin out, spread, stretch, supplement, take, uncoil, unfold, unfurl, unroll, widen, yield.

antonym shorten.

extension *n.* accretion, addendum, addition, adjunct, amplification, annexe, appendage, appendix, augmentation, branch, broadening, continuation, delay, development, dilatation, distension, el, elongation, enhancement, enlargement, expansion, extent, increase, lengthening, postponement, prolongation, protraction, spread, stretching, supplement, widening, wing.

extensive *adj.* all-inclusive, broad, capacious, commodious, comprehensive, expanded, expansive, extended, far-flung, far-reaching, general, great, huge, large, large-scale, lengthy, long, pervasive, prevalent, protracted, roomy, spacious, sweeping, thorough, thoroughgoing, universal, unrestricted, vast, voluminous, wholesale, wide, widespread.

antonyms narrow, restricted.

extent *n.* amount, amplitude, area, bounds, breadth, bulk, compass, degree, dimension(s), duration, expanse, expansion, length, magnitude, measure, play, proportions, quantity, range, reach, scope, size, sphere, spread, stretch, sweep, term, time, volume, width.

extenuate *v.* decrease, diminish, excuse, lessen, minimise, mitigate, moderate, modify, palliate, qualify, reduce, soften, temper, weaken.

extenuating *adj.* exculpatory, extenuative, extenuatory, justifying, mitigating, moderating, palliative, qualifying.

exterior *n.* appearance, aspect, coating, covering, externals, façade, face, finish, outside,

shell, skin, superficies, surface.
antonym interior.
adj. alien, exotic, external, extraneous, extrinsic, foreign, outer, outermost, outside, outward, peripheral, superficial, surface, surrounding.
antonym interior.

exterminate *v.* abolish, annihilate, deracinate, destroy, eliminate, eradicate, extirpate, massacre, wipe out.

extermination *n.* annihilation, deracination, destruction, elimination, eradication, extirpation, genocide, massacre.

external *adj.* alien, apparent, exoteric, exotic, exterior, extern, externe, extramural, extraneous, extrinsic, foreign, independent, outer, outermost, outside, outward, superficial, surface, visible.
antonym internal.

extinct *adj.* abolished, dead, defunct, doused, ended, exterminated, extinguished, gone, inactive, lost, obsolete, out, quenched, terminated, vanished, void.
antonyms extant, living.

extinction *n.* abolition, annihilation, death, destruction, eradication, excision, extermination, extinguishment, extirpation, obliteration, oblivion, quietus.

extinguish *v.* abolish, annihilate, destroy, douse, dout, eliminate, end, eradicate, erase, expunge, exterminate, extirpate, kill, obscure, put out, quench, remove, slake, smother, snuff out, stifle, suppress.

extirpate *v.* abolish, annihilate, cut out, deracinate, destroy, eliminate, eradicate, erase, expunge, exterminate, extinguish, remove, root out, uproot, wipe out.

extol *v.* acclaim, applaud, celebrate, commend, cry up, eulogise, exalt, glorify, laud, magnify, panegyrise, praise, puff.
antonyms blame, denigrate.

extort *v.* blackmail, bleed, bully, coerce, exact, extract, force, milk, squeeze, wrest, wring.

extortion *n.* blackmail, coercion, compulsion, demand, exaction, exorbitance, expensiveness, force, milking, oppression, overcharging, rapacity.

extortionate *adj.* blood-sucking, exacting, excessive, exorbitant, extorsive, extortive, extravagant, grasping, hard, harsh, immoderate, inflated, inordinate, oppressive, outrageous, preposterous, rapacious, rigorous, severe, sky-high, unreasonable, usurious.
antonym reasonable.

extra *adj.* accessory, added, additional, ancillary, auxiliary, excess, extraneous, for good measure, fresh, further, gash, inessential, leftover, more, needless, new, other, redundant, reserve, spare, supererogatory, superfluous, supernumerary, supplemental, supplementary, surplus, unnecessary, unneeded, unused.
antonym integral.
n. accessory, addendum, addition, adjunct, affix, appendage, appurtenance, attachment,

bonus, complement, extension, lagniappe, plus(s)age, supernumerary, supplement.
adv. especially, exceptionally, extraordinarily, extremely, particularly, remarkably, uncommonly, unusually.

extract *v.* abstract, choose, cite, cull, decoct, deduce, derive, develop, distil, draw, draw out, educe, elicit, enucleate, evoke, evolve, evulse, exact, express, extirpate, gather, get, glean, obtain, quote, reap, remove, select, uproot, withdraw, wrest, wring.
antonym insert.
n. abstract, apozem, citation, clip, clipping, concentrate, cutting, decoction, decocture, distillate, distillation, essence, excerpt, juice, passage, quotation, selection.

extraction *n.* ancestry, birth, blood, derivation, descent, distillation, drawing, educt, enucleation, extirpation, family, lineage, origin, parentage, pedigree, pulling, race, removal, separation, stock, withdrawal.
antonym insertion.

extraneous *adj.* accidental, additional, adventitious, alien, exotic, exterior, external, extra, extrinsic, foreign, immaterial, impertinent, inadmissible, inapplicable, inapposite, inappropriate, inapt, incidental, inessential, irrelevant, needless, non-essential, peripheral, redundant, strange, superfluous, supplementary, tangential, unconnected, unessential, unnecessary, unneeded, unrelated.
antonym integral.

extraordinary *adj.* amazing, bizarre, curious, exceptional, fantastic, marvellous, notable, noteworthy, odd, outstanding, particular, peculiar, phenomenal, rare, remarkable, significant, singular, special, strange, striking, surprising, uncommon, uncontemplated, unfamiliar, unheard-of, unimaginable, unique, unprecedented, unusual, unwonted, weird, wonderful.
antonyms commonplace, ordinary.

extravagance *n.* absurdity, dissipation, exaggeration, excess, exorbitance, folly, hyperbole, immoderation, improvidence, lavishness, outrageousness, overspending, preposterousness, prodigality, profligacy, profusion, recklessness, squandering, unreasonableness, unrestraint, unthrift, unthriftiness, waste, wastefulness, wildness.
antonyms moderation, thrift.

extravagant *adj.* absurd, costly, exaggerated, excessive, exorbitant, expensive, extortionate, fanciful, fancy, fantastic, flamboyant, flashy, foolish, garish, gaudy, grandiose, hyperbolic, hyperbolical, immoderate, improvident, imprudent, inordinate, lavish, ornate, ostentatious, outrageous, outré, overpriced, preposterous, pretentious, prodigal, profligate, reckless, showy, spendthrift, steep, thriftless, unreasonable, unrestrained, unthrifty, wasteful, wild.
antonyms moderate, thrifty.

extravaganza *n.* display, féerie, pageant, show, spectacle, spectacular.

extravert *see* **extrovert** .

extreme *adj.* acute, deep-dyed, dire, double-dyed, downright, Draconian, drastic, egregious, exaggerated, exceptional, excessive, exquisite, extraordinary, extravagant, fanatical, faraway, far-off, farthest, final, great, greatest, harsh, high, highest, immoderate, inordinate, intemperate, intense, last, maximum, out-and-out, outermost, outrageous, radical, red-hot, remarkable, remotest, rigid, severe, sheer, stern, strict, supreme, terminal, ultimate, ultra, unbending, uncommon, uncompromising, unconventional, unreasonable, unusual, utmost, utter, uttermost, worst, zealous.
antonyms mild, moderate.
n. acme, apex, apogee, boundary, climax, consummation, depth, edge, end, excess, extremity, height, limit, maximum, minimum, nadir, peak, pinnacle, pole, termination, top, ultimate, utmost, zenith.

extremely *adv.* acutely, awfully, exceedingly, exceptionally, excessively, extraordinarily, greatly, highly, inordinately, intensely, markedly, mortal, passing, quite, severely, terribly, too, too-too, ultra, uncommonly, unusually, utterly, very.

extremism *n.* fanaticism, radicalism, terrorism, ultraism, zeal, zealotism, zealotry.
antonym moderation.

extremist *n.* die-hard, fanatic, militant, radical, terrorist, ultra, ultraconservative, zealot.
antonym moderate.

extremity *n.* acme, acuteness, adversity, apex, apogee, border, bound, boundary, brim, brink, climax, consummation, crisis, crunch, depth, disaster, edge, emergency, end, excess, exigency, extreme, foot, frontier, hand, hardship, height, limit, margin, maximum, minimum, nadir, peak, pinnacle, plight, pole, rim, setback, terminal, termination, terminus, tip, top, trouble, ultimate, utmost, verge, zenith.

extricate *v.* clear, deliver, disembarrass, disembrangle, disembroil, disengage, disentangle, disintricate, free, liberate, release, relieve, remove, rescue, withdraw.
antonym involve.

extrinsic *adj.* accidental, alien, exotic, exterior, external, extraneous, foreign, imported, inessential, non-essential, outside, superficial.
antonym essential.

extroversion *n.* amiability, amicability, extraversion, exuberance, friendliness, heartiness, sociability, viscerotonia.

extrovert *adj.* amiable, amicable, extravert, exuberant, friendly, hail-fellow-well-met, hearty, outgoing, social, viscerotonic.
antonym introvert.
n. joiner, life and soul of the party, mixer, socialiser.
antonyms introvert, loner.

exuberance *n.* abundance, animation, buoyancy, cheerfulness, copiousness, eagerness, ebullience, effervescence, effusiveness, energy, enthusiasm, exaggeration, excessiveness, excitement, exhilaration, fulsomeness, high spirits, lavishness, life, liveliness, lushness, luxuriance, pizzazz, plenitude, prodigality, profusion, rankness, richness, spirit, sprightliness, superabundance, superfluity, vigour, vitality, vivacity, zest.
antonyms apathy, lifelessness, scantiness.

exuberant *adj.* abundant, animated, baroque, buoyant, cheerful, copious, eager, ebullient, effervescent, effusive, elated, energetic, enthusiastic, exaggerated, excessive, excited, exhilarated, fulsome, high-spirited, lavish, lively, lush, luxuriant, overdone, overflowing, plenteous, plentiful, prodigal, profuse, rambunctious, rank, rich, sparkling, spirited, sprightly, superabundant, superfluous, teeming, vigorous, vivacious, zestful.
antonyms apathetic, lifeless, scant.

exude *v.* bleed, discharge, display, emanate, emit, excrete, exhibit, flow out, issue, leak, manifest, ooze, perspire, radiate, secrete, seep, show, sweat, trickle, weep, well.

exult *v.* boast, brag, celebrate, crow, delight, gloat, glory, jubilate, rejoice, relish, revel, taunt, triumph.

exultant *adj.* cock-a-hoop, delighted, elated, exulting, gleeful, joyful, joyous, jubilant, over the moon, overjoyed, rejoicing, revelling, transporting, triumphant.
antonym depressed.

exultation *n.* boasting, bragging, celebration, crowing, delight, elation, glee, gloating, glory, glorying, joy, joyfulness, joyousness, jubilation, merriness, paean, rejoicing, revelling, transport, triumph.
antonym depression.

eye *n.* appreciation, belief, discernment, discrimination, eyeball, glim, judgement, keeker, mind, opinion, optic, orb, peeper, perception, recognition, taste, viewpoint.
v. contemplate, examine, eye up, gaze at, glance at, inspect, leer at, look at, make eyes at, observe, ogle, peruse, regard, scan, scrutinise, stare at, study, survey, view, watch.

eye-catching *adj.* arresting, attractive, beautiful, captivating, gorgeous, imposing, impressive, showy, spectacular, striking, stunning.
antonyms plain, unattractive.

eyeful *n.* beauty, dazzler, knockout, show, sight, sight for sore eyes, spectacle, stunner, view, vision.

eyeglasses *n.* glasses, lorgnette, lorgnon, monocle, pince-nez, specs, spectacles.

eyesight *n.* observation, perception, sight, view, vision.

eyesore *n.* atrocity, blemish, blight, blot, disfigurement, disgrace, dissight, horror, mess, monstrosity, sight, ugliness.

eye-witness *n.* beholder, bystander, looker-on, observer, onlooker, passer-by, spectator, viewer, watcher, witness.

F

fable *n.* allegory, apologue, fabliau, fabrication, fairy story, falsehood, fantasy, fib, fiction, figment, invention, legend, lie, Märchen, myth, narrative, old wives' tale, parable, romance, saga, story, tale, tall story, untruth, yarn.

fabled *adj.* fabulous, famed, famous, feigned, fictional, legendary, mythical, renowned, storied.
antonym unknown.

fabric *n.* cloth, constitution, construction, foundations, framework, infrastructure, make-up, material, organisation, structure, stuff, textile, texture, web.

fabricate *v.* assemble, build, coin, concoct, construct, create, devise, erect, fake, falsify, fashion, feign, forge, form, frame, invent, make, manufacture, shape, trump up.

fabrication *n.* assemblage, assembly, building, cock-and-bull story, concoction, construction, erection, fable, fairy story, fake, falsehood, fiction, figment, forgery, frame-up, invention, lie, manufacture, myth, production, story, untruth.
antonym truth.

fabulous *adj.* amazing, apocryphal, astounding, breathtaking, fabled, false, fantastic, feigned, fictitious, imaginary, immense, inconceivable, incredible, invented, legendary, marvellous, mythical, phenomenal, renowned, spectacular, superb, unbelievable, unreal, wonderful.
antonyms moderate, real, small.

façade *n.* appearance, cloak, cover, disguise, exterior, face, front, frontage, guise, mask, pretence, semblance, show, veil, veneer.

face *n.* air, appearance, aspect, assurance, audacity, authority, boatrace, boldness, brass neck, cheek, confidence, countenance, cover, dial, dignity, disguise, display, effrontery, expression, exterior, façade, facet, favour, features, front, frown, gall, grimace, honour, image, impudence, kisser, lineaments, look, mask, metope, moue, mug, nerve, outside, phiz, phizog, physiognomy, pout, prestige, presumption, pretence, reputation, sauce, scowl, self-respect, semblance, show, side, smirk, snoot, standing, status, surface, visage.
v. clad, coat, confront, cope with, cover, deal with, defy, dress, encounter, experience, finish, front, give on to, level, line, meet, oppose, overlay, overlook, sheathe, surface, tackle, veneer.

face to face à deux, confronting, eye to eye, eyeball to eyeball, in confrontation, opposite, tête-à-tête, vis-à-vis.

face up to accept, acknowledge, come to terms with, confront, cope with, deal with, meet head-on, recognise, square up to, stand up to.

face-lift *n.* cosmetic surgery, plastic surgery, redecoration, renovation, restoration, rhytidectomy.

facet *n.* angle, aspect, characteristic, face, feature, part, phase, plane, point, side, slant, surface.

facetious *adj.* amusing, comical, droll, facete, flippant, frivolous, funny, humorous, jesting, jocose, jocular, merry, playful, pleasant, tongue-in-cheek, unserious, waggish, witty.
antonym serious.

facile *adj.* adept, adroit, complaisant, cursory, dexterous, easy, effortless, fluent, glib, hasty, light, plausible, proficient, quick, ready, shallow, simple, skilful, slick, smooth, superficial, uncomplicated, yielding.
antonyms clumsy, implausible, profound.

facilitate *v.* assist, ease, expedite, forward, further, grease, help, promote, speed up.

facilities *n.* amenity, appliance, convenience, equipment, means, mod cons, opportunity, prerequisites, resource.

facility *n.* ability, adeptness, adroitness, bent, dexterity, ease, efficiency, effortlessness, expertness, fluency, gift, knack, proficiency, quickness, readiness, skilfulness, skill, smoothness, talent, turn.

facing *n.* cladding, coating, façade, false front, overlay, reinforcement, revetment, skin, surface, trimming, veneer.

facsimile *n.* carbon, carbon copy, copy, duplicate, image, mimeograph, photocopy, Photostat®, print, replica, repro, reproduction, transcript, Xerox®.

fact *n.* act, actuality, certainty, circumstance, datum, deed, detail, event, fait accompli, feature, gospel, happening, incident, item, occurrence, particular, point, reality, specific, truth.

faction[1] *n.* band, bloc, cabal, cadre, camp, caucus, clique, coalition, combination, confederacy, contingent, coterie, crowd, division, gang, ginger group, group, junta, lobby, minority, party, pressure group, ring, section, sector, set, splinter group, splinter party, troop.

faction[2] *n.* conflict, disagreement, discord, disharmony, dissension, disunity, division, divisiveness, fighting, friction, infighting, quarrelling, rebellion, sedition, strife, tumult, turbulence.
antonyms agreement, peace.

factious *adj.* conflicting, contentious, disputatious, dissident, divisive, insurrectionary,

litigious, malcontent, mutinous, partisan, quarrelling, quarrelsome, rebellious, refractory, rival, sectarian, seditious, troublemaking, tumultuous, turbulent, warring.
antonyms calm, co-operative.

factitious *adj.* affected, artificial, assumed, contrived, counterfeit, engineered, fabricated, fake, false, imitation, insincere, made-up, manufactured, mock, phoney, pinchbeck, put-on, sham, simulated, spurious, supposititious, synthetic, unnatural, unreal.
antonym genuine.

factor *n.* agent, aspect, cause, circumstance, component, consideration, deputy, determinant, element, estate manager, influence, item, joker, middleman, parameter, part, point, reeve, steward, thing, unknown quantity.

factors *n.* considerations, details, pros and cons.

factory *n.* hacienda, manufactory, mill, plant, shop, shop-floor, works.

factotum *n.* do-all, famulus, handyman, jack-of-all-trades, Johnnie a'thing, maid-of-all-work, Man (or Girl) Friday, odd-jobman, orra man.

facts *n.* data, details, gen, info, information, story, the low-down, the score.

factual *adj.* accurate, authentic, circumstantial, close, correct, credible, detailed, exact, faithful, genuine, literal, objective, precise, real, straight, sure, true, unadorned, unbiased, veritable.
antonym false.

faculties *n.* capabilities, functions, intelligence, powers, reason, senses, wits.

faculty[1] *n.* academics, department, discipline, lecturers, profession, school, staff.

faculty[2] *n.* ability, adroitness, aptitude, bent, brain-power, capability, capacity, cleverness, dexterity, facility, gift, knack, power, propensity, readiness, skill, talent, turn.

faculty[3] *n.* authorisation, authority, licence, prerogative, privilege, right.

fad *n.* affectation, craze, crotchet, fancy, fashion, mania, mode, rage, trend, vogue, whim.

fade *v.* blanch, bleach, blench, decline, die, dim, diminish, disappear, discolour, disperse, dissolve, droop, dull, dwindle, ebb, etiolate, evanesce, fail, fall, flag, languish, pale, perish, shrivel, vanish, wane, wilt, wither, yellow.

faded *adj.* bleached, dim, discoloured, dull, etiolated, indistinct, lustreless, pale, passé, past one's best, washed-out.
antonym bright.

faeces *n.* dregs, droppings, dung, excrement, excreta, ordure, scat, sediment, stools.

fag *n.* bind, bore, bother, chore, drag, inconvenience, irritation, nuisance, pest.

fagged *adj.* all in, beat, exhausted, fatigued, jaded, jiggered, knackered, on one's last legs, wasted, weary, worn out, zonked.
antonym refreshed.

fail *v.* abandon, cease, come to grief, conk out, crack up, crash, cut out, decline, desert, die, disappoint, droop, dwindle, fade, fall, flop,

flub, flunk, fold, forget, forsake, founder, fudge, give out, give up, go bankrupt, go bust, go to the wall, go under, gutter, languish, lay an egg, let down, miscarry, misfire, miss, miss one's trip, neglect, omit, peter out, plough, sink, smash, underachieve, underperform, wane, weaken.
antonyms gain, improve, prosper, succeed.

failing *n.* blemish, blind spot, decay, decline, defect, deficiency, deterioration, drawback, error, failure, fault, flaw, foible, frailty, hamartia, imperfection, lapse, miscarriage, misfortune, peccadillo, shortcoming, weakness.
antonyms advantage, strength.
adj. collapsing, decaying, declining, deteriorating, drooping, dwindling, dying, flagging, languishing, moribund, waning, weak, weakening.
antonyms thriving, vigorous.
prep. in default of, in the absence of, lacking, wanting, without.

failure *n.* abortion, also-ran, bankruptcy, breakdown, bummer, collapse, crash, cropper, damp squib, dead duck, decay, decline, default, defeat, deficiency, dereliction, deterioration, disappointment, downfall, dud, failing, fiasco, flivver, flop, folding, frost, frustration, goner, incompetent, insolvency, loser, loss, miscarriage, neglect, negligence, no-hoper, non-performance, omission, remissness, ruin, shortcoming, slip-up, stoppage, turkey, unsuccess, wash-out, wreck.
antonym success.

faint *adj.* bleached, delicate, dim, distant, dizzy, drooping, dull, enervated, exhausted, faded, faltering, fatigued, feeble, feint, giddy, hazy, hushed, ill-defined, indistinct, languid, lethargic, light, light-headed, low, muffled, muted, muzzy, remote, slight, soft, subdued, thin, unenthusiastic, vague, vertiginous, weak, whispered, woozy.
antonyms clear, strong.
v. black out, collapse, droop, drop, flag, flake out, keel over, pass out, swoon.
n. blackout, collapse, deliquium, swoon, syncope, unconsciousness.

faint-hearted *adj.* diffident, faint-heart, half-hearted, hen-hearted, irresolute, lily-livered, spiritless, timid, timorous, weak.
antonym courageous.

fair[1] *adj.* adequate, all right, average, beauteous, beautiful, bonny, bright, clean, clear, clement, cloudless, comely, decent, disinterested, dispassionate, dry, equal, equitable, even-handed, favourable, fine, handsome, honest, honourable, impartial, just, lawful, legitimate, lovely, mediocre, middling, moderate, not bad, objective, OK, on the level, passable, pretty, proper, reasonable, respectable, satisfactory, so-so, square, sunny, sunshiny, tolerable, trustworthy, unbiased, unclouded, unprejudiced, upright, well-favoured.
antonyms cloudy, inclement, poor, unfair.

fair[2] *adj.* blond(e), fair-haired, fair-headed, flaxen, light, tow-headed.
antonym dark.

fair[3] *n.* bang, bazaar, carnival, expo, exposition, festival, fête, gaff, gala, kermis, market, show.

fairly *adv.* absolutely, adequately, deservedly, equitably, ex aequo, fully, honestly, impartially, justly, moderately, objectively, plainly, positively, pretty, properly, quite, rather, really, reasonably, somewhat, tolerably, unbiasedly, veritably.
antonym unfairly.

fairness *n.* decency, disinterestedness, equitableness, equity, impartiality, justice, legitimacy, legitimateness, rightfulness, rightness, unbiasedness, uprightness.
antonym unfairness.

fairy *n.* brownie, buggane, elf, fay, fée, hob, hobgoblin, leprechaun, Mab, peri, pisky, pixie, Robin Goodfellow, rusalka, sprite.

fairy tale cock-and-bull story, fabrication, fairy story, fantasy, fiction, folk-tale, invention, lie, Märchen, Munch(h)ausen, myth, romance, tall story, untruth.

fairyland *n.* féerie, never-never-land, toyland.

faith *n.* allegiance, assurance, belief, church, communion, confidence, constancy, conviction, credence, credit, creed, denomination, dependence, dogma, faithfulness, fealty, fidelity, honesty, honour, loyalty, persuasion, pledge, promise, reliance, religion, sincerity, trust, truth, truthfulness, uberrima fides, vow, word, word of honour.
antonyms mistrust, treachery, unfaithfulness.

faithful *adj.* accurate, attached, card-carrying, close, constant, convinced, dependable, devoted, exact, just, leal, loyal, precise, reliable, soothfast, soothful, staunch, steadfast, strict, true, true-blue, true-hearted, trusty, truthful, unswerving, unwavering.
antonyms disloyal, inaccurate, treacherous.
n. adherents, believers, brethren, communicants, congregation, followers, supporters.

faithfulness *n.* accuracy, adherence, closeness, constancy, dependability, devotion, exactness, fealty, fidelity, justice, loyalty, scrupulousness, staunchness, strictness, trustworthiness, truth.
antonyms disloyalty, inaccuracy, treachery.

faithless *adj.* adulterous, delusive, disloyal, doubting, false, false-hearted, fickle, inconstant, perfidious, punic, recreant, traitorous, treacherous, unbelieving, unfaithful, unreliable, untrue, untrustworthy, untruthful.
antonyms believing, faithful.

faithlessness *n.* adultery, apostasy, betrayal, disloyalty, fickleness, inconstancy, infidelity, perfidy, treachery, unfaithfulness.
antonyms belief, faithfulness.

fake *v.* affect, assume, copy, counterfeit, fabricate, feign, forge, phon(e)y, pretend, put on, sham, simulate.
n. charlatan, copy, forgery, fraud, hoax, imitant, imitation, impostor, mountebank,

phon(e)y, reproduction, sham, simulation.
adj. affected, artificial, assumed, bastard, bogus, counterfeit, ersatz, false, forged, hyped up, imitation, mock, phon(e)y, pinchbeck, pretended, pseudo, reproduction, sham, simulated, spurious.
antonym genuine.

fall *v.* abate, backslide, become, befall, capitulate, cascade, chance, collapse, come about, come to pass, crash, decline, decrease, depreciate, descend, die, diminish, dive, drop, drop down, dwindle, ebb, err, fall away, fall off, fall out, flag, give in, give up, give way, go a purler, go astray, go down, happen, incline, keel over, lapse, lessen, measure one's length, meet one's end, nose-dive, occur, offend, perish, pitch, plummet, plunge, push, resign, settle, sin, sink, slope, slump, souse, stumble, subside, succumb, surrender, take place, topple, transgress, trespass, trip, trip over, tumble, yield, yield to temptation.
antonym rise.
n. capitulation, collapse, cropper, cut, death, decline, declivity, decrease, defeat, degradation, descent, destruction, diminution, dip, dive, downfall, downgrade, drop, dwindling, failure, incline, lapse, lessening, lowering, nose-dive, overthrow, plummet, plunge, pusher, reduction, resignation, ruin, sin, slant, slip, slope, slump, souse, spill, surrender, transgression, tumble, voluntary.
antonym rise.

fall apart break, crumble, decay, decompose, disband, disintegrate, disperse, dissolve, rot, shatter.

fall asleep doze off, drop off, nod off.

fall back on have recourse to, look to, resort to, turn to, use.

fall for accept, be taken in by, swallow.

fall guy dupe, patsy, scapegoat, victim.

fall in cave in, collapse, come down, crumble, give way, sink.

fall in with accept, acquiesce, agree with, assent, come across, comply, concur with, co-operate with, go along with, meet, support.

fall off decelerate, decline, decrease, deteriorate, drop, slacken, slow, slump, wane, worsen.

fall on assail, assault, attack, descend on, lay into, pounce on, snatch.

fall out[1] altercate, argue, bicker, clash, differ, disagree, fight, quarrel, squabble.
antonym agree.

fall out[2] befall, chance, happen, occur, result, take place.

fall through collapse, come to nothing, fail, fizzle out, founder, miscarry.
antonym succeed.

fall to apply oneself, begin, commence, get stuck in, set about, start.

fallacious *adj.* casuistical, deceptive, delusive, delusory, erroneous, false, fictitious, illogical, illusory, incorrect, misleading, mistaken, sophistic, sophistical, spurious, untrue, wrong.

antonyms correct, true.

fallacy *n.* casuistry, deceit, deception, deceptiveness, delusion, error, falsehood, faultiness, flaw, illusion, inconsistency, misapprehension, misconception, mistake, sophism, sophistry, untruth.
antonym truth.

fallible *adj.* errant, erring, frail, human, ignorant, imperfect, mortal, uncertain, weak.
antonym infallible.

fallow *adj.* dormant, idle, inactive, inert, resting, uncultivated, undeveloped, unplanted, unsown, untilled, unused.

false *adj.* artificial, bastard, bogus, concocted, counterfeit, deceitful, deceiving, deceptive, delusive, dishonest, dishonourable, disloyal, double-dealing, double-faced, duplicitous, erroneous, ersatz, faithless, fake, fallacious, false-hearted, faulty, feigned, fictitious, forged, fraudulent, hypocritical, illusive, imitation, improper, inaccurate, incorrect, inexact, invalid, lying, mendacious, misleading, mistaken, mock, perfidious, postiche, pretended, pseud, pseudo, sham, simulated, spurious, synthetic, treacherous, treasonable, trumped-up, truthless, two-faced, unfaithful, unfounded, unreal, unreliable, unsound, untrue, untrustworthy, untruthful, wrong.
antonyms honest, reliable, true.

falsehood *n.* deceit, deception, dishonesty, dissimulation, fable, fabrication, fib, fiction, inexactitude, inveracity, lie, mendacity, misstatement, perjury, prevarication, pseudery, story, unfact, untruth, untruthfulness.
antonyms truth, truthfulness.

falsification *n.* adulteration, alteration, change, deceit, dissimulation, distortion, forgery, misrepresentation, perversion, tampering.

falsify *v.* adulterate, alter, belie, cook, counterfeit, distort, doctor, fake, forge, garble, misrepresent, misstate, pervert, sophisticate, take liberties with, tamper with.

falter *v.* break, fail, flag, flinch, halt, hem and haw, hesitate, shake, stammer, stumble, stutter, totter, tremble, vacillate, waver.

faltering *adj.* broken, failing, flagging, hesitant, irresolute, stammering, stumbling, tentative, timid, uncertain, unsteady, weak.
antonyms firm, strong.

fame *n.* celebrity, credit, eminence, esteem, glory, honour, illustriousness, kudos, name, prominence, renown, reputation, repute, stardom.

famed *adj.* acclaimed, celebrated, famous, noted, recognised, renowned, well-known, widely-known.
antonym unknown.

familiar *adj.* abreast, accustomed, acquainted, amicable, au courant, au fait, aware, bold, chummy, close, common, common-or-garden, confidential, conscious, conventional, conversant, cordial, customary, disrespectful, domestic, easy, everyday, forward, free, free-and-easy, frequent, friendly, household, impudent, informal, intimate, intrusive, knowledgeable, mundane, near, open, ordinary, overfree, presuming, presumptuous, private, recognisable, relaxed, repeated, routine, stock, unceremonious, unconstrained, unreserved, versed, well-known.
antonyms formal, reserved, unfamiliar, unversed.

familiarise *v.* acclimatise, accustom, brief, coach, habituate, instruct, inure, prime, school, season, train.

familiarity *n.* acquaintance, acquaintanceship, awareness, boldness, cheek, closeness, conversance, disrespect, ease, experience, fellowship, forwardness, freedom, friendliness, grasp, impertinence, impudence, informality, intimacy, liberties, liberty, licence, naturalness, openness, presumption, sociability, unceremoniousness, understanding.
antonyms formality, reservation, unfamiliarity.

family *n.* ancestors, ancestry, birth, blood, brood, children, clan, class, classification, descendants, descent, dynasty, extraction, folk, forebears, forefathers, genealogy, genre, group, house, household, issue, kin, kind, kindred, kinsmen, kith and kin, line, lineage, ménage, network, offspring, parentage, pedigree, people, progeny, quiverful, race, relations, relatives, sept, stemma, stirps, strain, subdivision, system, tribe.

family tree ancestry, extraction, genealogy, line, lineage, pedigree, stemma, stirps.

famine *n.* dearth, destitution, hunger, scarcity, starvation, want.
antonym plenty.

famished *adj.* famishing, hungry, ravening, ravenous, starved, starving, voracious.
antonym sated.

famous *adj.* acclaimed, celebrated, conspicuous, distinguished, eminent, excellent, famed, far-famed, glorious, great, honoured, illustrious, legendary, lionised, notable, noted, prominent, remarkable, renowned, signal, well-known.
antonym unknown.

fan[1] *v.* aggravate, agitate, air-condition, air-cool, arouse, blow, cool, enkindle, excite, impassion, increase, provoke, refresh, rouse, stimulate, stir up, ventilate, whip up, winnow, work up.
n. air-conditioner, blower, extractor fan, flabellum, propeller, punkah, vane, ventilator.

fan[2] *n.* adherent, admirer, aficionado, buff, devotee, enthusiast, fiend, follower, freak, groupie, lover, rooter, supporter, zealot.

fanatic *n.* activist, addict, bigot, demoniac, devotee, energumen, enthusiast, extremist, fiend, freak, militant, visionary, zealot.

fanatical *adj.* bigoted, burning, demoniac, demoniacal, enthusiastic, extreme, fervent, fervid, frenzied, immoderate, mad, obsessive, overenthusiastic, passionate, rabid, visionary, wild, zealous.
antonyms moderate, unenthusiastic.

fanaticism *n.* bigotry, dedication, devotion, enthusiasm, extremism, fervidness, fervour, immoderacy, immoderateness, immoderation, infatuation, madness, monomania, obsessiveness, overenthusiasm, single-mindedness, zeal, zealotism, zealotry.
antonym moderation.

fanciful *adj.* airy-fairy, capricious, chimeric(al), curious, extravagant, fabulous, fairy-tale, fantastic, ideal, imaginary, imaginative, metaphysical, mythical, poetic, romantic, unreal, vaporous, visionary, whimsical, wild.
antonym ordinary.

fancy *v.* be attracted to, believe, conceive, conjecture, crave, desire, dream of, favour, go for, guess, hanker after, have an eye for, imagine, infer, like, long for, lust after, picture, prefer, reckon, relish, suppose, surmise, take a liking to, take to, think, think likely, whim, wish for, yearn for, yen for.
antonym dislike.
n. caprice, chim(a)era, conception, daydream, delusion, desire, dream, fantasy, fondness, hankering, humour, idea, image, imagination, impression, impulse, inclination, liking, nightmare, notion, partiality, penchant, phantasm, predilection, preference, relish, thought, urge, vapour, velleity, vision, whim.
antonyms dislike, fact, reality.
adj. baroque, capricious, chimerical, decorated, decorative, delusive, elaborate, elegant, embellished, extravagant, fanciful, fantastic, far-fetched, illusory, ornamented, ornate, rococo, whimsical.
antonym plain.

fanfare *n.* fanfarade, fanfaronade, flourish, trump, trumpet call, tucket.

fang *n.* prong, tang, tooth, tusk, venom-tooth.

fantasise *v.* build castles in the air, daydream, dream, hallucinate, imagine, invent, live in a dream, romance.

fantastic *adj.* absurd, ambitious, capricious, chimerical, comical, eccentric, enormous, excellent, exotic, extravagant, extreme, fanciful, fantasque, far-fetched, first-rate, freakish, grandiose, great, grotesque, illusory, imaginative, implausible, incredible, irrational, ludicrous, mad, marvellous, odd, out of this world, outlandish, outré, overwhelming, peculiar, phantasmagorical, preposterous, quaint, queer, ridiculous, rococo, sensational, severe, strange, superb, tremendous, unlikely, unreal, unrealistic, visionary, weird, whimsical, wild, wonderful.
antonyms ordinary, plain, poor.

fantasy *n.* apparition, caprice, creativity, daydream, delusion, dream, dreamery, fancy, fantasia, fantasque, flight of fancy, hallucination, illusion, imagination, invention, mirage, nightmare, originality, phantasy, pipe-dream, reverie, vision, whims(e)y.
antonym reality.

far *adv.* a good way, a long way, afar, considerably, decidedly, deep, extremely, greatly, incomparably, miles, much.
antonym near.
adj. distal, distant, faraway, far-flung, far-off, far-removed, further, god-forsaken, long, opposite, other, outlying, out-of-the-way, remote, removed.
antonyms close, nearby.

far and wide all about, broadly, everywhere, extensively, far and near, widely, worldwide.

faraway *adj.* absent, absent-minded, abstracted, distant, dreamy, far, far-flung, far-off, lost, outlying, remote.
antonyms alert, nearby.

farce *n.* absurdity, buffoonery, burlesque, comedy, commedia dell'arte, exode, joke, low comedy, mockery, nonsense, parody, ridiculousness, satire, sham, slapstick, travesty.

farcical *adj.* absurd, amusing, comic, derisory, diverting, droll, facetious, funny, laughable, ludicrous, nonsensical, preposterous, ridiculous, risible, silly, slapstick, stupid.
antonym sensible.

fare[1] *n.* charge, cost, fee, passage, passenger, pick-up, price, traveller.

fare[2] *n.* board, commons, diet, eatables, food, meals, menu, provisions, rations, sustenance, table, victuals.

fare[3] *v.* be, do, get along, get on, go, go on, happen, make out, manage, proceed, prosper, turn out.

farewell *n.* adieu, departure, good-bye, leave-taking, parting, send-off, valediction.
antonym hello.
adj. final, parting, valedictory.
interj. aloha, bye-bye, cheers, ciao, good-bye.

far-fetched *adj.* crazy, doubtful, dubious, fantastic, forced, implausible, improbable, incredible, preposterous, strained, unbelievable, unconvincing, unlikely, unnatural, unrealistic.
antonym plausible.

farm *n.* acreage, acres, bowery, croft, farmstead, grange, holding, homestead, kolkhoz, land, mains, plantation, ranch, smallholding, station.
v. cultivate, operate, plant, till, work the land.

farmer *n.* agriculturist, agronomist, countryman, crofter, gebur, husbandman, smallholder, yeoman.

farming *n.* agriculture, agronomy, crofting, husbandry.

farrago *n.* dog's breakfast, gallimaufry, hash, hotchpotch, jumble, medley, mélange, miscellany, mishmash, mixture, pot-pourri, salmagundi.

far-reaching *adj.* broad, consequential, extensive, important, momentous, pervasive, significant, sweeping, widespread.
antonym insignificant.

far-sighted *adj.* acute, canny, cautious, circumspect, discerning, far-seeing, judicious, politic, prescient, provident, prudent, sage, shrewd, wise.
antonyms imprudent, unwise.

fascinate v. absorb, allure, beguile, bewitch, captivate, charm, delight, enchant, engross, enrapture, enravish, enthrall, entrance, hypnotise, infatuate, intrigue, mesmerise, rivet, spellbind, transfix.
antonym bore.

fascinated adj. absorbed, beguiled, bewitched, captivated, charmed, engrossed, enthralled, entranced, hooked, hypnotised, infatuated, mesmerised, smitten, spellbound.
antonyms bored, uninterested.

fascinating adj. alluring, bewitching, captivating, charming, compelling, delightful, enchanting, engaging, engrossing, enticing, gripping, interesting, intriguing, irresistible, mesmerising, ravishing, riveting, seductive, witching.
antonyms boring, uninteresting.

fascination n. allure, attraction, charm, enchantment, glamour, interest, lure, magic, magnetism, pull, sorcery, spell, witchery.
antonym boredom.

fascism n. absolutism, authoritarianism, autocracy, dictatorship, Hitlerism, totalitarianism.

fascist n. absolutist, authoritarian, autocrat, Blackshirt, Hitlerist, Hitlerite, totalitarian. adj. absolutist, authoritarian, autocratic, fascistic, Hitlerist, Hitlerite, totalitarian.

fashion n. appearance, attitude, beau monde, configuration, convention, craze, custom, cut, demeanour, dernier cri, description, fad, figure, form, guise, haut ton, haute couture, high society, jet set, kind, latest, line, look, make, manner, method, mode, model, mould, pattern, rage, shape, sort, style, trend, type, usage, vogue, way.
v. accommodate, adapt, adjust, alter, construct, contrive, create, design, fit, forge, form, make, manufacture, mould, shape, suit, tailor, work.

fashionable adj. à la mode, alamode, all the rage, chic, chichi, contemporary, current, customary, funky, genteel, in, in vogue, latest, modern, modish, popular, prevailing, smart, snazzy, stylish, swagger, tippy, ton(e)y, ton(n)ish, trendsetting, trendy, up-to-date, up-to-the-minute, usual, with it.
antonym unfashionable.

fast[1] adj. accelerated, brisk, fleet, flying, hasty, hurried, mercurial, nippy, quick, rapid, spanking, speedy, swift, winged.
antonym slow.
adv. apace, hastily, hell for leather, hurriedly, like a flash, like a shot, posthaste, presto, quickly, rapidly, speedily, swiftly, ventre à terre.
antonym slowly.

fast[2] adj. close, constant, fastened, firm, fixed, fortified, immovable, impregnable, lasting, loyal, permanent, secure, sound, staunch, steadfast, tight, unflinching, unwavering.
antonyms impermanent, loose.
adv. close, deeply, firmly, fixedly, near, rigidly, securely, soundly, sound(ly), tightly, unflinchingly.

antonym loosely.

fast[3] adj. dissipated, dissolute, extravagant, immoral, intemperate, licentious, loose, profligate, promiscuous, rakehell, rakehelly, rakish, reckless, self-indulgent, wanton, whorish, wild.
antonyms chaste, moral.

fast[4] v. abstain, bant, diet, go hungry, starve. n. abstinence, diet, fasting, starvation, xerophagy.
antonyms gluttony, self-indulgence.

fasten v. affix, aim, anchor, attach, belay, bend, bind, bolt, chain, clamp, concentrate, connect, direct, fix, focus, grip, infibulate, join, lace, link, lock, nail, rivet, seal, secure, spar, tie, unite.
antonym unfasten.

fasten together interdigitate, interlink, interlock, join, link, unite.
antonyms unfasten, untie.

fastened adj. anchored, attached, bolted, chained, clamped, closed, fixed, joined, knotted, linked, locked, lockfast, nailed, sealed, secured, shut, tied.

fastening n. bond, catch, clasp, clip, copula, fastness, hasp, holder, hook, latch, latchet, link, lock, nexus, tach(e), tie, vinculum.

fastidious adj. choosy, critical, dainty, difficult, discriminating, finical, finicky, fussy, hypercritical, meticulous, overnice, particular, pernickety, picky, precise, punctilious, squeamish.
antonym undemanding.

fasting n. abstinence, banting, dieting, reducing, self-denial, slimming, starvation, xerophagy.
antonyms gluttony, self-indulgence.

fat adj. abdominous, adipose, affluent, beefy, blowzy, corpulent, cushy, elephantine, fatling, fatty, fertile, fleshed, fleshy, flourishing, fozy, fruitful, greasy, gross, heavy, jammy, lucrative, lush, obese, oily, oleaginous, overweight, paunchy, pinguid, plump, poddy, podgy, portly, pot-bellied, productive, profitable, prosperous, pudgy, remunerative, rich, roly-poly, rotund, round, solid, squab, stout, suety, thriving, tubbish, tubby, well-upholstered.
antonyms thin, unproductive.
n. adipose tissue, blubber, brown fat, cellulite, corpulence, degras, embonpoint, fatness, flab, obesity, overweight, paunch, pot (belly), speck.

fatal adj. baleful, baneful, calamitous, catastrophic, deadly, destructive, disastrous, final, incurable, killing, lethal, malignant, mortal, mortiferous, mortific, pernicious, ruinous, terminal, vital.
antonym harmless.

fatality n. casualty, deadliness, death, disaster, lethalness, loss, mortality, unavoidability.

fate n. chance, cup, death, destiny, destruction, divine will, doom, downfall, end, fortune, future, horoscope, issue, joss, karma, kismet, lot, Moira, nemesis, outcome, portion, predestination, predestiny, providence, ruin, stars, upshot, weird.

fated *adj.* destined, doomed, foreordained, ineluctable, inescapable, inevitable, predestined, pre-elected, preordained, sure, unavoidable, written.
antonym avoidable.

fateful *adj.* critical, crucial, deadly, decisive, destructive, disastrous, fatal, important, lethal, momentous, ominous, portentous, ruinous, significant.
antonym unimportant.

Fates *n.* Fatal Sisters, Moirai, Norns, Parcae, Providence, Three Sisters, Weird Sisters.

fathead *n.* ass, booby, dimwit, dolt, dope, dumb-cluck, dumbo, dunderhead, fool, goose, idiot, imbecile, jackass, nincompoop, nitwit, numskull, twerp, twit.

father *n.* abbé, ancestor, architect, author, begetter, confessor, creator, curé, dad, daddy, elder, forebear, forefather, founder, generant, genitor, governor, inventor, leader, maker, old boy, old man, originator, pa, padre, papa, pappy, parent, pastor, pater, paterfamilias, patriarch, patron, pop, poppa, pops, predecessor, priest, prime mover, procreator, progenitor, senator, sire.
v. beget, conceive, create, dream up, engender, establish, found, get, institute, invent, originate, procreate, produce, sire.

fatherland *n.* home, homeland, mother-country, motherland, native land, old country.

fatherly *adj.* affectionate, avuncular, benevolent, benign, forbearing, indulgent, kind, kindly, paternal, patriarchal, protective, supportive, tender.
antonyms cold, harsh, unkind.

fathom *v.* comprehend, deduce, divine, estimate, gauge, get to the bottom of, grasp, interpret, measure, penetrate, plumb, plummet, probe, see, sound, understand, work out.

fatigue *v.* do in, drain, exhaust, fag, jade, knacker, overtire, shatter, tire, weaken, wear out, weary, whack.
antonym refresh.
n. debility, decay, degeneration, ennui, failure, heaviness, languor, lethargy, listlessness, overtiredness, tiredness.
antonyms energy, freshness.

fatigued *adj.* all in, beat, bushed, dead-beat, exhausted, fagged, jaded, jiggered, knackered, overtired, tired, tired out, wasted, weary, whacked, zonked.
antonym refreshed.

fatness *n.* bulk, bulkiness, corpulence, embonpoint, flab, flesh, fleshiness, girth, grossness, heaviness, obesity, overweight, podginess, portliness, rotundity, size, stoutness, tubbiness, weight.

fatten *v.* bloat, broaden, build up, coarsen, cram, distend, expand, feed, feed up, fertilise, nourish, overfeed, pinguefy, spread, stuff, swell, thicken, thrive.

fatty *adj.* adipose, fat, greasy, oily, oleaginous, suet(t)y.

n. fatso, fustilugs, gor-belly, heavyweight, horse-godmother, podge, pudding, pudge, roly-poly.

fatuity *n.* absurdity, asininity, brainlessness, daftness, denseness, fatuousness, folly, foolishness, idiocy, imbecility, inanity, insanity, ludicrousness, lunacy, mindlessness, stupidity.
antonym sense.

fatuous *adj.* absurd, asinine, brainless, daft, dense, dull, fatuitous, foolish, idiotic, imbecile, inane, ludicrous, lunatic, mindless, moony, moronic, puerile, silly, stupid, vacuous, weak-minded, witless.
antonym sensible.

fault *n.* accountability, blemish, blunder, boner, boob, booboo, culpability, defect, deficiency, delict, delinquency, demerit, disdemeanour, dislocation, drawback, error, failing, flaw, frailty, goof, hamartia, imperfection, inaccuracy, indiscretion, infirmity, lack, lapse, liability, misconduct, misdeed, mistake, negligence, offence, omission, oversight, peccadillo, responsibility, shortcoming, sin, slip, slip-up, snag, solecism, transgression, trespass, weakness, wrong.
antonyms advantage, strength.
v. blame, call to account, censure, criticise, find fault with, impugn, pick a hole in someone's coat, pick at, pick holes in.
antonym praise.

fault-finder *n.* carper, caviller, grumbler, hairsplitter, hypercritic, kvetch(er), nagger, niggler, nit-picker, pettifogger.

fault-finding *n.* carping, cavilling, fingerpointing, grumbling, hair-splitting, hypercriticism, kvetching, nagging, niggling, nitpicking, ultracrepidation.
antonym praise.
adj. captious, carping, cavilling, censorious, critical, grumbling, hypercritical, nagging, pettifogging, querulous, ultracrepidarian.
antonym complimentary.

faultless *adj.* accurate, blameless, classic, correct, exemplary, faithful, flawless, foolproof, guiltless, immaculate, impeccable, innocent, irreproachable, model, perfect, pure, sinless, spotless, stainless, unblemished, unspotted, unsullied, untainted, word-perfect.
antonym imperfect.

faulty *adj.* bad, blemished, broken, casuistic, damaged, defective, erroneous, fallacious, flawed, illogical, impaired, imperfect, imprecise, inaccurate, incorrect, invalid, malfunctioning, out of order, specious, unsound, weak, wrong.

faux pas blunder, boner, boob, booboo, clanger, gaffe, gaucherie, goof, impropriety, indiscretion, solecism.

favour *n.* acceptance, approbation, approval, backing, badge, benefit, bias, boon, championship, courtesy, decoration, esteem, favouritism, friendliness, gift, good turn, goodwill, grace, indulgence, keepsake, kindness, knot, love-token, memento, obligement, partiality, patronage, present, regard, rosette, service, smile, souvenir, support, token.

antonym disfavour.

v. abet, accommodate, advance, advocate, aid, approve, assist, back, befriend, champion, choose, commend, countenance, ease, encourage, esteem, extenuate, facilitate, fancy, have in one's good books, help, indulge, like, oblige, opt for, pamper, patronise, prefer, promote, resemble, spare, spoil, succour, support, take after, take kindly to, value.

antonyms disfavour, hinder, thwart.

favourable *adj.* advantageous, affirmative, agreeable, amicable, appropriate, approving, auspicious, beneficial, benign, convenient, encouraging, enthusiastic, fair, Favonian, fit, friendly, good, helpful, hopeful, kind, opportune, positive, promising, propitious, reassuring, roseate, suitable, sympathetic, timely, understanding, welcoming, well-disposed, well-minded, white.

antonym unfavourable.

favourably *adv.* advantageously, agreeably, approvingly, auspiciously, benignly, conveniently, enthusiastically, fortunately, genially, graciously, helpfully, opportunely, profitably, propitiously, sympathetically, well.

antonym unfavourably.

favoured *adj.* advantaged, blessed, chosen, elite, favourite, lucky, pet, predilect, predilected, preferred, privileged, recommended, selected.

favourite *adj.* best-loved, choice, dearest, esteemed, favoured, pet, preferred.

antonyms hated, unfavourite.

n. beloved, blue-eyed boy, choice, darling, dear, form horse, idol, pet, pick, preference, teacher's pet, the apple of one's eye, whitehead, whiteheaded boy.

antonym pet hate.

favouritism *n.* bias, biasedness, injustice, jobs for the boys, nepotism, old school tie, one-sidedness, partiality, partisanship, preference, preferential treatment.

antonym impartiality.

fawn[1] *v.* bootlick, bow and scrape, court, crawl, creep, cringe, curry favour, dance attendance, flatter, grovel, ingratiate oneself, kneel, kowtow, pay court, smarm, toady, truckle.

fawn[2] *adj.* beige, buff, khaki, sand-coloured, sandy.

fawning *adj.* abject, bootlicking, crawling, cringing, deferential, flattering, grovelling, knee-crooking, obsequious, servile, slavish, sycophantic, toad-eating, toadying, toadyish, unctuous.

antonyms cold, proud.

fear *n.* agitation, alarm, anxiety, apprehension, apprehensiveness, awe, bogey, bugbear, concern, consternation, cravenness, danger, dismay, disquietude, distress, doubt, dread, foreboding(s), fright, funk, heart-quake, horror, likelihood, misgiving(s), nightmare, panic, phobia, phobism, qualms, reverence, risk, solicitude, spectre, suspicion, terror, timidity, tremors, trepidation, unease, uneasiness, veneration, wonder, worry.

antonyms courage, fortitude.

v. anticipate, apprehend, dread, expect, foresee, respect, reverence, shudder at, suspect, take fright, tremble, venerate, worry.

fear for tremble for, worry about.

fearful[1] *adj.* afraid, alarmed, anxious, apprehensive, diffident, faint-hearted, feared, frightened, hesitant, intimidated, jittery, jumpy, nervous, nervy, panicky, pusillanimous, scared, shrinking, tense, timid, timorous, uneasy.

antonym courageous.

fearful[2] *adj.* appalling, atrocious, awful, dire, distressing, dreadful, fearsome, ferly, frightful, ghastly, grievous, grim, gruesome, hair-raising, hideous, horrendous, horrible, horrific, monstrous, shocking, terrible, unspeakable.

antonym delightful.

fearless *adj.* aweless, bold, brave, confident, courageous, daring, dauntless, doughty, gallant, game, gutsy, heroic, impavid, indomitable, intrepid, lion-hearted, plucky, unabashed, unafraid, unapprehensive, unblenching, unblinking, undaunted, unflinching, valiant, valorous.

antonyms afraid, timid.

fearlessness *n.* boldness, bravery, confidence, courage, dauntlessness, guts, indomitability, intrepidity, intrepidness, lion-heartedness, nerve, pluck, pluckiness, prowess, valour.

antonyms fear, timidness.

fearsome *adj.* alarming, appalling, aweinspiring, awesome, awful, daunting, dismaying, formidable, frightening, frightful, hair-raising, horrendous, horrible, horrific, horrifying, menacing, terrible, unco, unnerving.

antonym delightful.

feasible *adj.* achievable, attainable, likely, possible, practicable, practical, realisable, reasonable, viable, workable.

antonym impossible.

feast *n.* banquet, barbecue, beanfeast, beano, binge, blow-out, carousal, carouse, celebration, delight, dinner, enjoyment, entertainment, epulation, festival, fête, gala day, gaudy, gratification, holiday, holy day, jollification, junket, pig, pleasure, repast, revels, saint's day, spread, treat.

v. delight, eat one's fill, entertain, gladden, gorge, gormandise, gratify, indulge, overindulge, regale, rejoice, stuff, stuff one's face, thrill, treat, wine and dine.

feat *n.* accomplishment, achievement, act, attainment, deed, exploit, gest(e), performance.

feather *n.* aigrette, egret, penna, pinion, plume, plumula, plumule, quill.

feathery *adj.* downy, feathered, featherlike, fluffy, pennaceous, penniform, plumate, plumed, plumose, plumy, wispy.

feature *n.* article, aspect, attraction, attribute, character, characteristic, column, comment, draw, facet, factor, hallmark, highlight, innovation, item, lineament, mark, peculiarity, piece, point, property, quality, report, special, speciality, specialty, story, trait.
v. accentuate, emphasise, headline, highlight, play up, present, promote, push, recommend, show, spotlight, star.

features *n.* countenance, face, lineaments, looks, mug, phiz, phizog, physiognomy.

febrile *adj.* burning, delirious, febrific, fevered, feverish, fiery, flushed, hot, inflamed, pyretic.

feckless *adj.* aimless, étourdi(e), feeble, futile, gormless, hopeless, incompetent, ineffectual, irresponsible, shiftless, useless, weak, worthless.
antonyms efficient, sensible.

fecund *adj.* feracious, fertile, fructiferous, fructuous, fruitful, productive, prolific, teeming.
antonym infertile.

fecundity *n.* feracity, fertility, fructiferousness, fruitfulness, productiveness.
antonym infertility.

fed up annoyed, blue, bored, brassed off, browned off, cheesed off, depressed, discontented, dismal, dissatisfied, down, gloomy, glum, scunnered, sick and tired, tired, weary.
antonym contented.

federate *v.* amalgamate, associate, combine, confederate, integrate, join together, league, syndicate, unify, unite.
antonyms disunite, separate.

federation *n.* alliance, amalgamation, association, Bund, coalition, combination, confederacy, confederation, copartnership, copartnery, entente, federacy, league, syndicate, union.

fee *n.* account, bill, charge, compensation, emolument, hire, honorarium, pay, payment, recompense, remuneration, retainer, reward, terms, toll.

feeble *adj.* debilitated, delicate, doddering, effete, enervated, enfeebled, exhausted, failing, faint, flat, flimsy, forceless, frail, fushionless, inadequate, incompetent, indecisive, ineffective, ineffectual, inefficient, inform, insignificant, insufficient, lame, languid, paltry, poor, powerless, puny, shilpit, sickly, silly, slight, tame, thin, unconvincing, vacillating, weak, weakened, weakly.
antonyms strong, worthy.

feeble-minded *adj.* addle-pated, cretinised, cretinoid, cretinous, deficient, dim-witted, dull, dumb, half-witted, idiotic, imbecilic, irresolute, lacking, moronic, retarded, simple, slow on the uptake, slow-witted, soft in the head, stupid, two bricks short of a load, vacant, weak-minded.
antonyms bright, intelligent.

feebleness *n.* debility, delicacy, effeteness, enervation, etiolation, exhaustion, faintness, flimsiness, forcelessness, foziness, frailness,

frailty, inadequacy, incapacity, incompetence, indecisiveness, ineffectualness, infirmity, insignificance, insufficiency, lameness, languor, lassitude, sickliness, weakness.
antonyms strength, weariness.

feed *v.* augment, bolster, cater for, dine, eat, encourage, fare, foster, fuel, graze, grub, nourish, nurture, pasture, provide for, provision, strengthen, subsist, supply, sustain, victual.
n. banquet, feast, fodder, food, forage, meal, nosh, pasturage, pasture, provender, repast, silage, spread, tuck-in, victuals.

feed in inject, input, key in, supply.

feed on consume, devour, eat, exist on, live on, partake of.

feel *v.* appear, believe, caress, consider, deem, empathise, endure, enjoy, experience, explore, finger, fondle, fumble, go through, grope, handle, have, have a hunch, hold, intuit, judge, know, manipulate, maul, notice, observe, paw, perceive, reckon, resemble, seem, sense, sound, stroke, suffer, take to heart, test, think, touch, try, undergo.
n. bent, feeling, finish, gift, impression, knack, quality, sense, surface, texture, touch, vibes.

feel for be sorry for, bleed for, commiserate (with), compassionate, condole, empathise with, pity, sympathise with.

feel like desire, fancy, want.

feeler *n.* advance, antenna, approach, ballon d'essai, horn, overture, probe, tentacle, trawl, trial balloon.

feeling *n.* (a)esthesia, (a)esthesis, affection, air, ambience, appreciation, apprehension, ardour, atmosphere, aura, compassion, concern, consciousness, emotion, empathy, Empfindung, feel, fervour, fondness, heat, hunch, idea, impression, inclination, inkling, instinct, intensity, mood, notion, opinion, passion, perception, pity, point of view, presentiment, quality, sensation, sense, sensibility, sensitivity, sentiment, sentimentality, suspicion, sympathy, touch, understanding, vibes, vibrations, view, warmth.

feelings *n.* affections, ego, emotions, passions, self-esteem, sensitivities, susceptibilities.

feign *v.* act, affect, assume, counterfeit, devise, dissemble, dissimulate, fabricate, fake, forge, imitate, invent, make a show of, pretend, put on, sham, simulate.

feigned *adj.* affected, artificial, assumed, counterfeit, fabricated, fake, false, imitation, insincere, personated, pretend, pretended, pseudo, sham, simulated, spurious.
antonyms genuine, sincere.

feint *n.* artifice, blind, bluff, deception, distraction, dodge, dummy, expedient, gambit, manoeuvre, mock-assault, play, pretence, ruse, stratagem, subterfuge, wile.

felicitous *adj.* apposite, appropriate, apropos, apt, delightful, fitting, happy, inspired, neat, opportune, pat, propitious, prosperous, suitable, timely, well-chosen, well-timed, well-

turned.
antonyms inappropriate, inept.
felicity *n.* applicability, appropriateness, aptness, becomingness, blessedness, blessing, bliss, blissfulness, delectation, delight, ecstasy, effectiveness, eloquence, grace, happiness, joy, propriety, suitability, suitableness.
antonyms inappropriateness, ineptitude, sadness.
feline *adj.* catlike, graceful, leonine, seductive, sensual, sinuous, sleek, slinky, smooth, stealthy.
fell[1] *v.* cut down, demolish, flatten, floor, hew down, lay level, level, prostrate, raze, strike down.
fell[2] *adj.* baneful, barbarous, bloody, cruel, deadly, destructive, fatal, ferocious, fierce, grim, implacable, inhuman, maleficent, malevolent, malicious, malign, malignant, merciless, mortal, nefarious, noxious, pernicious, pestilential, pitiless, relentless, ruinous, ruthless, sanguinary, savage, vicious.
antonyms benign, gentle, kind.
fellow[1] *n.* bloke, boy, buffer, bugger, cat, chal, chap, character, codger, cove, cuss, customer, dandiprat, dog, fucker, gadgie, gink, guy, hangdog, individual, Johnny, joker, josser, kipper, man, person, punter.
fellow[2] *n.* associate, brother, colleague, companion, compeer, comrade, counterpart, co-worker, double, equal, fellow-member, friend, like, match, mate, member, partner, peer, twin.
adj. associate, associated, co-, like, related, similar.
fellow-feeling *n.* commiseration, compassion, empathy, sympathy, understanding.
fellowship *n.* amity, association, brotherhood, camaraderie, club, communion, companionability, companionableness, companionship, endowment, familiarity, fraternisation, fraternity, guild, intercourse, intimacy, kindliness, league, order, sisterhood, sociability, society, sodality.
female *adj.* distaff, feminal, feminine, petticoat, womanish, womanly, yin.
antonym male.
femaleness *n.* feminality, femineity, femininity, feminineness, femininity, feminity.
antonym maleness.
feminine *adj.* delicate, effeminate, effete, gentle, girlish, graceful, ladylike, modest, petticoat, sissy, soft, tender, unmanly, unmasculine, weak, womanish, womanly.
antonym masculine.
femininity *n.* delicacy, effeminacy, effeteness, feminineness, gentleness, girlishness, muliebrity, sissiness, softness, unmanliness, womanhood, womanishness, womanliness, Yin.
antonym masculinity.
feminism *n.* female emancipation, women's emancipation, women's liberation, women's movement, women's rights.
femme fatale charmer, enchantress, seductress, siren, temptress, vamp.

fen *n.* bog, marsh, morass, moss, quag, quagmire, slough, swamp.
fence[1] *n.* barricade, barrier, defence, guard, hedge, paling, palisade, railings, rampart, sepiment, sept, shield, stockade, wall, windbreak.
v. bound, circumscribe, confine, coop, defend, encircle, enclose, fortify, guard, hedge, pen, protect, restrict, secure, separate, surround.
fence[2] *v.* beat about the bush, cavil, digladiate, dodge, equivocate, evade, hedge, parry, prevaricate, pussyfoot, quibble, shift, stonewall, tergiversate.
fencing[1] *n.* iaido, kendo, swordplay, swordsmanship.
fencing[2] *n.* beating about the bush, double talk, equivocation, evasiveness, hedging, parrying, prevarication, pussyfooting, quibbling, stonewalling, tergiversation, weasel-words.
fend for look after, maintain, provide for, shift for, support, sustain.
fend off avert, beat off, defend, deflect, hold at bay, keep off, parry, repel, repulse, resist, shut out, stave off, ward off.
feral *adj.* bestial, brutal, brutish, fell, ferae naturae, ferine, ferocious, fierce, savage, unbroken, uncultivated, undomesticated, untamed, vicious, wild.
antonym tame.
ferment *v.* agitate, boil, brew, bubble, concoct, effervesce, excite, fester, foam, foment, froth, heat, incite, inflame, leaven, provoke, rise, rouse, seethe, smoulder, stir up, work, work up.
n. agitation, brouhaha, commotion, disruption, excitement, fever, frenzy, furore, glow, heat, hubbub, imbroglio, stew, stir, tumult, turbulence, turmoil, unrest, uproar, yeast, zymosis.
antonym calm.
ferocious *adj.* barbaric, barbarous, bloodthirsty, bloody, brutal, brutish, catamountain, cruel, fearsome, feral, fiendish, fierce, homicidal, inhuman, merciless, murderous, pitiless, predatory, rapacious, ravening, relentless, ruthless, sadistic, sanguinary, savage, truculent, vicious, violent, wild.
antonyms gentle, mild.
ferocity *n.* barbarity, bloodthirstiness, brutality, cruelty, ferity, ferociousness, fiendishness, fierceness, inhumanity, murderousness, rapacity, ruthlessness, sadism, savageness, savagery, truculence, viciousness, wildness.
antonyms gentleness, mildness.
ferret out dig up, disclose, discover, disinter, drive out, elicit, extract, find, hunt down, nose out, root out, run to earth, smell out, sniff out, sus out, trace, track down, unearth, worm out.
ferry *v.* carry, chauffeur, convey, drive, move, remove, run, shift, ship, shuttle, taxi, transport.
fertile *adj.* abundant, fat, fecund, feracious, flowering, fructiferous, fructuous, frugiferous, fruit-bearing, fruitful, generative, lush,

luxuriant, plenteous, plentiful, potent, productive, prolific, rich, teeming, uberous, virile, yielding.
antonyms arid, barren.

fertilisation *n.* dressing, dunging, enrichment, fecundation, implantation, impregnation, insemination, manuring, mulching, pollination, procreation, propagation, top-dressing.

fertilise *v.* compost, dress, dung, enrich, fecundate, feed, fructify, impregnate, inseminate, manure, mulch, pollinate, top-dress.

fertiliser *n.* compost, dressing, dung, guano, manure, marl, plant-food.

fertility *n.* abundance, fatness, fecundity, feracity, fruitfulness, lushness, luxuriance, plenteousness, potency, productiveness, prolificity, prolificness, richness, uberty, virility.
antonyms aridity, barrenness.

fervent *adj.* animated, ardent, devout, eager, earnest, emotional, empressé, energetic, enthusiastic, excited, fervid, fiery, full-blooded, heartfelt, impassioned, intense, passionate, perfervid, spirited, vehement, vigorous, warm, whole-hearted, zealous.

fervour *n.* animation, ardour, eagerness, earnestness, empressment, energy, enthusiasm, excitement, fervency, fervidity, fervidness, hwyl, intensity, passion, spirit, unction, unctuousness, vehemence, verve, vigour, warmth, zeal.
antonym apathy.

fester *v.* chafe, decay, discharge, gall, gather, irk, maturate, putrefy, rankle, smoulder, suppurate, ulcerate.
antonyms dissipate, heal.

festering *n.* discharging, galling, gathering, infected, inflamed, mattering, mattery, maturating, poisonous, purulent, pussy, putrescent, rankling, septic, smouldering, suppurating, ulcerated, venomous, virulent.

festival *n.* anniversary, carnival, celebration, commemoration, eisteddfod, entertainment, feast, festa, festivities, fête, field day, fiesta, gala, holiday, holy day, jubilee, junketing, merry-make, merrymaking, merry-night, mod, puja, saint's day, treat.

festive *adj.* carnival, celebratory, cheery, Christmassy, convivial, cordial, en fête, festal, festivous, gala, gay, gleeful, happy, hearty, holiday, jolly, jovial, joyful, joyous, jubilant, merry, mirthful, rollicking, sportive, uproarious.
antonyms gloomy, sober, sombre.

festivities *n.* bacchanalia, banqueting, carousal, celebration, entertainment, feasting, festival, fun and games, glorification, jollification, jollities, junketings, party, rejoicings, revelries, revels.

festivity *n.* amusement, conviviality, enjoyment, feasting, festal, fun, gaiety, jollification, jollity, joviality, joyfulness, junketing, merriment, merrymaking, mirth, pleasure, revelry, sport, wassail.

festoon *n.* chaplet, decoration, garbe, garland, lei, swag, swathe, wreathe.

v. adorn, array, bedeck, bedizen, beribbon, deck, decorate, drape, garland, garnish, hang, swathe, wreath.

fetch *v.* be good for, bring, bring in, carry, conduct, convey, deliver, draw, earn, elicit, escort, evoke, get, go for, lead, make, obtain, produce, realise, retrieve, sell for, transport, uplift, utter, yield.

fetch up arrive, come, come to a halt, end up, finish, finish up, halt, land, reach, stop, turn up.

fetching *adj.* alluring, attractive, beguiling, captivating, charming, cute, disarming, enchanting, enticing, fascinating, pretty, sweet, taking, winning, winsome.
antonym repellent.

fête *n.* bazaar, carnival, fair, festival, gala, garden party, sale of work.

v. banquet, bring out the red carpet for, entertain, honour, lionise, make much of, regale, treat, welcome, wine and dine.

fetid *adj.* corrupt, disgusting, filthy, foul, malodorous, mephitic, nauseating, noisome, noxious, odorous, offensive, rancid, rank, reeking, sickly, smelly, stinking.
antonym fragrant.

fetish *n.* amulet, charm, cult object, fixation, idée fixe, idol, image, ju-ju, mania, obsession, periapt, phylactery, talisman, thing, totem.

fetter *v.* bind, chain, confine, curb, encumber, entrammel, gyve, hamper, hamshackle, hamstring, hobble, manacle, pinion, restrain, restrict, shackle, tie (up), trammel, truss.
antonym free.

fetters *n.* bilboes, bondage, bonds, bracelets, captivity, chains, check, constraint, curb, gyve, gyves, hampers, hamshackle, handcuffs, hindrance, hobble, hopple, inhibition, irons, manacles, obstruction, restraint, shackles, trammel.

feud *n.* animosity, antagonism, argument, bad blood, bickering, bitterness, conflict, contention, disagreement, discord, dispute, dissension, enmity, estrangement, faction, feuding, grudge, hostility, ill will, quarrel, rivalry, row, strife, variance, vendetta.
antonyms agreement, peace.

v. altercate, argue, be at odds, bicker, brawl, clash, contend, dispute, duel, fight, quarrel, row, squabble, war, wrangle.
antonym agree.

fever *n.* agitation, calenture, delirium, ecstasy, excitement, febricity, febricula, febricule, ferment, fervour, feverishness, flush, frenzy, heat, intensity, passion, pyrexia, restlessness, temperature, turmoil, unrest.

fevered *adj.* burning, febrile, feverish, feverous, fever-ridden, fiery, flushed, hectic, hot, pyretic, pyrexial, pyrexic.
antonym cool.

feverish *adj.* agitated, anxious, burning, distracted, eager, excited, fanatical, febrile, fevered, feverous, flurried, flushed, flustered, frantic, frenetic, frenzied, hasty, hectic, hot,

hurried, impatient, inflamed, nervous, obsessive, overwrought, pyretic, restless.
antonyms calm, cool.

feverishness *n.* agitation, bustle, commotion, distraction, excitement, febricity, febrility, ferment, fever, flurry, flush, franticness, frenzy, fuss, haste, hurry, kerfuffle, pother, pyrexia, restlessness, stir, turmoil.
antonyms calmness, coolness.

few *adj.* few and far between, hard to come by, in short supply, inadequate, inconsiderable, infrequent, insufficient, meagre, negligible, rare, scant, scanty, scarce, scattered, sparse, sporadic, thin, uncommon.
pron. a couple, handful, not many, oddments, one or two, scarcely any, scattering, small number, small quantity, some, sprinkling.

fewness *n.* dearth, inadequacy, infrequency, insufficiency, lack, negligibility, paucity, rareness, rarity, scantiness, scarceness, scarcity, sparseness, thinness, uncommonness, want.
antonyms abundance, glut.

fiancé(e) *n.* betrothed, bridegroom-to-be, bride-to-be, husband-to-be, intended, wife-to-be.

fiasco *n.* bummer, calamity, catastrophe, collapse, cropper, damp squib, debacle, disaster, failure, flivver, flop, mess, non-success, rout, ruin, turkey, unsuccess, wash-out.
antonym success.

fiat *n.* authorisation, command, decree, dictate, dictum, diktat, directive, edict, injunction, mandate, OK, order, ordinance, permission, precept, prescript, proclamation, sanction, ukase, warrant.

fib *n.* concoction, evasion, falsehood, fantasy, fiction, invention, lie, misrepresentation, prevarication, story, tale, untruth, white lie, whopper, yarn.
v. dissemble, evade, fabricate, falsify, fantasise, invent, lie, prevaricate, sidestep.

fibre *n.* backbone, bast, calibre, character, courage, determination, essence, fibril, filament, filasse, funicle, grit, guts, nature, nerve, pile, pluck, quality, resolution, sinew, spirit, stamina, staple, strand, strength, substance, temperament, tenacity, tendril, texture, thread, toughness.

fibrous *adj.* fibred, fibriform, fibrillar, fibrillary, fibrillate, fibrillose, fibrillous, fibroid, filamentous, filiform, filose, funicular, funiculate, penicillate, sinewy, stringy, tendinous, thread-like, wiry.

fickle *adj.* capricious, changeable, disloyal, dizzy, erratic, faithless, fitful, flighty, fluctuating, inconstant, irresolute, mercurial, mutable, quicksilver, treacherous, unfaithful, unpredictable, unreliable, unstable, unsteady, vacillating, variable, volage, volageous, volatile, wind-changing.
antonym constant.

fickleness *n.* capriciousness, changeability, changeableness, disloyalty, faithlessness, fitfulness, flightiness, inconstancy, mutability, treachery, unfaithfulness, unpredictability,

unreliability, unsteadiness, volatility.
antonym constancy.

fiction *n.* canard, cock-and-bull story, concoction, fable, fabrication, falsehood, fancy, fantasy, feuilleton, fib, figment, imagination, improvisation, invention, legend, lie, myth, novel, parable, romance, story, story-telling, tale, tall story, untruth, whopper, yarn.
antonym truth.

fictional *adj.* fabulous, imaginary, invented, legendary, made-up, mythical, non-existent, unreal.
antonyms real, true.

fictitious *adj.* apocryphal, artificial, assumed, bogus, counterfeit, fabricated, false, fanciful, feigned, fictive, fraudulent, imaginary, imagined, improvised, invented, made-up, make-believe, mythical, non-existent, spurious, supposed, suppositional, supposititious, unreal, untrue.
antonyms genuine, real.

fiddle[1] *v.* cheat, cook, cook the books, diddle, fidget, finagle, finger, fix, gerrymander, graft, interfere, juggle, manoeuvre, mess around, play, racketeer, swindle, tamper, tinker, toy, trifle, wangle.
n. chicanery, con, fix, fraud, graft, monkey-business, racket, rip-off, sharp practice, swindle, trickery, wangle.

fiddle[2] *n.* viol, viola, viola da braccio, viola da spalla, viola d'amore, violin.

fiddling *adj.* footling, futile, insignificant, negligible, paltry, pettifogging, petty, trifling, trivial.
antonyms important, significant.

fidelity *n.* accuracy, adherence, allegiance, authenticity, closeness, constancy, correspondence, dedication, dependability, devotedness, devotion, dutifulness, exactitude, exactness, faith, faithfulness, fealty, incorruptibility, integrity, lealty, loyalty, preciseness, precision, reliability, scrupulousness, staunchness, steadfastness, true-heartedness, trustworthiness.
antonyms inaccuracy, inconstancy, treachery.

fidget *v.* bustle, chafe, fiddle, fidge, fike, fret, jerk, jiggle, jitter, jump, mess about, play around, squirm, toy, twitch, worry.
n. agitation, anxiety, creeps, discomposure, edginess, fidgetiness, fidgets, heebie-jeebies, jimjams, jitteriness, jitters, jumpiness, nerves, nerviness, nervousness, restlessness, shakes, twitchiness, unease, uneasiness, willies.

fidgety *adj.* agitated, frisky, impatient, jerky, jittery, jumpy, nervous, nervy, on edge, restive, restless, skittish, twitchy, uneasy.
antonym still.

field[1] *n.* arena, battlefield, battleground, glebe, grassland, green, greensward, lawn, lay, lea, mead, meadow, padang, paddock, pasture, pitch, playing-field, theatre.

field[2] *n.* applicants, candidates, competition, competitors, contenders, contestants, entrants, opponents, opposition, possibilities, runners.

field³ *n.* area, bailiwick, ball park, bounds, confines, department, discipline, domain, environment, forte, limits, line, métier, period, pidgin, province, purview, range, scope, speciality, specialty, territory.

field⁴ *v.* answer, catch, cope with, deal with, deflect, handle, parry, pick up, receive, retrieve, return, stop.

fiend *n.* addict, aficionado, barbarian, beast, brute, degenerate, demon, devil, devotee, enthusiast, evil spirit, fanatic, freak, ghoul, goblin, hellhound, hobgoblin, incubus, lamia, maniac, monster, nut, ogre, Satan, savage, succubus.

fiendish *adj.* accursed, atrocious, baleful, black-hearted, cruel, damnable, demoniac, devilish, diabolic, diabolical, hellish, impious, implacable, infernal, inhuman, malefic, maleficent, malevolent, malicious, malign, malignant, Mephistophelean, Mephistophelic, mischievous, monstrous, nefarious, satanic, savage, ungodly, unspeakable, vicious, vile, wicked.

fierce *adj.* baleful, barbarous, blustery, boisterous, brutal, cruel, cut-throat, dangerous, fearsome, fell, feral, ferocious, fiery, frightening, furious, grim, howling, intense, keen, menacing, merciless, murderous, passionate, powerful, raging, relentless, savage, stern, stormy, strong, tempestuous, threatening, truculent, tumultuous, uncontrollable, unrelenting, untamed, vicious, violent, wild.
antonyms calm, gentle, kind.

fiercely *adv.* ardently, bitterly, fanatically, ferociously, furiously, implacably, intensely, keenly, menacingly, mercilessly, murderously, passionately, relentlessly, savagely, sternly, tempestuously, tigerishly, tooth and nail, viciously, violently, wildly, zealously.
antonyms gently, kindly.

fierceness *n.* ardour, avidity, bitterness, bluster, destructiveness, fanaticism, fearsomeness, ferocity, fervidness, fervour, fieriness, intensity, keenness, mercilessness, passion, relentlessness, roughness, ruthlessness, savageness, savagery, sternness, storminess, strength, tempestuousness, turbulence, viciousness, violence, wildness, zeal.
antonyms gentleness, kindness.

fiery *adj.* ablaze, afire, aflame, aglow, ardent, blazing, burning, choleric, excitable, febrile, fervent, fervid, fevered, feverish, fierce, flaming, flushed, glowing, heated, hot, hot-headed, impatient, impetuous, impulsive, inflamed, irascible, irritable, passionate, peppery, perfervid, precipitate, red-hot, sultry, torrid, truculent, violent, volcanic.
antonyms cold, impassive.

fight *v.* altercate, argue, assault, battle, bear arms against, bicker, box, brawl, clash, close, combat, conduct, conflict, contend, contest, cross swords, defy, dispute, do battle, engage, exchange blows, fence, feud, grapple, joust, lock horns, measure strength, measure

swords, mell, mix it, oppose, prosecute, quarrel, resist, scrap, scuffle, skirmish, spar, squabble, stand up to, strive, struggle, take the field, tilt, tussle, wage, wage war, war, withstand, wrangle, wrestle.
n. action, affray, altercation, argument, barney, battle, belligerence, bicker, bout, brawl, brush, clash, combat, conflict, contest, courage, dispute, dissension, dogfight, duel, encounter, engagement, fisticuffs, fracas, fray, free-for-all, gameness, hostilities, joust, luctation, mêlée, mettle, militancy, monomachy, passage of arms, pluck, pugnacity, quarrel, rammy, resilience, resistance, riot, row, ruck, rumble, scrap, scuffle, set-to, skirmish, spirit, strength, struggle, tenacity, tussle, war.

fight back¹ defend oneself, give as good as one gets, put up a fight, reply, resist, retaliate, retort.

fight back² bottle up, contain, control, curb, hold back, hold in check, repress, resist, restrain, suppress.

fight off beat off, hold off, keep at bay, put to flight, rebuff, repel, repress, repulse, resist, rout, stave off, ward off.

fight shy of avoid, disdain, eschew, give a wide berth, keep at arm's length, shun, spurn, steer clear of.

fighter *n.* adventurer, antagonist, battler, belligerent, boxer, brave, bruiser, champion, combatant, contender, contestant, disputant, fighting man, filibuster, free lance, gladiator, man-at-arms, mercenary, militant, prize-fighter, pugilist, soldier, soldier of fortune, swordsman, trouper, warrior, wrestler.

fighting *adj.* aggressive, argumentative, bellicose, belligerent, combative, contentious, disputatious, fierce, hawkish, martial, militant, militaristic, pugnacious, quarrelsome, sabre-rattling, truculent, warfaring, warlike.
n. battle, bloodshed, boxing, brawling, clash, combat, conflict, encounter, engagement, fisticuffs, fray, handicuffs, hostilities, mêlée, quarrelling, scuffle, scuffling, struggle, war, warfare, wrangling, wrestling.

figment *n.* concoction, creation, deception, delusion, fable, fabrication, falsehood, fancy, fiction, illusion, improvisation, invention, mare's nest, production, work.

figurative *adj.* allegorical, analogous, descriptive, embellished, emblematic, emblematical, fanciful, florid, flowery, metaphorical, ornate, parabolic, pictorial, picturesque, poetical, representative, symbolic, symbolical, tropical, typical.
antonym literal.

figure *n.* amount, body, build, celebrity, character, chassis, cipher, configuration, conformation, cost, depiction, design, device, diagram, digit, dignitary, drawing, embellishment, emblem, form, frame, illustration, image, leader, motif, notability, notable, number, numeral, outline, pattern, personage, personality, physique, presence, price, proportions, representation, shadow, shape, sign, silhouette, sketch, somebody, sum, symbol, torso, total, trope, value.

v. act, add, appear, believe, calculate, compute, count, estimate, feature, guess, judge, opine, reckon, sum, surmise, tally, think, tot up, work out.

figure of speech conceit, concetto, figure, image, imagery, rhetorical device, trope, turn of phrase.

figure out calculate, comprehend, compute, decipher, excogitate, explain, fathom, make out, puzzle out, reason out, reckon, resolve, see, understand, work out.

figured *adj.* adorned, decorated, embellished, marked, ornamented, patterned, printed, sprigged, variegated.
antonym plain.

figurehead *n.* bust, carving, cipher, dummy, front man, image, leader, man of straw, mouthpiece, name, nominal head, nonentity, puppet, straw man, titular head, token.

filament *n.* cilium, fibre, fibril, file, funicle, hair, pile, staple, strand, string, thread, whisker, wire.

filch *v.* abstract, borrow, crib, drib, embezzle, fake, finger, half-inch, lift, misappropriate, nick, palm, peculate, pilfer, pinch, plagiarise, prig, purloin, rip off, snaffle, snitch, steal, swipe, take, thieve.

file[1] *v.* abrade, burnish, furbish, grate, hone, pare, plane, polish, rasp, refine, rub (down), sand, scour, scrape, shape, shave, smooth, trim, whet.

file[2] *n.* binder, cabinet, case, date, documents, dossier, folder, information, portfolio, record.

v. capture, document, enter, memorise, pigeonhole, process, record, register, slot in, store.

file[3] *n.* column, cortège, line, list, procession, queue, row, stream, string, trail, train.

v. defile, march, parade, stream, trail, troop.

filial *adj.* affectionate, daughterly, devoted, dutiful, fond, loving, loyal, respectful, son-like, sonly.
antonyms disloyal, unfilial.

filibuster[1] *n.* delay, hindrance, impediment, obstruction, peroration, postponement, procrastination, speechifying.

v. delay, hinder, impede, obstruct, perorate, prevent, procrastinate, put off, speechify.
antonym expedite.

filibuster[2] *n.* adventurer, buccaneer, corsair, free lance, freebooter, pirate, rover, sea rat, sea-robber, sea-rover, soldier of fortune.

filigree *n.* fret-work, interlace, lace, lacework, lattice, lattice-work, scrollwork, tracery, wirework.

fill *v.* assign, block, bung, charge, clog, close, congest, cork, cram, crowd, discharge, drench, engage, englut, engorge, execute, fulfil, furnish, glut, gorge, hold, imbue, impregnate, inflate, load, occupy, officiate, overspread, pack, perform, permeate,

pervade, plug, replenish, sate, satiate, satisfy, saturate, seal, soak, stock, stop, stuff, suffuse, supply, surfeit, swell, take up.
antonyms clear, empty.

n. abundance, ample, enough, plenty, sufficiency, sufficient.

fill in acquaint, act for, advise, answer, apprise, brief, bring up to date, complete, deputise, fill out, inform, put wise, replace, represent, stand in, sub, substitute, understudy.

filling *n.* contents, filler, grouting, infill, infilling, innards, inside, insides, nogging, padding, rubble, stuffing, wadding.

adj. ample, big, bulky, generous, heavy, large, nutritious, satisfying, solid, square, substantial, sustaining, tidy.
antonym insubstantial.

fillip *n.* boost, flick, goad, impetus, incentive, prod, push, shove, spice, spur, stimulus, zest.
antonym damper.

film[1] *n.* bloom, blur, cloud, coat, coating, covering, dusting, gauze, glaze, haze, haziness, integument, layer, membrane, mist, opacity, pellicle, screen, scum, sheet, skin, tissue, veil, web, weft.

v. blear, blur, cloud, dull, glaze, haze, mist, screen, veil.

film[2] *n.* documentary, epic, feature film, flick, horse-opera, motion picture, movie, oldie, picture, short, spaghetti western, video, western.

v. photograph, shoot, take, video, videotape.

filmy *adj.* cobwebby, delicate, diaphanous, fine, flimsy, floaty, fragile, gauzy, gossamer, gossamery, insubstantial, light, see-through, sheer, shimmering, thin, translucent, transparent.
antonym opaque.

filter *v.* clarify, dribble, escape, exude, filtrate, leach, leak, ooze, penetrate, percolate, purify, refine, screen, seep, sieve, sift, strain, transpire, transude, trickle, well.

n. colander, gauze, membrane, mesh, riddle, sieve, sifter, strainer.

filth *n.* bilge, carrion, coarseness, colluvies, contamination, coprolalia, coprophilia, corruption, crud, defilement, dirt, dirty-mindedness, dung, excrement, excreta, faeces,, faex, filthiness, foulness, garbage, grime, grossness, gunge, impurity, indecency, muck, nastiness, obscenity, ordure, pollution, pornography, putrefaction, putrescence, refuse, scatology, sewage, slime, sludge, smut, smuttiness, soil, sordes, sordidness, squalor, sullage, uncleanness, vileness, vulgarity.
antonyms cleanliness, decency, purity.

filthy *adj.* Augean, base, bawdy, begrimed, black, blackened, blue, coarse, contemptible, coprolaliac, coprophilous, corrupt, depraved, despicable, dirty, dirty-minded, faecal, feculent, foul, foul-mouthed, grimy, gross, grubby, impure, indecent, lavatorial, lewd, licentious, low, mean, miry, mucky, muddy, nasty, nasty-minded, obscene, offensive, polluted, pornographic, putrid, scatological, scurrilous, slimy, smoky, smutty, sooty, sordid, squalid, suggestive, swinish, unclean, unwashed, vicious, vile, vulgar.

antonyms clean, decent, inoffensive, pure.

final *adj.* absolute, clinching, closing, concluding, conclusive, conclusory, decided, decisive, definite, definitive, desinent, desinential, determinate, dying, eleventh-hour, end, eventual, finished, incontrovertible, irrefragable, irrefutable, irrevocable, last, last-minute, latest, settled, terminal, terminating, ultimate, undeniable.

finale *n.* climax, close, conclusion, crescendo, crowning glory, culmination, curtain, dénouement, epilogue, final curtain, finis, last act, supreme moment.

finalise *v.* agree, clinch, complete, conclude, decide, dispose of, finish, get signed and sealed, get taped, resolve, round off, seal, settle, sew up, tie up, work out, wrap up.

finality *n.* certitude, conclusiveness, conviction, decidedness, decisiveness, definiteness, firmness, inevitability, inevitableness, irreversibility, irrevocability, resolution, ultimacy, unavoidability.

finally *adv.* absolutely, at last, at length, completely, conclusively, convincingly, decisively, definitely, eventually, for ever, for good, for good and all, in conclusion, in the end, inescapably, inexorably, irreversibly, irrevocably, lastly, once and for all, permanently, ultimately.

finance *n.* accounting, accounts, banking, business, commerce, economics, investment, money, money management, stock market, trade.

v. back, bail out, bankroll, capitalise, float, fund, guarantee, habilitate, pay for, set up, subsidise, support, underwrite.

finances *n.* affairs, assets, bank account, bread, budget, capital, cash, coffers, dibs, fisc, funds, income, liquidity, money, moolah, purse, resources, revenue, spondulicks, wealth, wherewithal.

financial *adj.* budgetary, chrematistic, commercial, economic, fiscal, monetary, money, pecuniary.

financier *n.* banker, broker, cambist, financialist, gnome, investor, money-maker, speculator, stockbroker.

find *v.* achieve, acquire, ascertain, attain, bring, catch, chance on, come across, consider, contribute, cough up, descry, detect, discover, earn, encounter, espy, experience, expose, ferret out, furnish, gain, get, hit on, judge, learn, light on, locate, meet, note, notice, observe, obtain, perceive, procure, provide, reach, realise, recognise, recover, rediscover, regain, remark, repossess, retrieve, spot, stumble on, supply, think, track down, turn up, uncover, unearth, win.

n. acquisition, asset, bargain, catch, coup, discovery, good buy, unconsidered trifle.

find fault bitch, carp, cavil, censure, complain,
criticise, depreciate, disparage, gripe, hyper-criticise, kvetch, nag, niggle, nitpick, pick holes, pull to pieces, quarrel with, quibble, reprove, take to task, ultracrepidate.

antonym praise.

find out ascertain, catch, detect, dig up, disclose, discover, establish, expiscate, expose, learn, note, observe, perceive, realise, reveal, rumble, show up, speir, sus out, tumble to, uncover, unmask.

finding *n.* award, breakthrough, conclusion, decision, decree, discovery, evidence, find, judgement, pronouncement, recommendation, verdict.

fine[1] *adj.* abstruse, acceptable, acute, admirable, agreeable, all right, attractive, balmy, beau, beaut, beautiful, bonny, brave, braw, bright, brilliant, choice, clear, clement, cloudless, convenient, critical, cutting, dainty, dandy, delicate, diaphanous, discriminating, dry, elegant, elusive, excellent, exceptional, expensive, exquisite, fair, fastidious, fine-drawn, first-class, first-rate, flimsy, four-square, fragile, gauzy, good, good-looking, goodly, gorgeous, gossamer, great, hair-splitting, handsome, honed, hunky-dory, impressive, intelligent, jake, keen, light, lovely, magnificent, masterly, minute, nice, OK, ornate, outstanding, pleasant, polished, powdery, precise, pure, quick, rare, refined, robust, satisfactory, select, sensitive, sharp, sheer, showy, skilful, skilled, slender, small, smart, solid, splendid, sterling, strong, sturdy, stylish, sublime, subtle, suitable, sunny, superior, supreme, tasteful, tenuous, thin, tickety-boo, unalloyed, virtuoso, well-favoured, wiredrawn.

fine[2] *v.* amerce, mulct, penalise, punish, sting.

n. amercement, amerciament, damages, forfeit, forfeiture, mulct, penalty, punishment.

finery *n.* bedizenment, decorations, frills and furbelows, frippery, gaud, gaudery, gauds, gear, gewgaws, glad rags, jewellery, ornaments, showiness, splendour, Sunday best, trappings.

finesse *n.* address, adeptness, adroitness, artfulness, artifice, cleverness, craft, deftness, delicacy, diplomacy, discretion, elegance, expertise, gracefulness, know-how, neatness, polish, quickness, refinement, savoir-faire, skill, sophistication, subtlety, tact.

v. bluff, evade, manipulate, manoeuvre, trick.

finger *v.* caress, feel, fiddle with, fondle, handle, manipulate, maul, meddle with, palpate, paw, play about with, stroke, touch, toy with.

n. claw, digit, digital, index, phalanges, talon.

finical *adj.* choosy, dainty, dandified, dandyish, fastidious, finicky, foppish, fussy, natty, neat, nice, nipperty-tipperty, particular, pernickety, precise.

finicky *adj.* choosy, critical, dainty, delicate, difficult, fastidious, finical, finicking, fussy, hypercritical, meticulous, nice, nit-picking, overnice, particular, pernickety, scrupulous, squeamish, tricky.

antonyms easy, easy-going.

finish *v.* accomplish, achieve, annihilate, best, buff, burnish, cease, close, coat, complete, conclude, consume, consummate, culminate, deal with, defeat, destroy, devour, discharge, dispatch, dispose of, do, drain, drink, eat, elaborate, empty, encompass, end, execute, exhaust, expend, exterminate, face, finalise, fulfil, get rid of, gild, hone, kill, lacquer, overcome, overpower, overthrow, perfect, polish, put an end to, put the last hand to, refine, round off, rout, ruin, settle, smooth, smooth off, sophisticate, spend, stain, stop, terminate, texture, use (up), veneer, wax, wind up, worst, zap.

n. annihilation, appearance, bankruptcy, burnish, cessation, close, closing, completion, conclusion, coup de grâce, culmination, cultivation, culture, curtain, curtains, death, defeat, dénouement, elaboration, end, end of the road, ending, finale, gloss, grain, liquidation, lustre, patina, perfection, polish, refinement, ruin, shine, smoothness, sophistication, surface, termination, texture, wind-up.

finished *adj.* accomplished, bankrupt, clapped-out, classic, consummate, cultivated, defeated, done, done for, doomed, drained, elegant, empty, exhausted, expert, faultless, flawless, impeccable, jiggered, lost, masterly, napoo, overpast, perfected, played out, polished, professional, proficient, refined, ruined, skilled, smooth, sophisticated, spent, through, undone, urbane, virtuoso, washed up, wrecked, zonked.

antonyms coarse, crude, unfinished.

finite *adj.* bounded, calculable, circumscribed, compassable, definable, delimited, demarcated, fixed, limited, measurable, restricted, terminable.

antonym infinite.

fire *n.* animation, ardour, bale-fire, barrage, blaze, bombardment, bonfire, brio, broadside, burning, cannonade, combustion, conflagration, dash, eagerness, earnestness, élan, enthusiasm, excitement, feeling, fervency, fervidity, fervidness, fervour, feu de joie, fierceness, flak, flames, force, fusillade, hail, heat, impetuosity, inferno, intensity, life, light, lustre, passion, radiance, salvo, scintillation, shelling, sniping, sparkle, spirit, splendour, verve, vigour, virtuosity, vivacity, volley, warmth, zeal.

v. activate, animate, arouse, boot out, cashier, depose, detonate, discharge, dismiss, eject, electrify, enkindle, enliven, excite, explode, galvanise, give marching orders, give the bum's rush, hurl, ignite, impassion, incite, inflame, inspire, inspirit, kindle, launch, let off, light, loose, put a match to, quicken, rouse, sack, send off, set alight, set fire to, set off, set on fire, shell, shoot, show the door, stimulate, stir, touch off, trigger off, whet.

firearm *n.* automatic, gun, handgun, musket, musketoon, muzzle-loader, muzzler, pistol, revolver, rifle, shooter, shooting-iron, shotgun, weapon.

fireworks *n.* devils, explosions, feux d'artifice, firecrackers, gerbes, hysterics, illuminations, maroon, pyrotechnics, rage, rockets, rows, sparks, storm, temper, trouble, uproar.

firm[1] *adj.* abiding, adamant, anchored, balanced, braced, cast-iron, cemented, changeless, committed, compact, compressed, concentrated, congealed, constant, convinced, crisp, definite, dense, dependable, determined, dogged, durable, embedded, enduring, established, fast, fastened, fixed, grounded, hard, hardened, immovable, impregnable, indurate, inelastic, inflexible, iron-hearted, jelled, jellified, motionless, obdurate, reliable, resolute, resolved, rigid, robust, secure, secured, set, settled, solid, solidified, stable, stationary, staunch, steadfast, steady, stiff, strict, strong, sturdy, substantial, sure, taut, tight, true, unalterable, unassailable, unbending, unchanging, undeviating, unfaltering, unflinching, unmoved, unmoving, unshakable, unshakeable, unshaken, unshifting, unswerving, unwavering, unyielding, well-knit.

antonyms infirm, soft, unsound.

firm[2] *n.* association, business, company, concern, conglomerate, corporation, enterprise, establishment, house, institution, organisation, outfit, partnership, set-up, syndicate.

firmly *adv.* compactly, decisively, definitely, determinedly, doggedly, enduringly, foursquare, immovably, inflexibly, motionlessly, resolutely, robustly, securely, solidly, squarely, stably, staunchly, steadfastly, steadily, strictly, strongly, sturdily, surely, tightly, unalterably, unchangeably, unflinchingly, unshakeably, unwaveringly.

antonyms hesitantly, uncertainly, unsoundly.

firmness *n.* changelessness, compactness, constancy, conviction, density, dependability, determination, doggedness, durability, fixedness, fixity, hardness, immovability, impregnability, indomitability, inelasticity, inflexibility, obduracy, reliability, resistance, resolution, resolve, rigidity, solidity, soundness, stability, staunchness, steadfastness, steadiness, stiffness, strength, strength of will, strictness, sureness, tautness, tension, tightness, will, will-power.

antonyms infirmity, uncertainty, unsoundness.

first *adj.* basic, cardinal, chief, earliest, eldest, elementary, embryonic, foremost, fundamental, head, highest, initial, introductory, key, leading, maiden, main, oldest, opening, original, paramount, predominant, preeminent, premier, primal, primary, prime, primeval, primitive, primordial, principal, prior, pristine, rudimentary, ruling, senior, sovereign, uppermost.

adv. at the outset, before all else, beforehand, early on, firstly, in preference, in the beginning, initially, originally, primarily, rather, sooner, to begin with, to start with.

first name baptismal name, Christian name, font name, forename, given name.

first-born *adj.* aîné(e), eigne, elder, eldest, older, primogenit, senior.

first-fruits *n.* annates, primitiae, tribute.

firsthand *adj.* direct, immediate, personal, straight from the horse's mouth. *antonyms* hearsay, indirect.

first-rate *adj.* A1, admirable, crack, élite, excellent, exceptional, exclusive, fine, first-class, jake, leading, matchless, nonpareil, outstanding, peerless, prime, second-to-none, splendid, superb, superior, superlative, tip-top, top, top-flight, top-notch, tops. *antonym* inferior.

fiscal *adj.* budgetary, bursal, economic, financial, monetary, money, pecuniary, treasury.

fish *v.* angle, cast, delve, elicit, hint, hunt, invite, seek, solicit, trawl, troll.
n. aquatic, chap, drip, fellow.

fish out come up with, dredge up, extract, extricate, find, haul up, produce.

fish out of water freak, horse marine, maverick, misfit, nonconformist, rogue, square peg in a round hole. *antonym* conformist.

fisherman *n.* angler, fisher, peter-man, piscator, piscatorian, rod-fisher, rodman, rodsman, rodster.

fishing *n.* angling, fishery, halieutics, piscary, trawling, trolling.
adj. halieutic, piscatorial, piscatory.

fishy *adj.* doubtful, dubious, fish-like, funny, glassy, implausible, improbable, irregular, odd, piscatorial, piscatory, pisciform, piscine, queer, questionable, rummy, shady, suspect, suspicious, unlikely, vacant. *antonyms* honest, legitimate.

fissile *adj.* cleavable, divisible, easily split, fissionable, fissive, flaky, scissile, separable, severable.

fission *n.* breaking, cleavage, division, parting, rending, rupture, schism, scission, severance, splitting.

fissure *n.* breach, break, chasm, chink, cleavage, cleft, crack, cranny, crevasse, crevice, fault, foramen, fracture, gap, gash, grike, hole, interstice, opening, rent, rift, rupture, scissure, slit, split, sulcus, vein.

fist *n.* duke, mitt, nieve, paw, pud, puddy.

fit¹ *adj.* able, able-bodied, adapted, adequate, apposite, appropriate, apt, becoming, blooming, capable, commensurate, competent, condign, convenient, correct, deserving, due, eligible, equipped, expedient, fit as a fiddle, fitted, fitting, hale, hale and hearty, healthy, in fine fettle, in good form, in good nick, in good shape, in good trim, in the pink, meet, prepared, proper, qualified, ready, right, robust, satisfactory, seemly, sound, strapping, strong, sturdy, suitable, suited, trained, trim, well, well-suited, worthy. *antonym* unfit.
v. accommodate, accord, adapt, adjust,

agree, alter, arrange, assimilate, belong, change, concur, conform, correspond, dispose, dovetail, fashion, fay, figure, follow, gee, go, harmonise, interlock, join, match, meet, modify, place, position, reconcile, shape, suit, tally.

fit out accommodate, accoutre, arm, caparison, equip, kit out, outfit, prepare, provide, rig out, supply.

fit² *n.* access, attack, bout, burst, caprice, convulsion, eruption, exies, explosion, fancy, humour, mood, outbreak, outburst, paroxysm, seizure, spasm, spell, storm, surge, whim.

fitful *adj.* broken, desultory, disturbed, erratic, fluctuating, haphazard, intermittent, irregular, occasional, spasmodic, sporadic, uneven, unstable, unsteady, variable. *antonyms* regular, steady.

fitfully *adv.* desultorily, erratically, haphazardly, in fits and starts, in snatches, intermittently, interruptedly, irregularly, off and on, spasmodically, sporadically, unevenly, unsteadily. *antonyms* regularly, steadily.

fitness *n.* adaptation, adequacy, applicability, appropriateness, aptness, competence, condition, eligibility, haleness, health, healthiness, pertinence, preparedness, propriety, qualifications, readiness, robustness, seemliness, strength, suitability, vigour. *antonym* unfitness.

fitted *adj.* accoutred, adapted, appointed, armed, booted and spurred, built-in, caparisoned, equipped, fit, furnished, kitted, outfitted, permanent, prepared, provided, qualified, rigged out, right, suitable, supplied, tailor-made. *antonym* unfitted.

fitting *adj.* apposite, appropriate, apt, becoming, comme il faut, condign, correct, decent, decorous, deserved, desirable, harmonious, meet, merited, proper, right, seasonable, seemly, suitable. *antonym* unsuitable.
n. accessory, attachment, component, connection, fitment, fixture, part, piece, unit.

fittings *n.* accessories, accoutrements, appointments, appurtenances, conveniences, equipment, extras, fitments, fixtures, furnishings, furniture, plenishing, trimmings.

fivefold *adj.* pentaploid, quintuple, quintuplicate.

fix¹ *v.* adjust, agree on, anchor, appoint, arrange, arrive at, attach, bind, cement, conclude, confirm, congeal, connect, consolidate, correct, couple, decide, define, determine, direct, embed, establish, fasten, fiddle, finalise, firm, focus, freeze, glue, harden, implant, inculcate, influence, install, irradicate, limit, link, locate, make, manipulate, manoeuvre, mend, nail, name, ordain, pin, place, plant, point, position, prearrange, preordain, produce, regulate, repair, resolve, restore, rigidify, rigidise, rivet, root, seal, seat, secure, see to, set, settle, solidify, sort,

sort out, specify, stabilise, stick, stiffen, straighten, swing, thicken, tidy, tie.

n. corner, difficulty, dilemma, embarrassment, hole, jam, mess, muddle, nineholes, pickle, plight, predicament, quagmire, quandary, scrape, spot.

fix up accommodate, agree on, arrange (for), bring about, equip, fix, furnish, lay on, organise, plan, produce, provide, settle, sort out, supply.

fix² *n.* dose, hit, injection, jag, score, shot, slug.

fixation *n.* complex, compulsion, fetish, hangup, idée fixe, infatuation, mania, monomania, obsession, preoccupation, thing.

fixed *adj.* agreed, anchored, arranged, attached, decided, definite, determinate, entrenched, established, fast, fiddled, fiducial, firm, framed, immovable, inflexible, ingrained, intent, invariable, lasting, level, manipulated, packed, permanent, planned, put-up, radicate, resolute, resolved, rigged, rigid, rooted, secure, set, settled, standing, steadfast, steady, sure, unalterable, unbending, unblinking, unchanging, undeviating, unflinching, unvarying, unwavering, unyielding.
antonyms alterable, variable.

fixity *n.* determination, doggedness, fixedness, intentness, perseverance, persistence, resoluteness, resolve, stability, steadiness, strength, tenacity.

fizz *v.* bubble, effervesce, fizzle, froth, fume, hiss, sizzle, sparkle, spit, sputter.

fizzle out abort, collapse, come to nothing, die away, die down, disappear, dissipate, evaporate, fail, fall through, fold, peter out, stop, subside, taper off.

fizzy *adj.* aerated, bubbling, bubbly, carbonated, effervescent, frothy, gassy, sparkling.

flabbergasted *adj.* amazed, astonished, astounded, bowled over, confounded, dazed, disconcerted, dumbfounded, nonplussed, overcome, overwhelmed, speechless, staggered, stunned, stupefied.

flabbiness *n.* bloat, bloatedness, embonpoint, fat, flab, flaccidity, flesh, fleshiness, heaviness, laxness, limpness, looseness, overweight, pendulousness, plumpness, slackness.
antonyms firmness, leanness, strength.

flabby *adj.* baggy, drooping, effete, enervated, feckless, feeble, flaccid, fleshy, floppy, fushionless, hanging, impotent, ineffective, ineffectual, inert, lax, limp, loose, nerveless, pendulous, plump, sagging, slack, sloppy, spineless, toneless, unfit, weak, yielding.
antonyms firm, lean, strong.

flaccid *adj.* clammy, drooping, flabby, floppy, hypotonic, inert, lax, limp, loose, nerveless, relaxed, sagging, slack, soft, toneless, weak.
antonym firm.

flaccidity *n.* clamminess, droopiness, flabbiness, floppiness, limpness, looseness, nervelessness, slackness, softness, tonelessness.
antonym firmness.

flag¹ *v.* abate, decline, degenerate, deteriorate, die, diminish, droop, dwindle, ebb, fade, fail,

faint, fall (off), falter, flop, languish, lessen, peter out, sag, sink, slow, slump, subside, succumb, taper off, tire, wane, weaken, weary, wilt.
antonym revive.

flag² *n.* banderole, banner, burgee, colours, ensign, fanion, gonfalon, jack, Jolly Roger, labarum, oriflamme, pennant, pennon, pen(n)oncel(le), standard, streamer, vane.

v. docket, hail, indicate, label, mark, motion, note, salute, signal, tab, tag, warn, wave.

flagellation *n.* beating, castigation, chastisement, flaying, flogging, lashing, scourging, thrashing, vapulation, verberation, whaling, whipping.

flagging *adj.* declining, decreasing, deteriorating, diminishing, drooping, dwindling, ebbing, fading, failing, faltering, lessening, sagging, sinking, slowing, subsiding, tiring, waning, weakening, wilting.
antonyms returning, reviving.

flagrant *adj.* arrant, atrocious, audacious, barefaced, blatant, bold, brazen, conspicuous, crying, egregious, enormous, flagitious, flaunting, glaring, heinous, immodest, infamous, notorious, open, ostentatious, outrageous, overt, rank, scandalous, shameless, unashamed, undisguised.
antonyms covert, secret.

flail *v.* beat, scutch, swinge, thrash, thresh, whip.

flair *n.* ability, accomplishment, acumen, aptitude, chic, dash, discernment, elegance, facility, faculty, feel, genius, gift, knack, mastery, nose, panache, skill, style, stylishness, talent, taste.
antonym ineptitude.

flak *n.* abuse, animadversions, aspersions, bad press, brickbats, censure, complaints, condemnation, criticism, disapprobation, disapproval, disparagement, fault-finding, hostility, invective, opposition, stick, strictures.

flake *n.* chip, disc, flaught, floccule, flocculus, lamina, layer, paring, peeling, scale, shaving, sliver, squama, wafer.

v. blister, chip, delaminate, desquamate, exfoliate, peel, scale.

flaky *adj.* desquamative, desquamatory, dry, exfoliative, furfuraceous, laminar, layered, scabrous, scaly, scurfy.

flamboyance *n.* brilliance, colour, dash, élan, extravagance, glamour, ostentation, panache, pizzazz, showiness, style, theatricality.
antonyms diffidence, restraint.

flamboyant *adj.* baroque, brilliant, colourful, dashing, dazzling, elaborate, exciting, extravagant, flashy, florid, gaudy, glamorous, jaunty, ornate, ostentatious, rich, showy, striking, stylish, swashbuckling, theatrical.
antonyms modest, restrained.

flame *v.* beam, blaze, burn, flare, flash, glare, glow, radiate, shine.

n. affection, ardour, beau, blaze, brightness, enthusiasm, fervency, fervour, fire, flake, flammule, heart-throb, intensity, keenness, light, lover, passion, radiance, sweetheart, warmth, zeal.

flaming *adj.* ablaze, afire, alight, angry, ardent, aroused, blazing, brilliant, burning, fervid, fiery, frenzied, glowing, hot, impassioned, intense, raging, red, red-hot, scintillating, smouldering, vehement, vivid.

flammable *adj.* combustible, combustive, deflagrable, ignitable, inflammable.
antonyms fire-resistant, flameproof, incombustible, non-flammable, non-inflammable.

flange *n.* flanch, flare, lip, rim, skirt, splay.

flank *n.* edge, flitch, ham, haunch, hip, loin, quarter, side, thigh, wing.
v. accompany, border, bound, confine, edge, fringe, line, screen, skirt, wall.

flap[1] *v.* agitate, beat, dither, flacker, flaff, flaffer, flail, flutter, fuss, panic, shake, swing, swish, thrash, thresh, vibrate, wag, wave.
n. agitation, commotion, dither, fluster, flutter, fuss, kerfuffle, pother, state, stew, sweat, tizzy, twitter.

flap[2] *n.* aileron, apron, cover, fly, fold, lapel, lappet, lug, overlap, skirt, slat, tab, tag, tail.

flare *v.* blaze, burn (up), burst, dazzle, erupt, explode, flame, flash, flicker, flutter, fulgurate, glare, waver.
n. bell-bottom, blaze, broadening, burst, dazzle, flame, flanch, flange, flash, flicker, glare, gore, splay, widening.
flare out broaden, flanch, flaunch, splay, spread out, widen.
flare up blaze, blow one's top, erupt, explode, fly off the handle, lose one's cool.

flash *v.* blaze, bolt, brandish, coruscate, dart, dash, display, exhibit, expose, flare, flaunt, flicker, flourish, fly, fulgurate, fulminate, glare, gleam, glint, glisten, glitter, light, race, scintillate, shimmer, shoot, show, sparkle, speed, sprint, streak, sweep, twinkle, whistle.
n. blaze, bluette, burst, coruscation, dazzle, demonstration, display, flare, flaught, flicker, fulguration, gleam, hint, instant, jiff, jiffy, manifestation, moment, outburst, ray, scintillation, second, shaft, shake, shimmer, show, sign, spark, sparkle, split second, streak, touch, trice, twinkle, twinkling.

flashing *adj.* coruscant, coruscating, dancing, flaring, flickering, fulgid, fulgurant, fulgurous, glittering, lambent, scintillating, sparkling, twinkling.
antonym steady.

flashy *adj.* bold, brassy, cheap, flamboyant, flash, garish, gaudy, glamorous, glittery, glitzy, jazzy, loud, meretricious, obtrusive, ostentatious, raffish, rakish, ritzy, showy, snazzy, tacky, tasteless, tawdry, tig(e)rish, tinselly, vulgar.
antonyms plain, simple, tasteful.

flask *n.* carafe, flacket, lekythos, matrass, pocket-pistol.

flat[1] *adj.* even, horizontal, lamellar, lamelliform, level, levelled, low, outstretched, planar, plane, prone, prostrate, reclining, recumbent, smooth, spread-eagled, supine, unbroken, uniform.

n. lowland, marsh, morass, moss, mud flat, plain, shallow, shoal, strand, swamp.
flat out all out, at full speed, at full tilt, at top speed, double-quick, for all one is worth, hell for leather, posthaste.

flat[2] *adj.* bored, boring, burst, collapsed, dead, deflated, depressed, dull, empty, flavourless, insipid, jejune, lacklustre, lifeless, monotonous, pointless, prosaic, punctured, spiritless, stale, tedious, uninteresting, unpalatable, vapid, watery, weak.

flat[3] *adj.* absolute, categorical, direct, downright, explicit, final, fixed, out-and-out, peremptory, plain, point-blank, positive, straight, total, uncompromising, unconditional, unequivocal, unqualified.
antonym equivocal.
adv. absolutely, categorically, completely, entirely, exactly, point-blank, precisely, totally, utterly.

flat[4] *n.* apartment, bed-sit, bed-sitter, maison(n)ette, pad, penthouse, pied-à-terre, rooms, tenement.

flatly *adv.* absolutely, categorically, completely, peremptorily, point-blank, positively, uncompromisingly, unconditionally, unhesitatingly.

flatness *n.* boredom, dullness, emptiness, evenness, horizontality, insipidity, languor, levelness, monotony, smoothness, staleness, tastelessness, tedium, uniformity, vapidity.

flatten *v.* compress, crush, demolish, even out, fell, floor, iron out, knock down, level, overwhelm, planish, plaster, prostrate, raze, roll, slight, smooth, squash, subdue, trample.

flatter *v.* adulate, become, beslobber, blandish, blarney, butter up, cajole, claw, collogue, compliment, court, enhance, eulogise, fawn, flannel, fleech, gloze, humour, inveigle, laud, play up to, praise, sawder, set off, show to advantage, soap, soft-soap, soothe, suit, sweet-talk, sycophantise, wheedle.
antonym criticise.

flatterer *n.* adulator, back-scratcher, bootlicker, earwig, encomiast, eulogiser, fawner, flunkey, groveller, incenser, lackey, sycophant, toady.
antonyms critic, opponent.

flattering *adj.* adulatory, becoming, complimentary, effective, effusive, enhancing, favourable, fawning, fulsome, gnathonic, gratifying, honeyed, honey-tongued, ingratiating, kind, laudatory, obsequious, servile, smooth-spoken, smooth-tongued, sugared, sugary, sycophantic, unctuous.
antonyms candid, uncompromising, unflattering.

flattery *n.* adulation, backscratching, blandishment, blarney, bootlicking, butter, cajolement, cajolery, eulogy, fawning, flannel, flapdoodle, fleechment, fulsomeness, ingratiation, obsequiousness, servility, soap, soft sawder, soft soap, sugar, sweet talk, sycophancy, sycophantism, taffy, toadyism, unctuousness.
antonym criticism.

flatulence n. borborygmus, eructation, flatulency, flatus, gas, gassiness, pomposity, prolixity, turgidity, ventosity, wind, windiness.

flatulent v. gassy, pompous, prolix, swollen, turgid, ventose, windy.

flaunt v. air, boast, brandish, dangle, display, disport, exhibit, flash, flourish, parade, show off, sport, vaunt, wield.

flavour n. aroma, aspect, character, essence, extract, feel, feeling, flavouring, hint, odour, piquancy, property, quality, relish, sapidity, savour, savouriness, seasoning, smack, soupçon, stamp, style, suggestion, tang, taste, tastiness, tinge, tone, touch, zest, zing.
v. contaminate, ginger up, imbue, infuse, lace, leaven, season, spice, taint.

flavourful adj. delicious, flavorous, flavoursome, high-tasted, palatable, sapid, savoury, tasty, toothsome.
antonyms insipid, tasteless.

flavouring n. essence, extract, seasoning, spirit, tincture, zest.

flaw n. blemish, breach, break, cleft, crack, craze, crevice, defect, disfigurement, failing, fallacy, fault, fissure, fracture, hamartia, imperfection, lapse, macula, mark, mistake, rent, rift, shortcoming, slip, speck, split, spot, tear, weakness, wreath.

flawed adj. blemished, broken, chipped, cracked, damaged, defective, disfigured, erroneous, faulty, imperfect, marked, marred, spoilt, unsound, vicious, vitiated.
antonyms flawless, perfect.

flawless adj. faultless, immaculate, impeccable, intact, irreproachable, perfect, sound, spotless, stainless, unblemished, unbroken, undamaged, unsullied, whole.
antonyms flawed, imperfect.

flay v. castigate, excoriate, execrate, flench, flog, lambast, pull to pieces, revile, scourge, skin, skin alive, tear a strip off, upbraid.

flea-ridden adj. crawling, decrepit, dingy, flea-bitten, fly-blown, frowsty, grotty, grubby, infested, insalubrious, lousy, mangy, mean, moth-eaten, mucky, pediculous, run-down, scabby, scruffy, scurfy, sleazy, slummy, sordid, squalid, tatty, unhealthy, unhygienic.
antonym salubrious.

fleck v. bespeckle, besprinkle, dapple, dot, dust, freak, mark, mottle, speckle, spinkle, spot, stipple, streak, variegate.
n. dot, freak, macula, mark, point, speck, speckle, spot, streak.

fledgling n. apprentice, beginner, chick, greenhorn, learner, neophyte, nestling, newcomer, novice, novitiate, recruit, rookie, tenderfoot, trainee, tyro.

flee v. abscond, avoid, beat a hasty retreat, bolt, bunk (off), cut and run, decamp, depart, escape, fly, get away, leave, make off, make oneself scarce, scarper, scram, shun, skedaddle, split, take flight, take it on the lam, take off, take to one's heels, vamoose, vanish, withdraw.
antonyms stand, stay.

fleece v. bilk, bleed, cheat, clip, con, defraud, diddle, mulct, overcharge, plunder, rifle, rip off, rob, rook, shear, skin, soak, squeeze, steal, sting, swindle.

fleecy adj. downy, eriophorous, floccose, flocculate, fluffy, hairy, lanuginose, nappy, pilose, shaggy, soft, velvety, woolly.
antonyms bald, smooth.

fleet[1] n. argosy, armada, escadrille, flota, flotilla, navy, squadron, task force.

fleet[2] adj. expeditious, fast, flying, light-footed, mercurial, meteoric, nimble, quick, rapid, speedy, swift, velocipede, winged.
antonym slow.

fleeting adj. brief, disappearing, ephemeral, evanescent, flitting, flying, fugacious, fugitive, impermanent, momentary, passing, short, short-lived, temporary, transient, transitory, vanishing.
antonym lasting.

fleetness n. celerity, dispatch, expedition, expeditiousness, light-footedness, nimbleness, quickness, rapidity, speed, speediness, swiftness, velocity.
antonym sluggishness.

flesh n. animality, beef, blood, body, brawn, carnality, corporeality, dead-meat, family, fat, fatness, flesh and blood, food, human nature, kin, kindred, kinsfolk, kith and kin, matter, meat, physicality, pulp, relations, relatives, sensuality, substance, tissue.

fleshiness n. adiposity, chubbiness, corpulence, embonpoint, flabbiness, heaviness, obesity, plumpness, portliness, stoutness, tubbiness.

fleshly adj. animal, bestial, bodily, brutish, carnal, corporal, corporeal, earthly, earthy, erotic, human, lustful, material, mundane, physical, secular, sensual, terrestrial, wordly.
antonym spiritual.

fleshy adj. ample, beefy, brawny, carneous, carnose, chubby, chunky, corpulent, fat, flabby, hefty, meaty, obese, overweight, paunchy, plump, podgy, portly, rotund, stout, tubby, well-padded.
antonym thin.

flex v. angle, bend, bow, contract, crook, curve, double up, ply, tighten.
antonyms extend, straighten.

flexibility n. adaptability, adjustability, agreeability, amenability, bendability, complaisance, elasticity, flexion, give, pliability, pliancy, resilience, spring, springiness, suppleness, tensility.
antonym inflexibility.

flexible adj. accommodating, adaptable, adjustable, agreeable, amenable, bendable, biddable, complaisant, compliant, discretionary, docile, double-jointed, ductile, elastic, flexile, gentle, limber, lissome, lithe, loose-limbed, manageable, mobile, mouldable, open, plastic, pliable, pliant, responsive, springy, stretchy, supple, tensile, tractable, variable, whippy, willowy, withy, yielding.
antonym inflexible.

flibbertigibbet n. backfisch, bird-brain, butterfly,

featherbrain, fizgig, flapper, giddy goat, madcap, rattle-brain, rattle-head, rattle-pate, scatterbrain, tearaway.

flick v. bat, click, dab, fillip, flap, flicker, flip, flirt, hit, jab, peck, rap, strike, tap, touch, whip.
n. click, fillip, flap, flip, flutter, jab, peck, rap, tap, touch.

flick through flip, glance, riffle, scan, skim, skip, thumb.

flicker v. coruscate, flare, flash, flutter, glimmer, gutter, quiver, scintillate, shimmer, sparkle, twinkle, vibrate, waver.
n. atom, breath, coruscation, drop, flare, flash, gleam, glimmer, glint, indication, inkling, iota, scintillation, spark, trace, vestige.

flickering n. coruscant, coruscating, guttering, lambent, sparkling, twinkling, unsteady.

flight[1] n. aeronautics, air transport, air travel, aviation, cloud, echelon, escadrille, flip, flock, flying, formation, journey, mounting, soaring, squadron, swarm, trip, unit, volitation, voyage, wing, winging.

flight[2] n. breakaway, departure, escape, exit, exodus, fleeing, getaway, guy, hegira, retreat, running away.

flightiness n. capriciousness, changeability, dizziness, fickleness, flippancy, frivolity, giddiness, inconstancy, irresponsibility, levity, lightness, mercurialness, volatility, wildness.
antonym steadiness.

flighty adj. bird-brained, bird-witted, capricious, changeable, dizzy, fickle, frivolous, giddy, hare-brained, impetuous, impulsive, inconstant, irresponsible, light-headed, mercurial, rattle-brained, rattle-headed, rattle-pated, scatterbrained, silly, skittish, thoughtless, unbalanced, unstable, unsteady, volage, volageous, volatile, whisky-frisky, wild.
antonym steady.

flimsy adj. cardboard, chiffon, cobwebby, delicate, diaphanous, ethereal, feeble, fragile, frail, frivolous, gauzy, gimcrack, gossamer, implausible, inadequate, insubstantial, light, makeshift, meagre, poor, rickety, shaky, shallow, sheer, slight, superficial, thin, transparent, trivial, unconvincing, unsatisfactory, unsubstantial, vaporous, weak.
antonym sturdy.

flinch v. baulk, blench, cower, cringe, draw back, duck, flee, quail, quake, recoil, retreat, shake, shirk, shiver, shrink, shudder, shy away, start, swerve, tremble, wince, withdraw.

fling v. bung, cant, cast, catapult, chuck, heave, hurl, jerk, let fly, lob, pitch, precipitate, propel, send, shoot, shy, sling, slug, souse, throw, toss.
n. attempt, bash, binge, cast, crack, gamble, go, heave, indulgence, lob, pitch, shot, spree, stab, throw, toss, trial, try, turn, venture, whirl.

flip v. cast, fillip, flap, flick, jerk, pitch, snap, spin, throw, toss, turn, twirl, twist.
n. bob, fillip, flap, flick, jerk, toss, turn, twirl, twist.

flippancy n. cheek, cheekiness, disrespect, disrespectfulness, frivolity, glibness, impertinence, irreverence, levity, persiflage, pertness, sauciness, superficiality.
antonym earnestness.

flippant adj. brash, cheeky, cocky, disrespectful, flip, frivolous, glib, impertinent, impudent, irreverent, malapert, nonchalant, offhand, pert, pococurante, rude, saucy, superficial, unserious.
antonym earnest.

flirt v. chat up, coquet, dally, ogle, philander, tease.
n. chippy, coquet(te), gillet, gillflirt, heartbreaker, hussy, philanderer, tease, trifler, wanton.

flirt with consider, dabble in, entertain, make up to, play with, toy with, trifle with, try.

flirtation n. affair, amorousness, amour, chatting up, coquetry, dalliance, dallying, intrigue, philandering, sport, teasing, toying, trifling.

flirtatious adj. amorous, arch, come-hither, come-on, coquettish, coy, flirty, loose, promiscuous, provocative, sportive, teasing, wanton.

flit v. beat, bob, dance, dart, elapse, flash, fleet, flutter, fly, pass, skim, slip, speed, volitate, whisk, wing.

flitting adj. bobbing, dancing, darting, ephemeral, fleet, fleeting, flittering, fluttering, skimming, volitant.

float v. bob, drift, glide, hang, hover, initiate, launch, poise, promote, ride, sail, set up, slide, swim, waft.
antonym sink.

floating adj. afloat, bobbing, buoyant, buoyed up, fluctuating, free, migratory, movable, ocean-going, sailing, swimming, unattached, uncommitted, unfixed, unsinkable, unsubmerged, variable, wandering, water-borne.

flock v. bunch, cluster, collect, congregate, converge, crowd, gather, gravitate, group, herd, huddle, mass, swarm, throng, troop.
n. assembly, bevy, collection, colony, company, congregation, convoy, crowd, drove, flight, gaggle, gathering, group, herd, horde, host, mass, multitude, pack, shoal, skein, swarm, throng.

flog v. beat, birch, breech, chastise, drive, drub, flagellate, flay, hide, knout, k(o)urbash, larrup, lash, overexert, overtax, overwork, punish, push, scourge, strain, swish, tat, tax, thrash, trounce, vapulate, verberate, welt, whack, whale, whang, whip, whop.

flogging n. beating, caning, drubbing, flagellation, flaying, hiding, horsewhipping, lashing, scourging, thrashing, trouncing, vapulation, verberation, whaling, whipping, whopping.

flood v. bog down, brim, choke, deluge, drench, drown, engulf, fill, flow, glut, gush, immerse, inundate, overflow, oversupply, overwhelm, pour, rush, saturate, soak, submerge, surge, swamp, swarm, sweep.

n. abundance, alluvion, bore, cataclysm, debacle, deluge, diluvion, diluvium, downpour, eagre, flash flood, flow, freshet, glut, inundation, multitude, outpouring, overflow, plethora, profusion, rush, spate, stream, superfluity, tide, torrent.
antonyms dearth, drought, trickle.

floor *n.* base, basis, deck, étage, landing, level, stage, storey, tier.
v. baffle, beat, bewilder, confound, conquer, defeat, discomfit, disconcert, down, dumbfound, frustrate, nonplus, overthrow, overwhelm, perplex, prostrate, puzzle, stump, stun, throw, trounce, worst.

flop *v.* bomb, close, collapse, dangle, droop, drop, fail, fall, fall flat, flap, flump, fold, founder, hang, misfire, plump, sag, slump, topple, tumble.
n. balls-up, cock-up, debacle, disaster, failure, fiasco, loser, no go, non-starter, turkey, wash-out.

floppy *adj.* baggy, dangling, droopy, flabby, flaccid, flapping, flappy, flopping, hanging, limp, loose, pendulous, sagging, soft.
antonym firm.

flora *n.* botany, herbage, plantage, plant-life, plants, vegetable kingdom, vegetation.

florid *adj.* baroque, blowzy, bombastic, busy, coloratura, elaborate, embellished, euphuistic, figurative, flamboyant, flourishy, flowery, flushed, fussy, grandiloquent, high-coloured, high-falutin(g), high-flown, melismatic, ornate, overelaborate, purple, raddled, red, rococo, rubicund, ruddy.
antonyms pale, plain.

flotsam *n.* debris, detritus, jetsam, junk, oddments, scum, sweepings, waveson, wreckage.

flounce *v.* bob, bounce, fling, jerk, spring, stamp, storm, throw, toss, twist.
n. falbala, frill, fringe, furbelow, ruffle, trimming, valance.

flounder *v.* blunder, bungle, falter, flail, fumble, grope, muddle, plunge, stagger, struggle, stumble, thrash, toss, tumble, wallop, wallow, welter.

flourish[1] *v.* advance, bloom, blossom, boom, burgeon, develop, do well, flower, get on, grow, increase, mushroom, progress, prosper, succeed, thrive, wax.
antonyms fail, languish.

flourish[2] *v.* brandish, display, flaunt, flutter, parade, shake, sweep, swing, swish, twirl, vaunt, wag, wave, wield.
n. arabesque, brandishing, ceremony, curlicue, dash, decoration, display, élan, embellishment, fanfare, ornament, ornamentation, panache, parade, paraph, pizzazz, plume, shaking, show, sweep, twirling, wave.

flourishing *adj.* blooming, booming, burgeoning, developing, going strong, in the pink, lush, luxuriant, mushrooming, progressing, prospering, rampant, rank, riotous, successful, thriving.
antonyms failing, languishing.

flout *v.* affront, contemn, defy, deride, disregard, insult, jeer at, mock, outrage, reject, ridicule, scoff at, scorn, scout, spurn, taunt.
antonym respect.

flow *v.* arise, bubble, cascade, circulate, course, deluge, derive, distil, drift, emanate, emerge, flood, glide, gush, inundate, issue, move, originate, overflow, pour, proceed, purl, result, ripple, roll, run, rush, slide, slip, spew, spill, spring, spurt, squirt, stream, surge, sweep, swirl, teem, well, whirl.
n. abundance, cascade, course, current, deluge, drift, effluence, efflux, effusion, emanation, flood, flowage, flux, fluxion, gush, outflow, outpouring, plenty, plethora, spate, spurt, stream, succession, tide, train, wash.

flower *n.* best, bloom, blossom, choice, cream, crème de la crème, efflorescence, élite, fleuret, fleuron, floret, floscule, floweret, freshness, height, pick, prime, vigour.
v. blossom, blow, burgeon, dehisce, effloresce, flourish, mature, open, unfold.

flowering *adj.* blooming, bloomy, blossoming, efflorescent, florescent.
n. anthesis, blooming, blossoming, burgeoning, development, florescence, flourishing, flowerage, maturing.

flowery *adj.* affected, baroque, elaborate, embellished, euphuistic, fancy, figurative, floral, floriated, florid, fulsome, high-flown, ornate, overelaborate, overwrought, rhetorical, Wardour Street.
antonym plain.

flowing *adj.* abounding, brimming, cantabile, cascading, continuous, cursive, easy, facile, falling, flooded, fluent, full, gushing, overrun, prolific, rich, rolling, rushing, smooth, streaming, surging, sweeping, teeming, unbroken, uninterrupted, voluble.
antonyms hesitant, interrupted.

fluctuate *v.* alter, alternate, change, ebb and flow, float, hesitate, oscillate, pendulate, rise and fall, seesaw, shift, shuffle, sway, swing, undulate, vacillate, vary, veer, waver.

fluctuating *adj.* capricious, changeable, fickle, fluctuant, irresolute, mutable, oscillating, oscillatory, rising and falling, swaying, swinging, unstable, unsteady, vacillant, vacillating, vacillatory, variable, wavering.
antonym stable.

fluctuation *n.* alternation, ambivalence, capriciousness, change, ficklessness, inconstancy, instability, irresolution, oscillation, shift, swing, unsteadiness, vacillation, variability, variableness, variation, wavering.

fluency *n.* articulateness, assurance, command, control, ease, eloquence, facility, facundity, glibness, readiness, slickness, smoothness, volubility.
antonym incoherence.

fluent *adj.* articulate, easy, effortless, eloquent, facile, flowing, fluid, glib, mellifluous, natural, ready, smooth, smooth-talking, voluble, well-versed.
antonym tongue-tied.

fluff *n.* down, dust, dustball, floccus, flosh, floss, flue, fug, fuzz, lint, nap, oose, pile.
v. balls up, botch, bungle, cock up, fumble, mess up, muddle, muff, screw up, spoil.
antonym bring off.

fluffy *adj.* downy, eriophorous, feathery, fleecy, floccose, flocculate, flossy, fuzzy, gossamer, hairy, lanuginose, lanuginous, nappy, oozy, shaggy, silky, soft, velvety, woolly.
antonym smooth.

fluid *adj.* adaptable, adjustable, aqueous, changeable, diffluent, easy, elegant, feline, flexible, floating, flowing, fluctuating, fluent, fluidal, fluidic, graceful, inconstant, indefinite, liquefied, liquid, melted, mercurial, mobile, molten, mutable, protean, running, runny, shifting, sinuous, smooth, unstable, watery.
antonyms solid, stable.
n. humour, juice, liquid, liquor, sanies, sap, solution.

fluke *n.* accident, blessing, break, chance, coincidence, fortuity, freak, lucky break, quirk, serendipity, stroke, windfall.

fluky *adj.* accidental, chance, chancy, coincidental, fortuitous, fortunate, freakish, incalculable, lucky, serendipitous, uncertain.

flummox *v.* baffle, bamboozle, befuddle, bewilder, confound, confuse, defeat, fox, mystify, nonplus, perplex, puzzle, stump, stymie.

flummoxed *adj.* at a loss, at sea, baffled, befuddled, bewildered, confounded, confused, foxed, mystified, nonplussed, perplexed, puzzled, stumped, stymied.

flunkey *n.* assistant, boot-licker, creature, cringer, drudge, footman, hanger-on, healer, lackey, manservant, menial, minion, slave, toady, tool, underling, valet, yes-man.

flurry *n.* ado, agitation, burst, bustle, commotion, disturbance, excitement, ferment, flap, flaw, fluster, flutter, furore, fuss, gust, hubbub, hurry, kerfuffle, outbreak, pother, spell, spurt, squall, stir, to-do, tumult, upset, whirl.
v. abash, agitate, bewilder, bother, bustle, confuse, disconcert, discountenance, disturb, fluster, flutter, fuss, hassle, hurry, hustle, perturb, rattle, ruffle, unsettle, upset.

flush[1] *v.* blush, burn, colour, crimson, flame, glow, go red, mantle, redden, rouge, suffuse.
antonym pale.
n. bloom, blush, colour, freshness, glow, redness, rosiness, rud, vigour.

flush[2] *v.* cleanse, douche, drench, eject, empty, evacuate, expel, hose, rinse, swab, syringe, wash.
adj. abundant, affluent, full, generous, in funds, lavish, liberal, moneyed, overflowing, prodigal, prosperous, rich, rolling, wealthy, well-heeled, well-off, well-supplied, well-to-do.

flush[3] *adj.* even, flat, level, plane, smooth, square, true.

flush[4] *v.* discover, disturb, drive out, force out, rouse, run to earth, start, uncover.

flushed *adj.* ablaze, aflame, aglow, animated, aroused, blowzy, blushing, burning, crimson, elated, embarrassed, enthused, excited, exhilarated, exultant, febrile, feverish, glowing, hectic, high, hot, inspired, intoxicated, red, rosy, rubicund, ruddy, sanguine, scarlet, thrilled.
antonym pale.

fluster *v.* abash, agitate, bother, bustle, confound, confuse, discombobulate, disconcert, discountenance, disturb, embarrass, excite, faze, flurry, hassle, heat, hurry, perturb, pother, pudder, rattle, ruffle, unnerve, unsettle, upset.
antonym calm.
n. agitation, bustle, commotion, discomposure, distraction, disturbance, dither, embarrassment, faze, flap, flurry, flutter, furore, kerfuffle, perturbation, ruffle, state, tizzy, turmoil.
antonym calm.

fluted *adj.* chamfered, channelled, corrugated, furrowed, gouged, grooved, ribbed, ridged, rutted, valleculate.

flutter *v.* agitate, bat, beat, dance, discompose, flap, flichter, flicker, flit, flitter, fluctuate, hover, palpitate, quiver, ripple, ruffle, shiver, toss, tremble, vibrate, volitate, wave, waver.
n. agitation, commotion, confusion, discomposure, dither, excitement, flurry, fluster, nervousness, palpitation, perturbation, quiver, quivering, shiver, shudder, state, tremble, tremor, tumult, twitching, upset, vibration, volitation.

fluttering *adj.* beating, dancing, flapping, flickering, flitting, hovering, palpitating, quivering, tossing, trembling, volitant, waving.

flux *n.* alteration, change, chaos, development, flow, fluctuation, fluidity, instability, modification, motion, movement, mutability, mutation, stir, transition, unrest.
antonym stability.

fly[1] *v.* abscond, aviate, avoid, bolt, career, clear out, dart, dash, decamp, disappear, display, elapse, escape, flap, flee, flit, float, flutter, get away, glide, hare, hasten, hasten away, hedge-hop, hightail it, hoist, hover, hurry, light out, mount, operate, pass, pilot, race, raise, retreat, roll by, run, run for it, rush, sail, scamper, scarper, scoot, shoot, show, shun, skim, soar, speed, sprint, take flight, take off, take to one's heels, take wing, tear, vamoose, volitate, wave, whisk, whiz, wing, zoom.
fly at assail, assault, attack, fall upon, go for, have at, light into, pitch into, rush at.
fly in the face of affront, defy, disobey, flout, insult, oppose.

fly[2] *adj.* alert, artful, astute, canny, careful, cunning, knowing, nobody's fool, on the ball, prudent, sagacious, sharp, shrewd, smart, wide-awake.

fly-by-night *adj.* brief, cowboy, discreditable, disreputable, dubious, ephemeral, here today - gone tomorrow, impermanent, irresponsi-

ble, questionable, shady, short-lived, undependable, unreliable, untrustworthy.
antonym reliable.

flying *adj.* airborne, brief, express, fast, flapping, fleet, fleeting, floating, fluttering, fugacious, fugitive, gliding, hasty, hovering, hurried, mercurial, mobile, rapid, rushed, short-lived, soaring, speedy, streaming, transitory, vanishing, volant, volatic, volitant, volitational, volitorial, waving, wind-borne, winged, winging.

foam *n.* barm, bubbles, effervescence, foaminess, froth, frothiness, head, lather, scum, spume, spumescence, suds.
v. boil, bubble, effervesce, fizz, froth, lather, spume.

foamy *adj.* barmy, bubbly, foaming, frothy, lathery, spumescent, spumous, spumy, sudsy.

fob off appease, deceive, dump, foist, get rid of, give a sop to, impose, inflict, palm off, pass off, placate, put off, stall, unload.

focus *n.* axis, centre, centre of attraction, core, crux, cynosure, focal point, headquarters, heart, hinge, hub, kernel, linchpin, nucleus, pivot, target.
v. aim, centre, concentrate, concentre, converge, direct, fix, focalise, home in, join, meet, rivet, spotlight, zero in, zoom in.

fodder *n.* browsing, feed, food, foodstuff, forage, fuel, nourishment, pabulum, provand, provend, provender, proviant, rations, silage.

foe *n.* adversary, antagonist, enemy, foeman, ill-wisher, opponent, rival.
antonym friend.

fog *n.* bewilderment, blanket, blindness, brume, confusion, daze, gloom, haze, London particular, miasma, mist, muddle, murk, murkiness, obscurity, pea-souper, perplexity, puzzlement, smog, stupor, trance, vagueness.
v. becloud, bedim, befuddle, bewilder, blanket, blind, cloud, confuse, darken, daze, dim, dull, mist, muddle, obfuscate, obscure, perplex, shroud, steam up, stupefy.

fog(e)y *n.* anachronism, antique, archaism, dodo, eccentric, fossil, fuddy-duddy, mossback, mumpsimus, oddity, period piece, relic, square, stick-in-the-mud.

foggy *adj.* beclouded, befuddled, bewildered, blurred, blurry, brumous, clouded, cloudy, confused, dark, dazed, dim, grey, hazy, indistinct, misty, muddled, muggish, muggy, murky, muzzy, nebulous, obscure, shadowy, smoggy, stupefied, stupid, unclear, vague, vaporous.
antonym clear.

foible *n.* crotchet, defect, eccentricity, failing, fault, habit, idiosyncrasy, imperfection, infirmity, oddity, oddness, peculiarity, quirk, shortcoming, strangeness, weakness.

foil[1] *v.* baffle, balk, check, checkmate, circumvent, counter, defeat, disappoint, elude, frustrate, nullify, obstruct, outsmart, outwit, spike (someone's) guns, stop, stump, thwart.
antonym abet.

foil[2] *n.* antithesis, background, balance, complement, contrast, relief, setting.

foist *v.* fob off, force, get rid of, impose, insert, insinuate, interpolate, introduce, palm off, pass off, thrust, unload, wish on.

fold *v.* bend, clasp, close, collapse, crash, crease, crimp, crumple, dog-ear, double, embrace, enclose, enfold, entwine, envelop, fail, fake, gather, go bust, hug, intertwine, overlap, pleat, ply, shut down, tuck, wrap, wrap up.
n. bend, corrugation, crease, crimp, duplicature, furrow, knife-edge, layer, overlap, pleat, ply, turn, wimple, wrinkle.

folder *n.* binder, envelope, file, folio, holder, portfolio.

foliage *n.* foliation, foliature, frondescence, greenery, leafage, verdure, vernation.

folk *n.* clan, family, kin, kindred, kinfolk, kinsmen, nation, people, race, society, tribe.
adj. ancestral, ethnic, indigenous, national, native, traditional, tribal.

folklore *n.* fables, folk-tales, legends, lore, mythology, myths, superstitions, tales, tradition.

follow *v.* accompany, accord, act according to, appreciate, arise, attend, catch, catch on, chase, come after, come next, comply, comprehend, conform, cultivate, dangle, develop, dog, emanate, ensue, escort, fathom, get, get the picture, grasp, haunt, heed, hound, hunt, imitate, keep abreast of, live up to, mind, note, obey, observe, pursue, realise, regard, result, second, see, shadow, stag, stalk, succeed, supersede, supervene, supplant, support, tag along, tail, track, trail, twig, understand, watch.
antonyms desert, precede.

follow through complete, conclude, consummate, continue, finish, fulfil, implement, pursue, see through.

follow up check out, consolidate, continue, investigate, pursue, reinforce, substantiate.

follower *n.* acolyte, adherent, admirer, Anthony, apostle, attendant, backer, believer, buff, cohort, companion, convert, devotee, disciple, emulator, fan, fancier, freak, galloglass, habitué, hanger-on, heeler, helper, henchman, imitator, lackey, minion, partisan, poodle-dog, poursuivant, pupil, representative, retainer, running dog, servitor, sidekick, supporter, tantony, votary, worshipper.
antonyms leader, opponent.

following *adj.* coming, consecutive, consequent, consequential, ensuing, later, next, resulting, sequent, subsequent, succeeding, successive.
n. audience, backing, circle, claque, clientèle, coterie, entourage, fans, followers, patronage, public, retinue, suite, support, supporters, train.

folly[1] *n.* absurdity, craziness, daftness, fatuity, foolishness, idiocy, illogicality, imbecility, imprudence, indiscretion, insanity, irrationality, irresponsibility, lunacy, madness, moonraking, moria, nonsense, preposterousness, rashness, recklessness, senselessness, silliness, stupidity, unreason, unwisdom.

antonym prudence.

folly[2] *n.* belvedere, gazebo, monument, tower, whim.

foment *v.* activate, agitate, arouse, brew, encourage, excite, foster, goad, incite, instigate, kindle, promote, prompt, provoke, quicken, raise, rouse, spur, stimulate, stir up, whip up, work up.

antonym quell.

fomenter *n.* abettor, agitator, demagogue, firebrand, incendiary, inciter, instigator, mob-orator, rabble-rouser, troublemaker, tub-thumper.

fond *adj.* absurd, adoring, affectionate, amorous, caring, credulous, deluded, devoted, doting, empty, foolish, indiscreet, indulgent, loving, naive, over-optimistic, sanguine, tender, uxorious, vain, warm.

antonyms hostile, realistic.

fond of addicted to, attached to, enamoured of, hooked on, keen on, partial to, predisposed towards, stuck on, sweet on.

fondle *v.* caress, cocker, coddle, cuddle, dandle, lallygag, pat, pet, smuggle, stroke.

fondly *adv.* absurdly, adoringly, affectionately, credulously, dearly, foolishly, indulgently, lovingly, naïvely, over-optimistically, sanguinely, stupidly, tenderly, vainly.

fondness *n.* affection, attachment, devotion, engouement, enthusiasm, fancy, inclination, kindness, leaning, liking, love, partiality, penchant, predilection, preference, soft spot, susceptibility, taste, tenderness, weakness.

antonym aversion.

food *n.* aliment, ambrosia, board, bread, cheer, chow, comestibles, commons, cooking, cuisine, diet, eatables, eats, edibles, fare, feed, fodder, foodstuffs, forage, grub, larder, meat, menu, nosh, nourishment, nouriture, nutriment, nutrition, pabulum, pap, prog, provand, provend, provender, proviant, provisions, rations, refreshment, scoff, scran, stores, subsistence, sustenance, table, tack, tommy, tuck, tucker, viands, victuals, vittles, vivers.

fool *n.* ass, bécasse, berk, besom-head, bête, bird-brain, blockhead, bonehead, boodle, buffethead, buffoon, burk, butt, capocchia, Charlie, chump, clodpate, clot, clown, cluck, comic, coxcomb, cuckoo, daftie, daw, dawcock, dimwit, dizzard, Dogberry, dolt, dope, dottle, droll, drongo, dumb-bell, dumb-cluck, dumbo, dunce, dunderhead, dunderpate, dupe, easy mark, fall guy, fathead, fon, galah, gaupus, git, goon, goop, goose, greenhorn, gudgeon, gull, halfwit, harlequin, idiot, ignoramus, illiterate, imbecile, jackass, Jack-fool, jerk, jester, jobernowl, josh, joskin, leather-head, loggerhead, log-head, loon, madhaun, merry-andrew, mooncalf, moron, motley, mug, nig-nog, nincompoop, ninny, nit, nitwit, nong, noodle, numskull, pierrot, pot-head, prat, prick, punchinello, sap, saphead, sawney, schmo, schmuck, silly, silly-billy, simpleton, soft, soft-head, softie,

softy, stooge, stupe, stupid, sucker, tomfool, Tom-noddy, turnip, twerp, twit, wally, want-wit, wimp, witling, wooden-head, yap, zany, zombie.

v. act dido, act the fool, act up, bamboozle, be silly, beguile, bluff, cavort, cheat, clown, con, cozen, cut capers, daff, deceive, delude, diddle, dupe, feign, fiddle, fon, frolic, gull, have on, hoax, hoodwink, horse around, jest, joke, kid, lark, meddle, mess, mess about, mislead, monkey, play, play the fool, play the goat, play up, pretend, put one over on, string, string along, swindle, take in, tamper, tease, toy, trick, trifle.

fool about dawdle, idle, kill time, lark, lark about, mess about, play about, trifle.

foolery *n.* antics, buffoonery, capers, carry-on, childishness, clowning, desipience, dido, drollery, espièglerie, farce, folly, fooling, high jinks, horseplay, larks, mischief, monkey tricks, nonsense, practical jokes, pranks, shenanigans, silliness, tomfoolery, waggery, zanyism.

foolhardy *adj.* adventurous, bold, dare-devil, hot-headed, ill-advised, ill-considered, impetuous, imprudent, incautious, irresponsible, madcap, precipitate, rash, reckless, temerarious, unheeding, unwary, venturesome, venturous.

antonym cautious.

fooling *n.* bluffing, buffoonery, clownishness, desipience, drollery, farce, jesting, joking, kidding, kidology, mockery, nonsense, pretence, shamming, skylarking, teasing, tricks, trifling, waggery, zanyism.

foolish *adj.* absurd, brainless, cockle-brained, crazy, daft, desipient, doited, doltish, dotish, dottled, dunderheaded, étourdi(e), fatuous, glaikit, gudgeon, half-baked, half-witted, hare-brained, idiotic, idle-headed, ill-advised, illaudable, ill-considered, ill-judged, imbecile, imbecilic, imprudent, incautious, indiscreet, inept, injudicious, insipient, lean-witted, ludicrous, mad, moronic, nonsensical, potty, ridiculous, senseless, short-sighted, silly, simple, simple-minded, sottish, stupid, tomfool, unintelligent, unreasonable, unwise, weak, wet, witless.

antonym wise.

foolishly *adv.* absurdly, fatuously, fondly, idiotically, ill-advisedly, imprudently, incautiously, indiscreetly, ineptly, injudiciously, mistakenly, ridiculously, senselessly, short-sightedly, stupidly, unwisely.

antonym wisely.

foolishness *n.* absurdity, bunk, bunkum, claptrap, étourderie, folly, foolery, imprudence, inanity, incaution, incautiousness, indiscretion, ineptitude, insipience, irresponsibility, malarkey, niaiserie, nonsense, rubbish, silliness, stupidity, unreason, unwisdom, weakness.

antonyms prudence, wisdom.

foolproof *adj.* certain, fail-safe, guaranteed, idiot-proof, infallible, never-failing, safe,

sure-fire, unassailable, unbreakable.
antonym unreliable.

footing *n*. base, basis, condition, conditions, establishment, foot-hold, foundation, grade, ground, groundwork, installation, position, purchase, rank, relations, relationshp, settlement, standing, state, status, terms.

footnotes *n*. annotations, apparatus criticus, commentary, marginalia, notes, scholia.

footprint *n*. footmark, spoor, trace, track, trail, vestige.

footstep *n*. footfall, plod, step, tramp, tread, trudge.

fop *n*. beau, coxcomb, dandy, dude, exquisite, Jack-a-dandy, Jessie, macaroni, muscadin, musk-cat, pansy, peacock, petit maître, popinjay, spark, swell.

foppish *adj*. affected, coxcombical, dainty, dandiacal, dandified, dandyish, dapper, dressy, finical, la-di-da, natty, overdressed, preening, prinking, spruce, vain.
antonym unkempt.

for dear life desperately, energetically, for all one is worth, intensely, strenuously, urgently, vigorously, with might and main.

for example eg, exempli gratia, par exemple, zum Beispiel.

for fun facetiously, for kicks, for thrills, in jest, jokingly, light-heartedly, mischievously, playfully, roguishly, sportively, teasingly, tongue in cheek.

for good finally, for ever, irreparably, irreversibly, irrevocably, once and for all, permanently, sine die.

for good measure as a bonus, as an extra, besides, gratis, in addition, into the bargain, to boot.

for love for nothing, for pleasure, free of charge, freely, gratis, voluntarily.

for love or money by any means, ever, for anything, on any condition, under any circumstances.

for the most part chiefly, commonly, generally, in the main, largely, mainly, mostly, on the whole, principally, usually.

for the present for a while, for now, for the moment, for the nonce, for the time being, in the interim, in the meantime, pro tem, pro tempore, provisionally, temporarily.

for the time being for now, for the moment, for the nonce, for the present, in the meantime, meantime, meanwhile, pro tem, pro tempore, temporarily.

forage *n*. étape, feed, fodder, food, foodstuffs, pabulum, pasturage, provender.
v. cast about, explore, hunt, plunder, prog, raid, ransack, rummage, scavenge, scour, scrounge, search, seek.

foray *n*. depredation, descent, excursion, incursion, inroad, invasion, irruption, offensive, raid, razzia, reconnaissance, sally, sortie, spreagh, swoop.

forbear *v*. abstain, avoid, cease, decline, desist, eschew, hesitate, hold, hold back, keep from, omit, pause, refrain, restrain oneself, stay, stop, withhold.

forbearance *n*. abstinence, avoidance, clemency, endurance, indulgence, leniency, lenity, longanimity, long-suffering, mildness, moderation, patience, refraining, resignation, restraint, self-control, sufferance, temperance, tolerance, toleration.
antonym intolerance.

forbearing *adj*. clement, easy, forbearant, forgiving, indulgent, lenient, longanimous, long-suffering, merciful, mild, moderate, patient, restrained, self-controlled, tolerant.
antonyms intolerant, merciless.

forbid *v*. ban, block, contraindicate, debar, deny, disallow, exclude, hinder, inhibit, interdict, outlaw, preclude, prevent, prohibit, proscribe, refuse, rule out, veto.
antonym allow.

forbidden *adj*. banned, barred, debarred, disallowed, interdit, out of bounds, outlawed, prohibited, proscribed, taboo, verboten, vetoed.

forbidding *adj*. abhorrent, awesome, daunting, formidable, frightening, gaunt, grim, hostile, inhospitable, menacing, off-putting, ominous, repellent, repulsive, sinister, threatening, unapproachable, unfriendly.
antonyms approachable, congenial.

force[1] *n*. aggression, arm-twisting, beef, big stick, bite, coercion, cogency, compulsion, constraint, drive, duress, dynamism, effect, effectiveness, efficacy, emphasis, energy, enforcement, fierceness, foison, forcefulness, fushion, impact, impetus, impulse, incentive, influence, intensity, jism, life, mailed fist, might, momentum, motivation, muscle, persistence, persuasiveness, potency, power, pressure, punch, shock, steam, stimulus, strength, stress, validity, vehemence, vigour, violence, vis, vitality, weight.
v. bulldoze, coerce, compel, constrain, drag, drive, exact, extort, impel, impose, lean on, make, necessitate, obligate, oblige, press, press-gang, pressure, pressurise, prise, propel, push, strong-arm, thrust, urge, wrench, wrest, wring.

force[2] *n*. army, battalion, body, corps, detachment, detail, division, effective, enomoty, host, legion, patrol, phalanx, regiment, squad, squadron, troop, unit, Wehrmacht.

forced *adj*. affected, artificial, compulsory, contrived, enforced, false, feigned, insincere, involuntary, laboured, mandatory, obligatory, stiff, stilted, strained, synthetic, unnatural, unspontaneous, wooden.
antonyms spontaneous, voluntary.

forceful *adj*. cogent, compelling, convincing, domineering, drastic, dynamic, effective, emphatic, energetic, persuasive, pithy, potent, powerful, strong, telling, urgent, vigorous, weighty.
antonym feeble.

forcible *adj*. active, aggressive, coercive, cogent, compelling, compulsory, drastic, effective, efficient, energetic, forceful, impressive, mighty, pithy, potent, powerful, strong,

telling, urgent, vehement, violent, weighty.
antonym feeble.

forcibly *adv.* against one's will, by main force, compulsorily, emphatically, obligatorily, under compulsion, under duress, vehemently, vigorously, violently, willy-nilly.

ford *n.* causeway, crossing, drift.

forebear *n.* ancestor, antecedent, antecessor, father, forefather, forerunner, predecessor, primogenitor, progenitor.
antonym descendant.

forebode *v.* augur, betoken, foreshadow, foreshow, foretell, foretoken, forewarn, import, indicate, omen, portend, predict, presage, prognosticate, promise, signify, warn.

foreboding *n.* anticipation, anxiety, apprehension, apprehensiveness, augury, boding, chill, dread, fear, foreshadowing, foretoken, hoodoo, intuition, misgiving, omen, portent, prediction, prefigurement, premonition, presage, presentiment, prodrome, prodromus, prognostication, sign, token, warning, worry.

forecast *v.* augur, bode, calculate, conjecture, divine, estimate, expect, foresee, foretell, plan, predict, prognosticate, prophesy.
n. augury, conjecture, foresight, forethought, guess, guesstimate, outlook, planning, prediction, prognosis, prognostication, projection, prophecy.

forefather *n.* ancestor, antecedent, antecessor, father, forebear, forerunner, predecessor, primogenitor, primogenitrix, procreator, progenitor, progenitress, progenitrix.
antonym descendant.

forefront *n.* avant-garde, centre, firing line, fore, foreground, front, front line, lead, prominence, spearhead, van, vanguard.
antonym rear.

forego *see* **forgo** .

foregoing *adj.* above, aforementioned, antecedent, anterior, earlier, former, preceding, previous, prior, prodromal, prodromic.

foregone *adj.* anticipated, cut-and-dried, foreseen, inevitable, open and shut, predetermined, predictable.
antonym unpredictable.

foreground *n.* centre, fore, forefront, front, limelight, prominence.
antonym background.

forehead *n.* brow, front, metope, temples.

foreign *adj.* adventitious, adventive, alien, borrowed, distant, exotic, external, extraneous, extrinsic, fremd, imported, incongruous, irrelevant, outlandish, outside, overseas, remote, strange, tramontane, unassimilable, uncharacteristic, unfamiliar, unknown, unnative, unrelated.
antonym native.

foreigner *n.* alien, Ausländer, barbarian, dago, étranger, étrangère, immigrant, incomer, metic, newcomer, outlander, stranger, uitlander, wog, wop.
antonym native.

foreknowledge *n.* clairvoyance, foresight, forewarning, precognition, premonition, presci-

ence, prevision, prognostication, second sight.

foreman *n.* charge-hand, charge-man, gaffer, ganger, gangsman, overman, overseer, oversman, steward, straw boss, supervisor.

foremost *adj.* cardinal, central, chief, first, front, headmost, highest, inaugural, initial, leading, main, paramount, pre-eminent, primary, prime, principal, salient, supreme, uppermost.

foreordain *v.* appoint, destine, doom, fate, foredoom, ordain, prearrange, predestine, predetermine, preordain.

foreordained *adj.* appointed, foredoomed, prearranged, predestined, predetermined, predevote, preordained.

forerunner *n.* ancestor, announcer, antecedent, antecessor, envoy, forebear, foregoer, foretoken, harbinger, herald, indication, omen, portent, precursor, predecessor, premonition, prodrome, prodromus, progenitor, prognostic, prototype, sign, token, vauntcourier.
antonyms aftermath, result.

foresee *v.* anticipate, augur, divine, envisage, expect, forebode, forecast, foreknow, foretell, predict, previse, prognosticate, prophesy, vaticinate.

foreshadow *v.* adumbrate, anticipate, augur, betoken, bode, forebode, forepoint, foreshow, foresignify, foretoken, imply, import, indicate, omen, portend, predict, prefigure, presage, promise, prophesy, signal.

foresight *n.* anticipation, care, caution, circumspection, far-sightedness, forethought, perspicacity, precaution, preparedness, prescience, prevision, providence, provision, prudence, readiness, vision.
antonym improvidence.

forest *n.* greenwood, monte, plantation, urman, wood, woodland.

forestall *v.* anticipate, avert, balk, circumvent, frustrate, head off, hinder, intercept, obstruct, obviate, parry, preclude, pre-empt, prevent, thwart, ward off.
antonyms encourage, facilitate.

forester *n.* gamekeeper, woodman, woodsman, woodward.

forestry *n.* afforestation, arboriculture, dendrology, forestation, silviculture, woodcraft, woodmanship.

foretaste *n.* example, foretoken, forewarning, indication, pregustation, prelibation, prelude, preview, sample, specimen, trailer, warning, whiff.

foretell *v.* adumbrate, augur, bode, forebode, forecast, foresay, foreshadow, foreshow, forespeak, forewarn, portend, predict, presage, presignify, prognosticate, prophesy, signify, soothsay, vaticinate.

forethought *n.* anticipation, circumspection, far-sightedness, foresight, precaution, preparation, providence, provision, prudence.
antonym improvidence.

foretold *adj.* forecast, foreshown, forespoken,

predicted, prophesied, written.
antonym unforeseen.

forever *adv.* always, ceaselessly, constantly, continually, endlessly, eternally, everlastingly, evermore, for all time, for good and all, for keeps, in perpetuity, in saecula saeculorum, incessantly, interminably, permanently, perpetually, persistently, till the cows come home, till the end of time, unremittingly, world without end.

forewarn *v.* admonish, advise, alert, apprise, caution, dissuade, previse, tip off.

foreword *n.* exordium, introduction, preamble, preface, preliminary, proem, prolegomenon, prologue.
antonyms epilogue, postscript.

forfeit *n.* amercement, damages, escheat, fine, forfeiture, loss, mulct, penalisation, penalty, surrender.
v. abandon, forgo, give up, lose, relinquish, renounce, sacrifice, surrender.

forfeiture *n.* attainder, confiscation, déchéance, escheat, forgoing, giving up, loss, relinquishment, sacrifice, sequestration, surrender.

forge¹ *v.* beat out, cast, coin, construct, contrive, copy, counterfeit, create, devise, fabricate, fake, falsify, fashion, feign, form, frame, hammer out, imitate, invent, make, mould, shape, simulate, work.

forge² *v.* advance, gain ground, improve, make great strides, make headway, press on, proceed, progress, push on.

forger *n.* coiner, contriver, counterfeiter, creator, deviser, fabricator, faker, falsifier, framer, truqueur.

forgery *n.* coining, counterfeit, counterfeiting, dud, fake, falsification, fraud, fraudulence, imitation, phoney, sham, stumer.
antonym original.

forget *v.* consign to oblivion, discount, dismiss, disregard, fail, ignore, lose sight of, misremember, neglect, omit, overlook, think no more of, unlearn.
antonym remember.

forgetful *adj.* absent-minded, amnesiac, amnesic, careless, dreamy, heedless, inattentive, lax, neglectful, negligent, oblivious, unmindful, unretentive.
antonyms attentive, heedful.

forgetfulness *n.* absent-mindedness, abstraction, amnesia, carelessness, dreaminess, heedlessness, inattention, lapse, laxness, Lethe, oblivion, obliviousness, obliviscence, woolgathering.
antonyms attentiveness, heedfulness.

forgivable *adj.* excusable, innocent, minor, pardonable, petty, slight, trifling, venial.
antonym unforgivable.

forgive *v.* absolve, acquit, condone, exculpate, excuse, exonerate, let off, overlook, pardon, remit, shrive.
antonym censure.

forgiveness *n.* absolution, acquittal, amnesty, condonation, exculpation, exoneration, mercy, pardon, remission, shrift, shriving.

antonyms blame, censure.

forgiving *adj.* clement, compassionate, forbearing, humane, indulgent, lenient, magnanimous, merciful, mild, remissive, soft-hearted, sparing, tolerant.
antonym censorious.

forgo, forego *v.* abandon, abjure, abstain from, cede, do without, eschew, forfeit, give up, pass up, refrain from, relinquish, renounce, resign, sacrifice, surrender, waive, yield.
antonyms claim, indulge in, insist on.

forgotten *adj.* blotted out, buried, bygone, disregarded, ignored, irrecoverable, irretrievable, lost, neglected, obliterated, omitted, out of mind, overlooked, past, past recall, past recollection, unrecalled, unremembered, unretrieved.
antonym remembered.

fork *v.* bifurcate, branch, branch off, divaricate, diverge, divide, part, ramify, separate, split.
n. bifurcation, branching, divarication, divergence, division, furcation, intersection, junction, ramification, separation, split.

forked *adj.* bifurcate, branched, branching, divaricated, divided, forficate, furcal, furcate, furcular, pronged, ramified, split, tined, zigzag.

forlorn *adj.* abandoned, abject, bereft, cheerless, comfortless, deserted, desolate, desperate, destitute, disconsolate, forgotten, forsaken, friendless, helpless, homeless, hopeless, lonely, lost, miserable, pathetic, piteous, pitiable, pitiful, unhappy, woebegone, woeful, wretched.
antonym hopeful.

form *v.* accumulate, acquire, appear, arrange, assemble, bring up, build, combine, compose, comprise, concoct, constitute, construct, contract, contrive, create, crystallise, cultivate, design, develop, devise, discipline, dispose, draw up, educate, establish, evolve, fabricate, fashion, forge, formulate, found, frame, group, grow, hatch, instruct, invent, make, make up, manufacture, materialise, model, mould, organise, pattern, plan, produce, put together, rear, rise, school, serve as, settle, shape, take shape, teach, train.
n. anatomy, appearance, application, arrangement, behaviour, being, body, build, cast, ceremony, character, class, condition, conduct, configuration, construction, convention, custom, cut, description, design, document, etiquette, fashion, fettle, figure, fitness, formality, format, formation, frame, framework, genre, Gestalt, grade, guise, harmony, health, kind, manifestation, manner, manners, matrix, method, mode, model, mould, nature, nick, order, orderliness, organisation, outline, paper, pattern, person, physique, plan, practice, procedure, proportion, protocol, questionnaire, rank, ritual, rule, schedule, semblance, shape, sheet, silhouette, sort, species, spirits, stamp, structure, style, symmetry, system, trim, type, variety, way.

formal *adj.* academic, aloof, approved, ceremo-

nial, ceremonious, conventional, correct, exact, explicit, express, fixed, full-dress, impersonal, lawful, legal, methodical, nominal, official, perfunctory, precise, prescribed, prim, punctilious, recognised, regular, reserved, rigid, ritualistic, set, solemn, starch, starched, starchy, stiff, stiff-necked, stilted, strict, unbending.
antonym informal.

formality *n.* ceremoniousness, ceremony, convenance, convention, conventionality, correctness, custom, decorum, etiquette, form, formalism, gesture, matter of form, politeness, politesse, procedure, propriety, protocol, punctilio, red tape, rite, ritual.
antonym informality.

format *n.* appearance, arrangement, configuration, construction, dimensions, form, lay-out, look, make-up, pattern, plan, shape, structure, style, type.

formation *n.* accumulation, appearance, arrangement, compilation, composition, configuration, constitution, construction, creation, crystallisation, design, development, disposition, emergence, establishment, evolution, fabrication, figure, format, forming, generation, genesis, grouping, manufacture, organisation, pattern, production, rank, shaping, structure.

formative *adj.* controlling, determinative, determining, developmental, dominant, guiding, impressionable, influential, malleable, mouldable, moulding, pliant, sensitive, shaping, susceptible.
antonym destructive.

former *adj.* above, aforementioned, aforesaid, ancient, antecedent, anterior, bygone, departed, earlier, erstwhile, ex-, first mentioned, foregoing, late, long ago, of yore, old, old-time, one-time, past, preceding, pre-existent, previous, prior, pristine, quondam, sometime, umwhile, whilom.
antonyms current, future, later, present, prospective, subsequent.

formerly *adv.* already, at one time, before, earlier, erstwhile, heretofore, hitherto, lately, once, previously, umwhile, while-ere, whilom.
antonyms currently, later, now, presently, subsequently.

formidable *adj.* alarming, appalling, arduous, awesome, challenging, colossal, dangerous, daunting, difficult, dismaying, dreadful, enormous, fearful, frightening, frightful, great, horrible, huge, impressive, indomitable, intimidating, leviathan, mammoth, menacing, mighty, onerous, overwhelming, powerful, puissant, redoubtable, shocking, staggering, terrific, terrifying, threatening, toilsome, tremendous.
antonyms easy, genial.

formless *adj.* amorphous, chaotic, confused, disorganised, inchoate, incoherent, indefinite, indeterminate, indigest, nebulous, shapeless, unformed, unshaped, vague.

antonyms definite, orderly.

formula *n.* blueprint, code, form, formulary, method, modus operandi, password, precept, prescription, principle, procedure, recipe, rite, ritual, rubric, rule, rule of thumb, way, wording.

formulate *v.* block out, codify, create, define, detail, develop, devise, evolve, express, form, frame, invent, originate, particularise, plan, specify, systematise, work out.

forsake *v.* abandon, abdicate, cast off, desert, discard, disown, forgo, forswear, give up, jettison, jilt, leave, leave in the lurch, quit, reject, relinquish, renounce, repudiate, surrender, throw over, turn one's back on, vacate, yield.
antonyms resume, revert to.

forsaken *adj.* abandoned, cast off, deserted, desolate, destitute, discarded, disowned, forlorn, friendless, ignored, isolated, jilted, left in the lurch, lonely, lorn, lovelorn, marooned, outcast, rejected, shunned, solitary.

forswear *v.* abandon, abjure, burn one's faggot, deny, disavow, disclaim, disown, drop, forgo, forsake, give up, lie, perjure oneself, recant, reject, renegue, renounce, repudiate, retract, swear off.
antonym revert to.

fort *n.* acropolis, blockhouse, camp, castle, citadel, fastness, fortification, fortress, garrison, hill-fort, rath, redoubt, station, stronghold, tower.

forte *n.* aptitude, bent, gift, long suit, métier, skill, speciality, strength, strong point, talent.
antonyms inadequacy, weak point.

forthcoming[1] *adj.* accessible, approaching, at hand, available, coming, expected, future, imminent, impending, obtainable, projected, prospective, ready.

forthcoming[2] *adj.* chatty, communicative, conversational, expansive, frank, free, informative, loquacious, open, sociable, talkative, unreserved.
antonyms bygone, distant, lacking, reserved.

forthright *adj.* above-board, blunt, bold, candid, direct, four-square, frank, open, outspoken, plain-speaking, plain-spoken, straightforward, straight-from-the-shoulder, trenchant, unequivocal.
antonyms devious, tactful.

forthwith *adv.* at once, directly, eftsoons, immediately, incontinent, instanter, instantly, posthaste, pronto, quickly, right away, straightaway, tout de suite, without delay.

fortification *n.* abatis, bastion, bulwark, buttressing, castle, citadel, defence, earthwork, embattlement, entrenchment, fastness, fort, fortress, keep, munition, outwork, protection, rampart, redoubt, reinforcement, stockade, strengthening, stronghold.

fortify *v.* boost, brace, bulwark, buttress, cheer, confirm, embattle, embolden, encourage, entrench, garrison, hearten, invigorate, lace, load, mix, munify, protect, reassure, re-

inforce, secure, shore up, spike, steel, stiffen, strengthen, support, sustain.
antonyms dilute, weaken.

fortitude *n.* backbone, bottle, braveness, bravery, courage, dauntlessness, determination, endurance, fearlessness, firmness, grit, guts, hardihood, indomitability, intrepidity, long-suffering, patience, perseverance, pluck, resoluteness, resolution, staying power, stout-heartedness, strength, strength of mind, valour.
antonyms cowardice, weakness.

fortress *n.* alcázar, burg, castle, citadel, fastness, fortification, kasbah, stronghold.

fortuitous *adj.* accidental, adventitious, arbitrary, casual, chance, coincidental, contingent, felicitous, fluky, fortunate, happy, incidental, lucky, providential, random, serendipitous, unexpected, unforeseen, unintentional, unplanned.
antonym intentional.

fortunate *adj.* advantageous, auspicious, blessed, bright, convenient, encouraging, favourable, favoured, felicitous, fortuitous, golden, happy, helpful, lucky, opportune, profitable, promising, propitious, prosperous, providential, rosy, serendipitous, successful, timely, well-off, well-timed.
antonym unfortunate.

fortunately *adv.* happily, luckily, providentially.
antonym unfortunately.

fortune[1] *n.* affluence, assets, bomb, bundle, estate, income, king's ransom, means, mint, opulence, packet, pile, possessions, property, prosperity, riches, treasure, wealth.

fortune[2] *n.* accident, adventures, chance, circumstances, contingency, cup, destiny, doom, expectation, experience, fate, fortuity, hap, happenstance, hazard, history, kismet, life, lot, luck, portion, providence, star, success, weird.

fortune-telling *n.* augury, chiromancy, crystal-gazing, divination, dukkeripen, palmistry, prediction, prognostication, prophecy, second sight.

forward[1] *adj.* advance, advanced, early, enterprising, first, fore, foremost, forward-looking, front, go-ahead, head, leading, onward, precocious, premature, progressive, well-advanced, well-developed.
antonym retrograde.
adv. ahead, en avant, forth, forwards, into view, on, onward, out, outward, to light, to the fore, to the surface.
antonym backward.
v. accelerate, advance, aid, assist, back, dispatch, encourage, expedite, facilitate, favour, foster, freight, further, hasten, help, hurry, post, promote, route, send, send on, ship, speed, support, transmit.
antonyms impede, obstruct.

forward[2] *adj.* assertive, assuming, audacious, bare-faced, bold, brash, brass-necked, brazen, brazen-faced, cheeky, confident, familiar, fresh, impertinent, impudent, malapert, officious, overweening, pert, presuming, presumptuous, pushy.
antonym diffident.

forward-looking *adj.* avant-garde, dynamic, enlightened, enterprising, far-sighted, go-ahead, goey, go-getting, innovative, liberal, modern, progressive, reforming.
antonyms conservative, retrograde.

forwardness *n.* assurance, audacity, boldness, brashness, brazenness, cheek, cheekiness, impertinence, impudence, malapertness, overconfidence, pertness, presumption, presumptuousness.
antonyms reserve, retiring.

fossilised *adj.* anachronistic, antediluvian, antiquated, archaic, archaistic, dead, démodé, extinct, exuvial, inflexible, obsolete, old-fashioned, old-fog(e)yish, ossified, out of date, outmoded, passé, petrified, prehistoric, stony, superannuated.
antonym up-to-date.

foster *v.* accommodate, bring up, care for, cherish, cultivate, encourage, entertain, feed, foment, harbour, make much of, nourish, nurse, nurture, promote, raise, rear, stimulate, support, sustain, take care of.
antonyms discourage, neglect.

foul *adj.* abhorrent, abominable, abusive, bad, base, blasphemous, blue, blustery, choked, coarse, contaminated, crooked, despicable, detestable, dirty, disagreeable, disfigured, disgraceful, disgusting, dishonest, dishonourable, entangled, fetid, filthy, foggy, foul-mouthed, fraudulent, gross, hateful, heinous, impure, indecent, inequitable, infamous, iniquitous, lewd, loathsome, low, malodorous, mephitic, murky, nasty, nauseating, nefarious, noisome, notorious, obscene, offensive, polluted, profane, putrid, rainy, rank, repulsive, revolting, rotten, rough, scandalous, scatological, scurrilous, shady, shameful, smutty, squalid, stinking, stormy, sullied, tainted, unclean, underhand, unfair, unfavourable, unjust, unsportsmanlike, untidy, vicious, vile, virose, vulgar, wet, wicked, wild.
antonyms clean, fair, pure, worthy.
v. befoul, begrime, besmear, besmirch, block, catch, choke, clog, contaminate, defile, dirty, ensnare, entangle, foul up, jam, pollute, smear, snarl, soil, stain, sully, taint, twist.
antonyms clean, clear, disentangle.

foul play chicanery, corruption, crime, deception, dirty work, double-dealing, duplicity, fraud, funny business, jiggery-pokery, perfidy, roguery, sharp practice, skulduggery, treachery, villainy.
antonyms fair play, justice.

foul-mouthed *adj.* abusive, blasphemous, coarse, foul-spoken, obscene, offensive, profane.

found *v.* base, bottom, build, constitute, construct, create, endow, erect, establish, fix, ground, inaugurate, initiate, institute, organise, originate, plant, raise, rest, root, set up, settle, start, sustain.

foundation *n.* base, basis, bedrock, bottom, endowment, establishment, fond, footing, ground, groundwork, inauguration, institution, organisation, setting up, settlement, substance, substratum, substructure, underpinning.

founder[1] *n.* architect, author, beginner, benefactor, builder, constructor, designer, endower, establisher, father, framer, generator, initiator, institutor, inventor, maker, organiser, originator, patriarch.

founder[2] *v.* abort, break down, collapse, come to grief, come to nothing, fail, fall, fall through, go lame, lurch, miscarry, misfire, sink, sprawl, stagger, stick, stumble, submerge, subside, trip.

foundling *n.* enfant trouvé, orphan, outcast, stray, urchin, waif.

fountain *n.* fons et origo, font, fount, fountainhead, gerbe, inspiration, jet, origin, reservoir, source, spout, spray, spring, waterworks, well, well-head, well-spring.

fourfold *adj.* quadruple, quadruplex, quadruplicate, tetraploid.

four-square *adv.* firmly, frankly, honestly, resolutely, squarely.
adj. firm, forthright, frank, honest, immovable, resolute, solid, steady, strong, unyielding.
antonyms uncertain, wavering.

fox *n.* cunning devil, Lowrie, Lowrie-tod, reynard, sly one, slyboots, tod, Tod-Lowrie.

foxy *adj.* artful, astute, canny, crafty, cunning, devious, fly, guileful, knowing, sharp, shrewd, sly, tricky, vulpine, wily.
antonyms naïve, open.

foyer *n.* antechamber, anteroom, entrance hall, hall, lobby, reception, vestibule.

fracas *n.* affray, aggro, bagarre, barney, brawl, disturbance, Donnybrook, fight, free-for-all, mêlée, quarrel, riot, row, ruckus, ruction, rumpus, scrimmage, scuffle, shindy, trouble, uproar.

fractious *adj.* awkward, captious, choleric, crabbed, crabby, cross, crotchety, fretful, froward, grouchy, irritable, peevish, pettish, petulant, quarrelsome, querulous, recalcitrant, refractory, testy, touchy, unruly.
antonyms complaisant, placid.

fracture *n.* breach, break, cleft, crack, fissure, gap, opening, rent, rift, rupture, schism, scission, split.
v. break, crack, rupture, splinter, split.
antonym join.

fragile *adj.* breakable, brittle, dainty, delicate, feeble, fine, flimsy, frail, frangible, infirm, insubstantial, shattery, slight, weak.
antonyms durable, robust, tough.

fragility *n.* breakableness, brittleness, delicacy, feebleness, frailty, frangibility, infirmity, weakness.
antonyms durability, robustness, strength.

fragment *n.* bit, cantlet, chip, flinder, fraction, frazzle, fritter, morceau, morsel, ort, part, particle, piece, portion, remnant, scrap, shard, shatter, sheave, shiver, shred, sliver.
v. break, break up, come apart, come to pieces, crumble, disintegrate, disunite, divide, fractionalise, fritter, shatter, shiver, splinter, split, split up.
antonyms hold together, join.

fragmentary *adj.* bitty, broken, disconnected, discrete, disjointed, fractionary, incoherent, incomplete, partial, piecemeal, scattered, scrappy, separate, sketchy, unsystematic.
antonym complete.

fragrance *n.* aroma, balm, balminess, bouquet, fragrancy, odour, perfume, redolence, scent, smell.

fragrant *adj.* aromatic, balmy, balsamy, odoriferous, odorous, perfumed, redolent, suaveolent, sweet, sweet-scented, sweet-smelling.
antonyms smelly, unscented.

frail *adj.* breakable, brittle, decrepit, delicate, feeble, flimsy, fragile, frangible, infirm, insubstantial, puny, slight, tender, unchaste, unsound, vulnerable, weak.
antonyms firm, robust, strong, tough.

frailty *n.* blemish, defect, deficiency, failing, fallibility, fault, feebleness, flaw, foible, frailness, imperfection, infirmity, peccability, peccadillo, peccancy, puniness, shortcoming, susceptibility, unchasteness, unchastity, vice, weakness.
antonyms firmness, robustness, strength, toughness.

frame *v.* assemble, block out, build, case, compose, conceive, concoct, constitute, construct, contrive, cook up, devise, draft, draw up, enclose, enframe, fabricate, fashion, forge, form, formulate, hatch, institute, invent, make, manufacture, map out, model, mould, mount, plan, put together, redact, set up, shape, sketch, surround, trap, victimise.
n. anatomy, body, bodyshell, bodywork, build, carcass, casing, chassis, construction, fabric, flake, form, framework, monture, morphology, mount, mounting, physique, scaffolding, scheme, setting, shell, skeleton, structure, system.

frame of mind attitude, disposition, fettle, humour, mood, morale, outlook, spirit, state, temper, vein.

frame-up *n.* fabrication, fit-up, fix, put-up job, trap, trumped-up charge.

framework *n.* bare bones, core, fabric, foundation, frame, gantry, groundwork, plan, schema, shell, skeleton, structure.

franchise *n.* authorisation, charter, concession, exemption, freedom, immunity, liberty, prerogative, privilege, right, suffrage, vote.

frank *adj.* artless, blunt, candid, direct, downright, forthright, four-square, free, honest, ingenuous, open, outright, outspoken, plain, plain-spoken, simple-hearted, sincere, straight, straightforward, transparent, truthful, unconcealed, undisguised, unreserved, unrestricted.
antonyms evasive, insincere.

frankly *adv.* bluntly, candidly, directly, freely, honestly, in truth, openly, plainly, straight, to be frank, to be honest, unreservedly, without reserve.
antonyms evasively, insincerely.

frankness *n.* bluntness, candour, forthrightness, franchise, ingenuousness, openness, outspokenness, plain speaking, truthfulness, unreserve.

frantic *adj.* berserk, beside oneself, desperate, distracted, distraught, fraught, frenetic, frenzied, furious, hairless, hectic, mad, overwrought, raging, raving, wild.
antonym calm.

fraternise *v.* affiliate, associate, concur, consort, cooperate, forgather, hobnob, mingle, mix, socialise, sympathise, unite.
antonyms ignore, shun.

fraternity *n.* association, brotherhood, camaraderie, circle, clan, club, companionship, company, comradeship, confraternity, confrère, fellowship, fratry, guild, kinship, league, set, society, sodality, union.

fraud¹ *n.* artifice, cheat, chicane, chicanery, craft, deceit, deception, double-dealing, duplicity, fake, forgery, guile, hoax, humbug, imposture, sham, sharp practice, spuriousness, swindling, swiz, swizzle, take-in, treachery, trickery.

fraud² *n.* bluffer, charlatan, cheat, counterfeit, double-dealer, hoaxer, impostor, malingerer, mountebank, phoney, pretender, pseud, quack, swindler.

fraudulent *adj.* bogus, counterfeit, crafty, criminal, crooked, deceitful, deceptive, dishonest, double-dealing, duplicitous, false, knavish, phoney, sham, specious, spurious, swindling, treacherous.
antonyms genuine, honest.

fraught *adj.* abounding, accompanied, agitated, anxious, attended, bristling, charged, difficult, distracted, distressed, distressing, emotive, filled, full, heavy, hotching, laden, replete, stuffed, tense, tricky, troublesome, trying, uptight, worrisome.
antonyms calm, untroublesome.

fray *n.* affray, bagarre, barney, battle, brawl, broil, clash, combat, conflict, disturbance, Donnybrook, dust-up, fight, free-for-all, mêlée, quarrel, rammy, riot, row, ruckus, ruction, rumble, rumpus, scuffle, set-to, shindy.

frayed *adj.* edgy, frazzled, on edge, ragged, shreddy, tattered, threadbare, worn.
antonyms calm, tidy.

freak¹ *n.* aberration, abnormality, abortion, anomaly, caprice, crotchet, fad, fancy, folly, grotesque, humour, irregularity, lusus naturae, malformation, misgrowth, monster, monstrosity, mutant, oddity, queer fish, quirk, rara avis, sport, teratism, turn, twist, vagary, weirdie, weirdo, whim, whimsy.
adj. aberrant, abnormal, atypical, bizarre, capricious, erratic, exceptional, fluky, fortuitous, odd, queer, surprise, unaccountable,

unexpected, unforeseen, unparalleled, unpredictable, unpredicted, unusual.
antonyms common, expected.

freak² *n.* addict, aficionado, buff, devotee, enthusiast, fan, fanatic, fiend, monomaniac, nut, votary.

freakish *adj.* aberrant, abnormal, arbitrary, capricious, changeable, erratic, fanciful, fantastic, fitful, freakful, freaky, grotesque, malformed, monstrous, odd, outlandish, outré, preternatural, strange, teratoid, unconventional, unpredictable, unusual, vagarious, vagarish, wayward, weird, whimsical.
antonym ordinary.

freckle *n.* fernitickle, heatspot, lentigo.

free *adj.* able, allowed, at large, at leisure, at liberty, autarchic, autonomous, available, bounteous, bountiful, buckshee, casual, charitable, clear, complimentary, cost-free, dégagé, democratic, disengaged, eager, easy, emancipated, empty, extra, familiar, footloose, forward, frank, free and easy, free of charge, generous, gratis, hospitable, idle, independent, informal, laid-back, lavish, lax, leisured, liberal, liberated, loose, munificent, natural, off the hook, on the house, on the loose, open, open-handed, permitted, prodigal, relaxed, self-governing, self-ruling, solute, sovereign, spare, spontaneous, unattached, unbidden, unbowed, unceremonious, uncommitted, unconstrained, unemployed, unencumbered, unengaged, unfettered, unforced, unhampered, unhindered, unimpeded, uninhabited, uninhibited, unobstructed, unoccupied, unpaid, unpent, unpreoccupied, unregimented, unregulated, unrestrained, unrestricted, unsparing, unstinting, untrammelled, unused, vacant, willing, without charge.
antonyms attached, confined, costly, formal, mean, niggardly, restricted, tied.
adv. abundantly, copiously, for free, for love, for nothing, freely, gratis, idly, loosely, without charge.
antonym meanly.
v. absolve, affranchise, clear, debarrass, declassify, decolonise, decontrol, deliver, disburden, discage, discharge, disembarrass, disembrangle, disenchain, disengage, disenslave, disentangle, disenthral, disimprison, disprison, emancipate, exempt, extricate, let go, liberate, loose, manumit, ransom, release, relieve, rescue, rid, set free, turn loose, unbind, unburden, uncage, unchain, undo, unfetter, unhand, unleash, unlock, unloose, unmanacle, unmew, unpen, unshackle, unstick, untether, untie, unyoke.
antonyms confine, enslave, imprison.

free hand authority, carte-blanche, discretion, freedom, latitude, liberty, permission, power, scope.

free of devoid of, exempt from, immune to, innocent of, lacking, not liable to, safe from, sans, unaffected by, unencumbered by, untouched by, without.

freebooter *n.* bandit, brigand, buccaneer,

cateran, filibuster, highwayman, looter, marauder, moss-trooper, pillager, pirate, plunderer, raider, reiver, robber, rover.

freedom *n.* abandon, ability, affranchisement, autonomy, boldness, brazenness, candour, carte-blanche, deliverance, directness, discretion, disrespect, ease, elbow-room, emancipation, exemption, facility, familiarity, flexibility, forwardness, frankness, free rein, home rule, immunity, impertinence, impunity, independence, informality, ingenuousness, lack of restraint or reserve, latitude, laxity, leeway, liberty, Liberty Hall, licence, manumission, openness, opportunity, overfamiliarity, play, power, presumption, privilege, range, release, scope, self-government, uhuru, unconstraint.
antonyms confinement, reserve, restriction.

freely *adv.* abundantly, amply, bountifully, candidly, cleanly, copiously, easily, extravagantly, frankly, generously, lavishly, liberally, loosely, of one's own accord, open-handedly, openly, plainly, readily, smoothly, spontaneously, sponte sua, unchallenged, unreservedly, unstintingly, voluntarily, willingly.
antonyms evasively, meanly, roughly, under duress.

free-thinker *n.* agnostic, deist, doubter, esprit fort, infidel, rationalist, sceptic, unbeliever.

free-will *n.* autarky, autonomy, election, freedom, independence, liberty, self-determination, self-sufficiency, spontaneity, volition.

freeze *v.* benumb, chill, congeal, enfreeze, fix, glaciate, harden, hold, ice, ice over, inhibit, peg, rigidify, shelve, solidify, stiffen, stop, suspend.
n. abeyance, discontinuation, embargo, freeze-up, frost, halt, interruption, moratorium, postponement, shut-down, standstill, stay, stoppage, suspension.

freezing *adj.* arctic, biting, bitter, brumous, chill, chilled, chilly, cutting, frigorific, frosty, gelid, glacial, icy, numbing, penetrating, polar, raw, Siberian, wintry.
antonyms hot, warm.

freight *n.* bulk, burden, cargo, carriage, charge, consignment, contents, conveyance, fee, goods, haul, lading, load, merchandise, pay-load, shipment, tonnage, transportation.

frenetic *adj.* demented, distraught, excited, fanatical, frantic, frenzical, frenzied, hyperactive, insane, mad, maniacal, obsessive, overwrought, phrenetic, unbalanced, wild.
antonyms calm, placid.

frenzied *adj.* agitated, convulsive, distracted, distraught, excited, feverish, frantic, frenetic, frenzical, furious, hysterical, mad, maniacal, must, musty, rabid, uncontrolled, wild.
antonyms calm, placid.

frenzy *n.* aberration, agitation, bout, burst, convulsion, delirium, derangement, distraction, fit, fury, hysteria, insanity, lunacy, madness, mania, must, oestrus, outburst, paroxysm, passion, rage, seizure, spasm,

transport, turmoil.
antonyms calm, placidness.

frequency *n.* constancy, frequence, frequentness, oftenness, periodicity, prevalence, recurrence, repetition.
antonym infrequency.

frequent[1] *adj.* common, commonplace, constant, continual, customary, everyday, familiar, habitual, incessant, numerous, persistent, recurrent, recurring, regular, reiterated, repeated, usual.
antonym infrequent.

frequent[2] *v.* associate with, attend, crowd, hang about, hang out at, haunt, haunt about, patronise, resort, visit.

frequenter *n.* client, customer, denizen, habitué, haunter, patron, regular.

frequently *adv.* commonly, continually, customarily, habitually, many a time, many times, much, oft, often, oftentimes, over and over, persistently, repeatedly.
antonyms infrequently, seldom.

fresh *adj.* added, additional, alert, artless, auxiliary, blooming, bold, bouncing, bracing, brazen, bright, brisk, callow, cheeky, chipper, clean, clear, cool, crisp, crude, dewy, different, disrespectful, energetic, extra, fair, familiar, flip, florid, forward, further, glowing, green, hardy, healthy, impudent, inexperienced, innovative, insolent, inventive, invigorated, invigorating, keen, latest, lively, malapert, modern, modernistic, more, natural, new, new-fangled, novel, original, other, pert, presumptuous, pure, raw, recent, refreshed, refreshing, renewed, rested, restored, revived, rosy, ruddy, saucy, span, spanking, sparkling, spick, sprightly, spry, stiff, supplementary, sweet, unblown, unconventional, uncultivated, undimmed, unhackneyed, unjaded, unjaundiced, unpolluted, unsoured, unspoilt, untrained, untried, unusual, unwarped, unwearied, up-to-date, verdant, vernal, vigorous, virescent, vital, vivid, warm, wholesome, young, youthful.
antonyms experienced, faded, old hat, polite, stale, tired.

freshen *v.* air, enliven, liven, purify, refresh, reinvigorate, restore, resuscitate, revitalise, spruce up, tart up, titivate, ventilate, vernalise.
antonym tire.

freshman *n.* bajan, bejant, first-year, fresher, pennal, sophomore, underclassman.

freshness *n.* bloom, brightness, cleanness, clearness, dewiness, fraîcheur, glow, newness, novelty, originality, shine, sparkle, vigour, virescence, wholesomeness.
antonyms staleness, tiredness.

fret *v.* abrade, agitate, agonise, annoy, bother, brood, chafe, chagrin, corrode, distress, disturb, eat into, erode, fray, gall, goad, grieve, harass, irk, irritate, nag, nettle, peeve, pique, provoke, rankle, repine, rile, ripple, rub, ruffle, torment, trouble, vex, wear, wear away, worry.

antonym calm.

fretful adj. cantankerous, captious, complaining, cross, crotchety, edgy, fractious, irritable, peevish, petulant, querulous, short-tempered, snappish, snappy, splenetic, testy, thrawn, touchy, uneasy.
antonym calm.

friable adj. brittle, crisp, crumbly, murly, powdery, pulverisable.
antonyms clayey, solid.

friar n. mendicant, monk, religieux, religionary, religioner, religious.

friction n. abrasion, animosity, antagonism, attrition, bad blood, bad feeling, bickering, chafing, conflict, contention, disagreement, discontent, discord, disharmony, dispute, dissension, erosion, fretting, grating, hostility, ill-feeling, incompatibility, irritation, limation, opposition, quarrelling, rasping, resentment, resistance, rivalry, rubbing, scraping, wearing away, wrangling, xerotripsis.

friend n. Achates, adherent, advocate, ally, alter ego, associate, backer, benefactor, boon companion, bosom friend, buddy, china, chum, cobber, companion, comrade, confidant, crony, familiar, gossip, intimate, mate, paisano, pal, partisan, partner, patron, playmate, side-kick, soul mate, supporter, well-wisher.
antonym enemy.

friendless adj. abandoned, alienated, alone, deserted, estranged, forlorn, forsaken, isolated, lonely, lonely-heart, lonesome, ostracised, shunned, solitary, unattached, unbefriended, unbeloved, unfriended, unloved.

friendliness n. affability, amiability, approachability, companionability, congeniality, conviviality, Gemütlichkeit, geniality, kindliness, matyness, neighbourliness, sociability, warmth.
antonyms coldness, unsociableness.

friendly adj. affable, affectionate, amiable, amicable, approachable, attached, attentive, auspicious, beneficial, benevolent, benign, chummy, close, clubby, companionable, comradely, conciliatory, confiding, convivial, cordial, familiar, Favonian, favourable, fond, fraternal, gemütlich, genial, good, helpful, intimate, kind, kindly, maty, neighbourly, outgoing, palsy-walsy, peaceable, propitious, receptive, sociable, sympathetic, thick, welcoming, well-disposed.
antonyms cold, unsociable.

friendship n. affection, affinity, alliance, amity, attachment, benevolence, closeness, concord, familiarity, fellowship, fondness, friendliness, goodwill, harmony, intimacy, love, neighbourliness, rapport, regard.
antonym enmity.

fright n. alarm, apprehension, consternation, dismay, dread, eyesore, fear, fleg, funk, horror, mess, monstrosity, panic, quaking, scare, scarecrow, shock, sight, spectacle, sweat, terror, the shivers, trepidation.

frighten v. affray, affright, affrighten, alarm, appal, cow, daunt, dismay, fleg, intimidate, petrify, scare, scare stiff, shock, spook, startle, terrify, terrorise, unman, unnerve.
antonyms calm, reassure.

frightened adj. affrighted, affrightened, afraid, alarmed, cowed, dismayed, frightsome, frozen, panicky, petrified, scared, scared stiff, startled, terrified, terrorised, terror-stricken, unnerved, windy.
antonyms calm, courageous.

frightening adj. alarming, appalling, bloodcurdling, daunting, dismaying, dreadful, fearful, fearsome, hair-raising, horrifying, intimidating, menacing, scary, shocking, spine-chilling, spooky, terrifying, traumatic, unnerving.
antonym reassuring.

frightful adj. alarming, appalling, awful, dire, disagreeable, dread, dreadful, fearful, fearsome, frightsome, ghastly, great, grim, grisly, gruesome, harrowing, hideous, horrendous, horrible, horrid, insufferable, macabre, petrifying, shocking, terrible, terrific, terrifying, traumatic, unnerving, unpleasant, unspeakable.
antonyms agreeable, pleasant.

frigid adj. aloof, arctic, austere, brumous, chill, chilly, cold, cold-hearted, cool, forbidding, formal, frore, frost-bound, frosty, frozen, gelid, glacial, icy, lifeless, passionless, passive, repellent, rigid, stand-offish, stiff, unanimated, unapproachable, unbending, unfeeling, unloving, unresponsive, wintry.
antonyms responsive, warm.

frigidity n. aloofness, austerity, chill, chilliness, cold-heartedness, coldness, frostiness, iciness, impassivity, lifelessness, passivity, stiffness, unapproachability, unresponsiveness, wintriness.
antonyms responsiveness, warmth.

frill n. flounce, furbelow, gathering, orphrey, purfle, ruche, ruching, ruff, ruffle, trimming, tuck, valance.

frills n. accessories, additions, affectation, decoration, embellishment, extras, fanciness, fandangles, finery, frilliness, frippery, froth, frothery, frou-frous, gewgaws, mannerisms, nonsense, ornamentation, ostentation, superfluities, tomfoolery, trimmings.

frilly adj. fancy, flouncy, frothy, lacy, ornate, overornate, ruched, ruffled.
antonyms plain, unadorned.

fringe n. borderline, edge, fimbriation, frisette, limits, march, marches, margin, outskirts, perimeter, periphery.
adj. alternative, unconventional, unofficial, unorthodox.
v. border, edge, enclose, fimbriate, skirt, surround, trim.

fringed adj. bordered, edged, fimbriated, fringy, tasselled, tasselly, trimmed.

frippery n. adornments, baubles, decorations, fanciness, fandangles, finery, flashiness, foppery, frilliness, frills, froth, frothery, fussiness, gaudiness, gewgaws, glad rags, knick-

knacks, meretriciousness, nonsense, ornaments, ostentation, pretentiousness, showiness, tawdriness, trifles, trinkets, trivia, triviality.
antonym plainness.

frisk[1] *v.* bounce, caper, cavort, curvet, dance, frolic, gambol, hop, jump, leap, pirouette, play, prance, rollick, romp, skip, sport, trip.

frisk[2] *v.* check, inspect, search, shake down.

frisky *adj.* bouncy, buckish, coltish, frolicsome, gamesome, high-spirited, kittenish, lively, playful, rollicking, romping, skittish, spirited, sportive.
antonym quiet.

fritter *v.* blow, dissipate, idle, misspend, run through, squander, waste.

frivolity *n.* childishness, flightiness, flippancy, flummery, folly, frivolousness, froth, fun, gaiety, giddiness, jest, levity, lightheartedness, lightness, nonsense, puerility, shallowness, silliness, skittishness, superficiality, trifling, triviality.
antonym seriousness.

frivolous *adj.* childish, dizzy, empty-headed, extravagant, facetious, flighty, flip, flippant, foolish, giddy, idle, ill-considered, impractical, jocular, juvenile, light, light-minded, petty, pointless, puerile, shallow, silly, skittish, superficial, trifling, trivial, unimportant, unserious, vacuous, vain.
antonym serious.

frizzy *adj.* corrugated, crimped, crisp, curled, curly, frizzed, wiry.
antonym straight.

frolic *v.* caper, cavort, cut capers, frisk, gambol, gammock, lark, make merry, play, rollick, romp, skylark, sport, wanton.
n. amusement, antic, drollery, escapade, fun, gaiety, gambado, gambol, game, gammock, gilravage, high jinks, lark, merriment, prank, razzle-dazzle, revel, rig, romp, skylarking, sport, spree.

frolicsome *adj.* coltish, espiègle, frisky, gamesome, gay, kittenish, kitteny, lively, merry, playful, rollicking, sportive, sprightly, wanton.
antonym quiet.

from hand to mouth dangerously, from day to day, improvidently, in poverty, insecurely, necessitously, on the breadline, precariously, uncertainly.

from time to time at times, every now and then, every so often, intermittently, now and then, occasionally, on occasion, once in a while, sometimes, spasmodically, sporadically.
antonym constantly.

front *n.* air, anterior, appearance, aspect, bearing, beginning, blind, countenance, cover, cover-up, demeanour, disguise, expression, exterior, façade, face, facing, fore, forefront, foreground, forepart, front line, frontage, head, lead, manner, mask, metope, mien, obverse, pretence, pretext, show, top, van, vanguard.
antonym back.

adj. anterior, anticous, first, fore, foremost, head, lead, leading.
antonyms back, last, least, posterior.
v. confront, face, look over, meet, oppose, overlook.

frontier *n.* borderland, borderline, bound, boundary, bourn(e), confines, edge, limit, march, marches, perimeter, verge.
adj. backwoods, limitrophe, outlying, pioneering.

frost *n.* coldness, disappointment, failure, freeze, freeze-up, hoar-frost, rime.

frosty *adj.* chilly, cold, discouraging, frigid, frozen, hoar, ice-capped, icicled, icy, off-putting, rimy, stand-offish, stiff, unfriendly, unwelcoming, wintry.
antonym warm.

froth *n.* bubbles, effervescence, foam, frivolity, frothery, head, lather, scum, spume, suds, triviality.
v. bubble, effervesce, ferment, fizz, foam, lather.

frothy *adj.* barmy, bubbling, bubbly, empty, foaming, foamy, frilly, frivolous, insubstantial, light, slight, spumescent, spumous, spumy, sudsy, trifling, trivial, trumpery, vain.
antonym flat.

frown *v.* glare, glower, grimace, lower, scowl.
n. dirty look, glare, glower, grimace, moue, scowl.

frown on deprecate, disapprove of, discountenance, discourage, dislike, look askance at, object to, take a dim view of.
antonym approve of.

frowzy *adj.* blowzed, blowzy, dirty, dishevelled, draggle-tailed, frumpish, frumpy, messy, slatternly, sloppy, slovenly, sluttish, ungroomed, unkempt, untidy, unwashed.
antonym well-groomed.

frozen *adj.* arctic, chilled, fixed, frigid, frore, frosted, icebound, ice-cold, ice-covered, icy, in abeyance, numb, pegged, petrified, rigid, rooted, shelved, solidified, stiff, stock-still, stopped, suspended, turned to stone.
antonym warm.

frugal *adj.* abstemious, careful, cheese-paring, economical, meagre, niggardly, parsimonious, penny-wise, provident, prudent, saving, sparing, Spartan, thrifty, ungenerous.
antonym wasteful.

frugality *n.* carefulness, conservation, economising, economy, frugalness, good management, husbandry, providence, prudence, thrift, thriftiness.
antonym wastefulness.

fruit *n.* advantage, benefit, consequence, crop, effect, fruitage, fruitery, harvest, outcome, produce, product, profit, result, return, reward, yield.

fruitful *adj.* abundant, advantageous, beneficial, copious, effective, fecund, feracious, fertile, flush, fructiferous, fructuous, gainful, plenteous, plentiful, productive, profitable, profuse, prolific, rewarding, rich, spawning, successful, teeming, uberous, useful, well-

spent, worthwhile.
antonyms barren, fruitless.

fruitfulness *n.* fecundity, feracity, fertility, productiveness, profitability, uberty, usefulness.
antonym fruitlessness.

fruition *n.* accomplishment, actualisation, attainment, completion, consummation, enjoyment, fulfilment, materialisation, maturation, maturity, perfection, realisation, ripeness, success.
antonym failure.

fruitless *adj.* abortive, barren, bootless, futile, hopeless, idle, ineffectual, pointless, profitless, unavailing, unfruitful, unproductive, unprofitable, unsuccessful, useless, vain.
antonyms fruitful, successful.

fruity *adj.* bawdy, blue, full, indecent, indelicate, juicy, mellow, racy, resonant, rich, ripe, risqué, salacious, saucy, sexy, smutty, spicy, suggestive, titillating, vulgar.
antonyms decent, light.

frump *n.* dowd, dowdy, draggle-tail, fright, Judy, mopsy, scarecrow, slattern, sloven, slut.

frumpish badly-dressed, blowzed, blowzy, dated, dingy, dowdy, drab, dreary, frumpy, ill-dressed, out of date.
antonyms chic, well-groomed.

frustrate *v.* baffle, balk, block, bugger, check, circumvent, confront, counter, countermine, crab, defeat, depress, disappoint, discourage, dishearten, foil, forestall, inhibit, neutralise, nullify, scotch, spike, stymie, thwart.
antonyms fulfil, further, promote.

frustrated *adj.* disappointed, discontented, discouraged, disheartened, embittered, foiled, irked, resentful, scunnered, thwarted.
antonym fulfilled.

frustration *n.* annoyance, balking, circumvention, contravention, curbing, disappointment, dissatisfaction, failure, foiling, irritation, non-fulfilment, non-success, obstruction, resentment, thwarting, vexation.
antonyms fulfilment, furthering, promoting.

fuddled *adj.* bemused, confused, drunk, groggy, hazy, inebriated, intoxicated, muddled, mused, muzzy, sozzled, stupefied, tipsy, woozy.
antonyms clear, sober.

fuddy-duddy *n.* back number, carper, conservative, dodo, fogey, fossil, museum piece, old fog(e)y, square, stick-in-the-mud, stuffed shirt.
adj. carping, censorious, old-fashioned, old-fog(e)yish, prim, stick-in-the-mud, stuffy.
antonym up-to-date.

fudge *v.* avoid, cook, dodge, equivocate, evade, fake, falsify, fiddle, fix, hedge, misrepresent, shuffle, stall.

fuel *n.* ammunition, eilding, encouragement, fodder, food, incitement, material, means, nourishment, provocation.
v. charge, encourage, fan, feed, fire, incite, inflame, nourish, stoke up, sustain.
antonyms damp down, discourage.

fug *n.* fetidity, fetidness, fetor, frowst, frowstiness, fustiness, reek, staleness, stink, stuffiness.
antonym airiness.

fuggy *adj.* airless, close, fetid, foul, frowsty, fusty, noisome, noxious, stale, stuffy, suffocating, unventilated.
antonym airy.

fugitive *n.* deserter, escapee, refugee, runagate, runaway.
adj. brief, elusive, ephemeral, evanescent, fleeing, fleeting, flitting, flying, fugacious, intangible, momentary, passing, short, short-lived, temporary, transient, transitory, unstable.
antonym permanent.

fulfil *v.* accomplish, achieve, answer, carry out, complete, comply with, conclude, conform to, consummate, discharge, effect, effectuate, execute, fill, finish, implement, keep, meet, obey, observe, perfect, perform, realise, satisfy.
antonyms break, defect, fail, frustrate.

fulfilment *n.* accomplishment, achievement, attainment, bringing about, carrying out, completion, consummation, crowning, discharge, discharging, effecting, effectuation, end, implementation, observance, perfection, performance, realisation, success.
antonyms failure, frustration.

full *adj.* abundant, adequate, all-inclusive, ample, baggy, brimful, brimming, broad, buxom, capacious, chock-a-block, chock-full, clear, complete, comprehensive, copious, crammed, crowded, curvaceous, deep, detailed, distinct, entire, exhaustive, extensive, filled, generous, gorged, intact, jammed, large, loaded, loud, maximum, occupied, orotund, packed, plenary, plenteous, plentiful, plump, replete, resonant, rich, rounded, sated, satiated, satisfied, saturated, stocked, sufficient, taken, thorough, unabbreviated, unabridged, uncut, unedited, unexpurgated, voluminous, voluptuous.
antonyms empty, incomplete.

full-blooded *adj.* gutsy, hearty, lusty, mettlesome, red-blooded, thoroughbred, vigorous, virile, whole-hearted.

full-grown *adj.* adult, developed, full-aged, full-blown, full-scale, grown-up, marriageable, mature, nubile, of age, ripe.
antonyms undeveloped, young.

fullness *n.* abundance, adequateness, ampleness, broadness, clearness, completeness, comprehensiveness, copiousness, curvaceousness, dilation, distension, enlargement, entirety, extensiveness, fill, glut, loudness, orotundity, plenitude, plenty, pleroma, profusion, repletion, resonance, richness, roundness, satiety, saturation, strength, sufficiency, swelling, totality, tumescence, vastness, voluptuousness, wealth, wholeness.
antonyms emptiness, incompleteness.

full-scale *adj.* all-encompassing, all-out, comprehensive, exhaustive, extensive, full-dress, in-depth, intensive, major, proper, sweeping, thorough, thoroughgoing, wide-ranging. *antonym* partial.

fully *adv.* absolutely, abundantly, adequately, altogether, amply, completely, comprehensively, enough, entirely, every inch, from first to last, heart and soul, in all respects, intimately, perfectly, plentifully, positively, quite, satisfactorily, sufficiently, thoroughly, totally, utterly, wholly, without reserve. *antonym* partly.

fully-fledged *adj.* experienced, full-blown, full-fledged, graduate, mature, professional, proficient, qualified, senior, trained. *antonym* inexperienced.

fulminate *v.* animadvert, criticise, curse, denounce, detonate, fume, inveigh, protest, rage, rail, thunder, vilipend, vituperate. *antonym* praise.

fulmination *n.* condemnation, denunciation, detonation, diatribe, invective, obloquy, philippic, reprobation, thundering, tirade. *antonym* praise.

fulsome *adj.* adulatory, cloying, effusive, excessive, extravagant, fawning, gross, immoderate, ingratiating, inordinate, insincere, nauseating, nauseous, offensive, overdone, rank, saccharine, sickening, smarmy, sycophantic, unctuous. *antonym* sincere.

fumble *v.* botch, bumble, bungle, faff, flail, flounder, fluff, footer, grope, misfied, mishandle, mismanage, muff, mumble, paw, scrabble, spoil.

fume *v.* boil, chafe, fizz, get steamed up, give off, rage, rant, rave, reek, seethe, smoke, smoulder, storm.

fumes *n.* effluvium, exhalation, exhaust, gas, haze, mephitis, miasma, pollution, reek, smog, smoke, stench, vapour.

fumigate *v.* cleanse, deodorise, disinfect, purify, sanitise, sterilise.

fuming *adj.* angry, boiling, enraged, fizzing, incensed, raging, roused, seething, spitting, steamed up. *antonym* calm.

fun *n.* amusement, buffoonery, cheer, clowning, distraction, diversion, enjoyment, entertainment, foolery, frolic, gaiety, game, gammock, high jinks, horseplay, jesting, jocularity, joking, jollification, jollity, joy, junketing, merriment, merrymaking, mirth, nonsense, play, playfulness, pleasure, recreation, romp, skylarking, sport, teasing, tomfoolery, treat, waggery, whoopee.

function[1] *n.* activity, business, capacity, charge, concern, duty, employment, exercise, faculty, job, mission, occupation, office, operation, part, post, province, purpose, raison d'être, responsibility, role, situation, task. *v.* act, be in running order, behave, do duty, functionate, go, officiate, operate, perform, run, serve, work.

function[2] *n.* affair, dinner, do, gathering, junket, luncheon, party, reception, shindig.

functional *adj.* hard-wearing, operational, operative, plain, practical, serviceable, useful, utilitarian, utility, working. *antonyms* effective, inoperative, ornate, useless.

functionary *n.* bureaucrat, dignitary, employee, office-bearer, office-holder, officer, official.

functionless *adj.* aimless, decorative, futile, hollow, idle, inactive, inert, irrelevant, needless, otiose, pointless, redundant, superfluous, useless. *antonym* useful.

fund *n.* cache, capital, endowment, foundation, hoard, kitty, mine, pool, repository, reserve, reservoir, source, stack, stock, store, storehouse, supply, treasury, vein, well. *v.* back, capitalise, endow, finance, float, promote, stake, subsidise, support, underwrite.

fundamental *adj.* axiomatic, basal, basic, basilar, cardinal, central, constitutional, crucial, elementary, essential, first, important, indispensable, integral, intrinsic, key, keynote, necessary, organic, primal, primary, prime, principal, rudimentary, underlying, vital. *antonym* advanced. *n.* axiom, basic, cornerstone, essential, first principle, law, principle, rudiment, rule, sine qua non.

fundamentally *adv.* à fond, at bottom, at heart, au fond, basically, essentially, intrinsically, primarily, radically.

fundamentals *n.* basics, brass tacks, business, nitty-gritty, practicalities.

funds *n.* backing, bread, capital, cash, dough, finance, hard cash, money, moola(h), pelf, ready money, resources, savings, spondulicks, the ready, the wherewithal.

funeral *n.* burial, inhumation, interment, obit, obsequies.

funereal *adj.* dark, deathlike, depressing, dirgelike, dismal, dreary, exequial, feral, funebral, funebrial, gloomy, grave, lamenting, lugubrious, mournful, sad, sepulchral, solemn, sombre, woeful. *antonyms* happy, lively.

funk *v.* balk at, blench, chicken out of, cop out, dodge, duck out of, flinch from, recoil from, shirk from.

funnel *v.* channel, conduct, convey, direct, filter, move, pass, pour, siphon, transfer.

funny *adj.* a card, a caution, a scream, absurd, amusing, comic, comical, curious, diverting, droll, dubious, entertaining, facetious, farcical, funny ha-ha, funny peculiar, hilarious, humorous, jocose, jocular, jolly, killing, laughable, ludicrous, mirth-provoking, mysterious, odd, peculiar, perplexing, puzzling, queer, remarkable, rich, ridiculous, riotous, risible, side-splitting, silly, slapstick, strange, suspicious, unusual, waggish, weird, witty. *antonyms* sad, solemn, unamusing, unfunny.

fur *n.* coat, down, fell, fleece, flix, flue, hide, pelage, pelt, skin, wool.

Furies *n.* Dirae, Erinyes, Eumenides, Furiae, Semnai.

furious *adj.* acharné, agitated, angry, boiling, boisterous, enraged, fierce, fizzing, frantic, frenzied, fuming, furibund, impetuous, incensed, infuriated, intense, livid, mad, maddened, maenadic, raging, savage, stormy, tempestuous, tumultuous, turbulent, up in arms, vehement, violent, waxy, wild, wrathful, wroth.
antonyms calm, pleased.

furnish *v.* afford, appoint, bedight, bestow, decorate, endow, equip, fit out, fit up, give, grant, offer, outfit, present, provide, provision, reveal, rig, stake, stock, store, suit, supply.
antonym divest.

furniture *n.* appliances, appointments, appurtenances, chattels, effects, equipment, fittings, furnishing, goods, household goods, movables, plenishing, possessions, things.

furore *n.* commotion, craze, disturbance, enthusiasm, excitement, flap, frenzy, fury, fuss, hullabaloo, mania, outburst, outcry, rage, stir, to-do, tumult, uproar.
antonym calm.

furrow *n.* chamfer, channel, corrugation, crease, crow's-foot, flute, fluting, groove, hollow, line, rut, seam, trench, vallecula, wrinkle.
v. corrugate, crease, draw together, flute, knit, seam, wrinkle.

furrowed *adj.* channelled, corrugated, exarate, fluted, gouged, grooved, ribbed, ridged, rutted, seamed, vallecular, valleculate, wrinkled.

further *adj.* additional, distant, extra, far, fresh, more, new, opposite, other, supplementary.
v. accelerate, advance, aid, assist, champion, contribute to, ease, encourage, expedite, facilitate, forward, foster, hasten, help, patronise, plug, promote, push, speed, succour.
antonyms frustrate, stop.

furtherance *n.* advancement, advancing, advocacy, backing, boosting, carrying-out, championship, promoting, promotion, prosecution, pursuit.

furthermore *adv.* additionally, also, as well, besides, further, in addition, into the bargain, likewise, moreover, not to mention, to boot, too, what's more.

furthest *adj.* extreme, farthest, furthermost, most distant, outermost, outmost, remotest, ultimate, uttermost.
antonym nearest.

furtive *adj.* back-door, backstairs, clandestine, cloaked, conspiratorial, covert, hidden, secret, secretive, skulking, slinking, sly, sneaking, sneaky, stealthy, surreptitious, underhand.
antonym open.

fury[1] *n.* anger, desperation, ferocity, fierceness, force, frenzy, impetuosity, intensity, ire, madness, passion, power, rage, savagery, severity, tempestuousness, turbulence, vehemence, violence, wax, wrath.
antonym calm.

fury[2] *n.* bacchante, hag, harridan, hell-cat, shrew, spitfire, termagant, virago, vixen.

fuse *v.* agglutinate, amalgamate, ankylose, blend, coalesce, combine, commingle, federate, integrate, intermingle, intermix, join, meld, melt, merge, smelt, solder, unite, weld.

fusillade *n.* barrage, broadside, burst, discharge, fire, hail, mitraille, outburst, salvo, volley.

fusion *n.* alloy, amalgam, amalgamation, blend, blending, coalescence, commingling, commixture, federation, integration, liquefaction, liquefying, melting, merger, merging, mixture, smelting, synthesis, union, uniting, welding.

fuss *n.* ado, agitation, bother, brouhaha, bustle, coil, commotion, confusion, difficulty, display, doodah, excitement, fantigue, fash, fidget, fikery, flap, flurry, fluster, flutter, furore, hassle, hoo-ha, hurry, kerfuffle, objection, palaver, pother, pudder, row, squabble, stew, stir, to-do, trouble, unrest, upset, worry.
antonym calm.
v. bustle, chafe, complain, emote, fash, fidget, flap, fret, fume, niggle, pother, pudder, take pains, worry.

fussiness *n.* busy-ness, choosiness, daintiness, elaborateness, faddiness, faddishness, fastidiousness, finicality, finicalness, meticulousness, niceness, niggling, particularity, perfectionism, pernicketiness.
antonym unfastidiousness.

fuss-pot *n.* fantod, fidget, fuss-budget, hypercritic, nit-picker, old woman, perfectionist, worrier.

fussy *adj.* busy, chichi, choosy, cluttered, dainty, difficult, discriminating, exacting, faddish, faddy, fastidious, finical, finicking, finicky, finikin, hard to please, niggling, nippertytipperty, nit-picking, old womanish, oldmaidish, overdecorated, overelaborate, overparticular, particular, pernickety, picky, squeamish.
antonyms plain, uncritical, undemanding.

fustiness *n.* airlessness, closeness, dampness, frowst, frowstiness, fug, fust, mouldiness, mustiness, staleness, stuffiness.
antonym airiness.

fusty *adj.* airless, antediluvian, antiquated, archaic, close, damp, dank, frowsty, fuggy, ill-smelling, malodorous, mildewed, mildewy, mouldering, mouldy, musty, old-fashioned, old-fog(e)yish, outdated, out-of-date, passé, rank, stale, stuffy, unventilated.
antonyms airy, chic, up-to-date.

futile *adj.* abortive, barren, bootless, empty, forlorn, fruitless, hollow, idle, ineffectual, nugatory, otiose, pointless, profitless, Sisyphean, sterile, trifling, trivial, unavailing, unimportant, unproductive, unprofitable, unsuccessful, useless, vain, valueless, worthless.
antonyms fruitful, profitable.

futility *n.* aimlessness, bootlessness, emptiness,

fruitlessness, hollowness, idleness, ineffectiveness, otioseness, pointlessness, triviality, unimportance, uselessness, vanity.
antonyms fruitfulness, profitability.

future *n.* expectation, futurition, futurity, hereafter, outlook, prospects.
antonym past.
adj. approaching, coming, designate, destined, eventual, expected, fated, forthcoming, impending, in the offing, later, prospective,

rising, subsequent, to be, to come, ultimate, unborn.
antonym past.

fuzz *n.* down, fibre, flock, floss, flue, fluff, fug, hair, lint, nap, ooze, pile.

fuzzy *adj.* bleary, blurred, blurry, distanceless, distorted, downy, faint, fluffy, frizzy, hazy, ill-defined, indistinct, linty, muffled, napped, shadowy, unclear, unfocused, vague, woolly.
antonyms base, distinct.

G

gab v. babble, blabber, blather, blether, buzz, chatter, drivel, gossip, jabber, jaw, prattle, talk, tattle, yabber, yak, yatter.

n. blab, blarney, blethering, blethers, chat, chatter, chitchat, conversation, drivel, gossip, loquacity, palaver, prattle, prattling, small talk, tête-à-tête, tittle-tattle, tongue-wagging, yabber, yackety-yak, yak, yatter.

gabble v. babble, blab, blabber, blether, cackle, chatter, gaggle, gibber, gush, jabber, prattle, rattle, splutter, spout, sputter, yabber, yatter.

n. babble, blabber, blethering, cackling, chatter, drivel, gibberish, jargon, nonsense, prattle, twaddle, waffle, yabber, yatter.

gad about dot about, gallivant, ramble, range, roam, rove, run around, stray, traipse, wander.

gadabout n. gallivanter, pleasure-seeker, rambler, rover, runabout, stravaiger, wanderer.

gadget n. appliance, contraption, contrivance, device, doodad, gimmick, gismo, gizmo, invention, jiggumbob, jigjam, jigmaree, novelty, thing, thingumajig, tool, widget.

gaffe n. bloomer, blunder, boner, boob, boo-boo, brick, clanger, faux pas, gaucherie, goof, howler, indiscretion, mistake, slip, solecism.

gaffer n. boss, foreman, ganger, manager, overman, overseer, superintendent, supervisor.

gag[1] v. choke, choke up, curb, disgorge, gasp, heave, muffle, muzzle, puke, quiet, retch, silence, spew, stifle, still, stop up, suppress, throttle, throw up, vomit.

gag[2] n. funny, hoax, jest, joke, one-liner, pun, quip, wisecrack, witticism.

gaiety n. animation, blitheness, blithesomeness, brightness, brilliance, celebration, cheerfulness, colour, colourfulness, conviviality, effervescence, elation, exhilaration, festivity, fun, galliardise, gaudiness, glee, glitter, good humour, high spirits, hilarity, joie de vivre, jollification, jollity, joviality, joyousness, light-heartedness, liveliness, merriment, merrymaking, mirth, revelry, revels, show, showiness, sparkle, sprightliness, vivacity.
antonyms drabness, dreariness, sadness.

gaily adv. blithely, brightly, brilliantly, cheerfully, colourfully, fancily, flamboyantly, flashily, gaudily, gleefully, happily, joyfully, joyously, light-heartedly, merrily, showily.
antonyms dully, sadly.

gain v. achieve, acquire, advance, arrive at, attain, avail, bag, bring in, capture, clear, collect, come to, earn, enlist, gather, get, get to, glean, harvest, impetrate, improve,

increase, make, net, obtain, pick up, procure, produce, profit, progress, reach, realise, reap, secure, win, win over, yield.
antonym lose.

n. accretion, achievement, acquisition, advance, advancement, advantage, attainment, benefit, bunce, dividend, earnings, emolument, growth, headway, improvement, income, increase, increment, lucre, proceeds, produce, profit, progress, pudding, return, rise, winnings, yield.
antonyms loss, losses.

gain on approach, catch up, catch up with, close with, come up with, encroach on, leave behind, level with, narrow the gap, outdistance, overtake, widen the gap.

gain time delay, drag one's feet, procrastinate, stall, temporise.

gainful adj. advantageous, beneficial, feracious, fructuous, fruitful, lucrative, moneymaking, paying, productive, profitable, remunerative, rewarding, useful, worthwhile.
antonym useless.

gains n. booty, bunce, earnings, fruits, gainings, loaves and fishes, pickings, prize, proceeds, profits, revenue, takings, velvet, winnings.
antonym losses.

gainsay v. contradict, contravene, controvert, deny, disaffirm, disagree with, dispute, nay-say.
antonym agree.

gait n. bearing, carriage, manner, pace, step, stride, tread, walk.

gala n. carnival, celebration, festival, festivity, fête, glorification, jamboree, jubilee, Mardi Gras, pageant, party, procession.

gale n. blast, burst, cyclone, eruption, explosion, fit, howl, hurricane, outbreak, outburst, peal, ripsnorter, shout, shriek, squall, storm, tempest, tornado, typhoon.

gall[1] n. acrimony, animosity, animus, antipathy, assurance, bad blood, bile, bitterness, brass, brass neck, brazenness, cheek, effrontery, enmity, hostility, impertinence, impudence, insolence, malevolence, malice, malignity, neck, nerve, presumption, presumptuousness, rancour, sauciness, sourness, spite, spleen, venom, virulence.
antonyms friendliness, modesty, reserve.

gall[2] v. abrade, aggravate, annoy, bark, bother, chafe, exasperate, excoriate, fret, get, get to, graze, harass, hurt, irk, irritate, nag, nettle, peeve, pester, plague, provoke, rankle, rile, rub raw, ruffle, scrape, skin, vex.

gallant adj. attentive, august, bold, brave, chivalrous, courageous, courteous, courtly,

daring, dashing, dauntless, dignified, doughty, elegant, fearless, game, gentlemanly, glorious, gracious, grand, heroic, high-spirited, honourable, imposing, indomitable, intrepid, lion-hearted, lofty, magnanimous, magnificent, manful, manly, mettlesome, noble, plucky, polite, splendid, stately, valiant, valorous.
antonyms cowardly, craven, ungentlemanly.
n. admirer, adventurer, beau, blade, boyfriend, buck, cavalier, champion, cicisbeo, dandy, daredevil, escort, fop, hero, knight, ladies' man, lady-killer, lover, paramour, suitor, wooer.

gallantry *n.* attention, attentiveness, audacity, boldness, bravery, chivalry, courage, courageousness, courteousness, courtesy, courtliness, daring, dauntlessness, derring-do, elegance, fearlessness, gentlemanliness, graciousness, heroism, intrepidity, manliness, mettle, nerve, nobility, pluck, politeness, politesse, prowess, spirit, valiance, valour.
antonyms cowardice, ungentlemanliness.

gallery *n.* arcade, art-gallery, balcony, circle, gods, grandstand, loggia, museum, passage, pawn, spectators, walk.

galley *n.* bireme, long-ship, lymphad, quadrireme, quinquereme, trireme.

galling *adj.* aggravating, annoying, bitter, bothersome, exasperating, harassing, humiliating, infuriating, irksome, irritating, nettling, plaguing, provoking, rankling, vexatious, vexing.
antonym pleasing.

gallivant *v.* dot about, gad about, ramble, range, roam, rove, run around, stravaig, stray, traipse, travel, wander.

gallop *v.* bolt, career, dart, dash, fly, gal(l)umph, hasten, hie, hurry, lope, race, run, rush, scud, shoot, speed, sprint, tear, zoom.

gallows *n.* dule-tree, hempen caudle, nubbing-cleat, scaffold, the rope.

galore *adv.* aplenty, everywhere, heaps of, in abundance, in numbers, in profusion, lots of, millions of, stacks of, to spare, tons of.
antonym scarce.

galvanise *v.* animate, arouse, awaken, electrify, excite, fire, inspire, invigorate, jolt, move, prod, provoke, quicken, shock, spur, startle, stimulate, stir, thrill, vitalise, wake.
antonym retard.

gambit *n.* artifice, device, manoeuvre, move, ploy, stratagem, trick, wile.

gamble *v.* back, bet, chance, gaff, game, have a flutter, hazard, play, punt, risk, speculate, stake, stick one's neck out, take a chance, try one's luck, venture, wager.
n. bet, chance, flutter, leap in the dark, lottery, punt, risk, speculation, uncertainty, venture, wager.

gambler *n.* better, gaffer, gamester, punter, throwster, wagerer.

gambol *v.* bounce, bound, caper, cavort, curvet, cut a caper, frisk, frolic, hop, jump, prance, rollick, skip.

n. antic, bound, caper, frisk, frolic, gambado, hop, jump, prance, skip, spring.

game[1] *n.* adventure, amusement, business, competition, contest, design, device, distraction, diversion, enterprise, entertainment, event, frolic, fun, jest, joke, lark, line, main, match, meeting, merriment, merry-making, occupation, pastime, plan, play, plot, ploy, proceeding, recreation, romp, round, scheme, sport, stratagem, strategy, tactic, tournament, trick, undertaking.

game[2] *n.* animals, bag, flesh, game-birds, meat, prey, quarry, spoils.

game[3] *adj.* bold, brave, courageous, dauntless, desirous, disposed, dogged, eager, fearless, gallant, gamy, heroic, inclined, interested, intrepid, persevering, persistent, plucky, prepared, ready, resolute, spirited, spunky, unflinching, valiant, valorous, willing.
antonyms cowardly, unwilling.

game[4] *adj.* bad, crippled, deformed, disabled, gammy, gouty, hobbling, incapacitated, injured, lame, maimed.

gamekeeper *n.* keeper, venerer, verderer, warden.

gamut *n.* area, catalogue, compass, field, range, scale, scope, series, spectrum, sweep.

gang *n.* band, circle, clique, club, coffle, company, core, coterie, crew, crowd, group, herd, horde, lot, mob, pack, party, ring, set, shift, squad, team, troupe.

gangling *adj.* angular, awkward, bony, gangly, gauche, gawky, lanky, loose-jointed, rangy, raw-boned, skinny, spindly, tall, ungainly.

gangster *n.* bandit, brigand, crook, desperado, heavy, hood, hoodlum, mobster, racketeer, robber, rough, ruffian, thug, tough.

gaol *see* **jail**.

gap *n.* blank, breach, break, chink, cleft, crack, cranny, crevice, diastema, difference, disagreement, discontinuity, disparateness, disparity, divergence, divide, hiatus, hole, inconsistency, interlude, intermission, interruption, interspace, interstice, interval, lacuna, lull, opening, pause, recess, rent, rift, space, vacuity, void.

gape *v.* crack, dehisce, gawk, gawp, goggle, open, split, stare, wonder, yawn.

gaping *adj.* broad, cavernous, dehiscent, fatiscent, great, hiant, open, ringent, vast, wide, yawning.
antonym tiny.

garage *n.* lock-up, petrol station, service station.

garb *n.* accoutrements, apparel, appearance, array, aspect, attire, clothes, clothing, costume, covering, cut, dress, fashion, garment, gear, guise, habiliment, habit, look, mode, outfit, raiment, robes, style, uniform, vestments, wear.
v. apparel, array, attire, clothe, cover, dress, habilitate, rig out, robe.

garbage *n.* bits and pieces, debris, detritus, dross, filth, gash, junk, litter, muck, odds and ends, offal, refuse, rubbish, scourings, scraps, slops, sweepings, swill, trash, waste.

garble v. confuse, corrupt, distort, doctor, edit, falsify, jumble, misinterpret, misquote, misreport, misrepresent, misstate, mistranslate, mix up, muddle, mutilate, pervert, slant, tamper with, twist.
antonym decipher.

garden n. backyard, garth, orchard, park, plot, yard.

gargantuan adj. big, Brobdingnag(ian), colossal, elephantine, enormous, giant, gigantic, huge, immense, large, leviathan, mammoth, massive, monstrous, monumental, mountainous, prodigious, titanic, towering, tremendous, vast.
antonym small.

gargoyle n. grotesque, spout.

garish adj. brassy, brummagem, cheap, criant, flash, flashy, flaunting, flaunty, gaudy, glaring, glittering, glitzy, loud, meretricious, raffish, showy, tasteless, tawdry, vulgar.
antonyms modest, plain, quiet.

garland n. bays, chaplet, coronal, crown, festoon, honours, laurels, lei, stemma, swag, wreath.
v. adorn, crown, deck, engarland, festoon, wreathe.

garments n. apparel, array, attire, clothes, clothing, costume, dress, duds, garb, gear, get-up, habiliment, habit, outfit, raiment, robes, togs, uniform, vestments, wear.

garner v. accumulate, amass, assemble, collect, cull, deposit, gather, hoard, husband, lay up, put by, reserve, save, stockpile, store, stow away, treasure.
antonym dissipate.

garnish v. adorn, beautify, bedeck, deck, decorate, embellish, enhance, furnish, grace, ornament, set off, trim.
antonym divest.
n. adornment, decoration, embellishment, enhancement, garnishment, garnishry, garniture, ornament, ornamentation, relish, trim, trimming.

garrison n. armed force, barracks, base, camp, casern(e), command, detachment, encampment, fort, fortification, fortress, post, station, stronghold, troops, unit, zareba.
v. assign, defend, furnish, guard, man, mount, occupy, place, position, post, protect, station.

garrulity n. babble, babbling, chatter, chattering, chattiness, diffuseness, effusiveness, gabbiness, garrulousness, gassing, gift of the gab, glibness, long-windedness, loquaciousness, loquacity, prating, prattle, prolixity, prosiness, talkativeness, verbosity, volubility, windiness, wordiness.
antonyms taciturnity, terseness.

garrulous adj. babbling, chattering, chatty, diffuse, effusive, gabby, gassy, glib, gossiping, gushing, glitzy, long-winded, loquacious, mouthy, prating, prattling, prolix, prosy, talkative, verbose, voluble, windy, wordy, yabbering.
antonyms taciturn, terse.

gash v. cleave, cut, gouge, incise, lacerate, nick, notch, rend, score, slash, slit, split, tear, wound.
n. cleft, cut, gouge, incision, laceration, nick, notch, rent, score, slash, slit, split, tear, wound.

gasp v. blow, breathe, choke, ejaculate, gulp, pant, puff, utter.
n. blow, breath, ejaculation, exclamation, gulp, pant, puff.

gate n. barrier, door, doorway, entrance, exit, gateway, opening, passage, port, portal, portcullis, wicket.

gather v. accumulate, amass, assemble, assume, build, clasp, collect, conclude, congregate, convene, crop, cull, deduce, deepen, draw, embrace, enfold, enlarge, expand, flock, fold, foregather, garner, glean, group, grow, harvest, heap, hear, heighten, hoard, hold, hug, increase, infer, intensify, learn, make, marshal, mass, muster, pick, pile up, pleat, pluck, pucker, rake up, reap, rise, round up, ruche, ruffle, select, shirr, stockpile, surmise, swell, thicken, tuck, understand, wax.
antonyms dissipate, scatter.

gathering n. accumulation, acquisition, aggregate, assemblage, assembly, collection, company, concentration, conclave, concourse, congregation, congress, convention, convocation, crowd, fest, flock, gain, galère, get-together, group, heap, hoard, jamboree, kgotla, knot, mass, meeting, moot, muster, omnium-gatherum, party, pile, procurement, rally, round-up, rout, stock, stockpile, throng, turn-out.
antonym scattering.

gauche adj. awkward, clumsy, farouche, gawky, graceless, ignorant, ill-bred, ill-mannered, inelegant, inept, insensitive, maladroit, tactless, uncultured, ungainly, ungraceful, unpolished, unsophisticated.
antonym graceful.

gaucherie n. awkwardness, bad taste, bloomer, blunder, boner, boob, brick, clanger, clumsiness, faux pas, gaffe, gaucheness, goof, gracelessness, ignorance, ill-breeding, indiscretion, inelegance, ineptness, insensitivity, maladroitness, mistake, slip, solecism, tactlessness.
antonym elegance.

gaudy adj. bright, brilliant, brummagem, chintzy, flash, flashy, florid, garish, gay, glaring, glitzy, loud, meretricious, ostentatious, raffish, showy, tasteless, tawdry, tinsel(ly), vulgar.
antonyms drab, plain, quiet.

gauge[1] v. adjudge, adjust, appraise, ascertain, assess, calculate, check, compute, count, determine, estimate, evaluate, figure, guess, judge, measure, rate, reckon, value, weigh.
n. basis, criterion, example, exemplar, guide, guideline, indicator, measure, meter, micrometer, model, pattern, rule, sample, standard, test, touchstone, yardstick.

gauge[2] n. bore, calibre, capacity, degree, depth, extent, height, magnitude, measure, scope, size, span, thickness, width.

gaunt *adj.* angular, attenuated, bare, bleak, bony, cadaverous, desolate, dismal, dreary, emaciated, forbidding, forlorn, grim, haggard, hagged, harsh, hollow-eyed, lank, lean, meagre, pinched, rawboned, scraggy, scrawny, skeletal, skinny, spare, thin, wasted.
antonyms hale, plump.

gauzy *adj.* delicate, diaphanous, filmy, flimsy, gossamer, insubstantial, light, see-through, sheer, thin, transparent, unsubstantial.
antonyms heavy, thick.

gawk *v.* gape, gaup, gaze, goggle, look, ogle, stare.

gawky *adj.* awkward, clownish, clumsy, gangling, gauche, loutish, lumbering, lumpish, maladroit, oafish, uncouth, ungainly, ungraceful.
antonym graceful.

gay[1] *adj.* animated, blithe, boon, bright, brilliant, carefree, cavalier, cheerful, colourful, convivial, debonair, festive, flamboyant, flashy, fresh, frivolous, frolicsome, fun-loving, gamesome, garish, gaudy, glad, gleeful, happy, hilarious, insouciant, jolly, jovial, joyful, joyous, lifesome, light-hearted, lightsome, lively, merry, playful, pleasure-seeking, rakish, riant, rich, rollicking, rorty, showy, sparkish, sparkling, sportive, sunny, tit(t)upy, vivacious, vivid, waggish.
antonyms gloomy, sad.

gay[2] *adj.* bent, dikey, homosexual, lesbian, queer.
antonyms heterosexual, straight.
n. dike, homo, homosexual, lesbian, poof, queer, sapphist.
antonym heterosexual.

gaze *v.* contemplate, gape, gaup, gawp, look, ogle, regard, stare, view, watch.
n. gaup, gawp, look, stare.

gazebo *n.* belvedere, hut, pavilion, shelter, summer-house.

gazette *n.* despatch, journal, magazine, newspaper, news-sheet, notice, organ, paper, periodical.

gear *n.* accessories, accoutrements, affair, apparatus, apparel, armour, array, attire, baggage, belongings, business, clothes, clothing, cog, costume, doings, dress, effects, equipment, garb, garments, gearing, get-up, habit, harness, instruments, kit, luggage, machinery, matter, mechanism, outfit, paraphernalia, possessions, rigging, rig-out, stuff, supplies, tackle, things, togs, tools, trappings, traps, wear, works.
v. adapt, adjust, equip, fit, harness, rig, suit, tailor.

gears *n.* cams, cam-wheels, cogs, cogwheels, engrenage, gear-wheels, mechanism, workings, works.

gelatinous *adj.* congealed, gluey, glutinous, gooey, gummy, jellied, jellified, jelly, jelly-form, jelly-like, mucilaginous, rubbery, sticky, viscid, viscous.

gem *n.* angel, bijou, brick, flower, honey, jewel, masterpiece, pearl, pick, pièce de résistance, precious stone, prize, stone, treasure.

gen *n.* background, data, details, facts, info, information, low-down.

genealogy *n.* ancestry, background, blood-line, derivation, descent, extraction, family, family tree, line, lineage, pedigree, progeniture, stemma, stirps, stock, strain.

general *adj.* accepted, accustomed, across-the-board, all-inclusive, approximate, blanket, broad, catholic, collective, common, comprehensive, conventional, customary, ecumenic, ecumenical, encyclop(a)edic, everyday, extensive, generic, habitual, ill-defined, imprecise, inaccurate, indefinite, indiscriminate, inexact, loose, miscellaneous, normal, ordinary, panoramic, popular, prevailing, prevalent, public, regular, sweeping, total, typical, universal, unspecific, usual, vague, widespread.
antonyms limited, novel, particular.
n. chief, c-in-c, commander, commander in chief, generalissimo, hetman, leader, marshal, officer.

generality *n.* approximateness, breadth, catholicity, commonness, comprehensiveness, ecumenicity, extensiveness, generalisation, impreciseness, indefiniteness, inexactness, looseness, miscellaneity, popularity, prevalence, sweeping statement, universality, vagueness.
antonyms detail, exactness, particular, uncommonness.

generally *adv.* approximately, as a rule, broadly, by and large, characteristically, chiefly, commonly, conventionally, customarily, extensively, for the most part, habitually, in the main, largely, mainly, mostly, normally, on average, on the whole, ordinarily, popularly, predominantly, principally, publicly, regularly, typically, universally, usually, widely.
antonym rarely.

generate *v.* beget, breed, bring about, cause, create, engender, father, form, gender, give rise to, initiate, make, originate, procreate, produce, propagate, spawn, whip up.
antonym prevent.

generation *n.* age, age group, begetting, breed, breeding, creation, crop, day, days, engendering, engenderment, engend(r)ure, epoch, era, formation, generating, genesis, geniture, origination, period, procreation, production, progeniture, propagation, reproduction, time, times.

generic *adj.* all-inclusive, blanket, collective, common, comprehensive, general, inclusive, sweeping, universal, wide.
antonym particular.

generosity *n.* beneficence, benevolence, big-heartedness, bounteousness, bounty, charity, goodness, high-mindedness, kindness, large-heartedness, liberality, magnanimity, munificence, nobleness, open-handedness, soft-heartedness, unselfishness, unsparingness.
antonyms meanness, selfishness.

generous *adj.* abundant, ample, beneficent,

benevolent, big-hearted, bounteous, bountiful, charitable, copious, disinterested, free, full, good, high-minded, hospitable, kind, large-hearted, large-minded, lavish, liberal, lofty, magnanimous, munificent, noble, openhanded, overflowing, plentiful, princely, rich, soft-boiled, soft-hearted, ungrudging, unreproachful, unresentful, unselfish, unsparing, unstinted, unstinting.
antonyms mean, selfish.

genesis *n.* beginning, birth, commencement, creation, dawn, engendering, formation, foundation, founding, generation, inception, initiation, origin, outset, propagation, root, source, start.
antonym end.

genial *adj.* affable, agreeable, amiable, cheerful, cheery, congenial, convivial, cordial, easygoing, expansive, friendly, glad, goodnatured, happy, hearty, jolly, jovial, joyous, kind, kindly, merry, pleasant, sunny, sunshiny, warm, warm-hearted.
antonym cold.

geniality *n.* affability, agreeableness, amiability, cheerfulness, cheeriness, congenialness, conviviality, cordiality, friendliness, gladness, good nature, happiness, heartiness, jollity, joviality, kindliness, kindness, mirth, openness, pleasantness, sunniness, warmheartedness, warmth.
antonym coldness.

genie *adj.* demon, (d)jinni, fairy, jann, jinnee, spirit.

genitals *n.* fanny, genitalia, private parts, privates, pudenda, pudendum, pussy, quim, yoni.

genius[1] *n.* adept, brain, expert, intellect, maestro, master, master-hand, mastermind, pastmaster, virtuoso.

genius[2] *n.* ability, aptitude, bent, brightness, brilliance, capacity, endowment, faculty, flair, gift, inclination, intellect, knack, propensity, talent, turn.

genius[3] *n.* daemon, double, genie, ka, spirit.

genocide *n.* ethnocide, extermination, massacre, slaughter.

genre *n.* brand, category, character, class, fashion, genus, group, kind, race, school, sort, species, strain, style, type, variety.

genteel *adj.* aristocratic, civil, courteous, courtly, cultivated, cultured, elegant, fashionable, formal, gentlemanly, graceful, ladylike, mannerly, polished, polite, refined, respectable, stylish, urbane, well-bred, well-mannered.
antonyms crude, rough, unpolished.

Gentile *n.* goy.

gentility *n.* aristocracy, blue blood, breeding, civility, courtesy, courtliness, cultivation, culture, decorum, elegance, elite, etiquette, formality, gentilesse, gentle birth, gentlefolk, gentrice, gentry, good family, high birth, mannerliness, manners, nobility, nobles, polish, politeness, propriety, rank, refinement, respectability, upper class, urbanity.
antonyms crudeness, discourteousness,

roughness.

gentle *adj.* amiable, aristocratic, balmy, benign, biddable, bland, broken, calm, canny, clement, compassionate, courteous, cultured, docile, easy, elegant, genteel, gentlemanlike, gentlemanly, gradual, high-born, humane, imperceptible, kind, kindly, ladylike, lamblike, lenient, light, low, maidenly, manageable, meek, merciful, mild, moderate, muted, noble, pacific, peaceful, placid, polished, polite, quiet, refined, serene, slight, slow, smooth, soft, soothing, sweet, sweettempered, tame, temperate, tender, tractable, tranquil, untroubled, upper-class, wellborn, well-bred.
antonyms crude, rough, unkind, unpolished.

gentleman *n.* duniewassal, gemman, gent, gentilhomme, hidalgo, sahib, Señor, Signor(e), sir.

gentlemanly *adj.* civil, civilised, courteous, cultivated, gallant, genteel, gentlemanlike, gentlewomanly, honourable, mannerly, noble, obliging, polished, polite, refined, reputable, suave, urbane, well-bred, wellmannered.
antonyms impolite, rough.

gentry *n.* aristocracy, elite, gens de condition, gentility, gentlefolk, nobility, nobles, quality, squirearchy, upper class.

genuine *adj.* actual, artless, authentic, bona fide, candid, earnest, frank, heartfelt, honest, kosher, legitimate, natural, original, pukka, pure, real, simon-pure, sincere, sound, sterling, sure-enough, true, unadulterate(d), unaffected, unalloyed, unfeigned, unsophisticated, veritable.
antonyms artificial, insincere.

genus *n.* breed, category, class, division, genre, group, kind, order, race, set, sort, species, taxon, type.

geography *n.* chorography, layout, lie.

geology *n.* geognosy, geogony, geotectonics.

germ *n.* bacterium, beginning, bud, bug, cause, egg, embryo, microbe, micro-organism, nucleus, origin, ovule, ovum, root, rudiment, seed, source, spark, spore, sprout, virus, zyme.

germane *adj.* akin, allied, applicable, apposite, appropriate, apropos, apt, cognate, connected, fitting, kin, kindred, material, pertinent, proper, related, relevant, suitable.
antonym irrelevant.

germinal *adj.* developing, embryonic, preliminary, rudimentary, seminal, undeveloped.

germinate *v.* bud, develop, generate, grow, originate, pullulate, root, shoot, sprout, swell, vegetate.

gestation *n.* conception, development, drafting, evolution, incubation, maturation, planning, pregnancy, ripening.

gesticulate *v.* gesture, indicate, motion, point, sign, signal, wave.

gesticulation *n.* ch(e)ironomy, motion, sign, signal, wave.

gesture *n.* act, action, gesticulation, indication,

motion, sign, signal, wave.

v. gesticulate, indicate, motion, point, sign, signal, wave.

get *v.* achieve, acquire, affect, annoy, arouse, arrange, arrest, arrive, attain, baffle, bag, become, bother, bring, bug, capture, catch, coax, collar, come, come by, come down with, communicate with, comprehend, confound, contact, contract, contrive, convince, earn, excite, fathom, fetch, fix, follow, gain, glean, grab, grow, hear, impetrate, impress, induce, influence, inherit, irk, irritate, make, make it, manage, move, mystify, net, nonplus, notice, obtain, perceive, perplex, persuade, pick up, pique, prevail upon, procure, puzzle, reach, realise, reap, receive, secure, see, seize, stimulate, stir, stump, succeed, sway, take, touch, trap, turn, twig, understand, upset, vex, wangle, wax, wheedle, win.

antonyms lose, misunderstand, pacify.

get a move on get cracking, get going, go to it, hurry (up), jump to it, make haste, shake a leg, speed up, step on it.

antonym slow down.

get across bring home to, communicate, convey, cross, ford, impart, negotiate, put over, transmit, traverse.

get ahead advance, flourish, get there, go places, make good, make it, progress, prosper, succeed, thrive.

antonyms fail, fall behind.

get along cope, develop, fare, get by, get on, harmonise, hit it off, make (a) shift, make out, manage, progress, shift, survive.

antonym argue.

get at acquire, annoy, attack, attain, blame, bribe, buy off, carp, corrupt, criticise, find fault with, hint, imply, influence, intend, irritate, make fun of, mean, mock, nag, pervert, pick on, poke fun at, suborn, suggest, tamper with, taunt.

antonym praise.

get away break out, decamp, depart, disappear, escape, flee, get out, leave, run away.

get back get even, get one's own back (on), recoup, recover, regain, repossess, retaliate, retrieve, return, revenge oneself (on), revert, revisit.

get by contrive, cope, exist, fare, get along, make both ends meet, manage, negotiate, pass muster, shift, subsist, survive.

get down alight, depress, descend, disembark, dishearten, dismount, dispirit, lower, sadden.

antonyms board, encourage.

get even even the score, get one's own back, pay back, reciprocate, repay, requite, revenge oneself, settle the score.

get in alight, appear, arrive, collect, come, embark, enter, gather in, include, infiltrate, insert, interpose, land, mount, penetrate, take.

antonym get out.

get off alight, depart, descend, detach, disembark, dismount, doff, escape, exit, learn, leave, remove, shed, swot up.

antonyms arrive, board, put on.

get on advance, agree, ascend, board, climb, concur, cope, embark, fare, get along, harmonise, hit it off, make out, manage, mount, proceed, progress, prosper, succeed.

antonyms alight, argue.

get out alight, break out, clear out, decamp, deliver, escape, evacuate, extricate oneself, flee, flit, free oneself, leave, produce, publish, quit, scarper, vacate, withdraw.

antonym board.

get out of avoid, dodge, escape, evade, shirk, skive.

get over communicate, convey, cross, defeat, explain, ford, get the better of, impart, master, overcome, pass, put across, recover from, shake off, surmount, survive, traverse.

get ready arrange, fix up, get psyched up, gird one's loins, inspan, prepare, psych oneself up, ready, rehearse, set out.

get rid of dispense with, dispose of, do away with, dump, eject, eliminate, expel, jettison, remove, rid oneself of, shake off, unload.

antonyms accumulate, acquire.

get round bypass, cajole, circumvent, coax, convert, edge, evade, outmanoeuvre, persuade, prevail upon, skirt, talk over, talk round, wheedle.

get the better of beat, best, defeat, outdo, outfox, outsmart, outwit, surpass, worst.

get the hang of absorb, comprehend, grasp, understand.

get the message catch on, comprehend, get it, get the point, see, take the hint, twig, understand.

antonym misunderstand.

get there advance, arrive, go places, make good, make it, prosper, succeed.

get together accumulate, assemble, collaborate, collect, congregate, convene, converge, gather, join, meet, muster, rally, unite.

get under one's skin annoy, get, get to, infuriate, irk, irritate, needle, nettle.

antonym pacify.

get up arise, arrange, ascend, climb, fix up, increase, learn, memorise, mount, organise, rise, scale, stand.

getaway *n.* break, break-out, decampment, escape, flight, start.

get-together *n.* do, function, gabfest, gathering, party, reception, social, soirée.

gewgaw *n.* bagatelle, bauble, bijou, gaud, gimcrack, kickshaw(s), knick-knack, novelty, plaything, toy, trifle, trinket.

ghastly *adj.* ashen, cadaverous, deathlike, deathly, dreadful, frightful, ghostly, grim, grisly, gruesome, hideous, horrendous, horrible, horrid, livid, loathsome, lurid, pale, pallid, repellent, shocking, spectral, terrible, terrifying, wan.

antonym delightful.

ghost *n.* apparition, astral body, duppy, eidolon, fetch, glimmer, gytrash, hint, jumby, larva, lemur, manes, phantasm, phantom, possibility, revenant, semblance, shade, shadow, simulacrum, soul, spectre, spirit, spook, suggestion, trace, umbra, visitant, white-lady.

ghostly *adj.* chthonian, eerie, eldritch, faint, ghostlike, illusory, insubstantial, phantasmal, phantom, spectral, spooky, supernatural, uncanny, unearthly, weird, wraith-like.

ghoulish *adj.* grisly, gruesome, macabre, morbid, revolting, sick, unhealthy, unwholesome.

giant *n.* behemoth, colossus, Goliath, Hercules, jotun, leviathan, monster, Patagonian, titan. *adj.* Atlantean, Babylonian, Brobdingnag(ian), colossal, cyclopean, elephantine, enormous, gargantuan, gigantean, gigantesque, gigantic, huge, immense, jumble, king-size, large, leviathan, mammoth, monstrous, Patagonian, prodigious, rounceval, titanic, vast.

gibber *v.* babble, blab, blabber, blather, cackle, cant, chatter, claptrap, gabble, jabber, prattle.

gibberish *n.* abracadabra, babble, balderdash, blather, drivel, gabble, gobbledegook, jabber, jabberwock(y), jargon, mumbo-jumbo, nonsense, prattle, slipslop, twaddle, yammer. *antonym* sense.

gibe *see* **jibe** .

giddiness *n.* dizziness, faintness, lightheadedness, nausea, vertigo, wobbliness, wooziness.

giddy *adj.* capricious, careless, changeable, changeful, dizzy, dizzying, erratic, faint, fickle, flighty, frivolous, heedless, impulsive, inconstant, irresolute, irresponsible, lightheaded, reckless, reeling, scatterbrained, scatty, silly, thoughtless, unbalanced, unstable, unsteady, vacillating, vertiginous, volage, volageous, volatile, wild. *antonyms* sensible, sober.

gift *n.* ability, aptitude, attribute, benefaction, benificence, bent, bequest, bonus, boon, bounty, cadeau, capability, capacity, contribution, cumshaw, deodate, dolly, donary, donation, donative, douceur, earnest, endowment, faculty, flair, foy, freebie, genius, grant, gratuity, knack, largess(e), legacy, manna, offering, power, present, sop, talent, turn, xenium.

gifted *adj.* able, accomplished, ace, adroit, bright, brilliant, capable, clever, expert, ingenious, intelligent, masterly, skilful, skilled, talented. *antonym* dull.

gigantic *adj.* Atlantean, Babylonian, Brobdingnag(ian), colossal, cyclopean, elephantine, enormous, gargantuan, giant, herculean, huge, immense, leviathan, mammoth, monstrous, Patagonian, prodigious, rounceval, stupendous, titanic, tremendous, vast. *antonym* small.

giggle *v.* chortle, chuckle, laugh, snigger, tee-hee, titter. *n.* chortle, chuckle, fou rire, laugh, snigger, tee-hee, titter.

gild *v.* adorn, array, beautify, bedeck, brighten, coat, deck, dress up, embellish, embroider,

enhance, enrich, festoon, garnish, grace, ornament, paint, trim.

gilded *adj.* gilt, gold, golden, inaurate.

gimcrack *adj.* cheap, rubbishy, shoddy, tawdry, trashy, trumpery. *antonyms* solid, well-made.

gimmick *n.* angle, attraction, contrivance, device, dodge, gadget, gambit, gizmo, manoeuvre, ploy, scheme, stratagem, stunt, trick.

gin *n.* mother's ruin (mothers' ruin).

gingerly *adv.* carefully, cautiously, charily, circumspectly, daintily, delicately, fastidiously, gently, hesitantly, reluctantly, squeamishly, suspiciously, timidly, warily. *antonyms* carelessly, roughly.

gipsy *see* **gypsy** .

gird *v.* belt, bind, blockade, brace, encircle, enclose, encompass, enfold, engird, environ, enzone, fortify, girdle, hem in, pen, prepare, ready, ring, steel, surround.

girdle *n.* band, belt, ceinture, cestus, cincture, cingulum, corset, cummerbund, fillet, sash, waistband, zona, zone, zonule. *v.* bind, bound, encirle, enclose, encompass, engird, environ, enzone, gird, gird round, go round, hem, ring, surround.

girl *n.* backfisch, bird, chick, chicken, chit, colleen, damsel, daughter, demoiselle, filly, fizgig, flapper, flibbertigibbet, floosie, fluff, fräulein, gal, giglet, girl-friend, gouge, grisette, judy, lass, lassie, maid, maiden, miss, moppet, peach, piece, popsy(-wopsy), quean, quine, sheila, sweetheart, wench.

girth *n.* band, belly-band, bulk, circumference, measure, saddle-band, size, strap.

gist *n.* core, direction, drift, essence, force, idea, import, marrow, matter, meaning, nub, pith, point, quintessence, sense, significance, substance.

give *v.* accord, administer, admit, allow, announce, award, bend, bestow, break, cause, cede, collapse, commit, communicate, concede, confer, consign, contribute, deliver, demonstrate, devote, display, do, donate, emit, engender, entrust, evidence, fall, furnish, grant, hand, hand over, impart, indicate, issue, lead, lend, make, make over, manifest, notify, occasion, offer, pay, perform, permit, present, produce, proffer, pronounce, provide, publish, recede, relinquish, render, retire, set forth, show, sink, state, supply, surrender, transmit, utter, vouchsafe, yield. *antonyms* hold out, take, withstand.

give away betray, disclose, divulge, expose, grass, inform on, leak, let out, let slip, rat, reveal, uncover.

give in capitulate, collapse, comply, concede, crack, give way, quit, submit, surrender, yield. *antonym* hold out.

give off discharge, emit, exhale, exude, outpour, pour out, produce, release, send out, throw out, vent.

give on to lead to, open on to, overlook.

give out announce, broadcast, communicate, discharge, disseminate, emit, exhale, exude, give off, impart, notify, outpour, pour out, produce, publish, release, send out, transmit, utter, vent.
antonym take in.

give rise to breed, bring about, bring on, cause, effect, engender, generate, produce, provoke, result in.

give up abandon, capitulate, cease, cede, cut out, desist, despair, forswear, hand over, leave off, quit, relinquish, renounce, resign, stop, surrender, throw in the towel, throw up the sponge, waive.
antonym hold out.

give way accede, acquiesce, back down, bend, break (down), cave in, cede, collapse, concede, crack, crumple, fall, give ground, give place, sink, submit, subside, withdraw, yield.
antonyms hold out, withstand.

give-and-take *n.* adaptability, compliance, flexibility, giff-gaff, good-will, willingness.

given *adj.* addicted, admitted, agreed, apt, bestowed, disposed, granted, inclined, liable, likely, prone, specified.

glacial *adj.* antagonistic, arctic, biting, bitter, brumous, chill, chilly, cold, freezing, frigid, frore, frosty, frozen, gelid, hostile, icy, inimical, piercing, polar, raw, Siberian, stiff, unfriendly, wintry.
antonym warm.

glad *adj.* animated, blithe, blithesome, bright, cheerful, cheering, cheery, chuffed, contented, delighted, delightful, felicitous, gay, gleeful, gratified, gratifying, happy, jocund, jovial, joyful, joyous, merry, over the moon, overjoyed, pleasant, pleased, pleasing, willing.
antonym sad.

gladden *v.* brighten, cheer, delight, elate, enliven, exhilarate, gratify, hearten, please, rejoice.
antonym sadden.

gladly *adv.* blithely, blithesomely, cheerfully, fain, freely, gaily, gleefully, happily, jovially, joyfully, joyously, merrily, readily, willingly, with good grace, with pleasure.
antonyms sadly, unwillingly.

gladness *n.* animation, blitheness, blithesomeness, brightness, cheerfulness, delight, felicity, gaiety, glee, happiness, high spirits, hilarity, jollity, joy, joyousness, mirth, pleasure.
antonym sadness.

glamorous *adj.* alluring, attractive, beautiful, bewitching, captivating, charming, classy, dazzling, elegant, enchanting, entrancing, exciting, fascinating, glittering, glossy, gorgeous, lovely, prestigious, smart.
antonyms boring, drab, plain.

glamour *n.* allure, appeal, attraction, beauty, bewitchment, charm, enchantment, fascination, magic, magnetism, prestige, ravishment, witchery.

glance[1] *v.* browse, dip, flip, gaze, glimpse, leaf, look, peek, peep, riffle, scan, skim, thumb, touch on, view.
n. allusion, coup d'oeil, dekko, gander, glimpse, look, mention, once over, peek, peep, reference, squint, view.

glance[2] *v.* bounce, brush, cannon, carom, coruscate, flash, gleam, glimmer, glint, glisten, glister, glitter, graze, rebound, reflect, ricochet, shimmer, shine, skim, twinkle.

glare *v.* blaze, coruscate, dazzle, flame, flare, frown, glower, look daggers, lower, scowl, shine.
n. black look, blaze, brilliance, dazzle, dirty look, flame, flare, flashiness, floridness, frown, gaudiness, glow, glower, light, look, loudness, lower, scowl, showiness, stare, tawdriness.

glaring *adj.* audacious, blatant, blazing, bright, conspicuous, dazzling, dreadful, egregious, flagrant, flashy, florid, garish, glowing, gross, horrendous, loud, manifest, obvious, open, outrageous, outstanding, overt, patent, rank, terrible, unconcealed, visible.
antonyms dull, hidden, minor.

glass *n.* beaker, crystal, goblet, lens, looking-glass, magnifying glass, pane, pocket-lens, roemer, rummer, schooner, tumbler, vitrics, window.

glass case display cabinet, vitrine, vivarium, Wardian case.

glassiness *n.* vitreosity, vitreousness.

glassware *n.* crystal, glass, vitrics.

glassy *adj.* blank, clear, cold, dazed, dull, empty, expressionless, fixed, glasslike, glazed, glazy, glossy, hyaline, icy, lifeless, shiny, slick, slippery, smooth, transparent, vacant, vitreous, vitriform.

glaze *v.* burnish, coat, crystallise, enamel, furbish, gloss, lacquer, polish, varnish.
n. coat, enamel, finish, gloss, lacquer, lustre, patina, polish, shine, varnish.

gleam *n.* beam, brightness, brilliance, coruscation, flash, flicker, glimmer, glint, gloss, glow, hint, inkling, lustre, ray, sheen, shimmer, sparkle, splendour, suggestion, trace.
v. coruscate, flare, flash, glance, glimmer, glint, glisten, glister, glitter, glow, scintillate, shimmer, shine, sparkle.

gleaming *adj.* ablaze, bright, brilliant, burnished, glistening, glowing, lustrous, polished, shining.
antonym dull.

glean *v.* accumulate, amass, collect, cull, find out, garner, gather, harvest, learn, pick (up), reap, select.

glee *n.* cheerfulness, delight, elation, exhilaration, exuberance, exultation, fun, gaiety, gladness, gratification, hilarity, jocularity, jollity, joviality, joy, joyfulness, joyousness, liveliness, merriment, mirth, pleasure, sprightliness, triumph, verve.

gleeful *adj.* beside oneself, cheerful, cock-a-hoop, delighted, elated, exuberant, exultant, gay, gleesome, gratified, happy, jovial, joyful,

joyous, jubilant, merry, mirthful, over the moon, overjoyed, pleased, triumphant.
antonym sad.

glib *adj.* artful, easy, facile, fast-talking, fluent, garrulous, insincere, logodaedalic, plausible, quick, ready, slick, slippery, smooth, smooth-spoken, smooth-tongued, suave, talkative, voluble.
antonyms implausible, tongue-tied.

glibness *n.* logodaedaly, plausibility, slickness, smoothness, suaveness, suavity.

glide *v.* coast, drift, float, flow, fly, glissade, roll, run, sail, skate, skim, slide, slip, soar, volplane.

glimmer *v.* blink, flicker, gleam, glint, glisten, glitter, glow, shimmer, shine, sparkle, twinkle.
n. blink, flicker, gleam, glimmering, glint, glow, grain, hint, inkling, ray, shimmer, sparkle, suggestion, trace, twinkle.

glimpse *n.* glance, gliff, glim, glisk, look, peek, peep, sight, sighting, squint.
v. descry, espy, sight, spot, spy, view.

glint *v.* flash, gleam, glimmer, glitter, reflect, shine, sparkle, twinkle.
n. flash, gleam, glimmer, glimmering, glitter, shine, sparkle, twinkle, twinkling.

glisten *v.* coruscate, flash, glance, glare, gleam, glimmer, glint, glister, glitter, scintillate, shimmer, shine, sparkle, twinkle.

glitter *v.* coruscate, flare, flash, glare, gleam, glimmer, glint, glisten, scintillate, shimmer, shine, spangle, sparkle, twinkle.
n. beam, brightness, brilliance, clinquant, display, flash, gaudiness, glamour, glare, gleam, lustre, pageantry, radiance, scintillation, sheen, shimmer, shine, show, showiness, sparkle, splendour, tinsel.

gloat *v.* crow, exult, eye, glory, ogle, rejoice, relish, revel in, rub it in, triumph, vaunt.

global *adj.* all-encompassing, all-inclusive, all-out, comprehensive, encylopaedic, exhaustive, general, globular, international, pandemic, planetary, spherical, thorough, total, unbounded, universal, unlimited, world, world-wide.
antonyms limited, parochial.

globe *n.* ball, earth, orb, planet, round, roundure, sphere, world.

globular *adj.* globate, globated, globoid, globous, globulous, orbicular, round, spherical, spheroid.

globule *n.* bead, bubble, drop, droplet, globulet, particle, pearl, pellet, vesicle, vesicula.

gloom *n.* blackness, blues, cloud, cloudiness, damp, dark, darkness, dejection, depression, desolation, despair, despondency, dimness, downheartedness, dullness, dusk, duskiness, gloominess, glumness, low spirits, melancholy, misery, murk, murkiness, obscurity, sadness, shade, shadow, sorrow, twilight, unhappiness, woe.
antonym brightness.

gloominess *n.* cheerlessness, darkness, dejection, depression, despondency, dreariness,

dullness, gloom, glumness, melancholy, mirkiness, misery, moroseness, mumps, murkiness, pessimism.
antonym brightness.

gloomy *adj.* bad, black, blue, chapfallen, cheerless, comfortless, crepuscular, crestfallen, dark, darksome, dejected, delightless, depressing, despondent, dim, disheartening, dismal, dispirited, dispiriting, down, down in the dumps, down in the mouth, down-beat, downcast, downhearted, dreary, dreich, dull, dusky, gloomful, glum, joyless, long-faced, long-visaged, low-spirited, melancholy, mirk(y), miserable, moody, morose, murk(y), obscure, overcast, pessimistic, sad, saddening, saturnine, sepulchral, shadowy, sombre, Stygian, sullen, tenebrous.
antonym bright.

glorification *n.* doxology, exaltation, glorifying, idolising, magnification, panegyric, praise, praising, romanticising.
antonyms blame, vilification.

glorify *v.* adore, adorn, aggrandise, apotheosise, augment, beatify, bless, canonise, celebrate, deify, dignify, elevate, enhance, ennoble, enshrine, eulogise, exalt, extol, honour, hymn, idolise, illuminate, immortalise, laud, lift up, magnify, panegyrise, praise, raise, revere, sanctify, venerate, worship.
antonyms denounce, vilify.

glorious *adj.* beautiful, bright, brilliant, celebrated, dazzling, delightful, distinguished, divine, drunk, effulgent, elated, elevated, eminent, enjoyable, excellent, famed, famous, fine, gorgeous, grand, great, heavenly, honoured, illustrious, intoxicated, magnificent, majestic, marvellous, noble, noted, pleasurable, radiant, renowned, resplendent, shining, splendid, sublime, superb, tipsy, triumphant, wonderful.
antonyms dreadful, inglorious, plain, unknown.

glory *n.* adoration, beauty, benediction, blessing, brightness, brilliance, celebrity, dignity, distinction, effulgence, eminence, exaltation, fame, gloire, gloria, gorgeousness, grandeur, gratitude, greatness, heaven, homage, honour, illustriousness, immortality, kudos, laudation, lustre, magnificence, majesty, nobility, pageantry, pomp, praise, prestige, radiance, renown, resplendence, richness, splendour, sublimity, thanksgiving, triumph, veneration, worship.
antonyms blame, restraint.
v. boast, crow, delight, exult, gloat, pride oneself, rejoice, relish, revel, triumph.

gloss[1] *n.* appearance, brightness, brilliance, burnish, façade, front, gleam, lustre, mask, polish, semblance, sheen, shine, show, surface, varnish, veneer, window-dressing.
gloss over camouflage, conceal, disguise, double-glaze, explain away, gild, glaze over, hide, mask, smooth over, veil, whitewash.

gloss[2] *n.* annotation, comment, commentary, elucidation, explanation, footnote, interpretation, note, postillation, scholion, scholium, translation.

v. annotate, comment, construe, elucidate, explain, interpret, postil, postillate, translate.

glossary *n.* dictionary, idioticon, lexicon, phrase-book, vocabulary, word-book, word-list.

glossy *adj.* bright, brilliant, burnished, enamelled, glacé, glassy, glazed, lustrous, polished, sheeny, shining, shiny, silken, silky, sleek, smooth.

antonym mat(t).

glow *n.* ardour, bloom, blush, brightness, brilliance, burning, earnestness, effulgence, enthusiasm, excitement, fervour, flush, gleam, glimmer, gusto, impetuosity, incandescence, intensity, lambency, light, luminosity, passion, phosphorescence, radiance, reddening, redness, rosiness, splendour, vehemence, vividness, warmth.

v. blush, brighten, burn, colour, fill, flush, gleam, glimmer, glowing, radiate, redden, shine, smoulder, thrill, tingle.

glower *v.* frown, glare, look daggers, lower, scowl.

n. black look, dirty look, frown, glare, look, lower, scowl, stare.

glowing *adj.* adulatory, aglow, beaming, bright, complimentary, ecstatic, enthusiastic, eulogistic, flaming, florid, flushed, gleamy, lambent, laudatory, luminous, panegyrical, rave, red, rhapsodic, rich, ruddy, suffused, vibrant, vivid, warm.

antonyms dull, restrained.

glue *n.* adhesive, cement, fish-glue, gum, isinglass, mucilage, paste, size.

v. affix, agglutinate, cement, fix, gum, paste, seal, stick.

gluey *adj.* adhesive, glutinous, gummy, sticky, viscid, viscous.

glum *adj.* chapfallen, churlish, crabbed, crestfallen, dejected, doleful, down, gloomy, glumpish, glumpy, gruff, grumpy, ill-humoured, low, moody, morose, pessimistic, saturnine, sour, sulky, sullen, surly.

antonyms ecstatic, happy.

glut *n.* excess, overabundance, oversupply, pleroma, saturation, superabundance, superfluity, surfeit, surplus.

antonyms lack, scarcity.

v. choke, clog, cram, deluge, englut, fill, flesh, flood, gorge, inundate, overfeed, overload, oversupply, sate, satiate, saturate, stuff.

glutinous *adj.* adhesive, cohesive, emplastic, gluey, gummy, mucilaginous, ropy, sticky, viscid, viscous.

glutton *n.* cormorant, free-liver, gannet, gobbler, gorger, gormandiser, gourmand, guzzler, hog, omnivore, pig, trencherman, whale.

antonym ascetic.

gluttonous *adj.* edacious, esurient, gluttonish, gormandising, greedy, gutsy, hoggish, insatiable, omnivorous, piggish, rapacious, ravenous, ventripotent, voracious.

antonyms abstemious, ascetic.

gluttony *n.* edacity, esurience, gormandising, go(u)rmandise, go(u)rmandism, greed, greediness, gulosity, insatiability, omnivorousness, piggishness, rapaciousness, rapacity, voraciousness, voracity.

antonyms abstinence, asceticism.

gnarled *adj.* contorted, distorted, gnarly, gnarred, knarred, knotted, knotty, knurled, leathery, rough, rugged, twisted, weatherbeaten, wrinkled.

gnaw *v.* bite, chew, consume, devour, distress, eat, erode, fret, harry, haunt, munch, nag, nibble, niggle, plague, prey, trouble, wear, worry.

go *v.* accord, advance, agree, avail, beat it, blend, chime, complement, concur, conduce, connect, contribute, correspond, decamp, decease, depart, develop, die, disappear, elapse, eventuate, expire, extend, fare, fit, flow, function, gee, happen, harmonise, incline, jib, journey, lapse, lead, lead to, leave, levant, make for, match, mosey, move, naff off, nip, operate, pass, pass away, perform, perish, proceed, progress, rate, reach, repair, result, retreat, roll, run, sally, scram, serve, shift, shove off, slip, sod off, span, spread, stretch, suit, take one's leave, tend, travel, trot, vanish, wag, walk, wend, withdraw, work.

n. animation, attempt, bid, crack, drive, dynamism, effort, energy, essay, force, get-up-and-go, life, oomph, pep, shot, spirit, stab, try, turn, verve, vigour, vim, vitality, vivacity, whack, whirl, zest.

go about address, approach, begin, circulate, get abroad, journey, set about, tackle, travel, undertake, wander.

go ahead advance, begin, continue, march on, move, proceed, progress.

go at argue, attack, blame, criticise, impugn, set about, turn on.

go away bugger off, decamp, depart, disappear, eff off, exit, fuck off, get lost, hop it, imshi, leave, piss off, recede, retreat, scat, scram, vanish, withdraw.

go back backslide, desert, forsake, renege, repudiate, retract, retreat, return, revert.

go by adopt, elapse, flow, follow, heed, observe, pass, proceed, trust.

go down collapse, decline, decrease, degenerate, deteriorate, drop, fail, fall, founder, go under, lose, set, sink, submerge, submit, succumb.

go far advance, blaze a trail, do well, progress, succeed.

go for admire, assail, assault, attack, be into, choose, clutch at, dig, enjoy, fall on, favour, fetch, hold with, like, lunge at, obtain, prefer, reach, seek, set about.

go ill with destroy, endanger, harm, imperil, injure, jeopardise, put at hazard, put at risk, ruin.

go in for adopt, embrace, engage in, enter, enter for, espouse, follow, participate in, practise, pursue, take part in, take up, undertake.

go into analyse, begin, check out, consider, delve into, develop, discuss, dissect, enter, examine, inquire into, investigate, make a study of, participate in, probe, pursue, review, scrutinise, study, sus out, undertake. **go mad** go bonkers, go crazy, go nuts, take leave of one's senses.

go missing be nowhere to be found, disappear, get lost, scarper, vamoose, vanish.

go off abscond, blow up, decamp, depart, deteriorate, detonate, dislike, explode, fire, happen, leave, occur, part, proceed, quit, rot, turn, vamoose, vanish.

go on behave, blether, chatter, continue, endure, happen, last, last out, occur, persist, prattle, proceed, ramble on, stay, waffle, witter.

go out depart, die out, exit, expire, fade out, leave, obsolesce.

go over detail, examine, inspect, list, overname, peruse, read, recall, recapitulate, rehearse, reiterate, review, revise, scan, skim, study.

go through bear, brave, check, consume, endure, examine, exhaust, experience, explore, face, hunt, investigate, look, rehearse, search, squander, suffer, tolerate, undergo, use, withstand.

go to bed bed down, go to sleep, hit the hay, hit the sack, kip, kip down, retire, turn in.

go together accord, agree, chime, fit, gee, harmonise, jibe, match.

go to pieces break down, capitulate, collapse, crack up, crumble, crumple, disintegrate, fall apart, lose control, lose one's head.

go to seed decay, decline, degenerate, deteriorate, go downhill, go to pot, go to waste, underachieve.

go to the dogs be ruined, degenerate, deteriorate, fail, go down the drain, go to pot, go to rack and ruin.

go under close down, collapse, default, die, drown, fail, fold, founder, go down, sink, submerge, succumb.

go with accompany, agree, blend, chime, complement, concur, correspond, court, date, fit, gee, go steady, harmonise, jibe, match, suit.

go wrong boob, break, break down, come to grief, come to nothing, come ungummed, come unstuck, conk out, cut out, err, fail, fall through, flop, go astray, go off the rails, go on the blink, go phut, lapse, malfunction, miscarry, misfire, sin, slip up.

goad n. fillip, impetus, incentive, incitement, irritation, jab, motivation, poke, pressure, prod, push, spur, stimulation, stimulus, thrust, urge.

v. annoy, arouse, badger, bullyrag, chivvy, drive, egg on, exasperate, exhort, harass, hassle, hector, hound, impel, incite, infuriate, instigate, irritate, lash, madden, nag, needle, persecute, prick, prod, prompt, propel, push, spur, stimulate, sting, urge, vex, worry.

go-ahead n. agreement, assent, authorisation,

clearance, consent, fiat, green light, leave, OK, permission, sanction.

antonyms ban, embargo, moratorium, veto. adj. ambitious, avant-garde, enterprising, goey, go-getting, pioneering, progressive, up-and-coming.

antonyms sluggish, unenterprising.

goal n. aim, ambition, aspiration, bourn(e), design, destination, destiny, end, grail, intention, limit, mark, object, objective, purpose, target.

goat-like adj. capriform, caprine, concupiscent, foolish, giddy, goatish, hircine, horny, lascivious, libidinous, lustful, randy, silly.

gobble v. bolt, consume, cram, devour, gorge, gulp, guttle, guzzle, hog, put away, shovel, slabber, stuff, swallow, wire into, wolf.

go-between n. agent, broker, contact, dealer, factor, informer, intermediary, internuncio, liaison, mediator, medium, messenger, middleman, ombudsman, pander, pimp, procuress.

goblet n. balloon glass, brandy-glass, chalice, drinking-cup, hanap, Paris goblet, quaich, rummer, tass, wine-glass.

goblin n. barghest, bogey, bogle, brownie, bugbear, demon, esprit follet, fiend, gremlin, hobgoblin, imp, kelpie, kobold, lubber fiend, nis, nix, nixie, red-cap, red-cowl, spirit, sprite.

God, god n. Allah, avatar, Brahma, deity, divinity, genius, Godhead, Holy One, idol, Jah, Jehovah, joss, Jove, kami, lar, Lord, Lord God, monad, Mumbo-jumbo, numen, penates, power, Providence, spirit, the Almighty, the Creator, tutelar, tutelary, Yahweh, Zeus.

god-forsaken adj. abandoned, backward, benighted, bleak, deserted, desolate, dismal, dreary, forlorn, gloomy, isolated, lonely, miserable, neglected, remote, unfrequented, wretched.

antonym congenial.

godless adj. atheistic, depraved, evil, heathen, impious, irreligious, irreverent, nullifidian, pagan, profane, sacrilegious, ungodly, unholy, unprincipled, unrighteous, wicked.

antonyms godly, pious.

godlike adj. celestial, deiform, divine, exalted, heavenly, saintly, sublime, superhuman, theomorphic, transcendent.

godly adj. blameless, devout, god-fearing, good, holy, innocent, pious, pure, religious, righteous, saintly, virtuous.

antonyms godless, impious.

godsend n. blessing, boon, fluke, lucky break, manna, miracle, stroke of luck, windfall.

antonyms blow, bolt from the blue, bombshell, setback.

going-over n. analysis, beating, buffeting, castigation, chastisement, check, check-up, chiding, doing, dressing-down, drubbing, examination, inspection, investigation, lecture, probe, rebuke, reprimand, review, row, scolding, scrutiny, study, survey, thrashing, thumping, treatment, trouncing, whipping.

golden *adj.* advantageous, aureate, auric, auspicious, best, blissful, blond(e), bright, brilliant, delightful, excellent, fair, favourable, favoured, flaxen, flourishing, glorious, happy, inaurate, invaluable, joyful, lustrous, opportune, precious, priceless, promising, propitious, prosperous, resplendent, rich, rosy, shining, successful, timely, valuable, xanthous, yellow.

goldmine *n.* dripping roast, Golconda, gold-dust, golden goose, widow's cruse.

gone *adj.* absent, astray, away, broken, bygone, closed, concluded, consumed, dead, deceased, defunct, departed, disappeared, done, elapsed, ended, extinct, finished, kaput, lacking, lost, missed, missing, over, over and done with, past, pregnant, spent, used, vanished, wanting.

goo *n.* crud, glaur, grease, grime, gunge, gunk, matter, mire, muck, mud, ooze, scum, slime, sludge, slush, stickiness.

good *adj.* able, acceptable, accomplished, adept, adequate, admirable, adroit, advantageous, agreeable, altruistic, amiable, ample, appropriate, approved, approving, auspicious, authentic, balmy, beneficent, beneficial, benevolent, benign, bona fide, bonzer, boshta, bosker, bright, brotherly, budgeree, buoyant, calm, capable, capital, charitable, cheerful, choice, clear, clever, cloudless, commendable, competent, complete, congenial, considerate, convenient, convivial, correct, decorous, dependable, deserving, dexterous, dutiful, eatable, efficient, enjoyable, entire, estimable, ethical, excellent, exemplary, expert, extensive, fair, favourable, fine, first-class, first-rate, fit, fitting, friendly, full, genuine, gracious, gratifying, great, happy, healthy, helpful, honest, honourable, humane, kind, kindly, large, legitimate, long, loyal, mannerly, merciful, meritorious, mild, moral, nice, noble, nourishing, nutritious, obedient, obliging, opportune, orderly, pious, pleasant, pleasing, pleasurable, polite, positive, praiseworthy, precious, presentable, professional, proficient, profitable, proper, propitious, rattling, real, reliable, right, righteous, safe, salubrious, salutary, satisfactory, satisfying, seemly, serviceable, sizeable, skilful, skilled, solid, sound, special, splendid, substantial, sufficient, suitable, sunny, super, superior, sustaining, talented, tested, thorough, tranquil, true, trustworthy, uncorrupted, untainted, upright, useful, valid, valuable, virtuous, well-behaved, well-disposed, well-mannered, whole, wholesome, worthwhile, worthy.

n. advantage, avail, behalf, behoof, benefit, boon, convenience, excellence, gain, goodness, interest, merit, morality, probity, profit, rectitude, right, righteousness, service, uprightness, use, usefulness, virtue, weal, welfare, well-being, worth, worthiness.

good health *interj.* à votre santé, cheers, Gesundheit, kia-ora, prosit, salud, salute,
your health.

n. haleness, hardiness, health, healthiness, heartiness, lustiness, robustness, soundness, strength, vigour, vitality.

antonyms ill health, invalidism.

good-bye *n., interj.* adieu, adiós, arrivederci, au revoir, auf Wiedersehen, chin-chin, ciao, farewell, leave-taking, parting, valediction, valedictory.

good-for-nothing *n.* black sheep, bum, drone, idler, layabout, lazy-bones, loafer, lorel, losel, mauvais sujet, ne'er-do-well, profligate, rapscallion, reprobate, scapegrace, vaurien, waster, wastrel.

antonyms achiever, success, winner.

adj. do-nothing, feckless, idle, indolent, irresponsible, lorel, losel, no-good, profligate, reprobate, slothful, useless, worthless.

antonyms conscientious, successful.

good-humoured *adj.* affable, amiable, approachable, blithe, cheerful, congenial, expansive, genial, good-tempered, happy, jocund, jovial, pleasant.

antonym ill-humoured.

good-looking *adj.* attractive, beautiful, bonny, comely, easy on the eye, fair, handsome, personable, presentable, pretty, well-favoured, well-looking, well-proportioned, well-set-up.

antonyms ill-favoured, plain, ugly.

good-luck charm amulet, periapt, phylactery, porte-bonheur, talisman.

antonym evil eye.

goodly *adj.* ample, considerable, good, large, significant, sizeable, substantial, sufficient, tidy.

antonym inadequate.

good-natured *adj.* agreeable, amenable, approachable, benevolent, broad-minded, friendly, gentle, good-hearted, helpful, kind, kind-hearted, kindly, neighbourly, open-minded, sympathetic, tolerant, warm-hearted.

antonym ill-natured.

goodness *n.* advantage, altruism, beneficence, benefit, benevolence, condescension, excellence, fairness, friendliness, generosity, goodwill, graciousness, honesty, honour, humaneness, humanity, integrity, justness, kindliness, kindness, mercy, merit, morality, nourishment, nutrition, piety, probity, quality, rectitude, righteousness, salubriousness, superiority, unselfishness, uprightness, value, virtue, wholesomeness, worth.

antonyms badness, inferiority, wickedness.

goods *n.* appurtenances, bags and baggage, belongings, chattels, commodities, effects, furnishings, furniture, gear, merchandise, movables, paraphernalia, plenishing, possessions, property, stock, stuff, traps, vendibles, wares.

goodwill *n.* altruism, amity, benevolence, compassion, earnestness, favour, friendliness, friendship, generosity, heartiness, kindliness, loving-kindness, sincerity, sympathy, zeal.

antonym ill-will.

goody-goody *adj.* pious, priggish, sanctimonious, self-righteous, ultra-virtuous, unctuous.

gooey *adj.* clarty, gluey, glutinous, gummy, gungy, maudlin, mawkish, mucilaginous, sentimental, slushy, soft, sticky, syrupy, tacky, thick, viscid, viscous.

gooseberry *n.* goosegob, goosegog, groser, groset, third person.

gooseflesh *n.* creeps, duck bumps, formication, goose bumps, goose-pimples, grue, heebie-jeebies, horripilation, horrors, shivers, shudders.

gore¹ *n.* blood, bloodiness, bloodshed, butchery, carnage, cruor, grume, slaughter.

gore² *v.* impale, penetrate, pierce, rend, spear, spit, stab, stick, transfix, wound.
n. flare, gair, godet, gusset.

gorge¹ *n.* abyss, barranca, canyon, chasm, cleft, clough, defile, fissure, gap, gulch, gully, pass, ravine.

gorge² *v.* bolt, cram, devour, feed, fill, fill one's face, glut, gluttonise, gobble, gormandise, gulp, guzzle, hog, make a pig of oneself, overeat, ravin, sate, satiate, stuff, surfeit, swallow, wolf.
antonym abstain.

gorgeous *adj.* attractive, beautiful, bright, brilliant, dazzling, delightful, elegant, enjoyable, exquisite, fine, flamboyant, glamorous, glittering, glorious, good, good-looking, grand, lovely, luxuriant, luxurious, magnificent, opulent, pleasing, ravishing, resplendent, rich, showy, splendid, splendiferous, stunning, sumptuous, superb.
antonyms dull, plain, seedy.

gory *adj.* blood-soaked, bloodstained, bloodthirsty, bloody, brutal, ensanguined, murderous, sanguinary, sanguineous, sanguinolent, savage.

gospel *n.* certainty, credo, creed, doctrine, evangel, fact, kerygma, message, news, revelation, teaching, testament, tidings, truth, verity.

gossamer *adj.* airy, cobwebby, delicate, diaphanous, fine, flimsy, gauzy, insubstantial, light, sheer, shimmering, silky, thin, translucent, transparent.
antonyms heavy, opaque, thick.

gossip¹ *n.* blether, bush telegraph, causerie, chinwag, chitchat, clash, clish-clash, clishmaclaver, gup, hearsay, idle talk, jaw, newsmongering, prattle, report, rumour, scandal, schmooze, small talk, tittle-tattle, yackety-yak.

gossip² *n.* babbler, blatherskite, blether, bletherskate, busybody, chatterbox, chatterer, gossip-monger, newsmonger, nosy parker, prattler, quidnunc, rumourer, scandalmonger, tabby, talebearer, tattler, telltale, whisperer.
v. blather, blether, bruit, chat, clash, gabble, jaw, prattle, rumour, tattle, tell tales, whisper.

gouge *v.* chisel, claw, cut, dig, extract, force,
gash, grave, groove, hack, hollow, incise, scoop, score, scratch, slash.
n. cut, furrow, gash, groove, hack, hollow, incision, notch, scoop, score, scratch, slash, trench.

gourmand *n.* cormorant, free-liver, gannet, glutton, gorger, gormandiser, guzzler, hog, omnivore, pig, trencherman, whale.
antonym ascetic.

gourmet *n.* arbiter elegantiae, arbiter elegantiarum, bon vivant, bon viveur, connoisseur, dainty eater, epicure, epicurean, gastronome, gastronomer, gastrosoph, gastrosopher.
antonym omnivore.

govern *v.* administer, allay, bridle, check, command, conduct, contain, control, curb, decide, determine, direct, discipline, guide, influence, inhibit, lead, manage, master, order, oversee, pilot, preside, quell, regulate, reign, restrain, rule, steer, subdue, superintend, supervise, sway, tame, underlie.

governess *n.* companion, duenna, gouvernante, guide, instructress, mentor, teacher, tutoress, tutress.

governing *adj.* commanding, dominant, dominative, guiding, leading, overriding, predominant, prevailing, reigning, ruling, supreme, transcendent, uppermost.

government *n.* administration, authority, charge, command, conduct, control, direction, domination, dominion, Establishment, executive, governance, guidance, kingcraft, law, management, ministry, polity, powers-that-be, raj, régime, regimen, regulation, restraint, rule, sovereignty, state, statecraft, superintendence, supervision, surveillance, sway.

governor *n.* adelantado, administrator, alcalde, alderman, boss, chief, commander, commissioner, comptroller, controller, corrector, director, executive, gubernator, hakim, head, leader, manager, naik, overseer, ruler, superintendent, supervisor, vali.

gown *n.* costume, creation, dress, dressing-gown, frock, garb, garment, habit, kirtle, négligé, robe.

grab *v.* affect, annex, appropriate, bag, capture, catch, catch hold of, clutch, collar, commandeer, grasp, grip, impress, latch on to, nab, pluck, ramp, rap, seize, snap up, snatch, strike, usurp.

grace¹ *n.* attractiveness, beauty, benefaction, beneficence, benevolence, benignity, benison, breeding, charity, charm, clemency, comeliness, compassion, compassionateness, consideration, courtesy, cultivation, decency, decorum, deftness, ease, elegance, eloquence, etiquette, favour, finesse, fluency, forgiveness, generosity, goodness, goodwill, gracefulness, graciousness, indulgence, kindliness, kindness, leniency, lenity, love, loveliness, mannerliness, manners, mercifulness, mercy, merit, pardon, pleasantness, poise, polish, propriety, quarter, refinement, reprieve, shapeliness, tact, tastefulness, unction, virtue.

v. adorn, beautify, bedeck, deck, decorate, dignify, distinguish, dress, elevate, embellish, enhance, enrich, favour, garnish, glorify, honour, ornament, prettify, set off, trim.

antonyms deface, detract from, spoil.

grace[2] *n.* benediction, benedictus, blessing, consecration, prayer, thanks, thanksgiving.

graceful *adj.* agile, balletic, beautiful, becoming, charming, comely, deft, easy, elegant, facile, feat, feline, fine, flowing, fluid, gainly, genty, gracile, lightsome, natural, pleasing, pliant, slender, smooth, suave, supple, tasteful, willowish, willowy.

antonym graceless.

graceless *adj.* awkward, barbarous, boorish, brazen, clumsy, coarse, crude, forced, gauche, gawky, ill-mannered, improper, incorrigible, indecorous, inelegant, inept, loutish, reprobate, rough, rude, shameless, uncouth, ungainly, ungraceful, unmannerly, unsophisticated, untutored, vulgar.

antonym graceful.

gracious *adj.* accommodating, affable, affluent, amenable, amiable, beneficent, benevolent, benign, benignant, charitable, chivalrous, civil, compassionate, complaisant, condescending, considerate, cordial, courteous, courtly, elegant, friendly, grand, hospitable, indulgent, kind, kindly, lenient, loving, luxurious, merciful, mild, obliging, pleasant, pleasing, polite, refined, sweet, well-mannered.

antonym ungracious.

gradation *n.* ablaut, arrangement, array, classification, degree, depth, grade, grading, grouping, level, mark, measurement, notch, ordering, place, point, position, progress, progression, rank, sequence, series, shading, sorting, stage, step, succession.

grade *n.* acclivity, bank, brand, category, class, condition, dan, declivity, degree, downgrade, echelon, gradation, gradient, group, hill, incline, level, mark, notch, order, place, position, quality, rank, rise, rung, size, slope, stage, station, step, upgrade.

v. arrange, blend, brand, categorise, class, classify, docket, evaluate, group, label, mark, order, pigeonhole, range, rank, rate, shade, size, sort, type, value.

gradient *n.* acclivity, bank, decline, declivity, downgrade, grade, hill, incline, rise, slope, upgrade.

gradual *adj.* cautious, continuous, deliberate, even, gentle, graduated, leisurely, measured, moderate, piecemeal, progressive, regular, slow, steady, step-by-step, successive, unhurried.

antonyms precipitate, sudden.

gradually *adv.* bit by bit, by degrees, cautiously, drop by drop, evenly, gently, gingerly, imperceptibly, in penny numbers, inch by inch, inchmeal, little by little, moderately, piece by piece, piecemeal, progressively, slowly, steadily, step by step, unhurriedly.

graduate[1] *v.* arrange, calibrate, classify, grade, group, make the grade, mark off, measure out, order, pass, proportion, qualify, range, rank, regulate, sort.

graduate[2] *n.* alumna, alumnus, bachelor, diplomate, diplômé, diplômée, doctor, fellow, graduand, licentiate, literate, master, member.

graft *n.* bud, engraft, engraftation, engraftment, heteroplasty, imp, implant, implantation, insert, scion, shoot, splice, sprout, transplant.

v. engraft, implant, insert, join, splice, transplant.

grain *n.* atom, bit, cereals, corn, crumb, doit, fibre, fragment, granule, grist, grits, iota, jot, kernel, marking, mite, modicum, molecule, morsel, mote, nap, ounce, panic, particle, pattern, piece, scintilla, scrap, scruple, seed, smidgeon, spark, speck, surface, suspicion, texture, trace, weave, whit.

grammarian *n.* grammaticaster, grammatist, linguist, linguistician, philologist, Priscianist.

grand *adj.* A1, admirable, affluent, ambitious, august, chief, condescending, dignified, elevated, eminent, exalted, excellent, fine, first-class, first-rate, glorious, gracious, grandiose, great, haughty, head, highest, illustrious, imperious, imposing, impressive, large, leading, lofty, lordly, luxurious, magnificent, main, majestic, marvellous, monumental, noble, opulent, ostentatious, outstanding, palatial, patronising, pompous, pre-eminent, pretentious, princely, principal, regal, senior, smashing, splendid, stately, striking, sublime, sumptuous, super, superb, supreme, wonderful.

grandeur *n.* augustness, dignity, graciousness, gravitas, greatness, hauteur, imperiousness, importance, loftiness, magnificence, majesty, morgue, nobility, pomp, splendour, state, stateliness, sublimity.

antonyms humbleness, lowliness, simplicity.

grandfather *n.* gaffer, goodsire, grandad, grand(d)addy, grandpa, grandsire, granfer, gutcher.

grandiloquence *n.* affectation, bombast, euphuism, fustian, Gongorism, magniloquence, orotundity, pomposity, pretentiousness, rhetoric, turgidity.

antonyms plainness, restraint, simplicity.

grandiloquent *adj.* bombastic, euphuistic, flowery, fustian, Gongoristic, grandiloquous, high-flown, high-sounding, inflated, magniloquent, orotund, pompous, pretentious, rhetorical, swollen, turgid.

antonyms plain, restrained, simple.

grandiose *adj.* affected, ambitious, bombastic, euphuistic, extravagant, flamboyant, grand, high-flown, imposing, impressive, lofty, magnificent, majestic, monumental, ostentatious, pompous, ponderous, pretentious, showy, stately, Wagnerian, weighty.

antonym unpretentious.

grandmother *n.* gammer, gran, grandma, grandmama, granny.

grant *v.* accede to, accord, acknowledge, admit, agree to, allocate, allot, allow, apportion, assign, award, bestow, cede, concede, confer, consent to, convey, deign, dispense, donate, give, impart, permit, present, provide, transfer, transmit, vouchsafe, yield.
antonyms deny, refuse.
n. accord, admission, allocation, allotment, allowance, annuity, award, benefaction, bequest, boon, bounty, bursary, concession, donation, endowment, gift, honorarium, present, scholarship, subsidy, subvention.

granular *adj.* crumbly, grainy, granulase, granulated, granulous, gravelly, gritty, murly, rough, sabulose, sabulous, sandy.

granule *n.* atom, bead, crumb, fragment, grain, iota, jot, molecule, particle, pellet, scrap, seed, speck.

graph *n.* chart, diagram, grid, histogram, table.

graphic *adj.* blow-by-blow, clear, cogent, delineated, delineative, descriptive, detailed, diagrammatic, drawn, explicit, expressive, forcible, illustrative, lively, lucid, pictorial, picturesque, representational, seen, specific, striking, telling, visible, visual, vivid.
antonyms impressionistic, vague.

grapple *v.* attack, battle, catch, clash, clasp, clinch, close, clutch, combat, come to grips, confront, contend, cope, deal with, encounter, engage, face, fasten, fight, grab, grasp, grip, gripe, hold, hug, lay hold, make fast, seize, snatch, struggle, tackle, tussle, wrestle.
antonyms avoid, evade.

grasp *v.* catch, catch on, clasp, clinch, clutch, comprehend, follow, get, grab, grapple, grip, gripe, hold, lay hold of, realise, savvy, see, seize, snatch, twig, understand.
n. acquaintance, apprehension, awareness, capacity, clasp, clutches, compass, competence, comprehension, control, conversance, conversancy, embrace, expertness, extent, familiarity, grip, hold, holt, intimacy, ken, knowledge, mastery, perception, possession, power, range, reach, realisation, scope, sway, sweep, tenure, understanding.

grasping *adj.* acquisitive, avaricious, close-fisted, covetous, greedy, mean, mercenary, miserly, niggardly, parsimonious, penny-pinching, rapacious, selfish, stingy, tight-fisted, usurious.
antonym generous.

grass *n.* fog, foggage, grama, grassland, green, greensward, hay, herbage, lawn, pasturage, pasture, sward, turf, verdure.

grasshopper *n.* cicada, cigale, cricket, grig, locust.

grassland *n.* downs, lay, lea, ley, llano, meadow, meadowland, pampas, pasture, prairie, savanna, steppe, sward, veldt.

grate *v.* aggravate, annoy, chafe, comminute, creak, exasperate, fret, gall, get on one's nerves, granulate, gride, grind, irk, irritate, jar, mince, nettle, peeve, pulverise, rankle, rasp, rub, scrape, scratch, set one's teeth on edge, shred, triturate, vex.

grateful *adj.* appreciative, aware, beholden, indebted, mindful, obligated, obliged, sensible, thankful.
antonym ungrateful.

gratification *n.* contentment, delight, elation, enjoyment, fruition, fulfilment, glee, indulgence, joy, jubilation, kicks, pleasure, recompense, relish, reward, satisfaction, thrill, triumph.
antonym frustration.

gratify *v.* appease, cater to, content, delight, favour, fulfil, gladden, humour, indulge, pander to, please, pleasure, recompense, requite, satisfy, thrill.
antonyms frustrate, thwart.

grating[1] *adj.* annoying, cacophonous, disagreeable, discordant, displeasing, grinding, harsh, horrisonant, irksome, irritating, jarring, rasping, raucous, scraping, squeaky, strident, unharmonious, unmelodious, unpleasant, vexatious.
antonyms harmonious, pleasing.

grating[2] *n.* grid, grill, grille, hack, heck, lattice, lattice-work, treillage, treille, trellis, trelliswork.

gratitude *n.* acknowledgement, appreciation, awareness, gratefulness, indebtedness, mindfulness, obligation, recognition, thankfulness, thanks.
antonym ingratitude.

gratuitous *adj.* assumed, baseless, buckshee, causeless, complimentary, free, gratis, groundless, irrelevant, needless, spontaneous, superfluous, unasked-for, uncalled-for, undeserved, unearned, unfounded, unjustified, unmerited, unnecessary, unpaid, unprovoked, unrewarded, unsolicited, unwarranted, voluntary, wanton.
antonyms justified, reasonable.

gratuity *n.* baksheesh, beer-money, benefaction, bonus, boon, bounty, dash, donation, donative, douceur, drink-money, gift, lagniappe, largess, perquisite, pourboire, present, recompense, reward, tip, Trinkgeld.

grave[1] *n.* barrow, burial-place, burying-place, cairn, cist, crypt, long home, mausoleum, pit, sepulchre, tomb, vault.

grave[2] *adj.* acute, Catonian, critical, crucial, dangerous, depressing, dignified, disquieting, dour, dull, earnest, exigent, gloomy, grim, grim-faced, hazardous, heavy, important, leaden, long-faced, momentous, muted, perilous, ponderous, preoccupied, pressing, quiet, reserved, restrained, sad, sage, saturnine, sedate, serious, severe, significant, sober, solemn, sombre, staid, subdued, thoughtful, threatening, unsmiling, urgent, vital, weighty.
antonyms cheerful, light, slight, trivial.

gravel *n.* chesil, grail, hogging, shingle.

gravelly *adj.* ginny, glareous, grainy, granular, grating, gritty, gruff, guttural, harsh, hoarse, pebbly, sabulose, sabulous, shingly, throaty.
antonyms clear, fine, powdery.

graveyard *n.* boneyard, burial-ground, burial-place, burying-place, cemetery, churchyard, God's acre, Golgotha, necropolis.

gravitate v. descend, drop, fall, head for, incline, lean, move, precipitate, settle, sink, tend.

gravity n. acuteness, consequence, demureness, dignity, earnestness, exigency, gloom, gravitas, grimness, hazardousness, importance, magnitude, moment, momentousness, perilousness, ponderousness, reserve, restraint, sedateness, seriousness, severity, significance, sobriety, solemnity, sombreness, thoughtfulness, urgency, weightiness.

antonyms gaiety, levity, triviality.

graze[1] v. batten, browse, crop, feed, fodder, pasture.

graze[2] v. abrade, bark, brush, chafe, gride, rub, scart, score, scotch, scrape, scratch, shave, skim, skin, touch.

n. abrasion, score, scrape, scratch.

grease n. dope, dripping, fat, gunge, lard, oil, ointment, sebum, tallow, unction, unguent, wax.

greasy adj. fatty, fawning, glib, grovelling, ingratiating, lardy, oily, oleaginous, sebaceous, slick, slimy, slippery, smarmy, smeary, smooth, sycophantic, tallowy, toadying, unctuous, waxy.

great adj. able, ace, active, adept, admirable, adroit, august, big, bulky, capital, celebrated, chief, colossal, consequential, considerable, crack, critical, crucial, decided, devoted, dignified, distinguished, eminent, enormous, enthusiastic, exalted, excellent, excessive, expert, extended, extensive, extravagant, extreme, fab, fabulous, famed, famous, fantastic, fine, finished, first-rate, generous, gigantic, glorious, good, grand, grave, great-hearted, grievous, heavy, heroic, high, high-minded, huge, idealistic, illustrious, immense, important, impressive, inordinate, invaluable, jake, keen, large, leading, lengthy, lofty, long, magnanimous, main, major, mammoth, manifold, marked, marvellous, massive, masterly, momentous, multitudinous, munificent, noble, nonpareil, notable, noteworthy, noticeable, outstanding, paramount, ponderous, precious, pre-eminent, priceless, primary, princely, principal, prodigious, proficient, prolific, prolonged, prominent, pronounced, protracted, remarkable, renowned, senior, serious, significant, skilful, skilled, strong, stupendous, sublime, superb, superior, superlative, swingeing, talented, terrific, tremendous, valuable, vast, virtuoso, voluminous, weighty, wonderful, zealous.

antonyms insignificant, pusillanimous, small, unimportant.

greatly adv. abundantly, considerably, enormously, exceedingly, extremely, highly, hugely, immensely, impressively, markedly, mightily, much, notably, noticeably, powerfully, remarkably, significantly, substantially, tremendously, vastly.

greatness n. amplitude, bulk, celebrity, dignity, distinction, eminence, excellence, fame,

force, generosity, genius, glory, grandeur, gravity, great-heartednes, heaviness, heroism, high-mindedness, hugeness, idealism, illustriousness, immensity, import, importance, intensity, largeness, length, loftiness, lustre, magnanimity, magnitude, majesty, mass, moment, momentousness, nobility, nobleness, note, potency, power, prodigiousness, renown, seriousness, significance, size, stateliness, strength, sublimity, superbness, urgency, vastness, weight.

antonyms insignificance, pettiness, pusillanimity, smallness.

greed n. acquisitiveness, anxiety, avidity, covetousness, craving, cupidity, desire, eagerness, edacity, esurience, esuriency, gluttony, gormandising, gormandism, gourmandise, greediness, gulosity, hunger, insatiability, insatiableness, itchy palm, land-hunger, longing, plutolatry, rapacity, ravenousness, selfishness, voraciousness, voracity.

antonym abstemiousness.

greedy adj. acquisitive, anxious, avaricious, avid, covetous, craving, curious, desirous, eager, edacious, esurient, gare, gluttonish, gluttonous, gormandising, grasping, gripple, gutsy, hoggery, hoggish, hungry, impatient, insatiable, itchy-palmed, land-grabbing, piggish, rapacious, ravenous, selfish, ventripotent, voracious.

antonym abstemious.

green adj. blooming, budding, callow, covetous, credulous, emerald, envious, flourishing, fresh, glaucous, grassy, grudging, gullible, ignorant, ill, immature, inexperienced, inexpert, ingenuous, innocent, jealous, leafy, naive, nauseous, new, pale, pliable, raw, recent, resentful, sick, starry-eyed, supple, tender, unhealthy, unpractised, unripe, unseasoned, unsophisticated, untrained, untried, unversed, verdant, verdurous, vert, virescent, virid, viridescent, vitreous, wan, wet behind the ears, young.

n. common, grass, greensward, lawn, sward, turf.

greenery n. foliage, greenness, greenth, vegetation, verdancy, verdure, virescence, viridescence, viridity.

greenhorn n. apprentice, beginner, catechumen, fledgling, ignoramus, ingénué, initiate, Johnnie raw, learner, naïf, neophyte, newcomer, novice, novitiate, recruit, rookie, simpleton, tenderfoot, tyro.

antonyms old hand, veteran.

greenhouse n. conservatory, glasshouse, hothouse, nursery, pavilion, vinery.

greet v. accost, acknowledge, address, compliment, hail, hallo, halloo, meet, receive, salute, wave to, welcome.

antonym ignore.

greeting n. accost, acknowledgement, address, aloha, hail, kiss of peace, reception, salaam, salutation, salute, salve, the time of day, welcome.

greetings n. best wishes, civilities, compliments,

devoirs, formalities, good wishes, love, regards, respects, salutations.

gregarious *adj.* affable, chummy, companionable, convivial, cordial, extrovert, friendly, outgoing, pally, sociable, social, warm.
antonym unsociable.

grey *adj.* aged, ancient, anonymous, ashen, bloodless, characterless, cheerless, cloudy, colourless, dark, depressing, dim, dismal, drab, dreary, dull, elderly, experienced, glaucous, gloomy, grège, greige, griseous, grizzle, grizzled, hoar, hoary, indistinct, leaden, liard, livid, mature, murksome, murky, neutral, old, overcast, pale, pallid, sunless, uncertain, unclear, unidentifiable, venerable, wan.

grid *n.* graticule, grating, gridison, grill, grille, lattice.

grief *n.* ache, affliction, agony, anguish, bereavement, blow, burden, dejection, desiderium, desolation, distress, dole, grievance, heartache, heartbreak, lamentation, misery, mournfulness, mourning, pain, regret, remorse, sadness, sorrow, suffering, tragedy, trial, tribulation, trouble, woe.
antonym happiness.

grief-stricken *adj.* afflicted, agonised, broken, broken-hearted, crushed, desolate, despairing, devastated, disconsolate, distracted, grieving, heartbroken, inconsolable, mourning, overcome, overwhelmed, sad, sorrowful, sorrowing, stricken, unhappy, woebegone, wretched.
antonym overjoyed.

grievance *n.* affliction, beef, bitch, charge, complaint, damage, distress, gravamen, grief, gripe, grouse, hardship, injury, injustice, moan, peeve, resentment, sorrow, trial, tribulation, trouble, unhappiness, wrong.

grieve *v.* ache, afflict, agonise, bemoan, bewail, complain, crush, cut to the quick, deplore, distress, disturb, eat one's heart out, harrow, hurt, injure, lament, mourn, pain, regret, rue, sadden, sorrow, suffer, upset, wail, weep, wound.

grieved *adj.* abashed, affronted, ashamed, desolated, displeased, distressed, horrified, hurt, injured, offended, pained, sad, saddened, shocked, sorry, upset, wounded.

grievous *adj.* appalling, atrocious, burdensome, calamitous, damaging, deplorable, devastating, distressing, dreadful, flagrant, glaring, grave, harmful, heart-rending, heavy, heinous, hurtful, injurious, intolerable, lamentable, monstrous, mournful, offensive, oppressive, outrageous, overwhelming, painful, pitiful, plightful, severe, shameful, shocking, sorrowful, tragic, unbearable, wounding.

grievously *adv.* appallingly, badly, deplorably, dernly, desperately, distressingly, dreadfully, gravely, heinously, lamentably, monstrously, outrageously, painfully, seriously, severely, shamefully, shockingly, unforgivably.

grim *adj.* adamant, cruel, doom-laden, dour,

fearsome, ferocious, fierce, forbidding, formidable, frightening, frightful, ghastly, grisly, gruesome, harsh, hideous, horrible, horrid, implacable, merciless, morose, relentless, repellent, resolute, ruthless, severe, shocking, sinister, stern, sullen, surly, terrible, unpleasant, unrelenting, unwelcome, unyielding.
antonyms benign, congenial, pleasant.

grimace *n.* face, fit of the face, frown, moue, mouth, pout, scowl, smirk, sneer, wry face.
v. fleer, frown, girn, make a face, mop, mop and mow, mouth, mow, mug, pout, scowl, smirk, sneer.

grime *n.* dirt, filth, muck, smut, soot, squalor.

grimy *adj.* begrimed, besmeared, besmirched, contaminated, dirty, filthy, foul, grubby, murky, reechy, smudgy, smutty, soiled, sooty, squalid.
antonyms clean, pure.

grind *v.* abrade, beaver, bray, comminute, crush, drudge, file, gnash, granulate, grate, grit, kibble, labour, levigate, lucubrate, mill, polish, pound, powder, pulverise, sand, scrape, sharpen, slave, smooth, sweat, swot, toil, triturate, whet.
n. chore, drudgery, exertion, grindstone, labour, round, routine, slavery, sweat, task, toil.

grind down afflict, crush, harass, harry, hound, oppress, persecute, plague, trouble, tyrannise.

grip *n.* acquaintance, clasp, clutches, comprehension, control, domination, embrace, grasp, handclasp, hold, influence, keeping, mastery, perception, possession, power, purchase, sway, tenure, understanding.
v. absorb, catch, clasp, clutch, compel, divert, engross, enthral, entrance, fascinate, grasp, hold, involve, latch on to, mesmerise, rivet, seize, spellbind, thrill, vice.

gripe *v.* beef, bellyache, bitch, carp, complain, groan, grouch, grouse, grumble, moan, nag, whine, whinge.
n. ache, aching, affliction, beef, bitch, colic, collywobbles, complaint, cramps, distress, grievance, griping, groan, grouch, grouse, grumble, moan, objection, pain, pang, pinching, spasm, stomach-ache, twinge.

gripping *adj.* absorbing, compelling, compulsive, diverting, engrossing, enthralling, entrancing, exciting, fascinating, riveting, spellbinding, suspenseful, thrilling, unputdownable.

grisly *adj.* abominable, appalling, awful, dreadful, eldritch, frightful, ghastly, grim, gruesome, hair-raising, hideous, horrible, horrid, macabre, shocking, sickening, terrible, terrifying, weird.
antonym delightful.

grit[1] *n.* chesil, dust, grail, gravel, hogging, pebbles, sand, shingle, swarf.
v. clench, gnash, grate, grind, lock.

grit[2] backbone, bottle, bravery, courage, determination, doggedness, foison, fortitude, fushion, gameness, guts, hardihood, mettle, nerve, perseverance, pluck, resolution, spine, spirit, spunk, stamina, staying power, tenacity, toughness.

gritty *adj.* abrasive, brave, courageous, determined, dogged, dusty, game, grainy, granular, gravelly, hardy, mettlesome, pebbly, plucky, resolute, rough, sabulose, sabulous, sandy, shingly, spirited, spunky, steadfast, tenacious, tough.

antonyms fine, smooth, spineless.

grizzle *v.* cry, fret, girn, mewl, pule, sniffle, snivel, snuffle, whimper, whine, whinge.

grizzled *adj.* canescent, grey, grey-haired, grey-headed, greying, griseous, grizzly, hoar, hoary, pepper-and-salt.

groan *n.* complaint, cry, moan, objection, outcry, protest, sigh, wail.

antonym cheer.

v. complain, cry, lament, moan, object, protest, sigh, wail.

antonym cheer.

grocer *n.* dealer, épicier, greengrocer, Italian warehouseman, purveyor, spicer, storekeeper, supplier, victualler.

groggy *adj.* befuddled, confused, dazed, dizzy, dopey, faint, fuddled, knocked-up, muzzy, punch-drunk, reeling, shaky, stunned, stupefied, unsteady, weak, wobbly, woozy.

antonym lucid.

groom *v.* brush, clean, coach, curry, dress, drill, educate, neaten, nurture, preen, prepare, prime, primp, prink, ready, school, smarten, spruce up, tart up, tend, tidy, titivate, train, turn out, tutor.

groove *n.* canal, cannelure, chamfer, channel, chase, cut, cutting, flute, furrow, gutter, hollow, indentation, kerf, rabbet, rebate, rigol, rut, score, scrobe, sulcus, trench, vallecula.

antonym ridge.

grooved *adj.* chamfered, channelled, exarate, fluted, furrowed, rabbeted, rutted, scored, scrobiculate, sulcal, sulcate.

antonym ridged.

grope *v.* cast about, feel, feel about, feel up, finger, fish, flounder, fumble, goose, grabble, probe, scrabble, search.

gross [1] *adj.* apparent, arrant, bawdy, bestial, big, blatant, blue, boorish, broad, brutish, bulky, callous, coarse, colossal, corpulent, crass, crude, cumbersome, dense, downright, dull, earthy, egregious, fat, flagrant, foul, glaring, great, grievous, heavy, heinous, huge, hulking, ignorant, immense, imperceptive, improper, impure, indecent, indelicate, insensitive, large, lewd, low, lumpish, manifest, massive, obese, obscene, obtuse, obvious, offensive, outrageous, outright, overweight, plain, rank, ribald, rude, sensual, serious, shameful, shameless, sheer, shocking, slow, sluggish, smutty, tasteless, thick, uncivil, uncouth, uncultured, undiscriminating, undisguised, unfeeling, unmitigated, unseemly, unsophisticated, unwieldy, utter, vulgar.

antonyms delicate, fine, seemly, slight.

gross [2] *n.* aggregate, bulk, entirety, sum, total, totality, whole.

adj. aggregate, all-inclusive, complete, entire, inclusive, total, whole.

v. accumulate, aggregate, bring, earn, make, rake in, take, total.

grossness *n.* bawdiness, bestiality, bigness, blatancy, brutishness, bulkiness, coarseness, corpulence, crassness, crudity, earthiness, egregiousness, fatness, flagrancy, foulness, greatness, grievousness, grossièreté, heaviness, hugeness, ignorance, immensity, impurity, incivility, indecency, indelicacy, insensitivity, licentiousness, lumpishness, obesity, obscenity, obtuseness, obviousness, offensiveness, rankness, ribaldry, rudeness, sensuality, seriousness, shamefulness, shamelessness, sluggishness, smut, smuttiness, tastelessness, thickness, uncouthness, unseemliness, unwieldiness, vulgarity.

antonyms delicacy, fineness, seemliness, slightness.

grotesque *adj.* absurd, antic, bizarre, deformed, distorted, extravagant, fanciful, fantastic, freakish, gruesome, hideous, incongruous, laughable, ludicrous, macabre, malformed, misshapen, monstrous, odd, outlandish, preposterous, ridiculous, rococo, strange, ugly, unnatural, unsightly, weird.

n. bizarrerie, extravaganza, fantastic figure, gargoyle, gobbo, grotesquerie, manikin.

grotto *n.* catacomb, cave, cavern, chamber, dene-hole, grot, souterrain, subterranean (chamber), subterrene, underground chamber.

grouch *v.* beef, bellyache, bitch, carp, complain, find fault, gripe, grouse, grumble, moan, whine, whinge.

antonym acquiesce.

n. belly-acher, churl, complainer, complaint, crab, crosspatch, crotcheteer, curmudgeon, fault-finder, grievance, gripe, grouse, grouser, grumble, grumbler, malcontent, moan, moaner, murmer, murmurer, mutterer, objection, whiner, whinge, whinger.

grouchy *adj.* bad-tempered, cantankerous, captious, churlish, complaining, cross, crotchety, discontented, dissatisfied, grumbling, grumpy, ill-tempered, irascible, irritable, mutinous, peevish, petulant, querulous, sulky, surly, testy, truculent.

antonym contented.

ground *n.* arena, background, ball-park, bottom, clay, clod, deck, dirt, dry land, dust, earth, field, foundation, land, loam, mould, park, pitch, sod, soil, solum, stadium, surface, terra firma, terrain, turf.

v. acquaint with, base, build up, coach, drill, establish, familiarise with, fix, found, inform, initiate, instruct, introduce, prepare, set, settle, teach, train, tutor.

groundless *adj.* absurd, baseless, chimerical, empty, false, gratuitous, idle, illusory, imaginary, irrational, unauthorised, uncalled-for,

unfounded, unjustified, unproven, unprovoked, unreasonable, unsubstantiated, unsupported, unwarranted.
antonyms justified, reasonable.

grounds[1] *n.* acres, area, country, district, domain, estate, fields, gardens, habitat, holding, land, park, property, realm, surroundings, terrain, territory, tract.

grounds[2] *n.* account, argument, base, basis, call, cause, excuse, factor, foundation, inducement, justification, motive, occasion, premise, pretext, principle, rationale, reason, score, vindication.

grounds[3] *n.* deposit, dregs, grouts, lees, precipitate, precipitation, sediment, settlings.

groundwork *n.* base, basis, cornerstone, essentials, footing, foundation, fundamentals, homework, preliminaries, preparation, research, spadework, underpinnings.

group *n.* accumulation, aggregation, assemblage, association, band, batch, bracket, bunch, category, caucus, circle, class, classification, classis, clique, clump, cluster, clutch, cohort, collection, collective, combination, company, conclave, conglomeration, congregation, constellation, core, coterie, covey, crowd, detachment, faction, formation, front, galère, gang, gathering, Gemeinschaft, genus, grouping, knot, lot, nexus, organisation, pack, parti, party, pop-group, set, shower, species, squad, squadron, team, troop.
v. arrange, assemble, associate, assort, band, bracket, categorise, class, classify, cluster, collect, congregate, consort, deploy, dispose, fraternise, gather, get together, link, marshal, mass, order, organise, range, sort.

grouse *v.* beef, belly-ache, bitch, carp, complain, find fault, fret, fuss, gripe, grouch, grumble, moan, mutter, whine, whinge.
antonym acquiesce.
n. belly-ache, complaint, grievance, gripe, grouch, grumble, moan, murmur, mutter, objection, peeve, whine, whinge.

grove *n.* arbour, avenue, bosk, bosket, brake, coppice, copse, covert, hurst, plantation, spinney, thicket, wood, woodland.

grovel *v.* abase oneself, backscratch, bootlick, cower, crawl, creep, cringe, crouch, defer, demean oneself, fawn, flatter, kowtow, sneak, sycophantise, toady.

grovelling *adj.* backscratching, bootlicking, fawning, flattering, ingratiating, obsequious, sycophantic, wormy.
antonyms outspoken, straightforward.

grow *v.* advance, arise, augment, become, branch out, breed, broaden, burgeon, cultivate, develop, diversify, enlarge, evolve, expand, extend, farm, flourish, flower, germinate, get, heighten, improve, increase, issue, mature, multiply, nurture, originate, produce, progress, proliferate, propagate, prosper, raise, ripen, rise, shoot, spread, spring, sprout, stem, stretch, succeed, swell, thicken, thrive, turn, vegetate, wax, widen.
antonyms decrease, fail, halt.

growing *adj.* accrescent, blossoming, broadening, burgeoning, crescent, crescive, deepening, developing, elongating, enlarging, escalating, expanding, extending, flourishing, heightening, increasing, increscent, intumescent, lengthening, maturing, mounting, multiplying, proliferating, rising, spreading, swelling, thickening, thriving, tumescent, waxing, widening.
antonyms decreasing, failing, stagnant, static, waning.

growl *v.* gnar, gnarl, gnarr, knar, snap, snarl, yap.

grown-up *adj.* adult, full-grown, fully-fledged, fully-grown, mature, of age.
antonyms childish, immature.
n. adult, gentleman, lady, man, woman.
antonym child.

growth *n.* accrescence, accretion, advance, advancement, aggrandisement, augmentation, auxesis, broadening, change, crop, cultivation, development, diversification, enlargement, evolution, excrement, excrescence, expansion, extension, flowering, gall, germination, growing, heightening, improvement, increase, intumescence, lump, maturation, multiplication, outgrowth, produce, production, progress, proliferation, prosperity, protuberance, ripening, rise, shooting, sprouting, stretching, success, swelling, thickening, transformation, tumour, vegetation, waxing, widening.
antonyms decrease, failure, stagnation, stoppage.

grub[1] *v.* burrow, delve, dig, explore, ferret, forage, grout, hunt, investigate, nose, probe, pull up, root, rootle, rummage, scour, uproot.
n. caterpillar, chrysalis, larva, maggot, nymph, pupa, worm.

grub[2] *n.* chow, commons, eats, edibles, fodder, food, nosh, provisions, rations, scoff, sustenance, victuals.

grubby *adj.* crummy, dirty, filthy, fly-blown, frowzy, grimy, manky, mean, messy, mucky, scruffy, seedy, shabby, slovenly, smutty, soiled, sordid, squalid, unkempt, untidy, unwashed.
antonyms clean, smart.

grudge *n.* animosity, animus, antagonism, antipathy, aversion, bitterness, dislike, enmity, envy, grievance, hard feelings, hate, ill-will, jealousy, malevolence, malice, pique, rancour, resentment, spite.
antonyms favour, regard.
v. begrudge, covet, dislike, envy, mind, niggard, object to, regret, repine, resent, stint, take exception to.
antonyms applaud, approve.

grudging *adj.* cautious, guarded, half-hearted, hesitant, reluctant, secret, unenthusiastic, unwilling.

gruelling *adj.* arduous, backbreaking, brutal, crushing, demanding, difficult, exhausting, fatiguing, fierce, grinding, hard, hard-going, harsh, laborious, punishing, severe, stern,

stiff, strenuous, taxing, tiring, tough, trying, uphill, wearing, wearying.
antonym easy.

gruesome *adj*. abominable, awful, chilling, eldritch, fearful, fearsome, ghastly, grim, grisly, grooly, hideous, horrible, horrid, horrific, horrifying, loathsome, macabre, monstrous, repellent, repugnant, repulsive, shocking, sick, spine-chilling, terrible, weird.
antonyms charming, congenial.

gruff *adj*. abrupt, bad-tempered, bearish, blunt, brusque, churlish, crabbed, croaking, crusty, curt, discourteous, gravelly, grouchy, grumpy, guttural, harsh, hoarse, husky, ill-humoured, ill-natured, impolite, low, rasping, rough, rude, sour, sullen, surly, throaty, uncivil, ungracious, unmannerly.
antonyms clear, courteous, sweet.

grumble *v*. beef, bellyache, bitch, bleat, carp, chunter, complain, croak, find fault, gripe, grouch, grouse, growl, gurgle, moan, murmur, mutter, nark, repine, roar, rumble, whine.
antonym acquiesce.
n. beef, bitch, bleat, complaint, grievance, gripe, grouch, grouse, growl, gurgle, moan, murmur, muttering, objection, roar, rumble, whinge.

grumpy *adj*. bad-tempered, cantankerous, churlish, crabbed, cross, crotchety, discontented, grouchy, grumbling, ill-tempered, irritable, mutinous, peevish, petulant, querulous, sulky, sullen, surly, testy, truculent.
antonyms civil, contented.

guarantee *n*. assurance, attestation, bond, certainty, collateral, covenant, earnest, endorsement, guaranty, insurance, oath, pledge, promise, security, surety, testimonial, undertaking, voucher, warranty, word, word of honour.
v. answer for, assure, avouch, certify, ensure, insure, maintain, make certain, make sure of, pledge, promise, protect, secure, swear, underwrite, vouch for, warrant.

guarantor *n*. angel, backer, bailsman, bondsman, covenanter, guarantee, referee, sponsor, supporter, surety, underwriter, voucher, warrantor.

guard *v*. be on the qui vive, be on the watch, beware, conserve, cover, defend, escort, keep, look out, mind, oversee, patrol, police, preserve, protect, safeguard, save, screen, secure, sentinel, shelter, shield, supervise, tend, ward, watch.
n. attention, backstop, barrier, buffer, bulwark, bumper, care, caution, convoy, custodian, defence, defender, escort, guarantee, heed, lookout, minder, pad, patrol, picket, precaution, protection, protector, rampart, safeguard, screen, security, sentinel, sentry, shield, vigilance, wall, warder, wariness, watch, watchfulness, watchman.

guarded *adj*. cagey, careful, cautious, circumspect, discreet, disingenuous, non-committal, prudent, reserved, restrained, reticent,

secretive, suspicious, uncommunicative, unforthcoming, wary, watchful.
antonyms frank, whole-hearted.

guardian *n*. attendant, champion, conservator, curator, custodian, defender, depositary, depository, escort, fiduciary, guard, keeper, minder, preserver, protector, trustee, warden, warder.

guardianship *n*. aegis, attendance, care, companionship, curatorship, custodianship, custody, defence, escort, guard, guidance, hands, keeping, patronage, protection, safekeeping, trust, trusteeship, wardenry, wardenship, wardship.

guerrilla *n*. bushwhacker, franc-tireur, freedom-fighter, guerrillero, haiduck, irregular, maquisard, partisan, resistance fighter, sniper.

guess *v*. assume, believe, conjecture, dare say, deem, divine, estimate, fancy, fathom, feel, guesstimate, hazard, hypothesise, imagine, intuit, judge, opine, penetrate, predict, reckon, solve, speculate, suppose, surmise, suspect, think, work out.
n. assumption, belief, conjecture, fancy, feeling, guesstimate, hypothesis, intuition, judgement, notion, opinion, prediction, reckoning, shot (in the dark), speculation, supposition, surmise, suspicion, theory.

guesswork *n*. assumption, conjecture, estimation, intuition, presumption, presupposition, reckoning, speculation, supposition, surmise, suspicion, theory.

guest *n*. boarder, caller, company, freeloader, habitué, lodger, parasite, regular, roomer, visitant, visitor.

guest-house *n*. boarding-house, hospice, hospitium, hostel, hostelry, hotel, inn, pension, rooming-house, xenodochium.

guidance *n*. advice, aegis, auspices, clues, conduct, control, counsel, counselling, direction, government, guidelines, help, illumination, indications, instruction, leadership, management, pointers, recommendation, regulation, steering, teaching.

guide *v*. accompany, advise, attend, command, conduct, control, convoy, counsel, direct, educate, escort, govern, handle, head, influence, instruct, lead, manage, manoeuvre, oversee, pilot, point, regulate, rule, shape, shepherd, steer, superintend, supervise, sway, teach, train, usher, vector.
n. ABC, adviser, attendant, beacon, catalogue, chaperon, cicerone, clue, companion, conductor, controller, counsellor, courier, criterion, director, directory, dragoman, escort, example, exemplar, guide-book, guideline, handbook, ideal, index, indication, informant, inspiration, instructions, key, landmark, leader, lodestar, manual, mark, marker, master, mentor, model, monitor, paradigm, pilot, pointer, praxis, sign, signal, signpost, standard, steersman, teacher, template, usher, vade-mecum.

guiding *adj*. advisory, consultant, consultative, consultatory, consulting, controlling, counselling, directorial, directory, formative, governing, influential, instructional, instructive, managing, monitoring, piloting, shepherding, steering, supervisory, tutorial.

guild *n.* association, brotherhood, chapel, club, company, corporation, fellowship, fraternity, incorporation, league, lodge, order, organisation, society, union.

guile *n.* art, artfulness, artifice, cleverness, craft, craftiness, cunning, deceit, deception, deviousness, disingenuity, duplicity, gamesmanship, knavery, ruse, slyness, treachery, trickery, trickiness, wiliness.
antonyms artlessness, guilelessness.

guileful *adj.* artful, clever, crafty, cunning, deceitful, devious, disingenuous, duplicitous, foxy, sly, sneaky, treacherous, tricky, underhand, wily.
antonyms artless, guileless.

guileless *adj.* artless, candid, direct, frank, genuine, honest, ingenuous, innocent, naïve, natural, open, simple, sincere, straightforward, transparent, trusting, truthful, unreserved, unsophisticated, unworldly.
antonyms artful, guileful.

guilt *n.* blamability, blame, blameworthiness, compunction, conscience, contrition, criminality, culpability, delinquency, disgrace, dishonour, guiltiness, guilty conscience, infamy, iniquity, mens rea, regret, remorse, responsibility, self-condemnation, self-reproach, self-reproof, shame, sinfulness, stigma, wickedness, wrong.
antonyms innocence, shamelessness.

guiltless *adj.* blameless, clean, clear, immaculate, impeccable, inculpable, innocent, irreproachable, pure, sinless, spotless, unimpeachable, unspotted, unsullied, untainted, untarnished.
antonyms guilty, tainted.

guilty *adj.* ashamed, blamable, blameworthy, compunctious, conscience-stricken, contrite, convicted, criminal, culpable, delinquent, errant, erring, evil, felonious, guilt-ridden, hangdog, illicit, iniquitous, nefarious, nocent, offending, penitent, regretful, remorseful, repentant, reprehensible, responsible, rueful, shamefaced, sheepish, sinful, sorry, wicked, wrong.
antonyms guiltless, innocent.

guise *n.* air, appearance, aspect, behaviour, custom, demeanour, disguise, dress, façade, face, fashion, features, form, front, likeness, manner, mask, mode, pretence, semblance, shape, show.

gulf *n.* abyss, basin, bay, bight, breach, chasm, cleft, gap, gorge, opening, rent, rift, separation, split, void, whirlpool.

gull *n.* maw, mew, seagull, sea-mew.

gullet *n.* craw, crop, maw, oesophagus, the Red Lane, throat, weasand.

gullibility *n.* credulity, glaikitness, innocence, naïvety, simplicity, trustfulness, verdancy.
antonym astuteness.

gullible *adj.* born yesterday, credulous, foolish, glaikit, green, innocent, naïve, trusting, unsuspecting, verdant.
antonym astute.

gully *n.* channel, ditch, donga, geo, gio, gulch, gutter, ravine, watercourse.

gulp *v.* bolt, choke, devour, gasp, gobble, gollop, gormandise, guzzle, knock back, quaff, stifle, stuff, swallow, swig, swill, toss off, wolf.
antonyms nibble, sip.
n. draught, mouthful, slug, swallow, swig.

gum *n.* adhesive, cement, glue, goo, mucilage, paste, resin, sap.
v. affix, block, cement, clog, fix, glue, paste, seal, stick.

gumboil *n.* abscess, parulis, swelling.

gummy *adj.* adhesive, gluey, gooey, sticky, tacky, viscid, viscous.

gumption *n.* ability, acumen, acuteness, astuteness, cleverness, common sense, discernment, enterprise, horse sense, initiative, mother wit, nous, resourcefulness, sagacity, savvy, shrewdness, smeddum, spirit, wit(s).
antonym foolishness.

gun *n.* equaliser, gat, heater, peacemaker, persuader, piece, pistol, shooter, shooting-iron, tool.

gunman *n.* assassin, bandit, bravo, desperado, gangster, gunsel, gunslinger, hatchet man, hit man, killer, mobster, murderer, shootist, sniper, terrorist, thug.

gurgle *v.* babble, bubble, burble, crow, guggle, lap, murmur, plash, purl, ripple, splash.
n. babble, guggle, murmur, purl, ripple.

guru *n.* authority, instructor, leader, luminary, maharishi, master, mentor, pundit, sage, Svengali, swami, teacher, tutor.

gush *v.* babble, blather, burst, cascade, chatter, drivel, effuse, enthuse, flood, flow, jabber, jet, pour, run, rush, spout, spurt, stream, yatter.
n. babble, burst, cascade, chatter, ebullition, effusion, eruption, exuberance, flood, flow, jet, outburst, outflow, rush, spout, spurt, stream, tide, torrent.

gushing *adj.* cloying, effusive, emotional, excessive, fulsome, gushy, mawkish, over-enthusiastic, saccharine, sentimental, sickly.
antonyms restrained, sincere.

gust *n.* blast, blow, breeze, burst, flaught, flaw, flurry, gale, puff, rush, squall, williwaw.
v. blast, blow, bluster, breeze, puff, squall.

gusto *n.* appetite, appreciation, brio, delight, élan, enjoyment, enthusiasm, exhilaration, exuberance, fervour, liking, pleasure, relish, savour, verve, zeal, zest.
antonyms apathy, distaste.

gusty *adj.* blowy, blustering, blustery, breezy, gustful, squally, stormy, tempestuous, windy.
antonym calm.

gut *v.* clean, clean out, despoil, disembowel, draw, dress, empty, eviscerate, exenterate, gill, pillage, plunder, ransack, ravage, rifle, sack, strip.
adj. basic, deep-seated, emotional, heartfelt,

innate, instinctive, intuitive, involuntary, natural, spontaneous, strong, unthinking, visceral.

gutless *adj.* abject, chicken, chicken-hearted, chicken-livered, cowardly, craven, faint-hearted, feeble, irresolute, lily-livered, spineless, submissive, timid, weak.
antonym courageous.

guts *n.* audacity, backbone, belly, boldness, bottle, bowels, courage, daring, endurance, entrails, forcefulness, grit, hardihood, innards, insides, intestines, inwards, mettle, nerve, paunch, pluck, spirit, spunk, stamina, staying power, stomach, tenacity, toughness, viscera.
antonym spinelessness.

gutsy *adj.* bold, brave, courageous, determined, gallant, game, indomitable, lusty, mettlesome, passionate, plucky, resolute, spirited, staunch.
antonyms quiet, timid.

gutter *n.* channel, conduit, ditch, drain, duct, grip, kennel, pipe, rigol(l), sluice, trench, trough, tube.

guttersnipe *n.* gamin, mudlark, ragamuffin, street Arab, tatterdemalion, urchin, waif.

guttural *adj.* deep, grating, gravelly, gruff, harsh, hoarse, husky, low, rasping, rough, thick, throaty.
antonym dulcet.

guy *n.* bloke, buffer, cat, chap, codger, cove, customer, fellow, individual, josser, lad, man, oik, person, punter, youth.

guzzle *v.* bolt, carouse, cram, devour, gobble, gormandise, stuff, wolf.

gypsy *n.* Bohemian, diddicoy, faw, gipsy, gitana, gitano, nomad, rambler, roamer, Romany, rover, tink, tinker, traveller, tsigane, tzigany, vagabond, vagrant, wanderer, Zigeuner, Zincalo, Zingaro.

gyrate *v.* circle, gyre, pirouette, revolve, rotate, spin, spiral, twirl, whirl.

gyrating *adj.* gyral, gyrant, revolving, rotating, spinning, twirling, whirling.

gyration *n.* convolution, pirouette, revolution, rotation, spin, spinning, spiral, twirl, vertigo, whirl, whirling.

H

habit[1] *n.* accustomedness, addiction, assuetude, bent, constitution, convention, custom, dependence, diathesis, disposition, fixation, frame of mind, habitude, inclination, make-up, manner, mannerism, mode, mores, nature, obsession, practice, proclivity, propensity, quirk, routine, rule, second nature, tendency, usage, vice, way, weakness, wont.

habit[2] *n.* apparel, attire, clothes, clothing, dress, garb, garment, habiliment.

habitat *n.* abode, domain, element, environment, home, locality, surroundings, terrain, territory.

habitation *n.* abode, cottage, domicile, dwelling, dwelling-place, home, house, hut, inhabitance, inhabitancy, inhabitation, living quarters, lodging, mansion, occupancy, occupation, quarters, residence, tenancy.

habitual *adj.* accustomed, chronic, common, confirmed, constant, customary, established, familiar, fixed, frequent, hardened, ingrained, inveterate, natural, normal, ordinary, persistent, recurrent, regular, routine, standard, traditional, usual, wonted.
antonym occasional.

habituate *v.* acclimatise, accustom, break in, condition, discipline, familiarise, harden, inure, school, season, tame, train.

habitué *n.* denizen, frequenter, patron, regular, regular customer.

hack[1] *v.* bark, chop, cough, cut, gash, haggle, hew, kick, lacerate, mangle, mutilate, notch, rasp, slash.
n. bark, chop, cough, cut, gash, notch, rasp, slash.

hack[2] *adj.* banal, hackneyed, mediocre, pedestrian, poor, stereotyped, tired, undistinguished, uninspired, unoriginal.
n. crock, drudge, horse, jade, journalist, nag, paper-stainer, penny-a-liner, scribbler, slave.

hackneyed *adj.* banal, clichéd, common, commonplace, corny, hack, hand-me-down, overworked, pedestrian, percoct, played-out, run-of-the-mill, second-hand, stale, stereotyped, stock, threadbare, time-worn, tired, trite, unoriginal, worn-out.
antonyms arresting, new.

hack-work *n.* drudgery, pot-boiler.

haemorrhoids *n.* emerods, piles.

hag *n.* battle-axe, beldame, crone, fury, harpy, harridan, ogress, shrew, termagant, virago, vixen, witch.

haggard *adj.* cadaverous, careworn, drawn, emaciated, gaunt, ghastly, hagged, hollow-eyed, pinched, shrunken, thin, wan, wasted, wrinkled.

antonym hale.

haggle *v.* bargain, barter, bicker, cavil, chaffer, dicker, dispute, higgle, palter, quarrel, squabble, wrangle.

hail[1] *n.* barrage, bombardment, rain, shower, storm, torrent, volley.
v. assail, barrage, batter, bombard, pelt, rain, shower, storm, volley.

hail[2] *v.* acclaim, accost, acknowledge, address, applaud, call, cheer, exalt, flag down, glorify, greet, halloo, honour, salute, shout, signal to, wave, welcome.
n. call, cry, halloo, holla, shout.

hair *n.* locks, mane, mop, shock, tresses, vibrissa, villus.
hair removal depilation, electrolysis, epilation.

hair-do *n.* coiffure, cut, haircut, hairstyle, perm, set, style.

hairdresser *n.* barber, coiffeur, coiffeuse, friseur, hair-stylist, stylist.

hairless *adj.* bald, bald-headed, beardless, clean-shaven, depilated, desperate, frantic, glabrate, glabrous, shorn, tonsured.
antonym hairy.

hairpiece *n.* postiche, wig.

hair-raising *adj.* alarming, bloodcurdling, breathtaking, creepy, eerie, exciting, frightening, ghastly, ghostly, horrifying, petrifying, scary, shocking, spine-chilling, startling, terrifying, thrilling.
antonym calming.

hair's-breadth *n.* fraction, hair, inch, jot, whisker.
antonym mile.

hair-splitting *adj.* captious, carping, cavilling, fault-finding, fine, finicky, nice, niggling, nit-picking, overnice, over-refined, pettifogging, quibbling, subtle, word-splitting.
antonym unfussy.

hairy *adj.* bearded, bewhiskered, bushy, crinigerous, crinite, crinose, dangerous, dicey, difficult, fleecy, furry, hazardous, hirsute, hispid, lanuginose, lanuginous, perilous, pilose, pilous, risky, scaring, shaggy, stubbly, tricky, villose, villous, woolly.
antonyms bald, clean-shaven.

halcyon *adj.* balmy, calm, carefree, flourishing, gentle, golden, happy, mild, pacific, peaceful, placid, prosperous, quiet, serene, still, tranquil, undisturbed.
antonym stormy.

hale *adj.* able-bodied, athletic, blooming, fit, flourishing, healthy, hearty, in fine fettle, in the pink, robust, sound, strong, vigorous, well, youthful.

antonym ill.

half *n.* bisection, division, fifty per cent, fraction, half-back, half-share, hemisphere, portion, section, segment, term.
adj. divided, fractional, halved, incomplete, limited, moderate, part, partial, semi-.
antonym whole.
adv. barely, imperfectly, in part, inadequately, incompletely, partially, partly, slightly.
antonym completely.

half-baked *adj.* brainless, crazy, foolish, harebrained, ill-conceived, ill-judged, impractical, senseless, short-sighted, silly, stupid, unplanned.
antonym sensible.

half-breed, half-caste *n.* griff(e), mestee, mestiza, mestizo, metif, métis, métisse, miscegen, miscegene, miscegine, mongrel, mulatta, mulatto, mulattress, mustee, quadroon, quarter-blood, quarteroon, quintroon, zambo.

half-hearted *adj.* apathetic, cool, indifferent, lackadaisical, lacklustre, listless, lukewarm, neutral, passive, perfunctory, uninterested.
antonym enthusiastic.

halfway *adv.* barely, imperfectly, in the middle, incompletely, midway, moderately, nearly, partially, partly, rather, slightly.
antonym completely.
adj. central, equidistant, incomplete, intermediate, mid, middle, midway, partial, part-way.
antonym complete.

half-wit *n.* cretin, dimwit, dolt, dullard, dunce, dunderhead, fool, gaupus, idiot, imbecile, moron, nitwit, nut, simpleton, underwit, witling.
antonym brain.

half-witted *adj.* addle-brained, barmy, batty, crazy, cretinous, dull, dull-witted, feeble-minded, foolish, idiotic, moronic, nuts, nutty, silly, simple, simple-minded, stupid, two bricks short of a load.
antonym clever.

hall *n.* assembly-room, auditorium, aula, basilica, chamber, concert-hall, concourse, corridor, entrance-hall, entry, foyer, hallway, lobby, salon, saloon, vestibule.

hallmark *n.* authentication, badge, brand-name, device, emblem, endorsement, indication, mark, seal, sign, stamp, symbol, trademark.

hallo! *see* hello.

hallowed *adj.* age-old, beatified, blessed, consecrated, dedicated, established, holy, honoured, inviolable, revered, sacred, sacrosanct, sanctified.

hallucinate *v.* aberrate, daydream, envision, fantasise, freak out, imagine, trip.

hallucination *n.* aberration, apparition, delusion, dream, fantasy, figment, illusion, mirage, phantasmagoria, pink elephants, vision.

halo *n.* aura, aureola, aureole, corona, gloria, gloriole, glory, halation, nimbus, radiance.

halt *v.* arrest, block, break off, call it a day, cease, check, curb, desist, draw up, end, impede, obstruct, pack it in, quit, rest, stem, stop, terminate, wait.
antonyms assist, continue, start.
n. arrest, break, close, end, étape, impasse, interruption, pause, stand, standstill, stop, stoppage, termination, way point.
antonyms continuation, start.

halting *adj.* awkward, broken, faltering, hesitant, imperfect, laboured, stammering, stumbling, stuttering, uncertain.
antonym fluent.

halve *v.* bisect, cut down, divide, go Dutch, lessen, reduce, share, split.

halved *adj.* bisected, dimidiate, divided, split.

hammer *v.* bang, beat, clobber, defeat, din, dolly, drive, drive home, drub, drum, form, grind, hit, impress upon, instruct, knock, make, malleate, pan, repeat, shape, slate, thrash, trounce, worst.
n. beetle, gavel, madge, mall, mallet, maul, monkey.

hammer out accomplish, bring about, complete, contrive, excogitate, fashion, finish, negotiate, produce, settle, sort out, thrash out.

hamper *v.* bind, cramp, cumber, curb, curtail, distort, embarrass, encumber, entangle, fetter, frustrate, hamshackle, hamstring, handicap, hinder, hobble, hold up, impede, interfere with, obstruct, pinch, prevent, restrain, restrict, shackle, slow down, tangle, thwart, trammel.
antonyms aid, expedite.

hamstrung *adj.* balked, crippled, disabled, foiled, frustrated, handicapped, helpless, hors de combat, incapacitated, paralysed, stymied.

hand[1] *n.* ability, agency, aid, applause, art, artistry, assistance, calligraphy, cheirography, clap, daddle, direction, fist, flipper, handwriting, help, influence, mitt, ovation, palm, part, participation, paw, penmanship, pud, puddy, script, share, skill, support.
v. aid, assist, conduct, convey, deliver, give, guide, help, lead, offer, pass, present, provide, transmit, yield.

hand down bequeath, give, grant, pass on, transfer, will.

hand in glove allied, in cahoots, in collusion, in league, intimate.

hand out deal out, disburse, dish out, dispense, disseminate, distribute, give out, mete, share out.

hand over deliver, donate, fork out, present, release, relinquish, surrender, turn over, yield.
antonym retain.

hand[2] *n.* artificer, artisan, craftsman, employee, farm-hand, hired man, hireling, labourer, operative, orra man, redneck, worker, workman.

handbook *n.* Baedeker, book of words, companion, guide, guidebook, instruction book, manual, vade-mecum.

handcuff *v.* fasten, fetter, manacle, secure, shackle, tie.

handcuffs *n.* bracelets, cuffs, darbies, fetters,

manacles, mittens, shackles, wristlets.

handful *n.* few, scattering, smattering, sprinkling, wheen.
antonym lot.

handicap *n.* barrier, block, defect, disability, disadvantage, drawback, encumbrance, hindrance, impairment, impediment, impost, limitation, millstone, obstacle, odds, penalty, restriction, shortcoming, stumbling-block.
antonyms assistance, benefit.
v. burden, disadvantage, encumber, hamper, hamstring, hinder, impede, limit, restrict, retard.
antonyms assist, further.

handicraft *n.* art, artisanship, craft, craftsmanship, handiwork, skill, workmanship.

handiness *n.* accessibility, adroitness, aptitude, availability, cleverness, closeness, convenience, deftness, dexterity, efficiency, expertise, knack, practicality, proficiency, proximity, skill, usefulness, workability.
antonym clumsiness.

handiwork *n.* achievement, artefact, craft, creation, design, doing, handicraft, handwork, invention, product, production, result, work.

handkerchief *n.* fogle, handkercher, hanky, monteith, mouchoir, nose-rag, romal, rumal, sudary, wipe.

handle *n.* ear, grip, haft, handfast, handgrip, heft, helve, hilt, knob, lug, stock, wythe.
v. administer, carry, conduct, control, cope with, deal in, deal with, direct, discourse, discuss, feel, finger, fondle, grasp, guide, hold, manage, manipulate, manoeuvre, market, maul, operate, paw, pick up, poke, sell, steer, stock, supervise, touch, trade, traffic in, treat, use, wield.

handling *n.* administration, approach, conduct, direction, discussion, management, manipulation, operation, running, transaction, treatment.

hand-out[1] *n.* alms, charity, dole, freebie, issue, largess(e), share, share-out.

hand-out[2] *n.* bulletin, circular, free sample, leaflet, literature, press release, statement.

hand-picked *adj.* choice, chosen, elect, elite, picked, recherché, screened, select, selected.

hands *n.* authority, care, charge, command, control, custody, disposal, guardianship, guidance, jurisdiction, keeping, possession, power, supervision, tutelage.

hands down easily, effortlessly, in a canter, with ease.
antonym with difficulty.

handsome *adj.* abundant, admirable, ample, attractive, beau, becoming, bountiful, braw, comely, considerable, elegant, feat(e)ous, featuous, featurely, fine, generous, good-looking, graceful, gracious, large, liberal, magnanimous, majestic, personable, plentiful, seemly, sizeable, stately, well-favoured, well-looking, well-proportioned, well-set-up.
antonyms mean, stingy, ugly.

handsomely *adv.* abundantly, amply, bounti-

fully, generously, lavishly, liberally, magnanimously, munificently, plentifully, richly, unsparingly, unstintingly.
antonym stingily.

handwriting *n.* cacography, calligraphy, cheirography, fist, hand, longhand, penmanship, scrawl, script.

handy *adj.* accessible, adept, adroit, at hand, available, clever, close, convenient, deft, dexterous, expert, helpful, manageable, near, nearby, neat, nimble, practical, proficient, ready, serviceable, skilful, skilled, useful.
antonyms clumsy, inconvenient, unwieldy.

handyman *n.* DIYer, factotum, famulus, hobjobber, Jack-of-all-trades, man-of-the-world, odd-jobman, orra man.

hang *v.* adhere, attach, bow, cling, cover, dangle, deck, decorate, depend, drape, drift, droop, drop, execute, fasten, fix, float, furnish, gibbet, hold, hover, incline, lean, loll, lower, remain, rest, sag, stick, string up, suspend, supercollate, swing, trail, weep.

hang about/around associate with, dally, frequent, haunt, linger, loiter, resort, roam, tarry, waste time.

hang back demur, hesitate, hold back, recoil, shy away.

hang fire delay, hang back, hold back, hold on, procrastinate, stall, stick, stop, vacillate, wait.
antonym press on.

hang on carry on, cling, clutch, continue, depend on, endure, grasp, grip, hang fire, hang in there, hinge, hold fast, hold on, hold out, hold the line, persevere, persist, remain, rest, stop, turn on, wait.
antonym give up.

hang over impend, loom, menace, threaten.

hangdog *adj.* abject, browbeaten, cowed, cringing, defeated, downcast, furtive, guilty, miserable, shamefaced, sneaking, wretched.
antonym bold.

hanger-on *n.* camp follower, dependant, follower, freeloader, lackey, leech, minion, parasite, sponger, sycophant, toad-eater, toady.

hanging[1] *adj.* dangling, drooping, flapping, flopping, floppy, loose, pendent, pendulous, pensile, suspended, swinging, unattached, undecided, unresolved, unsettled, unsupported.

hanging[2] *n.* dossal, dossel, drape, drapery, drop, drop-scene, frontal.

hangman *n.* Jack Ketch.

hang-out *n.* den, dive, haunt, home, howf(f), joint, local, resort, watering-hole.

hangover *n.* after-effects, crapulence, katzenjammer.

hang-up *n.* block, difficulty, idée fixe, inhibition, mental block, obsession, preoccupation, problem, thing.

hank *n.* coil, fank, length, loop, piece, roll, skein.

hanker for/after covet, crave, desire, hunger for, itch for, long for, lust after, pine for, thirst for, want, wish, yearn for, yen for.

antonym dislike.

hankering *n.* craving, desire, hunger, itch, longing, pining, thirst, urge, wish, yearning, yen.
antonym dislike.

hanky-panky *n.* cheating, chicanery, deception, devilry, dishonesty, funny business, jiggery-pokery, knavery, machinations, mischief, monkey business, nonsense, shenanigans, subterfuge, trickery, tricks.
antonym openness.

haphazard *adj.* accidental, aimless, arbitrary, careless, casual, chance, disorderly, disorganised, flukey, hit-or-miss, indiscriminate, promiscuous, random, slapdash, slipshod, unmethodical, unsystematic.
antonyms deliberate, planned.

hapless *adj.* cursed, ill-fated, ill-starred, jinxed, luckless, miserable, star-crossed, unfortunate, unhappy, unlucky, wretched.
antonym lucky.

happen *v.* appear, arise, befall, chance, come about, crop up, develop, ensue, eventuate, fall out, follow, materialise, occur, result, supervene, take place, transpire, turn out.
happen on chance on, come on, discover, find, hit on, light on, stumble on.

happening *n.* accident, adventure, affair, case, chance, circumstance, episode, event, experience, incident, occasion, occurrence, phenomenon, proceeding, scene.

happily *adv.* agreeably, appropriately, aptly, auspiciously, blithely, by chance, cheerfully, contentedly, delightedly, enthusiastically, favourably, felicitously, fittingly, fortunately, freely, gaily, gladly, gleefully, gracefully, heartily, joyfully, joyously, luckily, merrily, opportunely, perhaps, propitiously, providentially, seasonably, successfully, willingly.
antonym unhappily.

happiness *n.* beatitude, blessedness, bliss, cheer, cheerfulness, cheeriness, chirpiness, contentment, delight, ecstasy, elation, enjoyment, exuberance, felicity, gaiety, gladness, high spirits, joy, joyfulness, jubilation, light-heartedness, merriment, pleasure, satisfaction, well-being.
antonym unhappiness.

happy *adj.* advantageous, appropriate, apt, auspicious, befitting, blessed, blest, blissful, blithe, chance, cheerful, content, contented, convenient, delighted, ecstatic, elated, enviable, favourable, felicitous, fit, fitting, fortunate, glad, gratified, gruntled, idyllic, jolly, joyful, joyous, jubilant, lucky, merry, opportune, over the moon, overjoyed, pleased, promising, propitious, satisfactory, Saturnian, seasonable, starry-eyed, successful, sunny, thrilled, timely, well-timed.
antonym unhappy.

happy medium aurea mediocritas, golden mean, juste milieu.
antonym excess.

happy-go-lucky *adj.* blithe, carefree, casual, cheerful, devil-may-care, easy-going, heed-less, improvident, insouciant, irresponsible, light-hearted, nonchalant, reckless, unconcerned, untroubled, unworried.
antonyms anxious, wary.

harangue *n.* address, declamation, diatribe, discourse, exhortation, homily, lecture, oration, paternoster, peroration, philippic, sermon, speech, spiel, tirade.
v. address, declaim, descant, exhort, hold forth, lecture, monolog(u)ise, orate, perorate, preach, rant, rhetorise, sermonise, spout.

harass *v.* annoy, badger, bait, beleaguer, bother, chivvy, distress, disturb, exasperate, exhaust, fatigue, harry, hassle, hound, perplex, persecute, pester, plague, tease, tire, torment, trash, trouble, vex, wear out, weary, worry.
antonym assist.

harassed *adj.* careworn, distraught, distressed, harried, hassled, hounded, pestered, plagued, pressured, pressurised, strained, stressed, tormented, troubled, vexed, worried.
antonym carefree.

harassment *n.* aggravation, annoyance, badgering, bedevilment, bother, distress, hassle, irritation, molest, molestation, nuisance, persecution, pestering, pressuring, torment, trouble, vexation.
antonym assistance.

harbinger *n.* avant-courier, forerunner, foretoken, herald, indication, messenger, omen, portent, precursor, presage, sign, warning.

harbour *n.* anchorage, asylum, covert, destination, haven, marina, port, refuge, roadstead, sanctuary, sanctum, security, shelter.
v. believe, cherish, cling to, conceal, entertain, foster, hide, hold, imagine, lodge, maintain, nurse, nurture, protect, retain, secrete, shelter, shield.

hard *adj.* acrimonious, actual, adamantine, alcoholic, angry, antagonistic, arduous, backbreaking, baffling, bare, bitter, burdensome, calamitous, callous, cast-iron, cold, compact, complex, complicated, cruel, crusty, dark, definite, dense, difficult, disagreeable, disastrous, distressing, driving, exacting, exhausting, fatiguing, fierce, firm, flinty, forceful, formidable, grievous, grim, habit-forming, hard-hearted, harsh, heavy, Herculean, hostile, impenetrable, implacable, indisputable, inflexible, intolerable, intricate, involved, irony, knotty, laborious, marbly, obdurate, painful, perplexing, pitiless, plain, powerful, puzzling, rancorous, resentful, rigid, rigorous, ruthless, sclerous, severe, shrewd, solid, stern, stiff, stony, strenuous, strict, strong, stubborn, tangled, thorny, toilsome, tough, undeniable, unfathomable, unfeeling, ungentle, unjust, unkind, unpleasant, unrelenting, unsparing, unsympathetic, unvarnished, unyielding, uphill, verified, violent, wearying.
antonyms harmless, kind, mild, nonalcoholic, pleasant, pleasing, soft, yielding.
adv. agonisingly, assiduously, badly, bitterly,

close, completely, determinedly, diligently, distressingly, doggedly, earnestly, energetically, fiercely, forcefully, forcibly, fully, hardly, harshly, heavily, industriously, intensely, intently, keenly, laboriously, near, painfully, persistently, powerfully, rancorously, reluctantly, resentfully, roughly, severely, sharply, slowly, sorely, steadily, strenuously, strongly, uneasily, untiringly, vigorously, violently, with difficulty.
antonyms gently, mildly, moderately, unenthusiastically.

hard and fast binding, fixed, immutable, incontrovertible, inflexible, invariable, rigid, set, strict, stringent, unalterable, unchangeable, unchanging.
antonym flexible.

hard up bankrupt, broke, bust, cleaned out, destitute, impecunious, impoverished, in the red, penniless, penurious, poor, short, skint, strapped for cash.
antonym rich.

hard-bitten *adj.* callous, case-hardened, cynical, down-to-earth, hard-boiled, hard-headed, hard-nosed, matter-of-fact, practical, realistic, ruthless, shrewd, tough, unsentimental.
antonym callow.

hard-core *adj.* blatant, dedicated, die-hard, dyed-in-the-wool, explicit, extreme, intransigent, obstinate, rigid, staunch, steadfast.
antonym moderate.

harden *v.* accustom, anneal, bake, brace, brutalise, buttress, cake, case-harden, concrete, fortify, freeze, gird, habituate, indurate, inure, nerve, reinforce, sclerose, season, set, solidify, steel, stiffen, strengthen, toughen, train.
antonym soften.

hardened *adj.* accustomed, chronic, fixed, habitual, habituated, incorrigible, inured, inveterate, irredeemable, obdurate, reprobate, seasoned, set, shameless, toughened, unfeeling.
antonyms callow, soft.

hardening *n.* annealing, clotting, coagulation, congealing, sclerosis, setting, solidifying, vulcanisation.

hard-headed *adj.* astute, clear-thinking, cool, hard-boiled, level-headed, practical, pragmatic, realistic, sensible, shrewd, tough, unsentimental.
antonym unrealistic.

hard-hearted *adj.* callous, cold, cruel, hard, heartless, indifferent, inhuman, insensitive, intolerant, iron-hearted, marble-breasted, marble-hearted, merciless, pitiless, stony, uncaring, uncompassionate, unfeeling, unkind, unsympathetic.
antonyms kind, merciful.

hard-hitting *adj.* condemnatory, critical, forceful, no-holds-barred, strongly-worded, tough, unsparing, vigorous.
antonym mild.

hardihood *n.* assurance, audacity, backbone, boldness, bottle, bravery, courage, daring,

determination, effrontery, firmness, foolhardiness, grit, guts, hardiness, impertinence, impetuousness, intrepidity, mettle, nerve, pluck, prowess, rashness, recklessness, resolution, spirit, spunk, strength, temerity.
antonyms sense, timidity.

hardiness *n.* boldness, courage, fortitude, hardihood, intrepidity, resilience, resolution, robustness, ruggedness, sturdiness, toughness, valour.
antonym timidity.

hardline *adj.* definite, extreme, immoderate, inflexible, intransigent, militant, tough, uncompromising, undeviating, unyielding.
antonym moderate.

hardly *adv.* barely, by no means, faintly, harshly, infrequently, just, no way, not at all, not quite, only, only just, roughly, scarcely, severely, with difficulty.
antonyms easily, very.

hardness *n.* coldness, difficulty, firmness, harshness, inhumanity, insensitivity, laboriousness, pitilessness, rigidity, severity, solidity, steel, sternness, toughness.
antonyms ease, mildness, softness.

hard-pressed *adj.* hard-pushed, harrassed, harried, pushed, under pressure, up against it, with one's back to the wall.
antonym untroubled.

hardship *n.* adversity, affliction, austerity, burden, calamity, destitution, difficulty, fatigue, grievance, labour, misery, misfortune, need, oppression, persecution, privation, strait, suffering, toil, torment, trial, tribulation, trouble, want.
antonym ease.

hard-wearing *adj.* durable, resilient, rugged, stout, strong, sturdy, tough.
antonym delicate.

hard-working *adj.* assiduous, busy, conscientious, diligent, energetic, indefatigable, industrious, sedulous, workaholic, zealous.
antonym lazy.

hardy *adj.* audacious, bold, brave, brazen, courageous, daring, firm, fit, foolhardy, hale, headstrong, healthy, hearty, heroic, impudent, intrepid, lusty, manly, plucky, rash, reckless, resolute, robust, rugged, sound, Spartan, stalwart, stout, stout-hearted, strong, sturdy, tough, valiant, valorous, vigorous.
antonyms unhealthy, weak.

hare-brained *adj.* asinine, careless, daft, empty-headed, flighty, foolish, giddy, half-baked, harum-scarum, headlong, heedless, inane, mindless, rash, reckless, scatter-brained, scatty, unstable, unsteady, wild.
antonym sensible.

harem *n.* gynaeceum, seraglio, serai(l), women's quarters, zenana.

hark *v.* attend, give ear, hear, hearken, listen, mark, note, notice, pay attention, pay heed.
hark back go back, recall, recollect, regress, remember, revert.

harlot *n.* call-girl, fallen woman, hussy, loon,

loose fish, loose woman, lorette, Paphian, pro, prostitute, scrubber, street-walker, strumpet, tart, tramp, whore.

harm *n.* abuse, damage, detriment, disservice, evil, hurt, ill, immorality, impairment, iniquity, injury, loss, mischief, misfortune, scathe, sin, sinfulness, vice, wickedness, wrong.
antonyms benefit, service.

v. abuse, blemish, damage, hurt, ill-treat, ill-use, impair, injure, maltreat, mar, molest, ruin, scathe, spoil, wound.
antonyms benefit, improve.

harmful *adj.* baleful, baneful, damaging, deleterious, destructive, detrimental, disadvantageous, evil, hurtful, injurious, noxious, pernicious, pestful, pestiferous, pestilent, scatheful.
antonym harmless.

harmless *adj.* gentle, innocent, innocuous, innoxious, inoffensive, non-toxic, safe, scatheless, unharmed, uninjured, unobjectionable, unscathed.
antonym harmful.

harmonious *adj.* according, agreeable, amicable, compatible, concinnous, concordant, congenial, congruous, consonant, consonous, co-ordinated, cordial, correspondent, dulcet, euharmonic, euphonic, euphonious, eurhythmic, friendly, harmonic, harmonising, matching, mellifluous, melodious, musical, sweetsounding, sympathetic, symphonious, tuneful.
antonym inharmonious.

harmonise *v.* accommodate, accord, adapt, agree, arrange, attune, blend, chime, cohere, compose, co-ordinate, correspond, jibe, match, reconcile, suit, tally, tone.
antonym clash.

harmony *n.* accord, agreement, amicability, amity, balance, chime, compatibility, concinnity, concord, conformity, congruity, consensus, consistency, consonance, co-operation, co-ordination, correspondence, correspondency, diapason, euphony, eurhythmy, fitness, friendship, goodwill, like-mindedness, melodiousness, melody, parallelism, peace, rapport, suitability, symmetry, sympathy, tune, tunefulness, unanimity, understanding, unity.
antonym discord.

harness *n.* equipment, gear, reins, straps, tack, tackle, trappings.
v. apply, channel, control, couple, employ, exploit, make use of, mobilise, saddle, turn to account, use, utilise, yoke.

harp on (about) dwell on, labour, press, reiterate, renew, repeat.

harpoon *n.* arrow, barb, dart, grains, spear, trident.

harpy *n.* gold-digger, harriden, man-eater, vamp, vampire.

harridan *n.* battle-axe, dragon, fury, gorgon, harpy, hell-cat, nag, scold, shrew, tartar, termagant, virago, vixen, witch, Xanthippe.

harried *adj.* agitated, anxious, beset, bothered, distressed, hag-ridden, harassed, hard-pressed, hassled, plagued, pressured, pressurised, ravaged, tormented, troubled, worried.
antonym untroubled.

harrow *v.* agonise, daunt, dismay, distress, harass, lacerate, perturb, rack, rend, tear, torment, torture, vex, wound, wring.
antonyms assuage, hearten.

harrowing *adj.* agonising, alarming, chilling, distressing, disturbing, excruciating, frightening, heart-rending, lacerant, nerve-racking, racking, soaring, terrifying, tormenting, traumatic.
antonyms calming, heartening.

harry *v.* annoy, badger, bedevil, chivvy, depredate, despoil, devastate, disturb, fret, harass, hassle, maraud, molest, persecute, pester, pillage, plague, plunder, raid, ravage, rob, sack, tease, torment, trouble, vex, worry.
antonyms aid, calm.

harsh *adj.* abrasive, abusive, austere, bitter, bleak, brutal, coarse, comfortless, croaking, crude, cruel, discordant, dissonant, dour, Draconian, glaring, grating, grim, guttural, hard, jarring, pitiless, punitive, rasping, raucous, relentless, rough, ruthless, scabrous, severe, sharp, Spartan, stark, stern, strident, stringent, unfeeling, ungentle, unkind, unmelodious, unpleasant, unrelenting.
antonyms mild, smooth, soft.

harshness *n.* abrasiveness, acerbity, acrimony, asperity, austerity, bitterness, brutality, churlishness, coarseness, crudity, hardness, ill-temper, rigour, roughness, severity, sourness, starkness, sternness, strictness.
antonyms mildness, softness.

harum-scarum *adj.* careless, erratic, flighty, giddy, haphazard, hare-brained, hasty, ill-considered, impetuous, imprudent, irresponsible, precipitate, rash, reckless, scatter-brained, scatty, wild.
antonym sensible.

harvest *n.* collection, consequence, crop, effect, fruition, harvesting, harvest-time, hockey, ingathering, inning, produce, product, reaping, result, return, vendage, yield.
v. accumulate, acquire, amass, collect, garner, gather, mow, pick, pluck, reap.

hash[1] *n.* botch, confusion, cow's arse, fuck-up, hotchpotch, jumble, mess, mishmash, mix-up, muddle, shambles.

hash[2] *n.* goulash, hotpot, lob's course, lobscouse, stew.

hash[3] *see* **hashish** .

hashish *n.* bhang, cannabis, charas, churrus, dope, ganja, grass, hash, hemp, marijuana, pot.

hassle *n.* altercation, argument, bickering, bother, difficulty, disagreement, dispute, fight, inconvenience, nuisance, problem, quarrel, squabble, struggle, trial, trouble, tussle, upset, wrangle.
antonyms agreement, peace.
v. annoy, badger, bother, bug, chivvy, harass, harry, hound, pester.

antonyms assist, calm.

haste *n.* alacrity, briskness, bustle, celerity, dispatch, expedition, fleetness, hastiness, hurry, hustle, impetuosity, nimbleness, precipitance, precipitancy, precipitateness, precipitation, promptitude, quickness, rapidity, rapidness, rashness, recklessness, rush, speed, swiftness, urgency, velocity.
antonyms care, deliberation, slowness.

hasten *v.* accelerate, advance, bolt, dash, dispatch, expedite, fly, gallop, goad, haste, have it on one's toes, hightail it, hurry, make haste, precipitate, press, quicken, race, run, rush, scurry, scuttle, speed, speed up, sprint, step on it, step up, tear, trot, urge.
antonym dawdle.

hastily *adv.* apace, chop-chop, double-quick, fast, heedlessly, hurriedly, impetuously, impulsively, posthaste, precipitately, promptly, quickly, rapidly, rashly, recklessly, speedily, straightaway.
antonyms carefully, deliberately, slowly.

hasty *adj.* brief, brisk, brusque, cursory, eager, excited, expeditious, fast, fiery, fleet, fleeting, foolhardy, headlong, heedless, hot-headed, hot-tempered, hurried, impatient, impetuous, impulsive, indiscreet, irascible, irritable, passing, passionate, perfunctory, precipitant, precipitate, prompt, quick-tempered, rapid, rash, reckless, rushed, short, snappy, speedy, subitaneous, superficial, swift, thoughtless, urgent.
antonyms careful, deliberate, placid, slow.

hat *n.* beret, biretta, boater, bonnet, bowler, cap, lid, night-cap, poke-bonnet, skull-cap, sombrero, sou'wester, titfer, top-hat, trilby, yarmulka.

hatch *v.* breed, brood, conceive, concoct, contrive, cook up, design, develop, devise, dream up, incubate, originate, plan, plot, project, scheme, think up.

hate *v.* abhor, abominate, despise, detest, dislike, execrate, loathe, spite.
antonym like.
n. abhorrence, abomination, animosity, animus, antagonism, antipathy, averseness, aversion, detestation, dislike, enmity, execration, hatred, hostility, loathing, odium, odium theologicum.
antonym like.

hateful *adj.* abhorrent, abominable, damnable, despicable, detestable, disgusting, execrable, forbidding, foul, hateworthy, heinous, horrible, loathsome, obnoxious, odious, offensive, repellent, repugnant, repulsive, revolting, vile.
antonym pleasing.

hatred *n.* abomination, animosity, animus, antagonism, antipathy, aversion, despite, detestation, dislike, enmity, execration, hate, ill-will, misandry, misanthropy, odium, repugnance, revulsion.
antonym like.

haughtiness *n.* airs, aloofness, arrogance, conceit, contempt, contemptuousness, disdain, hauteur, insolence, loftiness, pomposity, pride, snobbishness, snootiness, superciliousness.
antonyms friendliness, humility.

haughty *adj.* arrogant, assuming, cavalier, conceited, contemptuous, disdainful, fastuous, high, high and mighty, highty-tighty, hoity-toity, imperious, lofty, overweening, proud, scornful, snobbish, snooty, stiff-necked, stomachful, stuck-up, supercilious, superior, uppish.
antonyms friendly, humble.

haul *v.* bouse, carry, cart, convey, drag, draw, hale, heave, hump, lug, move, pull, tow, trail, transport, trice, tug.
n. booty, bunce, catch, drag, find, gain, harvest, heave, loot, pull, spoils, swag, takings, tug, yield.

haunches *n.* buttocks, huckles, hucks, hunkers, nates, thighs.

haunt *v.* beset, frequent, obsess, plague, possess, prey on, recur, repair, resort, torment, trouble, visit, walk.
n. den, gathering-place, hangout, howf(f), meeting place, rendezvous, resort, stamping ground.

haunted *adj.* cursed, eerie, ghostly, hag-ridden, jinxed, obsessed, plagued, possessed, preoccupied, spooky, tormented, troubled, worried.

haunting *adj.* disturbing, eerie, evocative, indelible, memorable, nostalgic, persistent, poignant, recurrent, recurring, unforgettable.
antonym unmemorable.

have *v.* accept, acquire, allow, bear, beget, cheat, comprehend, comprise, consider, contain, deceive, deliver, dupe, embody, endure, enjoy, entertain, experience, feel, fool, gain, get, give birth to, hold, include, keep, obtain, occupy, outwit, own, permit, possess, procure, produce, put up with, receive, retain, secure, suffer, sustain, swindle, take, tolerate, trick, undergo.

have done with be through with, cease, desist, finish with, give up, stop, throw over, wash one's hands of.

have to be compelled, be forced, be obliged, be required, have got to, must, ought, should.

haven *n.* anchorage, asylum, harbour, hithe, port, refuge, retreat, roads, roadstead, sanctuary, sanctum, shelter.

havoc *n.* carnage, chaos, confusion, damage, depopulation, desolation, despoliation, destruction, devastation, disorder, disruption, mayhem, rack and ruin, ravages, ruin, shambles, slaughter, waste, wreck.

hawk[1] *v.* bark, cry, market, offer, peddle, sell, tout, vend.

hawk[2] *n.* buzzard, falcon, goshawk, haggard, t(i)ercel, warmonger.

hawker *n.* barrow-boy, cheap-jack, colporteur, coster, costermonger, crier, huckster, pedlar, vendor.

haywire *adj.* amiss, chaotic, confused, crazy, disarranged, disordered, disorganised, erratic, kaput, mad, shambolic, tangled, topsy-turvy, wild.

antonyms correct, in order.

hazard *n.* accident, chance, coincidence, danger, death-trap, endangerment, fluke, imperilment, jeopardy, luck, mischance, misfortune, mishap, peril, risk, threat.

antonym safety.

v. advance, attempt, chance, conjecture, dare, endanger, expose, gamble, imperil, jeopardise, offer, presume, proffer, risk, speculate, stake, submit, suggest, suppose, threaten, venture, volunteer.

hazardous *adj.* chancy, dangerous, dicey, difficult, fraught, hairy, haphazard, insecure, perilous, precarious, risky, thorny, ticklish, uncertain, unpredictable, unsafe.

antonyms safe, secure.

haze *n.* cloud, dimness, film, fog, mist, nebulosity, obscurity, smog, smokiness, steam, unclearness, vapour.

hazy *adj.* blurry, clouded, cloudy, dim, distanceless, dull, faint, foggy, fuzzy, ill-defined, indefinite, indistinct, loose, milky, misty, muddled, muzzy, nebulous, obscure, overcast, smoky, uncertain, unclear, vague, veiled.

antonyms clear, definite.

head *n.* ability, apex, aptitude, bean, beginning, bonce, boss, brain, brains, branch, capacity, cape, captain, caput, category, chief, chieftain, chump, class, climax, commander, commencement, conclusion, conk, cop, cranium, crest, crisis, crown, culmination, department, director, division, end, faculty, flair, fore, forefront, foreland, front, godfather, head teacher, heading, headland, headmaster, headmistress, height, intellect, intelligence, knowledge box, leader, loaf, manager, master, mastermind, mentality, mind, nab, napper, nob, noddle, nut, origin, pate, peak, pitch, point, principal, promontory, rise, sconce, section, skull, source, start, subject, summit, superintendent, supervisor, talent, tête, thought, tip, top, topic, topknot, turning-point, understanding, upperworks, van, vanguard, vertex.

antonyms foot, subordinate, tail.

adj. arch, chief, dominant, first, foremost, front, highest, leading, main, pre-eminent, premier, prime, principal, supreme, top, topmost.

v. aim, cap, command, control, crown, direct, govern, guide, lead, make a beeline, make for, manage, oversee, point, precede, rule, run, steer, superintend, supervise, top, turn.

head for aim for, direct towards, gravitate towards, make for, point to, steer for, turn for, zero in on.

head off avert, deflect, distract, divert, fend off, forestall, intercept, interpose, intervene, parry, prevent, stop, ward off.

head over heels completely, intensely, recklessly, thoroughly, uncontrollably, utterly, wholeheartedly, wildly.

headache *n.* bane, bother, cephalalgia, hassle, hemicrania, inconvenience, migraine, neuralgia, nuisance, problem, trouble, vexation, worry.

heading *n.* caption, category, class, division, headline, lemma, name, rubric, section, superscription, title.

headland *n.* bill, bluff, cape, cliff, foreland, head, morro, mull, naze, point, promontory.

headlong *adj.* breakneck, dangerous, hasty, head-first, head-foremost, head-on, hell-for-leather, impetuous, impulsive, inconsiderate, precipitate, reckless, thoughtless.

adv. hastily, head first, head foremost, head-on, heedlessly, hell for leather, helter-skelter, hurriedly, lickety-split, pell-mell, precipitately, rashly, thoughtlessly, wildly.

head-man *n.* captain, chief, leader, muqaddam, ruler, sachem.

headquarters *n.* base camp, head office, high command, HQ, nerve centre, praetorium.

headstrong *adj.* bull-headed, contrary, foolhardy, fractious, froward, heedless, imprudent, impulsive, intractable, mulish, obstinate, perverse, pig-headed, rash, reckless, self-willed, stubborn, ungovernable, unruly, wilful.

antonyms biddable, docile, obedient.

headway *n.* advance, improvement, inroad(s), progress, progression, way.

heady *adj.* exciting, exhilarating, hasty, impetuous, impulsive, inconsiderate, inebriant, intoxicating, overpowering, potent, precipitate, rash, reckless, spirituous, stimulating, strong, thoughtless, thrilling.

heal *v.* alleviate, ameliorate, balsam, compose, conciliate, cure, harmonise, mend, patch up, physic, reconcile, regenerate, remedy, restore, salve, settle, soothe, treat.

healing *adj.* analeptic, assuaging, comforting, curative, emollient, epulotic, gentle, lenitive, medicinal, mild, mitigative, palliative, remedial, restorative, restoring, sanative, sanatory, soothing, styptic, therapeutic, vulnerary.

health *n.* condition, constitution, fettle, fitness, form, good condition, haleness, heal, healthiness, robustness, salubrity, shape, soundness, state, strength, tone, vigour, weal, welfare, well-being.

antonyms disease, infirmity.

healthy *adj.* active, beneficial, blooming, bracing, fine, fit, flourishing, good, hale (and hearty), hardy, healthful, health-giving, hearty, hygienic, in fine feather, in fine fettle, in fine form, in good condition, in good shape, in the pink, invigorating, nourishing, nutritious, physically fit, robust, salubrious, salutary, salutiferous, sound, strong, sturdy, vigorous, well, wholesome.

antonyms diseased, ill, infirm, sick, unhealthy.

heap *n.* accumulation, acervation, aggregation, bing, clamp, cock, collection, cumulus, hoard, lot, mass, mound, mountain, pile, ruck, stack, stockpile, store.

v. accumulate, amass, assign, augment, bank, bestow, build, burden, collect, confer, gather, hoard, increase, lavish, load, mound, pile, shower, stack, stockpile, store.

heaps *n.* a lot, abundance, great deal, lashings, load(s), lots, mass, millions, mint, ocean(s), oodles, plenty, pot(s), quantities, scores, stack(s), tons.

hear *v.* acknowledge, ascertain, attend, catch, discover, eavesdrop, examine, find, gather, hark, hearken, heed, investigate, judge, learn, listen, overhear, pick up, try, understand.

hearing *n.* audience, audition, auditory, auditory range, ear, ear-shot, inquest, inquiry, inquisition, interview, investigation, perception, range, reach, review, sound, trial.

hearsay *n.* bruit, buzz, gossip, grapevine, on-dit, report, rumour, talk, talk of the town, tittle-tattle, word of mouth.

heart *n.* affection, benevolence, boldness, bravery, centre, character, compassion, concern, core, courage, crux, disposition, emotion, essence, feeling, fortitude, guts, hub, humanity, inclination, kernel, love, marrow, mettle, middle, mind, nature, nerve, nerve centre, nub, nucleus, pith, pity, pluck, purpose, quintessence, resolution, root, sentiment, soul, spirit, spunk, sympathy, temperament, tenderness, ticker, understanding, will.

heart and soul absolutely, completely, devotedly, eagerly, entirely, gladly, heartily, unreservedly, wholeheartedly.

heartache *n.* affliction, agony, anguish, bitterness, dejection, despair, despondency, distress, grief, heartbreak, heart-sickness, pain, remorse, sorrow, suffering, torment, torture.

heartbreak *n.* agony, anguish, dejection, desolation, despair, grief, misery, pain, sorrow, suffering.

antonyms elation, joy, relief.

heartbreaking *adj.* agonising, bitter, desolating, disappointing, distressing, grievous, harrowing, heart-rending, pitiful, poignant, sad, tragic.

antonyms heartening, heartwarming, joyful.

heartbroken *adj.* broken-hearted, crestfallen, crushed, dejected, desolate, despondent, disappointed, disconsolate, disheartened, dispirited, down, downcast, grieved, heart-sick, miserable, woebegone.

antonyms delighted, elated.

hearten *v.* animate, assure, buck up, buoy up, cheer, comfort, console, embolden, encourage, gladden, incite, inspire, inspirit, pep up, reassure, revivify, rouse, stimulate.

antonym dishearten.

heart-felt *adj.* ardent, cordial, deep, devoted, devout, earnest, fervent, genuine, hearty, honest, impassioned, infelt, profound, sincere, unfeigned, warm, whole-hearted.

antonyms false, insecure.

heartily *adv.* absolutely, completely, cordially, deeply, eagerly, earnestly, enthusiastically, feelingly, genuinely, gladly, profoundly, resolutely, sincerely, thoroughly, totally, unfeignedly, very, vigorously, warmly, zealously.

heartless *adj.* brutal, callous, cold, cold-blooded, cold-hearted, cruel, hard, hard-hearted, harsh, inhuman, merciless, pitiless, stern, uncaring, unfeeling, unkind.

antonyms considerate, kind, merciful, sympathetic.

heart-rending *adj.* affecting, distressing, harrowing, heartbreaking, moving, pathetic, piteous, pitiful, poignant, sad, tear-jerking, tragic.

heart-throb *n.* dreamboat, mantinée idol, pin-up, star.

heartwarming *adj.* affecting, cheering, encouraging, gladsome, gratifying, heartening, moving, pleasing, rewarding, satisfying, touching, warming.

antonym heart-breaking.

hearty *adj.* active, affable, ample, ardent, cordial, doughty, eager, earnest, ebullient, effusive, energetic, enthusiastic, exuberant, filling, friendly, generous, genial, genuine, hale, hardy, healthy, heartfelt, honest, jovial, nourishing, real, robust, sincere, sizeable, solid, sound, square, stalwart, strong, substantial, true, unfeigned, unreserved, vigorous, warm, well, whole-hearted.

antonyms cold, emotionless.

heat *n.* agitation, ardour, calefaction, earnestness, excitement, fervour, fever, fieriness, fury, hotness, impetuosity, incandescence, intensity, passion, sizzle, sultriness, swelter, torridity, vehemence, violence, warmness, warmth, zeal.

antonyms cold(ness), coolness.

v. animate, calefy, chafe, excite, flush, glow, impassion, inflame, inspirit, reheat, rouse, stimulate, stir, toast, warm up.

antonyms chill, cool.

heated *adj.* acrimonious, angry, bitter, excited, fierce, fiery, frenzied, furious, impassioned, intense, passionate, perfervid, raging, stormy, tempestuous, vehement, violent.

antonym dispassionate.

heathen *n.* barbarian, gentile, idolator, idolatress, infidel, nations, nullifidian, pagan, philistine, savage, unbeliever.

antonym believer.

adj. barbaric, gentile, godless, heathenish, idolatrous, infidel, irreligious, nullifidian, pagan, philistine, savage, uncivilised, unenlightened.

antonyms Christian, godly.

heave *v.* billow, breathe, cast, chuck, dilate, drag, elevate, exhale, expand, fling, gag, groan, haul, heft, hitch, hoist, hurl, let fly, lever, lift, palpitate, pant, pitch, puff, pull, raise, retch, rise, send, sigh, sling, sob, spew, surge, suspire, swell, throb, throw, throw up, toss, tug, vomit, yomp.

heaven *n.* bliss, ecstasy, Elysian fields, Elysium, empyrean, enchantment, ether, felicity, fiddler's green, firmament, happiness, happy

hunting-ground(s), hereafter, Land of the Leal, next world, nirvana, paradise, rapture, sky, Swarga, transport, utopia, Valhalla, welkin, Zion.
antonym hell.

heavenly *adj.* alluring, ambrosial, angelic, beatific, beautiful, blessed, blest, blissful, celestial, delightful, divine, empyrean, entrancing, exquisite, extra-terrestrial, glorious, godlike, holy, immortal, lovely, paradisaic-(al), paradisal, paradisean, paradisial, paradisian, paradisic, rapturous, ravishing, seraphic, sublime, superhuman, supernal, supernatural, Uranian, wonderful.
antonym hellish.

heavens *n.* ether, firmament, sky, the blue, the wild blue yonder, welkin.

heavily *adv.* awkwardly, closely, clumsily, compactly, completely, considerably, copiously, decisively, deep, deeply, dejectedly, densely, dully, excessively, fast, frequently, gloomily, hard, heftily, laboriously, painfully, ponderously, profoundly, roundly, sluggishly, solidly, sound, soundly, thick, thickly, thoroughly, to excess, utterly, weightily, woodenly.
antonym lightly.

heaviness *n.* arduousness, burdensomeness, deadness, dejection, depression, despondency, drowsiness, dullness, gloom, gloominess, glumness, gravity, grievousness, heftiness, languor, lassitude, melancholy, numbness, onerousness, oppression, oppressiveness, ponderousness, sadness, seriousness, severity, sleepiness, sluggishness, somnolence, torpor, weight, weightiness.
antonyms lightness, liveliness.

heavy *adj.* abundant, apathetic, boisterous, bulky, burdened, burdensome, clumpy, complex, considerable, copious, crestfallen, deep, dejected, depressed, despondent, difficult, disconsolate, downcast, drowsy, dull, encumbered, excessive, gloomy, grave, grieving, grievous, hard, harsh, hefty, inactive, indolent, inert, intolerable, laborious, laden, large, leaden, listless, loaded, lumping, lumpish, massive, melancholy, onerous, oppressed, oppressive, ponderous, portly, profound, profuse, rough, sad, serious, severe, slow, sluggish, solemn, sorrowful, squabbish, stodgy, stormy, stupid, tedious, tempestuous, torpid, turbulent, vexatious, violent, wearisome, weighted, weighty, wild, wooden.
antonyms airy, insignificant, light.

heavy-handed *adj.* autocratic, awkward, bungling, clumsy, domineering, graceless, hamfisted, ham-handed, harsh, inconsiderate, inept, inexpert, insensitive, maladroit, oppressive, overbearing, tactless, thoughtless, unsubtle.

heavy-hearted *adj.* crushed, depressed, despondent, discouraged, disheartened, downcast, downhearted, forlorn, glum, heart-sick, heart-sore, melancholy, miserable, morose, mournful, sad, sorrowful.

antonym light-hearted.

heckle *v.* bait, barrack, catcall, disrupt, gibe, interrupt, jeer, pester, shout down, taunt.

hectic *adj.* animated, boisterous, chaotic, excited, fast, fevered, feverish, flurrying, flustering, frantic, frenetic, frenzied, furious, heated, rapid, riotous, rumbustious, tumultuous, turbulent, wild.
antonym leisurely.

hector *v.* badger, bluster, boast, browbeat, bully, bullyrag, chivvy, harass, huff, intimidate, menace, nag, provoke, roister, threaten, worry.

hedge *n.* barrier, boundary, compensation, counterbalance, dike, dyke, guard, hay, hedgerow, insurance, protection, quickset, screen, wind-break.
v. block, circumscribe, confine, cover, dodge, duck, equivocate, fortify, guard, hem in, hinder, insure, obstruct, protect, quibble, restrict, safeguard, shield, sidestep, stall, temporise, waffle.

hedonism *n.* dolce vita, epicureanism, epicurism, gratification, luxuriousness, pleasure-seeking, self-indulgence, sensualism, sensuality, sybaritism, voluptuousness.
antonym asceticism.

hedonist *n.* bon vivant, epicure, epicurean, pleasure-seeker, sensualist, swinger, sybarite, voluptuary.
antonym ascetic.

hedonistic *adj.* epicurean, luxurious, pleasure-seeking, self-indulgent, swinging, sybaritic, voluptuous.
antonyms ascetic, austere.

heed *n.* animadversion, attention, care, caution, consideration, ear, heedfulness, mind, note, notice, reck, regard, respect, thought, watchfulness.
antonyms inattention, indifference, unconcern.
v. animadvert, attend, consider, follow, listen, mark, mind, note, obey, observe, regard, take notice of.
antonyms disregrad, ignore.

heedful *adj.* attentive, careful, cautious, chary, circumspect, mindful, observant, prudent, regardful, vigilant, wary, watchful.
antonym heedless.

heedless *adj.* careless, étourdi(e), foolhardy, imprudent, inattentive, incautious, incurious, inobservant, neglectful, negligent, oblivious, precipitate, rash, reckless, thoughtless, uncaring, unconcerned, unheedful, unheedy, unmindful, unobservant, unthinking.
antonym heedful.

heel *n.* blackguard, bounder, cad, crust, end, hallux, hock, remainder, rotter, rump, scoundrel, spur, stub, stump, swine.

hefty *adj.* ample, awkward, beefy, big, brawny, bulky, burly, colossal, cumbersome, forceful, heavy, hulking, husky, large, massive, muscular, ponderous, powerful, robust, solid, strapping, strong, substantial, thumping, tremendous, unwieldy, vigorous, weighty.

antonyms slight, small.

height *n.* acme, altitude, apex, apogee, ceiling, celsitude, climax, crest, crown, culmination, degree, dignity, elevation, eminence, exaltation, extremity, grandeur, highness, hill, limit, loftiness, maximum, mountain, ne plus ultra, peak, pinnacle, prominence, stature, summit, tallness, top, ultimate, utmost, uttermost, vertex, zenith.
antonym depth.

heighten *v.* add to, aggrandise, aggravate, amplify, augment, elevate, enhance, ennoble, exalt, greaten, improve, increase, intensify, magnify, raise, sharpen, strengthen, uplift.
antonyms decrease, diminish.

heinous *adj.* abhorrent, abominable, atrocious, awful, evil, execrable, facinorous, flagrant, grave, hateful, hideous, immitigable, infamous, iniquitous, monstrous, nefarious, odious, outrageous, revolting, shocking, unspeakable, vicious, villainous.

heir *n.* beneficiary, co-heir, heiress, heritor, inheritor, inheritress, inheritrix, parcener, scion, successor.

hell *n.* Abaddon, abyss, Acheron, affliction, agony, anguish, Erebus, Gehenna, Hades, hellfire, infernal regions, inferno, lower regions, Malebolge, martyrdom, misery, nether world, nightmare, ordeal, suffering, Tartarus, Tophet, torment, trial, underworld, wretchedness.
antonym heaven.

hell-bent *adj.* bent, determined, dogged, fixed, inflexible, intent, intransigent, obdurate, resolved, set, settled, tenacious, unhesitating, unwavering.

hellish *adj.* abominable, accursed, atrocious, barbarous, cruel, damnable, damned, demoniacal, detestable, devilish, diabolical, execrable, fiendish, infernal, inhuman, monstrous, nefarious, Stygian, sulphurous, vicious, wicked.
antonym heavenly.

hello *interj.* chin-chin, ciao, hail, hi, hiya, how-do-you-do, howdy, salve, what cheer, wotcher.
antonym good-bye.

helm *n.* command, control, direction, driving seat, leadership, reins, rudder, rule, saddle, tiller, wheel.

help¹ *v.* abet, abstain, aid, alleviate, ameliorate, assist, avoid, back, befriend, bestead, control, co-operate, cure, ease, eschew, facilitate, forbear, heal, hinder, improve, keep from, lend a hand, mitigate, prevent, promote, rally round, refrain from, relieve, remedy, resist, restore, save, second, serve, shun, stand by, succour, support, withstand.
antonym hinder.
n. adjuvant, advice, aid, aidance, assistance, avail, benefit, co-operation, guidance, leg up, service, support, use, utility.
antonym hindrance.

help² *n.* assistant, daily, employee, hand, helper, worker.

helper *n.* abettor, adjutant, aide, aider, ally,

assistant, attendant, auxiliary, coadjutor, collaborator, colleague, deputy, girl Friday, helpmate, man Friday, mate, PA, partner, person Friday, right-hand man, Samaritan, second, subsidiary, supporter.

helpful *adj.* accommodating, adjuvant, advantageous, beneficent, beneficial, benevolent, caring, considerate, constructive, co-operative, favourable, fortunate, friendly, furthersome, kind, neighbourly, practical, productive, profitable, serviceable, supportive, sympathetic, timely, useful.
antonyms futile, useless, worthless.

helping *n.* amount, dollop, piece, plateful, portion, ration, serving, share.

helpless *adj.* abandoned, adynamic, aidless, debilitated, defenceless, dependent, destitute, disabled, exposed, feeble, forlorn, friendless, impotent, incapable, incompetent, infirm, paralysed, powerless, unfit, unprotected, vulnerable, weak.
antonyms competent, enterprising, independent, resourceful, strong.

helpmate *n.* assistant, associate, better half, companion, consort, helper, helpmeet, husband, other half, partner, spouse, support, wife.

helter-skelter *adv.* carelessly, confusedly, hastily, headlong, hurriedly, impulsively, pellmell, rashly, recklessly, wildly.
adj. anyhow, confused, disordered, disorganised, haphazard, higgledy-piggledy, hit-or-miss, jumbled, muddled, random, topsy-turvy, unsystematic.

hem *n.* border, edge, fringe, margin, skirt, trimming.
v. beset, border, circumscribe, confine, edge, enclose, engird, environ, fimbriate, gird, hedge, restrict, skirt, surround.

hence *adv.* accordingly, ergo, therefore, thus.

henceforth *adv.* hence, henceforward, hereafter, hereinafter.

henchman *n.* aide, associate, attendant, bodyguard, cohort, crony, follower, gallo(w)glass, heavy, heeler, house-carl, jackal, led captain, minder, minion, myrmidon, right-hand man, running dog, satellite, sidekick, subordinate, supporter.

henpeck *v.* badger, browbeat, bully, carp, cavil, chide, chivvy, criticise, domineer, find fault, harass, hector, intimidate, nag, niggle, pester, scold, torment.

henpecked *adj.* browbeaten, bullied, cringing, dominated, intimidated, meek, subject, subjugated, timid.
antonym dominant.

herald *n.* courier, crier, forerunner, harbinger, indication, messenger, omen, precursor, sign, signal, token, vaunt-courier.
v. advertise, announce, broadcast, forebode, foretoken, harbinger, indicate, pave the way, portend, precede, presage, proclaim, prognosticate, promise, publicise, publish, show, trumpet, usher in.

heraldry *n.* arms, badge, blazonry, crest, emblazonry, emblem, ensign, (e)scutcheon,

hatchment, insignia, pageantry, regalia.
herculean *adj.* arduous, athletic, brawny, colossal, daunting, demanding, difficult, enormous, exacting, exhausting, formidable, gigantic, great, gruelling, hard, heavy, huge, husky, laborious, large, mammoth, massive, mighty, muscular, onerous, powerful, prodigious, rugged, sinewy, stalwart, strapping, strenuous, strong, sturdy, titanic, toilsome, tough, tremendous.
herd *n.* assemblage, canaille, collection, cowherd, crowd, crush, drove, flock, herdboy, herdsman, horde, mass, mob, multitude, populace, press, rabble, riff-raff, shepherd, swarm, the hoi polloi, the masses, the plebs, throng, vulgus.
v. assemble, associate, collect, congregate, drive, flock, force, gather, goad, guard, guide, huddle, lead, muster, protect, rally, shepherd, spur, watch.
herdsman *n.* cowherd, cowman, drover, grazier, stockman, vaquero, wrangler.
here and there from pillar to post, hither and thither, passim, sporadically, to and fro.
hereafter *adv.* eventually, hence, henceforth, henceforward, in future, later.
n. after-life, Elysian fields, happy hunting-ground, heaven, life after death, next world.
hereditary *adj.* ancestral, bequeathed, congenital, family, genetic, handed down, inborn, inbred, inheritable, inherited, patrimonial, traditional, transmissible, transmittable, transmitted, willed.
heresy *n.* apostasy, dissidence, error, free-thinking, heterodoxy, iconoclasm, impiety, revisionism, schism, unorthodoxy.
antonym orthodoxy.
heretic *n.* apostate, dissenter, dissident, free-thinker, nonconformist, renegade, revisionist, schismatic, sectarian, separatist.
antonym conformist.
heretical *adj.* free-thinking, heterodox, iconoclastic, idolatrous, impious, infidel, irreverent, rationalistic, revisionist, schismatic.
antonyms conformist, conventional, orthodox.
heritage *n.* bequest, birthright, deserts, due, endowment, estate, history, inheritance, legacy, lot, past, patrimony, portion, record, share, tradition.
hermetic *adj.* airtight, hermetical, sealed, shut, watertight.
hermit *n.* anchoret, anchorite, ascetic, eremite, monk, recluse, solitaire, solitarian, solitary, stylite.
hero *n.* celebrity, champion, conqueror, exemplar, goody, heart-throb, idol, male lead, paragon, protagonist, star, superstar, victor.
heroic *adj.* bold, brave, classic, classical, courageous, daring, dauntless, doughty, elevated, epic, exaggerated, extravagant, fearless, gallant, game, grand, grandiose, gritty, high-flown, Homeric, inflated, intrepid, legendary, lion-hearted, mythological, spunky, stout-hearted, undaunted, valiant, valorous.

antonyms cowardly, pusillanimous, timid.
heroin *n.* horse, shit, smack.
heroine *n.* celebrity, female lead, goddess, ideal, idol, protagonist, star, superstar.
heroism *n.* boldness, bravery, courage, courageousness, daring, derring-do, fearlessness, fortitude, gallantry, gameness, grit, intrepidity, prowess, spirit, valour.
antonyms cowardice, pusillaniminity, timidity.
hero-worship *n.* admiration, adoration, adulation, deification, idealisation, idolisation, veneration.
hesitancy *n.* demur, disinclination, doubt, doubtfulness, dubiousness, dubitance, dubitation, indecision, irresolution, misgiving, qualm, reluctance, reservation, swithering, uncertainty, unwillingness, wavering.
antonyms certainty, willingness.
hesitant *adj.* diffident, dilatory, doubtful, half-hearted, halting, hesitating, hesitative, hesitatory, irresolute, reluctant, sceptical, shy, swithering, timid, uncertain, unsure, vacillating, wavering.
antonyms resolute, staunch.
hesitate *v.* balk, be reluctant, be uncertain, be unwilling, boggle, delay, demur, dither, doubt, dubitate, falter, fumble, halt, haver, pause, scruple, shillyshally, shrink from, stammer, stumble, stutter, swither, think twice, vacillate, wait, waver.
hesitation *n.* delay, demurral, doubt, dubiety, faltering, fumbling, hesitancy, indecision, irresolution, misdoubt, misgiving(s), qualm(s), reluctance, scruple(s), second thought(s), stammering, stumbling, stuttering, swithering, uncertainty, unwillingness, vacillation.
antonyms alacrity, assurance, eagerness.
heterodox *adj.* dissident, free-thinking, heretical, iconoclastic, revisionist, schismatic, unorthodox, unsound.
antonym orthodox.
heterogeneous *adj.* assorted, catholic, contrary, contrasted, different, discrepant, disparate, dissimilar, divergent, diverse, diversified, incongruous, miscellaneous, mixed, motley, multiform, opposed, polymorphic, unlike, unrelated, varied.
antonym homogeneous.
hew *v.* axe, carve, chop, cut, fashion, fell, form, hack, lop, make, model, sculpt, sculpture, sever, shape, smooth, split.
heyday *n.* bloom, boom time, florescence, floruit, flower, flowering, golden age, pink, prime, salad days, vigour.
hiatus *n.* aperture, blank, breach, break, chasm, discontinuance, discontinuity, gap, interruption, interval, lacuna, lapse, opening, rift, space, void.
hidden *adj.* abstruse, cabbalistic(al), clandestine, close, concealed, covered, covert, cryptic, dark, de(a)rn, delitescent, doggo, hermetic, hermetical, latent, mysterious, mystic, mystical, obscure, occult, recondite,

secret, shrouded, ulterior, unapparent, unseen, veiled.

antonyms open, showing.

hide[1] *v.* abscond, bury, cache, camouflage, cloak, conceal, cover, disguise, earth, eclipse, ensconce, feal, go to ground, go underground, hole up, keep dark, lie low, mask, obscure, occult, screen, secrete, shadow, shelter, shroud, stash, suppress, take cover, tappice, veil, withhold.

antonyms display, reveal, show.

hide[2] *n.* deacon, fell, flaught, nebris, pelt, skin.

hide-away *n.* cloister, haven, hideout, hiding-place, nest, refuge, retreat, sanctuary.

hidebound *adj.* conventional, entrenched, narrow, narrow-minded, rigid, set, set in one's ways, strait-laced, ultra-conservative, unprogressive.

antonyms liberal, unconventional.

hideous *adj.* abominable, appalling, awful, detestable, disgusting, dreadful, frightful, gash, gashful, gashly, ghastly, grim, grisly, grotesque, gruesome, horrendous, horrible, horrid, loathsome, macabre, monstrous, odious, repulsive, revolting, shocking, sickening, terrible, terrifying, ugly, ugsome, unsightly.

antonym beautiful.

hideout *n.* den, hide-away, hiding-place, hole, lair, retreat, shelter.

hiding[1] *n.* beating, caning, drubbing, flogging, hammering, larruping, lathering, leathering, licking, spanking, tanning, thrashing, walloping, whaling, whipping.

hiding[2] *n.* camouflage, concealment, de(a)rn, disguise, screening, secretion, veiling.

hiding-place *n.* den, haven, hide-away, hideout, hole, lair, lurking-place, mew, priest hole, refuge, retreat, sanctuary, starting-hole, stash.

hierarchy *n.* echelons, grading, peck(ing) order, ranking, scale, strata.

higgledy-piggledy *adv.* any old how, anyhow, confusedly, haphazardly, helter-skelter, indiscriminately, pell-mell, topsy-turvy.

adj. confused, disorderly, disorganised, haphazard, indiscriminate, jumbled, muddled, topsy-turvy.

high *adj.* acute, altissimo, alto, arch, arrogant, boastful, boisterous, bouncy, bragging, capital, cheerful, chief, consequential, costly, dear, delirious, despotic, distinguished, domineering, elated, elevated, eminent, euphoric, exalted, excessive, excited, exhilarated, exorbitant, expensive, extraordinary, extravagant, extreme, exuberant, freaked out, gamy, grand, grave, great, haughty, high-pitched, important, inebriated, influential, intensified, intoxicated, joyful, lavish, leading, lighthearted, lofty, lordly, luxurious, merry, mountain(s)-high, niffy, orthian, ostentatious, overbearing, penetrating, piercing, piping, pongy, powerful, prominent, proud, rich, ruling, serious, sharp, shrill, significant, soaring, soprano, spaced out, steep, stiff, stoned, strident, strong, superior, tainted,

tall, towering, treble, tripping, tumultuous, turbulent, tyrannical, vainglorious, whiffy.

antonyms deep, low, lowly, short.

n. apex, apogee, delirium, ecstasy, euphoria, height, intoxication, level, peak, record, summit, top, trip, zenith.

antonyms low, nadir.

high and dry abandoned, bereft, destitute, helpless, marooned, stranded.

high and mighty arrogant, cavalier, conceited, disdainful, haughty, imperious, overbearing, overweening, self-important, snobbish, stuck-up, superior.

high society aristocracy, beautiful people, crème de la crème, éite, gentry, grand monde, haut monde, jet set, nobility, upper crust.

antonym hoi polloi.

high spirits boisterousness, bounce, buoyancy, exhilaration, exuberance, good cheer, hilarity, joie de vivre, liveliness, sparkle, vivacity.

high-born *adj.* aristocratic, blue-blooded, gentle, noble, patrician, pedigreed, thoroughbred, well-born, well-connected.

highbrow *n.* aesthete, boffin, Brahmin, brain, egghead, intellectual, long-hair, mandarin, mastermind, savant, scholar.

adj. bookish, brainy, cultivated, cultured, deep, intellectual, long-haired, serious, sophisticated.

antonym lowbrow.

high-class *adj.* A1, choice, classy, de luxe, elite, exclusive, first-rate, high-quality, posh, quality, select, superior, tiptop, top-flight, tops, U, upper-class.

antonyms mediocre, ordinary.

highest *adj.* apical, apogaeic, peak, record, top, topmost, upmost, uppermost, zenithal.

antonyms bottom(most), lowest.

high-falutin(g) *adj.* affected, big, bombastic, florid, grandiose, high-flown, high-sounding, la(h)-di-da(h), lofty, magniloquent, pompous, pretentious, supercilious, swanky.

high-flown *adj.* elaborate, elevated, exaggerated, extravagant, florid, grandiose, high-falutin(g), inflated, la(h)-di-da(h), lofty, magniloquent, overblown, pretentious, turgid.

high-handed *adj.* arbitrary, autocratic, bossy, despotic, dictatorial, discourteous, disdainful, domineering, imperious, inconsiderate, oppressive, overbearing, peremptory, self-willed, tyrannical, wilful.

highlight *n.* best, climax, cream, feature, focal point, focus, high point, high spot, peak, zenith.

v. accent, accentuate, emphasise, feature, focus on, illuminate, play up, point up, set off, show up, spotlight, stress, underline.

highly *adv.* appreciatively, approvingly, considerably, decidedly, eminently, enthusiastically, exceptionally, extraordinarily, extremely, favourably, greatly, immensely, supremely, tremendously, vastly, very, warmly, well.

highly-strung *adj.* edgy, excitable, irascible, irritable, jittery, nervous, nervy, neurotic, restless, sensitive, skittish, stressed, taut,

temperamental, tense.
antonyms calm, relaxed.

high-minded *adj.* elevated, ethical, fair, good, honourable, idealistic, lofty, magnanimous, moral, noble, principled, pure, righteous, scrupulous, upright, virtuous, worthy.
antonyms immoral, unscrupulous.

high-powered *adj.* aggressive, driving, dynamic, effective, energetic, enterprising, forceful, go-ahead, go-getting, industrious, vigorous.

high-priced *adj.* costly, dear, excessive, exorbitant, expensive, extortionate, high, pricy, steep, stiff, unreasonable.
antonym cheap.

high-quality *adj.* blue-chip, choice, classy, de luxe, gilt-edged, quality, select, superior, tiptop, top-class.

high-sounding *adj.* affected, artificial, bombastic, extravagant, flamboyant, florid, grandiloquent, grandiose, high-flown, magniloquent, orotund, ostentatious, overblown, pompous, ponderous, pretentious, stilted, strained.

high-spirited *adj.* animated, boisterous, bold, bouncy, daring, dashing, ebullient, effervescent, energetic, exuberant, frolicsome, lively, mettlesome, peppy, sparkling, spirited, spunky, vibrant, vital, vivacious.
antonyms downcast, glum.

highwayman *n.* bandit, bandolero, footpad, knight of the road, land-pirate, rank-rider, robber.

hijack *v.* commandeer, expropriate, kidnap, seize, skyjack, snatch, steal.

hike *v.* back-pack, footslog, hoof it, leg it, plod, ramble, tramp, treck, trudge, walk.
n. march, plod, ramble, tramp, trek, trudge, walk.

hilarious *adj.* amusing, comical, convivial, entertaining, funny, gay, happy, humorous, hysterical, jolly, jovial, joyful, joyous, killing, merry, mirthful, noisy, rollicking, side-splitting, uproarious.
antonyms grave, serious.

hilarity *n.* amusement, boisterousness, cheerfulness, conviviality, entertainment, exhilaration, exuberance, frivolity, gaiety, glee, high spirits, jollification, jollity, joviality, joyousness, laughter, levity, merriment, mirth, uproariousness.
antonyms gravity, seriousness.

hill *n.* acclivity, berg, brae, butte, climb, dod, down, drift, elevation, eminence, fell, gradient, heap, height, hillock, hilltop, how, hummock, incline, knoll, knowe, kop, koppie, law, mamelon, mesa, mound, mount, pike, pile, prominence, rise, slope, stack, tor.

hillock *n.* barrow, dune, hummock, knap, knoll, knowe, monticulus, mote, motte, mound, tump.

hilt *n.* grip, haft, handgrip, handle, heft, helve.

hind *adj.* after, back, caudal, hinder, posterior, rear, tail.
antonym fore.

hinder *v.* arrest, check, counteract, debar, delay, deter, embar, encumber, forelay, frustrate,

hamper, hamstring, handicap, hold back, hold up, impede, interrupt, obstruct, oppose, prevent, retard, slow down, stop, stymie, thwart, trammel.
antonyms aid, assist, help.

hindmost *adj.* concluding, endmost, final, furthest, lag, last, rearmost, remotest, tail, terminal, trailing, ultimate.
antonym foremost.

hindrance *n.* bar, barrier, check, demurrage, deterrent, difficulty, drag, drawback, encumbrance, handicap, hitch, impediment, interruption, limitation, obstacle, obstruction, pull-back, remora, restraint, restriction, snag, stoppage, stumbling-block, trammel.
antonyms aid, assistance, help.

hinge *v.* be contingent, centre, depend, hang, pivot, rest, revolve around, turn.
n. articulation, condition, foundation, garnet, joint, premise, principle.

hint *n.* advice, allusion, breath, clue, dash, help, implication, indication, inkling, innuendo, insinuation, intimation, mention, pointer, reminder, scintilla, sign, signal, soupçon, speck, subindication, suggestion, suspicion, taste, tinge, tip, tip-off, touch, trace, undertone, whiff, whisper, wrinkle.
v. allude, imply, indicate, inkle, innuendo, insinuate, intimate, mention, prompt, subindicate, suggest, tip off.

hinterland *n.* back-blocks, back-country, backveld, hinderland, interior.

hip *n.* buttocks, croup, haunch, hindquarters, huck, huckle, loin, pelvis, posterior, rump.

hippy *n.* beatnik, bohemian, drop-out, flower child, hippie.

hire *v.* appoint, book, charter, commission, employ, engage, lease, let, rent, reserve, retain, sign up, take on.
antonyms dismiss, fire.
n. charge, cost, fare, fee, price, rent, rental, toll.

hire-purchase *n.* easy terms, never-never.

hirsute *adj.* bearded, bewhiskered, bristly, crinigerous, crinite, crinose, hairy, hispid, shaggy, unshaven.
antonyms bald, hairless.

hiss *n.* boo, buzz, catcall, contempt, derision, hissing, hoot, jeer, mockery, raspberry, sibilance, sibilation, whistle.
v. boo, catcall, condemn, damn, decry, deride, hoot, jeer, mock, rasp, revile, ridicule, shrill, sibilate, siffle, wheeze, whirr, whiss, whistle, whiz.

historic *adj.* celebrated, consequential, epoch-making, extraordinary, famed, famous, momentous, notable, outstanding, red-letter, remarkable, renowned, significant.

historical *adj.* actual, archival, attested, authentic, documented, factual, real, traditional, verifiable.

history *n.* account, annals, antecedents, antiquity, autobiography, biography, chronicle, chronology, days of old, days of yore, genealogy, memoirs, narration, narrative, olden days, recapitulation, recital, record, relation, saga, story, tale, the past.

histrionic *adj.* affected, artificial, bogus, dramatic, forced, ham, insincere, melodramatic, ranting, sensational, theatrical, unnatural.

histrionics *n.* dramatics, overacting, performance, ranting and raving, scene, staginess, tantrums, temperament, theatricality.

hit *v.* accomplish, achieve, affect, arrive at, attain, bang, bash, batter, beat, belt, bump, clip, clobber, clock, clonk, clout, collide with, crown, cuff, damage, devastate, flog, frap, fustigate, gain, impinge on, influence, knock, lob, move, overwhelm, prop, punch, reach, secure, slap, slog, slosh, slug, smack, smash, smite, sock, strike, swat, thump, touch, volley, wallop, whack, wham, whap, w(h)op, wipe.
n. blow, bump, clash, clout, collision, cuff, impact, knock, rap, sell-out, sensation, shot, slap, slog, slosh, smack, smash, sock, stroke, success, swipe, triumph, venue, wallop, winner.

hit back recalcitrate, reciprocate, retaliate.
hit on arrive at, chance on, contrive, discover, guess, invent, light on, realise, stumble on.
hit out assail, attack, castigate, condemn, criticise, denounce, inveigh, lash, lay about one, rail.

hitch *v.* attach, connect, couple, fasten, harness, heave, hike (up), hitch-hike, hoi(c)k, hoist, jerk, join, pull, tether, thumb a lift, tie, tug, unite, yank, yoke.
antonyms unfasten, unhitch.
n. catch, check, delay, difficulty, drawback, hiccup, hindrance, hold-up, impediment, mishap, problem, snag, stick, stoppage, trouble.

hitherto *adv.* beforehand, heretofore, previously, so far, thus far, till now, until now, up to now.

hit-or-miss *adj.* aimless, apathetic, casual, cursory, disorganised, haphazard, indiscriminate, lackadaisical, perfunctory, random, undirected, uneven.

hoard *n.* accumulation, cache, fund, heap, mass, pile, profusion, reserve, reservoir, stockpile, store, supply, treasure-trove.
v. accumulate, amass, cache, coffer, collect, deposit, garner, gather, hive, husband, lay up, put by, reposit, save, stash away, stockpile, store, treasure.
antonyms spend, squander, use.

hoarder *n.* collector, gatherer, magpie, miser, niggard, squirrel.

hoarse *adj.* croaky, discordant, grating, gravelly, growling, gruff, guttural, harsh, husky, rasping, raspy, raucous, rough, throaty.
antonyms clear, smooth.

hoary *adj.* aged, ancient, antiquated, antique, canescent, frosty, grey, grey-haired, grizzled, hoar, old, senescent, silvery, venerable, white, white-haired.

hoax *n.* bam, cheat, cod, con, deception, fast one, fraud, grift, hum, huntiegowk, hunt-the-gowk, imposture, joke, josh, leg-pull, practical joke, prank, put-on, quiz, ruse, spoof, string, swindle, trick.
v. bam, bamboozle, befool, bluff, cod, con, deceive, delude, dupe, fool, gammon, gull, have on, hoodwink, hornswoggle, hum, lead on, pull someone's leg, spoof, string, stuff, swindle, take for a ride, trick.

hoaxer *n.* bamboozler, grifter, hoodwinker, humbug, joker, mystifier, practical joker, prankster, quiz, quizzer, spoofer, trickster.

hobble *v.* clog, dodder, falter, fasten, fetter, halt, hamshackle, hamstring, hirple, limp, restrict, shackle, shamble, shuffle, stagger, stumble, tie, totter.

hobby *n.* avocation, diversion, pastime, pursuit, recreation, relaxation, sideline.

hobgoblin *n.* apparition, bog(e)y, bugaboo, bugbear, goblin, hob, imp, spectre, spirit, sprite.

hobnob *v.* associate, consort, fraternise, hang about, keep company, mingle, mix, pal around, socialise.

hocus-pocus *n.* abracadabra, artifice, cant, cheat, chicanery, conjuring, deceit, deception, delusion, finesse, gibberish, gobbledegook, hoax, humbug, imposture, jargon, jugglery, legerdemain, mumbo-jumbo, nonsense, prestidigitation, rigmarole, sleight of hand, swindle, trickery, trompe-l'oeil.

hogwash *n.* balderdash, bilge, bunk, bunkum, claptrap, drivel, eyewash, hooey, nonsense, piffle, rot, rubbish, tar(r)adiddle, tosh, trash, tripe, twaddle.

hoi polloi *n.* admass, canaille, citizenry, commonalty, riff-raff, the common people, the great unwashed, the herd, the masses, the plebs, the populace, the proles, the proletariat, the rabble, the third estate.
antonyms aristocracy, élite, nobility.

hoist *v.* elevate, erect, heave, jack up, lift, raise, rear, uplift, upraise.
n. crane, davit, elevator, jack, lift, tackle, winch.

hoity-toity *adj.* arrogant, conceited, disdainful, haughty, high and mighty, lofty, overweening, pompous, proud, scornful, snobbish, snooty, stuck-up, supercilious, toffee-nosed, uppish, uppity.

hold *v.* accommodate, account, adhere, apply, arrest, assemble, assume, be in force, be the case, bear, believe, bond, brace, call, carry, carry on, celebrate, check, clasp, cleave, clinch, cling, clip, clutch, comprise, conduct, confine, consider, contain, continue, convene, cradle, curb, deem, delay, detain, embrace, endure, enfold, entertain, esteem, exist, grasp, grip, have, hold good, imprison, judge, keep, last, maintain, occupy, operate, own, persevere, persist, possess, preside over, presume, prop, reckon, regard, remain, remain true, remain valid, resist, restrain, retain, run, seat, shoulder, solemnise, stand up, stay, stick, stop, summon, support, suspend, sustain, take, think, view, wear.
n. anchorage, asendancy, authority, clasp,

clout, clutch, control, dominance, dominion, foothold, footing, grasp, grip, holt, influence, leverage, mastery, prop, pull, purchase, stay, support, sway, vantage.

hold back check, control, curb, desist, forbear, inhibit, refuse, repress, restrain, retain, stifle, suppress, withhold.

antonym release.

hold forth declaim, descant, discourse, go on, harangue, lecture, orate, preach, sermonise, speak, speechify, spiel, spout.

hold off avoid, defer, delay, fend off, keep off, postpone, put off, rebuff, refrain, repel, repulse, stave off, wait.

hold out continue, endure, extend, give, hang on, last, offer, persevere, persist, porrect, present, proffer, stand fast.

hold over adjourn, defer, delay, postpone, put off, shelve, suspend.

hold up brace, delay, detain, display, endure, exhibit, hinder, impede, last, lift, present, raise, retard, show, slow, stop, survive, sustain, waylay, wear.

hold water bear scrutiny, convince, make sense, pass the test, ring true, wash, work.

hold with accept, agree to, approve of, countenance, go along with, subscribe to, support.

holder *n.* bearer, case, container, cover, cradle, custodian, housing, incumbent, keeper, occupant, owner, possessor, proprietor, purchaser, receptacle, rest, sheath, stand.

holdings *n.* assets, bonds, estate, investments, land, possessions, property, real estate, resources, securities, shares, stocks.

hold-up[1] *n.* bottle-neck, delay, difficulty, gridlock, hitch, obstruction, setback, snag, stoppage, (traffic) jam, trouble, wait.

hold-up[2] *n.* heist, robbery, stick-up.

hole *n.* aperture, breach, break, burrow, cave, cavern, cavity, chamber, covert, crack, defect, den, depression, dilemma, dimple, discrepancy, dive, dump, earth, error, excavation, eyelet, fallacy, fault, fissure, fix, flaw, foramen, fovea, gap, hollow, hovel, imbroglio, inconsistency, jam, joint, lair, loophole, mess, nest, opening, orifice, outlet, perforation, pit, pocket, pore, predicament, puncture, quandary, rent, retreat, scoop, scrape, shaft, shelter, slum, split, spot, tangle, tear, tight spot, vent, ventage.

hole-and-corner *adj.* back-door, backstairs, back-stairs, clandestine, covert, furtive, hugger-mugger, hush-hush, secret, secretive, sneaky, stealthy, surreptitious, underhand, under-the-counter.

antonyms open, public.

holiday *n.* anniversary, break, celebration, exeat, feast, festival, festivity, fête, furlough, gala, hols, leave, recess, respite, rest, sabbatical, saint's day, time off, vacation.

holier-than-thou *adj.* complacent, goody-goody, pietistic(al), pious, priggish, religiose, sanctimonious, self-approving, self-righteous, self-satisfied, smug, unctuous.

antonyms humble, meek.

holiness *n.* blessedness, devoutness, divinity, evangelicism, godliness, halidom, pietism, piety, priggishness, purity, religiosity, religiousness, righteousness, sacredness, saintliness, sanctimoniousness, sanctity, self-righteousness, spirituality, unctuosity, unctuousness, virtuousness.

antonyms impiety, wickedness.

holler *n., v.* bawl, bellow, call, cheer, clamour, cry, hail, halloo, hollo, howl, hurrah, huzzah, roar, shout, shriek, whoop, yell, yelp, yowl.

hollow *adj.* artificial, cavernous, concave, coreless, cynical, deaf, deceitful, deceptive, deep, deep-set, depressed, dished, dull, empty, expressionless, faithless, false, famished, flat, fleeting, flimsy, fruitless, futile, gaunt, glenoid(al), hungry, hypocritical, indented, insincere, lantern-jawed, low, meaningless, muffled, muted, pointless, Pyrrhic, ravenous, reverberant, rumbling, sepulchral, specious, starved, sunken, toneless, treacherous, unavailing, unfilled, unreal, unreliable, unsound, useless, vacant, vain, void, weak, worthless.

n. basin, bottom, bowl, cave, cavern, cavity, channel, concave, concavity, coomb, crater, cup, dale, dell, den, dent, depression, dimple, dingle, dint, dish, druse, excavation, fossa, fossula, fovea, foveola, foveole, geode, gilgie, glen, gnamma hole, groove, hole, hope, how(e), indentation, invagination, pit, trough, umbilicus, vacuity, valley, vlei, well, womb.

v. burrow, channel, dent, dig, dint, dish, excavate, furrow, gouge, groove, indent, pit, scoop.

holocaust *n.* annihilation, carnage, conflagration, destruction, devastation, extermination, extinction, flames, genocide, hecatomb, immolation, inferno, mass murder, massacre, pogrom, sacrifice, slaughter.

holy *adj.* blessed, consecrated, dedicated, devout, divine, evangelical, evangelistic, faithful, god-fearing, godly, good, hallowed, perfect, pietistic, pious, pure, religiose, religious, righteous, sacred, sacrosanct, saintly, sanctified, sanctimonious, spiritual, sublime, unctuous, venerable, venerated, virtuous.

antonyms impious, unsanctified, wicked.

homage *n.* acknowledgement, admiration, adoration, adulation, allegiance, awe, deference, devotion, duty, esteem, faithfulness, fealty, fidelity, honour, loyalty, obeisance, praise, recognition, regard, respect, reverence, service, tribute, veneration, worship.

home *n.* abode, almshouse, asylum, birthplace, blighty, clinic, domicile, dwelling, dwelling-place, element, environment, family, fireside, habitat, habitation, haunt, hearth, home ground, home town, homestead, hospice, hospital, house, household, institution, native heath, nest, nursing-home, old people's home, pad, pied-à-terre, range, residence,

roof, sanatorium, stamping-ground, territory.
adj. candid, central, direct, domestic, domiciliary, familiar, family, household, incisive, inland, internal, intimate, local, national, native, penetrating, plain, pointed, unanswerable, uncomfortable, wounding.

homeland *n.* fatherland, mother country, motherland, native country, native heath, native land, native soil.

homeless *adj.* abandoned, destitute, disinherited, displaced, dispossessed, down-and-out, exiled, forlorn, forsaken, houseless, itinerant, outcast, unsettled, vagabond, wandering.
n. derelicts, dossers, down-and-outs, nomads, squatters, tramps, travellers, vagrants.

homely *adj.* comfortable, comfy, congenial, cosy, domestic, easy, everyday, familiar, folksy, friendly, gemütlich, homelike, homespun, hom(e)y, informal, intimate, modest, natural, ordinary, plain, relaxed, simple, snug, unaffected, unassuming, unpretentious, unsophisticated, welcoming.
antonyms formal, unfamiliar.

Homeric *adj.* epic, grand, heroic, imposing, impressive, Virgilian.

homesickness *n.* Heimweh, mal du pays, nostalgia, nostomania.
antonym wanderlust.

homespun *adj.* amateurish, artless, coarse, crude, folksy, homely, home-made, inelegant, plain, rough, rude, rustic, unpolished, unrefined, unsophisticated.
antonym sophisticated.

homicidal *adj.* blood-thirsty, deadly, death-dealing, lethal, maniacal, mortal, murderous, sanguinary, violent.

homicide *n.* assassin, assassination, bloodshed, cut-throat, killer, killing, liquidator, manslaughter, murder, murderer, slayer, slaying.

homily *n.* address, discourse, harangue, heart-to-heart, lecture, postil, preachment, sermon, spiel, talk.

homogeneity *n.* agreement, akinness, analogousness, comparability, consistency, consonancy, correspondence, identicalness, likeness, oneness, resemblance, sameness, similarity, similitude, uniformity.
antonyms difference, disagreement.

homogeneous *adj.* akin, alike, analogous, cognate, comparable, consistent, consonant, harmonious, identical, indiscrete, kindred, of a piece, similar, uniform, unvarying.
antonym different.

homologous *adj.* analogous, comparable, correspondent, corresponding, equivalent, like, matching, parallel, related, similar.
antonyms different, dissimilar.

homosexual *n.* catamite, dike, dyke, fag, fairy, fruit, Ganymede, gunsel, homophile, invert, les, lesbian, lez, Nancy, paederast, poof, pooftah, poove, puff, punk, queen, queer, sapphist, tribade, urning.
antonyms heterosexual, straight.
adj. bent, camp, dikey, dykey, fruity, gay, homoerotic, lesbian, paederastic, poofy,

poovy, queer, sapphic.
antonyms heterosexual, straight.

homosexuality *n.* gayness, homoeroticism, homoerotism, homosexualism, paederasty, poovery, queerdom, sapphism, tribadism, tribady.
antonym heterosexuality.

hone *v.* edge, file, grind, point, polish, rasp, sharpen, strop, whet.

honest *adj.* above-board, authentic, bona fide, candid, chaste, conscientious, decent, direct, equitable, ethical, fair, fair and square, forthright, four-square, frank, genuine, high-minded, honourable, humble, impartial, ingenuous, jake, just, law-abiding, legitimate, modest, objective, on the level, open, outright, outspoken, plain, plain-hearted, proper, real, reliable, reputable, respectable, scrupulous, seemly, simple, sincere, soothfast, square, straight, straightforward, true, trustworthy, trusty, truthful, undisguised, unequivocal, unfeigned, unreserved, upright, veracious, virtuous, well-gotten, well-won, white.
antonyms covert, devious, dishonest, dishonourable.

honestly *adv.* by fair means, candidly, cleanly, conscientiously, directly, dispassionately, equitably, ethically, fairly, frankly, honourably, in all sincerity, in good faith, justly, lawfully, legally, legitimately, objectively, on the level, openly, outright, plainly, really, scrupulously, sincerely, straight, straight out, truly, truthfully, undisguisedly, unreservedly, uprightly, verily.
antonyms dishonestly, dishonourably.

honesty *n.* artlessness, bluntness, candour, equity, even-handedness, explicitness, fairness, faithfulness, fidelity, frankness, genuineness, honour, incorruptibility, integrity, justness, morality, objectivity, openness, outspokenness, plain-heartedness, plainness, plain-speaking, probity, rectitude, reputability, scrupulousness, sincerity, sooth, squareness, straightforwardness, straightness, trustworthiness, truthfulness, unreserve, uprightness, veracity, verity, virtue.
antonyms deviousness, dishonesty.

honorary *adj.* complimentary, ex officio, formal, honorific, honoris causa, in name only, nominal, titular, unofficial, unpaid, virtute officii.
antonyms gainful, paid, salaried, waged.

honour *n.* acclaim, accolade, acknowledgement, admiration, adoration, chastity, commendation, compliment, credit, decency, deference, dignity, distinction, duty, elevation, esteem, fairness, favour, good name, goodness, homage, honesty, honorificabilitudinity, honourableness, innocence, integrity, kudos, laudation, laurels, loyalty, modesty, morality, pleasure, praise, principles, privilege, probity, purity, rank, recognition, rectitude, regard, renown, reputation, repute, respect, reverence, righteousness, self-respect, tri-

bute, trust, trustworthiness, uprightness, veneration, virginity, virtue, worship.
antonyms disgrace, dishonour, obloquy.
v. accept, acclaim, acknowledge, admire, adore, applaud, appreciate, carry out, cash, celebrate, clear, commemorate, commend, compliment, credit, crown, decorate, dignify, discharge, esteem, exalt, execute, fulfil, glorify, hallow, homage, keep, laud, laureate, lionise, observe, pass, pay, pay homage, perform, praise, prize, remember, respect, revere, reverence, take, value, venerate, worship.
antonyms betray, debase, disgrace, dishonour.

honourable *adj.* creditable, distinguished, eminent, equitable, estimable, ethical, fair, great, high-minded, honest, illustrious, irreproachable, just, meritorious, moral, noble, prestigious, principled, proper, renowned, reputable, respectable, respected, right, righteous, sincere, straight, true, trustworthy, trusty, unexceptionable, upright, upstanding, venerable, virtuous, worthful, worthy.
antonyms dishonest, dishonourable, unworthy.

honours *n.* awards, crowns, decorations, dignities, distinctions, laurels, prizes, rewards, titles, trophies.
antonyms aspersions, indignities.

hood *n.* capeline, capuche, cowl, domino.

hoodwink *v.* bamboozle, befool, blear, cheat, con, cozen, deceive, delude, dupe, fool, gammon, gull, gyp, have on, hoax, impose, mislead, rook, seel, swindle, take in, trick.

hoof *n.* cloot, cloven hoof, foot, trotter, ungula.

hoofed *adj.* cloven-footed, cloven-hoofed, ungulate, unguligrade.

hook *n.* agraffe, barb, catch, clasp, fastener, fluke, hamulus, hasp, holder, link, lock, peg, sickle, snag, snare, springe, trap, uncus.
v. bag, catch, clasp, collar, enmesh, ensnare, entangle, entrap, fasten, fix, grab, hasp, hitch, nab, secure, snare, trap.

hooked *adj.* addicted, adunc, aquiline, barbed, beaked, beaky, bent, curled, curved, devoted, enamoured, falcate, hamate, hamose, hamous, hamular, hamulate, obsessed, sickle-shaped, uncate, unciform, uncinate.

hooligan *n.* apache, bovver boy, delinquent, hood, hoodlum, lout, mobster, ned, rough, roughneck, rowdy, ruffian, thug, tityre-tu, tough, toughie, vandal, yob, yobbo.

hoop *n.* annulus, bail, band, circlet, gird, girdle, loop, ring, round, wheel.

hoot *n.* beep, boo, call, card, catcall, caution, cry, hiss, howl, jeer, laugh, raspberry, scream, shout, shriek, toot, whistle, whoop, yell.
v. beep, boo, catcall, condemn, cry, decry, deride, explode, hiss, howl down, jeer, ridicule, scream, shout, shriek, toot, ululate, whistle, whoop, yell, yell at.

hop *v.* bound, caper, dance, fly, frisk, hitch, hobble, jump, leap, limp, nip, prance, skip, spring, vault.

n. ball, barn-dance, bounce, bound, crossing, dance, flight, jump, leap, skip, social, spring, step, trip, vault.

hope *n.* ambition, anticipation, aspiration, assumption, assurance, belief, confidence, conviction, desire, dream, expectancy, expectation, faith, hopefulness, longing, optimism, promise, prospect, wish.
antonyms apathy, despair, pessimism.
v. anticipate, aspire, assume, await, believe, contemplate, desire, expect, foresee, long, reckon on, rely, trust, wish.
antonym despair.

hopeful *adj.* assured, auspicious, bright, bullish, buoyant, cheerful, confident, encouraging, expectant, favourable, heartening, optimistic, promising, propitious, reassuring, rosy, sanguine.
antonyms despairing, discouraging, pessimistic.
n. great white hope, white hope, wunderkind.

hopefully *adv.* all being well, bullishly, conceivably, confidently, deo volente, eagerly, expectantly, expectedly, feasibly, optimistically, probably, sanguinely, with a bit of luck.

hopeless *adj.* defeatist, dejected, demoralised, despairing, desperate, despondent, disconsolate, downhearted, foolish, forlorn, futile, helpless, impossible, impracticable, inadequate, incompetent, incorrigible, incurable, ineffectual, irredeemable, irremediable, irreparable, irreversible, lost, madcap, past cure, pessimistic, pointless, poor, reckless, unachievable, unattainable, useless, vain, woebegone, worthless, wretched.
antonyms curable, hopeful, optimistic.

horde *n.* band, bevy, concourse, crew, crowd, drove, flock, gang, herd, host, mob, multitude, pack, press, swarm, throng, troop.

horizon *n.* compass, ken, perspective, prospect, purview, range, realm, scope, skyline, sphere, stretch, verge, vista.

hornless *adj.* muley, polled.

horny[1] *adj.* callous, ceratoid, corneous, corny.

horny[2] *adj.* ardent, concupiscent, lascivious, lecherous, libidinous, lickerish, lubricious, lustful, priapic, randy, ruttish.
antonyms cold, frigid.

horrible *adj.* abhorrent, abominable, appalling, atrocious, awful, beastly, bloodcurdling, cruel, disagreeable, dreadful, fearful, fearsome, frightful, ghastly, grim, grisly, gruesome, heinous, hideous, horrid, horrific, loathsome, macabre, nasty, repulsive, revolting, shameful, shocking, terrible, terrifying, unkind, unpleasant, weird.
antonyms agreeable, pleasant.

horrid *adj.* abominable, alarming, appalling, awful, beastly, bloodcurdling, cruel, despicable, disagreeable, disgusting, dreadful, formidable, frightening, hair-raising, harrowing, hateful, hideous, horrible, horrific, mean, nasty, odious, offensive, repulsive, revolting, shocking, terrible, terrifying, unkind, unpleasant.

antonyms agreeable, lovely, pleasant.

horrific *adj*. appalling, awful, dreadful, frightening, frightful, ghastly, grim, grisly, hairraising, harrowing, horrendous, horrifying, scaring, shocking, spine-chilling, terrifying.

horrify *v*. abash, affright, alarm, appal, disgust, dismay, frighten, harrow, intimidate, outrage, petrify, scandalise, scare, shock, sicken, startle, terrify, unnerve.

antonyms delight, gratify, please.

horror *n*. abhorrence, abomination, alarm, antipathy, apprehension, aversion, awe, awfulness, consternation, detestation, disgust, dismay, dread, fear, fright, frightfulness, ghastliness, gooseflesh, goose-pimples, grimness, hatred, hideousness, horripilation, loathing, outrage, panic, repugnance, revulsion, shock, terror.

horror-struck *adj*. aghast, appalled, frightened, horrified, horror-stricken, petrified, shocked, stunned.

antonyms delighted, pleased.

horse *n*. bayard, bronc(h)o, brumby, caple, cayuse, charger, cob, crock, cuddy, destrier, dobbin, garran, gee-gee, hack, hackney, hobbler, hobby, horseflesh, hoss, jade, jennet, mare, mount, mustang, nag, pad, palfrey, pony, stallion, steed, tit, waler, war-horse, warragal.

horse sense brains, common sense, gumption, head, judgement, mother wit, native intelligence, nous, practicality, sense.

antonym stupidity.

horse-cloth *n*. caparison, horse-blanket, housing, manta, trap, trappings.

horseman *n*. broncobuster, buckaroo, cavalier, cavalryman, cowboy, dragoon, equestrian, gaucho, horse-soldier, hussar, jockey, rider.

horsemanship *n*. equestrianism, equitation, haute école, manège.

horseplay *n*. buffoonery, capers, clowning, desipience, fooling, fooling around, fun and games, high jinks, pranks, romping, rough-and-tumble, rough-housing, rough-stuff, rumpus, skylarking.

horse-trainer *n*. breaker, broncobuster, cowboy, handler, hippodamist, horse-breaker, horsetamer, trainer.

hortatory *adj*. didactic, edifying, encouraging, exhortative, exhortatory, heartening, homiletic, hortative, incitative, inspiriting, instructive, pep, practical, preceptive, stimulating.

horticulture *n*. arboriculture, cultivation, floriculture, gardening.

hospitable *adj*. accessible, amenable, amicable, approachable, bountiful, congenial, convivial, cordial, couthie, friendly, gemütlich, generous, genial, gracious, kind, liberal, liv(e)able, open-minded, receptive, responsive, sociable, tolerant, welcoming.

antonyms hostile, inhospitable.

hospital *n*. clinic, lazaret, lazaretto, leprosarium, leproserie, leprosery, sanatorium.

hospitality *n*. cheer, congeniality, conviviality, cordiality, friendliness, generosity, graciousness, open-handedness, sociability, warmth, welcome.

antonyms hostility, inhospitality.

host[1] *n*. anchor-man, announcer, compère, emcee, entertainer, innkeeper, landlord, link man, master of ceremonies, MC, presenter, proprietor, visitee.

v. compère, introduce, present.

host[2] *n*. army, array, band, company, drove, horde, legion, multitude, myriad, pack, swarm, throng.

hostel *n*. boarding-house, dormitory, doss-house, flophouse, Gasthaus, Gasthof, guesthouse, hospice, hospital, hospitium, hostelry, hotel, inn, residence, xenodochium, youth hostel.

hostile *adj*. adverse, alien, antagonistic, anti, antipathetic, bellicose, belligerent, contrary, ill-disposed, inhospitable, inimical, malevolent, opposed, opposite, oppugnant, rancorous, unfriendly, ungenial, unkind, unpropitious, unsympathetic, unwelcoming, warlike.

antonyms friendly, sympathetic.

hostilities *n*. battle, bloodshed, conflict, encounter, fighting, state of war, strife, war, warfare.

hostility *n*. abhorrence, animosity, animus, antagonism, antipathy, aversion, breach, detestation, disaffection, dislike, enmity, estrangement, hate, hatred, ill-will, malevolence, malice, opposition, resentment, unfriendliness.

antonyms friendliness, sympathy.

hot *adj*. acrid, animated, approved, ardent, biting, blistering, boiling, burning, candent, clever, close, dangerous, eager, excellent, excited, exciting, favoured, febrile, fervent, fervid, fevered, feverish, fierce, fiery, flaming, fresh, heated, hotheaded, impetuous, impulsive, in demand, in vogue, incandescent, inflamed, intense, irascible, latest, lustful, near, new, passionate, peppery, perfervid, piping, piquant, popular, pungent, quick, raging, recent, risky, roasting, scalding, scorching, searing, sensual, sharp, sizzling, skilful, sought-after, spicy, steaming, stormy, strong, sultry, sweltering, torrid, touchy, tropical, vehement, violent, voluptuous, warm, zealous.

antonyms calm, cold, mild, moderate.

hot air balderdash, blather, blether, bluster, bombast, bosh, bullshit, bunk, bunkum, cant, claptrap, emptiness, flatulence, foam, froth, gas, guff, jejuneness, nonsense, rant, vapour, verbiage, wind, words.

antonym wisdom.

hotbed *n*. breeding-ground, cradle, den, forcing-house, hive, nest, nidus, nursery, school, seedbed.

hot-blooded *adj*. ardent, bold, eager, excitable, fervent, fiery, heated, high-spirited, homothermous, impetuous, impulsive, lustful, lusty, passionate, perfervid, precipitate, rash, sensual, spirited, temperamental, warm-blooded, wild.

antonyms cool, dispassionate.

hotchpotch *n*. collection, commixture, confusion, congeries, conglomeration, farrago, gallimaufry, hash, jumble, medley, mélange, mess, miscellany, mishmash, mix, mixture, olio, olla-podrida, omnium gatherum, pot-pourri.

hotel n. auberge, boarding-house, doss-house, flophouse, Gasthaus, Gasthof, guest-house, hostelry, hydro, hydropathic, inn, motel, pension, pub, public house, tavern.

hotfoot adv. at top speed, hastily, helter-skelter, hurriedly, in haste, pell-mell, posthaste, quickly, rapidly, speedily, without delay.
antonyms dilatorily, slowly.

hothead n. daredevil, desperado, hotspur, madcap, madman, tearaway, terror.

hotheaded adj. daredevil, fiery, foolhardy, hasty, headstrong, hot-tempered, impetuous, impulsive, intemperate, madcap, over-eager, precipitate, quick-tempered, rash, reckless, unruly, volatile.
antonyms calm, cool.

hothouse n. conservatory, glasshouse, greenhouse, nursery, plant-house, vinery.

hot-tempered adj. choleric, explosive, fiery, hasty, irascible, irritable, petulant, quick-tempered, short-tempered, testy, violent, volcanic, wrathy.
antonyms calm, cool, imperturbable.

hound v. badger, chase, chivvy, drive, dun, goad, harass, harry, hunt (down), impel, importune, persecute, pester, prod, provoke, pursue.

house n. abode, ancestry, biggin, blood, building, business, clan, company, concern, domicile, dwelling, dynasty, edifice, establishment, family, family tree, firm, gens, habitation, home, homestead, hostelry, hotel, household, inn, kindred, line, lineage, lodgings, maison, maison(n)ette, ménage, organisation, outfit, parliament, partnership, pied-à-terre, public house, race, residence, roof, stem, tavern, tribe.
v. accommodate, bed, billet, board, contain, cover, domicile, domiciliate, harbour, hold, keep, lodge, place, protect, put up, quarter, sheathe, shelter, store, take in.

household n. establishment, family, family circle, home, house, ménage, set-up.
adj. common, domestic, domiciliary, established, everyday, familiar, family, home, ordinary, plain, well-known.

householder n. franklin, freeholder, goodman, head of the household, home-owner, housefather, landlord, occupant, occupier, owner, property owner, proprietor, resident, tenant.

housekeeper n. châtelaine, concièrge, gouvernante, home economist, housewife, ladyhelp.

houseman n. house-physician, house-surgeon, intern(e), resident.

house-trained adj. domesticated, house-broken, tame, tamed, well-mannered.
antonym unsocial.

housewife n. consort, hausfrau, home economist, homemaker, housekeeper, hussif, mate.

housing n. accommodation, case, casing, container, cover, covering, dwellings, enclosure, habitation, holder, homes, houses, living quarters, matrix, protection, roof, sheath, shelter.

hovel n. bothy, but-and-ben, cabin, cot, croft, cruve, den, doghole, dump, hole, hut, hutch, shack, shanty, shed.

hover v. alternate, dally, dither, drift, falter, flap, float, fluctuate, flutter, fly, hang, hang about, hesitate, impend, linger, loom, menace, oscillate, pause, poise, seesaw, threaten, vacillate, waver.

however conj. anyhow, but, even so, howbeit, in spite of that, natheless, nevertheless, nonetheless, notwithstanding, still, though, yet.

howl n. bay, bellow, clamour, cry, groan, holler, hoot, outcry, roar, scream, shriek, ululation, wail, yell, yelp, yowl.
v. bellow, cry, holler, hoot, lament, quest, roar, scream, shout, shriek, ululate, wail, waul, weep, yawl, yell, yelp.

howler n. bêtise, bloomer, blunder, boner, bull, clanger, error, gaffe, malapropism, mistake, solecism.

hub n. axis, centre, core, focal point, focus, heart, linchpin, middle, nave, nerve centre, pivot.

hubbub n. ado, agitation, babel, bedlam, brouhaha, chaos, clamour, coil, confusion, din, disorder, disturbance, hue and cry, hullabaloo, hurly-burly, kerfuffle, noise, palaver, pandemonium, racket, riot, rowdedow, rowdydow, ruckus, ruction, rumpus, tumult, turbulence, uproar, upset.
antonym calm.

huckster n. barker, chapman, dealer, haggler, hawker, packman, pedlar, pitcher, salesman, tinker, vendor.

huddle n. clump, clutch, conclave, confab, conference, confusion, crowd, discussion, disorder, heap, jumble, knot, mass, meeting, mess, muddle.
v. cluster, conglomerate, congregate, converge, crouch, crowd, cuddle, curl up, flock, gather, gravitate, hunch, nestle, press, ruck, snuggle, throng.
antonym disperse.

hue n. aspect, cast, character, colour, complexion, dye, light, nuance, shade, tincture, tinge, tint, tone.

hue and cry ado, brouhaha, chase, clamour, furore, howls, hullabaloo, humdudgeon, outcry, pursuit, ruction, rumpus, uproar.

huff n. anger, bad mood, mood, passion, pet, pique, sulks, tiff.

huffy adj. angry, crabbed, cross, crotchety, crusty, disgruntled, grumpy, hoity-toity, huffish, irritable, miffed, miffy, moody, moping, morose, offended, peevish, pettish, petulant, querulous, resentful, shirty, short, snappy, sulky, surly, testy, touchy, waspish.
antonyms cheery, happy.

hug v. cherish, clasp, cling to, cuddle, embrace, enclose, enfold, follow, grip, hold, lock,

nurse, retain, skirt, squeeze.
n. clasp, clinch, cuddle, embrace, squeeze.
huge *adj.* Babylonian, Brobdingnagian, bulky, colossal, Cyclopean, enormous, extensive, gargantuan, giant, gigantean, gigantesque, gigantic, great, gross, immense, jumbo, large, leviathan, mammoth, massive, monumental, mountainous, Patagonian, prodigious, rounceval, stupendous, swingeing, thundering, titanic, tremendous, unwieldy, vast, walloping, whacking.
antonyms dainty, tiny.
hugeness *n.* bulkiness, enormousness, extensiveness, gigantism, greatness, grossness, immensity, largeness, massiveness, overdevelopment, overgrowth, prodigiousness, size, stupendousness, tremendousness, unwieldiness, vastness.
antonyms daintiness, smallness.
hulk *n.* clod, derelict, frame, hull, lout, lubber, lump, oaf, ox, shell, shipwreck, wreck.
hulking *adj.* awkward, bulky, cloddish, clodhopping, clumsy, cumbersome, galumphing, gross, hulky, loutish, lubberly, lumbering, lumpish, massive, oafish, overgrown, ponderous, ungainly, unwieldy.
antonyms delicate, small.
hull[1] *n.* body, casing, covering, frame, framework, hulk, skeleton, structure.
hull[2] *n.* capsule, epicarp, husk, legume, peel, pod, rind, shell, shuck, skin, theca.
v. husk, pare, peel, shell, shuck, skin, strip, trim.
hullabaloo *n.* agitation, babel, bedlam, brouhaha, chaos, clamour, commotion, confusion, din, disturbance, furore, fuss, hubbub, hue and cry, hurly-burly, kerfuffle, noise, outcry, pandemonium, panic, racket, ruckus, ruction, rumpus, to-do, tumult, turmoil, uproar.
hum *v.* bombilate, bombinate, bum, bustle, buzz, croon, drone, lilt, move, mumble, murmur, pulsate, pulse, purr, sing, stir, susurrate, throb, thrum, vibrate, whirr, zoom.
n. bombilation, bombination, bustle, busyness, buzz, drone, mumble, murmur, noise, pulsation, pulse, purr, purring, singing, stir, susurration, susurrus, throb, thrum, vibration, whirr.
human *adj.* anthropoid, approachable, compassionate, considerate, fallible, fleshly, forgivable, hominoid, humane, kind, kindly, man-like, mortal, natural, reasonable, susceptible, understandable, understanding, vulnerable.
antonym inhuman.
n. body, child, creature, hominid, homo sapiens, human being, individual, living soul, man, mortal, person, soul, wight, woman.
humane *adj.* beneficent, benevolent, benign, charitable, civilising, clement, compassionate, forbearing, forgiving, gentle, good, good-natured, human, humanising, kind, kind-hearted, kindly, lenient, loving, magnanimous, merciful, mild, sympathetic, tender, understanding.

antonym inhumane.
humanise *v.* break, civilise, cultivate, domesticate, edify, educate, enlighten, improve, mellow, polish, reclaim, refine, soften, tame, temper.
antonym brutalise.
humanitarian *adj.* altruistic, beneficent, benevolent, charitable, compassionate, humane, philanthropic, philanthropical, public-spirited.
n. altruist, benefactor, do-gooder, Good Samaritan, philanthrope, philanthropist.
antonyms egoist, self-seeker.
humanitarianism *n.* beneficence, benevolence, charitableness, charity, compassionateness, do-goodery, generosity, goodwill, humanism, loving-kindness, philanthropy.
antonyms egoism, self-seeking.
humanity *n.* altruism, benevolence, benignity, brotherly love, charity, compassion, everyman, fellow-feeling, flesh, generosity, gentleness, goodwill, Homo sapiens, human nature, human race, humankind, humanness, kind-heartedness, kindness, loving-kindness, man, mandom, mankind, men, mercy, mortality, people, philanthropy, sympathy, tenderness, tolerance, understanding.
antonym inhumanity.
humble *adj.* common, commonplace, courteous, deferential, demiss, docile, homespun, humdrum, insignificant, low, low-born, lowly, mean, meek, modest, obedient, obliging, obscure, obsequious, ordinary, plebeian, polite, poor, respectful, self-effacing, servile, simple, submissive, subservient, supplicatory, unassertive, unassuming, undistinguished, unimportant, unostentatious, unpretending, unpretentious.
antonyms assertive, important, pretentious, proud.
v. abase, abash, break, bring down, bring low, chagrin, chasten, confound, crush, debase, deflate, degrade, demean, discomfit, discredit, disgrace, humiliate, lower, mortify, reduce, shame, sink, subdue, take down a peg.
antonyms exalt, raise.
humbleness *n.* abjectness, courtesy, deference, fawning, grovelling, heepishness, insignificance, lowliness, meanness, meekness, modestness, modesty, obscurity, obsequiousness, ordinariness, politeness, respectfulness, servility, simplicity, slavishness, smarminess, submissiveness, subservience, unimportance, unpretentiousness.
antonyms assertiveness, pride.
humbly *adv.* deferentially, diffidently, docilely, heepishly, meekly, modestly, obsequiously, respectfully, servilely, simply, submissively, subserviently, unassumingly, unpretentiously.
antonyms confidently, defiantly.
humbug *n.* baloney, blague, bluff, bounce, bullshit, bunk, bunkum, cant, charlatan, charlatanry, cheat, claptrap, con, con man,

deceit, deception, dodge, eyewash, faker, feint, fraud, fudge, gaff, gammon, hoax, hollowness, hype, hypocrisy, imposition, impostor, imposture, mountebank, nonsense, phoney, pretence, pseud, quack, quackery, rubbish, ruse, sham, shenanigans, swindle, swindler, trick, trickery, trickster, wile.
v. bamboozle, befool, beguile, cajole, cheat, cozen, deceive, delude, dupe, fool, gammon, gull, hoax, hoodwink, impose, mislead, swindle, trick.

humdrum *adj*. boring, commonplace, dreary, droning, dull, everyday, humble, monotonous, mundane, ordinary, prosy, repetitious, routine, tedious, tiresome, uneventful, uninteresting, unvaried, wearisome.
antonyms exceptional, unusual.

humid *adj*. clammy, damp, dank, moist, muggy, soggy, steamy, sticky, sultry, vaporous, watery, wet.
antonym dry.

humidity *n*. clamminess, damp, dampness, dankness, dew, humidness, moistness, moisture, mugginess, sogginess, steaminess, vaporosity, vaporousness, wetness.
antonym dryness.

humiliate *v*. abase, abash, bring low, chagrin, chasten, confound, crush, debase, deflate, degrade, discomfit, discredit, disgrace, embarrass, humble, mortify, shame, subdue, undignify.
antonyms boost, dignify, exalt, vindicate.

humiliating *adj*. chastening, crushing, deflating, degrading, discomfiting, disgraceful, disgracing, embarrassing, humbling, humiliant, humiliative, humiliatory, ignominious, inglorious, mortifying, shaming, snubbing.
antonyms gratifying, triumphant.

humiliation *n*. abasement, affront, chagrin, condescension, deflation, degradation, discomfiture, discrediting, disgrace, dishonour, embarrassment, humbling, ignominy, indignity, mortification, put-down, rebuff, resignation, shame, snub.
antonyms gratification, triumph.

humility *n*. deference, diffidence, humbleness, lowliness, meekness, modesty, obedience, resignation, self-abasement, servility, submissiveness, unassertiveness, unpretentiousness.
antonym pride.

hummock *n*. barrow, elevation, hillock, hump, knoll, mound, prominence.

humorist *n*. buffoon, clown, comedian, comédienne, comic, droll, eccentric, entertainer, funny man, jester, joker, parodist, satirist, wag, wisecracker, wit, zany.

humorous *adj*. absurd, amusing, comic, comical, entertaining, facetious, farcical, funny, hilarious, humoristic, jocose, jocular, laughable, ludicrous, merry, playful, pleasant, Rabelaisian, satirical, side-splitting, waggish, whimsical, wisecracking, witty, zany.
antonym humourless.

humour *n*. amusement, badinage, banter, bent, bias, caprice, choler, comedy, conceit, dis-

position, drollery, facetiousness, fancy, farce, frame of mind, fun, funniness, gags, jesting, jests, jocoseness, jocosity, jocularity, jokes, joking, ludicrousness, melancholy, mood, phlegm, pleasantries, propensity, quirk, raillery, repartee, spirits, temper, temperament, vagary, vein, whim, wisecracks, wit, witticisms, wittiness.
v. accommodate, appease, coax, comply with, cosset, favour, flatter, go along with, gratify, indulge, mollify, pamper, spoil.
antonym thwart.

humourless *adj*. austere, boring, crass, dour, dry, dull, glum, heavy-going, inflated, mirthless, morose, obtuse, self-important, tedious, thick, thick-skinned, unamused, unamusing, unfunny, unwitty.
antonyms humorous, witty.

hump *n*. bulge, bump, excrescence, hunch, knob, lump, mound, projection, prominence, protrusion, protuberance, swelling.
v. arch, carry, curve, heave, hoist, hunch, lift, lug, shoulder, yomp.

humpback *n*. crookback, gibbosity, gibbus, gobbo, hunchback, kyphosis, Quasimodo, torticollis, wry-neck.

hump-backed *adj*. crookbacked, crooked, deformed, gibbous, humped, hunchbacked, hunched, kyphotic, misshapen, stooped.
antonyms straight, upright.

humped *adj*. arched, bent, crooked, curved, gibbous, hunched.
antonyms flat, straight.

hunch *n*. feeling, guess, guesswork, idea, impression, inkling, intuition, premonition, presentiment, suspicion.
v. arch, bend, crouch, curl up, curve, draw in, huddle, hump, shrug, squat, stoop, tense.

hunger *n*. appetence, appetency, appetite, craving, desire, emptiness, esurience, esuriency, famine, greediness, hungriness, itch, lust, rapacity, ravenousness, starvation, voracity, yearning, yen, yird-hunger.
antonyms appeasement, satisfaction.
v. ache, crave, desire, hanker, itch, long, lust, pine, starve, thirst, want, wish, yearn.

hungry *adj*. aching, appetitive, athirst, avid, covetous, craving, desirous, eager, empty, esurient, famished, famishing, greedy, hollow, hungerful, keen, lean, longing, peckish, ravenous, sharp-set, starved, starving, underfed, undernourished, voracious, yearning.
antonyms replete, satisfied.

hunk *n*. block, chunk, clod, dod, dollop, gobbet, lump, mass, piece, slab, wedge, wodge.

hunt *v*. chase, chevy, course, dog, ferret, forage, gun for, hound, investigate, look for, pursue, rummage, scour, search, seek, stalk, track, trail.
n. battue, chase, chevy, hue and cry, hunting, investigation, pursuit, quest, search, venation.

hunted *adj*. angst-ridden, careworn, desperate, distraught, gaunt, haggard, hag-ridden, harassed, harried, henpecked, persecuted, stricken, terror-stricken, tormented, worn, worried. *antonym* serene.

hunting *adj.* cynegetic, venatic, venatical, venatorial.

huntsman *n.* chaser, chasseur, hunter, jaeger, jäger, montero, venator, venerer, woodman, woodsman.

hurdle *n.* barricade, barrier, complication, difficulty, fence, handicap, hedge, hindrance, impediment, jump, obstacle, obstruction, problem, snag, stumbling-block, wall.

hurl *v.* cast, catapult, chuck, dash, fire, fling, heave, launch, let fly, pitch, project, propel, send, shy, sling, throw, toss.

hurly-burly *n.* agitation, bedlam, brouhaha, bustle, chaos, commotion, confusion, disorder, distraction, frenzy, furore, hassle, hubbub, hustle, storm and stress, Sturm und Drang, tumult, turbulence, turmoil, upheaval.

hurricane *n.* baguio, cordonazo, cyclone, gale, squall, storm, tempest, tornado, twister, typhoon, whirlwind, willy-willy.

hurried *adj.* breakneck, brief, careless, cursory, hasty, headlong, hectic, passing, perfunctory, precipitate, quick, rushed, shallow, short, slapdash, speedy, superficial, swift, unthorough.
antonym leisurely.

hurry *v.* accelerate, belt, bustle, dash, dispatch, expedite, festinate, fly, get a move on, goad, hasten, hightail it, hump, hustle, jump to it, look lively, move, pike, quicken, rush, scoot, scurry, scutter, scuttle, shake a leg, shift, speed up, step on it, step on the gas, urge.
antonyms dally, delay.
n. bustle, celerity, commotion, dispatch, expedition, flurry, haste, precipitance, precipitancy, precipitation, promptitude, quickness, rush, scurry, speed, sweat, urgency.
antonyms calm, leisureliness.

hurt *v.* abuse, ache, afflict, aggrieve, annoy, bruise, burn, damage, disable, distress, grieve, harm, impair, injure, maim, maltreat, mar, pain, sadden, smart, spoil, sting, throb, tingle, torture, upset, wound.
n. abuse, bruise, damage, detriment, disadvantage, discomfort, distress, harm, injury, lesion, loss, mischief, pain, pang, scathe, sore, soreness, suffering, wound, wrong.
adj. aggrieved, annoyed, bruised, crushed, cut, damaged, displeased, grazed, harmed, huffed, injured, maimed, miffed, offended, pained, piqued, rueful, sad, saddened, scarred, scraped, scratched, wounded.

hurtful *adj.* catty, cruel, cutting, damaging, derogatory, destructive, detrimental, disadvantageous, distressing, harmful, humiliating, injurious, malefactory, malefic, maleficent, malicious, malificious, malignant, mean, mischievous, nasty, nocuous, pernicious, pestful, pestiferous, pestilent(ial), pointed, prejudicial, scathing, spiteful, unkind, upsetting, vicious, wounding.
antonyms helpful, kind.

hurtle *v.* bowl, charge, chase, crash, dash, fly, plunge, race, rattle, rush, scoot, scramble, shoot, speed, spin, spurt, tear.

husband[1] *v.* budget, conserve, economise, eke out, hoard, ration, save, save up, store, use sparingly.
antonyms squander, waste.

husband[2] *n.* Benedick, consort, goodman, hubby, man, married man, mate, old man, spouse.

husbandry *n.* agriculture, agronomics, agronomy, conservation, cultivation, economy, farming, frugality, good housekeeping, land management, management, thrift, thriftiness, tillage.
antonym wastefulness.

hush *v.* calm, compose, mollify, mute, muzzle, quieten, settle, shush, silence, soothe, still.
antonyms disturb, rouse.
n. calm, calmness, peace, peacefulness, quiet, quietness, repose, serenity, silence, still, stillness, tranquillity.
antonyms clamour, uproar.
interj. belt up, euphemeite, favete linguis, hold your tongue, leave it out, not another word, pipe down, quiet, say no more, shush, shut up, ssh, stow it, unberufen, wheesht, whisht.

hush up conceal, cover up, gag, keep dark, muzzle, smother, soft-pedal, squash, stifle, suppress.
antonym publicise.

hush-hush *adj.* classified, confidential, hushy, restricted, secret, top-secret, under wraps, unpublished.
antonyms open, public.

husk *n.* bark, bract, bran, case, chaff, covering, glume, hull, pod, rind, shell, shuck, tegmen.

huskiness *n.* croakiness, dryness, gruffness, gutturalness, harshness, hoarseness, roughness, throatiness.
antonym clarity.

husky[1] *adj.* croaking, croaky, gruff, guttural, harsh, hoarse, low, rasping, raucous, rough, roupy, throaty.

husky[2] *adj.* beefy, brawny, burly, hefty, muscular, powerful, rugged, stocky, strapping, strong, sturdy, thickset, tough.

hussy *n.* baggage, broad, floozy, jade, minx, piece, scrubber, slut, strumpet, tart, temptress, tramp, trollop, vamp, wanton, wench.

hustle *v.* bustle, crowd, elbow, force, frogmarch, haste, hasten, hurry, impel, jog, jostle, pressgang, pressure, push, rush, shove, thrust.

hut *n.* booth, bothan, bothy, cabin, caboose, crib, den, hogan, hovel, kraal, lean-to, shack, shanty, shebang, shed, shelter, shiel, shieling, tilt.

hybrid *n.* amalgam, combination, composite, compound, conglomerate, cross, crossbreed, half-blood, half-breed, heterogeny, mixture, mongrel, mule, pastiche.
adj. bastard, combined, composite, compound, cross, heterogeneous, hybridous,

hyphenated, mixed, mongrel, mule, patchwork.
antonyms pure, pure-bred.
hybridity *n.* bastardisation, compositeness, cross-breeding, crossing, heterogeneity, hybridism, interbreeding, pastiche.
antonym purity.
hygiene *n.* asepsis, cleanliness, disinfection, hygienics, purity, salubriousness, salubrity, salutariness, sanitariness, sanitation, sterility, wholesomeness.
antonyms filth, insanitariness.
hygienic *adj.* aseptic, clean, cleanly, disinfected, germ-free, healthy, pure, salubrious, salutary, sanitary, sterile, wholesome.
antonym unhygenic.
hymn *n.* anthem, cantata, canticle, canticum, carol, chant, choral(e), dithyramb, doxology, introit, mantra(m), motet, offertory, paean, paraphrase, psalm, song of praise.
hype *n.* advertisement, advertising, ballyhoo, build-up, deception, fuss, kidology, plugging, publicity, puffing, racket, razzmatazz.
hyperbole *n.* enlargement, exaggeration, excess, extravagance, magnification, overkill, overplay, overstatement.
antonyms meiosis, understatement.
hypercritical *adj.* captious, carping, cavilling, censorious, exceptious, fault-finding, finicky, fussy, hair-splitting, niggling, nit-picking, over-particular, pedantic, pernickety, quibbling, strict, ultracrepidarian, Zoilean.
antonyms tolerant, uncritical.
hypnotic *adj.* compelling, dazzling, fascinating, irresistible, magnetic, mesmeric, mesmerising, narcotic, opiate, sleep-inducing, somniferous, soothing, soporific, spellbinding.
hypnotise *v.* bewitch, captivate, dazzle, entrance, fascinate, magnetise, mesmerise, spellbind, stupefy.
hypnotism *n.* animal magnetism, hypnosis, hypnotherapy, mesmerism, suggestion.
hypochondria *n.* hypochondrianism, hypochondriasis, neurosis, valetudinarianism.
hypochondriac *n.* hypochondriast, valetudinarian.

adj. hypochondriacal, neurotic, valetudinarian.
hypocrisy *n.* cant, deceit, deceitfulness, deception, dissembling, double-talk, duplicity, falsity, imposture, insincerity, lip-service, pharisaicalness, pharisaism, phariseeism, phoneyness, pietism, pretence, quackery, sanctimoniousness, self-righteousness, speciousness, Tartuffism, two-facedness.
antonyms humility, sincerity.
hypocrite *n.* canter, charlatan, deceiver, dissembler, fraud, Holy Willie, impostor, mountebank, Pharisee, phon(e)y, pretender, pseud, pseudo, Tartuffe, whited sepulchre.
hypocritical *adj.* canting, deceitful, deceptive, dissembling, double-faced, duplicitous, false, fraudulent, hollow, insincere, Pecksniffian, pharisaic(al), phoney, pietistic, sanctimonious, self-pious, self-righteous, specious, spurious, Tartuffian, Tartuffish, two-faced.
antonyms genuine, humble, sincere.
hypothesis *n.* assumption, conjecture, guess, postulate, postulatum, premise, premiss, presumption, proposition, starting-point, supposition, theory, thesis.
hypothetical *adj.* academic, assumed, conjectural, imaginary, postulated, proposed, putative, speculative, supposed, suppositional, theoretical.
antonyms actual, real.
hysteria *n.* agitation, frenzy, hysterics, hysteromania, instability, madness, neurosis, panic, psychoneurosis, unreason.
antonyms calm, composure, reason.
hysterical *adj.* berserk, comical, crazed, distracted, distraught, falling about, farcical, frantic, frenzied, hairless, hilarious, mad, neurotic, overwrought, priceless, psychoneurotic, psychosomatic, raving, side-splitting, uncontrollable, uproarious.
antonyms calm, composed.
hysterics *n.* drama, dramatics, emotionalism, emotionality, histrionics, melodrama, (screaming) habdabs.

I

ice *n.* chill, chilliness, coldness, distance, formality, frazil, frigidity, frost, frostiness, ice-cream, iciness, icing, reserve, rime, stiffness, verglas.
v. freeze, frost, glaciate, glaze.

ice-cold *adj.* algid, arctic, biting, bitter, chilled to the bone, freezing, frigid, frozen, frozen to the marrow, gelid, glacial, icy, icy cold, raw, refrigerated.

iced *adj.* frappé(e), frosted, glazed.

icon *n.* figure, idol, ikon, image, portrait, portrayal, representation, symbol.

iconoclasm *n.* criticism, demythologisation, denunciation, disabusing, dissent, dissidence, heresy, irreverence, opposition, questioning, radicalism, scepticism, subversion, unbelief, undeceiving.
antonyms credulity, trustfulness.

iconoclast *n.* critic, denouncer, denunciator, dissenter, dissident, heretic, idoloclast, image-breaker, opponent, questioner, radical, rebel, sceptic, unbeliever.
antonyms believer, devotee.

iconoclastic *adj.* critical, denunciatory, dissentient, dissident, heretical, impious, innovative, irreverent, questioning, radical, rebellious, sceptical, subversive.
antonyms trustful, uncritical, unquestioning.

icy *adj.* algid, aloof, arctic, biting, bitter, chill, chilling, chilly, cold, distant, forbidding, formal, freezing, frigid, frore, frost-bound, frosty, frozen over, gelid, glacial, glassy, hoar, hostile, ice-cold, indifferent, raw, reserved, rimy, slippery, slippy, steely, stiff, stony, unfriendly.

idea *n.* abstraction, aim, approximation, archetype, belief, clue, conceit, concept, conception, conceptualisation, conclusion, conjecture, construct, conviction, design, doctrine, end, essence, estimate, fancy, form, guess, guesstimate, hint, hypothesis, idée fixe, image, import, impression, inkling, intention, interpretation, intimation, judgement, meaning, monomania, notion, object, opinion, pattern, perception, plan, purpose, reason, recept, recommendation, scheme, sense, significance, solution, suggestion, surmise, suspicion, teaching, theory, thought, type, understanding, view, viewpoint, vision.

ideal *n.* archetype, criterion, dreamboat, epitome, example, exemplar, image, last word, model, ne plus ultra, nonpareil, paradigm, paragon, pattern, perfection, pink of perfection, principle, prototype, standard, type.
adj. abstract, archetypal, best, classic, complete, conceptual, consummate, fanciful, highest, hypothetical, imaginary, impractical, model, optimal, optimum, perfect, quintessential, supreme, theoretical, transcendent, transcendental, unattainable, unreal, Utopian, visionary.

idealisation *n.* apotheosis, ennoblement, exaltation, glorification, romanticisation, romanticising, worship.

idealise *v.* apotheosise, deify, ennoble, exalt, glorify, romanticise, utopianise, worship.
antonyms caricature, travesty.

idealism *n.* impracticality, perfectionism, romanticism, utopianism, utopism.
antonyms pragmatism, realism.

idealist *n.* dreamer, perfectionist, romantic, romanticist, utopian, utopianiser, utopiast, utopist, visionary.
antonyms pragmatist, realist.

idealistic *adj.* impracticable, impractical, optimistic, perfectionist, quixotic, romantic, starry-eyed, unrealistic, utopian, visionary.
antonyms pragmatic, realistic.

idée fixe complex, fixation, fixed idea, hang-up, leitmotiv, monomania, obsession.

identical *adj.* alike, clonal, coincident, corresponding, duplicate, equal, equivalent, identic, indistinguishable, interchangeable, like, matching, monozygotic, same, self-same, synonymous, twin.
antonym different.

identifiable *adj.* ascertainable, detectable, discernible, distinguishable, known, noticeable, perceptible, recognisable, unmistakable.
antonyms indefinable, unfamiliar, unidentifiable, unknown.

identification *n.* association, cataloguing, classifying, connection, credentials, detection, diagnosis, documents, empathy, fellow-feeling, ID, involvement, labelling, naming, papers, pinpointing, rapport, recognition, relating, relationship, sympathy.

identify *v.* catalogue, classify, detect, diagnose, distinguish, finger, know, label, make out, name, pick out, pinpoint, place, recognise, single out, specify, spot, tag.
identify with ally with, associate with, connect with, empathise with, equate with, feel for, relate to, respond to.

identity *n.* accord, coincidence, correspondence, empathy, existence, haecceity, individuality, oneness, particularity, personality, quiddity, rapport, sameness, self, selfhood, singularity, unanimity, uniqueness, unity.

ideologist *n.* ideologue, theorist, thinker, visionary.

ideology *n.* belief(s), convictions, creed, doctrine(s), dogma, ethic, faith, ideas, metaphysics, philosophy, principles, speculation, tenets, Weltanschauung, world view.

idiocy *n.* amentia, asininity, cretinism, dementia, fatuity, fatuousness, folly, foolishness, imbecility, inanity, insanity, irrationality, lunacy, mental deficiency, senselessness, silliness, stupidity, tomfoolery.
antonyms sanity, wisdom.

idiom *n.* colloquialism, expression, idiolect, idiotism, jargon, language, locution, parlance, phrase, regionalism, set phrase, style, talk, turn of phrase, usage, vernacular.

idiomatic *adj.* colloquial, correct, dialectal, dialectical, grammatical, idiolectal, idiolectic, native, vernacular.
antonym unidiomatic.

idiosyncrasy *n.* characteristic, eccentricity, feature, freak, habit, kink, mannerism, oddity, oddness, peculiarity, quirk, singularity, trait.

idiosyncratic *adj.* characteristic, distinctive, eccentric, individual, individualistic, inimitable, odd, peculiar, quirky, typical.
antonyms common, general.

idiot *n.* ament, ass, blockhead, booby, cretin, cuckoo, dimwit, dolt, dumbbell, dummy, dunderhead, fat-head, featherbrain, fool, golem, half-wit, imbecile, mental defective, mooncalf, moron, natural, nidget, nig-nog, nincompoop, nitwit, nong, noodle, omadhaun, saphead, schlep, schmo, schmuck, simpleton, thick, thickhead.

idiotic *adj.* asinine, crazy, cretinous, daft, dumb, fat-headed, fatuous, foolhardy, foolish, hairbrained, half-witted, harebrained, idiotical, imbecile, imbecilic, inane, insane, loony, lunatic, moronic, nutty, screwy, senseless, simple, stupid, tomfool, unintelligent.
antonyms sane, sensible.

idle *adj.* abortive, bootless, dead, dormant, dronish, empty, foolish, frivolous, fruitless, futile, good-for-nothing, groundless, inactive, indolent, ineffective, ineffectual, inoperative, jobless, lackadaisical, lazy, mothballed, nugatory, of no avail, otiose, pointless, purposeless, redundant, shiftless, slothful, sluggish, stationary, superficial, torpid, trivial, unavailing, unbusy, unemployed, unproductive, unsuccessful, unused, useless, vain, work-shy, worthless.
antonyms active, effective, purposeful.
v. coast, dally, dawdle, drift, fool, fritter, kill time, lallygag, laze, lie up, loiter, lounge, potter, rest on one's laurels, shirk, skive, slack, take it easy, tick over, vegetate, waste, while.
antonyms act, work.

idleness *n.* dolce far niente, ease, flânerie, idlesse, inaction, inactivity, indolence, inertia, inoccupation, laziness, lazing, leisure, loafing, pottering, shiftlessness, skiving, sloth, slothfulness, sluggishness, torpor, unemployment, vegetating.
antonyms activity, employment.

idler *n.* clock-watcher, dawdler, dodger, do-naught, donnat, donnot, do-nothing, do-nought, drone, fainéant, flâneur, good-for-nothing, laggard, layabout, lazybones, loafer, lotus-eater, lounger, malingerer, shirker, skiver, slacker, sloth, slouch, sluggard, waster, wastrel.

idling *adj.* dawdling, drifting, loafing, pottering, resting, resting on one's oars, shirking, skiving, taking it easy, ticking over.

idol *n.* beloved, darling, deity, favourite, fetish, god, graven image, hero, icon, image, joss, ju-ju, mammet, Mumbo-jumbo, pet, pin-up, superstar.

idolater *n.* admirer, adorer, devotee, iconolater, idolatress, idolist, idol-worshipper, votary, worshipper.

idolatrous *adj.* adoring, adulatory, idolising, idol-worshipping, reverential, uncritical, worshipful.

idolatry *n.* adoration, adulation, deification, exaltation, glorification, hero-worship, iconolatry, idolising, idolism, mammetry, whoredom.
antonym vilification.

idolise *v.* admire, adore, apotheosise, deify, dote on, exalt, glorify, hero-worship, iconise, lionise, love, revere, reverence, venerate, worship.
antonym vilify.

idyllic *adj.* arcadian, charming, delightful, halcyon, happy, heavenly, idealised, innocent, pastoral, peaceful, picturesque, rustic, unspoiled.
antonym disagreeable.

ignite *v.* burn, catch fire, combust, conflagrate, fire, flare up, inflame, kindle, light, set alight, set fire to, spark off, touch off.
antonym quench.

ignoble *adj.* abject, base, base-born, caddish, common, contemptible, cowardly, craven, dastardly, degenerate, degraded, despicable, disgraceful, dishonourable, heinous, humble, infamous, low, low-born, lowly, mean, petty, plebeian, shabby, shameless, unworthy, vile, vulgar, worthless, wretched.
antonyms honourable, noble.

ignominious *adj.* abject, crushing, degrading, despicable, discreditable, disgraceful, dishonourable, disreputable, humiliating, indecorous, inglorious, mortifying, scandalous, shameful, sorry, undignified.
antonyms honourable, triumphant.

ignominy *n.* contempt, degradation, discredit, disgrace, dishonour, disrepute, humiliation, indignity, infamy, mortification, obloquy, odium, opprobrium, reproach, scandal, shame, stigma.
antonyms credit, honour.

ignoramus *n.* ass, blockhead, bonehead, booby, dolt, donkey, duffer, dullard, dunce, fool, ignaro, illiterate, know-nothing, lowbrow, num(b)skull, simpleton.
antonyms high-brow, intellectual, scholar.

ignorance *n.* benightedness, blindness, crassness, denseness, greenness, illiteracy, illiter-

ateness, inexperience, innocence, naïvety, nescience, oblivion, unawareness, unconsciousness, unfamiliarity.
antonyms knowledge, wisdom.

ignorant *adj.* as thick as two short planks, benighted, blind, bookless, clueless, crass, dense, green, gross, half-baked, idealess, ill-informed, illiterate, ill-versed, inexperienced, innocent, innumerate, insensitive, know-nothing, naïve, nescient, oblivious, pig-ignorant, stupid, thick, unacquainted, unaware, unconscious, uncultivated, uneducated, unenlightened, unidea'd, uninformed, uninitiated, uninstructed, unknowing, unlearned, unlettered, unread, unscholarly, unschooled, untaught, untrained, untutored, unwitting.
antonyms knowlegeable, wise.

ignore *v.* blink, cold-shoulder, cut, disregard, neglect, omit, overlook, pass over, pay no attention to, pidgeon-hole, reject, send to Coventry, set aside, shut one's eyes to, slight, take no notice of, turn a blind eye to, turn a deaf ear to, turn one's back on.
antonym note.

ilk *n.* brand, breed, cast cut, character, class, description, kidney, kind, make, sort, stamp, style, type, variety.

ill¹ *adj.* ailing, dicky, diseased, frail, funny, indisposed, infirm, laid up, not up to snuff, off-colour, on the sick list, out of sorts, peelie-wally, poorly, queasy, queer, seedy, sick, under the weather, unhealthy, unwell, valetudinarian.
antonym well.
n. affliction, ailment, complaint, disease, disorder, illness, indisposition, infection, infirmity, malady, malaise, sickness.

ill² *adj.* acrimonious, adverse, antagonistic, bad, cantankerous, cross, damaging, deleterious, detrimental, difficult, disturbing, evil, foul, harmful, harsh, hateful, hostile, hurtful, inauspicious, incorrect, inimical, iniquitous, injurious, malevolent, malicious, ominous, reprehensible, ruinous, sinister, sullen, surly, threatening, unfavourable, unfortunate, unfriendly, unhealthy, unkind, unlucky, unpromising, unpropitious, unwholesome, vile, wicked, wrong.
antonyms beneficial, fortunate, good, kind.
n. abuse, affliction, badness, cruelty, damage, depravity, destruction, evil, harm, hurt, ill-usage, injury, malice, mischief, misery, misfortune, pain, sorrow, suffering, trial, tribulation, trouble, unpleasantness, wickedness, woe.
antonym benefit.
adv. amiss, badly, by no means, hard, hardly, inauspiciously, insufficiently, poorly, scantily, scarcely, unfavourably, unluckily, wrongfully.
antonym well.

ill at ease anxious, awkward, disquieted, disturbed, edgy, embarrassed, fidgety, hesitant, like a cat on hot bricks, nervous, on edge, on tenterhooks, restless, self-conscious,

strange, tense, uncomfortable, uneasy, unrelaxed, unsettled, unsure, worried.
antonym at ease.

ill-advised *adj.* daft, foolhardy, foolish, hasty, hazardous, ill-considered, ill-judged, impolitic, imprudent, inappropriate, incautious, indiscreet, injudicious, misguided, overhasty, rash, reckless, short-sighted, thoughtless, unseemly, unwise, wrong-headed.
antonym sensible.

ill-assorted *adj.* discordant, incompatible, incongruous, inharmonious, misallied, mismatched, uncongenial, unsuited.
antonym harmonious.

ill-bred *adj.* bad-mannered, boorish, churlish, coarse, crass, crude, discourteous, ill-mannered, impolite, indelicate, non-U, rude, uncivil, uncivilised, uncouth, ungallant, ungentlemanly, ungracious, unladylike, unmannerly, unrefined, vulgar.
antonym urbane.

ill-considered *adj.* careless, follish, hasty, heedless, ill-advised, ill-judged, improvident, imprudent, injudicious, overhasty, precipitate, rash, unwise.
antonym sensible.

ill-defined *adj.* blurred, blurry, dim, fuzzy, hazy, imprecise, indefinite, indistinct, nebulous, shadowy, unclear, vague, woolly.
antonym clear.

ill-disposed *adj.* against, antagonistic, anti, antipathetic, averse, hostile, inimical, opposed, unco-operative, unfriendly, unsympathetic, unwelcoming.
antonym well-disposed.

illegal *adj.* actionable, banned, black-market, contraband, criminal, felonious, forbidden, illicit, outlawed, pirate, prohibited, proscribed, unauthorised, unconstitutional, under-the-counter, unlawful, unlicensed, wrongful, wrongous.
antonym legal.

illegality *n.* crime, criminality, felony, illegitimacy, illicitness, lawlessness, unconstitutionality, unlawfulness, wrong, wrongfulness, wrongness.
antonym legality.

illegible *adj.* crabbed, faint, hieroglyphic, indecipherable, indistinct, obscure, scrawled, undecipherable, unreadable.
antonym legible.

illegitimacy *n.* bar-sinister, bastardism, bastardy, baton-sinister, illegality, illicitness, irregularity, unconstitutionality, unlawfulness.
antonym legitimacy.

illegitimate *adj.* bastard, born on the wrong side of the blanket, born out of wedlock, fatherless, illegal, illicit, illogical, improper, incorrect, invalid, misbegotten, natural, spurious, unauthorised, unconstitutional, unfathered, unjustifiable, unjustified, unlawful, unsanctioned, unsound, unwarrantable, unwarranted.
antonym legitimate.

ill-fated *adj.* blighted, doomed, forlorn, hapless,

ill-omened, ill-starred, infaust, luckless, star-crossed, unfortunate, unhappy, unlucky.
antonym unlucky.

ill-favoured *adj.* hideous, homely, plain, repulsive, ugly, unattractive, unlovely, unprepossessing, unsightly.
antonym beautiful.

ill-feeling *n.* animosity, animus, antagonism, bad blood, bitterness, disgruntlement, dissatisfaction, dudgeon, enmity, frustration, grudge, hard-feelings, hostility, ill-will, odium, offence, rancour, resentment, sourness, spite.
antonyms friendship, goodwill.

ill-humour *n.* acrimony, choler, crabbiness, crassness, disagreeableness, dishumour, distemper, grumpiness, irascibility, moroseness, petulance, spleen, sulkiness, the dods.
antonym amiability.

ill-humoured *adj.* acrimonious, bad-tempered, cantankerous, crabbed, crabby, cross, cross-grained, disagreeable, grumpy, huffy, impatient, irascible, irritable, moody, morose, peevish, petulant, sharp, snappish, snappy, sulky, sullen, tart, testy, waspish.
antonym amiable.

illiberal *adj.* bigoted, close-fisted, hidebound, intolerant, mean, miserly, narrow-minded, niggardly, parsimonious, petty, prejudiced, reactionary, small-minded, sordid, stingy, tight, tightfisted, uncharitable, ungenerous, verkrampte.
antonym liberal.

illiberality *n.* bigotry, intolerance, meanness, miserliness, narrow-mindedness, narrowness, niggardliness, parsimony, pettiness, prejudice, small-mindedness, stinginess.
antonym liberality.

illicit *adj.* black, black-market, bootleg, clandestine, contraband, criminal, felonious, forbidden, furtive, guilty, illegal, illegitimate, ill-gotten, immoral, improper, inadmissible, prohibited, unauthorised, unlawful, unlicensed, unsanctioned, wrong.
antonyms legal, licit.

illiterate *adj.* analphabetic, benighted, ignorant, uncultured, uneducated, unlettered, untaught, untutored.
antonym literate.

ill-judged *adj.* daft, foolhardy, foolish, hasty, ill-advised, ill-considered, impolitic, imprudent, incautious, indiscreet, injudicious, misguided, overhasty, rash, reckless, short-sighted, unwise, wrong-headed.
antonym sensible.

ill-mannered *adj.* badly-behaved, boorish, churlish, coarse, crude, discourteous, ill-behaved, ill-bred, impolite, insensitive, insolent, loutish, rude, uncivil, uncouth, ungallant, unmannerly.
antonym polite.

ill-natured *adj.* bad-tempered, churlish, crabbed, cross, cross-grained, disagreeable, disobliging, malevolent, malicious, malignant, mean, nasty, perverse, petulant, spiteful, sulky, sullen, surly, unfriendly, unkind,

unpleasant, vicious, vindictive.
antonym good-natured.

illness *n.* affliction, ailment, attack, complaint, disability, disease, disorder, distemper, dyscrasia, idiopathy, ill-being, ill-health, indisposition, infirmity, malady, malaise, sickness.
antonym health.

illogical *adj.* absurd, fallacious, faulty, Fifish, illegitimate, inconclusive, inconsistent, incorrect, invalid, Irish, irrational, meaningless, senseless, sophistical, specious, spurious, unreasonable, unscientific, unsound.
antonym logical.

illogicality *n.* absurdity, fallaciousness, fallacy, inconsistency, invalidity, Irishness, irrationality, senselessness, speciousness, unreason, unsoundness.
antonym logicality.

ill-omened *adj.* doomed, ill-fated, inauspicious, infaust, star-crossed, unfortunate, unhappy, unlucky.
antonym fortunate.

ill-tempered *adj.* bad-tempered, choleric, cross, curt, grumpy, ill-humoured, ill-natured, impatient, irascible, irritable, sharp, spiteful, testy, tetchy, touchy, vicious, vixenish, vixenly.
antonym good-tempered.

ill-timed *adj.* awkward, crass, inappropriate, inconvenient, inept, inopportune, tactless, unseasonable, untimely, unwelcome, wrong-timed.
antonym well-timed.

ill-treat *v.* abuse, damage, harass, harm, harry, ill-use, injure, maltreat, manhandle, mishandle, mistreat, misuse, neglect, oppress, wrong.
antonym care for.

ill-treatment *n.* abuse, damage, harm, ill-use, injury, maltreatment, manhandling, mishandling, mistreatment, misuse, neglect.
antonym care.

illuminate *v.* adorn, beacon, brighten, clarify, clear up, decorate, edify, elucidate, enlighten, explain, illumine, illustrate, instruct, irradiate, light, light up, limn, miniate, ornament.
antonyms darken, deface, divest.

illuminating *adj.* edifying, enlightening, explanatory, helpful, informative, instructive, revealing, revelatory.
antonym unhelpful.

illumination *n.* adornment, awareness, beam, brightening, brightness, clarification, decoration, edification, enlightenment, insight, inspiration, instruction, light, lighting, lights, limning, miniation, ornamentation, perception, radiance, ray, revelation, splendour, understanding.
antonym darkness.

illusion *n.* apparition, chimera, daydream, deception, delusion, error, fallacy, fancy, fantasy, figment, hallucination, ignis fatuus, maya, mirage, misapprehension, misconception, phantasm, semblance, will-o'-the-wisp.
antonym reality.

illusory *adj.* apparent, Barmecidal, beguiling,

chimerical, deceitful, deceptive, deluding, delusive, fallacious, false, hallucinatory, illusive, misleading, mistaken, seeming, sham, unreal, unsubstantial, untrue, vain.
antonym real.

illustrate *v.* adorn, clarify, decorate, demonstrate, depict, draw, elucidate, emphasise, exemplify, exhibit, explain, illuminate, instance, interpret, miniate, ornament, picture, show, sketch.

illustrated *adj.* decorated, embellished, illuminated, miniated, pictorial.

illustration *n.* adornment, analogy, case, case in point, clarification, decoration, delineation, demonstration, drawing, elucidation, example, exemplification, explanation, figure, graphic, half-tone, instance, interpretation, photograph, picture, plate, representation, sketch, specimen.

illustrative *adj.* delineative, descriptive, diagrammatic, explanatory, explicatory, expository, graphic, illustrational, illustratory, interpretive, pictorial, representative, sample, specimen, typical.

illustrious *adj.* brilliant, celebrated, distinguished, eminent, exalted, excellent, famed, famous, glorious, great, magnificent, noble, notable, noted, outstanding, prominent, remarkable, renowned, resplendent, signal, splendid.
antonyms inglorious, shameful.

ill-will *n.* acrimony, animosity, animus, antagonism, antipathy, aversion, bad blood, dislike, enmity, envy, grudge, hard feelings, hatred, hostility, malevolence, malice, odium, rancour, resentment, spite, unfriendliness, venom.
antonyms friendship, good-will.

image *n.* appearance, conceit, concept, conception, counterpart, dead ringer, Doppelgänger, double, effigies, effigy, eidolon, eikon, facsimile, figure, icon, idea, idol, impression, likeness, perception, picture, portrait, reflection, replica, representation, semblance, similitude, simulacrum, spit, spitting image, statue, trope.

imaginable *adj.* believable, comprehensible, conceivable, credible, likely, plausible, possible, predictable, supposable, thinkable, visualisable.
antonym unimaginable.

imaginary *adj.* assumed, Barmecidal, chimerical, dreamlike, fancied, fanciful, fictional, fictitious, hallucinatory, hypothetical, ideal, illusive, illusory, imagined, insubstantial, invented, legendary, made-up, mythological, non-existent, phantasmal, shadowy, supposed, unreal, unsubstantial, visionary.
antonym real.

imagination *n.* chimera, conception, creativity, enterprise, fancy, idea, ideality, illusion, image, imaginativeness, ingenuity, innovativeness, innovatoriness, insight, inspiration, invention, inventiveness, notion, originality, resourcefulness, supposition, unreality,

vision, wit, wittiness.
antonyms reality, unimaginativeness.

imaginative *adj.* clever, creative, dreamy, enterprising, fanciful, fantastic, fertile, ingenious, innovative, inspired, inventive, original, poetical, resourceful, visionary, vivid.
antonym unimaginative.

imagine *v.* apprehend, assume, believe, conceive, conceptualise, conjecture, conjure up, create, deduce, deem, devise, dream up, envisage, envision, fancy, fantasise, frame, gather, guess, ideate, infer, invent, judge, picture, plan, project, realise, scheme, suppose, surmise, suspect, take it, think, think of, think up, visualise.

imbalance *n.* bias, disparity, disproportion, imparity, inequality, lopsidedness, partiality, top-heaviness, unequalness, unevenness, unfairness.
antonym parity.

imbecile *n.* ament, blockhead, bungler, clown, cretin, dolt, dotard, fool, half-wit, idiot, moron, thickhead.
adj. anile, asinine, doltish, fatuous, feeble-minded, foolish, idiotic, imbecilic, inane, ludicrous, moronic, senile, simple, stupid, thick, witless.
antonyms intelligent, sensible.

imbecility *n.* amentia, anility, asininity, childishness, cretinism, fatuity, foolishness, idiocy, inanity, incompetency, senility, stupidity.
antonyms intelligence, sense.

imbibe *v.* absorb, acquire, assimilate, consume, drink, drink in, gain, gather, gulp, ingest, knock back, lap up, quaff, receive, sink, sip, soak in, soak up, swallow, swig, take in.

imbroglio, embroglio *n.* confusion, difficulty, dilemma, embroilment, entanglement, involvement, mess, muddle, quandary, scrape, tangle.

imbue *v.* bathe, colour, dye, fill, impregnate, inculcate, infuse, ingrain, instil, moisten, permeate, pervade, saturate, stain, steep, suffuse, tinge, tint.

imitate *v.* affect, ape, burlesque, caricature, clone, copy, copy-cat, counterfeit, do, duplicate, echo, emulate, follow, follow suit, forge, impersonate, mimic, mirror, mock, monkey, parody, parrot, personate, repeat, reproduce, send up, simulate, spoof, take off, travesty.

imitation *n.* apery, aping, copy, counterfeit, counterfeiting, duplication, echoing, echopraxia, echopraxis, fake, forgery, impersonation, impression, likeness, mimesis, mimicry, mockery, parody, reflection, replica, reproduction, resemblance, sham, simulation, substitution, take-off, travesty.
adj. artificial, dummy, ersatz, man-made, mock, phoney, pinchbeck, pseudo, repro, reproduction, sham, simulated, synthetic.
antonym genuine.

imitative *adj.* apish, copied, copycat, copying, derivative, echoic, mimetic, mimicking, mock, onomatopoeic, parodistic, parrot-like, plagiarised, pseudo, put-on, second-hand, simulated, unoriginal.

imitator *n.* ape, aper, copier, copy-cat, echo, epigone, follower, impersonator, impressionist, mimic, parodist, parrot.

immaculate *adj.* blameless, clean, faultless, flawless, guiltless, impeccable, incorrupt, innocent, neat, perfect, pure, scrupulous, sinless, spick-and-span, spotless, spruce, stainless, trim, unblemished, uncontaminated, undefiled, unexceptionable, unpolluted, unsullied, untainted, untarnished, virtuous.
antonyms contaminated, spoiled.

immaterial *adj.* airy, disembodied, ethereal, extraneous, ghostly, impertinent, inapposite, inconsequential, inconsiderable, incorporeal, inessential, insignificant, insubstantial, irrelevant, metaphysical, minor, spiritual, trifling, trivial, unimportant, unnecessary, unsubstantial.
antonyms important, material, solid.

immature *adj.* adolescent, babyish, callow, childish, crude, green, immatured, imperfect, inexperienced, infantile, jejune, juvenile, premature, puerile, raw, under-age, undeveloped, unfinished, unfledged, unformed, unripe, unseasonable, untimely, young.
antonym mature.

immaturity *n.* babyishness, callowness, childishness, crudeness, crudity, greenness, immatureness, imperfection, inexperience, juvenility, prematureness, prematurity, puerility, rawness, unpreparedness, unripeness.
antonym maturity.

immeasurable *adj.* bottomless, boundless, endless, illimitable, immense, immensurable, incalculable, inestimable, inexhaustible, infinite, limitless, measureless, unbounded, unfathomable, unlimited, unmeasureable, vast.
antonym limited.

immediacy *n.* directness, imminence, instancy, instantaneity, promptness, simultaneity, spontaneity, swiftness.
antonym remoteness.

immediate *adj.* actual, adjacent, close, contiguous, current, direct, existing, extant, instant, instantaneous, near, nearest, neighbouring, next, on hand, present, pressing, primary, prompt, proximate, recent, unhesitating, up-to-date, urgent.
antonym distant.

immediately *adv.* at once, closely, directly, ek dum, forthwith, incontinent, instantly, lickety-split, nearly, now, off the top of one's head, on the instant, posthaste, promptly, pronto, right away, straight away, straight off, straight way, tout de suite, unhesitatingly, without delay.
antonyms eventually, never.

immemorial *adj.* age-old, ancestral, ancient, archaic, fixed, hoary, long-standing, time-honoured, traditional.
antonym recent.

immense *adj.* Brobdingnag(ian), colossal, cyclopean, elephantine, enormous, extensive, giant, gigantic, great, herculean, huge, illimitable, immeasurable, infinite, interminable, jumbo, large, limitless, mammoth, massive, monstrous, monumental, prodigious, rounceval, stupendous, Titanesque, titanic, tremendous, vast.
antonym minute.

immensity *n.* bulk, enormousness, expanse, extent, greatness, hugeness, infinity, magnitude, massiveness, scope, size, sweep, vastness.
antonym minuteness.

immerse *v.* bathe, demerge, demerse, dip, douse, duck, dunk, plunge, sink, submerge, submerse.

immersed *adj.* absorbed, buried, busy, consumed, deep, engrossed, involved, occupied, preoccupied, rapt, sunk, taken up, wrapped up.

immersion *n.* absorption, baptism, bathe, concentration, demersion, dip, dipping, dousing, ducking, dunking, involvement, plunging, preoccupation, submersion.

immigrant *n.* incomer, newcomer, settler, wetback.
antonym emigrant.

immigrate *v.* come in, migrate, move in, remove, resettle, settle.
antonym emigrate.

imminence *n.* approach, immediacy, impendency, instancy, menace, propinquity, threat.
antonym remoteness.

imminent *adj.* afoot, approaching, at hand, brewing, close, coming, forthcoming, gathering, impending, in the air, in the offing, looming, menacing, near, nigh, overhanging, threatening.
antonym far-off.

immobile *adj.* at a standstill, at rest, cataplectic, expressionless, fixed, frozen, immobilised, immotile, immovable, motionless, rigid, riveted, rooted, solid, stable, static, stationary, stiff, still, stock-still, stolid, unexpressive, unmoving.
antonyms mobile, moving.

immobilise *v.* cripple, disable, fix, freeze, halt, paralyse, stop, transfix.
antonym mobilise.

immobility *n.* disability, firmness, fixedness, fixity, immovability, inertness, motionlessness, stability, steadiness, stillness.
antonym mobility.

immoderate *adj.* distemperate, egregious, enormous, exaggerated, excessive, exorbitant, extravagant, extreme, hubristic, inordinate, intemperate, over the top, profligate, steep, uncalled-for, unconscionable, uncontrolled, undue, unjustified, unreasonable, unrestrained, unwarranted, wanton.
antonym moderate.

immoderately *adv.* exaggeratedly, excessively, exorbitantly, extravagantly, extremely, inordinately, unduly, unjustifiably, unreasonably, unrestrainedly, wantonly, without measure.

antonym moderately.

immoderation n. excess, exorbitance, extravagance, immoderateness, intemperance, over-indulgence, prodigality, unreason, unrestraint.

antonym moderation.

immodest adj. bawdy, bold, brass-necked, brazen, coarse, depraved, forward, fresh, gross, immoral, improper, impudent, impure, indecent, indecorous, indelicate, lewd, obscene, pushy, revealing, risqué, shameless, titillating, unblushing, unchaste, unmaidenly.

antonym modest.

immodesty n. audacity, bawdiness, boldness, brass, coarseness, forwardness, gall, impudence, impurity, indecorousness, indecorum, indelicacy, lewdness, obscenity, shamelessness, temerity.

antonym modesty.

immoral adj. abandoned, bad, corrupt, debauched, degenerate, depraved, dishonest, dissolute, evil, foul, impure, indecent, iniquitous, lecherous, lewd, licentious, nefarious, obscene, pornographic, profligate, reprobate, sinful, unchaste, unethical, unprincipled, unrighteous, unscrupulous, vicious, vile, wanton, wicked, wrong.

antonym moral.

immorality n. badness, corruption, debauchery, depravity, dissoluteness, evil, iniquity, libertinage, licence, licentiousness, profligacy, sin, turpitude, vice, wickedness, wrong.

antonym morality.

immortal adj. abiding, ambrosial, constant, deathless, endless, enduring, eternal, everlasting, imperishable, incorruptible, indestructable, lasting, perennial, perpetual, sempiternal, timeless, undying, unfading, unforgettable.

antonym mortal.

n. deity, divinity, genius, god, goddess, great, hero, Olympian.

immortalise v. apotheosise, celebrate, commemorate, deify, enshrine, eternalise, eternise, exalt, glorify, hallow, memorialise, perpetuate, solemnise.

immortality n. athanasy, celebrity, deathlessness, deification, endlessness, eternity, everlasting life, fame, glorification, gloriousness, glory, greatness, incorruptibility, indestructibility, perpetuity, renown, timelessness.

antonym mortality.

immovable adj. adamant, constant, determined, entrenched, fast, firm, fixed, immutable, impassive, inflexible, jammed, marble-constant, moveless, obdurate, obstinate, resolute, rooted, secure, set, stable, stationary, steadfast, stony, stuck, unbudgeable, unchangeable, unimpressionable, unmovable, unshakable, unshaken, unwavering, unyielding.

antonym movable.

immune adj. clear, exempt, free, insusceptible, insusceptive, invulnerable, proof, protected, resistant, safe, unaffected, unsusceptible.

antonym susceptible.

immunisation n. injection, inoculation, jab, jag, protection, vaccination.

immunise v. inject, inoculate, protect, safeguard, vaccinate.

immunity n. amnesty, charter, exemption, exoneration, franchise, freedom, immunisation, indemnity, insusceptibility, invulnerability, liberty, licence, mithridatism, prerogative, privilege, protection, release, resistance, right.

antonym susceptibility.

immure v. cage, cloister, confine, enclose, enwall, imprison, incarcerate, jail, shut up, wall in.

antonym free.

immutability n. changelessness, constancy, durability, fixedness, immutableness, invariability, permanence, stability, unalterableness, unchangeableness.

antonym mutability.

immutable adj. abiding, changeless, constant, enduring, fixed, inflexible, invariable, lasting, permanent, perpetual, sacrosanct, solid, stable, steadfast, unalterable, unchangeable.

antonym mutable.

imp n. brat, demon, devil, flibbertigibbet, gamin, minx, prankster, rascal, rogue, scamp, sprite, trickster, urchin.

impact n. aftermath, bang, blow, brunt, bump, burden, collision, concussion, consequences, contact, crash, effect, force, impression, influence, jolt, knock, knock-on effect, meaning, power, repercussions, shock, significance, smash, stroke, thrust, thump, weight.
v. clash, collide, crash, crush, fix, hit, press together, strike, wedge.

impair v. blunt, craze, damage, debilitate, decrease, deteriorate, devalue, diminish, enervate, enfeeble, harm, hinder, injure, lessen, mar, reduce, spoil, undermine, vitiate, weaken, worsen.

antonym enhance.

impaired adj. damaged, defective, faulty, flawed, imperfect, poor, unsound, vicious, vitiated.

antonym enhanced.

impairment n. damage, deterioration, disablement, dysfunction, fault, flaw, harm, hurt, injury, reduction, ruin, vitiation.

antonym enhancement.

impale v. ga(u)nch, lance, perforate, pierce, puncture, run through, skewer, spear, spike, spit, stick, transfix.

impalpable adj. airy, delicate, disembodied, elusive, fine, imperceptible, inapprehensible, incorporeal, indistinct, insubstantial, intangible, shadowy, tenuous, thin, unsubstantial.

antonym palpable.

impalpably adv. imperceptibly, insensibly, intangibly, slightly.

antonym perceptibly.

imparity n. bias, disparity, disproportion, imbalance, inequality, inequity, partiality, unequalness, unevenness, unfairness.

antonym parity.

impart *v.* accord, afford, bestow, communicate, confer, contribute, convey, disclose, discover, divulge, give, grant, hand over, lend, make known, offer, pass on, relate, reveal, tell, yield.

impartial *adj.* crossbench, detached, disinterested, dispassionate, equal, equitable, even-handed, fair, just, neutral, non-discriminating, non-partisan, objective, open-minded, umcommitted, unbiased, unprejudiced.
antonym biased.

impartiality *n.* detachment, disinterest, disinterestedness, dispassion, equality, equity, even-handedness, fairness, neutrality, nonpartisanship, objectivity, open-mindedness, unbiasedness.
antonym bias.

impassable *adj.* blocked, closed, impenetrable, invious, obstructed, pathless, trackless, unnavigable, unpassable.
antonym passable.

impasse *n.* blind alley, cul-de-sac, dead end, deadlock, halt, nonplus, stalemate, stand-off, standstill.

impassioned *adj.* animated, ardent, blazing, enthusiastic, excited, fervent, fervid, fiery, furious, glowing, heated, inflamed, inspired, intense, passionate, rousing, spirited, stirring, vehement, vigorous, violent, vivid, warm.
antonyms apathetic, mild.

impassive *adj.* aloof, apathetic, blockish, callous, calm, composed, cool, dispassionate, emotionless, expressionless, immobile, impassible, imperturbable, indifferent, inscrutable, insensible, insusceptible, laid back, phlegmatic, poker-faced, reserved, serene, stoical, stolid, unconcerned, unemotional, unexcitable, unfeeling, unimpressible, unmoved, unruffled.
antonyms moved, responsive, warm.

impassivity *n.* aloofness, calmness, composure, coolness, dispassion, impassibility, impassiveness, imperturbability, indifference, inscrutability, insensibility, phlegm, sang-froid, stoicism, stolidity.
antonyms compassion, responsiveness, warmth.

impatience *n.* agitation, anxiety, avidity, avidness, eagerness, edginess, haste, hastiness, heat, impetuosity, intolerance, irritability, irritableness, nervousness, rashness, restiveness, restlessness, shortness, snappishness, testiness, uneasiness, vehemence.
antonym patience.

impatient *adj.* abrupt, brusque, chafing, champing at the bit, curt, demanding, eager, edgy, fretful, hasty, headlong, hot-tempered, impetuous, intolerant, irritable, precipitate, quick-tempered, restless, snappy, testy, vehement, violent.
antonym patient.

impeach *v.* accuse, arraign, blame, cast doubt on, censure, challenge, charge, denounce,

disparage, grass on, impugn, indict, peach on, question, tax.

impeachment *n.* accusation, arraignment, charge, disparagement, indictment.

impeccable *adj.* blameless, exact, exquisite, flawless, immaculate, incorrupt, innocent, irreproachable, perfect, precise, pure, scrupulous, sinless, stainless, unblemished, unerring, unimpeachable.
antonym flawed.

impecunious *adj.* broke, cleaned out, destitute, impoverished, indigent, insolvent, penniless, penurious, poor, poverty-stricken, skint, stony.
antonym rich.

impede *v.* bar, block, brake, check, clog, curb, delay, disrupt, hamper, hinder, hobble, hold up, let, obstruct, restrain, retard, slow, stop, thwart, trammel.
antonym aid.

impediment *n.* bar, barrier, block, burr, check, clog, curb, defect, difficulty, encumbrance, hindrance, let, log, obstacle, obstruction, snag, stammer, stumbling-block, stutter.
antonym aid.

impel *v.* actuate, chivvy, compel, constrain, drive, excite, force, goad, incite, induce, influence, inspire, instigate, motivate, move, oblige, poke, power, prod, prompt, propel, push, spur, stimulate, urge.
antonym dissuade.

impending *adj.* approaching, brewing, close, collecting, coming, forthcoming, gathering, hovering, imminent, in store, looming, menacing, near, nearing, threatening.
antonym remote.

impenetrable *adj.* arcane, baffling, cabbalistic, cryptic, dark, dense, enigmatic(al), fathomless, hermetic, hidden, impassable, impermeable, impervious, incomprehensible, indiscernible, inexplicable, inscrutable, inviolable, mysterious, obscure, solid, thick, unfathomable, unintelligible, unpiercable.
antonyms imtelligible, penetrable.

impenitence *n.* defiance, hard-heartedness, impeniency, incorrigibility, obduracy, recidivism, stubbornness.
antonym penitence.

impenitent *adj.* defiant, hardened, incorrigible, obdurate, recidivisitic, remorseless, unabashed, unashamed, uncontrite, unreformed, unregenerate, unremorseful, unrepentant.
antonym penitent.

imperative *adj.* authoritative, autocratic, bossy, commanding, compulsory, crucial, dictatorial, domineering, essential, exigent, high-handed, imperious, indispensable, insistent, lordly, magisterial, obligatory, peremptory, pressing, tyrannical, tyrannous, urgent, vital.
antonyms humble, optional.

imperceptible *adj.* faint, fine, gradual, impalpable, inapparent, inappreciable, inaudible, inconsensequential, indiscernible, indistinguishable, infinitesimal, insensible, invisible,

microscopic, minute, shadowy, slight, small, subtle, tiny, undetectable, unnoticeable.
antonym perceptible.

imperceptibly *adv.* inappreciably, indiscernibly, insensibly, invisibly, little by little, slowly, subtly, unnoticeably, unobtrusively, unseen.
antonym perceptibly.

imperceptive *adj.* crass, dim, dull, impercipient, insensitive, obtuse, superficial, unappreciative, unaware, undiscerning, unobservant, unseeing.
antonym perceptive.

imperfect *adj.* abortive, broken, damaged, defective, deficient, faulty, flawed, impaired, incomplete, inexact, limited, partial, patchy, rudimentary, unfinished, unideal.
antonym perfect.

imperfection *n.* blemish, blot, blotch, crack, defect, deficiency, dent, failing, fallibility, fault, flaw, foible, frailty, glitch, inadequacy, incompleteness, insufficiency, peccadillo, shortcoming, stain, taint, weakness.
antonyms asset, perfection.

imperial *adj.* august, exalted, grand, great, imperatorial, imperious, kingly, lofty, magnificent, majestic, noble, princely, queenly, regal, royal, sovereign, superior, supreme.

imperialism *n.* acquisitiveness, adventurism, colonianism, empire-building, expansionism.

imperil *v.* compromise, endanger, expose, hazard, jeopardise, risk, threaten.

imperious *adj.* arrogant, authoritative, autocratic, bossy, commanding, demanding, despotic, dictatorial, domineering, exacting, haughty, high-and-mighty, high-handed, imperative, lordly, magisterial, overbearing, overweening, peremptory, tyrannical, tyrannous.
antonym humble.

imperishable *adj.* abiding, deathless, enduring, eternal, everlasting, immortal, incorruptible, indestructible, inextinguishable, perennial, permanent, perpetual, undying, unfading, unforgettable.
antonym perishable.

impermanent *adj.* brief, elusive, ephemeral, evanescent, fleeting, fly-by-night, flying, fugacious, fugitive, inconstant, momentary, mortal, passing, perishable, short-lived, temporary, transient, transitory, unfixed, unsettled, unstable.
antonym permanent.

impermeable *adj.* damp-proof, hermetic, impassable, impenetrable, impervious, nonporous, proof, resistant, waterproof, water-repellent, water-resistant.
antonym permeable.

impersonal *adj.* aloof, bureaucratic, businesslike, cold, detached, dispassionate, faceless, formal, frosty, glassy, inhuman, neutral, official, remote, unfriendly, unsympathetic.
antonym friendly.

impersonate *v.* act, ape, caricature, do, imitate, masquerade as, mimic, mock, parody, personate, pose as, take off.

impersonation *n.* apery, aping, burlesque,

caricature, imitation, impression, mimicry, parody, take-off.

impertinence *n.* assurance, audacity, backchat, boldness, brass, brazenness, cheek, discourtesy, disrespect, effrontery, forwardness, impoliteness, impudence, incivility, insolence, malapertness, nerve, pertness, politeness, presumption, rudeness, sauce, sauciness.

impertinent *adj.* bold, brattish, brazen, bumptious, cheeky, discourteous, disrespectful, forward, fresh, ill-mannered, impolite, impudent, insolent, interfering, malapert, pert, presumptuous, rude, saucy, uncivil, unmannerly.
antonym polite.

imperturbability *n.* calmness, complacency, composure, coolness, equanimity, self-possession, tranquility.
antonyms jitteriness, touchiness.

imperturbable *adj.* calm, collected, complacent, composed, cool, equanimous, impassible, optimistic, sanguine, sedate, self-possessed, stoical, tranquil, unexcitable, unflappable.
antonyms jittery, touchy.

impervious *adj.* closed, damp-proof, hermetic, immune, impassable, impenetrable, impermeable, imperviable, invulnerable, resistant, sealed, unaffected, unmoved, unreceptive, unswayable, untouched.
antonyms pervious, responsive.

impetuosity *n.* dash, élan, haste, hastiness, impetuousness, impulsiveness, precipitancy, precipitateness, rashness, vehemence, violence.
antonym circumspection.

impetuous *adj.* ardent, bull-headed, eager, furious, hasty, headlong, impassioned, impulsive, overhasty, passionate, precipitate, rash, spontaneous, tearaway, unplanned, unpremeditated, unreflecting, unrestrained, unthinking.
antonym circumspect.

impetuously *adv.* impulsively, passionately, precipitately, rashly, recklessly, spontaneously, unthinkingly, vehemently.
antonym circumspectly.

impetus *n.* drive, energy, force, goad, impulse, impulsion, incentive, momentum, motivation, motive, power, push, spur, stimulus.

impiety *n.* blasphemy, godlessness, hubris, iniquity, irreligion, irreverence, profaneness, profanity, sacrilege, sacrilegiousness, sinfulness, ungodliness, unholiness, unrighteousness, wickedness.
antonym piety.

impinge *v.* affect, clash, collide, dash, encroach, enter, hit, influence, infringe, intrude, invade, obtrude, strike, touch, touch on, trespass, violate.

impious *adj.* blasphemous, godless, hubristic, iniquitous, irreligious, irreverent, profane, sacrilegious, sinful, ungodly, unholy, unrighteous, wicked.
antonym pious.

impish *adj.* arch, devilish, elfin, frolicsome, gamin, mischievous, naughty, pranksome, puckish, rascally, roguish, sportive, tricksome, tricksy, waggish, wanton, wicked.

impishness *n.* archness, devilry, deviltry, gaminerie, mischief, naughtiness, puckishness, roguery, roguishness, sportiveness, waggishness, wickedness.

implacability *n.* implacableness, inexorability, inflexibility, instransigence, intractability, irreconcilability, mercilessness, pitilessness, rancorousness, relentlessness, remorselessness, ruthlessness, unforgivingness, vengefulness.
antonym placability.

implacable *adj.* cruel, immovable, inappeasable, inexorable, inflexible, intractable, intransigent, irreconcilable, merciless, pitiless, rancorous, relentless, remorseless, ruthless, unappeasable, unbending, uncompromising, unforgiving, unrelenting, unyielding.
antonym placable.

implant *v.* embed, fix, graft, inculcate, infix, infuse, ingraft, inoculate, inseminate, insert, inset, instil, place, plant, root, sow.

implausible *adj.* dubious, far-fetched, flimsy, improbable, incredible, suspect, thin, transparent, unbelievable, unconvincing, unlikely, unplausible, unreasonable, weak.
antonym plausible.

implement *n.* agent, apparatus, appliance, device, gadget, gimmick, gismo, instrument, tool, utensil.
v. accomplish, bring about, carry out, complete, discharge, do, effect, enforce, execute, fulfil, perfect, perform, realise.

implementation *n.* accomplishment, carrying out, completion, discharge, effecting, enforcement, execution, fulfilling, fulfilment, performance, performing, realisation.

implicate *v.* associate, compromise, connect, embroil, entangle, include, incriminate, inculpate, involve, throw suspicion on.
antonyms absolve, exonerate.

implicated *adj.* associated, compromised, embroiled, entangled, incriminated, inculpated, involved, suspected.
antonym exonerated.

implication *n.* association, assumption, conclusion, connection, entanglement, hint, incrimination, inference, innuendo, insinuation, involvement, meaning, overtone, presupposition, ramification, repercusssion, significance, signification, suggestion, undertone.

implicit *adj.* absolute, constant, contained, entire, firm, fixed, full, implied, inherent, latent, presupposed, steadfast, tacit, total, undeclared, understood, unhesitating, unqualified, unquestioning, unreserved, unshakable, unshaken, unspoken, wholehearted.
antonym explicit.

implicitly *adv.* absolutely, by implication, completely, firmly, unconditionally, unhesitatingly, unquestioningly, unreservedly, utterly.

antonym explicitly.

implied *adj.* assumed, hinted, implicit, indirect, inherent, insinuated, suggested, tacit, undeclared, understood, unexpressed, unspoken, unstated.
antonym stated.

implore *v.* ask, beg, beseech, crave, entreat, importune, plead, pray, solicit, supplicate, wheedle.

imply *v.* betoken, connote, denote, entail, evidence, hint, import, indicate, insinuate, intimate, involve, mean, point to, presuppose, require, signify, suggest.
antonym state.

impolite *adj.* abrupt, bad-mannered, boorish, churlish, clumsy, coarse, cross, discourteous, disrespectful, gauche, ill-bred, ill-mannered, indecorous, indelicate, inept, insolent, loutish, rough, rude, uncivil, uncourteous, ungallant, ungentlemanly, ungracious, unladylike, unmannerly, unrefined.
antonym polite.

impoliteness *n.* abruptness, bad manners, boorishness, churlishness, clumsiness, coarseness, crassness, discourtesy, disrespect, gaucherie, incivility, indelicacy, ineptitude, insolence, rudeness, unmannerliness.
antonym politeness.

impolitic *adj.* daft, foolish, ill-advised, illjudged, imprudent, indiscreet, inexpedient, injudicious, maladroit, misguided, rash, undiplomatic, unwise.
antonym politic.

import *n.* bearing, consequence, drift, essence, gist, implication, importance, intention, magnitude, meaning, message, moment, nub, purport, sense, significance, substance, thrust, weight.
v. betoken, bring in, imply, indicate, introduce, mean, purport, signify.

importance *n.* concern, concernment, consequence, consideration, distinction, eminence, esteem, gravitas, import, influence, interest, mark, moment, momentousness, pith, preeminence, prestige, prominence, significance, signification, standing, status, substance, usefulness, value, weight, worth.
antonym unimportance.

important *adj.* basic, eminent, essential, farreaching, foremost, grave, heavy, high-level, high-ranking, influential, key, keynote, large, leading, material, meaningful, momentous, notable, noteworthy, on the map, outstanding, powerful, pre-eminent, primary, prominent, relevant, salient, seminal, serious, signal, significant, substantial, urgent, valuable, valued, weighty.
antonym unimportant.

importunate *adj.* impatient, insistent, persistent, pertinacious, pressing, tenacious, urgent, wheedlesome, wheedling, whilly, whillywha(w).

importune *v.* badger, beset, besiege, cajole, dun, earwig, entreat, flagitate, harass, hound, pester, plague, plead with, press, solicit, urge.

importunity *n.* cajolery, entreaties, harassment, insistence, persistence, solicitation, urgency, urging.

impose[1] *v.* appoint, burden, charge (with), decree, dictate, encumber, enforce, enjoin, establish, exact, fix, impone, inflict, institute, introduce, lay, levy, ordain, place, prescribe, promulgate, put, saddle, set.

impose[2] *v.* butt in, encroach, foist, force oneself, gate crash, horn in, impone, interpose, intrude, obtrude, presume, take liberties, trespass.

impose on abuse, deceive, exploit, fool, hoodwink, mislead, play on, take advantage of, trick, use.

imposing *adj.* august, commanding, dignified, distinguished, effective, grand, grandiose, impressive, majestic, ortund, pompous, stately, striking.

antonyms modest, unimposing.

imposition[1] *n.* application, decree, exaction, infliction, introduction, levying, promulgation.

imposition[2] *n.* burden, charge, cheek, constraint, deception, duty, encroachment, intrusion, levy, liberty, lines, presumption, punishment, task, tax.

impossibility *n.* hopelessness, impracticability, inability, inconceivability, unattainableness, unobtainableness, untenability, unviability.

antonym possibility.

impossible *adj.* absurd, hopeless, impracticable, inadmissible, inconceivable, insoluble, intolerable, ludicrous, outrageous, preposterous, unacceptable, unachievable, unattainable, ungovernable, unobtainable, unreasonable, untenable, unthinkable, unviable, unworkable.

antonym possible.

impostor *n.* charlatan, cheat, con man, deceiver, faitor, fake, fraud, grifter, hypocrite, impersonator, mountebank, phoney, pretender, quack, rogue, sham, swindler, trickster.

imposture *n.* artifice, cheat, con, con trick, counterfeit, deception, fraud, grift, hoax, impersonation, quackery, swindle, trick.

impotence *n.* disability, enervation, feebleness, frailty, helplessness, impuissance, inability, inadequacy, incapacity, incompetence, ineffectiveness, inefficacy, inefficiency, infirmity, ligature, paralysis, powerlessness, resourcelessness, uselessness, weakness.

antonym strength.

impotent *adj.* disabled, enervated, feeble, frail, helpless, impuissant, inadequate, incapable, incapacitated, incompetent, ineffective, infirm, paralysed, powerless, resourceless, unable, unmanned, weak.

antonyms potent, strong.

impoverish *v.* bankrupt, beggar, break, denude, depauperate, deplete, diminish, drain, exhaust, pauperise, reduce, ruin, weaken.

antonym enrich.

impoverished *adj.* arid, bankrupt, barren, decayed, denuded, depauperate(d), depleted, destitute, distressed, drained, empty, exhausted, impecunious, in reduced circumstances, indigent, jejune, necessitous, needy, on the rocks, penurious, poor, poorly off, reduced, skint, spent, straitened.

antonym rich.

impracticability *n.* futility, hopelessness, impossibility, impracticality, impracticality, infeasibility, unsuitableness, unviability, unworkability, uselessness.

antonym practicability.

impracticable *adj.* awkward, doctrinaire, impossible, impractical, inapplicable, inconvenient, infeasible, unachievable, unattainable, unfeasible, unpractical, unserviceable, unsuitable, unworkable, useless, visionary.

antonym practicable.

impractical *adj.* academic, idealistic, impossible, impracticable, inoperable, ivory-tower, nonviable, romantic, starry-eyed, unbusinesslike, unrealistic, unserviceable, unworkable, visionary, wild.

antonym practical.

impracticality *n.* hopelessness, idealism, impossibility, infeasibility, romanticism, unworkability, unworkableness.

antonym practicality.

imprecation *n.* abuse, anathema, blasphemy, curse, denunciation, execration, malediction, profanity, vilification, vituperation.

imprecise *adj.* ambiguous, careless, equivocal, estimated, fluctuating, hazy, ill-defined, inaccurate, indefinite, indeterminate, inexact, inexplicit, loose, rough, sloppy, unprecise, unscholarly, unscientific, vague, woolly.

antonym precise.

impregnable *adj.* fast, fortified, immovable, impenetrable, impugnable, indestructible, invincible, invulnerable, secure, solid, strong, unassailable, unbeatable, unconquerable.

antonym vulnerable.

impregnate *v.* fecundate, fertilise, fill, fructify, imbrue, imbue, infuse, inseminate, knock up, percolate, permeate, pervade, saturate, soak, steep, suffuse.

impregnation *n.* fecundation, fertilisation, fertilising, fructification, fructifying, imbruement, imbruing, imbuing, insemination, saturation.

impress *v.* affect, emboss, emphasise, engrave, excite, fix, grab, imprint, inculcate, indent, influence, inspire, instil, make one's mark, mark, move, namedrop, print, slay, stamp, stand out, stir, strike, sway, touch, wow.

impressed *adj.* affected, épris, excited, grabbed, imprinted, indented, influenced, marked, moved, stamped, stirred, struck, taken, touched, turned on.

antonym unimpressed.

impression[1] *n.* awareness, belief, concept, consciousness, conviction, effect, fancy, feeling, hunch, idea, impact, influence, memory, notion, opinion, reaction, recollection, sense, suspicion, sway.

impression[2] *n.* dent, edition, engram, engramma, hollow, impress, imprint, imprinting, incuse, indentation, issue, mark, niello, outline, pressure, printing, stamp, stamping.

impression[3] *n.* apery, aping, burlesque, imitation, impersonation, parody, send-up, take-off.

impressionability *n.* greenness, impressibility, ingenuousness, naïvety, receptiveness, receptivity, sensitivity, suggestibility, susceptibility, vulnerability.

impressionable *adj.* gullible, impressible, ingenuous, naïve, open, receptive, responsive, sensitive, suggestible, susceptible, vulnerable.

impressive *adj.* affecting, effective, exciting, forcible, foudroyant, frappant, imposing, moving, powerful, stirring, striking, touching. *antonym* unimpressive.

imprint *n.* badge, brand mark, impression, indentation, logo, mark, print, sign, stamp. *v.* brand, engrave, etch, fix, impress, mark, print, stamp.

imprison *v.* cage, confine, constrain, detain, encage, enchain, immure, incarcerate, intern, jail, lock up, put away, quod, send down. *antonym* free.

imprisoned *adj.* bars, behind, caged, captive, confined, doing bird, doing time, immured, incarcerated, jailed, locked up, put away, sent down. *antonym* free.

imprisonment *n.* bird, confinement, custody, detention, durance, duress(e), enchainment, incarceration, internment, porridge, quod. *antonym* freedom.

improbability *n.* doubt, doubtfulness, dubiety, dubiousness, far-fetchedness, implausibility, uncertainty, unlikelihood, unlikeliness. *antonym* probability.

improbable *adj.* doubtful, dubious, fanciful, far-fetched, implausible, preposterous, questionable, tall, unbelievable, uncertain, unconvincing, unlikely, weak. *antonym* probable.

impromptu *adj.* ad-lib, autoschediastic, extemporaneous, extempore, extemporised, improvised, off the cuff, off-hand, offhand, spontaneous, unpremeditated, unprepared, unrehearsed, unscripted, unstudied. *antonyms* planned, rehearsed. *adv.* ad lib, extempore, off the cuff, off the top of one's head, on the spur of the moment, spontaneously. *n.* autoschediasm, extemporisation, improvisation, voluntary.

improper *adj.* abnormal, erroneous, false, illegitimate, ill-timed, impolite, inaccurate, inadmissible, inapplicable, inapposite, inappropriate, inapt, incongruous, incorrect, indecent, indecorous, indelicate, infelicitous, inopportune, irregular, malapropos, off-colour, out of place, risqué, smutty, suggestive, unbecoming, uncalled-for, unfit, unfitting, unmaidenly, unparliamentary, unprintable, unquotable, unrepeatable, unseasonable, unseemly, unsuitable, unsuited, untoward, unwarranted, vulgar, wrong.

antonym proper.

impropriety *n.* bad taste, blunder, faux pas, gaffe, gaucherie, immodesty, incongruity, indecency, indecorousness, indecorum, lapse, mistake, slip, solecism, unseemliness, unsuitability, vulgarity. *antonym* propriety.

improve *v.* advance, ameliorate, amend, augment, better, correct, culture, develop, embourgeoise, enhance, gentrify, help, increase, look up, meliorate, mend, mend one's ways, perk up, pick up, polish, progress, rally, recover, rectify, recuperate, reform, rise, touch up, turn over a new leaf, turn the corner, up, upgrade. *antonyms* decline, diminish.

improvement *n.* advance, advancement, amelioration, amendment, augmentation, bettering, betterment, correction, development, embourgeoisement, enhancement, furtherance, gain, gentrification, increase, melioration, progress, rally, recovery, rectification, reformation, rise, upswing. *antonyms* decline, retrogression.

improvidence *n.* carelessness, extravagance, fecklessness, heedlessness, imprudence, Micawberism, negligence, prodigality, profligacy, thriftlessness, wastefulness. *antonym* thrift.

improvident *adj.* careless, feckless, heedless, imprudent, Micawberish, negligent, prodigal, profligate, reckless, shiftless, spendthrift, thoughtless, thriftless, underprepared, uneconomical, unprepared, unthrifty, wasteful. *antonym* thrifty.

improving *adj.* convalescing, edifying, educational, instructive, meliorative, on the mend, recuperating, uplifting. *antonyms* harmful, unedifying.

improvisation *n.* ad-lib, ad-libbing, autoschediasm, expedient, extemporising, impromptu, invention, makeshift, spontaneity, vamp.

improvise *v.* ad-lib, autoschediaze, coin, concoct, contrive, devise, extemporise, improvisate, invent, make do, play it by ear, throw together, vamp.

improvised *adj.* ad-lib, extemporaneous, extempore, extemporised, improvisational, improvisatory, makeshift, off-the-cuff, spontaneous, unprepared, unrehearsed. *antonym* rehearsed.

imprudence *n.* carelessness, folly, foolhardiness, foolishness, haste, hastiness, heedlessness, improvidence, inadvisability, incaution, incautiousness, inconsiderateness, indiscretion, irresponsibility, rashness, recklessness, short-sightedness, temerity. *antonym* prudence.

imprudent *adj.* careless, foolhardy, foolish, hasty, heedless, ill-advised, ill-considered, ill-judged, impolitic, improvident, incautious, inconsiderate, indiscreet, injudicious, irresponsible, overhasty, rash, reckless, short-sighted, temerarious, unthinking, unwise.

antonym prudent.

impudence *n.* assurance, audacity, backchat, boldness, brass neck, brazenness, cheek, chutzpah, effrontery, face, impertinence, impudicity, insolence, lip, malapertness, neck, nerve, pertness, presumption, presumptuousness, rudeness, sauciness, shamelessness.

antonym politeness.

impudent *adj.* audacious, bold, bold-faced, brazen, brazen-faced, cheeky, cocky, forward, fresh, immodest, impertinent, insolent, malapert, pert, presumptuous, rude, saucy, shameless.

antonym polite.

impugn *v.* assail, attack, call in question, challenge, criticise, dispute, oppose, question, resist, revile, traduce, vilify, vilipend, vituperate.

antonym praise.

impulse *n.* caprice, catalyst, conatus, desire, drive, feeling, force, impetus, incitement, inclination, influence, instinct, momentum, motive, movement, notion, passion, pressure, push, resolve, stimulus, surge, thrust, urge, whim, wish.

impulsive *adj.* hasty, headlong, impetuous, instinctive, intuitive, passionate, precipitant, precipitate, quick, rash, reckless, spontaneous, unconsidered, unpredictable, unpremeditated.

antonym cautious.

impulsiveness *n.* haste, hastiness, impetuosity, impetuousness, precipitateness, precipitation, rashness, recklessness.

antonym caution.

impunity *n.* amnesty, dispensation, excusal, exemption, freedom, immunity, liberty, licence, permission, security.

antonym liability.

impure *adj.* admixed, adulterated, alloyed, carnal, coarse, contaminated, corrupt, debased, defiled, dirty, feculent, filthy, foul, gross, immodest, immoral, indecent, indelicate, infected, lascivious, lewd, licentious, lustful, mixed, obscene, polluted, prurient, salacious, smutty, sullied, tainted, turbid, unchaste, unclean, unrefined, unwholesome, vicious, vitiated.

antonyms chaste, pure.

impurity *n.* admixture, adulteration, befoulment, carnality, coarseness, contaminant, contamination, corruption, defilement, dirt, dirtiness, dross, feculence, filth, foreign body, foreign matter, foulness, grime, grossness, immodesty, immorality, indecency, infection, lasciviousness, lewdness, licentiousness, mark, mixture, obscenity, pollutant, pollution, prurience, salaciousness, scum, smuttiness, spot, stain, taint, turbidity, turbidness, unchastity, uncleanness, vulgarity.

antonyms chasteness, purity.

imputable *adj.* ascribable, attributable, blameable, chargeable, referable, traceable.

imputation *n.* accusation, arrogation, ascription, aspersion, attribution, blame, censure, charge, insinuation, reproach, slander, slur, suggestion.

impute *v.* accredit, ascribe, assign, attribute, charge, credit, put down to, refer.

in a state agitated, anxious, distressed, disturbed, flustered, hassled, het up, in a stew, in a tizzy, panic-stricken, ruffled, steamed up, troubled, upset, worked up, worried.

antonym calm.

in a word briefly, concisely, in a nutshell, in short, succinctly, to be brief, to put it briefly, to sum up.

antonym at length.

in abeyance dormant, hanging fire, on ice, pending, shelved, suspended.

in addition additionally, also, as well, besides, further, furthermore, into the bargain, moreover, over and above, to boot, too, withal.

in advance ahead, beforehand, earlier, in front, in the forefront, in the lead, in the van, previously, sooner.

antonyms behind, later.

in ambush embusqué, lying in wait.

in camera behind closed doors, hugger-mugger, in private, in secret, privately, secretly, sub rosa, under the rose.

antonym openly.

in confidence in private, privately, secretly, sub rosa, under the rose.

in conflict at daggers drawn, at loggerheads, at odds, at variance, at war, disagreeing, disunited, in disagreement, opposed.

antonyms at peace, in agreement.

in crowds gregatim, in droves, in flocks, in force, in herds, in hordes, in large numbers, in strength, in troops.

antonym in penny numbers.

in depth comprehensively, exhaustively, extensively, in detail, intensively, thoroughly.

antonyms broadly, superficially.

in detail comprehensively, exhaustively, in depth, in particular, inside out, item by item, particularly, point by point, thoroughly.

antonyms broadly, superficially.

in difficulties in a hole, in dire straights, in the shit, up shit creek, up the creek, up the pole.

in effect actually, effectively, essentially, for practical purposes, in actuality, in fact, in reality, in the end, in truth, really, to all intents and purposes, virtually, when all is said and done.

in fact actually, en effet, in point of fact, in reality, in truth, indeed, really, truly.

in favour of all for, backing, for, on the side of, pro, supporting, to the advantage of.

antonym against.

in force binding, current, effective, gregatim, in crowds, in droves, in flocks, in hordes, in large numbers, in operation, in strength, on the statute book, operative, valid, working.

antonym inoperative.

in French Gallice.

in front ahead, before, first, in advance, in the

van, leading, preceding, to the fore.
antonym behind.

in full completely, entirely, in its entirety, in total, in toto, unabridged, uncut, wholly.
antonyms partially, partly.

in German Germanice.

in good part cheerfully, cordially, good-naturedly, laughingly, well.
antonyms angrily, touchily.

in Greek Graece.

in gross en bloc, en masse, in aggregate, in bulk, in toto, wholesale.
antonym retail.

in hiding concealed, doggo, hidden, latitant.

in keeping appropriate, befitting, fit, fitting, harmonious, in harmony, of a piece, suitable.
antonym inappropriate.

in kind in like manner, similarly, tit for tat.

in Latin Latine.

in league allied, collaborating, conniving, conspiring, hand in glove, in cahoots, in collusion.
antonym at odds.

in love besotted, charmed, doting, enamoured, enraptured, hooked, infatuated, smitten.

in motion afoot, functioning, going, in progress, moving, on the go, operational, running, sailing, travelling, under way.
antonym stationary.

in my opinion for my money, me judice.

in order acceptable, all right, allowed, appropriate, arranged, called for, correct, done, fitting, in sequence, neat, OK, orderly, permitted, right, shipshape, suitable, tidy.
antonyms disallowed, out of order.

in order to intending to, so that, to, with a view to, with the intention of, with the purpose of.

in part a little, in some measure, part way, partially, partly, slightly, somewhat, to a certain extent, to some degree.
antonym wholly.

in particular distinctly, especially, exactly, expressly, in detail, particularly, specifically.

in passing accidentally, by the by(e), by the way, en passant, incidentally.

in penny numbers in dribs and drabs, in ones and twos.
antonyms in crowds, in force.

in person as large as life, bodily, in propria persona, personally.

in pieces broken, burst, damaged, disintegrated, in bits, in smithereens, kaput, piecemeal, ruined, shattered, smashed.

in place of as a replacement for, as a substitute for, as an alternative to, in exchange for, in lieu of, instead of.

in principle en principe, ideally, in essence, in theory, theoretically.

in private behind closed doors, hugger-mugger, in camera, in confidence, in secret, privately, secretly, sub rosa, under the rose.
antonym openly.

in progress going on, happening, occurring, proceeding, under way.

in proportion pro rata.

in public coram populo, for all to see, in full view, in open view, in the open, openly, publicly.
antonyms in camera, in secret.

in return en revanche.

in secret hugger-mugger, in confidence, in gremio, in pectore, in petto, inly, inwardly, on the q.t., on the quiet, sub rosa, under the rose.
antonym openly.

in spite of despite, notwithstanding.

in the interest(s) of for the sake of, on behalf of, on the part of, to the advantage of, to the benefit of.

in the light of bearing/keeping in mind, because of, considering, in view of, taking into account.

in the making budding, coming, developing, emergent, growing, nascent, potential, up and coming.

in the middle of among, busy with, during, engaged in, in the midst of, in the process of, occupied with, surrounded by, while.

in the midst of among, during, in the middle of, in the thick of, surrounded by.

in the money affluent, flush, loaded, opulent, prosperous, rich, rolling in it, wealthy, well-heeled, well-off, well-to-do.
antonym poor.

in the mood disposed, in the right frame of mind, inclined, interested, keen, minded, of a mind, willing.

in the offing at hand, close at hand, coming up, imminent, in sight, on the horizon, on the way.
antonym far off.

in the red bankrupt, in arrears, in debt, insolvent, on the rocks, overdrawn.
antonym in credit.

in the right justified, right.
antonym in the wrong.

in the wrong at fault, blameworthy, guilty, in error, mistaken, to blame.
antonym in the right.

in toto as a whole, completely, entirely, in its entirety, in total, totally, unabridged, uncut, wholly.

in two minds dithering, hesitant, hesitating, shilly-shallying, swithering, uncertain, undecided, unsure, vacillating, wavering.
antonym certain.

in vain bootlessly, fruitlessly, ineffectually, to no avail, unsuccessfully, uselessly, vainly.
antonym successfully.

inability *n.* disability, disqualification, handicap, impotence, inadequacy, incapability, incapacity, incompetence, ineptitude, ineptness, powerlessness, weakness.
antonym ability.

inaccessible *adj.* impassible, isolated, remote, solitary, unapproachable, unattainable, uncom(e)atable, unfrequented, unget-at-able, unreachable.
antonym accessible.

inaccuracy *n.* blunder, boob, carelessness, corrigendum, defect, erratum, erroneous-

ness, error, fault, faultiness, howler, imprecision, incorrectness, inexactness, looseness, miscalculation, mistake, slip, unreliability.
antonym accuracy.

inaccurate *adj.* careless, defective, discrepant, erroneous, faulty, imprecise, in error, incorrect, inexact, loose, mistaken, out, unfaithful, unreliable, unrepresentative, unsound, wide of the mark, wild, wrong.
antonym accurate.

inaccurately *adv.* carelessly, clumsily, imprecisely, inexactly, loosely, unfaithfully, unreliably, wildly.
antonym accurately.

inaction *n.* dormancy, idleness, immobility, inactivity, inertia, rest, stagnation, stasis, torpidity, torpor.
antonym activeness.

inactivate *v.* cripple, disable, immobilise, knock the bottom out of, mothball, paralyse, scupper, stabilise, stop.
antonym activate.

inactive *adj.* abeyant, dormant, dull, idle, immobile, indolent, inert, inoperative, jobless, kicking one's heels, latent, lazy, lethargic, low-key, mothballed, out of service, out of work, passive, quiet, sedentary, sleepy, slothful, slow, sluggish, somnolent, stagnant, stagnating, torpid, unemployed, unoccupied, unused.
antonym active.

inactivity *n.* abeyance, abeyancy, dilatoriness, dolce far niente, dormancy, dullness, heaviness, hibernation, idleness, immobility, inaction, indolence, inertia, inertness, languor, lassitude, laziness, lethargy, passivity, quiescence, sloth, sluggishness, stagnation, stasis, torpor, unemployment, vegetation.
antonym activeness.

inadequacy *n.* dearth, defect, defectiveness, deficiency, failing, faultiness, imperfection, inability, inadequateness, inaptness, incapacity, incompetence, incompetency, incompleteness, ineffectiveness, ineffectuality, ineffectualness, inefficacy, inefficiency, insufficiency, lack, meagreness, paucity, poverty, scantiness, shortage, shortcoming, skimpiness, unfitness, unsuitableness, want, weakness.
antonym adequacy.

inadequate *adj.* defective, deficient, faulty, imperfect, inapt, incapable, incommensurate, incompetent, incomplete, ineffective, ineffectual, inefficacious, inefficient, insubstantial, insufficient, leaving a little/a lot/much to be desired, meagre, niggardly, scanty, short, sketchy, skimpy, sparse, unequal, unfitted, unqualified, wanting.
antonym adequate.

inadequately *adv.* badly, carelessly, imperfectly, insufficiently, meagrely, poorly, scantily, sketchily, skimpily, sparsely, thinly.
antonym adequately.

inadmissable *adj.* disallowed, immaterial, improper, inappropriate, incompetent, irrele-

vant, prohibited, unacceptable, unallowable, unqualified.
antonym admissible.

inadvertence *n.* blunder, boob, boo-boo, carelessness, clanger, error, heedlessness, inadvertency, inattention, inconsideration, inobservance, mistake, neglect, negligence, oversight, remissness, thoughtlessness.
antonym care.

inadvertent *adj.* accidental, careless, chance, heedless, inattentive, negligent, thoughtless, unguarded, unheeding, unintended, unintentional, unplanned, unpremeditated, unthinking, unwitting.
antonym deliberate.

inadvertently *adv.* accidentally, by accident, by mistake, carelessly, heedlessly, involuntarily, mistakenly, negligently, remissly, thoughtlessly, unguardedly, unintentionally, unthinkingly, unwittingly.
antonym deliberately.

inadvisable *adj.* daft, foolish, ill-advised, ill-judged, impolitic, imprudent, incautious, indiscreet, inexpedient, injudicious, misguided, unwise.
antonym advisable.

inalienable *adj.* absolute, entailed, imprescriptible, indefeasible, infrangible, inherent, inviolable, non-negotiable, non-transferable, permanent, sacrosanct, unassailable, unremovable, untransferable.
antonym impermanent.

inane *adj.* asinine, daft, drippy, empty, fatuous, foolish, frivolous, futile, idiotic, imbecilic, mindless, nutty, puerile, senseless, silly, stupid, trifling, unintelligent, vacuous, vain, vapid, worthless.
antonym sensible.

inanimate *adj.* abiotic, dead, defunct, dormant, dull, exanimate, extinct, heavy, inactive, inert, inorganic, insensate, insentient, leaden, lifeless, listless, slow, spiritless, stagnant, torpid.
antonyms alive, animate, lively, living.

inanity *n.* asininity, bêtise, daftness, drippiness, emptiness, fatuity, folly, foolishness, frivolity, imbecility, puerility, senselessness, silliness, vacuity, vapidity, waffle.
antonym sense.

inapplicable *adj.* inapposite, inappropriate, inapt, inconsequent, irrelevant, unrelated, unsuitable, unsuited.
antonym applicable.

inappropriate *adj.* disproportionate, ill-fitted, ill-suited, ill-timed, improper, incongruous, infelicitous, malapropos, out of place, tactless, tasteless, unbecoming, unbefitting, unfit, unfitting, unseemly, unsuitable, untimely.
antonym appropriate.

inappropriately *adv.* malapropos, tactlessly, tastelessly.
antonym appropriately.

inapt *adj.* awkward, clumsy, crass, dull, gauche, ill-fitted, ill-suited, ill-timed, inapposite, inappropriate, incompetent, inept, inexpert,

infelicitous, inopportune, maladroit, slow, stupid, tactless, unapt, unfortunate, unhappy, unsuitable, unsuited.
antonym apt.

inaptitude *n.* awkwardness, clumsiness, crassness, inaptness, incompetence, inopportuneness, maladroitness, tactlessness, unfitness, unreadiness, unsuitableness.
antonym aptitude.

inarticulacy *n.* inarticulateness, incoherence, mumbling, speechlessness, tongue-tiedness, unintelligibility.
antonym articulacy.

inarticulate *adj.* blurred, dumb, dysarthric, dysphasic, dyspraxic, faltering, halting, hesitant, incoherent, incomprehensible, indistinct, muffled, mumbled, mute, silent, speechless, tongue-tied, unclear, unintelligible, unspoken, unuttered, unvoiced, voiceless, wordless.
antonym articulate.

inattention *n.* absence of mind, absentmindedness, carelessness, daydreaming, disregard, dwam, forgetfulness, heedlessness, inadvertence, inattentiveness, neglect, preoccupation, wool-gathering.
antonym attentiveness.

inattentive *adj.* absent-minded, careless, deaf, distracted, distrait, dreaming, dreamy, heedless, inadvertent, neglectful, negligent, preoccupied, regardless, remiss, unheeding, unmindful, unobservant, vague.
antonym attentive.

inaudible *adj.* faint, imperceptible, indistinct, low, muffled, mumbled, mumbling, muted, noiseless, out of earshot, silent.
antonym audible.

inaugural *adj.* consecratory, dedicatory, exordial, first, initial, introductory, launching, maiden, opening.

inaugurate *v.* begin, christen, commence, commission, consecrate, dedicate, enthrone, han(d)sel, induct, initiate, install, instate, institute, introduce, invest, kick off, launch, open, ordain, originate, set up, start, start off, usher in.

inauguration *n.* consecration, enthronement, han(d)sel, induction, initiation, installation, installing, institution, investiture, launch, launching, opening, setting up.

inauspicious *adj.* bad, black, discouraging, ill-boding, ill-omened, ominous, threatening, unfavourable, unfortunate, unlucky, unpromising, unpropitious, untoward.
antonym auspicious.

inborn *adj.* congenital, connate, hereditary, inbred, ingenerate, ingrained, inherent, inherited, innate, instinctive, intuitive, native, natural.
antonym learned.

inbred *adj.* connate, constitutional, ingenerate, ingrained, inherent, innate, native, natural.
antonym learned.

inbreeding *n.* endogamy, homogamy.

incalculable *adj.* boundless, countless, enormous, immense, incomputable, inestimable, infinite, innumerable, limitless, measureless, numberless, uncountable, unforeseeable, unlimited, unmeasureable, unpredictable, untold, vast.
antonym limited.

incantation *n.* abracadabra, chant, charm, conjuration, formula, hex, invocation, mantra(m), rune, spell.

incapable *adj.* disqualified, drunk, feeble, helpless, impotent, inadequate, incompetent, ineffective, ineffectual, inept, insufficient, powerless, tipsy, unable, unfit, unfitted, unqualified, weak.
antonyms capable, sober.

incapacitate *v.* cripple, disable, disqualify, hamstring, immobilise, lay up, paralyse, prostrate, put out of action, scupper, unfit.
antonyms facilitate, set up.

incapacitated *adj.* disqualified, drunk, hamstrung, immobilised, indisposed, laid up, out of action, prostrate, scuppered, tipsy, unfit, unwell.
antonym operative.

incapacity *n.* disability, disqualification, feebleness, impotence, inability, inadequacy, incapability, incompetency, ineffectiveness, powerlessness, unfitness, weakness.
antonym capability.

incapsulate *see* encapsulate .

incarcerate *v.* cage, commit, confine, coop up, detain, encage, gaol, immure, impound, imprison, intern, jail, lock up, put away, restrain, restrict, send down, wall in.
antonym free.

incarceration *n.* bondage, captivity, confinement, custody, detention, imprisonment, internment, jail, restraint, restriction.
antonym freedom.

incarnate *adj.* embodied, made flesh, personified, typified.

incarnation *n.* avatar, embodiment, exemplification, impersonation, manifestation, personification, type.

incautious *adj.* careless, hasty, heedless, ill-advised, ill-judged, improvident, imprudent, impulsive, inconsiderate, indiscreet, injudicious, negligent, overhasty, precipitate, rash, reckless, thoughtless, unchary, unguarded, unthinking, unwary, wareless.
antonym cautious.

incendiary[1] *n.* arsonist, firebug, fire- raiser, pétroleur, pétroleuse, pyromaniac.

incendiary[2] *n.* agitator, demagogue, firebrand, insurgent, rabble-rouser, revolutionary.
adj. dissentious, inciting, inflammatory, proceleusmatic, proleptic, provocative, rabble-rousing, seditious, subversive.
antonym calming.

incense[1] *n.* adulation, aroma, balm, bouquet, fragrance, homage, joss-stick, perfume, scent, worship.

incense[2] *v.* anger, enrage, exasperate, excite, inflame, infuriate, irritate, madden, make one see red, make one's blood boil, make one's hackles rise, provoke, raise one's hackles, rile. *antonym* calm.

incensed *adj.* angry, enraged, exasperated, fuming, furibund, furious, in a paddy, indignant, infuriated, irate, ireful, mad, maddened, on the warpath, steamed up, up in arms, waxy, wrathful. *antonym* calm.

incentive *n.* bait, carrot, cause, consideration, encouragement, enticement, impetus, impulse, inducement, lure, motivation, motive, reason, reward, spur, stimulant, stimulus. *antonym* disincentive.

inception *n.* beginning, birth, commencement, dawn, inauguration, initiation, installation, kick-off, origin, outset, rise, start. *antonym* end.

incessant *adj.* ceaseless, constant, continual, continuous, endless, eternal, everlasting, interminable, never-ending, non-stop, perpetual, persistent, relentless, unbroken, unceasing, unending, unrelenting, unremitting, weariless. *antonym* intermittent.

incidence *n.* amount, commonness, degree, extent, frequency, occurrence, prevalence, range, rate.

incident *n.* adventure, affaire, brush, circumstance, clash, commotion, confrontation, contretemps, disturbance, episode, event, fight, happening, mishap, occasion, occurrence, scene, skirmish.

incidental *adj.* accidental, accompanying, ancillary, attendant, casual, chance, concomitant, contingent, contributory, fortuitous, incident, inconsequential, inessential, irrelevant, minor, non-essential, occasional, odd, random, related, secondary, subordinate, subsidiary. *antonym* essential.

incidentally *adv.* accidentally, by chance, by the by(e), by the way, casually, digressively, en passant, fortuitously, in passing, parenthetically.

incidentals *n.* contingencies, epiphenomena, extras, odds and ends. *antonym* essentials.

incinerate *v.* burn, char, cremate, reduce to ashes.

incipient *adj.* beginning, commencing, developing, embryonic, inceptive, inchoate, nascent, originating, rudimentary, starting. *antonym* developed.

incise *v.* carve, chisel, cut, cut into, engrave, etch, gash.

incised *adj.* carved, cut, engraved, intagliated.

incision *n.* cut, discission, gash, incisure, insection, notch, opening, slash, slit.

incisive *adj.* acid, acute, astucious, astute, biting, caustic, cutting, keen, mordant, penetrating, perceptive, perspicacious, piercing, sarcastic, sardonic, satirical, severe, sharp, tart, trenchant. *antonym* woolly.

incisiveness *n.* acidity, astucity, astuteness,

keenness, penetration, perspicacity, pungency, sarcasm, sharpness, tartness, trenchancy. *antonym* woolliness.

incite *v.* abet, animate, drive, egg on, encourage, excite, foment, goad, impel, inflame, instigate, prompt, provoke, put up to, rouse, set on, solicit, spur, stimulate, stir up, urge, whip up. *antonym* restrain.

incitement *n.* abetment, agitation, encouragement, goad, hortation, impetus, impulse, inducement, instigation, motivation, motive, prompting, provocation, spur, stimulus. *antonyms* check, discouragement.

inciting *adj.* exciting, incendiary, inflammatory, proceleusmatic, protreptic, protreptical, provocative, rabble-rousing. *antonym* calming.

incivility *n.* bad manners, boorishness, coarseness, discourteousness, discourtesy, disrespect, ill-breeding, impoliteness, inurbanity, roughness, rudeness, unmannerliness, vulgarity. *antonym* civility.

inclemency *n.* bitterness, boisterousness, callousness, cruelty, harshness, mercilessness, pitilessness, rawness, rigour, roughness, severity, storminess, tyranny, unfeelingness, ungeniality. *antonym* clemency.

inclement *adj.* bitter, boisterous, callous, cruel, draconian, foul, harsh, intemperate, merciless, pitiless, rigorous, rough, severe, stormy, tempestuous, tyrannical, unfeeling, ungenial, unmerciful. *antonym* clement.

inclination[1] *n.* affection, aptitude, bent, bias, clinamen, desire, disposition, fancy, fondness, ingenium, leaning, liking, month's mind, partiality, penchant, predilection, predisposition, prejudice, proclivity, proneness, propensity, stomach, taste, tendency, turn, turn of mind, velleity, wish. *antonym* disinclination.

inclination[2] *n.* angle, bend, bending, bow, bowing, clinamen, deviation, gradient, incline, leaning, nod, pitch, slant, slope, tilt.

incline[1] *v.* affect, bias, dispose, influence, nod, persuade, predispose, prejudice, stoop, sway.

incline[2] *v.* bend, bevel, bow, cant, deviate, diverge, lean, slant, slope, tend, tilt, tip, veer. *n.* acclivity, ascent, brae, declivity, descent, dip, grade, gradient, hill, ramp, rise, slope.

inclined *adj.* apt, bent, disposed, given, liable, likely, minded, oblique, of a mind, predisposed, prone, sloping, tilted, willing. *antonym* flat.

inclose *see* enclose .

include *v.* add, allow for, comprehend, comprise, connote, contain, cover, embody, embrace, enclose, encompass, incorporate, involve, number among, rope in, subsume, take in, take into account. *antonyms* exclude, ignore.

inclusion *n.* addition, incorporation, insertion,

involvement.

antonym exclusion.

inclusive *adj.* across-the-board, all in, all-embracing, blanket, catch-all, compendious, comprehensive, full, general, overall, sweeping, umbrella.

antonyms exclusive, narrow.

incognito *adj.* disguised, in disguise, masked, unknown, unrecognisable, unrecognised, veiled.

antonyms openly, undisguised.

incoherence *n.* confusion, disconnectedness, disjointedness, illogicality, inarticulateness, inconsistency, unintelligibility, wildness.

antonym coherence.

incoherent *adj.* confused, disconnected, disjointed, dislocated, disordered, inarticulate, inconsequent, inconsistent, jumbled, loose, muddled, rambling, stammering, stuttering, unconnected, unco-ordinated, unintelligible, unjointed, wandering, wild.

antonym coherent.

incombustible *adj.* fireproof, fire-resistant, flameproof, flame-resistant, non-flammable, non-inflammable.

antonym combustible.

income *n.* earnings, gains, interest, means, pay, proceeds, profits, receipts, returns, revenue, salary, takings, wages, yield.

antonym expenses.

incoming *adj.* accruing, approaching, arriving, coming, ensuing, entering, homeward, landing, new, next, returning, succeeding.

antonym outgoing.

incommensurate *adj.* disproportionate, excessive, extravagant, extreme, inadequate, inequitable, inordinate, insufficient, unequal.

antonym appropriate.

incommunicable *adj.* indescribable, ineffable, inexpressible, unimpartable, unspeakable, unutterable.

antonym expressible.

incomparable *adj.* brilliant, inimitable, matchless, paramount, peerless, superb, superlative, supreme, transcendent, unequalled, unmatched, unparalleled, unrivalled.

antonyms poor, run-of-the-mill.

incomparably *adv.* brilliantly, by far, eminently, far and away, immeasurably, superbly, superlatively.

antonyms poorly, slightly.

incompatibility *n.* antagonism, clash, conflict, difference, discrepancy, disparateness, disparity, incongruity, inconsistency, irreconcilability, mismatch, uncongeniality.

antonym compatibility.

incompatible *adj.* antagonistic, antipathetic, clashing, conflicting, contradictory, discordant, discrepant, disparate, ill-assorted, incongruous, inconsistent, inconsonant, inharmonious, irreconcilable, mismatched, uncongenial, unsuitable, unsuited.

antonym compatible.

incompetence *n.* bungling, inability, inadequacy, incapability, incapacity, incompetency, in-

effectiveness, ineffectuality, ineffectualness, inefficiency, ineptitude, ineptness, insufficiency, stupidity, unfitness, uselessness.

antonym competence.

incompetent *adj.* bungling, floundering, incapable, incapacitated, ineffective, ineffectual, inept, inexpert, insufficient, stupid, unable, unfit, unfitted, unskilful, useless.

antonym competent.

incomplete *adj.* broken, defective, deficient, fragmentary, imperfect, incondite, inexhaustive, insufficient, lacking, part, partial, short, unaccomplished, undeveloped, undone, unexecuted, unfinished, wanting.

antonym complete.

incomprehensible *adj.* above one's head, all Greek, arcane, baffling, beyond one's comprehension, beyond one's grasp, double-Dutch, enigmatic, impenetrable, inapprehensible, inconceivable, inscrutable, mysterious, obscure, opaque, perplexing, puzzling, unfathomable, unimaginable, unintelligible, unthinkable.

antonym comprehensible.

inconceivable *adj.* implausible, incogitable, incredible, mind-boggling, out of the question, staggering, unbelievable, unheard-of, unimaginable, unknowable, unthinkable.

antonym conceivable.

inconclusive *adj.* ambiguous, indecisive, indeterminate, open, uncertain, unconvincing, undecided, unsatisfying, unsettled, vague.

antonym conclusive.

incongruity *n.* conflict, discrepancy, disparity, dissociability, dissociableness, inappropriateness, inaptness, incompatibility, inconcinnity, inconsistency, inharmoniousness, unsuitability.

antonyms consistency, harmoniousness.

incongruous *adj.* absurd, conflicting, contradictory, contrary, disconsonant, discordant, dissociable, extraneous, improper, inappropriate, inapt, incoherent, incompatible, inconcinnous, inconsistent, out of keeping, out of place, unbecoming, unsuitable, unsuited.

antonyms consistent, harmonious.

inconsequential *adj.* illogical, immaterial, inconsequent, inconsiderable, insignificant, minor, negligible, paltry, petty, trifling, trivial, unimportant.

antonym important.

inconsiderable *adj.* exiguous, inconsequential, insignificant, light, minor, negligible, petty, piddling, piffling, slight, small, small-time, trifling, trivial, unimportant, unnoticeable.

antonym considerable.

inconsiderate *adj.* careless, imprudent, indelicate, insensitive, intolerant, rash, rude, self-centred, selfish, tactless, thoughtless, unconcerned, ungracious, unkind, unthinking.

antonym considerate.

inconsiderateness *n.* carelessness, étourderie, indelicacy, insensitivity, rudeness, selfishness, tactlessness, thoughtlessness, unconcern,

unkindness.
antonym considerateness.

inconsistency *n.* changeableness, contrariety, disagreement, discrepancy, disparity, divergence, fickleness, incompatibility, incongruity, inconsonance, inconstancy, instability, paradox, unpredictability, unreliability, unsteadiness, variance.
antonym consistency.

inconsistent *adj.* at odds, at variance, capricious, changeable, conflicting, contradictory, contrary, discordant, discrepant, erratic, fickle, incoherent, incompatible, incongruous, inconstant, irreconcilable, irregular, unpredictable, unstable, unsteady, variable, varying.
antonym constant.

inconsistently *adv.* contradictorily, differently, eccentrically, erratically, illogically, inequably, randomly, unequally, unfairly, unpredictably, variably.
antonym consistently.

inconsolable *adj.* brokenhearted, desolate, desolated, despairing, devastated, disconsolate, heartbroken, wretched.
antonym consolable.

inconspicuous *adj.* camouflaged, hidden, insignificant, low-key, modest, muted, ordinary, plain, quiet, retiring, unassuming, unnoticeable, unobtrusive, unostentatious.
antonym conspicuous.

inconstant *adj.* capricious, changeable, changeful, erratic, fickle, fluctuating, inconsistent, irresolute, mercurial, moonish, mutable, uncertain, undependable, unreliable, unsettled, unstable, unsteady, vacillating, variable, varying, volatile, wavering, wayward.
antonym constant.

incontestable *adj.* certain, clear, evident, incontrovertible, indisputable, indubitable, irrefutable, obvious, self-evident, sure, undeniable, unquestionable.
antonym uncertain.

incontinence *n.* enuresis.

incontinent *adj.* debauched, dissipated, dissolute, enuretic, lascivious, lecherous, lewd, licentious, loose, lustful, profligate, promiscuous, unbridled, unchaste, unchecked, uncontrollable, uncontrolled, ungovernable, ungoverned, unrestrained, wanton.
antonym continent.

incontrovertible *adj.* certain, clear, established, evident, incontestable, indisputable, indubitable, irrefutable, positive, self-evident, sure, undeniable, unquestionable, unshakable.
antonym uncertain.

inconvenience *n.* annoyance, awkwardness, bother, cumbersomeness, difficulty, disadvantage, disruption, disturbance, disutility, drawback, fuss, hindrance, nuisance, trouble, uneasiness, unhandiness, unsuitableness, untimeliness, unwieldiness, upset, vexation.
antonym convenience.

v. bother, disaccommodate, discommode, disrupt, disturb, irk, put out, put to trouble, trouble, upset.

antonym convenience.

inconvenient *adj.* annoying, awkward, bothersome, cumbersome, difficult, disadvantageous, disturbing, embarrassing, inopportune, tiresome, troublesome, unhandy, unmanageable, unseasonable, unsocial, unsuitable, untimely, untoward, unwieldy, vexatious.
antonym convenient.

incorporate *v.* absorb, amalgamate, assimilate, blend, coalesce, combine, consolidate, embody, fuse, incarnate, include, integrate, merge, mix, subsume, unite.
antonyms separate, split off.

incorporation *n.* absorption, amalgamation, assimilation, association, blend, coalescence, company, federation, fusion, inclusion, integration, merger, society, unification, unifying.
antonyms separation, splitting off.

incorporeal *adj.* bodiless, ethereal, ghostly, illusory, intangible, phantasmal, phantasmic, spectral, spiritual, unfleshy, unreal.
antonym real.

incorrect *adj.* erroneous, false, faulty, flawed, illegitimate, imprecise, improper, inaccurate, inappropriate, inexact, mistaken, out, specious, ungrammatical, unidiomatic, unsuitable, untrue, wrong.
antonym correct.

incorrectness *n.* erroneousness, error, fallacy, falseness, faultiness, illegitimacy, impreciseness, imprecision, impropriety, inaccuracy, inexactness, speciousness, ungrammaticalness, unsoundness, unsuitability, wrongness.
antonym correctness.

incorrigible *adj.* hardened, hopeless, impenitent, incurable, indocile, intractable, inveterate, irreclaimable, irredeemable, irreformable, unreformable, unreformed, unteachable.
antonym reformable.

incorruptibility *n.* honesty, honour, integrity, justness, nobility, probity, uprightness, virtue.
antonym corruptibility.

incorruptible *adj.* everlasting, honest, honourable, imperishable, incorrupt, just, straight, trustworthy, unbribable, undecaying, upright.
antonym corruptible.

increase *v.* add to, advance, aggrandise, amplify, augment, boost, build up, develop, dilate, eke, eke out, enhance, enlarge, escalate, expand, extend, greaten, grow, heighten, inflate, intensify, magnify, mount, multiply, proliferate, prolong, pullulate, raise, snowball, soar, spread, step up, strengthen, swell, wax.
antonym decrease.

n. accrescence, addition, augment, augmentation, auxesis, boost, development, enlargement, escalation, expansion, extension, gain, growth, increment, intensification, proliferation, rise, step-up, surge, upsurge, upsurgence, upturn.
antonym decrease.

increasing *adj.* accrescent, addititious, advancing, broadening, crescent, crescive, developing, expanding, growing, intensifying, mounting, rising, rocketing, sprouting, waxing, widening.
antonym decreasing.

incredible *adj.* absurd, amazing, astonishing, astounding, extraordinary, fabulous, far-fetched, great, implausible, impossible, improbable, inconceivable, inspired, marvellous, preposterous, prodigious, superb, superhuman, unbelievable, unimaginable, unthinkable, wonderful.
antonyms believable, run-of-the-mill.

incredulity *n.* disbelief, distrust, doubt, doubting, incredulousness, scepticism, unbelief.
antonym credulity.

incredulous *adj.* disbelieving, distrustful, doubtful, doubting, dubious, mistrustful, sceptical, suspicious, unbelieving, uncertain, unconvinced.
antonym credulous.

increment *n.* accretion, accrual, accrument, addendum, addition, advancement, augmentation, enlargement, expansion, extension, gain, growth, increase, step up, supplement.
antonym decrease.

incriminate *v.* accuse, arraign, blame, charge, criminate, impeach, implicate, inculpate, indict, involve, point the finger at, recriminate, stigmatise.
antonym exonerate.

incubator *n.* eccaleobion, hatchery.

incubus *n.* affliction, angst, burden, cacod(a)emon, cross, demon, devil, dread, ephialtes, evil spirit, fear, fiend, load, nightmare, oppression, pressure, sorrow, spirit, stress, succubus, trial, worry.

inculcate *v.* drill into, drum into, engrain, hammer into, implant, impress, indoctrinate, infuse, instil, teach.

inculpate *v.* accuse, blame, censure, charge, connect, criminate, drag into, impeach, implicate, incriminate, involve, recriminate.
antonym exonerate.

incumbent *adj.* binding, compulsory, mandatory, necessary, obligatory, prescribed, up to.

incur *v.* arouse, bring upon, contract, draw, earn, expose oneself to, gain, induce, meet with, provoke, run up, suffer.

incurable *adj.* dyed-in-the-wool, fatal, hopeless, immedicable, incorrigible, inoperable, inveterate, irrecoverable, irremediable, recidivistic, remediless, terminal, unmedicinable, untreatable.
antonym curable.

incurious *adj.* apathetic, careless, inattentive, indifferent, unconcerned, uncurious, unenquiring, uninquiring, uninquisitive, uninterested, unreflective.
antonym curious.

incursion *n.* attack, foray, infiltration, inroads, invasion, irruption, penetration, raid.

indebted *adj.* beholden, grateful, in debt, obligated, obliged, thankful.

indecency *n.* bawdiness, coarseness, crudity, foulness, grossness, immodesty, impropriety, impurity, indecorum, indelicacy, lewdness, licentiousness, obscenity, outrageousness, pornography, Rabelaisianism, smut, smuttiness, unseemliness, vileness, vulgarity.
antonyms decency, modesty.

indecent *adj.* blue, coarse, crude, dirty, filthy, foul, gross, immodest, improper, impure, indecorous, indelicate, lewd, licentious, near the knuckle, offensive, outrageous, pornographic, Rabelaisian, salacious, scatological, smutty, tasteless, unbecoming, uncomely, unseemly, vile, vulgar.
antonyms decent, modest.

indecipherable *adj.* crabbed, cramped, illegible, indistinct, indistinguishable, tiny, unclear, unintelligible, unreadable.
antonym readable.

indecision *n.* ambivalence, doubt, hesitancy, hesitation, indecisiveness, irresoluteness, irresolution, shilly-shallying, swither, uncertainty, vacillation, wavering.
antonym decisiveness.

indecisive *adj.* doubtful, faltering, hesitating, hung, in two minds, inconclusive, indefinite, indeterminate, irresolute, pussyfooting, swithering, tentative, uncertain, unclear, undecided, undetermined, unsure, vacillating, wavering.
antonym decisive.

indecorous *adj.* boorish, churlish, coarse, crude, ill-bred, immodest, impolite, improper, indecent, rough, rude, tasteless, uncivil, uncouth, undignified, unmannerly, unseemly, untoward, vulgar.
antonym decorous.

indeed *adv.* actually, certainly, doubtlessly, forsooth, positively, really, strictly, to be sure, truly, undeniably, undoubtedly, verily, veritably.

indefatigable *adj.* assiduous, diligent, dogged, inexhaustible, patient, persevering, pertinacious, relentless, sedulous, tireless, undying, unfailing, unflagging, unremitting, unresting, untireable, untiring, unweariable, unwearied, unwearying.
antonyms flagging, slothful.

indefensible *adj.* faulty, inexcusable, insupportable, unforgivable, unjustifiable, unjustified, unpardonable, untenable, unwarrantable, wrong.
antonym defensible.

indefinable *adj.* dim, hazy, impalpable, indescribable, indistinct, inexpressible, nameless, obscure, subtle, unclear, unrealised, vague.
antonym definable.

indefinite *adj.* ambiguous, confused, doubtful, equivocal, evasive, general, ill-defined, imprecise, indeterminate, indistinct, inexact, loose, obscure, uncertain, unclear, undecided, undefined, undetermined, unfixed, unfocus(s)ed, unformed, unformulated, unknown, unlimited, unresolved, unsettled, vague.

antonyms clear, limited.

indefinitely *adv.* ad infinitum, continually, endlessly, eternally, for ever, for life, sine die, time without end, world without end.

indelible *adj.* enduring, indestructible, ineffaceable, ineradicable, inerasable, inexpungible, inextirpable, ingrained, lasting, permanent, unerasable.
antonyms erasable, impermanent.

indelicacy *n.* bad taste, coarseness, crudity, grossness, immodesty, impropriety, indecency, obscenity, offensiveness, rudeness, smuttiness, suggestiveness, tastelessness, underniceness, vulgarity.
antonym delicacy.

indelicate *adj.* blue, coarse, crude, embarrassing, gross, immodest, improper, indecent, indecorous, low, obscene, off-colour, offensive, risqué, rude, suggestive, tasteless, unbecoming, unmaidenly, unseemly, untoward, vulgar, warm.
antonym delicate.

indemnify *v.* compensate, endorse, exempt, free, guarantee, insure, pay, protect, reimburse, remunerate, repair, repay, requite, satisfy, secure, underwrite.

indemnity *n.* amnesty, compensation, excusal, exemption, guarantee, immunity, impunity, insurance, privilege, protection, redress, reimbursement, remuneration, reparation, requital, restitution, satisfaction, security.

indent[1] *v.* cut, dent, dint, mark, nick, notch, pink, scallop, serrate.

indent[2] *v.* ask for, demand, order, request, requisition.

indentation *n.* bash, cut, dent, depression, dimple, dint, dip, hollow, jag, nick, notch, pit.

indented *adj.* dancetté, dented, impressed, notched, zigzag.

independence *n.* affranchisement, autarchy, autarky, autonomy, decolonisation, freedom, home rule, individualism, liberty, manumission, self-determination, self-government, self-reliance, self-rule, self-sufficiency, separation, sovereignty, uhuru, unconventionality.
antonyms conventionality, dependence.

independent *adj.* absolute, autarchical, autocephalous, autogenous, autonomous, bold, crossbench, decontrolled, free, individualistic, liberated, non-aligned, one's own man, self-contained, self-determining, self-governing, self-reliant, self-sufficient, self-supporting, separate, separated, sovereign, unaided, unbiased, unconnected, unconstrained, uncontrolled, unconventional, unrelated, upon one's legs.
antonyms conventional, dependent, timid.

independently *adv.* alone, autonomously, by oneself, individually, on one's own, on one's tod, separately, solo, unaided.
antonym together.

indescribable *adj.* incommunicable, indefinable, ineffable, inexpressible, phraseless, unutterable.
antonym describable.

indestructible *adj.* abiding, durable, enduring, eternal, everlasting, immortal, imperishable, incorruptible, indissoluble, infrangible, lasting, permanent, unbreakable, unfading.
antonyms breakable, mortal.

indeterminacy *n.* impreciseness, inconclusiveness, indefiniteness, inexactness, openendedness, uncertainty, vagueness.
antonym definiteness.

indeterminate *adj.* imprecise, inconclusive, indefinite, inexact, open-ended, uncertain, undecided, undefined, undetermined, unfixed, unspecified, unstated, unstipulated, vague.
antonyms exact, limited.

index *n.* clue, guide, hand, indication, indicator, mark, needle, pointer, sign, symptom, table, token.

indicate *v.* add up to, bespeak, betoken, denote, designate, display, evince, express, imply, manifest, mark, point out, point to, read, record, register, reveal, show, signify, specify, suggest, telegraph, tip.

indicated *adj.* advisable, called-for, desirable, necessary, needed, recommended, required, suggested.

indication *n.* clue, endeixis, evidence, explanation, forewarning, hint, index, inkling, intimation, manifestation, mark, note, omen, portent, prognostic, sign, signal, signpost, suggestion, symptom, warning.

indicative *adj.* denotative, exhibitive, indicatory, indicial, significant, suggestive, symptomatic.

indicator *n.* display, gauge, gnomon, guide, index, mark, marker, meter, pointer, sign, signal, signpost, symbol, winker.

indict *v.* accuse, arraign, charge, criminate, impeach, incriminate, prosecute, recriminate, summon, summons, tax.
antonym exonerate.

indictment *n.* accusation, allegation, charge, crimination, impeachment, incrimination, prosecution, recrimination, summons.
antonym exoneration.

indifference *n.* aloofness, apathy, callousness, coldness, coolness, detachment, disinterestedness, dispassion, disregard, equity, heedlessness, impartiality, inattention, insignificance, irrelevance, latitudinarianism, negligence, neutrality, objectivity, pococurant(e)ism, stoicalness, unconcern, unimportance.
antonyms bias, interest.

indifferent *adj.* aloof, apathetic, average, callous, careless, cold, cool, detached, disinterested, dispassionate, distant, equitable, fair, heedless, immaterial, impartial, impervious, inattentive, incurious, insignificant, jack easy, mediocre, middling, moderate, neutral, non-aligned, objective, ordinary, passable, perfunctory, pococurante, regardless, so-so, unbiased, uncaring, unconcerned, undistinguished, unenquiring, unenthusiastic, unexcited, unimportant, unimpressed, uninspired, uninterested, uninvolved, unmoved,

unprejudiced, unresponsive, unsympathetic.
antonyms biased, interested.

indigence *n*. deprivation, destitution, distress, necessity, need, penury, poverty, privation, want.
antonym affluence.

indigenous *adj*. aboriginal, autochthonous, home-grown, indigene, local, native, original.
antonym foreign.

indigent *adj*. destitute, impecunious, impoverished, in forma pauperis, in want, necessitous, needy, penniless, penurious, poor, poverty-stricken, straitened.
antonym affluent.

indigestion *n*. cardialgia, dyspepsia, dyspepsy, heartburn, water-brash.

indignant *adj*. angry, annoyed, disgruntled, exasperated, fuming, furibund, furious, heated, huffy, in a paddy, in a wax, incensed, irate, livid, mad, marked, miffed, peeved, provoked, resentful, riled, scornful, sore, waxy, wrathful, wroth.
antonym pleased.

indignation *n*. anger, exasperation, fury, ire, pique, rage, resentment, scorn, umbrage, wax, wrath.
antonym pleasure.

indignity *n*. abuse, affront, contempt, contumely, disgrace, dishonour, disrespect, humiliation, incivility, injury, insult, obloquy, opprobrium, outrage, reproach, slight, snub.
antonym honour.

indirect *adj*. ancillary, backhanded, circuitous, circumlocutory, collateral, contingent, crooked, devious, incidental, meandering, mediate, oblique, periphrastic, rambling, roundabout, secondary, slanted, subsidiary, tortuous, unintended, wandering, winding, zigzag.
antonym direct.

indirectly *adv*. circumlocutorily, deviously, hintingly, obliquely, periphrastically, roundaboutedly, roundaboutly, second-hand.
antonym directly.

indiscernible *adj*. hidden, impalpable, imperceptible, indistinct, indistinguishable, invisible, minuscule, minute, tiny, unapparent, undiscernible.
antonym clear.

indiscreet *adj*. careless, foolish, hasty, heedless, ill-advised, ill-considered, ill-judged, impolitic, imprudent, incautious, injudicious, naïve, rash, reckless, tactless, temerarious, temerous, undiplomatic, unthinking, unwise.
antonym discreet.

indiscretion *n*. boob, brick, error, faux pas, folly, foolishness, gaffe, imprudence, mistake, rashness, recklessness, slip, slip of the tongue, tactlessness, temerity.
antonym discretion.

indiscriminate *adj*. aimless, careless, chaotic, confused, desultory, general, haphazard, higgledy-piggledy, hit or miss, indiscriminating, indiscriminative, jumbled, mingled, miscellaneous, mixed, mongrel, motley, prom-

iscuous, random, sweeping, uncritical, undifferentiated, undiscriminating, undistinguishable, unmethodical, unparticular, unselective, unsystematic, wholesale.
antonyms deliberate, selective.

indiscriminately *adv*. carelessly, haphazardly, in the mass, randomly, unsystematically, wholesale, without fear or favour.
antonyms deliberately, selectively.

indispensable *adj*. basic, crucial, essential, imperative, key, necessary, needed, needful, required, requisite, vital.
antonym unnecessary.

indisposed[1] *adj*. ailing, ill, laid up, poorly, sick, sickly, under the weather, unwell.
antonym well.

indisposed[2] *adj*. averse, disinclined, loath, not of a mind (to), not willing, reluctant, unwilling.
antonym inclined.

indisposition[1] *n*. ailment, illness, sickness.
antonym health.

indisposition[2] *n*. aversion, disinclination, dislike, distaste, hesitancy, reluctance, unwillingness.
antonym inclination.

indisputable *adj*. absolute, certain, evident, incontestable, incontrovertible, indubitable, irrebuttable, irrefragable, irrefutable, positive, sure, unanswerable, unassailable, undeniable, unquestionable.
antonym doubtful.

indissoluble *adj*. abiding, binding, enduring, eternal, fixed, imperishable, incorruptible, indestructible, inseparable, inviolable, lasting, permanent, sempiternal, solid, unbreakable.
antonym impermanent.

indistinct *adj*. ambiguous, bleary, blurred, confused, dim, distant, doubtful, faint, fuzzy, hazy, ill-defined, indefinite, indeterminate, indiscernible, indistinguishable, misty, muffled, mumbled, obscure, shadowy, slurred, unclear, undefined, unintelligible, vague.
antonym distinct.

indistinguishable *adj*. alike, identical, interchangeable, same, tantamount, twin.
antonyms distinguishable, unlike.

individual *n*. being, bloke, body, chap, character, creature, fellow, individuum, mortal, party, person, personage, punter, soul.
adj. characteristic, discrete, distinct, distinctive, exclusive, identical, idiosyncratic, own, particular, peculiar, personal, personalised, proper, respective, separate, several, single, singular, special, specific, unique.

individualism *n*. anarchism, egocentricity, egoism, free-thinking, free-thought, independence, libertarianism, originality, self-direction, self-interest, self-reliance.
antonym conventionality.

individualist *n*. anarchist, free-thinker, independent, libertarian, lone wolf, loner, maverick, nonconformist, original.
antonym conventionalist.

individualistic *adj*. anarchistic, characteristic,

distinctive, egocentric, egoistic, iconoclastic, idiosyncratic, independent, individual, libertarian, non-conformist, original, particular, self-reliant, special, typical, unconventional, unique.
antonym conventionalistic.

individuality *n.* character, discreteness, distinction, distinctiveness, haecceity, originality, peculiarity, personality, separateness, singularity, unicity, uniqueness.
antonym sameness.

individually *adv.* independently, particularly, separately, seriatim et privatim, severally, singly.
antonym together.

indivisible *adj.* impartible, indiscerptible, inseparable, undividable.
antonym divisible.

indoctrinate *v.* brainwash, catechise, drill, ground, imbue, initiate, instruct, school, teach, train.

indoctrination *n.* brainwashing, catechesis, catechetics, inculcation, instruction, schooling, training.

indolence *n.* do-nothingism, fainéance, heaviness, idleness, inactivity, inertia, inertness, languidness, languor, laziness, lethargy, shirking, slacking, sloth, sluggishness, torpidity, torpidness, torpitude, torpor.
antonyms activeness, enthusiasm, industriousness.

indolent *adj.* fainéant, idle, inactive, inert, lackadaisical, languid, lazy, lethargic, listless, lumpish, slack, slothful, slow, sluggard, sluggish, torpid.
antonyms active, enthusiastic, industrious.

indomitable *adj.* bold, intrepid, invincible, resolute, staunch, steadfast, unbeatable, unconquerable, undaunted, unflinching, untameable, unyielding.
antonyms compliant, timid.

indoor *adj.* inside, umbratile, umbratilous.
antonym outdoor.

indubitable *adj.* certain, evident, incontestable, incontrovertible, indisputable, irrebuttable, irrefragable, irrefutable, obvious, sure, unanswerable, unarguable, undeniable, undoubtable, undoubted, unquestionable, veritable.
antonym arguable.

induce *v.* actuate, bring about, cause, convince, draw, effect, encourage, engender, generate, get, give rise to, impel, incite, influence, instigate, lead to, move, occasion, persuade, press, prevail upon, produce, prompt, talk into.

inducement *n.* attraction, bait, carrot, cause, come-on, consideration, encouragement, impulse, incentive, incitement, influence, lure, motive, reason, reward, spur, stimulus.
antonym disincentive.

induct *v.* consecrate, enthrone, inaugurate, initiate, install, introduce, invest, ordain, swear in.

induction *n.* conclusion, consecration, deduc-

tion, enthronement, generalisation, inauguration, inference, initiation, installation, institution, introduction, investiture, ordination.

indulge *v.* baby, cocker, coddle, cosset, favour, foster, give in to, go along with, gratify, humour, mollycoddle, pamper, pander to, pet, regale, satiate, satisfy, spoil, treat (oneself), yield to.

indulge in give free rein to, give oneself up to, give way to, luxuriate in, revel in, wallow in.

indulgence *n.* appeasement, courtesy, excess, extravagance, favour, forbearance, good will, gratification, immoderateness, immoderation, intemperance, intemperateness, kindness, leniency, luxury, pampering, partiality, patience, permissiveness, privilege, prodigality, profligacy, profligateness, satiation, satisfaction, self-gratification, self-indulgence, spoiling, tolerance, treat, understanding.
antonyms moderation, strictness.

indulgent *adj.* complaisant, compliant, easygoing, favourable, fond, forbearing, gentle, gratifying, intemperate, kind, kindly, lenient, liberal, mild, permissive, prodigal, self-indulgent, tender, tolerant, understanding.
antonyms moderate, strict.

industrialist *n.* baron, boss, capitalist, captain of industry, financier, magnate, manufacturer, mill-owner, producer, tycoon.

industrious *adj.* active, assiduous, busy, conscientious, deedy, diligent, energetic, hard-working, laborious, persevering, persistent, productive, purposeful, sedulous, steady, tireless, zealous.
antonym indolent.

industriously *adv.* assiduously, conscientiously, diligently, doggedly, hard, perseveringly, sedulously, steadily, with one's nose to the grindstone.
antonym indolently.

industry *n.* activity, application, assiduity, business, commerce, determination, diligence, effort, labour, manufacturing, perseverance, persistence, production, tirelessness, toil, trade, vigour, zeal.
antonym indolence.

inebriate *v.* addle, animate, arouse, carry away, excite, exhilarate, fire, fuddle, intoxicate, stimulate, stupefy.
antonyms dampen, sober up.

inebriated *adj.* befuddled, blind drunk, blotto, drunk, glorious, half seas over, half-cut, half-drunk, in one's cups, incapable, inebriate, intoxicated, legless, merry, paralytic, pie-eyed, plastered, sloshed, smashed, sozzled, stoned, stotious, three sheets in the wind, tight, tipsy, tired and emotional, under the influence.
antonym sober.

inebriation *n.* drunkenness, inebriety, insobriety, intemperance, intoxication, sottishness, tipsiness.
antonym sobriety.

inedible *adj.* deadly, harmful, inesculent, injurious, noxious, poisonous, uneatable.

antonym edible.
ineducable *adj.* incorrigible, indocile, unteach-able.
antonym educable.
ineffable *adj.* incommunicable, indescribable, inexpressible, unimpartible, unspeakable, un-utterable.
antonym describable.
ineffective, ineffectual *adj.* abortive, barren, bootless, emasculate, feeble, fruitless, futile, idle, impotent, inadequate, incompetent, ineffective, ineffectual, inefficacious, in-efficient, inept, lame, powerless, unavailing, unproductive, useless, vain, void, weak, worthless.
antonyms effective, effectual.
inefficacy *n.* futility, inadequacy, ineffective-ness, ineffectuality, ineffectualness, unpro-ductiveness, uselessness.
antonym efficacy.
inefficiency *n.* carelessness, disorganisation, incompetence, muddle, negligence, slack-ness, sloppiness, waste, wastefulness.
antonym efficiency.
inefficient *adj.* incompetent, inept, inexpert, money-wasting, negligent, slipshod, sloppy, time-wasting, unworkmanlike, wasteful.
antonym efficient.
inelegant *adj.* awkward, barbarous, clumsy, coarse, crass, crude, gauche, graceless, indelicate, laboured, rough, uncourtly, un-couth, uncultivated, ungainly, ungraceful, unpolished, unrefined, unsophisticated.
antonym elegant.
ineligible *adj.* disqualified, improper, inapprop-riate, incompetent, objectionable, unaccept-able, undesirable, unequipped, unfit, un-fitted, unqualified, unsuitable, unworthy.
antonym eligible.
inept *adj.* absurd, awkward, bungling, cack-handed, clumsy, fatuous, futile, gauche, improper, inappropriate, inapt, incompetent, inexpert, infelicitous, irrelevant, maladroit, malapropos, meaningless, ridiculous, unfit, unhandy, unskilful, unworkmanlike.
antonyms adroit, apt.
ineptitude *n.* absurdity, clumsiness, crassness, fatuity, futility, gaucheness, gaucherie, in-appropriateness, incapacity, incompetence, ineptness, inexpertness, irrelevance, point-lessness, stupidity, unfitness, unhandiness, uselessness.
antonyms aptitude, skill.
inequality *n.* bias, difference, disparity, disprop_ortion, dissimilarity, diversity, imparity, in-adequacy, irregularity, preferentiality, pre-judice, unequalness, unevenness.
antonym equality.
inequitable *adj.* biased, discriminatory, one-sided, partial, partisan, preferential, pre-judiced, unequal, unfair, unjust, wrongful.
antonym equitable.
inequity *n.* abuse, bias, discrimination, in-justice, maltreatment, mistreatment, one-sidedness, partiality, prejudice, unfairness,

unjustness.
antonym equity.
inert *adj.* apathetic, dead, dormant, dull, idle, immobile, inactive, inanimate, indolent, insensible, lazy, leaden, lifeless, motionless, nerveless, numb, passive, quiescent, sense-less, slack, sleepy, slothful, sluggish, somno-lent, static, still, torpid, unmoving, unreact-ing, unresponsive.
antonyms alive, animated.
inertia *n.* accedia, accidie, apathy, deadness, drowsiness, dullness, idleness, immobility, inactivity, indolence, insensibility, languor, lassitude, laziness, lethargy, listlessness, ner-velessness, numbness, passivity, sleepiness, sloth, sluggishness, somnolence, stillness, stupor, torpor, unresponsiveness.
antonyms activity, liveliness.
inescapable *adj.* certain, destined, fated, ineluct-able, inevitable, inexorable, irrevocable, sure, unalterable, unavoidable, unprevent-able.
antonym escapable.
inessential *adj.* accidental, dispensable, expend-able, extraneous, extrinsic, irrelevant, need-less, non-essential, optional, redundant, secondary, spare, superfluous, surplus, un-asked-for, uncalled-for, unessential, unim-portant, unnecessary.
antonym essential.
n. accessory, appendage, expendable, extra, extravagance, luxury, non-essential, super-fluity, trimming.
antonym essential.
inestimable *adj.* immeasurable, immense, incal-culable, incomputable, infinite, invaluable, measureless, precious, priceless, prodigious, uncountable, unfathomable, unlimited, un-told, vast.
antonym insignificant.
inevitable *adj.* assured, automatic, certain, compulsory, decreed, destined, fated, fixed, ineluctable, inescapable, inexorable, irrevoc-able, mandatory, necessary, obligatory, ordained, settled, sure, unalterable, unavert-able, unavoidable, unpreventable, unshunn-able.
antonyms alterable, avoidable, uncertain.
inevitably *adv.* automatically, certainly, incon-testably, ineluctably, inescapably, necessari-ly, of necessity, perforce, surely, unavoidably.
inexact *adj.* erroneous, fuzzy, imprecise, inaccu-rate, incorrect, indefinite, indeterminate, indistinct, lax, loose, muddled, woolly.
antonym exact.
inexactitude *n.* blunder, error, impreciseness, imprecision, inaccuracy, incorrectness, inde-finiteness, inexactness, laxness, looseness, misalculation, mistake, woolliness.
antonym exactitude.
inexcusable *adj.* blameworthy, indefensible, inexpiable, intolerable, outrageous, repre-hensible, shameful, unacceptable, unforgiv-able, unjustifiable, unpardonable, unwarrant-able.

antonyms excusable, venial.

inexhaustible *adj.* abundant, bottomless, boundless, copious, endless, exhaustless, illimitable, indefatigable, infinite, lavish, limitless, measureless, never-ending, never-failing, tireless, unbounded, undaunted, unfailing, unflagging, unlimited, untiring, unwearied, unwearying.
antonym limited.

inexorable *adj.* adamant, cruel, hard, harsh, immovable, implacable, ineluctable, inescapable, inflexible, intransigent, irreconcilable, irresistible, irrevocable, merciless, obdurate, pitiless, relentless, remorseless, severe, unalterable, unappeasable, unavertable, unbending, uncompromising, unrelenting, unyielding.
antonyms flexible, lenient, yielding.

inexorably *adv.* implacably, ineluctably, inescapably, irresistibly, irrevocably, mercilessly, pitilessly, relentlessly, remorselessly, resistlessly.

inexpedient *adj.* detrimental, disadvantageous, foolish, ill-advised, ill-chosen, ill-judged, impolitic, impractical, imprudent, inadvisable, inappropriate, indiscreet, injudicious, misguided, senseless, unadvisable, undesirable, undiplomatic, unfavourable, unsuitable, unwise, wrong.
antonym expedient.

inexpensive *adj.* bargain, bon marché, budget, cheap, economical, low-cost, low-priced, modest, reasonable, uncostly.
antonym expensive.

inexperience *n.* callowness, greenness, ignorance, inexpertness, innocence, naïvety, nescience, newness, rawness, strangeness, unexpertness, unfamiliarity, unsophistication, verdancy.
antonym experience.

inexperienced *adj.* amateur, callow, fresh, green, immature, inexpert, innocent, nescient, new, raw, unaccustomed, unacquainted, unbearded, unfamiliar, unpractical, unpractised, unschooled, unseasoned, unskilled, unsophisticated, untrained, untravelled, untried, unused, unversed, verdant.
antonym experienced.

inexpert *adj.* amateurish, awkward, blundering, bungling, clumsy, incompetent, inept, maladroit, unhandy, unpractised, unprofessional, unskilful, unskilled, untaught, untrained, untutored, unworkmanlike.
antonym expert.

inexplicable *adj.* baffling, enigmatic, impenetrable, incomprehensible, incredible, inscrutable, insoluble, intractable, miraculous, mysterious, mystifying, puzzling, strange, unaccountable, unexplainable, unfathomable, unintelligible, unsolvable.
antonym explicable.

inexplicably *adv.* bafflingly, incomprehensibly, incredibly, miraculously, mysteriously, mystifyingly, puzzlingly, strangely, unaccountably, unexplainably.

antonym explicably.

inexpressible *adj.* incommunicable, indefinable, indescribable, ineffable, nameless, undescribable, unsayable, unspeakable, untellable, unutterable.

inexpressive *adj.* bland, blank, dead-pan, emotionless, empty, expressionless, immobile, impassive, inanimate, inscrutable, lifeless, poker-faced, stolid, stony, unexpressive, vacant.
antonym expressive.

inextinguishable *adj.* deathless, enduring, eternal, everlasting, immortal, imperishable, indestructible, irrepressible, lasting, unconquerable, undying, unquellable, unquenchable, unsuppressible.
antonyms impermanent, perishable.

inextricably *adv.* indissolubly, indistinguishably, inseparably, intricately, irresolubly, irretrievably, irreversibly.

infallibility *n.* accuracy, dependability, faultlessness, impeccability, inerrancy, inevitability, irrefutability, irreproachability, omniscience, perfection, reliability, safety, supremacy, sureness, trustworthiness, unerringness.
antonym fallibility.

infallible *adj.* accurate, certain, dependable, fail-safe, faultless, foolproof, impeccable, inerrable, inerrant, irreproachable, omniscient, perfect, reliable, sound, sure, sure-fire, trustworthy, unbeatable, unerring, unfailing, unfaltering, unfaulty, unimpeachable.
antonym fallible.

infamous *adj.* abhorrent, abominable, atrocious, base, dastardly, despicable, detestable, discreditable, disgraceful, dishonourable, disreputable, egregious, execrable, facinorous, flagitious, hateful, heinous, ignoble, ignominious, ill-famed, iniquitous, knavish, loathsome, monstrous, nefarious, notorious, odious, opprobrious, outrageous, scandalous, scurvy, shameful, shocking, vile, villainous, wicked.
antonym glorious.

infamy *n.* atrocity, baseness, crime, dastardliness, depravity, discredit, disgrace, dishonour, disrepute, enormity, ignominy, improbity, notoriety, obloquy, odium, opprobrium, outrageousness, scandal, shame, stain, stigma, turpitude, villainy, wickedness.
antonym glory.

infancy *n.* babyhood, beginnings, birth, childhood, commencement, cradle, dawn, embryonic stage, emergence, genesis, inception, origins, outset, start, youth.
antonym adulthood.

infant *n.* babe, babe in arms, baby, bairn, bambino, child, neonate, nipper, nurseling, papoose, suckling, tiny, toddler, tot, wean, weanling, youngling.
antonym adult.
adj. baby, childish, dawning, developing, early, emergent, growing, immature, inchoate, incipient, initial, juvenile, nascent, newborn, rudimentary, unfledged, unformed,

young, youthful.
antonym adult.

infantile *adj.* adolescent, babyish, childish, immature, juvenile, puerile, tender, undeveloped, young, youthful.
antonyms adult, mature.

infatuated *adj.* befooled, beguiled, besotted, bewitched, captivated, crazy, deluded, enamoured, enraptured, fascinated, fixated, hypnotised, intoxicated, mad, mesmerised, obsessed, possessed, ravished, smitten, spellbound.
antonyms disenchanted, indifferent.

infatuation *n.* besottedness, crush, dotage, engouement, fascination, fixation, folly, fondness, intoxication, madness, mania, obsession, passion, possession.
antonyms disenchantment, indifference.

infect *v.* affect, blight, canker, contaminate, corrupt, defile, enthuse, influence, inject, inspire, pervert, poison, pollute, taint, touch, vitiate.

infection *n.* contagion, contamination, corruption, defilement, disease, epidemic, illness, inflammation, influence, miasma, pestilence, poison, pollution, sepsis, septicity, taint, virus.

infectious *adj.* catching, communicable, contagious, contaminating, corrupting, deadly, defiling, epidemic, infective, miasmic, miasmous, pestilential, poisoning, poisonous, polluting, spreading, transmissible, transmittable, venemous, virulent, vitiating.

infelicitous *adj.* gauche, ill-timed, inappropriate, inopportune, maladroit, tactless, unapt, unfortunate, unhappy, unsuitable, untimely.
antonym felicitous.

infelicity *n.* despair, gaucheness, inappositeness, inappropriateness, inaptness, incongruity, inopportuneness, misery, misfortune, sadness, sorrow, tactlessness, unfortunateness, unhappiness, unsuitability, untimeliness, woe, wretchedness, wrongness.
antonyms aptness, felicity, happiness.

infer *v.* assume, conclude, conjecture, construe, deduce, derive, extract, extrapolate, gather, presume, surmise, understand.

inference *n.* assumption, conclusion, conjecture, consequence, construction, corollary, deduction, extrapolation, illation, interpretation, presumption, reading, surmise.

inferior *adj.* bad, crummy, dog, grotty, humble, imperfect, indifferent, junior, lesser, low, lower, low-grade, mean, mediocre, menial, minor, one-horse, paravail, poor, poorer, provant, schlock, secondary, second-class, second-rate, shoddy, slipshod, slovenly, subordinate, subsidiary, substandard, under, underneath, undistinguished, unsatisfactory, unworthy, worse.
antonym superior.
n. junior, menial, minion, subordinate, underling, understrapper, vassal.
antonym superior.

inferiority *n.* badness, baseness, deficiency, humbleness, imperfection, inadequacy, insignificance, lowliness, meanness, mediocrity, shoddiness, slovenliness, subordination, subservience, unimportance, unworthiness, worthlessness.
antonym superiority.

infernal *adj.* accursed, Acherontic, chthonian, chthonic, damnable, damned, demonic, devilish, diabolical, fiendish, Hadean, hellish, malevolent, malicious, Mephistophelian, Plutonian, satanic, Stygian, Tartarean, underworld.
antonym heavenly.

infertile *adj.* acarpous, arid, barren, dried-up, effete, infecund, infructuous, non-productive, parched, sterile, unbearing, unfruitful, unproductive.
antonym fertile.

infertility *n.* aridity, aridness, barrenness, effeteness, infecundity, sterility, unfruitfulness, unproductiveness.
antonym fertility.

infest *v.* beset, flood, infiltrate, invade, overrun, overspread, penetrate, permeate, pervade, ravage, swarm, throng.

infested *adj.* alive, beset, bristling, crawling, infiltrated, lousy, overrun, overspread, permeated, pervaded, plagued, ravaged, ridden, swarming, teeming, vermined, verminy.

infidel *n.* atheist, disbeliever, free-thinker, giaour, heathen, heretic, iconoclast, irreligionist, nullifidian, pagan, sceptic, unbeliever.
antonym believer.

infidelity *n.* adultery, apostasy, bad faith, betrayal, cheating, disbelief, disloyalty, duplicity, faithlessness, false-heartedness, falseness, iconoclasm, irreligion, perfidy, recreancy, renegation, scepticism, traitorhood, traitorousness, treachery, unbelief, unfaithfulness.
antonym fidelity.

infiltrate *v.* creep into, filter, infilter, insinuate, interpenetrate, intrude, penetrate, percolate, permeate, pervade, sift.

infiltration *n.* entr(y)ism, insinuation, interpenetration, intrusion, penetration, percolation, permeation, pervasion.

infiltrator *n.* entr(y)ist, insinuator, intruder, penetrator, seditionary, spy, subversive, subverter.

infinite *adj.* absolute, bottomless, boundless, countless, enormous, eternal, everlasting, fathomless, illimitable, immeasurable, immense, incomputable, inestimable, inexhaustible, interminable, limitless, measureless, never-ending, numberless, perpetual, stupendous, total, unbounded, uncountable, uncounted, unfathomable, untold, vast, wide.
antonym finite.

infinitesimal *adj.* atomic, exiguous, imperceptible, inappreciable, inconsiderable, insignificant, microscopic, minuscule, minute, negli-

gible, paltry, teeny, tiny, unnoticeable, wee.
antonyms significant, substantial.

infinity *n.* boundlessness, countlessless, endlessness, eternity, everlasting, everlastingness, illimitibleness, immeasurableness, immensity, inexhaustibility, infinitude, interminableness, limitlessness, perpetuity, vastness.
antonyms finiteness, limitation.

infirm *adj.* ailing, crippled, debilitated, decrepit, dicky, doddering, doddery, enfeebled, failing, faltering, feeble, fickle, frail, hesitant, indecisive, insecure, irresolute, lame, poorly, sickly, unreliable, wavering, weak, wobbly.
antonyms healthy, strong.

infirmity *n.* ailment, complaint, debility, decrepitude, defect, deficiency, dickiness, disease, disorder, failing, fault, feebleness, foible, frailty, ill health, illness, imperfection, instability, malady, sickliness, sickness, vulnerability, weakness.
antonyms health, strength.

inflame *v.* aggravate, agitate, anger, arouse, embitter, enkindle, enrage, exacerbate, exasperate, excite, fan, fire, foment, fuel, galvanise, heat, ignite, impassion, incense, increase, infatuate, infuriate, intensify, intoxicate, kindle, madden, provoke, ravish, rile, rouse, stimulate, worsen.
antonyms cool, quench.

inflamed *adj.* angry, chafing, enraged, erythematous, excited, festering, fevered, heated, hot, impassioned, incensed, infected, poisoned, red, septic, sore, swollen.

inflammable *adj.* burnable, choleric, combustible, deflagrable, flammable, incendiary, irascible, piceous, pyrophorous, short-tempered, volatile.
antonyms flame-proof, incombustible, non-flammable, non-inflammable.

inflammation *n.* abscess, burning, empyema, erythema, heat, infection, painfulness, rash, redness, sepsis, septicity, sore, soreness, tenderness.

inflammatory *adj.* anarchic, demagogic, explosive, fiery, incendiary, incitative, inflaming, instigative, insurgent, intemperate, provocative, rabble-rousing, rabid, riotous, seditious.
antonyms calming, pacific.

inflate *v.* aerate, aggrandise, amplify, balloon, bloat, blow out, blow up, bombast, boost, dilate, distend, enlarge, escalate, exaggerate, expand, increase, puff out, puff up, pump up, swell, tumefy.
antonym deflate.

inflated *adj.* ballooned, bloated, blown up, bombastic, dilated, distended, euphuistic, exaggerated, flatulent, grandiloquent, magniloquent, ostentatious, overblown, pompous, puffed out, swollen, tumefied, tumid, turgid.
antonym deflated.

inflation *n.* aggrandisement, ballooning, bloating, dilation, distension, enhancement, enlargement, escalation, expansion, extension, hyperinflation, increase, intensification, rise, spread, swelling, tumefaction.

antonym deflation.

inflexibility *n.* fixity, hardness, immovability, immutability, immutableness, inelasticity, intractability, intransigence, obduracy, obstinacy, rigidity, steeliness, stiffness, stringency, stubbornness, unsuppleness.
antonym flexibility.

inflexible *adj.* adamant, dyed-in-the-wool, entrenched, fast, firm, fixed, hard, hardened, immovable, immutable, implacable, inelastic, inexorable, intractable, intransigent, iron, non-flexible, obdurate, obstinate, relentless, resolute, rigid, rigorous, set, steadfast, steely, stiff, strict, stringent, stubborn, taut, unaccommodating, unadaptable, unbending, unchangeable, uncompromising, unpliable, unpliant, unsupple, unyielding.
antonym flexible.

inflict *v.* administer, afflict, apply, burden, deal, deliver, enforce, exact, force, impose, lay, levy, mete, perpetrate, visit, wreak.

infliction *n.* administration, affliction, burden, castigation, chastisement, exaction, imposition, nemesis, penalty, perpetration, punishment, retribution, trouble, visitation, worry, wreaking.

influence *n.* agency, ascendancy, authority, bias, charisma, clout, connections, control, credit, direction, domination, drag, effect, éminence grise, good offices, guidance, hold, importance, leverage, magnetism, mastery, power, pressure, prestige, pull, reach, rule, scope, spell, standing, strength, string-pulling, sway, teaching, training, weight, wire-pulling.
v. affect, alter, arouse, bias, change, control, direct, dispose, dominate, edge, guide, head, impel, impress, incite, incline, induce, instigate, manipulate, manoeuvre, modify, motivate, move, persuade, point, predispose, prompt, pull, pull wires, rouse, strings, sway, teach, train, weigh with.

influential *adj.* ascendant, authoritative, charismatic, cogent, compelling, controlling, dominant, dominating, effective, efficacious, forcible, guiding, important, instrumental, leading, momentous, moving, persuasive, potent, powerful, significant, strong, telling, weighty, well-placed.
antonym ineffectual.

influenza *n.* dog's disease, flu, grip, grippe.

influx *n.* access, accession, arrival, consignment, convergence, flood, flow, incursion, inflow, inrush, instreaming, inundation, invasion, rush.

inform[1] *v.* acquaint, advise, apprise, brief, clue up, communicate, enlighten, fill in, illuminate, impart, instruct, intimate, leak, notify, teach, tell, tip off, wise up.

inform on accuse, betray, blab, blow the whistle, clype, denounce, denunciate, dob (in), grass, incriminate, inculpate, nark, peach, rat, sing, snitch, squeal, tell on, whistle.

inform[2] *v.* animate, characterise, endue, fill, illuminate, imbue, inspire, invest, irradiate, light up, permeate, suffuse, typify.

informal *adj.* approachable, casual, colloquial, congenial, cosy, easy, familiar, free, homely, irregular, natural, relaxed, relaxing, simple, unbuttoned, unceremonious, unconstrained, unofficial, unorthodox, unpretentious, unsolemn.
antonym formal.

informality *n.* approachability, casualness, congeniality, cosiness, ease, familiarity, freedom, homeliness, irregularity, naturalness, relaxation, simplicity, unceremoniousness, unpretentiousness.
antonym formality.

informally *adj.* casually, colloquially, confidentially, cosily, easily, en famille, familiarly, freely, on the quiet, privately, simply, unceremoniously, unofficially.
antonym formally.

information *n.* advices, blurb, briefing, bulletin, bumf, clues, communiqué, data, databank, database, dope, dossier, enlightenment, facts, gen, illumination, info, input, instruction, intelligence, knowledge, low-down, message, news, notice, report, tidings, word.

informative *adj.* chatty, communicative, constructive, edifying, educational, enlightening, forthcoming, gossipy, illuminating, informatory, instructive, newsy, revealing, revelatory, useful, valuable.
antonym uninformative.

informed *adj.* abreast, acquainted, au courant, au fait, authoritative, briefed, clued up, conversant, enlightened, erudite, expert, familiar, filled in, genned up, hep, in the know, knowledgeable, learned, posted, primed, scholarly, trained, up to date, versed, well-informed, well-read, well-researched.
antonyms ignorant, unaware.

informer *n.* betrayer, canary, denouncer, denunciator, fink, fiz(z)gig, grass, Judas, nark, singer, sneak, snitch(er), snout, squeak, squealer, stool pigeon, stoolie, supergrass.

infrequent *adj.* exceptional, intermittent, occasional, rare, scanty, sparse, spasmodic, sporadic, uncommon, unusual.
antonym frequent.

infringe *v.* break, contravene, defy, disobey, encroach, flout, ignore, infract, intrude, invade, overstep, transgress, trespass, violate.

infringement *n.* breach, contravention, defiance, encroachment, evasion, infraction, intrusion, invasion, non-compliance, non-observance, transgression, trespass, violation.

infuriate *v.* anger, antagonise, bug, enrage, exasperate, incense, irritate, madden, provoke, put someone's back up, rile, rouse, vex.
antonyms calm, mollify.

infuriated *adj.* agitated, angry, beside oneself, enraged, exasperated, flaming, furious, heated, incensed, irate, irritated, maddened, provoked, roused, vexed, violent, wild.
antonyms calm, gratified, pleased.

infuriating *adj.* aggravating, annoying, exasper-

ating, frustrating, galling, intolerable, irritating, maddening, mortifying, pesky, pestiferous, pestilential, provoking, thwarting, unbearable, vexatious.
antonyms agreeable, pleasing.

infuse *v.* breathe into, brew, draw, imbue, impart to, implant, inculcate, inject, inspire, instil, introduce, leach, macerate, saturate, soak, steep.

infusion *n.* brew, implantation, inculcation, infusing, instillation, leachate, maceration, soaking, steeping.

ingenious *adj.* adroit, bright, brilliant, clever, crafty, creative, cunning, daedal, Daedalian, daedalic, dedalian, deft, dexterous, fertile, Gordian, Heath-Robinson, imaginative, innovative, intricate, inventive, masterly, original, pretty, ready, resourceful, shrewd, skilful, sly, subtle.
antonyms clumsy, unimaginative.

ingenuity *n.* adroitness, cleverness, cunning, deftness, faculty, flair, genius, gift, ingeniousness, innovativeness, invention, inventiveness, knack, originality, resourcefulness, sharpness, shrewdness, skill, slyness, turn.
antonyms clumsiness, dullness.

ingenuous *adj.* artless, candid, childlike, frank, guileless, honest, innocent, naïf, naïve, open, plain, simple, sincere, trustful, trusting, unreserved, unsophisticated, unstudied.
antonyms artful, sly.

ingenuousness *n.* artlessness, candour, frankness, guilelessness, innocence, naïvety, openness, trustfulness, unreserve, unsophisticatedness.
antonyms artfulness, slyness, subterfuge.

inglorious *adj.* discreditable, disgraceful, dishonourable, disreputable, humiliating, ignoble, ignominious, infamous, mortifying, obscure, shameful, unheroic, unhonoured, unknown, unsuccessful, unsung.
antonym glorious.

ingrain *v.* dye, embed, engrain, entrench, fix, imbue, implant, impress, imprint, infix, instil, root.

ingrained *adj.* constitutional, deep-rooted, deep-seated, entrenched, fixed, fundamental, hereditary, immovable, inborn, inbred, inbuilt, indelible, ineradicable, infixed, inherent, intrinsic, inveterate, permanent, rooted.
antonym superficial.

ingratiate *v.* blandish, crawl, curry, favour, fawn, flatter, get in with, grovel, insinuate, suck up, toady, worm.

ingratiating *adj.* bland, bootlicking, crawling, fawning, flattering, obsequious, servile, smooth-tongued, suave, sycophantic, time-serving, toadying, unctuous, whilly, whilly-wha(w).

ingratitude *n.* thanklessness, unappreciativeness, ungraciousness, ungratefulness.
antonym gratitude.

ingredient *n.* component, constituent, element, factor, part.

inhabit *v.* abide, bide, dwell, habit, live, lodge,

make one's home, occupy, people, populate, possess, reside, settle, settle in, stay, take up one's abode, tenant.

inhabitant n. aborigine, autochthon, burgher, citizen, denizen, dweller, habitant, indigene, indweller, inmate, lodger, native, occupant, occupier, resident, residentiary, resider, settler, tenant.

inhabited adj. colonised, developed, held, lived-in, occupied, overrun, peopled, populated, possessed, settled, tenanted.
antonym uninhabited.

inhalation n. breath, breathing, inhaling, inspiration, respiration, spiration, suction, toke.

inhale v. breathe in, draw, draw in, inbreathe, inspire, respire, suck in, toke, whiff.

inharmonious adj. antipathetic, atonal, cacophonous, clashing, conficting, discordant, dissonant, grating, harsh, horrisonant, incompatible, inconsonant, jangling, jarring, raucous, strident, tuneless, unharmonious, unmelodious, unmusical, untuneful.
antonym harmonious.

inherent adj. basic, characteristic, congenital, connate, essential, fundamental, hereditary, immanent, inborn, inbred, inbuilt, ingrained, inherited, innate, instinctive, instrinsic, inwrought, native, natural.

inherit v. accede to, assume, be bequeathed, be left, come in for, come into, fall heir to, receive, succeed to.

inheritance n. accession, bequest, birthright, descent, heredity, heritage, heritament, legacy, patrimony, succession.

inheritor n. beneficiary, co-heir, co-heiress, coheritor, devisee, heir, heiress, heritor, heritrix, inheritress, inheritrix, legatee, recipient, reversionary, successor.

inhibit v. arrest, bar, bridle, check, constrain, cramp, curb, debar, discourage, forbid, frustrate, hinder, hold, impede, interfere with, obstruct, prevent, prohibit, repress, restrain, stanch, stem, stop, suppress, thwart.

inhibited adj. bashful, constrained, diffident, frustrated, guarded, repressed, reserved, reticent, self-conscious, shamefaced, shy, strained, subdued, tense, uptight, withdrawn.
antonym uninhibited.

inhibition n. bar, check, constraint, embargo, hang-up, hindrance, impediment, interdict, interference, obstacle, obstruction, prohibition, repression, reserve, restraint, restriction, reticence, self-consciousness, shyness, suppression.
antonym freedom.

inhospitable adj. antisocial, bare, barren, bleak, cold, cool, desolate, forbidding, hostile, inimical, intolerant, sterile, unaccommodating, uncivil, uncongenial, unfavourable, unfriendly, ungenerous, uninhabitable, unkind, unneighbourly, unreceptive, unsociable, unwelcoming, xenophobic.
antonyms favourable, hospitable.

inhospitality n. coldness, coolness, hostility,

incivility, inimicality, intolerance, uncongeniality, unfriendliness, unkindness, unneighbourliness, unreceptiveness, unsociability, xenophobia.
antonym hospitality.

inhuman adj. animal, barbaric, barbarous, bestial, brutal, brutish, callous, cold-blooded, cruel, diabolical, fiendish, heartless, inhumane, insensate, merciless, pitiless, remorseless, ruthless, savage, sublime, unfeeling, vicious.
antonym human.

inhumane adj. brutal, callous, cold-hearted, cruel, heartless, indurate, inhuman, insensitive, pitiless, uncaring, uncompassionate, unfeeling, unkind, unsympathetic.
antonym humane.

inhumanity n. atrocity, barbarism, barbarity, brutality, brutishness, callousness, coldbloodedness, cold-heartedness, cruelty, hardheartedness, heartlessness, pitilessness, ruthlessness, sadism, unkindness, viciousness.
antonym humanity.

inimical adj. adverse, antagonistic, antipathetic, contrary, destructive, disaffected, harmful, hostile, hurtful, ill-disposed, inhospitable, injurious, intolerant, noxious, opposed, oppugnant, pernicious, repugnant, unfavourable, unfriendly, unwelcoming.
antonyms favourable, friendly, sympathetic.

inimitable adj. consummate, distinctive, exceptional, incomparable, matchless, nonpareil, peerless, sublime, superlative, supreme, unequalled, unexampled, unique, unmatched, unparalleled, unrivalled, unsurpassable, unsurpassed.

iniquitous adj. abominable, accursed, atrocious, awful, base, criminal, dreadful, evil, facinorous, flagitious, heinous, immoral, infamous, nefarious, nefast, reprehensible, reprobate, sinful, unjust, unrighteous, vicious, wicked.
antonym virtuous.

iniquity n. abomination, baseness, crime, enormity, evil, evil-doing, heinousness, impiety, infamy, injustice, misdeed, offence, sin, sinfulness, ungodliness, unrighteousness, vice, viciousness, wickedness, wrong, wrongdoing.
antonym virtue.

initial adj. beginning, commencing, early, embryonic, first, formative, inaugural, inauguratory, inceptive, inchoate, incipient, infant, introductory, opening, original, primary.
antonym final.

initially adv. at first, at the beginning, at the outset, at the start, first, first of all, firstly, in the beginning, introductorily, originally, prefatorily, to begin with, to start with.
antonym finally.

initiate v. activate, actuate, begin, cause, coach, commence, inaugurate, indoctrinate, induce, induct, instate, institute, instruct, introduce, invest, launch, open, originate, prompt, start, stimulate, teach, train.

n. authority, beginner, catechumen, cognoscente, connoisseur, convert, entrant, epopt, expert, insider, learner, member, newcomer, novice, novitiate, probationer, proselyte, recruit, sage, savant, tenderfoot, tiro.

initiation *n.* admission, commencement, début, enrolment, entrance, entry, inauguration, inception, induction, installation, instatement, instruction, introduction, investiture, reception, rite of passage.

initiative *n.* advantage, ambition, drive, dynamism, energy, enterprise, forcefulness, get-up-and-go, goeyness, innovativeness, inventiveness, lead, move, originality, prompting, push, recommendation, resource, resourcefulness, suggestion.

inject *v.* add, bring, fix, hit, infuse, inoculate, insert, instil, interject, introduce, jab, mainline, pop, shoot, shoot up, skin-pop, vaccinate.

injection *n.* dose, fix, hit, infusion, inoculation, insertion, interjection, introduction, jab, mainlining, popping, shot, skin-popping, vaccination, vaccine.

injudicious *adj.* foolish, hasty, ill-advised, ill-judged, ill-timed, impolitic, imprudent, inadvisable, incautious, inconsiderate, indiscreet, inexpedient, misguided, rash, stupid, unthinking, unwise, wrong-headed.
antonym judicious.

injunction *n.* admonition, behest, command, dictate, direction, directive, enjoinment, exhortation, instruction, interdict, mandate, order, precept, ruling.

injure *v.* abuse, aggrieve, blemish, blight, break, cripple, damage, deface, disable, disfigure, disserve, harm, hurt, ill-treat, impair, maim, maltreat, mar, ruin, scathe, spoil, tarnish, undermine, vandalise, vitiate, weaken, wound, wrong.

injured *adj.* abused, aggrieved, blemished, broken, cut to the quick, defamed, disabled, disgruntled, displeased, grieved, hurt, ill-treated, insulted, lamed, long-suffering, maligned, maltreated, misused, offended, pained, put out, stung, tarnished, undermined, unhappy, upset, vilified, weakened, wounded, wronged.

injurious *adj.* adverse, bad, baneful, calumnious, corrupting, damaging, deleterious, destructive, detrimental, disadvantageous, harmful, hurtful, iniquitous, insulting, libellous, mischievous, noxious, pernicious, prejudicial, ruinous, slanderous, unconducive, unhealthy, unjust, wrongful.
antonyms beneficial, favourable.

injury *n.* abuse, annoyance, damage, damnification, detriment, disservice, evil, grievance, harm, hurt, ill, impairment, injustice, insult, lesion, loss, mischief, noyance, prejudice, ruin, scathe, trauma, vexation, wound, wrong.

injustice *n.* bias, discrimination, disparity, favouritism, imposition, inequality, inequit-

ableness, inequity, iniquity, one-sidedness, oppression, partiality, partisanship, prejudice, unevenness, unfairness, unjustness, unlawfulness, unreason, wrong.
antonym justice.

inkling *n.* allusion, clue, conception, earthly, faintest, foggiest, glimmering, hint, idea, indication, intimation, notion, pointer, sign, suggestion, suspicion, umbrage, whisper.

inlaid *adj.* damascened, empaestic, enchased, set, studded, tessellated.

inland *adj.* central, domestic, inner, interior, internal, up-country.

inlay *n.* damascene, emblema, tessellation.

inlet *n.* bay, bight, cove, creek, entrance, fjord, fleet, hope, ingress, opening, passage, wick.

inmost *adj.* basic, buried, central, closest, dearest, deep, deepest, esoteric, essential, hidden, innermost, intimate, personal, private, secret.

inn *n.* albergo, alehouse, auberge, caravanserai, hostelry, hotel, howff, khan, local, public, public house, roadhouse, saloon, serai, tavern.

innards *n.* entera, entrails, gralloch, guts, insides, interior, intestines, inwards, mechanism, organs, umbles, viscera, vitals, works.

innate *adj.* basic, congenital, connate, constitutional, essential, fundamental, immanent, inborn, inbred, ingenerate, ingrained, inherent, inherited, instinctive, intrinsic, intuitive, native, natural.

inner *adj.* central, concealed, emotional, esoteric, essential, hidden, inly, inside, interior, internal, intimate, inward, mental, middle, personal, private, psychical, psychological, secret, spiritual.
antonyms outer, patent.

innkeeper *n.* aubergiste, boniface, host, hostess, hotelier, hotel-keeper, innholder, landlady, landlord, mine host, padrone, publican, restaurateur.

innocence *n.* artlessness, blamelessness, chastity, credulousness, freshness, greenness, guilelessness, guiltlessness, gullibility, harmlessness, honesty, ignorance, incorruptibility, incorruption, inexperience, ingenuousness, innocuity, innocuousness, inoffensiveness, irreproachability, naïvety, naturalness, nescience, probity, purity, righteousness, simplicity, sinlessness, stainlessness, trustfulness, unawareness, unfamiliarity, unimpeachability, unsophistication, unworldliness, virginity, virtue.
antonyms experience, guilt, knowledge.

innocent *adj.* Arcadian, artless, benign, bereft of, blameless, canny, chaste, childlike, clear, credulous, dewy-eyed, faultless, frank, free of, fresh, green, guileless, guiltless, gullible, harmless, honest, immaculate, impeccable, incorrupt, ingenuous, innocuous, inoffensive, intact, irreproachable, naïve, natural, nescient, open, pristine, pure, righteous, simple, sinless, spotless, stainless, trustful, trusting,

unblemished, uncontaminated, unimpeachable, unobjectionable, unoffending, unsullied, unsuspicious, untainted, untouched, unworldly, verdant, virginal, well-intentioned, well-meaning, well-meant.
antonyms experienced, guilty, knowing.
n. babe, babe in arms, beginner, child, greenhorn, infant, ingénu, ingénue, neophyte, tenderfoot.
antonyms connoisseur, expert.

innocently *adv.* artlessly, blamelessly, credulously, harmlessly, ingenuously, innocuously, inoffensively, like a lamb to the slaughter, simply, trustfully, trustingly, unoffendingly, unsuspiciously.

innocuous *adj.* bland, harmless, hypo-allergenic, innocent, innoxious, inoffensive, non-irritant, safe, unimpeachable, unobjectionable.
antonym harmful.

innovation *n.* alteration, change, departure, introduction, modernisation, modernism, neologism, neoterism, newness, novation, novelty, progress, reform, variation.

innovative *adj.* adventurous, bold, daring, enterprising, fresh, go-ahead, goey, imaginative, inventive, modernising, new, on the move, original, progressive, reforming, resourceful, revolutionary.
antonyms conservative, unimaginative.

innuendo *n.* aspersion, hint, implication, imputation, insinuation, intimation, overtone, slant, slur, suggestion, whisper.

innumerable *adj.* countless, incalculable, incomputable, infinite, many, multitudinous, myriad, numberless, numerous, uncountable, uncounted, unnumbered, untold.

inoculate *v.* immunise, inject, jag, protect, safeguard, vaccinate.

inoculation *n.* immunisation, injection, jag, protection, shot, vaccination.

inoffensive *adj.* gentle, harmless, humble, innocent, innocuous, innoxious, mild, mousy, non-provocative, peaceable, quiet, retiring, unassertive, unobjectionable, unobtrusive, unoffending.
antonyms malicious, offensive.

inoperable *adj.* impracticable, impractical, intractable, irremovable, non-viable, unrealistic, unworkable.
antonyms operable, practicable.

inoperative *adj.* broken, broken-down, defective, hors de combat, idle, ineffective, ineffectual, inefficacious, invalid, non-active, non-functioning, nugatory, out of action, out of commission, out of order, out of service, unserviceable, unused, unworkable, useless.
antonym operative.

inopportune *adj.* clumsy, ill-chosen, ill-timed, inappropriate, inauspicious, inconvenient, infelicitous, malapropos, mistimed, tactless, unfortunate, unpropitious, unseasonable, unsuitable, untimely, wrong-timed.
antonym opportune.

inordinate *adj.* disproportionate, excessive, exorbitant, extravagant, hubristic, immoderate, intemperate, overweening, preposterous, prohibitive, unconscionable, undue, unreasonable, unrestrained, unwarranted.
antonyms moderate, reasonable.

input *v.* capture, code, feed in, insert, key in, process, store.

inquietude *n.* agitation, anxiety, apprehension, discomposure, disquiet, disquietude, jumpiness, nervousness, perturbation, restlessness, solicitude, unease, uneasiness, worry.
antonym composure.

inquire *v.* ask, catechise, delve, enquire, examine, explore, inspect, interrogate, investigate, look into, probe, query, quest, question, reconnoitre, scout, scrutinise, search, speir.

inquirer *n.* explorer, interrogator, investigator, querist, quester, questioner, researcher, searcher, seeker, student.

inquiring *adj.* analytical, curious, doubtful, eager, inquisitive, interested, interrogatory, investigative, investigatory, nosy, outward-looking, probing, prying, questing, questioning, sceptical, searching, wondering, zetetic.
antonym incurious.

inquiry *n.* enquiry, examination, exploration, inquest, interrogation, investigation, perquisition, post-mortem, probe, query, question, research, scrutiny, search, study, survey, witch-hunt, zetetic.

inquisition *n.* catechism, cross-examination, cross-questioning, examination, grilling, inquest, inquiry, interrogation, investigation, questioning, quizzing, third degree, witch-hunt.

inquisitive *adj.* curious, eager, inquiring, intrusive, investigative, meddlesome, nosy, peeping, peering, probing, prying, questing, questioning, snooping, snoopy.
antonym incurious.

inroad *n.* advance, encroachment, foray, impingement, incursion, intrusion, invasion, irruption, onslaught, raid, sally, sortie, trespass.

insane *adj.* barmy, batty, bizarre, bonkers, brainsick, cracked, crackers, crazed, cuckoo, daft, delirious, demented, deranged, distracted, disturbed, fatuous, foolish, idiotic, impractical, irrational, irresponsible, loony, loopy, lunatic, mad, manic, mental, mentally ill, non compos mentis, nuts, nutty, preposterous, psychotic, queer, schizoid, schizophrenic, screwy, senseless, stupid, touched, unbalanced, unhinged.
antonym sane.

insanitary *adj.* contaminated, dirty, disease-ridden, feculent, filthy, foul, impure, infected, infested, insalubrious, insalutary, noisome, noxious, polluted, unclean, unhealthful, unhealthy, unhygienic, unsanitary.
antonym sanitary.

insanity *n.* aberration, alienation, amentia, brainsickness, brainstorm, craziness, delirium, dementia, derangement, folly, frenzy, infatuation, irresponsibility, lunacy, madness,

mania, mental illness, neurosis, preposterousness, psychoneurosis, psychosis, senselessness, stupidity.
antonym sanity.

insatiable *adj.* esurient, gluttonous, greedy, immoderate, incontrollable, inordinate, insatiate, intemperate, persistent, quenchless, rapacious, ravenous, unappeasable, uncurbable, unquenchable, unsatisfiable, voracious.
antonym moderate.

inscribe[1] *v.* carve, cut, engrave, etch, grave, impress, imprint, incise, stamp.

inscribe[2] *v.* address, autograph, dedicate, enlist, enrol, enter, record, register, sign, write.

inscription *n.* autograph, caption, dedication, engraving, epigraph, epitaph, label, legend, lettering, saying, signature, words.

inscrutable *adj.* baffling, blank, cryptic, deadpan, deep, enigmatic, esoteric, expressionless, hidden, impassive, impenetrable, incomprehensible, inexplicable, mysterious, pokerfaced, sphinx-like, undiscoverable, unexplainable, unfathomable, unintelligible, unknowable, unsearchable.
antonyms clear, comprehensible, expressive.

insecure *adj.* afraid, anxious, apprehensive, dangerous, defenceless, diffident, exposed, expugnable, flimsy, frail, hazardous, insubstantial, jerry-built, loose, nervous, perilous, precarious, pregnable, rickety, rocky, shaky, shoogly, uncertain, unconfident, uneasy, unguarded, unprotected, unsafe, unshielded, unsound, unstable, unsteady, unsure, vulnerable, weak, wobbly, worried.
antonyms confident, safe, secure.

insecurity *n.* anxiety, apprehension, danger, defencelessness, diffidence, dubiety, fear, flimsiness, frailness, hazard, instability, nervousness, peril, precariousness, ricketiness, risk, shakiness, uncertainty, uneasiness, unsafeness, unsafety, unsteadiness, unsureness, vulnerability, weakness, worry.
antonyms confidence, safety, security.

insensibility *n.* apathy, blindness, callousness, coma, crassness, deafness, dullness, indifference, inertness, insensitivity, lethargy, nervelessness, numbness, oblivion, thoughtlessness, torpor, unawareness, unconsciousness.
antonyms consciousness, sensibilty.

insensible[1] *adj.* anaesthetised, apathetic, blind, callous, cataleptic, cold, deaf, dull, hardhearted, impassive, impercipient, impervious, indifferent, inert, insensate, marble, nerveless, numb, numbed, oblivious, senseless, stupid, torpid, unaffected, unaware, unconscious, unfeeling, unmindful, unmoved, unnoticing, unobservant, unresponsive, unsusceptible, untouched.
antonyms conscious, sensible.

insensible[2] *adj.* imperceivable, imperceptible, inappreciable, minuscule, minute, negligible, tiny, unnoticeable.
antonym appreciable.

insensitive *adj.* blunted, callous, crass, dead, hardened, immune, impenetrable, impercep-

tive, impercipient, impervious, indifferent, insusceptible, obtuse, pachydermatous, proof, resistant, tactless, thick-skinned, tough, unaffected, uncaring, unconcerned, unfeeling, unimpressionable, unmoved, unreactive, unresponsive, unsensitive, unsusceptible.
antonym sensitive.

insensitivity *n.* bluntness, callousness, crassness, hard-headedness, hypalgesia, hypalgia, impenetrability, imperceptiveness, impercipience, imperviousness, indifference, obtuseness, tactlessness, unconcern, unresponsiveness.
antonym sensitivity.

inseparable *adj.* bosom, close, conjoined, devoted, impartible, inalienable, indiscerptible, indissociable, indissoluble, individuate, indivisible, inextricable, inseverable, intimate, undividable.
antonym separable.

insert *v.* embed, engraft, enter, immit, implant, infix, inset, intercalate, interject, interlaminate, interlard, interleave, interline, interpolate, interpose, introduce, intromit, let in, place, pop in, put, put in, set, stick in.
n. ad, advertisement, empiecement, enclosure, engraftment, godet, graft, gusset, implant, insertion, inset, notice.

insertion *n.* addition, entry, implant, inclusion, insert, inset, intercalation, interpolation, introduction, intromission, intrusion, supplement.

inside *n.* content, contents, interior.
adv. indoors, inly, internally, inwardly, privately, secretly, within.
adj. classified, confidential, esoteric, exclusive, hush-hush, inner, innermost, interior, internal, intramural, inward, private, restricted, secret.

insides *n.* belly, bowels, entera, entrails, gut, guts, innards, organs, stomach, viscera, vitals.

insidious *adj.* artful, crafty, crooked, cunning, deceitful, deceptive, designing, devious, disingenuous, duplicitous, furtive, guileful, intriguing, Machiavellian, slick, sly, smooth, sneaking, stealthy, subtle, surreptitious, treacherous, tricky, wily.

insight *n.* acumen, acuteness, apprehension, awareness, comprehension, discernment, grasp, ingenuity, intelligence, intuition, intuitiveness, judgement, knowledge, observation, penetration, perception, percipience, perspicacity, sensitivity, shrewdness, understanding, vision, wisdom.

insightful *adj.* acute, astute, discerning, intelligent, knowledgeable, observant, penetrating, perceptive, percipient, perspicacious, prudent, sagacious, sage, shrewd, understanding, wise.
antonym superficial.

insignia *n.* badge, brand, crest, decoration, emblem, ensign, hallmarks, mark, regalia, signs, symbol, trademark.

insignificance *n.* immateriality, inconsequence,

inconsequentiality, insubstantiality, irrelevance, meaninglessness, meanness, negligibility, nugatoriness, paltriness, pettiness, tininess, triviality, unimportance, worthlessness. *antonym* significance.

insignificant *adj.* dinky, flimsy, humble, immaterial, inappreciable, inconsequential, inconsiderable, insubstantial, irrelevant, meagre, meaningless, Mickey Mouse, minor, negligible, nondescript, nonessential, nugatory, paltry, petty, piddling, scanty, scrub, tiny, trifling, trivial, unimportant, unsubstantial. *antonym* significant.

insincere *adj.* artificial, canting, deceitful, deceptive, devious, dishonest, disingenuous, dissembling, dissimulating, double-dealing, duplicitous, evasive, faithless, false, hollow, hypocritical, lip-deep, lying, mendacious, perfidious, phoney, pretended, synthetic, two-faced, unfaithful, ungenuine, untrue, untruthful. *antonym* sincere.

insincerity *n.* artificiality, cant, deceitfulness, deviousness, dishonesty, disingenuousness, dissembling, dissimulation, duplicity, evasiveness, faithlessness, falseness, falsity, hollowness, hypocrisy, lip service, mendacity, perfidy, phoniness, pretence, untruthfulness. *antonym* sincerity.

insinuate *v.* allude, get at, hint, imply, indicate, innuendo, intimate, suggest.

insinuate oneself curry favour, get in with, ingratiate, sidle, work, worm, wriggle.

insinuation *n.* allusion, aspersion, hint, implication, infiltration, ingratiating, innuendo, intimation, introduction, slant, slur, suggestion.

insipid *adj.* anaemic, banal, bland, characterless, colourless, dilute, drab, dry, dull, fade, flat, flavourless, insulse, jejune, lash, lifeless, limp, missish, missy, monotonous, pointless, prosaic, prosy, savourless, spiritless, stale, tame, tasteless, trite, unappetising, unimaginative, uninteresting, unsavoury, vapid, watery, weak, wearish, weedy, wishy-washy. *antonyms* appetising, piquant, punchy, tasty.

insipidity *n.* anaemicness, banality, blandness, characterlessness, colournessness, diluteness, drabness, dryness, dullness, fadeur, flatness, jejuneness, jejunity, lifelessness, limpness, monotony, prosiness, spiritlessness, staleness, tameness, tastelessness, triteness, vapidity, wateriness, weakness, weediness. *antonyms* character, liveliness, piquancy, punch, tastiness.

insist *v.* assert, asseverate, aver, claim, contend, demand, dwell on, emphasise, harp on, hold, maintain, persist, reiterate, repeat, request, require, stand firm, stress, swear, urge, vow.

insistence *n.* advice, assertion, averment, certainty, contention, demand, determination, emphasis, encouragement, entreaty, exhortation, firmness, importunity, instance, persistence, persuasion, pressing, reiteration, solicitations, stress, urgency, urging.

insistent *adj.* demanding, dogged, emphatic, exigent, forceful, importunate, incessant, peremptory, persevering, persistent, pressing, relentless, tenacious, unrelenting, unremitting, urgent.

insobriety *n.* crapulence, drunkenness, inebriation, inebriety, intemperance, intoxication, tipsiness. *antonym* sobriety.

insolence *n.* abuse, arrogance, assurance, audacity, backchat, boldness, cheek, cheekiness, chutzpah, contemptuousness, contumely, defiance, disrespect, effrontery, forwardness, gall, gum, hubris, impertinence, impudence, incivility, insubordination, lip, malapertness, offensiveness, pertness, presumption, presumptuousness, rudeness, sauce, sauciness. *antonyms* politeness, respect.

insolent *adj.* abusive, arrogant, bold, brazen, cheeky, contemptuous, contumelious, defiant, disrespectful, forward, fresh, hubristic, impertinent, impudent, insubordinate, insulting, malapert, pert, presumptuous, rude, saucy, uncivil. *antonyms* polite, respectful.

insoluble *adj.* baffling, impenetrable, indecipherable, inexplicable, inextricable, intractable, mysterious, mystifying, obscure, perplexing, unaccountable, unexplainable, unfathomable, unsolvable. *antonym* explicable.

insolvency *n.* bankruptcy, default, failure, liquidation, ruin. *antonym* solvency.

insolvent *adj.* bankrupt, broke, bust, defaulting, destitute, failed, flat broke, in queer street, on the rocks, ruined. *antonym* solvent.

insomnia *n.* insomnolence, restlessness, sleeplessness, wakefulness. *antonym* sleep.

insouciance *n.* airiness, breeziness, carefreeness, ease, flippancy, heedlessness, indifference, jauntiness, light-heartedness, nonchalance, pococurantism, unconcern. *antonyms* anxiety, care.

insouciant *adj.* airy, breezy, buoyant, carefree, casual, easy-going, flippant, gay, happy-go-lucky, heedless, indifferent, jaunty, light-hearted, nonchalant, pococurante, sunny, unconcerned, untroubled, unworried. *antonyms* anxious, careworn.

inspect *v.* audit, check, examine, give the once-over, investigate, look over, oversee, peruse, reconnoitre, scan, scrutinise, search, study, superintend, supervise, survey, vet, visit.

inspection *n.* audit, autopsy, check, check-up, examination, investigation, once-over, postmortem, reconnaissance, review, scan, scrutiny, search, superintendence, supervision, surveillance, survey, vidimus, visitation.

inspector *n.* censor, checker, conner, controller, critic, examiner, investigator, overseer, reviewer, scrutineer, scrutiniser, superintendent, supervisor, surveyor, tester, viewer.

inspiration *n.* afflation, afflatus, Aganippe, arousal, awakening, brainstorm, brain-wave, creativity, elevation, encouragement, enthusiasm, estro, exaltation, genius, Hippocrene, hwyl, illumination, influence, insight, muse, Muse, revelation, spur, stimulation, stimulus, Svengali, taghairm.

inspire *v.* activate, animate, arouse, encourage, enkindle, enliven, enthuse, excite, fill, galvanise, hearten, imbue, influence, infuse, inhale, inspirit, instil, motivate, produce, quicken, spark off, spur, stimulate, stir, trigger.

inspired *adj.* afflated, aroused, brilliant, dazzling, elated, enthralling, enthused, enthusiastic, exalted, exciting, exhilarated, fired, galvanised, impressive, invigorated, memorable, outstanding, possessed, reanimated, stimulated, superlative, thrilled, thrilling, uplifted, wonderful.
antonyms dull, uninspired.

inspiring *adj.* affecting, emboldening, encouraging, exciting, exhilarating, heartening, inspiriting, invigorating, moving, rousing, stimulating, stirring, uplifting.
antonyms dull, uninspiring.

inspirit *v.* animate, cheer, embolden, encourage, enliven, exhilarate, fire, galvanise, gladden, hearten, incite, inspire, invigorate, move, nerve, quicken, refresh, reinvigorate, rouse, stimulate.

instability *n.* capriciousness, changeableness, fickleness, fitfulness, flimsiness, fluctuation, fluidity, frailty, imbalance, impermanence, inconstancy, insecurity, insolidity, irresolution, mutability, oscillation, precariousness, restlessness, shakiness, transience, uncertainty, undependableness, unpredictability, unreliability, unsafeness, unsoundness, unsteadiness, vacillation, variability, volatility, wavering, weakness.
antonym stability.

instal(l) *v.* consecrate, ensconce, establish, fix, inaugurate, induct, instate, institute, introduce, invest, lay, locate, lodge, ordain, place, plant, position, put, set, set up, settle, site, situate, station.

installation *n.* base, consecration, equipment, establishment, fitting, inauguration, induction, instalment, instatement, investiture, location, machinery, ordination, placing, plant, positioning, post, siting, station, system.

instalment *n.* chapter, consignment, delivery, division, episode, fascicule, heft, part, portion, repayment, section.

instance[1] *n.* case, case in point, citation, example, illustration, occasion, occurrence, precedent, sample, situation, time.
v. adduce, cite, mention, name, point to, quote, refer to, specify.

instance[2] *n.* advice, application, behest, demand, entreaty, exhortation, importunity, impulse, incitement, initiative, insistence, instigation, pressure, prompting, request, solicitation, urging.

instant *n.* flash, jiffy, juncture, minute, mo, moment, occasion, point, second, shake, split second, tick, time, trice, twinkling, two shakes.
adj. convenience, direct, fast, immediate, instantaneous, on-the-spot, precooked, prompt, quick, rapid, ready-mixed, split-second, unhesitating, urgent.

instantaneous *adj.* direct, immediate, instant, on-the-spot, prompt, rapid, unhesitating.
antonym eventual.

instantaneously *adv.* at once, directly, forthwith, immediately, instantly, on the spot, promptly, rapidly, straight away, there and then, unhesitatingly.
antonym eventually.

instantly *adv.* at once, directly, ek dum, forthwith, immediately, instantaneously, now, on the spot, pronto, quick-sticks, right away, straight away, there and then, tout de suite, without delay.
antonym eventually.

instead *adv.* alternatively, as a substitute, as an alternative, in lieu, in preference, preferably, rather.

instead of as proxy for, in default of, in lieu of, in place of, in preference to, on behalf of, rather than.

instigate *v.* actuate, cause, encourage, excite, foment, generate, impel, incite, influence, initiate, inspire, kindle, move, persuade, prompt, provoke, rouse, set on, spur, start, stimulate, stir up, urge, whip up.

instigation *n.* behest, bidding, encouragement, incentive, incitement, initiative, insistence, instance, prompting, urging.

instigator *n.* agent provocateur, agitator, firebrand, fomenter, goad, incendiary, inciter, leader, mischief-maker, motivator, prime mover, provoker, ringleader, spur, troublemaker.

instil *v.* din into, engender, engraft, imbue, implant, impress, inculcate, infix, infuse, inject, insinuate, introduce.

instinct *n.* ability, aptitude, faculty, feel, feeling, flair, gift, gut feeling, gut reaction, id, impulse, intuition, knack, nose, predisposition, proclivity, sixth sense, talent, tendency, urge.

instinctive *adj.* automatic, gut, immediate, impulsive, inborn, inherent, innate, instinctual, intuitional, intuitive, involuntary, mechanical, native, natural, reflex, spontaneous, unlearned, unpremeditated, unthinking, visceral.
antonyms conscious, deliberate, voluntary.

instinctively *adv.* automatically, intuitively, involuntarily, mechanically, naturally, spontaneously, unthinkingly, without thinking.
antonyms consciously, deliberately, voluntarily.

institute[1] *v.* appoint, begin, commence, constitute, create, enact, establish, fix, found,

inaugurate, induct, initiate, install, introduce, invest, launch, open, ordain, organise, originate, pioneer, set up, settle, start.
antonyms abolish, cancel, discontinue.

institute[2] *n.* custom, decree, doctrine, dogma, edict, firman, indiction, irade, law, maxim, precedent, precept, principle, regulation, rescript, rule, tenet, ukase.

institute[3] *n.* academy, association, college, conservatory, foundation, guild, institution, organisation, poly, polytechnic, school, seminary, society.

institution[1] *n.* constitution, creation, enactment, establishment, formation, foundation, founding, inception, initiation, installation, introduction, investiture, organisation, protectory.

institution[2] *n.* convention, custom, fixture, law, practice, ritual, rule, tradition, usage.

institution[3] *n.* academy, college, concern, corporation, establishment, foundation, hospital, institute, organisation, school, seminary, society, university.

institutional *adj.* accepted, bureaucratic, cheerless, clinical, cold, conventional, customary, drab, dreary, dull, established, establishment, forbidding, formal, impersonal, institutionary, monotonous, orthodox, regimented, ritualistic, routine, set, societal, uniform, unwelcoming.
antonyms individualistic, unconventional.

instruct *v.* acquaint, advise, apprise, bid, brief, catechise, charge, coach, command, counsel, direct, discipline, drill, educate, enjoin, enlighten, ground, guide, inform, mandate, notify, order, school, teach, tell, train, tutor.

instruction *n.* apprenticeship, briefing, catechesis, catechising, coaching, command, direction, directive, discipline, drilling, education, enlightenment, grounding, guidance, information, injunction, lesson(s), mandate, order, preparation, ruling, schooling, teaching, training, tuition, tutelage.

instructions *n.* advice, book of words, commands, directions, guidance, handbook, information, key, legend, orders, recommendations, rules.

instructive *adj.* cautionary, didactic, edificatory, edifying, educational, educative, educatory, enlightening, helpful, illuminating, improving, inculcative, informative, instructional, revealing, useful.
antonym unenlightening.

instructor *n.* adviser, catechiser, catechist, coach, demonstrator, edifier, Egeria, exponent, guide, guru, instructress, maharishi, master, mentor, mistress, pedagogue, preceptor, schoolmaster, schoolmistress, teacher, trainer, tutor.

instrument *n.* agency, agent, apparatus, appliance, cat's-paw, channel, contraption, contrivance, device, doodad, dupe, factor, force, gadget, implement, means, mechanism, medium, organ, pawn, puppet, tool, utensil, vehicle, way, widget.

instrumental *adj.* active, assisting, auxiliary,

conducive, contributive, contributory, helpful, helping, implemental, influential, involved, subsidiary, useful.
antonyms obstructive, unhelpful.

insubordinate *adj.* contumacious, defiant, disobedient, disorderly, fractious, impertinent, impudent, insurgent, mutinous, rebellious, recalcitrant, refractory, riotous, rude, seditious, turbulent, undisciplined, ungovernable, unruly.
antonyms docile, obedient.

insubordination *n.* defiance, disobedience, impertinence, impudence, indiscipline, insurrection, mutinousness, mutiny, rebellion, recalcitrance, revolt, riotousness, rudeness, sedition, ungovernability.
antonyms docility, obedience.

insubstantial *adj.* chimerical, ephemeral, false, fanciful, feeble, flimsy, frail, idle, illusory, imaginary, immaterial, incorporeal, moonshine, poor, slight, tenuous, thin, unreal, vaporous, weak, windy, yeasty.
antonyms real, strong.

insufferable *adj.* detestable, dreadful, hateful, impossible, insupportable, intolerable, loathsome, outrageous, unbearable, unendurable, unliv(e)able, unspeakable.
antonyms pleasant, tolerable.

insufficiency *n.* dearth, deficiency, inadequacy, inadequateness, lack, need, paucity, poverty, scantiness, scarcity, shortage, sparsity, want.
antonyms excess, sufficiency.

insufficient *adj.* deficient, inadequate, incapable, incommensurate, lacking, scanty, scarce, short, sparse, wanting.
antonyms excessive, sufficient.

insular *adj.* blinkered, circumscribed, closed, contracted, cut off, detached, illiberal, inward-looking, isolated, limited, narrow, narrow-minded, parish-pump, parochial, petty, prejudiced, provincial, xenophobic.
antonym cosmopolitan.

insularity *n.* isolation, narrow-mindedness, parochiality, parochialness, prejudice, xenophobia.
antonyms open-mindedness, openness.

insulate *v.* cocoon, cushion, cut off, isolate, protect, quarantine, separate off, sequester, shield.

insulation *n.* cushioning, deadening, deafening, padding, protection, stuffing.

insult *v.* abuse, affront, call names, fling/throw mud at, give offence to, injure, libel, miscall, offend, outrage, revile, slag, slander, slight, snub, vilify, vilipend.
antonyms compliment, honour.
n. abuse, affront, aspersion, contumely, indignity, insolence, libel, offence, outrage, rudeness, slander, slap in the face, slight, snub.
antonyms compliment, honour.

insulting *adj.* abusive, affronting, contemptuous, degrading, disparaging, insolent, libellous, offensive, rude, scurrilous, slanderous, slighting.

antonyms complimentary, respectful.

insuperable *adj.* formidable, impassable, insurmountable, invincible, overwhelming, unconquerable.

antonym surmountable.

insupportable *adj.* detestable, dreadful, hateful, indefensible, insufferable, intenable, intolerable, invalid, loathesome, unbearable, unendurable, unjustifiable, untenable.

antonym bearable.

insuppressible *adj.* energetic, go-getting, incorrigible, irrepressible, lively, obstreperous, uncontrollable, ungovernable, unruly, unstoppable, unsubduable.

antonym suppressible.

insurance *n.* assurance, cover, coverage, guarantee, indemnification, indemnity, policy, premium, protection, provision, safeguard, security, warranty.

insure *v.* assure, cover, guarantee, indemnify, protect, underwrite, warrant.

insurer *n.* assurer, underwriter.

insurgent *n.* insurrectionist, mutineer, partisan, rebel, resister, revolter, revoluntionist, revolutionary, rioter.

adj. disobedient, insubordinate, insurrectionary, mutinous, partisan, rebellious, revolting, revolutionary, riotous, seditious.

insurmountable *adj.* hopeless, impassable, impossible, insuperable, invincible, overwhelming, unclimable, unconquerable, unscalable, unsurmountable.

antonym surmountable.

insurrection *n.* coup, inqilab, insurgence, insurgency, mutiny, putsch, rebellion, revolt, revolution, riot, rising, sedition, uprising.

intact *adj.* all in one piece, complete, entire, inviolate, perfect, scatheless, sound, together, unbroken, undamaged, undefiled, unharmed, unhurt, unimpaired, uninjured, unscathed, untouched, unviolated, virgin, whole.

antonyms broken, damaged, harmed.

intaglio *n.* diaglyph.

intangible *adj.* airy, bodiless, dim, elusive, ethereal, evanescent, impalpable, imperceptible, incorporeal, indefinite, insubstantial, invisible, shadowy, unreal, unsubstantial, vague.

antonyms real, tangible.

integral *adj.* basic, complete, component, constituent, elemental, entire, essential, full, fundamental, indispensable, intact, intrinsic, necessary, requisite, undivided, unitary, whole.

antonyms accessory, partial.

integrate *v.* accommodate, amalgamate, assimilate, blend, coalesce, combine, commingle, desegregate, fuse, harmonise, incorporate, intermix, join, knit, merge, mesh, mix, unite.

antonym separate.

integrated *adj.* cohesive, concordant, connected, desegregated, harmonious, interrelated, part and parcel, unified, unsegregated, unseparated.

antonym unintegrated.

integration *n.* amalgamation, assimilation, blending, combining, commingling, desegregation, fusing, harmony, incorporation, mixing, unification.

antonym separation.

integrity *n.* candour, coherence, cohesion, completeness, entireness, goodness, honesty, honour, incorruptibility, principle, probity, purity, rectitude, righteousness, soundness, unity, uprightness, virtue, wholeness.

antonyms dishonesty, incompleteness, unreliability.

intellect *n.* brain, brain power, brains, egghead, genius, highbrow, intellectual, intelligence, judgement, mind, nous, reason, sense, thinker, understanding.

intellectual *adj.* bookish, cerebral, deep-browed, discursive, highbrow, intelligent, mental, noetic, rational, scholarly, studious, thoughtful.

antonym low-brow.

n. academic, egghead, headpiece, highbrow, mastermind, thinker.

antonym low-brow.

intelligence *n.* acuity, acumen, advice, alertness, aptitude, brain power, brains, brightness, capacity, cleverness, comprehension, data, discernment, disclosure, facts, findings, gen, grey matter, information, intellect, intellectuality, knowledge, low-down, mind, news, notice, notification, nous, penetration, perception, quickness, reason, report, rumour, tidings, tip-off, understanding, word.

antonym foolishness.

intelligent *adj.* acute, alert, apt, brainy, bright, clever, deep-browed, discerning, enlightened, instructed, knowing, penetrating, perspicacious, quick, quick-witted, rational, razorsharp, sharp, smart, thinking, well-informed.

antonyms foolish, unintelligent.

intelligentsia *n.* academics, brains, eggheads, eggmass, highbrows, illuminati, intellectuals, literati.

intelligibility *n.* clarity, clearness, comprehensibility, comprehensibleness, distinctness, explicitness, lucidity, lucidness, plainness, precision, simplicity.

antonym unintelligibility.

intelligible *adj.* clear, comprehensible, decipherable, distinct, fathomable, lucid, open, penetrable, plain, understandable.

antonym unintelligible.

intemperance *n.* crapulence, drunkenness, excess, extravagance, immoderation, inebriation, insobriety, intoxication, licence, overindulgence, self-indulgence, unrestraint.

antonym temperance.

intemperate *adj.* drunken, excessive, extravagant, extreme, immoderate, incontinent, inordinate, intoxicated, irrestrainable, licentious, over the top, passionate, prodigal, profligate, self-indulgent, severe, tempestuous, unbridled, uncontrollable, ungovernable, unrestrained, violent, wild.

antonym temperate.

intend *v.* aim, consign, contemplate, design, destine, determine, earmark, have a mind, mark out, mean, meditate, plan, project, propose, purpose, scheme, set apart.

intended *adj.* betrothed, deliberate, designate, designated, destined, future, intentional, planned, proposed, prospective.
antonym accidental.
n. betrothed, fiancé, fiancée, husband-to-be, wife-to-be.

intense *adj.* acute, agonising, ardent, burning, close, concentrated, consuming, eager, earnest, energetic, fanatical, fervent, fervid, fierce, forceful, forcible, great, harsh, heightened, impassioned, intensive, keen, passionate, powerful, profound, severe, strained, strong, vehement.
antonyms apathetic, mild.

intensely *adv.* ardently, deeply, extremely, fervently, fiercely, greatly, passionately, profoundly, strongly, very.
antonym mildly.

intensification *n.* acceleration, building-up, build-up, deepening, escalation, exacerbescence, heightening, increase, worsening.
antonym lessening.

intensify *v.* add to, aggravate, boost, concentrate, deepen, emphasise, enhance, escalate, exacerbate, fire, fuel, heighten, hot up, increase, magnify, quicken, redouble, reinforce, sharpen, step up, strengthen, whet, whip up.
antonyms damp down, die down.

intensity *n.* accent, ardour, concentration, depth, earnestness, emotion, energy, excess, extremity, fanaticism, fervency, fervour, fierceness, fire, force, intenseness, keenness, passion, potency, power, severity, strain, strength, tension, vehemence, vigour, voltage.

intensive *adj.* all-out, comprehensive, concentrated, demanding, detailed, exhaustive, in detail, in-depth, thorough, thoroughgoing.
antonym superficial.

intent *adj.* absorbed, alert, attentive, bent, committed, concentrated, concentrating, determined, eager, earnest, engrossed, fixed, hell-bent, industrious, intense, mindful, occupied, piercing, preoccupied, rapt, resolute, resolved, set, steadfast, steady, watchful, wrapped up.
antonyms absent-minded, distracted.
n. aim, design, end, goal, intention, meaning, object, objective, plan, purpose.

intention *n.* aim, concept, design, end, end in view, goal, idea, intent, meaning, object, objective, plan, point, purpose, scope, target, view.

intentional *adj.* calculated, deliberate, designed, intended, meant, planned, prearranged, preconcerted, premediated, purposed, studied, wilful.
antonym accidental.

intentionally *adv.* by design, deliberately,

designedly, meaningly, on purpose, wilfully, with malice aforethought.
antonym accidentally.

intently *adv.* attentively, carefully, closely, fixedly, hard, keenly, searchingly, staringly, steadily, watchfully.
antonym absent-mindedly.

inter *v.* bury, entomb, inhume, inurn, lay to rest, sepulchre.
antonym exhume.

interbreed *v.* cross, cross-breed, hybridise, miscegenate.

interbreeding *n.* cross-breeding, crossing, hybridisation, miscegenation.

intercede *v.* advocate, arbitrate, interpose, intervene, mediate, plead, speak.

intercept *v.* arrest, block, catch, check, cut off, deflect, delay, frustrate, head off, impede, interrupt, obstruct, retard, seize, stop, take, thwart.

intercession *n.* advocacy, agency, beseeching, entreaty, good offices, intervention, mediation, plea, pleading, prayer, solicitation, supplication.

interchange *n.* alternation, crossfire, exchange, interplay, intersection, junction, reciprocation, trading.

interchangeable *adj.* commutable, equal, equivalent, exchangeable, identical, reciprocal, similar, standard, synonymous, the same, transposable.
antonym different.

intercourse[1] *n.* association, commerce, communication, communion, congress, connection, contact, conversation, converse, correspondence, dealings, intercommunication, traffic, truck.

intercourse[2] *n.* carnal knowledge, coition, coitus, copulation, embraces, greens, intimacy, love-making, sex, sexual relations, venery.

interdict *v.* ban, bar, debar, disallow, forbid, outlaw, preclude, prevent, prohibit, proscribe, rule out, veto.
antonym allow.
n. ban, disallowance, injunction, interdiction, prohibition, proscription, taboo, veto.
antonym permission.

interest *n.* activity, advantage, affair, affection, attention, attentiveness, attraction, authority, bag, benefit, business, care, claim, commitment, concern, consequence, curiosity, diversion, finger, gain, good, hobby, importance, influence, investment, involvement, line of country, matter, moment, note, notice, participation, pastime, portion, preoccupation, profit, pursuit, regard, relaxation, relevance, right, share, significance, stake, study, suspicion, sympathy, weight.
antonyms boredom, irrelevance.
v. affect, amuse, attract, concern, divert, engage, engross, fascinate, intrigue, involve, move, touch, warm.
antonym bore.

interested *adj.* affected, attentive, attracted, biased, concerned, curious, drawn, engros-

sed, fascinated, implicated, intent, involved, keen, partisan, predisposed, prejudiced, responsive, simulated.
antonyms apathetic, indifferent, unaffected.
interesting *adj.* absorbing, amusing, amusive, appealing, attractive, compelling, curious, engaging, engrossing, entertaining, gripping, intriguing, provocative, stimulating, thought-provoking, unusual, viewable, visitable.
antonym boring.
interfere *v.* block, butt in, clash, collide, conflict, cramp, frustrate, hamper, handicap, hinder, impede, inhibit, interlope, intermeddle, interpose, intervene, intrude, meddle, obstruct, poke one's nose in, stick one's oar in, tamper, trammel.
antonyms assist, forbear.
interference *n.* clashing, collision, conflict, do-goodery, do-goodism, impedance, intervention, intrusion, meddlesomeness, meddling, mush, obstruction, opposition, prying, statics, white noise.
antonyms assistance, forbearance.
interim *adj.* acting, caretaker, improvised, intervening, makeshift, permanent, pro tem, provisional, stand-in, stop-gap, temporary.
n. interregnum, interval, meantime, meanwhile.
interior *adj.* central, domestic, hidden, home, inland, inly, inner, inside, internal, intimate, inward, mental, pectoral, personal, private, remote, secret, spiritual, up-country.
antonyms exterior, external.
n. bowels, centre, core, heart, heartland, hinterland, inside, up-country.
interject *v.* call, cry, exclaim, interjaculate, interpolate, interpose, interrupt, introduce, shout.
interjection *n.* call, cry, ejaculation, exclamation, interpolation, interposition, shout.
interlace *v.* braid, cross, enlace, entwine, interlock, intermix, intersperse, intertwine, interweave, interwreathe, knit, plait, reticulate, twine.
interlink *v.* clasp together, interconnect, intergrow, interlock, intertwine, interweave, knit, link, link together, lock together, mesh.
antonym separate.
interlock *v.* interdigitate, intertwine, lock together.
interloper *n.* gate-crasher, intruder, trespasser, uninvited guest.
interlude *n.* break, breathing-space, breathing-time, breathing-while, delay, episode, halt, hiatus, intermission, interval, pause, respite, rest, spell, stop, stoppage, wait.
intermarriage *n.* miscegenation.
intermediary *n.* agent, broker, entrepreneur, go-between, in-between, internuncio, mediator, middleman, ombudsman, ombudswoman.
intermediate *adj.* halfway, in-between, intermediary, interposed, intervening, mean, medial, median, mid, middle, midway, transitional.
antonym extreme.

interment *n.* burial, burying, funeral, inhumation, obsequies, obsequy, sepulture.
antonym exhumation.
interminable *adj.* boundless, ceaseless, dragging, endless, everlasting, immeasurable, infinite, limitless, long, long-drawn-out, long-winded, never-ending, perpetual, prolix, protracted, unbounded, unlimited, wearisome.
antonym limited.
intermingle *v.* amalgamate, blend, combine, commingle, commix, fuse, interlace, intermix, interweave, merge, mix, mix together, mix up.
antonym separate.
intermission *n.* break, breather, breathing-space, breathing-while, cessation, entr'acte, interlude, interruption, interval, let-up, lull, pause, recess, remission, respite, rest, stop, stoppage, suspense, suspension.
intermittent *adj.* broken, discontinuous, fitful, irregular, occasional, periodic, periodical, punctuated, recurrent, recurring, remittent, spasmodic, sporadic, stop-go.
antonym continuous.
intern *v.* confine, detain, hold, imprison, jail.
antonym free.
internal *adj.* domestic, in-house, inner, inside, interior, intimate, inward, private, subjective.
antonym external.
international *adj.* cosmopolitan, general, global, intercontinental, interterritorial, universal, worldwide.
antonym parochial.
internecine *adj.* bloody, civil, deadly, destructive, exterminating, exterminatory, family, fatal, internal, internecive, mortal, murderous, ruinous.
interplay *n.* exchange, give-and-take, interaction, interchange, meshing, reciprocation, reciprocity.
interpolate *v.* add, insert, intercalate, interjaculate, interject, introduce.
interpolation *n.* addition, aside, insert, insertion, intercalation, interjaculation, interjection, introduction.
interpose *v.* come between, insert, intercede, interfere, interjaculate, interject, interrupt, intervene, introduce, intrude, mediate, offer, place between, step in, thrust in.
antonym forbear.
interpret *v.* adapt, clarify, construe, decipher, decode, define, elucidate, explain, explicate, expound, paraphrase, read, render, solve, take, throw light on, translate, understand, unfold.
interpretation *n.* anagoge, anagogy, analysis, clarification, construction, diagnosis, elucidation, exegesis, explanation, explication, exposition, meaning, performance, portrayal, reading, rendering, rendition, sense, signification, translation, understanding, version.
interpretative *adj.* clarificatory, exegetic, explanatory, explicatory, expository, hermeneutic, interpretive.

interpreter *n.* annotator, commentator, dobhash, dragoman, elucidator, exegete, exegetist, exponent, expositor, hermeneutist, interpretress, linguister, munshi, scholiast, translator, truchman, ulema.

interrogate *v.* ask, catechise, cross-examine, cross-question, debrief, enquire, examine, give (someone) the third degree, grill, inquire, investigate, pump, question, quiz.

interrogation *n.* catachesis, cross-examination, cross-questioning, enquiry, examination, grilling, inquiry, inquisition, probing, questioning, third degree.

interrogative *adj.* catechetical, curious, erotetic, inquiring, inquisitional, inquisitive, inquisitorial, interrogatory, questioning, quizzical.

interrupt *v.* barge in, break, break in, break off, butt in, check, cut, cut off, cut short, delay, disconnect, discontinue, disjoin, disturb, disunite, divide, heckle, hinder, hold up, interfere, interjaculate, interject, intrude, obstruct, punctuate, separate, sever, stay, stop, suspend.
antonym forbear.

interrupted *adj.* broken, cut off, disconnected, discontinuous, disturbed, incomplete, intermittent, uneven, unfinished.
antonyms complete, continuous.

interruption *n.* break, cessation, Derby dog, disconnection, discontinuance, disruption, dissolution, disturbance, disuniting, division, halt, hiatus, hindrance, hitch, impediment, intrusion, obstacle, obstruction, pause, separation, severance, stop, stoppage, suspension.

intersect *v.* bisect, criss-cross, cross, cut, cut across, decussate, divide, divide up, meet.

intersection *n.* bisection, crossing, crossroads, decussation, division, interchange, junction.

intersperse *v.* diversify, dot, interlard, intermix, pepper, scatter, sprinkle.

intertwine *v.* braid, convolute, cross, entwine, interlace, intertangle, intertwist, interweave, interwreathe, inweave, link, reticulate, twist.

interval *n.* break, delay, distance, entr'acte, gap, hiatus, in-between, interim, interlude, intermission, interspace, interstice, meantime, meanwhile, opening, pause, period, playtime, rest, season, space, spell, term, time, wait.

intervene *v.* arbitrate, befall, ensue, happen, intercede, interfere, interpose oneself, interrupt, intrude, involve, mediate, occur, step in, succeed, supervene, take a hand.

intervening *adj.* between, interjacent, interposing, intervenient, mediate.

intervention *n.* agency, intercession, interference, interposition, intervening, intrusion, mediation.

interview *n.* audience, conference, consultation, dialogue, evaluation, inquiry, inquisition, meeting, oral, oral examination, press conference, talk, viva.
v. examine, interrogate, question, viva.

interviewer *n.* examiner, inquisitor, inquisitress, interlocutor, interrogant, interrogator, investigator, questioner, reporter.

interweave *v.* blend, braid, criss-cross, cross, interlace, intertangle, intertwine, intertwist, interwork, interwreathe, reticulate, splice.

interweaving *n.* interramification, intertangling, intertwining, intertwisting.

interwoven *adj.* blended, connected, entwined, inmixed, interconnected, interlaced, interlocked, intermingled, intertangled, intertwisted, interworked, interwreathed, interwrought, knit.

intestinal *adj.* abdominal, coeliac, duodenal, ileac, internal, stomachic, visceral.

intestines *n.* bowels, chitterlings, entrails, guts, innards, insides, offal, umbles, viscera, vitals.

intimacy *n.* brotherliness, closeness, coition, coitus, confidence, confidentiality, copulating, copulation, familiarity, fornication, fraternisation, friendship, intercourse, sexual intercourse, sisterliness, understanding.

intimate[1] *v.* allude, announce, communicate, declare, hint, impart, imply, indicate, insinuate, state, suggest, tell.

intimate[2] *adj.* as thick as thieves, bosom, cherished, close, confidential, cosy, dear, deep, deep-seated, detailed, exhaustive, friendly, gremial, informal, innermost, internal, near, palsy-walsy, penetrating, personal, private, privy, profound, secret, warm.
antonyms cold, distant, unfriendly.
n. Achates, associate, bosom buddy, buddy, china, chum, comrade, confidant, confidante, crony, familiar, friend, mate, mucker, pal, repository.
antonym stranger.

intimately *adv.* affectionately, closely, confidentially, confidingly, exhaustively, familiarly, fully, in detail, inside out, personally, tenderly, thoroughly, warmly.
antonyms coldly, distantly.

intimation *n.* allusion, announcement, communication, declaration, hint, indication, inkling, insinuation, notice, reminder, statement, suggestion, warning.

intimidate *v.* alarm, appal, browbeat, bulldoze, bully, coerce, cow, daunt, dishearten, dismay, dispirit, frighten, lean on, overawe, psych out, put the frighteners on, scare, subdue, terrify, terrorise, threaten.
antonym persuade.

intimidation *n.* arm-twisting, browbeating, bullying, coercion, fear, menaces, pressure, terror, terrorisation, terrorising, threats.
antonym persuasion.

intolerable *adj.* beyond the pale, excruciating, impossible, insufferable, insupportable, painful, unbearable, unendurable.
antonym tolerable.

intolerance *n.* bigotry, chauvinism, discrimination, dogmatism, fanaticism, illiberality, impatience, jingoism, narrow-mindedness, narrowness, opinionativeness, prejudice, racialism, racism, xenophobia.
antonym tolerance.

intolerant *adj.* bigoted, chauvinistic, dictatorial,

dogmatic, fanatical, illiberal, impatient, narrow, narrow-minded, opinionated, opinionative, opinioned, persecuting, prejudiced, racialist, racist, small-minded, uncharitable.
antonym tolerant.

intonation *n.* accentuation, cadence, chant, incantation, inflection, mantra(m), modulation, tone.

intone *v.* chant, croon, declaim, intonate, monotone, pronounce, recite, sing, utter.

intoxicate *n.* addle, befuddle, elate, excite, exhilarate, fuddle, inebriate, inflame, stimulate, stupefy.
antonym sober.

intoxicated *adj.* blotto, canned, cut, disguised in liquor, dizzy, drunk, drunken, ebriate, ebriated, ebriose, elated, enraptured, euphoric, excited, exhilarated, fuddled, glorious, half seas over, high, in one's cups, incapable, inebriate, inebriated, infatuated, legless, lit up, looped, pickled, pissed, pixil(l)ated, plastered, sent, sloshed, smashed, sozzled, stewed, stiff, stimulated, stoned, stotious, three sheets in the wind, tight, tipsy, under the influence, up the pole, zonked.
antonym sober.

intoxicating *adj.* alcoholic, dizzy, euphoric, exciting, exhilarating, heady, inebriant, intoxicant, spirituous, stimulating, strong, thrilling.
antonym sobering.

intoxication *n.* delirium, drunkenness, ebriety, ebriosity, elation, euphoria, exaltation, excitement, exhilaration, inebriation, inebriety, infatuation, insobriety, tipsiness.
antonym sobriety.

intractability *n.* awkwardness, cantankerousness, contrariness, incorrigibility, indiscipline, indocility, mulishness, obduracy, obstinacy, perverseness, perversity, pigheadedness, stubbornness, unamenability, unco-operativeness, ungovernability, waywardness.
antonym amenability.

intractable *adj.* awkward, bull-headed, cantankerous, contrary, difficult, fractious, haggard, headstrong, incurable, insoluble, intransigent, obdurate, obstinate, perverse, pigheaded, refractory, self-willed, stubborn, unamenable, unbending, unco-operative, undisciplined, ungovernable, unmanageable, unruly, unyielding, wayward, wild, wilful.
antonym amenable.

intransigent *adj.* hardline, immovable, intractable, irreconcilable, obdurate, obstinate, stubborn, tenacious, tough, unamenable, unbending, unbudgeable, uncompromising, unpersuadable, unyielding, uppity.
antonym amenable.

intrepid *adj.* audacious, bold, brave, courageous, daring, dashing, dauntless, doughty, fearless, gallant, game, gutsy, heroic, lion-hearted, nerveless, plucky, resolute, stalwart, stout-hearted, unafraid, undashed, undaunted, unflinching, valiant, valorous.

antonyms cowardly, timid.

intrepidness *n.* audacity, boldness, bravery, courage, daring, dauntlessness, doughtiness, fearlessness, fortitude, gallantry, guts, heroism, intrepidity, lion-heartedness, nerve, pluck, prowess, spirit, stout-heartedness, undauntedness, valour.
antonyms cowardice, timidity.

intricacy *n.* complexedness, complexity, complexness, complication, convolutions, elaborateness, entanglement, intricateness, involution, involvement, knottiness, obscurity.
antonym simplicity.

intricate *adj.* Byzantine, complex, complicated, convoluted, daedal(e), Daedalian, daedalic, dedal, dedalian, difficult, elaborate, entangled, fancy, Gordian, involved, knotty, labyrinthine, perplexing, rococo, sophisticated, tangled, tortuous.
antonym simple.

intrigue[1] *v.* attract, charm, fascinate, interest, puzzle, rivet, tantalise, tickle one's fancy, titillate.
antonym bore.

intrigue[2] *n.* affair, amour, brigue, cabal, chicanery, collusion, conspiracy, double-dealing, intimacy, knavery, liaison, machination, machination(s), manipulation, manoeuvre, plot, romance, ruse, scheme, sharp practice, stratagem, string-pulling, trickery, wheeler-dealing, wile, wire-pulling.
v. connive, conspire, machinate, manoeuvre, plot, scheme.

intriguer *n.* conniver, intrigant(e), Machiavellian, machinator, plotter, schemer, wangler, wheeler-dealer, wire-puller.

intriguing *adj.* beguiling, compelling, diverting, exciting, fascinating, interesting, puzzling, tantalising, titillating.
antonyms boring, uninteresting.

intrinsic *adj.* basic, basically, built-in, central, congenital, constitutional, constitutionally, elemental, essential, essentially, fundamental, fundamentally, genuine, inborn, inbred, inherent, intrinsically, inward, native, natural, underlying.
antonym extrinsic.

introduce *v.* acquaint, add, advance, air, announce, begin, bring in, bring up, broach, commence, conduct, establish, familiarise, found, inaugurate, initiate, inject, insert, institute, interpolate, interpose, launch, lead in, lead into, moot, offer, open, organise, pioneer, preface, present, propose, put forward, put in, recommend, set forth, start, submit, suggest, throw in, ventilate.
antonym take away.

introduction *n.* addition, baptism, commencement, debut, establishment, exordium, foreword, inauguration, induction, initiation, insertion, institution, interpolation, intro, launch, lead-in, opening, overture, pioneering, preamble, preface, preliminaries, prelude, presentation, prodrome, prodromus, proem, prolegomena, prolegomenon, pro-

logue, prooemion, prooemium.
antonym withdrawal.

introductory *adj.* early, elementary, exordial, first, inaugural, initial, initiatory, opening, precursory, prefatory, preliminary, preparatory, proemial, prolegomenary, prolegomenous, prolusory, starting.

introspection *n.* brooding, heart-searching, introversion, self-analysis, self-examination, self-observation, soul-searching.

introspective *adj.* brooding, contemplative, introverted, inward-looking, meditative, pensive, ruminative, subjective, thoughtful.
antonym outward-looking.

introverted *adj.* indrawn, intervertive, introspective, introversive, inward-looking, self-centred, self-contained, withdrawn.
antonym extraverted.

intrude *v.* aggress, butt in, encroach, infringe, interfere, interrupt, meddle, obtrude, trespass, violate.
antonyms stand back, withdraw.

intruder *n.* burglar, Derby dog, gate-crasher, infiltrator, interloper, invader, prowler, raider, snooper, trespasser.

intrusion *n.* aggression, encroachment, incursion, infringement, ingression, interference, interruption, invasion, trespass, violation.
antonym withdrawal.

intrusive *adj.* disturbing, forward, impertinent, importunate, interfering, invasive, meddlesome, nosy, obtrusive, officious, presumptuous, pushy, uncalled-for, unwanted, unwelcome.
antonyms unintrusive, welcome.

intuition *n.* discernment, feeling, gut feeling, hunch, insight, instinct, perception, presentiment, sixth sense.
antonym reasoning.

intuitive *adj.* innate, instinctive, instinctual, involuntary, spontaneous, unreflecting, untaught.
antonym reasoned.

inundate *v.* bury, deluge, drown, engulf, fill, flood, glut, immerse, overflow, overrun, overwhelm, submerge, swamp.

inundation *n.* deluge, deluvion, deluvium, flood, glut, overflow, tidal wave, torrent.
antonym trickle.

inure *v.* accustom, desensitise, familiarise, flesh, habituate, harden, strengthen, temper, toughen, train.

invade *v.* assail, assault, attack, burst in, come upon, descend upon, encroach, enter, fall upon, infest, infringe, irrupt, occupy, overrun, overspread, penetrate, pervade, raid, rush into, seize, swarm over, violate.
antonym withdraw.

invader *n.* aggressor, attacker, intruder, raider, trespasser.

invalid[1] *adj.* ailing, bedridden, disabled, feeble, frail, ill, infirm, invalidish, poorly, sick, sickly, valetudinarian, valetudinary, weak.
antonym healthy.

n. case, convalescent, patient, sufferer,

valetudinarian, valetudinary.

invalid[2] *adj.* baseless, fallacious, false, ill-founded, illogical, incorrect, inoperative, irrational, nugatory, null, null and void, unfounded, unscientific, unsound, untrue, void, worthless.
antonym valid.

invalidate *v.* abrogate, annul, cancel, nullify, overrule, overthrow, quash, rescind, undermine, undo, vitiate, weaken.
antonym validate.

invalidity *n.* fallaciousness, fallacy, falsity, illogicality, inconsistency, incorrectness, invalidness, irrationality, sophism, speciousness, unsoundness, voidness.

invaluable *adj.* costly, exquisite, inestimable, precious, priceless, valuable.
antonym worthless.

invariable *adj.* changeless, consistent, constant, fixed, immutable, inflexible, permanent, regular, rigid, set, static, unalterable, unchangeable, unchanging, unfailing, uniform, unvarying, unwavering.
antonym variable.

invariably *adv.* always, consistently, customarily, habitually, inevitably, perpetually, regularly, unfailingly, without exception, without fail.
antonym variably.

invasion *n.* aggression, assault, attack, breach, encroachment, foray, incursion, infiltration, infraction, infringement, inroad, intrusion, irruption, offensive, onslaught, raid, seizure, usurpation, violation.
antonym withdrawal.

invective *n.* abuse, berating, billingsgate, castigation, censure, contumely, denunciation, diatribe, flyting, obloquy, philippic, philippic(s), reproach, revilement, sarcasm, scolding, tirade, tongue-lashing, vilification, vituperation.
antonym praise.

inveigh *v.* berate, blame, castigate, censure, condemn, denounce, expostulate, flite, fulminate, lambast, rail, recriminate, reproach, scold, sound off, tongue-lash, upbraid, vituperate.
antonym praise.

inveigle *v.* allure, bamboozle, beguile, cajole, coax, con, decoy, ensnare, entice, entrap, lead on, lure, manipulate, manoeuvre, persuade, seduce, sweet-talk, wheedle, wile.
antonym force.

invent *v.* coin, conceive, concoct, contrive, cook up, create, design, devise, discover, dream up, fabricate, formulate, frame, imagine, improvise, make up, originate, think up, trump up.

invention *n.* brainchild, coinage, contraption, contrivance, contrivement, creation, creativeness, creativity, deceit, design, development, device, discovery, excogitation, fabrication, fake, falsehood, fantasy, fib, fiction, figment of (someone's) imagination, forgery, gadget, genius, imagination, ingenuity, inspiration,

inventiveness, inveracity, lie, originality, prevarication, resourcefulness, sham, story, tall story, untruth, yarn.
antonym truth.

inventive *adj.* creative, daedal(e), Daedalian, daedalic, dedal, excogitative, fertile, gifted, imaginative, ingenious, innovative, inspired, original, resourceful.
antonym uninventive.

inventor *n.* architect, author, builder, coiner, creator, designer, father, framer, inventress, maker, originator.

inventory *n.* account, catalogue, equipment, file, list, listing, record, register, roll, roster, schedule, stock.

inverse *adj.* contrary, converse, inverted, opposite, reverse, reversed, transposed, upside down.

inversion *n.* antipode, antithesis, contraposition, contrariety, contrary, hysteron-proteron, opposite, reversal, transposal, transposition.

invert *v.* capsize, introvert, inverse, overturn, reverse, transpose, turn turtle, turn upside down, upset, upturn.
antonym right.

invest *v.* adopt, advance, authorise, charge, consecreate, devote, empower, endow, endue, enthrone, establish, inaugurate, induct, install, lay out, license, ordain, provide, put in, sanction, sink, spend, supply, vest.
antonym divest.

investigate *v.* consider, examine, explore, go into, inquire into, inspect, look into, probe, scrutinise, search, see how the land lies, sift, study, suss out.

investigation *n.* analysis, enquiry, examination, exploration, fact finding, hearing, inquest, inquiry, inspection, probe, research, review, scrutiny, search, study, survey, witch-hunt, zetetic.

investigative *adj.* fact-finding, heuristic, inspecting, investigating, research, researching, zetetic.

investigator *n.* detective, dick, examiner, gumshoe, inquirer, inquisitor, private detective, private eye, researcher, shamus, sleuth, sleuth-hound.

investiture *n.* admission, coronation, enthronement, inauguration, induction, installation, instatement, investing, investment, ordination.

investment *n.* ante, asset, besieging, blockade, contribution, investing, investiture, siege, speculation, stake, transaction, venture.

inveterate *adj.* chronic, confirmed, deep-dyed, deep-rooted, deep-seated, diehard, dyed-in-the-wool, entrenched, established, habitual, hard-core, hardened, incorrigible, incurable, ineradicable, ingrained, irreformable, long-standing, obstinate.
antonym impermanent.

invidious *adj.* discriminating, discriminatory, hateful, objectionable, obnoxious, odious, offensive, repugnant, slighting, undesirable.
antonym desirable.

invigorate *v.* animate, brace, buck up, energise, enliven, exhilarate, fortify, freshen, galvanise, harden, inspirit, liven up, nerve, pep up, perk up, quicken, refresh, rejuvenate, revitalise, stimulate, strengthen, vitalise, vivify.
antonyms dishearten, weary.

invigorating *adj.* bracing, energising, exhilarating, fresh, generous, healthful, inspiriting, refreshing, rejuvenating, rejuvenative, restorative, salubrious, stimulating, tonic, uplifting, vivifying.
antonyms disheartening, wearying.

invincible *adj.* impenetrable, impregnable, indestructible, indomitable, inseparable, insuperable, invulnerable, irreducible, unassailable, unbeatable, unconquerable, unreducible, unsurmountable, unyielding.
antonym beatable.

inviolability *n.* holiness, inalienability, inviolableness, inviolacy, invulnerability, sacredness, sacrosanctness, sanctity.
antonym violability.

inviolable *adj.* hallowed, holy, inalienable, intemerate, sacred, sacrosanct, unalterable.
antonym violable.

inviolate *adj.* entire, intact, pure, sacred, stainless, unbroken, undefiled, undisturbed, unhurt, uninjured, unpolluted, unprofaned, unstained, unsullied, untouched, virgin, whole.
antonym sullied.

invisible *adj.* concealed, disguised, hidden, imperceptible, inappreciable, inconspicuous, indetectable, indiscernible, infinitesimal, microscopic, out of sight, unperceivable, unseeable, unseen.
antonym visible.

invitation *n.* allurement, asking, begging, bidding, call, challenge, come-on, coquetry, enticement, exhortation, glad eye, incitement, inducement, invite, overture, provocation, request, solicitation, summons, supplication, temptation.

invite *v.* allure, ask, ask for, attract, beckon, beg, bid, bring on, call, court, draw, encourage, entice, lead, provoke, request, seek, solicit, summon, tempt, welcome.
antonyms force, order.

inviting *adj.* alluring, appealing, appetising, attractive, beguiling, captivating, delightful, engaging, enticing, fascinating, intriguing, magnetic, mouthwatering, pleasing, seductive, tantalising, tempting, warm, welcoming, winning.
antonym uninviting.

invocation *n.* appeal, beseeching, conjuration, entreaty, epiclasis, imploration, petition, prayer, supplication.

invoke *v.* adjure, appeal to, apply, base on, beg, beseech, call upon, conjure, conjure up, entreat, implement, implore, initiate, petition, pray, put into effect, refer to, resort to, solicit, supplicate, use.

involuntary *adj.* automatic, blind, compulsory, conditioned, forced, instinctive, instinctual,

obligatory, reflex, reluctant, spontaneous, unconscious, uncontrolled, unintentional, unthinking, unwilled, unwilling, vegetative.
antonym voluntary.

involve *v.* absorb, affect, associate, bind, commit, comprehend, comprise, compromise, concern, connect, contain, cover, draw in, embrace, engage, engross, entail, grip, hold, implicate, imply, include, incorporate, incriminate, inculpate, mean, mix up, necessitate, number among, preoccupy, presuppose, require, rivet, take in, touch.

involved *adj.* anfractuous, caught up/in, complex, complicated, concerned, confusing, convoluted, difficult, elaborate, implicated, in on, intricate, knotty, labyrinthine, mixed up in/with, occupied, participating, sophisticated, tangled, tortuous.
antonyms simple, uninvolved.

involvement *n.* association, commitment, complexity, complication, concern, connection, dedication, difficulty, embarrassment, entanglement, imbroglio, implication, interest, intricacy, participation, problem, ramification, responsibility.

invulnerability *n.* impenetrability, inviolability, safety, security, strength, unassailability.
antonym vulnerability.

invulnerable *adj.* impenetrable, indestructible, insusceptible, invincible, proof against, safe, secure, unassailable, unwoundable.
antonym vulnerable.

inward *adj.* confidential, entering, hidden, inbound, incoming, inflowing, ingoing, inly, inmost, inner, innermost, inpouring, inside, interior, internal, penetrating, personal, private, privy, secret.
antonyms external, outward.

inwardly *adv.* at heart, deep down, in gremio, in pectore, in petto, inly, inside, privately, secretly, to oneself, within.
antonyms externally, outwardly.

iota *n.* atom, bit, drop, grain, hint, jot, mite, particle, scintilla, scrap, smidgeon, soupçon, speck, tittle, trace, whit.

IOU *n.* debenture.

irascibility *n.* asperity, bad temper, cantankerousness, choler, crabbiness, crossness, edginess, fieriness, ill-temper, impatience, irritability, irritation, petulance, shortness, snappishness, testiness, touchiness.
antonym placidness.

irascible *adj.* bad-tempered, cantankerous, choleric, crabbed, crabby, cross, hasty, hot-tempered, ill-natured, ill-tempered, iracund, iracundulous, irritable, narky, peppery, petulant, prickly, quick-tempered, short-tempered, testy, touchy, volcanic.
antonym placid.

irate *adj.* angered, angry, annoyed, enraged, exasperated, fuming, furibund, furious, gusty, in a paddy, incensed, indignant, infuriated, ireful, irritated, livid, mad, piqued, provoked, riled, up in arms, waxy, worked up, wrathful, wroth.
antonym calm.

ire *n.* anger, annoyance, choler, displeasure, exasperation, fury, indignation, passion, rage, wax, wrath.
antonym calmness.

iridescence *n.* glittering, iridisation, opalescence, reflet, shimmering.

iridescent *adj.* glittering, iridial, iridian, irisated, irised, nacreous, opalescent, opaline, pearly, polychromatic, prismatic, rainbow, rainbow-coloured, rainbow-like, shimmering, shot.

iris *n.* flag, fleur-de-lis, gladdon.

Irish *adj.* green, Hibernian, Milesian.

irk *v.* aggravate, annoy, bug, disgust, distress, gall, get, get to, irritate, miff, nettle, peeve, provoke, put out, rile, rub up the wrong way, ruffle, vex, weary.
antonym please.

irksome *adj.* aggravating, annoying, boring, bothersome, burdensome, disagreeable, exasperating, infuriating, irritating, tedious, tiresome, troublesome, vexatious, vexing, wearisome.
antonym pleasing.

iron *adj.* adamant, cruel, fast-binding, fixed, grating, hard, harsh, heavy, immovable, implacable, indomitable, inflexible, insensitive, obdurate, rigid, robust, steel, steely, strong, tough, unbending, unyielding.
antonyms pliable, weak.
v. flatten, press, smooth, uncrease.
n. flatiron, goose.

iron out clear up, deal with, eliminate, eradicate, erase, expedite, fix, get rid of, harmonise, put right, reconcile, resolve, settle, smooth over, solve, sort out, straighten out.

ironic *adj.* contemptuous, derisive, incongruous, ironical, irrisory, mocking, paradoxical, sarcastic, sardonic, satirical, scoffing, scornful, sneering, wry.

irons *n.* bilboes, bonds, chains, fetters, gyves, manacles, shackles, trammels.

irony *n.* asteism, contrariness, incongruity, irrision, mockery, paradox, sarcasm, satire.

irradiate *v.* brighten, enlighten, expose, illume, illuminate, illumine, light up, lighten, radiate, shine on.

irrational *adj.* aberrant, absurd, alogical, brainless, crazy, demented, foolish, illogical, injudicious, insane, mindless, muddleheaded, nonsensical, preposterous, raving, senseless, silly, unreasonable, unreasoning, unsound, unstable, unthinking, unwise, wild.
antonym rational.

irrationality *n.* absurdity, brainlessness, illogicality, insanity, lunacy, madness, preposterousness, senselessness, unreason, unreasonableness, unsoundness.
antonym rationality.

irreconcilable *adj.* clashing, conflicting, hardline, implacable, incompatible, incongruous, inconsistent, inexorable, inflexible, intransigent, opposed, unappeasable, uncompromising, unreconcilable.
antonym reconcilable.

irrecoverable *adj.* irreclaimable, irredeemable, irremediable, irreparable, irretrievable, lost, unrecoverable, unsalvageable, unsavable.
antonym recoverable.

irrefutable *adj.* apod(e)ictic, certain, impregnable, incontestable, incontrovertible, indisputable, indubitable, invincible, irrebuttable, irrefragable, irresistible, sure, unanswerable, unassailable, undeniable, ungainsayable, unquestionable.
antonym refutable.

irregular *adj.* abnormal, anomalistic(al), anomalous, asymmetrical, broken, bumpy, capricious, craggy, crooked, difform, disconnected, disorderly, eccentric, erratic, exceptional, extraordinary, extravagant, fitful, fluctuating, fragmentary, haphazard, holey, immoderate, improper, inappropriate, incondite, inordinate, intermittent, jagged, lopsided, lumpy, occasional, odd, patchy, peculiar, pitted, queer, quirky, ragged, random, rough, serrated, shifting, snatchy, spasmodic, sporadic, uncertain, unconventional, unequal, uneven, unofficial, unorthodox, unprocedural, unpunctual, unsteady, unsuitable, unsymmetrical, unsystematic, unusual, variable, wavering.
antonyms conventional, regular, smooth.

irregularity *n.* aberration, abnormality, anomaly, asymmetry, breach, bumpiness, confusion, crookedness, desultoriness, deviation, difformity, disorderliness, disorganisation, eccentricity, freak, haphazardness, heterodoxy, jaggedness, lop-sidedness, lumpiness, malfunction, malpractice, oddity, patchiness, peculiarity, raggedness, randomness, roughness, singularity, uncertainty, unconventionality, unevenness, unorthodoxy, unpunctuality, unsteadiness.
antonyms conventionality, regularity, smoothness.

irregularly *adv.* anyhow, by fits and starts, disconnectedly, eccentrically, erratically, fitfully, haphazardly, intermittently, jerkily, now and again, occasionally, off and on, spasmodically, unevenly, unmethodically.
antonym regularly.

irrelevance *n.* inappositeness, inappropriateness, inaptness, inconsequence, irrelevancy, unimportance.
antonym relevance.

irrelevant *adj.* alien, extraneous, foreign, immaterial, impertinent, inapplicable, inapposite, inappropriate, inapt, inconsequent, inessential, peripheral, tangential, unapt, unconnected, unnecessary, unrelated.
antonym relevant.

irreligious *adj.* agnostic, atheistic, blasphemous, free-thinking, godless, heathen, heathenish, iconoclastic, impious, irreverent, nullifidian, pagan, profane, rationalistic, sacrilegious, sceptical, sinful, unbelieving, undevout, ungodly, unholy, unreligious, unrighteous, wicked.
antonyms pious, religious.

irremediable *adj.* deadly, fatal, final, hopeless, incorrigible, incurable, inoperable, irrecoverable, irredeemable, irreparable, irretrievable, irreversible, mortal, remediless, terminal, unmedicinable.
antonym remediable.

irremovable *adj.* durable, fast, fixed, immovable, indestructible, ineradicable, ingrained, inoperable, obdurate, obstinate, permanent, persistent, rooted, set, stuck.
antonym removable.

irreparable *adj.* incurable, irreclaimable, irrecoverable, irremediable, irretrievable, irreversible, unrepairable.
antonyms recoverable, remediable.

irreplaceable *adj.* essential, indispensable, inimitable, invaluable, matchless, peerless, priceless, sublime, unique, unmatched, vital.
antonym replaceable.

irrepressible *adj.* boisterous, bubbling over, buoyant, ebullient, effervescent, inextinguishable, insuppressible, resilient, uncontainable, uncontrollable, ungovernable, uninhibited, unmanageable, unquenchable, unrestrainable, unstoppable.
antonyms depressed, depressive, despondent, resistible.

irreproachable *adj.* blameless, faultless, guiltless, immaculate, impeccable, inculpable, innocent, irreprehensible, irreprovable, perfect, pure, reproachless, stainless, taintless, unblemished, unimpeachable.
antonyms blameworthy, culpable.

irresistible *adj.* alluring, beckoning, beguiling, charming, compelling, enchanting, fascinating, imperative, ineluctable, inescapable, inevitable, inexorable, overmastering, overpowering, overwhelming, potent, pressing, ravishing, resistless, seductive, tempting, unavoidable, uncontrollable, urgent.
antonyms avoidable, resistible.

irresolute *adj.* dithering, doubtful, faint-hearted, fickle, fluctuating, half-hearted, hesitant, hesitating, indecisive, infirm, shifting, shilly-shallying, swithering, tentative, undecided, undetermined, unsettled, unstable, unsteady, vacillating, variable, wavering, weak.
antonym resolute.

irresolution *n.* dithering, faint-heartedness, fluctuation, half-heartedness, hesitancy, hesitation, inconsistency, inconstancy, indecisiveness, infirmity, infirmness, shifting, shilly-shally, shilly-shallying, tentativeness, uncertainty, unsteadiness, vacillation, wavering.
antonym resolution.

irresponsible *adj.* carefree, careless, feather-brained, feckless, flibbertigibbit, flighty, footloose, giddy, harebrained, harum-scarum, heedless, ill-considered, immature, light-hearted, madcap, negligent, rash, reckless, scatter-brained, shiftless, thoughtless, undependable, unreliable, untrustworthy, wild.
antonym responsible.

irretrievable *adj.* damned, hopeless, irrecoverable, irredeemable, irremediable, irrepar-

able, irreversible, irrevocable, lost, unrecallable, unrecoverable, unsalvageable.
antonyms recoverable, reversible.

irreverence *n.* blasphemy, cheek, cheekiness, derision, discourtesy, disrespect, disrespectfulness, flippancy, godlessness, iconoclasm, impertinence, impiety, impudence, levity, mockery, profanity, sauce.
antonym reverence.

irreverent *adj.* blasphemous, cheeky, contemptuous, derisive, discourteous, disrespectful, flip, flippant, godless, iconoclastic, impertinent, impious, impudent, mocking, profane, rude, sacrilegious, saucy, tongue-in-cheek.
antonym reverent.

irreversible *adj.* final, hopeless, immedicable, incurable, inoperable, irremediable, irreparable, irretrievable, irrevocable, lasting, lost, permanent, remediless, unalterable, unmedicinable.
antonyms curable, remediable, reversible.

irrevocable *adj.* changeless, fated, fixed, hopeless, immutable, inexorable, invariable, irremediable, irrepealable, irretrievable, irreversible, predestined, predetermined, settled, unalterable, unchangeable.
antonyms alterable, flexible, mutable, reversible.

irrigate *v.* dampen, flood, humect, humify, inundate, moisten, water, wet.

irritability *n.* edge, edginess, erethism, fractiousness, fretfulness, hypersensitivity, ill-humour, ill-temper, impatience, irascibility, peevishness, petulance, prickliness, testiness, tetchiness, touchiness.
antonyms bonhomie, cheerfulness, complacence, good humour.

irritable *adj.* bad-tempered, cantankerous, captious, choleric, crabbed, crabby, cross, crotchety, crusty, edgy, feisty, fractious, fretful, hasty, hypersensitive, ill-humoured, ill-tempered, impatient, irascible, narky, peevish, petulant, prickly, querulous, short, short-tempered, snappish, snappy, snarling, sore, tense, testy, te(t)chy, thin-skinned, touchy.
antonyms cheerful, complacent.

irritant *n.* annoyance, bore, bother, goad, menace, nuisance, pain, pest, pin-prick, plague, provocation, rankle, tease, thorn in the flesh, trouble, vexation.
antonyms pleasure, sop, sweetness.

irritate *v.* acerbate, aggravate, anger, annoy, bedevil, bother, bug, chafe, emboil, enrage, exacerbate, exasperate, faze, fret, get on one's nerves, get to, give the pip, gravel, grig, harass, incense, inflame, infuriate, intensify, irk, needle, nettle, offend, pain, peeve, pester, pique, provoke, put out, rankle, rile, rouse, rub, ruffle, vex.
antonyms gratify, mollify, placate, please.

irritated *adj.* angry, annoyed, bothered, cross, discomposed, displeased, edgy, exasperated, fazed, flustered, harassed, impatient, irked, irritable, nettled, peeved, piqued, put out,

ratty, riled, roused, ruffled, uptight, vexed.
antonyms composed, gratified, pleased.

irritating *adj.* abrasive, aggravating, annoying, bothersome, displeasing, disturbing, galling, infuriating, irksome, maddening, nagging, pesky, pesterous, pestful, pestiferous, pestilent, pestilential, plaguey, provoking, thorny, troublesome, trying, upsetting, urticant, vexatious, vexing, worrisome.
antonyms pleasant, pleasing.

irritation *n.* aggravation, anger, annoyance, crossness, displeasure, dissatisfaction, exasperation, fury, goad, impatience, indignation, irritability, irritant, nuisance, pain, pain in the neck, pest, pin-prick, provocation, rankle, resentment, shortness, snappiness, tease, testiness, vexation, wrath.
antonyms pleasure, satisfaction.

island *n.* ait, atoll, cay, eyot, holm, inch, isle, islet, key.

isolate *v.* abstract, cut off, detach, disconnect, divorce, exclude, identify, insulate, keep apart, ostracise, pinpoint, quarantine, remove, seclude, segregate, separate, sequester, set apart.
antonyms assimilate, incorporate.

isolated *adj.* abnormal, anomalous, atypical, backwoods, deserted, detached, dissociated, eremitic, exceptional, freak, godforsaken, hermitical, hidden, incommunicado, insular, lonely, monastic, outlying, out-of-the-way, random, reclusive, remote, retired, secluded, single, solitary, special, sporadic, unfrequented, unique, unrelated, untrodden, untypical, unusual, unvisited.
antonyms populous, typical.

isolation *n.* aloofness, detachment, disconnection, dissociation, exile, insularity, insulation, lazaretto, loneliness, quarantine, reclusion, remoteness, retirement, seclusion, segregation, self-sufficiency, separation, solitariness, solitude, withdrawal.

issue[1] *n.* affair, argument, concern, controversy, crux, debate, matter, point, problem, question, subject, topic.

issue[2] *n.* announcement, broadcast, circulation, copy, delivery, dispersal, dissemination, distribution, edition, emanation, flow, granting, handout, impression, instalment, issuance, issuing, number, printing, promulgation, propagation, publication, release, supply, supplying, vent.
v. announce, broadcast, circulate, deal out, deliver, distribute, emit, give out, mint, produce, promulgate, publicise, publish, put out, release, supply.

issue[3] *n.* conclusion, consequence, culmination, dénouement, effect, end, finale, outcome, pay-off, product, result, termination, upshot.
v. arise, burst forth, debouch, emanate, emerge, flow, leak, originate, proceed, rise, spring, stem.

issue[4] *n.* brood, children, descendants, heirs, offspring, progeny, scions, seed, young.

itch *v.* crawl, prickle, tickle, tingle, yuke.

n. cacoethes, craving, desire, eagerness, formication, hankering, hunger, irritation, itchiness, keenness, longing, lust, passion, prickling, scabies, tingling, yearning, yen.

itching *adj.* aching, avid, burning, dying, eager, greedy, hankering, impatient, inquisitive, itch, longing, raring, spoiling.

itchy *adj.* avaricious, eager, edgy, fidgety, greedy, impatient, restive, restless, roving, unsettled, yuky.

item *n.* account, article, aspect, bulletin, component, consideration, detail, element, entry, factor, feature, ingredient, matter, minute, note, notice, object, paragraph, particular, piece, point, report, thing.

itemise *v.* count, detail, document, enumerate, instance, inventory, list, mention, number, overname, particularise, record, specify, tabulate.

itinerancy *n.* drifting, nomadism, peregrination, roaming, rootlessness, roving, travelling, vagabondism, vagrancy, wandering, wanderlust, wayfaring.

itinerant *adj.* ambulatory, drifting, journeying, migratory, nomadic, peregrinatory, peripatetic, rambling, roaming, rootless, roving, travelling, vagabond, vagrant, wandering, wayfaring. *antonyms* settled, stationary.

n. diddicoy, dusty-foot, gypsy, hobo, nomad, perigrinator, peripatetic, piepowder, pilgrim, Romany, tinker, toe-rag, tramp, traveller, vagabond, vagrant, wanderer, wayfarer.

itinerary *n.* circuit, course, journey, line, plan, programme, route, schedule, tour.

J

jab *v.* dig, elbow, jag, lunge, nudge, poke, prod, punch, push, shove, stab, tap, thrust.

jabber *v.* babble, blather, blether, chatter, drivel, gab, gabble, gash, jaw, mumble, prate, rabbit, ramble, tattle, witter, yap.

jacket *n.* blouson, case, casing, coat, cover, covering, envelope, folder, jerkin, jupon, mackinaw, sheath, shell, skin, wrap, wrapper, wrapping.

jackpot *n.* award, big time, bonanza, kitty, pool, pot, prize, reward, stakes, winnings.

jade *n.* baggage, broad, draggle-tail, floosie, harridan, hussy, nag, shrew, slattern, slut, strumpet, tart, trollop, vixen, wench.

jaded *adj.* blunted, bored, cloyed, disjaskit, dulled, effete, exhausted, fagged, fatigued, played-out, satiated, spent, surfeited, tired, tired out, weary.
antonyms fresh, refreshed.

jag *n.* barb, denticle, dentil, notch, point, projection, protrusion, snag, spur, tooth.

jagged *adj.* barbed, broken, craggy, denticulate, hackly, indented, irregular, notched, pointed, ragged, ridged, rough, saw-edged, serrate, serrated, snagged, snaggy, spiked, spiky, toothed, uneven.
antonym smooth.

jail, gaol *n.* borstal, bridewell, brig, calaboose, can, cells, choky, clink, cooler, coop, custody, guardhouse, hoos(e)gow, house of correction, inside, jailhouse, jankers, jug, lock-up, nick, pen, penitentiary, pokey, porridge, prison, quod, reformatory, slammer, stir, tollbooth.
v. confine, detain, immure, impound, imprison, incarcerate, intern, lock up, quod, send down.

jailer, gaoler *n.* captor, guard, keeper, prison officer, screw, turnkey, warden, warder.

jam[1] *v.* block, clog, compact, confine, congest, cram, crowd, crush, force, obstruct, pack, press, ram, sandwich, squash, squeeze, stall, stick, stuff, throng, thrust, vice, wedge.
n. bottle-neck, concourse, crowd, crush, gridlock, herd, horde, mass, mob, multitude, pack, press, swarm, throng, traffic jam.

jam[2] *n.* bind, contretemps, difficulty, dilemma, fix, hitch, hole, hot water, imbroglio, impasse, pickle, plight, predicament, quandary, scrape, spot, straits, tangle, tight corner, trouble.

jam[3] *n.* confiture, confyt, conserve, jelly, marmalade, preserve, spread.

jamboree *n.* carnival, carouse, celebration, convention, festival, festivity, fête, field day, frolic, gathering, get-together, jubilee, junket, merriment, party, potlatch, rally, revelry, shindig, spree.

jangle *v.* chime, clank, clash, clatter, jar, jingle, rattle, upset, vibrate.
n. cacophony, clang, clangour, clash, din, dissonance, jar, racket, rattle, reverberation, stridence, stridency, stridor.
antonyms euphony, harmony.

janitor *n.* caretaker, concierge, custodian, doorkeeper, doorman, janitress, janitrix, ostiary, porter.

jar[1] *n.* amphora, aquamanile, bellarmine, can, carafe, container, crock, cruet, cruse, ewer, flagon, jug, kang, mug, olla, pitcher, pot, receptacle, stamnos, stoup, urn, vase, vessel.

jar[2] *v.* agitate, annoy, clash, convulse, disagree, discompose, disturb, grate, grind, interfere, irk, irritate, jangle, jolt, nettle, offend, quarrel, rasp, rattle, rock, shake, upset, vibrate.
n. clash, disagreement, discord, dissonance, grating, irritation, jangle, jolt, quarrel, rasping, wrangling.

jargon *n.* argot, balderdash, baragouin, bunkum, cant, dialect, diplomatese, double-Dutch, drivel, gabble, gibberish, gobbledegook, gobbledygook, Greek, idiom, jive, lingo, mumbo-jumbo, nonsense, palaver, parlance, patois, rigmarole, slang, tongue, twaddle, vernacular.

jarring *adj.* cacophonous, discordant, dissonant, disturbing, grating, horrisonant, irritating, jangling, jolting, rasping, strident, upsetting.

jaundiced *adj.* biased, bitter, cynical, disbelieving, distorted, distrustful, envious, hostile, jaded, jealous, misanthropic, partial, pessimistic, preconceived, prejudiced, resentful, sceptical, suspicious.
antonyms fresh, naïve, optimistic.

jaunty *adj.* airy, breezy, buoyant, carefree, cheeky, chipper, dapper, debonair, gay, high-spirited, insouciant, lively, perky, self-confident, showy, smart, sparkish, sprightly, spruce, trim.
antonyms anxious, depressed, dowdy, seedy.

jaw[1] *n.* chops, dewlap, flews, jaws, mandible, masticator, maw, maxilla, mouth, muzzle, proboscis, trap.

jaw[2] *v.* abuse, babble, censure, chat, chatter, criticise, gab, gabble, gossip, lecture, prate, revile, scold, talk.
n. chat, chinwag, conversation, discussion, gab, gossip, natter, talk.

jazz *n.* bebop, blues, boogie, boogie-woogie, crap, Dixieland, guff, hard rock, heavy metal, lies, New Wave, ragtime, rhythm, rock, spiel, swing, talk.

jazzy *adj.* animated, avant-garde, bold, fancy, flashy, gaudy, goey, lively, smart, snazzy, spirited, stylish, swinging, vivacious, wild, zestful.
antonyms conservative, prosaic, square.

jealous *adj.* anxious, apprehensive, attentive, careful, covetous, desirous, emulous, envious, green, green-eyed, grudging, guarded, heedful, invidious, mistrustful, possessive, proprietorial, protective, resentful, rival, solicitous, suspicious, vigilant, wary, watchful, zealous.

jealousy *n.* covetousness, distrust, emulation, envy, grudge, heart-burning, ill-will, mistrust, possessiveness, resentment, spite, suspicion, vigilance, watchfulness, zelotypia.

jeer *v.* banter, barrack, chaff, contemn, deride, explode, fleer, flout, flyte, gibe, heckle, hector, knock, mock, rail, razz, ridicule, scoff, sneer, taunt, twit.
n. abuse, aspersion, catcall, chaff, derision, dig, fleer, flyte, flyting, gibe, hiss, hoot, mockery, raillery, raspberry, ridicule, scoff, sneer, taunt, thrust.

jejune *adj.* arid, banal, barren, callow, childish, colourless, dry, dull, empty, foolish, immature, impoverished, inane, insipid, juvenile, meagre, naïve, pointless, prosaic, puerile, senseless, silly, simple, spiritless, trite, uninteresting, unoriginal, unsophisticated, vapid, wishy-washy.
antonyms mature, meaningful.

jell *v.* coagulate, congeal, crystallise, finalise, form, gee, gel, gelatinate, gelatinise, harden, jelly, materialise, set, solidify, take form, take shape, thicken.
antonym disintegrate.

jeopardise *v.* chance, endanger, expose, gamble, hazard, imperil, jeopard, menace, risk, stake, threaten, venture.
antonyms protect, safeguard.

jeopardy *n.* danger, endangerment, exposure, hazard, imperilment, insecurity, liability, peril, plight, precariousness, risk, venture, vulnerability.
antonyms safety, security.

jerk[1] *n.* bounce, jog, jolt, lurch, pluck, pull, shrug, throw, thrust, tug, tweak, twitch, wrench, yank.
v. bounce, flirt, jigger, jog, jolt, jounce, lurch, peck, pluck, pull, shrug, throw, thrust, tug, tweak, twitch, wrench, yank.

jerk[2] *n.* bum, clod, clot, clown, creep, dimwit, dolt, dope, fool, halfwit, idiot, klutz, ninny, prick, schlep, schmo, schmuck, twit.

jerky *adj.* bouncy, bumpy, convulsive, disconnected, fitful, incoherent, jolting, jumpy, rough, shaky, spasmodic, tremulous, twitchy, uncontrolled, unco-ordinated.
antonym smooth.

jerry-built *adj.* cheap, cheapjack, defective, faulty, flimsy, insubstantial, ramshackle, rickety, shoddy, slipshod, unsubstantial.
antonyms firm, stable, substantial.

jersey *n.* guernsey, jumper, lammy, pullover, sweater, sweat-shirt, woolly.

jest *n.* banter, bon mot, clowning, cod, crack, desipience, foolery, fooling, fun, gag, hoax, jape, jeu d'esprit, joke, josh, kidding, leg-pull, pleasantry, prank, quip, sally, sport, trick, trifling, waggery, wisecrack, witticism.
v. banter, chaff, clown, deride, fool, gibe, jeer, joke, josh, kid, mock, quip, scoff, tease, trifle.

jester *n.* buffoon, clown, comedian, comic, droll, fool, goliard, harlequin, humorist, joculator, joker, juggler, merry-andrew, merryman, motley, mummer, pantaloon, patch, prankster, quipster, wag, wit, zany.

jet[1] *n.* atomiser, flow, fountain, gush, issue, nose, nozzle, rose, rush, spout, spray, sprayer, spring, sprinkler, spurt, squirt, stream, surge.

jet[2] *adj.* atramentous, black, coal-black, ebon, ebony, inky, jetty, pitch-black, pitchy, raven, sable, sloe, sooty.

jetsam *n.* jetsom, jetson, lagan, waif, wreckage.

jettison *v.* abandon, chuck, discard, ditch, dump, eject, expel, heave, offload, scrap, unload.
antonyms load, take on.

jetty *n.* breakwater, dock, groyne, jutty, mole, pier, quay, wharf.

jewel *n.* bijou, brilliant, charm, find, flower, gaud, gem, gemstone, humdinger, locket, masterpiece, ornament, paragon, pearl, precious stone, pride, prize, rarity, rock, sparkler, stone, treasure, wonder.

jewellery *n.* bijouterie, bijoux, finery, gauds, gemmery, gems, jewels, ornaments, regalia, treasure, trinkets.

Jezebel *n.* Delilah, femme fatale, harlot, hussy, jade, man-eater, scarlet woman, seductress, temptress, vamp, wanton, whore, witch.

jib *v.* back off, balk, recoil, refuse, retreat, shrink, stall, stop short.

jibe *v.* deride, fleer, flout, jeer, mock, rail, ridicule, scoff, scorn, sneer, taunt, twit.
n. barb, crack, derision, dig, fleer, fling, jeer, mockery, poke, quip, raillery, ridicule, sarcasm, scoff, slant, sneer, taunt, thrust.

jiffy *n.* flash, instant, minute, moment, no time, sec, second, split second, tick, trice, twinkling, two shakes, two ticks, whiff.
antonym age.

jig *v.* bob, bobble, bounce, caper, hop, jerk, jiggle, jounce, jump, prance, shake, skip, twitch, wiggle, wobble.

jigger *v.* balls up, botch up, break, bugger up, destroy, kibosh, louse up, make a pig's ear of, queer, ruin, scupper, spoil, undermine, vitiate, wreck.

jiggery-pokery *n.* chicanery, deceit, deception, dishonesty, fraud, funny business, hanky-panky, monkey-business, subterfuge, trickery.

jiggle *v.* agitate, bounce, fidget, jerk, jig, jog, joggle, shake, shift, shimmy, twitch, waggle, wiggle, wobble.

jilt *v.* abandon, betray, brush off, chuck, deceive, desert, discard, ditch, drop, forsake,

reject, repudiate, spurn, throw over.
antonym cleave to.

jingle[1] *v.* chime, chink, clatter, clink, jangle, rattle, ring, tink, tinkle, tintinnabulate.
n. clang, clangour, clink, rattle, reverberation, ringing, tink, tinkle, tintinnabulation.

jingle[2] *n.* chant, chime, chorus, couplet, ditty, doggerel, limerick, melody, poem, rhyme, song, tune, verse.

jingoism *n.* chauvinism, flag-waving, imperialism, insularity, nationalism, parochialism, patriotism, xenophobia.

jinx *n.* black magic, charm, curse, evil eye, gremlin, hex, hoodoo, jettatura, Jonah, plague, spell, voodoo.
v. bedevil, bewitch, curse, doom, hex, hoodoo, plague.

jitters *n.* anxiety, fidgets, habdabs, heebiejeebies, jimjams, nerves, nervousness, tenseness, the creeps, the shakes, the shivers, the willies.

jittery *adj.* agitated, anxious, edgy, fidgety, flustered, jumpy, nervous, panicky, perturbed, quaking, quivering, shaky, shivery, trembling, uneasy.
antonyms calm, composed, confident.

job *n.* activity, affair, allotment, assignment, batch, business, calling, capacity, career, charge, chore, commission, concern, consignment, contract, contribution, craft, duty, employment, enterprise, errand, function, livelihood, lot, message, métier, mission, occupation, office, output, part, piece, place, portion, position, post, proceeding, product, profession, project, province, pursuit, responsibility, role, share, situation, stint, task, trade, undertaking, venture, vocation, work.

jobless *adj.* idle, inactive, laid off, on the dole, out of work, unemployed, unoccupied, unused, workless.
antonym employed.

jockey *v.* cajole, coax, ease, edge, engineer, finagle, induce, inveigle, manage, manipulate, manoeuvre, negotiate, wheedle.

jocose *adj.* blithe, comical, droll, facetious, funny, humorous, jesting, jocular, jocund, jovial, joyous, lepid, merry, mirthful, mischievous, playful, pleasant, sportive, teasing, waggish, witty.
antonym morose.

jocular *adj.* amusing, arch, blithe, comical, desipient, droll, entertaining, facetious, frolicsome, funny, humorous, jesting, jocose, jocund, joking, jolly, jovial, merry, playful, roguish, sportive, teasing, waggish, whimsical, witty.
antonym serious.

jocularity *n.* absurdity, comicality, desipience, drollery, facetiousness, fooling, gaiety, hilarity, humour, jesting, jocoseness, jocosity, jolliness, joviality, laughter, merriment, playfulness, pleasantry, roguishness, sport, sportiveness, teasing, waggery, waggishness, whimsicality, whimsy, wit.

jog[1] *v.* activate, arouse, bounce, jar, jerk,

joggle, jolt, jostle, jounce, nudge, poke, prod, prompt, push, remind, rock, shake, shove, stimulate, stir.
n. jerk, jiggle, jolt, nudge, poke, prod, push, reminder, shake, shove.

jog[2] *v, n.* bump, canter, dogtrot, jogtrot, lope, lumber, pad, run, trot.

joie de vivre blitheness, bounce, buoyancy, cheerfulness, ebullience, enjoyment, enthusiasm, gaiety, get-up-and-go, gusto, joy, joyfulness, merriment, mirth, pleasure, relish, zest.
antonym depression.

join *v.* abut, accompany, accrete, add, adhere, adjoin, affiliate, alligate, amalgamate, annex, append, associate, attach, border, border on, butt, cement, coincide, combine, compaginate, conglutinate, conjoin, conjugate, connect, couple, dock, enlist, enrol, enter, fasten, knit, link, march with, marry, meet, merge, reach, sign up, splice, team, tie, touch, unite, verge on, yoke.
antonyms leave, separate.

join in chip in, contribute, co-operate, help, lend a hand, muck in, partake, participate, pitch in.

join up enlist, enroll, enter, sign up, take the king's shilling.

joint[1] *n.* articulation, commissure, connection, geniculation, gimmel, ginglymus, gomphosis, hinge, intersection, junction, juncture, knot, nexus, node, seam, union.
adj. adjunct, amalgamated, collective, combined, communal, concerted, consolidated, co-operative, co-ordinated, joined, mutual, shared, united.
v. articulate, carve, connect, couple, cut up, dismember, dissect, divide, fasten, fit, geniculate, join, segment, sever, sunder, unite.

joint[2] *n.* dance-hall, dive, haunt, honky-tonk, jerry-shop, night-club, place, pub.

joint[3] *n.* reefer, roach, stick.

jointed *adj.* articulate, geniculate(d), gimmelled.

joke *n.* buffoon, butt, clown, conceit, concetto, frolic, fun, funny, gag, guy, hoot, jape, jest, jeu d'esprit, lark, laughing-stock, play, pun, quip, quirk, sally, simpleton, sport, target, whimsy, wisecrack, witticism, yarn, yell.
v. banter, chaff, clown, deride, fool, frolic, gambol, jest, kid, laugh, mock, quip, ridicule, spoof, taunt, tease, wisecrack.

joke-book *n.* jest-book, Joe Miller.

joker *n.* buffoon, card, character, clown, comedian, comic, droll, humorist, jester, joculator, jokesmith, kidder, prankster, sport, trickster, wag, wit.

jollification *n.* beanfeast, beano, celebration, frolic, jollity, junket, knees-up, merriment, merry-making, party, rave-up, shindig, spree, thrash.
antonym lamentation.

jolly *adj.* blithe, blithesome, buxom, carefree, cheerful, cheery, convivial, exuberant, festive, frisky, frolicsome, funny, gay, gladsome, happy, hearty, hilarious, jaunty, jocund, jovial, joyful, joyous, jubilant, merry, mirthful, playful, sportive, sprightly, sunny. *antonym* sad.

jolt *v.* astonish, bounce, bump, discompose, disconcert, dismay, disturb, jar, jerk, jog, jostle, jounce, knock, nonplus, perturb, push, shake, shock, shove, stagger, startle, stun, surprise, upset.
n. blow, bolt from the blue, bombshell, bump, hit, impact, jar, jerk, jog, jump, lurch, quiver, reversal, setback, shake, shock, start, surprise, thunderbolt.

jostle *v.* bump, butt, crowd, elbow, force, hustle, jog, joggle, jolt, press, push, rough up, scramble, shake, shoulder, shove, squeeze, throng, thrust.

jot *n.* ace, atom, bit, detail, fraction, gleam, glimmer, grain, hint, iota, mite, morsel, particle, scintilla, scrap, smidgen, speck, tittle, trace, trifle, whit.
jot down enter, list, note, record, register, scribble, take down, write down.

journal *n.* book, chronicle, commonplace, daily, daybook, diary, ephemeris, gazette, log, magazine, monthly, newspaper, organ, paper, periodical, publication, record, register, review, tabloid, waste-book, weekly.

journalism *n.* copy-writing, correspondence, feature-writing, Fleet Street, fourth estate, gossip-writing, Grub Street, news, press, reportage, reporting, writing.

journalist *n.* broadcaster, chronicler, columnist, commentator, contributor, correspondent, diarist, feature-writer, hack, newshound, newsman, newspaperman, news-writer, periodicalist, pressman, reporter, scribe, stringer, sub, subeditor.

journey *n.* career, course, excursion, expedition, eyre, hadj, itinerary, jaunt, odyssey, outing, passage, peregrination, pilgrimage, progress, raik, ramble, route, safari, tour, travel, trek, trip, voyage, wanderings.
v. fare, fly, gallivant, go, jaunt, peregrinate, proceed, ramble, range, roam, rove, safari, tour, tramp, travel, traverse, trek, voyage, wander, wend.

journeyer *n.* hadji, peregrinator, pilgrim, rambler, tourist, traveller, trekker, tripper, viator, voyager, wanderer, wayfarer.

joust *n.* contest, encounter, engagement, pas d'armes, skirmish, tilt, tournament, tourney, trial.

jovial *adj.* affable, airy, animated, blithe, buoyant, cheery, convivial, cordial, ebullient, expansive, Falstaffian, gay, glad, happy, hilarious, jaunty, jocose, jocund, jolly, jubilant, merry, mirthful.
antonyms morose, sad, saturnine.

joviality *n.* affability, buoyancy, cheerfulness, cheeriness, ebullience, fun, gaiety, gladness, glee, happiness, hilarity, jollity, merriment, mirth.
antonyms moroseness, sadness.

joy *n.* blessedness, bliss, charm, delight, ecstasy, elation, exaltation, exultation, felicity, festiv-

ity, gaiety, gem, gladness, gladsomeness, glee, gratification, happiness, hilarity, jewel, joyance, joyfulness, joyousness, pleasure, pride, prize, rapture, ravishment, satisfaction, seel, transport, treasure, treat, triumph, wonder.
antonyms mourning, sorrow.

joyful *adj.* blithe, blithesome, delighted, ecstatic, elated, enraptured, glad, gladsome, gratified, happy, jocund, jolly, jovial, jubilant, light-hearted, merry, pleased, rapturous, satisfied, seely, transported, triumphant.
antonyms mournful, sorrowful.

joyless *adj.* bleak, cheerless, dejected, depressed, despondent, discouraged, discouraging, dismal, dispirited, doleful, dour, downcast, dreary, forlorn, gloomy, glum, grim, miserable, sad, sombre, sunless, unhappy.
antonym joyful.

joyous *adj.* cheerful, ecstatic, festal, festive, frabjous, glad, gladsome, gleeful, happy, joyful, jubilant, merry, rapturous.
antonym sad.

jubilant *adj.* celebratory, delighted, elated, enraptured, euphoric, excited, exuberant, exultant, flushed, glad, gratified, joyous, over the moon, overjoyed, rejoicing, thrilled, triumphal, triumphant.
antonyms defeated, depressed.

jubilation *n.* celebration, ecstasy, elation, euphoria, excitement, exultation, festivity, jamboree, jollification, joy, jubilee, triumph.
antonyms depression, lamentation.

jubilee *n.* anniversary, carnival, celebration, commemoration, festival, festivity, fête, gala, holiday.

Judas *n.* betrayer, deceiver, quisling, renegade, tergiversator, traitor, turncoat.

judge *n.* adjudicator, alcalde, arbiter, arbiter elegantiae, arbitrator, arbitratrix, assessor, authority, beak, connoisseur, critic, Daniel, deemster, dempster, doomster, elegantiarum, evaluator, expert, hakim, justice, justiciar, justiciary, Law Lord, magistrate, mediator, moderator, pundit, referee, umpire, virtuoso, wig.
v. adjudge, adjudicate, appraise, appreciate, arbitrate, ascertain, assess, conclude, condemn, consider, criticise, decern, decide, decree, determine, dijudicate, discern, distinguish, doom, esteem, estimate, evaluate, examine, find, gauge, mediate, opine, rate, reckon, referee, review, rule, sentence, sit, try, umpire, value.

judgement *n.* acumen, appraisal, arbitration, arrêt, assessment, assize, award, belief, common sense, conclusion, conviction, damnation, decision, decree, decreet, deduction, determination, diagnosis, discernment, discretion, discrimination, doom, enlightenment, estimate, expertise, fate, fetwa, finding, intelligence, mediation, misfortune, opinion, order, penetration, perceptiveness, percipience, perspicacity, prudence, punishment, result, retribution, ruling, sagacity, sense, sentence, shrewdness, taste, understanding, valuation, verdict, view, virtuosity, wisdom.

judicial adj. critical, decretory, discriminating, distinguished, forensic, impartial, judiciary, juridical, legal, magisterial, magistral, official.

judicious adj. acute, astute, canny, careful, cautious, circumspect, considered, diplomatic, discerning, discreet, discriminating, enlightened, expedient, informed, percipient, perspicacious, politic, prescient, prudent, rational, reasonable, sagacious, sage, sane, sapient, sensible, shrewd, skilful, sober, sound, thoughtful, wary, well-advised, well-judged, well-judging, wise.
antonym injudicious.

jug n. amphora, aquamanile, bellarmine, blackjack, carafe, churn, container, crock, ewer, flagon, jar, pitcher, stoup, urn, vessel.

juggle v. alter, change, cook, disguise, doctor, fake, falsify, fix, hocus-pocus, manipulate, manoeuvre, misrepresent, modify, rig, tamper with.

juice n. essence, extract, fluid, latex, liquid, liquor, nectar, sap, secretion, serum, succus.

juicy adj. colourful, gamy, interesting, lactiferous, lush, moist, naughty, provocative, racy, risqué, salacious, sappy, scatological, sensational, serous, spicy, succose, succous, succulent, suggestive, vivid, watery.
antonym dry.

jumble v. confuse, disarrange, disarray, disorder, disorganise, mingle-mangle, mix, mix up, muddle, shuffle, tangle, tumble, wuzzle.
antonym order.
n. agglomeration, chaos, clutter, collection, confusion, congeries, conglomeration, disarrangement, disarray, disorder, farrago, gallimaufry, hotch-potch, medley, mess, mingle-mangle, miscellany, mishmash, mixture, mix-up, muddle, olio, olla-podrida, pastiche, pot-pourri, raffle, salad.

jumbled adj. chaotic, confused, disarrayed, disordered, disorganised, mingle-mangle, miscellaneous, mixed-up, muddled, shuffled, tangled, tumbled, unsorted, untidy.
antonym orderly.

jump[1] v. bounce, bound, caper, clear, dance, frisk, frolic, gambol, hop, hurdle, jig, leap, pounce, prance, skip, spring, vault.
n. bounce, bound, capriole, curvet, dance, frisk, frolic, gambado, hop, jeté, leap, pounce, prance, saltation, skip, spring, vault.

jump[2] v. avoid, bypass, digress, disregard, evade, ignore, leave out, miss, omit, overshoot, pass over, skip, switch.
n. breach, break, gap, hiatus, interruption, interval, lacuna, lapse, omission, saltation, saltus, switch.

jump[3] v. advance, appreciate, ascend, boost, escalate, gain, hike, increase, mount, rise, spiral, surge.
n. advance, ascent, augmentation, boost, escalation, increase, increment, mounting, rise, upsurge, upturn.

jump[4] v. flinch, jerk, jump out of one's skin, leap in the air, quail, recoil, resile, shrink, start, wince.
n. jar, jerk, jolt, lurch, quiver, shiver, shock, spasm, start, swerve, twitch, wrench.

jump[5] n. barricade, barrier, fence, gate, hedge, hurdle, impediment, obstacle, pons asinorum, rail.

jump at accept, agree to, fall for, grab, pounce on, seize, snatch, swallow, swoop on.
antonym recoil.

jump on berate, blame, castigate, censure, chide, criticise, fly at, flyte, rate, rebuke, reprimand, reproach, reprove, revile, scold, tick off, upbraid.

jumper n. guernsey, jersey, lammy, pullover, sweater, sweat-shirt, woolly.

jumping adj. desultory, disconnected, incoherent, jumpy, salient, saltatorial, saltatorious, saltatory, saltigrade, unco-ordinated.

jumpy adj. agitated, anxious, apprehensive, discomposed, edgy, fidgety, jittery, nervous, nervy, restive, restless, shaky, tense, tremulous, uneasy.
antonyms calm, composed.

junction n. abutment, combination, confluence, conjunction, connection, coupling, disemboguement, intersection, interstice, join, joining, joint, juncture, linking, meeting-point, nexus, seam, union.

juncture n. bond, conjunction, connection, convergence, crisis, crux, emergency, intersection, join, joining, junction, link, minute, moment, nexus, occasion, period, point, predicament, seam, stage, time, union, weld.

junior adj. inferior, lesser, lower, minor, puisne, secondary, subordinate, subsidiary, younger.
antonym senior.

junk n. clutter, debris, detritus, dregs, garbage, litter, oddments, refuse, rejectamenta, rubbish, rummage, scrap, trash, waste, wreckage.

junta n. cabal, camarilla, cartel, clique, combination, conclave, confederacy, convocation, coterie, council, crew, faction, gang, league, oligarchy, party, ring, set.

jurisdiction n. area, authority, bailiwick, bounds, cognisance, command, control, domination, dominion, field, influence, judicature, orbit, power, prerogative, province, range, reach, rule, scope, sovereignty, sphere, sway, verge, zone.

jury n. jurors, jurymen, jurywomen, panel, tales, talesmen, veniremen.

just adj. accurate, apposite, appropriate, apt, blameless, condign, conscientious, correct, decent, deserved, disinterested, due, equitable, even-handed, exact, fair, fair-minded, faithful, fitting, four-square, good, honest, honourable, impartial, impeccable, irreproachable, justified, lawful, legitimate, merited, normal, precise, proper, pure, reasonable, regular, right, righteous, rightful, sound, suitable, true, unbiased, unimpeachable, unprejudiced, upright, virtuous, well-deserved.

antonym unjust.

justice[1] *n.* amends, appositeness, appropriateness, compensation, correction, dharma, equitableness, equity, fairness, honesty, impartiality, integrity, justifiableness, justness, law, legality, legitimacy, nemesis, penalty, propriety, reasonableness, recompense, rectitude, redress, reparation, requital, right, rightfulness, rightness, satisfaction.
antonym injustice.

justice[2] *n.* beak, JP, judge, Justice of the Peace, justiciar, magistrate.

justifiable *adj.* acceptable, allowable, defensible, excusable, explainable, explicable, fit, forgivable, justified, lawful, legitimate, licit, maintainable, pardonable, proper, reasonable, right, sound, tenable, understandable, valid, vindicable, warrantable, warranted, well-founded.
antonyms culpable, illicit, unjustifiable.

justification *n.* absolution, apology, approval, authorisation, basis, defence, exculpation, excuse, exoneration, explanation, extenuation, foundation, grounds, mitigation, palliation, plea, rationalisation, reason, substance, vindication, warrant.

justify *v.* absolve, acquit, condone, confirm, defend, establish, exculpate, excuse, exonerate, explain, forgive, legalise, legitimise, maintain, pardon, substantiate, support, sustain, uphold, validate, vindicate, warrant.

justly *adv.* accurately, condignly, conscientiously, correctly, duly, equally, equitably, evenhandedly, fairly, honestly, impartially, lawfully, legitimately, objectively, properly, rightfully, rightly.
antonym unjustly.

jut *v.* beetle, bulge, extend, impend, overhang, poke, project, protrude, stick out.
antonym recede.

juvenile *n.* adolescent, boy, child, girl, halfling, infant, kid, minor, young person, youngster, youth.
antonym adult.
adj. adolescent, babyish, boyish, callow, childish, girlish, immature, impressionable, inexperienced, infantile, jejune, puerile, tender, undeveloped, unsophisticated, young, youthful.
antonym mature.

juxtaposition *n.* adjacency, closeness, contact, contiguity, immediacy, nearness, propinquity, proximity, vicinity.
antonyms dissociation, separation.

K

kaleidoscopic *adj.* changeable, ever-changing, fluctuating, fluid, manifold, many-coloured, many-splendoured, mobile, motley, multicoloured, multifarious, poikilitic, polychromatic, polychrome, variegated.
antonyms dull, monochrome, monotonous.

kaput *adj.* broken, conked out, dead, defunct, destroyed, extinct, fini, finished, phut, ruined, smashed, undone, wrecked.

keel over black out, capsize, collapse, crumple, drop, faint, fall, founder, go out like a light, overturn, pass out, stagger, swoon, topple over, upset.

keen *adj.* acid, acute, anxious, ardent, argute, assiduous, astute, avid, biting, brilliant, canny, caustic, clever, cutting, devoted, diligent, discerning, discriminating, eager, earnest, ebullient, edged, enthusiastic, fervid, fierce, fond, forthright, gleg, impassioned, incisive, industrious, intense, intent, mordant, penetrating, perceptive, perfervid, perspicacious, piercing, pointed, pungent, quick, razorlike, sagacious, sapient, sardonic, satirical, scathing, sedulous, sensitive, sharp, shrewd, shrill, tart, trenchant, wise, zealous.
antonyms apathetic, blunt, dull.

keenness *n.* acerbity, anxiety, ardour, assiduity, astuteness, avidity, avidness, canniness, cleverness, diligence, discernment, eagerness, earnestness, ebullience, enthusiasm, fervour, forthrightness, harshness, impatience, incisiveness, industriousness, industry, insight, intensity, intentness, mordancy, passion, penetration, perfervidity, pungency, rigour, sagacity, sapience, sedulity, sensitivity, severity, sharpness, shrewdness, sternness, trenchancy, virulence, wisdom, zeal, zest.
antonyms apathy, bluntness, dullness.

keep[1] *v.* accumulate, amass, carry, collect, conserve, control, deal in, deposit, furnish, garner, hang on to, heap, hold, hold on to, maintain, pile, place, possess, preserve, retain, stack, stock, store.

keep an eye on guard, keep tabs on, keep under surveillance, look after, look to, monitor, observe, regard, scrutinise, supervise, survey, watch.

keep at be steadfast, beaver away at, carry on, complete, continue, drudge, endure, finish, grind, labour, last, maintain, persevere, persist, plug away at, remain, slave, slog at, stay, stick at, toil.
antonyms abandon, neglect.

keep on carry on, continue, endure, hold on, keep at it, last, maintain, persevere, persist, prolong, remain, retain, soldier on, stay, stay the course.

keep on at badger, chivvy, dun, go on at, harass, harry, importune, nag, pester, plague, pursue.

keep one's distance avoid, be aloof, give a wide berth, keep at arm's length, keep oneself to oneself, shun, withdraw.

keep secret conceal, dissemble, hide, keep back, keep dark, keep under one's hat, keep under wraps, suppress, wash one's dirty linen at home.
antonym reveal.

keep track of follow, grasp, keep up with, monitor, oversee, plot, record, trace, track, understand, watch.

keep up be on a par with, compete, contend, continue, emulate, equal, keep pace, maintain, match, pace, persevere, preserve, rival, support, sustain, vie.

keep[2] *v.* be responsible for, board, care for, defend, feed, foster, guard, have charge of, have custody of, look after, maintain, manage, mind, nourish, nurture, operate, protect, provide for, provision, safeguard, shelter, shield, subsidise, support, sustain, tend, victual, watch, watch over.
n. board, food, livelihood, living, maintenance, means, nourishment, nurture, subsistence, support, upkeep.

keep[3] *v.* arrest, block, check, constrain, control, curb, delay, detain, deter, hamper, hamstring, hinder, hold, hold back, hold up, impede, inhibit, interfere with, keep back, limit, obstruct, prevent, restrain, retard, shackle, stall, trammel, withhold.

keep back censor, check, conceal, constrain, control, curb, delay, hide, hold back, hush up, impede, limit, prohibit, quell, ration, reserve, restrain, restrict, retain, retard, stifle, stop, suppress, withhold.

keep in bottle up, conceal, confine, control, detain, hide, inhibit, keep back, quell, restrain, retain, stifle, stop up, suppress.
antonyms declare, release.

keep[4] *v.* adhere to, celebrate, commemorate, comply with, fulfil, hold, honour, keep faith with, keep up, maintain, obey, observe, perform, perpetuate, recognise, respect, ritualise, solemnise.

keep[5] *n.* castle, citadel, donjon, dungeon, fastness, fort, fortress, motte, peel-house, peel-tower, stronghold, tower.

keeper *n.* attendant, caretaker, conservator, conservatrix, curator, custodian, defender, gaoler, governor, guard, guardian, inspector, jailer, mahout, nab, overseer, steward, superintendent, supervisor, surveyor, warden, warder.

keeping *n.* accord, accordance, aegis, agreement, auspices, balance, care, charge, compliance, conformity, congruity, consistency, correspondence, cure, custody, guardianship, harmony, keep, maintenance, obedience, observance, patronage, possession, proportion, protection, safe-keeping, supervision, surveillance, trust, tutelage, ward.

keepsake *n.* emblem, favour, memento, pledge, relic, remembrance, reminder, souvenir, token.

keg *n.* barrel, butt, cask, drum, firkin, hogshead, puncheon, round, rundlet, tierce, tun, vat.

ken *n.* acquaintance, appreciation, awareness, cognisance, compass, comprehension, field, grasp, knowledge, notice, perception, range, reach, realisation, scope, sight, understanding, view, vision.

kerchief *n.* babushka, bandana, cravat, fichu, headscarf, headsquare, kaffiyeh, madras, neck-cloth, neckerchief, scarf, shawl, square, sudary, veronica.

kernel *n.* core, essence, germ, gist, grain, heart, marrow, nitty-gritty, nub, pith, seed, substance.

key *n.* answer, clavis, clue, code, crib, cue, digital, explanation, glossary, guide, index, indicator, interpretation, lead, means, pointer, secret, sign, solution, table, translation.
adj. basic, cardinal, central, chief, core, crucial, decisive, essential, fundamental, hinge, important, leading, main, major, pivotal, principal, salient.
key in capture, input, load, process, store.

keynote *n.* accent, centre, core, emphasis, essence, flavour, flavour of the month, gist, heart, kernel, leitmotiv, marrow, motif, pith, stress, substance, theme.

keystone *n.* base, basis, core, cornerstone, crux, foundation, fundamental, ground, linchpin, mainspring, motive, principle, quoin, root, source, spring.

kick *v.* abandon, boot, break, desist from, drop, foot, give up, leave off, leave out, punt, quit, spurn, stop, toe.
n. bite, buzz, dash, élan, enjoyment, excitement, feeling, force, fun, gratification, gusto, intensity, panache, pep, pizzazz, pleasure, power, punch, pungency, relish, snap, sparkle, stimulation, strength, tang, thrill, verve, vitality, zest, zing, zip.
kick off begin, break the ice, commence, get under way, inaugurate, initiate, introduce, open, open the proceedings, set the ball rolling, start.
kick out chuck out, defenestrate, discharge, dismiss, eject, evict, expel, get rid of, give the bum's rush, oust, reject, remove, sack, throw out, toss out.

kick-off *n.* beginning, bully-off, commencement, face-off, inception, introduction, opening, outset, start, word go.

kid [1] *n.* babe, baby, bairn, bambino, boy, child, dandiprat, girl, halfling, infant, juvenile, kiddy, lad, nipper, shaver, stripling, teenager, tot, wean, whippersnapper, youngster, youth.

kid [2] *v.* bamboozle, befool, beguile, con, cozen, delude, dupe, fool, gull, have on, hoax, hoodwink, humbug, jest, joke, josh, mock, pretend, pull someone's leg, put one over on, rag, ridicule, tease, trick.

kidnap *v.* abduct, capture, hijack, rape, remove, seize, skyjack, snatch, steal.

kidnapped *adj.* abducted, enlevé, hijacked, rapt, seized, stolen.

kidnapping *n.* abduction, child-stealing, enlevement, kidnap, plagium, rape, seizure.

kill *v.* abolish, annihilate, assassinate, beguile, bump off, butcher, cancel, cease, deaden, defeat, destroy, dispatch, do away with, do in, do to death, eliminate, eradicate, execute, exterminate, extinguish, extirpate, fill, finish off, halt, kibosh, knock off, knock on the head, liquidate, mar, martyr, massacre, murder, napoo, neutralise, nip in the bud, nullify, obliterate, occupy, pass, pip, put to death, quash, quell, rub out, ruin, scotch, slaughter, slay, smite, smother, spoil, stifle, still, stonker, stop, suppress, top, veto, vitiate, while away, zap.
n. climax, conclusion, coup de grâce, death, death-blow, dénouement, dispatch, end, finish, mop-up, shoot-out.

killer *n.* assassin, butcher, cut-throat, destroyer, executioner, exterminator, fratricide, gunman, hatchet man, hit-man, homicide, infanticide, liquidator, matricide, murderer, parricide, patricide, regicide, ripper, shootist, slaughterer, slayer, sororicide, triggerman, uxoricide.

killing [1] *n.* assassination, bloodshed, carnage, elimination, ethnocide, execution, extermination, fatality, fratricide, homicide, infanticide, liquidation, mactation, manslaughter, massacre, matricide, murder, parricide, patricide, pogrom, regicide, slaughter, slaying, sororicide, thuggee, uxoricide.
adj. deadly, death-dealing, deathly, debilitating, enervating, exhausting, fatal, fatiguing, final, lethal, lethiferous, mortal, mortiferous, murderous, prostrating, punishing, tiring, vital.

killing [2] *n.* big hit, bomb, bonanza, bunce, clean-up, coup, fortune, gain, hit, lucky break, profit, success, windfall, winner.

killing [3] *adj.* absurd, amusing, comical, funny, hilarious, ludicrous, side-splitting, uproarious.

killjoy *n.* complainer, cynic, dampener, damper, grouch, misery, moaner, pessimist, prophet of doom, sceptic, spoil-sport, trouble-mirth, Weary Willie, wet blanket, whiner.
antonyms enthusiast, optimist, sport.

kin *n.* affines, affinity, blood, clan, connection, connections, consanguinity, cousins, extraction, family, flesh and blood, kindred, kinsfolk, kinship, kinsmen, kith, lineage, people, relations, relationship, relatives, stock, tribe.

adj. affine, akin, allied, close, cognate, congener, connected, consanguine, consanguineous, interconnected, kindred, linked, near, related, similar, twin.

kind[1] *n.* brand, breed, category, character, class, description, essence, family, genus, habit, ilk, kidney, manner, mould, nature, persuasion, race, set, sort, species, stamp, style, temperament, type, variety.

kind[2] *adj.* accommodating, affectionate, altruistic, amiable, amicable, avuncular, beneficent, benevolent, benign, benignant, bonhomous, boon, bounteous, bountiful, brotherly, charitable, clement, compassionate, congenial, considerate, cordial, courteous, diplomatic, fatherly, friendly, generous, gentle, giving, good, gracious, hospitable, humane, indulgent, kind-hearted, kindly, lenient, loving, mild, motherly, neighbourly, obliging, philanthropic, propitious, sisterly, soft-boiled, soft-hearted, sweet, sympathetic, tactful, tender-hearted, thoughtful, understanding.

antonyms cruel, inconsiderate, unhelpful.

kind-hearted *adj.* altruistic, amicable, benign, big-hearted, compassionate, considerate, generous, good-hearted, good-natured, gracious, helpful, humane, humanitarian, kind, kindly, obliging, philanthropic, sympathetic, tender-hearted, warm, warm-hearted.

antonym ill-natured.

kindle *v.* activate, actuate, agitate, animate, arouse, awaken, deflagrate, enkindle, exasperate, excite, fan, fire, foment, ignite, incite, induce, inflame, initiate, inspire, inspirit, light, provoke, rouse, set alight, sharpen, stimulate, stir, thrill.

kindliness *n.* amiability, beneficence, benevolence, benignity, charity, compassion, friendliness, generosity, kindness, loving-kindness, sympathy, warmth.

antonyms cruelty, meanness, unkindness.

kindly *adj.* benefic, beneficent, beneficial, benevolent, benign, charitable, comforting, compassionate, cordial, favourable, generous, genial, gentle, giving, good-natured, good-willy, hearty, helpful, indulgent, kind, mild, patient, pleasant, polite, sympathetic, tender, warm.

adv. agreeably, charitably, comfortingly, considerately, cordially, generously, gently, graciously, indulgently, patiently, politely, tenderly, thoughtfully.

antonyms cruel, inconsiderate, uncharitable, unpleasant.

kindness *n.* affection, aid, aloha, altruism, amiability, assistance, benefaction, beneficence, benevolence, benignity, bonhomie, bounty, charity, chivalry, clemency, compassion, cordiality, courtesy, favour, forbearance, friendliness, gallantry, generosity, gentilesse, gentleness, good will, goodness, grace, help, hospitality, humaneness, humanity, indulgence, kindliness, liberality, loving-kindness, magnanimity, mildness, muni-

ficence, obligingness, patience, philanthropy, service, tenderness, tolerance, understanding.

antonyms cruelty, illiberality, inhumanity.

kindred *n.* affines, affinity, clan, connections, consanguinity, family, flesh, folk, kin, kinsfolk, kinship, kinsmen, lineage, people, relations, relationship, relatives.

adj. affiliated, affine, akin, allied, cognate, common, congenial, connected, corresponding, kin, like, matching, related, similar.

king *n.* boss, chief, chieftain, doyen, emperor, kingpin, leading light, luminary, majesty, monarch, overlord, paramount, patriarch, potentate, prince, royalet, ruler, sovereign, supremo, suzerain.

kingdom *n.* area, commonwealth, country, division, domain, dominion, dynasty, empire, field, land, monarchy, nation, palatinate, principality, province, realm, reign, royalty, sovereignty, sphere, state, territory, tract.

kingly *adj.* august, basilical, glorious, grand, grandiose, imperial, imperious, imposing, lordly, majestic, monarchical, noble, regal, royal, sovereign, splendid, stately, sublime, supreme.

kink[1] *n.* bend, coil, complication, corkscrew, crick, crimp, defect, dent, difficulty, entanglement, flaw, hitch, imperfection, indentation, knot, loop, tangle, twist, wrinkle.

v. bend, coil, crimp, curl, tangle, twist, wrinkle.

kink[2] *n.* caprice, crotchet, eccentricity, fetish, foible, freak, idiosyncracy, idiosyncrasy, oddity, quirk, singularity, vagary, whim.

kinky[1] *adj.* coiled, crimped, crumpled, curled, curly, frizzy, tangled, twisted, wrinkled.

kinky[2] *adj.* bizarre, capricious, crotchety, degenerate, depraved, deviant, eccentric, freakish, idiosyncratic, licentious, odd, outlandish, peculiar, perverted, queer, quirky, strange, unconventional, unnatural, warped, weird, whimsical.

kinsfolk *n.* affines, clan, connections, cousins, family, kin, kindred, kinsmen, relations, relatives.

kinship *n.* affinity, alliance, association, bearing, community, conformity, connection, consanguinity, correspondence, kin, relation, relationship, similarity.

kinsman *n.* affine, cousin, relation, relative.

kiosk *n.* bookstall, booth, box, cabin, counter, hut, news-stand, stall, stand.

kismet *n.* destiny, doom, fate, fortune, joss, karma, lot, portion, predestiny, providence, weird.

kiss[1] *v.* buss, canoodle, neck, osculate, peck, salute, smooch, snog.

n. buss, osculation, peck, plonker, salute, smack, smacker, snog.

kiss[2] *v.* brush, caress, fan, glance, graze, lick, scrape, touch.

kit *n.* accoutrements, apparatus, appurtenances, baggage, effects, equipage, equipment, gear, impedimenta, implements, instruments, luggage, matériel, muniments, outfit, paraphernalia, provisions, rig, rig-out, set, supplies, tackle, tools, trappings, traps, utensils.

kit out accoutre, arm, deck out, dight, dress, equip, fit out, fix up, furnish, habilitate, outfit, prepare, supply.

kittenish *adj.* arch, coquettish, coy, cute, flirtatious, frisky, frolicsome, playful, sportive.
antonym staid.

knack *n.* ability, adroitness, aptitude, bent, capacity, dexterity, expertise, expertness, facility, faculty, flair, forte, genius, gift, handiness, hang, ingenuity, propensity, quickness, skilfulness, skill, talent, trick, trick of the trade, turn.

knapsack *n.* backpack, bag, dufflebag, haversack, musette, pack, rucksack, tuckerbag.

knave *n.* bastard, blackguard, blighter, bounder, cheat, dastard, drôle, fripon, rapscallion, rascal, reprobate, rogue, rotter, scallywag, scamp, scapegrace, scoundrel, stinker, swindler, swine, varlet, villain.

knavery *n.* chicanery, corruption, deceit, deception, devilry, dishonesty, double-dealing, duplicity, fraud, friponnerie, hanky-panky, imposture, knavishness, mischief, monkeybusiness, rascality, roguery, ropery, trickery, villainy.

knavish *adj.* contemptible, corrupt, damnable, dastardly, deceitful, deceptive, devilish, dishonest, dishonourable, fiendish, fraudulent, furciferous, lying, mischievous, rascally, reprobate, roguish, scoundrelly, unprincipled, unscrupulous, villainous, wicked.
antonyms honest, honourable, scrupulous.

knead *v.* form, knuckle, manipulate, massage, mould, ply, press, rub, shape, squeeze, work.

kneel *v.* fall to one's knees, genuflect.

knell *n.* chime, knoll, peel, ringing, sound, tintinnabulation, toll.

knickers *n.* bloomers, breeks, briefs, Directoire knickers, drawers, knickerbockers, panties, pants, smalls, underwear.

knick-knack *n.* bagatelle, bauble, bibelot, bric-à-brac, gadget, gaud, gewgaw, gimcrack, gismo, jimjam, kickshaw, object of virtu, plaything, pretty, pretty-pretty, quip, rattletrap, toy, trifle, trinket, whigmaleerie, whimwham.

knife *n.* blade, carver, chiv, cutter, dagger, dah, flick-knife, jack-knife, machete, parang, pen-knife, pocket-knife, skean, skene, skenedhu, skene-occle, switchblade, whittle.
v. cut, impale, lacerate, pierce, rip, slash, stab, wound.

knight *n.* cavalier, champion, chevalier, freelance, gallant, horseman, kemper, kemperyman, knight-at-arms, knight-errant, man-at-arms, preux chevalier, ritter, soldier, warrior.

knightly *adj.* bold, chivalrous, courageous, courtly, dauntless, gallant, gracious, heroic, honourable, intrepid, noble, soldierly, valiant, valorous.
antonyms cowardly, ignoble, ungallant.

knit *v.* ally, bind, connect, crease, crotchet, fasten, furrow, heal, interlace, intertwine, join, knot, link, loop, mend, secure, tie, unite, weave, wrinkle.

knob *n.* boll, boss, bump, caput, door-handle, knot, knub, knurl, lump, nub, projection, protrusion, protuberance, snib, stud, swell, swelling, tuber, tumour, umbo.

knock[1] *v.* buffet, clap, cuff, ding, hit, knobble, (k)nubble, punch, rap, slap, smack, smite, strike, thump, thwack.
n. blow, box, chap, clip, clout, con, cuff, hammering, rap, slap, smack, thump.

knock about[1] associate, go around, loaf, ramble, range, roam, rove, saunter, traipse, travel, wander.

knock about[2] abuse, bash, batter, beat up, biff, bruise, buffet, damage, hit, hurt, maltreat, manhandle, maul, mistreat.

knock down batter, clout, demolish, destroy, fell, floor, level, pound, prop, raze, smash, wallop, wreck.

knock off[1] cease, clock off, clock out, complete, conclude, finish, pack (it) in, stop, terminate.

knock off[2] deduct, filch, nick, pilfer, pinch, purloin, rob, steal, take away, thieve.

knock off[3] assassinate, bump off, do away with, do in, kill, liquidate, murder, rub out, slay, waste.

knock up achieve, build, construct, erect, make.
antonym demolish.

knock[2] *v.* abuse, belittle, carp, cavil, censure, condemn, criticise, deprecate, disparage, find fault, lambaste, run down, slam, vilify, vilipend.
n. blame, censure, condemnation, criticism, defeat, failure, rebuff, rejection, reversal, setback, stricture.
antonyms boost, praise.

knockout *n.* bestseller, coup de grâce, hit, kayo, KO, sensation, smash, smash-hit, stunner, success, triumph, winner.
antonyms flop, loser.

knoll *n.* barrow, hill, hillock, hummock, knowe, koppie, mound.

knot *v.* bind, entangle, entwine, knit, loop, secure, tangle, tether, tie, weave.
n. aggregation, bond, bow, braid, bunch, burl, clump, cluster, collection, connection, gnar, gnarl, heap, hitch, joint, knag, knar, knarl, ligature, loop, mass, pile, rosette, tie, tuft.

knotty *adj.* anfractuous, baffling, bumpy, Byzantine, complex, complicated, difficult, gnarled, hard, intricate, knobby, knotted, mystifying, nodose, nodous, nodular, perplexing, problematical, puzzling, rough, rugged, thorny, tricky, troublesome.

know *v.* apprehend, comprehend, discern, distinguish, experience, fathom, identify, intuit, ken, learn, make out, notice, perceive, realise, recognise, see, tell, undergo, understand, wist.

know-all *n.* Besserwisser, clever-clogs, smart Alec, smarty-pants.

know-how *n.* ability, adroitness, aptitude, capability, dexterity, experience, expertise, faculty, flair, gumption, ingenuity, knack, knowledge, proficiency, savoir-faire, savvy, skill, talent.

knowing *adj.* acute, astute, aware, clever, competent, conscious, cunning, discerning, downy, eloquent, experienced, expert, expressive, gnostic, gnostical, hep, intelligent, meaningful, perceptive, qualified, sagacious, shrewd, significant, skilful, well-informed.
antonyms ignorant, obtuse.

knowingly *adv.* consciously, deliberately, designedly, intentionally, on purpose, purposely, studiedly, wilfully, wittingly.

knowledge *n.* ability, acquaintance, acquaintanceship, apprehension, book-learning, booklore, cognisance, cognition, comprehension, consciousness, cum-savvy, discernment, education, enlightenment, erudition, familiarity, gnosis, grasp, information, instruction, intelligence, intimacy, judgement, know-how, learning, multiscience, notice, pansophy, recognition, scholarship, schooling, science, tuition, understanding, wisdom.
antonym ignorance.

knowledgeable *adj.* acquainted, au courant, au fait, aware, book-learned, bright, cognisant, conscious, conversant, educated, erudite, experienced, familiar, in the know, intelligent, learned, lettered, scholarly, well-informed.
antonym ignorant.

known *adj.* acknowledged, admitted, avowed, celebrated, commonplace, confessed, familiar, famous, manifest, noted, obvious, patent, plain, published, recognised, well-known.

knuckle under accede, acquiesce, capitulate, defer, give in, give way, submit, succumb, surrender, truckle, yield.

kowtow *v.* bow, court, cringe, defer, fawn, flatter, genuflect, grovel, kneel, pander, suck up, toady, truckle.

kudos *n.* acclaim, applause, distinction, esteem, fame, glory, honour, laudation, laurels, plaudits, praise, prestige, regard, renown, repute.

L

label *n.* badge, brand, categorisation, characterisation, classification, company, description, docket, epithet, mark, marker, sticker, tag, tally, ticket, trademark.
v. brand, call, categorise, characterise, class, classify, define, describe, designate, docket, dub, identify, mark, name, stamp, tag.

laborious *adj.* arduous, assiduous, backbreaking, burdensome, difficult, diligent, fatiguing, forced, hard, hard-working, heavy, herculean, indefatigable, industrious, laboured, onerous, operose, painstaking, persevering, ponderous, sedulous, strained, strenuous, tireless, tiresome, toilsome, tough, unflagging, uphill, wearing, wearisome.
antonyms easy, effortless, relaxing, simple.

labour[1] *n.* chore, donkey-work, drudgery, effort, employees, exertion, grind, hands, industry, job, labor improbus, labourers, moil, pains, painstaking, slog, sweat, task, toil, undertaking, work, workers, workforce, workmen.
antonyms ease, leisure, relaxation, rest.
v. drudge, endeavour, grind, heave, moil, pitch, plod, roll, slave, strive, struggle, suffer, sweat, toil, toss, travail, work.
antonyms idle, laze, loaf, lounge.

labour[2] *n.* birth, childbirth, contractions, delivery, labour pains, pains, parturition, throes, travail.
v. dwell on, elaborate, overdo, overemphasise, overstress, strain.

laboured *adj.* affected, awkward, complicated, contrived, difficult, forced, heavy, overdone, overwrought, ponderous, stiff, stilted, strained, studied, unnatural.
antonyms easy, natural.

labourer *n.* drudge, farm-hand, hand, hireling, hobbler, hobo, hodman, hunky, husbandman, land-girl, manual worker, navvy, redneck, worker, working man, workman.

labyrinth *n.* circumvolution, coil, complexity, complication, convolution, entanglement, Gordian knot, intricacy, jungle, maze, perplexity, puzzle, riddle, tangle, windings.

labyrinthine *adj.* Byzantine, complex, confused, convoluted, Daedalian, dedalian, faveolate, Gordian, intricate, involved, knotty, mazy, mizmaze, perplexing, puzzling, tangled, tortuous, winding.
antonyms simple, straightforward.

lace[1] *n.* crochet, dentelle, filigree, mesh-work, netting, open-work, tatting.

lace[2] *n.* bootlace, cord, lanyard, shoe-lace, string, thong, tie.
v. attach, bind, close, do up, fasten,
intertwine, interweave, interwork, string, thread, tie.

lace[3] *v.* add to, fortify, intermix, mix in, spike.

lacerate *v.* afflict, claw, cut, distress, gash, ga(u)nch, harrow, jag, lancinate, maim, mangle, rend, rip, slash, tear, torment, torture, wound.

laceration *n.* cut, gash, injury, lancination, maim, mutilation, rent, rip, slash, tear, wound.

lachrymose *adj.* crying, dolorous, lugubrious, mournful, sad, sobbing, tearful, teary, weeping, weepy, woeful.
antonyms happy, laughing.

lack *n.* absence, dearth, deficiency, deprivation, destitution, emptiness, insufficiency, need, privation, scantiness, scarcity, shortage, shortcoming, shortness, vacancy, void, want.
antonyms abundance, profusion.
v. miss, need, require, want.

lackadaisical *adj.* abstracted, apathetic, dreamy, dronish, dull, enervated, fainéant, half-hearted, idle, indifferent, indolent, inert, languid, languorous, lazy, lethargic, limp, listless, spiritless, supine.
antonyms active, dynamic, energetic, vigorous.

lackey *n.* attendant, creature, fawner, flatterer, flunky, footman, gofer, hanger-on, instrument, manservant, menial, minion, parasite, pawn, servitor, sycophant, toady, tool, valet, yes-man.

lacking *adj.* defective, deficient, flawed, impaired, inadequate, minus, missing, needing, sans, short of, wanting, without.

lacklustre *adj.* boring, dim, drab, dry, dull, flat, leaden, lifeless, lustreless, mundane, muted, prosaic, sombre, spiritless, unimaginative, uninspired, vapid.
antonyms brilliant, polished.

laconic *adj.* brief, close-mouthed, compact, concise, crisp, curt, pithy, sententious, short, succinct, taciturn, terse.
antonyms garrulous, verbose, wordy.

lacuna *n.* blank, break, cavity, gap, hiatus, omission, space, void.

lad *n.* boy, bucko, callant, chap, fellow, guy, halfling, juvenile, kid, laddie, schoolboy, shaver, stripling, youngster, youth.

laden *adj.* burdened, charged, chock-a-block, chock-full, encumbered, fraught, full, hampered, jammed, loaded, oppressed, packed, stuffed, taxed, weighed down, weighted.
antonym empty.

la-di-da *adj.* affected, conceited, foppish, high-falutin(g), mannered, mincing, over-refined, posh, precious, pretentious, put-on, snobbish, snooty, stuck-up, toffee-nosed, too-too.

ladies' man Casanova, Don Juan, gigolo, lady-killer, libertine, muff, poodle-faker, womaniser.

ladle v. bail, dip, dish, lade, scoop, shovel, spoon.

ladle out disburse, dish out, distribute, dole out, hand out.

lady n. begum, dame, damsel, don(n)a, Frau, gentlewoman, hidalga, madam(e), matron, memsahib, milady, noblewoman, Señora, signora, woman.

lady-killer n. Casanova, Don Juan, heartbreaker, ladies' man, libertine, Lothario, philanderer, rake, roué, stud, wolf, womaniser.

ladylike adj. courtly, cultured, decorous, elegant, genteel, matronly, modest, polite, proper, queenly, refined, respectable, well-bred.

lag v. dawdle, delay, hang back, idle, linger, loiter, mosey, saunter, shuffle, straggle, tarry, trail.
antonym lead.

laggard n. dawdler, idler, lingerer, loafer, loiterer, lounger, saunterer, slowcoach, slowpoke, slug-a-bed, sluggard, snail, straggler.
antonyms dynamo, go-getter, livewire.

lagoon n. bayou, bog, fen, haff, lake, marsh, pond, pool, shallows, shoal, swamp.

laid up bedridden, disabled, hors de combat, housebound, ill, immobilised, incapacitated, injured, on the sick list, out of action, sick.

laid-back adj. at ease, calm, casual, cool, easy-going, free and easy, passionless, relaxed, unflappable, unhurried, untroubled, unworried.
antonyms tense, uptight.

lair n. burrow, den, earth, form, hideout, hole, nest, refuge, retreat, roost, sanctuary, stronghold.

lake n. lagoon, loch, lochan, lough, mere, reservoir, tarn.

lam v. batter, beat, clout, hit, knock, lambaste, leather, pelt, pound, pummel, strike, thrash, thump.

lambast v. beat, berate, bludgeon, castigate, censure, cudgel, drub, flay, flog, leather, rebuke, reprimand, roast, scold, strike, thrash, upbraid, whip.

lambent adj. brilliant, dancing, flickering, fluttering, gleaming, glistening, glowing, incandescent, licking, light, luminous, lustrous, radiant, refulgent, shimmering, sparkling, touching, twinkling.

lame adj. crippled, defective, disabled, disappointing, feeble, flimsy, game, half-baked, halt, handicapped, hobbling, inadequate, insufficient, limping, poor, thin, unconvincing, unsatisfactory, weak.
v. cripple, damage, disable, hamstring, hobble, hurt, incapacitate, injure, maim, wing.

lament v. bemoan, bewail, beweep, complain, deplore, grieve, keen, mourn, regret, sorrow, wail, weep, yammer.
antonyms celebrate, rejoice.
n. complaint, coronach, dirge, dumka, elegy, jeremiad, keening, lamentation, moan, moaning, monody, plaint, requiem, threnody, ululation, wail, wailing.

lamentable adj. deplorable, disappointing, distressing, funest, grievous, inadequate, insufficient, low, meagre, mean, miserable, mournful, pitiful, poor, regrettable, sorrowful, tragic, unfortunate, unsatisfactory, woeful, wretched.

lamentation n. deploration, dirge, grief, grieving, jeremiad, keen, keening, lament, moan, mourning, plaint, sobbing, sorrow, ululation, wailing, weeping.
antonyms celebration, rejoicing.

laminate v. coat, cover, exfoliate, face, flake, foliate, layer, plate, separate, split, stratify, veneer.

lamp n. beacon, flare, floodlight, lampad, lantern, light, limelight, searchlight, torch, veilleuse.

lampoon n. burlesque, caricature, mickey-take, parody, Pasquil, Pasquin, pasquinade, satire, send-up, skit, spoof, squib, take-off.
v. burlesque, caricature, make fun of, mock, parody, Pasquil, Pasquin, pasquinade, ridicule, satirise, send up, spoof, squib, take off, take the mickey out of.

lampooner n. caricaturist, parodist, pasquilant, pasquiler, pasquinader, satirist.

land[1] n. country, countryside, dirt, distrcit, earth, estate, farmland, fatherland, ground, grounds, loam, motherland, nation, property, province, real estate, realty, region, soil, terra firma, territory, tract.
v. alight, arrive, berth, bring, carry, cause, come to rest, debark, deposit, disembark, dock, drop, end up, plant, touch down, turn up, wind up.

land[2] v. achieve, acquire, capture, gain, get, net, obtain, secure, win.

landlord n. freeholder, host, hotelier, hotelkeeper, innkeeper, lessor, letter, owner, proprietor, publican.
antonym tenant.

landmark n. beacon, boundary, cairn, feature, milestone, monument, signpost, turning-point, watershed.

lands n. acreage, acres, demesne, estate(s), grounds, manor, policies, spread.

landscape n. aspect, countryside, outlook, panorama, prospect, scene, scenery, view, vista.

landslide n. avalanche, earthfall, éboulement, landslip, lauwine, rock-fall.
adj. decisive, emphatic, overwhelming, runaway.

lane n. alley(way), avenue, boreen, byroad, byway, channel, driveway, footpath, footway, gut, loan, passage(way), path(way), towpath, vennel, way, wynd.

language n. argot, cant, conversation, dialect,

diction, discourse, expression, idiolect, idiom, interchange, jargon, langue, lingo, lingua franca, parlance, parole, patois, phraseology, phrasing, speech, style, talk, terminology, tongue, utterance, vernacular, vocabulary, wording.

languid *adj.* debilitated, drooping, dull, enervated, faint, feeble, heavy, inactive, indifferent, inert, lackadaisical, languorous, lazy, lethargic, limp, listless, pining, sickly, slow, sluggish, spiritless, torpid, unenthusiastic, uninterested, weak, weary.
antonyms alert, lively, vivacious.

languish *v.* brood, decline, desire, despond, droop, fade, fail, faint, flag, grieve, hanker, hunger, long, mope, pine, repine, rot, sicken, sigh, sink, sorrow, suffer, sulk, want, waste, waste away, weaken, wilt, wither, yearn.
antonym flourish.

languishing *adj.* brooding, declining, deteriorating, dreamy, drooping, droopy, fading, failing, flagging, longing, lovelorn, lovesick, melancholic, moping, nostalgic, pensive, pining, sickening, sinking, soulful, sulking, tender, wasting away, weak, weakening, wilting, wistful, withering, woebegone, yearning.
antonyms flourishing, thriving.

languor *n.* apathy, asthenia, calm, debility, dreaminess, drowsiness, enervation, ennui, faintness, fatigue, feebleness, frailty, heaviness, hush, indolence, inertia, lassitude, laziness, lethargy, listlessness, lull, oppressiveness, relaxation, silence, sleepiness, sloth, stillness, torpor, weakness, weariness.
antonyms alacrity, gusto.

lank *adj.* attenuated, drooping, dull, emaciated, flabby, flaccid, gaunt, lanky, lean, lifeless, limp, long, lustreless, rawboned, scraggy, scrawny, skinny, slender, slim, spare, straggling, thin.
antonym burly.

lanky *adj.* angular, bony, gangling, gangly, gaunt, loose-jointed, rangy, rawboned, scraggy, scrawny, spare, tall, thin, twiggy, weedy.
antonyms short, squat.

lap[1] *v.* drink, lick, sip, sup, tongue.

lap[2] *v.* gurgle, plash, purl, ripple, slap, slosh, splash, swish, wash.

lap[3] *n.* ambit, circle, circuit, course, distance, loop, orbit, round, tour.
v. cover, encase, enfold, envelop, fold, surround, swaddle, swathe, turn, twist, wrap.

lapse *n.* aberration, backsliding, break, caducity, decline, descent, deterioration, drop, error, failing, fall, fault, gap, indiscretion, intermission, interruption, interval, lull, mistake, negligence, omission, oversight, passage, pause, relapse, slip.
v. backslide, decline, degenerate, deteriorate, drop, end, expire, fail, fall, run out, sink, slide, slip, stop, terminate, worsen.

lapsed *adj.* discontinued, ended, expired, finished, invalid, obsolete, out of date, outdated, outworn, run out, unrenewed.

larceny *n.* burglary, expropriation, heist, misappropriation, pilfering, piracy, purloining, robbery, stealing, theft.

large *adj.* abundant, ample, big, broad, bulky, capacious, colossal, comprehensive, considerable, copious, decuman, enormous, extensive, full, generous, giant, gigantic, goodly, grand, grandiose, great, huge, immense, jumbo, king-sized, liberal, man-sized, massive, monumental, Patagonian, plentiful, plonking, roomy, sizeable, spacious, spanking, substantial, sweeping, swingeing, tidy, vast, wide.
antonyms diminutive, little, slight, small, tiny.

largely *adv.* abundantly, by and large, chiefly, considerably, extensively, generally, greatly, highly, mainly, mostly, predominantly, primarily, principally, widely.

largeness *n.* bigness, breadth, broadness, bulk, bulkiness, dimension, enormity, enormousness, expanse, extent, greatness, heaviness, heftiness, height, immensity, magnitude, mass, massiveness, measure, mightiness, obesity, prodigiousness, size, vastness, wideness, width.
antonym smallness.

large-scale *adj.* broad, country-wide, epic, expansive, extensive, far-reaching, global, nation-wide, sweeping, vast, wholesale, wide, wide-ranging.
antonym minor.

largess(e) *n.* aid, allowance, alms, benefaction, bequest, bounty, charity, donation, endowment, generosity, gift, grant, handout, liberality, munificence, open-handedness, philanthropy, present.
antonym meanness.

lark *n.* antic, caper, escapade, fling, fredaine, frolic, fun, gambol, game, gammock, guy, jape, mischief, prank, revel, rollick, romp, skylark, spree.
v. caper, cavort, frolic, gambol, gammock, play, rollick, romp, skylark, sport.

lascivious *adj.* bawdy, blue, coarse, crude, dirty, horny, indecent, lecherous, lewd, libidinous, licentious, lustful, obscene, offensive, Paphian, pornographic, prurient, randy, ribald, salacious, scurrilous, sensual, smutty, suggestive, tentiginous, unchaste, voluptuous, vulgar, wanton.

lash[1] *n.* blow, cat, cat-o'-nine-tails, hit, quirt, stripe, stroke, swipe, whip.
v. attack, beat, belabour, berate, birch, buffet, castigate, censure, chastise, criticise, dash, drum, flagellate, flay, flog, hammer, hit, horsewhip, knock, lace, lam, lambast, lampoon, larrup, pound, ridicule, satirise, scold, scourge, smack, strike, tear into, thrash, upbraid, welt, whip.

lash[2] *v.* affix, bind, fasten, join, make fast, rope, secure, strap, tether, tie.

lass *n.* bird, chick, colleen, damsel, girl, lassie, maid, maiden, miss, quean, quine, schoolgirl.

lassitude *n.* apathy, drowsiness, dullness, enervation, ennui, exhaustion, fatigue, heaviness,

languor, lethargy, listlessness, oscitancy, prostration, sluggishness, tiredness, torpor, weariness.
antonyms energy, vigour.
last[1] *adj.* aftermost, closing, concluding, conclusive, definitive, extreme, final, furthest, hindmost, latest, rearmost, remotest, terminal, ultimate, utmost.
antonyms first, initial.
adv. after, behind, finally, ultimately.
antonyms first, firstly.
n. close, completion, conclusion, curtain, end, ending, finale, finish, termination.
antonyms beginning, start.
last word[1] final decision, final say, ultimatum.
last word[2] best, cream, crème de la crème, dernier cri, latest, ne plus ultra, perfection, pick, quintessence, rage, ultimate, vogue.
last[2] *v.* abide, carry on, continue, endure, hold on, hold out, keep (on), perdure, persist, remain, stand up, stay, survive, wear.
last-ditch *adj.* all-out, desperate, eleventh-hour, final, frantic, heroic, last-gasp, straining, struggling.
lasting *adj.* abiding, continuing, deep-rooted, durable, enduring, immutable, indelible, indestructible, lifelong, long-standing, long-term, perennial, permanent, perpetual, sempiternal, unceasing, unchanging, undying, unending.
antonyms ephemeral, fleeting, short-lived.
lastly *adv.* finally, in conclusion, in fine, in the end, to sum up, ultimately.
antonym firstly.
latch *n.* bar, bolt, catch, fastening, hasp, hook, lock, sneck.
latch on to apprehend, attach oneself to, comprehend, twig, understand.
late[1] *adj.* behind, behind-hand, belated, delayed, dilatory, last-minute, overdue, slow, tardy, unpunctual.
antonyms early, punctual.
adv. behind-hand, belatedly, dilatorily, formerly, recently, slowly, tardily, unpunctually.
antonyms early, punctually.
late[2] *adj.* dead, deceased, defunct, departed, ex-, former, old, past, preceding, previous.
lately *adv.* formerly, heretofore, latterly, recently.
lateness *n.* belatedness, delay, dilatoriness, retardation, tardiness, unpunctuality.
antonym earliness.
latent *adj.* concealed, delitescent, dormant, hidden, inherent, invisible, lurking, potential, quiescent, secret, underlying, undeveloped, unexpressed, unrealised, unseen, veiled.
antonyms active, live, patent.
later *adv.* after, afterwards, next, sequentially, subsequently, successively, thereafter.
antonym earlier.
lateral *adj.* edgeways, flanking, marginal, oblique, side, sideward, sideways.
antonym central.
latest *adj.* current, fashionable, in, modern, newest, now, ultimate, up-to-date, up-to-the-minute, with it.
antonym earliest.
lather[1] *n.* bubbles, foam, froth, shampoo, soap, soap-suds, suds.
v. foam, froth, shampoo, soap, whip up.
lather[2] *n.* agitation, dither, fever, flap, fluster, flutter, fuss, pother, state, stew, sweat, tizzy, twitter.
lather[3] *v.* beat, cane, drub, flog, lambast, lash, leather, strike, thrash, whip.
latitude *n.* breadth, clearance, compass, elbow-room, extent, field, freedom, indulgence, laxity, leeway, liberty, licence, play, range, reach, room, scope, space, span, spread, sweep, width.
latrine *n.* bog, head, jakes, outhouse, privy, rear, toilet.
latter *adj.* closing, concluding, ensuing, last, last-mentioned, later, latest, modern, recent, second, succeeding, successive.
antonym former.
latterly *adv.* hitherto, lately, of late, recently.
antonym formerly.
lattice *n.* espalier, fret-work, grate, grating, grid, grille, lattice-work, mesh, network, open-work, reticulation, tracery, trellis, web.
laud *v.* acclaim, applaud, approve, celebrate, extol, glorify, hail, honour, magnify, praise.
antonyms blame, condemn, curse, damn.
laudable *adj.* admirable, commendable, creditable, estimable, excellent, exemplary, meritorious, of note, praiseworthy, sterling, worthy.
antonyms damnable, execrable.
laudation *n.* acclaim, acclamation, accolade, adulation, blessing, celebrity, commendation, devotion, encomion, encomium, eulogy, extolment, glorification, glory, homage, kudos, paean, panegyric, praise, reverence, tribute, veneration.
antonyms condemnation, criticism.
laudatory *adj.* acclamatory, adulatory, approbatory, approving, celebratory, commendatory, complimentary, encomiastic(al), epaenetic, eulogistic, glorifying, panegyrical.
antonym damning.
laugh *v.* cachinnate, chortle, chuckle, crease up, fall about, giggle, guffaw, snicker, snigger, split one's sides, te(e)hee, titter.
antonym cry.
n. belly-laugh, card, case, caution, chortle, chuckle, clown, comedian, comic, cure, entertainer, giggle, guffaw, hoot, humorist, joke, lark, scream, snicker, snigger, te(e)hee, titter, wag, wit.
laugh at belittle, deride, jeer, lampoon, make fun of, mock, ridicule, scoff at, scorn, take the mickey out of, taunt.
laugh off belittle, brush aside, dismiss, disregard, ignore, make little of, minimise, pooh-pooh, shrug off.
laughable *adj.* absurd, amusing, comical, derisive, derisory, diverting, droll, farcical, funny, gelastic, hilarious, humorous, laughworthy,

ludicrous, mirthful, mockable, nonsensical, preposterous, ridiculous, risible.

antonyms impressive, serious, solemn.

laughing *adj.* cackling, cheerful, cheery, chortling, chuckling, giggling, gleeful, guffawing, happy, jocund, jolly, jovial, merry, mirthful, riant, rident, snickering, sniggering, tittering.

laughing-stock *n.* Aunt Sally, butt, derision, fair game, figure of fun, pointing-stock, target, victim.

laughter *n.* amusement, asbestos gelos, cachinnation, chortling, chuckling, convulsions, fou rire, giggling, glee, guffawing, hilarity, Homeric laughter, horselaugh, laughing, merriment, mirth, tittering.

launch *v.* begin, cast, commence, discharge, dispatch, embark on, establish, fire, float, found, inaugurate, initiate, instigate, introduce, open, project, propel, send off, set in motion, start, throw.

lavatory *n.* bathroom, bog, can, cloakroom, cludge, comfort station, convenience, dike, draught-house, dunnakin, dunny, dyke, earth-closet, garderobe, Gents, George, head(s), jakes, john, Ladies, latrine, lav, loo, office, powder-room, privy, public convenience, smallest room, toilet, urinal, washroom, water-closet, WC.

lavish *adj.* abundant, bountiful, copious, effusive, exaggerated, excessive, extravagant, exuberant, free, generous, gorgeous, immoderate, improvident, intemperate, liberal, lush, luxuriant, munificent, open-handed, opulent, plentiful, princely, prodigal, profuse, prolific, sumptuous, thriftless, unlimited, unreasonable, unrestrained, unstinting, wasteful, wild.

antonyms economical, frugal, parsimonious, scanty, sparing, thrifty.

v. bestow, deluge, dissipate, expend, heap, pour, shower, spend, squander, waste.

law *n.* act, axiom, brocard, canon, charter, code, command, commandment, constitution, consuetudinary, covenant, criterion, decree, dharma, edict, enactment, formula, institute, jurisprudence, order, ordinance, precept, principle, regulation, rule, standard, statute.

antonym chance.

law-abiding *adj.* compliant, decent, dutiful, good, honest, honourable, lawful, obedient, orderly, peaceable, peaceful, upright.

antonym lawless.

law-breaker *n.* convict, criminal, crook, culprit, delinquent, felon, infractor, miscreant, offender, outlaw, sinner, transgressor, trespasser, wrong-doer.

lawful *adj.* allowable, authorised, constitutional, hal(l)al, kosher, legal, legalised, legitimate, licit, permissible, proper, rightful, valid, warranted.

antonyms illegal, illicit, lawless, unlawful.

lawless *adj.* anarchic(al), chaotic, disorderly, felonious, insubordinate, insurgent, mutinous, rebellious, reckless, riotous, ruleless, seditious, unbridled, ungoverned, unrestrained, unruly, wild.

antonym lawful.

lawlessness *n.* anarchy, chaos, disorder, insurgency, mobocracy, mob-rule, ochlocracy, piracy, racketeering, rent-a-mob.

antonym order.

lawsuit *n.* action, argument, case, cause, contest, dispute, litigation, proceedings, process, prosecution, suit, trial.

lawyer *n.* advocate, attorney, barrister, counsel, counsellor, green-bag, jurisconsult, law-agent, lawmonger, legist, solicitor.

lax *adj.* broad, careless, casual, derelict, easy-going, flabby, flaccid, general, imprecise, inaccurate, indefinite, inexact, lenient, loose, neglectful, negligent, overindulgent, remiss, shapeless, slack, slipshod, soft, vague, wide, wide-open, yielding.

antonyms rigid, strict, stringent.

laxative *n.* aperient, cathartic, eccoprotic, loosener, purgative, purge, salts.

adj. aperient, cathartic, eccoprotic, lenitive, purgative.

laxness *n.* carelessness, freedom, heedlessness, imprecision, indifference, indulgence, laissez-faire, latitude, latitudinarianism, laxism, laxity, leniency, looseness, neglect, negligence, nonchalance, permissiveness, slackness, sloppiness, slovenliness, softness, tolerance.

antonyms severity, strictness.

lay[1] *v.* advance, allay, alleviate, allocate, allot, appease, apply, arrange, ascribe, assess, assign, assuage, attribute, bet, burden, calm, charge, concoct, contrive, deposit, design, devise, dispose, encumber, establish, gamble, hatch, hazard, impose, impute, leave, locate, lodge, offer, organise, place, plan, plant, plot, posit, position, prepare, present, put, quiet, relieve, risk, saddle, set, set down, set out, settle, soothe, spread, stake, still, submit, suppress, tax, wager, work out.

lay aside abandon, cast aside, discard, dismiss, pigeon-hole, postpone, put aside, put off, reject, shelve, store.

lay bare disclose, divulge, exhibit, exhume, explain, expose, reveal, show, uncover, unveil.

lay down affirm, assert, assume, couch, discard, drop, establish, formulate, give, give up, ordain, postulate, prescribe, relinquish, state, stipulate, surrender, yield.

lay down the law crack down, dictate, dogmatise, emphasise, pontificate, read the riot act, rule the roost.

lay hands on acquire, assault, attack, beat up, bless, clasp, clutch, confirm, consecrate, discover, find, get, get hold of, grab, grasp, grip, lay hold of, lay into, ordain, seize, set on, unearth.

lay in accumulate, amass, build up, collect, gather, glean, hoard, stock up, stockpile, store (up).

lay into assail, attack, belabour, berate, chastise, lambast, let fly at, pitch into, set about, slam, tear into, turn on.

lay it on butter up, exaggerate, flatter, overdo it, overpraise, soft-soap, sweet-talk.

lay off axe, cease, desist, discharge, dismiss, drop, give it a rest, give over, give up, leave alone, leave off, let go, let up, make redundant, oust, pay off, quit, stop, withhold.

lay on contribute, furnish, give, provide, set up, supply.

lay out arrange, demolish, design, disburse, display, exhibit, expend, fell, flatten, fork out, give, invest, knock out, pay, plan, set out, shell out, spend, spread out.

lay up accumulate, amass, garner, hive, hoard, hospitalise, incapacitate, keep, preserve, put away, salt away, save, squirrel away, store up, treasure.

lay waste depredate, desolate, despoil, destroy, devastate, pillage, rape, ravage, raze, ruin, sack, spoil, vandalise.

lay² *adj.* amateur, inexpert, laic, laical, non-professional, non-specialist, secular.

lay³ *n.* ballad, canzone(t), lyric, madrigal, ode, poem, roundelay, song.

layabout *n.* beachcomber, good-for-nothing, idler, laggard, loafer, lounger, ne'er-do-well, shirker, skiver, slug-a-bed, waster.

layer *n.* bed, blanket, coat, coating, cover, covering, film, folium, lame, lamella, lamina, mantle, plate, ply, row, seam, sheet, stratum, table, thickness, tier, touch.

layman *n.* amateur, layperson, outsider, parishioner.

lay-off *n.* discharge, dismissal, redundancy, unemployment.

layout *n.* arrangement, blueprint, design, draft, formation, geography, map, outline, plan, sketch.

laze *v.* idle, lie around, loaf, loll, lounge, sit around.

laziness *n.* dilatoriness, faineance, fainéancy, idleness, inactivity, indolence, otiosity, pococurant(e)ism, slackness, sloth, slothfulness, slowness, sluggishness, tardiness.
antonym industriousness.

lazy *adj.* dormant, drowsy, idle, inactive, indolent, inert, languid, languorous, lethargic, otiose, remiss, shiftless, slack, sleepy, slobby, slothful, slow, slow-moving, sluggish, somnolent, torpid, work-shy.
antonyms active, diligent, energetic, industrious.

lazy-bones *n.* hallion, idler, laggard, loafer, lounger, shirker, skiver, sleepy-head, slouch, slug-a-bed, sluggard.

leach *v.* drain, extract, filter, filtrate, lixiviate, osmose, percolate, seep, strain.

lead *v.* antecede, cause, command, conduct, direct, dispose, draw, escort, exceed, excel, experience, govern, guide, have, head, incline, induce, influence, live, manage, outdo, outstrip, pass, persuade, pilot, precede, preside over, prevail, prompt, spend, steer, supervise, surpass, transcend, undergo, usher.
antonym follow.

n. advance, advantage, clue, direction, edge, example, first place, guidance, guide, hint, indication, leadership, margin, model, precedence, primacy, principal, priority, protagonist, starring role, start, suggestion, supremacy, tip, title role, trace, van, vanguard.
adj. chief, first, foremost, head, leading, main, premier, primary, prime, principal, star.

lead off begin, commence, get going, inaugurate, initiate, kick off, open, start, start off, start out, start the ball rolling.

lead on beguile, deceive, draw on, entice, hoax, inveigle, lure, persuade, seduce, string along, tempt, trick.

lead to bring about, bring on, cause, conduce, contribute to, produce, result in, tend towards.

lead up to approach, intimate, introduce, make advances, make overtures, overture, pave the way, prepare (the way) for.

leaden *adj.* ashen, burdensome, crushing, cumbersome, dingy, dismal, dreary, dull, gloomy, grey, greyish, heavy, humdrum, inert, laboured, lacklustre, languid, lead, lifeless, listless, lowering, lustreless, onerous, oppressive, overcast, plodding, sluggish, sombre, spiritless, stiff, stilted, wooden.

leader *n.* bell-wether, boss, captain, chief, chieftain, commander, conductor, coryphaeus, counsellor, director, doyen, figurehead, flagship, guide, head, mahatma, principal, ringleader, ruler, skipper, superior, supremo.
antonym follower.

leadership *n.* administration, authority, command, control, direction, directorship, domination, guidance, hegemony, influence, initiative, management, pre-eminence, premiership, running, superintendency, supremacy, sway.

leading *adj.* chief, dominant, first, foremost, governing, greatest, highest, main, number one, outstanding, paramount, pre-eminent, primary, principal, ruling, superior, supreme.
antonym subordinate.

leaf *n.* blade, bract, calyx, cotyledon, flag, folio, foliole, frond, needle, pad, page, sepal, sheet.
v. browse, flip, glance, riffle, skim, thumb (through).

leaflet *n.* advert, bill, booklet, brochure, circular, handbill, handout, pamphlet.

leafy *adj.* bosky, dasyphyllous, foliose, frondescent, frondose, green, leafed, leaved, shaded, shady, verdant, wooded, woody.

league *n.* alliance, association, band, Bund, cartel, category, class, coalition, combination, combine, compact, confederacy, confederation, consortium, federation, fellowship, fraternity, group, guild, level, partnership, sorority, syndicate, union.
v. ally, amalgamate, associate, band, collaborate, combine, confederate, consort, join forces, unite.

leak *n.* aperture, chink, crack, crevice, disclosure, divulgence, drip, fissure, hole, leakage, leaking, oozing, opening, percolation, perforation, puncture, seepage.

v. discharge, disclose, divulge, drip, escape, exude, give away, let slip, let the cat out of the bag, make known, make public, make water, ooze, pass, pass on, percolate, reveal, seep, spill, spill the beans, tell, trickle, weep.

leaky *adj.* cracked, holey, leaking, perforated, permeable, porous, punctured, split, waterlogged.

lean[1] *v.* bend, confide, count on, depend, favour, incline, list, prefer, prop, recline, rely, repose, rest, slant, slope, tend, tilt, tip, trust.

lean[2] *adj.* angular, bare, barren, bony, emaciated, gaunt, inadequate, infertile, lank, meagre, pitiful, poor, rangy, scanty, scragged, scraggy, scrawny, skinny, slender, slim, slink(y), spare, sparse, thin, unfruitful, unproductive, wiry.

antonyms fat, fleshy.

lean on force, persuade, pressurise, put pressure on.

leaning *n.* aptitude, bent, bias, disposition, inclination, liking, partiality, penchant, predilection, proclivity, proneness, propensity, susceptibility, taste, tendency, velleity.

leap *v.* advance, bounce, bound, caper, capriole, cavort, clear, curvet, escalate, frisk, gambol, hasten, hop, hurry, increase, jump, jump (over), reach, rocket, rush, skip, soar, spring, surge, vault.

antonyms drop, fall, sink.

n. bound, caper, capriole, curvet, escalation, frisk, hop, increase, jump, rise, sally, skip, spring, surge, upsurge, upswing, vault, volt(e).

learn *v.* acquire, ascertain, assimilate, attain, cognise, con, detect, determine, discern, discover, find out, gather, get off pat, grasp, hear, imbibe, learn by heart, master, memorise, pick up, see, understand.

learned *adj.* academic, adept, blue, cultured, erudite, experienced, expert, highbrow, intellectual, lettered, literate, proficient, sage, scholarly, skilled, versed, well-informed, well-read, wise.

antonyms ignorant, illiterate, uneducated.

learner *n.* abecedarian, alphabetarian, apprentice, beginner, catechumen, cheechako, disciple, neophyte, novice, pupil, scholar, student, tenderfoot, trainee, tyro.

learning *n.* acquirements, attainments, culture, edification, education, enlightenment, erudition, information, knowledge, letters, literature, lore, research, scholarship, schoolcraft, schooling, study, tuition, wisdom.

lease *v.* charter, farm out, hire, let, loan, rent, sublet.

leash *n.* check, control, curb, discipline, hold, lead, lyam, rein, restraint, tether.

least *adj.* fewest, last, lowest, meanest, merest, minimum, minutest, poorest, slightest, smallest, tiniest.

antonym most.

leathery *adj.* coriaceous, corious, durable, hard, hardened, leathern, rough, rugged, tough, wrinkled.

leave[1] *v.* abandon, allot, assign, bequeath, cause, cease, cede, commit, consign, decamp, depart, deposit, desert, desist, disappear, do a bunk, drop, entrust, exit, flit, forget, forsake, generate, give over, give up, go, go away, hand down, leave behind, levant, move, produce, pull out, quit, refer, refrain, relinquish, renounce, retire, set out, stop, surrender, take off, transmit, will, withdraw.

antonym arrive.

leave off abstain, break off, cease, desist, discontinue, end, give over, halt, knock off, lay off, quit, refrain, stop, terminate.

leave out bar, cast aside, count out, cut (out), disregard, eliminate, except, exclude, ignore, neglect, omit, overlook, pass over, reject.

leave[2] *n.* allowance, authorisation, concession, consent, dispensation, exeat, freedom, furlough, holiday, indulgence, liberty, permission, sabbatical, sanction, time off, vacation.

antonyms refusal, rejection.

leaven *v.* elevate, expand, ferment, imbue, inspire, lighten, permeate, pervade, quicken, raise, stimulate, suffuse, work.

leavings *n.* bits, detritus, dregs, dross, fragments, left-overs, orts, pieces, refuse, remains, remnants, residue, scraps, spoil, sweepings, waste.

lecher *n.* adulterer, Casanova, debauchee, Don Juan, fornicator, goat, lewdsby, lewdster, libertine, libidinist, profligate, rake, roué, satyr, seducer, sensualist, wanton, whoremonger, wolf, womaniser.

lecherous *adj.* carnal, concupiscent, goatish, lascivious, lewd, libidinous, licentious, lickerish, liquorish, lubricous, lustful, prurient, randy, raunchy, salacious, unchaste, wanton, womanising.

lechery *n.* carnality, concupiscence, debauchery, goatishness, lasciviousness, lecherousness, leching, lewdness, libertinism, libidinousness, licentiousness, lubricity, lust, lustfulness, profligacy, prurience, rakishness, randiness, raunchiness, salaciousness, sensuality, wantonness, womanising.

lecture *n.* address, castigation, censure, chiding, discourse, disquisition, dressing-down, going-over, harangue, instruction, lesson, prelection, rebuke, reprimand, reproof, scolding, speech, talk, talking-to, telling-off, wigging.

v. address, admonish, berate, carpet, castigate, censure, chide, discourse, expound, harangue, hold forth, lucubrate, prelect, rate, reprimand, reprove, scold, speak, talk, teach, tell off.

lecturer *n.* declaimer, expounder, haranguer, lector, orator, pedagogue, preacher, prelector, sermoniser, speaker, speechifier, speechmaker, talker, teacher, tutor.

ledge *n.* berm, mantle, projection, ridge, shelf, shelve, sill, step.

leech *n.* bloodsucker, freeloader, hanger-on,

parasite, sponger, sycophant, usurer.

leer v. eye, fleer, gloat, goggle, grin, ogle, smirk, squint, stare, wink.

n. grin, ogle, smirk, squint, stare, wink.

leery adj. careful, cautious, chary, distrustful, doubting, dubious, guarded, sceptical, shy, suspicious, uncertain, unsure, wary.

lees n. deposit, draff, dregs, grounds, precipitate, refuse, residue, sediment, settlings.

leeway n. elbow-room, latitude, play, room, scope, space.

left adj. communist, left-hand, leftist, left-wing, liberal, port, progressive, radical, red, sinistral, socialist.

antonym right.

left-handed adj. ambiguous, awkward, dubious, equivocal, gauche, sinistral, southpaw, unlucky.

antonym right-handed.

left-overs n. dregs, fag-end, leavings, oddments, odds and ends, orts, refuse, remainder, remains, remnants, residue, scraps, surplus, sweepings.

leg n. brace, gam, lap, limb, member, part, pin, portion, prop, section, segment, shank, stage, stretch, stump, support, upright.

legacy n. bequest, birthright, devise, endowment, estate, gift, heirloom, hereditament, heritage, heritance, inheritance, patrimony.

legal adj. above-board, allowable, allowed, authorised, constitutional, forensic, judicial, juridical, lawful, legalised, legitimate, licit, permissible, proper, rightful, sanctioned, valid, warrantable.

antonym illegal.

legalise v. allow, approve, authorise, decriminalise, legitimate, legitimise, license, permit, sanction, validate, warrant.

legality n. admissibleness, constitutionality, lawfulness, legitimacy, permissibility, rightfulness, validity.

antonym illegality.

legate n. ambassador, delegate, depute, deputy, emissary, envoy, exarch, messenger, nuncio.

legatee n. beneficiary, co-heir(ess), devisee, heir, inheritor, inheritrix, recipient.

legation n. commission, consulate, delegation, deputation, embassy, ministry, mission, representation.

legend n. caption, celebrity, cipher, code, device, fable, fiction, folk-tale, household name, inscription, key, luminary, marvel, motto, myth, narrative, phenomenon, prodigy, saga, spectacle, story, tale, tradition, wonder.

legendary adj. apocryphal, celebrated, fabled, fabulous, famed, famous, fanciful, fictional, fictitious, illustrious, immortal, mythical, renowned, romantic, storied, story-book, traditional, unhistoric(al), well-known.

legerdemain n. artfulness, artifice, chicanery, contrivance, craftiness, cunning, deception, feint, hocus-pocus, manipulation, manoeuvring, prestidigitation, sleight of hand, subterfuge, thaumaturgics, trickery.

legible adj. clear, decipherable, discernible, distinct, intelligible, neat, readable.

antonym illegible.

legion n. army, battalion, brigade, cohort, company, division, drove, force, horde, host, mass, multitude, myriad, number, regiment, swarm, throng, troop.

adj. countless, illimitable, innumerable, multitudinous, myriad, numberless, numerous.

legislate v. authorise, codify, constitute, constitutionalise, enact, establish, ordain, prescribe.

legislation n. act, authorisation, bill, charter, codification, constitutionalisation, enactment, law, law-making, measure, prescription, regulation, ruling, statute.

legislative adj. congressional, judicial, juridical, jurisdictional, jurisdictive, law-giving, law-making, ordaining, parliamentary, senatorial.

legislator n. law-giver, law-maker, nomothete, parliamentarian.

legislature n. assembly, chamber, congress, diet, governing body, house, parliament, senate.

legitimate adj. acknowledged, admissible, authentic, authorised, correct, genuine, just, justifiable, kosher, lawful, legal, legit, licit, logical, proper, real, reasonable, rightful, sanctioned, sensible, statutory, true, true-born, valid, warranted, well-founded.

antonym illegitimate.

v. authorise, charter, entitle, legalise, legitimise, license, permit, sanction.

legitimise v. authorise, charter, entitle, legalise, legitimate, license, permit, sanction.

leisure n. breather, ease, freedom, holiday, let-up, liberty, opportunity, pause, quiet, recreation, relaxation, respite, rest, retirement, spare time, time off, vacation.

antonyms toil, work.

leisurely adj. carefree, comfortable, deliberate, easy, gentle, indolent, laid-back, lazy, lingering, loose, relaxed, restful, slow, tranquil, unhasty, unhurried.

antonyms hectic, hurried, rushed.

lend v. add, advance, afford, bestow, confer, contribute, furnish, give, grant, impart, lease, loan, present, provide, supply.

antonym borrow.

lend a hand aid, assist, do one's bit, give a helping hand, help, help out, pitch in.

lend an ear give ear, hearken, heed, listen, pay attention, take notice.

length n. distance, duration, elongation, extensiveness, extent, lengthiness, longitude, measure, operoseness, operosity, period, piece, portion, prolixity, protractedness, reach, section, segment, space, span, stretch, tediousness, term.

lengthen v. continue, draw out, eke, eke out, elongate, expand, extend, increase, pad out, prolong, prolongate, protract, spin out, stretch.

antonym shorten.

lengthwise adv. endlong, endways, endwise, horizontally, lengthways, vertically.

lengthy *adj.* diffuse, drawn-out, extended, interminable, lengthened, long, long-drawn-out, long-winded, loquacious, marathon, overlong, prolix, prolonged, protracted, rambling, tedious, verbose, voluble.
antonym short.

leniency *n.* clemency, compassion, forbearance, gentleness, indulgence, lenience, lenity, mercy, mildness, moderation, permissiveness, soft-heartedness, softness, tenderness, tolerance.
antonym severity.

lenient *adj.* clement, compassionate, easy-going, forbearing, forgiving, gentle, indulgent, kind, merciful, mild, soft, soft-hearted, sparing, tender, tolerant.
antonym severe.

lenitive *adj.* alleviating, alleviative, assuaging, calmative, calming, easing, mitigating, mitigative, mollifying, palliative, relieving, soothing.
antonym irritant.

lens *n.* eye, eyeglass, eye-piece, glass, loupe, magnifying-glass, monocle, ocular.

leper *n.* lazar, outcast, pariah, undesirable, untouchable.

lesbian *n.* butch, dike, gay, homophile, homosexual, les, lez(z), lezzy, sapphist, tribade.
adj. butch, dikey, gay, homosexual, sapphic, tribadic.

lesion *n.* abrasion, bruise, contusion, cut, gash, hurt, impairment, injury, scrape, scratch, sore, trauma, wound.

lessen *v.* abate, abridge, bate, contract, curtail, deaden, decrease, de-escalate, degrade, die down, diminish, dwindle, ease, erode, fail, flag, impair, lighten, lower, minimise, moderate, narrow, reduce, shrink, slack, slow down, weaken.
antonym increase.

lessening *n.* abatement, bating, contraction, curtailment, deadening, decline, decrease, de-escalation, diminution, dwindling, ebbing, erosion, failure, flagging, let-up, minimisation, moderation, petering out, reduction, shrinkage, slackening, waning, weakening.
antonym increase.

lesser *adj.* inferior, lower, minor, secondary, slighter, smaller, subordinate.
antonym greater.

lesson *n.* admonition, assignment, censure, chiding, class, coaching, deterrent, drill, example, exemplar, exercise, homework, instruction, lection, lecture, message, model, moral, pericope, period, practice, precept, punishment, reading, rebuke, recitation, reprimand, reproof, schooling, scolding, task, teaching, tutorial, tutoring, warning.

let[1] *v.* agree to, allow, authorise, cause, charter, consent to, empower, enable, entitle, give leave, give permission, give the go-ahead, give the green light, grant, hire, lease, make, OK, permit, rent, sanction, tolerate.
antonym forbid.

let down abandon, betray, desert, disappoint, disenchant, disillusion, dissatisfy, fail, fall short.
antonym satisfy.

let go free, liberate, manumit, release, set free, unhand.
antonyms catch, imprison.

let in accept, admit, include, incorporate, receive, take in, welcome.
antonym bar.

let off absolve, acquit, detonate, discharge, dispense, emit, excuse, exempt, exonerate, explode, exude, fire, forgive, give off, ignore, leak, pardon, release, spare.
antonym punish.

let on act, admit, counterfeit, disclose, dissemble, dissimulate, divulge, feign, give away, leak, let out, make believe, make known, make out, pretend, profess, reveal, say, simulate.
antonym keep mum.

let out betray, discharge, disclose, emit, free, give, give vent to, leak, let fall, let go, let slip, liberate, make known, produce, release, reveal, utter.
antonym keep in.

let up abate, cease, decrease, diminish, ease, ease up, end, halt, moderate, slacken, stop, subside.
antonym continue.

let slip blab, blurt out, come out with, disclose, divulge, give away, leak, let out, let the cat out of the bag, reveal.
antonym keep mum.

let[2] *n.* check, constraint, hindrance, impediment, interference, obstacle, obstruction, prohibition, restraint, restriction.
antonym assistance.

let-down *n.* anticlimax, betrayal, blow, desertion, disappointment, disillusionment, frustration, lemon, set-back, wash-out.
antonym satisfaction.

lethal *adj.* baleful, dangerous, deadly, deathful, deathly, destructive, devastating, fatal, lethiferous, mortal, mortiferous, murderous, noxious, pernicious, poisonous, virulent.
antonym harmless.

lethargic *adj.* apathetic, comatose, debilitated, drowsy, dull, enervated, heavy, hebetant, hebetated, hebetudinous, inactive, indifferent, inert, languid, lazy, lethargic, listless, sleepy, slothful, slow, sluggish, somnolent, stupefied, torpid.
antonym lively.

lethargy *n.* apathy, drowsiness, dullness, hebetation, hebetude, hebetudinosity, inaction, indifference, inertia, languor, lassitude, listlessness, sleepiness, sloth, slowness, sluggishness, stupor, torpidity, torpor.
antonym liveliness.

letter[1] *n.* acknowledgement, answer, billet, chit, communication, da(w)k, dispatch, encyclical, epistle, epistolet, line, message, missive, note, reply.

letter[2] *n.* character, grapheme, lexigram, logogram, logograph, sign, symbol.

lettered *adj.* accomplished, cultivated, cultured, educated, erudite, highbrow, informed, knowledgeable, learned, literary, literate, scholarly, studied, versed, well-educated, well-read.
antonym ignorant.

letters *n.* academia, belles-lettres, books, culture, erudition, humanities, learning, literature, scholarship, writing.

let-up *n.* abatement, break, breather, cessation, interval, lessening, lull, pause, recess, remission, respite, slackening.
antonym continuation.

level[1] *adj.* aligned, balanced, calm, champaign, commensurate, comparable, consistent, equable, equal, equivalent, even, even-tempered, flat, flush, horizontal, neck and neck, on a par, plain, proportionate, smooth, stable, steady, uniform.
antonyms behind, uneven, unstable.
v. aim, beam, bulldoze, couch, demolish, destroy, devastate, direct, equalise, even out, flatten, flush, focus, knock down, lay low, plane, point, pull down, raze, smooth, tear down, train, wreck.
n. altitude, bed, class, degree, echelon, elevation, floor, grade, height, horizontal, layer, plain, plane, position, rank, stage, standard, standing, status, storey, stratum, zone.

level[2] *v.* admit, avow, come clean, confess, divulge, open up, tell.
antonym prevaricate.

level-headed *adj.* balanced, calm, collected, commonsensical, composed, cool, dependable, even-tempered, reasonable, sane, self-possessed, sensible, steady, together, unflappable.

lever *n.* bar, crowbar, handle, jemmy, joy-stick.
v. dislodge, force, heave, jemmy, move, prise, pry, purchase, raise, shift.

leverage *n.* advantage, ascendancy, authority, clout, force, influence, pull, purchase, rank, strength, weight.

leviathan *n.* behemoth, colossus, giant, hulk, mammoth, monster, sea-monster, Titan, whale.

levity *n.* buoyancy, facetiousness, fickleness, flightiness, flippancy, frivolity, giddiness, irreverence, light-heartedness, silliness, skittishness, triviality, whifflery.
antonyms seriousness, sobriety.

levy *v.* assemble, call, call up, charge, collect, conscript, demand, exact, gather, impose, mobilise, muster, press, raise, summon, tax.
n. assessment, collection, contribution, duty, exaction, excise, fee, gathering, imposition, impost, subscription, tariff, tax, toll.

lewd *adj.* bawdy, blue, Cyprian, dirty, harlot, impure, indecent, lascivious, libidinous, licentious, loose, lubric, lubrical, lubricious, lubricous, lustful, obscene, pornographic, profligate, salacious, smutty, unchaste, vile, vulgar, wanton, wicked.
antonyms chaste, polite.

lewdness *n.* bawdiness, carnality, crudity, debauchery, depravity, impurity, indecency, lasciviousness, lechery, licentiousness, lubricity, lustfulness, obscenity, pornography, priapism, profligacy, randiness, salaciousness, smut, smuttiness, unchastity, vulgarity, wantonness.
antonyms chasteness, politeness.

lexicographer *n.* dictionary-writer, glossarist, lexiconist, vocabulist.

lexicon *n.* dictionary, encyclopaedia, glossary, phrase-book, vocabulary, word-book, word-list.

liability *n.* accountability, albatross, answerability, arrears, burden, culpability, debit, debt, disadvantage, drag, drawback, duty, encumbrance, handicap, hindrance, impediment, inconvenience, indebtedness, likeliness, millstone, minus, nuisance, obligation, onus, responsibility.
antonyms asset(s), unaccountability.

liable *adj.* accountable, amenable, answerable, apt, bound, chargeable, disposed, exposed, inclined, likely, obligated, open, predisposed, prone, responsible, subject, susceptible, tending, vulnerable.
antonyms unaccountable, unlikely.

liaison *n.* affair, amour, communication, conjunction, connection, contact, entanglement, interchange, intermediary, intrigue, link, love affair, romance, union.

liar *n.* Ananias, bouncer, deceiver, fabricator, falsifier, fibber, perjurer, prevaricator, storyteller.

libel *n.* aspersion, calumny, defamation, denigration, obloquy, slander, slur, smear, vilification, vituperation.
antonym praise.
v. blacken, calumniate, defame, derogate, malign, revile, slander, slur, smear, traduce, vilify, vilipend, vituperate.
antonym praise.

libellous *adj.* aspersive, aspersory, calumniatory, calumnious, defamatory, defaming, derogatory, false, injurious, malicious, maligning, scurrilous, slanderous, traducing, untrue, vilifying, vituperative.
antonyms laudative, praising.

liberal *adj.* abundant, advanced, altruistic, ample, beneficent, bounteous, bountiful, broad, broad-minded, catholic, charitable, copious, enlightened, flexible, free, free-handed, general, generous, handsome, high-minded, humanistic, humanitarian, indulgent, inexact, kind, large-hearted, latitudinarian, lavish, lenient, libertarian, loose, magnanimous, munificent, open-handed, open-hearted, permissive, plentiful, profuse, progressive, radical, reformist, rich, tolerant, unbiased, unbigoted, unprejudiced, unstinting, verligte, Whig, Whiggish.
antonyms conservative, illiberal, mean, narrow-minded.

liberalism *n.* free-thinking, humanitarianism, latitudinarianism, libertarianism, progressiv-

ism, radicalism, Whiggery, Whiggism.
antonyms conservatism, narrow-mindedness.
liberality *n.* altruism, beneficence, benevolence, bounty, breadth, broad-mindedness, candour, catholicity, charity, free-handedness, generosity, impartiality, kindness, large-heartedness, largess(e), latitude, liberalism, libertarianism, magnanimity, munificence, open-handedness, open-mindedness, permissiveness, philanthropy, progressivism, tolerance, toleration.
antonyms illiberality, meanness.
liberate *v.* affranchise, deliver, discharge, disenthral, emancipate, free, let go, let loose, let out, manumit, ransom, redeem, release, rescue, set free, uncage, unchain, unfetter, unpen, unshackle.
antonyms enslave, imprison, restrict.
liberating *adj.* eleutherian, emancipatory, freeing, redeeming.
antonym restricting.
liberation *n.* deliverance, emancipation, enfranchisement, freedom, freeing, liberating, liberty, manumission, ransoming, redemption, release, uncaging, unchaining, unfettering, unpenning, unshackling.
antonyms enslavement, imprisonment, restriction.
liberator *n.* deliverer, emancipator, freer, manumitter, ransomer, redeemer, rescuer, saviour.
antonyms enslaver, jailer.
libertarian *n.* anarchist, free-thinker, libertine.
adj. anarchistic.
liberties *n.* audacity, disrespect, familiarity, forwardness, impertinence, impropriety, impudence, insolence, misuse, overfamiliarity, presumption, presumptuousness.
antonyms politeness, respect.
libertine *n.* debauchee, gay deceiver, lecher, loose fish, loose-liver, lovelace, profligate, rake, reprobate, roué, seducer, sensualist, voluptary, womaniser.
liberty *n.* authorisation, autonomy, carte-blanche, dispensation, emancipation, exemption, franchise, free rein, freedom, immunity, independence, latitude, leave, liberation, licence, permission, prerogative, privilege, release, right, sanction, self-determination, sovereignty.
antonyms imprisonment, restriction, slavery.
libidinous *adj.* carnal, concupiscent, cupidinous, debauched, impure, incontinent, lascivious, lecherous, lewd, lickerish, loose, lustful, prurient, randy, ruttish, salacious, sensual, unchaste, wanton, wicked.
antonyms modest, temperate.
library *n.* Athenaeum, bibliotheca, genizah, reading-room, reference-room, stack, study.
libretto *n.* book, lines, lyrics, script, text, words.
licence[1] *n.* authorisation, authority, carte blanche, certificate, charter, dispensation, entitlement, exemption, freedom, immunity, imprimatur, independence, indult, latitude, leave, liberty, permission, permit, privilege,

right, self-determination, warrant.
antonyms banning, dependence, restriction.
licence[2] *n.* abandon, amorality, anarchy, debauchery, disorder, dissipation, dissoluteness, excess, immoderation, impropriety, indulgence, intemperance, irresponsibility, lawlessness, laxity, profligacy, unruliness.
antonyms decorum, temperance.
license *v.* accredit, allow, authorise, certificate, certify, commission, empower, entitle, permit, sanction, warrant.
antonym ban.
licentious *adj.* abandoned, cupidinous, debauched, disorderly, dissolute, immoral, impure, lascivious, lax, lewd, libertine, libidinous, lickerish, lubric, lubrical, lubricious, lubricous, lustful, profligate, promiscuous, sensual, uncontrollable, uncontrolled, uncurbed, unruly, wanton.
licentiousness *n.* abandon, cupidinousness, debauchery, dissipation, dissoluteness, lechery, lewdness, libertinism, libidinousness, lubriciousness, lubricity, lust, lustfulness, priapism, profligacy, promiscuity, prurience, salaciousness, salacity, wantonness.
antonyms modesty, temperance.
lick[1] *v.* brush, dart, flick, lap, play over, smear, taste, tongue, touch, wash.
n. bit, brush, dab, hint, little, sample, smidgeon, speck, spot, stroke, taste, touch.
lick one's lips anticipate, drool over, enjoy, relish, savour.
lick[2] *v.* beat, best, defeat, excel, flog, outdo, outstrip, overcome, rout, skelp, slap, smack, spank, strike, surpass, thrash, top, trounce, vanquish, wallop.
lick[3] *n.* clip, gallop, pace, rate, speed.
licking *n.* beating, defeat, drubbing, flogging, hiding, skelping, smacking, spanking, tanning, thrashing, trouncing, whipping.
lie[1] *v.* dissimulate, equivocate, fabricate, falsify, fib, forswear oneself, invent, misrepresent, perjure, prevaricate.
n. bam, bounce, caulker, cram, crammer, cretism, deceit, fabrication, falsehood, falsification, falsity, fib, fiction, flam, invention, inveracity, mendacity, plumper, prevarication, stretcher, tar(r)adiddle, untruth, whacker, white lie, whopper.
antonym truth.
lie[2] *v.* be, belong, couch, dwell, exist, extend, inhere, laze, loll, lounge, recline, remain, repose, rest, slump, sprawl, stretch out.
lie low go to earth, hide, hide away, hide out, hole up, keep a low profile, lie doggo, lurk, skulk, take cover.
lie in wait for ambuscade, ambush, forelay, skulk, waylay.
life *n.* activity, animation, autobiography, behaviour, being, biography, breath, brio, career, conduct, confessions, continuance, course, creatures, duration, élan vital, energy, entity, essence, existence, fauna, flora and fauna, get-up-and-go, go, growth, heart, high spirits, history, life story, life-blood, life-style,

lifetime, liveliness, memoirs, oomph, organisms, sentience, soul, span, sparkle, spirit, story, the world, this mortal coil, time, verve, viability, vigour, vita, vital flame, vital spark, vitality, vivacity, way of life, wildlife, zest.

lifeless *adj.* abiotic, apathetic, bare, barren, cold, colourless, comatose, dead, deceased, defunct, desert, dull, empty, extinct, flat, heavy, hollow, inanimate, inert, insensate, insensible, insipid, lacklustre, lethargic, listless, nerveless, out cold, out for the count, passive, pointless, slow, sluggish, spent, spiritless, static, sterile, stiff, torpid, unconscious, uninhabited, unproductive, waste, wooden. *antonyms* alive, lively.

lifelike *adj.* authentic, exact, expressive, faithful, graphic, natural, photographic, pictorial, picturesque, real, realistic, true, true-to-life, undistorted, vivid. *antonyms* inexact, unnatural.

lifelong *adj.* abiding, constant, deep-rooted, deep-seated, enduring, entrenched, inveterate, lasting, lifetime, long-lasting, longstanding, perennial, permanent, persistent. *antonyms* impermanent, temporary.

lifetime *n.* career, course, day(s), existence, floruit, life, life span, period, span, time.

lift[1] *v.* advance, ameliorate, annul, appropriate, arrest, ascend, boost, buoy up, cancel, climb, collar, copy, countermand, crib, dignify, disappear, disperse, dissipate, draw up, elevate, end, enhance, exalt, half-inch, heft, hoist, improve, mount, nab, nick, pick up, pilfer, pinch, pirate, plagiarise, pocket, promote, purloin, raise, rear, relax, remove, rescind, revoke, rise, steal, stop, take, terminate, thieve, up, upgrade, uplift, upraise, vanish. *antonyms* drop, fall, impose, lower. *n.* boost, encouragement, fillip, pick-me-up, reassurance, shot in the arm, spur, uplift. *antonym* discouragement.

lift[2] *n.* drive, hitch, ride, run, transport.

lift[3] *n.* elevator, escalator, hoist, paternoster.

ligature *n.* band, bandage, binding, bond, connection, cord, ligament, link, rope, strap, string, thong, tie, tourniquet.

light[1] *n.* beacon, blaze, brightness, brilliance, bulb, candle, cockcrow, dawn, day, daybreak, daylight, daytime, effulgence, flame, flare, flash, glare, gleam, glim, glint, glow, illumination, incandescence, lambency, lamp, lampad, lantern, lighter, lighthouse, luminescence, luminosity, lustre, match, morn, morning, phosphorescence, radiance, ray, refulgence, scintillation, shine, sparkle, star, sunrise, sunshine, taper, torch, window, Yang. *antonym* darkness. *v.* animate, beacon, brighten, cheer, fire, floodlight, ignite, illuminate, illumine, inflame, irradiate, kindle, light up, lighten, put on, set alight, set fire to, switch on, turn on. *antonyms* darken, extinguish. *adj.* bleached, blond, bright, brilliant, faded,

faint, fair, glowing, illuminated, lightful, lightsome, lucent, luminous, lustrous, pale, pastel, shining, sunny, well-lit. *antonym* dark.

light[2] *n.* angle, approach, aspect, attitude, awareness, clue, comprehension, context, elucidation, enlightenment, example, exemplar, explanation, hint, illustration, information, insight, interpretation, knowledge, model, paragon, point of view, slant, understanding, viewpoint.

light[3] *adj.* agile, airy, amusing, animated, blithe, buoyant, carefree, cheerful, cheery, crumbly, delicate, delirious, digestible, diverting, dizzy, easy, effortless, entertaining, facile, faint, fickle, flimsy, friable, frivolous, frugal, funny, gay, gentle, giddy, graceful, humorous, idle, imponderous, inconsequential, inconsiderable, indistinct, insignificant, insubstantial, light-footed, light-headed, light-hearted, lightweight, lithe, lively, loose, manageable, merry, mild, minute, moderate, modest, nimble, pleasing, porous, portable, reeling, restricted, sandy, scanty, simple, slight, small, soft, spongy, sprightly, sunny, superficial, thin, tiny, trifling, trivial, unchaste, undemanding, underweight, unexacting, unheeding, unsteady, unsubstantial, untaxing, volatile, wanton, weak, witty, worthless. *antonyms* clumsy, harsh, heavy, important, sad, severe, sober, solid, stiff.

light on chance on, come across, discover, encounter, find, happen upon, hit on, spot, stumble on.

lighten[1] *v.* beacon, brighten, illume, illuminate, illumine, light up, shine. *antonym* darken.

lighten[2] *v.* alleviate, ameliorate, assuage, brighten, buoy up, cheer, disburden, disencumber, ease, elate, encourage, facilitate, gladden, hearten, inspire, inspirit, lessen, lift, mitigate, perk up, reduce, relieve, revive, unload, uplift. *antonyms* burden, depress, oppress.

light-fingered *adj.* crafty, crooked, dishonest, furtive, pilfering, shifty, sly, thieving, thievish. *antonym* honest.

light-footed *adj.* active, agile, buoyant, feat, graceful, lightsome, lithe, nimble, sprightly, spry, swift, tripping, winged. *antonyms* clumsy, slow.

light-giving *adj.* luciferous, luminant, luminiferous, luminous.

light-headed *adj.* bird-brained, delirious, dizzy, faint, feather-brained, fickle, flighty, flippant, foolish, frivolous, giddy, hazy, inane, shallow, silly, superficial, thoughtless, trifling, unsteady, vacuous, vertiginous, woozy. *antonym* sober.

light-hearted *adj.* blithe, blithesome, bright, carefree, cheerful, effervescent, elated, frolicsome, gay, glad, gleeful, happy-go-lucky, insouciant, jocund, jolly, jovial, joyful, joyous, light-spirited, merry, perky, playful,

sunny, untroubled, upbeat.
antonym sad.

lighthouse *n.* fanal, pharos.

lightly *adv.* airily, breezily, carelessly, delicately, easily, effortlessly, facilely, faintly, flippantly, frivolously, gaily, gently, gingerly, heedlessly, indifferently, moderately, readily, simply, slightingly, slightly, softly, sparingly, sparsely, thinly, thoughtlessly, timidly, wantonly.
antonyms heavily, soberly.

lightness *n.* agility, airiness, animation, blitheness, buoyancy, cheerfulness, cheeriness, crumbliness, delicacy, delicateness, facileness, faintness, fickleness, flimsiness, frivolity, gaiety, grace, idleness, inconsequentiality, indistinctness, insignificance, legerity, levity, light-heartedness, litheness, liveliness, mildness, minuteness, moderation, nimbleness, porosity, porousness, sandiness, scantiness, slightness, triviality, wantonness.
antonyms clumsiness, harshness, heaviness, importance, sadness, severity, sobriety, solidness, stiffness.

lightning *n.* thunderbolt, thunder-dart, wildfire.

lightweight *adj.* inconsequential, insignificant, negligible, nugatory, paltry, petty, slight, trifling, trivial, unimportant, worthless.
antonyms important, major.

like[1] *adj.* akin, alike, allied, analogous, approximating, cognate, corresponding, equivalent, homologous, identical, parallel, related, relating, resembling, same, similar.
antonym unlike.
n. counterpart, equal, fellow, match, opposite number, parallel, peer, twin.
prep. in the same manner as, on the lines of, similar to.

like[2] *v.* admire, adore, appreciate, approve, care to, cherish, choose, choose to, delight in, desire, dig, enjoy, esteem, fancy, feel inclined, go a bundle on, go for, hold dear, love, prefer, prize, relish, revel in, select, take a shine to, take kindly to, take to, want, wish.
antonym dislike.
n. cup of tea, favourite, liking, love, partiality, penchant, predilection, preference.
antonym dislike.

likeable *adj.* agreeable, amiable, appealing, attractive, charming, congenial, engaging, friendly, genial, loveable, nice, pleasant, pleasing, sympathetic, winning, winsome.
antonym disagreeable.

likelihood *n.* chance, liability, likeliness, possibility, probability, prospect, reasonableness, verisimilitude.
antonym unlikeliness.

likely *adj.* acceptable, agreeable, anticipated, appropriate, apt, befitting, believable, bright, credible, disposed, expected, fair, favourite, feasible, fit, foreseeable, hopeful, inclined, liable, odds-on, on the cards, plausible, pleasing, possible, predictable, probable, promising, prone, proper, qualified, reasonable, suitable, tending, up-and-coming, verisimilar.

antonyms unlikely, unsuitable.
adv. doubtlessly, in all probability, like as not, like enough, no doubt, odds on, presumably, probably, very like.

like-minded *adj.* agreeing, compatible, harmonious, in accord, in agreement, in harmony, in rapport, of one mind, of the same mind, unanimous.
antonym disagreeing.

liken *v.* associate, compare, equate, juxtapose, link, match, parallel, relate, set beside.

likeness *n.* affinity, appearance, copy, correspondence, counterpart, delineation, depiction, effigies, effigy, facsimile, form, guise, image, model, photograph, picture, portrait, replica, representation, reproduction, resemblance, semblance, similarity, similitude, simulacrum, study.
antonym unlikeness.

likewise *adv.* also, besides, by the same token, eke, further, furthermore, in addition, moreover, similarly, too.
antonym contrariwise.

liking *n.* affection, affinity, appreciation, attraction, bent, bias, desire, favour, fondness, inclination, love, partiality, penchant, predilection, preference, proneness, propensity, satisfaction, soft spot, stomach, taste, tendency, weakness.
antonym dislike.

lilt *n.* air, beat, cadence, measure, rhythm, song, sway, swing.

lily-white *adj.* chaste, incorrupt, innocent, irreproachable, milk-white, pure, spotless, uncorrupt, uncorrupted, unsullied, untainted, untarnished, virgin, virtuous.
antonym corrupt.

limb *n.* appendage, arm, bough, branch, extension, extremity, fork, leg, member, offshoot, part, projection, ramus, spur, wing.

limber *adj.* agile, elastic, flexible, flexile, graceful, lissom, lithe, loose-jointed, loose-limbed, plastic, pliable, pliant, supple.
antonym stiff.

limber up exercise, loosen up, prepare, warm up, work out.
antonym stiffen up.

limelight *n.* attention, big time, celebrity, fame, prominence, public notice, publicity, recognition, renown, stardom, the public eye, the spotlight.

limit *n.* bitter end, border, bound, boundary, bourne(e), brim, brink, ceiling, check, compass, confines, curb, cut-off point, deadline, edge, end, extent, frontier, limitation, maximum, mete, obstruction, outrance, perimeter, periphery, precinct, restraint, restriction, rim, saturation point, termination, terminus, terminus a quo, terminus ad quem, threshold, ultimate, utmost, verge.
v. bound, check, circumscribe, condition, confine, constrain, curb, delimit, delimitate, demarcate, fix, hem in, hinder, ration, restrain, restrict, specify.
antonyms extend, free.

limitation *n.* block, check, condition, constraint, control, curb, definitude, delimitation, demarcation, disadvantage, drawback, impediment, obstruction, qualification, reservation, restraint, restriction, snag.
antonyms asset, extension, furtherance.
limited *adj.* borné, bounded, checked, circumscribed, confined, constrained, controlled, cramped, curbed, defined, determinate, diminished, finite, fixed, hampered, hemmed in, inadequate, insufficient, minimal, narrow, reduced, restricted, short, unsatisfactory.
antonym limitless.
limitless *adj.* boundless, countless, endless, illimitable, illimited, immeasurable, immense, immensurable, incalculable, inexhaustible, infinite, measureless, never-ending, numberless, unbounded, undefined, unending, unlimited, untold, vast.
antonym limited.
limp[1] *v.* dot, falter, halt, hamble, hirple, hitch, hobble, hop, shamble, shuffle.
n. claudication, hitch, hobble, lameness.
limp[2] *adj.* debilitated, drooping, enervated, exhausted, flabby, flaccid, flexible, flexile, floppy, hypotonic, lax, lethargic, limber, loose, pliable, pooped, relaxed, slack, soft, spent, tired, toneless, weak, worn out.
antonym strong.
limpid *adj.* bright, clear, comprehensible, crystal-clear, crystalline, glassy, hyaline, intelligible, lucid, pellucid, pure, still, translucent, transparent, unruffled, untroubled.
antonyms muddy, ripply, turbid, unintelligible.
line[1] *n.* band, bar, border, borderline, boundary, cable, chain, channel, column, configuration, contour, cord, crease, crocodile, crow's foot, dash, demarcation, disposition, edge, features, figure, filament, file, firing line, formation, front, front line, frontier, furrow, groove, limit, mark, outline, position, procession, profile, queue, rank, rope, row, rule, score, scratch, sequence, series, silhouette, stipe, strand, streak, string, stroke, tail, thread, trail, trenches, underline, wire, wrinkle.
v. border, bound, crease, cut, draw, edge, fringe, furrow, hatch, inscribe, mark, rank, rim, rule, score, skirt, verge.
line up align, arrange, array, assemble, dispose, engage, fall in, form ranks, hire, lay on, marshal, obtain, order, organise, prepare, procure, produce, queue up, range, regiment, secure, straighten.
line[2] *n.* activity, approach, area, avenue, axis, belief, business, calling, course, course of action, department, direction, employment, field, forte, ideology, interest, job, line of country, method, occupation, path, policy, position, practice, procedure, profession, province, pursuit, route, scheme, specialisation, specialism, speciality, specialty, system, track, trade, trajectory, vocation.
line[3] *n.* ancestry, breed, family, lineage,
pedigree, race, stirps, stock, strain, succession.
line[4] *n.* card, clue, hint, indication, information, lead, letter, memo, memorandum, message, note, postcard, report, word.
line[5] *v.* ceil, cover, encase, face, fill, reinforce, strengthen, stuff.
lineage *n.* ancestors, ancestry, birth, breed, descendants, descent, extraction, family, forebears, forefathers, genealogy, heredity, house, line, offspring, pedigree, progeny, race, stirp(s), stock, succession.
lineaments *n.* appearance, aspect, configuration, countenance, face, features, lines, outline(s), physiognomy, traits, visage.
lined *adj.* feint, furrowed, lineate(d), lineolate, ruled, wizened, worn, wrinkled.
antonyms smooth, unlined.
linen *n.* bed-linen, napery, sheets, table-linen, white goods.
lines[1] *n.* appearance, configuration, contour, convention, cut, example, model, outline, pattern, plan, principle, procedure, shape, style.
lines[2] *n.* book, libretto, part, script, text, words.
lines[3] *n.* cross-hatching, hatching, shading.
line-up *n.* arrangement, array, bill, cast, queue, row, selection, team.
linger *v.* abide, continue, dally, dawdle, delay, dilly-dally, endure, hang around, hang on, hold out, idle, lag, last out, loiter, persist, procrastinate, remain, stay, stop, survive, tarry, wait.
antonyms leave, rush.
lingerie *n.* frillies, inexpressibles, linen, smalls, underclothes, underclothing, undergarments, underlinen, underset, unmentionables.
lingering *adj.* dragging, long-drawn-out, persistent, prolonged, protracted, remaining, slow.
antonym quick.
lingo *n.* argot, cant, dialect, idiom, jargon, language, parlance, patois, patter, speech, talk, terminology, tongue, vernacular, vocabulary.
linguist *n.* linguistic scientist, linguistician, verbalist, vocabularian.
liniment *n.* balm, balsam, cream, embrocation, emollient, lotion, ointment, salve, unguent, wash.
lining *n.* backing, encasement, inlay, interfacing, interlining, padding, stiffening.
link *n.* association, attachment, bond, communication, component, connection, constituent, division, element, joint, knot, liaison, member, part, piece, relationship, tie, tie-up, union.
v. associate, attach, bind, bracket, catenate, concatenate, connect, couple, fasten, identify, join, relate, tie, unite, yoke.
antonyms separate, unfasten.
link up ally, amalgamate, connect, dock, hook up, join, join forces, merge, team up, unify.
antonym separate.
link-up *n.* alliance, amalgamation, association, connection, merger, tie-in, union.

antonym separation.

lion-hearted *adj.* bold, brave, courageous, daring, dauntless, dreadless, gallant, heroic, intrepid, resolute, stalwart, stout-hearted, valiant, valorous.
antonym cowardly.

lionise *v.* acclaim, adulate, aggrandise, celebrate, eulogise, exalt, fête, glorify, hero-worship, honour, idolise, magnify, praise, sing the praises of.
antonym vilify.

lion-like *adj.* leonine, lion-hearted, lionly.

lip[1] *n.* border, brim, brink, edge, margin, rim, verge.

lip[2] *n.* backchat, cheek, effrontery, impertinence, impudence, insolence, rudeness, sauce.
antonym politeness.

liquefaction *n.* deliquescence, dissolution, dissolving, fusion, liquefying, melting, thawing.
antonym solidification.

liquefy *v.* deliquesce, dissolve, fluidise, flux, fuse, liquesce, liquidise, melt, run, smelt, thaw.
antonym solidify.

liquid *n.* drink, fluid, juice, liquor, lotion, potation, sap, solution.
adj. aqueous, clear, convertible, dulcet, flowing, fluid, limpid, liquefied, mellifluent, mellifluous, melted, molten, negotiable, running, runny, serous, shining, smooth, soft, sweet, thawed, translucent, transparent, watery, wet.
antonyms harsh, solid.

liquidate *v.* abolish, annihilate, annul, assassinate, bump off, cancel, cash, clear, destroy, discharge, dispatch, dissolve, do away with, do in, eliminate, exterminate, finish off, honour, kill, massacre, murder, pay, pay off, realise, remove, rub out, sell off, sell up, settle, silence, square, terminate, wipe out.

liquor[1] *n.* aguardiente, alcohol, booze, drink, fire-water, grog, hard stuff, hooch, intoxicant, juice, jungle juice, potation, rotgut, spirits, strong drink, tape.

liquor[2] *n.* broth, essence, extract, gravy, infusion, juice, liquid, stock.

lissom(e) *adj.* agile, flexible, graceful, light, limber, lithe, lithesome, loose-jointed, loose-limbed, nimble, pliable, pliant, supple, willowy.
antonym stiff.

list[1] *n.* catalogue, directory, enumeration, file, index, inventory, invoice, leet, listing, litany, matricula, record, register, roll, schedule, series, syllabus, table, tabulation, tally.
v. alphabeticise, bill, book, catalogue, enrol, enter, enumerate, file, index, itemise, note, record, register, schedule, set down, tabulate, write down.

list[2] *v.* cant, careen, heel, heel over, incline, lean, slope, tilt, tip.
n. cant, leaning, slant, slope, tilt.

listen *v.* attend, get a load of, give ear, give heed to, hang on (someone's) words, hang on (someone's) lips, hark, hear, hearken, heed, keep one's ears open, lend an ear, mind, obey, observe, pay attention, pin back one's ears, prick up one's ears, take notice.

listless *adj.* apathetic, bored, depressed, enervated, ennuyed, heavy, impassive, inattentive, indifferent, indolent, inert, languid, languishing, lethargic, lifeless, limp, lymphatic, mopish, sluggish, spiritless, supine, torpid, uninterested, vacant.
antonym lively.

listlessness *n.* accidie, acedia, apathy, enervation, ennui, inattention, indifference, indolence, languidness, languor, lethargy, lifelessness, sloth, sluggishness, spiritlessness, supineness, torpidity, torpor.
antonym liveliness.

litany *n.* account, catalogue, enumeration, invocation, list, narration, narrative, petition, prayer, recital, recitation, refrain, repetition, supplication, tale.

literacy *n.* ability, articulacy, articulateness, cultivation, culture, education, erudition, intelligence, knowledge, learning, proficiency, scholarship.
antonym illiteracy.

literal *adj.* accurate, actual, boring, close, colourless, down-to-earth, dull, exact, factual, faithful, genuine, matter-of-fact, plain, prosaic, prosy, real, simple, strict, true, unexaggerated, unimaginative, uninspired, unvarnished, verbatim, word-for-word.
antonym loose.

literally *adv.* actually, closely, exactly, faithfully, literatim, plainly, precisely, really, simply, strictly, to the letter, truly, verbatim, word for word.
antonym loosely.

literary *adj.* bookish, cultivated, cultured, erudite, formal, learned, lettered, literate, refined, scholarly, well-read.
antonym illiterate.

literature *n.* belles-lettres, blurb, brochure(s), bumf, circular(s), hand-out(s), information, leaflet(s), letters, lore, pamphlet(s), paper(s), writings.

lithe *adj.* double-jointed, flexible, flexile, limber, lissom(e), lithesome, loose-jointed, loose-limbed, pliable, pliant, supple.
antonym stiff.

litigant *n.* claimant, complainant, contender, contestant, disputant, litigator, party, plaintiff.

litigation *n.* action, case, contention, lawsuit, process, prosecution, suit.

litigious *adj.* argumentative, belligerent, contentious, disputable, disputatious, quarrelsome.
antonym easy-going.

litter[1] *n.* clutter, confusion, debris, detritus, disarray, disorder, fragments, jumble, mess, muck, refuse, rubbish, scatter, scoria, shreds, untidiness, wastage.
v. bestrew, clutter, derange, disarrange, disorder, mess up, scatter, strew.
antonym tidy.

litter[2] *n.* brood, family, offspring, progeny, quiverful, young.

litter[3] *n.* couch, palanquin, stretcher.

little *adj.* babyish, base, brief, cheap, diminutive, dwarf, elfin, fleeting, hasty, immature, inconsiderable, infant, infinitesimal, insignificant, insufficient, junior, Lilliputian, meagre, mean, microscopic, miniature, minor, minute, negligible, paltry, passing, petite, petty, piccaninny, pint-size(d), pygmy, scant, short, short-lived, skimpy, slender, small, sparse, tiny, transient, trifling, trivial, undeveloped, unimportant, wee, young.
antonyms important, large, long.
adv. barely, hardly, infrequently, rarely, scarcely, seldom.
antonyms frequently, greatly.
n. bit, dab, dash, drib, fragment, hint, modicum, particle, pinch, snippet, speck, spot, taste, touch, trace, trifle.
antonym lot.

little by little bit by bit, by degrees, gradually, imperceptibly, in penny numbers, piecemeal, progressively, slowly, step by step.
antonyms all at one go, quickly.

liturgical *adj.* ceremonial, eucharistic, formal, hieratic, ritual, sacerdotal, sacramental, solemn.
antonym secular.

liturgy *n.* celebration, ceremony, form, formula, office, rite, ritual, sacrament, service, usage, worship.

live[1] *v.* abide, breathe, continue, draw breath, dwell, earn a living, endure, exist, fare, feed, get along, hang out, inhabit, last, lead, lodge, make ends meet, pass, persist, prevail, remain, reside, settle, stay, subsist, survive.
antonyms cease, die.

live it up celebrate, go on the spree, have a ball, make merry, make whoopee, paint the town red, revel.

live[2] *adj.* active, alert, alight, alive, animate, blazing, breathing, brisk, burning, connected, controversial, current, dynamic, earnest, energetic, existent, glowing, hot, ignited, lively, living, pertinent, pressing, prevalent, relevant, sentient, smouldering, topical, unsettled, vigorous, vital, vivid, wide-awake.
antonyms apathetic, dead, out.

liveable *adj.* acceptable, adequate, bearable, comfortable, endurable, habitable, inhabitable, possible, satisfactory, sufferable, supportable, tolerable, worthwhile.
antonyms unbearable, uninhabitable.

liveable with bearable, companionable, compatible, congenial, gemütlich, harmonious, passable, sociable, tolerable.
antonyms impossible, unbearable.

livelihood *n.* employment, income, job, living, maintenance, means, occupation, subsistence, support, sustenance, work.

liveliness *n.* activity, animation, boisterousness, brio, briskness, dynamism, energy, entrain, gaiety, quickness, smartness, spirit, sprightliness, vitality, vivacity.

antonyms apathy, inactivity.

livelong complete, enduring, entire, full, long, protracted, whole.
antonym partial.

lively *adj.* active, agile, alert, animated, astir, blithe, blithesome, breezy, bright, brisk, buckish, bustling, busy, buxom, buzzing, canty, cheerful, chipper, chirpy, colourful, crowded, energetic, eventful, exciting, forceful, frisky, frolicsome, galliard, gay, invigorating, keen, lifesome, lightsome, merry, moving, nimble, perky, quick, racy, refreshing, skittish, sparkling, spirited, sprightly, spry, stimulating, stirring, swinging, tit(t)upy, vigorous, vivacious, vivid, zippy.
antonyms apathetic, inactive, moribund.

liven up animate, brighten, buck up, energise, enliven, hot up, invigorate, pep up, perk up, put life into, rouse, stir, stir up, vitalise, vivify.
antonyms deaden, dishearten.

liverish *adj.* crabbed, crabby, crotchety, crusty, disagreeable, grumpy, ill-humoured, irascible, irritable, peevish, snappy, splenetic, testy, tetchy.
antonyms calm, easy-going.

livery *n.* apparel, attire, clothes, clothing, costume, dress, garb, habit, raiment, regalia, suit, uniform, vestments.

live-wire ball of fire, cricket, dynamo, go-getter, grig, hustler, life and soul of the party, self-starter.
antonym wet blanket.

livid[1] *adj.* angry, beside oneself, boiling, enraged, exasperated, fuming, furibund, furious, incensed, indignant, infuriated, irate, ireful, mad, outraged, waxy.
antonym calm.

livid[2] *adj.* angry, ashen, black-and-blue, blanched, bloodless, bruised, contused, discoloured, doughy, greyish, leaden, pale, pallid, pasty, purple, wan, waxen, waxy.
antonyms healthy, rosy.

living *adj.* active, alive, animated, breathing, existing, live, lively, strong, vigorous, vital.
antonyms dead, sluggish.
n. being, benefice, existence, income, job, life, livelihood, maintenance, occupation, profession, property, subsistence, support, sustenance, way of life, work.

load *n.* affliction, albatross, bale, burden, cargo, consignment, encumbrance, freight, goods, lading, millstone, onus, oppression, pressure, shipment, trouble, weight, worry.
v. adulterate, burden, charge, cram, doctor, drug, encumber, fill, fortify, freight, hamper, heap, lade, oppress, overburden, pack, pile, prime, saddle with, stack, stuff, trouble, weigh down, weight, worry.

loaded *adj.* affluent, artful, biased, burdened, charged, distorted, drugged, drunk, fixed, flush, freighted, full, high, inebriated, insidious, intoxicated, laden, manipulative, moneyed, prejudicial, primed, rich, rolling, tight, tipsy, tricky, under the influence, wealthy, weighted, well-heeled, well-off, well-to-do.

antonyms poor, sober, straightforward, unloaded.

loads *n.* a million, dozens, heaps, hordes, hundreds, lots, millions, scores, thousands, tons.

loaf[1] *n.* block, cake, cube, lump, mass, slab.

loaf[2] *v.* idle, laze, lie around, loiter, loll, lounge around, mooch, moon, stand about, take it easy.

antonym toil.

loaf[3] *n.* brains, chump, common sense, gumption, head, noddle, nous, sense, smeddum.

loafer *n.* beachcomber, bludger, bum, bummer, burn, corner-boy, do-nothing, drone, idler, layabout, lazybones, lounge-lizard, lounger, ne'er-do-well, shirker, skiver, sluggard, time-waster, wastrel.

antonym worker.

loan *n.* accommodation, advance, allowance, calque, credit, lend-lease, loan translation, loan-word, mortgage, touch.

v. accommodate, advance, allow, credit, lend, let out, oblige.

antonym borrow.

lo(a)th *adj.* against, averse, backward, counter, disinclined, grudging, hesitant, indisposed, opposed, reluctant, resisting, unwilling.

antonym willing.

loathe *v.* abhor, abominate, despise, detest, dislike, execrate, hate, keck.

antonym like.

loathing *n.* abhorrence, abomination, antipathy, aversion, detestation, disgust, dislike, execration, hatred, horror, nausea, odium, repugnance, repulsion, revulsion.

antonym liking.

loathsome *adj.* abhorrent, abominable, detestable, disgusting, execrable, hateful, horrible, loathful, nasty, nauseating, obnoxious, odious, offensive, repellent, repugnant, repulsive, revolting, vile.

antonym likeable.

lob *v.* chuck, fling, heave, launch, lift, loft, pitch, shy, throw, toss.

lobby[1] *v.* call for, campaign for, demand, influence, persuade, press for, pressure, promote, pull strings, push for, solicit, urge.

n. ginger group, pressure group.

lobby[2] *n.* anteroom, corridor, entrance hall, foyer, hall, hallway, passage, passageway, porch, vestibule, waiting-room.

local *adj.* community, confined, district, limited, narrow, neighbourhood, parish, parochial, provincial, pump, regional, restricted, small-town, vernacular, vicinal.

antonym far-away.

n. denizen, inhabitant, native, resident, yokel.

antonym incomer.

locale *n.* area, locality, location, locus, place, position, scene, setting, site, spot, venue, zone.

localise *v.* ascribe, assign, circumscribe, concentrate, confine, contain, delimit, delimitate,

limit, narrow down, pin-point, restrain, restrict, specify, zero in on.

locality *n.* area, district, locale, location, neck of the woods, neighbourhood, place, position, region, scene, setting, site, spot, vicinity, zone.

locate *v.* detect, discover, establish, find, fix, identify, lay one's hands on, pin-point, place, put, run to earth, seat, set, settle, situate, track down, unearth.

location *n.* bearings, locale, locus, place, point, position, site, situation, spot, ubiety, venue, whereabouts.

lock[1] *n.* bolt, clasp, fastening, padlock, sneck.

v. bolt, clasp, clench, close, clutch, disengage, embrace, encircle, enclose, engage, entangle, entwine, fasten, grapple, grasp, hug, join, latch, link, mesh, press, seal, secure, shut, sneck, unite, unlock.

lock out ban, bar, debar, exclude, keep out, ostracise, refuse admittance to, shut out.

lock together interdigitate, interlock.

lock up cage, close up, confine, detain, enlock, imprison, incarcerate, jail, pen, secure, shut, shut in, shut up.

antonym free.

lock[2] *n.* curl, plait, ringlet, strand, tress, tuft.

lock-up *n.* brig, can, cell, clink, cooler, gaol, garage, hoos(e)gow, jail, jug, pen, penitentiary, prison, quod, tolbooth.

locomotion *n.* action, ambulation, headway, motion, movement, moving, progress, progression, travel, travelling.

locution *n.* accent, articulation, cliché, collocation, diction, expression, idiom, inflection, intonation, phrase, phrasing, style, term, turn of phrase, wording.

lodge *n.* abode, assemblage, association, branch, cabin, chalet, chapter, club, cot, cot-house, cottage, den, gang-hut, gatehouse, group, haunt, house, hunting-lodge, hut, lair, meeting-place, retreat, shelter, society.

v. accommodate, billet, board, deposit, dig, entertain, file, get stuck, harbour, imbed, implant, lay, place, put, put on record, put up, quarter, register, room, set, shelter, sojourn, stay, stick, stop, submit.

lodger *n.* boarder, guest, inmate, paying guest, renter, resident, roomer, tenant.

lodgings *n.* abode, accommodation, apartments, billet, boarding, digs, dwelling, gite, habitation, pad, quarters, residence, rooms, shelter.

lofty *adj.* arrogant, condescending, dignified, disdainful, distinguished, elevated, esteemed, exalted, grand, haughty, high, high and mighty, illustrious, imperial, imposing, lordly, majestic, noble, patronising, proud, raised, renowned, sky-high, snooty, soaring, stately, sublime, supercilious, superior, tall, toffee-nosed, towering.

antonyms humble, low(ly), modest.

log[1] *n.* billet, block, bole, chunk, loggat, stump, timber, trunk.

log[2] *n.* account, chart, daybook, diary, journal, listing, logbook, record, tally.

v. book, chart, note, record, register, report, tally, write down, write in, write up.

logic *n.* argumentation, deduction, dialectic(s), ratiocination, rationale, rationality, reason, reasoning, sense.

logical *adj.* clear, cogent, coherent, consistent, deducible, elenctic, judicious, necessary, obvious, pertinent, plausible, rational, reasonable, relevant, sensible, sound, valid, well-founded, well-grounded, well-organised, wise.

antonyms illogical, irrational.

logistics *n.* co-ordination, engineering, management, masterminding, orchestration, organisation, planning, plans, strategy.

loins *n.* genitalia, manliness, potency, power, reins, strength, virility.

loiter *v.* dally, dawdle, delay, dilly-dally, hang about, idle, lag, lallygag, linger, loaf, loll, lollygag, mooch, mouch, saunter, skulk, stroll.

loll *v.* dangle, depend, droop, drop, flap, flop, hang, lean, loaf, lounge, recline, relax, sag, slouch, slump, sprawl.

lone *adj.* deserted, isolated, lonesome, one, only, separate, separated, single, sole, solitary, unaccompanied, unattached, unattended.

antonym accompanied.

loneliness *n.* aloneness, desolation, forlornness, friendlessness, isolation, lonesomeness, seclusion, solitariness, solitude.

lonely *adj.* abandoned, alone, apart, companionless, destitute, estranged, forlorn, forsaken, friendless, isolated, lonely-heart, lonesome, outcast, out-of-the-way, remote, secluded, sequestered, solitary, unfrequented, uninhabited, untrodden.

loner *n.* hermit, individualist, lone wolf, maverick, outsider, pariah, recluse, solitary, solitudinarian.

lonesome *adj.* cheerless, companionless, deserted, desolate, dreary, forlorn, friendless, gloomy, isolated, lone, lonely, solitary.

long *adj.* dragging, elongated, expanded, expansive, extended, extensive, far-reaching, interminable, late, lengthy, lingering, long-drawn-out, marathon, prolonged, protracted, slow, spread out, stretched, sustained, tardy.

antonyms abbreviated, brief, fleeting, short.

long for covet, crave, desire, dream of, hanker for, hunger after, itch for, lust after, pine, thirst for, want, wish, yearn for, yen for.

long-drawn-out *adj.* interminable, lengthy, long-drawn, long-winded, marathon, overextended, overlong, prolix, prolonged, protracted, spun out, tedious.

antonyms brief, curtailed.

longing *n.* ambition, aspiration, coveting, craving, desire, hankering, hungering, itch, thirst, urge, wish, yearning, yen.

adj. anxious, appetence, appetency, ardent, avid, craving, desiderium, desirous, eager, hungry, languishing, pining, wishful, wistful, yearning.

long-lasting *adj.* abiding, continuing, enduring, entrenched, established, evergreen, imperishable, lifelong, long-lived, long-standing, perdurable, permanent, prolonged, protracted, unchanging, unfading.

antonyms ephemeral, short-lived, transient.

long-lived *adj.* durable, enduring, lasting, longevous, long-lasting, long-standing, macrobian, macrobiotic.

antonyms brief, ephemeral, short-lived.

long-standing *adj.* abiding, enduring, established, fixed, hallowed, long-established, long-lasting, long-lived, time-honoured, traditional.

long-suffering *adj.* easy-going, forbearant, forbearing, forgiving, patient, placid, resigned, stoical, tolerant, uncomplaining.

long-winded *adj.* circumlocutory, diffuse, discursive, garrulous, lengthy, long-drawn-out, overlong, prolix, prolonged, rambling, repetitious, tedious, verbose, voluble, wordy.

antonyms brief, compact, curt, terse.

long-windedness *n.* diffuseness, discursiveness, garrulity, lengthiness, longueur, macrology, prolixity, repetitiousness, tediousness, verbosity, volubility, wordiness.

antonyms brevity, curtness.

look *v.* appear, behold, consider, contemplate, display, evidence, examine, exhibit, eye, gape, gawk, gawp, gaze, get a load of, glance, goggle, inspect, observe, ogle, peep, regard, rubberneck, scan, scrutinise, see, seem, show, stare, study, survey, take a butcher's, take a gander, take shufti, view, watch.

n. air, appearance, aspect, bearing, butcher's, cast, complexion, countenance, decko, demeanour, effect, examination, expression, eyeful, eye-glance, face, fashion, gander, gaze, glance, glimpse, guise, inspection, look-see, manner, mien, observation, once-over, peek, review, semblance, shufti, sight, squint, survey, view.

look after attend to, care for, chaperon, guard, keep an eye on, mind, nurse, protect, supervise, take care of, take charge of, tend, watch.

antonym neglect.

look down on contemn, despise, disdain, hold in contempt, look down one's nose at, misprise, pooh-pooh, scorn, sneer at, spurn, turn one's nose up at.

antonyms approve, esteem.

look for forage for, hunt, hunt for, hunt out, quest, search for, seek.

look forward to anticipate, await, count on, envisage, envision, expect, hope for, long for, look for, wait for.

look into check out, delve into, examine, explore, fathom, follow up, go into, inquire about, inspect, investigate, look over, plumb, probe, research, scrutinise, study.

look like resemble, take after.

look out be careful, be on the qui vive, beware, keep an eye out, keep one's eyes peeled, keep one's eyes skinned, pay attention, watch out.

look out on face, front, front on, give on (to), overlook.

look over cast an eye over, check, examine, flick through, give a once-over, inspect, look through, monitor, peruse, scan, view.

look to/for anticipate, await, count on, expect, hope for, reckon on, rely on.

look up[1] call on, drop by, drop in on, find, hunt for, look in on, pay a visit to, research, search for, seek out, stop by, track down, visit.

look up[2] ameliorate, come on, get better, improve, meliorate, perk up, pick up, progress, shape up.

look up to admire, esteem, have a high opinion of, honour, respect, revere.

look-alike *n.* clone, dead ringer, doppel-gänger, double, living image, replica, ringer, spit, spit and image, spitting image, twin.

look-out *n.* affair, beacon, business, citadel, concern, funeral, guard, post, problem, readiness, sentinal, sentry, tower, vedette, vigil, watch, watchman, watch-tower, weather-eye, worry.

loom *v.* appear, bulk, dominate, emerge, hang over, hover, impend, materialise, menace, mount, overhang, overshadow, overtop, rise, soar, take shape, threaten, tower.

loop *n.* arc, bend, circle, coil, convolution, curl, curve, eyelet, hoop, kink, loophole, noose, ring, spiral, turn, twirl, twist, whorl.
v. bend, braid, circle, coil, connect, curl, curve round, encircle, fold, gird, join, knot, roll, spiral, turn, twist.

loophole *n.* aperture, avoidance, escape, evasion, excuse, get-out, let-out, opening, plea, pretence, pretext, slot, subterfuge.

loose[1] *adj.* baggy, crank, diffuse, disconnected, disordered, easy, floating, free, hanging, ill-defined, imprecise, inaccurate, indefinite, indistinct, inexact, insecure, loosened, movable, rambling, random, relaxed, released, shaky, slack, slackened, sloppy, solute, unattached, unbound, unconfined, unfastened, unfettered, unrestricted, unsecured, untied, vague, wobbly.
antonyms close, compact, precise, strict, taut, tense, tight.
v. absolve, detach, disconnect, disengage, ease, free, let go, liberate, loosen, release, set free, slacken, unbind, unbrace, unclasp, uncouple, undo, unfasten, unhand, unleash, unlock, unloose, unmew, unmoor, unpen, untie.
antonyms bind, fasten, fix, secure.

loose[2] *adj.* abandoned, careless, debauched, disreputable, dissipated, dissolute, fast, heedless, immoral, imprudent, lax, lewd, libertine, licentious, negligent, profligate, promiscuous, rash, thoughtless, unchaste, unmindful, wanton.
antonyms strict, stringent, tight.

loosen *v.* deliver, detach, free, let go, let out, liberate, release, separate, set free, slacken, unbind, undo, unfasten, unloose, unloosen, unstick, untie.

antonym tighten.

loosen up ease up, go easy, lessen, let up, mitigate, moderate, relax, soften, unbend, weaken.

loot *n.* boodle, booty, cache, goods, haul, plunder, prize, riches, spoils, swag.
v. burglarise, despoil, maraud, pillage, plunder, raid, ransack, ravage, rifle, rob, sack.

lop *v.* abscind, chop, clip, crop, curtail, cut, detach, detruncate, dock, hack, prune, sever, shorten, trim, truncate.

lope *v.* bound, canter, gallop, lollop, run, spring, stride.

lop-sided *adj.* askew, asymmetrical, awry, cockeyed, crooked, disproportionate, ill-balanced, off balance, one-sided, out of true, squint, tilting, unbalanced, unequal, uneven, warped.
antonyms balanced, straight, symmetrical.

loquacious *adj.* babbling, blathering, chattering, chatty, gabby, garrulous, gassy, gossipy, multiloquent, multiloquous, talkative, voluble, wordy.
antonyms succinct, taciturn, terse.

loquacity *n.* chattiness, effusiveness, garrulity, gassiness, multiloquence, multiloquy, talkativeness, volubility.
antonyms succinctness, taciturnity, terseness.

lord *n.* baron, commander, count, daimio, duke, earl, governor, Herr, king, leader, liege, liege-lord, master, monarch, noble, nobleman, overlord, peer, potentate, prince, ruler, seigneur, seignior, sovereign, superior, suzerain, viscount.

lord it over act big, boss around, domineer, oppress, order around, pull rank, put on airs, repress, swagger, tyrannise.

lordly *adj.* aristocratic, arrogant, authoritarian, condescending, despotic, dictatorial, dignified, disdainful, domineering, exalted, gracious, grand, haughty, high and mighty, high-handed, hoity-toity, imperial, imperious, lofty, majestic, masterful, noble, overbearing, patronising, princely, proud, regal, stately, stuck-up, supercilious, swanky, toffee-nosed, tyrannical.
antonyms humble, low(ly), mean.

lore *n.* beliefs, doctrine, erudition, experience, know-how, knowledge, learning, letters, mythus, saws, sayings, scholarship, schooling, teaching, traditions, wisdom.

lorry *n.* camion, double-bottom, drag, drawbar outfit, float, juggernaut, pick-up, truck.

lose *v.* capitulate, come a cropper, come to grief, consume, default, deplete, displace, dissipate, dodge, drain, drop, duck, elude, escape, evade, exhaust, expend, fail, fall short, forfeit, forget, get the worst of, give (someone) the slip, lap, lavish, leave behind, lose out on, misfile, mislay, misplace, miss, misspend, outdistance, outrun, outstrip, overtake, pass, pass up, shake off, slip away, squander, stray from, suffer defeat, take a licking, throw off, use up, wander from,

waste, yield.
antonyms gain, make, win.
loser *n*. also-ran, bum, bum steer, bummer, dud, failure, flop, lemon, no-hoper, runner-up, sucker, underdog, wash-out.
antonym winner.
loss *n*. bereavement, cost, damage, debit, debt, defeat, deficiency, deficit, depletion, deprivation, destruction, detriment, disadvantage, disappearance, failure, forfeiture, harm, hurt, impairment, injury, losing, losings, misfortune, privation, ruin, shrinkage, squandering, waste, write-off.
antonyms benefit, gain.
losses *n*. casualties, dead, death toll, disprofit, fatalities, missing, wounded.
lost *adj*. abandoned, abolished, absent, absorbed, abstracted, adrift, annihilated, astray, baffled, bewildered, confused, consumed, corrupt, damned, demolished, depraved, destroyed, devastated, disappeared, disoriented, dissipated, dissolute, distracted, dreamy, engrossed, entranced, eradicated, exterminated, fallen, forfeited, frittered away, irreclaimable, licentious, misapplied, misdirected, mislaid, misplaced, missed, missing, misspent, misused, mystified, obliterated, off-course, off-track, perished, perplexed, preoccupied, profligate, puzzled, rapt, ruined, spellbound, squandered, strayed, unrecallable, unrecapturable, unrecoverable, untraceable, vanished, wanton, wasted, wayward, wiped out, wrecked.
antonym found.
lot *n*. accident, allowance, assortment, batch, chance, collection, consignment, crowd, cut, destiny, doom, fate, fortune, group, hazard, jing-bang, parcel, part, percentage, piece, plight, portion, quantity, quota, ration, set, share, weird.
loth *see* **loath** .
lotion *n*. balm, cream, embrocation, fomentation, liniment, salve, solution.
lots *n*. a great deal, abundance, oodles, scade, tons.
lottery *n*. chance, draw, gamble, hazard, raffle, risk, sweepstake, toss-up, uncertainty, venture.
loud *adj*. blaring, blatant, boisterous, booming, brash, brassy, brazen, clamorous, coarse, crass, crude, deafening, ear-piercing, ear-splitting, flamboyant, flashy, garish, gaudy, glaring, high-sounding, loud-mouthed, lurid, noisy, offensive, ostentatious, piercing, raucous, resounding, rowdy, showy, sonorous, stentorian, streperous, strepitant, strident, strong, tasteless, tawdry, thundering, tumultuous, turbulent, vehement, vocal, vociferous, vulgar.
antonyms low, quiet, soft.
loudly *adv*. clamorously, deafeningly, fortissimo, lustily, noisily, resoundingly, shrilly, streperously, strepitantly, stridently, strongly, uproariously, vehemently, vigorously, vocally, vociferously.

antonyms quietly, softly.
loudmouth *n*. big mouth, blusterer, boaster, Bobadil, brag, braggadocio, braggart, Drawcansir, gasbag, swaggerer, windbag.
loud-voiced *adj*. full-throated, leather-lunged, penetrating, piercing, roaring, sonorous, stentorian.
antonyms quiet, soft.
lounge *v*. dawdle, idle, kill time, laze, lie about, lie back, loaf, loiter, loll, potter, recline, relax, slump, sprawl, take it easy, waste time.
n. day-room, drawing-room, parlour, sitting-room.
lour, lower *v*. be brewing, blacken, cloud over, darken, frown, give a dirty look, glare, glower, impend, look daggers, loom, menace, scowl, threaten.
louring, lowering *adj*. black, brooding, browning, clouded, cloudy, dark, darkening, forbidding, foreboding, gloomy, glowering, grey, grim, heavy, impending, menacing, minatory, ominous, overcast, scowling, sullen, surly, threatening.
lousy *adj*. awful, bad, base, contemptible, crap, despicable, dirty, hateful, inferior, lice-infested, lice-ridden, low, mean, miserable, no good, pedicular, pediculous, poor, rotten, second-rate, shoddy, slovenly, terrible, trashy, vicious, vile.
antonyms excellent, superb.
lout *n*. bear, booby, boor, bull-calf, bumpkin, calf, chuckle-head, churl, clod, dolt, gawk, hallion, hick, hob, hobbledehoy, jake, lob, lubber, lummox, oaf, swad, yahoo, yob, yobbo.
loutish *adj*. bearish, boorish, bungling, churlish, clodhopping, coarse, doltish, gawky, gross, ill-bred, ill-mannered, lubberly, lumpen, lumpish, oafish, rough, stolid, swinish, uncouth, unmannerly.
lovable *adj*. adorable, amiable, attractive, captivating, charming, cuddly, delightful, enchanting, endearing, engaging, fetching, likable, lovely, pleasing, sweet, taking, winning, winsome.
antonym hateful.
love *v*. adore, adulate, appreciate, cherish, delight in, desire, dote on, enjoy, fancy, hold dear, idolise, like, prize, relish, savour, take pleasure in, think the world of, treasure, want, worship.
antonyms detest, hate, loathe.
n. adoration, adulation, affection, agape, aloha, amity, amorosity, amorousness, ardour, attachment, delight, devotion, enjoyment, fondness, friendship, inclination, infatuation, liking, partiality, passion, rapture, regard, relish, soft spot, taste, tenderness, warmth, weakness.
antonyms detestation, hate, loathing.
love-affair *n*. affair, amour, grande passion, intrigue, liaison, love, mania, passion, relationship, romance.
loveless *adj*. cold, cold-hearted, disliked, forsaken, friendless, frigid, hard, heartless, icy,

insensitive, lovelorn, passionless, unappreciated, uncherished, unfeeling, unfriendly, unloved, unloving, unresponsive, unvalued. *antonym* passionate.

lovely *adj.* admirable, adorable, agreeable, amiable, attractive, beautiful, captivating, charming, comely, delightful, enchanting, engaging, enjoyable, exquisite, graceful, gratifying, handsome, idyllic, nice, pleasant, pleasing, pretty, sweet, taking, winning. *antonyms* hideous, ugly, unlovely.

love-making *n.* carnal knowledge, coition, coitus, congress, copulation, courtship, dalliance, foreplay, gallantry, intercourse, intimacy, mating, sexual intercourse, sexual relations, sexual union, venery.

lover *n.* admirer, amoretto, amorist, amoroso, beau, beloved, bon ami, boyfriend, Casanova, fancy man, fancy woman, fiancé(e), flame, gigolo, girlfriend, inamorata, inamorato, mistress, paramour, philanderer, suitor, swain, sweetheart.

lovesick *adj.* desiring, infatuated, languishing, longing, lovelorn, mashed, pining, yearning.

loving *adj.* affectionate, amative, amatorial, amatorian, amatorious, amorous, ardent, cordial, dear, demonstrative, devoted, doting, fond, friendly, kind, passionate, solicitous, tender, warm, warm-hearted.

low [1] *adj.* abject, base, base-born, blue, brassed off, browned off, cheap, coarse, common, contemptible, crude, dastardly, debilitated, deep, deficient, degraded, dejected, depleted, depraved, depressed, despicable, despondent, disgraceful, disheartened, dishonourable, disreputable, down, down in the dumps, downcast, dying, economical, exhausted, fed up, feeble, forlorn, frail, gloomy, glum, gross, humble, hushed, ignoble, ill, ill-bred, inadequate, inexpensive, inferior, insignificant, little, low-born, low-grade, lowly, low-lying, meagre, mean, mediocre, meek, menial, miserable, moderate, modest, morose, muffled, muted, nasty, obscene, obscure, paltry, plain, plebeian, poor, prostrate, puny, quiet, reasonable, reduced, rough, rude, sad, scant, scurvy, second-rate, servile, shallow, shoddy, short, simple, sinking, small, soft, sordid, sparse, squat, stricken, stunted, subdued, substandard, sunken, trifling, unbecoming, undignified, unhappy, unpretentious, unrefined, unworthy, vile, vulgar, weak, whispered, worthless. *antonyms* elevated, high, lofty, noble.

low point all-time low, low-watermark, nadir, perigee.

low [2] *v.* bellow, moo.

low-born *adj.* mean-born, plebeian, unexalted.

lowbrow *adj.* crude, ignorant, rude, uncultivated, uncultured, uneducated, unlearned, unlettered, unrefined, unscholarly. *antonym* highbrow.

low-down *n.* dope, gen, info, information, inside story, intelligence, news.

lower [1] *adj.* inferior, insignificant, junior, lesser,

low-level, lowly, minor, secondary, second-class, smaller, subordinate, subservient, under, unimportant.

v. abase, abate, belittle, condescend, couch, curtail, cut, debase, decrease, degrade, deign, demean, demolish, depress, devalue, diminish, discredit, disgrace, downgrade, drop, fall, humble, humiliate, lessen, let down, minimise, moderate, prune, raze, reduce, sink, slash, soften, stoop, submerge, take down, tone down. *antonyms* elevate, increase, raise, rise.

lower [2] *see* **lour** .

lowering *see* **louring** .

low-grade *adj.* bad, cheap-jack, inferior, poor, second-class, second-rate, substandard, third-rate. *antonyms* good, quality.

low-key *adj.* low-pitched, muffled, muted, quiet, restrained, slight, soft, subdued, understated.

lowly *adj.* average, common, docile, dutiful, homespun, humble, ignoble, inferior, low-born, mean, mean-born, meek, mild, modest, obscure, ordinary, plain, plebeian, poor, proletarian, simple, submissive, subordinate, unassuming, unexalted, unpretentious. *antonyms* lofty, noble.

low-minded *adj.* coarse, crude, depraved, dirty, disgusting, filthy, foul, gross, immoral, indecent, obscene, rude, scurril(e), smutty, uncouth, vulgar. *antonym* high-minded.

low-spirited *adj.* apathetic, blue, brassed off, browned off, dejected, depressed, despondent, down, down in the dumps, down-hearted, fed up, gloomy, glum, heavy-hearted, low, miserable, moody, pissed off, sad, unhappy. *antonyms* cheerful, high-spirited.

loyal *adj.* attached, constant, dependable, devoted, dutiful, faithful, honest, leal, patriotic, sincere, staunch, steadfast, true, true-blue, true-hearted, trustworthy, trusty, unswerving, unwavering. *antonyms* disloyal, traitorous.

loyalty *n.* allegiance, constancy, dependability, devotion, faithfulness, fealty, fidelity, honesty, lealty, patriotism, reliability, sincerity, staunchness, steadfastness, true-heartedness, trueness, trustiness, trustworthiness. *antonyms* disloyalty, treachery.

lozenge *n.* cough-drop, jujube, pastille, tablet, troche, trochiscus, trochisk.

lubberly *adj.* awkward, blundering, bungling, churlish, clodhopping, clownish, clumsy, coarse, crude, dense, doltish, gawky, heavy-handed, loutish, lumbering, lumpen, lumpish, oafish, obtuse, uncouth, ungainly.

lubricate *v.* grease, lard, oil, smear, wax.

lucid *adj.* beaming, bright, brilliant, clear, clear-cut, clear-headed, compos mentis, comprehensible, crystalline, diaphanous, distinct, effulgent, evident, explicit, glassy, gleaming, intelligible, limpid, luminous, obvious, pellucid, perspicuous, plain, pure, radiant, rational, reasonable, resplendent, sane, sensible,

shining, sober, sound, translucent, transparent.
antonyms dark, murky, unclear.
luck *n.* accident, blessing, break, chance, destiny, fate, fluke, fortuity, fortune, godsend, good fortune, hap, happenstance, hazard, jam, joss, prosperity, serendipity, stroke, success, windfall.
antonym misfortune.
luckily *adv.* feliciter, fortuitously, fortunately, haply, happily, opportunely, propitiously, providentially.
antonym unfortunately.
luckless *adj.* calamitous, catastrophic, cursed, disastrous, doomed, fey, hapless, hopeless, ill-fated, ill-starred, jinxed, star-crossed, unfortunate, unhappy, unlucky, unpropitious, unsuccessful.
antonym lucky.
lucky *adj.* advantageous, adventitious, auspicious, blessed, canny, charmed, favoured, fluk(e)y, fortuitous, fortunate, jammy, opportune, propitious, prosperous, providential, serendipitous, successful, timely.
antonyms luckless, unlucky.
lucky dip bran tub, grab-bag.
lucrative *adj.* advantageous, fecund, fertile, fruitful, gainful, paying, productive, profitable, remunerative, well-paid.
antonym unprofitable.
lucre *n.* gain(s), mammon, money, moolah, pelf, profit, riches, spoils, velvet, wealth.
ludicrous *adj.* absurd, amusing, burlesque, comic, comical, crazy, drôle, droll, farcical, funny, incongruous, laughable, nonsensical, odd, outlandish, preposterous, ridiculous, risible, silly, zany.
lug *v.* carry, drag, haul, heave, hump, humph, pull, tote, tow, yank.
luggage *n.* baggage, bags, cases, gear, impedimenta, paraphernalia, suitcases, things, traps, trunks.
lugubrious *adj.* dismal, doleful, dreary, funereal, gloomy, glum, melancholy, morose, mournful, sad, sepulchral, serious, sombre, sorrowful, Wertherian, woebegone, woeful.
antonyms cheerful, jovial, merry.
lukewarm *adj.* apathetic, cold, cool, half-hearted, indifferent, laodicean, Laodicean, lew, phlegmatic, tepid, unconcerned, unenthusiastic, uninterested, unresponsive, warm.
lull *v.* abate, allay, calm, cease, compose, decrease, diminish, dwindle, ease off, hush, let up, lullaby, moderate, pacify, quell, quiet, quieten down, sedate, slacken, soothe, still, subdue, subside, tranquillise, wane.
antonym agitate.
n. calm, calmness, hush, let-up, pause, peace, quiet, respite, silence, stillness, tranquillity.
antonym agitation.
lullaby *n.* berceuse, cradle-song, Wiegenlied.
lumber[1] *n.* bits and pieces, clutter, jumble, junk, odds and ends, refuse, rubbish, trash, trumpery.
v. burden, charge, encumber, hamper,

impose, land, load, saddle.
lumber[2] *v.* clump, galumph, plod, shamble, shuffle, stump, trudge, trundle, waddle.
lumbering *adj.* awkward, blundering, bovine, bumbling, clumsy, elephantine, heavy, heavy-footed, hulking, lubberly, lumpish, massive, overgrown, ponderous, ungainly, unwieldy.
antonyms agile, nimble.
luminary *n.* celebrity, dignitary, leader, leading light, lion, notable, personage, star, superstar, VIP, worthy.
luminescent *adj.* bright, effulgent, fluorescent, glowing, luciferous, luminous, phosphorescent, radiant, shining.
luminous *adj.* bright, brilliant, glowing, illuminated, lighted, lit, lucent, luminescent, luminiferous, lustrous, radiant, resplendent, shining, vivid.
lump[1] *n.* ball, bulge, bump, bunch, cake, chuck, chump, chunk, clod, cluster, cyst, dab, daud, dod, gob, gobbet, group, growth, hunch, hunk, (k)nub, (k)nubble, lob, mass, nugget, piece, protrusion, protuberance, spot, swelling, tuber, tumescence, tumour, wedge, wen, wodge.
v. coalesce, collect, combine, consolidate, group, mass, unite.
lump[2] *v.* bear (with), brook, endure, put up with, stand, stomach, suffer, swallow, take, thole, tolerate.
lumpish *adj.* awkward, boorish, bovine, bungling, clumsy, doltish, dull-witted, elephantine, gawky, heavy, lethargic, lumbering, oafish, obtuse, stolid, stupid, ungainly.
lumpy *adj.* bumpy, bunched, cloggy, clotted, curdled, grainy, granular, knobbly, nodose, nodous, nodular, nodulose, nodulous.
antonyms even, smooth.
lunacy *n.* aberration, absurdity, craziness, dementia, derangement, folly, foolhardiness, foolishness, idiocy, imbecility, insanity, madness, mania, moon-madness, moonraking, psychosis, senselessness, stupidity, tomfoolery.
antonym sanity.
lunatic *n.* bug, loony, madman, maniac, nut, nutcase, nutter, psychopath.
adj. barmy, bonkers, crazy, daft, demented, deranged, insane, irrational, mad, maniacal, moon-stricken, moon-struck, nuts, psychotic, unhinged.
antonyms sane, sensible.
lunch *n.* dejeune, déjeuner, luncheon, nooning, nuncheon, tiffin.
lunge *v.* bound, charge, cut, dash, dive, fall upon, grab (at), hit (at), jab, leap, pitch into, plunge, poke, pounce, set upon, stab, strike (at), thrust.
n. charge, cut, jab, pass, pounce, spring, stab, swing, swipe, thrust, venue.
lurch *v.* heave, lean, list, pitch, reel, rock, roll, stagger, stumble, sway, tilt, totter, wallow, weave, welter.
lure *v.* allure, attract, beckon, decoy, draw, ensnare, entice, inveigle, invite, lead on,

seduce, tempt, trepan.

n. allurement, attraction, bait, carrot, come-on, decoy, enticement, inducement, magnet, siren, song, temptation, train.

lurid *adj.* ashen, bloody, disgusting, exaggerated, fiery, flaming, ghastly, glaring, glowering, gory, graphic, grim, grisly, gruesome, intense, livid, loud, macabre, melodramatic, pale, pallid, revolting, sallow, sanguine, savage, sensational, shocking, startling, unrestrained, violent, vivid, wan.

lurk *v.* crouch, hide, hide out, lie in wait, lie low, prowl, skulk, slink, sneak, snook, snoop.

luscious *adj.* appetising, delectable, delicious, honeyed, juicy, luxuriant, luxurious, mouth-watering, palatable, rich, savoury, scrumptious, succulent, sweet, tasty, toothsome, yummy.

antonym austere.

lush *adj.* abundant, dense, elaborate, extravagant, flourishing, grand, green, juicy, lavish, luxuriant, luxurious, opulent, ornate, overgrown, palatial, plush, prolific, rank, ripe, ritzy, succulent, sumptuous, superabundant, teeming, tender, verdant.

lust *n.* appetence, appetency, appetite, avidity, carnality, concupiscence, covetousness, craving, cupidity, desire, greed, Kama, Kamadeva, lasciviousness, lechery, lewdness, libido, licentiousness, longing, passion, prurience, randiness, salaciousness, sensuality, thirst, wantonness.

lust after crave, desire, have hot-pants for, have the hots for, hunger for, need, slaver over, thirst for, want, yearn for, yen for.

lustful *adj.* carnal, concupiscent, craving, goatish, hankering, horny, lascivious, lecherous, lewd, libidinous, licentious, passionate, prurient, randy, raunchy, ruttish, sensual, unchaste, venerous, wanton.

lustily *adv.* forcefully, hard, loudly, powerfully, robustly, stoutly, strongly, vigorously, with all one's might, with might and main.

antonym weakly.

lustiness *n.* energy, haleness, hardihood, hardiness, health, healthiness, power, robustness, stoutness, strength, sturdiness, toughness, vigour, virility.

lustre *n.* brightness, brilliance, burnish, dazzle, distinction, effulgence, fame, gleam, glint, glitter, glory, gloss, glow, gorm, honour, illustriousness, lambency, luminousness, prestige, radiance, renown, resplendence, sheen, shimmer, shine, sparkle, water.

lustrous *adj.* bright, burnished, dazzling, gleaming, glistening, glittering, glossy, glowing, lambent, luminous, radiant, shimmering, shining, shiny, sparkling.

antonyms dull, lacklustre, matt.

lusty *adj.* blooming, brawny, energetic, gutsy, hale, healthy, hearty, in fine fettle, muscular, powerful, red-blooded, robust, rugged, stalwart, stout, strapping, strong, sturdy, vigorous, virile.

antonyms effete, weak.

luxuriance *n.* abundance, copiousness, denseness, excess, exuberance, fecundity, fertility, lavishness, lushness, profusion, rankness, richness, sumptuousness.

luxuriant *adj.* abundant, ample, baroque, copious, dense, elaborate, excessive, extravagant, exuberant, fancy, fecund, fertile, festooned, flamboyant, florid, flowery, lavish, lush, opulent, ornate, overflowing, plenteous, plentiful, prodigal, productive, profuse, prolific, rank, rich, riotous, rococo, sumptuous, superabundant, teeming, thriving.

antonyms barren, infertile.

luxuriate *v.* abound, bask, bloom, burgeon, delight, enjoy, flourish, grow, have a ball, indulge, live high off the hog, live the life of Riley, prosper, relish, revel, thrive, wallow, wanton.

luxurious *adj.* comfortable, costly, deluxe, epicurean, expensive, hedonistic, lavish, magnificent, opulent, pampered, plush, plushy, rich, ritzy, self-indulgent, sensual, splendid, sumptuous, sybaritic, voluptuous, well-appointed.

antonyms ascetic, austere, economical, frugal, scant(y), spartan.

luxury *n.* affluence, bliss, comfort, delight, dolce vita, enjoyment, extra, extravagance, fleshpots, flesh-pottery, frill, gratification, hedonism, indulgence, milk and honey, non-essential, opulence, pleasure, richness, satisfactiion, splendour, sumptuousness, treat, voluptuousness, well-being.

antonym essential.

lying *adj.* accumbent, deceitful, decumbent, dishonest, dissembling, double-dealing, duplicitous, false, guileful, mendacious, perfidious, treacherous, two-faced, untruthful.

antonyms honest, truthful.

n. deceit, dishonesty, dissimulation, double-dealing, duplicity, fabrication, falsity, fibbing, guile, mendacity, perjury, prevarication, pseudology, ùntruthfulness.

antonyms honesty, truthfulness.

lyrical *adj.* carried away, ecstatic, effusive, emotional, enthusiastic, expressive, impassioned, inspired, musical, passionate, poetic, rapturous, rhapsodic.

lyrics *n.* book, libretto, text, words.

M

macabre *adj.* cadaverous, deathlike, deathly, dreadful, eerie, frightening, frightful, ghastly, ghostly, ghoulish, grim, grisly, gruesome, hideous, horrible, horrid, morbid, sick, weird.

macerate *v.* blend, liquefy, mash, pulp, soak, soften, steep.

Machiavellian *adj.* amoral, artful, astute, calculating, crafty, cunning, cynical, deceitful, designing, double-dealing, foxy, guileful, intriguing, opportunist, perfidious, scheming, shrewd, sly, underhand, unscrupulous, wily.

machinate *v.* conspire, contrive, design, devise, engineer, finagle, hatch, intrigue, invent, manoeuvre, plan, plot, scheme, work.

machination *n.* artifice, cabal, conspiracy, design, device, dodge, finagling, intrigue, manoeuvre, plot, ploy, ruse, scheme, shenanigans, stratagem, trick.

machine *n.* agency, agent, apparatus, appliance, automaton, contraption, contrivance, device, engine, gadget, gizmo, instrument, machinery, mechanism, organisation, party, puppet, robot, set-up, structure, system, tool, zombi(e).

machine-gun *n.* Bren (gun), gatling-gun, mitrailleur, mitrailleuse, pompom, tommy-gun.

machinery *n.* agency, apparatus, channels, enginery, equipment, gear, instruments, kit, machine, mechanism, organisation, procedure, structure, system, tackle, tools, works.

mad *adj.* abandoned, aberrant, absurd, agitated, angry, ardent, avid, bananas, barmy, bats, batty, berserk, boisterous, bonkers, crackers, crazed, crazy, cuckoo, daft, delirious, demented, deranged, devoted, distracted, dotty, ebullient, enamoured, energetic, enraged, enthusiastic, exasperated, excited, fanatical, fond, foolhardy, foolish, frantic, frenetic, frenzied, fuming, furious, gay, gyte, have bats in the belfry, hooked, impassioned, imprudent, in a paddy, incensed, infatuated, infuriated, insane, irate, irrational, irritated, keen, livid, loony, loopy, ludicrous, lunatic, madcap, mental, moon-stricken, moonstruck, non compos mentis, nonsensical, nuts, nutty, off one's chump, off one's head, off one's nut, off one's rocker, off one's trolley, out of one's mind, possessed, preposterous, psychotic, rabid, raging, raving, resentful, riotous, round the bend, round the twist, screwball, screwy, senseless, unbalanced, uncontrolled, unhinged, unreasonable, unrestrained, unsafe, unsound, unstable, up the pole, waxy, wild, wrathful, zealous.
antonyms lucid, rational, sane.

madcap *adj.* bird-brained, crazy, flighty, foolhardy, hare-brained, heedless, hotheaded, ill-advised, imprudent, impulsive, lively, rash, reckless, silly, thoughtless, wild.

madden *v.* annoy, craze, dement, dementate, derange, enrage, exasperate, incense, inflame, infuriate, irritate, provoke, unhinge, upset, vex.
antonyms calm, pacify, please.

made-up *adj.* fabricated, fairy-tale, false, fictional, imaginary, invented, make-believe, mythical, specious, trumped-up, unreal, untrue.

madhouse *n.* asylum, Babel, bedlam, chaos, disarray, disorder, funny farm, loony bin, nut-house, pandemonium, snake-pit, turmoil, uproar.

madly *adv.* absurdly, crazily, deliriously, dementedly, desperately, devotedly, distractedly, energetically, exceedingly, excessively, excitedly, extremely, fanatically, foolishly, frantically, frenziedly, furiously, hastily, hurriedly, hysterically, insanely, intensely, irrationally, like mad, ludicrously, nonsensically, passionately, quickly, rabidly, rapidly, recklessly, senselessly, speedily, to distraction, unreasonably, violently, wildly.

madman *n.* bedlamite, détraqué, furioso, loony, lunatic, madling, maniac, mattoid, mental case, nut, nutcase, nutter, psycho, psychopath, psychotic, schizo, screwball.

madness *n.* abandon, aberration, absurdity, agitation, anger, ardour, craze, craziness, daftness, delusion, dementia, demoniacism, demonomania, derangement, distraction, enthusiasm, exasperation, excitement, fanaticism, folie, folly, fondness, foolhardiness, foolishness, frenzy, furore, fury, infatuation, insanity, intoxication, ire, keenness, lunacy, lycanthropy, mania, monomania, moonmadness, moonraking, nonsense, passion, preposterousness, psychopathy, psychosis, rage, raving, riot, unrestraint, uproar, wildness, wrath, zeal.
antonym sanity.

maelstrom *n.* bedlam, chaos, Charybdis, confusion, disorder, mess, pandemonium, tumult, turmoil, uproar, vortex, whirlpool.

maestro *n.* expert, genius, master, prodigy, virtuoso, wizard.

magazine[1] *n.* fanzine, journal, monthly, pamphlet, paper, periodical, quarterly, weekly.

magazine[2] *n.* ammunition dump, arsenal, depot, ordnance, powder-room, store, storehouse.

magic *n.* allurement, black art, charm, conjuring, conjury, diablerie, enchantment, fascination, glamour, goety, gramary(e), hocus-

pocus, hoodoo, illusion, jiggery-pokery, jugglery, legerdemain, magnetism, medicine, necromancy, occultism, prestidigitation, sleight of hand, sorcery, sortilege, spell, thaumaturgics, thaumaturgism, thaumaturgy, theurgy, trickery, voodoo, witchcraft, wizardry, wonder-work.
adj. bewitching, charismatic, charming, enchanting, entrancing, fascinating, goetic, hermetic, magical, magnetic, marvellous, miraculous, mirific, mirifical, sorcerous, spellbinding, spellful.

magician *n.* archimage, conjurer, conjuror, enchanter, enchantress, genius, illusionist, maestro, mage, Magian, magus, marvel, miracle-worker, necromancer, prestidigitator, prestigiator, sorcerer, spellbinder, thaumaturge, theurgist, virtuoso, warlock, witch, witch-doctor, wizard, wonder-monger, wonder-worker.

magisterial *adj.* arrogant, assertive, authoritarian, authoritative, bossy, commanding, despotic, dictatorial, domineering, high-handed, imperious, lordly, masterful, overbearing, peremptory.

magistrate *n.* aedile, bailiff, bail(l)ie, beak, JP, judge, jurat, justice, justice of the peace, mittimus, queer cuffin, stipendiary, tribune.

magnanimity *n.* beneficence, big-heartedness, bountifulness, charitableness, charity, generosity, high-mindedness, largess(e), liberality, munificence, nobility, open-handedness, selflessness, unselfishness.
antonym meanness.

magnanimous *adj.* altruistic, beneficent, big, big-hearted, bountiful, charitable, free, generous, great-hearted, handsome, high-minded, kind, kindly, large-hearted, large-minded, liberal, munificent, noble, open-handed, philanthropic, selfless, ungrudging, unselfish, unstinting.
antonyms mean, paltry, petty.

magnate *n.* aristocrat, baron, bashaw, big cheese, big noise, big shot, big wheel, bigwig, captain of industry, chief, fat cat, grandee, leader, magnifico, merchant, mogul, nabob, noble, notable, personage, plutocrat, prince, tycoon, VIP.

magnet *n.* appeal, attraction, bait, draw, enticement, lodestone, lure, solenoid.
antonym repellent.

magnetic *adj.* absorbing, alluring, attractive, captivating, charismatic, charming, enchanting, engrossing, entrancing, fascinating, gripping, hypnotic, irresistible, mesmerising, seductive.
antonyms repellent, repugnant, repulsive.

magnetism *n.* allure, appeal, attraction, attractiveness, charisma, charm, draw, drawing power, enchantment, fascination, grip, hypnotism, lure, magic, mesmerism, power, pull, seductiveness, spell.

magnification *n.* aggrandisement, amplification, augmentation, blow-up, boost, build-up, deepening, dilation, enhancement, enlarge-ment, exaggeration, expansion, extolment, heightening, increase, inflation, intensification, lionisation.
antonyms diminution, reduction.

magnificence *n.* brilliance, glory, gorgeousness, grandeur, grandiosity, impressiveness, luxuriousness, luxury, majesty, nobility, opulence, pomp, resplendence, splendour, stateliness, sublimity, sumptuousness.
antonyms modesty, plainness, simplicity.

magnificent *adj.* august, brilliant, elegant, elevated, exalted, excellent, fine, glorious, gorgeous, grand, grandiose, imposing, impressive, lavish, luxurious, majestic, noble, opulent, outstanding, plush, posh, princely, regal, resplendent, rich, ritzy, splendid, stately, sublime, sumptuous, superb, superior, transcendent.
antonyms humble, modest, plain, simple.

magnify *v.* aggrandise, aggravate, amplify, augment, blow up, boost, build up, deepen, dilate, dramatise, enhance, enlarge, exaggerate, expand, greaten, heighten, increase, inflate, intensify, lionise, overdo, overemphasise, overestimate, overplay, overrate, overstate, praise.
antonyms belittle, play down.

magniloquence *n.* bombast, euphuism, fustian, grandiloquence, loftiness, orotundity, pomposity, pretentiousness, rhetoric, turgidity.
antonyms simplicity, straightforwardness.

magniloquent *adj.* bombastic, declamatory, elevated, euphuistic, exalted, fustian, grandiloquent, high-flown, high-sounding, lofty, orotund, overblown, pompous, pretentious, rhetorical, sonorous, stilted, turgid.
antonyms simple, straightforward.

magnitude *n.* amount, amplitude, bigness, brightness, bulk, capacity, consequence, dimensions, eminence, enormousness, expanse, extent, grandeur, greatness, hugeness, immensity, importance, intensity, largeness, mark, mass, measure, moment, note, proportions, quantity, significance, size, space, strength, vastness, volume, weight.
antonym smallness.

magnum opus Almagest, chef d'oeuvre, masterpiece, master-work, pièce de résistance.

maid *n.* abigail, bonne, damsel, dresser, femme de chambre, fille de chambre, gentlewoman, girl, handmaiden, housemaid, lady's maid, lass, lassie, maiden, maid-of-all-work, maidservant, miss, nymph, servant, serving-maid, soubrette, tirewoman, tiring-woman, virgin, waitress, wench.

maiden *n.* damozel, damsel, demoiselle, girl, lass, lassie, maid, may, miss, nymph, virgin, wench.
adj. chaste, female, first, fresh, inaugural, initial, initiatory, intact, introductory, new, pure, unbroached, uncaptured, undefiled, unmarried, unpolluted, untapped, untried, unused, unwed, virgin, virginal.
antonyms defiled, deflowered, unchaste.

maidenly *adj.* becoming, chaste, decent, decorous, demure, gentle, girlish, modest, proper, pure, reserved, seemly, undefiled, vestal, virginal, virtuous.

antonym immodest.

mail *n.* correspondence, da(w)k, delivery, letters, packages, parcels, post.

v. air-mail, dispatch, forward, post, send.

maim *v.* cripple, disable, hack, haggle, hamstring, hurt, impair, incapacitate, injure, lame, mangle, mar, mutilate, savage, wound.

antonyms heal, repair.

main¹ *adj.* absolute, brute, capital, cardinal, central, chief, critical, crucial, direct, downright, entire, essential, extensive, first, foremost, general, great, head, leading, mere, necessary, outstanding, paramount, particular, predominant, pre-eminent, premier, primary, prime, principal, pure, sheer, special, staple, supreme, undisguised, utmost, utter, vital.

antonyms minor, unimportant.

n. effort, foison, force, might, potency, power, puissance, strength, vigour.

antonym weakness.

main² *n.* cable, channel, conduit, duct, line, pipe.

mainly *adv.* above all, as a rule, chiefly, especially, for the most part, generally, in general, in the main, largely, mostly, on the whole, overall, predominantly, primarily, principally, substantially, usually.

mainspring *n.* cause, driving force, fountainhead, generator, impulse, incentive, inspiration, motivation, motive, origin, prime mover, source, wellspring.

mainstay *n.* anchor, backbone, bulwark, buttress, linchpin, pillar, prop, support.

mainstream *adj.* accepted, average, conventional, established, general, normal, orthodox, received, regular, standard.

antonyms heterodox, peripheral.

maintain *v.* advocate, affirm, allege, argue, assert, asseverate, aver, avouch, avow, back, care for, carry on, champion, claim, conserve, contend, continue, declare, defend, fight for, finance, hold, insist, justify, keep, keep up, look after, make good, nurture, observe, perpetuate, plead for, practise, preserve, profess, prolong, provide, retain, stand by, state, supply, support, sustain, take care of, uphold, vindicate.

antonyms deny, neglect, oppose.

maintenance *n.* aliment, alimony, allowance, care, conservation, continuance, continuation, defence, food, keep, keeping, livelihood, living, nurture, perpetuation, preservation, prolongation, protection, provision, repairs, retainment, subsistence, supply, support, sustainment, sustenance, sustention, upkeep.

antonym neglect.

majestic *adj.* august, awesome, dignified, distinguished, elevated, exalted, grand, grandiose, imperial, imperious, imposing, impressive, kingly, lofty, magisterial, magni-

ficent, monumental, noble, pompous, princely, queenly, regal, royal, splendid, stately, sublime, superb.

antonyms unimportant, unimpressive.

majesty *n.* augustness, awesomeness, dignity, exaltedness, glory, grandeur, impressiveness, kingliness, loftiness, magnificence, majesticness, nobility, pomp, queenliness, regalness, resplendence, royalty, splendour, state, stateliness, sublimity.

antonyms unimportance, unimpressiveness.

major *adj.* better, bigger, chief, critical, crucial, elder, grave, great, greater, higher, important, key, keynote, larger, leading, main, most, notable, older, outstanding, pre-eminent, radical, senior, serious, significant, superior, supreme, uppermost, vital, weighty.

antonym minor.

majority *n.* adulthood, bulk, manhood, mass, maturity, plurality, preponderance, seniority, superiority, the many, womanhood, years of discretion.

antonyms childhood, minority.

make *v.* accomplish, acquire, act, add up to, amount to, appoint, arrive at, assemble, assign, attain, beget, bring about, build, calculate, carry out, catch, cause, clear, coerce, compel, compose, conclude, constitute, constrain, construct, contract, contribute, convert, create, designate, do, dragoon, draw up, drive, earn, effect, elect, embody, enact, engage in, engender, establish, estimate, execute, fabricate, fashion, fix, flow, force, forge, form, frame, gain, gar, gauge, generate, get, give rise to, impel, induce, install, invest, judge, lead to, manufacture, meet, mould, net, nominate, oblige, obtain, occasion, ordain, originate, pass, perform, practise, press, pressurise, prevail upon, proceed, produce, prosecute, put together, reach, reckon, render, require, secure, shape, smith(y), suppose, synthesise, take in, tend, think, turn, win.

antonyms dismantle, lose, persuade.

n. brand, build, character, composition, constitution, construction, cut, designation, disposition, form, formation, humour, kind, make-up, manner, manufacture, mark, model, nature, shape, sort, stamp, structure, style, temper, temperament, texture, type, variety.

make believe act, dream, enact, fantasise, feign, imagine, play, play-act, pretend.

make do cope, get along, get by, improvise, make out, manage, muddle through, scrape by, survive.

make eyes at flirt, give (someone) the come-on, leer at, make sheep's eyes at, ogle.

make for aim for, conduce to, contribute to, facilitate, favour, forward, further, head for, promote.

make fun of deride, lampoon, laugh at, make sport of, mock, parody, poke fun at, queer, quiz, rag, rib, ridicule, roast, rot, satirise, scoff at, send up, sneer at, take off, taunt.

antonym praise.

make inroads into consume, eat away, eat into, eat up, encroach upon, get on with, make progress with, progress with.
antonym add to.

make it arrive, come through, get on, prosper, pull through, reach, succeed, survive.
antonym fail.

make love canoodle, copulate, cuddle, embrace, enjoy, fuck, gender, go to bed, neck, pet, romance, screw, smooch.

make merry carouse, celebrate, feast, frolic, junket, make whoopee, paint the town red, revel, whoop it up.

make no difference be six and half a dozen, count for nothing, cut no ice.

make off abscond, beat a hasty retreat, bolt, clear off, cut and run, decamp, depart, flee, fly, have it on one's toes, leave, make away, run away, run for it, run off, take to one's heels.

make off with abduct, appropriate, carry off, filch, kidnap, knock off, nab, nick, pilfer, pinch, purloin, run away, run off with, steal, swipe, walk off with.
antonym bring.

make one's mark get on, make good, make it, make the big-time, prosper, succeed.
antonym fail.

make out assert, claim, complete, comprehend, decipher, demonstrate, describe, descry, detect, discern, discover, distinguish, draw up, espy, fare, fathom, fill in, fill out, follow, get on, grasp, imply, infer, inscribe, let on, make as if, manage, perceive, pretend, prosper, prove, realise, recognise, represent, see, show, succeed, survive, thrive, understand, work out, write, write out.
antonym fail.

make sense of apprehend, comprehend, fathom, figure out, grasp, make head or tail of, make much of, make out, understand.

make tracks beat it, dash, dash off, depart, disappear, go, hit the road, hurry, leave, make off, scram, set out, split, take off.

make up[1] arrange, coin, collect, complement, complete, compose, comprise, concoct, constitute, construct, cook up, create, devise, dream up, fabricate, feign, fill, form, formulate, frame, hatch, invent, meet, originate, parcel, put together, repair, supplement, supply, trump up, write.

make up[2] bury the hatchet, call it quits, come to terms, forgive and forget, make peace, mend one's fences, settle, settle differences, shake hands.

make up for atone for, balance, compensate, expiate, make amends for, offset, recompense, redeem, redress, requite.

make up one's mind choose, decide, determine, resolve, settle.
antonym waver.

make up to butter up, chat up, court, curry favour with, fawn on, flirt with, make overtures to, toady to, woo.

make-believe *n.* charade, dream, fantasy, imagination, play-acting, pretence, role-play, unreality.
antonym reality.
adj. dream, fantasised, fantasy, feigned, imaginary, imagined, made-up, mock, pretend, pretended, sham, simulated, unreal.
antonym real.

maker *n.* architect, author, builder, constructor, contriver, creator, director, fabricator, framer, manufacturer, producer.
antonym dismantler.

makeshift *adj.* band-aid, expedient, haywire, improvised, make-do, provisional, rough and ready, stop-gap, substitute, temporary.
antonyms finished, permanent.
n. band-aid, expedient, fig-leaf, shift, stop-gap, substitute.

make-up[1] *n.* cosmetics, fard, fucus, greasepaint, maquillage, paint, powder, war paint, white-face.

make-up[2] *n.* arrangement, assembly, build, cast, character, complexion, composition, configuration, constitution, construction, disposition, figure, form, format, formation, make, nature, organisation, stamp, structure, style, temper, temperament.

making *n.* assembly, building, composition, construction, creation, fabrication, forging, making, manufacture, modelling, moulding, production.
antonym dismantling.

makings *n.* beginnings, capability, capacity, earnings, income, ingredients, materials, possibilities, potential, potentiality, proceeds, profits, promise, qualities, returns, revenue, takings.

maladjusted *adj.* alienated, confused, disturbed, estranged, hung-up, muddled, neurotic, unstable.
antonym well-adjusted.

maladministration *n.* blundering, bungling, corruption, dishonesty, incompetence, inefficiency, malfeasance, malpractice, malversation, misconduct, misfeasance, misgovernment, mismanagement, misrule, stupidity.

maladroit *adj.* awkward, bungling, cack-handed, clumsy, gauche, graceless, ham-fisted, ill-timed, inconsiderate, inelegant, inept, inexpert, insensitive, tactless, thoughtless, undiplomatic, unhandy, unskilful, untoward.
antonyms adroit, tactful.

malady *n.* affliction, ailment, breakdown, complaint, disease, disorder, illness, indisposition, infirmity, malaise, sickness.
antonym health.

malaise *n.* angst, anguish, anxiety, depression, discomfort, disquiet, distemper, doldrums, enervation, future shock, illness, indisposition, lassitude, melancholy, sickness, unease, uneasiness, weakness.
antonyms happiness, well-being.

malapropos *adj.* ill-timed, inapposite, inappropriate, inapt, inopportune, misapplied, tactless, uncalled-for, unseemly, unsuitable, untimely.

antonyms appropriate, tactful.
adv. inappositely, inappropriately, inaptly, inopportunely, tactlessly, unseasonably, unsuitably.
antonyms appropriately, tactfully.
malapropism *n.* Dogberryism, misapplication, misuse.
malcontent *adj.* belly-aching, disaffected, discontented, disgruntled, dissatisfied, dissentious, factious, ill-disposed, morose, rebellious, resentful, restive, unhappy, unsatisfied.
antonym contented.
n. agitator, belly-acher, complainer, grouch, grouser, grumbler, mischief-maker, moaner, rebel, troublemaker.
male *adj.* bull, cock, dog, manlike, manly, masculine, virile.
antonym female.
n. boy, bull, cock, daddy, dog, father, man.
antonym female.
malediction *n.* anathema, anathematisation, curse, damnation, damning, denunciation, execration, imprecation, malison.
antonyms blessing, praise.
malefactor *n.* convict, criminal, crook, culprit, delinquent, evil-doer, felon, law-breaker, miscreant, misfeasor, offender, outlaw, transgressor, villain, wrong-doer.
maleficent *adj.* baleful, deleterious, destructive, detrimental, evil, harmful, hurtful, injurious, malefactory, malefic, maleficial, malign, malignant, noxious, pernicious.
antonyms beneficent, harmless.
malevolence *n.* bitterness, hate, hatred, hostility, ill-will, malice, maliciousness, malignance, malignancy, malignity, rancour, spite, spitefulness, vengefulness, venom, viciousness, vindictiveness.
antonym benevolence.
malevolent *adj.* baleful, bitter, despiteful, evil-minded, hostile, ill-natured, malicious, malign, malignant, pernicious, rancorous, spiteful, vengeful, venomous, vicious, vindictive.
antonym benevolent.
malformation *n.* crookedness, deformity, distortion, irregularity, misshape, misshapenness, warp, warpedness, warping.
malformed *adj.* abnormal, bent, contorted, crooked, deformed, distorted, imperfect, irregular, misshapen, twisted, warped.
antonym perfect.
malfunction *n.* breakdown, defect, failure, fault, flaw, glitch, impairment.
v. break down, fail, go wrong, misbehave.
malice *n.* animosity, animus, bad blood, bitterness, despite, enmity, hate, hatred, ill-will, malevolence, maliciousness, malignity, rancour, spite, spitefulness, spleen, vengefulness, venom, viciousness, vindictiveness.
antonym kindness.
malicious *adj.* baleful, bitchy, bitter, catty, despiteful, evil-minded, hateful, ill-natured, injurious, malevolent, malignant, mis-

chievous, pernicious, rancorous, resentful, sham, spiteful, vengeful, venomous, vicious.
antonyms kind, thoughtful.
malign *adj.* bad, baleful, baneful, deleterious, destructive, evil, harmful, hostile, hurtful, injurious, malevolent, malignant, noxious, pernicious, venomous, vicious, wicked.
antonym benign.
v. abuse, badmouth, blacken the name of, calumniate, defame, denigrate, derogate, disparage, harm, injure, libel, revile, run down, slander, smear, traduce, vilify, vilipend.
antonym praise.
malignant *adj.* baleful, bitter, cancerous, cankered, dangerous, deadly, destructive, devilish, evil, fatal, harmful, hostile, hurtful, inimical, injurious, irremediable, malevolent, malicious, malign, pernicious, spiteful, uncontrollable, venomous, vicious, viperish, viperous, virulent.
antonyms harmless, kind.
malignity *n.* animosity, animus, bad blood, balefulness, bitterness, deadliness, destructiveness, gall, harmfulness, hate, hatred, hostility, hurtfulness, ill-will, malevolence, malice, maliciousness, perniciousness, rancour, spite, vengefulness, venom, viciousness, vindictiveness, virulence, wickedness.
antonyms harmlessness, kindness.
malinger *v.* dodge, loaf, shirk, skive, slack, swing the lead.
antonym toil.
malingerer *n.* dodger, lead-swinger, loafer, shirker, skiver, slacker.
antonym toiler.
malleable *adj.* adaptable, biddable, compliant, ductile, governable, impressionable, manageable, plastic, pliable, pliant, soft, tractable, tractile, workable.
antonyms intractable, unworkable.
malnutrition *n.* anorexia (nervosa), hunger, inanition, starvation, undernourishment.
antonym nourishment.
malodorous *adj.* evil-smelling, f(o)etid, foul-smelling, mephitic, miasmal, miasmatic, miasmatous, miasmic, miasmous, nauseating, niffy, noisome, offensive, putrid, rank, reeking, smelly, stinking.
antonym sweet-smelling.
malpractice *n.* abuse, dereliction, malversation, misbehaviour, misconduct; misdeed, mismanagement, negligence, offence, transgression.
maltreat *v.* abuse, bully, damage, harm, hurt, ill-treat, injure, mistreat, misuse, mousle.
antonym care for.
maltreatment *n.* abuse, bullying, harm, ill-treatment, ill-usage, ill-use, injury, mistreatment, misuse.
antonym care.
mammoth *adj.* Brobdingnag, Brobdingnagian, colossal, enormous, formidable, gargantuan, giant, gigantic, herculean, huge, immense, leviathan, massive, mighty, monumental, mountainous, prodigious, rounceval, stupen-

dous, titanic, vast.
antonym small.

man[1] *n.* adult, attendant, beau, bloke, body, boyfriend, cat, chap, chiel, employee, fellow, follower, gentleman, guy, hand, hireling, hombre, human, human being, husband, individual, lover, male, manservant, partner, person, retainer, servant, soldier, spouse, subject, subordinate, valet, vassal, worker, workman.
v. crew, fill, garrison, occupy, operate, people, staff, take charge of.

man in the street homme moyen sensuel, John Doe, Tom Dick or Harry.

man of fashion bean, buck, dandy, homme du monde, swell toff.

man of straw Jack-straw, nobody, straw man.

man[2] *n.* Homo sapiens, human race, humanity, humankind, humans, mankind, mortals, people.

manacle *v.* bind, chain, check, clap in irons, confine, constrain, curb, fetter, gyve, hamper, hamstring, handcuff, inhibit, put in chains, restrain, shackle, trammel.
antonym unshackle.

manacles *n.* bonds, bracelets, chains, fetters, gyves, handcuffs, irons, shackles.

manage *v.* accomplish, administer, arrange, bring about, bring off, carry on, command, concert, conduct, contrive, control, cope, cope with, deal with, direct, dominate, effect, engineer, fare, get along, get by, get on, govern, guide, handle, influence, make do, make out, manipulate, muddle through, operate, oversee, pilot, ply, preside over, rule, run, shift, solicit, stage-manage, steer, succeed, superintend, supervise, survive, train, use, wield.
antonym fail.

manageable *adj.* amenable, biddable, compliant, controllable, convenient, docile, easy, governable, handy, submissive, tamable, tractable, wieldable, wieldy.
antonym unmanageable.

management *n.* administration, board, bosses, care, charge, command, conduct, control, direction, directorate, directors, employers, executive, executives, governance, government, governors, guidance, handling, managers, manipulation, operation, oversight, rule, running, stewardry, superintendence, supervision, supervisors.

manager *n.* administrator, boss, comptroller, conductor, controller, director, executive, factor, gaffer, governor, head, impresario, organiser, overseer, proprietor, steward, superintendent, supervisor.

mandate *n.* authorisation, authority, bidding, charge, command, commission, decree, dedimus, directive, edict, fiat, firman, injunction, instruction, irade, order, precept, rescript, right, sanction, ukase, warrant.

mandatory *adj.* binding, compulsory, imperative, necessary, obligatory, required, requisite.

antonym optional.

manful *adj.* bold, brave, courageous, daring, determined, gallant, hardy, heroic, indomitable, intrepid, lion-hearted, manly, noble, noble-minded, powerful, resolute, stalwart, stout, stout-hearted, strong, unflinching, valiant, vigorous.
antonyms half-hearted, timid.

manfully *adv.* boldly, bravely, courageously, desperately, determinedly, gallantly, hard, heroically, intrepidly, nobly, pluckily, powerfully, resolutely, stalwartly, steadfastly, stoutly, strongly, unflinchingly, valiantly, vigorously.
antonyms half-heartedly, timidly.

mangle *v.* butcher, crush, cut, deform, destroy, disfigure, distort, hack, haggle, lacerate, maim, mar, maul, mutilate, rend, ruin, spoil, tear, twist, wreck.

mangy *adj.* dirty, grotty, mean, moth-eaten, ratty, scabby, scruffy, seedy, shabby, shoddy, squalid, tatty.
antonyms clean, neat, spruce.

manhandle *v.* carry, haul, heave, hump, knock about, lift, maltreat, manoeuvre, maul, mishandle, mistreat, misuse, paw, pull, push, rough up, shove, tug.

manhood *n.* adulthood, bravery, courage, determination, firmness, fortitude, hardihood, machismo, manfulness, manliness, masculinity, maturity, mettle, resolution, spirit, strength, valour, virility.
antonym timidity.

mania *n.* aberration, cacoethes, compulsion, craving, craze, craziness, delirium, dementia, derangement, desire, disorder, enthusiasm, fad, fetish, fixation, frenzy, infatuation, insanity, itch, lunacy, madness, obsession, partiality, passion, preoccupation, rage, thing.

maniac *n.* détraqué(e), enthusiast, fan, fanatic, fiend, freak, fruit-cake, loony, lunatic, madman, madwoman, nutcase, nutter, psycho, psychopath.

manic *adj.* berserk, crazed, crazy, demented, deranged, frenzied, insane, lunatic, mad, maniacal, psychotic, raving, screwy, unbalanced, unhinged, wild.
antonym sane.

manifest *adj.* apparent, clear, conspicuous, distinct, evident, glaring, noticeable, obvious, open, palpable, patent, plain, unconcealed, undeniable, unmistakable, visible.
antonym unclear.
v. demonstrate, display, establish, evidence, evince, exhibit, expose, illustrate, prove, reveal, set forth, show.
antonym hide.

manifestation *n.* appearance, demonstration, disclosure, display, exhibition, exposure, expression, indication, instance, mark, mass-meeting, materialisation, procession, reflex, revelation, show, sign, sit-in, symptom, token.

manifesto *n.* declaration, platform, policies,

policy, pronunciamento.

manifold *adj*. abundant, assorted, copious, diverse, diversified, kaleidoscopic, many, multifarious, multifold, multiple, multiplex, multiplied, multitudinous, numerous, varied, various.
antonym simple.

manipulate *v*. conduct, control, cook, direct, employ, engineer, gerrymander, guide, handle, influence, juggle with, manoeuvre, negotiate, operate, ply, shuffle, steer, use, wield, work.

mankind *n*. Everyman, fellow-men, Homo sapiens, human race, humanity, humankind, man, mandom, mortality, people.

manliness *n*. boldness, bravery, courage, fearlessness, firmness, hardihood, heroism, independence, intrepidity, machismo, manfulness, manhood, masculinity, mettle, resolution, stalwartness, stout-heartedness, valour, vigour, virility.
antonyms timidity, unmanliness.

manly *adj*. bold, brave, courageous, daring, dauntless, fearless, gallant, hardy, heroic, macho, male, manful, masculine, muscular, noble, powerful, resolute, robust, stalwart, stout-hearted, strapping, strong, sturdy, valiant, valorous, vigorous, virile.
antonyms timid, unmanly.

man-made *adj*. artificial, ersatz, imitation, manufactured, simulated, synthetic.
antonym natural.

manner *n*. address, air, appearance, approach, aspect, bearing, behaviour, brand, breed, category, character, comportment, conduct, custom, demeanour, deportment, description, fashion, form, genre, habit, kind, line, look, means, method, mien, mode, nature, practice, presence, procedure, process, routine, sort, style, tack, tenor, tone, type, usage, variety, way, wise, wont.

mannered *adj*. affected, artificial, euphuistic, posed, precious, pretentious, pseudo, put-on, stilted.
antonym natural.

mannerism *n*. characteristic, feature, foible, habit, idiosyncrasy, peculiarity, quirk, stiltedness, trait, trick.

mannerly *adj*. civil, civilised, courteous, decorous, deferential, formal, genteel, gentlemanly, gracious, ladylike, polished, polite, refined, respectful, well-behaved, well-bred, well-mannered.
antonym unmannerly.

manners *n*. bearing, behaviour, breeding, carriage, ceremony, comportment, conduct, courtesy, decorum, demeanour, deportment, etiquette, formalities, mores, polish, politeness, politesse, proprieties, protocol, p's and q's, refinement, social graces.
antonyms impoliteness, indecorousness.

mannish *adj*. butch, hoydenish, masculine, tomboyish, unfeminine, unladylike, unwomanly, viraginian, viraginous, viragoish, virilescent.

antonym womanish.

mannishness *n*. butchness, hoydenism, masculinity, unfemininity, unladylikeness, unwomanliness, virilescence, virilism.
antonym womanishness.

manoeuvre *n*. action, artifice, device, dodge, exercise, gambit, intrigue, machination, move, movement, operation, plan, plot, ploy, ruse, scheme, stratagem, subterfuge, tactic, trick.
v. contrive, deploy, devise, direct, drive, engineer, exercise, guide, handle, intrigue, jockey, machinate, manage, manipulate, move, navigate, negotiate, pilot, plan, plot, pull strings, scheme, steer, wangle.

man-of-all-work *n*. factotum, famulus, handyman, hobjobber, odd-jobman, orra man, servant.

manor *n*. barony, big house, château, hall, Hof, schloss, seat, vill.

manse *n*. glebe-house, vicarage.

manservant *n*. butler, gentleman's gentleman, retainer, valet, valet-de-chambre.

mansion *n*. abode, big house, castle, château, dwelling, habitation, hall, home, house, manor, manor-house, residence, schloss, seat, villa.

mantle *n*. blanket, canopy, cape, cloak, cloud, cover, covering, curtain, envelope, hood, mantlet, pall, pelerine, pelisse, screen, shawl, shroud, veil, wrap.

manual¹ *n*. bible, book of words, companion, enchi(e)ridion, guide, guide-book, handbook, instructions, primer, vade-mecum.

manual² *adj*. hand, hand-operated, human, physical.

manufacture *v*. assemble, build, churn out, compose, concoct, construct, cook up, create, devise, fabricate, forge, form, hatch, invent, make, make up, mass-produce, mould, process, produce, shape, think up, trump up, turn out.
n. assembly, construction, creation, fabrication, facture, formation, making, mass-production, production.

manufacturer *n*. builder, constructor, creator, fabricant, fabricator, factory-owner, industrialist, maker, mill-owner, producer.

manure *n*. compost, droppings, dung, fertiliser, guano, muck, ordure.

manuscript *n*. autograph, deed, document, handwriting, holograph, palimpsest, parchment, scroll, text, vellum.

many *adj*. abundant, copious, countless, divers, frequent, innumerable, manifold, multifarious, multifold, multitudinous, myriad, n, numerous, profuse, sundry, umpteen, umpty, varied, various, zillion.
antonym few.

map *n*. atlas, chart, graph, mappemond, plan, plot, street plan.

mar *v*. blemish, blight, blot, damage, deface, detract from, disfigure, foul up, harm, hurt, impair, injure, maim, mangle, mutilate, pollute, ruin, scar, spoil, stain, sully, taint,

tarnish, temper, vitiate, wreck.
antonym enhance.
maraud *v.* depredate, despoil, forage, foray, harry, loot, pillage, plunder, raid, ransack, ravage, reive, sack, spoliate.
marauder *n.* bandit, brigand, buccaneer, cateran, corsair, depredator, freebooter, mosstrooper, outlaw, pillager, pirate, plunderer, raider, ravager, reiver, robber, spoliater.
march *v.* countermarch, file, flounce, goosestep, pace, parade, slog, stalk, stride, strut, stump, tramp, tread, walk.
n. advance, career, demo, demonstration, development, evolution, footslog, gait, hike, pace, parade, passage, procession, progress, progression, step, stride, tramp, trek, walk.
margin *n.* allowance, border, bound, boundary, brim, brink, compass, confine, edge, extra, latitude, leeway, limit, marge, perimeter, periphery, play, rand, rim, room, scope, side, skirt, space, surplus, verge.
antonyms centre, core.
marginal *adj.* bordering, borderline, doubtful, infinitesimal, insignificant, low, minimal, minor, negligible, peripheral, slight, small.
antonyms central, core.
marijuana *n.* bhang, cannabis, charas (churrus), dope, ganja, grass, greens, hash, hashish, hemp, kif, mary jane, pot, tea, weed.
marina *n.* dock, harbour, mooring, port, yacht station.
marine *adj.* maritime, nautical, naval, oceangoing, oceanic, pelagic, salt-water, sea, seafaring, sea-going, thalassian, thalassic.
n. galoot, leather-neck, sailor.
mariner *n.* bluejacket, deckhand, hand, Jack Tar, matelot, matlo(w), navigator, sailor, salt, sea-dog, seafarer, seaman, tar.
marital *adj.* conjugal, connubial, hymeneal, hymenean, married, matrimonial, nuptial, sponsal, spousal, wedded.
maritime *adj.* coastal, littoral, marine, nautical, naval, oceanic, pelagic, sea, seafaring, seaside, thalassian, thalassic.
mark *n.* aim, badge, blaze, blemish, blot, blotch, brand, bruise, character, characteristic, consequence, criterion, dent, device, dignity, distinction, earmark, emblem, eminence, end, evidence, fame, feature, fingermark, footmark, footprint, goal, hallmark, importance, impression, incision, index, indication, influence, label, level, line, lineament, marque, measure, nick, norm, notability, note, noteworthiness, notice, object, objective, pock, prestige, print, proof, purpose, quality, regard, scar, scratch, seal, sign, smudge, splotch, spot, stain, stamp, standard, standing, streak, symbol, symptom, target, token, trace, track, trail, vestige, yardstick.
v. appraise, assess, attend, betoken, blemish, blot, blotch, brand, bruise, characterise, correct, denote, dent, distinguish, evaluate, evince, exemplify, grade, hearken, heed, identify, illustrate, impress, imprint, label, list, listen, mind, nick, note, notice, observe,

print, regard, remark, scar, scratch, show, smudge, splotch, stain, stamp, streak, take to heart, traumatise, watch.
marked *adj.* apparent, clear, considerable, conspicuous, decided, distinct, doomed, emphatic, evident, glaring, indicated, manifest, notable, noted, noticeable, obvious, outstanding, patent, prominent, pronounced, remarkable, salient, signal, striking, strong, suspected, watched.
antonyms slight, unnoticeable.
market *n.* bazaar, demand, fair, market-place, mart, need, outlet, shop, souk.
v. hawk, peddle, retail, sell, vend.
antonym buy.
marketable *adj.* in demand, merchantable, salable, sellable, sought after, vendible, wanted.
antonym unsalable.
marksman *n.* bersagliere, crack shot, dead shot, sharpshooter, sniper.
maroon *v.* abandon, cast away, desert, isolate, leave, put ashore, strand.
antonym rescue.
marriage *n.* alliance, amalgamation, association, confederation, coupling, espousal, link, match, matrimony, matronage, matronhood, merger, nuptials, spousage, spousals, union, wedding, wedlock.
antonym divorce.
married *adj.* conjugal, connubial, hitched, husbandly, joined, marital, matrimonial, nuptial, spliced, spousal, united, wed, wedded, wifely, wived, yoked.
antonyms divorced, single.
marrow *n.* core, cream, essence, gist, heart, kernel, nub, pith, quick, quintessence, soul, spirit, stuff, substance.
marry *v.* ally, bond, espouse, get hitched, get spliced, join, jump the broomstick, knit, link, match, merge, splice, tie, tie the knot, unify, unite, wed, wive, yoke.
antonyms divorce, separate.
marsh *n.* bayou, bog, carr, fen, maremma, marshland, morass, moss, muskeg, quagmire, slough, slump, soak, swale, swamp, wetland.
marshal *v.* align, arrange, array, assemble, collect, conduct, convoy, deploy, dispose, draw up, escort, gather, group, guide, lead, line up, muster, order, organise, rank, shepherd, take, usher.
marshy *adj.* boggy, fennish, fenny, miry, paludal, paludinal, paludine, paludinous, quaggy, slumpy, spongy, swampy, waterlogged, wet.
antonym solid.
martial *adj.* bellicose, belligerent, brave, combative, heroic, militant, military, soldierly, warlike.
antonym pacific.
martinet *n.* disciplinarian, formalist, slavedriver, stickler, tyrant.
martyrdom *n.* agony, anguish, death, excruciation, ordeal, persecution, suffering, torment, torture, witness.

marvel *n.* genius, miracle, non(e)such, phenomenon, portent, prodigy, sensation, spectacle, whiz, wonder.

v. gape, gaze, goggle, wonder.

marvellous *adj.* amazing, astonishing, astounding, beyond belief, breathtaking, épatant, excellent, extraordinary, fabulous, fantastic, glorious, great, implausible, improbable, incredible, magnificent, miraculous, mirific(al), phenomenal, prodigious, remarkable, sensational, singular, smashing, spectacular, splendid, stupendous, super, superb, surprising, terrific, unbelievable, unlikely, wonderful, wondrous.

antonyms ordinary, plausible, run-of-the-mill.

masculine *adj.* bold, brave, butch, gallant, hardy, macho, male, manlike, manly, mannish, muscular, powerful, red-blooded, resolute, robust, stout-hearted, strapping, strong, tomboyish, vigorous, virile.

antonym feminine.

masculinity *n.* butchness, hoydenism, maleness, manhood, manliness, mannishness, potency, sexuality, tomboyishness, unladylikeness, unwomanliness, virileness, virilescence, virilism, virility, Yang.

antonym femininity.

mash *v.* beat, champ, comminute, crush, grind, pound, pulverise, pummel, smash, triturate.

mask *n.* blind, camouflage, cloak, concealment, cover, cover-up, disguise, domino, façade, false face, front, guise, pretence, screen, semblance, show, veil, veneer, visard-mask, visor, vizard.

v. camouflage, cloak, conceal, cover, disguise, hide, obscure, screen, shield, veil.

antonym uncover.

masked *adj.* camouflaged, cloaked, concealed, covered, disguised, screened, shielded, shrouded, visored, vizarded.

antonyms uncovered, unshielded.

masquerade *n.* cloak, costume, costume ball, counterfeit, cover, cover-up, deception, disguise, dissimulation, domino, fancy dress party, front, guise, imposture, mask, masked ball, masque, mummery, pose, pretence, put-on, revel, screen, subterfuge.

v. disguise, dissemble, dissimulate, impersonate, mask, pass oneself off, play, pose, pretend, profess.

mass[1] *n.* accumulation, aggregate, aggregation, assemblage, band, batch, block, body, bulk, bunch, chunk, collection, combination, concretion, congeries, conglomeration, crowd, dimension, entirety, extensity, group, heap, horde, host, hunk, lion's share, load, lot, lump, magnitude, majority, mob, number, piece, pile, preponderance, quantity, size, stack, sum, sum total, throng, totality, troop, welter, whole.

adj. across-the-board, blanket, comprehensive, extensive, general, indiscriminate, large-scale, pandemic, popular, sweeping, wholesale, widespread.

antonym limited.

v. assemble, cluster, collect, congregate, crowd, for(e)gather, gather, muster, rally.

antonym separate.

mass[2] *n.* communion, eucharist, holy communion, Lord's Supper, Lord's Table, nagmaal.

massacre *n.* annihilation, blood bath, butchery, carnage, decimation, extermination, holocaust, killing, murder, slaughter.

v. annihilate, butcher, decimate, exterminate, kill, mow down, murder, slaughter, slay, wipe out.

massage *n.* effleurage, kneading, malaxage, malaxation, manipulation, petrissage, rubbing, rub-down.

v. knead, manipulate, rub, rub down.

mass-book *n.* breviary, missal, prayer-book, service-book.

massive *adj.* big, bulky, colossal, cyclopean, enormous, extensive, gargantuan, gigantic, great, heavy, hefty, huge, hulking, immense, imposing, impressive, jumbo, mammoth, monster, monstrous, monumental, ponderous, rounceval, solid, substantial, titanic, vast, weighty, whacking, whopping.

antonyms slight, small.

master *n.* ace, adept, baas, boss, bwana, captain, chief, commander, controller, dab hand, deacon, director, doyen, employer, expert, genius, governor, guide, guru, head, Herr, instructor, lord, maestro, manager, overlord, overseer, owner, past master, pedagogue, preceptor, principal, pro, ruler, schoolmaster, skipper, superintendent, swami, teacher, tutor, virtuoso, wizard.

antonyms amateur, learner, pupil, servant, slave.

adj. ace, adept, chief, controlling, crack, expert, foremost, grand, great, leading, main, masterly, predominant, prime, principal, proficient, skilful, skilled.

antonyms copy, subordinate, unskilled.

v. acquire, bridle, check, command, conquer, control, curb, defeat, direct, dominate, get the hang of, govern, grasp, learn, manage, overcome, quash, quell, regulate, rule, subdue, subjugate, suppress, tame, triumph over, vanquish.

master race Herrenvolk.

masterful *adj.* adept, adroit, arrogant, authoritative, autocratic, bossy, clever, consummate, crack, deft, despotic, dexterous, dictatorial, domineering, excellent, expert, exquisite, fine, finished, first-rate, high-handed, imperious, magisterial, masterly, overbearing, overweening, peremptory, powerful, professional, self-willed, skilful, skilled, superior, superlative, supreme, tyrannical.

antonyms clumsy, humble, unskilful.

masterly *adj.* adept, adroit, clever, consummate, crack, dexterous, excellent, expert, exquisite, fine, finished, first-rate, magistral, masterful, skilful, skilled, superb, superior, superlative, supreme.

antonyms clumsy, poor, unskilled.

mastermind *v.* conceive, design, devise, direct,

dream up, forge, frame, hatch, manage, organise, originate, plan.

n. architect, authority, brain(s), creator, director, engineer, genius, intellect, manager, organiser, originator, planner, prime mover, virtuoso.

masterpiece *n.* chef d'oeuvre, classic, jewel, magnum opus, master-work, museum-piece, pièce de résistance, tour de force.

mastery *n.* ability, acquirement, advantage, ascendancy, attainment, authority, cleverness, command, comprehension, conquest, control, conversancy, deftness, dexterity, domination, dominion, expertise, familiarity, finesse, grasp, know-how, knowledge, preeminence, proficiency, prowess, rule, skill, superiority, supremacy, sway, triumph, understanding, upper hand, victory, virtuosity, whip-hand.

antonyms clumsiness, unfamiliarity.

masticate *v.* champ, chew, crunch, eat, knead, manducate, munch, ruminate.

masturbate *v.* frig, jerk off, play with oneself, toss (it) off, wank.

masturbation *n.* auto-eroticism, frig, frigging, frottage, onanism, self-abuse, self-stimulation, tribadism, tribady, wanking.

mat *n.* carpet, doormat, drugget, felt, rug, under-felt, underlay.

match¹ *n.* bout, competition, contest, game, main, test, trial, venue.

v. compete, contend, oppose, pit against, rival, vie.

match² *n.* affiliation, alliance, combination, companion, complement, copy, counterpart, couple, dead ringer, double, duet, duplicate, equal, equivalent, fellow, like, look-alike, marriage, mate, pair, pairing, parallel, partnership, peer, replica, ringer, rival, spit, spitting image, tally, twin, union.

v. accompany, accord, adapt, agree, ally, blend, combine, compare, co-ordinate, correspond, couple, emulate, equal, fit, gee, go together, go with, harmonise, join, link, marry, mate, measure up to, pair, relate, rival, suit, tally, team, tone with, unite, yoke.

antonyms clash, separate.

match³ *n.* Congreve-match, fuse, fusee, light, lucifer, lucifer-match, safety match, spill, taper, vesta, vesuvian.

matching *adj.* analogous, comparable, co-ordinating, corresponding, double, duplicate, equal, equivalent, homochromous, identical, like, parallel, pared, same, similar, toning, twin.

antonyms clashing, different.

matchless *adj.* consummate, excellent, exquisite, incomparable, inimitable, nonpareil, peerless, perfect, superlative, supreme, unequalled, unique, unmatched, unparalleled, unrivalled, unsurpassed.

antonyms commonplace, poor.

mate *n.* assistant, associate, better half, buddy, china, chum, colleague, companion, compeer, comrade, confidant(e), co-worker, crony, double, fellow, fellow-worker, fere, friend, gossip, helper, helpmate, helpmeet, husband, match, pal, partner, repository, side-kick, spouse, subordinate, twin, wife.

v. breed, copulate, couple, join, marry, match, pair, wed, yoke.

material *n.* body, cloth, constituents, data, element, evidence, fabric, facts, information, literature, matter, notes, stuff, substance, textile, work.

adj. applicable, apposite, apropos, bodily, central, concrete, consequential, corporeal, essential, fleshly, germane, grave, gross, hylic, important, indispensable, key, meaningful, momentous, non-spiritual, palpable, pertinent, physical, relevant, serious, significant, substantial, tangible, vital, weighty, worldly.

antonyms ethereal, immaterial.

materialise *v.* appear, arise, happen, occur, take shape, turn up.

antonym disappear.

materialism *n.* hylicism, hylism, mammon, mammonism, money-grubbing.

materialist *n.* hylicist, hylist, mammonite, money-grubber, mug-hunter, pot-hunter.

materialistic *adj.* banausic, Kensington, mammonist, mammonistic, mercenary, money-grubbing.

antonym spiritual.

materially *adv.* basically, considerably, essentially, fundamentally, gravely, greatly, much, palpably, physically, seriously, significantly, substantially, tangibly.

antonym insignificantly.

maternal *adj.* loving, matronal, motherly, protective.

antonym paternal.

mating *n.* breeding, coition, copulating, copulation, coupling, fusing, jointing, matching, pangamy, service, sexual intercourse, tupping, twinning, uniting.

matrimonial *adj.* conjugal, connubial, marital, marriage, married, nuptial, sponsal, spousal, wedded, wedding.

matrimony *n.* espousals, marriage, nuptials, sponsalia, spousage, spousal, wedlock.

matron *n.* dame, dowager, matriarch.

matted *adj.* knotted, tangled, tangly, tousled, uncombed.

antonyms tidy, untangled.

matter¹ *n.* affair, amount, argument, body, business, complication, concern, consequence, context, difficulty, distress, episode, event, hyle, import, importance, incident, issue, material, moment, note, occurrence, problem, proceeding, purport, quantity, question, sense, significance, situation, stuff, subject, substance, sum, text, thesis, thing, topic, transaction, trouble, upset, weight, worry.

antonym insignificance.

v. count, make a difference, mean something, signify.

matter² *n.* discharge, purulence, pus, secretion,

suppuration.

v. discharge, secrete.

matter-of-fact *adj.* deadpan, direct, down-to-earth, dry, dull, emotionless, flat, lifeless, literal, mundane, plain, prosaic, sober, unembellished, unimaginative, unsentimental, unvarnished.

antonym emotional.

mattress *n.* futon, pallet, palliasse.

mature *adj.* adult, complete, due, fit, full-blown, full-grown, fully fledged, grown, grown-up, matured, mellow, nubile, perfect, perfected, prepared, ready, ripe, ripened, seasoned, well-thought-out.

antonym immature.

v. accrue, age, bloom, come of age, develop, fall due, grow up, maturate, mellow, perfect, ripen, season.

maturity *n.* adulthood, completion, experience, fullness, majority, manhood, maturation, matureness, nubility, perfection, readiness, ripeness, wisdon, womanhood.

antonym immaturity.

maudlin *adj.* drunk, emotional, fuddled, half-drunk, icky, lachrymose, mawkish, mushy, sentimental, sickly, slushy, soppy, tearful, tipsy, weepy.

antonym matter-of-fact.

maul *v.* abuse, batter, beat, beat up, claw, ill-treat, knock about, lacerate, maltreat, mangle, manhandle, molest, paw, pummel, rough up, thrash.

maunder *v.* babble, blather, blether, chatter, drivel, gabble, grumble, mutter, prattle, rabbit, ramble, witter.

maw *n.* abyss, chasm, craw, crop, gulf, gullet, jaws, mouth, stomach, throat.

mawkish *adj.* disgusting, emotional, feeble, flat, foul, gushy, icky, insipid, jejune, loathsome, maudlin, mushy, nauseous, offensive, schmaltzy, sentimental, sickly, slushy, soppy, squeamish, stale, vapid.

antonyms matter-of-fact, pleasant.

maxim *n.* adage, aphorism, apophthegm, axiom, byword, epigram, gnome, mot, motto, precept, proverb, rule, saw, saying, sentence.

maximum *adj.* biggest, greatest, highest, largest, maximal, most, paramount, supreme, topmost, utmost.

antonym minimum.

n. apogee, ceiling, crest, extremity, height, most, ne plus ultra, peak, pinnacle, summit, top (point), upper limit, utmost, zenith.

antonym mimimum.

maybe *adv.* haply, happen, mayhap, peradventure, perchance, perhaps, possibly.

antonym definitely.

maze *n.* confusion, convolutions, imbroglio, intricacy, labyrinth, meander, mesh, mizmaze, puzzle, snarl, tangle, web.

meadow *n.* field, haugh, holm, inch, lea, ley, mead, pasture.

meagre *adj.* barren, bony, deficient, emaciated, exiguous, gaunt, hungry, inadequate, infertile, insubstantial, lank, lean, little, negligible,

paltry, penurious, poor, puny, scanty, scraggy, scrawny, scrimpy, short, skimpy, skinny, slender, slight, small, spare, sparse, starved, thin, underfed, unfruitful, unproductive, weak.

antonyms fertile, substantial.

meal[1] *n.* banquet, barbecue, beanfeast, beano, blow-out, breakfast, brunch, chota-hazri, collation, déjeuner, déjeuner à la fourchette, dinner, feast, lunch, luncheon, nosh, nosh-up, petit déjeuner, picnic, repast, scoff, snack, supper, tea, tiffin(g), tuck-in.

meal[2] *n.* farina, flour, grits, oatmeal, powder.

mealy-mouthed *adj.* equivocal, euphemistic, flattering, glib, hestitant, indirect, mincing, overdelicate, over-squeamish, plausible, prim, reticent, smooth-tongued.

mean[1] *adj.* abject, bad-tempered, base, base-born, beggarly, callous, cheese-paring, churlish, close, close-fisted, close-handed, common, contemptible, degraded, despicable, disagreeable, disgraceful, dishonourable, down-at-heel, excellent, fast-handed, good, great, hard-hearted, hostile, humble, ignoble, illiberal, inconsiderable, inferior, insignificant, low, low-born, lowly, malicious, malignant, mean-spirited, menial, mercenary, mingy, miserable, miserly, modest, narrow-minded, nasty, near, niggardly, obscure, one-horse, ordinary, paltry, parsimonious, penny-pinching, penurious, petty, plebeian, poor, proletarian, pusillanimous, rude, run-down, scrub, scurvy, seedy, selfish, servile, shabby, shameful, skilful, slink, small-minded, snippy, sordid, sour, squalid, stingy, tawdry, tight, tight-fisted, undistinguished, unfriendly, ungenerous, ungiving, unhandsome, unpleasant, vicious, vile, vulgar, wretched.

antonyms generous, kind, noble, superior.

mean[2] *v.* adumbrate, aim, aspire, augur, betoken, cause, connote, contemplate, convey, denote, design, desire, destine, drive at, engender, entail, express, fate, fit, foreshadow, foretell, get at, give rise to, herald, hint, imply, indicate, insinuate, intend, involve, lead to, make, match, necessitate, omen, plan, portend, predestine, preordain, presage, produce, promise, propose, purport, purpose, represent, result in, say, set out, signify, spell, stand for, suggest, suit, symbolise, want, wish.

mean[3] *adj.* average, half-way, intermediate, medial, median, medium, middle, middling, moderate, normal, standard.

antonym extreme.

n. aurea mediocritas, average, balance, compromise, golden mean, happy medium, median, middle, middle course, middle way, mid-point, norm, via media.

antonym extreme.

meander *v.* amble, curve, ramble, snake, stravaig, stray, stroll, turn, twist, wander, wind, zigzag.

meandering *adj.* circuitous, convoluted,

indirect, meandrous, roundabout, serpentine, sinuous, snaking, tortuous, twisting, wandering, winding.
antonym straight.

meaning *n.* aim, connotation, construction, denotation, design, drift, end, explanation, force, gist, goal, idea, implication, import, intention, interpretation, matter, message, object, plan, point, purport, purpose, sense, significance, signification, substance, thrust, trend, upshot, validity, value, worth.
adj. eloquent, expressive, important, material, meaningful, pointed, pregnant, purposeful, relevant, serious, significant, speaking, suggestive, useful, valid, warning, worthwhile.

meaningless *adj.* absurd, aimless, empty, expressionless, futile, hollow, inane, inconsequential, insignificant, insubstantial, nonsense, nonsensical, nugatory, pointless, purposeless, senseless, trifling, trivial, unmeaning, useless, vain, valueless, worthless.
antonym meaningful.

meanness *n.* abjectness, baseness, beggarliness, churlishness, close-fistedness, close-handedness, contemptibleness, degradation, despicableness, disagreeableness, disgracefulness, dishonourableness, humbleness, illiberality, insignificance, lowliness, malice, maliciousness, malignity, mean-spiritedness, minginess, miserliness, narrow-mindedness, nastiness, niggardliness, obscurity, paltriness, parsimony, penuriousness, pettiness, poorness, pusillanimity, rudeness, scurviness, seediness, selfishness, servility, shabbiness, shamefulness, sordidness, sourness, squalor, stinginess, tawdriness, tight-fistedness, unfriendliness, unpleasantness, viciousness, vileness, wretchedness.
antonyms generosity, kindness, nobility, superiority.

means *n.* ability, affluence, agency, avenue, capacity, capital, channel, course, estate, expedient, fortune, funds, income, instrument, machinery, measure, medium, method, mode, money, process, property, resources, riches, substance, way, wealth, wherewithal.

meantime, meanwhile *advs.* at the same time, concurrently, en attendant, for now, for the moment, in the interim, in the interval, in the meantime, in the meanwhile, simultaneously.

measly *adj.* beggarly, contemptible, meagre, mean, mingy, miserable, miserly, niggardly, paltry, pathetic, petty, piddling, pitiful, poor, puny, scanty, skimpy, stingy, trivial, ungenerous.

measurable *adj.* appreciable, assessable, computable, determinable, fathomable, gaugeable, material, mensurable, perceptible, quantifiable, quantitative, significant.
antonym measureless.

measure *n.* act, action, allotment, allowance, amount, amplitude, beat, bill, bounds, cadence, capacity, control, course, criterion, deed, degree, démarche, enactment, exam-

ple, expedient, extent, foot, gauge, jigger, law, limit, limitation, magnitude, manoeuvre, means, method, metre, model, moderation, norm, portion, procedure, proceeding, proportion, quantity, quota, range, ration, reach, resolution, restraint, rhythm, rule, scale, scope, share, size, standard, statute, step, system, test, touchstone, verse, yardstick.
v. admeasure, appraise, assess, calculate, calibrate, choose, compute, determine, estimate, evaluate, fathom, gauge, judge, mark out, measure off, measure out, plumb, quantify, rate, size, sound, step, survey, value, weigh.

measure off circumscribe, delimit, demarcate, determine, fix, lay down, lay off, limit, mark out, measure (out), pace out.

measure out allot, apportion, assign, deal out, dispense, distribute, divide, dole out, hand out, issue, measure (off), mete out, parcel out, pour out, proportion, share out.

measure up do, fill the bill, make the grade, pass muster, shape up, suffice.

measure up to compare with, equal, match, meet, rival, touch.

measured *adj.* calculated, considered, constant, deliberate, dignified, even, exact, gauged, grave, leisurely, metronomic, modulated, planned, precise, predetermined, premeditated, quantified, reasoned, regular, regulated, sedate, slow, sober, solemn, standard, stately, steady, studied, unhurried, uniform, verified, well-thought-out.

measureless *adj.* bottomless, boundless, endless, immeasurable, immense, incalculable, inestimable, infinite, innumerable, limitless, unbounded, vast.
antonym measurable.

measurement *n.* amount, amplitude, appraisal, appreciation, area, assessment, calculation, calibration, capacity, computation, depth, dimension, estimation, evaluation, extent, gauging, height, judgement, length, magnitude, mensuration, metage, size, survey, valuation, volume, weight, width.

meat[1] *n.* aliment, charqui, cheer, chow, comestibles, eats, fare, flesh, food, grub, jerk, nourishment, nutriment, provender, provisions, rations, subsistence, sustenance, viands, victuals.

meat[2] *n.* core, crux, essence, fundamentals, gist, heart, kernel, marrow, nub, nucleus, pith, point, substance.

meaty *adj.* beefy, brawny, burly, fleshy, hearty, heavy, husky, interesting, matterful, meaningful, muscular, nourishing, pithy, profound, rich, significant, solid, strapping, sturdy, substantial.

mechanic *n.* artificer, engineer, machinist, mechanician, operative, operator, opificer, repairman, technician.

mechanical *adj.* automated, automatic, cold, cursory, dead, dull, emotionless, habitual, impersonal, instinctive, involuntary, lacklustre, lifeless, machine-driven, machine-like, matter-of-fact, perfunctory, routine, spiritless, unanimated, unconscious, unfeeling, unthinking.

mechanism *n.* action, agency, apparatus, appliance, components, contrivance, device, execution, functioning, gadgetry, gears, innards, instrument, machine, machinery, means, medium, method, motor, operation, performance, procedure, process, structure, system, technique, tool, workings, works.

medal *n.* award, decoration, gong, honour, medalet, medallion, prize, reward, trophy.

meddle *v.* interfere, interlope, interpose, intervene, intrude, mell, pry, put one's oar in, tamper.

meddlesome *adj.* interfering, intruding, intrusive, meddling, mischievous, officious, prying, ultracrepidarian.

medi(a)eval *adj.* antediluvian, antiquated, antique, archaic, old-fashioned, old-world, outmoded, primitive, unenlightened.

mediate *v.* arbitrate, conciliate, incubate, intercede, interpose, intervene, moderate, negotiate, reconcile, referee, resolve, settle, step in, umpire.

mediation *n.* arbitration, conciliation, good offices, intercession, interposition, intervention, negotiation, parley, reconciliation.

mediator *n.* advocate, arbiter, arbitrator, go-between, honest broker, interceder, intermediary, interventor, judge, middleman, moderator, negotiator, ombudsman, ombudswoman, peacemaker, referee, umpire.

medical *adj.* Hippocratic, iatric(al), medicinal.

medical practitioner allopath, consultant, doc, doctor, feldsher, GP, healer, homeopath, intern, medico, MO, physician, sawbones, surgeon.

medicinal *adj.* adjuvant, analeptic, curative, healing, homeopathic, medical, medicamental, medicamentary, remedial, restorative, roborant, sanatory, therapeutic.

medicine[1] *n.* cure, diapente, diatessaron, drug, electuary, elixir, febrifuge, Galenical, materia medica, medicament, medication, nostrum, panacea, physic, remedy, specific, tincture, vermifuge.

medicine[2] *n.* acupuncture, allopathy, homeopathy, leech-craft, surgery, therapeutics.

medicine-man *n.* angek(k)ok, mystery-man, shaman, witch-doctor.

mediocre *adj.* amateurish, average, commonplace, indifferent, inferior, insignificant, mean, medium, middling, ordinary, passable, pedestrian, run-of-the-mill, second-rate, soso, undistinguished, unexceptional, uninspired.

antonyms excellent, exceptional, extraordinary.

mediocrity *n.* amateurishness, cipher, indifference, inferiority, insignificance, lightweight, nobody, nonentity, ordinariness, poorness, second-rater, unimportance.

meditate *v.* be in a brown study, cerebrate,

cogitate, consider, contemplate, deliberate, devise, excogitate, intend, mull over, muse, plan, ponder, purpose, reflect, ruminate, scheme, speculate, study, think, think over.

meditation *n.* brown study, cerebration, cogitation, concentration, contemplation, excogitation, musing, pondering, reflection, reverie, ruminating, rumination, speculation, study, thought.

meditative *adj.* cogitative, contemplative, deliberative, museful, pensive, reflective, ruminant, ruminative, studious, thoughtful.

medium[1] *adj.* average, fair, intermediate, mean, medial, median, mediocre, middle, middling, midway, standard.

n. aurea mediocritas, average, centre, compromise, golden mean, happy medium, mean, middle, middle ground, midpoint, via media, way.

medium[2] *n.* agency, avenue, base, channel, excipient, form, instrument, instrumentality, means, mode, organ, vehicle, way.

medium[3] *n.* clairvoyant, psychic, spiritist, spiritualist.

medium[4] *n.* ambience, atmosphere, circumstances, conditions, element, environment, habitat, influences, milieu, setting, surroundings.

medley *n.* assortment, collection, confusion, conglomeration, farrago, galimatias, gallimaufry, hodge-podge, hotchpotch, jumble, macaroni, macédoine, mélange, minglemangle, miscellany, mishmash, mixture, olio, olla-podrida, omnium-gatherum, pastiche, patchwork, pot-pourri, quodlibet, salmagundi.

meek *adj.* acquiescent, compliant, deferential, docile, forbearing, gentle, humble, longsuffering, mild, modest, patient, peaceful, resigned, slavish, soft, spineless, spiritless, subdued, submissive, tame, timid, unambitious, unassuming, unpretentious, unresisting, weak, yielding.

antonyms arrogant, rebellious.

meekness *n.* acquiescence, compliance, deference, docility, forbearance, gentleness, humbleness, humility, long-suffering, lowliness, mildness, modesty, patience, peacefulness, resignation, self-abasement, selfdisparagement, self-effacement, softness, spinelessness, spiritlessness, submission, submissiveness, tameness, timidity, weakness.

antonym arrogance.

meet *v.* abut, adjoin, answer, assemble, bear, bump into, chance on, collect, come across, come together, comply, confront, congregate, connect, contact, convene, converge, cross, discharge, encounter, endure, equal, experience, face, find, forgather, fulfil, gather, go through, gratify, handle, happen on, intersect, join, link up, match, measure up to, muster, perform, rally, rencontre, rencounter, run across, run into, satisfy, suffer, touch, undergo, unite.

meeting *n.* abutment, assembly, assignation,

audience, company, conclave, concourse, conference, confluence, confrontation, congregation, conjunction, consult, conventicle, convention, convergence, convocation, crossing, encounter, engagement, forum, gathering, gemot, get-together, gorsedd, indaba, intersection, introduction, junction, meet, moot, rally, rencontre, rencounter, rendezvous, reunion, session, synod, tryst, union, watersmeet.

meeting-point n. confluence, convergence, convergency, crossroads, interface, intersection, junction, watersmeet.

megalomania n. conceitedness, delusions of grandeur, folie de grandeur, overestimation, self-importance.

melancholy adj. blue, dejected, depressed, despondent, disconsolate, dismal, dispirited, doleful, down, down in the dumps, down in the mouth, downcast, down-hearted, gloomy, glum, heavy-hearted, hipped, joyless, low, low-spirited, lugubrious, melancholic, miserable, moody, mournful, pensieroso, pensive, sad, sombre, sorrowful, splenific, unhappy, woebegone, woeful.
antonyms cheerful, gay, happy, joyful.
n. blues, dejection, depression, despondency, dole, dolour, gloom, gloominess, glumness, low spirits, pensiveness, sadness, sorrow, unhappiness, woe.
antonym exhilaration.

mélange n. assortment, confusion, farrago, galimatias, gallimaufry, hash, hodge-podge, hotch-potch, jumble, medley, mingle-mangle, miscellany, mishmash, mix, mixed bag, mixture, olio, omnium-gatherum, pastiche, potpourri, salmagundi.

mêlée n. affray, battle royal, brawl, broil, dogfight, donnybrook, fight, fracas, fray, free-for-all, ruckus, ruction, rumpus, scrimmage, scrum, scuffle, set-to, stramash, tussle.

mellifluous adj. canorous, dulcet, euphonious, honeyed, mellow, silvery, smooth, soft, soothing, sweet, sweet-sounding, tuneful.
antonyms discordant, grating, harsh.

mellow adj. cheerful, cordial, delicate, dulcet, elevated, expansive, full, full-flavoured, genial, happy, jolly, jovial, juicy, mature, mellifluous, melodious, merry, perfect, placid, relaxed, rich, ripe, rounded, serene, smooth, soft, sweet, tipsy, tranquil, well-matured.
antonyms immature, unripe.
v. improve, mature, perfect, ripen, season, soften, sweeten, temper.

melodious adj. arioso, canorous, concordant, dulcet, euphonious, harmonious, melodic, musical, silvery, sonorous, sweet-sounding, tuneful.
antonyms discordant, grating, harsh.

melodramatic adj. blood-and-thunder, exaggerated, hammy, histrionic, overdone, overdramatic, overemotional, overwrought, sensational, stagy, theatrical.

melody n. air, aria, arietta, arriette, euphony,

harmony, melisma, melodiousness, music, musicality, refrain, song, strain, theme, tune, tunefulness.

melt v. deliquesce, diffuse, disarm, dissolve, flux, fuse, liquate, liquefy, mollify, relax, soften, thaw, touch, uncongeal, unfreeze.
antonyms freeze, harden, solidify.

melt away dematerialise, disappear, disperse, dissolve, evanesce, evaporate, fade, vanish.

member n. appendage, arm, associate, component, constituent, element, extremity, fellow, initiate, leg, limb, organ, part, portion, representative.

membership n. adherence, allegiance, associates, body, enrolment, fellows, fellowship, members, participation.

membrane n. diaphragm, fell, film, hymen, integument, partition, septum, skin, tissue, veil, velum.

memento n. keepsake, memorial, record, relic, remembrance, reminder, souvenir, token, trophy.

memoir n. account, biography, essay, journal, life, monograph, narrative, record, register, report.

memoirs n. annals, autobiography, chronicles, confessions, diary, experiences, journals, life, life story, memories, personalia, recollections, records, reminiscences, transactions.

memorable adj. catchy, celebrated, distinguished, extraordinary, famous, historic, illustrious, important, impressive, marvellous, momentous, notable, noteworthy, outstanding, remarkable, signal, significant, striking, unforgettable.
antonym forgettable.

memorial n. cairn, cromlech, dolmen, martyry, mausoleum, memento, menhir, monument, plaque, record, remembrance, souvenir, stone.
adj. celebratory, commemorative, monumental.

memorise v. con, learn, learn by heart, learn by rote, learn off, mug up, swot up.
antonym forget.

memory n. celebrity, commemoration, fame, glory, honour, memorial, name, recall, recollection, remembrance, reminiscence, renown, reputation, repute, retention.
antonym forgetfulness.

menace v. alarm, browbeat, bully, comminate, cow, frighten, impend, intimidate, loom, lour (lower), terrorise, threaten.
n. annoyance, commination, danger, hazard, intimidation, jeopardy, nuisance, peril, pest, plague, scare, terror, threat, troublemaker, warning.

menacing adj. alarming, Damoclean, dangerous, frightening, impending, intimidating, intimidatory, looming, louring (lowering), minacious, minatory, ominous, portentous, threatening.

mend v. ameliorate, amend, better, bushel, cobble, convalesce, correct, cure, darn, emend, fix, heal, improve, patch, recover,

rectify, recuperate, refit, reform, remedy, renew, renovate, repair, restore, retouch, revise, solder.
antonyms break, destroy, deteriorate.
n. clout, darn, patch, repair, stitch.

mendacious *adj.* deceitful, deceptive, dishonest, duplicitous, fallacious, false, fraudulent, insincere, inveracious, lying, perfidious, perjured, untrue, untruthful, unveracious.
antonyms honest, truthful.

mendacity *n.* deceit, deceitfulness, dishonesty, distortion, duplicity, falsehood, falsification, fraudulence, insincerity, inveracity, lie, lying, mendaciousness, misrepresentation, perfidy, perjury, untruth, untruthfulness, unveracity.
antonyms honesty, truthfulness.

mendicant *adj.* begging, cadging, petitionary, scrounging, supplicant.
n. almsman, beachcomber, beggar, bum, cadger, hobo, moocher, panhandler, pauper, scrounger, tramp, vagabond, vagrant.

menial *adj.* abject, attending, base, boring, degrading, demeaning, dull, fawning, grovelling, helping, humble, humdrum, ignoble, ignominious, low, lowly, mean, obsequious, routine, servile, slavish, sorry, subservient, sycophantic, unskilled, vile.
n. attendant, creature, dog's-body, domestic, drudge, eta, flunky, labourer, lackey, peon, serf, servant, skivvy, slave, underling.

menstruation *n.* catamenia, courses, flow, menorrhoea, menses, monthlies, period, the curse, the usual.

mensuration *n.* assessment, calculation, calibration, computation, estimation, evaluation, measurement, measuring, metage, survey, surveying, valuation.

mental[1] *adj.* abstract, cerebral, cognitive, conceptual, ideational, ideative, intellectual, noetic, rational, theoretical.
antonym physical.

mental[2] *adj.* crazy, deranged, disturbed, insane, loony, loopy, lunatic, mad, psychiatric, psychotic, unbalanced, unstable.
antonyms balanced, sane.

mentality *n.* attitude, brains, capacity, character, comprehension, disposition, endowment, faculty, frame of mind, intellect, IQ, make-up, mind, outlook, personality, psychology, rationality, understanding, wit.

mentally *adv.* emotionally, intellectually, inwardly, psychologically, rationally, subjectively, temperamentally.

mention *v.* acknowledge, adduce, advise, allude to, apprise, bring up, broach, cite, communicate, declare, disclose, divulge, hint at, impart, intimate, make known, name, point out, recount, refer to, report, reveal, speak of, state, tell, touch on.
n. acknowledgement, allusion, announcement, citation, indication, notification, observation, recognition, reference, remark, tribute.

mentioned *adj.* above-mentioned, aforesaid, cited, fore-cited, forementioned, forenamed,

fore-quoted, foresaid, quoted, reported, stated.

mentor *n.* adviser, coach, counsellor, guide, guru, instructor, pedagogue, swami, teacher, tutor.

menu *n.* bill of fare, card, carte du jour, list, tariff.

mercantile *adj.* commercial, marketable, merchantable, sal(e)able, trade, trading.

mercenary *adj.* acquisitive, avaricious, bought, covetous, grasping, greedy, hack, hired, mammonish, mammonistic, materialistic, meretricious, money-grubbing, paid, sordid, venal.
n. condottiere, free companion, free-lance, hireling, landsknecht, lansquenet, merc, soldier of fortune.

merchandise *n.* cargo, commodities, freight, goods, produce, products, shipment, staples, stock, stock in trade, truck, vendibles, wares.
v. carry, deal in, distribute, market, peddle, retail, sell, supply, trade, traffic in, vend.

merchant *n.* broker, dealer, jobber, négociant, retailer, salesman, seller, shopkeeper, trader, tradesman, trafficker, vendor, wholesaler.

merciful *adj.* beneficent, benignant, clement, compassionate, condolent, forbearing, forgiving, generous, gracious, humane, humanitarian, kind, lenient, liberal, mild, pitying, soft, sparing, sympathetic, tender-hearted.
antonyms cruel, merciless.

merciless *adj.* barbarous, callous, cruel, hard, hard-hearted, harsh, heartless, implacable, inexorable, inhuman, inhumane, pitiless, relentless, remorseless, ruthless, severe, unappeasable, unforgiving, unmerciful, unpitying, unsparing.
antonym merciful.

mercurial *adj.* active, capricious, changeable, erratic, fickle, flighty, gay, impetuous, impulsive, inconstant, irrepressible, light-hearted, lively, mobile, spirited, sprightly, temperamental, unpredictable, unstable, variable, volatile.
antonym saturnine.

mercy *n.* benevolence, blessing, boon, charity, clemency, compassion, favour, forbearance, forgiveness, godsend, grace, humanitarianism, kindness, leniency, pity, quarter, relief.
antonyms cruelty, revenge.

mere *adj.* absolute, bare, common, complete, entire, paltry, petty, plain, pure, pure and simple, sheer, simple, stark, unadulterated, unmitigated, unmixed, utter, very.

merge *v.* amalgamate, blend, coalesce, combine, commingle, confederate, consolidate, converge, fuse, incorporate, intermix, join, liquesce, meet, meld, melt into, mingle, mix, unite.

merger *n.* amalgamation, coalescence, coalition, combination, confederation, consolidation, fusion, incorporation, union.

merit *n.* advantage, asset, claim, credit, desert, due, excellence, good, goodness, integrity, justification, quality, right, strong point,

talent, value, virtue, worth, worthiness.
antonyms demerit, fault.
v. deserve, earn, incur, justify, rate, warrant.
merited *adj.* appropriate, condign, deserved, due, earned, entitled, fitting, just, justified, rightful, warranted, worthy.
antonyms inappropriate, unjustified.
meritorious *adj.* admirable, commendable, creditable, deserving, estimable, excellent, exemplary, good, honourable, laudable, praiseworthy, right, righteous, virtuous, worthful, worthy.
antonym unworthy.
merriment *n.* amusement, conviviality, elation, exhilaration, festivity, frolic, fun, gaiety, glee, hilarity, jocosity, jocularity, jocundity, jollity, joviality, laughter, levity, liveliness, merry-making, mirth, revelry, sport, waggery.
antonyms gloom, gravity, sadness, seriousness.
merry *adj.* amusing, blithe, blithesome, boon, carefree, cheerful, chirpy, comic, comical, convivial, crank, elevated, facetious, festive, frolicsome, fun-loving, funny, gay, glad, gleeful, happy, heartsome, hilarious, humorous, jocular, jocund, jolly, joyful, joyous, light-hearted, mellow, mirthful, rollicking, rorty, saturnalian, sportful, sportive, squiffy, tiddly, tipsy, vivacious.
antonyms gloomy, glum, grave, melancholy, serious, sober, sombre.
merry-go-round *n.* carousel, joy-wheel, roundabout, whirligig.
merrymaking *n.* carousal, carouse, carousing, celebration, conviviality, festivity, fun, gaiety, gil(l)ravage, jollification, mafficking, mallemaroking, merriment, mollie, party, rejoicings, revel, revelry.
mesh *n.* entanglement, lattice, net, netting, network, plexus, reticulation, snare, tangle, toils, tracery, trap, web.
v. catch, combine, come together, connect, co-ordinate, dovetail, engage, enmesh, entangle, fit, harmonise, inmesh, interlock, knit.
mesmerise *v.* benumb, captivate, enthral, entrance, fascinate, grip, hypnotise, magnetise, spellbind, stupefy.
mess *n.* bollocks, botch, chaos, clutter, cock-up, confusion, difficulty, dilemma, dirtiness, disarray, disorder, disorganisation, fix, guddle, hash, imbroglio, jam, jumble, litter, mishmash, mix-up, muddle, muss(e), perplexity, pickle, plight, predicament, shambles, shemozzle, soss, stew, turmoil, untidiness, yuck.
antonyms order, tidiness.
v. befoul, besmirch, clutter, dirty, disarrange, disarray, dishevel, foul, litter, muss(e), pollute, tousle.
antonyms order, tidy.
mess about amuse oneself, arse about, dabble, fiddle, footle, interfere, meddle, mess around, mess on, muck about, play, play about, play around, potter, tamper, tinker, toy, trifle.
mess up botch, bungle, disrupt, jumble, make

a hash of, muck up, muddle, spoil, tangle.
mess with fiddle with, interfere, meddle with, play with, tamper with, tangle with, tinker with.
message *n.* bulletin, cable, commission, communication, communiqué, dépêche, dispatch, errand, idea, import, intimation, job, letter, meaning, memorandum, mission, missive, moral, note, notice, point, purport, send, task, theme, tidings, word.
messenger *n.* agent, ambassador, bearer, carrier, courier, delivery boy, emissary, envoy, errand-boy, go-between, harbinger, herald, in-between, internuncio, mercury, nuncio, runner, send, vaunt-courier.
messy *adj.* chaotic, cluttered, confused, dirty, dishevelled, disordered, disorganised, grubby, littered, muddled, shambolic, sloppy, slovenly, unkempt, untidy, yucky.
antonyms neat, ordered, tidy.
metamorphose *v.* alter, change, convert, modify, mutate, remake, remodel, reshape, transfigure, transform, translate, transmogrify, transmute, transubstantiate.
metamorphosis *n.* alteration, change, changeover, conversion, modification, mutation, rebirth, transfiguration, transformation, translation, transmogrification, transmutation, transubstantiation.
metaphor *n.* allegory, analogy, apologue, emblem, figure of speech, image, symbol, trope.
metaphorical *adj.* allegorical, emblematic, emblematical, figurative, Pickwickian, symbolic, tropical.
metaphysical *adj.* abstract, abstruse, basic, deep, esoteric, essential, eternal, fundamental, general, high-flown, ideal, immaterial, impalpable, incorporeal, insubstantial, intangible, intellectual, oversubtle, philosophical, profound, recondite, speculative, spiritual, subjective, supernatural, theoretical, transcendental, universal, unreal, unsubstantial.
mete out administer, allot, apportion, assign, deal out, dispense, distribute, divide out, dole out, hand out, measure out, parcel out, portion, ration out, share out.
meteor *n.* aerolite, aerolith, bolide, comet, fire-ball, meteorite, meteoroid, shooting-star.
meteoric *adj.* brief, brilliant, dazzling, fast, instantaneous, momentary, overnight, rapid, spectacular, speedy, sudden, swift.
meteorologist *n.* climatologist, met-man, weatherman, weather-prophet.
method *n.* approach, arrangement, course, design, fashion, form, manner, mode, modus operandi, order, orderliness, organisation, pattern, plan, planning, practice, procedure, process, programme, purpose, regularity, routine, rule, scheme, structure, style, system, technique, way.
methodical *adj.* business-like, deliberate, disciplined, efficient, meticulous, neat, ordered, orderly, organised, painstaking, planned, precise, punctilious, regular, scrupulous,

structured, systematic, tidy.
antonyms confused, desultory, irregular.
meticulous *adj.* accurate, detailed, exact, fastidious, fussy, microscopic, nice, painstaking, particular, perfectionist, precise, punctilious, scrupulous, strict, thorough.
antonyms careless, slapdash.
métier *n.* calling, craft, field, forte, line, occupation, profession, pursuit, speciality, specialty, sphere, trade, vocation.
metropolis *n.* capital, city, megalopolis.
mettle *n.* ardour, boldness, bottle, bravery, calibre, character, courage, daring, disposition, fire, fortitude, gallantry, gameness, ginger, grit, guts, hardihood, heart, indomitability, kidney, life, make-up, nature, nerve, pith, pluck, quality, resolution, resolve, spirit, spunk, stamp, temper, temperament, valour, vigour.
mew *v.* caterwaul, meow, mewl, miaow, miaul, pule, whine.
mewl *v.* blubber, cry, girn, grizzle, pule, snivel, whimper, whine, whinge.
miasma *n.* effluvium, fetor, mephitis, odour, pollution, reek, smell, stench, stink.
miasmal *adj.* fetid, foul, insalubrious, malodorous, mephitic, miasm(at)ic, miasm(at)ous, noisome, noxious, polluted, putrid, reeking, smelly, stinking, unwholesome.
microbe *n.* bacillus, bacterium, bug, germ, micro-organism, pathogen, virus.
microscopic *adj.* imperceptible, indiscernible, infinitesimal, invisible, minuscule, minute, negligible, tiny.
antonyms huge, vast.
midday *n.* lunchtime, noon, noonday, noontide, twelve.
middle *adj.* central, halfway, inner, inside, intermediate, intervening, mean, medial, median, mediate, medium, mid, middle-bracket.
n. aurea mediocritas, centre, focus, golden mean, halfway mark, halfway point, happy medium, heart, inside, mean, middle way, midpoint, midriff, midsection, midst, thick, via media, waist.
antonyms beginning, border, edge, end, extreme.
middle-class *adj.* bourgeois, conventional, preppy, suburban.
middleman *n.* broker, distributor, entrepreneur, fixer, go-between, intermediary, negotiator, retailer.
middling *adj.* adequate, average, fair, indifferent, mean, median, mediocre, medium, moderate, modest, OK, ordinary, passable, run-of-the-mill, so-so, tolerable, unexceptional, unremarkable.
midget *n.* dwarf, gnome, homuncule, homunculus, manikin, minikin, minnow, pygmy, shrimp, Tom Thumb.
antonym giant.
adj. dwarf, Lilliputian, little, miniature, pocket, pocket-sized, pygmy, small, teeny, tiny.

antonym giant.
midst *n.* bosom, centre, core, depths, epicentre, heart, hub, interior, middle, mid-point, thick.
midway *adv.* betwixt and between, halfway, in the middle, partially.
mien *n.* air, appearance, aspect, aura, bearing, carriage, complexion, countenance, demeanour, deportment, look, manner, presence, semblance.
miffed *adj.* aggrieved, annoyed, chagrined, disgruntled, displeased, hurt, in a huff, irked, irritated, narked, nettled, offended, piqued, put out, resentful, upset, vexed.
antonyms chuffed, delighted, pleased.
might *n.* ability, capability, capacity, clout, efficacy, efficiency, energy, force, heftiness, muscularity, potency, power, powerfulness, prowess, puissance, strength, sway, valour, vigour.
mightily *adv.* decidedly, energetically, exceedingly, extremely, forcefully, greatly, highly, hugely, intensely, lustily, manfully, much, powerfully, strenuously, strongly, very, very much, vigorously.
mighty *adj.* bulky, colossal, doughty, enormous, forceful, gigantic, grand, great, hardy, hefty, huge, immense, indomitable, large, lusty, manful, massive, monumental, muscular, potent, powerful, prodigious, puissant, robust, stalwart, stout, strapping, strenuous, strong, stupendous, sturdy, titanic, towering, tremendous, vast, vigorous.
antonyms frail, weak.
migrant *n.* drifter, emigrant, globe-trotter, gypsy, immigrant, itinerant, land-louper, nomad, rover, tinker, transient, traveller, vagrant, wanderer.
adj. drifting, globe-trotting, gypsy, immigrant, itinerant, migratory, nomadic, roving, shifting, transient, travelling, vagrant, wandering.
migrate *v.* drift, emigrate, journey, move, roam, rove, shift, transhume, travel, trek, voyage, wander.
migration *n.* diaspora, emigration, journey, movement, roving, shift, transhumance, travel, trek, Völkerwanderung, voyage, wandering.
migratory *adj.* gipsy, itinerant, migrant, nomadic, peripatetic, roving, shifting, transient, transitory, travelling, vagrant, wandering.
mild *adj.* amiable, balmy, bland, calm, clement, compassionate, docile, easy, easy-going, equable, forbearing, forgiving, gentle, indulgent, kind, lenient, meek, mellow, merciful, moderate, pacific, passive, peaceable, placid, pleasant, serene, smooth, soft, temperate, tender, tranquil, warm.
antonyms fierce, harsh, stormy, strong, violent.
mildewy *adj.* fetid, fusty, mucedinous, mucid, musty, rotten.
mildness *n.* blandness, calmness, clemency, docility, forbearance, gentleness, indulgence, kindness, leniency, lenity, meekness, mellow-

ness, moderation, passivity, placidity, smoothness, softness, temperateness, tenderness, tractability, tranquillity, warmth.
antonyms ferocity, harshness, strength, violence.

mil(e)ometer *n.* hodometer, perambulator, tachograph, waywiser.

milieu *n.* arena, background, element, environment, locale, location, medium, scene, setting, sphere, surroundings.

militant *adj.* active, aggressive, assertive, belligerent, combating, combative, contending, embattled, fighting, hawkish, pugnacious, vigorous, warring.
n. activist, aggressor, belligerent, combatant, fighter, partisan, struggler, warrior.

military *adj.* armed, martial, service, soldierlike, soldierly, warlike.
n. armed forces, army, forces, services, soldiers, soldiery.

militate against contend, count against, counter, counteract, oppose, resist, tell against, weigh against.

militate for advance, aid, back, further, help, promote, speak for.

militia *n.* fencibles, minutemen, National Guard, reserve, reservists, Territorial Army, train-band, yeomanry.

milk *v.* bleed, drain, draw off, emulge, exploit, express, extract, impose on, press, pump, siphon, squeeze, tap, use, wring.

milk-and-water *adj.* bland, feeble, innocuous, insipid, jejune, tasteless, vapid, weak, wishy-washy.

milksop *n.* chinless wonder, coward, milquetoast, Miss Nancy, molly, mollycoddle, namby-pamby, pansy, sissy, weakling.

milky *adj.* alabaster, albescent, chalky, clouded, cloudy, milk-white, opaque, white, whitish.

mill[1] *n.* ball-mill, crusher, grinder, quern.
v. comminute, crush, granulate, grate, grind, pound, powder, press, pulverise, roll.

mill[2] *n.* factory, foundry, plant, shop, works.

mill[3] *v.* crowd, scurry, seethe, swarm, throng, wander.

millstone *n.* affliction, burden, drag, encumbrance, grindstone, load, quernstone, weight.

mime *n.* dumb show, gesture, mimicry, mummery, pantomime.
v. act out, gesture, impersonate, mimic, represent, signal, simulate.

mimic *v.* ape, caricature, echo, imitate, impersonate, look like, mirror, parody, parrot, personate, resemble, simulate, take off.
n. caricaturist, copy, copy-cat, imitator, impersonator, impressionist, parodist, parrot.
adj. echoic, fake, imitation, imitative, make-believe, mimetic, mock, pseudo, sham, simulated.

mimicry *n.* apery, burlesque, caricature, copying, imitating, imitation, impersonation, impression, mimesis, mimicking, mockery, parody, parrotry, take-off.

mince[1] *v.* chop, crumble, cut, dice, grind, hash.

n. hachis, hash.

mince[2] *v.* diminish, euphemise, extenuate, hold back, moderate, palliate, play down, soften, spare, suppress, tone down, weaken.

mince[3] *v.* attitudinise, ponce, pose, posture, simper.

mincing *adj.* affected, coxcombic(al), dainty, effeminate, foppish, lah-di-dah, minikin, nice, niminy-piminy, poncy, precious, pretentious, ripperty-tipperty, sissy.

mind[1] *n.* attention, attitude, belief, bent, brains, concentration, desire, disposition, fancy, feeling, genius, grey matter, head, imagination, inclination, inner, intellect, intellectual, intelligence, intention, judgement, leaning, marbles, memory, mentality, notion, opinion, outlook, point of view, psyche, purpose, rationality, reason, recollection, remembrance, sanity, sense, senses, sensorium, sensory, sentiment, spirit, tendency, thinker, thinking, thoughts, understanding, urge, view, will, wish, wits.

mind's eye contemplation, head, imagination, memory, mind, recollection, remembrance.

mind[2] *v.* care, demur, disapprove, dislike, object, resent, take offence.

mind[3] *v.* adhere to, attend, attend to, be careful, be on one's guard, comply with, ensure, follow, guard, have charge of, heed, keep an eye on, listen to, look after, make certain, mark, note, notice, obey, observe, pay attention, pay heed to, regard, respect, take care, take care of, take heed, tend, watch.

mind out be careful, be on one's guard, beware, keep one's eyes open, look out, pay attention, take care, watch, watch out.

mindful *adj.* alert, alive (to), attentive, aware, careful, chary, cognisant, compliant, conscious, heedful, obedient, regardful, remindful, respectful, sensible, thoughtful, wary, watchful.
antonyms heedless, inattentive, mindless.

mindless *adj.* asinine, automatic, brainless, brutish, careless, foolish, forgetful, gratuitous, heedless, idiotic, illogical, imbecilic, inattentive, irrational, mechanical, moronic, neglectful, negligent, oblivious, obtuse, stupid, thoughtless, unintelligent, unmindful, unreasoning, unthinking, witless.
antonyms intelligent, mindful, thoughtful.

mine[1] *n.* abundance, coalfield, colliery, deposit, excavation, fund, hoard, lode, pit, reserve, sap, shaft, source, stock, store, supply, treasury, trench, tunnel, vein, wealth, wheal.
v. delve, dig for, dig up, excavate, extract, hew, quarry, remove, sap, subvert, tunnel, undermine, unearth, weaken.

mine[2] *n.* bomb, depth charge, egg, explosive, land-mine.

miner *n.* coal-miner, collier, pitman.

mingle *v.* alloy, associate, blend, circulate, coalesce, combine, commingle, compound, hobnob, intermingle, intermix, interweave, join, marry, mell, merge, mix, rub shoulders, socialise, unite.

miniature *adj.* baby, diminutive, dwarf, Lilliputian, little, midget, mini, minuscule, minute, pint-size(d), pocket, pocket-sized, pygmy, reduced, scaled-down, small, tiny, toy, wee.
antonym giant.

minimal *adj.* least, littlest, minimum, minuscule, minute, nominal, slightest, smallest, token.

minimise *v.* abbreviate, attenuate, belittle, curtail, decrease, decry, deprecate, depreciate, diminish, discount, disparage, make light of, make little of, play down, prune, reduce, shrink, underestimate, underrate.
antonym maximise.

minimum *n.* bottom, least, lowest point, nadir, slightest.
antonym maximum.
adj. least, littlest, lowest, minimal, slightest, smallest, tiniest, weeniest, weest.
antonym maximum.

minion *n.* arse-licker, backscratcher, bootlicker, creature, darling, dependant, favourite, flatterer, flunky, follower, hanger-on, heeler, henchman, hireling, lackey, lickspittle, myrmidon, parasite, pet, sycophant, toady, underling, yes-man.

minister *n.* administrator, agent, aide, ambassador, assistant, churchman, clergyman, cleric, delegate, diplomat, divine, ecclesiastic, envoy, executive, Levite, office-holder, official, parson, pastor, plenipotentiary, preacher, priest, servant, subordinate, underling, vicar, vizier.
v. accommodate, administer, attend, cater to, nurse, pander to, serve, take care of, tend.

ministration *n.* aid, assistance, care, favour, help, patronage, relief, service, succour, supervision, support.

ministry [1] *n.* administration, bureau, cabinet, council, department, office.

ministry [2] *n.* holy orders, the church, the priesthood.

minor *adj.* inconsequential, inconsiderable, inferior, insignificant, junior, lesser, light, negligible, paltry, petty, piddling, secondary, second-class, slight, small, smaller, subordinate, trifling, trivial, unclassified, unimportant, younger.
antonym major.

minstrel *n.* bard, joculator, jongleur, musician, rhymer, rimer, singer, troubadour.

mint *v.* cast, coin, construct, devise, fabricate, fashion, forge, invent, make, make up, manufacture, monetise, produce, punch, stamp, strike.
adj. brand-new, excellent, first-class, fresh, immaculate, perfect, unblemished, undamaged, untarnished.
n. bomb, bundle, fortune, heap, million, packet, pile, stack.

minuscule *adj.* diminutive, fine, infinitesimal, itsy-bitsy, Lilliputian, little, microscopic, miniature, minute, teensy-weensy, teeny, tiny.
antonyms gigantic, huge.

minute [1] *n.* flash, instant, jiff, jiffy, mo, moment, sec, second, shake, tick, trice.

minute [2] *adj.* close, critical, detailed, diminutive, exact, exhaustive, fine, inconsiderable, infinitesimal, itsy-bitsy, Lilliputian, little, meticulous, microscopic, miniature, minim, minuscule, negligible, painstaking, paltry, petty, picayune, piddling, precise, punctilious, puny, slender, slight, small, tiny, trifling, trivial, unimportant.
antonyms gigantic, huge, immense.

minutely *adv.* closely, critically, exactly, exhaustively, in detail, meticulously, painstakingly, precisely, scrupulously, systematically, with a fine-tooth comb.

minutes *n.* details, memorandum, notes, proceedings, record(s), tapes, transactions, transcript.

minutiae *n.* details, niceties, particulars, subtleties, trifles, trivialities.

minx *n.* baggage, coquette, flirt, harpy, harridan, hoyden, hussy, jade, tomboy, wanton.

miracle *n.* deus ex machina, marvel, miraculum, phenomenon, prodigy, thaumaturgy, wonder, wonder-work.

miraculous *adj.* amazing, astonishing, astounding, extraordinary, incredible, inexplicable, magical, marvellous, otherworldly, phenomenal, preternatural, prodigious, stupendous, superhuman, supernatural, thaumaturgic, unaccountable, unbelievable, wonderful, wondrous.
antonyms natural, normal.

mirage *n.* fata Morgana, hallucination, illusion, optical illusion, phantasm.

mire *n.* bog, difficulties, dirt, fen, glaur, marsh, morass, muck, mud, ooze, quag, quagmire, slime, swamp, trouble.

mirror *n.* copy, double, glass, hand-glass, image, keeking-glass, likeness, looking-glass, pocket-glass, reflection, reflector, replica, representation, speculum, spit and image, spitting image, twin.
v. copy, depict, echo, emulate, follow, imitate, mimic, reflect, represent, show.

mirth *n.* amusement, cheerfulness, festivity, frolic, fun, gaiety, gladness, glee, hilarity, jocosity, jocularity, jocundity, jollity, joviality, joyousness, laughter, levity, merriment, merrymaking, pleasure, rejoicing, revelry, sport.
antonyms gloom, glumness, melancholy.

mirthful *adj.* amused, amusing, blithe, cheerful, cheery, festive, frolicsome, funny, gay, glad, gladsome, happy, hilarious, jocose, jocund, jolly, jovial, laughable, laughing, light-hearted, merry, playful, sportive, uproarious, vivacious.
antonyms gloomy, glum, melancholy, mirthless.

miry *adj.* boggy, dirty, fenny, glaury, marshy, mucky, muddy, oozy, slimy, swampy.

misadventure *n.* accident, calamity, cataclysm, catastrophe, debacle, disaster, failure, ill fortune, ill luck, mischance, misfortune, mishap, reverse, setback, tragedy.

misanthropic *adj.* antisocial, cynical, egoistic, inhumane, malevolent, surly, unfriendly, unsociable, unsympathetic.
antonym philanthropic.

misanthropy *n.* antisociality, cynicism, egoism, inhumanity, malevolence, unsociableness.
antonym philanthropy.

misapply *v.* abuse, exploit, misappropriate, misemploy, misuse, pervert.

misapprehend *v.* get the wrong idea, miscomprehend, misconceive, misconstrue, misinterpret, misknow, misread, mistake, misunderstand.
antonym apprehend.

misapprehension *n.* delusion, error, fallacy, misacceptation, misconception, misconstruction, misinterpretation, misreading, mistake, misunderstanding.
antonym apprehension.

misappropriate *v.* abuse, defalcate, embezzle, misapply, misspend, misuse, peculate, pervert, pocket, steal, swindle.

misappropriation *n.* defalcation, embezzlement, misapplication, misuse, peculation, pocketing, stealing, theft.

misbegotten *adj.* abortive, dishonest, disreputable, hare-brained, ill-advised, ill-conceived, ill-gotten, illicit, monstrous, poorly thought-out, purloined, shady, stolen, unlawful.

misbehave *v.* act up, carry on, get up to mischief, kick over the traces, mess about, muck about, offend, transgress, trespass.
antonym behave.

misbehaviour *n.* disobedience, impropriety, incivility, indiscipline, insubordination, mayhem, misconduct, misdeeds, misdemeanour, monkey business, naughtiness, rudeness, shenanigans.

misbelief *n.* delusion, error, fallacy, heresy, heterodoxy, miscreance, unorthodoxy.

miscalculate *v.* blunder, boob, err, get wrong, misjudge, overestimate, overrate, overvalue, slip up, underestimate, underrate, undervalue.

miscarriage *n.* abortion, botch, breakdown, casualty, disappointment, error, failure, misadventure, mischance, misfire, mishap, mismanagement, perversion, thwarting, undoing.
antonym success.

miscarry *v.* abort, bite the dust, come to grief, come to nothing, fail, fall through, flounder, gang agley, misfire, warp.
antonym succeed.

miscellaneous *adj.* assorted, confused, diverse, diversified, farraginous, heterogeneous, indiscriminate, jumbled, manifold, many, mingled, mixed, motley, multifarious, multiform, omnifarious, promiscuous, sundry, varied, various.

miscellany *n.* anthology, assortment, collection, diversity, farrago, gallimaufry, hash, hotchpotch, jumble, medley, mélange, mixed bag, mixture, olla-podrida, omnium-gatherum, pot-pourri, salmagundi, variety.

mischance *n.* accident, bad break, blow, calamity, contretemps, disaster, ill-chance, ill-fortune, ill-luck, infelicity, misadventure, misfortune, mishap, tragedy.

mischief[1] *n.* bane, damage, detriment, devilment, deviltry, diablerie, disruption, evil, harm, hurt, impishness, injury, misbehaviour, misfortune, monkey business, naughtiness, pranks, roguery, roguishness, shenanigans, trouble, waggery, waywardness.

mischief[2] *n.* devil, imp, monkey, nuisance, pest, rapscallion, rascal, rascallion, rogue, scallywag, scamp, tyke, villain.
antonym angel.

mischievous *adj.* arch, bad, damaging, deleterious, destructive, detrimental, elfish, elvan, elvish, evil, exasperating, frolicsome, harmful, hurtful, impish, injurious, malicious, malignant, naughty, pernicious, playful, puckish, rascally, roguish, sinful, spiteful, sportive, teasing, tricksy, troublesome, vexatious, vicious, wayward, wicked.
antonyms good, well-behaved.

misconceive *v.* misapprehend, misconstrue, misinterpret, misjudge, misread, mistake, misunderstand.

misconception *n.* delusion, error, fallacy, misapprehension, misconstruction, misreading, misunderstanding, the wrong end of the stick.

misconduct *n.* delinquency, dereliction, hanky-panky, immorality, impropriety, malfeasance, malpractice, malversation, misbehaviour, misdemeanour, misfeasance, mismanagement, naughtiness, rudeness, transgression, wrong-doing.

misconstruction *n.* delusion, misapprehension, misinterpretation, misreading, mistake, misunderstanding.

misconstrue *v.* misapprehend, misconceive, misinterpret, misjudge, misread, misreckon, mistake, mistranslate, misunderstand, take the wrong way.

miscreant *n.* blackguard, caitiff, criminal, dastard, evil-doer, knave, malefactor, mischief-maker, profligate, rascal, reprobate, rogue, scallywag, scamp, scapegrace, scoundrel, sinner, trouble-maker, vagabond, varlet, villain, wretch, wrong-doer.
antonym worthy.

misdeed *n.* crime, delict, delinquency, error, fault, felony, malefice, misconduct, misdemeanour, offence, peccadillo, sin, transgression, trespass, villainy, wrong.

misdemeanour *n.* delict, fault, indiscretion, infringement, lapse, malfeasance, misbehaviour, misconduct, misdeed, offence, peccadillo, transgression, trespass.

miser *n.* cheapskate, curmudgeon, hunks, mammonist, meanie, money-grubber, muck-worm, niggard, penny-pincher, pinchfist, pinchgut, pinchpenny, save-all, screw, Scrooge, skinflint, snudge, tightwad.
antonym spendthrift.

miserable *adj.* abject, anguished, bad, broken-hearted, caitiff, cheerless, contemptible, crestfallen, crushed, dejected, deplorable, depressed, depressive, desolate, despicable, despondent, destitute, detestable, disconsolate, disgraceful, dismal, distressed, doleful, dolorous, down, downcast, dreary, forlorn, gloomy, glum, grief-stricken, hapless, heartbroken, ignominious, impoverished, indigent, joyless, lachrymose, lamentable, low, luckless, lugubrious, meagre, mean, melancholic, melancholy, mournful, needy, niggardly, paltry, pathetic, penniless, piteous, pitiable, pitiful, poor, sad, scanty, scurvy, shabby, shameful, sordid, sorrowful, sorrowing, sorry, squalid, star-crossed, stricken, tearful, unhappy, vile, woebegone, worthless, wretched. *antonyms* cheerful, comfortable, generous, honourable, noble.

miserliness *n.* avarice, cheese-paring, churlishness, close-fistedness, covetousness, frugality, meanness, minginess, misery, nearness, niggardliness, parsimony, penny-pinching, penuriousness, stinginess, thrift, thriftiness, tight-fistedness. *antonyms* generosity, lavishness, prodigality.

miserly *adj.* avaricious, beggarly, cheese-paring, close, close-fisted, close-handed, covetous, curmudgeonly, gare, grasping, grudging, illiberal, mean, mercenary, mingy, money-grubbing, near, niggardly, parsimonious, penny-pinching, penurious, sordid, sparing, stingy, thrifty, tight-fisted, ungenerous. *antonyms* generous, lavish, prodigal, spendthrift.

misery[1] *n.* abjectness, adversity, affliction, agony, anguish, bale, bane, bitter pill, blow, burden, calamity, catastrophe, cross, curse, depression, desolation, despair, destitution, disaster, discomfort, distress, dole, dolour, extremity, gloom, grief, hardship, heartache, heartbreak, humiliation, indigence, living death, load, melancholia, melancholy, misfortune, mortification, need, oppression, ordeal, penury, poverty, privation, prostration, sadness, sordidness, sorrow, squalor, suffering, torment, torture, trial, tribulation, trouble, unhappiness, want, woe, wretchedness.

misery[2] *n.* grouch, Jeremiah, Job's comforter, killjoy, moaner, pessimist, prophet of doom, ray of sunshine, sourpuss, spoil-sport, Weary Willie, wet blanket, whiner, whinger. *antonym* sport.

misfire *v.* abort, bomb, come a cropper, come to grief, fail, fall flat, fall short, fall through, fizzle out, flop, founder, go phut, go wrong, miscarry. *antonym* succeed.

misfit *n.* drop-out, eccentric, fish out of water, horse marine, individual, lone wolf, loner, maverick, nonconformist, odd man out, oddball, rogue, square peg in a round hole, weirdo. *antonym* conformist.

misfortune *n.* accident, adversity, affliction, bad luck, blow, buffet, calamity, catastrophe, disaster, failure, grief, hardship, harm,

ill-luck, infelicity, infortune, loss, misadventure, mischance, misery, mishap, reverse, setback, sorrow, tragedy, trial, tribulation, trouble, woe. *antonyms* luck, success.

misgiving *n.* anxiety, apprehension, backward glance, compunction, distrust, doubt, dubiety, fear, hesitation, misdoubt, niggle, presentiment, qualm, reservation, scruple, second thoughts, suspicion, uncertainty, unease, worry. *antonym* confidence.

misguided *adj.* deluded, erroneous, foolish, ill-advised, ill-considered, ill-judged, imprudent, incautious, injudicious, misconceived, misled, misplaced, mistaken, rash, unreasonable, unsuitable, unwarranted, unwise. *antonym* sensible.

mishandle *v.* balls up, bollocks, botch, bungle, fumble, make a balls of, make a hash of, make a mess of, make a pig's ear of, mess up, misguggle, misjudge, mismanage, mousle, muff, screw up. *antonyms* cope, manage.

mishap *n.* accident, adversity, balls-up, calamity, contretemps, disaster, hiccup, ill-fortune, ill-luck, misadventure, mischance, misfortune, misventure, setback.

mishmash *n.* conglomeration, farrago, gallimaufry, hash, hotchpotch, jumble, medley, mess, muddle, olio, olla-podrida, pastiche, pot-pourri, salad, salmagundi.

misinform *v.* bluff, deceive, give a bum steer, hoodwink, lead up the garden path, misdirect, misguide, mislead, mistell, mizzle, snow, take for a ride.

misinformation *n.* baloney, bluff, bum steer, disinformation, dope, eyewash, guff, hype, lies, misdirection, misleading, nonsense.

misinterpret *v.* distort, garble, get the wrong end of the stick, misappreciate, misapprehend, misconceive, misconstruct, misconstrue, misjudge, misread, misrepresent, mistake, misunderstand, pervert, warp, wrest.

misjudge *v.* miscalculate, miscount, misestimate, misinterpret, misprise, mistake, overestimate, overrate, underestimate, underrate, undervalue.

mislay *v.* lose, lose sight of, misplace, miss.

mislead *v.* beguile, bluff, deceive, delude, fool, give a bum steer, hoodwink, lead up the garden path, misadvise, misdirect, misguide, misinform, mizzle, pull the wool over someone's eyes, snow, take for a ride, take in.

misleading *adj.* ambiguous, biased, casuistical, confusing, deceitful, deceptive, delusive, delusory, disingenuous, distorted, equivocatory, evasive, fallacious, false, falsidical, loaded, mendacious, sophistical, specious, spurious, tricky, unreliable. *antonyms* authentic, authoritative, informative, plain, unequivocal.

mismanage *v.* balls up, bollocks, botch, bungle, fluff, foul up, louse up, make a hash of, make a mess of, maladminister, mangle, mar, mess up, misconduct, misdirect, misgovern, mishandle, misjudge, misrule, misspend, muff, screw up, squander, waste.

mismatched *adj.* antipathetic, clashing, discordant, disparate, ill-assorted, incompatible, incongruous, irregular, misallied, mismated, unmatching, unreconcilable, unsuited.
antonyms compatible, matching.

misogynist *n.* anti-feminist, male chauvinist, male supremacist, misogamist, sexist, womanhater.
antonym feminist.

misplace *v.* lose, misapply, misassign, misfile, mislay, miss.

misprint *n.* corrigendum, erratum, error, literal, mistake, transposition, typo.

misprise *v.* belittle, depreciate, disparage, hold cheap, look down on, mistake, misunderstand, slight, underestimate, underrate, undervalue.
antonyms appreciate, understand.

misquote *v.* distort, falsify, garble, misremember, misreport, misrepresent, misstate, muddle, pervert, twist.

misrepresent *v.* belie, bend, disguise, distort, exaggerate, falsify, garble, load, minimise, miscolour, misconstrue, misinterpret, misquote, misstate, pervert, slant, twist.

misrule *n.* anarchy, chaos, confusion, disorder, disorganisation, indiscipline, lawlessness, maladministration, misgovernment, mismanagement, riot, tumult, turbulence, turmoil, unreason.

miss[1] *v.* avoid, bypass, circumvent, err, escape, evade, fail, forego, jump, lack, leave out, let go, let slip, lose, miscarry, mistake, obviate, omit, overlook, pass over, pass up, sidestep, skip, slip, trip.
n. blunder, error, failure, fault, fiasco, flop, lack, lacuna, loss, mistake, need, omission, oversight, want.
miss out bypass, dispense with, disregard, ignore, jump, leave out, omit, pass over, skip.

miss[2] *v.* grieve for, lack, lament, long for, mourn, need, pine for, regret, sorrow for, want, wish, yearn for.

miss[3] *n.* backfisch, child, damsel, demoiselle, flapper, Fraülein, girl, girly, Jungfrau, junior miss, kid, lass, lassie, mademoiselle, maid, maiden, missy, Ms, nymphet, schoolgirl, spinster, teenager, young thing.

missal *n.* breviary, euchologion, formulary, mass-book, office-book, prayer-book, service-book, Triodion.

misshapen *adj.* contorted, crippled, crooked, deformed, distorted, grotesque, ill-made, ill-proportioned, malformed, monstrous, thrawn, twisted, ugly, ungainly, unshapely, unsightly, warped, wry.
antonyms regular, shapely.

missile *n.* arrow, ball, bomb, dart, flying bomb, grenade, projectile, rocket, shaft, shell, shot, torpedo, V-bomb, weapon.

missing *adj.* absent, astray, disappeared, gone, lacking, lost, minus, misgone, mislaid, misplaced, strayed, unaccounted-for, wanting.
antonyms found, present.

mission *n.* aim, assignment, business, calling, campaign, charge, commission, crusade, delegation, deputation, duty, embassy, errand, goal, job, legation, mandate, ministry, object, office, operation, purpose, pursuit, quest, raison d'être, remit, task, task force, trust, undertaking, vocation, work.

missionary *n.* ambassador, apostle, campaigner, champion, crusader, emissary, envoy, evangelist, exponent, gospeller, preacher, promoter, propagandist, proselytiser, teacher.

missish *adj.* affected, arch, bossy, coy, demanding, flighty, giggly, girlish, hoity-toity, impossible, indulged, obstinate, self-willed, sentimental, silly, spoilt, squeamish, wilful.

missive *n.* bulletin, communication, communiqué, dispatch, epistle, letter, line, memo, memorandum, message, note, report.

misspent *adj.* dissipated, frittered away, idle, idled away, misapplied, misused, prodigal, profitless, squandered, thrown away, unprofitable, wasted.
antonym profitable.

misstate *v.* distort, falsify, garble, misquote, misrelate, misremember, misreport, misrepresent, mistell, pervert, twist.

mist *n.* brume, cloud, condensation, dew, dimness, drizzle, exhalation, film, fog, haar, haze, mizzle, roke, smir, smog, spray, steam, vapour, veil, water-smoke.
v. becloud, bedim, befog, blur, cloud, dim, film, fog, glaze, obscure, steam up, veil.
antonym clear.

mistake *n.* aberration, bêtise, bish, bloomer, blunder, boner, boob, boo-boo, clanger, clinker, corrigendum, erratum, error, fallacy, false move, fault, faux pas, floater, folly, gaffe, gaucherie, goof, howler, inaccuracy, indiscretion, inexactitude, lapse, lapsus, lapsus calami, lapsus linguae, lapsus memoriae, literal, malapropism, misapprehension, miscalculation, misconception, misjudgement, misprint, misprision, mispronunciation, misreading, misspelling, misunderstanding, mumpsimus, oversight, scape, slip, slip-up, solecism, stumer, tactlessness, trespass.
v. blunder, confound, confuse, err, get the wrong end of the stick, goof, misapprehend, miscalculate, misconceive, misconstrue, misinterpret, misjudge, misobserve, misprise, misrate, misread, misreckon, misunderstand, slip up.

mistaken *adj.* deceived, deluded, erroneous, fallacious, false, faulty, ill-judged, inaccurate, inappropriate, inauthentic, incorrect, inexact, misguided, misinformed, misinstructed, mislead, misprised, off base, unfair, unfounded, unjust, unsound, untrue, wide of the mark, wrong.
antonyms correct, justified.

mistakenly *adv.* by mistake, erroneously, fallaciously, falsely, inaccurately, inappropriately, incorrectly, misguidedly, unfairly, unjustly, wrongly.

antonyms appropriately, correctly, fairly, justly.

mistimed *adj.* ill-timed, inconvenient, infelicitous, inopportune, malapropos, tactless, unfortunate, unseasonable, unsynchronised, untimely.

antonym opportune.

mistreat *v.* abuse, batter, brutalise, bully, harm, hurt, ill-treat, ill-use, injure, knock about, maltreat, manhandle, maul, mishandle, misuse, molest, rough up.

antonym pamper.

mistreatment *n.* abuse, battering, brutalisation, bullying, cruelty, harm, ill-treatment, ill-usage, ill-use, injury, maltreatment, manhandling, mauling, mishandling, misuse, molestation, unkindness.

antonyms cosseting, pampering.

mistress *n.* amante, canary-bird, châtelaine, concubine, courtesan, demi-mondaine, doxy, fancy woman, girlfriend, hetaira, inamorata, kept woman, lady, lady-love, lover, odalisque, owner, paramour, popsy, proprietress, teacher, woman.

mistrust *n.* apprehension, caution, chariness, distrust, doubt, dubiety, fear, hesitancy, misdoubt, misgiving, reservations, scepticism, suspicion, uncertainty, wariness.

antonym trust.

v. be wary of, beware, disbelieve, distrust, doubt, fear, fight shy of, look askance at, misdoubt, mislippen, question, suspect.

antonym trust.

mistrustful *adj.* apprehensive, cautious, chary, cynical, distrustful, doubtful, dubious, fearful, hesitant, leery, sceptical, shy, suspicious, uncertain, wary.

antonym trustful.

misty *adj.* blear, bleared, bleary, blurred, blurry, cloudy, dark, dim, faint, foggy, fuzzy, gauzy, hazy, indistinct, mistful, murky, muzzy, nebulous, obscure, opaque, roky, smoky, translucent, unclear, vague, veiled.

antonyms bright, clear.

misunderstand *v.* get the wrong end of the stick, get wrong, misapprehend, miscomprehend, misconceive, misconstrue, misesteem, mishear, misinterpret, misjudge, misknow, misprise, misread, miss the point, mistake, take up wrong(ly).

antonyms grasp, understand.

misunderstanding *n.* argument, breach, clash, conflict, difference, difficulty, disagreement, discord, disharmony, dispute, dissension, error, malentendu, misacceptation, misapprehension, misconception, misconstruction, misinterpretation, misjudgement, misknowledge, misprision, misreading, mistake, mix-up, quarrel, rift, rupture, squabble, variance.

antonyms agreement, reconciliation.

misunderstood *adj.* ill-judged, misappreciated, misconstrued, misheard, misinterpreted, mis-

judged, misprised, misread, misrepresented, mistaken, unappreciated, unrecognised.

misuse *n.* abusage, abuse, barbarism, catachresis, corruption, desecration, dissipation, distortion, exploitation, harm, ill-treatment, ill-usage, injury, malappropriation, malapropism, maltreatment, manhandling, misapplication, misappropriation, misemployment, mistreatment, misusage, perversion, profanation, prostitution, solecism, squandering, wastage, waste.

v. abuse, brutalise, corrupt, desecrate, dissipate, distort, exploit, harm, ill-treat, ill-use, injure, malappropriate, maltreat, manhandle, maul, misapply, misappropriate, misemploy, mistreat, molest, overload, overtax, pervert, profane, prostitute, squander, strain, waste, wrong.

mite *n.* atom, grain, iota, jot, modicum, morsel, ounce, scrap, smidgen, spark, trace, whit.

mitigate *v.* abate, allay, alleviate, appease, assuage, attemper, blunt, calm, check, decrease, diminish, dull, ease, extenuate, lenify, lessen, lighten, moderate, modify, mollify, pacify, palliate, placate, quiet, reduce, remit, slake, soften, soothe, still, subdue, temper, tone down, weaken.

antonyms aggravate, exacerbate, increase.

mitigating *adj.* exculpatory, extenuating, extenuative, justificatory, justifying, lenitive, mitigative, mitigatory, modifying, palliating, palliative, qualifying, vindicating.

mitigation *n.* abatement, allaying, alleviation, appeasement, assuagement, decrease, diminution, easement, extenuation, lessening, moderation, mollification, palliation, qualification, reduction, relief, remission, tempering.

antonyms aggravation, exacerbation, increase.

mix *v.* allay, alloy, amalgamate, associate, blend, coalesce, combine, commingle, commix, compound, consort, contemper, cross, dash, fold in, fraternise, fuse, hobnob, homogenise, immingle, incorporate, intermingle, intermix, interweave, join, jumble, mell, merge, mingle, shuffle, socialise, synthesise, unite.

antonym separate.

n. alloy, amalgam, assortment, blend, combination, composite, compound, conglomerate, fusion, medley, mishmash, mixture, pastiche, synthesis.

mix in admix, blend, immingle, immix, incorporate, infiltrate, infuse, inject, interject, interlard, intermingle, interpolate, intersperse, introduce, merge.

antonyms extract, isolate.

mix up bewilder, blend, combine, complicate, confound, confuse, disturb, embroil, entangle, fluster, garble, implicate, involve, jumble, mix, muddle, perplex, puzzle, scramble, snarl up, upset.

mixed *adj.* alloyed, amalgamated, ambivalent, assorted, blended, combined, composite, compound, cosmopolitan, crossbred, diverse, diversified, ecumenical, equivocal, fused, heterogeneous, hybrid, incorporated, indecisive, integrated, interbred, interdenominational, international, joint, linsey-woolsey, mingled, miscegenate, miscellaneous, mongrel, mongrelly, motley, polyglot, promiscuous, uncertain, united, unsegregated, varied.

mixed up bewildered, chaotic, complicated, confused, désorienté, disordered, disoriented, distracted, distraught, disturbed, maladjusted, mingle-mangle, muddled, perplexed, puzzled, upset.

mixer[1] *n.* busybody, disrupter, interferer, makebate, meddler, mischief-maker, stirrer, subversive, trouble-maker.
antonym peacemaker.

mixer[2] *n.* everybody's friend, extrovert, joiner, life and soul of the party, socialiser.
antonyms introvert, loner, recluse.

mixing *n.* amalgamation, association, blending, coalescence, combination, fraternisation, fusion, hybridisation, interbreeding, intercourse, interflow, intermingling, minglement, miscegenation, socialising, synthesis, union.
antonym separation.

mixture *n.* admixture, alloy, amalgam, amalgamation, association, assortment, blend, brew, coalescence, combination, combine, composite, compost, compound, concoction, conglomeration, cross, fusion, galimatias, gallimaufry, half-breed, hotchpotch, hybrid, jumble, macédoine, medley, mélange, miscegen, miscegenation, miscellany, mix, mixed bag, mongrel, olio, olla-podrida, omnium-gatherum, pastiche, pot-pourri, salad, salmagundi, synthesis, union, variety.

mix-up *n.* balls-up, chaos, complication, confusion, disorder, fankle, foul-up, jumble, mess, mistake, misunderstanding, muddle, nonsense, snafu, snarl-up, tangle.

moan *n.* beef, belly-ache, bitch, complaint, gripe, groan, grouch, grouse, grumble, howl, keen, lament, lamentation, sigh, snivel, sob, sough, ululation, wail, whimper, whine, whinge.
v. beef, belly-ache, bemoan, bewail, bitch, carp, complain, deplore, grieve, gripe, groan, grouch, grouse, grumble, howl, keen, lament, mourn, sigh, snivel, sob, sough, ululate, wail, weep, whimper, whine, whinge, wuther.
antonym rejoice.

mob *n.* assemblage, bevy, body, canaille, class, collection, common herd, commonalty, company, crew, crowd, drove, faex populi, flock, galère, gang, gathering, great unwashed, group, herd, hoi polloi, horde, host, jingbang, lot, many-headed beast, many-headed monster, mass, masses, mobile, multitude, pack, plebs, populace, press, rabble, rent-a-crowd, rent-a-mob, riff-raff, rout, scum, set, swarm, throng, tribe, troop, vulgus.
v. besiege, charge, cram, crowd, crowd round, descend on, fill, jam, jostle, overrun, pack,

pester, set upon, surround, swarm round.
antonym shun.

mobile *adj.* active, agile, ambulatory, animated, changeable, changing, energetic, ever-changing, expressive, flexible, fluid, itinerant, lively, locomobile, locomotive, mercurial, migrant, motile, movable, moving, nimble, peripatetic, portable, roaming, roving, supple, travelling, vagile, vivacious, wandering.
antonym immobile.

mobilise *v.* activate, animate, assemble, call up, enlist, galvanise, levy, marshal, muster, organise, prepare, rally, ready, shift, stir, summon.

mobility *n.* agility, animation, expressiveness, flexibility, locomobility, locomotion, locomotivity, motility, motion, motivity, movability, movableness, portability, suppleness, vagility, vivacity.
antonyms immobility, inflexibility, rigidity.

mob-rule *n.* lynch-law, mobocracy, ochlocracy, Reign of Terror.

mock *v.* ape, baffle, befool, burlesque, caricature, chaff, cheat, counterfeit, debunk, deceive, defeat, defy, delude, deride, disappoint, disparage, dupe, elude, explode, fleer, flout, foil, fool, frustrate, guy, imitate, insult, jeer, lampoon, laugh at, laugh in (someone's) face, laugh to scorn, make fun of, make sport of, mimic, parody, parrot, poke fun at, queer, quiz, ridicule, satirise, scoff, scorn, send up, sneer, take the mickey, taunt, tease, thwart, travesty, twit.
antonyms flatter, praise.
adj. artificial, bogus, counterfeit, dummy, ersatz, fake, faked, false, feigned, forged, fraudulent, imitation, phoney, pinchbeck, pretended, pseudo, sham, simulated, spurious, synthetic.

mocker *n.* derider, detractor, fleerer, flouter, iconoclast, jeerer, lampooner, lampoonist, pasquinader, reviler, ridiculer, satirist, scoffer, scorner, sneerer, tease, tormentor, vilifier.
antonyms flatterer, supporter.

mockery *n.* apology, burlesque, caricature, contempt, contumely, deception, derision, disappointment, disdain, disrespect, farce, fleer, gibes, iconoclasm, imitation, insults, invective, irrision, jeering, joke, lampoon, lampoonery, let-down, mickey-taking, mimesis, mimicry, misrepresentation, parody, pasquinade, pretence, quiz, ridicule, sarcasm, satire, scoffing, scorn, send-up, sham, spoof, take-off, travesty, wisecracks.

mocking *adj.* contemptuous, contumelious, cynical, derisive, derisory, disdainful, disrespectful, iconoclastic, impudent, insulting, irreverent, irrisory, sarcastic, sardonic, satiric, satirical, scoffing, scornful, snide, taunting.
antonym laudatory.

mode *n.* approach, condition, convention, course, craze, custom, dernier cri, fad, fashion, form, latest thing, look, manner, method, plan, practice, procedure, process, quality, rage, rule, state, style, system, technique, trend, vein, vogue, way.

model *n*. archetype, configuration, copy, criterion, design, draft, dummy, embodiment, epitome, example, exemplar, facsimile, form, gauge, ideal, image, imitation, kind, loadstar, manikin, mannequin, maquette, mark, miniature, mock-up, mode, mould, original, paradigm, paragon, pattern, personification, plan, poser, praxis, prototype, replica, representation, sitter, sketch, standard, style, subject, template, touchstone, type, variety, version, yardstick.

adj. archetypal, complete, consummate, dummy, exemplary, facsimile, ideal, illustrative, imitation, miniature, par excellence, paradigmatic, perfect, prototypal, prototypical, representative, standard, typical.

v. base, carve, cast, create, design, display, fashion, form, make, mould, pattern, plan, sculpt, shape, show off, sport, wear, work.

moderate *adj*. abstemious, average, calm, centrist, continent, controlled, cool, deliberate, disciplined, equable, fair, fairish, frugal, gentle, indifferent, judicious, limited, mediocre, medium, middle-of-the-road, middling, mild, modest, non-extreme, ordinary, passable, peaceable, quiet, rational, reasonable, restrained, sensible, sober, softshell(ed), so-so, steady, temperate, unexceptional, well-regulated.

v. abate, allay, alleviate, appease, assuage, attemper, blunt, calm, chasten, check, control, curb, cushion, decrease, diminish, dwindle, ease, lenify, lessen, mitigate, modify, modulate, pacify, palliate, play down, quiet, regulate, repress, restrain, slake, soften, soft-pedal, subdue, subside, tame, temper, tone down.

moderately *adv*. fairly, frugally, gently, in moderation, modestly, passably, pretty, quite, rather, reasonably, slightly, soberly, somewhat, sparingly, to a certain degree, to a certain extent, to some extent, tolerably, unpretentiously, within limits, within measure, within reason.

antonym immoderately.

moderation *n*. abatement, abstemiousness, alleviation, aurea mediocritas, calmness, caution, chastity, composure, continence, control, coolness, decrease, diminution, discipline, discretion, easing, equanimity, extenuation, fairness, golden mean, judiciousness, justice, justness, let-up, mildness, mitigation, moderateness, modification, modulation, palliation, reasonableness, reduction, restraint, self-control, sobriety, temperance, via media.

antonyms increase, intemperance.

modern *adj*. advanced, avant-garde, contemporary, current, emancipated, fashionable, fresh, go-ahead, goey, innovative, inventive, jazzy, late, latest, mod, modernistic, modish, neoteric, new, newfangled, novel, present, present-day, progressive, recent, stylish,

trendy, twentieth-century, up-to-date, up-to-the-minute, with-it.

antonyms antiquated, old.

modernise *v*. do up, improve, modify, neoterise, progress, redesign, reform, refresh, refurbish, regenerate, rejuvenate, remake, remodel, renew, renovate, revamp, streamline, tart up, transform, update.

antonym regress.

modernity *n*. contemporaneity, currency, fashionableness, freshness, goeyness, innovation, innovativeness, newness, novelty, originality, recentness.

antonyms antiquatedness, antiquity.

modest *adj*. bashful, blushing, chaste, chastened, coy, demure, diffident, discreet, fair, humble, limited, maidenly, meek, middling, moderate, ordinary, proper, quiet, reserved, reticent, retiring, seemly, self-conscious, self-effacing, shamefaced, shy, simple, small, timid, unassuming, unexceptional, unpresuming, unpresumptuous, unpretending, unpretentious, verecund.

antonyms conceited, immodest, pretentious, vain.

modesty *n*. aidos, bashfulness, coyness, decency, demureness, diffidence, discreetness, humbleness, humility, meekness, propriety, quietness, reserve, reticence, seemliness, self-effacement, shamefacedness, shamefastness, shyness, simplicity, timidity, unobtrusiveness, unpretentiousness.

antonyms conceit, immodesty, vanity.

modicum *n*. atom, bit, crumb, dash, drop, fragment, grain, hint, inch, iota, little, mite, ounce, particle, pinch, scrap, shred, speck, suggestion, tinge, touch, trace.

modification *n*. adjustment, alteration, change, limitation, moderation, modulation, mutation, qualification, refinement, reformation, restriction, revision, tempering, variation.

modify *v*. abate, adapt, adjust, allay, alter, attemper, change, convert, improve, lessen, limit, lower, moderate, modulate, qualify, recast, redesign, redo, reduce, refashion, reform, remodel, reorganise, reshape, restrain, restrict, revise, rework, soften, temper, tone down, transform, vary.

modish *adj*. à la mode, all the rage, avant-garde, chic, contemporary, current, fashionable, goey, hip, in, jazzy, latest, mod, modern, modernistic, now, smart, stylish, trendy, up-to-the-minute, vogue, voguish, with-it.

antonyms dowdy, old-fashioned.

modulate *v*. adjust, alter, attune, balance, harmonise, inflect, lower, moderate, regulate, soften, tone, tune, vary.

antonyms increase, raise.

modulation *n*. accent, adjustment, alteration, inflection, inflexion, intonation, moderation, regulation, shade, shift, tone, tuning, variation.

modus operandi manner, method, operation, plan, practice, praxis, procedure, process, rule, rule of thumb, system, technique, way.

mogul *n.* baron, bashaw, big cheese, big gun, big noise, big pot, big shot, big wheel, bigwig, grandee, magnate, magnifico, Mr Big, nabob, notable, panjandrum, personage, potentate, supremo, top dog, tycoon, VIP.
antonym nobody.

moist *adj.* clammy, damp, dampish, dampy, dank, dewy, dripping, drizzly, humid, marshy, muggy, rainy, soggy, swampy, tearful, vaporous, watery, wet, wettish.
antonyms arid, dry.

moisten *v.* bedew, damp, dampen, embrocate, humect, humectate, humidify, humify, imbue, irrigate, lick, madefy, moistify, moisturise, slake, soak, water, wet.
antonym dry.

moistening *n.* dampening, damping, humectation, humidification, humification, irrigation, moisturisation, soaking, watering, wetting.
antonym drying.
adj. dampening, damping, humectant, humective, moisturising.
antonym drying.

moisture *n.* damp, dampness, dankness, dew, humidity, humour, liquid, mugginess, perspiration, sweat, tears, vapour, water, wateriness, wet, wetness.
antonym dryness.

mole[1] *n.* barrier, breakwater, dike, dyke, embankment, groyne, jetty, jutty, pier.

mole[2] *n.* moudiewart, mouldwarp.

mole[3] *n.* agent, double agent, infiltrator, secret agent, spy.

molest *v.* abuse, accost, afflict, annoy, assail, attack, badger, beset, bother, bug, disturb, faze, harass, harm, harry, hassle, hector, hound, hurt, ill-treat, injure, irritate, maltreat, manhandle, mistreat, persecute, pester, plague, tease, torment, trouble, upset, vex, worry.

mollify *v.* abate, allay, appease, assuage, blunt, calm, compose, conciliate, cushion, ease, lessen, lull, mellow, mitigate, moderate, modify, pacify, placate, propitiate, quell, quiet, relax, relieve, soften, soothe, sweeten, temper.
antonyms aggravate, anger.

mollycoddle *v.* baby, coddle, cosset, indulge, mother, overprotect, pamper, pander to, pet, ruin, spoil, spoon-feed.
antonyms ill-treat, neglect.

moment[1] *n.* breathing-while, flash, hour, instant, jiff, jiffy, juncture, less than no time, minute, mo, point, second, shake, split second, stage, tick, time, trice, twink, twinkling.

moment[2] *n.* concern, consequence, gravity, import, importance, note interest, seriousness, significance, substance, value, weight, weightiness, worth.
antonym insignificance.

momentarily *adv.* briefly, fleetingly, for a moment, for a second, for an instant, temporarily.

momentary *adj.* brief, elusive, ephemeral,

evanescent, fleeting, flying, fugitive, hasty, momentaneous, passing, quick, short, short-lived, temporary, transient, transitory.
antonyms lasting, permanent.

momentous *adj.* apocalyptic, consequential, critical, crucial, decisive, earth-shaking, epoch-making, eventful, fateful, grave, historic, important, major, pivotal, serious, significant, tremendous, vital, weighty.
antonym insignificant.

momentum *n.* drive, energy, force, impact, impetus, impulse, incentive, power, propulsion, push, speed, stimulus, strength, thrust, urge, velocity.

monarch *n.* despot, dynast, emperor, empress, king, potentate, prince, princess, queen, ruler, sovereign, tyrant.

monarchy *n.* absolutism, autocracy, despotism, empire, kingdom, kinghood, kingship, majesty, monocracy, princedom, princehood, principality, principate, realm, royalism, rule, sovereignty, tyranny.

monastery *n.* abbey, ashram, béguinage, Charterhouse, Chartreuse, cloister, coenobium, convent, fratery, fratry, friary, house, lamasery, nunnery, priory, vihara, wat.

monastic *adj.* anchoritic, ascetic, austere, celibate, cloistered, cloistral, coenobitic, contemplative, conventual, eremital, eremitic, hermitical, monachal, monasterial, monastical, monkish, recluse, reclusive, secluded, sequestered, withdrawn.
antonyms gregarious, materialistic, worldly.

monasticism *n.* anchoritsm, asceticism, austerity, coenobitism, eremitism, monachism, monkery, monkhood, recluseness, reclusion, seclusion.

monetary *adj.* budgetary, bursal, capital, cash, economic, financial, fiscal, money, pecuniary.

money *n.* akkas, akkers, baksheesh, banco, banknotes, bankroll, boodle, brass, bread, capital, cash, chips, coin, currency, dibs, dough, dumps, fat, filthy lucre, fonds, funds, gelt, gold, gravy, greens, hard cash, hard money, legal tender, lolly, loot, mazuma, mint-sauce, money of account, moolah, oof, pelf, readies, ready money, rhino, riches, scrip, shekels, siller, silver, specie, spondulix (spondulicks), stumpy, sugar, the needful, the ready, the wherewithal, tin, wealth.

money-box *n.* cash-box, chest, coffer, penny-pig, pig, piggy-bank, safe.

moneyed, monied *adj.* affluent, comfortable, flush, loaded, opulent, prosperous, rich, rolling, stinking, warm, wealthy, well-heeled, well-off, well-to-do.
antonym impoverished.

money-grubber *n.* mammonist, mammonite, muck-worm, quaestuary.

money-grubbing *adj.* acquisitive, grasping, mammonish, mammonistic, mercenary, miserly, quaestuary.

mongrel *n.* bigener, cross, crossbreed, half-breed, hybrid, lurcher, mule, mutt, yellow-dog.

adj. bastard, crossbred, half-breed, hybrid, ill-defined, mixed, mongrelly, nondescript.
antonyms pedigree, pure-bred.
monitor *n.* adviser, detector, guide, invigilator, overseer, prefect, recorder, scanner, screen, supervisor, watchdog.
v. check, detect, follow, keep an eye on, keep track of, keep under surveillance, note, observe, oversee, plot, record, scan, supervise, survey, trace, track, watch.
monk *n.* beghard, béguin, brother, cloisterer, coenobite, contemplative, conventual, frate, frater, friar, gyrovague, hermit, mendicant, monastic, religieux, religionary, religioner, religious.
monkey[1] *n.* ape, primate, simian.
monkey[2] *n.* ass, butt, devil, dupe, fool, imp, jackanapes, laughing-stock, mug, rapscallion, rascal, rogue, scallywag, scamp.
v. fiddle, fidget, fool, interfere, meddle, mess, play, potter, tamper, tinker, trifle.
monkey business carry-on, chicanery, clowning, dishonesty, foolery, hanky-panky, jiggery-pokery, jugglery, legerdemain, mischief, monkey tricks, pranks, shenanigans, skulduggery, sleight-of-hand, tomfoolery, trickery.
antonyms honesty, probity.
monochrome *adj.* black-and-white, monochroic, monochromatic, monotone, monotonous, sepia, unicolor, unicolorate, unicolorous, unicolour, unicoloured.
antonym kaleidoscopic.
monocle *n.* eyeglass, glass, quiz, quizzing-glass.
monogamous *adj.* monandrous, monogamic, monogynous.
antonyms bigamous, polygamous.
monogamy *n.* monandry, monogyny.
antonyms bigamy, polygamy.
monolingual *adj.* monoglot, unilingual.
antonym polyglot.
monolith *n.* megalith, menhir, sarsen, shaft, standing stone.
monolithic *adj.* colossal, faceless, giant, gigantic, huge, immobile, immovable, inflexible, intractable, massive, monumental, rigid, solid, undifferentiated, unvaried, vast.
monologue *n.* harangue, homily, lecture, oration, sermon, soliloquy, speech, spiel.
antonyms conversation, dialogue, discussion.
monomania *n.* bee in one's bonnet, fanaticism, fetish, fixation, hobby-horse, idée fixe, mania, neurosis, obsession, ruling passion, thing.
monopolise *v.* appropriate, control, corner, dominate, engross, hog, occupy, preoccupy, take over, take up, tie up.
antonym share.
monopoly *n.* ascendancy, control, corner, domination, exclusive right, monopsony, sole right.
monotheism *n.* henotheism, unitarianism.
antonym polytheism.
monotonous *adj.* boring, colourless, droning, dull, flat, humdrum, monochrome, plodding, prosaic, repetitious, repetitive, routine, samey, soul-destroying, tedious, tiresome,

toneless, unchanging, uneventful, uniform, uninflected, unvaried, unvarying, wearisome.
antonyms colourful, lively, varied.
monotony *n.* boredom, colourlessness, dullness, flatness, humdrumness, monotonousness, prosaicness, repetitiousness, repetitiveness, routine, routineness, sameness, tediousness, tedium, tiresomeness, uneventfulness, uniformity, wearisomeness.
antonyms colour, liveliness.
monster *n.* abortion, barbarian, basilisk, beast, behemoth, bogeyman, brute, centaur, chimera, cockatrice, colossus, Cyclops, demon, devil, fiend, freak, giant, Gorgon, harpy, hellhound, hippocampus, hippogriff, Hydra, jabberwock, kraken, lamia, leviathan, lindworm, mammoth, manticore, Medusa, Minotaur, miscreation, monstrosity, mutant, ogre, ogress, prodigy, rye-wolf, savage, Sphinx, teratism, titan, villain, wivern.
adj. Brobdingnagian, colossal, cyclopean, enormous, gargantuan, giant, gigantic, huge, immense, jumbo, mammoth, massive, monstrous, prodigious, rounceval, stupendous, titanic, tremendous, vast.
antonym minute.
monstrosity *n.* abnormality, abortion, atrocity, dreadfulness, enormity, evil, eyesore, freak, frightfulness, heinousness, hellishness, hideousness, horror, loathsomeness, miscreation, monster, mutant, obscenity, ogre, prodigy, teras, teratism.
monstrous *adj.* abhorrent, abnormal, atrocious, colossal, criminal, cruel, cyclopean, deformed, devilish, diabolical, disgraceful, dreadful, egregious, elephantine, enormous, evil, fiendish, foul, freakish, frightful, gargantuan, giant, gigantic, great, grotesque, gruesome, heinous, hellish, hideous, horrendous, horrible, horrific, horrifying, huge, hulking, immense, infamous, inhuman, intolerable, loathsome, malformed, mammoth, massive, miscreated, misshapen, monster, obscene, odious, outrageous, prodigious, rounceval, satanic, scandalous, shocking, stupendous, teratoid, terrible, titanic, towering, tremendous, unnatural, vast, vicious, villainous, wicked.
monthly *adj.* mensal, menstrual, mensual.
monument *n.* ancient monument, antiquity, barrow, cairn, cenotaph, commemoration, cross, dolmen, evidence, gravestone, headstone, marker, martyry, mausoleum, memento, memorial, obelisk, pillar, prehistoric monument, record, relic, remembrance, reminder, shaft, shrine, statue, testament, token, tombstone, tumulus, witness.
monumental *adj.* abiding, awe-inspiring, awesome, catastrophic, classic, colossal, commemorative, conspicuous, cyclopean, durable, egregious, enduring, enormous, epoch-making, funerary, gigantic, great, historic, horrible, huge, immense, immortal, important, imposing, impressive, indefensible, lasting, magnificent, majestic, massive,

memorable, memorial, monolithic, notable, outstanding, overwhelming, prodigious, significant, staggering, statuary, stupendous, terrible, tremendous, vast, whopping. *antonyms* insignificant, unimportant.

mood *n.* blues, caprice, depression, disposition, doldrums, dumps, fit, frame of mind, grumps, humour, melancholy, pique, spirit, state of mind, sulk, temper, tenor, the sulks, vein, whim.

moody *adj.* angry, atrabilious, broody, cantankerous, capricious, cast-down, changeable, choleric, crabbed, crabby, cranky, cross, crotchety, crusty, dejected, depressive, dismal, doleful, dour, downcast, erratic, faddish, fickle, fitful, flighty, gloomy, glum, huffish, huffy, ill-humoured, impulsive, inconstant, introspective, introvert, irascible, irritable, lugubrious, melancholy, mercurial, miserable, mopy, morose, peevish, pensive, petulant, piqued, sad, saturnine, short-tempered, splenetic, sulky, sullen, temperamental, testy, touchy, unpredictable, unsociable, unstable, unsteady, volatile, waspish. *antonyms* cheerful, equable.

moon[1] *v.* brood, daydream, dream, fantasise, idle, languish, loaf, mooch, mope, pine, potter.

moon[2] *n.* crescent, Cynthia, demilune, Diana, full moôn, half-moon, lune, lunule, meniscus, Paddy's lantern, Phoebe, Selene.

moon-like *adj.* crescent, crescentic, lunar, lunate, lunular, meniscoid, moon-shaped, moony, selenic.

moonshine[1] *n.* baloney, blather, blether, bosh, bullshit, bunk, bunkum, claptrap, crap, eyewash, gas, guff, havers, hogwash, hot air, nonsense, piffle, rot, rubbish, stuff, tarradiddle, tommyrot, tosh, tripe, twaddle. *antonym* sense.

moonshine[2] *n.* bootleg, hoo(t)ch, pot(h)een.

moor[1] *v.* anchor, berth, bind, dock, drop anchor, fasten, fix, hitch, lash, secure, tie up. *antonym* loose.

moor[2] *n.* brae, downs, fell, heath, moorland, muir, upland, wold.

moot *v.* advance, argue, bring up, broach, debate, discuss, introduce, pose, propose, propound, put forward, submit, suggest, ventilate.
adj. academic, arguable, contestable, controversial, crucial, debatable, disputable, disputed, doubtful, insoluble, knotty, open, open to debate, problematic, questionable, undecided, undetermined, unresolvable, unresolved, unsettled, vexed.

moot point controversial issue, crux, difficulty, knot, poser, problem, question mark, stumbling-block, vexata quaestio, vexed question.

mop *n.* head of hair, mane, mass, mat, shock, sponge, squeegee, swab, tangle, thatch.
v. absorb, clean, soak, sponge, swab, wash, wipe.

mop up absorb, account for, clean up, eliminate, finish off, neutralise, round up,

secure, soak up, sponge, swab, take care of, tidy up, wash, wipe.

mope *v.* agonise, boody, brood, despair, despond, droop, fret, grieve, idle, languish, mooch, moon, pine, sulk.
n. depressive, grouch, grump, introvert, killjoy, melancholiac, melancholic, misery, moaner, moper, mopus, pessimist, Weary Willie.

moral *adj.* blameless, chaste, clean-living, decent, equitable, ethical, good, high-minded, honest, honourable, incorruptible, innocent, just, meritorious, moralistic, noble, principled, proper, pure, responsible, right, righteous, square, straight, temperate, upright, upstanding, virtuous. *antonym* immoral.
n. adage, aphorism, apophthegm, dictum, epigram, gnome, import, lesson, maxim, meaning, message, motto, point, precept, proverb, saw, saying, significance, teaching.

morale *n.* confidence, esprit de corps, heart, mettle, mood, resolve, self-esteem, spirit, spirits, state of mind, temper.

moralise *v.* discourse, edify, ethicise, lecture, pontificate, pontify, preach, sermonise.

morality *n.* chastity, conduct, decency, deontology, equity, ethicality, ethicalness, ethics, ethos, goodness, habits, honesty, ideals, integrity, justice, manners, morals, mores, philosophy, principle, principles, probity, propriety, rationale, rectitude, righteousness, standards, tightness, uprightness, virtue. *antonym* immorality.

morals *n.* behaviour, conduct, deontics, deontology, equity, ethics, ethos, habits, ideals, integrity, manners, morality, mores, principles, probity, propriety, rectitude, scruples, standards.

morass *n.* bog, can of worms, chaos, clutter, confusion, fen, flow, jam, jumble, marsh, marshland, mess, mire, mix-up, moss, muddle, quag, quagmire, quicksand, slough, swamp, tangle.

moratorium *n.* ban, delay, embargo, freeze, halt, postponement, respite, standstill, stay, stoppage, suspension. *antonyms* go-ahead, green light.

morbid *adj.* ailing, brooding, corrupt, deadly, diseased, dreadful, ghastly, ghoulish, gloomy, grim, grisly, gruesome, hideous, horrid, hypochondriacal, infected, lugubrious, macabre, malignant, melancholy, neurotic, pathological, peccant, pessimistic, putrid, sick, sickly, sombre, unhealthy, unsalubrious, unsound, unwholesome, vicious, Wertherian.

mordant *adj.* acerbic, acid, acidic, acidulous, acrimonious, astringent, biting, bitter, caustic, corrosive, cutting, edged, harsh, incisive, mordacious, pungent, sarcastic, scathing, sharp, stinging, trenchant, venomous, vicious, waspish, wounding. *antonyms* gentle, sparing.

more *adj.* added, additional, alternative, extra, fresh, further, increased, new, other, renewed, repeated, spare, supplementary.

adv. again, better, further, longer.

moreover *adv.* additionally, also, as well, besides, further, furthermore, in addition, into the bargain, likewise, may I add, more, more to the point, to boot, too, what is more, withal.

morgue *n.* deadhouse, mortuary.

moribund *adj.* at a standstill, caducous, collapsing, comatose, crumbling, dead and alive, declining, doomed, dwindling, dying, ebbing, fading, failing, in extremis, obsolescent, on one's last legs, on the way out, senile, stagnant, stagnating, waning, wasting away, weak, with one foot in the grave.

antonyms alive, flourishing, lively, nascent.

morning *n.* ack emma, am, break of day, cock-crow, dawn, daybreak, daylight, dayspring, first thing, foreday, forenoon, morn, sunrise, sun-up.

adj. antemeridian, auroral, aurorean, dawn, forenoon, matinal, matutinal, matutive.

moron *n.* ass, blockhead, bonehead, clot, cretin, daftie, dimwit, dolt, dope, dumbbell, dummy, dunce, dunderhead, fool, halfwit, idiot, imbecile, klutz, mental defective, mooncalf, muttonhead, natural, nong, numbskull, schmo, schmuck, simpleton, thickhead, vegetable, zombie.

moronic *adj.* asinine, brainless, cretinous, daft, defective, dimwitted, doltish, dopey, foolish, gormless, halfwitted, idiotic, imbecilic, lacking, mindless, retarded, simple, simpleminded, stupid, subnormal, thick, unintelligent.

morose *adj.* blue, cheerless, churlish, crabbed, crabby, cross, crusty, depressed, dour, down, gloomy, glum, grim, grouchy, gruff, grum, huffy, humourless, ill-humoured, ill-natured, ill-tempered, low, melancholy, misanthropic, moody, mournful, perverse, pessimistic, saturnine, sour, stern, sulky, sullen, surly, taciturn, testy, unsociable.

antonyms cheerful, communicative.

morsel *n.* atom, bit, bite, bonne-bouche, crumb, fraction, fragment, grain, modicum, morceau, mouthful, nibble, part, piece, scrap, segment, slice, smidgen, snack, soupçon, taste, titbit.

mortal *adj.* agonising, awful, bodily, corporeal, deadly, deathful, dire, earthly, enormous, ephemeral, extreme, fatal, fleshly, grave, great, human, impermanent, implacable, intense, irreconcilable, lethal, lethiferous, mortiferous, passing, perishable, relentless, remorseless, severe, sublunary, sworn, temporal, terrible, transient, unrelenting, worldly.

antonym immortal.

n. being, body, creature, earthling, human, human being, individual, man, person, sublunar, sublunary, woman.

antonyms god, immortal.

mortality *n.* bloodshed, caducity, carnage, corruptibility, death, destruction, ephemerality, fatality, humanity, humans, impermanence, killing, mankind, mortals, perishabil-

ity, temporality, transience, transitoriness.

antonym immortality.

mortgage *v.* dip, pawn, pledge, put in hock.

n. bond, debenture, lien, loan, pledge, security, wadset.

mortification *n.* abasement, annoyance, ascesis, asceticism, chagrin, chastening, confounding, conquering, control, corruption, defeat, denial, discipline, discomfiture, dissatisfaction, embarrassment, festering, gangrene, humiliation, ignominy, loss of face, necrosis, overthrow, punishment, putrescence, shame, subjugation, vexation.

mortified *adj.* abashed, affronted, annoyed, ashamed, chagrined, chastened, confounded, crushed, dead, decayed, deflated, discomfited, displeased, embarrassed, gangrenous, humbled, humiliated, necrotic, put out, put to shame, putrefied, putrid, rotted, rotten, shamed, vexed.

antonyms elated, jubilant.

mortify *v.* abase, abash, affront, annoy, chagrin, chasten, confound, conquer, control, corrupt, crush, deflate, deny, die, disappoint, discipline, discomfit, embarrass, fester, gangrene, humble, humiliate, macerate, necrose, put to shame, putrefy, shame, subdue, vex.

mortifying *adj.* chastening, crushing, discomfiting, embarrassing, humbling, humiliating, ignominious, overwhelming, punishing, salutary, shaming, thwarting.

mortuary *n.* deadhouse, funeral parlour, morgue.

mostly *adv.* as a rule, characteristically, chiefly, commonly, customarily, feckly, for the most part, generally, largely, mainly, normally, on the whole, particularly, predominantly, primarily, principally, typically, usually.

mote *n.* atom, grain, iota, jot, mite, particle, speck, spot, trace.

moth-eaten *adj.* ancient, antiquated, archaic, dated, decayed, decrepit, dilapidated, mangy, moribund, mothed, mouldy, musty, obsolete, old-fashioned, outdated, outworn, ragged, seedy, shabby, stale, tattered, threadbare, worn-out.

antonyms fresh, new.

mother *n.* dam, generatrix, genetrix, ma, mam, mama, mamma, mammy, mater, materfamilias, mom, momma, mommy, mum, mummy, old lady, old woman.

v. baby, bear, care for, cherish, cosset, foster, fuss over, indulge, nurse, nurture, overprotect, pamper, produce, protect, raise, rear, spoil, tend.

antonym neglect.

motherly *adj.* affectionate, caring, comforting, fond, gentle, indulgent, kind, kindly, loving, maternal, protective, solicitous, tender, warm.

antonyms indifferent, neglectful, uncaring.

motif *n.* concept, decoration, design, device, figure, form, idea, leitmotiv, logo, notion, ornament, pattern, shape, strain, subject, theme.

motion *n.* action, change, dynamics, flow, flux, gesticulation, gesture, inclination, kinesics, kinetics, locomotion, mechanics, mobility, motility, move, movement, nod, passage, passing, progress, proposal, proposition, recommendation, sign, signal, submission, suggestion, transit, travel, wave.

v. beckon, direct, gesticulate, gesture, nod, sign, signal, usher, wave.

motionless *adj.* at a standstill, at rest, calm, fixed, frozen, halted, immobile, inanimate, inert, lifeless, moveless, paralysed, resting, rigid, stagnant, standing, static, stationary, still, stock-still, transfixed, unmoved, unmoving.

antonym active.

motivate *v.* actuate, arouse, bring, cause, draw, drive, encourage, impel, incite, induce, inspire, inspirit, instigate, kindle, lead, move, persuade, prompt, propel, provoke, push, spur, stimulate, stir, trigger, urge.

antonyms deter, prevent.

motivation *n.* ambition, desire, drive, hunger, impulse, incentive, incitement, inducement, inspiration, instigation, interest, momentum, motive, persuasion, provocation, push, reason, spur, stimulus, urge, wish.

antonyms discouragement, prevention.

motive *n.* cause, consideration, design, desire, encouragement, ground(s), impulse, incentive, incitement, inducement, influence, inspiration, intention, mainspring, motivation, object, occasion, purpose, rationale, reason, spur, stimulus, thinking, urge.

antonyms deterrent, discouragement, disincentive.

adj. activating, actuating, agential, driving, impelling, initiating, motivating, moving, operative, prompting, propellent.

antonyms deterrent, inhibitory, preventive.

motley *adj.* assorted, chequered, disparate, dissimilar, diverse, diversified, haphazard, heterogeneous, ill-assorted, kaleidoscopic, mingled, miscellaneous, mixed, multicoloured, particoloured, patchwork, polychromatic, polychrome, polychromous, promiscuous, rainbow, unlike, varied, variegated.

antonyms homogeneous, monochrome, uniform.

mottled *adj.* blotchy, brindled, chequered, dappled, flecked, freaked, freckled, jaspé, marbled, piebald, pied, poikilitic, skewbald, speckled, spotted, stippled, streaked, tabby, variegated, veined, watered.

antonyms monochrome, plain, uniform.

motto *n.* adage, apophthegm, byword, catchword, cry, dictum, epigraph, formula, gnome, golden rule, ichthys, maxim, precept, proverb, rule, saw, saying, sentence, slogan, watchword.

mould[1] *n.* arrangement, brand, build, calibre, cast, character, configuration, construction, cut, design, die, fashion, form, format, frame, framework, ilk, kidney, kind, line, make, matrix, model, nature, pattern, quality, shape, sort, stamp, structure, style, template, type.

v. affect, carve, cast, construct, control, create, design, direct, fashion, fit, forge, form, hew, influence, make, model, sculpt, sculpture, shape, stamp, work.

mould[2] *n.* black, black spot, blight, fungus, mildew, mouldiness, must, mustiness, rust.

mould[3] *n.* clods, dirt, dust, earth, ground, humus, loam, soil.

moulder *v.* corrupt, crumble, decay, decompose, disintegrate, humify, perish, rot, turn to dust, waste.

mouldy *adj.* bad, blighted, corrupt, decaying, fusty, mildewed, mucedinous, mucid, muggish, muggy, musty, putrid, rotten, rotting, spoiled, stale, vinewed.

antonyms fresh, wholesome.

mound *n.* agger, bank, barrow, bing, bulwark, drift, dune, earthwork, elevation, embankment, heap, hill, hillock, hummock, knoll, mote, motte, pile, rampart, rick, ridge, rise, stack, tuffet, tumulus, tussock, yardang.

mount *v.* accumulate, arise, ascend, bestride, build, clamber up, climb, climb on, climb up on, copulate, cover, deliver, display, emplace, enchase, escalade, escalate, exhibit, fit, frame, get astride, get on, get up, get up on, go up, grow, horse, increase, install, intensify, jump on, launch, lift, multiply, pile up, place, position, prepare, produce, put in place, put on, ready, ride, rise, rocket, scale, set, set in motion, set off, set up, soar, stage, straddle, swell, tower, tread.

n. backing, base, fixture, foil, frame, horse, monture, mounting, pedestal, podium, setting, stand, steed, support.

mountain *n.* abundance, alp, backlog, ben, berg, elevation, eminence, fell, heap, height, mass, massif, mound, mount, Munro, peak, pile, reserve, stack, ton.

mountainous *adj.* alpine, daunting, enormous, formidable, gigantic, great, gross, high, highland, hilly, huge, hulking, immense, mammoth, mighty, monumental, ponderous, prodigious, rocky, rugged, soaring, steep, towering, unwieldy, upland.

antonyms easy, flat, small.

mountebank *n.* charlatan, cheat, con man, confidence, fake, fraud, huckster, impostor, phoney, pretender, pseud, quack, quacksalver, rogue, spieler, swindler, trickster.

mourn *v.* bemoan, bewail, beweep, deplore, grieve, keen, lament, miss, regret, rue, sorrow, wail, weep.

antonyms bless, rejoice.

mourner *n.* bereaved, griever, keener, mute, sorrower.

mournful *adj.* afflicting, broken-hearted, calamitous, cast-down, cheerless, chopfallen, dearnful, dejected, deplorable, depressed, desolate, disconsolate, dismal, distressing, doleful, dolorous, downcast, funereal, gloomy, griefstricken, grieving, grievous, heartbroken, heavy, heavy-hearted, joyless, lachrymose, lamentable, long-faced, long-visaged, lugub-

rious, melancholy, miserable, painful, piteous, plaintive, plangent, rueful, sad, sombre, sorrowful, stricken, tragic, unhappy, woeful, woesome.
antonyms cheerful, joyful.

mourning *n.* bereavement, black, desolation, grief, grieving, keening, lamentation, sackcloth and ashes, sadness, sorrow, wailing, weeds, weeping, widow's weeds, woe.
antonym rejoicing.

mouse-like *adj.* cowering, diffident, diminutive, mous(e)y, murine, shy, timid, timorous.

mous(e)y *adj.* brownish, characterless, colourless, diffident, drab, dull, indeterminate, ineffectual, mouse-like, plain, quiet, self-effacing, shy, timid, timorous, unassertive, unforthcoming, uninteresting, withdrawn.
antonyms assertive, bright, extrovert, irrepressible.

moustache *n.* excrement, face fungus, handlebar moustache, mustachio, mustachios, toothbrush moustache, walrus, whiskers.

mouth[1] *n.* aperture, cake-hole, cavity, chops, crevice, débouché, debouchment, debouchure, disemboguement, door, embouchure, entrance, estuary, gateway, gob, inlet, jaws, kisser, lips, mandibles, maw, moue, opening, orifice, outlet, portal, potato-trap, pout, proboscis, rattle-trap, scowl, threshold, trap, vent.
v. articulate, declaim, elegise, enunciate, form, pronounce, shape, spout, utter, whisper.

mouth[2] *n.* backchat, boasting, braggadocio, bragging, cheek, effrontery, gas, hot air, impudence, insolence, lip, rudeness, sauce.

mouthful *n.* bit, bite, bonne bouche, drop, forkful, gob, gobbet, gulp, morsel, sample, sip, slug, spoonful, sup, swallow, taste, titbit.

mouthpiece *n.* agent, delegate, fugleman, journal, organ, propagandist, representative, spokesman, spokeswoman.

movable *adj.* adjustable, alterable, changeable, detachable, flexible, mobile, portable, portative, transferable, transportable.
antonyms fixed, immovable.

movables *n.* belongings, chattels, effects, furniture, gear, goods, impedimenta, plenishings, possessions, property, stuff, things, traps.

move *v.* activate, actuate, adjust, advance, advise, advocate, affect, agitate, budge, carry, cause, change, cover the ground, decamp, depart, disturb, drift, drive, ease, edge, excite, flit, get, give rise to, go, go away, gravitate, impel, impress, incite, induce, influence, inspire, instigate, jiggle, lead, leave, locomote, make strides, march, migrate, motivate, move house, operate, persuade, proceed, progress, prompt, propel, propose, pull, push, put forward, quit, recommend, relocate, remove, rouse, run, set going, shift, shove, start, stimulate, stir, submit, suggest, switch, take, touch, transfer, transport, transpose, turn, urge, walk.
n. act, action, deed, démarche, dodge,

draught, flit, flitting, go, manoeuvre, measure, migration, motion, movement, ploy, relocation, removal, ruse, shift, step, stratagem, stroke, tack, tactic, transfer, turn.

movement *n.* act, action, activity, advance, agitation, beat, cadence, campaign, change, crusade, current, development, displacement, division, drift, drive, evolution, exercise, faction, flow, front, gesture, ground swell, group, grouping, innards, machinery, manoeuvre, measure, mechanism, metre, motion, move, moving, operation, organisation, pace, part, party, passage, progress, progression, rhythm, section, shift, steps, stir, stirring, swing, tempo, tendency, transfer, trend, workings, works.

movie *n.* feature, film, flick, motion picture, picture, silent, talkie, video.

movies *n.* cinema, film, films, flicks, pictures, silver screen.

moving *adj.* affecting, ambulant, ambulatory, arousing, dynamic, emotional, emotive, exciting, impelling, impressive, inspirational, inspiring, locomobile, mobile, motile, motivating, movable, pathetic, persuasive, poignant, portable, propelling, running, stimulating, stimulative, stirring, touching, unfixed.
antonyms fixed, stationary, unemotional.

mow *v.* clip, crop, cut, scythe, shear, trim.

mow down butcher, cut down, cut to pieces, decimate, massacre, shoot down, slaughter.

much *adv.* considerably, copiously, decidedly, exceedingly, frequently, greatly, often.
adj. a lot of, abundant, ample, considerable, copious, great, plenteous, plenty of, siz(e)able, substantial.
n. heaps, lashings, loads, lots, oodles, plenty, scads.
antonym little.

muck *n.* dirt, droppings, dung, faeces, filth, gunge, gunk, manure, mire, mud, ooze, ordure, scum, sewage, slime, sludge.

muck up botch, bungle, make a mess of, make a muck of, mar, mess up, muff, ruin, screw up, spoil, waste.

mucky *adj.* begrimed, bespattered, dirty, filthy, grimy, messy, miry, mud-caked, muddy, oozy, soiled, sticky.
antonym clean.

mucous *adj.* gelatinous, glutinous, gummy, mucilaginous, slimy, snotty, viscid, viscous.

mud *n.* adobe, clabber, clay, dirt, fango, glaur, mire, ooze, silt, slab, sleech, slob, sludge, slush.

muddle *v.* befuddle, bewilder, confound, confuse, daze, disarrange, disorder, disorganise, disorient(ate), fuddle, fuzzle, jumble, make a mess of, mess, mix up, mull, perplex, scramble, spoil, stupefy, tangle.
n. bollocks, chaos, clutter, cock-up, confusion, daze, disarray, disorder, disorganisation, fankle, guddle, jumble, mess, mix-up, mull, perplexity, pie, plight, predicament, puddle, snarl-up, tangle.

muddle through cope, get along, get by, make

muddled *adj.* at sea, befuddled, bewildered, chaotic, confused, dazed, disarrayed, disordered, disorganised, disorient(at)ed, higgledy-piggledy, incoherent, jumbled, loose, messy, mixed-up, muddle-headed, perplexed, puzzle-headed, scrambled, stupefied, tangled, unclear, vague, woolly.

muddy *adj.* bespattered, blurred, boggy, clarty, cloudy, confused, dingy, dirty, dredgy, drumly, dull, foul, fuzzy, glaury, grimy, grouty, hazy, impure, indistinct, marshy, miry, mucky, mud-caked, muddled, opaque, quaggy, slabby, sleechy, sloppy, soiled, swampy, turbid, unclear, vague, woolly.
antonyms clean, clear.
v. bedash, bedaub, begrime, bespatter, cloud, dirty, smear, smirch, soil.
antonym clean.

muff *v.* botch, bungle, fluff, mess up, mishit, mismanage, miss, spoil.

muffle *v.* cloak, conceal, cover, damp down, dampen, deaden, disguise, dull, envelop, gag, hood, hush, mask, mute, muzzle, quieten, shroud, silence, soften, stifle, suppress, swaddle, swathe, wrap up.
antonym amplify.

mug[1] *n.* beaker, cup, flagon, jug, pot, stoup, tankard, toby jug.

mug[2] *n.* chump, fool, gull, innocent, mark, muggins, sap, saphead, simpleton, soft touch, sucker.

mug[3] *n.* clock, countenance, dial, face, features, mush, phiz(og), puss, visage.

mug up bone up, con, cram, get up, study, swot.

mug[4] *v.* attack, bash, batter, beat up, garrotte, jump (on), mill, rob, roll, set upon, steal from, waylay.

muggy *adj.* clammy, close, damp, humid, moist, oppressive, sticky, stuffy, sudorific, sultry, sweltering.
antonym dry.

mulish *adj.* bull-headed, cross-grained, defiant, difficult, headstrong, inflexible, intractable, intransigent, obstinate, perverse, pig-headed, recalcitrant, refractory, rigid, self-willed, stiff-necked, stubborn, unreasonable, wilful, wrong-headed.

mull *v.* chew, con, consider, contemplate, deliberate, examine, meditate, muse on, ponder, reflect on, review, ruminate, study, think about, think over, weigh up.

multifarious *adj.* different, diverse, diversified, legion, manifold, many, miscellaneous, multiform, multiple, multiplex, multitudinous, numerous, sundry, varied, variegated.

multiple *adj.* collective, manifold, many, multifarious, multiplex, multitudinous, numerous, several, sundry, various.

multiplicity *n.* abundance, array, diversity, heaps, host, loads, lot, lots, manifoldness, mass, multeity, myriad, number, numerousness, oodles, piles, profusion, scores, stacks, tons, variety.

multiply *v.* accumulate, augment, boost, breed, build up, expand, extend, increase, intensify, proliferate, propagate, reproduce, spread.
antonyms decrease, lessen.

multitude *n.* army, assemblage, assembly, collection, commonalty, concourse, congregation, crowd, herd, hive, hoi polloi, horde, host, legion, lot, lots, mass, mob, myriad, people, populace, proletariat, public, rabble, sea, swarm, throng.
antonyms handful, scattering.

multitudinous *adj.* abounding, abundant, considerable, copious, countless, great, infinite, innumerable, legion, manifold, many, myriad, numerous, profuse, swarming, teeming, umpteen.

mum *adj.* close-lipped, close-mouthed, dumb, mute, quiet, reticent, secretive, silent, tight-lipped, uncommunicative, unforthcoming.

mumbo-jumbo *n.* abracadabra, cant, chant, charm, claptrap, conjuration, double talk, gibberish, gobbledegook, hocus-pocus, humbug, incantation, jargon, magic, mummery, nonsense, rigmarole, rite, ritual, spell, superstition.

munch *v.* champ, chew, chomp, crunch, eat, masticate, scrunch.

mundane *adj.* banal, commonplace, day-to-day, earthly, everyday, fleshly, human, humdrum, material, mortal, ordinary, prosaic, routine, secular, subastral, sublunar(y), temporal, terrestrial, workaday, worldly.
antonyms cosmic, extraordinary, supernatural.

municipal *adj.* borough, burgh(al), city, civic, community, public, town, urban.

municipality *n.* borough, burgh, city, département, ment, department, district, precinct, town, township.

munificence *n.* beneficence, benevolence, bounteousness, bounty, generosity, generousness, hospitality, largess(e), liberality, magnanimousness, open-handedness, philanthropy.
antonym meanness.

munificent *adj.* beneficent, benevolent, big-hearted, bounteous, bountiful, free-handed, generous, hospitable, lavish, liberal, magnanimous, open-handed, philanthropical, princely, rich, unstinting.
antonym mean.

murder *n.* agony, assassination, bloodshed, butchery, carnage, danger, deicide, difficulty, filicide, fractricide, hell, homicide, infanticide, killing, manslaughter, massacre, misery, ordeal, parricide, patricide, slaying, trial, trouble.
v. abuse, assassinate, bump off, burke, butcher, destroy, dispatch, do in, drub, eliminate, hammer, hit, kill, mangle, mar, massacre, misuse, rub out, ruin, slaughter, slay, spoil, thrash, waste.

murderer *n.* assassin, butcher, cut-throat, filicide, hit-man, homicide, killer, matricide, parricide, patricide, slaughterer, slayer.

murderous *adj.* ardous, barbarous, bloodthirsty,

bloody, brutal, cruel, cut-throat, dangerous, deadly, death-dealing, destructive, devastating, difficult, exhausting, fatal, fell, ferocious, harrowing, hellish, internecine, killing, lethal, sanguinary, sapping, savage, slaughterous, strenuous, unpleasant, withering.

murky *adj.* cloudy, dark, dim, dismal, dreary, dull, dusky, enigmatic, foggy, gloomy, grey, misty, mysterious, obscure, overcast, veiled.
antonyms bright, clear.

murmur *n.* babble, brool, burble, buzz, buzzing, complaint, croon, drone, grumble, humming, moan, mumble, muttering, purl, purling, purr, rumble, susurrus, undertone, whisper, whispering.
v. babble, burble, burr, buzz, drone, gurgle, hum, mumble, mutter, purl, purr, rumble.

murmuring *adj.* buzzing, droning, mumbling, murmurous, muttering, purring, rumbling, whispering.
n. buzz(ing), drone, mumble, mumbling, murmuration, muttering, purr(ing), rumble, rumbling, susurrus, whisper(ing).

muscle *n.* brawn, clout, depressor, force, forcefulness, levator, might, potency, power, sinew, stamina, strength, sturdiness, tendon, thew, weight.
muscle in butt in, elbow one's way in, force one's way in, impose oneself, jostle, push in, shove, strongarm.

muscular *adj.* athletic, beefy, brawny, hefty, husky, lusty, powerful, powerfully-built, robust, sinewy, stalwart, strapping, strong, sturdy, vigorous, well-knit, wiry.
antonyms delicate, feeble, flabby, puny, weak.

muse *v.* brood, chew, cogitate, consider, contemplate, diliberate, dream, meditate, mull over, ponder, reflect, review, ruminate, speculate, think, think over, weigh.

mush *n.* corn, dough, hogwash, mash, mawkishness, pap, paste, pulp, schmaltz, sentimentality, slush, swill.

mushroom *v.* boom, burgeon, expand, flourish, grow, increase, luxuriate, proliferate, shoot up, spread, spring up, sprout.
n. champignon, chanterelle, fungus, morel, pixy-stool, puffball, toadstool.

mushy *adj.* doughy, maudlin, mawkish, pappy, pulpous, pulpy, saccharine, schmaltzy, sentimental, sloppy, slushy, soft, squashy, squelchy, squidgy, sugary, syrupy, weepy, wet.

musical *adj.* canorous, dulcet, euphonious, Euterpean, harmonious, lilting, lyrical, melodic, melodious, sweet-sounding, tuneful.
antonym unmusical.

musician *n.* accompanist, bard, composer, conductor, instrumentalist, minstrel, performer, player, singer, vocalist.

musing *n.* absent-mindedness, abstraction, brown study, cerebration, cogitation, contemplation, daydreaming, dreaming, introspection, meditation, ponderment, reflection, reverie, rumination, thinking, woolgathering.

must *n.* basic, duty, essential, fundamental, imperative, necessity, obligation, prerequisite, provision, requirement, requisite, sine qua non, stipulation.

muster *v.* assemble, call together, call up, collect, come together, congregate, convene, convoke, enrol, gather, group, marshal, mass, meet, mobilise, rally, round up, summon, throng.
n. assemblage, assembly, collection, concourse, congregation, convention, convocation, gathering, mass, meeting, mobilisation, rally, round-up, throng.

musty *adj.* airless, ancient, antediluvian, antiquated, banal, clichéd, dank, decayed, dull, foughty, frowsty, fusty, hackneyed, hoary, mildewed, mildewy, moth-eaten, mouldy, mucedinous, mucid, obsolete, old, old-fashioned, smelly, stale, stuffy, threadbare, trite, vinewed, worn-out.

mutability *n.* alterability, changeableness, interchangeability, permutability, variability, variation.

mutable *adj.* adaptable, alterable, changeable, changing, fickle, flexible, inconsistent, inconstant, interchangeable, irresolute, permutable, uncertain, undependable, unreliable, unsettled, unstable, unsteady, vacillating, variable, volatile, wavering.
antonyms constant, invariable, permanent.

mutation *n.* alteration, anomaly, change, deviant, deviation, evolution, metamorphosis, modification, mutant, transfiguration, transformation, variation, vicissitude.

mute *adj.* aphonic, dumb, mum, noiseless, silent, speechless, unexpressed, unpronounced, unspeaking, unspoken, voiceless, wordless.
antonyms articulate, vocal, voluble.
v. dampen, deaden, lower, moderate, muffle, silence, soften, soft-pedal, subdue, tone down.

muted *adj.* dampened, dull, faint, low-key, muffled, quiet, soft, stifled, suppressed.

mutilate *v.* adulterate, amputate, bowdlerise, butcher, censor, cut, cut to pieces, cut up, damage, detruncate, disable, disfigure, dismember, distort, expurgate, hack, hamble, injure, lacerate, lame, maim, mangle, mar, spoil.

mutilation *n.* amputation, bowdlerisation, damage, detruncation, disfigurement, dismembering, maiming.

mutinous *adj.* bolshie, bolshy, contumacious, disobedient, insubordinate, insurgent, rebellious, recusant, refractory, revolutionary, riotous, seditious, subversive, turbulent, ungovernable, unmanageable, unruly.
antonyms compliant, dutiful, obedient.

mutiny *n.* defiance, disobedience, insubordination, insurrection, putsch, rebellion, resistance, revolt, revolution, riot, rising, strike, uprising.
v. disobey, protest, rebel, resist, revolt, rise up, strike.

mutt *n.* cur, dog, dolt, drongo, dunderhead, fool, idiot, ignoramus, imbecile, mongrel, moron, nong, sap, saphead, thickhead.

mutter *v.* chunter, complain, grouch, grouse, grumble, mumble, murmur, mussitate, rumble.

mutual *adj.* common, communal, complementary, exchanged, interchangeable, interchanged, joint, reciprocal, reciprocated, requited, returned, shared.

muzzle *n.* bit, curb, gag, guard, jaws, mouth, nose, snaffle, snout.

v. censor, choke, curb, gag, mute, restrain, silence, stifle, suppress.

muzzy *adj.* addled, befuddled, bewildered, blurred, confused, dazed, hazy, muddled, mused, tipsy.

antonym clear.

myopic *adj.* half-blind, near-sighted, short-sighted.

antonym far-sighted.

myriad *adj.* boundless, countless, immeasurable, incalculable, innumerable, limitless, multitudinous, untold.

n. army, flood, horde, host, millions, mountain, multitude, scores, sea, swarm, thousands, throng.

mysterious *adj.* abstruse, arcane, baffling, concealed, covert, cryptic, curious, dark, enigmatic, furtive, hidden, impenetrable, incomprehensible, inexplicable, inscrutable, insoluble, mystical, mystifying, obscure, perplexing, puzzling, recondite, secret, secretive, strange, uncanny, unfathomable, unsearchable, veiled, weird.

antonyms comprehensible, frank, straightforward.

mystery *n.* arcanum, conundrum, enigma, problem, puzzle, question, riddle, secrecy, secret.

mystical *adj.* abstruse, arcane, cab(b)alistic(al), cryptic, enigmatical, esoteric, hidden, inscrutable, metaphysical, mysterious, mystic, occult, otherworldly, paranormal, preternatural, supernatural, transcendental.

mystify *v.* baffle, bamboozle, beat, bewilder, confound, confuse, escape, metagrabolise, metagrobolise, perplex, puzzle, stump.

mystique *n.* appeal, awe, charisma, charm, fascination, glamour, magic, spell.

myth *n.* allegory, delusion, fable, fairy tale, fancy, fantasy, fiction, figment, illusion, legend, old wives' tale, parable, saga, story, superstition, tradition, untruism.

mythical *adj.* fabled, fabricated, fabulous, fairy-tale, fanciful, fantasy, fictitious, imaginary, invented, legendary, made-up, make-believe, mythological, non-existent, pretended, unhistoric(al), unreal.

antonyms actual, historical, real, true.

mythological *adj.* fabulous, folkloric, legendary, mythic, mythical, traditional.

mythology *n.* folklore, folk-tales, legend, lore, myths, mythus, tales, tradition(s).

N

nab *v.* apprehend, arrest, capture, catch, collar, grab, nail, nick, seize, snatch.

nabob *n.* bigwig, billionaire, celebrity, Croesus, financier, luminary, magnate, millionaire, multimillionaire, panjandrum, personage, tycoon, VIP.

nadir *n.* all-time low, bottom, depths, low point, lowest point, low-watermark, minimum, rock bottom, zero.
antonyms acme, apex, peak, zenith.

nag[1] *v.* annoy, badger, berate, chivvy, goad, harass, harry, henpeck, irritate, kvetch, pain, pester, plague, scold, torment, upbraid, vex.
n. harpy, harridan, kvetch(er), scold, shrew, tartar, termagant, virago.

nag[2] *n.* hack, horse, jade, keffel, plug, rip, Rosinante.

nagging *adj.* continuous, critical, distressing, irritating, painful, persistent, scolding, shrewish, tormenting, upsetting, worrying.

nail *v.* apprehend, attach, beat, capture, catch, clinch, collar, fasten, fix, hammer, join, nab, nick, pin, secure, seize, tack.
n. brad, hobnail, nail, peg, pin, rivet, screw, skewer, spike, staple, tack, tacket.

naïve *adj.* artless, callow, candid, childlike, confiding, credulous, dewy-eyed, facile, frank, green, guileless, gullible, ingenuous, innocent, jejune, natural, open, simple, simplistic, trusting, unaffected, uncritical, unpretentious, unsophisticated, unsuspecting, unsuspicious, unworldly, verdant, wide-eyed.
antonyms experienced, sophisticated.

naïvety *n.* artlessness, callowness, candour, credulity, experience, frankness, guilelessness, gullibility, inexperience, ingenuousness, innocence, naturalness, openness, simplicity, sophistication.

naked *adj.* adamic, bare, blatant, defenceless, denuded, disrobed, divested, evident, exposed, helpless, in puris naturalibus, in the altogether, in the buff, insecure, manifest, mother-naked, nude, open, overt, patent, plain, simple, skyclad, stark, starkers, stark-naked, stripped, unadorned, unarmed, unclothed, unconcealed, uncovered, undisguised, undraped, undressed, unexaggerated, unguarded, unmistakable, unprotected, unqualified, unvarnished, vulnerable.
antonyms clothed, concealed, covered.

nakedness *n.* baldness, bareness, nudity, openness, plainness, simplicity, starkness, the altogether, the buff, undress.

namby-pamby *adj.* anaemic, colourless, feeble, insipid, mawkish, pretty-pretty, prim, prissy, sentimental, spineless, vapid, weak, weedy, wet, wishy-washy.

name *n.* acronym, agname, agnomen, appellation, character, cognomen, compellation, compellative, credit, denomination, designation, distinction, eminence, epithet, esteem, fame, handle, honour, moni(c)ker, nickname, note, praise, renown, reputation, repute, sobriquet, stage name, term, title, to-name.
v. appoint, baptise, bename, betitle, call, choose, christen, cite, classify, cognominate, commission, denominate, designate, dub, entitle, identify, label, mention, nominate, select, specify, style, term, title.

named *adj.* appointed, baptised, called, chosen, christened, cited, classified, commissioned, denominated, designated, dit, dubbed, entitled, identified, known as, labelled, mentioned, nominated, onymous, picked, selected, singled out, specified, styled, termed.
antonym nameless.

nameless *adj.* abominable, anonymous, dreadful, fearsome, horrendous, horrible, incognito, indescribable, ineffable, inexpressible, innominate, obscure, terrible, undesignated, undistinguished, unheard-of, unknown, unmentionable, unnamed, unspeakable, unsung, untitled, unutterable.
antonym named.

namely *adv.* ie, specifically, that is, that is to say, to wit, videlicet, viz.

nap[1] *v.* catnap, doze, drop off, drowse, kip, nod, nod off, rest, sleep, snooze.
n. catnap, forty winks, kip, rest, shuteye, siesta, sleep.

nap[2] *n.* down, downiness, fibre, fuzz, grain, pile, shag, weave.

nappy *n.* diaper, doily, hipping, napkin, serviette, towel.

narcissistic *adj.* conceited, egocentric, egomaniacal, ego(t)istic, self-centred, self-loving, vain.

narcotic *n.* anaesthetic, analgesic, anodyne, drug, hop, kef, opiate, pain-killer, sedative, tranquilliser.
adj. analgesic, calming, dulling, hypnotic, Lethean, numbing, pain-killing, sedative, somniferous, somnific, soporific, stupefacient, stupefactive, stupefying.

nark *v.* annoy, bother, bug, exasperate, gall, get, irk, irritate, miff, nettle, peeve, pip, pique, provoke, rile.

narrate *v.* chronicle, describe, detail, recite,

recount, rehearse, relate, repeat, report, set forth, state, tell, unfold.

narration *n.* description, enarration, explanation, reading, recital, recountal, rehearsal, relation, story-telling, telling, voice-over.

narrative *n.* account, chronicle, detail, history, parable, report, statement, story, tale.

narrator *n.* annalist, author, bard, chronicler, commentator, raconteur, reciter, relater, relator, reporter, story-teller, writer.

narrow *adj.* attenuated, avaricious, biased, bigoted, circumscribed, close, confined, constricted, contracted, cramped, dogmatic, exclusive, fine, illiberal, incapacious, intolerant, limited, meagre, mean, mercenary, narrow-minded, near, niggardly, partial, pinched, prejudiced, reactionary, restricted, scanty, select, simplistic, slender, slim, small-minded, spare, straitened, tapering, thin, tight, ungenerous.
antonyms broad, liberal, tolerant, wide.
v. circumscribe, constrict, constringe, diminish, limit, reduce, simplify, straiten, tighten.
antonyms broaden, increase, loosen, widen.

narrowing *n.* attenuation, compression, constipation, constriction, contraction, curtailment, emaciation, reduction, stenosis, tapering, thinning.
antonyms broadening, widening.

narrowly *adv.* barely, by a hair's breadth, by a whisker, carefully, closely, just, only just, painstakingly, precisely, scarcely, scrutinisingly, strictly.

narrow-minded *adj.* biased, bigoted, blinkered, borné, conservative, hidebound, illiberal, insular, intolerant, mean, opinionated, parochial, petty, prejudiced, provincial, reactionary, short-sighted, small-minded, strait-laced.
antonym broad-minded.

narrowness *n.* attentuation, closeness, constriction, crowdedness, exclusiveness, insularity, limitation, meagreness, narrow-mindedness, nearness, parochialism, restrictedness, slenderness, thinness, tightness.
antonyms breadth, width.

nascent *adj.* advancing, budding, developing, embryonic, evolving, growing, incipient, naissant, rising, young.
antonym dying.

nastiness *n.* defilement, dirtiness, disagreeableness, filth, filthiness, foulness, impurity, indecency, licentiousness, malice, meanness, obscenity, offensiveness, pollution, porn, pornography, ribaldry, smuttiness, spitefulness, squalor, uncleanliness, unpleasantness, unsavouriness, waspishness.

nasty *adj.* abusive, annoying, bad, bad-tempered, base, critical, dangerous, despicable, dirty, disagreeable, disgusting, distasteful, filthy, foul, gross, horrible, impure, indecent, lascivious, lewd, licentious, loathsome, low-down, malicious, malodorous, mean, mephitic, nauseating, noisome, objectionable, obnoxious, obscene, odious, offensive, painful, polluted, pornographic,

repellent, repugnant, ribald, serious, severe, sickening, smutty, spiteful, unappetising, unpleasant, unsavoury, vicious, vile, waspish.
antonyms agreeable, clean, decent, pleasant.

nation *n.* citizenry, commonwealth, community, country, people, population, race, realm, society, state, tribe.

national *adj.* civil, countrywide, domestic, general, governmental, internal, nationwide, public, social, state, widespread.
n. citizen, indigene, inhabitant, native, resident, subject.

nationalism *n.* allegiance, chauvinism, ethnocentricity, fealty, jingoism, loyalty, nationality, patriotism, xenophobia, xenophoby.

nationalistic *adj.* chauvinistic, ethnocentrist, jingoistic, loyal, patriotic, xenophobic.

nationality *n.* birth, clan, ethnic group, nation, race, tribe.

native *adj.* aboriginal, autochthonous, built-in, congenital, domestic, endemic, genuine, hereditary, home, home-born, home-bred, home-grown, home-made, inborn, inbred, indigene, indigenous, ingrained, inherent, inherited, innate, instinctive, intrinsic, inveterate, local, mother, natal, natural, original, real, vernacular.
n. aborigine, autochthon, citizen, countryman, dweller, indigene, inhabitant, national, resident.
antonyms foreigner, outsider, stranger.

nativity *n.* birth, childbirth, delivery, parturition.

natter *v.* blather, blether, chatter, confab, confabulate, gab, gabble, gossip, jabber, jaw, prate, prattle, talk.
n. blather, blether, chat, chinwag, chitchat, confab, confabulation, conversation, gab, gabble, gabfest, gossip, jabber, jaw, palaver, prattle, talk.

natty *adj.* chic, dapper, elegant, fashionable, neat, ritzy, smart, snazzy, spruce, stylish, swanky, trim.

natural *adj.* artless, candid, characteristic, common, congenital, constitutional, essential, everyday, frank, genuine, inborn, indigenous, ingenuous, inherent, innate, instinctive, intuitive, legitimate, logical, natal, native, normal, open, ordinary, organic, plain, pure, real, regular, simple, spontaneous, typical, unaffected, unbleached, unforced, unlaboured, unlearned, unmixed, unpolished, unpretentious, unrefined, unsophisticated, unstudied, untaught, usual, whole.
antonyms abnormal, affected, alien, artificial, pretended, unnatural.

naturalise *v.* acclimate, acclimatise, acculturate, accustom, adapt, adopt, domesticate, endenizen, enfranchise, familiarise, habituate.

naturalistic *adj.* graphic, lifelike, natural, photographic, realistic, real-life, representational, true-to-life.

naturally *adj.* absolutely, artlessly, as a matter of course, candidly, certainly, customarily, frankly, genuinely, informally, normally, of course, plainly, simply, spontaneously, typically, unaffectedly, unpretentiously.

naturalness n. artlessness, candidness, frankness, genuineness, informality, ingenuousness, openness, plainness, pureness, purity, realism, simpleness, simplicity, spontaneity, spontaneousness, unaffectedness, unpretentiousness, wholeness.

nature[1] n. attributes, category, character, complexion, constitution, cosmos, creation, description, disposition, earth, environment, essence, features, humour, inbeing, inscape, kind, make-up, mood, outlook, quality, sort, species, style, temper, temperament, traits, type, universe, variety, world.

nature[2] n. country, countryside, landscape, natural history, scenery.

naught n. nil, nothing, nothingness, nought, zero, zilch.

naughty adj. annoying, bad, bawdy, blue, disobedient, exasperating, fractious, impish, improper, lewd, misbehaved, mischievous, obscene, off-colour, perverse, playful, refractory, remiss, reprehensible, ribald, risqué, roguish, sinful, smutty, teasing, vulgar, wayward, wicked, worthless.
antonyms good, polite, well-behaved.

nausea n. abhorrence, aversion, biliousness, disgust, loathing, motion sickness, qualm(s), queasiness, repugnance, retching, revulsion, sickness, squeamishness, vomiting.

nauseate v. disgust, horrify, offend, repel, repulse, revolt, sicken, turn one's stomach.

nauseating adj. abhorrent, detestable, disgusting, distasteful, fulsome, loathsome, nauseous, offensive, repugnant, repulsive, revolting, sickening.

nautical adj. boating, marine, maritime, naval, oceanic, sailing, seafaring, sea-going, yachting.

naval adj. marine, maritime, nautical, sea.

navel n. belly-button, centre, hub, middle, omphalos, tummy-button, umbilicus.

navigate v. con, cross, cruise, direct, drive, guide, handle, helm, journey, manoeuvre, pilot, plan, plot, sail, skipper, steer, voyage.

navigation n. aviation, cruising, helmsmanship, pilotage, sailing, seamanship, steering, voyaging.

navigator n. helmsman, mariner, pilot, seaman.

navvy n. digger, ganger, labourer, worker, workman.

navy n. argosy, armada, fleet, flota, flotilla, navarchy, ships, warships.

near adj. accessible, adjacent, adjoining, akin, allied, alongside, approaching, at close quarters, attached, beside, bordering, close, connected, contiguous, dear, familiar, forthcoming, handy, imminent, impending, in the offing, intimate, looming, near-at-hand, nearby, neighbouring, next, nigh, on the cards, proximal, related, touching.
antonyms distant, far, remote.

near thing close shave, narrow escape, nasty moment, near miss.

nearby adj. accessible, adjacent, adjoining, convenient, handy, near, neighbouring.
antonym faraway.
adv. at close quarters, close at hand, near, not far away, within reach.

nearly adv. about, all but, almost, approaching, approximately, as good as, closely, just about, not quite, practically, pretty much, pretty well, roughly, virtually, well-nigh.

nearness n. accessibility, availability, chumminess, closeness, contiguity, dearness, familiarity, handiness, immediacy, imminence, intimacy, juxtaposition, propinquity, proximity, vicinity.

neat adj. accurate, adept, adroit, agile, apt, clean-cut, clever, dainty, deft, dexterous, dinky, efficient, effortless, elegant, expert, fastidious, genty, graceful, handy, methodical, nice, nimble, orderly, practised, precise, pure, shipshape, skilful, smart, spick-and-span, spruce, straight, stylish, systematic, tiddley, tidy, trig, trim, uncluttered, undiluted, unmixed, well-judged.
antonyms disordered, disorderly, messy, untidy.

neaten v. arrange, clean up, groom, put to rights, smarten, straighten, tidy, trim.

neatly adv. accurately, adeptly, adroitly, agilely, aptly, cleverly, daintily, deftly, dexterously, efficiently, effortlessly, elegantly, expertly, fastidiously, featly, gracefully, handily, methodically, nicely, nimbly, precisely, skilfully, smartly, sprucely, stylishly, systematically, tidily.
antonyms inelegantly, inexpertly, unskilfully, untidily.

neatness n. accuracy, adeptness, adroitness, agility, aptness, cleverness, daintiness, deftness, dexterity, disorderliness, efficiency, elegance, expertness, fastidiousness, grace, gracefulness, handiness, inelegance, methodicalness, niceness, nicety, nimbleness, orderliness, preciseness, precision, skilfulness, skill, smartness, spruceness, straightness, style, stylishness, tidiness, trimness, untidyness.

nebulous adj. ambiguous, amorphous, cloudy, confused, dim, fuzzy, hazy, imprecise, indefinite, indeterminate, indistinct, misty, murky, obscure, shadowy, shapeless, uncertain, unclear, unformed, unspecific, vague.
antonym clear.

necessarily adv. accordingly, automatically, axiomatically, by definition, certainly, compulsorily, consequently, incontrovertibly, ineluctably, inescapably, inevitably, inexorably, naturally, nolens volens, of course, of necessity, perforce, therefore, thus, willy-nilly.

necessary adj. certain, compulsory, de rigueur, essential, fated, imperative, indispensable, ineluctable, inescapable, inevitable, inexorable, mandatory, needed, needful, obligatory, required, requisite, unavoidable, vital.
antonyms inessential, unimportant, un-

necessary.

necessitate *v.* call for, coerce, compel, constrain, demand, entail, force, impel, involve, oblige, require.

necessities *n.* essentials, exigencies, fundamentals, indispensables, needs, requirements.

necessity *n.* ananke, compulsion, demand, desideratum, destiny, destitution, essential, exigency, extremity, fate, fundamental, indigence, indispensability, inevitability, inexorableness, necessary, need, needfulness, obligation, penury, poverty, prerequisite, privation, requirement, requisite, sine qua non, want.

neck *n.* halse, nape, scrag, scruff.

necklace *n.* carcanet, chain, choker, gorget, lavallière, locket, negligée, pendant, rivière, torc, torque.

necromancy *n.* black art, black magic, conjuration, demonology, divination, enchantment, hoodoo, magic, sorcery, thaumaturgy, voodoo, witchcraft, witchery, wizardry.

need *v.* call for, crave, demand, lack, miss, necessitate, require, want.
n. besoin, demand, deprivation, desideratum, destitution, distress, egence, egency, emergency, essential, exigency, extremity, impecuniousness, inadequacy, indigence, insufficiency, lack, longing, necessity, neediness, obligation, paucity, penury, poverty, privation, requirement, requisite, shortage, urgency, want, wish.
antonym sufficiency.

needed *adj.* called for, compulsory, desired, essential, lacking, necessary, obligatory, required, requisite, wanted.
antonyms unnecessary, unneeded.

needful *adj.* essential, indispensable, necessary, needed, needy, required, requisite, stipulated, vital.
antonyms excess, needless, superfluous.

needle *v.* aggravate, annoy, bait, goad, harass, irk, irritate, nag, nettle, pester, prick, prod, provoke, rile, ruffle, spur, sting, taunt, torment.

needless *adj.* causeless, dispensable, excessive, expendable, gratuitous, groundless, inessential, non-essential, pointless, purposeless, redundant, superfluous, uncalled-for, unessential, unnecessary, unwanted, useless.
antonyms necessary, needful.

needy *adj.* deprived, destitute, disadvantaged, impecunious, impoverished, indigent, penniless, penurious, poor, poverty-stricken, underprivileged.
antonyms affluent, wealthy, well-off.

ne'er-do-well *n.* black sheep, good-for-nothing, idler, layabout, loafer, scapegallows, vaurien, waster, wastrel.

nefarious *adj.* abominable, atrocious, base, criminal, depraved, detestable, dreadful, evil, execrable, foul, heinous, horrible, infamous, infernal, iniquitous, monstrous, odious, opprobrious, satanic, shameful, sinful, unholy, vicious, vile, villainous, wicked.

antonym exemplary.

negate *v.* abrogate, annul, cancel, contradict, countermand, deny, disallow, disprove, gainsay, invalidate, neutralise, nullify, oppose, quash, refute, repeal, rescind, retract, reverse, revoke, void, wipe out.
antonym affirm.

negation *n.* antithesis, cancellation, contradiction, contrary, converse, counterpart, denial, disavowal, disclaimer, inverse, neutralisation, nullification, opposite, rejection, renunciation, repeal, reverse, veto.
antonym affirmation.

negative *adj.* annulling, antagonistic, apathetic, below zero, colourless, contradictory, contrary, counteractive, cynical, denying, dissenting, gloomy, invalidating, jaundiced, neutralising, nullifying, opposing, pessimistic, refusing, rejecting, unco-operative, unenthusiastic, uninterested, unwilling, weak.
antonyms optimistic, positive.
n. contradiction, denial, opposite, refusal.

neglect *v.* contemn, disdain, disprovide, disregard, forget, ignore, leave alone, let slide, omit, overlook, pass by, pigeon-hole, rebuff, scorn, shirk, skimp, slight, spurn.
antonyms cherish, nurture, treasure.
n. carelessness, default, dereliction, disdain, disregard, disrespect, failure, forgetfulness, heedlessness, inattention, indifference, laches, laxity, laxness, neglectfulness, negligence, oversight, slackness, slight, slovenliness, unconcern.

neglected *adj.* abandoned, derelict, disregarded, overgrown, unappreciated, uncared-for, uncultivated, underestimated, undervalued, unhusbanded, unmaintained, untended, untilled, unweeded.
antonyms cherished, treasured.

neglectful *adj.* careless, disregardful, forgetful, heedless, inattentive, indifferent, lax, negligent, oblivious, remiss, thoughtless, uncaring, unmindful.
antonyms attentive, careful.

negligence *n.* carelessness, default, dereliction, disregard, failure, forgetfulness, heedlessness, inadvertence, inattention, inattentiveness, indifference, laxity, laxness, neglect, neglectfulness, omission, oversight, remissness, shortcoming, slackness, slight, stupidity, thoughtlessness.
antonyms attentiveness, care, regard.

negligent *adj.* careless, cursory, disregardful, forgetful, inattentive, indifferent, lax, neglectful, nonchalant, offhand, regardless, remiss, slack, thoughtless, uncareful, uncaring, unmindful, unthinking.
antonyms attentive, careful, heedful, scrupulous.

negligible *adj.* imperceptible, inconsequential, insignificant, minor, minute, neglectable, nugatory, petty, small, trifling, trivial, unimportant.
antonym significant.

negotiate *v.* adjudicate, arbitrate, arrange,

bargain, broke, clear, conciliate, confer, consult, contract, cross, deal, debate, discuss, get past, handle, manage, mediate, parley, pass, settle, surmount, transact, traverse, treat, work out.

negotiation *n.* arbitration, bargaining, debate, diplomacy, discussion, mediation, transaction, wheeler-dealing.

negotiator *n.* adjudicator, ambassador, arbitrator, broker, delegate, diplomat, go-between, intermediary, mediator, moderator.

neigh *v.* bray, hinny, whinny.

neighbourhood *n.* community, confines, district, environs, locale, locality, precincts, proximity, purlieus, quarter, region, surroundings, vicinage, vicinity.

neighbouring *adj.* abutting, adjacent, adjoining, bordering, connecting, contiguous, near, nearby, nearest, next, surrounding, vicinal.
antonyms distant, faraway, remote.

neighbourly *adj.* amiable, chummy, civil, companionable, considerate, friendly, genial, helpful, hospitable, kind, obliging, sociable, social, solicitous, well-disposed.

nemesis *n.* destiny, destruction, fate, punishment, retribution, vengeance.

nerve *n.* audacity, boldness, bottle, brass, bravery, brazenness, cheek, chutzpah, coolness, courage, daring, determination, effrontery, endurance, energy, fearlessness, firmness, force, fortitude, gall, gameness, grit, guts, hardihood, impertinence, impudence, insolence, intrepidity, mettle, might, pluck, resolution, sauce, spirit, spunk, steadfastness, temerity, vigour, will.
antonyms cowardice, weakness.
v. bolster, brace, embolden, encourage, fortify, hearten, invigorate, steel, strengthen.
antonym unnerve.

nerveless *adj.* afraid, cowardly, debilitated, enervated, feeble, flabby, inert, nervous, slack, spineless, timid, unnerved, weak.
antonyms bold, grave, strong.

nerve-racking *adj.* annoying, difficult, disquieting, distressing, frightening, harassing, harrowing, maddening, stressful, tense, trying, worrisome, worrying.

nerves *n.* anxiety, fretfulness, (h)abdabs, heebie-jeebies, nervousness, strain, stress, tension, worry.

nervous *adj.* agitated, anxious, apprehensive, edgy, excitable, fearful, fidgety, flustered, hesitant, highly-strung, high-strung, hysterical, jittery, jumpy, nervy, neurotic, on edge, shaky, tense, timid, timorous, twitchy, uneasy, uptight, weak, windy, worried.
antonyms bold, calm, confident, cool, relaxed.

nervousness *n.* agitation, anxiety, disquiet, excitability, fluster, (h)abdabs, heebiejeebies, perturbation, tension, timidity, touchiness, tremulousness, vapours, willies, worry.
antonyms calmness, coolness.

nervy *adj.* agitated, anxious, excitable, fidgety,

jittery, jumpy, nervous, on edge, restless, tense, unquiet.
antonyms calm, relaxed.

nest *n.* breeding-ground, burrow, den, drey, earth, form, formicary, haunt, hideaway, hotbed, nid(e), nidus, refuge, resort, retreat.

nest-egg *n.* bottom drawer, cache, deposit, fund(s), reserve(s), savings, store.

nestle *v.* cuddle, curl up, ensconce, huddle, nuzzle, snuggle.

nestling *adj.* baby, chick, fledgling, suckling, weanling.

net[1] *n.* drag, drag-net, drift, drift-net, drop-net, lattice, mesh, netting, network, open-work, reticulum, tracery, web.
v. apprehend, bag, benet, capture, catch, enmesh, ensnare, entangle, nab, trap.

net[2] *adj.* after tax, clear, final, lowest, nett.
v. accumulate, bring in, clear, earn, gain, make, obtain, realise, reap, receive, secure.

nether *adj.* basal, below, beneath, bottom, inferior, infernal, lower, Plutonian, Stygian, under, underground.

nettle *v.* annoy, chafe, discountenance, exasperate, fret, goad, harass, incense, irritate, needle, pique, provoke, ruffle, sting, tease, vex.

nettled *adj.* aggrieved, angry, annoyed, chafed, cross, exasperated, galled, goaded, harassed, huffy, incensed, irritable, irritated, miffed, needled, peeved, peevish, piqued, provoked, riled, ruffled, stung, vexed.

network *n.* arrangement, channels, circuitry, complex, convolution, grid, grill, interconnections, labyrinth, maze, mesh, meshwork, net, nexus, organisation, plexus, rete, reticulation, structure, system, tracks, web.

neurosis *n.* abnormality, affliction, derangement, deviation, disturbance, instability, maladjustment, obsession, phobia.

neurotic *adj.* abnormal, anxious, compulsive, deviant, disordered, distraught, disturbed, maladjusted, manic, morbid, nervous, obsessive, overwrought, unhealthy, unstable, wearisome.
antonyms normal, stable.

neuter *v.* caponise, castrate, doctor, dress, emasculate, fix, geld, spay.

neutral *adj.* colourless, disinterested, dispassionate, dull, even-handed, expressionless, impartial, indeterminate, indifferent, indistinct, indistinguishable, intermediate, non-aligned, non-committal, nondescript, non-partisan, unbia(s)sed, uncommitted, undecided, undefined, uninvolved, unprejudiced.
antonyms biased, prejudiced.

neutralise *v.* cancel, counteract, counterbalance, counterpoise, frustrate, invalidate, negate, nullify, offset, undo.

neutrality *n.* detachment, disinterest, disinterestedness, impartiality, impartialness, non-alignment, non-intervention, non-involvement, unbiasedness.

never *adv.* at no time, Greek calends, not at all, not on your life, not on your Nellie, on no

account, under no circumstances, when pigs fly.
antonym always.

never-ending *adj.* boundless, ceaseless, constant, continual, continuous, eternal, everlasting, incessant, interminable, non-stop, permanent, perpetual, persistent, relentless, Sisyphean, unbroken, unceasing, unchanging, uninterrupted, unremitting.
antonyms fleeting, transitory.

nevertheless *adv.* anyhow, anyway, but, even so, however, nonetheless, notwithstanding, regardless, still, yet.

new *adj.* added, advanced, altered, changed, contemporary, current, different, extra, fresh, improved, latest, modern, modernised, modernistic, modish, more, newborn, newfangled, novel, original, recent, redesigned, renewed, restored, supplementary, topical, trendy, ultra-modern, unfamiliar, unknown, unused, unusual, up-to-date, up-to-the-minute, virgin.
antonyms hackneyed, old, outdated, out-of-date, usual.

newcomer *n.* alien, arrival, arriviste, beginner, colonist, foreigner, immigrant, incomer, Johnny-come-lately, novice, outsider, parvenu, settler, stranger.

newfangled *adj.* contemporary, fashionable, futuristic, gimmicky, modern, modernistic, new, novel, recent, trendy.
antonym old-fashioned.

newly *adv.* afresh, anew, freshly, just, lately, latterly, recently.

newness *n.* freshness, innovation, novelty, oddity, originality, recency, strangeness, unfamiliarity, uniqueness, unusualness.
antonyms oldness, ordinariness.

news *n.* account, advice, bulletin, communiqué, disclosure, dispatch, exposé, gen, gossip, hearsay, information, intelligence, latest, leak, release, report, revelation, rumour, scandal, statement, story, tidings, update, word.

newspaper *n.* daily, gazette, journal, organ, paper, periodical, publication, rag, sheet, tabloid.

newsworthy *adj.* arresting, important, interesting, notable, noteworthy, remarkable, reportable, significant, stimulating, unusual.

next *adj.* adjacent, adjoining, closest, consequent, ensuing, following, later, nearest, neighbouring, sequent, sequential, subsequent, succeeding.
antonyms preceding, previous.
adv. afterwards, later, subsequently, then, thereafter.

nibble *n.* bit, bite, crumb, morsel, peck, piece, snack, soupçon, taste, titbit.
v. bite, eat, gnaw, knap, knapple, munch, nip, nosh, peck, pickle.

nice *adj.* accurate, agreeable, amiable, attractive, careful, charming, commendable, courteous, critical, cultured, dainty, delicate, delightful, discriminating, exact, exacting,

fastidious, fine, finical, friendly, genteel, good, kind, lik(e)able, meticulous, neat, particular, pleasant, pleasurable, polite, precise, prepossessing, punctilious, purist, refined, respectable, rigorous, scrupulous, strict, subtle, tidy, trim, virtuous, well-bred, well-mannered.
antonyms careless, disagreeable, haphazard, nasty, unpleasant.

nicely *adv.* acceptably, accurately, agreeable, amiably, attractively, carefully, charmingly, commendably, courteously, critically, daintily, delicately, delightfully, discriminatingly, elegantly, exactingly, exactly, fastidiously, finely, genteelly, kindly, lik(e)ably, meticulously, neatly, pleasantly, pleasingly, pleasurably, politely, precisely, prepossessingly, respectably, rigorously, scrupulously, strictly, subtly, tidily, trimly, virtuously, well.
antonyms carelessly, disagreeably, haphazardly, nastily, unpleasantly.

niceness *n.* accuracy, agreeableness, amiability, attractiveness, care, carefulness, charm, courtesy, daintiness, delicacy, delightfulness, discrimination, exactitude, exactness, fastidiousness, fineness, friendliness, gentility, goodness, kindness, lik(e)ableness, meticulousness, neatness, pleasantness, pleasurableness, politeness, preciseness, precision, punctilio, punctiliousness, purism, refinement, respectability, rigorousness, rigour, scrupulosity, scrupulousness, strictness, subtleness, subtlety, tidiness, trimness, virtue.
antonyms carelessness, disagreeableness, haphazardness, nastiness, unpleasantness.

nicety *n.* accuracy, daintiness, delicacy, discrimination, distinction, exactness, fastidiousness, finesse, finicality, meticulousness, minuteness, nuance, precision, punctilio, quiddit(y), refinement, subtlety.

niche[1] *n.* alcove, corner, cubby, cubby-hole, hollow, nook, opening, recess.

niche[2] *n.* calling, métier, pigeon-hole, place, position, slot, vocation.

nick[1] *n.* chip, cut, damage, dent, indent, indentation, mark, notch, scar, score, scratch, snick.
v. chip, cut, damage, dent, indent, mark, notch, scar, score, scratch, snick.

nick[2] *v.* finger, knap, knock off, lag, pilfer, pinch, snitch, steal.

nickname *n.* cognomen, diminutive, epithet, familiarity, label, moni(c)ker, pet name, sobriquet.

nifty *adj.* adroit, agile, apt, chic, clever, deft, enjoyable, excellent, neat, nippy, pleasing, quick, sharp, smart, spruce, stylish.

niggardliness *n.* avarice, avariciousness, beggarliness, cheese-paring, closeness, covetousness, frugality, grudgingness, inadequacy, insufficiency, meagreness, meanness, mercenariness, miserableness, miserliness, nearness, paltriness, parsimony, penuriousness, scantiness, skimpiness, smallness, sordidness, sparingness, stinginess, thrift, tight-fistedness,

ungenerousness, wretchedness.
antonyms bountifulness, generosity.

niggardly *adj.* avaricious, beggarly, cheese-paring, close, covetous, frugal, grudging, hard-fisted, inadequate, insufficient, meagre, mean, mercenary, miserable, miserly, near, paltry, parsimonious, penurious, scanty, skimpy, small, sordid, sparing, stinging, stingy, tight-fisted, ungenerous, ungiving, wretched.
antonyms bountiful, generous.

night *n.* dark, darkmans, darkness, dead of night, hours of darkness, night-time.
antonyms day, daytime.

nightclub *n.* cabaret, club, disco, discotheque, nightspot, niterie, nitery, watering-hole.

nightfall *n.* crepuscule, dusk, eve, evening, eventide, gloaming, moonrise, sundown, sunset, twilight, vespers.
antonyms dawn, sunrise.

nightmare *n.* bad dream, ephialtes, hallucination, horror, incubus, ordeal, succubus, torment, trial, tribulation.

nightmarish *adj.* agonising, alarming, creepy, disturbing, dreadful, fell, frightening, harrowing, horrible, horrific, scaring, terrifying, unreal.

nihilism *n.* abnegation, agnosticism, anarchy, atheism, cynicism, denial, disbelief, disorder, emptiness, lawlessness, negation, negativism, non-existence, nothingness, nullity, oblivion, pessimism, rejection, renunciation, repudiation, scepticism, terrorism.

nihilist *n.* agitator, agnostic, anarchist, antinomian, atheist, cynic, disbeliever, extremist, negationist, negativist, pessimist, revolutionary, sceptic, terrorist.

nil *n.* duck, goose-egg, love, naught, nihil, none, nothing, zero.

nimble *adj.* active, agile, alert, brisk, deft, dexterous, light-foot(ed), lissom(e), lively, nippy, proficient, prompt, quick, quick-witted, ready, smart, sprightly, spry, swift, volant.
antonyms awkward, clumsy.

nimbleness *n.* adroitness, agility, alacrity, alertness, deftness, dexterity, finesse, grace, legerity, lightness, niftiness, nippiness, skill, smartness, sprightliness, spryness.

nimbly *adv.* actively, acutely, agilely, alertly, briskly, deftly, dexterously, easily, fast, featly, fleetly, proficiently, promptly, quickly, quick-wittedly, readily, sharply, smartly, snappily, speedily, spryly, swiftly.
antonyms awkwardly, clumsily.

nincompoop *n.* blockhead, dimwit, dolt, dunce, fool, idiot, ignoramus, ninny, nitwit, noodle, numskull, sap, saphead, simpleton.

nip[1] *v.* bite, catch, check, clip, compress, grip, nibble, pinch, snag, snap, sneap, snip, squeeze, tweak, twitch.

nip[2] *n.* dram, draught, drop, finger, mouthful, peg, portion, shot, sip, slug, snifter, soupçon, sup, swallow, taste.

nipple *n.* breast, dug, mamilla, pap, teat, tit,
titty, udder.

nippy[1] *adj.* astringent, biting, chilly, nipping, pungent, sharp, stinging.

nippy[2] *adj.* active, agile, fast, nimble, quick, speedy, sprightly, spry.
antonym slow.

nirvana *n.* bliss, ecstasy, exaltation, joy, paradise, peace, serenity, tranquillity.

nit-picking *adj.* captious, carping, cavilling, finicky, fussy, hair-splitting, hypercritical, pedantic, pettifogging, quibbling.

nitwit *n.* dimwit, drongo, dummy, fool, half-wit, nincompoop, ninny, numskull, simpleton.

no doubt admittedly, assuredly, certainly, doubtless, doubtlessly, presumably, probably, surely, unquestionably.

nob *n.* aristocrat, big shot, bigwig, fat cat, nabob, personage, toff, VIP.

nobble *v.* bribe, disable, filch, get at, grab, hamper, handicap, incapacitate, influence, injure, intimidate, knock off, nick, outwit, pilfer, pinch, purloin, snitch, steal, swipe, take, weaken.

nobility *n.* aristocracy, dignity, élite, eminence, excellence, generosity, gentry, grandeur, greatness, high society, honour, illustriousness, incorruptibility, integrity, loftiness, lords, magnanimity, magnificence, majesty, nobleness, nobles, patricians, peerage, stateliness, sublimity, superiority, uprightness, virtue, worthiness.
antonyms baseness, proletariat.

noble *n.* aristocrat, baron, gentilhomme, grand seigneur, lord, nobleman, patrician, peer.
antonyms pleb, prole.
adj. aristocratic, august, blue-blooded, dignified, distinguished, elevated, eminent, excellent, generous, gentle, grand, great, high-born, honourable, honoured, imposing, impressive, lofty, lordly, magnanimous, magnificent, majestic, patrician, splendid, stately, titled, upright, virtuous, worthy.
antonyms base, ignoble, low-born.

nobody *n.* also-ran, cipher, lightweight, man of straw, menial, minnow, nonentity, no-one, nothing, Walter Mitty.
antonym somebody.

nod *v.* acknowledge, agree, assent, beckon, bob, bow, concur, dip, doze, droop, drowse, duck, gesture, indicate, nap, salute, sign, signal, sleep, slip up, slump.
n. acknowledgement, beck, cue, gesture, greeting, indication, salute, sign, signal.

node *n.* bud, bump, burl, caruncle, growth, knob, knot, lump, nodule, process, protuberance, swelling.

noise *n.* babble, ballyhoo, blare, brattle, chirm, clamour, clash, clatter, coil, commotion, cry, din, fracas, hubbub, outcry, pandemonium, racket, row, sound, talk, tumult, uproar.
antonyms quiet, silence.
v. advertise, announce, bruit, circulate, gossip, publicise, repeat, report, rumour.

noiseless *adj.* hushed, inaudible, mous(e)y, mute, muted, quiet, silent, soundless, still.

antonyms loud, noisy.

noisome *adj.* bad, baneful, deleterious, disgusting, fetid, foul, fulsome, harmful, hurtful, injurious, malodorous, mephitic, mischievous, noxious, offensive, pernicious, pestiferous, pestilential, poisonous, putrid, reeking, smelly, stinking, unhealthy, unwholesome.
antonyms balmy, pleasant, wholesome.

noisy *adj.* boisterous, cacophonous, chattering, clamorous, clangorous, deafening, ear-piercing, ear-splitting, horrisonant, loud, obstreperous, piercing, plangent, rackety, riotous, strepitant, strident, tumultuous, turbulent, uproarious, vocal, vociferous.
antonyms peaceful, quiet, silent.

nom de plume alias, allonym, assumed name, nom de guerre, pen name, pseudonym.

nomad *n.* drifter, itinerant, migrant, rambler, roamer, rover, traveller, vagabond, vagrant, wanderer.

nomadic *adj.* drifting, gypsy, itinerant, migrant, migratory, peregrinating, peripatetic, roaming, roving, travelling, unsettled, vagrant, wandering.

nomenclature *n.* classification, codification, locution, naming, phraseology, taxonomy, terminology, vocabulary.

nominal *adj.* fainéant, formal, inconsiderable, insignificant, minimal, ostensible, pretended, professed, puppet, purported, self-styled, small, so-called, soi-disant, supposed, symbolic, theoretical, titular, token, trifling, trivial.
antonyms actual, genuine, real, true.

nominate *v.* appoint, assign, choose, commission, designate, elect, elevate, empower, mention, name, present, propose, put up, recommend, select, submit, suggest, term.

nomination *n.* appointment, choice, designation, election, proposal, recommendation, selection, submission, suggestion.

nominee *n.* appointee, assignee, candidate, contestant, entrant, protégé, runner.

non compos mentis crazy, deranged, insane, mentally ill, of unsound mind, unbalanced, unhinged.
antonyms sane, stable.

non-aligned *adj.* impartial, independent, neutral, uncommitted, undecided.

nonchalance *n.* aplomb, calm, composure, cool, equanimity, imperturbability, indifference, insouciance, pococurant(e)ism, sang-froid, self-possession, unconcern.
antonyms anxiousness, worriedness.

nonchalant *adj.* airy, apathetic, blasé, calm, careless, casual, collected, cool, detached, dispassionate, impassive, indifferent, insouciant, offhand, pococurante, unconcerned, unemotional, unperturbed.
antonyms anxious, careful, concerned, worried.

non-committal *adj.* ambiguous, careful, cautious, circumspect, cunctatious, cunctative, cunctatory, discreet, equivocal, evasive, guarded, indefinite, neutral, politic, reserved,

tactful, temporising, tentative, unrevealing, vague, wary.

nonconformist *n.* deviant, dissenter, dissentient, eccentric, heretic, iconoclast, individualist, maverick, oddball, protester, radical, rebel, seceder, secessionist.
antonym conformist.

nonconformity *n.* deviation, dissent, eccentricity, heresy, heterodoxy, secession, unconventionality.
antonym conformity.

nondescript *adj.* commonplace, dull, featureless, indeterminate, mousy, ordinary, plain, unclassified, undistinctive, undistinguished, unexceptional, uninspiring, uninteresting, unmemorable, unremarkable, vague.

none *pron.* nil, nobody, no-one, not any, not one, zero, zilch.

nonentity *n.* cipher, dandiprat, drip, drongo, earthworm, gnatling, lightweight, mediocrity, nobody.

non-essential *adj.* dispensable, excessive, expendable, extraneous, extrinsic(al), inessential, peripheral, superfluous, supplementary, unimportant, unnecessary.
antonym essential.

none-the-less *adv.* even so, howbeit, however, natheless, nevertheless, notwithstanding, yet.

non-existence *n.* illusiveness, insubstantiality, unbeing, unreality.
antonym existence.

non-existent *adj.* chimerical, fancied, fictional, hallucinatory, hypothetical, illusory, imaginary, imagined, immaterial, incorporeal, insubstantial, legendary, missing, mythical, null, unreal.
antonyms actual, existing, real.

non-flammable *adj.* fire-proof, fire-resistant, flame-resistant, incombustible, uninflammable.
antonyms flammable, inflammable.

non-partisan *adj.* detached, dispassionate, even-handed, impartial, independent, neutral, objective, unbiased, unprejudiced.
antonym partisan.

nonplus *v.* astonish, astound, baffle, bewilder, confound, confuse, discomfit, disconcert, discountenance, dismay, dumbfound, embarrass, flabbergast, flummox, mystify, perplex, puzzle, stump, stun, take aback.

nonsense *n.* absurdity, balderdash, balls, baloney, bilge, blah, blather, blethers, bollocks, bombast, bosh, bull, bullshit, bunk, bunkum, claptrap, cobblers, codswallop, crap, double-Dutch, drivel, fadaise, faddle, fandangle, fatuity, fiddle-de-dee, fiddle-faddle, fiddlesticks, flapdoodle, folly, foolishness, fudge, gaff, galimatias, gammon, gas and gaiters, gibberish, gobbledygook, havers, hogwash, hooey, inanity, jabberwock(y), jest, ludicrousness, moonshine, no-meaning, piffle, pulp, ridiculousness, rot, rubbish, senselessness, silliness, squish, squit, stuff, stultiloquence, stupidity, tar(r)adiddle, tommy-rot, tosh, trash, twaddle, twattle,

unreason, waffle.
antonym sense.
nonsensical *adj.* absurd, crazy, daft, fatuous, foolish, inane, incomprehensible, irrational, ludicrous, meaningless, ridiculous, senseless, silly.
antonyms logical, sensible.
non-stop *adj.* ceaseless, constant, continuous, direct, endless, incessant, interminable, never-ending, on-going, relentless, round-the-clock, steady, unbroken, unceasing, unending, unfaltering, uninterrupted, unrelenting, unremitting.
antonyms intermittent, occasional.
adv. ceaselessly, constantly, continuously, directly, endlessly, incessantly, interminably, relentlessly, round-the-clock, steadily, unbrokenly, unceasingly, unendingly, unfalteringly, uninterruptedly, unrelentingly, unremittingly.
antonyms imtermittently, occasionally.
non-violent *adj.* dov(e)ish, irenic, pacifist, passive, peaceable, peaceful.
antonym violent.
nook *n.* alcove, cavity, corner, cranny, crevice, cubby-hole, hide-out, ingle-nook, nest, niche, opening, recess, retreat, shelter.
norm *n.* average, bench-mark, canon, criterion, mean, measure, model, pattern, reference, rule, standard, type, yardstick.
normal *adj.* accustomed, acknowledged, average, common, common-or-garden, conventional, habitual, mainstream, natural, ordinary, par for the course, popular, rational, reasonable, regular, routine, run-of-the-mill, sane, standard, straight, typical, usual, well-adjusted.
antonyms abnormal, irregular, odd, peculiar.
normality *n.* accustomedness, adjustment, balance, commonness, conventionality, naturalness, ordinariness, popularity, rationality, reason, regularity, routine, routineness, sanity, typicality, usualness.
antonyms abnormality, irregularity, oddity, peculiarity.
normally *adv.* as a rule, characteristically, commonly, habitually, ordinarily, regularly, straight, typically, usually.
antonym abnormally.
northern *adj.* Arctic, boreal, hyperborean, north, northerly, polar, septentrional.
antonym southern.
nose *n.* beak, bill, boko, conk, hooter, neb, proboscis, schnozzle, snitch, snout.
v. detect, inquire, interface, intrude, meddle, nudge, nuzzle, pry, push, scent, search, shove, smell, sniff, snoop.
nose-dive *n.* dive, drop, header, plummet, plunge, purler.
v. dive, drop, plummet, plunge, submerge.
nosegay *n.* bouquet, boutonnièe, corsage, posy, spray.
nos(e)y *adj.* curious, eavesdropping, inquisitive, interfering, intermeddling, intrusive, meddlesome, officious, prying, snooping.

nostalgia *n.* Heimweh, homesickness, longing, mal du pays, pining, regret, regretfulness, remembrance, reminiscence, wistfulness, yearning.
nostalgic *adj.* emotional, homesick, longing, maudlin, regretful, romantic, sentimental, wistful.
nosy *see* **nosey** .
not bad all right, average, fair, fair to middling, moderate, OK, passable, reasonable, respectable, satisfactory, so-so, tolerable.
notability *n.* celebrity, dignitary, distinction, eminence, esteem, fame, luminary, magnate, notable, personage, renown, somebody, VIP, worthy.
antonym nonentity.
notable *adj.* celebrated, conspicuous, distinguished, eminent, evident, extraordinary, famous, impressive, manifest, marked, memorable, noteworthy, noticeable, notorious, outstanding, overt, pre-eminent, pronounced, rare, remarkable, renowned, signal, striking, uncommon, unusual, well-known.
antonyms commonplace, ordinary, usual.
n. celebrity, dignitary, luminary, notability, personage, somebody, VIP, worthy.
antonyms nobody, nonentity.
notably *adv.* conspicuously, distinctly, eminently, especially, impressively, markedly, noticeably, outstandingly, particularly, remarkably, signally, strikingly, uncommonly.
notation *n.* alphabet, characters, code, noting, record, script, shorthand, signs, symbols, system.
notch *n.* cleft, cut, degree, grade, incision, indentation, insection, kerf, level, mark, nick, score, sinus, snip, step.
v. cut, gimp, indent, mark, nick, raffle, scallop, score, scratch.
notch up achieve, gain, make, record, register, score.
notched *adj.* crenellate(d), emarginate, eroded, erose, jagged, jaggy, pinked, serrate(d), serrulate(d).
note *n.* annotation, apostil(le), billet, celebrity, character, comment, communication, consequence, distinction, eminence, epistle, epistolet, fame, gloss, heed, indication, jotting, letter, line, mark, memo, memorandum, message, minute, notice, observation, prestige, record, regard, remark, reminder, renown, reputation, signal, symbol, token.
v. denote, designate, detect, enter, indicate, mark, mention, notice, observe, perceive, record, register, remark, see, witness.
noted *adj.* acclaimed, celebrated, conspicuous, distinguished, eminent, famous, great, illustrious, notable, notorious, prominent, recognised, renowned, respected, well-known.
notes *n.* draft, impressions, jottings, outline, record, report, sketch, synopsis.
noteworthy *adj.* exceptional, extraordinary, important, notable, on the map, outstanding, remarkable, significant, unusual, visitable.

antonyms commonplace, ordinary, unexceptional, usual.

nothing *n.* bagatelle, cipher, damn all, emptiness, naught, nix, nobody, nonentity, nonexistence, nothingness, nought, nullity, sweet Fanny Adams, (sweet) fuck all, trifle, void, zero.

antonyms everything, something.

nothingness *n.* nihilism, nihility, non-existence, nullity, oblivion, vacuum.

notice *v.* descry, detect, discern, distinguish, espy, heed, mark, mind, note, observe, perceive, remark, see, spot.

antonyms ignore, overlook.

n. advertisement, advice, affiche, announcement, attention, bill, civility, cognisance, comment, communication, consideration, criticism, heed, instruction, intelligence, intimation, news, note, notification, observation, order, poster, regard, respect, review, sign, warning.

noticeable *adj.* appreciable, clear, conspicuous, distinct, dramatic, evident, manifest, measurable, observable, obvious, perceptible, plain, significant, striking, unmistakable.

antonyms hidden, insignificant, obscure.

notification *n.* advice, alert, announcement, declaration, disclosure, information, intelligence, message, notice, publication, revelation, statement, telling, warning.

notify *v.* acquaint, advise, alert, announce, apprise, declare, disclose, inform, publish, reveal, tell, warn.

notion *n.* apprehension, belief, caprice, conceit, concept, conception, concetto, construct, desire, fancy, idea, image, impression, impulse, inclination, inkling, judgement, knowledge, opinion, sentiment, understanding, view, whim, wish.

notional *adj.* abstract, classificatory, conceptual, fanciful, hypothetical, ideational, imaginary, speculative, thematic, theoretical, unfounded, unreal, visionary.

antonym real.

notoriety *n.* disfame, dishonour, disrepute, esclandre, infamy, obloquy, opprobrium, scandal.

notorious *adj.* arrant, blatant, dishonourable, disreputable, egregious, flagrant, glaring, infamous, obvious, open, opprobrious, overt, patent, scandalous, undisputed.

notoriously *adv.* arrantly, blatantly, dishonourably, disreputably, egregiously, flagrantly, glaringly, infamously, notably, obviously, openly, opprobriously, overtly, particularly, patently, scandalously, spectacularly, undisputedly.

notwithstanding *adv.* although, despite, howbeit, however, natheless, nevertheless, nonetheless, though, withal, yet.

nought *n.* naught, nil, nix, nothing, nothingness, zero, zilch.

nourish *v.* attend, cherish, comfort, cultivate, encourage, feed, foster, furnish, harbour, maintain, nurse, nurture, promote, supply, support, sustain, tend.

nourishing *adj.* alimentative, beneficial, good, healthful, health-giving, nutritious, nutritive, substantial, wholesome.

nourishment *n.* aliment, diet, food, goodness, nutriment, nutrition, pabulum, provender, sustenance, viands, victuals.

novel *adj.* different, fresh, imaginative, innovative, new, original, rare, singular, strange, surprising, uncommon, unconventional, unfamiliar, unusual.

antonyms familiar, ordinary.

n. fiction, narrative, romance, saga, story, tale, yarn.

novelty *n.* bagatelle, bauble, curiosity, freshness, gadget, gewgaw, gimcrack, gimmick, innovation, knick-knack, memento, neoterism, newness, oddity, originality, peculiarity, souvenir, strangeness, surprise, trifle, trinket, unfamiliarity, uniqueness.

novice *n.* amateur, apprentice, beginner, catechumen, convert, cub, griffin, Johnny-raw, learner, neophyte, newcomer, novitiate, probationer, proselyte, pupil, tiro.

antonyms doyen, expert, professional.

now *adv.* at once, at present, directly, ek dum, immediately, instanter, instantly, next, nowadays, presently, promptly, straightaway, these days.

now and then at times, desultorily, from time to time, infrequently, intermittently, now and again, occasionally, on and off, on occasion, once in a while, periodically, sometimes, spasmodically, sporadically.

nowadays *adv.* any more, as things are, at the moment, now, these days, today.

noxious *adj.* baneful, corrupting, deadly, deleterious, destructive, detrimental, foul, harmful, hurtful, injurious, insalubrious, mephitic(al), morbiferous, morbific, noisome, pernicious, pestilential, poisonous, unhealthy, unwholesome.

antonyms innocuous, wholesome.

nuance *n.* degree, distinction, gradation, hint, nicety, overtone, refinement, shade, soupçon, subtlety, suggestion, suspicion, tinge, touch, trace.

nub *n.* centre, core, crux, essence, gist, heart, kernel, nitty-gritty, nucleus, pith, point.

nubile *adj.* marriageable, ripe, sexy, voluptuous.

nucleus *n.* basis, centre, core, crux, focus, heart, heartlet, kernel, nub, pivot.

nude *adj.* au naturel, bare, disrobed, exposed, in one's birthday suit, in puris naturalibus, in the altogether, in the buff, naked, starkers, stark-naked, stripped, unattired, unclad, unclothed, uncovered, undraped, undressed, without a stitch.

antonyms clothed, covered, dressed.

nudge *v, n.* bump, dig, jog, poke, prod, prompt, push, shove, touch.

nudity *n.* bareness, déshabillé, dishabille, nakedness, nudism, undress.

nugatory *adj.* bootless, futile, inadequate, inconsequential, ineffectual, inoperative, insignificant, invalid, null and void, trifling, trivial, unavailing, useless, vain, valueless, worthless.

antonyms important, significant.

nugget *n.* chunk, clump, hunk, lump, mass, piece, wodge.

nuisance *n.* annoyance, bore, bother, désagre-´ment, drag, drawback, inconvenience, inflic-tion, irritation, offence, pain, pest, plague, problem, trouble, vexation.

null *adj.* characterless, immaterial, incorporeal, ineffectual, inoperative, invalid, non-existent, powerless, useless, vain, valueless, void, worthless.

antonym valid.

nullify *v.* abate, abolish, abrogate, annul, cancel, counteract, countervail, invalidate, negate, neutralise, quash, repeal, rescind, revoke, undermine, veto, vitiate, void.

antonym validate.

nullity *n.* characterlessness, immateriality, in-corporeality, ineffectualness, invalidity, non-existence, powerlessness, uselessness, void-ness, worthlessness.

antonym validity.

numb *adj.* benumbed, dead, deadened, frozen, immobilised, insensate, insensible, insensi-tive, paralysed, stunned, stupefied, torpid, unfeeling.

antonym sensitive.

v. anaesthetise, benumb, deaden, dull, freeze, immobilise, obtund, paralyse, stun, stupefy.

antonym sensitise.

number[1] *n.* aggregate, amount, character, collection, company, count, crowd, digit, figure, folio, horde, index, integer, many, multitude, numeral, quantity, several, sum, throng, total, unit.

v. account, add, apportion, calculate, com-pute, count, enumerate, include, inventory, reckon, tell, total.

number[2] *n.* copy, edition, impression, imprint, issue, printing, volume.

numberless *adj.* countless, endless, infinite, innumerable, multitudinous, myriad, un-counted, unnumbered, unsummed, untold.

numbness *n.* anaesthetisation, deadness, dull-ness, insensateness, insensibility, insensitiv-ity, paralysis, stupefaction, torpor, unfeeling-ness.

antonym sensitivity.

numeral *n.* character, cipher, digit, figure, folio, integer, number.

numerous *adj.* abundant, copious, divers, many, multitudinous, myriad, plentiful, profuse, several, sundry.

antonyms few, scanty.

numerousness *n.* abundance, copiousness, manifoldness, multeity, multiplicity, multi-tudinousness, plentifulness, plurality, pro-fusion.

antonyms scantiness, scarcity.

numskull *n.* blockhead, bonehead, buffoon, clot, dimwit, dolt, dope, drongo, dullard, dummy, dunce, dunderhead, fathead, fool, sap, saphead, simpleton, thickhead, twit.

nun *n.* abbess, anchoress, ancress, bride of Christ, canoness, mother superior, prioress, sister, vestal, vowess.

nunnery *n.* abbey, cloister, convent, priory.

nuptial *adj.* bridal, conjugal, connubial, epitha-lamial, epithalamic, hymeneal, marital, matri-monial, wedded, wedding.

nuptials *n.* bridal, espousal, marriage, matri-mony, spousals, wedding.

nurse *v.* breast-feed, care for, cherish, cultivate, encourage, feed, foster, harbour, keep, nourish, nurture, preserve, promote, succour, suckle, support, sustain, tend, treat, wet-nurse.

n. amah, district-nurse, home-nurse, mammy, nanny, nursemaid, sister of mercy, wet nurse.

nurture *n.* care, cultivation, development, diet, discipline, education, food, instruction, nour-ishment, rearing, training, upbringing.

v. bring up, care for, cultivate, develop, discipline, educate, feed, instruct, nourish, nurse, rear, school, support, sustain, tend, train.

nut[1] *n.* kernel, pip, seed, stone.

nut[2] *n.* brain, crackpot, crank, eccentric, head, head-banger, loony, lunatic, madman, man-iac, mind, nutcase, nutter, psychopath, reason, senses.

nutriment *n.* aliment, diet, food, foodstuff, nourishment, nutrition, pabulum, provender, subsistence, support, sustenance.

nutrition *n.* eutrophy, food, nourishment, nutriment, sustenance.

nutritious *adj.* alimental, alimentative, bene-ficial, good, healthful, health-giving, invigor-ating, nourishing, nutritive, strengthening, substantial, wholesome.

antonyms bad, unwholesome.

nuts *adj.* bananas, batty, crazy, demented, deranged, eccentric, insane, irrational, loony, loopy, mad, nutty, psychopathic, unbalanced, unhinged.

antonym sane.

nuts and bolts basics, bits and pieces, compo-nents, details, essentials, fundamentals, nitty-gritty, practicalities.

nuzzle *v.* burrow, cuddle, fondle, nestle, nudge, pet, snuggle.

nymph *n.* damsel, dryad, girl, hamadryad, lass, maid, maiden, naiad, oread, sprite, sylph, undine.

O

oaf *n.* baboon, blockhead, bonehead, booby, brute, clod, dolt, dullard, dummy, dunce, fool, galoot, gawk, goon, gorilla, half-wit, hick, hobbledehoy, hulk, idiot, imbecile, lout, lummox, moron, nincompoop, oik, sap, schlemiel, schlep, simpleton, yob.

oafish *adj.* blockish, Boeotian, boneheaded, boorish, bovine, brutish, crass, dense, dim, dimwitted, doltish, dull, dumb, heavy, loutish, lubberly, lumbering, moronic, obtuse, schleppy, stupid, thick.

oasis *n.* enclave, haven, island, refuge, resting-place, retreat, sanctuary, sanctum, watering-hole.

oath *n.* affirmation, assurance, avowal, blasphemy, bond, curse, cuss, expletive, imprecation, malediction, pledge, plight, profanity, promise, swear-word, vow, word, word of honour.

obdurate *adj.* adamant, callous, dogged, firm, fixed, flinty, hard, hard-hearted, harsh, immovable, implacable, inexorable, inflexible, intransigent, iron, mulish, obstinate, perverse, pig-headed, relentless, stiff-necked, stony, stubborn, unbending, unfeeling, unrelenting, unshakable, unyielding.
antonyms submissive, tender.

obedience *n.* accordance, acquiescence, agreement, allegiance, amenableness, compliance, conformability, deference, docility, dutifulness, duty, observance, passivity, respect, reverence, submission, submissiveness, subservience, tractability.
antonym disobedience.

obedient *adj.* acquiescent, amenable, biddable, compliant, deferential, docile, duteous, dutiful, law-abiding, observant, passive, regardful, respectful, sequacious, submissive, subservient, tractable, unquestioning, unresisting, well-trained, yielding.
antonyms disobedient, rebellious, refractory, unruly, wilful.

obeisance *n.* bow, congé, curts(e)y, deference, genuflection, homage, kowtow, respect, reverence, salaam, salutation, salute.

obese *adj.* bulky, corpulent, Falstaffian, fat, fleshy, gross, heavy, outsize, overweight, paunchy, plump, podgy, ponderous, portly, pursy, roly-poly, rotund, stout, tubby.
antonyms skinny, slender, thin.

obesity *n.* bulk, chubbiness, corpulence, embonpoint, fatness, fleshiness, grossness, middle-age(d) spread, overweight, portliness, stoutness, tubbiness.
antonyms skinniness, slenderness, thinness.

obey *v.* abide by, act upon, adhere to, be ruled by, bow to, carry out, comply, conform, defer (to), discharge, embrace, execute, follow, fulfil, give in, give way, heed, implement, keep, knuckle under, mind, observe, perform, respond, serve, submit, surrender, take orders from, toe the line, yield.
antonym disobey.

object [1] *n.* aim, article, body, butt, design, end, entity, fact, focus, goal, idea, intent, intention, item, motive, objective, phenomenon, point, purpose, raison d'être, reality, reason, recipient, target, thing, victim, visible.

object [2] *v.* argue, complain, demur, dissent, expostulate, oppose, protest, rebut, refuse, repudiate, take exception.
antonyms accede, acquiesce, agree, assent.

objection *n.* cavil, censure, challenge, complaint, counter-argument, demur, doubt, exception, niggle, opposition, protest, remonstrance, scruple.
antonyms agreement, assent.

objectionable *adj.* abhorrent, antisocial, deplorable, despicable, detestable, disagreeable, dislik(e)able, displeasing, distasteful, exceptionable, indecorous, insufferable, intolerable, loathsome, noxious, obnoxious, offensive, regrettable, repugnant, unacceptable, undesirable, unpleasant, unseemly.
antonyms acceptable, pleasant, welcome.

objective *adj.* calm, detached, disinterested, dispassionate, equitable, even-handed, fair, impartial, impersonal, judicial, just, open-minded, sensible, sober, unbiased, uncoloured, unemotional, unimpassioned, uninvolved, unprejudiced.
antonyms biased, subjective.
n. aim, ambition, aspiration, design, destination, end, goal, intention, mark, object, prize, purpose, target.

objectivity *n.* detachment, disinterest, disinterestedness, dispassion, equitableness, even-handedness, impartiality, impersonality, open mind, open-mindedness.
antonyms bias, subjectivity.

obligation *n.* accountability, accountableness, agreement, bond, burden, charge, commitment, compulsion, contract, debt, duty, engagement, indebtedness, liability, must, obstriction, onus, promise, requirement, responsibility, stipulation, trust, understanding.
antonyms choice, discretion.

obligatory *adj.* binding, bounden, coercive, compulsory, de rigueur, enforced, essential, imperative, mandatory, necessary, required, requisite, statutory, unavoidable.

antonym optional.

oblige *v.* accommodate, assist, benefit, bind, coerce, compel, constrain, do a favour, favour, force, gratify, help, impel, indulge, make, necessitate, obligate, please, require, serve.

obliged *adj.* appreciative, beholden, bound, compelled, constrained, forced, grateful, gratified, in debt (to), indebted, obligated, required, thankful, under an obligation, under compulsion.

obliging *adj.* accommodating, agreeable, aidful, amiable, civil, complaisant, considerate, co-operative, courteous, eager, friendly, good-natured, helpful, kind, polite, willing. *antonyms* inconsiderate, unhelpful, unkind.

oblique *adj.* angled, aslant, at an angle, back-handed, circuitous, circumlocutory, evasive, inclined, indirect, roundabout, sidelong, slanted, slanting, sloped, sloping, tilted, transverse.

obliquely *adv.* askance, askant, aslant, aslope, at an angle, circuitously, diagonally, evasively, in a roundabout way, indirectly, not in so many words, slantwise.

obliterate *v.* annihilate, blot out, cancel, delete, destroy, efface, eradicate, erase, expunge, extirpate, rub out, vaporise, wipe out.

obliteration *n.* annihilation, blotting out, deletion, effacement, elimination, eradication, erasure, expunction, extirpation, rasure.

oblivion *n.* abeyance, blackness, coma, darkness, disregard, eclipse, extinction, forgetfulness, insensibility, Lethe, limbo, neglect, nothingness, obliviousness, obscurity, stupor, unawareness, unconsciousness, void. *antonyms* awareness, consciousness.

oblivious *adj.* blind, careless, comatose, deaf, disregardful, forgetful, heedless, ignorant, inattentive, insensible, neglectful, negligent, nescient, regardless, unaware, unconcerned, unconscious, unmindful, unobservant. *antonyms* aware, conscious.

obloquy *n.* abuse, animadversion, aspersion, attack, bad press, blame, calumny, censure, contumely, criticism, defamation, detraction, discredit, disfavour, disgrace, dishonour, humiliation, ignominy, infamy, invective, odium, opprobrium, reproach, shame, slander, stigma, vilification.

obnoxious *adj.* abhorrent, abominable, detestable, disagreeable, disgusting, dislik(e)able, foul, fulsome, hateful, horrid, insufferable, loathsome, nasty, nauseating, nauseous, noisome, objectionable, odious, offensive, repellent, reprehensible, repugnant, repulsive, revolting, sickening, unpleasant. *antonyms* agreeable, lik(e)able, pleasant.

obscene *adj.* atrocious, barrack-room, bawdy, blue, coarse, dirty, disgusting, evil, Fescennine, filthy, foul, gross, heinous, immodest, immoral, improper, impure, indecent, lewd, licentious, loathsome, loose, offensive, outrageous, pornographic, prurient, Rabelaisian, ribald, salacious, scabrous, scurrilous, shame-less, shocking, sickening, smutty, suggestive, unchaste, unwholesome, vile, wicked. *antonyms* clean, decent, decorous.

obscenity *n.* abomination, affront, atrocity, bawdiness, blight, blueness, coarseness, dirtiness, evil, expletive, facetiae, filthiness, foulness, four-letter word, grossness, immodesty, impropriety, impurity, indecency, indelicacy, lewdness, licentiousness, offence, outrage, pornography, profanity, prurience, salacity, scurrility, smut, smuttiness, suggestiveness, swear-word, vileness, vulgarism.

obscure *adj.* abstruse, ambiguous, arcane, blurred, caliginous, clear as mud, clouded, cloudy, concealed, confusing, cryptic, deep, Delphic, dim, doubtful, dusky, enigmatic, esoteric, faint, gloomy, hazy, hermetic, hidden, humble, incomprehensible, inconspicuous, indefinite, indistinct, inglorious, intricate, involved, little-known, lowly, minor, misty, murky, mysterious, nameless, obfuscated, occult, opaque, oracular, out-of-the-way, recondite, remote, riddling, shadowy, shady, sombre, tenebr(i)ous, tenebrose, twilight, unclear, undistinguished, unheard-of, unhonoured, unimportant, unknown, unlit, unnoted, unobvious, unrenowned, unseen, unsung, vague, veiled. *antonyms* clear, definite, explicit, famous, lucid.

v. bedim, befog, block out, blur, cloak, cloud, conceal, cover, darken, dim, disguise, dull, eclipse, hide, mask, muddy, obfuscate, overshadow, screen, shade, shadow, shroud, veil. *antonyms* clarify, illuminate.

obscurity *n.* abstruseness, ambiguity, complexity, darkness, dimness, dusk, duskiness, fogginess, gloom, haze, haziness, impenetrability, incomprehensibility, inconspicuousness, indistinctness, ingloriousness, insignificance, intricacy, lowliness, mirk, mirkiness, murk, murkiness, mysticism, namelessness, reconditeness, shadowiness, shadows, unimportance, vagueness. *antonyms* clarity, fame, lucidity.

obsequious *adj.* abject, cringing, deferential, dough-faced, fawning, flattering, grovelling, ingratiating, knee-crooking, menial, oily, servile, slavish, slimy, smarmy, submissive, subservient, sycophantic, toadying, unctuous. *antonym* assertive.

observable *adj.* apparent, appreciable, clear, detectable, discernable, evident, measurable, noticeable, obvious, open, patent, perceivable, perceptible, recognisable, significant, visible.

observance *n.* adherence, attention, celebration, ceremonial, ceremony, compliance, custom, discharge, fashion, form, formality, fulfilment, heeding, honouring, notice, obedience, observation, orthodoxy, performance, practice, rite, ritual, service, tradition.

observant *adj.* alert, attentive, eagle-eyed, eagle-sighted, falcon-eyed, heedful, mindful,

perceptive, percipient, quick, sharp-eyed, vigilant, watchful, wide-awake.
antonyms inattentive, unobservant.

observation *n.* annotation, attention, cognition, comment, consideration, discernment, examination, experience, finding, information, inspection, knowledge, monitoring, note, notice, obiter dictum, opinion, perception, pronouncement, reading, reflection, remark, review, scrutiny, study, surveillance, thought, utterance, watching.

observe *v.* abide by, adhere to, animadvert, celebrate, commemorate, comment, comply, conform to, contemplate, declare, detect, discern, discover, espy, follow, fulfil, heed, honour, keep, keep an eye on, keep tabs on, mention, mind, monitor, note, notice, obey, opine, perceive, perform, regard, remark, remember, respect, say, scrutinise, see, solemnise, spot, state, study, surveille, survey, view, watch, witness.
antonyms break, miss, overlook, violate.

observer *n.* beholder, bystander, commentator, discerner, eyewitness, looker-on, noter, onlooker, spectator, spotter, viewer, watcher, witness.

obsess *v.* bedevil, consume, dominate, engross, grip, haunt, hold, monopolise, nag, plague, possess, preoccupy, prey on, rule, torment.

obsessed *adj.* bedevilled, beset, dominated, gripped, hag-ridden, haunted, hounded, hung up on, immersed in, in the grip of, infatuated, plagued, preoccupied.
antonyms detached, indifferent, unconcerned.

obsession *n.* bee in one's bonnet, complex, enthusiasm, fetish, fixation, hang-up, idée fixe, infatuation, mania, monomania, phobia, preoccupation, ruling passion, thing, zelotypia.

obsessive *adj.* besetting, compulsive, consuming, fixed, gripping, haunting, maddening, nagging, tormenting, unforgettable.

obsolescent *adj.* ag(e)ing, declining, disappearing, dying out, fading, moribund, on the decline, on the wane, on the way out, past its prime, waning.

obsolete *adj.* anachronistic, ancient, antediluvian, antiquated, antique, archaic, bygone, dated, dead, démodé, discarded, disused, extinct, fogram, horse-and-buggy, musty, old, old hat, old-fashioned, out, out of date, outmoded, outworn, passé, superannuated.
antonyms contemporary, current, modern, new, up-to-date.

obstacle *n.* bar, barrier, boyg, catch, check, chicane, difficulty, drawback, hindrance, hitch, hurdle, impediment, interference, interruption, obstruction, pons asinorum, remora, snag, stop, stumbling-block, stumbling-stone.
antonyms advantage, help.

obstinacy *n.* doggedness, firmness, frowardness, inflexibility, intransigence, mulishness, obduracy, perseverance, persistence, pertinacity, perversity, pig-headedness, resoluteness, stubbornness, tenacity, wilfulness, wrong-headedness.
antonyms co-operativeness, flexibility, submissiveness.

obstinate *adj.* bullet-headed, bull-headed, bullish, camelish, contumacious, determined, dogged, firm, headstrong, immovable, inflexible, intractable, intransigent, mulish, obdurate, opinionated, persistent, pertinacious, perverse, pervicacious, pig-headed, recalcitrant, refractory, restive, rusty, self-willed, steadfast, stomachful, strong-minded, stubborn, sturdy, tenacious, unadvisable, unyielding, uppity, wilful, wrong-headed.
antonyms co-operative, flexible, pliant, submissive.

obstreperous *adj.* boisterous, clamorous, disorderly, intractable, loud, noisy, out of hand, rackety, rambunctious, rampaging, raucous, refractory, restive, riotous, rip-roaring, roistering, roisterous, rough, rowdy, stroppy, tempestuous, tumultuous, turbulent, uncontrolled, undisciplined, unmanageable, unruly, uproarious, vociferous, wild.
antonyms calm, disciplined, quiet.

obstruct *v.* arrest, bar, barricade, block, check, choke, clog, crab, cumber, curb, cut off, frustrate, hamper, hamstring, hide, hinder, hold up, impede, inhibit, interfere with, interrupt, mask, obscure, occlude, prevent, restrict, retard, shield, shut off, slow down, stall, stonewall, stop, stuff, thwart, trammel.
antonym help.

obstruction *n.* bar, barricade, barrier, blockage, check, difficulty, filibuster, hindrance, impediment, snag, stop, stoppage, trammel, traverse.
antonym help.

obstructive *adj.* awkward, blocking, delaying, difficult, hindering, inhibiting, restrictive, stalling, unaccommodating, unco-operative, unhelpful.
antonym helpful.

obtain[1] *v.* achieve, acquire, attain, come by, compass, earn, gain, get, impetrate, procure, secure.

obtain[2] *v.* be in force, be prevalent, be the case, exist, hold, prevail, reign, rule, stand.

obtainable *adj.* accessible, achievable, at hand, attainable, available, on call, on tap, procurable, ready, realisable, to be had.
antonym unobtainable.

obtrusive *adj.* blatant, forward, importunate, interfering, intrusive, manifest, meddling, nosy, noticeable, obvious, officious, prominent, protruding, protuberant, prying, pushy.
antonym unobtrusive.

obtuse *adj.* blunt, boneheaded, crass, dense, dopey, dull, dull-witted, dumb, imperceptive, impercipient, inattentive, insensitive, retarded, rounded, slow, stolid, stupid, thick, thick-skinned, uncomprehending, unintelligent.
antonyms bright, sharp.

obviate v. anticipate, avert, counter, counteract, divert, forestall, preclude, prevent, remove.

obvious adj. apparent, clear, conspicuous, discernible, distinct, evident, glaring, indisputable, manifest, noticeable, open, open-and-shut, overt, palpable, patent, perceptible, plain, prominent, pronounced, recognisable, self-evident, self-explanatory, straightforward, transparent, unconcealed, undeniable, undisguised, unmistakable, unsubtle, visible.
antonyms obscure, unclear.

obviously adv. certainly, clearly, distinctly, evidently, manifestly, of course, palpably, patently, plainly, undeniably, unmistakably, unquestionably, visibly, without doubt.

occasion n. affair, call, case, cause, celebration, chance, convenience, event, excuse, experience, ground(s), incident, inducement, influence, instance, justification, moment, motive, occurrence, opening, opportunity, prompting, provocation, reason, time.
v. bring about, bring on, cause, create, effect, elicit, engender, evoke, generate, give rise to, induce, influence, inspire, lead to, make, originate, persuade, produce, prompt, provoke.

occasional adj. casual, desultory, fitful, incidental, infrequent, intermittent, irregular, odd, periodic, rare, scattered, sporadic, uncommon.
antonym frequent.

occasionally adv. at intervals, at times, every so often, from time to time, infrequently, irregularly, now and again, now and then, off and on, on and off, on occasion, once in a while, periodically, sometimes, sporadically.
antonym frequently.

occult adj. abstruse, arcane, cabbalistic, concealed, esoteric, faint, hidden, impenetrable, invisible, magical, mysterious, mystic, mystical, mystifying, obscure, preternatural, recondite, secret, supernatural, unknown, unrevealed, veiled.
v. conceal, cover (up), enshroud, hide, mask, obscure, screen, shroud, veil.
antonym reveal.

occultism n. black magic, diabolism, magic, mysticism, sorcery, spiritualism, supernaturalism, the black arts, witchcraft.

occupancy n. domiciliation, habitation, holding, inhabitancy, occupation, ownership, possession, residence, tenancy, tenure, term, use.

occupant n. addressee, denizen, holder, householder, incumbent, indweller, inhabitant, inmate, lessee, occupier, resident, squatter, tenant, user.

occupation[1] n. absorption, activity, business, calling, craft, employment, job, line, post, profession, pursuit, trade, vocation, walk of life, work.

occupation[2] n. billet, conquest, control, habitation, holding, invasion, occupancy, possession, residence, seizure, subjugation, takeover, tenancy, tenure, use.

occupied adj. absorbed, busy, employed, engaged, engrossed, full, hard at it, in use, inhabited, lived-in, peopled, settled, taken, tenanted, tied up, unavailable, working.
antonym unoccupied.

occupy v. absorb, amuse, beguile, busy, capture, conquer, cover, divert, dwell in, employ, engage, engross, ensconce oneself in, entertain, establish oneself in, fill, garrison, hold, immerse, inhabit, interest, invade, involve, keep, keep busy, live in, monopolise, overrun, own, permeate, pervade, possess, preoccupy, reside in, seize, stay in, take over, take possession of, take up, tenant, tie up, use, utilise.

occur v. appear, arise, be found, be met with, be present, befall, betide, chance, come about, come off, come to pass, crop up, develop, eventuate, exist, happen, intervene, manifest itself, materialise, obtain, result, show itself, take place, transpire, turn up.

occur to come to mind, come to one, cross one's mind, dawn on, enter one's head, present itself, spring to mind, strike one, suggest itself.

occurrence n. action, adventure, affair, appearance, case, circumstance, development, episode, event, existence, happening, incident, instance, manifestation, materialisation, proceeding, transaction.

ocean n. briny, main, profound, sea, the deep, the drink.

odd[1] adj. abnormal, atypical, bizarre, curious, deviant, different, eccentric, exceptional, extraordinary, fantastic, freak, freakish, freaky, funky, funny, irregular, kinky, outlandish, peculiar, quaint, queer, rare, remarkable, singular, strange, uncanny, uncommon, unconventional, unexplained, unusual, weird, whimsical.
antonym normal.

odd[2] adj. auxiliary, casual, fragmentary, ill-matched, incidental, irregular, left-over, lone, miscellaneous, occasional, periodic, random, remaining, seasonal, single, solitary, spare, sundry, surplus, uneven, unmatched, unpaired, varied, various.

oddity n. abnormality, anomaly, bizarreness, card, character, crank, curiosity, eccentricity, extraordinariness, freak, freakishness, idiosyncrasy, incongruity, irregularity, kink, maverick, misfit, oddball, oddness, outlandishness, peculiarity, phenomenon, queerness, quirk, quizziness, rara avis, rarity, screwball, singularity, strangeness, unconventionality, unnaturalness, weirdie, weirdo.

oddment n. bit, end, fragment, leftover, offcut, patch, remnant, scrap, shred, sliver, snippet.

odds n. advantage, allowance, ascendancy, balance, chances, difference, discrepancy, disparity, dissimilarity, distinction, edge, lead, likelihood, probability, superiority.

odds and ends bits, bits and pieces, debris, flotsam and jetsam, junk, leavings, litter, oddments, odds and sods, remnants, rubbish, scraps, tatt.

odious *adj*. abhorrent, abominable, annoying, detestable, disgusting, execrable, foul, hateful, heinous, horrible, horrid, insufferable, loathsome, obnoxious, offensive, repellent, repugnant, repulsive, revolting, unpleasant, vile.
antonym pleasant.

odium *n*. abhorrence, animosity, antipathy, censure, condemnation, contempt, detestation, disapprobation, disapproval, discredit, disfavour, disgrace, dishonour, dislike, disrepute, execration, hatred, infamy, obloquy, opprobrium, reprobation, shame.

odorous *adj*. aromatic, balmy, fragrant, odoriferous, perfumed, pungent, redolent, scented, sweet-smelling.
antonym odourless.

odour *n*. air, aroma, atmosphere, aura, bouquet, breath, emanation, essence, exhalation, flavour, fragrance, perfume, quality, redolence, scent, smell, spirit, stench, stink.

odyssey *n*. journey, travels, wandering.

of course certainly, definitely, doubtlessly, indubitably, naturally, no doubt, obviously, undoubtedly.

off *adj*. abnormal, absent, bad, below par, cancelled, decomposed, disappointing, disheartening, displeasing, finished, gone, high, inoperative, mouldy, poor, postponed, quiet, rancid, rotten, slack, sour, substandard, turned, unavailable, unsatisfactory, wrong.
adv. apart, aside, at a distance, away, elsewhere, out.

off and on fitfully, from time to time, intermittently, now and again, now and then, occasionally, on and off, once in a while, periodically, sometimes, sporadically.

off guard napping, unprepared, unready, unwary, with one's defences down, with one's pants down.

off the cuff ad lib, extempore, impromptu, improvised, offhand, spontaneous, spontaneously, unofficially, unprepared, unrehearsed, unscripted.

off the hook acquitted, cleared, exonerated, in the clear, scot free, vindicated.

off the record confidential, confidentially, private, privately, sub rosa, unofficial, unofficially.
antonym officially.

off-colour *adj*. faded, ill, indecent, indisposed, off form, out of sorts, pasty-faced, peaky, peelie-wally, poorly, queasy, sick, under the weather, unwell.

off-duty *adj*. at leisure, at liberty, free, not at work, off, off work, on holiday.

offence *n*. affront, anger, annoyance, crime, delict, delinquency, displeasure, fault, hard feelings, harm, huff, hurt, indignation, indignity, infraction, infringement, injury, injustice, insult, ire, lapse, misdeed, misdemeanour, needle, outrage, peccadillo, pique, put-down, resentment, sin, slight, snub, transgression, trespass, umbrage, violation,

wrath, wrong, wrong-doing.

offend *v*. affront, annoy, disgruntle, disgust, displease, fret, gall, hip, hurt, insult, irritate, miff, nauseate, outrage, pain, pique, provoke, repel, repulse, rile, sicken, slight, snub, transgress, turn off, upset, vex, violate, wound, wrong.
antonym please.

offended *adj*. affronted, disgruntled, disgusted, displeased, huffy, in a huff, miffed, outraged, pained, piqued, put out, resentful, smarting, stung, upset, wounded.
antonym pleased.

offender *n*. criminal, culprit, delinquent, guilty party, law-breaker, malefactor, miscreant, misfeasor, sinner, transgressor, wrong-doer.

offensive *adj*. abominable, abusive, aggressive, annoying, attacking, detestable, disagreeable, discourteous, disgusting, displeasing, disrespectful, embarrassing, grisly, impertinent, insolent, insulting, intolerable, invading, irritating, loathsome, nasty, nauseating, noisome, objectionable, obnoxious, odious, rank, repellent, repugnant, revolting, rude, sickening, uncivil, unmannerly, unpalatable, unpleasant, unsavoury, vile.
antonyms defensive, pleasing.
n. attack, drive, onslaught, push, raid, sortie, thrust.

offer *v*. advance, afford, bid, extend, furnish, give, hold out, make available, move, present, proffer, propose, propound, provide, put forth, put forward, show, submit, suggest, tender, volunteer.
n. approach, attempt, bid, endeavour, essay, overture, presentation, proposal, proposition, submission, suggestion, tender.

offering *n*. contribution, donation, gift, oblation, present, sacrifice, subscription, xenium.

offhand *adj*. abrupt, aloof, brusque, careless, casual, cavalier, curt, glib, informal, offhanded, perfunctory, take-it-or-leave-it, unappreciative, uncaring, unceremonious, unconcerned, uninterested.
antonyms calculated, planned.
adv. at once, extempore, immediately, off the cuff, off the top of one's head, straightaway.

office *n*. appointment, bath, business, capacity, charge, commission, duty, employment, function, obligation, occupation, place, post, responsibility, role, room, service, situation, station, trust, work.

officer *n*. administrator, agent, appointee, bureaucrat, dignitary, executive, functionary, office-holder, official, public servant, representative.

offices *n*. advocacy, aegis, aid, auspices, backing, back-up, favour, help, intercession, intermediation, intervention, mediation, patronage, recommendation, referral, support, word.

official *adj*. accredited, approved, authentic, authenticated, authorised, authoritative, bona fide, certified, ex cathedra, formal, legitimate, licensed, proper, sanctioned.
antonym unofficial.

n. agent, bureaucrat, executive, fonctionnaire, functionary, gauleiter, hakim, intendant, jack-in-office, mandarin, office-bearer, officer, representative.

officiate *v.* adjudicate, chair, conduct, emcee, manage, oversee, preside, referee, serve, superintend, umpire.

officious *adj.* bustling, dictatorial, forward, impertinent, inquisitive, interfering, intermeddling, intrusive, meddlesome, meddling, mischievous, obtrusive, opinionated, over-zealous, pragmatical, pushy, self-important.

offish *adj.* aloof, cool, haughty, standoffish, stuck-up, unsociable.

antonyms friendly, sociable.

off-key *adj.* discordant, dissonant, inappropriate, indecent, inharmonious, jarring, out of keeping, out of tune, unsuitable.

offload *v.* deposit, disburden, discharge, drop, dump, get rid of, jettison, shift, transfer, unburden, unload, unship.

off-putting *adj.* daunting, demoralising, discomfiting, disconcerting, discouraging, disheartening, dismaying, dispiriting, disturbing, formidable, frustrating, intimidating, unnerving, unsettling, upsetting.

offset *v.* balance out, cancel out, compare, compensate for, counteract, counterbalance, counterpoise, countervail, juxtapose, make up for, neutralise.

n. balance, compensation, counterbalance, counterweight, equipoise, equivalent, redress.

offshoot *n.* adjunct, appendage, arm, branch, by-product, development, embranchment, limb, outgrowth, spin-off, sprout, spur.

offspring *n.* brood, child, children, creation, descendant, descendants, family, fry, heir, heirs, issue, kids, litter, progeny, quiverful, result, scion, seed, spawn, successor, successors, young.

antonym parent(s).

often *adv.* again and again, frequently, generally, habitually, many a time, much, oft, over and over, regularly, repeatedly, time after time, time and again.

antonym seldom.

ogle *v.* eye, eye up, leer, look, make eyes at, stare.

ogre *n.* bogey, bogeyman, bogle, boyg, bugaboo, bugbear, demon, devil, giant, humgruffi(a)n, monster, spectre.

oik *n.* bloke, bounder, cad, chap, ignoramus, twerp.

oil *v.* anoint, embrocate, grease, lubricate.

n. balm, cream, grease, liniment, lotion, lubricant, ointment, oleum, salve, unguent.

oily *adj.* fatty, flattering, fulsome, glib, greasy, hypocritical, obsequious, oiled, oleaginous, plausible, sebaceous, servile, slippery, smarmy, smeary, smooth, swimming, unctuous.

ointment *n.* balm, balsam, cerate, cream, demulcent, embrocation, emollient, liniment, lotion, salve, unction, unguent.

okay *adj.* acceptable, accurate, adequate, all right, approved, convenient, correct, fair, fine, good, in order, not bad, OK, passable, permitted, reasonable, right as rain, satisfactory, tolerable.

n. agreement, approbation, approval, assent, authorisation, consent, endorsement, go-ahead, green light, OK, permission, sanction, say-so, seal of approval, support.

v. accredit, agree to, approve, authorise, consent to, endorse, give the go-ahead to, give the green light to, OK, pass, rubber-stamp, sanction, validate.

interj. agreed, all right, fine, OK, right, very good, very well, yes.

old *adj.* aboriginal, aged, age-old, ancient, antediluvian, antiquated, antique, archaic, bygone, cast-off, crumbling, dated, decayed, decrepit, done, earlier, early, elderly, erstwhile, ex-, experienced, familiar, former, grey, grey-haired, grizzled, hackneyed, hardened, hoary, immemorial, long-established, long-standing, mature, obsolete, of old, of yore, Ogygian, olden, old-fashioned, one-time, original, out of date, outdated, outmoded, over the hill, passé, patriarchal, practised, preadamic(al), prehistoric, previous, prim(a)eval, primitive, primordial, pristine, quondam, remote, senescent, senile, skilled, stale, superannuated, time-honoured, time-worn, traditional, unfashionable, unoriginal, venerable, versed, veteran, vintage, worn-out.

antonym young.

old age advancing years, age, agedness, Anno Domini, dotage, e(i)ld, second childhood, senescence, senility, twilight of one's life.

antonym youth.

old man boss, elder, elder statesman, employer, father, gaffer, geezer, grandfather, grey, greybeard, hoarhead, husband, OAP, old codger, old stager, oldster, old-timer, patriarch, senior citizen, white-beard.

old woman bag, complainer, crone, fag(g)ot, fuss-pot, gammer, grandam, grannam, granny, grouch, grumbler, hag, mother, old dear, wet, wife, wimp.

old-fashioned *adj.* ancient, antiquated, archaic, arriéré, behind the times, corny, dated, dead, démodé, fog(e)yish, fusty, horse-and-buggy, musty, neanderthal, obsolescent, obsolete, old hat, old-fog(e)yish, old-time, out of date, outdated, outmoded, passé, past, retro, square, superannuated, unfashionable.

antonyms contemporary, modern, up-to-date.

old-world *adj.* archaic, ceremonious, chivalrous, conservative, courtly, formal, gallant, old-fashioned, picturesque, quaint, traditional.

Olympian *adj.* elevated, exalted, glorious, godlike, Jovian, lofty, majestic, rarefied, splendid, sublime.

omen *n.* augury, auspice, boding, foreboding, foretoken, freit, indication, portent, premonition, presage, prognostic, prognostication, sign, straw in the wind, warning, writing on the wall.

ominous *adj.* baleful, bodeful, dark, fateful, inauspicious, menacing, minatory, portentous, premonitory, presageful, sinister, threatening, unpromising, unpropitious. *antonym* auspicious.

omission *n.* avoidance, bowdlerisation, default, ellipsis, exclusion, failure, forgetfulness, gap, lack, neglect, oversight. *antonyms* addition, inclusion.

omit *v.* disregard, drop, edit out, eliminate, exclude, fail, forget, give something a miss, leave out, leave undone, let slide, miss out, neglect, overlook, pass over, pretermit, skip. *antonyms* add, include.

omnibus *adj.* all-embracing, compendious, comprehensive, encyclop(a)edic, inclusive, wide-ranging. *antonym* selective.

omnipotence *n.* divine right, invincibility, mastery, plenipotence, sovereignty, supremacy. *antonym* impotence.

omnipotent *adj.* all-powerful, almighty, plenipotent, supreme. *antonym* impotent.

omnipresent *adj.* pervasive, ubiquitary, ubiquitous, universal.

omniscient *adj.* all-knowing, all-seeing, pansophic.

on and off discontinuously, fitfully, from time to time, intermittently, now and again, now and then, off and on, on occasion, periodically, sometimes, spasmodically, sporadically.

on duty at work, busy, engaged, working. *antonym* off.

on edge apprehensive, eager, edgy, excited, ill at ease, impatient, irascible, irritable, keyed up, nervous, on tenterhooks, tense, touchy, uptight. *antonym* relaxed.

on fire ablaze, aflame, alight, ardent, blazing, burning, eager, enthusiastic, excited, fiery, fired, flaming, ignited, in flames, inspired, kindled, passionate.

on guard alert, cautious, chary, circumspect, excubant, on the alert, on the lookout, on the qui vive, prepared, ready, vigilant, wary, watchful, wide awake.

on one's last legs at death's door, dying, exhausted, fading fast, failing, moribund, with one foot in the grave, worn out.

on one's own alone, by oneself, independently, isolated, off one's own bat, on one's tod, singly, unaccompanied, unaided, unassisted.

on purpose deliberately, designedly, intentionally, knowingly, premeditatedly, purposely, wilfully, wittingly. *antonym* accidentally.

on the ball alert, attentive, aware, in touch, informed, on one's toes, quick, wide awake.

on the dot exactly, on time, precisely, promptly, punctually, spot on, to the minute.

on the fence between two stools, dithering, irresolute, shilly-shallying, uncertain, uncom-

mitted, undecided, unsure, vacillating.

on the increase accelerating, escalating, expanding, growing, increasing, multiplying, proliferating, rising, spreading. *antonym* on the wane.

on the level above board, candid, fair, frank, genuine, honest, open, sincere, square, straight, straightforward, up front.

on the mend convalescent, convalescing, healing, improving, recovering, recuperating, reviving.

on the move active, advancing, astir, moving, on the go, progressing, stirring, succeeding.

on the rampage amok, berserk, frenzied, in a frenzy, rampageous(ly), rampant(ly), riotous(ly), violent(ly), wild(ly).

on the scrap-heap discarded, ditched, dumped, forgotten, jettisoned, redundant, rejected, written off.

on the sly clandestinely, covertly, furtively, on the q.t., privately, secretly, surreptitiously, underhandedly. *antonym* openly.

on the spur of the moment capriciously, impetuously, impromptu, impulsively, on impulse, on the spot, thoughtlessly, unpremeditatedly, unthinkingly.

on the wane declining, degenerating, deteriorating, dropping, dwindling, ebbing, fading, lessening, moribund, obsolescent, on its last legs, on the decline, on the way out, subsiding, tapering off, weakening, withering. *antonym* on the increase.

on the whole all in all, all things considered, as a rule, by and large, for the most part, generally, generally speaking, in general, in the main, mostly, predominantly.

on thin ice at risk, in jeopardy, insecure, open to attack, precarious, unsafe, vulnerable.

on top of the world ecstatic, elated, exhilarated, exultant, happy, on cloud nine, over the moon, overjoyed, thrilled.

once *adv.* at one time, formerly, heretofore, in the old days, in the past, in times gone by, in times past, long ago, once upon a time, previously.

once (and) for all conclusively, decisively, definitively, finally, for good, for the last time, permanently, positively.

once in a blue moon hardly ever, infrequently, rarely, seldom.

oncoming *adj.* advancing, approaching, forthcoming, gathering, imminent, impending, looming, onrushing, upcoming.

one *adj.* alike, compatible, complete, entire, equal, harmonious, identical, like-minded, united, whole.

oneness *n.* completeness, consistency, distinctness, identicalness, identity, individuality, sameness, singleness, unicity, unity, wholeness.

onerous *adj.* backbreaking, burdensome, crushing, demanding, difficult, exacting, exhausting, exigent, formidable, grave, hard, heavy, herculean, laborious, oppressive,

responsible, taxing, troublesome, weighty.
antonyms easy, light.

one-sided *adj.* asymmetrical, biased, coloured, discriminatory, inequitable, lopsided, partial, partisan, prejudiced, unequal, unfair, unilateral, unjust.
antonym impartial.

one-time *adj.* erstwhile, ex-, former, late, previous, quondam, sometime, umquhile, whilom.

ongoing *adj.* advancing, continuing, continuous, current, developing, evolving, extant, growing, in progress, lasting, progressing, successful, unfinished, unfolding.

onlooker *n.* bystander, eye-witness, looker-on, observer, rubber-neck, spectator, viewer, watcher, witness.

only *adv.* at most, barely, exclusively, just, merely, purely, simply, solely.
adj. exclusive, individual, lone, single, sole, solitary, unique.

onrush *n.* career, cascade, charge, flood, flow, onset, onslaught, push, rush, stampede, stream, surge.

onset *n.* assault, attack, beginning, charge, commencement, inception, kick-off, onrush, onslaught, outbreak, outset, start.
antonyms end, finish.

onslaught *n.* assault, attack, barrage, blitz, bombardment, charge, offensive, onrush, onset.

onus *n.* burden, duty, encumbrance, liability, load, obligation, responsibility, task.

onward(s) *adv.* ahead, beyond, forth, forward, frontward(s), in front, on.
antonym backward(s).

oodles *n.* abundance, bags, heaps, lashings, loads, lots, masses, oodlins, tons.
antonym scarcity.

oomph *n.* animation, bounce, energy, enthusiasm, exuberance, get-up-and-go, pep, pizzazz, sex-appeal, sparkle, vigour, vitality, vivacity, zing.

ooze *v.* bleed, discharge, drain, dribble, drip, drop, emit, escape, exude, filter, leach, leak, osmose, overflow with, percolate, seep, strain, sweat, transude, weep.
n. alluvium, deposit, mire, muck, mud, sediment, silt, slime, sludge.

oozy *adj.* dewy, dripping, miry, moist, mucky, muddy, slimy, sloppy, sludgy, sweaty, uliginous, weeping.

opacity *n.* cloudiness, density, dullness, filminess, impermeability, milkiness, murkiness, obfuscation, obscurity, opaqueness, unclearness.
antonym transparency.

opaque *adj.* abstruse, baffling, clouded, cloudy, cryptic, difficult, dim, dull, enigmatic, filmy, fuliginous, hazy, impenetrable, incomprehensible, inexplicable, lustreless, muddied, muddy, murky, obfuscated, obscure, turbid, unclear, unfathomable, unintelligible.
antonym transparent.

open *adj.* above-board, accessible, agape, airy,

ajar, apparent, arguable, artless, available, avowed, bare, barefaced, blatant, bounteous, bountiful, candid, champaign, clear, conspicuous, debatable, disinterested, downright, evident, expanded, exposed, extended, extensive, fair, filigree, flagrant, frank, free, fretted, gaping, general, generous, guileless, holey, honest, honeycombed, impartial, ingenuous, innocent, lacy, liberal, lidless, loose, manifest, moot, munificent, natural, navigable, noticeable, objective, obvious, overt, passable, plain, porous, public, receptive, revealed, rolling, sincere, spacious, spongy, spread out, sweeping, transparent, unbarred, unbiased, unclosed, uncluttered, uncommitted, unconcealed, unconditional, uncovered, uncrowded, undecided, undefended, undisguised, unenclosed, unengaged, unfastened, unfenced, unfolded, unfortified, unfurled, unlidded, unlocked, unobstructed, unoccupied, unprejudiced, unprotected, unqualified, unreserved, unresolved, unrestricted, unroofed, unsealed, unsettled, unsheltered, unwalled, vacant, visible, wide, wide-open, yawning.
antonyms closed, shut.
v. begin, clear, come apart, commence, crack, disclose, divulge, exhibit, explain, expose, inaugurate, initiate, launch, lay bare, ope, pour out, rupture, separate, set in motion, show, split, spread (out), start, throw wide, unbar, unbare, unblock, unclose, uncork, uncover, undo, unfasten, unfold, unfurl, unlatch, unlid, unlock, unroll, unseal, unshutter.
antonyms close, shut.

open to accessible, disposed, exposed, liable, susceptible, vulnerable.

open-air *adj.* alfresco, hypaethral, outdoor, plein-air.
antonym indoor.

open-and-shut *adj.* obvious, simple, straightforward.

open-handed *adj.* bountiful, eleemosynary, free, generous, large-hearted, lavish, liberal, munificent, unstinting.
antonym tight-fisted.

opening *n.* adit, aperture, beginning, birth, breach, break, chance, chasm, chink, cleft, commencement, crack, dawn, fissure, fistula, foramen, gap, hole, inauguration, inception, initiation, interstice, kick-off, launch, launching, occasion, onset, opportunity, orifice, ostiole, outset, perforation, place, rent, rupture, slot, space, split, start, vacancy, vent, vista.
antonyms closing, closure.
adj. beginning, commencing, early, first, inaugural, inauguratory, inceptive, initial, initiatory, introductory, maiden, primary.
antonym closing.

openly *adv.* blatantly, brazenly, candidly, face to face, flagrantly, forthrightly, frankly, glaringly, in full view, in public, overtly, plainly, publicly, shamelessly, unabashedly, unashamedly, unhesitatingly, unreservedly, wantonly.

antonyms secretly, slyly.

open-minded *adj.* broad, broad-minded, catholic, dispassionate, enlightened, free, impartial, latidutinarian, liberal, objective, reasonable, receptive, tolerant, unbiased, unprejudiced.

antonyms bigoted, intolerant, prejudiced.

open-mouthed *adj.* amazed, astounded, clamorous, dumbfounded, edacious, expectant, flabbergasted, greedy, spellbound, thunderstruck, voracious.

operate *v.* act, function, go, handle, manage, manoeuvre, perform, run, serve, use, utilise, work.

operation *n.* action, activity, affair, agency, assault, business, campaign, course, deal, effect, effort, employment, enterprise, exercise, force, influence, instrumentality, manipulation, manoeuvre, motion, movement, performance, procedure, proceeding, process, surgery, transaction, undertaking, use, utilisation, working.

operational *adj.* functional, going, in service, in working order, on duty, operative, prepared, ready, usable, viable, workable, working.

antonym out of order.

operative *adj.* active, crucial, current, effective, efficient, engaged, functional, functioning, important, in action, in force, in operation, indicative, influential, key, operational, relevant, serviceable, significant, standing, workable.

antonym inoperative.

n. artisan, employee, hand, labourer, machinist, mechanic, operator, worker.

operator *n.* administrator, conductor, contractor, dealer, director, driver, handler, machinator, machinist, manager, manipulator, mechanic, mover, operant, operative, practitioner, punter, shyster, speculator, technician, trader, wheeler-dealer, worker.

opiate *n.* anodyne, bromide, depressant, downer, drug, narcotic, nepenthe, pacifier, sedative, soporific, stupefacient, tranquilliser.

opine *v.* believe, conceive, conclude, conjecture, declare, guess, judge, presume, say, suggest, suppose, surmise, suspect, think, venture, volunteer.

opinion *n.* assessment, belief, conception, conjecture, conventional wisdom, doxy, estimation, feeling, idea, idée reçue, impression, judgement, mind, notion, perception, persuasion, point of view, sentiment, stance, tenet, theory, view, voice, vox pop, vox populi.

opinionated *adj.* adamant, biased, bigoted, bull-headed, cocksure, dictatorial, doctrinaire, dogmatic, high-dried, inflexible, obdurate, obstinate, overbearing, partisan, pigheaded, prejudiced, self-assertive, single-minded, stubborn, uncompromising, wilful.

antonym open-minded.

opponent *n.* adversary, antagonist, challenger, competitor, contestant, disputant, dissen-

tient, dissident, enemy, foe, objector, opposer, opposition, rival.

antonyms ally, proponent.

opportune *adj.* advantageous, appropriate, apt, auspicious, convenient, favourable, felicitous, fit, fitting, fortunate, good, happy, lucky, pertinent, proper, propitious, seasonable, suitable, timely, well-timed.

antonym inopportune.

opportunism *n.* expediency, exploitation, Machiavellianism, making hay while the sun shines, pragmatism, realism, Realpolitik, taking advantage, trimming, unscrupulousness.

opportunity *n.* break, chance, convenience, hour, moment, occasion, opening, scope, shot, time, turn.

oppose *v.* bar, beard, breast, check, combat, compare, confront, contradict, contrary, contrast, contravene, controvert, counter, counterattack, counterbalance, defy, face, fight, fly in the face of, gainsay, hinder, obstruct, pit against, play off, prevent, recalcitrate, resist, stand up to, take a stand against, take issue with, thwart, withstand.

antonyms favour, support.

opposed *adj.* against, agin, antagonistic, anti, antipathetic, antithetical, clashing, conflicting, contrary, contrasted, dissentient, hostile, in opposition, incompatible, inimical, opposing, opposite.

antonym in favour.

opposing *adj.* antagonistic, antipathetic, clashing, combatant, conflicting, contentious, contrary, disputatious, enemy, hostile, incompatible, irreconcilable, opposed, opposite, oppugnant, rival, warring.

opposite *adj.* adverse, antagonistic, antipodal, antipodean, antithetical, conflicting, contradictory, contrary, contrasted, corresponding, different, differing, diverse, facing, fronting, hostile, inconsistent, inimical, irreconcilable, opposed, reverse, unlike.

antonym same.

n. antipode(s), antipole, antithesis, contradiction, contrary, converse, inverse, reverse.

antonym same.

opposition *n.* antagonism, antagonist, clash, colluctation, competition, contraposition, contrariety, counteraction, counter-stand, counter-time, counter-view, disapproval, foe, hostility, obstruction, obstructiveness, opponent, other side, polarity, prevention, resistance, rival, syzygy, unfriendliness.

antonyms co-operation, support.

oppress *v.* abuse, afflict, burden, crush, depress, dispirit, harass, harry, lie hard on, lie heavy on, maltreat, overpower, overwhelm, persecute, sadden, subdue, subjugate, suppress, torment, trample, tyrannise, vex, weigh heavy.

oppressed *adj.* abused, browbeaten, burdened, disadvantaged, downtrodden, enslaved, harassed, henpecked, maltreated, misused, persecuted, prostrate, slave, subject, subjugated, troubled, tyrannised, underprivileged. *antonym* free.

oppression *n.* abuse, brutality, calamity, cruelty, hardship, harshness, injury, injustice, jackboot, liberticide, maltreatment, misery, persecution, severity, subjection, suffering, tyranny.

oppressive *adj.* airless, brutal, burdensome, close, cruel, despotic, grinding, harsh, heavy, inhuman, intolerable, muggy, onerous, overbearing, overpowering, overwhelming, repressive, severe, stifling, stuffy, suffocating, sultry, torrid, tyrannical, unendurable, unjust. *antonym* gentle.

oppressor *n.* autocrat, bully, coercionist, despot, dictator, harrier, intimidator, liberticide, persecutor, scourge, slave-driver, taskmaster, tormentor, tyrant.

opprobrious *adj.* abusive, calumniatory, calumnious, contemptuous, contumelious, damaging, defamatory, derogatory, dyslogistic, insolent, insulting, invective, offensive, scandalous, scurrilous, vitriolic, vituperative.

opprobrium *n.* calumny, censure, contumely, debasement, degradation, discredit, disfavour, disgrace, dishonour, disrepute, ignominy, infamy, obloquy, odium, reproach, scurrility, shame, slur, stigma.

opt *v.* choose, decide (on), elect, go for, plump for, prefer, select, single out.

optimistic *adj.* assured, bright, bullish, buoyant, cheerful, confident, encouraged, expectant, heartened, hopeful, idealistic, Panglossian, Panglossic, positive, sanguine, upbeat, Utopian. *antonym* pessimistic.

optimum *adj.* A1, best, choicest, highest, ideal, optimal, peak, perfect, superlative, top. *antonym* worst.
n. best, peak, zenith.

option *n.* alternative, choice, election, possibility, preference, selection.

optional *adj.* discretionary, elective, extra, open, possible, unforced, voluntary. *antonym* compulsory.

opulence *n.* abundance, affluence, copiousness, cornucopia, easy street, fortune, fullness, lavishness, luxuriance, luxury, plenty, pleroma, profusion, prosperity, riches, richness, sumptuousness, superabundance, wealth. *antonyms* penury, poverty.

opulent *adj.* abundant, affluent, copious, lavish, luxuriant, luxurious, moneyed, plentiful, profuse, prolific, prosperous, rich, sumptuous, superabundant, wealthy, well-heeled, well-off, well-to-do. *antonyms* penurious, poor.

opus *n.* brainchild, composition, creation, lucubration, oeuvre, piece, production, work.

oracle *n.* adviser, answer, augur, augury, authority, divination, guru, high priest, mastermind, mentor, prediction, prognostication, prophecy, prophet, pundit, python, revelation, sage, seer, sibyl, soothsayer, vision, wizard.

oracular *adj.* ambiguous, arcane, auspicious, authoritative, cryptic, Delphic, dictatorial, dogmatic, equivocal, grave, haruspical, mantic, mysterious, obscure, ominous, portentous, positive, predictive, prescient, prognostic, prophetic, pythonic, sage, sibylline, significant, two-edged, vatic, vaticinal, venerable, wise.

oral *adj.* acroamatic(al), spoken, unwritten, verbal, vocal. *antonym* written.

orate *v.* declaim, discourse, harangue, hold forth, pontificate, sermonise, speak, speechify, talk.

oration *n.* address, declamation, discourse, éloge, harangue, homily, lecture, sermon, speech, spiel.

orator *n.* declaimer, demagogue, lecturer, phrasemaker, phraseman, phrasemonger, phraser, public speaker, rhetorician, speaker, spellbinder, spieler.

oratorical *adj.* bombastic, Ciceronian, declamatory, Demosthenic, elocutionary, eloquent, grandiloquent, high-flown, magniloquent, rhetorical, silver-tongued, smooth-tongued, sonorous.

oratory *n.* declamation, diction, elocution, eloquence, grandiloquence, public speaking, rhetoric, speech, speechifying, speechmaking.

orb *n.* ball, circle, globe, globule, mound, ring, round, sphere, spherule.

orbit *n.* ambit, circle, circumgyration, circumvolution, compass, course, cycle, domain, ellipse, influence, path, range, reach, revolution, rotation, scope, sphere, sphere of influence, sweep, track, trajectory.
v. circle, circumnavigate, circumvolve, encircle, revolve.

orchestrate *v.* arrange, compose, concert, co-ordinate, fix, integrate, organise, prepare, present, score, stage-manage.

ordain *v.* anoint, appoint, call, consecrate, decree, destine, dictate, elect, enact, enjoin, fate, fix, foredoom, foreordain, frock, instruct, intend, invest, lay down, legislate, nominate, order, predestine, predetermine, prescribe, pronounce, require, rule, set, will.

ordeal *n.* affliction, agony, anguish, nightmare, pain, persecution, suffering, test, torture, trial, tribulation(s), trouble(s).

order[1] *n.* application, arrangement, array, behest, booking, calm, categorisation, chit, classification, codification, command, commission, control, cosmos, decree, dictate, diktat, direction, directive, discipline, disposal, disposition, eutaxy, grouping, harmony, injunction, instruction, law, law and order, layout, line, line-up, mandate, method, neatness, ordering, orderliness, ordinance, organisation, pattern, peace, placement, plan, precept, progression, propriety, quiet, regularity, regulation, request, requisition, reservation, rule, sequence, series, stipula-

tion, structure, succession, symmetry, system, tidiness, tranquillity.
antonym disorder.

v. adjure, adjust, align, arrange, authorise, bid, book, catalogue, charge, class, classify, command, conduct, control, decree, direct, dispose, enact, engage, enjoin, group, instruct, lay out, manage, marshal, neaten, ordain, organise, prescribe, put to rights, regulate, request, require, reserve, sort out, systematise, tabulate, tidy.
antonym disorder.

order[2] *n.* association, breed, brotherhood, cast, caste, class, community, company, degree, family, fraternity, genre, genus, grade, guild, hierarchy, ilk, kind, league, lodge, organisation, pecking order, phylum, position, rank, sect, sisterhood, society, sodality, sort, species, status, subclass, tribe, type, union.

orderly *adj.* businesslike, controlled, cosmic, decorous, disciplined, in order, law-abiding, methodical, neat, non-violent, peaceable, quiet, regular, restrained, ruly, scientific, shipshape, systematic, systematised, tidy, trim, well-behaved, well-organised, well-regulated.
antonym disorderly.

ordinance *n.* canon, ceremony, command, decree, dictum, directive, edict, enactment, fiat, injunction, institution, law, observance, order, practice, precept, prescript, regulation, rite, ritual, rule, ruling, sacrament, statute, usage.

ordinarily *adv.* as a rule, commonly, conventionally, customarily, familiarly, generally, habitually, in general, normally, usually.

ordinary *adj.* accustomed, average, common, common-or-garden, commonplace, conventional, customary, established, everyday, fair, familiar, habitual, homespun, household, humble, humdrum, inconsequential, indifferent, inferior, mean, mediocre, modest, normal, pedestrian, plain, prevailing, prosaic, quotidian, regular, routine, run-of-the-mill, settled, simple, standard, stock, typical, undistinguished, unexceptional, unmemorable, unpretentious, unremarkable, usual, wonted, workaday.
antonyms extraordinary, special, unusual.

ordnance *n.* arms, artillery, big guns, cannon, guns, matériel, missil(e)ry, munitions, weapons.

ordure *n.* dirt, dung, excrement, filth.

organ *n.* agency, channel, device, element, forum, harmonium, hurdy-gurdy, implement, instrument, journal, kist of whistles, means, medium, member, mouthpiece, newspaper, paper, part, periodical, process, publication, structure, tool, unit, vehicle, viscus, voice.

organic *adj.* anatomical, animate, biological, biotic, constitutional, formal, fundamental, inherent, innate, integral, integrated, live, living, methodical, natural, ordered, organised, structural, structured, systematic, systematised.

organisation *n.* arrangement, assembling, assembly, association, body, business, chemistry, combine, company, composition, concern, confederation, configuration, conformation, consortium, constitution, construction, co-ordination, corporation, design, disposal, federation, firm, format, formation, formulation, framework, group, grouping, institution, league, make-up, management, method, methodology, organism, outfit, pattern, plan, planning, regulation, running, standardisation, structure, structuring, syndicate, system, unity, whole.
antonym disorganisation.

organise *v.* arrange, catalogue, classify, codify, constitute, construct, co-ordinate, dispose, establish, form, frame, group, marshal, pigeonhole, regiment, run, see to, set up, shape, structure, systematise, tabulate.
antonym disorganise.

organised *adj.* arranged, neat, orderly, planned.
antonym disorganised.

organism *n.* animal, being, body, cell, creature, entity, living thing, structure.

orgy *n.* bacchanal, bacchanalia, binge, bout, carousal, debauch, excess, indulgence, love-in, overindulgence, revel, revelry, saturnalia, splurge, spree, surfeit.

orient *v.* acclimatise, accommodate, adapt, adjust, align, familiarise, get one's bearings, habituate, orientate.

orientation *n.* acclimatisation, adaptation, adjustment, assimilation, attunement, bearings, collimation, co-ordination, direction, familiarisation, introduction, location, position, sense of direction, settling in.

orifice *n.* aperture, cleft, hole, inlet, mouth, opening, perforation, pore, rent, slit, vent.

origin *n.* ancestry, base, basis, beginning, beginnings, birth, cause, commencement, creation, dawning, derivation, descent, emergence, etymology, etymon, extraction, family, fons et origo, font, foundation, fountain, fountain-head, genesis, heritage, inauguration, inception, incunabula, launch, lineage, occasion, origination, outset, parentage, paternity, pedigree, provenance, root, roots, source, spring, start, stirps, stock, well-spring.
antonyms end, termination.

original *adj.* aboriginal, archetypal, authentic, autochthonous, commencing, creative, earliest, early, embryonic, fertile, first, first-hand, fresh, genuine, imaginative, infant, ingenious, initial, innovative, innovatory, introductory, inventive, master, new, novel, opening, primal, primary, primigenial, primitical, primitive, primordial, pristine, prototypical, resourceful, rudimentary, seminal, starting, unborrowed, unconventional, unhackneyed, unprecedented, unusual.
antonym unoriginal.

n. archetype, case, character, cure, eccentric, master, model, nonconformist, oddity, paradigm, pattern, prototype, queer fish, standard, type, weirdo.

originality *n.* boldness, cleverness, creative spirit, creativeness, creativity, daring, eccentricity, freshness, imagination, imaginativeness, individuality, ingenuity, innovation, innovativeness, inventiveness, newness, novelty, resourcefulness, singularity, unconventionality, unorthodoxy.

originally *adv.* at first, at the outset, at the start, by birth, by derivation, first, in origin, in the beginning, initially.

originate *v.* arise, be born, begin, come, commence, conceive, create, derive, develop, discover, emanate, emerge, establish, evolve, flow, form, formulate, generate, give birth to, inaugurate, initiate, institute, introduce, invent, issue, launch, pioneer, proceed, produce, result, rise, set up, spring, start, stem.
antonyms end, terminate.

originator *n.* architect, author, creator, designer, father, founder, generator, innovator, inventor, mother, pioneer, prime mover, the brains.

ornament *n.* accessory, adornment, bauble, decoration, doodah, embellishment, fallal, fandangle, figgery, flower, frill, furbelow, garnish, gaud, honour, jewel, leading light, pride, treasure, trimming, trinket.
v. adorn, beautify, bedizen, bespangle, brighten, caparison, deck, decorate, dress up, embellish, festoon, garnish, gild, grace, prettify, prink, trim.

ornamental *adj.* attractive, beautifying, decorative, embellishing, flashy, for show, grandiose, showy.

ornamentation *n.* adornment, decoration, elaboration, embellishment, embroidery, fallalery, frills, garniture, ornateness.

ornate *adj.* arabesque, aureate, baroque, beautiful, bedecked, busy, convoluted, decorated, elaborate, elegant, fancy, florid, flowery, fussy, ornamented, rococo, sumptuous.
antonyms austere, plain.

oro(ro)tund *adj.* dignified, imposing, magniloquent, pompous, pretentious.

orthodox *adj.* accepted, approved, conformist, conventional, correct, customary, doctrinal, established, kosher, official, received, sound, traditional, true, usual, well-established.
antonym unorthodox.

orthodoxy *n.* authenticity, authoritativeness, authority, conformism, conformity, conventionality, devotion, devoutness, faithfulness, inflexibility, properness, received wisdom, soundness, traditionalism, trueness.

oscillate *v.* fluctuate, librate, seesaw, sway, swing, vacillate, vary, vibrate, waver, wigwag, yo-yo.

oscillation *n.* fluctuation, instability, seesawing, shilly-shallying, swing, swinging, vacillation, variation, wavering.

ossified *adj.* bony, fixed, fossilised, frozen, hardened, indurate(d), inflexible, petrified, rigid, rigidified, solid, stiff.

ostensible *adj.* alleged, apparent, avowed, exhibited, manifest, outward, plausible, presumed, pretended, professed, purported, put-on, seeming, so-called, specious, superficial, supposed.

ostensibly *adv.* apparently, professedly, purportedly, reputedly, seemingly, supposedly.

ostentation *n.* affectation, boasting, display, exhibitionism, flamboyance, flashiness, flaunting, flourish, foppery, pageantry, parade, pomp, pretension, pretentiousness, show, showiness, showing off, swank, tinsel, trappings, vaunting, window-dressing.
antonym unpretentiousness.

ostentatious *adj.* aggressive, boastful, conspicuous, extravagant, fastuous, flamboyant, flash, flashy, garish, gaudy, loud, obtrusive, pretentious, self-advertising, showy, splashy, swanking, swanky, vain, vulgar.
antonyms quiet, restrained.

ostracise *v.* avoid, banish, bar, black, blackball, blacklist, boycott, cast out, cold-shoulder, cut, debar, disfellowship, exclude, excommunicate, exile, expatriate, expel, reject, segregate, send to Coventry, shun, snub.
antonyms accept, receive, reinstate, welcome.

ostracism *n.* avoidance, banishment, boycott, cold-shouldering, disfellowship, exclusion, excommunication, exile, expulsion, isolation, proscription, rejection.
antonyms acceptance, reinstatement, welcome.

other *adj.* added, additional, alternative, auxiliary, contrasting, different, differing, dissimilar, distinct, diverse, extra, fresh, further, more, new, remaining, separate, spare, supplementary, unrelated.

otherworldly *adj.* absent-minded, bemused, dreamy, ethereal, fey, preoccupied, rapt.
antonyms mundane, solid, substantial, worldly.

ounce *n.* atom, crumb, drop, grain, iota, jot, modicum, morsel, particle, scrap, shred, speck, spot, trace, whit.

oust *v.* depose, disinherit, dislodge, displace, dispossess, drive out, eject, evict, expel, overthrow, replace, supplant, throw out, topple, turn out, unseat, upstage.
antonyms ensconce, install, reinstate, settle.

out[1] *adj.* abroad, absent, away, disclosed, elsewhere, evident, exposed, gone, manifest, not at home, outside, public, revealed.
out of bounds banned, barred, disallowed, forbidden, off-limits, prohibited, taboo.
out of date antiquated, archaic, behind the times, dated, fogram, horse-and-buggy, moribund, obsolete, old, old hat, old-fashioned, outmoded, passé.
antonyms fashionable, modern, new.
out of doors alfresco, en plein air, out, outdoors, outside.
antonym indoors.
out of focus blurred, blurry, fuzzy, hazy, ill-defined, indistinct, muzzy.
antonyms clear, sharp.

out of order broken, broken down, burst, conked out, gone phut, haywire, in disrepair, inoperative, kaput, non-functional, on the blink, out of commission.
antonym serviceable.

out of place disarranged, in disorder, inappropriate, malapropos, tactless, topsy-turvy, unbecoming, unfitting, unseemly, unsuitable.
antonyms appropriate, apropos.

out of sorts below par, depressed, down in the dumps, down in the mouth, fed up, gloomy, ill, moody, mops and brooms, off-colour, peelie-wally, poorly, sick, under the weather.
antonyms cheerful, well.

out of the blue all of a sudden, suddenly, unexpectedly.

out of the wood(s) home and dry, in the clear, on dry land, out of danger, out of difficulty, safe, safe and sound, secure.
antonyms insecure, vulnerable.

out of this world excellent, fabulous, fantastic, great, incredible, indescribable, marvellous, phenomenal, remarkable, superb, unbelievable, wonderful.
antonyms mundane, ordinary.

out of work idle, jobless, laid off, on the dole, redundant, unemployed, workless.
antonyms busy, employed, occupied.

out² *adj.* antiquated, banned, blacked, dated, dead, démodé, disallowed, ended, excluded, exhausted, expired, extinguished, finished, forbidden, impossible, not on, old hat, old-fashioned, out of date, passé, square, taboo, unacceptable, unfashionable, used up.
antonyms acceptable, fashionable, in.

out-and-out *adj.* absolute, arrant, complete, consummate, downright, dyed-in-the-wool, inveterate, outright, perfect, thoroughgoing, total, uncompromising, unmitigated, unqualified, utter, whole-hog.

outbreak *n.* burst, ebullition, epidemic, eruption, excrescence, explosion, flare-up, flash, outburst, pompholyx, rash, spasm, upsurge.

outburst *n.* access, attack, boutade, discharge, eruption, explosion, fit, fit of temper, flare-up, gale, gush, outbreak, outpouring, paroxysm, seizure, spasm, storm, surge, volley.

outcast *n.* abject, castaway, derelict, exile, leper, outsider, pariah, persona non grata, refugee, reject, reprobate, unperson, untouchable, vagabond, wretch.
antonyms favourite, idol.

outclass *v.* beat, eclipse, excel over, leave standing, outdistance, outdo, outrank, outrival, outshine, outstrip, overshadow, put in the shade, surpass, top, transcend.

outcome *n.* after-effect, aftermath, conclusion, consequence, effect, end, end result, harvest, issue, pay-off, result, sequel, upshot.

outcry *n.* clamour, commotion, complaint, cry, exclamation, flap, howl, hue and cry, hullaballoo, noise, outburst, protest, row, scream, screech, uproar, vociferation, yell.

outdated *adj.* antediluvian, antiquated, antique,

archaic, behind the times, dated, démodé, fogram, obsolescent, obsolete, old-fashioned, out of date, out of style, outmoded, passé, square, unfashionable, unmodish.
antonyms fashionable, modern, modish.

outdistance *v.* leave behind, leave standing, outpace, outrun, outstrip, overhaul, overtake, pass, pull ahead of, shake off, surpass.

outdo *v.* beat, best, eclipse, excel over, get the better of, outclass, outdistance, outfox, out-Herod, outmanoeuvre, outshine, outsmart, outstrip, outwit, overcome, surpass, top, transcend.

outdoor *adj.* alfresco, extraforaneous, open-air, out-of-door(s), outside.
antonym indoor.

outer *adj.* distal, distant, exterior, external, further, outlying, outside, outward, peripheral, remote, superficial, surface.
antonyms central, inner, mesial, proximal.

outface *v.* beard, brave, brazen out, confront, defy, outstare, stare down.
antonyms capitulate, succumb.

outfit¹ *n.* accoutrements, clothes, costume, ensemble, equipage, equipment, garb, gear, get-up, kit, paraphernalia, rig, rig-out, set-out, suit, togs, trappings, turn-out.
v. accoutre, apparel, appoint, attire, equip, fit out, fit up, furnish, kit out, provision, stock, supply, turn out.

outfit² *n.* business, clan, clique, company, corps, coterie, crew, firm, galère, gang, group, organisation, set, set-out, set-up, squad, team, unit.

outfitter *n.* clothier, costumer, costumier, couturier, couturière, dressmaker, haberdasher, modiste, sartor, tailor.

outflow *n.* debouchment, discharge, disembogüement, drainage, ebb, effluence, effluent, effluvium, efflux, effluxion, effusion, emanation, emergence, gush, jet, outfall, outpouring, rush, spout.

outflowing *adj.* debouching, discharging, effluent, emanant, gushing, leaking, rushing, spurting.

outgoing *adj.* affable, approachable, chatty, communicative, cordial, demonstrative, departing, easy, ex-, expansive, extrovert, former, friendly, genial, gregarious, informal, last, open, past, retiring, sociable, sympathetic, unreserved, warm, withdrawing.
antonyms incoming, introvert, new, unsociable.

outgoings *n.* costs, disbursal, disbursement, expenditure, expenses, outlay, overheads, spending.
antonym income.

outgrowth *n.* consequence, effect, emanation, excrescence, offshoot, product, protuberance, shoot, sprout, swelling.

outing *n.* excursion, expedition, jaunt, picnic, pleasure trip, ramble, spin, trip, wayzgoose.

outlandish *adj.* alien, barbarous, bizarre, eccentric, exotic, extraordinary, fantastic, foreign, grotesque, odd, outré, preposterous, queer,

strange, unheard-of, weird.
antonyms familiar, ordinary.

outlandishness *n.* bizarreness, eccentricity, exoticness, grotesqueness, oddness, peregrinity, queerness, strangeness, weirdness.
antonyms commonplaceness, familiarity.

outlast *v.* come through, outlive, outstay, ride, survive, weather.

outlaw *n.* bandit, brigand, bushranger, cateran, dacoit, desperado, freebooter, fugitive, highwayman, klepht, marauder, outcast, outsider, pariah, proscript, robber.
v. ban, banish, bar, condemn, debar, decitizenise, disallow, embargo, exclude, excommunicate, forbid, illegalise, illegitimate, interdict, prohibit, proscribe, waive.
antonyms allow, legalise.

outlawed *adj.* banished, banned, condemned, disallowed, embargoed, excommunicated, hors la loi, proscribed.

outlay *n.* cost, disbursal, disbursement, expenditure, expenses, investment, outgoings, payment, price.
antonym income.

outlet *n.* avenue, channel, débouché, debouchment, duct, egress, emissary, exit, femerall, market, opening, orifice, outfall, release, safety valve, vent, way out.
antonyms entry, inlet.

outline *n.* bare facts, configuration, contorno, contour, croquis, delineation, draft, drawing, figure, form, frame, framework, lay-out, lineament(s), plan, profile, recapitulation, résumé, rough, run-down, scenario, schema, shape, silhouette, skeleton, sketch, summary, synopsis, thumbnail sketch, tracing.
v. adumbrate, delineate, draft, plan, recapitulate, rough out, sketch, summarise, trace.

outlive *v.* come through, live through, outlast, survive, weather.
antonym predecease.

outlook *n.* angle, aspect, attitude, expectations, forecast, frame of mind, future, look-out, panorama, perspective, point of view, prognosis, prospect, scene, slant, standpoint, vantage-point, view, viewpoint, views, vista.

outlying *adj.* distant, far-away, far-flung, far-off, forane, further, outer, outlandish, peripheral, provincial, remote.
antonyms central, inner.

outmanoeuvre *v.* beat, circumvent, get the better of, outdo, outflank, outfox, outgeneral, outsmart, outthink, outwit, put the dead wood on.

outmoded *adj.* anachronistic, antediluvian, antiquated, antique, archaic, behind the times, bygone, dated, démodé, fogram, fossilised, horse-and-buggy, obsolescent, obsolete, olden, old-fashioned, old-fogeyish, out of date, outworn, passé, square, superannuated, superseded, unfashionable, unmodish, unusable.
antonyms fashionable, fresh, modern, modish, new.

out-of-the-way *adj.* abnormal, abstruse, curious,

distant, exceptional, extraordinary, far-away, far-flung, far-off, inaccessible, isolated, little-known, lonely, obscure, odd, outlandish, outlying, peculiar, remote, secluded, strange, uncommon, unfamiliar, unfrequented, ungetat-able, unusual.

outpace *v.* beat, outdistance, outdo, outrun, outstrip, overhaul, overtake, pass, surpass.

outpouring *n.* cascade, debouchment, débouchure, deluge, disemboguement, effluence, efflux, effusion, emanation, flow, flux, logorrhoea, outflow, spate, spurt, stream, torrent, word salad.

output *n.* achievement, manufacture, outturn, print-out, product, production, productivity, read-out, yield.
antonyms input, outlay.

outrage *n.* hurt, abuse, affront, anger, atrocity, barbarism, crime, desecration, disgrace, enormity, evil, fury, grand guignol, horror, indignation, indignity, inhumanity, injury, insult, offence, profanation, rape, ravishing, resentment, scandal, shock, violation, violence, wrath.
v. abuse, affront, astound, defile, desecrate, disgust, épater le bourgeois, incense, infuriate, injure, insult, madden, make someone's blood boil, maltreat, offend, rape, ravage, ravish, repel, scandalise, shock, violate.

outrageous *adj.* abominable, atrocious, barbaric, beastly, disgraceful, egregious, excessive, exorbitant, extortionate, extravagant, flagrant, godless, heinous, horrible, immoderate, infamous, inhuman, iniquitous, inordinate, monstrous, nefarious, offensive, preposterous, scandalous, shocking, steep, turbulent, unconscionable, ungodly, unholy, unreasonable, unspeakable, villainous, violent, wicked.
antonyms acceptable, irreproachable.

outrider *n.* advance guard, attendant, bodyguard, escort, guard, harbinger, herald, precursor, scout, squire, vanguard.

outright *adj.* absolute, arrant, categorical, complete, consummate, definite, direct, downright, flat, out-and-out, perfect, point-blank, pure, straightforward, thorough, thoroughgoing, total, uncompromising, unconditional, undeniable, unequivocal, unmitigated, unqualified, utter, wholesale.
antonyms ambiguous, indefinite, provisional.
adv. absolutely, at once, cleanly, completely, directly, explicitly, immediately, instantaneously, instantly, on the spot, openly, positively, straight away, straightaway, straightforwardly, there and then, thoroughly, unhesitatingly, without restraint.

outrun *v.* beat, exceed, excel, leave behind, lose, outdistance, outdo, outpace, outstrip, overhaul, overtake, pass, shake off, surpass.

outset *n.* beginning, commencement, early days, forthgoing, inauguration, inception, kick-off, opening, start.
antonyms conclusion, end, finish.

outshine *v.* beat, best, dwarf, eclipse, excel,

outclass, outdo, outrank, outstrip, overshadow, put in the shade, surpass, top, transcend, upstage.

outside[1] *adj.* exterior, external, extraforaneous, extramural, extraneous, extreme, outdoor, outer, outermost, outward, superficial, surface.

antonym inside.

n. cover, exterior, façade, face, front, skin, superficies, surface, topside.

antonym inside.

prep. furth, outwith, without.

outside[2] *adj.* distant, faint, infinitesimal, marginal, minute, negligible, remote, slight, slim, small, unlikely.

antonyms likely, real, substantial.

outsider *n.* alien, foreigner, immigrant, incomer, interloper, intruder, layman, misfit, newcomer, non-member, non-resident, observer, odd man out, outcast, outlander, outlier, settler, stranger.

antonyms inhabitant, insider, local, member, native, resident, specialist.

outskirts *n.* borders, boundary, edge, environs, faubourgs, fringes, margin, periphery, purlieus, suburbia, suburbs, vicinity.

antonyms centre, city-centre.

outsmart *v.* beat, best, deceive, dupe, get the better of, outfox, outmanoeuvre, outperform, out-think, outwit, trick.

outspoken *adj.* abrupt, blunt, candid, direct, explicit, forthright, frank, free, open, plain-spoken, pointed, Rabelaisian, rude, sharp, trenchant, unceremonious, unequivocal, unreserved.

antonyms diplomatic, tactful.

outspread *adj.* expanded, extended, fanned out, flared, open, opened, outstretched, spread out, stretched, unfolded, unfurled, wide, wide-open.

outstanding[1] *adj.* ace, arresting, celebrated, conspicuous, distinguished, egregious, eminent, excellent, exceptional, extraordinary, eye-catching, great, important, impressive, marked, memorable, notable, noteworthy, pre-eminent, prominent, prosilient, remarkable, salient, signal, singular, special, striking, superior, superlative, surpassing.

antonyms ordinary, unexceptional.

outstanding[2] *adj.* due, left, ongoing, open, over, owing, payable, pending, remaining, uncollected, undone, unpaid, unresolved, unsettled.

outstrip *v.* beat, best, better, eclipse, exceed, excel, gain on, leave behind, leave standing, outclass, outdistance, outdo, outpace, outperform, outrun, outshine, overhaul, overtake, pass, surpass, top, transcend.

outward *adj.* alleged, apparent, avowed, evident, exterior, external, noticeable, observable, obvious, ostensible, outer, outside, professed, public, superficial, supposed, surface, visible.

antonyms inner, private.

outwardly *adv.* apparently, at first sight,

evidently, externally, in appearance, officially, on the surface, ostensibly, seemingly, superficially, supposedly, to all appearances, to the eye.

antonyms internally, inwardly, privately.

outweigh *v.* cancel out, compensate for, eclipse, make up for, outbalance, overcome, override, overrule, predominate, preponderate, prevail over, take precedence over, tip the scales in favour of, transcend.

outwit *v.* beat, best, better, cheat, circumvent, deceive, defraud, dupe, get the better of, gull, make a monkey of, outfox, outmanoeuvre, outsmart, outthink, swindle, trick.

outworn *adj.* abandoned, antiquated, clichéd, defunct, discredited, disused, exhausted, fogeyish, fogram, hackneyed, horse-and-buggy, moth-eaten, obsolete, out of date, outdated, outmoded, overused, rejected, stale, superannuated, threadbare, tired, trite, worn-out.

antonyms fresh, new.

oval *adj.* egg-shaped, ellipsoidal, elliptical, lens-shaped, lenticular, lentiform, lentoid, obovate, obovoid, ovate, oviform, ovoid, ovoidal, vulviform.

ovation *n.* acclaim, acclamation, applause, bravos, cheering, cheers, clapping, éclat, laudation, plaudits, praises, tribute.

antonyms abuse, boos, catcalls, mockery.

over[1] *adj.* accomplished, bygone, closed, completed, concluded, done with, ended, finished, forgotten, gone, in the past, past, settled, up.

over[2] *prep.* above, exceeding, in charge of, in command of, in excess of, more than, on, on top of, superior to, upon.

adv. above, aloft, beyond, extra, in addition, in excess, left, on high, overhead, remaining, superfluous, surplus, unclaimed, unused, unwanted.

over and above added to, along with, as well as, besides, in addition to, let alone, not to mention, on top of, plus, together with.

over and over (again) ad infinitum, ad nauseam, again and again, continually, endlessly, frequently, often, repeatedly, seventy times seven, time and (time) again.

over the top a bit much, excessive, histrionic, immoderate, inordinate, overdone, too much, uncalled-for.

overabundance *n.* embarras de choix, embarras de richesse, excess, glut, oversupply, plethora, profusion, superabundance, superfluity, surfeit, surplus, too much of a good thing.

antonyms dearth, lack.

overact *v.* emote, exaggerate, ham, ham up, overdo, overplay.

antonyms underact, underplay.

overall *adj.* all-embracing, all-inclusive, all-over, blanket, broad, complete, comprehensive, general, global, inclusive, total, umbrella.

antonyms narrow, short-term.

adv. by and large, generally speaking, in

general, in the long term, on the whole.

overalls *n.* boiler-suit, coverall, dungarees, work-wear.

overawe *v.* abash, alarm, awe, browbeat, cow, daunt, disconcert, dismay, frighten, intimidate, petrify, scare, terrify, unnerve.
antonym reassure.

overbalance *v.* capsize, fall over, keel over, lose (one's) balance, lose one's footing, overset, overturn, slip, tip over, topple over, trip, tumble, turn turtle, upset.

overbearing *adj.* arrogant, autocratic, bossy, cavalier, despotic, dictatorial, dogmatic, domineering, haughty, high and mighty, high-handed, imperious, lordly, magisterial, officious, oppressive, overweening, peremptory, pompous, supercilious, superior, tyrannical.
antonyms modest, unassertive, unassuming.

overcast *adj.* black, clouded, clouded over, cloudy, dark, darkened, dismal, dreary, dull, grey, hazy, leaden, lowering, murky, sombre, sunless, threatening.
antonyms bright, clear, sunny.

overcharge *v.* cheat, diddle, do, extort, fleece, mulct, rip off, rook, short-change, sting, surcharge.
antonym undercharge.

overcome *v.* beat, best, better, conquer, crush, defeat, expugn, lick, master, overpower, overthrow, overwhelm, prevail, rise above, subdue, subjugate, surmount, survive, triumph over, vanquish, weather, worst.
adj. affected, beaten, bowled over, broken, defeated, exhausted, overpowered, overwhelmed, speechless, swept off one's feet.

over-confident *adj.* arrogant, brash, cocksure, cocky, foolhardy, hubristic, incautious, overoptimistic, overweening, presumptuous, rash, sanguine, temerarious, uppish.
antonyms cautious, diffident.

overcritical *adj.* captious, carping, cavilling, fault-finding, hair-splitting, hard to please, hypercritical, nit-picking, over-nice, overparticular, pedantic, pernickety, purist, ultracrepidarian, Zoilean.
antonyms easygoing, tolerant, uncritical.

overcrowded *adj.* chock-a-block, chock-full, choked, congested, crammed full, hotching, jam-packed, overloaded, overpopulated, packed, packed out, seething, swarming.
antonyms deserted, empty.

overdo *v.* do to death, exaggerate, gild the lily, go to extremes, go too far, labour, lay it on thick, overact, overexert, overindulge, overplay, overreach, overstate, overtax, overuse, overwork.
antonyms neglect, underuse.

overdone *adj.* burnt, burnt to a cinder, charred, dried up, effusive, exaggerated, excessive, fulsome, histrionic, immoderate, inordinate, over the top, overcooked, overelaborate, overplayed, overstated, percoct, preposterous, spoiled, supererogatory, undue, unnecessary.

antonyms raw, underdone, underplayed, understated.

overdue *adj.* behind schedule, behindhand, belated, delayed, late, owing, slow, tardy, unpunctual.
antonym early.

overeat *v.* binge, eat like a horse, gluttonise, gorge, gormandise, guzzle, make a pig of oneself, overindulge, pack away, stuff, stuff oneself.
antonyms abstain, starve.

overeating *n.* bingeing, bulimia, gluttony, gormandise, gormandism, gourmandise, gourmandism, guzzling, hyperphagia, overindulgence.
antonyms abstemiousness, abstention.

overemphasise *v.* belabour, exaggerate, labour, overdramatise, overstress.
antonyms belittle, minimise, underplay, understate.

overexert oneself break a leg, burn the candle at both ends, drive oneself too hard, fatigue, knock oneself out, overdo it, overstrain oneself, overtax oneself, overtire oneself, overwork, push oneself too hard, strain oneself, wear oneself out, work oneself to death.
antonyms idle, laze.

overflow *v.* brim over, bubble over, cover, deluge, discharge, drown, flood, inundate, pour over, shower, soak, spill, spray, submerge, surge, swamp, well over.
n. flood, inundation, overabundance, overspill, spill, superfluity, surplus.

overflowing *adj.* abounding, bountiful, brimful, copious, inundant, plenteous, plentiful, profuse, rife, superabundant, swarming, teeming, thronged.
antonyms lacking, scarce.

overgrowth *n.* escalation, hypertrophy, overabundance, overdevelopment, superabundance.
antonyms decline, failure, shrinkage, wasting.

overhang *v.* beetle, bulge, extend, impend, jut, loom, menace, project, protrude, stick out, threaten.

overhanging *adj.* beetling, jutting, pensile, projecting, protruding.

overhaul[1] *v.* check, do up, examine, fix, inspect, mend, recondition, re-examine, repair, restore, service, survey.
n. check, check-up, examination, going-over, inspection, reconditioning, repair, restoration, service.

overhaul[2] *v.* gain on, outpace, outstrip, overtake, pass, pull ahead of.

overhead *adv.* above, aloft, on high, up above, upward.
antonyms below, underfoot.
adj. aerial, elevated, overhanging, roof, upper.
antonyms floor, ground, underground.

overheads *n.* burden, expenses, oncost, operating costs, outgoings, running costs.
antonyms income, profit.

overheated *adj*. agitated, excited, fiery, flaming, impassioned, inflamed, overexcited, overwrought, passionate, roused.
antonyms calm, cool, dispassionate, impassive.

overheating *n*. heatstroke, hyperpyrexia, hyperthermia, sunstroke.
antonyms chill, hypothermia.

overindulge *v*. binge, booze, debauch, gluttonise, gorge, gormandise, guzzle.
antonym abstain.

overindulgence *n*. binge, debauch, excess, immoderation, intemperance, overeating, surfeit.
antonyms abstemiousness, abstention.

overjoyed *adj*. delighted, delirious, ecstatic, elated, enraptured, euphoric, in raptures, joyful, jubilant, on cloud nine, over the moon, rapturous, thrilled, tickled pink, transported.
antonyms disappointed, sad.

overlap *v*. coincide, cover, flap over, imbricate, overlay, overlie, shingle.

overlapping *adj*. coinciding, covering, imbricated, layered, limbous, overlying, shingled.

overload *v*. burden, encumber, oppress, overburden, overcharge, overtax, saddle, strain, surcharge, tax, weigh down.

overlook[1] *v*. condone, disregard, excuse, forget, forgive, ignore, let pass, let ride, miss, neglect, omit, pardon, pass, pass over, skip, slight, turn a blind eye to, wink at.
antonyms animadvert, note, notice, penalise, record, remember.

overlook[2] *v*. command a view of, face, front on to, give upon, look on to.

overlooked *adj*. unconsidered, unheeded, unhonoured, unnoted, unprized, unregarded, unremarked, unvalued.
antonyms appreciated, prized, sought-after, valued.

overly *adv*. exceedingly, excessively, immoderately, inordinately, over, too, unduly, unreasonably.
antonyms inadequately, insufficiently.

over-nice *adj*. finical, nit-picking, overfastidious, over-meticulous, overparticular, overprecise, overscrupulous, oversensitive, oversubtle, pernickety, rose-water.
antonyms casual, uncritical.

overpower *v*. beat, best, conquer, crush, defeat, floor, immobilise, master, overcome, overthrow, overwhelm, quell, subdue, subjugate, vanquish.

overpowering *adj*. compelling, convincing, extreme, forceful, insuppressible, invincible, irrefutable, irrepressible, irresistible, nauseating, oppressive, overwhelming, powerful, sickening, strong, suffocating, telling, unbearable, uncontrollable.

overrate *v*. blow up, magnify, make too much of, overestimate, overpraise, overprize, oversell, overvalue.
antonym underrate.

override *v*. abrogate, annul, cancel, countermand, disregard, ignore, nullify, outweigh,

overrule, quash, rescind, reverse, ride roughshod over, set aside, supersede, trample, upset, vanquish.

overriding *adj*. cardinal, compelling, determining, dominant, essential, final, first, major, number one, overruling, paramount, pivotal, predominant, prevailing, primary, prime, prior, ruling, supreme, ultimate.
antonyms insignificant, unimportant.

overrule *v*. abrogate, annul, cancel, countermand, disallow, invalidate, outvote, override, overturn, recall, repeal, rescind, reverse, revoke, set aside, veto, vote down.
antonyms allow, approve.

overrun[1] *v*. choke, infest, inundate, invade, occupy, overflow, overgrow, overspread, overwhelm, permeate, ravage, run riot, spread over, surge over, swamp, swarm over.
antonyms desert, evacuate.

overrun[2] *v*. exceed, overdo, overshoot, overstep.

overseas *adj*. exotic, foreign, outland, outlandish, ultramarine.
antonyms domestic, home.
adv. abroad, in/to foreign climes, in/to foreign parts.
n. foreign climes, foreign parts, outland, outremer.
antonym home.

overseer *n*. boss, chief, foreman, forewoman, gaffer, headman, manager, master, super, superintendent, superior, supervisor, surveyor, workmaster, workmistress.

overshadow *v*. adumbrate, becloud, bedim, blight, cloud, darken, dim, dominate, dwarf, eclipse, excel, mar, obfuscate, obscure, outshine, outweigh, protect, put in the shade, rise above, ruin, shelter, spoil, surpass, tower above, veil.

oversight[1] *n*. administration, care, charge, control, custody, direction, guidance, handling, inspection, keeping, management, responsibility, superintendence, supervision, surveillance.

oversight[2] *n*. blunder, boob, carelessness, delinquency, error, fault, inattention, lapse, laxity, mistake, neglect, omission, slip, slip-up.

overt *adj*. apparent, avowed, evident, manifest, observable, obvious, open, patent, plain, professed, public, unconcealed, undisguised, visible.
antonyms covert, secret.

overtake *v*. befall, catch up with, come upon, draw level with, engulf, happen, hit, outdistance, outdo, outstrip, overhaul, pass, pull ahead of, strike.

overthrow *v*. abolish, beat, bring down, conquer, crush, defeat, demolish, depose, destroy, dethrone, displace, knock down, level, master, oust, overcome, overpower, overturn, overwhelm, raze, ruin, subdue, subjugate, subvert, topple, unseat, upset, vanquish.
antonyms install, reinstate.

n. bouleversement, confounding, defeat, deposition, destruction, dethronement, discomfiture, disestablishment, displacement, dispossession, downfall, end, fall, humiliation, labefactation, labefaction, ousting, prostration, rout, ruin, subjugation, subversion, suppression, undoing, unseating.

overtone *n.* association, connotation, feeling, flavour, hint, implication, innuendo, intimation, nuance, sense, slant, something, suggestion, undercurrent.

overture *n.* advance, approach, introduction, invitation, motion, move, offer, opening, (opening) gambit, opening move, prelude, proposal, proposition, signal, suggestion, tender.

overturn *v.* abolish, abrogate, annul, capsize, countermand, depose, destroy, invalidate, keel over, knock down, knock over, overbalance, overset, overthrow, quash, repeal, rescind, reverse, set aside, spill, tip over, topple, tumble, unseat, upend, upset, upturn.

overused *adj.* bromidic, clichéd, commonplace, hackneyed, platitudinous, played out, stale, stereotyped, threadbare, tired, trite, unoriginal, worn.
antonyms fresh, original.

overweening *adj.* arrogant, cavalier, cocksure, cocky, conceited, egotistical, excessive, extravagant, haughty, high-handed, hubristic, immoderate, inflated, insolent, lordly, opinionated, overblown, pompous, presumptuous, proud, self-confident, supercilious, swollen, uppish, vain, vainglorious.
antonyms diffident, unassuming.

overweight *adj.* ample, bulky, buxom, chubby, chunky, corpulent, fat, flabby, fleshy, gross, heavy, hefty, huge, massive, obese, outsize, plump, podgy, portly, pot-bellied, stout, tubby, well-padded, well-upholstered.
antonyms emaciated, skinny, thin, underweight.

overwhelm *v.* bowl over, bury, confuse, crush, cut to pieces, defeat, deluge, destroy, devastate, engulf, floor, inundate, knock for six, massacre, overcome, overpower, overrun, prostrate, rout, snow under, stagger, submerge, swamp.

overwhelming *adj.* breathtaking, crushing, devastating, foudroyant, insuppressible, invincible, irrepressible, irresistible, overpowering, shattering, stunning, towering, uncontrollable, vast.
antonyms insignificant, negligible, resistible.

overwork *v.* burden, burn the midnight oil, exhaust, exploit, fatigue, oppress, overburden, overload, overstrain, overtax, overuse, prostrate, strain, sweat, tax, wear out, weary, work one's fingers to the bone.

overwrought *adj.* agitated, beside oneself, distracted, emotional, excited, frantic, keyed up, on edge, overcharged, overexcited, overheated, overworked, stirred, strung up, tense, uptight, worked up, wound up.
antonyms calm, cool, impassive.

owing *adj.* due, in arrears, outstanding, overdue, owed, payable, unpaid, unsettled.

owing to as a result of, because of, imputable to, on account of, thanks to.

own[1] *adj.* idiosyncratic, individual, inimitable, particular, personal, private.

own[2] *v.* acknowledge, admit, agree, allow, avow, concede, confess, disclose, enjoy, grant, have, hold, keep, possess, recognise, retain.

own up admit, come clean, confess, make a clean breast of it, spill the beans, tell the truth.

owner *n.* franklin, freeholder, holder, laird, landlady, landlord, lord, master, mistress, possessor, proprietor, proprietress, proprietrix.

ownership *n.* dominion, freehold, possession, proprietary rights, proprietorship, right of possession, title.

ox *n.* bison, buffalo, bullock, clod, dolt, gaur, g(a)yal, lout, oaf, steer.

P

pace *n*. celerity, clip, gait, lick, measure, momentum, motion, movement, progress, quickness, rapidity, rate, speed, step, stride, tempo, time, tread, velocity, walk.
v. count, determine, march, mark out, measure, pad, patrol, pound, step, stride, tramp, tread, walk.

pacific *adj*. appeasing, calm, complaisant, conciliatory, diplomatic, dovelike, dovish, eirenic, equable, friendly, gentle, halcyon, irenic, mild, nonbelligerent, nonviolent, pacificatory, pacifist, peaceable, peaceful, peace-loving, peacemaking, placatory, placid, propitiatory, quiet, serene, smooth, still, tranquil, unruffled.
antonyms aggressive, belligerent, contentious, pugnacious.

pacifism *n*. non-violence, pacificism, passive resistance, satyagraha.

pacifist *n*. conchie, conscientious objector, dove, pacificist, passive resister, peace-lover, peacemonger, peacenik, satyagrahi.
antonyms hawk, warmonger.

pacify *v*. allay, ameliorate, appease, assuage, calm, chasten, compose, conciliate, crush, humour, lull, moderate, mollify, placate, propitiate, put down, quell, quiet, repress, silence, smooth down, soften, soothe, still, subdue, tame, tranquillise.
antonyms aggravate, anger.

pack *n*. assemblage, back-pack, bale, band, boodle, bunch, bundle, burden, collection, company, crew, crowd, deck, drove, fardel, flock, galère, gang, group, haversack, herd, kit, kitbag, knapsack, load, lot, Matilda, mob, outfit, package, packet, parcel, rucksack, set, troop, truss.
v. batch, bundle, burden, charge, compact, compress, cram, crowd, empocket, fill, jam, load, mob, package, packet, press, ram, steeve, store, stow, stuff, tamp, throng, thrust, wedge.

package *n*. agreement, amalgamation, arrangement, bale, box, carton, combination, consignment, container, deal, entity, kit, pack, packet, parcel, proposal, proposition, unit, whole.
v. batch, box, pack, pack up, packet, parcel, parcel up, wrap, wrap up.

packed *adj*. brimful, brim-full, chock-a-block, chock-full, congested, cram-full, crammed, crowded, filled, full, hotching, jammed, jam-packed, overflowing, overloaded, seething, swarming.
antonyms deserted, empty.

packet[1] *n*. bag, carton, case, container, pack, package, packing, parcel, poke, wrapper, wrapping.

packet[2] *n*. a bob or two, bomb, bundle, fortune, king's ransom, lot, lots, mint, pile, pot, pots, pretty penny, small fortune, tidy sum.

pack-horse *n*. beast of burden, led horse, pack-animal, sumpter, sumpter-horse.

pact *n*. agreement, alliance, arrangement, bargain, bond, cartel, compact, concord, concordat, contract, convention, covenant, deal, entente, league, protocol, treaty, understanding.
antonyms breach, disagreement, quarrel.

pad[1] *n*. block, buffer, cushion, jotter, notepad, pillow, protection, pulvillus, pulvinar, stiffening, stuffing, tablet, wad, writing-pad.
v. cushion, fill, line, pack, protect, shape, stuff, wrap.
pad out amplify, augment, bombast, eke, elaborate, expand, fill out, flesh out, inflate, lengthen, protract, spin out, stretch.

pad[2] *n*. foot, footprint, paw, print, sole.

pad[3] *n*. apartment, flat, hang-out, home, penthouse, place, quarters, room, rooms.

pad[4] *v*. lope, move, run, step, tiptoe, tramp, tread, trudge, walk.

padding *n*. bombast, circumlocution, filling, hot air, packing, perissology, prolixity, stuffing, verbiage, verbosity, wadding, waffle, wordiness.

paddle[1] *n*. oar, scull, sweep.
v. oar, ply, propel, pull, row, scull, steer.

paddle[2] *v*. dabble, plash, slop, splash, stir, trail, wade.

paddy *n*. bate, fit of temper, fury, paddywhack, passion, pet, rage, taking, tantrum, temper, tiff, wax.

paean *n*. anthem, dithyramb, doxology, encomium, eulogy, hymn, ovation, panegyric, psalm.
antonyms denunciation, satire.

pagan *n*. atheist, Gentile, heathen, idolater, infidel, nullifidian, polytheist, unbeliever.
antonym believer.
adj. atheistic, Gentile, godless, heathen, heathenish, idolatrous, infidel, irreligious, nullifidian, polytheistic.

page[1] *n*. chapter, episode, epoch, era, event, folio, incident, leaf, period, phase, point, recto, sheet, side, stage, time, verso.

page[2] *n*. attendant, bell-boy, bellhop, boy, buttons, cupbearer, footboy, footman, pageboy, servant, squire.
v. announce, bid, call, call out, preconise, seek, send for, summon.

pageant *n*. display, extravaganza, masque,

parade, play, procession, representation, ritual, scene, show, spectacle, tableau, tableau vivant.

pageantry *n.* ceremony, display, drama, extravagance, glamour, glitter, grandeur, magnificence, melodrama, ostentation, parade, pomp, show, showiness, spectacle, splash, splendour, state, theatricality.

pail *n.* bail, bucket, churn, piggin, tub.

pain *n.* ache, affliction, aggravation, agony, anguish, annoyance, bitterness, bore, bother, burden, cramp, discomfort, distress, dole, dolour, drag, grief, gyp, headache, heartache, heartbreak, hurt, irritation, lancination, misery, nuisance, pang, pest, smart, soreness, spasm, suffering, tenderness, throb, throe, torment, torture, tribulation, trouble, twinge, vexation, woe, wretchedness.
v. afflict, aggrieve, agonise, annoy, chagrin, cut to the quick, disappont, disquiet, distress, exasperate, gall, grieve, harass, hurt, irritate, nettle, rile, sadden, torment, torture, vex, worry, wound, wring.
antonyms gratify, please.

pained *adj.* aggrieved, chagrined, cut to the quick, cut up, disappointed, distressed, galled, grieved, hurt, injured, miffed, nettled, offended, reproachful, saddened, stung, upset, wounded.
antonyms gratified, pleased.

painful *adj.* aching, achy, afflictive, agonising, arduous, difficult, disagreeable, distasteful, distressing, doloriferous, dolorific, excruciating, grievous, hard, harrowing, laborious, lancinating, saddening, severe, smarting, sore, tedious, tender, troublesome, trying, unpleasant, vexatious.
antonyms easy, painless.

painfully *adv.* alarmingly, clearly, deplorably, distressingly, dreadfully, excessively, markedly, pitiably, pitifully, sadly, unfortunately, woefully, wretchedly.

painkiller *n.* alleviative, anaesthetic, analgesic, anodyne, drug, lenitive, palliative, paregoric, remedy, sedative.
antonym irritant.

painless *adj.* downhill, easy, effortless, fast, pain-free, plain sailing, quick, simple, trouble-free, undemanding.
antonyms difficult, painful.

pains *n.* assiduity, assiduousness, birth-pangs, bother, care, contractions, diligence, effort, industry, labour, sedulity, sedulousness, throes, trouble.

painstaking *adj.* assiduous, careful, conscientious, dedicated, devoted, diligent, earnest, exacting, hardworking, industrious, meticulous, perfectionist, persevering, punctilious, scrupulous, sedulous, strenuous, thorough, thoroughgoing.
antonyms careless, negligent.

paint *n.* colour, colouring, cosmetics, distemper, dye, emulsion, enamel, glaze, greasepaint, lacquer, lake, make-up, maquillage, oils, pigment, primer, stain, tint, undercoat,

warpaint, wash, water-colour, whitewash.
v. apply, coat, colour, cover, daub, decorate, delineate, depict, describe, distemper, evoke, glaze, lacquer, limn, picture, portray, recount, render, represent.

painter *n.* artist, colourist, dauber, delineator, depicter, limner, miniaturist, oil-painter, water-colourist.

painting *n.* aquarelle, daubery, depiction, fresco, illustration, kakemono, landscape, miniature, mural, oil, oil-painting, picture, portrait, portraiture, portrayal, representation, scene, seascape, still life, tablature, water-colour.

pair *n.* brace, combination, couple, doublet, doubleton, duad, duo, dyad, match, span, twins, two of a kind, twosome, yoke.
v. bracket, couple, join, link, marry, match, match up, mate, pair off, put together, splice, team, twin, wed, yoke.
antonyms dissever, sever.

paired *adj.* associated, bracketed, coupled, didymous, double, in twos, joined, linked, matched, mated, twinned, yoked.
antonym single.

pal *n.* amigo, buddy, china, chum, companion, comrade, confidant(e), crony, friend, gossip, intimate, mate, partner, side-kick, soul mate.
antonym enemy.

palace *n.* alcázar, basilica, château, dome, palazzo, schloss.
antonym hovel.

palatable *adj.* acceptable, agreeable, appetising, attractive, enjoyable, fair, pleasant, sapid, satisfactory, savoury, tasty, toothsome.
antonyms unacceptable, unpleasant.

palate *n.* appetite, appreciation, enjoyment, gout, gusto, heart, liking, relish, stomach, taste, zest.

palatial *adj.* de luxe, grand, grandiose, illustrious, imposing, luxurious, magnificent, majestic, opulent, plush, posh, regal, spacious, splendid, stately, sumptuous, swanky.
antonyms cramped, poky.

palaver *n.* activity, babble, blather, blether, business, bustle, carry-on, chatter, colloquy, confab, conference, confusion, discussion, fuss, fuss about nothing, get-together, hubbub, natter, parley, performance, pow-wow, prattle, procedure, rigmarole, session, song and dance, to-do, tongue-wagging, yak.
v. blab, blather, blether, chatter, confab, confer, discuss, gabble, jabber, jaw, natter, parley, powwow, prattle, tattle, yak.

pale *adj.* anaemic, ashen, ashy, bleached, bloodless, chalky, colourless, dim, etiolated, faded, faint, feeble, inadequate, light, lily-livered, pallid, pasty, poor, sallow, thin, wan, washed-out, waxy, weak, whey-faced, white, white-livered, whitish.
antonym ruddy.
v. blanch, decrease, dim, diminish, dull, etiolate, fade, lessen, whiten.
antonyms blush, colour.

palisade *n.* barricade, bulwark, defence, enclosure, fence, fortification, paling, palisado, stockade.

pall[1] *n.* check, cloud, cold water, damp, damper, dismay, gloom, mantle, melancholy, shadow, shroud, sindon, veil.

pall[2] *v.* bore, cloy, glut, jade, lose savour, satiate, sicken, surfeit, tire, weary.

palliate *v.* abate, allay, alleviate, assuage, cloak, conceal, cover, diminish, ease, excuse, extenuate, lenify, lessen, lighten, minimise, mitigate, moderate, mollify, relieve, soften, soothe, temper.

palliative *adj.* alleviative, anodyne, assuasive, calmative, calming, demulcent, lenitive, mitigative, mitigatory, mollifying, paregoric, sedative, soothing.

antonym irritant.

n. analgesic, anodyne, calmative, demulcent, lenitive, painkiller, paregoric, sedative, tranquilliser.

pallid *adj.* anaemic, ashen, ashy, bloodless, cadaverous, colourless, doughy, etiolated, insipid, lifeless, livid, pale, pasty, pasty-faced, peelie-wally, sallow, spiritless, sterile, tame, tired, uninspired, vapid, wan, waxen, waxy, whey-faced, whitish.

antonyms high-complexioned, ruddy, vigorous.

pallor *n.* bloodlessness, chalkiness, etiolation, paleness, pallidness, sallowness, wanness, whiteness.

antonym ruddiness.

pally *adj.* affectionate, chummy, close, familiar, friendly, intimate, palsy, palsy-walsy, thick.

antonym unfriendly.

palm *n.* hand, mitt, paw, vola.

v. appropriate, conceal, grab, half-inch, nick, sneak, snitch.

palm off fob off, foist, foist off, impose, offload, pass off, thrust, unload.

palmistry *n.* chirognomy, chiromancy, fortune-telling, palm reading.

palmy *adj.* carefree, flourishing, fortunate, glorious, golden, halcyon, happy, joyous, luxurious, prosperous, salad, thriving, triumphant.

palpable *adj.* apparent, blatant, clear, concrete, conspicuous, evident, manifest, material, obvious, open, overt, patent, plain, real, solid, substantial, tangible, touchable, unmistakable, visible.

antonyms elusive, impalpable, imperceptible, intangible.

palpitate *v.* beat, flutter, pitapat, pit-pat, pitter-patter, pittypat, pound, pulsate, pulse, quiver, shiver, throb, thump, tremble, vibrate.

palsied *adj.* agued, arthritic, atonic, crippled, debilitated, disabled, helpless, paralysed, paralytic, rheumatic, sclerotic, shaking, shaky, shivering, spastic, trembling, tremulous.

paltry *adj.* base, beggarly, contemptible, derisory, despicable, inconsiderable, insignificant, jitney, low, meagre, mean, minor, miserable,

negligible, pettifogging, petty, picayunish, piddling, piffling, pimping, pitiful, poor, puny, rubbishy, slight, small, sorry, tinpot, trifling, trivial, two-bit, twopenny-halfpenny, unimportant, worthless, wretched.

antonyms significant, substantial.

pamper *v.* baby, cocker, coddle, cosset, fondle, gratify, humour, indulge, mollycoddle, mother, overindulge, pet, spoil.

antonyms ill-treat, neglect.

pampered *adj.* coddled, cosseted, high-fed, indulged, mollycoddled, overfed, petted, spoilt.

antonyms abused, neglected.

pamphlet *n.* booklet, broadside, brochure, chapbook, folder, leaflet, tract, tractate, treatise.

pan[1] *n.* casserole, container, fryer, marmite, pancheon, pot, saucepan, skillet, spider, stewpot, vessel, wok.

v. censure, criticise, flay, hammer, knock, pick to pieces, pull to pieces, roast, rubbish, slam, slate.

antonym praise.

pan out be exhausted, come to an end, culminate, eventuate, happen, result, turn out, work out, yield.

pan[2] *v.* circle, follow, move, scan, sweep, swing, track, traverse, turn.

panacea *n.* catholicon, cure-all, diacatholicon, elixir, nostrum, panpharmacon, theriac, treacle.

panache *n.* brio, dash, élan, enthusiasm, flair, flamboyance, flourish, grand manner, ostentation, pizzazz, spirit, style, swagger, theatricality, verve, vigour, zest.

pandemonium *n.* babel, bedlam, chaos, clamour, commotion, confusion, din, disorder, Donnybrook, frenzy, hubbub, hue and cry, hullaballoo, racket, ruckus, ruction, rumpus, to-do, tumult, turbulence, turmoil, uproar.

antonyms calm, order, peace.

pander *v.* cater to, furnish, gratify, indulge, pamper, please, provide, purvey, satisfy.

n. bawd, go-between, mack, pimp, ponce, procurer, procuress, white-slaver, whoremaster, whoremonger.

panegyric *n.* accolade, citation, commendation, encomium, eulogium, eulogy, homage, paean, praise, tribute.

antonym censure.

adj. commendatory, complimentary, encomiastic, eulogistic, favourable, flattering, glowing, laudatory, panegyrical, praiseful, praising.

antonyms censorious, damning.

panel *n.* compartment, rectangle, strip, table.

panelling *n.* dado, panel-work, wainscot, wainscot(t)ing.

pang *n.* ache, agony, anguish, crick, discomfort, distress, gripe, pain, prick, spasm, stab, sting, stitch, throe, twinge, twitch, wrench.

panic *n.* agitation, alarm, consternation, dismay, fear, fright, hassle, horror, hysteria, scare, terror, tizzy, to-do.

antonyms assurance, confidence.

v. alarm, get one's knickers in a twist, go to pieces, lose one's cool, lose one's nerve, overreact, put the wind up, scare, startle, terrify, unnerve.

antonyms reassure, relax.

panic-stricken *adj.* affrighted, aghast, agitated, alarmed, appalled, fearful, frenzied, frightened, horrified, horror-stricken, hysterical, in a cold sweat, panicky, perturbed, petrified, scared, scared stiff, startled, stunned, stupefied, terrified, terror-stricken, unnerved.

antonyms confident, laid-back, relaxed.

panoply *n.* armour, array, attire, dress, equipment, garb, gear, get-up, insignia, raiment, regalia, show, trappings, turn-out.

panorama *n.* bird's-eye view, overview, perspective, prospect, scene, scenery, spectacle, survey, view, vision, vista.

panoramic *adj.* bird's-eye, comprehensive, extensive, far-reaching, gazy, general, inclusive, overall, panned, scenic, sweeping, universal, wide, widespread.

antonym limited.

pansy *n.* fag, faggot, homo, homosexual, Jessie, milksop, Miss Nancy, molly, mollycoddle, namby-pamby, poof, poofter, queen, queer.

pant *v.* ache, blow, breathe, covet, crave, desire, flaff, gasp, hanker, heave, huff, hunger, long, palpitate, pine, puff, sigh, thirst, throb, want, wheeze, yearn, yen.

n. gasp, huff, puff, throb, wheeze.

panting *adj.* anxious, breathless, eager, gasping, impatient, out of breath, puffed, puffed out, puffing, short-winded, winded.

pantomime *n.* charade, dumb-show, galantry show, panto.

pants *n.* briefs, drawers, knickers, panties, shorts, slacks, trews, trousers, trunks, underpants, undershorts, Y-fronts.

paper *n.* analysis, archive, article, assignment, authorisation, certificate, composition, credential, critique, daily, deed, diary, dissertation, document, dossier, essay, examination, file, gazette, instrument, journal, letter, monograph, news, newspaper, notepaper, organ, rag, record, report, script, stationery, study, thesis, treatise.

papery *adj.* delicate, flimsy, fragile, frail, insubstantial, light, lightweight, paper-thin, thin, translucent.

papism *n.* papery, papistry, Roman Catholicism.

papist *n.* Catholic, Fenian, papisher, Roman Catholic.

adj. Catholic, Fenian, papish, popish, Roman Catholic.

par *n.* accordance, average, balance, correspondence, equal footing, equality, equilibrium, equivalence, level, mean, median, norm, parity, similarity, standard, usual.

parable *n.* allegory, apologue, exemplum, fable, homily, lesson, story.

parade *n.* array, cavalcade, ceremony, column, corso, display, exhibition, flaunting, march, motorcade, ostentation, pageant, panache,

pizzazz, pomp, procession, promenade, review, show, spectacle, train, vaunting.

v. air, brandish, defile, display, exhibit, flaunt, make a show of, march, peacock, process, show, show off, strut, swagger, vaunt.

paradigm *n.* archetype, example, exemplar, framework, ideal, model, original, pattern, prototype.

paradise *n.* bliss, City of God, delight, Eden, Elysian fields, Elysium, felicity, garden of delights, Garden of Eden, heaven, heavenly kingdom, Land o' the Leal, Olympus, Promised Land, seventh heaven, utopia, Valhalla, Zion.

antonyms Hades, hell.

paradox *n.* absurdity, ambiguity, anomaly, contradiction, enigma, equivocation, incongruity, inconsistency, mystery, oddity, puzzle, riddle.

paradoxical *adj.* absurd, ambiguous, baffling, conflicting, confounding, contradictory, enigmatic, equivocal, Gilbertian, illogical, impossible, improbable, incongruous, inconsistent, puzzling, self-contradictory.

paragon *n.* apotheosis, archetype, crème de la crème, criterion, cynosure, epitome, exemplar, ideal, jewel, masterpiece, model, non(e)such, nonpareil, paradigm, pattern, prototype, quintessence, standard, the bee's knees.

paragraph *n.* clause, item, notice, part, passage, portion, section, subdivision, subsection.

parallel *adj.* akin, aligned, alongside, analogous, co-extensive, collateral, connate, correspondent, corresponding, equidistant, homologous, like, matching, resembling, similar, uniform.

antonyms divergent, separate.

n. analogue, analogy, comparison, corollary, correlation, correspondence, counterpart, duplicate, equal, equivalent, homologue, likeness, match, parallelism, resemblance, similarity, twin.

v. agree, compare, conform, correlate, correspond, duplicate, emulate, equal, match.

antonyms diverge, separate.

paralyse *v.* anaesthetise, arrest, benumb, clamp down on, cripple, debilitate, disable, freeze, halt, immobilise, incapacitate, lame, numb, obtund, petrify, stun, stupefy, torpefy, transfix.

paralysis *n.* arrest, break-down, halt, hemiplegia, immobility, monoplegia, palsy, paraplegia, paresis, quadriplegia, shut-down, stagnation, standstill, stoppage, torpor.

paralytic[1] *adj.* crippled, disabled, hemiplegic, immobile, immobilised, incapacitated, lame, monoplegic, numb, palsied, paralysed, quadriplegic.

paralytic[2] *adj.* canned, drunk, inebriated, intoxicated, legless, pie-eyed, pissed, plastered, sloshed, smashed, stewed, stoned, stotious, three sheets in the wind.

antonym (stone-cold) sober.

parameter *n.* boundary, constant, criterion, framework, guideline, indication, limit, limitation, restriction, specification, variable.

paramount *adj.* capital, cardinal, chief, dominant, eminent, first, foremost, highest, main, outstanding, predominant, pre-eminent, premier, primary, prime, principal, superior, supreme, topmost, top-rank.
antonyms inferior, last, lowest.

paramour *n.* beau, concubine, courtesan, doxy, fancy man, fancy woman, hetaira, inamorata, kept woman, lover, mistress, woman.

paranoia *n.* delusions, megalomania, monomania, obsession, psychosis.

parapet *n.* barbican, bartisan, bastion, battlement, bulwark, fortification, rampart.

paraphernalia *n.* accessories, accoutrements, apparatus, appurtenances, baggage, belongings, bits and pieces, clobber, clutter, effects, equipage, equipment, gear, impedimenta, material, odds and ends, stuff, tackle, things, trappings, traps.

paraphrase *n.* farse, gloss, interpretation, recapitulation, rehash, rendering, rendition, rephrasing, restatement, rewording, translation, version.
v. farse, gloss, interpret, recapitulate, rehash, render, rephrase, restate, reword, translate.

parasite *n.* bloodsucker, cadger, endophyte, endozoon, entozoon, epiphyte, epizoan, epizoon, free-loader, hanger-on, leech, lick-trencher, scrounger, sponge, sponger, sucker.

parasitic *adj.* biogenous, bloodsucking, cadging, epizoan, epizoic, free-loading, leechlike, parasitical, scrounging, sponging.

parcel *n.* band, batch, bunch, bundle, carton, collection, company, crew, crowd, da(w)k, gang, group, lot, pack, package, packet, plot, portion, property, quantity, set, tract.
v. bundle, collect, pack, package, tie up, wrap.
parcel out allocate, allot, apportion, carve up, deal out, dispense, disperse, distribute, divide, dole out, mete, portion out, separate, share out.

parch *v.* blister, burn, dehydrate, desiccate, dry up, exsiccate, roast, scorch, sear, shrivel, wither.

parched *adj.* arid, dehydrated, dried up, drouthy, dry, scorched, shrivelled, thirsty, waterless, withered.

parchment *n.* certificate, charter, diploma, document, palimpsest, scroll, vellum.

pardon *v.* absolve, acquit, amnesty, condone, emancipate, exculpate, excuse, exonerate, forgive, free, let off, liberate, overlook, release, remit, reprieve, respite, vindicate.
n. absolution, acquittal, allowance, amnesty, compassion, condonation, discharge, excuse, exoneration, forgiveness, grace, humanity, indulgence, mercy, release, remission, reprieval, reprieve.

pardonable *adj.* allowable, condonable, dispensable, excusable, forgivable, justifiable, minor, permissible, remissible, understandable, venial, warrantable.
antonym inexcusable.

pare *v.* clip, crop, cut, cut back, decrease, diminish, dock, flaught, float, lop, peel, prune, reduce, retrench, shave, shear, skin, skive, trim.

parent *n.* architect, author, begetter, cause, creator, father, forerunner, generant, genetrix, genitor, guardian, mother, origin, originator, procreator, progenitor, progenitress, progenitrix, prototype, root, sire, source.

parentage *n.* affiliation, ancestry, birth, derivation, descent, extraction, family, filiation, line, lineage, origin, paternity, pedigree, race, source, stirps, stock.

parenthetic *adj.* adventitious, bracketed, elucidative, explanatory, extraneous, extrinsic, in parenthesis, incidental, inserted, interposed, intervening, parenthetical, qualifying.
antonyms basic, original.

pariah *n.* black sheep, castaway, exile, Ishmael, leper, outcast, outlaw, undesirable, unperson, untouchable.

paring *n.* clipping, cutting, flake, flaught, fragment, peel, peeling, rind, shaving, shred, skin, slice, sliver, snippet.

parish *n.* brethren, church, churchgoers, community, congregation, district, flock, fold, parishioners, vicariate.

parity *n.* affinity, agreement, analogy, conformity, congruence, congruity, consistency, consonance, correspondence, equality, equivalence, likeness, par, parallelism, resemblance, sameness, semblance, similarity, similitude, uniformity, unity.

park[1] *n.* estate, garden, grounds, paddock, parkland, pleasance, pleasure garden, reserve, woodland.

park[2] *v.* deposit, dump, leave, position, station.

parlance *n.* argot, cant, diction, idiom, jargon, language, lingo, phraseology, speech, talk, tongue.

parley *n.* colloquy, confab, conference, council, deliberation, dialogue, discussion, get-together, meeting, negotiation, palaver, pow-wow, talk(s), tête-à-tête.
v. confabulate, confer, consult, deliberate, discuss, get together, negotiate, palaver, powwow, speak, talk.

parliament *n.* assembly, conclave, congress, convocation, council, Dail, diet, house, legislature, senate, talking-shop, Tynwald.

parliamentary *adj.* congressional, deliberative, governmental, law-making, legislative, legislatorial, senatorial.

parlour *n.* drawing-room, living-room, lounge, sitting-room.

parochial *adj.* blinkered, confined, incestuous, insular, inward-looking, limited, narrow, narrow-minded, parish-pump, petty, provincial, restricted, small-minded.

parochialism *n.* insularity, narrow-mindedness, pettiness, provincialism.

parody n. burlesque, caricature, imitation, lampoon, mimicry, pasquinade, satire, send-up, skit, spoof, take-off.

v. burlesque, caricature, lampoon, mimic, pasquinade, satirise, send up, spoof, take off, travesty.

paroxysm n. attack, convulsion, eruption, explosion, fit, flare-up, outbreak, outburst, seizure, spasm, tantrum.

parrot n. ape, copy-cat, imitator, mimic, phraser, repeater.

v. ape, copy, echo, imitate, mimic, rehearse, reiterate, repeat.

parrot-fashion adv. automatically, by rote, mechanically, mindlessly, unthinkingly.

parry v. avert, avoid, block, circumvent, deflect, divert, dodge, duck, evade, fence, fend off, field, forestall, obviate, rebuff, repel, repulse, shun, sidestep, stave off, ward off.

parsimonious adj. cheese-paring, close, close-fisted, close-handed, frugal, grasping, mean, mingy, miserable, miserly, money-grubbing, niggardly, penny-pinching, penny-wise, penurious, saving, scrimpy, sparing, stingy, stinting, tight-fisted.

antonyms generous, liberal, open-handed.

parsimony n. frugality, meanness, minginess, niggardliness, penny-pinching, stinginess, tight-fistedness.

antonyms generosity, liberality.

parson n. churchman, clergyman, cleric, divine, ecclesiastic, incumbent, Jack-priest, man of God, mar-text, minister, padre, pastor, preacher, priest, rector, reverend, vicar.

part n. airt, area, behalf, bit, branch, business, capacity, cause, character, charge, clause, complement, component, concern, constituent, department, district, division, duty, element, faction, factor, fraction, fragment, function, heft, ingredient, interest, involvement, limb, lines, lot, member, module, neck of the woods, neighbourhood, office, organ, particle, partwork, party, piece, place, portion, quarter, region, responsibility, role, scrap, section, sector, segment, share, side, slice, task, territory, tip of the iceberg, unit, vicinity, work.

v. break, break up, cleave, come apart, depart, detach, disband, disconnect, disjoin, dismantle, disperse, disunite, divide, go, go away, leave, part company, quit, rend, scatter, separate, sever, split, split up, sunder, take leave, tear, withdraw.

part with abandon, cede, discard, forgo, give up, jettison, let go of, relinquish, renounce, sacrifice, surrender, yield.

partake v. be involved, engage, enter, participate, share, take part.

partake of consume, drink, eat, evince, evoke, have, manifest, receive, share, show, suggest, take.

partial¹ adj. fragmentary, imperfect, incomplete, inexhaustive, limited, part, uncompleted, unfinished.

antonyms complete, exhaustive, total.

partial² adj. affected, biased, coloured, discriminatory, ex parte, influenced, interested, one-sided, partisan, predisposed, prejudiced, tendentious, unfair, unjust.

antonyms disinterested, fair, unbiased.

partial to crazy about, daft about, fond of, keen on, mad about, taken with.

partiality n. affinity, bias, discrimination, favouritism, fondness, inclination, liking, love, partisanship, penchant, predilection, predisposition, preference, prejudice, proclivity, propensity, soft spot, taste, weakness.

antonyms dislike, justice.

partially adv. fractionally, in part, incompletely, partly, somewhat.

participant n. associate, contributor, co-operator, helper, member, partaker, participator, party, shareholder, worker.

participate v. be involved, co-operate, engage, enter, join, muck in, partake, perform, share, take part.

participation n. a piece of the action, assistance, contribution, co-operation, involvement, mucking in, partaking, partnership, sharing.

particle n. atom, atom(y), bit, corn, crumb, drop, electron, grain, iota, jot, kaon, mite, molecule, morsel, mote, neutrino, neutron, piece, pion, proton, scrap, shred, sliver, smidgen, speck, tittle, whit.

parti-coloured adj. motley, piebald, polychromatic, polychromic, variegated, versicoloured.

antonyms monochromatic, plain.

particular¹ adj. blow-by-blow, circumstantial, detailed, distinct, especial, exact, exceptional, express, itemised, marked, minute, notable, noteworthy, painstaking, peculiar, precise, remarkable, selective, several, singular, special, specific, thorough, uncommon, unique, unusual, very.

antonym general.

n. circumstance, detail, fact, feature, item, point, specific, specification.

particular² adj. choosy, critical, dainty, demanding, discriminating, exacting, fastidious, finical, finicky, fussy, meticulous, nice, overnice, perjink, pernickety, picky.

antonym casual.

particularise v. detail, enumerate, individualise, individuate, itemise, specify, stipulate.

particularity n. accuracy, carefulness, characteristic, choosiness, circumstance, detail, distinctiveness, fact, fastidiousness, feature, fussiness, idiosyncrasy, individuality, instance, item, mannerism, meticulousness, peculiarity, point, precision, property, quirk, singularity, thoroughness, trait, uniqueness.

particularly adv. decidedly, distinctly, especially, exceptionally, explicitly, expressly, extraordinarily, in particular, markedly, notably, noticeably, outstandingly, peculiarly, remarkably, singularly, specifically, surprisingly, uncommonly, unusually.

parting n. adieu, breaking, departure, detachment, disjunction, disunion, divergence,

division, farewell, going, goodbye, leave-taking, partition, rift, rupture, separation, severance, split, valediction.
antonyms convergence, meeting.
adj. closing, concluding, deathbed, departing, dying, farewell, final, last, stirrup, valedictory.
antonyms arriving, first.

partisan *n.* adherent, backer, champion, devotee, disciple, factionary, factionist, follower, guerrilla, irregular, party-man, stalwart, supporter, upholder, votary.
adj. biased, discriminatory, factional, guerrilla, interested, irregular, one-sided, partial, predisposed, prejudiced, resistance, sectarian, tendentious, underground.

partisanship *n.* bias, factionalism, fanaticism, partiality, partyism, sectarianism.

partition[1] *n.* allocation, allotment, apportionment, distribution, dividing, division, part, portion, rationing out, section, segregation, separation, severance, share, splitting.
v. allocate, allot, apportion, assign, divide, parcel out, portion, section, segment, separate, share, split up, subdivide.

partition[2] *n.* barrier, diaphragm, dissepiment, divider, hallan, membrane, room-divider, screen, septum, traverse, wall.
v. bar, divide, fence off, screen, separate, wall off.

partly *adv.* halfway, in part, incompletely, moderately, partially, relatively, slightly, somewhat, to a certain degree, to a certain extent, up to a point.
antonyms completely, in toto, totally.

partner *n.* accomplice, ally, associate, bedfellow, butty, collaborator, colleague, companion, comrade, confederate, consort, co-partner, gigolo, helper, helpmate, helpmeet, husband, mate, participant, side-kick, spouse, team-mate, wife.

partnership *n.* affiliation, alliance, association, brotherhood, combination, combine, companionship, company, conglomerate, connection, co-operation, co-operative, co-partnership, corporation, fellowship, firm, fraternity, house, interest, participation, sharing, society, syndicate, union.

parts *n.* ability, accomplishments, attributes, calibre, capabilities, endowments, expertise, faculties, genius, gifts, intellect, intelligence, skill, talents.

party[1] *n.* assembly, at-home, bash, beanfeast, beano, ceilidh, celebration, do, drag, drum, entertainment, -fest, festivity, function, gathering, get-together, hooley, hoot(e)-nanny, housewarming, hurricane, jollification, knees-up, rave-up, reception, rout, shindig, social, soirée, thrash.

party[2] *n.* alliance, association, band, body, bunch, cabal, caucus, clique, coalition, combination, company, confederacy, contingent, contractor, coterie, crew, defendant, detachment, faction, gang, gathering, group, grouping, individual, junto, league, litigant,

participant, person, plaintiff, set, side, squad, team, unit.

parvenu *n.* arriviste, climber, new rich, nouveau riche, pretender, upstart, vulgarian.
adj. nouveau riche, upstart, vulgarian.

pass[1] *v.* accept, adopt, answer, approve, authorise, beat, befall, beguile, blow over, cease, come up, come up to scratch, convey, declare, decree, defecate, delate, deliver, depart, develop, devote, die, die away, disappear, discharge, disregard, dissolve, do, dwindle, ebb, elapse, eliminate, employ, empty, enact, end, establish, evacuate, evaporate, exceed, excel, exchange, excrete, expel, experience, expire, express, fade, fall out, fill, flow, get through, give, go, go beyond, go by, go past, graduate, hand, happen, ignore, impersonate, lapse, leave, legislate, melt away, miss, move, neglect, occupy, occur, omit, ordain, outdistance, outdo, outstrip, overlook, overtake, pass muster, proceed, pronounce, qualify, ratify, roll, run, sanction, send, serve as, skip, spend, succeed, suffer, suffice, suit, surmount, surpass, take place, terminate, throw, transcend, transfer, transmit, undergo, utter, validate, vanish, void, waft, wane, while away.

pass[2] *n.* advances, approach, authorisation, chit, condition, feint, identification, jab, juncture, laissez-passer, licence, lunge, overture, passport, permission, permit, pinch, play, plight, predicament, proposition, push, safe-conduct, situation, stage, state, state of affairs, straits, suggestion, swing, thrust, ticket, warrant.

pass away croak, decease, die, expire, give up the ghost, kick the bucket, pass on, pass over, peg out, snuff it.

pass by disregard, forget, ignore, leave, miss, neglect, omit, overlook, pass over, pretermit.

pass muster be adequate, be up to scratch, fill the bill, make the grade, measure up, qualify.

pass off come to an end, counterfeit, die away, disappear, dismiss, disregard, emit, evaporate, fade out, fake, feign, give off, go off, happen, ignore, occur, palm off, pass by, send forth, take place, turn out, utter, vanish, vaporise, wink at.

pass out[1] black out, die, drop, faint, flake out, keel over, lose consciousness, swoon.

pass out[2] deal out, dispense, distribute, dole out, give out, hand out, share out.

pass over ignore, neglect, omit, overlook, pretermit.

pass[3] *n.* canyon, col, defile, gap, gha(u)t, gorge, halse, nek, ravine.

passable *adj.* acceptable, adequate, admissible, all right, allowable, average, clear, fair, mediocre, middling, moderate, navigable, OK, open, ordinary, presentable, so-so, tolerable, traversable, unblocked, unexceptional, unobstructed.

passably *adv.* after a fashion, fairly, moderately, rather, reasonably, relatively, somewhat, tolerably.

passage *n.* acceptance, access, adit, advance, allowance, authorisation, avenue, change, channel, citation, clause, close, communication, conduit, conversion, corridor, course, crossing, deambulatory, doorway, drift, dromos, duct, enactment, entrance, entrance hall, establishment, excerpt, exit, extract, fistula, flow, freedom, gallery, gut, hall, hallway, journey, lane, legalisation, legislation, lobby, motion, movement, opening, orifice, paragraph, part, passageway, passing, path, permission, piece, portion, progress, progression, quotation, ratification, reading, right, road, route, safe-conduct, section, sentence, spiracle, text, thorough, thoroughfare, tour, transit, transition, trek, trip, vent, verse, vestibule, visa, vista, voyage, warrant, way.

passageway *n.* aisle, alley, corridor, entrance, exit, hall, hallway, lane, lobby, passage, pend, vennel, wynd.

passé *adj.* antiquated, dated, démodé, obsolete, old hat, old-fashioned, out, outdated, outmoded, out-of-date, outworn, past one's best, unfashionable.
antonyms fashionable, in.

passenger *n.* commuter, fare, hitch-hiker, pillionist, pillion-rider, rider, traveller.

passer-by *n.* bystander, looker-on, onlooker, spectator, witness.

passing *adj.* brief, casual, cursory, ephemeral, evanescent, fleeting, fly-by-night, fugitive, glancing, hasty, impermanent, momentary, quick, shallow, shirt, short, short-lived, slight, superficial, temporary, transient, transitory.
antonyms long-lasting, permanent.
n. death, decease, demise, end, expiration, finish, loss, quietus, termination.

passion *n.* adoration, affection, anger, animation, ardour, attachment, avidity, bug, chafe, concupiscence, craving, craze, dander, desire, eagerness, emotion, enthusiasm, excitement, fancy, fascination, feeling, fervency, fervour, fire, fit, flare-up, fondness, frenzy, fury, heat, idol, indignation, infatuation, intensity, ire, itch, joy, keenness, love, lust, mania, monomania, obsession, outburst, paroxysm, rage, rapture, resentment, spirit, storm, transport, vehemence, verve, vivacity, warmth, wax, wrath, zeal, zest.
antonyms calm, coolness, self-possession.

passionate *adj.* amorous, animated, ardent, aroused, choleric, desirous, eager, emotional, enthusiastic, erotic, excitable, excited, fervent, fervid, fierce, fiery, frenzied, heartfelt, hot, hot-headed, hot-tempered, impassioned, impetuous, impulsive, incensed, inflamed, inspirited, intense, irascible, irate, irritable, loving, lustful, peppery, quick-tempered, sensual, sexy, stormy, strong, sultry, tempestuous, torrid, vehement, violent, wanton, warm, wild, zealous.
antonyms frigid, laid-back, phlegmatic.

passionless *adj.* apathetic, callous, calm, cold, cold-blooded, cold-hearted, detached, dispassionate, emotionless, frigid, frosty, icy, impartial, impassive, inappetent, indifferent, insensible, neutral, restrained, uncaring, unemotional, unfeeling, uninvolved, unloving, unresponsive, withdrawn.
antonyms caring, sensitive, sympathetic.

passive *adj.* acquiescent, compliant, docile, enduring, impassive, inactive, indifferent, indolent, inert, lifeless, long-suffering, non-participating, non-violent, patient, quiescent, receptive, resigned, submissive, supine, unaffected, unassertive, uninvolved, unresisting.
antonyms active, involved, lively.

passive resistance non-violence, satyagraha, vis inertiae.

passport *n.* authorisation, laissez-passer, pass, permit, visa.

password *n.* countersign, open sesame, parole, shibboleth, signal, watchword.

past *adj.* accomplished, ancient, bygone, completed, defunct, done, early, elapsed, ended, erstwhile, extinct, finished, foregone, forgotten, former, gone, gone by, late, long-ago, no more, olden, over, over and done with, preceding, previous, prior, quondam, recent, spent, vanished.
n. antiquity, auld lang syne, background, days of yore, dossier, experience, former times, good old days, history, life, old times, olden days, track record, yesteryear.

past one's best not what one was, over the hill, passé.

paste *n.* adhesive, cement, dope, dough, glue, gum, mastic, mucilage, pastry, putty.
v. beat, cement, fasten, fix, glue, gum, hammer, stick, thrash, thump, whitewash.

pastel *adj.* delicate, faint, gentle, light, muted, pale, soft, soft-hued, subdued.
n. chalk, crayon, drawing, pastille, sketch, vignette, wood.

pastiche *n.* blend, composition, farrago, gallimaufry, hotchpotch, medley, mélange, miscellany, mixture, motley, olla-podrida, patchwork, pot-pourri.

pastille *n.* confection, cough drop, cough sweet, jujube, lozenge, pastel, sweet, tablet, troche.

pastime *n.* activity, amusement, avocation, distraction, diversion, divertisement, entertainment, game, hobby, play, recreation, relaxation, sport, Zeitvertreib.
antonyms business, employment, occupation, vocation, work.

pastmaster *n.* ace, adept, artist, dab hand, expert, old hand, proficient, virtuoso, wizard.
antonym incompetent.

pastor *n.* canon, churchman, clergyman, cleric, divine, ecclesiastic, minister, parson, prebendary, priest, rector, vicar.

pastoral *adj.* agrarian, Arcadian, bucolic, clerical, countrified, country, ecclesiastical, georgic, idyllic, ministerial, priestly, rural, rustic, simple.
antonyms oppidan, urban.

pasture *n.* alp, eddish, grass, grassland, grazing, lay, lea, ley, machair, mead, meadow, pasturage, pasture-land, raik, shieling.

pasty *adj.* anaemic, doughy, gluey, glutinous, mucilaginous, pale, pallid, pasty-faced, peelie-wally, sallow, sickly, starchy, sticky, unhealthy, viscous, wan, waxy, whey-faced.
antonyms healthy, rubicund.

pat *v.* caress, clap, dab, fondle, pet, rub, slap, stroke, tap, touch.
n. cake, caress, clap, dab, lump, piece, portion, slap, stroke, tap, touch.
adv. exactly, faultlessly, flawlessly, fluently, glibly, just right, off pat, opportunely, perfectly, plumb, precisely, relevantly, seasonably.
antonyms imprecisely, wrongly.
adj. apposite, appropriate, apropos, apt, automatic, easy, facile, felicitous, fitting, glib, happy, neat, pertinent, ready, relevant, right, simplistic, slick, smooth, spot-on, suitable, to the point, well-chosen.
antonyms irrelevant, unsuitable.

patch *n.* area, bit, clout, ground, land, lot, parcel, piece, plot, scrap, shred, spot, stretch, tract.
v. botch, cover, fix, mend, reinforce, repair, sew up, stitch, vamp.

patchwork *n.* confusion, farrago, gallimaufry, hash, hotchpotch, jumble, medley, mishmash, mixture, pastiche.

patchy *adj.* bitty, erratic, fitful, incongruous, inconsistent, inharmonious, irregular, maculate, random, sketchy, spotty, uneven, variable, varying.
antonyms consistent, even, regular, uniform.

patent *adj.* apparent, blatant, clear, clear-cut, conspicuous, downright, evident, explicit, flagrant, glaring, indisputable, manifest, obvious, open, ostensible, overt, palpable, transparent, unconcealed, unequivocal, unmistakable.
antonyms hidden, opaque.
n. certificate, copyright, invention, licence, privilege, registered trademark.

paternal *adj.* benevolent, concerned, fatherlike, fatherly, indulgent, patrilineal, patrimonial, patroclinic, patroclinous, protective, solicitous, vigilant.

paternity *n.* authorship, descent, extraction, family, fatherhood, fathership, lineage, origination, parentage.

path *n.* avenue, course, direction, footpath, footway, gate, pad, passage, pathway, procedure, ridgeway, road, route, towpath, track, trail, walk, walkway, way.

pathetic *adj.* affecting, contemptible, crummy, deplorable, dismal-looking, distressing, feeble, heartbreaking, heart-rending, inadequate, lamentable, meagre, melting, miserable, moving, paltry, petty, piteous, pitiable, pitiful, plaintive, poignant, poor, puny, rubbishy, sad, sorry, tender, touching, trashy, uninteresting, useless, woebegone, woeful, worthless.

antonyms admirable, cheerful.

pathos *n.* inadequacy, misery, pitiableness, pitifulness, plaintiveness, poignancy, sadness.

patience *n.* calmness, composure, constancy, cool, diligence, endurance, equanimity, forbearance, fortitude, long-suffering, perseverance, persistence, resignation, restraint, self-control, serenity, stoicism, submission, sufferance, tolerable, toleration.
antonyms impatience, intolerance.

patient[1] *adj.* accommodating, calm, composed, enduring, even-tempered, forbearing, forgiving, indulgent, lenient, long-suffering, mild, persevering, persistent, philosophical, quiet, resigned, restrained, self-controlled, self-possessed, serene, stoical, submissive, tolerant, uncomplaining, understanding, untiring.
antonyms impatient, intolerant.

patient[2] *n.* case, client, invalid, sufferer.

patois *n.* argot, cant, dialect, jargon, lingo, lingua franca, patter, slang, vernacular.

patriarch *n.* elder, father, founder, grand old man, grandfather, greybeard, paterfamilias, sire.

patrician *n.* aristocrat, gentleman, grandee, noble, nobleman, peer.
antonyms commoner, pleb.
adj. aristocratic, blue-blooded, gentle, high-born, high-class, lordly, noble, thoroughbred, well-born.
antonyms common, humble.

patrimony *n.* bequest, birthright, estate, heritage, inheritance, legacy, portion, revenue, share.

patriot *n.* chauvinist, flag-waver, jingo, jingoist, loyalist, nationalist.

patriotic *adj.* chauvinistic, flag-waving, jingoish, jingoistic, loyal, nationalistic.

patriotism *n.* chauvinism, flag-waving, jingoism, loyalty, nationalism.

patrol *n.* defence, garrison, guard, guarding, policing, protecting, roundvigilance, sentinel, surveillance, watch, watching, watchman.
v. cruise, go the rounds, guard, inspect, perambulate, police, range, tour.

patron *n.* advocate, backer, benefactor, buyer, champion, client, customer, defender, fautor, frequenter, friend, guardian, habitué, helper, Maecenas, partisan, philanthropist, protector, regular, shopper, sponsor, subscriber, supporter, sympathiser.

patronage *n.* aegis, aid, assistance, backing, benefaction, business, championship, clientèle, commerce, custom, encouragement, help, participation, promotion, sponsorship, subscription, support, sustenance, trade, trading, traffic.

patronise *v.* assist, back, befriend, encourage, foster, frequent, fund, habituate, help, humour, maintain, promote, shop at, sponsor, support, talk down to.

patronising *adj.* condescending, contemptuous, disdaining, gracious, haughty, high-handed, imperious, lofty, overbearing, snobbish, stooping, supercilious, superior, toffee-nosed.

antonym humble.

patter[1] *v.* beat, pat, pelt, pitapat, pit-pat, pitter-patter, pittypat, rat-a-rat, scurry, scuttle, skip, spatter, tap, tiptoe, trip.

n. pattering, pitapat, pit-pat, pitter-patter, pittypat, tapping.

patter[2] *n.* argot, cant, chatter, gabble, glib talk, jabber, jargon, line, lingo, monologue, patois, pitch, prattle, slang, spiel, vernacular, yak.

pattern *n.* archetype, arrangement, criterion, cynosure, decoration, delineation, design, device, diagram, examplar, example, figuration, figure, Gestalt, guide, instructions, kind, method, model, motif, norm, order, orderliness, original, ornament, ornamentation, paradigm, paragon, plan, prototype, sample, sequence, shape, sort, specimen, standard, stencil, style, system, template, type, variety.

v. copy, decorate, design, emulate, follow, form, imitate, match, model, mould, order, shape, stencil, style, trim.

patterned *adj.* decorated, figured, moiré, ornamented, printed, stamped, watered.

paucity *n.* dearth, deficiency, exiguousness, fewness, insufficiency, lack, meagreness, paltriness, poverty, rarity, scantiness, scarcity, shortage, slenderness, slightness, smallness, sparseness, sparsity, want.

antonym abundance.

paunch *n.* abdomen, beer-belly, beer-gut, belly, bread-basket, corporation, pot, pot-belly.

paunchy *adj.* adipose, corpulent, fat, podgy, portly, pot-bellied, pudgy, rotund, tubby.

pauper *n.* bankrupt, beggar, church-mouse, down-and-out, have-not, indigent, insolvent, mendicant.

pause *v.* break, cease, cut, delay, desist, discontinue, halt, hesitate, interrupt, rest, take a break, take a breather, take five, wait, waver.

n. abatement, break, breather, caesura, cessation, delay, discontinuance, dwell, gap, halt, hesitation, interlude, intermission, interruption, interval, let-up, lull, respite, rest, slackening, stay, stoppage, suspension, wait.

pave *v.* asphalt, concrete, cover, flag, floor, macadamise, revet, slab, surface, tar, tile.

pavement *n.* bed, causeway, floor, footway, pavé, sidewalk.

paw *v.* grab, manhandle, maul, mishandle, molest.

n. foot, forepaw, hand, pad, pud, puddy.

pawn[1] *n.* cat's-paw, creature, dupe, instrument, plaything, puppet, stooge, tool, toy.

pawn[2] *v.* deposit, dip, gage, hazard, hock, impawn, impignorate, lay in lavender, mortgage, pledge, pop, stake, wager.

n. hostage, security.

pawnbroker *n.* gombeen-man, lender, money-lender, uncle, usurer.

pawnshop *n.* leaving-shop, mont-de-piété, monte de pietà, pop-shop.

pay *v.* ante, benefit, bestow, bring in, clear, compensate, cough up, disburse, discharge, extend, foot, get even with, give, grant, honour, indemnify, liquidate, meet, offer, pay out, present, produce, proffer, profit, punish, reciprocate, recompense, reimburse, remit, remunerate, render, repay, requite, return, reward, serve, settle, square, square up, yield.

n. allowance, compensation, consideration, earnings, emoluments, fee, hire, honorarium, income, payment, recompense, reimbursement, remuneration, reward, salary, stipend, takings, wages.

pay back avenge, chasten, get even with, get one's own back, punish, reciprocate, recompense, refund, reimburse, repay, retaliate, return, settle up, settle with, square.

pay for answer for, atone, compensate, face the music, get one's deserts, make amends, suffer.

pay off clear, discharge, dismiss, fire, lay off, liquidate, sack, satisfy, settle, square, succeed, work.

pay out cough up, disburse, dish out, expend, fork out, hand over, lay out, render, shell out, spend.

payable *adj.* due, in arrears, mature, obligatory, outstanding, owed, owing, receivable, unpaid.

payment *n.* advance, alimony, ante, consideration, defrayal, deposit, discharge, fee, hire, instalment, outlay, paying, portion, premium, remittance, remuneration, reward, settlement, sub, wage.

pay-off *n.* climax, clincher, conclusion, consequence, crunch, culmination, day of reckoning, dénouement, judgement, moment of truth, outcome, punch-line, reimbursement, result, retribution, reward, settlement, upshot.

peace *n.* accord, agreement, amity, armistice, calm, calmness, cease-fire, composure, conciliation, concord, contentment, frith, harmony, hush, pacification, pax, peacefulness, placidity, quiet, quietude, relaxation, repose, rest, serenity, silence, stillness, tranquillity, treaty, truce.

antonyms disagreement, disturbance, war.

peace studies irenology.

peaceable *adj.* amiable, amicable, compatible, conciliatory, douce, dovish, easy-going, friendly, gentle, inoffensive, mild, non-belligerent, pacific, peaceful, peace-loving, placid, unwarlike.

antonyms belligerent, offensive.

peaceful *adj.* amicable, at peace, becalmed, calm, conciliatory, friendly, gentle, halcyon, harmonious, irenic (eirenic), non-violent, pacific, peaceable, peace-loving, placatory, placid, quiet, restful, serene, still, tranquil, unagitated, undisturbed, unruffled, untroubled, unwarlike.

antonyms disturbed, noisy, troubled.

peacemaker *n.* appeaser, arbitrator, conciliator, interceder, intercessor, mediator, mediatress, mediatrix, pacifier, peacemonger.

peacemaking *adj.* appeasing, conciliatory,

irenic(al), mediating, mediative, mediatorial, mediatory, pacific.

peace-pipe *n.* calumet, pipe of peace.

peak *n.* acme, aiguille, apex, apogee, brow, climax, crest, crown, culmination, cuspid, high point, maximum, ne plus ultra, pinnacle, point, summit, tip, top, visor, zenith.
antonyms nadir, trough.
v. climax, come to a head, culminate, spire, tower.

peaky *adj.* drooping, emaciated, ill, off-colour, pale, peelie-wally, pinched, poorly, shilpit, sick, sickly, under the weather, unwell, wan, washed-out, wilting.
antonyms healthy, in the pink.

peal *n.* blast, carillon, chime, clamour, clang, clangour, clap, clash, crash, resounding, reverberation, ring, ringing, roar, rumble, sound, tintinnabulation.
v. chime, clash, crack, crash, resonate, resound, reverberate, ring, roar, roll, rumble, sound, tintinnabulate, toll, vibrate.

peanut *n.* goober, ground-nut, monkey-nut.

peanuts *n.* chickenfeed, pennies, pittance.

peasant *n.* boor, bumpkin, churl, countryman, fellah, hind, jungli, kulak, lout, moujik, mujik, muzhik, oaf, oik, provincial, rustic, swain, yokel.
antonym sophisticate.

pebble *n.* agate, chip, gallet, stone.

peccadillo *n.* boob, delinquency, error, fault, indiscretion, infraction, lapse, misdeed, misdemeanour, slip, slip-up.

peck *n.* criticism, food, jab, kiss, strike.
v. eat, jab, kiss, nibble.

peculiar[1] *adj.* abnormal, bizarre, curious, eccentric, exceptional, extraordinary, far-out, freakish, funky, funny, odd, offbeat, outlandish, out-of-the-way, quaint, queer, singular, strange, uncommon, unconventional, unusual, way-out, weird.
antonyms normal, ordinary.

peculiar[2] *adj.* appropriate, characteristic, discriminative, distinct, distinctive, distinguishing, endemic, idiosyncratic, individual, local, particular, personal, private, quintessential, restricted, special, specific, unique.
antonyms general, uncharacteristic.

peculiarity *n.* abnormality, attribute, bizarreness, characteristic, distinctiveness, eccentricity, exception, feature, foible, freakishness, idiosyncrasy, kink, mannerism, mark, oddity, particularity, property, quality, queerness, quirk, singularity, speciality, trait, whimsicality.

pecuniary *adj.* commercial, financial, fiscal, monetary, nummary, nummulary.

pedagogue *n.* dogmatist, dominie, don, educationalist, educationist, educator, instructor, master, mistress, pedant, preceptor, schoolmaster, schoolmistress, teacher.

pedagogy *n.* instruction, pedagogics, teaching, training, tuition, tutelage.

pedant *n.* casuist, doctrinaire, dogmatist, Dryasdust, gerund-grinder, grammaticaster, gram-

matist, hair-splitter, literalist, mandarin, nit-picker, pedagogue, pettifogger, precisian, quibbler, scholastic, vocabularian.

pedantic *adj.* abstruse, academic, bookish, cavilling, didactic, donnish, erudite, finical, formal, fussy, hair-splitting, learned, nit-picking, particular, pedagogic, perfectionist, pompous, precise, punctilious, scholastic, schoolmasterly, sententious, stilted.
antonyms casual, imprecise, informal.

pedantry *n.* bookishness, cavilling, finicality, hair-splitting, pedagogism, pedagoguery, pedagoguishness, pedantism, pomposity, punctiliousness, quibbling, stuffiness.

peddle *v.* dilly-dally, flog, hawk, huckster, idle, loiter, market, piddle, push, retail, sell, tout, trade, trifle, vend.

pedestal *n.* base, dado, foot, foundation, mounting, pier, platform, plinth, podium, socle, stand, support, understructure.

pedestrian *n.* footslogger, foot-traveller, voetganger, walker.
adj. banal, boring, commonplace, dull, flat, humdrum, indifferent, mediocre, mundane, ordinary, plodding, prosaic, run-of-the-mill, stodgy, tolerable, unimaginative, uninspired, uninteresting.
antonyms bright, brilliant, exciting, imaginative.

pedigree *n.* ancestry, blood, breed, derivation, descent, dynasty, extraction, family, family tree, genealogy, heritage, line, lineage, parentage, race, stemma, stirps, stock, succession.

pedigreed *adj.* aristocratic, full-blooded, pedigree, pure-bred, thoroughbred.

pedlar *n.* boxwallah, chapman, cheap-jack, colporteur, gutter-man, gutter-merchant, hawker, huckster, seller, street-trader, vendor, walker, yagger.

peek *v.* glance, keek, look, peep, peer, spy.
n. blink, dekko, gander, glance, glimpse, keek, look, look-see, peep, shufti.

peel *v.* decorticate, denude, desquamate, flake (off), pare, scale, skin, strip (off), undress.
n. epicarp, exocarp, integument, peeling, rind, skin, zest.

peep *v.* blink, emerge, glimpse, issue, keek, peek, peer.
n. blink, dekko, gander, glim, glimpse, keek, look, look-see, peek, shufti.

peephole *n.* aperture, chink, cleft, crack, crevice, fissure, hole, interstice, keyhole, opening, pinhole, slit, spy-hole.

peer[1] *v.* appear, blink, emerge, examine, gaze, inspect, peep, scan, scrutinise, snoop, spy, squint.

peer[2] *n.* aristocrat, baron, count, duke, earl, lord, marquess, marquis, noble, nobleman, thane, viscount.

peer[3] *n.* compeer, counterpart, equal, equipollent, equivalent, fellow, like, match.

peerage *n.* aristocracy, lords and ladies, nobility, patriciate, top drawer, upper crust.

peeress *n.* baroness, countess, dame, duchess,

lady, marchioness, noblewoman, viscountess.

peerless *adj.* beyond compare, excellent, incomparable, matchless, nonpareil, outstanding, paramount, second to none, superlative, supreme, unbeatable, unequalled, unexcelled, unique, unmatched, unparalleled, unrivalled, unsurpassed.

peeved *adj.* annoyed, exasperated, galled, irked, irritated, miffed, narked, nettled, pipped, piqued, put out, riled, sore, upset, vexed.

peevish *adj.* acrimonious, cantankerous, captious, childish, churlish, crabbed, cross, crotchety, crusty, dorty, fractious, frampold, franzy, fretful, grumpy, hipped, ill-natured, ill-tempered, irritable, miffy, perverse, pettish, petulant, querulous, ratty, short-tempered, snappy, splenetic, sulky, sullen, surly, testy, touchy, waspish.

antonym good-tempered.

peevishness *n.* acrimony, captiousness, ill-temper, irritability, perversity, pet, petulance, pique, protervity, querulousness, testiness.

peg *v.* attach, control, fasten, fix, freeze, insert, join, limit, mark, pierce, score, secure, set, stabilise.

n. dowel, hook, knob, marker, pin, post, stake, thole(-pin), toggle.

peg away apply oneself, beaver away, hang in, keep at it, persevere, persist, plod along, plug away, stick at it, work away.

pejorative *adj.* bad, belittling, condemnatory, damning, debasing, deprecatory, depreciatory, derogatory, detractive, detractory, disparaging, negative, slighting, uncomplimentary, unflattering, unpleasant.

antonyms complimentary, laudatory.

pell-mell *adv.* feverishly, full tilt, hastily, heedlessly, helter-skelter, hurriedly, hurry-scurry, impetuously, posthaste, precipitously, rashly, recklessly.

adj. chaotic, confused, disordered, disorganised, haphazard, indiscriminate, scrambled, tumultuous.

pelt[1] *v.* assail, batter, beat, belabour, belt, bombard, bucket, career, cast, charge, dash, hit, hurl, hurry, pepper, pour, pummel, rain cats and dogs, rush, shoot, shower, sling, speed, strafe, strike, tear, teem, thrash, throw, wallop, whiz.

pelt[2] *n.* coat, fell, fleece, fur, hide, skin.

pen[1] *v.* author, compose, draft, jot down, scribble, write.

pen name alias, allonym, nom de plume, pseudonym.

pen[2] *n.* cage, coop, crib, cru(i)ve, enclosure, fold, hutch, stall, sty.

v. cage, confine, coop, corral, crib, enclose, fence, hedge, hem in, hurdle, mew (up), shut up.

penal servitude bird, lag, porridge, stretch, time.

penalise *v.* amerce, correct, disadvantage, discipline, handicap, mulct, punish.

antonym reward.

penalty *n.* amende, amercement, disadvantage,

fine, forfeit, forfeiture, handicap, mulct, price, punishment, retribution.

antonym reward.

penance *n.* atonement, mortification, penalty, placation, propitiation, punishment, reparation, sackcloth and ashes.

penchant *n.* affinity, bent, bias, disposition, fondness, inclination, leaning, liking, partiality, predilection, predisposition, preference, proclivity, proneness, propensity, soft spot, taste, tendency, turn.

antonym dislike.

pendant *n.* drop, lavaliere, locket, medallion, necklace.

pendent *adj.* dangling, drooping, hanging, nutant, pendulous, pensile, suspended, swinging.

pending *adj.* awaiting, forthcoming, hanging, imminent, impending, in the balance, in the offing, on the back burner, undecided, undetermined, unfinished, unsettled.

antonyms finished, settled.

pendulous *adj.* dangling, drooping, droopy, hanging, pendent, sagging, suspended, swaying, swinging.

penetrable *adj.* accessible, clear, comprehensible, explicable, fathomable, intelligible, open, passable, permeable, pervious, porous, understandable.

antonym impenetrable.

penetrate *v.* affect, bore, come across, come home, comprehend, decipher, diffuse, discern, enter, fathom, get through to, get to the bottom of, grasp, impress, infiltrate, perforate, permeate, pervade, pierce, prick, probe, seep, sink, stab, strike, suffuse, touch, understand, unravel.

penetrating *adj.* acute, astute, biting, carrying, critical, discerning, discriminating, harsh, incisive, intelligent, intrusive, keen, observant, penetrative, perceptive, percipient, perspicacious, pervasive, piercing, profound, pungent, quick, sagacious, searching, sharp, sharp-witted, shrewd, shrill, stinging, strong.

antonyms gentle, obtuse, soft.

penetration *n.* acumen, acuteness, astuteness, discernment, entrance, entry, incision, inroad, insight, interpenetration, invasion, keenness, perception, perforation, perspicacity, piercing, puncturing, sharpness, shrewdness, wit.

peninsula *n.* cape, chersonese, doab, mull, point, tongue.

penis *n.* cock, dick, John Thomas, knob, membrum virile, pecker, phallus, pizzle, prick, rod, shaft, tool, winkle.

penitence *n.* compunction, contrition, regret, regretfulness, remorse, repentance, rue, self-reproach, shame, sorrow.

penitent *adj.* abject, apologetic, atoning, conscience-stricken, contrite, humble, in sackcloth and ashes, regretful, remorseful, repentant, rueful, sorrowful, sorry.

antonym unrepentant.

penniless *adj.* bankrupt, broke, bust(ed),

cleaned out, destitute, flat broke, impecunious, impoverished, indigent, moneyless, necessitous, needy, obolary, on one's uppers, on the rocks, penurious, poor, poverty-stricken, ruined, skint, stoney-broke, strapped.
antonyms rich, wealthy.

pennon *n.* banderol(e), banner, burgee, ensign, gonfalon, jack, oriflamme, pencel, pencil, pennant, pensel, streamer.

penny-pincher *n.* meany, miser, niggard, pinchfist, pinchgut, pinchpenny, screw, Scrooge, skinflint.

penny-pinching *adj.* cheeseparing, close, frugal, mean, mingy, miserly, near, niggardly, parsimonious, scrimping, stingy, tight-fisted, ungenerous.
antonyms generous, open-handed.

pension *n.* allowance, annuity, benefit, maintenance, stipend, superannuation.

pensive *adj.* absent-minded, absorbed, cogitative, contemplative, dreamy, grave, meditative, melancholy, musing, preoccupied, reflective, ruminative, serious, sober, solemn, thoughtful, wistful.

pent-up *adj.* bottled-up, bridled, checked, constrained, curbed, inhibited, repressed, restrained, smothered, stifled, suppressed.

penurious *adj.* beggarly, bust(ed), cheeseparing, close, close-fisted, deficient, destitute, flat broke, frugal, grudging, impecunious, impoverished, inadequate, indigent, meagre, mean, miserable, miserly, near, needy, niggardly, obolary, paltry, parsimonious, penniless, poor, poverty-stricken, scanty, skimping, stingy, tight-fisted, ungenerous.
antonyms generous, wealthy.

penury *n.* beggary, dearth, deficiency, destitution, indigence, lack, mendicancy, mendicity, need, paucity, pauperism, poverty, privation, scantiness, scarcity, shortage, sparseness, straitened circumstances, straits, want.
antonym prosperity.

people *n.* citizens, clan, commonalty, community, crowd, demos, family, folk, general public, gens, grass roots, hoi polloi, human beings, humanity, humans, inhabitants, mankind, many-headed beast, many-headed monster, masses, mob, mortals, multitude, nation, persons, plebs, populace, population, public, punters, rabble, race, rank and file, the herd, the million, tribe.
v. colonise, inhabit, occupy, populate, settle, tenant.

pep *n.* animation, energy, exuberance, get-up-and-go, gusto, high spirits, life, liveliness, pizzazz, spirit, verve, vigour, vim, vitality, vivacity, zip.
pep up animate, energise, enliven, excite, exhilarate, inspire, invigorate, jazz up, quicken, stimulate, vitalise, vivify.

peppery *adj.* astringent, biting, caustic, choleric, fiery, grumpy, hot, hot-tempered, incisive, irascible, irritable, nippy, piquant, pungent, quick-tempered, sarcastic, sharp, snappish,

spicy, stinging, testy, touchy, trenchant, waspish.

perceive *v.* appreciate, apprehend, be aware of, behold, catch, comprehend, conclude, deduce, descry, discern, discover, distinguish, espy, feel, gather, get, grasp, intuit, know, learn, make out, note, observe, realise, recognise, remark, see, sense, spot, understand.

perceptible *adj.* apparent, appreciable, clear, conspicuous, detectable, discernible, distinct, distinguishable, evident, noticeable, observable, obvious, palpable, perceivable, recognisable, salient, tangible, visible.
antonym imperceptible.

perception *n.* Anschauung, apprehension, awareness, conception, consciousness, discernment, feeling, grasp, idea, impression, insight, intellection, notion, observation, recognition, sensation, sense, taste, understanding, uptake.

perceptive *adj.* able to see through a millstone, acute, alert, astute, aware, discerning, insightful, observant, penetrating, percipient, perspicacious, quick, responsive, sagacious, sapient, sensitive, sharp.
antonym unobservant.

perch *v.* alight, balance, drop, land, light, rest, roost, settle, sit on.

percipience *n.* acuity, acuteness, alertness, astuteness, awareness, discernment, insight, intuition, judgement, penetration, perception, perspicacity, sagacity, sensitivity, understanding.

percipient *adj.* alert, alive, astute, aware, discerning, discriminating, intelligent, judicious, knowing, penetrating, perceptive, perspicacious, quick-witted, sharp, wide-awake.
antonyms obtuse, unaware.

percolate *v.* drain, drip, exude, filter, filtrate, leach, leak, ooze, osmose, penetrate, permeate, pervade, seep, strain, transfuse.

perdition *n.* condemnation, damnation, destruction, doom, downfall, hell, hellfire, ruin, ruination.

peregrination *n.* excursion, expedition, exploration, globe-trotting, journey, odyssey, roaming, roving, tour, travel, travelling, trek, trekking, trip, voyage, wandering, wayfaring.

peremptory *adj.* abrupt, absolute, arbitrary, assertive, authoritative, autocratic, binding, bossy, categorical, commanding, compelling, curt, decisive, dictatorial, dogmatic, domineering, final, high-handed, imperative, imperious, incontrovertible, intolerant, irrefutable, obligatory, overbearing, summary, undeniable.

perennial *adj.* abiding, ceaseless, chronic, constant, continual, continuing, deathless, enduring, eternal, evergreen, everlasting, immortal, imperishable, incessant, inveterate, lasting, lifelong, never-ending, never-failing, permanent, perpetual, persistent, recurrent, sempiternal, unceasing, unchanging, undying, unfailing, uninterrupted.

perfect *adj.* absolute, accomplished, accurate, adept, blameless, close, complete, completed, consummate, copybook, correct, entire, exact, excellent, experienced, expert, faithful, faultless, finished, flawless, full, ideal, immaculate, impeccable, irreproachable, masterly, model, polished, practised, precise, pure, right, sheer, skilful, skilled, splendid, spotless, spot-on, strict, sublime, superb, superlative, supreme, true, unadulterated, unalloyed, unblemished, unerring, unimpeachable, unmarred, unmitigated, untarnished, utter, whole.
antonyms flawed, imperfect.
v. accomplish, achieve, carry out, complete, consummate, effect, elaborate, finish, fulfil, perfectionate, perform, realise, refine.

perfection *n.* accomplishment, achievement, acme, completeness, completion, consummation, crown, evolution, exactness, excellence, exquisiteness, flawlessness, fulfilment, ideal, integrity, maturity, nonpareil, paragon, perfectness, pinnacle, precision, purity, realisation, sublimity, superiority, wholeness.
antonyms flaw, imperfection.

perfectionist *n.* formalist, idealist, precisian, precisionist, purist, stickler.

perfectly *adv.* absolutely, admirably, altogether, completely, consummately, entirely, exquisitely, faultlessly, flawlessly, fully, ideally, impeccably, incomparably, irreproachably, quite, superbly, superlatively, supremely, thoroughly, to perfection, totally, unimpeachably, utterly, wholly, wonderfully.
antonyms imperfectly, partially.

perfidious *adj.* corrupt, deceitful, dishonest, disloyal, double-dealing, double-faced, duplicitous, faithless, false, Machiavellian, Punic, recreant, traitorous, treacherous, treasonous, two-faced, unfaithful, untrustworthy.
antonyms faithful, honest, loyal.

perfidy *n.* betrayal, deceit, disloyalty, double-dealing, duplicity, faithlessness, falsity, infidelity, perfidiousness, Punic faith, traitorousness, treachery, treason.
antonyms faithfulness, honesty, loyalty.

perforate *v.* bore, drill, hole, honeycomb, penetrate, pierce, prick, punch, puncture, stab.

perforated *adj.* bored, drilled, ethmoid, fenestrate(d), fenestrial, foraminous, holed, pierced, porous, punched, punctured.

perforation *n.* bore, cut, dotted line, fenestration, hole, prick, puncture, slit, space.

perforce *adv.* inevitably, necessarily, of necessity, unavoidably, willy-nilly.

perform *v.* accomplish, achieve, act, appear as, bring about, bring off, carry out, complete, depict, discharge, do, effect, enact, execute, fulfil, function, functionate, manage, observe, play, present, produce, pull off, put on, render, represent, satisfy, stage, transact, work.

performance *n.* accomplishment, account,

achievement, act, acting, action, appearance, behaviour, bother, business, carrying out, carry-on, completion, conduct, consummation, discharge, efficiency, execution, exhibition, exploit, feat, fulfilment, functioning, fuss, gig, implementation, interpretation, melodrama, operation, play, portrayal, practice, presentation, production, rendition, representation, rigmarole, running, show, to-do, work, working.

performer *n.* actor, actress, artiste, moke, mummer, play-actor, player, Thespian, trouper.

perfume *n.* aroma, attar, balm, balminess, bouquet, cologne, essence, fragrance, incense, odour, redolence, scent, smell, sweetness, toilet water.

perfunctory *adj.* automatic, brief, careless, cursory, heedless, hurried, inattentive, indifferent, mechanical, negligent, offhand, routine, sketchy, slipshod, slovenly, stereotyped, superficial, wooden.
antonym cordial.

perhaps *adv.* conceivably, feasibly, happen, maybe, mayhap, peradventure, perchance, possibly, you never know.

peril *n.* danger, exposure, hazard, imperilment, insecurity, jeopardy, menace, pitfall, risk, threat, uncertainty, vulnerability.
antonyms safety, security.

perilous *adj.* chancy, dangerous, desperate, dicey, difficult, dire, exposed, hairy, hazardous, menacing, parlous, precarious, risky, threatening, unsafe, unsure, vulnerable.
antonyms safe, secure.

perimeter *n.* ambit, border, borderline, boundary, bounds, circumference, confines, edge, fringe, frontier, limit, margin, periphery.
antonyms centre, heart, middle.

period[1] *n.* aeon, age, course, cycle, date, days, end, epoch, era, generation, interval, season, space, span, spell, stage, stint, stop, stretch, term, time, turn, while, years.

period[2] *n.* menses, menstrual flow, menstruation, monthlies, the curse.

periodic *adj.* cyclic, cyclical, desultory, etesian, infrequent, intermittent, occasional, periodical, recurrent, regular, repeated, seasonal, spasmodic, sporadic.

periodical *n.* gazette, journal, magazine, monthly, organ, paper, publication, quarterly, review, serial, weekly.

peripatetic *adj.* ambulant, ambulatory, itinerant, journeying, migrant, mobile, nomadic, roaming, roving, travelling, vagabond, vagrant, wandering.
antonym fixed.

peripheral *adj.* borderline, exterior, external, incidental, inessential, irrelevant, marginal, minor, outer, outermost, outlying, outside, perimetric, secondary, superficial, surface, tangential, unimportant, unnecessary.
antonyms central, crucial.

periphery *n.* ambit, border, boundary, brim, brink, circuit, circumference, edge, fringe,

hem, margin, outskirts, perimeter, rim, skirt, verge.
antonyms centre, nub.

perish *v.* collapse, croak, crumble, decay, decline, decompose, decrease, die, disappear, disintegrate, end, expire, fall, moulder, pass away, rot, vanish, waste, wither.

perishable *adj.* biodegradable, corruptible, decomposable, destructible, fast-decaying, fast-deteriorating, short-lived, unstable.

perjury *n.* false oath, false statement, false swearing, false witness, falsification, forswearing, mendacity.

perk *n.* benefit, bonus, bunce, dividend, extra, freebie, fringe benefit, perquisite, plus.

perk up brighten, buck up, cheer up, improve, liven up, look up, pep up, rally, recover, recuperate, revive, take heart, upturn.

perky *adj.* animated, bouncy, bright, bubbly, buoyant, cheerful, cheery, effervescent, gay, jaunty, lively, peppy, spirited, sprightly, sunny, vivacious.
antonyms cheerless, dull, gloomy.

permanence *n.* constancy, continuance, continuity, deathlessness, dependability, durability, duration, endurance, finality, fixedness, fixity, immortality, imperishability, indestructibility, lastingness, longevity, perdurability, permanency, perpetuity, stability, survival.
antonym impermanence.

permanent *adj.* abiding, constant, durable, enduring, everlasting, fixed, immutable, imperishable, indestructible, ineffaceable, ineradicable, inerasable, invariable, lasting, long-lasting, perennial, perpetual, persistent, stable, standing, steadfast, unchanging, unfading.
antonyms ephemeral, fleeting, temporary.

permanently *adv.* always, ceaselessly, constantly, continually, endlessly, eternally, ever more, everlastingly, for keeps, forever, once and for all, umremittingly, unendingly.
antonym temporarily.

permeable *adj.* absorbent, absorptive, passable, penetrable, pervious, porous, spongeous, spongy.
antonyms impermeable, watertight.

permeate *v.* charge, fill, filter through, imbue, impenetrate, impregnate, infiltrate, interfuse, interpenetrate, pass through, penetrate, percolate, pervade, saturate, seep through, soak through.

permissible *adj.* acceptable, admissible, all right, allowable, allowed, authorised, kosher, lawful, leal, legit, legitimate, licit, OK, permitted, proper, sanctioned.
antonym prohibited.

permission *n.* allowance, approval, assent, authorisation, consent, dispensation, freedom, go-ahead, green light, imprimatur, indult, leave, liberty, licence, permit, sanction, sufferance.
antonym prohibition.

permissive *adj.* acquiescent, complaisant, easy-going, forbearing, free, indulgent, latitudinarian, lax, lenient, liberal, open-minded, overindulgent, tolerant.
antonym strict.

permit *v.* admit, agree, allow, authorise, consent, empower, enable, endorse, endure, give leave, grant, let, warrant.
antonym prohibit.

n. authorisation, carnet, liberty, licence, pass, passport, permission, sanction, visa, warrant.
antonym prohibition.

permutation *n.* alteration, change, commutation, shift, transformation, transmutation, transposition, transubstantiation.

pernicious *adj.* bad, baleful, baneful, damaging, dangerous, deadly, deleterious, destructive, detrimental, evil, fatal, harmful, hurtful, injurious, maleficent, malevolent, malicious, malign, malignant, noisome, noxious, offensive, pestilent, poisonous, ruinous, toxic, unhealthy, unwholesome, venomous, wicked.
antonym innocuous.

pernickety *adj.* careful, carping, detailed, exacting, fastidious, fiddly, fikish, fiky, fine, finical, finicky, fussy, hair-splitting, nice, nit-picking, over-precise, painstaking, particular, punctilious, tricky.

peroration *n.* closing remarks, conclusion, recapitulation, recapping, reiteration, summary, summing-up.

perpendicular *adj.* plumb, precipitous, sheer, straight, upright, vertical.
antonym horizontal.

perpetrate *v.* carry out, commit, do, effect, enact, execute, inflict, perform, practise, wreak.

perpetual *adj.* abiding, ceaseless, constant, continual, continuous, deathless, endless, enduring, eternal, everlasting, immortal, incessant, infinite, interminable, lasting, never-ending, never-failing, perennial, permanent, persistent, recurrent, repeated, sempiternal, unceasing, unchanging, undying, unending, unfailing, unflagging, uninterrupted, unremitting, unvarying.
antonyms ephemeral, intermittent, transient.

perpetuate *v.* commemorate, continue, eternalise, immortalise, keep alive, keep up, maintain, preserve, protract, sustain.

perplex *v.* baffle, befuddle, beset, bewilder, complicate, confound, confuse, dumbfound, embrangle, encumber, entangle, gravel, hobble, involve, jumble, mix up, muddle, mystify, nonplus, pother, pudder, puzzle, stump, tangle, thicken, throw.

perplexed *adj.* at a loss, baffled, bamboozled, bewildered, confounded, disconcerted, fuddled, muddled, mystified, puzzled, worried.

perplexing *adj.* amazing, baffling, bewildering, complex, complicated, confusing, difficult, distractive, enigmatic, hard, inexplicable, intricate, involved, knotty, labyrinthine, mysterious, mystifying, paradoxical, puzzling, strange, taxing, thorny, unaccountable, vexatious, weird.
antonyms easy, simple.

perplexity *n.* bafflement, bewilderment, complexity, confusion, difficulty, dilemma, enigma, incomprehension, intricacy, involvement, labyrinth, mystery, mystification, nonplus, obfuscation, obscuration, obscurity, paradox, puzzle, puzzlement, snarl, stupefaction.

perquisite *n.* ap(p)anage, baksheesh, benefit, bonus, dividend, extra, fringe benefit, gratuity, perk, plus, tip.

persecute *v.* afflict, annoy, badger, bait, bother, castigate, crucify, distress, dragoon, harass, haze, hound, hunt, ill-treat, injure, maltreat, martyr, molest, oppress, pester, pursue, tease, torment, torture, tyrannise, vex, victimise, worry.
antonyms accommodate, humour, indulge, pamper.

persecution *n.* abuse, baiting, bashing, castigation, discrimination, maltreatment, molestation, oppression, punishment, subjugation, suppression, torture, tyranny.

perseverance *n.* abidance, assiduity, constancy, dedication, determination, diligence, doggedness, endurance, indefatigability, persistence, pertinacity, purposefulness, resolution, sedulity, stamina, steadfastness, tenacity.

persevere *v.* adhere, carry on, continue, endure, go on, hang on, hold fast, hold on, keep going, persist, plug away, pursue, remain, soldier on, stand firm, stick at.
antonyms desist, discontinue, give up, stop.

persist *v.* abide, carry on, continue, endure, insist, keep at it, last, linger, perdure, persevere, remain, stand fast, stand firm.
antonyms desist, stop.

persistence *n.* assiduity, assiduousness, constancy, determination, diligence, doggedness, endurance, grit, indefatigableness, perseverance, pertinacity, pluck, resolution, sedulity, stamina, steadfastness, tenacity, tirelessness.

persistent *adj.* assiduous, constant, continual, continuous, determined, dogged, endless, enduring, fixed, hydra-headed, immovable, incessant, indefatigable, indomitable, interminable, never-ending, obdurate, obstinate, perpetual, persevering, pertinacious, relentless, repeated, resolute, steadfast, steady, stubborn, tenacious, tireless, unflagging, unrelenting, unremitting, zealous.

person *n.* being, bod, body, cat, chal, character, codger, cookie, customer, human, human being, individual, individuum, living soul, party, soul, specimen, type, wight.

persona *n.* character, façade, face, front, image, mask, part, personality, public face, role.

personable *adj.* affable, agreeable, amiable, attractive, charming, good-looking, handsome, lik(e)able, nice, outgoing, pleasant, pleasing, presentable, warm, winning.
antonyms disagreeable, unattractive.

personage *n.* big shot, celebrity, dignitary, headliner, luminary, name, notable, personality, public figure, somebody, VIP, worthy.

personal *adj.* bodily, corporeal, corporeal,

derogatory, disparaging, exclusive, exterior, idiosyncratic, individual, inimitable, insulting, intimate, material, nasty, offensive, own, particular, peculiar, pejorative, physical, private, privy, slighting, special, tête-à-tête.
antonyms general, public, universal.

personality *n.* attraction, attractiveness, celebrity, character, charisma, charm, disposition, dynamism, humour, identity, individuality, lik(e)ableness, magnetism, make-up, nature, notable, personage, pleasantness, psyche, selfhood, selfness, star, temper, temperament, traits.

personally *adv.* alone, idiosyncratically, independently, individually, privately, solely, specially, subjectively.

personification *n.* delineation, embodiment, image, incarnation, likeness, manifestation, portrayal, recreation, representation, semblance.

personify *v.* embody, epitomise, exemplify, express, hypostatise, image, incarnate, mirror, personise, represent, symbolise, typify.

personnel *n.* crew, employees, helpers, human resources, liveware, manpower, members, people, staff, workers, workforce.

perspective *n.* angle, aspect, attitude, context, objectivity, outlook, overview, panorama, proportion, prospect, relation, scene, slant, view, vista.

perspicacious *adj.* acute, alert, astute, aware, clear-eyed, clear-sighted, clever, discerning, far-sighted, keen, observant, penetrating, perceptive, percipient, sagacious, sharp, sharp-witted, shrewd.
antonyms obtuse, unobservant.

perspicacity *n.* acuity, acumen, acuteness, brains, cleverness, discernment, discrimination, insight, keenness, penetration, perceptiveness, percipience, perspicaciousness, perspicuity, sagaciousness, sagacity, sharpness, shrewdness, wit.

perspicuity *n.* clarity, clearness, comprehensibility, comprehensibleness, distinctness, explicitness, intelligibility, limpidity, limpidness, lucidity, penetrability, plainness, precision, straightforwardness, transparency.

perspicuous *adj.* apparent, clear, comprehensible, crystal-clear, distinct, explicit, intelligible, limpid, lucid, manifest, obvious, plain, self-evident, straightforward, transparent, unambiguous, understandable.

perspiration *n.* dew, diaphoresis, exudation, hidrosis, moisture, sudor, sweat, wetness.

perspire *v.* drip, exude, glow, secrete, sudate, sweat, swelter.

persuadable *adj.* acquiescent, agreeable, amenable, compliant, flexible, impressionable, malleable, persuasible, pliable, receptive, susceptive.
antonyms firm, inflexible, stubborn.

persuade *v.* actuate, advise, allure, bring round, cajole, coax, convert, convince, counsel, entice, impel, incite, induce, influence, inveigle, lead on, lean on, prevail upon, prompt, satisfy, sway, sweet-talk, talk into, urge, win over.

antonyms discourage, dissuade.

persuasion *n.* belief, blandishment, cajolery, camp, certitude, cogency, come-on, conversion, conviction, credo, creed, cult, denomination, enticement, exhortation, faction, faith, force, inducement, influence, inveiglement, opinion, party, persuasiveness, potency, power, pull, school (of thought), sect, side, suasion, sweet talk, tenet, views, wheedling.

persuasive *adj.* cogent, compelling, convincing, credible, effective, eloquent, forceful, honeyed, impelling, impressive, inducing, influential, logical, moving, persuasory, plausible, potent, sound, telling, touching, valid, weighty, whilly, whillywha(w), winning.

pert *adj.* bold, brash, brisk, cheeky, daring, dicacious, flip, flippant, forward, fresh, gay, impertinent, impudent, insolent, jaunty, lively, nimble, perky, presumptuous, saucy, smart, spirited, sprightly, tossy.

antonyms coy, shy.

pertain *v.* appertain, apply, be appropriate, be part of, be relevant, bear on, befit, belong, come under, concern, refer, regard, relate.

pertinacious *adj.* determined, dogged, headstrong, inflexible, intractable, mulish, obdurate, obstinate, persevering, persistent, perverse, purposeful, relentless, resolute, self-willed, strong-willed, stubborn, tenacious, uncompromising, unyielding, wilful.

pertinent *adj.* ad rem, admissible, analogous, applicable, apposite, appropriate, apropos, apt, befitting, fit, fitting, germane, material, pat, proper, relevant, suitable, to the point, to the purpose.

antonyms inappropriate, irrelevant, unsuitable.

pertness *n.* audacity, boldness, brashness, brass, brazenness, bumptiousness, cheek, cheekiness, chutzpah, cockiness, didacity, effrontery, forwardness, freshness, impertinence, impudence, insolence, presumption, rudeness, sauciness.

perturb *v.* aerate, agitate, alarm, bother, confuse, disarrange, discompose, disconcert, discountenance, disorder, disquiet, disturb, faze, feeze, fluster, muddle, ruffle, trouble, unsettle, upset, vex, worry.

antonyms compose, reassure.

perturbed *adj.* agitated, alarmed, anxious, discomposed, disconcerted, disturbed, fearful, flurried, flustered, nervous, restless, shaken, troubled, uncomfortable, uneasy, unsettled, upset, worried.

antonym unperturbed.

perusal *n.* browse, check, examination, inspection, look, read, run-through, scrutiny, study.

peruse *v.* browse, check, examine, inspect, look through, pore over, read, scan, scrutinise, study, vet.

pervade *v.* affect, charge, diffuse, extend, fill, imbue, infuse, osmose, overspread, penetrate, percolate, permeate, saturate, suffuse.

pervasive *adj.* common, diffuse, extensive, general, immanent, inescapable, omnipresent, permeating, pervading, prevalent, rife, ubiquitous, universal, widespread.

perverse *adj.* abnormal, balky, camstairy, cantankerous, churlish, contradictory, contrary, contumacious, crabbed, cross, cross-grained, cussed, delinquent, depraved, deviant, disobedient, dogged, fractious, froward, headstrong, ill-natured, ill-tempered, improper, incorrect, intractable, intransigent, miscreant, mulish, obdurate, obstinate, peevish, petulant, pig-headed, rebellious, recalcitrant, refractory, spiteful, stroppy, stubborn, surly, thrawn, thwart, troublesome, unhealthy, unmanageable, unreasonable, unyielding, uppity, wayward, wilful, wrong-headed, wry.

antonyms normal, reasonable.

perversion *n.* aberration, abnormality, anomaly, corruption, debauchery, depravity, deviance, deviancy, deviation, distortion, falsification, immorality, kink, kinkiness, misapplication, misinterpretation, misrepresentation, misuse, paraphilia, twisting, unnaturalness, vice, vitiation, wickedness.

perversity *n.* contradictoriness, contrariness, contumacy, cussedness, frowardness, gee, intransigence, obduracy, protervity, refractoriness, waywardness, wrong-headedness.

pervert *v.* abuse, bend, corrupt, debase, debauch, degrade, deprave, distort, divert, falsify, garble, lead astray, misapply, misconstrue, misinterpret, misrepresent, misuse, subvert, twist, vitiate, warp, wrest.

n. debauchee, degenerate, deviant, paraphiliac, vert, weirdo.

perverted *adj.* aberrant, abnormal, corrupt, debased, debauched, depraved, deviant, distorted, evil, freakish, immoral, impaired, kinky, misguided, queer, sick, twisted, unhealthy, unnatural, vicious, vitiated, warped, wicked.

pessimism *n.* cynicism, dejection, depression, despair, despondency, distrust, doomwatch, gloom, gloominess, glumness, hopelessness, melancholy, Weltschmerz.

antonym optimism.

pessimist *n.* Cassandra, cynic, defeatist, dismal Jimmy, doomster, doomwatcher, gloom and doom merchant, killjoy, melancholic, wet blanket, worrier.

antonym optimist.

pessimistic *adj.* bleak, cynical, dark, defeatist, dejected, depressed, despairing, despondent, dismal, distrustful, downhearted, fatalistic, gloomy, glum, hopeless, melancholy, misanthropic, morose, resigned, sad, worried.

antonym optimistic.

pest *n.* annoyance, bane, blight, bore, bother, bug, canker, curse, irritation, nuisance, pain (in the neck), scourge, thorn in one's flesh, trial, vexation.

pester *v.* annoy, badger, bedevil, bother, bug, chivvy, disturb, dog, drive round the bend, drive up the wall, fret, get at, harass, harry, hassle, hector, hound, irk, nag, pick on, plague, ride, torment, worry.

pestilent *adj.* annoying, bothersome, catching, communicable, contagious, contaminated, corrupting, deleterious, destructive, detrimental, diseased, disease-ridden, evil, galling, harmful, infected, infectious, injurious, irksome, irritating, morbiferous, morbific, pernicious, plague-ridden, plagu(e)y, ruinous, tainted, tiresome, vexing, vicious.

pestilential *adj.* annoying, catching, contagious, contaminated, dangerous, deadly, deleterious, destructive, detrimental, disease-ridden, evil, foul, harmful, hazardous, infectious, injurious, malignant, morbiferous, morbific, noxious, pernicious, pesky, pestiferous, poisonous, ruinous, troublesome, venomous.

pet *n.* darling, dautie, dilling, doll, duck, ewe-lamb, favourite, idol, jewel, treasure, whitehead.
adj. cherished, dearest, favoured, favourite, particular, preferred, special.
v. baby, canoodle, caress, coddle, cosset, cuddle, daut, dote on, fondle, indulge, kiss, mollycoddle, neck, pamper, pat, smooch, snog, spoil, stroke.

peter out cease, dissolve, dwindle, ebb, evaporate, fade, fail, stop, taper off, wane.

petite *adj.* bijou, dainty, delicate, dinky, elfin, little, slight, small.
antonyms big, large.

petition *n.* address, appeal, application, boon, entreaty, imploration, invocation, plea, prayer, request, rogation, round robin, solicitation, suit, supplication.
v. appeal, ask, beg, beseech, bid, call upon, crave, entreat, implore, memorialise, plead, pray, press, solicit, sue, supplicate, urge.

pet-name *n.* diminutive, endearment, hypocorisma, nickname.

petrified *adj.* aghast, appalled, benumbed, dazed, dumbfounded, fossilised, frozen, horrified, horror-stricken, numb, ossified, scared stiff, shocked, speechless, stunned, stupefied, terrified, terror-stricken.

petrify *v.* amaze, appal, astonish, astound, benumb, calcify, confound, dumbfound, fossilise, gorgonise, harden, horrify, immobilise, numb, paralyse, set, solidify, stun, stupefy, terrify, transfix, turn to stone.

petticoat *n.* crinoline, farthingale, half-slip, jupon, kirtle, slip, underskirt.

pettifogging *adj.* captious, casuistic, cavilling, circumlocutory, equivocating, hair-splitting, mean, niggling, nit-picking, over-refined, paltry, petty, quibbling, sophistical, sophisticated, subtle.

pettish *adj.* cross, fractious, fretful, grumpy, huffy, ill-humoured, irritable, peevish, petulant, querulous, snappish, splenetic, sulky, tetchy, thin-skinned, touchy, waspish.

petty *adj.* cheap, contemptible, grudging, inconsiderable, inessential, inferior, insignificant, junior, lesser, little, lower, mean, measly, minor, negligible, one-horse, paltry, picayune, picayunish, piddling, pimping, poking, poky, secondary, shabby, slight, small, small-minded, spiteful, stingy, subordinate, trifling, trivial, ungenerous, unimportant.
antonyms generous, important, large-hearted, significant, vital.

petulance *n.* bad temper, crabbedness, crabbiness, ill-humour, ill-temper, irritability, peevishness, pettishness, pique, procacity, querulousness, spleen, sulkiness, sullenness, waspishness.

petulant *adj.* bad-tempered, captious, cavilling, crabbed, cross, crusty, fretful, ill-humoured, impatient, irascible, irritable, moody, peevish, perverse, pettish, procacious, querulous, snappish, sour, sulky, sullen, ungracious, waspish.

phantom *n.* apparition, chimera, eidolon, figment (of the imagination), ghost, hallucination, illusion, manes, phantasm(a), revenant, shade, simulacrum, spectre, spirit, spook, vision, wraith.

pharisaical *adj.* canting, formal, goody-goody, holier-than-thou, hypocritical, insincere, moralising, pharisaic, pietistic, preachy, sanctimonious, self-righteous, Tartuf(f)ian, Tartuf(f)ish.

pharisee *n.* canter, dissembler, dissimulator, fraud, Holy Willie, humbug, hypocrite, phoney, pietist, Tartuf(f)e, whited sepulchre.

phase *n.* aspect, chapter, condition, development, juncture, period, point, position, season, spell, stage, state, step, time.
phase out close, deactivate, dispose of, ease off, eliminate, get rid of, remove, replace, run down, taper off, terminate, wind down, withdraw.

phenomenal *adj.* amazing, exceptional, extraordinary, fantastic, marvellous, miraculous, outstanding, prodigious, remarkable, sensational, singular, stupendous, uncommon, unique, unparalleled, unusual, wondrous.

phenomenon *n.* appearance, circumstance, curiosity, episode, event, fact, happening, incident, marvel, miracle, occurrence, prodigy, rarity, sensation, sight, spectacle, wonder.

philanderer *n.* Casanova, dallier, Don Juan, flirt, gallant, gay deceiver, ladies' man, lady-killer, libertine, Lothario, playboy, stud, trifler, venerean, wencher, wolf, womaniser.

philanthropic *adj.* alms-giving, altruistic, beneficent, benevolent, benignant, bounteous, bountiful, charitable, eleemosynary, gracious, humane, humanitarian, kind, kind-hearted, kindly, munificent, public-spirited.
antonym misanthropic.

philanthropist *n.* alms-giver, altruist, angel, benefactor, contributor, donor, giver, good fairy, humanitarian, patron.
antonyms misanthrope, misanthropist.

philanthropy *n.* agape, alms-giving, altruism,

beneficence, benevolence, benignity, bounty, brotherly love, charitableness, charity, generosity, humanitarianism, kind-heartedness, liberality, munificence, open-handedness, patronage, public-spiritedness, unselfishness.

Philistine *n.* Babbit, barbarian, Boeotian, boor, bourgeois, Goth, ignoramus, lout, lowbrow, vulgarian, yahoo.
antonym aesthete.
adj. Boeotian, boorish, bourgeois, crass, ignorant, lowbrow, tasteless, uncultivated, uncultured, uneducated, unlettered, unread, unrefined.

philosopher *n.* deipnosophist, dialectician, epistemologist, logician, metaphysician, sage, theorist, thinker, vocabularian.

philosophical *adj.* abstract, analytical, calm, collected, composed, cool, dispassionate, equanimous, erudite, impassive, imperturbable, learned, logical, metaphysical, patient, philosophic, rational, resigned, sagacious, serene, stoical, theoretical, thoughtful, tranquil, unruffled, wise.

philosophy *n.* aesthetics, attitude, beliefs, convictions, doctrine, epistemology, ideology, knowledge, logic, metaphysics, principle, rationale, rationalism, reason, reasoning, tenets, thinking, thought, values, viewpoint, Weltanschauung, wisdom, world-view.

phlegmatic *adj.* apathetic, bovine, cold, dull, frigid, heavy, impassive, imperturbable, indifferent, lethargic, listless, lymphatic, matter-of-fact, nonchalant, placid, sluggish, stoical, stolid, unconcerned, undemonstrative, unemotional.
antonyms demonstrative, passionate.

phobia *n.* anxiety, aversion, detestation, dislike, distaste, dread, fear, hang-up, hatred, horror, loathing, neurosis, obsession, phobism, repulsion, revulsion, terror, thing.
antonyms liking, love.

phoney *adj.* affected, assumed, bogus, counterfeit, fake, false, forged, imitation, pseudo, put-on, quack, quacksalving, sham, spurious, trick.
antonyms real, true.
n. counterfeit, fake, faker, forgery, fraud, humbug, imposter, mountebank, pretender, pseud, quack, sham.

phosphorescent *adj.* bright, glowing, luminescent, luminous, noctilucent, noctilucous, radiant, refulgent.

photograph *n.* ambrotype, angiogram, daguerreotype, ferrotype, image, likeness, photo, picture, print, shot, slide, snap, snapshot, transparency.
v. film, record, shoot, snap, take, video.

photographic *adj.* accurate, cinematic, detailed, exact, faithful, filmic, graphic, lifelike, minute, natural, naturalistic, pictorial, precise, realistic, representational, retentive, visual, vivid.

phrase *n.* construction, expression, idiom, locution, mention, motto, remark, saying, tag, utterance.

v. couch, express, formulate, frame, present, pronounce, put, say, style, term, utter, voice, word.

phraseology *n.* argot, cant, diction, expression, idiom, language, parlance, patois, phrase, phrasing, speech, style, syntax, wording.

physical *adj.* actual, bodily, carnal, concrete, corporal, corporeal, earthly, fleshly, incarnate, material, mortal, natural, palpable, real, sensible, solid, somatic, substantial, tangible, visible.
antonyms mental, spiritual.

physician *n.* doc, doctor, doctor of medicine, general practitioner, GP, hakim, healer, houseman, intern, leech, MD, medic, medical practitioner, medico, registrar, specialist.

physiognomy *n.* clock, countenance, dial, face, features, look, mug, phiz, phizog, visage, visnomy.

physique *n.* body, build, chassis, constitution, figure, form, frame, make-up, shape, structure.

pick *v.* break into, break open, choose, collect, crack, cull, cut, decide on, elect, embrace, espouse, fix upon, foment, gather, harvest, incite, instigate, opt for, pluck, prise, provoke, pull, screen, select, settle on, sift out, single out, start.
antonym reject.
n. best, brightest and best, choice, choicest, choosing, cream, crème de la crème, decision, elect, élite, flower, option, preference, pride, prize, selection, tops.

pick at nibble, peck, play with, toy with.

pick off detach, drill, hit, kill, plug, remove, shoot, strike.

pick on badger, bait, blame, bully, carp at, cavil at, criticise, find fault with, get at, nag, needle, quibble with, tease, torment.

pick out choose, cull, differentiate, discriminate, distinguish, hand-pick, notice, perceive, recognise, select, separate, single out, tell apart.

pick up acquire, apprehend, arrest, bust, buy, call for, collar, collect, come across, fetch, find, gain, gain ground, garner, gather, grasp, happen on, hoist, improve, learn, lift, master, mend, nab, nick, obtain, perk up, pinch, pull in, purchase, raise, rally, recover, recuperate, run in, score, snap up, uplift.

picket *n.* demonstrator, dissenter, guard, lookout, outpost, pale, paling, palisade, patrol, peg, picketer, post, protestor, scout, sentinel, sentry, spotter, stake, stanchion, upright, vedette, watchman.
v. blockade, boycott, corral, demonstrate, enclose, fence, hedge in, palisade, pen in, protest.

pickings *n.* booty, bunce, earnings, gravy, loot, plunder, proceeds, profits, returns, rewards, spoils, take, yield.

pickle *n.* bind, crisis, difficulty, dilemma, exigency, fix, hot water, jam, pinch, predicament, quandary, scrape, spot, straits, tight spot.

v. conserve, cure, marinade, preserve, steep.

pick-me-up *n.* boost, cordial, fillip, refreshment, restorative, roborant, shot in the arm, stimulant, tonic.

pick-pocket *n.* dip, diver, file, pick-purse, snatcher, wire.

picnic[1] *n.* excursion, fête champêtre, outdoor meal, outing, wayzgoose.

picnic[2] *n.* child's play, cinch, doddle, piece of cake, pushover, sinecure, snap, walkover.

pictorial *adj.* diagrammatic, expressive, graphic, illustrated, picturesque, representational, scenic, schematic, striking, vivid.

picture *n.* account, archetype, carbon copy, copy, dead ringer, delineation, depiction, description, double, drawing, duplicate, effigy, embodiment, engraving, epitome, essence, film, flick, graphic, illustration, image, impression, kakemono, likeness, living image, lookalike, motion picture, movie, painting, personification, photograph, portrait, portrayal, print, re-creation, replica, report, representation, ringer, scene, similitude, sketch, spit, spitting image, tablature, table, twin, vraisemblance.
v. conceive of, delineate, depict, describe, draw, envisage, envision, illustrate, image, imagine, paint, photograph, portray, render, represent, see, show, sketch, visualise.

picturesque *adj.* attractive, beautiful, charming, colourful, descriptive, graphic, pretty, quaint, scenic, striking, vivid.

piebald *adj.* brindled, dappled, flecked, mottled, pied, skewbald, speckled, spotted.

piece *n.* allotment, article, bit, case, chunk, component, composition, constituent, creation, division, element, example, fraction, fragment, instance, item, length, mammock, morsel, mouthful, objet d'art, occurrence, offcut, part, piecemeal, portion, production, quantity, sample, scrap, section, segment, share, shred, slice, snippet, specimen, stroke, study, work, work of art.
piece together assemble, attach, compose, fit, fix, join, mend, patch, repair, restore, unite.

pièce de résistance *n.* chef-d'oeuvre, jewel, magnum opus, masterpiece, masterwork, prize, showpiece.

piecemeal *adv.* at intervals, bit by bit, by degrees, fitfully, in dribs and drabs, in penny numbers, intermittently, little by little, parcel-wise, partially, slowly.
antonyms completely, entirely, wholly.
adj. discrete, fragmentary, intermittent, interrupted, partial, patchy, scattered, unsystematic.
antonyms complete, entire, whole, wholesale.

pied *adj.* brindle(d), dappled, flecked, irregular, motley, mottled, multicoloured, particoloured, piebald, skewbald, spotted, streaked, varicoloured, variegated.

pier *n.* buttress, column, jetty, jutty, landing-place, pile, piling, pillar, post, promenade, quay, support, upright, wharf.

pierce *v.* affect, barb, bore, comprehend, discern, discover, drift, drill, enter, excite, fathom, grasp, gride, hurt, impale, lancinate, move, pain, penetrate, perforate, pink, prick, probe, prog, puncture, realise, rouse, run through, see, spike, stab, stick into, sting, stir, strike, thrill, thrust, touch, transfix, transpierce, understand, wound.

pierced *adj.* impaled, perforated, pertusate, pertuse(d), punctured, stung.

piercing *adj.* acute, agonising, alert, algid, arctic, aware, biting, bitter, cold, ear-piercing, ear-splitting, excruciating, exquisite, fierce, freezing, frore, frosty, gelid, high-pitched, intense, keen, loud, nipping, nippy, numbing, painful, penetrating, perceptive, perspicacious, powerful, probing, quick-witted, racking, raw, searching, severe, sharp, shattering, shooting, shrewd, shrill, Siberian, stabbing, wintry.

piety *n.* devotion, devoutness, dutifulness, duty, faith, godliness, grace, holiness, piousness, religion, religiosity, reverence, saintliness, sanctity, veneration.
antonym impiety.

piffle *n.* balderdash, balls, bullshit, bunk, bunkum, codswallop, drivel, guff, hooey, nonsense, poppycock, rot, rubbish, tarradiddle, tommy-rot, tosh, trash, tripe, twaddle.

pig *n.* animal, beast, boar, boor, brute, glutton, gormandiser, go(u)rmand, greedy guts, grunter, guzzler, hog, piggy, piglet, porker, shoat, slob, sloven, sow, swine.

pigeonhole *n.* box, category, class, classification, compartment, cubbyhole, cubicle, locker, niche, place, section, slot.
v. alphabetise, catalogue, characterise, classify, codify, compartmentalise, defer, file, label, postpone, put off, shelve, slot, sort, typecast.

pig-headed *adj.* bull-headed, contrary, cross-grained, dense, froward, inflexible, intractable, intransigent, mulish, obstinate, perverse, self-willed, stiff-necked, stubborn, stupid, unyielding, wilful, wrong-headed.
antonyms flexible, tractable.

pigment *n.* colour, colo(u)rant, colouring, colouring matter, dye, dyestuff, hue, paint, stain, tempera, tincture, tint.

pile[1] *n.* accumulation, assemblage, assortment, bing, bomb, building, cock, collection, edifice, erection, fortune, heap, hoard, mass, mint, money, mound, mountain, mow, packet, pot, stack, stockpile, structure, wealth.
v. accumulate, amass, assemble, build up, charge, climb, collect, crowd, crush, flock, flood, gather, heap, hoard, jam, load up, mass, pack, rush, stack, store, stream.

pile[2] *n.* bar, beam, column, foundation, pier, piling, pill, post, rib, stanchion, support, upright.

pile[3] *n.* down, fur, fuzz, fuzziness, hair, nap, plush, shag.

piles[1] *n.* a great deal, a lot, loads, millions, oceans, oodles, quantities, stacks.

piles[2] *n.* haemorrhoids.

pilfer *v.* appropriate, embezzle, filch, finger, help oneself to, knock off, lift, mooch, nick, peculate, pickle, pinch, purloin, rifle, rob, steal, thieve.

pilgrim *n.* crusader, hadji, palmer, peregrine, traveller, wanderer, wayfarer.

pilgrimage *n.* crusade, excursion, expedition, hadj, journey, mission, odyssey, peregrination, tour, trip.

pill *n.* ball, bolus, capsule, contraceptive, globule, pellet, pilule, tablet.

pillage *v.* depredate, despoil, freeboot, loot, maraud, plunder, raid, ransack, ravage, raze, reive, rifle, rob, sack, spoil, spoliate, strip, vandalise.

n. booty, depredation, devastation, harrying, loot, marauding, plunder, rapine, robbery, sack, seizure, spoils, spoliation.

pillar *n.* balluster, bastion, cippus, column, leader, leading light, mainstay, mast, pier, pilaster, piling, post, prop, rock, shaft, stanchion, support, supporter, tower of strength, upholder, upright, worthy.

pillory *v.* brand, cast a slur on, denounce, hold up to shame, lash, mock, pour scorn on, ridicule, show up, stigmatise.

pilot *n.* airman, aviator, captain, conductor, coxswain, director, flier, guide, helmsman, hobbler, hoveller, leader, lodesman, navigator, steersman.

v. boss, conduct, control, direct, drive, fly, guide, handle, lead, manage, navigate, operate, run, shepherd, steer.

adj. experimental, model, test, trial.

pimp *n.* bawd, fancy man, fleshmonger, go-between, mack, pander, panderer, procurer, white-slaver, whoremaster, whoremonger.

pimple *n.* black-head, boil, papula, papule, plook, pustule, quat, spot, swelling, whelk, zit.

pin *v.* affix, attach, fasten, fix, hold down, hold fast, immobilise, join, nail, pinion, press, restrain, secure, tack.

n. bolt, breastpin, brooch, clip, fastener, nail, peg, rivet, screw, spike, spindle, stick pin, tack, tie-pin.

pin down bind, compel, confine, constrain, designate, determine, fix, force, hold, hold down, home in on, identify, immobilise, locate, make, nail, nail down, name, pinpoint, press, pressurise, specify, tie down, zero in on.

pincers *n.* forceps, forfex, tweezers.

pinch *v.* afflict, apprehend, arrest, bust, chafe, check, collar, compress, confine, cramp, crush, distress, do, economise, filch, grasp, hurt, knap, knock off, lay, lift, nab, nick, nip, oppress, pain, pick up, pilfer, press, prig, pull in, purloin, rob, run in, scrimp, skimp, snaffle, snatch, sneap, snitch, spare, squeeze, steal, stint, swipe, tweak.

n. bit, crisis, dash, difficulty, emergency, exigency, hardship, jam, jot, mite, necessity, nip, oppression, pass, pickle, plight, predicament, pressure, soupçon, speck, squeeze, strait, stress, taste, tweak.

pinched *adj.* careworn, drawn, gaunt, haggard, narrowed, peaky, starved, straightened, thin, worn.

pine *v.* ache, covet, crave, decay, decline, desire, droop, dwindle, dwine, fade, flag, hanker, hunger, languish, long, peak, sicken, sigh, sink, thirst, waste, weaken, wilt, wish, wither, yearn, yen.

pinion *v.* bind, chain, confine, fasten, fetter, hobble, immobilise, manacle, pin down, shackle, tie, truss.

pink[1] *n.* acme, best, extreme, flower, height, peak, perfection, summit, tiptop, top.

adj. flushed, reddish, rose, roseate, rosy, salmon.

pink[2] *v.* crenellate, incise, notch, perforate, prick, punch, scallop, score, serrate.

pinnacle *n.* acme, apex, apogee, cap, cone, crest, crown, eminence, height, needle, obelisk, peak, pyramid, spire, steeple, summit, top, turret, vertex, zenith.

pin-point *v.* define, distinguish, home in on, identify, locate, place, spot, zero in on.

pint-size *adj.* diminutive, dwarf, little, midget, miniature, pocket, pocket-sized, small, tiny, wee.

antonyms giant, huge.

pioneer *n.* coloniser, colonist, developer, explorer, founder, founding father, frontiersman, innovator, leader, settler, trail-blazer, voortrekker, way-maker.

v. blaze a trail, create, develop, discover, establish, found, initiate, instigate, institute, invent, launch, lead, open up, originate, prepare, start.

pious *adj.* dedicated, devoted, devout, God-fearing, godly, good, goody-goody, holier-than-thou, holy, hypocritical, moral, pietistic, religiose, religious, reverent, righteous, saintly, sanctimonious, self-righteous, spiritual, unctuous, virtuous.

antonym impious.

pipe *n.* briar, clay, conduit, conveyor, duct, fife, fistula, flue, hookah, horn, hose, kalian, line, main, meerschaum, overflow, passage, pipeline, tooter, tube, whistle.

v. carry, channel, cheep, chirp, conduct, convey, funnel, peep, play, sing, siphon, sound, supply, tootle, transmit, trill, tweet, twitter, warble, whistle.

pipe-dream *n.* castle in Spain, castle in the air, chimera, daydream, delusion, dream, fantasy, mirage, notion, reverie, romance, vagary.

pipeline *n.* channel, conduit, conveyor, duct, line, passage, pipe, tube.

pipsqueak *n.* creep, hobbledehoy, nobody, nonentity, nothing, oik, squirt, twerp, upstart, whippersnapper.

antonym somebody.

piquancy *n.* bite, colour, edge, excitement, flavour, ginger, interest, juice, kick, pep, pepperiness, pizzazz, punch, pungency, raciness, relish, sharpness, spice, spiciness, spirit, tang, vigour, vitality, zest, zip.

piquant *adj.* biting, interesting, lively, peppery, poignant, provocative, pungent, racy, salty, savoury, scintillating, sharp, sparkling, spicy, spirited, stimulating, stinging, tangy, tart, zesty.
antonyms banal, jejune.

pique *n.* annoyance, displeasure, grudge, huff, irritation, miff, offence, pet, resentment, umbrage, vexation.
v. affront, annoy, arouse, displease, excite, gall, galvanise, get, goad, incense, irk, irritate, kindle, miff, mortify, nettle, offend, peeve, provoke, put out, rile, rouse, spur, stimulate, sting, stir, vex, whet, wound.

piracy *n.* bootlegging, buccaneering, freebooting, hijacking, infringement, plagiarism, rapine, robbery, stealing, theft.

pirate *n.* buccaneer, corsair, filibuster, freebooter, infringer, marauder, marque, picaroon, plagiariser, plagiarist, raider, rover, salleeman, sea-rat, sea-robber, sea-rover, sea-wolf, water-rat.
v. appropriate, borrow, copy, crib, lift, nick, pinch, plagiarise, poach, reproduce, steal.

pirouette *n.* gyration, pivot, spin, turn, twirl, whirl.
v. gyrate, pivot, spin, turn, twirl, whirl.

pistol *n.* dag, derringer, gat, gun, hand-gun, iron, Luger, piece, revolver, rod, sidearm, six-shooter.

pit *n.* abyss, alveole, alveolus, cavity, chasm, coal-mine, crater, dent, depression, dimple, excavation, gulf, hole, hollow, indentation, mine, oubliette, pock-mark, pothole, trench, variole.
pit against match, oppose, set against.

pitch *v.* bung, cast, chuck, dive, drop, erect, fall headlong, fix, fling, flounder, heave, hurl, launch, lob, locate, lurch, peck, place, plant, plunge, raise, roll, set up, settle, sling, stagger, station, throw, topple, toss, tumble, wallow, welter.
n. angle, cant, degree, dip, gradient, ground, harmonic, height, incline, level, line, modulation, park, patter, playing-field, point, sales talk, slope, sound, spiel, sports field, steepness, summit, tilt, timbre, tone.

pitch-dark *adj.* black, dark, inky, jet-black, pitch-black, pitchy, Stygian, unilluminated, unlit.

pitcher *n.* bottle, can, container, crock, ewer, jack, jar, jug, urn, vessel.

piteous *adj.* affecting, deplorable, distressing, doleful, doloriferous, dolorific, grievous, heartbreaking, heart-rending, lamentable, miserable, mournful, moving, pathetic, pitiable, pitiful, plaintive, poignant, sad, sorrowful, touching, woeful, wretched.

pitfall *n.* catch, danger, difficulty, downfall, drawback, hazard, peril, pit, snag, snare, stumbling-block, trap.

pith *n.* consequence, core, crux, depth, essence, force, gist, gravamen, heart, import, importance, kernel, marrow, matter, meat, moment, nub, point, power, quintessence, salient point, significance, strength, substance, value, weight.

pithy *adj.* aphoristic, apo(ph)thegmatic(al), brief, cogent, compact, concise, epigrammatic, expressive, forceful, laconic, matterful, meaningful, pointed, short, succinct, telling, terse, trenchant.
antonyms prolix, verbose, wordy.

pitiable *adj.* contemptible, distressed, distressful, distressing, doleful, grievous, lamentable, miserable, mournful, pathetic, piteous, poor, sad, sorry, woeful, woesome, wretched.

pitiful *adj.* abject, base, beggarly, contemptible, deplorable, despicable, distressing, grievous, heartbreaking, heart-rending, hopeless, inadequate, insignificant, lamentable, low, mean, miserable, paltry, pathetic, piteous, pitiable, ruthful, sad, scurvy, shabby, sorry, vile, woeful, worthless, wretched.

pitiless *adj.* brutal, callous, cold-blooded, cold-hearted, cruel, flinty, hard-hearted, harsh, heartless, implacable, inexorable, inhuman, merciless, obdurate, relentless, ruthless, uncaring, unfeeling, unmerciful, unpitying, unsympathetic.
antonyms compassionate, gentle, kind, merciful.

pittance *n.* chicken-feed, crumb, drop (in the ocean), mite, modicum, peanuts, trifle.

pitted *adj.* blemished, dented, dinted, gouged, holey, indented, lacunose, marked, nicked, notched, pock-marked, pocky, potholed, punctuate, punctuated, riddled, rough, rutty, scarred, scratched.

pity *n.* charity, clemency, commiseration, compassion, condolence, crime, crying shame, fellow-feeling, forbearance, kindness, mercy, misfortune, regret, ruth, shame, sin, sympathy, tenderness, understanding.
antonyms cruelty, disdain, scorn.
v. absolve, bleed for, commiserate with, condole with, feel for, forgive, grieve for, pardon, reprieve, sympathise with, weep for.

pivot *n.* axis, axle, centre, focal point, fulcrum, heart, hinge, hub, kingpin, linchpin, spindle, swivel.
v. depend, hang, hinge, lie, rely, revolve, rotate, spin, swing, swivel, turn, twirl.

pivotal *adj.* axial, central, climactic, critical, crucial, decisive, determining, focal, vital.

pixie *n.* brownie, elf, fairy, goblin, leprechaun, pisky, sprite.

placard *n.* advertisement, affiche, bill, poster, public notice, sandwich-board, sticker.

placate *v.* appease, assuage, calm, conciliate, humour, lull, mollify, pacify, propitiate, quiet, satisfy, soothe, win over.
antonyms anger, enrage, incense, infuriate.

placatory *adj.* appeasing, conciliatory, pacificatory, peace-making, propitiative, propitiatory.

place *n.* abode, accommodation, affair, apartment, appointment, area, berth, billet, charge, city, concern, district, domicile, duty, dwelling, employment, flat, function, grade, home, house, job, locale, locality, location, locus, manor, mansion, neighbourhood, pad, point, position, post, prerogative, property, quarter, rank, region, residence, responsibility, right, role, room, seat, site, situation, space, spot, station, status, stead, town, venue, vicinity, village, whereabouts.

v. allocate, appoint, arrange, assign, associate, bung, charge, class, classify, commission, deposit, dispose, dump, entrust, establish, fix, give, grade, group, identify, install, know, lay, locate, order, plant, position, put, put one's finger on, rank, recognise, remember, rest, set, settle, situate, sort, stand, station, stick.

placement *n.* appointment, arrangement, assignment, classification, deployment, disposition, distribution, emplacement, employment, engagement, installation, locating, location, ordering, positioning, ranking, stationing.

placid *adj.* calm, collected, composed, cool, equable, even, even-tempered, gentle, halcyon, imperturbable, level-headed, mild, peaceful, quiet, reposeful, restful, self-possessed, serene, still, tranquil, undisturbed, unexcitable, unmoved, unruffled, untroubled. *antonyms* agitated, jumpy.

plagiarise *v.* appropriate, borrow, counterfeit, crib, infringe, lift, pirate, reproduce, steal, thieve.

plagiarism *n.* appropriation, borrowing, copying, counterfeiting, cribbing, infringement, lifting, piracy, reproduction, theft.

plagiarist *n.* Autolycus, copier, imitator, pirate, robber, thief.

plague *n.* affliction, aggravation, annoyance, bane, blight, bother, calamity, cancer, contagion, curse, death, disease, epidemic, evil, infection, irritant, nuisance, pain, pandemic, pest, pestilence, problem, scourge, thorn in the flesh, torment, trial, vexation, visitation. *v.* afflict, annoy, badger, bedevil, bother, distress, disturb, fret, harass, harry, hassle, haunt, hound, molest, pain, persecute, pester, tease, torment, torture, trouble, vex.

plain *adj.* apparent, artless, austere, bare, basic, blunt, candid, clear, clinical, common, commonplace, comprehensible, direct, discreet, distinct, downright, even, everyday, evident, flat, forthright, frank, frugal, guileless, home-bred, homely, homespun, honest, ill-favoured, ingenuous, legible, level, lowly, lucid, manifest, modest, muted, obvious, open, ordinary, outspoken, patent, penny-plain, plane, pure, restrained, self-coloured, severe, simple, sincere, smooth, Spartan, stark, straightforward, transparent, ugly, unadorned, unaffected, unambiguous, unattractive, unbeautiful, understandable, undistinguished, unelaborate, unembellished, unfigured, unhandsome, unlovely, unmistakable, unobstructed, unornamented, unpatterned, unprepossessing, unpretentious, untrimmed, unvarnished, visible, whole-coloured, workaday. *antonyms* abstruse, attractive, elaborate,

exaggerated, ostentatious, rich, striking, unclear.

n. flat, grassland, llano, lowland, maidan, plateau, prairie, steppe, tableland, vega, veld(t).

plain-spoken *adj.* blunt, candid, direct, downright, explicit, forthright, frank, honest, open, outright, outspoken, straightforward, truthful, unequivocal.

plaintive *adj.* disconsolate, dismal, doleful, dolorous, grief-stricken, grievous, heart-rending, melancholy, mournful, pathetic, piteous, pitiful, rueful, sad, sorrowful, wistful, woebegone, woeful.

plan *n.* blueprint, chart, contrivance, delineation, design, device, diagram, drawing, idea, illustration, layout, map, method, plot, procedure, programme, project, proposal, proposition, representation, scenario, schedule, scheme, sketch, strategy, suggestion, system.

v. aim, arrange, complot, concoct, conspire, contemplate, contrive, design, devise, draft, envisage, foreplan, foresee, formulate, frame, intend, invent, mean, organise, outline, plot, prepare, propose, purpose, represent, scheme.

plane[1] *n.* class, condition, degree, echelon, footing, level, position, rank, rung, stage, stratum.

adj. even, flat, flush, horizontal, level, plain, planar, regular, smooth, uniform.

plane[2] *n.* aeroplane, aircraft, airliner, bomber, fighter, glider, jet, jumbo, jumbo jet, sea-plane, swing-wing, VTOL.

v. fly, glide, sail, skate, skim, volplane, wing.

plangent *adj.* clangorous, deep, loud, mournful, plaintive, resonant, resounding, reverberating, ringing, sonorous, vibrant.

plant[1] *n.* bush, flower, herb, shrub, vegetable, weed, wort.

v. bury, establish, fix, found, imbed, implant, inlay, insert, inset, institute, lodge, put in the ground, root, scatter, seed, set, set out, settle, sow, transplant.

plant[2] *n.* apparatus, equipment, factory, foundry, gear, machinery, mill, shop, works, workshop, yard.

plaque *n.* badge, brooch, cartouche, medal, medallion, panel, plaquette, plate, shield, slab, tablet.

plaster *n.* bandage, cataplasm, dressing, gypsum, mortar, plaster of Paris, sticking-plaster, stucco.

v. bedaub, besmear, coat, cover, daub, overlay, parge, parget, smear, spread, teer.

plastic *adj.* compliant, docile, ductile, fictile, flexible, impressionable, malleable, manageable, mouldable, pliable, pliant, receptive, responsive, soft, supple, tractable. *antonyms* inflexible, rigid.

plasticity *n.* flexibility, malleability, pliability, pliableness, pliancy, softness, suppleness, tractability. *antonyms* inflexibility, rigidity.

plate 473 **pleasant**

plate *n.* ashet, charger, course, dish, helping, illustration, lame, lamella, lath, layer, lithograph, palette, panel, platter, portion, print, scale, serving, sheet, slab, trencher.

v. anodise, coat, cover, electroplate, face, galvanise, gild, laminate, nickel, overlay, platinise, silver, tin, veneer, zinc, zinc(k)ify.

plateau *n.* grade, highland, level, mesa, plane, stability, stage, table, tableland, upland.

platform *n.* dais, estrade, gantry, manifesto, objective(s), party line, podium, policy, principle, programme, rostrum, stage, stand, tenet(s).

platitude *n.* banality, bromide, chestnut, cliché, commonplace, inanity, stereotype, truism.

platitudinous *adj.* banal, clichéd, commonplace, corny, dull, flat, hack, hackneyed, overworked, set, stale, stereotyped, stock, tired, trite, truistic, vapid, well-worn.

platonic *adj.* ideal, idealistic, incorporeal, intellectual, non-physical, spiritual, transcendent.

platoon *n.* battery, company, group, outfit, patrol, squad, squadron, team.

platter *n.* ashet, charger, dish, meat-plate, plate, salver, tray, trencher.

plaudits *n.* acclaim, acclamation, accolade, applause, approbation, approval, clapping, commendation, congratulations, hand, hurrahs, kudos, ovation, praise, standing ovation.

plausible *adj.* believable, colourable, conceivable, convincing, credible, facile, fair-spoken, glib, likely, persuasive, possible, probable, reasonable, smooth, smooth-talking, smooth-tongued, specious, tenable, voluble.

antonyms implausible, improbable, unlikely.

play *v.* act, bet, caper, challenge, chance, compete, contend, execute, fiddle, fidget, flirt, fool around, frisk, frolic, gamble, gambol, hazard, impersonate, interfere, lilt, participate, perform, personate, portray, punt, represent, revel, risk, rival, romp, speculate, sport, string along, take, take on, take part, take the part of, trifle, vie with, wager.

antonym work.

n. action, activity, amusement, caper, comedy, diversion, doodle, drama, elbowroom, employment, entertainment, exercise, farce, foolery, frolic, fun, function, gambling, gambol, game, gaming, give, humour, jest, joking, lark, latitude, leeway, margin, masque, motion, movement, operation, pastime, performance, piece, prank, range, recreation, romp, room, scope, show, space, sport, sweep, swing, teasing, tragedy, transaction, working.

play around dally, flirt, fool, mess around, philander, trifle, womanise.

play ball collaborate, co-operate, go along, play along, reciprocate, respond, show willing.

play by ear ad-lib, extemporise, improvisate, improvise.

play down gloss over, make light of, make little of, minimise, soft-pedal, underplay, underrate, undervalue.

play for time delay, drag one's feet, filibuster, hang fire, hesitate, procrastinate, stall, temporise.

play havoc with confuse, demolish, destroy, devastate, disorganise, disrupt, mess up, ruin, wreck.

play on abuse, capitalise on, exploit, milk, misuse, profit by, take advantage of, trade on, turn to account, utilise.

play the fool act the (giddy) goat, clown around, fool around, horse around, mess about, mess on, monkey around, skylark.

play the game acquiesce, conform, keep in step, play by the rules, play fair, toe the line, yield.

play up accentuate, begin, bother, emphasise, exaggerate, fool, highlight, hurt, magnify, make a fool of, malfunction, overemphasise, pain, spotlight, start, stress, strike up, trouble.

play up to blandish, bootlick, butter up, fawn, flatter, ingratiate oneself, soft-soap, suck up to, toady.

playboy *n.* debauchee, ladies' man, lady-killer, libertine, man about town, philanderer, rake, roué, socialite, womaniser.

player *n.* actor, actress, artist(e), bandsman, competitor, contestant, cricketer, entertainer, footballer, instrumentalist, musician, participant, performer, sportsman, sportswoman, Thespian, trouper.

playful *adj.* arch, cheerful, coltish, coquettish, coy, espiègle, flirtatious, frisky, frolicsome, gamesome, gay, good-natured, humorous, impish, jesting, jokey, joking, joyous, kittenish, kitteny, larkish, larky, lively, merry, mischievous, puckish, reasing, roguish, rollicking, spirited, sportive, sprightly, tongue-in-cheek, toyish, toysome, vivacious, waggish.

antonyms serious, stern.

playmate *n.* buddy, chum, companion, comrade, friend, marrow, neighbour, pal, playfellow.

plaything *n.* amusement, bauble, game, gewgaw, gimcrack, pastime, puppet, toy, trifle, trinket.

playwright *n.* dramatist, dramaturge, dramaturgist, screen-writer, scriptwriter.

plea *n.* action, allegation, apology, appeal, begging, cause, claim, defence, entreaty, excuse, explanation, extenuation, imploration, intercession, invocation, justification, overture, petition, placit(um), prayer, pretext, request, suit, supplication, vindication.

plead *v.* adduce, allege, appeal, argue, ask, assert, beg, beseech, crave, entreat, implore, importune, maintain, moot, petition, put forward, request, solicit, supplicate.

pleasant *adj.* acceptable, affable, agreeable, amene, amiable, amusing, charming, cheerful, cheery, congenial, cool, delectable, delightful, delightsome, engaging, enjoyable, fine, friendly, genial, good-humoured, gra-

tifying, likeable, listenable, lovely, nice, pleasing, pleasurable, refreshing, satisfying, sunshiny, toothsome, welcome, winsome.
antonyms distasteful, nasty, repugnant, unpleasant.

pleasantry *n.* badinage, banter, bon mot, jest, joke, persiflage, quip, sally, witticism.

please *v.* amuse, captivate, charm, cheer, choose, content, delight, desire, enchant, entertain, gladden, go for, gratify, humour, indulge, like, opt, prefer, rejoice, satisfy, see fit, suit, think fit, tickle, tickle pink, want, will, wish.
antonyms anger, annoy, displease.

pleased *adj.* chuffed, contented, delighted, elated, euphoric, glad, gratified, gruntled, happy, in high spirits, over the moon, satisfied, thrilled, tickled, tickled pink.
antonyms annoyed, displeased.

pleasing *adj.* acceptable, agreeable, amiable, amusing, attractive, charming, congenial, delightful, engaging, enjoyable, entertaining, good, gratifying, likable, nice, pleasurable, polite, satisfying, welcome, winning.
antonym unpleasant.

pleasurable *adj.* agreeable, amusing, congenial, delightful, diverting, enjoyable, entertaining, fun, good, gratifying, groovy, lovely, nice, pleasant, welcome.
antonyms bad, disagreeable.

pleasure *n.* amusement, bliss, choice, comfort, command, complacency, contentment, delectation, delight, desire, diversion, ease, enjoyment, gladness, gratification, happiness, inclination, joy, mind, option, preference, purpose, recreation, satisfaction, solace, will, wish.
antonyms displeasure, pain, sorrow, trouble.

pleat *v.* crease, crimp, flute, fold, gather, goffer, plait, pucker, shirr, tuck.

plebeian *adj.* base, coarse, common, ignoble, low, low-born, lower-class, mean, non-U, peasant, proletarian, uncultivated, unrefined, vulgar, working-class.
antonyms aristocratic, noble, patrician.
n. common man, commoner, man in the street, peasant, pleb, prole, proletarian, roturier, worker.
antonyms aristocrat, noble, patrician.

plebiscite *n.* ballot, poll, referendum, straw poll, vote.

pledge *n.* assurance, bail, bond, collateral, covenant, deposit, earnest, gage, guarantee, health, oath, pawn, promise, security, surety, toast, undertaking, vow, wadset(t), warrant, word, word of honour.
v. bind, contract, drink to, engage, ensure, gage, guarantee, mortgage, plight, promise, secure, swear, toast, undertake, vouch, vow.

plenary *adj.* absolute, complete, entire, full, general, integral, open, sweeping, thorough, unconditional, unlimited, unqualified, unrestricted, whole.

plenipotentiary *n.* ambassador, dignitary, emissary, envoy, legate, minister, nuncio, plenipo.

plenitude *n.* abundance, amplitude, bounty, completeness, copiousness, cornucopia, entireness, excess, fullness, plenteousness, plentifulness, plenty, plethora, profusion, repletion, wealth.
antonym scarcity.

plenteous *adj.* abounding, abundant, ample, bounteous, bountiful, bumper, copious, fertile, fruitful, generous, inexhaustible, infinite, lavish, liberal, luxuriant, overflowing, plentiful, productive, profuse, prolific.
antonym scarce.

plentiful *adj.* abounding, abundant, ample, bounteous, bountiful, bumper, complete, copious, fertile, fruitful, generous, inexhaustible, infinite, lavish, liberal, luxuriant, overflowing, plenteous, productive, profuse, prolific.
antonyms rare, scanty, scarce.

plenty *n.* abundance, affluence, copiousness, enough, fertility, fruitfulness, fund, heap(s), lots, luxury, mass, masses, milk and honey, mine, mountain(s), oodles, opulence, pile(s), plenitude, plenteousness, plentifulness, plethora, profusion, prosperity, quantities, quantity, stack(s), store, sufficiency, volume, wealth.
antonyms lack, need, scarcity, want.

plethora *n.* excess, glut, overabundance, overful(l)ness, profusion, superabundance, superfluity, surfeit, surplus.

pliability *n.* adaptability, amenability, bendability, compliance, docility, ductility, elasticity, flexibility, impressionableness, malleability, mobility, plasticity, pliancy, suggestibility, susceptibility, tractableness.
antonyms inflexibilty, rigidity.

pliable *adj.* accommodating, adaptable, bendable, bendy, compliant, docile, ductile, flexible, impressionable, influenceable, limber, lithe, malleable, manageable, persuadable, plastic, pliant, receptive, responsive, suggestible, supple, susceptible, tractable, yielding.
antonyms inflexible, rigid.

pliant *adj.* adaptable, bendable, bendy, biddable, compliant, ductile, easily led, flexible, impressionable, influenceable, lithe, manageable, persuadable, plastic, pliable, supple, susceptible, tractable, whippy, yielding.
antonyms inflexible, intractable.

plight[1] *n.* case, circumstances, condition, difficulty, dilemma, extremity, galère, hole, jam, perplexity, pickle, predicament, quandary, scrape, situation, spot, state, straits, trouble.

plight[2] *n.* affiance, contract, covenant, engage, guarantee, pledge, promise, propose, swear, vouch, vow.

plod *v.* clump, drag, drudge, grind, grub, labour, lumber, moil, peg, persevere, plough through, plug, slog, soldier on, stomp, sweat, toil, tramp, tread, trudge.

plodder *n.* drudge, dullard, mug, sap, slogger, toiler.

antonym high-flier.

plot[1] *n.* action, cabal, conspiracy, covin, design, intrigue, machination(s), narrative, outline, plan, scenario, scheme, story, story line, stratagem, subject, theme, thread.

v. brew, cabal, calculate, chart, collude, compass, compute, conceive, concoct, conspire, contrive, cook up, design, devise, draft, draw, frame, hatch, imagine, intrigue, lay, locate, machinate, manoeuvre, map, mark, outline, plan, project, scheme.

plot[2] *n.* allotment, area, erf, green, ground, lot, parcel, patch, tract.

plotter *n.* caballer, conspirator, intriguer, Machiavellian, machinator, schemer, strategist.

plough *v.* break, cultivate, dig, furrow, ridge, spade, till.

ploy *n.* artifice, contrivance, device, dodge, gambit, game, manoeuvre, move, ruse, scheme, stratagem, subterfuge, tactic, trick, wile.

pluck[1] *n.* backbone, boldness, bottle, bravery, courage, determination, fortitude, gameness, grit, guts, hardihood, heart, intrepidity, mettle, nerve, resolution, spirit, spunk, tenacity.

pluck[2] *v.* catch, clutch, collect, depilate, deplume, displume, draw, evulse, gather, harvest, jerk, pick, plunk, pull, pull off, pull out, snatch, strum, thrum, tug, twang, tweak, unplume, yank.

plucky *adj.* bold, brave, courageous, daring, doughty, game, gamy, gritty, gutsy, hardy, heroic, intrepid, mettlesome, spirited, spunky, tenacious, unflinching, valiant.

antonyms feeble, weak.

plug *n.* advert, advertisement, bung, cake, chew, cork, dook, dossil, dottle, good word, hype, mention, pigtail, publicity, puff, push, quid, spigot, spile, stopper, stopple, studdle, tamp(i)on, twist, wad.

v. advertise, block, build up, bung, choke, close, cork, cover, drudge, fill, grind, hype, labour, mention, pack, peg away, plod, promote, publicise, puff, push, seal, slog, stop, stop up, stopper, stopple, stuff, tamp, toil.

plum *n.* bonus, cushy number, find, pick, prize, sinecure, treasure.

adj. best, choice, cushy, first-class, prize.

plumb *n.* lead, plumb bob, plummet, sinker, weight.

adv. bang, dead, exactly, perpendicularly, precisely, slap, spot-on, square, up and down, vertically.

v. delve, explore, fathom, gauge, investigate, mark, measure, penetrate, probe, search, sound, unravel.

plume *n.* aigrette, crest, feather, pappus, pinion, quill, tuft.

plume oneself on boast about, congratulate oneself, exult in, pat oneself on the back, pique oneself, preen oneself, pride oneself.

plummet *v.* crash, descend, dive, drop, fall, hurtle, nose-dive, plunge, stoop, swoop, tumble.

antonym soar.

plump[1] *adj.* beefy, burly, buxom, chopping, chubby, corpulent, dumpy, embonpoint, endomorphic, fat, fleshy, full, matronly, obese, podgy, portly, roly-poly, rotund, round, stout, tubby, well-upholstered.

antonyms skinny, thin.

plump[2] *v.* collapse, descend, drop, dump, fall, flop, sink, slump.

adv. abruptly, directly, straight.

plump for back, choose, favour, opt for, select, side with, support.

plumpness *n.* chubbiness, corpulence, embonpoint, fatness, fleshiness, obesity, podginess, portliness, pudginess, rotundity, stoutness, tubbiness.

antonyms skinniness, thinness.

plunder *v.* depredate, despoil, devastate, loot, pillage, raid, ransack, ravage, reive, rifle, rob, sack, spoil, spoliate, steal, strip.

n. booty, despoilment, ill-gotten gains, loot, pickings, pillage, prey, prize, rapine, spoils, swag.

plunge *v.* career, cast, charge, dash, demerge, demerse, descend, dip, dive, dive-bomb, dook, douse, drop, fall, go down, hurtle, immerse, jump, lurch, nose-dive, pitch, plummet, rush, sink, submerge, swoop, tear, throw, tumble.

n. collapse, descent, dive, dook, drop, fall, immersion, jump, submersion, swoop, tumble.

plurality *n.* bulk, diversity, galaxy, majority, mass, most, multiplicity, multitudinousness, numerousness, preponderance, profusion, variety.

plus *n.* advantage, asset, benefit, bonus, credit, extra, gain, good point, perk, surplus.

antonym minus.

plush *adj.* affluent, costly, de luxe, lavish, luxurious, luxury, opulent, palatial, rich, ritzy, sumptuous.

plutocrat *n.* billionaire, capitalist, Croesus, Dives, fat cat, magnate, millionaire, moneybags, multimillionaire, rich man, tycoon.

ply[1] *v.* assail, beseige, beset, bombard, carry on, employ, exercise, feed, follow, furnish, handle, harass, importune, manipulate, practise, press, provide, pursue, supply, swing, urge, utilise, wield, work at.

ply[2] *n.* bend, fold, layer, leaf, sheet, strand, thickness.

poach *v.* appropriate, encroach, infringe, intrude, pilfer, plunder, rob, steal, trespass.

pocket *n.* bag, compartment, envelope, hollow, pouch, receptacle, reticule, sack.

adj. abridged, compact, concise, dwarf, little, mini, miniature, pint-size(d), portable, potted, small.

v. appropriate, filch, help oneself to, impocket, lift, nick, pilfer, pinch, purloin, snaffle, steal, take.

pockmark n. blemish, pit, pock, pockpit, scar.

pod n. case, hull, husk, legume, shell, shuck.

podgy adj. chubby, chunky, corpulent, dumpy, fat, fleshy, paunchy, plump, roly-poly, rotund, squat, stout, stubby, stumpy, tubby. antonym skinny.

podium n. dais, platform, rostrum, stage, stand.

poem n. acrostic, ballad(e), dit(t), ditty, eclogue, elegy, epicede, epicedium, epinicion, epithalamion, epithalamium, fabliau, genethliac(on), idyll, jingle, lay, limerick, lipogram, lyric, madrigal, monody, ode, palinode, rhyme, song, sonnet, verse, verselet, verset, versicle.

poet n. bard, iambist, iambographer, idyllist, lyricist, makar, maker, Meistersinger, metrician, metricist, minnesinger, minstrel, monodist, odist, Parnassian, poetaster, poeticule, rhymer, rhymester, rhymist, rimer, skald, verse-man, verse-monger, verser, verse-smith, versificator, versifier, verslibrist.

poetic adj. artistic, elegiac, flowing, graceful, lyric, lyrical, metrical, moving, rhythmical. antonym prosaic.

poetry n. free verse, gay science, iambics, lyrics, macaronics, muse, Parnassus, pennill, poems, poesy, rhyme, rhyming, vers libre, verse, versing.

poignancy n. bitterness, emotion, emotionalism, evocativeness, feeling, intensity, keenness, painfulness, pathos, piquancy, piteousness, plaintiveness, pungency, sadness, sentiment, sharpness, tenderness.

poignant adj. acrid, acute, affecting, agonising, biting, bitter, caustic, distressing, heartbreaking, heart-rending, intense, keen, moving, painful, pathetic, penetrating, piercing, piquant, pointed, pungent, sad, sarcastic, severe, sharp, stinging, tender, touching, upsetting.

point[1] n. aim, aspect, attribute, burden, characteristic, circumstance, condition, core, crux, degree, design, detail, dot, drift, end, essence, extent, facet, feature, full stop, gist, goal, import, instance, instant, intent, intention, item, juncture, location, mark, marrow, matter, meaning, moment, motive, nicety, nub, object, objective, particular, peculiarity, period, pith, place, position, property, proposition, purpose, quality, question, reason, respect, score, side, site, speck, spot, stage, station, stop, subject, tally, text, theme, thrust, time, trait, unit, use, usefulness, utility.

v. aim, denote, designate, direct, draw attention to, hint, indicate, level, show, signal, signify, suggest, train.

point of view angle, approach, attitude, belief, judgement, opinion, orientation, outlook, perspective, position, slant, stance, standpoint, view, viewpoint.

point out allude to, bring up, call attention to, identify, indicate, mention, remind, reveal, show, specify.

point up accentuate, emphasise, headline, spotlight, stress, underline, underscore.

point[2] n. apex, bill, cacumen, cape, end, fastigium, foreland, head, headland, neb, ness, nib, promontory, prong, spike, spur, summit, tang, tine, tip, top.

point-blank adj. abrupt, blunt, categorical, direct, downright, explicit, express, forthright, plain, plain-spoken, straightforward, unreserved.

adv. bluntly, brusquely, candidly, directly, explicitly, forthrightly, frankly, openly, plainly, straight, straightforwardly, unequivocally.

pointed adj. accurate, acicular, aciform, aculeate(d), acuminate, acute, barbed, biting, cuspidate, cutting, edged, fastigiate(d), incisive, keen, lanceolate(d), lancet, lanciform, mucronate, penetrating, pertinent, sharp, telling, trenchant.

pointer n. advice, caution, fingerpost, guide, hand, hint, indication, indicator, information, needle, recommendation, suggestion, tip, warning.

pointless adj. absurd, aimless, bootless, fruitless, futile, inane, ineffectual, irrelevant, meaningless, nonsensical, profitless, senseless, silly, stupid, unavailing, unbeneficial, unproductive, unprofitable, useless, vague, vain, worthless. antonyms meaningful, profitable.

poise n. aplomb, assurance, calmness, collectedness, composure, cool, coolness, dignity, elegance, equanimity, equilibrium, grace, presence, presence of mind, sangfroid, savoir-faire, self-possession, serenity.

v. balance, float, hang, hold, hover, librate, position, support, suspend.

poised adj. calm, collected, composed, cool, dignified, expectant, graceful, nonchalant, prepared, ready, self-confident, self-possessed, serene, suave, unruffled, urbane, waiting.

poison n. aconite, aconitum, bane, blight, cancer, canker, contagion, contamination, corruption, malignancy, miasma, toxin, venom, virus.

v. adulterate, contaminate, corrupt, defile, deprave, empoison, envenom, infect, kill, murder, pervert, pollute, subvert, taint, undermine, vitiate, warp.

poisonous adj. aconitic, baleful, baneful, corruptive, deadly, evil, fatal, lethal, malicious, mephitic, mortal, noxious, pernicious, pestiferous, pestilential, toxic, venomous, vicious, virose, virous, virulent.

poke v. butt, butt in, dig, elbow, hit, interfere, intrude, jab, meddle, nose, nudge, peek, prod, prog, pry, punch, push, shove, snoop, stab, stick, tamper, thrust.

n. butt, dig, dunt, jab, nudge, prod, punch, shove, thrust.

poke fun at chaff, guy, jeer, make fun of, mock, parody, prog, rag, rib, ridicule, send up, spoof, take the mickey, tease.

poky adj. confined, cramped, crowded, incommodious, narrow, small, tight, tiny.

antonym spacious.

polarity *n.* ambivalence, contradiction, contrariety, dichotomy, duality, oppositeness, opposition, paradox.

pole[1] *n.* bar, lug, mast, post, rod, shaft, spar, staff, stake, standard, stang, stick.

pole[2] *n.* antipode, extremity, limit, terminus, (ultima) Thule.

poles apart at opposite extremes, incompatible, irreconcilable, like chalk and cheese, like night and day, worlds apart.

polemic *n.* argument, controversy, debate, dispute.
adj. argumentative, contentious, controversial, disputatious, eristic(al), polemical.

polemicist *n.* arguer, contender, controversialist, debater, disputant, disputer, logomachist, polemist.

polemics *n.* argument, argumentation, contention, controversy, debate, disputation, dispute, logomachy.

police *n.* boys in blue, constabulary, fuzz, gendarmerie, law, myrmidons of the law, (the) Old Bill.
v. check, control, defend, guard, keep a check on, keep guard over, keep in order, keep the peace, monitor, observe, oversee, patrol, protect, regulate, stand guard over, supervise, watch.

policeman *n.* beetle-crusher, bluebottle, bobby, bogey, bull, catchpole, constable, cop, copper, crusher, flatfoot, flic, fuzz, garda, gendarme, gumshoe, hammer(-beak), headborough, mountie, officer, peeler, pig, rozzer, sepoy, slop.

policy *n.* action, approach, code, course, custom, discretion, good sense, guideline, line, plan, position, practice, procedure, programme, protocol, prudence, rule, sagacity, scheme, shrewdness, stance, stratagem, theory, wisdom.

polish *v.* brighten, brush up, buff, burnish, clean, correct, cultivate, emend, emery, enhance, file, finish, furbish, improve, lustre, perfect, planish, refine, rub, rub up, shine, shine up, slick, slicken, smooth, touch up, wax.
antonyms dull, tarnish.
n. breeding, brightness, brilliance, class, cultivation, elegance, eutrapelia, expertise, finesse, finish, glaze, gloss, grace, lustre, perfectionism, politesse, proficiency, refinement, savoir-faire, sheen, smoothness, sophistication, sparkle, style, suavity, urbanity, varnish, veneer, wax.
antonyms clumsiness, dullness, gaucherie.

polish off bolt, bump off, consume, devour, dispose of, down, eat, eliminate, finish, gobble, kill, liquidate, murder, put away, rub out, shift, stuff, wolf.

polished *adj.* accomplished, adept, bright, burnished, civilised, courtly, cultivated, educated, elegant, expert, faultless, fine, finished, flawless, furbished, genteel, glassy, gleaming, glossy, graceful, gracious, impeccable, lustrous, masterly, outstanding, perfected,

polite, professional, refined, sheeny, shining, skilful, slippery, smooth, sophisticated, suave, superlative, urbane, well-bred.
antonyms clumsy, dull, gauche, inexpert, tarnished.

polite *adj.* affable, attentive, civil, civilised, complaisant, considerate, cordial, courteous, courtly, cultured, deferential, diplomatic, discreet, elegant, genteel, gentlemanly, gracious, Grandisonian, ladylike, mannerly, obliging, polished, refined, respectful, tactful, thoughtful, urbane, well-behaved, well-bred, well-mannered.
antonyms impolite, uncultivated.

politeness *n.* attention, civility, complaisance, considerateness, cordiality, courtesy, courtliness, cultivation, culture, deference, diplomacy, discretion, elegance, gentilesse, gentility, gentlemanliness, grace, graciousness, mannerliness, manners, polish, refinement, respect, respectfulness, tact, thoughtfulness.
antonym impoliteness.

politic *adj.* advantageous, advisable, artful, astute, canny, crafty, cunning, designing, diplomatic, discreet, expedient, ingenious, intriguing, judicious, Machiavellian, opportune, prudent, sagacious, sage, scheming, sensible, shrewd, sly, subtle, tactful, unscrupulous, wise.
antonym impolitic.

politician *n.* agitator, legislator, Machiavellian, machinator, manipulator, Member of Parliament, MP, opportunist, politicaster, politico, statesman, statist, stirrer, tactician, wheeler-dealer.

politics *n.* affairs of state, civics, diplomacy, government, ideology, Machiavellianism, Machiavellism, machination, Machtpolitik, manipulation, political science, polity, power-politics, Realpolitik, statecraft, statesmanship, Weltpolitik, wheeler-dealing.

poll[1] *n.* ballot, canvass, census, count, figures, kite-flying, plebiscite, returns, sampling, straw-poll, survey, tally, vote, voting.

poll[2] *v.* clip, dishorn, dod, pollard, shear, trim.

pollute *v.* adulterate, befoul, besmirch, canker, contaminate, corrupt, debase, debauch, defile, deprave, desecrate, dirty, dishonour, foul, infect, mar, poison, profane, soil, spoil, stain, sully, taint, violate, vitiate.

pollution *n.* adulteration, befouling, contamination, corruption, defilement, desecration, dirtying, foulness, impurity, infection, profanation, soilure, stain, taint, uncleanness, violation, vitiation.
antonyms purification, purity.

polychromatic *adj.* kaleidoscopic, many-coloured, many-hued, motley, mottled, multicoloured, parti-coloured, poikilitic, polychrome, rainbow, varicoloured, variegated.
antonyms monochromatic, monochrome.

polyglot *adj.* cosmopolitan, international, multilingual, multiracial, polyglottal, polyglottic.
antonym monoglot.

n. linguist, multilinguist.

polymath *n.* all-rounder, know-all, mine of information, oracle, pansophist, polyhistor, Renaissance man, walking encyclopaedia.
antonym ignoramus.

pomp *n.* ceremonial, ceremoniousness, ceremony, display, éclat, flourish, formality, grandeur, grandiosity, magnificence, ostentation, pageant, pageantry, parade, pomposity, ritual, show, solemnity, splendour, state, vainglory.
antonyms austerity, simplicity.

pomposity *n.* affectation, airs, arrogance, bombast, euphuism, fustian, grandiloquence, grandiosity, loftiness, magniloquence, oro(ro)tundity, pompousness, pontificating, portentousness, preachiness, presumption, pretension, pretentiousness, ranting, rhetoric, self-importance, stuffiness, turgidity, vainglory, vanity.
antonyms economy, simplicity.

pompous *adj.* affected, aldermanlike, aldermanly, arrogant, bloated, bombastic, budge, chesty, euphuistic, flatulent, fustian, grandiloquent, grandiose, high-flown, imperious, inflated, magisterial, magniloquent, oro(ro)tund, ostentatious, overbearing, overblown, pontifical, portentous, pretentious, prosy, ranting, self-important, stilted, supercilious, turgid, vainglorious, windy.
antonyms economical, modest, simple, unaffected, unassuming.

ponder *v.* analyse, brood, cerebrate, cogitate, comtemplate, consider, deliberate, examine, excogitate, give thought to, incubate, mediate, mull over, muse, ponderate, puzzle over, ratiocinate, reason, reflect, ruminate over, study, think, volve, weigh.

ponderous *adj.* awkward, bulky, clumsy, cumbersome, cumbrous, dreary, dull, elephantine, graceless, heavy, heavy-footed, heavy-handed, hefty, huge, humourless, laborious, laboured, lifeless, long-winded, lumbering, massive, pedantic, pedestrian, plodding, portentous, prolix, slow-moving, stilted, stodgy, stolid, tedious, unwieldy, verbose, weighty.
antonyms delicate, light, simple.

ponderousness *n.* gravitas, heaviness, humourlessness, laboriousness, seriousness, stodginess, stolidity, tedium, unwieldiness, weightiness.
antonyms delicacy, lightness, subtlety.

poniard *n.* bodkin, dagger, dirk, misericord, skene, stiletto, stylet.

pontifical *adj.* apostolic, bloated, condescending, didactic, dogmatic, ecclesiastical, homiletical, imperious, magisterial, overbearing, papal, pompous, portentous, preachy, prelatic, pretentious, self-important, sermonising.
antonyms reticent, unassuming.

pontificate *v.* declaim, dogmatise, expound, harangue, hold forth, lay down the law, lecture, moralise, perorate, pontify, preach, pronounce, sermonise, sound off.

pooh-pooh *v.* belittle, brush aside, deride, disdain, dismiss, disparage, disregard, make little of, minimise, play down, reject, ridicule, scoff, scorn, slight, sneer, sniff at, spurn, turn up one's nose at.
antonyms consider, exaggerate, magnify, regard.

pool[1] *n.* dub, lake, lasher, leisure pool, linn, mere, pond, puddle, splash, stank, swimming bath, swimming pool, tarn, water-hole, watering-hole.

pool[2] *n.* accumulation, bank, cartel, collective, combine, consortium, funds, group, jackpot, kitty, pot, purse, reserve, ring, stakes, syndicate, team, trust.
v. amalgamate, chip in, combine, contribute, dob in, merge, muck in, put together, share.

poor[1] *adj.* badly off, bankrupt, beggared, beggarly, broke, deficient, destitute, distressed, embarrassed, exiguous, hard up, impecunious, impoverished, in reduced circumstances, inadequate, indigent, insufficient, lacking, meagre, miserable, moneyless, necessitious, needy, niggardly, obolary, on one's beam-ends, on one's uppers, on the rocks, pauperised, penniless, penurious, pinched, pitiable, poverty-stricken, reduced, scanty, skimpy, skint, slight, sparse, stony-broke, straitened, without means, without the wherewithal.
antonyms affluent, opulent, rich, wealthy.

poor[2] *adj.* bad, bare, barren, below par, depleted, exhausted, faulty, feeble, fruitless, grotty, humble, imperfect, impoverished, inferior, infertile, insignificant, jejune, low-grade, lowly, mean, mediocre, modest, paltry, pathetic, pitiful, plain, ropy, rotten, rubbishy, second-rate, shabby, shoddy, sorry, spiritless, sterile, substandard, third-rate, trivial, unfruitful, unimpressive, unproductive, unsatisfactory, valueless, weak, worthless.
antonym superior.

poor[3] *adj.* accursed, cursed, forlorn, hapless, ill-fated, luckless, miserable, pathetic, pitiable, star-crossed, unfortunate, unhappy, unlucky, wretched.
antonym lucky.

poorly *adv.* badly, crudely, faultily, feebly, inadequately, incompetently, inexpertly, inferiorly, insufficiently, meanly, rottenly, shabbily, shoddily, unjustly, unsatisfactorily, unsuccessfully.
antonym well.
adj. ailing, below par, dicky, frail, groggy, ill, indisposed, off colour, out of sorts, rotten, seedy, shaky, sick, sickly, under the weather, unhealthy, unwell.
antonyms healthy, robust, well.

pop *v.* appear, bang, bulge, burst, call, come, crack, drop, drop in, explode, go, go bang, go off, go phut, insert, jump, nip, protrude, push, put, report, shove, slide, slip, snap, spring, step, stick, thrust, tuck, visit.
n. bang, burst, crack, explosion, noise, report,

snap.

pope n. Bishop of Rome, His Holiness, Holy Father, papa, pontiff, sovereign pontiff, Vicar of Christ.

popinjay n. beau, buck, coxcomb, dandy, dude, exquisite, fop, fopling, jackanapes, macaroni, pansy, peacock, princox, spark, swell, toff.
antonyms he-man, macho.

poppycock n. babble, balderdash, balls, baloney, bullshit, bunk, bunkum, drivel, eyewash, gibberish, gobbledegook, guff, hooey, nonsense, rot, rubbish, tommyrot, tosh, trash, twaddle.
antonym sense.

populace n. canaille, common herd, commonalty, crowd, general public, hoi polloi, inhabitants, masses, mob, multitude, people, plebs, proletariat, public, punters, rabble, rank and file, throng, vulgus.
antonyms aristocracy, élite, nobility.

popular adj. accepted, approved, celebrated, common, conventional, current, democratic, demotic, famous, fashionable, favoured, favourite, fêted, general, household, idolised, in, in demand, in favour, liked, lionised, modish, overpopular, overused, prevailing, prevalent, public, sought-after, standard, stock, trite, ubiquitous, universal, vernacular, voguey, voguish, vulgar, well-liked, widespread.
antonyms exclusive, unpopular, unusual.

popularise v. debase, democratise, disseminate, familiarise, give currency to, propagate, simplify, spread, universalise, vulgarise.
antonym discredit.

popularity n. acceptance, acclaim, adoration, adulation, approbation, approval, celebrity, currency, esteem, fame, favour, glory, idolisation, kudos, lionisation, mass appeal, recognition, regard, renown, reputation, repute, vogue, worship.
antonym unpopularity.

popularly adv. commonly, conventionally, customarily, generally, in the vernacular, ordinarily, regularly, traditionally, universally, usually, vernacularly, vulgarly, widely.

populate v. colonise, establish oneself in, habit, inhabit, live in, occupy, overrun, people, put down roots in, settle, tenant.

population n. citizenry, citizens, community, denizens, folk, inhabitants, natives, occupants, people, populace, residents, society.

populous n. crawling, crowded, frequented, overpeopled, overpopulated, packed, populated, swarming, teeming, thickly populated, thronged.
antonyms deserted, unfrequented.

pore v. brood, con, contemplate, devour, dwell on, examine, go over, peruse, ponder, read, scan, scrutinise, study.

pornographic adj. bawdy, blue, coarse, dirty, filthy, girlie, gross, indecent, lewd, nudie, obscene, off-colour, offensive, porn, porno, prurient, risqué, salacious, smutty.
antonyms innocent, inoffensive.

pornography n. bawdiness, dirt, erotica, facetiae, filth, grossness, indecency, obscenity, porn, porno, sexploitation, smut.

porous adj. absorbent, absorptive, cellular, foraminous, foveate, honeycombed, penetrable, permeable, pervious, pitted, spongelike, spongy.
antonyms impermeable, impervious.

port n. anchorage, harbour, harbourage, haven, hithe, roads, roadstead, seaport.

portable adj. carriageable, compact, convenient, handy, light, lightweight, manageable, movable, portatile, portative, transportable.
antonyms fixed, immovable.

portend v. adumbrate, announce, augur, bespeak, betoken, bode, forebode, forecast, foreshadow, foretell, foretoken, forewarn, harbinger, herald, indicate, omen, point to, predict, presage, prognosticate, promise, signify, threaten, warn of.

portent n. augury, foreboding, forecast, forerunner, foreshadowing, forewarning, harbinger, indication, omen, precursor, prefiguration, premonition, presage, presentiment, prodrome, prognostic, prognostication, sign, signification, threat, warning.

portentous adj. alarming, amazing, astounding, awe-inspiring, bloated, charged, consequential, crucial, earth-shaking, epoch-making, extraordinary, fateful, heavy, important, menacing, minatory, miraculous, momentous, ominous, phenomenal, pompous, ponderous, pontifical, pregnant, prodigious, remarkable, significant, sinister, solemn, threatening.
antonyms insignificant, unimportant, unimpressive.

porter[1] n. baggage attendant, baggage man, bearer, caddie, carrier.

porter[2] n. caretaker, commissionaire, concierge, door-keeper, doorman, doors-man, dvornik, gatekeeper, huissier, janitor, porteress, portress.

portion n. allocation, allotment, allowance, assignment, bit, cup, destiny, division, fate, fortune, fraction, fragment, helping, kismet, lot, luck, measure, meed, moiety, morsel, parcel, part, piece, quantity, quota, rake-off, ration, scrap, section, segment, serving, share, slice, something, tranche, whack.
v. allocate, allot, apportion, assign, carve up, deal, distribute, divide, divvy up, dole, parcel, partion, partition, share out, slice up.

portliness n. ampleness, beefiness, chubbiness, corpulence, dumpiness, embonpoint, fleshiness, fullness, heaviness, obesity, paunchiness, plumpness, rotundity, roundness, stoutness, tubbiness.

portly adj. ample, beefy, bulky, chubby, corpulent, dumpy, embonpoint, fat, fleshy, full, gaucie, heavy, large, obese, overweight, paunchy, plump, rotund, round, stout, tubby.
antonyms slight, slim.

portrait n. account, caricature, characterisation, depiction, description, icon, image, likeness, miniature, mug shot, painting, photograph, picture, portraiture, portrayal, profile, representation, sketch, thumbnail, vignette.

portray v. act, capture, characterise, delineate, depict, describe, draw, emblazon, encapsulate, evoke, figure, illustrate, impersonate, limn, paint, personate, personify, picture, play, present, render, represent, sketch, suggest.

portrayal n. characterisation, delineation, depiction, description, evocation, hypotyposis, impersonation, interpretation, performance, picture, presentation, rendering, representation, sketch.

pose v. advance, affect, arrange, assert, attitudinise, claim, feign, impersonate, masquerade, model, pass oneself off, place, posit, position, posture, present, pretend, profess to be, propound, put, put forward, put on an act, set, sham, sit, state, strike an attitude, submit. n. act, affectation, air, attitude, bearing, con, façade, front, mark, masquerade, mien, position, posture, pretence, role, sham, stance, take-in.

poser[1] n. brain-teaser, chinese puzzle, conundrum, enigma, mystery, problem, puzzle, question, riddle, vexed question.

poser[2] n. attitudiniser, poseur, poseuse, posturer, posturist.

poseur n. attitudiniser, charlatan, con, exhibitionist, impostor, masquerader, mountebank, phoney, poser, poseuse, posturer, posturist, pseud, quack.

posh adj. classy, de-luxe, elegant, exclusive, fashionable, grand, high-class, lavish, luxurious, luxury, opulent, plummy, ritzy, select, smart, stylish, sumptuous, swanky, swell, swish, up-market, upper-class.
antonyms cheap, inferior.

posit v. advance, assert, assume, pose, postulate, predicate, presume, propound, put forward, state, submit.

position n. angle, area, arrangement, attitude, bearings, belief, berth, billet, capacity, character, circumstances, condition, deployment, disposition, duty, employment, function, grade, importance, job, level, locale, locality, location, niche, occupation, office, opinion, outlook, pass, perspective, pinch, place, placement, placing, plight, point, point of view, pose, positioning, post, posture, predicament, prestige, rank, reference, reputation, role, set, setting, site, situation, slant, slot, spot, stance, stand, standing, standpoint, state, station, stature, status, ubiety, view, viewpoint, whereabouts.
v. arrange, array, deploy, dispose, fix, lay out, locate, place, pose, put, range, set, settle, stand, stick.

positive adj. absolute, actual, affirmative, arrant, assertive, assured, authoritative, beneficial, categorical, certain, clear, clear-cut, cocksure, complete, conclusive, concrete, confident, constructive, consummate, convinced, decided, decisive, definite, direct, dogmatic, downright, effective, efficacious, emphatic, explicit, express, firm, forceful, forward-looking, helpful, hopeful, incontestable, incontrovertible, indisputable, irrefragable, irrefutable, open-and-shut, opinionated, optimistic, out-and-out, peremptory, perfect, practical, productive, progressive, promising, rank, real, realistic, resolute, secure, self-evident, sheer, stubborn, sure, thorough, thoroughgoing, uncompromising, undeniable, unequivocal, unmistakable, unmitigated, unquestioning, useful, utter.
antonyms indecisive, indefinite, negative, uncertain.

positively adv. absolutely, assuredly, authoritatively, categorically, certainly, conclusively, constructively, decisively, definitely, dogmatically, emphatically, expressly, finally, firmly, incontestably, incontrovertibly, indisputably, surely, uncompromisingly, undeniably, unequivocally, unmistakably, unquestionably.

possess v. acquire, be endowed with, control, dominate, enjoy, have, hold, obtain, occupy, own, possess oneself of, seize, take, take over, take possession of.

possessed adj. bedevilled, berserk, besotted, bewitched, consumed, crazed, cursed, demented, dominated, enchanted, entêté, frenzied, hag-ridden, haunted, infatuated, maddened, mesmerised, obsessed, raving.

possession n. colony, control, custody, dependency, dominion, enjoyment, fruition, hold, mandate, occupancy, occupation, ownership, proprietorship, protectorate, province, tenure, territory, title.

possessions n. assets, belongings, chattels, effects, estate, goods, goods and chattels, junk, meum et tuum, movables, paraphernalia, property, riches, stuff, things, traps, wealth, worldly wealth.

possessive adj. acquisitive, clinging, covetous, dominating, domineering, grasping, jealous, overprotective, proprietorial, selfish.
antonyms generous, sharing, unassertive.

possibilities n. advantages, capabilities, expectations, potential, potentiality, promise, prospects, talent.
antonyms disadvantages, liabilities.

possibility n. achievability, chance, conceivability, feasibility, hazard, hope, liability, likelihood, odds, plausibility, potentiality, practicability, probability, prospect, realisability, risk, workableness.
antonym impossibility.

possible adj. accomplishable, achievable, alternative, attainable, available, conceivable, credible, doable, feasible, hopeful, hypothetical, imaginable, likely, on, potential, practicable, probable, promising, realisable, tenable, viable, workable.
antonym impossible.

possibly adv. at all, by any chance, by any means, Deo volente, DV, God willing, haply, happen, hopefully, in any way, maybe, mayhap, peradventure, perchance, perhaps, very like(ly).

post[1] *n.* baluster, banister, column, leg, newel, pale, palisade, picket, pier, pillar, pin, pole, shaft, stake, stanchion, standard, stock, strut, support, upright.

v. advertise, affix, announce, denounce, display, make known, placard, preconise, proclaim, promulgate, publicise, publish, report, stick up.

post[2] *n.* appointment, assignment, beat, berth, billet, employment, incumbency, job, office, place, position, situation, station, vacancy.

v. appoint, assign, establish, locate, move, place, position, put, second, send, shift, situate, station, transfer.

post[3] *n.* collection, delivery, dispatch, mail, postal service, uplifting.

v. acquaint, advise, apprise, brief, dispatch, fill in on, inform, keep posted, mail, notify, report to, send, transmit.

poster *n.* advertisement, affiche, announcement, bill, handbill, notice, placard, sign, sticker.

posterior *adj.* after, back, behind, dorsal, ensuing, following, hind, hinder, later, latter, posticous, rear, rearward, subsequent, succeeding.

antonyms anterior, front, previous.

n. backside, behind, bottom, bum, buttocks, haunches, hinder end, hindquarters, rear, rump, seat, tail.

posterity *n.* children, descendants, epigons, family, future, heirs, issue, offspring, progeny, scions, seed, successors.

antonyms ancestors, antiquity, forebears, past.

posthaste *adv.* at once, directly, double-quick, ek dum, full tilt, hastily, immediately, promptly, pronto, quickly, speedily, straightaway, swiftly, with all speed.

antonyms eventually, gradually, slowly.

postman *n.* letter-carrier, mail-carrier, post, postie.

postmortem *n.* analysis, autopsy, dissection, examination, necropsy, review.

postpone *v.* adjourn, defer, delay, freeze, hold over, pigeonhole, prorogue, put back, put off, put on ice, shelve, suspend, table, waive.

antonyms advance, forward.

postponed *adj.* adjourned, deferred, frozen, in abeyance, on ice, pigeonholed, shelved, suspended.

antonym advanced.

postponement *n.* adjournment, deferment, deferral, delay, freeze, moratorium, prorogation, put-off, respite, stay, suspension.

postscript *n.* addendum, addition, afterthought, afterword, appendix, codicil, epilogue, PS, supplement.

antonyms introduction, prologue.

postulate *v.* advance, assume, hypothesise, lay down, posit, predicate, presuppose, propose, stipulate, suppose, take for granted, theorise.

posture *n.* attitude, bearing, carriage, decubitus, disposition, mien, port, pose, position, set, stance.

v. affect, attitudinise, pose, put on airs, show off, strike attitudes, strut.

posy *n.* bouquet, boutonniere, buttonhole, corsage, inscription, motto, nosegay, spray, verse, verselet.

pot *n.* basin, beaker, bowl, coffee-pot, crock, crucible, cruse, cupel, flask, gallipot, jar, marmite, pan, pig, pipkin, planter, receptacle, samovar, teapot, test, urn, vase, vessel.

potato *n.* murphy, pratie, praty, spud, tater, tattie.

pot-bellied *adj.* bloated, corpulent, distended, fat, gor-bellied, obese, overweight, paunchy, portly, tubby.

pot-belly *n.* beer belly, belly, corporation, gor-belly, gut, paunch, pot, spare tyre.

potency *n.* authority, capacity, cogency, control, effectiveness, efficaciousness, efficacy, energy, force, headiness, influence, kick, might, muscle, persuasiveness, potential, power, puissance, punch, strength, sway, vigour.

antonyms impotence, weakness.

potent *adj.* authoritative, cogent, commanding, compelling, convincing, dominant, dynamic, effective, efficacious, eloquent, forceful, formidable, heady, impressive, influential, intoxicating, mighty, moving, persuasive, powerful, puissant, pungent, strong, telling, vigorous, weighty.

antonyms impotent, weak.

potentate *n.* chief, chieftain, despot, dictator, dynast, emperor, empress, head of state, king, leader, mogul, monarch, overlord, prince, queen, ruler, sovereign, tyrant.

potential *adj.* budding, concealed, conceivable, dormant, embryonic, future, hidden, imaginable, in embryo, in posse, inherent, latent, likely, possible, probable, promising, prospective, undeveloped, unrealised.

n. ability, aptitude, capability, capacity, flair, possibility, potentiality, power, talent, the makings, what it takes, wherewithal.

potentiality *n.* ability, aptitude, capability, capacity, likelihood, possibilities, potential, promise, prospect, virtuality.

potion *n.* beverage, brew, concoction, cup, dose, draught, drink, electuary, elixir, medicine, mixture, philtre, potation, tonic, treacle.

pot-pourri *n.* collection, combination, gallimaufry, hotchpotch, jumble, medley, mélange, miscellany, mixture, motley, olio, olla-podrida, pastiche, patchwork, salad, salmagundi.

potter *v.* dabble, da(c)ker, dodder, fettle, fiddle, fidget, footle, fribble, frig, fritter, mess about, mooch, moon, tinker.

pottery *n.* ceramics, china, China-ware, crockery, delf, earthenware, pig, porcelain, stoneware, terra cotta, ware.

adj. ceramic, china, clay, earthenware, fictile, figuline, porcelain, stoneware, wally.

potty *adj.* bananas, barmy, bonkers, crackers, crazy, daft, demented, dippy, dotty, eccentric, foolish, footling, insignificant, nuts, nutty, petty, piddling, silly, soft, touched, trifling, trivial.

pouch *n.* bag, container, marsupium, pocket, poke, purse, reticule, sac, sack, sporran, wallet.

pounce *v.* ambush, attack, dash at, dive on, drop, fall upon, grab, jump, leap at, lunge at, snatch, spring, strike, swoop.
n. assault, attack, bound, dive, grab, jump, leap, lunge, spring, swoop.

pound[1] *v.* bang, bash, baste, batter, beat, belabour, bray, bruise, clobber, clomp, clump, comminute, crush, drum, hammer, levigate, march, palpitate, pelt, powder, pulsate, pulse, pulverise, pummel, smash, stomp, strike, strum, thrash, throb, thrum, thud, thump, thunder, tramp, triturate.

pound[2] *n.* compound, corral, enclosure, fank, fold, pen, yard.

pour *v.* bucket, cascade, course, crowd, decant, effuse, emit, exude, flow, gush, rain, rain cats and dogs, run, rush, sheet, spew, spill, spout, stream, swarm, teem, throng, tumble.
pour out debouch, decant, discharge, disembogue, disgorge, embogue, emit, issue, lave, spew forth.

pout *v.* glower, grimace, lower, mope, pull a face, scowl, sulk.
antonyms grin, smile.
n. glower, grimace, long face, moue, scowl.
antonyms grin, smile.

poverty *n.* aridity, bareness, barrenness, beggary, dearth, deficiency, depletion, destitution, distress, exhaustion, hardship, ill-being, impoverishment, inadequacy, indigence, infertility, insolvency, insufficiency, jejuneness, lack, meagreness, necessitousness, necessity, need, paucity, pauperism, pennilessness, penury, poorness, poortith, privation, proletarianism, scarcity, shortage, sterility, thinness, unfruitfulness, want.
antonyms affluence, fertility, fruitfulness, riches, richness.

poverty-stricken *adj.* bankrupt, beggared, broke, destitute, distressed, impecunious, impoverished, indigent, necessitous, needy, obolary, on one's beam-ends, on one's uppers, penniless, penurious, poor, skint, stony, stony-broke, strapped.
antonyms affluent, rich.

powder *n.* bran, dust, pounce, pulvil, pulville, pulvil(l)io, talc, triturate.
v. bray, comminute, cover, crush, dredge, dust, granulate, grind, levigate, pestle, pound, pulverise, scatter, sprinkle, strew, triturate.

powdery *adj.* chalky, crumbling, crumbly, dry, dusty, fine, friable, grainy, granular, levigate, loose, powder, pulverised, pulverous, pulverulent, sandy.

power *n.* ability, ascendancy, autarchy, authorisation, authority, brawn, capability, capacity, clout, clutches, command, competence, competency, control, dominance, domination, dominion, efficiency, energy, faculty, force, forcefulness, heavy metal, hegemony, imperium, influence, intensity, juice, kami, licence, mana, mastery, might, muscle, omnipotence, plenipotence, potency, potential, prerogative, privilege, right, rule, sovereignty, strength, supremacy, sway, teeth, vigour, virtue, vis, voltage, vroom, warrant, weight.

powerful *adj.* ascendant, authoritative, cogent, commanding, compelling, controlling, convincing, dominant, effective, effectual, energetic, forceful, forcible, impressive, influential, leading, masterful, mighty, muscular, omnipotent, persuasive, plutocratic, potent, pre-eminent, prepotent, prevailing, puissant, robust, souped-up, sovereign, stalwart, strapping, strong, sturdy, supreme, telling, vigorous, weighty, winning.
antonyms impotent, ineffective, weak.

powerfully *adv.* cogently, convincingly, forcefully, forcibly, hard, impressively, mightily, persuasively, potently, strongly, tellingly, vigorously, with might and main.

powerless *adj.* adynamic, debilitated, defenceless, dependent, disabled, effete, feeble, frail, helpless, impotent, incapable, incapacitated, ineffective, ineffectual, inefficacious, inerm, infirm, nerveless, paralysed, prostrate, subject, tied, unarmed, vulnerable, weak, weak-headed.
antonyms commanding, potent, powerful.

practicability *n.* feasibility, handiness, operability, possibility, practicality, use, usefulness, utility, value, viability, workability, workableness.
antonym impracticability.

practicable *adj.* accomplishable, achievable, attainable, compassable, doable, effectible, feasible, negotiable, passable, performable, possible, viable, workable.
antonym impracticable.

practical *adj.* accomplished, active, applicative, applied, businesslike, commonsense, commonsensical, down-to-earth, efficient, empirical, everyday, expedient, experienced, experimental, factual, feasible, functional, hardheaded, hard-nosed, material, matter-of-fact, mundane, nuts-and-bolts, ordinary, practicable, practive, pragmatic, proficient, qualified, realistic, seasoned, sensible, serviceable, skilled, sound, trained, unsentimental, useful, utilitarian, workable, workaday, working.
antonym impractical.

practicality *n.* basics, common sense, experience, feasibility, nitty-gritty, nuts and bolts, practicability, practicalities, practicalness, practice, pragmatism, realism, sense, serviceability, soundness, usefulness, utility, workability.

practically[1] *adv.* actually, all but, almost, essentially, fundamentally, in effect, in practice, in principle, just about, nearly, not quite, pretty nearly, pretty well, very nearly, virtually, well-nigh.

practically[2] *adv.* clearly, from a commonsense

angle, matter-of-factly, rationally, realistically, reasonably, sensibly, unsentimentally.

practice *n.* action, application, business, career, clientèle, convention, custom, discipline, drill, dry run, dummy run, effect, exercise, experience, habit, ism, method, mode, modus operandi, operation, patronage, performance, policy, practic, practicalities, practicum, praxis, preparation, procedure, profession, rehearsal, repetition, routine, rule, run-through, study, system, tradition, training, usage, use, vocation, way, wont, work, work-out.

practise *v.* apply, carry out, discipline, do, drill, enact, engage in, execute, exercise, follow, implement, live up to, observe, perfect, perform, ply, prepare, pursue, put into practice, rehearse, repeat, run through, study, train, undertake, warm up.

practised *adj.* able, accomplished, consummate, experienced, expert, finished, highly-developed, knowing, knowledgeable, perfected, proficient, qualified, refined, seasoned, skilled, trained, versed, veteran, well-trained.

antonyms inexpert, unpractised.

pragmatic *adj.* businesslike, efficient, factual, hard-headed, opportunistic, practical, realistic, sensible, unidealistic, unsentimental, utilitarian.

antonyms idealistic, romantic, unrealistic.

pragmatism *n.* hard-headedness, humanism, opportunism, practicalism, practicality, realism, unidealism, utilitarianism.

antonyms idealism, romanticism.

pragmatist *n.* humanist, opportunist, practicalist, realist, utilitarian.

antonyms idealist, romantic.

praise *n.* acclaim, acclamation, accolade, acknowledgement, adoration, adulation, applause, approbation, approval, bouquet, cheering, commend, commendation, compliment, compliments, congratulation, devotion, encomium, eulogium, eulogy, extolment, flattery, glory, homage, honour, kudos, laud, laudation, ovation, panegyric, plaudit, puff, rave, recognition, salvoes, testimonial, thanks, thanksgiving, tribute, worship.

antonyms criticism, revilement.

v. acclaim, acknowledge, admire, adore, applaud, approve, belaud, bless, celebrate, cheer, compliment, congratulate, cry up, eulogise, exalt, extol, flatter, give thanks to, glorify, hail, honour, laud, magnify, panegyrise, pay tribute to, promote, puff, rave over, recognise, tout, wax lyrical, worship.

antonyms criticise, revile.

praiseworthy *adj.* admirable, commendable, creditable, deserving, estimable, excellent, exemplary, fine, honourable, laudable, meritorious, reputable, sterling, worthy.

antonyms discreditable, dishonourable, ignoble.

praising adj, adulatory, approbatory, approving, commendatory, complimentary, congra-

tulatory, encomiastic, eulogistic, favourable, flattering, laudative, laudatory, panegyric, plauditory, promotional, recommendatory, worshipful.

antonyms condemnatory, critical.

prance *v.* bound, caper, capriole, caracole, cavort, curvet, dance, frisk, frolic, gambol, jump, leap, parade, prank, prankle, romp, show off, skip, spring, stalk, strut, swagger, swank, vault.

prank *n.* antic, caper, dido, escapade, fredaine, frolic, galliardise, guy, jape, joke, lark, piece of mischief, practical joke, rig, spree, stunt, trick, vagary.

prate *v.* babble, blather, bleat, blether, boast, brag, burble, chatter, drivel, gab, gas, haver, jabber, jaw, maunder, palaver, prattle, ramble, witter, yak.

prattle *v.* babble, blather, blether, chat, chatter, clack, clash, drivel, gabble, gossip, jabber, patter, rattle, twitter, witter.

n. bavardage, bletheration, blethers, chat, chatter, clack, clash, claver, drivel, foolishness, gab, gabnash, gibberish, gossip, gup, haverings, havers, hot air, jaw, maundering, nashgab, nonsense, prating, talk, tattle.

prattler *n.* babbler, blabbermouth, blatherskite, blether, bletherskate, chatterbox, chatterer, gabbler, gabnash, gossip, loudmouth, magpie, nashgab, pie, prater, prattlebox, rattlebrain, talker, tatler, tattler, windbag.

antonym clam.

pray *v.* adjure, ask, beg, beseech, call on, crave, entreat, implore, importune, invoke, obsecrate, petition, plead, press, request, solicit, sue, supplicate, urge.

prayer *n.* appeal, collect, communion, devotion, entreaty, invocation, kyrie, kyrie eleison, litany, orison, paternoster, petition, plea, request, solicitation, suffrage, suit, supplication.

prayer-book *n.* breviary, euchologion, euchologue, euchology, ma(c)hzor, missal, ordinal.

preach *v.* address, admonish, advocate, ethicise, evangelise, exhort, harangue, lecture, moralise, orate, pontificate, pontify, preachify, prose, sermonise, urge.

preacher *n.* canter, clergyman, devil-dodger, evangelist, homilist, mar-text, minister, missionary, moraliser, parson, pontificater, predicant, pulpite(e)r, ranter, revivalist, sermoniser.

preachiness *n.* cant, didacticism, dogmatism, moralising, pharisaism, pietism, pomposity, portentousness, preachment, pulpitry, religiosity, sanctimoniousness, sanctimony, self-righteousness, sermonising.

preaching *n.* doctrine, dogma, evangel, evangelism, exhortation, gospel, homiletics, homilies, instruction, kerygma, message, pontificating, precepts, sermonising, sermons, teaching.

preachy *adj.* canting, didactic, dogmatic, edifying, exhortatory, holier-than-thou, homiletic, hortatory, moralising, pharisaic, pietistic, pontifical, pontificating, preceptive, religiose, sanctimonious, self-righteous, sermonising.

preamble *n.* exordium, foreword, introduction, lead-in, overture, preface, preliminaries, prelude, preparation, proem, prolegomenon, prologue.

antonyms epilogue, postscript.

precarious *adj.* chancy, dangerous, delicate, dicey, dodgy, doubtful, dubious, hairy, hazardous, iffy, insecure, parlous, periculous, perilous, problematic, risky, shaky, slippery, ticklish, tricky, uncertain, unpredictable, unreliable, unsafe, unsettled, unstable, unsteady, unsure, vulnerable.

antonyms certain, safe, secure.

precaution *n.* anticipation, backstop, buffer, care, caution, circumspection, foresight, forethought, insurance, preparation, prophylaxis, protection, providence, provision, prudence, safeguard, safety measure, security, surety, wariness.

precautionary *adj.* anticipatory, cautious, foresighted, foresightful, judicious, preliminary, preparatory, preventive, prophylactic, protective, provident, provisional, prudent, safety, self-protective.

precede *v.* antecede, antedate, anticipate, come first, forerun, front, go before, head, herald, introduce, lead, preface, prefix, prelude, premise, prevene, take precedence.

antonym follow.

precedence *n.* antecedence, first place, lead, pre-eminence, preference, pride of place, primacy, priority, rank, seniority, superiority, supremacy.

precedent *n.* antecedent, authority, citation, criterion, example, exemplar, guideline, instance, judgement, model, paradigm, past instance, pattern, prototype, ruling, standard, yardstick.

preceding *adj.* above, aforementioned, aforesaid, antecedent, anterior, earlier, foregoing, former, past, precedent, precursive, previous, prior, supra.

antonyms following, later.

precept *n.* axiom, behest, bidding, byword, canon, charge, command, commandment, convention, decree, dictum, direction, directive, guideline, injunction, institute, instruction, law, mandate, maxim, motto, order, ordinance, principle, regulation, rubric, rule, saying, sentence, statute.

precinct *n.* area, banlieue, bound, boundary, confine, district, division, enclosure, limit, quarter, section, sector, zone.

precincts *n.* area, borders, bounds, confines, district, environs, limits, locality, milieu, neighbourhood, purlieus, region, surrounds, vicinity.

preciosity *n.* affectation, alembication, artificiality, chichi, floweriness, Marivaudage, overrefinement, tweeness.

precious *adj.* adored, affected, artificial, beloved, cherished, chichi, choice, costly, darling, dear, dearest, expensive, exquisite,

fastidious, favourite, fine, flowery, greenery-yallery, idolised, inestimable, invaluable, irreplaceable, loved, namby-pamby, over-nice, over-refined, priceless, prized, rare, recherché, treasured, twee, valuable, valued.

precipice *n.* bluff, brink, cliff, cliff face, crag, drop, escarp, escarpment, height, krantz, scarp, steep.

precipitate *v.* accelerate, advance, bring on, cast, cause, chuck, discharge, drive, expedite, fling, further, hasten, hurl, hurry, induce, launch, occasion, pitch, press, project, quicken, speed, throw, trigger.

adj. abrupt, breakneck, brief, frantic, Gadarene, hasty, headlong, heedless, hotheaded, hurried, impatient, impetuous, impulsive, incautious, indiscreet, madcap, pell-mell, plunging, precipitous, quick, quixotic, rapid, rash, reckless, rushing, sudden, swift, unannounced, unexpected, violent.

antonym cautious.

precipitous *adj.* abrupt, dizzy, giddy, high, perpendicular, sheer, steep, vertiginous.

antonyms gradual, sloping.

précis *n.* abbreviation, abridgement, abstract, aperçu, compendium, condensation, conspectus, contraction, digest, encapsulation, epitome, outline, résumé, run-down, sketch, summary, synopsis, table.

v. abbreviate, abridge, abstract, compress, condense, contract, digest, encapsulate, epitomise, outline, shorten, sum up, summarise, synopsise.

antonyms amplify, expand.

precise *adj.* absolute, accurate, actual, authentic, blow-by-blow, buckram, careful, ceremonious, clear-cut, correct, definite, delimitative, determinate, distinct, exact, explicit, express, expressis verbis, factual, faithful, fastidious, finical, finicky, fixed, formal, identical, literal, meticulous, minute, nice, particular, prim, punctilious, puritanical, rigid, scrupulous, specific, strict, succinct, unequivocal, verbatim, word-for-word.

antonym imprecise.

precisely *adv.* absolutely, accurately, bang, blow by blow, correctly, dead, distinctly, exactly, expressis verbis, just, just so, literally, minutely, plumb, slap, smack, square, squarely, strictly, verbatim, word for word.

precision *n.* accuracy, care, correctness, definiteness, detail, exactitude, exactness, explicitness, expressness, faithfulness, fastidiousness, fidelity, meticulousness, minuteness, neatness, niceness, nicety, particularity, preciseness, punctilio, punctiliousness, rigour, scrupulosity, specificity.

antonym imprecision.

preclude *v.* avoid, check, debar, eliminate, exclude, forestall, hinder, inhibit, obviate, prevent, prohibit, restrain, rule out, stop.

antonyms incur, involve.

precocious *adj.* advanced, ahead, bright, clever, developed, fast, forward, gifted, mature, precocial, premature, quick, smart.

antonym backward.

preconceive *v.* anticipate, assume, conceive, conceptualise, envisage, ideate, imagine, picture, presume, presuppose, project, visualise.

preconception *n.* anticipation, assumption, bias, conjecture, notion, predisposition, prejudice, prenotion, prepossession, presumption, presupposition.

precondition *n.* essential, must, necessity, need, prerequisite, proviso, requirement, requisite, sine qua non, stipulation.

precursor *n.* antecedent, forebear, forerunner, harbinger, herald, indication, messenger, originator, pathfinder, pioneer, predecessor, prodrome, prodromus, sign, trail-blazer, usher, vanguard, warning, way-maker.
antonyms after-effect, aftermath.

precursory *adj.* antecedent, anterior, introductory, preambulatory, preceding, precursive, prefatory, preliminary, preludial, prelusive, premonitory, preparatory, prevenient, previous, prior, prodromal, warning.
antonyms following, resulting, subsequent.

predatory *adj.* acquisitive, avaricious, carnivorous, covetous, despoiling, greedy, hunting, lupine, marauding, pillaging, plundering, predacious, predative, preying, rapacious, raptatorial, raptorial, ravaging, ravening, thieving, voracious, vulturine, vulturous, wolfish.

predecessor *n.* ancestor, antecedent, antecessor, forebear, forefather, forerunner, precursor, progenitor.
antonyms descendant, successor.

predestination *n.* ananke, destiny, doom, election, fate, foreordainment, foreordination, karma, lot, necessity, portion, predestiny, predetermination, preordainment, preordination, weird.

predestine *v.* destine, doom, fate, foredoom, foreordain, intend, mean, predestinate, predetermine, pre-elect, preordain.

predetermined *adj.* agreed, cut and dried, decided beforehand, deliberate, fixed, foregone, foreordained, prearranged, preordained, preplanned, set, set up, settled.

predicament *n.* can of worms, corner, crisis, dilemma, embarrassment, emergency, fix, galère, hole, hot water, impasse, jam, kettle of fish, mess, pickle, pinch, plight, quandary, scrape, situation, spot, state, trouble.

predicate *v.* affirm, assert, aver, avouch, avow, base, build, contend, declare, establish, found, ground, maintain, posit, postulate, premise, proclaim, rest, state.

predict *v.* augur, auspicate, divine, forebode, forecast, foresay, foresee, foreshow, forespeak, foretell, portend, presage, prognosticate, project, prophesy, second-guess, soothsay, vaticinate.

predictable *adj.* anticipated, calculable, certain, dependable, determinate, expected, finite, foregone, foreseeable, foreseen, imaginable, likely, presumable, probable, reliable, sure.

antonym unpredictable.

prediction *n.* augury, auspication, divination, forecast, fortune-telling, prognosis, prognostication, prophecy, second sight, soothsaying, vaticination.

predictive *adj.* augural, diagnostic, divinatory, foretelling, prognostic, prophetic.

predilection *n.* affection, affinity, bent, bias, enthusiasm, fancy, fondness, inclination, leaning, liking, love, partiality, penchant, predisposition, preference, proclivity, proneness, propensity, soft spot, taste, tendency, weakness.
antonyms antipathy, disinclination.

predispose *v.* affect, bias, dispose, head, incline, induce, influence, lead, lean, make, make liable, prejudice, prepare, prime, prompt, sway.

predisposed *adj.* agreeable, amenable, biased, disposed, favourable, inclined, liable, minded, not unwilling, nothing loth, prejudiced, prepared, prone, ready, subject, susceptible, well-disposed, willing.

predisposition *n.* bent, bias, disposition, inclination, leaning, liability, likelihood, mind, penchant, potentiality, predilection, preference, prejudice, proclivity, proneness, propensity, susceptibility, tendency, vulnerability, willingness.

predominance *n.* ascendancy, control, dominance, dominion, edge, hegemony, hold, influence, leadership, mastery, numbers, paramountcy, power, prepollence, prepollency, preponderance, prepotence, prepotency, prevalence, superiority, supremacy, sway, upper hand, weight.
antonyms ineffectiveness, weakness.

predominant *adj.* ascendant, capital, chief, controlling, dominant, forceful, important, influential, leading, main, paramount, potent, powerful, prepollent, preponderant, prepotent, prevailing, prevalent, primary, prime, principal, prominent, ruling, sovereign, strong, superior, supreme.
antonyms ineffective, lesser, minor, weak.

predominate *v.* dominate, obtain, outnumber, outweigh, override, overrule, overshadow, preponderate, prevail, reign, rule, tell, transcend.

pre-eminence *n.* distinction, excellence, fame, incomparability, matchlessness, paramountcy, peerlessness, predominance, prestige, prominence, renown, repute, superiority, supremacy, transcendence.

pre-eminent *adj.* chief, consummate, distinguished, excellent, exceptional, facile princeps, foremost, incomparable, inimitable, leading, matchless, nonpareil, outstanding, paramount, passing, peerless, predominant, prominent, renowned, superior, superlative, supreme, surpassing, transcendent, unequalled, unmatched, unrivalled, unsurpassed.
antonyms undistinguished, unknown.

pre-eminently *adv.* conspicuously, eminently, emphatically, especially, exceptionally, exclusively, incomparably, inimitably, matchlessly, notably, par excellence, particularly, peerlessly, signally, singularly, strikingly, superlatively, supremely, surpassingly.

pre-empt *v.* acquire, anticipate, appropriate, arrogate, assume, bag, forestall, secure, seize, usurp.

preen *v.* adorn, array, beautify, clean, deck, do up, doll up, dress up, fig out, groom, plume, prank, prettify, primp, prink, slick, spruce up, tart up, titivate, trick out, trim.

preen (oneself) bask, congratulate, exult, gloat, pique, plume, pride.

preface *n.* exordium, foreword, intro, introduction, preamble, preliminaries, prelims, prelude, proem, prolegomena, prolegomenon, prologue, prooemion, prooemium.
antonyms afterthought, epilogue, postscript.
v. begin, introduce, launch, lead up to, open, precede, prefix, prelude, premise, start.
antonyms append, complete, finish.

prefatory *adj.* antecedent, exordial, explanatory, introductory, opening, preambulatory, precursory, prefatorial, preliminary, preludial, prelusive, prelusory, preparatory, proemial, prolegomenal.
antonyms closing, final.

prefect *n.* administrator, monitor, praefect, praeposter, prepositor, supervisor.

prefer[1] *v.* adopt, advocate, back, be partial to, choose, desire, elect, endorse, fancy, favour, go for, incline towards, like better, opt for, pick, plump for, recommend, select, single out, support, want, wish, would rather, would sooner.
antonym reject.

prefer[2] *v.* bring, file, lodge, place, present, press.

prefer[3] *v.* advance, aggrandise, dignify, elevate, exalt, promote, raise, upgrade.
antonym demote.

preferable *adj.* advantageous, advisable, best, better, choice, chosen, desirable, eligible, expedient, favoured, nicer, preferred, stronger, superior, worthier.
antonyms ineligible, inferior, undesirable.

preferably *adv.* first, for choice, for preference, rather, sooner.

preference[1] *n.* choice, desire, election, fancy, favourite, first choice, inclination, liking, option, partiality, pick, predilection, selection, wish.

preference[2] *n.* advantage, favour, favouritism, precedence, preferential treatment, priority, special consideration, special treatment.

preferential *adj.* advantageous, better, biased, favourable, favoured, partial, partisan, prior, privileged, special, superior.
antonym equal.

preferment *n.* advancement, aggrandisement, betterment, dignity, elevation, exaltation, furtherance, improvement, promotion, rise, step up, upgrading.
antonym demotion.

preferred *adj.* approved, authorised, choice,

chosen, desired, favoured, predilect, recommended, sanctioned, selected.
antonyms rejected, undesirable.

pregnancy *n.* child-bearing, conception, family way, fertilisation, gestation, gravidity, impregnation.

pregnant[1] *adj.* big, big-bellied, enceinte, expectant, expecting, gravid, impregnated, in an interesting condition, in the club, in the family way, in the pudding club, parturient, preggers, teeming, with child.

pregnant[2] *adj.* charged, eloquent, expressive, full, heavy, loaded, meaning, meaningful, ominous, pithy, pointed, significant, suggestive, telling, weighty.
antonym jejune.

prehistoric *adj.* ancient, antediluvian, antiquated, archaic, earliest, early, fogram, hoary, obsolete, Ogygian, old, outmoded, out-of-date, primeval, primitive, primordial.
antonym modern.

prejudge *v.* anticipate, assume, forejudge, judge prematurely, predetermine, prejudicate, presume, presuppose.

prejudice[1] *n.* bias, bigotry, chauvinism, discrimination, injustice, intolerance, narrow-mindedness, partiality, partisanship, preconception, prejudgement, racism, sexism, unfairness, viewiness, warp.
antonyms fairness, tolerance.
v. bias, colour, condition, distort, incline, indoctrinate, influence, jaundice, load, poison, predispose, prepossess, slant, sway, warp, weight.

prejudice[2] *n.* damage, detriment, disadvantage, harm, hurt, impairment, injury, loss, mischief, ruin, vitiation, wreck.
antonyms advantage, benefit.
v. damage, harm, hinder, hurt, impair, injure, mar, ruin, spoil, undermine, vitiate, wreck.
antonyms advance, benefit, help.

prejudiced *adj.* biased, bigoted, chauvinist, conditioned, discriminatory, distorted, ex parte, illiberal, influenced, intolerant, jaundiced, loaded, narrow-minded, one-sided, opinionated, partial, partisan, prepossessed, racist, sexist, subjective, unenlightened, unfair, verkrampte, viewy, warped, weighted.
antonyms fair, tolerant.

prejudicial *adj.* counter-productive, damaging, deleterious, detrimental, disadvantageous, harmful, hostile, hurtful, inimical, injurious, mischievous, noxious, pernicious, ruinous, undermining, unfavourable.
antonyms advantageous, beneficial.

preliminaries *n.* basics, beginning, first round, formalities, foundations, groundwork, initiation, introduction, opening, preamble, preface, prelims, prelude, preparation, proem, prolegomena, rudiments, start.

preliminary *adj.* earliest, early, embryonic, exordial, experimental, exploratory, first, inaugural, initial, initiative, initiatory, introductory, opening, pilot, precursory, prefatory, prelusive, preparatory, primary, prior,

qualifying, test, trial.
antonyms closing, final.
prelude *n*. beginning, commencement, curtain-raiser, exordium, foreword, inroduction, intro, opener, overture, praeludium, preamble, precursor, preface, preliminary, preludio, prelusion, preparation, prodrome, proem, prolegomenon, prologue, prooemion, prooemium, start, taster, verset, Vorspiel.
antonyms aftermath, epilogue, postscript.
premature *adj*. abortive, early, embryonic, forward, green, half-formed, hasty, ill-considered, ill-timed, immature, imperfect, impulsive, incomplete, inopportune, overhasty, precipitate, precocious, preterm, previous, rash, raw, undeveloped, unfledged, unripe, unseasonable, untimely.
antonyms late, tardy.
premeditated *adj*. aforethought, calculated, cold-blooded, conscious, considered, contrived, deliberate, intended, intentional, planned, plotted, prearranged, predetermined, prepense, preplanned, studied, wilful.
antonyms spontaneous, unpremeditated.
premeditation *n*. deliberateness, deliberation, design, determination, forethought, intention, malice aforethought, planning, plotting, prearrangement, predetermination, purpose, scheming.
antonyms impulse, spontaneity.
premier *n*. chancellor, chief minister, first minister, head of government, prime minister, secretary of state.
adj. arch, cardinal, chief, earliest, first, foremost, head, highest, initial, leading, main, original, paramount, pre-eminent, primary, prime, principal, supreme, top.
premiere *n*. début, first night, opening, opening night.
premise *v*. assert, assume, hypothesise, lay down, posit, postulate, predicate, presuppose, state, stipulate, take as true.
n. argument, assertion, assumption, ground, hypothesis, postulate, postulation, predication, premiss, presupposition, proposition, statement, stipulation, supposition, thesis.
premises *n*. building, establishment, estate, grounds, office, place, property, site.
premonition *n*. anxiety, apprehension, fear, feeling, foreboding, forewarning, hunch, idea, intuition, misgiving, niggle, omen, portent, presage, presentiment, sign, suspicion, unease, uneasiness, warning, worry.
preoccupation *n*. absence of mind, absent-mindedness, absorption, abstraction, brown study, concern, daydreaming, distraction, engrossment, enthusiasm, fixation, hang-up, hobby-horse, idée fixe, immersion, inattention, inattentiveness, musing, oblivion, obliviousness, obsession, pensiveness, raptness, reverie, wool-gathering.
preoccupied *adj*. absent-minded, absorbed, abstracted, daydreaming, distracted, distrait, engrossed, entêté, faraway, fixated, heedless, immersed, intent, oblivious, obsessed,

pensive, rapt, taken up, unaware, visited, wrapped up.
preordain *v*. destine, doom, fate, foreordain, prearrange, predestine, predetermine.
preparation[1] *n*. alertness, anticipation, arrangement, assignment, basics, development, expectation, foresight, foundation, groundwork, homework, imposition, lesson, measure, plan, precaution, preliminaries, prep, preparedness, provision, readiness, revision, rudiments, safeguard, schoolwork, study, task.
preparation[2] *n*. application, composition, compound, concoction, lotion, medicine, mixture, potion, tincture.
preparatory *adj*. basic, elementary, exordial, fundamental, initial, introductory, opening, prefatory, preliminary, preparative, primary, proemial, rudimentary.
preparatory to before, in advance of, in anticipation of, in expectation of, previous to, prior to.
prepare *v*. accoutre, adapt, adjust, anticipate, arrange, assemble, boun, brace, brief, busk, coach, compose, concoct, confect, construct, contrive, develop, devise, dispose, do one's homework, draft, draw up, dress, equip, fashion, fettle, fit, fit out, fix up, forearm, form, fortify, furnish, get up, gird, groom, instruct, limber up, make, make ready, outfit, plan, practise, predispose, prime, produce, provide, psych up, ready, rehearse, rig out, steel, strengthen, supply, train, trim, warm up.
prepare oneself brace oneself, fortify oneself, get psyched up, gird oneself, limber up, psych oneself up, ready oneself, steel oneself.
prepared *adj*. able, arranged, briefed, disposed, expectant, fit, forearmed, inclined, minded, planned, predisposed, primed, psyched up, ready, set, waiting, well-rehearsed, willing, word-perfect.
antonyms unprepared, unready.
preparedness *n*. alertness, anticipation, expectancy, fitness, order, preparation, readiness.
antonym unreadiness.
preponderance *n*. ascendancy, bulk, dominance, domination, dominion, extensiveness, force, lion's share, majority, mass, power, predominance, prevalence, superiority, supremacy, sway, weight.
preponderant *adj*. ascendant, controlling, dominant, extensive, foremost, greater, important, larger, overriding, overruling, paramount, predominant, prevailing, prevalent, significant, superior.
preponderate *v*. dominate, outnumber, override, overrule, predominate, prevail, rule, tell, turn the balance, turn the scale, weigh with.
prepossessing *adj*. alluring, amiable, appealing, attractive, beautiful, bewitching, captivating, charming, delightful, disarming, enchanting, engaging, fair, fascinating, fetching, good-looking, handsome, inviting, likable, lovable,

magnetic, pleasing, striking, taking, winning, winsome.

antonyms unattractive, unprepossessing.

prepossession *n.* absorption, bias, engrossment, inclination, leaning, liking, partiality, predilection, predisposition, prejudice, preoccupation.

preposterous *adj.* absurd, asinine, bizarre, crazy, derisory, excessive, exorbitant, extravagant, extreme, fatuous, foolish, imbecile, impossible, inane, incredible, insane, intolerable, irrational, laughable, ludicrous, monstrous, nonsensical, outrageous, ridiculous, risible, senseless, shocking, unbelievable, unconscionable, unreasonable, unthinkable.

antonym reasonable.

prerequisite *adj.* basic, essential, fundamental, imperative, indispensable, mandatory, necessary, needed, needful, obligatory, required, requisite, vital.

antonym unnecessary.

n. condition, essential, imperative, must, necessity, precondition, provision, proviso, qualification, requirement, requisite, sine qua non.

antonym extra.

prerogative *n.* advantage, authority, birthright, carte blanche, choice, claim, droit, due, exemption, immunity, liberty, licence, perquisite, privilege, right, sanction, title.

presage *v.* adumbrate, augur, betoken, bode, divine, feel, forebode, forecast, forefeel, foreknow, forepoint, foresee, foreshadow, foretell, forethink, foretoken, forewarn, intuit, omen, point to, portend, predict, previse, prognosticate, prophesy, sense, signify, soothsay, vaticinate, warn.

n. apprehension, augury, auspice, bad vibes, bodement, boding, feeling, foreboding, forecast, forewarning, harbinger, intimation, intuition, misgiving, omen, portent, prediction, premonition, presentiment, prodrome, prodromus, prognostic, prognostication, prophecy, sign, warning.

prescience *n.* clairvoyance, far-sightedness, foreknowledge, foresight, precognition, prevision, prophecy, propheticness, second sight.

prescient *adj.* clairvoyant, discerning, divinatory, divining, far-seeing, far-sighted, foreknowing, foresighted, mantic, perceptive, previsional, prophetic, psychic.

antonym imperceptive.

prescribe *v.* appoint, assign, command, decree, define, dictate, direct, enjoin, fix, impose, lay down, limit, ordain, order, require, rule, set, set bounds to, specify, stipulate.

prescribed *adj.* assigned, decreed, formulary, laid down, ordained, set, specified, stipulated.

prescription *n.* direction, drug, formula, instruction, medicine, mixture, preparation, recipe, remedy, treatment.

prescriptive *adj.* authoritarian, customary, dictatorial, didactic, dogmatic, legislating, preceptive, prescribing, rigid.

presence *n.* air, apparition, appearance, aspect, attendance, aura, bearing, carriage, closeness, companionship, company, comportment, demeanour, ease, existence, ghost, habitation, inhabitance, manifestation, mien, nearness, neighbourhood, occupancy, personality, poise, propinquity, proximity, residence, revenant, self-assurance, shade, spectre, spirit, statuesqueness, vicinity.

antonym absence.

presence of mind alertness, aplomb, calmness, composure, cool, coolness, gumption, imperturbability, level-headedness, nous, quickness, sang-froid, self-assurance, self-command, self-possession, wits.

antonyms agitation, confusion.

present[1] *adj.* at hand, attending, available, contemporary, current, existent, extant, here, immediate, instant, near, ready, there, to hand.

antonyms absent, out-of-date, past.

present[2] *v.* acquaint with, adduce, advance, award, bestow, confer, declare, demonstrate, display, donate, entrust, exhibit, expound, extend, furnish, give, grant, hand over, hold out, introduce, mount, offer, porrect, pose, produce, proffer, put on, raise, recount, relate, show, stage, state, submit, suggest, tender.

antonym take.

n. benefaction, boon, bounty, cadeau, compliment, donation, endowment, favour, gift, grant, gratuity, largess, nuzzer, offering, prezzie, refresher.

presentable *adj.* acceptable, becoming, clean, decent, neat, passable, proper, respectable, satisfactory, suitable, tidy, tolerable.

antonyms unpresentable, untidy.

presentation *n.* appearance, arrangement, award, bestowal, conferral, delivery, demonstration, display, donation, exhibition, exposition, giving, introduction, investiture, offering, pageant, performance, production, rendition, representation, show, staging, submission.

present-day *adj.* contemporary, current, existing, fashionable, hodiernal, living, modern, present, up-to-date.

antonyms future, past.

presenter *n.* anchorman, compère, frontman, host, master of ceremonies, MC.

presentiment *n.* anticipation, apprehension, bad vibes, expectation, fear, feeling, forebodement, foreboding, forecast, forethought, hunch, intuition, misgiving, premonition, presage.

presently *adv.* anon, before long, by and by, directly, immediately, in a minute, shortly, soon.

preservation *n.* conservation, defence, keeping, maintenance, perpetuation, protection, retention, safeguarding, safekeeping, safety, salvation, security, storage, support, upholding, upkeep.

antonyms destruction, ruination.

preserve *v.* care for, confect, conserve, continue,

defend, embalm, entreasure, guard, keep, maintain, perpetuate, protect, retain, safeguard, save, secure, shelter, shield, store, sustain, uphold.

antonyms destroy, ruin.

n. area, confection, confiture, conserve, domain, field, game park, game reserve, jam, jelly, konfyt, marmalade, pigeon, realm, reservation, reserve, safari park, sanctuary, specialism, speciality, specialty, sphere, thing.

preside *v.* administer, chair, conduct, control, direct, govern, head, lead, manage, officiate, run, supervise.

press[1] *v.* adpress, afflict, appress, assail, beg, beset, besiege, calendar, clasp, cluster, compel, compress, condense, constrain, crowd, crush, demand, depress, disquiet, dun, embrace, encircle, enfold, enforce, enjoin, entreat, exhort, finish, flatten, flock, force, force down, gather, harass, hasten, herd, hug, hurry, implore, importune, insist on, iron, jam, mangle, mash, mill, petition, plague, plead, pressurise, push, reduce, rush, seethe, smooth, squeeze, steam, stuff, sue, supplicate, surge, swarm, throng, torment, trouble, urge, vex, worry.

antonyms expand, hang back, lighten, relieve.

n. bunch, bustle, crowd, crush, demand, flock, hassle, herd, horde, host, hurry, mob, multitude, pack, pressure, push, strain, stress, swarm, throng, urgency.

press[2] *n.* columnists, correspondents, Fleet Street, fourth estate, hacks, journalism, journalists, news media, newsmen, newspapers, paparazzi, papers, photographers, pressmen, reporters, writers.

pressed *adj.* browbeaten, bullied, coerced, constrained, forced, harassed, hurried, pressured, pressurised, pushed, rushed, short.

antonyms unhurried, well-off.

pressing *adj.* burning, constraining, crowding, crucial, essential, exigent, high-priority, imperative, important, importunate, serious, thronging, urgent, vital.

antonyms trivial, unimportant.

pressure *n.* adversity, affliction, burden, coercion, compressing, compression, compulsion, constraint, crushing, demands, difficulty, distress, exigency, force, hassle, heat, heaviness, hurry, influence, load, obligation, power, press, pression, squeezing, strain, stress, sway, urgency, weight.

v. browbeat, bulldoze, bully, coerce, compel, constrain, dragoon, drive, force, impel, induce, lean on, oblige, persuade, press, pressurise, squeeze.

pressurise *v.* browbeat, bulldoze, bully, coerce, compel, constrain, dragoon, drive, force, impel, induce, lean on, oblige, persuade, press, pressure, squeeze.

prestige *n.* authority, cachet, celebrity, clout, credit, distinction, eminence, esteem, fame, honour, importance, influence, kudos, pull,

regard, renown, reputation, standing, stature, status, weight.

antonyms humbleness, unimportance.

prestigious *adj.* blue-chip, celebrated, eminent, esteemed, exalted, great, illustrious, important, imposing, impressive, influential, prominent, renowned, reputable, respected, upmarket.

antonyms humble, modest.

presumably *adv.* apparently, as like as not, doubtless, doubtlessly, in all likelihood, in all probability, most likely, no doubt, probably, seemingly.

presume *v.* assume, bank on, believe, conjecture, count on, dare, depend on, go so far, have the audacity, hypothesise, hypothetise, infer, make bold, make so bold, posit, postulate, presuppose, rely on, suppose, surmise, take for granted, take it, take the liberty, think, trust, undertake, venture.

presumption[1] *n.* assurance, audacity, boldness, brass, brass neck, cheek, effrontery, forwardness, gall, impudence, insolence, neck, nerve, presumptuousness, temerity.

antonyms humility, politeness.

presumption[2] *n.* anticipation, assumption, basis, belief, chance, conjecture, grounds, guess, hypothesis, likelihood, opinion, plausibility, premiss, presupposition, probability, reason, supposition, surmise.

presumptive *adj.* assumed, believable, believed, conceivable, credible, designate, expected, hypothetical, inferred, likely, plausible, possible, probable, prospective, reasonable, supposed, understood.

antonyms known, unlikely.

presumptuous *adj.* arrogant, audacious, bigheaded, bold, conceited, foolhardy, forward, impertinent, impudent, insolent, overconfident, over-familiar, overweening, presuming, pushy, rash, uppish.

antonym modest.

presuppose *v.* accept, assume, consider, imply, posit, postulate, premise, presume, suppose, take for granted.

presupposition *n.* assumption, belief, hypothesis, preconception, premise, premiss, presumption, supposition, theory.

pretence *n.* acting, affectation, aim, allegation, appearance, artifice, blague, bounce, charade, claim, cloak, colour, cover, deceit, deception, display, excuse, fabrication, façade, faking, falsehood, feigning, garb, guise, humbug, invention, make-believe, mask, masquerade, posing, posturing, pretentiousness, pretext, profession, pseudery, purpose, ruse, semblance, sham, show, simulation, subterfuge, trickery, veil, veneer, wile.

antonyms honesty, openness, reason.

pretend *v.* act, affect, alge, allege, aspire, assume, claim, counterfeit, dissemble, dissimulate, fake, falsify, feign, go through the motions, imagine, impersonate, make believe, pass oneself off, profess, purport, put on, sham, simulate, suppose.

pretended *adj.* alleged, avowed, bogus, counterfeit, fake, false, feigned, fictitious, imaginary, ostensible, phoney, pretend, professed, pseudo, purported, sham, so-called, specious, spurious, supposed, supposititious. *antonym* real.

pretender *n.* aspirant, claimant, claimer, pretendant.

pretension *n.* affection, airs, aspiration, assertion, assumption, claim, conceit, demand, hypocrisy, ostentation, pomposity, pretence, pretentiousness, pretext, profession, self-importance, show, showiness, snobbery, snobbishness, vainglory, vanity. *antonyms* humility, modesty, simplicity, straightforwardness.

pretentious *adj.* affected, ambitious, assuming, bombastic, chichi, conceited, euphemistic, exaggerated, extravagant, flaunting, grandiloquent, grandiose, highfalutin, high-flown, high-sounding, hollow, inflated, magniloquent, mannered, oro(ro)tund, ostentatious, overambitious, overassuming, pompous, showy, snobbish, specious, uppish, vainglorious. *antonyms* humble, modest, simple, straightforward.

pretentiousness *n.* attitudinising, flamboyance, floridness, floweriness, ostentation, posing, posturing, pretension, pseudery, show, theatricality. *antonyms* humbleness, modesty, simplicity, straightforwardness.

pretext *n.* appearance, cloak, cover, device, excuse, guise, mask, ploy, pretence, rationale, ruse, semblance, show, simulation, umbrage, veil.

prettify *v.* adorn, beautify, bedeck, deck, deck out, decorate, do up, doll up, embellish, garnish, gild, ornament, primp, prink up, smarten up, tart up, titivate, trick out, trim. *antonyms* mar, uglify.

pretty *adj.* appealing, attractive, beautiful, bijou, bonny, charming, comely, cute, dainty, delicate, elegant, fair, fine, good-looking, graceful, lovely, neat, nice, personable, pleasing, sightly, tasteful, trim. *antonyms* tasteless, ugly. *adv.* fairly, moderately, passably, quite, rather, reasonably, somewhat, tolerably.

prevail *v.* abound, obtain, overcome, overrule, predominate, preponderate, reign, rule, succeed, triumph, win. *antonym* lose.

prevail upon bring round, convince, dispose, dissuade, incline, induce, influence, persuade, prompt, sway, talk into, talk out of, talk round, win over.

prevailing *adj.* common, controlling, current, customary, dominant, established, fashionable, general, in style, in vogue, influential, main, mainstream, operative, ordinary, popular, predominating, preponderating, prepotent, prevalent, principal, ruling, set, usual,

widespread. *antonyms* minor, uncommon.

prevalence *n.* acceptance, ascendancy, commonness, currency, frequency, hold, mastery, omnipresence, pervasiveness, popularity, predominance, preponderance, primacy, profusion, regularity, rule, sway, ubiquity, universality. *antonym* uncommonness.

prevalent *adj.* accepted, ascendant, common, commonplace, compelling, current, customary, dominant, epidemic, established, everyday, extensive, frequent, general, governing, habitual, popular, powerful, predominant, prevailing, rampant, regnant, rife, successful, superior, ubiquitous, universal, usual, victorious, widespread. *antonyms* subordinate, uncommon.

prevaricate *v.* cavil, deceive, dodge, equivocate, evade, fib, hedge, lie, palter, quibble, shift, shuffle, temporise, tergiversate.

prevarication *n.* cavil, cavillation, cavilling, deceit, deception, equivocation, evasion, falsehood, falsification, fibbing, fib(s), half-truth, lie, misrepresentation, pretence, quibbling, tergiversation, untruth.

prevaricator *n.* Ananias, casuist, caviller, deceiver, dissembler, dodger, equivocator, evader, fibber, hypocrite, liar, pettifogger, quibbler, sophist.

prevent *v.* anticipate, avert, avoid, balk, bar, block, check, counteract, debar, defend against, foil, forestall, frustrate, hamper, head off, hinder, impede, inhibit, intercept, obstruct, obviate, preclude, restrain, stave off, stop, stymie, thwart, ward off. *antonyms* cause, foster, help.

prevention *n.* anticipation, avoidance, bar, check, deterrence, elimination, forestalling, forethought, frustration, hindrance, impediment, interruption, obstacle, obstruction, obviation, precaution, preclusion, prophylaxis, safeguard, stoppage, thwarting. *antonyms* causing, fostering, help.

preventive *adj.* counteractive, deterrent, hampering, hindering, impeding, inhibitory, obstructive, precautionary, prevenient, preventative, prophylactic, protective, shielding. *antonyms* causative, fostering. *n.* block, condom, deterrent, hindrance, impediment, neutraliser, obstacle, obstruction, prevention, prophylactic, protection, protective, remedy, safeguard, shield. *antonyms* cause, encouragement, incitement.

previous *adj.* antecedent, anterior, arranged, earlier, erstwhile, ex-, foregoing, former, one-time, past, preceding, precipitate, premature, prior, quondam, sometime, umwhile, untimely, whilom. *antonyms* later, timely.

previously *adv.* before, beforehand, earlier, formerly, heretofore, hitherto, once. *antonym* later.

prey *n.* booty, dupe, fall guy, game, kill, mark, mug, plunder, quarry, target, victim.

prey on blackmail, bleed, bully, burden, devour, distress, eat, eat away, exploit, feed on, gnaw at, haunt, hunt, intimidate, live off, moth-eat, oppress, seize, take advantage of, terrorise, trouble, victimise, waste, weigh down, weigh heavily, worry.

price *n.* amount, assessment, bill, bounty, charge, consequences, cost, damage, estimate, expenditure, expense, fee, figure, levy, odds, outlay, payment, penalty, rate, reward, sacrifice, sum, toll, valuation, value, worth.
v. assess, cost, estimate, evaluate, offer, put, rate, valorise, value.

priceless[1] *adj.* beyond price, cherished, costly, dear, expensive, incalculable, incomparable, inestimable, invaluable, irreplaceable, precious, prized, rare, rich, treasured, without price.
antonyms cheap, run-of-the-mill.

priceless[2] *adj.* a hoot, a scream, absurd, amusing, comic, droll, funny, hilarious, killing, rib-tickling, ridiculous, riotous, risible, side-splitting.

price-list *n.* catalogue, menu, price(s)-current.

pric(e)y *adj.* costly, dear, excessive, exorbitant, expensive, extortionate, high-priced, over the odds, steep.
antonym cheap.

prick *v.* bite, bore, itch, jab, jag, pain, perforate, pierce, pink, point, prickle, prog, punch, puncture, raise, rise, smart, stab, sting, thorn, tingle, touch, trouble.
n. jag, pang, perforation, pinhole, prickle, prog, puncture, smart, spasm, sting, twinge, wound.

prickle *n.* acantha, barb, formication, needle, point, smart, spike, spine, spur, thorn, tickle, tingle, tingling.
v. itch, jab, nick, nip, prick, smart, sting, tingle.

prickly *adj.* acanaceous, aculeate(d), barbed, brambly, bristly, cantankerous, complicated, crawling, difficult, echinate, edgy, fractious, grumpy, intricate, involved, irritable, itchy, jaggy, knotty, peevish, pettish, petulant, pricking, prickling, scratchy, sharp, short-tempered, smarting, spiny, stinging, tetchy, thorny, ticklish, tingling, touchy, tricky, troublesome, trying, waspish.
antonyms easy-going, simple, smooth.

pricy *see* pric(e)y .

pride *n.* amour-propre, arrogance, best, big-headedness, boast, choice, conceit, cream, delight, dignity, egotism, élite, flower, gem, glory, gratification, haughtiness, hauteur, high spirits, honour, hubris, jewel, joy, loftiness, magnificence, mettle, morgue, ostentation, pick, pleasure, presumption, pretension, pretentiousness, pride and joy, prize, satisfaction, self-esteem, self-importance, self-love, self-respect, smugness, snobbery, splendour, superciliousness, treasure, vainglory, vanity.
antonym humility.

pride (oneself on) boast, brag, congratulate

oneself, crow, exult, flatter oneself, glory, pat oneself on the back, pique, plume, preen, revel, take pride, vaunt.
antonyms belittle, humble.

priest *n.* abbé, churchman, clergyman, cleric, curate, divine, ecclesiast, ecclesiastic, father, father confessor, flamen, holy man, Jack-priest, lama, Levite, Magus, man of God, man of the cloth, mar-text, masspriest, minister, padre, priestling, vicar.

priestess *n.* abbess, beguine, canoness, clergywoman, deaconess, mambo, nun, prioress, religious, sister, vestal.

priestly *adj.* Aaronic(al), canonical, clerical, ecclesiastical, flaminical, hieratic, pastoral, priestlike, sacerdotal.

prig *n.* goody-goody, holy Joe, Holy Willie, Mrs Grundy, old maid, precisian, prude, puritan.

priggish *adj.* goody-goody, holier-than-thou, narrow-minded, pedantic, prim, prudish, pudibund, puritanical, self-righteous, self-satisfied, smug, starchy, stiff, stuffy.
antonyms broad-minded, informal.

prim *adj.* demure, fastidious, formal, fussy, governessy, old-maidish, old-maidist, particular, perjink, po-faced, precise, priggish, prissy, proper, prudish, pudibund, puritanical, school-marmish, sedate, starchy, stiff, strait-laced.
antonyms broad-minded, informal.

primacy *n.* ascendancy, command, dominance, dominion, leadership, paramoun(t)cy, pre-eminence, seniority, sovereignty, superiority, supremacy.
antonym inferiority.

primal *adj.* central, chief, earliest, first, fundamental, greatest, highest, initial, main, major, original, paramount, primary, prime, primeval, primitive, primordial, principal, pristine.
antonyms later, minor.

primarily *adv.* at first, basically, chiefly, especially, essentially, fundamentally, generally, initially, mainly, mostly, originally, principally.
antonym secondarily.

primary *adj.* aboriginal, basic, beginning, best, capital, cardinal, chief, dominant, earliest, elemental, elementary, essential, first, first-formed, first-made, fundamental, greatest, highest, initial, introductory, leading, main, original, paramount, primal, prime, primeval, primigenial, primitial, primitive, primordial, principal, pristine, radical, rudimentary, simple, top, ultimate, underlying.
antonym secondary.

prime[1] *adj.* basic, best, capital, chief, choice, earliest, excellent, first-class, first-rate, fundamental, highest, leading, main, original, predominant, pre-eminent, primary, principal, quality, ruling, select, selected, senior, superior, top, underlying.
antonyms minor, secondary, second-rate.
n. beginning, flowering, height, heyday, maturity, morning, opening, peak, perfec-

tion, spring, springtide, springtime, start, zenith.

prime[2] *v.* brief, charge, clue up, coach, cram, fill, fill in, gen up, groom, inform, notify, post up, prepare, train.

primer *n.* Donat, introduction, manual, prodrome, prodromus, text-book.

primeval *adj.* ancient, earliest, early, first, Ogygian, old, original, prehistoric, primal, primitial, primitive, primordial, pristine.
antonyms developed, later, modern.

primitive *adj.* aboriginal, barbarian, barbaric, childlike, crude, earliest, early, elementary, first, naïve, neanderthal, original, primal, primary, primeval, primordial, pristine, rough, rude, rudimentary, savage, simple, uncivilised, uncultivated, undeveloped, unrefined, unsophisticated, untrained, untutored.
antonyms advanced, civilised, developed.

primordial *adj.* basic, earliest, elemental, first, first-formed, first-made, fundamental, original, prehistoric, primal, primeval, primigenial, primitial, primitive, pristine, radical.
antonyms developed, later, modern.

prince *n.* lord, mogul, monarch, nabob, nawab, potentate, ruler, sovereign.

princely *adj.* august, bounteous, bountiful, dignified, generous, gracious, grand, imperial, imposing, lavish, liberal, lofty, magnanimous, magnificent, majestic, munificent, noble, open-handed, regal, rich, royal, sovereign, stately, sumptuous.
antonyms humble, mean.

principal[1] *adj.* capital, cardinal, chief, controlling, decuman, dominant, essential, first, foremost, highest, key, leading, main, paramount, pre-eminent, primary, prime, strongest, truncal.
antonyms least, lesser, minor.
n. boss, chief, dean, director, first violin, head, head teacher, headmaster, headmistress, lead, leader, master, prima ballerina, prima donna, rector, star, superintendent.

principal[2] *n.* assets, capital, capital funds, money.

principality *n.* princedom, principate.

principally *adv.* above all, chiefly, especially, mainly, mostly, particularly, predominantly, primarily.

principle *n.* assumption, attitude, axiom, belief, canon, code, conscience, credo, criterion, dictum, doctrine, dogma, duty, element, ethic, formula, fundamental, golden rule, honour, institute, integrity, law, maxim, moral, morality, morals, opinion, precept, principium, probity, proposition, rectitude, rule, scruples, standard, tenet, truth, uprightness, verity.
antonyms corruption, wickedness.

principled *adj.* clear, clear-cut, conscientious, correct, decent, ethical, high-minded, honourable, just, logical, moral, rational, reasoned, righteous, right-minded, scrupulous, sensible, thought-out, upright, virtuous.
antonym unprincipled.

print *v.* engrave, impress, imprint, issue, mark, produce, publish, put to bed, reproduce, run off, stamp, write.
n. book, characters, copy, dab, engraving, face, fingerprint, font, fount, impression, lettering, letters, magazine, mould, newspaper, newsprint, periodical, photo, photograph, picture, publication, reproduction, stamp, type, typeface, typescript.

prior *adj.* aforementioned, antecedent, anterior, earlier, foregoing, former, preceding, pre-existent, previous.
antonym later.

prior to before, earlier than, preceding, preparatory to, previous to.
antonym after.

priority *n.* precedence, pre-eminence, preference, prerogative, privilege, rank, right of way, seniority, superiority, supremacy, the lead.
antonyms inferiority, subordinateness.

priory *n.* abbey, béguinage, cloister, convent, monastery, nunnery, religious house.

prise *see* prize .

prison *n.* bagnio, bastille, borstal(l), bridewell, brig, cage, calaboose, can, cell, chok(e)y, clink, confinement, cooler, coop, dungeon, gaol, glasshouse, gulag, hoos(e)gow, house of correction, imprisonment, jail, jug, lock-up, panopticon, penal institution, penitentiary, pokey, porridge, prison-house, prison-ship, quod, slammer, slink, stalag, stir, tank, tol(l)booth.

prisoner *n.* canary-bird, captive, collegian, con, convict, detainee, détenu(e), forçat, hostage, inmate, internee, jail-bird, lag.

prissy *adj.* effeminate, fastidious, finicky, fussy, old-maidish, overnice, po-faced, precious, prim, prim and proper, prudish, pudibund, school-marmish, squeamish, starchy, strait-laced.
antonyms broad-minded, informal.

pristine *adj.* earliest, first, former, initial, original, primal, primary, primeval, primigenial, primitial, primitive, primordial, uncorrupted, undefiled, unspoiled, unsullied, untouched, virgin.
antonyms developed, later, spoiled.

privacy *n.* clandestineness, concealment, confidentiality, isolation, privateness, quietness, quietude, retirement, retreat, seclusion, secrecy, separateness, sequestration, solitude.
antonym publicness.

private *adj.* clandestine, closet, concealed, confidential, exclusive, home-felt, hush-hush, in camera, independent, individual, inside, intimate, intraparietal, inward, isolated, off the record, own, particular, personal, privy, reserved, retired, secluded, secret, separate, sequestrated, solitary, special, unofficial, withdrawn.
antonyms open, public.
n. enlisted man, private soldier, squaddy, swad, swaddy, tommy, Tommy Atkins.

private detective pinkerton, private eye,

private investigator, shamus.

private parts fanny, genitalia, genitals, privates, pudenda, pussy, quim.

privateer *n.* buccaneer, corsair, freebooter, marque, pirate, sea-robber, sea-wolf.

privation *n.* affliction, austerity, destitution, distress, hardship, indigence, lack, loss, misery, necessary, need, neediness, penury, poverty, suffering, want.
antonyms affluence, wealth.

privatise *v.* denationalise.
antonym nationalise.

privilege *n.* advantage, benefit, birthright, claim, concession, droit, due, entitlement, franchise, freedom, immunity, liberty, licence, prerogative, right, sanction, title.
antonym disadvantage.

privileged *adj.* advantaged, allowed, authorised, élite, empowered, entitled, exempt(ed), favoured, free, granted, honoured, indulged, licensed, permitted, powerful, ruling, sanctioned, special, vested.
antonyms disadvantaged, under-privileged.

privy *n.* bog, cloaca, closet, cludge, earth-closet, head, John, latrine, lavatory, loo, reredorter, toilet, water-closet.
adj. confidential, hidden, hush-hush, intimate, off the record, personal, private, secret, top secret.
antonym public.
privy to apprised of, aware of, cognisant of, in on, in the know, informed about, wise to.
antonym unaware.

prize[1] *n.* accolade, aim, ambition, award, conquest, desire, gain, goal, haul, honour, hope, jackpot, premium, purse, reward, stake(s), trophy, windfall, winnings.
adj. award-winning, best, champion, excellent, first-rate, outstanding, top, top-notch, winning.
antonym second-rate.
v. appreciate, cherish, esteem, hold dear, revere, reverence, set store by, treasure, value.
antonyms despise, undervalue.

prize[2] *n.* booty, capture, loot, pickings, pillage, plunder, spoils, trophy.

prize[3], **prise** *v.* force, jemmy, lever, pry, winkle.

prize-winner *n.* champ, champion, cup-winner, dux, medallist, prize-man, winner.

probability *n.* assumption, chance, chances, expectation, liability, likelihood, likeliness, odds, presumption, prospect.
antonym improbability.

probable *adj.* apparent, credible, feasible, likely, odds-on, on the cards, plausible, possible, presumed, reasonable, seeming, verisimilar.
antonym improbable.

probably *adv.* as likely as not, doubtless, happen, in all likelihood, in all probability, likely, maybe, most likely, perhaps, possibly, presumably.
antonym improbably.

probation *n.* apprenticeship, examination, initiation, noviciate, proof, test, testing, trial, trial period.

probe *v.* examine, explore, go into, investigate, look into, pierce, poke, prod, query, scrutinise, search, sift, sound, test, verify.
n. bore, detection, drill, examination, exploration, inquest, inquiry, investigation, research, scrutiny, study, test.

probity *n.* equity, fairness, fidelity, goodness, honesty, honour, honourableness, integrity, justice, morality, rectitude, righteousness, sincerity, trustworthiness, truthfulness, uprightness, virtue, worth.
antonym improbity.

problem *n.* boyg, brain-teaser, complication, conundrum, difficulty, dilemma, disagreement, dispute, doubt, enigma, no laughing matter, poser, predicament, puzzle, quandry, question, riddle, trouble, vexata quaestio, vexed question.
adj. delinquent, difficult, intractable, perverse, refractory, uncontrollable, unmanageable, unruly.
antonyms manageable, well-behaved.

problematic *adj.* chancy, debatable, doubtful, dubious, enigmatic, moot, problematical, puzzling, questionable, tricky, uncertain, unestablished, unsettled, unsure.
antonym certain.

procedure *n.* action, conduct, course, custom, form, formula, method, modus operandi, move, operation, performance, plan of action, policy, practice, process, routine, scheme, step, strategy, system, transaction.

proceed *v.* advance, arise, carry on, come, continue, derive, emanate, ensue, flow, follow, go ahead, issue, move on, originate, press on, progress, result, set in motion, spring, start, stem.
antonyms retreat, stop.

proceedings *n.* account, action, affair, affairs, annals, archives, business, course of action, dealings, deeds, doings, event(s), matters, measures, minutes, moves, procedure, process, records, report, steps, transactions, undertaking.

proceeds *n.* earnings, emoluments, gain, income, motser, motza, produce, products, profit, receipts, returns, revenue, takings, yield.
antonyms losses, outlay.

process[1] *n.* action, advance, case, course, course of action, development, evolution, formation, growth, manner, means, measure, method, mode, movement, operation, performance, practice, procedure, proceeding, progress, progression, stage, step, suit, system, transaction, trial, unfolding.
v. alter, convert, deal with, digitise, dispose of, fulfil, handle, prepare, refine, transform, treat.

process[2] *n.* node, nodosity, nodule, projection, prominence, protuberance, protusion.

processing *n.* conversion, datamation, handling, preparation, refinement.

procession *n.* cavalcade, column, concatenation,

cortege, course, cycle, file, march, motorcade, parade, run, sequence, series, skimmington, string, succession, train.

proclaim *v.* advertise, affirm, announce, annunciate, blaze, blazon, circulate, declare, enounce, enunciate, give out, herald, indicate, make known, preconise, profess, promulgate, publish, show, testify, trumpet.

proclamation *n.* announcement, annunciation, ban, declaration, decree, edict, firman, hatti-sherif, indiction, interlocution, irade, manifesto, notice, notification, proclaim, promulgation, pronouncement, pronunciamento, publication, ukase.

proclivity *n.* bent, bias, disposition, facility, inclination, leaning, liability, liableness, penchant, predilection, predisposition, proneness, propensity, tendency, weakness. *antonym* disinclination.

procrastinate *v.* adjourn, dally, defer, delay, dilly-dally, drag one's feet, gain time, penelopise, play for time, postpone, prolong, protract, put off, retard, stall, temporise. *antonyms* advance, proceed.

procrastination *n.* dallying, deferral, delaying, dilly-dallying, stalling, temporising.

procreate *v.* beget, breed, conceive, engender, father, generate, mother, produce, propagate, reproduce, sire, spawn.

procure *v.* acquire, appropriate, bag, buy, come by, earn, effect, find, gain, get, induce, lay hands on, obtain, pander, pick up, pimp, purchase, secure, win. *antonym* lose.

procurer *n.* bawd, madam, pander, panderer, pimp, procuress, white-slaver, whoremonger.

prod *v.* dig, drive, egg on, elbow, goad, impel, incite, jab, motivate, move, nudge, poke, prick, prog, prompt, propel, push, rouse, shove, spur, stimulate, urge. *n.* boost, cue, dig, elbow, jab, nudge, poke, prog, prompt, push, reminder, shove, signal, stimulus.

prodigal *adj.* bounteous, bountiful, copious, excessive, extravagant, exuberant, immoderate, improvident, intemperate, lavish, luxuriant, profligate, profuse, reckless, spendthrift, squandering, sumptuous, superabundant, teeming, unsparing, unthrift, unthrifty, wanton, wasteful. *antonyms* modest, parsimonious, thrifty. *n.* big spender, profligate, spendall, spendthrift, squanderer, waster, wastrel.

prodigality *n.* abandon, abundance, amplitude, bounteousness, bounty, copiousness, dissipation, excess, extravagance, exuberance, immoderation, intemperance, lavishness, luxuriance, plenteousness, plenty, profligacy, profusion, recklessness, richness, squandering, sumptuousness, unthrift, unthriftiness, wantonness, waste, wastefulness. *antonyms* modesty, parsimony, thrift.

prodigious *adj.* abnormal, amazing, astounding, colossal, enormous, exceptional, extraordinary, fabulous, fantastic, flabbergasting, giant,

gigantic, huge, immeasurable, immense, impressive, inordinate, mammoth, marvellous, massive, miraculous, monstrous, monumental, phenomenal, remarkable, spectacular, staggering, startling, striking, stupendous, tremendous, unusual, vast, wonderful. *antonyms* commonplace, small, unremarkable.

prodigy *n.* abnormality, child genius, curiosity, freak, genius, grotesque, marvel, matermind, miracle, monster, monstrosity, mutation, phenomenon, rara avis, rarity, sensation, spectacle, talent, whiz, whiz kid, wizard, wonder, wonder child, wonder-work, wunderkind.

produce[1] *v.* advance, afford, bear, beget, breed, bring forth, cause, compose, construct, create, deliver, demonstrate, develop, direct, effect, engender, exhibit, fabricate, factify, factuate, furnish, generate, give, give rise to, invent, make, manufacture, mount, occasion, offer, originate, present, provoke, put forward, put on, render, result in, show, stage, supply, throw, yield. *antonyms* consume, result from. *n.* crop, harvest, product, yield.

produce[2] *v.* continue, elongate, extend, lengthen, prolong, protract.

producer *n.* director, farmer, grower, impresario, maker, manager, manufacturer, presenter, régisseur.

product *n.* artefact, commodity, concoction, consequence, creation, effect, facture, fruit, goods, invention, issue, legacy, merchandise, offshoot, offspring, outcome, output, produce, production, result, returns, spin-off, upshot, work, yield. *antonym* cause.

production *n.* assembly, construction, creation, direction, fabrication, facture, formation, fructification, making, management, manufacture, manufacturing, origination, preparation, presentation, producing, staging. *antonym* consumption.

productive *adj.* advantageous, beneficial, constructive, creative, dynamic, effective, energetic, fecund, fertile, fructiferous, fructuous, fruitful, gainful, generative, gratifying, inventive, plentiful, producing, profitable, prolific, rewarding, rich, teeming, uberous, useful, valuable, vigorous, voluminous, worthwhile. *antonyms* fruitless, unproductive.

productivity *n.* abundance, output, production, productiveness, uberty, work-rate, yield. *antonym* unproductiveness.

profane *adj.* abusive, blasphemous, coarse, crude, disrespectful, filthy, forbidden, foul, godless, heathen, idolatrous, impious, impure, irreligious, irreverent, lay, obscene, pagan, sacrilegious, secular, sinful, temporal, terefa(h), unclean, unconsecrated, ungodly, unhallowed, unholy, uninitiated, unsanctified, vulgar, wicked, worldly. *antonyms* initiated, permitted, religious, sacred.

v. abuse, contaminate, debase, defile, degrade, desecrate, misemploy, misuse, pervert, pollute, prostitute, violate, vitiate.

antonym revere.

profanity *n.* abuse, blasphemy, curse, cursing, execration, expletive, four-letter word, impiety, imprecation, inquination, irreverence, malediction, obscenity, profaneness, sacrilege, swearing, swear-word.

antonyms politeness, reverence.

profess *v.* acknowledge, admit, affirm, allege, announce, assert, asseverate, aver, avow, certify, claim, confess, confirm, declare, enunciate, fake, feign, maintain, make out, own, pretend, proclaim, propose, propound, purport, sham, state, vouch.

professed *adj.* acknowledged, avowed, certified, confirmed, declared, ostensible, pretended, proclaimed, purported, self-acknowledged, self-confessed, self-styled, so-called, soi-disant, supposed, would-be.

profession *n.* acknowledgement, affirmation, assertion, attestation, avowal, business, calling, career, claim, confession, declaration, employment, job, line (of work), manifesto, métier, occupation, office, position, sphere, statement, testimony, vocation, vow, walk of life.

professional *adj.* adept, competent, crack, efficient, experienced, expert, finished, masterly, polished, practised, proficient, qualified, skilled, slick, trained, virtuoso, virtuosic, well-skilled.

antonyms amateur, unprofessional.

n. adept, authority, dab hand, expert, maestro, master, pastmaster, pro, proficient, specialist, virtuoso, wizard.

proffer *v.* advance, extend, hand, hold out, offer, present, propose, propound, submit, suggest, tender, volunteer.

proficiency *n.* ability, accomplishment, aptitude, competence, conversancy, dexterity, expertise, expertness, facility, finesse, knack, know-how, mastery, skilfulness, skill, talent, virtuosity.

antonyms clumsiness, incompetence.

proficient *adj.* able, accomplished, adept, apt, capable, clever, competent, conversant, efficient, experienced, expert, gifted, masterly, qualified, skilful, skilled, talented, trained, versed, virtuose, virtuosic.

antonyms clumsy, incompetent.

profile *n.* analysis, biography, biopic, characterisation, chart, contour, diagram, drawing, examination, figure, form, graph, outline, portrait, review, shape, side view, silhouette, sketch, study, survey, table, thumbnail sketch, vignette.

profit *n.* a fast buck, advancement, advantage, avail, benefit, boot, bottom line, bunce, earnings, emoluments, fruit, gain, gelt, good, graft, gravy, grist, interest, melon, percentage, proceeds, receipts, return, revenue, surplus, takings, use, value, velvet, winnings, yield.

antonym loss.

v. advance, advantage, aid, avail, benefit, better, boot, contribute, gain, help, improve, line one's pockets, promote, serve, stand in good stead.

antonyms harm, hinder.

profit by/from capitalise on, cash in on, exploit, learn from, put to good use, reap the benefit of, take advantage of, turn to account, turn to advantage, use, utilise.

antonym lose by.

profitable *adj.* advantageable, advantageous, beneficial, commercial, cost-effective, emolumental, emolumentary, fruitful, gainful, lucrative, money-making, paying, plummy, productive, remunerative, rewarding, serviceable, useful, utile, valuable, worthwhile.

antonym unprofitable.

profiteer *n.* exploiter, extortioner, extortionist, racketeer.

v. exploit, extort, fleece, make a fast buck, make a quick killing, overcharge, racketeer.

profiteering *n.* exploitation, extortion, Rachmanism, racketeering.

profitless *adj.* bootless, fruitless, futile, gainless, idle, ineffective, ineffectual, pointless, thankless, unavailing, unproductive, unprofitable, unremunerative, useless, vain, worthless.

antonym profitable.

profligacy *n.* abandon, corruption, debauchery, degeneracy, depravity, dissipation, dissoluteness, excess, extravagance, immorality, improvidence, lavishness, laxity, libertinism, licentiousness, prodigality, promiscuity, recklessness, squandering, unrestraint, unthrift, unthriftiness, wantonness, waste, wastefulness.

antonyms morality, parsimony, thrift, uprightness.

profligate *adj.* abandoned, corrupt, Cyprian, debauched, degenerate, depraved, dissipated, dissolute, extravagant, immoderate, immoral, improvident, iniquitous, libertine, licentious, loose, prodigal, promiscuous, reckless, shameless, spendthrift, squandering, unprincipled, vicious, vitiated, wanton, wasteful, whorish, wicked, wild.

antonyms moral, parsimonious, thrifty, upright.

n. debauchee, degenerate, libertine, prodigal, racketeer, rake, reprobate, roué, spendthrift, squanderer, waster, wastrel.

profound *adj.* abject, absolute, abstruse, abysmal, acute, awful, bottomless, cavernous, complete, consummate, deep, deep-seated, discerning, erudite, exhaustive, extensive, extreme, far-reaching, fathomless, great, heartfelt, heart-rending, hearty, intense, keen, learned, penetrating, philosophical, pronounced, recondite, sagacious, sage, serious, sincere, skilled, subtle, thoroughgoing, thoughtful, total, utter, weighty, wise, yawning.

antonyms mild, shallow, slight.

profoundly *adv.* abjectly, acutely, awfully, deeply, dreadfully, extremely, greatly, heartily, intensely, keenly, seriously, sincerely, thoroughly.
antonym slightly.

profundity *n.* abstruseness, acuity, acumen, depth, erudition, extremity, insight, intelligence, intensity, learning, penetration, perceptiveness, perspecuity, perspicacity, profoundness, sagacity, seriousness, severity, strength, wisdom.
antonym shallowness.

profuse *adj.* abundant, ample, bountiful, copious, excessive, extravagant, exuberant, fulsome, generous, immoderate, largehanded, lavish, liberal, luxuriant, openhanded, over the top, overflowing, plentiful, prodigal, prolific, teeming, unstinting.
antonyms sparing, sparse.

profusion *n.* abundance, bounty, copiousness, cornucopia, excess, extravagance, exuberance, glut, lavishness, luxuriance, multitude, plenitude, pleroma, plethora, prodigality, quantity, riot, superabundance, superfluity, surplus, wealth.
antonyms sparingness, sparsity.

progenitor *n.* ancestor, antecedent, begetter, father, forebear, forefather, forerunner, founder, instigator, mother, originator, parent, precursor, predecessor, primogenitor, procreator, source.

progeny *n.* breed, children, descendants, family, issue, lineage, offspring, posterity, quiverful, race, scions, seed, stock, young.

prognosis *n.* diagnosis, expectation, forecast, outlook, prediction, prognostication, projection, prospect, speculation, surmise.

prognosticate *v.* augur, betoken, divine, forebore, forecast, foreshadow, foretell, harbinger, herald, indicate, portend, predict, presage, prophesy, soothsay.

prognostication *n.* expectation, forecast, horoscope, prediction, prognosis, projection, prophecy, speculation, surmise.

programme *n.* agenda, broadcast, curriculum, design, line-up, list, listing, order of events, order of the day, performance, plan, plan of action, presentation, procedure, production, project, schedule, scheme, show, syllabus, transmission.
v. arrange, bill, book, brainwash, design, engage, formulate, itemise, lay on, line up, list, map out, plan, prearrange, schedule, work out.

progress *n.* advance, advancement, amelioration, betterment, breakthrough, circuit, continuation, course, development, gain, growth, headway, improvement, increase, journey, movement, passage, procession, progression, promotion, step forward, way.
antonyms decline, deterioration.
v. advance, ameliorate, better, blossom, come on, continue, develop, forge ahead, gain, gather momentum, grow, improve, increase, make headway, make strides, mature, pro-

ceed, prosper, travel.
antonyms decline, deteriorate.

progression *n.* advance, advancement, chain, concatenation, course, cycle, furtherance, gain, headway, order, progress, sequence, series, string, succession.
antonyms decline, deterioration.

progressive *adj.* accelerating, advanced, advancing, avant-garde, continuing, continuous, developing, dynamic, enlightened, enterprising, escalating, forward-looking, go-ahead, growing, increasing, intensifying, liberal, modern, ongoing, radical, reactionary, reformist, regressive, revolutionary, up-and-coming.

prohibit *v.* ban, bar, constrain, debar, disallow, forbid, hamper, hinder, impede, interdict, obstruct, outlaw, preclude, prevent, proscribe, restrict, rule out, stop, veto.
antonym permit.

prohibited *adj.* banned, barred, disallowed, embargoed, forbidden, interdicted, proscribed, taboo, verboten, vetoed.
antonym permitted.

prohibition *n.* ban, bar, constraint, disallowance, embargo, exclusion, forbiddal, forbiddance, injunction, interdict, interdiction, negation, obstruction, prevention, proscription, restruction, veto.
antonym permission.

prohibitionist *n.* abolitionist, dry, pussyfoot, teetotaller.

prohibitive *adj.* excessive, exorbitant, extortionate, forbidding, impossible, preposterous, prohibiting, prohibitory, proscriptive, repressive, restraining, restrictive, sky-high, steep, suppressive.
antonyms encouraging, reasonable.

project *n.* activity, assignment, conception, design, enterprise, idea, job, occupation, plan, programme, proposal, purpose, scheme, task, undertaking, venture, work.
v. beetle, bulge, calculate, cast, contemplate, contrive, design, devise, discharge, draft, estimate, exsert, extend, extrapolate, extrude, fling, forecast, frame, gauge, hurl, jut, launch, map out, outline, overhang, plan, predetermine, predict, propel, prophesy, propose, protrude, purpose, reckon, scheme, shoot, stand out, stick out, throw, transmit.

projectile *n.* ball, bullet, grenade, missile, mortar-bomb, rocket, shell, shot.

projecting *adj.* beetling, exsertile, extrusive, extrusory, overhanging, protrudent, protruding, protrusive.

projection *n.* blueprint, bulge, calculation, computation, diagram, eaves, estimate, estimation, extrapolation, forecast, jut, jutty, ledge, map, nab, outjet, outjut, outline, overhang, plan, prediction, process, prominence, protrusion, protuberance, reckoning, representation, ridge, shelf, sill.

proletariat *n.* canaille, common people, commonalty, commoners, great unwashed, herd, hoi polloi, lower classes, masses, mob, plebs, proles, rabble, working class.

proliferate v. breed, burgeon, escalate, expand, exuberate, increase, multiply, mushroom, run riot, snowball.

antonym dwindle.

proliferation n. build-up, concentration, duplication, escalation, expansion, extension, increase, intensification, multiplication, mushrooming, snowballing, spread.

antonym decrease.

prolific adj. abounding, abundant, bountiful, copious, fecund, fertile, fertilising, fruitful, generative, luxuriant, productive, profuse, rank, reproductive, rich, teeming, voluminous.

antonyms infertile, scarce.

prolix adj. diffuse, digressive, discursive, lengthy, long, long-winded, prolonged, prosy, protracted, rambling, tedious, tiresome, verbose, windy, wordy.

antonym succinct.

prolixity n. boringness, circuity, diffuseness, discursiveness, long-windedness, macrology, maundering, pleonasm, prosiness, rambling, tediousness, verbiage, verboseness, verbosity, wandering, windiness, wordiness.

antonym succinctness.

prologue n. exordium, foreword, introduction, preamble, preface, preliminary, prelude, proem, prolegomena, prooemion, prooemium.

prolong v. continue, delay, drag out, draw out, extend, lengthen, lengthen out, perpetuate, produce, protract, spin out, stretch.

antonym shorten.

promenade[1] n. boulevard, esplanade, front, parade, prom, sea-front, terrace, walkway.

promenade[2] n. airing, breather, constitutional, saunter, stroll, turn, walk, walkabout.

v. flaunt, mosey, parade, perambulate, sally forth, saunter, stroll, strut, swagger, walk.

prominence[1] n. bulge, bump, cliff, crag, crest, elevation, headland, height, hummock, hump, jutting, lump, mound, pinnacle, process, projection, prominency, promontory, protrusion, protuberance, rise, spur, swelling.

prominence[2] n. celebrity, conspicuousness, distinction, eminence, fame, greatness, importance, markedness, name, notability, outstandingness, precedence, pre-eminence, prestige, rank, reputation, salience, specialness, standing, top billing, visibility, weight.

antonyms inconspicuousness, unimportance.

prominent adj. beetling, bulging, celebrated, chief, conspicuous, distinguished, eminent, eye-catching, famous, foremost, important, jutting, leading, main, noted, noticeable, obtrusive, obvious, outstanding, popular, pre-eminent, projecting, pronounced, protruding, protrusive, protuberant, remarkale, renowned, respected, salient, standing out, striking, top, unmistakable, weighty, well-known.

antonyms inconspicuous, unimportant.

promiscuity n. abandon, amorality, debauchery, depravity, dissipation, immorality, laxity, laxness, lechery, libertinism, licentiousness, looseness, permissiveness, profligacy, promiscuousness, protervity, wantonness, whoredom, whoring, whorishness.

antonym chastity.

promiscuous adj. abandoned, accidental, careless, casual, chaotic, confused, debauched, disordered, dissipated, dissolute, diverse, fast, haphazard, heterogeneous, ill-assorted, immoral, indiscriminate, intermingled, intermixed, jumbled, libertine, licentious, loose, mingled, miscellaneous, mixed, motley, of easy virtue, profligate, random, unbridled, unchaste, uncontrolled, undiscriminating, unselective, wanton, whoremasterly, whorish, wild.

antonyms chaste, controlled, selective.

promise v. assure, augur, bespeak, betoken, bid fair, contract, denote, engage, guarantee, hint at, indicate, look like, pledge, plight, predict, presage, prophesy, stipulate, suggest, swear, take an oath, undertake, vouch, vow, warrant.

n. ability, aptitude, assurance, bond, capability, capacity, commitment, compact, covenant, engagement, flair, guarantee, oath, pledge, pollicitation, potential, talent, undertaking, vow, word, word of honour.

promised land land of milk and honey, paradise, Shangri-la, Zion.

promising adj. able, auspicious, bright, encouraging, favourable, gifted, good, hopeful, likely, propitious, reassuring, rising, rosy, talented, up-and-coming.

antonym unpromising.

promontory n. cape, foreland, head, headland, hoe, mull, nab, naze, ness, peninsula, point, projection, ridge, spur.

promote v. advance, advertise, advocate, aggrandise, aid, assist, back, blazon, boost, champion, contribute to, develop, dignify, elevate, encourage, endorse, espouse, exalt, forward, foster, further, help, honour, hype, kick upstairs, nurture, plug, popularise, prefer, publicise, puff, push, raise, recommend, sell, sponsor, stimulate, support, trumpet, upgrade, urge.

antonyms demote, disparage, obstruct.

promotion n. advancement, advertising, advocacy, aggrandisement, backing, ballyhoo, boosting, campaign, cultivation, development, elevation, encouragement, ennoblement, espousal, exaltation, fanfare, furtherance, honour, hype, plugging, preferment, propaganda, publicity, puffery, pushing, rise, support, trumpeting, upgrading.

antonyms demotion, disparagement, obstruction.

prompt[1] adj. alert, brisk, eager, early, efficient, expeditious, immediate, instant, instantaneous, on time, punctual, quick, rapid, ready, responsive, smart, speedy, swift, timely, timeous, unhesitating, willing.

antonym slow.

adv. exactly, on the dot, promptly, punctually, sharp, to the minute.

prompt[2] *v.* advise, assist, call forth, cause, cue, elicit, evoke, give rise to, impel, incite, induce, inspire, instigate, motivate, move, occasion, prod, produce, provoke, remind, result in, spur, stimulate, urge.

antonym dissuade.

n. cue, help, hint, instigation, jog, jolt, prod, reminder, spur, stimulus.

prompting *n.* admonition, advice, assistance, encouragement, hint, incitement, influence, jogging, persuasion, pressing, pressure, prodding, protreptic, pushing, reminder, reminding, suggestion, urging.

antonym dissuasion.

promptly *adv.* directly, ek dum, forthwith, immediately, instantly, on time, posthaste, pronto, punctually, quickly, speedily, swiftly, unhesitatingly.

promptness *n.* alacrity, alertness, briskness, dispatch, eagerness, expedition, haste, promptitude, punctuality, quickness, readiness, speed, swiftness, willingness.

antonym tardiness.

promulgate *v.* advertise, announce, broadcast, circulate, communicate, declare, decree, disseminate, issue, notify, preconise, proclaim, promote, publicise, publish, spread.

promulgation *n.* announcement, communication, declaration, dissemination, issuance, proclamation, promulgating, publication, publicising.

prone[1] *adj.* apt, bent, disposed, given, inclined, liable, likely, predisposed, propense, subject, susceptible, tending, vulnerable.

antonym unlikely.

prone[2] *adj.* face down, flat, full-length, horizontal, procumbent, prostrate, recumbent, stretched.

antonym upright.

proneness *n.* aptness, bent, bias, disposition, inclination, leaning, liability, penchant, proclivity, propensity, susceptibility, tendency, weakness.

antonym dislike.

prong *n.* fork, grain, point, projection, spike, spur, tine, tip.

pronounce *v.* accent, affirm, announce, articulate, assert, breathe, declaim, declare, decree, deliver, enunciate, judge, proclaim, say, sound, speak, stress, utter, vocalise, voice.

pronounceable *adj.* articulable, enunciable, expressible, sayable, speakable, utterable, vocable.

antonym unpronounceable.

pronounced *adj.* broad, clear, conspicuous, decided, definite, distinct, evident, marked, noticeable, obvious, positive, striking, strong, unmistakable.

antonyms unnoticeable, vague.

pronouncement *n.* announcement, assertion, declaration, decree, dictum, edict, ipse dixit, ipsissima verba, judgement, manifesto, noti-

fication, proclamation, promulgation, pronunciamento, statement.

pronunciation *n.* accent, accentuation, articulation, diction, elocution, enunciation, inflection, intonation, modulation, speech, stress.

proof *n.* assay, attestation, authentication, certification, confirmation, corroboration, demonstration, documentation, evidence, examination, experiment, ordeal, scrutiny, substantiation, test, testimony, trial, verification, voucher.

adj. impenetrable, impervious, proofed, rainproof, repellent, resistant, strong, tight, treated, waterproof, weatherproof, windproof.

antonyms permeable, untreated.

prop *v.* bolster, buttress, lean, maintain, rest, set, shore, stand, stay, strut, support, sustain, truss, underpin, uphold.

n. brace, buttress, mainstay, stanchion, stay, strut, studdle, support, truss.

propaganda *n.* advertising, agitprop, ballyhoo, brainwashing, hype, promotion, publicity, puffery, puffs.

propagandist *n.* advocate, canvasser, evangelist, indoctrinator, pamphleteer, plugger, promoter, proponent, proselytiser, publicist.

propagate *v.* beget, breed, broadcast, circulate, diffuse, disseminate, engender, generate, increase, multiply, proclaim, procreate, produce, proliferate, promote, promulgate, provine, publicise, publish, reproduce, spawn, spread, transmit.

propagation *n.* breeding, circulation, communication, diffusion, dissemination, distribution, generation, increase, issuance, multiplication, procreation, proliferation, promotion, promulgation, reproduction, spawning, spread, spreading, transmission.

propel *v.* drive, force, impel, launch, push, send, shoot, shove, start, thrust, waft.

antonyms slow, stop.

propensity *n.* aptness, bent, bias, disposition, foible, inclination, leaning, liability, penchant, predisposition, proclivity, proneness, readiness, susceptibility, tendency, weakness.

antonym disinclination.

proper *adj.* accepted, accurate, appropriate, apt, becoming, befitting, characteristic, conventional, correct, decent, decorous, established, exact, fit, fitting, formal, genteel, gentlemanly, gradely, graithly, individual, kosher, ladylike, legitimate, mannerly, meet, orthodox, own, particular, peculiar, perjink, personal, polite, precise, prim, prissy, punctilious, refined, respectable, respective, right, sedate, seemly, special, specific, suitable, suited, well-becoming, well-beseeming.

antonyms common, general, improper.

property[1] *n.* acres, assets, belongings, building(s), capital, chattels, effects, estate, freehold, goods, holding, holdings, house(s), land, means, meum et tuum, possessions, real estate, realty, resources, riches, title, wealth.

property[2] *n.* ability, affection, attribute, characteristic, feature, hallmark, idiosyncrasy, mark, peculiarity, quality, trait, virtue.

prophecy *n.* augury, divination, forecast, foretelling, hariolation, prediction, prognosis, prognostication, revelation, second-sight, soothsaying, taghairm, vaticination.

prophesy *v.* augur, divine, forecast, foresee, foretell, forewarn, hariolate, predict, presage, prognosticate, soothsay, vaticinate.

prophet *n.* augur, Cassandra, clairvoyant, divinator, diviner, forecaster, foreteller, Nostradamus, oracle, prognosticator, prophesier, seer, sibyl, soothsayer, tipster, vaticinator.

prophet of doom Cassandra, doomwatcher, Jeremiah, pessimist.

prophetic *adj.* augural, divinatory, fatidical, fey, foreshadowing, mantic, oracular, predictive, presaging, prescient, prognostic, sibylline, vatic, vaticidal.

antonym unprophetic.

propinquity *n.* adjacency, affiliation, affinity, blood, closeness, connection, consanguinity, contiguity, kindredness, kindredship, kinship, nearness, neighbourhood, proximity, relation, relationship, tie, vicinity.

antonym remoteness.

propitiate *v.* appease, conciliate, mollify, pacify, placate, reconcile, satisfy, soothe.

antonyms anger, provoke.

propitiation *n.* appeasement, conciliation, mollification, pacification, pacifying, peacemaking, placation, reconciliation.

antonyms angering, provocation.

propitiatory *adj.* appeasing, assuaging, conciliatory, mollifying, pacificatory, pacifying, peacemaking, placative, placatory, propitiative, reconciliatory, soothing.

antonym provocative.

propitious *adj.* advantageous, auspicious, beneficial, benevolent, benign, bright, encouraging, favourable, fortunate, friendly, gracious, happy, kindly, lucky, opportune, promising, prosperous, reassuring, rosy, timely, well-disposed.

antonym inauspicious.

proponent *n.* advocate, apologist, backer, champion, defender, enthusiast, exponent, friend, partisan, patron, proposer, propounder, subscriber, supporter, upholder, vindicator.

antonym opponent.

proportion *n.* agreement, amount, balance, congruity, correspondence, cut, distribution, division, eurhythmy, fraction, harmony, measure, part, percentage, quota, ratio, relationship, segment, share, symmetry.

antonyms disproportion, imbalance.

proportional *adj.* balanced, commensurate, comparable, compatible, consistent, correspondent, corresponding, equitable, even, fair, just, logistical, proportionate.

antonyms disproportionate, unjust.

proportionally *adv.* commensurately, comparably, correspondingly, evenly, pro rata, proportionately.

antonym disproportionately.

proportions *n.* amplitude, breadth, bulk, capacity, dimensions, expanse, extent, magnitude, measurements, range, scope, size, volume.

proposal *n.* bid, design, draft, manifesto, motion, offer, outline, overture, plan, platform, presentation, proffer, programme, project, proposition, recommendation, scheme, sketch, suggestion, suit, tender, terms.

propose *v.* advance, aim, bring up, design, enunciate, have in mind, intend, introduce, invite, lay before, mean, move, name, nominate, pay suit, plan, pop the question, present, proffer, propound, purpose, put forward, put up, recommend, scheme, submit, suggest, table, tender.

antonyms oppose, withdraw.

proposition *n.* manifesto, motion, plan, programme, project, proposal, recommendation, scheme, suggestion, tender.

v. accost, solicit.

propound *v.* advance, advocate, contend, enunciate, lay down, move, postulate, present, propose, put forward, set forth, submit, suggest.

antonym oppose.

proprietor *n.* châtelaine, deed holder, freeholder, landlady, landlord, landowner, owner, possessor, proprietary, proprietress, proprietrix, title-holder.

propriety *n.* appropriateness, aptness, becomingness, breeding, correctness, courtesy, decency, decorum, delicacy, etiquette, fitness, gentlemanliness, manners, modesty, politeness, protocol, punctilio, rectitude, refinement, respectability, rightness, seemliness, suitableness.

antonym impropriety.

proprieties *n.* civilities, conventions, decencies, decorum, etiquette, niceties, protocol, p's and q's, social graces.

antonym boorishness.

propulsion *n.* drive, impetus, impulse, impulsion, momentum, power, pressure, push, thrust.

prosaic *adj.* banal, boring, bromidic, commonplace, dry, dull, everyday, flat, hackneyed, humdrum, matter-of-fact, mundane, ordinary, pedestrian, routine, stale, tame, trite, unimaginative, uninspired, uninspiring, unpoetical, vapid, workaday.

antonyms imaginative, interesting.

proscribe *v.* attant, ban, banish, bar, black, blackball, boycott, censure, condemn, damn, denounce, deport, doom, embargo, exclude, excommunicate, exile, expatriate, expel, forbid, interdict, ostracise, outlaw, prohibit, reject.

antonyms admit, allow.

proscription *n.* attainder, ban, banishment, bar, barring, boycott, censure, condemnation, damning, denunciation, deportation, ejection, embargo, eviction, exclusion, excommunication, exile, expatriation, expulsion,

interdict, ostracism, outlawry, prohibition, rejection.
antonyms admission, allowing.

prosecute *v.* arraign, bring suit against, bring to trial, carry on, conduct, continue, direct, discharge, engage in, execute, follow through, indict, litigate, manage, perform, persevere, persist, practise, prefer charges, pursue, put on trial, see through, sue, summon, take to court, try, work at.
antonym desist.

proselytise *v.* bring into the fold, bring to God, convert, evangelise, make converts, persuade, propagandise, spread the gospel, win over.

prospect *n.* calculation, chance, contemplation, expectation, future, hope, landscape, likelihood, odds, opening, outlook, panorama, perspective, plan, possibility, presumption, probability, promise, proposition, scene, sight, spectacle, thought, view, vision, vista.
antonym unlikelihood.
v. explore, fossick, nose, quest, search, seek, survey.

prospective *adj.* anticipated, approaching, awaited, coming, designate, designated, destined, eventual, expected, forthcoming, future, imminent, intended, likely, possible, potential, soon-to-be, to come, -to-be.
antonyms agreed, current.

prospectus *n.* account, announcement, catalogue, conspectus, list, manifesto, outline, pamphlet, plan, platform, programme, scheme, syllabus, synopsis.

prosper *v.* advance, bloom, boom, burgeon, fare well, flourish, flower, get on, grow rich, make good, progress, succeed, thrive, turn out well.
antonym fail.

prosperity *n.* affluence, boom, ease, fortune, good fortune, luxury, plenty, prosperousness, riches, success, the good life, weal, wealth, well-being.
antonym poverty.

prosperous *adj.* affluent, blooming, booming, burgeoning, flourishing, fortunate, in the money, lucky, moneyed, opulent, palmy, profitable, rich, successful, thriving, wealthy, well-heeled, well-off, well-to-do.
antonym poor.

prostitute *n.* bawd, brass, broad, call-girl, cocotte, courtesan, dolly-mop, drab, fallen woman, fille de joie, fille des rues, floosie, grande cocotte, harlot, hooker, hustler, loon, loose woman, loose-fish, lorette, moll, Paphian, pro, punk, street-walker, strumpet, tart, trollop, trull, vizard-mask, wench, white slave, whore, woman of the town, working girl.
v. cheapen, debase, degrade, demean, devalue, misapply, misuse, pervert, profane.

prostitution *n.* harlotry, meretriciousness, street-walking, the game, the oldest profession, vice, whoredom, whoring.

prostrate *adj.* abject, brought to one's knees, crushed, defenceless, dejected, depressed, desolate, disarmed, done, drained, exhausted, fagged, fallen, flat, helpless, horizontal, impotent, inconsolable, knackered, kowtowing, overcome, overwhelmed, paralysed, pooped, powerless, procumbent, prone, reduced, shattered, spent, worn out.
antonyms elated, erect, hale, happy, strong, triumphant.
v. crush, depress, disarm, drain, exhaust, fag out, fatigue, knacker, lay low, overcome, overthrow, overturn, overwhelm, paralyse, poop, reduce, ruin, sap, shatter, tire, wear out, weary.
antonyms elate, exalt, strengthen.

prostrate oneself abase oneself, bend the knee, bow down, cringe, grovel, kneel, kowtow, submit.
antonym exalt oneself.

prostration *n.* abasement, bow, collapse, dejection, depression, desolation, despair, despondency, exhaustion, genuflection, grief, helplessness, kneeling, kowtow, obeisance, paralysis, slough of despond, submission, weakness, weariness.
antonyms elation, exaltation, happiness, triumph.

protagonist *n.* advocate, champion, chief character, exponent, hero, heroine, lead, leader, mainstay, prime mover, principal, proponent, standard-bearer, supporter.

protean *adj.* amoebic, changeable, ever-changing, inconstant, many-sided, mercurial, multiform, mutable, polymorphic, polymorphous, variable, volatile.
antonyms stable, unchanging.

protect *v.* care for, chaperon, convoy, cover, cover up for, defend, escort, guard, harbour, keep, look after, preserve, safeguard, save, screen, secure, shelter, shield, stand guard over, support, watch over.
antonyms attack, threaten.

protection *n.* aegis, armour, backstop, barrier, buffer, bulwark, care, charge, cover, custody, defence, guard, guardianship, guarding, preservation, protecting, refuge, safeguard, safekeeping, safety, screen, security, shelter, shield, umbrella, wardship.
antonyms attack, threat.

protective *adj.* careful, conservationist, covering, custodial, defensive, fatherly, insulating, jealous, maternal, motherly, paternal, possessive, safeguarding, sheltering, shielding, tutelary, vigilant, warm, watchful.
antonyms aggressive, threatening.

protector *n.* advocate, benefactor, bodyguard, champion, counsel, defender, father-figure, guard, guardian, patron, protectress, protectrix, safeguard.
antonyms attacker, threat.

protégé(e) *n.* blue-eyed boy, charge, dependant, discovery, pupil, student, ward, white-headed boy.
antonym guardian.

protest *n.* complaint, declaration, demur, demurral, dharna, disapproval, dissent,

formal complaint, objection, obtestation, outcry, protestation, remonstrance.
antonym acceptance.

v. affirm, argue, assert, asseverate, attest, avow, complain, contend, cry out, declare, demonstrate, demur, disagree, disapprove, expostulate, insist, maintain, object, obtest, oppose, profess, remonstrate, squawk, take exception, testify, vow.
antonym accept.

protestation *n.* affirmation, asseveration, assurance, avowal, complaint, declaration, disagreement, dissent, expostulation, oath, objection, outcry, pledge, profession, protest, remonstrance, remonstration, statement, vow.

protestor *n.* agitator, demonstrator, dissenter, dissident, rebel, remonstrant, remonstrator.

protocol *n.* conventions, courtesies, customs, decorum, etiquette, formalities, good form, manners, politesse, procedure, propriety, p's and q's.
antonym boorishness.

prototype *n.* archetype, example, exemplar, mock-up, model, original, paradigm, pattern, precedent, standard, type.

protract *v.* continue, draw out, extend, keep going, lengthen, prolong, spin out, stretch out, sustain.
antonym shorten.

protracted *adj.* dragged out, drawn-out, extended, interminable, lengthy, long, long-drawn-out, overlong, prolix, prolonged, wearisome, wordy.
antonym shortened.

protrude *v.* bulge, come through, exsert, extend, extrude, jut, obtrude, point, pop, project, protuberate, stand out, start, stick out, strout.

protruding *adj.* astrut, exsertive, extrusive, extrusory, jutting, prominent, protrudent, protrusive, protuberant, proud.
antonyms flat, flush.

protrusion *n.* bulge, bump, jut, lump, outgrowth, process, projection, protuberance, swelling.

protuberance *n.* apophysis, bulb, bulge, bump, excrescence, knob, lump, mamelon, mamilla, outgrowth, process, projection, prominence, protrusion, swelling, tuber, tubercle, tumour, umbo, venter, wart, welt.

protuberant *adj.* astrut, beetling, bulbous, bulging, bunched, exsertive, extrusive, extrusory, gibbous, jutting, popping, prominent, protrudent, protruding, protrusive, proud, swelling, swollen.
antonym flat.

proud *adj.* appreciative, arrogant, august, boastful, conceited, content, contented, disdainful, distinguished, egotistical, eminent, exalted, glad, glorious, grand, gratified, gratifying, great, haughty, high and mighty, honoured, illustrious, imperious, imposing, lofty, lordly, magnificent, majestic, memorable, misproud, noble, orgulous, overbearing, overweening, pleased, pleasing, presump-

tuous, prideful, red-letter, rewarding, satisfied, satisfying, self-important, self-respecting, snobbish, snobby, snooty, splendid, stately, stuck-up, supercilious, toffee-nosed, vain.
antonym humble.

provable *adj.* attestable, confirmable, corroborable, demonstrable, establishable, evincible, testable, verifiable.
antonym unprovable.

prove *v.* analyse, ascertain, assay, attest, authenticate, bear out, check, confirm, corroborate, demonstrate, determine, document, establish, evidence, evince, examine, experience, experiment, justify, show, substantiate, suffer, test, try, turn out, verify.
antonyms discredit, disprove, falsify.

proven *adj.* accepted, attested, authentic, certified, checked, confirmed, corroborated, definite, dependable, established, proved, reliable, tested, tried, trustworthy, undoubted, valid, verified.
antonym unproven.

provenance *n.* birthplace, derivation, origin, provenience, source.

provender *n.* comestibles, eatables, eats, edibles, fare, feed, fodder, food, foodstuffs, forage, groceries, grub, nosh, provand, proviant, provisions, rations, supplies, sustenance, victuals.

proverb *n.* adage, aphorism, apophthegm, bromide, byword, dictum, gnome, maxim, precept, saw, saying.

proverbial *adj.* accepted, acknowledged, apophthegmatic, archetypal, axiomatic, bromidic, conventional, current, customary, famed, famous, legendary, notorious, self-evident, time-honoured, traditional, typical, unquestioned, well-known.

provide *v.* accommodate, add, afford, anticipate, arrange for, bring, cater, contribute, determine, equip, forearm, furnish, give, impart, lay down, lend, outfit, plan for, prepare for, present, produce, provision, render, require, serve, specify, state, stipulate, stock up, suit, supply, take measures, take precautions, yield.
antonyms remove, take.

provide for dower, endow, fend, keep, maintain, support, sustain.
antonyms ignore, neglect.

providence *n.* care, caution, destiny, discretion, divine intervention, far-sightedness, fate, foresight, forethought, fortune, God's will, karma, kismet, perspicacity, predestination, predetermination, presence of mind, prudence.
antonym improvidence.

provident *adj.* canny, careful, cautious, discreet, economical, equipped, far-seeing, far-sighted, frugal, imaginative, long-sighted, prudent, sagacious, shrewd, thrifty, vigilant, wary, well-prepared, wise.
antonym improvident.

providential *adj.* convenient, fortuitous, fortun-

ate, happy, heaven-sent, lucky, opportune, timely, welcome.
antonym untimely.

provider *n.* angel, benefactor, breadwinner, donor, earner, funder, giver, mainstay, source, supplier, supporter, wage-earner.

providing *conj.* as long as, contingent upon, given, on condition, on the assumption, on the understanding, provided, subject to, with the proviso.

province *n.* area, bailiwick, business, capacity, charge, colony, concern, county, department, dependency, district, division, domain, duty, employment, field, function, line, orbit, part, pigeon, post, region, responsibility, role, section, sphere, territory, tract, zone.

provincial *adj.* bucolic, country, home-grown, homespun, insular, inward-looking, limited, local, mofussil, narrow, narrow-minded, parish-pump, parochial, rural, rustic, small-minded, small-town, uninformed, unsophisticated.
antonyms sophisticated, urban.

provincialism *n.* insularity, localism, narrow-mindedness, parochialism, provinciality, regionalism, sectionalism.
antonym sophistication.

provision *n.* accoutrement, agreement, arrangement, catering, clause, condition, demand, equipping, fitting out, furnishing, plan, prearrangement, precaution, preparation, prerequisite, providing, proviso, purveyance, purveying, requirement, specification, stipulation, supplying, term, victualling.
antonyms neglect, removal.

provisional *adj.* conditional, contingent, interim, limited, pro tem, provisory, qualified, stop-gap, temporary, tentative, transitional.
antonyms definite, fixed, permanent.

provisionally *adv.* for the time being, interim, meanwhile, pro tem, pro tempore.

provisions *n.* comestibles, eatables, eats, edibles, fare, food, foodstuff, groceries, grub, piece, prog, provand, provender, proviant, rations, stores, supplies, sustenance, viands, viaticum, victuallage, victuals, vittles.

proviso *n.* clause, condition, limitation, provision, qualification, requirement, reservation, restriction, rider, small print, stipulation.

provisory *adj.* conditional, interim, provisional, qualified, temporary, tentative.
antonyms definite, fixed, permanent.

provocation *n.* affront, aggravation, annoyance, casus belli, cause, challenge, dare, grievance, grounds, incitement, indignity, inducement, injury, instigation, insult, justification, motivation, motive, offence, reason, red rag, stimulus, taunt, vexation.

provocative *adj.* abusive, aggravating, alluring, annoying, arousing, challenging, disturbing, erotic, exciting, galling, goading, incensing, insulting, inviting, offensive, outrageous, provocatory, provoking, seductive, sexy, stimulating, suggestive, tantalising, tempting.
antonyms pacificatory, unprovocative.

provoke *v.* affront, aggravate, anger, annoy, cause, chafe, elicit, enrage, evoke, exasperate, excite, fire, gall, generate, give rise to, incense, incite, induce, inflame, infuriate, inspire, instigate, insult, irk, irritate, kindle, madden, motivate, move, occasion, offend, pique, precipitate, produce, promote, prompt, put out, rile, rouse, stimulate, stir, vex.
antonyms pacify, please, result.

provoking *adj.* aggravating, annoying, exasperating, galling, infuriating, irking, irksome, irritating, maddening, obstructive, offensive, pesky, pestiferous, tiresome, vexatious, vexing.
antonyms pacificatory, pleasing.

prow *n.* bow(s), cut-water, fore, forepart, front, head, nose, prore, stem.
antonym stern.

prowess *n.* ability, accomplishment, adeptness, adroitness, aptitude, attainment, bravery, command, daring, dauntlessness, dexterity, doughtiness, excellence, expertise, expertness, facility, genius, heroism, mastery, skill, talent, valour.
antonyms clumsiness, mediocrity.

prowl *v.* creep, cruise, hunt, lurk, nose, patrol, range, roam, rove, scavenge, search, skulk, slink, sneak, snook, stalk, steal.

proximity *n.* adjacency, closeness, contiguity, juxtaposition, nearness, neighbourhood, propinquity, proximation, vicinity.
antonym remoteness.

proxy *n.* agent, attorney, delegate, deputy, factor, representative, stand-in, substitute, surrogate.

prude *n.* Mrs Grundy, old maid, prig, puritan, school-marm, Victorian.

prudence *n.* canniness, care, caution, circumspection, common sense, discretion, economy, far-sightedness, foresight, forethought, frugality, good sense, heedfulness, husbandry, judgement, judiciousness, planning, policy, precaution, preparedness, providence, sagacity, saving, thrift, vigilance, wariness, wisdom.
antonym imprudence.

prudent *adj.* canny, careful, cautious, circumspect, discerning, discreet, economical, far-sighted, frugal, judicious, politic, provident, sagacious, sage, sensible, shrewd, sparing, thrifty, vigilant, wary, well-advised, wise, wise-hearted.
antonym imprudent.

prudish *adj.* demure, narrow-minded, old-maidish, overmodest, overnice, po-faced, priggish, prim, prissy, proper, pudibund, puritanical, school-marmish, squeamish, starchy, strait-laced, stuffy, ultra-virtuous, Victorian.
antonyms easy-going, lax.

prudishness *n.* Grundyism, old-maidishness, overmodesty, priggishness, primness, prissiness, prudery, pudibundity, puritanism, squeamishness, starchiness, strictness, stuffiness.

antonym laxness.

prune *v.* clip, cut, dehorn, dock, lop, pare, reduce, shape, shorten, snip, trim.

prurient *adj.* concupiscent, cupidinous, desirous, dirty, erotic, indecent, itching, lascivious, lecherous, lewd, libidinous, lickerish, lustful, obscene, pornographic, salacious, smutty, voyeuristic.

antonym decent.

pry *v.* delve, dig, ferret, interfere, intrude, meddle, nose, peep, peer, poke, poke one's nose in, snoop.

antonym mind one's own business.

prying *adj.* curious, inquisitive, interfering, intrusive, meddlesome, meddling, nosy, peering, peery, snooping, snoopy, spying.

antonym uninquisitive.

psalm *n.* canticle, chant, hymn, paean, paraphrase, song.

pseud *n.* fraud, humbug, phoney, poser, poseur, trendy.

pseudo *adj.* artificial, bogus, counterfeit, ersatz, fake, false, imitation, mock, phoney, pretended, pseud, quasi-, sham, spurious, ungenuine.

antonym genuine.

pseudonym *n.* alias, allonym, anonym, assumed name, false name, incognito, monicker, nom de guerre, nom de plume, pen name, stage name.

psyche *n.* anima, awareness, consciousness, individuality, intellect, intelligence, mind, personality, pneuma, self, soul, spirit, subconscious, understanding.

psychiatrist *n.* analyst, headshrinker, psychoanalyser, psychoanalyst, psychologist, psychotherapist, shrink, therapist, trickcyclist.

psychic *adj.* clairvoyant, cognitive, extrasensory, intellectual, mental, mystic, mystical, occult, preternatural, psychogenic, psychological, spiritual, spiritualistic, supernatural, telekinetic, telepathic.

psychological *adj.* affective, cerebral, cognitive, emotional, imaginary, intellectual, irrational, mental, psychosomatic, subconscious, subjective, unconscious, unreal.

psychology *n.* brains, craft, craftiness, cunning, psychiatry, psychics, slyness, subtlety, wiliness.

psychopath *n.* lunatic, madman, maniac, psycho, psychotic, sociopath.

psychotic *adj.* certifiable, demented, deranged, insane, lunatic, mad, mental, psychopathic, unbalanced.

antonym sane.

puberty *n.* adolescence, juvenescence, maturity, nubility, pubescence, teens, youth.

antonyms childhood, immaturity.

public *adj.* accessible, acknowledged, circulating, civic, civil, common, communal, community, exposed, general, important, known, national, notorious, obvious, open, overt, patent, plain, popular, prominent, published,

recognised, respected, social, state, universal, unrestricted, well-known, widespread.

antonym private.

n. audience, buyers, citizens, clientèle, commonalty, community, country, electorate, everyone, followers, following, masses, multitude, nation, patrons, people, populace, population, punters, society, supporters, voters.

public house alehouse, bar, bierkeller, bodega, boozer, brasserie, cantina, dram-shop, hostelry, inn, jerry-shop, local, lush-house, pot-house, pot-shop, pub, roadhouse, taphouse, tavern, tippling-house, vaults.

publican *n.* barman, inn-keeper, mine host, padrone, taverner.

publication *n.* advertisement, airing, announcement, appearance, book, booklet, broadcasting, brochure, declaration, disclosure, dissemination, divulgation, handbill, issue, leaflet, magazine, newspaper, notification, pamphlet, periodical, proclamation, promulgation, publishing, publishment, reporting, vent.

publicise *v.* advertise, blaze, blazon, broadcast, hype, plug, promote, puff, push, spotlight, spread about, write off.

antonym keep secret.

publicity *n.* advertising, attention, ballyhoo, boost, build-up, hype, plug, press, promotion, public notice, puff, puffery, réclame, splash.

antonym secrecy.

public-spirited *adj.* altruistic, charitable, community-minded, conscientious, generous, humanitarian, philanthropic, unselfish.

antonym selfish.

publish *v.* advertise, announce, bring out, broadcast, circulate, communicate, declare, diffuse, disclose, distribute, divulgate, divulge, evulgate, issue, leak, part, print, proclaim, produce, promulgate, publicise, reveal, spread, vent.

antonym keep secret.

pucker *v.* compress, contract, crease, crinkle, crumple, furrow, gather, purse, ruck, ruckle, ruffle, screw up, shirr, shrivel, tighten, wrinkle.

n. crease, crinkle, crumple, fold, ruck, ruckle, shirr, wrinkle.

puckered *adj.* creased, gathered, pursy, rucked, ruckled, wrinkled.

antonym smooth.

puckish *adj.* frolicsome, impish, mischievous, naughty, pawky, playful, roguish, sly, sportive, teasing, waggish, whimsical.

antonym solemn.

pudding *n.* afters, dessert, dumpling, pud, sweet.

puddle *n.* dub, plash, plashet, pool, slop, sop, soss.

pudenda *n.* fanny, genitalia, genitals, private parts, privates, pussy, quim.

puerile *adj.* babyish, childish, foolish, immature, inane, infantile, irresponsible, jejune, juvenile, naïve, petty, ridiculous, silly, trifling,

trivial, weak.
antonym mature.
puff *n.* advertisement, blast, breath, commendation, drag, draught, emanation, flurry, gust, mention, plug, pull, smoke, waft, whiff.
v. bloat, blow, breathe, dilate, distend, drag, draw, exhale, expand, gasp, gulp, hype, inflate, inhale, pant, plug, praise, promote, publicise, pull, push, smoke, suck, swell, waft, wheeze, whiff, whiffle.
puffed *adj.* breathless, done in, exhausted, gasping, out of breath, panting, winded.
antonym vigorous.
puffed up arrogant, big-headed, full of oneself, high and mighty, prideful, proud, swollen-headed, too big for one's boots.
antonym modest.
puffy *adj.* bloated, distended, enlarged, inflamed, inflated, oedematous, puffed up, pursy, swollen.
antonym flat.
pugilism *n.* boxing, fighting, fistiana, prize-fighting, the fancy, the noble art, the noble science, the prize-ring, the ring.
pugilist *n.* boxer, bruiser, fighter, prize-fighter, pug, pugil.
pugnacious *adj.* aggressive, antagonistic, argumentative, bellicose, belligerent, choleric, combative, contentious, disputatious, hostile, hot-tempered, irascible, petulant, quarrelsome.
antonym easy-going.
puke *v.* disgorge, heave, posset, regurgitate, retch, spew, throw up, vomit.
pull *v.* attract, cull, dislocate, drag, draw, draw out, entice, extract, gather, haul, jerk, lure, magnetise, pick, pluck, remove, rend, rip, schlep, sprain, strain, stretch, take out, tear, tow, track, trail, tug, tweak, uproot, weed, whang, wrench, yank.
antonyms deter, push, repel.
n. advantage, allurement, attraction, clout, drag, drawing power, effort, exertion, force, forcefulness, influence, inhalation, jerk, leverage, lure, magnetism, muscle, power, puff, seduction, tug, twitch, weight, yank.
antonyms deterring, push, repelling.
pull a face frown, glower, grimace, knit one's brows, lower, pout, scowl, sulk.
pull a fast one on cheat, con, deceive, defraud, grift, hoodwink, put one over on, sting, swindle, take for a ride, trick.
pull apart attack, carp at, criticise, dismember, divellicate, find fault, flay, knock, lay into, pan, part, pick holes in, pull to pieces, run down, separate, slam, slate, sunder.
antonym praise.
pull down bulldoze, demolish, destroy, dismantle, knock down, raze, remove.
antonym put up.
pull in arrest, arrive, attract, bring in, bust, clear, collar, come in, draw, draw in, draw up, earn, gain, gross, make, nab, nail, net, park, pinch, pocket, reach, run in, stop, take home.
antonyms lose, pull away, repel.

pull off accomplish, achieve, bring off, carry out, manage, succeed, swing.
antonym fail.
pull out abandon, depart, draw out, evacuate, evulse, leave, quit, retreat, withdraw.
antonym join.
pull someone's leg chaff, deceive, fool, make fun of, tease, trick.
pull the wool over someone's eyes bamboozle, con, deceive, delude, dupe, fool, hoodwink, lead up the garden path, pull a fast one on, put one over on, snow, take in, trick.
pull through rally, recover, recuperate, survive, weather.
antonym fail.
pull together collaborate, co-operate, team up, work together.
antonym fight.
pull up admonish, brake, carpet, castigate, draw in, draw up, halt, lift, raise, rebuke, reprimand, reprove, stop, take to task, tell off, tick off, uproot.
pulp *n.* flesh, marrow, mash, mush, pap, paste, pomace, soft part, triturate.
v. crush, liquidise, mash, pulverise, squash.
pulpit *n.* dais, lectern, platform, rostrum, soap-box, wood.
pulpy *adj.* fleshy, mushy, pappy, sloppy, soft, squashy, succulent.
antonym hard.
pulsate *v.* beat, drum, hammer, oscillate, palpitate, pound, pulse, quiver, throb, thud, thump, tick, vibrate.
pulsating *adj.* oscillating, palpitating, pulsatile, pulsative, pulsatory, pulsing, vibratile, vibrating, vibrative.
pulsation *n.* ictus, oscillation, palpitation, vibration, vibratiuncle.
pulse *n.* beat, beating, drumming, oscillation, pulsation, rhythm, stroke, throb, throbbing, thudding, vibration.
v. beat, drum, pulsate, throb, thud, tick, vibrate.
pulverise *v.* annihilate, bray, comminute, crush, defeat, demolish, destroy, flatten, granulate, grind, hammer, levigate, mill, pestle, pound, smash, triturate, vanquish, wreck.
pummel *v.* bang, batter, beat, fib, hammer, knock, nevel, pound, punch, strike, thump.
pump *v.* catechise, cross-examine, debrief, drive, force, grill, inject, interrogate, pour, probe, push, question, quiz, send, supply.
pump out bail out, drain, draw off, empty, force out, siphon.
pump up blow up, dilate, distend, inflate, puff up.
pun *n.* clinch, double entendre, equivoke, jeu de mots, paronomasia, paronomasy, play on words, quip, witticism.
punch[1] *v.* bash, biff, bop, box, clout, fib, hit, plug, pummel, slam, slug, smash, sock, strike, wallop.
n. bash, biff, bite, blow, bop, clout, drive, effectiveness, force, forcefulness, hit, impact, jab, knock, knuckle sandwich, lander,

muzzler, panache, pizzazz, plug, point, sock, thump, verve, vigour, wallop.
antonym feebleness.

punch[2] *v.* bore, cut, drill, perforate, pierce, pink, prick, puncture, stamp.

punch-drunk *adj.* befuddled, confused, dazed, dizzy, groggy, punchy, reeling, slap-happy, staggering, stupefied, unsteady, woozy.

punch-up *n.* argument, brawl, ding-dong, Donnybrook, dust-up, fight, free-for-all, row, ruckus, scrap, set-to, shindy, stand-up fight.

punchy *adj.* aggressive, dynamic, effective, forceful, incisive, lively, powerful, spirited, vigorous, zappy.
antonyms feeble, weak.

punctilio *n.* ceremony, convention, delicacy, distinction, exactitude, exactness, fine point, finickiness, formality, meticulousness, nicety, particular, particularity, preciseness, precision, punctiliousness, refinement, scrupulousness, strictness.
antonyms boorishness, informality.

punctilious *adj.* careful, ceremonious, conscientious, exact, finicky, formal, formalist, fussy, meticulous, nice, overnice, particular, precise, proper, scrupulous, strict.
antonyms boorish, easy-going, informal.

punctual *adj.* early, exact, in good time, on the dot, on time, precise, prompt, punctilious, strict, timely, up to time.
antonym unpunctual.

punctuality *n.* promptitude, promptness, readiness, regularity, strictness.
antonym unpunctuality.

punctually *adv.* on the dot, on time, precisely, prompt, promptly, sharp.
antonym unpunctually.

punctuate *v.* accentuate, break, emphasise, interject, interrupt, intersperse, pepper, point, sprinkle.

puncture *n.* break, cut, fissure, flat, flat tyre, hole, leak, nick, opening, perforation, rupture, slit.
v. bore, cut, deflate, discourage, disillusion, flatten, humble, nick, penetrate, perforate, pierce, prick, rupture, take down a peg or two.

pundit *n.* authority, buff, deipnosophist, expert, guru, maestro, master, teacher.

pungent *adj.* acid, acrid, acrimonious, acute, aromatic, barbed, biting, bitter, caustic, cutting, fell, hot, incisive, keen, mordant, painful, penetrating, peppery, piercing, piquant, poignant, pointed, sarcastic, scathing, seasoned, sharp, sour, spicy, stinging, stringent, strong, tangy, tart, telling, trenchant.
antonyms feeble, mild, tasteless.

punish *v.* abuse, amerce, batter, beat, castigate, chasten, chastise, correct, crucify, discipline, flog, give a lesson to, give someone laldie, harm, hurt, injure, keelhaul, knee-cap, lash, maltreat, manhandle, masthead, misuse, oppress, penalise, rough up, scour, scourge, sort, strafe, trounce.

punishable *adj.* blameworthy, chargeable, convictable, criminal, culpable, indictable,

unlawful.

punishing *adj.* arduous, backbreaking, burdensome, demanding, exhausting, fatiguing, grinding, gruelling, hard, strenuous, taxing, tiring, wearing.
antonym easy.

punishment *n.* abuse, beating, chastening, chastisement, come-uppance, correction, damnation, deserts, discipline, jankers, kneecapping, laldie, maltreatment, manhandling, medicine, pain, pay-off, penalty, penance, punition, retribution, sanction, toco, torture, victimisation.

punitive *adj.* penal, punitory, retaliative, retaliatory, retributive, revengeful, vindictive.

punter *n.* backer, better, bloke, buffer, chap, client, cove, customer, fellow, gambler, guy, individual, josser, oik, person, shaver.

puny *adj.* diminutive, dwarfish, feeble, frail, inconsequential, inferior, insignificant, little, meagre, minor, paltry, petty, piddling, pimping, reckling, runted, runtish, runty, sickly, stunted, tiny, trifling, trivial, underfed, undersized, undeveloped, weak, weakly, worthless.
antonyms important, large, strong.

pupil *n.* beginner, catechumen, disciple, learner, neophyte, novice, protégé, scholar, schoolboy, schoolgirl, student, tiro, tutee.
antonym teacher.

puppet *n.* cat's-paw, creature, doll, dupe, figurehead, gull, instrument, marionette, mouthpiece, pawn, quisling, stooge, tool.

puppet-show *n.* bunraku, fantoccini, Punch and Judy show, puppet-play, puppetry.

puppy *n.* braggart, cub, jackanapes, popinjay, pup, shaver, whelp, whippersnapper.

purchase *v.* achieve, acquire, attain, buy, earn, gain, invest in, obtain, pay for, procure, ransom, realise, secure, win.
antonym sell.
n. acquisition, advantage, asset, buy, edge, emption, foothold, footing, gain, grasp, grip, hold, influence, investment, lever, leverage, possession, property, ransoming, support, toehold.
antonym sale.

purchaser *n.* buyer, chap, chapman, client, consumer, customer, emptor, hirer, shopper, vendee.

pure *adj.* absolute, abstract, academic, antiseptic, authentic, blameless, chaste, clean, clear, disinfected, flawless, genuine, germ-free, guileless, high-minded, honest, hygienic, immaculate, innocent, intemerate, maidenly, modest, natural, neat, pasteurised, perfect, philosophical, real, refined, sanitary, Saturnian, sheer, simple, sincere, snow-white, speculative, spiritous, spotless, stainless, sterile, sterilised, straight, taintless, theoretical, thorough, true, unadulterate, unadulterated, unalloyed, unblemished, uncontaminated, uncorrupted, undefiled, unmingled, unmitigated, unmixed, unpolluted, unqualified, unsoiled, unspoilt, unspotted, un-

stained, unsullied, untainted, untarnished, upright, utter, virgin, virginal, virginly, virtuous, wholesome.
antonyms adulterated, applied, defiled, immoral, impure, polluted, tainted.

pure-bred *adj.* blooded, full-blooded, pedigree, pedigreed, pure-blood, pure-blooded, thoroughbred.
antonyms cross-bred, hybrid, mixed, mongrel.

purely *adv.* absolutely, completely, entirely, exclusively, just, merely, only, plainly, sheerly, simply, solely, thoroughly, totally, utterly, wholly.

purgation *n.* abstersion, catharsis, cleansing, clearing, depuration, evacuation, exculpation, exoneration, justification, purge, purging, purification, riddance, ridding, vindication.

purgative *n.* abstersive, aperient, cathartic, clyster, depurative, diacatholicon, eccoprotic, emetic, enema, evacuant, laxative, purge.
adj. abstersive, aperient, cathartic, cathartical, cleansing, depurative, eccoprotic, evacuant, laxative, purging.

purge *v.* absolve, absterge, catharise, clean out, cleanse, clear, dismiss, eject, eradicate, exonerate, expel, expiate, exterminate, extract, forgive, get rid of, kill, liquidate, oust, pardon, purify, remove, rid, root out, scour, wash, wipe out.
n. aperient, catharsis, cathartic, clyster, depurative, ejection, elimination, emetic, enema, eradication, expulsion, extermination, laxative, liquidation, purgative, removal, witch hunt.

purification *n.* absolution, beneficiation, catharsis, clarification, cleaning, cleansing, decontamination, deodorisation, depuration, desalination, disinfection, epuration, filtration, fumigation, furbishing, lustration, lustre, lustrum, mundification, purgation, redemption, refinement, sanctification, sanitisation.
antonyms contamination, defilement, pollution.

purify *v.* absolve, beneficiate, catharise, chasten, clarify, clean, cleanse, decontaminate, deodorise, depurate, desalinate, disinfect, epurate, filter, fumigate, furbish, lustrate, mundify, redeem, refine, sanctify, sanitise, shrive, sublimise, wash.
antonyms contaminate, defile, pollute.

purifying *adj.* cathartic, cleansing, depurative, lustral, mundificative, purgative, purging, purificatory, refining.
antonyms contaminating, defiling, polluting.

purism *n.* Atticism, austerity, classicism, fastidiousness, formalism, fussiness, orthodoxy, over-precision, pedantry, restraint, strictness.
antonyms liberality, open-mindedness, tolerance.

purist *n.* Atticist, classicist, formalist, grammaticaster, grammatist, mandarin, nit-picker, pedant, precisian, precisianist, precisionist, quibbler, stickler, vocabularian.

antonym liberal.
adj. austere, captious, fastidious, finicky, fussy, hypercritical, nit-picking, over-exact, over-fastidious, over-meticulous, over-particular, over-precise, pedantic, puristic, quibbling, strict, uncompromising.
antonyms liberal, open-minded, tolerant.

puritan *n.* bluenose, disciplinarian, fanatic, kill-joy, moralist, pietist, prude, rigorist, spoil-sport, zealot.
antonyms hedonist, libertarian.
adj. ascetic, austere, disciplinarian, hard-line, hide-bound, intolerant, moralistic, narrow, narrow-minded, prim, prudish, puritanical, self-disciplined, severe, stern, strait-laced, strict, uncompromising.
antonyms broad-minded, hedonistic, indulgent, liberal.

puritanical *adj.* abstemious, abstinent, ascetic, austere, bigoted, disapproving, disciplinarian, fanatical, narrow, narrow-minded, prim, proper, prudish, puritan, rigid, severe, stern, stiff, strait-laced, strict, stuffy, uncompromising, zealous.
antonyms broad-minded, hedonistic, indulgent, liberal.

puritanism *n.* abstemiousness, abstinence, asceticism, austerity, bigotry, fanaticism, narrowmindedness, narrowness, priggishness, primness, propriety, prudishness, rigidity, rigorousness, self-denial, self-discipline, severity, sternness, stiffness, strictness, uncompromisingness, zealotry.
antonyms broad-mindedness, hedonism, indulgence, liberality.

purity *n.* blamelessness, chasteness, chastity, clarity, classicism, cleanliness, clearness, decency, faultlessness, fineness, genuineness, immaculateness, incorruption, innocence, integrity, morality, piety, pureness, rectitude, refinement, sanctity, simplicity, sincerity, spotlessness, stainlessness, truth, unspottedness, untaintedness, uprightness, virginity, virtue, virtuousness, wholesomeness.
antonyms immorality, impurity.

purlieus *n.* banlieue, borders, bounds, confines, environs, fringes, limits, neighbourhood, outskirts, perimeter, periphery, precincts, suburbs, vicinity.

purloin *v.* abstract, appropriate, filch, finger, half-inch, lift, nick, nobble, palm, pilfer, pinch, pocket, prig, remove, rob, snaffle, snitch, steal, swipe, take, thieve.

purport *v.* allege, argue, assert, betoken, claim, convey, declare, denote, express, give out, imply, import, indicate, intend, maintain, mean, portend, pose as, pretend, proclaim, profess, seem, show, signify, suggest.
n. bearing, direction, drift, gist, idea, implication, import, meaning, point, significance, spirit, substance, tendency, tenor, theme, thrust.

purpose *n.* advantage, aim, ambition, aspiration, assiduity, avail, benefit, constancy, contemplation, decision, dedication, design, determination, devotion, drive, effect, end, firmness, function, gain, goal, good, hope, idea, ideal, intention, motive, object, objective, outcome, persistence, pertinacity, plan, point, principle, profit, project, rationale, reason, resolution, resolve, result, return, scheme, service, single-mindedness, steadfastness, target, telos, tenacity, use, usefulness, utility, view, vision, will, wish, zeal.

v. aim, aspire, contemplate, decide, design, desire, determine, ettle, intend, mean, meditate, plan, propose, resolve.

purposeful *adj.* assiduous, decided, deliberate, determined, firm, fixed, hormic, motivated, persevering, persistent, pertinacious, positive, purposive, resolute, resolved, sedulous, settled, single-minded, steadfast, strong-willed, teleological, tenacious, unfaltering, unswerving.

antonym purposeless.

purposeless *adj.* aimless, empty, goalless, gratuitous, motiveless, needless, nonsensical, objectless, pointless, senseless, thoughtless, unasked-for, uncalled-for, unnecessary, useless, vacuous, vain, wanton.

antonym purposeful.

purposely *adv.* by design, calculatedly, consciously, deliberately, designedly, expressly, intentionally, knowingly, on purpose, premeditatedly, specifically, wilfully, with malice aforethought.

antonyms impulsively, spontaneously, unpremeditatedly.

purse *n.* award, burse, coffers, exchequer, finances, fisc, funds, means, money, moneybag, monkey-bag, pocket-book, portemonnaie, pouch, prize, resources, reward, sporran, treasury, wallet, wealth.

v. close, compress, contract, draw together, pucker, tighten, wrinkle.

pursuance *n.* accomplishment, achievement, completion, discharge, effecting, effectuation, execution, following, fulfilment, performance, prosecution, pursuing.

pursue *v.* accompany, adhere to, aim at, aim for, aspire to, attend, bedevil, beset, besiege, carry on, chase, check out, conduct, continue, course, court, cultivate, desire, dog, engage in, follow, follow up, go for, gun for, harass, harry, haunt, hold to, hound, hunt, inquire into, investigate, keep on, maintain, perform, persecute, persevere in, persist in, plague, ply, practise, proceed, prosecute, purpose, seek, set one's cap at, shadow, stalk, strive for, tackle, tail, track, trail, try for, wage, woo.

antonyms eschew, shun.

pursuit[1] *n.* chase, chevy, hounding, hue and cry, hunt, hunting, inquiry, investigation, quest, search, seeking, stalking, tracking, trail, trailing.

pursuit[2] *n.* activity, craft, hobby, interest, line, occupation, parergon, pastime, pleasure, side-line, speciality, vocation.

purvey *v.* cater, communicate, deal in, dissemi-

nate, furnish, pass on, propagate, provide, provision, publicise, publish, put about, retail, sell, spread, stock, supply, trade in, transmit, victual.

purveyor *n.* communicator, dealer, disseminator, propagater, provider, provisor, retailer, stockist, supplier, trader, transmitter, victualler.

push *v.* advance, advertise, boost, browbeat, bulldoze, bully, coerce, constrain, depress, dragoon, drive, edge, egg on, elbow, encourage, expedite, force, hurry, hype, incite, influence, inveigle, jockey, jog, joggle, jostle, manhandle, manoeuvre, oblige, peddle, persuade, plug, poke, press, prod, promote, propagandise, propel, publicise, puff, ram, shoulder, shove, speed, spur, squeeze, thrust, urge, wedge, whang.

n. advance, ambition, assault, attack, bunt, butt, charge, determination, discharge, dismissal, drive, dynamism, effort, energy, enterprise, go, impetus, impulse, initiative, jolt, knock, notice, nudge, offensive, one's books, one's cards, one's marching orders, onset, onslaught, poke, pressure, prod, shove, the axe, the boot, the bum's rush, the chop, the sack, thrust, vigour, vim, vitality, zip.

push off depart, go away, leave, make a move, make tracks, move, push along, shift, shove off.

pushed *adj.* harassed, hard-pressed, hard-up, harried, hurried, in difficulties, pinched, pressed, rushed, short of, strapped, stretched, under pressure.

pushing *adj.* aggressive, ambitious, assertive, bold, brash, bumptious, determined, driving, dynamic, enterprising, forceful, forward, go-ahead, high-powered, impertinent, intrusive, presumptuous, purposeful, pushful, pushy, resourceful, self-assertive, thrusting.

antonyms conservative, diffident, unassertive, unassuming, unenterprising.

push-over *n.* child's play, cinch, doddle, dupe, easy mark, fall guy, gull, mug, picnic, piece of cake, sinecure, sitting duck, sitting target, soft mark, soft touch, stooge, sucker, walk-over.

antonyms challenge, labour.

pushy *adj.* aggressive, ambitious, arrogant, assertive, assuming, bold, bossy, brash, bumptious, forceful, forward, loud, obtrusive, offensive, officious, over-confident, presumptuous, pushing, self-assertive.

antonyms quiet, restrained, unassertive, unassuming.

pusillanimity *n.* cowardliness, cravenness, faint-heartedness, fearfulness, feebleness, gutlessness, poltroonery, recreancy, spinelessness, timidity, timorousness, weakness, yellow-streak.

pusillanimous *adj.* caitiff, chicken, chicken-hearted, cowardly, craven, faint-hearted, fearful, feeble, gutless, lily-livered, mean-spirited, poltroon, recreant, scared, spineless, timid, timorous, unassertive, unenterprising, weak, weak-kneed, yellow.

antonyms ambitious, courageous, forceful, strong.

pussyfoot *v.* beat about the bush, creep, equivocate, hedge, mess about, pad, prevaricate, prowl, sidestep, slink, steal, tergiversate, tiptoe.

pustule *n.* abscess, blister, boil, bulla, carbuncle, eruption, fester, furuncle, gathering, impostume, papilla, papule, pimple, pock, ulcer, whelk, whitlow.

put *v.* advance, apply, assign, bring, bring forward, cast, commit, condemn, consign, constrain, couch, deploy, deposit, dispose, drive, employ, enjoin, establish, express, fit, fix, fling, force, formulate, forward, frame, heave, hurl, impel, impose, induce, inflict, land, lay, levy, lob, make, oblige, offer, park, phrase, pitch, place, plonk, pose, position, post, present, propose, push, render, require, rest, send, set, set down, settle, situate, state, station, subject, submit, suggest, tender, throw, thrust, toss, utter, voice, word, write.

put across bring home to, communicate, convey, explain, express, get through to, put over, spell out.

put an end to abolish, annihilate, annul, cancel, check, destroy, discontinue, jugulate, kibosh, knock on the head, nullify, put a stop to, put paid to, put the kibosh on, put the lid on, put the mockers on, stem, stop, terminate.

put aside[1] cache, deposit, hoard, keep, lay by, put by, reserve, retain, salt away, save, set aside, stash, stockpile, store, stow.

put aside[2] abandon, bury, discard, discount, dispense with, disregard, forget, ignore, set aside.

put away certify, commit, consume, divorce, eat, imprison, institutionalise, kill, put aside, remove, renounce, replace, repudiate, return, save, shift, store, tidy, wolf.

put back delay, postpone, replace, repulse, reschedule, return.

put down[1] enter, inscribe, log, note, record, register, report, state, transcribe, write down.

put down[2] abash, condemn, crush, defeat, deflate, degrade, destroy, dismiss, disparage, humble, humiliate, kill, mortify, put to sleep, quash, quell, reject, repress, shame, silence, slight, snub, suppress, take down a peg, topple.

put down[3] ascribe, assign, attribute, impute.

put forward advance, introduce, move, nominate, offer, present, press, proffer, propose, recommend, submit, suggest, table, tender.

put in enter, input, insert, key in.

put off abash, confuse, daunt, defer, delay, demoralise, deter, discomfit, disconcert, discourage, dishearten, dismay, dispirit, dissuade, distress, divert, nonplus, perturb, postpone, put out, rattle, reschedule, throw, unnerve, unsettle.

antonym encourage.

put on add, affect, affix, apply, assume,

attach, back, bet, deceive, do, don, dress, fake, feign, gain, impose, increase by, lay, make believe, mislead, mount, place, present, pretend, produce, sham, show, simulate, stage, stake, wager.

put one's finger on discover, find out, hit the nail on the head, hit upon, identify, indicate, isolate, locate, pin down, pinpoint, place, recall, remember.

put out affront, anger, announce, annoy, bother, broadcast, circulate, confound, discomfit, discommode, discompose, disconcert, discountenance, dislocate, dismiss, disturb, douse, embarrass, exasperate, exert, expel, extinguish, give out, harass, hurt, impose on, incommode, inconvenience, irk, irritate, issue, nettle, offend, perturb, produce, provoke, publish, quench, release, smother, trouble, upset, vex.

put the wind up agitate, alarm, daunt, discourage, frighten, panic, perturb, scare, sound the alarm, startle, unnerve.

antonym reassure.

put through accomplish, achieve, bring off, conclude, effect, execute, finalise, manage.

put to death execute, exterminate, kill, liquidate, martyr.

put to shame disgrace, eclipse, humble, humiliate, outclass, outdo, outstrip, shame, show up, surpass.

put up accommodate, advance, assemble, board, build, construct, entertain, erect, fabricate, float, give, house, invest, lodge, nominate, offer, pay, pledge, present, propose, provide, put forward, quarter, raise, recommend, shelter, submit, supply.

put up to abet, encourage, goad, incite, instigate, prompt, urge.

antonyms discourage, dissuade.

put up with abide, allow, bear, brook, endure, lump, stand, stand for, stomach, suffer, swallow, take, take lying down, thole, tolerate.

antonyms object to, protest against, reject.

put upon exploit, impose on, inconvenience, take a loan of, use.

put wise alert, apprise, clue in, fill in, inform, intimate to, make wise to, notify, put in the picture, tell, tip off, warn, wise up.

putative *adj.* alleged, assumed, conjectural, hypothetical, imputed, presumed, presumptive, reported, reputative, reputed, supposed, suppositional, supposititious.

put-down *n.* affront, dig, disparagement, gibe, humiliation, insult, rebuff, sarcasm, slap in the face, slight, sneer, snub.

put-off *n.* constraint, curb, damper, deterrent, discouragement, disincentive, hindrance, obstacle, restraint.

antonyms encouragement, incentive.

putrefy *v.* addle, corrupt, decay, decompose, deteriorate, fester, foost, gangrene, go bad, mortify, mould, necrose, perish, rot, spoil, stink, taint.

putrescent *adj.* decaying, decomposing, festering, mephitic, perishing, putrefying, rotting, stinking.

putrid *adj.* addle, addled, bad, contaminated, corrupt, decayed, decomposed, fetid, foosty, foul, gangrenous, mephitic, mouldy, necrosed, noisome, off, putrefied, rancid, rank, reeking, rotten, rotting, sphacelate(d), spoiled, stinking, tainted.
antonyms fresh, wholesome.

put-upon *adj.* abused, beset, exploited, harassed, harried, henpecked, ill-used, imposed on, inconvenienced, overworked, persecuted.

puzzle[1] *v.* baffle, bamboozle, beat, bewilder, confound, confuse, fickle, floor, flummox, gravel, metagrobolise, mystify, nonplus, perplex, pother, pudder, stump, worry.
n. acrostic, anagram, brain-teaser, confusion, conundrum, crossword, difficulty, dilemma, enigma, knot, koan, logogram, logograph, logogriph, maze, mind-bender, mystery, paradox, poser, problem, quandary, question, rebus, riddle, Sphinx, tickler.

puzzle[2] *v.* brood, cogitate, consider, deliberate, figure, meditate, mull over, muse, ponder, rack one's brains, ratiocinate, reason, ruminate, study, think, wonder, worry.

puzzle out clear up, crack, decipher, decode, excogitate, figure out, metagrobolise, reason out, resolve, see, solve, sort out, think out, unravel, unriddle, untangle, work out.

puzzled *adj.* at a loss, at sea, baffled, bamboozled, beaten, bemused, bewildered, confounded, confused, disorientated, doubtful, flummoxed, in a haze, lost, mixed up, mizzled, mystified, nonplussed, perplexed, stuck, stumped, stymied, uncertain.
antonyms certain, clear.

puzzlement *n.* astonishment, bafflement, bamboozlement, bewilderment, confusion, disorientation, doubt, doubtfulness, incertitude, mystification, perplexity, surprise, uncertainty, wonder.
antonyms certainty, clarity, lucidity.

puzzling *adj.* abstruse, ambiguous, baffling, bewildering, bizarre, cabalistic, circuitous, confusing, cryptic, curious, enigmatic, equivocal, impenetrable, inexplicable, intricate, involved, knotty, labyrinthine, mindbending, mind-boggling, misleading, mysterious, mystical, mystifying, peculiar, perplexing, queer, riddling, Sphynx-like, strange, tangled, tortuous, unaccountable, unclear, unfathomable.

pygmy *n.* dwarf, fingerling, half-pint, homunculus, hop-o'-my-thumb, Lilliputian, manikin, midget, runt, shrimp, thumbling, Tom Thumb.
antonym giant.
adj. baby, diminutive, dwarf, dwarfish, elfin, half-pint, Lilliputian, midget, miniature, minuscule, minute, pint-sized, pocket, pygmaean, small, stunted, tiny, toy, undersized, wee.
antonym gigantic.

pyromaniac *n.* arsonist, firebug, fire-raiser, incendiary, pétroleur, pétroleuse.

Q

quack *n.* charlatan, cowboy, empiric, fake, fraud, humbug, impostor, masquerader, medicaster, mountebank, phoney, pretender, pseud, quacksalver, sham, spieler, swindler, trickster, witch-doctor.
adj. bogus, counterfeit, fake, false, fraudulent, phoney, pretended, sham, so-called, spurious, supposed, unqualified.
antonym genuine.

quackery *n.* charlatanism, charlatanry, empiricism, fraud, fraudulence, humbug, imposture, mountebankery, mountebankism, phoniness, sham.

quaff *v.* booze, carouse, down, drain, drink, gulp, guzzle, imbibe, knock back, swallow, swig, swill, tipple, tope, toss off.
n. bevvy, cup, dram, draught, drink, jorum, slug, snifter, swig.

quagmire *n.* bog, everglade, fen, marsh, mire, morass, moss, mudflat, quag, quicksand, slough, swamp.

quail *v.* back away, blanch, blench, cower, droop, faint, falter, flinch, quake, recoil, shake, shrink, shudder, shy away, tremble, wince.

quaint *adj.* absurd, antiquated, antique, bizarre, charming, curious, droll, eccentric, fanciful, fantastic, freaky, funky, Heath-Robinson, ingenious, odd, old-fashioned, old-time, old-world, peculiar, picturesque, queer, rum, singular, strange, unconventional, unusual, weird, whimsical.

quake *v.* convulse, heave, jolt, move, pulsate, quail, quiver, rock, shake, shiver, shudder, sway, throb, totter, tremble, vibrate, waver, wobble.

qualification[1] *n.* ability, accomplishment, adequacy, aptitude, attribute, capability, capacity, certification, competence, eligibility, fitness, skill, suitability, suitableness, training.

qualification[2] *n.* adaptation, adjustment, allowance, caveat, condition, criterion, exception, exemption, limitation, modification, objection, provision, proviso, reservation, restriction, stipulation.

qualified[1] *adj.* able, accomplished, adept, adequate, capable, certificated, certified, competent, efficient, eligible, equipped, experienced, expert, fit, habilitated, knowledgeable, licensed, practised, proficient, skilful, talented, trained.
antonym unqualified.

qualified[2] *adj.* bounded, cautious, circumscribed, conditional, confined, contingent, equivocal, guarded, limitative, limited, modificatory, modified, provisional, qualificatory, reserved, restricted.

qualify[1] *v.* authorise, capacitate, certificate, empower, endow, equip, fit, graduate, habilitate, permit, prepare, sanction, shape, train.
antonym unfit.

qualify[2] *v.* abate, adapt, adjust, alleviate, assuage, categorise, characterise, circumscribe, classify, define, delimit, describe, designate, diminish, distinguish, ease, lessen, limit, mitigate, moderate, modify, modulate, reduce, regulate, restrain, restrict, soften, temper, vary, weaken.

quality *n.* aspect, attribute, calibre, character, characteristic, class, complexion, condition, constitution, deal, description, distinction, essence, excellence, feature, fineness, grade, kidney, kind, make, mark, merit, nature, peculiarity, position, pre-eminence, property, rank, refinement, sort, standing, status, superiority, talent, timbre, tone, trait, value, water, worth.

qualm *n.* anxiety, apprehension, compunction, disquiet, doubt, fear, hesitation, misgiving, pang, presentiment, regret, reluctance, remorse, scruple, twinge, uncertainty, unease, uneasiness, worry.

quandary *n.* bewilderment, confusion, corner, difficulty, dilemma, doubt, embarrassment, entanglement, fix, hole, imbroglio, impasse, jam, kettle of fish, mess, perplexity, plight, predicament, problem, puzzle, uncertainty.

quantity *n.* aggregate, allotment, amount, breadth, bulk, capacity, content, dosage, expanse, extent, greatness, length, lot, magnitude, mass, measure, number, part, portion, proportion, quantum, quota, share, size, spread, strength, sum, total, volume, weight.

quarantine *n.* detention, isolation, lazaret, lazaretto, segregation.

quarrel *n.* affray, altercation, argument, barney, beef, bicker, brattle, brawl, breach, breeze, broil, clash, commotion, conflict, contention, controversy, coolness, debate, difference, disagreement, discord, disputation, dispute, dissension, dissidence, disturbance, dust-up, estrangement, feud, fight, fracas, fratch, fray, misunderstanding, row, rupture, schism, scrap, shouting match, slanging match, spat, split, squabble, strife, tiff, tumult, vendetta, wrangle.
antonyms agreement, harmony.
v. altercate, argue, be at loggerheads, be at variance, bicker, brawl, carp, cavil, clash, contend, differ, disagree, dispute, dissent, fall out, fight, find fault, object, pick holes,

question, row, spar, spat, squabble, take exception, tiff, vitilitigate, wrangle.
antonym agree.

quarrelling *n.* altercation, argumentation, argy-bargying, bickering, contention, discord, disharmony, disputation, dissension, feuding, rowing, strife, variance, vitilitigation, wrangling.
antonyms concord, harmony.
adj. at loggerheads, at odds, at variance, bickering, contending, discordant, dissentient, feuding, fighting, rowing, scrapping, squabbling, waring, wrangling.
antonyms amicable, friendly.

quarrelsome *adj.* altercative, antagonistic, argumentative, bellicose, belligerent, cantankerous, captious, choleric, combative, contentious, contrary, cross, disputatious, fractious, ill-tempered, irascible, irritable, peevish, perverse, petulant, pugnacious, querulous, stroppy, testy, truculent, turbulent, wranglesome.
antonyms peaceable, placid.

quarry *n.* game, goal, kill, object, objective, prey, prize, target, victim.

quarter[1] *n.* area, direction, district, division, locality, location, neighbourhood, part, place, point, position, province, quartier, region, section, sector, side, spot, station, territory, vicinity, zone.

quarter[2] *n.* clemency, compassion, favour, forgiveness, grace, indulgence, leniency, mercy, pardon, pity.

quarter[3] *n.* fardel, forpit, fourth, quartern, term.
v. decussate, divide in four, quadrisect.

quarter[4] *v.* accommodate, bed, billet, board, house, install, lodge, place, post, put up, shelter, station.

quarters *n.* abode, accommodation, apartment, barracks, billet, cantonment, caserne, chambers, digs, domicile, dwelling, habitation, lodging, lodgings, post, quarterage, residence, rooms, station.

quash *v.* annul, cancel, crush, declare null and void, defeat, disannul, disenact, invalidate, nullify, overrule, overthrow, quell, repress, rescind, reverse, revoke, set aside, squash, subdue, suppress, void.
antonyms confirm, justify, reinstate, vindicate.

quaver *v.* break, crack, flicker, flutter, oscillate, pulsate, quake, quiver, shake, shudder, tremble, trill, twitter, vibrate, warble.
n. break, quaveriness, quiver, shake, sob, throb, tremble, trembling, tremolo, tremor, trill, vibration, vibrato, warble.

quay *n.* dock, harbour, jetty, levee, pier, wharf.

queasy *adj.* bilious, dizzy, faint, giddy, green, groggy, ill, indisposed, nauseated, off-colour, qualmish, qualmy, queer, sick, sickened, squeamish, unwell.

queen *n.* beauty, belle, consort, diva, doyenne, empress, goddess, grande dame, idol, maharani, mistress, monarch, nonpareil, prima donna, princess, rani, ruler, sovereign, star, sultana, tsarina, Venus.

queenly *adj.* dignified, gracious, grand, imperial, imperious, majestic, noble, regal, royal, sovereign, stately.
antonym undignified.

queer *adj.* aberrant, abnormal, absurd, anomalous, atypical, bizarre, cranky, crazy, curious, daft, demented, deranged, deviant, disquieting, dizzy, doubtful, droll, dubious, eccentric, eerie, eldritch, erratic, exceptional, extraordinary, faint, fanciful, fantastic, fey, fishy, freakish, funny, giddy, grotesque, homosexual, idiosyncratic, ill, irrational, irregular, light-headed, mad, mysterious, odd, offbeat, outlandish, outré, peculiar, preternatural, puzzling, quaint, queasy, questionable, reeling, remarkable, rum, screwy, shady, shifty, singular, strange, suspect, suspicious, touched, unaccountable, unbalanced, uncanny, uncommon, unconventional, uneasy, unhinged, unnatural, unorthodox, unusual, unwell, unwonted, weird.
antonyms common, ordinary, straightforward, unexceptional, usual.
v. botch, cheat, endanger, foil, frustrate, harm, impair, imperil, injure, jeopardise, mar, ruin, spoil, stymie, thwart, upset, wreck.

queerness *n.* aberrance, abnormality, absurdity, anomalousness, atypicalness, bizarreness, crankiness, craziness, curiousness, deviance, drollness, dubiety, dubiousness, eccentricity, eeriness, fishiness, grotesqueness, idiosyncrasy, individuality, irrationality, irregularity, light-headedness, madness, mysteriousness, mystery, oddity, oddness, outlandishness, peculiarity, puzzle, quaintness, shadiness, shiftiness, singularity, strangeness, suspiciousness, uncanniness, uncommonness, unconventionality, unnaturalness, unorthodoxy, unusualness, unwontedness.

quell *v.* allay, alleviate, appease, assuage, blunt, calm, compose, conquer, crush, deaden, defeat, dull, extinguish, hush, mitigate, moderate, mollify, overcome, overpower, pacify, put down, quash, quench, quiet, reduce, silence, soothe, squash, stifle, subdue, subjugate, suppress, vanquish.

quench *v.* allay, appease, check, cool, crush, damp down, destroy, douse, end, extinguish, overcome, put out, quash, quell, sate, satisfy, silence, slake, smother, snuff out, stifle, suppress.

querulous *adj.* cantankerous, captious, carping, cavilling, censorious, complaining, crabbed, critical, cross, cross-grained, crusty, discontented, dissatisfied, exacting, fault-finding, fretful, fussy, grouchy, grumbling, hypercritical, intolerant, irascible, irritable, peevish, perverse, petulant, plaintive, quarrelsome, querimonious, sour, testy, thrawn, waspish, whingeing, whining.
antonyms contented, equable, placid, uncomplaining.

querulousness *n.* cantankerousness, captiousness, censoriousness, crabbedness, criticalness, crossness, crustiness, discontent, discon-

tentedness, dissatisfaction, fault-finding, fretfulness, fussiness, grouchiness, intolerance, irrascibility, irritability, peevishness, perversity, petulance, querimony, sourness, testiness, waspishness.
antonyms contentedness, equableness, placidity.

query *v.* ask, be sceptical of, call in question, challenge, disbelieve, dispute, distrust, doubt, enquire, misdoubt, mistrust, quarrel with, question, suspect.
antonym accept.
n. demand, doubt, hesitation, inquiry, misdoubt, misgiving, objection, problem, quaere, question, quibble, reservation, scepticism, suspicion, uncertainty.

quest *n.* adventure, crusade, enterprise, expedition, exploration, hunt, inquiry, investigation, journey, mission, pilgrimage, pursuit, search, undertaking, venture, voyage.

question *v.* ask, be sceptical of, catechise, challenge, controvert, cross-examine, debrief, disbelieve, dispute, distrust, doubt, enquire, examine, grill, impugn, interpellate, interrogate, interview, investigate, misdoubt, mistrust, oppose, probe, pump, quarrel with, query, quiz, suspect.
n. argument, confusion, contention, controversy, debate, difficulty, dispute, doubt, dubiety, erotema, erotesis, examination, inquiry, interpellation, interrogation, investigation, issue, misdoubt, misgiving, motion, point, problem, proposal, proposition, quaere, query, quibble, scepsis, subject, theme, topic, uncertainty.

questionable *adj.* arguable, borderline, controversial, debatable, disputable, doubtful, dubious, dubitable, equivocal, fishy, iffy, impugnable, moot, problematical, queer, shady, suspect, suspicious, uncertain, undetermined, unproven, unreliable, unsettled, vexed.
antonyms certain, indisputable, straightforward.

questioner *n.* agnostic, catechiser, catechist, disbeliever, doubter, examiner, inquirer, inquisitor, interlocutor, interrogator, interviewer, investigator, sceptic.

questionnaire *n.* answer-sheet, catechism, form, questionary, quiz, test.

queue *n.* file, line, line-up, order, procession, sequence, series, string, succession, tail, tail-back, train.

quibble *v.* carp, cavil, chop logic, equivocate, pettifog, prevaricate, shift, split hairs.
n. carriwitchet, casuistry, cavil, complaint, criticism, equivocation, equivoke, evasion, niggle, objection, pettifoggery, prevarication, query, quiddit, quiddity, quillet, quip, quirk, sophism, subterfuge.

quibbler *n.* casuist, caviller, chop-logic, criticaster, equivocator, hair-splitter, logic-chopper, niggler, nit-picker, pettifogger, sophist.

quibbling *adj.* ambiguous, captious, carping, casuistic, cavilling, critical, equivocating,

evasive, hair-splitting, logic-chopping, niggling, nit-picking, overnice, pettifogging, quidditative, sophistical.

quick *adj.* able, active, acute, adept, adroit, agile, alert, animated, apt, astute, awake, brief, bright, brisk, clever, cursory, deft, dexterous, discerning, energetic, expeditious, express, fast, fleet, flying, hasty, headlong, hurried, immediate, instant, instantaneous, intelligent, keen, lively, nifty, nimble, nippy, penetrating, perceptive, perfunctory, precipitate, prompt, quick-witted, rapid, ready, receptive, responsive, sharp, shrewd, skilful, smart, snappy, speedy, spirited, sprightly, spry, sudden, summary, swift, unhesitating, vivacious, wide-awake, winged.
antonyms dull, slow.

quicken *v.* accelerate, activate, advance, animate, arouse, dispatch, energise, enliven, excite, expedite, galvanise, hasten, hurry, impel, incite, inspire, invigorate, kindle, precipitate, reactivate, refresh, reinvigorate, resuscitate, revitalise, revive, revivify, rouse, sharpen, speed, stimulate, strengthen, vitalise, vivify.
antonyms dull, retard.

quickly *adv.* abruptly, at a rate of knots, at the double, before you can say Jack Robinson, briskly, by leaps and bounds, cursorily, ek dum, expeditiously, express, fast, hastily, hell for leather, hotfoot, hurriedly, immediately, instantaneously, instantly, lickety-split, like a bat out of hell, perfunctorily, posthaste, promptly, pronto, quick, rapidly, readily, soon, speedily, swiftly, unhesitatingly.
antonyms slowly, tardily, thoroughly.

quickness *n.* acuteness, agility, alertness, aptness, astuteness, briskness, deftness, dexterity, expedition, hastiness, immediacy, instantaneousness, intelligence, keenness, liveliness, nimbleness, penetration, precipitation, promptitude, promptness, quick-wittedness, rapidity, readiness, receptiveness, sharpness, shrewdness, speed, speediness, suddenness, summariness, swiftness, turn of speed.
antonyms dullness, slowness, tardiness.

quick-tempered *adj.* choleric, excitable, explosive, fiery, hot-tempered, impatient, impulsive, irascible, irritable, petulant, quarrelsome, shrewish, snappy, splenetic, temperamental, testy, touchy, volcanic, waspish.
antonyms cool, dispassionate.

quick-witted *adj.* acute, alert, astute, bright, clever, crafty, ingenious, intelligent, keen, nimble-witted, penetrating, perceptive, ready-witted, resourceful, sharp, shrewd, smart, wide-awake, witty.
antonyms dull, slow, stupid.

quiescent *adj.* asleep, calm, dormant, in abeyance, inactive, inert, latent, motionless, passive, peaceful, placid, quiet, reposeful, resting, serene, silent, sleeping, smooth, still, tranquil, undisturbed, untroubled.
antonym active.

quiet *adj.* calm, composed, conservative, contemplative, contented, docile, dumb, even-tempered, gentle, hushed, inaudible, isolated, lonely, low, low-pitched, meek, mild, modest, motionless, noiseless, pacific, passive, peaceable, peaceful, placid, plain, private, removed, reserved, restful, restrained, retired, retiring, secluded, secret, sedate, self-contained, sequestered, serene, shy, silent, simple, smooth, sober, soft, soundless, still, stilly, subdued, taciturn, thoughtful, tranquil, uncommunicative, unconversable, undisturbed, uneventful, unexcitable, unexciting, unforthcoming, unfrequented, uninterrupted, unobtrusive, untroubled.

antonyms busy, noisy, obtrusive.

n. calm, calmness, ease, hush, lull, peace, quiescence, quietness, quietude, repose, rest, serenity, silence, stillness, tranquillity.

antonyms bustle, disturbance, noise.

quieten *v.* abate, allay, alleviate, appease, assuage, blunt, calm, compose, deaden, diminish, dull, hush, lull, mitigate, mollify, muffle, mute, pacify, palliate, quell, quiet, reduce, silence, smooth, sober, soothe, stifle, still, stop, subdue, tranquillise.

antonyms aggravate, discompose, disturb, exacerbate.

quietly *adv.* calmly, composedly, confidentially, contentedly, demurely, diffidently, dispassionately, docilely, gently, humbly, inaudibly, meekly, mildly, modestly, mutely, noiselessly, obediently, patiently, peacefully, placidly, privately, secretly, serenely, silently, softly, soundlessly, surreptitiously, tranquilly, undemonstratively, unobtrusively, unostentatiously, unpretentiously.

antonyms noisily, obtrusively.

quietness *n.* calm, calmness, composure, dullness, hush, inactivity, inertia, lull, peace, placidity, quiescence, quiet, quietude, repose, serenity, silence, still, stillness, tranquillity, uneventfulness.

antonyms activity, bustle, commotion, disturbance, noise, racket.

quietus *n.* acquittance, coup de grâce, death, death-blow, death-stroke, decease, demise, discharge, dispatch, end, extinction, finishing stroke, quittance, silencing.

quilt *n.* bed quilt, bedcover, bedspread, comforter, counterpane, coverlet, Downie®, duvet, eiderdown, Federbett.

quintessence *n.* core, distillation, embodiment, essence, exemplar, extract, gist, heart, kernel, marrow, pattern, pith, quiddity, soul, spirit, sum and substance.

quintessential *adj.* archetypical, complete, consummate, definitive, entire, essential, ideal, perfect, prototypical, ultimate.

quip *n.* bon mot, carriwitchet, crack, epigram, gag, gibe, jest, jeu d'esprit, joke, mot, one-liner, pleasantry, quirk, retort, riposte, sally, wisecrack, witticism.

v. gag, gibe, jest, joke, quirk, retort, riposte, wisecrack.

quirk *n.* aberration, caprice, characteristic, curiosity, eccentricity, fancy, fetish, foible,

freak, habit, idiosyncrasy, kink, mannerism, oddity, oddness, peculiarity, singularity, trait, turn, twist, vagary, warp, whim.

quisling *n.* betrayer, collaborationist, collaborator, fifth columnist, Judas, puppet, renegade, traitor, turncoat.

quit *v.* abandon, abdicate, apostatise, cease, conclude, decamp, depart, desert, disappear, discontinue, drop, end, exit, forsake, give up, go, halt, leave, relinquish, renege, renounce, repudiate, resign, retire, stop, surrender, suspend, vamoose, vanish, withdraw.

quit of clear of, discharged from, done with, finished with, free of, released from, rid of.

quite *adv.* absolutely, comparatively, completely, entirely, exactly, fairly, fully, moderately, perfectly, precisely, rather, relatively, somewhat, totally, utterly, wholly.

quits *adj.* equal, even, level, square.

quitter *n.* apostate, defector, delinquent, deserter, rat, recreant, renegade, shirker, skiver.

quiver *v.* agitate, bicker, convulse, flichter, flicker, flutter, oscillate, palpitate, pulsate, quake, quaver, shake, shiver, shudder, tremble, vibrate, wobble.

n. convulsion, flicker, flutter, oscillation, palpitation, pulsation, shake, shiver, shudder, spasm, throb, tic, tremble, tremor, vibration, wobble.

quixotic *adj.* chivalrous, extravagant, fanciful, fantastical, idealistic, impetuous, impracticable, impulsive, romantic, starry-eyed, unrealistic, unworldly, Utopian, visionary.

antonyms hard-headed, practical, realistic.

quiz *n.* catechism, examination, investigation, questioning, questionnaire, test.

v. ask, catechise, cross-examine, cross-question, debrief, examine, grill, interrogate, investigate, pump, question.

quizzical *adj.* amused, arch, bantering, curious, humorous, inquiring, mocking, questioning, sardonic, satirical, sceptical, teasing, waggish, whimsical.

quizzicality *n.* archness, humorousness, humour, mockery, satiricalness, scepticism, teasing, waggishness, whimsicality.

quota *n.* allocation, allowance, assignment, cut, part, percentage, portion, proportion, quotum, ration, share, slice, whack.

quotation[1] *n.* citation, crib, cutting, excerpt, extract, gobbet, locus classicus, passage, piece, quote, reference, remnant.

quotation[2] *n.* charge, cost, estimate, figure, price, quote, rate, tender.

quote *v.* adduce, attest, cite, detail, echo, Hansardise, instance, name, parrot, recall, recite, recollect, refer to, repeat, reproduce, retell.

quoted *adj.* above-mentioned, cited, fore-cited, forementioned, instanced, referred to, reported, reproduced, stated.

quotidian *adj.* common, commonplace, customary, daily, day-to-day, diurnal, everyday, habitual, normal, ordinary, recurrent, regular, repeated, routine, workaday.

R

rabbit *n.* bunny, bunny rabbit, cony, cottontail, daman, dassie, hyrax.

rabble *n.* canaille, clamjamphrie, colluvies, commonalty, commoners, crowd, doggery, dregs, faex populi, galère, herd, hoi polloi, horde, masses, mob, peasantry, plebs, populace, proles, proletariat, raffle, raggle-taggle, rag-tag (and bobtail), rascality, riffraff, scum, swarm, tagrag, throng, trash.
antonyms aristocracy, elite, nobility.

rabble-rouser *n.* agitator, demagogue, firebrand, fomenter, incendiary, mischief-maker, mob-orator, ringleader, troublemaker, tub-thumper.

Rabelaisian *adj.* barrack-room, bawdy, blue, broad, coarse, earthy, extravagant, exuberant, gross, indecent, lewd, lusty, racy, ribald, risqué, robust, salacious, satirical, scabrous, uninhibited, unrestrained, vulgar.

rabid *adj.* berserk, bigoted, crazed, extreme, fanatical, fervent, frantic, frenzied, furious, hydrophobic, hysterical, infuriated, intemperate, intolerant, irrational, mad, maniacal, narrow-minded, obsessive, overzealous, raging, unreasoning, violent, wild, zealous.

rabies *n.* hydrophobia, rabidity, rabidness.

race[1] *n.* chase, competition, contention, contest, corso, dash, derby, foot-race, marathon, pursuit, quest, rat race, regatta, rivalry, scramble, sprint, steeplechase.
v. career, compete, contest, dart, dash, fly, gallop, hare, hasten, hurry, run, rush, speed, sprint, tear, zoom.

race[2] *n.* ancestry, blood, breed, clan, descent, family, folk, house, issue, kin, kindred, line, lineage, nation, offspring, people, progeny, seed, stirps, stock, strain, tribe, type.

race-course *n.* circuit, circus, course, dromos, hippodrome, race-track, route, speedway, track, turf.

racial *adj.* ancestral, avital, ethnic, ethnological, folk, genealogical, genetic, inherited, national, tribal.

raciness *n.* animation, bawdiness, boisterousness, breeziness, buoyancy, doubtfulness, dubiousness, dynamism, ebullience, energy, exhilaration, freshness, gaminess, indecency, indelicacy, jauntiness, lewdness, naughtiness, piquancy, pungency, relish, ribaldry, richness, salaciousness, sharpness, smuttiness, spiciness, suggestiveness, tanginess, tastiness, zest, zestfulness.

rack[1] *n.* frame, framework, gantry, gondola, hack, shelf, stand, structure.

rack[2] *n.* affliction, agony, anguish, distress, misery, pain, pangs, persecution, suffering, torment, torture.
v. afflict, agonise, convulse, crucify, distress, excruciate, harass, harrow, lacerate, oppress, pain, shake, strain, stress, stretch, tear, torment, torture, wrench, wrest, wring.

racket[1] *n.* babel, ballyhoo, clamour, clangour, commotion, din, disturbance, fuss, hubbub, hullabaloo, hurly-burly, kerfuffle, noise, outcry, pandemonium, row, shouting, tumult, uproar.

racket[2] *n.* business, con, deception, dodge, fiddle, fraud, game, scheme, swindle, trick.

racy *adj.* animated, bawdy, blue, boisterous, breezy, broad, buoyant, distinctive, doubtful, dubious, dynamic, ebullient, energetic, entertaining, enthusiastic, exciting, exhilarating, gamy, heady, immodest, indecent, indelicate, jaunty, lewd, lively, naughty, piquant, pungent, Rabelaisian, ribald, rich, risqué, salacious, sharp, smutty, sparkling, spicy, spirited, stimulating, strong, suggestive, tangy, tasty, vigorous, zestful.
antonyms dull, ponderous.

radiance *n.* brightness, brilliance, delight, effulgence, gaiety, glare, gleam, glitter, glow, happiness, incandescence, joy, lambency, light, luminosity, lustre, pleasure, rapture, refulgence, resplendence, shine, splendour, warmth.

radiant *adj.* aglow, alight, beaming, beamish, beamy, beatific, blissful, bright, brilliant, delighted, ecstatic, effulgent, gleaming, glittering, glorious, glowing, happy, illuminated, incandescent, joyful, joyous, lambent, luminous, lustrous, profulgent, rapturous, refulgent, resplendent, shining, sparkling, splendid, sunny.
antonym dull.

radiate *v.* branch, diffuse, disseminate, divaricate, diverge, emanate, emit, eradiate, gleam, glitter, issue, pour, scatter, shed, shine, spread, spread out.

radiation *n.* emanation, emission, insolation, rays.

radical *adj.* basic, complete, comprehensive, constitutional, deep-seated, entire, essential, excessive, extreme, extremist, fanatical, far-reaching, fundamental, inherent, innate, intrinsic, native, natural, organic, primary, profound, revolutionary, rooted, severe, sweeping, thorough, thoroughgoing, total, violent.
antonym superficial.
n. extremist, fanatic, jacobin, left-winger, militant, reformer, reformist, revolutionary.

raffish *adj.* bohemian, careless, casual, cheap,

coarse, dashing, devil-may-care, disreputable, dissipated, dissolute, flamboyant, flashy, garish, gaudy, gross, improper, jaunty, loud, meretricious, rakish, showy, sporty, tasteless, tawdry, trashy, uncouth, vulgar.

antonyms decorous, proper, sedate, staid.

raffle *n.* draw, lottery, sweep, sweepstake, tombola.

rag *v.* badger, bait, bullyrag, chaff, chiack, haze, jeer, mock, rib, ridicule, taunt, tease, torment, twit.

ragamuffin *n.* dandiprat, gamin, guttersnipe, mudlark, scarecrow, street arab, tatterdemalion, urchin, waif.

ragbag *n.* assemblage, confusion, hotchpotch, jumble, medley, miscellany, mixture, olio, olla podrida, omnium-gatherum, pastiche, pot-pourri, salad.

rage *n.* agitation, anger, bate, chafe, conniption, craze, dernier cri, enthusiasm, fad, fashion, frenzy, fury, ire, madness, mania, obsession, paddy, passion, style, tantrum, vehemence, violence, vogue, wrath.

v. chafe, explode, fret, fulminate, fume, inveigh, ramp, rampage, rant, rave, seethe, storm, surge, thunder.

ragged *adj.* broken, deckled, desultory, disorganised, down-at-heel, duddie, erratic, fragmented, frayed, irregular, jagged, motheaten, notched, patchy, raguly, rent, ripped, rough, rugged, scraggy, serrated, shabby, shaggy, tattered, tattery, tatty, threadbare, torn, uneven, unfinished, unkempt, worn-out.

raging *adj.* enraged, fizzing, frenzied, fulminating, fuming, furibund, furious, incensed, infuriated, irate, ireful, mad, rabid, rampageous, raving, seething, wrathful.

rags *n.* clouts, duddery, duds, raggedness, remnants, shreds, tats, tatters.

raid *n.* attack, break-in, bust, descent, foray, incursion, inroad, invasion, irruption, onset, onslaught, razzia, sally, seizure, sortie, strike, swoop.

v. attack, bust, descend on, do, forage, foray, invade, loot, maraud, pillage, plunder, ransack, reive, rifle, rush, sack.

raider *n.* attacker, brigand, cateran, depredator, despoiler, forager, freebooter, invader, looter, marauder, pirate, plunderer, ransacker, reiver, robber, rustler, sacker, thief.

rail *v.* abuse, arraign, attack, castigate, censure, criticise, decry, denounce, fulminate, inveigh, jeer, mock, revile, ridicule, scoff, upbraid, vituperate, vociferate.

railing *n.* balustrade, barrier, fence, paling, parapet, rail, rails.

raillery *n.* badinage, banter, chaff, chiacking, diatribe, dicacity, invective, irony, jeering, jesting, joke, joking, kidding, mockery, persiflage, pleasantry, ragging, repartee, ribbing, ridicule, satire, sport, teasing.

railway *n.* line, metro, permanent way, railroad, rails, subway, track, tramway, tube, underground.

rain *n.* cloudburst, deluge, downpour, drizzle,

fall, flood, hail, mizzle, precipitation, raindrops, rainfall, rains, serein, shower, spate, squall, stream, torrent, volley.

v. bestow, bucket, deluge, deposit, drizzle, drop, expend, fall, heap, lavish, mizzle, pour, shower, spit, sprinkle, teem.

rainbow *n.* arc, iris, prism, spectrum.

adj. iridescent, irisated, irised, kaleidoscopic, nacreous, opalescent, prismatic, rainbow-like, shot, spectral, variegated.

antonym monochrome.

rainy *adj.* damp, dripping, drizzly, hyetal, mizzly, pluviose, pluvious, showery, wet.

antonym dry.

raise *v.* abandon, activate, advance, aggrade, aggrandise, aggravate, amplify, arouse, assemble, augment, awaken, boost, breed, broach, build, cause, collect, construct, create, cultivate, develop, discontinue, elate, elevate, emboss, embourgeoise, end, engender, enhance, enlarge, erect, escalate, evoke, exaggerate, exalt, excite, foment, form, foster, gather, gentrify, get, grow, heave, heighten, hoist, incite, increase, inflate, instigate, intensify, introduce, kindle, levy, lift, loft, magnify, mass, mobilise, moot, motivate, muster, nurture, obtain, occasion, originate, pose, prefer, produce, promote, propagate, provoke, rally, rear, recruit, reinforce, relinquish, remove, sky, start, strengthen, sublime, suggest, terminate, up, upgrade, uplift.

antonyms debase, decrease, degrade, dismiss, lower, reduce, suppress.

raised *adj.* applied, appliqué, cameo, embossed, relief, rilievo.

antonyms engraved, incised, intaglio.

raising *n.* abandonment, advancement, aggradation, ascension, assumption, breeding, construction, development, elation, elevation, enhancement, erection, exaltation, fostering, increase, intensification, levitation, lifting, mobilisation, nurture, preferment, promotion, rearing, recruitment, rise, rising, upgrading, upping.

rake[1] *v.* accumulate, amass, bombard, collect, comb, drag, enfilade, examine, gather, graze, harrow, haul in, hoe, hunt, make, pepper, ransack, remove, scan, scour, scrape, scratch, scrutinise, search, strafe, sweep.

rake[2] *n.* blood, debauchee, degenerate, dissolute, hedonist, lecher, libertine, loose-liver, playboy, pleasure-seeker, prodigal, profligate, rakehell, roué, sensualist, spendthrift, swinger, voluptuary.

antonyms ascetic, puritan.

rakish *adj.* abandoned, breezy, dapper, dashing, debauched, debonair, degenerate, depraved, devil-may-care, dissipated, dissolute, flamboyant, flashy, immoral, jaunty, lecherous, libertine, licentious, loose, natty, prodigal, profligate, raffish, sharp, sinful, smart, snazzy, sporty, stylish, wanton.

rally[1] *v.* assemble, bunch, cheer, cluster, collect, congregate, convene, embolden, encourage, gather, hearten, improve, marshal, mass, mobilise, muster, organise, pick up, rally round, reassemble, recover, recuperate, reform, regroup, reorganise, revive, round up, summon, unite.

n. assembly, comeback, concourse, conference, congregation, convention, convocation, gathering, improvement, jamboree, meeting, recovery, recuperation, regrouping, renewal, reorganisation, resurgence, reunion, revival, stand.

rally[2] *v.* chaff, mock, rag, rib, ridicule, send up, taunt, tease, twit.

ram *v.* beat, butt, cram, crash, crowd, dash, drive, drum, force, hammer, hit, impact, jam, pack, pound, pun, slam, smash, strike, stuff, tamp, thrust.

ramble *v.* amble, babble, chatter, digress, divagate, dodder, drift, expatiate, maunder, meander, perambulate, peregrinate, range, roam, rove, saunter, snake, straggle, stravaig, stray, stroll, traipse, walk, wander, wind, zigzag.

n. divagation, excursion, hike, perambulation, peregrination, roaming, roving, saunter, stroll, tour, traipse, trip, walk.

rambler *n.* drifter, globe-trotter, hiker, peregrinator, roamer, rover, stroller, walker, wanderer, wayfarer.

rambling *adj.* circuitous, desultory, diffuse, digressive, disconnected, discursive, disjointed, excursive, incoherent, irregular, long-drawn-out, long-winded, periphrastic, prolix, sprawling, spreading, straggling, trailing, wordy.

antonym direct.

ramification *n.* branch, complication, consequence, development, dichotomy, divarication, division, excrescence, extension, fork, offshoot, outgrowth, ramulus, ramus, result, sequel, subdivision, upshot.

ramp *n.* grade, gradient, incline, rise, slope.

rampage *v.* rage, rant, rave, run amuck, run riot, run wild, rush, storm, tear.

n. destruction, frenzy, furore, fury, rage, storm, tempest, tumult, uproar, violence.

rampant *adj.* aggressive, dominant, epidemic, erect, excessive, exuberant, fierce, flagrant, luxuriant, outrageous, prevalent, prodigal, profuse, raging, rampaging, rank, rearing, rife, riotous, standing, unbridled, unchecked, uncontrollable, uncontrolled, ungovernable, unrestrained, upright, vehement, violent, wanton, widespread, wild.

rampart *n.* barricade, bastion, breastwork, bulwark, defence, earthwork, embankment, fence, fort, fortification, guard, parapet, security, stronghold, vallum, wall.

ramshackle *adj.* broken-down, crumbling, decrepit, derelict, dilapidated, flimsy, haywire, jerry-built, rickety, shaky, tottering, tumbledown, unsafe, unsteady.

antonyms solid, stable.

ranch *n.* estancia, estate, farm, hacienda, plantation, station.

rancid *adj.* bad, fetid, foul, frowsty, fusty, musty, off, putrid, rank, reasty, rotten, sour, stale, strong-smelling, tainted.

antonym sweet.

rancorous *adj.* acrimonious, bitter, hostile, implacable, malevolent, malignant, resentful, spiteful, splenetic, vengeful, venomous, vindictive, virulent.

rancour *n.* acrimony, animosity, animus, antipathy, bitterness, enmity, grudge, hate, hatred, hostility, ill-feeling, ill-will, malevolence, malice, malignity, resentfulness, resentment, spite, spleen, venom, vindictiveness.

random *adj.* accidental, adventitious, aimless, arbitrary, casual, chance, desultory, fortuitous, haphazard, incidental, indiscriminate, purposeless, scattershot, spot, stray, unfocused, unplanned, unpremeditated.

antonyms deliberate, systematic.

randy *adj.* amorous, aroused, concupiscent, goatish, horny, hot, lascivious, lecherous, lustful, raunchy, satyric, sexy, turned-on.

range *n.* amplitude, area, assortment, band, bounds, chain, class, collection, compass, confines, diapason, distance, domain, extent, field, file, gamut, kind, latitude, limits, line, lot, orbit, order, palette, parameters, province, purview, radius, raik, rank, reach, row, scale, scope, selection, sequence, series, sort, span, spectrum, sphere, string, sweep, tessitura, tier, variety.

v. aim, align, arrange, array, bracket, catalogue, categorise, class, classify, cruise, direct, dispose, explore, extend, file, fluctuate, go, grade, group, level, order, pigeonhole, point, raik, ramble, rank, reach, roam, rove, run, straggle, stravaig, stray, stretch, stroll, sweep, train, traverse, wander.

rangy *adj.* gangling, lanky, leggy, long-legged, rawboned, skinny, weedy.

antonyms compact, dumpy.

rank[1] *n.* caste, class, classification, column, condition, degree, dignity, division, echelon, estate, état, file, formation, grade, group, level, line, nobility, order, position, quality, range, row, series, sort, standing, station, status, stratum, tier, type.

v. align, arrange, array, class, classify, dispose, grade, locate, marshal, order, organise, place, position, range, sort.

rank[2] *adj.* absolute, abundant, abusive, arrant, atrocious, bad, blatant, coarse, complete, crass, dense, disagreeable, disgusting, downright, egregious, excessive, extravagant, exuberant, fetid, filthy, flagrant, flourishing, foul, fusty, gamy, glaring, gross, indecent, lush, luxuriant, mephitic, musty, nasty, noisome, noxious, obscene, off, offensive, out-and-out, outrageous, productive, profuse, pungent, putrid, rampant, rancid, repulsive, revolting, scurrilous, sheer, shocking, stale, stinking, strong-smelling, thorough, thoroughgoing, total, undisguised, unmitigated, utter, vigorous, vulgar.

antonyms sparse, sweet.

rankle *v.* anger, annoy, chafe, embitter, fester, gall, irk, irritate, nettle, peeve, rile.

ransack *v.* comb, depredate, despoil, explore, gut, loot, maraud, pillage, plunder, raid, rake, ravage, rifle, rummage, sack, scour, search, strip.

ransom *n.* deliverance, liberation, money, payment, pay-off, price, redemption, release, rescue.

v. buy out, deliver, extricate, liberate, redeem, release, rescue.

rant *v.* bellow, bluster, cry, declaim, mouth it, rave, roar, shout, slang-whang, spout, vociferate, yell.

n. bluster, bombast, declamation, diatribe, fanfaronade, harangue, philippic, rhetoric, storm, tirade, vociferation.

rap *v.* bark, castigate, censure, chat, confabulate, converse, crack, criticise, discourse, flirt, hit, knock, pan, reprimand, scold, strike, talk, tap.

n. blame, blow, castigation, censure, chat, chiding, clout, colloquy, confabulation, conversation, crack, dialogue, discourse, discussion, knock, punishment, rebuke, reprimand, responsibility, sentence, talk, tap.

rapacious *adj.* avaricious, esurient, extortionate, grasping, greedy, insatiable, marauding, plundering, predatory, preying, ravening, ravenous, usurious, voracious, vulturine, vulturish, vulturous, wolfish, wolvish.

rapacity *n.* avarice, avidity, cupidity, esurience, esuriency, graspingness, greed, greediness, insatiableness, predatoriness, rapaciousness, ravenousness, shark's manners, usury, voraciousness, voracity, wolfishness.

rape *n.* abuse, defilement, deflowering, depredation, desecration, despoilment, despoliation, maltreatment, outrage, perversion, pillage, plundering, rapine, ravaging, ravishment, sack, spoliation, violation.

v. assault, despoil, loot, pillage, plunder, ransack, ravish, sack, spoliate, stuprate, violate.

rapid *adj.* brisk, expeditious, express, fast, fleet, flying, hasty, headlong, hurried, precipitate, prompt, quick, speedy, swift, tantivy.

antonyms leisurely, slow, sluggish.

rapidity *n.* alacrity, briskness, celerity, dispatch, expedition, expeditiousness, fleetness, haste, hurry, precipitateness, promptitude, promptness, quickness, rush, speed, speediness, swiftness, velocity.

antonym slowness.

rapidly *adv.* briskly, expeditiously, fast, hastily, hurriedly, lickety-split, precipitately, promptly, quickly, speedily, swiftly.

antonym slowly.

rapids *n.* dalles, white water, wild water.

rapine *n.* depredation, despoilment, despoliation, looting, marauding, pillage, plunder, ransacking, rape, ravaging, robbery, sack, sacking, seizure, spoliation, theft.

rapport *n.* affinity, bond, compatibility, empathy, harmony, link, relationship, sympathy, understanding.

rapprochement *n.* agreement, détente, harmonisation, reconcilement, reconciliation, reunion, softening.

rapscallion *n.* blackguard, cad, cur, disgrace, good-for-nothing, knave, ne'er-do-well, rascal, reprobate, rogue, scallywag, scamp, scoundrel, wastrel, wretch.

rapt *adj.* absorbed, beatific, bewitched, captivated, charmed, delighted, ecstatic, enchanted, engrossed, enraptured, enthralled, entranced, fascinated, gripped, held, intent, preoccupied, rapturous, ravished, spellbound, transported.

rapture *n.* beatitude, bliss, delectation, delight, ecstasy, enthusiasm, entrancement, euphoria, exaltation, felicity, happiness, joy, ravishment, rhapsody, spell, transport.

rapturous *adj.* blissful, delighted, ecstatic, enthusiastic, entranced, euphoric, exalted, happy, joyful, joyous, overjoyed, ravished, rhapsodic, transported.

rare *adj.* admirable, choice, curious, excellent, exceptional, exquisite, extreme, few, fine, great, incomparable, infrequent, invaluable, peerless, precious, priceless, recherché, rich, scarce, singular, sparse, sporadic, strange, superb, superlative, uncommon, unusual.

antonyms abundant, common, usual.

rarefied *adj.* clannish, cliquish, elevated, esoteric, exalted, exclusive, high, lofty, noble, occult, private, refined, select, spiritual, sublime.

rarely *adv.* atypically, exceptionally, extraordinarily, finely, hardly, infrequently, little, notably, remarkably, seldom, singularly, uncommonly, unusually.

antonyms frequently, often.

raring *adj.* agog, athirst, avid, desperate, eager, enthusiastic, impatient, itching, keen, longing, ready, willing, yearning.

rarity *n.* choiceness, curio, curiosity, excellence, exquisiteness, find, fineness, gem, incomparability, incomparableness, infrequency, object of virtu, one-off, pearl, peerlessness, preciousness, pricelessness, quality, richness, scarcity, shortage, singularity, sparseness, strangeness, treasure, uncommonness, unusualness, value, worth.

antonyms commonness, commonplace.

rascal *n.* blackguard, caitiff, cullion, devil, disgrace, good-for-nothing, hellion, hempy, imp, knave, loon, lorel, losel, miscreant, ne'er-do-well, rake, ra(p)scallion, reprobate, rogue, scallywag, scamp, scoundrel, skeesicks, spalpeen, toe-rag, toe-ragger, varmint, villain, wastrel, wretch.

rascally *adj.* bad, base, crooked, dishonest, disreputable, evil, furciferous, good-for-nothing, knavish, low, mean, reprobate, scoundrelly, unscrupulous, vicious, villainous, wicked.

rash[1] *adj.* adventurous, audacious, brash, careless, foolhardy, harebrained, harum-

scarum, hasty, headlong, headstrong, heedless, helter-skelter, hot-headed, ill-advised, ill-considered, impetuous, imprudent, impulsive, incautious, indiscreet, injudicious, insipient, madcap, precipitant, precipitate, premature, reckless, slap-dash, temerarious, temerous, thoughtless, unguarded, unthinking, unwary, venturesome.
antonyms calculating, careful, considered, wary.

rash² *n.* epidemic, eruption, exanthem(a), flood, hives, nettlerash, outbreak, plague, pompholyx, series, spate, succession, urticaria, wave.

rashness *n.* adventurousness, audacity, brashness, carelessness, foolhardiness, hastiness, heedlessness, incaution, incautiousness, indiscretion, precipitance, precipitation, precipitency, recklessness, temerity, thoughtlessness.
antonyms carefulness, cautiousness.

rasp *n.* croak, grating, grinding, harshness, hoarseness, scrape, scratch.
v. abrade, croak, excoriate, file, grate, grind, irk, irritate, jar, rub, sand, scour, scrape.

rasping *adj.* creaking, croaking, croaky, grating, gravelly, gruff, harsh, hoarse, husky, jarring, raspy, raucous, rough, scratchy, stridulant.

rat *n.* cad, ratfink, renegade, swine, turncoat.

rate¹ *n.* basis, charge, class, classification, cost, degree, dues, duty, fee, figure, gait, grade, hire, measure, pace, percentage, position, price, proportion, quality, rank, rating, ratio, reckoning, relation, scale, speed, standard, status, tariff, tax, tempo, time, toll, value, velocity, worth.
v. adjudge, admire, appraise, assess, class, classify, consider, count, deserve, esteem, estimate, evaluate, figure, grade, judge, measure, measure up, merit, perform, rank, reckon, regard, respect, value, weigh.

rate² *v.* admonish, berate, blame, castigate, censure, chide, criticise, lecture, rebuke, reprimand, reprove, roast, scold, tongue-lash, upbraid.

rather *adv.* a bit, fairly, instead, kind of, moderately, noticeably, preferably, pretty, quite, relatively, significantly, slightly, somewhat, sooner, sort of, very.

ratify *v.* affirm, approve, authenticate, authorise, bind, certify, confirm, corroborate, endorse, establish, homologate, legalise, recognise, sanction, sign, uphold, validate.
antonyms reject, repudiate.

rating¹ *n.* class, classification, degree, designation, estimate, evaluation, grade, grading, order, placing, position, rank, rate, sort, sorting, standing, status.

rating² *n.* castigation, chiding, dressing-down, lecture, rebuke, reprimand, reproof, roasting, row, scolding, telling-off, ticking-off, tongue-lashing, upbraiding, wigging.

ratio *n.* arrangement, balance, correlation, correspondence, equation, fraction, percentage, proportion, quotient, rate, relation,

relationship.

ration *n.* allocation, allotment, allowance, amount, dole, helping, measure, part, portion, provision, quota, share.
v. allocate, allot, apportion, budget, conserve, control, deal, dispense, distribute, dole, issue, limit, mete, restrict, save, supply.

rational *adj.* balanced, cerebral, cognitive, compos mentis, dianoetic, enlightened, intelligent, judicious, logical, lucid, normal, ratiocinative, realistic, reasonable, reasoning, sagacious, sane, sensible, sound, thinking, well-founded, well-grounded, wise.
antonyms crazy, illogical, irrational.

rationale *n.* excuse, exposition, grounds, logic, motivation, philosophy, pretext, principle, raison d'être, reasons, theory.

rationalise *v.* elucidate, excuse, extenuate, justify, reason out, reorganise, resolve, streamline, trim, vindicate.

rations *n.* commons, étape, food, prog, provender, provisions, stores, supplies.

rattle *v.* bang, bounce, bump, clank, clatter, clitter, crepitate, discomfit, discompose, disconcert, discountenance, disturb, faze, frighten, jangle, jiggle, jolt, jounce, perturb, scare, shake, upset, vibrate.

rattle off anote, enumerate, itemise, list, recite, reel off, rehearse, repeat, run through.

rattle on blether, cackle, chatter, gab, gabble, gibber, jabber, prate, prattle, rabbit on, witter, ya(c)k.

ratty *adj.* angry, annoyed, crabbed, cross, impatient, irritable, peeved, short, short-tempered, snappy, testy, touchy.
antonyms calm, patient.

raucous *adj.* grating, harsh, hoarse, husky, loud, noisy, rasping, rough, rusty, strident.

ravage *v.* demolish, depredate, desolate, despoil, destroy, devastate, gut, lay waste, loot, pillage, plunder, ransack, raze, ruin, sack, shatter, spoil, wreck.
n. damage, defilement, demolition, depredation, desecration, desolation, destruction, devastation, havoc, pillage, plunder, rapine, ruin, ruination, spoliation, waste, wreckage.

ravaged *adj.* battle-torn, desolate, destroyed, devastated, ransacked, shattered, spoilt, war-torn, war-wasted, war-worn, wrecked.
antonym unspoilt.

rave *v.* babble, declaim, fulminate, fume, harangue, rage, ramble, rant, roar, splutter, storm, thunder.
adj. ecstatic, enthusiastic, excellent, fantastic, favourable, laudatory, wonderful.

ravenous *adj.* avaricious, covetous, devouring, esurient, famished, ferocious, gluttonous, grasping, greedy, insatiable, insatiate, predatory, rapacious, ravening, starved, starving, voracious, wolfish, wolvish.

rave-up *n.* bash, blow-out, carousal, celebration, debauch, do, orgy, party, shindig, thrash, wing-ding.

ravine *n.* arroyo, canyon, chine, clough, defile, flume, gap, gorge, grike, gulch, gully, khor, khud, kloof, linn, lin(n), pass.

raving *adj.* berserk, bonkers, crazed, crazy, delirious, frantic, frenzied, furious, hysterical, insane, irrational, mad, manic, rabid, raging, wild.

ravish *v.* abuse, captivate, charm, deflorate, deflower, delight, enchant, enrapture, entrance, fascinate, outrage, overjoy, rape, spellbind, transport, violate.

ravishing *adj.* alluring, beautiful, bewitching, charming, dazzling, delightful, enchanting, entrancing, gorgeous, lovely, radiant, seductive, stunning.

raw *adj.* abraded, bare, basic, biting, bitter, bleak, bloody, blunt, brutal, callow, candid, chafed, chill, chilly, coarse, cold, crude, damp, frank, freezing, fresh, grazed, green, harsh, ignorant, immature, inexperienced, naked, natural, new, open, organic, piercing, plain, realistic, rough, scraped, scratched, sensitive, skinned, sore, tender, unadorned, uncooked, undisciplined, undisguised, undressed, unfinished, unpleasant, unpractised, unprepared, unprocessed, unrefined, unripe, unseasoned, unskilled, untrained, untreated, untried, unvarnished, verdant, wet.
antonyms cooked, experienced, refined.

ray *n.* bar, beam, flash, flicker, gleam, glimmer, glint, hint, indication, scintilla, shaft, spark, stream, trace.

raze *v.* bulldoze, delete, demolish, destroy, dismantle, efface, erase, expunge, extinguish, extirpate, flatten, level, obliterate, remove, ruin.

re *prep.* about, anent, apropos, concerning, regarding, respecting, touching, with reference to, with regard to.

reach *v.* amount to, arrive at, attain, contact, drop, fall, get to, grasp, hand, land at, make, move, pass, rise, sink, stretch, strike, touch. *n.* ambit, capacity, command, compass, distance, extension, extent, grasp, influence, jurisdiction, latitude, mastery, power, purview, range, scope, spread, stretch, sweep.

react *v.* acknowledge, act, answer, behave, emote, function, operate, proceed, reply, respond, work.

reaction *n.* acknowledgement, answer, antiperistasis, backwash, compensation, conservatism, counteraction, counterbalance, counterbuff, counterpoise, counter-revolution, feedback, obscurantism, recoil, reply, response, swingback.

reactionary *adj.* blimpish, conservative, counter-revolutionary, obscurantist, obstructive, reactionist, rightist.
antonyms progressive, radical, revolutionary.
n. Colonel Blimp, conservative, counter-revolutionary, die-hard, obscurantist, obstructionist, reactionist, rightist, right-winger.
antonyms progressive, radical, revolutionary.

read *v.* announce, comprehend, con, construe, decipher, declaim, deliver, discover, display, indicate, interpret, peruse, pore over, recite, record, refer to, register, scan, see, show, speak, study, understand, utter.

readable *adj.* clear, compelling, comprehensible, compulsive, decipherable, enjoyable, entertaining, enthralling, gripping, intelligible, interesting, legible, plain, pleasant, understandable, unputdownable.
antonyms illegible, unreadable.

readily *adv.* cheerfully, eagerly, easily, effortlessly, fain, freely, gladly, lief, promptly, quickly, smoothly, speedily, unhesitatingly, voluntarily, willingly.

readiness *n.* adroitness, alacrity, aptitude, aptness, dexterity, eagerness, ease, facility, fitness, gameness, handiness, inclination, keenness, maturity, preparation, preparedness, promptitude, promptness, quickness, rapidity, ripeness, skill, willingness.

reading *n.* book-learning, conception, construction, edification, education, emendation, erudition, examination, grasp, homily, impression, inspection, interpretation, knowledge, learning, lecture, lesson, performance, pericope, perusal, recital, rendering, rendition, review, scholarship, scrutiny, sermon, study, treatment, understanding, version.

ready *adj.* à la main, about, accessible, acute, ad manum, adroit, agreeable, alert, apt, arranged, astute, available, bright, clever, close, completed, convenient, deft, dexterous, disposed, eager, expert, facile, fit, game, glad, handy, happy, inclined, intelligent, keen, liable, likely, minded, near, on call, on tap, organised, overflowing, perceptive, predisposed, prepared, present, primed, prompt, prone, quick, quick-witted, rapid, resourceful, ripe, set, sharp, skilful, smart, willing.
antonyms unprepared, unready.
v. alert, arrange, equip, order, organise, prepare, prime, set.

real *adj.* absolute, actual, authentic, bona fide, certain, dinkum, dinky-di(e), essential, existent, factual, genuine, heartfelt, honest, intrinsic, legitimate, positive, right, rightful, simon-pure, sincere, substantial, substantive, sure-enough, tangible, thingy, true, unaffected, unfeigned, valid, veritable.
antonyms imaginary, unreal.

realisation *n.* accomplishment, achievement, actualisation, appreciation, apprehension, awareness, cognisance, completion, comprehension, conception, consciousness, consummation, effectuation, fulfilment, grasp, imagination, perception, recognition, understanding.

realise *v.* accomplish, achieve, acquire, actualise, appreciate, apprehend, catch on, clear, complete, comprehend, conceive, consummate, do, earn, effect, effectuate, fulfil, gain, get, grasp, imagine, implement, make, net, obtain, perform, produce, recognise, reify, take in, twig, understand.

realism *n.* actuality, practicality, pragmatism, rationality, saneness, sanity, sensibleness.

realistic *adj.* authentic, businesslike, clear-eyed,

clear-sighted, common-sense, detached, down-to-earth, faithful, genuine, graphic, hard-headed, level-headed, lifelike, matter-of-fact, natural, naturalistic, objective, practical, pragmatic, rational, real, real-life, representational, sensible, sober, true, truthful, unromantic, unsentimental.
antonyms fanciful, impractical, irrational, unrealistic.

reality *n.* actuality, authenticity, certainty, corporeality, fact, factuality, genuineness, materiality, nitty-gritty, palpability, realism, tangibility, truth, validity, verisimilitude, verity.

really *adv.* absolutely, actually, assuredly, categorically, certainly, essentially, genuinely, indeed, intrinsically, positively, surely, truly, undoubtedly, verily.

realm *n.* area, bailiwick, branch, country, department, domain, dominion, empire, field, jurisdiction, kingdom, land, monarchy, orbit, principality, province, region, sphere, state, territory, world, zone.

reap *v.* acquire, collect, crop, cut, derive, gain, garner, gather, get, harvest, mow, obtain, realise, secure, win.

rear[1] *n.* back, backside, bottom, buttocks, croup, end, hindquarters, posterior, rearguard, rump, stern, tail.
antonym front.
adj. aft, after, back, following, hind, hindmost, last.
antonym front.

rear[2] *v.* breed, build, construct, cultivate, educate, elevate, erect, fabricate, foster, grow, hoist, lift, loom, nurse, nurture, parent, raise, rise, soar, tower, train.

rearrange *v.* adjust, alter, rejig, rejigger, reorder, reposition, shift, vary.

reason *n.* aim, apologia, apology, apprehension, argument, basis, bounds, brains, case, cause, common sense, comprehension, consideration, defence, design, end, excuse, explanation, exposition, goal, ground, grounds, gumption, impetus, incentive, inducement, intellect, intention, judgement, justification, limits, logic, mentality, mind, moderation, motive, nous, object, occasion, propriety, purpose, ratiocination, rationale, rationality, reasonableness, reasoning, sanity, sense, sensibleness, soundness, target, understanding, vindication, warrant, wisdom.
v. conclude, deduce, infer, intellectualise, ratiocinate, resolve, solve, syllogise, think, work out.
reason with argue, debate, dispute, dissuade, expostulate, make representations, move, persuade, protest, remonstrate, talk, urge.

reasonable *adj.* acceptable, advisable, arguable, average, believable, credible, equitable, fair, fit, honest, inexpensive, intelligent, judicious, just, justifiable, logical, moderate, modest, OK, passable, plausible, possible, practical, proper, rational, reasoned, right, sane, satisfactory, sensible, sober, sound, tenable,

tolerable, viable, well-advised, well-thought-out, wise.
antonyms crazy, extravagant, irrational, outrageous, unreasonable.

reasoned *adj.* clear, judicious, logical, methodical, rational, sensible, sound, systematic, well-thought-out.
antonyms illogical, unsystematic.

reasoning *n.* analysis, argument, case, cogitation, deduction, explication, exposition, hypothesis, interpretation, logic, proof, ratiocination, reason, supposition, thinking, thought.

reassure *v.* bolster, brace, comfort, encourage, hearten, inspirit, nerve, rally.

rebate *n.* allowance, bonus, deduction, discount, reduction, refund, repayment.

rebel *v.* defy, disobey, dissent, flinch, kick over the traces, mutiny, recoil, resist, revolt, rise up, run riot, shrink.
n. apostate, dissenter, heretic, insurgent, insurrectionary, Jacobin, malcontent, mutineer, nonconformist, revolutionary, revolutionist, schismatic, secessionist.
adj. insubordinate, insurgent, insurrectionary, malcontent(ed), mutinous, rebellious, revolutionary.

rebellion *n.* apostasy, defiance, disobedience, dissent, heresy, inqilab, insubordination, insurgence, insurgency, insurrection, Jacquerie, mutiny, nonconformity, resistance, revolt, revolution, rising, schism, uprising.

rebellious *adj.* contumacious, defiant, difficult, disaffected, disloyal, disobedient, disorderly, incorrigible, insubordinate, insurgent, insurrectionary, intractable, malcontent(ed), mutinous, obstinate, rebel, recalcitrant, refractory, resistant, revolutionary, seditious, turbulent, ungovernable, unmanageable, unruly.
antonyms obedient, submissive.

rebirth *n.* reactivation, reanimation, regeneration, reincarnation, rejuvenation, renaissance, renascence, renewal, restoration, resurgence, resurrection, revitalisation, revival.

rebound *v.* backfire, boomerang, bounce, misfire, recoil, redound, resile, resound, return, ricochet.
n. back-wash, bounce, reflection, repercussion, return, reverberation, ricochet.

rebuff *v.* cold-shoulder, cut, decline, deny, discourage, put someone's nose out of joint, refuse, reject, repulse, resist, slight, snub, spurn, turn down.
n. brush-off, check, cold shoulder, defeat, denial, discouragement, flea in one's ear, noser, opposition, refusal, rejection, repulse, rubber, set-down, slight, snub.

rebuild *v.* haussmannise, reassemble, reconstruct, re-edify, refashion, remake, remodel, renovate, restore.
antonyms demolish, destroy.

rebuke *v.* admonish, berate, blame, carpet, castigate, censure, chide, countercheck, jobe, keelhaul, lecture, lesson, rate, reprehend, reprimand, reproach, reprove, scold, slap

down, tell off, tick off, trim, trounce, upbraid.
antonyms compliment, praise.

n. admonition, blame, castigation, censure, countercheck, dressing-down, lecture, reprimand, reproach, reproof, reproval, row, slap, telling-off, ticking-off, tongue-lashing, wigging.
antonyms compliment, praise.

rebut *v.* confute, defeat, discredit, disprove, explode, give the lie to, invalidate, negate, overturn, quash, refute.

rebuttal *n.* confutation, defeat, disproof, invalidation, negation, overthrow, refutation.

recalcitrant *adj.* contrary, contumacious, defiant, disobedient, insubordinate, intractable, obstinate, refractory, renitent, stubborn, uncontrollable, unco-operative, ungovernable, unmanageable, unruly, unsubmissive, unwilling, wayward, wilful.
antonym amenable.

recall *v.* abjure, annul, cancel, cast one's mind back, countermand, evoke, mind, nullify, place, recognise, recollect, remember, repeal, rescind, retract, revoke, withdraw.
n. abrogation, annulment, cancellation, memory, nullification, recision, recollection, remembrance, repeal, rescission, retraction, revocation, withdrawal.

recant *v.* abjure, abrogate, apostatise, deny, disavow, disclaim, disown, forswear, recall, renounce, repudiate, rescind, retract, revoke, unsay, withdraw.

recantation *n.* abjuration, apostasy, denial, disavowal, disclaimer, disownment, renunciation, repudiation, retractation, retraction, revocation, revoke, withdrawal.

recapitulate *v.* give a resumé, recap, recount, reiterate, repeat, restate, review, summarise.

recede *v.* abate, decline, decrease, diminish, dwindle, ebb, fade, lessen, regress, retire, retreat, retrogress, return, shrink, sink, slacken, subside, wane, withdraw.
antonyms advance, proceed.

receipt *n.* acceptance, acknowledgement, counterfoil, delivery, receiving, reception, recipience, slip, stub, ticket, voucher.

receipts *n.* gains, gate, income, proceeds, profits, return, take, takings.

receive *v.* accept, accommodate, acquire, admit, apprehend, bear, collect, derive, encounter, entertain, experience, gather, get, greet, hear, meet, obtain, perceive, pick up, react to, respond to, suffer, sustain, take, undergo, welcome.
antonyms donate, give.

receiver *n.* beneficiary, donee, Fagin, fence, handset, radio, recipient, tuner, wireless.
antonym donor.

recent *adj.* contemporary, current, fresh, late, latter, latter-day, modern, neoteric(al), new, novel, present-day, up-to-date, young.
antonyms dated, old, out-of-date.

recently *adv.* currently, freshly, lately, latterly, newly.

receptacle *n.* container, holder, pantechnicon,

repository, reservatory, vessel.

reception *n.* acceptance, acknowledgement, admission, do, durbar, entertainment, function, greeting, levee, party, reaction, receipt, receiving, recipience, recognition, response, shindig, soirée, treatment, welcome.

receptive *adj.* accessible, alert, amenable, approachable, bright, favourable, friendly, hospitable, interested, open, open-minded, perceptive, responsive, sensitive, suggestible, susceptible, sympathetic, welcoming.

recess *n.* alcove, apse, apsidiole, bay, break, cavity, cessation, closure, corner, depression, embrasure, holiday, hollow, indentation, intermission, interval, loculus, niche, nook, oriel, respite, rest, vacation.

recesses *n.* bowels, depths, heart, innards, interior, penetralia, reaches, retreats.

recession *n.* decline, depression, downturn, slump, stagflation.
antonyms boom, upturn.

recherché *adj.* abstruse, arcane, choice, esoteric, exotic, far-fetched, rare, refined, select.
antonym commonplace.

recipe *n.* directions, formula, ingredients, instructions, method, prescription, procedure, process, programme, receipt, system, technique.

recipient *n.* assignee, beneficiary, donee, grantee, legatee, receiver, suscipient.
antonyms donor, giver.

reciprocal *adj.* alternate, complementary, correlative, corresponding, equivalent, give-and-take, interchangeable, interdependent, mutual, reciprocative, reciprocatory, shared.

reciprocate *v.* alternate, barter, correspond, equal, exchange, interchange, match, reply, requite, respond, return, swap, trade.

recital *n.* account, convert, description, detailing, enumeration, interpretation, narration, narrative, performance, reading, recapitulation, recitation, rehearsal, relation, rendering, rendition, repetition, statement, story, tale, telling.

recitation *n.* lecture, narration, party piece, passage, performance, piece, reading, recital, rendering, rendition, telling.

recite *v.* articulate, declaim, deliver, describe, detail, enumerate, itemise, narrate, orate, perform, recapitulate, recount, rehearse, relate, repeat, speak, tell.

reckless *adj.* careless, daredevil, devil-may-care, foolhardy, harebrained, hasty, headlong, heedless, ill-advised, imprudent, inattentive, incautious, indiscreet, irresponsible, madcap, mindless, negligent, precipitate, rantipole, rash, regardless, tearaway, thoughtless, wild.
antonyms calculating, careful, cautious.

recklessness *n.* carelessness, foolhardiness, gallowsness, heedlessness, imprudence, inattention, incaution, irresponsibleness, irresponsibility, madness, mindlessness, motorway madness, negligence, rashness, thoughtlessness.
antonym carefulness.

reckon v. account, add up, adjudge, appraise, assess, assume, believe, calculate, compute, conjecture, consider, count, deem, enumerate, esteem, estimate, evaluate, expect, fancy, gauge, guess, hold, imagine, judge, number, opine, rate, regard, suppose, surmise, tally, think, total.

reckon on bank, calculate, count, depend, figure on, hope for, rely, trust in.

reckon with anticipate, bargain for, consider, cope, deal, expect, face, foresee, handle, plan for, take into account, treat.

reckoning n. account, adding, addition, bill, calculation, charge, computation, count, counting, doom, due, enumeration, estimate, judgement, retribution, score, settlement, summation, working.

reclaim v. impolder, recapture, recover, redeem, reform, regain, regenerate, reinstate, rescue, restore, retrieve, salvage.

recline v. couch, lean, lie, loll, lounge, repose, rest, sprawl, stretch out.

recluse n. anchoress, anchoret, anchorite, ancress, ascetic, eremite, hermit, monk, solitaire, solitarian, solitary, stylite.

reclusive adj. anchoretic(al), anchoritic(al), ascetic, cloistered, eremitic, hermitical, isolated, monastic, recluse, retiring, secluded, sequestered, solitary, withdrawn.

recognise v. accept, acknowledge, admit, allow, appreciate, approve, avow, concede, confess, grant, greet, honour, identify, know, notice, own, perceive, place, realise, recall, recollect, remember, respect, salute, see, spot, understand, wot.

recognition n. acceptance, acknowledgement, admission, allowance, appreciation, approval, avowal, awareness, cognisance, confession, detection, discovery, enlightenment, gratitude, greeting, honour, identification, notice, perception, realisation, recall, recollection, remembrance, respect, salute, understanding.

recoil v. backfire, boomerang, falter, flinch, kick, misfire, quail, react, rebound, redound, resile, shrink.

n. backlash, kick, reaction, rebound, redound(ing), repercussion.

recollect v. call up, cast one's mind back, mind, place, recall, remember, reminisce.

recollection n. image, impression, memory, recall, remembrance, reminiscence, souvenir.

recommend v. advance, advise, advocate, approve, commend, counsel, endorse, enjoin, exhort, plug, praise, propose, puff, suggest, urge, vouch for.

antonyms disapprove, veto.

recommendation n. advice, advocacy, approbation, approval, blessing, commendation, counsel, endorsement, plug, praise, proposal, puff, reference, sanction, suggestion, testimonial, urging.

antonyms disapproval, veto.

recompense v. compensate, guerdon, indemnify, pay, redress, reimburse, remunerate, repay,

requite, reward, satisfy.

n. amends, compensation, damages, emolument, guerdon, indemnification, indemnity, pay, payment, remuneration, reparation, repayment, requital, restitution, return, reward, satisfaction, wages.

reconcile v. accept, accommodate, accord, adjust, appease, compose, conciliate, harmonise, pacify, placate, propitiate, rectify, resign, resolve, reunite, settle, square, submit, yield.

antonym estrange.

reconciliation n. accommodation, adjustment, agreement, appeasement, compromise, conciliation, détente, harmony, pacification, propitiation, rapprochement, reconcilement, rectification, reunion, settlement, understanding.

antonyms estrangement, separation.

recondite adj. abstruse, arcane, cabbalistic, complicated, concealed, dark, deep, difficult, esoteric, hidden, intricate, involved, mysterious, mystical, obscure, occult, profound, secret.

antonyms simple, straightforward.

recondition v. fix, overhaul, refurbish, remodel, renew, renovate, repair, restore, revamp, sort.

reconnaissance n. examination, exploration, inspection, investigation, observation, patrol, probe, recce, reconnoitring, scan, scouting, scrutiny, survey.

reconnoitre v. case, examine, explore, inspect, investigate, observe, patrol, probe, recce, scan, scout, scrutinise, spy out, survey.

reconsider v. modify, reassess, re-examine, rethink, review, revise, think better of, think over, think twice.

reconstruct v. reassemble, rebuild, recreate, re-establish, refashion, reform, reformulate, regenerate, remake, remodel, renovate, reorganise, restore.

record n. account, album, annals, archives, background, career, chronicle, curriculum vitae, diary, disc, document, documentation, dossier, entry, EP, evidence, file, form, forty-five, gramophone record, history, journal, log, LP, memoir, memorandum, memorial, minute, noctuary, performance, platter, recording, register, release, remembrance, report, single, talky, testimony, trace, tracing, track record, witness.

v. annalise, chalk up, chronicle, contain, cut, diarise, document, enregister, enrol, enter, indicate, inscribe, log, minute, note, preserve, read, register, report, say, score, show, tape, tape-record, transcribe, video, video-tape, wax.

recorder n. annalist, archivist, chronicler, chronographer, chronologer, clerk, diarist, historian, registrar, score-keeper, scorer, scribe, stenographer.

recording n. cut, disc, gramophone record, performance, record, recordation, release, tape, video.

recount *v.* communicate, delineate, depict, describe, detail, enumerate, narrate, portray, recite, rehearse, relate, repeat, report, tell.

recoup *v.* compensate, indemnify, make good, recover, redeem, refund, regain, reimburse, remunerate, repay, requite, retrieve, satisfy.

recourse *n.* access, alternative, appeal, choice, expedient, option, refuge, remedy, resort.

recover *v.* convalesce, heal, improve, mend, pick up, pull through, rally, recapture, reclaim, recoup, recuperate, redeem, regain, repair, replevy, repossess, restore, retake, retrieve, revive.
antonyms forfeit, lose, worsen.

recovery *n.* amelioration, betterment, convalescence, healing, improvement, mending, rally, recapture, reclamation, recoupment, recuperation, redemption, rehabilitation, repair, repossession, restoration, retrieval, revival, upturn.
antonyms forfeit, loss, worsening.

recreation *n.* amusement, distraction, diversion, enjoyment, entertainment, exercise, fun, games, hobby, leisure activity, pastime, play, pleasure, refreshment, relaxation, relief, sport.

recrimination *n.* accusation, bickering, counterattack, counterblast, countercharge, namecalling, quarrel, retaliation, retort, squabbling.

recruit *v.* augment, draft, engage, enlist, enrol, gather, headhunt, impress, levy, mobilise, muster, obtain, procure, proselytise, raise, refresh, reinforce, renew, replenish, restore, strengthen, supply, trawl.
n. apprentice, beginner, conscript, convert, draftee, greenhorn, helper, initiate, learner, neophyte, nig-nog, novice, proselyte, rookie, trainee, tyro, yob.

rectify *v.* adjust, amend, correct, distil, emend, fix, improve, mend, purify, redress, refine, reform, remedy, repair, right, separate, square, straighten.

rectitude *n.* accuracy, correctness, decency, equity, exactness, goodness, honesty, honour, incorruptibility, integrity, irreproachability, justice, morality, precision, principle, probity, righteousness, rightness, scrupulousness, sinlessness, soundness, unimpeachability, uprightness, verity, virtue.

recumbent *adj.* flat, horizontal, leaning, lounging, lying, prone, prostrate, reclining, resting, sprawling, supine.
antonyms erect, upright.

recuperate *v.* convalesce, get better, improve, mend, pick up, rally, recoup, recover, regain, revive.
antonym worsen.

recur *v.* persist, reappear, repeat, return.

recurrent *adj.* continued, cyclical, frequent, habitual, haunting, periodic, recurring, regular, repeated, repetitive.

recycle *v.* reclaim, reconstitute, reprocess, reuse, salvage, save.

red *adj.* bay, bloodshot, bloodstained, bloody, blooming, blushing, cardinal, carmine, carroty, cherry, chestnut, coral, crimson, damask, embarrassed, ensanguined, flame-coloured, flaming, florid, flushed, foxy, glowing, gory, gules, healthy, horseflesh, incarnadine, inflamed, Judas-coloured, lateritious, maroon, pink, reddish, rose, roseate, rosy, rubicund, rubied, rubineous, rubious, ruby, ruby-red, ruddy, sandy, sanguine, scarlet, shamefaced, suffused, titian, vermeil, vermilion, wine.

red-blooded *adj.* hearty, lively, lusty, manly, robust, strong, vigorous, virile, vital.

redden *v.* blush, colour, crimson, flush, rubefy, suffuse.

reddish *adj.* bloodshot, ginger, pink, rosy, rubicund, ruddy, rufescent, rufous, russet, sandy.

redeem *v.* absolve, acquit, atone for, cash (in), change, compensate for, defray, deliver, discharge, emancipate, exchange, extricate, free, fulfil, keep, liberate, make good, make up for, meet, offset, outweigh, perform, ransom, reclaim, recoup, recover, recuperate, redress, regain, rehabilitate, reinstate, repossess, repurchase, rescue, retrieve, salvage, satisfy, save, trade in.

redemption *n.* amends, atonement, compensation, deliverance, discharge, emancipation, exchange, expiation, fulfilment, liberation, performance, ransom, reclamation, recovery, rehabilitation, reinstatement, release, reparation, repossession, repurchase, rescue, retrieval, salvation, trade-in.

redolent *adj.* aromatic, evocative, fragrant, odorous, perfumed, remindful, reminiscent, scented, suggestive, sweet-smelling.

redoubtable *adj.* courageous, doughty, dreadful, fearful, fearsome, formidable, heroic, mighty, powerful, resolute, strong, terrible, valiant.

redound *v.* accrue, conduce, contribute, effect, ensue, rebound, recoil, reflect, resile, result, tend.

redress *v.* adjust, amend, balance, correct, ease, expiate, mend, recompense, rectify, reform, regulate, relieve, remedy, repair, square.
n. aid, amends, assistance, atonement, compensation, correction, cure, ease, expiation, help, indemnification, justice, payment, quittance, recompense, rectification, relief, remedy, reparation, requital, restitution, satisfaction.
antonyms boost, fatten, increase.

reduce *v.* abate, abridge, bankrupt, break, cheapen, conquer, contract, curtail, cut, debase, decimate, decrease, degrade, demote, deoxidate, deoxidise, depress, diet, dilute, diminish, discount, downgrade, drive, force, humble, humiliate, impair, impoverish, lessen, lower, master, moderate, overpower, pauperise, rebate, ruin, scant, shorten, slake, slash, slenderise, slim, subdue, trim, truncate, vanquish, weaken.
antonyms boost, fatten, increase, upgrade.

reduction *n.* abbreviation, abridgement, abstraction, alleviation, attenuation, compression, condensation, constriction, contraction, curtailment, cut, cutback, decline, decrease, deduction, degradation, demotion, deoxidation, deoxidisation, deposal, depreciation, devaluation, diminution, discount, drop, easing, ellipsis, limitation, loss, miniature, mitigation, moderation, modification, muffling, muting, narrowing, rebate, rebatement, refund, restriction, shortening, shrinkage, slackening, softening, subtraction, summarisation, summary, syncope.

antonyms enlargement, improvement, increase.

redundancy *n.* battology, excess, pleonasm, prolixity, repetition, superfluity, surplus, tautology, uselessness, verbosity, wordiness.

redundant *adj.* de trop, diffuse, excessive, extra, inessential, inordinate, padded, periphrastic, pleonastical, prolix, repetitious, supererogatory, superfluous, supernumerary, surplus, tautological, unemployed, unnecessary, unneeded, unwanted, verbose, wordy.

antonyms concise, essential, necessary.

reef *n.* cay, key, ridge, sand-bank, sand-bar.

reek *v.* exhale, fume, hum, pong, smell, smoke, stink.

n. effluvium, exhalation, fetor, fume(s), malodour, mephitis, odour, pong, smell, smoke, stench, stink, vapour.

reel *v.* gyrate, lurch, pitch, revolve, rock, roll, spin, stagger, stumble, sway, swim, swirl, totter, twirl, waver, wheel, whirl, wobble.

refer *v.* accredit, adduce, advert, allude, apply, ascribe, assign, attribute, belong, cite, commit, concern, consign, consult, credit, deliver, direct, go, guide, hint, impute, invoke, look up, mention, pertain, point, recommend, relate, send, speak of, submit, touch on, transfer, turn to.

referee *n.* adjudicator, arbiter, arbitrator, arbitratrix, arbitress, judge, ref, umpire.

v. adjudicate, arbitrate, judge, ref, umpire.

reference *n.* allusion, applicability, bearing, certification, character, citation, concern, connection, consideration, credentials, endorsement, illustration, instance, mention, note, quotation, recommendation, regard, relation, remark, respect, testimonial.

refine *v.* chasten, civilise, clarify, cultivate, distil, elevate, exalt, filter, hone, improve, perfect, polish, process, purify, rarefy, spiritualise, sublimise, subtilise, temper.

refined *adj.* Attic, Augustan, civil, civilised, clarified, clean, courtly, cultivated, cultured, delicate, discerning, discriminating, distilled, elegant, exact, fastidious, filtered, fine, genteel, gentlemanly, gracious, ladylike, nice, polished, polite, precise, processed, punctilious, pure, purified, sensitive, sophisticated, sublime, subtle, urbane, well-bred, well-mannered.

antonyms brutish, coarse, earthy, rude, vulgar.

refinement *n.* breeding, chastity, civilisation, civility, clarification, cleansing, courtesy, courtliness, cultivation, culture, delicacy, discrimination, distillation, elegance, fastidiousness, filtering, fineness, finesse, finish, gentility, grace, graciousness, manners, nicety, nuance, polish, politeness, politesse, precision, processing, purification, rarefaction, rectification, sophistication, style, subtlety, taste, urbanity.

antonyms coarseness, earthiness, vulgarity.

reflect *v.* bespeak, cogitate, communicate, consider, contemplate, deliberate, demonstrate, display, echo, evince, exhibit, express, imitate, indicate, manifest, meditate, mirror, mull (over), muse, ponder, reproduce, return, reveal, ruminate, show, think, wonder.

reflection *n.* aspersion, censure, cerebration, cogitation, consideration, contemplation, counterpart, criticism, deliberation, derogation, echo, idea, image, impression, imputation, meditation, musing, observation, opinion, pondering, reflex, reproach, rumination, slur, study, thinking, thought, view.

reflective *adj.* absorbed, cogitating, contemplative, deliberative, dreamy, meditative, pensive, pondering, reasoning, ruminative, thoughtful.

reform *v.* ameliorate, amend, better, correct, emend, improve, mend, purge, rebuild, reclaim, reconstitute, reconstruct, rectify, regenerate, rehabilitate, remodel, renovate, reorganise, repair, restore, revamp, revolutionise.

n. amelioration, amendment, betterment, correction, improvement, purge, rectification, rehabilitation, renovation, shake-out.

reformer *n.* do-gooder, revolutionary, whistleblower.

refractory *adj.* balky, cantankerous, contentious, contumacious, difficult, disobedient, disputatious, headstrong, intractable, mulish, obstinate, perverse, recalcitrant, resistant, restive, stubborn, uncontrollable, uncooperative, unmanageable, unruly, wilful.

antonyms co-operative, malleable, obedient.

refrain[1] *v.* abstain, avoid, cease, desist, eschew, forbear, leave off, quit, renounce, stop, swear off.

refrain[2] *n.* burden, chorus, epistrophe, falderal, melody, song, tune, undersong, wheel.

refresh *v.* brace, cheer, cool, energise, enliven, freshen, inspirit, jog, prod, prompt, reanimate, reinvigorate, rejuvenate, renew, renovate, repair, replenish, restore, revitalise, revive, revivify, stimulate.

antonyms exhaust, tire.

refreshing *adj.* bracing, cooling, different, energising, fresh, inspiriting, invigorating, new, novel, original, refrigerant, restorative, revivifying, stimulating, thirst-quenching.

antonyms exhausting, tiring.

refreshment *n.* enlivenment, freshening, reanimation, reinvigoration, renewal, renovation, repair, restoration, revitalisation, revival, stimulation.

refreshments *n.* aliment, drinks, food, provisions, snacks, sustenance, titbits.

refrigerate *v.* chill, congeal, cool, freeze.
antonyms heat, warm.

refuge *n.* asylum, bolthole, funk-hole, harbour, haven, hide-away, hideout, holt, protection, resort, retreat, sanctuary, security, shelter.

refugee *n.* absconder, deserter, displaced person, émigré, escapee, exile, fugitive, runaway.

refulgent *adj.* beaming, bright, brilliant, gleaming, glistening, glittering, irradiant, lambent, lustrous, radiant, resplendent, shining.

refund *v.* rebate, reimburse, repay, restore, return.
n. rebate, reimbursement, repayment, return.

refurbish *v.* mend, overhaul, recondition, re-equip, refit, remodel, renovate, repair, restore, revamp.

refusal *n.* choice, consideration, defiance, denial, incompliance, nay-say, negation, no, opportunity, option, rebuff, rejection, repudiation.
antonym acceptance.

refuse¹ *v.* decline, deny, nay-say, reject, repel, repudiate, spurn, withhold.
antonyms accept, allow.

refuse² *n.* chaff, dregs, dross, excrementa, garbage, hogwash, husks, junk, lag(s), landfill, leavings, lees, left-overs, litter, mullock, offscourings, rejectamenta, riddlings, rubbish, scum, sediment, slops, sordes, sullage, sweepings, tailings, trash, waste, wastrel.

refutation *n.* confutation, disproof, elenchus, negation, overthrow, rebuttal.

refute *v.* confute, counter, discredit, disprove, give the lie to, negate, overthrow, rebut, silence.

regain *v.* reattain, recapture, reclaim, recoup, recover, redeem, re-establish, repossess, retake, retrieve, return to.

regal *adj.* kingly, magnificent, majestic, monarch(i)al, monarchic(al), noble, princely, proud, queenly, royal, sovereign, stately.

regale *v.* amuse, captivate, delight, divert, entertain, fascinate, feast, gratify, ply, refresh, serve.

regard *v.* account, adjudge, attend, behold, believe, concern, consider, deem, esteem, estimate, eye, heed, hold, imagine, interest, judge, mark, mind, note, notice, observe, pertain to, rate, relate to, remark, respect, scrutinise, see, suppose, think, treat, value, view, watch.
antonyms despise, disregard.
n. account, advertence, advertency, affection, aspect, attachment, attention, bearing, care, concern, connection, consideration, deference, detail, esteem, feature, gaze, glance, heed, honour, item, look, love, matter, mind, note, notice, particular, point, reference, relation, relevance, reputation, repute, respect, scrutiny, stare, store, sympathy, thought.
antonyms contempt, disapproval, disregard.

regardful *adj.* attentive, aware, cany, careful, circumspect, considerate, dutiful, heedful, mindful, observant, respectful, thoughtful, watchful.
antonyms heedless, inattentive, regardless, unobservant.

regarding *prep.* about, apropos, as regards, as to, concerning, in re, in respect of, in the matter of, on the subject of, re, respecting, touching, with reference to, with regard to.

regardless *adj.* disregarding, heedless, inattentive, inconsiderate, indifferent, neglectful, negligent, nonchalant, rash, reckless, remiss, uncaring, unconcerned, unmindful.
antonyms attentive, heedful, regardful.
adv. anyhow, anyway, come what may, despite everything, in any case, nevertheless, no matter what, nonetheless, willy-nilly.

regards *n.* compliments, devoirs, greetings, respects, salutations.

regenerate *v.* change, inspirit, invigorate, reawaken, reconstitute, reconstruct, re-establish, refresh, reinvigorate, rejuvenate, renew, renovate, reproduce, restore, revive, revivify, uplift.

regeneration *n.* homomorphosis, reconstitution, reconstruction, re-establishment, reinvigoration, rejuvenation, renewal, renovation, reproduction, restoration.

regime *n.* administration, command, control, establishment, government, leadership, management, reign, rule, system.

regiment *n.* band, battery, body, brigade, cohort, company, crew, gang, group, platoon, squadron.

regimented *adj.* controlled, co-ordinated, disciplined, methodical, ordered, organised, regulated, severe, standardised, stern, strict, systematic.
antonyms disorganised, free, lax, loose.

region *n.* area, clime, country, district, division, domain, expanse, field, land, locality, neighbourhood, part, place, province, quarter, range, realm, scope, section, sector, sphere, terrain, terrene, territory, tract, vicinity, world, zone.

regional *adj.* district, local, localised, parochial, provincial, sectional, zonal.

register *n.* almanac, annals, archives, catalogue, chronicle, diary, file, ledger, list, log, matricula, memorandum, notitia, record, roll, roster, schedule.
v. bespeak, betray, catalogue, chronicle, display, enlist, enrol, enter, exhibit, express, indicate, inscribe, list, log, manifest, mark, note, read, record, reflect, reveal, say, score, show, sign on.

registrar *n.* administrator, annalist, archivist, cataloguer, chronicler, clerk, greffier, protocolist, recorder, secretary.

regress *v.* backslide, degenerate, deteriorate, ebb, lapse, recede, relapse, retreat, retrocede, retrogress, return, revert, wane.
antonym progress.

regret *v.* bemoan, bewail, deplore, grieve,

lament, miss, mourn, repent, rue, sorrow.

n. bitterness, compunction, contrition, disappointment, grief, lamentation, penitence, remorse, repentance, ruefulness, self-reproach, shame, sorrow.

regretful *adj.* apologetic, ashamed, conscience-stricken, contrite, disappointed, mournful, penitent, remorseful, repentant, rueful, sad, sorrowful, sorry.

antonyms impenitent, unashamed.

regrettable *adj.* deplorable, disappointing, distressing, ill-advised, lamentable, pitiable, sad, shameful, sorry, unfortunate, unhappy, unlucky, woeful, wrong.

antonyms fortunate, happy.

regular *adj.* approved, balanced, bona fide, classic, common, commonplace, consistent, constant, consuetudinary, conventional, correct, customary, daily, dependable, efficient, established, even, everyday, fixed, flat, formal, habitual, level, methodical, normal, official, ordered, orderly, ordinary, orthodox, periodic, prevailing, proper, rhythmic, routine, sanctioned, set, smooth, standard, standardised, stated, steady, straight, symmetrical, systematic, time-honoured, traditional, typical, uniform, unvarying, usual.

antonyms irregular, sporadic, unconventional.

regulate *v.* adjust, administer, arrange, balance, conduct, control, direct, fit, govern, guide, handle, manage, moderate, modulate, monitor, order, organise, oversee, regiment, rule, run, settle, square, superintend, supervise, systematise, tune.

regulation *n.* adjustment, administration, arrangement, commandment, control, decree, dictate, direction, edict, governance, government, law, management, modulation, order, ordinance, precept, prodecure, regimentation, requirement, rule, statute, supervision, tuning.

adj. accepted, customary, mandatory, normal, official, prescribed, required, standard, stock, usual.

regurgitate *v.* disgorge, puke, regorge, spew, throw up, vomit.

rehabilitate *v.* adjust, clear, convert, mend, normalise, rebuild, recondition, reconstitute, reconstruct, redeem, redintegrate, re-establish, reform, reinstate, reintegrate, reinvigorate, renew, renovate, restore, save.

rehash *n.* rearrangement, rejig, rejigging, reshuffle, restatement, reworking, rewrite.

v. alter, change, rearrange, refashion, rejig, rejigger, reshuffle, restate, rework, rewrite.

rehearsal *n.* account, catalogue, description, drill, dry-run, enumeration, list, narration, practice, preparation, reading, recital, recounting, relation, run-through, telling.

rehearse *v.* act, delineate, depict, describe, detail, drill, enumerate, list, narrate, practise, prepare, ready, recite, recount, relate, repeat, review, run through, spell out, study, tell, train, trot out.

reign *n.* ascendancy, command, control, dominion, empire, hegemony, influence, monarchy, power, rule, sovereignty, supremacy, sway.

v. administer, authority, command, govern, influence, kingship, obtain, predominate, prevail, rule.

reimburse *v.* compensate, indemnify, recompense, refund, remunerate, repay, requite, restore, return, square up.

rein *n.* brake, bridle, check, check-rein, control, curb, harness, hold, overcheck, restraint, restriction.

v. arrest, bridle, check, control, curb, halt, hold, hold back, limit, restrain, restrict, stop.

reincarnation *n.* metempsychosis, palingenesis, rebirth, transmigration.

reinforce *v.* augment, bolster, buttress, emphasise, fortify, harden, increase, prop, recruit, steel, stiffen, strengthen, stress, supplement, support, toughen, underline.

antonyms undermine, weaken.

reinforcement *n.* addition, amplification, augmentation, brace, buttress, emphasis, enlargement, fortification, hardening, increase, prop, shore, stay, strengthening, supplement, support.

reinforcements *n.* auxiliaries, back-up, reserves, support.

reinstate *v.* reappoint, recall, re-establish, rehabilitate, reinstall, replace, restore, return.

reiterate *v.* ding, iterate, recapitulate, repeat, resay, restate, retell.

reject *v.* athetise, condemn, decline, deny, despise, disallow, discard, eliminate, exclude, explode, jettison, jilt, pip, rebuff, refuse, renounce, repel, reprobate, repudiate, repulse, scrap, spike, spurn, veto.

antonyms accept, select.

n. cast-off, discard, failure, second.

rejection *n.* athetesis, brush-off, dear John letter, denial, dismissal, elimination, exclusion, rebuff, refusal, renunciation, repudiation, veto.

antonyms acceptance, selection.

rejoice *v.* celebrate, delight, exult, glory, joy, jubilate, maffick, revel, triumph.

rejoicing *n.* celebration, cheer, delight, elation, exultation, festivity, gaiety, gladness, happiness, joy, jubilation, mafficking, mallemaroking, merrymaking, revelry, triumph.

rejoin *v.* answer, quip, repartee, reply, respond, retort, riposte.

rejoinder *n.* answer, come-back, counter, countercharge, counter-claim, quip, repartee, reply, response, retort, riposte.

rejuvenate *v.* reanimate, recharge, refresh, regenerate, reinvigorate, rekindle, renew, restore, revitalise, revivify.

relapse *v.* backslide, degenerate, deteriorate, fade, fail, lapse, regress, retrogress, revert, sicken, sink, weaken, worsen.

n. backsliding, deterioration, hypostrophe, lapse, recidivism, recurrence, regression, retrogression, reversion, setback, weakening,

St. Mary's Church, Doddington

Order of Service

for the Marriage of

Joanne Chambers

and

Andrew Forgan

Saturday, 3rd September, 1988,
at 3.30 p.m.

ORDER OF SERVICE

BRIDAL MARCH "Lohengrin"   Wagner

HYMN

I danced in the morning when the world was begun,
And I danced in the moon and the stars and the sun,
And I came down from heaven and I danced on the earth;
At Bethlehem I had my birth.

Dance then wherever you may be;
I am the Lord of the Dance, said he,
And I'll lead you all, wherever you may be,
And I'll lead you all in the dance, said he.

I danced for the scribe and the pharisee,
But they would not dance and they wouldn't follow me;
I danced for the fishermen, for James and John;
They came with me and the dance went on.

I danced on the sabbath and I cured the lame:
The holy people said it was a shame.
They whipped and they stripped and they hung me high,
And they left me there on a cross to die.

I danced on a Friday when the sky turned black;
It's hard to dance with the devil on your back.
They buried my body and they thought I'd gone;
But I am the dance and I still go on.

They cut me down and I leapt up high;
I am the life that'll never, never die;
I'll live in you if you'll live in me:
I am the Lord of the Dance, said he.

THE MARRIAGE

THE ACCLAMATIONS

Priest: Blessed are you, heavenly Father:
All: You give joy to bridegroom and bride.
Priest: Blessed are you, Lord Jesus Christ:
All: You have brought new life to mankind.
Priest: Blessed are you, Holy Spirit of God:
All: You have brought us together in love.
Priest: Blessed be Father, Son and Holy Spirit:
All: One God, to be praised for ever. Amen.

HYMN

Lord of all hopefulness, Lord of all joy,
Whose trust, ever childlike, no cares could destroy:
Be there at our waking, and give us, we pray,
Your bliss in our hearts, Lord, at the break of the day.

Lord of all eagerness, Lord of all faith,
Whose strong hands were skilled at the plane and the lathe:
Be there at our labours, and give us, we pray,
Your strength in our hearts, Lord, at the noon of the day.

Lord of all kindliness, Lord of all grace,
Your hands swift to welcome, your arms to embrace:
Be there at our homing, and give us, we pray,
Your love in our hearts, Lord, at the eve of the day.

Lord of all gentleness, Lord of all calm,
Whose voice is contentment, whose presence is balm:
Be there at our sleeping, and give us, we pray,
Your peace in our hearts, Lord, at the end of the day!

REGISTRATION

READING

1 Corinthians, Verse 13

ADDRESS

THE PRAYERS

Priest: As our Saviour taught us, so we pray.

All:

Our Father in heaven
Hallowed be your name
Your Kingdom come
Your will be done
On earth as in heaven.
Give us today our daily bread
Forgive us our sins
As we forgive those who sin against us.
Lead us not into temptation
But deliver us from evil,
For the kingdom, the power and the glory are yours
Now and forever. Amen.

HYMN

Lord Jesus Christ,
You have come to us,
You are one with us,
   Mary's Son;
Cleansing our souls from all their sin,
Pouring your love and goodness in;
Jesus, our love for you we sing,
   Living Lord.

Lord Jesus Christ,
Now and every day
Teach us how to pray,
   Son of God.
You have commanded us to do
This in remembrance, Lord, of you:
Into our lives your power breaks through,
   Living Lord.

Lord Jesus Christ,
You have come to us,
Born as one of us,
   Mary's Son.
Led out to die on Calvary,
Risen from death to set us free,
Living Lord Jesus, help us see
   You are Lord.

Lord Jesus Christ,
I would come to you,
Live my life for you,
   Son of God.
All your commands I know are true,
Your many gifts will make me new,
Into my life your power breaks through,
   Living Lord.

THE BLESSING

WEDDING MARCH   Mendelssohn

worsening.

relate *v.* ally, appertain, apply, associate, chronicle, concern, connect, co-ordinate, correlate, couple, describe, detail, empathise, feel for, identify with, impart, join, link, narrate, pertain, present, recite, recount, refer, rehearse, report, sympathise, tell, understand.

related *adj.* accompanying, affiliated, affine(d), agnate, akin, allied, associated, cognate, concomitant, connected, consanguine, consanguineous, correlated, interconnected, joint, kin, kindred, linked.
antonyms different, unconnected, unrelated.

relation *n.* account, affiliation, affine, affinity, agnate, agnation, application, bearing, bond, comparison, connection, consanguinity, correlation, description, german, interdependence, kin, kindred, kinship, kinsman, kinswoman, link, narration, narrative, pertinence, propinquity, recital, recountal, reference, regard, relationship, relative, report, sib, similarity, story, tale, tie-in.

relations *n.* affairs, associations, clan, communications, connections, contact, dealings, doings, family, interaction, intercourse, kin, kindred, kinsmen, liaison, meetings, rapport, relationship, relatives, terms, tribe, truck.

relationship *n.* affaire, association, bond, communications, conjunction, connection, contract, correlation, dealings, exchange, intercourse, kinship, liaison, link, parallel, proportion, rapport, ratio, similarity, tie-up.

relative *adj.* allied, applicable, apposite, appropriate, appurtenant, apropos, associated, comparative, connected, contingent, correlative, corresponding, dependent, germane, interrelated, pertinent, proportionate, reciprocal, related, relevant, respective.
n. cognate, connection, german, kinsman, kinswoman, relation, sib.

relatively *adv.* comparatively, fairly, quite, rather, somewhat.

relax *v.* abate, diminish, disinhibit, ease, ebb, lessen, loosen, lower, mitigate, moderate, reduce, relieve, remit, rest, slacken, soften, tranquillise, unbend, unclench, unwind, weaken.
antonyms intensify, tighten.

relaxation *n.* abatement, amusement, délassement, détente, diminution, disinhibition, distraction, easing, emollition, enjoyment, entertainment, fun, leisure, lessening, let-up, moderation, pleasure, recreation, reduction, refreshment, rest, slackening, weakening.
antonyms intensification, tension.

relaxed *adj.* calm, carefree, casual, collected, composed, cool, down-beat, easy-going, even-tempered, happy-go-lucky, informal, insouciant, laid-back, mellow, mild, nonchalant, placid, serene, together, tranquil, unhurried.
antonyms edgy, nervous, stiff, tense, uptight.

relay *n.* broadcast, communication, dispatch, message, programme, relief, shift, transmission, turn.
v. broadcast, carry, communicate, rebroadcast, send, spread, supply, transmit.

release *v.* absolve, acquit, break, circulate, declassify, decontrol, deliver, discage, discharge, disengage, disenthral, disimprison, disinhibit, disoblige, dispense, disprison, disseminate, distribute, drop, emancipate, exempt, excuse, exonerate, extricate, free, furlough, issue, launch, liberate, loose, manumit, present, publish, unbind, uncage, unchain, undo, unfasten, unfetter, unhand, unleash, unloose, unmew, unpen, unshackle, untie, unveil.
antonyms check, detain.
n. absolution, acquittal, acquittance, announcement, deliverance, delivery, discharge, disimprisonment, disinhibition, dispensation, emancipation, exemption, exoneration, freedom, issue, let-off, liberation, liberty, manumission, offering, proclamation, publication, quittance, relief.
antonym detention.

relegate *v.* assign, banish, consign, delegate, demote, deport, dispatch, downgrade, eject, entrust, exile, expatriate, expel, refer, transfer.
antonym promote.

relent *v.* acquiesce, capitulate, drop, ease, fall, forbear, give in, melt, relax, slacken, slow, soften, unbend, weaken, yield.

relentless *adj.* cruel, fierce, grim, hard, harsh, implacable, incessant, inexorable, inflexible, merciless, non-stop, persistent, pitiless, punishing, remorseless, ruthless, stern, sustained, unabated, unbroken, uncompromising, undeviating, unfaltering, unflagging, unforgiving, unrelenting, unrelieved, unremitting, unstoppable, unyielding.
antonyms submissive, yielding.

relevant *adj.* ad rem, admissable, applicable, apposite, appropriate, appurtenant, apt, congruous, fitting, germane, material, pertinent, proper, related, relative, significant, suitable, suited.
antonym irrelevant.

reliable *adj.* certain, constant, copper-bottomed, dependable, faithful, honest, predictable, regular, responsible, safe, solid, sound, stable, staunch, sure, true, trustworthy, trusty, unfailing, upright, white.
antonyms doubtful, suspect, unreliable, untrustworthy.

reliance *n.* assurance, belief, confidence, credence, credit, dependence, faith, trust.

relic *n.* fragment, keepsake, memento, potsherd, remembrance, remnant, scrap, souvenir, survival, token, trace, vestige.

relief *n.* abatement, aid, alleviation, assistance, assuagement, balm, break, breather, comfort, cure, deliverance, diversion, ease, easement, help, let-up, load off one's mind, mitigation, palliation, refreshment, relaxation, release, remedy, remission, respite, rest, solace, succour, support, sustenance.

relieve *v.* abate, aid, alleviate, appease, assist, assuage, break, brighten, calm, comfort, console, cure, deliver, diminish, discharge, disembarrass, disencumber, dull, ease, exempt, free, help, interrupt, lighten, mitigate, mollify, palliate, relax, release, salve, slacken, soften, solace, soothe, spell, stand in for, substitute for, succour, support, sustain, take over from, take the place of, unburden, vary.
antonyms aggravate, intensify.

religious *adj.* church-going, conscientious, devotional, devout, divine, doctrinal, exact, faithful, fastidious, God-fearing, godly, holy, meticulous, pious, punctilious, pure, reverent, righteous, rigid, rigorous, sacred, scriptural, scrupulous, sectarian, spiritual, strict, theological, unerring, unswerving.
antonyms irreligious, lax, ungodly.

relinquish *n.* abandon, abdicate, cede, desert, discard, drop, forgo, forsake, hand over, leave, quit, release, renounce, repudiate, resign, surrender, vacate, waive, yield.
antonyms keep, retain.

relish *v.* appreciate, degust, enjoy, fancy, lap up, like, prefer, revel in, savour, taste.
n. appetiser, appetite, appreciation, condiment, enjoyment, fancy, flavour, fondness, gout, gusto, liking, love, partiality, penchant, piquancy, predilection, sauce, savour, seasoning, smack, spice, stomach, tang, taste, trace, zest.

reluctance *n.* aversion, backwardness, disinclination, dislike, distaste, hesitancy, indisposition, loathing, recalcitrance, repugnance, unwillingness.
antonyms eagerness, willingness.

reluctant *adj.* averse, backward, disinclined, grudging, hesitant, indisposed, loath, loathful, loth, recalcitrant, renitent, slow, squeamish, unenthusiastic, unwilling.
antonyms eager, willing.

rely *v.* bank, bet, count, depend, lean, reckon, swear by, trust.

remain *v.* abide, bide, cling, continue, delay, dwell, endure, last, linger, persist, prevail, rest, sojourn, stand, stay, survive, tarry, wait.
antonyms depart, go, leave.

remainder *n.* balance, dregs, excess, leavings, remanent, remanet, residuum, rest, surplus, trace, vestige(s).

remaining *adj.* abiding, extant, lasting, left, lingering, outstanding, persisting, residual, surviving, unfinished, unspent, unused.

remains *n.* ashes, balance, body, cadaver, carcass, corpse, crumbs, debris, detritus, dregs, fragments, leavings, left-overs, oddments, pieces, relics, reliquiae, remainder, remnants, residue, rest, scraps, traces, vestiges.

remark *v.* animadvert, comment, declare, espy, heed, mark, mention, note, notice, observe, perceive, reflect, regard, say, see, state.
n. acknowledgement, assertion, attention, comment, consideration, declaration, heed, mention, notice, observation, opinion, recognition, reflection, regard, say, statement, thought, utterance, word.

remarkable *adj.* amazing, conspicuous, distinguished, exceptional, extraordinary, famous, impressive, miraculous, notable, noteworthy, odd, outstanding, phenomenal, pre-eminent, prominent, rare, signal, singular, strange, striking, surprising, unco, uncommon, unusual, wonderful.
antonyms average, commonplace, ordinary.

remedy *n.* antidote, corrective, counteractive, countermeasure, cure, magistery, medicament, medicine, nostrum, panacea, physic, prescript, redress, relief, restorative, solution, specific, therapy, treatment.
v. alleviate, ameliorate, assuage, control, correct, counteract, cure, ease, fix, heal, help, mitigate, palliate, put right, rectify, redress, reform, relieve, repair, restore, solve, soothe, treat.

remember *v.* commemorate, place, recall, recognise, recollect, reminisce, retain, summon up, think back.
antonym forget.

remembrance *n.* anamnesis, commemoration, keepsake, memento, memorial, memory, mind, monument, recall, recognition, recollection, recordation, regard, relic, remembrancer, reminder, reminiscence, retrospect, souvenir, testimonial, thought, token.

remind *v.* bring to mind, call to mind, call up, cue, hint, jog one's memory, prompt, put in mind, refresh one's memory.

reminder *n.* aide-mémoire, cue, hint, memo, memorandum, nudge, prompt(ing), suggestion.

reminisce *v.* hark back, look back, recall, recollect, remember, retrospect, review, think back.

reminiscence *n.* anecdote, memoir, memory, personalia, recall, recollection, reflection, remembrance, retrospection, review.

reminiscent *adj.* evocative, nostalgic, redolent, remindful, similar, suggestive.

remiss *adj.* careless, culpable, delinquent, derelict, dilatory, fainéant, forgetful, heedless, inattentive, indifferent, lackadaisical, lax, neglectful, negligent, regardless, slack, slipshod, sloppy, slothful, slow, tardy, thoughtless, unmindful.
antonyms careful, scrupulous.

remission *n.* abatement, abeyance, absolution, acquittal, alleviation, amelioration, amnesty, decrease, diminution, discharge, ebb, excuse, exemption, exoneration, forgiveness, indulgence, lessening, let-up, lull, moderation, pardon, reduction, relaxation, release, relinquishment, reprieve, respite, slackening, suspension.

remit *v.* abate, alleviate, cancel, decrease, defer, delay, desist, desist from, diminish, dispatch, dwindle, forbear, forward, halt, mail, mitigate, moderate, post, postpone, put back, reduce, relax, repeal, rescind, send, send back, shelve, sink, slacken, soften, stop,

suspend, transfer, transmit, wane, weaken.
n. authorisation, brief, guidelines, instructions, orders, responsibility, scope, terms of reference.

remittance *n.* allowance, consideration, dispatch, fee, payment, sending.

remnant *n.* balance, bit, end, fent, fragment, hangover, left-overs, piece, remainder, remains, remane(n)t, residue, residuum, rest, rump, scrap, shred, survival, trace, vestige.

remonstrance *n.* complaint, exception, expostulation, grievance, objection, petition, protest, protestation, reprimand, reproof.

remonstrate *v.* argue, challenge, complain, dispute, dissent, expostulate, gripe, object, protest.

remorse *n.* anguish, bad conscience, compassion, compunction, contrition, grief, guilt, penitence, pity, regret, repentance, ruefulness, ruth, self-reproach, shame, sorrow.

remorseful *adj.* apologetic, ashamed, chastened, compunctious, conscience-stricken, contrite, guilt-ridden, guilty, penitent, regretful, repentant, rueful, sad, sorrowful, sorry.
antonyms impenitent, remorseless.

remorseless *adj.* callous, cruel, hard, hard-hearted, harsh, implacable, inexorable, inhumane, merciless, pitiless, relentless, ruthless, savage, stern, undeviating, unforgiving, unmerciful, unrelenting, unremitting, unstoppable.
antonyms remorseful, sorry.

remote *adj.* abstracted, alien, aloof, backwoods, cold, detached, distant, doubtful, dubious, extraneous, extrinsic, faint, far, faraway, far-off, foreign, god-forsaken, immaterial, implausible, inaccessible, inconsiderable, indifferent, introspective, introverted, irrelevant, isolated, lonely, meagre, negligible, outlying, out-of-the-way, outside, poor, removed, reserved, secluded, slender, slight, slim, small, standoffish, unconnected, uninterested, uninvolved, unlikely, unrelated, withdrawn.
antonyms adjacent, close, nearby, significant.

removal *n.* ablation, abstraction, demigration, departure, dislodgement, dismissal, displacement, dispossession, ejection, elimination, eradication, erasure, expulsion, expunction, extraction, flitting, metastasis, move, purge, purging, relocation, riddance, stripping, subtraction, transfer, uprooting, withdrawal.

remove *v.* ablate, abolish, abstract, amove, amputate, assassinate, delete, depart, depose, detach, dethrone, discharge, dislodge, dismiss, displace, doff, efface, eject, eliminate, erase, execute, expunge, extract, flit, flit (move house), guy, kill, liquidate, move, murder, oust, purge, quit, relegate, relocate, shave, shear, shed, shift, sideline, strike, subduct, transfer, transmigrate, transport, unseat, vacate, withdraw.

remunerate *v.* compensate, fee, guerdon, indemnify, pay, recompense, redress, reimburse, repay, requite, reward.

remuneration *n.* compensation, earnings, emolument, fee, guerdon, income, indemnity, pay, payment, profit, recompense, reimbursement, remittance, reparation, repayment, retainer, return, reward, salary, stipend, wages.

remunerative *adj.* fruitful, gainful, lucrative, moneymaking, paying, profitable, rewarding, rich, worthwhile.

renaissance *n.* awakening, new birth, new dawn, reappearance, reawakening, rebirth, recrudescence, re-emergence, regeneration, rejuvenation, renascence, renewal, restoration, resurgence, resurrection, revival.

renascent *adj.* born-again, reanimated, reawakened, reborn, redivivus, re-emergent, renewed, resurgent, resurrected, revived.

rend *v.* afflict, anguish, break, burst, cleave, crack, dissever, distress, disturb, disunite, divide, fracture, hurt, lacerate, pain, pierce, pull, rip, rive, rupture, separate, sever, shatter, smash, splinter, split, stab, sunder, tear, torment, wound, wrench, wring.

render *v.* act, cede, clarify, construe, contribute, deliver, depict, display, do, evince, exchange, exhibit, explain, furnish, give, give back, give up, hand over, interpret, leave, make, make up, manifest, melt, pay, perform, play, portray, present, provide, put, relinquish, repay, represent, reproduce, restate, restore, return, show, show forth, submit, supply, surrender, swap, tender, trade, transcribe, translate, yield.

rendezvous *n.* appointment, assignation, date, engagement, haunt, meeting, meeting-place, resort, tryst, trysting-place, venue.
v. assemble, collect, convene, converge, gather, meet, muster, rally.

rendition *n.* arrangement, construction, delivery, depiction, execution, explanation, interpretation, metaphrase, metaphrasis, performance, portrayal, presentation, reading, rendering, transcription, translation, version.

renegade *n.* apostate, backslider, betrayer, defector, deserter, dissident, mutineer, outlaw, rebel, recreant, renegado, renegate, runaway, tergiversator, traitor, turncoat.
antonyms adherent, disciple, follower.
adj. apostate, backsliding, disloyal, dissident, mutinous, outlaw, perfidious, rebel, rebellious, recreant, runaway, traitorous, unfaithful.

renegue *v.* apostatise, cross the floor, default, renege, renig, repudiate, welsh.

renew *v.* continue, extend, mend, modernise, overhaul, prolong, reaffirm, recommence, recreate, re-establish, refashion, refit, refresh, refurbish, regenerate, rejuvenate, remodel, renovate, reopen, repair, repeat, replace, replenish, restate, restock, restore, resume, revitalise, transform.

renewal *n.* instauration, kiss of life, recommencement, reconditioning, reconstitution, reconstruction, recreation, recruit, recruital, refurbishment, reinvigoration, reiteration, rejuvenation, renovation, repair, replenishment, resumption, resurrection, resuscitation, revitalisation, revivification.

renounce v. abandon, abdicate, abjure, abnegate, decline, deny, discard, disclaim, disown, disprofess, eschew, forgo, forsake, forswear, put away, quit, recant, reject, relinquish, repudiate, resign, spurn.

renovate v. do up, furbish, improve, modernise, overhaul, recondition, reconstitute, recreate, refit, reform, refurbish, rehabilitate, remodel, renew, repair, restore, revamp.

renovation n. face-lift, improvement, modernisation, reconditioning, refit, refurbishment, renewal, repair, restoration.

renown n. acclaim, celebrity, distinction, eminence, fame, glory, honour, illustriousness, kudos, lustre, mark, note, reputation, repute, stardom.

antonyms anonymity, obscurity.

renowned adj. acclaimed, celebrated, distinguished, eminent, esteemed, famed, famous, illustrious, notable, noted, pre-eminent, supereminent, well-known.

antonyms anonymous, obscure, unknown.

rent¹ n. fee, gale, hire, lease, payment, rental, tariff.

v. charter, farm out, hire, lease, let, sublet, take.

rent² n. breach, break, chink, cleavage, crack, dissension, disunion, division, flaw, gash, hole, opening, perforation, rift, rip, rupture, schism, slash, slit, split, tear.

renunciation n. abandonment, abdication, abjuration, abnegation, abstention, denial, disavowal, disclaimer, eschewal, forgoing, forswearing, recantation, rejection, relinquishment, repudiation, resignation, spurning, surrender, waiver.

repair¹ v. debug, fix, heal, mend, patch up, recover, rectify, redress, renew, renovate, restore, retrieve, square.

n. adjustment, condition, darn, fettle, form, improvement, mend, nick, overhaul, patch, restoration, shape, state.

repair² v. go, wend one's way, move, remove, resort, retire, turn, withdraw.

reparable adj. corrigible, curable, recoverable, rectifiable, remediable, restorable, retrievable, salvageable, savable.

antonym irreparable.

reparation n. amends, atonement, compensation, damages, indemnity, propitiation, recompense, redress, renewal, repair, requital, restitution, satisfaction, solatium.

repartee n. badinage, banter, jesting, persiflage, pleasantry, raillery, riposte, sally, waggery, wit, witticism, wittiness, wordplay.

repast n. collation, feed, food, meal, nourishment, refection, snack, spread, victuals.

repay v. avenge, compensate, get even with, make restitution, reciprocate, recompense, refund, reimburse, remunerate, requite, restore, retaliate, return, revenge, reward, settle the score, square.

repayment n. amends, avengement, compensation, rebate, reciprocation, recompense, redress, refund, reimbursement, remuneration, reparation, requital, restitution, retaliation, retribution, revenge, reward, ultion, vengeance.

repeal v. abolish, abrogate, annul, cancel, countermand, invalidate, nullify, quash, recall, rescind, reverse, revoke, set aside, void, withdraw.

antonyms enact, establish.

n. abolition, abrogation, annulment, cancellation, invalidation, nullification, quashing, rescinding, rescindment, rescission, reversal, revocation, withdrawal.

antonyms enactment, establishment.

repeat v. duplicate, echo, iterate, quote, rebroadcast, recapitulate, recite, re-do, rehearse, reiterate, relate, renew, replay, reproduce, rerun, reshow, restate, retell.

n. duplicate, echo, rebroadcast, recapitulation, reiteration, repetition, replay, reproduction, rerun, reshowing.

repeatedly adv. again and again, frequently, often, oftentimes, ofttimes, over and over, recurrently, time after time, time and (time) again.

repel v. check, confront, decline, disadvantage, disgust, fight, hold off, nauseate, offend, oppose, parry, rebuff, refuse, reject, repulse, resist, revolt, sicken, ward off.

antonym attract.

repellent adj. abhorrent, abominable, discouraging, disgusting, distasteful, hateful, horrid, loathsome, nauseating, noxious, obnoxious, odious, offensive, off-putting, rebarbative, repugnant, repulsive, revolting, sickening.

antonym attractive.

repent n. atone, bewail, deplore, lament, regret, relent, rue, sorrow.

repentance n. compunction, contrition, grief, guilt, metanoia, penitence, regret, remorse, self-reproach, sorriness, sorrow.

repentant adj. apologetic, ashamed, chastened, compunctious, contrite, penitent, regretful, remorseful, rueful, sorry.

antonym unrepentant.

repercussion n. aftermath, backlash, backwash, consequence, echo, rebound, recoil, result, reverberation, side effect.

repertory n. collection, list, range, repertoire, repository, reserve, reservoir, stock, store, supply.

repetition n. anaphora, dittography, duplication, echo, echolalia, epanalepsis, epanaphora, iteration, reappearance, recapitulation, recital, recurrence, redundancy, rehearsal, reiteration, relation, renewal, repeat, repetitiousness, replication, restatement, return, tautology.

repetitious adj. battological, long-winded, pleonastic(al), prolix, redundant, tautological, tedious, verbose, windy, wordy.

repetitive adj. boring, dull, interminable, mechanical, monotonous, recurrent, samey, tedious, unchanging, unvaried.

rephrase v. paraphrase, recast, reword, rewrite.

repine v. beef, brood, complain, fret, grieve, grouse, grumble, lament, languish, moan, mope, murmur, sulk.

replace v. deputise, follow, make good, oust, re-establish, reinstate, restore, substitute, succeed, supersede, supplant, supply.

replacement n. double, fill-in, proxy, replacer, stand-in, substitute, succedaneum, successor, surrogate, understudy.

replenish v. fill, furnish, provide, recharge, recruit, refill, reload, renew, replace, restock, restore, stock, supply, top up.

replete adj. abounding, brimful, brimming, charged, chock-a-block, chock-full, crammed, filled, full, full up, glutted, gorged, jammed, jam-packed, sated, satiated, stuffed, teeming, well-provided, well-stocked.

repletion n. completeness, fullness, glut, overfullness, plethora, satiation, satiety, superabundance, superfluity.

replica n. clone, copy, duplicate, facsimile, imitation, model, reproduction.

replicate v. ape, clone, copy, duplicate, follow, mimic, recreate, reduplicate, repeat, reproduce.

reply v. acknowledge, answer, counter, echo, react, reciprocate, rejoin, repartee, respond, retaliate, retort, return, riposte.
n. acknowledgement, answer, comeback, counter, echo, reaction, reciprocation, rejoinder, repartee, response, retaliation, retort, return, riposte.

report n. account, announcement, article, bang, blast, boom, bruit, character, communication, communiqué, crack, crash, declaration, description, detail, detonation, discharge, dispatch, esteem, explosion, fame, gossip, hearsay, information, message, narrative, news, noise, note, paper, piece, procès-verbal, recital, record, regard, relation, reputation, repute, reverberation, rumour, sound, statement, story, summary, tale, talk, tidings, version, word, write-up.
v. air, announce, appear, arrive, broadcast, bruit, circulate, come, communicate, cover, declare, describe, detail, document, mention, narrate, note, notify, proclaim, publish, recite, record, recount, relate, relay, state, tell.

reporter n. announcer, correspondent, hack, Jenkins, journalist, leg-man, newscaster, newshound, newspaperman, newspaperwoman, pressman, stringer, writer.

repose[1] n. aplomb, calm, calmness, composure, dignity, ease, equanimity, inactivity, peace, poise, quiet, quietness, quietude, relaxation, respite, rest, restfulness, self-possession, serenity, sleep, slumber, stillness, tranquillity.
antonyms activity, strain, stress.
v. laze, recline, relax, rest, sleep, slumber.

repose[2] v. confide, deposit, entrust, invest, lodge, place, put, set, store.

repository n. archive, depository, depot, empor-ium, magazine, promptuary, receptacle, repertory, store, storehouse, treasury, vault, warehouse.

reprehensible adj. bad, blamable, blameworthy, censurable, condemnable, culpable, delinquent, discreditable, disgraceful, errant, erring, ignoble, objectionable, opprobrious, remiss, shameful, unworthy.
antonyms creditable, good, praiseworthy.

represent v. act, appear as, be, betoken, delineate, denote, depict, depicture, describe, designate, embody, enact, epitomise, equal, evoke, exemplify, exhibit, express, illustrate, mean, outline, perform, personify, picture, portray, produce, render, reproduce, show, sketch, stage, symbolise, typify.

representation n. account, argument, bust, committee, delegates, delegation, delineation, depiction, description, embassy, exhibition, explanation, exposition, expostulation, icon, idol, illustration, image, likeness, model, narration, narrative, performance, petition, picture, play, portrait, portrayal, production, relation, remonstrance, resemblance, show, sight, sketch, spectacle, statue.

representative n. agent, archetype, commissioner, councillor, delegate, depute, deputy, embodiment, epitome, exemplar, member, MP, personification, proxy, rep, representant, salesman, spokesman, spokesperson, spokeswoman, traveller, type.
adj. archetypal, characteristic, chosen, delegated, elected, elective, emblematic, evocative, exemplary, illustrative, normal, symbolic, typical, usual.
antonyms atypical, unrepresentative.

repress v. bottle up, chasten, check, control, crush, curb, hamper, hinder, impede, inhibit, master, muffle, overcome, overpower, quash, quell, reprime, restrain, silence, smother, stifle, subdue, subjugate, suppress, swallow.

repression n. authoritarianism, censorship, coercion, constraint, control, denial, despotism, domination, gagging, inhibition, restraint, subjugation, suffocation, suppression, tyranny.

repressive adj. absolute, authoritarian, autocratic, coercive, despotic, dictatorial, harsh, iron-handed, oppressive, severe, tough, tyrannical.

reprieve v. abate, allay, alleviate, mitigate, palliate, pardon, redeem, relieve, rescue, respite.
n. abatement, abeyance, alleviation, amnesty, deferment, let-up, mitigation, palliation, pardon, postponement, redemption, relief, remission, rescue, respite, suspension.

reprimand n. admonition, blame, castigation, censure, dressing-down, jawbation, jobation, lecture, rebuke, reprehension, reproach, reproof, row, schooling, talking-to, telling-off, ticking-off, tongue-lashing, wigging.
v. admonish, bawl out, blame, bounce, castigate, censure, check, chide, jobe, keelhaul, lecture, lesson, rebuke, reprehend,

reproach, reprove, scold, slate, tongue-lash, upbraid.

reprisal *n.* counter-stroke, recaption, requital, retaliation, retribution, revenge, ultion, vengeance.

reproach *v.* abuse, blame, censure, chide, condemn, criticise, defame, discredit, disparage, dispraise, rebuke, reprehend, reprimand, reprove, scold, upbraid.

n. abuse, blame, blemish, censure, condemnation, contempt, disapproval, discredit, disgrace, dishonour, disrepute, ignominy, indignity, nayword, obloquy, odium, opprobrium, reproof, scorn, shame, slight, slut, stain, stigma, upbraiding.

reproachful *adj.* abusive, admonitory, aggrieved, castigatory, censorious, condemnatory, contemptuous, critical, disappointed, disapprõving, fault-finding, opprobrious, reproving, scolding, upbraiding.
antonym complimentary.

reprobate *adj.* abandoned, bad, base, condemnatory, corrupt, damned, degenerate, depraved, dissolute, hardened, immoral, incorrigible, profligate, reprobative, reprobatory, shameless, sinful, unprincipled, vile, wicked.
antonym upright.

n. blackguard, degenerate, evildoer, knave, miscreant, ne'er-do-well, outcast, pariah, profligate, rake, rakehell, rascal, rogue, roué, scamp, scoundrel, sinner, villain, wastrel, wretch, wrongdoer.

reproduce *v.* ape, breed, copy, duplicate, echo, emulate, facsimile, generate, imitate, match, mirror, multiply, parallel, parrot, print, procreate, proliferate, propagate, recreate, regurgitate, repeat, replicate, represent, simulate, spawn, transcribe.

reproduction *n.* amphimixis, breeding, copy, duplicate, ectype, facsimile, fructuation, gamogenesis, generation, imitation, increase, multiplication, picture, print, procreation, proliferation, propagation, replica.
antonym original.

reproductive *adj.* generative, genital, procreative, progenitive, propagative, sex, sexual.

reproof *n.* admonition, blame, castigation, censure, chiding, condemnation, criticism, dressing-down, rebuke, reprehension, reprimand, reproach, reproval, reproving, scolding, ticking-off, tongue-lashing, upbraiding.
antonym praise.

reprove *v.* abuse, admonish, berate, blame, censure, check, chide, condemn, rap, rate, rebuke, reprehend, reprimand, scold, upbraid.
antonym praise.

repudiate *v.* abandon, abjure, cast off, deny, desert, disaffirm, disavow, discard, disclaim, disown, disprofess, divorce, forsake, reject, renounce, rescind, retract, reverse, revoke.
antonyms admit, own.

repudiation *n.* abjuration, denial, disaffirmance, disaffirmation, disavowal, disclaimer, disowning, recantation, rejection, renouncement,

renunciation, retraction.
antonym acceptance.

repugnance *n.* abhorrence, abhorring, antipathy, aversion, disgust, dislike, disrelish, distaste, hatred, inconsistency, loathing, reluctance, repugnancy, repulsion, revulsion.
antonyms liking, pleasure.

repugnant *adj.* abhorrent, abominable, adverse, antagonistic, antipathetic, averse, contradictory, disgusting, distasteful, foul, hateful, horrid, hostile, incompatible, inconsistent, inimical, loathsome, nauseating, objectionable, obnoxious, odious, offensive, opposed, repellent, revolting, sickening, unacceptable, vile.
antonyms acceptable, consistent, pleasant.

repulse *v.* beat off, check, defeat, disdain, disregard, drive back, rebuff, refuse, reject, repel, snub, spurn.

n. check, defeat, disappointment, failure, rebuff, refusal, rejection, repudiation, reverse, snub, spurning.
antonyms acceptance, success.

repulsion *n.* abhorrence, aversion, detestation, disgust, disrelish, distaste, hatred, loathing, repellence, repellency, repugnance, revulsion.
antonym liking.

repulsive *adj.* abhorrent, abominable, cold, disagreeable, disgusting, distasteful, forbidding, foul, hateful, hideous, horrid, ill-faced, loathsome, nauseating, objectionable, obnoxious, odious, offensive, repellent, reserved, revolting, sickening, ugly, unpleasant, vile.
antonyms friendly, pleasant.

reputable *adj.* creditable, dependable, estimable, excellent, good, honourable, honoured, irreproachable, legitimate, principled, reliable, respectable, trustworthy, unimpeachable, upright, worthy.
antonyms disreputable, infamous.

reputation *n.* bad name, character, credit, distinction, esteem, estimation, fame, good name, honour, infamy, name, opinion, renown, repute, standing, stature.

repute *n.* celebrity, distinction, esteem, estimation, fame, good name, name, renown, reputation, standing, stature.
antonym infamy.

reputed *adj.* accounted, alleged, believed, considered, deemed, estimated, held, ostensible, putative, reckoned, regarded, reputative, rumoured, said, seeming, supposed, thought.
antonym actual.

reputedly *adv.* allegedly, apparently, ostensibly, reputatively, seemingly, supposedly.
antonym actually.

request *v.* ask, ask for, beg, beseech, demand, desire, entreat, impetrate, importune, petition, pray, requisition, seek, solicit, supplicate.

n. appeal, application, asking, begging, call, demand, desire, entreaty, impetration, petition, prayer, representation, requisition, solicitation, suit, supplication.

require v. ask, beg, beseech, bid, command, compel, constrain, crave, demand, desire, direct, enjoin, exact, force, instruct, involve, lack, make, miss, necessitate, need, oblige, order, request, take, want, wish.

required adj. compulsory, demanded, essential, mandatory, necessary, needed, obligatory, prescribed, recommended, requisite, set, stipulated, unavoidable, vital.
antonyms inessential, optional.

requirement n. demand, desideratum, essential, lack, must, necessity, need, precondition, prerequisite, provision, proviso, qualification, requisite, sine qua non, specification, stipulation, term, want.
antonym inessential.

requisite adj. essential, imperative, indispensable, mandatory, necessary, needed, needful, obligatory, prerequisite, required, vital.
antonyms inessential, optional.
n. condition, desiderative, desideratum, essential, must, necessity, need, precondition, prerequisite, requirement, sine qua non.
antonym inessential.

requisition v. appropriate, commandeer, confiscate, demand, occupy, put in for, request, seize, take.
n. application, appropriation, call, commandeering, demand, occupation, order, request, seizure, summons, takeover, use.

requital n. amends, compensation, indemnification, indemnity, payment, pay-off, quittance, recompense, redress, reparation, repayment, restitution, satisfaction.

requite v. avenge, compensate, pay, reciprocate, recompense, redress, reimburse, remunerate, repay, respond, retaliate, return, reward, satisfy.

rescind v. abrogate, annul, cancel, countermand, invalidate, negate, nullify, overturn, quash, recall, repeal, retract, reverse, revoke, void.
antonym enforce.

rescission n. abrogation, annulment, cancellation, invalidation, negation, nullification, recall, repeal, rescindment, retraction, reversal, revocation, voidance.
antonym enforcement.

rescue v. deliver, extricate, free, liberate, ransom, recover, redeem, release, salvage, save.
antonym capture.
n. deliverance, delivery, extrication, liberation, recovery, redemption, release, relief, salvage, salvation, saving.
antonym capture.

research n. analysis, delving, examination, experimentation, exploration, fact-finding, groundwork, inquiry, investigation, probe, quest, scrutiny, search, study.
v. analyse, examine, experiment, explore, ferret, investigate, probe, scrutinise, search, study.

researcher n. analyst, boffin, field worker, inquirer, inspector, investigator, student.

resemblance n. affinity, analogy, assonance, closeness, comparability, comparison, conformity, correspondence, counterpart, facsimile, image, kinship, likeness, parallel, parity, sameness, semblance, similarity, similitude.
antonym dissimilarity.

resemble v. approach, duplicate, echo, favour, mirror, parallel, take after.
antonym differ from.

resent v. begrudge, chafe at, dislike, grudge, grumble at, object to, take amiss, take exception to, take offence at, take the huff, take umbrage at.
antonyms accept, like.

resentful adj. aggrieved, angry, bitter, embittered, exasperated, grudging, huffish, huffy, hurt, incensed, indignant, irate, ireful, jealous, miffed, offended, peeved, piqued, put out, resentive, revengeful, stomachful, unforgiving, wounded.
antonym contented.

resentment n. anger, animosity, bitterness, disaffection, discontentment, displeasure, fury, grudge, huff, hurt, ill-feeling, ill-will, indignation, ire, irritation, malice, pique, rage, rancour, umbrage, vexation, vindictiveness, wrath.
antonym contentment.

reservation[1] n. arrière pensée, condition, demur, doubt, hesitancy, hesitation, inhibition, proviso, qualification, restraint, scepticism, scruple, second thought, stipulation.

reservation[2] enclave, homeland, park, preserve, reserve, sanctuary, territory, tract.

reserve[1] v. bespeak, book, conserve, defer, delay, engage, hoard, hold, husband, keep, postpone, prearrange, preserve, retain, save, secure, set apart, spare, stockpile, store, withhold.
antonym use up.
n. backlog, cache, capital, fund, hoard, park, preserve, reservation, reservoir, sanctuary, savings, stock, stockpile, store, substitute, supply, tract.

reserve[2] aloofness, constraint, coolness, formality, limitation, modesty, reluctance, reservation, restraint, restriction, reticence, secretiveness, shyness, silence, taciturnity.
antonyms friendliness, informality.
adj. additional, alternate, auxiliary, extra, secondary, spare, substitute.

reserved[1] adj. booked, bound, designated, destined, earmarked, engaged, fated, held, intended, kept, meant, predestined, restricted, retained, set aside, spoken for, taken.
antonym unreserved.

reserved[2] aloof, cautious, close-mouthed, cold, cool, demure, formal, modest, prim, restrained, reticent, retiring, secretive, shy, silent, stand-offish, taciturn, unapproachable, unclub(b)able, uncommunicative, uncompanionable, unconversable, undemonstrative, unforthcoming, unresponsive, unsociable.
antonyms friendly, informal.

reservoir n. accumulation, basin, container,

fund, holder, lake, pond, pool, receptacle, repository, reservatory, reserves, source, stock, stockpile, store, supply, tank.

reshuffle n. change, interchange, realignment, rearrangement, redistribution, regrouping, reorganisation, restructuring, revision, shake-up, upheaval.

v. change, interchange, realign, rearrange, redistribute, regroup, reorganise, restructure, revise, shake up, shift, shuffle.

reside v. abide, consist, dwell, exist, inhabit, inhere, lie, live, lodge, remain, settle, sit, sojourn, stay.

residence n. abode, country-house, country-seat, domicile, dwelling, habitation, hall, home, house, household, lodging, manor, mansion, occupancy, occupation, pad, palace, place, quarters, seat, sojourn, stay, tenancy, villa.

resident n. citizen, commorant, denizen, habitant, indweller, inhabitant, local, lodger, occupant, tenant.
antonym non-resident.
adj. dwelling, en poste, gremial, inhabiting, living, local, neighbourhood, permanent, settled.
antonym non-resident.

residential adj. commuter, exurban, suburban.
residential area commuter belt, dormitory town, exurbia, suburbia, suburbs.

residual adj. left-over, net(t), reliquary, remaining, residuary, residuous, unconsumed, unused, vestigial.
antonym core.

residue n. balance, difference, dregs, excess, extra, left-overs, overflow, overplus, remainder, remains, remnant, residuum, rest, surplus.
antonym core.

resign v. abandon, abdicate, cede, forgo, forsake, leave, quit, relinquish, renounce, sacrifice, stand down, surrender, vacate, waive, yield.
antonyms join, maintain.
resign oneself accede, accept, acquiesce, bow, comply, reconcile, submit, yield.
antonym resist.

resignation n. abandonment, abdication, acceptance, acquiescence, compliance, defeatism, demission, departure, endurance, forbearing, fortitude, leaving, non-resistance, notice, passivity, patience, relinquishment, renunciation, retirement, submission, sufferance, surrender.
antonym resistance.

resigned adj. acquiescent, compliant, defeatist, long-suffering, patient, stoical, subdued, submissive, unprotesting, unresisting.
antonym resisting.

resilience n. adaptability, bounce, buoyancy, elasticity, flexibility, give, hardiness, plasticity, pliability, recoil, spring, springiness, strength, suppleness, toughness, unshockability.
antonyms inflexibility, rigidity.

resilient adj. adaptable, bouncy, buoyant, elastic, flexible, hardy, irrepressible, plastic, pliable, springy, strong, supple, tough, unshockable.
antonyms downcast, rigid.

resist v. avoid, battle, check, combat, confront, counteract, countervail, curb, defy, dispute, fight back, forbear, forgo, hinder, oppose, recalcitrate, refuse, repel, thwart, weather, withstand.
antonyms accept, submit.

resistance n. antiperistasis, battle, combat, contention, counteraction, counter-stand, counter-time, defiance, fight, fighting, hindrance, impedance, impediment, intransigence, Maquis, obstruction, opposition, partisans, refusal, resistant, resistors, struggle, underground.
antonyms acceptance, submission.

resistant adj. antagonistic, combative, defiant, dissident, hard, hostile, impervious, insusceptible, intractible, intransigent, opposed, recalcitrant, renitent, resistive, stiff, strong, tough, unsusceptible, unwilling, unyielding.
antonyms compliant, yielding.

resolute adj. bold, constant, determined, dogged, firm, fixed, indissuadable, indivertible, inflexible, obstinate, persevering, purposeful, relentless, set, staunch, steadfast, stout, strong-minded, strong-willed, stubborn, sturdy, tenacious, unbending, undaunted, unflinching, unshakable, unshaken, unwavering.
antonym irresolute.

resolution n. aim, answer, boldness, constancy, courage, decision, declaration, dedication, dénouement, determination, devotion, doggedness, earnestness, end, energy, finding, firmness, fortitude, intent, intention, judgement, motion, obstinacy, outcome, perseverance, pertinacity, purpose, relentlessness, resoluteness, resolve, settlement, sincerity, solution, solving, staunchness, steadfastness, stubbornness, tenacity, unravelling, verdict, will power, zeal.
antonym indecision.

resolve v. agree, alter, analyse, anatomise, answer, banish, break up, change, clear, conclude, convert, crack, decide, design, determine, disentangle, disintegrate, dispel, dissect, dissipate, dissolve, elucidate, explain, fathom, fix, intend, liquefy, melt, metamorphose, purpose, reduce, relax, remove, separate, settle, solve, transform, transmute, undertake, unravel.
antonyms blend, waver.
n. boldness, conclusion, conviction, courage, decision, design, determination, earnestness, firmness, intention, objective, project, purpose, resoluteness, resolution, sense of purpose, steadfastness, undertaking, will power.
antonym indecision.

resonant adj. booming, canorous, echoing, full, plummy, resounding, reverberant, reverberating, rich, ringing, sonorous, vibrant.

antonym faint.

resort *v.* frequent, go, haunt, hie, repair, visit.
antonym avoid.
  n. alternative, chance, course, expedient,
haunt, health resort, hope, howf(f), possibility, recourse, reference, refuge, retreat, spa,
spot, watering-place.
  resort to employ, exercise, go so far as to,
lower oneself to, stoop to, use, utilise.

resound *v.* boom, echo, re-echo, resonate,
reverberate, ring, sound, thunder.

resounding *adj.* booming, conclusive, crushing,
decisive, echoing, full, plangent, powerful,
reboant, resonant, reverberating, rich, ringing, sonorous, sounding, thorough, vibrant,
vocal.
antonyms faint, slight.

resource *n.* ability, appliance, cache, capability,
cleverness, contrivance, course, device, expedient, hoard, ingenuity, initiative, inventiveness, means, quick-wittedness, reserve, resort, resourcefulness, shift, source, stockpile,
supply, talent.
antonym unimaginativeness.

resourceful *adj.* able, bright, capable, clever,
creative, fertile, imaginative, ingenious, innovative, inventive, originative, quick-witted,
sharp, slick, talented.

resourceless *adj.* feckless, feeble, fushionless,
helpless, hopeless, inadequate, shiftless,
useless.
antonym unimaginative.

resources *n.* assets, capital, fisc, funds, holdings,
materials, means, money, pelf, property,
purse, reserves, riches, supplies, wealth,
wherewithal.

respect *n.* admiration, appreciation, approbation, aspect, bearing, characteristic, connection, consideration, deference, detail, esteem,
estimation, facet, feature, homage, honour,
matter, particular, point, recognition, reference, regard, relation, reverence, sense,
veneration, way.
antonym disrespect.
  v. admire, appreciate, attend, esteem, follow,
heed, honour, notice, obey, observe, pay
homage to, recognise, regard, revere, reverence, value, venerate.
antonym scorn.

respectable *adj.* admirable, ample, appreciable,
clean-living, considerable, decent, decorous,
dignified, estimable, fair, good, goodly,
honest, honourable, large, passable, presentable, proper, reasonable, reputable, respected, seemly, sizable, substantial, tidy,
tolerable, upright, venerable, well-to-do,
worthy.
antonyms disreputable, miserly, unseemly.

respectful *adj.* civil, courteous, courtly, deferential, dutiful, filial, gracious, humble, mannerly, obedient, polite, regardful, reverent,
reverential, self-effacing, solicitous, submissive, subservient, well-mannered.
antonym disrespectful.

respecting *prep.* about, concerning, considering,
in respect of, regarding, with regard to, with
respect to.

respective *adj.* corresponding, individual, own,
particular, personal, relevant, separate, several, special, specific, various.

respects *n.* compliments, devoirs, duty, greetings, regards, salutations.

respite *n.* adjournment, break, breather, cessation, delay, gap, halt, hiatus, intermission,
interruption, interval, let-up, lull, moratorium, pause, postponement, recess, relaxation,
relief, remission, reprieve, rest, stay, suspension.

resplendent *adj.* beaming, bright, brilliant,
dazzling, effulgent, fulgent, gleaming, glittering, glorious, irradiant, luminous, lustrous,
radiant, refulgent, shining, splendid, splendiferous.
antonym dull.

respond *v.* acknowledge, answer, answer back,
come back, counter, react, reciprocate,
rejoin, reply, retort, return.

response *n.* acknowledgement, answer, comeback, counterblast, feedback, reaction,
rejoinder, reply, respond, retort, return,
riposte.
antonym query.

responsibility *n.* accountability, amenability,
answerability, authority, blame, burden, care,
charge, conscientiousness, culpability, dependability, duty, fault, guilt, importance,
level-headedness, liability, maturity, obligation, onus, power, rationality, reliability,
sense, sensibleness, soberness, stability, trust,
trustworthiness.
antonym irresponsibility.

responsible *adj.* accountable, adult, amenable,
answerable, authoritative, bound, chargeable, conscientious, culpable, decisionmaking, dependable, duty-bound, ethical,
executive, guilty, high, important, levelheaded, liable, mature, public-spirited, rational, reliable, right, sensible, sober, sound,
stable, steady, subject, trustworthy.
antonym irresponsible.

responsive *adj.* alive, awake, aware, forthcoming, impressionable, open, perceptive, reactive, receptive, respondent, responsorial,
sensitive, sharp, susceptible, sympathetic.
antonym unresponsive.

rest[1] *n.* base, break, breather, breathing-space,
breathing-time, breathing-while, calm, cessation, cradle, doze, halt, haven, holder,
holiday, idleness, inactivity, interlude, intermission, interval, leisure, lie-down, lie-in,
lodging, lull, motionlessness, nap, pause,
prop, refreshment, refuge, relaxation, relief,
repose, retreat, shelf, shelter, shut-eye, siesta,
sleep, slumber, snooze, somnolence, spell,
stand, standstill, stillness, stop, support,
tranquillity, trestle, vacation.
antonyms action, activity, restlessness.
  v. alight, base, cease, continue, depend,
desist, discontinue, doze, found, halt, hang,
hinge, idle, keep, land, lay, laze, lean, lie, lie

back, lie down, lie in, perch, prop, recline, relax, rely, remain, repose, reside, settle, sit, sleep, slumber, snooze, spell, stand, stay, stop, turn.
antonyms change, continue, work.

rest[2] *n.* balance, core, excess, left-overs, majority, others, remainder, remains, remnants, residue, residuum, rump, surplus.

restaurant *n.* automat, bistro, brasserie, buffet, café, cafeteria, diner, dining-car, dining-room, eatery, eating-house, grill-room, porter-house, snack bar, steak-house.

restful *adj.* calm, calming, comfortable, easeful, languid, pacific, peaceful, placid, quiet, relaxed, relaxing, serene, sleepy, soothing, tranquil, tranquillising, undisturbed, unhurried.
antonyms disturbed, disturbing.

restitution *n.* amends, compensation, damages, indemnification, indemnity, recompense, redress, refund, reimbursement, remuneration, reparation, repayment, requital, restoration, restoring, return, satisfaction.

restive *adj.* agitated, edgy, fidgety, fractious, fretful, impatient, jittery, jumpy, nervous, obstinate, recalcitrant, refractory, restless, uneasy, unquiet, unruly.
antonyms calm, relaxed.

restless *adj.* active, agitated, anxious, bustling, changeable, disturbed, edgy, fidgety, fitful, footloose, fretful, hurried, inconstant, irresolute, jumpy, moving, nervous, nomadic, restive, roving, shifting, sleepless, transient, troubled, turbulent, uneasy, unquiet, unresting, unruly, unsettled, unstable, unsteady, wandering, worried.
antonyms calm, relaxed.

restlessness *n.* activity, agitation, anxiety, bustle, disquiet, disturbance, edginess, fitfulness, fretfulness, heebie-jeebies, hurry, hurry-scurry, inconstancy, inquietude, insomnia, instability, jitters, jumpiness, movement, nervousness, restiveness, transience, turbulence, turmoil, uneasiness, unrest, unsettledness, wanderlust, worriedness.
antonyms calmness, relaxation.

restoration *n.* instauration, kiss of life, reconstruction, recovery, recruit, recruital, re-establishment, refreshment, refurbishing, rehabilitation, reinstallation, reinstatement, rejuvenation, renewal, renovation, repair, replacement, restitution, return, revitalisation, revival.
antonyms damage, removal, weakening.

restore *v.* fix, mend, reanimate, rebuild, recondition, reconstitute, reconstruct, recover, recruit, redintegrate, re-enforce, re-establish, refresh, refurbish, rehabilitate, reimpose, reinstate, reintroduce, rejuvenate, renew, renovate, repair, replace, retouch, return, revitalise, revive, revivify, strengthen.
antonyms damage, remove, weaken.

restrain *v.* arrest, bind, bit, bridle, chain, check, cohibit, confine, constrain, control, curb, curtail, debar, detain, fetter, govern, hamper,

hamshackle, handicap, harness, hinder, hold, imprison, inhibit, jail, keep, limit, manacle, muzzle, pinion, prevent, repress, restrict, stay, subdue, suppress, tie.
antonyms encourage, liberate.

restrained *adj.* calm, controlled, discreet, low-key, mild, moderate, muted, quiet, reasonable, reticent, self-controlled, soft, steady, subdued, tasteful, temperate, undemonstrative, understated, unemphatic, unobtrusive.
antonym unrestrained.

restraint *n.* arrest, ban, bondage, bonds, bridle, captivity, chains, check, coercion, cohibition, command, compulsion, confinement, confines, constraint, control, cramp, curb, curtailment, dam, detention, embargo, fetters, grip, hindrance, hold, imprisonment, inhibition, interdict, lid, limit, limitation, manacles, moderation, pinions, prevention, rein, restriction, self-control, self-discipline, self-possession, self-restraint, stint, straitjacket, suppression, taboo, tie.
antonym freedom.

restrict *v.* astrict, bound, circumscribe, condition, confine, constrain, contain, cramp, demarcate, hamper, handicap, impede, inhibit, limit, regulate, restrain, restringe, scant, thirl, tie.
antonyms broaden, encourage, free.

restriction *n.* check, condition, confinement, constraint, containment, control, curb, demarcation, handicap, inhibition, limitation, regulation, restraint, rule, squeeze, stint, stipulation.
antonyms broadening, encouragement, freedom.

result *n.* conclusion, consequence, decision, development, effect, end, end-product, event, fruit, issue, outcome, produce, reaction, sequel, termination, upshot.
antonyms beginning, cause.
v. appear, arise, culminate, derive, develop, emanate, emerge, end, ensue, eventuate, finish, flow, follow, happen, issue, proceed, spring, stem, terminate.
antonyms begin, cause.

resume *v.* continue, pick up, proceed, recommence, reinstitute, reopen, restart, take up.
antonym cease.

résumé *n.* abstract, digest, epitome, overview, précis, recapitulation, review, run-down, summary, synopsis.

resumption *n.* continuation, epanalepsis, re-establishment, renewal, reopening, restart, resurgence.
antonym cessation.

resurgence *n.* rebirth, recrudescence, re-emergence, renaissance, renascence, resumption, resurrection, return, revival, revivification, risorgimento.
antonym decrease.

resurrect *v.* come to life, disinter, reintroduce, renew, restore, revive.
antonyms bury, kill off, quash.

resurrection *n.* comeback, reactivation, reappearance, rebirth, renaissance, renascence, renewal, restoration, resurgence, resuscitation, return, revival, revivification.
antonyms burying, killing off, quashing.

resuscitate *v.* quicken, reanimate, reinvigorate, renew, rescue, restore, resurrect, revitalise, revive, revivify, save.

resuscitated *adj.* redintegrate(d), redivivus, restored, resurrected, revived.

retain *v.* absorb, commission, contain, detail, employ, engage, grasp, grip, hire, hold, hold back, keep, keep in mind, keep up, maintain, memorise, pay, preserve, recall, recollect, remember, reserve, restrain, save.
antonyms release, spend.

retainer[1] *n.* attendant, dependant, domestic, flunky, footman, galloglass, lackey, menial, servant, supporter, valet, vassal.

retainer[2] advance, deposit, fee, retaining fee.

retaliate *v.* fight back, get back at, get even with, get one's own back, give as good as one gets, hit back, reciprocate, repay in kind, return like for like, revenge oneself, strike back, take revenge.
antonyms accept, submit.

retaliation *n.* a taste of one's own medicine, counterblow, counterstroke, reciprocation, repayment, reprisal, requital, retort, retortion, retribution, revenge, tit for tat, vengeance.
antonyms acceptance, submission.

retard *v.* arrest, brake, check, clog, decelerate, defer, delay, detain, encumber, handicap, hinder, impede, keep back, obstruct, slow, stall.
antonym advance.

retardation *n.* deficiency, delay, dullness, hindering, hindrance, impeding, incapability, incapacity, lag, mental handicap, obstruction, retardment, slowing, slowness.
antonym advancement.

retch *v.* disgorge, gag, heave, puke, reach, regurgitate, spew, throw up, vomit.

retching *n.* gagging, nausea, puking, reaching, vomiting, vomiturition.

reticence *n.* muteness, quietness, reserve, restraint, secretiveness, silence, taciturnity, uncommunicativeness, unforthcomingness.
antonyms communicativeness, forwardness, frankness.

reticent *adj.* boutonné, close-lipped, close-mouthed, mum, mute, quiet, reserved, restrained, secretive, silent, taciturn, tight-lipped, uncommunicative, unforthcoming, unspeaking.
antonyms communicative, forward, frank.

retinue *n.* aides, attendants, cortège, entourage, escort, followers, following, personnel, servants, staff, suite, train.

retiral *n.* abdication, decumbiture, departure, exit, flight, resignation, retirement, retreat, withdrawal.
antonym advance.

retire *v.* decamp, depart, draw back, ebb, exit, leave, recede, remove, retreat, withdraw.
antonyms enter, join.

retired *adj.* emeritus, ex-, former, past.

retirement *n.* loneliness, obscurity, privacy, retiral, retreat, seclusion, solitude, withdrawal.
antonyms company, limelight.

retiring *adj.* bashful, coy, demure, diffident, humble, meek, modest, mousy, quiet, reclusive, reserved, reticent, self-effacing, shamefaced, shrinking, shy, timid, timorous, unassertive, unassuming.
antonyms assertive, forward.

retort *v.* answer, counter, rejoin, repartee, reply, respond, retaliate, return, riposte.
   n. answer, backword, come-back, quip, rejoinder, repartee, reply, response, riposte, sally.

retract *v.* abjure, cancel, deny, disavow, disclaim, disown, recall, recant, renounce, repeal, repudiate, rescind, reverse, revoke, unsay, unspeak, withdraw.
antonym maintain.

retreat *v.* depart, ebb, leave, quit, recede, recoil, retire, shrink, turn tail, withdraw.
antonym advance.
   n. asylum, den, departure, ebb, evacuation, flight, funk-hole, growlery, haunt, haven, hibernacle, hibernaculum, hideaway, privacy, refuge, resort, retirement, sanctuary, seclusion, shelter, withdrawal.
antonyms advance, company, limelight.

retrench *v.* curtail, cut, decrease, diminish, economise, husband, lessen, limit, pare, prune, reduce, save, slim down, trim.
antonym increase.

retrenchment *n.* contraction, cost-cutting, curtailment, cut, cutback, economy, pruning, reduction, run-down, shrinkage.
antonym increase.

retribution *n.* compensation, justice, Nemesis, payment, punishment, reckoning, recompense, redress, repayment, reprisal, requital, retaliation, revenge, reward, satisfaction, talion, vengeance.

retrieve *v.* fetch, make good, recall, recapture, recoup, recover, redeem, regain, repair, repossess, rescue, restore, return, salvage, save.
antonym lose.

retrograde *adj.* backward, declining, degenerative, denigrating, deteriorating, downward, inverse, negative, regressive, relapsing, retreating, retrogressive, reverse, reverting, waning, worsening.
antonym progressive.

retrogress *v.* backslide, decline, degenerate, deteriorate, drop, ebb, fall, recede, regress, relapse, retire, retreat, retrograde, return, revert, sink, wane, withdraw, worsen.
antonym progress.

retrogression *n.* decline, deterioration, drop, ebb, fall, recidivism, regress, relapse, retrogradation, return, worsening.
antonyms increase, progress.

retrospect *n.* afterthought, contemplation, hindsight, recollection, re-examination, reference, regard, remembrance, reminiscence, review, survey.
antonym prospect.

retrospective *adj.* backward-looking, retroactive, retro-operative.

return *v.* announce, answer, choose, communicate, convey, deliver, earn, elect, make, net, pick, reappear, rebound, reciprocate, recoil, recompense, recur, redound, re-establish, refund, reimburse, reinstate, rejoin, remit, render, repair, repay, replace, reply, report, requite, respond, restore, retort, retreat, revert, send, submit, transmit, volley, yield.
antonyms leave, take.

n. account, advantage, answer, benefit, comeback, compensation, form, gain, homecoming, income, interest, list, proceeds, profit, quip, reappearance, rebound, reciprocation, recoil, recompense, recrudescence, recurrence, redound, re-establishment, reimbursement, reinstatement, rejoinder, reparation, repayment, replacement, reply, report, requital, response, restoration, retaliation, retort, retreat, revenue, reversion, reward, riposte, sally, statement, summary, takings, yield.
antonyms disappearance, expense, loss, payment.

re-use *v.* reconstitute, recycle.

revamp *v.* do up, overhaul, rebuild, recast, recondition, reconstruct, refit, refurbish, rehabilitate, renovate, repair, restore, revise.

reveal *v.* announce, bare, betray, broadcast, communicate, disbosom, disclose, dismask, display, divulge, exhibit, expose, impart, leak, lift the lid off, manifest, open, proclaim, publish, show, tell, unbare, unbosom, uncover, unearth, unfold, unmask, unshadow, unveil.
antonym hide.

revel *v.* carouse, celebrate, live it up, make merry, paint the town red, push the boat out, raise the roof, roist, roister, whoop it up.
n. bacchanal, carousal, carouse, celebration, comus, debauch, festivity, gala, jollification, merry-make, merrymaking, party, saturnalia, spree.

revel in bask, crow, delight, gloat, glory, indulge, joy, lap up, luxuriate, rejoice, relish, savour, take pleasure, thrive on, wallow.
antonym dislike.

revelation *n.* announcement, apocalypse, betrayal, broadcasting, communication, disclosure, discovery, display, exhibition, exposé, exposition, exposure, giveaway, leak, manifestation, news, proclamation, publication, telling, uncovering, unearthing, unveiling.

reveller *n.* bacchanal, bacchant, carouser, celebrator, merrymaker, party-goer, pleasure-seeker, roister, roisterer, royster, roysterer, wassailer.

revelry *n.* carousal, carouse, celebration, debauch, debauchery, festivity, fun, jollification, jollity, merrymaking, party, revel-rout, riot, roistering, saturnalia, spree, wassail, wassailing, wassailry.
antonym sobriety.

revenge *n.* a dose/taste of one's own medicine, ravanche, reprisal, requital, retaliation, retribution, revengement, satisfaction, ultion, vengeance, vindictiveness.
v. avenge, even the score, get one's own back, get satisfaction, repay, requite, retaliate, vindicate.

revengeful *adj.* bitter, implacable, malevolent, malicious, malignant, merciless, pitiless, resentful, spiteful, unforgiving, unmerciful, vengeful, vindictive, wreakful.
antonym forgiving.

revenue *n.* gain, income, interest, proceeds, profits, receipts, returns, rewards, take, takings, yield.
antonym expenditure.

reverberate *v.* echo, rebound, recoil, re-echo, reflect, resound, ring, vibrate.

reverberation *n.* echo, rebound, recoil, re-echoing, reflection, resonance, resounding, ringing, vibration, wave.

reverberations *n.* consequences, effects, repercussions, results, ripples, shock wave.

revere *v.* adore, defer to, exalt, honour, pay homage to, respect, reverence, venerate, worship.
antonyms despise, scorn.

reverence *n.* admiration, adoration, awe, deference, devotion, dulia, esteem, genuflection, homage, honour, hyperdulia, latria, puja, respect, veneration, worship.
antonym scorn.
v. acknowledge, admire, adore, honour, respect, revere, venerate, worship.
antonyms despise, scorn.

reverent *adj.* adoring, awed, decorous, deferential, devout, dutiful, humble, loving, meek, pious, respectful, reverential, solemn, submissive.
antonym irreverent.

reverie *n.* absent-mindedness, abstraction, brown study, daydream, daydreaming, dreamery, inattention, musing, preoccupation, trance, woolgathering.

reversal *n.* abrogation, annulment, cancellation, countermanding, defeat, delay, difficulty, disaster, enantiodromia, misfortune, mishap, nullification, problem, repeal, rescinding, rescission, reverse, revocation, set-back, turnabout, turnaround, turnround, upset, U-turn, volte-face.
antonyms advancement, progress.

reverse *v.* alter, annul, back, backtrack, cancel, change, countermand, hark back, invalidate, invert, negate, overrule, overset, overthrow, overturn, quash, repeal, rescind, retract, retreat, revert, revoke, transpose, undo, up-end, upset.
antonym enforce.
n. adversity, affliction, antithesis, back, blow, check, contradiction, contrary, converse,

defeat, disappointment, failure, hardship, inverse, misadventure, misfortune, mishap, opposite, rear, repulse, reversal, setback, trial, underside, verso, vicissitude, woman. *adj.* backward, contrary, converse, inverse, inverted, opposite, verso.

revert *v.* backslide, lapse, recur, regress, relapse, resume, retrogress, return, reverse. *antonym* progress.

review *v.* assess, criticise, discuss, evaluate, examine, inspect, judge, reassess, recall, recapitulate, recollect, reconsider, re-evaluate, re-examine, rehearse, remember, rethink, revise, scrutinise, study, weigh. *n.* analysis, assessment, commentary, criticism, critique, evaluation, examination, journal, judgement, magazine, notice, periodical, reassessment, recapitulation, recension, reconsideration, re-evaluation, re-examination, report, rethink, retrospect, revision, scrutiny, study, survey.

reviewer *n.* arbiter, commentator, connoisseur, critic, essayist, judge, observer.

revile *v.* abuse, blackguard, calumniate, defame, denigrate, libel, malign, miscall, reproach, scorn, slander, smear, traduce, vilify, vilipend, vituperate. *antonym* praise.

revise *v.* alter, amend, change, correct, edit, emend, memorise, modify, recast, recense, reconsider, reconstruct, redo, re-examine, reread, revamp, review, rewrite, study, swot up, update.

revision *n.* alteration, amendment, change, correction, editing, emendation, homework, memorising, modification, recast, recasting, recension, reconstruction, re-examination, rereading, review, rewriting, rifacimento, studying, swotting, updating.

revitalise *v.* reactivate, reanimate, refresh, rejuvenate, renew, restore, resurrect, revive, revivify. *antonyms* dampen, suppress.

revival *n.* awakening, quickening, reactivation, reanimation, reawakening, rebirth, recrudescence, renaissance, renascence, renewal, restoration, resurgence, resurrection, resuscitation, revitalisation, revivification, risorgimento. *antonym* suppression.

revive *v.* animate, awaken, cheer, comfort, invigorate, quicken, rally, reactivate, reanimate, recover, refresh, rekindle, renew, renovate, restore, resuscitate, revitalise, revivify, rouse. *antonyms* suppress, weary.

revivify *v.* inspirit, invigorate, reactivate, reanimate, refresh, renew, restore, resuscitate, revive. *antonyms* dampen, depress.

reviving *adj.* bracing, enheartening, exhilarating, invigorating, reanimating, refreshening, regenerating, reinvigorating, revivescent, revivifying, reviviscent, stimulating, tonic. *antonyms* disheartening, exhausting.

revocation *n.* abolition, annulment, cancellation, countermanding, nullification, quashing, repeal, repealing, repudiation, rescinding, rescission, retractation, retraction, reversal, revoking, withdrawal. *antonym* enforcement.

revoke *v.* abolish, abrogate, annul, cancel, countermand, disclaim, dissolve, invalidate, negate, nullify, quash, recall, recant, renounce, repeal, repudiate, rescind, retract, reverse, withdraw. *antonym* enforce.

revolt[1] *n.* breakaway, defection, inqilab, insurgency, insurrection, Jacquerie, mutiny, putsch, rebellion, revolution, rising, secession, sedition, uprising. *antonym* submit. *v.* defect, mutiny, rebel, resist, riot, rise.

revolt[2] *v.* disgust, nauseate, offend, outrage, repel, repulse, scandalise, shock, sicken. *antonym* please.

revolting *adj.* abhorrent, abominable, appalling, disgusting, distasteful, fetid, foul, horrible, horrid, loathsome, nasty, nauseating, nauseous, noisome, obnoxious, obscene, offensive, repellent, repugnant, repulsive, shocking, sickening, sickly. *antonym* pleasant.

revolution *n.* cataclysm, change, circle, circuit, coup, coup d'état, cycle, gyration, innovation, inqilab, insurgency, Jacquerie, lap, metamorphosis, metanoia, mutiny, orbit, putsch, rebellion, reformation, revolt, rising, rotation, round, shift, spin, transformation, turn, upheaval, uprising, volution, wheel, whirl.

revolutionary *n.* anarchist, insurgent, insurrectionary, insurrectionist, Jacobin, mutineer, rebel, revolutionist, Trot, Trotskyite. *adj.* anarchistic, avant-garde, different, drastic, experimental, extremist, fundamental, innovative, insurgent, insurrectionary, mutinous, new, novel, progressive, radical, rebel, seditious, subversive, thoroughgoing. *antonyms* commonplace, establishment.

revolve *v.* circle, circumgyrate, circumvolve, gyrate, orbit, rotate, spin, turn, wheel, whirl.

revolver *n.* air-gun, firearm, gun, hand-gun, heater, peace-maker, piece, pistol, rod, shooter, six-shooter.

revolving *adj.* gyral, gyrating, gyratory, rotating, spinning, turning, whirling. *antonym* stationary.

revulsion *n.* abhorrence, abomination, aversion, detestation, disgust, dislike, distaste, hatred, loathing, recoil, repugnance, repulsion. *antonym* pleasure.

reward *n.* benefit, bonus, bounty, come-up(p)ance, compensation, desert, gain, guerdon, honour, meed, merit, payment, pay-off, premium, prize, profit, punishment, recompense, remuneration, repayment, requital, retribution, return, wages. *antonym* punishment. *v.* compensate, guerdon, honour, pay, recompense, remunerate, repay, requite.

antonym punish.

rewarding *adj.* advantageous, beneficial, edifying, enriching, fruitful, fulfilling, gainful, gratifying, pleasing, productive, profitable, remunerative, rewardful, satisfying, valuable, worthwhile.

antonym unrewarding.

rewording *n.* metaphrase, metaphrasis, paraphrase, rephrasing, revision.

rewrite *v.* correct, edit, emend, recast, redraft, revise, reword, rework.

rhetoric *n.* bombast, declamation, eloquence, fustian, grandiloquence, hyperbole, magniloquence, oratory, pomposity, rant, verbosity, wordiness.

rhetorical *adj.* artificial, bombastic, declamatory, false, flamboyant, flashy, florid, flowery, grandiloquent, high-flown, high-sounding, hyperbolic, inflated, insincere, linguistic, magniloquent, oratorical, over-decorated, pompous, pretentious, rhetoric, showy, silver-tongued, stylistic, verbal, verbose, windy.

antonym simple.

rhyme *n.* chime, ditty, doggerel, jingle, limerick, ode; poem, poesie, poetry, song, verse.

rhythm *n.* accent, beat, cadence, cadency, eurhythmy, flow, lilt, measure, metre, movement, pattern, periodicity, pulse, rhythmicity, swing, tempo, time.

rhythmic *adj.* cadenced, flowing, harmonious, lilting, melodious, metric, metrical, musical, periodic, pulsating, rhythmical, throbbing.

antonym unrhythmical.

rib *n.* band, bar, bone, costa, moulding, purlin(e), ribbing, ridge, shaft, support, vein, wale.

ribald *adj.* base, bawdy, blue, broad, coarse, derisive, earthy, filthy, foul-mouthed, gross, indecent, irrisory, jeering, licentious, low, mean, mocking, naughty, obscene, offcolour, Rabelaisian, racy, risqué, rude, scurrilous, smutty, vulgar.

antonym polite.

ribaldry *n.* baseness, bawdiness, billingsgate, coarseness, derision, earthiness, filth, grossness, indecency, jeering, licentiousness, lowness, mockery, naughtiness, obscenity, raciness, rudeness, scurrility, smut, smuttiness, vulgarity.

ribbon *n.* band, cord, fillet, hair-band, headband, jag, sash, shred, strip, taenia, tatter.

rich *adj.* abounding, abundant, affluent, ample, bright, copious, costly, creamy, deep, delicious, dulcet, elaborate, elegant, expensive, exquisite, exuberant, fatty, fecund, fertile, fine, flavoursome, flush, fruitful, full, fullbodied, full-flavoured, full-toned, gay, gorgeous, heavy, highly-flavoured, humorous, in the money, intense, juicy, laughable, lavish, loaded, ludicrous, luscious, lush, luxurious, mellifluous, mellow, moneyed, opulent, palatial, pecunious, plenteous, plentiful, plutocratic, precious, priceless, productive, prolific, propertied, property, prosper-

ous, resonant, ridiculous, risible, rolling, savoury, side-splitting, spicy, splendid, strong, succulent, sumptuous, superb, sweet, tasty, uberous, valuable, vibrant, vivid, warm, wealthy, well-heeled, well-off, well-provided, well-stocked, well-supplied, well-to-do.

antonyms harsh, miserly, plain, poor, simple, tasteless, thin, unfertile.

riches *n.* a long purse, abundance, affluence, assets, fortune, gold, mint, money, opulence, pelf, plenty, property, resources, richness, substance, treasure, uberty, wealth.

antonym poverty.

richly *adv.* amply, appropriately, condignly, elaborately, elegantly, expensively, exquisitely, fully, gorgeously, lavishly, luxuriously, opulently, palatially, properly, splendidly, suitably, sumptuously, thoroughly, well.

antonyms poorly, scantily.

rickety *adj.* broken, broken-down, decrepit, derelict, dilapidated, feeble, flimsy, frail, imperfect, infirm, insecure, jerry-built, precarious, ramshackle, shaky, shoogly, tottering, tottery, unsound, unstable, unsteady, weak, wobbly.

antonyms stable, strong.

rid *v.* clear, deliver, disabuse, disburden, disembarrass, disencumber, expel, free, purge, relieve, unburden.

antonym burden.

riddance *n.* clearance, deliverance, disposal, ejection, elimination, expulsion, extermination, freedom, purgation, release, relief, removal.

antonym burdening.

riddle[1] *n.* brain-teaser, charade, conundrum, enigma, logogram, logograph, logogriph, mystery, poser, problem, puzzle, rebus.

riddle[2] *v.* boult, corrupt, damage, fill, filter, impair, infest, invade, mar, pepper, perforate, permeate, pervade, pierce, puncture, screen, sieve, sift, spoil, strain, winnow.

n. boulter, sieve, strainer.

ride *v.* control, dominate, enslave, float, grip, handle, haunt, hurl, journey, manage, move, oppress, progress, sit, survive, travel, weather.

n. drive, hurl, jaunt, journey, lift, outing, spin, trip, whirl.

ridge *n.* arête, band, costa, crinkle, drum, drumlin, escarpment, eskar, hill, hog's back, hummock, lump, reef, ripple, saddle, wale, weal, welt, yardang, zastruga.

ridicule *n.* banter, chaff, derision, gibe, irony, irrision, jeering, jeers, laughter, mockery, raillery, sarcasm, satire, scorn, sneers, taunting.

antonym praise.

v. banter, burlesque, caricature, cartoon, chaff, crucify, deride, humiliate, jeer, josh, lampoon, mock, parody, pillory, pooh-pooh, queer, quiz, rib, satirise, scoff, send up, sneer at, take the mickey out of, taunt.

antonym praise.

ridiculous *adj.* absurd, comical, contemptible,

damfool, derisory, farcical, foolish, funny, hilarious, incredible, laughable, laughworthy, ludicrous, nonsensical, outrageous, preposterous, risible, silly, stupid, unbelievable.
antonym sensible.

riding-school *n.* manège, school of equitation.

rife *adj.* abounding, abundant, common, commonplace, current, epidemic, frequent, general, plentiful, prevailing, prevalent, raging, rampant, teeming, ubiquitous, universal, widespread.
antonym scarce.

riff-raff *n.* canaille, hoi polloi, mob, rabble, raffle, raggle-taggle, rag-tag, rag-tag and bobtail, rascality, rent-a-mob, scum, undesirables.

rifle[1] *v.* burgle, despoil, gut, loot, maraud, pillage, plunder, ransack, rob, rummage, sack, strip.

rifle[2] *n.* air-gun, bundook, carbine, firearm, firelock, flintlock, fusil, gun, musket, shotgun.

rift *n.* alienation, beach, breach, break, chink, cleavage, cleft, crack, cranny, crevice, difference, disaffection, disagreement, dissure, division, estrangement, fault, flaw, fracture, gap, opening, quarrel, schism, separation, space, split.
antonym unity.

rig[1] *v.* accoutre, equip, fit up, furnish, kit out, outfit, provision, supply.
n. accoutrements, apparatus, ensemble, equipage, equipment, fitments, fittings, fixtures, gear, machinery, outfit, tackle.
rig out accoutre, array, attire, caparison, clothe, costume, dress, dress up, equip, fit, fit out, fit up, furnish, kit out, outfit.
rig up arrange, assemble, build, construct, erect, fit up, fix up, improvise, knock up.
antonym dismantle.

rig[2] *v.* arrange, cook, doctor, engineer, fake, falsify, fiddle, fix, gerrymander, juggle, manipulate, tamper with, trump up.

right *adj.* absolute, accurate, admissible, advantageous, appropriate, authentic, balanced, becoming, characteristic, comme il faut, complete, compos mentis, conservative, correct, deserved, desirable, dexter, dextral, direct, done, due, equitable, ethical, exact, factual, fair, favourable, fine, fit, fitting, genuine, good, healthy, honest, honourable, ideal, just, lawful, lucid, moral, normal, opportune, out-and-out, perpendicular, precise, proper, propitious, rational, reactionary, real, reasonable, righteous, rightful, rightist, rightward, right-wing, sane, satisfactory, seemly, sound, spot-on, straight, suitable, thorough, thoroughgoing, Tory, true, unerring, unimpaired, upright, utter, valid, veracious, veritable, virtuous, well.
antonyms left, left-wing, mad, unfit, wrong.
adv. absolutely, accurately, advantageously, altogether, appropriate, aptly, aright, bang, befittingly, beneficially, completely, correctly, directly, entirely, ethically, exactly, factually, fairly, favourably, fittingly, fortun-

ately, genuinely, honestly, honourably, immediately, instantly, justly, morally, perfectly, precisely, promptly, properly, quickly, quite, righteously, rightward(s), satisfactorily, slap-bang, squarely, straight, straightaway, suitably, thoroughly, totally, truly, utterly, virtuously, well, wholly.
antonyms incorrectly, left, unfairly, wrongly.
n. authority, business, claim, droit, due, equity, freedom, good, goodness, honour, integrity, interest, justice, lawfulness, legality, liberty, licence, morality, permission, power, prerogative, privilege, propriety, reason, rectitude, righteousness, rightfulness, rightness, title, truth, uprightness, virtue.
antonyms depravity, wrong.
v. avenge, correct, fix, rectify, redress, repair, righten, settle, stand up, straighten, vindicate.
right away at once, chop-chop, directly, forthwith, immediately, instantly, now, promptly, right off, straight off, straightaway, straightway, this instant, tout de suite, without delay, without hesitation.
antonym eventually.

righteous *adj.* blameless, equitable, ethical, fair, God-fearing, good, guiltless, honest, honourable, incorrupt, just, law-abiding, moral, pure, saintly, sinless, upright, virtuous.
antonym unrighteous.
n. Holy Willies, just, Pharisees, saints, unco guid, well-doers.
antonym unrighteous.

righteousness *n.* blamelessness, dharma, equity, ethicalness, faithfulness, goodness, honesty, honour, integrity, justice, morality, probity, purity, rectitude, uprightness, virtue.
antonym unrighteousness.

rightful *adj.* authorised, bona fide, correct, de jure, due, just, lawful, legal, legitimate, licit, prescribed, proper, real, suitable, true, valid.
antonyms incorrect, unlawful.

rightfully *adv.* correctly, de jure, justifiably, justly, lawfully, legally, legitimately, properly, rightly.
antonyms incorrectly, unjustifiably.

right-handed *adj.* dext(e)rous.
antonym left-handed.

right-handedness *n.* dexterity, dextrality.
antonym left-handedness.

rigid *adj.* adamant, austere, cast-iron, exact, fixed, harsh, inflexible, intransigent, invariable, rigorous, set, severe, starch(y), stern, stiff, stony, strict, stringent, tense, unalterable, unbending, uncompromising, undeviating, unrelenting, unyielding.
antonym flexible.

rigmarole *n.* balderdash, bother, carry-on, gibberish, hassle, jargon, nonsense, palaver, performance, red tape, riddle-me-ree, to-do, trash, twaddle.

rigorous *adj.* accurate, austere, challenging, conscientious, demanding, exact, exacting, extreme, firm, hard, harsh, inclement, inflexible, inhospitable, meticulous, nice, painstaking, precise, punctilious, Rhadamanthine,

rigid, scrupulous, severe, stern, strict, stringent, thorough, tough, unsparing.
antonyms lenient, mild.

rigour *n.* accuracy, asperity, austerity, conscientiousness, exactitude, exactness, firmness, hardness, hardship, harshness, inflexibility, meticulousness, ordeal, preciseness, precision, privation, punctiliousness, rigidity, rigorism, rigourousness, sternness, strictness, stringency, suffering, thoroughness, trial.
antonyms leniency, mildness.

rig-out *n.* apparel, clobber, clothing, costume, dress, ensemble, garb, gear, get-up, habit, livery, outfit, raiment, rig, togs, uniform.

rile *v.* anger, annoy, bug, exasperate, gall, get, irk, irritate, miff, nark, nettle, peeve, pique, provoke, put out, upset, vex.
antonym soothe.

rim *n.* border, brim, brink, circumference, edge, lip, margin, skirt, verge.
antonym centre.

rind *n.* crust, epicarp, husk, integument, peel, skin, zest.

ring[1] *n.* annulation, annulet, annulus, arena, association, band, cabal, cartel, cell, circle, circuit, circus, clique, collar, collet, combine, coterie, crew, enclosure, gang, group, gyre, halo, hoop, knot, loop, mob, organisation, rink, round, rundle, syndicate.
v. circumscribe, encircle, enclose, encompass, gash, gird, girdle, mark, score, surround.

ring[2] *v.* bell, buzz, call, chime, clang, clink, peal, phone, resonate, resound, reverberate, sound, tang, telephone, ting, tinkle, tintinnabulate, toll.
n. buzz, call, chime, clang, clink, knell, peal, phone-call, tang, ting, tinkle, tintinnabulation.

ringleader *n.* bell-wether, brains, chief, fugleman, leader, spokesman.

rinse *v.* bathe, clean, cleanse, dip, sluice, splash, swill, synd, wash, wet.
n. bath, dip, dye, splash, tint, wash, wetting.

riot *n.* anarchy, bagarre, boisterousness, carousal, commotion, confusion, debauchery, disorder, display, disturbance, Donnybrook, émeute, excess, extravaganza, festivity, flourish, fray, frolic, high, insurrection, jinks, jollification, lawlessness, merry-make, merry-making, quarrel, revelry, riotousness, riotry, romp, rookery, rout, row, ruction, ruffle, shindig, shindy, show, splash, strife, tumult, turbulence, turmoil, uproar.
antonyms calm, order.
v. carouse, frolic, rampage, rebel, revel, revolt, rise up, roister, romp, run riot, run wild.

riotous *adj.* anarchic, boisterous, disorderly, insubordinate, insurrectionary, lawless, loud, luxurious, mutinous, noisy, orgiastic, rambunctious, rampageous, rebellious, refractory, roisterous, rollicking, rowdy, saturnalian, side-splitting, tumultuous, ungovernable, unrestrained, unruly, uproarious, violent, wanton, wild.

antonyms orderly, restrained.

rip *v.* burst, claw, cut, gash, hack, lacerate, rend, rupture, score, separate, slash, slit, split, tear.
n. cleavage, cut, gash, hole, laceration, rent, rupture, slash, slit, split, tear.

rip off cheat, con, defraud, diddle, do, dupe, exploit, filch, fleece, lift, mulct, overcharge, pilfer, pinch, rob, rogue, steal, sting, swindle, swipe, thieve, trick.

ripe *adj.* accomplished, auspicious, complete, developed, favourable, finished, grown, ideal, mature, mellow, opportune, perfect, prepared, promising, propitious, ready, right, ripened, seasoned, suitable, timely.
antonyms inopportune, untimely.

ripen *v.* age, burgeon, develop, mature, mellow, prepare, season.

rip-off *n.* cheat, con, con trick, daylight robbery, diddle, exploitation, fraud, robbery, sting, swindle, theft.

riposte *n.* answer, come-back, quip, rejoinder, repartee, reply, response, retort, return, sally.
v. answer, quip, reciprocate, rejoin, reply, respond, retort, return.

ripple *n.* babble, burble, disturbance, eddy, gurgle, lapping, pirl, purl, ripplet, undulation, wave, wimple.

rise *v.* advance, appear, arise, ascend, buoy, climb, crop up, emanate, emerge, enlarge, eventuate, flow, get up, grow, happen, improve, increase, intensify, issue, levitate, lift, mount, mutiny, occur, originate, progress, prosper, rebel, resist, revolt, slope, slope up, soar, spring, spring up, stand up, surface, swell, tower, volume, wax.
antonyms descend, fall.
n. acclivity, advance, advancement, aggrandisement, ascent, climb, elevation, hillock, improvement, incline, increase, increment, origin, progress, promotion, raise, rising, upsurge, upswing, upturn, upward turn.
antonyms descent, fall.

risible *adj.* absurd, amusing, comic, comical, droll, farcical, funny, hilarious, humorous, laughable, ludicrous, rib-tickling, ridiculous, side-splitting.
antonyms serious, unfunny.

rising *n.* émeute, insurrection, revolt, revolution, riot, uprising.
adj. advancing, approaching, ascending, assurgent, emerging, growing, increasing, intensifying, mounting, soaring, swelling.
antonym decreasing.

risk *n.* adventure, chance, danger, gamble, hazard, jeopardy, peril, possibility, speculation, uncertainty, venture.
antonyms certainty, safety.
v. adventure, chance, dare, endanger, gamble, hazard, imperil, jeopardise, speculate, venture.

risky *adj.* chancy, dangerous, dicey, dodgy, fraught, hazardous, perilous, precarious, riskful, touch-and-go, tricky, uncertain, unsafe.
antonym safe.

risqué *adj.* bawdy, blue, coarse, crude, daring, earthy, immodest, improper, indecent, indecorous, indelicate, naughty, near the knuckle, off colour, Rabelaisian, racy, ribald, suggestive.
antonym decent.

rite *n.* act, ceremonial, ceremony, custom, form, formality, liturgy, mystery, observance, office, ordinance, practice, procedure, ritual, sacrament, service, solemnity, usage, worship.

ritual *n.* ceremonial, ceremony, communion, convention, custom, form, formality, habit, liturgy, mystery, observance, ordinance, practice, prescription, procedure, rite, routine, sacrament, service, solemnity, tradition, usage, wont.
adj. ceremonial, ceremonious, conventional, customary, formal, formulary, habitual, prescribed, procedural, routine, stereotyped.
antonyms informal, unusual.

rival *n.* adversary, antagonist, challenger, collateral, compeer, competitor, contender, contestant, corrival, emulator, equal, equivalent, fellow, match, opponent, peer, rivaless.
antonyms associate, colleague, co-worker.
adj. competing, competitive, conflicting, corrival, emulating, emulous, opposed, opposing.
antonyms associate, co-operating.
v. compete, contend, emulate, equal, match, oppose, rivalise, vie with.
antonym co-operate.

rivalry *n.* antagonism, competition, competitiveness, conflict, contention, contest, duel, emulation, opposition, rivality, rivalship, struggle, vying.
antonym co-operation.

river *n.* beck, burn, creek, ea, flood, flow, gush, riverway, rush, spate, stream, surge, tributary, waterway.
adj. fluvial, riverain, riverine.

river-bank *n.* rivage.

river-mouth *n.* broads, delta, estuary, firth, frith, ostium.

riveting *adj.* absorbing, arresting, captivating, engrossing, enthralling, fascinating, gripping, hypnotic, magnetic, spellbinding.
antonym boring.

road *n.* Autobahn, autopista, autoroute, autostrada, avenue, boulevard, camino real, carriageway, clearway, course, crescent, direction, drift, drive, driveway, freeway, highway, lane, motorway, path, pathway, roadway, route, street, thoroughfare, track, way.

roam *v.* drift, meander, peregrinate, prowl, ramble, range, rove, squander, stravaig, stray, stroll, travel, walk, wander.
antonym stay.

roar *v.* bawl, bay, bell, bellow, blare, clamour, crash, cry, guffaw, hoot, howl, rumble, shout, thunder, vociferate, wuther, yell.
antonym whisper.
n. bellow, belly-laugh, blare, clamour, crash,

cry, guffaw, hoot, howl, outcry, rumble, shout, thunder, yell.
antonym whisper.

rob *v.* bereave, bunko, cheat, con, defraud, deprive, despoil, dispossess, do, flake, flimp, gyp, heist, hold up, loot, mill, pillage, plunder, raid, ramp, ransack, reive, rifle, rip off, roll, sack, sting, strip, swindle.
antonyms give, provide.

robber *n.* bandit, brigand, burglar, cateran, cheat, con man, dacoit, fraud, highwayman, hijacker, klepht, ladrone, land-pirate, latron, looter, motor-bandit, pirate, plunderer, raider, reiver, stealer, swindler, thief.

robbery *n.* burglary, dacoitage, dacoity, depredation, embezzlement, filching, fraud, heist, high toby, hold-up, larceny, low toby, pillage, plunder, purse-snatching, purse-taking, raid, rapine, rip-off, spoliation, stealing, stick-up, swindle, theft, thievery.

robe *n.* bathrobe, costume, dressing-gown, gown, habit, housecoat, peignoir, vestment, wrap, wrapper.
v. apparel, attire, clothe, drape, dress, garb, vest.

robot *n.* android, automaton, Dalek, golem, machine, zombie.

robust *adj.* able-bodied, athletic, boisterous, brawny, coarse, down-to-earth, earthy, fit, hale, hard-headed, hardy, healthy, hearty, husky, indecorous, lusty, muscular, overhearty, powerful, practical, pragmatic, raw, realistic, robustious, roisterous, rollicking, rough, rude, rugged, sensible, sinewy, sound, staunch, sthenic, stout, straightforward, strapping, strong, sturdy, thick-set, tough, unsubtle, vigorous, well.
antonyms mealy-mouthed, unhealthy, unrealistic, weak.

rock[1] *n.* anchor, boulder, bulwark, cornerstone, danger, foundation, hazard, logan, log(g)anstone, mainstay, obstacle, pebble, problem, protection, stone, support.

rock[2] *v.* astonish, astound, daze, dumbfound, jar, lurch, pitch, reel, roll, shake, shock, stagger, stun, surprise, sway, swing, tilt, tip, toss, wobble.

rocky[1] *adj.* craggy, flinty, hard, pebbly, rocklike, rough, rugged, stony.
antonyms smooth, soft.

rocky[2] *adj.* dizzy, doubtful, drunk, ill, inebriated, intoxicated, rickety, shaky, sick, sickly, staggering, tipsy, tottering, uncertain, undependable, unpleasant, unreliable, unsatisfactory, unstable, unsteady, unwell, weak, wobbly, wonky.
antonyms dependable, steady, well.

rod *n.* bar, baton, birch, cane, dowel, ferula, ferule, mace, pole, sceptre, shaft, spoke, staff, stick, strut, switch, verge, wand.

rogue *n.* blackguard, charlatan, cheat, con man, crook, deceiver, devil, fraud, Greek, knave, miscreant, mountebank, nasty piece/bit of work, ne'er-do-well, picaroon, rapscallion, rascal, reprobate, saltimbanco, scamp, scape-

gallows, scoundrel, sharper, swindler, vagrant, villain, wag.
antonym saint.

roguish *adj.* arch, bantering, cheeky, confounded, coquettish, criminal, crooked, deceitful, deceiving, dishonest, espiègle, fraudulent, frolicsome, hempy, impish, knavish, mischievous, playful, puckish, raffish, rascally, roguing, shady, sportive, swindling, unprincipled, unscrupulous, villainous, waggish.
antonyms honest, serious.

roguishly *adv.* archly, cheekily, coquettishly, en badinant, impishly, mischievously, playfully.
antonym seriously.

roguishness *n.* archness, badinage, bantering, cheekiness, coquettishness, deceitfulness, dishonesty, espièglerie, fraud, impishness, mischief, mischievousness, playfulness, roguery, tricks, unscrupulousness, villainy, waggishness.
antonym seriousness.

roister *v.* bluster, boast, brag, carouse, celebrate, frolic, make merry, paint the town red, revel, roist, rollick, romp, strut, swagger, whoop it up.

roisterer *n.* blusterer, boaster, braggart, carouser, ranter, reveller, roister, swaggerer.

roisterous *adj.* boisterous, clamorous, disorderly, exuberant, loud, noisy, obstreperous, roisting, rowdy, uproarious, wild.
antonyms orderly, restrained.

role *n.* capacity, character, duty, function, impersonation, job, job of work, part, portrayal, position, post, representation, task.

roll *v.* billow, bind, boom, coil, curl, drum, echo, elapse, enfold, entwine, envelop, even, flatten, flow, furl, grumble, gyrate, level, lumber, lurch, pass, peel, pivot, press, reel, resound, reverberate, revolve, roar, rock, rotate, rumble, run, smooth, spin, spread, stagger, swagger, swathe, sway, swing, swivel, thunder, toss, trill, trindle, trundle, tumble, turn, twirl, twist, undulate, volume, waddle, wallow, wander, welter, wheel, whirl, wind, wrap.
n. annals, ball, bobbin, boom, catalogue, census, chronicle, cycle, cylinder, directory, drumming, growl, grumble, gyration, index, inventory, list, notitia, record, reel, register, resonance, reverberation, revolution, roar, roller, roster, rotation, rumble, run, schedule, scroll, spin, spool, table, thunder, turn, twirl, undulation, volume, wheel, whirl.
roll up arrive, assemble, cluster, congregate, convene, forgather, gather.
antonyms leave, scatter.

rollicking *adj.* boisterous, carefree, cavorting, devil-may-care, exuberant, frisky, frolicsome, hearty, jaunty, jovial, joyous, lively, merry, playful, rip-roaring, roisterous, roisting, romping, spirited, sportive, sprightly, swashbuckling.
antonyms restrained, serious.

rolling *adj.* heaving, rippling, surging, undulant,

undulating, waving.
antonym flat.

roly-poly *adj.* buxom, chubby, fat, overweight, plump, podgy, pudgy, roll-about, rotund, roundabout, rounded, tubby.
antonym slim.

romance *n.* absurdity, adventure, affair(e), amour, attachment, charm, colour, exaggeration, excitement, fabrication, fairy tale, falsehood, fantasy, fascination, fiction, gest(e), glamour, idyll, intrigue, invention, legend, liaison, lie, love affair, love story, melodrama, mystery, novel, passion, relationship, sentiment, story, tale, tear-jerker.
v. exaggerate, fantasise, lie, overstate.

romantic *adj.* amorous, charming, chimerical, colourful, dreamy, exaggerated, exciting, exotic, extravagant, fabulous, fairy-tale, fanciful, fantastic, fascinating, fictitious, fond, glamorous, high-flown, idealistic, idyllic, imaginary, imaginative, impractical, improbable, legendary, lovey-dovey, loving, made-up, mushy, mysterious, passionate, picturesque, quixotic, romantical, sentimental, sloppy, soppy, starry-eyed, tender, unrealistic, utopian, visionary, whimsical, wild.
antonyms humdrum, practical, real, sober, unromantic.
n. Don Quixote, dreamer, idealist, romancer, sentimentalist, utopian, visionary.
antonym realist.

Romeo *n.* Casanova, Don Juan, gigolo, ladies' man, lady-killer, Lothario, lover.

romp *v.* caper, cavort, frisk, frolic, gambol, revel, rig, roister, rollick, skip, sport.
n. caper, frolic, lark, rig, spree.

rook *v.* bilk, cheat, clip, con, defraud, diddle, do, fleece, mulct, overcharge, rip off, soak, sting, swindle.

room *n.* allowance, apartment, area, capacity, chamber, chance, compartment, compass, elbow-room, expanse, extent, house-room, latitude, leeway, margin, occasion, office, opportunity, play, range, salon, saloon, scope, space, territory, volume.

roomy *adj.* ample, broad, capacious, commodious, extensive, generous, large, sizable, spacious, voluminous, wide.
antonym cramped.

root¹ *n.* base, basis, beginnings, bottom, cause, core, crux, derivation, essence, foundation, fountainhead, fundamental, germ, heart, mainspring, more, nub, nucleus, occasion, origin, radicle, radix, rhizome, root-cause, rootlet, seat, seed, source, starting point, stem, tuber.
v. anchor, embed, entrench, establish, fasten, fix, ground, implant, moor, set, sink, stick.
root and branch completely, entirely, finally, radically, thoroughly, totally, utterly, wholly.
antonyms not at all, slightly.

root² *v.* burrow, delve, dig, ferret, forage, grout, hunt, nose, poke, pry, rootle, rummage.
root out abolish, clear away, destroy, dig out, discover, efface, eliminate, eradicate, erase,

exterminate, extirpate, produce, remove, root up, turn up, uncover, unearth, uproot.
antonyms cover, establish.

rooted *adj.* confirmed, deep, deeply, deep-seated, entrenched, established, felt, firm, fixed, ingrained, radical, rigid, root-fast.
antonyms superficial, temporary.

roots *n.* background, beginning(s), birthplace, cradle, family, heritage, home, origins.

rope *n.* cable, cord, fake, hawser, lariat, lasso, line, marline, strand, warp, widdy.
v. bind, catch, fasten, hitch, lash, lasso, moor, pinion, tether, tie.

rope in embroil, engage, enlist, inveigle, involve, lure, persuade.
antonym keep out.

ropy *adj.* below par, deficient, inadequate, indifferent, inferior, off colour, poorly, rough, sketchy, stringy, substandard, unwell.
antonyms good, well.

roster *n.* bead-roll, list, listing, register, roll, rota, schedule, table.

rostrum *n.* dais, hustings, platform, podium, stage.

rosy *adj.* auspicious, blooming, blushing, bright, cheerful, encouraging, favourable, fresh, glowing, healthy-looking, hopeful, optimistic, pink, promising, reassuring, red, reddish, rose, roseate, rose-coloured, rose-hued, rose-like, rose-pink, rose-red, rose-scented, rosy-fingered, rubicund, ruddy, sunny.
antonyms depressed, depressing, sad.

rot *v.* corrode, corrupt, crumble, decay, decline, decompose, degenerate, deteriorate, disintegrate, fester, go bad, languish, moulder, perish, putrefy, ret, spoil, taint.
n. balderdash, blight, bosh, bunk, bunkum, canker, claptrap, codswallop, collapse, corrosion, corruption, decay, decomposition, deterioration, disintegration, drivel, flapdoodle, guff, hogwash, moonshine, mould, nonsense, poppycock, putrefaction, putrescence, rubbish, tommyrot, tosh, twaddle.

rotary *adj.* gyrating, gyratory, revolving, rotating, rotational, rotatory, spinning, turning, whirling.
antonym fixed.

rotate *v.* alternate, gyrate, interchange, pirouette, pivot, reel, revolve, spell, spin, switch, swivel, turn, twiddle, wheel.

rotation *n.* alternation, cycle, gyration, interchanging, orbit, pirouette, reel, revolution, sequence, spin, spinning, succession, switching, turn, turning, volution, wheel.

rotten *adj.* addle(d), bad, base, below par, bent, contemptible, corroded, corrupt, crooked, crumbling, crummy, decayed, decaying, deceitful, decomposed, decomposing, degenerate, deplorable, despicable, dirty, disagreeable, disappointing, dishonest, dishonourable, disintegrating, disloyal, faithless, festering, fetid, filthy, foul, grotty, ill-considered, ill-thought-out, immoral, inadequate, inferior, lousy, low-grade, manky, mean, mercenary, mouldering, mouldy, nasty, off

colour, perfidious, perished, poor, poorly, punk, putid, putrescent, putrid, rank, regrettable, ropy, rough, scurrilous, sick, sorry, sour, stinking, substandard, tainted, treacherous, unacceptable, unfortunate, unlucky, unpleasant, unsatisfactory, unsound, untrustworthy, unwell, venal, vicious, vile, wicked.
antonyms good, honest, practical, sensible, well.

rotter *n.* bastard, blackguard, blighter, bounder, cad, cur, dastard, fink, louse, rat, scoundrel, stinker, swine.
antonym saint.

rotund *adj.* bulbous, chubby, corpulent, fat, fleshy, full, globular, grandiloquent, heavy, magniloquent, obese, orbed, orbicular, orby, oro(ro)tund, plump, podgy, portly, resonant, rich, roly-poly, rotundate, round, rounded, sonorous, spheral, spheric, spherical, spherular, sphery, stout, tubby.
antonyms flat, gaunt, slim.

roué *n.* debauchee, lecher, libertine, profligate, rake, rakehell, sensualist, wanton.

rough *adj.* agitated, amorphous, approximate, arduous, austere, basic, bearish, bluff, blunt, boisterous, bristly, broken, brusque, bumpy, bushy, cacophonous, choppy, churlish, coarse, craggy, crude, cruel, cursory, curt, discordant, discourteous, dishevelled, disordered, drastic, estimated, extreme, foggy, formless, fuzzy, general, grating, gruff, hairy, hard, harsh, hasty, hazy, husky, ill, ill-bred, ill-mannered, imperfect, impolite, imprecise, inclement, incomplete, inconsiderate, indelicate, inexact, inharmonious, irregular, jagged, jarring, loutish, nasty, off colour, poorly, quick, rasping, raspy, raucous, raw, rocky, ropy, rotten, rough-and-ready, rowdy, rude, rudimentary, rugged, rusty, scabrous, severe, shaggy, shapeless, sharp, sick, sketchy, spartan, squally, stony, stormy, tangled, tempestuous, tough, tousled, tousy, turbulent, unceremonious, uncivil, uncomfortable, uncouth, uncultured, uncut, undressed, uneven, unfeeling, unfinished, ungracious, unjust, unmannerly, unmusical, unpleasant, unpolished, unprocessed, unrefined, unshaven, unshorn, untutored, unwell, unwrought, upset, vague, violent, wild.
antonyms accurate, calm, harmonious, mild, polite, smooth, well.
n. bruiser, bully, corner-boy, draft, hooligan, keelie, mock-up, model, outline, roughneck, rowdy, ruffian, sketch, thug, tough, yob, yobbo.

rough up bash, batter, beat up, do, knock about, maltreat, manhandle, mistreat, mug, thrash.

rough-and-ready *adj.* adequate, approximate, crude, impoverished, makeshift, provisional, sketchy, stop-gap, unpolished, unrefined.
antonyms exact, refined.

rough-and-tumble *n.* affray, bagarre, barney, brawl, Donnybrook, dust-up, fight, fracas, mêlée, punch-up, rookery, rout, ruction, ruffle, rumpus, scrap, scuffle, shindy, struggle.

roughen v. abrade, asperate, coarsen, granulate, graze, harshen, rough, scuff.
antonym smooth.

roughneck n. apache, bruiser, bully boy, corner-boy, hooligan, keelie, lout, Mohock, myrmidon, rough, rowdy, ruffian, thug, toe-rag, toe-ragger, tough.

round adj. ample, annular, ball-shaped, blunt, bowed, bulbous, candid, circular, complete, curved, curvilinear, cylindrical, direct, discoid, disc-shaped, entire, fleshy, frank, full, full-fleshed, globular, mellifluous, orbed, orbicular, orby, orotund, outspoken, plain, plump, resonant, rich, ring-shaped, roly-poly, rotund, rotundate, rounded, solid, sonorous, spheral, spheric, spherical, spherular, sphery, straightforward, unbroken, undivided, unmodified, whole.
antonyms evasive, niggardly, partial, thin.
n. ambit, ball, band, beat, bout, bullet, cartridge, circle, circuit, compass, course, cycle, disc, discharge, division, globe, lap, level, orb, period, ring, routine, schedule, sequence, series, session, shell, shot, sphere, spheroid, spherule, stage, succession, tour, turn.
v. bypass, circle, circumnavigate, encircle, flank, sail round, skirt, turn.

round off cap, close, complete, conclude, crown, end, finish, finish off, settle.
antonym begin.

round on abuse, assail, attack, bite (someone's) head off, retaliate, snap at, turn on.

round the bend barmy, batty, bonkers, crazy, cuckoo, daft, dotty, eccentric, insane, mad, nuts, nutty, off one's rocker, screwy.
antonym sane.

round up assemble, collect, drive, gather, gather in, group, herd, marshal, muster, rally.
antonym disperse.

roundabout adj. ambagious, circuitous, circumlocutory, devious, discursive, evasive, indirect, meandering, oblique, periphrastic, tortuous, twisting, winding.
antonyms direct, straight, straightforward.

roundly adv. bluntly, completely, fiercely, forcefully, frankly, intensely, openly, outspokenly, rigorously, severely, sharply, thoroughly, vehemently, violently.
antonym mildly.

round-up n. assembly, collation, collection, gathering, herding, marshalling, muster, overview, précis, rally, summary, survey.
antonym dispersal.

rouse v. agitate, anger, animate, arouse, awaken, bestir, call, disturb, enkindle, excite, exhilarating, firk, flush, galvanise, incite, inflame, instigate, move, provoke, rise, start, startle, stimulate, stir, suscitate, unbed, wake, whip up.
antonym calm.

rousing adj. brisk, electrifying, excitant, excitative, excitatory, exciting, exhilarating, hypno-

pompic, inflammatory, inspiring, lively, moving, spirited, stimulating, stirring, vigorous.
antonym calming.

rout n. beating, brawl, clamour, crowd, debacle, defeat, disturbance, Donnybrook, drubbing, flight, fracas, fuss, herd, hiding, licking, mob, overthrow, pack, rabble, riot, rookery, ruffle, ruin, shambles, stampede, thrashing.
antonyms calm, win.
v. beat, best, chase, conquer, crush, defeat, destroy, discomfit, dispel, drub, fleme, fley, hammer, lick, overthrow, scatter, thrash, worst.

route n. avenue, beat, circuit, course, direction, flightpath, itinerary, journey, passage, path, road, round, run, way.
v. convey, direct, dispatch, forward, send.

routine n. act, bit, custom, formula, grind, groove, heigh, jog-trot, line, method, order, pattern, performance, piece, practice, procedure, programme, spiel, usage, way, wont.
adj. banal, boring, clichéd, conventional, customary, day-by-day, dull, everyday, familiar, habitual, hackneyed, humdrum, mundane, normal, ordinary, predictable, run-of-the-mill, standard, tedious, tiresome, typical, unimaginative, uninspired, unoriginal, usual, wonted, workaday.
antonyms exciting, unusual.

rove v. cruise, drift, gallivant, meander, ramble, range, roam, stravaig, stray, stroll, traipse, waltz Matilda, wander.
antonym stay.

rover n. drifter, gadabout, gypsy, itinerant, nomad, rambler, ranger, stravaiger, transient, traveller, vagrant, wanderer.
antonym stay-at-home.

row[1] n. bank, colonnade, column, file, line, queue, range, rank, sequence, series, string, tier.

row[2] n. altercation, brawl, castigation, commotion, controversy, dispute, disturbance, Donnybrook, dressing-down, falling-out, fracas, fray, fuss, lecture, noise, quarrel, racket, rammy, reprimand, reproof, rhubarb, rollicking, rookery, rout, ruckus, ruction, ruffle, rumpus, scrap, shemozzle, shindig, shindy, slanging match, squabble, talking-to, telling-off, ticking-off, tiff, tongue-lashing, trouble, tumult, uproar.
antonym calm.
v. argue, argufy, brawl, dispute, fight, scrap, squabble, wrangle.

rowdy adj. boisterous, disorderly, loud, loutish, noisy, obstreperous, roisterous, roisting, rorty, rough, rumbustious, stroppy, unruly, uproarious, wild.
antonyms quiet, restrained.
n. brawler, corner-boy, hoodlum, hooligan, keelie, lout, rough, ruffian, tearaway, tough, yahoo, yob, yobbo.

royal adj. august, basilical, grand, imperial, impressive, kinglike, kingly, magnificent, majestic, monarchical, princely, queenlike, queenly, regal, sovereign, splendid, stately, superb, superior.

rub *v.* abrade, apply, caress, chafe, clean, embrocate, fray, grate, knead, malax, malaxate, massage, polish, put, scour, scrape, shine, smear, smooth, spread, stroke, wipe.
n. caress, catch, difficulty, drawback, hindrance, hitch, impediment, kneading, malaxage, malaxation, massage, obstacle, polish, problem, shine, snag, stroke, trouble, wipe.
rub out assassinate, cancel, delete, efface, erase, expunge, kill, murder, obliterate, remove.
rub up the wrong way anger, annoy, bug, get, get one's goat, get to, get under one's skin, irk, irritate, needle, niggle, peeve, vex.
antonym calm.

rubbish *n.* balderdash, balls, baloney, bosh, bunkum, clamjamphrie, claptrap, cobblers, codswallop, crap, dead-wood, debris, draff, drivel, dross, flotsam and jetsam, garbage, gibberish, gobbledegook, guff, havers, hogwash, junk, kibosh, kitsch, landfill, leavings, litter, lumber, moonshine, mullock, nonsense, offal, offscourings, offscum, piffle, poppycock, raffle, refuse, riddlings, rot, scoria, scrap, stuff, sullage, sweepings, tommyrot, tosh, trash, trashery, truck, trumpery, twaddle, vomit, waste.
antonym sense.

rubbish-dump *n.* kitchen-midden, landfill, laystall, tip.

rubbishy *adj.* brummagem, cheap, draffish, draffy, gimcrack, grotty, paltry, petty, shoddy, tatty, tawdry, third-rate, throw-away, trashy, twopenny-halfpenny, valueless, worthless.
antonym classy.

ruction *n.* altercation, brawl, commotion, dispute, disturbance, Donnybrook, fracas, fuss, quarrel, racket, rookery, rout, row, ruffle, rumpus, scrap, storm, to-do, trouble, uproar.
antonym calm.

ruddy *adj.* blooming, blushing, crimson, flammulated, florid, flushed, fresh, glowing, healthy, pink, red, reddish, roseate, rosehued, rose-pink, rosy, rosy-cheeked, rubicund, rubineous, rubious, ruby, sanguine, scarlet, sunburnt.
antonyms pale, unhealthy.

rude *adj.* abrupt, abusive, artless, barbarous, blunt, boorish, brusque, brutish, cheeky, churlish, coarse, crude, curt, discourteous, disrespectful, graceless, gross, harsh, ignorant, illiterate, ill-mannered, impertinent, impolite, impudent, inartistic, inconsiderate, inelegant, insolent, insulting, loutish, low, makeshift, oafish, obscene, offhand, peremptory, primitive, raw, rough, savage, scurrilous, sharp, short, simple, startling, sudden, uncivil, uncivilised, uncouth, uncultured, uneducated, ungracious, unmannerly, unpleasant, unpolished, unrefined, untutored, violent, vulgar.
antonyms graceful, polished, polite, smooth.

rudeness *n.* abruptness, abuse, abusiveness, bad manners, barbarism, bluntness, boorishness, brusqueness, cheek, churlishness, curtness, discourtesy, disrespect, grossièreté, ill-manners, impertinence, impoliteness, impudence, incivility, insolence, oafishness, sharpness, uncouthness, vulgarity.
antonym politeness.

rudimentary *adj.* abecedarian, basic, early, elementary, embryonic, fundamental, germinal, immature, inchoate, initial, introductory, primary, primitive, primordial, undeveloped, vestigial.
antonyms advanced, developed.

rudiments *n.* ABC, basics, beginnings, elements, essentials, foundation, fundamentals, germin, principia, principles, prolegomena.

rue *v.* bemoan, bewail, beweep, deplore, grieve, lament, mourn, regret, repent.
antonym rejoice.

rueful *adj.* conscience-stricken, contrite, dismal, doleful, grievous, long-visaged, lugubrious, melancholy, mournful, penitent, pitiable, pitiful, plaintive, regretful, remorseful, repentant, sad, self-reproachful, sorrowful, sorry, woebegone, woeful.
antonym glad.

ruffian *n.* apache, bruiser, brute, bully, bully-boy, corner-boy, cut-throat, hoodlum, hooligan, keelie, lout, miscreant, Mohock, myrmidon, plug-ugly, rascal, rogue, rough, roughneck, rowdy, scoundrel, thug, toe-rag, toe-ragger, tough, villain, yob, yobbo.

ruffle *v.* agitate, annoy, confuse, derange, disarrange, discompose, disconcert, dishevel, disorder, disquiet, disturb, fluster, harass, irritate, mess up, muss up, muss(e), nettle, peeve, perturb, rattle, rumple, stir, torment, tousle, trouble, unsettle, upset, vex, worry, wrinkle.
antonym smooth.

rugged *adj.* arduous, austere, barbarous, beefy, blunt, brawny, broken, bumpy, burly, churlish, crabbed, craggy, crude, demanding, difficult, dour, exacting, graceless, gruff, hale, hard, hard-featured, hardy, harsh, husky, irregular, jagged, laborious, muscular, ragged, rigorous, robust, rocky, rough, rude, severe, sour, stark, stern, strenuous, strong, sturdy, surly, taxing, tough, trying, uncompromising, uncouth, uncultured, uneven, unpolished, unrefined, vigorous, weather-beaten, weathered, worn.
antonyms easy, refined, smooth.

ruin *n.* bankruptcy, bouleversement, breakdown, collapse, crash, damage, decay, defeat, destitution, destruction, devastation, disintegration, disrepair, dissolution, downfall, failure, fall, havoc, heap, insolvency, nemesis, overthrow, ruination, subversion, undoing, Waterloo, wreck, wreckage.
antonyms development, reconstruction.
v. banjax, bankrupt, botch, break, crush, damage, defeat, demolish, destroy, devastate, disfigure, impoverish, injure, jigger, mangle,

mar, mess up, overthrow, overturn, overwhelm, pauperise, raze, scupper, scuttle, shatter, smash, spoil, unmake, unshape, wreck.

antonyms develop, restore.

ruinous *adj.* baleful, baneful, broken-down, calamitous, cataclysmic, catastrophic, crippling, deadly, decrepit, deleterious, derelict, destructive, devastating, dilapidated, dire, disastrous, extravagant, fatal, immoderate, injurious, murderous, noxious, pernicious, ramshackle, ruined, shattering, wasteful, withering.

antonym beneficial.

ruins *n.* chaos, debris, devastation, havoc, shambles.

rule *n.* administration, ascendancy, authority, axiom, canon, command, condition, control, convention, course, criterion, custom, decree, direction, domination, dominion, empire, form, formula, governance, government, guide, guideline, habit, influence, institute, jurisdiction, law, leadership, mastery, maxim, method, order, ordinance, policy, power, practice, precept, prescript, principle, procedure, raj, regime, regulation, reign, routine, ruling, standard, supremacy, sway, tenet, way, wont.

v. adjudge, adjudicate, administer, command, control, decide, decree, determine, direct, dominate, establish, find, govern, guide, judge, lead, manage, obtain, predominate, preponderate, prevail, pronounce, regulate, reign, resolve, settle.

rule out ban, debar, disallow, dismiss, eliminate, exclude, forbid, obviate, preclude, prevent, prohibit, proscribe, reject.

ruler *n.* commander, controller, emperor, empress, gerent, governor, gubernator, head of state, imperator, king, leader, lord, monarch, potentate, prince, princess, queen, sovereign, suzerain.

antonym subject.

ruling *n.* adjudication, decision, decree, finding, firman, hatti-sherif, indiction, interlocution, irade, judgement, pronouncement, resolution, ukase, verdict.

adj. boss, chief, commanding, controlling, dominant, governing, leading, main, predominant, pre-eminent, preponderant, prevailing, prevalent, principal, regnant, reigning, supreme, upper.

rum *adj.* abnormal, bizarre, curious, freakish, funny, funny-peculiar, odd, peculiar, queer, singular, strange, suspect, suspicious, unusual, weird.

rumbustious *adj.* boisterous, clamorous, disorderly, exuberant, loud, noisy, obstreperous, refractory, robust, roisterous, roisting, rorty, rough, rowdy, unmanageable, unruly, uproarious, wayward, wild, wilful.

antonyms quiet, restrained, sensible.

ruminate *v.* brood, chew over, chew the cud, cogitate, consider, contemplate, deliberate, meditate, mull over, muse, ponder, reflect,

revolve, think.

rummage *v.* delve, examine, explore, hunt, poke around, ransack, root, rootle, rout, search.

rumour *n.* breeze, bruit, bush telegraph, buzz, canard, fame, furphy, gossip, grapevine, hearsay, kite, news, on-dit, report, story, talk, tidings, underbreath, whisper, word.

v. bruit, circulate, gossip, publish, put about, report, say, tell, whisper.

rump *n.* backside, bottom, bum, buttocks, croup, dock, haunch, hindquarters, nache, posterior, rear, seat.

rumple *v.* crease, crinkle, crumple, crush, derange, dishevel, disorder, muss up, muss(e), pucker, ruffle, scrunch, tousle, wrinkle.

antonym smooth.

rumpus *n.* bagarre, barney, brouhaha, commotion, confusion, disruption, disturbance, Donnybrook, fracas, furore, fuss, kerfuffle, noise, rhubarb, rookery, rout, row, ruction, shemozzle, shindig, shindy, tumult, uproar.

antonym calm.

run *v.* abscond, administer, bear, beat it, bleed, bolt, boss, career, carry, cascade, challenge, circulate, clear out, climb, compete, conduct, contend, continue, control, convey, co-ordinate, course, creep, dart, dash, decamp, depart, direct, discharge, display, dissolve, drive to, escape, extend, feature, flee, flow, function, fuse, gallop, glide, go, gush, hare, hasten, head, hie, hotfoot, hurry, issue, jog, ladder, last, lead, leak, lie, liquefy, lope, manage, manoeuvre, mastermind, melt, mix, move, operate, oversee, own, pass, perform, ply, pour, print, proceed, propel, publish, race, range, reach, regulate, roll, rush, scamper, scarper, scramble, scud, scurry, skedaddle, skim, slide, speed, spill, spout, spread, sprint, stand, stream, stretch, superintend, supervise, tear, tick, trail, transport, unravel, work.

antonyms stay, stop.

n. application, category, chain, class, coop, course, current, cycle, dash, demand, direction, drift, drive, enclosure, excursion, flow, gallop, jaunt, jog, journey, joy, kind, ladder, lift, motion, movement, order, outing, passage, path, pen, period, pressure, progress, race, ride, rip, round, rush, season, sequence, series, snag, sort, spell, spin, sprint, spurt, streak, stream, stretch, string, tear, tendency, tenor, tide, trend, trip, type, variety, way.

run after chase, follow, pursue, stalk, tail.

antonym flee.

run away abscond, beat it, bolt, clear out, decamp, elope, escape, flee, scarper, scoot, scram, skedaddle, take it on the lam.

antonym stay.

run down belittle, capture, criticise, curtail, cut, debilitate, decrease, decry, defame, denigrate, disparage, drop, exhaust, hit, knock, knock over, reduce, revile, run over, strike, tire, trim, vilify, weaken.

antonyms increase, miss, praise.

run for it bolt, do a bunk, escape, flee, fly, have it on one's toes, make off, retreat, scarper, scram, skedaddle.
antonym stay.

run in apprehend, arrest, bust, collar, feel (someone's) collar, jail, lift, nab, nick, pick up, pinch.

run into bash, encounter, hit, meet, ram, strike.
antonym miss.

run off abscond, bleed, bolt, decamp, drain, duplicate, elope, escape, have it on one's toes, make off, print, produce, scarper, siphon, skedaddle, tap.
antonym stay.

run out cease, close, dry up, end, expire, fail, finish, terminate.

run over hit, knock down, overflow, rehearse, reiterate, review, run down, spill, strike, survey.

run riot cut loose, go on the rampage, kick over the traces, rampage, sow one's wild oats, spread.

run through blow, check, dissipate, examine, exhaust, fritter away, pierce, practise, read, rehearse, review, spit, squander, stab, stick, survey, transfix, waste.

run together amalgamate, blend, coalesce, combine, commingle, fuse, intermingle, intermix, join, merge, mingle, mix, unite.
antonym separate.

runaway *n.* absconder, deserter, escapee, escaper, fleer, fugitive, refugee, truant.
adj. escaped, fleeing, fugitive, loose, uncontrolled, wild.

rundown *n.* briefing, cut, decrease, drop, lessening, outline, précis, recap, reduction, résumé, review, run-through, sketch, summary, synopsis.

run-down *adj.* broken-down, debilitated, decrepit, dilapidated, dingy, drained, enervated, exhausted, fatigued, grotty, peaky, ramshackle, scabby, seedy, shabby, tumble-down, unhealthy, weak, weary, worn-out.
antonym well-kept.

run-in *n.* altercation, argument, brush, confrontation, contretemps, difference of opinion, dispute, dust-up, encounter, fight, quarrel, set-to, skirmish, tussle, wrangle.

runner[1] *n.* athlete, competitor, courier, harrier, jogger, messenger, miler, participant, sprinter.

runner[2] *n.* flagellum, offshoot, sarmentum, shoot, sprig, sprout, stem, stolon, tendril.

running *adj.* consecutive, constant, continuous, current, flowing, incessant, moving, perpetual, streaming, successive, together, unbroken, unceasing, uninterrupted.
antonyms broken, ceased, occasional.
n. administration, charge, competition, conduct, contention, contest, control, co-ordination, direction, functioning, going, leadership, maintenance, management, operation, organisation, pace, performance, regulation, superintendency, supervision, working.

runny *adj.* dilute, diluted, flowing, fluid, liquefied, liquid, melted, molten, watery.
antonym solid.

run-of-the-mill *adj.* average, common, commonplace, everyday, fair, mediocre, middling, modest, ordinary, passable, routine, tolerable, undistinguished, unexceptional, unexciting, unimaginative, unimpressive, unremarkable.
antonym exceptional.

rupture *n.* altercation, breach, break, breaking, burst, bust-up, cleavage, cleft, contention, crack, disagreement, disruption, dissolution, estrangement, falling-out, feud, fissure, fracture, hernia, hostility, quarrel, rent, rift, schism, split, splitting, tear.
v. break, burst, cleave, crack, disrupt, dissever, divide, fracture, puncture, rend, separate, sever, split, sunder, tear.

rural *adj.* agrarian, agrestic, agricultural, Arcadian, bucolic, countrified, country, forane, mofussil, pastoral, pr(a)edical, rustic, sylvan, yokelish.
antonym urban.

ruse *n.* artifice, blind, deception, device, dodge, hoax, imposture, manoeuvre, ploy, sham, stall, stratagem, subterfuge, trick, wile.

rush *v.* accelerate, attack, bolt, capture, career, charge, dart, dash, dispatch, expedite, fly, hasten, hightail it, hotfoot, hurry, hustle, overcome, press, push, quicken, race, run, scour, scramble, scurry, shoot, speed, speed up, sprint, stampede, storm, tear, wallop, w(h)oosh.
n. assault, charge, dash, dispatch, expedition, flow, haste, hurry, onslaught, push, race, scramble, speed, stampede, storm, streak, surge, swiftness, tantivy, tear, urgency.
adj. brisk, careless, cursory, emergency, expeditious, fast, hasty, hurried, prompt, quick, rapid, superficial, swift, urgent.

rush about rampage.

rust *n.* blight, corrosion, fungus, mildew, mould, must, oxidation, patina, rot, stain, verdigris.
v. atrophy, corrode, corrupt, decay, decline, degenerate, deteriorate, oxidise, rot, stagnate, tarnish.

rust-coloured *adj.* auburn, chestnut, copper, coppery, ginger, gingery, red, reddish, reddish-brown, russet, rusty, sandy, tawny, titian.

rustic *adj.* agrarian, agrestic, Arcadian, artless, awkward, boorish, bucolic, churlish, cloddish, clodhopping, clownish, clumsy, coarse, countrified, country, crude, georgic, graceless, hick, hodden, homely, homespun, loutish, lumpish, maladroit, oafish, pastoral, plain, provincial, rough, rude, rural, silvatic, silvestrian, simple, sylvan, unaffected, uncouth, uncultured, unmannerly, unpolished, unrefined, unsophisticated, yokelish.
antonyms cultivated, polished, sophisticated, urban, urbane.
n. boor, bumpkin, carl, chaw-bacon, chuff,

churl, clod, clodhopper, clown, Corydon, country cousin, countryman, countrywoman, hayseed, hick, hillbilly, hind, hob, Hobinoll, Hodge, kern, oaf, peasant, provincial, swain, yokel.

antonyms dandy, man-about-town, sophisticate.

rustle *v.* crackle, crepitate, susurrate, swish, whisper, whoosh.

n. crackle, crepitation, crepitus, crinkling, rustling, susurration, susurrus, swish, whisper, whispering, whoosh.

rusty *adj.* aeruginous, ancient, antiquated, antique, corroded, creaking, creaky, croaking, croaky, dated, deficient, discoloured, dull, encrusted, fogram, hoarse, impaired, old-fashioned, outmoded, oxidised, passé,

patinated, raucous, rough, rust-covered, rusted, sluggish, stagnated, stale, stiff, tarnished, time-worn, unpractised, weak.

rut *n.* channel, ditch, furrow, gouge, groove, gutter, habit, indentation, pattern, pothole, routine, score, sulcus, system, track, trough, vallecula, wheelmark.

v. channel, cut, furrow, gouge, groove, hole, indent, mark, score.

ruthless *adj.* adamant, adamantine, barbarous, brutal, callous, cruel, cut-throat, dog-eat-dog, ferocious, fierce, hard, hard-hearted, harsh, heartless, implacable, inexorable, inhuman, merciless, pitiless, relentless, remorseless, savage, severe, stern, stony, unfeeling, unmerciful, unpitying, unrelenting.

antonyms compassionate, merciful.

S

sable *adj.* black, coal-black, dark, dusky, ebon, ebony, inky, jet, jetty, midnight, pitch-black, pitch-dark, pitchy, reven, sombre.

sabotage *v.* cripple, damage, destroy, disable, disrupt, incapacitate, mar, nullify, ratten, scupper, subvert, thwart, undermine, vandalise, vitiate, wreck.
n. damage, destruction, disablement, disruption, impairment, marring, rattening, subversion, treachery, treason, undermining, vandalism, vitiation, wrecking.

sac *n.* bag, bladder, bursa, capsule, cyst, follicle, pocket, pod, pouch, saccule, theca, vesica, vesicle, vesicula.

saccharine *adj.* cloying, honeyed, maudlin, mawkish, nauseating, oversweet, schmaltzy, sentimental, sickly, sickly-sweet, sloppy, soppy, sugary, syrupy, treacly.
antonyms bitter, tart.

sack[1] *v.* axe, discharge, dismiss, fire, lay off, make redundant.
n. discharge, dismissal, notice, one's books, one's cards, one's marching orders, the axe, the boot, the bum's rush, the chop, the elbow, the push.

sack[2] *v.* demolish, depredate, desecrate, despoil, destroy, devastate, lay waste, level, loot, maraud, pillage, plunder, raid, rape, ravage, raze, rifle, rob, ruin, spoil, strip, waste.
n. depredation, desecration, despoliation, destruction, devastation, levelling, looting, marauding, pillage, plunder, plundering, rape, rapine, ravage, razing, ruin, waste.

sacred *adj.* blessed, consecrated, dedicated, devotional, divine, ecclesiastical, godly, hallowed, heavenly, holy, inviolable, inviolate, invulnerable, priestly, protected, religious, revered, sacrosanct, saintly, sanctified, secure, solemn, venerable, venerated.
antonyms mundane, profane, temporal.

sacredness *n.* divinity, godliness, holiness, inviolability, invulnerability, sacrosanctity, saintliness, sanctity, solemnity.
antonyms profaneness, worldliness.

sacrifice *v.* abandon, forego, forfeit, immolate, let go, lose, offer, relinquish, renounce, slaughter, surrender.
n. corban, destruction, hecatomb, holocaust, host, immolation, loss, mactation, oblation, offering, renunciation, surrender, victim, votive offering.

sacrificial *adj.* atoning, expiatory, oblatory, piacular, propitiatory, reparative, votive.

sacrilege *n.* blasphemy, defilement, desecration, disrespect, heresy, impiety, impiousness, irreverence, mockery, outrage, profanation, profaneness, profanity, violation.
antonyms piety, respect, reverence.

sacrilegious *adj.* blasphemous, desecrating, disrespectful, godless, heretical, impious, irreligious, irreverent, profanatory, profane, ungodly, unholy.
antonyms pious, respectful, reverent.

sacrosanct *adj.* hallowed, impregnable, inviolable, inviolate, sacred, sanctified, untouchable.

sad *adj.* bad, blue, calamitous, cheerless, chopfallen, crestfallen, crushed, dark, dejected, deplorable, depressed, depressing, desolated, despondent, disastrous, disconsolate, dismal, dispirited, distressed, distressing, doleful, dolesome, doloriferous, dolorific, doughy, dour, dowie, downcast, downhearted, drear, dreary, gloomy, glum, grave, grief-stricken, grieved, grieving, grievous, heart-rending, heavy, heavy-hearted, jawfallen, joyless, lachrymose, lamentable, long-faced, low, low-spirited, lugubrious, melancholy, miserable, mournful, moving, painful, pathetic, pensive, piteous, pitiable, pitiful, poignant, regrettable, serious, shabby, sober, sober-minded, sombre, sorrowful, sorry, sportless, stiff, tearful, touching, tragic, triste, uncheerful, unfortunate, unhappy, unsatisfactory, upsetting, wan, wistful, woebegone, woeful, wretched.
antonyms cheerful, fortunate, happy, lucky.

sadden *v.* aggrieve, dash, deject, depress, desolate, discourage, dishearten, dispirit, distress, grieve, hurt, oppress, upset.
antonyms cheer, delight, gratify, please.

saddle *v.* burden, charge, encumber, impose, land, load, lumber, task, tax.
n. demipique, pack-saddle, pigskin, pillion, seat.

sadism *n.* barbarity, bestiality, brutality, callousness, cruelty, heartlessness, inhumanity, malevolence, ruthlessness, sado-masochism, savagery, spite, unnaturalness, viciousness.

sadistic *adj.* barbarous, bestial, brutal, cruel, heartless, inhuman, malevolent, perverted, ruthless, savage, spiteful, unnatural, vicious.

sadness *n.* bleakness, cheerlessness, darkness, dejection, depression, desolation, despondency, disconsolateness, dismalness, distress, dole, dolefulness, dolour, gloominess, glumness, gravity, grief, joylessness, low spirits, lugubriousness, melancholy, misery, misfortune, mournfulness, pain, pathos, poignancy, regret, sombreness, sorrow, sorrowfulness, tearfulness, tragedy, unhappiness, wanness, wistfulness, woe, wretchedness.

antonyms cheerfulness, delight, happiness.

safe *adj*. alive and well, all right, cautious, certain, circumspect, conservative, dependable, discreet, foolproof, guarded, hale, harmless, immune, impregnable, innocuous, intact, invulnerable, non-poisonous, nontoxic, OK, out of harm's way, protected, proven, prudent, pure, realistic, reliable, scatheless, secure, sound, sure, tame, tested, tried, trustworthy, unadventurous, uncontaminated, undamaged, unfailing, unharmed, unhurt, uninjured, unscathed, wholesome.

antonyms exposed, harmful, unsafe, vulnerable.

n. cash-box, chest, coffer, deposit box, peter, repository, strongbox, vault.

safe-conduct *n*. authorisation, convoy, laissez-passer, licence, pass, passport, permit, safeguard, warrant.

safeguard *v*. assure, defend, guard, insure, preserve, protect, screen, secure, shelter, shield.

antonyms endanger, jeopardise.

n. armour, assurance, bulwark, convoy, cover, defence, escort, guarantee, guard, insurance, long-stop, Palladium, precaution, preventive, protection, security, shield, surety.

safekeeping *n*. aegis, care, charge, custody, guard, guardianship, keeping, lock and key, protection, supervision, surveillance, trust, tutelage, vigilance, ward, wardship, watch.

safety *n*. assurance, cover, deliverance, dependability, harmlessness, immunity, impregnability, invulnerability, protection, refuge, reliability, safeguard, salvation, sanctuary, security, shelter, sureness, via trita, via tuta.

antonyms danger, jeopardy.

adj. fail-safe, precautionary, preventative, protective.

sag *v*. bag, decline, dip, drag, droop, drop, dwindle, fail, fall, flag, give, give way, hang, settle, sink, slide, slip, slump, wane, weaken, wilt.

antonyms bulge, rise.

n. decline, depression, dip, downturn, drop, dwindling, fall, low, low point, reduction, slide, slip, slump.

antonyms peak, rise.

saga *n*. adventure, chronicle, epic, epopee, epopeia, epos, history, narrative, romance, roman-fleuve, soap opera, story, tale, yarn.

sagacious *adj*. able, acute, apt, astute, canny, cute, discerning, downy, far-sighted, fly, insightful, intelligent, judicious, knowing, long-headed, long-sighted, penetrating, perceptive, percipient, perspicacious, quick, sage, sapient, sharp, shrewd, smart, wary, wide-awake, wise.

antonyms foolish, obtuse, short-sighted.

sagacity *n*. acumen, acuteness, astuteness, canniness, discernment, foresight, insight, judgement, judiciousness, knowingness, penetration, percipience, perspicacity, prudence, sapience, sense, sharpness, shrewdness, understanding, wariness, wiliness, wisdom.

antonyms folly, foolishness, obtuseness.

sage *adj*. astute, canny, discerning, intelligent, judicious, knowing, knowledgeable, learned, perspicacious, politic, prudent, sagacious, sapient, sensible, wise.

antonym foolish.

n. authority, elder, expert, guru, hakam, maharishi, mahatma, master, Nestor, oracle, philosopher, pundit, rishi, savant, Solomon, Solon, teacher, wise man.

antonym ignoramus.

sail *v*. captain, cruise, drift, embark, float, fly, glide, navigate, pilot, plane, put to sea, scud, shoot, skim, skipper, soar, steer, sweep, take ship, voyage, waft, weigh anchor, wing.

sail into assault, attack, belabour, lambaste, lay into, let fly, set about, tear into, turn on.

sailor *n*. AB, able seaman, able-bodied seaman, galiongee, gob, hearty, Jack Tar, lascar, leatherneck, limey, marine, mariner, matelot, matlow, navigator, rating, salt, sea dog, sea-dog, seafarer, seaman, tar, tarpaulin, tarry-breeks, water-rat.

saintliness *n*. asceticism, blessedness, chastity, devoutness, faith, godliness, goodness, holiness, morality, piety, purity, righteousness, sanctity, self-denial, selflessness, self-sacrifice, spirituality, spotlessness, unselfishness, uprightness, virtue.

antonyms godlessness, unholiness, wickedness.

saintly *adj*. angelic, beatific, blameless, blessed, blest, celestial, devout, god-fearing, godly, holy, immaculate, innocent, pious, pure, religious, righteous, sainted, saintlike, seraphic, sinless, spotless, stainless, upright, virtuous, worthy.

antonyms godless, unholy, unrighteous, wicked.

sake *n*. account, advantage, aim, behalf, benefit, cause, consideration, end, gain, good, interest, motive, object, objective, principle, profit, purpose, reason, regard, respect, score, welfare, wellbeing.

salacious *adj*. bawdy, blue, carnal, coarse, concupiscent, erotic, horny, improper, indecent, lascivious, lecherous, lewd, libidinous, lickerish, lubricious, lustful, obscene, pornographic, prurient, randy, raunchy, ribald, ruttish, scurrilous, smutty, steamy, wanton.

antonyms clean, decent, proper.

salaried *adj*. emolumental, emolumentary, paid, remunerated, stipendiary, waged.

antonyms honorary, unpaid, voluntary.

salary *n*. earnings, emolument, honorarium, income, pay, remuneration, screw, stipend, wage, wages.

sale *n*. auction, deal, disposal, marketing, sell, selling, trade, traffic, transaction, vending, vendition, vendue.

saleable *adj*. desirable, marketable, merchantable, sought-after, vendible.

antonyms unmarketable, unsaleable.

salesperson *n.* bagman, clerk, counter-jumper, counter-skipper, sales assistant, salesclerk, salesgirl, saleslady, salesman, saleswoman, shop assistant, shop-boy, shopgirl, shopkeeper, vendeuse.

salient *adj.* arresting, chief, conspicuous, important, jutting, main, marked, noticeable, obvious, outstanding, principal, projecting, prominent, pronounced, protruding, remarkable, signal, significant, striking.

sallow *adj.* anaemic, bilious, colourless, pale, pallid, pasty, sickly, unhealthy, wan, yellowish.
antonyms rosy, sanguine.

sally¹ *v.* breeze, charge, erupt, foray, issue, mosey, promenade, rush, saunter, sortie, stroll, surge, venture.
antonym retreat.
n. assault, dash, drive, escapade, excursion, foray, frolic, incursion, jaunt, offensive, raid, rush, sortie, surge, thrust, trip, venture.
antonyms retire, retreat.

sally² *n.* bon mot, crack, jest, jeu d'esprit, joke, quip, retort, riposte, wisecrack, witticism.

salt *n.* acuteness, Attic salt, Attic wit, bite, dryness, flavour, liveliness, merum sal, pawkiness, piquancy, punch, pungency, relish, sarcasm, savour, seasoning, sharpness, smack, taste, trenchancy, vigour, wit, zest, zip.
adj. brackish, briny, saline, salted, saltish, salty.
antonym fresh.

salt away accumulate, amass, bank, cache, collect, hide, hoard, save, stash, stockpile, store up.
antonyms spend, squander.

salty *adj.* brackish, briny, colourful, dry, humorous, keen, lively, pawky, piquant, pungent, racy, saline, salsuginous, salt, salted, saltish, spicy, tangy, tart, witty, wry, zestful.

salubrious *adj.* beneficial, bracing, healthful, health-giving, healthy, hygienic, invigorating, refreshing, restorative, salutary, sanitary, wholesome.
antonyms insalubrious, unwholesome.

salutary *adj.* advantageous, beneficial, good, healthful, healthy, helpful, much-needed, practical, profitable, salubrious, seasonable, timely, useful, valuable, wholesome.

salutation *n.* address, greeting, homage, obeisance, respects, reverence, salaam, salute, welcome.

salute *v.* accost, acknowledge, address, bow, greet, hail, honour, kiss, knuckle, nod, recognise, salaam, wave, welcome.
n. acknowledgement, address, bow, gesture, greeting, hail, handclap, handshake, hello, kiss, nod, obeisance, recognition, reverence, salaam, salutation, salve, salvo, tribute, wave.

salvage *v.* conserve, glean, preserve, reclaim, recover, recuperate, redeem, repair, rescue, restore, retrieve, salve, save.
antonyms abandon, lose, waste.

salvation *n.* deliverance, escape, liberation, lifeline, preservation, reclamation, redemption, rescue, restoration, retrieval, safety, saving, soteriology.
antonyms damnation, loss.

salve *n.* application, balm, cream, dressing, embrocation, emollient, liniment, lotion, lubricant, medication, ointment, preparation, unguent.

same *adj.* aforementioned, aforesaid, alike, analogous, changeless, comparable, consistent, corresponding, duplicate, equal, equivalent, homologous, identical, indistinguishable, interchangeable, invariable, matching, mutual, reciprocal, selfsame, similar, substitutable, synonymous, twin, unaltered, unchanged, undiminished, unfailing, uniform, unvarying, very.
antonyms changeable, different, incompatible, inconsistent, variable.
n. ditto, the above-mentioned, the abovenamed, the aforementioned, the aforesaid.

sameness *n.* changelessness, consistency, déja vu, duplication, identicalness, identity, indistinguishability, invariability, likeness, monotony, oneness, predictability, repetition, resemblance, similarity, standardisation, tedium, uniformity.
antonyms difference, variety.

sample *n.* cross section, demonstration, ensample, example, exemplification, foretaste, free sample, freebie, illustration, indication, instance, model, pattern, representative, sign, specimen, swatch.
v. experience, inspect, investigate, pree, sip, taste, test, try.
adj. demonstration, illustrative, pilot, representative, specimen, test, trial.

sanctify *v.* anoint, bless, cleanse, consecrate, dedicate, divinify, divinise, exalt, hallow, make holy, purify, sanction.
antonyms defile, degrade, desecrate.

sanctimonious *adj.* canting, false, goody-goody, holier-than-thou, holy, hypocritical, moralising, pharisaical, pi, pietistic, pious, preaching, priggish, righteous, self-righteous, selfsatisfied, smug, superior, Tartuffian, Tartuffish, unctuous.
antonym humble.

sanctimoniousness *n.* cant, canting, complacency, holiness, humbug, hypocrisy, moralising, pharisaism, pietism, preachiness, priggishness, righteousness, self-righteousness, selfsatisfaction, smugness, Tartuffism, unctuousness.
antonym humility.

sanction *n.* accreditation, agreement, allowance, approbation, approval, authorisation, authority, backing, cachet, confirmation, countenance, endorsement, go-ahead, green light, imprimatur, licence, OK, permission, ratification, seal, support.
antonyms disapproval, veto.
v. accredit, allow, approve, authorise, back, confirm, countenance, countersign, endorse,

fiat, license, permit, ratify, support, underwrite, warrant.
antonyms disallow, disapprove, veto.
sanctions *n.* ban, boycott, embargo, interdict, penalty, prohibition, proscription, restrictions.
sanctity *n.* devotion, godliness, goodness, grace, holiness, inviolability, piety, purity, religiousness, righteousness, sacredness, sacrosanctity, saintliness, saintship, sanctitude, solemnity, spirituality, venerableness.
antonyms godlessness, impurity, secularity, unholiness, worldliness.
sanctuary *n.* adytum, altar, ark, asylum, chancel, church, delubrum, frith, grith, harbourage, haven, holy of holies, naos, presbytery, protection, refuge, retreat, sacrarium, sanctum, sanctum sanctorum, seclusion, shelter, shrine, tabernacle, temple.
sanctum *n.* cubby-hole, den, growlery, hideaway, holy of holies, refuge, retreat, sanctuary, sanctum sanctorum, shrine, snug, snuggery, study.
sand *n.* arena, beach, gravel, grit, sands, shore, strand.
sand-bank *n.* bar, cay, dune, hurst, key, reef, sand-bar, sand-hill, yardang.
sandy *adj.* arenaceous, auburn, coppery, ginger, gingerous, gingery, gritty, psammitic, red, reddish, reddish-yellow, rusty, tawny, titian, xanthous, yellow, yellowish, yellowy.
sane *adj.* all there, balanced, compos mentis, dependable, judicious, level-headed, lucid, moderate, normal, rational, reasonable, reliable, right-minded, sensible, sober, sound, stable.
sang-froid *n.* aplomb, assurance, calmness, composure, cool, cool-headedness, coolness, dispassion, equanimity, imperturbability, indifference, nerve, nonchalance, phlegm, poise, self-control, self-possession, unflappability.
antonyms discomposure, excitability, hysteria, panic.
sanguinary *adj.* bloodied, bloodthirsty, bloody, brutal, cruel, fell, gory, grim, merciless, murderous, pitiless, ruthless, savage.
sanguine[1] *adj.* animated, ardent, assured, buoyant, cheerful, confident, expectant, hopeful, lively, optimistic, over-confident, over-optimistic, Panglossian, roseate, spirited, unabashed, unappalled, unbowed.
antonyms cynical, depressive, gloomy, melancholy, pessimistic, realistic.
sanguine[2] *adj.* florid, flushed, fresh, fresh-complexioned, pink, red, rosy, rubicund, ruddy.
antonyms pale, sallow.
sanitary *adj.* aseptic, clean, disinfected, germ-free, healthy, hygienic, pure, salubrious, uncontaminated, unpolluted, wholesome.
antonyms insanitary, unwholesome.
sanity *n.* balance of mind, common sense, dependability, judiciousness, level-headedness, lucidity, normality, rationality,

reason, reasonableness, reliability, saneness, sense, soundness, stability.
antonyms foolishness, insanity.
sap *v.* bleed, deplete, devitalise, diminish, drain, enervate, exhaust, impair, reduce, rob, undermine, weaken.
antonyms build up, increase, strengthen.
sarcasm *n.* acidity, bitterness, contempt, cynicism, derision, diatribe, invective, irony, mockery, mordancy, satire, scorn, sneering, venom, vitriol.
sarcastic *adj.* acerbic, acid, acrimonious, biting, caustic, contemptuous, cutting, cynical, derisive, disparaging, incisive, ironical, mocking, mordant, sardonic, sarky, satirical, scathing, sharp, sharp-tongued, sneering, taunting, withering.
sardonic *adj.* biting, bitter, cynical, derisive, dry, heartless, ironical, jeering, malevolent, malicious, malignant, mocking, mordant, quizzical, sarcastic, satirical, scornful, sneering, wry.
sash *n.* baldric, belt, cincture, cummerbund, girdle, surcingle, vitta, waistband, zone.
Satan *n.* Abaddon, Apollyon, Beelzebub, Belial, Clootie, Cloots, Hornie, Lucifer, Mephistopheles, Old Nick, Prince of Darkness, The Adversary, The Devil, The Enemy, The Evil One, The Tempter.
satanic *adj.* accursed, black, demoniac, demoniacal, demonic, devilish, diabolic, diabolical, evil, fell, fiendish, hellish, infernal, inhuman, iniquitous, malevolent, malignant, Mephistophelian, satanical, wicked.
antonyms benevolent, benign, divine, godlike, godly, heavenly, holy.
sate *v.* cloy, fill, glut, gorge, gratify, overfill, satiate, satisfy, saturate, sicken, slake, surfeit, weary.
antonyms deprive, dissatisfy, starve.
satellite *n.* adherent, aide, attendant, dependant, disciple, follower, hanger-on, lackey, minion, moon, parasite, puppet, retainer, sidekick, sputnik, subordinate, sycophant, tributary, vassal, votary.
satiate *v.* cloy, engorge, glut, gorge, jade, nauseate, overfeed, overfill, sate, satisfy, slake, stuff, surfeit.
antonyms deprive, dissatisfy, underfeed.
satiety *n.* fullness, gratification, over-fullness, overindulgence, repleteness, repletion, satiation, satisfaction, saturation, surfeit.
satire *n.* burlesque, caricature, diatribe, invective, irony, lampoon, parody, Pasquil, Pasquin, pasquinade, raillery, ridicule, sarcasm, send-up, skit, spoof, squib, takeoff, travesty, wit.
satirical *adj.* biting, bitter, burlesque, caustic, cutting, cynical, derisive, Hudibrastic, iambic, incisive, ironical, irreverent, mocking, mordant, pungent, sarcastic, sardonic, satiric, taunting.
satirise *v.* abuse, burlesque, caricature, censure, criticise, deride, lampoon, make fun of, make sport of, mock, parody, Pasquil, Pasquin, pasquinade, pillory, ridicule, send up, squib,

take off, travesty.
antonyms acclaim, celebrate, honour.
satirist *n.* caricaturist, cartoonist, lampooner, lampoonist, mocker, parodist, pasquilant, pasquiler, pasquinader, ridiculer.
satisfaction *n.* achievement, amends, appeasing, assuaging, atonement, comfort, compensation, complacency, content, contentedness, contentment, conviction, damages, ease, enjoyment, fulfilment, fullness, gratification, guerdon, happiness, indemnification, justice, payment, pleasure, pride, quittance, recompense, redress, reimbursement, remuneration, reparation, repleteness, repletion, requital, resolution, restitution, reward, satiety, self-satisfaction, sense of achievement, settlement, vindication, well-being.
antonyms discontent, displeasure, dissatisfaction, frustration.
satisfactory *adj.* acceptable, adequate, all right, average, competent, fair, fit, OK, passable, proper, sufficient, suitable, tickety-boo, up to the mark.
antonyms inadequate, unacceptable, unsatisfactory.
satisfied *adj.* appeased, complacent, content, contented, convinced, full, happy, mollified, pacified, persuaded, pleased, positive, reassured, replete, sated, satiated, self-satisfied, smug, sure.
antonyms dissatisfied, hungry, unconvinced.
satisfy *v.* answer, appease, assuage, assure, atone, compensate, content, convince, delight, discharge, do, fill, fulfil, glut, gratify, guerdon, indemnify, indulge, meet, mollify, pacify, pay, persuade, placate, please, qualify, quench, quiet, reassure, recompense, reimburse, remunerate, replete, requite, reward, sate, satiate, serve, settle, slake, square up, suffice, surfeit.
antonyms disappoint, dissatisfy, fail, frustrate, thwart.
satisfying *adj.* cheering, convincing, cool, filling, fulfilling, gratifying, persuasive, pleasing, pleasurable, satisfactory.
antonyms dissatisfying, frustrating, thwarting, unsatisfactory.
saturate *v.* douse, drench, drouk, imbue, impregnate, infuse, permeate, ret, soak, souse, steep, suffuse, waterlog.
saturated *adj.* drenched, dripping, droukit, imbued, impregnated, permeated, soaked, soaking, sodden, sopping, soused, steeped, suffused, waterlogged, wringing.
saturnine *adj.* austere, dismal, dour, dull, gloomy, glum, grave, heavy, melancholy, mirthless, moody, morose, phlegmatic, severe, sombre, stern, taciturn, uncommunicative, withdrawn.
antonyms cheerful, jovial.
satyr *n.* faun, goat, lecher, Pan, philanderer, womaniser, wood-house, woodwose.
sauce *n.* archness, assurance, audacity, backchat, brass, brazenness, cheek, cheekiness, disrespect, disrespectfulness, flippancy, fresh-

ness, impertinence, impudence, insolence, irreverence, lip, malapertness, nerve, pertness, presumption, presumptuousness, rudeness, sass, sauciness.
antonyms politeness, respectfulness.
saucy *adj.* arch, audacious, cheeky, dashing, disdainful, disrespectful, flip, flippant, forward, fresh, gay, impertinent, impudent, insolent, irreverent, jaunty, lippy, malapert, natty, perky, pert, presumptuous, provocative, rakish, rude, sassy, sporty.
antonyms polite, respectful.
saunter *v.* amble, dacker, dally, dander, daunder, dawdle, linger, loiter, meander, mooch, mosey, perambulate, promenade, ramble, roam, rove, sally forth, stravaig, stroll, wander.
n. airing, amble, breather, constitutional, outing, perambulation, promenade, ramble, sally, stroll, turn, walk.
savage *adj.* barbarous, beastly, bestial, blistering, bloodthirsty, bloody, brutal, brutish, catamountain, cruel, devilish, diabolical, dog-eat-dog, fell, feral, ferocious, fierce, harsh, immane, inhuman, merciless, murderous, pitiless, primitive, ravening, rough, rude, rugged, ruthless, sadistic, sanguinary, uncivilised, uncultivated, undomesticated, uneducated, unenlightened, unsparing, untamed, untaught, vicious, wild.
antonyms benign, civilised, humane.
n. aboriginal, aborigine, ape, autochthon, barbarian, bear, beast, boor, brute, fiend, heathen, illiterate, indigene, lout, monster, native, oaf, philistine, primitive, roughneck, yahoo, yobbo.
v. attack, claw, hammer, lacerate, mangle, maul, pan, scarify, tear.
savagery *n.* barbarity, bestiality, bloodthirstiness, brutality, brutishness, cruelty, ferity, ferocity, fierceness, inhumanity, mercilessness, murderousness, pitilessness, primitiveness, roughness, ruthlessness, sadism, viciousness, wildness.
antonyms civilisation, civility, humanity.
savant *n.* authority, guru, intellectual, man of letters, master, mastermind, philosopher, pundit, rishi, sage, savante, scholar.
antonyms amateur, duffer, ignoramus.
save *v.* cache, collect, conserve, cut back, deliver, economise, free, gather, guard, hinder, hoard, hold, husband, keep, lay up, liberate, obviate, preserve, prevent, protect, put aside, put by, reclaim, recover, redeem, rescue, reserve, retain, retrench, safeguard, salt away, salvage, screen, shield, spare, squirrel, stash, store.
antonyms discard, spend, squander, waste.
saving *adj.* careful, compensatory, economical, extenuating, frugal, mitigating, qualifying, redeeming, soterial, sparing, thrifty.
n. bargain, conservation, cut, discount, economy, preservation, reclamation, redemption, reduction, rescue, retrenchment, salvage, salvation.

antonyms expense, loss, waste.

savings *n.* capital, fund, nest egg, reserve fund, reserves, resources, store.

saviour *n.* champion, defender, emancipator, guardian, knight-errant, liberator, messiah, preserver, protector, rescuer, salvation.
antonyms destroyer, enemy.

savoir-faire *n.* ability, accomplishment, address, assurance, capability, confidence, diplomacy, discretion, expertise, finesse, know-how, poise, tact, urbanity.
antonyms awkwardness, clumsiness, incompetence, inexperience.

savour *n.* excitement, fascination, flavour, interest, piquancy, relish, salt, sapor, smack, smell, spice, tang, taste, zest.
v. appreciate, dwell on, enjoy, gloat over, like, luxuriate in, partake, rehearse, relish, revel in.
antonyms shrink from, wince at.

savoury *adj.* agreeable, appetising, aromatic, dainty, decent, delectable, delicious, edifying, full-flavoured, gamy, good, gusty, honest, luscious, mouthwatering, palatable, piquant, reputable, respectable, rich, salubrious, scrumptious, spicy, tangy, tasty, toothsome, wholesome.
antonyms insipid, tasteless, unappetising.
n. appetiser, bonne bouche, canapé, hors d'oeuvre.

saw *n.* adage, aphorism, apophthegm, axiom, byword, commonplace, dictum, epigram, gnome, maxim, mot, proverb, saying.

say *v.* add, affirm, allege, announce, answer, assert, assume, bruit, claim, comment, communicate, conjecture, convey, declare, deliver, disclose, divulge, do, enunciate, estimate, express, guess, imagine, imply, intimate, judge, maintain, mention, opine, orate, perform, presume, pronounce, read, recite, reckon, rehearse, rejoin, remark, render, repeat, reply, report, respond, retort, reveal, rumour, signify, speak, state, suggest, surmise, tell, utter, voice.
n. authority, chance, clout, crack, go, influence, power, sway, turn, voice, vote, weight, word.

saying *n.* adage, aphorism, apophthegm, axiom, byword, dictum, gnome, maxim, mot, motto, precept, proverb, remnant, saw, slogan.

sayings *n.* analects, bon mots, dicta, gems, logia, mots, obiter dicta, quotations, quotes, remarks, remnants, tags, words of wisdom.

say-so *n.* affirmation, agreement, approval, assertion, asseveration, assurance, authorisation, authority, backing, consent, dictum, guarantee, OK, permission, ratification, sanction, word.

scald *v.* blister, burn, sear.

scale[1] *n.* calibration, compass, continuum, degree, degrees, extent, gamut, gradation, grading, graduation, hierarchy, ladder, measure, order, progression, proportion, range, ranking, ratio, reach, register, scope, sequence, series, spectrum, spread, steps.

v. adjust, level, move, proportion, prorate, regulate, shift.

scale[2] *n.* crust, encrustation, film, flake, furfur, lamella, lamina, layer, plate, scutellum, shield, squama, squamella, squamula, squamule.
v. clean, desquamate, exfoliate, flake, peel, scrape.

scale[3] *v.* ascend, clamber, climb, escalade, mount, scramble, shin up, surmount, swarm.

scaliness *n.* dandruff, flakiness, furfur, scabrousness, scurfiness, squamosity.

scaly *adj.* branny, desquamative, desquamatory, flaky, furfuraceous, furfurous, lepidote, leprose, leprous, scabby, scabrous, scurfy, squamose, squamous, squamulose.

scamp *n.* blighter, caitiff, devil, fripon, imp, knave, lorel, losel, mischief-maker, monkey, prankster, rascal, rogue, ruffian, scallywag, scapegrace, toe-rag, tyke, whippersnapper, wretch.

scamper *v.* chevy, dart, dash, fly, frisk, frolic, gambol, hasten, hurry, pelt, romp, run, rush, scoot, scurry, scuttle, skedaddle, sprint.

scan *v.* check, con, examine, glance through, investigate, pan, pan over, scrutinise, search, skim, survey, sweep.
n. check, examination, investigation, probe, review, screening, scrutiny, search, survey.

scandal *n.* abuse, aspersion, backbiting, calumniation, calumny, crime, defamation, detraction, dirt, discredit, disgrace, dishonour, embarrassment, enormity, evil, furore, gossip, gossiping, ignominy, infamy, muckraking, obloquy, odium, offence, opprobrium, outcry, outrage, reproach, rumours, shame, sin, slander, stigma, talk, tattle, traducement, uproar, Watergate, wrongdoing.

scandalise *v.* affront, appal, astound, disgust, dismay, horrify, nauseate, offend, outrage, repel, revolt, shock, sicken.

scandalmonger *n.* busybody, calumniator, defamer, gossip, gossip-monger, muck-raker, quidnunc, scandal-bearer, tabby, tabby-cat, tale-bearer, tattle, tattler, traducer.

scandalous *adj.* abominable, atrocious, calumnious, defamatory, disgraceful, disreputable, evil, exorbitant, extortionate, gamy, gossiping, immoderate, improper, infamous, libellous, monstrous, odious, opprobrious, outrageous, scurrilous, shameful, shocking, slanderous, unseemly, unspeakable, untrue.

scant *adj.* bare, deficient, hardly any, inadequate, insufficient, limited, little, little or no, minimal, sparse.
antonyms adequate, ample, sufficient.

scanty *adj.* bare, beggarly, deficient, exiguous, inadequate, insubstantial, insufficient, light, meagre, narrow, parsimonious, poor, restricted, scant, scrimp, scrimpy, short, shy, skimped, skimpy, slender, sparing, sparse, thin.
antonyms ample, plentiful, substantial.

scapegoat *n.* fall guy, patsy, victim, whipping-boy.

scapegrace *n*. blighter, good-for-nothing, imp, ne'er-do-well, rapscallion, rascal, reprobate, rogue, scallywag, scamp, toe-rag.

scar *n*. blemish, cicatrix, injury, lesion, mark, proud flesh, scar tissue, scarring, stigma, trauma, ulosis, wound.

v. brand, cicatrise, damage, disfigure, mark, stigmatise, traumatise.

scarce *adj*. deficient, few, infrequent, insufficient, lacking, rare, scanty, sparse, thin on the ground, uncommon, unusual, wanting.

antonyms common, copious, plentiful.

scarcely *adv*. barely, hardly, just and no more, not readily, not willingly, only just, scarce.

scarcity *n*. dearth, deficiency, infrequency, insufficiently, lack, niggardliness, paucity, poverty, rareness, rarity, scantiness, shortage, sparseness, uncommonness, want.

antonyms abundance, enough, glut, plenty, sufficiency.

scare *v*. affright, alarm, appal, daunt, dismay, frighten, gally, intimidate, panic, shock, startle, terrify, terrorise, unnerve.

antonym reassure.

n. agitation, alarm, alarm and despondency, alert, consternation, dismay, fright, hysteria, panic, shock, start, terror.

antonym reassurance.

scarecrow *n*. craw-bogle, craw-deil, crowboggart, crow-keeper, fright, gally-bagger, gally-crow, mess, sight, tatterdemalion.

scared *adj*. affrighted, affrightened, agitated, anxious, appalled, dismayed, fearful, frightened, nervous, panicky, panic-stricken, petrified, shaken, startled, terrified, worried.

antonyms confident, reassured.

scaremonger *n*. alarmist, Cassandra, doom and gloom merchant, doomsman, doomwatcher, jitterbug, pessimist, prophet of doom.

scarf *n*. babushka, boa, cravat, fichu, headscarf, headsquare, kerchief, muffler, neckerchief, necktie, shawl, stole, tawdry-lace.

scarper *v*. abscond, absquatulate, beat it, bolt, bunk off, clear off, decamp, depart, disappear, do a bunk, escape, flee, flit, go, hightail it, run away, run for it, scram, skedaddle, vamoose, vanish.

scary *adj*. alarming, anxious, bloodcurdling, chilling, creepy, disturbing, eldritch, frightening, hair-raising, hairy, horrendous, horrible, horrifying, intimidating, shocking, spine-chilling, spooky, terrifying, unnerving, upsetting, worrying.

scathing *adj*. acid, biting, bitter, brutal, caustic, critical, cutting, excoriating, harsh, lacerating, mordant, sarcastic, savage, scornful, searing, trenchant, unsparing, virulent, vitriolic, withering, wounding.

antonym complimentary.

scatter *v*. bestrew, break up, broadcast, diffuse, disband, disintegrate, disject, dispel, disperse, disseminate, dissipate, disunite, divide, fling, flurr, litter, propagate, separate, shower, sow, spatter, splutter, spread, sprinkle,

squander, strew.

antonyms collect, concentrate.

scatter-brained *adj*. bird-brained, careless, dizzy, empty-headed, feather-brained, flighty, forgetful, frivolous, giddy, inattentive, irresponsible, madcap, scatty, silly, slap-happy, thoughtless, undependable, unreliable.

antonyms careful, efficient, sensible, sober.

scattering *n*. break-up, diaspora, diffusion, disgregation, disjection, dispersal, dispersion, dissemination, dissipation, dissolution, few, fistful, handful, propagation, scatter, separation, smatter, smattering, sprinkling.

antonyms abundance, mass.

adj. disintegrative, dispersive, disseminative, dissipative, divisive.

antonym unifying.

scavenger *n*. Autolycus, cleaner, dustman, forager, garbage collector, raker, rummager, scavager, scrounger, street orderly, street-cleaner, sweeper.

scenario *n*. outline, plan, plot, projection, résumé, rundown, scheme, sequence, situation, skeleton, sketch, story line, summary, synopsis.

scene *n*. act, area, arena, backdrop, background, business, carry-on, chapter, circumstances, commotion, confrontation, display, disturbance, division, drama, environment, episode, exhibition, focus, fuss, incident, landscape, locale, locality, location, melodrama, milieu, mise en scène, outburst, pageant, panorama, part, performance, picture, place, position, prospect, representation, row, set, setting, show, sight, site, situation, spectacle, spot, stage, tableau, tantrum, to-do, upset, view, vista, whereabouts, world.

scenery *n*. backdrop, background, décor, flats, landscape, mise en scène, outlook, panorama, set, setting, sight, surroundings, terrain, tormentors, view, vista.

scenic *adj*. awe-inspiring, beautiful, breathtaking, grand, impressive, magnificent, panoramic, picturesque, pretty, spectacular, striking, stupendous.

antonyms dreary, dull, unspectacular.

scent *n*. aroma, bouquet, fragrance, fumet, odour, perfume, redolence, smell, spoor, trace, track, trail, waft, whiff.

antonym stink.

v. detect, discern, nose, nose out, perceive, recognise, sense, smell, sniff, sniff out.

scented *adj*. aromatic, fragrant, odoriferous, perfumed, redolent, sweet-smelling.

antonyms malodorous, noisome, stinking.

sceptic *n*. agnostic, atheist, cynic, disbeliever, doubter, doubting Thomas, nullifidian, Pyrrhonist, questioner, questionist, rationalist, scoffer, unbeliever.

antonym believer.

sceptical *adj*. cynical, disbelieving, distrustful, doubtful, doubting, dubious, hesitating, incredulous, mistrustful, pessimistic, questioning, quizzical, scoffing, suspicious, unbelieving, unconvinced, unpersuaded, untrustful.

antonyms convinced, naïve, trusting.

scepticism *n.* agnosticism, atheism, cynicism, disbelief, distrust, doubt, incredulity, pessimism, Pyrrhonism, rationalism, suspicion, unbelief, Voltairianism, Voltairism.
antonyms belief, faith, naïvety.

schedule *n.* agenda, calendar, catalogue, diary, form, inventory, itinerary, list, plan, programme, scheme, scroll, table, timetable.
v. appoint, arrange, book, list, organise, plan, programme, slot, table, time.

schematic *adj.* diagrammatic, diagrammatical, graphic, illustrative, representational, simplified, simplistic, symbolic.

scheme *n.* arrangement, blueprint, chart, codification, configuration, conformation, conspiracy, contrivance, dart, design, device, diagram, disposition, dodge, draft, game, idea, intrigue, lay-out, machinations, manoeuvre, method, outline, pattern, plan, plot, ploy, procedure, programme, project, proposal, proposition, racket, ruse, schedule, schema, shape, shift, stratagem, strategy, subterfuge, suggestion, system, tactics, theory.
v. collude, conspire, contrive, design, devise, frame, imagine, intrigue, machinate, manipulate, manoeuvre, mastermind, plan, plot, project, pull strings, pull wires, work out.

schemer *n.* conniver, deceiver, éminence grise, fox, intriguer, Machiavelli, Machiavellian, machinator, mastermind, plotter, politician, wangler, wheeler-dealer, wire-puller.

scheming *adj.* artful, calculating, conniving, crafty, cunning, deceitful, designing, devious, duplicitous, foxy, insidious, Machiavellian, slippery, sly, tricky, underhand, unscrupulous, wily.
antonyms artless, honest, open, transparent.

schism *n.* breach, break, cleavage, discord, disunion, division, estrangement, faction, quarrel, rift, rupture, sect, separation, severance, splinter group, splintering, split, sunderance.

scholar *n.* academe, academic, authority, bookman, bookworm, egghead, intellectual, man of letters, pupil, savant, scholastic, schoolboy, schoolchild, schoolgirl, schoolman, student.
antonyms dullard, dunce, ignoramus, illiterate, philistine.

scholarly *adj.* academic, analytical, bookish, clerk-like, clerkly, conscientious, critical, erudite, intellectual, knowledgeable, learned, lettered, scholastic, scientific, studious, well-read, wissenschaftlich.
antonyms illiterate, unscholarly.

scholarship[1] *n.* attainments, book-learning, education, erudition, insight, knowledge, learnedness, learning, lore, scholarliness, wisdom, Wissenschaft.

scholarship[2] *n.* award, bursary, endowment, exhibition, fellowship, grant.

scholastic *adj.* academic, analytical, bookish, learned, lettered, literary, pedagogic, pedantic, precise, scholarly, subtle.

school *n.* academy, adherents, alma mater, circle, class, clique, college, creed, denomination, department, devotees, disciples, discipline, doctrine, dogma, externat, faction, faculty, faith, followers, following, group, gymnasium, institute, institution, lycée, outlook, pedagoguery, persuasion, pupils, sect, seminary, set, students, teaching, view, votaries.
v. coach, discipline, drill, educate, habituate, harden, indoctrinate, instruct, inure, prepare, prime, train, tutor, verse.

schooling *n.* book-learning, booklore, coaching, drill, education, grounding, guidance, inculcation, indoctrination, instruction, preparation, schoolcraft, teaching, training, tuition.

schoolteacher *n.* dominie, educator, instructor, master, mistress, pedagogue, school-dame, school-ma'am, schoolmarm, schoolmaster, schoolmistress, teacher, usher.

science *n.* art, discipline, knowledge, ology, proficiency, skill, specialisation, technique, technology, Wissenschaft.

scientific *adj.* accurate, analytical, controlled, exact, mathematical, methodical, precise, scholarly, systematic, thorough, wissenschaftlich.

scintillate *v.* blaze, coruscate, flash, gleam, glint, glisten, glitter, shine, spark, sparkle, twinkle, wink.

scintillating *adj.* animated, blazing, blinding, bright, brilliant, coruscant, coruscating, dazzling, ebullient, exciting, flashing, glittering, lively, shining, sparkling, stimulating, vivacious, winking, witty.
antonym dull.

scion *n.* branch, child, descendant, graft, heir, imp, offshoot, offspring, shoot, slip, sprig, sprout, successor, twig.

scoff[1] *v.* belittle, deride, despise, fleer, flout, geck, gibe, jeer, knock, mock, poke fun, pooh-pooh, rail, revile, rib, ridicule, scorn, sneer, taunt, twit.
antonyms compliment, flatter, praise.

scoff[2] *v.* bolt, consume, cram, devour, fill one's face, gobble, gulp, guzzle, pig, put away, shift, wolf.
antonym abstain.
n. chow, comestibles, commons, eatables, eats, edibles, fare, feed, fodder, food, grub, meal, nosh, nosh-up, provisions, rations, scran, tuck, victuals.

scoffing *adj.* cynical, fiendish, Mephistophelian, sarcastic.

scold *v.* admonish, bawl out, berate, blame, castigate, censure, chide, find fault with, flyte, jaw, lecture, nag, rate, rebuke, remonstrate, reprimand, reproach, reprove, take to task, tell off, tick off, upbraid, vituperate, wig.
antonyms commend, praise.
n. battle-axe, beldam, fishwife, Fury, harridan, nag, shrew, termagant, virago, vixen, Xanthippe.

scolding *n.* a piece of one's mind, castigation,

dirdum, dressing-down, earful, flyting, jaw, jawbation, jawing, jobation, lecture, rebuke, reprimand, reproof, row, siserary, talking-to, telling-off, throughgoing, ticking-off, tongue-lashing, upbraiding, wigging.
antonym commendation.

scoop[1] *n.* backhoe, bail, bailer, bucket, dipper, lade, ladle, spoon.
v. bail, dig, dip, empty, excavate, gather, gouge, hollow, ladle, lift, pick up, remove, scrape, shovel, sweep.

scoop[2] *n.* coup, exclusive, exposé, inside story, latest, low-down, revelation, sensation.

scoot *v.* beat it, bolt, bowl, career, dart, dash, hurry, run, scamper, scarper, scud, scurry, scuttle, shoot, skedaddle, sprint, tootle, vamoose, zip.

scope *n.* ambit, application, area, breadth, capacity, compass, competence, confines, coverage, elbow-room, extent, freedom, latitude, liberty, opportunity, orbit, outlook, purview, range, reach, remit, room, space, span, sphere, terms of reference, tessitura.

scorch *v.* blacken, blister, burn, char, parch, roast, scald, sear, shrivel, singe, sizzle, torrefy, wither.

scorched *adj.* arid, baked, blackened, blistered, burnt, charred, cracked, parched, sear, seared, shrivelled, torrid, withered.

scorching *adj.* baking, blistering, boiling, broiling, burning, fiery, flaming, parching, red-hot, roasting, scalding, searing, sizzling, sweltering, torrid, tropical, withering.

score *n.* a bone to pick, account, amount, basis, bill, cause, charge, debt, due, gash, grade, gravamen, grievance, ground, grounds, grudge, injury, injustice, line, mark, notch, obligation, outcome, points, reason, reckoning, record, result, scratch, sum total, tab, tally, total, wrong.
v. achieve, adapt, amass, arrange, attain, be one up, benefit, chalk up, count, cut, deface, earn, engrave, furrow, gain, gouge, grave, graze, groove, hatch, have the advantage, have the edge, impress, incise, indent, knock up, make, make a hit, mark, nick, notch, notch up, orchestrate, profit, realise, record, register, scrape, scratch, set, slash, tally, total, win.
score out cancel, cross out, delete, efface, erase, expunge, obliterate, remove, strike out.
antonyms reinstate, restore.

scores *n.* crowds, droves, hosts, hundreds, legions, lots, masses, millions, multitudes, myriads, shoals, swarms.

scorn *n.* contempt, contemptuousness, contumely, derision, despite, disdain, disgust, dismissiveness, disparagement, geck, mockery, sarcasm, scornfulness, slight, sneer.
antonyms admiration, respect.
v. contemn, deride, despise, disdain, dismiss, flout, hold in contempt, laugh at, laugh in the face of, look down on, misprise, pooh-pooh, refuse, reject, scoff at, slight, sneer at, spurn.

antonyms admire, respect.

scornful *adj.* arrogant, contemptuous, contumelious, defiant, derisive, disdainful, dismissive, disparaging, haughty, insulting, jeering, mocking, sarcastic, sardonic, scathing, scoffing, slighting, sneering, supercilious, withering.
antonyms admiring, complimentary, respectful.

scornfully *adv.* arrogantly, contemptuously, derisively, disdainfully, dismissively, disparagingly, haughtily, scathingly, slightingly, sneeringly, superciliously, witheringly.
antonyms admiringly, respectfully.

scot-free *adj.* clear, ininjured, safe, scatheless, undamaged, unharmed, unhurt, unpunished, unrebuked, unreprimanded, unreproached, unscathed, without a scratch.

scoundrel *n.* blackguard, blighter, bounder, caitiff, cheat, cur, dastard, good-for-nothing, heel, hound, knave, louse, miscreant, ne'er-do-well, picaroon, rascal, rat, reprobate, rogue, rotter, ruffian, scab, scallywag, scamp, scapegrace, stinker, swine, vagabond, villain.

scour[1] *v.* abrade, buff, burnish, clean, cleanse, flush, furbish, polish, purge, rub, scrape, scrub, wash, whiten.

scour[2] *v.* beat, comb, drag, forage, go over, hunt, rake, ransack, search, turn upside-down.

scourge *n.* affliction, bane, cat, cat-o'-nine-tails, curse, evil, flagellum, infliction, knout, lash, menace, misfortune, penalty, pest, pestilence, plague, punishment, strap, switch, terror, thong, torment, visitation, whip.
antonyms benefit, blessing, boon, godsend.
v. afflict, beat, belt, cane, castigate, chastise, curse, devastate, discipline, excoriate, flagellate, flail, flog, harass, horsewhip, lambast, lash, lather, leather, plague, punish, tan, terrorise, thrash, torment, trounce, verberate, visit, wallop, whale, whip.

scout *v.* case, check out, do a recce, explore, hunt, investigate, look, observe, pickeer, probe, reconnoitre, search, seek, snoop, spy, spy out, survey, track, watch.
n. emissary, escort, lookout, outrider, pickeerer, precursor, reconnoitrer, spy, vanguard.

scowl *v.* frown, glare, glower, grimace, lower.
n. frown, glare, glower, grimace, moue.
antonyms beam, grin, smile.

scrabble *v.* clamber, claw, dig, grope, grub, paw, root, scramble, scrape, scratch.

scraggy *adj.* angular, bony, emaciated, gangling, gaunt, lank, lanky, lean, meagre, rawboned, scranny, scrawny, skinny, spare, undernourished, wasted.
antonyms plump, rounded, sleek.

scram *v.* beat it, bolt, clear off, clear out, depart, disappear, do a bunk, flee, get lost, go away, leave, quit, scarper, scoot, shove off, skedaddle, take to one's heels, vamoose.

scramble *v.* clamber, climb, contend, crawl, hasten, jostle, jumble, push, run, rush, scale, scrabble, shuffle, sprawl, strive, struggle, swarm, vie.

n. climb, commotion, competition, confusion, contention, free-for-all, hustle, mêlée, muddle, race, rat race, rivalry, rush, strife, struggle, trek, trial, tussle.

scrap[1] *n.* atom, bit, bite, crumb, fraction, fragment, grain, iota, junk, mite, modicum, morsel, mouthful, part, particle, piece, portion, remnant, shard, shred, sliver, snap, snatch, snippet, trace, vestige, waste, whit.

v. abandon, axe, break up, cancel, chuck, demolish, discard, ditch, drop, jettison, junk, shed, throw out, write off.

antonyms reinstate, restore, resume.

scrap[2] *n.* argument, bagarre, barney, battle, brawl, disagreement, dispute, dust-up, fight, quarrel, row, ruckus, ruction, rumpus, scuffle, set-to, shindy, squabble, tiff, wrangle.

antonyms agreement, peace.

v. argue, argufy, bicker, clash, fall out, fight, spat, squabble, wrangle.

antonym agree.

scrape *v.* abrade, bark, claw, clean, erase, file, grate, graze, grind, pinch, rasp, remove, rub, save, scour, scrabble, scratch, screech, scrimp, scuff, skimp, skin, squeak, stint.

n. abrasion, difficulty, dilemma, distress, fix, graze, mess, pickle, plight, predicament, pretty kettle of fish, rub, scratch, scuff, shave, spot, trouble.

scrappy *adj.* bitty, disjointed, fragmentary, incomplete, perfunctory, piecemeal, sketchy, slapdash, slipshod, superficial.

antonyms complete, finished.

scraps *n.* bits, leavings, leftovers, remains, scrapings.

scratch *v.* annul, cancel, claw, curry, cut, damage, delete, eliminate, erase, etch, grate, graze, incise, lacerate, mark, race, retire, rub, scarify, score, scrab, scrabble, scrape, withdraw.

n. blemish, claw mark, gash, graze, laceration, mark, race, scrape, streak.

adj. haphazard, impromptu, improvised, rough, rough-and-ready, unrehearsed.

antonym polished.

scrawl *n.* cacography, scrabble, scratch, scribble, squiggle, writing.

scrawny *adj.* angular, bony, emaciated, gaunt, lanky, lean, rawboned, scraggy, skeletal, skinny, thin, underfed, under-nourished.

antonym plump.

scream[1] *v.* bawl, clash, cry, holler, jar, roar, screak, screech, shriek, shrill, squeal, wail, yell, yelp, yowl.

n. howl, outcry, roar, screak, screech, shriek, squeal, wail, yell, yelp, yowl.

antonym whisper.

scream[2] *n.* card, caution, character, comedian, comic, cure, hoot, joker, laugh, riot, sensation, wit.

antonym bore.

screech *v.* cry, screak, scream, shriek, squawk, squeal, ululate, yelp.

antonym whisper.

screen *v.* broadcast, cloak, conceal, cover, cull, defend, evaluate, examine, filter, gauge, grade, guard, hide, mask, present, process, protect, riddle, safeguard, scan, shade, shelter, shield, show, shroud, sieve, sift, sort, veil, vet.

antonyms abat-jour, awning, canopy, cloak, concealment, cover, divider, guard, hallan, hedge, hoarding, mantle, mesh, net, partition, shade, shelter, shield, shroud, uncover.

screw *v.* adjust, bleed, cheat, coerce, compress, constrain, contort, contract, crumple, distort, extort, extract, fasten, force, oppress, pressurise, pucker, squeeze, tighten, turn, twist, wind, wrest, wring, wrinkle.

screw up botch, bungle, close, contort, contract, crumple, disrupt, distort, knot, louse up, make a hash of, mess up, mishandle, mismanage, pucker, queer, spoil, tighten, wrinkle.

antonyms manage, unscrew.

screwy *adj.* batty, cracked, crackers, crazy, daft, dotty, eccentric, mad, nutty, odd, queer, round the bend, round the twist, weird.

antonym sane.

scribble *v.* dash off, doodle, jot, pen, scratch, scrawl, write.

scribbler *n.* hack, ink-slinger, paper-stainer, pen-driver, penny-a-liner, pen-pusher, potboiler, quill-driver, quillman, writer.

scribe *n.* amanuensis, clerk, copyist, hierographer, notary, penman, scrivener, secretary, tabellion, writer.

scrimmage *n.* affray, bovver, brawl, disturbance, dust-up, fight, fray, free-for-all, mêlée, riot, row, scrap, scuffle, set-to, shindy, skirmish, squabble, stramash, struggle.

antonym calmness.

scrimp *v.* curtail, economise, limit, pinch, reduce, restrict, save, scrape, shorten, skimp, stint.

antonym spend.

script *n.* book, calligraphy, cheirography, copy, hand, handwriting, letters, libretto, lines, longhand, manuscript, penmanship, text, words, writing.

scripture *n.* Analects, Bhagavad Gita, Granth, Holy Bible, Holy Scripture, Holy Writ, Koran, New Testament, Old Testament, Pentateuch, shaster, shastra, sutra(s), the Bible, the Good Book, the Gospels, the Scriptures, the Word, the Word of God, Tripitaka, Upanishad(s), Veda(s), Zend-Avesta.

scroll *n.* inventory, list, parchment, roll, volume, volute.

Scrooge *n.* cheapskate, meanie, miser, money-grubber, niggard, penny-pincher, skinflint, tightwad.

antonym spendthrift.

scrounge *v.* beg, bludge, bum, cadge, freeload, purloin, sponge, wheedle.

scrounger *n.* bludger, bum, cadger, freeloader, parasite, sponger.

scrub *v.* abandon, abolish, cancel, clean,

cleanse, delete, discontinue, ditch, drop, forget, give up, rub, scour.

scruff *n.* draggle-tail, ragamuffin, ragbag, scarecrow, sloven, slut, tatterdemalion, tramp.

scruffy *adj.* disreputable, dog-eared, draggle-tailed, frowzy, grotty, ill-groomed, mangy, messy, ragged, run-down, scrubby, seedy, shabby, slatternly, slovenly, sluttish, squalid, tattered, ungroomed, unkempt, untidy.
antonyms tidy, well-dressed.

scrumptious *adj.* appetising, delectable, delicious, delightful, exquisite, luscious, magnificent, moreish, mouth-watering, succulent, yummy.
antonym unappetising.

scrunch *v.* champ, chew, crumple, crunch, crush, grate, grind, mash, squash.

scruple *v.* balk at, demur at, falter, hesitate, object to, recoil from, shrink from, stick at, vacillate, waver.
n. caution, compunction, difficulty, doubt, hesitation, misgiving, pang, perplexity, qualm, reluctance, squeamishness, uneasiness.

scrupulous *adj.* careful, conscientious, conscionable, exact, fastidious, honourable, meticulous, minute, moral, nice, painstaking, precise, principled, punctilious, rigorous, strict, upright.
antonym careless.

scrutinise *v.* analyse, dissect, examine, explore, give a once-over, inspect, investigate, peruse, probe, scan, search, sift, study.

scrutiny *n.* analysis, docimasy, examination, exploration, inquiry, inspection, investigation, once-over, perusal, search, sifting, study.

scud *v.* blow, dart, fly, hasten, race, sail, shoot, skim, speed.

scuff *v.* abrade, brush, drag, graze, rub, scratch, shuffle, skin.

scuffle *v.* clash, contend, fight, grapple, hocus, jostle, struggle, tussle.
n. affray, bagarre, barney, brawl, commotion, disturbance, dog-fight, fight, fray, ruck, ruckus, ruction, rumpus, scrap, set-to, tussle.

sculpt *v.* carve, chisel, cut, fashion, form, hew, model, mould, represent, sculp, sculpture, shape.

scum *n.* algae, canaille, crust, dregs, dross, film, froth, impurities, offscourings, offscum, pellicle, rabble, rag-tag and bobtail, riff-raff, rubbish, scruff, spume, sullage, trash, vomit.

scupper *v.* defeat, demolish, destroy, disable, overthrow, overwhelm, put a spanner in the works, ruin, torpedo, wreck.
antonyms advance, promote.

scurf *n.* dandruff, flakiness, furfur, scabrousness, scaliness.

scurfy *adj.* furfuraceous, furfurous, lepidote, leprose, leprous, scaberulous, scabrid, scabrous, scaly.

scurrility *n.* abuse, abusiveness, billingsgate, coarseness, grossness, indecency, invective, nastiness, obloquy, obscenity, offensiveness, rudeness, scurrilousness, vituperation, vulgarity.
antonym politeness.

scurrilous *adj.* abusive, coarse, defamatory, Fescennial, foul, foul-mouthed, gross, indecent, insulting, low, nasty, obscene, offensive, Rabelaisian, ribald, rude, salacious, scabrous, scandalous, slanderous, vituperative, vulgar.
antonym polite.

scurry *v.* dart, dash, fly, hurry, race, scamper, scoot, scud, scuttle, skedaddle, skelter, skim, sprint, trot, whisk.
antonym stroll.
n. flurry, hustle and bustle, scampering, whirl.
antonym calm.

scurvy *adj.* abject, bad, base, caddish, contemptible, despicable, dirty, dishonourable, ignoble, low, low-down, mean, pitiful, rotten, scabby, shabby, sorry, vile, worthless.
antonyms good, honourable.

scuttle *v.* bustle, hare, hasten, hurry, run, rush, scamper, scoot, scramble, scud, scurry, scutter, trot.
antonym stroll.

sea *n.* abundance, briny, deep, ditch, drink, expanse, main, mass, multitude, ocean, plethora, profound, profusion, waves.
adj. aquatic, marine, maritime, naval, ocean, ocean-going, oceanic, pelagic, salt, saltwater, sea-going.
antonyms air, land.

seafaring *adj.* marine, maritime, nautical, naval, oceanic, sailing.
antonym land.

seal *v.* assure, attest, authenticate, bung, clinch, close, conclude, confirm, consummate, cork, enclose, establish, fasten, finalise, plug, ratify, secure, settle, shake hands on, shut, stamp, stop, stopper, validate, waterproof.
antonym unseal.
n. assurance, attestation, authentication, bulla, confirmation, imprimatur, insignia, notification, ratification, sigil, signet, stamp.
seal off block up, close off, cut off, fence off, isolate, quarantine, segregate, shut off.
antonym open up.

sealed *adj.* closed, corked, hermetic, plugged, shut.
antonym unsealed.

seam *n.* closure, crack, furrow, joint, layer, line, lode, ridge, scar, stratum, suture, vein, wrinkle.

seaman *n.* AB, deck-hand, hand, Jack tar, lascar, matelot, matlo(w), sailor, seacunny, sea-dog, seafarer, steersman, tar.

seamy *adj.* corrupt, dark, degraded, disagreeable, disreputable, low, nasty, rough, sleazy, sordid, squalid, unpleasant, unwholesome.
antonyms pleasant, respectable.

sear *v.* blight, brand, brown, burn, cauterise, desiccate, dry up, harden, scorch, seal, shrivel, sizzle, wilt, wither.

search *v.* check, comb, examine, explore, ferret, frisk, inquire, inspect, investigate, jerque, look, probe, pry, quest, ransack, rifle, rummage, scour, scrutinise, sift, test.

n. examination, exploration, going-over, hunt, inquiry, inspection, investigation, perquisition, perscrutation, pursuit, quest, researches, rummage, scrutiny, zetetic.

searching *adj.* close, intent, keen, minute, penetrating, piercing, probing, quizzical, severe, sharp, thorough, zetetic.

antonyms superficial, vague.

seasickness *n.* mal de mer, nausea, queasiness.

season *n.* division, interval, period, span, spell, term, time.

v. acclimatise, accustom, anneal, colour, condiment, condition, discipline, enliven, flavour, habituate, harden, imbue, inure, lace, leaven, mature, mitigate, moderate, prepare, qualify, salt, spice, temper, toughen, train.

seasonable *adj.* appropriate, convenient, fit, opportune, providential, suitable, timely, timeous, welcome, well-timed.

antonym unseasonable.

seasoned *adj.* acclimatised, battle-scarred, experienced, hardened, long-serving, mature, old, practised, time-served, veteran, weathered, well-versed.

antonym novice.

seasoning *n.* condiment, dressing, flavouring, pepper, relish, salt, sauce, spice.

seat *n.* abode, axis, base, bed, bench, bottom, capital, cause, centre, chair, constituency, cradle, footing, foundation, ground, groundwork, headquarters, heart, house, hub, incumbency, location, mansion, membership, pew, place, residence, seat-stick, sedes, settle, shooting-stick, site, situation, source, stall, station, stool, throne.

v. accommodate, assign, contain, deposit, fit, fix, hold, install, locate, place, set, settle, sit, slot, take.

seating *n.* accommodation, chairs, gradin(e), places, room, seats.

seaweed *n.* gulf-weed, kelp, laver, laverbread, sargasso, sea-moss, sea-tang, sea-tangle, sea-ware, sea-wrack, varec(h), wrack.

secede *v.* apostatise, disaffiliate, leave, quit, resign, retire, separate, split off, withdraw.

antonyms join, unite with.

secession *n.* apostasy, break, defection, disaffiliation, schism, schismatics, seceders, seceding, split, withdrawal.

antonyms amalgamation, unification.

secluded *adj.* claustral, cloistered, cloistral, cut off, isolated, lonely, out-of-the-way, private, reclusive, remote, retired, sequestered, sheltered, solitary, umbratile, umbratilous, unfrequented.

antonyms busy, public.

seclusion *n.* concealment, hiding, isolation, privacy, purdah, recluseness, remoteness, retirement, retreat, shelter, solitude.

second[1] *adj.* additional, alternate, alternative, double, duplicate, extra, following, further, inferior, lesser, lower, next, other, repeated,

reproduction, secondary, subordinate, subsequent, succeeding, supplementary, supporting, twin.

n. assistant, backer, helper, supporter.

v. advance, agree with, aid, approve, assist, back, encourage, endorse, forward, further, help, promote, support.

second coming parousia.

second[2] *n.* instant, jiff, jiffy, minute, mo, moment, sec, tick, trice, twinkling.

secondary *adj.* alternate, auxiliary, back-up, consequential, contingent, derivative, derived, extra, indirect, inferior, lesser, lower, minor, relief, reserve, resultant, resulting, second, second-hand, second-rate, spare, subordinate, subsidiary, supporting, unimportant.

antonym primary.

second-class *adj.* déclassé(e), indifferent, inferior, mediocre, second-best, second-rate, undistinguished, uninspired, uninspiring.

second-hand *adj.* borrowed, derivative, hand-me-down, old, plagiarised, used, vicarious, worn.

antonym new.

second-rate *adj.* cheap, cheap and nasty, grotty, inferior, low-grade, mediocre, poor, rubbishy, shoddy, substandard, tacky, tawdry, undistinguished, uninspired, uninspiring.

antonym first-rate.

secrecy *n.* clandestineness, concealment, confidence, confidentiality, covertness, furtiveness, hugger-mugger, mystery, privacy, retirement, seclusion, secretiveness, silence, solitude, stealth, stealthiness, surreptitiousness.

antonym openness.

secret *adj.* abstruse, arcane, back-door, backstairs, cabbalistic(al), camouflaged, clandestine, classified, cloak-and-dagger, close, closet, concealed, conspiratorial, covered, covert, cryptic, deep, discreet, disguised, esoteric, furtive, hidden, hole-and-corner, hush-hush, inly, mysterious, occult, out-of-the-way, private, privy, recondite, reticent, retired, secluded, secretive, sensitive, shrouded, sly, stealthy, tête-à-tête, undercover, underground, underhand, under-the-counter, undisclosed, unfrequented, unknown, unpublished, unrevealed, unseen.

antonyms open, public.

n. arcanum, code, confidence, enigma, formula, key, mystery, recipe.

secretary *n.* assistant, clerk, famulus, girl Friday, PA, person Friday, personal assistant, stenographer, typist.

secrete[1] *v.* appropriate, bury, cache, conceal, cover, disguise, harbour, hide, screen, secure, shroud, stash away, stow, veil.

antonym reveal.

secrete[2] *v.* emanate, emit, extravasate, extrude, exude, osmose, secern, separate.

secretion *n.* discharge, emission, excretion, extravasation, exudation, osmosis, secernment.

secretive *adj.* cagey, close, close-lipped, close-mouthed, cryptic, deep, enigmatic, quiet, reserved, reticent, tight-lipped, uncommunicative, unforthcoming, withdrawn.
antonyms communicative, open.

secretly *adv.* clandestinely, confidentially, covertly, furtively, in camera, in confidence, in private, in secret, on the q.t., on the quiet, on the sly, privately, privily, quietly, stealthily, surreptitiously, unobserved.
antonym openly.

sect *n.* camp, denomination, division, faction, group, party, school, splinter group, subdivision, wing.

sectarian *adj.* bigoted, clannish, cliquish, doctrinaire, dogmatic, exclusive, factional, fanatic, fanatical, insular, limited, narrow, narrow-minded, parochial, partisan, rigid, ultra.
antonyms broad-minded, cosmopolitan, non-sectarian.
n. adherent, bigot, disciple, dogmatist, extremist, fanatic, fractionalist, partisan, zealot.

section *n.* area, article, component, cross section, department, district, division, fraction, fractionlet, fragment, instalment, part, passage, piece, portion, region, sample, sector, segment, slice, subdivision, wing, zone.
antonym whole.

sectional *adj.* class, divided, exclusive, factional, local, localised, partial, racial, regional, sectarian, separate, separatist.
antonyms general, universal.

sector *n.* area, category, district, division, part, quarter, region, section, stratum, subdivision, zone.
antonym whole.

secular *adj.* civil, laic, laical, lay, non-religious, profane, state, temporal, worldly.
antonym religious.

secularise *v.* deconsecrate.

secure *adj.* absolute, assured, certain, conclusive, confident, definite, dependable, easy, fast, fastened, firm, fixed, fortified, immovable, immune, impregnable, on velvet, over-confident, protected, reassured, reliable, safe, sheltered, shielded, solid, stable, steadfast, steady, sure, tight, unassailable, undamaged, unharmed, well-founded.
antonyms insecure, uncertain.
v. acquire, assure, attach, batten down, bolt, chain, ensure, fasten, fix, gain, get, get hold of, guarantee, insure, land, lash, lock, lock up, moor, nail, obtain, padlock, procure, rivet, seize.
antonyms lose, unfasten.

security *n.* assurance, asylum, care, certainty, collateral, confidence, conviction, cover, custody, defence, gage, guarantee, guards, hostage, immunity, insurance, pawn, pledge, positiveness, precautions, preservation, protection, refuge, reliance, retreat, safeguards, safe-keeping, safety, sanctuary, sureness, surety, surveillance, warranty.

antonym insecurity.

sedate *adj.* calm, collected, composed, cool, decorous, deliberate, demure, dignified, douce, earnest, grave, imperturbable, middle-aged, placed, proper, quiet, seemly, serene, serious, slow-moving, sober, solemn, staid, tranquil, unflappable, unruffled.
antonyms flippant, hasty, undignified.

sedative *adj.* allaying, anodyne, calmative, calming, depressant, lenitive, relaxing, soothing, soporific, tranquillising.
antonym rousing.
n. anodyne, calmative, downer, narcotic, opiate, quietive, sedative, sleeping-pill, tranquilliser.

sedentary *adj.* desk, desk-bound, inactive, motionless, seated, sedent, sitting, stationary, still, torpid, unmoving.
antonym active.

sediment *n.* deposit, draff, dregs, faeces, fecula, grounds, lees, precipitate, residium, settlings, warp.

sedition *n.* agitation, disloyalty, rabble-rousing, ruckus, rumpus, subversion, treason, tumult.
antonyms calm, loyalty.

seditious *adj.* disloyal, dissident, insubordinate, mutinous, rebellious, refractory, revolutionary, subversive, traitorous.
antonyms calm, loyal.

seduce *v.* allure, attract, beguile, betray, bewitch, corrupt, debauch, deceive, decoy, deflower, deprave, dishonour, ensnare, entice, inveigle, lure, mislead, ruin, tempt.

seducer *n.* cad, Casanova, charmer, deceiver, Don Juan, flirt, gay deceiver, goat, libertine, Lothario, philanderer, wolf, womaniser.

seduction *n.* allure, allurement, come-on, corruption, defloration, enticement, lure, ruin, seducement, snare, temptation.

seductive *adj.* alluring, attractive, beguiling, bewitching, captivating, come-hither, come-on, enticing, flirtatious, honeyed, inviting, irresistible, provocative, ravishing, seducing, sexy, siren, specious, tempting.
antonym unattractive.

seductress *n.* Circe, femme fatale, Lorelei, siren, temptress, vamp.

sedulous *adj.* assiduous, busy, conscientious, constant, determined, diligent, industrious, laborious, painstaking, persevering, persistent, resolved, tireless, unflagging, unremitting, untiring.
antonym half-hearted.

see *v.* accompany, anticipate, appreciate, ascertain, attend, behold, comprehend, consider, consult, court, date, decide, deem, deliberate, descry, determine, discern, discover, distinguish, divine, encounter, ensure, envisage, escort, espy, experience, fathom, feel, follow, foresee, foretell, get, glimpse, grasp, guarantee, heed, identify, imagine, interview, investigate, judge, know, lead, learn, look, make out, mark, meet, mind, note, notice, observe, perceive, picture, realise, receive, recognise, reflect, regard, show, sight, spot, take, understand, usher, view, visit, visualise, walk, witness.

see eye to eye accord, agree, coincide, concur, get along, get on, harmonise, jibe, speak the same language, subscribe.
antonym disagree.

see red blow one's top, blow up, boil, go mad, go off one's head, lose one's rag, lose one's temper.

see to arrange, attend to, deal with, do, fix, look after, manage, organise, repair, sort out, take care of, take charge of.

seed *n.* beginning, children, descendants, egg, embryo, germ, grain, heirs, inkling, issue, kernel, nucleus, offspring, ovule, ovum, pip, progeny, quiverful, race, scions, semen, source, spawn, sperm, spore, start, successors, suspicion.
antonym ancestors.

seedy *adj.* ailing, crummy, decaying, dilapidated, faded, grotty, grubby, ill, mangy, manky, off-colour, old, peelie-wally, poorly, run-down, scruffy, shabby, sickly, sleazy, slovenly, squalid, tatty, unkempt, unwell, worn.
antonyms posh, well.

seek *v.* aim, ask, aspire to, attempt, beg, busk, desire, endeavour, entreat, essay, follow, hunt, inquire, invite, petition, pursue, request, solicit, strive, try, want.

seeker *n.* chela, disciple, inquirer, novice, searcher, student, zetetic.

seem *v.* appear, look, look like, pretend, sound like.

seeming *adj.* apparent, appearing, illusory, ostensible, outward, pseudo, quasi-, specious, surface.
antonym real.

seemingly *adv.* allegedly, apparently, as far as one can see, on the face of it, on the surface, ostensibly, outwardly, superficially.
antonym really.

seemly *adj.* appropriate, attractive, becoming, befitting, comely, comme il faut, decent, decorous, fit, fitting, handsome, maidenly, meet, nice, proper, suitable, suited.
antonym unseemly.

seep *v.* exude, leak, ooze, osmose, percolate, permeate, soak, trickle, weep, well.

seepage *n.* exudation, leak, leakage, oozing, osmosis, percolation.

seer *n.* augur, prophet, sibyl, soothsayer, spaeman, spaewife.

seesaw *v.* alternate, fluctuate, oscillate, pitch, swing, teeter.
n. pendulum, wild mare.

seethe *v.* boil, bubble, churn, ferment, fizz, foam, foam at the mouth, froth, fume, hotch, marinate, rage, rise, saturate, simmer, smoulder, soak, souse, steep, storm, surge, swarm, swell, teem.

see-through *adj.* diaphanous, filmy, flimsy, gauzy, gossamer(y), sheer, translucent, transparent.
antonym opaque.

segment *n.* articulation, bit, compartment, division, part, piece, portion, section, slice, wedge.
antonym whole.
v. anatomise, cut up, divide, halve, separate, slice, split.

segregate *v.* cut off, discriminate against, dissociate, isolate, quarantine, separate, set apart.
antonym unite.

segregation *n.* apartheid, discrimination, isolation, quarantine, separation.
antonym unification.

seize *v.* abduct, annex, apprehend, appropriate, arrest, capture, catch, claw, clutch, cly, collar, commander, confiscate, crimp, distrain, distress, fasten, fix, for(e)hent, get, grab, grasp, grip, hijack, impound, nab, prehend, smug, snatch, take.
antonym let go.

seizure *n.* abduction, annexation, apprehension, arrest, attachment, attack, capture, commandeering, confiscation, convulsion, distraint, distress, fit, grabbing, paroxysm, spasm, taking.
antonym liberation.

seldom *adv.* infrequently, occasionally, rarely, scarcely.
antonym often.

select *v.* choose, cull, pick, prefer, single out.
adj. choice, élite, excellent, exclusive, first-class, first-rate, hand-picked, limited, picked, posh, preferable, prime, privileged, rare, selected, special, superior, top, top-notch.
antonyms general, second-rate.

selection *n.* anthology, assortment, choice, choosing, collection, line-up, medley, miscellany, option, palette, pick, potpourri, preference, range, variety.

selective *adj.* careful, discerning, discriminating, discriminatory, eclectic, élitist, particular.
antonym unselective.

self *n.* ego, egoity, I, identity, person, personality, soul.

self-assertive *adj.* aggressive, authoritarian, bossy, commanding, dictatorial, domineering, forceful, heavy-handed, high-handed, overbearing, overweening, peremptory, pushing, pushy.
antonym compliant.

self-assurance *n.* assurance, cockiness, cocksureness, confidence, overconfidence, positiveness, self-confidence, self-possession.
antonyms humility, unsureness.

self-assured *adj.* assured, cocksure, cocky, confident, overconfident, self-collected, self-possessed, sure of oneself.
antonyms humble, unsure.

self-centred *adj.* egotistic(al), narcissistic, self-absorbed, self-interested, selfish, self-seeking, self-serving.
antonym altruistic.

self-confidence *n.* aplomb, assurance, confidence, nerve, poise, self-assurance, self-possession, self-reliance.

antonyms humility, unsureness.

self-confident *adj.* assured, confident, fearless, poised, secure, self-assured, self-collected, self-possessed, self-reliant.
antonyms humble, unsure.

self-conscious *adj.* affected, awkward, bashful, coy, diffident, embarrassed, ill at ease, insecure, nervous, retiring, self-effacing, shamefaced, sheepish, shrinking, uncomfortable.
antonyms natural, unaffected.

self-control *n.* calmness, composure, cool, coolness, discipline, encraty, restraint, self-command, self-discipline, self-government, self-mastery, self-restraint, temperance, willpower.

self-denial *n.* abstemiousness, asceticism, moderation, renunciation, self-abandonment, self-abnegation, selflessness, self-renunciation, self-sacrifice, temperance, unselfishness.
antonym self-indulgence.

self-esteem *n.* amour-propre, dignity, pride, self-assurance, self-confidence, self-pride, self-regard, self-respect.
antonym humility.

self-evident *adj.* axiomatic, clear, incontrovertible, inescapable, manifest, obvious, undeniable, unquestionable.

self-glorification *n.* egotheism, egotism, self-admiration, self-advertisement, self-aggrandisement, self-exaltation.
antonym humility.

self-government *n.* autarchy, autonomy, democracy, home rule, independence, self-sovereignty.
antonym subjection.

self-importance *n.* arrogance, big-headedness, bumptiousness, cockiness, conceit, conceitedness, pomposity, pompousness, pushiness, self-consequence, self-opinion, vanity.
antonym humility.

self-important *adj.* arrogant, big-headed, bumptious, cocky, conceited, consequential, overbearing, pompous, pushy, self-consequent, strutting, swaggering, swollen-headed, vain.
antonym humble.

self-indulgence *n.* dissipation, dissoluteness, excess, extravagance, high living, incontinence, intemperance, profligacy, self-gratification, sensualism.
antonym self-denial.

self-indulgent *adj.* dissipated, dissolute, extravagant, intemperate, profligate, sensualistic.
antonym abstemious.

self-interest *n.* self, selfishness, self-love, self-regard, self-serving.
antonym selflessness.

selfish *adj.* egoistic, egoistical, egotistic, egotistical, greedy, mean, mercenary, narrow, self-centred, self-interested, self-seeking, self-serving.
antonym unselfish.

selfishness *n.* egoism, egotism, greed, meanness, self-centredness, self-interest, self-love, self-regard, self-seeking, self-serving.
antonym selflessness.

selfless *adj.* altruistic, generous, magnanimous, self-denying, self-forgetful, self-sacrificing, ungrudging, unselfish.
antonym selfish.

self-possessed *adj.* calm, collected, composed, confident, cool, poised, self-assured, self-collected, together, unruffled.
antonym worried.

self-possession *n.* aplomb, calmness, composure, confidence, cool, coolness, poise, sang-froid, self-command, self-confidence, unflappability.
antonym worry.

self-propelling *adj.* automobile, locomobile, self-moving.

self-reliance *n.* autarky, independence, self-sufficiency, self-support, self-sustainment, self-sustenance, self-sustentation.
antonym dependence.

self-reliant *adj.* autarkic(al), independent, self-sufficient, self-supporting, self-sustaining.
antonym dependent.

self-respect *n.* amour-propre, dignity, pride, self-assurance, self-confidence, self-esteem, self-pride, self-regard.
antonym self-doubt.

self-restraint *n.* abstemiousness, encraty, forbearance, moderation, patience, self-command, self-control, self-denial, self-discipline, self-government, temperance, willpower.
antonym licence.

self-righteous *adj.* complacent, goody-goody, holier-than-thou, hypocritical, pharisaical, pi, pietistic(al), pious, priggish, sanctimonious, self-satisfied, smug, superior, Tartuffian, Tartuffish.
antonym understanding.

self-righteousness *n.* goodiness, goody-goodiness, pharisaicalness, pharisaism, piousness, priggishness, sanctimoniousness.
antonyms humility, understanding.

self-sacrifice *n.* altruism, generosity, self-abandonment, self-abnegation, self-denial, selflessness, self-renunciation.
antonym selfishness.

self-satisfaction *n.* complacency, contentment, pride, self-appreciation, self-approbation, self-approval, smugness.
antonym humility.

self-satisfied *adj.* complacent, puffed up, self-approving, self-congratulatory, self-righteous, smug.
antonym humble.

self-seeking *adj.* acquisitive, calculating, careerist, fortune-hunting, gold-digging, mercenary, on the make, opportunistic, self-endeared, self-interested, selfish, self-loving, self-serving.
antonym altruistic.

self-styled *adj.* professed, pseudo, self-appointed, so-called, soi-disant, would-be.

self-supporting *adj.* autarkic(al), self-financing,

self-reliant, self-sufficient, self-sustaining.
antonym dependent.

self-willed *adj.* bloody-minded, cussed, headstrong, intractable, obstinate, opinionated, pig-headed, refractory, self-opinionated, self-opinionative, stiff-necked, stubborn, ungovernable, wilful.
antonym complaisant.

sell *v.* barter, cheat, convince, deal in, exchange, handle, hawk, impose on, market, merchandise, peddle, persuade, promote, retail, sell out, stock, surrender, trade, trade in, traffic in, trick, vend.
antonym buy.

sell out betray, double-cross, fail, fink on, rat on, sell down the river, stab in the back.
antonym back.

seller *n.* agent, dealer, merchant, rep, representative, retailer, salesgirl, saleslady, salesman, saleswoman, shopkeeper, storekeeper, tradesman, traveller, vendor.
antonym buyer.

selling *n.* dealing, marketing, merchandising, promotion, salesmanship, trading, traffic, transactions, vendition.
antonym buying.

semblance *n.* air, apparition, appearance, aspect, bearing, façade, figure, form, front, guise, image, likeness, mask, mien, pretence, resemblance, show, similarity, veneer.

semen *n.* jism, seed, spawn, sperm, spunk.

semicircle *n.* half-round, hemicycle.

seminal *adj.* creative, formative, imaginative, important, influential, innovative, major, original, productive, seminary.
antonym derivative.

seminary *n.* academy, college, institute, institution, school, training-college.

send *v.* broadcast, cast, charm, communicate, consign, convey, delight, deliver, direct, discharge, dispatch, electrify, emit, enrapture, enthrall, excite, exude, fire, fling, forward, grant, hurl, intoxicate, move, please, propel, radiate, ravish, remit, shoot, stir, thrill, titillate, transmit.

send for call for, call out, command, order, request, summon.
antonym dismiss.

send up burlesque, imitate, lampoon, mickeytake, mimic, mock, parody, satirise, spook, take off, take the mickey out of.

send-off *n.* departure, farewell, going-away, leave-taking, start, valediction.
antonym arrival.

send-up *n.* imitation, mickey-take, mockery, parody, satire, skit, spoof, take-off.

senile *adj.* anile, decrepit, doddering, doited, doting, failing, imbecile, senescent.

senility *n.* anility, caducity, decrepitude, dotage, eld, infirmity, paracme, second childhood, senescence, senile dementia.

senior *adj.* aîné(e), elder, first, higher, high-ranking, major, older, superior.
antonym junior.

seniority *n.* eldership, precedence, priority,

rank, standing, superiority.
antonym juniority.

sensation *n.* agitation, awareness, commotion, consciousness, emotion, Empfindung, excitement, feeling, furore, hit, impression, perception, scandal, sense, stir, surprise, thrill, tingle, vibes, vibrations, wow.

sensational *adj.* amazing, astounding, blood-and-thunder, breathtaking, dramatic, electrifying, excellent, exceptional, exciting, fabulous, gamy, hair-raising, horrifying, impressive, lurid, marvellous, melodramatic, mind-blowing, revealing, scandalous, sensationalistic, shocking, smashing, spectacular, staggering, startling, superb, thrilling.
antonym run-of-the-mill.

sense *n.* advantage, appreciation, atmosphere, aura, awareness, brains, clear-headedness, cleverness, consciousness, definition, denotation, direction, discernment, discrimination, drift, faculty, feel, feeling, gist, good, gumption, implication, import, impression, intelligence, interpretation, intuition, judgement, logic, marbles, meaning, message, mother wit, nous, nuance, opinion, perception, point, premonition, presentiment, purport, purpose, quickness, reason, reasonableness, sagacity, sanity, savvy, sensation, sensibility, sentiment, sharpness, significance, signification, smeddum, substance, tact, understanding, use, value, wisdom, wit(s), worth.
antonym foolishness.

v. appreciate, comprehend, detect, divine, feel, grasp, notice, observe, perceive, realise, suspect, understand.

senseless *adj.* absurd, anaesthetised, asinine, crazy, daft, deadened, dotty, fatuous, foolish, halfwitted, idiotic, illogical, imbecilic, inane, incongruous, inconsistent, insensate, insensible, irrational, ludicrous, mad, meaningless, mindless, moronic, nonsensical, numb, numbed, out, out for the count, pointless, ridiculous, silly, simple, stunned, stupid, unconscious, unfeeling, unintelligent, unreasonable, unwise.
antonym sensible.

sensibilities *n.* emotions, feelings, sensitivities, sentiments, susceptibilities.

sensibility *n.* appreciation, awareness, delicacy, discernment, insight, intuition, perceptiveness, responsiveness, sensitiveness, sensitivity, susceptibility, taste.
antonym insensibility.

sensible *adj.* appreciable, canny, considerable, delicate, discernable, discreet, discriminating, down-to-earth, far-sighted, intelligent, judicious, level-headed, matter-of-fact, noticeable, palpable, perceptible, practical, prudent, rational, realistic, reasonable, right-thinking, sagacious, sage, sane, senseful, shrewd, significant, sober, solid, sound, tangible, visible, well-advised, well-thought-out, wise.
antonyms imperceptible, senseless.

sensible of acquainted with, alive to, aware of, cognisant of, conscious of, convinced of, mindful of, observant of, sensitive to, understanding.
antonym unaware of.

sensitive *adj.* acute, controversial, delicate, fine, hyper(a)esthesic, hyper(a)esthetic, hyperconscious, impressionable, irritable, keen, perceptive, precise, reactive, responsive, secret, sensitised, sentient, susceptible, temperamental, tender, thin-skinned, touchy, umbrageous.
antonym insensitive.

sensitivity *n.* delicacy, hyper(a)esthesia, hyperconsciousness, reactiveness, reactivity, receptiveness, responsiveness, sensitiveness, susceptibility.
antonym insensitivity.

sensual *adj.* animal, bodily, carnal, epicurean, erotic, fleshly, lascivious, lecherous, lewd, libidinous, licentious, lustful, luxurious, pandemian, physical, randy, raunchy, self-indulgent, sexual, sexy, voluptuous, worldly.
antonyms ascetic, Puritan.

sensualist *n.* bon vivant, bon viveur, debauchee, epicure, Epicurean, gourmand, gourmet, hedonist, libertine, profligate, roué, sybarite, voluptuary.
antonyms ascetic, Puritan.

sensuality *n.* animal magnetism, animalism, carnality, debauchery, eroticism, gourmandise, lasciviousness, lecherousness, lewdness, libertinism, libidinousness, licentiousness, lustfulness, profligacy, prurience, salaciousness, sexiness, voluptuousness.
antonyms asceticism, Puritanism.

sensuous *adj.* epicurean, gratifying, hedonistic, lush, luxurious, pleasurable, rich, sensory, sumptuous, sybaritic, voluptuous.
antonyms ascetic, plain, simple.

sentence *n.* aphorism, apophthegm, condemnation, decision, decree, doom, gnome, judgement, maxim, opinion, order, pronouncement, ruling, saying, verdict.
v. condemn, doom, judge, pass judgement on, penalise, pronounce judgement on.

sententious *adj.* aphoristic, axiomatic, brief, canting, compact, concise, epigrammatic, gnomic, laconic, moralising, moralistic, pithy, pointed, pompous, ponderous, preachy, sanctimonious, short, succinct, terse.
antonyms humble, prolix.

sentient *adj.* aware, conscious, live, living, reactive, responsive, sensitive.
antonym insentient.

sentiment *n.* attitude, belief, emotion, emotionalism, feeling, idea, judgement, mawkishness, maxim, opinion, persuasion, romanticism, saying, sensibility, sentimentalism, sentimentality, slush, soft-heartedness, tenderness, thought, view.
antonyms hard-heartedness, straightforwardness.

sentimental *adj.* corny, dewy-eyed, drippy, emotional, gushing, gushy, gutbucket, impressionable, lovey-dovey, maudlin, mawkish, mushy, nostalgic, pathetic, romantic, rose-water, schmaltzy, simpering, sloppy, slushy, soft-hearted, tearful, tear-jerking, tender, too-too, touching, treacly, weepy, wertherian.
antonym unsentimental.

sentimentality *n.* bathos, corniness, emotionalism, gush, mawkishness, mush, nostalgia, pulp, romanticism, schmaltz, sentimentalism, sloppiness, slush, tenderness.

sentry *n.* guard, look-out, picket, sentinel, vedette, watch, watchman.

separable *adj.* detachable, discerptible, distinguishable, divisible, partible, scissile, severable.
antonym inseperable.

separate *v.* abstract, bifurcate, deglutinate, departmentalise, detach, disaffiliate, disally, discerp, disconnect, disentangle, disjoin, dislink, dispart, dissever, distance, disunite, divaricate, diverge, divide, divorce, eloi(g)n, estrange, exfoliate, isolate, part, part company, prescind, remove, secede, secern, seclude, segregate, sever, shear, split, split up, sunder, uncouple, winnow, withdraw.
antonyms join, unite.
adj. alone, apart, autonomous, detached, disconnected, discrete, disjointed, disjunct, disparate, distinct, divided, divorced, independent, individual, isolated, particular, several, single, solitary, sundry, unattached, unconnected.
antonyms attached, together.

separated *adj.* apart, disassociated, disconnected, disunited, divided, isolated, parted, segregated, separate, split up, sundered.
antonyms attached, together.

separately *adv.* alone, apart, discretely, discriminately, divisim, independently, individually, personally, severally, singly.
antonym together.

separating *adj.* discretive, disjunctive, divellent, dividing, divisive, divulsive, intervening, isolating, partitioning, segregating.
antonym unifying.

separation *n.* break, break-up, detachment, diaeresis, dialysis, diaspora, diastasis, discerption, disconnection, disengagement, disgregation, disjunction, disjuncture, disseverance, disseveration, disseverment, dissociation, disunion, division, divorce, estrangement, farewell, gap, leave-taking, parting, rift, segregation, severance, solution, split, split-up.
antonyms togetherness, unification.

septic *adj.* festering, infected, poisoned, purulent, putrefactive, putrefying, putrid, pyogenic, pyoid, suppurating.

sepulchral *adj.* cheerless, deep, dismal, funereal, gloomy, grave, hollow, lugubrious, melancholy, morbid, mournful, reverberating, sad, sepultural, sepulchrous, sombre, sonorous, woeful.
antonym cheerful.

sepulchre *n.* grave, mausoleum, tomb, vault.

sequel *n.* conclusion, consequence, continuation, development, end, follow-up, issue, outcome, pay-off, prequel, result, upshot.

sequence *n.* arrangement, chain, consequence, course, cycle, order, procession, progression, series, set, succession, track, train.

sequestered *adj.* backveld, cloistered, isolated, lonely, outback, out-of-the-way, private, quiet, remote, retired, secluded, unfrequented.
antonyms busy, frequented, public.

seraphic *adj.* angelic, beatific, blissful, celestial, divine, heavenly, holy, innocent, pure, saintly, seraphical, sublime.
antonym demonic.

serene *adj.* calm, composed, cool, halcyon, imperturbable, peaceful, placid, tranquil, unclouded, undisturbed, unflappable, unruffled, untroubled.
antonym troubled.

serenity *n.* calm, calmness, composure, cool, peace, peacefulness, placidity, quietness, quietude, stillness, tranquillity, unflappability.
antonyms anxiety, disruption.

serf *n.* bondmaid, bondservant, bond-slave, bon(d)sman, bond(s)-woman, helot, servant, slave, thrall, villein.
antonym master.

series *n.* arrangement, catena, chain, concatenation, consecution, course, cycle, enfilade, line, order, progression, run, scale, sequence, set, string, succession, train.

serious *adj.* acute, alarming, critical, crucial, dangerous, deep, deliberate, determined, difficult, earnest, far-reaching, fateful, genuine, grave, grim, heavy, honest, humourless, important, long-faced, momentous, pensive, pressing, resolute, resolved, sedate, severe, significant, sincere, sober, solemn, staid, stern, thoughtful, unsmiling, urgent, weighty, worrying.
antonyms facetious, light, slight, smiling, trivial.

seriously *adv.* acutely, badly, critically, dangerously, distressingly, earnestly, gravely, grievously, joking apart, severely, sincerely, solemnly, sorely, thoughtfully.
antonyms casually, slightly.

seriousness *n.* danger, earnestness, gravitas, gravity, humourless, importance, moment, sedateness, significance, sobriety, solemnity, staidness, sternness, urgency, weight.
antonyms casualness, slightness, triviality.

sermon *n.* address, dressing-down, exhortation, harangue, homily, lecture, preachment, talking-to.

sermonise *v.* preach, preachify.

sermonising *n.* pi-jaw, preachifying, preachment, pulpitry.

serpentine *adj.* coiling, crooked, meandering, serpentiform, sinuous, snakelike, snaking, snaky, tortuous, twisting, winding.
antonym straight.

serrated *adj.* notched, sawlike, saw-toothed, serrate, serratulate, serriform, serrulate(d), toothed.
antonym smooth.

serried *adj.* close, close-set, compact, crowded, dense, massed.
antonym scattered.

servant *n.* aia, amah, ancillary, attendant, ayah, bearer, boy, daily, day, day-woman, domestic, drudge, esne, flunkey, footman, galopin, garçon, gentleman's gentleman, gossoon, gyp, haiduk, handmaid, handmaiden, help, helper, hind, hireling, Jeeves, khidmutgar, kitchen-maid, knave, lackey, lady's maid, livery-servant, maid, maid of all work, maître d'hôtel, major-domo, man, manservant, menial, ministrant, retainer, scout, seneschal, servitor, skivvy, slave, slavey, steward, valet, vassal, woman.
antonyms master, mistress.

serve *v.* act, aid, answer, arrange, assist, attend, avail, complete, content, dance attendance, deal, deliver, discharge, distribute, do, fulfil, further, handle, help, minister to, oblige, observe, officiate, pass, perform, present, provide, satisfy, succour, suffice, suit, supply, undergo, wait on, work for.

service *n.* advantage, assistance, avail, availability, benefit, business, ceremony, check, disposal, duty, employ, employment, expediting, function, help, labour, maintenance, ministrations, observance, office, overhaul, performance, rite, servicing, set, supply, use, usefulness, utility, work, worship.
v. check, maintain, overhaul, recondition, repair, tune.

serviceable *adj.* advantageous, beneficial, convenient, dependable, durable, efficient, functional, hard-wearing, helpful, operative, plain, practical, profitable, simple, strong, tough, unadorned, usable, useful, utilitarian.
antonym unserviceable.

servile *adj.* abject, base, bootlicking, controlled, craven, cringing, fawning, grovelling, humble, low, mean, menial, obsequious, slavish, subject, submissive, subservient, sycophantic, toadying, toadyish, unctuous.
antonyms aggressive, bold.

servility *n.* abjection, abjectness, arse-licking, baseness, bootlicking, fawning, grovelling, meanness, obsequiousness, self-abasement, slavishness, submissiveness, subservience, sycophancy, toad-eating, toadyism, unctuousness.
antonyms aggressiveness, boldness.

servitude *n.* bondage, bonds, chains, enslavement, obedience, serfdom, slavery, subjugation, thraldom, thrall, vassalage, villeinage.
antonym freedom.

session *n.* assembly, conference, discussion, get-together, go, hearing, meeting, period, semester, sitting, term, year.

set[1] *v.* adjust, aim, allocate, allot, apply, appoint, arrange, assign, cake, conclude, condense, congeal, co-ordinate, crystallise, decline, decree, deposit, designate, determine, dip, direct, disappear, embed, establish, fasten, fix, fix up, gelatinise, harden, impose, install, jell, lay, locate, lodge, mount, name, ordain, park, place, plant, plonk, plump, position, prepare, prescribe, propound, put, rectify, regulate, resolve, rest, schedule, seat, settle, sink, situate, solidify, specify, spread, stake, station, stick, stiffen, subside, synchronise, thicken, turn, vanish.

n. attitude, bearing, carriage, fit, hang, inclination, mise-en-scène, position, posture, scene, scenery, setting, turn.

adj. agreed, appointed, arranged, artificial, conventional, customary, decided, definite, deliberate, entrenched, established, firm, fixed, formal, hackneyed, immovable, inflexible, intentional, prearranged, predetermined, prescribed, regular, rehearsed, rigid, routine, scheduled, settled, standard, stereotyped, stock, strict, stubborn, traditional, unspontaneous, usual.

antonyms free, movable, spontaneous, undecided.

set about assail, assault, attack, bash, beat up, begin, belabour, lambaste, mug, start, tackle, wade into.

set against alienate, balance, compare, contrast, disunite, divide, estrange, juxtapose, mix, oppose, weigh.

set apart choose, elect, peculiarise, put aside, separate.

set aside abrogate, annul, cancel, discard, dismiss, keep, keep back, lay aside, nullify, overrule, overturn, put aside, quash, reject, repudiate, reserve, reverse, save, select, separate.

set back delay, hamper, hinder, hold up, impede, interrupt, retard, slow.

set eyes on behold, clap eyes on, come across, come upon, encounter, lay eyes on, meet, meet with, notice, observe, see.

set free decontrol, deliver, disembarrass, disentangle, disimprison, disprison, emancipate, extricate, free, liberate, loose, manumit, ransom, release, rescue, rid, save, unpen.
antonyms confine, enslave.

set off depart, detonate, display, embark, enhance, explode, ignite, leave, light, make tracks, present, sally forth, show off, touch off, trigger off.

set on assail, assault, attack, beat up, fall upon, fly at, go for, incite, instigate, lay into, mug, pitch into, sail into, set about, set upon, turn on, urge.

set out arrange, array, begin, describe, detail, display, dispose, elaborate, elucidate, embark, exhibit, explain, lay out, make a move, make tracks, present, sally forth, set off, start, start out.

set up arrange, assemble, back, begin, boost, build, cheer, compose, construct, create, elate, elevate, erect, establish, finance, form, found, gratify, inaugurate, initiate, install, institute, introduce, organise, prearrange,

prepare, promote, raise, revivify, start, strengthen, subsidise.

set² *n.* apparatus, assemblage, assortment, band, batch, circle, class, clique, collection, company, compendium, coterie, covey, crew, crowd, faction, gang, group, kit, outfit, sect, sequence, series.

setback *n.* blow, check, defeat, delay, disappointment, hiccup, hitch, hold-up, misfortune, problem, rebuff, relapse, reverse, snag, throw-back, upset.
antonyms advance, advantage, boost, help.

setting *n.* adjustment, age, backcloth, backdrop, background, context, environment, frame, locale, location, milieu, mise en scène, mounting, period, perspective, position, scene, scenery, set, site, surround, surroundings.

setting-up *n.* creation, establishment, foundation, founding, inauguration, inception, institution, introduction, start.
antonyms abolition, termination.

settle *v.* adjust, agree, alight, appoint, arrange, bed, calm, choose, clear, colonise, compact, complete, compose, conclude, confirm, decide, decree, descend, determine, discharge, dispose, dower, drop, dwell, endow, establish, fall, fix, found, hush, inhabit, land, light, liquidate, live, lower, lull, occupy, ordain, order, pacify, pay, people, pioneer, plant, plump, populate, quell, quiet, quieten, quit, reassure, reconcile, relax, relieve, reside, resolve, sedate, sink, soothe, square, square up, subside, tranquillise.

settlement¹ *n.* accommodation, adjustment, agreement, allowance, arrangement, Ausgleich, clearance, clearing, completion, conclusion, confirmation, decision, defrayal, diktat, discharge, disposition, establishment, income, liquidation, payment, resolution, satisfaction, termination.

settlement² *n.* colonisation, colony, community, encampment, hamlet, immigration, kibbutz, nahal, occupation, outpost, peopling, plantation, population.

settlement³ *n.* compacting, drop, fall, sinkage, subsidence.

settler *n.* coloniser, colonist, frontiersman, immigrant, incomer, kibbutznik, newcomer, pioneer, planter, squatter.
antonym native.

set-to *n.* altercation, argument, argy-bargy, barney, brush, conflict, contest, disagreement, dust-up, exchange, fight, fracas, quarrel, row, scrap, spat, squabble, wrangle.

set-up *n.* arrangement, business, circumstances, conditions, ménage, organisation, régime, structure, system.

sever *v.* alienate, bisect, cleave, cut, detach, disconnect, disjoin, dissever, dissociate, dissolve, dissunder, disunite, divide, estrange, part, rend, separate, split, sunder, terminate.
antonyms join, unite.

several *adj.* assorted, different, discrete, disparate, distinct, divers, diverse, individual, many, particular, respective, separate, single, some, some few, specific, sundry, various.

severally *adv.* discretely, individually, particularly, respectively, separately, seriatim, specifically.

antonyms simultaneously, together.

severe *adj.* acute, arduous, ascetic, astringent, austere, biting, bitter, Catonian, caustic, chaste, classic, classical, cold, critical, cruel, cutting, dangerous, demanding, difficult, disapproving, distressing, dour, Draconian, Draconic, Dracontic, eager, exacting, extreme, fierce, flinty, forbidding, functional, grave, grim, grinding, hard, harsh, inclement, inexorable, intense, iron-handed, oppressive, pitiless, plain, punishing, relentless, restrained, Rhadamanthine, rigid, rigorous, satirical, scathing, serious, shrewd, simple, sober, Spartan, stern, strait-laced, strict, stringent, taxing, tight-lipped, tough, trying, unadorned, unbending, unembellished, ungentle, unrelenting, unsmiling, unsparing, unsympathetic, violent.

antonyms compassionate, kind, lenient, mild, sympathetic.

severely *adv.* acutely, austerely, badly, bitterly, coldly, critically, dangerously, disapprovingly, dourly, extremely, gravely, grimly, hard, harshly, rigorously, sharply, sorely, sternly, strictly, unsympathetically.

severity *n.* acuteness, asceticism, austerity, coldness, gravity, hardness, harshness, plainness, rigour, seriousness, severeness, sharpness, sternness, stringency, strictness, toughness, ungentleness.

antonyms compassion, kindness, leniency, mildness.

sex *n.* coition, coitus, congress, copulation, desire, fornication, gender, intercourse, intimacy, libido, lovemaking, nookie, reproduction, screw, sexual intercourse, sexual relations, sexuality, union, venery.

sex appeal allure, desirability, glamour, it, magnetism, nubility, oomph, seductiveness, sensuality, sex attraction, sexiness, voluptuousness.

sexless *adj.* asexual, neuter, parthenogenetic, undersexed, unfeminine, unmasculine, unsexed, unsexual.

sexpot *n.* enchantress, houri, Lolita, nymphet, seductress, sex goddess, siren.

sexton *n.* caretaker, fossor, grave-digger, grave-maker, sacristan, verger.

sexual *adj.* carnal, coital, erotic, gamic, genital, intimate, procreative, reproductive, sensual, sex, sex-related, venereal.

antonym asexual.

sexual intercourse carnal knowledge, coition, coitus, commerce, congress, consummation, copulation, coupling, fuck, fucking, greens, mating, nookie, penetration, pussy, screw, screwing, sex, shag, shagging, tail, union.

sexuality *n.* carnality, desire, eroticism, lust, sensuality, sexiness, sexual instincts, sexual urge, virility, voluptuousness.

sexy *adj.* arousing, beddable, come-hither, cuddly, curvaceous, epigamic, erotic, flirtatious, inviting, kissable, naughty, nubile, pornographic, provocative, provoking, seductive, sensual, sensuous, slinky, suggestive, titillating, virile, voluptuous.

antonym sexless.

shabby *adj.* cheap, contemptible, dastardly, despicable, dilapidated, dingy, dirty, dishonourable, disreputable, dog-eared, down-at-heel, faded, frayed, ignoble, low, low-down, low-life, low-lived, mangy, mean, moth-eaten, neglected, paltry, poking, poky, poor, ragged, raunchy, rotten, run-down, scruffy, seedy, shameful, shoddy, tacky, tattered, tatty, threadbare, ungentlemanly, unworthy, worn, worn-out.

antonyms honourable, smart.

shack *n.* bothy, but and ben, cabin, dump, hole, hovel, hut, hutch, lean-to, shanty, shed, shiel, shieling.

shackle *n.* bond, bracelets, chain, darbies, fetter, gyve, hamper, handcuff, hobble, iron, leg-iron, manacle, rope, shackles, tether, trammel.

v. bind, chain, constrain, embarrass, encumber, fetter, gyve, hamper, hamstring, handcuff, handicap, hobble, hogtie, impede, inhibit, limit, manacle, obstruct, pinion, restrain, restrict, secure, tether, thwart, tie, trammel.

shade *n.* amount, apparition, blind, canopy, colour, coolness, cover, covering, curtain, darkness, dash, degree, difference, dimness, dusk, eidolon, ghost, gloaming, gloom, gloominess, gradation, hint, hue, manes, murk, nuance, obscurity, phantasm, phantom, screen, semblance, semi-darkness, shadiness, shadow, shadows, shelter, shield, shroud, spectre, spirit, stain, suggestion, suspicion, tinge, tint, tone, trace, twilight, umbra, umbrage, variation, variety, veil, wraith.

v. cloud, conceal, cover, darken, dim, hide, inumbrate, mute, obscure, overshadow, protect, screen, shadow, shield, shroud, veil.

shadow *n.* affliction, blight, caliginosity, cloud, companion, cover, darkness, detective, dimness, dusk, ghost, gloaming, gloom, hint, image, inseparable, obscurity, pal, phantom, protection, remnant, representation, sadness, shade, shelter, sidekick, sleuth, spectre, spirit, suggestion, suspicion, tenebrity, tenebrosity, trace, umbrage, vestige.

v. darken, dog, follow, obscure, overhang, overshadow, screen, shade, shield, stalk, tail, tail-up, trail, watch.

shadowy *adj.* caliginous, crepuscular, dark, dim, dreamlike, dusky, faint, ghostly, gloomy, half-remembered, hazy, illusory, imaginary, impalpable, indistinct, intangible, murky, nebulous, obscure, shaded, shady, spectral, tenebrious, tenebrose, tenebrous, umbratile, umbratilous, undefined, unreal, unsubstantial, vague, wraithlike.

shady[1] *adj.* bosky, bowery, caliginous, cool, dark, dim, leafy, shaded, shadowy, tenebrous, umbrageous, umbratile, umbratilous, umbriferous, umbrose, umbrous.
antonyms bright, sunlit, sunny.

shady[2] *adj.* crooked, discreditable, dishonest, disreputable, dubious, fishy, louche, questionable, shifty, slippery, suspect, suspicious, underhand, unethical, unscrupulous, untrustworthy.
antonyms honest, trustworthy.

shaft *n.* arbor, arrow, barb, beam, cut, dart, gibe, gleam, haft, handle, missile, pole, ray, rod, shank, stem, stick, sting, streak, thrust, upright, well, winze.

shaggy *adj.* crinose, hairy, hirsute, long-haired, nappy, rough, tousled, tousy, unkempt, unshorn.
antonyms bald, shorn.

shake *n.* agitation, convulsion, disturbance, instant, jar, jerk, jiffy, jolt, jounce, moment, no time, pulsation, quaking, second, shiver, shock, shudder, tick, trembling, tremor, trice, twitch, vellication, vibration.
v. agitate, brandish, bump, churn, concuss, convulse, didder, discompose, distress, disturb, flourish, fluctuate, frighten, heave, impair, intimidate, jar, joggle, jolt, jounce, move, oscillate, quake, quiver, rattle, rock, rouse, shimmy, shiver, shock, shog, shudder, split, stir, succuss, sway, totter, tremble, twitch, undermine, unnerve, unsettle, upset, vellicate, vibrate, wag, waggle, wave, waver, weaken, wobble.

shake a leg get a move on, get cracking, hurry, look lively, step on it, stir one's stumps.

shake off dislodge, elude, get rid of, give the slip, leave behind, lose, outdistance, outpace, outstrip.

shake-up *n.* disturbance, rearrangement, reorganisation, reshuffle, upheaval.

shaky *adj.* dubious, faltering, inexpert, insecure, precarious, questionable, quivery, rickety, rocky, shoogly, suspect, tottering, tottery, uncertain, undependable, unreliable, unsound, unstable, unsteady, unsupported, untrustworthy, weak, wobbly.
antonyms firm, strong.

shallow *adj.* empty, flimsy, foolish, frivolous, idle, ignorant, meaningless, puerile, simple, skin-deep, slight, superficial, surface, trivial, unanalytical, unintelligent, unscholarly.
antonyms analytical, deep.

sham *n.* charlatan, counterfeit, feint, forgery, fraud, gold-brick, hoax, humbug, imitation, impostor, imposture, mountebank, phoney, pretence, pretender, pseud, stumer.
adj. artificial, bogus, Brummagem, counterfeit, ersatz, faked, false, feigned, imitation, mock, pasteboard, phoney, pinchbeck, pretended, pseud, pseudo, put-on, simulated, snide, spurious, synthetic.
antonym genuine.
v. affect, counterfeit, fake, feign, malinger, pretend, put on, simulate.

shaman *n.* angekkok, magician, medicine-man, pawaw, powwow, sorcerer, witch-doctor.

shambles *n.* anarchy, bedlam, chaos, confusion, disarray, disorder, disorganisation, havoc, madhouse, mess, muddle, pigsty, wreck.

shambling *adj.* awkward, clumsy, disjointed, loose, lumbering, lurching, shuffling, uncoordinated, ungainly, unsteady.
antonyms agile, neat, nimble, spry.

shame *n.* aidos, bashfulness, blot, chagrin, compunction, contempt, degradation, derision, discredit, disgrace, dishonour, disrepute, embarrassment, humiliation, ignominy, infamy, mortification, obloquy, odium, opprobrium, reproach, scandal, shamefacedness, stain, stigma.
antonyms distinction, honour, pride.
v. abash, blot, confound, debase, defile, degrade, discomfit, disconcert, discredit, disgrace, dishonour, embarrass, humble, humiliate, mortify, put to shame, reproach, ridicule, show up, smear, stain, sully, taint.
interj. fi donc, fie, fie upon you, for shame, fy, shame on you.

shamefaced *adj.* abashed, apologetic, ashamed, bashful, blushing, chagrined, conscience-stricken, contrite, diffident, discomfited, embarrassed, hesitant, humiliated, modest, mortified, pudibund, red-faced, remorseful, shamefast, sheepish, shrinking, shy, timid, uncomfortable.
antonyms proud, unashamed.

shameful *adj.* abominable, atrocious, base, contemptible, dastardly, degrading, discreditable, disgraceful, dishonourable, embarrassing, humiliating, ignominious, indecent, infamous, low, mean, mortifying, outrageous, reprehensible, scandalous, shaming, unbecoming, unworthy, vile, wicked.
antonyms creditable, honourable.

shameless *adj.* abandoned, abashless, audacious, barefaced, blatant, brash, brazen, corrupt, defiant, depraved, dissolute, flagrant, hardened, immodest, improper, impudent, incorrigible, indecent, insolent, ithyphallic, profligate, reprobate, unabashed, unashamed, unblushing, unprincipled, unscrupulous, wanton.
antonyms ashamed, contrite, shamefaced.

shanty *n.* bothy, cabin, hovel, hut, hutch, lean-to, shack, shed.

shape *n.* apparition, appearance, aspect, build, condition, configuration, conformation, contours, cut, dimensions, fettle, figure, form, format, frame, Gestalt, guise, health, kilter, likeness, lines, make, model, mould, outline, pattern, physique, profile, semblance, silhouette, state, template, trim.
v. accommodate, adapt, construct, create, define, develop, devise, embody, fashion, forge, form, frame, guide, make, model, modify, mould, plan, prepare, produce, redact, regulate, remodel.

shapeless *adj.* amorphous, asymmetrical, battered, characterless, dumpy, embryonic, formless, inchoate, indeterminate, indigest, irregular, misshapen, nebulous, undeveloped, unformed, unshapely, unstructured.

antonym shapely.

shapely *adj.* comely, curvaceous, elegant, featous, gainly, graceful, neat, pretty, trim, voluptuous, well-formed, well-proportioned, well-set-up, well-turned.

antonym shapeless.

share *v.* allot, apportion, assign, chip in, distribute, divide, divvy, divvy up, go Dutch, go fifty-fifty, go halves, muck in, partake, participate, split, whack.

n. a piece of the action, allotment, allowance, contribution, cut, dividend, division, divvy, due, finger, lot, part, portion, proportion, quota, ration, snap, snip, stint, whack.

share out allot, apportion, assign, distribute, divide up, give out, parcel out, prorate.

antonym monopolise.

shark *n.* chiseller, crook, extortioner, fleecer, parasite, politician, sharper, slicker, sponger, swindler, wheeler-dealer.

sharp *adj.* abrupt, acerbic, acicular, acid, acidulous, acrid, acrimonious, acute, alert, apt, artful, astute, barbed, biting, bitter, bright, burning, canny, caustic, chic, chiselled, classy, clear, clear-cut, clever, crafty, crisp, cunning, cutting, discerning, dishonest, distinct, dressy, eager, edged, excruciating, extreme, fashionable, fierce, fit, fly, harsh, honed, hot, hurtful, incisive, intense, jagged, keen, knife-edged, knifelike, knowing, long-headed, marked, natty, nimble-witted, noticing, observant, painful, penetrating, per-acute, perceptive, piercing, piquant, pointed, pungent, quick, quick-witted, rapid, razor-sharp, ready, sarcastic, sardonic, saw-edged, scathing, serrated, severe, sharpened, shooting, shrewd, sly, smart, snappy, snazzy, sour, spiky, stabbing, stinging, stylish, subtle, sudden, tart, trenchant, trendy, unblurred, undulled, unscrupulous, vinegary, violent, vitriolic, waspish, wily.

antonyms blunt, dull, mild, obtuse, slow, stupid.

adv. abruptly, exactly, on the dot, out of the blue, precisely, promptly, punctually, suddenly, unexpectedly.

sharpen *v.* acuminate, edge, file, grind, hone, strop, taper, whet.

antonym blunt.

sharpness *n.* acuity, acuteness, astuteness, discernment, eagerness, fierceness, incisiveness, intensity, keenness, observation, penetration, perceptiveness, pungency, quickness, severity, shrewdness, whet.

antonyms dullness, sloth.

sharp-sighted *adj.* eagle-eyed, gimlet-eyed, hawk-eyed, keen-sighted, lyncean, lynx-eyed, noticing, observant, perceptive.

antonyms short-sighted, unobservant.

shatter *v.* blast, blight, break, burst, crack, crush, demolish, destroy, devastate, disable, disshiver, dumbfound, exhaust, explode,

impair, implode, overturn, overwhelm, pulverise, ruin, shiver, smash, split, stun, torpedo, undermine, upset, wreck.

shattered *adj.* all in, crushed, dead beat, devastated, dog-tired, done in, exhausted, jiggered, knackered, overwhelmed, undermined, weary, worn out, zonked.

shattering *adj.* crushing, damaging, devastating, foudroyant, overwhelming, paralysing, severe, stunning.

shave *v.* barber, brush, crop, fleece, graze, pare, plane, plunder, scrape, shear, tonsure, touch, trim.

sheaf *n.* armful, bunch, bundle, dorlach, gait, garbe, truss.

sheath *n.* armour, carapace, case, casing, coat, coating, condom, covering, envelope, French letter, protective layer, rubber, safe, shell, sleeve, vagina, vaginula.

shed[1] *v.* afford, cast, cast off, diffuse, discard, drop, emit, exuviate, give, moult, pour, radiate, scatter, shower, slough, spill, throw.

shed light on clarify, clear up, effuse, elucidate, exfoliate, explain, illuminate, simplify.

shed[2] *n.* barn, hut, lean-to, lock-up, outhouse, shack.

shedding *n.* casting, diffusion, discarding, ecdysis, effusion, emission, exfoliation, exuviation, moulting, radiation, scattering, sloughing.

sheen *n.* brightness, brilliance, burnish, gleam, gloss, lustre, patina, polish, shimmer, shine, shininess.

antonyms dullness, tarnish.

sheep *n.* bell-wether, eanling, ewe, jumbuck, lamb, ram, tup, wether, yow.

sheepish *adj.* abashed, ashamed, chagrined, chastened, embarrassed, foolish, mortified, self-conscious, shamefaced, silly, uncomfortable.

antonym unabashed.

sheer[1] *adj.* abrupt, absolute, arrant, complete, downright, mere, out-and-out, perpendicular, precipitous, pure, rank, steep, thorough, thoroughgoing, total, unadulterated, unalloyed, unmingled, unmitigated, unqualified, utter, vertical.

sheer[2] diaphanous, fine, flimsy, gauzy, gossamer, pellucid, see-through, thin, translucent, transparent.

antonyms heavy, thick.

sheet *n.* blanket, broadsheet, broadside, circular, coat, covering, expanse, film, flyer, folio, handbill, handout, lamina, layer, leaf, leaflet, membrane, nappe, news-sheet, overlay, pane, panel, piece, plate, shroud, skin, slab, stratum, surface, veneer.

shelf *n.* bank, bar, bench, bracket, ledge, mantel, mantelpiece, platform, projection, reef, sandbank, sand-bar, shoal, step, terrace.

shell *n.* carapace, case, casing, chassis, covering, crust, dop, frame, framework, hull, husk, nacelle, pod, rind, shuck, skeleton, structure.

v. attack, barrage, batter, blitz, bomb,

bombard, cannonade, hull, husk, shuck, strafe, strike.

shell out ante, contribute, cough up, disburse, donate, expend, fork out, give, lay out, pay out, subscribe.

shelter v. accommodate, cover, defend, ensconce, guard, harbour, hide, protect, put up, safeguard, screen, shade, shadow, shield, shroud, skug.
antonym expose.
n. accommodation, aegis, asylum, bield, bunker, cover, covert, coverture, defence, dugout, funk-hole, guard, gunyah, harbourage, haven, lean-to, lee, lodging, protection, refuge, retreat, roof, safety, sanctuary, sconce, screen, screening, security, shade, shadow, shiel, umbrage, umbrella.
antonym exposure.

sheltered adj. cloistered, conventual, cosy, hermitic, isolated, lee, protected, quiet, reclusive, retired, screened, secluded, shaded, shielded, snug, unworldly, warm, withdrawn.
antonym exposed.

shelve v. defer, dismiss, freeze, halt, mothball, pigeonhole, postpone, put aside, put in abeyance, put off, put on ice, suspend, table.
antonyms expedite, implement.

shepherd n. guardian, herd, herdboy, herdgroom, herdsman, protector, shepherd boy, shepherdess, shepherdling.
v. conduct, convoy, escort, guide, herd, lead, marshal, steer, usher.

shield n. aegis, ancile, buckler, bulwark, cover, defence, escutcheon, guard, pelta, protection, rampart, safeguard, screen, scutum, shelter, targe, ward.
v. cover, defend, guard, protect, safeguard, screen, shade, shadow, shelter.
antonym expose.

shift v. adjust, alter, budge, change, dislodge, displace, fluctuate, manoeuvre, move, quit, rearrange, relocate, remove, reposition, rid, scoff, swallow, swerve, switch, transfer, transpose, vary, veer, wolf.
n. alteration, artifice, change, contrivance, craft, device, displacement, dodge, equivocation, evasion, expedient, fluctuation, manoeuvre, modification, move, permutation, rearrangement, removal, resource, ruse, shifting, sleight, stratagem, subterfuge, switch, transfer, trick, veering, wile.

shiftless adj. aimless, directionless, feckless, goalless, good-for-nothing, idle, incompetent, indolent, ineffectual, inefficient, inept, irresponsible, lackadaisical, lazy, resourceless, slothful, unambitious, unenterprising.
antonyms ambitious, aspiring, eager, enterprising.

shifty adj. contriving, crafty, deceitful, devious, dishonest, disingenuous, dubious, duplicitous, evasive, fly-by-night, furtive, scheming, shady, slippery, tricky, underhand, unprincipled, untrustworthy, wily.
antonyms honest, open.

shilly-shally v. dilly-dally, dither, falter, fluctuate, haver, hem and haw, hesitate, mess about, prevaricate, seesaw, shuffle, swither, teeter, vacillate, waver.

shimmer v. coruscate, gleam, glisten, glitter, phosphoresce, scintillate, twinkle.
n. coruscation, gleam, glimmer, glitter, glow, incandescence, iridescence, lustre, phosphorescence.

shimmering adj. aventurine, gleaming, glistening, glittering, glowing, incandescent, iridescent, luminous, lustrous, shining, shiny.
antonyms dull, matt.

shin v. ascend, clamber, climb, mount, scale, scramble, shoot, soar, swarm.

shine v. beam, brush, buff, burnish, coruscate, effulge, excel, flash, glare, gleam, glimmer, glisten, glitter, glow, lustre, polish, radiate, resplend, scintillate, shimmer, sparkle, stand out, star, twinkle.
n. brightness, burnish, effulgence, glare, glaze, gleam, gloss, glow, lambency, light, luminosity, lustre, patina, polish, radiance, sheen, shimmer, sparkle.

shininess n. brightness, burnish, effulgence, gleam, glitter, glossiness, lustre, polish, sheen, shine.
antonym dullness.

shining adj. beaming, bright, brilliant, celebrated, conspicuous, distinguished, effulgent, eminent, fulgent, gleaming, glistening, glittering, glorious, glowing, illustrious, lamping, leading, lucent, luminous, nitid, outstanding, profulgent, radiant, resplendent, rutilant, shimmering, sparkling, splendid, twinkling.

shiny adj. agleam, aglow, bright, burnished, gleaming, glistening, glossy, lustrous, nitid, polished, satiny, sheeny, shimmery, sleek.
antonyms dark, dull.

ship n. argosy, bark, barque, boat, ferry, galleon, galley, liner, prore, prow, steamer, tanker, trawler, vessel, yacht.

shipshape adj. businesslike, neat, orderly, seamanlike, spick-and-span, spruce, tidy, trig, trim, well-organised, well-planned, well-regulated.
antonyms disorderly, untidy.

shirk v. avoid, bludge, dodge, duck, duck out of, evade, funk, shun, sidestep, skive, skrimshank, slack, swing the lead.

shirker n. absentee, bludger, clock-watcher, dodger, embusqué, idler, layabout, loafer, malingerer, quitter, shirk, skiver, skrimshanker, slacker.

shiver v. palpitate, quake, quiver, shake, shudder, tremble, vibrate.
n. flutter, frisson, grue, quiver, shudder, start, thrill, tremble, trembling, tremor, twitch, vibration.

shivery adj. chilled, chilly, cold, fluttery, nervous, quaking, quivery, shaking, shuddery, trembly.

shoal n. assemblage, flock, horde, mass, mob, multitude, swarm, throng.

shock v. agitate, appal, astound, confound,

disgust, dismay, disquiet, horrify, jar, jolt, nauseate, numb, offend, outrage, paralyse, revolt, scandalise, shake, sicken, stagger, stun, stupefy, traumatise, unnnerve, unsettle. *antonyms* delight, gratify, please, reassure.

n. blow, bombshell, breakdown, clash, collapse, collision, concussion, consternation, dismay, distress, disturbance, encounter, fright, impact, jarring, jolt, perturbation, prostration, stupefaction, stupor, succussion, thunderbolt, trauma, turn, upset.
antonyms delight, pleasure.

shocking *adj.* abhorrent, abominable, appalling, astounding, atrocious, deplorable, detestable, disgraceful, disgusting, disquieting, distressing, dreadful, execrable, foul, frightful, ghastly, hideous, horrible, horrific, horrifying, insufferable, intolerable, loathsome, monstrous, nauseating, nefandous, odious, offensive, outrageous, repugnant, repulsive, revolting, scandalous, sickening, stupefying, unbearable, unspeakable.
antonyms acceptable, delightful, pleasant, satisfactory.

shoddy *adj.* cheap, cheap-jack, flimsy, gimcrack, inferior, junky, poor, rubbishy, second-rate, slipshod, tacky, tatty, tawdry, trashy, trumpery.
antonyms fine, well-made.

shoemaker *n.* bootmaker, cobbler, snab, snob, souter.

shoemaking *n.* bootmaking, cobblery, cobbling, gentle craft.

shoot[1] *v.* bag, blast, bolt, charge, dart, dash, discharge, dump, emit, enfilade, film, fire, flash, flung, gun down, hit, hurl, hurtle, kill, launch, open fire, photograph, pick off, plug, precipitate, project, propel, race, rake, rush, scoot, speed, spring, sprint, streak, take, tear, whisk, whiz, zap.

shoot[2] *n.* branch, bud, germen, offshoot, scion, slip, sprig, sprout, tendron, twig.
v. bolt, bud, burgeon, detonate, germinate, grow, shoot up, sprout, stretch, tower.

shop *n.* boutique, chain, dolly-shop, emporium, hypermarket, market, mart, store, supermarket, workshop.

shopping precinct arcade, complex, mall, market, plaza.

shore[1] *n.* beach, coast, foreshore, lakeside, littoral, margin, offing, promenade, rivage, sands, seaboard, sea-front, seashore, strand, waterfront, water's edge, waterside.

shore[2] *v.* brace, buttress, hold, prop, reinforce, shore up, stay, strengthen, support, underpin.

shorn *adj.* bald, beardless, crew-cut, cropped, deprived, nott, polled, shaved, shaven, stripped.

short *adj.* abbreviated, abridged, abrupt, blunt, brief, brittle, brusque, compendious, compressed, concise, crisp, crumbly, crusty, curt, curtailed, deficient, diminutive, direct, discourteous, dumpy, ephemeral, evanescent, fleeting, friable, gruff, impolite, inadequate, insufficient, lacking, laconic, limited, little,

low, meagre, momentary, murly, offhand, passing, petite, pithy, poor, précised, sawn-off, scant, scanty, scarce, sententious, sharp, shortened, short-handed, short-lived, short-term, slender, slim, small, snappish, snappy, sparse, squat, straight, succinct, summarised, summary, tart, terse, tight, tiny, transitory, uncivil, understaffed, unplentiful, wanting, wee.
antonyms adequate, ample, expansive, large, lasting, long, long-lived, polite, tall.

short of apart from, deficient in, except, lacking, less than, low on, missing, other than, pushed for, short on, wanting.

shortage *n.* absence, dearth, deficiency, deficit, failure, inadequacy, insufficiency, lack, leanness, meagreness, paucity, poverty, scantiness, scarcity, shortfall, sparseness, want, wantage.
antonyms abundance, sufficiency.

shortcoming *n.* defect, drawback, faible, failing, fault, flaw, foible, frailty, imperfection, inadequacy, weakness.

shorten *v.* abbreviate, abridge, crop, curtail, cut, decrease, diminish, dock, foreshorten, lessen, lop, précis, prune, reduce, take up, telescope, trim, truncate.
antonyms amplify, enlarge, lengthen.

shortened *adj.* abbreviated, abbreviatory, abridged, abstracted, compendious, condensed, summarised.
antonym amplified.

shorthand *n.* brachygraphy, phonography, stenography, tachygraphy.
antonym longhand.

short-lived *adj.* brief, caducous, ephemeral, evanescent, fleeting, fugacious, impermanent, momentary, passing, short, temporary, transient, transitory.
antonyms abiding, enduring, lasting, long-lived.

shortly *adv.* abruptly, anon, briefly, concisely, curtly, directly, laconically, presently, sharply, soon, succinctly, tartly, tersely.

short-sighted *adj.* careless, hasty, ill-advised, ill-considered, impolitic, impractical, improvident, imprudent, injudicious, myopic, near-sighted, unimaginative, unthinking.
antonyms far-sighted, hypermetropic, long-sighted.

short-tempered *adj.* choleric, crusty, fiery, hot-tempered, impatient, irascible, irritable, peppery, quick-tempered, ratty, testy, touchy.
antonyms calm, patient, placid.

short-winded *adj.* breathless, gasping, panting, peching, puffing, pursy.

shot[1] *n.* attempt, ball, bash, blast, bullet, cannon-ball, chance, conjecture, contribution, crack, discharge, dram, effort, endeavour, essay, go, guess, injection, lead, lob, marksman, opportunity, pellet, projectile, range, reach, shooter, shy, slug, spell, stab, stroke, surmise, throw, try, turn.
shot in the arm boost, encouragement, fillip,

fresh talent, impetus, lift, stimulus, uplift.

shot in the dark blind guess, conjecture, guess, guesswork, speculation.

shot[2] *adj.* iridescent, moiré, mottled, variegated, watered.

shoulder *v.* accept, assume, barge, bear, carry, elbow, jostle, press, push, shove, sustain, take on, thrust.

shout *n.* bay, bellow, belt, call, cheer, cry, roar, scream, shriek, yell.

v. bawl, bay, bellow, call, cheer, cry, holler, roar, scream, shriek, yell.

shove *v.* barge, crowd, drive, elbow, force, impel, jostle, press, propel, push, shoulder, thrust.

shove off beat it, clear off, clear out, depart, do a bunk, get lost, leave, push off, put out, scarper, scram, skedaddle, vamoose.

shovel *n.* backhoe, bail, bucket, scoop, spade.

v. convey, dredge, heap, ladle, load, move, scoop, shift, spade, spoon, toss.

show *v.* accompany, accord, assert, attend, attest, bestow, betray, clarify, conduct, confer, demonstrate, disclose, display, divulge, elucidate, escort, evidence, evince, exemplify, exhibit, explain, grant, guide, illustrate, indicate, instruct, lead, manifest, offer, present, prove, register, reveal, teach, usher, witness.

n. affectation, air, appearance, array, dash, demonstration, display, éclat, élan, entertainment, exhibition, exhibitionism, expo, exposition, extravaganza, façade, fair, féerie, flamboyance, gig, illusion, indication, likeness, manifestation, ostentation, pageant, pageantry, panache, parade, performance, pizzazz, plausibility, pose, presentation, pretence, pretext, production, profession, razzledazzle, representation, semblance, sight, sign, spectacle, swagger, view.

show off advertise, boast, brag, brandish, demonstrate, display, enhance, exhibit, flaunt, grandstand, parade, peacock, set off, strut, swagger, swank.

show up appear, arrive, come, disgrace, embarrass, expose, highlight, humiliate, lay bare, let down, mortify, pinpoint, reveal, shame, show, stand out, turn up, unmask.

show-down *n.* clash, climax, confrontation, crisis, culmination, dénouement, exposé, face-off.

shower[1] *n.* barrage, deluge, douche, downcome, drift, fusillade, hail, plethora, precipitation, rain, spout, stream, torrent, volley.

v. deluge, douche, douse, heap, inundate, lavish, load, overwhelm, pour, rain, sparge, spray, sprinkle.

shower[2] *n.* crew, galère, gang, mob, rabble.

showiness *n.* flamboyance, flashiness, glitter, glitz, ostentation, pizzazz, razzle-dazzle, razzmatazz, swank.

antonym restraint.

showing *n.* account, appearance, display, evidence, exhibition, impression, past performance, performance, presentation, re-cord, representation, show, staging, statement, track record.

adj. demonstrative, descriptive, elucidative, endeictic, explanatory, explicatory, illustrative, indicative, representative, revelatory, significant, symbolic.

showing-off *n.* boasting, braggadocio, bragging, egotism, exhibitionism, hokum, peacockery, self-advertisement, swagger, swank, vainglory.

antonym modesty.

showman *n.* entertainer, impresario, performer, publicist, ring-master, self-advertiser, show-off.

show-off *n.* boaster, braggadocio, braggart, egotist, exhibitionist, peacock, self-advertiser, swaggerer, swanker, vaunter.

showy *adj.* epideictic, euphuistic, flamboyant, flash, flashy, florid, flossy, garish, gaudy, glitzy, loud, ostentatious, pompous, pretentious, sparkish, specious, splashy, swanking, swanky, tawdry, tinselly.

antonyms quiet, restrained.

shred *n.* atom, bit, fragment, grain, iota, jot, mammock, mite, piece, rag, ribbon, scrap, sliver, snippet, tatter, trace, whit, wisp.

shrew *n.* bitch, dragon, Fury, harridan, henpecker, nag, scold, spitfire, termagant, virago, vixen, Xanthippe.

shrewd *adj.* acute, arch, argute, artful, astucious, astute, calculated, calculating, callid, canny, clever, crafty, cunning, discerning, discriminating, downy, far-seeing, far-sighted, fly, gnostic, intelligent, judicious, keen, knowing, long-headed, observant, perceptive, perspicacious, sagacious, sharp, sly, smart, well-advised, wily.

antonyms naïve, obtuse, unwise.

shrewdly *adv.* artfully, astutely, cannily, cleverly, craftily, far-sightedly, judiciously, knowingly, perceptively, perspicaciously, sagaciously, wisely.

shrewdness *n.* acumen, acuteness, astucity, astuteness, callidity, canniness, discernment, grasp, intelligence, judgement, penetration, perceptiveness, perspicacity, sagacity, sharpness, smartness, wisdom.

antonyms foolishness, naïvety, obtuseness.

shrewish *adj.* bad-tempered, captious, complaining, discontented, fault-finding, henpecking, ill-humoured, ill-natured, ill-tempered, nagging, peevish, petulant, quarrelsome, querulous, scolding, sharp-tongued, vixenish.

antonyms affectionate, peaceable, placid, supportive.

shriek *v.* bellow, caterwaul, cry, holler, howl, scream, screech, shout, squeal, wail, yell.

n. bellow, caterwaul, cry, howl, scream, screech, shout, squeal, wail.

shrill *adj.* acute, argute, carrying, ear-piercing, ear-splitting, high, high-pitched, penetrating, piercing, piping, screaming, screeching, screechy, sharp, strident, treble.

antonyms gentle, low, soft.

shrine n. chapel, dagoba, darga, delubrum, dome, fane, martyry, sanctuary, stupa, tabernacle, temple, tope, vimana.

shrink v. back away, balk, contract, cower, cringe, decrease, deflate, diminish, dwindle, flinch, lessen, narrow, quail, recoil, retire, shorten, shrivel, shun, shy away, wince, withdraw, wither, wrinkle.

antonyms embrace, expand, stretch, warm to.

shrivel v. burn, dehydrate, desiccate, dwindle, frizzle, gizzen, parch, pucker, scorch, sear, shrink, wilt, wither, wizen, wrinkle.

shrivelled adj. desiccated, dried up, dry, emaciated, gizzen, puckered, sere, shrunken, withered, wizened, wrinkled, writhled.

shroud v. blanket, cloak, conceal, cover, enshroud, envelop, enwrap, hide, screen, sheet, swathe, veil, wrap.

antonyms expose, uncover.

n. cerecloth, cerement, cloud, covering, grave-clothes, mantle, pall, screen, sindon, veil, winding-sheet.

shrouded adj. blanketed, cloaked, clouded, concealed, covered, enshrouded, enveloped, hidden, swathed, veiled, wrapped.

antonyms exposed, uncovered.

shrunken adj. cadaverous, contracted, emaciated, gaunt, reduced, shrivelled, shrunk.

antonyms full, generous, rounded, sleek.

shudder v. convulse, heave, quake, quiver, shake, shiver, tremble.

n. convulsion, frisson, grue, horror, quiver, spasm, trembling, tremor.

shuffle[1] v. drag, hobble, limp, scrape, scuff, scuffle, shamble.

shuffle[2] chop and change, confuse, disarrange, disorder, intermix, jumble, mix, rearrange, reorganise, shift, shift around, switch around.

shun v. avoid, cold-shoulder, elude, eschew, evade, ignore, ostracise, shy away from, spurn, steer clear of.

antonyms accept, embrace.

shut v. bar, bolt, cage, close, fasten, latch, lock, seal, secure, slam, spar.

antonym open.

shut down cease, close, discontinue, halt, inactivate, shut up, stop, suspend, switch off, terminate.

shut in box in, circumscribe, confine, enclose, hedge round, hem in, imprison, incarcerate.

shut off cut off, isolate, remove, seclude, segregate, separate, sequester.

shut out banish, bar, conceal, cover, debar, exclude, hide, lock out, mask, muffle, ostracise, screen, veil.

shut up cage, clam up, confine, coop up, gag, gaol, hold one's tongue, hush up, immure, imprison, incarcerate, intern, jail, muzzle, pipe down, silence.

shutter n. abat-jour, jalousie, louvre, screen.

shuttle v. alternate, commute, go to and fro, ply, seesaw, shunt, shuttlecock, travel.

shy adj. backward, bashful, cautious, chary, coy, diffident, distrustful, farouche, hesitant, inhibited, modest, mousy, nervous, reserved, reticent, retiring, self-conscious, self-effacing, shrinking, suspicious, timid, unassertive, wary.

antonyms bold, confident.

v. back away, balk, buck, flinch, quail, rear, recoil, shrink, start, swerve, wince.

shyness n. bashfulness, constraint, coyness, diffidence, hesitancy, inhibition, modesty, mousiness, nervousness, reticence, self-consciousness, timidity, timidness, timorousness.

antonyms boldness, confidence.

sibling n. brother, german, sib, sister, twin.

sibyl n. oracle, prophetess, Pythia, pythoness, seer, seeress, sorceress, wise woman.

sick adj. ailing, black, blasé, bored, diseased, disgusted, displeased, dog-sick, fed up, feeble, ghoulish, glutted, ill, indisposed, jaded, laid up, morbid, mortified, nauseated, pining, poorly, puking, qualmish, queasy, sated, satiated, sickly, tired, under the weather, unwell, vomiting, weak, weary.

antonyms healthy, well.

sicken v. disgust, nauseate, put off, repel, revolt, scunner, turn off.

antonyms attract, delight.

sickening adj. disgusting, distasteful, foul, loathsome, mephitic, offensive, putrid, repulsive, revolting, vile.

antonyms attractive, delightful, pleasing.

sickly adj. ailing, bilious, bloodless, cloying, delicate, faint, feeble, frail, icky, indisposed, infirm, lacklustre, languid, mawkish, nauseating, pallid, peaked, peaky, peelie-wally, pimping, pining, puly, revolting, saccharine, sweet, syrupy, treacly, unhealthy, wan, weak, weakly.

antonyms robust, sturdy.

sickness n. affliction, ailment, bug, complaint, derangement, disease, disorder, dwam, ill-health, illness, indisposition, infirmity, insanity, malady, nausea, pestilence, qualmishness, queasiness, vomiting.

antonym health.

side n. airs, angle, arrogance, aspect, bank, border, boundary, brim, brink, camp, cause, department, direction, division, edge, elevation, face, facet, faction, flank, flitch, fringe, gang, hand, insolence, light, limit, margin, opinion, ostentation, page, part, party, perimeter, periphery, position, pretentiousness, quarter, region, rim, sect, sector, slant, stand, standpoint, surface, team, twist, verge, view, viewpoint.

adj. flanking, incidental, indirect, irrelevant, lateral, lesser, marginal, minor, oblique, roundabout, secondary, subordinate, subsidiary.

side with agree with, befriend, favour, second, support, team up with, vote for.

sidelong adj. covert, indirect, oblique, sideward, sideways.

antonyms direct, overt.

sidestep v. avoid, bypass, circumvent, dodge, duck, elude, evade, find a way round, shirk,

skip, skirt.
antonym tackle.
sidetrack *v.* deflect, distract, divert, head off.
sideways *adv.* askance, crabwise, edgeways, edgewise, laterally, obliquely, sidelong, sidewards.
adj. oblique, side, sidelong, sideward, slanted.
sidle *v.* creep, edge, inch, ingratiate, insinuate, slink, sneak, steal, wriggle.
siesta *n.* catnap, doze, forty winks, nap, relaxation, repose, rest, sleep, snooze.
sieve *v.* boult, remove, riddle, separate, sift, strain.
n. boulter, colander, riddle, screen, sifter, strainer.
sift *v.* analyse, boult, discuss, examine, fathom, filter, investigate, pan, part, probe, review, riddle, screen, scrutinise, separate, sieve, sort, sprinkle, temse, winnow.
n. analysis, colation, examination, filtering, filtration, review, screening, separation, sort, sorting, straining.
sigh *n.* moan, sough, suspiration, wuther.
v. breathe, complain, grieve, lament, moan, sorrow, sough, suspire, wuther.
sigh for grieve, lament, languish, long, mourn, pine, weep, yearn.
sight *n.* appearance, apprehension, decko, display, estimation, exhibition, eye, eyes, eye-shot, eyeshot, eyesight, eyesore, field of vision, fright, gander, glance, glimpse, judgement, ken, look, mess, monstrosity, observation, opinion, pageant, perception, range, scene, seeing, show, spectacle, view, viewing, visibility, vision, vista.
v. behold, discern, distinguish, glimpse, observe, perceive, see, spot.
sights *n.* amenities, beauties, curiosities, features, marvels, Sehenswürdigkeiten, splendours, videnda, wonders.
sightseer *n.* excursionist, holidaymaker, rubberneck, tourist, tripper, visitor.
sign *n.* augury, auspice, badge, beck, betrayal, board, character, cipher, clue, device, emblem, ensign, evidence, figure, foreboding, forewarning, gesture, giveaway, grammalogue, hierogram, hint, indication, indicium, insignia, intimation, lexigram, logo, logogram, logograph, manifestation, mark, marker, miracle, note, notice, omen, placard, pointer, portent, presage, proof, reminder, representation, rune, signal, signature, signification, signpost, spoor, suggestion, symbol, symptom, token, trace, trademark, vestige, warning.
v. autograph, beckon, endorse, gesticulate, gesture, indicate, initial, inscribe, motion, signal, subscribe, wave.
sign over consign, convey, deliver, entrust, make over, surrender, transfer, turn over.
sign up appoint, contract, employ, engage, enlist, enrol, hire, join, join up, recruit, register, sign on, take on, volunteer.
signal *n.* alarm, alert, beacon, beck, cue, flare,

flash, gesture, go-ahead, griffin, impulse, indication, indicator, light, mark, OK, password, rocket, sign, tip-off, token, transmitter, waft, warning, watchword.
adj. conspicuous, distinguished, eminent, exceptional, extraordinary, famous, glorious, impressive, memorable, momentous, notable, noteworthy, outstanding, remarkable, significant, striking.
v. beckon, communicate, gesticulate, gesture, indicate, motion, nod, sign, telegraph, waft, wave.
signature *n.* autograph, endorsement, initials, inscription, mark, sign.
significance *n.* consequence, consideration, force, implication, implications, import, importance, impressiveness, interest, matter, meaning, message, moment, point, purport, relevance, sense, signification, solemnity, weight.
antonym unimportance.
significant *adj.* critical, denoting, eloquent, expressing, expressive, important, indicative, knowing, material, meaning, meaningful, momentous, noteworthy, ominous, pregnant, senseful, serious, solemn, suggestive, symbolic, symptomatic, vital, weighty.
antonyms meaningless, unimportant.
significantly *adj.* appreciably, considerably, critically, crucially, eloquently, knowingly, materially, meaningfully, meaningly, noticeably, perceptibly, suggestively, vitally.
signify *v.* announce, augur, betoken, carry weight, communicate, connote, convey, count, denote, evidence, exhibit, express, imply, indicate, intimate, matter, mean, omen, portend, presage, proclaim, represent, show, stand for, suggest, symbolise, transmit.
signpost *n.* clue, fingerpost, guidepost, handpost, pointer, sign, way-post.
silence *n.* calm, dumbness, hush, lull, muteness, noiselessness, obmutescence, peace, quiescence, quiet, quietness, reserve, reticence, secretiveness, speechlessness, stillness, taciturnity, uncommunicativeness.
v. deaden, dumbfound, extinguish, gag, muffle, muzzle, quell, quiet, quieten, stifle, still, strike dumb, subdue, suppress.
silent *adj.* aphonic, aphonous, dumb, hushed, idle, implicit, inaudible, inoperative, mum, mute, muted, noiseless, quiet, reticent, soundless, speechless, still, stilly, tacit, taciturn, tongue-tied, uncommunicative, understood, unexpressed, unforthcoming, unpronounced, unsounded, unspeaking, unspoken, voiceless, wordless.
antonyms loud, noisy, talkative.
silently *adv.* dumbly, ex tacito, inaudibly, mutely, noiselessly, quietly, soundlessly, speechlessly, tacitly, unheard, wordlessly.
silhouette *n.* configuration, delineation, form, outline, profile, shadow-figure, shadowgraph, shape.
silky *adj.* fine, satiny, silken, sleek, smooth, soft, velvety.

silly *adj.* absurd, addled, asinine, benumbed, bird-brained, brainless, childish, cuckoo, daft, dazed, dopey, drippy, fatuous, feather-brained, flighty, foolhardy, foolish, frivolous, giddy, groggy, hen-witted, idiotic, illogical, immature, imprudent, inane, inappropriate, inept, irrational, irresponsible, meaningless, mindless, muzzy, pointless, preposterous, puerile, ridiculous, scatter-brained, senseless, spoony, stunned, stupefied, stupid, unwise, witless.
antonyms collected, mature, sane, sensible, wise.
n. clot, dope, duffer, goose, half-wit, ignoramus, ninny, silly-billy, simpleton, twit, wally.

silt *n.* alluvium, deposit, mud, ooze, residue, sediment, sludge.
silt up block, choke, clog, congest, dam.

silvan *adj.* arboreous, bosky, forestal, forested, forestine, leafy, tree-covered, wooded, woodland.
antonym treeless.

similar *adj.* alike, analogous, close, comparable, compatible, congruous, corresponding, homogeneous, homogenous, homologous, related, resembling, self-like, uniform.
antonym different.

similarity *n.* affinity, agreement, analogy, closeness, coincidence, comparability, compatibility, concordance, congruence, correspondence, equivalence, homogeneity, likeness, relation, resemblance, sameness, similitude, uniformity.
antonym difference.

similarly *adv.* by analogy, by the same token, correspondingly, likewise, uniformly.

simmer *v.* boil, burn, fizz, fume, rage, seethe, smart, smoulder.
simmer down calm down, collect oneself, contain oneself, control oneself, cool down, cool off, recollect oneself, settle down, take it easy.

simpering *adj.* affected, arch, coy, giggling, missish, schoolgirlish, self-conscious, silly.

simple *adj.* artless, bald, basic, brainless, childlike, classic, classical, clean, clear, credulous, dense, direct, dumb, easy, elementary, feeble, feeble-minded, foolish, frank, green, guileless, half-witted, homely, honest, humble, idiot-proof, inelaborate, ingenuous, innocent, inornate, intelligible, lowly, lucid, manageable, modest, moronic, naïf, naive, naïve, naked, natural, obtuse, one-fold, plain, pure, rustic, Saturnian, shallow, silly, sincere, single, slow, Spartan, stark, straightforward, stupid, thick, unadorned, unaffected, unalloyed, unblended, uncluttered, uncombined, uncomplicated, undeniable, understandable, undisguised, undivided, unelaborate, unembellished, unfussy, uninvolved, unlearned, unmixed, unornate, unpretentious, unschooled, unskilled, unsophisticated, unsuspecting, unvarnished.
antonyms artful, clever, complicated, difficult, fancy, intricate.

simple-minded *adj.* addle-brained, artless, backward, brainless, cretinous, dim-witted, dopey, feeble-minded, foolish, goofy, idiot, idiotic, imbecile, moronic, natural, retarded, simple, stupid, unsophisticated.
antonyms bright, clever.

simpleton *n.* Abderite, blockhead, booby, daftie, dizzard, dolt, dope, dullard, dunce, dupe, flat, flathead, fool, gaby, gander, gomeril, goon, goop, goose, goose-cap, goosy, Gothamist, Gothamite, green goose, greenhorn, gump, gunsel, idiot, imbecile, jackass, Johnny, juggins, maffling, moron, nincompoop, ninny, ninny-hammer, numskull, soft-head, spoon, stupid, twerp.
antonym brain.

simplicity *n.* artlessness, baldness, candour, clarity, classicism, clearness, directness, ease, easiness, elementariness, guilelessness, innocence, intelligibility, modesty, naïveté, naïvety, naturalness, obviousness, openness, plainness, purity, restraint, simpleness, sincerity, straightforwardness, uncomplicatedness.
antonyms difficulty, guile, intricacy, sophistication.

simplify *v.* abridge, decipher, disentangle, facilitate, prune, reduce, streamline.
antonyms complicate, elaborate.

simplistic *adj.* naive, oversimplified, schematic, shallow, simple, superficial, sweeping, unanalytical.
antonyms analytical, detailed.

simply *adv.* absolutely, altogether, artlessly, baldly, clearly, completely, directly, easily, intelligibly, just, merely, modestly, naturally, obviously, only, plainly, purely, quite, really, simpliciter, sincerely, solely, straightforwardly, totally, unaffectedly, undeniably, unpretentiously, unquestionably, unreservedly, utterly, wholly.

simulate *v.* act, affect, assume, counterfeit, duplicate, echo, fabricate, fake, feign, imitate, mimic, parrot, pretend, put on, reflect, reproduce, sham.

simulated *adj.* artificial, assumed, bogus, fake, feigned, imitation, inauthentic, insincere, make-believe, man-made, mock, phoney, pinchbeck, pretended, pseudo, put-on, sham, spurious, substitute, synthetic, ungenuine.
antonyms genuine, real.

simultaneous *adj.* accompanying, coincident, coinciding, concomitant, concurrent, contemporaneous, parallel, synchronic, synchronous.
antonyms asynchronous, separate.

sin *n.* crime, damnation, debt, error, evil, fault, guilt, hamartia, impiety, iniquity, lapse, misdeed, offence, sinfulness, transgression, trespass, ungodliness, unrighteousness, wickedness, wrong, wrongdoing.
v. err, fall, fall from grace, go astray, lapse, misbehave, offend, stray, transgress, trespass.

sincere *adj.* artless, bona fide, candid, deep-felt, earnest, frank, genuine, guileless, heartfelt,

heart-whole, honest, natural, open, plain-hearted, plain-spoken, pure, real, serious, simple, simple-hearted, single-hearted, soulful, straightforward, true, true-hearted, truthful, unadulterated, unaffected, unfeigned, unmixed, wholehearted.
antonym insincere.

sincerely *adv.* earnestly, genuinely, honestly, in earnest, really, seriously, simply, truly, truthfully, unaffectedly, wholeheartedly.

sincerity *n.* artlessness, bona fides, candour, earnestness, frankness, genuineness, good faith, guilelessness, honesty, plain-heartedness, probity, seriousness, straightforwardness, truth, truthfulness, wholeheartedness.
antonym insincerity.

sinecure *n.* cinch, cushy job, doddle, gravy train, money for jam, picnic, plum job, soft option.

sinewy *adj.* athletic, brawny, lusty, muscular, powerful, robust, stringy, strong, sturdy, tendinous, vigorous, wiry.

sinful *adj.* bad, corrupt, criminal, depraved, erring, fallen, guilty, immoral, impious, iniquitous, irreligious, peccable, peccant, ungodly, unholy, unrighteous, unvirtuous, wicked, wrongful.
antonyms righteous, sinless.

sinfulness *n.* corruption, depravity, guilt, immorality, impiety, iniquity, peccability, peccancy, sin, transgression, ungodliness, unrighteousness, wickedness.
antonym righteousness.

sing *v.* betray, bizz, blow the whistle, cantillate, carol, caterwaul, chant, chirp, croon, finger, fink, grass, hum, inform, intone, lilt, melodise, peach, pipe, purr, quaver, rat, render, serenade, spill the beans, squeal, talk, trill, vocalise, warble, whine, whistle, yodel.
  sing out bawl, bellow, call, cooee, cry, halloo, holler, shout, yell.

singe *v.* blacken, burn, cauterise, char, scorch, sear.

singer *n.* balladeer, balladist, bard, cantabank, cantatrice, cantor, caroller, chanteuse, choirboy, choirgirl, choirman, chorister, crooner, diva, jongleur, Meistersinger, minstrel, precentor, prima donna, psalmodist, songster, troubadour, vocalist.

single *adj.* celibate, distinct, exclusive, free, individual, lone, man-to-man, one, one-fold, one-to-one, only, particular, separate, simple, sincere, single-minded, singular, sole, solitary, unattached, unblended, unbroken, uncombined, uncompounded, undivided, unique, unmarried, unmixed, unshared, unwed, wholehearted.
  single out choose, cull, distinguish, hand-pick, highlight, isolate, pick, pinpoint, select, separate, set apart.

single-handed *adj., adv.* alone, independently, solo, unaccompanied, unaided, unassisted.

single-minded *adj.* dedicated, determined, dogged, fixed, hell-bent, monomaniacal, resolute, steadfast, stubborn, tireless, undeviating, unswerving, unwavering.

singular *adj.* atypical, conspicuous, curious, eccentric, eminent, exceptional, extraordinary, individual, noteworthy, odd, out-of-the-way, outstanding, peculiar, pre-eminent, private, prodigious, proper, puzzling, queer, rare, remarkable, separate, single, sole, strange, uncommon, unique, unparalleled, unusual.
antonyms normal, usual.

singularity *n.* abnormality, curiousness, eccentricity, extraordinariness, idiosyncrasy, irregularity, oddity, oddness, oneness, particularity, peculiarity, queerness, quirk, strangeness, twist, unicity, uniqueness.
antonym normality.

singularly *adv.* bizarrely, conspicuously, especially, exceptionally, extraordinarily, notably, outstandingly, particularly, prodigiously, remarkably, signally, surprisingly, uncommonly, unusually.

sinister *adj.* dire, disquieting, evil, inauspicious, injurious, left, louche, malevolent, malign, malignant, menacing, ominous, threatening, underhand, unlucky.
antonyms harmless, innocent.

sink *v.* abandon, abate, abolish, bore, collapse, conceal, decay, decline, decrease, defeat, degenerate, degrade, delapse, descend, destroy, dig, diminish, dip, disappear, drill, drive, droop, drop, drown, dwindle, ebb, engulf, excavate, fade, fail, fall, finish, flag, founder, invest, lapse, lay, lessen, lower, merge, overwhelm, pay, penetrate, plummet, plunge, relapse, retrogress, ruin, sag, scupper, slip, slope, slump, stoop, submerge, subside, succumb, suppress, weaken, worsen.
antonyms float, rise, uplift.

sinless *adj.* faultless, guiltless, immaculate, impeccable, innocent, pure, unblemished, uncorrupted, undefiled, unspotted, unsullied, virtuous.
antonym sinful.

sinner *n.* backslider, evil-doer, malefactor, miscreant, offender, reprobate, transgressor, trespasser, wrong-doer.

sinuous *adj.* coiling, crooked, curved, curvy, lithe, mazy, meandering, serpentine, slinky, supple, tortuous, undulating, winding.
antonym straight.

sip *v.* delibate, sample, sup, taste.
  n. drop, mouthful, spoonful, swallow, taste, thimbleful.

siren *n.* charmer, Circe, femme fatale, houri, Lorelei, seductress, temptress, vamp, witch.

sissy *n.* baby, coward, milksop, mollycoddle, mummy's boy, namby-pamby, pansy, softy, weakling, wet.
  adj. cowardly, effeminate, feeble, namby-pamby, pansy, sissified, soft, unmanly, weak, wet.

sit *v.* accommodate, assemble, befit, brood, contain, convene, deliberate, hold, meet, officiate, perch, pose, preside, reside, rest, seat, settle.

site *n.* ground, location, lot, place, plot, position, setting, spot, station.

v. dispose, install, locate, place, position, set, situate, station.

sitting *n.* assembly, consultation, get-together, hearing, meeting, period, seat, session, spell.

situation *n.* ball-game, berth, case, circumstances, condition, employment, galère, job, kettle of fish, lie of the land, locale, locality, location, office, place, plight, position, post, predicament, rank, scenario, seat, setting, set-up, site, sphere, spot, state, state of affairs, station, status.

sizable *adj.* biggish, considerable, decent, decent-sized, goodly, large, largish, respectable, significant, substantial, tidy.

antonym small.

size *n.* amount, amplitude, bigness, bulk, dimensions, extent, greatness, height, hugeness, immensity, largeness, magnitude, mass, measurement(s), proportions, range, vastness, volume.

size up appraise, assess, evaluate, gauge, measure.

sizzle *v.* crackle, frizzle, fry, hiss, scorch, sear, spit, sputter.

skedaddle *v.* abscond, beat it, bolt, decamp, disappear, do a bunk, flee, hop it, run away, scarper, scoot, scram, split, vamoose.

skeletal *adj.* cadaverous, drawn, emaciated, fleshless, gaunt, haggard, hollow-cheeked, shrunken, skin-and-bone, wasted.

skeleton *n.* bare bones, draft, endoskeleton, frame, framework, outline, sketch, structure.

sketch *v.* block out, delineate, depict, draft, draw, outline, paint, pencil, plot, portray, represent, rough out.

n. croquis, delineation, design, draft, drawing, ébauche, esquisse, outline, plan, scenario, skeleton, vignette.

sketchily *adv.* cursorily, hastily, imperfectly, inadequately, incompletely, patchily, perfunctorily, roughly, vaguely.

antonym fully.

sketchy *adj.* bitty, crude, cursory, imperfect, inadequate, incomplete, insufficient, outline, perfunctory, rough, scrappy, skimpy, slight, superficial, unfinished, vague.

antonym full.

skilful *adj.* able, accomplished, adept, adroit, apt, canny, clever, competent, dexterous, experienced, expert, handy, masterly, nimble-fingered, practised, professional, proficient, quick, ready, skilled, tactical, trained.

antonyms awkward, clumsy, inept.

skill *n.* ability, accomplishment, adroitness, aptitude, art, cleverness, competence, dexterity, experience, expertise, expertness, facility, finesse, handiness, ingenuity, intelligence, knack, proficiency, quickness, readiness, savoir-faire, savvy, skilfulness, talent, technique, touch.

skilled *adj.* able, accomplished, crack, experienced, expert, masterly, practised, professional, proficient, schooled, skilful, trained.

antonym unskilled.

skim *v.* brush, coast, cream, dart, despumate, float, fly, glide, plane, sail, scan, separate, skip, soar.

skimp *v.* conserve, cut corners, economise, pinch, scamp, scant, scrimp, stint, withhold.

skimpy *adj.* beggarly, exiguous, inadequate, insufficient, meagre, measly, miserly, niggardly, scanty, short, sketchy, sparse, thin, tight.

antonym generous.

skin *n.* casing, coating, crust, deacon, epidermis, fell, film, hide, husk, integument, membrane, outside, peel, pellicle, pelt, rind, tegument.

v. abrade, bark, excoriate, flay, fleece, graze, peel, scrape, strip.

skin-deep *adj.* artificial, empty, external, meaningless, outward, shallow, superficial, surface.

skinflint *n.* cheese-parer, meanie, miser, niggard, penny-pincher, Scrooge, tightwad.

skinny *adj.* attenuate(d), emaciated, lean, scragged, scraggy, skeletal, skin-and-bone, thin, twiggy, underfed, undernourished, weedy.

antonym fat.

skip *v.* bob, bounce, caper, cavort, cut, dance, eschew, flisk, flit, frisk, gambol, hop, miss, omit, overleap, play truant, prance, trip.

skirmish *n.* affair, affray, battle, brush, clash, combat, conflict, contest, dust-up, encounter, engagement, fracas, incident, scrap, scrimmage, set-to, spat, tussle, velitation.

v. clash, collide, pickeer, scrap, tussle.

skirt *v.* avoid, border, bypass, circle, circumambulate, circumnavigate, circumvent, detour, edge, evade, flank, steer clear of.

skit *n.* burlesque, caricature, parody, satire, sketch, spoof, take-off, travesty, turn.

skittish *adj.* coltish, excitable, fickle, fidgety, frivolous, highly-strung, jumpy, kittenish, kitteny, lively, nervous, playful, restive.

skittles *n.* kettle-pins, kittle-pins, ninepins, pins, tenpins.

skive *v.* dodge, dodge the column, idle, malinger, shirk, skrimshank, skulk, slack, swing the lead.

skiver *n.* dodger, do-nothing, idler, loafer, malingerer, scrimshanker, shirker, slacker.

skulduggery *n.* chicanery, double-dealing, duplicity, fraudulence, jiggery-pokery, machinations, shenanigan(s), swindling, trickery, underhandedness, unscrupulousness.

skulk *v.* creep, lie in wait, loiter, lurk, pad, prowl, pussyfoot, slink, sneak.

sky *n.* air, ambient, atmosphere, azure, blue, empyrean, firmament, heavens, vault of heaven, welkin.

slab *n.* briquette, chunk, hunk, lump, piece, planch, portion, slice, wedge, wodge.

slack *adj.* baggy, crank, dull, easy, easy-going, flaccid, flexible, idle, inactive, inattentive, lax, lazy, limp, loose, neglectful, negligent, permissive, quiet, relaxed, remiss, slow, slow-moving, sluggish, tardy.

antonyms busy, diligent, quick, rigid, stiff,

taut.

n. excess, give, inactivity, leeway, looseness, play, relaxation, room.

v. dodge, idle, malinger, neglect, relax, shirk, skive, slacken.

slacken off abate, decrease, diminish, fail, flag, lessen, loosen, moderate, reduce, relax, release, slow, slow down, tire.

antonyms increase, quicken, tighten.

slacker *n.* clock-watcher, dawdler, dodger, do-nothing, embusqué, fainéant, good-for-nothing, idler, layabout, loafer, malingerer, passenger, shirk(er), skiver, skrimshanker.

slag *v.* abuse, berate, criticise, deride, insult, lambaste, malign, mock, slam, slang, slate.

slake *v.* abate, allay, assuage, deaden, extinguish, gratify, mitigate, moderate, moisten, quench, reduce, sate, satiate, satisfy, slacken, subside.

slam *v.* attack, bang, castigate, clap, crash, criticise, damn, dash, excoriate, fling, hurl, lambaste, pan, pillory, slate, smash, swap, swop, throw, thump, vilify.

slander *n.* aspersion, backbiting, calumniation, calumny, defamation, detraction, libel, misrepresentation, muck-raking, obloquy, scandal, smear, traducement, traduction.

v. asperse, backbite, calumniate, decry, defame, detract, disparage, libel, malign, muck-rake, scandalise, slur, smear, traduce, vilify, vilipend.

antonyms glorify, praise.

slanderous *adj.* abusive, aspersive, aspersory, calumnious, damaging, defamatory, libellous, malicious.

slang *v.* abuse, berate, castigate, excoriate, insult, lambaste, malign, revile, scold, slag, vilify, vituperate.

antonym praise.

slanging match altercation, argument, argy-bargy, barney, dispute, quarrel, row, set-to, shouting match, spat.

slant *v.* angle, bend, bevel, bias, cant, colour, distort, incline, lean, list, shelve, skew, slope, tilt, twist, warp, weight.

n. angle, attitude, bias, camber, declination, diagonal, emphasis, gradient, incline, leaning, obliquity, pitch, prejudice, rake, ramp, slope, tilt, viewpoint.

slanting *adj.* angled, askew, aslant, asymmetrical, bent, canted, cater-cornered, diagonal, inclined, oblique, sideways, skew-whiff, slanted, slantwise, sloping, tilted, tilting.

antonym level.

slap *n.* bang, blow, clap, clout, cuff, paddy-whack, skelp, smack, spank, wallop, whack.

v. bang, clap, clout, cuff, daub, hit, plaster, plonk, skelp, spank, spread, strike, whack.

adv. bang, dead, directly, exactly, plumb, precisely, right, slap-bang, smack.

slap down berate, keelhaul, rebuke, reprimand, restrain, squash, upbraid.

slap in the face affront, blow, humiliation, indignity, insult, put-down, rebuff, rebuke, rejection, repulse, snub.

slap-dash *adj.* careless, clumsy, disorderly, haphazard, hasty, hurried, last-minute, messy, negligent, offhand, perfunctory, rash, slipshod, sloppy, slovenly, thoughtless, thrown-together, untidy.

antonyms careful, orderly.

slap-happy *adj.* boisterous, casual, dazed, giddy, haphazard, happy-go-lucky, hit-or-miss, irresponsible, nonchalant, punch-drunk, reckless, reeling, slap-dash, woozy.

slapstick *n.* buffoonery, comedy, farce, horseplay, knockabout, tomfoolery.

slap-up *adj.* elaborate, excellent, first-class, first-rate, lavish, luxurious, magnificent, princely, splendid, sumptuous, superb, superlative.

slash *v.* criticise, cut, drop, gash, hack, lacerate, lash, lower, reduce, rend, rip, score, slit.

n. cut, gash, incision, laceration, lash, rent, rip, slit.

slashing *adj.* aggressive, biting, brutal, ferocious, harsh, savage, searing, unsparing, vicious.

slate *v.* abuse, berate, blame, castigate, censure, criticise, lambaste, pan, rebuke, reprimand, roast, scold, slag, slam, slang.

antonym praise.

slatternly *adj.* bedraggled, dirty, dowdy, draggle-tailed, frowzy, frumpish, frumpy, slipshod, sloppy, slovenly, sluttish, unclean, unkempt, untidy.

slaughter *n.* battue, blood-bath, bloodshed, butchery, carnage, extermination, holocaust, killing, liquidation, massacre, murder, slaying.

v. butcher, crush, defeat, destroy, exterminate, halal, hammer, kill, liquidate, massacre, murder, overwhelm, rout, scupper, slay, thrash, trounce, vanquish.

slave *n.* abject, bondservant, bond-slave, bond(s)man, bond(s)woman, captive, drudge, esne, helot, Mameluke, scullion, serf, servant, skivvy, slavey, thrall, vassal, villein.

v. drudge, grind, labour, skivvy, slog, struggle, sweat, toil.

slaver *v.* dribble, drivel, drool, salivate, slabber, slobber.

slavery *n.* bondage, captivity, duress(e), enslavement, impressment, serfdom, servitude, subjugation, thraldom, thrall, vassalage, yoke.

antonym freedom.

slavish *adj.* abject, base, conventional, cringing, despicable, fawning, grovelling, imitative, laborious, literal, low, mean, menial, obsequious, servile, strict, submissive, sycophantic, unimaginative, uninspired, unoriginal.

antonyms independent, original.

slay *v.* amuse, annihilate, assassinate, butcher, destroy, dispatch, eliminate, execute, exterminate, impress, kill, massacre, murder, rub out, slaughter, wow.

slaying *n.* annihilation, assassination, butchery, destruction, dispatch, elimination, extermination, killing, mactation, massacre, murder, shambles, slaughter.

sleazy *adj.* crummy, disreputable, low, run-down, seedy, sordid, squalid, tacky.

sleek *adj.* glossy, insinuating, lustrous, plausible, shiny, smooth, smug, well-fed, well-groomed.

sleep *v.* catnap, doss (down), doze, drop off, drowse, hibernate, nod off, repose, rest, slumber, snooze, snore.
n. coma, dormancy, doss, doze, forty winks, hibernation, nap, repose, rest, shut-eye, siesta, slumber(s), snooze, sopor.

sleepiness *n.* doziness, drowsiness, heaviness, lethargy, oscitancy, somnolence, torpor.
antonyms alertness, wakefulness.

sleeping *adj.* asleep, becalmed, daydreaming, dormant, dormient, hibernating, idle, inactive, inattentive, off guard, passive, slumbering, unaware.
antonyms alert, awake.

sleepless *adj.* alert, disturbed, insomniac, insomnious, restless, unsleeping, vigilant, wakeful, watchful, wide-awake.

sleeplessness *n.* insomnia, insomnolence, wakefulness.

sleep-walker *n.* noctambulist, somnambulist.

sleep-walking *n.* noctambulation, noctambulism, somnambulation, somnambulism.

sleepy *adj.* drowsy, dull, heavy, hypnotic, inactive, lethargic, quiet, slow, sluggish, slumb(e)rous, slumbersome, slumbery, somnolent, soporific, soporose, soporous, torpid.
antonyms alert, awake, restless, wakeful.

sleight of hand adroitness, artifice, dexterity, legerdemain, magic, manipulation, prestidigitation, skill, trickery.

slender *adj.* acicular, faint, feeble, flimsy, fragile, gracile, inadequate, inconsiderable, insufficient, lean, little, meagre, narrow, poor, remote, scanty, slight, slim, small, spare, svelte, sylph-like, tenuous, thin, thready, wasp-waisted, weak, willowish, willowy.
antonyms considerable, fat, thick.

sleuth *n.* bloodhound, detective, dick, gumshoe, private eye, private investigator, shadow, tail, tracker.

slice *n.* cut, frustum, helping, piece, portion, rasher, section, segment, share, sheave, shive, slab, sliver, tranche, wafer, wedge, whack, whang.
v. carve, chop, cut, divide, segment, sever, sliver, whittle.

slick *adj.* adroit, deft, dexterous, glib, meretricious, plausible, polished, professional, sharp, skilful, sleek, smooth, sophistical, specious, trim.
antonyms amateurish, clumsy, coarse.

slide *v.* coast, glide, glissade, lapse, skate, skim, slidder, slip, slither, toboggan, veer.

slight *adj.* delicate, feeble, flimsy, fragile, gracile, inconsiderable, insignificant, insubstantial, meagre, minor, modest, negligible, paltry, scanty, slender, slim, small, spare, superficial, trifling, trivial, unimportant, weak.

antonyms considerable, large, major, significant.
v. affront, cold-shoulder, cut, despise, disdain, disparage, disrespect, ignore, insult, neglect, scorn, snub.
antonyms compliment, flatter.
n. affront, contempt, discourtesy, disdain, disregard, disrespect, inattention, indifference, insult, neglect, rebuff, rudeness, slur, snub.

slighting *adj.* abusive, belittling, defamatory, derogatory, disdainful, disparaging, disrespectful, insulting, offensive, scornful, slanderous, supercilious, uncomplimentary.
antonym complimentary.

slim *adj.* ectomorphic, faint, gracile, lean, narrow, poor, remote, slender, slight, svelte, sylph-like, thin, trim.
antonyms chubby, fat, strong.
v. bant, diet, lose weight, reduce, slenderise.

slime *n.* bitumen, cludge, filth, gleet, glit, goo, gunk, mess, muck, mucus, mud, ooze.

slimy *adj.* clammy, creeping, disgusting, glutinous, grovelling, miry, mucous, muddy, obsequious, oily, oozy, servile, smarmy, soapy, sycophantic, toadying, uliginous, unctuous, viscous.

sling *v.* cast, catapult, chuck, dangle, fling, hang, heave, hurl, lob, pitch, shy, suspend, swing, throw, toss.
n. band, bandage, catapult, loop, parbuckle, strap, support.

slink *v.* creep, prowl, pussyfoot, sidle, skulk, slip, sneak, steal.

slinky *adj.* clinging, close-fitting, feline, figure-hugging, lean, sinuous, skin-tight, sleek.

slip¹ *v.* blunder, boob, conceal, creep, disappear, discharge, dislocate, elude, err, escape, fall, get away, glide, hide, lapse, loose, miscalculate, misjudge, mistake, skate, skid, slidder, slide, slink, slither, sneak, steal, trip.
n. bloomer, blunder, boob, error, failure, fault, imprudence, indiscretion, lapsus, lapsus calami, lapsus linguae, lapsus memoriae, mistake, omission, oversight, slip-up.

slip² *n.* certificate, coupon, cutting, offshoot, pass, piece, runner, scion, shoot, sliver, sprig, sprout, strip.

slipper *n.* flip-flop, loafer, moccasin, mule, pabouche, pantable, pantof(f)le, panton, pantoufle, pump, sandal.

slippery *adj.* crafty, cunning, devious, dishonest, duplicitous, evasive, false, foxy, glassy, greasy, icy, lubric(al), lubric(i)ous, perilous, shifty, skiddy, sliddery, slippy, smooth, sneaky, treacherous, tricky, two-faced, unpredictable, unreliable, unsafe, unstable, unsteady, untrustworthy.

slippy *adj.* elusive, evasive, greasy, icy, lubric(i)ous, smooth, uncertain, unstable.

slipshod *adj.* careless, casual, loose, negligent, slap-dash, sloppy, slovenly, unsystematic, untidy.
antonyms careful, fastidious, neat, tidy.

slit v. cut, gash, knife, lance, pierce, rip, slash, slice, split.

    n. cut, fent, fissure, gash, incision, opening, rent, split, tear, vent.

    adj. cut, pertusate, pertuse(d), rent, split, torn.

slither v. glide, skitter, slidder, slide, slink, slip, snake, undulate.

sliver n. chip, flake, fragment, paring, shaving, shiver, shred, slip, splinter.

slob n. boor, brute, churl, lout, oaf, philistine, sloven, yahoo, yob.

slobber v. dribble, drivel, drool, salivate, slabber, slaver, splutter, water at the mouth.

slog v. bash, belt, hit, labour, persevere, plod, plough through, slave, slosh, slug, smite, sock, strike, thump, toil, tramp, trek, trudge, wallop, work.

    n. effort, exertion, grind, hike, labour, struggle, tramp, trek, trudge.

slogan n. battle-cry, catch-phrase, catchword, chant, jingle, motto, rallying-cry, war cry, watchword.

slop v. overflow, slobber, slosh, spatter, spill, splash, splatter, wash away.

slope v. batter, delve, fall, incline, lean, pitch, rise, slant, tilt, verge, weather.

    n. bajada, brae, cant, declination, declivity, descent, downgrade, escarp, glacis, gradient, inclination, incline, ramp, rise, scarp, slant, tilt, versant.

sloping adj. acclivitous, acclivous, bevelled, canting, declivitous, declivous, inclined, inclining, leaning, oblique, slanting.

    antonym level.

sloppy adj. amateurish, banal, careless, clumsy, gushing, hit-or-miss, inattentive, mawkish, messy, mushy, schmaltzy, sentimental, slipshod, slovenly, sludgy, slushy, soppy, splashy, trite, unkempt, untidy, watery, weak, wet.

    antonyms careful, exact, precise.

slosh v. bash, biff, flounder, hit, plash, pour, punch, shower, slap, slog, slop, slug, sock, splash, spray, strike, swash, swipe, thump, thwack, wade, wallop.

slot n. aperture, channel, gap, groove, hole, niche, opening, place, position, slit, space, time, vacancy.

    v. adjust, assign, fit, insert, pigeonhole, place, position.

sloth n. accidie, acedia, fainéance, idleness, inactivity, indolence, inertia, laziness, listlessness, slackness, slothfulness, sluggishness, torpor.

    antonyms diligence, industriousness, sedulity.

slothful adj. do-nothing, fainéant, idle, inactive, indolent, inert, lazy, listless, skiving, slack, sluggish, torpid, workshy.

    antonyms diligent, industrious, sedulous.

slouch v. droop, hunch, loll, shamble, shuffle, slump, stoop.

slouching adj. careless, disorderly, heedless, loose, negligent, shambling, shuffling, slack, slap-dash, slatternly, slipshod, sloppy, unkempt, untidy.

slow adj. adagio, backward, behind, behindhand, boring, bovine, conservative, creeping, dawdling, dead, dead-and-alive, delayed, deliberate, dense, dilatory, dim, dull, dullwitted, dumb, easy, gradual, inactive, lackadaisical, laggard, lagging, late, lazy, leaden, leisurely, lingering, loitering, long-drawn-out, measured, obtuse, one-horse, pedetentous, plodding, ponderous, prolonged, protracted, quiet, retarded, slack, lagging, sleepy, slow-moving, slow-witted, sluggardly, sluggish, stagnant, stupid, tame, tardy, tedious, thick, time-consuming, uneventful, unhasty, unhurried, uninteresting, unproductive, unprogressive, unpunctual, unresponsive, wearisome.

    antonyms active, fast, quick, rapid, swift.

    v. brake, check, curb, decelerate, delay, detain, draw rein, handicap, hold up, lag, relax, restrict, retard.

    slow to averse, disinclined, hesitant, indisposed, loath, reluctant, unwilling.

slowly adv. adagio, gradually, inchmeal, larghetto, largo, lazily, leisurely, lento, ploddingly, ponderously, sluggishly, steadily, unhurriedly.

    antonym quickly.

sludge n. dregs, gunge, gunk, mire, muck, mud, ooze, residue, sediment, silt, slag, slime, slop, slush, swill.

sluggish adj. dull, heavy, inactive, indolent, inert, lethargic, lifeless, listless, lurdan, lymphatic, phlegmatic, slothful, slow, slow-moving, torpid, unresponsive.

    antonyms brisk, dynamic, eager, quick, vigorous.

sluggishness n. apathy, drowsiness, dullness, fainéance, heaviness, indolence, inertia, languor, lassitude, lethargy, listlessness, slothfulness, slowness, somnolence, stagnation, torpor.

    antonyms dynamism, eagerness, quickness.

sluice v. cleanse, drain, drench, flush, irrigate, slosh, swill, wash.

slumber v. doze, drowse, nap, repose, rest, sleep, snooze.

slummy adj. decayed, dirty, overcrowded, ramshackle, run-down, seedy, sleazy, sordid, squalid, wretched.

slump v. bend, collapse, crash, decline, deteriorate, droop, drop, fall, hunch, loll, plummet, plunge, sag, sink, slip, slouch, worsen.

    n. collapse, crash, decline, depreciation, depression, downturn, drop, failure, fall, falling-off, low, recession, reverse, stagnation, trough, worsening.

    antonym boom.

slur n. affront, aspersion, blot, brand, calumny, discredit, disgrace, innuendo, insinuation, insult, reproach, slander, slight, smear, stain, stigma.

slut n. dolly-map, drab, d(r)aggle-tail, dratchell, jade, slattern, sloven, trollop.

sly adj. arch, artful, astute, canny, clever, conniving, covert, crafty, cunning, devious, foxy, furtive, guileful, impish, insidious, knowing, mischievous, peery, roguish, scheming, secret, secretive, shifty, sleeky, stealthy, subtle, surreptitious, underhand, vulpine, wily.

antonyms frank, honest, open, straightforward.

smack *v.* box, clap, cuff, hit, pandy, pat, skelp, slap, sock, spank, strike, tap, thwack, whack.

n. blow, box, crack, cuff, hit, pandy, pat, skelp, slap, sock, spank, strike, tap, thwack, whack.

adv. directly, exactly, plumb, point-blank, precisely, right, slap, slap-bang, squarely, straight.

smack one's lips anticipate, delight in, drool over, enjoy, relish, savour.

small *adj.* bantam, base, dilute, diminutive, dwarf(ish), grudging, humble, illiberal, immature, inadequate, incapacious, inconsiderable, insignificant, insufficient, itsy-bitsy, lesser, limited, little, meagre, mean, mignon(ne), mini, miniature, minor, minuscule, minute, modest, narrow, negligible, paltry, petite, petty, pigmean, pint-size(d), pocket, pocket-sized, puny, pygmaean, pygmean, scanty, selfish, slight, small-scale, tichy, tiddl(e)y, tiny, trifling, trivial, undersized, unimportant, unpretentious, wee, young.

antonyms big, huge, large.

small-minded *adj.* bigoted, envious, grudging, hidebound, insular, intolerant, mean, narrow-minded, parochial, petty, rigid, ungenerous.

antonyms broad-minded, liberal, tolerant.

small-time *adj.* inconsequential, insignificant, minor, no-account, petty, piddling, unimportant.

antonyms important, major.

smarminess *n.* obsequiousness, oiliness, servility, suavity, sycophancy, toadying, unctuosity, unctuousness.

smarmy *adj.* bootlicking, crawling, fawning, fulsome, greasy, ingratiating, obsequious, oily, servile, smooth, soapy, suave, sycophantic, toadying, unctuous.

smart[1] *adj.* acute, adept, agile, apt, astute, bright, brisk, canny, chic, clever, cracking, dandy, effective, elegant, fashionable, fine, impertinent, ingenious, intelligent, jaunty, keen, lively, modish, natty, neat, nimble, nimble-witted, nobby, pert, pointed, quick, quick-witted, rattling, ready, ready-witted, saucy, sharp, shrewd, smart-alecky, snappy, spanking, spirited, spruce, stylish, swagger, swish, tippy, trim, vigorous, vivacious, well-appointed, witty.

antonyms dowdy, dumb, slow, stupid, unfashionable, untidy.

smart Alec(k) Besserwisser, clever clogs, clever dick, know-all, smart-arse, smarty-boots, smartypants, wise guy, wiseacre.

smart[2] *v.* burn, hurt, nip, pain, sting, throb, tingle, twinge.

adj. hard, keen, nipping, nippy, painful, piercing, resounding, sharp, stinging.

n. nip, pain, pang, smarting, soreness, sting, twinge.

smarten *v.* beautify, clean, groom, neaten, polish, primp, prink, spruce up, tidy.

smash *v.* break, collide, crash, crush, defeat, demolish, destroy, disintegrate, lay waste, overthrow, prang, pulverise, ruin, shatter, shiver, squabash, wreck.

n. accident, collapse, collision, crash, defeat, destruction, disaster, downfall, failure, pile-up, prang, ruin, shattering, smash-up.

smashing *adj.* braw, excellent, exhilarating, fab, fabulous, fantastic, first-class, first-rate, great, magnificent, marvellous, sensational, stupendous, super, superb, superlative, terrific, tremendous, wonderful.

smattering *n.* basics, bit, dash, elements, modicum, rudiments, smatter, soupçon, sprinkling.

smear *v.* asperse, bedaub, bedim, besmirch, blacken, blur, calumniate, coat, cover, dab, daub, dirty, drag (someone's) name through the mud, gaum, malign, patch, plaster, rub on, slubber, smarm, smudge, soil, spread over, stain, sully, tarnish, traduce, vilify.

n. blot, blotch, calumny, daub, defamation, gaum, libel, mudslinging, slander, smudge, splodge, streak, vilification, whispering campaign.

smell *n.* aroma, bouquet, fetor, fragrance, fumet(te), funk, malodour, mephitis, nose, odour, perfume, pong, redolence, scent, sniff, stench, stink, whiff.

v. be malodorous, hum, inhale, nose, pong, reek, scent, sniff, snuff, stink, stink to high heaven, whiff.

smelly *adj.* bad, evil-smelling, fetid, foul, foul-smelling, frowsty, funky, graveolent, high, malodorous, mephitic, noisome, off, pongy, putrid, reeking, stinking, strong, strong-smelling, whiffy.

smirk *n.* grin, leer, simper, sneer, snigger.

smitten *adj.* afflicted, beguiled, beset, bewitched, bowled over, burdened, captivated, charmed, enamoured, infatuated, plagued, struck, troubled.

smoke *n.* exhaust, film, fog, fume, funk, gas, mist, reek, roke, smog, vapour.

v. cure, dry, fume, fumigate, reek, roke, smoulder, vent.

smoky *adj.* begrimed, black, caliginous, grey, grimy, hazy, murky, reechy, reeky, roky, sooty, thick.

smooth *adj.* agreeable, bland, calm, classy, easy, effortless, elegant, equable, even, facile, fair-spoken, flat, flowing, fluent, flush, frictionless, glassy, glib, glossy, hairless, horizontal, ingratiating, level, levigate, mellow, mild, mirror-like, peaceful, persuasive, plain, plane, pleasant, polished, regular, rhythmic, serene, shiny, silken, silky, sleek, slick, slippery, smarmy, smug, soft, soothing, steady, suave, tranquil, unbroken, unctuous, undisturbed, uneventful, uniform, uninterrupted, unpuckered, unruffled, unrumpled, untroubled, unwrinkled, urbane, velvety, well-ordered.

antonyms coarse, harsh, irregular, rough, unsteady.

v. allay, alleviate, appease, assuage, calm, dub, ease, emery, extenuate, facilitate, flatten, iron, level, levigate, mitigate, mollify, palliate, plane, polish, press, slicken, soften, unknit, unwrinkle.

antonym roughen.

smoothly *adv.* calmly, easily, effortlessly, equably, evenly, fluently, ingratiatingly, legato, mildly, peacefully, pleasantly, serenely, slickly, soothingly, steadily, suavely, tranquilly.

smoothness *n.* calmness, ease, efficiency, effortlessness, evenness, facility, felicity, finish, flow, fluency, glassiness, glibness, levelness, lubricity, oiliness, placidity, polish, regularity, rhythm, serenity, silkiness, sleekness, slickness, smarminess, softness, stillness, suavity, unbrokenness, urbanity, velvetiness.

antonyms coarseness, harshness, roughness.

smooth-talking *adj.* bland, facile, glib, logodaedalic, persuasive, plausible, slick, smooth, suave.

smother *v.* choke, cocoon, conceal, cover, envelop, extinguish, heap, hide, inundate, muffle, overlie, overwhelm, repress, shower, shroud, snuff, stifle, strangle, suffocate, suppress, surround.

smoulder *v.* boil, burn, fester, fume, rage, seethe, simmer, smoke.

smudge *v.* blacken, blur, daub, dirty, mark, smear, smirch, soil, spot, stain.

n. blemish, blot, blur, smear, smut, smutch, spot, stain.

smug *adj.* cocksure, complacent, conceited, holier-than-thou, priggish, self-opinionated, self-righteous, self-satisfied, superior, unctuous.

antonym modest.

smuggler *n.* bootlegger, contrabandist, courier, moonshiner, mule, rum-runner, runner, wrecker.

smutty *adj.* bawdy, blue, coarse, crude, dirty, filthy, gross, improper, indecent, indelicate, lewd, obscene, off colour, pornographic, prurient, racy, raunchy, ribald, risqué, salacious, suggestive, vulgar.

antonyms clean, decent.

snack *n.* bite, break, elevens, elevenses, nacket, nibble, nocket, quick-lunch, refreshment(s), rere-supper, running-banquet, titbit, zakuska.

snag *n.* bug, catch, complication, difficulty, disadvantage, drawback, hitch, inconvenience, obstacle, problem, snub, stick, stumbling block.

v. catch, hole, ladder, rip, tear.

snap *v.* bark, bite, break, catch, chop, click, crack, crackle, crepitate, flash, grip, growl, knap, nip, pop, retort, seize, separate, snarl, snatch.

n. bite, break, crack, crackle, energy, fillip,

flick, get-up-and-go, go, grabe, liveliness, nip, pizazz, pop, vigour, zip.

adj. abrupt, immediate, instant, offhand, on-the-spot, sudden, unexpected, unpremeditated.

snap up grab, grasp, nab, pick up, pluck, pounce on, seize, snatch.

snappy *adj.* brusque, chic, crabbed, cross, dapper, edgy, fashionable, hasty, ill-natured, irritable, modish, natty, quick-tempered, smart, snappish, stylish, tart, testy, touchy, trendy, up-to-the-minute, waspish.

snare *v.* catch, ensnare, entrap, illaqueate, net, seize, springe, trap, trepan, wire.

n. catch, cobweb, gin, lime, lime-twig, net, noose, pitfall, springe, springle, toils, trap, wire.

snarl[1] *v.* complain, gnarl, gnar(r), growl, grumble, knar.

snarl[2] *v.* complicate, confuse, embroil, enmesh, entangle, entwine, jam, knot, muddle, ravel, tangle.

snarl-up *n.* confusion, entanglement, jumble, mess, mix-up, muddle, tangle, traffic jam.

snatch *v.* clutch, gain, grab, grasp, grip, kidnap, nab, pluck, pull, ramp, rap, rescue, seize, spirit, take, win, wrench, wrest.

n. bit, fraction, fragment, part, piece, section, segment, smattering, snippet, spell.

snazzy *adj.* attractive, dashing, fashionable, flamboyant, flashy, jazzy, raffish, ritzy, showy, smart, snappy, sophisticated, sporty, stylish, swinging, with-it.

antonyms drab, unfashionable.

sneak *v.* cower, cringe, grass on, inform on, lurk, pad, peach, sidle, skulk, slink, slip, smuggle, spirit, steal, tell tales.

n. informer, snake in the grass, sneaker, telltale.

adj. clandestine, covert, furtive, quick, secret, stealthy, surprise, surreptitious.

sneaking *adj.* contemptible, dim, furtive, half-formed, hidden, intuitive, mean, nagging, niggling, persistent, private, secret, sly, sneaky, suppressed, surreptitious, two-faced, uncomfortable, underhand, unexpressed, unvoiced, worrying.

sneaky *adj.* base, contemptible, cowardly, deceitful, devious, dishonest, disingenuous, double-dealing, furtive, guileful, low, low-down, malicious, mean, nasty, shady, shifty, slippery, sly, snide, unethical, unreliable, unscrupulous, untrustworthy.

antonyms honest, open.

sneer *v.* deride, disdain, fleer, gibe, jeer, laugh, look down on, mock, ridicule, scoff, scorn, sniff at, snigger.

n. derision, disdain, fleer, gibe, jeer, mockery, ridicule, scorn, smirk, snidery, snigger.

sneezing *adj.* errhine, sternutatory.

snide *adj.* base, cynical, derogatory, dishonest, disparaging, hurtful, ill-natured, insinuating, malicious, mean, nasty, sarcastic, scornful, sneering, spiteful, unkind.

sniff *v.* breathe, inhale, nose, smell, snuff,

snuffle, vent.

sniffy *adj.* condescending, contemptuous, disdainful, haughty, scoffing, sneering, supercilious, superior.

snigger *v., n.* giggle, laugh, sneer, snicker, snort, titter.

snip *v.* clip, crop, cut, nick, notch, prune, shave, slit, trim.
n. bargain, bit, clipping, fragment, giveaway, piece, scrap, shred, slit, snippet.

snippet *n.* fragment, part, particle, piece, portion, scrap, section, segment, shred, snatch.

snivelling *adj.* blubbering, crying, girning, grizzling, mewling, moaning, sniffling, snuffling, weeping, whimpering, whingeing, whining.

snobbery *n.* airs, arrogance, condescension, loftiness, lorliness, pretension, pride, side, snobbishness, snootiness, uppishness.

snobbish *adj.* arrogant, condescending, high and mighty, high-hat, hoity-toity, lofty, lordly, patronising, pretentious, snooty, stuck-up, superior, toffee-nosed, uppish, uppity, upstage.

snoop *v.* interfere, pry, sneak, spy.

snooper *n.* busybody, meddler, nosy parker, Paul Pry, pry, snoop, spy.

snooze *v.* catnap, doze, drowse, kip, nap, nod off, sleep.
n. catnap, doze, forty winks, kip, nap, shut-eye, siesta, sleep.

snout *n.* muzzle, neb, proboscis, schnozzle, snitch, trunk.

snub *v.* check, cold-shoulder, cut, humble, humiliate, mortify, rebuff, rebuke, shame, slight, sneap, squash, squelch, wither.
n. affront, brush-off, check, humiliation, insult, put-down, rebuff, rebuke, slap in the face, sneap.

snug *adj.* close, close-fitting, comfortable, comfy, compact, cosy, homely, intimate, neat, sheltered, trim, warm.

snuggle *v.* cuddle, embrace, hug, nestle, nuzzle.

so far hitherto, thus far, till now, to date.

soak *v.* bathe, damp, drench, imbue, immerse, infuse, interfuse, marinate, moisten, penetrate, permeate, saturate, sog, souse, steep, wet.

soaking *adj.* drenched, dripping, drookit, saturated, soaked, sodden, sopping, streaming, waterlogged, wringing.
antonym dry.

soar *v.* ascend, climb, escalate, fly, mount, plane, rise, rocket, tower, wing.
antonym plummet.

sob *v.* bawl, blubber, boohoo, cry, greet, howl, mewl, moan, shed tears, snivel, weep.

sober *adj.* abstemious, abstinent, calm, clear-headed, cold, composed, cool, dark, dispassionate, douce, drab, grave, level-headed, lucid, moderate, peaceful, plain, practical, quiet, rational, realistic, reasonable, restrained, sedate, serene, serious, severe, solemn, sombre, sound, staid, steady,

subdued, temperate, unexcited, unruffled.
antonyms drunk, excited, frivolous, gay, intemperate, irrational.

sobriety *n.* abstemiousness, abstinence, calmness, composure, continence, coolness, gravity, level-headedness, moderation, reasonableness, restraint, sedateness, self-restraint, seriousness, soberness, solemnity, staidness, steadiness, temperance.
antonyms drunkenness, excitement, frivolity.

so-called *adj.* alleged, nominal, ostensible, pretended, professed, self-styled, soi-disant, supposed.

sociability *n.* affability, chumminess, companionability, congeniality, conviviality, cordiality, friendliness, gregariousness, neighbourliness.

sociable *adj.* accessible, affable, approachable, chummy, companionable, conversable, convivial, cordial, familiar, friendly, genial, gregarious, neighbourly, outgoing, social, viscerotonic, warm.
antonyms unfriendly, unsociable, withdrawn.

social *adj.* collective, common, communal, community, companionable, friendly, general, gregarious, group, neighbourly, organised, public, sociable, societal.
n. ceilidh, do, gathering, get-together, hoolly, hoot(e)nanny, party.

socialise *v.* entertain, fraternise, get together, go out, hang out, mix, party.

socialism *n.* communism, leftism, Leninism, Marxism, Stalinism, Trotskyism, welfarism.

socialist *adj.* commie, communist, leftie, leftist, left-wing, pink, red, Trot, Trotskyist, Trotskyite.
n. commie, communist, leftie, leftist, left-winger, parlour pink, pink(o), red, Trot, Trotskyist, Trotskyite, welfarist.

society *n.* association, beau monde, brotherhood, camaraderie, circle, civilisation, club, companionship, company, corporation, culture, elite, fellowship, fraternity, fratry, friendship, gentry, Gesellschaft, group, guild, haut monde, humanity, institute, league, mankind, organisation, people, population, sisterhood, the nobs, the public, the smart set, the swells, the toffs, the top drawer, the world, union, upper classes, upper crust, Verein.

sodden *adj.* boggy, drenched, drookit, marshy, miry, saturated, soaked, soggy, sopping, waterlogged, wet.
antonym dry.

soft *adj.* balmy, bendable, bland, caressing, comfortable, compassionate, cottony, creamy, crumby, cushioned, cushiony, cushy, daft, delicate, diffuse, diffused, dim, dimmed, doughy, downy, ductile, dulcet, easy, easygoing, effeminate, elastic, faint, feathery, feeble-minded, flabby, flaccid, fleecy, flexible, flowing, fluid, foolish, furry, gelatinous, gentle, impressible, indulgent, kind, lash, lax, lenient, liberal, light, limp, low, malleable, mellifluous, mellow, melodious, mild, mouldable, murmured, muted, namby-pamby, non-alcoholic, overindulgent, pale, pampered, pastel, permissive, pitying, plastic, pleasant, pleasing, pliable, pulpy, quaggy, quiet, restful, sensitive, sentimental, shaded, silky, silly, simple, smooth, soothing, soppy, spineless, spongy, squashy, subdued, supple, swampy, sweet, sympathetic, temperate, tender, tender-hearted, undemanding, understated, unprotected, velvety, weak, whispered, yielding.

antonyms hard, harsh, heavy, loud, rigid, rough, severe, strict.

soft spot fondness, liking, partiality, penchant, weakness.

soften *v.* abate, allay, alleviate, anneal, appease, assuage, calm, cushion, digest, diminish, ease, emolliate, intenerate, lessen, lighten, lower, macerate, malax, malaxate, melt, mitigate, moderate, modify, mollify, muffle, palliate, quell, relax, soothe, still, subdue, temper.

soften up conciliate, disarm, melt, persuade, soft-soap, weaken, win over.

soft-hearted *adj.* benevolent, charitable, clement, compassionate, generous, indulgent, kind, merciful, sentimental, sympathetic, tender, tender-hearted, warm-hearted.

antonym hard-hearted.

soft-pedal *v.* de-emphasise, go easy, moderate, play down, subdue, tone down.

antonyms emphasise, play up.

soggy *adj.* boggy, dripping, heavy, moist, mushy, pulpy, saturated, soaked, sodden, sopping, soppy, spiritless, spongy, waterlogged.

soil[1] *n.* clay, country, dirt, dust, earth, glebe, ground, humus, land, loam, region, terra firma.

soil[2] *v.* bedaggle, bedraggle, befoul, begrime, besmirch, besmut, defile, dirty, foul, maculate, muddy, pollute, smear, spatter, spot, stain, sully, tarnish.

soiled *adj.* dirty, grimy, maculate, manky, polluted, spotted, stained, sullied, tarnished.

antonyms clean, immaculate.

sojourn *n.* peregrination, rest, stay, stop, stopover, visit.

v. abide, dwell, lodge, reside, rest, stay, stop, tabernacle, tarry.

solace *n.* alleviation, assuagement, comfort, consolation, relief, succour, support.

v. allay, alleviate, comfort, console, mitigate, soften, soothe, succour, support.

soldier *n.* buff-coat, buff-jerkin, fighter, gallo(w)glass, galoot, ghazi, GI, hoplite, Ironside, jackman, jäger, janissary, jawan, kern(e), lancer, landsknecht, lansquenet, leather-neck, Mameluke, man-at-arms, marine, poilu, redcoat, rifleman, sepoy, serviceman, soldado, squaddy, swad(dy), sweat, Tommy, trooper, warrior.

sole *adj.* alone, exclusive, individual, one, only, single, singular, solitary, unique.

antonyms multiple, shared.

solecism *n.* absurdity, anacoluthon, blunder, boo-boo, cacology, faux pas, gaffe, gaucherie, impropriety, incongruity, indecorum, lapse, mistake.

solely *adv.* alone, completely, entirely, exclusively, merely, only, single-handedly, singly, uniquely.

solemn *adj.* august, awed, awe-inspiring, ceremonial, ceremonious, devotional, dignified, earnest, formal, glum, grand, grave, hallowed, holy, imposing, impressive, majestic, momentous, pompous, portentous, religious, reverential, ritual, sacred, sanctified, sedate, serious, sober, sombre, staid, stately, thoughtful, venerable.

antonyms frivolous, gay, light-hearted.

solemnise *v.* celebrate, commemorate, dignify, honour, keep, observe.

solemnities *n.* celebration, ceremonial, ceremony, formalities, observance, proceedings, rite, ritual.

solemnity *n.* dignity, earnestness, grandeur, gravity, impressiveness, momentousness, portentousness, sacredness, sanctity, seriousness, stateliness.

antonym frivolity.

solicit *v.* ask, beg, beseech, canvass, crave, entreat, implore, importune, petition, pray, seek, sue, supplicate.

solicitor *n.* advocate, attorney, barrister, DA, law-agent, lawmonger, lawyer, notary (public), QC, silk.

solicitous *adj.* anxious, apprehensive, ardent, attentive, careful, caring, concerned, eager, earnest, fearful, troubled, uneasy, worried, zealous.

solicitude *n.* anxiety, attentiveness, care, concern, considerateness, consideration, disquiet, regard, uneasiness, worry.

solid *adj.* agreed, compact, complete, concrete, constant, continuous, cubic(al), decent, dense, dependable, estimable, firm, genuine, good, hard, law-abiding, level-headed, massed, pure, real, reliable, sensible, serious, sober, sound, square, stable, stocky, strong, sturdy, substantial, trusty, unalloyed, unanimous, unbroken, undivided, uninterrupted, united, unmixed, unshakeable, unvaried, upright, upstanding, wealthy, weighty, worthy.

antonyms broken, insubstantial, liquid.

solidarity *n.* accord, camaraderie, cohesion, concord(ance), consensus, consentaneity, esprit de corps, harmony, like-mindedness, soundness, stability, team spirit, unanimity, unification, unity.

antonyms discord, division, schism.

solidify *v.* cake, clot, coagulate, cohere, congeal, harden, jell, jellify, set.

antonyms dissolve, liquefy, soften.

solitary *adj.* alone, cloistered, companionless, de(a)rnful, desolate, friendless, hermitical, hidden, isolated, lone, lonely, lonesome, out-of-the-way, reclusive, remote, retired, secluded, separate, sequestered, single, sole, unfrequented, unsociable, unsocial, untrodden, unvisited.

antonyms accompanied, gregarious.

solitude n. aloneness, desert, emptiness, isolation, loneliness, privacy, reclusiveness, retirement, seclusion, waste, wasteland, wilderness.
antonym companionship.

solution n. answer, blend, clarification, compound, decipherment, dénouement, disconnection, dissolution, elucidation, emulsion, explanation, explication, key, liquefaction, melting, mix, mixture, resolution, result, solvent, solving, suspension, unfolding, unravelling.

solve v. answer, clarify, crack, decipher, disentangle, dissolve, elucidate, explain, expound, interpret, resolve, settle, unbind, unfold, unravel, work out.

sombre adj. dark, dim, dismal, doleful, drab, dull, dusky, funereal, gloomy, grave, joyless, lugubrious, melancholy, mournful, obscure, sad, sepulchral, shadowy, shady, sober, sombrous, subfusc.
antonyms bright, cheerful, happy.

somebody n. big noise, big shot, big wheel, bigwig, celebrity, dignitary, heavyweight, household name, luminary, magnate, mogul, nabob, name, notable, panjandrum, personage, quidam, star, superstar, VIP.
antonym nobody.

someday adv. eventually, one day, sometime, ultimately.
antonym never.

somehow adv. by fair means or foul, by hook or by crook, come hell or high water, come what may, one way or another.

sometimes adv. at times, from time to time, now and again, now and then, occasionally, off and on, once in a while, otherwhiles.
antonyms always, never.

somnolent adj. comatose, dozy, drowsy, half-awake, heavy-eyed, oscitant, sleepy, soporific, torpid.

son n. boy, descendant, disciple, inhabitant, lad(die), native, offspring.

song n. air, anthem, ballad, barcarol(l)e, canticle, cantilena, canto, canzone, canzonet, carol, chanson, chansonette, chant, chorus, ditty, elegy, epicede, epicedium, epinicion, epithalamion, epithalamium, fit, folk-song, hymn, lay, lied, lilt, lullaby, lyric, madrigal, melody, number, ode, paean, poem, psalm, shanty, strain, tune, volkslied, war-song, wassail.

song and dance ado, commotion, flap, furore, fuss, hoo-ha, kerfuffle, performance, pother, shindig, shindy, squall, stir, tizzy, to-do, tumult, variety, vaudeville.

songster n. balladeer, chanteuse, chorister, crooner, minstrel, singer, troubadour, vocalist, warbler.

sonorous adj. full, full-mouthed, full-throated, full-voiced, grandiloquent, high-flown, high-sounding, loud, oro(ro)tund, plangent, resonant, resounding, rich, ringing, rounded, sounding.

soon adv. anon, betimes, in a minute, in a short time, in the near future, presently, shortly.

soothe v. allay, alleviate, appease, assuage, calm, coax, comfort, compose, ease, hush, lull, mitigate, mollify, pacify, quiet, relieve, salve, settle, soften, still, tranquillise.
antonyms annoy, irritate, vex.

soothing adj. anetic, assuasive, balmy, balsamic, calming, demulcent, easeful, emollient, lenitive, palliative, relaxing, restful.
antonyms annoying, irritating, vexing.

soothsayer n. augur, Chaldee, diviner, foreteller, haruspex, prophet, seer, sibyl.

sophisticated adj. advanced, blasé, citified, complex, complicated, cosmopolitan, couth, cultivated, cultured, delicate, elaborate, highly-developed, intricate, jet-set, multifaceted, refined, seasoned, subtle, urbane, worldly, worldly-wise, world-weary.
antonyms artless, naïve, simple, unsophisticated.

sophistication n. culture, elegance, experience, finesse, poise, savoir-faire, savoir-vivre, urbanity, worldliness.
antonyms naïvety, simplicity.

sophistry n. casuistry, elenchus, fallacy, paralogism, quibble, sophism.

soporific adj. dormitive, hypnagogic, hypnic, hypnogenetic, hypnogenic, hypnogenous, hypnotic, poppied, sedative, sleep-inducing, sleepy, somniferous, somnolent, tranquillising.
antonyms invigorating, stimulating.
n. anaesthetic, hypnic, hypnotic, narcotic, opiate, sedative, tranquilliser.
antonym stimulant.

soppy adj. cloying, corny, daft, drippy, gushy, lovey-dovey, mawkish, mushy, pathetic, schmaltzy, sentimental, silly, slushy, soft, weepy.

sorcerer n. angek(k)ok, enchanter, mage, Magian, magician, magus, necromancer, reim-kennar, sorceress, voodoo, warlock, witch, wizard.

sorcery n. black art, black magic, charm, diablerie, divination, enchantment, hoodoo, incantation, magic, necromancy, pishogue, spell, voodoo, warlockry, witchcraft, witchery, witching, wizardry.

sordid adj. avaricious, base, corrupt, covetous, debauched, degenerate, degraded, despicable, dingy, dirty, disreputable, filthy, foul, grasping, low, mean, mercenary, miserly, niggardly, rapacious, seamy, seedy, selfish, self-seeking, shabby, shameful, sleazy, slovenly, slummy, squalid, tawdry, unclean, ungenerous, venal, vicious, vile, wretched.

sore adj. acute, afflicted, aggrieved, angry, annoyed, annoying, burning, chafed, critical, desperate, dire, distressing, extreme, grieved, grievous, harrowing, hurt, inflamed, irked, irritable, irritated, pained, painful, peeved, pressing, raw, reddened, resentful, sensitive, severe, sharp, smarting, stung, tender, touchy, troublesome, upset, urgent, vexed.
n. abscess, boil, canker, carbuncle, chafe,

gathering, inflammation, swelling, ulcer, wound.

sorrow *n.* affliction, anguish, blow, distress, dole, grief, hardship, heartache, heartbreak, lamentation, misery, misfortune, mourning, regret, ruth, sadness, trial, tribulation, trouble, unhappiness, woe, worry.
antonyms happiness, joy.
v. agonise, bemoan, bewail, beweep, grieve, lament, moan, mourn, pine, weep.
antonym rejoice.

sorrowful *adj.* affecting, afflicted, dejected, depressed, disconsolate, distressing, doleful, grievous, heartbroken, heart-rending, heavy-hearted, lamentable, lugubrious, melancholy, miserable, mournful, painful, piteous, rueful, ruthful, sad, sorry, tearful, unhappy, wae, woebegone, woeful, wretched.
antonyms happy, joyful.

sorry *adj.* abject, apologetic, base, commiserative, compassionate, conscience-stricken, contrite, deplorable, disconsolate, dismal, distressed, distressing, grieved, guilt-ridden, mean, melancholy, miserable, mournful, moved, paltry, pathetic, penitent, piteous, pitiable, pitiful, pitying, poor, regretful, remorseful, repentant, ruthful, sad, self-reproachful, shabby, shamefaced, sorrowful, sympathetic, unhappy, unworthy, vile, wretched.
antonym glad.

sort *n.* brand, breed, category, character, class, denomination, description, family, genre, genus, group, ilk, kidney, kind, make, nature, order, quality, race, species, stamp, style, type, variety.
v. arrange, assort, catalogue, categorise, choose, class, classify, distribute, divide, file, grade, group, neaten, order, rank, screen, select, separate, systematise, tidy.
sort out clarify, clear up, divide, organise, resolve, segregate, select, separate, sift, tidy up.

so-so *adj.* adequate, average, fair, fair to middling, indifferent, middling, moderate, neutral, not bad, OK, ordinary, passable, respectable, run-of-the-mill, tolerable, undistinguished, unexceptional.

soul *n.* alma, animation, ardour, being, body, courage, creature, element, embodiment, energy, essence, feeling, fervour, force, incarnation, individual, inner man, inspiration, inspirer, intellect, leader, life, man, mind, mortal, nobility, person, personification, pneuma, psyche, quintessence, reason, spirit, type, vital force, vitality, vivacity, woman.

soulful *adj.* eloquent, emotional, expressive, heartfelt, meaningful, mournful, moving, profound, sensitive.

soulless *adj.* callous, cold, cruel, dead, ignoble, inhuman, lifeless, mean, mean-spirited, mechanical, soul-destroying, spiritless, unfeeling, uninteresting, unkind, unsympathetic.

sound[1] *n.* description, din, earshot, hearing, idea, implication, impression, look, noise, range, report, resonance, reverberation, tenor, tone, utterance, voice.
v. announce, appear, articulate, chime, declare, echo, enunciate, express, knell, look, peal, pronounce, resonate, resound, reverberate, ring, seem, signal, toll, utter, voice.

sound[2] *adj.* complete, copper-bottomed, correct, deep, entire, established, fair, fere, firm, fit, hale, healthy, hearty, intact, just, level-headed, logical, orthodox, peaceful, perfect, proper, proven, prudent, rational, reasonable, recognised, reliable, reputable, responsible, right, right-thinking, robust, safe, secure, sensible, solid, solvent, stable, sturdy, substantial, thorough, tried-and-true, true, trustworthy, unbroken, undamaged, undisturbed, unhurt, unimpaired, uninjured, untroubled, valid, vigorous, wakeless, well-founded, well-grounded, whole, wise.
antonyms shaky, unfit, unreliable, unsound.

sound[3] *v.* examine, fathom, inspect, investigate, measure, plumb, probe, test.
sound out ask, canvass, examine, probe, pump, question.

sound[4] *n.* channel, estuary, firth, fjord, inlet, passage, strait, voe.

soup *n.* bisque, broth, chowder, consommé, julienne, potage.

sour *adj.* acerb(ic), acetic, acid, acidulated, acrid, acrimonious, bad, bitter, churlish, crabbed, curdled, cynical, disagreeable, discontented, embittered, fermented, grouchy, grudging, ill-natured, ill-tempered, inharmonious, jaundiced, off, peevish, pungent, rancid, rank, sharp, tart, turned, ungenerous, unpleasant, unsavoury, unsuccessful, unsweet, unwholesome, vinegarish, vinegary, waspish.
antonyms good-natured, sweet.
v. alienate, curdle, disenchant, embitter, envenom, exacerbate, exasperate, spoil.

source *n.* author, authority, begetter, beginning, cause, commencement, derivation, fons et origo, fountain-head, informant, klondike, milch-cow, mine, origin, originator, primordium, quarry, rise, spring, water-head, well-head, ylem.

sourpuss *n.* crosspatch, grouse, grumbler, grump, killjoy, kvetch, misery, shrew, whiner, whinger.

souse *v.* douse, drench, dunk, immerse, marinate, pickle, plunge, soak, steep.

souvenir *n.* fairing, gift, keepsake, memento, memory, relic, remembrance(r), reminder, token.

sovereign *n.* autarch, chief, dynast, emperor, empress, kaiser, king, monarch, potentate, prince, queen, ruler, shah, tsar.
adj. absolute, august, chief, dominant, effectual, efficacious, efficient, excellent, imperial, kingly, majestic, monarch(ic)al, paramount, predominant, principal, queenly, regal, royal, ruling, supreme, unlimited.

sovereignty *n.* ascendancy, domination, imperium, kingship, primacy, raj, regality, supremacy, suzerainty, sway.

sow *v.* broadcast, disseminate, drill, implant, inseminate, lodge, plant, scatter, seed, spread, strew.

space *n.* accommodation, amplitude, berth, blank, capacity, chasm, diastema, distance, duration, elbow-room, expanse, extension, extent, gap, house-room, interval, lacuna, leeway, margin, omission, period, place, play, room, scope, seat, spaciousness, span, time, volume.

spacious *adj.* ample, big, broad, capacious, comfortable, commodious, expansive, extensive, huge, large, roomy, sizable, uncrowded, vast, wide.
antonyms confined, cramped, narrow, small.

spadework *n.* donkey-work, drudgery, foundation, groundwork, labour, preparation.

span *n.* amount, compass, distance, duration, extent, length, period, reach, scope, spell, spread, stretch, term.
v. arch, bridge, cover, cross, encompass, extend, link, overarch, traverse, vault.

spank *v.* belt, cane, cuff, leather, slap, slipper, smack, tan, wallop, whack.

spanking *adj.* brand-new, brisk, energetic, fast, fine, gleaming, invigorating, lively, quick, smart, snappy, speedy, swift, vigorous.
antonym slow.

spar *v.* argue, bicker, contend, contest, dispute, fall out, scrap, skirmish, spat, squabble, tiff, wrangle, wrestle.

spare *adj.* additional, economical, emergency, extra, free, frugal, gash, gaunt, lank, lean, leftover, meagre, modest, odd, over, remaining, scanty, slender, slight, slim, sparing, superfluous, supernumerary, surplus, unoccupied, unused, unwanted, wiry.
antonyms corpulent, necessary, profuse.
v. afford, allow, bestow, give quarter, grant, leave, let off, pardon, part with, refrain from, release, relinquish.

sparing *adj.* careful, chary, cost-conscious, economical, frugal, lenten, prudent, saving, thrifty.
antonyms lavish, liberal, unsparing.

spark *n.* atom, flake, flare, flash, flaught, flicker, gleam, glint, hint, jot, scintilla, scintillation, scrap, spit, trace, vestige.
v. animate, cause, excite, inspire, kindle, occasion, precipitate, provoke, set off, start, stimulate, stir, trigger.

sparkle *v.* beam, bubble, coruscate, dance, effervesce, emicate, fizz, fizzle, flash, gleam, glint, glisten, glister, glitter, glow, scintillate, shimmer, shine, spark, twinkle, wink.
n. animation, brilliance, coruscation, dash, dazzle, effervescence, élan, emication, flash, flicker, gaiety, gleam, glint, glitter, life, panache, pizzazz, radiance, scintillation, spark, spirit, twinkle, vim, vitality, vivacity, wit, zip.

sparkling *adj.* animated, bubbly, carbonated, coruscating, effervescent, emicant, fizzy, flashing, gleaming, glistening, glittering, scintillating, twinkling, witty.
antonyms dull, flat.

sparse *adj.* infrequent, meagre, scanty, scarce, scattered, sporadic.
antonyms dense, lush, thick.

spartan *adj.* abstemious, abstinent, ascetic, austere, bleak, disciplined, extreme, frugal, hardy, joyless, plain, rigorous, self-denying, severe, stern, strict, stringent, temperate, unflinching.

spasm *n.* access, burst, contraction, convulsion, eruption, fit, frenzy, jerk, outburst, paroxysm, seizure, throe, twitch.

spasmodic *adj.* convulsive, erratic, fitful, intermittent, irregular, jerky, occasional, paroxysmal, sporadic.
antonyms continuous, uninterrupted.

spate *n.* deluge, epidemic, flood, flow, outpouring, rush, torrent.

spatter *v.* bedaub, bespatter, bespot, besprinkle, bestrew, daub, dirty, scatter, soil, speckle, splash, splodge, spray, sprinkle.

speak *v.* address, advert to, allude to, argue, articulate, breathe, comment on, communicate, converse, deal with, declaim, declare, discourse, discuss, enunciate, express, harangue, lecture, mention, plead, pronounce, refer to, say, speechify, spiel, state, talk, tell, utter, voice.

speak to accost, address, admonish, apostrophise, bring to book, dress down, lecture, rebuke, reprimand, scold, tell off, tick off, upbraid, warn.

speaker *n.* lecturer, mouthpiece, orator, prolocutor, speechifier, speech-maker, spieler, spokesman, spokesperson, spokeswoman.

spearhead *v.* front, head, initiate, launch, lead, pioneer.

special *adj.* appropriate, certain, characteristic, chief, choice, detailed, distinctive, distinguished, especial, exceptional, exclusive, extraordinary, festive, gala, important, individual, intimate, main, major, memorable, momentous, particular, peculiar, precise, primary, red-letter, select, significant, specialised, specific, uncommon, unique, unusual.
antonyms common, normal, ordinary, usual.

specialist *n.* adept, authority, connoisseur, consultant, expert, master, professional, proficient.

speciality *n.* bag, forte, métier, pièce de résistance, scene, special, specialty, strength.

species *n.* breed, category, class, collection, denomination, description, genus, group, kind, sort, type, variety.

specific *adj.* characteristic, clear-cut, definite, delimitative, distinguishing, especial, exact, explicit, express, limited, particular, peculiar, precise, special, unambiguous, unequivocal.
antonyms general, vague.

specification *n.* condition, description, detail, enumeration, item, itemisation, listing, particular, qualification, requirement, stipulation.

specify v. cite, define, delineate, describe, designate, detail, enumerate, indicate, individualise, itemise, list, mention, name, particularise, spell out, stipulate.

specimen n. copy, embodiment, ensample, example, exemplar, exemplification, exhibit, illustration, individual, instance, model, paradigm, pattern, person, proof, representative, sample, type.

specious adj. casuistic, deceptive, fallacious, false, misleading, pageant, plausible, sophistic, sophistical, unsound, untrue.
antonym valid.

speck n. atom, bit, blemish, blot, defect, dot, fault, flaw, fleck, grain, iota, jot, macula, mark, mite, modicum, mote, particle, shred, speckle, spot, stain, tittle, trace, whit.

speckled adj. brinded, brindle(d), dappled, dotted, flecked, fleckered, freckled, lentiginous, mottled, spotted, spotty, sprinkled, stippled.

spectacle n. curiosity, display, event, exhibition, extravaganza, marvel, pageant, parade, performance, phenomenon, scene, show, sight, wonder.

spectacles n. cheaters, eyeglasses, glasses, goggles, lorgnette, lorgnon, opera-glasses, pince-nez, specs.

spectacular adj. amazing, breathtaking, daring, dazzling, dramatic, eye-catching, fabulous, fantastic, grand, impressive, magnificent, marked, remarkable, sensational, splendid, staggering, striking, stunning.
antonyms ordinary, unspectacular.
n. display, extravaganza, pageant, show, spectacle.

spectator n. beholder, bystander, eye-witness, looker-on, observer, onlooker, passer-by, viewer, watcher, witness.
antonyms contestant, participant, player.

spectral adj. disembodied, eerie, ghostly, incorporeal, insubstantial, phantasmal, phantom, shadowy, spooky, supernatural, uncanny, unearthly, weird.

spectre n. apparition, ghost, larva, lemur, phantom(a), presence, revenant, shade, shadow, spirit, vision, wraith.

speculate v. cogitate, conjecture, consider, contemplate, deliberate, gamble, guess, hazard, hypothesise, meditate, muse, reflect, risk, scheme, suppose, surmise, theorise, venture, wonder.

speculation n. conjecture, consideration, contemplation, deliberation, flight of fancy, gamble, gambling, guess, guesswork, hazard, hypothesis, ideology, land-jobbing, opinion, risk, supposition, surmise, theory.

speculative adj. abstract, academic, chancy, conjectural, dicey, hazardous, hypothetical, iffish, iffy, notional, projected, risky, suppositional, tentative, theoretical, uncertain, unpredictable.

speech n. address, articulation, colloquy, communication, conversation, dialect, dialogue, diction, discourse, discussion, disquisition,

enunciation, harangue, homily, idiom, intercourse, jargon, language, lecture, lingo, oration, parlance, parole, peroration, say, spiel, talk, tongue, utterance, voice, winged words.

speechless adj. aghast, amazed, astounded, dazed, dumb, dumbfounded, dumbstruck, inarticulate, mum, mute, obmutescent, shocked, silent, thunderstruck, tongue-tied, wordless.

speed n. acceleration, celerity, dispatch, expedition, fleetness, haste, hurry, lick, momentum, pace, precipitation, quickness, rapidity, rush, swiftness, tempo, velocity.
v. advance, aid, assist, belt, bomb, boost, bowl along, career, dispatch, expedite, facilitate, flash, fleet, further, gallop, hasten, help, hurry, impel, lick, press on, promote, put one's foot down, quicken, race, rush, sprint, step on it, step on the gas, step on the juice, tear, urge, vroom, zap, zoom.
antonyms delay, hamper, restrain, slow.

speedily adv. fast, hastily, hurriedly, posthaste, promptly, quickly, rapidly, swiftly, ventre à terre.
antonym slowly.

speedy adj. clipping, expeditious, express, fast, fleet, hasty, headlong, hurried, immediate, nimble, precipitate, prompt, quick, rapid, summary, swift, winged, zappy.
antonyms dilatory, slow, tardy.

spell[1] n. bout, course, innings, interval, patch, period, season, stint, stretch, term, time, turn.

spell[2] n. abracadabra, allure, bewitchment, charm, conjuration, enchantment, exorcism, fascination, glamour, hex, incantation, jettatura, love-charm, magic, open sesame, paternoster, philtre, rune, sorcery, trance, weird, witchery.

spell[3] v. augur, herald, imply, indicate, mean, portend, presage, promise, signal, signify, suggest.

spell out clarify, elucidate, emphasise, explain, specify.

spellbound adj. bemused, bewitched, captivated, charmed, enchanted, enthralled, entranced, fascinated, gripped, hooked, mesmerised, possessed, rapt, transfixed, transported.

spend v. apply, bestow, blow, blue, concentrate, consume, cough up, deplete, devote, disburse, dispense, dissipate, drain, employ, empty, exhaust, expend, fill, fork out, fritter, invest, lavish, lay out, occupy, pass, pay out, shed, shell out, splash out, squander, use, use up, waste.
antonyms hoard, save.

spendthrift n. big spender, prodigal, profligate, spendall, spender, squanderer, unthrift, waster, wastrel.
antonyms hoarder, miser, saver.
adj. extravagant, improvident, prodigal, profligate, thriftless, wasteful.

spent adj. all in, burnt out, bushed, consumed, dead beat, debilitated, dog-tired, done in, drained, exhausted, expended, fagged (out), finished, gone, jiggered, knackered, played out, prostrate, shattered, tired out, used up, weakened, wearied, weary, whacked, worn out, zonked.

spew *v.* belch, disgorge, posset, puke, regurgitate, retch, spit out, throw up, vomit.

sphere *n.* ball, capacity, circle, compass, department, domain, employment, field, function, globe, globule, milieu, orb, province, range, rank, realm, scope, spheroid, spherule, station, stratum, territory.

spherical *adj.* globate, globed, globe-shaped, globoid, globose, globular, orbicular, rotund, round.

spice *n.* colour, excitement, flavouring, gusto, kick, life, pep, piquancy, relish, savour, seasoning, tang, zap, zest, zip.

spick and span clean, immaculate, neat, polished, scrubbed, shipshape, spotless, spruce, tidy, trim, well-kept.
antonyms dirty, untidy.

spicy *adj.* aromatic, flavoursome, fragrant, hot, improper, indecorous, indelicate, off-colour, piquant, pointed, pungent, racy, ribald, risqué, savoury, scandalous, seasoned, sensational, showy, suggestive, tangy, titillating, unseemly.
antonym bland.

spiel *v.* harangue, hold forth, lecture, orate, recite, sermonise, speechify, spout.
n. harangue, oration, patter, pitch, recital, sales patter, sermon, speech.

spike *n.* barb, nail, point, prong, spine, spire, tine.
v. block, foil, frustrate, impale, reject, spear, spit, stick, thwart.

spill *v.* discharge, disgorge, overflow, overturn, scatter, shed, slop, slosh, upset.
n. accident, cropper, fall, overturn, tumble, upset.

spill the beans blab, blow the gaff, give the game away, grass, inform, let the cat out of the bag, rat, split, squeal, tattle.

spin *v.* birl, concoct, develop, gyrate, gyre, hurtle, invent, narrate, pirouette, purl, recount, reel, relate, revolve, rotate, spirt, swim, swirl, tell, turn, twirl, twist, unfold, wheel, whirl.
n. agitation, commotion, drive, flap, gyration, hurl, panic, pirouette, revolution, ride, roll, run, state, tizzy, turn, twist, whirl.

spin out amplify, delay, extend, lengthen, maintain, pad out, prolong, prolongate, protract, sustain.

spindle *n.* arbor, axis, axle, fusee, pivot.

spindly *adj.* attenuate(d), gangling, gangly, lanky, leggy, skeletal, skinny, spidery, spindle-shanked, thin, twiggy, weedy.
antonyms stocky, thickset.

spine *n.* backbone, barb, needle, quill, rachis, ray, spicule, spiculum, spike, spur, vertebrae, vertebral column.

spine-chilling *adj.* bloodcurdling, eerie, frightening, hair-raising, horrifying, scary, spine-tingling, spooky, terrifying.

spineless *adj.* cowardly, faint-hearted, feeble, gutless, inadequate, ineffective, irresolute, lily-livered, soft, spiritless, squeamish, submissive, vacillating, weak, weak-kneed, weak-willed, wet, wishy-washy, yellow.
antonyms brave, strong.

spiny *adj.* acanthaceous, acanthous, briery, prickly, spicular, spiculate, spiniferous, spinigerous, spinose, spinous, thistly, thorny.

spiral *adj.* circular, cochlear, cochleate, coiled, corkscrew, gyral, gyroidal, helical, scrolled, spiraliform, voluted, volutoid, whorled, winding.
n. coil, convolution, corkscrew, curlicue, gyre, helix, screw, volute, volution, whorl.

spire *n.* cone, flèche, peak, pinnacle, point, shoot, spike, sprout, stalk, steeple, summit, tip, top.

spirit *n.* air, animation, apparition, ardour, Ariel, atmosphere, attitude, backbone, bravura, breath, brio, character, complexion, courage, daemon, dauntlessness, deva, disposition, div, djinni, earnestness, energy, enterprise, enthusiasm, entrain, Erdgeist, esprit follet, essence, familiar, faun, feeling, feelings, fire, foison, force, gameness, geist, genie, genius, genius loci, ghost, ghoul, gist, grit, guts, humour, intent, intention, jinnee, jinni, ka, kobold, life, liveliness, manito(u), marid, meaning, mettle, mood, morale, motivation, outlook, phantom, pneuma, psyche, purport, purpose, python, quality, resolution, resolve, revenant, sense, shade, shadow, soul, sparkle, spectre, spook, sprite, spunk, stout-heartedness, substance, sylph, temper, temperament, tenor, tone, verve, vigour, vision, vivacity, warmth, water-horse, water-nymph, water-rixie, water-sprite, Weltgeist, wili, will, will power, Zeitgeist, zest.
v. abduct, abstract, capture, carry, convey, kidnap, purloin, remove, seize, snaffle, steal, whisk.

spirited *adj.* active, animated, ardent, bold, courageous, energetic, game, gamy, high-spirited, lively, mettlesome, plucky, sparkling, sprightly, spunky, stomachful, vigorous, vivacious.
antonyms lazy, spiritless, timid.

spiritless *adj.* anaemic, apathetic, dejected, depressed, despondent, dispirited, droopy, dull, lacklustre, languid, lifeless, listless, low, melancholic, melancholy, mopy, torpid, unenthusiastic, unmoved, wishy-washy.
antonym spirited.

spirits *n.* alcohol, fire-water, hooch, liquor, moonshine, strong drink, strong liquor, the hard stuff.

spiritual *adj.* aery, devotional, divine, ecclesiastical, ethereal, ghostly, holy, immaterial, incorporeal, otherwordly, pneumatic, pure, religious, sacred, unfleshly, unworldly.
antonyms material, physical.

spit *v.* discharge, drizzle, eject, expectorate, hawk, hiss, spew, splutter, sputter.
n. dribble, drool, expectoration, phlegm,

saliva, slaver, spittle, sputum.

spite *n.* animosity, bitchiness, despite, gall, grudge, hate, hatred, ill-nature, malevolence, malice, malignity, pique, rancour, spitefulness, spleen, venom, viciousness.

antonyms affection, goodwill.

v. annoy, discomfit, gall, harm, hurt, injure, irk, irritate, needle, nettle, offend, peeve, pique, provoke, put out, vex.

spiteful *adj.* barbed, bitchy, catty, cruel, ill-disposed, ill-natured, malevolent, malicious, malignant, nasty, rancorous, snide, splenetic, vengeful, venomous, vindictive, waspish.

antonyms affectionate, charitable.

spitting image clone, dead ringer, dead spit, double, likeness, lookalike, picture, replica, ringer, spit, twin.

splash *v.* bathe, batter, bespatter, blazon, break, broadcast, buffet, dabble, dash, flaunt, flouse, floush, headline, paddle, plash, plaster, plop, plunge, publicise, shower, slop, slosh, smack, spatter, splodge, spray, spread, sprinkle, squirt, strew, strike, surge, tout, trumpet, wade, wallow, wash, wet.

n. burst, dash, display, effect, excitement, impact, ostentation, patch, publicity, sensation, spattering, splatter, splodge, splurge, stir, touch.

splash out invest in, lash out, push the boat out, spend, splurge.

spleen *n.* acrimony, anger, animosity, animus, bad temper, bile, biliousness, bitterness, gall, hatred, hostility, ill-humour, ill-will, malevolence, malice, malignity, peevishness, petulance, pique, rancour, resentment, spite, spitefulness, venom, vindictiveness, wrath.

splendid *adj.* admirable, beaming, bright, brilliant, costly, dazzling, excellent, exceptional, fantastic, fine, first-class, glittering, glorious, glowing, gorgeous, grand, great, heroic, illustrious, imposing, impressive, lavish, lustrous, luxurious, magnificent, marvellous, ornate, outstanding, pontific(al), radiant, rare, refulgent, remarkable, renowned, resplendent, rich, splendiferous, splend(o)rous, sterling, sublime, sumptuous, superb, supreme, tiptop, top-hole, top-notch, topping, wonderful.

antonyms drab, ordinary, run-of-the-mill.

splendour *n.* brightness, brilliance, ceremony, dazzle, display, effulgence, fulgo(u)r, glory, gorgeousness, grandeur, lustre, magnificence, majesty, pomp, radiance, refulgence, renown, resplendence, richness, show, solemnity, spectacle, stateliness, sumptuousness.

splenetic *adj.* acid, atrabilious, bilious, bitchy, choleric, churlish, crabbed, crabby, cross, envenomed, fretful, irascible, irritable, morose, peevish, petulant, rancorous, sour, spiteful, sullen, testy, touchy.

splice *v.* bind, braid, entwine, graft, interlace, interlink, intertwine, intertwist, interweave, join, knit, marry, mesh, plait, tie, unite, wed, yoke.

splinter *n.* chip, flake, flinder, fragment, needle, paring, shaving, sliver, spall, spicule, stob.

v. disintegrate, fracture, fragment, shatter, shiver, smash, split.

split *v.* allocate, allot, apportion, betray, bifurcate, branch, break, burst, cleave, crack, delaminate, disband, distribute, disunite, divaricate, diverge, divide, divulge, fork, gape, grass, halve, inform on, open, parcel out, part, partition, peach, rend, rip, separate, share out, skive, slash, slice up, slit, sliver, snap, spell, splinter, squeal.

n. breach, break, break-up, cleft, crack, damage, dichotomy, difference, discord, disruption, dissension, disunion, divergence, division, estrangement, fissure, gap, partition, race, rent, rift, rip, rupture, schism, scissure, separation, slash, slit, tear.

adj. ambivalent, bisected, broken, cleft, cloven, cracked, divided, dual, fractured, ruptured, twofold.

split hairs cavil, find fault, nit-pick, over-refine, pettifog, quibble.

split up break up, disband, dissolve, divorce, part, part company, separate.

spoil *v.* addle, baby, blemish, bugger, butcher, cocker, coddle, cosset, curdle, damage, debase, decay, decompose, deface, despoil, destroy, deteriorate, disfigure, go bad, go off, harm, impair, indulge, injure, jigger, louse up, mar, mildew, mollycoddle, pamper, plunder, putrefy, queer, rot, ruin, screw, spoon-feed, turn, upset, wreck.

spoils *n.* acquisitions, boodle, booty, gain, haul, loot, pickings, pillage, plunder, prey, prizes, rapine, spoliation, swag, winnings.

spoil-sport *n.* damper, dog in the manger, killjoy, mar-sport, meddler, misery, party-pooper, wet blanket, wowser.

spoken *adj.* declared, expressed, oral, phonetic, said, stated, told, unwritten, uttered, verbal, viva voce, voiced.

antonyms unspoken, written.

sponge *v.* cadge, freeload, mooch, scrounge, shool.

sponger *n.* bloodsucker, cadge, cadger, freeloader, hanger-on, leech, moocher, parasite, scrounger, smell-feast.

spongy *adj.* absorbent, bibulous, cushioned, cushiony, elastic, fozy, light, porous, springy.

sponsor *n.* angel, backer, godparent, guarantor, patron, promoter, surety, underwriter.

v. back, finance, fund, guarantee, patronise, promote, subsidise, underwrite.

spontaneous *adj.* extempore, free, impromptu, impulsive, instinctive, natural, ultroneous, unbidden, uncompelled, unconstrained, unforced, unhesitating, unlaboured, unpremeditated, unprompted, unstudied, untaught, voluntary, willing.

antonyms forced, planned, studied.

spontaneously *adv.* ex mero motu, ex proprio motu, extempore, freely, impromptu, impulsively, instinctively, of one's own accord, off the cuff, on impulse, unprompted, voluntarily, willingly.

spoof *n.* bluff, burlesque, caricature, con, deception, fake, game, hoax, joke, lampoon, leg-pull, mockery, parody, prank, satire, send-up, take-off, travesty, trick.

spooky *adj.* chilling, creepy, eerie, eldritch, frightening, ghostly, hair-raising, mysterious, scary, spine-chilling, supernatural, uncanny, unearthly, weird.

spoonerism *n.* marrowsky, transposition.

spoon-feed *v.* baby, cosset, featherbed, indulge, mollycoddle, pamper, spoil.

sporadic *adj.* erratic, infrequent, intermittent, irregular, isolated, occasional, random, scattered, spasmodic, uneven.
antonyms frequent, regular.

sport *n.* activity, amusement, badinage, banter, brick, buffoon, butt, dalliance, derision, diversion, entertainment, exercise, fair game, frolic, fun, game, jest, joking, kidding, laughing-stock, merriment, mirth, mockery, pastime, play, plaything, raillery, recreation, ridicule, sportsman, teasing.
v. caper, dally, display, disport, exhibit, flirt, frolic, gambol, philander, play, romp, show off, toy, trifle, wear.

sporting *adj.* considerate, fair, gentlemanly, sportsmanlike.
antonyms unfair, ungentlemanly, unsporting.

sportive *adj.* coltish, frisky, frolicsome, gamesome, gay, jaunty, joyous, kittenish, lively, merry, playful, prankish, rollicking, skittish, sprightly.

sporty *adj.* athletic, casual, energetic, flamboyant, flashy, gay, hearty, informal, jaunty, jazzy, loud, natty, outdoor, raffish, rakish, showy, snazzy, stylish, trendy.

spot *n.* bit, blemish, blot, blotch, daub, difficulty, discoloration, flaw, little, locality, location, macula, maculation, macule, mark, mess, morsel, pimple, place, plight, plook, point, position, predicament, pustule, quandary, scene, site, situation, smudge, speck, splash, stain, stigma, taint, trouble.
v. besmirch, blot, descry, detect, dirty, discern, dot, espy, fleck, identify, maculate, mark, mottle, observe, recognise, see, sight, soil, spatter, speckle, splodge, splotch, stain, sully, taint, tarnish.

spotless *adj.* blameless, chaste, faultless, flawless, gleaming, immaculate, innocent, irreproachable, pure, shining, snowy, spick and span, unblemished, unimpeachable, unstained, unsullied, untarnished, virgin, virginal, white.
antonyms dirty, impure, spotted.

spotlight *v.* accentuate, emphasise, feature, focus on, highlight, illuminate, point up, throw into relief.
n. attention, emphasis, fame, interest, limelight, notoriety, public eye.

spotted *adj.* brinded, brindle(d), dappled, dotted, flecked, fleckered, guttate(d), macled, macular, maculate, maculose, mottled, parded, pied, polka-dot, specked, speckled.

antonym spotless.

spotty *adj.* blotchy, pimpled, pimply, plooky, speckled, spotted.

spouse *n.* better half, companion, consort, fere, helpmate, husband, mate, partner, wife.

spout *v.* declaim, discharge, emit, erupt, expatiate, gush, jet, orate, pontificate, rabbit on, ramble (on), rant, sermonise, shoot, speechify, spiel, spray, spurt, squirt, stream, surge.
n. chute, fistula, fountain, gargoyle, geyser, jet, nozzle, outlet, rose, spray.

sprawl *v.* flop, loll, lounge, ramble, recline, repose, slouch, slump, spread, straggle, trail.

spray[1] *v.* atomise, diffuse, douse, drench, scatter, shower, sprinkle, wet.
n. aerosol, atomiser, drizzle, droplets, foam, froth, mist, moisture, spindrift, spoondrift, sprinkler.

spray[2] *n.* bough, branch, corsage, garland, shoot, sprig, wreath.

spread *v.* advertise, arrange, array, blazon, bloat, broadcast, broaden, bruit, cast, circulate, couch, cover, diffuse, dilate, dispread, disseminate, distribute, divulgate, divulge, effuse, escalate, expand, extend, fan out, furnish, lay, metastasise, multiply, mushroom, open, overlay, prepare, proclaim, proliferate, promulgate, propagate, publicise, publish, radiate, scatter, set, shed, sprawl, stretch, strew, swell, transmit, unfold, unfurl, unroll, widen.
antonyms close, compress, contain, fold.
n. advance, advancement, array, banquet, blow-out, compass, cover, development, diffusion, dispersion, dissemination, divulgation, divulgence, escalation, expanse, expansion, extent, feast, increase, period, proliferation, ranch, reach, repast, span, spreading, stretch, suffusion, sweep, term, transmission.

spree *n.* bacchanalia, bender, binge, blind, bum, carouse, debauch, fling, jag, jamboree, junketing, orgy, randan, razzle-dazzle, revel, splurge, tear.

sprightly *adj.* active, agile, airy, alert, animated, blithe, brisk, cheerful, energetic, frolicsome, gamesome, gay, hearty, jaunty, joyous, lively, nimble, perky, playful, spirited, sportive, spry, vivacious.
antonym inactive.

spring[1] *v.* appear, arise, bounce, bound, burgeon, come, dance, derive, descend, develop, emanate, emerge, grow, hop, issue, jump, leap, mushroom, originate, proceed, rebound, recoil, shoot up, sprout, start, stem, vault.
n. bounce, bounciness, bound, buck, buoyancy, elasticity, flexibility, gambado, give, hop, jump, leap, rebound, recoil, resilience, saltation, springiness, vault.

spring[2] *n.* beginning, cause, eye, fountain-head, origin, root, source, well, well-spring.

springy *adj.* bouncy, buoyant, elastic, flexible, resilient, rubbery, spongy, stretchy.
antonyms rigid, stiff.

sprinkle *v.* asperge, diversify, dot, dredge, dust, pepper, powder, scatter, seed, shower, sparge, spatter, spray, strew.

sprinkling *n.* admixture, dash, dusting, few, handful, scatter, scattering, smattering, sprinkle, touch, trace.

sprint *v.* belt, dart, dash, gallop, hare, hotfoot, race, run, scamper, shoot, tear, whiz.

sprite *n.* apparition, brownie, dryad, elf, fairy, goblin, imp, kelpie, leprechaun, naiad, nymph, pixie, pouke, puck, spirit, sylph.

sprout *v.* bud, develop, germinate, grow, pullulate, push, shoot, spring, vegetate.

spruce *adj.* dainty, dapper, elegant, natty, neat, sleek, slick, smart, smirk, trig, trim, well-groomed, well-turned-out.
antonyms dishevelled, untidy.

spruce up groom, neaten, preen, primp, smarten up, tidy, titivate.

spry *adj.* active, agile, alert, brisk, energetic, nimble, nippy, peppy, quick, ready, sprightly, supple.
antonyms doddering, inactive, lethargic.

spunk *n.* backbone, bottle, chutzpah, courage, gameness, grit, guts, heart, mettle, nerve, pluck, resolution, spirit, toughness.
antonym funk.

spur *v.* animate, drive, goad, impel, incite, poke, press, prick, prod, prompt, propel, stimulate, urge.
antonym curb.
n. fillip, goad, impetus, impulse, incentive, incitement, inducement, motive, prick, rowel, stimulus.
antonym curb.

spurious *adj.* adulterate, adulterine, apocryphal, artificial, bastard, bogus, contrived, counterfeit, deceitful, dog, fake, false, feigned, forged, illegitimate, imitation, mock, phoney, pretended, pseudo, sham, simulated, specious, suppositious, unauthentic.
antonyms authentic, genuine, real.

spurn *v.* cold-shoulder, contemn, cut, despise, disdain, disregard, rebuff, reject, repulse, scorn, slight, snub, turn down.
antonym embrace.

spurt *v.* burst, effuse, erupt, gush, jet, shoot, spew, squirt, surge.
n. access, burst, effusion, fit, rush, spate, surge.

spy *n.* beagle, double agent, fifth columnist, foreign agent, mole, scout, secret agent, secret service man, snooper, spook, undercover agent.
v. descry, discover, espy, glimpse, notice, observe, spot.

squabble *v.* argue, bicker, brawl, clash, dispute, fall out, fight, quarrel, row, scrap, spat, tiff, wrangle.
n. argument, barney, clash, disagreement, dispute, fight, rhubarb, row, scrap, set-to, spat, tiff.

squad *n.* band, brigade, company, crew, force, gang, group, outfit, team, troop.

squalid *adj.* broken-down, decayed, dingy, dirty, disgusting, fetid, filthy, foul, low, nasty, neglected, poverty-stricken, repulsive, run-down, seedy, sleazy, slovenly, slummy, sordid, uncared-for, unclean, unkempt.
antonyms clean, pleasant.

squall *n.* blow, drow, gale, gust, hurricane, storm, tempest, williwaw, wind-storm.

squally *adj.* blowy, blustery, gusty, rough, stormy, tempestuous, turbulent, wild, windy.

squalor *n.* decay, dinginess, filth, foulness, meanness, neglect, sleaziness, squalidness, wretchedness.

squander *v.* blow, blue, consume, dissipate, expend, fritter away, lavish, misspend, misuse, scatter, spend, splurge, throw away, waste.

square *v.* accommodate, accord, adapt, adjust, agree, align, appease, balance, bribe, conform, correspond, corrupt, discharge, fit, fix, harmonise, level, liquidate, match, quit, reconcile, regulate, rig, satisfy, settle, suborn, suit, tailor, tally, true.
adj. above-board, bourgeois, broad, complete, conservative, conventional, decent, equitable, ethical, even, exact, fair, fitting, full, genuine, honest, just, old-fashioned, on the level, opposed, orthodox, quadrate, right-angled, satisfying, solid, straight, straightforward, strait-laced, stuffy, suitable, thick-set, traditional, true, unequivocal, upright.
n. antediluvian, conformer, conformist, conservative, conventionalist, die-hard, fuddy-duddy, (old) fogy, stick-in-the-mud, traditionalist.

squash *v.* annihilate, compress, crowd, crush, distort, flatten, humiliate, mash, pound, press, pulp, quash, quell, silence, smash, snub, squelch, stamp, suppress, trample.
antonyms elongate, stretch.

squashy *adj.* mushy, pappy, pulpy, soft, spongy, squelchy, squishy, yielding.
antonym firm.

squat *adj.* chunky, dumpy, fubby, short, squabby, stocky, stubby, stumpy, thickset.
antonyms lanky, slender.
v. absquatulate, bend, camp out, crouch, hunch, hunker, ruck, settle, stoop.

squawk *v.* cackle, complain, crow, cry, grouse, hoot, protest, screech, shriek, squeal, yelp.

squeak *v.* chirk, peep, pipe, shrill, squeal, whine, yelp.

squeal *n.* scream, screech, shriek, ululation, wail, yell, yelp, yowl.
v. betray, blab, complain, grass, inform on, moan, peach, protest, rat on, scream, screech, shout, shriek, shrill, snitch, squawk, ululate, wail, yelp.

squeamish *adj.* coy, delicate, fastidious, finicky, nauseous, particular, prissy, prudish, punctilious, qualmish, queasy, queer, reluctant, scrupulous, sick, sickish, strait-laced.

squeeze *v.* bleed, chirt, clasp, clutch, compress, cram, crowd, crush, cuddle, embrace, enfold, extort, force, grip, hug, jam, jostle, lean on, milk, nip, oppress, pack, pinch, press, pressurise, ram, scrounge, squash, strain, stuff, thrust, wedge, wrest, wring.

n. clasp, congestion, crowd, crush, embrace, grasp, handclasp, hold, hug, jam, press, pressure, restriction, squash.

squint *adj.* askew, aslant, awry, cockeyed, crooked, indirect, oblique, off-centre, skew-whiff, strabismic.

antonym straight.

squire *v.* accompany, attend, conduct, escort.

squirm *v.* agonise, fidget, flounder, move, shift, squiggle, twist, wiggle, wriggle, writhe.

squirt *v.* chirt, discharge, ejaculate, eject, emit, expel, jet, shoot, spout, spurt.

n. chirt, jet, spray, spurt.

stab *v.* bayonet, cut, dirk, gore, injure, jab, knife, pierce, pink, puncture, spear, stick, thrust, transfix, wound.

n. ache, attempt, endeavour, essay, gash, incision, jab, pang, pink, prick, puncture, rent, thrust, try, twinge, venture, wound.

stab in the back betray, deceive, double-cross, inform on, let down, sell out, slander.

stabbing *adj.* acute, lancinating, piercing, shooting, stinging.

stability *n.* constancy, durability, firmness, fixity, permanence, solidity, soundness, steadfastness, steadiness, strength, sturdiness.

antonyms insecurity, instability, unsteadiness, weakness.

stable *adj.* abiding, constant, deep-rooted, durable, enduring, established, fast, firm, fixed, immutable, invariable, lasting, permanent, reliable, secure, self-balanced, sound, static, steadfast, steady, strong, sturdy, sure, unalterable, unchangeable, unwavering, well-founded.

antonyms shaky, unstable, weak, wobbly.

stack *n.* accumulation, clamp, cock, heap, hoard, load, mass, mound, mountain, pile, ruck, stockpile.

v. accumulate, amass, assemble, gather, load, pile, save, stockpile, store.

staff *n.* caduceus, cane, crew, employees, lecturers, lituus, officers, organisation, personnel, pole, prop, rod, stave, teachers, team, wand, workers, workforce.

stage *n.* division, floor, juncture, lap, leg, length, level, period, phase, point, shelf, step, storey, subdivision, tier.

v. arrange, do, engineer, give, mount, orchestrate, organise, perform, present, produce, put on, stage-manage.

stagger *v.* alternate, amaze, astonish, astound, confound, daddle, daidle, dumbfound, falter, flabbergast, hesitate, lurch, nonplus, overlap, overwhelm, reel, shake, shock, step, stun, stupefy, surprise, sway, teeter, titubate, totter, vacillate, waver, wobble, zigzag.

stagnant *adj.* becalmed, brackish, lethargic, motionless, sluggish, stale, standing, still, torpid.

stagnate *v.* decay, decline, degenerate, deteriorate, fester, idle, languish, rot, rust, vegetate.

staid *adj.* calm, composed, decorous, demure, grave, quiet, sedate, self-restrained, serious, sober, sober-blooded, solemn, steady, Victorian.

antonyms debonair, frivolous, jaunty, sportive.

stain *v.* bedye, besmirch, blacken, blemish, blot, colour, contaminate, corrupt, defile, deprave, dirty, discolour, disgrace, distain, dye, imbue, mark, smutch, soil, spot, sully, taint, tarnish, tinge.

n. blemish, blot, discoloration, disgrace, dishonour, eye, infamy, reproach, shame, slur, smirch, smutch, soil, splodge, spot, stigma, tint.

stake[1] *n.* loggat, pale, paling, picket, pile, pole, post, spike, standard, stang, stave, stick.

v. brace, fasten, pierce, prop, secure, support, tether, tie, tie up.

stake out define, delimit, demarcate, keep an eye on, mark out, outline, reserve, stake off, survey, watch.

stake[2] *n.* ante, bet, chance, claim, concern, hazard, interest, investment, involvement, peril, pledge, prize, risk, share, venture, wager.

v. ante, bet, chance, gage, gamble, hazard, imperil, jeopardise, pledge, risk, venture, wager.

stale *adj.* antiquated, banal, cliché'd, cliché-ridden, common, commonplace, decayed, drab, dry, effete, faded, fetid, flat, fozy, fusty, hackneyed, hard, insipid, musty, old, old hat, overused, platitudinous, repetitious, sour, stagnant, stereotyped, tainted, tasteless, threadbare, trite, unoriginal, vapid, worn-out.

antonym fresh.

stalemate *n.* deadlock, draw, halt, impasse, standstill, stop, tie, zugzwang.

antonym progress.

stalk[1] *v.* approach, follow, haunt, hunt, march, pace, pursue, shadow, stride, strut, tail, track.

stalk[2] *n.* bole, branch, kex, shoot, spire, stem, sterigma, trunk.

stall[1] *v.* delay, equivocate, hedge, obstruct, penelopise, play for time, prevaricate, stonewall, temporise.

antonym advance.

stall[2] *n.* bay, bench, booth, compartment, cowshed, pew, seat, stable, table.

stalwart *adj.* athletic, beefy, brawny, daring, dependable, determined, hefty, husky, indomitable, intrepid, lusty, manly, muscular, redoubtable, resolute, robust, rugged, sinewy, staunch, stout, strapping, strong, sturdy, valiant, vigorous.

antonyms timid, weak.

stamina *n.* energy, fibre, force, grit, indefatigability, lustiness, power, resilience, resistence, staying power, strength, vigour.

antonym weakness.

stammer *v.* falter, gibber, hesitate, splutter, stumble, stutter.

stamp *v.* beat, brand, bray, categorise, characterise, crush, engrave, exhibit, fix, identify, impress, imprint, inscribe, label, mark, mint, mould, pound, print, pronounce, reveal, strike, trample.

n. attestation, authorisation, brand, breed, cast, character, cut, description, earmark, evidence, fashion, form, hallmark, impression, imprint, incuse, kind, mark, mould, sign, signature, sort, stomp, type.

stamp out crush, destroy, eliminate, end, eradicate, extinguish, extirpate, kill, quell, quench, scotch, suppress.

antonym encourage.

stampede *n.* charge, dash, debacle, flight, rout, rush, scattering, sprint.

v. charge, dash, flee, fly, gallop, hightail it, hot-foot it, run, rush, scurry, shoot, sprint, tear.

antonyms walk, wander.

stance *n.* angle, attitude, bearing, carriage, deportment, point of view, position, posture, stand, standpoint, station, viewpoint.

stanch *v.* arrest, block, check, dam, halt, plug, stay, stem, stop.

antonyms increase, promote.

stand *v.* abide, allow, bear, belong, brook, continue, cost, countenance, demur, endure, erect, exist, experience, halt, handle, hold, mount, obtain, pause, place, position, prevail, put, rank, remain, rest, rise, scruple, set, stay, stomach, stop, suffer, support, sustain, take, thole, tolerate, undergo, wear, weather, withstand.

antonym advance.

n. attitude, base, booth, bracket, cradle, dais, determination, erection, frame, grandstand, halt, holder, loss, opinion, place, platform, position, rack, rank, resistance, rest, stage, staging, stall, stance, standpoint, standstill, stay, stop, stop-over, stoppage, support, table, tub, vat, witness-box.

antonym progress.

stand by adhere to, back, befriend, champion, defend, hold to, reiterate, repeat, speak for, stick up for, support, uphold.

antonym let down.

stand down abdicate, cede, give away, give up, quit, resign, step down, withdraw.

antonyms ascend, join.

stand for bear, betoken, brook, champion, countenance, denote, embody, endure, epitomise, exemplify, indicate, mean, personify, represent, signify, suffer, symbolise, tolerate, typify, wear.

stand in for cover for, deputise for, hold the fort for, replace, substitute for, understudy.

stand out bulk large, catch the eye, jut out, project, stare one in the face, stick out, stick out a mile, stick out like a sore thumb.

stand up cohere, hold up, hold water, stand, wash.

stand up for champion, defend, fight for, side with, speak for, speak up for, stick up for, support, uphold.

antonym attack.

stand up to brave, confront, defy, endure, face, front, oppose, resist, withstand.

antonym give in to.

standard[1] *n.* average, bench-mark, canon, criterion, example, exempler, gauge, grade, guide, guideline, level, measure, model, norm, norma, pattern, principle, requirement, rule, sample, specification, touchstone, type, yardstick.

adj. accepted, approved, authoritative, average, basic, classic, customary, definitive, established, mainstream, normal, official, orthodox, popular, prevailing, recognised, regular, set, staple, stock, typical, usual.

antonyms abnormal, irregular, unusual.

standard[2] *n.* banner, colours, ensign, flag, gonfalon, gonfanon, labarum, pennant, pennon, rallying-point, streamer, vexillum.

standard-bearer *n.* cornet, ensign, gonfalonier, standard, vexillary.

standardise *v.* assimilate, equalise, institutionalise, mass-produce, normalise, regiment, stereotype.

antonym differentiate.

standards *n.* ethics, ideals, morals, principles.

standing *n.* condition, continuance, credit, duration, eminence, estimation, existence, experience, footing, position, rank, reputation, repute, seniority, station, status.

adj. erect, fixed, lasting, on one's feet, permanent, perpendicular, perpetual, rampant, regular, repeated, up-ended, upright, vertical.

antonyms horizontal, lying.

standing-stone *n.* megalith, menhir, monolith.

stand-offish *adj.* aloof, cold, distant, haughty, remote, reserved, unapproachable, uncommunicative, unsociable, untalkative.

antonym friendly.

standpoint *n.* angle, point of view, position, post, stance, station, vantage-point, viewpoint, Weltanschauung.

standstill *n.* arrest, cessation, dead-finish, deadlock, halt, hold-up, impasse, lapse, log-jam, lull, moratorium, pause, reprieve, respite, rest, stalemate, stay, stop, stoppage, termination.

antonym progress.

staple *adj.* basic, chief, essential, fundamental, key, leading, main, major, predominant, primary, principle.

antonym minor.

star[1] *n.* asterisk, asteroid, comet, étoile, meteor, meteorite, nova, planet, pulsar, quasar, red dwarf, red giant, satellite, shooting-star, starlet, sun, supernova, white dwarf.

star[2] *n.* celebrity, draw, idol, lead, leading, leading lady, leading man, luminary, main attraction, name, starlet, vedette.

adj. brilliant, celebrated, illustrious, leading, major, paramount, pre-eminent, principal, prominent, talented, well-known.

antonym minor.

starchy *adj.* ceremonious, conventional, formal, prim, punctilious, stiff, strait-laced, stuffy.

antonym informal.

stare *v.* gape, gawk, gawp, gaze, glare, goggle, look, watch.

n. fish-eye, gaze, glare, glower, leer, look, ogle, scowl.

stark *adj.* absolute, arrant, austere, bald, bare, barren, bleak, blunt, cold, consummate, depressing, desolate, downright, drear, dreary, entire, flagrant, forsaken, grim, harsh, out-and-out, palpable, patent, plain, pure, severe, sheer, simple, solitary, stern, stiff, strong, unadorned, unalloyed, unmitigated, unyielding, utter.

antonyms mild, slight.

adv. absolutely, altogether, clean, completely, entirely, quite, stoutly, totally, utterly, wholly.

antonyms mildly, slightly.

stark-naked *adj.* in one's birthday suit, in the altogether, in the buff, in the nude, in the raw, naked, nude, stark, starkers, stripped, unclad, undressed.

antonym clothed.

start *v.* activate, appear, arise, begin, blench, break away, commence, create, dart, depart, engender, establish, father, flinch, found, inaugurate, initiate, instigate, institute, introduce, issue, jerk, jump, kick off, launch, leave, open, originate, pioneer, recoil, sally forth, set off, set out, set up, shoot, shy, spring forward, twitch.

antonyms finish, stop.

n. advantage, backing, beginning, birth, break, chance, commencement, convulsion, dawn, edge, fit, foundation, inauguration, inception, initiation, introduction, jar, jump, kick-off, lead, onset, opening, opportunity, outburst, outset, spasm, sponsorship, spurt, twitch.

antonyms finish, stop.

startle *v.* affray, agitate, alarm, amaze, astonish, astound, electrify, flush, frighten, scare, shock, spook, start, surprise.

antonym calm.

startling *adj.* alarming, astonishing, astounding, dramatic, electric, electrifying, extraordinary, shocking, staggering, sudden, surprising, unexpected, unforeseen.

antonyms boring, calming, ordinary.

starvation *n.* famishment, hunger, inanition, malnutrition, underfeeding, undernourishment.

antonym plenty.

starve *v.* clem, deny, deprive, die, diet, fast, hunger, perish, refuse.

antonym provide.

starving *adj.* famished, hungering, hungry, ravenous, sharp-set, starved, underfed, undernourished.

antonym fed.

stash *v.* cache, closet, conceal, hide, hoard, lay up, salt away, save up, secrete, stockpile, stow.

antonyms bring out, uncover.

state[1] *v.* affirm, articulate, assert, asseverate, aver, declare, enumerate, explain, expound, express, formalise, formulate, formulise, present, propound, put, report, say, specify, voice.

n. attitude, bother, case, category, ceremony, circumstances, condition, dignity, display, flap, glory, grandeur, humour, majesty, mode, mood, panic, pass, phase, plight, pomp, position, pother, predicament, shape, situation, spirits, splendour, stage, station, style, tizzy.

antonym calmness.

state of affairs case, circumstances, condition, crisis, galère, juncture, kettle of fish, lie of the land, plight, position, predicament, situation.

state[2] *n.* body politic, commonwealth, country, federation, government, kingdom, land, leviathan, nation, republic, territory.

adj. ceremonial, ceremonious, formal, governmental, magnificent, national, official, pompous, public, solemn.

stately *adj.* august, ceremonious, deliberate, dignified, elegant, grand, imperial, imposing, impressive, Junoesque, kingly, lofty, majestic, measured, noble, pompous, princely, queenly, regal, royal, solemn.

antonyms informal, unimpressive.

statement *n.* account, announcement, bulletin, communication, communiqué, constatation, declaration, explanation, ipse dixit, ipsissima verba, proclamation, recital, relation, report, testimony, utterance, verbal.

statesman *n.* diplomat, Elder Statesman, GOM, homme d'état, politician.

static *adj.* changeless, constant, fixed, immobile, inert, motionless, resting, stable, stagnant, stationary, still, unmoving, unvarying.

antonyms active, dynamic, moving.

station *n.* appointment, base, business, calling, depot, employment, grade, habitat, headquarters, location, occupation, office, place, position, post, rank, seat, situation, sphere, stance, standing, standing-place, status, stopping-place.

v. appoint, assign, establish, fix, garrison, install, locate, post, send, set.

stationary *adj.* fixed, inert, moored, motionless, parked, resting, settled, standing, static, stock-still, unmoving.

antonym moving.

statue *n.* acrolith, bronze, bust, carving, caryatid, effigy, figure, figurine, head, idol, statuette, xoanon.

statuesque *adj.* dignified, imposing, majestic, regal, stately, statuary.

antonym small.

stature *n.* consequence, eminence, importance, prestige, prominence, rank, size, standing, weight.

antonym unimportance.

status *n.* character, condition, consequence, degree, distinction, eminence, grade, importance, position, prestige, rank, standing, state, weight.

antonym unimportance.

statute *n.* act, decree, edict, enactment, firman, hatti-sherif, indiction, interlocution, irade, law, ordinance, regulation, rescript, rule, ukase.[1]

staunch[1] *adj.* constant, dependable, faithful, firm, hearty, loyal, reliable, resolute, sound, steadfast, stout, strong, sure, true, true-blue, trustworthy, trusty, watertight, yeomanly, zealous.
antonyms unreliable, wavering, weak.

staunch[2] *same as* **stanch**.

stave off avert, delay, evade, fend off, foil, hold off, keep at bay, keep back, parry, ward off.
antonyms cause, encourage.

stay[1] *v.* abide, adjourn, allay, arrest, check, continue, curb, defer, delay, detain, discontinue, dwell, endure, halt, hinder, hold, hold out, hover, impede, last, linger, live, lodge, loiter, obstruct, pause, prevent, prorogue, remain, reside, restrain, settle, sojourn, stand, stop, suspend, tarry, visit, wait.
antonyms advance, leave.

n. continuance, deferment, delay, halt, holiday, pause, postponement, remission, reprieve, sojourn, stop, stopover, stopping, suspension, visit.

stay[2] *n.* brace, buttress, prop, reinforcement, shoring, stanchion, support.

v. buttress, prop, prop up, shore up, support, sustain.

steadfast *adj.* constant, dedicated, dependable, established, faithful, fast, firm, fixed, intent, loyal, perseverant, persevering, reliable, resolute, single-minded, stable, staunch, steady, unfaltering, unflinching, unswerving, unwavering.
antonyms unreliable, wavering, weak.

steady *adj.* balanced, calm, ceaseless, confirmed, consistent, constant, continuous, dependable, equable, even, faithful, firm, fixed, habitual, immovable, imperturbable, incessant, industrious, level-headed, non-stop, persistent, regular, reliable, rhythmic, safe, sedate, sensible, serene, serious-minded, settled, sober, stable, staid, steadfast, substantial, unbroken, unchangeable, unfaltering, unfluctuating, unhasting, unhasty, unhurried, uniform, uninterrupted, unremitting, unswerving, unvarying, unwavering.
antonyms unsteady, wavering.

v. balance, brace, firm, fix, secure, stabilise, support.

steal *v.* appropriate, bone, cly, convey, creep, embezzle, filch, flit, half-inch, heist, knap, knock off, lag, lift, mill, misappropriate, nab, nick, peculate, pilfer, pinch, pirate, plagiarise, poach, purloin, relieve someone of, rip off, shoplift, slink, slip, smouch, smug, snaffle, snatch, sneak, snitch, swipe, take, thieve, tiptoe.
antonym return.

stealing *n.* embezzlement, larceny, misappropriation, peculation, pilferage, pilfering, plagiarism, rip-off, robbery, shoplifting, theft, thievery, thieving.

stealth *n.* covertness, furtiveness, secrecy, slyness, sneakiness, stealthiness, surreptitiousness, unobtrusiveness.
antonym openness.

stealthy *adj.* cat-like, clandestine, covert, furtive, quiet, secret, secretive, skulking, sly, sneaking, sneaky, surreptitious, underhand.
antonym open.

steam *n.* condensation, dampness, fumes, haze, mist, moisture, roke, vapour.

steamboat *n.* packet, packet-boat, packet-ship, paddle-boat, paddle-steamer, puffer, steamer, steam-packet, steamship, steam-tug, steam-vessel, steam-yacht, vaporetto.

steamy *adj.* close, damp, gaseous, hazy, humid, misty, muggy, roky, steaming, stewy, sticky, sultry, sweaty, sweltering, vaporiform, vaporous, vapourish, vapoury.

steed *n.* charger, hack, horse, jade, mount, nag, Rosinante.

steel *v.* brace, fortify, harden, nerve, toughen.
antonym weaken.

steep[1] *adj.* abrupt, bluff, excessive, exorbitant, extortionate, extreme, headlong, high, overpriced, precipitous, sheer, stiff, uncalled-for, unreasonable.
antonyms gentle, moderate.

steep[2] *v.* brine, damp, drench, fill, imbrue, imbue, immerse, infuse, macerate, marinate, moisten, permeate, pervade, pickle, saturate, seethe, soak, souse, submerge, suffuse.

steer *v.* con, conduct, control, direct, govern, guide, pilot.

steer clear of avoid, bypass, circumvent, dodge, escape, eschew, evade, shun, skirt.
antonym seek.

stem[1] *n.* axis, branch, family, house, line, lineage, peduncle, race, shoot, stalk, stock, trunk.

stem from arise from, come from, derive from, develop from, emanate from, flow from, issue from, originate in, spring from.
antonym give rise to.

stem[2] *v.* check, contain, curb, dam, oppose, resist, restrain, stanch, stay, stop, tamp.
antonyms encourage, increase.

stench *n.* mephitis, odour, pong, reek, stink, whiff.

step *n.* act, action, advance, advancement, deed, degree, demarche, doorstep, expedient, footfall, footprint, footstep, gait, halfpace, impression, level, manoeuvre, means, measure, move, pace, phase, point, print, procedure, proceeding, process, progression, rank, remove, round, rung, stage, stair, stride, trace, track, tread, walk.

v. move, pace, stalk, stamp, tread, walk.

step by step gradatim, gradually, slowly.

step down abdicate, bow out, leave, quit, resign, retire, stand down, withdraw.
antonyms ascend, join.

step up accelerate, augment, boost, build up, escalate, increase, intensify, raise, speed up, up.
antonym decrease.

stereotype *n.* convention, formula, mould, pattern.
v. categorise, conventionalise, dub, mass-produce, pigeonhole, standardise, typecast.
antonym differentiate.

stereotyped *adj.* banal, cliché'd, cliché-ridden, conventional, corny, hackneyed, mass-produced, overused, platitudinous, stale, standard, standardised, stock, threadbare, tired, trite, unoriginal.
antonyms different, unconventional.

sterile *adj.* abortive, acarpous, antiseptic, aseptic, bare, barren, disinfected, dry, empty, fruitless, germ-free, infecund, pointless, sterilised, unfruitful, unimaginative, unproductive, unprofitable, unprolific.
antonyms fruitful, septic.

sterilise *v.* clean, cleanse, disinfect, fumigate, purify.
antonyms contaminate, infect.

sterility *n.* asepsis, atocia, barrenness, cleanness, fruitlessness, futility, impotence, ineffectiveness, inefficacy, pointlessness, purity, unfecundity, unfruitfulness, uselessness.
antonyms fertility, fruitfulness.

sterling *adj.* authentic, excellent, first-class, genuine, great, pure, real, sound, standard, substantial, superlative, true, worthy.
antonyms false, poor.

stern *adj.* austere, authoritarian, bitter, cruel, flinty, forbidding, frowning, grim, hard, harsh, inflexible, relentless, rigid, rigorous, serious, severe, stark, steely, strict, unrelenting, unsmiling, unsparing, unyielding.
antonym mild.

stew *v.* agonise, boil, braise, fret, fricassee, fuss, jug, perspire, seethe, simmer, sweat, swelter, worry.
n. agitation, bother, bouillabaisse, chowder, daube, fluster, fret, fuss, goulash, hash, lobscouse, pot-au-feu, pother, ragout, tizzy, worry.

steward *n.* chamberlain, dewan, factor, grieve, homme d'affaires, maître d'hôtel, major-domo, manciple, marshal.

stick[1] *v.* abid, adhere, affix, attach, bind, bond, bulge, catch, cement, cleave, cling, clog, deposit, dig, drop, endure, extend, fasten, fix, fuse, glue, gore, hold, insert, install, jab, jam, join, jut, lay, linger, lodge, obtrude, paste, penetrate, persist, pierce, pin, place, plant, plonk, poke, position, prod, project, protrude, puncture, put, put up with, remain, set, show, snag, spear, stab, stand, stay, stomach, stop, store, stuff, take, thole, thrust, tolerate, transfix, weld.
antonym unstick.

stick at[1] continue, heng on in, keep at, persevere in, persist, plug away at.
antonym give up.

stick at[2] balk, demur, doubt, draw the line at, hesitate, pause, recoil, scruple, shrink from, stop at.

stick to adhere to, cleave to, honour, keep to, persevere in, stand by.

antonyms give up, quit.

stick up for champion, defend, speak for, speak up for, stand up for, support, take the part or side of, uphold.
antonym attack.

stick[2] *n.* baton, bavin, birch, bludgeon, branch, cane, lathi, lug, pole, quarterstaff, rod, sceptre, staff, stake, stave, switch, twig, waddy, wand, whip, withy.

stick[3] *n.* abuse, blame, criticism, flak, hostility, punishment, reproof.
antonym praise.

stickiness *n.* adhesiveness, gaum, glueyness, glutinousness, goo, gooeyness, gumminess, syrupiness, tack, tackiness, viscidity.

stick-in-the-mud *adj.* antediluvian, antiquated, conservative, fogram, fogyish, fossilised, outmoded, unadventurous, Victorian.
antonyms adventurous, modern.
n. conservative, fog(e)y, fogram, fogramite, fossil.

stickler *n.* fanatic, fusspot, maniac, martinet, nut, pedant, perfectionist, precisianist, purist.

sticky *adj.* adhesive, awkward, claggy, clammy, clinging, clingy, cloggy, close, dauby, delicate, difficult, discomforting, embarrassing, gluey, glutinous, gooey, gummy, hairy, humid, muggy, nasty, oppressive, painful, smeary, sultry, sweltering, syrupy, tacky, tenacious, thorny, tricky, unpleasant, viscid, viscous.
antonyms cool, dry, easy.

stiff *adj.* arduous, arthritic, artificial, austere, awkward, brisk, brittle, buckram, budge, ceremonious, chilly, clumsy, cold, constrained, creaky, crude, cruel, difficult, drastic, exacting, excessive, extreme, fatiguing, firm, forced, formal, formidable, fresh, graceless, great, hard, hardened, harsh, heavy, inelastic, inelegant, inexorable, inflexible, jerky, laborious, laboured, mannered, oppressive, pertinaceous, pitiless, pokerish, pompous, powerful, priggish, prim, punctilious, resistant, rheumaticky, rigid, rigorous, severe, sharp, solid, solidified, stand-offish, starch(y), stark, stilted, strict, stringent, strong, stubborn, taut, tense, tight, toilsome, tough, trying, unbending, uneasy, ungainly, ungraceful, unnatural, unrelaxed, unsupple, unyielding, uphill, vigorous, wooden.
antonyms flexible, graceful, informal, mild.

stiffen *v.* ankylose, brace, coagulate, congeal, crystallise, harden, jell, reinforce, rigidify, rigidise, set, solidify, starch, tauten, tense, thicken.

stiff-necked *adj.* arrogant, contumacious, haughty, obstinate, opinionated, proud, stubborn, uncompromising.
antonyms flexible, humble.

stifle *v.* asphyxiate, check, choke, curb, dampen, extinguish, hush, muffle, prevent, repress, restrain, silence, smother, stop, strangle, suffocate, suppress.
antonym encourage.

stigma *n.* blemish, blot, brand, disgrace,

dishonour, imputation, mark, reproach, shame, slur, smirch, spot, stain.
antonym credit.

stigmatise *v.* brand, condemn, denounce, discredit, fame, label, mark, pillory, vilify, vilipend.
antonym praise.

still *adj.* calm, hushed, inert, lifeless, motionless, noiseless, pacific, peaceful, placid, quiet, restful, serene, silent, smooth, stagnant, stationary, stilly, tranquil, undisturbed, unruffled, unstirring.
antonyms agitated, busy, disturbed, noisy.
v. allay, alleviate, appease, calm, hold back, hush, lull, pacify, quiet, quieten, restrain, settle, silence, smooth, soothe, subdue, tranquillise.
antonyms agitate, stir up.
n. hush, peace, peacefulness, quiet, quietness, silence, stillness, tranquillity.
antonyms agitation, disturbance, noise.
adv. but, even so, even then, however, nevertheless, nonetheless, notwithstanding, yet.

stilted *adj.* artificial, bombastic, constrained, forced, grandiloquent, high-flown, high-sounding, inflated, laboured, mannered, pedantic, pompous, pretentious, stiff, unnatural, wooden.
antonyms flowing, fluent.

stimulant *n.* analeptic, bracer, excitant, hype, incitant, oestrus, pep pill, pick-me-up, restorative, reviver, tonic, upper, whetstone.
antonym depressant.

stimulate *v.* animate, arouse, encourage, fan, fire, foment, get psyched up, goad, hop up, hype up, impel, incite, inflame, instigate, jog, prompt, provoke, psych oneself up, quicken, rouse, spur, titillate, urge, whet.
antonym discourage.

stimulating *adj.* excitant, excitative, excitatory, exciting, exhilarating, galvanic, inspiring, intriguing, provocative, provoking, rousing, stirring, thought-provoking.
antonyms boring, depressing, uninspiring.

stimulus *n.* carrot, encouragement, fillip, ginger, goad, incentive, incitement, inducement, prick, provocation, spur.
antonym discouragement.

sting *v.* anger, burn, cheat, con, defraud, do, fleece, gall, hurt, incense, inflame, infuriate, nettle, overcharge, pain, pique, provoke, rile, rip off, smart, swindle, tingle, urticate, wound.
antonym soothe.
n. agony, anguish, bite, bitterness, distress, goad, incentive, incitement, nip, prick, pungency, smarting, spur, stimulus, tingle, torment, torture, woe.

stinging *adj.* aculeate(d), burning, nippy, smarting, tingling, urent, urticant.
antonyms mild, soothing.

stingy *adj.* avaricious, cheeseparing, close-fisted, covetous, illiberal, inadequate, insufficient, meagre, mean, measly, mingy, miserly, near,

niggardly, parsimonious, penny-pinching, penurious, save-all, scanty, scrimping, small, tightfisted, ungenerous, ungiving.
antonym generous.

stink *v.* niff, pong, reek, whiff.
n. brouhaha, commotion, disturbance, fetor, foulness, fuss, hubbub, malodour, mephitis, niff, odour, pong, row, rumpus, scandal, stench, stir, to-do, uproar, upset, whiff.

stinker *n.* affliction, beast, bounder, cad, creep, cur, dastard, difficulty, fink, heel, horror, impediment, plight, poser, predicament, problem, rat, rotter, scab, scoundrel, shocker, sod, swine.

stinking *adj.* boozed, canned, contemptible, disgusting, drunk, fetid, foul-smelling, graveolent, grotty, ill-smelling, intoxicated, low, low-down, malodorous, mean, mephitic, noisome, pissed, plastered, pongy, reeking, rotten, smashed, smelly, sozzled, stenchy, stewed, stoned, unpleasant, vile, whiffy, wretched.
antonyms good, pleasant, sober.

stint *n.* assignment, bit, period, quota, share, shift, spell, stretch, term, time, tour, trick, turn.
v. begrudge, economise, pinch, save, scrimp, skimp on, withhold.

stipulate *v.* agree, contract, covenant, engage, guarantee, insist upon, lay down, pledge, postulate, promise, provide, require, settle, specify.
antonym imply.

stipulation *n.* agreement, clause, condition, contract, engagement, precondition, prerequisite, provision, proviso, qualification, requirement, restriction, settlement, sine qua non, small print, specification, term.
antonym implication.

stir *v.* affect, agitate, beat, bestir, budge, disturb, electrify, emove, excite, fire, flutter, hasten, inspire, look lively, mix, move, quiver, rustle, shake, shake a leg, thrill, touch, tremble.
antonyms bore, calm, stay.
n. activity, ado, agitation, bustle, commotion, disorder, disturbance, excitement, ferment, flurry, fuss, hustle and bustle, movement, to-do, toing and froing, tumult, uproar.
antonym calm.

stir up animate, arouse, awaken, excite, incite, inflame, instigate, jog, kindle, mix, prompt, provoke, quicken, raise, spur, stimulate, urge.
antonyms calm, discourage.

stirring *adj.* animating, dramatic, emotive, exciting, exhilarating, heady, impassioned, inspiring, intoxicating, lively, martial, moving, rousing, spirited, stimulating, thrilling.
antonyms calming, uninspiring.

stock *n.* ancestry, array, assets, assortment, background, beasts, block, breed, cache, capital, cattle, choice, commodities, descent, equipment, estimation, extraction, family, flocks, forebears, fund, funds, goods, handle, herds, hoard, horses, house, inventory, investment, kindred, line, lineage, livestock, log, merchandise, parentage, pedigree, post, property, race, range, repertoire, repute, reserve, reservoir, selection, sheep, source, stem, stockpile, store, strain, stump, supply, trunk, type, variety, wares.

adj. banal, basic, bromidic, cliché'd, commonplace, conventional, customary, formal, hackneyed, ordinary, overused, regular, routine, run-of-the-mill, set, standard, staple, stereotyped, traditional, trite, usual, worn-out.

antonym original.

v. deal in, handle, keep, sell, supply, trade in.

stock up accumulate, amass, equip, fill, furnish, gather, hoard, lay in, pile up, provision, replenish, save, store (up), supply.

stocky *adj.* chunky, dumpy, mesomorphic, short, solid, stubby, stumpy, sturdy, thickset.

antonyms skinny, tall.

stodgy *adj.* boring, dull, filling, formal, fuddy-duddy, heavy, laboured, leaden, solemn, spiritless, staid, starchy, stuffy, substantial, tedious, turgid, unenterprising, unexciting, unimaginative, uninspired.

antonyms exciting, informal, light.

stoical *adj.* calm, cool, dispassionate, impassive, imperturbable, indifferent, long-suffering, patient, philosophic(al), phlegmatic, resigned, stoic, stolid.

antonyms anxious, depressed, furious, irascible.

stoicism *n.* acceptance, ataraxia, ataraxy, calmness, dispassion, fatalism, forbearance, fortitude, impassivity, imperturbability, indifference, long-suffering, patience, resignation, stolidity.

antonyms anxiety, depression, fury.

stolid *adj.* apathetic, beefy, blockish, bovine, doltish, dull, heavy, impassive, lumpish, obtuse, slow, stoic(al), stupid, unemotional, wooden.

antonyms interested, lively.

stomach *n.* abdomen, appetite, belly, breadbasket, craw, desire, gizzard, gut, inclination, inner man, inside(s), king's-hood, little Mary, maw, mind, paunch, pot, potbelly, relish, spare tyre, taste, tummy.

v. abide, bear, endure, submit to, suffer, swallow, take, thole, tolerate.

stone *n.* boulder, cobble, concretion, endocarp, flagstone, gem, gemstone, gravestone, headstone, jewel, kernel, lapis, pebble, pip, pit, rock, seed, set(t), slab, tombstone.

stone circle henge, peristalith.

stony *adj.* adamant, blank, callous, chilly, expressionless, frigid, hard, heartless, hostile, icy, indifferent, inexorable, lapideous, lapilliform, lithoid(al), merciless, obdurate, pitiless, steely, stonelike, unfeeling, unforgiving, unresponsive.

antonyms forgiving, friendly, soft-hearted.

stooge *n.* butt, cat's paw, dupe, fall guy, foil, henchman, lackey, patsy, pawn, puppet.

stoop *v.* bend, bow, couch, crouch, descend, duck, hunch, incline, kneel, lean, squat.

n. droop, inclination, round-shoulderedness, sag, slouch, slump.

stoop to condescend, deign, descend, go so far as, go so low as, lower oneself, resort, sink, vouchsafe.

stop *v.* arrest, bar, block, break, cease, check, close, conclude, desist, discontinue, embar, end, finish, forestall, frustrate, halt, hinder, impede, intercept, intermit, interrup, knock off, leave off, lodge, obstruct, pack (it) in, pack in, pack up, pause, plug, poop out, prevent, quit, refrain, repress, rest, restrain, scotch, seal, silence, sojourn, stall, staunch, stay, stem, stymie, suspend, tarry, terminate.

antonyms advance, continue, start.

n. bar, block, break, bung, cessation, check, conclusion, control, depot, destination, discontinuation, end, finish, halt, hindrance, impediment, plug, rest, sojourn, stage, standstill, statation, stay, stop-over, stoppage, termination, terminus, ventage, visit.

antonyms continuation, start.

interj. avast, cease, cut it out, desist, easy, give over, halt, hang on, hold it, hold on, hold your horses, lay off, leave it out, refrain, stop it, wait, wait a minute, whoa.

stop-gap *n.* expedient, improvisation, makeshift, resort, shift, substitute.

adj. emergency, expediential, impromptu, improvised, makeshift, provisional, rough-and-ready, temporary.

antonyms finished, permanent.

stoppage *n.* abeyance, arrest, blockage, check, close, closure, curtailment, cut-off, deduction, desistance, discontinuance, halt, hartal, hindrance, interruption, lay-off, obstruction, occlusion, shut-down, sit-in, standstill, stasis, stopping, strike, walk-out.

antonyms continuation, start.

stopper *n.* bung, cork, plug, stopple.

store *v.* accumulate, cupboard, deposit, garner, hive, hoard, husband, keep, lay aside, lay by, lay in lavender, lay up, put aside, reserve, salt away, save, stash, stock, stockpile, treasure.

antonym use.

n. abundance, accumulation, cache, cupboard, depository, emporium, esteem, fund, hoard, keeping, lot, market, mart, mine, outlet, panary, plenty, plethora, provision, quantity, repository, reserve, reservoir, shop, stock, stockpile, storehouse, storeroom, supermarket, supply, value, warehouse, wealth.

antonym scarcity.

storehouse *n.* armoury, arsenal, barn, cellar, depository, depot, elevator, entrepot, étape, fund, garderobe, garner, granary, hold, larder, pantry, repertory, repository, silo, treasury, vault, warehouse.

storey *n.* deck, étage, flight, floor, level, stage, stratum, tier.

storm *n.* agitation, anger, assault, attack, blast, blitz, blitzkrieg, blizzard, clamour, commotion, cyclone, disturbance, dust-devil, furore,

gale, gust, haboob, hubbub, hurricane, offensive, onset, onslaught, outbreak, outburst, outcry, paroxysm, passion, roar, row, rumpus, rush, sandstorm, squall, stir, strife, tempest, tornado, tumult, turmoil, violence, whirlwind.
antonym calm.
v. assail, assault, beset, bluster, charge, complain, expugn, flounce, fly, fume, rage, rant, rave, rush, scold, stalk, stamp, stomp, thunder.

stormy *adj.* blustering, blustery, boisterous, choppy, dirty, foul, gustful, gusty, oragious, raging, rough, squally, tempestuous, turbulent, wild, windy.
antonym calm.

story *n.* account, ancedote, article, chronicle, episode, fable, fairy-tale, falsehood, feature, fib, fiction, historiette, history, legend, lie, Märchen, myth, narration, narrative, news, novel, plot, recital, record, relation, report, romance, scoop, spiel, tale, untruth, version, yarn.

storyteller *n.* anecdotist, author, bard, chronicler, clype, fabulist, fibber, liar, narrator, novelist, raconteur, raconteuse, romancer, tell-tale.

stout *adj.* able-bodied, athletic, beefy, big, bold, brave, brawny, bulky, burly, chopping, corpulent, courageous, dauntless, doughty, embonpoint, enduring, fat, fearless, fleshy, gallant, hardy, heavy, hulking, husky, intrepid, lion-hearted, lusty, manly, muscular, obese, overweight, plucky, plump, portly, resolute, robust, rotund, stalwart, strapping, strong, sturdy, substantial, thick, tough, tubby, valiant, valorous, vigorous.
antonyms slim, timid, weak.

stove *n.* calefactor, chauffer, cockle, cooker, furnace, grill, heater, kiln, oven, range.

stow *v.* bundle, cram, deposit, dump, jam, load, pack, secrete, sling, stash, store, stuff, tuck.
antonym unload.

straggle *v.* amble, dilly-dally, drift, lag, loiter, ramble, range, roam, rove, scatter, spread, stray, string out, trail, wander.

straggly *adj.* aimless, disorganised, drifting, irregular, loose, rambling, random, spreading, straggling, straying, strung out, untidy.
antonyms grouped, organised, tidy.

straight *adj.* accurate, aligned, arranged, authentic, balanced, blunt, bourgeois, candid, consecutive, conservative, continuous, conventional, decent, direct, downright, equitable, erect, even, fair, forthright, frank, honest, honourable, horizontal, just, law-abiding, level, near, neat, non-stop, normal, orderly, organised, orthodox, outright, perpendicular, plain, plumb, point-blank, pure, reliable, respectable, right, running, settled, shipshape, short, smooth, solid, square, straightforward, successive, sustained, through, tidy, traditional, true, trustworthy, unadulterated, undeviating, undiluted, uninterrupted, unmixed, unqualified,

unrelieved, unswerving, upright, vertical.
antonyms circuitous, dilute, dishonest, evasive, indirect, roundabout.
adv. candidly, directly, frankly, honestly, outspokenly, point-blank, upright.

straightaway *adv.* at once, directly, immediately, instanter, instantly, now, right away, straightway, there and then, this minute, tout de suite.
antonym eventually.

straighten *v.* arrange, neaten, order, untwist.
antonyms bend, twist.

straighten out clear up, correct, disentangle, rectify, regularise, resolve, settle, sort out, unfankle, unsnarl, work out.
antonym muddle.

straightforward *adj.* candid, clear-cut, direct, easy, elementary, forthright, genuine, guileless, honest, open, open-and-shut, penny-plain, routine, simple, sincere, truthful, uncomplicated, undemanding.
antonyms complicated, devious, evasive.

strain[1] *v.* compress, distend, drive, embrace, endeavour, exert, express, extend, fatigue, filter, injure, labour, overtax, overwork, percolate, pull, purify, restrain, retch, riddle, screen, seep, separate, sieve, sift, sprain, squeeze, stretch, strive, struggle, tauten, tax, tear, tighten, tire, tug, twist, weaken, wrench, wrest, wrick.
n. anxiety, burden, effort, exertion, force, height, injury, key, pitch, pressure, pull, sprain, stress, struggle, tautness, tension, wrench.

strain[2] *n.* ancestry, blood, descent, extraction, family, humour, lineage, manner, pedigree, race, spirit, stem, stock, streak, style, suggestion, suspicion, temper, tendency, tone, trace, trait, vein, way.

strained *adj.* artificial, awkward, constrained, difficult, embarrassed, epitonic, false, forced, laboured, self-conscious, stiff, tense, uncomfortable, uneasy, unnatural, unrelaxed.
antonym natural.

strains *n.* air, lay, measure, melody, song, theme, tune.

strait *n.* channel, gat, gut, kyle, narrows, sound.

straitened *adj.* difficult, distressed, embarrassed, impoverished, limited, poor, reduced, restricted.
antonyms easy, well-off.

strait-laced *adj.* moralistic, narrow, narrow-minded, old-maidish, prim, proper, prudish, puritanical, strict, stuffy, upright, Victorian.
antonyms broad-minded, easy-going.

straits *n.* crisis, difficulty, dilemma, distress, embarrassment, emergency, extremity, hardship, hole, mess, perplexity, plight, poverty, predicament.

strand *n.* fibre, fibril, fibrilla, filament, length, lock, rope, string, thread, tress, twist.

stranded *adj.* abandoned, aground, ashore, beached, grounded, helpless, high and dry, homeless, in the lurch, marooned, penniless, shipwrecked, wrecked.

strange *adj.* abnormal, alien, astonishing, awkward, bewildered, bizarre, curious, disorientated, disoriented, eccentric, eerie, exceptional, exotic, extraordinary, fantastic(al), ferly, foreign, frain, fremd, fremit, funny, irregular, lost, marvellous, mystifying, new, novel, odd, out-of-the-way, peculiar, perplexing, queer, rare, remarkable, remote, singular, sinister, unaccountable, unacquainted, uncanny, unco, uncomfortable, uncommon, unexplained, unexplored, unfamiliar, unheard of, unknown, untried, unversed, weird, wonderful.
antonyms comfortable, common, familiar, ordinary.

strangeness *n.* abnormalism, abnormality, abnormity, bizarreness, bizarrerie, eccentricity, eeriness, exoticness, extraordinariness, fantasticality, fantasticalness, irregularity, oddity, oddness, peculiarity, queerness, singularity, uncanniness.
antonym ordinariness.

stranger *n.* alien, foreigner, fraim, fremd, fremit, guest, incomer, newcomer, nonmember, outlander, unknown, visitor.
antonyms local, native.

strangle *n.* asphyxiate, choke, constrict, gag, garrotte, inhibit, jugulate, repress, smother, stifle, strangulate, suffocate, suppress, throttle.

strap *n.* belt, leash, thong, tie, vitta.
v. beat, belt, bind, buckle, fasten, flog, lash, scourge, secure, tie, truss, whip.

strapping *adj.* beefy, big, brawny, burly, hefty, hulking, hunky, husky, powerful, robust, stalwart, strong, sturdy, well-built.
antonym puny.

stratagem *n.* artifice, device, dodge, feint, fetch, intrigue, manoeuvre, plan, plot, ploy, ruse, ruse de guerre, scheme, subterfuge, trick, wile.

strategic *adj.* calculated, cardinal, critical, crucial, decisive, deliberate, diplomatic, important, key, planned, politic, strategetical, vital.
antonym unimportant.

strategy *n.* approach, design, manoeuvring, plan, planning, policy, procedure, programme, scheme, way.

stratum *n.* bed, bracket, caste, category, class, grade, group, layer, level, lode, rank, region, seam, station, stratification, table, tier, vein.

stray *v.* deviate, digress, diverge, drift, err, get lost, meander, ramble, range, roam, rove, straggle, wander (off).
adj. abandoned, accidental, chance, erratic, forwandered, freak, homeless, lost, odd, random, roaming, scattered, vagrant.

streak *n.* band, dash, element, freak, layer, line, slash, smear, strain, strip, stripe, stroke, touch, trace, vein.
v. band, dart, daub, flash, fleck, fly, gallop, hurtle, slash, smear, speed, sprint, striate, stripe, sweep, tear, whistle, whizz, zoom.

streaked *adj.* banded, barred, brinded, brindle(d), flecked, fleckered, lined, streaky, striate, veiny.

stream *n.* beck, brook, burn, course, creek, current, drift, flow, freshet, ghyll, gill, gush, outpouring, rill, rillet, river, rivulet, run, runnel, rush, surge, tide, torrent, tributary.
v. cascade, course, emit, flood, flow, glide, gush, issue, pour, run, shed, spill, spout, surge, well out.

streamer *n.* banner, ensign, flag, gonfalon, gonfanon, pennant, pennon, plume, ribbon, standard.

streamlined *adj.* efficient, graceful, modernised, organised, rationalised, sleek, slick, smooth, smooth-running, superior, time-saving, up-to-the-minute, well-run.
antonyms clumsy, inefficient, old-fashioned.

street *n.* avenue, boulevard, carriageway, corso, crescent, drive, gate, highway, lane, prospect, road, roadway, row, terrace, thoroughfare.

strength *n.* advantage, anchor, asset, backbone, brawn, brawniness, cogency, concentration, courage, effectiveness, efficacy, energy, firmness, foison, force, fortitude, fushion, health, intensity, lustiness, mainstay, might, muscle, potency, power, resolution, robustness, security, sinew, spirit, stamina, stoutness, sturdiness, thew, toughness, vehemence, vigour, virtue.
antonyms timidness, weakness.

strengthen *v.* afforce, bolster, brace, buttress, confirm, consolidate, corroborate, edify, encourage, enhance, establish, fortify, harden, hearten, heighten, increase, intensify, invigorate, justify, nerve, nourish, reinforce, rejuvenate, restore, steel, stiffen, substantiate, support, toughen.
antonym weaken.

strenuous *adj.* active, arduous, bold, demanding, determined, eager, earnest, energetic, exhausting, hard, Herculean, laborious, persistent, resolute, spirited, strong, taxing, tireless, toilful, toilsome, tough, uphill, urgent, vigorous, warm, zealous.
antonyms easy, effortless.

stress *n.* accent, accentuation, anxiety, beat, burden, emphasis, emphaticalness, force, hassle, importance, oppression, pressure, significance, strain, tautness, tension, trauma, urgency, weight, worry.
antonym relaxation.
v. accentuate, belabour, emphasise, repeat, strain, tauten, underline, underscore.
antonym relax.

stretch *n.* area, bit, distance, exaggeration, expanse, extensibility, extension, extent, period, reach, run, space, spell, spread, stint, strain, sweep, term, time, tract.
v. cover, distend, elongate, expand, extend, inflate, lengthen, pull, rack, reach, spread, strain, swell, tauten, tighten, unfold, unroll.
antonyms relax, squeeze.

stretch one's legs exercise, go for a walk, move about, promenade, stroll, take a breather, take a walk, take the air.

stretch out hold out, lie down, porrect, put out, reach, relax, stretch forth.
antonym draw back.

strew *v.* bespread, besprinkle, bestrew, disperse, litter, scatter, spread, sprinkle, toss.
antonym gather.

stricken *adj.* affected, afflicted, expunged, hit, injured, smitten, struck, wounded.
antonym unaffected.

strict *adj.* absolute, accurate, austere, authoritarian, close, complete, exact, faithful, firm, harsh, meticulous, no-nonsense, particular, perfect, precise, religious, restricted, rigid, rigorous, scrupulous, severe, stern, stringent, thoroughgoing, total, true, unsparing, utter, Victorian.
antonyms easy-going, flexible, mild.

strictness *n.* accuracy, austerity, authoritarianism, exactness, firmness, harshness, martinetism, meticulousness, rigidity, rigidness, rigorousness, rigour, scrupulousness, severity, sternness, stringency, stringentness.
antonyms flexibility, mildness.

stricture *n.* animadversion, blame, censure, criticism, flak, rebuke, reproof.
antonym praise.

strident *adj.* cacophonous, clamorous, clashing, discordant, grating, harsh, jangling, jarring, loud, rasping, raucous, screeching, shrill, stridulant, stridulous, unmusical, vociferous.
antonyms quiet, sweet.

strife *n.* animosity, battle, bickering, brigue, colluctation, combat, conflict, contention, contest, contestation, controversy, discord, dissension, friction, quarrel, rivalry, row, squabbling, struggle, warfare, wrangling.
antonym peace.

strike *n.* attack, buffet, hartal, hit, mutiny, raid, refusal, stoppage, thump, walk-out, wallop, work-to-rule.
v. achieve, affect, afflict, arrange, assail, assault, assume, attack, attain, bang, beat, bop, box, buff, buffet, cancel, chastise, clap, clash, clobber, clout, clump, cob, coin, collide with, cuff, dart, dash, delete, devastate, discover, dismantle, douse, down tools, drive, dunt, effect, encounter, find, force, hammer, hit, impel, impress, interpose, invade, knock, mutiny, penetrate, pierce, pound, print, punish, ratify, reach, register, remove, revolt, seem, shoot, slap, slat, smack, smite, sock, stamp, stumble across, stumble upon, surrender, swap, swipe, swop, thrust, thump, touch, trap, turn up, uncover, unearth, walk out, wallop, wham, work to rule, zap.

strike down afflict, assassinate, destroy, kill, murder, ruin, slay, smite.

strike out cancel, cross out, delete, efface, erase, excise, expunge, remove, score off, score out, strike off, strike through.
antonym add.

striking *adj.* arresting, astonishing, conspicuous, dazzling, distingué(e), extraordinary, forcible, foudroyant, frappant, impressive, memorable, noticeable, outstanding, salient, stunning, wonderful.
antonym unimpressive.

string *n.* bunch, chain, cord, fibre, file, line, number, procession, queue, row, sequence, series, strand, succession, train, twine.
v. festoon, hang, link, loop, sling, stretch, suspend, thread, tie up.

string along[1] accompany, agree, assent, collaborate, co-operate, go along.
antonym dissent.

string along[2] bluff, deceive, dupe, fool, hoax, humbug, play (someone) false, play fast and loose with, put one over on, take (someone) for a ride.

string out disperse, extend, fan out, lengthen, protract, space out, spread out, straggle, stretch out, wander.
antonyms gather, shorten.

stringent *adj.* binding, demanding, exacting, flexible, inflexible, mild, rigid, rigorous, severe, strict, tight, tough.

strings *n.* catches, conditions, limitations, obligations, prerequisites, provisos, qualifications, requirements, restrictions, stipulations.

stringy *adj.* chewy, fibrous, gristly, ropy, sinewy, tough, wiry.
antonym tender.

strip[1] *v.* bare, clear, defoliate, denude, deprive, despoil, devest, disadorn, disembellish, disgarnish, disinvest, disleaf, disleave, dismantle, displenish, disrobe, divest, doff, empty, excoriate, excorticate, expose, gut, husk, lay bare, loot, peel, pillage, plunder, ransack, rob, sack, skin, spoil, unclothe, uncover, undress, widow.
antonyms cover, provide.

strip[2] *n.* band, belt, bit, fillet, lath, list, piece, ribbon, sash, screed, shred, slat, slip, spline, strake, strap, swathe, thong, tongue, vitta.

stripe *n.* band, bar, belt, chevron, flash, fleck, striation, vitta.

striped *adj.* banded, barred, streaky, striated, stripy, vittate.

stripling *n.* adolescent, boy, fledgling, hobbledehoy, lad, shaver, teenager, youngling, youngster, young'un, youth.

strive *v.* attempt, compete, contend, endeavour, fight, labour, push oneself, strain, struggle, toil, try, work.

stroke *n.* accomplishment, achievement, apoplexy, attack, blow, clap, collapse, effleurage, feat, fit, flourish, hit, knock, move, movement, pat, rap, seizure, shock, swap, swop, thump.
v. caress, clap, fondle, pat, pet, rub.

stroll *v.* amble, da(c)ker, dander, dawdle, mosey, promenade, ramble, saunter, stooge, toddle, wander.
n. airing, constitutional, dawdle, excursion, promenade, ramble, saunter, toddle, turn, walk.

stroller *n.* dawdler, flâneur, rambler, saunterer, walker, wanderer.

strong *adj.* acute, aggressive, athletic, beefy, biting, bold, brave, brawny, bright, brilliant, burly, capable, clear, clear-cut, cogent, compelling, competent, concentrated, convincing, courageous, dazzling, dedicated, deep, deep-rooted, determined, distinct, drastic, durable, eager, effective, efficient, emphasised, excelling, extreme, fast-moving, fervent, fervid, fierce, firm, forceful, forcible, formidable, glaring, great, grievous, gross, hale, hard, hard-nosed, hard-wearing, hardy, heady, healthy, hearty, heavy-duty, Herculean, highly-flavoured, highly-seasoned, hot, intemperate, intense, intoxicating, keen, loud, lusty, marked, muscular, nappy, numerous, offensive, overpowering, persuasive, petrous, piquant, pithy, plucky, pollent, potent, powerful, pungent, pure, rank, redoubtable, reinforced, resilient, resolute, resourceful, robust, self-assertive, severe, sharp, sinewy, sound, spicy, stalwart, stark, staunch, steadfast, sthenic, stout, stouthearted, strapping, stressed, sturdy, substantial, telling, tenacious, thewy, tough, trenchant, undiluted, unmistakable, unseemly, unyielding, urgent, vehement, violent, virile, vivid, weighty, well-armed, well-built, well-established, well-founded, well-knit, well-protected, well-set, well-versed, zealous. *antonyms* mild, weak.

strong point advantage, aptitude, asset, bag, bent, forte, gift, long suit, métier, speciality, specialty, strength, strong suit, talent, thing.

strongarm *adj.* aggressive, bullying, coercive, forceful, intimidatory, oppressive, physical, terror, threatening, thuggish, violent. *antonym* gentle.

stronghold *n.* bastion, bulwark, castle, centre, citadel, fastness, fort, fortress, hedgehog, keep, redoubt, refuge.

strong-minded *adj.* determined, firm, independent, iron-willed, resolute, steadfast, strong-willed, tenacious, unbending, uncompromising, unwavering. *antonym* weak-willed.

stroppy *adj.* awkward, bad-tempered, bloody-minded, cantankerous, difficult, obstreperous, perverse, quarrelsome, refractory, rowdy, unco-operative, unhelpful. *antonyms* co-operative, sweet-tempered.

structural *adj.* configurational, constructional, design, formational, organisational, tectonic.

structure *n.* arrangement, building, compages, configuration, conformation, construction, contexture, design, edifice, erection, fabric, form, formation, make-up, organisation, pile, set-up.

v. arrange, assemble, build, construct, design, form, organise, shape.

struggle *v.* agonise, battle, compete, contend, fight, grapple, labour, scuffle, strain, strive, toil, work, wrestle. *antonyms* give in, rest.

n. agon, agony, battle, brush, clash, combat, conflict, contest, effort, encounter, exertion, grind, hostilities, labour, luctation, pains, scramble, skirmish, strife, toil, tussle, work.

antonyms ease, submission.

strut *v.* brank, cock, parade, peacock, prance, stalk, swagger.

stub *n.* butt, counterfoil, dog-end, doup, end, fag-end, remnant, snub, stump, tail, tail-end.

stubborn *adj.* bull-headed, contumacious, cross-grained, difficult, dogged, dour, fixed, headstrong, inflexible, intractable, intransigent, mulish, obdurate, obstinate, opinionated, persistent, pertinacious, pig-headed, recalcitrant, refractory, rigid, self-willed, stiff, stiff-necked, tenacious, unbending, unmanageable, unshakable, unyielding, wilful. *antonym* compliant.

stubby *adj.* bristling, bristly, chunky, dumpy, knobbly, knubbly, knubby, nubbly, nubby, prickly, rough, short, squat, stocky, stubbly, stumpy, thickset. *antonyms* long, tall, thin.

stuck *adj.* baffled, beaten, cemented, fast, fastened, firm, fixed, glued, joined, nonplussed, stumped, stymied. *antonym* loose.

stuck on crazy about, dotty about, enthusiastic about, infatuated with, keen on, mad on, nuts on, obsessed with, wild about. *antonym* indifferent to.

stuck-up *adj.* arrogant, big-headed, conceited, condescending, exclusive, haughty, high and mighty, hoity-toity, overweening, patronising, prideful, proud, snobbish, snooty, swollen-headed, toffee-nosed, uppish, uppity. *antonym* humble.

studded *adj.* bejewelled, bespangled, dotted, flecked, ornamented, scattered, set, spangled, speckled, spotted, sprinkled.

student *n.* apprentice, bajan, bejant, bookman, chela, co-ed, collegianer, contemplator, disciple, fresher, freshman, learner, observer, pupil, scholar, seminarist, soph, sophomore, undergraduate, undergraduette.

studied *adj.* calculated, conscious, deliberate, forced, intentional, over-elaborate, planned, premeditated, purposeful, unnatural, voulu, wilful. *antonyms* natural, unplanned.

studio *n.* atelier, school, workroom, workshop.

studious *adj.* academic, assiduous, attentive, bookish, careful, diligent, eager, earnest, hard-working, heedful, intellectual, intent, meditative, reflective, scholarly, sedulous, serious, solicitous, thoughtful. *antonym* lazy.

study *v.* analyse, cogitate, con, consider, contemplate, cram, deliberate, dig, examine, investigate, learn, lucubrate, meditate, mug up, peruse, ponder, pore over, read, read up, research, scan, scrutinise, survey, swot.

n. analysis, application, attention, cogitation, consideration, contemplation, cramming, critique, examination, inclination, inquiry, inspection, interest, investigation, learning, lessons, lucubration, memoir, monograph, prolusion, reading, report, research, reverie, review, scrutiny, survey, swotting, thesis, thought, zeal.

stuff v. binge, bombast, compress, cram, crowd, fill, force, gobble, gorge, gormandise, guzzle, jam, load, overindulge, pack, pad, push, ram, sate, satiate, shove, squeeze, steeve, stodge, stow, trig, wedge.
antonyms nibble, unload.

n. belongings, clobber, cloth, effects, equipment, essence, fabric, furniture, gear, goods, impedimenta, junk, kit, luggage, material, materials, matériel, matter, objects, paraphernalia, pith, possessions, provisions, quintessence, staple, substance, tackle, textile, things, trappings.

stuffing n. bombast, farce, farcing, filler, force-meat, kapok, packing, quilting, wadding.

stuffy adj. airless, close, conventional, deadly, dreary, dull, fetid, fogram, fogyish, frowsty, frowzy, fuggy, fusty, heavy, humourless, muggy, musty, old-fashioned, oppressive, poking, poky, pompous, priggish, prim, staid, stale, stifling, stilted, stodgy, strait-laced, suffocating, sultry, uninteresting, unventilated, Victorian.
antonyms airy, informal, interesting, modern.

stultify v. benumb, blunt, dull, hebetate, invalidate, negate, nullify, numb, smother, stifle, stupefy, suppress, thwart.
antonyms prove, sharpen.

stultifying adj. dulling, hebetant, hebetating, numbing, stupefying.
antonym electrifying.

stumble v. blunder, fall, falter, flounder, fluff, hesitate, lurch, reel, slip, stagger, stammer, stutter, titubate, trip.
stumble on blunder upon, chance upon, come across, discover, encounter, find, happen upon, light upon.

stumbling-block n. bar, barrier, crux, difficulty, hindrance, hurdle, impediment, obstacle, obstruction, pons asinorum, snag.
antonym boost.

stump v. baffle, bamboozle, bewilder, clomp, clump, confound, confuse, defeat, dumbfound, flummox, foil, lumber, mystify, nonplus, outwit, perplex, plod, puzzle, stamp, stomp, stop, stymie, trudge.
antonym assist.
stump up contribute, cough up, donate, fork out, hand over, pay, pay out, pay up, shell out.
antonym receive.

stumped adj. baffled, bamboozled, floored, flummoxed, nonplussed, perplexed, stuck, stymied.

stumpy adj. chunky, dumpy, dwarf, dwarfish, heavy, short, squat, stocky, stubby, thick, thickset.
antonyms long, tall, thin.

stun v. amaze, astonish, astound, bedeafen, bewilder, confound, confuse, daze, deafen, dumbfound, flabbergast, overcome, overpower, shock, stagger, stupefy.

stung adj. angered, bitten, exasperated, goaded, hurt, incensed, irked, needled, nettled,

peeved, piqued, resentful, roused, wounded.
antonym soothed.

stunned adj. astounded, dazed, devastated, dumbfounded, flabbergasted, floored, numb, shocked, staggered, stupefied.
antonym indifferent.

stunner n. beauty, charmer, dazzler, dish, dolly, eye-catcher, eyeful, femme fatale, good-looker, heart-throb, honey, knock-out, looker, lovely, peach, sensation, siren, smasher, stotter, wow.
antonym dog.

stunning adj. beautiful, brilliant, dazing, dazzling, devastating, gorgeous, great, heavenly, impressive, lovely, marvellous, ravishing, remarkable, sensational, smashing, spectacular, stotting, striking, wonderful.
antonyms poor, ugly.

stunt[1] n. act, campaign, deed, enterprise, exploit, feat, feature, gest(e), performance, tour de force, trick, turn.

stunt[2] v. arrest, check, dwarf, hamper, hinder, impede, restrict, slow, stop.
antonym promote.

stunted adj. diminutive, dwarfed, dwarfish, little, runtish, runty, small, tiny, undersized.
antonyms large, sturdy.

stupefaction n. amaze, amazement, astonishment, awe, bafflement, bewilderment, wonder, wonderment.

stupefy v. amaze, astound, baffle, benumb, bewilder, confound, daze, drowse, dumbfound, hocus, numb, shock, stagger, stun.

stupendous adj. amazing, astounding, breathtaking, colossal, enormous, fabulous, fantastic, gigantic, huge, marvellous, mind-blowing, mind-boggling, overwhelming, phenomenal, prodigious, staggering, stunning, superb, tremendous, vast, wonderful.
antonym unimpressive.

stupid adj. anserine, asinine, beef-brained, beef-witted, blockish, Boeotian, boobyish, boring, bovine, brainless, clueless, crackbrained, cretinous, cuckoo, damfool, dazed, deficient, dense, dim, doltish, donnart, donnered, dopey, dovie, dozy, drippy, dull, dumb, fat-witted, foolish, fozy, futile, gaumless, glaikit, gormless, groggy, gullible, half-baked, half-witted, hammer-headed, idiotic, ill-advised, imbecilic, inane, indiscreet, insensate, insensible, insulse, irrelevant, irresponsible, laughable, ludicrous, lumpen, lurdan, meaningless, mindless, moronic, naïve, nonsensical, obtuse, opaque, pointless, puerile, punch-drunk, rash, semiconscious, senseless, short-sighted, simple, simple-minded, slow, slow-witted, sluggish, stolid, stunned, stupefied, thick, thick-headed, thick-witted, trivial, unintelligent, unthinking, vacuous, vapid, witless, wooden-headed.
antonyms alert, clever.

stupidity n. absurdity, asininity, bétise, brainlessness, crassitude, crassness, denseness, dimness, dopiness, doziness, dullness, dumb-

ness, duncery, fatuity, fatuousness, feeble-mindedness, folly, foolhardiness, foolishness, futility, goosery, idiocy, imbecility, impracticality, inanity, indiscretion, ineptitude, insipience, irresponsibility, ludicrousness, lunacy, madness, naïveté, naivety, obtuseness, oscitancy, pointlessness, puerility, rashness, senselessness, silliness, simplicity, slowness, thick-headedness, thickness, vapidity.
antonyms alertness, cleverness.

stupor *n.* coma, daze, inertia, insensibility, kef, lethargy, numbness, stupefaction, torpor, trance, unconsciousness, wonder.
antonym alertness.

sturdy *adj.* athletic, brawny, determined, durable, firm, flourishing, hardy, hearty, husky, lusty, muscular, obstinate, powerful, resolute, robust, secure, solid, stalwart, staunch, steadfast, stout, strong, substantial, vigorous, well-built, well-made.
antonyms decrepit, puny.

stutter *v.* falter, hesitate, mumble, splutter, stammer, stumble.

style *n.* affluence, appearance, approach, bon ton, category, chic, comfort, cosmopolitanism, custom, cut, dash, design, diction, dressiness, dress-sense, ease, élan, elegance, expression, fashion, fashionableness, flair, flamboyance, form, genre, grace, grandeur, hand, haut ton, kind, luxury, manner, method, mode, panache, pattern, phraseology, phrasing, pizzazz, polish, rage, refinement, savoir-faire, smartness, sophistication, sort, spirit, strain, stylishness, taste, technique, tenor, tone, treatment, trend, type, urbanity, variety, vein, vogue, way, wording.
antonym inelegance.
v. adapt, address, arrange, call, christen, create, cut, denominate, design, designate, dress, dub, entitle, fashion, label, name, shape, tailor, term, title.

stylish *adj.* á la mode, chic, chichi, classy, dapper, dressy, fashionable, groovy, in vogue, modish, natty, polished, smart, snappy, snazzy, trendy, urbane, voguish.
antonym unstylish.

stylus *n.* gnomon, graphium, graver, hand, index, needle, pen, pointer, probe, style.

stymie *v.* baffle, balk, bamboozle, confound, defeat, flummox, foil, frustrate, hinder, mystify, nonplus, puzzle, snooker, stump, thwart.
antonym assist.

suave *adj.* affable, agreeable, bland, charming, civilised, courteous, diplomatic, gracious, obliging, pleasing, polite, smooth, smooth-tongued, soft-spoken, sophisticated, unctuous, urbane, worldly.
antonym unsophisticated.

suavity *n.* blandness, charm, sophistication, unctuosity, unctuousness, urbanity.
antonym coarseness.

subaquatic *adj.* demersal, subaqua, subaqueous, submarine, submersed, undersea, underwater.

subconscious *adj.* hidden, inner, innermost, intuitive, latent, repressed, subliminal, suppressed, unconscious.
antonym conscious.
n. id, super-ego, unconscious, underself.

subdue *v.* allay, break, check, conquer, control, crush, damp, dampen, daunt, defeat, discipline, humble, master, mellow, moderate, overcome, overpower, overrun, quell, quieten, reduce, repress, soften, soft-pedal, subact, subject, suppress, tame, trample, vanquish.
antonym arouse.

subdued *adj.* abated, chastened, crestfallen, dejected, dim, downcast, grave, hushed, low-key, muted, quiet, repentant, repressed, restrained, sad, serious, shaded, sober, soft, solemn, sombre, subfusc, subtle, unobtrusive.
antonyms aroused, lively.

subject *n.* affair, business, case, chapter, citizen, client, dependant, ground, issue, liegeman, matter, mind, national, object, participant, patient, point, question, subordinate, substance, theme, topic, vassal, victim.
antonym master.
adj. answerable, captive, cognisable, conditional, contingent, dependent, disposed, enslaved, exposed, heteronomous, inferior, liable, obedient, open, prone, satellite, subjugated, submissive, subordinate, subservient, susceptible, vulnerable.
antonyms free, insusceptible, superior.
v. expose, lay open, subdue, submit, subordinate, treat.

subjection *n.* bondage, captivity, chains, crushing, defeat, domination, enslavement, mastery, oppression, quelling, servitude, shackles, slavery, subduing, subjugation, thraldom, thrall, vassalage.

subjective biased, emotional, idiosyncratic, individual, instinctive, introspective, intuitive, personal, prejudiced.
antonym objective.

subjugate *v.* conquer, crush, defeat, enslave, enthrall, master, overcome, overpower, overthrow, quell, reduce, subdue, suppress, tame, thrall, vanquish.
antonym free.

sublimate *v.* channel, divert, elevate, exalt, heighten, purify, redirect, refine, sublime, transfer, transmute, turn.
antonym let out.

sublime *adj.* Dantean, Dantesque, elevated, eminent, empyreal, empyrean, exalted, glorious, grand, great, high, imposing, lofty, magnificent, majestic, noble, transcendent.
antonym lowly.

submerge *v.* deluge, demerge, dip, drown, duck, dunk, engulf, flood, immerse, implunge, inundate, overflow, overwhelm, plunge, sink, submerse, swamp.
antonym surface.

submerged *adj.* concealed, demersal, demersed, drowned, hidden, immersed, inundated, obscured, subaquatic, subaqueous, submarine, submersed, sunk, sunken, swamped, undersea, underwater, unseen.

submission *n.* acquiescence, argument, assent, capitulation, compliance, contention, deference, docility, entry, meekness, obedience, passivity, presentation, proposal, resignation, resignedness, submissiveness, submitting, suggestion, surrender, tendering, tractability, yielding.
antonym intractability.

submissive *adj.* abject, accommodating, acquiescent, amenable, biddable, bootlicking, complaisant, compliant, deferential, docile, dutiful, humble, ingratiating, malleable, meek, obedient, obeisant, obsequious, passive, patient, pliant, resigned, subdued, subservient, supine, tractable, uncomplaining, unresisting, yielding.
antonym intractable.

submit *v.* accede, acquiesce, advance, agree, argue, assert, bend, bow, capitulate, claim, commit, comply, contend, defer, endure, knuckle under, move, present, proffer, propose, propound, put, refer, state, stoop, succumb, suggest, surrender, table, tender, tolerate, volunteer, yield.
antonym struggle.

subnormal *adj.* cretinous, ESN, feeble-minded, imbecilic, inferior, low, moronic, retarded, slow, unteachable.
antonym gifted.

subordinate *adj.* ancillary, auxiliary, dependent, inferior, junior, lesser, lower, menial, minor, secondary, servient, subject, subservient, subsidiary, supplementary.
antonym superior.
n. adjunct, aide, assistant, attendant, dependant, inferior, junior, second, second banana, stooge, sub, subaltern, underdog, underling, underman, under-workman, weakling.
antonym superior.

subordination *n.* inferiority, servitude, subjection, submission, subservience.
antonym superiority.

subscribe *v.* acquiesce, advocate, agree, approve, consent, contribute, cough up, countenance, donate, endorse, fork out, give, offer, pledge, promise, shell out, support.

subscription *n.* abonnement, contribution, donation, dues, fee, gift, offering, payment.

subsequent *adj.* after, consequent, consequential, ensuing, following, later, postliminary, postliminous, resulting, succeeding.
antonym previous.

subsequently *adv.* after, afterwards, consequently, later.
antonym previously.

subservient *adj.* abject, accessory, ancillary, auxiliary, bootlicking, conducive, cringing, deferential, dough-faced, helpful, inferior, instrumental, obsequious, serviceable, servile, slavish, subject, submissive, subordinate, subsidiary, sycophantic, truckling, useful.
antonyms domineering, rebellious, unhelpful.

subside *v.* abate, collapse, decline, decrease,

descend, diminish, drop, dwindle, ease, ebb, fall, lessen, lower, moderate, quieten, recede, settle, sink, slacken, slake, wane.
antonym increase.

subsidence *n.* abatement, decline, decrease, de-escalation, descent, detumescence, diminution, ebb, lessening, settlement, settling, sinking, slackening.
antonym increase.

subsidiary *adj.* adjective, aiding, ancillary, assistant, auxiliary, branch, contributory, co-operative, helpful, lesser, minor, secondary, serviceable, subordinate, subservient, succursal, supplemental, supplementary, useful.
antonym chief.
n. affiliate, branch, division, offshoot, part, section.

subsidise *v.* aid, back, finance, fund, promote, sponsor, support, underwrite.

subsidy *n.* aid, allowance, assistance, backing, contribution, finance, grant, help, sponsorship, subvention, support.

subsist *v.* continue, endure, exist, hold out, inhere, last, live, remain, survive.

subsistence *n.* aliment, existence, food, keep, livelihood, living, maintenance, nourishment, prog, provision, rations, support, survival, sustenance, upkeep, victuals.

substance *n.* actuality, affluence, assets, body, burden, concreteness, consistence, element, entity, essence, estate, fabric, force, foundation, gist, gravamen, ground, hypostasis, import, material, matter, meaning, means, nitty-gritty, pith, property, reality, resources, significance, solidity, stuff, subject, subject-matter, texture, theme, wealth.

substandard *adj.* damaged, imperfect, inadequate, inferior, poor, second-rate, shoddy, tawdry, unacceptable.
antonym first-rate.

substantial *adj.* actual, ample, big, bulky, considerable, corporeal, durable, enduring, essential, existent, firm, full-bodied, generous, goodly, hefty, important, large, massive, material, positive, real, significant, sizable, solid, sound, stout, strong, sturdy, tidy, true, valid, weighty, well-built, worthwhile.
antonyms insignificant, small.

substantially *adv.* essentially, largely, materially, significantly, to all intents and purposes.
antonym slightly.

substantiate *v.* affirm, authenticate, confirm, corroborate, embody, establish, prove, support, validate, verify.
antonym disprove.

substitute *v.* change, commute, exchange, interchange, replace, subrogate, swap, switch.
n. agent, alternate, depute, deputy, equivalent, ersatz, locum, locum tenens, makeshift, proxy, relief, replacement, replacer, reserve, stand-by, stop-gap, sub, succedaneum, supply, surrogate, temp, vicar.
adj. acting, additional, alternative, ersatz,

proxy, replacement, reserve, second, surrogate, temporary, vicarious.
substitute for act for, cover for, deputise, double for, fill in for, relieve, stand in for, sub.
substitution *n*. change, exchange, interchange, replacement, swap, swapping, switch, switching.
subterfuge *n*. artifice, deception, deviousness, dodge, duplicity, evasion, excuse, expedient, machination, manoeuvre, ploy, pretence, pretext, quibble, ruse, scheme, shift, stall, stratagem, trick.
antonyms honesty, openness.
subtle *adj*. artful, astute, crafty, cunning, deep, delicate, designing, devious, discriminating, elusive, faint, fine-drawn, fine-spun, impalpable, implied, indirect, ingenious, insinuated, intriguing, keen, Machiavellian, nice, obstruse, over-refined, penetrating, profound, rarefied, refined, scheming, shrewd, slight, sly, sophisticated, tenuous, understated, wily.
antonyms open, unsubtle.
subtlety *n*. acumen, acuteness, artfulness, astuteness, cleverness, craftiness, cunning, delicacy, deviousness, discernment, discrimination, finesse, guile, intricacy, nicety, openness, penetration, refinement, sagacity, skill, slyness, sophistication, unsubtlety, wiliness.
subtract *v*. debit, deduct, detract, diminish, remove, withdraw.
antonyms add, add to.
suburbs *n*. banlieue, commuter belt, dormitory, environs, exurbia, faubourg, neighbourhood, outskirts, precincts, purlieus, stockbroker belt, suburbia, villadom.
antonyms centre, heart.
subversive *adj*. destructive, disruptive, incendiary, inflammatory, insurrectionary, overthrowing, perversive, riotous, seditious, treasonous, underground, undermining.
antonym loyal.
n. deviationist, dissident, fifth columnist, freedom fighter, insurrectionary, quisling, saboteur, seditionary, seditionist, terrorist, traitor.
subvert *v*. confound, contaminate, corrupt, debase, demolish, demoralise, deprave, destroy, disrupt, invalidate, overturn, pervert, poison, raze, ruin, sabotage, undermine, upset, vitiate, wreck.
antonyms boost, uphold.
subway *n*. métro, tube, underground.
succeed *v*. arrive, ensue, fadge, flourish, follow, make good, make it, prosper, result, supervene, thrive, triumph, work.
antonyms fail, precede.
succeed to accede, come into, enter upon, inherit, replace, supersede, take over.
antonyms abdicate, precede.
succeeding *adj*. coming, ensuing, following, later, next, subsequent, successive, to come.
antonym previous.
success *n*. ascendancy, bestseller, celebrity, eminence, fame, fortune, happiness, hit, luck,

prosperity, sensation, somebody, star, triumph, VIP, well-doing, winner.
antonym failure.
successful *adj*. acknowledged, bestselling, booming, efficacious, favourable, flourishing, fortunate, fruitful, lucky, lucrative, moneymaking, paying, profitable, prosperous, rewarding, satisfactory, satisfying, thriven, thriving, top, unbeaten, victorious, wealthy, well-doing.
antonym unsuccessful.
successfully *adv*. beautifully, famously, fine, great, swimmingly, victoriously, well.
antonym unsuccessfully.
succession *n*. accession, assumption, chain, concatenation, continuation, course, cycle, descendants, descent, elevation, flow, inheritance, line, lineage, order, procession, progression, race, run, sequence, series, train.
successive *adj*. consecutive, following, in succession, sequent, succeeding.
succinct *adj*. brief, compact, compendious, concise, condensed, gnomic, laconic, pithy, short, summary, terse.
antonym wordy.
succour *v*. aid, assist, befriend, comfort, encourage, foster, help, help out, nurse, relieve, support.
antonym undermine.
n. aid, assistance, comfort, help, helping hand, ministrations, relief, support.
succulent *adj*. fleshy, juicy, luscious, lush, mellow, moist, mouthwatering, rich, sappy.
antonym dry.
succumb *v*. capitulate, collapse, deteriorate, die, fall, give in, knuckle under, submit, surrender, yield.
antonym overcome.
suck *v*. absorb, drain, draw in, extract, imbibe.
sucker *n*. butt, cat's-paw, dupe, fool, mark, mug, patsy, pushover, sap, stooge, victim.
sucking-up *n*. arse-licking, bootlicking, currying favour, fawning, flattering, ingratiating, toadying, truckling.
sudden *adj*. abrupt, hasty, hurried, impulsive, prompt, quick, rapid, rash, snap, startling, subitaneous, swift, unexpected, unforeseen, unusual.
antonym slow.
suddenness *n*. abruptness, haste, hastiness, hurriedness, impulsiveness.
antonym slowness.
sue *v*. apply, beg, beseech, charge, entreat, indict, petition, plead, prosecute, solicit, summon, supplicate.
suffer *v*. ache, agonise, allow, bear, brook, deteriorate, endure, experience, feel, grieve, hurt, let, permit, sorrow, support, sustain, tolerate, undergo.
suffering *n*. ache, affliction, agony, anguish, discomfort, distress, hardship, martyrdom, misery, ordeal, pain, pangs, torment, torture.
suffice *v*. answer, content, do, measure up, satisfy, serve.
sufficiency *n*. adequacy, adequateness, compe-

tence, conceit, enough, enow, plenty, quantum sufficit, satiety, sufficience.
antonym insufficiency.
sufficient *adj.* adequate, competent, effective, enough, satisfactory, sufficing, well-off, well-to-do.
antonyms insufficient, poor.
suffocate *v.* asphyxiate, choke, smother, stifle, strangle, throttle.
suffuse *v.* bathe, colour, cover, flood, imbue, infuse, mantle, permeate, pervade, redden, steep, transfuse.
suggest *v.* advise, advocate, connote, evoke, hint, imply, indicate, inkle, innuendo, insinuate, intimate, move, propose, recommend.
antonyms demonstrate, order.
suggestion *n.* breath, hint, incitement, indication, innuendo, insinuation, intimation, motion, plan, proposal, proposition, recommendation, suspicion, temptation, trace, whisper.
antonyms demonstration, order.
suggestive *adj.* bawdy, blue, evocative, expressive, immodest, improper, indecent, indelicate, indicative, insinuating, meaning, offcolour, provocative, prurient, racy, redolent, reminiscent, ribald, risqué, rude, smutty, spicy, titillating, unseemly.
antonyms clean, unevocative.
suicide *n.* felo de se, hara-kiri, self-destruction, self-immolation, self-murder, self-slaughter, suttee.
suit *v.* accommodate, adapt, adjust, agree, answer, become, befit, correspond, do, fashion, fit, gee, gratify, harmonise, match, modify, please, proportion, satisfy, tailor, tally.
antonyms clash, displease.
n. action, addresses, appeal, attentions, case, cause, clothing, costume, courtship, dress, ensemble, entreaty, get-up, habit, invocation, kind, lawsuit, outfit, petition, prayer, proceeding, prosecution, request, rig-out, series, trial, type.
suitability *n.* appositeness, appropriateness, aptness, fitness, fittingness, opportuneness, rightness, timeliness.
antonym unsuitability.
suitable *adj.* acceptable, accordant, adequate, applicable, apposite, appropriate, apt, becoming, befitting, competent, conformable, congenial, congruent, consonant, convenient, correspondent, due, fit, fitting, opportune, pertinent, proper, relevant, right, satisfactory, seemly, square, suited, well-becoming, well-beseeming.
antonym unsuitable.
suitably *adv.* acceptably, accordingly, appropriately, fitly, fittingly, properly, quite.
antonym unsuitably.
suite *n.* apartment, attendants, collection, entourage, escort, followers, furniture, household, retainers, retinue, rooms, sequence, series, servants, set, train.
suitor *n.* admirer, beau, follower, pretendant, swain, wooer, young man.

sulk *v.* boody, brood, grouch, grump, mope, pet, pout.
sulky *adj.* aloof, churlish, cross, disgruntled, grouty, ill-humoured, moody, morose, perverse, pettish, petulant, put out, resentful, sullen.
antonym cheerful.
sullen *adj.* baleful, brooding, cheerless, cross, dark, dismal, dull, farouche, gloomy, glowering, glum, heavy, lumpish, malignant, moody, morose, obstinate, perverse, silent, sombre, sour, stubborn, sulky, surly, unsociable.
antonym cheerful.
sullenness *n.* brooding, glowering, glumness, heaviness, moodiness, moroseness, sourness, sulkiness, surliness.
antonym cheerfulness.
sully *v.* befoul, besmirch, blemish, contaminate, darken, defile, dirty, disgrace, dishonour, distain, mar, pollute, spoil, spot, stain, taint, tarnish.
antonyms cleanse, honour.
sultry *adj.* close, come-hither, erotic, hot, humid, indecent, lurid, muggy, oppressive, passionate, provocative, seductive, sensual, sexy, sticky, stifling, stuffy, sweltering, torrid, voluptuous.
antonyms cold, cool.
sum *n.* aggregate, amount, completion, culmination, entirety, height, quantity, reckoning, result, score, substance, sum total, summary, tally, total, totality, whole.
sum up close, conclude, perorate, précis, recapitulate, review, summarise.
summarily *adv.* abruptly, arbitrarily, expeditiously, forthwith, hastily, immediately, peremptorily, promptly, speedily, swiftly.
summarise *v.* abbreviate, abridge, condense, encapsulate, epitomise, outline, précis, review, shorten, sum up.
antonym expand (on).
summary *n.* abridgement, abstract, compendium, digest, epitome, essence, extract, outline, précis, recapitulation, résumé, review, rundown, summation, summing-up, synopsis.
adj. arbitrary, brief, compact, compendious, concise, condensed, cursory, expeditious, hasty, laconic, perfunctory, pithy, short, succinct.
antonym lengthy.
summer-house *n.* belvedere, gazebo, pavilion.
summit *n.* acme, apex, apogee, crown, culmination, head, height, peak, pinnacle, point, top, zenith.
antonyms bottom, nadir.
summon *v.* accite, arouse, assemble, beckon, bid, call, cite, convene, convoke, gather, hist, invite, invoke, mobilise, muster, preconise, rally, rouse.
antonym dismiss.
sumptuous *adj.* costly, dear, expensive, extravagant, gorgeous, grand, lavish, luxurious, magnificent, opulent, plush, posh, princely, rich, ritzy, splendid, superb.

antonym mean.

sun *n.* daystar, star, sun-disc, sunlight, sunshine.
v. bake, bask, brown, insolate, sunbathe, tan.

sunbathe *v.* bake, bask, brown, insolate, take the sun, tan.

sunburnt *adj.* blistered, bronzed, brown, burnt, peeling, red, ruddy, scarlet, tanned, weather-beaten.
antonym pale.

sunder *v.* chop, cleave, cut, dissever, dissunder, divide, part, separate, sever, split.
antonym join.

sundry *adj.* a few, assorted, different, divers, miscellaneous, separate, several, some, varied, various.

sunk *adj.* done for, doomed, finished, lost, ruined, up the creek, up the spout.

sunken *adj.* buried, concave, depressed, drawn, emaciated, gaunt, haggard, hollow, hollowed, immersed, lower, recessed, submerged.

sunless *adj.* bleak, cheerless, cloudy, dark, depressing, dismal, dreary, gloomy, grey, hazy, overcast, sombre.
antonym sunny.

sunny *adj.* beaming, blithe, bright, brilliant, buoyant, cheerful, cheery, clear, cloudless, fine, genial, happy, joyful, light-hearted, luminous, optimistic, pleasant, radiant, smiling, summery, sun-bright, sunlit, sunshiny.
antonym gloomy.

sunrise *n.* aurora, cock-crow, crack of dawn, dawn, daybreak, daylight, dayspring, sun-up.

sunset *n.* crepuscule, dusk, evening, eventide, gloaming, nightfall, sundown, twilight.

super *adj.* excellent, glorious, incomparable, magnificent, marvellous, matchless, outstanding, peerless, sensational, smashing, superb, terrific, top-notch, wizard, wonderful.
antonym poor.

superannuated *adj.* aged, antiquated, decrepit, fogram, moribund, obsolete, old, past it, pensioned off, put out to grass, retired, senile, superannuate.
antonym young.

superb *adj.* admirable, breathtaking, choice, clipping, excellent, exquisite, fine, first-rate, gorgeous, grand, magnificent, marvellous, splendid, superior, unrivalled.
antonym poor.

supercilious *adj.* arrogant, condescending, contemptuous, disdainful, haughty, highty-tighty, hoity-toity, imperious, insolent, lofty, lordly, overbearing, patronising, proud, scornful, snooty, snotty, snouty, stuck-up, toffee-nosed, uppish, uppity, upstage, vainglorious.
antonym humble.

superficial *adj.* apparent, casual, cosmetic, cursory, desultory, empty, empty-headed, evident, exterior, external, frivolous, hasty, hurried, lightweight, nodding, ostensible, outward, passing, perfunctory, peripheral, seeming, shallow, silly, sketchy, skin-deep, slapdash, slight, surface, trivial, unanalytical, unreflective.

antonym detailed.

superficially *adv.* apparently, externally, ostensibly, seemingly.
antonym in depth.

superfluity *n.* excess, exuberance, glut, perissology, pleonasm, plethora, postiche, redundancy, superabundance, surfeit, surplus.
antonym lack.

superfluous *adj.* de trop, excess, excessive, extra, needless, otiose, pleonastic(al), postiche, redundant, remaining, residuary, spare, superabundant, supererogatory, supernumerary, surplus, uncalled-for, unnecessary, unneeded, unneedful, unwanted.
antonym necessary.

superhuman *adj.* divine, great, herculean, heroic, immense, paranormal, phenomenal, preternatural, prodigious, stupendous, supernatural, valiant.
antonyms average, ordinary.

superintend *v.* administer, control, direct, guide, inspect, manage, overlook, oversee, run, steer, supervise.

superintendence *n.* administration, care, charge, control, direction, government, guidance, inspection, management, supervision, surveillance.

superintendent *n.* administrator, chief, conductor, controller, curator, director, gaffer, governor, inspector, manager, overseer, supervisor.

superior *adj.* admirable, airy, better, choice, condescending, de luxe, disdainful, distinguished, excellent, exceptional, exclusive, fine, first-class, first-rate, good, grander, greater, haughty, high-class, higher, highty-tighty, hoity-toity, lofty, lordly, par excellence, patronising, predominant, preferred, pretentious, prevailing, respectable, snobbish, snooty, snotty, snouty, stuck-up, supercilious, superordinate, surpassing, top-flight, top-notch, transcendent, unrivalled, upper, uppish, uppity, upstage, worthy.
antonyms humble, inferior.
n. boss, chief, director, foreman, gaffer, manager, principal, senior, supervisor.
antonyms inferior, junior.

superiority *n.* advantage, ascendancy, edge, excellence, lead, predominance, preeminence, preponderance, prevalence, supremacy, vis major.
antonym inferiority.

superlative *adj.* consummate, crack, excellent, greatest, highest, magnificent, matchless, nonpareil, outstanding, peerless, supreme, surpassing, transcendent, unbeatable, unbeaten, unparalleled, unrivalled, unsurpassed.
antonym poor.

superman *n.* colossus, giant, Übermensch.

supernatural *adj.* abnormal, dark, ghostly, hidden, hyperphysical, metaphysical, miraculous, mysterious, mystic, occult, paranormal, phantom, preternatural, psychic, spectral, spiritual, superlunary, supersensible, super-

sensory, uncanny, unearthly, unnatural.
antonym natural.

supernumerary *adj.* excess, excessive, extra, extraordinary, redundant, spare, superfluous, surplus.
antonym necessary.

supersede *v.* annul, displace, oust, overrule, remove, replace, succeed, supplant, supplement, suspend, usurp.

superstition *n.* Aberglaube, delusion, fable, fallacy, illusion, myth, old wives' tale, voodooism.

superstitious *adj.* delusive, fallacious, false, fetishistic, groundless, illusory, voodooistic.

supervise *v.* administer, conduct, control, direct, general, handle, inspect, keep tabs on, manage, oversee, preside over, run, superintend.

supervision *n.* administration, auspices, care, charge, control, direction, guidance, instruction, leading-strings, management, oversight, stewardship, superintendence, surveillance.

supervisor *n.* administrator, boss, chief, foreman, gaffer, inspector, manager, overseer, steward, superintendent.

supervisory *adj.* administrative, directorial, executive, managerial, overseeing, superintendent.

supine *adj.* apathetic, bored, careless, flat, heedless, horizontal, idle, inactive, incurious, indifferent, indolent, inert, languid, lazy, lethargic, listless, negligent, passive, prostrate, recumbent, resigned, slothful, sluggish, spineless, spiritless, torpid, uninterested, unresisting.
antonyms alert, upright.

supplant *v.* displace, dispossess, oust, overthrow, remove, replace, supersede, topple, undermine, unseat.

supple *adj.* bending, double-jointed, elastic, flexible, limber, lithe, loose-limbed, plastic, pliable, pliant, whippy, willowish, willowy.
antonym rigid.

supplement *n.* addendum, addition, appendix, codicil, complement, extra, insert, postscript, pull-out, sequel, supplemental, supplementary, suppletion.
v. add, add to, augment, complement, eke, eke out, extend, fill up, reinforce, supply, top up.
antonym deplete.

supplementary *adj.* accompanying, additional, ancillary, auxiliary, complementary, extra, secondary, supplemental, suppletive, suppletory.
antonym core.

suppliant *adj.* begging, beseeching, craving, entreating, imploring, importunate, supplicating.
n. applicant, petitioner, pleader, postulant, suitor, supplicant.

supplication *n.* appeal, entreaty, invocation, orison, petition, plea, pleading, prayer, request, rogation, solicitation, suit, supplicat.

supplicatory *adj.* begging, beseeching, imploring, imprecatory, petitioning, precative, precatory, supplicating.

supplier *n.* dealer, hawker, Italian warehouseman, pedlar, provider, purveyor, retailer, seller, shop-keeper, sutler, vendor, vivandier, vivandière, wholesaler.

supplies *n.* equipment, food, foodstuffs, materials, matériel, necessities, provender, provisions, rations, stores, victuals, vittles.

supply *v.* afford, contribute, endow, equip, fill, furnish, give, grant, minister, outfit, produce, provide, purvey, replenish, satisfy, stock, store, victual, yield.
antonym take.
n. cache, fund, hoard, materials, necessities, provender, provisions, quantity, rations, reserve, reservoir, service, source, stake, stock, stockpile, store, stores.
antonym lack.

support *v.* adminiculate, advocate, aid, appui, appuy, assist, authenticate, back, bear, bolster, brace, brook, buttress, carry, champion, cherish, confirm, corroborate, countenance, crutch, defend, document, endorse, endure, finance, foster, fund, help, hold, keep, maintain, nourish, promote, prop, rally round, reinforce, second, stand (for), stay, stomach, strengthen, strut, submit, subsidise, substantiate, succour, suffer, sustain, take (someone's) part, thole, tolerate, underpin, underwrite, uphold, verify.
antonyms contradict, oppose.
n. abutment, adminicle, aid, aidance, approval, appui, assistance, back, backbone, backer, backing, backstays, backstop, blessing, brace, championship, comfort, comforter, crutch, encouragement, foundation, friendship, fulcrum, furtherance, help, jockstrap, keep, lining, livelihood, loyalty, mainstay, maintenance, patronage, pillar, post, prop, protection, relief, second, sheet-anchor, shore, stanchion, stay, stiffener, subsistence, succour, supporter, supportment, supporture, sustenanace, sustenance, underpinning, upkeep.
antonym opposition.

supporter *n.* adherent, advocate, ally, apologist, bottle-holder, champion, co-worker, defender, fan, follower, friend, heeler, helper, patron, seconder, sponsor, upholder, well-wisher.
antonym opponent.

supportive *adj.* attentive, caring, encouraging, helpful, reassuring, sympathetic, understanding.
antonym discouraging.

suppose *v.* assume, believe, calculate, conceive, conclude, conjecture, consider, expect, fancy, guess, hypothesise, hypothetise, imagine, infer, judge, opine, posit, postulate, presume, presuppose, pretend, surmise, think.
antonym know.

supposed *adj.* accepted, alleged, assumed, conjectured, hypothetical, imagined, presumed, presupposed, professed, putative,

reported, reputed, rumoured.
antonym known.
supposed to expected to, intended to, meant to, obliged to, required to.
supposedly *adv.* allegedly, assumedly, avowedly, hypothetically, ostensibly, presumably, professedly, purportedly, theoretically.
antonym really.
supposition *n.* assumption, conjecture, doubt, guess, guesstimate, guesswork, hypothesis, idea, notion, opinion, postulate, presumption, speculation, surmise, theory.
antonym knowledge.
suppress *v.* censor, check, conceal, conquer, contain, crush, extinguish, muffle, muzzle, overpower, overthrow, quash, quell, repress, restrain, silence, smother, snuff out, squelch, stamp out, stifle, stop, strangle, subdue, submerge, vote down, withhold.
antonyms encourage, incite.
suppression *n.* censorship, check, clampdown, crackdown, crushing, dissolution, elimination, extinction, inhibition, prohibition, quashing, quelling, smothering, termination.
antonyms encouragement, incitement.
suppurate *v.* discharge, fester, gather, matter, maturate, ooze, weep.
suppuration *n.* diapyesis, festering, mattering, pus, pussiness.
supremacy *n.* ascendancy, dominance, domination, dominion, hegemony, lordship, mastery, paramountcy, predominance, pre-eminence, primacy, sovereignty, sway.
supreme *adj.* cardinal, chief, consummate, crowning, culminating, extreme, final, first, foremost, greatest, head, highest, incomparable, leading, matchless, nonpareil, paramount, peerless, predominant, pre-eminent, prevailing, prime, principal, second-to-none, sovereign, superlative, surpassing, top, transcendent, ultimate, unbeatable, unbeaten, unsurpassed, utmost, world-beating.
antonyms lowly, poor, slight.
sure *adj.* accurate, assured, bound, certain, clear, confident, convinced, decided, definite, dependable, effective, fast, firm, fixed, foolproof, guaranteed, honest, indisputable, ineluctable, inescapable, inevitable, infallible, irrevocable, persuaded, positive, precise, reliable, safe, satisfied, secure, solid, stable, steadfast, steady, sure-fire, trustworthy, trusty, undeniable, undoubted, unerring, unfailing, unmistakable, unswerving, unwavering.
antonyms doubtful, unsure.
surely *adv.* assuredly, certainly, confidently, definitely, doubtlessly, firmly, indubitably, inevitably, inexorably, safely, undoubtedly, unquestionably.
surety *n.* bail, bond, bondsman, certainty, deposit, guarantee, guarantor, hostage, indemnity, insurance, mortgagor, pledge, safety, security, sponsor, warrant, warranty.
surface *n.* covering, day, exterior, façade, face, facet, grass, outside, plane, side, skin, superficies, top, veneer, working-surface,

worktop.
antonym interior.
adj. apparent, exterior, external, outer, outside, outward, superficial.
antonym interior.
v. appear, come to light, emerge, materialise, rise, transpire.
antonyms disappear, sink.
surfeit *n.* bellyful, excess, glut, overindulgence, plethora, satiety, superabundance, superfluity.
antonym lack.
v. cram, fill, glut, gorge, overcloy, overfeed, overfill, satiate, stuff.
surge *v.* billow, eddy, gush, heave, rise, roll, rush, seethe, swell, swirl, tower, undulate.
n. access, billow, breaker, efflux, flood, flow, gurgitation, gush, intensification, outpouring, roller, rush, swell, uprush, upsurge, wave.
surly *adj.* bearish, brusque, chuffy, churlish, crabbed, cross, crusty, curmudgeonly, grouchy, gruff, grum, gurly, ill-natured, morose, perverse, sulky, sullen, testy, uncivil, ungracious.
antonym pleasant.
surmise *v.* assume, conclude, conjecture, consider, deduce, fancy, guess, imagine, infer, opine, presume, speculate, suppose, suspect.
antonym know.
n. assumption, conclusion, conjecture, deduction, guess, hypothesis, idea, inference, notion, opinion, possibility, presumption, speculation, supposition, suspicion, thought.
antonym certainty.
surmount *v.* conquer, exceed, get over, master, overcome, surpass, triumph over, vanquish.
surpass *v.* beat, best, ding, eclipse, exceed, excel, outdo, outshine, outstrip, override, overshadow, surmount, top, tower above, transcend.
surpassing *adj.* exceptional, extraordinary, incomparable, inimitable, matchless, outstanding, phenomenal, rare, supreme, transcendent, unrivalled, unsurpassed.
antonym poor.
surplus *n.* balance, excess, overplus, remainder, residue, superabundance, superfluity, surfeit, surplusage.
antonym lack.
adj. excess, extra, odd, redundant, remaining, spare, superfluous, unused.
antonym essential.
surprise *v.* amaze, astonish, astound, bewilder, confuse, disconcert, dismay, flabbergast, nonplus, stagger, startle, stun.
n. amazement, astonishment, bewilderment, bombshell, dismay, eye-opener, incredulity, jolt, revelation, shock, start, stupefaction, wonder.
antonym composure.
surprised *adj.* amazed, astonished, confounded, disconcerted, incredulous, nonplussed, open-mouthed, shocked, speechless, staggered, startled, thunderstruck.

antonyms composed, unsurprised.

surprising *adj.* amazing, astonishing, astounding, extraordinary, incredible, marvellous, remarkable, staggering, startling, stunning, unexpected, unlooked-for, unusual, unwonted, wonderful.

antonyms expected, unsurprising.

surrender *v.* abandon, capitulate, cede, concede, forego, give in, give up, quit, relinquish, remise, renounce, resign, submit, succumb, waive, yield.

antonym fight on.

n. appeasement, capitulation, déchéance, delivery, Munich, relinquishment, remise, rendition, renunciation, resignation, submission, white flag, yielding.

surreptitious *adj.* behind-door, clandestine, covert, fraudulent, furtive, secret, sly, sneaking, stealthy, unauthorised, underhand, veiled.

antonym open.

surrogate *n.* deputy, proxy, replacement, representative, stand-in, substitute.

surround *v.* begird, besiege, compass, embosom, encase, encincture, encircle, enclose, encompass, envelop, environ, girdle, invest, ring.

surrounding *adj.* adjacent, adjoining, ambient, bordering, circumambient, circumjacent, encircling, enclosing, environing, environmental, nearby, neighbouring.

surroundings *n.* ambience, background, entourage, environment, environs, locale, location, milieu, neighbourhood, setting, vicinity.

surveillance *n.* care, charge, check, control, direction, guardianship, inspection, monitoring, observation, regulation, scrutiny, stewardship, superintendence, supervision, vigilance, watch.

survey *v.* appraise, assess, consider, contemplate, estimate, examine, inspect, measure, observe, peruse, plan, plot, prospect, reconnoitre, research, review, scan, scrutinise, study, supervise, surview, triangulate, view.

n. appraisal, assessment, conspectus, examination, geodesy, inquiry, inspection, measurement, overview, perusal, review, sample, scrutiny, study, triangulation.

surveying *n.* geodesy, geodetics, measurement, triangulation.

surveyor *n.* assessor, examiner, geodesist, inspector.

survive *v.* endure, exist, last, last out, live, live out, live through, outlast, outlive, ride, stay, subsist, weather, withstand.

antonym succumb.

susceptibility *n.* defencelessness, liability, openness, predisposition, proclivity, proneness, propensity, responsiveness, sensitivity, suggestibility, tendency, vulnerability, weakness.

antonyms impregnability, resistance.

susceptible *adj.* defenceless, disposed, given, impressible, impressionable, inclined, liable, open, predisposed, pregnable, prone, receptive, responsive, sensitive, subject, suggesti-

ble, tender, vulnerable.

antonyms impregnable, resistant.

suspect *v.* believe, call in question, conclude, conjecture, consider, distrust, doubt, fancy, feel, guess, infer, mistrust, opine, speculate, suppose, surmise.

adj. debatable, dodgy, doubtful, dubious, fishy, questionable, suspicious, unauthoritative, unreliable.

antonyms acceptable, innocent, straightforward.

suspend *v.* adjourn, append, arrest, attach, cease, dangle, debar, defer, delay, disbar, discontinue, dismiss, expel, freeze, hang, hold off, interrupt, postpone, shelve, sideline, stay, swing, unfrock, withhold.

antonyms continue, expedite, reinstate, restore.

suspended *adj.* dangling, hanging, pendent, pending, pensile, put on ice, shelved.

suspense *n.* anticipation, anxiety, apprehension, doubt, excitement, expectancy, expectation, incertitude, indecision, insecurity, irresolution, tension, uncertainty, wavering.

antonyms certainty, knowledge.

suspension *n.* abeyance, abeyancy, adjournment, break, cessation, deferment, deferral, delay, diapause, disbarment, discontinuation, dormancy, intermission, interruption, moratorium, postponement, remission, respite, standstill, stay.

antonyms continuation, reinstatement, restoration.

suspicion *n.* apprehension, chariness, conjecture, distrust, doubt, glimmer, guess, hint, hunch, idea, impression, intuition, jealousy, misgiving, mistrust, notion, presentiment, qualm, scepticism, shade, shadow, soupçon, strain, streak, suggestion, supposition, surmise, suspiciousness, tinge, touch, trace, wariness.

antonym trust.

suspicious *adj.* apprehensive, chary, distrustful, dodgy, doubtful, dubious, fishy, incredulous, irregular, jealous, louche, mistrustful, peculiar, queer, questionable, sceptical, shady, suspect, suspecting, unbelieving, uneasy, wary.

antonyms innocent, trustful, unexceptionable.

sustain *v.* aid, approve, assist, bear, carry, comfort, confirm, continue, endorse, endure, experience, feel, foster, help, hold, keep going, maintain, nourish, nurture, prolong, protract, provide for, ratify, relieve, sanction, stay, suffer, support, survive, sustenate, undergo, uphold, validate, verify, withstand.

sustained *adj.* constant, continuous, long-drawn-out, non-stop, perpetual, prolonged, protracted, steady, unremitting.

antonyms broken, intermittent, interrupted, occasional, spasmodic.

sustenance *n.* aliment, board, comestibles, commons, eatables, edibles, étape, fare, food, freshments, livelihood, maintenance, nourishment, nutriment, pabulum, provender, provisions, rations, refection, subsistence, support, viands, victuals.

svelte *adj.* elegant, graceful, lissom, lithe, polished, shapely, slender, slinky, smooth, sophisticated, streamlined, sylphlike, urbane, willowy.

antonyms bulky, ungainly.

swagger *v.* bluster, boast, brag, brank, bully, cock, crow, gasconade, hector, parade, prance, roist, roister, strut, swank.

n. arrogance, bluster, boastfulness, boasting, braggadocio, display, fanfaronade, gasconade, gasconism, ostentation, rodomontade, show, showing off, swank, vainglory.

antonyms diffidence, modesty, restraint.

swaggerer *n.* attitudiniser, blusterer, boaster, braggadocio, braggart, fanfaron, gascon, gasconader, loudmouth, peacock, poser, poseur, poseuse, posturer, rodomontader, roister, roisterer, scaramouch, show-off, strutter, swank, swashbuckler, whiffler.

swallow *v.* absorb, accept, assimilate, believe, buy, consume, devour, down, drink, eat, englut, engulf, gulp, imbibe, ingest, ingurgitate, knock back, quaff, stifle, suppress, swig, swill, wash down.

swallow up absorb, consume, deplete, dissipate, drain, eat up, engulf, envelop, exhaust, gobble up, guzzle, ingurgitate, overrun, overwhelm, use up, waste.

swamp *n.* bog, dismal, everglades, fen, marsh, mire, morass, moss, quagmire, quicksands, slough, vlei.

v. beset, besiege, capsise, deluge, drench, engulf, flood, inundate, overload, overwhelm, saturate, sink, submerge, waterlog.

swampy *adj.* boggy, fenny, marish, marshy, miry, mushy, paludal, quaggy, soggy, squelchy, uliginous, waterlogged, wet.

antonyms arid, dehydrated, dry.

swank *v.* attitudinise, boast, parade, posture, preen oneself, show off, strut, swagger.

n. boastfulness, conceit, conceitedness, display, ostentation, pretentiousness, self-advertisement, show, showing-off, swagger, vainglory.

antonyms modesty, restraint.

swanky *adj.* de luxe, epideictic, exclusive, expensive, fancy, fashionable, flash, flashy, glamorous, grand, lavish, luxurious, ostentatious, plush, plushy, posh, pretentious, rich, ritzy, showy, smart, stylish, sumptuous, swish.

antonyms discreet, unobtrusive.

swap, swop *v.* bandy, barter, exchange, interchange, substitute, switch, trade, traffic, transpose.

swarm *n.* army, bevy, concourse, crowd, drove, flock, herd, horde, host, mass, mob, multitude, myriad, shoal, throng.

v. congregate, crowd, flock, flood, mass, stream, throng.

swarm with abound, bristle, crawl, hotch, teem.

swarthy *adj.* black, brown, dark, dark-complexioned, dark-skinned, dusky, swart, swarth, tawny.

antonyms fair, pale.

swashbuckling *adj.* adventurous, bold, daredevil, dashing, exciting, flamboyant, gallant, lusty, mettlesome, rip-roaring, robust, roisterous, spirited, swaggering.

antonyms tame, unadventurous, unexciting.

swastika *n.* fylfot, gammadion, gammation, Hakenkreuz.

swathe *v.* bandage, bind, cloak, drape, enshroud, envelop, enwrap, fold, furl, lap, sheathe, shroud, swaddle, wind, wrap.

antonyms unwind, unwrap.

sway *v.* affect, bend, control, direct, divert, dominate, fluctuate, govern, guide, incline, induce, influence, lean, lurch, oscillate, overrule, persuade, rock, roll, swerve, swing, titter, veer, wave.

n. ascendency, authority, cloud, command, control, dominion, government, hegemony, influence, jurisdiction, leadership, power, predominance, preponderance, rule, sovereignty, sweep, swerve, swing.

swear[1] *v.* affirm, assert, asseverate, attest, avow, declare, depose, insist, promise, testify, vow, warrant.

swear[2] *v.* blaspheme, blind, curse, cuss, eff, imprecate, maledict, take the Lord's name in vain, turn the air blue.

swearing *n.* bad language, billingsgate, blasphemy, coprolalia, cursing, cussing, effing and blinding, expletives, foul language, imprecations, maledictions, profanity.

swear-word *n.* blasphemy, curse, expletive, four-letter word, imprecation, oath, obscenity, profanity.

sweat *n.* agitation, anxiety, chore, dew, diaphoresis, distress, drudgery, effort, exudation, fag, flap, hidrosis, labour, panic, perspiration, strain, sudation, sudor, worry.

v. agonise, chafe, exude, fret, glow, perspirate, perspire, swelter, worry.

sweaty *adj.* clammy, damp, glowing, moist, perspiring, sticky, sudorous, sweating.

antonyms cool, dry.

sweep *v.* brush, career, clean, clear, dust, flounce, fly, glance, glide, hurtle, pass, remove, sail, scud, skim, tear, whisk, zoom.

n. arc, bend, clearance, compass, curve, expanse, extent, gesture, impetus, move, movement, onrush, range, scope, span, stretch, stroke, sweep, swing, vista.

sweeping *adj.* across-the-board, all-embracing, all-inclusive, blanket, broad, comprehensive, exaggerated, extensive, far-reaching, global, indiscriminate, overdrawn, oversimplified, overstated, radical, simplistic, thoroughgoing, unanalytical, unqualified, wholesale, wide, wide-ranging.

sweepstake *n.* draw, lottery, sweep, sweepstakes.

sweet[1] *adj.* affectionate, agreeable, amiable, appealing, aromatic, attractive, balmy, beautiful, beloved, benign, charming, cherished, clean, cloying, darling, dear, dearest, delightful, dulcet, engaging, euphonic, euphonious, fair, fragrant, fresh, gentle, gracious, harmonious, honeyed, icky, kin, lovable, luscious, mellow, melodious, melting, mild, musical, new, perfumed, pet, precious, pure, redolent, saccharine, sickly, silver-toned, silvery, soft, suave, sugary, sweetened, sweet-smelling, sweet-sounding, sweet-tempered, syrupy, taking, tender, toothsome, treasured, tuneful, unselfish, wholesome, winning, winsome.

antonyms acid, bitter, cacophonous, discordant, malodorous, salty, sour, unpleasant.

n. afters, dessert, pudding, second course, sweet course.

sweet[2] *n.* bonbon, candy, comfit, confect, confection, confectionery, sweetie, sweetmeat.

sweeten *v.* alleviate, appease, cushion, dulcify, edulcorate, honey, mellow, mollify, pacify, soften, soothe, sugar, sugar-coat, take the sting out of, temper.

antonyms aggravate, embitter, jaundice.

sweetheart *n.* admirer, beau, beloved, betrothed, boyfriend, darling, dear, dona, Dulcinea, flame, follower, girlfriend, inamorata, inamorato, lady-love, leman, love, lover, Romeo, steady, suitor, swain, sweetie, truelove, valentine.

sweetness *n.* amiability, balminess, charm, dulcitude, euphony, fragrance, freshness, harmony, kindness, love, loveliness, lusciousness, mellowness, suavity, succulence, sugariness, sweet temper, syrup, tenderness, winsomeness.

antonyms acidity, bitterness, cacophony, nastiness, saltness, sourness.

sweet-smelling *adj.* ambrosial, aromatic, balmy, fragrant, odoriferous, odorous, perfumed, redolent, sweet-scented.

antonyms fetid, malodorous.

swell[1] *v.* aggravate, augment, balloon, belly, billow, blab, bloat, boll, bulb, bulge, dilate, distend, enhance, enlarge, expand, extend, fatten, grow, heave, heighten, hove, increase, intensify, intumesce, louden, mount, protrude, reach a crescendo, rise, strout, surge, tumefy, volume.

antonyms contract, dwindle, shrink.

n. billow, bore, bulge, distension, eagre, enlargement, loudening, rise, surge, swelling, undulation, wave.

swell[2] *n.* adept, beau, bigwig, blade, cockscomb, dandy, dude, fop, nob, popinjay, toff.

antonyms down-and-out, scarecrow, tramp.

adj. de luxe, dude, exclusive, fashionable, flashy, grand, posh, ritzy, smart, stylish, swanky.

antonyms seedy, shabby.

swelling *n.* blister, boll, botch, bruise, bulb, bulge, bump, dilation, distension, emphysema, enlargement, gall, gathering, gout, inflammation, intumescence, lump, oedema, protuberance, puffiness, tuber, tubercle,

tumescence, tumour, venter.

sweltering *adj.* airless, baking, broiling, burning, hot, humid, oppressive, perspiring, scorching, steamy, stifling, suffocating, sultry, sweating, torrid, tropical.

antonyms airy, breezy, chilly, cold, cool, fresh.

swerve *v.* bend, carve, deflect, deviate, diverge, incline, sheer, shift, skew, stray, sway, swing, turn, veer, wander, warp, wind.

swift *adj.* abrupt, agile, expeditious, express, fast, fleet, fleet-footed, flying, hurried, light-heeled, light-legged, limber, nimble, nimble-footed, nippy, precipitate, prompt, quick, rapid, ready, short, spanking, speedy, sudden, winged.

antonyms slow, sluggish, tardy.

swiftly *adj.* at full tilt, double-quick, expeditiously, express, fast, hotfoot, hurriedly, instantly, posthaste, promptly, quickly, rapidly, speedily.

antonyms slowly, tardily.

swiftness *n.* alacrity, celerity, dispatch, expedition, fleetness, immediacy, immediateness, instantaneity, promptness, quickness, rapidity, readiness, speed, speediness, suddenness, velocity.

antonyms delay, slowness, tardiness.

swill *v.* consume, drain, drink, gulp, guzzle, imbibe, knock back, quaff, swallow, swig, toss off.

n. hogwash, mash, mush, offal, pigswill, refuse, scourings, slops, waste.

swill out cleanse, drench, flush, rinse, sluice, wash down, wash out.

swimming-pool *n.* Jacuzzi®, leisure pool, lido, swimming-bath, swimming-pond.

swimsuit *n.* bathers, bathing-costume, bathing-dress, bathing-suit, bikini, cossie, maillot, swimming costume, swimwear, trunks.

swindle *v.* bamboozle, bilk, bunko, cheat, chicane, chouse, con, deceive, defraud, diddle, do, dupe, finagle, financier, fleece, grift, gyp, hand someone a lemon, hornswoggle, overcharge, ramp, rip off, rook, sell smoke, sell someone a pup, skelder, trick.

n. chicanery, con, deceit, deception, double-dealing, fiddle, fraud, gold-brick, grift, gyp, imposition, knavery, racket, rip-off, roguery, scam, sharp practice, shenanigans, skin-game, swizz, swizzle, trickery.

swindler *n.* charlatan, cheat, chicaner, con man, escroc, fraud, fraudster, grifter, impostor, jackman, knave, mountebank, rascal, rogue, rook, shark, sharper, slicker, spieler, trickster.

swine *n.* beast, boar, boor, brute, cad, heel, pig, reptile, rotter, scoundrel.

swing *v.* arrange, brandish, control, dangle, fix, fluctuate, hang, hurl, influence, librate, oscillate, pendulate, rock, suspend, sway, swerve, vary, veer, vibrate, wave, whirl.

n. fluctuation, impetus, libration, motion, oscillation, rhythm, scope, stroke, sway, swaying, sweep, sweeping, vibration, waving.

swing round curve, gyrate, pivot, revolve, rotate, spin, swivel, turn, twirl, wheel.

swingeing *adj.* Draconian, drastic, excessive, exorbitant, extortionate, harsh, heavy, huge, oppressive, punishing, severe, stringent, thumping.
antonym mild.

swinging *adj.* contemporary, dynamic, fashionable, fast, groovy, hip, jet-setting, lively, modern, stylish, toney, trendy, up-to-date, up-to-the-minute, with it.
antonyms old-fashioned, square.

swipe *v.* appropriate, clip, filch, half-inch, hit, lift, pilfer, pinch, purloin, slap, slosh, snaffle, snitch, sock, steal, strike, thwack, wallop, whack.
n. blow, clip, clout, cuff, gobble, gowff, slap, smack, thwack, wallop, whack.

swirl *v.* agitate, boil, churn, eddy, purl, scud, spin, surge, swish, twirl, twist, wheel, whirl.

swish¹ *v.* birch, brandish, flog, flourish, lash, rustle, swing, swirl, swoosh, thrash, twirl, wave, whip, whirl, whisk, whistle, whiz(z), whoosh.

swish² *adj.* de luxe, dude, elegant, exclusive, fashionable, flash, grand, plush, posh, ritzy, smart, sumptuous, swanky, swell.
antonyms seedy, shabby.

switch¹ *v.* change, change course, change direction, chop and change, deflect, deviate, divert, exchange, interchange, put, rearrange, replace, shift, shunt, substitute, swap, trade, turn, veer.
n. about-turn, alteration, change, change of direction, exchange, interchange, shift, substitution, swap.
switch off inactivate, put off, turn off.

switch² *v.* birch, flog, jerk, lash, swish, twitch, wave, whip, whisk.
n. birch, cane, jerk, rod, whip, whisk.

swivel *v.* gyrate, pirouette, pivot, revolve, rotate, spin, swing round, turn, twirl, wheel.

swollen *adj.* bloated, bolled, bulbous, distended, dropsical, emphysematous, enlarged, inflamed, intumescent, oedematose, oedematous, puffed up, puffy, tumescent, tumid, turgid, ventricose, ventricous.
antonyms contracted, emaciated, shrunken.

swoop *v.* descend, dive, drop, fall, lunge, pounce, rush, stoop, sweep.
n. attack, descent, drop, lunge, onslaught, plunge, pounce, rush, stoop, sweep.

swop *see* **swap** .

sword *n.* bilbo, blade, broadsword, claymore, cutlass, foil, gladius, machete, rapier, sabre, schiavone, scimitar.

sworn *adj.* attested, confirmed, devoted, eternal, implacable, inveterate, relentless.

swot *v.* bone up, burn the midnight oil, con, cram, dig, learn, lucubrate, memorise, mug up, pore over, revise, study, work.
n. bluestocking, bookworm, crammer, dig, worker.
antonym idler.

sybarite *n.* bon vivant, epicure, epicurean,

hedonist, one of the idle rich, parasite, playboy, pleasurer, pleasure-seeker, sensualist, voluptuary.
antonyms ascetic, toiler.

sybaritic *adj.* easy, epicurean, hedonistic, Lucullan, luxurious, parasitic, pleasure-loving, pleasure-seeking, self-indulgent, sensual, voluptuous.
antonym ascetic.

sycophancy *n.* adulation, arse-licking, backscratching, bootlicking, cringing, fawning, flattery, grovelling, kowtowing, obsequiousness, servility, slavishness, toadyism, truckling.

sycophant *n.* arse-licker, backscratcher, bootlicker, cringer, fawner, flatterer, groveller, hanger-on, lickspittle, parasite, slave, sponger, toad-eater, toady, truckler, yes-man.

sycophantic *adj.* arse-licking, backscratching, bootlicking, cringing, fawning, flattering, grovelling, ingratiating, obsequious, parasitical, servile, slavish, slimy, smarmy, time-serving, toad-eating, toadying, truckling, unctuous.

syllabus *n.* course, curriculum, plan, programme, schedule, table.

syllogism *n.* argument, deduction, epicheirema, proposition.

sylph-like *adj.* elegant, graceful, lithe, slender, slight, slim, streamlined, svelte, willowy.
antonyms bulky, plump.

symbiotic *adj.* commensal, co-operative, emphytic, endophytic, epizoan, epizoic, epizootic, interactive, interdependent, synergetic.

symbol *n.* badge, character, emblem, figure, grammalogue, ideogram, ideograph, image, logo, logogram, logograph, mandala, mark, representation, rune, sign, token, type.

symbolic *adj.* allegorical, allusive, aniconic, emblematic, figurative, metaphorical, representative, ritual, significant, symbolical, token, typical.

symbolise *v.* allude to, betoken, connote, denote, emblem, emblematise, emblemise, exemplify, mean, personate, personify, represent, signify, typify.

symmetrical *adj.* balanced, corresponding, isometric, parallel, proportional, regular, well-balanced, well-proportioned, well-rounded.
antonyms asymmetrical, irregular.

symmetry *n.* agreement, balance, correspondence, evenness, form, harmony, isometry, order, parallelism, proportion, regularity.
antonyms asymmetry, irregularity.

sympathetic *adj.* affectionate, agreeable, appreciative, caring, comforting, commiserating, companionable, compassionate, compatible, concerned, congenial, consoling, empathetic, empathic, exorable, feeling, friendly, interested, kind, kindly, like-minded, pitying, responsive, supportive, tender, understanding, warm, warm-hearted, well-intentioned.
antonyms antipathetic, callous, indifferent, unsympathetic.

sympathetically *adv.* appreciatively, comfortingly, compassionately, consolingly, feelingly, kindly, pityingly, responsively, sensitively, supportively, understandingly, warmheartedly, warmly.

sympathise *v.* agree, commiserate, condole, empathise, feel for, identify with, pity, rap, respond to, side with, understand.

antonyms disapprove, dismiss, disregard, ignore, oppose.

sympathiser *n.* adherent, admirer, backer, condoler, fan, fellow-traveller, friend in need, partisan, supporter, well-wisher.

antonyms enemy, opponent.

sympathy *n.* affinity, agreement, comfort, commiseration, compassion, condolement, condolence, condolences, congeniality, correspondence, empathy, fellow-feeling, harmony, pity, rapport, responsiveness, tenderness, thoughtfulness, understanding, warmth.

antonyms callousness, disharmony, incompatibility, indifference.

symptom *n.* concomitant, diagnostic, evidence, expression, feature, indication, manifestation, mark, note, sign, syndrome, token, warning.

symptomatic *adj.* associated, characteristic, indicative, suggestive, typical.

syndicate *n.* alliance, bloc, cartel, combination, combine, group, ring.

synonymous *adj.* co-extensive, comparable, corresponding, equal, equivalent, exchangeable, identical, identified, interchangeable, parallel, similar, substitutable, tantamount, the same.

antonyms antonymous, dissimilar, opposite.

synopsis *n.* abridgement, abstract, aperçu, compendium, condensation, conspectus, digest, epitome, outline, précis, recapitulation, résumé, review, run-down, sketch, summary, summation.

synthesis *n.* alloy, amalgam, amalgamation, blend, coalescence, combination, composite, compound, fusion, integration, pastiche, unification, union, welding.

synthesise *v.* amalgamate, blend, coalesce, combine, compound, fuse, integrate, manufacture, merge, unify, unite, weld.

antonyms analyse, resolve, separate.

synthetic *adj.* artificial, bogus, ersatz, fake, imitation, man-made, manufactured, mock, pseud, pseudo, put-on, sham, simulated.

antonyms genuine, real.

syphilis *n.* clap, French pox, gonorrhoea, pip, pox, venereal disease.

system *n.* arrangement, classification, co-ordination, logic, method, methodicalness, methodology, mode, modus operandi, orderliness, organisation, plan, practice, procedure, process, regularity, routine, rule, scheme, set-up, structure, systematisation, tabulation, taxis, taxonomy, technique, theory, usage.

systematic *adj.* businesslike, efficient, habitual, intentional, logical, methodical, ordered, orderly, organised, planned, precise, standardised, systematical, systematised, well-ordered, well-planned.

antonyms disorderly, inefficient, unsystematic.

systematise *v.* arrange, classify, dispose, make uniform, methodise, order, organise, rationalise, regiment, regulate, schematise, standardise, tabulate.

T

tab *n.* docket, flag, flap, label, marker, sticker, tag, ticket.

tabby *adj.* banded, brindled, mottled, streaked, striped, stripy, variegated, wavy.

table *n.* agenda, altar, bench, board, catalogue, chart, counter, diagram, diet, digest, fare, flat, flatland, food, graph, index, inventory, list, mahogany, paradigm, plain, plan, plateau, record, register, roll, schedule, slab, spread, stall, stand, syllabus, synopsis, table-land, victuals.
v. postpone, propose, put forward, submit, suggest.

tableau *n.* diorama, picture, portrayal, representation, scene, spectacle, tableau vivant, vignette.

taboo *adj.* accursed, anathema, banned, forbidden, inviolable, outlawed, prohibited, proscribed, sacrosanct, unacceptable, unmentionable, unthinkable, verboten.
antonym acceptable.
n. anathema, ban, curse, disapproval, interdict, interdiction, prohibition, proscription, restriction.

tabulate *v.* arrange, catalogue, categorise, chart, classify, codify, index, list, order, range, sort, systematise, table, tabularise.

tacit *adj.* implicit, implied, inferred, silent, ulterior, undeclared, understood, unexpressed, unprofessed, unspoken, unstated, unuttered, unvoiced, voiceless, wordless.
antonyms explicit, express, spoken, stated.

taciturn *adj.* aloof, antisocial, cold, distant, dumb, mute, quiet, reserved, reticent, saturnine, silent, tight-lipped, uncommunicative, unconversable, unforthcoming, withdrawn.
antonyms communicative, forthcoming, sociable, talkative.

tack *n.* approach, attack, bearing, course, direction, drawing-pin, heading, line, loop, method, nail, path, pin, plan, procedure, route, staple, stitch, tactic, thumb-tack, tin-tack, way.
v. add, affix, annex, append, attach, baste, fasten, fix, join, nail, pin, staple, stitch, tag.

tackle¹ *n.* accoutrements, apparatus, equipment, gear, harness, implements, outfit, paraphernalia, rig, rigging, tackling, tools, trappings.
v. harness.

tackle² *n.* attack, block, challenge, interception, intervention, stop.
v. attempt, begin, block, challenge, clutch, confront, deal with, embark upon, encounter, engage in, essay, face up to, grab, grapple with, grasp, halt, intercept, seize, set about,

stop, take on, throw, try, undertake, wade into.
antonyms avoid, side-step.

tacky *adj.* adhesive, cheap, gimcrack, gluey, gummy, messy, nasty, scruffy, seedy, shabby, shoddy, sleazy, sticky, tasteless, tatty, tawdry, vulgar, wet.

tact *n.* address, adroitness, consideration, delicacy, diplomacy, discernment, discretion, finesse, grace, judgement, perception, prudence, savoir-faire, sensitivity, skill, thoughtfulness, understanding.
antonyms clumsiness, indiscretion, tactlessness.

tactful *adj.* careful, considerate, delicate, diplomatic, discerning, discreet, graceful, judicious, perceptive, polished, polite, politic, prudent, sensitive, skilful, subtle, thoughtful, understanding.
antonym tactless.

tactic *n.* approach, course, device, line, manoeuvre, means, method, move, ploy, policy, ruse, scheme, shift, stratagem, subterfuge, tack, trick, way.

tactical *adj.* adroit, artful, calculated, clever, cunning, diplomatic, judicious, politic, prudent, shrewd, skilful, smart, strategic.
antonym impolitic.

tactician *n.* brain, campaigner, co-ordinator, director, mastermind, orchestrator, planner, politician, strategist.

tactics *n.* approach, campaign, game plan, line of attack, manoeuvres, moves, plan, plan of campaign, plans, ploys, policy, procedure, shifts, stratagems, strategy.

tactless *adj.* blundering, boorish, careless, clumsy, discourteous, gauche, hurtful, ill-timed, impolite, impolitic, imprudent, inappropriate, inconsiderate, indelicate, indiscreet, inept, insensitive, maladroit, rough, rude, thoughtless, uncivil, undiplomatic, unfeeling, unkind, unsubtle.
antonym tactful.

tactlessness *n.* bad timing, boorishness, clumsiness, discourtesy, gaucherie, impoliteness, indelicacy, indiscretion, ineptitude, insensitivity, maladdress, maladroitness, rudeness, thoughtlessness.
antonym tact.

tag¹ *n.* aglet, aiglet, aiguillette, appellation, dag, designation, docket, epithet, flap, identification, label, mark, marker, name, note, slip, sticker, tab, tally, ticket.
v. add, adjoin, affix, annex, append, call, christen, designate, dub, earmark, fasten, identify, label, mark, name, nickname, style,

tack, term, ticket.

tag along accompany, attend, dog, follow, hang round, shadow, tail, trail.

tag² *n.* dictum, fadaise, gnome, gobbet, maxim, moral, motto, proverb, quotation, quote, remnant, saw, saying.

tail *n.* appendage, backside, behind, bottom, bum, buttocks, conclusion, croup, detective, empennage, end, extremity, file, follower, fud, line, posterior, queue, rear, rear end, retinue, rump, scut, suite, tailback, tailpiece, tailplane, train.

v. dog, follow, keep with, shadow, spy on, stalk, track, trail.

tail off decrease, die, die out, drop, dwindle, fade, fail, fall away, peter out, tail away, taper off, wane.

antonyms grow, increase.

tailless *adj.* acaudal, acaudate, anurous, ecaudate, excaudate, Manx.

tailor *n.* clothier, costumer, costumier, couturier, couturière, darzi, dressmaker, modiste, outfitter, seamstress, whipcat, whip-stitch.

v. accommodate, adapt, adjust, alter, convert, cut, fashion, fit, modify, mould, shape, style, suit, trim.

tailor-made *adj.* bespoke, custom-built, custommade, fitted, ideal, made-to-measure, perfect, right, suitable, suited.

antonyms ill-adapted, unsuitable.

taint *v.* adulterate, besmirch, blacken, blemish, blight, blot, brand, contaminate, corrupt, damage, defile, deprave, dirty, disgrace, dishonour, envenom, foul, infect, muddy, poison, pollute, ruin, shame, smear, smirch, soil, spoil, stain, stigmatise, sully, tarnish, vitiate.

n. blemish, blot, contagion, contamination, corruption, defect, disgrace, dishonour, fault, flaw, infamy, infection, obloquy, odium, opprobrium, pollution, shame, smear, smirch, spot, stain, stigma.

take *v.* abduct, abide, abstract, accept, accommodate, accompany, acquire, adopt, appropriate, arrest, ascertain, assume, attract, bear, believe, betake, bewitch, blight, book, brave, bring, brook, buy, call for, captivate, capture, carry, cart, catch, charm, clutch, conduct, consider, consume, contain, convey, convoy, deduct, deem, delight, demand, derive, detract, do, drink, eat, effect, eliminate, enchant, endure, engage, ensnare, entrap, escort, execute, fascinate, ferry, fetch, filch, gather, glean, grasp, grip, guide, haul, have, have room for, hire, hold, imbibe, ingest, inhale, lead, lease, make, measure, misappropriate, necessitate, need, nick, observe, obtain, operate, perceive, perform, photograph, pick, pinch, please, pocket, portray, presume, purchase, purloin, receive, regard, remove, rent, require, reserve, secure, seize, select, stand, steal, stomach, strike, subtract, succeed, suffer, swallow, swipe, thole, tolerate, tote, transport, undergo, understand, undertake, usher, weather, win, withstand,

work.

n. catch, gate, haul, income, proceeds, profits, receipts, return, revenue, takings, yield.

take aback astonish, astound, bewilder, disconcert, dismay, flabbergast, floor, nonplus, stagger, startle, stun, surprise, upset.

take apart analyse, disassemble, dismantle, resolve, take down, take to pieces.

take back deny, disavow, disclaim, eat one's words, recant, reclaim, regain, renounce, repossess, repudiate, retract, unsay, withdraw.

take down deflate, demolish, disassemble, dismantle, humble, humiliate, level, lower, minute, mortify, note, put down, raze, record, reduce, set down, strike, transcribe, unstep, write.

take effect be effective, become operative, begin, come into force, work.

take heart brighten up, buck up, cheer up, perk up, rally, revive.

antonym despond.

take in absorb, accommodate, admit, annex, appreciate, assimilate, bamboozle, bilk, bluff, cheat, comprehend, comprise, con, contain, cover, cozen, deceive, digest, do, dupe, embrace, enclose, encompass, fool, furl, grasp, gull, hoodwink, imagine, include, incorporate, kid, mislead, realise, receive, shelter, subdue, swindle, tighten, trick, understand.

take issue call in question, challenge, disagree, dispute, object, oppose, quarrel, question, take exception.

take it ill be miffed, be offended, miff, object, protest, take the huff.

take off beat it, bloom, burgeon, caricature, decamp, depart, disappear, discard, divest, doff, drop, expand, flourish, go, imitate, lampoon, leave, mimic, mock, parody, remove, satirise, scarper, send up, soar, spoof, strip, take wing, travesty, vamoose.

take offence be miffed, miff, sulk, take it ill, take the huff.

take on accept, acquire, assume, complain, contend with, employ, engage, enlist, enrol, face, fight, grieve, hire, lament, oppose, retain, tackle, undertake, vie with.

take part associate oneself, be instrumental, be involved, join, partake, participate, play a part, share, take a hand.

take pity on feel compassion for, forgive, give quarter, have mercy on, melt, pardon, pity, relent, reprieve, show mercy, spare.

take place befall, betide, come about, come off, come to pass, fall, happen, occur.

take stock appraise, assess, estimate, size up, survey, weigh up.

take the plunge commit oneself, cross the Rubicon, decide, pop the question.

take to task blame, censure, criticise, lecture, rebuke, reprimand, reproach, reprove, scold, tell off, tick off, upbraid.

antonyms commend, praise.

take up absorb, accept, adopt, affect, arrest,

assume, begin, borrow, carry on, consume, continue, cover, engage in, engross, fasten, fill, interrupt, lift, monopolise, occupy, proceed, raise, recommence, restart, resume, secure, start, use up.

take-off *n.* burlesque, caricature, imitation, lampoon, mickey-take, mimicry, parody, spoof, travesty.

takeover *n.* amalgamation, coalition, combination, coup, incorporation, merger.

taking *adj.* alluring, appealing, attractive, beguiling, captivating, catching, charming, compelling, delightful, enchanting, engaging, fascinating, fetching, intriguing, pleasing, prepossessing, winning, winsome.
antonyms repellent, repulsive, unattractive.
n. agitation, alarm, coil, commotion, consternation, flap, fuss, panic, passion, pother, state, sweat, tiz-woz, tizzy, turmoil, wax.

takings *n.* earnings, emoluments, gain, gate, haul, income, pickings, proceeds, profits, receipts, returns, revenue, take, yield.

tale *n.* account, anecdote, fable, fabrication, falsehood, fib, fiction, legend, lie, Märchen, Munchausen, myth, narration, narrative, old wives' tale, relation, report, rigmarole, romance, rumour, saga, spiel, story, superstition, tall story, tradition, untruth, yarn.

talent *n.* ability, aptitude, bent, capacity, endowment, faculty, feel, flair, forte, genius, gift, knack, long suit, nous, parts, power, strength.
antonyms inability, ineptitude, weakness.

talented *adj.* able, accomplished, adept, adroit, apt, artistic, brilliant, capable, clever, deft, gifted, ingenious, inspired, well-endowed.
antonyms clumsy, inept, maladroit.

talisman *n.* abraxas, amulet, charm, fetish, juju, mascot, periapt, phylactery, telesm.

talk *v.* articulate, blab, blether, chat, chatter, chinwag, commune, communicate, confabulate, confer, converse, crack, gab, gossip, grass, inform, jaw, natter, negotiate, palaver, parley, prate, prattle, rap, say, sing, speak, squeak, squeal, utter, verbalise, witter.
n. address, argot, bavardage, blather, blether, causerie, chat, chatter, chinwag, chitchat, clash, claver, colloquy, conclave, confab, confabulation, conference, consultation, conversation, crack, dialect, dialogue, discourse, discussion, disquisition, dissertation, gab, gossip, gup, harangue, hearsay, jargon, jaw, jawing, language, lecture, lingo, meeting, natter, negotiation, oration, palabra, palaver, parley, patois, rap, rumour, seminar, sermon, slang, speech, spiel, symposium, tittle-tattle, utterance, words.

talk big bluster, boast, brag, crow, exaggerate, swank, vaunt.

talk into bring round, coax, convince, encourage, overrule, persuade, sway, win over.
antonym dissuade.

talk out of caution, deter, discourage, dissuade, expostulate, head off, protest, put

off, remonstrate, urge against.

talkative *adj.* chatty, communicative, conversational, effusive, expansive, forthcoming, gabby, garrulous, gossipy, long-tongued, long-winded, loquacious, prating, prolix, unreserved, verbose, vocal, voluble, wordy.
antonyms reserved, taciturn.

talker *n.* chatterbox, communicator, conversationalist, lecturer, orator, speaker, speechmaker.

talking-to *n.* criticism, dressing-down, earful, jaw, jawbation, lecture, rebuke, reprimand, reproach, reproof, row, scolding, slating, telling-off, ticking-off, wigging.
antonyms commendation, congratulation, praise.

tall *adj.* absurd, big, dubious, elevated, embellished, exaggerated, far-fetched, giant, grandiloquent, great, high, implausible, improbable, incredible, lanky, leggy, lofty, overblown, preposterous, remarkable, soaring, steep, topless, towering, unbelievable, unlikely.
antonyms low, reasonable, short, small.

tallness *n.* altitude, height, loftiness, procerity, stature.

tally *v.* accord, agree, coincide, compute, concur, conform, correspond, figure, fit, harmonise, jibe, mark, match, parallel, reckon, record, register, square, suit, tie in, total.
antonyms differ, disagree.
n. account, count, counterfoil, counterpart, credit, duplicate, label, mark, match, mate, notch, reckoning, record, score, stub, tab, tag, tick, total.

tame *adj.* amenable, anaemic, biddable, bland, bloodless, boring, broken, compliant, cultivated, disciplined, docile, domesticated, dull, feeble, flat, gentle, humdrum, insipid, lifeless, manageable, meek, obedient, prosaic, spiritless, subdued, submissive, tedious, tractable, unadventurous, unenterprising, unexciting, uninspired, uninspiring, uninteresting, unresisting, vapid, wearisome.
antonyms exciting, rebellious, unmanageable, wild.
v. break in, bridle, calm, conquer, curb, discipline, domesticate, enslave, gentle, house-train, humble, master, mellow, mitigate, mute, pacify, quell, repress, soften, subdue, subjugate, suppress, temper, train.

tamper *v.* alter, bribe, cook, corrupt, damage, fiddle, fix, influence, interfere, intrude, juggle, manipulate, meddle, mess, rig, tinker.

tang *n.* aroma, bite, flavour, hint, kick, overtone, piquancy, pungency, reek, savour, scent, smack, smell, suggestion, taste, tinge, touch, trace, whiff.

tangible *adj.* actual, concrete, corporeal, definite, discernible, evident, manifest, material, objective, observable, palpable, perceptible, physical, positive, real, sensible, solid, substantial, tactile, touchable.
antonym intangible.

tangle *n.* burble, coil, complication, confusion, convolution, embroglio, embroilment, entanglement, fankle, fix, imbroglio, jam, jumble, jungle, knot, labyrinth, mass, mat, maze, mesh, mess, mix-up, muddle, raffle, snarl, snarl-up, twist, web.
v. catch, coil, confuse, convolve, embroil, enmesh, ensnare, entangle, entrap, hamper, implicate, interlace, interlock, intertwine, intertwist, interweave, involve, jam, knot, mat, mesh, muddle, snarl, trap, twist.
antonym disentangle.

tangled *adj.* complex, complicated, confused, convoluted, dishevelled, entangled, intricate, involved, jumbled, knotted, knotty, matted, messy, mixed-up, scrambled, snarled, tortuous, tousled, twisted.
antonyms clear, free.

tangy *adj.* biting, bitter, fresh, gamy, piquant, pungent, savoury, sharp, spicy, strong, tart.
antonym insipid.

tank[1] *n.* aquarium, basin, cistern, container, reservoir, vat.

tank[2] *n.* armoured car, armoured vehicle, panzer.

tantalise *v.* baffle, bait, balk, disappoint, entice, frustrate, lead on, play upon, provoke, taunt, tease, thwart, titillate, torment, torture.
antonym satisfy.

tantamount *adj.* as good as, commensurate, equal, equivalent, synonymous, the same as, virtually.

tantrum *n.* bate, fit, flare-up, fury, hysterics, outburst, paddy, paroxysm, rage, scene, storm, temper, wax.

tap[1] *v.* beat, chap, drum, knock, pat, rap, strike, tat, touch.
n. beat, chap, knock, pat, rap, rat-tat, touch.

tap[2] *n.* bug, bung, faucet, plug, receiver, spigot, spile, spout, stop-cock, stopper, valve.
v. bleed, broach, bug, drain, exploit, milk, mine, open, pierce, quarry, siphon, unplug, use, utilise, wiretap.

tape *n.* band, binding, magnetic tape, riband, ribbon, strip, tape-measure.
v. assess, bind, measure, record, seal, secure, stick, tape-record, video, wrap.

taper[2] *v.* attenuate, decrease, die away, die out, dwindle, fade, lessen, narrow, peter out, reduce, slim, subside, tail off, thin, wane, weaken.
antonyms increase, swell, widen.

taper[2] *n.* bougie, candle, spill, wax-light, wick.

tardily *adv.* at the eleventh hour, at the last minute, belatedly, late, late in the day, slowly, sluggishly, unpunctually.
antonyms promptly, punctually.

tardiness *n.* belatedness, dawdling, delay, dilatoriness, lateness, procrastination, slowness, sluggishness, unpunctuality.
antonyms promptness, punctuality.

tardy *adj.* backward, behindhand, belated, dawdling, delayed, dilatory, eleventh-hour, lag, last-minute, late, loitering, overdue, procrastinating, retarded, slack, slow, slug-

gish, unpunctual.
antonyms prompt, punctual.

target *n.* aim, ambition, bull's-eye, butt, destination, end, goal, intention, jack, mark, object, objective, prey, prick, purpose, quarry, scapegoat, victim.

tariff *n.* assessment, bill of fare, charges, customs, duty, excise, impost, levy, menu, price list, rate, schedule, tax, toll.

tarnish *v.* befoul, blacken, blemish, blot, darken, dim, discolour, dislustre, dull, mar, rust, soil, spoil, spot, stain, sully, taint.
antonyms brighten, enhance, polish up.
n. blackening, blemish, blot, discoloration, film, patina, rust, spot, stain, taint.
antonyms brightness, polish.

tarry *v.* abide, bide, dally, dawdle, delay, dwell, lag, linger, loiter, pause, remain, rest, sojourn, stay, stop, wait.

tart[1] *n.* pastry, pie, quiche, tartlet.

tart[2] *adj.* acerb, acerbic, acid, acidulous, acrimonious, astringent, barbed, biting, bitter, caustic, cutting, incisive, piquant, pungent, sardonic, scathing, sharp, short, sour, tangy, trenchant, vinegary.

tart[3] *n.* broad, call girl, drab, fallen woman, fille de joie, fille publique, floosie, harlot, hooker, prostitute, slut, street-walker, strumpet, trollop, whore.

task *n.* assignment, aufgabe, burden, business, charge, chore, darg, duty, employment, enterprise, exercise, imposition, job, job of work, labour, mission, occupation, pensum, toil, undertaking, work.
v. burden, charge, commit, encumber, entrust, exhaust, load, lumber, oppress, overload, push, saddle, strain, tax, test, weary.

taste *n.* appetite, appreciation, bent, bit, bite, choice, correctness, cultivation, culture, dash, decorum, delicacy, desire, discernment, discretion, discrimination, drop, elegance, experience, fancy, finesse, flavour, fondness, gout, grace, gustation, inclination, judgement, leaning, liking, morsel, mouthful, nibble, nicety, nip, palate, partiality, penchant, perception, polish, politeness, predilection, preference, propriety, refinement, relish, restraint, sample, sapor, savour, sensitivity, sip, smack, smatch, soupçon, spoonful, style, swallow, tact, tactfulness, tang, tastefulness, titbit, touch.
v. assay, degust, degustate, differentiate, discern, distinguish, encounter, experience, feel, know, meet, nibble, perceive, relish, sample, savour, sip, smack, test, try, undergo.

tasteful *adj.* aesthetic, artistic, beautiful, charming, comme il faut, correct, cultivated, cultured, delicate, discreet, discriminating, elegant, exquisite, fastidious, graceful, handsome, harmonious, judicious, polished, refined, restrained, smart, stylish, well-judged.
antonym tasteless.

tasteless *adj.* barbaric, bland, boring, cheap, coarse, crass, crude, dilute, dull, flashy, flat,

flavourless, garish, gaudy, graceless, gross, improper, inartistic, indecorous, indelicate, indiscreet, inelegant, inharmonious, insipid, low, mild, rude, stale, tacky, tactless, tame, tatty, tawdry, thin, uncouth, undiscriminating, uninspired, uninteresting, unseemly, untasteful, vapid, vulgar, watered-down, watery, weak, wearish.
antonym tasteful.

tasting *n.* assay, assessment, gustation, sampling, testing, trial.

tasty *adj.* appetising, delectable, delicious, flavorous, flavourful, flavoursome, gusty, luscious, mouthwatering, palatable, piquant, sapid, saporous, savoury, scrumptious, succulent, toothsome, yummy.
antonyms disgusting, insipid, tasteless.

tattered *adj.* duddie, frayed, in shreds, lacerated, ragged, raggy, rent, ripped, tatty, threadbare, torn.
antonyms neat, trim.

tatters *n.* duddery, duds, flitters, rags, ribbons, shreds.

tattle *v.* babble, blab, blather, blether, chat, chatter, clash, claver, gab, gash, gossip, jabber, natter, prate, prattle, talk, tittle-tattle, yak, yap.
n. babble, blather, blether, chat, chatter, chitchat, clash, claver, gossip, hearsay, jabber, prattle, rumour, talk, tittle-tattle, yak, yap.

tattler *n.* busybody, gossip, newsmonger, quidnunc, rumour-monger, scandalmonger, talebearer, tale-teller, tell-tale.

taunt *v.* bait, chiack, deride, fleer, flout, flyte, gibe, insult, jeer, mock, provoke, reproach, revile, rib, ridicule, sneer, tease, torment, twit.
n. barb, catcall, censure, cut, derision, dig, fling, gibe, insult, jeer, poke, provocation, reproach, ridicule, sarcasm, sneer, teasing.

taut *adj.* contracted, rigid, strained, stressed, stretched, tense, tensed, tight, tightened, unrelaxed.
antonyms loose, relaxed, slack.

tautological *adj.* iterative, otiose, pleonastic, redundant, repetitious, repetitive, superfluous, truistic.
antonyms economical, succinct.

tautology *n.* duplication, iteration, otioseness, perissology, pleonasm, redundancy, repetition, repetitiousness, repetitiveness, superfluity.
antonyms economy, succinctness.

tavern *n.* alehouse, bar, boozer, bush, dive, doggery, fonda, hostelry, inn, joint, local, pub, public house, roadhouse, tap-house.

tawdry *adj.* brummagem, cheap, cheap-jack, flashy, garish, gaudy, gimcrack, gingerbread, glittering, meretricious, pinchbeck, plastic, raffish, showy, tacky, tasteless, tatty, tinsel, tinselly, vulgar.
antonyms excellent, fine, superior.

tawny *adj.* fawn, fulvid, fulvous, golden, sandy, tan, xanthous, yellow.

tax *n.* agistment, assessment, burden, charge, contribution, customs, demand, drain, duty, excise, geld, imposition, impost, levy, load, octroi, pressure, rate, scat, scot, strain, tariff, tithe, toll, tribute, weight.
v. accuse, arraign, assess, blame, burden, censure, charge, demand, drain, enervate, exact, exhaust, extract, geld, impeach, impose, impugn, incriminate, load, overburden, overtax, push, rate, reproach, sap, strain, stretch, task, tithe, try, weaken, weary.

taxi *n.* cab, fiacre, hackney-coach, hansom-cab, taxicab.

taxing *adj.* burdensome, demanding, draining, enervating, exacting, exhausting, heavy, onerous, punishing, stressful, tiring, tough, trying, wearing, wearisome.
antonyms easy, gentle, mild.

teach *v.* accustom, advise, coach, counsel, demonstrate, direct, discipline, drill, edify, educate, enlighten, ground, guide, impart, implant, inculcate, inform, instil, instruct, school, show, train, tutor, verse.

teacher *n.* abecedarian, coach, dominie, don, educator, guide, guru, instructor, khodja, kindergartener, kindergärtner, lecturer, luminary, maharishi, master, mentor, mistress, pedagogue, professor, pundit, schoolmarm, schoolmaster, schoolmistress, schoolteacher, trainer, tutor, usher.

teaching *n.* didactics, doctrine, dogma, education, gospel, grounding, indoctrination, instruction, pedagoguism, pedagogy, precept, principle, schooling, tenet, training, tuition.

team *n.* band, body, bunch, company, crew, écurie, équipe, gang, group, line-up, pair, set, shift, side, span, squad, stable, troupe, yoke.
v. combine, couple, join, link, match, yoke.

team up band together, combine, co-operate, join, unite.

teamwork *n.* collaboration, co-operation, co-ordination, esprit de corps, fellowship, joint effort, team spirit.
antonyms disharmony, disunity.

tear *v.* belt, bolt, career, charge, claw, dart, dash, dilacerate, divide, drag, fly, gallop, gash, grab, hurry, lacerate, mangle, mutilate, pluck, pull, race, rend, rip, rive, run, rupture, rush, scratch, seize, sever, shoot, shred, snag, snatch, speed, split, sprint, sunder, wrench, wrest, yank, zoom.
n. hole, laceration, rent, rip, run, rupture, scratch, snag, split.

tearaway *n.* daredevil, delinquent, good-for-nothing, hoodlum, hooligan, hothead, madcap, rascal, rough, roughneck, rowdy, ruffian, tityre-tu, tough.

tearful *adj.* blubbering, crying, distressing, dolorous, emotional, lachrymose, lamentable, maudlin, mournful, pathetic, pitiable, pitiful, poignant, sad, sobbing, sorrowful, upsetting, weeping, weepy, whimpering, woeful.

tears *n.* blubbering, crying, distress, lamentation, mourning, pain, regret, sadness, sobbing, sorrow, wailing, water-drops, water-works, weeping, whimpering, woe.

tease v. aggravate, annoy, badger, bait, banter, bedevil, chaff, chip, gibe, goad, grig, guy, irritate, josh, mock, needle, pester, plague, provoke, rag, rib, ridicule, take a rise out of, tantalise, taunt, torment, twit, vex, worry.

technique n. address, adroitness, approach, art, artistry, course, craft, craftsmanship, delivery, executancy, execution, expertise, facility, fashion, knack, know-how, manner, means, method, mode, modus operandi, performance, procedure, proficiency, skill, style, system, touch, way.

tedious adj. annoying, banal, boring, deadly, drab, dreary, dreich, dull, fatiguing, humdrum, irksome, laborious, lifeless, long-drawn-out, longsome, long-spun, monotonous, prosaic, prosy, soporific, tiring, unexciting, uninteresting, vapid, wearisome.
antonyms exciting, interesting.

tedium n. banality, boredom, drabness, dreariness, dullness, ennui, lifelessness, monotony, prosiness, routine, sameness, tediousness, vapidity.

teem v. abound, bear, brim, bristle, burst, increase, multiply, overflow, overspill, produce, proliferate, pullulate, swarm.
antonyms lack, want.

teeming adj. abundant, alive, brimful, brimming, bristling, bursting, chock-a-block, chock-full, crawling, fruitful, full, numerous, overflowing, packed, pregnant, proliferating, pullulating, replete, swarming, thick.
antonyms lacking, rare, sparse.

teenage adj. adolescent, immature, juvenile, pubescent, teen, young, youthful.

teenager n. adolescent, bobbysoxer, boy, girl, juvenile, minor, youth.

teeny adj. diminutive, microscopic, miniature, minuscule, minute, teensy-weensy, teeny-weeny, tichy, tiny, tottie, wee.

teeter v. balance, lurch, pitch, pivot, rock, seesaw, stagger, sway, titubate, totter, tremble, waver, wobble.

teetotaller n. abstainer, nephalist, non-drinker, Rechabite, water-drinker.

telegram n. cable, telegraph, telemessage, telex, wire.

telegraph n. cable, radiotelegraph, telegram, teleprinter, telex, wire.
v. cable, send, signal, telex, transmit, wire.

telepathy n. clairvoyance, ESP, mind-reading, sixth sense, thought transference.

telephone n. blower, dog and bone, handset, line, phone.
v. buzz, call, call up, contact, dial, get in touch, get on the blower, give someone a tinkle, phone, ring (up).

telescope v. abbreviate, abridge, compress, concertina, condense, contract, crush, curtail, cut, reduce, shorten, shrink, squash, trim, truncate.

television n. boob tube, goggle-box, idiot box, receiver, set, small screen, telly, the box, the tube, TV, TV set.

tell v. acquaint, announce, apprise, authorise, bid, calculate, chronicle, command, communicate, comprehend, compute, confess, count, depict, describe, differentiate, direct, discern, disclose, discover, discriminate, distinguish, divulge, enjoin, enumerate, express, foresee, identify, impart, inform, instruct, mention, militate, narrate, notify, number, order, portray, predict, proclaim, reckon, recount, register, rehearse, relate, report, require, reveal, say, see, speak, state, summon, tally, understand, utter, weigh.

tell off bawl out, berate, censure, chide, dress down, lecture, objurgate, rebuke, reprimand, reproach, reprove, scold, take to task, tear off a strip, tick off, upbraid.

telling-off n. bawling-out, castigation, dressing-down, jawbation, jawing, jobation, lecture, rebuke, reprimand, reproach, reproof, row, scolding, tongue-lashing.

temerity n. assurance, audacity, boldness, brass neck, chutzpah, daring, effrontery, forwardness, gall, heedlessness, impudence, impulsiveness, intrepidity, nerve, pluck, rashness, recklessness.
antonym caution.

temper n. anger, annoyance, attitude, bait, calm, calmness, character, composure, constitution, cool, coolness, disposition, equanimity, fury, heat, humour, ill-humour, irascibility, irritability, irritation, mind, moderation, mood, nature, paddy, passion, peevishness, pet, petulance, rage, resentment, sang-froid, self-control, surliness, taking, tantrum, temperament, tenor, tranquillity, vein, wax, wrath.
v. abate, admix, allay, anneal, assuage, calm, harden, indurate, lessen, mitigate, moderate, modify, mollify, palliate, restrain, soften, soothe, strengthen, toughen.

temperament n. anger, bent, character, complexion, constitution, crasis, disposition, excitability, explosiveness, hot-headedness, humour, impatience, make-up, mettle, moodiness, moods, nature, outlook, personality, petulance, quality, soul, spirit, stamp, temper, tendencies, tendency, volatility.

temperamental adj. capricious, congenital, constitutional, emotional, erratic, excitable, explosive, fiery, highly-strung, hot-headed, hypersensitive, impatient, inborn, inconsistent, ingrained, inherent, innate, irritable, mercurial, moody, natural, neurotic, over-emotional, passionate, petulant, sensitive, touchy, undependable, unpredictable, unreliable, volatile, volcanic.
antonyms calm, serene, steady.

temperance n. abstemiousness, abstinence, continence, discretion, forbearance, moderation, prohibition, restraint, self-abnegation, self-control, self-denial, self-discipline, self-restraint, sobriety, teetotalism.
antonyms excess, intemperance.

temperate adj. abstemious, abstinent, agreeable,

balanced, balmy, calm, clement, composed, continent, controlled, cool, dispassionate, equable, even-tempered, fair, gentle, mild, moderate, pleasant, reasonable, restrained, sensible, sober, soft, stable.
antonyms excessive, extreme, intemperate.

tempest *n.* bourasque, commotion, cyclone, disturbance, ferment, furore, gale, hurricane, squall, storm, tornado, tumult, typhoon, upheaval, uproar.

tempestuous *adj.* agitated, blustery, boisterous, breezy, emotional, excited, feverish, furious, gusty, heated, hysterical, impassioned, intense, passionate, raging, squally, stormy, troubled, tumultuous, turbulent, uncontrolled, violent, wild, windy.
antonyms calm, quiet.

temple *n.* church, delubrum, fane, haffet, joss-house, mandir(a), masjid, monopteron, monopteros, mosque, pagoda, sanctuary, shrine, tabernacle, vihara, wat.

tempo *n.* beat, cadence, measure, metre, pace, pulse, rate, rhythm, speed, time, velocity.

temporal *adj.* carnal, civil, earthly, evanescent, fleeting, fleshly, fugacious, fugitive, impermanent, lay, material, momentary, mortal, mundane, passing, profane, secular, short-lived, sublunary, temporary, terrestrial, transient, transitory, unspiritual, worldly.
antonym spiritual.

temporarily *adv.* briefly, fleetingly, for the nonce, for the time being, in the interim, momentarily, pro tem, transiently, transitorily.
antonym permanently.

temporary *adj.* brief, ephemeral, evanescent, fleeting, fugacious, fugitive, impermanent, interim, makeshift, momentary, passing, pro tem, pro tempore, provisional, short-lived, stop-gap, transient, transitory.
antonyms everlasting, permanent.

temporise *v.* delay, equivocate, hang back, hum and haw, pause, play for time, procrastinate, stall, tergiversate.

tempt *v.* allure, attract, bait, coax, dare, decoy, draw, enamour, entice, incite, inveigle, invite, lure, provoke, risk, seduce, tantalise, test, try, woo.
antonyms discourage, dissuade.

temptation *n.* allurement, appeal, attraction, attractiveness, bait, blandishments, coaxing, come-on, decoy, draw, enticement, fascination, forbidden fruit, inducement, invitation, lure, persuasion, pull, seduction, snare.

tempting *adj.* alluring, appetising, attractive, enticing, inviting, lickerish, liquorish, mouth-watering, seductive, tantalising, temptatious.
antonyms unattractive, uninviting.

temptress *n.* Circe, coquette, Delilah, enchantress, femme fatale, flirt, seductress, siren, sorceress, vamp.

tenable *adj.* arguable, believable, credible, defendable, defensible, justifiable, maintainable, plausible, rational, reasonable, sound, supportable, viable.

antonyms indefensible, unjustifiable, untenable.

tenacious *adj.* adamant, adhesive, clinging, coherent, cohesive, determined, dogged, fast, firm, forceful, gluey, glutinous, inflexible, intransigent, mucilaginous, obdurate, obstinate, persistent, pertinacious, resolute, retentive, single-minded, solid, staunch, steadfast, sticky, strong, strong-willed, stubborn, sure, tight, tough, unshakeable, unswerving, unwavering, unyielding, viscous.
antonyms loose, slack, weak.

tenacity *n.* adhesiveness, application, clinginess, coherence, cohesiveness, determination, diligence, doggedness, fastness, firmness, force, forcefulness, indomitability, inflexibility, intransigence, obduracy, obstinacy, perseverance, persistence, pertinacity, power, resoluteness, resolution, resolve, retention, retentiveness, single-mindedness, solidity, solidness, staunchness, steadfastness, stickiness, strength, stubbornness, toughness, viscosity.
antonyms looseness, slackness, weakness.

tenancy *n.* holding, incumbency, lease, leasehold, occupancy, occupation, possession, renting, residence, tenure.

tenant *n.* gavelman, inhabitant, landholder, leaseholder, lessee, occupant, occupier, renter, resident.

tend¹ *v.* affect, aim, bear, bend, conduce, contribute, go, gravitate, head, incline, influence, lead, lean, move, point, trend, verge.

tend² *v.* attend, comfort, control, cultivate, feed, guard, handle, keep, maintain, manage, minister to, nurse, nurture, protect, serve, succour.
antonym neglect.

tendency *n.* bearing, bent, bias, conatus, course, direction, disposition, drift, drive, heading, inclination, leaning, liability, movement, partiality, penchant, predilection, predisposition, proclivity, proneness, propensity, purport, readiness, susceptibility, tenor, thrust, trend, turning.

tender¹ *adj.* aching, acute, affectionate, affettuoso, amoroso, amorous, benevolent, breakable, bruised, callow, caring, chary, compassionate, complicated, considerate, dangerous, delicate, difficult, emotional, evocative, feeble, fond, fragile, frail, gentle, green, humane, immature, impressionable, inexperienced, inflamed, irritated, kind, loving, merciful, moving, new, painful, pathetic, pitiful, poignant, raw, risky, romantic, scrupulous, sensitive, sentimental, smarting, soft, soft-hearted, sore, sympathetic, tender-hearted, ticklish, touching, touchy, tricky, vulnerable, warm, warm-hearted, weak, young, youthful.
antonyms callous, chewy, hard, harsh, rough, severe, tough.

tender² *v.* advance, extend, give, offer, present, proffer, propose, submit, suggest, volunteer.
n. bid, currency, estimate, medium, money,

offer, payment, proffer, proposal, proposition, specie, submission, suggestion.

tender-hearted adj. affectionate, benevolent, benign, caring, compassionate, considerate, feeling, fond, gentle, humane, kind, kind-hearted, kindly, loving, merciful, mild, pitying, responsive, sensitive, sentimental, soft-hearted, sympathetic, warm, warmhearted.

antonyms callous, cruel, hard-hearted, unfeeling.

tenderness n. ache, aching, affection, amorousness, attachment, benevolence, bruising, callowness, care, compassion, consideration, delicateness, devotion, discomfort, feebleness, fondness, fragility, frailness, gentleness, greenness, humaneness, humanity, immaturity, impressionableness, inexperience, inflammation, irritation, kindness, liking, love, loving-kindness, mercy, newness, pain, painfulness, pity, rawness, sensitiveness, sensitivity, sentimentality, soft-heartedness, softness, soreness, sweetness, sympathy, tenderheartedness, vulnerability, warmheartedness, warmth, weakness, youth, youthfulness.

antonyms cruelty, hardness, harshness.

tenet n. article of faith, belief, canon, conviction, credo, creed, doctrine, dogma, maxim, opinion, precept, presumption, principle, rule, teaching, thesis, view.

tenor n. aim, burden, course, direction, drift, essence, evolution, gist, intent, meaning, path, point, purport, purpose, sense, spirit, substance, tendency, theme, trend, way.

tense adj. anxious, apprehensive, edgy, electric, exciting, fidgety, jittery, jumpy, moving, nerve-racking, nervous, overwrought, restless, rigid, strained, stressful, stretched, strung up, taut, tight, uneasy, uptight, worrying.

antonyms calm, lax, loose, relaxed.

v. brace, contract, strain, stretch, tauten, tighten.

antonyms loosen, relax.

tension n. anxiety, apprehension, edginess, hostility, nervousness, pressure, restlessness, rigidity, stiffness, strain, straining, stress, stretching, suspense, tautness, tightness, tone, unease, worry.

antonyms calm(ness), laxness, looseness, relaxation.

tent n. big top, canvas, marquee, marquise, tabernacle, tepee, wigwam, y(o)urt.

tentative adj. cautious, conjectural, diffident, doubtful, experimental, faltering, hesitant, indefinite, peirastic, provisional, speculative, timid, uncertain, unconfirmed, undecided, unformulated, unsettled, unsure.

antonyms conclusive, decisive, definite, final.

tenuous adj. attenuated, delicate, doubtful, dubious, fine, flimsy, gossamer, insignificant, insubstantial, nebulous, questionable, rarefied, shaky, sketchy, slender, slight, slim, thin, weak.

antonyms significant, strong, substantial.

tenure n. habitation, holding, incumbency, occupancy, occupation, possession, proprietorship, residence, tenancy, term, time.

tepid adj. apathetic, cool, half-hearted, indifferent, lew, lukewarm, unenthusiastic, warmish.

antonyms animated, cold, hot, passionate.

tergiversation n. apostasy, defection, desertion, equivocation, fencing, hedging, prevarication, shilly-shallying, vacillation, wavering.

term[1] n. appellation, denomination, designation, epithet, epitheton, expression, locution, name, phrase, title, word.

v. call, denominate, designate, dub, entitle, label, name, style, tag, title.

term[2] n. bound, boundary, close, conclusion, confine, course, culmination, duration, end, finish, fruition, half, interval, limit, period, season, session, space, span, spell, terminus, time, while.

terminal adj. bounding, concluding, deadly, desinent, desinential, extreme, fatal, final, incurable, killing, last, lethal, limiting, mortal, ultimate, utmost.

antonym initial.

n. boundary, depot, end, extremity, limit, termination, terminus.

terminate v. abort, cease, close, complete, conclude, cut off, discontinue, drop, end, expire, finish, issue, lapse, result, stop, wind up.

antonyms begin, initiate, start.

termination n. abortion, cessation, close, completion, conclusion, consequence, dénouement, discontinuation, effect, end, ending, expiry, finale, finis, finish, issue, result, wind-up.

antonyms beginning, initiation, start.

terminology n. argot, cant, jargon, language, lingo, nomenclature, patois, phraseology, terms, vocabulary, words.

terminus n. boundary, close, depot, destination, end, extremity, furthermost point, garage, goal, limit, station, target, termination.

terms n. agreement, charges, compromise, conditions, fees, footing, language, particulars, payment, phraseology, position, premises, price, provisions, provisos, qualifications, rates, relations, relationship, specifications, standing, status, stipulations, terminology, understanding.

terrain n. country, countryside, ground, land, landscape, territory, topography.

terrestrial adj. earthly, global, mundane, subastral, sublunary, tellurian, terrene, worldly.

antonyms cosmic, empyreal, heavenly.

terrible adj. abhorrent, appalling, awful, bad, beastly, dangerous, desperate, dire, disgusting, distressing, dread, dreaded, dreadful, extreme, fearful, foul, frightful, god-awful, gruesome, harrowing, hateful, hideous, horrendous, horrible, horrid, horrific, horrifying, loathsome, monstrous, obnoxious, odious, offensive, outrageous, poor, repulsive, revolting, rotten, serious, severe, shocking, unpleasant, vile.

antonyms great, pleasant, superb, wonderful.

terribly *adv.* awfully, decidedly, desperately, exceedingly, extremely, frightfully, gravely, greatly, much, seriously, shockingly, thoroughly, very.

terrific *adj.* ace, amazing, awesome, awful, breathtaking, brilliant, dreadful, enormous, excellent, excessive, extreme, fabulous, fantastic, fearful, fierce, fine, gigantic, great, harsh, horrific, huge, intense, magnificent, marvellous, monstrous, outstanding, prodigious, sensational, severe, smashing, stupendous, super, superb, terrible, tremendous, wonderful.

terrified *adj.* alarmed, appalled, awed, dismayed, frightened, horrified, horror-struck, intimidated, panic-stricken, petrified, scared.

terrify *v.* affright, alarm, appal, awe, dismay, frighten, horrify, intimidate, petrify, scare, shock, terrorise.

territorial *adj.* area, district, domainal, geographical, localised, regional, sectional, topographic, zonal.

territory *n.* area, bailiwick, country, dependency, district, domain, jurisdiction, land, park, preserve, province, region, sector, state, terrain, tract, zone.

terror *n.* affright, alarm, anxiety, awe, blue funk, bogeyman, bugbear, consternation, devil, dismay, dread, fear, fiend, fright, horror, intimidation, monster, panic, rascal, rogue, scourge, shock, tearaway.

terrorise *v.* alarm, appal, awe, browbeat, bully, coerce, dismay, frighten, horrify, intimidate, menace, oppress, petrify, scare, shock, strongarm, terrify, threaten.

terse *adj.* abrupt, aphoristic, brief, brusque, clipped, compact, concise, condensed, crisp, curt, economical, elliptical, epigrammatic, gnomic, incisive, laconic, neat, pithy, sententious, short, snappy, succinct.

antonyms long-winded, prolix, repetitious.

test *v.* analyse, assay, assess, check, examine, experiment, investigate, prove, screen, try, verify.

n. analysis, assessment, attempt, catechism, check, evaluation, examination, hurdle, investigation, moment of truth, ordeal, pons asinorum, probation, proof, shibboleth, trial, try-out.

testament *n.* attestation, demonstration, devise, earnest, evidence, exemplification, proof, testimony, tribute, will, witness.

testicles *n.* balls, bollocks, gonads, goolies, knackers, nuts, pills, stones.

testify *v.* affirm, assert, asseverate, attest, avow, certify, corroborate, declare, depone, depose, evince, show, state, swear, vouch, witness.

testimonial *n.* certificate, character, commendation, credential, endorsement, gift, memorial, plug, recommendation, reference, tribute.

testimony *n.* affidavit, affirmation, asseveration, attestation, avowal, confirmation, corrobora-

tion, declaration, demonstration, deposition, evidence, indication, information, manifestation, profession, proof, statement, submission, support, verification, witness.

testy *adj.* bad-tempered, cantankerous, captious, carnaptious, crabbed, cross, crusty, fretful, grumpy, impatient, inflammable, irascible, irritable, peevish, peppery, petulant, quarrelsome, quick-tempered, short-tempered, snappish, snappy, splenetic, sullen, tetchy, touchy, waspish.

antonyms even-tempered, good-humoured.

tether *n.* bond, chain, cord, fastening, fetter, halter, lead, leash, line, restraint, rope, shackle.

v. bind, chain, fasten, fetter, lash, leash, manacle, picket, restrain, rope, secure, shackle, tie.

text *n.* argument, body, contents, lection, libretto, matter, motif, paragraph, passage, reader, reading, script, sentence, source, subject, textbook, theme, topic, verse, wordage, wording, words.

texture *n.* character, composition, consistency, constitution, fabric, feel, grain, quality, structure, surface, tissue, weave, weftage, woof.

thankful *adj.* appreciative, beholden, contented, grateful, indebted, obliged, pleased, relieved.

antonyms thankless, unappreciative, ungrateful.

thankless *adj.* fruitless, unappreciated, ungrateful, unprofitable, unrecognised, unrequited, unrewarding, useless.

antonym rewarding.

thanks *n.* acknowledgement, appreciation, credit, grace, gratefulness, gratitude, recognition, thank-offering, thanksgiving.

interj. cheers, danke (schön), gracias, gramercy, grand merci, grazie, merci, merci beaucoup, merci bien, ta.

thanks to as a result of, because of, by reason of, due to, in consequence of, on account of, owing to, through.

thaw *v.* defreeze, defrost, dissolve, liquefy, melt, soften, unbend, uncongeal, unfreeze, unthaw, warm.

antonym freeze.

the end beyond endurance, enough, insufferable, intolerable, the final blow, the last straw, the limit, the worst, too much, unbearable, unendurable.

the limit enough, it, the end, the final blow, the last straw, the worst.

the masses hoi polloi, the admass, the common people, the commonalty, the crowd, the majority, the many, the multitude, the people, the plebs, the proles, the proletariat, the rank and file.

theatre *n.* amphitheatre, auditorium, hall, lyceum, odeon, opera house, penny gaff, playhouse.

theatrical *adj.* affected, artificial, ceremonious, dramatic, dramaturgic, exaggerated, extravagant, hammy, histrionic, mannered, melodramatic, ostentatious, overdone, pompous, scenic, showy, stagy, stilted, theatric, Thespian, unreal.

theft *n.* abstraction, embezzlement, fraud, heist, kleptomania, larceny, pilfering, plunderage, purloining, rip-off, robbery, stealing, thievery, thieving.

thematic *adj.* conceptual, notional, taxonomic, classificatory.

theme *n.* argument, burden, composition, dissertation, essay, exercise, idea, keynote, leitmotiv, lemma, matter, motif, mythos, paper, subject, subject-matter, text, thesis, topic, topos.

theological *adj.* divine, doctrinal, ecclesiastical, hierological, religious.

theorem *n.* deduction, dictum, formula, hypothesis, postulate, principle, proposition, rule, statement, thesis.

theoretical *adj.* abstract, academic, conjectural, doctrinaire, doctrinal, hypothetical, ideal, impractical, on paper, pure, speculative. *antonyms* applied, concrete, practical.

theorise *v.* conjecture, formulate, guess, hypothesise, postulate, project, propound, speculate, suppose.

theory *n.* abstraction, assumption, conjecture, guess, hypothesis, ism, philosophy, plan, postulation, presumption, proposal, scheme, speculation, supposition, surmise, system, thesis. *antonyms* certainty, practice.

therapeutic *adj.* ameliorative, analeptic, beneficial, corrective, curative, good, healing, recuperative, remedial, restorative, salubrious, salutary, sanative, tonic. *antonym* harmful.

therapy *n.* cure, healing, prophylaxis, tonic, treatment.

therefore *adv.* accordingly, as a result, consequently, ergo, for that reason, hence, so, then, thence, thus.

thesaurus *n.* dictionary, encyclopedia, lexicon, repository, storehouse, synonymicon, synonymy, treasury, vocabulary, wordbook.

thesis *n.* argument, assumption, composition, contention, disquisition, dissertation, essay, hypothesis, idea, monograph, opinion, paper, postulate, premiss, proposal, proposition, statement, subject, supposition, surmise, theme, theory, topic, tract, tractate, treatise, view.

thick *adj.* abundant, brainless, brimming, bristling, broad, bulky, bursting, chock-a-block, chock-full, chummy, close, clotted, coagulated, compact, concentrated, condensed, confidential, covered, crass, crawling, crowded, decided, deep, dense, devoted, dim-witted, distinct, distorted, dopey, dull, excessive, familiar, fat, foggy, frequent, friendly, full, gross, guttural, heavy, hoarse, husky, impenetrable, inarticulate, indistinct, insensitive, inseparable, intimate, marked, matey, moronic, muffled, numerous, obtuse, opaque, packed, pally, pronounced, replete,

rich, slow, slow-witted, solid, soupy, squabbish, strong, stupid, substantial, swarming, teeming, thick-headed, throaty, turbid, wide. *antonyms* brainy, clever, slender, slight, slim, thin, watery.
n. centre, focus, heart, hub, middle, midst.

thicken *v.* cake, clot, coagulate, condense, congeal, deepen, gel, incrassate, inspissate, jell, set. *antonym* thin.

thicket *n.* bosket, brake, clump, coppice, copse, covert, dead-finish, greave, grove, macchie, maquis, spinney, wood, woodland.

thickhead *n.* blockhead, bonehead, chump, clot, dimwit, dolt, dope, dullard, dummy, dunce, dunderhead, fathead, fool, idiot, imbecile, moron, nitwit, numskull, pinhead, thick, twit.

thick-headed *adj.* asinine, blockheaded, brainless, dense, dim-witted, doltish, dopey, dull-witted, idiotic, imbecilic, moronic, obtuse, slow, slow-witted, stupid, thick. *antonyms* brainy, clever, intelligent, sharp.

thickness *n.* body, breadth, bulk, bulkiness, density, diameter, layer, ply, sheet, spissitude, stratum, viscosity, width. *antonym* thinness.

thickset *adj.* beefy, brawny, bulky, burly, dense, heavy, muscular, nuggety, powerful, solid, squabbish, squabby, squat, stocky, strong, stubby, sturdy, thick, well-built. *antonym* lanky.

thick-skinned *adj.* callous, case-hardened, hard-boiled, hardened, impervious, insensitive, inured, obdurate, pachydermatous, stolid, tough, unfeeling. *antonym* thin-skinned.

thief *n.* abactor, Autolycus, bandit, burglar, cheat, cracksman, crook, cut-purse, embezzler, filcher, house-breaker, kleptomaniac, ladrone, land-rat, larcener, larcenist, latron, mugger, pickpocket, pilferer, plunderer, prigger, purloiner, robber, shop-lifter, snatch-purse, St Nicholas's clerk, stealer, swindler.

thieve *v.* abstract, cheat, embezzle, filch, half-inch, heist, knock off, lift, misappropriate, nick, peculate, pilfer, pinch, plunder, poach, purloin, rip off, rob, steal, swindle, swipe.

thieving *n.* banditry, burglary, crookedness, embezzlement, larceny, mugging, peculation, pilferage, pilfering, piracy, plundering, robbery, shop-lifting, stealing, theft, thievery.

thievish *adj.* crooked, dishonest, fraudulent, furacious, larcenous, light-fingered, piratical, predatory, rapacious, sticky-fingered, thieving.

thin *adj.* attenuate, attenuated, bony, deficient, delicate, diaphanous, dilute, diluted, emaciated, feeble, filmy, fine, fine-drawn, flimsy, gaunt, gossamer, inadequate, insubstantial, insufficient, lanky, lean, light, meagre, narrow, poor, rarefied, runny, scant, scanty, scarce, scattered, scragged, scraggy, scrawny, see-through, shallow, sheer, skeletal, skimpy, skinny, slender, slight, slim, spare, sparse,

spindly, superficial, tenuous, translucent, transparent, unconvincing, undernourished, underweight, unsubstantial, washy, watery, weak, wishy-washy, wispy.
antonyms broad, dense, fat, solid, strong, thick.
v. attenuate, decrassify, dilute, diminish, emaciate, extenuate, prune, rarefy, reduce, refine, trim, water down, weaken, weed out.

thing *n.* act, action, affair, apparatus, article, aspect, attitude, being, body, circumstance, concept, contrivance, creature, deed, detail, device, dislike, entity, event, eventuality, facet, fact, factor, feat, feature, fetish, fixation, gadget, hang-up, happening, idée fixe, implement, incident, instrument, item, liking, machine, mania, matter, means, mechanism, monomania, object, obsession, occurrence, part, particular, phenomenon, phobia, point, portion, possession, preoccupation, problem, proceeding, quirk, something, statement, substance, thought, tool.

things *n.* baggage, belongings, bits and pieces, clobber, clothes, effects, equipment, gear, goods, impedimenta, junk, luggage, odds and ends, paraphernalia, possessions, stuff, traps, utensils.

think *v.* anticipate, be under the impression, believe, brood, calculate, cerebrate, cogitate, conceive, conclude, consider, contemplate, deem, deliberate, design, determine, envisage, esteem, estimate, expect, foresee, hold, ideate, imagine, intellectualise, judge, meditate, mull over, muse, ponder, presume, purpose, ratiocinate, reason, recall, reckon, recollect, reflect, regard, remember, revolve, ruminate, suppose, surmise.
n. assessment, cogitation, consideration, contemplation, deliberation, meditation, reflection.

think much of admire, esteem, prize, rate, respect, set store by, think highly of, value.
antonym abominate.

think over chew over, consider, contemplate, meditate, mull over, ponder, reflect upon, ruminate, weigh up.

think up conceive, concoct, contrive, create, design, devise, dream up, imagine, improvise, invent, visualise.

thinkable *adj.* cogitable, conceivable, feasible, imaginable, likely, possible, reasonable, supposable.
antonym unthinkable.

thinker *n.* brain, ideologist, imaginist, intellect, mastermind, philosopher, sage, theorist.

thinking *n.* assessment, cogitation, conclusions, conjecture, idea, judgement, opinion, outlook, philosophy, position, ratiocination, reasoning, theory, thoughts, view.
adj. analytical, cerebral, contemplative, cultured, dianoetic, intelligent, meditative, philosophical, ratiocinative, rational, reasoning, reflective, sophisticated, thoughtful.

thin-skinned *adj.* hypersensitive, irascible, irritable, sensitive, snappish, soft, susceptible,

tender, testy, touchy, vulnerable.
antonym thick-skinned.

third-rate *adj.* bad, cheap and nasty, cheap-jack, duff, indifferent, inferior, low-grade, mediocre, poor, ropy, shoddy.

thirst *n.* appetite, craving, desire, drought, drouth, drouthiness, dryness, eagerness, hankering, hunger, hydromania, keenness, longing, lust, passion, thirstiness, yearning, yen.

thirsty *adj.* adry, appetitive, arid, athirst, avid, burning, craving, dehydrated, desirous, drouthy, dry, dying, eager, greedy, hankering, hungry, hydropic, itching, longing, lusting, parched, thirsting, yearning.

thorn *n.* acantha, affliction, annoyance, bane, barb, bother, curse, doorn, irritant, irritation, nuisance, pest, plague, prickle, scourge, spike, spine, torment, torture, trouble.

thorny *adj.* acanthous, awkward, barbed, bristly, difficult, fraught, harassing, hard, irksome, pointed, prickly, problematic, sharp, spiky, spinous, spiny, sticky, ticklish, tough, troublesome, trying, unpleasant, upsetting, vexatious, vexed, worrying.

thorough *adj.* absolute, all-embracing, all-inclusive, arrant, assiduous, careful, complete, comprehensive, conscientious, deep-seated, downright, efficient, entire, exhaustive, full, in-depth, intensive, meticulous, out-and-out, painstaking, perfect, pure, root-and-branch, scrupulous, sheer, sweeping, thoroughgoing, total, unmitigated, unqualified, utter.
antonyms careless, haphazard, partial.

thoroughfare *n.* access, avenue, boulevard, concourse, highway, motorway, passage, passageway, road, roadway, street, turnpike, way.

thoroughly *adv.* à fond, absolutely, assiduously, carefully, completely, comprehensively, conscientiously, downright, efficiently, entirely, every inch, exhaustively, fully, inside out, intensively, meticulously, painstakingly, perfectly, point-device (-devise), quite, root and branch, scrupulously, sweepingly, totally, utterly, with a fine-tooth comb.
antonyms carelessly, haphazardly, partially.

though *conj.* albeit, allowing, although, even if, granted, howbeit, notwithstanding, while.
adv. all the same, even so, for all that, however, in spite of that, nevertheless, nonetheless, notwithstanding, still, yet.

thought *n.* aim, anticipation, anxiety, aspiration, assessment, attention, attentiveness, belief, brainwork, care, cerebration, cogitation, compassion, concept, conception, concern, conclusion, conjecture, considerateness, consideration, contemplation, conviction, dash, deliberation, design, dream, estimation, excogitation, expectation, heed, hope, idea, intention, introspection, jot, judgement, kindness, little, meditation, mentation, muse, musing, notion, object, opinion, plan, prospect, purpose, reflection, regard, resolution, rumination, scrutiny, solicitude, study, sympathy, thinking, thoughtfulness, touch, trifle, view, whisker.

thoughtful *adj.* absorbed, abstracted, astute, attentive, canny, careful, caring, cautious, circumspect, considerate, contemplative, deliberate, deliberative, discreet, heedful, helpful, introspective, kind, kindly, meditative, mindful, musing, pensieroso, pensive, prudent, rapt, reflective, ruminative, serious, solicitous, studious, thinking, unselfish, wary, wistful.
antonym thoughtless.

thoughtless *adj.* absent-minded, careless, étourdi(e), foolish, heedless, ill-considered, impolite, imprudent, inadvertent, inattentive, inconsiderate, indiscreet, injudicious, insensitive, mindless, neglectful, negligent, rash, reckless, regardless, remiss, rude, selfish, silly, stupid, tactless, uncaring, undiplomatic, unkind, unmindful, unobservant, unreflecting, unthinking.
antonym thoughtful.

thraldom *n.* bondage, enslavement, serfdom, servitude, slavery, subjection, subjugation, vassalage, ville(i)nage.
antonym freedom.

thrash *v.* beat, belt, bethump, bethwack, birch, cane, chastise, clobber, crush, defeat, drub, flagellate, flail, flog, hammer, heave, horsewhip, jerk, lam, lambaste, larrup, lather, lay into, leather, maul, overwhelm, paste, plunge, punish, quilt, rout, scourge, slaughter, spank, squirm, swish, tan, thresh, toss, towel, trim, trounce, wallop, whale, whap, whip, writhe.
thrash out debate, discuss, negotiate, resolve, settle, solve.

thrashing *n.* beating, belting, caning, chastisement, defeat, dressing, drubbing, flogging, hammering, hiding, laldie, lamming, lashing, leathering, mauling, pasting, punishment, quilting, rout, strap-oil, tanning, trouncing, whaling, whipping, whopping.

thread *n.* cotton, course, direction, drift, fibre, filament, film, fimbria, line, motif, plot, story-line, strain, strand, string, tenor, theme, yarn.
v. ease, inch, meander, pass, string, weave, wind.

threadbare *adj.* clichéd, cliché-ridden, commonplace, conventional, corny, down-at-heel, frayed, hackneyed, moth-eaten, old, overused, overworn, ragged, scruffy, shabby, stale, stereotyped, stock, tattered, tatty, tired, trite, used, well-worn, worn, worn-out.
antonyms fresh, luxurious, new, plush.

thread-like *adj.* fibriform, fibrillar(y), fibrillate(d), filaceous, filamentary, filamentous, filiform, filose, fine, slender, stringy, thin, thready.

threat *n.* commination, danger, foreboding, foreshadowing, frighteners, hazard, menace, omen, peril, portent, presage, risk, sabre-rattling, warning.

threaten *v.* browbeat, bully, comminate, cow, endanger, forebode, foreshadow, impend, imperil, intimidate, jeopardise, menace, portend, presage, pressurise, terrorise, warn.

threatening *adj.* baleful, bullying, cautionary, comminatory, Damoclean, grim, inauspicious, intimidatory, menacing, minacious, minatory, ominous, sinister, terrorising, warning.

threesome *n.* trey, triad, trilogy, trine, trinity, trio, triple, triplet, triplex, triptych, triumvirate, triune, troika.

threshold *n.* beginning, brink, dawn, door, door-sill, door-stead, doorstep, doorway, entrance, inception, minimum, opening, outset, sill, start, starting-point, verge.

thrift *n.* carefulness, conservation, economy, frugality, husbandry, parsimony, prudence, saving, thriftiness.
antonyms profligacy, waste.

thriftless *adj.* dissipative, extravagant, improvident, imprudent, lavish, prodigal, profligate, spendthrift, unthrifty, wasteful.
antonym thrifty.

thrifty *adj.* careful, conserving, economical, frugal, parsimonious, provident, prudent, saving, sparing.
antonyms prodigal, profligate, thriftless, wasteful.

thrill *n.* adventure, buzz, charge, flutter, fluttering, frisson, glow, kick, pleasure, quiver, sensation, shudder, stimulation, throb, tingle, titillation, tremble, tremor, vibration.
v. arouse, electrify, excite, flush, flutter, glow, move, quake, quiver, send, shake, shudder, stimulate, stir, throb, tingle, titillate, tremble, vibrate, wow.

thrilling *adj.* electrifying, exciting, exhilarating, gripping, hair-raising, heart-stirring, quaking, rip-roaring, riveting, rousing, sensational, shaking, shivering, shuddering, soul-stirring, stimulating, stirring, trembling, vibrating.

thrive *v.* advance, bloom, blossom, boom, burgeon, develop, flourish, gain, grow, increase, profit, prosper, succeed, wax.
antonyms die, fail, languish, stagnate.

thriving *adj.* affluent, blooming, blossoming, booming, burgeoning, comfortable, developing, flourishing, growing, healthy, prosperous, successful, wealthy, well.
antonyms ailing, dying, failing, languishing, stagnating.

throat *n.* craw, fauces, gorge, gullet, halse, oesophagus, the Red Lane, thropple, throttle, weasand, windpipe.

throaty *adj.* deep, gruff, guttural, hoarse, husky, low, rasping, raucous, thick.

throb *v.* beat, palpitate, pound, pulsate, pulse, thump, vibrate.
n. beat, palpitation, pounding, pulsating, pulsation, pulse, thump, thumping, vibration, vibrato.

throe *n.* convulsion, fit, pain, pang, paroxysm, seizure, spasm, stab.

throes *n.* agony, anguish, death-agony, distress, pain, suffering, torture, travail.

throng *n.* assemblage, bevy, concourse, congregation, crowd, crush, flock, herd, horde, host, jam, mass, mob, multitude, pack, press, swarm.

v. bunch, congregate, converge, cram, crowd, fill, flock, herd, jam, mill around, pack, press, swarm.

throttle *v.* asphyxiate, choke, control, gag, garrotte, inhibit, silence, smother, stifle, strangle, strangulate, suppress.

through *prep.* as a result of, because of, between, by, by means of, by reason of, by virtue of, by way of, during, in, in and out of, in consequence of, in the middle of, past, thanks to, throughout, using, via.

adj. completed, direct, done, ended, express, finished, non-stop, terminated.

through and through altogether, completely, entirely, from top to bottom, fully, thoroughly, to the core, totally, unreservedly, utterly, wholly.

throughout *adv.* everywhere, extensively, ubiquitously, widely.

throw *v.* astonish, baffle, bemuse, bring down, cast, chuck, confound, confuse, defeat, discomfit, disconcert, dislodge, dumbfound, elance, execute, fell, fling, floor, heave, hurl, jaculate, launch, lob, overturn, perform, perplex, pitch, produce, project, propel, put, send, shy, sling, slug, toss, unhorse, unsaddle, unseat, upset, whang.

n. attempt, cast, chance, essay, fling, gamble, hazard, heave, lob, pitch, projection, put, shy, sling, spill, toss, try, venture, wager.

throw away blow, blue, cast off, discard, dispense with, dispose of, ditch, dump, fritter away, jettison, lose, reject, scrap, squander, waste.

antonyms keep, preserve, rescue, salvage.

throw dust in the eyes of con, confuse, cozen, deceive, delude, dupe, fool, have on, hoodwink, mislead, take in.

throw off abandon, cast off, confuse, discard, disconcert, disturb, doff, drop, shake off, throw, unsaddle, unseat, unsettle, upset.

throw out confuse, diffuse, discard, disconcert, dismiss, disseminate, disturb, ditch, dump, egurgitate, eject, emit, evict, expel, give off, jettison, radiate, reject, scrap, throw, turf out, turn down, unhouse, unsettle, upset, utter.

throw over abandon, chuck, desert, discard, drop, finish with, forsake, jilt, leave, quit, reject.

throw up abandon, chuck, disgorge, egurgitate, give up, heave, jack in, leave, produce, puke, quit, regurgitate, relinquish, renounce, resign, retch, reveal, spew, vomit.

throwaway *adj.* careless, casual, cheap, disposable, offhand, passing, undramatic, unemphatic.

thrust *v.* bear, butt, drive, force, impel, intrude, jab, jam, lunge, pierce, plunge, poke, press, prod, propel, push, ram, shove, stab, stick, urge, wedge.

n. drive, flanconade, impetus, lunge, momentum, poke, prod, prog, push, shove, stab, stoccado.

thud *n.* clonk, clump, clunk, crash, knock, smack, thump, thwack, wallop, wham.

v. bash, clonk, clump, clunk, crash, knock, smack, thump, thunder, thwack, wallop, wham.

thug *n.* animal, assassin, bandit, bangster, bruiser, bully-boy, cut-throat, gangster, goon, gorilla, heavy, highbinder, hood, hoodlum, hooligan, killer, mugger, murderer, robber, ruffian, tough.

thumb one's nose at cock a snook at, deride, flout, guy, jeer at, laugh at, mock, ridicule, scoff.

thumb through browse through, flick through, flip through, glance at, leaf through, peruse, riffle through, scan, skim.

thumbnail *adj.* brief, compact, concise, miniature, pithy, quick, short, small, succinct.

thumbs down disapproval, negation, no, rebuff, refusal, rejection, turn-down.

antonym thumbs up.

thumbs up acceptance, affirmation, approval, encouragement, go-ahead, green light, OK, sanction, yes.

antonym thumbs down.

thump *n.* bang, blow, box, clout, clunk, crash, cuff, knock, rap, smack, thud, thwack, wallop, whack.

v. bang, batter, beat, belabour, box, clout, crash, cuff, daud, ding, dunt, dush, hit, knock, lambaste, pound, rap, smack, strike, thrash, throb, thud, thwack, wallop, whack.

thumping *adj.* big, colossal, enormous, excessive, exorbitant, gargantuan, gigantic, great, huge, immense, impressive, mammoth, massive, monumental, terrific, thundering, titanic, towering, tremendous, whooping.

antonyms insignificant, petty, piddling, trivial.

thunder *n.* boom, booming, clap, cracking, crash, crashing, detonation, explosion, pealing, roll, rumble, rumbling.

v. bark, bellow, blast, boom, clap, crack, crash, curse, declaim, denounce, detonate, explode, fulminate, inveigh, peal, rail, resound, reverberate, roar, rumble, shout, threaten, yell.

thundering *adj.* enormous, excessive, great, monumental, remarkable, tremendous, unmitigated.

thunderous *adj.* booming, deafening, earsplitting, loud, noisy, resounding, reverberating, roaring, stentorian, tumultuous.

thunderstruck *adj.* agape, aghast, amazed, astonished, astounded, dazed, dumbfounded, flabbergasted, floored, flummoxed, nonplussed, open-mouthed, paralysed, petrified, shocked, staggered, stunned.

thus *adv.* accordingly, as follows, consequently, ergo, hence, in this way, like so, like this, so, then, therefore, thuswise.

thwack v. bash, beat, buffet, clout, cuff, flog, hit, slap, smack, thump, wallop, whack.

   n. bash, blow, buffet, cloud, cuff, slap, smack, thump, wallop, whack.

thwart v. baffle, balk, check, defeat, foil, frustrate, hinder, impede, obstruct, oppose, outwit, prevent, spite, stonker, stop, stymie, transverse, traverse.

   antonyms abet, aid, assist.

tic *n.* jerk, spasm, tic douloureux, twitch.

tick *n.* clack, click, clicking, dash, flash, instant, jiffy, mark, minute, moment, sec, second, shake, stroke, tap, tapping, tick-tick, tick-tock, trice, twinkling.

   v. beat, choose, clack, click, indicate, mark (off), select, tally, tap.

tick off bawl out, berate, censure, chide, haul over the coals, keelhaul, lecture, rebuke, reprimand, reproach, reprove, scold, take to task, tear off a strip, tell off, upbraid.

   antonym praise.

ticket *n.* card, certificate, coupon, docket, label, marker, pass, slip, sticker, tab, tag, tessera, token, voucher.

tickle v. amuse, cheer, delight, divert, enchant, entertain, excite, gratify, please, thrill, titillate.

ticklish *adj.* awkward, critical, delicate, difficult, dodgy, hazardous, nice, precarious, risky, sensitive, thorny, touchy, tricky, uncertain, unstable, unsteady.

   antonyms easy, straightforward.

tide *n.* course, current, direction, drift, ebb, flow, flux, movement, stream, tendency, tenor, trend.

tidings *n.* advice, bulletin, communication, dope, gen, greetings, information, intelligence, message, news, report, word.

tidy *adj.* ample, businesslike, clean, cleanly, considerable, fair, generous, good, goodly, handsome, healthy, large, largish, methodical, neat, ordered, orderly, respectable, shipshape, siz(e)able, spick, spick-and-span, spruce, substantial, systematic, trim, uncluttered, well-groomed, well-kept.

   antonyms disorganised, untidy.

   v. arrange, clean, fettle, groom, neaten, order, spruce up, straighten.

tie v. attach, bind, confine, connect, draw, equal, fasten, hamper, hinder, hold, interlace, join, knot, lash, ligature, limit, link, match, moor, oblige, restrain, restrict, rope, secure, strap, tether, truss, unite.

   n. affiliation, allegiance, band, bond, commitment, connection, contest, copula, cord, dead heat, deadlock, draw, duty, encumbrance, fastening, fetter, fixture, game, hindrance, joint, kinship, knot, liaison, ligature, limitation, link, match, obligation, relationship, restraint, restriction, rope, stalemate, string.

tie up attach, bind, conclude, end, engage, engross, finish off, lash, ligate, moor, occupy, pinion, restrain, rope, secure, settle, terminate, tether, truss, wind up, wrap up.

tie-in *n.* affiliation, association, connection,

co-ordination, hook-up, liaison, link, relation, relationship, tie-up.

tier *n.* band, belt, echelon, floor, gradin(e), layer, level, line, rank, row, stage, storey, stratification, stratum, zone.

tiff *n.* barney, difference, disagreement, dispute, falling-out, huff, ill-humour, pet, quarrel, row, scrap, set-to, spat, squabble, sulk, tantrum, temper, words.

tight[1] *adj.* close, close-fitting, compact, competent, constricted, cramped, dangerous, difficult, even, evenly-balanced, fast, firm, fixed, grasping, harsh, hazardous, hermetic, impervious, inflexible, mean, miserly, narrow, near, niggardly, parsimonious, penurious, perilous, precarious, precise, problematic, proof, rigid, rigorous, sealed, secure, severe, snug, sound, sparing, stern, sticky, stiff, stingy, stretched, strict, stringent, taut, tense, ticklish, tight-fisted, tough, tricky, trig, troublesome, uncompromising, unyielding, watertight, well-matched, worrisome.

   antonyms lax, loose, slack.

tight[2] *adj.* blotto, drunk, half cut, half-seas-over, in one's cups, inebriated, intoxicated, pickled, pie-eyed, pissed, plastered, smashed, sozzled, stewed, stoned, three sheets in the wind, tiddly, tipsy, under the influence.

   antonym sober.

tighten v. close, constrict, constringe, cramp, crush, fasten, fix, narrow, rigidify, screw, secure, squeeze, stiffen, stretch, tauten, tense.

   antonyms loosen, relax.

tight-fisted *adj.* cheese-paring, close, close-fisted, grasping, mean, mingy, miserly, niggardly, parsimonious, penny-pinching, penurious, sparing, stingy, tight.

   antonym generous.

tight-lipped *adj.* close-lipped, close-mouthed, mum, mute, quiet, reserved, reticent, secretive, silent, taciturn, uncommunicative, unforthcoming.

   antonyms garrulous, talkative.

till v. cultivate, dig, dress, plough, work.

tilt v. attack, cant, clash, contend, duel, encounter, fight, heel, incline, joust, lean, list, overthrow, pitch, slant, slope, spar, tip.

   n. angle, cant, clash, combat, duel, encounter, fight, inclination, incline, joust, list, lists, pitch, set-to, slant, slope, thrust, tournament, tourney.

timber *n.* beams, boarding, boards, forest, logs, planking, planks, trees, wood.

timbre *n.* colour, klang, resonance, ring, tonality, tone, voice quality.

time *n.* age, beat, chronology, date, day, duration, epoch, era, generation, heyday, hour, instance, interval, juncture, life, life-span, lifetime, measure, metre, occasion, peak, period, point, rhythm, season, space, span, spell, stage, stretch, tempo, term, tide, while.

   v. clock, control, count, judge, measure, meter, regulate, schedule, set.

time and again frequently, many times, often, on many occasions, over and over again, recurrently, repeatedly, time after time.

time-honoured *adj.* accustomed, age-old, ancient, conventional, customary, established, fixed, historic, long-established, old, traditional, usual, venerable.

timeless *adj.* abiding, ageless, amaranthine, ceaseless, changeless, deathless, endless, enduring, eternal, everlasting, immortal, immutable, imperishable, indestructible, lasting, permanent, perpetual, persistent, undying.

timely *adj.* appropriate, convenient, judicious, opportune, prompt, propitious, punctual, seasonable, suitable, tempestive, well-timed. *antonyms* ill-timed, inappropriate, unfavourable.

timetable *n.* agenda, calendar, curriculum, diary, list, listing, programme, roster, rota, schedule.

time-worn *adj.* aged, ancient, broken-down, bromidic, cliché'd, dated, decrepit, dog-eared, hackneyed, hoary, lined, old hat, out of date, outworn, passé, ragged, ruined, run-down, shabby, stale, stock, threadbare, tired, trite, weathered, well-worn, worn, wrinkled. *antonyms* fresh, new.

timid *adj.* afraid, apprehensive, bashful, cowardly, coy, diffident, faint-hearted, fearful, hen-hearted, irresolute, modest, mousy, nervous, pavid, pusillanimous, retiring, shrinking, shy, spineless, timorous. *antonyms* audacious, bold, brave.

timorous *adj.* afraid, apprehensive, aspen, bashful, cowardly, coy, diffident, faint-hearted, fearful, inadventurous, irresolute, modest, mousy, nervous, pusillanimous, retiring, shrinking, shy, tentative, timid, trembling. *antonyms* assertive, assured, bold.

tincture *n.* aroma, colour, dash, flavour, hint, hue, seasoning, shade, smack, stain, suggestion, tinct, tinge, tint, touch, trace.

v. colour, dye, flavour, imbue, infuse, permeate, scent, season, stain, suffuse, tinge, tint.

tinge *n.* bit, cast, colour, dash, drop, dye, flavour, pinch, shade, smack, smatch, smattering, sprinkling, stain, suggestion, tinct, tincture, tint, touch, trace, wash.

v. colour, dye, encolour, imbue, shade, stain, suffuse, tint.

tingle *v.* dindle, itch, prickle, ring, sting, thrill, throb, tickle, vibrate.

n. frisson, gooseflesh, goose-pimples, itch, itching, pins and needles, prickling, quiver, shiver, stinging, thrill, tickle, tickling.

tinker *v.* dabble, fiddle, meddle, monkey, play, potter, putter, toy, trifle.

n. botcher, bungler, diddicoy, fixer, itinerant, mender.

tinsel *adj.* brummagem, cheap, clinquant, flashy, gaudy, gimcrack, meretricious, ostentatious, pinchbeck, plastic, sham, showy, specious,

superficial, tawdry, trashy.

n. artificiality, clinquant, display, flamboyance, frippery, garishness, gaudiness, glitter, insignificance, meaninglessness, ostentation, pinchbeck, pretension, sham, show, spangle, triviality, worthlessness.

tint *n.* cast, colour, dye, hint, hue, rinse, shade, stain, streak, suggestion, tinct, tincture, tinge, tone, touch, trace, wash.

v. affect, colour, dye, influence, rinse, stain, streak, taint, tincture, tinge.

tiny *adj.* diminutive, dwarfish, infinitesimal, insignificant, itsy-bitsy, Lilliputian, little, microscopic, mini, miniature, minute, negligible, petite, pint-size(d), pocket, puny, pygmy, slight, small, teensy, teentsy, teeny, teeny-weeny, tiddl(e)y, tottie, totty, trifling, wee, weeny. *antonyms* big, immense.

tip[1] *n.* acme, apex, cap, crown, end, extremity, ferrule, head, nib, peak, pinnacle, point, summit, top.

v. cap, crown, finish, pinnacle, poll, pollard, prune, surmount, top.

tip[2] *v.* cant, capsize, ditch, dump, empty, heel, incline, lean, list, overturn, pour out, slant, spill, tilt, topple over, unload, up-end, upset.

n. bing, coup, dump, midden, refuse-heap, rubbish-heap, slag-heap.

tip[3] *n.* baksheesh, clue, forecast, gen, gift, gratuity, hint, information, inside information, lagniappe, perquisite, pointer, pourboire, refresher, suggestion, tip-off, warning, word, word of advice, wrinkle.

v. advise, caution, forewarn, inform, remunerate, reward, suggest, tell, warn.

tipple *v.* bib, drink, imbibe, indulge, quaff, swig, tope.

n. alcohol, booze, drink, liquor, poison, wet.

tippler *n.* bibber, boozer, dipso(maniac), drinker, drunk, drunkard, inebriate, lush, soak, sot, sponge, toper, wine-bag.

tipsy *adj.* a peg too low, a pip out, cockeyed, corny, drunk, elevated, fuddled, happy, mellow, merry, moony, moppy, mops and brooms, nappy, pixil(l)ated, rocky, screwed, screwy, slewed, sprung, squiff(y), tiddled, tiddley, tiddly, tight, totty, wet, woozy. *antonym* sober.

tirade *n.* abuse, denunciation, diatribe, fulmination, harangue, invective, lecture, outburst, philippic, rant.

tire *v.* annoy, betoil, bore, cook, drain, droop, enervate, exasperate, exhaust, fag, fail, fatigue, flag, harass, irk, irritate, jade, knacker, sink, weary. *antonyms* energise, enliven, exhilarate, invigorate, refresh.

tired *adj.* all in, awearied, aweary, beat, bone-weary, bushed, clapped-out, clichéd, conventional, corny, dead-beat, disjaskit, dog-tired, drained, drooping, drowsy, enervated, épuisé(e), exhausted, fagged, familiar, fatigued, flagging, forfairn, forfough(t)en, forjeskit, hackneyed, jaded, knackered, old,

outworn, shagged, shattered, sleepy, spent, stale, stock, threadbare, trite, weary, well-worn, whacked, worn out.
antonyms active, energetic, fresh, lively, rested.

tireless *adj.* determined, diligent, energetic, indefatigable, industrious, resolute, sedulous, unflagging, untiring, unwearied, vigorous.
antonyms tired, unenthusiastic, weak.

tiresome *adj.* annoying, boring, bothersome, dull, exasperating, fatiguing, flat, irksome, irritating, laborious, monotonous, pesky, tedious, troublesome, trying, uninteresting, vexatious, wearing, wearisome.
antonyms easy, interesting, stimulating.

tiring *adj.* arduous, demanding, draining, enervating, enervative, exacting, exhausting, fagging, fatiguing, laborious, strenuous, tough, wearing, wearying.

tiro *n.* apprentice, beginner, catechumen, freshman, greenhorn, initiate, learner, neophyte, novice, novitiate, pupil, starter, student, tenderfoot, trainee.
antonyms old hand, veteran.

tissue *n.* accumulation, agglomeration, collection, combination, concatenation, conglomeration, fabric, fabrication, gauze, mass, mesh, network, pack, paper, series, structure, stuff, texture, tissue-paper, web.

tit for tat a Roland for an Oliver, counterblow, counterbuff, countercharge, lex talionis, measure for measure, quid pro quo, requital, retaliation, revenge, talion.

titan *n.* Atlas, colossus, giant, Hercules, leviathan, superman.

titanic *adj.* Brobdingnagian, colossal, cyclopean, enormous, giant, gigantic, herculean, huge, immense, jumbo, mammoth, massive, mighty, monstrous, monumental, mountainous, prodigious, stupendous, towering, vast.
antonyms insignificant, small.

titbit *n.* appetiser, bonne bouche, dainty, delicacy, goody, morsel, scrap, snack, tidbit, treat.

tithe *n.* assessment, duty, impost, levy, rent, tariff, tax, tenth, toll, tribute.
v. assess, charge, give, hand over, levy, pay, rate, take in, tax.

titillate *v.* arouse, captivate, excite, interest, intrigue, provoke, stimulate, tantalise, tease, thrill, tickle, turn on.

titillating *adj.* arousing, captivating, exciting, interesting, intriguing, lewd, lurid, provocative, sensational, stimulating, suggestive, teasing, thrilling.

titivate *v.* doll up, make up, prank, preen, primp, prink, refurbish, smarten up, tart up, touch up.

title *n.* appellation, caption, championship, claim, crown, denomination, designation, entitlement, epithet, handle, heading, inscription, label, laurels, legend, letterhead, moniker, name, nickname, nom de plume, ownership, prerogative, privilege,

pseudonym, right, sobriquet, style, term.
v. call, christen, designate, dub, entitle, label, name, style, term.

titter *v.* chortle, chuckle, giggle, laugh, mock, snigger, tee-hee.

tittle-tattle *n.* babble, blather, blether, cackle, chatter, chitchat, clishmaclaver, gossip, hearsay, jaw, natter, prattle, rumour, twaddle, ya(c)k, yackety-yak.
v. babble, blather, blether, cackle, chat, chatter, chitchat, gossip, jaw, natter, prattle, tell tales, witter, ya(c)k, yackety-yak.

titular *adj.* formal, honorary, nominal, puppet, putative, so-called, token.

to a fault excessively, immoderately, in the extreme, needlessly, out of all proportion, over the top, overly, overmuch, preposterously, ridiculously, to extremes, unduly.

to a man bar none, every one, nem con, one and all, unanimously, without exception.

to a turn correctly, exactly, perfectly, precisely, to perfection.

to all intents and purposes as good as, practically, pretty much, pretty well, virtually.

to be reckoned with consequential, considerable, formidable, important, influential, powerful, significant, strong, weighty.

to the full completely, entirely, fully, thoroughly, to the utmost, utterly.

to the hilt absolutely, completely, entirely, fully, totally, wholly.

to the letter accurately, exactly, literally, literatim, precisely, spot on, strictly, word for word.

to the point applicable, apposite, appropriate, apropos, apt, brief, fitting, germane, pertinent, pithy, pointed, relevant, short, suitable, terse.
antonym irrelevant.

toady *n.* arse-licker, bootlicker, clawback, crawler, creep, fawner, flatterer, flunkey, groveller, hanger-on, jackal, Jenkins, lackey, lick-platter, lickspittle, lick-spittle, minion, nark, parasite, pick-thank, running dog, spaniel, sucker, sycophant, toad-eater, truckler, tuft-hunter, yes-man.
v. bootlick, bow and scrape, butter up, crawl, creep, cringe, curry favour, fawn, flatter, grovel, kiss the feet, kowtow, suck up, truckle.

toast[1] *v.* broil, brown, grill, heat, roast, warm.

toast[2] *n.* compliment, darling, drink, favourite, grace cup, health, hero, heroine, pledge, salutation, salute, tribute, wassail.

to-do *n.* agitation, bother, brouhaha, bustle, commotion, disturbance, excitement, flap, flurry, furore, fuss, hoo-ha, performance, pother, quarrel, ruction, rumpus, stew, stir, stramash, tumult, turmoil, unrest, uproar.

together *adv.* all at once, arranged, as one, as one man, at the same time, cheek by jowl, closely, collectively, concurrently, consecutively, contemporaneously, continuously, en masse, fixed, hand in glove, hand in hand, in a body, in a row, in concert, in co-operation, in fere, in mass, in succession, in unison, jointly, mutually, on end, ordered, organised, pari passu, settled, shoulder to shoulder, side by side, simultaneously, sorted out, straight, successively.

antonym separately.

adj. calm, commonsensical, composed, cool, down-to-earth, level-headed, sensible, stable, well-adjusted, well-balanced, well-organised.

toil *n.* application, donkey-work, drudgery, effort, elbow grease, exertion, graft, industry, labor improbus, labour, pains, slog, sweat, travail, yakka.

v. drudge, graft, grind, grub, labour, persevere, plug away, slave, slog, strive, struggle, sweat, tew, work.

toiler *n.* donkey, drudge, grafter, labourer, menial, navvy, slave, slogger, struggler, workaholic, worker, workhorse, workman.

antonyms idler, loafer, shirker.

toilet *n.* ablutions, bathing, bathroom, bog, can, closet, comfort station, convenience, dressing, gents', grooming, john, ladies', latrine, lavatory, loo, outhouse, powder-room, privy, reredorter, rest-room, smallest room, thunder-box, toilette, urinal, washroom, water closet, WC.

toilsome *adj.* arduous, backbreaking, burdensome, difficult, fatiguing, hard, herculean, laborious, painful, severe, strenuous, taxing, tedious, tiresome, tough, uphill, wearisome.

token *n.* badge, clue, demonstration, earnest, evidence, expression, index, indication, keepsake, manifestation, mark, memento, memorial, note, proof, remembrance, reminder, representation, sign, souvenir, symbol, tessera, testimony, voucher, warning.

adj. emblematic, hollow, inconsiderable, minimal, nominal, perfunctory, superficial, symbolic.

tolerable *adj.* acceptable, adequate, all right, allowable, average, bearable, endurable, fair, fair to middling, indifferent, liv(e)able, mediocre, middling, not bad, OK, ordinary, passable, run-of-the-mill, so-so, sufferable, supportable, unexceptional.

antonym intolerable.

tolerance *n.* allowance, broad-mindedness, charity, endurance, fluctuation, forbearance, fortitude, hardiness, hardness, indulgence, lenity, magnanimity, open-mindedness, patience, permissiveness, play, resilience, resistance, rope, stamina, sufferance, swing, sympathy, toughness, variation.

antonyms bigotry, intolerance, narrow-mindedness, prejudice.

tolerant *adj.* biddable, broad-minded, catholic, charitable, complaisant, compliant, easy-going, fair, forbearing, indulgent, kind-hearted, latitudinarian, lax, lenient, liberal, long-suffering, magnanimous, open-minded, patient, permissive, soft, sympathetic, understanding, unprejudiced.

antonyms biased, bigoted, intolerant, prejudiced, unsympathetic.

tolerate *v.* abear, abide, accept, admit, allow, bear, brook, condone, connive at, countenance, endure, indulge, permit, pocket, put up with, receive, sanction, stand, stomach, suffer, swallow, take, thole, turn a blind eye to, undergo, wear, wink at.

toleration *n.* acceptance, allowance, condonation, connivance, endurance, indulgence, permissiveness, sanction, sufferance, tholing, wearing.

toll[1] *v.* announce, call, chime, clang, knell, peal, ring, send, signal, sound, strike, summon, warn.

toll[2] *n.* assessment, charge, cost, customs, damage, demand, duty, fee, impost, inroad, levy, loss, payment, penalty, rate, tariff, tax, tithe, tribute.

tomb *n.* burial-place, catacomb, cenotaph, crypt, dolmen, grave, mastaba, mausoleum, sepulchre, sepulture, speos, vault.

tomboy *n.* gamine, gilp(e)y, hempy, hoyden, minx, randie, randy, romp.

tombstone *n.* gravestone, headstone, marker, memorial, monument, stone.

tome *n.* book, opus, volume, work.

tomfoolery *n.* balderdash, baloney, bilge, bosh, buffoonery, bunk, bunkum, childishness, claptrap, clowning, foolishness, hogwash, hooey, horseplay, idiocy, inanity, larking about, larks, messing about, messing on, nonsense, poppycock, rot, rubbish, shenanigans, silliness, skylarking, stupidity, tommy-rot, tosh, trash, twaddle.

tone *n.* accent, air, approach, aspect, attitude, cast, character, colour, drift, effect, emphasis, feel, force, frame, grain, harmony, hue, inflection, intonation, klang, manner, modulation, mood, note, pitch, quality, shade, spirit, strength, stress, style, temper, tenor, timbre, tinge, tint, tonality, vein, volume.

v. blend, harmonise, intone, match, sound, suit.

tone down alleviate, assuage, dampen, dim, mitigate, moderate, modulate, palliate, play down, reduce, restrain, soften, soft-pedal, subdue, temper.

tone up brighten, freshen, invigorate, limber up, shape up, sharpen up, touch up, trim, tune up.

tongue *n.* argot, articulation, clack, clapper, dialect, discourse, idiom, language, languet(te), lath, lingo, parlance, patois, red rag, speech, talk, utterance, vernacular, voice.

tongue-tied *adj.* dumb, dumbstruck, inarticulate, mute, silent, speechless, voiceless.

antonyms garrulous, talkative, voluble.

tonic *n.* analeptic, boost, bracer, cordial, fillip, inspiration, livener, pick-me-up, refresher, restorative, roborant, shot in the arm, stimulant.

too[1] *adv.* also, as well, besides, further, in addition, into the bargain, likewise, moreover, to boot, what's more.

too[2] *adv.* excessively, exorbitantly, extremely,

immoderately, inordinately, over, overly, ridiculously, to excess, to extremes, unduly, unreasonably, very.

tool *n.* agency, agent, apparatus, appliance, cat's-paw, contraption, contrivance, creature, device, dupe, flunkey, front, gadget, hireling, implement, instrument, intermediary, jackal, lackey, machine, means, medium, minion, pawn, puppet, stooge, toady, utensil, vehicle, weapon, widget.
v. chase, cut, decorate, fashion, machine, ornament, shape, work.

tooth *n.* cog, denticle, denticulation, dentil, fang, incisor, jag, masticator, molar, prong, tush, tusk.

toothless *adj.* edentate, edentulous, fangless, gummy, powerless.

toothsome *adj.* agreeable, ambrosial, appetising, dainty, delectable, delicious, flavoursome, luscious, mouthwatering, nice, palatable, sapid, savoury, scrumptious, sweet, tasty, tempting, yummy.
antonyms disagreeable, unpleasant.

top *n.* acme, apex, apogee, cacumen, cap, cop, cork, cover, crest, crown, culmen, culmination, head, height, high point, lead, lid, meridian, peak, pinnacle, stopper, summit, upside, vertex, zenith.
antonyms base, bottom, nadir.
adj. best, chief, crack, crowning, culminating, dominant, elite, finest, first, foremost, greatest, head, highest, lead, leading, pre-eminent, prime, principal, ruling, sovereign, superior, topmost, upmost, upper, upper-most.
v. ascend, beat, best, better, cap, climb, command, cover, crest, crown, decorate, eclipse, exceed, excel, finish, finish off, garnish, head, lead, outdo, outshine, outstrip, roof, rule, scale, surmount, surpass, tip, transcend.

topic *n.* issue, lemma, matter, motif, point, question, subject, subject-matter, talking-point, text, theme, thesis.

topical *adj.* contemporary, current, familiar, newsworthy, popular, relevant, up-to-date, up-to-the-minute.

topmost *adj.* apical, dominant, foremost, highest, leading, loftiest, maximum, paramount, principal, supreme, top, upper, uppermost.
antonyms bottom, bottommost, lowest.

topple *v.* capsize, collapse, oust, overbalance, overthrow, overturn, totter, tumble, unseat, upset.

topsy-turvy *adj.* arsy-versy, backside-foremost, chaotic, confused, disarranged, disorderly, disorganised, inside-out, jumbled, messy, mixed-up, untidy, upside-down.
antonyms ordered, tidy.

torch *n.* brand, cresset, firebrand, flambeau, flashlight, lampad, link.

torment *v.* afflict, agitate, agonise, annoy, bedevil, bother, chivvy, crucify, devil, distort, distress, excruciate, harass, harrow, harry, hound, irritate, nag, pain, persecute, pester,

plague, provoke, rack, tease, torture, trouble, vex, worry, wrack.
n. affliction, agony, angst, anguish, annoyance, bane, bother, distress, harassment, hassle, hell, irritation, misery, nag, nagging, nuisance, pain, persecution, pest, plague, provocation, scourge, suffering, torture, trouble, vexation, worry.

torn *adj.* cut, dithering, divided, havering, irresolute, lacerated, ragged, rent, ripped, slit, split, swithering, uncertain, undecided, unsure, vacillating, wavering.

tornado *n.* cyclone, gale, hurricane, monsoon, squall, storm, tempest, twister, typhoon, whirlwind.

torpid *adj.* apathetic, benumbed, dormant, drowsy, dull, fainéant, hebetudinous, inactive, indolent, inert, lackadaisical, languid, languorous, lazy, lethargic, listless, lymphatic, motionless, numb, passive, slothful, slow, slow-moving, sluggish, somnolent, stagnant, supine.
antonyms active, lively, vigorous.

torpor *n.* accidie, acedia, apathy, dormancy, drowsiness, dullness, hebetude, inactivity, inanition, indolence, inertia, inertness, languor, laziness, lethargy, listlessness, numbness, passivity, sloth, sluggishness, somnolence, stagnancy, stupidity, stupor, torpidity.
antonyms activity, animation, vigour.

torrent *n.* barrage, cascade, deluge, downpour, effusion, flood, flow, gush, outburst, rush, spate, stream, tide, volley.

torrid *adj.* ardent, arid, blistering, boiling, broiling, burning, dried, dry, emotional, erotic, fervent, fiery, hot, intense, parched, parching, passionate, scorched, scorching, sexy, sizzling, steamy, stifling, sultry, sweltering, tropical.
antonym arctic.

tortuous *adj.* ambagious, ambiguous, bent, Byzantine, circuitous, complicated, convoluted, crooked, cunning, curved, deceptive, devious, indirect, involved, mazy, meandering, misleading, roundabout, serpentine, sinuous, tricky, twisted, twisting, winding, zigzag.
antonyms straight, straightforward.

torture *v.* afflict, agonise, crucify, distress, excruciate, harrow, lacerate, martyr, martyrise, pain, persecute, rack, torment, wrack.
n. affliction, agony, anguish, distress, gyp, hell, laceration, martyrdom, misery, pain, pang(s), persecution, rack, suffering, torment.

toss *v.* agitate, cant, cast, chuck, disturb, fling, flip, heave, hurl, jiggle, joggle, jolt, labour, launch, lob, lurch, pitch, project, propel, rock, roll, shake, shy, sling, thrash, throw, tumble, wallow, welter, wriggle, writhe.
n. cast, chuck, fling, lob, pitch, shy, sling, throw.

tot *n.* baby, bairn, child, dram, finger, infant, measure, mite, nip, shot, slug, snifter, toddler, toothful, wean.

tot up add (up), calculate, compute, count (up), reckon, sum, tally, total.

total *n.* aggregate, all, amount, ensemble, entirety, lot, mass, sum, totality, whole.
adj. absolute, all-out, complete, comprehensive, consummate, downright, entire, full, gross, integral, out-and-out, outright, perfect, root-and-branch, sheer, sweeping, thorough, thoroughgoing, unconditional, undisputed, undivided, unmitigated, unqualified, utter, whole, whole-hog.
antonyms limited, partial, restricted.
v. add (up), amount to, come to, count (up), reach, reckon, sum (up), tot up.

totalitarian *adj.* authoritarian, despotic, dictatorial, monocratic, monolithic, omnipotent, one-party, oppressive, tyrannous, undemocratic.
antonym democratic.

totality *n.* aggregate, all, completeness, cosmos, entireness, entirety, everything, fullness, pleroma, sum, total, universe, whole, wholeness.

totally *adv.* absolutely, completely, comprehensively, consummately, entirely, fully, perfectly, quite, thoroughly, unconditionally, undisputedly, undividedly, unmitigatedly, utterly, wholeheartedly, wholly.
antonym partially.

totter *v.* daddle, daidle, falter, lurch, quiver, reel, rock, shake, stagger, stumble, sway, teeter, titter, tremble, waver.

touch *n.* ability, acquaintance, adroitness, approach, art, artistry, awareness, bit, blow, brush, caress, characteristic, command, communication, contact, correspondence, dash, deftness, detail, direction, drop, effect, facility, familiarity, feel, feeling, flair, fondling, hand, handiwork, handling, hint, hit, influence, intimation, jot, knack, manner, mastery, method, palpation, pat, pinch, push, skill, smack, smattering, soupçon, speck, spot, stroke, style, suggestion, suspicion, tactility, tap, taste, technique, tig, tincture, tinge, trace, trademark, understanding, virtuosity, way, whiff.
v. abut, adjoin, affect, attain, border, brush, caress, cheat, compare with, concern, consume, contact, converge, disturb, drink, eat, equal, feel, finger, fondle, graze, handle, hit, hold a candle to, impress, influence, inspire, interest, mark, match, meet, melt, move, palp, palpate, parallel, pat, pertain to, push, reach, regard, rival, soften, stir, strike, stroke, tap, tat, tinge, upset, use, utilise.

touch off actuate, arouse, begin, cause, fire, foment, ignite, inflame, initiate, light, provoke, set off, spark off, trigger (off).

touch on allude to, broach, cover, deal with, mention, refer to, remark on, speak of.

touch up arouse, brush up, enhance, finish off, fondle, improve, patch up, perfect, polish up, renovate, retouch, revamp, round off, stimulate, titivate.

touch-and-go *adj.* close, critical, dangerous, dodgy, hairy, hazardous, near, nerve-racking, offhand, parlous, perilous, precarious, risky, sticky, tricky.

touched *adj.* affected, barmy, batty, bonkers, crazy, cuckoo, daft, disturbed, dotty, eccentric, impressed, mad, melted, moved, nuts, nutty, softened, stirred, swayed, upset.

touchiness *n.* bad temper, captiousness, crabbedness, grouchiness, grumpiness, irascibility, irritability, peevishness, pettishness, petulance, surliness, testiness, tetchiness.

touching *adj.* affecting, emotional, emotive, haptic, heartbreaking, libant, melting, moving, pathetic, piteous, pitiable, pitiful, poignant, sad, stirring, tender.

touchstone *n.* bench-mark, criterion, gauge, measure, norm, proof, standard, yardstick.

touchy *adj.* bad-tempered, captious, crabbed, cross, feisty, grouchy, grumpy, huffy, irascible, irritable, miffy, peevish, pettish, petulant, querulous, quick-tempered, snippety, snuffy, sore, splenetic, surly, testy, tetchy, thin-skinned.
antonyms calm, imperturbable, serene, unflappable.

tough *adj.* adamant, arduous, bad, baffling, brawny, butch, callous, cohesive, difficult, durable, exacting, exhausting, firm, fit, hard, hard-bitten, hard-boiled, hardened, hardnosed, hardy, herculean, inflexible, intractable, irksome, knotty, laborious, lamentable, leathery, merciless, obdurate, obstinate, perplexing, pugnacious, puzzling, refractory, regrettable, resilient, resistant, resolute, rigid, rough, ruffianly, rugged, ruthless, seasoned, severe, solid, stalwart, stern, stiff, stout, strapping, strenuous, strict, strong, stubborn, sturdy, tenacious, thorny, troublesome, unbending, unforgiving, unfortunate, unlucky, unyielding, uphill, vicious, vigorous, violent.
antonyms brittle, delicate, fragile, liberal, soft, tender, vulnerable, weak.
n. bravo, bruiser, brute, bully, bully-boy, bully-rook, gorilla, hooligan, rough, roughneck, rowdy, ruffian, thug, yob, yobbo.

toughness *n.* arduousness, callousness, difficulty, durability, firmness, fitness, grit, hardiness, hardness, inflexibility, intractability, laboriousness, obduracy, obstinacy, pugnacity, resilience, resistance, rigidity, roughness, ruggedness, ruthlessness, severity, solidity, sternness, stiffness, strength, strenuousness, strictness, sturdiness, tenacity, viciousness.
antonyms fragility, liberality, softness, vulnerability, weakness.

tour *n.* circuit, course, drive, excursion, expedition, jaunt, journey, outing, peregrination, progress, ride, round, trip.
v. drive, explore, journey, ride, sightsee, travel, visit.

tourist *n.* emmet, excursionist, globe-trotter, grockle, holidaymaker, journeyer, rubberneck, sightseer, sojourner, traveller, tripper, voyager.

tournament n. championship, competition, contest, event, joust, lists, match, meeting, series, tourney.

tourniquet n. garrot.

tousled adj. disarranged, dishevelled, disordered, messed up, ruffled, rumpled, tangled, tumbled.

tow v. drag, draw, haul, lug, pull, tote, trail, transport, trawl, tug, yank.

towards adv. a little short of, about, almost, approaching, close to, coming up to, concerning, for, getting on for, in the direction of, in the vicinity of, just before, nearing, nearly, on the way to, regarding, to, -wards, with regard to, with respect to.

tower n. barbican, bastille, bastion, belfry, castle, citadel, column, donjon, fort, fortification, fortress, keep, minar, minaret, mirador, obelisk, pillar, refuge, skyscraper, steeple, stronghold, turret.

v. ascend, dominate, exceed, loom, mount, overlook, overtop, rear, rise, soar, surpass, top, transcend, uprise.

towering adj. burning, colossal, elevated, excessive, extraordinary, extreme, fiery, gigantic, great, high, immoderate, imposing, impressive, inordinate, intemperate, intense, lofty, magnificent, mighty, monumental, outstanding, overpowering, paramount, passionate, prodigious, soaring, sublime, superior, supreme, surpassing, tall, transcendent, vehement, violent.

antonyms minor, small, trivial.

town n. borough, bourg, burg, burgh, city, metropolis, municipality, settlement, township.

antonym country.

town-dweller n. burgher, citizen, oppidan, townsman, towny, urbanite.

antonyms country-dweller, rustic.

toxic adj. baneful, deadly, harmful, lethal, morbific, noxious, pernicious, pestilential, poisonous, septic, unhealthy.

antonym harmless.

toy n. bauble, doll, game, gewgaw, kickshaw(s), knick-knack, plaything, trifle, trinket.

v. dally, fiddle, flirt, play, potter, putter, sport, tinker, trifle, wanton.

trace n. bit, dash, drop, evidence, footmark, footprint, footstep, hint, indication, iota, jot, mark, path, record, relic, remains, remnant, scintilla, shadow, sign, smack, soupçon, spoor, spot, suggestion, survival, suspicion, tincture, tinge, token, touch, track, trail, trifle, vestige, whiff.

v. ascertain, chart, copy, delineate, depict, detect, determine, discover, draw, find, follow, map, mark, outline, pursue, record, seek, shadow, show, sketch, stalk, track, trail, traverse, unearth, write.

track n. course, drift, footmark, footprint, footstep, line, mark, orbit, path, pathway, piste, rail, rails, ridgeway, road, scent, sequence, slot, spoor, tack, trace, trail, train, trajectory, wake, wavelength, way.

v. chase, dog, follow, hunt, pursue, shadow, spoor, stalk, tail, trace, trail, travel, traverse.

track down apprehend, capture, catch, dig up, discover, expose, ferret out, find, hunt down, run to earth, sniff out, trace, unearth.

tract[1] n. area, district, estate, expanse, extent, lot, plot, quarter, region, section, stretch, territory, zone.

tract[2] n. booklet, brochure, discourse, disquisition, dissertation, essay, homily, leaflet, monograph, pamphlet, sermon, tractate, treatise.

tractable adj. amenable, biddable, complaisant, compliant, controllable, docile, ductile, fictile, governable, malleable, manageable, obedient, persuadable, plastic, pliable, pliant, submissive, tame, tractile, willing, workable, yielding.

antonyms headstrong, intractable, obstinate, refractory, stubborn, unruly, wilful.

traction n. adhesion, drag, draught, drawing, friction, grip, haulage, propulsion, pull, pulling, purchase, resistance.

trade n. avocation, barter, business, calling, clientele, commerce, commodities, craft, custom, customers, deal, dealing, employment, exchange, interchange, job, line, market, métier, occupation, patrons, profession, public, pursuit, shopkeeping, skill, swap, traffic, transactions, truck.

v. bargain, barter, commerce, deal, do business, exchange, peddle, swap, switch, traffic, transact, truck.

trademark n. badge, brand, crest, emblem, hallmark, identification, idiograph, insignia, label, logo, logotype, name, sign, symbol.

trader n. barrow-boy, barterer, broker, buyer, dealer, marketer, merchandiser, merchant, seller, sutler.

tradesman n. artisan, craftsman, dealer, journeyman, mechanic, merchant, retailer, seller, shopkeeper, shopman, vendor, workman.

tradition n. convention, custom, customs, folklore, habit, institution, lore, praxis, ritual, usage, usance, way, wony.

traditional adj. accustomed, ancestral, conventional, customary, established, fixed, folk, historic, long-established, new, old, oral, time-honoured, tralaticious, transmitted, unconventional, unwritten, usual.

traduce v. abuse, asperse, blacken, calumniate, decry, defame, denigrate, deprecate, depreciate, detract, disparage, knock, malign, misrepresent, revile, run down, slag, slander, smear, vilify.

traducer n. abuser, asperser, calumniator, defamer, denigrator, deprecator, detractor, disparager, knocker, mud-slinger, slanderer, smearer, vilifier.

traffic n. barter, business, commerce, communication, dealing, dealings, doings, exchange, freight, intercourse, movement, passengers, peddling, relations, toing and froing, trade, transport, transportation, truck, vehicles.

v. bargain, barter, deal, do business, exchange, intrigue, market, merchandise, peddle, trade, truck.

trafficker *n.* broker, dealer, merchant, monger, peddler, trader.

tragedy *n.* adversity, affliction, blow, calamity, catastrophe, disaster, misfortune, unhappiness.

antonyms prosperity, success, triumph.

tragic *adj.* anguished, appalling, awful, calamitous, catastrophic, deadly, dire, disastrous, doleful, dreadful, fatal, grievous, heartbreaking, heart-rending, ill-fated, ill-starred, lamentable, miserable, mournful, pathetic, pitiable, ruinous, sad, shocking, sorrowful, thespian, unfortunate, unhappy, woeful, wretched.

antonyms comic, successful, triumphant.

trail *v.* chase, dangle, dawdle, drag, draw, droop, extend, follow, hang, haul, hunt, lag, linger, loiter, pull, pursue, shadow, stalk, straggle, stream, sweep, tail, tow, trace, track, traipse.

n. abature, appendage, drag, footpath, footprints, footsteps, mark, marks, path, road, route, scent, spoor, stream, tail, trace, track, train, wake, way.

trail away decrease, die away, diminish, disappear, dwindle, fade (away), fall away, lessen, peter out, shrink, sink, subside, tail off, taper off, trail off, weaken.

train *v.* aim, coach, direct, discipline, drill, educate, excercise, focus, guide, improve, instruct, lesson, level, point, prepare, rear, rehearse, school, teach, tutor.

n. appendage, attendants, caravan, chain, choo-choo, column, concatenation, convoy, cortege, course, court, entourage, file, followers, following, household, lure, order, process, procession, progression, retinue, sequence, series, set, staff, string, succession, suite, tail, trail.

trainer *n.* coach, drill-master, handler, instructor, teacher, tutor, walker.

training *n.* coaching, discipline, dressage, education, exercise, grounding, guidance, instruction, manège, practice, preparation, schooling, teaching, tuition, tutelage, upbringing, working-out.

traipse *v.* plod, slouch, trail, tramp, trudge.

n. plod, slog, tramp, trek, trudge.

trait *n.* attribute, characteristic, feature, idiosyncrasy, lineament, mannerism, peculiarity, quality, quirk, thew.

traitor *n.* apostate, back-stabber, betrayer, deceiver, defector, deserter, double-crosser, fifth columnist, informer, Judas, miscreant, nithing, proditor, quisling, rebel, renegade, turncoat.

traitorous *adj.* apostate, dishonourable, disloyal, double-crossing, double-dealing, faithless, false, perfidious, proditorious, renegade, seditious, treacherous, treasonable, unfaithful, untrue.

antonyms faithful, loyal, patriotic.

trajectory *n.* course, flight, line, path, route, track, trail.

trammel *n.* bar, block, bond, chain, check, clog, curb, fetter, hamper, handicap, hindrance, impediment, obstacle, rein, shackle, stumbling-block.

v. bar, block, capture, catch, check, clog, curb, enmesh, ensnare, entrammel, entrap, fetter, hamper, handicap, hinder, impede, inhibit, net, pinion, restrain, restrict, shackle, snag, tie.

tramp *v.* crush, footslog, hike, march, plod, ramble, range, roam, rove, slog, stamp, stomp, stump, toil, traipse, trample, tread, trek, trudge, walk, yomp.

n. clochard, derelict, dosser, down-and-out, drifter, drummer, footfall, footstep, hike, hobo, march, piker, plod, ramble, slog, stamp, toe-rag(ger), tread, trek, vagabond, vagrant, weary willie.

trample *v.* crush, flatten, hurt, infringe, insult, squash, stamp, tread, violate.

trance *n.* abstraction, catalepsy, daze, dream, ecstasy, muse, rapture, reverie, spell, stupefaction, stupor, unconsciousness.

tranquil *adj.* at peace, calm, composed, cool, disimpassioned, dispassionate, pacific, peaceful, placid, quiet, reposeful, restful, sedate, serene, still, undisturbed, unexcited, unperturbed, unruffled, untroubled.

antonyms agitated, disturbed, noisy, troubled.

tranquillise *v.* calm, compose, lull, narcotise, opiate, pacify, quell, quiet, relax, sedate, soothe.

antonyms agitate, disturb, upset.

tranquilliser *n.* barbiturate, bromide, downer, narcotic, opiate, opium, sedative.

tranquillity *n.* ataraxia, ataraxy, calm, calmness, composure, coolness, equanimity, hush, imperturbability, peace, peacefulness, placidity, quiet, quietness, quietude, repose, rest, restfulness, sedateness, serenity, silence, stillness.

antonyms agitation, disturbance, noise.

transact *v.* accomplish, carry on, carry out, conclude, conduct, discharge, dispatch, do, enact, execute, handle, manage, negotiate, perform, prosecute, settle.

transaction *n.* action, affair, arrangement, bargain, business, coup, deal, deed, enterprise, event, execution, matter, negotiation, occurrence, proceeding, undertaking.

transactions *n.* affairs, annals, concerns, doings, goings-on, minutes, proceedings, record.

transcend *v.* eclipse, exceed, excel, outdo, outrival, outshine, outstrip, overleap, overstep, overtop, surmount, surpass.

transcendence *n.* ascendancy, excellence, greatness, incomparability, matchlessness, paramoun(t)cy, predominance, pre-eminence, sublimity, superiority, supremacy, transcendency.

transcendent *adj.* consummate, exceeding, extraordinary, foremost, incomparable, matchless, peerless, pre-eminent, sublime, superior, transcendental, unequalled, unique, unparalleled, unrivalled, unsurpassed.

transcribe v. copy, engross, exemplify, interpret, note, record, render, reproduce, rewrite, take down, tape, tape-record, transfer, translate, transliterate.

transcript n. carbon, copy, duplicate, manuscript, note, notes, record, recording, reproduction, transcription, translation, transliteration, version.

transfer v. carry, cede, change, consign, convey, decal, decant, demise, displace, grant, hand over, move, relocate, remove, second, shift, translate, transmit, transplant, transport, transpose.
n. change, changeover, crossover, decantation, displacement, handover, move, relocation, removal, shift, switch, switch-over, transference, translation, transmission, transposition, virement.

transfigure v. alter, apotheosise, change, convert, exalt, glorify, idealise, metamorphose, transform, translate, transmute.

transfix v. engross, fascinate, fix, hold, hypnotise, impale, mesmerise, paralyse, petrify, pierce, puncture, skewer, spear, spellbind, spike, spit, stick, stun, transpierce.
antonym bore.

transform v. alter, change, convert, metamorphose, reconstruct, remodel, renew, revolutionise, transfigure, translate, transmogrify, transmute, transverse.
antonym preserve.

transformation n. alteration, change, conversion, metamorphosis, metanoia, metastasis, renewal, revolution, sea-change, transfiguration, translation, transmogrification, transmutation.
antonym preservation.

transfuse v. imbue, instil, permeate, pervade, suffuse, transfer.

transgress v. breach, break, contravene, defy, disobey, encroach, err, exceed, infringe, lapse, misbehave, offend, overstep, sin, trespass, violate.
antonym obey.

transgression n. breach, contravention, crime, debt, encroachment, error, fault, infraction, infringement, iniquity, lapse, misbehaviour, misdeed, misdemeanour, offence, peccadillo, peccancy, sin, trespass, violation, wrong, wrongdoing.

transgressor n. criminal, culprit, debtor, delinquent, evil-doer, felon, lawbreaker, malefactor, miscreant, offender, sinner, trespasser, villain, wrong-doer.

transience n. brevity, briefness, caducity, deciduousness, ephemerality, evanescence, fleetingness, fugacity, fugitiveness, impermanence, shortness, transitoriness.
antonym permanence.

transient adj. brief, caducous, deciduous, ephemeral, evanescent, fleeting, flying, fugacious, fugitive, impermanent, momentary,

passing, short, short-lived, short-term, temporary, transitory.
antonym permanent.

transit n. alteration, carriage, cartage, carting, change, changeover, conversion, conveyance, crossing, haulage, motion, movement, passage, portage, shift, shipment, transfer, transition, transport, transportation, travel, traverse.

transition n. alteration, change, changeover, conversion, development, evolution, flux, metabasis, metamorphosis, metastasis, passage, passing, progress, progression, shift, transformation, transit, transmutation, upheaval.
antonyms beginning, end.

transitional adj. changing, developmental, fluid, intermediate, metabatic, passing, provisional, temporary, transition, transitionary, unsettled.
antonyms final, initial.

transitory adj. brief, deciduous, ephemeral, evanescent, fleeting, flying, fugacious, fugitive, impermanent, momentary, passing, short, short-lived, short-term, temporary, transient, vanishing.
antonym lasting.

translate v. alter, carry, change, construe, convert, convey, decipher, decode, do, do up, elucidate, enrapture, explain, improve, interpret, metamorphose, move, paraphrase, remove, render, renovate, send, simplify, spell out, transcribe, transfer, transfigure, transform, transliterate, transmogrify, transmute, transplant, transport, transpose, turn.

translation n. alteration, change, conversion, conveyance, crib, decoding, elucidation, explanation, gloss, interpretation, metamorphosis, metaphrase, metaphrasis, move, paraphrase, removal, rendering, rendition, rephrasing, rewording, simplification, transcription, transference, transfiguration, transformation, transliteration, transmutation, transposition, version.

translator n. dragoman, exegete, exegetist, glossarist, glossator, glosser, interpreter, linguist, metaphrast, paraphraser, paraphrast.

translucent adj. clear, diaphanous, limpid, lucent, pellucid, translucid, transparent.
antonym opaque.

transmigration n. metempsychosis, Pythagoreanism, rebirth, reincarnation, transformation.

transmission n. broadcast, broadcasting, carriage, communication, conveyance, diffusion, dispatch, dissemination, passage, programme, relaying, remission, sending, shipment, show, showing, signal, spread, trajection, transfer, transference, transit, transport, transportation.
antonym reception.

transmit v. bear, broadcast, carry, communicate, convey, diffuse, dispatch, disseminate, forward, impart, network, radio, relay, remit,

send, spread, traject, transfer, transport.
antonym receive.

transmute *v.* alter, change, convert, metamorphose, remake, transfigure, transform, translate, transmogrify, transverse.
antonym retain.

transparency[1] *n.* apparentness, candidness, clarity, clearness, diaphanousness, directness, distinctness, explicitness, filminess, forthrightness, frankness, gauziness, limpidity, limpidness, obviousness, openness, patentness, pellucidity, pellucidness, perspicuousness, plainness, sheerness, straightforwardness, translucence, translucency, translucidity, transparence, unambiguousness, visibility, water.
antonyms ambiguity, opacity, unclearness.

transparency[2] *n.* photograph, picture, plate, slide.

transparent *adj.* apparent, candid, clear, crystalline, diaphanous, dioptric, direct, distinct, easy, evident, explicit, filmy, forthright, frank, gauzy, hyaline, hyaloid, ingenuous, limpid, lucent, lucid, manifest, obvious, open, patent, pellucid, perspicuous, plain, plainspoken, recognisable, see-through, sheer, straight, straightforward, translucent, transpicuous, unambiguous, understandable, undisguised, unequivocal, visible.
antonyms ambiguous, opaque, unclear.

transpire *v.* appear, arise, befall, betide, chance, come out, come to light, emerge, happen, leak out, occur, take place, turn up.

transplant *v.* displace, pot on, relocate, remove, repot, resettle, shift, transfer, uproot.
antonym leave.

transport *v.* banish, bear, bring, captivate, carry, carry away, convey, delight, deport, ecstasise, electrify, enchant, enrapture, entrance, exile, fetch, haul, move, ravish, remove, run, ship, spellbind, take, transfer, waft.
antonyms bore, leave.
n. bliss, carriage, cartage, carting, conveyance, delight, ecstasy, enchantment, euphoria, happiness, haulage, heaven, rapture, ravishment, removal, shipment, shipping, transference, transportation, vehicle, waterage.
antonym boredom.

transportation *n.* carriage, cartage, carting, conveyance, haulage, postage, transfer, transport, transportal.

transpose *v.* alter, change, exchange, interchange, metathesise, move, rearrange, relocate, reorder, shift, substitute, swap, switch, transfer.
antonym leave.

transverse *adj.* cross, crossways, crosswise, diagonal, oblique, transversal.

transvestism *n.* cross-dressing, drag, eonism, travesty.

trap *n.* ambush, artifice, bunker, danger, deception, device, gin, hazard, net, noose, pitfall, ruse, snare, spring, springe, springle, stratagem, subterfuge, toils, trap-door, trepan, trick, trickery, wile.
v. ambush, beguile, benet, catch, corner, deceive, dupe, enmesh, ensnare, entrap, illaqueate, inveigle, lime, snare, take, tangle, trepan, trick.

trapped *adj.* ambushed, beguiled, caught, cornered, deceived, duped, ensnared, illaqueated, inveigled, netted, snared, stuck, surrounded, trepanned, tricked.
antonym free.

trapper *n.* backwoodsman, frontiersman, hunter, huntsman, voyageur.

trappings *n.* accompaniments, accoutrements, adornments, clothes, decorations, dress, equipment, finery, fittings, fixtures, fripperies, furnishings, gear, housings, livery, ornaments, panoply, paraphernalia, raiment, things, trimmings.

trash *n.* balderdash, draff, dregs, drivel, dross, garbage, hogwash, inanity, junk, kitsch, litter, nonsense, offscourings, offscum, refuse, riddlings, rot, rubbish, scoria, sullage, sweepings, trashery, tripe, trumpery, twaddle, waste.
antonym sense.

trashy *adj.* brummagem, catchpenny, cheap, cheap-jack, flimsy, grotty, inferior, kitschy, meretricious, pinchbeck, rubbishy, shabby, shoddy, tawdry, third-rate, tinsel, worthless.
antonym first-rate.

trauma *n.* agony, anguish, damage, disturbance, hurt, injury, jolt, lesion, ordeal, pain, scar, shock, strain, suffering, torture, upheaval, upset, wound.
antonyms healing, relaxation.

traumatic *adj.* agonising, damaging, distressing, disturbing, frightening, hurtful, injurious, painful, scarring, shocking, unpleasant, upsetting, wounding.
antonyms healing, relaxed, relaxing.

travail *n.* birth-pangs, childbirth, distress, drudgery, effort, exertion, grind, hardship, labour, labour pains, pain, slavery, slog, strain, stress, suffering, sweat, tears, throes, toil, tribulation.
antonym rest.

travel *v.* carry, commute, cross, excursionise, go, hump the bluey, journey, locomote, move, peregrinate, proceed, progress, ramble, roam, rove, tour, traverse, trek, voyage, walk, wander, wayfare, wend.
antonym stay.

traveller *n.* agent, drummer, excursionist, explorer, globetrotter, gypsy, hiker, holidaymaker, itinerant, journeyer, migrant, nomad, passenger, peregrinator, rep, representative, salesman, saleswoman, tinker, tourist, tripper, vagrant, viator, voyager, wanderer, wayfarer.

travelling *adj.* itinerant, migrant, migratory, mobile, movable, moving, multivagrant, nomadic, on the move, peripatetic, roaming, roving, touring, vagrant, viatorial, wandering, wayfaring.
antonyms fixed, stay-at-home.

travels *n.* excursion, expedition, globetrotting, journey, passage, peregrination, ramble, tour, travel, trip, voyage, walk, wanderings, wayfare.

travel-worn *adj.* footsore, jet-lagged, saddle-sore, travel-weary, waygone, wayworn, weary.
antonym fresh.

traverse *v.* balk, bridge, check, consider, contradict, contravene, counter, counteract, cover, cross, deny, dispute, examine, eye, frustrate, hinder, impede, inspect, investigate, move, negotiate, obstruct, oppose, peregrinate, ply, range, review, roam, scan, scrutinise, span, study, swing, thwart, turn, wander.
antonyms aid, confirm.

travesty *n.* apology, botch, burlesque, caricature, distortion, lampoon, mockery, parody, perversion, send-up, sham, take-off.
v. burlesque, caricature, deride, distort, lampoon, mock, parody, pervert, pillory, ridicule, send up, sham, spoof, take off.

treacherous *adj.* dangerous, deceitful, deceptive, disloyal, double-crossing, double-dealing, double-hearted, double-tongued, duplicitous, faithless, false, hazardous, icy, perfidious, perilous, precarious, proditorious, proditory, Punic, recreant, risky, slippery, slippy, traitorous, treasonable, tricky, unfaithful, unreliable, unsafe, unstable, untrue, untrustworthy.
antonyms dependable, loyal.

treacherously *adv.* deceitfully, disloyally, faithlessly, falsely, perfidiously.
antonym loyally.

treachery *n.* betrayal, disloyalty, double-cross, double-dealing, duplicity, faithlessness, falseness, infidelity, Judas-kiss, laesa majestas, Medism, perfidiousness, perfidy, Punic faith, Punica fides, trahison, treason.
antonyms dependability, loyalty.

tread *v.* crush, hike, march, oppress, pace, pad, plod, press, quell, repress, squash, stamp, step, stride, subdue, subjugate, suppress, tramp, trample, trudge, walk, walk on.
n. footfall, footstep, gait, pace, step, stride, walk.

tread on someone's toes affront, annoy, bruise, discommode, disgruntle, hurt, inconvenience, infringe, injure, irk, offend, upset, vex.
antonym soothe.

treason *n.* disaffection, disloyalty, duplicity, laesa majestas, lese-majesty, mutiny, perfidy, sedition, subversion, trahison, traitorousness, treachery.
antonym loyalty.

treasonable *adj.* disloyal, false, insurrectionary, mutinous, perfidious, seditious, subversive, traitorous, treacherous.
antonym loyal.

treasure *n.* cash, darling, ewe-lamb, flower, fortune, funds, gem, gold, jewel, jewels, money, nonpareil, paragon, pearl, precious, pride and joy, prize, riches, valuables, wealth.
v. adore, cherish, esteem, idolise, love, preserve, prize, revere, value, venerate, worship.
antonym disparage.

treasurer *n.* bursar, cashier, purser, quaestor.

treasury *n.* assets, bank, cache, capital, chrestomathy, coffers, corpus, exchequer, finances, fisc, funds, hoard, money, Parnassus, repository, resources, revenues, store, storehouse, thesaurus, vault.

treat *n.* banquet, celebration, delight, enjoyment, entertainment, excursion, feast, fun, gift, gratification, joy, outing, party, pleasure, refreshment, satisfaction, surprise, thrill, wayzgoose.
antonym drag.
v. attend to, bargain, care for, confer, consider, contain, deal with, discourse upon, discuss, doctor, entertain, feast, give, handle, manage, medicament, medicate, medicine, negotiate, nurse, parley, provide, regale, regard, stand, use.

treatise *n.* disquisition, dissertation, essay, exposition, monograph, pamphlet, pandect, paper, prolegomena, prolusion, study, thesis, tract, tractate, work, writing.

treatment *n.* care, conduct, cure, deal, dealing, discussion, handling, healing, management, manipulation, medication, medicine, prescript, reception, regimen, remedy, surgery, therapeutics, therapy, usage, use.

treble *adj.* high, high-pitched, piping, sharp, shrill, threefold, triple.
antonym deep.

treaty *n.* agreement, alliance, bargain, bond, compact, concordat, contract, convention, covenant, entente, negotiation, pact.

tree *n.* arbor, bush, conifer, cross, evergreen, frutex, gallows, pollard, sampling, seedling, shrub.

trek *n.* expedition, footslog, hike, journey, march, migration, odyssey, safari, slog, tramp, walk.
v. footslog, hike, journey, march, migrate, plod, range, roam, rove, slog, traipse, tramp, trudge, yomp.

tremble *v.* heave, oscillate, quake, quiver, rock, shake, shiver, shudder, teeter, totter, vibrate, wobble.
n. heart-quake, oscillation, quake, quiver, shake, shiver, shudder, tremblement, tremor, vibration.
antonym steadiness.

trembling *n.* heart-quake, oscillation, quaking, quavering, quivering, rocking, shakes, shaking, shivering, shuddering, tremblement, trepidation, vibration.
antonym steadiness.

tremendous *adj.* ace, amazing, appalling, awe-inspiring, awesome, awful, colossal, deafening, dreadful, enormous, excellent, exceptional, extraordinary, fabulous, fantastic, fearful, formidable, frightful, gargantuan, gigantic, great, herculean, huge, immense, incredible, mammoth, marvellous, monstrous, prodigious, sensational, spectacular, stupendous, super, terrible, terrific, titanic, towering, vast, whopping, wonderful.

antonyms boring, dreadful, run-of-the-mill, tiny.

tremor *n.* agitation, earthquake, quake, quaking, quaver, quavering, quiver, quivering, shake, shaking, shiver, shock, thrill, tremble, trembling, trepidation, trillo, vibration, wobble.

antonym steadiness.

tremulous *adj.* afraid, agitated, agog, anxious, aspen, excited, fearful, frightened, jittery, jumpy, nervous, quavering, quivering, quivery, scared, shaking, shivering, timid, trembling, trembly, tremulant, trepid, trepidant, vibrating, wavering.

antonyms calm, firm.

trench *n.* channel, cut, ditch, drain, earthwork, entrenchment, excavation, fosse, furrow, grip, gullet, gutter, pit, rill, sap, trough, waterway.

trenchant *adj.* acerbic, acid, acidulous, acute, astringent, biting, caustic, clear, clear-cut, cogent, crisp, cutting, distinct, driving, effective, effectual, emphatic, energetic, explicit, forceful, forthright, hurtful, incisive, keen, mordant, penetrating, piquant, pointed, potent, powerful, pungent, sarcastic, scratching, severe, sharp, strong, tart, unequivocal, vigorous.

antonym woolly.

trend *n.* bias, course, craze, current, dernier cri, direction, dirt, fad, fashion, flow, inclination, leaning, look, mode, rage, style, tendency, thing, vogue.

trendy *adj.* fashionable, funky, groovy, in, latest, modish, stylish, up to the minute, voguish, with it.

antonym unfashionable.

trepidation *n.* agitation, alarm, anxiety, apprehension, butterflies, cold sweat, consternation, dismay, disquiet, disturbance, dread, emotion, excitement, fear, fright, jitters, misgivings, nervousness, palpitation, perturbation, qualms, quivering, shaking, trembling, tremor, unease, uneasiness, worry.

antonym calm.

trespass *v.* encroach, err, infringe, injure, intrude, invade, obtrude, offend, poach, sin, transgress, violate, wrong.

antonyms keep to, obey.

n. breach, contravention, crime, debt, delinquency, encroachment, error, evil-doing, fault, infraction, infringement, iniquity, injury, intrusion, invasion, misbehaviour, misconduct, misdeed, misdemeanour, offence, poaching, sin, transgression, wrong-doing.

trespasser *n.* criminal, debtor, delinquent, evil-doer, infringer, interloper, intruder, invader, malefactor, offender, poacher, sinner, transgressor, wrong-doer.

tress *n.* braid, bunch, curl, lock, pigtail, plait, queue, ringlet, tail.

trial *n.* adversity, affliction, assay, attempt, audition, bane, bother, burden, check, contest, crack, distress, effort, endeavour, examination, experience, experiment, go, grief, hardship, hassle, hearing, irritation, litigation, load, misery, nuisance, ordeal, pain, pest, plague, probation, proof, shot, sorrow, stab, suffering, taster, temptation, test, testing, tribulation, tribunal, trouble, try, trying, unhappiness, venture, vexation, whack, woe, worry, wretchedness.

antonyms happiness, rest.

adj. dry, dummy, experimental, exploratory, pilot, probationary, provisional, testing.

triangular *adj.* cuneiform, three-cornered, three-sided, trigonal, trigonic, trigonous, trilateral.

tribal *adj.* class, ethnic, family, gentilitial, gentilitian, gentilitious, group, narrow, native, parochial, primitive, savage, sectarian, sectional, uncivilised, uncultured.

tribe *n.* blood, branch, caste, clan, class, division, dynasty, family, gens, group, house, ilk, nation, people, phratry, race, seed, sept, stock.

tribulation *n.* adversity, affliction, blow, burden, care, curse, distress, grief, heartache, misery, misfortune, ordeal, pain, reverse, sorrow, suffering, travail, trial, trouble, unhappiness, vexation, woe, worry, wretchedness.

antonyms happiness, rest.

tribunal *n.* bar, bench, court, examination, hearing, inquisition, trial.

tribute *n.* accolade, acknowledgement, annates, applause, charge, commendation, compliment, contribution, cornage, credit, customs, duty, encomium, esteem, eulogy, excise, first-fruits, gavel, gift, gratitude, homage, honour, horngeld, impost, laudation, offering, panegyric, payment, praise, ransom, recognition, respect, subsidy, tax, testimonial, testimony, toll.

antonym blame.

trice *n.* flash, instant, jiff, jiffy, minute, moment, sec, second, shake, tick, twinkling, whiff.

trick *n.* antic, art, artifice, cantrip, caper, characteristic, chicane, command, con, craft, deceit, deception, device, dodge, dog-trick, expedient, expertise, feat, feint, foible, fraud, frolic, gag, gambol, gift, gimmick, habit, hang, hoax, idiosyncrasy, imposition, imposture, jape, joke, josh, knack, know-how, legerdemain, leg-pull, mannerism, manoeuvre, peculiarity, ploy, practical joke, practice, prank, put-on, quirk, quiz, rig, ruse, secret, shot, skill, sleight, spell, stall, stratagem, stunt, subterfuge, swindle, technique, toy, trait, trap, trinket, turn, wile.

adj. artificial, bogus, counterfeit, ersatz, fake, false, feigned, forged, imitation, mock, pretend, sham.

antonym genuine.

v. bamboozle, beguile, cheat, con, cozen, deceive, defraud, delude, diddle, dupe, fool, gull, hoax, hocus-pocus, hoodwink, hornswoggle, illude, lead on, mislead, outwit, pull a fast one on, pull someone's leg, sell, swindle, trap.

trick out adorn, array, attire, bedeck, bedizen, decorate, do up, doll up, dress up, ornament, prank, prink, spruce up, tart up, trick up.

trickery *n.* cheating, chicanery, con, conveyance, deceit, deception, dishonesty, dodgery, double-dealing, dupery, flim-flam, fraud, funny business, guile, hanky-panky, hoax, hocus-pocus, imposture, jiggery-pokery, jugglery, monkey business, pretence, shennanigans, skulduggery, sleight, sleight-of-hand, swindling, trickstering.
antonym honesty.

trickle *v.* dribble, drip, drop, exude, filter, gutter, leak, ooze, percolate, run, seep.
antonyms gush, stream.
n. drib, dribble, driblet, dribs and drabs, drip, seepage.
antonyms gush, stream.

trickster *n.* cheat, con man, cozener, deceiver, diddler, fraud, hoaxer, impostor, joker, pretender, quiz, quizzer, swindler, tregetour, tricker.

tricky *adj.* artful, complicated, crafty, cunning, deceitful, deceptive, delicate, devious, difficult, foxy, Gordian, knotty, legerdemain, problematic, risky, scheming, slippery, sly, sticky, subtle, thorny, ticklish, touch-and-go, trickish, tricksome, tricksy, wily.
antonyms easy, honest.

trifle *n.* bagatelle, bauble, bit, concetto, dash, drop, falderal, finicality, foolishness, gewgaw, jot, knick-knack, little, nonsense, nothing, pinch, plaything, spot, touch, toy, trace, trinket, triviality, whigmaleerie, whim-wham.
v. coquet, dabble, dally, dawdle, faddle, fiddle-faddle, flirt, fool, fribble, fritter, frivol, idle, meddle, niggle, palter, play, play with, sport, toy, wanton, waste.

trifler *n.* dallier, dilettante, fribbler, futilitarian, good-for-nothing, idler, layabout, loafer, ne'er-do-well, piddler, waster.

trifles *n.* inessentials, minor considerations, minutiae, nugae, trivia, trivialities.
antonym essentials.

trifling *adj.* empty, footling, foozling, fribbling, fribblish, frivolous, idle, inconsiderable, insignificant, minuscule, negligible, nugatory, paltry, petty, piddling, piffling, puny, shallow, silly, slight, small, tiny, trivial, unimportant, valueless, worthless.
antonym important.
n. desipience, fiddling, fooling, footling, frivolity, piddling, piffling, whifflery.

trigger *v.* activate, actuate, cause, elicit, generate, initiate, produce, prompt, provoke, set off, spark off, start.
n. catch, goad, lever, release, spur, stimulus, switch.

trill *v.* cheep, chirp, chirrup, sing, tweet, twitter, warble, whistle.

trim *adj.* clean-limbed, compact, dapper, natty, neat, orderly, shipshape, slender, slim, smart, smirk, soigné, spick-and-span, spruce, streamlined, svelte, trig, well-dressed, well-groomed, willowy.
antonym scruffy.
v. adjust, adorn, arrange, array, balance, barb, barber, beautify, bedeck, clip, crop, curtail, cut, decorate, distribute, dock, dress, dub, embellish, embroider, garnish, lop, order, ornament, pare, prepare, prune, settle, shave, shear, tidy, trick.
n. adornment, array, attire, border, clipping, condition, crop, cut, decoration, disposition, dress, edging, embellishment, equipment, fettle, fitness, fittings, form, frill, fringe, garnish, gear, health, humour, nick, order, ornament, ornamentation, piping, pruning, repair, shape, shave, shearing, situation, state, temper, trappings, trimming.

trimmer *n.* time-server, vicar of Bray, weathercock.

trimming *n.* adornment, border, braid, decoration, edging, embellishment, falbala, fimbriation, frill, fringe, frou-frou, furbelow, garnish, ornamentation, passament, passementerie, piping, trim.

trimmings *n.* accessories, accompaniments, additions, appurtenances, clippings, cuttings, ends, extras, frills, garnish, ornaments, paraphernalia, parings, remnants, shavings, trappings.

trinity *n.* threefoldness, threesome, triad, trilogy, trio, tripersonality, triple, triplet, triumvirate, triune, triunity, troika.

trinket *n.* bagatelle, bauble, bibelot, bijou, doodad, fairing, gewgaw, gimcrack, kickshaws, knick-knack, nothing, ornament, toy, trifle, trinkum-trankum, whigmaleerie, whimwham.

trio *n.* terzetto, threesome, triad, trilogy, trine, trinity, triple, triplet, triptych, triumvirate, triune.

trip *n.* blunder, boob, errand, error, excursion, expedition, fall, faux pas, foray, indiscretion, jaunt, journey, lapse, misstep, outing, ramble, run, skip, slip, step, stumble, tour, travel, voyage.
v. activate, blunder, boob, caper, confuse, dance, disconcert, engage, err, fall, flip, flit, frisk, gambol, go, hop, lapse, miscalculate, misstep, pull, ramble, release, set off, skip, slip, slip up, spring, stumble, switch on, throw, tilt up, tip up, tour, trap, travel, tumble, unsettle, voyage.

tripe *n.* balderdash, balls, blah, bosh, bullshit, bunkum, claptrap, drivel, garbage, guff, hogwash, inanity, nonsense, poppycock, rot, rubbish, tosh, trash, trumpery, twaddle.
antonym sense.

triple *adj.* ternal, three-branched, threefold, three-ply, three-way, treble, trigeminal, trinal, trinary, tripartite, triplex, triplicate, triploid.
n. threefoldness, threesome, triad, trilogy, trine, trinity, trio, triplet, triplicity, triumvirate, triune, triunity.

v. treble, triplicate.

triplet *n.* tercet, terzetta, threesome, triad, trilling, trilogy, trin, trine, trinity, trio, triple, triplicity, tripling, triumvirate, triune, troika.

tripper *n.* emmet, excursionist, grockle, holiday-maker, sightseer, tourist, voyager.

trite *adj.* banal, bromidic, cliché'd, common, commonplace, corny, dull, hack, hackneyed, Mickey Mouse, ordinary, overworn, pedestrian, routine, run-of-the-mill, stale, stereotyped, stock, threadbare, tired, uninspired, unoriginal, well-trodden, well-worn, worn, worn out.
antonym original.

triumph *n.* accomplishment, achievement, ascendancy, attainment, conquest, coup, elation, exultation, feat, happiness, hit, joy, jubilation, masterstroke, mastery, pride, rejoicing, sensation, smash, smash-hit, success, tour de force, victory, walk-away, walk-over, win.
antonym disaster.
v. best, celebrate, crow, defeat, dominate, exult, gloat, glory, have the last laugh, humble, humiliate, jubilate, overcome, overwhelm, prevail, prosper, rejoice, revel, subdue, succeed, swagger, vanquish, win.
antonym fail.

triumphant *adj.* boastful, celebratory, cock-a-hoop, conquering, dominant, elated, epinikian, exultant, gloating, glorious, joyful, jubilant, proud, rejoicing, successful, swaggering, triumphal, undefeated, victorious, winning.
antonyms defeated, humble.

trivia *n.* details, irrelevancies, minutiae, nugae, pap, trifles, trivialities.
antonym essentials.

trivial *adj.* commonplace, dinky, everyday, frivolous, incidental, inconsequential, inconsiderable, insignificant, little, meaningless, Mickey Mouse, minor, negligible, nugatory, paltry, pettifogging, petty, piddling, piffling, puny, slight, small, snippety, trifling, trite, unimportant, valueless, worthless.
antonym significant.

trivialise *v.* belittle, depreciate, devalue, minimise, play down, scoff at, underestimate, underplay, undervalue.
antonym exalt.

triviality *n.* detail, frivolity, futility, inconsequence, inconsequentiality, insignificance, littleness, meaninglessness, minor matter, negligibility, nothing, nugatoriness, paltriness, pettiness, slightness, smallness, technicality, trifle, triteness, unimportance, valuelessness, worthlessness.
antonyms essential, importance.

troop *n.* assemblage, band, body, bunch, company, contingent, crew, crowd, division, drove, flock, gang, gathering, group, herd, horde, multitude, pack, squad, squadron, swarm, team, throng, trip, troop, unit.
v. crowd, flock, go, march, pack, parade, stream, swarm, throng, traipse, turn.

troops *n.* army, men, military, servicemen, soldiers, soldiery.

trophy *n.* award, booty, cup, laurels, memento, memorial, prize, souvenir, spoils.

tropical *adj.* equatorial, hot, humid, lush, luxuriant, steamy, stifling, sultry, sweltering, torrid.
antonyms arctic, cold, cool, temperate.

trot *v.* bustle, canter, jog, lope, pace, run, scamper, scurry, scuttle.
n. canter, jog, jog-trot, lope, run.

trot out adduce, bring forward, bring up, drag up, exhibit, recite, rehearse, reiterate, relate, repeat.

troubadour *n.* balladeer, cantabank, jongleur, minnesinger, minstrel, poet, singer, trouvère, trouveur.

trouble *n.* affliction, agitation, ailment, annoyance, anxiety, attention, bother, care, commotion, complaint, concern, danger, defect, difficulty, dilemma, disability, discontent, discord, disease, disorder, disquiet, dissatisfaction, distress, disturbance, effort, exertion, failure, grief, heartache, illness, inconvenience, irritation, labour, malfunction, mess, misfortune, nuisance, pain, pains, pest, pickle, predicament, problem, row, scrape, solicitude, sorrow, spot, strife, struggle, suffering, thought, torment, travail, trial, tribulation, tumult, uneasiness, unrest, upheaval, upset, vexation, woe, work, worry.
antonyms calm, peace.
v. afflict, agitate, annoy, bother, burden, discomfort, discommode, discompose, disconcert, disquiet, distress, disturb, fash, fret, grieve, harass, incommode, inconvenience, molest, muddy, pain, perplex, perturb, pester, plague, sadden, torment, upset, vex, worry.
antonyms help, reassure.

troublemaker *n.* agent provocateur, agitator, bell-wether, bolshevik, bovver boy, firebrand, heller, incendiary, instigator, meddler, mischief-maker, rabble-rouser, ringleader, stirrer, tub-thumper.
antonym peace-maker.

troublesome *adj.* annoying, arduous, bothersome, burdensome, demanding, difficult, disorderly, fashious, harassing, hard, importunate, inconvenient, insubordinate, irksome, irritating, laborious, oppressive, pestilential, plaguesome, plaguy, rebellious, recalcitrant, refractory, rowdy, spiny, taxing, thorny, tiresome, tricky, trying, turbulent, uncooperative, undisciplined, unruly, upsetting, vexatious, violent, wearisome, worrisome, worrying.
antonyms easy, helpful, polite.

trough *n.* back, channel, conduit, crib, depression, ditch, duct, flume, furrow, gully, gutter, hollow, manger, trench, tub.

trounce *v.* beat, best, censure, clobber, crush, drub, hammer, lick, overwhelm, paste, punish, rebuke, rout, slaughter, thrash, whale, whitewash.

troupe *n.* band, cast, company, group, set, troop.

trouper *n.* actor, artiste, entertainer, old hand, performer, player, Roscius, theatrical, thespian, veteran.

trousers *n.* bags, bloomers, breeches, breeks, culottes, denims, ducks, dungarees, flannels, indescribables, inexpressibles, jeans, knickerbockers, lederhosen, Levis®, pantaloons, pants, pedal-pushers, plus-fours, shorts, slacks, trews, trunk-breeches, trunk-hose, unmentionables, unutterables.

truancy *n.* absence, dodging, malingering, shirking, skiving.
antonyms attendance, effort.

truant *n.* absentee, deserter, dodger, hookey, malingerer, runaway, shirker, skiver, wag.
adj. absent, malingering, missing, runaway, skiving.
v. desert, dodge, malinger, play truant, shirk, skive, skive off.

truce *n.* armistice, break, cease-fire, cessation, intermission, interval, let-up, lull, moratorium, peace, respite, rest, stay, suspension, treaty, Truce of God.
antonym hostilities.

truck[1] *n.* business, commerce, communication, connection, contact, dealings, exchange, intercourse, relations, trade, traffic.

truck[2] *n.* barrow, bogie, camion, cart, drag, float, hand-cart, lorry, trailer, trolley, van, wag(g)on, water-cart, water-wagon, wheelbarrow.

truculent *adj.* aggressive, antagonistic, bad-tempered, bellicose, belligerent, combative, contentious, cross, defiant, fierce, hostile, ill-tempered, obstreperous, pugnacious, quarrelsome, savage, scrappy, sullen, violent.
antonyms co-operative, good-natured.

trudge *v.* clump, footslog, hike, labour, lumber, march, mush, plod, slog, stump, traipse, tramp, trek, walk.
n. footslog, haul, hike, march, mush, slog, traipse, tramp, trek, walk.

true *adj.* absolute, accurate, actual, apod(e)ictic, authentic, bona fide, confirmed, conformable, constant, correct, corrected, dedicated, devoted, dutiful, exact, factual, faithful, fast, firm, genuine, honest, honourable, legitimate, loyal, natural, perfect, precise, proper, pure, real, right, rightful, sincere, sooth, spot-on, square, staunch, steady, true-blue, true-born, true-hearted, trustworthy, trusty, truthful, typical, unerring, unswerving, upright, valid, veracious, veridical, veritable.
antonyms faithless, false, inaccurate.
adv. accurately, correctly, exactly, faithfully, honestly, perfectly, precisely, properly, rightly, truly, truthfully, unerringly, veraciously, veritably.
antonyms falsely, inaccurately.

true-blue *adj.* card-carrying, committed, confirmed, constant, dedicated, devoted, dyed-in-the-wool, faithful, loyal, orthodox, staunch, true, trusty, uncompromising, unwavering.
antonyms superficial, wavering.

truism *n.* axiom, bromide, cliché, commonplace, platitude, saw, truth, verity.

truly *adv.* accurately, authentically, constantly, correctly, devotedly, dutifully, en verité, exactly, exceptionally, extremely, factually, faithfully, fegs, firmly, genuinely, greatly, honestly, honourably, in good sooth, in reality, in truth, indeed, indubitably, legitimately, loyally, precisely, properly, really, rightly, sincerely, soothly, staunchly, steadfastly, steadily, truthfully, undeniably, veraciously, verily, veritably, very.
antonyms faithlessly, falsely, incorrectly, slightly.

trump up *v.* concoct, contrive, cook up, create, devise, fabricate, fake, invent, make up.

trumped-up *adj.* concocted, contrived, cooked-up, fabricated, fake, faked, false, falsified, invented, made-up, phoney, spurious, untrue.
antonym genuine.

trumpery *adj.* brummagem, cheap, flashy, grotty, meretricious, nasty, pinchbeck, rubbishy, shabby, shoddy, tawdry, trashy, trifling, useless, valueless, worthless.
antonym first-rate.

trumpet *n.* bellow, blare, blast, bray, bugle, call, clarion, cry, honk, horn, roar.
v. advertise, announce, bellow, blare, blast, bray, broadcast, call, extol, honk, preconise, proclaim, publish, roar, shout, tout.

truncate *v.* abbreviate, clip, crop, curtail, cut, cut short, lop, maim, pare, prune, shorten, trim.
antonym lengthen.

truncheon *n.* baton, club, cosh, cudgel, knobkerrie, life-preserver, night-stick, shillela(g)h, staff.

trunk[1] *n.* bin, box, case, chest, coffer, crate, Gladstone bag, kist, locker, portmanteau, suitcase.

trunk[2] *n.* body, bole, frame, shaft, stalk, stem, stock, torso, tube.

trunk[3] *n.* nose, proboscis, snout.

truss *v.* bind, bundle, fasten, hogtie, pack, pinion, secure, strap, tether, tie.
antonym untie.
n. bale, bandage, beam, binding, brace, bundle, buttress, joist, prop, shore, stanchion, stay, strut, support.

trust *n.* affiance, assurance, belief, care, certainty, certitude, charge, confidence, conviction, credence, credit, custody, duty, expectation, faith, fidelity, guard, guardianship, hope, obligation, protection, reliance, responsibility, safekeeping, trusteeship, uberrima fides.
antonym mistrust.
v. assign, assume, bank on, believe, command, commit, confide, consign, count on, credit, delegate, depend on, entrust, expect, give, hope, imagine, presume, rely on, suppose, surmise, swear by.
antonym mistrust.

trustee *n.* administrator, agent, custodian, depositary, executor, executrix, fiduciary, guardian, keeper.

trusting *adj.* confiding, credulous, gullible, innocent, naïve, optimistic, simple, trustful, unguarded, unquestioning, unsuspecting, unsuspicious, unwary.
antonyms cautious, distrustful.

trustworthy *adj.* authentic, dependable, ethical, four-square, honest, honourable, level-headed, mature, principled, reliable, responsible, righteous, sensible, steadfast, true, trusty, truthful, upright.
antonym unreliable.

trusty *adj.* dependable, faithful, firm, honest, loyal, reliable, responsible, solid, staunch, steady, straightforward, strong, supportive, true, trustworthy, upright.
antonym unreliable.

truth *n.* accuracy, actuality, axiom, candour, certainty, constancy, dedication, devotion, dutifulness, exactness, fact, facts, factuality, factualness, faith, faithfulness, fidelity, frankness, genuineness, historicity, honesty, integrity, law, legitimacy, loyalty, maxim, naturalism, precision, realism, reality, sooth, truism, truthfulness, uprightness, validity, veracity, verdicality, verity.
antonym falsehood.

truthful *adj.* accurate, candid, correct, exact, faithful, forthright, frank, honest, literal, naturalistic, plain-spoken, precise, realistic, reliable, sincere, sooth, soothfast, soothful, straight, straightforward, true, trustworthy, veracious, veridicous, verist, veristic, veritable.
antonym untruthful.

truthfulness *n.* candour, frankness, honesty, openness, righteousness, sincerity, straightness, uprightness, veracity, verism.
antonym untruthfulness.

try *v.* adjudge, adjudicate, afflict, aim, annoy, appraise, attempt, catechise, endeavour, essay, evaluate, examine, experiment, hear, inconvenience, inspect, investigate, irk, irritate, pain, plague, prove, sample, seek, strain, stress, strive, struggle, taste, tax, test, tire, trouble, undertake, upset, venture, vex, wear out, weary.
n. appraisal, attempt, bash, crack, effort, endeavour, essay, evaluation, experiment, fling, go, inspection, sample, shot, stab, taste, taster, test, trial, whack.
try out appraise, check out, evaluate, inspect, sample, taste, test, try on.

trying *adj.* aggravating, annoying, arduous, bothersome, difficult, distressing, exasperating, fatiguing, hard, irksome, irritating, searching, severe, stressful, taxing, testing, tiresome, tough, troublesome, upsetting, vexing, wearisome.
antonym calming.

tub *n.* back, barrel, basin, bath, bathtub, bucket, butt, cask, hogshead, keeve, keg, kid, kit, pail, puncheon, stand, tun, vat.

tubby *adj.* buxom, chubby, corpulent, fat, obese, overweight, paunchy, plump, podgy, portly, pudgy, roly-poly, stout, well-upholstered.
antonym slim.

tube *n.* channel, conduit, cylinder, duct, hose, inlet, main, outlet, pipe, shaft, spout, trunk, vas.

tuberculosis *n.* consumption, phthisis, TB.

tubular *adj.* pipelike, pipy, tubate, tubelike, tubiform, tubulate, tubulous, vasiform.

tuck[1] *v.* cram, crease, fold, gather, insert, push, stuff.
n. crease, fold, gather, pinch, pleat, pucker.

tuck[2] *n.* comestibles, eats, food, grub, nosh, prog, scoff, victuals, vittles.
tuck in devour, dine, eat, eat up, fall to, feast, gobble, gorge, scoff, sup.

tuft *n.* beard, bunch, clump, cluster, collection, crest, dag, daglock, dollop, floccule, flocculus, floccus, flock, knot, shock, tassle, topknot, truss, tussock.

tug *v.* drag, draw, haul, heave, jerk, jigger, lug, pluck, pull, tow, wrench, yank.
n. drag, haul, heave, jerk, pluck, pull, tow, traction, wrench, yank.

tuition *n.* education, instruction, lessons, pedagogics, pedagogy, schooling, teaching, training, tutelage, tutoring.

tumble *v.* disorder, drop, fall, flop, jumble, overthrow, pitch, plummet, roll, rumple, stumble, topple, toss, trip up.
n. collapse, drop, fall, flop, plunge, roll, spill, stumble, toss, trip.

tumbler[1] *n.* acrobat, contortionist, gymnast, voltigeur.

tumbler[2] *n.* beaker, cup, drinking-glass, glass, goblet, mug, schooner.

tumbledown *adj.* broken-down, crumbling, crumbly, decrepit, dilapidated, disintegrating, ramshackle, rickety, ruined, ruinous, shaky, tottering.
antonym well-kept.

tumid *adj.* affected, bloated, bombastic, bulbous, bulging, distended, enlarged, euphuistic, flowery, fulsome, fustian, grandiloquent, grandiose, high-flown, inflated, magniloquent, oro(ro)tund, overblown, pompous, pretentious, protuberant, puffed up, puffy, sesquipedalian, stilted, swollen, tumescent, turgid.
antonyms flat, simple.

tumour *n.* cancer, carcinoma, growth, lump, lymphoma, melanoma, myeloma, neoplasm, sarcoma, swelling, tubercle, tubercule, tuberculoma, tuberculum.

tumult *n.* ado, affray, agitation, altercation, bedlam, brattle, brawl, brouhaha, bustle, clamour, coil, commotion, deray, din, disorder, disturbance, Donnybrook, émeute, excitement, fracas, hubbub, hullabaloo, outbreak, pandemonium, quarrel, racket, riot, rookery, rout, row, ruction, ruffle, stir, stramash, strife, turmoil, unrest, upheaval, uproar.

antonym calm.

tumultuous *adj*. agitated, boisterous, clamorous, confused, disorderly, disturbed, excited, fierce, hectic, irregular, lawless, noisy, obstreperous, passionate, raging, restless, riotous, rowdy, rumbustious, stormy, tempestuous, troubled, turbulent, unrestrained, unruly, uproarious, violent, vociferous, wild. *antonym* calm.

tune *n*. agreement, air, attitude, concert, concord, consonance, demeanour, disposition, euphony, frame of mind, harmony, melisma, melody, mood, motif, pitch, song, strain, sympathy, temper, theme, unison.
v. adapt, adjust, attune, harmonise, pitch, regulate, set, synchronise, temper.

tuneful *adj*. canorous, catchy, euphonious, harmonious, mellifluous, mellow, melodic, melodious, musical, pleasant, sonorous. *antonym* tuneless.

tuneless *adj*. atonal, cacophonous, clashing, discordant, dissonant, harsh, horrisonant, unmelodic, unmelodious, unmusical. *antonym* tuneful.

tunnel *n*. burrow, channel, chimney, drift, flue, gallery, hole, passage, passageway, sap, shaft, subway, underpass.
v. burrow, dig, excavate, mine, penetrate, sap, undermine.

turbid *adj*. clouded, cloudy, confused, dense, dim, disordered, feculent, foggy, foul, fuzzy, hazy, impure, incoherent, muddled, muddy, murky, opaque, roily, thick, unclear, unsettled. *antonym* clear.

turbulence *n*. agitation, boiling, chaos, commotion, confusion, disorder, disruption, instability, pandemonium, roughness, storm, tumult, turmoil, unrest, upheaval. *antonym* calm.

turbulent *adj*. agitated, anarchic, blustery, boiling, boisterous, choppy, confused, disordered, disorderly, foaming, furious, insubordinate, lawless, mutinous, obstreperous, raging, rebellious, refractory, riotous, rough, rowdy, seditious, stormy, tempestuous, tumultuous, unbridled, undisciplined, ungovernable, unruly, unsettled, unstable, uproarious, violent, wild. *antonym* calm.

turf *n*. clod, divot, glebe, grass, green, sod, sward.
turf out banish, bounce, chuck out, discharge, dismiss, dispossess, eject, elbow, evict, expel, fire, fling out, give the elbow to, kick out, oust, sack, throw out, turn out.

turgid *adj*. affected, bloated, bombastic, bulging, congested, dilated, distended, extravagant, flowery, fulsome, fustian, grandiloquent, grandiose, high-flown, inflated, magniloquent, oro(ro)tund, ostentatious, overblown, pompous, pretentious, protuberant, puffy, sesquipedalian, stilted, swollen, tumescent, tumid, windy. *antonyms* flat, simple.

turmoil *n*. agitation, bedlam, brouhaha, bustle, chaos, combustion, commotion, confusion, disorder, disquiet, disturbance, Donnybrook, dust, émeute, ferment, flurry, hubbub, hubbuboo, noise, pandemonium, pother, pudder, rookery, rout, row, ruffle, stir, stour, stramash, strife, tracasserie, trouble, tumult, turbulence, uproar, violence, welter. *antonym* calm.

turn *v*. adapt, alter, apostatise, appeal, apply, approach, become, caracol, change, circle, construct, convert, corner, curdle, defect, deliver, depend, desert, divert, double, execute, fashion, fit, form, frame, go, gyrate, hang, hinge, infatuate, influence, issue, look, make, metamorphose, mould, move, mutate, nauseate, negotiate, pass, perform, persuade, pivot, prejudice, remodel, renege, resort, retract, return, reverse, revolve, roll, rotate, shape, shift, sicken, sour, spin, spoil, swerve, switch, swivel, taint, transfigure, transform, translate, transmute, twirl, twist, upset, veer, wheel, whirl, write.
n. act, action, airing, aptitude, bend, bent, bias, bout, caracol, cast, chance, change, circle, circuit, constitutional, crack, crankle, crisis, culmination, curve, cycle, deed, departure, deviation, direction, distortion, drift, drive, excursion, exigency, fashion, favour, fling, form, format, fright, gesture, go, guise, gyration, heading, innings, jaunt, make-up, manner, mode, mould, occasion, opportunity, outing, performance, performer, period, pivot, promenade, reversal, revolution, ride, rotation, round, saunter, scare, service, shape, shift, shock, shot, spell, spin, start, stint, stroll, style, succession, surprise, swing, tendency, time, trend, trick, try, turning, twist, uey, U-turn, vicissitude, walk, warp, way, whack, whirl.
turn away avert, deflect, depart, deviate, discharge, dismiss. *antonym* accept.
turn back beat off, do a uey, drive back, drive off, force back, go back, rebuff, repel, repulse, resist, retrace one's steps, return, revert. *antonyms* go on, stay.
turn down decline, diminish, fold, invert, lessen, lower, muffle, mute, quieten, rebuff, refuse, reject, repudiate, soften, spurn. *antonyms* accept, turn up.
turn in deliver, enter, give back, give up, go to bed, hand in, hand over, hit the sack, register, retire, return, submit, surrender, tender. *antonyms* get up, give out, keep.
turn inside out evaginate, evert, extravert, introvert.
turn of events affair, galère, happening, incident, occurrence, outcome, phenomenon, result.
turn of phrase diction, expression, idiom, locution, metaphor, phraseology, saying, style.
turn off alienate, bore, branch off, cut out,

depart from, deviate, discourage, disenchant, disgust, dismiss, displease, divert, irritate, kill, leave, nauseate, offend, put off, put out, quit, repel, shut, shut down, sicken, stop, switch off, turn out, unplug.
antonym turn on.

turn on activate, arouse, assail, assault, attack, attract, balance, depend, energise, excite, expose, fall on, hang, hinge, ignite, inform, initiate, introduce, pivot, please, rest, round on, rouse, show, start, start up, stimulate, switch on, thrill, titillate, trip, turn against, work up.
antonym turn off.

turn out accoutre, apparel, appear, assemble, attend, attire, banish, become, cashier, clean out, clear, clothe, come, come about, crop up, deport, develop, discharge, dishome, dishouse, dismiss, displant, dispossess, dress, drive out, drum out, emerge, empty, end up, eventuate, evict, evolve, expel, fabricate, finish, fire, fit, gather, go, happen, kick out, make, manufacture, muster, oust, outfit, process, produce, result, sack, show up, switch off, throw out, transpire, turf out, turn off, turn up, unplug, unseat.
antonyms stay away, turn on.

turn over activate, assign, break up, capsize, commend, commit, consider, contemplate, crank, deliberate, deliver, dig, examine, give over, give up, hand over, keel over, mull over, overturn, pass on, plough, ponder, reflect on, render, reverse, revolve, rob, ruminate, start up, surrender, switch on, think about, think over, transfer, upend, upset, yield.
antonym stand firm.

turn over a new leaf amend, begin anew, change, change one's ways, improve, mend one's ways, pull one's socks up, reform.
antonym persist.

turn tail escape, flee, hightail it, make off, retreat, run away, run for it, run off, scarper, skedaddle, take off, take to one's heels, vamoose.
antonym stand firm.

turn up amplify, appear, arrive, attend, boost, come, crop up, dig up, disclose, discover, disgust, enhanse, expose, find, increase, intensify, invert, pop up, raise, reveal, show, show up, transpire, unearth.
antonyms stay away, turn down.

turncoat *n.* apostate, backslider, blackleg, defector, deserter, fink, rat, recreant, renegade, renegate, scab, seceder, tergiversator, traitor.

turning *n.* bend, crossroads, curve, flexure, fork, junction, turn, turn-off.

turning-point *n.* change, climacteric, crisis, crossroads, crux, cusp, moment of truth, watershed.

turn-out *n.* array, assemblage, assembly, attendance, attire, audience, company, congregation, costume, crowd, dress, equipage, equipment, gate, gear, get-up, number, outfit, output, outturn, product, production, productivity, rig-out, team, throng, turnover, volume, yield.

turnover *n.* business, change, flow, income, movement, output, outturn, production, productivity, profits, replacement, volume, yield.

turpitude *n.* badness, baseness, corruption, corruptness, criminality, degeneracy, depravity, evil, flagitiousness, foulness, immorality, iniquity, nefariousness, rascality, sinfulness, viciousness, vileness, villainy, wickedness.
antonym honour.

tussle *v.* battle, brawl, compete, contend, fight, grapple, scramble, scrap, scuffle, struggle, vie, wrestle.
n. battle, bout, brawl, competition, conflict, contention, contest, dust-up, fight, fracas, fray, mêlée, punch-up, race, scramble, scrap, scrimmage, scrum, scuffle, set-to, struggle.

tutelage *n.* aegis, care, charge, custody, education, eye, guardianship, guidance, instruction, patronage, preparation, protection, schooling, teaching, tuition, vigilance, wardship.

tutor *n.* coach, director of studies, educator, governor, guardian, guide, guru, instructor, lecturer, master, mentor, preceptor, répétiteur, supervisor, teacher.
v. coach, control, direct, discipline, drill, edify, educate, guide, instruct, lecture, school, supervise, teach, train.

tutorial *n.* class, lesson, seminar, teach-in.
adj. coaching, didactic, educative, educatory, guiding, instructional, teaching.

twaddle *n.* balderdash, balls, blather, blether, bunk, bunkum, chatter, claptrap, drivel, fadaise, gabble, garbage, gobbledegook, gossip, guff, havers, hogwash, hot air, inanity, nonsense, piffle, poppycock, rigmarole, rot, rubbish, stuff, tattle, tosh, trash, trumpery, waffle.
antonym sense.

tweak *v, n.* jerk, nip, pull, punch, snatch, squeeze, tug, twist, twitch.

twee *adj.* affected, bijou, cute, dainty, kitschy, precious, pretty, quaint, sentimental, sweet.

tweezers *n.* forceps, pincers, tongs, vulsella.

twiddle *v.* adjust, fiddle, finger, jiggle, juggle, swivel, turn, twirl, twist, wiggle.

twig[1] *n.* branch, offshoot, ramulus, shoot, spray, spring, stick, wattle, whip, withe, withy.

twig[2] *v.* catch on, comprehend, cotton on, fathom, get, grasp, rumble, savvy, see, tumble to, understand.

twilight *n.* crepuscle, crepuscule, decline, demi-jour, dimness, dusk, ebb, evening, eventide, gloaming, half-light, sundown, sunset.
adj. crepuscular, darkening, declining, dim, dying, ebbing, evening, final, last, shadowy.

twin *n.* clone, corollary, counterpart, doppelgänger, double, duplicate, fellow, gemel, likeness, lookalike, match, mate, ringer.
adj. balancing, corresponding, didymous, double, dual, duplicate, geminate, geminous,

identical, matched, matching, paired, parallel, symmetrical, twofold.

v. combine, couple, join, link, match, pair, yoke.

twine *n.* cord, string, twist, yarn.

v. bend, braid, coil, curl, encircle, entwine, interlace, interweave, knit, loop, meander, plait, snake, spiral, splice, surround, tie, twist, weave, wind, wrap, wreathe, wriggle, zigzag.

twinge *n.* bite, gripe, pain, pang, pinch, prick, qualm, spasm, stab, stitch, throb, throe, tweak, twist, twitch.

twinkle *v.* blink, coruscate, flash, flicker, gleam, glint, glisten, glitter, scintillate, shimmer, shine, sparkle, vibrate, wink.

n. amusement, blink, coruscation, flash, flicker, gleam, glimmer, glistening, glitter, glittering, light, quiver, scintillation, shimmer, shine, spark, sparkle, wink.

twinkling *adj.* blinking, bright, coruscating, flashing, flickering, gleaming, glimmering, glistening, glittering, nitid, polished, scintillating, shimmering, shining, sparkling, twinkling, winking.

n. flash, instant, jiff, jiffy, mo, moment, no time, sec, second, shake, tick, trice, twinkle, two shakes.

twirl *v.* birl, coil, gyrate, gyre, pirouette, pivot, revolve, rotate, spin, swivel, turn, twiddle, twist, wheel, whirl, wind.

n. coil, convulsion, gyration, gyre, helix, pirouette, revolution, rotation, spin, spiral, turn, twiddle, twist, wheel, whirl, whorl.

twirling *adj.* gyral, gyratory, pirouetting, pivotal, pivoting, revolving, rotating, rotatory, spinning, swivelling, whirling.

twist *v.* alter, change, coil, contort, corkscrew, crankle, crinkle, crisp, curl, distort, encircle, entangle, entwine, garble, intertwine, misquote, misrepresent, pervert, pivot, revolve, rick, screw, spin, sprain, squirm, strain, swivel, turn, tweak, twine, warp, weave, wigwag, wind, wrap, wreathe, wrench, wrest, wrick, wriggle, wring, writhe.

n. aberration, arc, bend, bent, braid, break, change, characteristic, coil, confusion, contortion, convolution, crankle, curl, curlicue, curve, defect, deformation, development, distortion, eccentricity, entanglement, fault, flaw, foible, hank, idiosyncrasy, imperfection, intortion, jerk, kink, knot, meander, mess, mix-up, nuance, oddity, peculiarity, plug, proclivity, pull, quid, quirk, revelation, roll, screw, slant, snarl, spin, sprain, squiggle, surprise, swivel, tangle, tortion, trait, turn, twine, undulation, variation, warp, wind, wrench, wrest, zigzag.

twist someone's arm bulldoze, bully, coerce, dragoon, force, intimidate, lean on, persuade, pressurise.

twisted *adj.* bent, biased, bitter, coiled, contorted, convoluted, curled, deformed, deviant, devious, distorted, garbled, intertwined, intorted, jaundiced, misshapen, perverse, perverted, quirky, thrawn, torqued, tortile, tortuous, unnatural, warped, wound, woven, wry.

antonyms straight, straightforward.

twister *n.* blackguard, cheat, con man, crook, deceiver, fraud, phoney, rogue, rotter, scoundrel, swindler, trickster.

twit [1] *v.* banter, berate, blame, censure, chiack, deride, jeer, mock, rib, scorn, taunt, tease, upbraid.

twit [2] *n.* ass, blockhead, buffoon, chump, clot, clown, dope, fool, halfwit, idiot, muggins, nincompoop, ninny, nitwit, noodle, silly ass, simpleton, twerp.

twitch *v.* blink, flutter, jerk, jump, pinch, pluck, pull, snatch, tug, tweak, vellicate, yank.

n. blink, convulsion, flutter, jerk, jump, pluck, pull, spasmytic, subsultus, tremor, tweak, twinge, vellication.

twitter *v.* chatter, cheep, chirp, chirrup, giggle, prattle, simper, sing, snigger, titter, trill, tweet, warble, whistle.

n. agitation, anxiety, call, chatter, cheeping, chirping, chirruping, cry, dither, excitement, flurry, fluster, flutter, nervousness, song, tizz, tizzy, trill, tweeting, warble.

two-faced *adj.* deceitful, deceiving, devious, dissembling, double-dealing, double-tongued, duplicitous, false, hypocritical, insincere, Janus-faced, lying, mendacious, perfidious, treacherous, untrustworthy.

antonyms candid, frank, honest.

tycoon *n.* baron, big cheese, big noise, big shot, capitalist, captain of industry, Croesus, Dives, entrepreneur, fat cat, financier, gold-bug, industrialist, magnate, mogul, nabob, plutocrat, potentate, supremo.

type [1] *n.* archetype, breed, category, class, classification, description, designation, emblem, embodiment, epitome, essence, example, exemplar, form, genre, group, ilk, insignia, kidney, kind, mark, model, order, original, paradigm, pattern, personification, prototype, quintessence, sort, species, specimen, stamp, standard, strain, subdivision, variety.

type [2] *n.* case, characters, face, font, fount, lettering, print, printing.

typhoon *n.* baguio, cordonazo, cyclone, hurricane, squall, storm, tempest, tornado, twister, whirlwind, willy-willy.

typical *adj.* archetypal, average, characteristic, classic, conventional, distinctive, essential, illustrative, indicative, model, normal, orthodox, quintessential, representative, standard, stock, symptomatic, usual, vintage.

antonyms atypical, untypical.

typify *v.* characterise, embody, encapsulate, epitomise, exemplify, illustrate, incarnate, personify, represent, symbolise.

tyrannical *adj.* absolute, arbitrary, authoritarian, autocratic, coercive, despotic, dictatorial, domineering, high-handed, imperious, inexorable, iron-handed, magisterial, Neronian, oppressive, overbearing, overpowering, overweening, peremptory, ruthless, severe,

tyrannous, unjust, unreasonable.
antonyms liberal, tolerant.

tyrannise *v.* browbeat, bully, coerce, crush, dictate, domineer, enslave, intimidate, lord it, oppress, subjugate, terrorise.

tyranny *n.* absolutism, authoritarianism, autocracy, coercion, despotism, dictatorship, harshness, high-handedness, imperiousness, injustice, liberticide, monocracy, oppression, peremptoriness, relentlessness, ruthlessness.
antonyms democracy, liberality.

tyrant *n.* absolutist, authoritarian, autocrat, bully, despot, dictator, Hitler, liberticide, martinet, monarch, oppressor, satrap, slave-driver, sovereign, taskmaster.

tyro *see* **tiro** .

U

ubiquitous *adj.* all-over, common, commonly-encountered, ever-present, everywhere, frequent, global, omnipresent, pervasive, universal.
antonym rare.

ubiquity *n.* commonness, frequency, omnipresence, pervasiveness, popularity, prevalence, universality.
antonym rarity.

ugliness *n.* danger, deformity, disgrace, enormity, evil, frightfulness, heinousness, hideosity, hideousness, homeliness, horridness, horror, menace, monstrosity, monstrousness, nastiness, offensiveness, plainness, repulsiveness, unattractiveness, unloveliness, unpleasantness, unsightliness, vileness.
antonyms beauty, charm, goodness, pleasantness.

ugly *adj.* angry, bad-tempered, dangerous, dark, disagreeable, disgusting, distasteful, evil, evil-favoured, forbidding, frightful, hagged, haggish, hard-favoured, hard-featured, hideous, homely, horrid, ill-faced, ill-favoured, ill-looking, malevolent, menacing, misshapen, monstrous, nasty, objectionable, offensive, ominous, plain, repugnant, repulsive, revolting, shocking, sinister, spiteful, sullen, surly, terrible, threatening, truculent, unattractive, unlovely, unpleasant, unprepossessing, unsightly, vile.
antonyms beautiful, charming, good, pretty.

ulcer *n.* abscess, canker, fester, impostume, noma, sore, ulceration.

ulterior *adj.* concealed, covert, hidden, personal, private, secondary, secret, selfish, undisclosed, unexpressed.
antonyms declared, overt.

ultimate *adj.* basic, conclusive, consummate, decisive, elemental, end, eventual, extreme, final, fundamental, furthest, greatest, highest, last, maximum, paramount, perfect, primary, radical, remotest, superlative, supreme, terminal, topmost, utmost.
n. consummation, culmination, daddy of them all, dinger, epitome, extreme, granddaddy, greatest, height, peak, perfection, summit.

ultimately *adv.* after all, at last, basically, eventually, finally, fundamentally, in origin, in the end, originally, primarily, sooner or later.

ultra *adj.* avant-garde, excessive, extravagant, extreme, fanatical, immoderate, rabid, radical, revolutionary, way-out.

ultra- *adv.* especially, exceptionally, excessively, extra, extraordinarily, extremely, remarkably, unusually.

ululate *v.* cry, holler, hoot, howl, keen, lament, moan, mourn, scream, screech, sob, wail, weep.

umbrage *n.* anger, chagrin, disgruntlement, displeasure, grudge, high dudgeon, huff, indignation, offence, pique, resentment, sulks.

umbrella *n.* aegis, agency, brolly, chatta, cover, en tout cas, gamp, mush, mushroom, parasol, patronage, protection, sunshade, umbel.

umpire *n.* adjudicator, arbiter, arbitrator, daysman, judge, linesman, mediator, moderator, ref, referee.
v. adjudicate, arbitrate, call, control, judge, moderate, ref, referee.

umpteen *adj.* a good many, a thousand, considerable, countless, innumerable, millions, n, numerous, plenty, uncounted.
antonym few.

unabashed *adj.* blatant, bold, brazen, composed, confident, unawed, unblushing, unconcerned, undaunted, undismayed, unembarrassed.
antonyms abashed, sheepish.

unable *adj.* impotent, inadequate, incapable, incompetent, ineffectual, powerless, unequipped, unfit, unfitted, unqualified.
antonym able.

unabridged *adj.* complete, entire, full, full-length, uncondensed, uncut, unexpurgated, unshortened, whole.
antonym abridged.

unacceptable *adj.* before the pale, disagreeable, displeasing, distasteful, improper, inadmissible, insupportable, objectionable, offensive, ugly, undesirable, unpleasant, unsatisfactory, unwelcome.
antonym acceptable.

unaccommodating *adj.* disobliging, inflexible, intransigent, obstinate, perverse, rigid, stubborn, unbending, uncomplaisant, uncompromising, unco-operative, unyielding.
antonyms flexible, obliging.

unaccompanied *adj.* a cappella, alone, lone, solo, unattended, unescorted.
antonym accompanied.

unaccountable *adj.* astonishing, baffling, extraordinary, impenetrable, incomprehensible, inexplicable, inscrutable, mysterious, odd, peculiar, puzzling, singular, strange, uncommon, unexplainable, unfathomable, unheard-of, unintelligible, unusual, unwonted.
antonyms accountable, explicable.

unaccustomed *adj.* different, green, inexperienced, new, remarkable, special, strange, surprising, unacquainted, uncommon, unex-

pected, unfamiliar, unpractised, unprecedented, unused, unusual, unwonted.
antonyms accustomed, customary.

unacquainted *adj.* ignorant, strange, unaccustomed, unfamiliar.

unadorned *adj.* austere, outright, plain, restrained, severe, simple, stark, straightforward, undecorated, unembellished, unornamented, unvarnished.
antonyms decorated, embellished, ornate.

unaffected[1] *adj.* aloof, impervious, naïf, natural,
proof, spontaneous, unaltered, unchanged,
unimpressed, unmoved, unresponsive, untouched.
antonyms affected, unnatural.

unaffected[2] *adj.* artless, blasé, genuine, honest,
indifferent, ingenuous, naive, plain, simple,
sincere, straightforward, unassuming, unconcerned, unpretentious, unsophisticated, unspoilt, unstudied.
antonyms affected, impressed, moved.

unafraid *adj.* confident, daring, dauntless,
fearless, imperturbable, intrepid, unshakeable.
antonym afraid.

unalterable *adj.* final, fixed, immutable, inflexible, invariable, permanent, rigid, steadfast,
unchangeable, unchanging, unyielding.
antonyms alterable, flexible.

unanimity *n.* accord, agreement, chorus, concert, concord, concurrence, consensus, consent, correspondence, harmony, like-
mindedness, unison, unity.
antonyms disagreement, disunity.

unanimous *adj.* agreed, common, concerted,
concordant, harmonious, in accord, in agreement, joint, united.
antonyms disunited, split.

unanimously *adv.* at one man, by common
consent, conjointly, in concert, nem con,
unopposed, without exception, without opposition.

unanswerable *adj.* absolute, conclusive, final,
incontestable, incontrovertible, indisputable,
irrefragable, irrefutable, unarguable, undeniable.
antonyms answerable, refutable.

unappetising *adj.* disagreeable, distasteful, insipid, off-putting, tasteless, unappealing,
unattractive, unexciting, uninteresting, uninviting, unpalatable, unpleasant, unsavoury.
antonym appetising.

unapproachable *adj.* aloof, distant, forbidding,
formidable, frigid, godforsaken, inaccessible,
remote, reserved, stand-offish, unbending,
unfriendly, un-get-at-able, unreachable, unsociable, withdrawn.
antonym approachable.

unapt *adj.* inapplicable, inapposite, inappropriate, inapt, malapropos, unfit, unfitted, unseasonable, unsuitable, unsuited, untimely.
antonym apt.

unarmed *adj.* assailable, defenceless, exposed,
helpless, inerm, open, pregnable, un-
armoured, unprotected, vulnerable, weak,
weaponless.
antonym armed.

unashamed *adj.* impenitent, open, shameless,
unabashed, unconcealed, undisguised, unrepentant.

unasked *adj.* gratuitous, spontaneous, unbidden, undemanded, undesired, uninvited,
unprompted, unrequested, unsolicited, unsought, unwanted, voluntary.
antonyms invited, solicited.

unassailable *adj.* absolute, conclusive, impregnable, incontestable, incontrovertible, indisputable, invincible, inviolable, invulnerable,
irrefutable, positive, proven, sacrosanct,
secure, sound, undeniable, well-armed, well-
fortified.
antonym assailable.

unassertive *adj.* backward, bashful, diffident,
meek, mousy, quiet, retiring, self-effacing,
shy, timid, timorous, unassuming.
antonym assertive.

unassuming *adj.* diffident, humble, meek,
modest, natural, quiet, restrained, retiring,
self-effacing, simple, unassertive, unobtrusive, unostentatious, unpresuming, unpretentious.
antonyms assuming, presumptuous, pretentious.

unattached *adj.* autonomous, available, fancy-
free, footloose, free, independent, non-
aligned, single, unaffilated, uncommitted,
unengaged, unmarried, unspoken for.
antonyms attached, committed, engaged.

unattended *adj.* abandoned, alone, disregarded,
ignored, unaccompanied, unescorted, unguarded, unsupervised, unwatched.
antonyms attended, escorted.

unattractive *adj.* disagreeable, disgusting, distasteful, homely, ill-favoured, objectionable,
offensive, off-putting, plain, repellent, ugly,
unappealing, unappetising, uncomely, undesirable, unexciting, uninviting, unlovely,
unpalatable, unpleasant, unprepossessing,
unsavoury, unsightly, unwelcome.
antonym attractive.

unauthorised *adj.* illegal, illicit, irregular,
unlawful, unofficial, unsanctioned, unwarranted.
antonym authorised.

unavailing *adj.* abortive, barren, bootless,
fruitless, futile, idle, ineffective, ineffectual,
inefficacious, pointless, unproductive, unprofitable, unsuccessful, useless, vain.
antonyms productive, successful.

unavoidable *adj.* certain, compulsory, fated,
ineluctable, inescapable, inevitable, inexorable, mandatory, necessary, obligatory.
antonym avoidable.

unaware *adj.* blind, deaf, forgetful, heedless,
ignorant, incognisant, oblivious, unconscious,
unenlightened, uninformed, unknowing, unmindful, unsuspecting, unsuspicious.
antonym aware.

unawares *adv.* aback, abruptly, accidentally,
by surprise, imperceptibly, inadvertently,

insidiously, mistakenly, off guard, on the hop, suddenly, unconsciously, unexpectedly, unintentionally, unknowingly, unprepared, unthinkingly, unwittingly.

unbalanced *adj.* asymmetrical, biased, crazy, demented, deranged, disturbed, dysharmonic, eccentric, erratic, inequitable, insane, irrational, irregular, lopsided, lunatic, mad, off-balance, off-centre, one-sided, partial, partisan, prejudiced, shaky, touched, unequal, uneven, unfair, unhinged, unjust, unsound, unstable, unsteady, wobbly.
antonym balanced.

unbearable *adj.* insufferable, insupportable, intolerable, outrageous, unacceptable, unendurable, unspeakable.
antonyms acceptable, bearable.

unbeatable *adj.* indomitable, invincible, matchless, nonpareil, supreme, unconquerable, unstoppable, unsurpassable.
antonyms inferior, weak.

unbeaten *adj.* supreme, triumphant, unbowed, unconquered, undefeated, unsubdued, unsurpassed, unvanquished, victorious, winning.
antonyms defeated, vanquished.

unbecoming *adj.* discreditable, dishonourable, ill-suited, improper, inappropriate, incongruous, indecorous, indelicate, offensive, tasteless, unattractive, unbefitting, unfit, unflattering, unmaidenly, unmeet, unseemly, unsightly, unsuitable, unsuited.
antonyms becoming, seemly.

unbelief *n.* agnosticism, atheism, disbelief, distrust, doubt, incredulity, scepticism.
antonyms belief, faith.

unbelievable *adj.* astonishing, far-fetched, implausible, impossible, improbable, inconceivable, incredible, outlandish, preposterous, questionable, staggering, unconvincing, unimaginable, unlikely, unthinkable.
antonyms believable, credible.

unbeliever *n.* agnostic, atheist, disbeliever, doubter, doubting Thomas, infidel, nullifidian, sceptic.
antonyms believer, supporter.

unbelieving *adj.* disbelieving, distrustful, doubtful, doubting, dubious, incredulous, nullifidian, sceptical, suspicious, unconvinced, unpersuaded.
antonyms credulous, trustful.

unbend *v.* loosen up, relax, straighten, thaw, unbutton, uncoil, uncurl, unfreeze.
antonyms stiffen, withdraw.

unbending *adj.* aloof, distant, firm, forbidding, formal, formidable, hard-line, inflexible, intransigent, reserved, resolute, Rhadamanthine, rigid, severe, stiff, strict, stubborn, tough, uncompromising, unyielding.
antonyms approachable, friendly, relaxed.

unbiased *adj.* disinterested, dispassionate, equitable, even-handed, fair, fair-minded, impartial, independent, just, neutral, objective, open-minded, uncoloured, uninfluenced, unprejudiced.
antonym biased.

unbidden *adj.* free, spontaneous, unasked, unforced, uninvited, unprompted, unsolicited, unwanted, unwelcome, voluntary, willing.
antonyms invited, solicited.

unbind *v.* free, liberate, loose, loosen, release, unchain, undo, unfasten, unfetter, unloose, unloosen, unshackle, untie, unyoke.
antonyms bind, restrain.

unblemished *adj.* clear, flawless, immaculate, irreproachable, perfect, pure, spotless, unflawed, unimpeachable, unspotted, unstained, unsullied, untarnished.
antonyms blemished, flawed, imperfect.

unblinking *adj.* assured, calm, composed, cool, emotionless, fearless, impassive, imperturbable, steady, unafraid, unemotional, unfaltering, unflinching, unshrinking, unwavering.
antonyms cowed, faithful, fearful.

unblushing *adj.* amoral, blatant, bold, brazen, conscience-proof, immodest, shameless, unabashed, unashamed, unembarrassed.
antonyms abashed, ashamed.

unborn *adj.* awaited, coming, embryonic, expected, foetal, future, hereafter, in utero, later, subsequent, succeeding.

unbosom *v.* admit, bare, confess, confide, disburden, disclose, divulge, lay bare, let out, pour out, reveal, tell, unburden, uncover.
antonyms conceal, suppress.

unbounded *adj.* absolute, boundless, endless, immeasurable, infinite, lavish, limitless, prodigal, unbridled, unchecked, unconstrained, uncontrolled, unlimited, unrestrained, vast.
antonym limited.

unbreakable *adj.* armoured, durable, indestructible, infrangible, lasting, permanent, proof, resistant, rugged, shatter-proof, solid, strong, tough, toughened.
antonyms breakable, fragile.

unbridled *adj.* excessive, immoderate, intemperate, licentious, profligate, rampant, riotous, unchecked, unconstrained, uncontrolled, uncurbed, ungovernable, ungoverned, unrestrained, unruly, violent, wanton.

unbroken *adj.* ceaseless, complete, constant, continuous, endless, entire, incessant, intact, integral, perpetual, progressive, serried, solid, successive, total, unbowed, unceasing, undivided, unimpaired, uninterrupted, unremitting, unsubdued, untamed, whole.
antonyms cowed, fitful, intermittent.

unburden *v.* confess, confide, disburden, discharge, disclose, discumber, disencumber, empty, lay bare, lighten, offload, pour out, relieve, reveal, tell all, unbosom, unload.
antonyms conceal, hide, suppress.

uncalled-for *adj.* gratuitous, inappropriate, needless, undeserved, unheeded, unjust, unjustified, unmerited, unnecessary, unprovoked, unwanted, unwarranted, unwelcome.
antonym timely.

uncanny *adj.* astonishing, astounding, bizarre, creepy, eerie, eldritch, exceptional, extraordinary, fantastic, incredible, inspired, miraculous, mysterious, preternatural, prodigious, queer, remarkable, scary, singular, spooky, strange, supernatural, unaccountable, unco, unearthly, unerring, unheard-of, unnatural, unusual, weird.

uncaring *adj.* callous, inconsiderate, indifferent, negligent, unconcerned, unfeeling, uninterested, unmoved, unresponsive, unsympathetic.
antonyms concerned, solicitous.

unceasing *adj.* ceaseless, constant, continual, continuing, continuous, endless, incessant, never-ending, non-stop, perpetual, persistent, relentless, unbroken, unending, unfailing, uninterrupted, unrelenting, unremitting.
antonyms intermittent, spasmodic.

uncertain *adj.* ambiguous, ambivalent, chancy, changeable, conjectural, dicky, doubtful, dubious, erratic, fitful, hazardous, hazy, hesitant, iffy, in the lap of the gods, incalculable, inconstant, indefinite, indeterminate, indistinct, insecure, irregular, irresolute, on the knees of the gods, precarious, problematic, questionable, risky, shaky, slippy, speculative, unclear, unconfirmed, undecided, undetermined, unfixed, unforeseeable, unpredictable, unreliable, unresolved, unsettled, unsure, vacillating, vague, variable, wavering.
antonym certain.

uncertainty *n.* ambiguity, bewilderment, confusion, diffidence, dilemma, doubt, dubiety, hesitancy, hesitation, incalculability, inconclusiveness, indecision, insecurity, irresolution, misgiving, peradventure, perplexity, puzzlement, qualm, quandary, risk, scepticism, unpredictability, vagueness.
antonym certainty.

unchallengeable *adj.* absolute, conclusive, final, impregnable, inappellable, incontestable, incontrovertible, indisputable, irrefragable, irrefutable.
antonyms contestable, inconclusive.

unchangeable *adj.* changeless, eternal, final, immutable, intransmutable, irreversible, permanent, unchanging.
antonym changeable.

unchanging *adj.* abiding, changeless, constant, continuing, enduring, eternal, fixed, immutable, imperishable, lasting, permanent, perpetual, phaseless, steadfast, steady, unchanged, unfading, unvarying.
antonyms changeable, changing.

uncharitable *adj.* callous, captious, cruel, hard-hearted, hypercritical, inhumane, insensitive, mean, merciless, pitiless, stingy, unchristian, unfeeling, unforgiving, unfriendly, ungenerous, unkind, unsympathetic.
antonym charitable.

uncharted *adj.* foreign, mysterious, new, novel, strange, undiscovered, unexplored, unfamiliar, unknown, unplumbed, virgin.
antonyms familiar, well-known.

unchaste *adj.* defiled, depraved, dishonest, dissolute, fallen, immodest, immoral, impure,

lewd, licentious, loose, promiscuous, wanton.
antonym chaste.

uncivil *adj.* abrupt, bad-mannered, bearish, boorish, brusque, churlish, curt, discourteous, disrespectful, gruff, ill-bred, ill-mannered, impolite, rude, surly, uncouth, ungracious, unmannerly.
antonym civil.

uncivilised *adj.* antisocial, barbarian, barbaric, barbarous, boorish, brutish, churlish, coarse, gross, heathenish, ill-bred, illiterate, philistine, primitive, savage, tramontane, uncouth, uncultivated, uncultured, uneducated, unpolished, unsophisticated, untamed, vulgar, wild.
antonym civilised.

unclassifiable *adj.* doubtful, elusive, etypic(al), ill-defined, indefinable, indefinite, indescribable, indeterminate, indistinct, uncertain, unconformable, undefinable, unidentifiable, vague.
antonyms conformable, definable, identifiable.

unclean *adj.* contaminated, corrupt, defiled, dirty, evil, filthy, foul, impure, insalubrious, nasty, polluted, soiled, spotted, stained, sullied, tainted, unhygienic, unwholesome.
antonym clean.

unclear *adj.* ambiguous, as clear as mud, dim, doubtful, dubious, equivocal, hazy, indefinite, indescernible, indistinguishable, multivocal, obscure, uncertain, vague.
antonym clear.

unclothed *adj.* bare, disrobed, en cuerpo, in one's birthday suit, in the altogether, in the buff, naked, nude, stark naked, starkers, stripped, unclad, undressed.
antonyms clothed, dressed.

uncomfortable *adj.* awkward, bleak, confused, conscience-stricken, cramped, disagreeable, discomfited, discomfortable, discomposed, disquieted, distressed, disturbed, embarrassed, hard, ill-fitting, incommodious, irritating, painful, poky, self-conscious, sheepish, troubled, troublesome, uneasy.
antonyms comfortable, easy.

uncommitted *adj.* available, fancy-free, floating, free, neutral, non-aligned, non-partisan, unattached, undecided, uninvolved.
antonym committed.

uncommon *adj.* abnormal, atypical, bizarre, curious, distinctive, exceptional, extraordinary, incomparable, infrequent, inimitable, notable, noteworthy, novel, odd, outstanding, peculiar, queer, rare, recherché, remarkable, scarce, singular, special, strange, superior, unfamiliar, unparalleled, unprecedented, unusual, unwonted.
antonym common.

uncommonly *adv.* abnormally, exceptionally, extremely, infrequently, occasionally, outstandingly, particularly, peculiarly, rarely, remarkably, seldom, singularly, strangely, unusually, very.
antonyms commonly, frequently.

uncommunicative *adj.* brief, close, curt, guarded, laconic, reserved, reticent, retiring, secretive, short, shy, silent, taciturn, tight-lipped, unforthcoming, unresponsive, unsociable, withdrawn.
antonym communicative.

uncompromising *adj.* decided, die-hard, firm, hard-core, hard-line, hardshell, inexorable, inflexible, intransigent, obdurate, obstinate, rigid, steadfast, strict, stubborn, tough, unaccommodating, unbending, unyielding.
antonyms flexible, open-minded.

unconcealable *adj.* clear, insistent, insuppressible, irrepressible, manifest, obvious, plain, uncontrollable, undistinguishable.

unconcealed *adj.* admitted, apparent, blatant, conspicuous, evident, frank, ill-concealed, manifest, naked, noticeable, obvious, open, overt, patent, self-confessed, unashamed, undistinguished, visible.
antonyms hidden, secret.

unconcern *n.* aloofness, apathy, callousness, detachment, indifference, insouciance, jauntiness, negligence, nonchalance, pococurantism, remoteness, uninterestedness.
antonym concern.

unconcerned *adj.* aloof, apathetic, blithe, callous, carefree, careless, complacent, composed, cool, detached, dispassionate, distant, easy, incurious, indifferent, insouciant, joco, nonchalant, oblivious, pococurante, relaxed, serene, uncaring, uninterested, uninvolved, unmoved, unperturbed, unruffled, unsympathetic, untroubled, unworried.
antonym concerned.

unconditional *adj.* absolute, categorical, complete, downright, entire, full, implicit, out-and-out, outright, plenary, positive, thoroughgoing, total, unequivocal, unlimited, unqualified, unreserved, unrestricted, utter, whole-hearted.
antonym conditional.

unconformity *n.* disconformity, discontinuity, irregularity, unconformability.
antonym conformability.

uncongenial *adj.* antagonistic, antipathetic, disagreeable, discordant, displeasing, distasteful, incompatible, unappealing, unattractive, uninviting, unpleasant, unsavoury, unsuited, unsympathetic.
antonym congenial.

unconnected *adj.* detached, disconnected, disjointed, divided, illogical, incoherent, independent, irrational, irrelevant, separate, unattached, unrelated.
antonyms connected, relevant.

unconquerable *adj.* enduring, indomitable, ingrained, insuperable, insurmountable, inveterate, invincible, irrepressible, irresistible, overpowering, unbeatable, undefeatable, unyielding.
antonyms weak, yielding.

unconscionable *adj.* amoral, criminal, excessive, exorbitant, extravagant, extreme, immoderate, inordinate, outrageous, preposterous, unethical, unjustifiable, unpardonable, unprincipled, unreasonable, unscrupulous, unwarrantable.

unconscious *adj.* accidental, automatic, blind to, comatose, concussed, deaf to, heedless, ignorant, inadvertent, innate, insensible, instinctive, involuntary, knocked out, latent, oblivious, out, out cold, out for the count, reflex, repressed, senseless, stunned, subconscious, subliminal, suppressed, unaware, unintended, unintentional, unknowing, unmindful, unsuspecting, unwitting.
antonym conscious.

unconstraint *n.* abandon, freedom, laissez-aller, laissez-faire, liberality, openness, relaxation, unreserve, unrestraint.

uncontrollable *adj.* frantic, furious, intractable, irrepressible, irresistible, irrestrainable, mad, masterless, recalcitrant, refractory, strong, ungovernable, unmanageable, unruly, violent, wild.
antonyms controllable, manageable.

uncontrolled *adj.* boisterous, furious, masterless, rampant, riotous, unbridled, unchecked, uncurbed, undisciplined, ungoverned, unhindered, unrestrained, unruly, untrammelled, violent, wild.
antonyms contained, controlled.

unconventional *adj.* abnormal, alternative, atypical, bizarre, bohemian, different, eccentric, freakish, idiosyncratic, individual, individualistic, informal, irregular, nonconforming, odd, offbeat, original, spacy, unconformable, unorthodox, unusual, wayout, wayward.
antonym conventional.

unconvincing *adj.* doubtful, dubious, feeble, fishy, flimsy, implausible, improbable, inconclusive, lame, questionable, specious, suspect, tall, thin, unlikely, unpersuasive, weak.
antonyms convincing, plausible.

unco-ordinated *adj.* awkward, bumbling, clodhopping, clumsy, desultory, diffuse, disjointed, disorganised, graceless, inept, lumbering, maladroit, unconcerted, ungainly, ungraceful.
antonyms concerted, graceful, systematic.

uncouth *adj.* awkward, barbarian, barbaric, boorish, clownish, clumsy, coarse, crude, gauche, gawky, graceless, gross, ill-mannered, loutish, lubberly, oafish, rough, rude, rustic, uncivilised, uncultivated, ungainly, unrefined, unseemly, vulgar.
antonyms polished, polite, refined, urbane.

uncover *v.* bare, detect, disclose, discover, dismask, disrobe, divulge, exhume, expose, leak, lift the lid off, open, reveal, show, strip, unearth, unmask, unveil, unwrap.
antonyms conceal, cover, suppress.

uncritical *adj.* accepting, credulous, indiscriminate, naïve, superficial, trusting, undiscerning, undiscriminating, unexacting, unfussy, unscholarly, unselective, unthinking.
antonyms critical, discriminating, sceptical.

unctuous *adj.* fawning, glib, greasy, gushing, ingratiating, insincere, obsequious, oily, pietistic, plausible, religiose, sanctimonious, slick, smarmy, smooth, suave, sycophantic.

uncultivated *adj.* fallow, incult, natural, rough, uncultured, wild.
antonym cultivated.

uncultured *adj.* awkward, boorish, coarse, crude, hick, raw, rustic, uncivilised, uncouth, uncultivated, unrefined, unsophisticated.
antonym cultured.

undaunted *adj.* bold, brave, courageous, dauntless, fearless, gallant, indomitable, intrepid, resolute, steadfast, unbowed, undashed, undeterred, undiscouraged, undismayed, unfaltering, unflinching, unperturbed, unshrinking.
antonyms cowed, timorous.

undecided *adj.* ambivalent, debatable, dithering, doubtful, dubious, hesitant, in two minds, indefinite, irresolute, moot, open, pending, swithering, tentative, torn, uncertain, uncommitted, unconcluded, undetermined, unfixed, unsettled, unsure, vague, vexed, wavering.
antonyms certain, decided, definite.

undecorated *adj.* austere, classical, functional, inornate, plain, severe, simple, stark, unadorned, unembellished, unornamented.
antonyms decorated, ornate.

undefended *adj.* defenceless, exposed, expugnable, inerm, naked, open, pregnable, unarmed, unfortified, unguarded, unprotected, vulnerable.
antonyms armed, defended, fortified.

undefiled *adj.* chaste, clean, clear, flawless, immaculate, intact, intemerate, inviolate, pure, sinless, spotless, unblemished, unsoiled, unspotted, unstained, unsullied, virginal.

undefined *adj.* formless, hazy, ill-defined, imprecise, indefinite, indeterminate, indistinct, inexact, nebulous, shadowy, tenuous, unclear, unexplained, unspecified, vague, woolly.
antonyms definite, precise.

undemonstrative *adj.* aloof, cold, contained, cool, distant, formal, impassive, phlegmatic, reserved, restrained, reticent, stiff, stolid, unbending, uncommunicative, unemotional, unresponsive, withdrawn.
antonym demonstrative.

undeniable *adj.* certain, clear, evident, incontestable, incontrovertible, indisputable, indubitable, irrefragable, irrefutable, manifest, obvious, patent, proven, sound, sure, unassailable, undoubted, unmistakable, unquestionable.

undependable *adj.* capricious, changeable, erratic, fair-weather, fickle, inconsistent, inconstant, irresponsible, mercurial, treacherous, uncertain, unpredictable, unreliable, unstable, untrustworthy, variable.
antonyms dependable, reliable.

under *prep.* belonging to, below, beneath, governed by, included in, inferior to, junior to, lead by, less than, lower than, secondary to, subject to, subordinate to, subservient to, underneath.
adv. below, beneath, down, downward, less, lower.

under an obligation beholden, bound, duty-bound, grateful, honour-bound, in debt to, in honour bound, indebted, obligated, obliged, thankful.

under the weather ailing, below par, groggy, hung over, ill, indisposed, mops and brooms, nauseous, off-colour, out of sorts, peelie-wally, poorly, queer, seedy, sick, squeamish, the worse for wear.

under way afoot, begun, going, in motion, in operation, in progress, launched, moving, on the go, on the move, started.

underclothes *n.* frillies, lingerie, smalls, underclothing, undergarments, underlinen, underwear, undies, unmentionables.

undercover *adj.* clandestine, concealed, confidential, covert, furtive, hidden, hush-hush, intelligence, private, secret, spy, stealthy, surreptitious, underground.
antonyms open, unconcealed.

undercurrent *n.* atmosphere, aura, cross-current, drift, eddy, feeling, flavour, hint, movement, murmur, overtone, rip, riptide, sense, suggestion, tendency, tenor, tide, tinge, trend, underflow, undertone, undertow, vibes, vibrations.

undercut *v.* excavate, gouge out, hollow out, mine, sacrifice, scoop out, underbid, undercharge, undermine, underprice, undersell.

underestimate *v.* belittle, dismiss, fail to appreciate, minimise, miscalculate, misprise, sell short, underrate, undervalue.
antonyms exaggerate, overestimate.

undergo *v.* bear, brook, endure, experience, run the gauntlet, stand, submit to, suffer, sustain, weather, withstand.

underground *adj.* alternative, avant-garde, buried, clandestine, concealed, covered, covert, experimental, hidden, hypogeal, hypogean, hypogene, hypogeous, radical, revolutionary, secret, subterranean, subversive, surreptitious, undercover.
n. métro, subway, tube.

undergrowth *n.* bracken, brambles, briars, brush, brushwood, firth, frith, ground cover, scrub, underbrush.

underhand *adj.* clandestine, crafty, crooked, deceitful, deceptive, devious, dishonest, dishonourable, fraudulent, furtive, immoral, improper, shady, shifty, sly, sneaky, stealthy, surreptitious, treacherous, underhanded, unethical, unscrupulous.
antonym above board.

underline *v.* accentuate, emphasise, highlight, italicise, labour, mark, point up, press, reiterate, stress, underscore, urge.
antonyms play down, soft-pedal.

underling *n.* flunkey, hireling, inferior, lackey, menial, minion, nobody, nonentity, retainer, servant, slave, subordinate, understrapper, weakling.

antonyms boss, leader, master.

underlying *adj.* basal, basic, concealed, elementary, essential, fundamental, hidden, intrinsic, latent, lurking, primary, prime, root, subjacent, substratal, substructural, veiled.

undermine *v.* debilitate, disable, erode, excavate, impair, mar, mine, sabotage, sap, subvert, threaten, tunnel, undercut, vitiate, weaken, wear away.
antonyms fortify, strengthen.

underprivileged *adj.* deprived, destitute, disadvantaged, impecunious, impoverished, needy, poor, poverty-stricken.
antonyms affluent, fortunate, privileged.

underrate *v.* belittle, depreciate, discount, dismiss, disparage, misprise, underestimate, undervalue.
antonyms exaggerate, overrate.

undersell *v.* cut, depreciate, disparage, mark down, play down, reduce, slash, undercharge, undercut, understate.

undersized *adj.* achondroplastic, atrophied, dwarfed, dwarfish, miniature, minute, puny, pygmy, runtish, runty, small, stunted, tiny, underdeveloped, underweight.
antonyms big, oversized, overweight.

understand *v.* accept, appreciate, apprehend, assume, believe, commiserate, comprehend, conceive, conclude, cotton on, discern, fathom, follow, gather, get, get the message, get the picture, grasp, hear, know, learn, penetrate, perceive, presume, realise, recognise, savvy, see, see daylight, suppose, sympathise, think, tolerate, tumble, twig.
antonym misunderstand.

understanding *n.* accord, agreement, appreciation, awareness, belief, comprehension, conclusion, discernment, estimation, grasp, idea, impression, insight, intellect, intellection, intelligence, interpretation, judgement, knowledge, notion, opinion, pact, penetration, perception, reading, sense, view, viewpoint, wisdom.
adj. accepting, compassionate, considerate, discerning, forbearing, forgiving, kind, kindly, loving, patient, perceptive, responsive, sensitive, sympathetic, tender, tolerant.
antonyms impatient, insensitive, intolerant, unsympathetic.

understate *v.* belittle, dismiss, make light of, make little of, minimise, play down, soft-pedal, underplay, undersell.

understatement *n.* dismissal, litotes, meiosis, minimisation, restraint, underplaying.

understood *adj.* accepted, assumed, axiomatic, implicit, implied, inferred, presumed, tacit, unspoken, unstated, unwritten.

understudy *n.* alternate, deputy, double, fill-in, replacement, reserve, stand-in, substitute.

undertake *v.* accept, agree, assume, attempt, bargain, begin, commence, contract, covenant, embark on, endeavour, engage, guarantee, pledge, promise, shoulder, stipulate, tackle, try.

undertaker *n.* funeral director, funeral

furnisher, mortician.

undertaking *n.* adventure, affair, assurance, attempt, business, commitment, effort, emprise, endeavour, enterprise, game, operation, pledge, project, promise, task, venture, vow, word.

undertone *n.* atmosphere, current, feeling, flavour, hint, murmur, suggestion, tinge, touch, trace, undercurrent, undervoice, whisper.

undervalue *v.* depreciate, discount, dismiss, disparage, disprize, minimise, misjudge, misprice, misprise, underestimate, underrate.
antonyms exaggerate, overrate.

underwater *adj.* subaquatic, subaqueous, submarine, submerged, sunken, undersea.

underwear *n.* frillies, lingerie, smalls, underclothes, underclothing, undergarments, underlinen, undies, unmentionables.

underweight *adj.* emaciated, half-starved, puny, skinny, thin, undernourished, undersized.
antonym overweight.

underworld *n.* Avernus, criminal fraternity, gangland, gangsterland, Hades, hell, nether world, the Inferno.

underwrite *v.* approve, authorise, back, consent, countenance, countersign, endorse, finance, fund, guarantee, initial, insure, okay, sanction, sign, sponsor, subscribe, subsidise, validate.

undesirable *adj.* disagreeable, disliked, disreputable, distasteful, dreaded, objectionable, obnoxious, offensive, repugnant, unacceptable, unattractive, unpleasant, unpopular, unsavoury, unsuitable, unwanted, unwelcome, unwished-for.
antonym desirable.

undeveloped *adj.* dwarfed, embryonic, immature, inchoate, latent, potential, primordial, stunted, unformed.
antonyms developed, mature.

undignified *adj.* foolish, improper, inappropriate, indecorous, inelegant, infra dig, petty, unbecoming, ungentlemanly, unladylike, unrefined, unseemly, unsuitable.
antonym dignified.

undisciplined *adj.* disobedient, disorganised, obstreperous, uncontrolled, unpredictable, unreliable, unrestrained, unruly, unschooled, unsteady, unsystematic, untrained, wayward, wild, wilful.
antonym disciplined.

undisguised *adj.* apparent, blatant, confessed, evident, explicit, frank, genuine, ill-concealed, manifest, naked, obvious, open, out-and-out, outright, overt, patent, stark, thoroughgoing, transparent, unadorned, unashamed, unconcealed, unmistakable, utter, whole-hearted.
antonyms concealed, hidden, secret.

undisguisedly *adj.* blatantly, frankly, obviously, openly, outright, overtly, patently, transparently, unreservedly.
antonym secretly.

undisputed *adj.* accepted, acknowledged, cer-

tain, conclusive, incontestable, incontroverti-ble, indisputable, irrefragable, irrefutable, recognised, sure, unchallenged, uncontested, undeniable, undoubted, unequivocal, unmis-takable, unquestioned.
antonyms dubious, uncertain.

undistinguished *adj.* banal, commonplace, ev-eryday, indifferent, inferior, mediocre, ordin-ary, pedestrian, prosaic, run-of-the-mill, so-so, unexceptional, unexciting, unimpress-ive, unremarkable.
antonyms distinguished, exceptional.

undisturbed *adj.* calm, collected, composed, equable, even, motionless, placid, quiet, serene, tranquil, unaffected, unconcerned, uninterrupted, unperturbed, unruffled, un-touched, untroubled.
antonyms disturbed, interrupted.

undivided *adj.* combined, complete, concen-trated, concerted, entire, exclusive, full, individuate, solid, thorough, tight-knit, unanimous, unbroken, united, whole, whole-hearted.

undo *v.* annul, cancel, defeat, destroy, disen-gage, dislink, invalidate, loose, loosen, mar, neutralise, nullify, offset, open, overturn, quash, reverse, ruin, separate, shatter, spoil, subvert, unbutton, undermine, unfasten, unlink, unlock, unloose, unloosen, untie, unwind, unwrap, upset, vitiate, wreck.
antonym fasten.

undoing *n.* besetting sin, blight, collapse, curse, defeat, destruction, disgrace, downfall, hamartia, humiliation, misfortune, over-throw, overturn, reversal, ruin, ruination, shame, tragic fault, trouble, weakness.

undomesticated *adj.* ferae naturae, feral, natu-ral, savage, uncivilised, unhouseproud, un-housewifely, unmaternal, unmotherly, un-practical, untamed, wild.
antonyms domesticated, home-loving, tame.

undone[1] *adj.* betrayed, destroyed, lost, ruined.

undone[2] *adj.* forgotten, incomplete, left, neglected, omitted, outstanding, unaccom-plished, uncompleted, unfinished, unfulfilled, unperformed.
antonyms accomplished, complete, done.

undone[3] *adj.* loose, open, unbraced, unbut-toned, unfastened, unlaced, unlocked, un-tied.
antonyms fastened, secured.

undoubted *adj.* acknowledged, certain, definite, evident, incontrovertible, indisputable, in-dubitable, obvious, patent, sure, unchal-lenged, undisputed, unquestionable, unques-tioned.

undoubtedly *adv.* assuredly, certainly, definite-ly, doubtless, indubitably, of course, surely, undeniably, unmistakably, unquestionably.

undreamed-of *adj.* astonishing, inconceivable, incredible, miraculous, undreamt, unex-pected, unforeseen, unheard-of, unhoped-for, unimagined, unsuspected.

undress *v.* disrobe, divest, peel off, remove, shed, strip, take off.

n. déshabillé, disarray, dishabille, nakedness, nudity.

undressed *adj.* disrobed, en cuerpo, naked, nude, stark naked, starkers, stripped, unclad, unclothed.

undue *adj.* disproportionate, excessive, extrava-gant, extreme, immoderate, improper, in-ordinate, intemperate, needless, overmuch, supererogatory, uncalled-for, undeserved, unnecessary, unreasonable, unseemly, un-warranted.
antonym reasonable.

undulate *v.* billow, heave, ripple, rise and fall, roll, surge, swell, wave.

undulating *adj.* billowing, flexuose, flexuous, rippling, rolling, sinuous, undate, undulant, wavy.
antonym flat.

unduly *adv.* disproportionately, excessively, extravagantly, immoderately, inordinately, over, overly, overmuch, too, unjustifiably, unnecessarily, unreasonably.
antonym reasonably.

undutiful *adj.* careless, defaulting, delinquent, disloyal, neglectful, negligent, remiss, slack, unfilial.
antonym dutiful.

undutifulness *n.* default, defection, delinquency, dereliction, desertion, disloyalty, incivism, neglect, negligence, remissness.
antonyms dutifulness, loyalty.

undying *adj.* abiding, constant, continuing, deathless, eternal, everlasting, immortal, imperishable, indestructible, inextinguish-able, infinite, lasting, perennial, permanent, perpetual, sempiternal, undiminished, unen-ding, unfading.
antonyms impermanent, inconstant.

unearth *v.* detect, dig up, discover, disinter, dredge up, excavate, exhume, expose, ferret out, find, reveal, uncover.

unearthly *adj.* abnormal, eerie, eldritch, ethereal, extraordinary, ghostly, haunted, heavenly, nightmarish, other-worldly, phan-tom, preternatural, spectral, spine-chilling, strange, sublime, supernatural, uncanny, ungodly, unreasonable, weird.

uneasiness *n.* agitation, alarm, anxiety, apprehension, apprehensiveness, dis-ease, disquiet, doubt, dysphoria, inquietude, mis-giving, nervousness, perturbation, qualms, suspicion, unease, worry.
antonyms calm, composure.

uneasy *adj.* agitated, anxious, apprehensive, awkward, constrained, discomposed, dis-quieting, disturbed, disturbing, edgy, impa-tient, insecure, jittery, nervous, niggling, on edge, perturbed, precarious, restive, restless, shaky, strained, tense, troubled, troubling, uncomfortable, unquiet, unsettled, unstable, upset, upsetting, worried, worrying.
antonyms calm, composed.

uneconomic *adj.* loss-making, non-profit-making, uncommercial, unprofitable.
antonyms economic, profitable.

uneducated *adj.* benighted, ignorant, illiterate, low-brow, philistine, uncultivated, uncultured, uninstructed, unlessoned, unlettered, unread, unschooled, untaught.
antonym educated.

unembellished *adj.* austere, bald, bare, functional, modest, plain, severe, simple, stark, unadorned, undecorated, unelaborated, unornamented, unvarnished.
antonyms embellished, ornate.

unemotional *adj.* apathetic, cold, cool, dispassionate, impassive, indifferent, laid-back, low-key, objective, passionless, phlegmatic, reserved, undemonstrative, unexcitable, unfeeling, unimpassioned, unresponsive.
antonyms emotional, excitable.

unemphatic *adj.* down-beat, played-down, soft-pedalled, underplayed, understated, unobtrusive, unostentatious.

unemployed *adj.* idle, jobless, on the dole, out of work, redundant, resting, unoccupied, workless.
antonym employed.

unending *adj.* ceaseless, constant, continual, endless, eternal, everlasting, incessant, interminable, never-ending, perpetual, unceasing, undying, unrelenting, unremitting.
antonyms intermittent, transient.

unendurable *adj.* insufferable, insupportable, intolerable, overwhelming, shattering, unbearable.
antonyms bearable, endurable.

unenthusiastic *adj.* apathetic, blasé, bored, cool, half-hearted, indifferent, laodicean, lukewarm, neutral, nonchalant, unimpressed, uninterested, unmoved, unresponsive.
antonym enthusiastic.

unenviable *adj.* disagreeable, painful, thankless, uncomfortable, uncongenial, undesirable, unpalatable, unpleasant, unsavoury.
antonyms desirable, enviable.

unequal *adj.* asymmetrical, different, differing, disparate, disproportionate, dissimilar, ill-equipped, ill-matched, inadequate, incapable, incompetent, insufficient, irregular, unbalanced, uneven, unlike, unmatched, variable, varying.
antonym equal.

unequalled *adj.* exceptional, incomparable, inimitable, matchless, nonpareil, paramount, peerless, pre-eminent, supreme, surpassing, transcendent, unmatched, unparalleled, unrivalled, unsurpassed.

unequivocal *adj.* absolute, certain, clear, clear-cut, crystal-clear, decisive, definite, direct, distinct, evident, explicit, express, incontrovertible, indubitable, manifest, plain, positive, straight, unambiguous, uncontestable, unmistakable.
antonyms ambiguous, vague.

unerring *adj.* accurate, certain, dead, exact, faultless, impeccable, infallible, perfect, sure, uncanny, unfailing.
antonym fallible.

unerringly *adv.* accurately, bang, dead, infall-

ibly, unfailingly.

unethical *adj.* dirty, discreditable, dishonest, dishonourable, disreputable, illegal, illicit, immoral, improper, shady, underhand, unfair, unprincipled, unprofessional, unscrupulous, wrong.
antonym ethical.

uneven *adj.* accidented, asymmetrical, broken, bumpy, changeable, desultory, disparate, erratic, fitful, fluctuating, ill-matched, inconsistent, intermittent, irregular, jerky, lop-sided, odd, one-sided, patchy, rough, spasmodic, unbalanced, unequal, unfair, unsteady, variable.
antonym even.

uneventful *adj.* boring, commonplace, dull, humdrum, monotonous, ordinary, quiet, routine, tame, tedious, unexceptional, unexciting, uninteresting, unmemorable, unremarkable, unvaried.
antonyms eventful, memorable.

unexampled *adj.* incomparable, never before seen, novel, unequalled, unheard-of, unique, unmatched, unparalleled, unprecedented.

unexceptional *adj.* average, commonplace, conventional, indifferent, insignificant, mediocre, normal, ordinary, pedestrian, run-of-the-mill, typical, undistinguished, unimpressive, unmemorable, unremarkable, usual.
antonyms exceptional, impressive.

unexcitable *adj.* calm, composed, contained, cool, dispassionate, easy-going, impassive, imperturbable, laid-back, passionless, phlegmatic, relaxed, self-possessed, serene, unimpassioned.
antonym excitable.

unexpected *adj.* abrupt, accidental, amazing, astonishing, chance, fortuitous, startling, sudden, surprising, unaccustomed, unanticipated, unforeseen, unlooked-for, unpredictable, unusual, unwonted.
antonyms expected, normal, predictable.

unexpectedly *adv.* abruptly, by chance, ex improviso, fortuitously, out of the blue, suddenly, surprisingly, unpredictably, without warning.

unexpressive *adj.* blank, dead-pan, emotionless, expressionless, immobile, impassive, inexpressive, inscrutable, vacant.
antonyms expressive, mobile.

unfading *adj.* abiding, durable, enduring, fadeless, fast, immarcescible, imperishable, lasting, undying, unfailing.
antonyms changeable, transient.

unfailing *adj.* certain, constant, dependable, faithful, infallible, loyal, reliable, staunch, steadfast, steady, sure, true, undying, unfading.
antonyms fickle, impermanent, transient.

unfair *adj.* arbitrary, biased, bigoted, crooked, discriminatory, dishonest, dishonourable, inequitable, one-sided, partial, partisan, prejudiced, uncalled-for, undeserved, unethical, unjust, unmerited, unprincipled, unscrupulous, unsporting, unwarranted, wrongful. *antonym* fair.

unfairness *n.* bias, bigotry, discrimination, inequity, injustice, maldistribution, one-sidedness, partiality, partisanship, prejudice. *antonyms* equity, fairness.

unfaithful *adj.* adulterous, deceitful, dishonest, disloyal, faithless, false, false-hearted, fickle, godless, inconstant, perfidious, recreant, traitorous, treacherous, treasonable, two-timing, unbelieving, unchaste, unreliable, untrue, untrustworthy. *antonyms* faithful, loyal.

unfaltering *adj.* constant, firm, fixed, indefatigable, pertinacious, resolute, steadfast, steady, tireless, unfailing, unflagging, unflinching, unswerving, untiring, unwavering. *antonyms* faltering, uncertain, wavering.

unfamiliar *adj.* alien, curious, different, foreign, new, novel, out-of-the-way, strange, unaccustomed, unacquainted, uncharted, uncommon, unconversant, unexplored, unknown, unpractised, unskilled, unusual, unversed. *antonyms* customary, familiar.

unfashionable *adj.* antiquated, dated, démodé, demoded, dismoded, fogram, obsolete, old hat, old-fashioned, out, out of date, outmoded, passé, square, unpopular. *antonym* fashionable.

unfasten *v.* detach, disconnect, loosen, open, separate, uncouple, undo, unlace, unlock, unloose, unloosen, untie. *antonym* fasten.

unfathomable *adj.* abstruse, baffling, bottomless, deep, esoteric, fathomless, hidden, immeasurable, impenetrable, incomprehensible, indecipherable, inexplicable, mysterious, profound, unknowable, unplumbed, unsounded. *antonyms* comprehensible, explicable, penetrable.

unfavourable *adj.* adverse, bad, contrary, critical, disadvantageous, discouraging, hostile, ill-suited, inauspicious, infelicitous, inimical, inopportune, low, negative, ominous, poor, threatening, uncomplimentary, unfortunate, unfriendly, unlucky, unpromising, unpropitious, unseasonable, unsuited, untimely, untoward. *antonym* favourable.

unfeeling *adj.* apathetic, callous, cold, cruel, hard, hardened, hard-hearted, harsh, heartless, inhuman, insensitive, pitiless, soulless, stony, uncaring, unsympathetic. *antonym* concerned.

unfeigned *adj.* frank, genuine, heartfelt, natural, pure, real, sincere, spontaneous, unaffected, unforced, whole-hearted. *antonyms* feigned, insincere, pretended.

unfettered *adj.* free, unbridled, unchecked, unconfined, unconstrained, unhampered, unhindered, uninhibited, unrestrained, unshackled, untrammelled. *antonyms* constrained, fettered.

unfinished *adj.* bare, crude, deficient, half-done,

imperfect, incomplete, incondite, lacking, natural, raw, rough, rude, sketchy, unaccomplished, uncompleted, undone, unfulfilled, unpolished, unrefined, wanting. *antonyms* finished, polished, refined.

unfit *adj.* debilitated, decrepit, feeble, flabby, flaccid, hypotonic, ill-adapted, ill-equipped, inadequate, inappropriate, incapable, incompetent, ineffective, ineligible, unequal, unhealthy, unprepared, unqualified, unsuitable, unsuited, untrained, useless. *antonyms* competent, fit, suitable.

unflagging *adj.* constant, fixed, indefatigable, never-failing, persevering, persistent, single-minded, staunch, steady, tireless, unceasing, undeviating, unfailing, unfaltering, unremitting, unswerving, untiring. *antonyms* faltering, inconstant.

unflappable *adj.* calm, collected, composed, cool, equable, impassive, imperturbable, level-headed, phlegmatic, self-possessed, unexcitable, unruffled, unworried. *antonyms* excitable, nervous, temperamental.

unflattering *adj.* blunt, candid, critical, honest, outspoken, unbecoming, uncomplimentary, unfavourable, unprepossessing. *antonyms* complimentary, flattering.

unflinching *adj.* bold, constant, determined, firm, fixed, resolute, stalwart, staunch, steadfast, steady, sure, unblinking, unfaltering, unshaken, unshrinking, unswerving, unwavering. *antonyms* cowed, scared.

unfold *v.* clarify, describe, develop, disclose, disentangle, divulge, elaborate, evolve, expand, explain, flatten, grow, illustrate, mature, open, present, reveal, show, spread, straighten, stretch out, uncoil, uncover, undo, unfurl, unravel, unroll, unwrap. *antonyms* fold, suppress, withhold, wrap.

unforeseen *adj.* abrupt, accidental, fortuitous, startling, sudden, surprise, surprising, unanticipated, unavoidable, unexpected, unheralded, unlooked-for, unpredicted. *antonyms* expected, predictable.

unforgettable *adj.* exceptional, extraordinary, historic, impressive, memorable, momentous, notable, noteworthy. *antonyms* unexceptional, unmemorable.

unforgivable *adj.* deplorable, disgraceful, indefensible, inexcusable, reprehensible, shameful, unconscionable, unjustifiable, unpardonable, unwarrantable. *antonyms* forgivable, venial.

unforgiven *adj.* unabsolved, unredeemed, unregenerate, unrepentant, unshrived, unshriven. *antonyms* absolved, forgiven.

unfortunate *adj.* adverse, calamitous, cursed, deplorable, disadventurous, disastrous, doomed, hapless, hopeless, ill-advised, ill-fated, ill-starred, ill-timed, inappropriate, infelicitous, inopportune, lamentable, luckless, poor, regrettable, ruinous, star-crossed, tactless, unbecoming, unfavourable, unhappy, unlucky, unprosperous, unsuccessful,

unsuitable, untimely, untoward, wretched.
antonym fortunate.

unfortunately *adv.* miserabile dictu, regrettably, sad to relate, sad to say, sadly, unhappily, unluckily, worse luck.
antonym fortunately.

unfounded *adj.* baseless, fabricated, false, gratuitous, groundless, idle, spurious, trumped-up, unjustified, unmerited, unproven, unsubstantiated, unsupported.
antonym justified.

unfrequented *adj.* deserted, desolate, godforsaken, isolated, lone, lonely, remote, secluded, sequestered, solitary, uninhabited, unvisited.
antonyms busy, crowded, populous.

unfriendly *adj.* alien, aloof, antagonistic, chilly, cold, critical, disagreeable, distant, hostile, ill-disposed, inauspicious, inhospitable, inimical, quarrelsome, sour, stand-offish, surly, unapproachable, unbending, uncongenial, unfavourable, unneighbourly, unsociable, unwelcoming.
antonyms agreeable, amiable, friendly.

unfrock *v.* degrade, demote, depose, disfrock, disgown, dismiss, suspend.
antonyms reinstate, restore.

unfruitful *adj.* arid, barren, exhausted, fruitless, impoverished, infecund, infertile, infructuous, sterile, unproductive, unprofitable, unprolific, unrewarding.
antonym fruitful.

ungainly *adj.* awkward, clumsy, gangling, gauche, gawky, inelegant, loutish, lubberly, lumbering, slouching, unco-ordinated, uncouth, unwieldy.
antonyms elegant, graceful.

ungirded *adj.* discinct, unbelted, ungirt, unprepared, unready.

ungodly *adj.* blasphemous, corrupt, depraved, dreadful, godless, horrendous, immoral, impious, intolerable, irreligious, outrageous, profane, sinful, unearthly, unreasonable, unseasonable, unseemly, unsocial, vile, wicked.

ungovernable *adj.* disorderly, masterless, rebellious, refractory, uncontrollable, ungoverned, unmanageable, unrestrainable, unruly, wild.

ungracious *adj.* bad-mannered, boorish, churlish, discourteous, disrespectful, graceless, ill-bred, impolite, offhand, rude, uncivil, unmannerly.
antonyms gracious, polite.

ungrateful *adj.* heedless, ill-mannered, ingrate, selfish, thankless, unappreciative, ungracious, unmindful.
antonym grateful.

unguarded[1] *adj.* careless, foolhardy, foolish, heedless, ill-considered, impolitic, imprudent, incautious, indiscreet, rash, thoughtless, uncircumspect, undiplomatic, unheeding, unthinking, unwary.
antonyms cautious, guarded.

unguarded[2] *adj.* defenceless, exposed, pregnable, undefended, unpatrolled, unprotected, vulnerable.
antonyms guarded, protected.

unhandy *adj.* awkward, bungling, cack-handed, clumsy, cumbersome, fumbling, heavy-handed, ill-contrived, incompetent, inconvenient, inept, inexpert, maladroit, unco-ordinated, unskilful, unwieldy.
antonyms adroit, deft, handy.

unhappy *adj.* awkward, blue, clumsy, contentless, crestfallen, cursed, dejected, depressed, despondent, disconsolate, dismal, dispirited, down, downcast, gauche, gloomy, hapless, ill-advised, ill-chosen, ill-fated, ill-omened, ill-timed, inappropriate, inapt, inept, infelicitous, injudicious, long-faced, luckless, lugubrious, malapropos, melancholy, miserable, mournful, sad, sorrowful, sorry, tactless, uneasy, unfortunate, unlucky, unsuitable, wretched.
antonyms fortunate, happy.

unharmed *adj.* intact, safe, scot-free, sound, undamaged, unhurt, unimpaired, uninjured, unscarred, unscathed, untouched, whole.
antonyms damaged, harmed, impaired.

unhealthy *adj.* ailing, bad, baneful, corrupt, corrupting, degrading, deleterious, delicate, demoralising, detrimental, epinosic, feeble, frail, harmful, infirm, insalubrious, insalutary, insanitary, invalid, morbid, noisome, noxious, polluted, poorly, sick, sickly, undesirable, unhygienic, unsound, unwell, unwholesome, weak.
antonyms healthy, hygienic, robust, salubrious.

unheard-of *adj.* disgraceful, extreme, inconceivable, new, novel, obscure, offensive, out of the question, outrageous, preposterous, shocking, singular, unacceptable, unbelievable, undiscovered, undreamed-of, unexampled, unfamiliar, unimaginable, unique, unknown, unprecedented, unregarded, unremarked, unsung, unthinkable, unthought-of, unusual.
antonyms famous, normal, usual.

unheeded *adj.* disobeyed, disregarded, forgotten, ignored, neglected, overlooked, unnoticed, unobserved, unremarked.
antonyms heeded, noted, observed.

unheralded *adj.* surprise, unadvertised, unannounced, unexpected, unforeseen, unnoticed, unproclaimed, unpublicised, unrecognised, unsung.
antonyms advertised, publicised, trumpeted.

unhesitating *adj.* automatic, immediate, implicit, instant, instantaneous, prompt, ready, resolute, spontaneous, steadfast, unfaltering, unquestioning, unreserved, unswerving, unwavering, whole-hearted.
antonyms hesitant, tentative, uncertain.

unhinge *v.* confuse, craze, derange, disorder, distract, drive mad, madden, unbalance, unnerve, unsettle, upset.

unholy *adj.* appalling, base, corrupt, depraved, dishonest, evil, heinous, immoral, iniquitous, irreligious, outrageous, profane, shocking,

sinful, taboo, unconscionable, unearthly, ungodly, unnatural, unreasonable, vile, wicked.
antonyms godly, holy, pious, reasonable.

unhoped-for *adj.* incredible, surprising, unanticipated, unbelievable, undreamed-of, unexpected, unforeseen, unimaginable, unlooked-for.

unhurried *adj.* calm, deliberate, easy, easygoing, laid-back, leisurely, relaxed, sedate, slow.
antonyms hasty, hurried.

unicorn *n.* monoceros.

unidentified *adj.* anonymous, incognito, mysterious, nameless, unclaimed, unclassified, unfamiliar, unknown, unmarked, unnamed, unrecognised, unspecified.
antonyms identified, known, named.

unification *n.* alliance, amalgamation, coalescence, coalition, combination, confederation, enosis, federation, fusion, incorporation, merger, union, uniting.
antonyms separation, split.

uniform *n.* costume, dress, garb, gear, habit, insignia, livery, outfit, regalia, regimentals, rig, robes, suit.
adj. alike, consistent, constant, equable, equal, even, homochromous, homogeneous, homomorphic, homomorphous, identical, like, monochrome, montonous, of a piece, regular, same, selfsame, similar, smooth, unbroken, unchanging, undeviating, unvarying.
antonyms changing, colourful, varied.

uniformity *n.* constancy, drabness, dullness, evenness, flatness, homogeneity, homomorphism, invariability, monotony, regularity, sameness, similarity, similitude, tedium.
antonyms difference, dissimilarity, variation.

unify *v.* amalgamate, bind, combine, confederate, consolidate, federate, fuse, join, marry, merge, unite, weld.
antonyms separate, split.

unifying *adj.* combinatory, consolidative, esemplastic, henotic, reconciling, unific, uniting.
antonym divisive.

unimaginable *adj.* fantastic, impossible, inconceivable, incredible, indescribable, ineffable, mind-boggling, unbelievable, undreamed-of, unheard-of, unhoped-for, unknowable, unthinkable.

unimaginative *adj.* banal, barren, blinkered, commonplace, derivative, dry, dull, hackneyed, lifeless, matter-of-fact, myopic, ordinary, pedestrian, predictable, prosaic, routine, short-sighted, tame, uncreative, uninspired, unoriginal.
antonyms imaginative, original.

unimpeachable *adj.* blameless, faultless, immaculate, impeccable, irreproachable, perfect, spotless, unassailable, unblemished, unchallengeable, unexceptionable, unquestionable.
antonyms blameworthy, faulty.

unimpeded *adj.* all-round, clear, free, open, unblocked, unchecked, unconstrained, unhampered, unhindered, uninhibited, unrestrained, untrammelled.
antonyms hampered, impeded.

unimportant *adj.* immaterial, inconsequential, insignificant, irrelevant, low-ranking, Mickey Mouse, minor, minuscule, negligible, nugatory, off the map, paltry, paravail, petty, slight, small-time, trifling, trivial, worthless.
antonym important.

unimpressive *adj.* average, commonplace, dull, indifferent, mediocre, undistinguished, unexceptional, uninteresting, unremarkable, unspectacular.
antonyms impressive, memorable, notable.

uninhibited *adj.* abandoned, candid, emancipated, frank, free, informal, instinctive, liberated, natural, open, relaxed, spontaneous, unbridled, unchecked, unconstrained, uncontrolled, uncurbed, unrepressed, unreserved, unrestrained, unrestricted, unselfconscious.
antonyms constrained, inhibited, repressed.

uninspired *adj.* boring, commonplace, dull, humdrum, indifferent, ordinary, pedestrian, prosaic, stale, stock, trite, undistinguished, unexciting, unimaginative, uninspiring, uninteresting, unoriginal.
antonyms inspired, original.

unintelligent *adj.* brainless, dense, dull, dumb, empty-headed, fatuous, foolish, gormless, half-witted, obtuse, silly, slow, stupid, thick, unreasoning, unthinking.
antonym intelligent.

unintelligible *adj.* double Dutch, garbled, illegible, inapprehensible, inarticulate, incoherent, incomprehensible, indecipherable, indistinct, jumbled, meaningless, muddled, unfathomable.
antonym intelligible.

unintentional *adj.* accidental, fortuitous, inadvertent, involuntary, unconscious, undeliberate, unintended, unpremeditated, unthinking, unwitting.
antonyms deliberate, intentional.

uninterested *adj.* apathetic, blasé, bored, distant, impassive, incurious, indifferent, listless, pococurante, unconcerned, unenthusiastic, uninvolved, unresponsive.
antonyms concerned, enthusiastic, interested, responsive.

uninteresting *adj.* boring, commonplace, corny, drab, dreary, dry, dull, flat, humdrum, monotonous, tame, tedious, tiresome, uneventful, unexciting, unimpressive, uninspiring, wearisome.
antonyms exciting, interesting.

uninterrupted *adj.* constant, continual, continuous, non-stop, peaceful, prolonged, quiet, steady, sustained, unbroken, undisturbed, unending.
antonyms broken, intermittent.

uninvited *adj.* unasked, unbidden, unsolicited, unsought, unwanted, unwelcome.
antonyms invited, solicited.

uninviting *adj.* disagreeable, distasteful, offensive, off-putting, repellent, repulsive, unappealing, unappetising, unattractive, undesirable, unpleasant, unsavoury, unwelcoming.
antonyms inviting, welcome.

uninvolved *adj.* disengaged, fancy-free, footloose, free, heart-free, heart-whole, independent, unattached, uncommitted, unengaged, unhampered, unhindered, untrammelled.
antonyms attached, committed.

union *n.* accord, agreement, alliance, amalgam, amalgamation, Anschluss, association, blend, Bund, coalition, coition, coitus, combination, compact, concord, concrescence, concurrence, confederacy, confederation, conjugation, conjunction, copulation, couplement, coupling, enosis, federation, fusion, harmony, intercourse, junction, juncture, league, marriage, matrimony, mixture, symphysis, synthesis, unanimity, unison, uniting, unity, wedlock.
antonyms alienation, disunity, estrangement, separation.

unique *adj.* incomparable, inimitable, lone, matchless, nonpareil, one-off, only, peerless, single, sole, solitary, sui generis, unequalled, unexampled, unmatched, unparalleled, unprecedented, unrivalled.
antonym commonplace.

unison *n.* accord, accordance, aggreement, concert, concord, co-operation, harmony, homophony, monophony, unanimity, unity.
antonyms disharmony, polyphony.

unit *n.* ace, assembly, component, constituent, detachment, element, entity, Gestalt, group, item, measure, measurement, member, module, monad, monas, one, part, piece, portion, quantity, section, segment, system, whole.

unite *v.* accrete, ally, amalgamate, associate, band, blend, coadunate, coalesce, combine, confederate, conglutinate, conjoin, conjugate, consolidate, cooperate, couple, fay, fuse, incorporate, join, join forces, league, link, marry, merge, pool, splice, unify, wed.
antonyms separate, sever.

united *adj.* affiliated, agreed, allied, collective, combined, concerted, concordant, conjoined, conjoint, conjunctive, corporate, in accord, in agreement, leagued, like-minded, one, pooled, unanimous, unified.
antonyms differing, disunited, separated, unco-ordinated.

unity *n.* accord, agreement, community, concord, concurrence, consensus, entity, harmony, integrity, oneness, peace, singleness, solidarity, unanimity, unification, union, wholeness.
antonyms disagreement, disunity.

universal *adj.* across-the-board, all-embracing, all-inclusive, all-round, catholic, common, ecumenic, ecumenical, entire, general, global, omnipresent, total, ubiquitous, unlimited, whole, widespread, worldwide.

universality *n.* all-inclusiveness, commonness, completeness, comprehensiveness, entirety, generalisation, generality, predominance, prevalence, totality, ubiquity.

universally *adv.* always, everywhere, invariably, ubiquitously, uniformly.

universe *n.* cosmos, creation, firmament, heavens, macrocosm, nature, world.

university *n.* academia, academy, Athenaeum, college, institute, multiversity, varsity.

unjust *adj.* biased, gratuitous, groundless, inequitable, one-sided, partial, partisan, prejudiced, undeserved, unethical, unfair, unjustified, unmerited, wrong, wrongful.
antonym just.

unjustifiable *adj.* excessive, immoderate, indefensible, inexcusable, outrageous, steep, unacceptable, unforgivable, unjust, unpardonable, unreasonable, unwarrantable, wrong.
antonym justifiable.

unkempt *adj.* bedraggled, blowsy, disarranged, dishevelled, disordered, frowsy, mal soigné, messy, mop-headed, ratty, rumpled, scruffy, shabby, shaggy, slatternly, sloppy, slovenly, sluttish, tousled, uncombed, ungroomed, untidy.
antonyms neat, tidy.

unkind *adj.* callous, cruel, disobliging, hard-hearted, harsh, inconsiderate, inhuman, inhumane, insensitive, malevolent, malicious, mean, nasty, spiteful, thoughtless, unamiable, uncaring, uncharitable, unchristian, unfeeling, unfriendly, unsympathetic.
antonyms considerate, kind.

unkindness *n.* callousness, cruelty, disobligingness, hard-heartedness, harshness, ill-turn, inhumanity, insensitivity, maliciousness, meanness, spite, uncharitableness, unfriendliness.
antonyms friendship, kindness.

unknowable *adj.* in the lap of the gods, incalculable, incognisable, infinite, on the knees of the gods, unascertainable, unfathomable, unforeseeable, unimaginable, unpredictable, untold.

unknown *adj.* alien, anonymous, concealed, dark, foreign, hidden, humble, incognito, mysterious, nameless, new, obscure, secret, strange, uncharted, undisclosed, undiscovered, undistinguished, unexplored, unfamiliar, unheard-of, unidentified, unnamed, unrecognised, unsung, untold.
antonyms familiar, known.

unladylike *adj.* boyish, coarse, hoydenish, ill-bred, impolite, indelicate, inelegant, rough, rude, tomboyish, uncivil, unfeminine, ungracious, unmannerly, unrefined, unseemly.
antonyms ladylike, seemly.

unlawful *adj.* actionable, banned, criminal, forbidden, illegal, illegitimate, illicit, outlawed, prohibited, unauthorised, unconstitutional, unlicensed, unsanctioned.
antonym lawful.

unleash *v.* free, loose, release, unloose, untether, untie.

antonym restrain.

unlettered *adj.* ignorant, illiterate, uneducated, unlearned, unlessoned, unschooled, untaught, untutored.
antonym educated.

unlike *adj.* contrasted, different, difform, disparate, dissimilar, distinct, divergent, diverse, ill-matched, incompatible, opposed, opposite, unequal, unrelated.
antonyms related, similar.

unlikely *adj.* doubtful, dubious, faint, implausible, improbable, incredible, questionable, remote, slight, suspect, suspicious, tall, unbelievable, unconvincing, unexpected, unimaginable.
antonyms likely, plausible.

unlikeness *n.* contrast, difference, disparity, dissemblance, dissimilarity, divergence, diversity, incompatibility.
antonym similarity.

unlimited *adj.* absolute, all-encompassing, boundless, complete, countless, endless, extensive, full, great, illimitable, immeasurable, immense, incalculable, infinite, limitless, total, unbounded, uncircumscribed, unconditional, unconstrained, unfettered, unhampered, unqualified, unrestricted, vast.
antonyms circumscribed, limited.

unload *v.* disburden, discharge, discumber, disencumber, disload, dump, empty, offload, relieve, unburden, unpack.

unlock *v.* bare, disengage, free, open, release, unbar, unbolt, undo, unfasten, unlatch.
antonyms fasten, lock.

unlooked-for *adj.* chance, fortuitous, fortunate, lucky, surprise, surprising, unanticipated, undreamed-of, unexpected, unforeseen, unhoped-for, unpredicted, unthought-of.
antonyms expected, predictable.

unloved *adj.* detested, disliked, forsaken, hated, loveless, neglected, rejected, spurned, uncared-for, uncherished, unpopular, unwanted.
antonyms beloved, loved.

unlucky *adj.* cursed, disastrous, doomed, hapless, ill-fated, ill-omened, ill-starred, inauspicious, infaust, jinxed, left-handed, luckless, mischanceful, miserable, ominous, unfavourable, unfortunate, unhappy, unsuccessful, untimely, wretched.
antonym lucky.

unman *v.* daunt, demoralise, discourage, disman, dispirit, effeminate, effeminise, emasculate, emolliate, enervate, enfeeble, evirate, intimidate, unnerve, weaken.
antonyms brace, nerve, steel.

unmanageable *adj.* awkward, bulky, cumbersome, difficult, disorderly, fractious, inconvenient, intractable, obstreperous, recalcitrant, refractory, stroppy, uncontrollable, uncooperative, unhandy, unruly, unwieldy, wild.
antonyms docile, manageable.

unmanly *adj.* chicken-hearted, cowardly, craven, dishonourable, effeminate, epicene, feeble, ignoble, namby-pamby, sissy, soft,

weak, weak-kneed, weedy, wet, womanish, yellow.
antonym manly.

unmannerly *adj.* badly-behaved, bad-mannered, boorish, discourteous, disrespectful, graceless, ill-bred, ill-mannered, impolite, lowbred, rude, uncivil, uncouth, ungracious.
antonym polite.

unmarried *adj.* available, bachelor, celibate, fancy-free, footloose, maiden, single, unattached, unwed, unwedded, virgin.
antonym married.

unmask *v.* bare, detect, disclose, discover, dismask, expose, reveal, show, uncloak, uncover, unveil.

unmatched *adj.* beyond compare, consummate, incomparable, matchless, nonpareil, paramount, peerless, supreme, unequalled, unexampled, unparalleled, unrivalled, unsurpassed.

unmentionable *adj.* abominable, disgraceful, disreputable, immodest, indecent, innominable, nefandous, scandalous, shameful, shocking, taboo, unnameable, unspeakable, unutterable.

unmerciful *adj.* brutal, callous, cruel, hard, heartless, implacable, merciless, pitiless, relentless, remorseless, ruthless, sadistic, uncaring, unfeeling, unrelenting, unsparing.
antonym merciful.

unmethodical *adj.* confused, desultory, disorderly, haphazard, illogical, immethodical, irregular, muddled, random, unco-ordinated, unorganised, unsystematic.
antonym methodical.

unmindful *adj.* blind, careless, deaf, forgetful, heedless, inattentive, indifferent, lax, neglectful, negligent, oblivious, regardless, remiss, slack, unaware, unconscious, unheeding.
antonyms aware, heedful, mindful.

unmistakable *adj.* certain, clear, conspicuous, crystal-clear, decided, distinct, evident, explicit, glaring, indisputable, manifest, obvious, palpable, patent, plain, positive, pronounced, sure, unambiguous, undeniable, undisputed, unequivocal, unquestionable.
antonyms ambiguous, unclear.

unmitigated *adj.* absolute, arrant, complete, consummate, downright, grim, harsh, intense, oppressive, out-and-out, outright, perfect, persistent, pure, rank, relentless, sheer, thorough, thoroughgoing, unabated, unalleviated, unbroken, undiminished, unmodified, unqualified, unredeemed, unrelenting, unrelieved, unremitting, utter.

unmoved *adj.* adamant, cold, determined, dispassionate, dry-eyed, fast, firm, impassive, indifferent, inflexible, obdurate, phlegmatic, resolute, resolved, steadfast, steady, unaffected, unchanged, undeviating, unfeeling, unimpressed, unresponsive, unshaken, untouched, unwavering.
antonyms affected, moved, shaken.

unnatural *adj.* aberrant, abnormal, absonant, affected, anomalous, artificial, assumed,

bizarre, brutal, callous, cataphysical, cold-blooded, contrived, cruel, disnatured, evil, extraordinary, factitious, false, feigned, fiendish, forced, freakish, heartless, inhuman, insincere, irregular, laboured, mannered, monstrous, odd, outlandish, perverse, perverted, phoney, queer, ruthless, sadistic, savage, self-conscious, stagy, stiff, stilted, strained, strange, studied, supernatural, theatrical, unaccountable, uncanny, unfeeling, unspontaneous, unusual, wicked.
antonyms acceptable, natural, normal.

unnecessary *adj.* dispensable, expendable, inessential, needless, non-essential, otiose, pleonastic, redundant, supererogatory, superfluous, supernumerary, tautological, uncalled-for, unjustified, unneeded, useless.
antonyms indispensable, necessary.

unnerve *adj.* confound, daunt, demoralise, disconcert, discourage, dishearten, dismay, dispirit, fluster, frighten, intimidate, rattle, scare, shake, unhinge, unman, upset, worry.
antonyms brace, nerve, steel.

unnoticed *adj.* disregarded, ignored, neglected, overlooked, passed over, unconsidered, undiscovered, unheeded, unobserved, unperceived, unrecognised, unrecorded, unremarked, unseen.
antonyms noted, remarked.

unobtrusive *adj.* humble, inconspicuous, low-key, meek, modest, quiet, restrained, retiring, self-effacing, subdued, unassertive, unassuming, unemphatic, unnoticeable, unostentatious, unpretentious.
antonyms obtrusive, ostentatious.

unobtrusively *adv.* inconspicuously, modestly, on the q.t., on the quiet, quietly, surreptitiously, unostentatiously.
antonyms obtrusively, ostentatiously.

unoccupied *adj.* disengaged, empty, free, idle, inactive, jobless, unemployed, uninhabited, untenanted, vacant, workless.
antonyms busy, occupied.

unofficial *adj.* confidential, illegal, informal, personal, private, ulterior, unauthorised, unconfirmed, undeclared, wildcat.
antonym official.

unoriginal *adj.* cliché-ridden, copied, cribbed, derivative, derived, second-hand, stale, trite, unimaginative, uninspired.
antonyms imaginative, original.

unorthodox *adj.* abnormal, alternative, fringe, heterodox, irregular, nonconformist, unconventional, unusual, unwonted.
antonyms conventional, orthodox.

unpaid *adj.* due, free, honorary, outstanding, overdue, owing, payable, unremunerative, unsalaried, unsettled, voluntary.
antonym paid.

unpalatable *adj.* bitter, disagreeable, displeasing, distasteful, inedible, insipid, offensive, repugnant, unappetising, unattractive, uneatable, unenviable, unpleasant, unrelished, unsavoury.
antonyms palatable, pleasant.

unparalleled *adj.* consummate, exceptional, incomparable, matchless, peerless, rare, singular, superlative, supreme, surpassing, unequalled, unexampled, unique, unmatched, unprecedented, unrivalled, unsurpassed.

unpardonable *adj.* deplorable, disgraceful, indefensible, inexcusable, irremissible, outrageous, scandalous, shameful, shocking, unconscionable, unforgivable.
antonyms forgivable, understandable.

unperturbed *adj.* calm, collected, composed, cool, impassive, placid, poised, self-possessed, serene, tranquil, undisturbed, unexcited, unflinching, unflustered, unruffled, untroubled, unworried.
antonyms anxious, perturbed.

unpleasant *adj.* abhorrent, bad, disagreeable, displeasing, distasteful, god-awful, ill-natured, irksome, nasty, objectionable, obnoxious, repulsive, rocky, sticky, traumatic, troublesome, unattractive, unpalatable.
antonym pleasant.

unpleasantness *n.* annoyance, bother, embarrassment, esclandre, furore, fuss, ill-feeling, nastiness, scandal, trouble, upset.

unpolished *adj.* coarse, crude, home-bred, rough, rough and ready, rude, sketchy, uncivilised, uncouth, uncultivated, uncultured, unfashioned, unfinished, unrefined, unsophisticated, unworked, vulgar.
antonyms finished, polished, refined.

unpopular *adj.* avoided, detested, disliked, hated, neglected, rejected, shunned, undesirable, unfashionable, unloved, unsought-after, unwanted, unwelcome.
antonyms fashionable, popular.

unprecedented *adj.* abnormal, exceptional, extraordinary, freakish, new, novel, original, remarkable, revolutionary, singular, unexampled, unheard-of, unknown, unparalleled, unrivalled, unusual.

unpredictable *adj.* chance, changeable, doubtful, erratic, fickle, fluky, iffy, in the lap of the gods, inconstant, on the knees of the gods, random, scatty, unforeseeable, unreliable, unstable, variable.
antonym predictable.

unprejudiced *adj.* balanced, detached, dispassionate, enlightened, even-handed, fair, fair-minded, impartial, just, non-partisan, objective, open-minded, unbiased, uncoloured.
antonyms narrow-minded, prejudiced.

unpremeditated *adj.* extempore, fortuitous, impromptu, impulsive, offhand, off-the-cuff, spontaneous, spur-of-the-moment, unintentional, unplanned, unprepared, unrehearsed.
antonym premeditated.

unprepared *adj.* ad-lib, extemporaneous, half-baked, ill-considered, improvised, incomplete, napping, off-the-cuff, spontaneous, surprised, unawares, unfinished, ungirded, unplanned, unready, unrehearsed, unsuspecting.
antonyms prepared, ready.

unpretentious *adj.* homely, honest, humble,

modest, natural, penny-plain, plain, simple, straightforward, unaffected, unassuming, unimposing, unobtrusive, unostentatious, unpretending, unsophisticated, unspoiled.
antonym pretentious.

unprincipled *adj.* amoral, corrupt, crooked, deceitful, devious, discreditable, dishonest, dishonourable, immoral, underhand, unethical, unprofessional, unscrupulous.
antonym ethical.

unproductive *adj.* arid, barren, bootless, dry, fruitless, futile, idle, ineffective, inefficacious, infertile, otiose, sterile, unavailing, unfruitful, unprofitable, unprolific, unremunerative, unrewarding, useless, vain, valueless, worthless.
antonyms fertile, productive.

unprofessional *adj.* amateur, amateurish, improper, inadmissible, incompetent, inefficient, inexperienced, inexpert, lax, negligent, unacceptable, unbecoming, unethical, unfitting, unprincipled, unseemly, unskilled, untrained, unworthy.
antonyms professional, skilful.

unpromising *adj.* adverse, depressing, discouraging, dispiriting, doubtful, gloomy, inauspicious, ominous, unfavourable, unpropitious.
antonym promising.

unprotected *adj.* defenceless, exposed, helpless, inerm, liable, naked, open, pregnable, unarmed, unattended, undefended, unfortified, unguarded, unsheltered, unshielded, unvaccinated, vulnerable.
antonyms immune, protected, safe.

unprovable *adj.* indemonstrable, indeterminable, unascertainable, undemonstrable, unverifiable.
antonym verifiable.

unqualified *adj.* absolute, categorical, complete, consummate, downright, ill-equipped, incapable, incompetent, ineligible, out-and-out, outright, thorough, thoroughgoing, total, uncertificated, unconditional, unfit, unmitigated, unmixed, unprepared, unreserved, unrestricted, untrained, utter, whole-hearted.
antonyms conditional, tentative.

unquestionable *adj.* absolute, certain, clear, conclusive, definite, faultless, flawless, incontestable, incontrovertible, indisputable, indubitable, irrefutable, manifest, obvious, patent, self-evident, sure, unchallenged, undeniable, unequivocal, unmistakable.
antonyms dubious, questionable.

unquestioning *adj.* implicit, questionless, unconditional, unhesitating, unqualified, whole-hearted.
antonym doubtful.

unravel *v.* disentangle, explain, extricate, figure out, free, interpret, penetrate, puzzle out, ravel out, resolve, separate, solve, sort out, undo, unknot, untangled, unwind, work out.
antonyms complicate, tangle.

unreal *adj.* academic, artificial, chimerical, fabulous, fairy-tale, fake, false, fanciful, fantastic, fictitious, hypothetical, illusory,

imaginary, immaterial, impalpable, insincere, insubstantial, intangible, made-up, make-believe, mock, moonshiny, mythical, nebulous, ostensible, phantasmagorical, pretended, seeming, sham, storybook, synthetic, vaporous, visionary.
antonyms genuine, real.

unrealistic *adj.* half-baked, idealistic, impracticable, impractical, improbable, quixotic, romantic, starry-eyed, theoretical, unworkable.
antonyms pragmatic, realistic.

unreasonable *adj.* absurd, arbitrary, biased, blinkered, capricious, cussed, erratic, excessive, exorbitant, extortionate, extravagant, far-fetched, foolish, froward, headstrong, illogical, immoderate, inconsistent, irrational, mad, nonsensical, opinionated, perverse, preposterous, quirky, senseless, silly, steep, stupid, thrawn, uncalled-for, undue, unfair, unjust, unjustifiable, unjustified, unwarranted.
antonyms moderate, rational, reasonable.

unrecognisable *adj.* altered, changed, disguised, incognisable, incognito, unidentifiable, unknowable.

unrefined *adj.* boorish, coarse, crude, imperfect, inelegant, raw, rude, uncultivated, uncultured, unfinished, unperfected, unpolished, unpurified, unsophisticated, untreated, vulgar.
antonyms finished, refined.

unregenerate *adj.* abandoned, hardened, impenitent, incorrigible, intractable, obdurate, obstinate, persistent, recalcitrant, refractory, shameless, sinful, stubborn, unconverted, unreformed, unrepentant, wicked.
antonyms reformed, repentant.

unrelated *adj.* different, disparate, dissimilar, distinct, extraneous, inapplicable, inappropriate, irrelevant, unassociated, unconnected, unlike.
antonyms related, similar.

unrelenting *adj.* ceaseless, constant, continual, continuous, cruel, endless, implacable, incessant, inexorable, insistent, intransigent, merciless, perpetual, pitiless, relentless, remorseless, ruthless, steady, stern, tough, unabated, unalleviated, unbroken, unceasing, uncompromising, unmerciful, unremitting, unsparing.
antonyms intermittent, spasmodic.

unreliable *adj.* deceptive, delusive, disreputable, erroneous, fair-weather, fallible, false, implausible, inaccurate, inauthentic, irresponsible, mistaken, specious, uncertain, unconvincing, undependable, unsound, unstable, untrustworthy.
antonym reliable.

unremitting *adj.* assiduous, ceaseless, conscientious, constant, continual, continuous, diligent, incessant, indefatigable, perpetual, relentless, remorseless, sedulous, tireless, unabated, unbroken, unceasing, unrelenting.
antonym spasmodic.

unrepentant *adj.* callous, hardened, impenitent,

incorrigible, obdurate, shameless, unabashed, unashamed, unregenerate, unremorseful, unrepenting.

antonyms penitent, repentant.

unreserved *adj.* absolute, candid, complete, demonstrative, direct, entire, extrovert, forthright, frank, free, full, open, openhearted, outgoing, outspoken, total, unconditional, unhesitating, uninhibited, unlimited, unqualified, unrestrained, whole-hearted.

antonyms inhibited, tentative.

unreservedly *adv.* completely, entirely, outright, plump, unhesitatingly, utterly, wholeheartedly.

unresisting *adj.* docile, like a lamb to the slaughter, meek, obedient, passive, submissive.

antonyms protesting, resisting.

unresolved *adj.* doubtful, indefinite, moot, pending, problematical, unanswered, undecided, undetermined, unsettled, unsolved, up in the air, vague, vexed.

antonyms definite, determined.

unresponsive *adj.* aloof, apathetic, cool, echoless, indifferent, unaffected, uninterested, unmoved, unsympathetic.

antonyms responsive, sympathetic.

unrest *n.* agitation, anxiety, apprehension, disaffection, discontent, discord, disquiet, dissatisfaction, dissension, distress, perturbation, protest, rebellion, restlessness, sedition, strife, tumult, turmoil, unease, uneasiness, worry.

antonyms calm, peace.

unrestrained *adj.* abandoned, boisterous, free, immoderate, inordinate, intemperate, irrepressible, natural, rampant, unbounded, unbridled, unchecked, unconstrained, uncontrolled, unhindered, uninhibited, unrepressed, unreserved, uproarious.

antonym inhibited.

unrestricted *adj.* absolute, all-round, clear, free, free-for-all, free-wheeling, open, public, unbounded, uncircumscribed, unconditional, unhindered, unimpeded, unlimited, unobstructed, unopposed, unregulated.

antonyms limited, restricted.

unripe *adj.* green, immature, undeveloped, unready, unripened.

antonyms mature, ripe.

unrivalled *adj.* incomparable, inimitable, matchless, nonpareil, peerless, superlative, supreme, surpassing, unequalled, unexcelled, unmatched, unparalleled, unsurpassed, without equal.

unruffled *adj.* calm, collected, composed, cool, even, imperturbable, level, peaceful, placid, serene, smooth, tranquil, unbroken, undisturbed, unflustered, unmoved, unperturbed, untroubled.

antonyms anxious, troubled.

unruly *adj.* camstairy, disobedient, disorderly, fractious, headstrong, insubordinate, intractable, lawless, mutinous, obstreperous, rebellious, refractory, riotous, rowdy, ruleless, turbulent, uncontrollable, ungovernable, unmanageable, wayward, wild, wilful.

antonym manageable.

unsafe *adj.* dangerous, exposed, hazardous, insecure, parlous, perilous, precarious, risky, threatening, treacherous, uncertain, unreliable, unsound, unstable, vulnerable.

antonyms safe, secure.

unsaid *adj.* undeclared, unexpressed, unmentioned, unpronounced, unspoken, unstated, unuttered, unvoiced.

antonym spoken.

unsaleable *adj.* invendible, unmarketable, unsellable.

antonyms marketable, saleable.

unsatisfactory *adj.* deficient, disappointing, displeasing, dissatisfying, frustrating, inadequate, inferior, insufficient, leaving a lot to be desired, mediocre, poor, rocky, thwarting, unacceptable, unsatisfying, unsuitable, unworthy, weak.

antonym satisfactory.

unsavoury *adj.* disagreeable, distasteful, nasty, nauseating, objectionable, obnoxious, offensive, repellent, repugnant, repulsive, revolting, sickening, sordid, squalid, unappetising, unattractive, undesirable, unpalatable, unpleasant.

antonyms palatable, pleasant.

unscathed *adj.* intact, safe, scot-free, sound, unharmed, unhurt, uninjured, unmarked, unscarred, unscratched, untouched, whole.

antonyms harmed, injured.

unscrupulous *adj.* corrupt, crooked, cynical, discreditable, dishonest, dishonourable, immoral, improper, ruthless, shameless, unethical, unprincipled.

antonym scrupulous.

unseasonable *adj.* ill-timed, inappropriate, inopportune, intempestive, malapropos, mistimed, seasonable, timely, unsuitable, untimely.

unseasoned *adj.* green, unmatured, unprepared, unprimed, untempered, untreated.

unseat *v.* depose, dethrone, discharge, dishorse, dismiss, dismount, displace, disseat, oust, overthrow, remove, throw, topple, unhorse, unsaddle.

unseemly *adj.* discreditable, disreputable, improper, inappropriate, indecorous, indelicate, shocking, unbecoming, unbefitting, undignified, undue, ungentlemanly, unladylike, unrefined, unsuitable.

antonyms decorous, seemly.

unseen *adj.* concealed, hidden, invisible, lurking, obscure, overlooked, undetected, unnoticed, unobserved, unobtrusive, unperceived, veiled.

antonyms observed, visible.

unselfish *adj.* altruistic, charitable, dedicated, devoted, disinterested, generous, humanitarian, kind, liberal, magnanimous, noble, philanthropic, self-denying, selfless, self-sacrificing, single-eyed, ungrudging, unstinting.

antonym selfish.

unsentimental *adj.* cynical, hard as nails, hard-headed, level-headed, practical, pragmatic, realistic, shrewd, tough.
antonyms sentimental, soft.

unsettle *v.* agitate, bother, confuse, destabilise, discompose, disconcert, disorder, disturb, fluster, flutter, perturb, rattle, ruffle, shake, throw, trouble, unbalance, upset.
antonyms compose, settle.

unsettled *adj.* agitated, anxious, changeable, changing, confused, debatable, disorderly, disoriented, disturbed, doubtful, due, edgy, flustered, iffy, inconstant, insecure, moot, open, outstanding, overdue, owing, payable, pending, perturbed, problematical, restive, restless, shaken, shaky, tense, troubled, uncertain, undecided, undertermined, uneasy, unnerved, unpredictable, unresolved, unstable, unsteady, upset, variable.
antonyms certain, composed, settled.

unshakable *adj.* absolute, adamant, constant, determined, firm, fixed, immovable, resolute, stable, staunch, steadfast, sure, unassailable, unswerving, unwavering, well-founded.
antonym insecure.

unsheathe *v.* dissheathe, draw, evaginate, expose, reveal, uncover.
antonyms retract, sheathe.

unshod *adj.* barefooted, discalced, shoeless.
antonym shod.

unsightly *adj.* disagreeable, displeasing, hideous, horrid, off-putting, repellent, repugnant, repulsive, revolting, ugly, unattractive, unpleasant, unprepossessing.
antonym pleasing.

unskilful *adj.* amateurish, awkward, bungling, clumsy, fumbling, gauche, incompetent, inept, inexperienced, inexpert, maladroit, unapt, uneducated, unhandy, unpractised, unprofessional, unqualified, unskilled, untalented, untaught, untrained.
antonyms skilful, skilled.

unsociable *adj.* aloof, chilly, cold, distant, farouche, hostile, inconversable, inhospitable, introverted, reclusive, reserved, retiring, stand-offish, taciturn, uncommunicative, uncongenial, unforthcoming, unfriendly, unneighbourly, unsocial, withdrawn.
antonyms friendly, sociable.

unsolicited *adj.* gratuitous, spontaneous, unasked, uncalled-for, unforced, uninvited, unrequested, unsought, unwanted, unwelcome, voluntary.
antonyms invited, solicited.

unsophisticated *adj.* artless, childlike, funky, guileless, hick, homespun, inexperienced, ingenuous, innocent, naïve, natural, plain, simple, straightforward, unaffected, uncomplicated, uninvolved, unpretentious, unrefined, unspecialised, unspoilt, untutored, unworldly.
antonyms complex, pretentious, sophisticated.

unsound *adj.* ailing, defective, delicate,

deranged, dicky, diseased, erroneous, fallacious, fallible, false, faulty, flawed, frail, ill, ill-founded, illogical, insecure, invalid, shaky, specious, unbalanced, unhealthy, unhinged, unreliable, unsafe, unstable, unsteady, unwell, weak, wobbly.
antonyms safe, sound.

unsparing *adj.* abundant, bountiful, generous, hard, harsh, implacable, inexorable, lavish, liberal, merciless, munificent, open-handed, plenteous, prodigal, profuse, relentless, rigorous, ruthless, scathing, severe, stern, stringent, uncompromising, unforgiving, ungrudging, unmerciful, unstinting.
antonyms forgiving, mean, sparing.

unspeakable *adj.* abhorrent, abominable, appalling, dreadful, evil, execrable, frightful, heinous, horrible, inconceivable, indescribable, ineffable, inexpressible, loathsome, monstrous, nefandous, odious, overwhelming, repellent, shocking, unbelievable, unimaginable, unutterable, wonderful.

unspoilt *adj.* artless, innocent, intact, natural, perfect, preserved, scatheless, unaffected, unaltered, unassuming, unblemished, unchanged, undamaged, unharmed, unimpaired, unscathed, unsophisticated, unspoiled, unstudied, untouched, wholesome.
antonyms affected, spoilt.

unspoken *adj.* assumed, implicit, implied, inferred, mute, silent, speechless, tacit, undeclared, understood, unexpressed, unsaid, unspoken, unstated, unuttered, voiceless, wordless.
antonym explicit.

unstable *adj.* astable, capricious, changeable, erratic, fitful, fluctuating, inconsistent, inconstant, insecure, irrational, labile, precarious, rickety, risky, shoogly, slippy, ticklish, tottering, unpredictable, unsettled, unsteady, untrustworthy, vacillating, variable, volatile, wobbly.
antonyms stable, steady.

unsteady *adj.* changeable, dicky, erratic, flickering, flighty, fluctuating, frail, inconstant, infirm, insecure, irregular, precarious, reeling, rickety, shaky, shoogly, skittish, tittupy, tottering, totty, treacherous, tremulous, unreliable, unsafe, unstable, unsteeled, vacillating, variable, volatile, wavering, wobbly.
antonyms firm, steady.

unstinting *adj.* abounding, abundant, ample, bountiful, full, generous, large, lavish, liberal, munificent, plentiful, prodigal, profuse, ungrudging, unsparing.
antonyms grudging, mean.

unsubstantial *adj.* airy, chimerical, dreamlike, erroneous, fanciful, flimsy, fragile, frail, ill-founded, illusory, imaginary, immaterial, impalpable, inadequate, insubstantial, light, slight, superficial, tenuous, thin, unsound, unsupported, vaporous, visionary, weak.
antonyms real, valid.

unsubstantiated *adj.* debatable, dubious, questionable, unattested, unconfirmed, uncorro-

borated, unestablished, unproved, unproven, unsupported, unverified.
antonyms proved, proven.
unsuccessful *adj.* abortive, bootless, failed, foiled, fruitless, frustrated, futile, ill-fated, inadequate, ineffective, ineffectual, losing, luckless, manqué, otiose, sterile, thwarted, unavailing, unfortunate, unlucky, unproductive, unsatisfactory, useless, vain.
antonyms effective, successful.
unsuitable *adj.* improper, inapposite, inappropriate, inapt, incompatible, incongruous, inconsistent, indecorous, ineligible, infelicitous, malapropos, unacceptable, unbecoming, unbefitting, unfitting, unlikely, unseasonable, unseemly, unsuited.
antonyms seemly, suitable.
unsullied *adj.* clean, immaculate, intact, perfect, pristine, pure, spotless, stainless, unblackened, unblemished, uncorrupted, undefiled, unsoiled, unspoiled, unspotted, unstained, untarnished, untouched.
antonyms dirty, stained.
unsung *adj.* anonymous, disregarded, forgotten, neglected, obscure, overlooked, unacknowledged, uncelebrated, unhailed, unhonoured, unknown, unnamed, unrecognised, unrenowned.
antonyms famous, renowned.
unsure *adj.* agnostic, distrustful, doubtful, dubious, hesitant, insecure, irresolute, mistrustful, sceptical, suspicious, tentative, uncertain, unconvinced, undecided, unpersuaded.
antonyms resolute, sure.
unsurpassed *adj.* consummate, exceptional, incomparable, matchless, nonpareil, paramount, peerless, sublime, superlative, supreme, surpassing, transcendent, unequalled, unexcelled, unparalleled, unrivalled.
unsuspecting *adj.* childlike, confiding, credulous, green, gullible, inexperienced, ingenuous, innocent, naïve, trustful, trusting, unconscious, uncritical, unsuspicious, unwary, unwitting.
antonyms conscious, knowing.
unswerving *adj.* constant, dedicated, devoted, direct, firm, fixed, immovable, resolute, single-minded, staunch, steadfast, steady, sure, true, undeviating, unfaltering, unflagging, untiring, unwavering.
antonyms irresolute, tentative.
unsympathetic *adj.* antagonistic, antipathetic, apathetic, callous, cold, compassionless, cruel, hard, hard as nails, hard-hearted, harsh, heartless, indifferent, inhuman, insensitive, soulless, stony, uncharitable, uncompassionate, unconcerned, unfeeling, unkind, unmoved, unpitying, unresponsive.
antonyms compassionate, sympathetic.
unsystematic *adj.* chaotic, confused, desultory, disorderly, disorganised, haphazard, illogical, indiscriminate, irregular, jumbled, muddled, random, shambolic, slapdash, sloppy, uncoordinated, unmethodical, unorganised,

unplanned, untidy.
antonyms logical, systematic.
untamed *adj.* barbarous, ferae naturae, feral, fierce, haggard, savage, unbroken, undomesticated, unmellowed, untameable, wild.
antonyms domesticated, tame.
untangle *v.* disentangle, explain, extricate, ravel out, resolve, solve, undo, unravel, unsnarl.
antonyms complicate, tangle.
untarnished *adj.* bright, burnished, clean, glowing, immaculate, impeccable, intact, polished, pristine, pure, shining, spotless, stainless, unblemished, unimpeachable, unsoiled, unspoilt, unspotted, unstained, unsullied.
antonyms blemished, tarnished.
untenable *adj.* fallacious, flawed, illogical, indefensible, insupportable, rocky, shaky, unmaintainable, unreasonable, unsound, unsustainable.
antonyms sound, tenable.
unthinkable *adj.* absurd, illogical, implausible, impossible, improbable, incogitable, inconceivable, incredible, insupportable, outrageous, preposterous, shocking, unbelievable, unheard-of, unimaginable, unlikely, unreasonable.
unthinking *adj.* automatic, careless, heedless, impulsive, inadvertent, incautious, inconsiderate, indiscreet, insensitive, instinctive, mechanical, negligent, oblivious, rash, rude, selfish, senseless, tactless, thoughtless, unconscious, undiplomatic, unguarded, vacant, witless.
antonyms conscious, deliberate, witting.
untidy *adj.* bedraggled, chaotic, cluttered, dishevelled, disorderly, higgledy-piggledy, jumbled, littered, messy, muddled, ratty, raunchy, rumpled, scruffy, shambolic, slatternly, slipshod, sloppy, slovenly, sluttish, topsy-turvy, unkempt, unsystematic.
antonyms systematic, tidy.
untie *v.* free, loosen, release, unbind, undo, unfasten, unknot, unlace, unloose, unloosen, untether.
antonyms fasten, tie.
untimely *adj.* awkward, early, ill-timed, inappropriate, inauspicious, inconvenient, inopportune, intempestive, malapropos, mistimed, premature, unfortunate, unseasonable, unsuitable.
antonyms opportune, timely.
untiring *adj.* constant, dedicated, determined, devoted, dogged, incessant, indefatigable, patient, persevering, persistent, staunch, steady, tenacious, tireless, unfailing, unfaltering, unflagging, unremitting, unwearied.
antonym inconstant.
untold *adj.* boundless, countless, hidden, incalculable, indescribable, inexhaustible, inexpressible, infinite, innumerable, measureless, myriad, numberless, private, secret, uncountable, uncounted, undisclosed, undreamed-of, unimaginable, unknown, unnumbered, unpublished, unreckoned, unrecounted, unre-

lated, unrevealed, unthinkable, unutterable.

untouched *adj.* indifferent, intact, safe, scatheless, unaffected, unaltered, unconcerned, undamaged, unharmed, unhurt, unimpaired, unimpressed, uninjured, unmoved, unscathed, unstirred.
antonyms affected, impaired, moved.

untoward *adj.* adverse, annoying, awkward, contrary, disastrous, ill-timed, improper, inappropriate, inauspicious, inconvenient, indecorous, inimical, inopportune, irritating, ominous, troublesome, unbecoming, unexpected, unfavourable, unfitting, unfortunate, unlucky, unpropitious, unseemly, unsuitable, untimely, vexatious, worrying.
antonyms auspicious, suitable.

untrained *adj.* amateur, green, inexperienced, inexpert, raw, uneducated, unpractised, unprofessional, unqualified, unschooled, unskilled, untaught, untutored.
antonyms expert, trained.

untried *adj.* experimental, exploratory, innovative, innovatory, new, novel, unestablished, unproved, untested.
antonyms proven, tested.

untroubled *adj.* calm, composed, cool, impassive, peaceful, placid, serene, steady, tranquil, unconcerned, undisturbed, unexcited, unflappable, unflustered, unperturbed, unruffled, unstirred, unworried.
antonyms anxious, troubled.

untrue *adj.* deceitful, deceptive, deviant, dishonest, disloyal, distorted, erroneous, faithless, fallacious, false, forsworn, fraudulent, inaccurate, inconstant, incorrect, lying, mendacious, misleading, mistaken, perfidious, sham, specious, spurious, traitorous, treacherous, two-faced, unfaithful, untrustworthy, untruthful, wrong.
antonyms honest, true.

untrustworthy *adj.* capricious, deceitful, devious, dishonest, disloyal, dubious, duplicitous, fair-weather, faithless, false, fickle, fly-by-night, shady, slippery, treacherous, tricky, two-faced, undependable, unfaithful, unreliable, unsafe, untrue, untrusty.
antonyms reliable, trustworthy.

untruth *n.* deceit, deceitfulness, duplicity, fabrication, falsehood, falsification, falsism, falsity, fib, fiction, inexactitude, invention, inveracity, lie, lying, mendacity, perjury, prevarication, story, tale, trick, truthlessness, untruthfulness, whopper.
antonym truth.

untruthful *adj.* crooked, deceitful, deceptive, dishonest, dissembling, false, hypocritical, lying, mendacious, untrustworthy, unveracious.
antonym truthful.

untwine *v.* disentwine, uncoil, unravel, untwist, unwind.
antonyms twine, wind.

untwist *v.* detort, ravel out, uncoil, unravel, untwine, unwind.
antonym twist.

untutored *adj.* artless, ignorant, illiterate, inexperienced, inexpert, simple, uneducated, unlearned, unlessoned, unpractised, unrefined, unschooled, unsophisticated, untrained, unversed.
antonyms educated, trained.

unused *adj.* available, extra, fresh, idle, intact, left, left-over, new, pristine, remaining, unaccustomed, unconsumed, unemployed, unexploited, unfamiliar, untouched, unutilised.

unusual *adj.* abnormal, anomalous, atypical, bizarre, curious, different, eccentric, exceptional, extraordinary, odd, phenomenal, queer, rare, remarkable, singular, strange, surprising, uncommon, unconventional, unexpected, unfamiliar, unwonted.
antonyms normal, usual.

unutterable *adj.* egregious, extreme, indescribable, ineffable, nefandous, overwhelming, unimaginable, unspeakable.

unvarnished *adj.* bare, candid, frank, honest, naked, plain, pure, sheer, simple, sincere, stark, straightforward, unadorned, undisguised, unembellished.
antonyms disguised, embellished.

unveil *v.* bare, disclose, discover, disenshroud, divulge, expose, reveal, uncover, unfold, unshroud.
antonyms cover, hide.

unwanted *adj.* de trop, extra, otiose, outcast, rejected, superfluous, surplus, unasked, undesired, uninvited, unnecessary, unneeded, unrequired, unsolicited, unwelcome, useless.
antonyms necessary, needed, wanted.

unwarranted *adj.* baseless, gratuitous, groundless, indefensible, inexcusable, uncalled-for, unjust, unjustified, unprovoked, unreasonable, vain, wrong.
antonyms justifiable, warranted.

unwary *adj.* careless, credulous, hasty, heedless, imprudent, incautious, indiscreet, rash, reckless, thoughtless, unchary, uncircumspect, unguarded, unthinking, unwatchful.
antonyms cautious, wary.

unwavering *adj.* consistent, dedicated, determined, resolute, single-minded, staunch, steadfast, steady, sturdy, tenacious, undeviating, unfaltering, unflagging, unquestioning, unshakable, unshaken, unswerving, untiring.
antonyms fickle, wavering.

unwelcome *adj.* disagreeable, displeasing, distasteful, excluded, rejected, thankless, unacceptable, undesirable, uninvited, unpalatable, unpleasant, unpopular, unwanted, upsetting, worrying.
antonyms desirable, welcome.

unwell *adj.* ailing, ill, indisposed, mops and brooms, nohow, nohowish, off-colour, poorly, sick, sickly, unhealthy.
antonyms healthy, well.

unwholesome *adj.* anaemic, bad, corrupting, degrading, deleterious, demoralising, depraving, epinosic, evil, harmful, immoral, innutritious, insalubrious, insalutary, insanitary, junk, noxious, pale, pallid, pasty, perverting, poisonous, sickly, tainted, unhealthy, unhygienic, wan, wicked.

antonyms salubrious, wholesome.

unwieldy *adj.* awkward, bulky, burdensome, clumsy, cumbersome, cumbrous, gangling, hefty, hulking, inconvenient, massive, ponderous, ungainly, unhandy, unmanageable, weighty.

antonyms dainty, neat, petite.

unwilling *adj.* averse, disinclined, grudging, indisposed, laggard, loath, loathful, opposed, reluctant, resistant, slow, unenthusiastic.

antonyms enthusiastic, willing.

unwillingness *n.* backwardness, disinclination, hesitancy, indisposition, lack of enthusiasm, loathfulness, nolition, reluctance, slowness.

antonyms enthusiasm, willingness.

unwind *v.* calm down, detort, disentangle, quieten down, relax, slacken, uncoil, undo, unravel, unreel, unroll, unswathe, untwine, untwist, unwrap, wind down.

antonyms twist, wind.

unwise *adj.* foolhardy, foolish, ill-advised, ill-considered, ill-judged, impolitic, improvident, imprudent, inadvisable, indiscreet, inexpedient, injudicious, irresponsible, rash, reckless, senseless, short-sighted, silly, stupid, thoughtless, unintelligent.

antonyms prudent, wise.

unwitting *adj.* accidental, chance, ignorant, inadvertent, innocent, involuntary, unaware, unconscious, unintended, unintentional, unknowing, unmeant, unplanned, unsuspecting, unthinking.

antonyms conscious, deliberate, knowing, witting.

unwonted *adj.* atypical, exceptional, extraordinary, infrequent, peculiar, rare, singular, strange, unaccustomed, uncommon, uncustomary, unexpected, unfamiliar, unheard-of, unusual.

antonyms usual, wonted.

unworldly *adj.* abstract, celestial, ethereal, extramundane, extra-physical, extraterrestrial, green, idealistic, impractical, inexperienced, innocent, metaphysical, naïve, otherworldly, religious, spiritual, transcendental, unearthly, unsophisticated, visionary.

antonyms materialistic, practical, worldly.

unworried *adj.* collected, composed, downbeat, unabashed, undismayed, unperturbed, unruffled, untroubled.

antonym anxious.

unworthy *adj.* base, contemptible, degrading, desertless, discreditable, disgraceful, dishonourable, disreputable, ignoble, improper, inappropriate, ineligible, inferior, shameful, unbecoming, unbefitting, undeserving, unfitting, unprofessional, unseemly, unsuitable, unsuited.

antonyms commendable, worthy.

unwritten *adj.* accepted, conventional, customary, implicit, oral, recognised, tacit,

traditional, understood, unformulated, unrecorded, verbal, vocal, word-of-mouth.

antonyms recorded, written.

unyielding *adj.* adamant, determined, firm, hardline, immovable, implacable, inexorable, inflexible, intractable, intransigent, obdurate, obstinate, relentless, resolute, rigid, solid, staunch, steadfast, stubborn, tough, unbending, uncompromising, unrelenting, unwavering.

antonyms flexible, yielding.

up to one's eyes busy, engaged, inundated, overwhelmed, preoccupied, tied up.

antonyms free, idle.

up to scratch acceptable, adequate, capable, comme il faut, competent, OK, satisfactory, sufficient.

antonym unsatisfactory.

up-and-coming ambitious, assertive, eager, enterprising, go-getting, promising, pushing.

upbeat *adj.* bright, bullish, buoyant, cheerful, cheery, encouraging, favourable, forward-looking, heartening, hopeful, optimistic, positive, promising, rosy.

antonyms down-beat, gloomy.

upbraid *v.* admonish, berate, blame, carpet, castigate, censure, chide, condemn, criticise, dress down, jaw, lecture, rate, rebuke, reprimand, reproach, reprove, scold, take to task, tell off, tick off.

antonyms commend, praise.

upbringing *n.* breeding, bringing-up, care, cultivation, education, instruction, nurture, parenting, raising, rearing, tending, training.

update *v.* amend, correct, modernise, renew, renovate, revamp, revise.

upgrade *v.* advance, ameliorate, better, elevate, embourgeoise, enhance, gentilise, gentrify, improve, promote, raise.

antonyms degrade, downgrade.

upgrading *n.* advancement, amelioration, betterment, elevation, embourgeoisement, enhancement, gentrification, improvement, promotion.

upheaval *n.* cataclysm, chaos, confusion, disorder, disruption, disturbance, earthquake, eruption, overthrow, revolution, shake-up, turmoil, upset.

uphill *adj.* acclivious, acclivitous, arduous, ascending, climbing, difficult, exhausting, gruelling, hard, laborious, mounting, punishing, rising, strenuous, taxing, tough, upward, wearisome.

antonyms downhill, easy.

uphold *v.* advocate, aid, back, champion, countenance, defend, encourage, endorse, fortify, hold to, justify, maintain, promote, stand by, stengthen, support, sustain, vindicate.

upkeep *n.* care, conservation, expenditure, expenses, keep, maintenance, oncosts, operating costs, outgoing, outlay, overheads, preservation, repair, running, running costs, subsistence, support, sustenance.

antonym neglect.

uplift *v.* advance, ameliorate, better, boost, civilise, cultivate, edify, elate, elevate, enlighten, exalt, heave, hoist, improve, inspire, lift, raise, refine, upgrade.

n. advancement, betterment, boost, cultivation, edification, enhancement, enlightenment, enrichment, improvement, lift, refinement.

upper *adj.* elevated, eminent, exalted, greater, high, higher, important, loftier, senior, superior, top, topmost, uppermost.

antonyms inferior, junior, lower.

upper hand advantage, ascendancy, control, dominance, domination, dominion, edge, mastery, superiority, supremacy, sway.

upper-class *adj.* aristocratic, blue-blooded, educated, élite, exclusive, gentle, high-born, high-class, noble, patrician, swanky, top-drawer, well-born, well-bred.

antonyms humble, working-class.

uppermost *adj.* chief, dominant, first, foremost, greatest, highest, leading, loftiest, main, paramount, predominant, pre-eminent, primary, principal, prominent, supreme, top, topmost, upmost.

antonyms bottommost, lowest.

uppish *adj.* affected, arrogant, assuming, big-headed, bumptious, cocky, conceited, hoity-toity, impertinent, overweening, presumptuous, self-important, snobbish, stuck-up, supercilious, swanky, toffee-nosed, uppity.

antonyms diffident, unassertive.

upright *adj.* arrect, bluff, conscientious, erect, ethical, faithful, four-square, good, high-minded, honest, honourable, incorruptible, just, noble, perpendicular, principled, righteous, straight, straightforward, true, trustworthy, unimpeachable, upstanding, vertical, virtuous.

antonyms dishonest, flat, horizontal, prone, supine.

uprising *n.* inqilab, insurgence, insurgency, insurrection, mutiny, putsch, rebellion, revolt, revolution, rising, sedition, upheaval.

uproar *n.* brawl, brouhaha, clamour, commotion, confusion, din, disorder, furore, hubbub, hullabaloo, hurly-burly, katzenjammer, noise, outcry, pandemonium, racket, rammy, randan, riot, ruckus, ruction, rumpus, stramash, tumult, turbulence, turmoil.

uproarious *adj.* boisterous, clamorous, confused, convulsive, deafening, disorderly, gleeful, hilarious, hysterical, killing, loud, noisy, rib-tickling, riotous, rip-roaring, roistering, rollicking, rowdy, rowdy-dowdy, side-splitting, tempestuous, tumultuous, turbulent, unrestrained, wild.

antonym sedate.

uproot *v.* deracinate, destroy, disorient, displace, disroot, eliminate, eradicate, exile, exterminate, extirpate, grub up, remove, rip up, root out, weed out, wipe out.

upset *v.* agitate, bother, capsize, change, conquer, defeat, destabilise, discombobulate, discompose, disconcert, dismay, disorder,

disorganise, disquiet, distress, disturb, fluster, grieve, hip, overcome, overset, overthrow, overturn, perturb, ruffle, shake, spill, spoil, tip, topple, trouble, unnerve, unsteady.

n. agitation, bother, bug, complaint, defeat, disorder, disruption, disturbance, illness, indisposition, malady, purl, reverse, shake-up, shock, sickness, surprise, trouble, upheaval, worry.

adj. agitated, bothered, capsized, chaotic, choked, confused, disconcerted, dismayed, disordered, disquieted, distressed, disturbed, frantic, gippy, grieved, hurt, ill, messed up, muddled, overturned, overwrought, pained, poorly, qualmish, queasy, ruffled, shattered, sick, spilled, toppled, topsy-turvy, troubled, tumbled, worried.

upshot *n.* conclusion, consequence, culmination, end, event, finale, finish, issue, outcome, pay-off, result.

upside down at sixes and sevens, chaotic, confused, disordered, higgledy-piggledy, inverted, jumbled, muddled, overturned, topsy-turvy, upset, upturned, wrong side up.

antonym shipshape.

upstanding *adj.* erect, ethical, firm, four-square, good, hardy, healthy, hearty, honest, honourable, incorruptible, lusty, moral, principled, robust, stalwart, strong, sturdy, true, trustworthy, upright, vigorous.

antonyms puny, untrustworthy.

upstart *n.* arriviste, mushroom, nobody, nouveau riche, parvenu, social climber.

uptight *adj.* anxious, edgy, hung-up, irritated, nervy, prickly, tense, uneasy.

antonyms calm, cool, relaxed.

up-to-date *adj.* à la mode, all the rage, contemporary, current, fashionable, in, latest, modern, modish, newest, now, popular, smart, stylish, swinging, trendy, up-to-the-minute, vogue, voguish, with it.

antonym old-fashioned.

upturn *n.* advancement, amelioration, boost, improvement, increase, recovery, revival, rise, upsurge, upswing.

antonyms downturn, drop, setback.

urban *adj.* built-up, burghal, city, civic, inner-city, metropolitan, municipal, oppidan, town, urbanised.

antonyms country, rural, rustic.

urbane *adj.* bland, civil, civilised, cosmopolitan, courteous, cultivated, cultured, debonair, easy, elegant, mannerly, polished, refined, smooth, sophisticated, suave, well-bred, well-mannered.

antonyms gauche, uncouth.

urbanity *n.* blandness, charm, civility, courtesy, cultivation, culture, ease, elegance, eutrapelia, grace, mannerliness, polish, refinement, smoothness, sophistication, suavity, worldliness.

antonyms awkwardness, gaucheness.

urchin *n.* brat, gamin, gutter-snipe, kid, mudlark, ragamuffin, street Arab, tatterdemalion, waif.

urge *v.* advise, advocate, beg, beseech, champion, compel, constrain, counsel, drive, emphasise, encourage, entreat, exhort, force, goad, hasten, hist, impel, implore, incite, induce, instigate, nag, plead, press, propel, push, recommend, solicit, spur, stimulate, support, underline, underscore.
antonyms deter, dissuade.
n. compulsion, desire, drive, eagerness, fancy, impulse, inclination, itch, libido, longing, wish, yearning, yen.
antonym disinclination.

urgency *n.* exigence, exigency, extremity, gravity, hurry, imperativeness, importance, importunity, instancy, necessity, need, pressure, seriousness, stress.

urgent *adj.* clamorous, cogent, compelling, critical, crucial, eager, earnest, emergent, exigent, immediate, imperative, important, importunate, insistent, instant, intense, persistent, persuasive, pressing, top-priority.

urinal *n.* gents, pissoir.

urinate *v.* ease oneself, leak, make water, micturate, pass water, pee, piddle, piss, relieve oneself, spend a penny, stale, tinkle, wee, wee-wee.

urination *n.* emiction, micturition, run-off.

urine *n.* pee, piddle, piss, stale, water.

usable *adj.* available, current, exploitable, functional, operating, operational, practical, serviceable, utilisable, valid, working.
antonyms unusable, useless.

usage *n.* application, control, convention, custom, employment, etiquette, form, habit, handling, management, method, mode, operation, practice, procedure, protocol, régime, regulation, routine, rule, running, tradition, treatment, use, wont.

use *v.* apply, bring, consume, employ, enjoy, exercise, exhaust, expend, exploit, handle, manipulate, misuse, operate, ply, practise, spend, treat, usufruct, utilise, waste, wield, work.
n. advantage, application, avail, benefit, call, cause, custom, employment, end, enjoyment, exercise, good, habit, handling, help, meaning, mileage, necessity, need, object, occasion, operation, point, practice, profit, purpose, reason, service, treatment, usage, usefulness, usufruct, utility, value, way, wont, worth.

use up absorb, consume, deplete, devour, drain, eat into, exhaust, finish, fritter, sap, squander, swallow, waste.

used *adj.* accustomed, cast-off, dog-eared, familiar, hand-me-down, nearly new, reach-me-down, second-hand, shop-soiled, soiled, worn.
antonyms fresh, new, unused.

useful *adj.* advantageous, all-purpose, beneficial, convenient, effective, fruitful, general-purpose, handy, helpful, practical, productive, profitable, salutary, serviceable, valuable, worthwhile.
antonym useless.

useless *adj.* bootless, clapped-out, disadvantageous, effectless, feckless, fruitless, futile, hopeless, idle, impractical, incompetent, ineffective, ineffectual, inefficient, inept, of no use, pointless, profitless, shiftless, spastic, stupid, unavailing, unproductive, unworkable, vain, valueless, weak, worthless.
antonym useful.

uselessness *n.* futility, hopelessness, idleness, impracticality, incompetence, ineffectiveness, ineffectuality, ineptitude, inutility.
antonyms effectiveness, usefulness.

usher *n.* attendant, doorkeeper, escort, guide, huissier, usherette.
v. conduct, direct, escort, guide, lead, pilot, shepherd, steer.

usher in announce, herald, inaugurate, initiate, introduce, launch, precede, ring in.

usual *adj.* accepted, accustomed, common, constant, conventional, customary, everyday, expected, familiar, fixed, general, habitual, nomic, normal, ordinary, recognised, regular, routine, standard, stock, typical, unexceptional, wonted.
antonyms unheard-of, unusual.

usually *adv.* as a rule, by and large, chiefly, commonly, customarily, generally, generally speaking, habitually, in the main, mainly, mostly, normally, on the whole, ordinarily, regularly, routinely, traditionally, typically.
antonym exceptionally.

usurer *n.* extortionist, gombeen-man, loan-shark, money-lender, note-shaver, Shylock.

usurp *v.* annex, appropriate, arrogate, assume, commandeer, seize, steal, take, take over, wrest.

usury *n.* extortion, gombeen, interest, money-lending, usance.

utensil *n.* apparatus, contrivance, device, gadget, gismo, implement, instrument, tool.

utilise *v.* adapt, appropriate, employ, exploit, make use of, put to use, resort to, take advantage of, turn to account, use.

utilitarian *adj.* convenient, down-to-earth, effective, efficient, functional, lowly, practical, pragmatic, sensible, serviceable, unpretentious, useful.
antonyms decorative, impractical.

utilitarianism *n.* eudaemonism.

utility *n.* advantage, advantageousness, avail, benefit, convenience, efficacy, expedience, fitness, point, practicality, profit, satisfactoriness, service, serviceableness, use, usefulness, value.
antonym inutility.

utmost *adj.* extreme, farthest, final, first, greatest, highest, last, maximum, outermost, paramount, remotest, supreme, ultimate, uttermost.
n. best, hardest, maximum, most, uttermost.

Utopia *n.* bliss, Eden, Elysium, Erewhon, Garden of Eden, heaven, heaven on earth, paradise, seventh heaven, Shangri-la.

Utopian *adj.* airy, chimerical, dream, Elysian, fanciful, fantastic, ideal, idealistic, illusory, imaginary, impractical, perfect, romantic, unworkable, visionary, wishful.

utter[1] *adj.* absolute, arrant, complete, consummate, dead, downright, entire, out-and-out, perfect, sheer, stark, thorough, thoroughgoing, total, unalleviated, unmitigated, unqualified.

utter[2] *v.* articulate, declare, deliver, divulge, enounce, enunciate, express, proclaim, promulgate, pronounce, publish, reveal, say, sound, speak, state, tell, tongue, verbalise, vocalise, voice.

utterance *n.* announcement, articulation, comment, declaration, delivery, ejaculation, expression, gift of tongues, glossolalia, illocution, opinion, pronouncement, remark, speaking with tongues, speech, statement, verbalisation, vocalisation, vociferation.

utterly *adv.* absolutely, completely, dead, diametrically, entirely, extremely, fully, perfectly, thoroughly, totally, wholly.

U-turn *n.* about-turn, backtrack, enantiodromia, reversal, tergiversation, uey, volteface.

V

vacancy *n*. accommodation, emptiness, gap, job, opening, opportunity, place, position, post, room, situation, space, vacuity, vacuousness, vacuum, void.

vacant *adj*. absent, absent-minded, abstracted, available, blank, disengaged, dreaming, dreamy, empty, expressionless, free, idle, inane, inattentive, incurious, thoughtless, to let, unemployed, unengaged, unfilled, unoccupied, untenanted, unthinking, vacuous, void.
antonyms engaged, occupied.

vacate *v*. abandon, depart, evacuate, leave, quit, withdraw.

vacillate *v*. fluctuate, haver, hesitate, oscillate, shilly-shally, shuffle, sway, swither, temporise, tergiversate, waver.

vacillating *adj*. hesitant, irresolute, oscillating, shilly-shallying, shuffling, swithering, temporising, uncertain, unresolved, wavering.
antonyms resolute, unhesitating.

vacillation *n*. fluctuation, hesitancy, hesitation, inconstancy, indecision, indecisiveness, irresolution, shilly-shallying, temporisation, tergiversation, unsteadiness, wavering.

vacuity *n*. apathy, blankness, emptiness, inanity, incognisance, incomprehension, incuriosity, nothingness, space, vacuousness, vacuum, void.

vacuous *adj*. apathetic, blank, empty, idle, inane, incurious, stupid, uncomprehending, unfilled, unintelligent, vacant, void.

vacuum *n*. chasm, emptiness, gap, nothingness, space, vacuity, void.

vagabond *n*. beggar, bum, down-and-out, hobo, itinerant, land-louper, migrant, nomad, outcast, rascal, rover, runabout, runagate, tramp, vagrant, wanderer, wayfarer.

vagary *n*. caprice, crotchet, fancy, fegary, humour, megrim, notion, prank, quirk, whim, whimsy.

vagrant *n*. beggar, bum, gangrel, hobo, itinerant, land-louper, rolling stone, stroller, tramp, wanderer.
adj. footloose, homeless, itinerant, nomadic, roaming, rootless, roving, shiftless, travelling, vagabond, wandering.

vague *adj*. amorphous, blurred, dim, doubtful, evasive, fuzzy, generalised, hazy, ill-defined, imprecise, indefinite, indeterminate, indistinct, inexact, lax, loose, misty, nebulous, obscure, shadowy, uncertain, unclear, undefined, undetermined, unknown, unspecific, unspecified, woolly.
antonyms certain, clear, definite.

vaguely *adv*. absent-mindedly, dimly, faintly,

imprecisely, inexactly, obscurely, slightly, vacantly.

vagueness *n*. ambiguity, amorphousness, dimness, faintness, fuzziness, haziness, imprecision, inexactitude, looseness, obscurity, uncertainty, woolliness.
antonyms clarity, precision.

vain *adj*. abortive, affected, arrogant, baseless, bigheaded, conceited, egotistical, empty, fruitless, futile, groundless, hollow, idle, inflated, mindless, narcissistic, nugatory, ostentatious, overweening, peacockish, pointless, pretentious, proud, purposeless, self-important, self-satisfied, senseless, stuck-up, swaggering, swanky, swollen-headed, time-wasting, trifling, trivial, unavailing, unimportant, unproductive, unprofitable, unsubstantial, useless, vainglorious, vaporous, worthless.
antonyms modest, self-effacing.

valediction *n*. adieu, farewell, godspeed, goodbye, leave-taking, send-off, vale.
antonyms greeting, welcome.

valet *n*. body servant, gentleman's gentleman, man, man-servant, valet de chambre.

valetudinarian *adj*. delicate, feeble, frail, hypochondriac, infirm, invalid, neurotic, sickly, weakly.
antonym stoical.

valiant *adj*. bold, brave, courageous, dauntless, doughty, fearless, gallant, heroic, indomitable, intrepid, plucky, redoubtable, stalwart, staunch, stout, stout-hearted, valorous, worthy.
antonym cowardly.

valid *adj*. approved, authentic, binding, bona fide, cogent, conclusive, convincing, efficacious, efficient, genuine, good, just, lawful, legal, legitimate, logical, official, potent, powerful, proper, rational, reliable, sound, substantial, telling, weighty, well-founded, well-grounded.
antonym invalid.

validate *v*. attest, authenticate, authorise, certify, confirm, corroborate, endorse, legalise, ratify, substantiate, underwrite.

validity *n*. authority, cogency, force, foundation, grounds, justifiability, lawfulness, legality, legitimacy, logic, point, power, soundness, strength, substance, weight.
antonym invalidity.

valley *n*. clough, coomb, cwm, dale, dean, dell, den, depression, dingle, glen, graben, griff, gulch, hollow, hope, slade, strath, vale.

valorous *adj*. bold, brave, courageous, dauntless, doughty, fearless, gallant, hardy, heroic,

intrepid, lion-hearted, mettlesome, plucky, redoubtable, stalwart, valiant.
antonyms cowardly, weak.

valour *n.* boldness, bravery, courage, derring-do, doughtiness, fearlessness, fortitude, gallantry, hardiness, heroism, intrepidity, lion-heartedness, mettle, spirit.
antonyms cowardice, weakness.

valuable *adj.* advantageous, beneficial, blue-chip, cherished, costly, dear, esteemed, estimable, expensive, fruitful, handy, helpful, high-priced, important, invaluable, precious, prizable, prized, productive, profitable, serviceable, treasured, useful, valued, worthwhile, worthy.
antonyms useless, valueless.

valuation *n.* appraisement, assessment, computation, estimate, evaluation, survey.

value *n.* account, advantage, avail, benefit, cost, desirability, equivalent, good, help, importance, merit, price, profit, rate, significance, use, usefulness, utility, worth.
v. account, appraise, appreciate, apprize, assess, cherish, compute, esteem, estimate, evaluate, hold dear, price, prize, rate, regard, respect, survey, treasure.
antonyms disregard, neglect, undervalue.

valued *adj.* beloved, cherished, dear, esteemed, highly regarded, loved, prized, respected, treasured.

values *n.* ethics, morals, principles, standards.

vamoose *v.* absquatulate, clear off, decamp, disappear, do a bunk, make oneself scarce, quit, scarper, scram, skedaddle, vanish.

vanish *v.* dematerialise, depart, die out, disappear, disperse, dissolve, evanesce, evaporate, exit, fade, fizzle out, melt, peter out.
antonyms appear, materialise.

vanity *n.* affectation, airs, arrogance, bigheadedness, conceit, conceitedness, egotism, emptiness, frivolity, fruitlessness, fume, futility, hollowness, idleness, inanity, narcissism, ostentation, peacockery, pointlessness, pretension, pride, self-admiration, self-conceit, self-love, self-satisfaction, swollenheadedness, triviality, unreality, unsubstantiality, uselessness, vainglory, worthlessness.
antonyms modesty, worth.

vanquish *v.* beat, confound, conquer, crush, defeat, humble, master, overcome, overpower, overwhelm, quell, reduce, repress, rout, subdue, subjugate, triumph over.

vapid *adj.* banal, bland, bloodless, boring, colourless, dead, dull, flat, flavourless, insipid, jejune, lifeless, limp, stale, tame, tasteless, tedious, tiresome, trite, uninspiring, uninteresting, watery, weak, wishy-washy.
antonyms interesting, vigorous.

vaporous *adj.* brumous, chimerical, fanciful, flimsy, foggy, fumous, fumy, gaseous, insubstantial, misty, steamy, vain.
antonym substantial.

vapour *n.* breath, brume, damp, dampness, exhalation, fog, fumes, halitus, haze, miasm, miasma, mist, reek, roke, smoke, steam.

variable *adj.* capricious, chameleonic, changeable, fickle, fitful, flexible, fluctuating, inconstant, mercurial, moonish, mutable, protean, shifting, temperamental, unpredictable, unstable, unsteady, vacillating, varying, versiform, wavering.
antonym invariable.
n. factor, parameter.

variance *n.* difference, disagreement, discord, discrepancy, disharmony, dissension, dissent, divergence, division, inconsistency, quarrelling, strife, variation.
antonyms agreement, harmony.

variant *adj.* alternative, derived, deviant, different, divergent, exceptional, modified.
antonyms normal, standard, usual.
n. alternative, development, deviant, modification, rogue, sport, variation.

variation *n.* alteration, change, departure, deviation, difference, discrepancy, diversification, diversity, elaboration, inflection, innovation, modification, modulation, novelty, variety.
antonyms monotony, similitude, uniformity.

varied *adj.* accidented, assorted, different, diverse, heterogeneous, manifold, miscellaneous, mixed, motley, multifarious, sundry, various.
antonyms similar, uniform.

variegated *adj.* diversified, freaked, jaspé, many-coloured, motley, mottled, multicoloured, parti-coloured, pied, poikilific, polychrome, streaked, varicoloured, veined, versicoloured.
antonyms monochrome, plain.

variety *n.* array, assortment, brand, breed, category, change, class, collection, difference, discrepancy, diversification, diversity, intermixture, kind, make, manifoldness, many-sidedness, medley, miscellany, mixture, multifariousness, multiplicity, olio, olla-podrida, order, pot-pourri, range, sort, species, strain, type, variation:
antonyms monotony, similitude, uniformity.

various *adj.* assorted, different, differing, disparate, distinct, divers, diverse, diversified, heterogeneous, many, many-sided, miscellaneous, multifarous, omnifarous, several, sundry, varied, variegated, varying.

varnish *n.* coating, glaze, gloss, japan, lac, lacquer, polish, resin, shellac.

vary *v.* alter, alternate, change, depart, differ, disagree, diverge, diversify, fluctuate, inflect, intermix, modify, modulate, permutate, reorder, transform.

vase *n.* amphora, container, ewer, hydria, jar, jug, pitcher, urn, vessel.

vassal *n.* bondman, bondservant, bondsman, galloglass, liege, liegeman, retainer, serf, slave, subject, thrall, villein.

vassalage *n.* bondage, dependence, serfdom, servitude, slavery, subjection, subjugation, thraldom, villeinage.

vast *adj.* astronomical, boundless, capacious, colossal, cyclopean, enormous, extensive, far-flung, fathomless, gigantic, great, huge, illimitable, immeasurable, immense, limitless, mammoth, massive, measureless, monstrous, monumental, never-ending, prodigious, stupendous, sweeping, tremendous, unboudned, unlimited, vasty, voluminous, wide.

vat *n*. container, keeve, kier, tank, tub.

vault[1] *v*. bound, clear, hurdle, jump, leap, leap-frog, spring.

vault[2] *n*. arch, camera, cavern, cellar, concave, crypt, depository, mausoleum, repository, roof, span, strongroom, tomb, undercroft, wine-cellar.

vaunt *v*. blazon, boast, brag, crow, exult in, flaunt, parade, show off, trumpet.
antonyms belittle, minimise.

veer *v*. change, sheer, shift, swerve, tack, turn, wheel.

vegetables *n*. greens, greenstuff, legumes.

vegetarian *adj*. grass-eating, herbivorous, Pythagorean, vegan.

vegetate *v*. degenerate, deteriorate, go to seed, idle, languish, moulder, rust, rusticate, stagnate.

vehemence *n*. animation, ardour, eagerness, earnestness, emphasis, energy, enthusiasm, fervency, fervour, fire, force, forcefulness, heat, impetuosity, intensity, keenness, passion, urgency, verve, vigour, violence, warmth, zeal.
antonym indifference.

vehement *adj*. animated, ardent, eager, earnest, emphatic, enthusiastic, fervent, fervid, fierce, forceful, forcible, heated, impassioned, impetuous, intense, passionate, powerful, strong, urgent, violent, zealous.
antonyms apathetic, indifferent.

vehicle *n*. apparatus, channel, conveyance, means, mechanism, medium, organ.

veil *v*. cloak, conceal, cover, dim, disguise, dissemble, dissimulate, hide, mantle, mask, obscure, screen, shade, shadow, shield.
antonyms expose, uncover.
n. blind, cloak, cover, curtain, disguise, film, humeral, integument, mask, screen, shade, shroud, velum.

vein *n*. blood vessel, course, current, dash, frame of mind, hint, humour, lode, mode, mood, note, seam, strain, stratum, streak, stripe, style, temper, tenor, thread, tone, trait.

veined *adj*. freaked, jaspé, marbled, mottled, streaked, variegated.

velocity *n*. celerity, fleetness, impetus, pace, quickness, rapidity, rate, speed, swiftness.

venal *adj*. bent, bribable, buyable, corrupt, corruptible, grafting, mercenary, purchasable, simoniacal.
antonym incorruptible.

vendetta *n*. bad blood, bitterness, blood-feud, enmity, feud, quarrel, rivalry.

veneer *n*. appearance, coating, façade, front, gloss, guise, layer, mask, pretence, semblance, show, surface.

venerable *adj*. aged, august, dignified, esteemed, grave, honoured, respected, revered, reverenced, reverend, sage, sedate, venerated, wise, worshipful.

venerate *v*. adore, esteem, hallow, honour, respect, revere, reverence, worship.
antonyms anathematise, disregard, execrate.

veneration *n*. adoration, awe, deference, devotion, dulia, esteem, hyperdulia, latria, respect, reverence, worship.

vengeance *n*. avengement, lex talionis, reprisal, requital, retaliation, retribution, revanche, revenge, talion, tit for tat.
antonym forgiveness.

vengeful *adj*. avenging, implacable, punitive, rancorous, relentless, retaliatory, retributive, revanchist, revengeful, spiteful, unforgiving, vindictive.
antonym forgiving.

venial *adj*. excusable, forgivable, insignificant, minor, negligible, pardonable, slight, trifling, trivial.
antonyms mortal, unforgivable, unpardonable.

venom *n*. acrimony, bane, bitterness, gall, grudge, hate, hatred, ill-will, malevolence, malice, maliciousness, malignity, poison, rancour, spite, spitefulness, spleen, toxin, venin, vindictiveness, virulence, virus, vitrio.

venomous *adj*. baleful, baneful, envenomed, hostile, malicious, malign, malignant, mephitic, noxious, poison, poisonous, rancorous, savage, spiteful, toxic, vicious, vindictive, virulent, vitriolic.

vent *n*. aperture, blowhole, duct, hole, opening, orifice, outlet, passage, spiracle, split.
v. air, discharge, emit, express, let fly, release, unloose, utter, voice.

ventilate *v*. air, broadcast, debate, discuss, examine, expound, express.
antonym suppress.

venture *v*. advance, adventure, chance, dare, endanger, hazard, imperil, jeopardise, make bold, presume, put forward, risk, speculate, stake, suggest, take the liberty, volunteer, wager.
n. adventure, chance, endeavour, enterprise, fling, gamble, hazard, operation, project, risk, speculation, undertaking.

venturesome *adj*. adventurous, audacious, bold, courageous, daredevil, daring, dauntless, doughty, enterprising, fearless, intrepid, plucky, spirited.
antonyms pusillanimous, unenterprising.

veracious *adj*. accurate, credible, dependable, exact, factual, faithful, frank, genuine, honest, reliable, straightforward, true, trustworthy, truthful, veridical.
antonym untruthful.

veracity *n*. accuracy, candour, credibility, exactitude, frankness, honesty, integrity, precision, probity, rectitude, trustworthiness, truth, truthfulness, verity.
antonym untruthfulness.

verbal *adj*. lexical, oral, spoken, unwritten, verbatim, word-of-mouth.

verbatim *adv.* exactly, literally, precisely, to the letter, (verbatim et) literatim, word for word.

verbiage *n.* circumlocution, periphrasis, perissology, pleonasm, prolixity, repetition, verbosity.
antonyms economy, succinctness.

verbose *adj.* ambagious, circumlocutory, diffuse, garrulous, long-winded, loquacious, multiloquent, periphrastic, phrasy, pleonastic, prolix, windy, wordy.
antonyms economical, laconic, succinct.

verbosity *n.* garrulity, logorrhoea, long-windedness, loquaciousness, loquacity, multiloquy, prolixity, verbiage, verboseness, windiness, wordiness.
antonyms economy, succinctness.

verdant *adj.* fresh, graminaceous, gramineous, grassy, green, leafy, lush, virid, viridescent.

verdict *n.* adjudication, assessment, conclusion, decision, finding, judgement, opinion, sentence.

verdure *n.* foliage, grass, greenery, greenness, greenth, herbage, leafage, meadows, pasture, verdancy, vert, viridescence, viridity.

verge *n.* border, boundary, brim, brink, edge, edging, extreme, limit, lip, margin, roadside, threshold.
verge on approach, border on, come close to, near.

verification *n.* attestation, authentication, checking, confirmation, corroboration, proof, substantiation, validation.

verify *v.* attest, authenticate, check, confirm, corroborate, prove, substantiate, support, testify, validate.
antonyms discredit, invalidate.

verisimilitude *n.* authenticity, colour, credibility, likeliness, plausibility, realism, resemblance, ring of truth, semblance.
antonym implausibility.

verity *n.* actuality, authenticity, factuality, soundness, truth, truthfulness, validity, veracity.
antonym untruth.

vernacular *adj.* colloquial, common, endemic, indigenous, informal, local, mother, native, popular, vulgar.
n. argot, cant, dialect, idiom, jargon, language, lingo, parlance, patois, speech, tongue.

versatile *adj.* adaptable, adjustable, all-round, flexible, functional, general-purpose, handy, many-sided, multifaceted, multipurpose, protean, Renaissance, resourceful, variable.
antonym inflexible.

verse *n.* canto, doggerel, elegaics, fit, iambics, jingle, poesy, poetastery, poetry, rhyme, stanza, stave, strophe, verse-making, versemongering, versicle, versification.

versed *adj.* accomplished, acquainted, au fait, competent, conversant, experienced, familiar, knowledgeable, learned, practiced, proficient, qualified, seasoned, skilled.

versifier *n.* poet, poetaster, poetess, poeticule, rhymer, rhymester, rhymist, verse-maker,

verse-monger, verser, verse-smith, versificator.

version *n.* account, adaptation, design, form, interpretation, kind, model, paraphrase, portrayal, reading, rendering, rendition, style, translation, type, variant.

vertex *n.* acme, apex, apogee, crown, culmination, extremity, height, peak, pinnacle, summit, top, zenith.
antonym nadir.

vertical *adj.* erect, on end, perpendicular, upright, upstanding.
antonym horizontal.

vertigo *n.* dizziness, giddiness, light-headedness, megrim.

verve *n.* animation, brio, dash, élan, energy, enthusiasm, force, gusto, life, liveliness, pizzazz, punch, relish, sparkle, spirit, vigour, vim, vitality, vivacity, zeal, zip.
antonym apathy.

very *adv.* absolutely, acutely, awfully, decidedly, deeply, dogged, dooms, eminently, exceeding(ly), excessively, extremely, fell, gey, greatly, highly, jolly, noticeably, particularly, passing, rattling, really, remarkably, superlatively, surpassingly, terribly, truly, uncommonly, unusually, wonderfully.
antonyms hardly, scarcely, slightly.
adj. actual, appropriate, bare, exact, express, identical, mere, perfect, plain, precise, pure, real, same, selfsame, sheer, simple, unqualified, utter.

vessel *n.* barque, boat, canister, container, craft, holder, jar, pot, receptacle, ship, utensil.

vestibule *n.* anteroom, entrance, entrance-hall, entrance-way, foyer, hall, lobby, porch, portico.

vestige *n.* evidence, glimmer, hint, indication, print, relic, remainder, remains, remnant, residue, scrap, sign, suspicion, token, trace, track, whiff.

vestigial *adj.* functionless, imperfect, incomplete, reduced, rudimentary, surviving, undeveloped.

vet[1] *v.* appraise, audit, check, examine, inspect, investigate, review, scan, scrutinise, survey.

vet[2] *n.* dog-leech, farrier, hippiatrist, horse-doctor, horse-leech, veterinarian, veterinary, veterinary surgeon.

veteran *n.* master, old hand, old soldier, old stager, old-timer, pastmaster, pro, trouper, war-horse.
antonyms novice, recruit.
adj. adept, battle-scarred, experienced, expert, long-serving, masterly, old, practised, professional, proficient, seasoned.
antonyms inexperienced, raw.

veto *v.* ban, blackball, disallow, forbid, interdict, kill, negative, prohibit, reject, rule out, turn down.
antonyms approve, sanction.
n. ban, embargo, interdict, prohibition, rejection, thumbs down.
antonyms approval, assent.

vex *v.* afflict, aggravate, agitate, annoy, bother,

bug, chagrin, deave, displease, distress, disturb, exasperate, fret, gall, get (to), harass, hump, irritate, molest, needle, nettle, offend, peeve, perplex, pester, pique, plague, provoke, rile, spite, tease, torment, trouble, upset, worry.

antonym soothe.

vexation *n.* aggravation, anger, annoyance, bore, bother, chagrin, difficulty, displeasure, dissatisfaction, exasperation, frustration, fury, headache, irritant, misfortune, nuisance, pique, problem, trouble, upset, worry.

vexatious *adj.* afflicting, aggravating, annoying, bothersome, burdensome, disagreeable, disappointing, distressing, doggone, exasperating, fashious, harassing, infuriating, irksome, irritating, nagging, pesky, pestful, pestiferous, pestilent, plaguesome, plagu(e)y, provoking, teasing, tormenting, troublesome, trying, unpleasant, upsetting, worrisome, worrying.

antonyms pleasant, soothing.

vexed *adj.* afflicted, aggravated, agitated, annoyed, bedevilled, bored, bothered, chagrined, confused, contested, controversial, deaved, displeased, disputed, distressed, disturbed, exasperated, harassed, irritated, miffed, moot, nettled, peeved, perplexed, provoked, put out, riled, ruffled, tormented, troubled, upset, worried.

viable *adj.* achievable, applicable, feasible, operable, possible, practicable, usable, workable.

antonyms impossible, unworkable.

vibes *n.* ambience, atmosphere, aura, emanation, emotions, feel, feelings, reaction, response, vibrations.

vibrant *adj.* alive, animated, bright, colourful, dynamic, electric, electrifying, jazzy, oscillating, palpitating, peppy, pulsating, quivering, responsive, sensitive, sparkling, spirited, trembling, vivacious, vivid.

vibrate *v.* dinnle, dirl, fluctuate, judder, oscillate, pendulate, pulsate, pulse, quiver, resonate, reverberate, shake, shimmy, shiver, shudder, sway, swing, throb, tremble, undulate.

vibration *n.* diadrom, fremitus, frisson, judder, juddering, oscillation, pulsation, pulse, quiver, resonance, reverberation, shaking, shudder, throb, throbbing, trembling, tremor.

vicarious *adj.* acting, commissioned, delegated, deputed, empathetic, indirect, second-hand, substituted, surrogate.

vice *n.* bad habit, besetting sin, blemish, corruption, defect, degeneracy, depravity, evil, evil-doing, failing, fault, hamartia, immorality, imperfection, iniquity, profligacy, shortcoming, sin, venality, weakness, wickedness.

antonym virtue.

vicinity *n.* area, circumjacency, district, environs, locality, neighbourhood, precincts, propinquity, proximity, purlieus, vicinage.

vicious *adj.* abhorrent, atrocious, backbiting, bad, barbarous, bitchy, brutal, catty, corrupt, cruel, dangerous, debased, defamatory, depraved, diabolical, fiendish, foul, heinous, immoral, infamous, malicious, mean, monstrous, nasty, perverted, profligate, rancorous, savage, sinful, slanderous, spiteful, unprincipled, venomous, vile, vindictive, violent, virulent, vitriolic, wicked, worthless, wrong.

antonyms gentle, good, virtuous.

viciousness *n.* badness, bitchiness, brutality, corruption, cruelty, depravity, ferocity, immorality, malice, profligacy, rancour, savagery, sinfulness, spite, spitefulness, venom, virulence, wickedness.

antonyms gentleness, goodness, virtue.

vicissitude *n.* alteration, alternation, change, deviation, divergence, fluctuation, mutation, revolution, shift, turn, twist, variation.

victim *n.* casualty, dupe, fall guy, fatality, gull, innocent, mark, martyr, patsy, sacrifice, scapegoat, sitting target, sucker, sufferer.

victimise *v.* bully, cheat, deceive, defraud, discriminate against, dupe, exploit, fool, gull, hoodwink, oppress, persecute, pick on, prey on, swindle, use.

victor *n.* champ, champion, conqueror, first, prize-winner, subjugator, top dog, vanquisher, victor ludorum, victrix, winner.

antonyms loser, vanquished.

victorious *adj.* champion, conquering, first, prize-winning, successful, top, triumphant, unbeaten, winning.

antonyms losing, unsuccessful.

victory *n.* conquest, laurels, mastery, palm, prize, subjugation, success, superiority, triumph, vanquishment, win.

antonyms defeat, loss.

victuals *n.* aliment, bread, comestibles, eatables, eats, edibles, food, grub, meat, nosh, provisions, rations, stores, supplies, sustenance, viands, vittles.

vie *v.* compete, contend, contest, corrival, fight, rival, strive, struggle.

view *n.* aspect, attitude, belief, contemplation, conviction, display, estimation, examination, feeling, glimpse, impression, inspection, judgement, landscape, look, notions, opinion, outlook, panorama, perception, perspective, picture, prospect, scan, scene, scrutiny, sentiment, sight, spectacle, survey, viewing, vision, vista.

v. behold, consider, contemplate, deem, examine, explore, eye, inspect, judge, observe, perceive, read, regard, scan, speculate, survey, watch, witness.

viewer *n.* looker-in, observer, onlooker, spectator, watcher.

viewpoint *n.* angle, Anschauung, attitude, feeling, opinion, perspective, position, slant, stance, standpoint.

vigil *n.* lookout, pernoctation, sleeplessness, stake-out, wake, wakefulness, watch.

vigilance *n.* alertness, attentiveness, carefulness, caution, circumspection, guardedness, observation, wakefulness, watchfulness.

vigilant *adj.* alert, Argus-eyed, attentive, careful, cautious, circumspect, guarded, on one's guard, on one's toes, on the alert, on the lookout, on the qui vive, sleepless, unsleeping, wakeful, watchful, wide-awake.

antonyms careless, forgetful, lax, negligent.

vigorous *adj.* active, brisk, dynamic, effective, efficient, energetic, enterprising, flourishing, forceful, forcible, full-blooded, hale, hardy, healthy, hearty, intense, lively, lusty, mettlesome, powerful, red-blooded, robust, sound, spanking, spirited, stout, strenuous, strong, virile, vital, zippy.

antonyms feeble, lethargic, weak.

vigorously *adv.* briskly, eagerly, energetically, forcefully, hard, heartily, lustily, powerfully, strenuously, strongly.

antonyms feebly, weakly.

vigour *n.* activity, animation, dash, dynamism, energy, force, forcefulness, gusto, health, liveliness, might, oomph, pep, potency, power, punch, robustness, snap, soundness, spirit, stamina, strength, verve, vim, virility, vitality, zip.

antonyms impotence, sluggishness, weakness.

vile *adj.* abandoned, abject, appalling, bad, base, coarse, contemptible, corrupt, debased, degenerate, degrading, depraved, despicable, disgraceful, disgusting, earthly, evil, foul, horrid, humiliating, ignoble, impure, loathsome, low, mean, miserable, nasty, nauseating, nefarious, noxious, offensive, perverted, repellent, repugnant, repulsive, revolting, scabbed, scabby, scandalous, scurvy, shocking, sickening, sinful, ugly, vicious, vulgar, wicked, worthless, wretched.

vileness *n.* baseness, coarseness, corruption, degeneracy, depravity, dreadfulness, enormity, evil, foulness, meanness, noxiousness, offensiveness, outrage, profanity, ugliness, wickedness.

vilification *n.* abuse, aspersion, calumniation, calumny, contumely, criticism, defamation, denigration, disparagement, invective, mudslinging, revilement, scurrility, vituperation.

vilify *v.* abuse, asperse, bad-mouth, berate, calumniate, criticise, debase, decry, defame, denigrate, denounce, disparage, malign, revile, slander, smear, stigmatise, traduce, vilipend, vituperate.

antonyms adore, compliment, eulogise, glorify.

village *n.* clachan, community, dorp, hamlet, kampong, kraal, pueblo, settlement, township.

villain *n.* anti-hero, baddy, blackguard, bravo, caitiff, criminal, devil, evil-doer, heavy, knave, libertine, malefactor, miscreant, profligate, rapscallion, rascal, reprobate, rogue, scoundrel, wretch.

antonyms angel, goody, hero, heroine.

villainous *adj.* atrocious, bad, base, blackguardly, criminal, cruel, debased, degenerate, depraved, detestable, diabolical, disgraceful,

evil, fiendish, hateful, heinous, ignoble, infamous, inhuman, malevolent, mean, nefarious, opprobrious, outrageous, ruffianly, scoundrelly, sinful, terrible, thievish, vicious, vile, wicked.

antonyms angelic, good, heroic.

villainy *n.* atrocity, badness, baseness, crime, criminality, delinquency, depravity, devilry, iniquity, knavery, rascality, roguery, sin, turpitude, vice, viciousness, wickedness.

vindicate *v.* absolve, acquit, advocate, assert, clear, defend, establish, exculpate, excuse, exonerate, justify, maintain, rehabilitate, support, uphold, verify.

antonyms accuse, convict.

vindication *n.* apology, assertion, defence, exculpation, excuse, exoneration, extenuation, justification, maintenance, plea, rehabilitation, substantiation, support, verification.

antonyms accusation, conviction.

vindictive *adj.* implacable, malevolent, malicious, malignant, merciless, punitive, rancorous, relentless, resentful, retributive, revengeful, spiteful, unforgiving, unrelenting, vengeful, venomous.

antonyms charitable, forgiving, merciful.

vintage *n.* collection, crop, epoch, era, generation, harvest, origin, period, year.

adj. best, choice, classic, fine, mature, old, prime, quintessential, rare, ripe, select, superior, venerable, veteran.

violate *v.* abuse, assault, befoul, break, contravene, debauch, defile, desecrate, dishonour, disobey, disregard, flout, infract, infringe, invade, outrage, pollute, profane, rape, ravish, transgress.

antonyms obey, observe, uphold.

violation *n.* abuse, breach, contravention, defilement, desecration, disruption, encroachment, infraction, infringement, offence, profanation, rapine, sacrilege, spoliation, transgression, trespass.

antonyms obedience, observance.

violence *n.* abandon, acuteness, bestiality, bloodshed, bloodthirstiness, boisterousness, brutality, conflict, cruelty, destructiveness, ferocity, fervour, fierceness, fighting, force, frenzy, fury, harshness, hostilities, intensity, murderousness, passion, power, roughness, savagery, severity, sharpness, storminess, terrorism, thuggery, tumult, turbulence, vehemence, wildness.

antonyms passivity, peacefulness.

violent *adj.* acute, agonising, berserk, biting, bloodthirsty, blustery, boisterous, brutal, cruel, destructive, devastating, excruciating, extreme, fiery, forceful, forcible, furious, harsh, headstrong, homicidal, hot-headed, impetuous, intemperate, intense, maddened, maniacal, murderous, outrageous, painful, passionate, peracute, powerful, raging, riotous, rough, ruinous, savage, severe, sharp, strong, tempestuous, tumultuous, turbulent, uncontrollable, ungovernable, unrestrained, vehement, vicious, wild.

antonyms calm, gentle, moderate, passive, peaceful.

VIP *n.* big cheese, big name, big noise, big shot, bigwig, celebrity, dignitary, headliner, heavyweight, lion, luminary, notable, personage, somebody, star.

antonyms nobody, nonentity.

virago *n.* battle-axe, dragon, fury, gorgon, harridan, hell-cat, randy, scold, shrew, tartar, termagant, vixen, Xanthippe.

virgin *n.* bachelor, celibate, damsel, girl, maid, maiden, spinster, vestal, virgo intacta.

adj. chaste, fresh, immaculate, intact, maidenly, modest, new, pristine, pure, snowy, spotless, stainless, uncorrupted, undefiled, unsullied, untouched, unused, vestal, virginal.

virginal *adj.* celibate, chaste, fresh, immaculate, maidenly, pristine, pure, snowy, spotless, stainless, uncorrupted, undefiled, undisturbed, untouched, vestal, virgin, white.

virginity *n.* chasteness, chastity, maidenhead, maidenhood, purity, virtue.

virile *adj.* forceful, husky, lusty, macho, male, man-like, manly, masculine, potent, red-blooded, robust, rugged, strong, vigorous.

antonyms effeminate, impotent, weak.

virility *n.* huskiness, machismo, manhood, manliness, masculinity, potency, ruggedness, vigour.

antonyms effeminacy, impotence, weakness.

virtual *adj.* effective, essential, implicit, implied, indirect, potential, practical, tacit.

antonym actual.

virtually *adv.* almost, as good as, effectively, effectually, in effect, in essence, nearly, practically, to all intents and purposes.

virtue *n.* advantage, asset, attribute, chastity, credit, excellence, goodness, high-mindedness, honour, incorruptibility, innocence, integrity, justice, merit, morality, plus, probity, purity, quality, rectitude, redeeming feature, righteousness, strength, uprightness, virginity, worth, worthiness.

antonym vice.

virtuosity *n.* bravura, brilliance, éclat, expertise, finesse, finish, flair, mastery, panache, polish, skill, wizardry.

virtuoso *n.* ace, artist, crackerjack, dabster, genius, maestro, magician, master, prodigy, whiz, wizard.

adj. bravura, brilliant, crackerjack, dazzling, expert, masterly, wizard.

virtuous *adj.* blameless, celibate, chaste, clean-living, continent, ethical, excellent, exemplary, good, high-principled, honest, honourable, incorruptible, innocent, irreproachable, moral, praiseworthy, pure, righteous, spotless, unimpeachable, upright, virginal, worthy.

antonyms bad, dishonest, immoral, vicious, wicked.

virulence *n.* acrimony, antagonism, bitterness, deadliness, harmfulness, hatred, hostility, hurtfulness, infectiousness, malevolence,

malice, malignancy, poison, rancour, resentment, spite, spleen, toxicity, venom, viciousness, vindictiveness, virulency, vitriol.

virulent *adj.* acrimonious, baneful, bitter, deadly, envenomed, hostile, infective, injurious, lethal, malevolent, malicious, malignant, noxious, pernicious, poisonous, rancorous, resentful, septic, spiteful, splenetic, toxic, venomous, vicious, vindictive, vitriolic.

viscera *n.* bowels, chitterlings, entrails, gralloch, harigal(d)s, ha(r)slet, innards, insides, intestines, vitals.

viscous *adj.* adhesive, clammy, gelatinous, gluey, glutinous, gooey, gummy, mucilaginous, mucous, sticky, syrupy, tacky, tenacious, thick, treacly, viscid.

antonyms runny, thin, watery.

visible *adj.* apparent, aspectable, clear, conspicuous, detectable, discernible, discoverable, distinguishable, evident, manifest, noticeable, observable, obvious, open, palpable, patent, perceivable, perceptible, plain, unconcealed, undisguised, unmistakable.

antonym invisible.

vision *n.* apparition, chimera, concept, conception, construct, daydream, delusion, discernment, dream, eyes, eyesight, fantasy, far-sightedness, foresight, ghost, hallucination, idea, ideal, illusion, image, imagination, insight, intuition, mirage, penetration, perception, phantasm, phantasma, phantom, picture, prescience, revelation, seeing, sight, spectacle, spectre, view, wraith.

visionary *adj.* chimerical, delusory, dreaming, dreamy, fanciful, fantastic, ideal, idealised, idealistic, illusory, imaginary, impractical, moonshiny, prophetic, quixotic, romantic, speculative, starry-eyed, unreal, unrealistic, unworkable, utopian.

n. daydreamer, Don Quixote, dreamer, enthusiast, fantasist, idealist, mystic, prophet, rainbow-chaser, romantic, seer, theorist, utopian, zealot.

antonym pragmatist.

visit *v.* afflict, assail, attack, befall, call in, call on, drop in on, haunt, inspect, look in, look up, pop in, punish, see, smite, stay at, stay with, stop by, take in, trouble.

n. call, excursion, sojourn, stay, stop.

visitation *n.* appearance, bane, blight, calamity, cataclysm, catastrophe, disaster, examination, infliction, inspection, manifestation, nemesis, ordeal, punishment, retribution, scourge, trial, visit.

visitor *n.* caller, company, emmet, grockle, guest, holidaymaker, tourist, visitant.

vista *n.* enfilade, panorama, perspective, prospect, view.

visual *adj.* discernible, observable, ocular, optic, optical, perceptible, specular, visible.

visualise *v.* conceive, envisage, ideate, imagine, picture.

vital *adj.* alive, animate, animated, animating, basic, cardinal, critical, crucial, decisive, dynamic, energetic, essential, forceful, fund-

amental, generative, imperative, important, indispensable, invigorating, key, life-giving, life-or-death, live, lively, living, necessary, quickening, requisite, significant, spirited, urgent, vibrant, vigorous, vivacious, zestful.
antonyms inessential, peripheral, unimportant.

vitality *n.* animation, energy, exuberance, foison, go, life, liveliness, lustiness, oomph, pep, robustness, sparkle, stamina, strength, vigour, vim, vivaciousness, vivacity.

vitiate *v.* blemish, blight, contaminate, corrupt, debase, defile, deprave, deteriorate, devalue, harm, impair, injure, invalidate, mar, nullify, pervert, pollute, ruin, spoil, sully, taint, undermine.
antonym purify.

vitriolic *adj.* acerbic, acid, bitchy, biting, bitter, caustic, destructive, envenomed, malicious, sardonic, scathing, venomous, vicious, virulent, withering.

vituperate *v.* abuse, berate, blame, castigate, censure, denounce, rate, reproach, revile, slag, slam, slang, slate, upbraid, vilify.
antonyms applaud, eulogise, extol, praise.

vituperation *n.* abuse, blame, castigation, censure, contumely, diatribe, fault-finding, flak, invective, objurgation, obloquy, phillipic, rebuke, reprimand, reproach, revilement, scurrility, stick, vilification.
antonyms acclaim, eulogy, praise.

vituperative *adj.* abusive, belittling, calumniatory, censorious, defamatory, denunciatory, derogatory, fulminatory, harsh, insulting, malign, objurgatory, opprobrious, sardonic, scornful, scurrilous, withering.
antonym laudatory.

vivacious *adj.* animated, bubbling, bubbly, cheerful, chipper, ebullient, effervescent, frisky, frolicsome, gay, high-spirited, jolly, light-hearted, lively, merry, scintillating, sparkling, spirited, sportive, sprightly, vital.
antonym languid.

vivacity *n.* animation, brio, bubbliness, ebullience, effervescence, energy, friskiness, gaiety, high spirits, jollity, life, liveliness, pep, quickness, sparkle, spirit, sprightliness.
antonym languor.

vivid *adj.* active, animated, bright, brilliant, clear, colourful, distinct, dramatic, dynamic, eidetic, energetic, expressive, flamboyant, glowing, graphic, highly-coloured, intense, lifelike, lively, memorable, powerful, quick, realistic, rich, sharp, spirited, stirring, striking, strong, telling, vibrant, vigorous.
antonyms dull, lifeless.

vividness *n.* brightness, brilliancy, clarity, distinctness, glow, immediacy, intensity, life, liveliness, lucidity, radiance, realism, refulgence, resplendence, sharpness, sprightliness, strength.
antonyms dullness, lifelessness.

vixen *n.* beldam, bitch, fury, harpy, harridan, hell-cat, scold, shrew, spitfire, termagant, virago, Xanthippe.

vocabulary *n.* dictionary, glossary, idiom, idioticon, language, lexicon, lexis, nomenclature, thesaurus, word-book, words.

vocal *adj.* articulate, clamorous, eloquent, expressive, forthright, frank, free-spoken, noisy, oral, outspoken, plain-spoken, said, shrill, spoken, strident, uttered, vociferous, voiced.
antonyms inarticulate, quiet.

vocation *n.* bag, business, calling, career, employment, job, métier, mission, niche, office, post, profession, pursuit, role, trade, work.

vociferous *adj.* clamant, clamorous, loud, loud-mouthed, noisy, obstreperous, ranting, shouting, shrill, stentorian, strident, thundering, uproarious, vehement, vocal.
antonyms quiet, silent.

vogue *n.* acceptance, craze, currency, custom, day, dernier cri, fashion, fashionableness, favour, haut ton, last word, mode, popularity, prevalence, style, the latest, the rage, the thing, trend, usage, use.
adj. current, fashionable, in, modish, now, popular, prevalent, stylish, trendy, up-to-the-minute, voguish, with it.

voice *n.* agency, articulation, decision, expression, inflection, instrument, intonation, language, medium, mouthpiece, organ, part, say, sound, speech, spokesman, spokesperson, spokeswoman, tone, utterance, vehicle, view, vote, will, wish, words.
v. air, articulate, assert, bruit, convey, declare, disclose, divulge, enunciate, express, say, speak of, utter, ventilate.

void *adj.* bare, blank, cancelled, clear, dead, drained, emptied, empty, free, inane, ineffective, ineffectual, inoperative, invalid, nugatory, null, tenantless, unenforceable, unfilled, unoccupied, useless, vacant, vain, worthless.
antonyms full, valid.
n. blank, blankness, cavity, chasm, emptiness, gap, hiatus, hollow, lack, opening, space, vacuity, vacuum, want.
v. abnegate, annul, cancel, defecate, discharge, drain, eject, elimate, emit, empty, evacuate, invalidate, nullify, rescind.
antonyms fill, validate.

volatile *adj.* airy, changeable, erratic, explosive, fickle, flighty, gay, giddy, hot-headed, hot-tempered, inconstant, lively, mercurial, sprightly, temperamental, unsettled, unstable, unsteady, variable, volcanic.
antonyms constant, steady.

volition *n.* choice, choosing, determination, discretion, election, option, preference, purpose, resolution, taste, velleity, will.

volley *n.* barrage, blast, bombardment, burst, cannonade, discharge, enfilade, explosion, fusillade, hail, salvo, shower.

voluble *adj.* articulate, fluent, forthcoming, garrulous, glib, loquacious, talkative.

volume *n.* aggregate, amount, amplitude, bigness, body, book, bulk, capacity, compass, dimensions, fascic(u)le, heft, mass, part, publication, quantity, tome, total, treatise.

voluminous *adj.* abounding, ample, big, billowing, bulky, capacious, cavernous, commodious, copious, full, large, massive, prolific, roomy, vast.

antonyms scanty, slight.

voluntarily *adv.* by choice, consciously, deliberately, freely, intentionally, of one's own accord, of one's own free will, on one's own initiative, purposely, spontaneously, willingly.

antonyms involuntarily, unwillingly.

voluntary *adj.* conscious, deliberate, discretional, free, gratuitous, honorary, intended, intentional, optional, purposeful, purposive, spontaneous, unconstrained, unforced, unpaid, volunteer, wilful, willing.

antonyms compulsory, forced, involuntary, unwilling.

volunteer *v.* advance, communicate, extend, offer, present, proffer, propose, put forward, step forward, suggest, tender.

voluptuary *n.* bon vivant, debauchee, epicurean, hedonist, libertine, playboy, pleasure-seeker, profligate, sensualist, sybarite.

antonym ascetic.

voluptuous *adj.* ample, buxom, curvaceous, effeminate, enticing, epicurean, erotic, goluptious, hedonistic, licentious, luscious, luxurious, pleasure-loving, provocative, seductive, self-indulgent, sensual, shapely, sybaritic.

antonym ascetic.

voluptuousness *n.* buxomness, carnality, curvaceousness, licentiousness, lusciousness, opulence, seductiveness, sensuality, shapeliness.

antonym asceticism.

vomit *v.* bring up, cat, chunder, disgorge, egurgitate, eject, emit, heave, posset, puke, regurgitate, retch, sick up, spew out, spew up, throw up.

vomiting *n.* chundering, egurgitation, ejection, emesis, emission, puking, regurgitation, retching, sickness, spewing.

voracious *adj.* acquisitive, avid, devouring, edacious, gluttonous, greedy, hungry, insatiable, omnivorous, pantophagous, prodigious,

rapacious, ravening, ravenous, uncontrolled, unquenchable.

voracity *n.* acquisitiveness, avidity, eagerness, edacity, greed, hunger, pantophagy, rapacity, ravenousness.

vortex *n.* eddy, maelstrom, whirl, whirlpool, whirlwind.

votary *n.* addict, adherent, aficionado, believer, devotee, disciple, follower, monk.

vote *n.* ballot, election, franchise, plebiscite, poll, referendum, show of hands, suffrage.

v. ballot, choose, declare, elect, judge, opt, plump for, pronounce, propose, recommend, return, suggest.

vouch for affirm, assert, asseverate, attest to, avouch, back, certify, confirm, endorse, guarantee, support, swear to, uphold.

vouchsafe *v.* accord, bestow, cede, confer, deign, grant, impart, yield.

vow *v.* affirm, avouch, bename, consecrate, dedicate, devote, maintain, pledge, profess, promise, swear.

n. avouchment, oath, pledge, promise, troth.

voyage *n.* crossing, cruise, expedition, journey, passage, peregrination, travels, trip.

vulgar *adj.* banausic, blue, boorish, cheap and nasty, coarse, common, crude, dirty, flashy, gaudy, general, gross, ill-bred, impolite, improper, indecent, indecorous, indelicate, low, low-life, low-lived, low-minded, low-thoughted, nasty, native, naughty, ordinary, pandemian, plebby, plebeian, ribald, risque, rude, suggestive, tacky, tasteless, tawdry, uncouth, unmannerly, unrefined, vernacular.

antonyms correct, decent, elegant, noble, polite, refined.

vulgarian *n.* arriviste, barbarian, boor, nouveau riche, parvenu, philistine, upstart.

vulgarity *n.* coarseness, crudeness, crudity, dirtiness, gaudiness, grossness, indecency, indecorum, indelicacy, ribaldry, rudeness, suggestiveness, tastelessness, tawdriness.

antonyms decency, politeness.

vulnerable *adj.* accessible, assailable, defenceless, exposed, expugnable, pregnable, sensitive, susceptible, tender, thin-skinned, unprotected, weak, wide open.

antonyms protected, strong.

W

wacky *adj.* crazy, daft, eccentric, erratic, goofy, irrational, loony, loopy, nutty, odd, screwy, silly, unpredictable, wild, zany.
antonym sensible.

wad *n.* ball, block, bundle, chunk, hump, hunk, mass, pledget, plug, roll.

wadding *n.* cotton-wool, filler, lining, packing, padding, stuffing.

waddle *v.* rock, shuffle, sway, toddle, totter, wiggle, wobble.

waffle *v.* blather, fudge, jabber, prate, prattle, prevaricate, rabbit on, spout, witter on.
n. blather, gobbledegook, guff, jabber, nonsense, padding, prating, prattle, prolixity, verbiage, verbosity, wordiness.

waft *v.* bear, carry, convey, drift, float, ride, transmit, transport, whiffle, winnow.
n. breath, breeze, current, draught, puff, scent, whiff.

wag¹ *v.* bob, bobble, flutter, jiggle, nod, oscillate, pendulate, quiver, rock, shake, stir, vibrate, waggle, wave, wiggle.
n. bob, bobble, flutter, jiggle, nod, oscillation, quiver, shake, toss, vibration, waggle, wave, wiggle.

wag² *n.* banterer, card, clown, comedian, comic, droll, fool, humorist, jester, joker, wit.

wage *n.* allowance, compensation, earnings, emolument, fee, guerdon, hire, pay, payment, penny-fee, recompense, remuneration, reward, salary, screw, stipend, wage-packet, wages.
v. carry on, conduct, engage in, practise, prosecute, pursue, undertake.

wager *n.* bet, flutter, gage, gamble, hazard, pledge, punt, speculation, stake, venture.
v. bet, chance, gamble, hazard, lay, lay odds, pledge, punt, risk, speculate, stake, venture.

waggish *adj.* amusing, arch, bantering, comical, droll, espiègle, facetious, frolicsome, funny, humorous, impish, jesting, jocose, jocular, merry, mischievous, playful, puckish, risible, roguish, sportive, witty.
antonyms grave, serious, staid.

waggle *v.* bobble, flutter, jiggle, oscillate, shake, wag, wave, wiggle, wobble.
n. bobble, flutter, jiggle, oscillation, shake, wag, wave, wiggle, wobble.

wagon *n.* buggy, carriage, cart, dray, float, train, truck, tumbrel, van.

waif *n.* foundling, orphan, stray, wastrel.

wail *v.* bemoan, bewail, complain, cry, deplore, grieve, howl, keen, lament, mewl, moan, ululate, weep, yammer, yowl.
n. caterwaul, complaint, cry, grief, howl, keen, lament, lamentation, moan, ululation, weeping, yowl.

wait *v.* abide, dally, delay, hang fire, hesitate, hold back, hover, linger, loiter, mark time, pause, remain, rest, stay, tarry.
antonyms depart, go, leave.
n. delay, halt, hesitation, hiatus, hold-up, interval, pause, rest, stay.

waive *v.* abandon, defer, disclaim, forgo, postpone, relinquish, remit, renounce, resign, surrender.
antonyms claim, maintain.

waiver *n.* abandonment, abdication, deferral, disclaimer, postponement, relinquishment, remission, renunciation, resignation, surrender.

wake¹ *v.* activate, animate, arise, arouse, awake, awaken, bestir, enliven, excite, fire, galvanise, get up, kindle, provoke, quicken, rise, rouse, stimulate, stir, unbed.
antonyms relax, sleep.
n. death-watch, funeral, pernoctation, vigil, watch.

wake² *n.* aftermath, backwash, path, rear, track, trail, train, wash, waves.

wakeful *adj.* alert, alive, attentive, heedful, insomniac, observant, restless, sleepless, unblinking, unsleeping, vigilant, wary, watchful.
antonyms inattentive, sleepy, unwary.

waken *v.* activate, animate, arouse, awake, awaken, enliven, fire, galvanise, get up, ignite, kindle, quicken, rouse, stimulate, stir, whet.

walk *v.* accompany, advance, amble, convoy, escort, go by Shanks's pony, hike, hoof it, march, move, pace, pedestrianise, perambulate, plod, promenade, saunter, step, stride, stroll, take, traipse, tramp, tread, trek, trog, trudge.
n. aisle, alley, ambulatory, avenue, carriage, constitutional, esplanade, footpath, frescade, gait, hike, lane, mall, march, pace, path, pathway, pavement, pawn, perambulation, promenade, ramble, saunter, sidewalk, step, stride, stroll, trail, traipse, tramp, trek, trudge, turn.

walk of life activity, area, arena, calling, career, course, field, line, métier, profession, pursuit, sphere, trade, vocation.

walker *n.* ambulator, backpacker, footslogger, hiker, pedestrian, rambler, wayfarer.

walk-out *n.* industrial action, protest, rebellion, revolt, stoppage, strike.

walk-over *n.* child's play, cinch, doddle, picnic, piece of cake, pushover, snap, walk-away.

walkway *n.* ambulatory, esplanade, footpath,

lane, path, pathway, pavement, promenade, sidewalk.

wall *n.* bailey, barricade, barrier, block, breastwork, bulk-head, bulwark, dike, divider, dyke, embankment, enclosure, fence, fortification, hedge, impediment, membrane, obstacle, obstruction, palisade, panel, parapet, partition, rampart, screen, septum, stockade.

wallet *n.* bill-fold, case, holder, note-case, pochette, pocket-book, pouch, purse.

wallop *v.* batter, beat, belt, best, buffet, clobber, crush, defeat, drub, hammer, hit, lambaste, lick, paste, pound, pummel, punch, rout, slug, smack, strike, swat, swipe, thrash, thump, thwack, trounce, vanquish, whack, worst.
n. bash, belt, blow, haymaker, hit, kick, punch, slug, smack, swat, swipe, thump, thwack, whack.

wallow *v.* bask, delight, enjoy, flounder, glory, indulge, lie, lurch, luxuriate, relish, revel, roll, splash, stagger, stumble, tumble, wade, welter.

wan *adj.* anaemic, ashen, bleak, bloodless, cadaverous, colourless, dim, discoloured, faint, feeble, ghastly, livid, lurid, mournful, pale, pallid, pasty, sickly, waxen, weak, weary, whey-faced, white.

wand *n.* baton, mace, rod, sceptre, sprig, staff, stick, twig, verge, withe, withy.

wander *v.* aberrate, babble, cruise, depart, deviate, digress, divagate, diverge, drift, err, hump the bluey, lapse, meander, mill around, peregrinate, ramble, range, rave, roam, rove, saunter, squander, straggle, stravaig, stray, stroll, swerve, traipse, veer, wilder.
n. cruise, excursion, meander, peregrination, ramble, saunter, stroll, traipse.

wanderer *n.* drifter, gypsy, itinerant, nomad, rambler, ranger, rolling stone, rover, strag, straggler, stray, stroller, traveller, vagabond, vagrant, voyager.

wandering *n.* aberration, deviation, digression, divagation, divergence, drift(ing), evagation, journey(ing), meander(ing), odyssey, peregrination, travels, walkabout.
adj. aberrant, circumforaneous, drifting, homeless, itinerant, migratory, nomadic, peripatetic, rambling, rootless, roving, strolling, travelling, vagabond, vagrant, voyaging, wayfaring.

wane *v.* abate, atrophy, contract, decline, decrease, dim, diminish, droop, drop, dwindle, ebb, fade, fail, lessen, shrink, sink, subside, taper off, weaken, wither.
antonyms increase, wax.
n. abatement, atrophy, contraction, decay, decline, decrease, diminution, drop, dwindling, ebb, fading, failure, fall, lessening, sinking, subsidence, tapering off, weakening.
antonym increase.

wangle *v.* arrange, contrive, engineer, fiddle, finagle, fix, flam, manage, manipulate, manoeuvre, pull off, scheme, work, work the oracle.

want *v.* call for, covet, crave, demand, desiderate, desire, fancy, hanker after, hunger for, lack, long for, miss, need, pine for, require, thirst for, wish, yearn for, yen.
n. absence, appetite, besoin, craving, dearth, default, deficiency, demand, desideratum, desire, destitution, famine, fancy, hankering, hunger, indigence, insufficiency, lack, longing, necessity, need, neediness, paucity, pauperism, penury, poverty, privation, requirement, scantiness, scarcity, shortage, thirst, wish, yearning, yen.
antonyms abundance, plenty, riches.

wanting *adj.* absent, defective, deficient, disappointing, faulty, imperfect, inadequate, incomplete, inferior, insufficient, lacking, less, missing, patchy, poor, short, shy, sketchy, substandard, unsatisfactory, unsound.
antonyms adequate, sufficient.

wanton *adj.* abandoned, arbitrary, careless, coltish, cruel, dissipated, dissolute, evil, extravagant, fast, gratuitous, groundless, heedless, immoderate, immoral, intemperate, lavish, lecherous, lewd, libertine, libidinous, licentious, loose, lubricious, lustful, malevolent, malicious, motiveless, needless, outrageous, promiscuous, rakish, rash, reckless, senseless, shameless, spiteful, uncalled-for, unchaste, unjustifiable, unjustified, unprovoked, unrestrained, vicious, wicked, wild, wilful.
n. Casanova, debauchee, Don Juan, gammerstang, giglet, giglot, gillet, gillflirt, harlot, jillet, jillflirt, lecher, libertine, mort, profligate, prostitute, rake, roué, slut, strumpet, tart, trollop, voluptuary, whore.

war *n.* battle, bloodshed, combat, conflict, contention, contest, enmity, fighting, hostilities, hostility, jihad, strife, struggle, ultima ratio regum, warfare.
antonym peace.
v. battle, clash, combat, contend, contest, fight, skirmish, strive, struggle, take up arms, wage war.

war cry battle cry, rallying-cry, slogan, war-song, war-whoop, watchword.

warble *v.* chirp, chirrup, quaver, sing, trill, twitter, yodel.
n. call, chirp, chirrup, cry, quaver, song, trill, twitter.

ward *n.* apartment, area, care, charge, cubicle, custody, dependant, district, division, guardianship, keeping, minor, precinct, protection, protégé, pupil, quarter, room, safekeeping, vigil, watch, zone.

ward off avert, avoid, beat off, block, deflect, disperse, evade, fend off, forestall, parry, repel, repulse, stave off, thwart, turn aside, turn away.

warden *n.* administrator, captain, caretaker, castellan, châtelaine, concierge, curator, custodian, guardian, janitor, keeper, ranger, steward, superintendent, warder, watchman.

warder *n.* custodian, gaoler, guard, jailer,

keeper, prison officer, screw, turnkey, wardress.

wardrobe *n.* apparel, attire, closet, clothes, cupboard, garderobe, outfit.

warehouse *n.* depository, depot, entrepot, freightshed, godown, hong, repository, stockroom, store, storehouse.

wares *n.* commodities, goods, lines, manufactures, merchandise, produce, products, stock, stuff, vendibles.

warfare *n.* arms, battle, blows, combat, conflict, contention, contest, discord, fighting, hostilities, passage of arms, strife, struggle, war.
antonyms harmony, peace.

warily *adv.* apprehensively, cagily, carefully, cautiously, charily, circumspectly, distrustfully, gingerly, guardedly, hesitantly, leerily, suspiciously, uneasily, vigilantly, watchfully.
antonyms heedlessly, recklessly, thoughtlessly, unwarily.

wariness *n.* alertness, apprehension, attention, caginess, care, carefulness, caution, circumspection, discretion, distrust, foresight, heedfulness, hesitancy, mindfulness, prudence, suspicion, unease, vigilance, watchfulness.
antonyms heedlessness, recklessness, thoughtlessness.

warlike *adj.* aggressive, antagonistic, bellicose, belligerent, bloodthirsty, combative, hawkish, hostile, inimical, jingoistic, martial, militaristic, military, pugnacious, sabre-rattling, truculent, unfriendly.
antonym peaceable.

warlock *n.* conjurer, demon, enchanter, magician, magus, necromancer, sorcerer, witch, wizard.

warm *adj.* affable, affectionate, amiable, amorous, animated, ardent, balmy, calid, cheerful, cordial, dangerous, disagreeable, earnest, effusive, emotional, enthusiastic, excited, fervent, friendly, genial, glowing, happy, hazardous, hearty, heated, hospitable, impassioned, incalescent, intense, irascible, irritable, keen, kindly, lively, loving, lukewarm, passionate, perilous, pleasant, quick, sensitive, short, spirited, stormy, sunny, tender, tepid, thermal, touchy, tricky, uncomfortable, unpleasant, vehement, vigorous, violent, zealous.
antonyms cool, indifferent, unfriendly.
v. animate, awaken, excite, heat, heat up, interest, melt, mull, put some life into, reheat, rouse, stimulate, stir, thaw, turn on.
antonym cool.

warm-blooded *adj.* ardent, earnest, emotional, enthusiastic, excitable, fervent, homothermic, homothermous, hot-blooded, idiothermous, impetuous, lively, passionate, rash, red-blooded, spirited, vivacious.

warm-hearted *adj.* affectionate, ardent, compassionate, cordial, generous, genial, kindhearted, kindly, loving, sympathetic, tender, tender-hearted.
antonyms cold, unsympathetic.

warmth *n.* affability, affection, amorousness,

animation, ardour, calidity, cheerfulness, cordiality, eagerness, earnestness, effusiveness, empressement, enthusiasm, excitement, fervency, fervour, fire, happiness, heartiness, heat, hospitableness, hotness, intensity, kindliness, love, passion, spirit, tenderness, transport, vehemence, vigour, violence, warmness, zeal, zest.
antonyms coldness, coolness, unfriendliness.

warn *v.* admonish, advise, alert, apprise, caution, counsel, forewarn, inform, notify, put on one's guard, tip off.

warning *n.* admonishment, admonition, advance notice, advice, alarm, alert, augury, caution, caveat, forenotice, foretoken, forewarning, griffin, hint, larum, larum-bell, lesson, monition, notice, notification, omen, premonition, presage, prodrome, sign, signal, siren, threat, tip, tip-off, token, vigia, word, word to the wise.
adj. admonitory, aposematic, cautionary, in terrorem, monitive, monitory, ominous, premonitory, prodromal, prodromic, threatening.

warp *v.* bend, contort, deform, deviate, distort, kink, misshape, pervert, twist.
antonym straighten.
n. bend, bent, bias, contortion, deformation, deviation, distortion, irregularity, kink, perversion, quirk, turn, twist.

warrant *n.* authorisation, authority, commission, guarantee, licence, permission, permit, pledge, sanction, security, voucher, warranty.
v. affirm, answer for, approve, assure, attest, authorise, avouch, be bound, call for, certify, commission, declare, demand, empower, entitle, excuse, guarantee, justify, license, necessitate, permit, pledge, require, sanction, secure, underwrite, uphold, vouch for.

warrantable *adj.* accountable, allowable, defensible, excusable, justifiable, lawful, legal, necessary, permissible, proper, reasonable, right.
antonyms indefensible, unjustifiable, unwarrantable.

warranty *n.* assurance, authorisation, bond, certificate, contract, covenant, guarantee, justification, pledge.

warring *adj.* at daggers drawn, at war, belligerent, combatant, conflicting, contending, embattled, fighting, hostile, opposed, opposing.

warrior *n.* champion, combatant, fighter, fighting man, gallo(w)glass, ghazi, man-at-arms, soldier, wardog, war-horse.

wart *n.* excrescence, growth, lump, protuberance, verruca.

wary *adj.* alert, apprehensive, attentive, cagey, careful, cautious, chary, circumspect, distrustful, guarded, hawk-eyed, heedful, leery, on one's guard, on the lookout, on the qui vive, prudent, suspicious, vigilant, watchful, wide-awake.
antonyms careless, foolhardy, heedless, reckless, unwary.

wash[1] *v.* bath, bathe, clean, cleanse, launder, moisten, rinse, scrub, shampoo, shower, sluice, swill, wet.

n. a lick and a promise, ablution, bath, bathe, cleaning, cleansing, coat, coating, ebb and flow, film, flow, laundering, layer, overlay, rinse, roll, screen, scrub, shampoo, shower, souse, stain, suffusion, surge, sweep, swell, washing, wave.

wash one's hands abandon, abdicate responsibility, give up on, have nothing to do with, leave to one's own devices.

wash[2] *v.* bear examination, bear scrutiny, carry weight, hold up, hold water, pass muster, stand up, stick.

washed-out *adj.* all in, blanched, bleached, colourless, dead on one's feet, dog-tired, drained, drawn, etiolated, exhausted, faded, fatigued, flat, haggard, knackered, lacklustre, mat, pale, pallid, peelie-wally, spent, tired-out, wan, weary, worn-out.

wash-out *n.* disappointment, disaster, dud, failure, fiasco, flop, incompetent, lead balloon, lemon, loser, mess.

antonyms success, triumph, winner.

waspish *adj.* bad-tempered, bitchy, cantankerous, captious, crabbed, crabby, cross, crotchety, fretful, grouchy, grumpy, ill-tempered, irascible, irritable, peevish, peppery, pettish, petulant, prickly, snappish, splenetic, testy, touchy, waxy.

waste *v.* atrophy, blow, consume, corrode, crumble, debilitate, decay, decline, deplete, despoil, destroy, devastate, disable, dissipate, drain, dwindle, eat away, ebb, emaciate, enfeeble, exhaust, fade, fritter away, gnaw, lavish, lay waste, misspend, misuse, perish, pillage, prodigalise, rape, ravage, raze, rig, ruin, sack, sink, spend, spoil, squander, tabefy, throw away, undermine, wane, wanton, wear out, wither.

n. debris, desert, desolation, destruction, devastation, dissipation, dregs, dross, effluent, expenditure, extravagance, garbage, havoc, leavings, leftovers, litter, loss, misapplication, misuse, mullock, offal, offscouring(s), prodigality, ravage, recrement, refuse, rubbish, ruin, scrap, slops, solitude, spoilage, squandering, sweepings, trash, void, wastefulness, wasteland, wild, wilderness.

adj. bare, barren, desolate, devastated, dismal, dreary, empty, extra, left-over, superfluous, supernumerary, uncultivated, uninhabited, unproductive, unprofitable, unused, unwanted, useless, wild, worthless.

wasted *adj.* abandoned, atrophied, cadaverous, debauched, depleted, dissipated, dissolute, emaciated, exhausted, finished, gaunt, profligate, shrivelled, shrunken, spent, tabescent, tabid, wanton, war-worn, washed-out, withered.

antonyms healthy, robust.

wasteful *adj.* dissipative, extravagant, improvident, lavish, prodigal, profligate, ruinous, spendthrift, thriftless, uneconomical, un-

thrifty.

antonyms economical, frugal, thrifty.

wasteland *n.* barrenness, desert, solitude, void, waste, wilderness, wild(s).

waster *n.* drone, good-for-nothing, idler, layabout, loafer, lounger, malingerer, ne'er-do-well, profligate, shirker, skiver, spendthrift, wastrel.

antonym worker.

wasting *n.* atrophy, degeneration, dystrophy, emaciation, marasmus, tubefaction, tubes, tubescence.

adj. destroying, devastating, dystrophic, emaciating, enfeebling, marasmic, tubescent, tubetic, tubid.

antonym strengthening.

watch[1] *v.* attend, contemplate, eye, gaze at, guard, keep, keep an eye open, look, look after, look at, look on, look out, mark, mind, note, observe, ogle, pay attention, peer at, protect, regard, see, spectate, stare at, superintend, take care of, take heed, tend, view, wait.

n. alertness, attention, eye, heed, inspection, lookout, notice, observation, pernoctation, supervision, surveillance, vigil, vigilance, wake, watchfulness.

watch out have a care, keep a weather eye open, keep one's eyes open, keep one's eyes peeled, keep one's eyes skinned, mind oneself.

watch over defend, guard, keep an eye on, look after, mind, preserve, protect, shelter, shield, stand guard over, tend.

watch[2] *n.* chronometer, clock, ticker, tick-tick, tick-tock, timepiece, wristwatch.

watch-dog *n.* custodian, guard dog, guardian, house-dog, inspector, monitor, ombudsman, protector, scrutineer, vigilante.

watcher *n.* Argus, looker-on, lookout, member of the audience, observer, onlooker, peeping Tom, spectator, spy, viewer, voyeur, witness.

watchful *adj.* alert, attentive, cautious, circumspect, guarded, heedful, observant, on one's guard, on the lookout, on the qui vive, on the watch, suspicious, unmistaking, vigilant, wary, wide awake.

antonym inattentive.

watchfulness *n.* alertness, attention, attentiveness, caution, cautiousness, circumspection, heedfulness, suspicion, suspiciousness, vigilance, wariness.

antonym inattention.

watchman *n.* caretaker, custodian, guard, security guard, security man, wakeman.

watchword *n.* battle-cry, buzz-word, byword, catch phrase, catchword, countersign, magic word, maxim, motto, password, rallying-cry, shibboleth, signal, slogan.

water *n.* Adam's ale, Adam's wine, aqua, lake, ocean, rain, river, saliva, sea, stream, sweat, tears, urine.

v. adulterate, damp, dampen, dilute, douse, drench, drink, flood, hose, irrigate, moisten, soak, souse, spray, sprinkle, thin, water down, weaken.

antonyms dry out, purify, strengthen.

water down adulterate, dilute, mitigate, mix, qualify, soften, thin, tone down, water, weaken.

antonyms purify, strengthen.

water-closet *n.* bog, cludge, convenience, gents', head, john, ladies', lav, lavatory, loo, powder-room, privy, public convenience, toilet, urinal, wash-room, WC.

watercourse *n.* arroyo, channel, ditch, khor, river, stream, wadi, water-channel.

water-diviner *n.* dowser, water-finder.

waterfall *n.* cascade, cataract, chute, fall, force, lash, lin(n), torrent.

water-power *n.* white coal.

waterproof *adj.* coated, damp-proof, impermeable, impervious, proofed, rubberised, water-repellent, water-resistant.

antonym leaky.

watertight *adj.* airtight, firm, flawless, foolproof, hermetic, impregnable, incontrovertible, sound, unassailable, waterproof.

antonyms leaky, unsound.

watery *adj.* adulterated, aqueous, damp, dilute, diluted, flavourless, fluid, humid, hydatoid, insipid, liquid, marshy, moist, poor, rheumy, runny, soggy, squelchy, tasteless, tear-filled, tearful, thin, washy, watered-down, waterish, weak, weepy, wet, wishy-washy.

antonyms solid, strong.

wave[1] *v.* beckon, brandish, direct, flap, flourish, flutter, gesticulate, gesture, indicate, oscillate, quiver, ripple, shake, sign, signal, stir, sway, swing, undulate, waft, wag, waver, weave, wield.

wave[2] *n.* billow, breaker, comber, current, drift, flood, ground swell, movement, outbreak, rash, ripple, roller, rush, stream, surge, sweep, swell, tendency, tidal wave, trend, tsunami, undulation, unevenness, upsurge, water-wave, wavelet, white horse.

waver *v.* blow hot and cold, dither, falter, flicker, fluctuate, haver, hesitate, hum and haw, quiver, reel, rock, seesaw, shake, shilly-shally, sway, swither, totter, tremble, undulate, vacillate, vary, waffle, wave, weave, wobble.

antonyms decide, stand.

waverer *n.* ditherer, doubter, haverer, invertebrate, shilly-shallier, wobbler.

wavering *adj.* dithering, dithery, doubtful, doubting, havering, hesitant, in two minds, shilly-shallying.

antonym determined.

wavy *adj.* curly, curvy, flamboynat, ridged, ridgy, rippled, ripply, sinuate(d), sinuous, undate, undulate, undulated, winding, wrinkled, zigzag.

antonyms flat, smooth.

wax *v.* become, develop, dilate, enlarge, expand, fill out, grow, increase, magnify, mount, rise, swell.

antonym wane.

waxen *adj.* anaemic, ashen, bloodless, colour-

less, ghastly, livid, pale, pallid, wan, white, whitish.

antonym ruddy.

waxy *adj.* ceraceous, cereous, impressible, impressionable, pallid, pasty, soft, waxen.

way *n.* access, advance, aim, ambition, approach, aspect, avenue, channel, characteristic, choice, circumstance, condition, conduct, course, custom, demand, desire, detail, direction, distance, elbow-room, fashion, feature, fettle, gate, goal, habit, headway, highway, idiosyncrasy, journey, lane, length, manner, march, means, method, mode, movement, nature, opening, particular, passage, path, pathway, personality, plan, pleasure, point, practice, procedure, process, progress, respect, road, room, route, scheme, sense, shape, situation, space, state, status, street, stretch, style, system, technique, thoroughfare, track, trail, trait, usage, will, wish, wont.

way of life life-style, modus vivendi.

wayfarer *n.* bird of passage, dusty-foot, globetrotter, gypsy, itinerant, journeyer, nomad, piepowder, rover, traveller, trekker, viator, voyager, walker, wanderer.

antonyms resident, stay-at-home.

wayfaring *adj.* drifting, itinerant, journeying, multivagant, nomadic, peripatetic, rambling, roving, travelling, viatorial, voyaging, walking, wandering.

antonyms resident, stay-at-home.

waylay *v.* accost, ambush, attack, buttonhole, catch, hold up, intercept, lie in wait for, seize, set upon, surprise.

way-out *adj.* advanced, amazing, avant-garde, bizarre, crazy, eccentric, excellent, experimental, fantastic, far-out, freaky, great, marvellous, off-beat, outlandish, progressive, satisfying, tremendous, unconventional, unorthodox, unusual, weird, wild, wonderful.

antonym ordinary.

ways and means capability, capacity, capital, cash, funds, methods, procedure, reserves, resources, tools, way, wherewithal.

wayward *adj.* capricious, changeable, contrary, contumacious, cross-grained, disobedient, erratic, fickle, flighty, froward, headstrong, inconstant, incorrigible, insubordinate, intractable, mulish, obdurate, obstinate, perverse, rebellious, refractory, self-willed, stubborn, undependable, ungovernable, unmanageable, unpredictable, unruly, uppity, wilful.

antonyms complaisant, good-natured.

weak *adj.* anaemic, asthenic, atonic, cowardly, debile, debilitated, decrepit, defenceless, deficient, delicate, diluted, disturbant, dull, effete, enervated, exhausted, exposed, faint, faulty, feeble, fibreless, flimsy, fragile, frail, helpless, hollow, imperceptible, impotent, inadequate, inconclusive, indecisive, ineffective, ineffectual, infirm, insipid, invalid, irresolute, lacking, lame, languid, low, milk-and-water, muffled, namby-pamby,

pathetic, poor, powerless, puny, quiet, runny, shaky, shallow, sickly, slight, small, soft, spent, spineless, substandard, tasteless, tender, thin, timorous, toothless, unconvincing, under-strength, unguarded, unprotected, unresisting, unsafe, unsatisfactory, unsound, unsteady, unstressed, untenable, vulnerable, wanting, wasted, watery, weak-hearted, weak-kneed, weakly, weak-minded, weak-spirited, wishy-washy.
antonym strong.

weaken *v.* abate, adulterate, craze, cut, debase, debilitate, depress, dilute, diminish, disinvigorate, droop, dwindle, ease up, effeminate, effeminise, emasculate, enervate, enfeeble, fade, fail, flag, give way, impair, invalidate, lessen, lower, mitigate, moderate, reduce, sap, soften up, temper, thin, tire, undermine, wane, water down.
antonym strengthen.

weakening *n.* abatement, dilution, diminishment, dwindling, easing, fading, failing, flagging, labefactation, labefaction, lessening, lowering, moderation, reduction, waning.
antonym strengthening.

weakling *n.* coward, doormat, drip, milksop, milquetoast, mouse, sissy, softling, underdog, underling, wally, weed, wet, wimp, windlestraw, wraith.
antonyms hero, stalwart.

weakness *n.* Achilles' heel, asthenia, atonicity, atony, blemish, debility, decrepitude, defect, deficiency, enervation, enfeeblement, faible, failing, faintness, fault, feebleness, flaw, fondness, fragility, frailty, imperfection, impotence, inclination, infirmity, irresolution, lack, liking, passion, penchant, powerlessness, predilection, proclivity, proneness, shortcoming, soft spot, soft underbelly, underbelly, vulnerability, weakpoint, weediness.
antonyms dislike, strength.

weak-willed *adj.* complaisant, compliant, fainthearted, irresolute, persuadable, persuasible, pliable, pusillanimous, spineless, submissive, weak-hearted, weak-kneed, weak-minded.
antonym strong-willed.

weal *n.* cicatrice, cicatrix, contusion, mark, ridge, scar, streak, stripe, wale, welt, wheal, wound.

wealth *n.* abundance, affluence, assets, bounty, capital, cash, copiousness, cornucopia, estate, fortune, fullness, funds, golden calf, goods, klondike, lucre, mammon, means, money, opulence, pelf, plenitude, plenty, possessions, profusion, property, prosperity, resources, riches, richness, store, substance.
antonym poverty.

wealthy *adj.* affluent, comfortable, easy, filthy rich, flush, living in clover, loaded, moneyed, opulent, prosperous, rich, rolling in it, well-heeled, well-off, well-to-do.
antonym poor.

wear *v.* abrade, accept, allow, annoy, bear, bear up, believe, brook, carry, consume, corrode, countenance, deteriorate, display, don, drain, dress in, endure, enervate, erode, exasperate, exhibit, fall for, fatigue, fly, fray, grind, harass, have on, hold up, irk, last, permit, pester, put on, put up with, rub, show, sport, stand for, stand up, stomach, swallow, take, tax, tolerate, undermine, use, vex, waste, weaken, weary.
n. abrasion, apparel, attire, attrition, clothes, corrosion, costume, damage, depreciation, deterioration, dress, durability, employment, erosion, friction, garb, garments, gear, habit, mileage, outfit, service, things, use, usefulness, utility, wear and tear.

wear down abrade, chip away at, consume, corrode, diminish, erode, grind down, lessen, macerate, overcome, reduce, rub away, undermine.

wear off abate, abrade, decrease, diminish, disappear, dwindle, ebb, efface, fade, lessen, peter out, rub away, subside, wane, weaken.
antonym increase.

wear out consume, deteriorate, enervate, erode, exhaust, fag out, fatigue, fray, impair, knacker, prostrate, rub through, sap, tire (out), tucker (out), use up, wear through, weary.
antonyms refresh, replenish.

weariness *n.* drowsiness, enervation, ennui, exhaustion, fatigue, languor, lassitude, lethargy, listlessness, prostration, sleepiness, tiredness.
antonym freshness.

wearing *adj.* abradant, abrasive, exasperating, exhausting, fatiguing, irksome, oppressive, taxing, tiresome, tiring, trying, wearisome.
antonym refreshing.

wearisome *adj.* annoying, boring, bothersome, burdensome, dreary, dull, ennuying, exasperating, exhausting, fatiguing, humdrum, irksome, monotonous, oppressive, pestilential, prolix, prosaic, protracted, tedious, troublesome, trying, vexatious, weariful, wearing.
antonym refreshing.

weary *adj.* all in, arduous, awearied, aweary, beat, bored, browned-off, dead beat, dead on one's feet, discontented, dog-tired, drained, drooping, drowsy, enervated, enervative, ennuied, ennuyé, exhausted, fagged, fatigued, fed up, flagging, impatient, indifferent, irksome, jaded, knackered, laborious, sick, sick and tired, sleepy, spent, taxing, tired, tiresome, tiring, wayworn, wearied, wearing, wearisome, whacked, worn out.
antonyms excited, fresh, lively.
v. annoy, betoil, bore, bug, burden, debilitate, drain, droop, enervate, ennui, exasperate, fade, fag, fail, fatigue, irk, irritate, jade, plague, sap, sicken, tax, tire, tire out, wear out.

wearying *adj.* ennuying, exhausting, fatiguing, taxing, tiring, trying, wearing, wearisome.
antonym refreshing.

weather *n.* climate, conditions, rainfall, temperature.

v. brave, come through, endure, expose, harden, live through, overcome, pull through, resist, ride out, rise above, season, stand, stick out, suffer, surmount, survive, toughen, weather out, withstand.
antonym succumb.

weave *v.* blend, braid, build, construct, contrive, create, criss-cross, entwine, fabricate, fuse, incorporate, intercross, interdigitate, interlace, intermingle, intertwine, introduce, knit, make, mat, merge, plait, put together, spin, twist, unite, wind, zigzag.

weaver *n.* brabener, wabster, webster.

web *n.* interlacing, lattice, mesh, mesh-work, net, netting, network, palama, screen, snare, tangle, tela, texture, toils, trap, weave, webbing, weft.

wed *v.* ally, blend, coalesce, combine, commingle, dedicate, espouse, fuse, get hitched, interweave, join, jump the broomstick, link, marry, merge, splice, tie the knot, unify, unite, wive, yoke.
antonym divorce.

wedding *n.* bridal, espousals, marriage, matrimony, nuptials.
antonym divorce.
adj. bridal, epithalamial, epithalamic, hymeneal, hymenean, marriage, matrimonial, nuptial.

wedge *n.* block, chock, chunk, cleat, lump, wodge.
v. block, cram, crowd, force, jam, lodge, pack, push, ram, squeeze, stuff, thrust.
antonyms dislodge, space out, take out.

wedlock *n.* holy matrimony, marriage, matrimony, union.

wee *adj.* diminutive, insignificant, itsy-bitsy, Lilliputian, little, microscopic, midget, miniature, minuscule, minute, negligible, small, teeny, teeny-weeny, tiny, weeny.
antonym large.

weed *v.* hoe.

weed out eliminate, eradicate, extirpate, get rid of, purge, remove, root out.
antonyms add, fix, infiltrate.

weedy *adj.* feeble, frail, ineffectual, insipid, lanky, namby-pamby, puny, skinny, thin, undersized, ungainly, weak, weak-kneed, wet, wimpish.
antonym strong.

week *n.* hebdomad, sennight.

weekly *adv.* by the week, every week, hebdomadally, once a week.
adj. hebdomadal, hebdomadary.

weep *v.* bemoan, bewail, blub, blubber, boo-hoo, bubble, complain, cry, drip, exude, greet, keen, lament, leak, moan, mourn, ooze, pipe, pipe one's eye, pour forth, pour out, rain, snivel, sob, tune one's pipes, ululate, whimper, whinge.
antonym rejoice.
n. blub, bubble, cry, greet, lament, moan, snivel, sob.

weepie *n.* melodrama, sob-stuff, tear-jerker.

weepy *adj.* blubbering, crying, labile, lachrymose, sobbing, tearful, teary, weeping.
antonym dry-eyed.

weigh *v.* bear down, burden, carry weight, consider, contemplate, count, deliberate, evaluate, examine, give thought to, impress, matter, meditate on, mull over, oppress, ponder, ponderate, prey, reflect on, study, tell, think over.
antonyms cut no ice, hearten.

weigh down afflict, bear down, burden, depress, get down, load, oppress, overburden, overload, press down, trouble, weigh upon, worry.
antonyms hearten, lighten, refresh.

weigh up assess, chew over, cogitate, consider, contemplate, deliberate, discuss, examine, mull over, perpend, ponder, ruminate on, think over.

weight *n.* authority, avoirdupois, ballast, burden, clout, consequence, consideration, efficacy, emphasis, force, gravity, heaviness, heft, impact, import, importance, impressiveness, influence, load, mass, millstone, moment, onus, oppression, persuasiveness, ponderance, ponderancy, poundage, power, preponderance, pressure, significance, strain, substance, tonnage, value.
antonym lightness.
v. ballast, bias, burden, charge, encumber, freight, handicap, hold down, impede, keep down, load, oppress, overburden, slant, unbalance, weigh down.
antonym lighten.

weightless *adj.* airy, imponderous, insubstantial, light, unsubstantial.
antonym heavy.

weighty *adj.* backbreaking, burdensome, consequential, considerable, critical, crucial, crushing, cumbersome, demanding, dense, difficult, exacting, forcible, grave, heavy, hefty, important, leading, massive, momentous, onerous, oppressive, ponderous, portentous, respected, revered, serious, significant, solemn, substantial, taxing, worrisome, worrying.
antonyms trivial, unimportant.

weir *n.* dam, fence, garth, lash, wear.

weird *adj.* bizarre, creepy, eerie, eldritch, freakish, ghostly, grotesque, mysterious, odd, outlandish, preternatural, queer, spooky, strange, superlunar, supernatural, uncanny, unco, unearthly, unnatural, witching.
antonym normal.

weirdo *n.* crackpot, crank, cure, eccentric, freak, fruitcake, loony, nut, nutcase, nutter, oddball, queer fish, weirdie.

welcome *adj.* able, acceptable, accepted, agreeable, allowed, appreciated, delightful, desirable, entitled, free, gratifying, permitted, pleasant, pleasing, refreshing.
antonym unwelcome.
n. acceptance, greeting, hospitality, reception, red carpet, salaam, salutation.
v. accept, approve of, embrace, greet, hail, meet, receive, roll out the red carpet for.

antonyms reject, snub.

weld *v.* bind, bond, cement, connect, fuse, join, link, seal, solder, unite.
antonym separate.
n. bond, joint, seal, seam.

welfare *n.* advantage, benefit, good, happiness, heal, health, interest, profit, prosperity, success, weal, well-being.
antonym harm.

well[1] *n.* bore, cavity, fount, fountain, hole, lift-shaft, mine, pit, pool, repository, shaft, source, spring, waterhole, well-spring.
v. brim over, flood, flow, gush, jet, ooze, pour, rise, run, seep, spout, spring, spurt, stream, surge, swell, trickle.

well[2] *adv.* ably, abundantly, accurately, adeptly, adequately, admirably, agreeably, amply, approvingly, attentively, capitally, carefully, clearly, closely, comfortably, completely, conscientiously, considerably, correctly, deeply, easily, effectively, efficiently, expertly, fairly, famously, favourably, fittingly, flourishingly, fully, glowingly, graciously, greatly, happily, heartily, highly, intimately, justly, kindly, nicely, personally, pleasantly, possibly, proficiently, profoundly, properly, prosperously, readily, rightly, satisfactorily, skilfully, smoothly, splendidly, substantially, successfully, sufficiently, suitably, thoroughly, warmly.
antonym badly.
adj. A1, able-bodied, advisable, agreeable, bright, fine, fit, fitting, flourishing, fortunate, good, great, hale, happy, healthy, hearty, in fine fettle, in good health, lucky, on the top of the world, pleasing, profitable, proper, prudent, right, robust, satisfactory, sound, strong, thriving, up to par, useful.
antonyms bad, ill.

well done! brava, bravo, euge.

well-balanced *adj.* graceful, harmonious, judicious, level-headed, nutritious, proportional, rational, reasonable, sane, sensible, sober, sound, symmetrical, together, well-adjusted, well-proportioned.
antonym unbalanced.

well-being *n.* comfort, contentment, good, happiness, prosperity, weal, welfare.
antonyms discomfort, harm.

well-bred *adj.* aristocratic, blue-blooded, civil, courteous, courtly, cultivated, cultured, gallant, genteel, gentle, gentlemanly, highborn, ladylike, mannerly, noble, patrician, polished, polite, refined, titled, upper-crust, urbane, well-born, well-brought-up, well-mannered.
antonym ill-bred.

well-deserved *adj.* appropriate, condign, deserved, due, just, justified, meet, merited, rightful.
antonym undeserved.

well-disposed *adj.* agreeable, amicable, favourable, friendly, sympathetic, well-aimed, well-arranged, well-minded, well-placed.
antonym ill-disposed.

well-dressed *adj.* dapper, natty, neat, smart, spruce, tidy, trim, well-groomed.
antonym scruffy.

well-equipped *adj.* well-appointed, well-found.

well-known *adj.* celebrated, famed, familiar, famous, illustrious, notable, noted, popular, renowned.
antonym unknown.

well-off *adj.* affluent, comfortable, flourishing, flush, fortunate, in the money, loaded, lucky, moneyed, prosperous, rich, successful, thriving, warm, wealthy, well-heeled, well-to-do.
antonym poor.

well-thought-of *adj.* admired, esteemed, highly regarded, honoured, reputable, respected, revered, venerated, weighty.
antonym despised.

well-to-do *adj.* affluent, comfortable, flush, loaded, moneyed, prosperous, rich, warm, wealthy, well-heeled, well-off.
antonym poor.

well-wisher *n.* fan, supporter, sympathiser, well-willer.

well-worn *adj.* bromidic, commonplace, hackneyed, overused, stale, stereotyped, threadbare, timeworn, tired, trite.
antonym original.

welsh *v.* cheat, defraud, diddle, do, swindle, welch.

welt *n.* cicatrice, cicatrix, contusion, mark, ridge, scar, streak, stripe, wale, weal, wheal.

welter *v.* billow, flounder, heave, lie, pitch, roll, splash, stumble, toss, tumble, wade, wallow, writhe.
n. confusion, hotchpotch, jumble, mess, mish-mash, mixter-maxter, muddle, tangle, web.

wend one's way go, hike, meander, move, plod, proceed, progress, travel, trudge, walk, wander.
antonym stay.

werewolf *n.* lycanthrope, lycanthropist, werwolf.

western *adj.* Hesperian, occidental.
antonym eastern.
n. horse opera, spaghetti western.

wet *adj.* boggy, clammy, damp, dank, drenched, dripping, drizzling, effete, feeble, foolish, humid, ineffectual, irresolute, misty, moist, moistened, namby-pamby, pouring, raining, rainy, saturated, showery, silly, sloppy, soaked, soaking, sodden, soft, soggy, sopping, soppy, soused, spineless, spongy, teeming, timorous, waterlogged, watery, weak, weedy.
antonyms dry, resolute, strong.
n. clamminess, condensation, damp, dampness, drip, drizzle, humidity, liquid, milksop, milquetoast, moisture, rain, rains, sap, water, weakling, weed, wetness, wimp.
antonym dryness.
v. bedabble, bedew, bedrench, damp, dampen, dip, douse, drench, humidify, imbue, irrigate, moisten, saturate, sluice, soak, splash, spray, sprinkle, steep, water.
antonym dry.

wet behind the ears callow, green, immature, inexperienced, innocent, naïve, new, raw, untrained.
antonym experienced.

wetness *n.* clamminess, condensation, damp, dampness, dankness, humidity, liquid, moisture, soddenness, sogginess, water, wet.
antonym dryness.

wet-nurse *n.* amah.

whack *v.* bang, bash, beat, belabour, belt, biff, box, buffet, clobber, clout, cuff, hit, lambaste, rap, slap, slug, smack, sock, strike, thrash, thump, thwack, wallop, whale, whang.
n. allotment, attempt, bang, bash, belt, biff, bit, blow, box, buffet, clout, crack, cuff, cut, go, hit, part, portion, quota, rap, share, shot, slap, slug, smack, sock, stab, stroke, thump, thwack, try, turn, wallop, wham, whang.

wham *n.* bang, bash, blow, clout, concussion, hit, impact, slam, smack, splat, thump, thwack, wallop, whack, whang.

wharf *n.* dock, dockyard, jetty, landing-stage, marina, pier, quay, quayside.

what's-its-name *n.* dingus, doodad, jigamaree, jiggumbob, thingumajig, thingumbob, thingummy, what-d'ye-call-it, whatsit, what-you-may-call-it.

wheedle *v.* cajole, charm, coax, court, draw, entice, flatter, importune, inveigle, persuade, whilly, whillywha(w).
antonym force.

wheel *n.* birl, circle, gyration, pivot, revolution, roll, rotation, spin, turn, twirl, whirl.
v. birl, circle, gyrate, orbit, pirouette, revolve, roll, rotate, spin, swing, swivel, turn, twirl, whirl.

wheelbarrow *n.* ball-barrow, barrow, hand-cart, monotroch.

wheeze[1] *v.* cough, gasp, hiss, rasp, whiss, whistle, whiz(z).
n. cough, gasp, hiss, rasp, whistle, whiz(z).

wheeze[2] *n.* anecdote, catch-phrase, chestnut, crack, expedient, gag, idea, joke, one-liner, plan, ploy, practical joke, prank, ruse, scheme, story, stunt, trick, wrinkle.

whereabouts *n.* location, place, position, site, situation, vicinity.

wherewithal *n.* capital, cash, funds, means, money, necessary, readies, resources, supplies.

whet *v.* acuminate, arouse, awaken, file, grind, hone, incite, increase, kindle, pique, provoke, quicken, rouse, sharpen, stimulate, stir, strop, titillate.
antonyms blunt, dampen.

whiff *n.* aroma, blast, breath, draught, gale, gust, hint, niff, odour, pong, puff, reek, scent, smell, sniff, stench, stink.

whim *n.* caprice, chimera, conceit, concetto, crank, craze, crotchet, fad, fancy, fizgig, flam, freak, humour, impulse, maggot, notion, quirk, sport, urge, vagary, whims(e)y.

whimper *v.* blub, blubber, cry, girn, grizzle, mewl, moan, pule, snivel, sob, weep, whine, whinge.

n. girn, moan, snivel, sob, whine.

whimsical *adj.* capricious, chimeric(al), crotchety, curious, dotty, droll, eccentric, fanciful, fantastic(al), freakish, funny, Gilbertian, maggoty, mischievous, odd, peculiar, playful, quaint, queer, singular, unusual, waggish, weird, whimmy.
antonym sensible.

whine *n.* beef, belly-ache, complaint, cry, girn, gripe, grouch, grouse, grumble, moan, sob, wail, whimper.
v. beef, belly-ache, carp, complain, cry, girn, gripe, grizzle, grouch, grouse, grumble, kvetch, moan, sob, wail, whimper, whinge.

whinge *v.* beef, belly-ache, carp, complain, gripe, grouse, grumble, kvetch, moan.
n. beef, belly-ache, complaint, gripe, grouse, grumble, moan.

whip *v.* agitate, beat, best, birch, cane, castigate, clobber, compel, conquer, dart, dash, defeat, dive, drive, drub, flagellate, flash, flit, flog, flounce, fly, foment, goad, hammer, hound, incite, instigate, jambok, jerk, knout, k(o)urbash, lash, leather, lick, outdo, overcome, overpower, overwhelm, paddle, prick, prod, produce, provoke, pull, punish, push, quirt, remove, rout, rush, scourge, shoot, sjambok, snatch, spank, spur, stir, strap, switch, tan, tear, thrash, trounce, urge, whale, whisk, whop, worst.
n. birch, bullwhip, cane, cat, cat-o'-nine-tails, crop, flagellum, horsewhip, jambok, knout, k(o)urbash, lash, paddle, quirt, rawhide, riding-crop, scourge, sjambok, switch, thong.
whip up agitate, arouse, excite, foment, incite, inflame, instigate, kindle, provoke, psych up, stir up, work up.
antonyms dampen, deter.

whippersnapper *n.* hobbledehoy, nipper, shaver, whiffet.

whipping *n.* beating, belting, birching, caning, castigation, flagellation, flogging, hiding, lashing, leathering, paddling, punishment, quilting, spanking, tanning, thrashing.

whirl *v.* birl, circle, gyrate, gyre, pirouette, pivot, reel, revolve, roll, rotate, spin, swirl, swivel, turn, twirl, twist, wheel.
n. agitation, birl, bustle, circle, commotion, confusion, daze, dither, flurry, giddiness, gyration, gyre, hubbub, hubbuboo, hurly-burly, merry-go-round, pirouette, reel, revolution, roll, rotation, round, series, spin, stir, succession, swirl, tumult, turn, twirl, twist, uproar, vortex, wheel, whorl.
antonym calm.

whirling *adj.* birling, gyral, gyrating, gyratory, pirouetting, pivoting, reeling, revolving, rotating, spinning, turning, twirling, vertiginous, vortical, vorticular, vorticuse, vortiginous, wheeling.
antonym stationary.

whirlpool *n.* maelstrom, vortex, weel.

whirlwind *n.* cyclone, dust-devil, tornado, vortex, waterspout.
adj. hasty, headlong, impetuous, impulsive,

lightning, precipitate, quick, rapid, rash, short, speedy, split-second, swift. *antonyms* deliberate, slow.

whisk *v.* beat, brush, dart, dash, flick, fly, grab, hasten, hurry, race, rush, scoot, shoot, speed, sweep, swipe, tear, twitch, whip, wipe.
n. beater, brush, swizzle-stick.

whisker *n.* bristle, hair, hair's breadth, vibrissa.

whisk(e)y *n.* barley-bree, bourbon, John Barleycorn, malt, mountain dew, peat-reek, rye, Scotch, usquebaugh.

whisper *v.* breathe, buzz, divulge, gossip, hint, hiss, insinuate, intimate, murmur, rustle, sigh, sough, susurrate, tittle.
antonym shout.
n. breath, buzz, gossip, hint, hiss, innuendo, insinuation, murmur, report, rumour, rustle, shadow, sigh, sighing, soughing, soupçon, suggestion, suspicion, susurration, susurrus, swish, tinge, trace, underbreath, undertone, whiff, word.
antonym roar.

whistle *n.* call, cheep, chirp, hooter, siren, song, warble.
v. call, cheep, chirp, pipe, siffle, sing, warble, wheeze, whiss.

whit *n.* atom, bit, crumb, damn, dash, drop, fragment, grain, hoot, iota, jot, little, mite, modicum, particle, piece, pinch, scrap, shred, speck, tittle, trace.
antonym lot.

white *adj.* ashen, auspicious, bloodless, bright, canescent, Caucasian, clean, colourless, dealbate, favourable, ghastly, grey, grizzled, hoar, hoary, honest, immaculate, innocent, pale, pallid, pasty, pure, purified, reliable, silver, snowy, spotless, stainless, unblemished, unsullied, wan, waxen, whey-faced.
antonyms black, dark, dishonest, ruddy, unclean, unreliable.
n. albumen, gub, gubbah, honkie, whitey.

white-collar *adj.* clerical, executive, non-manual, office, professional, salaried.
antonyms blue-collar, manual.

whiten *v.* blanch, bleach, blench, decolour, etiolate, fade, pale, whitewash.
antonyms blacken, colour, darken.

whitewash[1] *n.* camouflage, concealment, cover-up, deception, extenuation.
antonym exposure.
v. camouflage, conceal, cover up, euphemise, extenuate, gloss over, make light of, suppress.
antonym expose.

whitewash[2] *v.* beat, best, clobber, crush, drub, hammer, lick, paste, thrash, trounce, whale.

whitlow *n.* paronychia.

whittle *v.* carve, consume, cut, destroy, diminish, eat away, erode, hew, pare, reduce, scrape, shape, shave, trim, undermine, wear away.

whole *adj.* better, complete, cured, entire, faultless, fit, flawless, full, good, hale, healed, healthy, in one piece, intact, integral, integrate, inviolate, mint, perfect, recovered, robust, sound, strong, total, unabbreviated, unabridged, unbroken, uncut, undamaged, undivided, unedited, unexpurgated, unharmed, unhurt, unimpaired, uninjured, unmutilated, unscathed, untouched, well.
antonyms damaged, ill, partial.
n. aggregate, all, ensemble, entirety, entity, everything, fullness, Gestalt, lot, piece, total, totality, unit, unity.
antonym part.

whole-hearted *adj.* committed, complete, dedicated, determined, devoted, earnest, emphatic, enthusiastic, genuine, heartfelt, hearty, passionate, real, sincere, true, unfeigned, unqualified, unreserved, unstinting, warm, whole-souled, zealous.
antonym half-hearted.

wholesale *adj.* broad, comprehensive, extensive, far-reaching, indiscriminate, mass, massive, sweeping, total, wide-ranging.
antonym partial.
adv. comprehensively, en bloc, extensively, indiscriminately, massively, totally.
antonym partially.

wholesome *adj.* advantageous, beneficial, clean, decent, edifying, exemplary, good, healthful, health-giving, healthy, helpful, honourable, hygienic, improving, innocent, invigorating, moral, nice, nourishing, nutritious, propitious, pure, respectable, righteous, salubrious, salutary, sanitary, uplifting, virtuous, worthy.
antonym unwholesome.

wholly *adv.* absolutely, all, altogether, completely, comprehensively, entirely, exclusively, fully, in toto, only, perfectly, solely, thoroughly, through and through, totally, utterly.
antonym partly.

whoop *v, n.* cheer, cry, holler, hoop, hoot, hurrah, roar, scream, shout, shriek, yell.

whooping-cough *n.* pertussis.

whopper *n.* colossus, cracker, fable, fabrication, fairy story, falsehood, giant, lie, monster, plumper, tall story, untruth.

whopping *adj.* big, enormous, extraordinary, giant, gigantic, great, huge, large, mammoth, massive, mighty, monstrous, monumental, prodigious, staggering, tremendous, whacking.
antonym tiny.

whore *n.* brass, broad, call girl, courtesan, demimondaine, demirep, drab, fallen woman, fille de joie, harlot, hooker, hustler, loon, loose fish, lorette, Paphian, prostitute, scarlet woman, strange woman, street-walker, strumpet, succubus, tart, tramp, trollop, waistcoateer, wench, woman of the town, working girl.

whorehouse *n.* bagnio, bawdy-house, bordello, brothel, cat-house, house of ill repute, knocking-shop, stew.

whorl *n.* coil, convolution, corkscrew, helix, spiral, turn, twist, vortex.

wicked *adj.* abandoned, abominable, acute, agonising, amoral, arch, atrocious, awful, bad, black-hearted, bothersome, corrupt, debased, depraved, destructive, devilish, difficult, dissolute, distressing, dreadful, egregious, evil, facinorous, fearful, fiendish, fierce, flagitious, foul, galling, guilty, harmful, heinous, immoral, impious, impish, incorrigible, inexpiable, iniquitous, injurious, intense, irreligious, mighty, mischievous, nasty, naughty, nefarious, nefast, offensive, painful, piacular, rascal-like, rascally, roguish, scandalous, severe, shameful, sinful, spiteful, terrible, troublesome, trying, ungodly, unpleasant, unprincipled, unrighteous, vicious, vile, villainous, worthless.

antonyms good, harmless, modest, upright.

wickedness *n*. abomination, amorality, atrocity, corruption, corruptness, depravity, devilishness, dissoluteness, enormity, evil, facinorousness, fiendishness, foulness, heinousness, immorality, impiety, iniquity, pravity, reprobacy, shamefulness, sin, sinfulness, unrighteousness, vileness, villainy.

antonym uprightness.

wickerwork *n*. basket-work, wattle, wattlework.

wide *adj*. ample, away, baggy, broad, capacious, catholic, commodious, comprehensive, diffuse, dilated, distant, distended, encyclopaedic, expanded, expansive, extensive, far-reaching, full, general, immense, inclusive, large, latitudinous, loose, off, off-course, off-target, outspread, outstretched, remote, roomy, spacious, sweeping, vast.

antonyms limited, narrow.

adv. aside, astray, off course, off target, off the mark, out.

antonym on target.

wide-awake *adj*. alert, astute, aware, conscious, fully awake, heedful, keen, observant, on one's toes, on the alert, on the ball, on the qui vive, quick-witted, roused, sharp, vigilant, wakened, wary, watchful.

antonym asleep.

widen *v*. broaden, dilate, distend, enlarge, expand, extend, open out, splay, spread, stretch.

antonym narrow.

wide-open *adj*. defenceless, expansive, exposed, gaping, indeterminate, open, outspread, outstretched, splayed, spread, susceptible, uncertain, unfortified, unpredictable, unprotected, unsettled, vulnerable, wide.

antonyms closed, narrow.

widespread *adj*. broad, common, epidemic, extensive, far-flung, far-reaching, general, pervasive, popular, prevailing, prevalent, rife, sweeping, universal, unlimited, wholesale.

antonyms limited, uncommon.

widowed *adj*. bereaved, viduous.

widowhood *n*. viduage, viduity.

width *n*. amplitude, beam, breadth, compass, diameter, extent, girth, measure, range, reach, scope, span, thickness, wideness.

wield *v*. apply, brandish, command, control,

employ, exercise, exert, flourish, handle, have, hold, maintain, manage, manipulate, ply, possess, swing, use, utilise, wave, weave.

wife *n*. better half, bride, consort, dutch, helpmate, helpmeet, little woman, mate, missis, missus, old lady, old woman, partner, rib, spouse, woman.

antonym husband.

wifely *adj*. uxorial.

wig *n*. caxon, dalmahoy, gizz, Gregorian, jas(e)y, jazy, jiz, merkin, peruke, postiche, tie-wig.

wiggle *v, n*. jerk, jiggle, shake, shimmy, squirm, twist, twitch, wag, waggle, wriggle, writhe.

wild *adj*. agrest(i)al, barbaric, barbarous, berserk, blustery, boisterous, brutish, chaotic, chimeric(al), choppy, crazed, crazy, daft, delirious, demented, desert, deserted, desolate, dishevelled, disordered, disorderly, eager, empty, enthusiastic, excited, extravagant, fantastic, ferae naturae, feral, feralised, ferine, ferocious, fierce, flighty, foolhardy, foolish, frantic, free, frenzied, furious, giddy, god-forsaken, howling, hysterical, ill-considered, impetuous, impracticable, imprudent, inaccurate, indigenous, intense, irrational, lawless, mad, madcap, maniacal, native, natural, noisy, nuts, outrageous, potty, preposterous, primitive, rabid, raging, rash, raving, reckless, riotous, rough, rowdy, rude, savage, self-willed, tempestuous, tousled, trackless, turbulent, unbridled, unbroken, uncheated, uncivilised, uncontrollable, uncontrolled, uncultivated, undisciplined, undomesticated, unfettered, ungovernable, uninhabited, unjustified, unkempt, unmanageable, unpopulated, unpruned, unrestrained, unruly, unsubstantiated, untamed, untidy, uproarious, violent, virgin, wayward, woolly.

antonyms civilised, peaceful, sane, sensible, tame, unenthusiastic.

wilderness *n*. clutter, confusion, congeries, desert, jumble, jungle, mass, maze, muddle, tangle, waste, wasteland, welter, wild, wildland.

wildlife *n*. animals, fauna.

wilds *n*. back-veld, desert, outback, the back of beyond, the boondocks, the middle of nowhere, the sticks, wasteland, wilderness.

wile *n*. artfulness, artifice, cheating, chicanery, contrivance, craft, craftiness, cunning, deceit, device, dodge, expedient, fraud, guile, hanky-panky, imposition, lure, manoeuvre, ploy, ruse, slyness, stratagem, subterfuge, trick, trickery.

antonym guilelessness.

wilful *adj*. adamant, bloody-minded, bull-headed, conscious, deliberate, determined, dogged, froward, headstrong, inflexible, intended, intentional, intractable, intransigent, mulish, obdurate, obstinate, persistent, perverse, pig-headed, purposeful, refractory, self-willed, stubborn, thrawn, uncompromising, unyielding, volitional, voluntary.

antonyms complaisant, good-natured.

will *n.* aim, attitude, choice, command, decision, declaration, decree, desire, determination, discretion, disposition, fancy, feeling, inclination, intention, mind, option, pleasure, preference, prerogative, purpose, resolution, resolve, testament, velleity, volition, willpower, wish, wishes.

v. bequeath, bid, cause, choose, command, confer, decree, desire, determine, devise, direct, dispose of, elect, give, leave, opt, ordain, order, pass on, resolve, transfer, want, wish.

willing *adj.* agreeable, amenable, biddable, compliant, consenting, content, desirous, disposed, eager, enthusiastic, favourable, game, happy, inclined, nothing lo(a)th, pleased, prepared, ready, so-minded, volitient, willing-hearted.

antonym unwilling.

willingly *adv.* by choice, cheerfully, eagerly, freely, gladly, happily, nothing lo(a)th, readily, unhesitatingly, voluntarily.

antonym unwillingly.

willingness *n.* agreeableness, agreement, complaisance, compliance, consent, desire, disposition, enthusiasm, favour, inclination, volition, will, wish.

antonym unwillingness.

will-o'-the-wisp *n.* fatuous fire, fen-fire, friar's lantern, ignis fatuus, wisp.

willowy *adj.* graceful, gracile, limber, lissom, lithe, lithesome, slender, slim, supple, svelte, sylph-like.

antonym buxom.

will-power *n.* determination, drive, grit, resolution, resolve, self-command, self-control, self-discipline, self-mastery, single-mindedness.

willy-nilly *adv.* compulsorily, necessarily, nolens volens, of necessity, perforce.

wilt *v.* atrophy, diminish, droop, dwindle, ebb, fade, fail, flag, flop, languish, melt away, sag, shrivel, sink, wane, weaken, wither.

antonym perk up.

wily *adj.* arch, artful, astute, cagey, crafty, crooked, cunning, deceitful, deceptive, designing, fly, foxy, guileful, intriguing, long-headed, Machiavellian, scheming, sharp, shifty, shrewd, sly, tricky, underhand, versute, wileful.

antonym guileless.

wimp *n.* clot, clown, drip, fool, jerk, marshmallow, milksop, nebbich, neb(b)ish, nyaff, sap, softy, wally, wet.

win *v.* accomplish, achieve, acquire, attain, bag, capture, catch, collect, come away with, conquer, earn, gain, get, net, obtain, overcome, pick up, prevail, procure, receive, secure, succeed, sweep the board, triumph.

antonym lose.

n. conquest, mastery, success, triumph, victory.

antonym defeat.

win over allure, attract, carry, charm, convert, convince, disarm, dissuade, induce, influence, persuade, prevail upon, sway, talk round.

wince *v.* blench, cower, cringe, draw back, flinch, funk, jerk, quail, recoil, shrink, start.

n. cringe, flinch, jerk, start.

wind[1] *n.* air, air-current, babble, blast, blather, bluster, boasting, breath, breeze, clue, current, cyclone, draught, flatulence, flatus, gab, gale, gas, gregale, gust, harmattan, hint, hot air, humbug, hurricane, idle talk, inkling, intimation, khamsin, levanter, libeccio, notice, puff, report, respiration, rumour, suggestion, talk, tidings, tornado, warning, whisper, williwaw, windiness, zephyr.

wind[2] *v.* bend, coil, curl, curve, deviate, encircle, furl, loop, meander, ramble, reel, roll, serpent, serpentine, serpentinise, snake, spiral, turn, twine, twist, wreath, zigzag.

n. bend, curve, meander, turn, twist, zigzag.

wind down decline, diminish, dwindle, lessen, quieten down, reduce, relax, slacken off, slow, slow down, subside, unwind.

antonyms increase, tense.

wind up close, close down, coil, conclude, crank up, end, end one's days, end up, excite, finalise, find oneself, finish, finish up, hoist, liquidate, raise, settle, terminate, tighten, work up, wrap up.

antonym begin.

wind-bag *n.* big-mouth, blether, boaster, bore, braggart, gas-bag, gossip, rodomontader.

winded *adj.* breathless, out of breath, out of puff, panting, pooped, puffed, puffed out.

antonym fresh.

windfall *n.* bonanza, find, godsend, jackpot, manna, pennies from heaven, stroke of luck, treasure-trove.

windiness *n.* borborygmus, breeziness, flatulence, flatulency, gassiness, gustiness, storminess, ventosity.

antonym calm.

winding *adj.* anfractuous, bending, circuitous, convoluted, crooked, curving, flexuose, flexuous, indirect, meandering, meandrous, roundabout, serpentine, sinuate(d), sinuous, spiral, tortuous, turning, twisting.

antonym straight.

window *n.* dormer, dormer-window, fenestella, fenestra, fenestral, glass, light, loop-light, lucarne, opening, oriel, oriel-window, pane, rosace, rose-window, skylight, ventana.

windpipe *n.* pharynx, throat, trachea, weasand.

wind-sock *n.* drogue, wind-cone, wind-sleeve.

windy *adj.* afraid, blowy, blustering, blustery, boastful, boisterous, bombastic, breezy, changeable, chicken, conceited, cowardly, diffuse, empty, fearful, flatulent, flatuous, frightened, garrulous, gusty, long-winded, loquacious, meandering, nervous, pompous, prolix, rambling, scared, squally, stormy, tempestuous, thrasonic, timid, turgid, ventose, verbose, wild, windswept, wordy.

antonyms calm, fearless, modest.

wine *n.* champagne, claret, plonk, port, rosé, vin, vin ordinaire, vinho verde, vino, vintage.

wine-glass *n.* flute, glass, goblet, schooner.

wine-grower *n.* vigneron, viniculturist, viticulturist.

wine-growing *n.* viniculture, viticulture.

wing *n.* adjunct, annexe, arm, branch, circle, clique, coterie, extension, faction, flank, group, grouping, mudguard, pinion, protection, section, segment, set, side.

v. clip, fleet, flit, fly, glide, hasten, hit, hurry, move, nick, pass, race, soar, speed, travel, wound, zoom.

wink *v.* bat, blink, flash, flicker, flutter, gleam, glimmer, glint, nictate, nictitate, pink, sparkle, twinkle.

n. blink, flash, flutter, gleam, glimmering, glint, hint, instant, jiffy, moment, nictation, nictitation, second, sparkle, split second, twinkle, twinkling.

winner *n.* champ, champion, conqueror, corker, cracker, daisy, dinger, first, humdinger, master, vanquisher, victor, world-beater, wow.

antonym loser.

winning *adj.* alluring, amiable, attractive, bewitching, captivating, charming, conquering, delectable, delightful, disarming, enchanting, endearing, engaging, fascinating, fetching, lovely, on top, pleasing, prepossessing, successful, sweet, taking, triumphant, unbeaten, undefeated, victorious, winsome.

antonyms losing, unappealing.

winnings *n.* booty, gains, motser, motza, prize(s), proceeds, profits, spoils, takings, velvet.

antonym losses.

winnow *v.* comb, cull, diffuse, divide, fan, part, screen, select, separate, sift, waft.

winsome *adj.* agreeable, alluring, amiable, attractive, bewitching, captivating, charming, cheerful, comely, delectable, disarming, enchanting, endearing, engaging, fair, fascinating, fetching, graceful, pleasant, pleasing, prepossessing, pretty, sweet, taking, winning.

antonym unattractive.

wintry *adj.* algid, bleak, brumous, cheerless, chilly, cold, desolate, dismal, freezing, frore, frosty, frozen, gelid, harsh, hibernal, hiemal, icy, rimy, Siberian, snowy, winterly.

antonym summery.

wipe *v.* absterge, brush, clean, clear, deterge, dicht, dry, dust, erase, mop, remove, rub, sponge, swab, take away, take off.

n. brush, dicht, lick, rub, swab.

wipe out abolish, annihilate, blot out, destroy, efface, eradicate, erase, expunge, exterminate, extirpate, massacre, obliterate, put paid to, raze.

antonym establish.

wire-pulling *n.* clout, conspiring, influence, intrigue, Machiavellianism, manipulation, plotting, pull, scheming.

wiry *adj.* bristly, lean, sinewy, stiff, strong, tough, withy.

antonym puny.

wisdom *n.* anthroposophy, astuteness, circumspection, comprehension, discernment, enlightenment, erudition, foresight, gnosis, intelligence, judgement, judiciousness, knowledge, learning, penetration, prudence, reason, sagacity, sapience, sence, sophia, understanding.

antonym folly.

wise *adj.* aware, clever, discerning, enlightened, erudite, informed, intelligent, judicious, knowing, long-headed, long-sighted, perceptive, politic, prudent, rational, reasonable, sagacious, sage, sapient, sensible, shrewd, sound, understanding, well-advised, well-informed.

antonym foolish.

wiseacre *n.* clever dick, smart Alec(k), smarty-pants, wise guy, wiseling.

wisecrack *n.* barb, funny, gag, jest, jibe, joke, one-liner, quip, witticism.

wish *v.* ask, aspire, bid, command, covet, crave, desiderate, desire, direct, greet, hanker, hope, hunger, instruct, long, need, order, require, thirst, want, whim, yearn, yen.

antonyms dislike, fear.

n. aspiration, bidding, command, desire, hankering, hope, hunger, inclination, intention, liking, order, request, thirst, urge, velleity, voice, want, whim, will, yearning, yen.

antonyms dislike, fear.

wishbone *n.* furcula, merry-thought.

wishy-washy *adj.* bland, feeble, flat, ineffective, ineffectual, insipid, jejune, namby-pamby, tasteless, thin, vapid, watered-down, watery, weak, wersh.

antonym strong.

wisp *n.* jag, lock, piece, shred, snippet, strand, thread, twist.

wispy *adj.* attenuate, attenuated, delicate, diaphanous, ethereal, faint, fine, flimsy, flyaway, fragile, frail, gossamer, insubstantial, light, thin, unsubstantial.

antonym substantial.

wistful *adj.* contemplative, disconsolate, dreaming, dreamy, forlorn, longing, meditative, melancholy, mournful, musing, pensive, reflective, sad, soulful, thoughtful, wishful, yearning.

wit *n.* acumen, badinage, banter, brains, card, cleverness, comedian, common sense, comprehension, conceit, discernment, drollery, epigrammatist, eutrapelia, facetiousness, farceur, fun, homme d'esprit, humorist, humour, ingenuity, insight, intellect, intelligence, jocularity, joker, judgement, levity, merum sal, mind, nous, perception, pleasantry, punster, quipster, raillery, reason, repartee, sense, smeddum, understanding, wag, wisdom, wit-cracker, wordplay.

antonyms seriousness, stupidity.

witch *n.* enchantress, galdregon, gyre-carline, hag, hex, lamia, magician, necromancer, occultist, pythoness, reim-kennar, sorceress, sortileger, weird, wise woman, witch-wife.

witchcraft *n.* black magic, conjuration, divination, enchantment, glamour, goety, incantation, invultuation, magic, myalism, necromancy, occultism, pishogue, sorcery, sortilege, sortilegy, spell, the black art, the occult, voodoo, witchery, witching, wizardry.

witch-doctor *n.* angek(k)ok, magician, medicine-man, shaman.

witch-hunt *n.* hounding, hue and cry, McCarthyism.

with it fashionable, groovy, hep, hip, in, modern, modish, progressive, trendy, up-to-date, up-to-the-minute, vogue.
antonym out-of-date.

withdraw *v.* abjure, absent oneself, back out, depart, disavow, disclaim, disengage, disenrol, disinvest, draw back, draw out, drop out, extract, fall back, go, go away, hive off, leave, pull back, pull out, recall, recant, remove, repair, rescind, retire, retract, retreat, revoke, secede, subduct, subtract, take away, take back, take off, unsay, waive.
antonyms advance, deposit, persist.

withdrawal *n.* abjuration, departure, disavowal, disclaimer, disengagement, disinvestment, Dunkirk, exit, exodus, extraction, recall, recantation, removal, repudiation, rescission, retirement, retraction, retreat, revocation, secession, waiver, withdrawment.
antonyms advance, deposit, persistence.

withdrawn *adj.* aloof, detached, distant, hidden, introvert, isolated, out-of-the-way, private, quiet, remote, reserved, retiring, secluded, shrinking, shy, silent, solitary, taciturn, uncommunicative, unforthcoming, unsociable.
antonym outgoing.

wither *v.* abash, blast, blight, decay, decline, desiccate, disintegrate, droop, dry, fade, humiliate, languish, miff, mortify, perish, put down, shame, shrink, shrivel, snub, wane, waste, welt, wilt.
antonyms boost, thrive.

wither away decrease, die, die off, disappear, dwindle, fade away, miff, shrink, shrivel, wilt.

withering *adj.* deadly, death-dealing, destructive, devastating, humiliating, killing, mortifying, murderous, scathing, scornful, searing, slaughterous, snubbing, wounding.
antonym supportive.

withhold *v.* check, conceal, deduct, detain, hide, keen, keep back, refuse, repress, reserve, resist, restrain, retain, sit on, suppress, suspend.
antonyms accord, give.

without delay at once, immediately, pronto, quick-stick(s), right away, straight away, straightway, there and then, tout de suite.

without doubt certainly, doubtless, no doubt, questionless, unquestionably.

without fail conscientiously, constantly, dependably, faithfully, like clockwork, predictably, punctually, regularly, reliably, religiously, unfailingly, without exception.
antonyms unpredictably, unreliably.

withstand *v.* bear, brave, combat, confront, cope

with, defy, endure, face, grapple with, hold off, hold one's ground, hold out, last out, oppose, put up with, resist, stand, stand fast, stand one's ground, stand up to, survive, take, take on, thwart, tolerate, weather.
antonyms collapse, yield.

witless *adj.* crazy, cretinous, daft, dull, empty-headed, foolish, gormless, half-witted, idiotic, imbecilic, inane, moronic, obtuse, senseless, silly, stupid.
antonym intelligent.

witness *n.* attestant, beholder, bystander, corroborator, deponent, eye-witness, looker-on, observer, onlooker, spectator, testifier, viewer, vouchee, voucher, watcher, witnesser.
v. attend, attest, bear out, bear witness, confirm, corroborate, countersign, depone, depose, endorse, look on, mark, note, notice, observe, perceive, see, sign, testify, view, watch.

wits *n.* acumen, astuteness, brains, cleverness, comprehension, faculties, gumption, ingenuity, intelligence, judgement, marbles, mother-wit, nous, reason, sense, understanding.
antonym stupidity.

witticism *n.* bon mot, epigram, jeu d'esprit, mot, one-liner, pleasantry, pun, quip, repartee, riposte, sally.

witty *adj.* amusing, brilliant, clever, comic, droll, epigrammatic, facetious, fanciful, funny, humorous, ingenious, jocular, lively, original, piquant, salty, sparkling, waggish, whimsical.
antonyms dull, unamusing.

wizard[1] *n.* conjurer, enchanter, mage, magician, magus, necromancer, occultist, reim-kennar, shaman, sorcerer, sortileger, thaumaturge, warlock, witch.

wizard[2] *n.* ace, adept, dabster, deacon, expert, genius, hotshot, maestro, master, prodigy, star, virtuoso, whiz.
antonym duffer.
adj. ace, brilliant, enjoyable, fab, fantastic, good, great, marvellous, sensational, smashing, super, superb, terrif, terrific, tiptop, top-hole, topping, tremendous, wonderful.
antonym rotten.

wizardry *n.* black magic, conjuration, divination, enchantment, glamour, goety, incantation, invultuation, magic, myalism, necromancy, occultism, pishogue, sorcery, sortilege, sortilegy, the black art, the occult, voodoo, warlockry, witchcraft, witchery, witching.

wizened *adj.* dried up, gnarled, lined, sere, shrivelled, shrunken, thin, weazen, weazened, withered, wizen, worn, wrinkled.
antonyms plump, smooth.

wobble *v.* dither, dodder, fluctuate, haver, heave, hesitate, oscillate, quake, rock, seesaw, shake, shilly-shally, sway, swither, teeter, totter, tremble, vacillate, vibrate, waver.
n. oscillation, quaking, rock, shake, tremble,

tremor, unsteadiness, vibration.

wobbly *adj.* doddering, doddery, rickety, shaky, shoogly, teetering, tottering, unbalanced, uneven, unsafe, unstable, unsteady, wonky. *antonym* stable.

woe *n.* adversity, affliction, agony, anguish, burden, curse, dejection, depression, disaster, distress, dole, dolour, dule, gloom, grief, hardship, heartache, heartbreak, melancholy, misery, misfortune, pain, sadness, sorrow, suffering, tears, trial, tribulation, trouble, unhappiness, wretchedness. *antonym* joy.

woebegone *adj.* blue, crestfallen, dejected, disconsolate, dispirited, doleful, down in the mouth, downcast, downhearted, forlorn, gloomy, grief-stricken, hangdog, long-faced, lugubrious, miserable, mournful, sad, sorrowful, tearful, tear-stained, troubled, wretched. *antonym* joyful.

woeful *adj.* agonising, appalling, awful, bad, calamitous, catastrophic, cruel, deplorable, disappointing, disastrous, disconsolate, disgraceful, distressing, doleful, dreadful, feeble, gloomy, grieving, grievous, heartbreaking, heart-rending, hopeless, inadequate, lamentable, lousy, mean, miserable, mournful, paltry, pathetic, piteous, pitiable, pitiful, plaintive, poor, rotten, sad, shocking, sorrowful, sorry, terrible, tragic, unhappy, woesome, wretched. *antonym* joyful.

wolf *n.* Casanova, dallier, Don Juan, ladies' man, lady-killer, lecher, Lothario, philanderer, Romeo, seducer, womaniser.

    wolf down bolt, cram, devour, gobble, gorge, gormandise, gulp, pack away, put away, scoff, shift, stuff. *antonym* nibble.

wolf-man *n.* lycanthrope, lycanthropist, werewolf.

woman *n.* bint, bird, bride, broad, chambermaid, char, charwoman, chick, dame, daughter, domestic, fair, female, feme, femme, Frau, gimmer, girl, girlfriend, handmaiden, housekeeper, kept woman, lady, lady-in-waiting, ladylove, lass, lassie, maid, maiden, maidservant, mate, miss, mistress, mort, old lady, partner, piece, placket, she, sheila, spouse, sweetheart, vrouw, wife, womanbody. *antonym* man.

womanhood *n.* muliebrity, woman, womankind, womenfolk(s), womenkind.

womaniser *n.* Casanova, dallier, Don Juan, ladies' man, lady-killer, lecher, Lothario, philanderer, Romeo, seducer, wolf.

womanising *n.* dalliance, lechery, philandering, venery, wenching, whoring.

womanly *adj.* female, feminine, ladylike, matronly, motherly, weak, womanish. *antonym* manly.

womb *n.* matrix, uterus.

women *n.* distaff side, muliebrity, muslin, womanhood, womankind, womenfolk(s),

womenkind.

wonder *n.* admiration, amaze, amazement, astonishment, awe, bewilderment, curiosity, fascination, marvel, miracle, nonpareil, phenomenon, portent, prodigy, rarity, sight, spectacle, stupefaction, surprise, wonderment, wunderkind. *antonyms* disinterest, ordinariness.

    v. ask oneself, boggle, conjecture, doubt, gape, gaup, gawk, inquire, marvel, meditate, ponder, puzzle, query, question, speculate, stare, think.

wonderful *adj.* ace, admirable, amazing, astonishing, astounding, awe-inspiring, awesome, brilliant, épatant, excellent, extraordinary, fab, fabulous, fantastic, great, incredible, magnificent, marvellous, miraculous, mirific(al), odd, oustanding, peculiar, phenomenal, remarkable, sensational, smashing, staggering, startling, strange, stupendous, super, superb, surprising, terrif, terrific, tiptop, top-hole, topping, tremendous, unheard-of, wizard, wondrous. *antonyms* ordinary, rotten.

wonders *n.* curiosities, magic, marvels, mirabilia, miracles, phenomena, prodigies, sights.

wonky *adj.* amiss, askew, awry, groggy, infirm, shaky, skew-whiff, squint, unsound, unsteady, weak, wobbly, wrong. *antonyms* stable, straight.

wont *adj.* accustomed, given, habituated, used. *n.* custom, habit, practice, routine, rule, use, way.

wonted *adj.* accustomed, common, conventional, customary, daily, familiar, frequent, habitual, normal, regular, routine, usual. *antonym* unwonted.

woo *v.* chase, court, cultivate, importune, look for, pay court to, pursue, seek, seek the hand of.

wood[1] *n.* hyle, lumber, planks, timber.

wood[2] *n.* bosk, coppice, copse, forest, grove, hanger, holt, hurst, plantation, thicket, trees, underwood, woodland, woods.

wooded *adj.* bosky, forested, nemorous, silvan, timbered, tree-covered, woody. *antonym* open.

wooden *adj.* awkward, blank, clumsy, colourless, deadpan, dense, dim, dim-witted, dull, dull-witted, emotionless, empty, expressionless, gauche, gawky, glassy, graceless, inelegant, inflexible, lifeless, ligneous, maladroit, muffled, oaken, obstinate, obtuse, rigid, slow, spiritless, stiff, stupid, thick, timber, treen, unbending, unemotional, ungainly, unresponsive, unyielding, vacant, woody, xyloid. *antonyms* bright, lively.

woodland *n.* boscage, forest, frith (firth), wood(s).

woody *adj.* bosky, forested, ligneous, sylvan, tree-covered, wooded, wooden, xyloid. *antonym* open.

wool *n.* down, fleece, floccus, fluff, hair, yarn.

woolly *adj.* blurred, clouded, confused, fleecy, floccose, flocculent, foggy, frizzy, fuzzy, hairy, hazy, ill-defined, indefinite, indistinct, lanate, laniferous, lanigerous, lanose, muddled, nappy, nebulous, shaggy, ulotrichous, unclear, vague, woolled, woollen, woolly-haired.

n. cardigan, guernsey, jersey, jumper, pullover, sweater.

woozy *adj.* befuddled, bemused, blurred, confused, dazed, dizzy, fuddled, nauseated, pickled, pixil(l)ated, rocky, tipsy, unsteady, vague, wobbly, woolly.

antonyms alert, sober.

word *n.* account, advice, affirmation, assertion, assurance, bidding, bulletin, chat, colloquy, command, commandment, comment, communication, communiqué, confab, confabulation, consultation, conversation, countersign, declaration, decree, dicky-bird, discussion, dispatch, edict, expression, firman, go-ahead, green light, guarantee, hatti-sherif, hint, information, intelligence, interlocution, intimation, lexigram, locution, mandate, message, news, notice, oath, order, palabra, parole, password, pledge, promise, remark, report, rescript, rumour, sign, signal, slogan, talk, term, tête-à-tête, tidings, ukase, undertaking, utterance, vocable, vow, war-cry, watch-word, will.

v. couch, explain, express, phrase, put, say, write.

wordiness *n.* logorrhoea, perissology, verbal diarrhoea, verbiage, wordage.

wording *n.* choice of words, diction, language, phraseology, phrasing, style, terminology, verbiage, wordage, words.

word-lover *n.* logodaedalus, philologist, philologue, verbalist, verbarian, vocabularian, wordsmith.

word-perfect *adj.* accurate, exact, faithful, letter-perfect, spot-on.

antonym inaccurate.

word-play *n.* paronomasia, punning, puns, repartee, wit, witticisms.

words *n.* altercation, argument, barney, bickering, contention, disagreement, dispute, libretto, lyrics, quarrel, row, run-in, set-to, squabble, text.

wordy *adj.* diffuse, discursive, garrulous, longiloquent, long-winded, loquacious, phrasy, pleonastic, prolix, rambling, verbose, windy.

antonyms concise, laconic.

work *n.* achievement, art, assignment, book, business, calling, chore, commission, composition, craft, creation, darg, deed, doings, drudgery, duty, effort, elbow grease, employ, employment, exertion, graft, grind, handiwork, industry, job, labour, line, livelihood, métier, occupation, oeuvre, office, opus, ouvrage, performance, piece, play, poem, production, profession, pursuit, service, skill, slog, stint, sweat, task, toil, trade, travail, undertaking, workload, workmanship.

antonyms hobby, play, rest.

v. accomplish, achieve, act, arrange, beaver, bring about, bring off, cause, contrive,

control, convulse, create, cultivate, dig, direct, drive, drudge, effect, encompass, execute, exploit, farm, fashion, fiddle, fix, force, form, function, go, graft, handle, implement, knead, labour, make, manage, manipulate, manoeuvre, mould, move, operate, peg away, perform, ply, process, progress, pull off, run, shape, slave, slog, sweat, swing, till, toil, twitch, use, wield, writhe.

antonyms fail, play, rest.

work on butter up, cajole, coax, dissuade, influence, inveigle, persuade, soft-soap, sweet-talk, talk round, wheedle.

work out accomplish, achieve, add up to, amount to, arrange, attain, calculate, clear up, come out, come to, construct, contrive, develop, devise, drill, effect, elaborate, evolve, excogitate, exercise, exhaust, expiate, figure out, flourish, form, formulate, go, happen, pan out, plan, practise, prosper, put together, puzzle out, reach, resolve, result, solve, succeed, train, turn out, warm up, win, worry out.

work up agitate, animate, arouse, elaborate, enkindle, excite, expand, foment, generate, incite, increase, inflame, instigate, move, rouse, spur, stir up, wind up.

workable *adj.* doable, effectible, feasible, possible, practicable, practical, realistic, viable.

antonym unworkable.

workaday *adj.* common, commonplace, dull, everyday, familiar, humdrum, labouring, mundane, ordinary, practical, prosaic, routine, run-of-the-mill, toiling, work-day, working.

antonym exciting.

worker *n.* artisan, craftsman, employee, hand, labourer, proletarian, staffer, tradesman, work-girl, workhorse, working man, working woman, workman, work-woman.

antonym idler.

workforce *n.* employees, hands, labour, labour force, personnel, shop-floor, staff, workers, workfolk(s), work-people.

working *n.* action, functioning, manner, method, operation, routine, running.

adj. active, employed, functioning, going, labouring, operational, operative, running.

antonyms idle, inoperative, retired, unemployed.

workings *n.* diggings, excavations, mine, pit, quarry, shaft.

workman *n.* artificer, artisan, craftsman, employee, hand, journeyman, labourer, mechanic, navvy, operative, tradesman, worker.

workmanlike *adj.* adept, careful, efficient, expert, masterly, painstaking, professional, proficient, satisfactory, skilful, skilled, thorough, workmanly.

antonym amateurish.

workmanship *n.* art, artistry, craft, craftsmanship, execution, expertise, facture, finish, handicraft, handiwork, manufacture, skill, technique, work.

work-mate *n.* associate, colleague, co-worker, fellow-worker, work-fellow, yoke-fellow, yoke-mate.

works[1] *n.* factory, foundry, mill, plant, shop, workshop.

works[2] *n.* actions, acts, books, canon, deeds, doings, oeuvre, output, plays, poetry, productions, writings.

works[3] *n.* action, gearing, guts, innards, insides, machinery, mechanism, movement, parts, workings.

workshop *n.* atelier, class, discussion group, factory, mill, plant, school, seminar, shop, studio, symposium, workroom, works.

world *n.* age, area, class, creation, days, division, domain, earth, environment, epoch, era, existence, field, globe, human race, humanity, humankind, kingdom, life, man, mankind, men, nature, people, period, planet, province, public, realm, society, sphere, star, system, terrene, times, universe, Welt.

worldly *adj.* ambitious, avaricious, blasé, carnal, cosmopolitan, covetous, earthly, experienced, fleshly, grasping, greedy, knowing, lay, materialistic, mundane, physical, politic, profane, secular, selfish, sophisticated, sublunary, temporal, terrene, terrestrial, unspiritual, urbane, worldly-minded, worldly-wise.
antonym unworldly.

worldwide *adj.* catholic, general, global, international, mondial, pandemic, ubiquitous, universal.
antonym local.

worn *adj.* attrite, bromidic, careworn, cliché'd, drawn, exhausted, fatigued, frayed, hackneyed, haggard, jaded, lined, pinched, played-out, ragged, shabby, shiny, spent, tattered, tatty, threadbare, tired, trite, wearied, weary, wizened, woe-wearied, woe-worn, worn-out.
antonyms fresh, new.

worn out all in, clapped out, clapped-out, dead on one's feet, decrepit, dog-tired, done, done in, épuisé(e), exhausted, fatigued, finished, fit to drop, forswunk, frayed, jiggered, knackered, moth-eaten, on its last legs, played-out, prostrate, ragged, shabby, spent, tattered, tatty, threadbare, tired, tired out, used, useless, warby, weary, worn, zonked.
antonym fresh.

worried *adj.* afraid, agonised, anxious, apprehensive, bothered, concerned, distracted, distraught, distressed, disturbed, fearful, frabbit, fretful, frightened, ill at ease, nervous, on edge, overwrought, perturbed, strained, tense, tormented, troubled, uneasy, unquiet, upset.
antonyms calm, unconcerned, unworried.

worrisome *adj.* agonising, anxious, apprehensive, bothersome, disquieting, distressing, disturbing, fretful, frightening, insecure, irksome, jittery, nail-biting, nervous, perturb-

ing, troublesome, uneasy, upsetting, vexing, worrying.
antonyms calm, reassuring, unworried.

worry *v.* agonise, annoy, attack, badger, bite, bother, brood, deave, disquiet, distress, disturb, faze, feeze, frab, fret, get one's knickers in a twist, gnaw at, go for, harass, harry, hassle, hector, importune, irritate, kill, lacerate, nag, perturb, pester, plague, savage, tantalise, tear, tease, torment, trouble, unsettle, upset, vex.
antonyms comfort, reassure.
n. agitation, annoyance, anxiety, apprehension, care, concern, disturbance, fear, irritation, misery, misgiving, perplexity, pest, plague, problem, stew, tew, tizz, tizzy, torment, trial, trouble, unease, vexation, woe, worriment.
antonyms comfort, reassurance.

worrying *adj.* anxious, disquieting, distressing, disturbing, harassing, nail-biting, perturbing, troublesome, trying, uneasy, unsettling, upsetting, worrisome.
antonym reassuring.

worsen *v.* aggravate, damage, decay, decline, degenerate, deteriorate, disimprove, exacerbate, go downhill, pejorate, retrogress, sink, take a turn for the worse.
antonym improve.

worsening *n.* decay, decline, degeneration, deterioration, exacerbation, pejoration, retrogression.
antonym improvement.

worship *v.* adore, adulate, deify, exalt, glorify, honour, idolatrise, idolise, kanticoy, laud, love, misworship, praise, pray to, respect, revere, reverence, venerate.
antonym despise.
n. adoration, adulation, deification, devotion(s), dulia, exaltation, glorification, glory, homage, honour, hyperdulia, image-worship, knee-drill, latria, latry, laudation, love, misdevotion, misworship, monolatry, praise, prayer(s), puja, regard, respect, reverence, will-worship.
antonym vilification.

worst *v.* beat, best, conquer, crush, defeat, drub, master, overcome, overpower, overthrow, subdue, subjugate, vanquish, whitewash.

worth *n.* aid, assistance, avail, benefit, cost, credit, desert(s), excellence, goodness, help, importance, merit, price, quality, rate, significance, use, usefulness, utility, value, virtue, worthiness.
antonym worthlessness.

worthless *adj.* abandoned, abject, base, beggarly, Brummagem, contemptible, depraved, despicable, draffish, draffy, futile, good-for-nothing, grotty, ignoble, ineffectual, insignificant, littleworth, meaningless, miserable, no use, no-account, nugatory, paltry, pointless, poor, rubbishy, scabbed, scabby, screwy, stramineous, trashy, trifling, trivial, unavailing, unimportant, unusable, useless, valueless, vaurien, vile, wretched.

antonym valuable.

worthwhile *adj.* beneficial, constructive, furthersome, gainful, good, helpful, justifiable, productive, profitable, useful, utile, valuable, worthy.

antonym useless.

worthy *adj.* admirable, appropriate, commendable, creditable, decent, dependable, deserving, estimable, excellent, fit, good, honest, honourable, laudable, meritorious, praiseworthy, reliable, reputable, respectable, righteous, suitable, upright, valuable, virtuous, worthwhile.

antonyms disreputable, unworthy.

n. big cheese, big noise, big pot, big shot, big-wig, dignitary, luminary, name, notable, personage.

wound *n.* anguish, cut, damage, distress, gash, grief, harm, heartbreak, hurt, injury, insult, laceration, lesion, offence, pain, pang, scar, shock, slash, slight, torment, torture, trauma.

v. annoy, bless, cut, cut to the quick, damage, distress, gash, grieve, harm, hit, hurt, injure, irritate, lacerate, mortify, offend, pain, pierce, pip, shock, slash, sting, traumatise, wing, wring someone's withers.

wraith *n.* apparition, ghost, larva, lemur, phantom, revenant, shade, spectre, spirit, spook.

wrangle *n.* altercation, argument, argy-bargy, barney, bickering, brawl, clash, contest, controversy, dispute, quarrel, row, set-to, slanging match, squabble, tiff, tussle.

antonym agreement.

v. altercate, argue, argufy, bicker, brawl, contend, digladiate, disagree, dispute, ergotise, fall out, fight, quarrel, row, scrap, squabble.

antonym agree.

wrap *v.* absorb, bind, bundle up, cloak, cocoon, cover, encase, enclose, enfold, envelop, fold, hap, immerse, muffle, pack, package, roll up, sheathe, shroud, surround, swathe, wind.

antonym unwrap.

n. cape, cloak, mantle, pelisse, robe, shawl, stole.

wrap up[1] bring to a close, complete, conclude, end, finish off, pack up, package, parcel, round off, terminate, wind up.

antonym begin.

wrap up[2] be quiet, hold one's tongue, hold one's wheesht, put a sock in it, shoosh, shut it, shut one's cakehole, shut one's face, shut one's mouth, shut one's trap, shut up, wheesht.

wrapper *n.* cover, dust-jacket, envelope, jacket, packaging, paper, sheath, sleeve, wrapping.

wrapping *n.* blister card, blister pack, bubble pack, carton, case, cellophane®, envelope, Jiffybag®, packaging, paper, silver-paper, swathe, tinfoil, wrappage.

wrath *n.* anger, bitterness, choler, displeasure, exasperation, fury, indignation, ire, irritation, passion, rage, resentment, spleen, temper.

antonyms calm, pleasure.

wrathful *adj.* angry, bitter, displeased, enraged, furibund, furious, gusty, in a paddy, incensed, indignant, infuriated, irate, ireful, on the warpath, raging, waxy, wrathy, wroth.

antonyms calm, pleased.

wreak *v.* bestow, bring about, carry out, cause, create, effect, execute, exercise, express, inflict, perpetrate, unleash, vent, visit, work.

wreath *n.* anadem, band, chaplet, coronet, crown, festoon, garland, lei, loop, ring.

wreathe *v.* adorn, coil, crown, encircle, enfold, entwine, envelop, enwrap, festoon, intertwine, interweave, surround, swathe, twine, twist, wind, wrap, writhe.

wreck *v.* break, crab, demolish, destroy, devastate, mar, play havoc with, ravage, ruin, shatter, smash, spoil, torpedo, write off.

antonyms repair, save.

n. derelict, desolation, destruction, devastation, disruption, hulk, mess, overthrow, ruin, ruination, shipwreck, undoing, write-off.

wreckage *n.* debris, flotsam, fragments, pieces, remains, rubble, ruin, waveson, wrack.

wrench *v.* distort, force, jerk, pull, rax, rick, rip, sprain, strain, tear, tug, twist, wrest, wring, yank.

n. ache, blow, jerk, monkey-wrench, pain, pang, pliers, pull, sadness, shock, sorrow, spanner, sprain, tear, tug, twist, upheaval, uprooting.

wrest *v.* extract, force, pervert, pull, seize, strain, take, twist, win, wrench, wring.

wrestle *v.* battle, combat, contend, contest, fight, grapple, scuffle, strive, struggle, tussle, vie.

wretch *n.* blackguard, cad, caitiff, cullion, cur, good-for-nothing, insect, miscreant, outcast, pilgarlick, profligate, rapscallion, rascal, rascallion, rat, rogue, rotter, ruffian, scoundrel, swine, vagabond, villain, wight, worm.

wretched *adj.* abject, base, broken-hearted, caitiff, calamitous, cheerless, comfortless, contemptible, crestfallen, dejected, deplorable, depressed, despicable, disconsolate, distressed, doggone, doleful, downcast, forlorn, gloomy, grotty, hapless, hopeless, inferior, low, low-down, mean, melancholy, miserable, paltry, pathetic, pesky, pitiable, pitiful, poor, ratty, scurvy, shabby, shameful, sorry, unfortunate, unhappy, vile, woebegone, woeful, worthless.

antonyms excellent, happy.

wriggle *v.* crawl, dodge, edge, extricate, jerk, jiggle, manoeuvre, scriggle, sidle, slink, snake, sneak, squiggle, squirm, talk one's way out, turn, twist, wag, waggle, wiggle, worm, writhe, zigzag.

n. jerk, jiggle, squirm, turn, twist, twitch, wag, waggle, wiggle.

wring *v.* coerce, distress, exact, extort, extract, force, hurt, lacerate, mangle, pain, pierce, rack, rend, screw, squeeze, stab, tear, torture, twist, wound, wrench, wrest.

wrinkle *n.* corrugation, crease, crinkle, crow's-foot, crumple, fold, furrow, gather, line, pucker, rumple, wimple.

v. corrugate, crease, crinkle, crumple, fold, furrow, gather, line, pucker, rivel, ruck, rumple, runkle, shrivel.

wrinkled *adj.* creased, crinkled, crinkly, crumpled, furrowed, puckered, ridged, rivelled, rugate, rugose, rugous, rumpled, wrinkly. *antonym* smooth.

writ *n.* court order, decree, subpoena, summons.

write *v.* compose, copy, correspond, create, draft, draw up, indite, inscribe, jot down, pen, record, screeve, scribble, scribe, set down, take down, tell, transcribe.

write off cancel, crash, cross out, destroy, disregard, scrub, smash up, wreck.

writer *n.* amanuensis, author, authoress, clerk, columnist, copyist, crime writer, detectivist, dialogist, diarist, diatribist, dramatist, dramaturg, dramaturgist, elegiast, elegist, encomiast, epigrammatist, epistler, epistolarian, epistoler, epistolist, epitapher, epitaphist, epitomist, essayist, farceur, fictionist, hack, librettist, littérateur, man of letters, memoirist, novelist, panegyrist, paper-stainer, pen, penman, penny-a-liner, penpusher, penwoman, periodicalist, playwright, prosaist, proseman, proser, prose-writer, quill-driver, scribbler, scribe, secretary, wordsmith, writeress.

writhe *v.* coil, contort, jerk, squirm, struggle, thrash, thresh, toss, twist, wiggle, wreathe, wriggle.

writing *n.* autography, belles-lettres, book, calligraphy, chirography, composition, document, exaration, hand, handwriting, letter, letters, literature, opus, penmanship, print, publication, scrawl, scribble, script, work.

written *adj.* documental, documentary, drawn up, recorded, set down, transcribed. *antonyms* unwritten, verbal.

wrong *adj.* abusive, amis, askew, awry, bad, blameworthy, criminal, crooked, defective, dishonest, dishonourable, erroneous, evil, fallacious, false, faulty, felonious, funny, illegal, illicit, immoral, improper, in error, in the wrong, inaccurate, inappropriate, inapt, incongruous, incorrect, indecorous, infelicitous, iniquitous, inner, inside, inverse, malapropos, misinformed, mistaken, off beam, off target, off-base, opposite, out, out of commission, out of order, reprehensible, reverse, sinful, unacceptable, unbecoming, unconventional, under, undesirable, unethical, unfair, unfitting, unhappy, unjust, unlawful, unseemly, unsound, unsuitable, untrue, wicked, wide of the mark, wrongful, wrongous. *antonym* right.

adv. amiss, askew, astray, awry, badly, erroneously, faultily, improperly, inaccurately, incorrectly, mistakenly, wrongly. *antonym* right.

n. abuse, crime, error, grievance, immorality, inequity, infraction, infringement, iniquity, injury, injustice, misdeed, offence, sin, sinfulness, transgression, trespass, unfairness, wickedness, wrong-doing. *antonym* right.

v. abuse, cheat, discredit, dishonour, harm, hurt, ill-treat, ill-use, impose on, injure, malign, maltreat, misrepresent, mistreat, oppress, traduce.

wrong-doer *n.* criminal, culprit, delinquent, evil-doer, felon, law-breaker, malefactor, miscreant, offender, sinner, transgressor, trespasser.

wrong-doing *n.* crime, delinquency, error, evil, fault, felony, immorality, iniquity, maleficence, mischief, misdeed, offence, sin, sinfulness, transgression, wickedness.

wrongful *adj.* blameworthy, criminal, dishonest, dishonourable, evil, felonious, illegal, illegitimate, illicit, immoral, improper, reprehensible, unethical, unfair, unjust, unlawful, wicked, wrong, wrongous. *antonym* rightful.

wrongly *adv.* badly, by mistake, erroneously, in error, inaccurately, incorrectly, mistakenly. *antonym* rightly.

wrought *adj.* beaten, decorative, fashioned, hammered, made, manufactured, ornamental, ornamented, ornate, shaped.

wry *adj.* askew, aslant, awry, contorted, crooked, deformed, distorted, droll, dry, ironic, mocking, pawky, perverse, sarcastic, sardonic, thrawn, twisted, uneven, warped. *antonym* straight.

X Y Z

xenophobia *n.* ethnocentrism, racialism, racism, xenophoby.
antonym xenomania.

xenophobic *adj.* ethnocentrist, parochial, racialist, racist.

ya(c)k *v.* blather, chatter, gab, gossip, jabber, jaw, prattle, run on, tattle, twattle, witter on, yap, yatter.
n. blah, blather, chat, chinwag, confab, gossip, hot air, jaw, prattle, twattle, ya(c)kety-ya(c)k, yatter.

yank *v., n.* haul, heave, jerk, pull, snatch, tug, wrench.

yap *v.* babble, blather, chatter, go on, gossip, jabber, jaw, prattle, talk, tattle, twattle, ya(c)k, yammer, yatter, yelp, yip.

yard *n.* court, court-yard, garden, garth, Hof, hypaethron, quad, quadrangle.

yardstick *n.* benchmark, comparison, criterion, gauge, measure, standard, touchstone.

yarn [1] *n.* abb, fibre, fingering, gimp, lisle, thread.

yarn [2] *n.* anecdote, cock-and-bull story, fable, fabrication, story, tale, tall story.

yawn *v.* gape, ga(u)nt, open, split.

yawning *adj.* cavernous, gaping, hiant, huge, vast, wide, wide-open.
antonym narrow.

yearly *adj.* annual, per annum, per year.
adv. annually, every year, once a year.

yearn for ache for, covet, crave, desire, hanker for, hunger for, itch for, languish for, long for, lust for, pant for, pine for, want, wish for, yen for.
antonym dislike.

yell *v.* bawl, bellow, holler, hollo, howl, roar, scream, screech, shout, shriek, squawl, squeal, whoop, yelp, yowl.
antonym whisper.
n. bellow, cry, holler, hollo, howl, roar, scream, screech, shriek, squawl, whoop, yelp.
antonym whisper.

yellow *adj.* flavescent, flaxen, fulvid, fulvous, gold, golden, lemon, primrose, saffron, vitellary, vitelline, xanthic, xanthochroic, xanthomelanous, xanthous.

yelp *v.* bark, bay, cry, yap, yell, yip, yowl.
n. bark, cry, yap, yell, yip, yowl.

yen *n.* craving, desire, hankering, hunger, itch, longing, lust, passion, thing, yearning.
antonym dislike.

yes *interj.* absolutely, affirmative, agreed, quite, right, uh-huh, yea, yeah, yep.
antonym no.

yes-man *n.* arse-licker, bootlicker, crawler, creature, lackey, minion, sycophant, toadeater, toady.

yesterday's *adj.* bygone, hesternal, passé, past, stale.
antonym tomorrow's.

yield [1] *v.* abandon, abdicate, accede, acquiesce, admit defeat, agree, allow, bow, capitulate, cave in, cede, comply, concede, consent, cry quits, give, give in, give way, go along with, grant, knuckle under, part with, permit, relinquish, resign, resign oneself, submit, succumb, surrender, throw in the towel.
antonym withstand.

yield [2] *v.* afford, bear, bring forth, bring in, earn, fructify, fructuate, fruit, furnish, generate, give, net, pay, produce, provide, return, supply.
n. crop, earnings, harvest, income, output, proceeds, produce, product, profit, return, revenue, takings.

yielding *adj.* accommodating, acquiescent, amenable, biddable, complaisant, compliant, docile, easy, elastic, flexible, obedient, obliging, pliable, pliant, quaggy, resilient, soft, spongy, springy, submissive, supple, tractable, unresisting.
antonyms obstinate, solid.

yobbo *n.* apache, corner-boy, hoodlum, hooligan, keelie, loafer, lout, rough, rowdy, ruffian, thug, tough, yahoo, yob.

yoke *n.* bond, bondage, burden, chain, coupling, enslavement, helotry, ligament, link, oppression, serfdom, service, servility, servitude, slavery, subjugation, thraldom, tie, vassalage.
v. bracket, connect, couple, enslave, harness, hitch, inspan, join, link, tie, unite.
antonym unhitch.

yokel *n.* boor, bucolic, bumpkin, clodhopper, corn-ball, country cousin, hick, hillbilly, jake, joskin, peasant, rustic.
antonyms sophisticate, towny.

young *adj.* adolescent, baby, callow, cub, early, fledgling, green, growing, immature, infant, junior, juvenile, little, new, recent, unblown, unfledged, youthful.
antonym old.
n. babies, brood, chicks, cubs, family, fledglings, issue, litter, little ones, offspring, progeny, quiverful.
antonym parents.

youngster *n.* boy, girl, juvenile, kid, lad, laddie, lass, lassie, nipper, shaver, teenybopper, urchin, young pup, youth.
antonym oldie.

youth *n.* adolescence, adolescent, boy, boyhood, colt, ephebe, ephebus, girlhood, halflin(g), hobbledehoy, immaturity, juvenescence, juvenile, kid, lad, salad days, shaveling, springal(d), stripling, swain, teenager, the young, young man, young people, young shaver, younger generation, youngster, younker.

antonyms old age, oldie.

youthful *adj.* active, boyish, childish, ephebic, fresh, girlish, immature, inexperienced, juvenescent, juvenile, lively, pubescent, puerile, sprightly, spry, vigorous, vivacious, well-preserved, young.

antonyms aged, languorous.

youthfulness *n.* freshness, juvenileness, juvenility, liveliness, sprightliness, spryness, vigour, vivaciousness, vivacity.

antonyms agedness, languor.

yowl *v.* bay, caterwaul, cry, howl, screech, squall, ululate, wail, yell, yelp.

n. cry, howl, screech, wail, yell, yelp.

yucky *adj.* beastly, dirty, disgusting, filthy, foul, grotty, horrible, messy, mucky, revolting, saccharine, sentimental, sickly, unpleasant.

antonym nice.

zany *adj.* amusing, clownish, comical, crazy, daft, droll, eccentric, funny, goofy, kooky, loony, madcap, nutty, screwy, wacky.

antonym serious.

n. buffoon, card, clown, comedian, cure, droll, fool, jester, joker, kook, laugh, merry-andrew, nut, nutcase, nutter, screwball, wag.

zeal *n.* ardour, dedication, devotion, eagerness, earnestness, enthusiasm, fanaticism, fervency, fervour, fire, gusto, keenness, militancy, passion, spirit, verve, warmth, zelotypia, zest.

antonym apathy.

zealot *n.* bigot, devotee, enthusiast, extremist, fanatic, fiend, freak, maniac, militant.

zealous *adj.* ardent, burning, devoted, eager, earnest, enthusiastic, fanatical, fervent, fervid, fired, gung-ho, impassioned, keen, militant, passionate, rabid, spirited.

antonym apathetic.

zenith *n.* acme, apex, apogee, climax, culmination, height, high point, meridian, peak, pinnacle, summit, top, vertex.

antonym nadir.

zero *n.* bottom, cipher, duck, goose-egg, love, nadir, naught, nil, nothing, nought.

zero in on aim for, concentrate on, converge on, direct at, fix on, focus on, head for, home in on, level at, pinpoint, train on.

zest *n.* appetite, charm, delectation, élan, enjoyment, flavour, gusto, interest, joie de vivre, keenness, kick, peel, piquancy, pungency, relish, rind, savour, smack, spice, tang, taste, zeal, zing.

antonym apathy.

zigzag *v.* meander, snake, wind, yaw.

adj. meandering, serpentine, sinuous, zigzagging, zigzaggy.

antonym straight.

zing *n.* animation, brio, dash, élan, energy, go, joie de vivre, life, liveliness, oomph, pizzazz, sparkle, spirit, vigour, vitality, zest, zip.

antonym listlessness.

zip *n.* brio, drive, élan, energy, enthusiasm, get-up-and-go, go, gusto, life, liveliness, oomph, pep, pizzazz, punch, sparkle, spirit, verve, vigour, vim, vitality, zest, zing.

antonym listlessness.

v. dash, flash, fly, gallop, hurry, race, rush, scoot, shoot, speed, tear, whiz, whoosh, zoom.

zone *n.* area, belt, district, region, section, sector, sphere, stratum, territory, tract, zona, zonule, zonulet.

zoo *n.* animal park, aquarium, aviary, menagerie, safari park, zoological gardens.

zoom *v.* buzz, dash, dive, flash, fly, gallop, hare, hurtle, pelt, race, rush, scoot, shoot, speed, streak, tear, whirl, whiz, whoosh, zip.

Appendices

Appendix I

Classified word-lists

air and space vehicles aerobus, aerodrome, aerodyne, aerohydroplane, aeroplane, aerostat, air-ambulance, air-bus, airship, all-wing aeroplane, amphibian, autogiro, balloon, biplane, blimp, bomber, cable-car, camel, canard, chopper, comsat, convertiplane, crate, delta-wing, dirigible, dive bomber, fan-jet, fighter, fire-balloon, flying boat, flying saucer, flying wing, glider, gondola, gyrocopter, gyroplane, helibus, helicopter, hoverbus, hovercar, hovercraft, hovertrain, hydro-aeroplane, hydrofoil, hydroplane, intercepter, jet, jetliner, jetplane, lem, microlight, module, monoplane, multiplane, plane, rocket, rocket-plane, runabout, sailplane, satellite, seaplane, space platform, space probe, space shuttle, spacecraft, spaceship, spitfire, sputnik, step-rocket, stol, strato-cruiser, stratotanker, swingtail cargo aircraft, swing-wing, tanker, taube, téléférique, tow-plane, tractor, triplane, troop-carrier, tube, tug, turbojet, turbo-jet, twoseater, UFO, warplane, zeppelin.

alphabets and writing systems Chalcidian alphabet, cuneiform, Cyrillic, devanagari, estrang(h)elo, finger-alphabet, futhark, Glagol, Glossic, Greek, Gurmukhi, hieroglyphs, hiragana, ideograph, kana, katakana, Kufic, linear A, linear B, logograph, nagari, naskhi, og(h)am, pictograph, Roman, runic, syllabary.

anatomical abductor, acromion, adductor, alvine, ancon, astragalus, atlas, aural, auricular, axilla, biceps, blade-bone, bone, brachial, bregma, buccal, calcaneum, calcaneus, capitate, cardiac, carpal, carpus, cartilage, cephalic, cerebral, cholecyst, clavicle, coccyx, c(o)eliac, collar-bone, concha, coracoid, crural, cuboid, cuneiform, deltoid, dental, derm, derma, dermal, dermic, diaphragm, diencephalon, digital, diploe, diverticulum, dorsal, dorsolumbar, dorsum, duodenal, duodenum, dura mater, earlap, elbow, enarthrosis, encephalic, encephalon, endocardiac, endocardial, endocardium, endocrinal, endocrine, epencephalic, epencephalon, epidermal, epidermic, epidermis, epididymis, epigastric, epigastrium, epiglottic, epiglottis, epithelium, eponychium, erythrocyte, ethmoid, extensor, Fallopian tubes, false rib, femur, fenestra ovalis, fenestra rotunda, fibula, flexor, floating rib, fontanel(le), fonticulus, foramen magnum, forearm, forebrain, forefinger, foreskin, fourchette, fr(a)enum, frontal, funiculus, funny bone, gastric, gastrocnemius, gena, genal, genial, genitalia, genu, gingival, glabella, glabellar, gladiolus, glossa, glossal, glottal, glottic, glottis, glut(a)eus, gnathal, gnathic, gonion, gracilis, gremial, gristle, groin, gula, gular, gullet, guttural, h(a)emal, haematic, hallux, ham, hamate, hamstring, helix, hepatic, hind-brain, hindhead, hip-bone, hip-girdle, hock, huckle-bone, humeral, humerus, hyoid, hypogastrium, hypothalamus, iliac, ilium, incus, inguinal, innominate, innominate bone, intercostal, ischium, jugular, labial, lachrymal, lacrimal, leucocyte, ligament, lumbar, lumbrical, lunate, luz, malar, malleolus, malleus, mamillar(y), mammary, mandible, mandibular, manubrium, marriage-bone, mastoid, maxilla, maxillary, membral, mental, merrythought, metacarpal, metatarsal, mons veneris, mount of Venus, muscle, nasal, nates,

anatomical *contd.*

navicular, neural, obturators, occipital, occiput, occlusal, occlusion, occlusor, ocular,
odontic, (o)esophagus, omentum, omohyoid, omoplate, optical, orbicularis,
orbit(a), origin, os innominatum, oscheal, oscular, ossicle, otic, otolith, palatal,
palatine, palpebral, parasphenoid, parietal, paroccipital, parotid, patella, patellar,
pecten, pectoral, pedal, pelvic girdle, pelvis, periotic, perone, phalanges, pisiform,
plantar, popliteal, poplitic, prefrontal, premaxilla, premaxillary, pronator, prootic,
prosencephalon, psoas, pubis, pudenda, pulmonary, quadriceps, radius, renal,
rhomboid, rib, rictal, sacrocostal, sacrum, sartorius, scaphoid, scapula, sesamoid,
shoulder-blade, shoulder-bone, skull, soleus, spade-bone, sphenoid, spine,
splinter-bone, stapes, sternum, stirrup-bone, supinator, sural, talus, tarsal, temporal,
tendon, thigh-bone, tibia, trapezium, trapezius, trapezoid, triceps, triquetral,
turbinal, tympanic, ulna, umbilicus, unguis, urachus, uterus, uvula, vagus, vas
deferens, velum, vermis, vertebra, vertebrae, vertex, vesica, voice-box, vomer,
vulva, windpipe, wisdom tooth, womb, wrist, xiphisternum, xiphoid, zygapophysis,
zygoma, zygomatic.

architecture and building abacus, abutment, acrolith, acroter, acroterial, acroterion,
acroterium, alcove, annulet, anta, antefix, araeostyle, architrave, ashlar, ashler,
astragal, baguette, bandelet, banderol(e), barge-board, barge-couple, barge-stones,
battlement, bellcote, bema, bratticing, canephor, canton, cartouche, caryatid,
Catherine-wheel, cavetto, centering, cinque-foil, concha, corbeil, corbel,
corner-stone, corona, cradling, crenel, crocket, crossette, cruck, cul-de-four, dado,
decorated, demi-bastion, demi-lune, dentil, diaconicon, diaper, diastyle, diglyph,
dimension work, dinette, dipteros, distyle, ditriglyph, dodecastyle, dog-leg(ged),
dogtooth, dome, domed, domical, donjon, Doric, dormer, double-glazing, doucine,
drawbridge, drawing-room, dreamhole, dressing, drip, dripstone, dromic, dromos,
drum, dry-stone, duplex, Early English, eaves, echinus, egg-and-anchor,
egg-and-dart, egg-and-tongue, egg-box, el, elevation, Elizabethan, embattlement,
embrasure, emplection, encarpus, engage, engaged, engrail, enneastyle, entresol,
epaule, epaulement, epistyle, eustyle, exedra, extrados, eye-catcher, façade, fan
tracery, fan vaulting, fanlight, fascia, fastigium, feathering, fenestella, fenestra,
fenestral, fenestration, festoon, fillet, finial, flamboyant, flèche, Flemish bond,
fletton, fleuron, foliation, fornicate, fortalice, French sash/window, frieze, fronton,
furring, fusarol(e), fust, gable, gablet, galilee, gambrel roof, gargoyle, gatehouse,
glacis, glyph, gopura(m), gorgerin, Gothic, gradin(e), griff(e), groin, groundplan,
groundsel, guilloche, gutta, hagioscope, half-timbered, hammer-beam,
hammer-brace, hance, hanging buttress, harling, haunch, haute époque, headstone,
heart, helix, herringbone, hexastyle, hip, hip-knob, holderbat, hood-mould(ing),
hypostyle, imbrex, imbricate, imbrication, imperial, impost, impostume,
intercolumniation, intrados, jamb, javelin, jerkinhead, knosp, lierne, linen-fold,
linen-scroll, lintel, mansard(-roof), mascaron, merlon, metope, modillion,
monostyle, mullion, muntin(g), mutule, Norman, oeil-de-boeuf, ogee,
opisthodomos, oriel, out-wall, ovolo, ox-eye, pagoda, pantile, parget, patera,
paternoster, patten, pediment, pilaster, pineapple, pinnacle, plafond, platband,
plateresque, plinth, poppy-head, predella, propylaeum, propylon, prostyle, pylon,
quatrefeuille, quatrefoil, queen-post, quirk, rear-arch, reglet, regula, rere-arch,
retrochoir, reredos, revet, rocaille, rococo, Romanesque, rood-loft, rood-screen,
rood-steeple, rood-tower, roof, roof-tree, rosace, rose, rosette, rotunda, roughcast,

architecture and building *contd.*

sacristy, skew-back, socle, soffit, solidum, spandrel, strap-work, stria, string-course, subbasal, surbase, swag, systyle, tabernacle-work, table, telamon, terrazzo, tierceron, tondino, toroid, torsel, torus, trabeation, tracery, triforium, trumeau, tympanum, vault, vaultage, vaulted, vaulting, Venetian mosaic, vermiculate(d), vice, vitrail, vitrailled, Vitruvian, volute, voussoir, wainscot, wall-plate, water-joint, water-table, weathering, xystus.

art abstract, abstraction, action painting, anaglyph, anastasis, anastatic, anthemion, aquarelle, bas relief, Bauhaus, camaieu, cire perdue, dadaism, decal, decoupage, Der Blaue Reiter, diaglyph, Die Brücke, diptych, dry-point, duotone, écorché, enamel, encaustic, engraving, etch, etchant, faience, fashion-plate, Fauve, Fauvism, fête champêtre, figurine, filigree, flambé, flannelgraph, Flemish, flesh-tint, Florentine, free-hand, fresco, fret, frit, futurism, futurist, gadroon, genre, gesso, glyptics, glyptography, Gobelin, gouache, graphic, graphics, graphium, graticulation, gravure, grecque, grisaille, gumption, hachure, hatch, hatching, haut relief, herm(a), historiated, hound's-tooth, intaglio, linocut, literalism, litho, lithochromatic(s), lithochromy, lithograph, lithoprint, lost wax, mandorla, meander, monotint, monotype, morbidezza, Parian, paysage, phylactery, pietra-dura, piqué, pochoir, pompier, putto, quattrocento, relievo, repoussage, repoussé, reserved, retroussage, rilievo, sculp(t), scumble, sea-piece, seascape, secco, serigraph, statuary, stipple, stylus, surrealism, symbolism, tachism(e), tempera, tenebrism, tessellated, tessera, tondo, trecento, triptych, ukiyo-e, velatura, Venetian mosaic, Venetian red, verditer, verism, vermiculate(d), versal, vitrail, vitraillist, vitrifacture, vitrine, vitro-di-trina, volute, vorticism, woodblock, wood-carving, woodcut, wood-engraving, xoanon, zoomorphic.

canonical hours compline, lauds, matins, none, orthros, prime, sext, terce, undern, vespers.

cattle breeds Africander, Alderney, Angus, Ankole, Ayrshire, Blonde d'Aquitaine, Brahman, Brown Swiss, cattabu, cattalo, Charol(l)ais, Chillingham, Devon, dexter, Durham, Friesian, Galloway, Guernsey, Hereford, Highland, Holstein, Jersey, Latvian, Limousin, Luing, Red Poll, Romagnola, Santa Gertrudis, short-horn, Simmenthaler, Teeswater, Ukrainian, Welsh Black.

cheeses Amsterdam, Bel Paese, Blarney, Bleu d'Auvergne, Blue Vinny, Boursin, Brie, Caboc, Caerphilly, Camembert, Carré, Cheddar, Cheshire, Chevrotin, Colwick, Coulommiers, Crowdie, Danish blue, Derby, Dolcelatte, Dorset Blue, double Gloucester, Dunlop, Edam, Emmental, Emment(h)al(er), Esrom, ewe-cheese, Feta, Fynbo, Gammelost, G(j)etost, Gloucester, Gorgonzola, Gouda, Grana, Grevé, Gruyère, Handkäse, Havarti, Herrgårdsost, Herve, Huntsman, Hushållsost, Islay, Jarlsberg, Killarney, Kryddost, Lancashire, Leicester, Limburg(er), Lymeswold, mouse-trap, mozzarella, Munster, Mysost, Neufchâtel, Parmesan, Petit Suisse, pipo creme, Pont-l'Éveque, Port(-du-)Salut, Prästost, Provolone, Pultost, Raclette, Red Windsor, Reggiano, ricotta, Romadur, Roquefort, sage Derby, Saint-Paulin, Samsø, sapsago, Stilton, stracchino, Tilsit(er), Vacherin, Wensleydale, Wexford.

chemical elements Actinium, Aluminium, Americium, Antimony, Argon, Arsenic, Astatine, Barium, Berkelium, Beryllium, Bismuth, Boron, Bromine, Cadmium, Caesium, Calcium, Californium, Carbon, Cerium, Chlorine, Chromium, Cobalt, Copper, Curium, Dysprosium, Einsteinium, Erbium, Europium, Fermium,

chemical elements *contd.*
Fluorine, Francium, Gadolinium, Gallium, Germanium, Gold, Hafnium, Hahnium, Helium, Holmium, Hydrogen, Indium, Iodine, Iridium, Iron, Krypton, Lanthanum, Lawrencium, Lead, Lithium, Lutetium, Magnesium, Manganese, Mendelevium, Mercury, Molybdenum, Neodymium, Neon, Neptunium, Nickel, Niobium, Nitrogen, Nobelium, Osmium, Oxygen, Palladium, Phosphorus, Platinum, Plutonium, Polonium, Potassium, Praseodymium, Promethium, Protoactinium, Radium, Radon, Rhenium, Rhodium, Rubidium, Ruthenium, Rutherfordium, Samarium, Scandium, Selenium, Silicon, Silver, Sodium, Strontium, Sulphur, Tantalum, Technetium, Tellurium, Terbium, Thallium, Thorium, Thulium, Tin, Titanium, Tungsten, Uranium, Vanadium, Xenon, Ytterbium, Yttrium, Zinc, Zirconium.

cloths, fabrics abaca, abb, alamode, alepine, alpaca, American cloth, angora, armozine, armure, arrasene, astrakhan, atlas, baft, bagging, Balbriggan, baldachin, balzarine, barathea, barege, barracan, batiste, batting, bayadère, bearskin, beaver, beige, bengaline, Binca®, blanket, blanketing, blonde(e)-lace, bobbinet, bobbin-lace, bombasine, bone-lace, botany, bouclé, bo(u)lting cloth, box-cloth, broadcloth, brocade, brocatel(le), broché, Brussels lace, buckram, buckskin, budge, buff, bunting, Burberry, burlap, burnet, burrel, butter-cloth, butter-muslin, byssus, caddis, calamanco, calico, cambric, cameline, camlet, candlewick, canvas, carmelite, carpeting, casement-cloth, cashmere, cassimere, catgut, (cavalry) twill, challis, chamois, chantilly (lace), charmeuse, cheesecloth, damask, damassin, delaine, denim, devil's dust, dhoti, d(h)urrie, diamanté, diaper, dimity, doe-skin, doily, domett, dornick, dowlas, drab, drabbet, drap-de-Berry, dreadnought, drill, droguet, drugget, duchesse lace, duck, duffel, dungaree, dupion, durant, Dutch carpet, ecru, éolienne, façonné, faille, far(r)andine, fearnought, felt, ferret, filet, flannel, flannelette, foulard, foulé, frieze, frocking, fustian, gaberdine, galatea, galloon, gambroon, gauze, genappe, georgette, gingham, Gobelin(s), gold-cloth, gold-lace, grass cloth, grenadine, grogram, grosgrain, guipure, gunny, gurrah, habit-cloth, haircloth, harn, Hessian, hodden, holland, homespun, Honiton, hopsack, horsehair, huckaback, humhum, jaconet, Jaeger®, jamdani, jean, jeanette, jersey, kalamkari, karakul, kente cloth, kersey, kerseymere, khader, khaki, kid, kidskin, kilt, kincob, kip-skin, lamé, lampas, lawn, leather, leather-cloth, leatherette, leghorn, leno, levant, Lincoln-green, linen, linsey, linsey-woolsey, llama, lockram, loden, longcloth, lovat, Lurex®, lustre, lustring, lutestring, mac(k)intosh, madras, mantling, marcella, marocain, maroquin, marquisette, mazarine, Mechlin, medley, melton, merino, Mexican, mignonette, mohair, moire, moleskin, monk's cloth, moreen, morocco, mourning-stuff, mousseline, mousseline-de-laine, mousseline-de-soie, Moygashel®, mull, mulmul(l), mungo, musk-rat, muslin, muslinet, musquash, nacarat, nainsook, nankeen, ninon, nitro-silk, nun's-veiling, nylon, oilcloth, organdie, organza, organzine, orleans, osnaburg, orris, ottoman, overcoating, paduasoy, paisley, panne, paper-cloth, paper-muslin, par(r)amatta, peau-de-soie, penistone, percale, percaline, perse, petersham, piña-cloth, pin-stripe, piqué, plaid, plush, point-lace, polycotton, poplin, poplinette, prunella, purple, quilting, rabanna, ratine (ratteen), raven('s)-duck, rep (repp), roan, russel, russel-cord, russet, sackcloth, sacking, sagathy, sail-cloth, samite, sarsenet, satara, sateen, satin, satinette, satin-sheeting, saxony, say, scarlet, schappe, scrim, seersucker, sendal, serge, shagreen, shalloon, shammy(-leather), shantung, sharkskin, sheepskin,

cloths, fabrics *contd.*

Shetland wool, shoddy, Sicilian, sicilienne, silesia, silk, slipper satin, soneri, split, sponge-cloth, spun silk, stammel, strouding, suede, suedette, suiting, surah, surat, swansdown, swan-skin, tabaret, tabbinet, tabby, taffeta, tamin(e), tamise, tammy, tarlatan, tarpaulin, tartan, tat, Tattersall (check), T-cloth, tentage, tent-cloth, terry, Terylene®, thibet, thickset, thrown-silk, thunder-and-lightning, ticken, tick(ing), tiffany, toile, toilinet(te), torchon lace, towelling, tram, tricot, troll(e)y, tulle, tusser(-silk), tweed, union, Valenciennes, veiling, Velcro®, velour(s), veloutine, velveret, velvet, velveteen, velveting, vicuña, voile, wadmal, waistcoating, watchet, waterwork, waxcloth, webbing, whipcord, wigan, wild silk, wincey, winceyette, wire gauze, woolsey, worcester, worsted, zanella, zephyr.

coins, currencies agora, antoninianus, as, asper, aureus, baht, balboa, bawbee, bekah, belga, bezant, bit, bod(d)le, bolivar, boliviano, bonnet-piece, broad(piece), buck, cardecu(e), Carolus, cash, cent, centavo, centime, chiao, colon, conto, cordoba, couter, crown, crusado, cruzeiro, dam, daric, deaner, décime, denarius, denier, Deutschmark, didrachm(a), dime, dinar, dirham, doit, dollar, double, doubloon, drachma, ducat, dupondius, duro, eagle, écu, eighteen-penny piece, escudo, farthing, fen, fifty-pence piece, fifty-penny piece, five-pence piece, five-penny piece, florin, forint, franc, geordie, gerah, gourde, groat, groschen, guinea, gulden, haler, half-crown, half-dollar, halfpenny, half-sovereign, heller, jacobus, jane, jitney, joe, joey, jo(h)annes, kina, knife-money, koban(g), kopeck, koruna, kreutzer, krona, krone, Krugerrand, kwacha, kyat, lek, lepton, leu, lev, lion, lira, litre, livre, louis, louis-d'or, mag, maik, make, manch, mancus, maravedi, mark, mawpus, merk, mil, millième, millime, milreis, mina, mite, mna, mohur, moidore, mopus, naira, napoleon, (naya) paisa, (new) cedi, ngwee, nickel, nicker, obang, obol, obolus, öre, øre, Paduan, pagoda, paolo, para, patrick, paul, peseta, pesewa, peso, pfennig, piastre, picayune, pice, piece of eight, pine-tree money, pistareen, pistole, pistolet, plack, portague, portcullis, pound, punt, qintar, quetzal, quid, rag, rand, real, red, red cent, reichsmark, reis, rial, rider, riel, ringgit, rix-dollar, riyal, rose-noble, r(o)uble, royal, ruddock, ruddy, rupee, rupiah, ryal, saw-buck, sceat(t), schilling, scudo, semis, semuncia, sen, sequin, sesterce, sestertium, sextans, shekel, shilling, silverling, sixpence, skilling, smacker, sol, soldo, solidus, sou, sovereign, spade-guinea, spur-royal, stater, sterling, stiver, sucre, sword-dollar, sycee, tael, taka, talent, tanner, tenner, tenpence, ten-pence piece, ten-penny piece, tester(n), testo(o)n, testril(l), tetradrachm, thaler, thick'un, thin'un, three-farthings, three-halfpence, threepence, threepenny bit/piece, tical, tick(e)y, tizzy, toman, turner, twenty-pence piece, twenty-penny piece, two bits, twopence, two-pence piece, two-penny piece, unicorn, ure, vellon, wakiki, wampum, won, xerafin, yen, yuan, zack, zecchino, zimbi, zloty, zuz, zwanziger.

collective nouns building of rooks, cast of hawks, cete of badgers, charm of goldfinches, chattering of choughs, clamour of rooks, clowder of cats, covert of coots, covey of partridges, down of hares, drift of swine, drove of cattle, dule of doves, exaltation of larks, fall of woodcock, fesnyng of ferrets, gaggle of geese, gam of whales, gang of elks, grist of bees, husk of hares, kindle of kittens, leap of leopards, leash of bucks, murder of crows, murmuration of starlings, muster of peacocks, mute of hounds, nide of pheasants, pace of asses, pod of seals, pride of lions, school of porpoises, siege (or sedge) of bitterns, skein of geese, skulk of foxes, sloth of bears, sounder of boars, spring of teals, stud of mares, team of ducks, tok of capercailzies, troop of kangaroos, walk of snipe, watch of nightingales.

collectors, enthusiasts abolitionist, ailurophile, antiquary, antivaccinationist, antivivisectionist, arachnologist, arctophile, audiophil(e), balletomane, bibliolatrist, bibliomane, bibliopegist, bibliophagist, bibliophile, bibliophilist, bicameralist, campanologist, canophilist, cartophile, cartophilist, cheirographist, coleopterist, conservationist, cynophilist, Dantophilist, deltiologist, discophile, dog-fancier, ecclesiologist, egger, entomologist, environmentalist, ephemerist, epicure, ex-librist, feminist, Francophile, Gallophile, gastronome, gemmologist, Germanophil(e), gourmet, herpetologist, hippophile, homoeopathist, iconophilist, incunabulist, Kremlinologist, lepidopterist, medallist, miscegenationist, monarchist, myrmecologist, negrophile, negrophilist, notaphilist, numismatist, oenophile, oenophilist, ophiophilist, orchidomaniac, ornithologist, orthoepist, orthographist, ostreiculturist, pangrammatist, Panhellenist, panislamist, Pan-Slavist, paragrammatist, paroemographer, perfectionist, philanthrope, philatelist, philhellene, phillumenist, philogynist, philologist, philologue, prohibitionist, pteridophilist, reincarnationist, Russophile, Russophilist, scripophile, scripophilist, sericulturist, Sinophile, Slavophile, spelaeologist, steganographist, stegophilist, supernaturalist, tege(s)tologist, timbrologist, timbromaniac, timbrophilist, tulipomane, tulipomaniac, Turcophile, ufologist, ultramontanist, vexillologist, virtuoso, vulcanologist, xenophile, zoophile, zoophilist.

colours anthochlore, anthocyan(in), anthoxanthin, aquamarine, argent, aurora, avocado, badious, Berlin blue, beryl, biscuit, black, blae, blood-red, blue, bottle-green, brick-red, buff, caesious, canary, caramel, carmine, carnation, celadon, celeste, cerise, cerulean, cervine, champagne, charcoal, cobalt-blue, coral, cyan, dove, drab, dun, Dutch pink, dwale, eau de Nil, ebony, emerald, fawn, feldgrau, ferrugin(e)ous, filemot, flame, flavescent, flaxen, flesh-colour, fulvous, fuscous, ginger, glaucous, gold, golden, green, greige (grège), grey (gray), gridelin, griseous, grizzle(d), gules, guly, hoar, horse-flesh, hyacinth, hyacinthine, ianthine, icterine, icteritious, incarnadine, indigo, isabel, isabella, isabelline, jacinth, khaki, lake, lateritious, lemon, lilac, lovat, lurid, luteolous, luteous, lutescent, magenta, mahogany, maize, mandarin(e), maroon, mauve, mazarine, miniate, minium, modena, morel, mouse-colour(ed), mous(e)y, mulberry, murrey, nacarat, Naples-yellow, nattier blue, Nile green, nut-brown, ochroleucous, off-white, orange, oxblood, Oxford blue, palatinate, pansy, peach, peach-bloom, peacock, peacock-blue, perse, philomot, piceous, pink, plum, plumbeous, pompadour, ponceau, pongee, porphyry, porraceous, puce, purple, purpure, pyrrhous, red, reseda, roan, rose, rose-coloured, rose-pink, rose-red, rosy, rubicund, rubied, rubiginous, rubineous, rubious, ruby, ruby-red, ruddy, rufescent, rufous, russet, rust-coloured, rusty, sable, saffron, sage, salmon, sand, sapphire, saxe blue, scarlet, sepia, siena, silver, sky, slate, smalt, straw, tan, taupe, tawny, tenné, Titian, tomato, tusser, Tyrian, ultramarine, vermeil, vermilion, vinous, violet, virescent, vitellary, vitreous, watchet, white, wine, xanthic, xanthous, yellow.

confections, dishes, foods angels-on-horseback, battalia pie, bir(i)yani, blanquette, Bombay duck, borsch(t), bouillabaisse, bubble-and-squeak, bummalo, burgoo, cannelloni, carbon(n)ade, cassoulet, cecils, charlotte russe, chilli con carné, chocolate vermicelli, chop-suey, chowder, chow-mein, cockaleekie, colcannon, consommé, Danish pastry, dariole, devil, devil's food cake, devils-on-horseback, Devonshire cream, diet-bread, dika-bread, dimsum, dough-boy, doughnut, dragée,

confections, dishes, foods *contd.*

drammock, duff, dumpling, dunderfunk, Eccles cake, éclair, Edinburgh rock, egg custard, enchilada, eryngo, escalope, escargot, faggot, fancy-bread, farle, fedelini, felafel, fettuc(c)ine, fishball, fishcake, fishfinger, flan, flapjack, floater, flummery, foie gras, fondant, fondue, forcemeat, fortune cookie, fraise, frankfurter, French bread, French dressing, French fry, French stick, French toast, fricandeau, fricassee, friedcake, fritter, fritto misto, friture, froise, fruit cocktail, fruit salad, fruitcake, frumenty, fu yung, fudge, fumado, galantine, game chips, garam masala, Garibaldi biscuit, gateau, gazpacho, gefilte fish, Genoa cake, ghee, ginger nut, gingerbread, gingersnap, gnocchi, gofer, goulash, graham bread, graham crackers, grits, gruel, guacamole, gumdrop, gundy, haberdine, haggis, halva(h), hamburger, hard sauce, hardbake, hardtack, hoe-cake, hominy, hoosh, hot dog, hot-cross-bun, hotpot, howtowdie, humbug, hummus, hundreds-and-thousands, hyson, jemmy, kedgeree, lardy-cake, laverbread, matelote, millefeuille(s), minestrone, mous(s)aka, na(a)n, navarin, olla-podrida, opsonium, paella, panada, pastrami, pavlova, pem(m)ican, pettitoes, pilaff, pilau, pinole, pirozhki, pizza, ploughman's lunch, plum-duff, plum-porridge, plum-pudding, poi, polenta, polony, popover, pop(p)adum, porterhouse(-steak), pot-au-feu, prairie-oyster, profiterole, prosciutto, pumpernickel, queen of puddings, queen's pudding, quenelle, quiche, ragout, ramekin, ratatouille, ravioli, remoulade, risotto, rissole, roly-poly pudding, Sachertorte, salmagundi, salmi(s), saltimbocca, sauce hollandaise, sauerkraut, scampi, schnitzel, sch(t)chi, Scotch woodcock, shepherd's pie, smørbrød, smörgåsbord, soufflé, spaghetti (alla) bolognese, spotted dick, spring roll, stovies, stroganoff, succotash, sukiyaki, summer pudding, sundae, sup(p)awn, sushi, syllabub, Tabasco®, tablet, taco, tamal(e), tandoori, tapioca, taramasalata, tempura, timbale, toad-in-the-hole, torte, tortellini, tortilla, trifle, tsamba, turtle-soup, tutti-frutti, tzimmes, velouté sauce, vermicelli, vichyssoise, vienna loaf, vienna steak, vindaloo, vol-au-vent, wafer, waffle, warden pie, wastel-bread, water-biscuit, water-gruel, welsh rabbit (rarebit), white sauce, white-pot, white-pudding, Wiener schnitzel, Wimpy®, wine-biscuit, wonder, Worcestershire sauce, wurst, yoghurt, Yorkshire pudding, zabaglione, Zwieback.

dances allemande, beguine, belly-dance, bergamask, black bottom, bolero, bossa nova, bourree, branle, breakdown, bunny-hug, cachucha, cakewalk, canary, cancan, carioca, carmagnole, carol, cha-cha, chaconne, Charleston, cinque-pace, Circassian circle, clogdance, conga, coranto, corroboree, cotill(i)on, country-dance, courant, cracovienne, csárdás (czardas), dos-à-dos (dosi-do), dump, écossaise, egg-dance, fading, fado, fandango, farruca, figure-dance, flamenco, fling, flip-flap(-flop), forlana, fox-trot, galliard, gallopade, galop, gavotte, gigue, gopak, habanera, haka, halling, haymaker, hey (hay), hey-de-guy, Highland fling, hoedown, hoolachan, hula-hula, jig, jitterbug, jive, jota, juba, kolo, lancers, loure, malagueña, mambo, matachin, maxixe, mazurka, minuet, Moresco, morris-dance, musette, onestep, Paduan, paso doble, passacaglia, passepied, passy-measure, Paul Jones, pavan(e), petronella, planxty, polacca, polka, polo, polonaise, poule, poussette, quadrille, quickstep, redowa, reel, r(h)umba, rigadoon, ring-dance, romaika, roundel, roundelay, roundle, rumba, saltarello, samba, sand-dance, saraband, schottische, sequidilla, shimmy(-shake), siciliano, spring, square-dance, stomp, strathspey, sword-dance, tamborin, tango, tap-dance, tarantella, the twist, toe-dance, tripudium, turkey-trot, two-step, Tyrolienne, valeta, valse, varsovienne, volta, waltz, war dance, zapateado, ziganka.

dog-breeds affenpinscher, badger-dog, basenji, basset(-hound), Bedlington (terrier), Blenheim spaniel, boar-hound, Border terrier, borzoi, Boston terrier, Briard, Brussels griffon, bull mastiff, bulldog, bull-terrier, cairn terrier, Cavalier King Charles spaniel, chihuahua, chow, clumber spaniel, coach-dog, cocker spaniel, collie, corgi, dachshund, Dalmatian, Dandie Dinmont, Dane, deerhound, dhole, dingo, Doberman(n) pinscher, elkhound, Eskimo dog, foxhound, fox-terrier, German police dog, German Shepherd dog, Great Dane, greyhound, griffon, harlequin, (Irish) water-spaniel, Jack Russell, keeshond, King Charles spaniel, Labrador, laika, lhasa apso, lurcher, lyam-hound, malemute, Maltese, mastiff, peke, Pekin(g)ese, pinscher, pointer, Pomeranian, poodle, pug, pug-dog, retriever, Rottweiler, saluki, Samoyed(e), sausage-dog, schipperke, schnauzer, Scotch-terrier, Sealyham, setter, sheltie, Shetland sheepdog, shih tzu, shough, Skye (terrier), spaniel, Spartan, spitz, St Bernard, staghound, Sussex spaniel, talbot, teckel, terrier, vizsla, volpino, warragal, water-dog, Weimaraner, whippet, wire-hair(ed terrier), wolf-dog, wolf-hound, Yorkshire terrier, zorro.

drinks, alcoholic absinth(e), aguardiente, akvavit, amontillado, anisette, apple-jack, aqua-mirabilis, aquavit, aqua-vitae, arak, Armagnac, arrack, audit ale, ava, bacharach, badminton, barley-bree, Beaujolais, Beaune, Benedictine, bingo, bishop, black velvet, bloody Mary, blue ruin, bourbon, brandy-pawnee, bride-ale, Bristol-milk, bucellas, bumbo, burgundy, Calvados, Campari, canary, catawba, Chablis, chain-lightning, Chambertin, Champagne, Chartreuse, cherry brandy, cherry-bounce, Chianti, chicha, cider, claret, claret-cup, cobbler, cobbler's punch, Cognac, Cointreau®, cold-without, Constantia, cool-tankard, cooper, cordial, corn-brandy, daiquiri, demerara, dog's-nose, dop, eau de vie, eau des creoles, egg-flap, eggnog, enzian, fine, fino, flip, four-ale, geneva, genevrette, geropiga, gimlet, gin, gin and it, gin-fizz, ginger wine, ginsling, glogg, gooseberry wine, grappa, Graves, grog, haoma, heavy wet, herb-beer, hermitage, hippocras, hock, hollands, hoo(t)ch, it, Johannisberger, John Barleycorn, John Collins, kaoliang, kava, kefir, kirsch, kirschwasser, k(o)umiss, kümmel, kvass, London particular, manzanilla, maraschino, marc brandy, Marcobrunner, Marsala, Martini®, Médoc, metheglin, mirabelle, mobbie, Moselle, mountain, mountain dew, muscat, muscatel, negus, Nipa, noyau, oenomel, Old Tom, oloroso, olykoek, Orvieto, ouzo, pastis, peach-brandy, Pernod®, perry, persico(t), Peter-see-me, pils(e)ner, plottie, pombe, port, pot(h)een, pousse-café, pulque, punch, purl, quetsch, ratafia, resinata, retsina, Rhine-wine, Riesling, Rioja, rosé, Rudesheimer, Rüdesheimer, rum, rumbo, rumfustian, rum-punch, rum-shrub, rye, rye-whisky, sack, sack-posset, sake, samshoo, sangaree, sangria, Sauterne(s), schiedam, schnapps, Scotch, shandy, sherry, sherry-cobbler, shrub, sidecar, Sillery, sling, slivovitz, sloe-gin, small beer, small-ale, sour, spruce-beer, St Julien, Steinberger, stengah, stinger, stingo, swipes, swizzle, tafia, Tarragona, tent, tequil(l)a, tipper, toddy, Tokay, Tom Collins, Tom-and-Jerry, twankay, twopenny, usquebaugh, vermouth, vin blanc, vin ordinaire, vin rosé, vinho verde, vodka, wassail, water-brose, whisk(e)y, whisky toddy, white wine, white-ale, Xeres, zythum.

French Revolutionary calendar Brumaire, Floréal, Frimaire, Fructidor, Germinal, Messidor, Nivôse, Pluviôse, Prairiel, Thermidor, Vendémiaire, Ventôse.

furniture, furnishings andiron, banquette, basket-chair, basketwork, bergama, bergamot, bolster, bonheur-du-jour, box-bed, bracket clock, brise-soleil, buffet,

furniture, furnishings *contd.*

buhl, bureau, cabriolet, camp-bed, canterbury, chair-bed, chaise-longue, chesterfield, cheval-glass, chiffonier, coaster, commode, continental quilt, credence (table/shelf), credenza, davenport, day-bed, desk, dinner-table, dinner-wagon, divan, dos-à-dos, drape, drawer, drawing-table, draw-leaf table, dresser, dressing-table, dumb-waiter, easy-chair, elbow-chair, electrolier, encoignure, escritoire, étagere, faldstool, fauteuil, fender, fender-stool, festoon-blind, fire-dog, fireguard, firescreen, four-poster, gasalier, girandole, girnel, guéridon, hallstand, hassock, hearth-rug, highboy, high-chair, hip-bath, humpty, jardinière, lectern, looking-glass, lounge, lounger, love-seat, lowboy, lug-chair, mirror, mobile, ottoman, overmantel, pelmet, pembroke (table), picture rail, piecrust table, pier-glass, pier-table, plaque, plenishings, pouf(fe), prie-dieu, pulpit, pulvinar, radiator, rocking chair, sag-bag, scatter rug/cushion, sconce, secretaire, settee, settle, settle-bed, sideboard, side-table, sofa, sofa-bed, sofa-table, squab, standard lamp, studio couch, swivel-chair, table, tallboy, tapestry, tatami, teapoy, tea-service, tea-set, tea-table, tea-tray, tea-trolley, tent-bed, tête-à-tête, toilet-table, toílet(te), torchère, tridarn, tringle, umbrella-stand, Vanitory®, vanity unit, vargueño, veilleuse, vis-à-vis, vitrine, wall-unit, wardrobe, washhand-stand, wash-stand, water bed, Welsh dresser, whatnot, writing-desk, writing-table.

garments, vestments aba, abaya, abba, abolla, achkan, acton, Afghan, alb, alpargata, amice, anorak, antigropelo(e)s, babouche, babushka, balaclava, Balbriggan, balibuntal, balmoral, bandan(n)a, bania(n), barret, basher, bashlyk, basinet, basque, basquine, bathing-costume, bauchle, beanie, bearskin, beaver, bed-jacket, bedsocks, beetle-crushers, belcher, benjamin, Bermuda shorts, Bermudas, bertha, bikini, billycock, biretta, blanket, blouson, blucher, boa, boater, bobbysock, bodice, body stocking, bolero, bomber jacket, bongrace, bonnet, bonnet-rouge, boob-tube, bootee, bottine, box-coat, bow-tie, bra, brassière, breeches, breeks, breton, broad-brim, brogue(s), buckskins, buff, buffalo-robe, buff-coat, buff-jerkin, bumfreezer, Burberry, burdash, burk(h)a, burnous(e), busby, bush jacket, bush shirt, buskin, bustle, bustle, bycoket, caftan, cagoul(e), calamanco, calash, calceamentum, calotte, calyptra, camiknickers, camise, camisole, capa, cape, capel(l)ine, capote, capuche, capuchin, carcanet, car-coat, cardigan, cardinal, carmagnole, cashmere, casque, cassock, casuals, catsuit, caul, cere-cloth, cerement, chadar, chaparajos, chapeau, chapeau-bras, chaperone, chapka, chaplet, chaps, chasuble, collar of esses, corset, corslet, cummerbund, dalmahoy, Dalmatic, décolletage, derby, diadem, diaper, dick(e)y, dinner-gown, dinner-jacket, dirndl, dishabille, dittos, divided skirt, djellaba(h), djibbah, dog-collar, Dolly Varden, dolman, donkey jacket, doublet, drainpipes, drapesuit, drawers, dreadnought, dress uniform, dress-coat, dress-improver, dressing-gown, dressing-jacket, dressing-sack, dress-shirt, dress-suit, dress-tie, duffel coat, dungarees, earmuffs, encolpion, epaulet(te), ephod, epitrachelion, espadrille, Eton collar, Eton jacket, Etons, evening dress, evening-dress, exomis, faldetta, falling band, fannel(l), fanon, farthingale, fascinator, fatigues, fedora, ferronnière, fez, fibula, fichu, filibeg, fillet, finnesko, flat-cap, flip-flop, fob, fontange, fore-and-after, fraise, French knickers, frock, frock-coat, frog, frontlet, fustanella, gaberdine, gaiter, galligaskins, galoshes, gamash, gambeson, garibaldi, gauchos, gay deceivers, gee-string (G-string), geneva bands, geta, gibus, gi(e), gilet, girandole, gizz, grego, gremial, g-suit, guernsey, gumboot, gum(shoe), habergeon, hacqueton, haik, hair-net, hair-piece, half-boot,

garments, vestments *contd.*

hat, hatband, hatpin, hattock, hauberk, havelock, headcloth, head-hugger,
headsquare, himation, hip-huggers, hipsters, hogger, Homburg, hood, hotpants,
housecoat, hug-me-tight, humeral veil, hummel, hunting cap, ihram, indescribables,
jabot, jacket, Jap-silk, jeans, jersey, jiz, jubbah (djibbah), jumper, jump-suit, jupon,
kabaya, kaffiyeh, kaftan, kagoul, kalpak, kalyptra, kamees, kanzu, kell, kerchief,
k(h)anga, k(h)urta, Kilmarnock, Kilmarnock cowl, kimono, kirtle, kiss-me,
kiss-me-quick, knickerbockers, knickers, lammy, lava-lava, lederhosen, leggings,
leghorn, leg-warmers, leotard, Levis®, liberty bodice, lingerie, loden, lounger,
lounge-suit, lungi, mac(k), mackinaw, mac(k)intosh, madras, manta, manteau,
mantilla, mantle, mantlet, manto, matinee, matinee jacket/coat, maud, mazarine,
mazarine hood, middy (blouse), mink, mitre, mitt, mitten, mob, mob-cap, mode,
modius, mohair, moleskins, monkey-jacket, monteith, montero, montero-cap,
morning-dress, morning-gown, mortar-board, Mother Hubbard, mourning-cloak,
mousquetaire, moz(z)etta, muff, muffin-cap, muffler, mutch, muu-muu, netherstock,
newmarket, nightingale, Nithsdale, Norfolk jacket, nubia, obi, omophorion, orarion,
orarium, overcoat, overgarment, Oxonian, paduasoy, paenula, pagri, paletot, pall,
palla, pallium, paludament, pantable, pantalets, pantaloons, panties, pantihose,
pantof(f)le, panton, pantoufle, pants, pants suit, pea-coat, pea-jacket, pearlies,
pectoral, pedal-pushers, pelerine, pelisse, pencil skirt, penitentials, peplos, peplum,
petasos, petersham, petticoat, petticoat, petticoat-breeches, ph(a)elonion, Phrygian
cap, picture-hat, pierrot, pilch, pileus, pill-box, pinafore, pinafore-dress,
pinafore-skirt, pinner, pixie-hood, plaid, plimsoll, plus-fours, plushes,
pneumonia-blouse, poke-bonnet, polonaise, polo-neck, poncho, pontificals,
pos(h)teen, powdering-gown, pressure-helmet, pressure-suit, pressure-waistcoat,
princess(e), pumps, puttee, rabato, raglan, raincoat, rami(e), Ramil(l)ie(s), ra-ra
skirt, rat-catcher, rational, rationals, rebater, rebato, redingote, reefer,
reefing-jacket, riding-breeches, riding-cloak, riding-clothes, riding-coat,
riding-glove, riding-habit, riding-hood, riding-robe, riding-skirt, riding-suit, robe,
robe-de-chambre, rochet, roll-neck sweater, roll-on, rompers, romper-suit,
roquelaure, ruff, rug-gown, sabot, sack, sack-coat, safari jacket, safari suit, sagum,
sailor-hat, sakkos, salopette, samfoo, sanbenito, sandal, sarafan, sari, sarong, sash,
sayon, scapular, scarf, scarpetto, schema, scotch bonnet, screen, sea-boots, sealskin,
semmit, separates, shako, shaps, shauchle, shawl, shawl-waistcoat, shift, shirt, shirt
dress, shirtwaist, shirtwaister, shoe, shooting-jacket, short-clothes, short-coats,
shortgown, shorts, shovel-hat, silk-hat, silly-how, singlet, siren suit, skeleton suit,
skin-tights, skirt, skullcap, slacks, slicker, sling-back, slip, slip-over, slipper(s),
slipslop, sloppy Joe, slop(s), slouch(-hat), small-clothes, smalls, smicket, smock,
smock-frock, smoking cap, smoking jacket, sneaker(s), snood, snow-boots,
snow-shoe(s), sock, sola(r) topi/helmet, solitaire, solleret, sombrero, sontag,
soubise, soutane, sou'-wester, space-suit, spat, spattee, spatterdash, spencer,
sphendone, sponge-bags, sporran, sports jacket, sports shirt, start-up, stays,
steenkirk, steeple-crown, steeple-hat, stephane, step-in, Stetson, sticharion, stock,
stockinet(te), stockingette, stocking(s), stola, stole, stomacher, stovepipe (hat),
strait-jacket, strait-waistcoat, straw (hat), string vest, string-tie, strip, stuff-gown,
subfusc, subucula, succinctorium, sun-bonnet, sundown, sun-dress, sunhat, sunsuit,
superhumeral, surcingle, surcoat, surplice, surtout, suspender-belt, suspenders,
swaddling-band/cloth/clothes, swagger-coat, swallow-tail, sweat band, sweat suit,

garments, vestments *contd.*

sweater, sweat-shirt, swimming costume, swimsuit, swimwear, sword-belt, tabard, taglioni, tail-coat, tails, taj, talar, talaria, tall hat, tallith, talma, tam, Tam O'Shanter, tammy, tanga, tank top, tarboosh, tarpaulin, tasse, tawdry-lace, tea-gown, Teddy suit, tee-shirt, ten-gallon hat, terai, thrum-cap, tiar(a), tie, tights, tile(-hat), tippet, toga, tonnag, top-boots, topcoat, topee, topi, topper, tops, toque, toreador pants, tournure, tower, toy, tozie, track shoe, track suit, trenchard, trench-coat, trencher-cap, trews, tricorn(e), trilby, trollopee, trot-cozy, trouser suit, trousers, trouse(s), trunk-breeches, trunk-hose, trunks, truss(es), trusty, T-shirt, tube-skirt, tunic, tunicle, tuque, turban, turtle-neck, tuxedo, twin-set, ugly, ulster, ulsterette, undercoat, underpants, undershorts, undervest, upper-stock, Vandyke (collar), vareuse, veil, veld(-)schoen, vest, victorine, visite, vitta, volet, waistcloth, waistcoat, wam(p)us, war bonnet, warm, watch cap, watch chain, Watteau bodice, weeper, wellie, wellington, wet-suit, whisk, white tie, wide-awake, wig, wimple, windcheater, windjammer, wing collar, winkle-pickers, woggle, wrap, wraparound, wrapover, wrapper, wrap-rascal, wristlet, wylie-coat, yarmulka, yashmak, Y-fronts, zamarra, zoot suit, zoster, zucchetto.

heraldry abatement, addorsed, affrontee, Albany Herald, allusive, annulet, armorist, assurgent, augmentation, baton-sinister, bendlet, bend-sinister, bendwise, bendy, bezant, bicorporate, billet, bordure, botoné, brisure, caboched, cabré, cadency, canting, canton, catherine-wheel, champ, chequy, chevron, chevrony, chief, coupé, debased, debruised, declinant, delf, device, dexter, difference, dimidiate, dismembered, displayed, dormant, double, doubling, dragonné, dwale, eightfoil, embattled, emblaze, emblazon, emblazoner, emblazonment, emblazonry, enarched, enarmed, engouled, engrail, engrailed, engrailment, enveloped, escrol(l), escutcheon, extendant, fess(e), fesse-point, fetterlock, field, fimbriate, fitché(e), flanch, flanched, flotant, fracted, fret, fructed, fur, fusil, gale, gamb, garb(e), gemel, gerbe, golp(e), gorged, grieced, g(u)ardant, gules, gyron, gyronny, hatchment, haurient, herisson, honour-point, impale, impalement, increscent, inescutcheon, interfretted, invected, jessant, langued, lioncel, lis, lozenge, lozengy, manche, mantling, martlet, mascle, mascled, masculy, moline, morné, morned, mounted, mullet, naiant, naissant, nombril, nowed, nowy, opinicus, or, orle, palewise, pall, passant, patonce, patté(e), pean, percussant, pheon, pile, point, pommelé, pommelled, pommetty, portate, portcullis, posé, potencé, potent, primrose, quarter, quartering, quarterly, queue, ragged staff, raguled, raguly, rampant, raping, rebate, regardant, respect, respectant, roundel, rustre, saltire, sans nombre, satyral, scarp, segreant, sej(e)ant, semé(e), square-pierced, statant, tenné, trangle, tressure, trippant, umbrated, undee, undifferenced, unguled, urinant, vair, vairé, verdoy, vert, voided, vol, volant, vorant, vuln, vulned, waved, weel, wivern, woodwose (wood-house).

herbs, spices amaracus, basil thyme, caraway seeds, cardamom, cassia, cayenne, chervil, chilli, chive, cinnamon, cloves, coriander, cum(m)in, dill, dittany, endive, eyebright, fennel, fenugreek, finoc(c)hio, galega, garlic, gentian, ginger, groundsel, hellebore, henbane, horehound, horseradish, Hyoscyamus, hyssop, isatis, juniper, lemon thyme, liquorice, lovage, lungwort, mace, marjoram, mint, motherwort, mustard, myrrh, nutmeg, oregano, orpine, paprika, parsley, peppermint, purslane, rampion, rape, rosemary, rue, saffron, sage, savory, stacte, tarragon, thyme, turmeric, vanilla, verbena, watercress, wintergreen, wormwood, woundwort, yerba.

jewels, gems agate, amber, amethyst, aquamarine, asteria, balas ruby, baroque, beryl, bloodstone, brilliant, cairngorm, cameo, carbuncle, chalcedony, chrysolite, coral, cornelian, crystal, diamond, draconites, emerald, fire-opal, garnet, girasol(e), grossular(ite), heliodor, hyacinth, hyalite, hydrophane, intaglio, jacinth, jade, jango(o)n, jasper, jet, lapis lazuli, ligure, marcasite, marquise, Mocha stone, moonstone, morganite, mother-of-pearl, nacre, olivet, olivine, onyx, opal, oriental amethyst, paragon, pearl, peridot(e), pyreneite, pyrope, Rhinestone, rhodolite, rose, rose-cut, rose-diamond, ruby, sapphire, sard, sardine, sardonyx, smaragd, topaz, tourmaline, turquoise, water-sapphire, wood-opal, yu, yu-stone, zircon.

Jewish calendar Ab, Abib, Adar, Adar Sheni, Elul, Hes(h)van, Iy(y)ar, Kislev, Nisan, S(h)ebat, Sivan, Tammuz, Tebet(h), Tis(h)ri, Veadar.

languages Aeolic, Afghan, Afrikaans, Akkadian, Albanian, Alemannic, Algonki(a)n, Altaic, Ameslan, Amharic, Anatolian, Anglo-Saxon, Arabic, Aramaic, Armenian, Armoric, Aryan, Assyrian, Attic, Austric, Austroasiatic, Austronesian, Avestan, Bahasa Indonesia, Balinese, Baltoslav(on)ic, Baluch(i), Bantu, Basque, Basuto, Bengali, Berber, Bohemian, bohunk, Breton, Brezonek, British, Brythonic, Bulgarian, Bulgaric, Burmese, B(y)elorussian, Cajun, Carib, Catalan, Celtic, Chaldaic, Cherokee, Chinese, Choctaw, Circassian, Cornish, creole, Croat(ian), Cushitic, Czech, Danish, Dardic, Doric, Dravidian, Dutch, Early English, English, Erse, Eskimo, Esperanto, Est(h)onian, Ethiopic, Etruscan, Euskarian, Fanti, Farsi, Finnish, Finno-Ugric (-Ugrian), Flemish, Franglais, French, Frisian, Gadhelic (Goidelic), Gaelic, Gaulish, Geëz (Giz), Gentoo, Georgian, German, Germanic, Greek, Guaraní, Gujarat(h)i, Gullah, Hausa, Hawaiian, Hebrew, Hellenic, Herero, High German, Hindi, Hindustani, Hittite, Hottentot, Hungarian, Icelandic, Idiom Neutral, Ido, I(g)bo, Indian, Indic, Indo-European, Indo-Germanic, In(n)uit, Interlingua, Ionic, Iranian, Iraqi, Irish, Iroquoian, Italian, Italic, Japanese, Kalmuck, Kanarese, Kannada, Karen, Kennick, Khmer, Koine, Kolarian, Kuo-yü, Kurdish, Ladin, Ladino, Lallans, Landsmaal, Langue d'oc, Langue d'oil, Langue d'oui, Laplandish, Lapp, Lappish, Latin, Latvian, Lettic, Lettish, lingua franca, lingua geral, Lithuanian, Low German, Magyar, Malagasy, Malay, Malayala(a)m, Maltese, Manchu, Mandaean, Mandarin, Mandingo, Manx, Maori, Marathi, Median, Melanesian, Mexican, Micmac, Middle English, Moeso-gothic, Mohawk, Mohican, Mon, Mongolian, Munda, Nahuatl, Neo, Newspeak, Norwegian, Novial, Nynorsk, Old English, Old Norse, Oriya, Oscan, Ostyak, Pali, Pawnee, Pehlevi, Pekin(g)ese, Pennsylvania Dutch, Persian, Persic, Phoenician, Pictish, pig Latin, Pilipino, Platt-Deutsch, Polabian, Polish, Portuguese, Prakrit, Provençal, Provinçal, Prussian, Punic, Punjabi, Pushtu, Quechua, Rabbinic, Rhaetic, Rhaeto-Romance, Rhaeto-Romanic, Rock English, rogues' Latin, Romaic, Romance, Romanes, Romanic, Roman(n)y, Romans(c)h, Rumanian, Russian, Russniak, Ruthenian, Sakai, Samnite, Samoyed(e), Sanskrit, Saxon, Scots, Scythian, Semitic, Serb(ian), Serbo-Croat(ian), Shan, Shona, Siamese, Sinhalese, Siouan, Slavonic, Slovak, Slovenian, Somali, Sorbian, Sorbish, Spanish, Sudanic, Sumerian, Suomi, Swahili, Swedish, Swiss, Syriac, Taal, Tagálog, Taino, Tamil, Tataric, Telugu, Teutonic, Thai, Tibetan, Tocharian, Tswana, Tuareg, Tungus(ian), Tupí, Turki, Turkish, Twi, Ugrian, Ugro-finnic, Ukrainian, Umbrian, Uralic, Urdu, Uzbeg, Vaudois, Vietnamese, Volapük, Volga-Baltic, Volscian, Welsh, Wendic, Wendish, West-Saxon, Wolof, Xhosa, Yakut, Yiddish, Yoruba, Zulu.

legal abate, abatement, absolvitor, abstract of title, acceptilation, accession, accessory, accessory after the fact, accessory before the fact, Acts of Adjournal, (ad)avizandum, adeem, adhere, adjudication, adminicle, administrator, afforce, alienee, alienor, allenarly, allodial, amicus curiae, amove, appointer, apprize, apprizer, assumpsit, attorn, back-bond, bairn's-part, capias, certiorari, chaud-mellé, cognosce, cognovit, compear, compulsitor, copyhold, cross-examine, decree absolute, decree nisi, decreet, decretals, decretist, dedimus, deed, deed of accession, defalcate, defeasance, defeasanced, defeasible, defendant, defender, deforce, deforcement, deforciant, delapidation, delate, delation, delator, delict, demurrer, deodand, detainer, detinue, devastavit, devest, diet, dimissory, disapply, disbar, disbench, discovert, discoverture, disentail, disgavel, disinherison, dispone, disponee, disposition, disseise, disseisin, disseisor, distinguish, distrain, distrainee, distrainer, distrainment, distrainor, distraint, distress, distringas, dittay, dole, donatary, droit, droit du Seigneur, duplicand, duply, dying declaration, easement, ejectment, embracer, embracery, emendals, emphyteusis, en ventre sa mère, enfeoff, enfeoffment, enjoin, enlevé, enlevement, entry, eric, escheat, escrow (escroll), escuage, esnecy, esrepe, essoin, estate, estop, estoppel, estover, estray, estreat, estrepement, examination, excamb, excambion, excambium, executry, exemplify, expromission, extend, extent, extinguishment, extract, extradition, facile, facility, factorise, faldage, felo de se, felony, feme, feme covert, feme sole, feoff, feoffee, feoffer (feoffor), feoffment, feu, feuar, fief, filacer, fire-bote, fiscal, folio, force and fear, force majeure, foreclose, foreclosure, forinsec, forisfamiliate, forjudge, frankalmoign, free-bench, frontager, fugitation, fungibles, garnishee, garnisheement, garnisher, gavelkind, gavelman, granter (grantor), grassum, hamesucken, hedge-bote, hide, homologation, horning, house-bote, hypothec, hypothecary, hypothecate, hypothecation, improbation, indenture, indict, indictee, indictment, induciae, infangthief, infeft, inquirendo, institorial, insucken, interlocutor, interplead, interpleader, interpose, irrepleviable, irreplevisable, ish, John Doe and Richard Roe, joinder, jointure, jus primae noctis, laches, law-agent, law-burrows, legitim, lenocinium, letters of administration, lien, life-rent, malfeasance, mens rea, mesne, messuage, misdemeanant, misfeasance, misfeasor, misprision, mittimus, mora, mortmain, multiplepoinding, nolle prosequi, nolo contendere, non-access, nonage, non-compearance, non-entry, nonsuit, non-user, notour, novalia, noverint, novodamus, noxal, obligant, obligation, obligor, obreption, onus probandi, ouster, outfangthief, overt act, owelty, oyer, pactum nudum, Pandect, panel, pernancy, personalty, pickery, plaint, plaintiff, porteous roll, portioner, practic, prima facie, privy, prorogate, pupil, quadruply, realty, recaption, recusation, reddendo, relator, relaxation, remise, replevin, replevy, repone, reprobator, res gestae, retour, retroact, retroactive, reverser, right of drip, rout, scutage, stillicide, supersedeas, supplicavit, surrebut, surrebuttal, surrebutter, surrejoin, surrejoinder, terminer, tolt, tort, tortfeasor, tortious, udal, udaller, ultimus haeres, unlaw, uses, usucapient, usucapion (usucaption), usucapt, usucaptible, usufruct, usufructuary, ultimogeniture, vacatur, venire (facias), venter, venue, vert, vest, vested, visne, voidable, voir dire, volunteer, wage, waive, waste, watch, watching brief, water-privilege, wit.

minerals adularia, aegirine, aegirite, alabandine, almandine, alum-shale, alum-slate, alum-stone, alunite, amazonite, amazon-stone, amianthus, amphibole, analcime, anatase, andesine, argil, arkose, asbestos, asparagus-stone, asphalt(um), aventurine,

minerals *contd.*

baetyl, balas, Barbados earth, barilla, baryta, barytes, basalt, Bath stone, bath-brick, bezoar, bitter-earth, bitter-spar, bitumen, blackjack, blacklead, blaes, blende, bloodstone, blue ground, blue John, blue vitriol, bluestone, Bologna phosphorus, borane, borax, borazon, boride, bornite, boulder-clay, breccia, Bristol-brick, Bristol-diamond, brown spar, brownstone, buhrstone, cacholong, caen-stone, cairngorm, calamine, calc-sinter, calcspar, calc-tuff, caliche, calp, Carborundum®, cat's-eye, cat-silver, cauk, celestine, cement-stone, ceruse, chalcedony, chalcedonyx, chalk, chert, Chile saltpetre, china clay, china stone, chrome-alum, chrome-spinel, chrysoberyl, chrysocolla, chrysoprase, chrysotile, cinnabar, cinnamon-stone, cipollino, corundum, cryolite, cymophane, dacite, dendrite, Derbyshire spar, diabase, diallage, dialogite, diaspore, diatomite, dice-coal, diopside, dioptase, diorite, dogger, dogtooth-spar, dolerite, dolomite, dopplerite, dropstone, dunite, dyscrasite, dysodyle, eagle-stone, earthflax, earthwax, eclogite, electric calamine, elvan, emery, encrinite, enhydrite, enhydros, epidiorite, epidosite, epidote, epistilbite, epsomite, erinite, erubescite, erythrite, euclase, eucrite, eudialyte, eutaxite, euxenite, fahlerz, fahlore, fakes, fayalite, fel(d)spar, felsite, felstone, flint, fluorite, fluorspar, franklinite, French chalk, fuchsite, fulgurite, fuller's earth, gabbro, gadolinite, gahnite, galena, galenite, gangue, gan(n)ister, garnet-rock, gibbsite, glance, glauberite, glauconite, glimmer, gmelinite, gneiss, goldstone, goslarite, gossan, göthite, granite, granitite, granodiorite, granophyre, granulite, graphic granite, graphite, green earth, greenockite, greensand, greenstone, greisen, greywacke, gummite, gypsum, haematite, hälleflinta, halloysite, harmotome, hatchettite, haüyne, heavy spar, hedyphane, hemimorphite, hepatite, hercynite, (h)essonite, heulandite, hiddenite, honey-stone, hornblende, hornfels, hornstone, horseflesh ore, humite, hyacinth, hyalophane, hypersthene, ice-spar, ice-stone, idocrase, ironstone, jacinth, keratophyre, kermes, kermesite, kieselguhr, kunkur, kupferschiefer, lamprophyre, lapis lazuli, lepidomelane, limestone, lithomarge, marlstone, meerschaum, mellite, mica, microlite, microlith, mispickel, morion, moss-agate, mundic, nail-head-spar, needle-tin, nepheline, nickel-bloom, nickel-ochre, Norway saltpetre, nosean, noselite, obsidian, omphacite, onyx, onyx-marble, orthoclase, orthophyre, ottrelite, ozokerite, peacock-ore, pencil-ore, pencil-stone, peperino, periclase, pericline, petuntse, pipeclay, pipestone, plagioclose, pleonaste, porphyry, potstone, prase, protogine, pyrites, quartz, realgar, rock-oil, rubicelle, ruby-spinel, rutile, saltpetre, sandstone, sanidine, sapphire, sapphire-quartz, sapphirine, sard, sardonyx, satin-spar, satin-stone, scaglia, schalstein, schiller-spar, schist, schorl, serpentine, serpentine(-rock), shale, shell-limestone, shell-marl, silica, silver-glance, sinter, slate, soapstone, spar, speiss-cobalt, spelter, sphene, spiegeleisen, spinel, spinel-ruby, spodumene, stinkstone, sunstone, surturbrand, swinestone, sylvine, tabular spar, tachylyte, talc, talc-schist, terne, terpene, terpineol, terra alba, terracotta, terra-japonica, terramara, terra-rossa, terra-sigillata, terts, thulia, tiger(s)-eye, till, tin-stone, toad-stone, tombac, touchstone, tourmaline, trass, travertin(e), tripoli, troutstone, tufa, tuff, Turkey hone, Turkey stone, turquoise, tutty, uinta(h)ite, umber, Uralian emerald, uralite, uraninite, uranite, uvarovite, vanadinite, variolite, variscite, veinstone, veinstuff, Venice talc, verd-antique, vesuvianite, vitrain, vivianite, vulpinite, wacke, wad(d), wallsend, wavellite, Wernerite, whet-slate, whewellite, whinstone, white pyrites, willemite, witherite, wolfram, wollastonite, wood-coal,

minerals *contd.*
wulfenite, wurtzite, zaratite, zarnich, zeolite, zeuxite, zinkenite, zircon, zoisite, zorgite.

musical instruments aeolian harp, aerophone, alpenhorn, alphorn, althorn, alto, Amati, American organ, apollonicon, archlute, arpeggione, atabal, autoharp, balalaika, bandore, banjulele, baryton(e), bass clarinet, bass drum, bass fiddle, bass horn, bass tuba, bass viol, basset horn, bazooka, bombard, bombardon, bongo (drum), bouzouki, buccina, bugle, buglet, bull fiddle, calliope, castanets, celeste, cello, cembalo, chair-organ, chalumeau, chamber organ, chikara, Chinese pavilion, chitarrone, chordophone, cinema-organ, cithara, cither(n), citole, cittern, clarichord, clarinet, clarion, clarsach, clave, clavichord, crwth, cymbal, cymbalo, decachord, dichord, didgeridoo, digitorium, double bass, drum, dulcimer, Dulcitone®, dumb-piano, echo, electric guitar, electric organ, euphonium, fagotto, fife, fipple-flute, flageolet, flügel, flügelhorn, flute, flûte-à-bec, flutina, French horn, gamelan, German flute, gimbard, gittern, glass harmonica, glockenspiel, grand piano, gu, guitar, gusla, Hammerklavier, hand-horn, hand-organ, harmonica, harmonicon, harmoniphone, harmonium, harp, harpsichord, hautboy, heckelphone, heptachord, horn, hornpipe, humstrum, hunting-horn, hurdy-gurdy, idiophone, jingling Johnny, kazoo, kent-bugle, keyboard(s), keybugle, klavier, koto, krummhorn, Kuh-horn, langsp(i)el, lituus, lur(e), lyra-viol, lyre, mandola, mandolin(e), mandora, maraca, marimba, marine trumpet, melodeon, metallophone, mirliton, monochord, Moog synthesizer, mouth-harp, mouth-organ, musette, musical glasses, naker, nose-flute, nun's-fiddle, oboe, oboe d'amore, oboe di caccia, ocarina, octachord, octave-flute, ophicleide, organ-harmonium, orpharion, orpheorion, pandora, panharmonicon, Pan-pipes, Pan's pipes, pantaleon, pianette, pianino, piano, piano-accordion, pianoforte, Pianola®, piano-organ, piffero, pipe, pipeless organ, pipe-organ, player piano, polyphon(e), posaune, psaltery, pyrophone, quint(e), racket(t), rebec(k), regal, rote, sackbut, salpinx, sambuca, sancho, sang, santir, sarangi, sarrusophone, sausage-bassoon, saxhorn, saxophone, seraphine, serinette, serpent, s(h)amisen, shawm, side-drum, sitar, small-pipes, sourdeline, sousaphone, spinet(te), squeeze-box, squiffer, steel drum, sticcado, stock-and-horn, strad, Stradivari(us), string bass, sultana, symphonion, symphony, synthesiser, syrinx, tabla, tabor, tabo(u)rin, tabret, tambour, tamboura, tambourine, tam-tam, testudo, tetrachord, theatre organ, theorbo, timbal, timbrel, timpano, tin whistle, traps, triangle, trichord, tromba marina, trombone, trump, trumpet, trumpet marine, tuba, tubular bells, tympan, uillean pipes, ukulele, vibraharp, vibraphone, vielle, vihuela, vina, viol, viola, viola da braccio, (viola da) gamba, viola da gamba, viola da spalla, viola d'amore, violin, violoncello, violone, virginal(s), vocalion, waldflute, waldhorn, Welsh harp, xylophone, zambomba, zampogna, zanze, zel, zinke, zither, zufolo.

parliaments Althing (Iceland), Cortes (Spain, Portugal), Dáil (Ireland), d(o)uma (Russia), ecclesia (Athens), Folketing (Denmark), House of Commons (UK), House of Keys (Isle of Man), House of Lords (UK), Knesset (Israel), Lagt(h)ing (Norway), Lagting (Norway), Landst(h)ing (Denmark), Landtag (Germany), Lok Sabha (India), Majlis (Iran), Odelst(h)ing (Norway), Oireachtas (Ireland), Parliament (UK), Pnyx (Athens), Porte (Turkey), Rajya Sabha (India), Reichsrat(h) (Austria), Reichstag (Germany), Rigsdag (Denmark), Riksdag (Sweden), Seanad (Ireland),

parliaments *contd.*
Senate (Rome, USA, etc.), Skupshtina (Yugoslavia), Sobranje (Bulgaria), Stort(h)ing (Norway), Tynwald (Isle of Man), witenagemot (England).

prosody Alcaic, alexandrine, amphibrach, amphibrachic, amphimacer, Anacreontic, anacrusis, anacrustic, anapaest, anapaestic, antibacchius, antispast, antispastic, antistrophe, Archilochian, arsis, Asclepiad, asynartete, atonic, bacchius, catalectic, choliamb, choree, choriamb, cinquain, cretic, dactyl, decastich, decasyllabic, decasyllable, dipody, dispondaic, dispondee, distich, disyllable, ditrochean, ditrochee, dizain, dochmiac, dochmius, dodecasyllabic, dodecasyllable, dolichurus, duan, ectasis, ecthlipsis, elide, elision, enjamb(e)ment, envoy, epic, epirrhema, epistrophe, epitrite, epode, epopee, epopoeia, epos, epyllion, extrametrical, eye-rhyme, false quantity, feminine caesura, feminine ending, feminine rhyme, fifteener, free verse, galliambic, g(h)azal, glyconic, gradus, haiku, head-rhyme, hendecasyllabic, hendecasyllable, hephthemimer, heptameter, heptapody, heptasyllabic, heterostrophic, heterostrophy, hexameter, hexametric(al), hexapody, hexastich, Hudibrastic, huitain, hypercatalectic, hypercatalexis, hypermetrical, iamb, iambus, ictus, Ionic, irrational, kyrielle, laisse, Leonine, limerick, limma, linked verse, logaoedic, long-measure, macaronic(s), masculine ending, masculine rhyme, meliboean, miurus, monometer, monorhyme, monostich, monostrophic, mora, outride, oxytone, pantoum, pentameter, pentastich, penthemimer, Pherecratean, Pherecratic, Pindaric, poulters' measure, proceleusmatic, pyrrhic, Pythian, quatorzain, quatrain, reported verses, rhopalic, rhyme-royal, rich rhyme, riding-rhyme, rime riche, rime suffisante, rondeau, rondel, rove-over, rubaiyat, run-on, Sapphics, scazon, semeion, senarius, septenarius, sestina, spondee, strophe, synaphe(i)a, tetrameter, tetrapody, tetrasemic, tetrastich, thesis, tirade, tribrach, trimeter, tripody, triseme, trochee, villanelle, virelay.

ranks in armed forces able seaman, acting sub-lieutenant, admiral, admiral of the fleet, air chief marshal, air commandant, air commodore, air vice marshal, aircraftman, air-marshal, brigadier, captain, chief officer, chief petty officer, chief technician, colonel, commandant, commander, commodore, corporal, field marshal, first officer, fleet chief petty officer, flight lieutenant, flight officer, flight sergeant, flying officer, general, group captain, group officer, junior seaman, junior technician, lance-corporal, lance-jack, lance-sergeant, leading aircraftman, leading seaman, lieutenant, lieutenant-colonel, lieutenant-commander, lieutenant-general, major, major-general, marshal, marshal of the Royal Air Force, master-at-arms, midshipman, ordinary seaman, petty officer, pilot officer, post-captain, private, purser, quartermaster, quartermaster-general, quartermaster-sergeant, quartermistress, rear-admiral, risaldar, ritt-master, second lieutenant, second officer, senior aircraftman, sergeant, sergeant-major, squadron leader, squadron officer, staff sergeant, sub-lieutenant, superintendent, third officer, vice admiral, warrant officer, wing commander, wing officer.

rhetoric abscission, alliteration, amoebaean, anacoluthia, anacoluthon, anadiplosis, anaphora, anaphoric, anastrophe, antimetabole, antimetathesis, antiphrasis, antiphrastic(al), antithesis, antithetic(al), antonomasia, aporia, asteism, asyndeton, auxesis, catachresis, chiasmus, climax, diallage, diegesis, dissimile, double entendre, dramatic irony, dysphemism, ecbole, echoic, ecphonesis, ellipsis, enallage, enantiosis, enumeration, epanadiplosis, epanalepsis, epanaphora, epanodos,

rhetoric *contd.*

epanorthosis, epexegesis, epiphonema, epizeuxis, erotema, erotetic, figure, flower, head-rhyme, hendiadys, holophrase, hypallage, hyperbaton, hyperbole, hypobole, hypostrophe, hypotyposis, hysteron-proteron, increment, irony, litotes, meiosis, metalepsis, metaphor, metonym, metonymy, mixed metaphor, onomatopoeia, oxymoron, parabole, paral(e)ipsis, parenthesis, prolepsis, simile, syllepsis, symploce, synchoresis, synchysis, synecdoche, synoeciosis, trope, vicious circle, zeugma.

titles of rulers abuna, adelantado, ag(h)a, alderman, amir, amman, amtman, ard-ri(gh), atabeg, atabek, ataman, atheling, ayatollah, Ban, beglerbeg, begum, bey, boyar, burgrave, caboceer, cacique, caliph, caudillo, Cid, Dan, Dauphin, Dauphine, Dauphiness, dey, diadochus, doge, duce, duke, ealdorman, elector, emir, emperor, empress, ethnarch, exarch, gospodar, Graf, Gräfin, grave, Great Mogul, harmost, heptarch, hospodar, huzoor, imperator, Inca, infanta, infante, jarl, kaid, kaiser, kalif, khan, khedive, king, kinglet, kingling, landgrave, landgravine, maharaja(h), maharani, mandarin, marchesa, marchese, marchioness, margrave, margravine, marquess, marquis, marquise, mikado, Mirza, Monseigneur, monsieur, Monsignor, Monsignore, mormaor, mpret, nabob, naik, nawab, nizam, nomarch, omrah, padishah, palatine, palsgrave, pasha, pendragon, pentarch, pharaoh, prince, prince-bishop, prince-imperial, princess, raja(h), rajpramukh, rana, rani, Rhinegrave, Rhinegravine, sachem, sagamore, satrap, shah, sheik(h), sherif, shogun, sirdar, sovereign, stad(t)holder, starosta, suba(h)dar, sultan, suzerain, taoiseach, theocrat, toiseach, toparch, tsar, tuchun, voivode, waldgrave.

tools about-sledge, aiguille, auger, auger-bit, awl, boaster, bodkin, bolster, bradawl, broach, bucksaw, burin, burr, buzz-saw, card, caschrom, caulking-iron, celt, centre-bit, chaser, chisel, chopper, clamp, cleaver, cold-chisel, cradle-scythe, crosscut-saw, crown-saw, diamond-drill, dibble, dividers, dolly, drawing-knife, draw-knife, drill, drove, els(h)in, extirpator, fillister, float, forceps, forfex, fork, fraise, frame-saw, fretsaw, gad, gang-saw, gavelock, gimlet, gouge, grapnel, grapple, graver, gurlet, hacksaw, hammer, handsaw, hawk, hay fork, hay knife, helve-hammer, hod, hoe, holing-axe, jackhammer, jack-plane, jointer, laster, level, levelling-rod, levelling-staff, loy, mace, madge, maker, mall, mallet, mattock, maul, monkey, moon-knife, mortar, muller, oliver, oustiti, pachymeter, pad-saw, palstave, panel saw, panga, paper-cutter, paper-knife, pattle, pecker, peel, pestle, pick, pickaxe, pincers, pinch, pinking-shears, piolet, pitchfork, plane, planer, plessor, plexor, pliers, plough, plow, plugger, plumb, plumb-line, plumb-rule, plummet, pocket-knife, pointel, pricker, priest, priming-iron, priming-wire, probang, probe, probing-scissors, prod, prog, pruning-bill, pruning-hook, pruning-knife, pruning-shears, prunt, punch, puncheon, punty, quadrant, quannet, rabble, rake, raspatory, reed-knife, repositor, retractor, ricker, rickstick, riddle, riffle, ripper, ripping-saw, ripple, rip-saw, risp, router, rule, ruler, sash-tool, saw, sax, scalpel, scauper, scissors, scoop, scooper, scorper, scraper, screwdriver, screwjack, screw-wrench, scribe(r), scutch(er), scythe, seam-set, serving-mallet, shave, shears, shovel, sickle, slane, slate-axe, slater, slicker, smoother, snap, snarling-iron, snarling-rod, snips, soldering-bolt, soldering-iron, spade, spanner, spider, spokeshave, spud, squeegee, stadda, stake, stapler, stapling-machine, steel, stithy, stone-hammer, stretching-iron, strickle, strigil, stubble-rake, style, stylet, swage,

tools *contd.*
swingle(-hand), switch, tedder, tenon-saw, threshel, thresher, thrust-hoe, tint-tool,
tongs, trepan, trowel, T-square, turfing-iron, turf-spade, turning-saw, tweezers, twist
drill, upright, van, vice, vulsella, waster, whip-saw, widener, wimble, wood-shears,
wortle, xyster, Y-level.

units of measurement acre, ampere, angstrom, anker, ardeb, are, arpent, arroba,
arshin, as, bar, barleycorn, barn, barrel, bath, baud, becquerel, bel, bigha, bit, Board
of Trade Unit/BTU, board-foot, boll, bolt, braccio, bushel, butt, cab, cable, calorie,
candela, candle, candy, carat, catty, cell, cental, centner, chain, chalder, chaldron,
ch(o)enix, chopin, chronon, clove, co(o)mb, cor, cord, coss, coulomb, cran, crith,
cubit, cumec, curie, cusec, cyathus, daraf, Debye (unit), degree, demy, dessiatine,
digit, dirham, dra(ch)m, dyne, ell, em, en, epha(h), erg, farad, faraday, fathom,
fermium, firkin, firlot, foot, fother, fou, furlong, gal, gallon, gerah, gilbert, gill, grain,
gram(me), hectare, henry, hertz, hin, hogshead, homer, hoppus foot,
hundredweight, inch, joule, kaneh, kantar, kelvin, k(h)at, kilderkin, kin, knot,
league, leaguer, li, liang, liard, ligne, link, lippy, lire, lisp(o)und, litre, log, lux,
maneh, maund, metre, mho, micrometre, micron, mile, mil(l), mina, minim, minute,
mna, modius, mole, morgen, muid, mutchkin, nail, neper, nepit, newton, nit
(information), nit (luminance), noggin, obol, oersted, ohm, oke, omer, ounce,
oxgang, parasang, pascal, peck, perch, picul, pin, pint, pipe, poise, pole, pood,
pound, poundal, quart, quarter, quartern, quintal, quire, radian, ream, rem, rod,
rood, rote, rotolo, run(d)let, rutherford, sabin, s(a)eculum, sazhen, scruple, second,
seer, semuncia, shekel, shippound, siemens, sievert, sone, span, square, stadium,
steradian, stere, stilb, stoke(s), stone, tael, talent, tare, tesla, therm, tical, tierce, tod,
toise, tola, ton, tonne, tonneau, tor, truss, tun, vara, verst, virgate, volt, watt, weber,
wey, yard, yardland, yojan.

vehicles aerotrain, air-car, amtrack, araba, arba, aroba, barouche, Bath chair,
berlin(e), bicycle, biga, bobsled, bobsleigh, bogie, boneshaker, brake, britzka,
brougham, bubble-car, buckboard, buckcart, buck-wagon, buggy, bus, cab, caboose,
cabriolet, caisson, calash, camper, car, caravan, caravanette, caroche, car(r)iole,
carry-all, catafalque, chair, chaise, chaise-cart, chapel cart, charabanc, chariot,
clarence, coach, convertible, conveyance, cycle, dandy-cart, dandy-horse, dennet,
désobligeante, dhooly, diesel, diligence, dilly, Dodgem(s)®, dog-cart, dogcart, dolly,
doolie, dormitory-car, drag, dray, dros(h)ky, duck, ekka, fiacre, fly, fork-lift truck,
four-in-hand, gharri, gig, glass-coach, go-kart, Green Goddess, gyrocar, gyrodyne,
hack, hackery, hackney-carriage/coach, hatchback, herdic, honey-cart,
honey-wag(g)on, hurley-hacket, ice-yacht, inside-car, jeep, jingle, jinricksha(w),
jitney, juggernaut, kago, kajawah, kart, kibitka, landau, landaulet(te), limousine,
litter, lorry, mail-cart, minibus, monorail, motor caravan, motor-bicycle, motor-bike,
motor-bus, motor-car, motor-coach, motor-cycle, motor-lorry, motor-scooter,
norimon, omnibus, outside-car, palanquin (palankeen), palki, pantechnicon, pedal
cycle, pedicab, people mover, phaeton, pick-up, pill-box, pincers, post-chaise, prairie
schooner, pulka, quadriga, rail-bus, rail-car, rail-motor, ricksha(w), roadster,
rockaway, runabout, safety bicycle, saloon-car, saloon-carriage, scooter, sedan,
sedan-chair, shandry(dan), shooting-brake, sidecar, single-decker, skateboard,
ski-bob, sled, sledge, sleeper, sleeping-car, sleeping-carriage, sleeping-coach, sleigh,
slip-carriage, slip-coach, slipe, snowmobile, snow-plough, sociable, solo, speedster,

725

vehicles *contd.*

spider, spring-carriage, spring-cart, squad car, stage-coach, stage-wagon, stanhope, station-wagon, steam-car, steam-carriage, steamer, steam-roller, stillage, stone boat, straddle carrier, street-car, sulky, surrey, tally-ho, tandem, tank, tank-car, tank-engine, tanker, tank-wagon, tarantas(s), tartana, tax(ed)-cart, taxi, taxicab, T-cart, telega, telpher, tender, thoroughbrace, through-train, tilbury, tim-whisk(e)y, tin Lizzie, tip, tip-cart, tipper, toboggan, tonga, tourer, touring-car, tractor, trailer, train, tram, tramway-car, transporter, transport-rider, trap, tricar, tricycle, trike, triplet, trishaw, troika, trolley, trolley-bus, trolley-car, troop-carrier, truck, tube, tumble-car(t), tumbrel, turbocar, two-decker, twoseater, two-wheeler, velocipede, vettura, victoria, village cart, vis-à-vis, volante, wag(g)on, wagonette, wagon-lit, wain, water-cart, water-wagon, weasel, wheelbarrow, wheel-chair, whisk(e)y, Whitechapel cart.

vessels, ships argosy, barca, barque, barquentine, bateau, bawley, Berthon-boat, bilander, billyboy, bireme, birlinn, boat, bomb-ketch, bomb-vessel, brig, brigantine, Bucentaur, budgerow, bum-boat, buss, butty, cabin cruiser, caique, canal-boat, canoe, caravel, Carley float, carrack, casco, cat, catamaran, catboat, clipper, coaster, cob(b)le, cockboat, cockleshell, cog, collier, commodore, coracle, corocore, corvette, cot, crare, crayer, currach, cutter, dandy, deep-sinker, destroyer, d(h)ow, dinghy, diving-bell, dogger, drake, dreadnought, dredger, drog(h)er, dromond, dugout, East-Indiaman, E-boat, faltboat, felucca, flatboat, floating battery, flyboat, flying bridge, fore-and-after, frigate, frigatoon, funny, gabbart, galleass, galleon, galley, gal(l)iot, gallivat, gay-you, geordie, gondola, grab, hatch boat, herringer, hooker, hovercraft, hoy, hydrofoil, hydroplane, hydrovane, ice-boat, Indiaman, iron-clad, jigger, jollyboat, junk, kayak, ketch, koff, laker, landing-craft, lapstreak, launch, liberty-ship, lighter, line-of-battle-ship, liner, long-boat, longship, lorcha, lugger, lymphad, mackinaw, masoolah, merchantman, mistico, monitor, monkey-boat, monohull, monoxylon, montaria, motor-boat, motor-launch, motor-ship, motoscafo, mud-boat, mudscow, multihull, nacelle, nuggar, outrigger, packet, packet-boat, packet-ship, pair-oar, patamar, pedalo, penteconter, periagua, peter-boat, pink, pinkie, pinky, pinnace, piragua, pirogue, pleasure-boat, pocket battleship, polacca, polacre, pontoon, powerboat, praam, pra(h)u, pram, privateer, puffer, pulwar, punt, puteli, quadrireme, quinquereme, randan, razee, river-boat, river-craft, row-barge, row-boat, rowing-boat, saic, sail-boat, sailing-boat, sailing-ship, salmon-coble, sampan, schooner, schuit, scooter, scow, scull, sculler, sea-boat, seaplane-carrier, settee, shallop, ship, ship-of-the-line, shore-boat, show-boat, skiff, sloop, sloop-of-war, smack, smuggler, snow, speed-boat, speedster, square rigger, steamboat, steamer, steam-launch, steam-packet, steamship, steam-tug, steam-vessel, steam-yacht, stern-wheeler, stew-can, sub, submarine, super-Dreadnought, supertanker, surface-craft, surf-board, surf-boat, surf-canoe, surfing-board, swamp boat, tanker, tartane(e), tender, tern, three-decker, three-master, tilt-boat, torpedo-boat, torpedo-boat destroyer, track-boat, tracker, trader, train ferry, tramp, transport-ship, trawler, trek-schuit, triaconter, trimaran, trireme, troop-carrier, trooper, troop-ship, tub, tug, tug-boat, turbine-steamer, turret-ship, two-decker, two-master, U-boat, umiak, vaporetto, vedette(-boat), vessel, wager-boat, warship, water-bus, well-boat, well-smack, whaleboat, whaler, wherry, whiff, windjammer, xebec, yacht, yawl, zabra.

weapons, armour A-bomb, ack-ack, aerodart, ailette, air rifle, amusette, an(e)lace, arbalest, arblast, Archibald, Archie, arcubalist, armet, arquebus(e), baldric(k), ballista, ballistic missile, bandolier, basilisk, baton gun, bazooka, beaver, bill, Biscayan, blackjack, blowgun, blowpipe, bludgeon, blunderbuss, boarding-pike, bodkin, Bofors gun, bolas, bomb, bombard, boomerang, bowie knife, brassard, breastplate, breech-loader, Bren (gun), bricole, brigandine, broadsword, brown Bess, brown bill, buckler, buckshot, bulldog, bullet, bundook, Bungalore torpedo, burganet, byrnie, caltrop, cannon, carbine, carronade, casque, cataphract, catapult, chain-armour, chain-mail, chamfrain, Chassepot, chausses, cheval-de-frise, chokebore, claymore, cluster-bomb, coal-box, co(e)horn, Colt, Congreve, corium, dag, dagger, dah, Damascus blade, Damascus sword, demi-cannon, demi-culverin, demi-lance, depth-bomb, depth-charge, dirk, dragoon, elephant gun, épée, escopette, Exocet®, express rifle, falchion, falconet, field gun, fire-arm, fire-arrow, firebomb, firelock, firepot, fission bomb, flail, flame-thrower, flick-knife, flintlock, foil, fougade, fougasse, four-pounder, fusee, fusil, Garand rifle, gatling-gun, gavelock, genouillère, gisarme, gladius, gorget, grapeshot, greave, Greek fire, grenade, gun, habergeon, hackbut, hacqueton, hailshot, halberd, half-pike, hand-grenade, hand-gun, han(d)jar, handstaff, harquebus, hauberk, H-bomb, heaume, helm, helmet, hielaman, howitzer, jack, jamb(e), jazerant, jesserant, Jethart staff, kris, lamboys, lame, lance, Lochaber-axe, Long Tom, machete, machine-gun, mangonel, martel, Martini (-Henry), matchlock, Mauser, Maxim(-gun), mesail, Mills bomb, Mills grenade, mine, mine-thrower, mini-rocket launcher, minnie, mitrailleur, mitrailleuse, morgenstern, morglay, morning-star, mor(r)ion, mortar, musket, musketoon, nulla-nulla, oerlikon, panga, partisan, pauldron, pavis(e), peasecod-cuirass, pederero, pelican, pelta, perrier, petrary, petronel, pickelhaube, pike, pilum, pistol, pistolet, placket, plastron, plate-armour, pocket-pistol, poitrel, pole-ax(e), poleyn, pompom, poniard, potgun, quarter-staff, queen's-arm, rapier, rerebrace, rest, revolver, rifle, rifle-grenade, sabaton, sabre, saker, sallet, saloon-pistol, saloon-rifle, sap, sarbacane, schiavone, schläger, scimitar, scorpion, scutum, serpentine, sharp, shell, shield, shillela(g)h, shortsword, shotgun, shrapnel, siege-artillery, siege-gun, siege-piece, singlestick, six-gun, six-shooter, skean(dhu), sling, slung-shot, small-arm, small-sword, smoke-ball, smoke-bomb, snickersnee, spadroon, sparth(e), spear, spear gun, splint-armour, spontoon, spring-gun, squid, steel, sten gun, Sterling, stern-chaser, stiletto, stone axe, stone-bow, stylet, submachine-gun, sumpit(an), switch-blade (knife), swivel-gun, sword, sword bayonet, sword-cane, sword-stick, tace, targe, target, taslet, tasse, tasset, testudo, three-pounder, threshel, throw-stick, time-bomb, toc emma, toggle-iron, tomahawk, tomboc, tommy-gun, tormentum, torpedo, tortoise, trecento, trench-mortar, trident, truncheon, tuille, tuillette, tulwar, turret-gun, twibill, vambrace, vamplate, V-bomb, visor, vou(l)ge, war-wolf, waster, water-cannon, water-pistol, Welsh hook, white-arm, Winchester (rifle), wind-gun, wo(o)mera(ng), yatag(h)an, zumbooruk.

wine-bottle sizes baby, balthasar, jeroboam, magnum, Methuselah, nebuchadnezzar, nip, rehoboam, Salmanazar.

zodiac signs Aquarius, Aries, Cancer, Capricorn, Gemini, Leo, Libra, Pisces, Sagittarius, Scorpio, Taurus, Virgo.

Appendix II

Words listed by suffix

-ast chiliast, diaskeuast, dicast, dikast, dynast, ecclesiast, ecdysiast, elegiast, encomiast, enthusiast, fantast, gymnasiast, gymnast, Hesychast, hypochondriast, iconoclast, idoloclast, metaphrast, orgiast, paederast, pancratiast, paraphrast, peltast, phantasiast, pleonast, scholiast, utopiast.

-aster criticaster, grammaticaster, medicaster, philosophaster, poetaster, politicaster, theologaster.

-cide aborticide, acaricide, algicide, aphicide, aphidicide, bacillicide, bactericide, biocide, deicide, ecocide, ethnocide, feticide, filicide, foeticide, fratricide, fungicide, genocide, germicide, giganticide, herbicide, homicide, infanticide, insecticide, larvicide, liberticide, matricide, menticide, molluscicide, ovicide, parasiticide, parasuicide, parricide, patricide, pesticide, prolicide, regicide, rodenticide, sororicide, spermicide, suicide, taeniacide, trypanocide, tyrannicide, uxoricide, vaticide, verbicide, vermicide, viricide, viticide, vulpicide, weedicide.

-cracy aristocracy, autocracy, bureaucracy, chrysocracy, cottonocracy, democracy, demonocracy, despotocracy, dollarocracy, doulocracy, dulocracy, ergatocracy, Eurocracy, gerontocracy, gynaecocracy, hagiocracy, hierocracy, isocracy, kakistocracy, meritocracy, millocracy, mobocracy, monocracy, nomocracy, ochlocracy, pantisocracy, pedantocracy, physiocracy, plantocracy, plutocracy, plutodemocracy, pornocracy, ptochocracy, slavocracy, snobocracy, squattocracy, stratocracy, technocracy, thalassocracy, thalattocracy, theocracy, timocracy.

-crat aristocrat, autocrat, bureaucrat, cosmocrat, democrat, hierocrat, meritocrat, millocrat, mobocrat, monocrat, ochlocrat, pantisocrat, pedantocrat, physiocrat, plutocrat, slavocrat, stratocrat, technocrat, theocrat.

-cratic aristocratic, autocratic, bureaucratic, cosmocratic, democratic, Eurocratic, gerontocratic, gynaecocratic, hierocratic, isocratic, meritocratic, mobocratic, monocratic, ochlocratic, pancratic, pantisocratic, pedantocratic, physiocratic, plutocratic, stratocratic, technocratic, theocratic, timocratic, undemocratic.

-cultural accultural, agricultural, arboricultural, crinicultural, cultural, floricultural, horticultural, piscicultural, subcultural, vinicultural, vocicultural.

-culture agriculture, apiculture, aquaculture, aquiculture, arboriculture, aviculture, culture, electroculture, floriculture, horticulture, mariculture, monoculture, ostreiculture, pisciculture, pomiculture, self-culture, sericiculture, sericulture, silviculture, stirpiculture, subculture, sylviculture, viniculture, viticulture, water-culture, zooculture.

-cyte athrocyte, cyte, erythrocyte, fibrocyte, gonocyte, granulocyte, haemocyte, leucocyte, lymphocyte, macrocyte, microcyte, oocyte, phagocyte, poikilocyte, spermatocyte, thrombocyte, thymocyte.

-dom Anglo-Saxondom, apedom, archdukedom, attorneydom, babeldom, babudom, bachelordom, beadledom, beggardom, birthdom, bishopdom, boredom, Bumbledom, chiefdom, Christendom, clerkdom, cockneydom, crippledom, cuckoldom, czardom, demirepdom, devildom, Dogberrydom, dolldom, dufferdom, dukedom, duncedom, earldom, enthraldom, fairydom, fandom, filmdom, flunkeydom, fogydom, freedom, fresherdom, Greekdom, gypsydom, halidom, heathendom, heirdom, hobbledehoydom, hobodom, junkerdom, kaiserdom, kingdom, kitchendom, leechdom, liegedom, mandom, martyrdom, masterdom, newspaperdom, niggerdom, noodledom, noveldom, officialdom, overfreedom, penny-wisdom, popedom, princedom, puppydom, puzzledom, Quakerdom, queendom, queerdom, rascaldom, rebeldom, sachemdom, saintdom, savagedom, Saxondom, scoundreldom, serfdom, sheikdom, sheikhdom, sheriffdom, Slavdom, spinsterdom, squiredom, stardom, subkingdom, swelldom, thanedom, thraldom, thralldom, topsyturvydom, tsardom, underkingdom, unwisdom, villadom, whoredom, wisdom, Yankeedom.

-ferous aluminiferous, amentiferous, antenniferous, argentiferous, auriferous, bacciferous, balsamiferous, bulbiferous, calciferous, carboniferous, celliferous, celluliferous, cheliferous, cobaltiferous, conchiferous, coniferous, coralliferous, corniferous, cruciferous, culmiferous, cupriferous, cupuliferous, diamantiferous, diamondiferous, doloriferous, dorsiferous, ferriferous, flagelliferous, flammiferous, floriferous, foraminiferous, fossiliferous, frondiferous, fructiferous, frugiferous, furciferous, garnetiferous, gemmiferous, glandiferous, glanduliferous, globuliferous, glumiferous, granuliferous, guaniferous, gummiferous, guttiferous, lactiferous, laniferous, laticiferous, lethiferous, luciferous, luminiferous, mammaliferous, mammiferous, manganiferous, manniferous, margaritiferous, melliferous, metalliferous, morbiferous, mortiferous, moschiferous, muciferous, nectariferous, nickeliferous, nubiferous, nuciferous, odoriferous, oleiferous, omniferous, ossiferous, oviferous, ovuliferous, ozoniferous, papilliferous, papuliferous, Permo-Carboniferous, pestiferous, petaliferous, petroliferous, piliferous, platiniferous, plumbiferous, polliniferous, pomiferous, poriferous, proliferous, pyritiferous, quartziferous, reptiliferous, resiniferous, rotiferous, sacchariferous, saliferous, salutiferous, sanguiferous, sebiferous, seminiferous, septiferous, siliciferous, soboliferous, somniferous, soporiferous, spiniferous, spinuliferous, splendiferous, staminiferous, stanniferous, stelliferous, stigmatiferous, stoloniferous, strombuliferous, styliferous, sudoriferous, tentaculiferous, thuriferous, titaniferous, tuberiferous, umbelliferous, umbriferous, unfossiliferous, uriniferous, vitiferous, vociferous, yttriferous, zinciferous, zinkiferous.

-gamy allogamy, apogamy, autogamy, bigamy, chalazogamy, chasmogamy, cleistogamy, clistogamy, cryptogamy, deuterogamy, dichogamy, digamy, endogamy, exogamy, geitonogamy, hercogamy, herkogamy, heterogamy, homogamy, hypergamy, isogamy, misogamy, monogamy, oogamy, pangamy, pantagamy, plasmogamy, plastogamy, polygamy, porogamy, siphonogamy, syngamy, trigamy, xenogamy, zoogamy.

-genesis abiogenesis, agamogenesis, anthropogenesis, autogenesis, biogenesis, blastogenesis, carcinogenesis, chondrogenesis, cytogenesis, diagenesis, diplogenesis, dynamogenesis, ectogenesis, electrogenesis, embryogenesis, epeirogenesis, epigenesis, gametogenesis, gamogenesis, haematogenesis, heterogenesis,

-genesis *contd.*
  histogenesis, homogenesis, hylogenesis, hypnogenesis, merogenesis, metagenesis, monogenesis, morphogenesis, mythogenesis, neogenesis, noogenesis, ontogenesis, oogenesis, organogenesis, orogenesis, orthogenesis, osteogenesis, paedogenesis, palingenesis, pangenesis, paragenesis, parthenogenesis, pathogenesis, perigenesis, petrogenesis, phylogenesis, phytogenesis, polygenesis, psychogenesis, pyogenesis, schizogenesis, spermatogenesis, sporogenesis, syngenesis, thermogenesis, xenogenesis.

-genic aesthesiogenic, allergenic, androgenic, anthropogenic, antigenic, biogenic, blastogenic, carcinogenic, cariogenic, cryogenic, dysgenic, ectogenic, electrogenic, endogenic, epeirogenic, erogenic, erotogenic, eugenic, genic, glycogenic, hallucinogenic, histogenic, hypnogenic, hysterogenic, iatrogenic, lactogenic, lysigenic, mammogenic, mutagenic, myogenic, neurogenic, odontogenic, oestrogenic, oncogenic, ontogenic, orogenic, orthogenic, osteogenic, pathogenic, photogenic, phytogenic, polygenic, psychogenic, pyogenic, pyrogenic, pythogenic, radiogenic, rhizogenic, saprogenic, schizogenic, somatogenic, spermatogenic, telegenic, teratogenic, thermogenic, tumorgenic, tumorigenic, visiogenic, zoogenic, zymogenic.

-gon chiliagon, decagon, dodecagon, endecagon, enneagon, hendecagon, heptagon, hexagon, isogon, nonagon, octagon, pentagon, perigon, polygon, tetragon, trigon.

-gram aerogram, anagram, anemogram, angiogram, audiogram, ballistocardiogram, barogram, cablegram, calligram, cardiogram, cartogram, centigram, centimetre-gram, chromatogram, chromogram, chronogram, cryptogram, dactylogram, decagram, decigram, dendrogram, diagram, echogram, electrocardiogram, electroencephalogram, encephalogram, engram, epigram, ergogram, ferrogram, harmonogram, hectogram, hexagram, hierogram, histogram, hologram, ideogram, indicator-diagram, isogram, kilogram, lexigram, lipogram, logogram, lymphogram, marconigram, marigram, meteorogram, microgram, monogram, myogram, nanogram, nephogram, neurogram, nomogram, organogram, oscillogram, pangram, paragram, parallelogram, pentagram, phonogram, photogram, phraseogram, pictogram, program, psychogram, pyelogram, radiogram, radiotelegram, röntgenogram, scintigram, seismogram, sialogram, skiagram, sociogram, spectrogram, spectroheliogram, sphenogram, sphygmogram, steganogram, stereogram, tachogram, telegram, tephigram, tetragram, thermogram, tomogram, trigram.

-graph Addressograph®, aerograph, airgraph, allograph, anemograph, apograph, audiograph, autograph, autoradiograph, ballistocardiograph, bar-graph, barograph, biograph, cardiograph, cathodograph, cerograph, chirograph, choreograph, chromatograph, chromolithograph, chromoxylograph, chronograph, cinematograph, coronagraph, coronograph, cryptograph, cyclograph, cymagraph, cymograph, diagraph, Dictograph®, digraph, dynamograph, eidograph, electrocardiograph, electroencephalograph, electrograph, electromyograph, ellipsograph, encephalograph, epigraph, ergograph, evaporograph, flannelgraph, glyphograph, harmonograph, hectograph, helicograph, heliograph, hierograph, hodograph, holograph, homograph, hydrograph, hyetograph, hyetometrograph, hygrograph, ideograph, idiograph, jellygraph, keraunograph, kinematograph,

-graph *contd.*

kinetograph, kymograph, lithograph, logograph, magnetograph, marconigraph, marigraph, meteorograph, micrograph, microphotograph, microseismograph, mimeograph, monograph, myograph, nephograph, nomograph, odograph, odontograph, oleograph, opisthograph, orthograph, oscillograph, pantograph, paragraph, pentagraph, phonautograph, phonograph, photograph, photolithograph, photomicrograph, phototelegraph, photozincograph, phraseograph, pictograph, planigraph, plethysmograph, polygraph, pseudograph, psychograph, pyrophotograph, radioautograph, radiograph, radiometeorograph, radiotelegraph, rotograph, seismograph, selenograph, serigraph, shadowgraph, skiagraph, spectrograph, spectroheliograph, sphygmograph, spirograph, steganograph, stenograph, stereograph, Stevengraph, stylograph, syngraph, tachograph, tachygraph, Telautograph®, telegraph, telephotograph, thermograph, thermometrograph, tomograph, torsiograph, trigraph, vectograph, vibrograph, xylograph, zincograph.

-graphy aerography, ampelography, angiography, anthropogeography, anthropography, areography, autobiography, autography, autoradiography, autotypography, ballistocardiography, bibliography, biogeography, biography, brachygraphy, cacography, calligraphy, cardiography, cartography, cathodography, ceramography, cerography, chalcography, chartography, cheirography, chirography, cholangiography, choregraphy, choreography, chorography, chromatography, chromolithography, chromotypography, chromoxylography, chronography, cinematography, cinemicrography, climatography, cometography, cosmography, cryptography, crystallography, dactyliography, dactylography, demography, dermatography, dermography, discography, dittography, doxography, echocardiography, ectypography, electrocardiography, electroencephalography, electrography, electromyography, electrophotography, encephalography, enigmatography, epigraphy, epistolography, ethnography, ferrography, filmography, geography, glossography, glyphography, glyptography, hagiography, haplography, heliography, heresiography, hierography, historiography, holography, horography, hydrography, hyetography, hymnography, hypsography, ichnography, ichthyography, iconography, ideography, lexicography, lexigraphy, lipography, lithography, logography, lymphography, mammography, metallography, microcosmography, micrography, microphotography, mimography, monography, morphography, myography, mythography, nomography, nosography, oceanography, odontography, oleography, opisthography, orchesography, oreography, organography, orography, orthography, osteography, palaeogeography, palaeography, palaeontography, pantography, paroemiography, pasigraphy, pathography, petrography, phonography, photography, photolithography, photomicrography, phototelegraphy, photoxylography, photozincography, physiography, phytogeography, phytography, pictography, polarography, polygraphy, pornography, prosopography, pseudepigraphy, pseudography, psychobiography, psychography, pterylography, pyelography, pyrography, pyrophotography, radiography, radiotelegraphy, reprography, rhyparography, röntgenography, scenography, scintigraphy, seismography, selenography, serigraphy, sialography, snobography, spectrography, sphygmography, steganography, stenography, stereography, stratigraphy, stylography, symbolography, tachygraphy, telautography, telegraphy,

-graphy *contd.*
telephotography, thalassography, thanatography, thaumatography, thermography, tomography, topography, typography, ultrasonography, uranography, urography, ventriculography, xerography, xeroradiography, xylography, xylopyrography, xylotypography, zincography, zoogeography, zoography.

-graphical autobiographical, bathygraphical, bathyorographical, bibliographical, biobibliographical, biogeographical, biographical, cacographical, calligraphical, cartographical, cerographical, chorographical, cinematographical, climatographical, cosmographical, geographical, glossographical, graphical, hagiographical, hierographical, historiographical, hydrographical, hyetographical, hygrographical, ichnographical, ideographical, lexicographical, lexigraphical, lithographical, logographical, monographical, myographical, oceanographical, oreographical, orographical, orthographical, palaeographical, palaeontographical, pantographical, paragraphical, pasigraphical, petrographical, photographical, physiographical, prosopographical, pseudepigraphical, psychobiographical, psychographical, pterylographical, seismographical, selenographical, spectrographical, stenographical, stereographical, stratigraphical, tachygraphical, topographical, typographical, xylographical, zincographical, zoogeographical, zoographical.

-hedron chiliahedron, decahedron, dihedron, dodecahedron, enneahedron, hemihedron, hexahedron, holohedron, icosahedron, icositetrahedron, leucitohedron, octahedron, octohedron, pentahedron, polyhedron, pyritohedron, rhombohedron, scalenohedron, tetrahedron, tetrakishexahedron, trapezohedron, triakisoctahedron, trihedron, trisoctahedron.

-hood adulthood, angelhood, apehood, apprenticehood, babyhood, bachelorhood, beadlehood, beasthood, bountihood, boyhood, brotherhood, cathood, childhood, Christhood, companionhood, cousinhood, cubhood, deaconhood, dollhood, drearihood, elfhood, fairyhood, falsehood, fatherhood, flapperhood, flesh-hood, gawkihood, gentlehood, gentlemanhood, gianthood, girlhood, godhood, hardihood, high-priesthood, hobbledehoyhood, hoghood, hoydenhood, idlehood, invalidhood, jealoushood, kinghood, kinglihood, knighthood, ladyhood, likelihood, livelihood, lustihood, maidenhood, maidhood, manhood, masterhood, matronhood, misshood, monkhood, motherhood, nationhood, needy-hood, neighbourhood, novicehood, nunhood, old-maidhood, orphanhood, pagehood, parenthood, popehood, priesthood, princehood, prophethood, puppyhood, queenhood, sainthood, selfhood, serfhood, sisterhood, spinsterhood, squirehood, statehood, swinehood, tabbyhood, thanehood, thinghood, traitorhood, unlikelihood, virginhood, waiterhood, widowerhood, widowhood, wifehood, wivehood, womanhood, youthhood.

-iac ammoniac, amnesiac, anaphrodisiac, anglomaniac, Anglophobiac, antaphrodisiac, anthomaniac, aphasiac, aphrodisiac, archgenethliac, bacchiac, bibliomaniac, cardiac, celiac, Cluniac, coeliac, coprolaliac, demoniac, dextrocardiac, Dionysiac, dipsomaniac, dochmiac, dysthymiac, egomaniac, elegiac, endocardiac, erotomaniac, etheromaniac, Genesiac, genethliac, haemophiliac, hebephreniac, heliac, hypochondriac, iliac, insomniac, intracardiac, Isiac, kleptomaniac, maniac, megalomaniac, melancholiac, melomaniac, monomaniac, morphinomaniac, mythomaniac, necrophiliac, neurastheniac, nymphomaniac, opsomaniac, orchidomaniac, paedophiliac, Pandemoniac, paradisiac, paranoiac, paraphiliac,

-iac *contd.*
paroemiac, pericardiac, phrenesiac, pyromaniac, sacroiliac, scopophiliac, scoriac, simoniac, symposiac, Syriac, theomaniac, theriac, timbromaniac, toxiphobiac, zodiac, zygocardiac.

-iatric chemiatric, chemopsychiatric, geriatric, hippiatric, kinesiatric, paediatric, psychiatric, psychogeriatric.

-iatry chemopsychiatry, geriatry, hippiatry, neuropsychiatry, orthopsychiatry, paediatry, podiatry, psychiatry.

-ician academician, acoustician, aeroelastician, aesthetician, arithmetician, audiometrician, beautician, biometrician, clinician, cosmetician, diagnostician, dialectician, dietician, econometrician, ekistician, electrician, geometrician, geopolitician, geriatrician, informatician, linguistician, logician, logistician, magician, magnetician, mathematician, mechanician, metaphysician, metrician, mortician, musician, obstetrician, optician, paediatrician, patrician, Paulician, phonetician, physician, politician, practician, psychogeriatrician, psychometrician, rhetorician, rubrician, statistician, systematician, tactician, technician, theoretician.

-ics acoustics, acrobatics, aerobatics, aerobics, aerodynamics, aeronautics, aerostatics, aesthetics, agogics, agonistics, ambisonics, apologetics, aquabatics, aquanautics, astrodynamics, astronautics, astrophysics, athletics, atmospherics, autonomics, avionics, axiomatics, ballistics, bioastronautics, biodynamics, bioethics, biomathematics, biomechanics, biometrics, bionics, bionomics, biophysics, biorhythmics, biosystematics, cacogenics, calisthenics, callisthenics, catacoustics, catallactics, cataphonics, catechetics, catoptrics, ceroplastics, chemotherapeutics, chrematistics, chromatics, civics, cliometrics, conics, cosmonautics, cosmopolitics, cryogenics, cryonics, cryophysics, cybernetics, cytogenetics, deontics, dermatoglyphics, diacoustics, diagnostics, dialectics, dianetics, didactics, dietetics, dioptrics, dogmatics, dramatics, dynamics, dysgenics, eclectics, econometrics, economics, ecumenics, ekistics, electrodynamics, electrokinetics, electromechanics, electronics, electrostatics, electrotechnics, electrotherapeutics, electrothermics, energetics, entoptics, environics, epigenetics, epistemics, epizootics, ergonomics, ethics, ethnolinguistics, eudaemonics, eudemonics, eugenics, eurhythmics, euthenics, exegetics, floristics, fluidics, forensics, genetics, geodetics, geodynamics, geophysics, geopolitics, geoponics, geostatics, geotectonics, geriatrics, gerontotherapeutics, glyptics, gnomonics, gnotobiotics, graphemics, graphics, gyrostatics, halieutics, haptics, harmonics, hedonics, hermeneutics, hermetics, hippiatrics, histrionics, homiletics, hydraulics, hydrodynamics, hydrokinetics, hydromagnetics, hydromechanics, hydroponics, hydrostatics, hydrotherapeutics, hygienics, hypersonics, hysterics, informatics, irenics, isagogics, isometrics, kinematics, kinesics, kinetics, linguistics, lithochromatics, liturgics, logistics, loxodromics, macrobiotics, macroeconomics, magnetics, magneto-hydrodynamics, magneto-optics, maieutics, mathematics, mechanics, melodics, metalinguistics, metamathematics, metaphysics, metapsychics, meteoritics, microeconomics, microelectronics, microphysics, mnemotechnics, mole-electronics, monostrophics, morphemics, morphophonemics, nautics, nucleonics, numismatics, obstetrics, olympics, onomastics, optics, optoelectronics, orchestics, orthodontics, orthodromics, orthogenics, orthopaedics, orthopedics, orthoptics, orthotics, paedeutics, paediatrics, paedodontics, paideutics, pantopragmatics, paralinguistics,

-ics *contd.*

party-politics, pataphysics, patristics, pedagogics, peptics, periodontics, pharmaceutics, pharmacodynamics, pharmacokinetics, phelloplastics, phonemics, phonetics, phonics, phonocamptics, phonotactics, photics, photochromics, photoelectronics, phototherapeutics, photovoltaics, physics, physiotherapeutics, plastics, pneumatics, pneumodynamics, polemics, politico-economics, politics, power-politics, problematics, prosthetics, prosthodontics, psychics, psychodynamics, psychogeriatrics, psycholinguistics, psychometrics, psychonomics, psychophysics, psychosomatics, psychotherapeutics, pyrotechnics, quadraphonics, quadrophonics, radionics, radiophonics, radiotherapeutics, rhythmics, robotics, semantics, semeiotics, semiotics, Semitics, sferics, significs, sociolinguistics, sonics, sophistics, spherics, sphragistics, statics, stereoptics, strategics, stylistics, subatomics, subtropics, syllabics, symbolics, synectics, systematics, tactics, technics, tectonics, telearchics, thaumaturgics, theatrics, therapeutics, thermionics, thermodynamics, thermotics, toponymics, toreutics, transonics, transsonics, ultrasonics, vitrics, zoiatrics, zootechnics, zymotechnics.

-iform aciform, acinaciform, aciniform, aeriform, alphabetiform, amoebiform, anguiform, anguilliform, antenniform, asbestiform, auriform, aviform, bacciform, bacilliform, biform, bursiform, cactiform, calcariform, calceiform, calyciform, cambiform, campaniform, campodeiform, cancriform, capriform, cauliform, cerebriform, cirriform, claviform, clypeiform, cobriform, cochleariform, coliform, colubriform, conchiform, coniform, coralliform, cordiform, corniform, corolliform, cotyliform, crateriform, cribriform, cristiform, cruciform, cteniform, cubiform, cucumiform, culiciform, cultriform, cumuliform, cuneiform, curviform, cyathiform, cylindriform, cymbiform, cystiform, deiform, dendriform, dentiform, digitiform, dolabriform, elytriform, ensiform, equisetiform, eruciform, falciform, fibriform, filiform, flabelliform, flagelliform, floriform, fringilliform, fungiform, fusiform, gangliform, gasiform, glandiform, granitiform, granuliform, hydatidiform, incisiform, infundibuliform, insectiform, janiform, jelliform, lamelliform, lanciform, lapilliform, larviform, lentiform, limaciform, linguiform, lumbriciform, lyriform, malleiform, mamilliform, mammiform, maniform, medusiform, mitriform, monadiform, moniliform, morbilliform, multiform, mummiform, muriform, mytiliform, napiform, natiform, naupliiform, nubiform, omniform, oviform, paliform, panduriform, papilliform, patelliform, pelviform, penicilliform, penniform, perciform, phialiform, piliform, pisciform, pisiform, placentiform, planuliform, plexiform, poculiform, proteiform, pulvilliform, pyriform, quadriform, radiciform, raduliform, raniform, reniform, restiform, retiform, sacciform, sagittiform, salpiform, scalariform, scalpelliform, scalpriform, scoleciform, scolopendriform, scutiform, scyphiform, securiform, septiform, serpentiform, spiniform, spongiform, squamiform, stalactiform, stalactitiform, stelliform, stratiform, strigiform, strobiliform, strombuliform, styliform, tauriform, tectiform, telescopiform, thalliform, triform, tuberiform, tubiform, tympaniform, umbraculiform, unciform, unguiform, uniform, vaporiform, variform, vasculiform, vasiform, vermiform, verruciform, versiform, villiform, viperiform, vitriform, vulviform, ypsiliform, zeolitiform.

-ism abnormalism, abolitionism, aboriginalism, absenteeism, absolutism, academicalism, academicism, accidentalism, achromatism, acosmism, acrobatism, acrotism, actinism, activism, Adamitism, adiaphorism, adoptianism, Adoptionism,

-ism *contd.*

adventurism, aeroembolism, aerotropism, aestheticism, Africanism, ageism, agnosticism, agrarianism, Albigensianism, albinism, albinoism, alcoholism, algorism, alienism, allelomorphism, allotropism, alpinism, altruism, amateurism, Americanism, ametabolism, amoralism, amorism, amorphism, anabaptism, anabolism, anachronism, anagrammatism, anarchism, anastigmatism, androdioecism, andromonoecism, aneurism, Anglicanism, anglicism, Anglo-Catholicism, aniconism, animalism, animatism, animism, annihilationism, antagonism, anthropomorphism, anthropomorphitism, anthropopathism, anthropophuism, anthropopsychism, antichristianism, anticivism, anticlericalism, antidisestablishmentarianism, anti-federalism, anti-Gallicanism, anti-Jacobinism, antinomianism, antiochianism, antiquarianism, anti-Semitism, antisepticism, antisocialism, antitheism, antitrinitarianism, antivaccinationism, antivivisectionism, anythingarianism, apheliotropism, aphorism, apism, aplanatism, apochromatism, apogeotropism, apoliticism, Apollinarianism, apostolicism, apriorism, Arabism, Aramaism, Arcadianism, archaicism, archaism, Arianism, aristocratism, Aristotelianism, Aristotelism, Arminianism, asceticism, asepticism, Asiaticism, aspheterism, asteism, asterism, astigmatism, asynchronism, asystolism, atavism, atheism, athleticism, Atlanticism, atomism, atonalism, atropism, Atticism, attorneyism, Augustinianism, Australianism, authorism, authoritarianism, autism, autochthonism, autoeroticism, autoerotism, automatism, automobilism, automorphism, autotheism, avant-gardism, Averrhoism, Averroism, Baalism, Baathism, Ba'athism, Babbitism, Babeeism, babelism, Babiism, Babism, babuism, bacchanalianism, bachelorism, Baconianism, Bahaism, bantingism, baptism, barbarism, bashawism, bastardism, bathmism, bedlamism, behaviourism, Benthamism, Bergsonism, Berkeleianism, bestialism, betacism, biblicism, bibliophilism, bilateralism, bilingualism, bimetallism, bipedalism, blackguardism, blepharism, bogeyism, bogyism, Bohemianism, bolshevism, Bonapartism, bonism, boobyism, Boswellism, botulism, Bourbonism, bowdlerism, bradyseism, braggartism, Brahmanism, Brahminism, Braidism, Briticism, Britishism, Brownism, bruxism, Buchmanism, Buddhism, bullyism, Burschenism, Byronism, Byzantinism, cabalism, cabbalism, Caesarism, caesaropapism, caffeinism, caffeism, Calvinism, cambism, Camorrism, cannibalism, capitalism, Carbonarism, careerism, Carlism, Carlylism, carnalism, Cartesianism, casualism, catabolism, catastrophism, catechism, catechumenism, Catharism, catheterism, catholicism, causationism, cauterism, cavalierism, Celticism, centenarianism, centralism, centripetalism, centrism, cerebralism, ceremonialism, chaldaism, characterism, charism, charlatanism, chartism, Chasidism, Chassidism, Chaucerism, chauvinism, chemism, chemotropism, chloralism, Christianism, chromaticism, churchism, Ciceronianism, cicisbeism, cinchonism, civism, classicism, clericalism, cliquism, clubbism, coalitionism, Cobdenism, cocainism, cockneyism, coenobitism, collectivism, collegialism, colloquialism, colonialism, commensalism, commercialism, communalism, communism, compatriotism, comstockism, Comtism, conacreism, conceptualism, concettism, concretism, confessionalism, confrontationism, Confucianism, Congregationalism, conservatism, consortism, constitutionalism, constructionism, constructivism, consubstantialism, consumerism, contact-metamorphism, continentalism, contortionism, contrabandism, conventionalism, conversationism, convictism, copyism, corporatism, corporealism,

-ism *contd.*

corybantism, cosmeticism, cosmism, cosmopolitanism, cosmopolitism, cosmotheism, cottierism, Couéism, courtierism, creatianism, creationism, cretinism, cretism, criticism, crotalism, cubism, cultism, curialism, cyclicism, cynicism, czarism, Dadaism, Daltonism, dandyism, Darwinism, deaf-mutism, decimalism, defeatism, deism, demagogism, demagoguism, demoniacism, demonianism, demonism, denominationalism, departmentalism, descriptivism, despotism, deteriorism, determinism, deviationism, devilism, diabolism, diachronism, diageotropism, diaheliotropism, dialecticism, diamagnetism, diaphototropism, diastrophism, diatropism, dichroism, dichromatism, dichromism, diclinism, dicrotism, didacticism, diffusionism, dilettanteism, dilettantism, dimerism, dimorphism, dioecism, diorism, diothelism, diphysitism, dirigism, dissenterism, dissolutionism, disyllabism, ditheism, ditheletism, dithelism, dithelitism, divisionism, Docetism, doctrinairism, doctrinarianism, Dogberryism, dogmatism, do-goodism, dolichocephalism, donatism, donnism, do-nothingism, Doricism, Dorism, dowdyism, draconism, dragonism, dramaticism, drudgism, druidism, dualism, dudism, dufferism, dunderheadism, dynamism, dyotheletism, dyothelism, dysphemism, ebionism, ebionitism, echoism, eclecticism, ecumenicalism, ecumenicism, ecumenism, Edwardianism, egalitarianism, egoism, egotheism, egotism, electromagnetism, electromerism, elementalism, elitism, Elizabethanism, embolism, emotionalism, empiricism, enantiomorphism, Encratism, encyclopaedism, endemism, Englishism, entrism, environmentalism, eonism, epicism, Epicureanism, epicurism, epiphenomenalism, epiphytism, epipolism, episcopalianism, episcopalism, equalitarianism, equestrianism, Erastianism, eremitism, erethism, ergotism, eroticism, erotism, erythrism, escapism, esotericism, esoterism, Essenism, essentialism, etacism, etherism, ethicism, ethnicism, ethnocentrism, eudaemonism, eugenism, euhemerism, eumerism, eunuchism, eunuchoidism, euphemism, euphuism, Eurocommunism, Europeanism, evangelicalism, evangelicism, evangelism, evolutionism, exclusionism, exclusivism, exhibitionism, existentialism, ex-librism, exorcism, exotericism, exoticism, expansionism, experientialism, experimentalism, expressionism, extensionalism, externalism, extremism, Fabianism, factionalism, faddism, fairyism, fakirism, falangism, familism, fanaticism, fantasticism, faradism, fascism, fatalism, Fauvism, favism, favouritism, Febronianism, federalism, femininism, feminism, Fenianism, fetichism, fetishism, feudalism, feuilletonism, fideism, fifth-monarchism, filibusterism, finalism, fissiparism, flagellantism, flunkeyism, fogyism, formalism, fortuitism, Fourierism, fractionalism, Froebelism, functionalism, fundamentalism, fusionism, futurism, gaelicism, Galenism, Gallicanism, gallicism, galvanism, gamotropism, ganderism, gangsterism, Gargantuism, gargarism, gargoylism, Gasconism, Gaullism, generationism, Genevanism, genteelism, gentilism, geocentricism, geomagnetism, geophagism, geotropism, Germanism, giantism, gigantism, Girondism, Gnosticism, Gongorism, gormandism, Gothicism, gourmandism, gradualism, Graecism, grammaticism, Grangerism, Grecism, gregarianism, griffinism, Grobianism, Grundyism, gynandrism, gynandromorphism, gynodioecism, gynomonoecism, gypsyism, gyromagnetism, haptotropism, Hasidism, Hassidism, heathenism, Hebraicism, Hebrewism, hectorism, hedonism, Hegelianism, hegemonism, heliotropism, Hellenism, helotism, hemihedrism, hemimorphism, henotheism, hermaphroditism, heroism, hetaerism, hetairism, heterochronism, heteroecism,

-ism *contd.*

heteromorphism, heterostylism, heterothallism, heurism, Hibernianism,
Hibernicism, hidalgoism, hierarchism, highbrowism, High-Churchism,
Hildebrandism, Hinduism, Hippocratism, hispanicism, historicism, historism,
histrionicism, histrionism, Hitlerism, Hobbesianism, Hobbianism, Hobbism,
hobbledehoyism, hobbyism, hobgoblinism, hoboism, holism, holohedrism,
holometabolism, holophytism, homeomorphism, homoeomorphism,
homoeroticism, homoerotism, homomorphism, homothallism, hooliganism,
hoydenism, humanism, humanitarianism, Humism, humoralism, hybridism,
hydrargyrism, hydrotropism, hylicism, hylism, hylomorphism, hylopathism,
hylotheism, hylozoism, hyperadrenalism, hyperbolism, hypercriticism,
hyperthyroidism, hyphenism, hypnotism, hypochondriacism, hypocorism,
hypognathism, hypothyroidism, Ibsenism, iconomaticism, iconophilism, idealism,
idiotism, idolism, illuminism, illusionism, imagism, immanentism, immaterialism,
immediatism, immersionism, immobilism, immoralism, imperialism, impossibilism,
impressionism, incendiarism, incivism, incorporealism, indeterminism,
indifferentism, individualism, industrialism, infallibilism, infantilism, inflationism,
Infralapsarianism, inquilinism, inspirationism, institutionalism, instrumentalism,
insularism, insurrectionism, intellectualism, interactionism, internationalism,
interventionism, intimism, intransigentism, intuitionalism, intuitionism, intuitivism,
invalidism, iodism, Ionism, iotacism, irenicism, Irishism, irrationalism, irredentism,
Irvingism, Islamism, ism, Ismailism, isochronism, isodimorphism, isolationism,
isomerism, isomorphism, isotropism, itacism, Italianism, italicism, Jacobinism,
Jacobitism, Jainism, Jansenism, Jesuitism, jingoism, jockeyism, Johnsonianism,
Johnsonism, journalism, Judaism, junkerism, kaiserism, Kantianism, Kantism,
katabolism, Kelticism, Keynesianism, klephtism, know-nothingism, Krishnaism,
labdacism, labialism, labourism, laconicism, laconism, ladyism, Lamaism,
Lamarckianism, Lamarckism, lambdacism, landlordism, Laodiceanism, larrikinism,
lathyrism, Latinism, latitudinarianism, laxism, leftism, legalism, leggism,
Leibnitzianism, Leibnizianism, Leninism, lesbianism, liberalism, liberationism,
libertarianism, libertinism, lichenism, lionism, lipogrammatism, Listerism,
literalism, literaryism, localism, Lollardism, Londonism, Low-Churchism, Luddism,
luminarism, Lutheranism, Lutherism, lyricism, lyrism, Lysenkoism, macarism,
Machiavellianism, Machiavellism, Magianism, Magism, magnetism, Magyarism,
Mahdiism, Mahdism, maidism, malapropism, Malthusianism, mammonism,
Manichaeanism, Manichaeism, Manicheanism, Manicheism, mannerism, Maoism,
Marcionitism, Marinism, martialism, martinetism, Marxianism, Marxism,
masochism, materialism, mathematicism, matriarchalism, maudlinism, Mazdaism,
Mazdeism, McCarthyism, mechanism, mediaevalism, medievalism, Medism,
melanism, meliorism, memoirism, Mendelism, mentalism, mephitism, mercantilism,
mercenarism, mercurialism, merism, merycism, mescalism, mesmerism,
mesocephalism, mesomerism, Messianism, metabolism, metachronism,
metamerism, metamorphism, metasomatism, metempiricism, meteorism,
methodism, metopism, Micawberism, Michurinism, micro-organism, microseism,
militarism, millenarianism, millenarism, millennianism, millenniarism, Miltonism,
minimalism, minimism, misoneism, Mithraicism, Mithraism, mithridatism,
modalism, moderatism, modernism, Mohammedanism, Mohammedism, Molinism,
monachism, monadism, monarchianism, monarchism, monasticism, monergism,

-ism *contd.*

monetarism, mongolism, mongrelism, monism, monkeyism, monochromatism, monoecism, monogenism, monolingualism, monometallism, monophysitism, monorchism, monosyllabism, monotheism, monotheletism, monothelism, monothelitism, Monroeism, Montanism, moralism, Moravianism, Morisonianism, Mormonism, morphinism, mosaicism, Mosaism, Moslemism, mountebankism, multiracialism, Munichism, municipalism, Muslimism, mutism, mutualism, myalism, mysticism, mythicism, mythism, namby-pambyism, nanism, Napoleonism, narcissism, narcotism, nationalism, nativism, naturalism, naturism, navalism, Nazaritism, Naziism, Nazism, necessarianism, necessitarianism, necrophilism, negativism, negroism, negrophilism, neoclassicism, neocolonialism, Neo-Darwinism, Neofascism, Neohellenism, Neo-Impressionism, Neo-Kantianism, Neo-Lamarckism, neologism, Neo-Malthusianism, neo-Nazism, neonomianism, neopaganism, neoplasticism, Neo-Plasticism, Neoplatonism, Neopythagoreanism, neoterism, neovitalism, nephalism, Nestorianism, neuroticism, neutralism, newspaperism, nicotinism, Nietzscheanism, niggerism, nihilism, noctambulism, Noetianism, nomadism, nominalism, nomism, northernism, notaphilism, nothingarianism, nothingism, Novatianism, novelism, nudism, nyctitropism, obeahism, obeism, obiism, objectivism, obscurantism, obsoletism, Occamism, occasionalism, Occidentalism, occultism, Ockhamism, odism, odylism, oecumenicalism, oecumenicism, oecumenism, officialism, old-maidism, onanism, oneirocriticism, onirocriticism, Ophism, Ophitism, opportunism, optimism, Orangeism, Orangism, organicism, organism, Orientalism, Origenism, Orleanism, orphanism, Orphism, orthognathism, orthotropism, ostracism, ostrichism, Owenism, pacificism, pacifism, Paddyism, paedobaptism, paedomorphism, paganism, palaeomagnetism, palladianism, paludism, panaesthetism, Pan-Africanism, Pan-Americanism, Pan-Arabism, panchromatism, pancosmism, panderism, panegoism, Pan-Germanism, Panhellenism, panislamism, panlogism, panpsychism, pansexualism, Pan-Slavism, pansophism, panspermatism, panspermism, Pantagruelism, pantheism, papalism, papism, parabaptism, parachronism, paragnathism, paraheliotropism, parallelism, paralogism, paramagnetism, paramorphism, parapsychism, parasitism, Parkinsonism, parliamentarism, Parnassianism, Parnellism, parochialism, Parseeism, Parsiism, Parsism, partialism, particularism, partyism, passivism, pasteurism, pastoralism, paternalism, patrialism, patriarchalism, patriarchism, patriotism, Patripassianism, patristicism, Paulinism, pauperism, pedagogism, pedagoguism, pedanticism, pedantism, pedestrianism, Pelagianism, pelmanism, pelorism, pennalism, penny-a-linerism, pentadactylism, pentamerism, pentaprism, peonism, perfectibilism, perfectionism, peripateticism, perpetualism, Persism, personalism, perspectivism, pessimism, petalism, Petrarchianism, Petrarchism, Petrinism, phaeism, phagocytism, phalansterianism, phalansterism, phallicism, phallism, pharisaism, phariseeism, phenakism, phenomenalism, phenomenism, philhellenism, philistinism, philosophism, phobism, phoneticism, phonetism, phosphorism, photism, photochromism, photoperiodism, phototropism, physicalism, physicism, physitheism, pianism, pietism, piezomagnetism, Pindarism, Pittism, plagiarism, plagiotropism, Platonicism, Platonism, plebeianism, pleiotropism, pleochroism, pleomorphism, plumbism, pluralism, Plutonism, Plymouthism, pococuranteism, pococurantism, poeticism, pointillism, polonism, polychroism, polycrotism,

-ism *contd.*

polydactylism, polygenism, polymastism, polymerism, polymorphism, polynomialism, polysyllabicism, polysyllabism, polysyllogism, polysyntheticism, polysynthetism, polytheism, Pooterism, populism, porism, Porphyrogenitism, positivism, possibilism, Post-Impressionism, post-millennialism, Poujadism, Powellism, practicalism, pragmatism, precisianism, predestinarianism, predeterminism, preferentialism, preformationism, prelatism, premillenarianism, premillennialism, Pre-Raphaelism, Pre-Raphaelitism, Presbyterianism, presentationism, preternaturalism, prettyism, priapism, priggism, primitivism, primordialism, probabiliorism, probabilism, prochronism, professionalism, prognathism, progressionism, progressism, progressivism, prohibitionism, proletarianism, propagandism, prophetism, prosaicism, prosaism, proselytism, prostatism, prosyllogism, protectionism, Protestantism, proverbialism, provincialism, prudentialism, Prussianism, psellism, psephism, pseudo-archaism, pseudoclassicism, pseudomorphism, psilanthropism, psychism, psychologism, psychopannychism, psychoticism, ptyalism, puerilism, pugilism, puppyism, purism, puritanism, Puseyism, pyrrhonism, Pythagoreanism, Pythagorism, Quakerism, quattrocentism, quietism, quixotism, rabbinism, Rabelaisianism, racemism, Rachmanism, racialism, racism, radicalism, Ramism, ranterism, rascalism, rationalism, reactionarism, realism, rebaptism, Rebeccaism, Rechabitism, recidivism, red-tapism, reductionism, reformism, regalism, regionalism, reincarnationism, relationism, relativism, religionism, Rembrandtism, representationalism, representationism, republicanism, restitutionism, restorationism, resurrectionism, reunionism, revanchism, revisionism, revivalism, revolutionism, rheotropism, rheumatism, rhopalism, rhotacism, Ribbonism, rigorism, ritualism, Romanism, romanticism, Rosicrucianism, Rosminianism, Rotarianism, routinism, rowdyism, royalism, ruffianism, ruralism, Russianism, Russophilism, Sabaism, Sabbatarianism, sabbatism, Sabellianism, Sabianism, sacerdotalism, sacramentalism, sacramentarianism, Sadduceeism, Sadducism, sadism, sado-masochism, saintism, Saint-Simonianism, Saint-Simonism, Saivism, Saktism, salvationism, Samaritanism, sanitarianism, sansculottism, sapphism, saprophytism, Saracenism, satanism, saturnism, Saxonism, scepticism, schematism, scholasticism, scientism, sciolism, Scotism, Scotticism, scoundrelism, scribism, scripturalism, scripturism, secessionism, sectarianism, sectionalism, secularism, self-criticism, self-hypnotism, selfism, semi-Arianism, semi-barbarism, Semi-Pelagianism, Semitism, sensationalism, sensationism, sensism, sensualism, sensuism, sentimentalism, separatism, serialism, servilism, servo-mechanism, sesquipedalianism, sexism, sexualism, Shaivism, shakerism, Shaktism, shamanism, shamateurism, Shiism, Shintoism, Shivaism, shunamitism, sigmatism, Sikhism, simplism, sinapism, sinecurism, singularism, Sinicism, Sinophilism, Sivaism, Slavism, snobbism, socialism, Socinianism, sociologism, Sofism, solarism, solecism, sol-faism, solidarism, solidism, solifidianism, solipsism, somatism, somnambulism, somniloquism, sophism, southernism, sovietism, specialism, speciesism, Spencerianism, Spinozism, spiritism, spiritualism, spoonerism, spread-eagleism, Stahlianism, Stahlism, Stakhanovism, Stalinism, stand-pattism, statism, stercoranism, stereoisomerism, stereotropism, stibialism, stigmatism, stoicism, strabism, structuralism, strychninism, strychnism, Stundism, subjectivism, sublapsarianism, subordinationism, substantialism, suburbanism, suffragism,

-ism *contd.*

Sufiism, Sufism, suggestionism, supernationalism, supernaturalism, superrealism, Supralapsarianism, supremacism, suprematism, surrealism, sutteeism, Swadeshism, swarajism, Swedenborgianism, swingism, sybaritism, sybotism, syllabism, syllogism, symbolism, symphilism, synaposematism, synchronism, syncretism, syndactylism, syndicalism, synecdochism, synergism, synoecism, syntheticism, Syriacism, Syrianism, systematism, tachism, tactism, Tammanyism, tantalism, Tantrism, Taoism, tarantism, Tartuffism, Tartufism, tautochronism, tautologism, tautomerism, teetotalism, teleologism, tenebrism, teratism, terminism, territorialism, terrorism, tetramerism, tetratheism, Teutonicism, Teutonism, textualism, thanatism, thaumaturgism, theanthropism, theatricalism, theatricism, theism, theomorphism, Theopaschitism, theophilanthropism, theosophism, therianthropism, theriomorphism, thermotropism, thigmotropism, Thomism, thrombo-embolism, thuggism, tigerism, Timonism, Titanism, Titoism, toadyism, tokenism, Toryism, totalitarianism, totemism, tourism, tractarianism, trade-unionism, traditionalism, Traducianism, traitorism, transcendentalism, transformism, transmigrationism, transsexualism, transvestism, transvestitism, traumatism, trialism, tribadism, tribalism, trichroism, trichromatism, tricrotism, triliteralism, trimorphism, Trinitarianism, trinomialism, tripersonalism, tritheism, triticism, trituberculism, trivialism, troglodytism, troilism, trophotropism, tropism, Trotskyism, truism, tsarism, tuism, Turcophilism, tutiorism, tutorism, tychism, ultra-Conservatism, ultraism, ultramontanism, undenominationalism, unicameralism, unidealism, uniformitarianism, unilateralism, unionism, unitarianism, universalism, unrealism, unsectarianism, unsocialism, untruism, uranism, utilitarianism, utopianism, utopism, Utraquism, vagabondism, Valentinianism, valetudinarianism, vampirism, vandalism, Vansittartism, Vaticanism, Vedism, veganism, vegetarianism, ventriloquism, verbalism, verism, vernacularism, Victorianism, vigilantism, vikingism, virilism, virtualism, vitalism, viviparism, vocalism, vocationalism, volcanism, Voltaireanism, Voltairianism, Voltairism, voltaism, voltinism, voluntarism, voluntaryism, voodooism, vorticism, voyeurism, vulcanism, vulgarism, vulpinism, vulturism, Wagnerianism, Wagnerism, Wahabiism, Wahabism, welfarism, werewolfism, Wertherism, werwolfism, Wesleyanism, westernism, Whiggism, whiteboyism, wholism, witticism, Wodenism, Wolfianism, xanthochroism, Yankeeism, yogism, zanyism, Zarathustrianism, Zarathustrism, zealotism, Zionism, Zoilism, zoism, Zolaism, zombiism, zoomagnetism, zoomorphism, zoophilism, zootheism, Zoroastrianism, Zwinglianism, zygodactylism, zygomorphism.

-itis adenitis, antiaditis, aortitis, appendicitis, arteritis, arthritis, balanitis, blepharitis, bronchitis, bursitis, carditis, cellulitis, cephalitis, ceratitis, cerebritis, cholecystitis, colitis, conchitis, conjunctivitis, crystallitis, cystitis, dermatitis, diaphragmatitis, diphtheritis, diverticulitis, duodenitis, encephalitis, endocarditis, endometritis, enteritis, fibrositis, gastritis, gastroenteritis, gingivitis, glossitis, hamarthritis, hepatitis, hysteritis, ileitis, iritis, keratitis, labyrinthitis, laminitis, laryngitis, lymphangitis, mastitis, mastoiditis, meningitis, metritis, myelitis, myocarditis, myositis, myringitis, nephritis, neuritis, onychitis, oophoritis, ophthalmitis, orchitis, osteitis, osteo-arthritis, osteomyelitis, otitis, ovaritis, panarthritis, pancreatitis, panophthalmitis, papillitis, parotiditis, parotitis, pericarditis, perigastritis, perihepatitis, perinephritis, perineuritis, periostitis, peritonitis, perityphlitis,

-itis *contd.*

pharyngitis, phlebitis, phrenitis, pleuritis, pneumonitis, poliomyelitis, polyneuritis, proctitis, prostatitis, pyelitis, pyelonephritis, rachitis, rectitis, retinitis, rhachitis, rhinitis, rhinopharyngitis, salpingitis, scleritis, sclerotitis, sinuitis, sinusitis, splenitis, spondylitis, staphylitis, stomatitis, strumitis, synovitis, syringitis, thrombo-phlebitis, thyroiditis, tonsilitis, tonsillitis, tracheitis, trachitis, tympanitis, typhlitis, ulitis, ureteritis, urethritis, uteritis, uveitis, uvulitis, vaginitis, valvulitis, vulvitis.

-latrous bibliolatrous, heliolatrous, ichthyolatrous, idolatrous, litholatrous, Mariolatrous, Maryolatrous, monolatrous, ophiolatrous, zoolatrous.

-latry angelolatry, anthropolatry, astrolatry, autolatry, bardolatry, bibliolatry, Christolatry, cosmolatry, demonolatry, dendrolatry, ecclesiolatry, epeolatry, geolatry, hagiolatry, heliolatry, hierolatry, ichthyolatry, iconolatry, idolatry, litholatry, lordolatry, Mariolatry, Maryolatry, monolatry, necrolatry, ophiolatry, physiolatry, plutolatry, pyrolatry, symbololatry, thaumatolatry, theriolatry, zoolatry.

-logical aerobiological, aerological, aetiological, agrobiological, agrological, agrostological, algological, alogical, amphibological, analogical, anthropological, arachnological, archaeological, astrological, atheological, audiological, autecological, axiological, bacteriological, batological, battological, biological, bryological, campanological, carcinological, cartological, chorological, Christological, chronological, climatological, codicological, conchological, cosmological, craniological, cryobiological, cryptological, cytological, demonological, dendrological, deontological, dermatological, dysteleological, ecclesiological, ecological, Egyptological, electrophysiological, embryological, entomological, epidemiological, epistemological, eschatological, ethnological, ethological, etymological, futurological, gastrological, gemmological, gemological, genealogical, genethlialogical, geochronological, geological, geomorphological, gerontological, glaciological, glossological, gnotobiological, graphological, gynaecological, hagiological, helminthological, hepaticological, herpetological, histological, histopathological, homological, horological, hydrobiological, hydrological, ichthyological, ideological, illogical, immunological, laryngological, limnological, lithological, logical, malacological, mammalogical, martyrological, metapsychological, meteorological, micrological, mineralogical, monological, morphological, musicological, mycological, myological, myrmecological, mythological, necrological, neological, nephological, nephrological, neurological, nomological, nosological, nostological, oceanological, odontological, oenological, ontological, ophiological, ophthalmological, oreological, ornithological, orological, osteological, paedological, palaeontological, palaeozoological, palynological, parapsychological, pathological, pedological, penological, pestological, petrological, phaenological, phenological, phenomenological, philological, phonological, phraseological, phrenological, phycological, physiological, phytological, phytopathological, pneumatological, poenological, pomological, posological, potamological, protozoological, psephological, psychobiological, psychological, radiological, reflexological, rheumatological, rhinological, scatological, sedimentological, seismological, selenological, serological, Sinological, sociobiological, sociological, somatological, soteriological, Sovietological, spectrological, spelaeological, stoechiological, stoicheiological, stoichiological, synecological, tautological, technological, teleological, teratological, terminological,

-logical *contd.*
theological, topological, toxicological, traumatological, trichological, tropological, typological, unlogical, untheological, urological, virological, volcanological, vulcanological, zóological, zoophytological, zymological.

-logous analogous, antilogous, dendrologous, heterologous, homologous, isologous, tautologous.

-logue aeglogue, analogue, apologue, catalogue, collogue, decalogue, dialogue, duologue, eclogue, epilogue, grammalogue, homologue, idealogue, ideologue, isologue, monologue, philologue, prologue, Sinologue, theologue, travelogue, trialogue.

-logy acarology, aerobiology, aerolithology, aerology, aetiology, agriology, agrobiology, agrology, agrostology, algology, amphibology, anaesthesiology, analogy, andrology, anemology, angelology, anthology, anthropobiology, anthropology, antilogy, apology, arachnology, archaeology, archeology, archology, aristology, Assyriology, astrogeology, astrology, atheology, atmology, audiology, autecology, autology, axiology, bacteriology, balneology, batology, battology, bibliology, bioecology, biology, biotechnology, brachylogy, bryology, bumpology, cacology, caliology, campanology, carcinology, cardiology, carphology, cartology, cetology, cheirology, chirology, choreology, chorology, Christology, chronobiology, chronology, cine-biology, climatology, codicology, cometology, conchology, coprology, cosmetology, cosmology, craniology, criminology, cryobiology, cryptology, cytology, dactyliology, dactylology, deltiology, demology, demonology, dendrochronology, dendrology, deontology, dermatology, diabology, diabolology, dialectology, diplomatology, dittology, docimology, dogmatology, dosiology, dosology, doxology, dyslogy, dysteleology, ecclesiology, eccrinology, ecology, edaphology, Egyptology, electrobiology, electrology, electrophysiology, electrotechnology, elogy, embryology, emmenology, endemiology, endocrinology, entomology, enzymology, epidemiology, epistemology, escapology, eschatology, ethnology, ethnomusicology, ethology, Etruscology, etymology, euchology, eulogy, exobiology, festilogy, festology, folk-etymology, futurology, gastroenterology, gastrology, gemmology, gemology, genealogy, genethlialogy, geochronology, geology, geomorphology, gerontology, gigantology, glaciology, glossology, glottology, gnomonology, gnoseology, gnosiology, gnotobiology, graphology, gynaecology, haematology, hagiology, hamartiology, haplology, heliology, helminthology, heortology, hepaticology, hepatology, heresiology, herpetology, heterology, hierology, hippology, histiology, histology, histopathology, historiology, homology, hoplology, horology, hydrobiology, hydrogeology, hydrology, hydrometeorology, hyetology, hygrology, hymnology, hypnology, ichnology, ichthyology, iconology, ideology, immunology, insectology, irenology, kidology, kinesiology, koniology, Kremlinology, laryngology, lepidopterology, lexicology, lichenology, limnology, lithology, liturgiology, macrology, malacology, malariology, mammalogy, Mariology, martyrology, Maryology, Mayology, menology, metapsychology, meteorology, methodology, microbiology, microclimatology, micrology, micro-meteorology, microtechnology, mineralogy, misology, monadology, monology, morphology, muscology, museology, musicology, mycetology, mycology, myology, myrmecology, mythology, necrology, nematology, neology, nephology, nephrology, neurobiology, neurohypnology, neurology,

-logy *contd.*

neuropathology, neurophysiology, neuroradiology, neurypnology, nomology, noology, nosology, nostology, numerology, numismatology, oceanology, odontology, oenology, olfactology, oncology, oneirology, onirology, ontology, oology, ophiology, ophthalmology, optology, orchidology, oreology, ornithology, orology, orthopterology, oryctology, osteology, otolaryngology, otology, otorhinolaryngology, ourology, paedology, palaeanthropology, palaeethnology, palaeichthyology, palaeoclimatology, palaeolimnology, palaeontology, palaeopedology, palaeophytology, palaeozoology, palillogy, palynology, pantheology, papyrology, paradoxology, paralogy, parapsychology, parasitology, paroemiology, pathology, patrology, pedology, pelology, penology, periodontology, perissology, pestology, petrology, phaenology, pharmacology, pharyngology, phenology, phenomenology, philology, phonology, photobiology, photogeology, phraseology, phrenology, phycology, physiology, phytology, phytopathology, planetology, plutology, pneumatology, podology, poenology, pomology, ponerology, posology, potamology, primatology, protistology, protozoology, psephology, pseudology, psychobiology, psychology, psychopathology, psychophysiology, pteridology, pyretology, pyroballogy, radiobiology, radiology, reflexology, rheology, rheumatology, rhinology, röntgenology, sarcology, satanology, scatology, Scientology, sedimentology, seismology, selenology, selenomorphology, semasiology, semeiology, semiology, serology, sexology, sindonology, Sinology, sitiology, sitology, skatology, sociobiology, sociology, somatology, soteriology, spectrology, spelaeology, sphagnology, sphygmology, spongology, stichology, stoechiology, stoicheiology, stoichiology, stomatology, storiology, symbology, symbolology, symptomatology, synchronology, synecology, synoecology, syphilology, systematology, tautology, technology, teleology, teratology, terminology, terotechnology, tetralogy, thanatology, theology, thermology, therology, thremmatology, timbrology, tocology, tokology, topology, toxicology, traumatology, tribology, trichology, trilogy, trophology, tropology, typhlology, typology, ufology, uranology, urbanology, urinology, urology, venereology, vexillology, victimology, vinology, virology, volcanology, vulcanology, xylology, zoopathology, zoophytology, zoopsychology, zymology.

-lysis analysis, atmolysis, autocatalysis, autolysis, bacteriolysis, catalysis, cryptanalysis, cytolysis, dialysis, electroanalysis, electrolysis, haematolysis, haemodialysis, haemolysis, histolysis, hydrolysis, hypno-analysis, leucocytolysis, microanalysis, narco-analysis, neurolysis, paralysis, photolysis, plasmolysis, pneumatolysis, proteolysis, psephoanalysis, psychoanalysis, pyrolysis, radiolysis, thermolysis, uranalysis, urinalysis, zincolysis, zymolysis.

-lytic analytic, anxiolytic, autocatalytic, autolytic, bacteriolytic, catalytic, dialytic, electrolytic, haemolytic, histolytic, hydrolytic, paralytic, photolytic, plasmolytic, pneumatolytic, proteolytic, psychoanalytic, pyrolytic, sympatholytic, tachylytic, thermolytic, unanalytic.

-mania acronymania, anglomania, anthomania, balletomania, bibliomania, Celtomania, demonomania, dipsomania, egomania, erotomania, etheromania, francomania, gallomania, hydromania, hypomania, hysteromania, Keltomania, kleptomania, mania, megalomania, melomania, methomania, metromania, monomania, morphinomania, mythomania, nostomania, nymphomania,

-mania *contd.*
    oenomania, opsomania, orchidomania, petalomania, phyllomania, potichomania, pteridomania, pyromania, squandermania, theatromania, theomania, timbromania, toxicomania, tulipomania, typomania, xenomania.

-mancy aeromancy, axinomancy, belomancy, bibliomancy, botanomancy, capnomancy, cartomancy, ceromancy, cheiromancy, chiromancy, cleromancy, coscinomancy, crithomancy, crystallomancy, dactyliomancy, gastromancy, geomancy, gyromancy, hieromancy, hydromancy, lampadomancy, lithomancy, myomancy, necromancy, nigromancy, oenomancy, omphalomancy, oneiromancy, oniromancy, onychomancy, ornithomancy, pyromancy, rhabdomancy, scapulimancy, spodomancy, tephromancy, theomancy, zoomancy.

-mantic cheiromantic, chiromantic, geomantic, hydromantic, myomantic, necromantic, ornithomantic, pyromantic, scapulimantic, spodomantic, theomantic, zoomantic.

-mathic chrestomathic, philomathic, polymathic.

-mathy chrestomathy, opsimathy, philomathy, polymathy.

-meter absorptiometer, accelerometer, acidimeter, actinometer, aerometer, alcoholometer, alkalimeter, altimeter, ammeter, anemometer, araeometer, areometer, arithmometer, atmometer, audiometer, auxanometer, auxometer, barometer, bathometer, bathymeter, bolometer, bomb-calorimeter, calorimeter, cathetometer, centimeter, chlorimeter, chlorometer, chronometer, clinometer, colorimeter, Comptometer®, coulombmeter, coulometer, craniometer, cryometer, cyanometer, cyclometer, decelerometer, declinometer, dendrometer, densimeter, densitometer, diagometer, diameter, diaphanometer, diffractometer, dimeter, dose-meter, dosimeter, drosometer, dynamometer, effusiometer, electrodynamometer, electrometer, endosmometer, ergometer, eriometer, evaporimeter, extensimeter, extensometer, fathometer, flowmeter, fluorimeter, fluorometer, focimeter, galactometer, galvanometer, gas-meter, gasometer, geometer, geothermometer, goniometer, gradiometer, gravimeter, harmonometer, heliometer, heptameter, hexameter, hodometer, hydrometer, hyetometer, hygrometer, hypsometer, iconometer, inclinometer, interferometer, isoperimeter, katathermometer, konimeter, kryometer, lactometer, luxmeter, lysimeter, machmeter, magnetometer, manometer, mekometer, meter, micrometer, microseismometer, mileometer, milometer, monometer, nephelometer, Nilometer, nitrometer, octameter, odometer, oenometer, ohmmeter, ombrometer, oncometer, ophthalmometer, opisometer, opsiometer, optometer, osmometer, oximeter, pachymeter, parameter, passimeter, pedometer, pelvimeter, pentameter, perimeter, permeameter, phonmeter, phonometer, photometer, piezometer, planimeter, planometer, plessimeter, pleximeter, pluviometer, pneumatometer, polarimeter, potentiometer, potometer, psychometer, psychrometer, pulsimeter, pulsometer, pycnometer, pyknometer, pyrheliometer, pyrometer, quantometer, radiogoniometer, radiometer, radiotelemeter, refractometer, rheometer, rhythmometer, saccharimeter, saccharometer, salimeter, salinometer, scintillometer, sclerometer, seismometer, semi-diameter, semiperimeter, sensitometer, slot-meter, solarimeter, spectrophotometer, speedometer, spherometer, sphygmomanometer, sphygmometer, spirometer, stactometer, stalagmometer, stereometer, strabismometer, strabometer, swingometer,

-meter *contd.*

sympiesometer, tacheometer, tachometer, tachymeter, taseometer, tasimeter, taximeter, telemeter, tellurometer, tetrameter, thermometer, Tintometer®, tonometer, torque-meter, tribometer, trigonometer, trimeter, trocheameter, trochometer, tromometer, udometer, urinometer, vaporimeter, variometer, viameter, vibrometer, viscometer, viscosimeter, voltameter, voltmeter, volumenometer, volumeter, volumometer, water-barometer, water-meter, water-thermometer, wattmeter, wavemeter, weatherometer, xylometer, zymometer, zymosimeter.

-metry acidimetry, aerometry, alcoholometry, alkalimetry, anemometry, anthropometry, araeometry, asymmetry, barometry, bathymetry, biometry, bolometry, calorimetry, chlorimetry, chlorometry, chronometry, clinometry, colorimetry, coulometry, craniometry, densimetry, densitometry, dissymmetry, dosimetry, dynamometry, electrometry, galvanometry, gasometry, geometry, goniometry, gravimetry, hodometry, horometry, hydrometry, hygrometry, hypsometry, iconometry, interferometry, isometry, isoperimetry, micrometry, microseismometry, nephelometry, noometry, odometry, ophthalmometry, optometry, pelvimetry, perimetry, photometry, planimetry, plessimetry, pleximetry, polarimetry, pseudosymmetry, psychometry, psychrometry, pyrometry, saccharimetry, seismometry, sociometry, spectrometry, spectrophotometry, spirometry, stalagmometry, stereometry, stichometry, stoechiometry, stoicheiometry, stoichiometry, symmetry, tacheometry, tachometry, tachymetry, telemetry, tensiometry, thermometry, trigonometry, unsymmetry, uranometry, viscometry, viscosimetry, zoometry.

-monger balladmonger, barber-monger, borough-monger, carpetmonger, cheese-monger, costardmonger, costermonger, fellmonger, fishmonger, flesh-monger, gossip-monger, ironmonger, lawmonger, love-monger, maxim-monger, meal-monger, miracle-monger, mystery-monger, newsmonger, panic-monger, peace-monger, pearmonger, peltmonger, phrasemonger, place-monger, prayer-monger, relic-monger, scandalmonger, scaremonger, sensation-monger, species-monger, starmonger, state-monger, system-monger, verse-monger, warmonger, whoremonger, wit-monger, wonder-monger.

-morphic actinomorphic, allelomorphic, allotriomorphic, anamorphic, anthropomorphic, automorphic, biomorphic, dimorphic, ectomorphic, enantiomorphic, endomorphic, ergatomorphic, gynandromorphic, hemimorphic, heteromorphic, homeomorphic, homoeomorphic, homomorphic, hylomorphic, idiomorphic, isodimorphic, isomorphic, lagomorphic, mesomorphic, metamorphic, monomorphic, morphic, ophiomorphic, ornithomorphic, paedomorphic, paramorphic, perimorphic, pleomorphic, polymorphic, protomorphic, pseudomorphic, tetramorphic, theomorphic, theriomorphic, trimorphic, xenomorphic, xeromorphic, zoomorphic, zygomorphic.

-morphous amorphous, anamorphous, anthropomorphous, dimorphous, enantiomorphous, gynandromorphous, heteromorphous, homeomorphous, homoeomorphous, homomorphous, isodimorphous, isomorphous, lagomorphous, mesomorphous, monomorphous, ophiomorphous, perimorphous, pleomorphous, polymorphous, pseudomorphous, rhizomorphous, tauromorphous, theriomorphous, trimorphous, xeromorphous, zygomorphous.

-onym acronym, anonym, antonym, autonym, cryptonym, eponym, exonym, heteronym, homonym, metonym, paronym, polyonym, pseudonym, synonym, tautonym, toponym, trionym.

-onymic acronymic, Hieronymic, homonymic, matronymic, metonymic, metronymic, patronymic, polyonymic, synonymic, toponymic.

-osis abiosis, acidosis, actinobacillosis, actinomycosis, aerobiosis, aeroneurosis, alkalosis, amaurosis, amitosis, anabiosis, anadiplosis, anaerobiosis, anamorphosis, anaplerosis, anastomosis, anchylosis, ankylosis, anthracosis, anthropomorphosis, antibiosis, apodosis, aponeurosis, apotheosis, arteriosclerosis, arthrosis, asbestosis, aspergillosis, ateleiosis, atherosclerosis, athetosis, autohypnosis, avitaminosis, bacteriosis, bagassosis, bilharziosis, biocoenosis, bromhidrosis, bromidrosis, brucellosis, byssinosis, carcinomatosis, carcinosis, chlorosis, cirrhosis, coccidiosis, cyanosis, cyclosis, dermatosis, diarthrosis, diorthosis, diverticulosis, dulosis, ecchymosis, enantiosis, enarthrosis, endometriosis, endosmosis, enosis, enteroptosis, epanadiplosis, epanorthosis, exosmosis, exostosis, fibrosis, fluorosis, furunculosis, gliomatosis, gnotobiosis, gomphosis, gummosis, haematosis, halitosis, hallucinosis, heliosis, heterosis, hidrosis, homeosis, homoeosis, homomorphosis, homozygosis, hydronephrosis, hyperhidrosis, hyperidrosis, hyperinosis, hypersarcosis, hypervitaminosis, hypinosis, hypnosis, hypotyposis, ichthyosis, kenosis, keratosis, ketosis, kurtosis, kyllosis, kyphosis, leishmaniosis, leptospirosis, leucocytosis, limosis, lipomatosis, lordosis, madarosis, marmarosis, meiosis, melanosis, metachrosis, metamorphosis, metempsychosis, miosis, mitosis, molybdosis, mononucleosis, monosis, morphosis, mucoviscidosis, mycosis, mycotoxicosis, myosis, myxomatosis, narcohypnosis, narcosis, necrobiosis, necrosis, nephroptosis, nephrosis, neurosis, onychocryptosis, ornithosis, osmidrosis, osmosis, osteoarthrosis, osteoporosis, otosclerosis, paedomorphosis, parabiosis, paraphimosis, parapsychosis, parasitosis, pediculosis, phagocytosis, phimosis, pholidosis, phytosis, pneumoconiosis, pneumokoniosis, pneumonokoniosis, pneumonoultramicroscopicsilicovolcanoconiosis, pollenosis, polyposis, porosis, proptosis, psilosis, psittacosis, psychoneurosis, psychosis, pterylosis, ptilosis, ptosis, pyrosis, resinosis, salmonellosis, sarcoidosis, sarcomatosis, sclerosis, scoliosis, self-hypnosis, siderosis, silicosis, sorosis, spirillosis, spirochaetosis, steatosis, stegnosis, stenosis, strongylosis, sycosis, symbiosis, symptosis, synarthrosis, synchondrosis, syndesmosis, synoeciosis, synostosis, syntenosis, syssarcosis, thanatosis, theriomorphosis, thrombosis, thylosis, thyrotoxicosis, torulosis, toxoplasmosis, trichinosis, trichophytosis, trichosis, trophobiosis, trophoneurosis, tuberculosis, tylosis, ulosis, urosis, virosis, visceroptosis, xerosis, zoonosis, zygosis, zymosis.

-path allopath, homeopath, homoeopath, kinesipath, naturopath, neuropath, osteopath, psychopath, sociopath, telepath.

-pathic allopathic, anthropopathic, antipathic, empathic, homoeopathic, hydropathic, idiopathic, kinesipathic, naturopathic, neuropathic, osteopathic, protopathic, psychopathic, sociopathic, telepathic.

-pathy allopathy, anthropopathy, antipathy, apathy, cardiomyopathy, dyspathy, empathy, enantiopathy, homeopathy, homoeopathy, hydropathy, idiopathy,

-pathy *contd.*
kinesipathy, myocardiopathy, naturopathy, neuropathy, nostopathy, osteopathy, psychopathy, sociopathy, sympathy, telepathy, theopathy, zoopathy.

-phage bacteriophage, macrophage, ostreophage, xylophage.

-phagous anthropophagous, autophagous, carpophagous, coprophagous, creophagous, endophagous, entomophagous, exophagous, geophagous, hippophagous, hylophagous, ichthyophagous, lithophagous, mallophagous, meliphagous, monophagous, myrmecophagous, necrophagous, omophagous, ophiophagous, ostreophagous, pantophagous, phyllophagous, phytophagous, polyphagous, rhizophagous, saprophagous, sarcophagous, scatophagous, theophagous, toxicophagous, toxiphagous, xylophagous, zoophagous.

-phagy anthropophagy, autophagy, coprophagy, dysphagy, endophagy, entomophagy, exophagy, geophagy, hippophagy, ichthyophagy, monophagy, mycophagy, omophagy, ostreophagy, pantophagy, polyphagy, sarcophagy, scatophagy, theophagy, xerophagy.

-phile ailurophile, arctophile, audiophile, bibliophile, cartophile, discophile, francophile, gallophile, Germanophile, gerontophile, halophile, hippophile, homophile, iodophile, lyophile, myrmecophile, necrophile, negrophile, oenophile, ombrophile, paedophile, psammophile, Russophile, scripophile, Sinophile, Slavophile, spermophile, thermophile, Turcophile, xenophile, zoophile.

-philia ailurophilia, anglophilia, canophilia, coprophilia, ephebophilia, Germanophilia, gerontophilia, haemophilia, necrophilia, paedophilia, paraphilia, scopophilia, scoptophilia, zoophilia.   ·

-philist bibliophilist, canophilist, cartophilist, Dantophilist, iconophilist, negrophilist, notaphilist, oenophilist, ophiophilist, pteridophilist, Russophilist, scripophilist, stegophilist, timbrophilist, zoophilist.

-phily acarophily, anemophily, bibliophily, cartophily, entomophily, halophily, hydrophily, myrmecophily, necrophily, notaphily, oenophily, ornithophily, photophily, scripophily, Sinophily, symphily, timbrophily, toxophily, xerophily.

-phobe ailurophobe, anglophobe, francophobe, gallophobe, Germanophobe, hippophobe, hygrophobe, lyophobe, negrophobe, ombrophobe, photophobe, Russophobe, Slavophobe, Turcophobe, xenophobe.

-phobia acrophobia, aerophobia, agoraphobia, ailurophobia, algophobia, anglophobia, astraphobia, astrapophobia, bathophobia, bibliophobia, canophobia, claustrophobia, cynophobia, dromophobia, ecophobia, ergophobia, gallophobia, hydrophobia, hypsophobia, monophobia, mysophobia, necrophobia, negrophobia, neophobia, nosophobia, nyctophobia, ochlophobia, panophobia, pantophobia, pathophobia, phonophobia, photophobia, Russophobia, satanophobia, scopophobia, sitiophobia, sitophobia, symmetrophobia, syphilophobia, taphephobia, taphophobia, thanatophobia, theophobia, toxicophobia, toxiphobia, triskaidecaphobia, triskaidekaphobia, xenophobia, zoophobia.

-phobic aerophobic, agoraphobic, anglophobic, claustrophobic, heliophobic, hydrophobic, lyophobic, monophobic, phobic, photophobic.

-phone aerophone, allophone, anglophone, Ansaphone®, audiphone, chordophone, detectophone, diaphone, dictaphone, diphone, earphone, Entryphone®, francophone, geophone, gramophone, harmoniphone, headphone, heckelphone, homophone, hydrophone, idiophone, interphone, kaleidophone, megaphone, metallophone, microphone, monotelephone, optophone, phone, photophone, Picturephone®, polyphone, pyrophone, radiogramophone, radiophone, radiotelephone, sarrusophone, saxophone, sousaphone, speakerphone, sphygmophone, stentorphone, telephone, theatrophone, triphone, vibraphone, videophone, videotelephone, viewphone, xylophone.

-phonic acrophonic, allophonic, anglophonic, antiphonic, aphonic, cacophonic, cataphonic, chordophonic, dodecaphonic, dysphonic, euphonic, gramophonic, homophonic, microphonic, monophonic, paraphonic, photophonic, quadraphonic, quadrophonic, radiophonic, stentorophonic, stereophonic, symphonic, telephonic, xylophonic.

-phony acrophony, antiphony, aphony, autophony, cacophony, colophony, dodecaphony, euphony, gramophony, homophony, laryngophony, monophony, photophony, polyphony, quadraphony, quadrophony, radiophony, radiotelephony, stereophony, symphony, tautophony, telephony.

-phorous discophorous, Eriophorous, galactophorous, hypophosphorous, mastigophorous, necrophorous, odontophorous, phosphorous, pyrophorous, rhynchophorous, sporophorous.

-phyte aerophyte, bryophyte, cormophyte, dermatophyte, ectophyte, endophyte, entophyte, epiphyte, gametophyte, geophyte, halophyte, heliophyte, heliosciophyte, holophyte, hydrophyte, hygrophyte, hylophyte, lithophyte, mesophyte, microphyte, neophyte, oophyte, osteophyte, phanerophyte, phreatophyte, protophyte, psammophyte, pteridophyte, saprophyte, schizophyte, spermaphyte, spermatophyte, spermophyte, sporophyte, thallophyte, tropophyte, xerophyte, zoophyte, zygophyte.

-saurus Allosaurus, Ankylosaurus, Apatosaurus, Atlantosaurus, brachiosaurus, brontosaurus, Ceteosaurus, Dolichosaurus, Ichthyosaurus, megalosaurus, Plesiosaurus, Stegosaurus, Teleosaurus, Titanosaurus, tyrannosaurus.

-scope aethrioscope, auriscope, baroscope, bathyscope, benthoscope, bioscope, bronchoscope, chromoscope, chronoscope, colposcope, cryoscope, cystoscope, dichrooscope, dichroscope, dipleidoscope, ebullioscope, electroscope, endoscope, engiscope, engyscope, epidiascope, episcope, fluoroscope, galvanoscope, gastroscope, gyroscope, hagioscope, helioscope, hodoscope, horoscope, hydroscope, hygroscope, iconoscope, iriscope, kaleidoscope, kinetoscope, koniscope, lactoscope, laparoscope, laryngoscope, lychnoscope, megascope, microscope, mutoscope, myringoscope, myrioscope, nephoscope, opeidoscope, ophthalmoscope, oscilloscope, otoscope, pantoscope, periscope, pharyngoscope, phenakistoscope, phonendoscope, polariscope, poroscope, praxinoscope, proctoscope, pseudoscope, pyroscope, radarscope, radioscope, rhinoscope, scintilloscope, scope, seismoscope, sigmoidoscope, somascope, spectrohelioscope, spectroscope, sphygmoscope, spinthariscope, statoscope, stereofluoroscope, stereoscope, stethoscope, stroboscope, tachistoscope, teinoscope, telescope, thermoscope, triniscope, ultramicroscope, vectorscope, Vertoscope®, vitascope.

-scopic autoscopic, bronchoscopic, cryoscopic, deuteroscopic, dichrooscopic, dichroscopic, ebullioscopic, electroscopic, endoscopic, gyroscopic, hagioscopic, helioscopic, horoscopic, hygroscopic, kaleidoscopic, laryngoscopic, macroscopic, megascopic, metoposcopic, microscopic, necroscopic, ophthalmoscopic, orthoscopic, pantoscopic, periscopic, poroscopic, rhinoscopic, seismoscopic, spectroscopic, stethoscopic, stroboscopic, submicroscopic, tachistoscopic, telescopic, thermoscopic, ultramicroscopic, zooscopic.

-scopy autoscopy, bronchoscopy, colposcopy, cranioscopy, cryoscopy, cystoscopy, dactyloscopy, deuteroscopy, ebullioscopy, endoscopy, episcopy, fluoroscopy, hepatoscopy, hieroscopy, horoscopy, laparoscopy, laryngoscopy, metoposcopy, microscopy, necroscopy, omoplatoscopy, oneiroscopy, oniroscopy, ophthalmoscopy, ornithoscopy, ouroscopy, pharyngoscopy, poroscopy, proctoscopy, radioscopy, retinoscopy, rhinoscopy, röntgenoscopy, skiascopy, spectroscopy, stereoscopy, stethoscopy, telescopy, tracheoscopy, ultramicroscopy, urinoscopy, uroscopy, zooscopy.

-ship abbotship, accountantship, acquaintanceship, administratorship, admiralship, advisership, aedileship, airmanship, aldermanship, amateurship, ambassadorship, apostleship, apprenticeship, archonship, assessorship, associateship, attorneyship, auditorship, augurship, authorship, bachelorship, bailieship, baillieship, bardship, barristership, bashawship, batsmanship, beadleship, bedellship, bedelship, benchership, bondmanship, brinkmanship, bursarship, bushmanship, butlership, cadetship, Caesarship, candidateship, captainship, cardinalship, catechumenship, censorship, chairmanship, chamberlainship, championship, chancellorship, chaplainship, chelaship, chiefship, chieftainship, citizenship, clanship, clerkship, clientship, clownship, coadjutorship, colleagueship, collectorship, colonelship, commandantship, commandership, commissaryship, commissionership, committeeship, companionship, compotationship, comradeship, conductorship, confessorship, connoisseurship, conservatorship, constableship, consulship, controllership, copartnership, co-rivalship, corporalship, counsellorship, countship, courtship, cousinship, cowardship, craftmanship, craftsmanship, creatorship, creatureship, curateship, curatorship, custodianship, deaconship, dealership, deanship, demyship, denizenship, devilship, dictatorship, directorship, discipleship, disfellowship, doctorship, dogeship, dogship, dollarship, donship, draftsmanship, dukeship, editorship, eldership, electorship, emperorship, endship, ensignship, entrepreneurship, envoyship, executorship, factorship, fathership, fellowship, foxship, freshmanship, friendship, gamesmanship, generalship, gentlemanship, giantship, gladiatorship, goddess-ship, godship, good-fellowship, governor-generalship, governorship, grandeeship, guardianship, guideship, hardship, headship, hectorship, heirship, heraldship, heroship, hership, hetmanship, horsemanship, hostess-ship, housewifeship, huntsmanship, inspectorship, interpretership, interrelationship, janitorship, jockeyship, judgeship, justiceship, kaisership, keepership, kindredship, kingship, kinship, knaveship, ladyship, lairdship, land-ownership, laureateship, leadership, lectorship, lectureship, legateship, legislatorship, librarianship, lieutenant-commandership, lieutenant-generalship, lieutenant-governorship, lieutenantship, lifemanship, logship, lordship, ludship, mageship, major-generalship, majorship, managership, marshalship, mastership, matronship, mayorship, mediatorship, membership, Messiahship, milk-kinship, minorship, mistress-ship, moderatorship, monitorship,

-ship *contd.*

multi-ownership, musicianship, noviceship, nunship, oarsmanship, one-upmanship, overlordship, ownership, partisanship, partnership, pastorship, patroonship, peatship, pendragonship, penmanship, physicianship, poetship, popeship, possessorship, postmastership, praetorship, preachership, precentorship, prefectship, prelateship, premiership, prenticeship, presbytership, presidentship, pretendership, priestship, primateship, primogenitureship, principalship, priorship, probationership, proconsulship, proctorship, procuratorship, professorship, progenitorship, prolocutorship, prophetship, proprietorship, prosectorship, protectorship, provostship, pursership, quaestorship, queenship, rajahship, rajaship, rangership, readership, recordership, rectorship, regentship, registrarship, relationship, residentiaryship, residentship, retainership, rivalship, rogueship, rulership, sachemship, saintship, salesmanship, scholarship, school-friendship, schoolmastership, scrivenership, seamanship, secretaryship, seigniorship, sempstress-ship, senatorship, seneschalship, serfship, sergeantship, serjeantship, servantship, servitorship, sextonship, sheriffship, showmanship, sibship, sizarship, soldiership, solicitorship, sonship, speakership, spectatorship, spinstership, sponsorship, sportsmanship, squireship, statesmanship, stewardship, studentship, subahship, subdeaconship, subeditorship, subinspectorship, subjectship, successorship, suffraganship, sultanship, superintendentship, superiorship, supervisorship, suretyship, surgeonship, surrogateship, surveyorship, survivorship, swordsmanship, teachership, tellership, tenantship, thaneship, thwartship, tide-waitership, township, traineeship, traitorship, treasurership, treeship, tribuneship, truantship, trusteeship, tutorship, twinship, umpireship, uncleship, under-clerkship, undergraduateship, under-secretaryship, unfriendship, ushership, vaivodeship, vergership, vicarship, vice-chairmanship, vice-chancellorship, vice-consulship, viceroyship, virtuosoship, viscountship, viziership, vizirship, voivodeship, waivodeship, wardenship, wardship, watermanship, Whigship, workmanship, worship, wranglership, writership, yachtsmanship.

-sophy anthroposophy, gastrosophy, gymnosophy, pansophy, philosophy, sciosophy, theosophy.

-stat aerostat, antistat, appestat, bacteriostat, barostat, chemostat, coccidiostat, coelostat, cryostat, gyrostat, haemostat, heliostat, humidistat, hydrostat, hygrostat, klinostat, pyrostat, rheostat, siderostat, thermostat.

-therapy actinotherapy, balneotherapy, chemotherapy, cryotherapy, curietherapy, electrotherapy, heliotherapy, hydrotherapy, hypnotherapy, immunotherapy, kinesitherapy, musicotherapy, narcotherapy, opotherapy, organotherapy, pelotherapy, phototherapy, physiotherapy, psychotherapy, pyretotherapy, radiotherapy, röntgenotherapy, serotherapy, serum-therapy, zootherapy.

-tomy adenectomy, adenoidectomy, anatomy, anthropotomy, appendectomy, appendicectomy, arteriotomy, autotomy, cephalotomy, cholecystectomy, cholecystotomy, colotomy, cordotomy, craniectomy, craniotomy, cystotomy, dichotomy, duodenectomy, embryotomy, encephalotomy, enterectomy, enterotomy, gastrectomy, gastrotomy, gingivectomy, glossectomy, hepatectomy, herniotomy, hysterectomy, hysterotomy, iridectomy, iridotomy, laparotomy, laryngectomy, laryngotomy, leucotomy, lipectomy, lithotomy, lobectomy, lobotomy, lumpectomy, mastectomy, microtomy, myringotomy,

-tomy *contd.*

necrotomy, nephrectomy, nephrotomy, neurectomy, neuroanatomy, neurotomy, oophorectomy, orchidectomy, orchiectomy, osteotomy, ovariotomy, pharyngotomy, phlebotomy, phytotomy, pleurotomy, pneumonectomy, pogonotomy, prostatectomy, rhytidectomy, salpingectomy, sclerotomy, splenectomy, stapedectomy, stereotomy, strabotomy, sympathectomy, symphyseotomy, symphysiotomy, syringotomy, tenotomy, tetrachotomy, thymectomy, tonsilectomy, tonsillectomy, tonsillotomy, tonsilotomy, topectomy, tracheotomy, trichotomy, tubectomy, ultramicrotomy, uterectomy, uterotomy, varicotomy, vasectomy, zootomy.

-urgy chemurgy, dramaturgy, electrometallurgy, hierurgy, hydrometallurgy, liturgy, metallurgy, micrurgy, theurgy, zymurgy.

-vorous apivorous, baccivorous, carnivorous, fructivorous, frugivorous, graminivorous, granivorous, herbivorous, insectivorous, lignivorous, mellivorous, myristicivorous, nucivorous, omnivorous, ossivorous, piscivorous, radicivorous, ranivorous, sanguinivorous, sanguivorous, vermivorous.

CHAMBERS ENGLISH DICTIONARY

The most up-to-date and comprehensive single-volume dictionary of international English.

The celebrated *Chambers Twentieth Century Dictionary* enjoyed an enviable reputation among all who studied and cared about the English language. Now the *Chambers English Dictionary* builds on this success with a wealth of new words and new definitions, all clearly and carefully presented and explained. For its breadth of coverage and clarity, with more definitions than any of its competitors, the new *Chambers English Dictionary* represents the outstanding dictionary choice of today.

- **15,000 new words and phrases**
- **190,000 references and 265,000 definitions**
- **Unrivalled coverage of literature and language, science and technology, law, business and finance, common idioms**
- **Easy-to-understand pronunciation guide, with minimum use of complicated symbols**

Standard Edition   1 85296 000 0   1808pp
Thumb Index Edition   1 85296 001 9

CHAMBERS
CAMBRIDGE

Chambers English Dictionary Range

A complete range of Chambers English Dictionaries is now available. From the Standard and Thumb Index editions right down to the Mini edition, the Chambers English Dictionary range represents the answer to everyone's dictionary needs.

CHAMBERS ENGLISH DICTIONARY
Standard · 1 85296 000 0   1808pp
Thumb Index Edition   1 85296 001 9

- **190,000 references**
- **265,000 definitions**
- **Literary words**
- **Scientific and technical terms**
- **Word origins**
- **Business and finance terms**
- **Word puzzlers' treasure chest**
- **Plain language definitions**
- **Easy pronunciation guide**
- **Useful appendices**

The most up-to-date and comprehensive single-volume dictionary of international English.
Essential for students, scholars, writers, journalists, librarians, publishers, scientists, lawyers, accountants, Scrabble® players, crossword solvers and setters.

CHAMBERS CONCISE DICTIONARY
Hardcover   1 85296 010 8   1216pp
Paperback   1 85296 011 6

- **121,000 references**
- **156,000 definitions**
- **Accurate and comprehensive**
- **Contemporary English**
- **Clear simple definitions**
- **Easy pronunciation guide**
- **Abbreviations and useful appendices**

An abridged version of *Chambers English Dictionary*. Ideal for everyday use by students and general readers who want the emphasis on the language of the 1980s. Has many of the features of the larger dictionary without its massive coverage of words. Extremely good value in compact form.

CHAMBERS
CAMBRIDGE

CHAMBERS POCKET DICTIONARY
Hardcover   1 85296 012 4   896pp

- **33,000 references**
- **50,000 definitions**
- **Simple definitions**
- **Clear layout**
- **Usage examples**
- **Easy pronunciation guide**
- **Abbreviations**

A particularly handy dictionary for school or office use. Sufficient number of headwords for everyday use with brief, clear definitions and examples to help with common writing problems. Well designed for quick reference.

CHAMBERS MINI DICTIONARY
Paperback   1 85296 014 0   640pp

- **24,000 references**
- **38,000 definitions**
- **Handy size**
- **Abbreviations**

A masterpiece of compression. Genuinely pocket or handbag size but with the range of a much larger dictionary.
Excellent value in easily transportable form. The ideal second dictionary to carry to school or office.

CHAMBERS
CAMBRIDGE

CHAMBERS
SCIENCE AND TECHNOLOGY DICTIONARY

Edited by PETER WALKER

Now revised for the first time in seventeen years, the world's leading single-volume scientific dictionary is a unique reference source for all branches of science.

- **45,000 entries**
- **Coverage of 100 fields, from computing and engineering to behavioural studies and medicine**
- **More than 40 internationally experienced contributors**
- **The standard reference book for scientists, researchers and students**

Hardcovers   1 85296 150 3   1024pp
Paperback   1 85296 151 1

CHAMBERS
CAMBRIDGE